THE NEW OXFORD ANNOTATED BIBLE

WITH THE APOCRYPHA
EXPANDED EDITION

REVISED STANDARD VERSION

AN ECUMENICAL STUDY BIBLE

THE NEW OXFORD ANNOTATED BIBLE WITH THE APOCRYPHA

REVISED STANDARD VERSION

*Containing the Second Edition of the New Testament
And an Expanded Edition of the Apocrypha*

EDITED BY

HERBERT G. MAY   BRUCE M. METZGER

NEW YORK   OXFORD UNIVERSITY PRESS

FOREWORD

THE NEW OXFORD ANNOTATED BIBLE WITH THE APOCRYPHA is presented in order to encourage the study and understanding of both the canonical Scriptures (the Old Testament and the New Testament) and the Old Testament Apocrypha. The Old Testament Apocrypha contains a rich variety of types of materials —historical writings, romantic tales, two fine examples of Wisdom literature, apocalyptic prophecy, late additions and supplements to Old Testament books. It provides valuable source materials for the understanding of the history and culture of post-Old Testament Judaism and for appreciating the background of the New Testament. For example, information from the inter-Testamental books bears upon such matters as the development of the sects of the Pharisees and the Sadducees, the growth of interest in the coming of the Messiah, the extension of beliefs concerning angels and demons, the dissemination of the doctrine of the resurrection—to mention only a few of the institutions and beliefs which are taken for granted in the New Testament, but of which there are only allusions in the Old Testament.

Although the Christian Churches have taken divergent attitudes toward the books of the Apocrypha and Catholics and Protestants have held differing views regarding their authority, the writings of the Apocrypha belong to the common heritage of the Church from Judaism, and they have been part of the great English translations of the Bible, including the King James Version of 1611, the English Revised Version of the last century, and now the Revised Standard Version. The Catholic Douay Version of 1609–1610, in accord with the Catholic view of the divine authority of these books, followed the standard Latin version (the Vulgate), of which it is a translation, in having these writings among or a part of the Old Testament books; the Protestant versions make a separate section of them. The original commission of the Standard Bible Committee, which was entrusted with making the Revised Standard Version, did not call for a revised translation of the Apocrypha. The motivation for producing the Revised Standard Version of the Apocrypha came from an obviously increasing desire of the Churches for it.

The Revised Standard Version has become an important instrument in the ecumenical dialogue among English-speaking Christians. Now, with the Second Edition of the translation of the New Testament and the translation of 3 and 4 Maccabees and Psalm 151, its contribution to the understanding of the Bible is even more significant. It is gratifying that this version of the Scriptures has received the hearty commendation of churchmen and scholars of all the major denominations of Christendom. The editors are particularly pleased that His Eminence, the late RICHARD CARDINAL CUSHING, Archbishop of Boston, Massachusetts, endorsed the first edition of THE OXFORD ANNOTATED BIBLE WITH THE APOCRYPHA, granting it the *imprimatur*. Likewise, His Eminence, ATHENAGORAS, Archbishop of Thyateira and Great Britain, has expressed his great satisfaction that, by the addition of 3 and 4 Maccabees and Psalm 151, there is now available in the Revised Standard Version the complete canon of the Septuagint Version which is in use among Orthodox Churches. Thus this edition can serve as a common Bible for Protestant, Roman Catholic, and Eastern Orthodox readers alike.

Special thanks must be expressed not only to the several contributors to the volume, but also to FATHER PHILIP J. KING, St. John's Seminary, Brighton, Massachusetts; FATHER W. VAN ETTEN CASEY, S.J., College of the Holy Cross, Worcester, Massachusetts; and FATHER EUGENE H. MALY, Mt. St. Mary's Seminary of the West, Norwood, Ohio, for valuable editorial advice and counsel.

HERBERT G. MAY
BRUCE M. METZGER

THE NUMBER AND SEQUENCE OF

THE BOOKS OF THE BIBLE

By Bruce M. Metzger

THE OLD TESTAMENT

ACCORDING TO JEWISH USAGE THE TWENTY-FOUR BOOKS of the Hebrew Scriptures fall into three divisions: the Law, the Prophets, and the Writings. The Prophets are divided into the Former Prophets and the Latter Prophets (the terms "former" and "latter" refer to their position in the list, and have no reference to date of composition). The books of Samuel, Kings, Chronicles, Ezra-Nehemiah were not divided by the Jews until the close of the Middle Ages. The twelve Minor Prophets are treated as one book. The two subdivisions of the Prophets therefore contain four books each. In most editions of the Hebrew Bible the sequence of the books is as follows:

THE LAW (five books):
   Genesis, Exodus, Leviticus, Numbers, Deuteronomy.

THE PROPHETS (eight books):
   Former Prophets: Joshua, Judges, Samuel (1 and 2), Kings (1 and 2).
   Latter Prophets:　Isaiah, Jeremiah, Ezekiel, the Twelve (= Hosea, Joel, Amos, Obadiah, Jonah, Micah, Nahum, Habakkuk, Zephaniah, Haggai, Zechariah, Malachi).

THE WRITINGS (eleven books):
   Psalms, Proverbs, Job, Song of Songs, Ruth, Lamentations, Ecclesiastes, Esther, Daniel, Ezra-Nehemiah, Chronicles (1 and 2).

In Protestant editions of the Bible the Old Testament follows the Hebrew text as regards content, but the books in the second and third divisions are rearranged in sequence and several are divided, making a total of thirty-nine.

In Roman Catholic editions the Old Testament contains the rearranged thirty-nine books of the Hebrew Scriptures plus seven others which are current in the official Latin Vulgate Bible and which Protestants include among the Apocrypha. (For a discussion of the reasons why Protestant and Roman Catholic Bibles differ in contents, see pp. ix–xvi of the section containing the Apocrypha at the close of the volume.) The order of these forty-six books in Vulgate manuscripts varies greatly; in fact, the manuscripts that have been examined disclose more than two hundred different ways of arranging the books. In current editions of

Roman Catholic Bibles (including the Douay Version, the Jerusalem Bible, and the New American Bible), Tobit and Judith stand after Nehemiah; 1 and 2 Maccabees, after Esther (except in the Douay Version, in which these books conclude the Old Testament); Wisdom and Ecclesiasticus, after the Song of Solomon; and Baruch, with the Letter of Jeremiah as ch. 6, after Lamentations. Furthermore, the books of Esther and Daniel are expanded by several additional chapters and parts of chapters, which Protestants regard as apocryphal. They comprise six Additions to the book of Esther and the following three supplements to the book of Daniel: the Prayer of Azariah and the Song of the Three Young Men, Susanna, and Bel and the Dragon.

In the original Douay Version of 1609–1610 an appendix after the close of the Old Testament contains three other books, 3 and 4 Esdras (called 1 and 2 Esdras by Protestants) and the Prayer of Manasseh. These are regarded as apocryphal by Roman Catholics as well as by Protestants. It is curious that in the Geneva Bible of 1560, widely used by the Puritans, the Prayer of Manasseh is included in the Old Testament between 2 Chronicles and Ezra, though in the table of contents it is designated as apocryphal.

The Greek Orthodox Church, which uses the Greek Septuagint Version as its official text, has generally been accustomed to follow the longer canon of the Old Testament, including in this case also the 151st Psalm and 3 Maccabees. The Seventh Ecumenical Council held at Nicaea in 787 and the Council convened by Basil in Constantinople in 869 quote certain Apocrypha as authoritative. On the other hand, writers who raised the issue concerning the limits of the canon, such as John of Damascus and Nicephorus, express views that coincide with those of Athanasius, who adhered to the Hebrew canon. In the Schism of 1054 the Apocrypha were not an issue, though they became such during the Protestant Reformation. At that time a short-lived attempt was made by Cyril Lucar, Patriarch of Constantinople, to promote the adoption of the Hebrew canon in the Greek Church. Subsequently, however, the Synod of Jerusalem (1672) condemned Cyril and expressly designated the books of Wisdom, Judith, Tobit, Bel and the Dragon, Susanna, Maccabees, and Ecclesiasticus as canonical.

By way of summary, the Roman Catholic Church and the Greek Orthodox Church agree in regarding as authoritative certain books which they call deuterocanonical and which Protestants call apocryphal. In addition the following books are considered apocryphal by Protestants and Roman Catholics, but are in the Greek canon when indicated.

1 Esdras (= Esdras A in the Greek canon; 3 Esdras in Appendix to Latin Vulgate).

2 Esdras (= 4 Esdras in Appendix to Latin Vulgate).

Prayer of Manasseh (in the Greek canon; in Appendix to Latin Vulgate).

Psalm 151 and 3 Maccabees (in the Greek canon; 4 Maccabees in Appendix to Greek canon).

The number and the sequence of the twenty-seven books of the New Testament are the same in Protestant and Roman Catholic editions of the English Bible.

A comparison of the extant manuscripts of the New Testament discloses that the early Church was accustomed to arrange them in four groups: (1) the Gospels, (2) the Acts and the General, or Catholic, Letters (that is, the seven letters which bear the names of James, Peter, John, and Jude), (3) the Pauline Letters, (4) the Apocalypse (as in the fifth-century codex Alexandrinus and many other manuscripts). Sometimes the Pauline Letters precede the Acts and General Letters, thus placing first the books which had earliest obtained canonical authority (as in the fourth-century codex Sinaiticus and the sixth-century codex Fuldensis).

Within each of the four groups there was a great variety of order. In the early Western Church the Gospel sequence most commonly followed was that of Matthew, John, Luke, Mark—namely, the Gospels attributed to apostles preceding those attributed to disciples of the apostles. The Letter to the Hebrews had no fixed place; sometimes it stood at the end of the Pauline Letters, sometimes between Paul's Letters to churches and those to individuals (that is, between 2 Thessalonians and 1 Timothy), and occasionally after Romans (as in the third-century Chester Beatty Papyrus) or after Galatians (as in an ancestor of the fourth-century codex Vaticanus, as is disclosed by the section numbers in Vaticanus). In the West the Letters of Peter were frequently placed first among the General Letters.

The current order of the Pauline and the General Letters seems to have been drawn up roughly in accord with length, the longest one in each group (Paul to churches, Paul to individuals, and General Letters) standing first and the shortest one, last.

THE BOOKS OF THE BIBLE
AND OF THE APOCRYPHA

The section that contains the books of the Apocrypha has its own pagination; in the following index "*Ap.*" is prefixed to page references within that section.

THE NEW OXFORD ANNOTATED BIBLE

REVISED STANDARD VERSION

THE NEW OXFORD ANNOTATED BIBLE

THE
HOLY BIBLE

REVISED STANDARD VERSION CONTAINING
THE OLD AND NEW TESTAMENTS

*Translated from the Original Languages
Being the Version Set Forth A.D. 1611
Revised A.D. 1881–1885 and A.D. 1901
Compared with the Most Ancient Authorities
And Revised A.D. 1946–1952
Second Edition of the New Testament A.D. 1971*

*Introductions, Comments, Cross References, General Articles,
Measures and Weights, Chronological Tables of Rulers, Maps, and Indexes*

EDITED BY

HERBERT G. MAY   BRUCE M. METZGER

NEW YORK   OXFORD UNIVERSITY PRESS

TABLE OF CONTENTS

THE EDITORS' PREFACE

TO THE NEW EDITION

AFTER A DECADE OF WIDESPREAD USE OF *The Oxford Annotated Bible,* the publishers have suggested that it be issued in a revised and enlarged edition which takes into account further advances made in Biblical studies and translation. Accordingly the editors have solicited from the contributors to the first edition any alterations which seemed to be necessary in the light of current research or in the interest of clarity of expression. All such alterations, along with greater or lesser changes introduced by the editors themselves, have been incorporated in the annotations, in the special articles, and in the maps. In addition, three new articles on various aspects of Bible study have been specially prepared for this edition.

The Second Edition of the translation of the New Testament (1971) profits from textual and linguistic studies published since the Revised Standard Version New Testament was first issued in 1946. Many proposals for modification were submitted to the Committee by individuals and by two denominational committees. All of these were given careful attention by the Committee.

Thus, the present volume, besides containing the most recent form of the Revised Standard Version of the Bible, which now includes the Second Edition of the New Testament, supplies the following helps.

1. General introductions to the Old Testament and to the New Testament present information regarding the literary divisions, the language, text, and canon of each Testament.

2. Each of the books of the Bible has an introduction dealing with its composition, authorship, date, and contents. Because of common problems of authorship and date, there is also an introduction to the first five books of the Old Testament (the Pentateuch).

3. Each chapter of the Bible is supplied with annotations which explain literary, historical, geographical, archaeological, and theological matters in the text. In addition to the comments there are selected cross references to other passages of Scripture which shed light upon the verse under consideration. The words in boldface type at the beginning of each section of the annotations serve as an outline of the subject matter of the Biblical text. Running heads at the top of each page indicate at a glance the general content or noteworthy passages.

4. Several special articles provide fuller information on (a) the use and understanding of the Bible; (b) modern approaches to Biblical study; (c) characteristics of Hebrew poetry; (d) literary forms in the Gospels; (e) the geography, history, and archaeology of Bible lands (including also tables of chronology and of measures and weights); and (f) the principal English

[vii]

versions of the Scriptures in the Tyndale-King James tradition.

5. An index of the chief annotations directs attention to comments on important names, institutions, and ideas in the Bible.

6. A set of the New Oxford Bible maps in full color, with an index to places mentioned on the maps, has been revised, incorporating changes and additions resulting from the intensive archaeological and geographical researches of the past decade.

The following persons contributed to THE NEW OXFORD ANNOTATED BIBLE:

The Introduction to the Old Testament was written by HERBERT G. MAY, Chairman, Revised Standard Version Bible Committee; Emeritus Professor of Old Testament Language and Literature, Oberlin College, Oberlin, Ohio, and The Divinity School, Vanderbilt University, Nashville, Tennessee; Visiting Professor, Yale University Divinity School, New Haven, Connecticut (1970–1971); and Distinguished Visiting Professor of Religion, Oberlin College (1972–1973).

The Introduction to the New Testament was written by BRUCE M. METZGER, Vice Chairman, Revised Standard Version Bible Committee; and George L. Collord Professor of New Testament Language and Literature, Princeton Theological Seminary, Princeton, New Jersey.

The introductions and annotations for individual books of the Bible were contributed by BERNHARD W. ANDERSON, Princeton Theological Seminary, Princeton, New Jersey (Genesis, Exodus, Leviticus, Numbers, and Deuteronomy; he also wrote the introduction to the Pentateuch); ROBERT C. DENTAN, General Theological Seminary, New York City (Joshua, Judges, Ruth, and Psalms); WILLIAM F. STINESPRING, Emeritus, The Divinity School, Duke University, Durham, North Carolina (1 and 2 Samuel, 1 and 2 Kings, and 1 and 2 Chronicles); the late ARTHUR JEFFERY, Columbia University, New York City (Ezra, Nehemiah, Esther, and Daniel); SAMUEL TERRIEN, Union Theological Seminary, New York City (Job); R. B. Y. SCOTT, Emeritus, Princeton University, Princeton, New Jersey (Proverbs, Ecclesiastes, Song of Solomon, and Lamentations); VICTOR R. GOLD, Pacific Lutheran Theological Seminary, Berkeley, California (Isaiah, Jeremiah, and Ezekiel); R. LANSING HICKS, Yale Divinity School, New Haven, Connecticut (the Twelve Minor Prophets—Hosea through Malachi); ELWYN E. TILDEN, Lafayette College, Easton, Pennsylvania (Matthew, Mark, and Luke); DONALD G. MILLER, Laurinburg Presbyterian Church, Laurinburg, North Carolina (the Gospel and the three Letters of John); SHERMAN E. JOHNSON, Emeritus, Church Divinity School of the Pacific, Berkeley, California (the Acts of the Apostles); JOHN KNOX, Emeritus, Union Theological Seminary, New York City (Romans, 1 and 2 Corinthians, and Philippians); WARREN A. QUANBECK, Luther Theological Seminary, St. Paul, Minnesota (1 and 2 Thessalonians, 1 and 2 Timothy,

Titus, James, 1 and 2 Peter, and Jude); and BRUCE M. METZGER (Galatians, Ephesians, Colossians, Philemon, Hebrews, and Revelation).

The special articles were prepared by the late H. H. ROWLEY, the University of Manchester, Manchester, England ("How to Read the Bible with Understanding"); ROLAND E. MURPHY, O. Carm., The Divinity School, Duke University, Durham, North Carolina ("Modern Approaches to Biblical Study"); GEORGE W. ANDERSON, University of Edinburgh, Scotland ("Characteristics of Hebrew Poetry"); BRUCE M. METZGER ("Literary Forms in the Gospels"); GEORGES A. BARROIS, St. Vladimir's Orthodox Theological Seminary, Tuckahoe, New York ("Survey of the Geography, History, and Archaeology of the Bible Lands"); and the late LUTHER A. WEIGLE, Dean of the Divinity School and Sterling Professor, Emeritus, Yale University, New Haven, Connecticut ("English Versions of the Bible: The Tyndale-King James Tradition").

The editors express their gratitude to all who are mentioned above, as well as to the staff and craftsmen of the Oxford University Press, who, under the guidance of Wilbur D. Ruggles, assisted in producing this annotated edition of the Holy Scriptures. May its varied helps prove useful in leading many readers to a deeper understanding of the Word of God.

HERBERT G. MAY
Old Testament Editor

BRUCE M. METZGER
New Testament Editor

PREFACE TO THE REVISED STANDARD VERSION

THE REVISED STANDARD VERSION of the Bible is an authorized revision of the American Standard Version, published in 1901, which was a revision of the King James Version, published in 1611.

The first English version of the Scriptures made by direct translation from the original Hebrew and Greek, and the first to be printed, was the work of William Tyndale. He met bitter opposition. He was accused of willfully perverting the meaning of the Scriptures, and his New Testaments were ordered to be burned as "untrue translations." He was finally betrayed into the hands of his enemies, and in October 1536, was publicly executed and burned at the stake.

Yet Tyndale's work became the foundation of subsequent English versions, notably those of Coverdale, 1535; Thomas Matthew (probably a pseudonym for John Rogers), 1537; the Great Bible, 1539; the Geneva Bible, 1560; and the Bishops' Bible, 1568. In 1582 a translation of the New Testament, made from the Latin Vulgate by Roman Catholic scholars, was published at Rheims.

The translators who made the King James Version took into account all of these preceding versions; and comparison shows that it owes something to each of them. It kept felicitous phrases and apt expressions, from whatever source, which had stood the test of public usage. It owed most, especially in the New Testament, to Tyndale.

The King James Version had to compete with the Geneva Bible in popular use; but in the end it prevailed, and for more than two and a half centuries no other authorized translation of the Bible into English was made. The King James Version became the "Authorized Version" of the English-speaking peoples.

The King James Version has with good reason been termed "the noblest monument of English prose." Its revisers in 1881 expressed admiration for "its simplicity, its dignity, its power, its happy turns of expression . . . the music of its cadences, and the felicities of its rhythm." It entered, as no other book has, into the making of the personal character and the public institutions of the English-speaking peoples. We owe to it an incalculable debt.

Yet the King James Version has grave defects. By the middle of the nineteenth century, the development of Biblical studies and the discovery of many manuscripts more ancient than those upon which the King James Version was based, made it manifest that these defects are so many and so serious as to call for revision of the English translation. The task was undertaken, by authority of the Church of England, in 1870. The English Revised Version of the Bible was published in 1881–1885; and the American Standard Version, its variant embodying the preferences of the American scholars associated in the work, was published in 1901.

[xi]

Because of unhappy experience with unauthorized publications in the two decades between 1881 and 1901, which tampered with the text of the English Revised Version in the supposed interest of the American public, the American Standard Version was copyrighted, to protect the text from unauthorized changes. In 1928 this copyright was acquired by the International Council of Religious Education, and thus passed into the ownership of the churches of the United States and Canada which were associated in this Council through their boards of education and publication.

The Council appointed a committee of scholars to have charge of the text of the American Standard Version and to undertake inquiry as to whether further revision was necessary. For more than two years the Committee worked upon the problem of whether or not revision should be undertaken; and if so, what should be its nature and extent. In the end the decision was reached that there is need for a thorough revision of the version of 1901, which will stay as close to the Tyndale-King James tradition as it can in the light of our present knowledge of the Hebrew and Greek texts and their meaning on the one hand, and our present understanding of English on the other.

In 1937 the revision was authorized by vote of the Council, which directed that the resulting version should "embody the best results of modern scholarship as to the meaning of the Scriptures, and express this meaning in English diction which is designed for use in public and private worship and preserves those qualities which have given to the King James Version a supreme place in English literature."

Thirty-two scholars have served as members of the Committee charged with making the revision, and they have secured the review and counsel of an Advisory Board of fifty representatives of the cooperating denominations. The Committee has worked in two sections, one dealing with the Old Testament and one with the New Testament. Each section has submitted its work to the scrutiny of the members of the other section; and the charter of the Committee requires that all changes be agreed upon by a two-thirds vote of the total membership of the Committee. The Revised Standard Version of the New Testament was published in 1946. The publication of the Revised Standard Version of the Bible, containing the Old and New Testaments, was authorized by vote of the National Council of the Churches of Christ in the U.S.A. in 1951.

The problem of establishing the correct Hebrew and Aramaic text of the Old Testament is very different from the corresponding problem in the New Testament. For the New Testament we have a large number of Greek manuscripts, preserving many variant forms of the text. Some of them were made only two or three centuries later than the original composition of the books. For the Old Testament only late manuscripts survive, all (with the exception of the Dead Sea texts of Isaiah and Habakkuk and some fragments of other books) based on a standardized form of the text established many centuries after the books were written.

The present revision is based on the consonantal Hebrew and Aramaic text as fixed early in the Christian era and revised by Jewish scholars (the "Masoretes") of the sixth to ninth centuries. The vowel signs, which were added by the Masoretes, are accepted also in the main, but where a more probable and convincing reading can be obtained by assuming different vowels, this has been done. No notes are given in such cases, because the vowel points are less ancient and reliable than the consonants.

Departures from the consonantal text of the best manuscripts have been made only where it seems clear that errors in copying had been made before the text was standardized. Most of the corrections adopted are based on the ancient versions (translations into Greek, Aramaic, Syriac, and Latin), which were made before the time of the Masoretic revision and therefore reflect earlier forms of the text. In every such instance a footnote specifies the version or versions from which the correction has been derived, and also gives a translation of the Masoretic Text.

Sometimes it is evident that the text has suffered in transmission, but none of the versions provides a satisfactory restoration. Here we can only follow the best judgment of competent scholars as to the most probable reconstruction of the original text. Such corrections are indicated in the footnotes by the abbreviation *Cn*, and a translation of the Masoretic Text is added.

The discovery of the meaning of the text, once the best readings have been established, is aided by many new resources for understanding the original languages. Much progress has been made in the historical and comparative study of these languages. A vast quantity of writings in related Semitic languages, some of them only recently discovered, has greatly enlarged our knowledge of the vocabulary and grammar of Biblical Hebrew and Aramaic. Sometimes the present translation will be found to render a Hebrew word in a sense quite different from that of the traditional interpretation. It has not been felt necessary in such cases to attach a footnote, because no change in the text is involved and it may be assumed that the new rendering was not adopted without convincing evidence. The analysis of religious texts from the ancient Near East has made clearer the significance of ideas and practices recorded in the Old Testament. Many difficulties and obscurities, of course, remain. Where the choice between two meanings is particularly difficult or doubtful, we have given an alternative rendering in a footnote. If in the judgment of the Committee the meaning of a passage is quite uncertain or obscure, either because of corruption in the text or because of the inadequacy of our present knowledge of the language, that fact is indicated by a note. It should not be assumed, however, that the Committee was entirely sure or unanimous concerning every rendering not so indicated. To record all minority views was obviously out of the question.

A major departure from the practice of the American Standard Version is the rendering of the Divine Name, the "Tetragrammaton." The American Standard Version used the term "Jehovah"; the King James Version had employed this in four places, but everywhere else, except in three cases where it was employed as part of a proper name, used the English word LORD (or in certain cases GOD) printed in capitals. The present revision returns to the procedure of the King James Version, which follows the precedent of the ancient Greek and Latin translators and the long established practice in the reading of the Hebrew scriptures in the synagogue. While it is almost if not quite certain that the Name was originally pronounced "Yahweh," this pronunciation was not indicated when the Masoretes added vowel signs to the consonantal Hebrew text. To the four consonants YHWH of the Name, which had come to be regarded as too sacred to be pronounced, they attached vowel signs indicating that in its place should be read the Hebrew word *Adonai* meaning "Lord" (or *Elohim* meaning "God"). The ancient Greek translators substituted the word *Kyrios* (Lord) for the Name. The Vulgate likewise used the Latin word *Dominus*. The form "Jehovah" is of late medieval origin; it is a combination of the consonants of the Divine Name and the vowels attached to it by the Masoretes but belonging to an entirely different word. The sound of Y is represented by J and the sound of W by V, as in Latin. For two reasons the Committee has returned to the more familiar usage of the King James Version: (1) the word "Jehovah" does not accurately represent any form of the Name ever used in Hebrew; and (2) the use of any proper name for the one and only God, as though there were other gods from whom He had to be distinguished, was discontinued in Judaism before the Christian era and is entirely inappropriate for the universal faith of the Christian Church.

The King James Version of the New Testament was based upon a Greek text that was marred by mistakes, containing the accumulated errors of fourteen centuries of manuscript copying. It was essentially the Greek text of the New Testament as edited by Beza, 1589, who closely followed that published by Erasmus, 1516–1535, which was based upon a few medieval manuscripts. The earliest and best of the eight manuscripts which Erasmus consulted was from the tenth century, and he made the least use of it because it differed most from the commonly received text; Beza had access to two manuscripts of great value, dating from the fifth and sixth centuries, but he made very little use of them because they differed from the text published by Erasmus.

We now possess many more ancient manuscripts of the New Testament, and are far better equipped to seek to recover the original wording of the Greek text. The evidence for the text of the books of the New Testament is better than for any other ancient book, both in the number of extant manuscripts and in the nearness of the date of some of these manuscripts to the date when the book was originally written.

The revisers in the 1870's had most of the evidence that we now have for the Greek text, though the most ancient of all extant manuscripts of the Greek New Testament were not discovered until 1931. But they lacked the resources which discoveries within the past eighty years have afforded for understanding the vocabulary, grammar and idioms of the Greek New Testament. An amazing body of Greek papyri has been unearthed in Egypt since the 1870's—private letters, official reports, wills, business accounts, petitions, and other such trivial, everyday recordings of the activities of human beings. In 1895 appeared the first of Adolf Deissmann's studies of these ordinary materials. He proved that many words which had hitherto been assumed to belong to what was called "Biblical Greek" were current in the spoken vernacular of the first century A.D. The New Testament was written in the Koiné, the common Greek which was spoken and understood practically everywhere throughout the Roman Empire in the early centuries of the Christian era. This development in the study of New Testament Greek has come since the work on the English Revised Version and the American Standard Version was done, and at many points sheds new light upon the meaning of the Greek text.

A major reason for revision of the King James Version, which is valid for both the Old Testament and the New Testament, is the change since 1611 in English usage. Many forms of expression have become archaic, while still generally intelligible—the use of thou, thee, thy, thine and the verb endings -est and -edst, the verb endings -eth and -th, it came to pass that, whosoever, whatsoever, insomuch that, because that, for that, unto, howbeit, peradventure, holden, aforetime, must needs, would fain, behooved, to you-ward, etc. Other words are obsolete and no longer understood by the common reader. The greatest problem, however, is presented by the English words which are still in constant use but now convey a different meaning from that which they had in 1611 and in the King James Version. These words were once accurate translations of the Hebrew and Greek Scriptures; but now, having changed in meaning, they have become misleading. They no longer say what the King James translators meant them to say.

Thus, the King James Version uses the word "let" in the sense of "hinder," "prevent" to mean "precede," "allow" in the sense of "approve," "communicate" for "share," "conversation" for "conduct," "comprehend" for "overcome," "ghost" for "spirit," "wealth" for "well-being," "allege" for "prove," "demand" for "ask," "take no thought" for "be not anxious," etc.

The Revised Standard Version of the Bible, containing the Old and New Testaments, was published on September 30, 1952, and has met with wide acceptance. This preface does not undertake to set forth in detail the lines along which the revision proceeded. That is done in pamphlets entitled *An Introduction to the Revised Standard Version of the Old Testament* and *An Introduction to the Revised Standard Version of the New Testament,* written by members of the Committee and designed to help the general public to understand the main principles which have guided this comprehensive revision of the King James and American Standard versions.

These principles were reaffirmed by the Committee in 1959, in connection with a study of criticisms and suggestions from various readers. As a result, a few changes were authorized for subsequent editions, most of them corrections of punctuation, capitalization, or footnotes. Some of them are changes of words or phrases made in the interest of consistency, clarity, or accuracy of translation.

The Revised Standard Version Bible Committee is a continuing body, holding its meetings at regular intervals. It has become both ecumenical and international, with Protestant and Catholic members, who come from Great Britain, Canada, and the United States.

The Second Edition of the translation of the New Testament (1971) profits from textual and linguistic studies published since the Revised Standard Version New Testament was first issued in 1946. Many proposals for modification were submitted to the Committee by individuals and by two denominational committees. All of these were given careful attention by the Committee.

Two passages, the longer ending of Mark (16.9–20) and the account of the woman caught in adultery (Jn 7.53–8.11), are restored to the text, separated from it by a blank space and accompanied by informative notes describing the various arrangements of the text in the ancient authorities. With new manuscript support two passages, Lk 22.19b–20 and 24.51b, are restored to the text, and one passage, Lk 22.43–44, is placed in the note, as is a phrase in Lk 12.39. Notes are added which indicate significant variations, additions, or omissions in the ancient authorities (Mt 9.34; Mk 3.16; 7.4; Lk 24.32,51, etc.). Among the new notes are those giving the equivalence of ancient coinage with the contemporary day's or year's wages of a laborer (Mt 18.24,28; 20.2; etc.). Some of the revisions clarify the meaning through rephrasing or reordering the text (see Mk 5.42; Lk 22.29–30; Jn 10.33; 1 Cor 3.9; 2 Cor 5.19; Heb 13.13). Even when the changes appear to be largely matters of English style, they have the purpose of presenting to the reader more adequately the meaning of the text (see Mt 10.8; 12.1; 15.29; 17.20; Lk 7.36; 11.17; 12.40; Jn 16.9; Rom 10.16; 1 Cor 12.24; 2 Cor 2.3; 3.5,6; etc.).

The Revised Standard Version Bible seeks to preserve all that is best in the English Bible as it has been known and used through the years. It is intended for use in public and private worship, not merely for reading and instruction. We have resisted the temptation to use phrases that are merely current usage, and have sought to put the message of the Bible in simple, enduring words that are worthy to stand in the great Tyndale-King James tradition. We are glad to say, with the King James translators: "Truly (good Christian Reader) we never thought from the beginning, that we should need to make a new Translation, nor yet to make of a bad one a good one . . . but to make a good one better."

The Bible is more than a historical document to be preserved. And it is more than a classic of English literature to be cherished and admired. It is a record of God's dealing with men, of God's revelation of Himself and His will. It records the life and work of Him in whom the Word of God became flesh and dwelt among men. The Bible carries its full message, not to those who regard it simply as a heritage of the past or praise its literary style, but to those who read it that they may discern and understand God's Word to men. That Word must not be disguised in phrases that are no longer clear, or hidden under words that have changed or lost their meaning. It must stand forth in language that is direct and plain and meaningful to people today. It is our hope and our earnest prayer that this Revised Standard Version of the Bible may be used by God to speak to men in these momentous times, and to help them to understand and believe and obey His Word.

THE BOOKS OF THE BIBLE

The Old Testament

The New Testament

ABBREVIATIONS OF THE BOOKS OF THE BIBLE

		PAGE				PAGE
Acts	The Acts	1319		Jude	Jude	1491
Am.	Amos	1107		1 Kg.	1 Kings	413
1 Chr.	1 Chronicles	495		2 Kg.	2 Kings	454
2 Chr.	2 Chronicles	530		Lam.	Lamentations	991
Col.	Colossians	1428		Lev.	Leviticus	122
1 Cor.	1 Corinthians	1380		Lk.	Luke	1240
2 Cor.	2 Corinthians	1398		Mal.	Malachi	1160
Dan.	Daniel	1067		Mic.	Micah	1123
Dt.	Deuteronomy	214		Mk.	Mark	1213
Ec.	Ecclesiastes	805		Mt.	Matthew	1171
Eph.	Ephesians	1417		Nah.	Nahum	1132
Est.	Esther	603		Neh.	Nehemiah	586
Ex.	Exodus	67		Num.	Numbers	160
Ezek.	Ezekiel	1000		Ob.	Obadiah	1118
Ezra	Ezra	573		1 Pet.	1 Peter	1474
Gal.	Galatians	1410		2 Pet.	2 Peter	1480
Gen.	Genesis	1		Phil.	Philippians	1423
Hab.	Habakkuk	1136		Philem.	Philemon	1453
Hag.	Haggai	1145		Pr.	Proverbs	769
Heb.	Hebrews	1455		Ps.	Psalms	656
Hos.	Hosea	1088		Rev.	Revelation	1493
Is.	Isaiah	822		Rom.	Romans	1361
Jas.	James	1469		Ru.	Ruth	325
Jer.	Jeremiah	908		1 Sam.	1 Samuel	330
Jg.	Judges	293		2 Sam.	2 Samuel	374
Jl.	Joel	1101		S. of S.	Song of Solomon	815
Jn.	John	1286		1 Th.	1 Thessalonians	1433
1 Jn.	1 John	1484		2 Th.	2 Thessalonians	1437
2 Jn.	2 John	1489		1 Tim.	1 Timothy	1440
3 Jn.	3 John	1490		2 Tim.	2 Timothy	1446
Job	Job	613		Tit.	Titus	1450
Jon.	Jonah	1120		Zech.	Zechariah	1148
Jos.	Joshua	263		Zeph.	Zephaniah	1140

MISCELLANEOUS ABBREVIATIONS

Other abbreviations used in the annotations throughout the Bible and in the notes to the books of the Old Testament are the following:

Ant.	Josephus, *Antiquities of the Jews*
Aram	Aramaic
B.J.	Josephus, *Jewish War* (*Bellum Judaïcum*)
Ch., chs.	Chapter, chapters
Cn	Correction; made where the text has suffered in transmission and the versions provide no satisfactory restoration but where the Standard Bible Committee agrees with the judgment of competent scholars as to the most probable reconstruction of the original text. The reader is referred to pp. xii–xiii for a statement of policy concerning text and notes.
e.g.	for example
Gk	Septuagint, Greek version of the Old Testament
Heb	Hebrew of the consonantal Masoretic Text of the Old Testament
i.e.	that is
Josephus	Flavius Josephus (Jewish historian, about A.D. 37 to about 95)
lit.	literally
Macc.	The book(s) of the Maccabees
Ms(s)	Manuscript(s)
MT	The Hebrew of the pointed Masoretic Text of the Old Testament
n.	note
Sam	Samaritan Hebrew text of the Old Testament
Syr	Syriac Version of the Old Testament
Tg	Targum
Vg	Vulgate, Latin Version of the Old Testament
v., vv.	Verse, verses

OTHER EXPLANATIONS

In the Old Testament the word LORD (printed in capital letters) represents the Divine name, Yahweh (for further information see pp. xiii–xiv).

In the annotations italics are used to designate the words which are quoted verbatim from the Scripture text. In the notes belonging to the Revised Standard Version (designated by italic letters and standing at the foot of the second column of the Scripture text) alternative renderings or readings are printed in italics.

In the annotations on the Synoptic Gospels (Matthew, Mark, and Luke) the cross references to parallel passages stand in parentheses immediately after the boldface heading of a new paragraph. For example, at the account of Jesus' transfiguration in Mk.9.2–8 the references to Mt.17.1–8 and Lk.9.28–36 indicate where the Synoptic

[xxi]

parallels are to be found; similar information is given at the passages in Matthew and Luke. A careful comparison of such parallel passages will often reveal the special emphases in each Synoptic account.

HOW TO LOOK UP REFERENCES

Jn.3.16	means the Gospel according to John, chapter 3, verse 16.
Is.9.1,6	means Isaiah, chapter 9, verse 1 and verse 6.
Rev.22.1–5	means Revelation, chapter 22, verses 1 to 5 inclusive.
Acts 8.4; 11.19	means Acts, chapter 8, verse 4; and chapter 11, verse 19 (of the same book).
See Heb.3.2 n.	means there is an annotation on Hebrews, chapter 3, verse 2. Both the Scripture passage and the annotation should be consulted.
v. 4a; v. 7b	means the first part of verse 4; the second part of verse 7.

The best commentary on the Bible is often some other text in the Bible: therefore it cannot be too strongly urged that, for the fullest comprehension of any one passage, all of the cross references should be looked up.

THE
OLD TESTAMENT

INTRODUCTION TO THE OLD TESTAMENT

THE OLD TESTAMENT may be described as the literary expression of the religious life of ancient Israel. More than a thousand years of time separate the earliest and the latest compositions in the Old Testament. It reflects a varied social, economic, political, religious, and geographical background; slave and free, the nomad and farmer, the oppressed poor and privileged landowners and rulers, proud empires and vassal states, the desert and the sown, rain-watered highlands and the great flood plains of the Nile and Tigris-Euphrates—these are among the settings of the drama of divine revelation. The Old Testament reflects the many facets of the life of Israel, and its literature takes many forms; in it are prose and poetry, myth and legend, folk tale and history, sacred hymns and a superb love song, religious and secular laws, proverbs of the wise and oracles of the prophets, epic poems, laments, parables, and allegories. Despite the variety in content as well as in viewpoint, there is a significant unity, centered in belief in the God of judgment and redemption, of justice and mercy, and springing out of the continuity and corporate nature of that people chosen by God to play the main role in the drama of revelation and from whom was to come Jesus of Nazareth. The Israelites were more history-conscious than any other people in the ancient world. Probably as early as the time of David and Solomon, out of a matrix of myth, legend, and history, there had appeared the earliest written form of the story of the saving acts of God from Creation to the conquest of the Promised Land, an account which later in modified form became a part of Scripture. But it was to be a long time before the idea of Scripture arose and the Old Testament took its present form.

The Jews reckoned three divisions within the Scriptures: the Law, the Prophets, and the Writings. The Law is the Pentateuch, the first five books, i.e. Genesis, Exodus, Leviticus, Numbers, and Deuteronomy. The Prophets consist of the Former Prophets and the Latter Prophets. The books of the Former Prophets are Joshua, Judges, Samuel, and Kings (1 and 2 Samuel are reckoned as one book, and so also 1 and 2 Kings). The Latter Prophets are Isaiah, Jeremiah, and Ezekiel (the "Major Prophets") and the book of the Twelve (the "Minor Prophets"—Hosea to Malachi). The remaining books belong to the Writings. In the Hebrew Bible, Ruth, Lamentations, and Daniel are placed among the Writings, a section which begins with the Psalms and ends with 1 and 2 Chronicles; this is in contrast with the English Bible, where the order is influenced by the Greek and Latin versions. Some have seen an allusion to this three-fold division in "the law of Moses and the prophets and the psalms" of Luke 24.44.

That the Bible was not written originally in English is a fact not always appreciated, and there are even those who are unaware of it. What we use is the translated Bible (see pp. 1551–1557). The New Testament was written in

Greek and the Old Testament in Hebrew, with the exception of parts of Daniel (2.4b–7.28) and Ezra (4.8–6.18; 7.12–26) and one verse in Jeremiah (10.11), which are in Aramaic. The translation of Hebrew and Aramaic presents distinctive and often difficult problems; they belong to the Semitic family of languages, to which Arabic, Assyrian and Babylonian, and Canaanite also belong, in contrast to Greek and English, which are Indo-European.

The text of the Old Testament, like that of the New Testament (see p. 1169), has occasionally suffered from copyists' errors and scribal emendations, some of which can be corrected in the light of the ancient versions; the notes of the RSV give many examples of this. The translator must also decide among variant readings in the Hebrew manuscripts themselves, a task complicated by the recent discovery of much earlier manuscripts of the Hebrew Old Testament than had previously been known. Before the time of the council of Jamnia, about A.D. 90–100, there did not exist a single standard text of the various books of Scripture regarded as possessing sole authority (a *textus receptus*). Rather, as the Dead Sea (Qumran) Scrolls afford evidence, there were variant recensions of the same Old Testament book. It is true that there was already in existence a form of that Hebrew text which was to be edited later by the Jewish scholars known as Masoretes (from about A.D. 600 to the 10th century) and their predecessors and which is the standard text used today, but there were also variant forms of the text. In contrast with this Qumran evidence of variant textual recensions, the Biblical manuscripts found further south in the Wilderness of Judea at Wadi Murabbaat and belonging to the early part of the second century A.D. (after A.D. 100) are strictly Masoretic (proto-Masoretic) in character, disclosing that by this time the standard text had been adopted. Although there are variants in the preserved manuscripts of the Masoretic Text, due largely to simple scribal errors, the Masoretic Text has been transmitted with incredible accuracy.

The books accepted as authoritative Scripture are spoken of as belonging to the "canon" (see p. 1169f.) of Scripture. If by canonical one means that a book must be regarded as having a special authority, that it is holy and inspired, that it is one of a strictly limited number of books, and that there is a single, standard text with its verbal form inviolable, then one cannot speak of a canon of Old Testament Scripture before about A.D. 100. Long before this, however, the Jews had their Scriptures.

The process by which the Jews became "the people of the Book" was gradual, and the development is shrouded in the mists of history and tradition. One might designate as their earliest Scripture "the book of the law" found in the Jerusalem temple in 621 B.C. and used as the basis for Josiah's reform. It is generally agreed that it is now incorporated within the present book of Deuteronomy (chs. 5[12?]–26; 28). Another landmark is "the book of the law of Moses" brought by Ezra from Babylonia in 458 (398 ?) B.C. (Ezra 7.6–10,14; Neh. chs. 8-10). This has been variously identified by scholars as the prototype or earlier form of that legislation which became the P Code in the Pentateuch, or the P Code itself, or the completed Pentateuch (see the Introduction to the Pentateuch). The date of the final compilation of the Pentateuch or Law, which was the first corpus or larger body of literature that came to be regarded by the Jews as authoritative Scripture, is uncertain, although some have conservatively dated it at the time of the Exile in the sixth century. Since the P Source is found in Genesis through Joshua, those responsible for the final form of the Pentateuch must have looked upon Joshua as a continuation of it, but because the career of Moses did not extend beyond Deuteronomy, only Genesis to Deuteronomy came to be regarded as Mosaic in origin, and so the Law was limited to the Pentateuch. Certainly before the middle of the third century B.C., when according to tradition the Pentateuch was first translated into Greek, it had achieved a primary status as the Scripture of the Jews. It was to retain this primary position even after the body of Scripture had been enlarged to include the Prophets and the Writings. When in the second century B.C. the Samaritans finally separated from Judaism, they retained the Pentateuch as their sole Scripture, preserving it in a script derived from the old Hebrew script which was revived in the Maccabean period.

Before the adoption of the Pentateuch as the Law of Moses, there had been compiled and edited in the spirit and diction of the Deuteronomic "school" the group of books consisting of Deuteronomy, Joshua, Judges, Samuel, and Kings, in much their present form. This may have occurred in two stages, i.e. shortly before the death of Josiah in 609 B.C. and during the Exile in the middle of the sixth century. Isaiah, Jeremiah, Ezekiel, and the book of the Twelve were edited and compiled during the post-exilic period. The process of compiling and editing the Latter Prophets is illustrated by the addition of chs. 40–66 to the book of Isaiah and chs. 9–14 to the prophecies of Zechariah, by the superscriptions giving information about the person and time of the prophet, and by certain additions and changes mentioned in the annotations in this volume. The editing was both an adaptation of the books of the prophets to the needs of the post-exilic period and a recognition of the relevance of the prophetic messages for contemporary as well as historic Israel. Just when the Former Prophets and the Latter Prophets came to be regarded as a definitely limited body of Scripture is not clear. Ben Sirach, the author of the apocryphal book of Ecclesiasticus, writing around 180 B.C., seems to have regarded his work as a continuation of the Prophets and the books of Wisdom. The grandson of Ben Sirach (in his Preface to Ecclesiasticus) refers to the three-fold division of Scripture as the Law, the Prophets, and the other or rest of the books, although he does not necessarily imply a closed canon. The Former Prophets perhaps came to be associated with the Latter Prophets because of allusions in the Former Prophets to prophetic figures and because of a tradition that they were composed largely by prophets. Such a tradition is suggested in 1 Chr.29.29; 2 Chr.9.29; 12.15; 13.22; 20.34; 26.22; 32.32.

In contrast with the Pentateuch, the Former Prophets, and the Latter Prophets, the books of the Writings contain less homogeneous materials. They were not edited in groups or combined as in the case of the other books, but circulated separately. This should be qualified by the recognition that 1 and 2 Chronicles, Ezra, and Nehemiah are a connected history and the work of a single author ("the Chronicler"). It was not until about A.D. 100 that the authority of disputed books among the Writings was settled.

Among many writings not included in the canon were the books of the Apocrypha, which are found in the Septuagint (see p. 1543), and which, with the exception of 1 and 2 Esdras, were composed in the last two centuries B.C., certainly before the council of Jamnia (about A.D. 100). They could not be accepted, in part because of the current conviction that the Old Testament canon was closed at the time of Ezra when prophetic revelation was supposed to have ceased, or because, in the case of some, they had been written in Greek or else had ceased to be copied in Hebrew and Aramaic after their translation into Greek. There was also probably no widespread demand for their canonization.

THE PENTATEUCH

THE PENTATEUCH (literally, the "five scrolls") comprises the so-called "five books of Moses," known in Jewish tradition as the Law or Torah. These books elaborate basic themes of Israel's tradition: the revelation to the patriarchs against the background of primeval history (Genesis), the exodus from Egypt (Exodus chs. 1–18); the giving of the law in connection with the Sinai covenant (Exodus chs. 19–40; Leviticus); and the Lord's guidance of his people through the wilderness toward the promised land (Numbers). The last book, Deuteronomy, which gives Moses' final address to Israel, represents a pause in the flow of the narratives toward the realization of the promise (Joshua).

The Pentateuch embraces a great diversity of material which reflects Israel's pilgrimage from the time of Abraham to the Exile. The whole tradition, however, has been shaped by basic themes found essentially in the confession of faith preserved in Dt.26.5–10 (compare Jos. ch. 24). The Pentateuch may be regarded as an elaboration of this creedal statement, according to the interests and insights of various circles of tradition. In the early monarchy (perhaps about 950 B.C.) a traditionist from Judah (J) first organized the traditions into a written epic. Sometime later (between about 900 to 750 B.C.) a traditionist from North Israel or Ephraim (E) presented another version of the sacred story. In the seventh century B.C. Deuteronomy (D) was published (2 Kg. chs. 22–23), although this version rests upon old traditions. And finally, about the time of the Exile, priestly writers (P) rounded out the expanded tradition with materials preserved by the Jerusalem priesthood.

Thus the Pentateuch took shape over a long period of time. It preserves not only the tones which reverberated in the Mosaic period, but the overtones of meaning perceived by subsequent generations. In tribute to the creative influence of Moses, the whole tradition in its manifold richness was ascribed to the leader to whom, Israel believed, God had spoken as to no other man.

THE FIRST BOOK OF MOSES COMMONLY CALLED

GENESIS

Genesis, meaning "beginning," covers the times from the creation (i.e. the beginning of history) to the Israelite sojourn in Egypt. The book falls naturally into two main sections: chs. 1–11 deal with primeval history; chs. 12–50 treat the history of the "fathers" of Israel. The latter section tells the stories of Abraham (chs. 12–25), of Isaac and his twin sons Esau and Jacob (chs. 26–36), and of Jacob's family, the chief member of which was Joseph (chs. 37–50).

Unlike the stories of primeval history, those of the patriarchs can be read against the background of the history of the Near East in the early part of the second millennium B.C. (2000–1500), as documented from extra-Biblical sources (see "Survey of . . . Bible Lands," § 6). The primary purpose of the whole book, however, is to narrate God's dealings with men and, in particular, to interpret Israel's special role in his historical plan. Thus the call of Abraham (12.1–3) is the great turning point. God's creation had been marred by man's persistent wickedness which not even the flood erased. Out of this fallible human material, however, God gradually separated one family line and eventually chose one man, Abraham, promising that he and his people would have a great historical destiny and would be instrumental in bringing divine blessing upon all the dispersed families of mankind.

The book is composed of three main literary traditions (Judean, Ephraimite, and Priestly; see Introduction to Pentateuch) and these, in turn, often preserve ancient oral tradition. Thus the voices of many generations unite in the affirmation that the only true God is the God of Abraham, Isaac, and Jacob, whose redemptive purpose, like the rainbow of his promise, spans the course of human history from its remote beginning to its unrealized future.

N THE BEGINNING God CREATED[a] the heavens and the earth. 2 The earth was without form and void, and darkness was upon the face of the deep; and the Spirit[b] of God was moving over the face of the waters.

3 And God said, "Let there be light"; and there was light. 4 And God saw that the light was good; and God separated the light from the darkness. 5 God called the light Day, and the darkness he called Night. And there was evening and there was morning, one day.

6 And God said, "Let there be a firmament in the midst of the waters, and let it separate the waters from the waters." 7 And God made the firmament and separated the waters which were under the firmament from the waters which were above the firmament. And it was so. 8 And God called the firmament Heaven. And there was evening and there was morning, a second day.

9 And God said, "Let the waters under the heavens be gathered together into one place, and let the dry land appear." And it was so. 10 God

a Or When God began to create   b Or wind

1.1–2.4a: The Priestly story of creation. Out of original chaos God created an orderly world in which he assigned a preeminent place to man. 1: Probably a preface to the whole story, though possibly introductory to v. 3: When God began to create (note a) . . . God said (compare 2.4b–7). The ancients believed the world originated from and was founded upon a watery chaos (the deep; compare Ps.24.1,2), portrayed as a dragon in various myths (Is.51.9). 3–5: Creation by the word of God (Ps.33.6–9) expresses God's absolute lordship and prepares for the doctrine of creation out of nothing (2 Macc.7.28). Light was created first (2 Cor.4.6), even before the sun, and was separated from night, a remnant of uncreated darkness (v. 2). Since the Jewish day began with sundown, the order is evening and morning. 6–8: A firmament, or solid dome (Job 37.18), separated the upper from the lower waters (Ex.20.4; Ps.148.4). See

called the dry land Earth, and the waters that were gathered together he called Seas. And God saw that it was good. [11] And God said, "Let the earth put forth vegetation, plants yielding seed, and fruit trees bearing fruit in which is their seed, each according to its kind, upon the earth." And it was so. [12] The earth brought forth vegetation, plants yielding seed according to their own kinds, and trees bearing fruit in which is their seed, each according to its kind. And God saw that it was good. [13] And there was evening and there was morning, a third day.

14 And God said, "Let there be lights in the firmament of the heavens to separate the day from the night; and let them be for signs and for seasons and for days and years, [15] and let them be lights in the firmament of the heavens to give light upon the earth." And it was so. [16] And God made the two great lights, the greater light to rule the day, and the lesser light to rule the night; he made the stars also. [17] And God set them in the firmament of the heavens to give light upon the earth, [18] to rule over the day and over the night, and to separate the light from the darkness. And God saw that it was good. [19] And there was evening and there was morning, a fourth day.

20 And God said, "Let the waters bring forth swarms of living creatures, and let birds fly above the earth across the firmament of the heavens." [21] So God created the great sea monsters and every living creature that moves, with which the waters swarm, according to their kinds, and every winged bird according to its kind. And God saw that it was good. [22] And God blessed them, saying, "Be fruitful and multiply and fill the waters in the seas, and let birds multiply on the earth." [23] And there was evening and there was morning, a fifth day.

24 And God said, "Let the earth bring forth living creatures according to their kinds: cattle and creeping things and beasts of the earth according to their kinds." And it was so. [25] And God made the beasts of the earth according to their kinds and the cattle according to their kinds, and everything that creeps upon the ground according to its kind. And God saw that it was good.

26 Then God said, "Let us make man in our image, after our likeness; and let them have dominion over the fish of the sea, and over the birds of the air, and over the cattle, and over all the earth, and over every creeping thing that creeps upon the earth." [27] So God created man in his own image, in the image of God he created him; male and female he created them. [28] And God blessed them, and God said to them, "Be fruitful and multiply, and fill the earth and subdue it; and have dominion over the fish of the sea and over the birds of the air and over every living thing that moves upon the earth." [29] And God said, "Behold, I

7.11 n. **9–10:** The *seas*, a portion of the watery chaos, were assigned boundaries at the edge of the earth (Ps.139.9; Pr.8.29), where they continue to menace God's creation (Jer.5.22; Ps. 104.7–9). **11–13:** *Vegetation* was created only indirectly by God; his creative command was directed to *the earth*. **14–19:** The sun, moon, and stars are not divine powers that control man's destiny, as was believed in antiquity, but are only *lights*. Implicitly worship of the heavenly host is forbidden (Dt.4.19; Zeph.1.5). **20–23:** The creation of birds and fishes. *Sea monsters*, see Pss.74.13; 104.25–26. **24–25:** God's command for the earth to *bring forth* (compare v. 11) suggests that the animals are immediately bound to *the ground* and only indirectly related to God, in contrast with man. **26–27:** The solemn divine decision emphasizes man's supreme place at the climax of God's creative work. **26:** The plural *us, our* (3.22; 11.7; Is.6.8) probably refers to the divine beings who compose God's heavenly court (1 Kg.22.19; Job 1.6). Made in *the image of God*, man is the creature through whom God manifests his rule on earth. The language reflects "royal theology" in which, as in Egypt, the king was the "image of God." **27:** *Him, them:* man was not created to be alone but is *male and female* (2.18–24). *Man*, the Hebrew word is "adam," a collective, referring to mankind. **28:** As God's representative, man is given *dominion*

have given you every plant yielding seed which is upon the face of all the earth, and every tree with seed in its fruit; you shall have them for food. ³⁰ And to every beast of the earth, and to every bird of the air, and to everything that creeps on the earth, everything that has the breath of life, I have given every green plant for food." And it was so. ³¹ And God saw everything that he had made, and behold, it was very good. And there was evening and there was morning, a sixth day.

2 Thus the heavens and the earth were finished, and all the host of them. ² And on the seventh day God finished his work which he had done, and he rested on the seventh day from all his work which he had done. ³ So God blessed the seventh day and hallowed it, because on it God rested from all his work which he had done in creation.

4 These are the generations of the heavens and the earth when they were created.

In the day that the LORD God made the earth and the heavens, ⁵ when no plant of the field was yet in the earth and no herb of the field had yet sprung up–for the LORD God had not caused it to rain upon the earth, and there was no man to till the ground; ⁶ but a mist^c went up from the earth and watered the whole face of the ground– ⁷ then the LORD God formed man of dust from the ground, and breathed into his nostrils the breath of life; and man became a living being. ⁸ And the LORD God planted a garden in Eden, in the east; and there he put the man whom he had formed. ⁹ And out of the ground the LORD God made to grow every tree that is pleasant to the sight and good for food, the tree of life also in the midst of the garden, and the tree of the knowledge of good and evil.

10 A river flowed out of Eden to water the garden, and there it divided and became four rivers. ¹¹ The name of the first is Pishon; it is the one which flows around the whole land of Hav′-ilah, where there is gold; ¹² and the gold of that land is good; bdellium and onyx stone are there. ¹³ The name of the second river is Gihon; it is the one which flows around the whole land of Cush. ¹⁴ And the name of the third river is Tigris, which flows east of Assyria. And the fourth river is the Euphra′tes.

15 The LORD God took the man and put him in the garden of Eden to till it and keep it. ¹⁶ And the LORD God commanded the man, saying, "You may freely eat of every tree of the garden; ¹⁷ but of the tree of the knowledge of good and evil you shall not eat, for in the day that you eat of it you shall die."

18 Then the LORD God said, "It is not good that the man should be alone;

c Or *flood*

(Ps.8.6–8). **29–30:** His dominion is limited, as shown by the vegetarian requirement, modified in Noah's time (9.2–3); it is to be benevolent and peaceful (compare Is.11.6–8). **31:** *Very good* (vv. 4,10,12. etc.), corresponding perfectly to God's purpose. **2.1–3:** The verb *rested* (Hebrew *"shabat"*) is the basis of the noun sabbath (Ex.31.12–17).

2.4b–3.24: The creation and the fall of man. This is a different tradition from that in 1.1–2.4a, as evidenced by the flowing style and the different order of events, e.g. man is created before vegetation, animals, and woman. **6:** *A mist* (or *flood*) probably refers to the water which surged up from the subterranean ocean, the source of fertility (49.25). **7:** The word-play on *man* ('adham) and *ground* ('adhamah) introduces a motif characteristic of this early tradition: man's relation to the ground from which he was *formed*, like a potter molds clay (Jer.18.6). Man is not body and soul (a Greek distinction) but is dust animated by the LORD God's *breath* or "spirit" which constitutes him *a living being* or psycho-physical self (Ps.104.29–30; Job 34.14–15). **8–9:** *Eden*, meaning "delight," is a "garden of God" (Is.51.3; Ezek.31.8–9; Jl.2.3) or divine park. **9:** The *tree of life* was believed to confer eternal life (3.22; see Pr.3.18 n.; Rev.22.2,14,19), as the *tree of the knowledge of good and evil* confers wisdom (see 2 Sam.14.17; Is.7.15). **10–14:** The rivers, springing from the subterranean ocean (v. 6), flowed out to the four corners of the known

I will make him a helper fit for him."
¹⁹ So out of the ground the Lord God formed every beast of the field and every bird of the air, and brought them to the man to see what he would call them; and whatever the man called every living creature, that was its name. ²⁰ The man gave names to all cattle, and to the birds of the air, and to every beast of the field; but for the man there was not found a helper fit for him. ²¹ So the Lord God caused a deep sleep to fall upon the man, and while he slept took one of his ribs and closed up its place with flesh; ²² and the rib which the Lord God had taken from the man he made into a woman and brought her to the man. ²³ Then the man said,

"This at last is bone of my bones
  and flesh of my flesh;
she shall be called Woman,ᵈ
  because she was taken out of
  Man."ᵉ

²⁴ Therefore a man leaves his father and his mother and cleaves to his wife, and they become one flesh. ²⁵ And the man and his wife were both naked, and were not ashamed.

3 Now the serpent was more subtle than any other wild creature that the Lord God had made. He said to the woman, "Did God say, 'You shall not eat of any tree of the garden'?" ² And the woman said to the serpent, "We may eat of the fruit of the trees of the garden; ³ but God said, 'You shall not eat of the fruit of the tree which is in the midst of the garden, neither shall you touch it, lest you die.'" ⁴ But the serpent said to the woman, "You will not die. ⁵ For God knows that when you eat of it your eyes will be opened, and you will be like God, knowing good and evil." ⁶ So when the woman saw that the tree was good for food, and that it was a delight to the eyes, and that the tree was to be desired to make one wise, she took of its fruit and ate; and she also gave some to her husband, and he ate. ⁷ Then the eyes of both were opened, and they knew that they were naked; and they sewed fig leaves together and made themselves aprons.

8 And they heard the sound of the Lord God walking in the garden in the cool of the day, and the man and his wife hid themselves from the presence of the Lord God among the trees of the garden. ⁹ But the Lord God called to the man, and said to him, "Where are you?" ¹⁰ And he said, "I heard the sound of thee in the garden, and I was afraid, because I was naked; and I hid myself." ¹¹ He said, "Who told you that you were naked? Have you eaten of the tree of which I commanded you not to eat?" ¹² The man said, "The woman whom thou gavest to be with me, she gave me fruit of the tree, and I ate." ¹³ Then the Lord God said to the woman, "What is this that you have done?" The woman said, "The serpent beguiled me, and I ate." ¹⁴ The Lord

ᵈ Heb *ishshah*   ᵉ Heb *ish*

historical world. **15–17:** Man is given a task: to *till* and *keep* the garden. The prohibition against eating the forbidden fruit (3.3) stresses God's lordship and man's obedience. **18:** *To be alone* is not good, for man is social by nature (see 1.27 n.). *A helper fit for him* means a partner who is suitable for him, who completes his being. **19:** Naming the animals signifies man's dominion over them (compare 1.28). **21–23:** The deep affinity between man and woman is portrayed in the statement that God made the woman from the man's *rib*. **24–25:** Sex is not regarded as evil but as a God-given impulse which draws man and woman together so that *they become one flesh*. **25:** The two were unashamedly *naked*, a symbol of their guiltless relation to God and to one another. **3.1–7:** The temptation begins with the insinuation of doubt (vv. 1–3), increases as suspicion is cast upon God's motive (vv. 4–5), and becomes irresistible when the couple sense the possibilities of freedom (v. 6). **1:** *The serpent*, one of the wild creatures, distinguished by uncanny wisdom (Mt.10.16); there is a hint of a seductive power in man's environment, hostile to God. **5:** *Like God:* perhaps "like gods" (Septuagint), the divine beings of the heavenly court (v. 22; 1.26 n.). *Knowing good and evil*, see 2.9 n. **7:** Bodily shame (2.25) symbolizes anxiety about broken relationship with God. **8–13:** Anxiety leads to a guilty attempt to hide from God (Ps.139.7–12), described anthropomorphically as strolling in his garden. **14–15:** The

God said to the serpent,
"Because you have done this,
  cursed are you above all cattle,
  and above all wild animals;
upon your belly you shall go,
  and dust you shall eat
  all the days of your life.
¹⁵ I will put enmity between you and
  the woman,
  and between your seed and her
    seed;
he shall bruise your head,
  and you shall bruise his heel."
¹⁶ To the woman he said,
"I will greatly multiply your pain in
  childbearing;
  in pain you shall bring forth
  children,
yet your desire shall be for your
  husband,
  and he shall rule over you."
¹⁷ And to Adam he said,
"Because you have listened to the
  voice of your wife,
  and have eaten of the tree
of which I commanded you,
  'You shall not eat of it,'
cursed is the ground because of you;
  in toil you shall eat of it all the
  days of your life;
¹⁸ thorns and thistles it shall bring
  forth to you;
  and you shall eat the plants of the
  field.
¹⁹ In the sweat of your face
  you shall eat bread

till you return to the ground,
  for out of it you were taken;
you are dust,
  and to dust you shall return."

20 The man called his wife's name Eve,*f* because she was the mother of all living. ²¹ And the LORD God made for Adam and for his wife garments of skins, and clothed them.

22 Then the LORD God said, "Behold, the man has become like one of us, knowing good and evil; and now, lest he put forth his hand and take also of the tree of life, and eat, and live for ever"– ²³ therefore the LORD God sent him forth from the garden of Eden, to till the ground from which he was taken. ²⁴ He drove out the man; and at the east of the garden of Eden he placed the cherubim, and a flaming sword which turned every way, to guard the way to the tree of life.

4 Now Adam knew Eve his wife, and she conceived and bore Cain, saying, "I have gotten*g* a man with the help of the LORD." ² And again, she bore his brother Abel. Now Abel was a keeper of sheep, and Cain a tiller of the ground. ³ In the course of time Cain brought to the LORD an offering of the fruit of the ground, ⁴ and Abel brought of the firstlings of his flock and of their fat portions. And the LORD had regard for Abel and his offering,

f The name in Hebrew resembles the word for *living*
g Heb *qanah*, get

---

curse contains an old explanation of why the serpent crawls rather than walks and why men are instinctively hostile to it. **16:** This divine judgment contains an old explanation of woman's pain in childbirth, her sexual *desire* for her husband (i.e. her motherly impulse, compare 30.1), and her subordinate position to man in ancient society. **17–19:** An explanation of man's struggle to eke an existence from the soil. Work is not essentially evil (2.15) but it becomes *toil* as a result of man's broken relationship with his Creator. **17:** The Hebrew word *Adam* is usually translated "man" in this story (see 1.27 n.). Note that the curse is upon the ground, not man. **19:** *Till you return to the ground:* The mortal nature of man was implicit in the circumstances of his origin (2.7); because of man's disobedience, God now makes death an inevitable fate that haunts man throughout life. **21:** *Garments of skins,* a sign of God's protective care even in the time of judgment (4.15). **22:** *Like one of us,* see 3.5 n. *The tree of life* (2.9) does not figure in the temptation story, which explicitly speaks of only one tree in the center of the garden (3.3–6, 11–12, 17). **24:** *The cherubim,* guardians of sacred areas (1 Kg.8.6–7), were represented as winged creatures like the Sphynx of Egypt, half human and half lion (Ezek.41.18–19). *A flaming sword* (compare Jer.47.6) was placed near the cherubim to remind banished man of the impossibility of overstepping his creaturely bounds (compare Ezek.28.13–16).

4.1–26: Cain, Abel, and Seth. 2–5: The story reflects the tension between farmers and semi-nomads, two different ways of life that are symbolized in the two types of offerings. No reason

⁵ but for Cain and his offering he had no regard. So Cain was very angry, and his countenance fell. ⁶ The LORD said to Cain, "Why are you angry, and why has your countenance fallen? ⁷ If you do well, will you not be accepted? And if you do not do well, sin is couching at the door; its desire is for you, but you must master it."

8 Cain said to Abel his brother, "Let us go out to the field."ʰ And when they were in the field, Cain rose up against his brother Abel, and killed him. ⁹ Then the LORD said to Cain, "Where is Abel your brother?" He said, "I do not know; am I my brother's keeper?" ¹⁰ And the LORD said, "What have you done? The voice of your brother's blood is crying to me from the ground. ¹¹ And now you are cursed from the ground, which has opened its mouth to receive your brother's blood from your hand. ¹² When you till the ground, it shall no longer yield to you its strength; you shall be a fugitive and a wanderer on the earth." ¹³ Cain said to the LORD, "My punishment is greater than I can bear. ¹⁴ Behold, thou hast driven me this day away from the ground; and from thy face I shall be hidden; and I shall be a fugitive and a wanderer on the earth, and whoever finds me will slay me." ¹⁵ Then the LORD said to him, "Not so!ⁱ If any one slays Cain, vengeance shall be taken on him sevenfold." And the LORD put a mark on Cain, lest any who came upon him should kill him. ¹⁶ Then Cain went away from the presence of the LORD, and dwelt in the land of Nod,ʲ east of Eden.

17 Cain knew his wife, and she conceived and bore Enoch; and he built a city, and called the name of the city after the name of his son, Enoch. ¹⁸ To Enoch was born Irad; and Irad was the father of Me-hu′ja-el, and Me-hu′ja-el the father of Me-thu′sha-el, and Me-thu′sha-el the father of Lamech. ¹⁹ And Lamech took two wives; the name of the one was Adah, and the name of the other Zillah. ²⁰ Adah bore Jabal; he was the father of those who dwell in tents and have cattle. ²¹ His brother's name was Jubal; he was the father of all those who play the lyre and pipe. ²² Zillah bore Tubal-cain; he was the forger of all instruments of bronze and iron. The sister of Tubal-cain was Na′amah.

23 Lamech said to his wives:

"Adah and Zillah, hear my voice;
    you wives of Lamech, hearken to
        what I say:
I have slain a man for wounding me,
    a young man for striking me.
²⁴ If Cain is avenged sevenfold,
    truly Lamech seventy-sevenfold."

25 And Adam knew his wife again, and she bore a son and called his name Seth, for she said, "God has appointed for me another child instead of Abel, for Cain slew him." ²⁶ To Seth also a son was born, and he called his name Enosh. At that time men began to call upon the name of the LORD.

ʰ Sam Gk Syr Compare Vg: Heb lacks *Let us go out to the field*
ⁱ Gk Syr Vg: Heb *Therefore*   ʲ That is *Wandering*

is given for the acceptance of Abel's offering (compare Ex.33.19). **7:** Perhaps the meaning is that Cain himself will be *accepted*, even though his offering is not, if his deed springs from the right motive. Sin is pictured as a predatory animal, *couching at the door*. **10–11:** Blood is sacred to God, for it is the seat of life (Dt.12.23) and cries *from the ground* for vindication. **13–14:** Cain concludes that exile from the farmland is also exile from the LORD's *face*, i.e. protective presence, exposing him to blood revenge. **15:** The "mark of Cain" was a protective mark, perhaps a tattoo, signifying divine mercy. **17:** Here Cain is not the ancestor of nomadic tribesmen (vv. 11–16) but the founder of sedentary culture. **19–22:** Cultural advance is evidenced by the three occupations of Lamech's sons: shepherds, musicians, and smiths. **23–24:** An ancient song, probably once sung in praise of Lamech, is here quoted to illustrate the development of wickedness from murder to measureless blood revenge. **25–26:** From Cain's genealogy the narrator returns to the sequel of Cain's banishment (vv. 11–16) and introduces the new line of Seth. **26b:** This tradition traces the worship of the LORD (Yahweh) back to the time of Adam's grandson, in contrast to other traditions which claim that the sacred name was introduced in Moses' time (Ex.3.13–15; 6.2–3).

5 This is the book of the generations of Adam. When God created man, he made him in the likeness of God. ² Male and female he created them, and he blessed them and named them Man when they were created. ³ When Adam had lived a hundred and thirty years, he became the father of a son in his own likeness, after his image, and named him Seth. ⁴ The days of Adam after he became the father of Seth were eight hundred years; and he had other sons and daughters. ⁵ Thus all the days that Adam lived were nine hundred and thirty years; and he died.

6 When Seth had lived a hundred and five years, he became the father of Enosh. ⁷ Seth lived after the birth of Enosh eight hundred and seven years, and had other sons and daughters. ⁸ Thus all the days of Seth were nine hundred and twelve years; and he died.

9 When Enosh had lived ninety years, he became the father of Kenan. ¹⁰ Enosh lived after the birth of Kenan eight hundred and fifteen years, and had other sons and daughters. ¹¹ Thus all the days of Enosh were nine hundred and five years; and he died.

12 When Kenan had lived seventy years, he became the father of Ma-hal'-alel. ¹³ Kenan lived after the birth of Ma-hal'alel eight hundred and forty years, and had other sons and daughters. ¹⁴ Thus all the days of Kenan were nine hundred and ten years; and he died.

15 When Ma-hal'alel had lived sixty-five years, he became the father of Jared. ¹⁶ Ma-hal'alel lived after the birth of Jared eight hundred and thirty years, and had other sons and daughters. ¹⁷ Thus all the days of Ma-hal'-alel were eight hundred and ninety-five years; and he died.

18 When Jared had lived a hundred and sixty-two years he became the father of Enoch. ¹⁹ Jared lived after the birth of Enoch eight hundred years, and had other sons and daughters. ²⁰ Thus all the days of Jared were nine hundred and sixty-two years; and he died.

21 When Enoch had lived sixty-five years, he became the father of Methu'-selah. ²² Enoch walked with God after the birth of Methu'selah three hundred years, and had other sons and daughters. ²³ Thus all the days of Enoch were three hundred and sixty-five years. ²⁴ Enoch walked with God; and he was not, for God took him.

25 When Methu'selah had lived a hundred and eighty-seven years, he became the father of Lamech. ²⁶ Methu'selah lived after the birth of Lamech seven hundred and eighty-two years, and had other sons and daughters. ²⁷ Thus all the days of Methu'-selah were nine hundred and sixty-nine years; and he died.

28 When Lamech had lived a hundred and eighty-two years, he became the father of a son, ²⁹ and called his name Noah, saying, "Out of the ground which the Lord has cursed this one shall bring us relief from our work and from the toil of our hands." ³⁰ Lamech lived after the birth of Noah five hundred and ninety-five years, and had

---

5.1–32: The generations from Adam to Noah. This priestly tradition bridges the times from the creation to the flood. **1:** *The book of the generations* was evidently a separate source from which the writer drew genealogical data (6.9; 10.1; 11.10,27; etc.). **1b–2:** See 1.26–28. **3:** The divine *likeness* (v. 1; see 1.26 n.) was continued in Adam's son Seth, born *in his own likeness*, and thus was transmitted to succeeding generations without effacement (9.6). Priestly tradition makes no reference to the account of the fall of man. **4–32:** Babylonian tradition also reckons ten heroes before the flood but ascribes fantastically higher ages. In Hebrew tradition the ages decrease from 900–1000 (Adam to Noah), to 200–600 (Noah to Abraham), to 100–200 (the patriarchs), to the normal three-score years and ten (Ps.90.10). This list is somehow related to the genealogy of Cain (4.17–21) as shown by the resemblance of some of the names. **24:** Babylonian tradition also reports that the seventh hero before the flood was taken by God, i.e. translated (2 Kg.2.11). **29:** This verse, the only connection with the early traditions of Eden (3.17–19) and Cain and Abel, anticipates the new age inaugurated with Noah (9.20).

other sons and daughters. ³¹ Thus all the days of Lamech were seven hundred and seventy-seven years; and he died.

32 After Noah was five hundred years old, Noah became the father of Shem, Ham, and Japheth.

6 When men began to multiply on the face of the ground, and daughters were born to them, ² the sons of God saw that the daughters of men were fair; and they took to wife such of them as they chose. ³ Then the Lord said, "My spirit shall not abide in man for ever, for he is flesh, but his days shall be a hundred and twenty years." ⁴ The Nephilim were on the earth in those days, and also afterward, when the sons of God came in to the daughters of men, and they bore children to them. These were the mighty men that were of old, the men of renown.

5 The Lord saw that the wickedness of man was great in the earth, and that every imagination of the thoughts of his heart was only evil continually. ⁶ And the Lord was sorry that he had made man on the earth, and it grieved him to his heart. ⁷ So the Lord said, "I will blot out man whom I have created from the face of the ground, man and beast and creeping things and birds of the air, for I am sorry that I have made them." ⁸ But Noah found favor in the eyes of the Lord.

9 These are the generations of Noah. Noah was a righteous man, blameless in his generation; Noah walked with God. ¹⁰ And Noah had three sons, Shem, Ham, and Japheth.

11 Now the earth was corrupt in God's sight, and the earth was filled with violence. ¹² And God saw the earth, and behold, it was corrupt; for all flesh had corrupted their way upon the earth. ¹³ And God said to Noah, "I have determined to make an end of all flesh; for the earth is filled with violence through them; behold, I will destroy them with the earth. ¹⁴ Make yourself an ark of gopher wood; make rooms in the ark, and cover it inside and out with pitch. ¹⁵ This is how you are to make it: the length of the ark three hundred cubits, its breadth fifty cubits, and its height thirty cubits. ¹⁶ Make a roof*k* for the ark, and finish it to a cubit above; and set the door of the ark in its side; make it with lower, second, and third decks. ¹⁷ For behold, I will bring a flood of waters upon the earth, to destroy all flesh in which is the breath of life from under heaven; everything that is on the earth shall die. ¹⁸ But I will establish my covenant with you; and you shall come into the ark, you, your sons, your wife, and your sons' wives with you. ¹⁹ And of every living thing of all flesh, you

k Or *window*

6.1–4: The birth of the Nephilim is related to demonstrate the increase of wickedness on the earth. **1:** This old fragment of mythology connects immediately with chs. 2–4. **2:** *The sons of God* were divine beings who belonged to the heavenly court (1.26 n.). **3:** Despite the lustful intrusion of divine beings into the human sphere, man did not become semi-divine (compare 3.22–24) but remained a mortal creature in whom the Lord's *spirit* dwells temporarily (see 2.7 n.). **4:** Originally the story accounted for *the Nephilim* (Num.13.33; Dt.2.10–11), men of gigantic stature whose superhuman power was thought to result from divine-human marriage.

6.5–8.22: The great flood. God's judgment took the form of a destructive flood, and his mercy was shown in saving a remnant with whom he made a new historical beginning. **5–8:** An introduction, belonging to the old literary tradition found in 2.4b–3.24; 4.1–26; 6.1–4. **5:** The *heart* includes the will and reason, as shown by its capacity for *imagination* of thought. **7:** The Biblical account is superficially similar to the Babylonian Gilgamesh Epic. The Biblical perspective, however, is basically different, for the flood was not the expression of polytheistic caprice but of God's judgment upon the *wickedness of man*. **9:** Noah was *a righteous man*, i.e. he stood in right relationship to God (15.6). **11–22:** A parallel version. It is generally recognized that an earlier and a later (priestly) tradition have been combined. **11:** The earth, once seen to be "good" (1.31), is called *corrupt* owing to man's *violence* or wilful, lawless deeds. **14–16:** In the Babylonian epic too, the hero is commanded to build a houseboat, sealing it with pitch. **15:** The dimensions: about 450 × 75 × 45 feet.

shall bring two of every sort into the ark, to keep them alive with you; they shall be male and female. ²⁰ Of the birds according to their kinds, and of the animals according to their kinds, of every creeping thing of the ground according to its kind, two of every sort shall come in to you, to keep them alive. ²¹ Also take with you every sort of food that is eaten, and store it up; and it shall serve as food for you and for them." ²² Noah did this; he did all that God commanded him.

7 Then the LORD said to Noah, "Go into the ark, you and all your household, for I have seen that you are righteous before me in this generation. ² Take with you seven pairs of all clean animals, the male and his mate; and a pair of the animals that are not clean, the male and his mate; ³ and seven pairs of the birds of the air also, male and female, to keep their kind alive upon the face of all the earth. ⁴ For in seven days I will send rain upon the earth forty days and forty nights; and every living thing that I have made I will blot out from the face of the ground." ⁵ And Noah did all that the LORD had commanded him.

6 Noah was six hundred years old when the flood of waters came upon the earth. ⁷ And Noah and his sons and his wife and his sons' wives with him went into the ark, to escape the waters of the flood. ⁸ Of clean animals, and of animals that are not clean, and of birds, and of everything that creeps on the ground, ⁹ two and two, male and female, went into the ark

with Noah, as God had commanded Noah. ¹⁰ And after seven days the waters of the flood came upon the earth.

11 In the six hundredth year of Noah's life, in the second month, on the seventeenth day of the month, on that day all the fountains of the great deep burst forth, and the windows of the heavens were opened. ¹² And rain fell upon the earth forty days and forty nights. ¹³ On the very same day Noah and his sons, Shem and Ham and Japheth, and Noah's wife and the three wives of his sons with them entered the ark, ¹⁴ they and every beast according to its kind, and all the cattle according to their kinds, and every creeping thing that creeps on the earth according to its kind, and every bird according to its kind, every bird of every sort. ¹⁵ They went into the ark with Noah, two and two of all flesh in which there was the breath of life. ¹⁶ And they that entered, male and female of all flesh, went in as God had commanded him; and the LORD shut him in.

17 The flood continued forty days upon the earth; and the waters increased, and bore up the ark, and it rose high above the earth. ¹⁸ The waters prevailed and increased greatly upon the earth; and the ark floated on the face of the waters. ¹⁹ And the waters prevailed so mightily upon the earth that all the high mountains under the whole heaven were covered; ²⁰ the waters prevailed above the mountains, covering them fifteen cubits deep. ²¹ And all flesh died that moved upon

7.1–10: This section is essentially a continuation of the early tradition (6.5–8). **2–3:** On clean and unclean animals, see Lev. ch. 11. (The priestly version mentions two animals of every sort [v. 9; 6.19], presuming that the clean-unclean distinction was introduced at Sinai.) **4:** The flood was caused by heavy rainfall, lasting *forty days and forty nights* (v. 12; compare the difference in the priestly version, v. 24). **11–24:** Largely from the priestly tradition. **11:** Here the flood was not caused by a rain storm but was a cosmic catastrophe resulting from opening the *windows of the heavens* (or the firmament) and the upsurging of the *fountains of the great deep* (or the subterranean watery chaos; see 1.6–8 n.). Thus the earth was threatened with a return to pre-creation chaos (1.2). **15:** The animals went in *two by two* (6.19; see 7.2 n.). **16b:** *The LORD shut him in,* a note from the early tradition, which delights in anthropomorphic touches. **18–20:** The waters covered *all the high mountains,* thus threatening a confluence of the upper and lower waters (1.6). Archaeological evidence suggests that traditions of a prehistoric flood covering the whole earth are heightened versions of local inundations, e.g. in the Tigris-

the earth, birds, cattle, beasts, all swarming creatures that swarm upon the earth, and every man; ²² everything on the dry land in whose nostrils was the breath of life died. ²³ He blotted out every living thing that was upon the face of the ground, man and animals and creeping things and birds of the air; they were blotted out from the earth. Only Noah was left, and those that were with him in the ark. ²⁴ And the waters prevailed upon the earth a hundred and fifty days.

8 But God remembered Noah and all the beasts and all the cattle that were with him in the ark. And God made a wind blow over the earth, and the waters subsided; ² the fountains of the deep and the windows of the heavens were closed, the rain from the heavens was restrained, ³ and the waters receded from the earth continually. At the end of a hundred and fifty days the waters had abated; ⁴ and in the seventh month, on the seventeenth day of the month, the ark came to rest upon the mountains of Ar'arat. ⁵ And the waters continued to abate until the tenth month; in the tenth month, on the first day of the month, the tops of the mountains were seen.

6 At the end of forty days Noah opened the window of the ark which he had made, ⁷ and sent forth a raven; and it went to and fro until the waters were dried up from the earth. ⁸ Then he sent forth a dove from him, to see if the waters had subsided from the face of the ground; ⁹ but the dove found no place to set her foot, and she returned to him to the ark, for the waters were still on the face of the whole earth. So he put forth his hand and took her

and brought her into the ark with him. ¹⁰ He waited another seven days, and again he sent forth the dove out of the ark; ¹¹ and the dove came back to him in the evening, and lo, in her mouth a freshly plucked olive leaf; so Noah knew that the waters had subsided from the earth. ¹² Then he waited another seven days, and sent forth the dove; and she did not return to him any more.

13 In the six hundred and first year, in the first month, the first day of the month, the waters were dried from off the earth; and Noah removed the covering of the ark, and looked, and behold, the face of the ground was dry. ¹⁴ In the second month, on the twenty-seventh day of the month, the earth was dry. ¹⁵ Then God said to Noah, ¹⁶ "Go forth from the ark, you and your wife, and your sons and your sons' wives with you. ¹⁷ Bring forth with you every living thing that is with you of all flesh–birds and animals and every creeping thing that creeps on the earth–that they may breed abundantly on the earth, and be fruitful and multiply upon the earth." ¹⁸ So Noah went forth, and his sons and his wife and his sons' wives with him. ¹⁹ And every beast, every creeping thing, and every bird, everything that moves upon the earth, went forth by families out of the ark.

20 Then Noah built an altar to the LORD, and took of every clean animal and of every clean bird, and offered burnt offerings on the altar. ²¹ And when the LORD smelled the pleasing odor, the LORD said in his heart, "I will never again curse the ground because of man, for the imagination of man's

Euphrates basin. **8.1–5:** In the main a continuation of the priestly tradition. Because God *remembered Noah*, he stayed the cosmic destruction by water from above and below (v. 2a). **4:** In the Babylonian epic the boat also rested on a mountain. *Ararat* (2 Kg.19.37; Jer.51.27) is the name of a region in Armenia. **6–12:** Essentially from the early tradition. In the Babylonian epic the hero sent out two birds, a dove and a swallow, each of which came back; the third, a raven, did not return. **13–19:** A continuation of the priestly account. **20–22:** The early tradition relates that Noah sacrificed *burnt offerings* (Lev. ch. 1) of clean animals (see 7.2–3 n.). In the Babylonian epic the hero offered sacrifices and "the gods smelt [compare v. 21] the goodly savor." For the curse, compare 3.17. Despite the evil *imagination of man's heart* (6.5), the LORD'S steadfast mercy will be expressed in the regularities of nature, *seedtime and harvest*, etc.

heart is evil from his youth; neither will I ever again destroy every living creature as I have done. ²² While the earth remains, seedtime and harvest, cold and heat, summer and winter, day and night, shall not cease."

9 And God blessed Noah and his sons, and said to them, "Be fruitful and multiply, and fill the earth. ² The fear of you and the dread of you shall be upon every beast of the earth, and upon every bird of the air, upon everything that creeps on the ground and all the fish of the sea; into your hand they are delivered. ³ Every moving thing that lives shall be food for you; and as I gave you the green plants, I give you everything. ⁴ Only you shall not eat flesh with its life, that is, its blood. ⁵ For your lifeblood I will surely require a reckoning; of every beast I will require it and of man; of every man's brother I will require the life of man. ⁶ Whoever sheds the blood of man, by man shall his blood be shed; for God made man in his own image. ⁷ And you, be fruitful and multiply, bring forth abundantly on the earth and multiply in it."

8 Then God said to Noah and to his sons with him, ⁹ "Behold, I establish my covenant with you and your descendants after you, ¹⁰ and with every living creature that is with you, the birds, the cattle, and every beast of the earth with you, as many as came out of the ark.ᴵ ¹¹ I establish my covenant with you, that never again shall all flesh be cut off by the waters of a flood, and never again shall there be a flood to destroy the earth." ¹² And God said, "This is the sign of the covenant which I make between me and you and every living creature that is with you, for all future generations: ¹³ I set my bow in the cloud, and it shall be a sign of the covenant between me and the earth. ¹⁴ When I bring clouds over the earth and the bow is seen in the clouds, ¹⁵ I will remember my covenant which is between me and you and every living creature of all flesh; and the waters shall never again become a flood to destroy all flesh. ¹⁶ When the bow is in the clouds, I will look upon it and remember the everlasting covenant between God and every living creature of all flesh that is upon the earth." ¹⁷ God said to Noah, "This is the sign of the covenant which I have established between me and all flesh that is upon the earth."

18 The sons of Noah who went forth from the ark were Shem, Ham, and Japheth. Ham was the father of Canaan. ¹⁹ These three were the sons of Noah; and from these the whole earth was peopled.

20 Noah was the first tiller of the soil. He planted a vineyard; ²¹ and he drank of the wine, and became drunk, and lay uncovered in his tent. ²² And Ham, the father of Canaan, saw the nakedness of his father, and told his two brothers outside. ²³ Then Shem

l Gk: Heb repeats *every beast of the earth*

9.1–19: God's covenant with Noah included all mankind under divine promise and law. **1:** The new age opened with a renewal of the blessing which had been given at creation (v. 7; compare 1.28). **3–6:** The command to exercise dominion (1.28–30) is qualified by the permission to eat animal flesh but not with *its life*, i.e. *its blood* (see 4.10–11 n.). The violence which had corrupted the earth (6.11) is restrained by a very old law against murder, the validity of which is grounded in the creation: man is made in God's *image* (1.26–27). These verses set forth the laws given to Noah, binding not only on Israel but on all men (Acts 15.20; 21.25). **8–11:** The preservation of the natural order from the waters of chaos is guaranteed by a *covenant* (see 17.2 n.). Unlike later covenants (ch. 17; Ex. ch. 24), this is a universal covenant with Noah, his *descendants*, and *every living creature*, for Noah's three sons (6.10; 9.18–19) are regarded as the ancestors of all the nations (see ch. 10). **13:** Ancients imagined the rainbow as God's weapon (bow) from which the lightnings of his arrows were shot (Ps.7.12–13; Hab.3.9–11). God places his weapon in the heavens as a *sign*, or visible token, that his wrath has abated.

9.18–27: Noah's curse upon Canaan. 20: In the new age, Noah was the *first tiller of the soil*. His success in agriculture fulfilled the prophecy made at his birth (5.29). **22:** Since the curse was later put on Canaan rather than Ham (v. 25), it is likely that Canaan was the actor originally.

and Japheth took a garment, laid it upon both their shoulders, and walked backward and covered the nakedness of their father; their faces were turned away, and they did not see their father's nakedness. 24 When Noah awoke from his wine and knew what his youngest son had done to him, 25 he said,

"Cursed be Canaan;
    a slave of slaves shall he be to
      his brothers."
26 He also said,
"Blessed by the LORD my God
    be Shem;*m*
and let Canaan be his slave.
27 God enlarge Japheth,
    and let him dwell in the tents
      of Shem;
    and let Canaan be his slave."

28 After the flood Noah lived three hundred and fifty years. 29 All the days of Noah were nine hundred and fifty years; and he died.

10 These are the generations of the sons of Noah, Shem, Ham, and Japheth; sons were born to them after the flood.

2 The sons of Japheth: Gomer, Magog, Madai, Javan, Tubal, Meshech, and Tiras. 3 The sons of Gomer: Ash'kenaz, Riphath, and Togar'mah. 4 The sons of Javan: Eli'shah, Tarshish, Kittim, and Do'danim. 5 From these the coastland peoples spread. These are the sons of Japheth*n* in their lands, each with his own lan-guage, by their families, in their nations.

6 The sons of Ham: Cush, Egypt, Put, and Canaan. 7 The sons of Cush: Seba, Hav'ilah, Sabtah, Ra'amah, and Sab'teca. The sons of Ra'amah: Sheba and Dedan. 8 Cush became the father of Nimrod; he was the first on earth to be a mighty man. 9 He was a mighty hunter before the LORD; therefore it is said, "Like Nimrod a mighty hunter before the LORD." 10 The beginning of his kingdom was Ba'bel, Erech, and Accad, all of them in the land of Shinar. 11 From that land he went into Assyria, and built Nin'eveh, Reho'both-Ir, Calah, and 12 Resen between Nin'eveh and Calah; that is the great city. 13 Egypt became the father of Ludim, An'amim, Leha'bim, Naph-tu'him, 14 Pathru'sim, Caslu'him (whence came the Philistines), and Caph'torim.

15 Canaan became the father of Sidon his first-born, and Heth, 16 and the Jeb'usites, the Amorites, the Gir'-gashites, 17 the Hivites, the Arkites, the Sinites, 18 the Ar'vadites, the Zem'arites, and the Ha'mathites. Afterward the families of the Canaanites spread abroad. 19 And the territory of the Canaanites extended from Sidon, in the direction of Gerar, as far as Gaza, and in the direction of Sodom,

m Or *Blessed be the* LORD, *the God of Shem*
n Compare verses 20, 31. Heb lacks *These are the sons of Japheth*

24: Here Noah's *youngest son* is clearly Canaan, not Ham as in v. 22. **25:** The curse implies that Canaan's subjugation to Israel was the result of Canaanite sexual perversions (Lev.18.24–30). **26:** *Shem,* 10.21. **27:** *Japheth,* 10.2–5. The verse may refer to the Philistines, one of the sea-peoples who dwelt *in the tents of Shem,* i.e. conquered the coast of Canaan.

10.1–32: The table of the nations provides a background of world history for the call of Abraham (ch. 12). **1:** This list, which connects with 5.32, was probably drawn from the book of generations (5.1). The original unity of mankind is represented by the view that all the nations originated from Noah's three sons (9.19). Although the various "families" were separated by language and land (vv. 5,20,31), the present list is arranged primarily on the basis of political rather than ethnic considerations. **2–5:** *The sons of Japheth* (9.27) had their political center in Asia Minor, the former territory of the Hittites (Heth, v. 15). The spread of the *coastland peoples,* including the Philistines (see 9.27 n.), reflects population movements in the Aegean area about 1200 B.C. **6–20:** *The sons of Ham* lived in the Egyptian orbit. *Canaan* is included because it was nominally under Egyptian control from 1500–1200 B.C. **8–12:** An old fragment of tradition relates how Nimrod, a successful warrior, built a kingdom in *Shinar* (Babylonia) and Assyria. **15–20:** *Heth* (the Hittites), who once established a powerful empire in Asia Minor, disappeared as a world power in the twelfth century B.C. Here they are mentioned along with other Canaanite peoples; e.g. the *Jebusites* (located around Jerusalem), the *Amorites* (natives of

Gomor'rah, Admah, and Zeboi'im, as far as Lasha. ²⁰ These are the sons of Ham, by their families, their languages, their lands, and their nations.

21 To Shem also, the father of all the children of Eber, the elder brother of Japheth, children were born. ²² The sons of Shem: Elam, Asshur, Arpach'shad, Lud, and Aram. ²³ The sons of Aram: Uz, Hul, Gether, and Mash. ²⁴ Arpach'shad became the father of Shelah; and Shelah became the father of Eber. ²⁵ To Eber were born two sons: the name of the one was Peleg,ᵒ for in his days the earth was divided, and his brother's name was Joktan. ²⁶ Joktan became the father of Almo'dad, Sheleph, Hazarma'veth, Jerah, ²⁷ Hador'am, Uzal, Diklah, ²⁸ Obal, Abim'a-el, Sheba, ²⁹ Ophir, Hav'ilah, and Jobab; all these were the sons of Joktan. ³⁰ The territory in which they lived extended from Mesha in the direction of Sephar to the hill country of the east. ³¹ These are the sons of Shem, by their families, their languages, their lands, and their nations.

32 These are the families of the sons of Noah, according to their genealogies, in their nations; and from these the nations spread abroad on the earth after the flood.

11 Now the whole earth had one language and few words. ² And as men migrated from the east, they found a plain in the land of Shinar and settled there. ³ And they said to one another, "Come, let us make bricks, and burn them thoroughly." And they had brick for stone, and bitumen for mortar. ⁴ Then they said, "Come, let us build ourselves a city, and a tower with its top in the heavens, and let us make a name for ourselves, lest we be scattered abroad upon the face of the whole earth." ⁵ And the LORD came down to see the city and the tower, which the sons of men had built. ⁶ And the LORD said, "Behold, they are one people, and they have all one language; and this is only the beginning of what they will do; and nothing that they propose to do will now be impossible for them. ⁷ Come, let us go down, and there confuse their language, that they may not understand one another's speech." ⁸ So the LORD scattered them abroad from there over the face of all the earth, and they left off building the city. ⁹ Therefore its name was called Ba'bel, because there the LORD confusedᵖ the language of all the earth; and from there the LORD scattered them abroad over the face of all the earth.

10 These are the descendants of Shem. When Shem was a hundred years old, he became the father of Arpach'-

o That is *Division*
p Compare Heb *balal*, confuse

the Palestinian hill country), the *Hivites* (perhaps Horites or Hurrians; see 34.2). **21–31:** *Shem* is the father of Semitic peoples, *the children of Eber,* that is, all "Hebrews," including those Hebrews who later became Israel. During 1500–1200 B.C. waves of Hebrews came into Syria-Palestine and eventually established states, such as *Aram* or Syria (v. 23), Moab, Edom, and Israel.

11.1–9: The tower of Babel. The LORD judged man's presumptuous effort by scattering the peoples and confusing their tongues. **1:** *One language,* compare 10.5,20,31. This tradition is clearly independent of and different from the table of nations. **2:** *Shinar,* 10.10. The *plain* is the Tigris-Euphrates basin. **4:** In the eyes of nomads Mesopotamian city culture was characterized by the ziggurat, a pyramidal temple tower whose summit was believed to be the gateway to heaven. **6:** 3.22. **7:** *Let us,* see 1.26 n. **8:** The enterprise, motivated by a Promethean desire for unity, fame, and security (v. 4), ended in misunderstanding and thus arose the various peoples. **9:** *Babel,* meaning "gate of God," is here interpreted by the Hebrew verb "confuse" (see note p). The story, now told to show the LORD's judgment upon the continuing sin of mankind, once explained the origin of languages and the cultural glory of Babylon, the center of Hammurabi's empire.

11.10–32: Genealogies to Abraham. The line of Shem (10.21–31) leads to Terah's three sons (v. 26) and narrows down to Abraham, showing how God chose Abraham and his seed from all the families of the earth. **10:** Here begin further quotations from the book of genealogies (5.1).

shad two years after the flood; [11] and Shem lived after the birth of Arpach'shad five hundred years, and had other sons and daughters.

12 When Arpach'shad had lived thirty-five years, he became the father of Shelah; [13] and Arpach'shad lived after the birth of Shelah four hundred and three years, and had other sons and daughters.

14 When Shelah had lived thirty years, he became the father of Eber; [15] and Shelah lived after the birth of Eber four hundred and three years, and had other sons and daughters.

16 When Eber had lived thirty-four years, he became the father of Peleg; [17] and Eber lived after the birth of Peleg four hundred and thirty years, and had other sons and daughters.

18 When Peleg had lived thirty years, he became the father of Re'u; [19] and Peleg lived after the birth of Re'u two hundred and nine years, and had other sons and daughters.

20 When Re'u had lived thirty-two years, he became the father of Serug; [21] and Re'u lived after the birth of Serug two hundred and seven years, and had other sons and daughters.

22 When Serug had lived thirty years, he became the father of Nahor; [23] and Serug lived after the birth of Nahor two hundred years, and had other sons and daughters.

24 When Nahor had lived twenty-nine years, he became the father of Terah; [25] and Nahor lived after the birth of Terah a hundred and nineteen years, and had other sons and daughters.

26 When Terah had lived seventy years, he became the father of Abram, Nahor, and Haran.

27 Now these are the descendants of Terah. Terah was the father of Abram, Nahor, and Haran; and Haran was the father of Lot. [28] Haran died before his father Terah in the land of his birth, in Ur of the Chalde'ans. [29] And Abram and Nahor took wives; the name of Abram's wife was Sar'ai, and the name of Nahor's wife, Milcah, the daughter of Haran the father of Milcah and Iscah. [30] Now Sar'ai was barren; she had no child.

31 Terah took Abram his son and Lot the son of Haran, his grandson, and Sar'ai his daughter-in-law, his son Abram's wife, and they went forth together from Ur of the Chalde'ans to go into the land of Canaan; but when they came to Haran, they settled there. [32] The days of Terah were two hundred and five years; and Terah died in Haran.

12 Now the LORD said to Abram, "Go from your country and your kindred and your father's house to the land that I will show you. [2] And I will make of you a great nation, and I will bless you, and make your name great, so that you will be a blessing. [3] I will bless those who bless you, and him who curses you I will curse; and by you all the families of the earth shall bless themselves."*q*

4 So Abram went, as the LORD had told him; and Lot went with him. Abram was seventy-five years old when he departed from Haran. [5] And

q Or in you all the families of the earth shall be blessed

27: *Abram*, see 17.5. 30: *Sarai*, see 17.15. 31: *Haran*, in northwest Mesopotamia, was Abraham's ancestral home according to 24.10 (compare 29.4). Extra-biblical sources show that several of the names in the genealogy, e.g. Peleg (v. 16), Serug (v. 20), Terah and Nahor (v. 24), were place-names in this region, variously called Paddan-aram or Aram-naharaim. The migration from Mesopotamia into Canaan was a phase of population movements in the early part of the second millennium B.C., occasioned by the influx of Amorites from the Arabian desert.

12.1–8: **God's call of Abraham** is sketched against the background of divided mankind. 1–3: Israel, represented by Abraham, is chosen to play a decisive role in God's historical purpose (Is.19.24; Acts 3.25–26; Rom.4.13). The promise includes receiving a land, becoming a great nation, and mediating blessing to other peoples. 1: *Your country*, see 11.31 n. 4: By breaking ties of land and kindred (v. 1) and responding obediently to the LORD's summons, Abraham

Abram took Sar'ai his wife, and Lot his brother's son, and all their possessions which they had gathered, and the persons that they had gotten in Haran; and they set forth to go to the land of Canaan. When they had come to the land of Canaan, [6] Abram passed through the land to the place at Shechem, to the oak[r] of Moreh. At that time the Canaanites were in the land. [7] Then the LORD appeared to Abram, and said, "To your descendants I will give this land." So he built there an altar to the LORD, who had appeared to him. [8] Thence he removed to the mountain on the east of Bethel, and pitched his tent, with Bethel on the west and Ai on the east; and there he built an altar to the LORD and called on the name of the LORD. [9] And Abram journeyed on, still going toward the Negeb.

10 Now there was a famine in the land. So Abram went down to Egypt to sojourn there, for the famine was severe in the land. [11] When he was about to enter Egypt, he said to Sar'ai his wife, "I know that you are a woman beautiful to behold; [12] and when the Egyptians see you, they will say, 'This is his wife'; then they will kill me, but they will let you live. [13] Say you are my sister, that it may go well with me because of you, and that my life may be spared on your account." [14] When Abram entered Egypt the Egyptians saw that the woman was very beautiful. [15] And when the princes of Pharaoh saw her, they praised her to Pharaoh. And the woman was taken into Pharaoh's house. [16] And for her sake he dealt well with Abram; and he had sheep, oxen, he-asses, menservants, maidservants, she-asses, and camels.

17 But the LORD afflicted Pharaoh and his house with great plagues because of Sar'ai, Abram's wife. [18] So Pharaoh called Abram, and said, "What is this you have done to me? Why did you not tell me that she was your wife? [19] Why did you say, 'She is my sister,' so that I took her for my wife? Now then, here is your wife, take her, and be gone." [20] And Pharaoh gave men orders concerning him; and they set him on the way, with his wife and all that he had.

13 So Abram went up from Egypt, he and his wife, and all that he had, and Lot with him, into the Negeb. 2 Now Abram was very rich in cattle, in silver, and in gold. [3] And he journeyed on from the Negeb as far as Bethel, to the place where his tent had been at the beginning, between Bethel and Ai, [4] to the place where he had made an altar at the first; and there Abram called on the name of the LORD. [5] And Lot, who went with Abram, also had flocks and herds and tents, [6] so that the land could not support both of them dwelling together; for their possessions were so great that they could not dwell together, [7] and there was strife between the herdsmen of Abram's cattle and the herdsmen of Lot's cattle. At that time the Canaanites and the Per'izzites dwelt in the land.

8 Then Abram said to Lot, "Let there be no strife between you and me,

r Or *terebinth*

---

typifies the man of faith (Heb.11.8). **6:** *Shechem*, located at the commercial crossroads of Canaan in the pass between Mount Ebal and Mount Gerizim, was a flourishing city during the second millennium B.C. (Jg. ch. 9). Nearby was *the oak of Moreh* ("oracle giver"), a sacred tree (35.4; Dt.11.30; Jos.24.26; Jg.9.37).

12.10–13.1: Sarah in jeopardy. God's promise of a posterity was temporarily eclipsed in Egypt where Sarah, the ancestress of Israel, was almost taken into Pharaoh's harem. **13:** Sarah was Abraham's *sister*, i.e. half-sister, according to 20.12. The narrative does not moralize about the white lie but rather portrays the LORD's rescue of Sarah from the jeopardy into which Abraham's self-interest had placed her (compare ch. 20; 26.1–11).

13.2–18: Abraham and Lot. The LORD's promise of the land hung in the balance of a decision, but providentially Lot, the ancestor of Moab, chose the region around Sodom. **5–7:** The patriarchs are represented as living a semi-nomadic life in the midst of the Canaanites; thus

and between your herdsmen and my herdsmen; for we are kinsmen. [9] Is not the whole land before you? Separate yourself from me. If you take the left hand, then I will go to the right; or if you take the right hand, then I will go to the left." [10] And Lot lifted up his eyes, and saw that the Jordan valley was well watered everywhere like the garden of the LORD, like the land of Egypt, in the direction of Zo'ar; this was before the LORD destroyed Sodom and Gomor'rah. [11] So Lot chose for himself all the Jordan valley, and Lot journeyed east; thus they separated from each other. [12] Abram dwelt in the land of Canaan, while Lot dwelt among the cities of the valley and moved his tent as far as Sodom. [13] Now the men of Sodom were wicked, great sinners against the LORD.

14 The LORD said to Abram, after Lot had separated from him, "Lift up your eyes, and look from the place where you are, northward and southward and eastward and westward; [15] for all the land which you see I will give to you and to your descendants for ever. [16] I will make your descendants as the dust of the earth; so that if one can count the dust of the earth, your descendants also can be counted. [17] Arise, walk through the length and the breadth of the land, for I will give it to you." [18] So Abram moved his tent, and came and dwelt by the oaks[s] of Mamre, which are at Hebron; and there he built an altar to the LORD.

14 In the days of Am'raphel king of Shinar, Ar'ioch king of Ella'sar, Ched-or-lao'mer king of Elam, and Tidal king of Goi'im, [2] these kings made war with Bera king of Sodom, Birsha king of Gomor'rah, Shinab king of Admah, Sheme'ber king of Zeboi'im, and the king of Bela (that is, Zo'ar). [3] And all these joined forces in the valley of Siddim (that is, the Salt Sea). [4] Twelve years they had served Ched-or-lao'mer, but in the thirteenth year they rebelled. [5] In the fourteenth year Ched-or-lao'mer and the kings who were with him came and subdued the Reph'aim in Ash'teroth-karna'im, the Zuzim in Ham, the Emim in Sha'veh-kiriatha'im, [6] and the Horites in their Mount Se'ir as far as El-paran on the border of the wilderness; [7] then they turned back and came to Enmish'pat (that is, Kadesh), and subdued all the country of the Amal'ekites, and also the Amorites who dwelt in Haz'azon-ta'mar. [8] Then the king of Sodom, the king of Gomor'rah, the king of Admah, the king of Zeboi'im, and the king of Bela (that is, Zo'ar) went out, and they joined battle in the Valley of Siddim [9] with Ched-or-lao'mer king of Elam, Tidal king of Goi'im, Am'raphel king of Shinar, and Ar'ioch king of Ella'sar, four kings against five. [10] Now the Valley of Siddim was full of bitumen pits; and as the kings of Sodom and Gomor'rah fled, some fell into them, and the rest fled to the mountain. [11] So the enemy took all the goods of Sodom and Gomor'rah, and all their provisions, and went their way; [12] they also took Lot, the son of Abram's brother, who dwelt in Sodom, and his goods, and departed.

13 Then one who had escaped came, and told Abram the Hebrew, who

s Or terebinths

adequate pasture land was vital to the *herdsmen*. **10:** The fertility of the *Jordan valley* is compared to *the garden of the* LORD (2.8–10) and the Nile valley. *Zoar*, 19.20–22. *Sodom and Gomorrah*, 19.1–29. **11:** Lot thus became the ancestor of Moab and Ammon (19.30–38). **14–17:** The promise of 12.7 is renewed. **18:** *Mamre* was an ancient sacred place, slightly north of Hebron, with which Abraham was associated.

14.1–24: An alliance of four eastern kings was defeated by Abraham's small forces. This independent tradition, which pictures Abraham as a military hero in the field of world politics, deviates from the usual portrayal of the patriarchs as peaceful semi-nomads. **1:** None of the kings can be identified with certainty. *Shinar*, 10.10. *Ellasar*, i.e. Larsa. **2–4:** The rebellious city-kings held sway in the region of the Dead Sea before its lower basin was covered with water. **5–7:** The object of the invasion may have been to secure the trade routes to Egypt and southern

was living by the oaks^s of Mamre the Amorite, brother of Eshcol and of Aner; these were allies of Abram. ^{14} When Abram heard that his kinsman had been taken captive, he led forth his trained men, born in his house, three hundred and eighteen of them, and went in pursuit as far as Dan. ^{15} And he divided his forces against them by night, he and his servants, and routed them and pursued them to Hobah, north of Damascus. ^{16} Then he brought back all the goods, and also brought back his kinsman Lot with his goods, and the women and the people.

17 After his return from the defeat of Ched-or-lao′mer and the kings who were with him, the king of Sodom went out to meet him at the Valley of Shaveh (that is, the King's Valley). ^{18} And Mel-chiz′edek king of Salem brought out bread and wine; he was priest of God Most High. ^{19} And he blessed him and said,

"Blessed be Abram by God Most High,
    maker of heaven and earth;
^{20} and blessed be God Most High,
    who has delivered your enemies into your hand!"

And Abram gave him a tenth of everything. ^{21} And the king of Sodom said to Abram, "Give me the persons, but take the goods for yourself." ^{22} But Abram said to the king of Sodom, "I have sworn to the LORD God Most High, maker of heaven and earth, ^{23} that I would not take a thread or a sandal-thong or anything that is yours,

lest you should say, 'I have made Abram rich.' ^{24} I will take nothing but what the young men have eaten, and the share of the men who went with me; let Aner, Eshcol, and Mamre take their share."

15 After these things the word of the LORD came to Abram in a vision, "Fear not, Abram, I am your shield; your reward shall be very great." ^{2} But Abram said, "O Lord GOD, what wilt thou give me, for I continue childless, and the heir of my house is Elie′zer of Damascus?" ^{3} And Abram said, "Behold, thou hast given me no offspring; and a slave born in my house will be my heir." ^{4} And behold, the word of the LORD came to him, "This man shall not be your heir; your own son shall be your heir." ^{5} And he brought him outside and said, "Look toward heaven, and number the stars, if you are able to number them." Then he said to him, "So shall your descendants be." ^{6} And he believed the LORD; and he reckoned it to him as righteousness.

7 And he said to him, "I am the LORD who brought you from Ur of the Chalde′ans, to give you this land to possess." ^{8} But he said, "O Lord GOD, how am I to know that I shall possess it?" ^{9} He said to him, "Bring me a heifer three years old, a she-goat three years old, a ram three years old, a turtledove, and a young pigeon." ^{10} And he brought him all these, cut them in two, and laid each half over against

s Or *terebinths*

Arabia. **13:** *Mamre* here is the name of a person (compare 13.18). **14:** *Dan* was known as Laish in the early period (Jg.18.29). **17:** *The King's Valley*, near Jerusalem (2 Sam.18.18). **18:** *Salem* is a name for Jerusalem (Ps.76.2), where in pre-Israelite times *God Most High* (El Elyon) was worshiped as the high god of the pantheon. **19–20:** Melchizedek, the priest of the Canaanite cult, blesses Abraham in the name of his god, *maker of heaven and earth.* **22:** Here *God Most High* is identified with the LORD, the God of Israel (Num.24.16; Ps.46.4). The mysterious Melchizedek was later interpreted messianically (Ps.110.4; Heb.7.1–17).

15.1–21: The covenant with Abraham. The LORD ratified his promise even though Abraham still had no heir. **1:** *Your shield*, i.e. divine protector (Ps.28.7; 33.20). Abraham's *reward* is his numerous posterity (13.14–17). **2–3:** Inscriptions from Nuzi in Mesopotamia (middle of the second millennium) show the law there stipulated that a slave could be adopted as the heir in case of childlessness, a practice which is apparently presupposed here. **6:** *He believed*, i.e. put his trust in the LORD's promise even when there was no tangible evidence. *Righteousness*, see 6.9 n.; 7.1. **7:** 11.31. The covenant ceremony described in vv. 7–12 and 17–18 rests on an early tradition, as evidenced by the ancient ritual of making a covenant by cutting animals in two

the other; but he did not cut the birds in two. [11] And when birds of prey came down upon the carcasses, Abram drove them away.

12 As the sun was going down, a deep sleep fell on Abram; and lo, a dread and great darkness fell upon him. [13] Then the LORD said to Abram, "Know of a surety that your descendants will be sojourners in a land that is not theirs, and will be slaves there, and they will be oppressed for four hundred years; [14] but I will bring judgment on the nation which they serve, and afterward they shall come out with great possessions. [15] As for yourself, you shall go to your fathers in peace; you shall be buried in a good old age. [16] And they shall come back here in the fourth generation; for the iniquity of the Amorites is not yet complete."

17 When the sun had gone down and it was dark, behold, a smoking fire pot and a flaming torch passed between these pieces. [18] On that day the LORD made a covenant with Abram, saying, "To your descendants I give this land, from the river of Egypt to the great river, the river Euphra'tes, [19] the land of the Ken'ites, the Ken'izzites, the Kad'monites, [20] the Hittites, the Per'izzites, the Reph'aim, [21] the Amorites, the Canaanites, the Gir'gashites and the Jeb'usites."

16 Now Sar'ai, Abram's wife, bore him no children. She had an Egyptian maid whose name was Hagar; [2] and Sar'ai said to Abram, "Behold now, the LORD has prevented me from bearing children; go in to my maid; it may be that I shall obtain children by her." And Abram hearkened to the voice of Sar'ai. [3] So, after Abram had dwelt ten years in the land of Canaan, Sar'ai, Abram's wife, took Hagar the Egyptian, her maid, and gave her to Abram her husband as a wife. [4] And he went in to Hagar, and she conceived; and when she saw that she had conceived, she looked with contempt on her mistress. [5] And Sar'ai said to Abram, "May the wrong done to me be on you! I gave my maid to your embrace, and when she saw that she had conceived, she looked on me with contempt. May the LORD judge between you and me!" [6] But Abram said to Sar'ai, "Behold, your maid is in your power; do to her as you please." Then Sar'ai dealt harshly with her, and she fled from her.

7 The angel of the LORD found her by a spring of water in the wilderness, the spring on the way to Shur. [8] And he said, "Hagar, maid of Sar'ai, where have you come from and where are you going?" She said, "I am fleeing from my mistress Sar'ai." [9] The angel of the LORD said to her, "Return to your mistress, and submit to her." [10] The angel of the LORD also said to her, "I will so greatly multiply your descendants that they cannot be numbered for multitude." [11] And the angel of the LORD said to her, "Behold, you are with child, and shall bear a son; you shall call his name Ish'mael;[t] because

t That is God hears

(Jer.34.17–19) and passing between the parts. **12:** Abraham fell into *a deep sleep* (compare 2.21), in which he received the revelation (Job 4.13; 33.15). **13–16:** An inserted tradition explains the delay in the fulfilment of the promise, referring to the Egyptian oppression for 400 years (Ex. 12.40) and the victorious Exodus. *The iniquity of the Amorites* (10.16) was the sexual corruption which led to their downfall (9.25 n.). **17–18:** Continuation of vv. 7–12. The presence of God is symbolized by fire (see Ex.3.2 n.) passing between the pieces. *A covenant,* see 17.2 n. The ideal boundaries of the promised land–from the brook of Egypt to the Euphrates–were those of David's empire (Dt.11.24; 2 Sam.8.3; compare 1 Kg.4.21; 8.65).

    16.1–16: The birth of Ishmael. 2: In antiquity both barrenness and fertility were traced to God (20.17–18; 30.2; 33.5; 1 Sam.1.6). According to ancient custom, a wife could give her maid to her husband and claim the child as her own (30.3,9). **4–6:** The inferior Hagar felt superior to Sarai and threatened to take her mistress's place (Pr.30.23) as the ancestress of Israel. **7:** Here *the angel of the LORD* is not a heavenly being subordinate to God but the LORD himself in earthly manifestation, as is clear from v. 13 (compare 21.17,19; Ex.14.19). **12:** *A wild ass of a man*

the LORD has given heed to your affliction. ¹² He shall be a wild ass of a man, his hand against every man and every man's hand against him; and he shall dwell over against all his kinsmen." ¹³ So she called the name of the LORD who spoke to her, "Thou art a God of seeing"; for she said, "Have I really seen God and remained alive after seeing him?"ᵘ ¹⁴ Therefore the well was called Beer-la'hai-roi;ᵛ it lies between Kadesh and Bered.

15 And Hagar bore Abram a son; and Abram called the name of his son, whom Hagar bore, Ish'mael. ¹⁶ Abram was eighty-six years old when Hagar bore Ish'mael to Abram.

17 When Abram was ninety-nine years old the LORD appeared to Abram, and said to him, "I am God Almighty;ʷ walk before me, and be blameless. ² And I will make my covenant between me and you, and will multiply you exceedingly." ³ Then Abram fell on his face; and God said to him, ⁴ "Behold, my covenant is with you, and you shall be the father of a multitude of nations. ⁵ No longer shall your name be Abram,ˣ but your name shall be Abraham;ʸ for I have made you the father of a multitude of nations. ⁶ I will make you exceedingly fruitful; and I will make nations of you, and kings shall come forth from you. ⁷ And I will establish my covenant between me and you and your descendants after you throughout their generations for an everlasting covenant, to be God to you and to your descendants after you. ⁸ And I will give to you, and to your descendants after you, the land of your sojournings, all the land of Canaan, for an everlasting possession; and I will be their God."

9 And God said to Abraham, "As for you, you shall keep my covenant, you and your descendants after you throughout their generations. ¹⁰ This is my covenant, which you shall keep, between me and you and your descendants after you: Every male among you shall be circumcised. ¹¹ You shall be circumcised in the flesh of your foreskins, and it shall be a sign of the covenant between me and you. ¹² He that is eight days old among you shall be circumcised; every male throughout your generations, whether born in your house, or bought with your money from any foreigner who is not of your offspring, ¹³ both he that is born in your house and he that is bought with your money, shall be circumcised. So shall my covenant be in your flesh an everlasting covenant. ¹⁴ Any uncircumcised male who is not circumcised in the flesh of his foreskin shall be cut off from his people; he has broken my covenant."

15 And God said to Abraham, "As for Sar'ai your wife, you shall not call

u Cn: Heb *have I even here seen after him who sees me?*
v That is *the well of one who sees and lives*
w Heb *El Shaddai*   x That is *exalted father*
y Here taken to mean *father of a multitude*

describes the bedouin freedom of the Ishmaelites in the southern wilderness (25.16–18). **13:** *The God of seeing* was the name of the deity of the sacred place, now identified with Israel's God. On Hagar's question, compare Ex.33.20; Jg.6.22–23; 13.22.
    17.1–27: The covenant of circumcision. This account from the priestly tradition is another version of the covenant with Abraham (compare the early tradition, 15.7–21). **1:** *God Almighty* (El Shaddai), meaning "God, the One of the Mountains," was a divine name current in the pre-Mosaic period (Ex.6.2–3). Perhaps it was brought with the patriarchs from Mesopotamia. **2:** Covenant is a term of relationship between a superior and an inferior party, the former "making" or "establishing" (v. 7) the bond (9.9–17). **5:** The new relationship involved receiving a new name, *Abraham* (a dialectal variant of Abram). The name, which means "the (divine) Father is exalted," is artificially explained by its similarity to the Hebrew for *father of a multitude*. The latter refers to the nations whose ancestry was traced to Abraham (v. 16; 28.3; 35.11; 48.4), e.g. Edomites and Ishmaelites. **8:** In the priestly view, the patriarchs were wanderers or sojourners who looked forward to their promised inheritance in Canaan (21.23; 23.4; 28.4; 36.7; 37.1; 47.9). **9–14:** To *keep* the covenant is to practice circumcision, an ancient rite which was practiced by some of Israel's neighbors and whose origin is explained by various traditions (Ex.4.24–26; Jos.5.2–9). Circumcision is an external *sign* (v. 11) of membership in the covenant commu-

her name Sar'ai, but Sarah shall be her name. [16] I will bless her, and moreover I will give you a son by her; I will bless her, and she shall be a mother of nations; kings of peoples shall come from her." [17] Then Abraham fell on his face and laughed, and said to himself, "Shall a child be born to a man who is a hundred years old? Shall Sarah, who is ninety years old, bear a child?" [18] And Abraham said to God, "O that Ish'mael might live in thy sight!" [19] God said, "No, but Sarah your wife shall bear you a son, and you shall call his name Isaac.[z] I will establish my covenant with him as an everlasting covenant for his descendants after him. [20] As for Ish'mael, I have heard you; behold, I will bless him and make him fruitful and multiply him exceedingly; he shall be the father of twelve princes, and I will make him a great nation. [21] But I will establish my covenant with Isaac, whom Sarah shall bear to you at this season next year."

[22] When he had finished talking with him, God went up from Abraham. [23] Then Abraham took Ish'mael his son and all the slaves born in his house or bought with his money, every male among the men of Abraham's house, and he circumcised the flesh of their foreskins that very day, as God had said to him. [24] Abraham was ninety-nine years old when he was circumcised in the flesh of his foreskin. [25] And Ish'mael his son was thirteen years old when he was circumcised in the flesh of his foreskin. [26] That very day Abraham and his son Ish'mael were circumcised; [27] and all the men of his house, those born in the house and those bought with money from a foreigner, were circumcised with him.

18 And the LORD appeared to him by the oaks[a] of Mamre, as he sat at the door of his tent in the heat of the day. [2] He lifted up his eyes and looked, and behold, three men stood in front of him. When he saw them, he ran from the tent door to meet them, and bowed himself to the earth, [3] and said, "My lord, if I have found favor in your sight, do not pass by your servant. [4] Let a little water be brought, and wash your feet, and rest yourselves under the tree, [5] while I fetch a morsel of bread, that you may refresh yourselves, and after that you may pass on–since you have come to your servant." So they said, "Do as you have said." [6] And Abraham hastened into the tent to Sarah, and said, "Make ready quickly three measures[b] of fine meal, knead it, and make cakes." [7] And Abraham ran to the herd, and took a calf, tender and good, and gave it to the servant, who hastened to prepare it. [8] Then he took curds, and milk, and the calf which he had prepared, and set it before them; and he stood by them under the tree while they ate.

[9] They said to him, "Where is Sarah your wife?" And he said, "She is in the tent." [10] The LORD said, "I will surely return to you in the spring, and Sarah your wife shall have a son." And Sarah was listening at the tent door behind him. [11] Now Abraham and Sarah were old, advanced in age; it had ceased to be with Sarah after the manner of women. [12] So Sarah laughed to herself, saying, "After I have grown old, and my husband is old, shall I have pleas-

z That is *he laughs*
a Or *terebinths*   b Heb *seahs*

---

nity. Unlike the Noachian covenant (9.9–17), the Abrahamic *covenant in your flesh* (v. 13) is binding on Israel only. **15:** *Sarah*, meaning "princess," is a variant of Sarai. **17:** 18.11–15. **18–20:** 16.10–12.

18.1–33: The LORD's visit to Abraham and Abraham's intercession for Sodom. 1: *The oaks of Mamre*, see 13.18 n. **2–8:** A fine description of oriental courtesy and hospitality. When the visitors appeared at the noontime siesta, Abraham did not recognize them as divine beings (Heb.13.2). The relation of the three men to the LORD (v. 1) is difficult. All three *angels* (19.1) may represent the LORD (see 16.7 n.); thus the plurality becomes a single person in vv. 10,13. On the other hand, v. 22 and 19.1 suggest that the LORD is one of the three, the other two being his attendants. **9–15:** Various traditions (17.17–19; 21.6) interpret the name of Isaac, meaning "he

ure?" ¹³ The LORD said to Abraham, "Why did Sarah laugh, and say, 'Shall I indeed bear a child, now that I am old?' ¹⁴ Is anything too hard*c* for the LORD? At the appointed time I will return to you, in the spring, and Sarah shall have a son." ¹⁵ But Sarah denied, saying, "I did not laugh"; for she was afraid. He said, "No, but you did laugh."

16 Then the men set out from there, and they looked toward Sodom; and Abraham went with them to set them on their way. ¹⁷ The LORD said, "Shall I hide from Abraham what I am about to do, ¹⁸ seeing that Abraham shall become a great and mighty nation, and all the nations of the earth shall bless themselves by him?*d* ¹⁹ No, for I have chosen*e* him, that he may charge his children and his household after him to keep the way of the LORD by doing righteousness and justice; so that the LORD may bring to Abraham what he has promised him." ²⁰ Then the LORD said, "Because the outcry against Sodom and Gomor′rah is great and their sin is very grave, ²¹ I will go down to see whether they have done altogether according to the outcry which has come to me; and if not, I will know."

22 So the men turned from there, and went toward Sodom; but Abraham still stood before the LORD. ²³ Then Abraham drew near, and said, "Wilt thou indeed destroy the righteous with the wicked? ²⁴ Suppose there are fifty righteous within the city; wilt thou then destroy the place and not spare it for the fifty righteous who are in it? ²⁵ Far be it from thee to do such a thing, to slay the righteous with the wicked, so that the righteous fare as the wicked!

Far be that from thee! Shall not the Judge of all the earth do right?" ²⁶ And the LORD said, "If I find at Sodom fifty righteous in the city, I will spare the whole place for their sake." ²⁷ Abraham answered, "Behold, I have taken upon myself to speak to the Lord, I who am but dust and ashes. ²⁸ Suppose five of the fifty righteous are lacking? Wilt thou destroy the whole city for lack of five?" And he said, "I will not destroy it if I find forty-five there." ²⁹ Again he spoke to him, and said, "Suppose forty are found there." He answered, "For the sake of forty I will not do it." ³⁰ Then he said, "Oh let not the Lord be angry, and I will speak. Suppose thirty are found there." He answered, "I will not do it, if I find thirty there." ³¹ He said, "Behold, I have taken upon myself to speak to the Lord. Suppose twenty are found there." He answered, "For the sake of twenty I will not destroy it." ³² Then he said, "Oh let not the Lord be angry, and I will speak again but this once. Suppose ten are found there." He answered, "For the sake of ten I will not destroy it." ³³ And the LORD went his way, when he had finished speaking to Abraham; and Abraham returned to his place.

19 The two angels came to Sodom in the evening; and Lot was sitting in the gate of Sodom. When Lot saw them, he rose to meet them, and bowed himself with his face to the earth, ² and said, "My lords, turn aside, I pray you, to your servant's house and spend the night, and wash your feet; then you may rise up early and go on your way." They said, "No;

c Or *wonderful*
d Or *in him all the nations of the earth shall be blessed*
e Heb *known*

---

laughs." **17–19:** Because Abraham is chosen for a special role (12.1–3), he is taken into the LORD's counsel (compare 6.13–22), for Sodom will become an example to future generations. **23–33:** Ancient Israelite thought, with its strong sense of communal solidarity, held that the wickedness of a few contaminates the whole community (Dt.21.1–9). Here the issue is put the other way around: can the righteousness of a few, even a minority of ten, have a saving influence upon the whole?

19.1–38: The destruction of Sodom and Gomorrah impressed itself deeply upon later generations as an example of God's total judgment upon appalling wickedness (Dt.29.23; Is.1.9; Jer.49.18; Am.4.11). **1:** *Two angels*, see 18.2–8 n. **4–11:** Compare the crime of Gibeah (Jg.19.22–

we will spend the night in the street."
³ But he urged them strongly; so they
turned aside to him and entered his
house; and he made them a feast, and
baked unleavened bread, and they ate.
⁴ But before they lay down, the men
of the city, the men of Sodom, both
young and old, all the people to the
last man, surrounded the house; ⁵ and
they called to Lot, "Where are the men
who came to you tonight? Bring them
out to us, that we may know them."
⁶ Lot went out of the door to the men,
shut the door after him, ⁷ and said, "I
beg you, my brothers, do not act so
wickedly. ⁸ Behold, I have two daughters who have not known man; let me
bring them out to you, and do to them
as you please; only do nothing to these
men, for they have come under the
shelter of my roof." ⁹ But they said,
"Stand back!" And they said, "This
fellow came to sojourn, and he would
play the judge! Now we will deal worse
with you than with them." Then they
pressed hard against the man Lot, and
drew near to break the door. ¹⁰ But the
men put forth their hands and brought
Lot into the house to them, and shut
the door. ¹¹ And they struck with
blindness the men who were at the
door of the house, both small and great,
so that they wearied themselves groping for the door.

12 Then the men said to Lot, "Have
you any one else here? Sons-in-law,
sons, daughters, or any one you have
in the city, bring them out of the place;
¹³ for we are about to destroy this
place, because the outcry against its
people has become great before the
LORD, and the LORD has sent us to destroy it." ¹⁴ So Lot went out and said
to his sons-in-law, who were to marry
his daughters, "Up, get out of this
place; for the LORD is about to destroy
the city." But he seemed to his sons-in-
law to be jesting.

15 When morning dawned, the
angels urged Lot, saying, "Arise, take
your wife and your two daughters who
are here, lest you be consumed in the
punishment of the city." ¹⁶ But he
lingered; so the men seized him and his
wife and his two daughters by the
hand, the LORD being merciful to him,
and they brought him forth and set
him outside the city. ¹⁷ And when they
had brought them forth, they*ᶠ* said,
"Flee for your life; do not look back or
stop anywhere in the valley; flee to the
hills, lest you be consumed." ¹⁸ And
Lot said to them, "Oh, no, my lords;
¹⁹ behold, your servant has found
favor in your sight, and you have
shown me great kindness in saving my
life; but I cannot flee to the hills, lest
the disaster overtake me, and I die.
²⁰ Behold, yonder city is near enough
to flee to, and it is a little one. Let me
escape there–is it not a little one?–
and my life will be saved!" ²¹ He said
to him, "Behold, I grant you this favor
also, that I will not overthrow the city
of which you have spoken. ²² Make
haste, escape there; for I can do nothing till you arrive there." Therefore
the name of the city was called Zo′ar.*ᵍ*
²³ The sun had risen on the earth
when Lot came to Zo′ar.

24 Then the LORD rained on Sodom
and Gomor′rah brimstone and fire
from the LORD out of heaven; ²⁵ and
he overthrew those cities, and all the
valley, and all the inhabitants of the
cities, and what grew on the ground.
²⁶ But Lot's wife behind him looked
back, and she became a pillar of salt.
²⁷ And Abraham went early in the

ᶠ Gk Syr Vg: Heb *he*   *ᵍ* That is *Little*

---

30). The episode is told to show the unbridled lusts of Sodom. **5:** *Know* refers to sexual relations
(v. 8), here homosexual. **8:** Once guests had eaten in his house, Lot had to obey the law of
oriental hospitality which guaranteed protection. Thus his proposal to hand over his daughters
showed his determination to put first his obligation as a host. **20–22:** *Zoar*, meaning "small,"
was a town at the southern end of the Dead Sea which survived the calamity. **24:** *Brimstone and
fire*, a memory of a catastrophe in remote times when seismic activity and the explosion of subterranean gases changed the face of the area, which was formerly fertile (13.10). **26:** An old
tradition to account for bizarre salt formations in the area such as may be seen today on

morning to the place where he had stood before the LORD; ²⁸ and he looked down toward Sodom and Gomor'rah and toward all the land of the valley, and beheld, and lo, the smoke of the land went up like the smoke of a furnace.

29 So it was that, when God destroyed the cities of the valley, God remembered Abraham, and sent Lot out of the midst of the overthrow, when he overthrew the cities in which Lot dwelt.

30 Now Lot went up out of Zo'ar, and dwelt in the hills with his two daughters, for he was afraid to dwell in Zo'ar; so he dwelt in a cave with his two daughters. ³¹ And the first-born said to the younger, "Our father is old, and there is not a man on earth to come in to us after the manner of all the earth. ³² Come, let us make our father drink wine, and we will lie with him, that we may preserve offspring through our father." ³³ So they made their father drink wine that night; and the first-born went in, and lay with her father; he did not know when she lay down or when she arose. ³⁴ And on the next day, the first-born said to the younger, "Behold, I lay last night with my father; let us make him drink wine tonight also; then you go in and lie with him, that we may preserve offspring through our father." ³⁵ So they made their father drink wine that night also; and the younger arose, and lay with him; and he did not know when she lay down or when she arose. ³⁶ Thus both the daughters of Lot were with child by their father. ³⁷ The first-born bore a son, and called his name Moab; he is the father of the Moabites to this day. ³⁸ The younger also bore a son, and called his name

Ben-ammi; he is the father of the Ammonites to this day.

20 From there Abraham journeyed toward the territory of the Negeb, and dwelt between Kadesh and Shur; and he sojourned in Gerar. ² And Abraham said of Sarah his wife, "She is my sister." And Abim'elech king of Gerar sent and took Sarah. ³ But God came to Abim'elech in a dream by night, and said to him, "Behold, you are a dead man, because of the woman whom you have taken; for she is a man's wife." ⁴ Now Abim'elech had not approached her; so he said, "Lord, wilt thou slay an innocent people? ⁵ Did he not himself say to me, 'She is my sister'? And she herself said, 'He is my brother.' In the integrity of my heart and the innocence of my hands I have done this." ⁶ Then God said to him in the dream, "Yes, I know that you have done this in the integrity of your heart, and it was I who kept you from sinning against me; therefore I did not let you touch her. ⁷ Now then restore the man's wife; for he is a prophet, and he will pray for you, and you shall live. But if you do not restore her, know that you shall surely die, you, and all that are yours."

8 So Abim'elech rose early in the morning, and called all his servants, and told them all these things; and the men were very much afraid. ⁹ Then Abim'elech called Abraham, and said to him, "What have you done to us? And how have I sinned against you, that you have brought on me and my kingdom a great sin? You have done to me things that ought not to be done." ¹⁰ And Abim'elech said to Abraham, "What were you thinking of, that you did this thing?" ¹¹ Abraham said, "I did it because I thought, There is no

Jebel Usdum. **30–38:** A story which explains the origin of the Moabites and Ammonites, neighbors of Israel.

20.1–18: Abraham and Sarah in Gerar. This story parallels that of 12.10–20 (compare 26.6–11). Here, however, the narrator is more concerned with the ethical problems involved. **1:** *From there*, i.e. Mamre (18.1). **2:** Compare 12.11–13. **3–7:** Ethically sensitive, the narrator insists that Abimelech was innocent, for he did not go near Sarah. **7:** To Abraham is attributed the intercessory role of *a prophet* (18.22–33; compare Num.12.13; 21.7; 1 Sam.12.19–23). **11–12:** Abraham's excuses. Marriage with a half-sister was permitted in ancient times (2 Sam.13.13) but

fear of God at all in this place, and
they will kill me because of my wife.
¹² Besides she is indeed my sister, the
daughter of my father but not the
daughter of my mother; and she became my wife. ¹³ And when God
caused me to wander from my father's
house, I said to her, 'This is the kindness you must do me: at every place
to which we come, say of me, He is
my brother.' " ¹⁴ Then Abim'elech
took sheep and oxen, and male and
female slaves, and gave them to Abraham, and restored Sarah his wife to
him. ¹⁵ And Abim'elech said, "Behold,
my land is before you; dwell where it
pleases you." ¹⁶ To Sarah he said,
"Behold, I have given your brother a
thousand pieces of silver; it is your
vindication in the eyes of all who are
with you; and before every one you
are righted." ¹⁷ Then Abraham prayed
to God; and God healed Abim'elech,
and also healed his wife and female
slaves so that they bore children. ¹⁸ For
the LORD had closed all the wombs of
the house of Abim'elech because of
Sarah, Abraham's wife.

21 The LORD visited Sarah as he had
said, and the LORD did to Sarah
as he had promised. ² And Sarah conceived, and bore Abraham a son in his
old age at the time of which God had
spoken to him. ³ Abraham called the
name of his son who was born to him,
whom Sarah bore him, Isaac. ⁴ And
Abraham circumcised his son Isaac
when he was eight days old, as God
had commanded him. ⁵ Abraham was
a hundred years old when his son Isaac
was born to him. ⁶ And Sarah said,
"God has made laughter for me; every
one who hears will laugh over me."
⁷ And she said, "Who would have said
to Abraham that Sarah would suckle

children? Yet I have borne him a son
in his old age."

8 And the child grew, and was
weaned; and Abraham made a great
feast on the day that Isaac was
weaned. ⁹ But Sarah saw the son of
Hagar the Egyptian, whom she had
borne to Abraham, playing with her
son Isaac.ʰ ¹⁰ So she said to Abraham, "Cast out this slave woman with
her son; for the son of this slave woman
shall not be heir with my son Isaac."
¹¹ And the thing was very displeasing
to Abraham on account of his son.
¹² But God said to Abraham, "Be not
displeased because of the lad and because of your slave woman; whatever
Sarah says to you, do as she tells you,
for through Isaac shall your descendants be named. ¹³ And I will make a
nation of the son of the slave woman
also, because he is your offspring."
¹⁴ So Abraham rose early in the morning, and took bread and a skin of
water, and gave it to Hagar, putting it
on her shoulder, along with the child,
and sent her away. And she departed,
and wandered in the wilderness of
Beer-sheba.

15 When the water in the skin was
gone, she cast the child under one of
the bushes. ¹⁶ Then she went, and sat
down over against him a good way off,
about the distance of a bowshot; for
she said, "Let me not look upon the
death of the child." And as she sat over
against him, the child lifted up his
voiceⁱ and wept. ¹⁷ And God heard
the voice of the lad; and the angel of
God called to Hagar from heaven, and
said to her, "What troubles you, Hagar? Fear not; for God has heard the
voice of the lad where he is. ¹⁸ Arise,

h Gk Vg: Heb lacks *with her son Isaac*
i Gk: Heb *she lifted up her voice*

later was forbidden (Lev.18.9,11; 20.17). **16:** *Vindication,* i.e. a gift to induce everyone to overlook the injury done to Sarah.
   21.1–21: Isaac and Ishmael. Although Isaac was designated to continue Abraham's line,
Ishmael too was promised a future. **4:** On circumcision, see 17.9–14 n. **6:** See 18.9–15 n. **9–10:**
The jealous mother could not stand seeing the two boys on the same level, even at play. **11–14:**
Compare Abraham's different attitude in the parallel story (ch. 16). **14:** *Beer-sheba* is the locale
of the Isaac stories, just as Abraham is associated primarily with Mamre or Hebron (see 13.18
n.). **17:** *The angel of God,* see 16.7 n. *God has heard:* a play on the name Ishmael, meaning "God

lift up the lad, and hold him fast with your hand; for I will make him a great nation." [19] Then God opened her eyes, and she saw a well of water; and she went, and filled the skin with water, and gave the lad a drink. [20] And God was with the lad, and he grew up; he lived in the wilderness, and became an expert with the bow. [21] He lived in the wilderness of Paran; and his mother took a wife for him from the land of Egypt.

22 At that time Abim'elech and Phicol the commander of his army said to Abraham, "God is with you in all that you do; [23] now therefore swear to me here by God that you will not deal falsely with me or with my offspring or with my posterity, but as I have dealt loyally with you, you will deal with me and with the land where you have sojourned." [24] And Abraham said, "I will swear."

25 When Abraham complained to Abim'elech about a well of water which Abim'elech's servants had seized, [26] Abim'elech said, "I do not know who has done this thing; you did not tell me, and I have not heard of it until today." [27] So Abraham took sheep and oxen and gave them to Abim'elech, and the two men made a covenant. [28] Abraham set seven ewe lambs of the flock apart. [29] And Abim'elech said to Abraham, "What is the meaning of these seven ewe lambs which you have set apart?" [30] He said, "These seven ewe lambs you will take

from my hand, that you may be a witness for me that I dug this well." [31] Therefore that place was called Beer-sheba;[j] because there both of them swore an oath. [32] So they made a covenant at Beer-sheba. Then Abim'elech and Phicol the commander of his army rose up and returned to the land of the Philistines. [33] Abraham planted a tamarisk tree in Beer-sheba, and called there on the name of the LORD, the Everlasting God. [34] And Abraham sojourned many days in the land of the Philistines.

22 After these things God tested Abraham, and said to him, "Abraham!" And he said, "Here am I." [2] He said, "Take your son, your only son Isaac, whom you love, and go to the land of Mori'ah, and offer him there as a burnt offering upon one of the mountains of which I shall tell you." [3] So Abraham rose early in the morning, saddled his ass, and took two of his young men with him, and his son Isaac; and he cut the wood for the burnt offering, and arose and went to the place of which God had told him. [4] On the third day Abraham lifted up his eyes and saw the place afar off. [5] Then Abraham said to his young men, "Stay here with the ass; I and the lad will go yonder and worship, and come again to you." [6] And Abraham took the wood of the burnt offering, and laid it on Isaac his son; and he took in his hand the fire and the knife.

j That is *Well of seven* or *Well of the oath*

---

hears" (16.11). **20:** Though Ishmael was not the heir of the promise, *God was with the lad*, destining him to be the ancestor of Bedouin tribes of the southern wilderness (16.12).

21.22–34: Abraham's dispute with Abimelech. This story contains two traditional explanations of the name Beer-sheba. According to one, Abimelech guaranteed Abraham's loyalty by an oath. Hence Beer-sheba means "well of the oath" (v. 31). According to the other (vv. 25–26, 28–30), a dispute over a well resulted in a covenant, seven ewe-lambs being taken in witness. Thus the alternate meaning, "Well of seven." **33:** *The Everlasting God* (El Olam) is an ancient divine name, once associated with the pre-Israelite sanctuary of Beer-sheba, which Israel adopted as a title for the LORD (Is.40.28). **34:** *The land of the Philistines* is an anachronism, for the Philistines came into Canaan after 1200 B.C. (see 10.2–5 n.).

22.1–19: The testing of Abraham. The present story portrays a miracle of faith: Abraham received back the promise after showing he had the faith to surrender his only heir. In its oldest form the story told how the Deity relaxed his claim upon the first-born and provided an animal for a substitute (Ex.13.2,11–16; 22.29; 34.19–20). **1:** *Tested*, i.e. put under trial to see whether he would obey in faith (12.4; compare Heb.11.17–19). **2:** *Moriah* is unknown. In 2 Chr.3.1 it is identified with Jerusalem. Samaritan tradition locates the scene on Mount Gerizim (Shechem;

So they went both of them together. ⁷ And Isaac said to his father Abraham, "My father!" And he said, "Here am I, my son." He said, "Behold, the fire and the wood; but where is the lamb for a burnt offering?" ⁸ Abraham said, "God will provide himself the lamb for a burnt offering, my son." So they went both of them together.

9 When they came to the place of which God had told him, Abraham built an altar there, and laid the wood in order, and bound Isaac his son, and laid him on the altar, upon the wood. ¹⁰ Then Abraham put forth his hand, and took the knife to slay his son. ¹¹ But the angel of the LORD called to him from heaven, and said, "Abraham, Abraham!" And he said, "Here am I." ¹² He said, "Do not lay your hand on the lad or do anything to him; for now I know that you fear God, seeing you have not withheld your son, your only son, from me." ¹³ And Abraham lifted up his eyes and looked, and behold, behind him was a ram, caught in a thicket by his horns; and Abraham went and took the ram, and offered it up as a burnt offering instead of his son. ¹⁴ So Abraham called the name of that place The LORD will provide;ᵏ as it is said to this day, "On the mount of the LORD it shall be provided."ˡ

15 And the angel of the LORD called to Abraham a second time from heaven, ¹⁶ and said, "By myself I have sworn, says the LORD, because you have done this, and have not withheld your son, your only son, ¹⁷ I will indeed bless you, and I will multiply your descendants as the stars of heaven and as the sand which is on the seashore. And your descendants shall possess the gate of their enemies, ¹⁸ and by your descendants shall all the nations of the earth bless themselves, because you have obeyed my voice." ¹⁹ So Abraham returned to his young men, and they arose and went together to Beersheba; and Abraham dwelt at Beersheba.

20 Now after these things it was told Abraham, "Behold, Milcah also has borne children to your brother Nahor: ²¹ Uz the first-born, Buz his brother, Kemu'el the father of Aram, ²² Chesed, Hazo, Pildash, Jidlaph, and Bethu'el." ²³ Bethu'el became the father of Rebekah. These eight Milcah bore to Nahor, Abraham's brother. ²⁴ Moreover, his concubine, whose name was Reumah, bore Tebah, Gaham, Tahash, and Ma'acah.

23 Sarah lived a hundred and twenty-seven years; these were the years of the life of Sarah. ² And Sarah died at Kir'iath-ar'ba (that is, Hebron) in the land of Canaan; and Abraham went in to mourn for Sarah and to weep for her. ³ And Abraham rose up from before his dead, and said to the Hittites, ⁴ "I am a stranger and a sojourner among you; give me property among you for a burying place, that I may bury my dead out of my sight." ⁵ The Hittites answered Abraham, ⁶ "Hear us, my lord; you are a mighty prince among us. Bury your dead in the choicest of our sepulchres; none of us will withhold from you his sepulchre, or hinder you from burying your dead." ⁷ Abraham rose and bowed to the Hittites, the people of the land. ⁸ And he said to them, "If you are willing that I should bury my dead out of my sight, hear me, and entreat for me Ephron the son of Zohar, ⁹ that he may give me the cave of Mach-pe'lah, which he owns; it is at the end of

k Or *see* *l* Or *he will be seen*

compare 12.6), three days' journey (22.4) from Beer-sheba (v. 19; 21.33). **11:** *The angel of the* LORD, see 16.7 n. **14:** *God will provide*, see v. 8. **20–24:** The descendants of Abraham's brother, Nahor (11.27–29). The purpose of this Aramean genealogy is to introduce Bethuel, Rebekah's father, thus preparing for ch. 24.

23.1–20: Abraham's purchase of a family burial place. **2:** *Kiriath-arba*, the older name of Hebron (Jos.14.15; 15.13; Jg.1.10). **3:** *The Hittites* belonged at that time to the pre-Israelite population, *the people of the land* (v. 7; see 10.15 n.). **4–16:** Legal transactions were handled by elders at the city gate (v. 10). **9:** Abraham insists on payment of *the full price* in order to obtain

his field. For the full price let him give it to me in your presence as a possession for a burying place." ¹⁰ Now Ephron was sitting among the Hittites; and Ephron the Hittite answered Abraham in the hearing of the Hittites, of all who went in at the gate of his city, ¹¹ "No, my lord, hear me; I give you the field, and I give you the cave that is in it; in the presence of the sons of my people I give it to you; bury your dead." ¹² Then Abraham bowed down before the people of the land. ¹³ And he said to Ephron in the hearing of the people of the land, "But if you will, hear me; I will give the price of the field; accept it from me, that I may bury my dead there." ¹⁴ Ephron answered Abraham, ¹⁵ "My lord, listen to me; a piece of land worth four hundred shekels of silver, what is that between you and me? Bury your dead." ¹⁶ Abraham agreed with Ephron; and Abraham weighed out for Ephron the silver which he had named in the hearing of the Hittites, four hundred shekels of silver, according to the weights current among the merchants.

17 So the field of Ephron in Mach-pe′lah, which was to the east of Mamre, the field with the cave which was in it and all the trees that were in the field, throughout its whole area, was made over ¹⁸ to Abraham as a possession in the presence of the Hittites, before all who went in at the gate of his city. ¹⁹ After this, Abraham buried Sarah his wife in the cave of the field of Mach-pe′lah east of Mamre (that is, Hebron) in the land of Canaan. ²⁰ The field and the cave that is in it were made over to Abraham as a possession for a burying place by the Hittites.

24 Now Abraham was old, well advanced in years; and the LORD had blessed Abraham in all things. ² And Abraham said to his servant, the oldest of his house, who had charge of all that he had, "Put your hand under my thigh, ³ and I will make you swear by the LORD, the God of heaven and of the earth, that you will not take a wife for my son from the daughters of the Canaanites, among whom I dwell, ⁴ but will go to my country and to my kindred, and take a wife for my son Isaac." ⁵ The servant said to him, "Perhaps the woman may not be willing to follow me to this land; must I then take your son back to the land from which you came?" ⁶ Abraham said to him, "See to it that you do not take my son back there. ⁷ The LORD, the God of heaven, who took me from my father's house and from the land of my birth, and who spoke to me and swore to me, 'To your descendants I will give this land,' he will send his angel before you, and you shall take a wife for my son from there. ⁸ But if the woman is not willing to follow you, then you will be free from this oath of mine; only you must not take my son back there." ⁹ So the servant put his hand under the thigh of Abraham his master, and swore to him concerning this matter.

10 Then the servant took ten of his master's camels and departed, taking all sorts of choice gifts from his master; and he arose, and went to Mesopota′mia, to the city of Nahor. ¹¹ And he made the camels kneel down outside the city by the well of water at the time of evening, the time when women go out to draw water. ¹² And he said, "O LORD, God

---

legal title to the land. **19:** The cave of Machpelah was the tomb of Abraham and Sarah (25.9–10), Isaac (35.27–29) and Rebekah (49.31), Jacob (50.13) and Leah (49.31).

24.1–67: Finding a wife for Isaac among kinsman in Haran. **2:** The servant was perhaps Abraham's major-domo, Eliezer (15.2). Putting the hand under the thigh, an old form of oath taking (47.29), reflected the view that the fountain of reproductivity was sacred to the deity (see 16.2 n.). **3:** Aloofness from the Canaanites was based upon fear of the corrupting influence of Canaanite religion (Ex.34.15–16; Dt.7.3–4). **7:** *His angel*, see 16.7 n. **10:** *The city of Nahor*, near Haran (see 11.31 n.). **12:** *Steadfast love* is a covenant term, referring to the faithful assistance and loyal love of the LORD towards those bound to him by covenant. The Hebrew word is

of my master Abraham, grant me success today, I pray thee, and show steadfast love to my master Abraham. [13] Behold, I am standing by the spring of water, and the daughters of the men of the city are coming out to draw water. [14] Let the maiden to whom I shall say, 'Pray let down your jar that I may drink,' and who shall say, 'Drink, and I will water your camels'–let her be the one whom thou hast appointed for thy servant Isaac. By this I shall know that thou hast shown steadfast love to my master."

15 Before he had done speaking, behold, Rebekah, who was born to Bethu'el the son of Milcah, the wife of Nahor, Abraham's brother, came out with her water jar upon her shoulder. [16] The maiden was very fair to look upon, a virgin, whom no man had known. She went down to the spring, and filled her jar, and came up. [17] Then the servant ran to meet her, and said, "Pray give me a little water to drink from your jar." [18] She said, "Drink, my lord"; and she quickly let down her jar upon her hand, and gave him a drink. [19] When she had finished giving him a drink, she said, "I will draw for your camels also, until they have done drinking." [20] So she quickly emptied her jar into the trough and ran again to the well to draw, and she drew for all his camels. [21] The man gazed at her in silence to learn whether the LORD had prospered his journey or not.

22 When the camels had done drinking, the man took a gold ring weighing a half shekel, and two bracelets for her arms weighing ten gold shekels, [23] and said, "Tell me whose daughter you are. Is there room in your father's house for us to lodge in?" [24] She said to him, "I am the daughter of Bethu'el the son of Milcah, whom she bore to Nahor." [25] She added, "We have both straw and provender enough, and room to lodge in." [26] The man bowed his head and worshiped

the LORD, [27] and said, "Blessed be the LORD, the God of my master Abraham, who has not forsaken his steadfast love and his faithfulness toward my master. As for me, the LORD has led me in the way to the house of my master's kinsmen."

28 Then the maiden ran and told her mother's household about these things. [29] Rebekah had a brother whose name was Laban; and Laban ran out to the man, to the spring. [30] When he saw the ring, and the bracelets on his sister's arms, and when he heard the words of Rebekah his sister, "Thus the man spoke to me," he went to the man; and behold, he was standing by the camels at the spring. [31] He said, "Come in, O blessed of the LORD; why do you stand outside? For I have prepared the house and a place for the camels." [32] So the man came into the house; and Laban ungirded the camels, and gave him straw and provender for the camels, and water to wash his feet and the feet of the men who were with him. [33] Then food was set before him to eat; but he said, "I will not eat until I have told my errand." He said, "Speak on."

34 So he said, "I am Abraham's servant. [35] The LORD has greatly blessed my master, and he has become great; he has given him flocks and herds, silver and gold, menservants and maidservants, camels and asses. [36] And Sarah my master's wife bore a son to my master when she was old; and to him he has given all that he has. [37] My master made me swear, saying, 'You shall not take a wife for my son from the daughters of the Canaanites, in whose land I dwell; [38] but you shall go to my father's house and to my kindred, and take a wife for my son.' [39] I said to my master, 'Perhaps the woman will not follow me.' [40] But he said to me, 'The LORD, before whom I walk, will send his angel with you and

prosper your way; and you shall take a wife for my son from my kindred and from my father's house; ⁴¹ then you will be free from my oath, when you come to my kindred; and if they will not give her to you, you will be free from my oath.'

42 "I came today to the spring, and said, 'O LORD, the God of my master Abraham, if now thou wilt prosper the way which I go, ⁴³ behold, I am standing by the spring of water; let the young woman who comes out to draw, to whom I shall say, "Pray give me a little water from your jar to drink," ⁴⁴ and who will say to me, "Drink, and I will draw for your camels also," let her be the woman whom the LORD has appointed for my master's son.'

45 "Before I had done speaking in my heart, behold, Rebekah came out with her water jar on her shoulder; and she went down to the spring, and drew. I said to her, 'Pray let me drink.' ⁴⁶ She quickly let down her jar from her shoulder, and said, 'Drink, and I will give your camels drink also.' So I drank, and she gave the camels drink also. ⁴⁷ Then I asked her, 'Whose daughter are you?' She said, 'The daughter of Bethu'el, Nahor's son, whom Milcah bore to him.' So I put the ring on her nose, and the bracelets on her arms. ⁴⁸ Then I bowed my head and worshiped the LORD, and blessed the LORD, the God of my master Abraham, who had led me by the right way to take the daughter of my master's kinsman for his son. ⁴⁹ Now then, if you will deal loyally and truly with my master, tell me; and if not, tell me; that I may turn to the right hand or to the left."

50 Then Laban and Bethu'el answered, "The thing comes from the LORD; we cannot speak to you bad or good. ⁵¹ Behold, Rebekah is before you, take her and go, and let her be the wife of your master's son, as the LORD has spoken."

52 When Abraham's servant heard their words, he bowed himself to the earth before the LORD. ⁵³ And the servant brought forth jewelry of silver and of gold, and raiment, and gave them to Rebekah; he also gave to her brother and to her mother costly ornaments. ⁵⁴ And he and the men who were with him ate and drank, and they spent the night there. When they arose in the morning, he said, "Send me back to my master." ⁵⁵ Her brother and her mother said, "Let the maiden remain with us a while, at least ten days; after that she may go." ⁵⁶ But he said to them, "Do not delay me, since the LORD has prospered my way; let me go that I may go to my master." ⁵⁷ They said, "We will call the maiden, and ask her." ⁵⁸ And they called Rebekah, and said to her, "Will you go with this man?" She said, "I will go." ⁵⁹ So they sent away Rebekah their sister and her nurse, and Abraham's servant and his men. ⁶⁰ And they blessed Rebekah, and said to her, "Our sister, be the mother of thousands of ten thousands; and may your descendants possess the gate of those who hate them!" ⁶¹ Then Rebekah and her maids arose, and rode upon the camels and followed the man; thus the servant took Rebekah, and went his way.

62 Now Isaac had come from*ⁿ* Beer-la'hai-roi, and was dwelling in the Negeb. ⁶³ And Isaac went out to meditate in the field in the evening; and he lifted up his eyes and looked, and behold, there were camels coming. ⁶⁴ And Rebekah lifted up her eyes, and when she saw Isaac, she alighted from the camel, ⁶⁵ and said to the servant, "Who is the man yonder, walking in the field to meet us?" The servant said, "It is my master." So she took her veil and covered herself. ⁶⁶ And the servant told Isaac all the things that he had done. ⁶⁷ Then Isaac brought her into the tent,*ᵒ* and took Rebekah, and she became his wife; and he loved her. So Isaac was comforted after his mother's death.

n Syr Tg: Heb *from coming to*
o Heb adds *Sarah his mother*

25 Abraham took another wife, whose name was Ketu′rah. ² She bore him Zimran, Jokshan, Medan, Mid′ian, Ishbak, and Shuah. ³ Jokshan was the father of Sheba and Dedan. The sons of Dedan were Asshu′rim, Letu′shim, and Le-um′mim. ⁴ The sons of Mid′ian were Ephah, Epher, Hanoch, Abi′da, and Elda′ah. All these were the children of Ketu′rah. ⁵ Abraham gave all he had to Isaac. ⁶ But to the sons of his concubines Abraham gave gifts, and while he was still living he sent them away from his son Isaac, eastward to the east country.

7 These are the days of the years of Abraham's life, a hundred and seventy-five years. ⁸ Abraham breathed his last and died in a good old age, an old man and full of years, and was gathered to his people. ⁹ Isaac and Ish′mael his sons buried him in the cave of Machpe′lah, in the field of Ephron the son of Zohar the Hittite, east of Mamre, ¹⁰ the field which Abraham purchased from the Hittites. There Abraham was buried, with Sarah his wife. ¹¹ After the death of Abraham God blessed Isaac his son. And Isaac dwelt at Beer-la′hai-roi.

12 These are the descendants of Ish′mael, Abraham's son, whom Hagar the Egyptian, Sarah's maid, bore to Abraham. ¹³ These are the names of the sons of Ish′mael, named in the order of their birth: Neba′ioth, the firstborn of Ish′mael; and Kedar, Adbeel, Mibsam, ¹⁴ Mishma, Dumah, Massa, ¹⁵ Hadad, Tema, Jetur, Naphish, and Ked′emah. ¹⁶ These are the sons of Ish′mael and these are their names, by their villages and by their encampments, twelve princes according to their tribes. ¹⁷ (These are the years of the life of Ish′mael, a hundred and thirty-seven years; he breathed his last and died, and was gathered to his kindred.) ¹⁸ They dwelt from Hav′ilah to Shur, which is opposite Egypt in the direction of Assyria; he settled*p* over against all his people.

19 These are the descendants of Isaac, Abraham's son: Abraham was the father of Isaac, ²⁰ and Isaac was forty years old when he took to wife Rebekah, the daughter of Bethu′el the Aramean of Paddanaram, the sister of Laban the Aramean. ²¹ And Isaac prayed to the LORD for his wife, because she was barren; and the LORD granted his prayer, and Rebekah his wife conceived. ²² The children struggled together within her; and she said, "If it is thus, why do I live?"*q* So she went to inquire of the LORD. ²³ And the LORD said to her,

"Two nations are in your womb,
and two peoples, born of you,
    shall be divided;
the one shall be stronger than the
    other,
    the elder shall serve the younger."
²⁴ When her days to be delivered were fulfilled, behold, there were twins in her womb. ²⁵ The first came forth red, all his body like a hairy mantle; so they called his name Esau. ²⁶ Afterward his brother came forth, and his hand had taken hold of Esau's heel; so his name was called Jacob.*r* Isaac was sixty years old when she bore them.

27 When the boys grew up, Esau was a skilful hunter, a man of the field,

p Heb *fell*
q Syr: Heb obscure
r That is *He takes by the heel* or *He supplants*

25.1–18: The death of Abraham. 1–6: The ancestry of Arabic tribes, including Midian (Ex.2.15b–22; 18.1), is traced to Abraham through his other wife, Keturah. **9:** See ch. 23. **12–18:** An excerpt from the book of generations (5.1). **16:** Like later Israel, the Ishmaelites were organized into twelve tribes, each with a tribal prince. **18:** 16.7,14.

25.19–34: The rivalry of Jacob (Israel) and Esau (Edom). 20: *Paddan-aram,* see 11.31 n. **21:** See 16.2 n. **22–23:** Rebekah went to a sanctuary *to inquire of the LORD* and received the oracular answer in v. 23. **25:** The Hebrew word *red* ('adhmoni) is a play on the word Edom ('edhom; v. 30); *hairy* (se'ar) is a play on Seir, the region of the Edomites (32.3). **26:** *Jacob* is interpreted by a play on the Hebrew word for "heel," i.e. "he takes by the heel" or "he supplants" (Hos. 12.3; Jer.9.4). **27–28:** The two boys typify the hunter and the shepherd, two rival ways of life

while Jacob was a quiet man, dwelling in tents. [28] Isaac loved Esau, because he ate of his game; but Rebekah loved Jacob.

29 Once when Jacob was boiling pottage, Esau came in from the field, and he was famished. [30] And Esau said to Jacob, "Let me eat some of that red pottage, for I am famished!" (Therefore his name was called Edom.[s]) [31] Jacob said, "First sell me your birthright." [32] Esau said, "I am about to die; of what use is a birthright to me?" [33] Jacob said, "Swear to me first."[t] So he swore to him, and sold his birthright to Jacob. [34] Then Jacob gave Esau bread and pottage of lentils, and he ate and drank, and rose and went his way. Thus Esau despised his birthright.

26 Now there was a famine in the land, besides the former famine that was in the days of Abraham. And Isaac went to Gerar, to Abim'elech king of the Philistines. [2] And the LORD appeared to him, and said, "Do not go down to Egypt; dwell in the land of which I shall tell you. [3] Sojourn in this land, and I will be with you, and will bless you; for to you and to your descendants I will give all these lands, and I will fulfil the oath which I swore to Abraham your father. [4] I will multiply your descendants as the stars of heaven, and will give to your descendants all these lands; and by your descendants all the nations of the earth shall bless themselves: [5] because Abraham obeyed my voice and kept my charge, my commandments, my statutes, and my laws."

6 So Isaac dwelt in Gerar. [7] When the men of the place asked him about his wife, he said, "She is my sister"; for he feared to say, "My wife," thinking, "lest the men of the place should kill me for the sake of Rebekah"; because she was fair to look upon. [8] When he had been there a long time, Abim'elech king of the Philistines looked out of a window and saw Isaac fondling Rebekah his wife. [9] So Abim'elech called Isaac, and said, "Behold, she is your wife; how then could you say, 'She is my sister'?" Isaac said to him, "Because I thought, 'Lest I die because of her.'" [10] Abim'elech said, "What is this you have done to us? One of the people might easily have lain with your wife, and you would have brought guilt upon us." [11] So Abim'elech warned all the people, saying, "Whoever touches this man or his wife shall be put to death."

12 And Isaac sowed in that land, and reaped in the same year a hundredfold. The LORD blessed him, [13] and the man became rich, and gained more and more until he became very wealthy. [14] He had possessions of flocks and herds, and a great household, so that the Philistines envied him. [15] (Now the Philistines had stopped and filled with earth all the wells which his father's servants had dug in the days of Abraham his father.) [16] And Abim'elech said to Isaac, "Go away from us; for you are much mightier than we."

17 So Isaac departed from there, and encamped in the valley of Gerar and dwelt there. [18] And Isaac dug again the wells of water which had been dug in the days of Abraham his father; for the Philistines had stopped them after the death of Abraham; and he gave them the names which his father had given them. [19] But when Isaac's servants dug in the valley and found there a well of springing water, [20] the herdsmen of Gerar quarreled

s That is *Red*　　*t* Heb *today*

(4.2). **31–34:** The *birthright* refers to the rights of the eldest son: leadership of the family and a double share of the inheritance (Dt.21.15–17). The caricature of Esau as a dull person, easily outwitted on an empty stomach, is intended to explain why Israel gained ascendancy over Edom (2 Sam.8.12–14; 2 Chr.25.11–24) even though the latter became a nation first (36.31–39).
　26.1–34: Stories about Isaac. 1: *The former famine,* 12.10. *The Philistines,* see 21.34 n. **3–5:** The promise, first given to Abraham (12.2–3,7), is reaffirmed to Isaac. **7–11:** 12.10–20 and ch. 20. **12–33:** Isaac is portrayed as a semi-nomad who settled down long enough to raise crops

with Isaac's herdsmen, saying, "The water is ours." So he called the name of the well Esek,[u] because they contended with him. 21 Then they dug another well, and they quarreled over that also; so he called its name Sitnah.[v] 22 And he moved from there and dug another well, and over that they did not quarrel; so he called its name Reho'both,[w] saying, "For now the LORD has made room for us, and we shall be fruitful in the land."

23 From there he went up to Beersheba. 24 And the LORD appeared to him the same night and said, "I am the God of Abraham your father; fear not, for I am with you and will bless you and multiply your descendants for my servant Abraham's sake." 25 So he built an altar there and called upon the name of the LORD, and pitched his tent there. And there Isaac's servants dug a well.

26 Then Abim'elech went to him from Gerar with Ahuz'zath his adviser and Phicol the commander of his army. 27 Isaac said to them, "Why have you come to me, seeing that you hate me and have sent me away from you?" 28 They said, "We see plainly that the LORD is with you; so we say, let there be an oath between you and us, and let us make a covenant with you, 29 that you will do us no harm, just as we have not touched you and have done to you nothing but good and have sent you away in peace. You are now the blessed of the LORD." 30 So he made them a feast, and they ate and drank. 31 In the morning they rose early and took oath with one another; and Isaac set them on their way, and they departed from him in peace. 32 That same day Isaac's servants

came and told him about the well which they had dug, and said to him, "We have found water." 33 He called it Shibah; therefore the name of the city is Beer-sheba to this day.

34 When Esau was forty years old, he took to wife Judith the daughter of Be-e'ri the Hittite, and Bas'emath the daughter of Elon the Hittite; 35 and they made life bitter for Isaac and Rebekah.

27 When Isaac was old and his eyes were dim so that he could not see, he called Esau his older son, and said to him, "My son"; and he answered, "Here I am." 2 He said, "Behold, I am old; I do not know the day of my death. 3 Now then, take your weapons, your quiver and your bow, and go out to the field, and hunt game for me, 4 and prepare for me savory food, such as I love, and bring it to me that I may eat; that I may bless you before I die."

5 Now Rebekah was listening when Isaac spoke to his son Esau. So when Esau went to the field to hunt for game and bring it, 6 Rebekah said to her son Jacob, "I heard your father speak to your brother Esau, 7 'Bring me game, and prepare for me savory food, that I may eat it, and bless you before the LORD before I die.' 8 Now therefore, my son, obey my word as I command you. 9 Go to the flock, and fetch me two good kids, that I may prepare from them savory food for your father, such as he loves; 10 and you shall bring it to your father to eat, so that he may bless you before he dies." 11 But Jacob said to Rebekah his mother, "Behold,

u That is *Contention*
v That is *Enmity*
w That is *Broad places* or *Room*

(v. 12) but also moved about to find pasturage and water for his flocks. **24:** *The God of Abraham*, the God of the patriarchs is not known in general or abstract terms but by his concrete, historical relations to particular persons (Ex.3.6). **28–30:** Compare 21.22–24. **32–33:** *Shibah*, another explanation of the name of Isaac's shrine, Beer-sheba (see 21.22–34 n.).

    27.1–45: Jacob cheats Esau out of the blessing. Here begins a cycle of stories about Jacob, the founder of the sanctuary of Bethel. **3:** For Esau as a hunter, see 25.27–34, an episode to which Jacob makes no reference. **4:** Death-bed blessings were important in the life and literature of ancient peoples (48.8–20; 49.1–28; Dt. ch. 33; Jos. ch. 23). It was believed that the blessing, like the curse (v. 12), released a power which effectively determined the character and destiny of the recipient (Num. ch. 22–24). **5–29:** The elements of deceit and even outright lying (v. 20)

my brother Esau is a hairy man, and I am a smooth man. ¹² Perhaps my father will feel me, and I shall seem to be mocking him, and bring a curse upon myself and not a blessing." ¹³ His mother said to him, "Upon me be your curse, my son; only obey my word, and go, fetch them to me." ¹⁴ So he went and took them and brought them to his mother; and his mother prepared savory food, such as his father loved. ¹⁵ Then Rebekah took the best garments of Esau her older son, which were with her in the house, and put them on Jacob her younger son; ¹⁶ and the skins of the kids she put upon his hands and upon the smooth part of his neck; ¹⁷ and she gave the savory food and the bread, which she had prepared, into the hand of her son Jacob.

18 So he went in to his father, and said, "My father"; and he said, "Here I am; who are you, my son?" ¹⁹ Jacob said to his father, "I am Esau your first-born. I have done as you told me; now sit up and eat of my game, that you may bless me." ²⁰ But Isaac said to his son, "How is it that you have found it so quickly, my son?" He answered, "Because the LORD your God granted me success." ²¹ Then Isaac said to Jacob, "Come near, that I may feel you, my son, to know whether you are really my son Esau or not." ²² So Jacob went near to Isaac his father, who felt him and said, "The voice is Jacob's voice, but the hands are the hands of Esau." ²³ And he did not recognize him, because his hands were hairy like his brother Esau's hands; so he blessed him. ²⁴ He said, "Are you really my son Esau?" He answered, "I am." ²⁵ Then he said, "Bring it to me, that I may eat of my son's game and bless you." So he brought it to him, and he ate; and he brought him wine, and he drank. ²⁶ Then his father Isaac said to him, "Come near and kiss me, my son."

²⁷ So he came near and kissed him; and he smelled the smell of his garments, and blessed him, and said,

"See, the smell of my son
　is as the smell of a field which the
　　LORD has blessed!
²⁸ May God give you of the dew of
　heaven,
　and of the fatness of the earth,
　and plenty of grain and wine.
²⁹ Let peoples serve you,
　and nations bow down to you.
Be lord over your brothers,
　and may your mother's sons bow
　　down to you.
Cursed be every one who curses you,
　and blessed be every one who
　　blesses you!"

30 As soon as Isaac had finished blessing Jacob, when Jacob had scarcely gone out from the presence of Isaac his father, Esau his brother came in from his hunting. ³¹ He also prepared savory food, and brought it to his father. And he said to his father, "Let my father arise, and eat of his son's game, that you may bless me." ³² His father Isaac said to him, "Who are you?" He answered, "I am your son, your first-born, Esau." ³³ Then Isaac trembled violently, and said, "Who was it then that hunted game and brought it to me, and I ate it all*ˣ* before you came, and I have blessed him?–yes, and he shall be blessed." ³⁴ When Esau heard the words of his father, he cried out with an exceedingly great and bitter cry, and said to his father, "Bless me, even me also, O my father!" ³⁵ But he said, "Your brother came with guile, and he has taken away your blessing." ³⁶ Esau said, "Is he not rightly named Jacob? For he has supplanted me these two times. He took away my birthright; and behold, now he has taken away my blessing." Then he said, "Have you not reserved a blessing for me?"

x Cn: Heb *of all*

---

mark this as a popular story; the sequel shows that later Jacob reaped the consequences of his action. **34:** To appreciate the pathos of the scene it must be remembered that the spoken blessing, like an arrow shot toward its goal, released a power which could not be retracted (see v. 33). **36:** *He has supplanted me,* see 25.26 n. **39:** This blessing inverts the meaning of the same

[37] Isaac answered Esau, "Behold, I have made him your lord, and all his brothers I have given to him for servants, and with grain and wine I have sustained him. What then can I do for you, my son?" [38] Esau said to his father, "Have you but one blessing, my father? Bless me, even me also, O my father." And Esau lifted up his voice and wept.

39 Then Isaac his father answered him:

"Behold, away from[y] the fatness of
   the earth shall your dwelling
   be,
and away from[y] the dew of
   heaven on high.
[40] By your sword you shall live,
   and you shall serve your brother;
but when you break loose
   you shall break his yoke from
   your neck."

41 Now Esau hated Jacob because of the blessing with which his father had blessed him, and Esau said to himself, "The days of mourning for my father are approaching; then I will kill my brother Jacob." [42] But the words of Esau her older son were told to Rebekah; so she sent and called Jacob her younger son, and said to him, "Behold, your brother Esau comforts himself by planning to kill you. [43] Now therefore, my son, obey my voice; arise, flee to Laban my brother in Haran, [44] and stay with him a while, until your brother's fury turns away; [45] until your brother's anger turns away, and he forgets what you have done to him; then I will send, and fetch you from there. Why should I be bereft of you both in one day?"

46 Then Rebekah said to Isaac, "I am weary of my life because of the Hittite women. If Jacob marries one of the Hittite women such as these, one of the women of the land, what good will my life be to me?" [1] Then Isaac called Jacob and blessed him, and charged him, "You shall not marry one of the Canaanite women. [2] Arise, go to Paddan-aram to the house of Bethu'el your mother's father; and take as wife from there one of the daughters of Laban your mother's brother. [3] God Almighty[z] bless you and make you fruitful and multiply you, that you may become a company of peoples. [4] May he give the blessing of Abraham to you and to your descendants with you, that you may take possession of the land of your sojournings which God gave to Abraham!" [5] Thus Isaac sent Jacob away; and he went to Paddan-aram to Laban, the son of Bethu'el the Aramean, the brother of Rebekah, Jacob's and Esau's mother.

6 Now Esau saw that Isaac had blessed Jacob and sent him away to Paddan-aram to take a wife from there, and that as he blessed him he charged him, "You shall not marry one of the Canaanite women," [7] and that Jacob had obeyed his father and his mother and gone to Paddan-aram. [8] So when Esau saw that the Canaanite women did not please Isaac his father, [9] Esau went to Ish'mael and took to wife, besides the wives he had, Ma'halath the daughter of Ish'mael Abraham's son, the sister of Neba'ioth.

10 Jacob left Beer-sheba, and went toward Haran. [11] And he came to a certain place, and stayed there that night, because the sun had set. Taking one of the stones of the place, he put it under his head and lay down in that place to sleep. [12] And he dreamed that there was a ladder set up on the earth, and the top of it reached to

[y] Or *of*   [z] Heb *El Shaddai*

words in v. 28, for the land of Edom was not fertile. **40:** In David's time Edom was subjugated (2 Sam.8.12–14) but it revolted under Solomon (1 Kg.11.14–22,25; compare 2 Kg.8.20–22).

27.46–28.22: Jacob's departure for Aram and his dream at Bethel. **46:** *Hittite women*, i.e. Canaanites (see 23.3 n. and 24.3 n.). **28.2:** *Paddan-aram*, see 11.31 n. **3:** *God Almighty*, see 17.1 n. **11:** Bethel was at this time unsettled. According to ancient belief, oracles could be received by sleeping in a holy place (1 Sam. ch. 3). **12:** Angels in a company are mentioned here and in 32.1–2 (compare 16.7; 21.17), suggesting the view of a retinue surrounding the heavenly King.

heaven; and behold, the angels of God were ascending and descending on it! [13] And behold, the LORD stood above it[a] and said, "I am the LORD, the God of Abraham your father and the God of Isaac; the land on which you lie I will give to you and to your descendants; [14] and your descendants shall be like the dust of the earth, and you shall spread abroad to the west and to the east and to the north and to the south; and by you and your descendants shall all the families of the earth bless themselves.[b] [15] Behold, I am with you and will keep you wherever you go, and will bring you back to this land; for I will not leave you until I have done that of which I have spoken to you." [16] Then Jacob awoke from his sleep and said, "Surely the LORD is in this place; and I did not know it." [17] And he was afraid, and said, "How awesome is this place! This is none other than the house of God, and this is the gate of heaven."

18 So Jacob rose early in the morning, and he took the stone which he had put under his head and set it up for a pillar and poured oil on the top of it. [19] He called the name of that place Bethel;[c] but the name of the city was Luz at the first. [20] Then Jacob made a vow, saying, "If God will be with me, and will keep me in this way that I go, and will give me bread to eat and clothing to wear, [21] so that I come again to my father's house in peace, then the LORD shall be my God, [22] and this stone, which I have set up for a pillar, shall be God's house; and of all that thou givest me I will give the tenth to thee."

29 Then Jacob went on his journey, and came to the land of the people of the east. [2] As he looked, he saw a well in the field, and lo, three flocks of sheep lying beside it; for out of that well the flocks were watered. The stone on the well's mouth was large, [3] and when all the flocks were gathered there, the shepherds would roll the stone from the mouth of the well, and water the sheep, and put the stone back in its place upon the mouth of the well.

4 Jacob said to them, "My brothers, where do you come from?" They said, "We are from Haran." [5] He said to them, "Do you know Laban the son of Nahor?" They said, "We know him." [6] He said to them, "Is it well with him?" They said, "It is well; and see, Rachel his daughter is coming with the sheep!" [7] He said, "Behold, it is still high day, it is not time for the animals to be gathered together; water the sheep, and go, pasture them." [8] But they said, "We cannot until all the flocks are gathered together, and the stone is rolled from the mouth of the well; then we water the sheep."

9 While he was still speaking with them, Rachel came with her father's sheep; for she kept them. [10] Now when Jacob saw Rachel the daughter of Laban his mother's brother, and the sheep of Laban his mother's brother, Jacob went up and rolled the stone

a Or *beside him*
b Or *be blessed*
c That is *The house of God*

13-15: The Deity identifies himself as *the God of Abraham* and *the God of Isaac* (see 26.24 n.) and renews the promise (12.2–3,7). **17:** An explanation of the name of Beth-el (*house of God*). *The gate of heaven* suggests the ancient view that a sanctuary was a place where God came down to meet the people, like Babel or "gate of God" (11.1–9). **18:** The *pillar* was a sacred stone, often found at ancient sanctuaries (Jos.24.26). Anointing the stone made it holy, that is, set it apart for the Deity (v. 22). **21:** The personal relationship with the LORD indicated in the expression *my God*, is characteristic of patriarchal religion. The patriarch chooses God in response to a personal revelation. **22:** The story explains the origin of the northern sanctuary at Bethel which flourished from the time of Jeroboam I (1 Kg.12.26–29) to its destruction by Josiah (2 Kg.23.15).

29.1–31.55: Jacob's success in Haran. 1: *The people of the east,* a general expression (11.2), is applied here to the Arameans. **8:** Local custom prevented use of the well until all rightful parties could be there to get their fair share; thus the stone covering was bigger than one man could

from the well's mouth, and watered the flock of Laban his mother's brother. [11] Then Jacob kissed Rachel, and wept aloud. [12] And Jacob told Rachel that he was her father's kinsman, and that he was Rebekah's son; and she ran and told her father.

13 When Laban heard the tidings of Jacob his sister's son, he ran to meet him, and embraced him and kissed him, and brought him to his house. Jacob told Laban all these things, [14] and Laban said to him, "Surely you are my bone and my flesh!" And he stayed with him a month.

15 Then Laban said to Jacob, "Because you are my kinsman, should you therefore serve me for nothing? Tell me, what shall your wages be?" [16] Now Laban had two daughters; the name of the older was Leah, and the name of the younger was Rachel. [17] Leah's eyes were weak, but Rachel was beautiful and lovely. [18] Jacob loved Rachel; and he said, "I will serve you seven years for your younger daughter Rachel." [19] Laban said, "It is better that I give her to you than that I should give her to any other man; stay with me." [20] So Jacob served seven years for Rachel, and they seemed to him but a few days because of the love he had for her.

21 Then Jacob said to Laban, "Give me my wife that I may go in to her, for my time is completed." [22] So Laban gathered together all the men of the place, and made a feast. [23] But in the evening he took his daughter Leah and brought her to Jacob; and he went in to her. [24] (Laban gave his maid Zilpah to his daughter Leah to be her maid.) [25] And in the morning, behold, it was Leah; and Jacob said to Laban, "What is this you have done to me? Did I not serve with you for Rachel? Why then have you deceived me?" [26] Laban said, "It is not so done in our country, to give the younger before the first-born. [27] Complete the week of this one, and we will give you the other also in return for serving me another seven years." [28] Jacob did so, and completed her week; then Laban gave him his daughter Rachel to wife. [29] (Laban gave his maid Bilhah to his daughter Rachel to be her maid.) [30] So Jacob went in to Rachel also, and he loved Rachel more than Leah, and served Laban for another seven years.

31 When the LORD saw that Leah was hated, he opened her womb; but Rachel was barren. [32] And Leah conceived and bore a son, and she called his name Reuben;[d] for she said, "Because the LORD has looked upon my affliction; surely now my husband will love me." [33] She conceived again and bore a son, and said, "Because the LORD has heard[e] that I am hated, he has given me this son also"; and she called his name Simeon. [34] Again she conceived and bore a son, and said, "Now this time my husband will be joined[f] to me, because I have borne him three sons"; therefore his name was called Levi. [35] And she conceived again and bore a son, and said, "This time I will praise[g] the LORD"; therefore she called his name Judah; then she ceased bearing.

30 When Rachel saw that she bore Jacob no children, she envied her sister; and she said to Jacob, "Give me children, or I shall die!" [2] Jacob's anger was kindled against Rachel, and

d That is *See, a son*   e Heb *shama*
f Heb *lawah*   g Heb *hodah*

---

lift (vv. 2–3). **17:** Leah's eyes were *weak*, i.e. lacking luster. **18:** Jacob asks for Rachel as a reward for service (compare Jos.15.16–17; 1 Sam.17.25; 18.17) instead of paying the usual marriage price (Ex.22.16–17; Dt.22.29). **23–25:** The exchange could be made because the bride was brought veiled to the bridegroom (24.65). **27:** *The week* refers to the week of marriage festivity (Jg.14.12). **29.31–30.24:** Jacob's eleven sons (for Benjamin's birth, see 35.16–18). The fanciful name-explanations, based on Hebrew word-plays (see notes *d* to *n*), reflect the rivalry of the two wives for Jacob's affection. The story assumes the twelve-tribe pattern of the Israelite confederacy, probably instituted in Joshua's time (Jos. ch. 24). **30.2–3:** See 16.2 n. **6:** *God has*

he said, "Am I in the place of God, who has withheld from you the fruit of the womb?" [3] Then she said, "Here is my maid Bilhah; go in to her, that she may bear upon my knees, and even I may have children through her." [4] So she gave him her maid Bilhah as a wife; and Jacob went in to her. [5] And Bilhah conceived and bore Jacob a son. [6] Then Rachel said, "God has judged me, and has also heard my voice and given me a son"; therefore she called his name Dan.[h] [7] Rachel's maid Bilhah conceived again and bore Jacob a second son. [8] Then Rachel said, "With mighty wrestlings I have wrestled[i] with my sister, and have prevailed"; so she called his name Naph'tali.

[9] When Leah saw that she had ceased bearing children, she took her maid Zilpah and gave her to Jacob as a wife. [10] Then Leah's maid Zilpah bore Jacob a son. [11] And Leah said, "Good fortune!" so she called his name Gad.[j] [12] Leah's maid Zilpah bore Jacob a second son. [13] And Leah said, "Happy am I! For the women will call me happy"; so she called his name Asher.[k]

[14] In the days of wheat harvest Reuben went and found mandrakes in the field, and brought them to his mother Leah. Then Rachel said to Leah, "Give me, I pray, some of your son's mandrakes." [15] But she said to her, "Is it a small matter that you have taken away my husband? Would you take away my son's mandrakes also?" Rachel said, "Then he may lie with you tonight for your son's mandrakes." [16] When Jacob came from the field in the evening, Leah went out to meet him, and said, "You must come in to me; for I have hired you with my son's mandrakes." So he lay with her that night. [17] And God hearkened to Leah, and she conceived and bore Jacob a fifth son. [18] Leah said, "God has given me my hire[l] because I gave my maid

to my husband"; so she called his name Is'sachar. [19] And Leah conceived again, and she bore Jacob a sixth son. [20] Then Leah said, "God has endowed me with a good dowry; now my husband will honor[m] me, because I have borne him six sons"; so she called his name Zeb'ulun. [21] Afterwards she bore a daughter, and called her name Dinah. [22] Then God remembered Rachel, and God hearkened to her and opened her womb. [23] She conceived and bore a son, and said, "God has taken away my reproach"; [24] and she called his name Joseph,[n] saying, "May the LORD add to me another son!"

[25] When Rachel had borne Joseph, Jacob said to Laban, "Send me away, that I may go to my own home and country. [26] Give me my wives and my children for whom I have served you, and let me go; for you know the service which I have given you." [27] But Laban said to him, "If you will allow me to say so, I have learned by divination that the LORD has blessed me because of you; [28] name your wages, and I will give it." [29] Jacob said to him, "You yourself know how I have served you, and how your cattle have fared with me. [30] For you had little before I came, and it has increased abundantly; and the LORD has blessed you wherever I turned. But now when shall I provide for my own household also?" [31] He said, "What shall I give you?" Jacob said, "You shall not give me anything; if you will do this for me, I will again feed your flock and keep it: [32] let me pass through all your flock today, removing from it every speckled and spotted sheep and every black lamb, and the spotted and speckled among the goats; and such shall be my wages. [33] So my honesty will answer for me later, when you come to look into my wages with you. Every one that is not speckled and spotted among the goats

h That is *He judged*   i Heb *niphtal*
j That is *Fortune*   k That is *Happy*
l Heb *sakar*   m Heb *zabal*   n That is *He adds*

---

judged me, i.e. has gotten justice for me. **14:** In antiquity *mandrakes*, roots of a potato-like plant, were thought to have aphrodisiac properties which stimulated conception. **32–36:** Since striped

and black among the lambs, if found with me, shall be counted stolen." [34] Laban said, "Good! Let it be as you have said." [35] But that day Laban removed the he-goats that were striped and spotted, and all the she-goats that were speckled and spotted, every one that had white on it, and every lamb that was black, and put them in charge of his sons; [36] and he set a distance of three days' journey between himself and Jacob; and Jacob fed the rest of Laban's flock.

37 Then Jacob took fresh rods of poplar and almond and plane, and peeled white streaks in them, exposing the white of the rods. [38] He set the rods which he had peeled in front of the flocks in the runnels, that is, the watering troughs, where the flocks came to drink. And since they bred when they came to drink, [39] the flocks bred in front of the rods and so the flocks brought forth striped, speckled, and spotted. [40] And Jacob separated the lambs, and set the faces of the flocks toward the striped and all the black in the flock of Laban; and he put his own droves apart, and did not put them with Laban's flock. [41] Whenever the stronger of the flock were breeding Jacob laid the rods in the runnels before the eyes of the flock, that they might breed among the rods, [42] but for the feebler of the flock he did not lay them there; so the feebler were Laban's, and the stronger Jacob's. [43] Thus the man grew exceedingly rich, and had large flocks, maidservants and menservants, and camels and asses.

31 Now Jacob heard that the sons of Laban were saying, "Jacob has taken all that was our father's; and from what was our father's he has gained all this wealth." [2] And Jacob saw that Laban did not regard him with favor as before. [3] Then the LORD said to Jacob, "Return to the land of your fathers and to your kindred, and I will be with you." [4] So Jacob sent and called Rachel and Leah into the field where his flock was, [5] and said to them, "I see that your father does not regard me with favor as he did before. But the God of my father has been with me. [6] You know that I have served your father with all my strength; [7] yet your father has cheated me and changed my wages ten times, but God did not permit him to harm me. [8] If he said, 'The spotted shall be your wages,' then all the flock bore spotted; and if he said, 'The striped shall be your wages,' then all the flock bore striped. [9] Thus God has taken away the cattle of your father, and given them to me. [10] In the mating season of the flock I lifted up my eyes, and saw in a dream that the he-goats which leaped upon the flock were striped, spotted, and mottled. [11] Then the angel of God said to me in the dream, 'Jacob,' and I said, 'Here I am!' [12] And he said, 'Lift up your eyes and see, all the goats that leap upon the flock are striped, spotted, and mottled; for I have seen all that Laban is doing to you. [13] I am the God of Bethel, where you anointed a pillar and made a vow to me. Now arise, go forth from this land, and return to the land of your birth.'" [14] Then Rachel and Leah answered him, "Is there any portion or inheritance left to us in our father's house? [15] Are we not regarded by him as foreigners? For he has sold us, and he has been using up the money given for us. [16] All the property which God has taken away from our father belongs to us and to our children; now then, whatever God has said to you, do."

17 So Jacob arose, and set his sons and his wives on camels; [18] and he drove away all his cattle, all his live-

---

or speckled coloration was unusual, Laban seemingly had nothing to lose. **37–40:** Ancient cattle-breeders believed that the female, at the time of conception, was influenced by visual impressions which affect the color of the offspring. Jacob produced striped animals by putting striped sticks before the females' eyes while they were breeding. **31.4–16:** Jacob discusses the situation with his wives because legally they belong to their *father's house* (v. 14), and are part

stock which he had gained, the cattle in his possession which he had acquired in Paddan-aram, to go to the land of Canaan to his father Isaac. ¹⁹ Laban had gone to shear his sheep, and Rachel stole her father's household gods. ²⁰ And Jacob outwitted Laban the Aramean, in that he did not tell him that he intended to flee. ²¹ He fled with all that he had, and arose and crossed the Euphra'tes, and set his face toward the hill country of Gilead.

22 When it was told Laban on the third day that Jacob had fled, ²³ he took his kinsmen with him and pursued him for seven days and followed close after him into the hill country of Gilead. ²⁴ But God came to Laban the Aramean in a dream by night, and said to him, "Take heed that you say not a word to Jacob, either good or bad."

25 And Laban overtook Jacob. Now Jacob had pitched his tent in the hill country, and Laban with his kinsmen encamped in the hill country of Gilead. ²⁶ And Laban said to Jacob, "What have you done, that you have cheated me, and carried away my daughters like captives of the sword? ²⁷ Why did you flee secretly, and cheat me, and did not tell me, so that I might have sent you away with mirth and songs, with tambourine and lyre? ²⁸ And why did you not permit me to kiss my sons and my daughters farewell? Now you have done foolishly. ²⁹ It is in my power to do you harm; but the God of your father spoke to me last night, saying, 'Take heed that you speak to Jacob neither good nor bad.' ³⁰ And now you have gone away because you longed greatly for your father's house, but why did you steal my gods?" ³¹ Jacob answered Laban, "Because I was afraid, for I thought that you would take your daughters from me by force. ³² Any one with whom

you find your gods shall not live. In the presence of our kinsmen point out what I have that is yours, and take it." Now Jacob did not know that Rachel had stolen them.

33 So Laban went into Jacob's tent, and into Leah's tent, and into the tent of the two maidservants, but he did not find them. And he went out of Leah's tent, and entered Rachel's. ³⁴ Now Rachel had taken the household gods and put them in the camel's saddle, and sat upon them. Laban felt all about the tent, but did not find them. ³⁵ And she said to her father, "Let not my lord be angry that I cannot rise before you, for the way of women is upon me." So he searched, but did not find the household gods.

36 Then Jacob became angry, and upbraided Laban; Jacob said to Laban, "What is my offense? What is my sin, that you have hotly pursued me? ³⁷ Although you have felt through all my goods, what have you found of all your household goods? Set it here before my kinsmen and your kinsmen, that they may decide between us two. ³⁸ These twenty years I have been with you; your ewes and your she-goats have not miscarried, and I have not eaten the rams of your flocks. ³⁹ That which was torn by wild beasts I did not bring to you; I bore the loss of it myself; of my hand you required it, whether stolen by day or stolen by night. ⁴⁰ Thus I was; by day the heat consumed me, and the cold by night, and my sleep fled from my eyes. ⁴¹ These twenty years I have been in your house; I served you fourteen years for your two daughters, and six years for your flock, and you have changed my wages ten times. ⁴² If the God of my father, the God of Abraham and the Fear of Isaac, had not been on my side, surely now you would have sent me away empty-handed. God saw

of the property (Ru.4.5,10). **19:** Possession of *the household gods* (1 Sam.19.13–17), according to ancient custom, insured a man's leadership of the family and his claim on the property. **35:** The narrator ridicules the idols upon which Rachel sat in her time of "uncleanness" (Lev.15.19–23). **42:** *The Fear of Isaac* (perhaps, the "Kinsman" of Isaac) is an old epithet for the God of the

my affliction and the labor of my hands,
and rebuked you last night."
43 Then Laban answered and said
to Jacob, "The daughters are my
daughters, the children are my children,
the flocks are my flocks, and all that
you see is mine. But what can I do this
day to these my daughters, or to their
children whom they have borne?
44 Come now, let us make a covenant, you and I; and let it be a witness between you and me." 45 So
Jacob took a stone, and set it up as a
pillar. 46 And Jacob said to his kinsmen, "Gather stones," and they took
stones, and made a heap; and they ate
there by the heap. 47 Laban called
it Je′gar-sahadu′tha:[o] but Jacob
called it Galeed.[p] 48 Laban said, "This
heap is a witness between you and me
today." Therefore he named it Galeed,
49 and the pillar[q] Mizpah,[r] for he
said, "The LORD watch between you
and me, when we are absent one from
the other. 50 If you ill-treat my
daughters, or if you take wives besides my daughters, although no man
is with us, remember, God is witness
between you and me."
51 Then Laban said to Jacob, "See
this heap and the pillar, which I have
set between you and me. 52 This heap
is a witness, and the pillar is a witness,
that I will not pass over this heap to
you, and you will not pass over this
heap and this pillar to me, for harm.
53 The God of Abraham and the God
of Nahor, the God of their father,
judge between us." So Jacob swore by
the Fear of his father Isaac, 54 and
Jacob offered a sacrifice on the mountain and called his kinsmen to eat
bread; and they ate bread and tarried
all night on the mountain.
55[s] Early in the morning Laban
arose, and kissed his grandchildren and
his daughters and blessed them; then
he departed and returned home.

32 Jacob went on his way and the
angels of God met him; 2 and
when Jacob saw them he said, "This is
God's army!" So he called the name
of that place Mahana′im.[t]
3 And Jacob sent messengers before
him to Esau his brother in the land of
Se′ir, the country of Edom, 4 instructing them, "Thus you shall say to my
lord Esau: Thus says your servant Jacob, 'I have sojourned with Laban, and
stayed until now; 5 and I have oxen,
asses, flocks, menservants, and maidservants; and I have sent to tell my
lord, in order that I may find favor in
your sight.'"
6 And the messengers returned to
Jacob, saying, "We came to your
brother Esau, and he is coming to meet
you, and four hundred men with him."
7 Then Jacob was greatly afraid and
distressed; and he divided the people
that were with him, and the flocks and
herds and camels, into two companies,
8 thinking, "If Esau comes to the one
company and destroys it, then the company which is left will escape."

o In Aramaic *The heap of witness*
p In Hebrew *The heap of witness*
q Compare Sam: Heb lacks *the pillar*
r That is *Watchpost* *s* Ch 32.1 in Heb
t Here taken to mean *Two armies*

fathers, appropriated as a title for Israel's God. **43:** Laban's argument presupposes the legality of a type of marriage in which the wife stays in her father's household and the husband must leave his family (Jg.14.2–3; 15.1). **44:** The story reflects a boundary covenant between Arameans and Israelites, both of whom laid claim to the area in Transjordan (v. 52). **46:** *They ate there*, a reference to the covenant meal (v. 54) at which, it was believed, the Deity was present. **47:** The stone-heap is given two names (see notes *o* and *p*), one in Laban's language (Aramaic) and one in Jacob's (Hebrew). **49:** The "Mizpah benediction" is a prayer that the Deity would oversee the treaty (since neither Jacob nor Laban could trust each other) and guarantee that both parties live up to the contract.

32.1–33.20: Jacob's reconciliation with Esau. Before re-entering the promised land, Jacob underwent a struggle which chastened his self-confidence and prepared him for a new relation with Esau. **1–2:** The *angels* or heavenly host (see 28.12 n.) constituted *God's army* (Jos.5.13–15; 2 Kg.6.17). *Mahanaim*, here explained by a word-play, was important in later Israelite history (2 Sam.2.8–9; 17.24–29; 1 Kg.4.14). **3:** *Seir*, the region of Edom in which apparently Esau had

9 And Jacob said, "O God of my father Abraham and God of my father Isaac, O LORD who didst say to me, 'Return to your country and to your kindred, and I will do you good,' ¹⁰ I am not worthy of the least of all the steadfast love and all the faithfulness which thou hast shown to thy servant, for with only my staff I crossed this Jordan; and now I have become two companies. ¹¹ Deliver me, I pray thee, from the hand of my brother, from the hand of Esau, for I fear him, lest he come and slay us all, the mothers with the children. ¹² But thou didst say, 'I will do you good, and make your descendants as the sand of the sea, which cannot be numbered for multitude.'"

13 So he lodged there that night, and took from what he had with him a present for his brother Esau, ¹⁴ two hundred she-goats and twenty he-goats, two hundred ewes and twenty rams, ¹⁵ thirty milch camels and their colts, forty cows and ten bulls, twenty she-asses and ten he-asses. ¹⁶ These he delivered into the hand of his servants, every drove by itself, and said to his servants, "Pass on before me, and put a space between drove and drove." ¹⁷ He instructed the foremost, "When Esau my brother meets you, and asks you, 'To whom do you belong? Where are you going? And whose are these before you?' ¹⁸ then you shall say, 'They belong to your servant Jacob; they are a present sent to my lord Esau; and moreover he is behind us.'" ¹⁹ He likewise instructed the second and the third and all who followed the

droves, "You shall say the same thing to Esau when you meet him, ²⁰ and you shall say, 'Moreover your servant Jacob is behind us.'" For he thought, "I may appease him with the present that goes before me, and afterwards I shall see his face; perhaps he will accept me." ²¹ So the present passed on before him; and he himself lodged that night in the camp.

22 The same night he arose and took his two wives, his two maids, and his eleven children, and crossed the ford of the Jabbok. ²³ He took them and sent them across the stream, and likewise everything that he had. ²⁴ And Jacob was left alone; and a man wrestled with him until the breaking of the day. ²⁵ When the man saw that he did not prevail against Jacob, he touched the hollow of his thigh; and Jacob's thigh was put out of joint as he wrestled with him. ²⁶ Then he said, "Let me go, for the day is breaking." But Jacob said, "I will not let you go, unless you bless me." ²⁷ And he said to him, "What is your name?" And he said, "Jacob." ²⁸ Then he said, "Your name shall no more be called Jacob, but Israel,ᵘ for you have striven with God and with men, and have prevailed." ²⁹ Then Jacob asked him, "Tell me, I pray, your name." But he said, "Why is it that you ask my name?" And there he blessed him. ³⁰ So Jacob called the name of the place Peni'el,ᵛ saying, "For I have seen God face to face, and yet my life is preserved." ³¹ The sun rose upon him as he passed

u That is *He who strives with God* or *God strives*
v That is *The face of God*

already settled (36.6–8). **3–21:** Although uncertain how his brother felt toward him after twenty years, the resourceful Jacob believed that he could get the situation into hand, either by saving half of his camp (vv. 6–8) or by winning Esau over with impressive gifts (vv. 13–21). **25:** Owing to his Herculean strength (29.10; compare 28.18), Jacob was winning the contest until his opponent sprained Jacob's thigh. **26:** The divine being had to vanish before sunrise–a mark of the antiquity of the tradition. **27:** In antiquity it was believed that a person's self was concentrated in his name (compare v. 29). **28:** Jacob's new name signified a new self: no longer was he the Supplanter (25.26; 27.36) but *Israel* (35.10), which probably means "God rules." This name, which later designated the Tribal Confederacy (see 33.20 n.), is interpreted to mean "He who strives with God" (Hos.12.3–4). *And with men* refers to Jacob's strife with Esau and Laban. **29:** The divine being refuses lest Jacob, by possessing the name, gain power over him (compare Ex.3.13–14; Jg.13.17). **30:** Jacob had feared to see Esau's face (v. 20; 33.10), but instead he saw

Penu'el, limping because of his thigh.
³² Therefore to this day the Israelites
do not eat the sinew of the hip which
is upon the hollow of the thigh, because
he touched the hollow of Jacob's thigh
on the sinew of the hip.

33 And Jacob lifted up his eyes
and looked, and behold, Esau
was coming, and four hundred men
with him. So he divided the children
among Leah and Rachel and the two
maids. ² And he put the maids with
their children in front, then Leah with
her children, and Rachel and Joseph
last of all. ³ He himself went on before
them, bowing himself to the ground
seven times, until he came near to his
brother.

4 But Esau ran to meet him, and
embraced him, and fell on his neck and
kissed him, and they wept. ⁵ And when
Esau raised his eyes and saw the
women and children, he said, "Who
are these with you?" Jacob said, "The
children whom God has graciously
given your servant." ⁶ Then the maids
drew near, they and their children,
and bowed down; ⁷ Leah likewise and
her children drew near and bowed
down; and last Joseph and Rachel drew
near, and they bowed down. ⁸ Esau
said, "What do you mean by all this
company which I met?" Jacob answered, "To find favor in the sight of
my lord." ⁹ But Esau said, "I have
enough, my brother; keep what you
have for yourself." ¹⁰ Jacob said, "No,
I pray you, if I have found favor in
your sight, then accept my present
from my hand; for truly to see your
face is like seeing the face of God, with
such favor have you received me.
¹¹ Accept, I pray you, my gift that is

brought to you, because God has dealt
graciously with me, and because I have
enough." Thus he urged him, and he
took it.

12 Then Esau said, "Let us journey
on our way, and I will go before you."
¹³ But Jacob said to him, "My lord
knows that the children are frail, and
that the flocks and herds giving suck
are a care to me; and if they are over-
driven for one day, all the flocks will
die. ¹⁴ Let my lord pass on before his
servant, and I will lead on slowly, according to the pace of the cattle which
are before me and according to the
pace of the children, until I come to
my lord in Se'ir."

15 So Esau said, "Let me leave
with you some of the men who are with
me." But he said, "What need is there?
Let me find favor in the sight of my
lord." ¹⁶ So Esau returned that day
on his way to Se'ir. ¹⁷ But Jacob journeyed to Succoth,ʷ and built himself
a house, and made booths for his cattle; therefore the name of the place is
called Succoth.

18 And Jacob came safely to the
city of Shechem, which is in the land of
Canaan, on his way from Paddan-
aram; and he camped before the city.
¹⁹ And from the sons of Hamor,
Shechem's father, he bought for a hundred pieces of moneyˣ the piece of
land on which he had pitched his tent.
²⁰ There he erected an altar and called
it El-El'ohe-Israel.ʸ

34 Now Dinah the daughter of
Leah, whom she had borne
to Jacob, went out to visit the
women of the land; ² and when

w That is *Booths*
x Heb *a hundred qesitah*
y That is *God, the God of Israel*

God *face to face* and was allowed to live (16.13; Ex.33.20). **32:** An explanation of the Israelite
taboo against eating the corresponding muscle of an animal. **33.10:** *Like seeing the face of God,*
who at Penuel also proved to be gracious (32.30). **18:** *Shechem,* see 12.6 n. **19:** *The Sons of Hamor*
were the ruling clan of the city (Jg.9.28), of Hivite (perhaps Horite or Hurrian) extraction (see
36.20 n.). *The piece of land* later became the traditional burial place of Joseph (Jos.24.32). **20:**
The worship of *El-Elohe-Israel* (see note y) apparently preceded the later establishment of a
twelve-tribe confederacy of Israel, presumably at Shechem (Jos. ch. 24), when El (the Semitic
word for "God") was succeeded by the LORD (Yahweh), the God of Israel.
   34.1–24: Shechem's violation of Dinah and its consequences. **1:** Dinah is mentioned elsewhere

Shechem the son of Hamor the Hivite, the prince of the land, saw her, he seized her and lay with her and humbled her. ³ And his soul was drawn to Dinah the daughter of Jacob; he loved the maiden and spoke tenderly to her. ⁴ So Shechem spoke to his father Hamor, saying, "Get me this maiden for my wife." ⁵ Now Jacob heard that he had defiled his daughter Dinah; but his sons were with his cattle in the field, so Jacob held his peace until they came. ⁶ And Hamor the father of Shechem went out to Jacob to speak with him. ⁷ The sons of Jacob came in from the field when they heard of it; and the men were indignant and very angry, because he had wrought folly in Israel by lying with Jacob's daughter, for such a thing ought not to be done.

⁸ But Hamor spoke with them, saying, "The soul of my son Shechem longs for your daughter; I pray you, give her to him in marriage. ⁹ Make marriages with us; give your daughters to us, and take our daughters for yourselves. ¹⁰ You shall dwell with us; and the land shall be open to you; dwell and trade in it, and get property in it." ¹¹ Shechem also said to her father and to her brothers, "Let me find favor in your eyes, and whatever you say to me I will give. ¹² Ask of me ever so much as marriage present and gift, and I will give according as you say to me; only give me the maiden to be my wife."

13 The sons of Jacob answered Shechem and his father Hamor deceitfully, because he had defiled their sister Dinah. ¹⁴ They said to them, "We cannot do this thing, to give our sister to one who is uncircumcised, for that would be a disgrace to us. ¹⁵ Only on this condition will we consent to you: that you will become as we are and every male of you be circumcised. ¹⁶ Then we will give our daughters to you, and we will take your daughters to ourselves, and we will dwell with you and become one people. ¹⁷ But if you will not listen to us and be circumcised, then we will take our daughter, and we will be gone."

18 Their words pleased Hamor and Hamor's son Shechem. ¹⁹ And the young man did not delay to do the thing, because he had delight in Jacob's daughter. Now he was the most honored of all his family. ²⁰ So Hamor and his son Shechem came to the gate of their city and spoke to the men of their city, saying, ²¹ "These men are friendly with us; let them dwell in the land and trade in it, for behold, the land is large enough for them; let us take their daughters in marriage, and let us give them our daughters. ²² Only on this condition will the men agree to dwell with us, to become one people: that every male among us be circumcised as they are circumcised. ²³ Will not their cattle, their property and all their beasts be ours? Only let us agree with them, and they will dwell with us." ²⁴ And all who went out of the gate of his city hearkened to Hamor and his son Shechem; and every male was circumcised, all who went out of the gate of his city.

25 On the third day, when they were sore, two of the sons of Jacob, Simeon and Levi, Dinah's brothers, took their swords and came upon the city unawares, and killed all the males. ²⁶ They slew Hamor and his son Shechem with the sword, and took

---

only in 30.21 and 46.15. *The women of the land,* i.e. Canaanite women. **2:** Here *Shechem* is the name of a person (33.19). The story portrays, in the guise of individuals, relations between the Canaanite city and early Hebrew tribes. *The sons of Hamor,* see 33.19 n. **7:** *Wrought folly in Israel* is an old expression for a crime affecting the whole tribal community of Israel (Dt.22.21; Jos.7.15; Jg.19.23–24; 20.6,10). **12:** *Marriage present,* Ex.22.16–17; Dt.22.29. **14–15:** Circumcision, see 17.9–14 n. **19:** The fact that Shechem *was most honored of all his family* and *the prince of the land* (v. 2) shows the ascendancy of this Canaanite city in the pre-Israelite period. **22–23:** *One people,* i.e. a kindred-group in which the Shechemites would have the leadership. **25–26:**

Dinah out of Shechem's house, and went away. [27] And the sons of Jacob came upon the slain, and plundered the city, because their sister had been defiled; [28] they took their flocks and their herds, their asses, and whatever was in the city and in the field; [29] all their wealth, all their little ones and their wives, all that was in the houses, they captured and made their prey. [30] Then Jacob said to Simeon and Levi, "You have brought trouble on me by making me odious to the inhabitants of the land, the Canaanites and the Per'izzites; my numbers are few, and if they gather themselves against me and attack me, I shall be destroyed, both I and my household." [31] But they said, "Should he treat our sister as a harlot?"

35 God said to Jacob, "Arise, go up to Bethel, and dwell there; and make there an altar to the God who appeared to you when you fled from your brother Esau." [2] So Jacob said to his household and to all who were with him, "Put away the foreign gods that are among you, and purify yourselves, and change your garments; [3] then let us arise and go up to Bethel, that I may make there an altar to the God who answered me in the day of my distress and has been with me wherever I have gone." [4] So they gave to Jacob all the foreign gods that they had, and the rings that were in their ears; and Jacob hid them under the oak which was near Shechem.

5 And as they journeyed, a terror from God fell upon the cities that were round about them, so that they did not pursue the sons of Jacob. [6] And Jacob came to Luz (that is, Bethel), which is in the land of Canaan, he and all the people who were with him, [7] and there he built an altar, and called the place El-bethel,*z* because there God had revealed himself to him when he fled from his brother. [8] And Deb'orah, Rebekah's nurse, died, and she was buried under an oak below Bethel; so the name of it was called Al'lon-bacuth.*a*

9 God appeared to Jacob again, when he came from Paddan-aram, and blessed him. [10] And God said to him, "Your name is Jacob; no longer shall your name be called Jacob, but Israel shall be your name." So his name was called Israel. [11] And God said to him, "I am God Almighty:*b* be fruitful and multiply; a nation and a company of nations shall come from you, and kings shall spring from you. [12] The land which I gave to Abraham and Isaac I will give to you, and I will give the land to your descendants after you." [13] Then God went up from him in the place where he had spoken with him. [14] And Jacob set up a pillar in the place where he had spoken with him, a pillar of stone; and he poured out a drink offering on it, and poured oil on it. [15] So Jacob called the name of the place where God had spoken with him, Bethel.

16 Then they journeyed from Bethel; and when they were still some

z That is God of Bethel
a That is Oak of weeping   b Heb El Shaddai

Simeon and Levi took the initiative because they were full brothers of Dinah. **30:** The violent action, which threatened the good relations of Jacob's family with the Canaanites, reflects events which forced Simeon and Levi out of the area and led to their decline in power (49.5–7).

35.1–29: Jacob's journey from Shechem to Mamre. 1: *Bethel*, 28.19–22. Verses 1–4 may reflect the custom of making a pilgrimage to the Bethel sanctuary (compare Jg.20.26–27). **2:** The worshipers had to undergo ceremonial purification, which involved changing garments and ablutions (Ex.19.10; Jos.7.13), and to renounce *foreign gods* (Jos.24.14–18,23), including the household gods (31.19). **4:** The earrings and other magical amulets belonged to foreign idolatry (Ex.32.2–3; Jg.8.24). *The oak*, i.e. of Moreh (12.6). **5:** *A terror from God*, an expression derived from ancient holy war (Ex.23.27; Jos.10.10), was a mysterious panic that paralyzed the enemy. **6–7:** 28.18–22. **9–13:** Another account of Jacob's receiving a new name (compare 32.24–30) and God's promise to him (28.13–15). **11:** *God Almighty*, see 17.1 n. **14–15:** A tradition parallel to 28.18–22. **16:** *Ephrath*, see v. 19 n. **18:** Dying in child-birth, Rachel gave an ominous name (see

distance from Ephrath, Rachel travailed, and she had hard labor. [17] And when she was in her hard labor, the midwife said to her, "Fear not; for now you will have another son." [18] And as her soul was departing (for she died), she called his name Ben-o'ni;[c] but his father called his name Benjamin.[d] [19] So Rachel died, and she was buried on the way to Ephrath (that is, Bethlehem), [20] and Jacob set up a pillar upon her grave; it is the pillar of Rachel's tomb, which is there to this day. [21] Israel journeyed on, and pitched his tent beyond the tower of Eder.

22 While Israel dwelt in that land Reuben went and lay with Bilhah his father's concubine; and Israel heard of it.

Now the sons of Jacob were twelve. [23] The sons of Leah: Reuben (Jacob's first-born), Simeon, Levi, Judah, Is'sachar, and Zeb'ulun. [24] The sons of Rachel: Joseph and Benjamin. [25] The sons of Bilhah, Rachel's maid: Dan and Naph'tali. [26] The sons of Zilpah, Leah's maid: Gad and Asher. These were the sons of Jacob who were born to him in Paddan-aram.

27 And Jacob came to his father Isaac at Mamre, or Kir'iath-ar'ba (that is, Hebron), where Abraham and Isaac had sojourned. [28] Now the days of Isaac were a hundred and eighty years. [29] And Isaac breathed his last; and he died and was gathered to his people, old and full of days; and his sons Esau and Jacob buried him.

36 These are the descendants of Esau (that is, Edom). [2] Esau took his wives from the Canaanites: Adah the daughter of Elon the Hittite, Oholiba'mah the daughter of Anah the son[e] of Zib'eon the Hivite, [3] and Bas'emath, Ish'mael's daughter, the sister of Neba'ioth. [4] And Adah bore to Esau, El'iphaz; Bas'emath bore Reu'el; [5] and Oholiba'mah bore Je'ush, Jalam, and Korah. These are the sons of Esau who were born to him in the land of Canaan.

6 Then Esau took his wives, his sons, his daughters, and all the members of his household, his cattle, all his beasts, and all his property which he had acquired in the land of Canaan; and he went into a land away from his brother Jacob. [7] For their possessions were too great for them to dwell together; the land of their sojournings could not support them because of their cattle. [8] So Esau dwelt in the hill country of Se'ir; Esau is Edom.

9 These are the descendants of Esau the father of the E'domites in the hill country of Se'ir. [10] These are the names of Esau's sons: El'iphaz the son of Adah the wife of Esau, Reu'el the son of Bas'emath the wife of Esau. [11] The sons of El'iphaz were Teman, Omar, Zepho, Gatam, and Kenaz. [12] (Timna was a concubine of El'iphaz, Esau's son; she bore Am'alek to El'iphaz.) These are the sons of Adah, Esau's wife. [13] These are the sons of Reu'el: Nahath, Zerah, Shammah, and Mizzah. These are the sons of Bas'emath, Esau's wife. [14] These are the sons of Oholiba'mah the daughter of Anah the son[f] of Zib'eon, Esau's wife: she bore to Esau Je'ush, Jalam, and Korah.

c That is *Son of my sorrow*
d That is *Son of the right hand* or *Son of the South*
e Sam Gk Syr: Heb *daughter*
f Gk Syr: Heb *daughter*

note c) to the child (see 1 Sam.4.21), although Jacob changed the name to a propitious one. *Benjamin* (see note d) refers either to the right hand as a symbol of power and fortune or to the tribe's position south of Ephraim. **19:** Here and in 48.7 (Ru.4.11; Mic.5.2) Ephrath is identified with Bethlehem. Another tradition located Rachel's grave in Benjaminite territory north of Jerusalem (1 Sam.10.2; Jer.31.15). **21–22:** This fragmentary account apparently told of an incident which resulted in Reuben's loss of prestige as the first-born son (49.3–4). **21:** From this point on the name *Israel* is often used to refer to Jacob (32.28).

36.1–43: Edomite lists. Some of this material (vv. 1–8,9–14,15–19,40–43) was apparently drawn from the book of generations (5.1). **1:** *Esau* (*Edom*), 25.21–28. **2–3:** Esau's wives, see 26.34; 28.8–9. **8:** *Seir*, or Edom (see 25.25 n.; 27.39–40).

15 These are the chiefs of the sons of Esau. The sons of El'iphaz the first-born of Esau: the chiefs Teman, Omar, Zepho, Kenaz, 16 Korah, Gatam, and Am'alek; these are the chiefs of El'iphaz in the land of Edom; they are the sons of Adah. 17 These are the sons of Reu'el, Esau's son: the chiefs Nahath, Zerah, Shammah, and Mizzah; these are the chiefs of Reu'el in the land of Edom; they are the sons of Bas'emath, Esau's wife. 18 These are the sons of Oholiba'mah, Esau's wife: the chiefs Je'ush, Jalam, and Korah; these are the chiefs born of Oholiba'mah the daughter of Anah, Esau's wife. 19 These are the sons of Esau (that is, Edom), and these are their chiefs.

20 These are the sons of Se'ir the Horite, the inhabitants of the land: Lotan, Shobal, Zib'eon, Anah, 21 Dishon, Ezer, and Dishan; these are the chiefs of the Horites, the sons of Se'ir in the land of Edom. 22 The sons of Lotan were Hori and Heman; and Lotan's sister was Timna. 23 These are the sons of Shobal: Alvan, Man'ahath, Ebal, Shepho, and Onam. 24 These are the sons of Zib'eon: A'iah and Anah; he is the Anah who found the hot springs in the wilderness, as he pastured the asses of Zib'eon his father. 25 These are the children of Anah: Dishon and Oholiba'mah the daughter of Anah. 26 These are the sons of Dishon: Hemdan, Eshban, Ithran, and Cheran. 27 These are the sons of Ezer: Bilhan, Za'avan, and Akan. 28 These are the sons of Dishan: Uz and Aran. 29 These are the chiefs of the Horites: the chiefs Lotan, Shobal, Zib'eon, Anah, 30 Dishon, Ezer, and Dishan; these are the chiefs of the Horites, according to their clans in the land of Se'ir.

31 These are the kings who reigned in the land of Edom, before any king reigned over the Israelites. 32 Bela the son of Be'or reigned in Edom, the name of his city being Din'habah. 33 Bela died, and Jobab the son of Zerah of Bozrah reigned in his stead. 34 Jobab died, and Husham of the land of the Te'manites reigned in his stead. 35 Husham died, and Hadad the son of Bedad, who defeated Mid'ian in the country of Moab, reigned in his stead, the name of his city being Avith. 36 Hadad died, and Samlah of Masre'kah reigned in his stead. 37 Samlah died, and Shaul of Reho'both on the Euphra'tes reigned in his stead. 38 Shaul died, and Ba'al-ha'nan the son of Achbor reigned in his stead. 39 Ba'al-ha'nan the son of Achbor died, and Hadar reigned in his stead, the name of his city being Pau; his wife's name was Mehet'abel, the daughter of Matred, daughter of Me'zahab.

40 These are the names of the chiefs of Esau, according to their families and their dwelling places, by their names: the chiefs Timna, Alvah, Jetheth, 41 Oholiba'mah, Elah, Pinon, 42 Kenaz, Teman, Mibzar, 43 Mag'diel, and Iram; these are the chiefs of Edom (that is, Esau, the father of Edom), according to their dwelling places in the land of their possession.

37 Jacob dwelt in the land of his father's sojournings, in the land of Canaan. 2 This is the history of the family of Jacob.

Joseph, being seventeen years old, was shepherding the flock with his brothers; he was a lad with the sons of Bilhah and Zilpah, his father's wives; and Joseph brought an ill report of them to their father. 3 Now Israel

---

20: *Horite* refers to the Hurrians, a non-Semitic people who migrated into Mesopotamia about 2000 B.C. and later formed an important element of the Canaanite population. **31–39:** Edom became a monarchy long (perhaps 150 years) before Israel did (Num. 20.14), a circumstance reflected in the tradition that Esau was the older brother although Jacob gained the ascendancy.

37.1–36: Joseph is sold into slavery. The narratives about Joseph, found in chs. 37; 39–47; and 50, constitute a single literary form or short story. **2:** The Joseph story is regarded as part of the history of Jacob, who died at the end of the saga (49.33). *The sons of Bilhah and Zilpah,* 30.1–13.

loved Joseph more than any other of his children, because he was the son of his old age; and he made him a long robe with sleeves. [4] But when his brothers saw that their father loved him more than all his brothers, they hated him, and could not speak peaceably to him.

5 Now Joseph had a dream, and when he told it to his brothers they only hated him the more. [6] He said to them, "Hear this dream which I have dreamed: [7] behold, we were binding sheaves in the field, and lo, my sheaf arose and stood upright; and behold, your sheaves gathered round it, and bowed down to my sheaf." [8] His brothers said to him, "Are you indeed to reign over us? Or are you indeed to have dominion over us?" So they hated him yet more for his dreams and for his words. [9] Then he dreamed another dream, and told it to his brothers, and said, "Behold, I have dreamed another dream; and behold, the sun, the moon, and eleven stars were bowing down to me." [10] But when he told it to his father and to his brothers, his father rebuked him, and said to him, "What is this dream that you have dreamed? Shall I and your mother and your brothers indeed come to bow ourselves to the ground before you?" [11] And his brothers were jealous of him, but his father kept the saying in mind.

12 Now his brothers went to pasture their father's flock near Shechem. [13] And Israel said to Joseph, "Are not your brothers pasturing the flock at Shechem? Come, I will send you to them." And he said to him, "Here I am." [14] So he said to him, "Go now, see if it is well with your brothers, and with the flock; and bring me word again." So he sent him from the valley of Hebron, and he came to Shechem. [15] And a man found him wandering in the fields; and the man asked him, "What are you seeking?" [16] "I am seeking my brothers," he said, "tell me, I pray you, where they are pasturing the flock." [17] And the man said, "They have gone away, for I heard them say, 'Let us go to Dothan.'" So Joseph went after his brothers, and found them at Dothan. [18] They saw him afar off, and before he came near to them they conspired against him to kill him. [19] They said to one another, "Here comes this dreamer. [20] Come now, let us kill him and throw him into one of the pits; then we shall say that a wild beast has devoured him, and we shall see what will become of his dreams." [21] But when Reuben heard it, he delivered him out of their hands, saying, "Let us not take his life." [22] And Reuben said to them, "Shed no blood; cast him into this pit here in the wilderness, but lay no hand upon him"–that he might rescue him out of their hand, to restore him to his father. [23] So when Joseph came to his brothers, they stripped him of his robe, the long robe with sleeves that he wore; [24] and they took him and cast him into a pit. The pit was empty, there was no water in it.

25 Then they sat down to eat; and looking up they saw a caravan of Ish′maelites coming from Gilead, with their camels bearing gum, balm, and myrrh, on their way to carry it down to Egypt. [26] Then Judah said to his brothers, "What profit is it if we slay our brother and conceal his blood? [27] Come, let us sell him to the Ish′maelites, and let not our hand be upon

---

3: *A long robe with sleeves* was a luxurious robe (2 Sam.13.18–19), different from the ordinary sleeveless tunic which reached to the knees. **5–11:** Joseph's two dreams were prophetic of his future elevation in Egypt (42.6; 50.18). **9:** *Eleven stars,* apparently the eleven constellations which ancients pictured in animal form. **12:** The previous scene is laid in Hebron (35.27), several days' journey from Jacob's pasture land *near Shechem* (33.18–20). **21:** *Reuben* may be a scribal mistake for Judah, Joseph's advocate in v. 26. **20:** *The pits* were open cisterns for storing rain water (Jer.38.6). **22:** The advice of Reuben and Judah reflects the ancient belief that blood cannot be "concealed" (v. 26) but cries out for requital (see 4.10–11 n.). **25–28:** Two traditions have been combined: according to one, Joseph was sold to *Ishmaelites;* according to the other,

him, for he is our brother, our own flesh." And his brothers heeded him. 28 Then Mid′ianite traders passed by; and they drew Joseph up and lifted him out of the pit, and sold him to the Ish′maelites for twenty shekels of silver; and they took Joseph to Egypt.

29 When Reuben returned to the pit and saw that Joseph was not in the pit, he rent his clothes 30 and returned to his brothers, and said, "The lad is gone; and I, where shall I go?" 31 Then they took Joseph's robe, and killed a goat, and dipped the robe in the blood; 32 and they sent the long robe with sleeves and brought it to their father, and said, "This we have found; see now whether it is your son's robe or not." 33 And he recognized it, and said, "It is my son's robe; a wild beast has devoured him; Joseph is without doubt torn to pieces." 34 Then Jacob rent his garments, and put sackcloth upon his loins, and mourned for his son many days. 35 All his sons and all his daughters rose up to comfort him; but he refused to be comforted, and said, "No, I shall go down to Sheol to my son, mourning." Thus his father wept for him. 36 Meanwhile the Mid′- ianites had sold him in Egypt to Pot′- i-phar, an officer of Pharaoh, the captain of the guard.

38 It happened at that time that Judah went down from his brothers, and turned in to a certain Adullamite, whose name was Hirah.

2 There Judah saw the daughter of a certain Canaanite whose name was Shua; he married her and went in to her, 3 and she conceived and bore a son, and he called his name Er. 4 Again she conceived and bore a son, and she called his name Onan. 5 Yet again she bore a son, and she called his name Shelah. She*g* was in Chezib when she bore him. 6 And Judah took a wife for Er his first-born, and her name was Tamar. 7 But Er, Judah's first-born, was wicked in the sight of the LORD; and the LORD slew him. 8 Then Judah said to Onan, "Go in to your brother's wife, and perform the duty of a brother-in-law to her, and raise up offspring for your brother." 9 But Onan knew that the offspring would not be his; so when he went in to his brother's wife he spilled the semen on the ground, lest he should give offspring to his brother. 10 And what he did was displeasing in the sight of the LORD, and he slew him also. 11 Then Judah said to Tamar his daughter-in-law, "Remain a widow in your father's house, till Shelah my son grows up"–for he feared that he would die, like his brothers. So Tamar went and dwelt in her father's house.

12 In course of time the wife of Judah, Shua's daughter, died; and when Judah was comforted, he went up to Timnah to his sheepshearers, he and his friend Hirah the Adullamite.

g Gk: Heb He

---

he was kidnapped by *Midianite traders* (v. 36). Dothan (a few miles north of Shechem), where Joseph found his brothers (v. 17), lay on the trade route from Syria to Egypt. **35:** *Sheol,* the underworld to which, it was believed, a man's shade went at death (2 Sam.12.23; Ps.115.17). Since this after-life was a shadowy existence, Jacob's going to his son there was not a comforting expectation. **36:** *Potiphar* is a form of Potiphera, the name of the Egyptian priest, of 41.45 and 46.20. It has been thought they may be the same person, one source designating him as captain of the guard, and another as a priest.

38.1–30: Judah and Tamar. This chapter, an interlude in the Joseph story, deals with a woman's part in the LORD's promise that Abraham will have a great posterity. **1:** *Adullamite,* a resident of Adullam near Bethlehem. **2:** The marriage with Shuah's daughter reflects territorial expansion of the tribe of Judah and the consequent intermarriage with Canaanites. **7:** The early and childless death of Er is attributed to a divine act, almost demonic in character. **8:** According to the ancient widespread custom of levirate marriage (Dt.25.5–10; compare Ru.4.1–12), *the duty of a brother-in-law* was to raise up a male descendant for his deceased brother and thus perpetuate his name and inheritance. **11:** Judah apparently feared that the death of his two sons resulted from Tamar's sinister power. A widow was supposed to return to her *father's house*

13 And when Tamar was told, "Your father-in-law is going up to Timnah to shear his sheep," 14 she put off her widow's garments, and put on a veil, wrapping herself up, and sat at the entrance to Enaim, which is on the road to Timnah; for she saw that Shelah was grown up, and she had not been given to him in marriage. 15 When Judah saw her, he thought her to be a harlot, for she had covered her face. 16 He went over to her at the road side, and said, "Come, let me come in to you," for he did not know that she was his daughter-in-law. She said, "What will you give me, that you may come in to me?" 17 He answered, "I will send you a kid from the flock." And she said, "Will you give me a pledge, till you send it?" 18 He said, "What pledge shall I give you?" She replied, "Your signet and your cord, and your staff that is in your hand." So he gave them to her, and went in to her, and she conceived by him. 19 Then she arose and went away, and taking off her veil she put on the garments of her widowhood.

20 When Judah sent the kid by his friend the Adullamite, to receive the pledge from the woman's hand, he could not find her. 21 And he asked the men of the place, "Where is the harlot[h] who was at Enaim by the wayside?" And they said, "No harlot[h] has been here." 22 So he returned to Judah, and said, "I have not found her; and also the men of the place said, 'No harlot[h] has been here.' " 23 And Judah replied, "Let her keep the things as her own, lest we be laughed at; you see, I sent this kid, and you could not find her."

24 About three months later Judah was told, "Tamar your daughter-in-law has played the harlot; and moreover she is with child by harlotry." And Judah said, "Bring her out, and let her be burned." 25 As she was being brought out, she sent word to her father-in-law, "By the man to whom these belong, I am with child." And she said, "Mark, I pray you, whose these are, the signet and the cord and the staff." 26 Then Judah acknowledged them and said, "She is more righteous than I, inasmuch as I did not give her to my son Shelah." And he did not lie with her again.

27 When the time of her delivery came, there were twins in her womb. 28 And when she was in labor, one put out a hand; and the midwife took and bound on his hand a scarlet thread, saying, "This came out first." 29 But as he drew back his hand, behold, his brother came out; and she said, "What a breach you have made for yourself!" Therefore his name was called Perez.[i] 30 Afterward his brother came out with the scarlet thread upon his hand; and his name was called Zerah.

39 Now Joseph was taken down to Egypt, and Pot'i-phar, an officer of Pharaoh, the captain of the guard, an Egyptian, bought him from the Ish'maelites who had brought him down there. 2 The LORD was with Joseph, and he became a successful man; and he was in the house of his master the Egyptian, 3 and his master

h Or *cult prostitute*   *i* That is *A breach*

(Ru.1.8–9; Lev.22.13). **14:** Suspecting that Judah's promise (v. 11) was insincere, Tamar took steps to make him perform the levirate duty. **15:** Tamar was taken to be a cult prostitute (see note *h* on v. 21), a devotee of the mother-goddess Ishtar. Prostitution was connected with the worship of the nature gods of fertility (Dt.23.18; 1 Kg.14.24; 2 Kg.23.7; Hos.4.13; Am.2.7). **18:** The signet was a ring or cylinder, often suspended around the neck by a cord and used to stamp one's "signature." **24:** In Israel stoning was the usual punishment for a harlot (Dt.22.23–24; compare Jn.8.5), although burning was prescribed for exceptional cases (Lev.21.9). **26:** Tamar is singled out for approval, for judged by the levirate obligation, she was *more righteous* (see 6.9 n.) than Judah. **27–30:** The birth of the twins (25.21–26) portrays the rivalry of Perez and Zerah, two clans of Judah (Num.26.19–22) who were partially Canaanite. Perez, the firstborn, was an ancestor of David (Ru.4.18–22).

39.1–23: Joseph's success, temptation, and imprisonment. **1:** This story continues from ch. 37,

saw that the LORD was with him, and that the LORD caused all that he did to prosper in his hands. [4] So Joseph found favor in his sight and attended him, and he made him overseer of his house and put him in charge of all that he had. [5] From the time that he made him overseer in his house and over all that he had the LORD blessed the Egyptian's house for Joseph's sake; the blessing of the LORD was upon all that he had, in house and field. [6] So he left all that he had in Joseph's charge; and having him he had no concern for anything but the food which he ate.

Now Joseph was handsome and good-looking. [7] And after a time his master's wife cast her eyes upon Joseph, and said, "Lie with me." [8] But he refused and said to his master's wife, "Lo, having me my master has no concern about anything in the house, and he has put everything that he has in my hand; [9] he is not greater in this house than I am; nor has he kept back anything from me except yourself, because you are his wife; how then can I do this great wickedness, and sin against God?" [10] And although she spoke to Joseph day after day, he would not listen to her, to lie with her or to be with her. [11] But one day, when he went into the house to do his work and none of the men of the house was there in the house, [12] she caught him by his garment, saying, "Lie with me." But he left his garment in her hand, and fled and got out of the house. [13] And when she saw that he had left his garment in her hand, and had fled out of the house, [14] she called to the men of her household and said to them, "See, he has brought among us a Hebrew to insult us; he came in to me to lie

with me, and I cried out with a loud voice; [15] and when he heard that I lifted up my voice and cried, he left his garment with me, and fled and got out of the house." [16] Then she laid up his garment by her until his master came home, [17] and she told him the same story, saying, "The Hebrew servant, whom you have brought among us, came in to me to insult me; [18] but as soon as I lifted up my voice and cried, he left his garment with me, and fled out of the house."

19 When his master heard the words which his wife spoke to him, "This is the way your servant treated me," his anger was kindled. [20] And Joseph's master took him and put him into the prison, the place where the king's prisoners were confined, and he was there in prison. [21] But the LORD was with Joseph and showed him steadfast love, and gave him favor in the sight of the keeper of the prison. [22] And the keeper of the prison committed to Joseph's care all the prisoners who were in the prison; and whatever was done there, he was the doer of it; [23] the keeper of the prison paid no heed to anything that was in Joseph's care, because the LORD was with him; and whatever he did, the LORD made it prosper.

40 Some time after this, the butler of the king of Egypt and his baker offended their lord the king of Egypt. [2] And Pharaoh was angry with his two officers, the chief butler and the chief baker, [3] and he put them in custody in the house of the captain of the guard, in the prison where Joseph was confined. [4] The captain of the guard charged Joseph with them, and he waited on them; and they continued for some time in custody. [5] And

---

and follows the tradition about the Ishmaelites (37.25). **5:** 30.27–30. **6:** For ritual reasons Potiphar took charge of his own food (43.32). **7–20:** The Egyptian "Tale of Two Brothers" also tells how a man rejected the advances of his brother's wife, who then laid false accusations against him and almost brought about his death at the hands of his brother. **21:** Strangely Joseph, a slave, was not executed for alleged adultery, for *the LORD was with him*, not only in success (v. 2) but also in adversity.

40.1–23: Joseph, the interpreter of dreams. 5: Since, according to ancient belief, dreams were

one night they both dreamed–the butler and the baker of the king of Egypt, who were confined in the prison–each his own dream, and each dream with its own meaning. 6 When Joseph came to them in the morning and saw them, they were troubled. 7 So he asked Pharaoh's officers who were with him in custody in his master's house, "Why are your faces downcast today?" 8 They said to him, "We have had dreams, and there is no one to interpret them." And Joseph said to them, "Do not interpretations belong to God? Tell them to me, I pray you."

9 So the chief butler told his dream to Joseph, and said to him, "In my dream there was a vine before me, 10 and on the vine there were three branches; as soon as it budded, its blossoms shot forth, and the clusters ripened into grapes. 11 Pharaoh's cup was in my hand; and I took the grapes and pressed them into Pharaoh's cup, and placed the cup in Pharaoh's hand." 12 Then Joseph said to him, "This is its interpretation: the three branches are three days; 13 within three days Pharaoh will lift up your head and restore you to your office; and you shall place Pharaoh's cup in his hand as formerly, when you were his butler. 14 But remember me, when it is well with you, and do me the kindness, I pray you, to make mention of me to Pharaoh, and so get me out of this house. 15 For I was indeed stolen out of the land of the Hebrews; and here also I have done nothing that they should put me into the dungeon."

16 When the chief baker saw that the interpretation was favorable, he said to Joseph, "I also had a dream: there were three cake baskets on my head, 17 and in the uppermost basket there were all sorts of baked food for Pharaoh, but the birds were eating it out of the basket on my head." 18 And Joseph answered, "This is its interpretation: the three baskets are three days; 19 within three days Pharaoh will lift up your head–from you!–and hang you on a tree; and the birds will eat the flesh from you."

20 On the third day, which was Pharaoh's birthday, he made a feast for all his servants, and lifted up the head of the chief butler and the head of the chief baker among his servants. 21 He restored the chief butler to his butlership, and he placed the cup in Pharaoh's hand; 22 but he hanged the chief baker, as Joseph had interpreted to them. 23 Yet the chief butler did not remember Joseph, but forgot him.

41 After two whole years, Pharaoh dreamed that he was standing by the Nile, 2 and behold, there came up out of the Nile seven cows sleek and fat, and they fed in the reed grass. 3 And behold, seven other cows, gaunt and thin, came up out of the Nile after them, and stood by the other cows on the bank of the Nile. 4 And the gaunt and thin cows ate up the seven sleek and fat cows. And Pharaoh awoke. 5 And he fell asleep and dreamed a second time; and behold, seven ears of grain, plump and good, were growing on one stalk. 6 And behold, after them sprouted seven ears, thin and blighted by the east wind. 7 And the thin ears swallowed up the seven plump and full ears. And Pharaoh awoke, and behold, it was a dream. 8 So in the morning his spirit

---

a channel of divine communication (1 Sam.28.6), the wise interpreter of dreams could discern the course of the future (37.5–10; Dan.2.26–28). **6–8:** Professional interpreters of dreams were unnecessary (41.16), for *interpretations belong to God* who knows and controls the events of the future. **13:** *Lift up your head,* i.e. graciously free you from prison (2 Kg.25.27). The same phrase is humorously applied to the baker's fate in v. 19. **15:** *Stolen,* 37.28.

41.1–57: **Joseph's elevation** as a result of his successful interpretation of Pharaoh's dreams. **1–2:** Egypt's fertility, symbolized by the sacred cows, was dependent upon the Nile. **6:** *The east wind,* the sirocco, a burning wind from the desert which withers vegetation (Hos.13.15). **8:** The narrator intends to demonstrate the superiority of Israel's God over heathen magic and wisdom

was troubled; and he sent and called for all the magicians of Egypt and all its wise men; and Pharaoh told them his dream, but there was none who could interpret it[j] to Pharaoh.

9 Then the chief butler said to Pharaoh, "I remember my faults today. [10] When Pharaoh was angry with his servants, and put me and the chief baker in custody in the house of the captain of the guard, [11] we dreamed on the same night, he and I, each having a dream with its own meaning. [12] A young Hebrew was there with us, a servant of the captain of the guard; and when we told him, he interpreted our dreams to us, giving an interpretation to each man according to his dream. [13] And as he interpreted to us, so it came to pass; I was restored to my office, and the baker was hanged."

14 Then Pharaoh sent and called Joseph, and they brought him hastily out of the dungeon; and when he had shaved himself and changed his clothes, he came in before Pharaoh. [15] And Pharaoh said to Joseph, "I have had a dream, and there is no one who can interpret it; and I have heard it said of you that when you hear a dream you can interpret it." [16] Joseph answered Pharaoh, "It is not in me; God will give Pharaoh a favorable answer." [17] Then Pharaoh said to Joseph, "Behold, in my dream I was standing on the banks of the Nile; [18] and seven cows, fat and sleek, came up out of the Nile and fed in the reed grass; [19] and seven other cows came up after them, poor and very gaunt and thin, such as I had never seen in all the land of Egypt. [20] And the thin and gaunt cows ate up the first seven fat cows, [21] but when they had eaten them no one would have known that they had eaten them, for they were still as gaunt as at the beginning. Then I awoke. [22] I also saw in my dream seven ears growing on one stalk, full and good;

[23] and seven ears, withered, thin, and blighted by the east wind, sprouted after them, [24] and the thin ears swallowed up the seven good ears. And I told it to the magicians, but there was no one who could explain it to me."

25 Then Joseph said to Pharaoh, "The dream of Pharaoh is one; God has revealed to Pharaoh what he is about to do. [26] The seven good cows are seven years, and the seven good ears are seven years; the dream is one. [27] The seven lean and gaunt cows that came up after them are seven years, and the seven empty ears blighted by the east wind are also seven years of famine. [28] It is as I told Pharaoh, God has shown to Pharaoh what he is about to do. [29] There will come seven years of great plenty throughout all the land of Egypt, [30] but after them there will arise seven years of famine, and all the plenty will be forgotten in the land of Egypt; the famine will consume the land, [31] and the plenty will be unknown in the land by reason of that famine which will follow, for it will be very grievous. [32] And the doubling of Pharaoh's dream means that the thing is fixed by God, and God will shortly bring it to pass. [33] Now therefore let Pharaoh select a man discreet and wise, and set him over the land of Egypt. [34] Let Pharaoh proceed to appoint overseers over the land, and take the fifth part of the produce of the land of Egypt during the seven plenteous years. [35] And let them gather all the food of these good years that are coming, and lay up grain under the authority of Pharaoh for food in the cities, and let them keep it. [36] That food shall be a reserve for the land against the seven years of famine which are to befall the land of Egypt, so that the land may not perish through the famine."

37 This proposal seemed good to

j Gk: Heb *them*

(Ex.8.18–19; 9.11; Dan.2.2–19; 5.8,15–28). **16:** Joseph denies having any occult art and ascribes his skill solely to God (see 40.6–8 n.). **32:** Two dreams with the same meaning (v. 25) show that the event is *fixed* or predestined by God. Note that this sense of God's overruling sovereignty does not evoke a fatalistic resignation but a practical plan of action (vv. 33–36). **38:** *The Spirit*

Pharaoh and to all his servants. [38] And Pharaoh said to his servants, "Can we find such a man as this, in whom is the Spirit of God?" [39] So Pharaoh said to Joseph, "Since God has shown you all this, there is none so discreet and wise as you are; [40] you shall be over my house, and all my people shall order themselves as you command; only as regards the throne will I be greater than you." [41] And Pharaoh said to Joseph, "Behold, I have set you over all the land of Egypt." [42] Then Pharaoh took his signet ring from his hand and put it on Joseph's hand, and arrayed him in garments of fine linen, and put a gold chain about his neck; [43] and he made him to ride in his second chariot; and they cried before him, "Bow the knee!"[k] Thus he set him over all the land of Egypt. [44] Moreover Pharaoh said to Joseph, "I am Pharaoh, and without your consent no man shall lift up hand or foot in all the land of Egypt." [45] And Pharaoh called Joseph's name Zaph'enath-pane'ah; and he gave him in marriage As'enath, the daughter of Poti'phera priest of On. So Joseph went out over the land of Egypt.

[46] Joseph was thirty years old when he entered the service of Pharaoh king of Egypt. And Joseph went out from the presence of Pharaoh, and went through all the land of Egypt. [47] During the seven plenteous years the earth brought forth abundantly, [48] and he gathered up all the food of the seven years when there was plenty[l] in the land of Egypt, and stored up food in the cities; he stored up in every city the food from the fields around it. [49] And Joseph stored up grain in great abundance, like the sand of the sea, until he ceased to measure it, for it could not be measured.

[50] Before the year of famine came, Joseph had two sons, whom As'enath, the daughter of Poti'phera priest of On, bore to him. [51] Joseph called the name of the first-born Manas'seh,[m] "For," he said, "God has made me forget all my hardship and all my father's house." [52] The name of the second he called E'phraim,[n] "For God has made me fruitful in the land of my affliction."

[53] The seven years of plenty that prevailed in the land of Egypt came to an end; [54] and the seven years of famine began to come, as Joseph had said. There was famine in all lands; but in all the land of Egypt there was bread. [55] When all the land of Egypt was famished, the people cried to Pharaoh for bread; and Pharaoh said to all the Egyptians, "Go to Joseph; what he says to you, do." [56] So when the famine had spread over all the land, Joseph opened all the storehouses,[o] and sold to the Egyptians, for the famine was severe in the land of Egypt. [57] Moreover, all the earth came to Egypt to Joseph to buy grain, because the famine was severe over all the earth.

42 When Jacob learned that there was grain in Egypt, he said to his sons, "Why do you look at one another?" [2] And he said, "Behold, I have heard that there is grain in Egypt; go down and buy grain for us there, that we may live, and not die." [3] So ten

k *Abrek*, probably an Egyptian word similar in sound to the Hebrew word meaning *to kneel*
l Sam Gk: Heb *which were*
m That is *Making to forget*
n From a Hebrew word meaning *to be fruitful*
o Gk Vg Compare Syr: Heb *all that was in them*

---

of God, the source of extraordinary powers (Ex.31.3; Num.27.18; Dan.5.11,14). **39–41:** Joseph was made prime minister, second only to Pharaoh in authority. During the period of Hyksos ascendancy in Egypt (about 1720–1550 B.C.), when the land was under pro-Semitic rule, conditions were favorable for a Hebrew to rise to such a position of leadership. **42:** *The signet ring* (see 38.18 n.) empowered Joseph to act as Pharaoh's representative (compare Est.3.10; 8.2). **45:** The installation rites, typically Egyptian, culminated with the bestowal of an Egyptian name. Joseph's adoption into the Egyptian court is further indicated by his marriage into the leading priesthood of *On* or Heliopolis. *Potiphera*, see 37.36 n. **46:** Joseph's slavery and imprisonment lasted thirteen years (37.2–3).

42.1–38: Joseph's brothers journey to Egypt during the famine. 5: See 12.10 n. **6:** *Bowed them-*

of Joseph's brothers went down to buy grain in Egypt. 4 But Jacob did not send Benjamin, Joseph's brother, with his brothers, for he feared that harm might befall him. 5 Thus the sons of Israel came to buy among the others who came, for the famine was in the land of Canaan.

6 Now Joseph was governor over the land; he it was who sold to all the people of the land. And Joseph's brothers came, and bowed themselves before him with their faces to the ground. 7 Joseph saw his brothers, and knew them, but he treated them like strangers and spoke roughly to them. "Where do you come from?" he said. They said, "From the land of Canaan, to buy food." 8 Thus Joseph knew his brothers, but they did not know him. 9 And Joseph remembered the dreams which he had dreamed of them; and he said to them, "You are spies, you have come to see the weakness of the land." 10 They said to him, "No, my lord, but to buy food have your servants come. 11 We are all sons of one man, we are honest men, your servants are not spies." 12 He said to them, "No, it is the weakness of the land that you have come to see." 13 And they said, "We, your servants, are twelve brothers, the sons of one man in the land of Canaan; and behold, the youngest is this day with our father, and one is no more." 14 But Joseph said to them, "It is as I said to you, you are spies. 15 By this you shall be tested: by the life of Pharaoh, you shall not go from this place unless your youngest brother comes here. 16 Send one of you, and let him bring your brother, while you remain in prison, that your words may be tested, whether

there is truth in you; or else, by the life of Pharaoh, surely you are spies." 17 And he put them all together in prison for three days.

18 On the third day Joseph said to them, "Do this and you will live, for I fear God: 19 if you are honest men, let one of your brothers remain confined in your prison, and let the rest go and carry grain for the famine of your households, 20 and bring your youngest brother to me; so your words will be verified, and you shall not die." And they did so. 21 Then they said to one another, "In truth we are guilty concerning our brother, in that we saw the distress of his soul, when he besought us and we would not listen; therefore is this distress come upon us." 22 And Reuben answered them, "Did I not tell you not to sin against the lad? But you would not listen. So now there comes a reckoning for his blood." 23 They did not know that Joseph understood them, for there was an interpreter between them. 24 Then he turned away from them and wept; and he returned to them and spoke to them. And he took Simeon from them and bound him before their eyes. 25 And Joseph gave orders to fill their bags with grain, and to replace every man's money in his sack, and to give them provisions for the journey. This was done for them.

26 Then they loaded their asses with their grain, and departed. 27 And as one of them opened his sack to give his ass provender at the lodging place, he saw his money in the mouth of his sack; 28 and he said to his brothers, "My money has been put back; here it is in the mouth of my sack!" At this their hearts failed them, and they

---

selves *before him*, thereby unwittingly fulfilling the prediction of Joseph's dream (v. 9; see 37.5–11 n.). **9–14:** The charge of espionage was natural, for Egypt's frontier, facing Canaan, was vulnerable to attack (Ex.1.10). **15–17:** The "testing" involved not only the verification of the brothers' words but also a discipline of suffering which would purge the evil of their hearts (compare v. 21). *By the life of Pharaoh*, an oath in the name of Pharaoh, who was revered as divine in Egypt. **21–22:** Once again the brothers have to announce to their father that misfortune has befallen one of his sons (compare ch. 37). Though they do not yet recognize Joseph, the similarity of the two situations evokes a feeling of guilt for their former behavior. **28:** They sense that divine retribution is behind the mysterious events. **38:** *Sheol*, see 37.35 n.

turned trembling to one another, saying, "What is this that God has done to us?"

29 When they came to Jacob their father in the land of Canaan, they told him all that had befallen them, saying, 30 "The man, the lord of the land, spoke roughly to us, and took us to be spies of the land. 31 But we said to him, 'We are honest men, we are not spies; 32 we are twelve brothers, sons of our father; one is no more, and the youngest is this day with our father in the land of Canaan.' 33 Then the man, the lord of the land, said to us, 'By this I shall know that you are honest men: leave one of your brothers with me, and take grain for the famine of your households, and go your way. 34 Bring your youngest brother to me; then I shall know that you are not spies but honest men, and I will deliver to you your brother, and you shall trade in the land.' "

35 As they emptied their sacks, behold, every man's bundle of money was in his sack; and when they and their father saw their bundles of money, they were dismayed. 36 And Jacob their father said to them, "You have bereaved me of my children: Joseph is no more, and Simeon is no more, and now you would take Benjamin; all this has come upon me." 37 Then Reuben said to his father, "Slay my two sons if I do not bring him back to you; put him in my hands, and I will bring him back to you." 38 But he said, "My son shall not go down with you, for his brother is dead, and he only is left. If harm should befall him on the journey that you are to make, you would bring down my gray hairs with sorrow to Sheol."

43 Now the famine was severe in the land. 2 And when they had eaten the grain which they had brought from Egypt, their father said to them, "Go again, buy us a little food." 3 But Judah said to him, "The man solemnly warned us, saying, 'You shall not see my face, unless your brother is with you.' 4 If you will send our brother with us, we will go down and buy you food; 5 but if you will not send him, we will not go down, for the man said to us, 'You shall not see my face, unless your brother is with you.' " 6 Israel said, "Why did you treat me so ill as to tell the man that you had another brother?" 7 They replied, "The man questioned us carefully about ourselves and our kindred, saying, 'Is your father still alive? Have you another brother?' What we told him was in answer to these questions; could we in any way know that he would say, 'Bring your brother down'?" 8 And Judah said to Israel his father, "Send the lad with me, and we will arise and go, that we may live and not die, both we and you and also our little ones. 9 I will be surety for him; of my hand you shall require him. If I do not bring him back to you and set him before you, then let me bear the blame for ever; 10 for if we had not delayed, we would now have returned twice."

11 Then their father Israel said to them, "If it must be so, then do this: take some of the choice fruits of the land in your bags, and carry down to the man a present, a little balm and a little honey, gum, myrrh, pistachio nuts, and almonds. 12 Take double the money with you; carry back with you the money that was returned in the mouth of your sacks; perhaps it was an oversight. 13 Take also your brother, and arise, go again to the man; 14 may God Almighty*p* grant you mercy before the man, that he may send back your other brother and Benjamin. If I am bereaved of my children, I am bereaved." 15 So the men took the present, and they took double

p Heb *El Shaddai*

43.1–34: The second journey to Egypt. 1–2: Simeon, left as a hostage in Egypt (vv. 14,23), is apparently forgotten, for the brothers return only when more grain is needed. **3–7:** 42.29–34. **13:** *God Almighty*, see 17.1 n.

the money with them, and Benjamin; and they arose and went down to Egypt, and stood before Joseph.

16 When Joseph saw Benjamin with them, he said to the steward of his house, "Bring the men into the house, and slaughter an animal and make ready, for the men are to dine with me at noon." 17 The man did as Joseph bade him, and brought the men to Joseph's house. 18 And the men were afraid because they were brought to Joseph's house, and they said, "It is because of the money, which was replaced in our sacks the first time, that we are brought in, so that he may seek occasion against us and fall upon us, to make slaves of us and seize our asses." 19 So they went up to the steward of Joseph's house, and spoke with him at the door of the house, 20 and said, "Oh, my lord, we came down the first time to buy food; 21 and when we came to the lodging place we opened our sacks, and there was every man's money in the mouth of his sack, our money in full weight; so we have brought it again with us, 22 and we have brought other money down in our hand to buy food. We do not know who put our money in our sacks." 23 He replied, "Rest assured, do not be afraid; your God and the God of your father must have put treasure in your sacks for you; I received your money." Then he brought Simeon out to them. 24 And when the man had brought the men into Joseph's house, and given them water, and they had washed their feet, and when he had given their asses provender, 25 they made ready the present for Joseph's coming at noon, for they heard that they should eat bread there.

26 When Joseph came home, they brought into the house to him the present which they had with them, and bowed down to him to the ground.

27 And he inquired about their welfare, and said, "Is your father well, the old man of whom you spoke? Is he still alive?" 28 They said, "Your servant our father is well, he is still alive." And they bowed their heads and made obeisance. 29 And he lifted up his eyes, and saw his brother Benjamin, his mother's son, and said, "Is this your youngest brother, of whom you spoke to me? God be gracious to you, my son!" 30 Then Joseph made haste, for his heart yearned for his brother, and he sought a place to weep. And he entered his chamber and wept there. 31 Then he washed his face and came out; and controlling himself he said, "Let food be served." 32 They served him by himself, and them by themselves, and the Egyptians who ate with him by themselves, because the Egyptians might not eat bread with the Hebrews, for that is an abomination to the Egyptians. 33 And they sat before him, the first-born according to his birthright and the youngest according to his youth; and the men looked at one another in amazement. 34 Portions were taken to them from Joseph's table, but Benjamin's portion was five times as much as any of theirs. So they drank and were merry with him.

44 Then he commanded the steward of his house, "Fill the men's sacks with food, as much as they can carry, and put each man's money in the mouth of his sack, 2 and put my cup, the silver cup, in the mouth of the sack of the youngest, with his money for the grain." And he did as Joseph told him. 3 As soon as the morning was light, the men were sent away with their asses. 4 When they had gone but a short distance from the city, Joseph said to his steward, "Up, follow after the men; and when you overtake them, say to them, 'Why have you returned evil for good? Why have you

---

23: The steward's words again stress the fundamental motif of the story: the working of divine providence. **29–30:** Joseph's heart *yearned* for Benjamin, his only full brother through Rachel. **32:** Laws of ritual purity required that Egyptians eat apart from foreigners.

44.1–34: Joseph puts his brothers to a final test. 1–2: The reference to the money harks back to the same motif in 42.25–28; here the real object of interest is Joseph's cup (v. 5). **5:** The

stolen my silver cup?*q* *5* Is it not from this that my lord drinks, and by this that he divines? You have done wrong in so doing.' "

6 When he overtook them, he spoke to them these words. *7* They said to him, "Why does my lord speak such words as these? Far be it from your servants that they should do such a thing! *8* Behold, the money which we found in the mouth of our sacks, we brought back to you from the land of Canaan; how then should we steal silver or gold from your lord's house? *9* With whomever of your servants it be found, let him die, and we also will be my lord's slaves." *10* He said, "Let it be as you say: he with whom it is found shall be my slave, and the rest of you shall be blameless." *11* Then every man quickly lowered his sack to the ground, and every man opened his sack. *12* And he searched, beginning with the eldest and ending with the youngest; and the cup was found in Benjamin's sack. *13* Then they rent their clothes, and every man loaded his ass, and they returned to the city.

14 When Judah and his brothers came to Joseph's house, he was still there; and they fell before him to the ground. *15* Joseph said to them, "What deed is this that you have done? Do you not know that such a man as I can indeed divine?" *16* And Judah said, "What shall we say to my lord? What shall we speak? Or how can we clear ourselves? God has found out the guilt of your servants; behold, we are my lord's slaves, both we and he also in whose hand the cup has been found." *17* But he said, "Far be it from me that I should do so! Only the man in whose

hand the cup was found shall be my slave; but as for you, go up in peace to your father."

18 Then Judah went up to him and said, "O my lord, let your servant, I pray you, speak a word in my lord's ears, and let not your anger burn against your servant; for you are like Pharaoh himself. *19* My lord asked his servants, saying, 'Have you a father, or a brother?' *20* And we said to my lord, 'We have a father, an old man, and a young brother, the child of his old age; and his brother is dead, and he alone is left of his mother's children; and his father loves him.' *21* Then you said to your servants, 'Bring him down to me, that I may set my eyes upon him.' *22* We said to my lord, 'The lad cannot leave his father, for if he should leave his father, his father would die.' *23* Then you said to your servants, 'Unless your youngest brother comes down with you, you shall see my face no more.' *24* When we went back to your servant my father we told him the words of my lord. *25* And when our father said, 'Go again, buy us a little food,' *26* we said, 'We cannot go down. If our youngest brother goes with us, then we will go down; for we cannot see the man's face unless our youngest brother is with us.' *27* Then your servant my father said to us, 'You know that my wife bore me two sons; *28* one left me, and I said, Surely he has been torn to pieces; and I have never seen him since. *29* If you take this one also from me, and harm befalls him, you will bring down my gray hairs in sorrow to Sheol.' *30* Now therefore, when

---

q Gk Compare Vg: Heb lacks *Why have you stolen my silver cup?*

---

cup was a sacred vessel used for divination, i.e. for magical prediction by observing the effects created when objects were thrown into the water contained therein. **15:** Having been initiated into Egyptian wisdom, Joseph can claim to practice divination, by which means the theft was discovered. **16:** Since the brothers acknowledge their collective guilt, Judah's words may refer not only to the theft but to their treatment of Joseph in his youth. **17:** Joseph tests his brothers to see whether, as in his case once, they will let Benjamin go into slavery and return to their father to justify the loss of another of his sons. **18–34:** Judah's speech, one of the finest prose pieces from Israel's early tradition, summarizes and epitomizes the whole sequence of events. **20:** The tragedy of Joseph's supposed death heightens the pathos; for of Jacob's two sons by Rachel, only Benjamin is left and Jacob's *life is bound up in the lad's life* (v. 30).

I come to your servant my father, and the lad is not with us, then, as his life is bound up in the lad's life, [31] when he sees that the lad is not with us, he will die; and your servants will bring down the gray hairs of your servant our father with sorrow to Sheol. [32] For your servant became surety for the lad to my father, saying, 'If I do not bring him back to you, then I shall bear the blame in the sight of my father all my life.' [33] Now therefore, let your servant, I pray you, remain instead of the lad as a slave to my lord; and let the lad go back with his brothers. [34] For how can I go back to my father if the lad is not with me? I fear to see the evil that would come upon my father."

45 Then Joseph could not control himself before all those who stood by him; and he cried, "Make every one go out from me." So no one stayed with him when Joseph made himself known to his brothers. [2] And he wept aloud, so that the Egyptians heard it, and the household of Pharaoh heard it. [3] And Joseph said to his brothers, "I am Joseph; is my father still alive?" But his brothers could not answer him, for they were dismayed at his presence.

4 So Joseph said to his brothers, "Come near to me, I pray you." And they came near. And he said, "I am your brother, Joseph, whom you sold into Egypt. [5] And now do not be distressed, or angry with yourselves, because you sold me here; for God sent me before you to preserve life. [6] For the famine has been in the land these two years; and there are yet five years in which there will be neither plowing nor harvest. [7] And God sent me before you to preserve for you a remnant on earth, and to keep alive for you many survivors. [8] So it was not you who sent me here, but God; and he has made me a father to Pharaoh, and lord of all his house and ruler over all the land of Egypt. [9] Make haste and go up to my father and say to him, 'Thus says your son Joseph, God has made me lord of all Egypt; come down to me, do not tarry; [10] you shall dwell in the land of Goshen, and you shall be near me, you and your children and your children's children, and your flocks, your herds, and all that you have; [11] and there I will provide for you, for there are yet five years of famine to come; lest you and your household, and all that you have, come to poverty.' [12] And now your eyes see, and the eyes of my brother Benjamin see, that it is my mouth that speaks to you. [13] You must tell my father of all my splendor in Egypt, and of all that you have seen. Make haste and bring my father down here." [14] Then he fell upon his brother Benjamin's neck and wept; and Benjamin wept upon his neck. [15] And he kissed all his brothers and wept upon them; and after that his brothers talked with him.

16 When the report was heard in Pharaoh's house, "Joseph's brothers have come," it pleased Pharaoh and his servants well. [17] And Pharaoh said to Joseph, "Say to your brothers, 'Do this: load your beasts and go back to the land of Canaan; [18] and take your father and your households, and come to me, and I will give you the best of the land of Egypt, and you shall

---

45.1–28: Joseph makes himself known to his brothers. 7–8: This passage sets forth the central theme of the Joseph story: events were directed by God's hand, not by human purposes. God graciously contrives to bring good out of evil; for the brothers, in selling Joseph into slavery, had unwittingly carried out God's will. **7:** Through Joseph God acted *to preserve life* (v. 5; 50.20), not only the life of famine-stricken Egyptians but also that of *a remnant*, that is, the family which is the bearer of the promise given to Abraham (12.2–3; 50.24). **8:** *A father to Pharaoh*, a title of the chief minister (Is.22.21; compare 1 Macc.11.32). **10:** *The land of Goshen*, the present Wadi Tumilat, a narrow strip of grazing land in the Delta. Since the settlers would be *near* Joseph, the assumption is that Pharaoh's capital was in the Delta region; this was the case during the Hyksos period (see 41.39–41 n.). **16–20:** According to Egyptian sources, it was not unusual for Pharaoh to permit Asiatics to settle in his country in time of famine.

eat the fat of the land.' ¹⁹ Command them' also, 'Do this: take wagons from the land of Egypt for your little ones and for your wives, and bring your father, and come. ²⁰ Give no thought to your goods, for the best of all the land of Egypt is yours.' "

21 The sons of Israel did so; and Joseph gave them wagons, according to the command of Pharaoh, and gave them provisions for the journey. ²² To each and all of them he gave festal garments; but to Benjamin he gave three hundred shekels of silver and five festal garments. ²³ To his father he sent as follows: ten asses loaded with the good things of Egypt, and ten she-asses loaded with grain, bread, and provision for his father on the journey. ²⁴ Then he sent his brothers away, and as they departed, he said to them, "Do not quarrel on the way." ²⁵ So they went up out of Egypt, and came to the land of Canaan to their father Jacob. ²⁶ And they told him, "Joseph is still alive, and he is ruler over all the land of Egypt." And his heart fainted, for he did not believe them. ²⁷ But when they told him all the words of Joseph, which he had said to them, and when he saw the wagons which Joseph had sent to carry him, the spirit of their father Jacob revived; ²⁸ and Israel said, "It is enough; Joseph my son is still alive; I will go and see him before I die."

46 So Israel took his journey with all that he had, and came to Beer-sheba, and offered sacrifices to the God of his father Isaac. ² And God spoke to Israel in visions of the night, and said, "Jacob, Jacob." And he said, "Here am I." ³ Then he said, "I am God, the God of your father;

do not be afraid to go down to Egypt; for I will there make of you a great nation. ⁴ I will go down with you to Egypt, and I will also bring you up again; and Joseph's hand shall close your eyes." ⁵ Then Jacob set out from Beer-sheba; and the sons of Israel carried Jacob their father, their little ones, and their wives, in the wagons which Pharaoh had sent to carry him. ⁶ They also took their cattle and their goods, which they had gained in the land of Canaan, and came into Egypt, Jacob and all his offspring with him, ⁷ his sons, and his sons' sons with him, his daughters, and his sons' daughters; all his offspring he brought with him into Egypt.

8 Now these are the names of the descendants of Israel, who came into Egypt, Jacob and his sons. Reuben, Jacob's first-born, ⁹ and the sons of Reuben: Hanoch, Pallu, Hezron, and Carmi. ¹⁰ The sons of Simeon: Jemu'-el, Jamin, Ohad, Jachin, Zohar, and Shaul, the son of a Canaanitish woman. ¹¹ The sons of Levi: Gershon, Kohath, and Merar'i. ¹² The sons of Judah: Er, Onan, Shelah, Perez, and Zerah (but Er and Onan died in the land of Canaan); and the sons of Perez were Hezron and Hamul. ¹³ The sons of Is'sachar: Tola, Puvah, Iob, and Shimron. ¹⁴ The sons of Zeb'ulun: Sered, Elon, and Jah'leel ¹⁵ (these are the sons of Leah, whom she bore to Jacob in Paddan-aram, together with his daughter Dinah; altogether his sons and his daughters numbered thirty-three). ¹⁶ The sons of Gad: Ziph'ion, Haggi, Shuni, Ezbon, Eri, Aro'di, and Are'li. ¹⁷ The sons of Asher: Imnah, Ishvah,

r Compare Gk Vg: Heb *you are commanded*

46.1–27: Jacob's migration to Egypt. 1: From Hebron (37.14) Jacob went first to *Beer-sheba*, the shrine associated with Isaac (26.23–25; 28.10). *The God of your father*, see 26.24 n. **2–4:** The descent into Egypt, which was to have decisive significance for Israel's history, was prompted not merely by Jacob's desire to see his long-lost son (45.28) but by divine revelation *in visions of the night*. **3:** As on a previous occasion (28.13–15), before Jacob left the land of the promise to go to a foreign land God renewed his promise to make him *a great nation* (12.2; 18.18) in Egypt (Ex.1.7). **4:** Only Jacob's corpse was returned from Egypt (50.4–14). However, according to Hebraic corporate thinking, the words *bring you up again* were fulfilled, for the father lived on in the person of his sons. **8–27:** This section, from a separate priestly tradition, contains a list of Jacob's descendants, based on the traditional number seventy (v. 27; Ex.1.5; Dt.10.22). Most

Ishvi, Beri'ah, with Serah their sister. And the sons of Beri'ah: Heber and Mal'chi-el [18] (these are the sons of Zilpah, whom Laban gave to Leah his daughter; and these she bore to Jacob–sixteen persons). [19] The sons of Rachel, Jacob's wife: Joseph and Benjamin. [20] And to Joseph in the land of Egypt were born Manas'seh and E'phraim, whom As'enath, the daughter of Poti'phera the priest of On, bore to him. [21] And the sons of Benjamin: Bela, Becher, Ashbel, Gera, Na'aman, Ehi, Rosh, Muppim, Huppim, and Ard [22] (these are the sons of Rachel, who were born to Jacob–fourteen persons in all). [23] The sons of Dan: Hushim. [24] The sons of Naph'tali: Jahzeel, Guni, Jezer, and Shillem [25] (these are the sons of Bilhah, whom Laban gave to Rachel his daughter, and these she bore to Jacob–seven persons in all). [26] All the persons belonging to Jacob who came into Egypt, who were his own offspring, not including Jacob's sons' wives, were sixty-six persons in all; [27] and the sons of Joseph, who were born to him in Egypt, were two; all the persons of the house of Jacob, that came into Egypt, were seventy.

28 He sent Judah before him to Joseph, to appear[s] before him in Goshen; and they came into the land of Goshen. [29] Then Joseph made ready his chariot and went up to meet Israel his father in Goshen; and he presented himself to him, and fell on his neck, and wept on his neck a good while. [30] Israel said to Joseph, "Now let me die, since I have seen your face and know that you are still alive." [31] Joseph said to his brothers and to his father's household, "I will go up and tell Pharaoh, and will say to him,

'My brothers and my father's household, who were in the land of Canaan, have come to me; [32] and the men are shepherds, for they have been keepers of cattle; and they have brought their flocks, and their herds, and all that they have.' [33] When Pharaoh calls you, and says, 'What is your occupation?' [34] you shall say, 'Your servants have been keepers of cattle from our youth even until now, both we and our fathers,' in order that you may dwell in the land of Goshen; for every shepherd is an abomination to the Egyptians."

47 So Joseph went in and told Pharaoh, "My father and my brothers, with their flocks and herds and all that they possess, have come from the land of Canaan; they are now in the land of Goshen." [2] And from among his brothers he took five men and presented them to Pharaoh. [3] Pharaoh said to his brothers, "What is your occupation?" And they said to Pharaoh, "Your servants are shepherds, as our fathers were." [4] They said to Pharaoh, "We have come to sojourn in the land; for there is no pasture for your servants' flocks, for the famine is severe in the land of Canaan; and now, we pray you, let your servants dwell in the land of Goshen." [5] Then Pharaoh said to Joseph, "Your father and your brothers have come to you. [6] The land of Egypt is before you; settle your father and your brothers in the best of the land; let them dwell in the land of Goshen; and if you know any able men among them, put them in charge of my cattle."

7 Then Joseph brought in Jacob his father, and set him before Pharaoh, and Jacob blessed Pharaoh. [8] And

s Sam Syr Compare Gk Vg: Heb *to show the way*

of the names of the ancestral clan leaders are found in the priestly list in Num. ch. 26. **27:** *Seventy*, the author includes Joseph and his two sons born in Egypt, as well as Jacob himself. **46.28–47.12: Jacob and his sons settle in Egypt. 28:** Judah is sent ahead because he is the chief spokesman (37.26; 43.3–10; 44.18–34). *Goshen*, see 45.10 n. **31–34:** Desiring to have his relatives near him in the Delta, Joseph advised his brothers to testify that they were shepherds; since this occupation was abominable to Egyptians in the interior (v. 34), Pharaoh would see the wisdom of setting them apart in the land of Goshen. **47.1–6:** Egyptian sources testify that the pharaohs possessed large herds and gave much attention to cattle-breeding. **7–12:** According to this

Pharaoh said to Jacob, "How many are the days of the years of your life?" [9] And Jacob said to Pharaoh, "The days of the years of my sojourning are a hundred and thirty years; few and evil have been the days of the years of my life, and they have not attained to the days of the years of the life of my fathers in the days of their sojourning." [10] And Jacob blessed Pharaoh, and went out from the presence of Pharaoh. [11] Then Joseph settled his father and his brothers, and gave them a possession in the land of Egypt, in the best of the land, in the land of Ram'eses, as Pharaoh had commanded. [12] And Joseph provided his father, his brothers, and all his father's household with food, according to the number of their dependents.

13 Now there was no food in all the land; for the famine was very severe, so that the land of Egypt and the land of Canaan languished by reason of the famine. [14] And Joseph gathered up all the money that was found in the land of Egypt and in the land of Canaan, for the grain which they bought; and Joseph brought the money into Pharaoh's house. [15] And when the money was all spent in the land of Egypt and in the land of Canaan, all the Egyptians came to Joseph, and said, "Give us food; why should we die before your eyes? For our money is gone." [16] And Joseph answered, "Give your cattle, and I will give you food in exchange for your cattle, if your money is gone." [17] So they brought their cattle to Joseph; and Joseph gave them food in exchange for the horses, the flocks, the herds, and

the asses: and he supplied them with food in exchange for all their cattle that year. [18] And when that year was ended, they came to him the following year, and said to him, "We will not hide from my lord that our money is all spent; and the herds of cattle are my lord's; there is nothing left in the sight of my lord but our bodies and our lands. [19] Why should we die before your eyes, both we and our land? Buy us and our land for food, and we with our land will be slaves to Pharaoh; and give us seed, that we may live, and not die, and that the land may not be desolate."

20 So Joseph bought all the land of Egypt for Pharaoh; for all the Egyptians sold their fields, because the famine was severe upon them. The land became Pharaoh's; [21] and as for the people, he made slaves of them*t* from one end of Egypt to the other. [22] Only the land of the priests he did not buy; for the priests had a fixed allowance from Pharaoh, and lived on the allowance which Pharaoh gave them; therefore they did not sell their land. [23] Then Joseph said to the people, "Behold, I have this day bought you and your land for Pharaoh. Now here is seed for you, and you shall sow the land. [24] And at the harvests you shall give a fifth to Pharaoh, and four fifths shall be your own, as seed for the field and as food for yourselves and your households, and as food for your little ones." [25] And they said, "You have saved our lives; may it please my lord, we will be slaves to Pharaoh." [26] So

---

t Sam Gk Compare Vg: Heb *he removed them to the cities*

priestly tradition, *Jacob blessed Pharaoh*, presumably with the blessing of welfare and long life. **9**: *The years of my sojourning*, see 17.8 n. Jacob's statement that his years had been *few and evil* reflects the view that there was an increasing shortening and troubling of man's life (see 5.4–32 n.). **11**: *The land of Rameses* (= Goshen), was named after Rameses II (see Ex.1.8,11 n.).

47.13–26: Joseph's agrarian program, involving a change in the Egyptian system of land-tenure. **14**: First, the people spent all their money for grain (compare 41.56). **15–17**: Next, in their desperation they exchanged all their cattle for food. **18–19**: Finally, they offered themselves and their lands to Pharaoh. **20–26**: The result was that former land-owners became tenants of Pharaoh, farming the land for him and paying him one-fifth of the produce as tax (v. 24). Temple lands were excepted (v. 22). Egyptian sources testify that such a feudalistic system was introduced between 1700–1500 B.C. **25**: The narrator does not intend to sanction absolutism but only to praise Joseph for his wisdom in delivering the people.

Joseph made it a statute concerning the land of Egypt, and it stands to this day, that Pharaoh should have the fifth; the land of the priests alone did not become Pharaoh's.

27 Thus Israel dwelt in the land of Egypt, in the land of Goshen; and they gained possessions in it, and were fruitful and multiplied exceedingly. 28 And Jacob lived in the land of Egypt seventeen years; so the days of Jacob, the years of his life, were a hundred and forty-seven years.

29 And when the time drew near that Israel must die, he called his son Joseph and said to him, "If now I have found favor in your sight, put your hand under my thigh, and promise to deal loyally and truly with me. Do not bury me in Egypt, 30 but let me lie with my fathers; carry me out of Egypt and bury me in their burying place." He answered, "I will do as you have said." 31 And he said, "Swear to me"; and he swore to him. Then Israel bowed himself upon the head of his bed.

48 After this Joseph was told, "Behold, your father is ill"; so he took with him his two sons, Manas'seh and E'phraim. 2 And it was told to Jacob, "Your son Joseph has come to you"; then Israel summoned his strength, and sat up in bed. 3 And Jacob said to Joseph, "God Almighty*u* appeared to me at Luz in the land of Canaan and blessed me, 4 and said to me, 'Behold, I will make you fruitful, and multiply you, and I will make of you a company of peoples, and will give this land to your descendants after you for an everlasting possession.' 5 And now your two sons, who were born to you in the land of Egypt before I came to you in Egypt, are mine; E'phraim and Manas'seh shall be mine, as Reuben and Simeon are. 6 And the offspring born to you after them shall be yours; they shall be called by the name of their brothers in their inheritance. 7 For when I came from Paddan, Rachel to my sorrow died in the land of Canaan on the way, when there was still some distance to go to Ephrath; and I buried her there on the way to Ephrath (that is, Bethlehem)."

8 When Israel saw Joseph's sons, he said, "Who are these?" 9 Joseph said to his father, "They are my sons, whom God has given me here." And he said, "Bring them to me, I pray you, that I may bless them." 10 Now the eyes of Israel were dim with age, so that he could not see. So Joseph brought them near him; and he kissed them and embraced them. 11 And Israel said to Joseph, "I had not thought to see your face; and lo, God has let me see your children also." 12 Then Joseph removed them from his knees, and he bowed himself with his face to the earth. 13 And Joseph took them both, E'phraim in his right hand toward Israel's left hand, and Manas'seh in his left hand toward Israel's right hand, and brought them near him. 14 And Israel stretched out

u Heb *El Shaddai*

47.27–48.22: Jacob's adoption and blessing of Ephraim and Manasseh. 29: *Put your hand under my thigh*, see 24.2 n. **31:** Joseph binds himself by oath to bury Jacob in his fathers' *burying place*, i.e. Machpelah (ch. 23; 49.29–30; 50.12–13). *Jacob bowed himself upon the head of his bed* (compare Heb.11.21), a gesture of reverence or gratitude (1 Kg.1.47). **48.3–4:** Jacob's adoption and blessing of Joseph's two sons are based on the divine promise given at Luz, or Bethel (35.9–13). **5–6:** By adopting his grandsons, Jacob gives them status equal to his eldest sons, Reuben and Simeon. The narrative accounts for the circumstance that "the house of Joseph" (Jos.17.17; 18.5; Jg.1.23,35) came to be divided into two tribes, Manasseh and Ephraim, each claiming full rank with the other tribes (49.22–26). **7:** 35.16–20. *Paddan(-aram)*, see 11.31 n. **12:** An adoption ceremony may be suggested by the boys' having been between or on Jacob's knees. **13–14:** Joseph brings Manasseh, his first-born, for the blessing of the right hand, but Jacob crosses his hands and puts his right hand on Ephraim, thereby giving him precedence. The narrator appeals to the ancient belief in the efficacy of the death-bed blessing (see 27.4 n.) to account for two facts: (1) Manasseh and Ephraim, located in the central hill country, were powerful tribes in early Israelite history; (2) the latter, during the period of the Judges and the

his right hand and laid it upon the head of E′phraim, who was the younger, and his left hand upon the head of Manas′-seh, crossing his hands, for Manas′seh was the first-born. 15 And he blessed Joseph, and said,

"The God before whom my fathers
  Abraham and Isaac walked,
the God who has led me all my life
  long to this day,
16 the angel who has redeemed me
  from all evil, bless the lads;
and in them let my name be perpetuated, and the name of my
  fathers Abraham and Isaac;
and let them grow into a multitude
  in the midst of the earth."

17 When Joseph saw that his father laid his right hand upon the head of E′phraim, it displeased him; and he took his father's hand, to remove it from E′phraim's head to Manas′seh's head. 18 And Joseph said to his father, "Not so, my father; for this one is the first-born; put your right hand upon his head." 19 But his father refused, and said, "I know, my son, I know; he also shall become a people, and he also shall be great; nevertheless his younger brother shall be greater than he, and his descendants shall become a multitude of nations." 20 So he blessed them that day, saying,

"By you Israel will pronounce blessings, saying,

'God make you as E′phraim and as
  Manas′seh' ";

and thus he put E′phraim before Manas′seh. 21 Then Israel said to Joseph, "Behold, I am about to die, but God will be with you, and will bring you again to the land of your fathers. 22 Moreover I have given to you rather than to your brothers one mountain slope[v] which I took from the hand of the Amorites with my sword and with my bow."

49 Then Jacob called his sons, and said, "Gather yourselves together, that I may tell you what shall befall you in days to come.
2 Assemble and hear, O sons of Jacob,
  and hearken to Israel your father.

3 Reuben, you are my first-born,
  my might, and the first fruits of
    my strength,
  pre-eminent in pride and
    pre-eminent in power.
4 Unstable as water, you shall not
    have pre-eminence
  because you went up to your
    father's bed;
  then you defiled it—you[w] went
    up to my couch!

5 Simeon and Levi are brothers;
  weapons of violence are their
    swords.

v Heb *shekem*, shoulder   *w* Gk Syr Tg: Heb *he*

---

early monarchy, gained pre-eminence over the "first-born" tribe that once ranked first in leadership. **15–16:** Jacob invokes God by a threefold description: the God before whom his fathers *walked* (17.1; 24.40), who *led* (lit. "shepherded"; Ps.23.1) him throughout his life, who *redeemed* him from evil (Is.48.20). *The angel*, see 16.7 n. According to ancient belief, *the name*, that is, the psychic life of the fathers, was to be perpetuated in the two boys. **20:** Another version of the blessing (compare vv. 15–16). *Israel* here refers not to Jacob but to the people (34.7). *As Ephraim and Manasseh*, i.e. as fruitful with offspring as these tribes. **21:** Joseph died in Egypt and his bones were brought back to Canaan (see 46.4 n.). **22:** In Hebrew *one mountain slope* (or "shoulder") is a play on the name Shechem, the important city which lay in the territory of Joseph (see 12.6 n.). *With my sword and with my bow* reflects a different tradition from that in 33.19–20, which reports Jacob's peaceful coming to Shechem, and ch. 34, which describes his protest against his sons' attack upon the city (34.25–30). *Amorites*, see 10.15–20 n.

49.1–28: Jacob's blessing on his twelve sons. This poem, apparently dating from the time of David (see vv. 8–12), portrays the character of the tribes in the person of their ancestor (Dt. ch. 33). Although regarded as Jacob's death-bed blessing (v. 28), this is not an altogether adequate description, for the poet sometimes speaks words of censure and even curse (e.g. v. 7). On death-bed blessings, see 27.4 n. **1–2:** The futuristic language, *what shall befall you in days to come*, is relevant to the Judah oracle (vv. 8–12); the other oracles, however, describe chiefly past events or present circumstances. **3–4:** Reuben the first born, whose territory lay east of the

⁶ O my soul, come not into their
    council;
  O my spirit,ˣ be not joined to
    their company;
for in their anger they slay men,
  and in their wantonness they
    hamstring oxen.
⁷ Cursed be their anger, for it is fierce;
  and their wrath, for it is cruel!
I will divide them in Jacob
  and scatter them in Israel.

⁸ Judah, your brothers shall praise
    you;
  your hand shall be on the neck of
    your enemies;
  your father's sons shall bow down
    before you.
⁹ Judah is a lion's whelp;
  from the prey, my son, you have
    gone up.
He stooped down, he couched as a
    lion,
  and as a lioness; who dares rouse
    him up?
¹⁰ The scepter shall not depart from
    Judah,
  nor the ruler's staff from between
    his feet,
until he comes to whom it belongs;ʸ
  and to him shall be the obedience
    of the peoples.
¹¹ Binding his foal to the vine
  and his ass's colt to the choice
    vine,

he washes his garments in wine
  and his vesture in the blood of
    grapes;
¹² his eyes shall be red with wine,
  and his teeth white with milk.

¹³ Zeb'ulun shall dwell at the shore
    of the sea;
  he shall become a haven for ships,
  and his border shall be at Sidon.

¹⁴ Is'sachar is a strong ass,
  crouching between the sheep-
    folds;
¹⁵ he saw that a resting place was good,
  and that the land was pleasant;
so he bowed his shoulder to bear,
  and became a slave at forced
    labor.

¹⁶ Dan shall judge his people
  as one of the tribes of Israel.
¹⁷ Dan shall be a serpent in the way,
  a viper by the path,
that bites the horse's heels
  so that his rider falls backward.
¹⁸ I wait for thy salvation, O Lᴏʀᴅ.

¹⁹ Raidersᶻ shall raid Gad,
  but he shall raid at their heels.

²⁰ Asher's food shall be rich,
  and he shall yield royal dainties.

x Or *glory*   y Syr Compare Tg: Heb *until Shiloh
comes* or *until he comes to Shiloh*   z Heb *gedud,* a
raiding troop

Dead Sea, was once a leading tribe but in early times was overcome by the Moabites (Jg.5.15–16;
Dt.33.6). **4:** *Your father's bed,* a reference to the ancestor's act of immorality (35.22), which
typifies the tribe's moral weakness and instability. **5–7:** Simeon and Levi are considered together,
for they led in the attack against Shechem with *weapons of violence* (34.25–30). Levi, once a full
tribe, came to be a priestly class (Ex.32.26–29; Dt.10.8–9). Simeon was eventually absorbed into
the tribe of Judah. **8–12:** This oracle reflects a situation, like that in David's time, when Judah
had pre-eminence over the tribes. **10:** The first part of the verse portrays Judah as a sovereign;
the second part, however, is very obscure (see note *y*). *To whom it belongs* refers to *the scepter,
the ruler's staff* (Num.24.17). *Until he comes* may mean that after the kingdom of Judah has
lasted for an indefinite time there will arise a messianic ruler who will command *the obedience
of the peoples* (Is.11.1–9). **11–12:** A picture of the marvelous fertility that will ensue. **13:** Zebulun
will have a favorable position, no longer shut up in the interior (Jos.19.10–16) but with access to
the Mediterranean Sea. Expansion into Asher's territory is assumed. **14–15:** Issachar is compared to a domesticated beast of burden, contented with a comfortable land and willing to
surrender political independence in subservience to the Canaanites. **16–18:** Dan will rise
to full tribal prestige by judging (i.e. getting justice for) his people. The Hebrew verb "judge"
involves a play on the word Dan. The comparison with *a serpent in the way* portrays the in-
sidious warfare of a small tribe in its rise to power. **19:** Gad, settled east of the Jordan just
above Reuben, is cited for bravery in repelling Ammonite and desert marauders (Jg. ch. 11).
20: Asher's land, situated on the coastal strip between Mount Carmel and Phoenicia, was so

²¹ Naph'tali is a hind let loose,
    that bears comely fawns.ᵃ

²² Joseph is a fruitful bough,
    a fruitful bough by a spring;
    his branches run over the wall.
²³ The archers fiercely attacked him,
    shot at him, and harassed him
        sorely;
²⁴ yet his bow remained unmoved,
    his arms ᵇ were made agile
    by the hands of the Mighty One of
        Jacob
    (by the name of the Shepherd,
        the Rock of Israel),
²⁵ by the God of your father who will
        help you,
    by God Almightyᵘ who will bless
        you
    with blessings of heaven above,
    blessings of the deep that couches
        beneath,
    blessings of the breasts and of the
        womb.
²⁶ The blessings of your father
    are mighty beyond the blessings
        of the eternal mountains,ᶜ
    the bounties of the everlasting
        hills;
    may they be on the head of Joseph,
    and on the brow of him who was
        separate from his brothers.

²⁷ Benjamin is a ravenous wolf,
    in the morning devouring the
        prey,
    and at even dividing the spoil."

28 All these are the twelve tribes of
Israel; and this is what their father said
to them as he blessed them, blessing
each with the blessing suitable to him.
²⁹ Then he charged them, and said
to them, "I am to be gathered to my
people; bury me with my fathers in the
cave that is in the field of Ephron the
Hittite, ³⁰ in the cave that is in the
field at Mach-pe'lah, to the east of
Mamre, in the land of Canaan, which
Abraham bought with the field from
Ephron the Hittite to possess as a
burying place. ³¹ There they buried
Abraham and Sarah his wife; there
they buried Isaac and Rebekah his wife;
and there I buried Leah– ³² the field
and the cave that is in it were purchased
from the Hittites." ³³ When Jacob
finished charging his sons, he drew
up his feet into the bed, and breathed
his last, and was gathered to his
people.

50 Then Joseph fell on his father's
face, and wept over him, and
kissed him. ² And Joseph commanded
his servants the physicians to embalm
his father. So the physicians embalmed
Israel; ³ forty days were required for
it, for so many are required for embalming. And the Egyptians wept for
him seventy days.

4 And when the days of weeping
for him were past, Joseph spoke to the
household of Pharaoh, saying, "If now
I have found favor in your eyes,
speak, I pray you, in the ears of Pharaoh, saying, ⁵ My father made me
swear, saying, 'I am about to die: in
my tomb which I hewed out for myself
in the land of Canaan, there shall you

a Or *who gives beautiful words*
b Heb *the arms of his hands*
u Heb *El Shaddai*
c Compare Gk: Heb *of my progenitors to*

---

rich that it yielded *royal dainties* (Dt.33.24). **21:** The comparison of Naphtali to *a hind let loose*
suggests the idea of freedom, agility, and vitality (compare Dt.33.23). **22–26:** A picture of the
prosperity and strength of the populous tribe of Joseph, apparently harking back to a time
before "the house of Joseph" was divided into the tribes of Manasseh and Ephraim, as in
Dt.33.13–17 (see Gen. ch. 48). **24:** *The Mighty One of Jacob*, a title of "the God of the fathers"
(v. 25a; Is.1.24; 49.26). **25:** *God Almighty*, see 17.1 n. *Blessings of heaven*, i.e. rain, dew, sun.
The deep that couches beneath (Dt.33.13), an allusion to the subterranean ocean (see 1.2,6),
believed to be the source of fertility (see 2.6 n.). **26:** The ancestral blessing surpasses even the
majesty and fertility of the hills of Ephraim. *Separate*, i.e. set apart by prestige and position.
    49.29–50.26: The death of Jacob and the final days of Joseph. 30–32: *Machpelah*, see ch. 23.
50.2–3: Embalming, an ancient Egyptian custom, was necessary if Jacob's body was to be
carried back to Canaan. Egyptians are said to have mourned for a king seventy-two days;
thus, out of respect for Joseph, Jacob was given a royal funeral. **5:** According to this fragment

bury me.' Now therefore let me go up, I pray you, and bury my father; then I will return." [6] And Pharaoh answered, "Go up, and bury your father, as he made you swear." [7] So Joseph went up to bury his father; and with him went up all the servants of Pharaoh, the elders of his household, and all the elders of the land of Egypt, [8] as well as all the household of Joseph, his brothers, and his father's household; only their children, their flocks, and their herds were left in the land of Goshen. [9] And there went up with him both chariots and horsemen; it was a very great company. [10] When they came to the threshing floor of Atad, which is beyond the Jordan, they lamented there with a very great and sorrowful lamentation; and he made a mourning for his father seven days. [11] When the inhabitants of the land, the Canaanites, saw the mourning on the threshing floor of Atad, they said, "This is a grievous mourning to the Egyptians." Therefore the place was named A'bel-mizraim;[d] it is beyond the Jordan. [12] Thus his sons did for him as he had commanded them; [13] for his sons carried him to the land of Canaan, and buried him in the cave of the field at Mach-pe'lah, to the east of Mamre, which Abraham bought with the field from Ephron the Hittite, to possess as a burying place. [14] After he had buried his father, Joseph returned to Egypt with his brothers and all who had gone up with him to bury his father.

15 When Joseph's brothers saw that their father was dead, they said, "It may be that Joseph will hate us and pay us back for all the evil which we did to him." [16] So they sent a message to Joseph, saying, "Your father gave this command before he died, [17] 'Say to Joseph, Forgive, I pray you, the transgression of your brothers and their sin, because they did evil to you.' And now, we pray you, forgive the transgression of the servants of the God of your father." Joseph wept when they spoke to him. [18] His brothers also came and fell down before him, and said, "Behold, we are your servants." [19] But Joseph said to them, "Fear not, for am I in the place of God? [20] As for you, you meant evil against me; but God meant it for good, to bring it about that many people should be kept alive, as they are today. [21] So do not fear; I will provide for you and your little ones." Thus he reassured them and comforted them.

22 So Joseph dwelt in Egypt, he and his father's house; and Joseph lived a hundred and ten years. [23] And Joseph saw E'phraim's children of the third generation; the children also of Machir the son of Manas'seh were born upon Joseph's knees. [24] And Joseph said to his brothers, "I am about to die; but God will visit you, and bring you up out of this land to the land which he swore to Abraham, to Isaac, and to Jacob." [25] Then Joseph took an oath of the sons of Israel, saying, "God will visit you, and you shall carry up my bones from here." [26] So Joseph died, being a hundred and ten years old; and they embalmed him, and he was put in a coffin in Egypt.

d That is *meadow* (or *mourning*) *of Egypt*

---

of tradition, Jacob hewed out a tomb for himself east of the Jordan (v. 10) and was buried there rather than at Machpelah (vv. 12–13). This explains why the funeral cortege detoured to Transjordan (vv. 10–11), though a main road led from Egypt along the coast to Beer-sheba. **18:** A recapitulation of the motif introduced at the beginning of the Joseph story (see 37.5–11 n.). **19–20:** The heart and climax of the Joseph story: Joseph asserts that only God can forgive and heal man's guilt, and he testifies to God's overruling providence which has already turned man's evil purposes to a good end (45.4–7). **23:** The children of *Machir*, Joseph's grandson, were *born upon his knees*, i.e. adopted as his descendants. Machir was the ancestor of a warlike clan of Manasseh which laid claim to Gilead (Num.32.39–40; Dt.3.15; Jg.5.14). **24:** An anticipation of the Exodus, based on the promise to the fathers. **25–26:** See Ex.13.19. According to tradition, Joseph was buried in Shechem (Jos.24.32; compare Gen.33.19; Acts 7.16).

EXODUS

In Israel's historical traditions the crucial event is the Exodus. Although Egyptian records make no reference to this border incident, there can be no doubt that Israel's faith rests upon an actual historical occurrence. Various lines of evidence point to the period of the 19th Dynasty (about 1350–1200 B.C.) as the most probable historical setting (see Ex.1.8 n.). The story unfolds against the background of Egyptian imperialism which motivated ambitious pharaohs to use Hebrew slaves as pawns in their scheme of world politics (see "Survey of . . . Bible Lands," § 7).

The book of Exodus bears witness to the religious meaning of what took place; namely, God's action to deliver a people from bondage and to bind them to himself in covenant. The book discloses an interweaving of traditions which preserve both the original Mosaic tradition and the interpretations of subsequent generations (see Introduction to Pentateuch). It falls into two major sections: (1) Israel's emancipation from Egyptian bondage and the pilgrimage to Sinai (chs. 1–18) and (2) Israel's sojourn at Sinai, where the covenant was made and the laws governing life and worship were promulgated (chs. 19–40).

At the center of the event stood Moses who was called to be the agent in delivering Israel from slavery, to be the interpreter of God's redemptive work, and to be the mediator of the covenant. Each tradition portrays him in a somewhat different light, but the whole account testifies to his massive influence upon subsequent history. Indeed, it was Moses who laid down the spiritual foundations of Israel's faith upon which later generations built.

THESE ARE THE NAMES OF THE sons of Israel who came to Egypt with Jacob, each with his household: ² Reuben, Simeon, Levi, and Judah, ³ Is'sachar, Zeb'ulun, and Benjamin, ⁴ Dan and Naph'tali, Gad and Asher. ⁵ All the offspring of Jacob were seventy persons; Joseph was already in Egypt. ⁶ Then Joseph died, and all his brothers, and all that generation. ⁷ But the descendants of Israel were fruitful and increased greatly; they multiplied and grew exceedingly strong; so that the land was filled with them.

8 Now there arose a new king over Egypt, who did not know Joseph. ⁹ And he said to his people, "Behold, the people of Israel are too many and too mighty for us. ¹⁰ Come, let us deal shrewdly with them, lest they multiply, and, if war befall us, they join our enemies and fight against us and escape from the land." ¹¹ Therefore they set taskmasters over them to afflict them with heavy burdens; and they built for Pharaoh store-cities, Pithom and Ra-am'ses. ¹² But the more they were oppressed, the more they multiplied and

---

1.1–22: Israel's bondage in Egypt. In spite of oppression, Abraham's descendants multiplied and prospered, in fulfilment of the divine promise (Gen.12.2; 15.5). **1–7:** Gen.35.23–26; 50.26. **5:** *Seventy persons,* Gen.46.8–27; Dt.10.22. The book of Exodus reflects the memory of decisive events with which Israel as a people identified itself in faith. The twelve-tribe confederacy was formed later and embraced tribes that had not been in Egypt (Jos. ch. 24). **6:** Over four centuries elapsed since Joseph's death (12.40; compare Gen.15.13). **7:** The promise concerning Abraham's numerous posterity was being fulfilled (Gen.17.1–8; see Ex.12.37 n.). *The land,* see Gen.45.10 n.; 47.11 n. **8:** Probably the allusion is to the new regime at the beginning of the 19th Dynasty under Seti I (1308–1290 B.C.) and Rameses II (1290–1224 B.C.). Hoping to regain Egypt's lost Asiatic empire, the pharaohs moved their capital from Thebes, where it had been during the 18th Dynasty, to the Delta. **9–10:** The presence of the Hebrews on Egypt's frontier was regarded as a security risk. **11:** *Store cities,* an allusion to the fortification of the area. The new capital, *Raamses* or Rameses (Zoan; Ps.78.12), was the former Hyksos capital (Avaris or Tanis) of Joseph's time (see Gen.45.10 n.; Num.13.22). As in the case of the pyramids, the work was carried out with the corvée (compare 1 Kg.5.13). **15:** *Hebrew,* an older and broader term

the more they spread abroad. And the Egyptians were in dread of the people of Israel. [13] So they made the people of Israel serve with rigor, [14] and made their lives bitter with hard service, in mortar and brick, and in all kinds of work in the field; in all their work they made them serve with rigor.

15 Then the king of Egypt said to the Hebrew midwives, one of whom was named Shiph'rah and the other Pu'ah, [16] "When you serve as midwife to the Hebrew women, and see them upon the birthstool, if it is a son, you shall kill him; but if it is a daughter, she shall live." [17] But the midwives feared God, and did not do as the king of Egypt commanded them, but let the male children live. [18] So the king of Egypt called the midwives, and said to them, "Why have you done this, and let the male children live?" [19] The midwives said to Pharaoh, "Because the Hebrew women are not like the Egyptian women; for they are vigorous and are delivered before the midwife comes to them." [20] So God dealt well with the midwives; and the people multiplied and grew very strong. [21] And because the midwives feared God he gave them families. [22] Then Pharaoh commanded all his people, "Every son that is born to the Hebrews[a] you shall cast into the Nile, but you shall let every daughter live."

2 Now a man from the house of Levi went and took to wife a daughter of Levi. [2] The woman conceived and bore a son; and when she saw that he was a goodly child, she hid him three months. [3] And when she could hide

him no longer she took for him a basket made of bulrushes, and daubed it with bitumen and pitch; and she put the child in it and placed it among the reeds at the river's brink. [4] And his sister stood at a distance, to know what would be done to him. [5] Now the daughter of Pharaoh came down to bathe at the river, and her maidens walked beside the river; she saw the basket among the reeds and sent her maid to fetch it. [6] When she opened it she saw the child; and lo, the babe was crying. She took pity on him and said, "This is one of the Hebrews' children." [7] Then his sister said to Pharaoh's daughter, "Shall I go and call you a nurse from the Hebrew women to nurse the child for you?" [8] And Pharaoh's daughter said to her, "Go." So the girl went and called the child's mother. [9] And Pharaoh's daughter said to her, "Take this child away, and nurse him for me, and I will give you your wages." So the woman took the child and nursed him. [10] And the child grew, and she brought him to Pharaoh's daughter, and he became her son; and she named him Moses,[b] for she said, "Because I drew him out[c] of the water."

11 One day, when Moses had grown up, he went out to his people and looked on their burdens; and he saw an Egyptian beating a Hebrew, one of his people. [12] He looked this way and that, and seeing no one he killed the Egyptian and hid him in the sand. [13] When he went out the next

a Sam Gk Tg: Heb lacks *to the Hebrews*
b Heb *Mosheh*   c Heb *mashah*

---

than Israelite (see Gen.10.21–31 n.), was often used when foreigners spoke to or about Abraham's people (Gen.39.14,17; 40.15). **19:** See vv. 7,12.

2.1–22: The infancy and early career of Moses. 1: It was probably the Joseph tribes that took part in the Exodus, although elements of the tribe of Levi were also in Egypt. **2–10:** Aspects of this story are paralleled in the legends of other national heroes, e.g. Sargon of Agade (about 2600 B.C.) who in infancy was saved from danger by being put in a basket of rushes sealed with pitch and floated on the river. **4:** Moses' sister was Miriam (Num.26.59). **10:** The name *Moses*, from an Egyptian word meaning "to beget a child" and perhaps once joined with the name of an Egyptian deity (compare the name Thut-mose), is explained by a Hebrew verb meaning "to draw out." The narrator sees divine providence at work, causing the evil design of Pharaoh to serve God's purpose. **11–14:** In spite of his Egyptian upbringing Moses identified himself

day, behold, two Hebrews were struggling together; and he said to the man that did the wrong, "Why do you strike your fellow?" ¹⁴ He answered, "Who made you a prince and a judge over us? Do you mean to kill me as you killed the Egyptian?" Then Moses was afraid, and thought, "Surely the thing is known." ¹⁵ When Pharaoh heard of it, he sought to kill Moses.

But Moses fled from Pharaoh, and stayed in the land of Mid'ian; and he sat down by a well. ¹⁶ Now the priest of Mid'ian had seven daughters; and they came and drew water, and filled the troughs to water their father's flock. ¹⁷ The shepherds came and drove them away; but Moses stood up and helped them, and watered their flock. ¹⁸ When they came to their father Reu'el, he said, "How is it that you have come so soon today?" ¹⁹ They said, "An Egyptian delivered us out of the hand of the shepherds, and even drew water for us and watered the flock." ²⁰ He said to his daughters, "And where is he? Why have you left the man? Call him, that he may eat bread." ²¹ And Moses was content to dwell with the man, and he gave Moses his daughter Zippo'rah. ²² She bore a son, and he called his name Gershom; for he said, "I have been a sojourner*d* in a foreign land."

23 In the course of those many days the king of Egypt died. And the people of Israel groaned under their bondage, and cried out for help, and their cry under bondage came up to God. ²⁴ And God heard their groaning, and God remembered his covenant with Abraham, with Isaac, and with Jacob. ²⁵ And God saw the people of Israel, and God knew their condition.

3 Now Moses was keeping the flock of his father-in-law, Jethro, the priest of Mid'ian; and he led his flock to the west side of the wilderness, and came to Horeb, the mountain of God. ² And the angel of the LORD appeared to him in a flame of fire out of the midst of a bush; and he looked, and lo, the bush was burning, yet it was not consumed. ³ And Moses said, "I will turn aside and see this great sight, why the bush is not burnt." ⁴ When the LORD saw that he turned aside to see, God called to him out of the bush, "Moses, Moses!" And he said, "Here am I." ⁵ Then he said, "Do not come near; put off your shoes from your feet, for the place on which you are standing is holy ground." ⁶ And he said, "I am the God of your father, the God of Abraham, the God of Isaac, and the God of Jacob." And Moses hid his face, for he was afraid to look at God.

7 Then the LORD said, "I have seen the affliction of my people who are in Egypt, and have heard their cry because of their taskmasters; I know their sufferings, ⁸ and I have come down to deliver them out of the hand

d Heb *ger*

---

with his people (Heb.11.24–25). **15:** The Midianites were distant blood relatives of Israel (Gen.25.2). **18:** "The priest of Midian" (v. 16) is usually called either Jethro (3.1; 4.18; 18.1) or Hobab (Num.10.29; Jg.4.11). *Reuel* was apparently his father (Num.10.29).

2.23–4.17: The call of Moses. In Midian the God of the fathers revealed himself to Moses and summoned him to be his agent in delivering Israel. **23:** *The king* was probably Seti I (see 1.8 n). The Israelites hoped that their condition would improve under the new regime, but Rameses II continued the oppressive building program. **24:** On the covenant with the fathers, see Gen.12.1–3; 17.1–14; 26.2–5. **3.1–6:** The theophany of the bush. **1:** *The mountain of God*, called both Horeb and Sinai, was probably a Midianite sacred place (see v. 5 n.). Its location is unknown, but tradition places it in the eastern part of the Sinaitic Peninsula. **2:** *The angel of the LORD*, see Gen.16.7 n. *Fire* was conceived to be the form of the divine appearance (Gen.15.17; Ex.19.18; Ps.104.3–4; Ezek.1.27). **5:** Moses unexpectedly found himself in a holy place (see v. 1 n.; Gen.28.16–17). The removal of sandals before entering a holy place was an ancient custom (Jos.5.15). **6:** *The God of your father*, see Gen.26.24 n. The vision of God veiled in fire aroused dread (33.20), for divine holiness was experienced as a mysterious power that threatened man's existence (19.10–13). **7–12:** The divine commission. **8:** Canaan was *a land flowing with*

God commissions Moses

of the Egyptians, and to bring them up out of that land to a good and broad land, a land flowing with milk and honey, to the place of the Canaanites, the Hittites, the Amorites, the Per'-izzites, the Hivites, and the Jeb'usites. 9 And now, behold, the cry of the people of Israel has come to me, and I have seen the oppression with which the Egyptians oppress them. 10 Come, I will send you to Pharaoh that you may bring forth my people, the sons of Israel, out of Egypt." 11 But Moses said to God, "Who am I that I should go to Pharaoh, and bring the sons of Israel out of Egypt?" 12 He said, "But I will be with you; and this shall be the sign for you, that I have sent you: when you have brought forth the people out of Egypt, you shall serve God upon this mountain."

13 Then Moses said to God, "If I come to the people of Israel and say to them, 'The God of your fathers has sent me to you,' and they ask me, 'What is his name?' what shall I say to them?" 14 God said to Moses, "I AM WHO I AM."e And he said, "Say this to the people of Israel, 'I AM has sent me to you.' " 15 God also said to Moses, "Say this to the people of Israel, 'The LORD,f the God of your fathers, the God of Abraham, the God of Isaac, and the God of Jacob, has sent me to you': this is my name for ever, and thus I am to be remembered throughout all generations. 16 Go and gather the elders of Israel together, and say to them, 'The LORD, the God of your fathers, the God of Abraham, of Isaac, and of Jacob, has appeared to me, saying, "I have observed you and what has been done to you in Egypt; 17 and I promise that I will bring you up out of the affliction of Egypt, to the land of the Canaanites, the Hittites, the Amorites, the Per'izzites, the Hivites, and the Jeb'usites, a land flowing with milk and honey." ' 18 And they will hearken to your voice; and you and the elders of Israel shall go to the king of Egypt and say to him, 'The LORD, the God of the Hebrews, has met with us; and now, we pray you, let us go a three days' journey into the wilderness, that we may sacrifice to the LORD our God.' 19 I know that the king of Egypt will not let you go unless compelled by a mighty hand.g 20 So I will stretch out my hand and smite Egypt with all the wonders which I will do in it; after that he will let you go. 21 And I will give this people favor in the sight of the Egyptians; and when you go, you shall not go empty, 22 but each woman shall ask of her neighbor, and of her who sojourns in her house, jewelry of silver and of gold, and clothing, and you shall put them on your sons and on your daughters; thus you shall despoil the Egyptians."

4 Then Moses answered, "But behold, they will not believe me or listen to my voice, for they will say,

e Or I AM WHAT I AM or I WILL BE WHAT I WILL BE
f The word LORD when spelled with capital letters, stands for the divine name, *YHWH*, which is here connected with the verb *hayah*, to be
g Gk Vg: Heb *no, not by a mighty hand*

---

milk and honey, foods that made it a paradise in the eyes of semi-nomads. On the pre-Israelite peoples, see Gen.10.15–20; Num.13.29. **11–12:** The first of Moses' four objections (v. 13; 4.1,10). God's word will be confirmed by *a sign* (compare Is.7.10–17), i.e. the return of Israel to Sinai for worship. A sign may be an extraordinary wonder (4.1–9) or an ordinary phenomenon. What makes it significant, and therefore miraculous, is that God's presence and power are disclosed to faith. **13–15:** Moses' second question assumes a polytheistic environment; thus he must know the identity of the God who is dealing with him. On the *name*, see Gen.32.27 n. **14:** I AM WHO I AM is an etymology of the Israelite name for God, YHWH, probably pronounced Yahweh. (The RSV, following ancient synagogue practice, substitutes "the LORD"; see the Preface, pp.xiii-xiv). YHWH is treated as a verbal form derived from "to be" and formulated in the first person because God is the speaker. Actually YHWH is a third person form and may mean "He causes to be." The name does not indicate God's eternal being but his action and presence in historical affairs. **15:** The name is here introduced for the first time (6.2–3; see Gen.4.26b n.). **21–22:** See 11.2–3; 12.35–36. **4.1–9:** This narrative reflects superstitious magic which flourished

'The LORD did not appear to you.' "
² The LORD said to him, "What is that
in your hand?" He said, "A rod."
³ And he said, "Cast it on the ground."
So he cast it on the ground, and it became a serpent; and Moses fled from it.
⁴ But the LORD said to Moses, "Put out
your hand, and take it by the tail"–
so he put out his hand and caught it,
and it became a rod in his hand–
⁵ "that they may believe that the LORD,
the God of their fathers, the God of
Abraham, the God of Isaac, and the
God of Jacob, has appeared to you."
⁶ Again, the LORD said to him, "Put
your hand into your bosom." And he
put his hand into his bosom; and when
he took it out, behold, his hand was
leprous, as white as snow. ⁷ Then God
said, "Put your hand back into your
bosom." So he put his hand back into
his bosom; and when he took it out,
behold, it was restored like the rest of
his flesh. ⁸ "If they will not believe
you," God said, "or heed the first sign,
they may believe the latter sign. ⁹ If
they will not believe even these two
signs or heed your voice, you shall take
some water from the Nile and pour it
upon the dry ground; and the water
which you shall take from the Nile will
become blood upon the dry ground."

10 But Moses said to the LORD,
"Oh, my Lord, I am not eloquent,
either heretofore or since thou hast
spoken to thy servant; but I am slow
of speech and of tongue." ¹¹ Then the
LORD said to him, "Who has made
man's mouth? Who makes him dumb,
or deaf, or seeing, or blind? Is it not I,
the LORD? ¹² Now therefore go, and

I will be with your mouth and teach
you what you shall speak." ¹³ But he
said, "Oh, my Lord, send, I pray, some
other person." ¹⁴ Then the anger of the
LORD was kindled against Moses and he
said, "Is there not Aaron, your brother,
the Levite? I know that he can speak
well; and behold, he is coming out to
meet you, and when he sees you he
will be glad in his heart. ¹⁵ And you
shall speak to him and put the words in
his mouth; and I will be with your
mouth and with his mouth, and will
teach you what you shall do. ¹⁶ He
shall speak for you to the people; and
he shall be a mouth for you, and you
shall be to him as God. ¹⁷ And you
shall take in your hand this rod, with
which you shall do the signs."

18 Moses went back to Jethro his
father-in-law and said to him, "Let me
go back, I pray, to my kinsmen in
Egypt and see whether they are still
alive." And Jethro said to Moses, "Go
in peace." ¹⁹ And the LORD said to
Moses in Mid'ian, "Go back to
Egypt; for all the men who were seeking your life are dead." ²⁰ So Moses
took his wife and his sons and set
them on an ass, and went back to the
land of Egypt; and in his hand Moses
took the rod of God.

21 And the LORD said to Moses,
"When you go back to Egypt, see that
you do before Pharaoh all the miracles
which I have put in your power; but I
will harden his heart, so that he will
not let the people go. ²² And you shall
say to Pharaoh, 'Thus says the LORD,
Israel is my first-born son, ²³ and I say
to you, "Let my son go that he may

---

in Egypt and claims that Moses was given power to excel these "secret arts" (7.11; 8.18–19;
9.11). **3**: 7.8–12. Serpent magic was practiced in Egypt from ancient times. The sign was the
reverse of a trick whereby a snake is made rigid by hypnotism, so that it can be picked up by the
tail. **10–17**: Aaron is designated as Moses' aide. **11**: Jer.1.6. In Hebraic thought human conditions were not ascribed to secondary causes but to God whose will is sovereign in all things
(Dt.32.39). **16**: The relation between God and his prophetic spokesman is analogous to the
relation between Moses and Aaron (7.1; compare 16.9).
4.18–31: Moses returns to Egypt to arouse the faith of his people. 20: Only one of Moses'
sons has been mentioned so far (2.22); see 18.3–4. **21**: Even Pharaoh's stubbornness, which
paradoxically was the expression of his own free will (8.15,32; 9.34), was foreknown (3.19) and
foreordained by God, thus indicating divine sovereignty in historical affairs (compare Is.6.10).
22: *Israel* (the people) is the LORD's *first-born son* among the nations, a pre-eminent rank based

serve me"; if you refuse to let him go, behold, I will slay your first-born son.' "

24 At a lodging place on the way the LORD met him and sought to kill him. [25] Then Zippo'rah took a flint and cut off her son's foreskin, and touched Moses' feet with it, and said, "Surely you are a bridegroom of blood to me!" [26] So he let him alone. Then it was that she said, "You are a bridegroom of blood," because of the circumcision.

27 The LORD said to Aaron, "Go into the wilderness to meet Moses." So he went, and met him at the mountain of God and kissed him. [28] And Moses told Aaron all the words of the LORD with which he had sent him, and all the signs which he had charged him to do. [29] Then Moses and Aaron went and gathered together all the elders of the people of Israel. [30] And Aaron spoke all the words which the LORD had spoken to Moses, and did the signs in the sight of the people. [31] And the people believed; and when they heard that the LORD had visited the people of Israel and that he had seen their affliction, they bowed their heads and worshiped.

5 Afterward Moses and Aaron went to Pharaoh and said, "Thus says the LORD, the God of Israel, 'Let my people go, that they may hold a feast to me in the wilderness.'" [2] But Pharaoh said, "Who is the LORD, that I should heed his voice and let Israel go? I do not know the LORD, and moreover I will not let Israel go." [3] Then they said, "The God of the Hebrews has met with us; let us go, we pray, a three days' journey into the wilderness, and sacrifice to the LORD our God, lest he fall upon us with pestilence or with the sword." [4] But the king of Egypt said to them, "Moses and Aaron, why do you take the people away from their work? Get to your burdens." [5] And Pharaoh said, "Behold, the people of the land are now many and you make them rest from their burdens!" [6] The same day Pharaoh commanded the taskmasters of the people and their foremen, [7] "You shall no longer give the people straw to make bricks, as heretofore; let them go and gather straw for themselves. [8] But the number of bricks which they made heretofore you shall lay upon them, you shall by no means lessen it; for they are idle; therefore they cry, 'Let us go and offer sacrifice to our God.' [9] Let heavier work be laid upon the men that they may labor at it and pay no regard to lying words."

10 So the taskmasters and the foremen of the people went out and said to the people, "Thus says Pharaoh, 'I will not give you straw. [11] Go yourselves, get your straw wherever you can find it; but your work will not be lessened in the least.'" [12] So the people were scattered abroad throughout all the land of Egypt, to gather stubble for straw. [13] The taskmasters were urgent, saying, "Complete your work, your daily task, as when there was straw." [14] And the foremen of the people of Israel, whom Pharaoh's taskmasters had set over them, were beaten, and were asked, "Why have you not

upon divine adoption or election (Jer.31.9; Hos.11.1). **23:** 11.5; 12.29–34. **24–26:** An archaic tradition which traces the origin of circumcision (compare Gen.17.9–14) to the Midianite wife of Moses. **24:** This verse reflects ancient belief in demonic attack (see Gen.38.7 n.), warded off by the timely performance of the rite. Originally circumcision was a puberty or marriage rite; *bridegroom of blood* (v. 26) is perhaps an old expression for a young man who was circumcised before marriage. **25:** Here it is assumed that the circumcision of the infant son was efficacious for Moses, who was evidently uncircumcised. *Feet,* a euphemism for the sexual organs (Is.7.20). **27:** *The mountain of God* (3.1), which Moses had already left (4.20).

5.1–6.1: The first audience with Pharaoh fails. 1: The petition is for a leave of absence for a pilgrimage to the sacred mountain (v. 3; 3.18). **2:** The contemptuous Pharaoh, whose absolute power was enforced by his deification in Egyptian religion, knew many gods; but this "god," the LORD, was unheard of and a request made in his name carried no authority. **9:** Compare 1 Kg.12.1–11. Pharaoh treats the request for a three-day journey as *lying words,* i.e. a ruse to

done all your task of making bricks today, as hitherto?"

15 Then the foremen of the people of Israel came and cried to Pharaoh, "Why do you deal thus with your servants? ¹⁶ No straw is given to your servants, yet they say to us, 'Make bricks!' And behold, your servants are beaten; but the fault is in your own people." ¹⁷ But he said, "You are idle, you are idle; therefore you say, 'Let us go and sacrifice to the LORD.' ¹⁸ Go now, and work; for no straw shall be given you, yet you shall deliver the same number of bricks." ¹⁹ The foremen of the people of Israel saw that they were in evil plight, when they said, "You shall by no means lessen your daily number of bricks." ²⁰ They met Moses and Aaron, who were waiting for them, as they came forth from Pharaoh; ²¹ and they said to them, "The LORD look upon you and judge, because you have made us offensive in the sight of Pharaoh and his servants, and have put a sword in their hand to kill us."

22 Then Moses turned again to the LORD and said, "O LORD, why hast thou done evil to this people? Why didst thou ever send me? ²³ For since I came to Pharaoh to speak in thy name, he has done evil to this people, and thou hast not delivered thy people at all." ¹ But the LORD said to Moses, "Now you shall see what I will do to Pharaoh; for with a strong hand he will send them out, yea, with a strong hand he will drive them out of his land."

2 And God said to Moses, "I am the LORD. ³ I appeared to Abraham, to Isaac, and to Jacob, as God Almighty,ʰ

but by my name the LORD I did not make myself known to them. ⁴ I also established my covenant with them, to give them the land of Canaan, the land in which they dwelt as sojourners. ⁵ Moreover I have heard the groaning of the people of Israel whom the Egyptians hold in bondage and I have remembered my covenant. ⁶ Say therefore to the people of Israel, 'I am the LORD, and I will bring you out from under the burdens of the Egyptians, and I will deliver you from their bondage, and I will redeem you with an outstretched arm and with great acts of judgment, ⁷ and I will take you for my people, and I will be your God; and you shall know that I am the LORD your God, who has brought you out from under the burdens of the Egyptians. ⁸ And I will bring you into the land which I swore to give to Abraham, to Isaac, and to Jacob; I will give it to you for a possession. I am the LORD.' " ⁹ Moses spoke thus to the people of Israel; but they did not listen to Moses, because of their broken spirit and their cruel bondage.

10 And the LORD said to Moses, ¹¹ "Go in, tell Pharaoh king of Egypt to let the people of Israel go out of his land." ¹² But Moses said to the LORD, "Behold, the people of Israel have not listened to me; how then shall Pharaoh listen to me, who am a man of uncircumcised lips?" ¹³ But the LORD spoke to Moses and Aaron, and gave them a charge to the people of Israel and to Pharaoh king of Egypt to bring the people of Israel out of the land of Egypt.

14 These are the heads of their
h Heb El Shaddai

leave the country permanently. **16:** The foremen diplomatically suggest that the fault lies with Pharaoh's subordinates, i.e. *your own people.* **21:** *The LORD . . . judge,* i.e. give Moses and Aaron due justice for worsening their plight.

6.2–7.7: The call of Moses and the appointment of Aaron are recapitulated in a priestly version (compare 3.1–4.17). **2–3:** See 3.14 n. The LORD (YHWH) is the same God who led the patriarchs but formerly he was known by another name, El Shaddai (see Gen.17.1 n.). **4:** The *covenant* is the Abrahamic covenant (Gen. ch. 17) which guaranteed possession of Canaan (v. 8). *Sojourners,* see Gen.17.8 n. **7:** *My people . . . your God,* a succinct statement of the meaning of the covenant relation (Hos.2.23; Jer.31.33). **12:** *Uncircumcised lips* are sealed lips; a vivid way of saying that Moses was a man poor in speech (4.10–16). The answer to Moses' question, inter-

fathers' houses: the sons of Reuben, the first-born of Israel: Hanoch, Pallu, Hezron, and Carmi; these are the families of Reuben. ¹⁵ The sons of Simeon: Jemu'el, Jamin, Ohad, Jachin, Zohar, and Shaul, the son of a Cana-anite woman; these are the families of Simeon. ¹⁶ These are the names of the sons of Levi according to their genera-tions: Gershon, Kohath, and Merar'i, the years of the life of Levi being a hundred and thirty-seven years. ¹⁷ The sons of Gershon: Libni and Shim'e-i, by their families. ¹⁸ The sons of Ko-hath: Amram, Izhar, Hebron, and Uz'ziel, the years of the life of Kohath being a hundred and thirty-three years. ¹⁹ The sons of Merar'i: Mahli and Mushi. These are the families of the Levites according to their generations. ²⁰ Amram took to wife Joch'ebed his father's sister and she bore him Aaron and Moses, the years of the life of Amram being one hundred and thirty-seven years. ²¹ The sons of Izhar: Korah, Nepheg, and Zichri. ²² And the sons of Uz'ziel: Mi'sha-el, Elza'-phan, and Sithri. ²³ Aaron took to wife Eli'sheba, the daughter of Ammin'-adab and the sister of Nahshon; and she bore him Nadab, Abi'hu, Elea'zar, and Ith'amar. ²⁴ The sons of Korah: Assir, Elka'nah, and Abi'asaph; these are the families of the Ko'rahites. ²⁵ Elea'zar, Aaron's son, took to wife one of the daughters of Pu'ti-el; and she bore him Phin'ehas. These are the heads of the fathers' houses of the Levites by their families.

26 These are the Aaron and Moses to whom the LORD said: "Bring out the people of Israel from the land of Egypt by their hosts." ²⁷ It was they who spoke to Pharaoh king of Egypt about bringing out the people of Israel

from Egypt, this Moses and this Aaron. 28 On the day when the LORD spoke to Moses in the land of Egypt, ²⁹ the LORD said to Moses, "I am the LORD; tell Pharaoh king of Egypt all that I say to you." ³⁰ But Moses said to the LORD, "Behold, I am of uncir-cumcised lips; how then shall Pharaoh 7 listen to me?" ¹ And the LORD said to Moses, "See, I make you as God to Pharaoh; and Aaron your brother shall be your prophet. ² You shall speak all that I command you; and Aaron your brother shall tell Phar-aoh to let the people of Israel go out of his land. ³ But I will harden Pharaoh's heart, and though I multiply my signs and wonders in the land of Egypt, ⁴ Pharaoh will not listen to you; then I will lay my hand upon Egypt and bring forth my hosts, my people the sons of Israel, out of the land of Egypt by great acts of judgment. ⁵ And the Egyptians shall know that I am the LORD, when I stretch forth my hand upon Egypt and bring out the people of Israel from among them." ⁶ And Moses and Aaron did so; they did as the LORD commanded them. ⁷ Now Moses was eighty years old, and Aaron eighty-three years old, when they spoke to Pharaoh.

8 And the LORD said to Moses and Aaron, ⁹ "When Pharaoh says to you, 'Prove yourselves by working a mir-acle,' then you shall say to Aaron, 'Take your rod and cast it down before Pharaoh, that it may become a ser-pent.' " ¹⁰ So Moses and Aaron went to Pharaoh and did as the LORD com-manded; Aaron cast down his rod be-fore Pharaoh and his servants, and it became a serpent. ¹¹ Then Pharaoh summoned the wise men and the sor-cerers; and they also, the magicians of

---

rupted by vv. 14–27, is found in v. 28 to 7.2. **14–27:** The purpose of the genealogy of Aaron and Moses is to trace priestly lineage from Levi, Jacob's son, to Aaron and through Aaron's third son, Eleazar, to Phinehas (Num. ch. 3). **14–16:** Gen.46.8–11. *Fathers' houses,* see Num.1.2–4 n. **28–30:** Continuation from v. 12. **7.1:** See 4.16 n. **2:** See 5.1 where both Moses and Aaron are to speak to the king; here the role of Aaron, the priest, is stressed. **3–4:** See 4.21 n. The *great acts of judgment* (6.6) are the signs and wonders.

    7.8–11.10: The ten plagues (Pss.78.44–51; 105.28–36). **8–13:** The preface to the contest with Pharaoh is drawn from priestly tradition (compare 4.1–5). Here Aaron is the chief actor and his

Egypt, did the same by their secret arts. ¹² For every man cast down his rod, and they became serpents. But Aaron's rod swallowed up their rods. ¹³ Still Pharaoh's heart was hardened, and he would not listen to them; as the LORD had said.

14 Then the LORD said to Moses, "Pharaoh's heart is hardened, he refuses to let the people go. ¹⁵ Go to Pharaoh in the morning, as he is going out to the water; wait for him by the river's brink, and take in your hand the rod which was turned into a serpent. ¹⁶ And you shall say to him, 'The LORD, the God of the Hebrews, sent me to you, saying, "Let my people go, that they may serve me in the wilderness; and behold, you have not yet obeyed." ¹⁷ Thus says the LORD, "By this you shall know that I am the LORD: behold, I will strike the water that is in the Nile with the rod that is in my hand, and it shall be turned to blood, ¹⁸ and the fish in the Nile shall die, and the Nile shall become foul, and the Egyptians will loathe to drink water from the Nile." ' " ¹⁹ And the LORD said to Moses, "Say to Aaron, 'Take your rod and stretch out your hand over the waters of Egypt, over their rivers, their canals, and their ponds, and all their pools of water, that they may become blood; and there shall be blood throughout all the land of Egypt, both in vessels of wood and in vessels of stone.' "

20 Moses and Aaron did as the LORD commanded; in the sight of Pharaoh and in the sight of his servants, he lifted up the rod and struck the water that was in the Nile, and all the water that was in the Nile turned to blood. ²¹ And the fish in the Nile died; and the Nile became foul, so that the Egyptians could not drink water from the Nile; and there was blood throughout all the land of Egypt. ²² But the magicians of Egypt did the same by their secret arts; so Pharaoh's heart remained hardened, and he would not listen to them; as the LORD had said. ²³ Pharaoh turned and went into his house, and he did not lay even this to heart. ²⁴ And all the Egyptians dug round about the Nile for water to drink, for they could not drink the water of the Nile.

25 Seven days passed after the LORD had struck the Nile. **8**ⁱ ¹ Then the LORD said to Moses, "Go in to Pharaoh and say to him, 'Thus says the LORD, "Let my people go, that they may serve me. ² But if you refuse to let them go, behold, I will plague all your country with frogs; ³ the Nile shall swarm with frogs which shall come up into your house, and into your bedchamber and on your bed, and into the houses of your servants and of your people,ʲ and into your ovens and your kneading bowls; ⁴ the frogs shall come up on you and on your people and on all your servants." ' " ⁵ᵏ And the LORD said to Moses, "Say to Aaron, 'Stretch out your hand with your rod over the rivers, over the canals, and over the pools, and cause frogs to come upon the land of Egypt!' " ⁶ So Aaron stretched out his hand over the waters of Egypt; and the frogs came up and covered the

i Ch 7.26 in Heb
j Gk: Heb *upon your people*
k Ch 8.1 in Heb

---

rod–not Moses'–is turned into a serpent or dragon. **14–24: First plague:** the pollution of the Nile. **15:** Moses was to meet Pharaoh *at the river's brink* with a challenge to Egyptian existence; for the Nile, believed to have its source in the subterranean ocean (see Gen.2.6 n.), was the source of life and fertility. **17–18:** The plague of blood apparently reflects a natural phenomenon of Egypt: namely, the reddish color of the Nile at its height in the summer owing to red particles of earth or perhaps minute organisms. **19:** The tendency to enhance the tradition is seen in the facts that here the rod is Aaron's (see 4.14; 7.2) and that all the water of Egypt is said to have been polluted. **22:** See v. 11.

7.25–8.15: Second plague: frogs. **8.3:** The mud of the Nile, after the seasonal overflowing, was a natural place for frogs to generate. Egypt has been spared more frequent occurrence of this pestilence by the frog-eating bird, the ibis. **5–7:** Another unit of tradition which extols

land of Egypt. ⁷ But the magicians did the same by their secret arts, and brought frogs upon the land of Egypt.

8 Then Pharaoh called Moses and Aaron, and said, "Entreat the LORD to take away the frogs from me and from my people; and I will let the people go to sacrifice to the LORD." ⁹ Moses said to Pharaoh, "Be pleased to command me when I am to entreat, for you and for your servants and for your people, that the frogs be destroyed from you and your houses and be left only in the Nile." ¹⁰ And he said, "Tomorrow." Moses said, "Be it as you say, that you may know that there is no one like the LORD our God. ¹¹ The frogs shall depart from you and your houses and your servants and your people; they shall be left only in the Nile." ¹² So Moses and Aaron went out from Pharaoh; and Moses cried to the LORD concerning the frogs, as he had agreed with Pharaoh.*ˡ* ¹³ And the LORD did according to the word of Moses; the frogs died out of the houses and courtyards and out of the fields. ¹⁴ And they gathered them together in heaps, and the land stank. ¹⁵ But when Pharaoh saw that there was a respite, he hardened his heart, and would not listen to them; as the LORD had said.

16 Then the LORD said to Moses, "Say to Aaron, 'Stretch out your rod and strike the dust of the earth, that it may become gnats throughout all the land of Egypt.'" ¹⁷ And they did so; Aaron stretched out his hand with his rod, and struck the dust of the earth, and there came gnats on man and beast; all the dust of the earth became gnats throughout all the land of Egypt. ¹⁸ The magicians tried by their secret arts to bring forth gnats, but they could not. So there were gnats on man and beast. ¹⁹ And the magicians said to Pharaoh, "This is the finger of God." But Pharaoh's heart was hardened, and he would not listen to them; as the LORD had said.

20 Then the LORD said to Moses, "Rise up early in the morning and wait for Pharaoh, as he goes out to the water, and say to him, 'Thus says the LORD, "Let my people go, that they may serve me. ²¹ Else, if you will not let my people go, behold, I will send swarms of flies on you and your servants and your people, and into your houses; and the houses of the Egyptians shall be filled with swarms of flies, and also the ground on which they stand. ²² But on that day I will set apart the land of Goshen, where my people dwell, so that no swarms of flies shall be there; that you may know that I am the LORD in the midst of the earth. ²³ Thus I will put a division*ᵐ* between my people and your people. By tomorrow shall this sign be."'" ²⁴ And the LORD did so; there came great swarms of flies into the house of Pharaoh and into his servants' houses, and in all the land of Egypt the land was ruined by reason of the flies.

25 Then Pharaoh called Moses and Aaron, and said, "Go, sacrifice to your God within the land." ²⁶ But Moses said, "It would not be right to do so; for we shall sacrifice to the LORD our God offerings abominable to the Egyptians. If we sacrifice offerings abominable to the Egyptians before their eyes, will they not stone us? ²⁷ We

ˡ Or *which he had brought upon Pharaoh*
ᵐ Gk Vg: Heb *set redemption*

Aaron the priest (7.19). **8:** *Entreat the LORD*, for the first time Pharaoh momentarily recognizes Israel's God. **9–11:** To enhance the wonder, Moses promises to pray that the scourge cease at a designated time.

8.16–32: Third and fourth plagues: gnats and flies. **16:** From ancient times stinging gnats or mosquitoes have plagued Egypt, especially in the autumn. The Nile, receding from its overflow, leaves stagnant pools of water in which the insects breed. On Aaron's rod, see 7.19; 8.5–7. **19:** This time the magicians are unable to match the feat and confess that *this is the finger of God* (31.18; Ps.8.3; Lk.11.20). **20–32:** The fourth plague is probably a variant of vv. 16–19. **22–23:** The sign was not just the coming of myriads of flies but the isolation of Goshen so that the scourge did not affect the Hebrews. **26:** Egypt had strong taboos against the religious prac-

must go three days' journey into the wilderness and sacrifice to the LORD our God as he will command us." 28 So Pharaoh said, "I will let you go, to sacrifice to the LORD your God in the wilderness; only you shall not go very far away. Make entreaty for me." 29 Then Moses said, "Behold, I am going out from you and I will pray to the LORD that the swarms of flies may depart from Pharaoh, from his servants, and from his people, tomorrow; only let not Pharaoh deal falsely again by not letting the people go to sacrifice to the LORD." 30 So Moses went out from Pharaoh and prayed to the LORD. 31 And the LORD did as Moses asked, and removed the swarms of flies from Pharaoh, from his servants, and from his people; not one remained. 32 But Pharaoh hardened his heart this time also, and did not let the people go.

9 Then the LORD said to Moses, "Go in to Pharaoh, and say to him, 'Thus says the LORD, the God of the Hebrews, "Let my people go, that they may serve me. 2 For if you refuse to let them go and still hold them, 3 behold, the hand of the LORD will fall with a very severe plague upon your cattle which are in the field, the horses, the asses, the camels, the herds, and the flocks. 4 But the LORD will make a distinction between the cattle of Israel and the cattle of Egypt, so that nothing shall die of all that belongs to the people of Israel." ' " 5 And the LORD set a time, saying, "Tomorrow the LORD will do this thing in the land." 6 And on the morrow the LORD did this thing; all the cattle of the Egyptians died, but of the cattle of the people of Israel not one died. 7 And Pharaoh sent, and behold,

not one of the cattle of the Israelites was dead. But the heart of Pharaoh was hardened, and he did not let the people go.

8 And the LORD said to Moses and Aaron, "Take handfuls of ashes from the kiln, and let Moses throw them toward heaven in the sight of Pharaoh. 9 And it shall become fine dust over all the land of Egypt, and become boils breaking out in sores on man and beast throughout all the land of Egypt." 10 So they took ashes from the kiln, and stood before Pharaoh, and Moses threw them toward heaven, and it became boils breaking out in sores on man and beast. 11 And the magicians could not stand before Moses because of the boils, for the boils were upon the magicians and upon all the Egyptians. 12 But the LORD hardened the heart of Pharaoh, and he did not listen to them; as the LORD had spoken to Moses.

13 Then the LORD said to Moses, "Rise up early in the morning and stand before Pharaoh, and say to him, 'Thus says the LORD, the God of the Hebrews, "Let my people go, that they may serve me. 14 For this time I will send all my plagues upon your heart, and upon your servants and your people, that you may know that there is none like me in all the earth. 15 For by now I could have put forth my hand and struck you and your people with pestilence, and you would have been cut off from the earth; 16 but for this purpose have I let you live, to show you my power, so that my name may be declared throughout all the earth. 17 You are still exalting yourself against my people, and will not let them go. 18 Be-

---

tices of foreigners (Gen.43.32). **28**: Pharaoh's further concession–permission to go just beyond the border–reflects his suspicion of Moses' intention (5.9).

9.1–12: Fifth and sixth plagues: cattle plague and boils. **3**: This plague, perhaps anthrax, seems to have resulted from conditions created by former plagues: disease spread by mosquitoes or flies. **4**: See 8.22–23 n. **5**: This time Pharaoh was given twenty-four hours notice. **8–12**: The sixth plague, boils or a similar skin outbreak (Dt.28.27), is parallel to the previous one, so far as the cattle are concerned. **13–35: Seventh plague:** hail and thunderstorm. **14**: *All my plagues upon your heart* is not clear but may refer to unleashing the full fury of heaven: thunder, hail, rain, and lightning (vv. 23,33). **15–16**: It is explained that the ineffectiveness of the plagues up to this point is not due to the LORD's weakness but to his patient determination to demon-

hold, tomorrow about this time I will cause very heavy hail to fall, such as never has been in Egypt from the day it was founded until now. [19] Now therefore send, get your cattle and all that you have in the field into safe shelter; for the hail shall come down upon every man and beast that is in the field and is not brought home, and they shall die." ' " [20] Then he who feared the word of the LORD among the servants of Pharaoh made his slaves and his cattle flee into the houses; [21] but he who did not regard the word of the LORD left his slaves and his cattle in the field.

22 And the LORD said to Moses, "Stretch forth your hand toward heaven, that there may be hail in all the land of Egypt, upon man and beast and every plant of the field, throughout the land of Egypt." [23] Then Moses stretched forth his rod toward heaven; and the LORD sent thunder and hail, and fire ran down to the earth. And the LORD rained hail upon the land of Egypt; [24] there was, hail, and fire flashing continually in the midst of the hail, very heavy hail, such as had never been in all the land of Egypt since it became a nation. [25] The hail struck down everything that was in the field throughout all the land of Egypt, both man and beast; and the hail struck down every plant of the field, and shattered every tree of the field. [26] Only in the land of Goshen, where the people of Israel were, there was no hail.

27 Then Pharaoh sent, and called Moses and Aaron, and said to them, "I have sinned this time; the LORD is in the right, and I and my people are in the wrong. [28] Entreat the LORD; for there has been enough of this thunder and hail; I will let you go, and you shall stay no longer." [29] Moses said to him,

"As soon as I have gone out of the city, I will stretch out my hands to the LORD; the thunder will cease, and there will be no more hail, that you may know that the earth is the LORD's. [30] But as for you and your servants, I know that you do not yet fear the LORD God." [31] (The flax and the barley were ruined, for the barley was in the ear and the flax was in bud. [32] But the wheat and the spelt were not ruined, for they are late in coming up.) [33] So Moses went out of the city from Pharaoh, and stretched out his hands to the LORD; and the thunder and the hail ceased, and the rain no longer poured upon the earth. [34] But when Pharaoh saw that the rain and the hail and the thunder had ceased, he sinned yet again, and hardened his heart, he and his servants. [35] So the heart of Pharaoh was hardened, and he did not let the people of Israel go; as the LORD had spoken through Moses.

10 Then the LORD said to Moses, "Go in to Pharaoh; for I have hardened his heart and the heart of his servants, that I may show these signs of mine among them, [2] and that you may tell in the hearing of your son and of your son's son how I have made sport of the Egyptians and what signs I have done among them; that you may know that I am the LORD."

3 So Moses and Aaron went in to Pharaoh, and said to him, "Thus says the LORD, the God of the Hebrews, 'How long will you refuse to humble yourself before me? Let my people go, that they may serve me. [4] For if you refuse to let my people go, behold, tomorrow I will bring locusts into your country, [5] and they shall cover the face of the land, so that no one can see the land; and they shall eat what is left to you after the hail, and they shall eat

strate his sovereignty (compare Rom.9.17). **26:** See vv. 6–7; 8.22–23 n. **27:** For the first time Pharaoh confesses that he is beaten, hoping thus to appease the foreign deity without making further concessions. **29:** The plagues bear witness to the fact that *the earth is the LORD's* (19.5; Ps.24.1), for the powers of nature serve his purpose. **31–32:** This parenthetical remark explains why there were still plants for the locusts to eat during the next plague and, incidentally, dates the seventh plague around the middle of January, when the crops begin to mature.

10.1–20: Eighth plague: locusts. **4–6:** Clouds of locusts were a familiar pestilence to farmers

every tree of yours which grows in the field, ⁶ and they shall fill your houses, and the houses of all your servants and of all the Egyptians; as neither your fathers nor your grandfathers have seen, from the day they came on earth to this day.' " Then he turned and went out from Pharaoh.

7 And Pharaoh's servants said to him, "How long shall this man be a snare to us? Let the men go, that they may serve the LORD their God; do you not yet understand that Egypt is ruined?" ⁸ So Moses and Aaron were brought back to Pharaoh; and he said to them, "Go, serve the LORD your God; but who are to go?" ⁹ And Moses said, "We will go with our young and our old; we will go with our sons and daughters and with our flocks and herds, for we must hold a feast to the LORD." ¹⁰ And he said to them, "The LORD be with you, if ever I let you and your little ones go! Look, you have some evil purpose in mind." ⁿ ¹¹ No! Go, the men among you, and serve the LORD, for that is what you desire." And they were driven out from Pharaoh's presence.

12 Then the LORD said to Moses, "Stretch out your hand over the land of Egypt for the locusts, that they may come upon the land of Egypt, and eat every plant in the land, all that the hail has left." ¹³ So Moses stretched forth his rod over the land of Egypt, and the LORD brought an east wind upon the land all that day and all that night; and when it was morning the east wind had brought the locusts. ¹⁴ And the locusts came up over all the land of Egypt, and settled on the whole country of Egypt, such a dense swarm of locusts as had never been before, nor ever shall be

again. ¹⁵ For they covered the face of the whole land, so that the land was darkened, and they ate all the plants in the land and all the fruit of the trees which the hail had left; not a green thing remained, neither tree nor plant of the field, through all the land of Egypt. ¹⁶ Then Pharaoh called Moses and Aaron in haste, and said, "I have sinned against the LORD your God, and against you. ¹⁷ Now therefore, forgive my sin, I pray you, only this once, and entreat the LORD your God only to remove this death from me." ¹⁸ So he went out from Pharaoh, and entreated the LORD. ¹⁹ And the LORD turned a very strong west wind, which lifted the locusts and drove them into the Red Sea; not a single locust was left in all the country of Egypt. ²⁰ But the LORD hardened Pharaoh's heart, and he did not let the children of Israel go.

21 Then the LORD said to Moses, "Stretch out your hand toward heaven that there may be darkness over the land of Egypt, a darkness to be felt." ²² So Moses stretched out his hand toward heaven, and there was thick darkness in all the land of Egypt three days; ²³ they did not see one another, nor did any rise from his place for three days; but all the people of Israel had light where they dwelt. ²⁴ Then Pharaoh called Moses, and said, "Go, serve the LORD; your children also may go with you; only let your flocks and your herds remain behind." ²⁵ But Moses said, "You must also let us have sacrifices and burnt offerings, that we may sacrifice to the LORD our God. ²⁶ Our cattle also must go with us; not a hoof shall be left behind, for we must take of them to serve the LORD our God, and

n Heb before your face

---

in the ancient Near East (see Joel). **7–11:** At the insistence of his impressed courtiers, Pharaoh attempts to negotiate before the twenty-four hour deadline (9.5); he offers to let only the men go, since adult males took part in the religious rites (23.17; 34.23; Dt.16.16). **13:** The miracle rests upon a natural phenomenon (14.21; Num.11.31); an *east wind* brought the locusts and, when the wind shifted, a *west wind* drove them into the Red Sea (v. 19).

10.21–29: Ninth plague: thick darkness. **21:** *A darkness to be felt* aptly describes conditions created by the hot wind, the "khamsin," which blows in from the desert during the spring (March-May), bringing with it so much dust and sand that the air is darkened and breathing becomes difficult. **23b:** Compare 8.22–23; 9.6–7,26.

we do not know with what we must serve the LORD until we arrive there." ²⁷ But the LORD hardened Pharaoh's heart, and he would not let them go. ²⁸ Then Pharaoh said to him, "Get away from me; take heed to yourself; never see my face again; for in the day you see my face you shall die." ²⁹ Moses said, "As you say! I will not see your face again."

11 The LORD said to Moses, "Yet one plague more I will bring upon Pharaoh and upon Egypt; afterwards he will let you go hence; when he lets you go, he will drive you away completely. ² Speak now in the hearing of the people, that they ask, every man of his neighbor and every woman of her neighbor, jewelry of silver and of gold." ³ And the LORD gave the people favor in the sight of the Egyptians. Moreover, the man Moses was very great in the land of Egypt, in the sight of Pharaoh's servants and in the sight of the people.

4 And Moses said, "Thus says the LORD: About midnight I will go forth in the midst of Egypt; ⁵ and all the first-born in the land of Egypt shall die, from the first-born of Pharaoh who sits upon his throne, even to the first-born of the maidservant who is behind the mill; and all the first-born of the cattle. ⁶ And there shall be a great cry throughout all the land of Egypt, such as there has never been, nor ever shall be again. ⁷ But against any of the people of Israel, either man or beast, not a dog shall growl; that you may know that the LORD makes a distinction between the Egyptians and Israel. ⁸ And

all these your servants shall come down to me, and bow down to me, saying, 'Get you out, and all the people who follow you.' And after that I will go out." And he went out from Pharaoh in hot anger. ⁹ Then the LORD said to Moses, "Pharaoh will not listen to you; that my wonders may be multiplied in the land of Egypt."

10 Moses and Aaron did all these wonders before Pharaoh; and the LORD hardened Pharaoh's heart, and he did not let the people of Israel go out of his land.

12 The LORD said to Moses and Aaron in the land of Egypt, ² "This month shall be for you the beginning of months; it shall be the first month of the year for you. ³ Tell all the congregation of Israel that on the tenth day of this month they shall take every man a lamb according to their fathers' houses, a lamb for a household; ⁴ and if the household is too small for a lamb, then a man and his neighbor next to his house shall take according to the number of persons; according to what each can eat you shall make your count for the lamb. ⁵ Your lamb shall be without blemish, a male a year old; you shall take it from the sheep or from the goats; ⁶ and you shall keep it until the fourteenth day of this month, when the whole assembly of the congregation of Israel shall kill their lambs in the evening.ᵒ ⁷ Then they shall take some of the blood, and put it on the two doorposts and the lintel of the houses in which they eat them. ⁸ They shall eat

o Heb *between the two evenings*

11.1–10: **The announcement of the final plague,** the death of the first-born (concluded in 12.29–32). **2–3:** The "spoliation of the Egyptians" (3.21–22; 12.35–36) is explained as evidence of the favor which Moses and the Israelites had gained in Egypt.
12.1–28: **The feasts of passover and unleavened bread. 1–13** (and vv. 43–49): This is priestly tradition concerning the passover, an ancient nomadic spring festival which Israel reinterpreted as a memorial of the LORD's deliverance of his people from Egypt (Dt.16.1–8; Num.9.1–14; Ezek.45.21–25). **2:** *This month* refers to Nisan (March-April) which in the post-exilic ecclesiastical calendar was *the beginning of months* (see Lev.23.5,23–25 n.). According to the older agricultural calendar, the new year began in the autumn (Ex.23.16; 34.22). **3–4:** Priestly tradition assumes that Israel in Egypt was already an organized *congregation* under the leadership of tribal princes (16.22). *Fathers' houses,* see Num.1.2–4 n. The passover was a nocturnal festival, celebrated during full moon (v. 8; see Is. 30.29). **7:** Blood, regarded as the deity's portion of the sacrifice (Lev.1.5), was smeared on the doorposts and the lintel, the holy places of the house

the flesh that night, roasted; with unleavened bread and bitter herbs they shall eat it. [9] Do not eat any of it raw or boiled with water, but roasted, its head with its legs and its inner parts. [10] And you shall let none of it remain until the morning, anything that remains until the morning you shall burn. [11] In this manner you shall eat it: your loins girded, your sandals on your feet, and your staff in your hand; and you shall eat it in haste. It is the LORD's passover. [12] For I will pass through the land of Egypt that night, and I will smite all the first-born in the land of Egypt, both man and beast; and on all the gods of Egypt I will execute judgments: I am the LORD. [13] The blood shall be a sign for you, upon the houses where you are; and when I see the blood, I will pass over you, and no plague shall fall upon you to destroy you, when I smite the land of Egypt.

14 "This day shall be for you a memorial day, and you shall keep it as a feast to the LORD; throughout your generations you shall observe it as an ordinance for ever. [15] Seven days you shall eat unleavened bread; on the first day you shall put away leaven out of your houses, for if any one eats what is leavened, from the first day until the seventh day, that person shall be cut off from Israel. [16] On the first day you shall hold a holy assembly, and on the seventh day a holy assembly; no work shall be done on those days; but what every one must eat, that only may be prepared by you. [17] And you shall observe the feast of unleavened bread, for on this very day I brought your hosts out of the land of Egypt: therefore you shall observe this day, throughout your generations, as an ordinance for ever. [18] In the first month, on the fourteenth day of the month at evening, you shall eat unleavened bread, and so until the twenty-first day of the month at evening. [19] For seven days no leaven shall be found in your houses; for if any one eats what is leavened, that person shall be cut off from the congregation of Israel, whether he is a sojourner or a native of the land. [20] You shall eat nothing leavened; in all your dwellings you shall eat unleavened bread."

21 Then Moses called all the elders of Israel, and said to them, "Select lambs for yourselves according to your families, and kill the passover lamb. [22] Take a bunch of hyssop and dip it in the blood which is in the basin, and touch the lintel and the two doorposts with the blood which is in the basin; and none of you shall go out of the door of his house until the morning. [23] For the LORD will pass through to slay the Egyptians; and when he sees the blood on the lintel and on the two doorposts, the LORD will pass over the door, and will not allow the destroyer to enter your houses to slay you. [24] You shall observe this rite as an ordinance for you and for your sons for ever. [25] And

---

(21.6; Dt.6.9), as a protection against the destroyer (vv. 22–23; see 4.24 n.). **11:** The feast must be eaten in readiness for the march, in commemoration of Israel's hasty exodus. **12–13:** Here *passover* is interpreted from a verb meaning "to pass over," referring to the LORD's passing over Israelite houses during the plague of the first-born (vv. 24–27). **14–20:** The feast of unleavened cakes, originally an agricultural festival held at the time of barley harvest, was also converted into an historical commemoration and came to be closely connected with the passover (Dt.16.1–8; Ezek.45.21–25). **14:** The passover was celebrated on the 14th of Nisan (v. 6); *this day* refers to the 15th (Lev.23.6; Num.28.17). The seven day festival is regarded as a continuation of the passover. **15:** The absence of leaven (yeast) is interpreted as due to hasty preparations for flight (vv. 34,39; Dt.16.3). Originally leaven, owing to its fermenting or corrupting power (23.18; Mt.16.6; 1 Cor.5.7), was regarded as a ritually unclean substance (compare Lev.2.11) which could contaminate the whole harvest. **18:** So closely is the festival combined with the passover that it is said to begin on the evening of the 14th, i.e. the night of the passover (see v. 14). **21–28:** An older tradition concerning the passover. **22:** See v. 7 n. *Hyssop*, the foliage of an aromatic plant. Because of its presumed magical powers, it was used for ritual purposes (Lev.14.4; Num.19.6,18; Ps.51.7). **23:** *The destroyer*, or the angel of death (2 Sam.24.16; Is.37.36), was regarded as a manifestation of the LORD's power.

when you come to the land which the LORD will give you, as he has promised, you shall keep this service. 26 And when your children say to you, 'What do you mean by this service?' 27 you shall say, 'It is the sacrifice of the LORD's passover, for he passed over the houses of the people of Israel in Egypt, when he slew the Egyptians but spared our houses.'" And the people bowed their heads and worshiped.

28 Then the people of Israel went and did so; as the LORD had commanded Moses and Aaron, so they did.

29 At midnight the LORD smote all the first-born in the land of Egypt, from the first-born of Pharaoh who sat on his throne to the first-born of the captive who was in the dungeon, and all the first-born of the cattle. 30 And Pharaoh rose up in the night, he, and all his servants, and all the Egyptians; and there was a great cry in Egypt, for there was not a house where one was not dead. 31 And he summoned Moses and Aaron by night, and said, "Rise up, go forth from among my people, both you and the people of Israel; and go, serve the LORD, as you have said. 32 Take your flocks and your herds, as you have said, and be gone; and bless me also!"

33 And the Egyptians were urgent with the people, to send them out of the land in haste; for they said, "We are all dead men." 34 So the people took their dough before it was leavened, their kneading bowls being bound up in their mantles on their shoulders. 35 The people of Israel had also done as Moses told them, for they had asked

of the Egyptians jewelry of silver and of gold, and clothing; 36 and the LORD had given the people favor in the sight of the Egyptians, so that they let them have what they asked. Thus they despoiled the Egyptians.

37 And the people of Israel journeyed from Ram'eses to Succoth, about six hundred thousand men on foot, besides women and children. 38 A mixed multitude also went up with them, and very many cattle, both flocks and herds. 39 And they baked unleavened cakes of the dough which they had brought out of Egypt, for it was not leavened, because they were thrust out of Egypt and could not tarry, neither had they prepared for themselves any provisions.

40 The time that the people of Israel dwelt in Egypt was four hundred and thirty years. 41 And at the end of four hundred and thirty years, on that very day, all the hosts of the LORD went out from the land of Egypt. 42 It was a night of watching by the LORD, to bring them out of the land of Egypt; so this same night is a night of watching kept to the LORD by all the people of Israel throughout their generations.

43 And the LORD said to Moses and Aaron, "This is the ordinance of the passover: no foreigner shall eat of it; 44 but every slave that is bought for money may eat of it after you have circumcised him. 45 No sojourner or hired servant may eat of it. 46 In one house shall it be eaten; you shall not carry forth any of the flesh outside the house; and you shall not break a bone

12.29–50: Israel's departure from Egypt. 29–32: The conclusion of the tenth plague (11.1–10). **33–34:** See v. 15 n. **35–36:** See 3.21–22 and 11.2–3. **37:** Rameses (1.11) and Succoth (13.20) were the starting places on Israel's itinerary (Num.33.5). *Six hundred thousand men on foot* (Num.11.21), in addition to women and children, is an exaggeration, for neither the land of Goshen nor the southern Palestinian wilderness could have supported so large a population (at least two and a half million). The number apparently reflects the census list in Num.1.17–46. **38:** The *mixed multitude* (Num.11.4) included other "Hebrews" (see 1.15 n.) or rootless people. **40:** If the four hundred and thirty years (see Gen.15.13; Acts 7.6 n.; Gal.3.17 n.) covers the total time of the Egyptian sojourn, then the descent into Egypt coincided with the Hyksos invasion (about 1720 B.C.; see Gen.45.10 n.) and the Exodus occurred during the reign of Rameses II, about 1290 B.C. (see 1.8 n.). **42:** The *night of watching* refers to the passover. **43–49:** A supplement to the priestly tradition about the passover (12.1–13). A *foreigner* (v. 43), a visiting *sojourner*, and a *hired servant* (v. 45) are excluded on the ground that they are related to other gods; however, the purchased slave who becomes a part of the family (v. 44) and the

of it. [47] All the congregation of Israel shall keep it. [48] And when a stranger shall sojourn with you and would keep the passover to the LORD, let all his males be circumcised, then he may come near and keep it; he shall be as a native of the land. But no uncircumcised person shall eat of it. [49] There shall be one law for the native and for the stranger who sojourns among you."

50 Thus did all the people of Israel; as the LORD commanded Moses and Aaron, so they did. [51] And on that very day the LORD brought the people of Israel out of the land of Egypt by their hosts.

13 The LORD said to Moses, [2] "Consecrate to me all the first-born; whatever is the first to open the womb among the people of Israel, both of man and of beast, is mine."

3 And Moses said to the people, "Remember this day, in which you came out from Egypt, out of the house of bondage, for by strength of hand the LORD brought you out from this place; no leavened bread shall be eaten. [4] This day you are to go forth, in the month of Abib. [5] And when the LORD brings you into the land of the Canaanites, the Hittites, the Amorites, the Hivites, and the Jeb'usites, which he swore to your fathers to give you, a land flowing with milk and honey, you shall keep this service in this month. [6] Seven days you shall eat unleavened bread, and on the seventh day there shall be a feast to the LORD. [7] Unleavened bread shall be eaten for seven days; no leavened bread shall be seen with you, and no leaven shall be seen with you in all your territory. [8] And you shall tell your son on that day, 'It is because of what the LORD did for me when I came out of Egypt.' [9] And it shall be to you as a sign on your hand and as a memorial between your eyes, that the law of the LORD may be in your mouth; for with a strong hand the LORD has brought you out of Egypt. [10] You shall therefore keep this ordinance at its appointed time from year to year.

11 "And when the LORD brings you into the land of the Canaanites, as he swore to you and your fathers, and shall give it to you, [12] you shall set apart to the LORD all that first opens the womb. All the firstlings of your cattle that are males shall be the LORD'S. [13] Every firstling of an ass you shall redeem with a lamb, or if you will not redeem it you shall break its neck. Every first-born of man among your sons you shall redeem. [14] And when in time to come your son asks you, 'What does this mean?' you shall say to him, 'By strength of hand the LORD brought us out of Egypt, from the house of bondage. [15] For when Pharaoh stubbornly refused to let us go, the LORD slew all the first-born in the land of Egypt, both the first-born of man and the first-born of cattle. Therefore I sacrifice to the LORD all the males that first open the womb; but all the first-born of my sons I redeem.' [16] It shall be as a mark on your hand or frontlets between your eyes; for by a strong hand the LORD brought us out of Egypt."

sojourner who resides permanently within Israel may eat the passover, if the *one law* of circumcision is kept (Gen.17.9–14).
13.1–16: The consecration of the first-born. 2: According to ancient belief, the devotion of the first-born of man and beast to God, the giver of fertility, was necessary for continuing increase and well-being (22.29b–30; Lev.27.26–27; Num.3.13; 8.17–18; 18.15). **3–10:** Old tradition about the feast of unleavened bread (compare the parallel priestly version, 12.14–20). **4:** *Abib*, the older name for the month of the Exodus (23.15; see 12.2 n.). **5:** See 3.8. **8:** In later times a man could tell *what the LORD did for me when I came out of Egypt*, for in worship the redemptive event was made present (12.26–27; see Dt.5.2–3 n.). **9:** See Dt.6.8. **11–16:** An old tradition about the consecration of the first-born. **13:** Unclean animals, of which the ass is typical (Lev. ch. 11; Dt. ch. 14), may be redeemed by substituting a lamb. In early times the custom arose of substituting an animal for the human first-born (34.19–20; compare Gen.22.13), although pagan human sacrifice persisted (1 Kg.16.34; 2 Kg.16.3; Ezek.20.26; Mic.6.7). **14–15:** The practice, rooted in ancient fertility beliefs, is here reinterpreted in the light of the Exodus.

17 When Pharaoh let the people go, God did not lead them by way of the land of the Philistines, although that was near; for God said, "Lest the people repent when they see war, and return to Egypt." 18 But God led the people round by the way of the wilderness toward the Red Sea. And the people of Israel went up out of the land of Egypt equipped for battle. 19 And Moses took the bones of Joseph with him; for Joseph had solemnly sworn the people of Israel, saying, "God will visit you; then you must carry my bones with you from here." 20 And they moved on from Succoth, and encamped at Etham, on the edge of the wilderness. 21 And the LORD went before them by day in a pillar of cloud to lead them along the way, and by night in a pillar of fire to give them light, that they might travel by day and by night; 22 the pillar of cloud by day and the pillar of fire by night did not depart from before the people.

14 Then the LORD said to Moses, 2 "Tell the people of Israel to turn back and encamp in front of Pi-ha-hi'roth, between Migdol and the sea, in front of Ba'al-ze'phon; you shall encamp over against it, by the sea. 3 For Pharaoh will say of the people of Israel, 'They are entangled in the land; the wilderness has shut them in.' 4 And I will harden Pharaoh's heart, and he will pursue them and I will get glory over Pharaoh and all his host; and the Egyptians shall know that I am the LORD." And they did so.

5 When the king of Egypt was told that the people had fled, the mind of Pharaoh and his servants was changed toward the people, and they said, "What is this we have done, that we have let Israel go from serving us?" 6 So he made ready his chariot and took his army with him, 7 and took six hundred picked chariots and all the other chariots of Egypt with officers over all of them. 8 And the LORD hardened the heart of Pharaoh king of Egypt and he pursued the people of Israel as they went forth defiantly. 9 The Egyptians pursued them, all Pharaoh's horses and chariots and his horsemen and his army, and overtook them encamped at the sea, by Pi-ha-hi'roth, in front of Ba'al-ze'phon.

10 When Pharaoh drew near, the people of Israel lifted up their eyes, and behold, the Egyptians were marching after them; and they were in great fear. And the people of Israel cried out to the LORD; 11 and they said to Moses, "Is it because there are no graves in Egypt that you have taken us away to die in the wilderness? What have you done to us, in bringing us out of Egypt? 12 Is not this what we said to you in Egypt, 'Let us alone and let us serve the Egyptians'? For it would have been better for us to serve the Egyptians than to die in the wilderness." 13 And Moses said to the people, "Fear not, stand firm, and see the salvation of the LORD, which he will work for you today; for the Egyptians whom you see today, you shall never see again. 14 The LORD will fight for you, and you have only to be still." 15 The LORD said to

---

13.17–14.22. Israel's deliverance. 17–18: *Philistines*, see Gen.21.34 n. The route mentioned was the main military road into Canaan. To avoid attack, the people were providentially led *round by the way of the wilderness*. On the *Red Sea*, see 14.2 n. 19: See Gen.50.25–26 n. 21–22: The *pillar of cloud* and the *pillar of fire* may reflect the ancient custom of carrying a burning brazier at the head of a marching army or caravan to indicate the line of march by day and night. Whatever the nature of the phenomenon originally, cloud and fire have become traditional ways of expressing God's presence and guidance (see 3.2 n.; 19.9; 33.9; 40.34–38; 1 Kg.8.10–11). 14.2: The places mentioned, like Etham (13.20), were probably Egyptian frontier fortresses. Apparently the Israelites were unable to break through and had to *turn back*, with the result that they were trapped (v. 3) between the water barrier and the Egyptian forces. The sea, known in Hebrew as the "sea of reeds," was not the Red Sea itself but a shallow body of water farther north, perhaps in the area of Lake Timsah. 11–12: See 15.24 n. 13–14: Viewed in faith, the victory was a mighty act of the LORD who was fighting for his people in a contest with the powerful

Moses, "Why do you cry to me? Tell the people of Israel to go forward. [16] Lift up your rod, and stretch out your hand over the sea and divide it, that the people of Israel may go on dry ground through the sea. [17] And I will harden the hearts of the Egyptians so that they shall go in after them, and I will get glory over Pharaoh and all his host, his chariots, and his horsemen. [18] And the Egyptians shall know that I am the LORD, when I have gotten glory over Pharaoh, his chariots, and his horsemen."

19 Then the angel of God who went before the host of Israel moved and went behind them; and the pillar of cloud moved from before them and stood behind them, [20] coming between the host of Egypt and the host of Israel. And there was the cloud and the darkness; and the night passed[p] without one coming near the other all night.

21 Then Moses stretched out his hand over the sea; and the LORD drove the sea back by a strong east wind all night, and made the sea dry land, and the waters were divided. [22] And the people of Israel went into the midst of the sea on dry ground, the waters being a wall to them on their right hand and on their left. [23] The Egyptians pursued, and went in after them into the midst of the sea, all Pharaoh's horses, his chariots, and his horsemen. [24] And in the morning watch the LORD in the pillar of fire and of cloud looked down upon the host of the Egyptians, and discomfited the host of the Egyptians, [25] clogging[q] their chariot wheels so that they drove heavily; and the Egyptians said, "Let us flee from before Israel; for the LORD fights for them against the Egyptians."

26 Then the LORD said to Moses, "Stretch out your hand over the sea, that the water may come back upon the Egyptians, upon their chariots, and upon their horsemen." [27] So Moses stretched forth his hand over the sea, and the sea returned to its wonted flow when the morning appeared; and the Egyptians fled into it, and the LORD routed[r] the Egyptians in the midst of the sea. [28] The waters returned and covered the chariots and the horsemen and all the host[s] of Pharaoh that had followed them into the sea; not so much as one of them remained. [29] But the people of Israel walked on dry ground through the sea, the waters being a wall to them on their right hand and on their left.

30 Thus the LORD saved Israel that day from the hand of the Egyptians; and Israel saw the Egyptians dead upon the seashore. [31] And Israel saw the great work which the LORD did against the Egyptians, and the people feared the LORD; and they believed in the LORD and in his servant Moses.

15 Then Moses and the people of Israel sang this song to the LORD, saying,

"I will sing to the LORD, for he has
　　triumphed gloriously;
　the horse and his rider[t] he has
　　thrown into the sea.
[2] The LORD is my strength and my
　　song,
　and he has become my salvation;
　this is my God, and I will praise him,
　　my father's God, and I will exalt
　　him.

p　Gk: Heb *and it lit up the night*
q　Or *binding.* Sam Gk Syr: Heb *removing*
r　Heb *shook off*
s　Gk Syr: Heb *to all the host*
t　Or *its chariot*

Pharaoh (v. 25). *Salvation,* see Gen.49.18. **19–20:** One tradition expresses the divine presence as *the angel of God* (see Gen.16.7 n.), another as the shining pillar of cloud (v. 24; see 13.21–22 n.). **21–29:** The divine victory was rooted in a natural phenomenon: during a storm the shallow waters were driven back by *a strong east wind* (v. 21), making it possible for the Israelites to cross on foot. Egyptian chariots, however, were mired in the mud and engulfed by the returning waters. Tradition heightened the miracle by attributing it to Moses' wonder-working rod (vv. 16,21a,26–27) and by saying that the waters stood up like walls (vv. 22b,29b).

15.1–21: Two songs of praise which celebrate the LORD's deliverance of his people. **1:** The song of Moses (vv. 1–18) is introduced by quoting the ancient song of Miriam (v. 21). **2:** See

3 The LORD is a man of war;
   the LORD is his name.

4 "Pharaoh's chariots and his host he
      cast into the sea;
   and his picked officers are sunk in
      the Red Sea.
5 The floods cover them;
   they went down into the depths
      like a stone.
6 Thy right hand, O LORD, glorious
      in power,
   thy right hand, O LORD, shatters
      the enemy.
7 In the greatness of thy majesty thou
      overthrowest thy adversaries;
   thou sendest forth thy fury, it
      consumes them like stubble.
8 At the blast of thy nostrils the
      waters piled up,
   the floods stood up in a heap;
   the deeps congealed in the heart
      of the sea.
9 The enemy said, 'I will pursue, I
      will overtake,
   I will divide the spoil, my desire
      shall have its fill of them.
   I will draw my sword, my hand
      shall destroy them.'
10 Thou didst blow with thy wind,
      the sea covered them;
   they sank as lead in the mighty
      waters.

11 "Who is like thee, O LORD, among
      the gods?
   Who is like thee, majestic in
      holiness,
   terrible in glorious deeds, doing
      wonders?

12 Thou didst stretch out thy right
      hand,
   the earth swallowed them.

13 "Thou hast led in thy steadfast love
      the people whom thou hast
      redeemed,
   thou hast guided them by thy
      strength to thy holy abode.
14 The peoples have heard, they
      tremble;
   pangs have seized on the
      inhabitants of Philistia.
15 Now are the chiefs of Edom
      dismayed;
   the leaders of Moab, trembling
      seizes them;
   all the inhabitants of Canaan have
      melted away.
16 Terror and dread fall upon them;
   because of the greatness of thy
      arm, they are as still as a stone,
   till thy people, O LORD, pass by,
   till the people pass by whom thou
      hast purchased.
17 Thou wilt bring them in, and plant
      them on thy own mountain,
   the place, O LORD, which thou
      hast made for thy abode,
   the sanctuary, O LORD, which thy
      hands have established.
18 The LORD will reign for ever and
      ever."

19 For when the horses of Pharaoh with his chariots and his horsemen went into the sea, the LORD brought back the waters of the sea upon them; but the people of Israel walked on dry ground in the midst of the sea. 20 Then Miriam, the proph-

---

14.13–14 n. *My father's God* refers to "the God of the fathers" (3.6). **3**: *A man of war*, i.e. Divine Warrior (Ps.24.8). In the following vv. Canaanite mythical motifs are used to confess the Lord's saving action in behalf of Israel (14.14,25). **4–10**: Recital of the Divine Warrior's victory at the Sea (Ps.78.12–13). **8–10**: The language seems influenced by the myth of a divine battle against the *sea*, the chaotic power hostile to God's rule (see Ps.77.16–19; 114.3–6; Hab. 3.8–15). **11**: The LORD's *glorious deeds* demonstrate that he is incomparable *among the gods* who compose his heavenly council (Pss.86.8; 89.7–8; Gen.1.26 n.). **13–17**: The guidance into Canaan. **13**: *Thy holy abode*, i.e. Canaan (Ps.78.54). **14**: *Philistia* was settled by the Philistines (Gen.21.32 n.) about 1175 B.C.; hence the poem was written afterwards. **15**: See Num.20.18–21; 21.13. **16**: *Purchased*, possibly "created." **17**: Canaan is described as the mythical cosmic mountain, Zaphon, where God has his *abode* and *sanctuary* (see Ps.48.1–3 n.). **19–21**: Miriam's victory dance. Miriam (Num.26.59) is called a prophetess (compare Jg.4.4) because of her ecstatic rousing of devotion to the LORD through song and dance. Compare 1 Sam.18.6–7).

etess, the sister of Aaron, took a timbrel in her hand; and all the women
went out after her with timbrels and
dancing. ²¹ And Miriam sang to them:
"Sing to the LORD, for he has
        triumphed gloriously;
the horse and his rider he has thrown
        into the sea."
22 Then Moses led Israel onward
from the Red Sea, and they went into
the wilderness of Shur; they went three
days in the wilderness and found no
water. ²³ When they came to Marah,
they could not drink the water of
Marah because it was bitter; therefore
it was named Marah.ᵘ ²⁴ And the people murmured against Moses, saying,
"What shall we drink?" ²⁵ And he
cried to the LORD; and the LORD
showed him a tree, and he threw it into
the water, and the water became sweet.
There the LORDᵛ made for them a
statute and an ordinance and there he
proved them, ²⁶ saying, "If you will
diligently hearken to the voice of the
LORD your God, and do that which is
right in his eyes, and give heed to his
commandments and keep all his statutes, I will put none of the diseases
upon you which I put upon the Egyptians; for I am the LORD, your healer."
27 Then they came to Elim, where
there were twelve springs of water and
seventy palm trees; and they encamped
there by the water.

16 They set out from Elim, and all
the congregation of the people of

Israel came to the wilderness of Sin,
which is between Elim and Sinai, on
the fifteenth day of the second month
after they had departed from the land
of Egypt. ² And the whole congregation
of the people of Israel murmured
against Moses and Aaron in the wilderness, ³ and said to them, "Would that
we had died by the hand of the LORD
in the land of Egypt, when we sat by the
fleshpots and ate bread to the full; for
you have brought us out into this
wilderness to kill this whole assembly
with hunger."
4 Then the LORD said to Moses,
"Behold, I will rain bread from heaven
for you; and the people shall go out and
gather a day's portion every day, that
I may prove them, whether they will
walk in my law or not. ⁵ On the sixth
day, when they prepare what they
bring in, it will be twice as much as
they gather daily." ⁶ So Moses and
Aaron said to all the people of Israel,
"At evening you shall know that it was
the LORD who brought you out of the
land of Egypt, ⁷ and in the morning
you shall see the glory of the LORD, because he has heard your murmurings
against the LORD. For what are we, that
you murmur against us?" ⁸ And Moses
said, "When the LORD gives you in the
evening flesh to eat and in the morning
bread to the full, because the LORD has
heard your murmurings which you
murmur against him—what are we?

u That is *Bitterness*   *v* Heb *he*

21: The Song of Miriam, one of the oldest poetic couplets in the Old Testament, was probably
composed by an eyewitness of the event.
15.22–16.36: Crises in the wilderness. In times of need, when faith was put to the test, Israel
perceived signs of the LORD's care and protection. **22:** *The wilderness of Shur*, identified with the
wilderness of Etham in Num.33.8, was on the border of Egypt. **24:** Israel's continual murmuring in the wilderness is a dominant theme of the tradition (16.2–3; 17.3; 32.1–4,25; Num.11.4–6;
12.1–2; 14.2–3; 16.13–14; 20.2–13; 21.4–5). **25:** It was believed that the leaves or bark of certain
trees had magical properties for sweetening or "healing" water (2 Kg.2.21). **26:** *Diseases*, i.e.
the Egyptian plagues. *Your healer*, Num.21.4–9; Dt.7.15; Ps.103.3. **16.1–36:** The provision of
food in the wilderness. **1:** *The wilderness of Sin* (17.1; Num.33.11–12), probably on the Sinaitic
Peninsula. **3:** The murmuring wanderers preferred the seasoned food of *the fleshpots of Egypt*
to the precarious freedom of the wilderness. **4:** *Prove*, i.e. test their faith by providing only a
portion sufficient for one day (see Dt.8.3,16; Mt.6.11). **5:** See vv. 22–30. **6–7:** *At evening* when
the quails come; *in the morning* when the manna is found (vv. 8,12). In the priestly view, *the
glory of the LORD* was an envelope of light (associated with the pillar of cloud and fire; see
13.21–22 n.) which veiled his being. Though men could not see God they could behold the

Your murmurings are not against us but against the LORD."

9 And Moses said to Aaron, "Say to the whole congregation of the people of Israel, 'Come near before the LORD, for he has heard your murmurings.' " [10] And as Aaron spoke to the whole congregation of the people of Israel, they looked toward the wilderness, and behold, the glory of the LORD appeared in the cloud. [11] And the LORD said to Moses, [12] "I have heard the murmurings of the people of Israel; say to them, 'At twilight you shall eat flesh, and in the morning you shall be filled with bread; then you shall know that I am the LORD your God.' "

13 In the evening quails came up and covered the camp; and in the morning dew lay round about the camp. [14] And when the dew had gone up, there was on the face of the wilderness a fine, flake-like thing, fine as hoarfrost on the ground. [15] When the people of Israel saw it, they said to one another, "What is it?"[w] For they did not know what it was. And Moses said to them, "It is the bread which the LORD has given you to eat. [16] This is what the LORD has commanded: 'Gather of it, every man of you, as much as he can eat; you shall take an omer apiece, according to the number of the persons whom each of you has in his tent.' " [17] And the people of Israel did so; they gathered, some more, some less. [18] But when they measured it with an omer, he that gathered much had nothing over, and he that gathered little had no lack; each gathered according to what he could eat. [19] And Moses said to them, "Let no man leave any of it till the morning." [20] But they did not listen to Moses; some left part of it till the morning, and it bred worms and became foul; and Moses was angry with

them. [21] Morning by morning they gathered it, each as much as he could eat; but when the sun grew hot, it melted.

22 On the sixth day they gathered twice as much bread, two omers apiece; and when all the leaders of the congregation came and told Moses, [23] he said to them, "This is what the LORD has commanded: 'Tomorrow is a day of solemn rest, a holy sabbath to the LORD; bake what you will bake and boil what you will boil, and all that is left over lay by to be kept till the morning.' " [24] So they laid it by till the morning, as Moses bade them; and it did not become foul, and there were no worms in it. [25] Moses said, "Eat it today, for today is a sabbath to the LORD; today you will not find it in the field. [26] Six days you shall gather it; but on the seventh day, which is a sabbath, there will be none." [27] On the seventh day some of the people went out to gather, and they found none. [28] And the LORD said to Moses, "How long do you refuse to keep my commandments and my laws? [29] See! The LORD has given you the sabbath, therefore on the sixth day he gives you bread for two days; remain every man of you in his place, let no man go out of his place on the seventh day." [30] So the people rested on the seventh day.

31 Now the house of Israel called its name manna; it was like coriander seed, white, and the taste of it was like wafers made with honey. [32] And Moses said, "This is what the LORD has commanded: 'Let an omer of it be kept throughout your generations, that they may see the bread with which I fed you in the wilderness, when I brought you out of the land of Egypt.' " [33] And Moses said to Aaron, "Take a jar, and

w Or *"It is manna."* Heb *man hu*

glory which signified his presence (40.34; Num.14.10b,22; 16.19; Ezek.11.23). **9–10:** *Before the LORD*, see vv. 33–34 n. **13–21:** An early tradition concerning the provision of bread (v. 15). **13:** On the quails, see Num.11.1–35. **14:** The description here (see also v. 31 and Num.11.7–9) corresponds fairly closely to the "honey-dew" excretion of two scale-insects which feed on the twigs of the tamarisk tree. **15:** The name of the food, *manna* (v. 31), is explained by an expression meaning "What is it?" For men of faith the answer was that the natural phenomenon was *bread which the LORD has given.* **22–36:** The provision of manna is the occasion for the insertion

put an omer of manna in it, and place it before the LORD, to be kept throughout your generations." ³⁴ As the LORD commanded Moses, so Aaron placed it before the testimony, to be kept. ³⁵ And the people of Israel ate the manna forty years, till they came to a habitable land; they ate the manna, till they came to the border of the land of Canaan. ³⁶ (An omer is the tenth part of an ephah.)

17 All the congregation of the people of Israel moved on from the wilderness of Sin by stages, according to the commandment of the LORD, and camped at Reph'idim; but there was no water for the people to drink. ² Therefore the people found fault with Moses, and said, "Give us water to drink." And Moses said to them, "Why do you find fault with me? Why do you put the LORD to the proof?" ³ But the people thirsted there for water, and the people murmured against Moses, and said, "Why did you bring us up out of Egypt, to kill us and our children and our cattle with thirst?" ⁴ So Moses cried to the LORD, "What shall I do with this people? They are almost ready to stone me." ⁵ And the LORD said to Moses, "Pass on before the people, taking with you some of the elders of Israel; and take in your hand the rod with which you struck the Nile, and go. ⁶ Behold, I will stand before you there on the rock at Horeb; and you shall

strike the rock, and water shall come out of it, that the people may drink." And Moses did so, in the sight of the elders of Israel. ⁷ And he called the name of the place Massah[x] and Mer'-ibah,[y] because of the faultfinding of the children of Israel, and because they put the LORD to the proof by saying, "Is the LORD among us or not?"

8 Then came Am'alek and fought with Israel at Reph'idim. ⁹ And Moses said to Joshua, "Choose for us men, and go out, fight with Am'alek; tomorrow I will stand on the top of the hill with the rod of God in my hand." ¹⁰ So Joshua did as Moses told him, and fought with Am'alek; and Moses, Aaron, and Hur went up to the top of the hill. ¹¹ Whenever Moses held up his hand, Israel prevailed; and whenever he lowered his hand, Am'alek prevailed. ¹² But Moses' hands grew weary; so they took a stone and put it under him, and he sat upon it, and Aaron and Hur held up his hands, one on one side, and the other on the other side; so his hands were steady until the going down of the sun. ¹³ And Joshua mowed down Am'alek and his people with the edge of the sword.

14 And the LORD said to Moses, "Write this as a memorial in a book and recite it in the ears of Joshua, that I will utterly blot out the remembrance

x That is *Proof*
y That is *Contention*

of priestly teaching concerning the sabbath, *a day of solemn rest* (31.15; 35.2). **33-34:** *Before the LORD*, i.e. before the ark. In priestly tradition the ark is sometimes designated by its chief contents, *the Testimony* or tablets of law (27.21; Lev.16.13; Num.17.4).
    17.1-16: Other trying experiences in the wilderness. 1-7: Israel's thirst was quenched with water from the rock (compare Num.20.2-13). **1:** *By stages*, see Num.33.1-49. **2-3:** See 15.24 n. *Put the LORD to proof*, i.e. challenged him to show that he was in their midst (v. 7b). **6:** Water lies below the limestone surface in the region of Sinai. **7:** The place is named both *Massah* from the Hebrew verb "test" and *Meribah* from the verb "find fault"–names which became memorials of Israel's faithlessness (Dt.6.16; 9.22; 33.8; Ps.95.8). Meribah was one of the springs at Kadesh (Num.20.13; 27.14; Dt.32.51). Marah (15.23) and Massah were evidently springs at the same oasis. Some traditions in 15.23-18.27 come from this oasis south of Beer-sheba (see Num.13.26 n.). **8-15:** The battle with the Amalekites. **8:** The Amalekites, a fierce desert tribe, claimed control of the wilderness in the region of Kadesh (Gen.14.7; Num.13.29; 14.25). **9-13:** *Choose for us men* implies holy war (v. 16) with a select group (compare Jg. ch. 7). The young warrior, Joshua, here mentioned for the first time, was at the head of the Israelite army. Moses, however, led the battle from a hilltop and ensured victory by the power of his rod and outstretched arms and perhaps by the power of the curse (Num.22.4-6). **10:** *Hur*, elsewhere mentioned only in 24.14. **14:** *Utterly blot out*, i.e. the foe will be subjected to the sacrificial ban,

of Am'alek from under heaven." [15] And Moses built an altar and called the name of it, The LORD is my banner, [16] saying, "A hand upon the banner of the LORD!^{z} The LORD will have war with Am'alek from generation to generation."

[18] Jethro, the priest of Mid'ian, Moses' father-in-law, heard of all that God had done for Moses and for Israel his people, how the LORD had brought Israel out of Egypt. [2] Now Jethro, Moses' father-in-law, had taken Zippo'rah, Moses' wife, after he had sent her away, [3] and her two sons, of whom the name of the one was Gershom (for he said, "I have been a sojourner^a in a foreign land"), [4] and the name of the other, Elie'zer^b (for he said, "The God of my father was my help, and delivered me from the sword of Pharaoh"). [5] And Jethro, Moses' father-in-law, came with his sons and his wife to Moses in the wilderness where he was encamped at the mountain of God. [6] And when one told Moses, "Lo,^{c} your father-in-law Jethro is coming to you with your wife and her two sons with her," [7] Moses went out to meet his father-in-law, and did obeisance and kissed him; and they asked each other of their welfare, and went into the tent. [8] Then Moses told his father-in-law all that the LORD had done to Pharaoh and to the Egyptians for Israel's sake, all the hardship that had come upon them in the way, and how the LORD had delivered them. [9] And Jethro rejoiced for all the good which the LORD had done to Israel, in

that he had delivered them out of the hand of the Egyptians.

[10] And Jethro said, "Blessed be the LORD, who has delivered you out of the hand of the Egyptians and out of the hand of Pharaoh. [11] Now I know that the LORD is greater than all gods, because he delivered the people from under the hand of the Egyptians,^{d} when they dealt arrogantly with them." [12] And Jethro, Moses' father-in-law, offered^e a burnt offering and sacrifices to God; and Aaron came with all the elders of Israel to eat bread with Moses' father-in-law before God.

[13] On the morrow Moses sat to judge the people, and the people stood about Moses from morning till evening. [14] When Moses' father-in-law saw all that he was doing for the people, he said, "What is this that you are doing for the people? Why do you sit alone, and all the people stand about you from morning till evening?" [15] And Moses said to his father-in-law, "Because the people come to me to inquire of God; [16] when they have a dispute, they come to me and I decide between a man and his neighbor, and I make them know the statutes of God and his decisions." [17] Moses' father-in-law said to him, "What you are doing is not good. [18] You and the people with you will wear yourselves out, for the thing is too heavy for you; you are not able to perform it alone. [19] Listen now to my voice; I will give you counsel, and

z Cn: Heb obscure   *a* Heb *ger*
b Heb *Eli*, my God, *ezer*, help   *c* Sam Gk Syr: Heb *I*
d Transposing the last clause of v. 10 to v. 11
e Syr Tg Vg: Heb *took*

a practice of holy war. **16:** The bitter feud with Amalek persisted (Num.24.20; Dt.25.17–19; 1 Sam.15.7–8; 27.8; ch. 30) until the foe was exterminated during the reign of Hezekiah (1 Chr.4.41–43).

    18.1–27: Jethro's visit. The priest of Midian celebrated a sacred meal and counseled Moses about the administration of law. **1:** *Jethro*, see 2.18 n. **2–4:** Zipporah and her sons (2.21–22) apparently had been sent back from Egypt to Midian. **5:** The narrative is out of order, for Israel reached *the mountain of God* later (19.2). **9–12:** This passage may imply that the priest of Midian was already a worshiper of the LORD (see 3.1 n.). As the priest of the cult, Jethro came to rejoice in the LORD's great deeds and to officiate at a cultic celebration. **12:** *Eat bread*, an allusion to a sacred meal held *before God* (24.9–11). Moses was not invited, perhaps because he had already been initiated into the cult (3.1–6). **13–27:** Jethro's plan for the reorganization of legal administration (compare Dt.1.9–18). **13:** Like a bedouin chief, Moses acted as judge in the people's disputes (2 Sam.15.1–6). **15–16:** *Inquire of God*, i.e. seek a verdict by oracle (Jg.4.

God be with you! You shall represent the people before God, and bring their cases to God; ²⁰ and you shall teach them the statutes and the decisions, and make them know the way in which they must walk and what they must do. ²¹ Moreover choose able men from all the people, such as fear God, men who are trustworthy and who hate a bribe; and place such men over the people as rulers of thousands, of hundreds, of fifties, and of tens. ²² And let them judge the people at all times; every great matter they shall bring to you, but any small matter they shall decide themselves; so it will be easier for you, and they will bear the burden with you. ²³ If you do this, and God so commands you, then you will be able to endure, and all this people also will go to their place in peace."

24 So Moses gave heed to the voice of his father-in-law and did all that he had said. ²⁵ Moses chose able men out of all Israel, and made them heads over the people, rulers of thousands, of hundreds, of fifties, and of tens. ²⁶ And they judged the people at all times; hard cases they brought to Moses, but any small matter they decided themselves. ²⁷ Then Moses let his father-in-law depart, and he went his way to his own country.

19 On the third new moon after the people of Israel had gone forth out of the land of Egypt, on that day they came into the wilderness of Sinai.

² And when they set out from Reph'-idim and came into the wilderness of Sinai, they encamped in the wilderness; and there Israel encamped before the mountain. ³ And Moses went up to God, and the LORD called to him out of the mountain, saying, "Thus you shall say to the house of Jacob, and tell the people of Israel: ⁴ You have seen what I did to the Egyptians, and how I bore you on eagles' wings and brought you to myself. ⁵ Now therefore, if you will obey my voice and keep my covenant, you shall be my own possession among all peoples; for all the earth is mine, ⁶ and you shall be to me a kingdom of priests and a holy nation. These are the words which you shall speak to the children of Israel."

7 So Moses came and called the elders of the people, and set before them all these words which the LORD had commanded him. ⁸ And all the people answered together and said, "All that the LORD has spoken we will do." And Moses reported the words of the people to the LORD. ⁹ And the LORD said to Moses, "Lo, I am coming to you in a thick cloud, that the people may hear when I speak with you, and may also believe you for ever."

Then Moses told the words of the people to the LORD. ¹⁰ And the LORD said to Moses, "Go to the people and consecrate them today and tomorrow, and let them wash their garments, ¹¹ and be ready by the third day; for

---

4–5). **21–22:** Moses was to deal with cases without legal precedent which required a special oracle (compare Dt.17.8–13); ordinary cases were to be handled by lay leaders (Num.11.16–17, 24–25) or appointed judges (compare Dt.16.18–20). *Rulers of thousands,* see Num.1.17–46 n.

19.1–25 (20.18–21): The theophany at Sinai. At the sacred mountain the LORD offered to make a covenant with Israel. **2:** *Sinai,* see 3.1 n. **3:** The account assumes that the LORD dwells in heaven, whence he "comes down" (v. 20; 3.8) to the mountain top for meeting with men (24.9–11). Compare the similar view reflected in the Babylonian temple-tower (Gen.11.1–9). **4:** *You have seen what I did,* the background and presupposition of the *covenant* (see Gen. 17.2 n.) is the LORD's mighty acts of deliverance. *On eagles' wings,* Dt.32.11–12. **5:** On Israel's side, the covenant rests upon a condition, *if you will obey my voice*–an allusion to the covenant laws to be given. *My own possession,* or "treasure," is a metaphor for Israel's special relationship to God. In freedom and grace he chose this people for his own (Dt.7.6; 14.2; 26.18), though all the earth belongs to him (Ex.9.29b). **6:** That which is holy is set apart as belonging to God; thus Israel is to be *a kingdom of priests and a holy nation,* consecrated for his service (see Is.61.6; 1 Pet.2.5,9). **7–8:** Compare 24.7. **9:** This tradition stresses Moses' role as the covenant mediator whom the people are to believe *for ever* (20.19; 24.1–2,9–11). **10–15:** In this tradition all the people are to prepare for participation in the covenant ceremony (24.3–8).

on the third day the LORD will come down upon Mount Sinai in the sight of all the people. ¹² And you shall set bounds for the people round about, saying, 'Take heed that you do not go up into the mountain or touch the border of it; whoever touches the mountain shall be put to death; ¹³ no hand shall touch him, but he shall be stoned or shot; whether beast or man, he shall not live.' When the trumpet sounds a long blast, they shall come up to the mountain." ¹⁴ So Moses went down from the mountain to the people, and consecrated the people; and they washed their garments. ¹⁵ And he said to the people, "Be ready by the third day; do not go near a woman."

16 On the morning of the third day there were thunders and lightnings, and a thick cloud upon the mountain, and a very loud trumpet blast, so that all the people who were in the camp trembled. ¹⁷ Then Moses brought the people out of the camp to meet God; and they took their stand at the foot of the mountain. ¹⁸ And Mount Sinai was wrapped in smoke, because the LORD descended upon it in fire; and the smoke of it went up like the smoke of a kiln, and the whole mountain quaked greatly. ¹⁹ And as the sound of the trumpet grew louder and louder, Moses spoke, and God answered him in thunder. ²⁰ And the LORD came down upon Mount Sinai, to the top of the mountain; and the LORD called

Moses to the top of the mountain, and Moses went up. ²¹ And the LORD said to Moses, "Go down and warn the people, lest they break through to the LORD to gaze and many of them perish. ²² And also let the priests who come near to the LORD consecrate themselves, lest the LORD break out upon them." ²³ And Moses said to the LORD, "The people cannot come up to Mount Sinai; for thou thyself didst charge us, saying, 'Set bounds about the mountain, and consecrate it.'" ²⁴ And the LORD said to him, "Go down, and come up bringing Aaron with you; but do not let the priests and the people break through to come up to the LORD, lest he break out against them." ²⁵ So Moses went down to the people and told them.

20 And God spoke all these words, saying,

2 "I am the LORD your God, who brought you out of the land of Egypt, out of the house of bondage.

3 "You shall have no other gods before*ᶠ* me.

4 "You shall not make for yourself a graven image, or any likeness of anything that is in heaven above, or that is in the earth beneath, or that is in the water under the earth; ⁵ you shall not bow down to them or serve them; for I the LORD your God am a jealous God, visiting the iniquity of the fathers upon the children to the third and the fourth generation of those who hate me,ᵍ but

f Or *besides*

12: The setting of bounds so that the people do not come near the mountain (v. 21) reflects the ancient view of holiness as a mysterious, threatening power with which the mountain is charged (see 3.6 n.; 2 Sam.6.6-9). No hand may touch the offender who has become affected with the contagion of holiness (Lev.6.27-28). **14-15:** Washing or changing of garments (Gen.35.2) and sexual abstinence (1 Sam.21.4-6) were forms of ceremonial purification. **16-19:** The theophany is portrayed primarily in the imagery of a violent thunderstorm (Jg.5.4-5; Pss.18.7-15; 29.3-9; etc.). This traditional language-"earthquake, wind, and fire" (1 Kg.19.11-13)-depicts the wonder and majesty of God's revelation. **16:** The trumpet (v. 13) was sounded on cultic occasions (2 Sam.6.15).

20.1-17: The Ten Commandments, the epitome of man's duties toward God and his neighbor. **1:** *These words,* i.e. "the ten words" or the Decalogue (34.28; Dt.4.13; 10.4). Originally each commandment was a short utterance (see vv. 13,14,15), lacking the explanatory comments found, e.g. in vv. 5,6,9-11. **2:** Jewish tradition considers this to be the first commandment. Actually it is a preface which summarizes the meaning of the Exodus, thus setting law within the context of God's redemptive action. **3:** The first commandment asserts that for Israel there shall be no other gods, because the LORD is *a jealous God* (v. 5; 34.14) who will tolerate no rivals for his people's devotion. **4-6:** Imageless worship of the LORD made Israel's faith unique in the

showing steadfast love to thousands of those who love me and keep my commandments.

7 "You shall not take the name of the LORD your God in vain; for the LORD will not hold him guiltless who takes his name in vain.

8 "Remember the sabbath day, to keep it holy. 9 Six days you shall labor, and do all your work; 10 but the seventh day is a sabbath to the LORD your God; in it you shall not do any work, you, or your son, or your daughter, your manservant, or your maidservant, or your cattle, or the sojourner who is within your gates; 11 for in six days the LORD made heaven and earth, the sea, and all that is in them, and rested the seventh day; therefore the LORD blessed the sabbath day and hallowed it.

12 "Honor your father and your mother, that your days may be long in the land which the LORD your God gives you.

13 "You shall not kill.

14 "You shall not commit adultery.

15 "You shall not steal.

16 "You shall not bear false witness against your neighbor.

17 "You shall not covet your neighbor's house; you shall not covet your neighbor's wife, or his manservant, or his maidservant, or his ox, or his ass, or anything that is your neighbor's."

18 Now when all the people perceived the thunderings and the lightnings and the sound of the trumpet and the mountain smoking, the people were afraid and trembled; and they stood afar off, 19 and said to Moses, "You speak to us, and we will hear; but let not God speak to us, lest we die." 20 And Moses said to the people, "Do not fear; for God has come to prove you, and that the fear of him may be before your eyes, that you may not sin."

21 And the people stood afar off, while Moses drew near to the thick darkness where God was. 22 And the LORD said to Moses, "Thus you shall say to the people of Israel: 'You have seen for yourselves that I have talked with you from heaven. 23 You shall not make gods of silver to be with me, nor shall you make for yourselves gods of gold. 24 An altar of earth you shall make for me and sacrifice on it your burnt offerings and your peace offerings, your sheep and your oxen; in every place where I cause my name to be remembered I will come to you and bless you. 25 And if you make me an altar of stone, you shall not build it of hewn stones; for if you wield your tool upon it you profane it. 26 And you shall not go up by steps to my altar, that your nakedness be not exposed on it.'

---

ancient world where natural powers were personified and statues of them (animal or human) were worshiped. Some interpreters consider vv. 3–6 as one commandment and divide v. 17 into two commandments. **7:** The third commandment prohibits the misuse of the LORD's name in magic, divination, or false swearing (Lev.19.12). It reflects the ancient view that knowledge of the name could be used to exert magical control (see Gen.32.27,29 n.). **8–11:** Keeping the sabbath *holy* means to observe it as a day separated from others, a segment of time belonging especially to God. **10:** 16.22–30. **11:** Compare Dt.5.15. **12:** 21.15,17; Dt.27.16. **13:** This commandment forbids murder (see Gen.9.5,6 n.), not the forms of killing authorized for Israel, e.g. war or capital punishment. **16:** This law demands telling the truth in a law suit involving the neighbor (23.1; Dt.19.15–21; 1 Kg.21.8–14). **17:** Some regard the first sentence as a separate commandment; however, *neighbor's house* probably includes what is enumerated in the second part of the verse: wife, manservant, etc. **18–21:** The conclusion to the theophany scene (ch. 19). The people request that Moses be the covenant mediator (see 19.9 n.) so that they need not hear God's law directly (compare Dt.5.4–5).

　20.22–23.33: The Covenant Code. These laws are largely neutral in regard to Israelite faith and presuppose a settled agricultural society. They reflect a situation after Israel's invasion of Canaan, when prevailing laws were borrowed and adapted to the covenant tradition. **22–26:** Cultic regulations. **23:** See 20.4–6 n. **24–26:** The Israelite altar, in contrast to pagan models, is to be the simplest kind and is to be built wherever the LORD *causes his name to be remembered*,

21 "Now these are the ordinances which you shall set before them. ² When you buy a Hebrew slave, he shall serve six years, and in the seventh he shall go out free, for nothing. ³ If he comes in single, he shall go out single; if he comes in married, then his wife shall go out with him. ⁴ If his master gives him a wife and she bears him sons or daughters, the wife and her children shall be her master's and he shall go out alone. ⁵ But if the slave plainly says, 'I love my master, my wife, and my children; I will not go out free,' ⁶ then his master shall bring him to God, and he shall bring him to the door or the doorpost; and his master shall bore his ear through with an awl; and he shall serve him for life.

7 "When a man sells his daughter as a slave, she shall not go out as the male slaves do. ⁸ If she does not please her master, who has designated her[g] for himself, then he shall let her be redeemed; he shall have no right to sell her to a foreign people, since he has dealt faithlessly with her. ⁹ If he designates her for his son, he shall deal with her as with a daughter. ¹⁰ If he takes another wife to himself, he shall not diminish her food, her clothing, or her marital rights. ¹¹ And if he does not do these three things for her, she shall go out for nothing, without payment of money.

12 "Whoever strikes a man so that he dies shall be put to death. ¹³ But if he did not lie in wait for him, but God let him fall into his hand, then I will appoint for you a place to which he may flee. ¹⁴ But if a man willfully attacks another to kill him treacherously, you shall take him from my altar, that he may die.

15 "Whoever strikes his father or his mother shall be put to death.

16 "Whoever steals a man, whether he sells him or is found in possession of him, shall be put to death.

17 "Whoever curses his father or his mother shall be put to death.

18 "When men quarrel and one strikes the other with a stone or with his fist and the man does not die but keeps his bed, ¹⁹ then if the man rises again and walks abroad with his staff, he that struck him shall be clear; only he shall pay for the loss of his time, and shall have him thoroughly healed.

20 "When a man strikes his slave, male or female, with a rod and the slave dies under his hand, he shall be punished. ²¹ But if the slave survives a day or two, he is not to be punished; for the slave is his money.

22 "When men strive together, and hurt a woman with child, so that there is a miscarriage, and yet no harm follows, the one who hurt her shall[h] be fined, according as the woman's husband shall lay upon him; and he shall pay as the judges determine. ²³ If

g Another reading is *so that he has not designated her*
h Heb *he shall*

i.e. chooses to reveal himself. Contrast the reform demanded in Dt.12.5–14. **21.1–11:** The rights of a slave (compare Dt.15.12–18). **1:** *Ordinances* refers to laws formulated (usually in the third person) to deal with various cases, in contrast to the apodictic or unconditional law of the Israelite theocracy (e.g. the Decalogue). These case laws reflect the agricultural way of life in Canaan (e.g. 22.5–6) and are similar in style and content to other legal codes of the ancient Near East. **2:** *Hebrew*, see Ex.1.15 n. An Israelite could go into servitude because of debts (Ex.22.1; Lev.25.39; 2 Kg.4.1). **6:** *To God*, i.e. the legal act had to be performed at the sacred doorpost of the house (see 12.7 n.), perhaps in the presence of the household gods (Gen.31.19). **7–11:** The rights of a female slave or concubine (compare Dt.15.12,17). **8:** *Redeemed*, i.e. by a relative or another buyer who pays the purchase price.

21.12–32: Laws protecting human beings. 12–14: A distinction is drawn between intentional and unintentional murder. As protection from the swift justice of the blood-avenger, the manslayer is guaranteed asylum (Num.35.12; Dt.4.41–43; 19.1–13; Jos. ch. 20), so that the case may be adjudicated soberly by legal authorities. The asylum in ancient times was at the altar (1 Kg.2.28–34). **17:** The curse, according to ancient belief, released an inexorable power (Num. 22.6), thus making it as serious to curse parents as to strike them. **22–25:** This lex talionis (see Lev.24.20) was not an expression of vengeance but a limitation upon measureless vengeance.

any harm follows, then you shall give life for life, ²⁴ eye for eye, tooth for tooth, hand for hand, foot for foot, ²⁵ burn for burn, wound for wound, stripe for stripe.

26 "When a man strikes the eye of his slave, male or female, and destroys it, he shall let the slave go free for the eye's sake. ²⁷ If he knocks out the tooth of his slave, male or female, he shall let the slave go free for the tooth's sake.

28 "When an ox gores a man or a woman to death, the ox shall be stoned, and its flesh shall not be eaten; but the owner of the ox shall be clear. ²⁹ But if the ox has been accustomed to gore in the past, and its owner has been warned but has not kept it in, and it kills a man or a woman, the ox shall be stoned, and its owner also shall be put to death. ³⁰ If a ransom is laid on him, then he shall give for the redemption of his life whatever is laid upon him. ³¹ If it gores a man's son or daughter, he shall be dealt with according to this same rule. ³² If the ox gores a slave, male or female, the owner shall give to their master thirty shekels of silver, and the ox shall be stoned.

33 "When a man leaves a pit open, or when a man digs a pit and does not cover it, and an ox or an ass falls into it, ³⁴ the owner of the pit shall make it good; he shall give money to its owner, and the dead beast shall be his.

35 "When one man's ox hurts another's, so that it dies, then they shall sell the live ox and divide the price of it; and the dead beast also they shall divide. ³⁶ Or if it is known that the ox has been accustomed to gore in the past, and its owner has not kept it in, he shall pay ox for ox, and the dead beast shall be his.

22 ⁱ "If a man steals an ox or a sheep, and kills it or sells it, he shall pay five oxen for an ox, and four sheep for a sheep.^j He shall make restitution; if he has nothing, then he shall be sold for his theft. ⁴ If the stolen beast is found alive in his possession, whether it is an ox or an ass or a sheep, he shall pay double.

2^k "If a thief is found breaking in, and is struck so that he dies, there shall be no bloodguilt for him; ³ but if the sun has risen upon him, there shall be bloodguilt for him.

5 "When a man causes a field or vineyard to be grazed over, or lets his beast loose and it feeds in another man's field, he shall make restitution from the best in his own field and in his own vineyard.

6 "When fire breaks out and catches in thorns so that the stacked grain or the standing grain or the field is consumed, he that kindled the fire shall make full restitution.

7 "If a man delivers to his neighbor money or goods to keep, and it is stolen out of the man's house, then, if the thief is found, he shall pay double. ⁸ If the thief is not found, the owner of the house shall come near to God, to show whether or not he has put his hand to his neighbor's goods.

9 "For every breach of trust, whether it is for ox, for ass, for sheep, for clothing, or for any kind of lost thing, of which one says, 'This is it,' the case of both parties shall come before God; he whom God shall condemn shall pay double to his neighbor.

10 "If a man delivers to his neighbor an ass or an ox or a sheep or any beast to keep, and it dies or is hurt or is driven away, without any one seeing it, ¹¹ an oath by the LORD shall be be-

i Ch 21.37 in Heb
j Restoring the second half of verse 3 with 4 to their place immediately following verse 1
k Ch 22.1 in Heb

21.33–22.17: Laws dealing with property. 33–36: These laws establish responsibility in cases of carelessness. **22:1–4:** Case laws regulating stealing. **2–3:** These verses may mean that if the invader is caught in the act (at night) he may be slain with impunity, but if he is slain in broad daylight there is blood guilt. **5–6:** Cases of neglect. **7–15:** Cases involving trusteeship. **9:** *Before God* (v. 8), i.e. to the sanctuary (possibly to the doorpost; 21.6) for an oracular decision or the

tween them both to see whether he has not put his hand to his neighbor's property; and the owner shall accept the oath, and he shall not make restitution. [12] But if it is stolen from him, he shall make restitution to its owner. [13] If it is torn by beasts, let him bring it as evidence; he shall not make restitution for what has been torn.

14 "If a man borrows anything of his neighbor, and it is hurt or dies, the owner not being with it, he shall make full restitution. [15] If the owner was with it, he shall not make restitution; if it was hired, it came for its hire.*l*

16 "If a man seduces a virgin who is not betrothed, and lies with her, he shall give the marriage present for her, and make her his wife. [17] If her father utterly refuses to give her to him, he shall pay money equivalent to the marriage present for virgins.

18 "You shall not permit a sorceress to live.

19 "Whoever lies with a beast shall be put to death.

20 "Whoever sacrifices to any god, save to the LORD only, shall be utterly destroyed.

21 "You shall not wrong a stranger or oppress him, for you were strangers in the land of Egypt. [22] You shall not afflict any widow or orphan. [23] If you do afflict them, and they cry out to me, I will surely hear their cry; [24] and my wrath will burn, and I will kill you with the sword, and your wives shall become widows and your children fatherless.

25 "If you lend money to any of my people with you who is poor, you shall not be to him as a creditor, and you shall not exact interest from him. [26] If ever you take your neighbor's garment in pledge, you shall restore it to him before the sun goes down; [27] for that is his only covering, it is his mantle for his body; in what else shall he sleep? And if he cries to me, I will hear, for I am compassionate.

28 "You shall not revile God, nor curse a ruler of your people.

29 "You shall not delay to offer from the fulness of your harvest and from the outflow of your presses.

"The first-born of your sons you shall give to me. [30] You shall do likewise with your oxen and with your sheep: seven days it shall be with its dam; on the eighth day you shall give it to me.

31 "You shall be men consecrated to me; therefore you shall not eat any flesh that is torn by beasts in the field; you shall cast it to the dogs.

23 "You shall not utter a false report. You shall not join hands with a wicked man, to be a malicious witness. [2] You shall not follow a multitude to do evil; nor shall you bear witness in a suit, turning aside after a multitude, so as to pervert justice; [3] nor shall you be partial to a poor man in his suit.

4 "If you meet your enemy's ox or his ass going astray, you shall bring it back to him. [5] If you see the ass of one who hates you lying under its burden, you shall refrain from leaving him with it, you shall help him to lift it up.*m*

l Or *it is reckoned in* (Heb *comes into*) *its hire*
m Gk: Heb obscure

---

sacred oath (v. 11; 1 Kg.8.31–32). **16–17:** This law is included here because it deals with a financial matter, the *marriage present* (Dt.22.29). Laws concerning sexual relations are found in Dt.22.13–30.

22.18–23.9: Miscellaneous social and cultic laws. The laws of vv. 18–20 (compare 21.12,15–17) are in the unconditional style of the Decalogue. **20:** Compare 20.3; Dt.13.12–18. **21–27:** Israel's God is the protector of the legally defenseless: the stranger (sojourner), orphan, widow, and poor. **25:** Being a farming people, Israel frowned upon the mercantile way of life (Hos.12.7–8) and specifically upon the exaction of interest from a fellow-Israelite (Lev.25.35–38). **26:** A loan with a garment as security could only be for the day, lest a poor man suffer (Dt.24.12–13; Am.2.8). **28:** Lev.24.15–16; 2 Sam.16.9; 1 Kg.2.8–9; 21.10. **29–30:** See 13.2 n. **31:** Flesh torn by beasts was regarded as unclean because it was not properly drained of blood (Lev.7.24; 17.15). **23.1–9:** Laws expounding Israel's sense of justice. **4–5:** Justice extends even to helping *your enemy* (Dt.22.1–4).

6 "You shall not pervert the justice due to your poor in his suit. [7] Keep far from a false charge, and do not slay the innocent and righteous, for I will not acquit the wicked. [8] And you shall take no bribe, for a bribe blinds the officials, and subverts the cause of those who are in the right.

9 "You shall not oppress a stranger; you know the heart of a stranger, for you were strangers in the land of Egypt.

10 "For six years you shall sow your land and gather in its yield; [11] but the seventh year you shall let it rest and lie fallow, that the poor of your people may eat; and what they leave the wild beasts may eat. You shall do likewise with your vineyard, and with your olive orchard.

12 "Six days you shall do your work, but on the seventh day you shall rest; that your ox and your ass may have rest, and the son of your bondmaid, and the alien, may be refreshed. [13] Take heed to all that I have said to you; and make no mention of the names of other gods, nor let such be heard out of your mouth.

14 "Three times in the year you shall keep a feast to me. [15] You shall keep the feast of unleavened bread; as I commanded you, you shall eat unleavened bread for seven days at the appointed time in the month of Abib, for in it you came out of Egypt. None shall appear before me empty-handed. [16] You shall keep the feast of harvest, of the first fruits of your labor, of what you sow in the field. You shall keep the feast of ingathering at the end of the year, when you gather in from the field the fruit of your labor. [17] Three times in the year shall all your males appear before the Lord GOD.

18 "You shall not offer the blood of my sacrifice with leavened bread, or let the fat of my feast remain until the morning.

19 "The first of the first fruits of your ground you shall bring into the house of the LORD your God.

"You shall not boil a kid in its mother's milk.

20 "Behold, I send an angel before you, to guard you on the way and to bring you to the place which I have prepared. [21] Give heed to him and hearken to his voice, do not rebel against him, for he will not pardon your transgression; for my name is in him.

22 "But if you hearken attentively to his voice and do all that I say, then I will be an enemy to your enemies and an adversary to your adversaries.

23 "When my angel goes before you, and brings you in to the Amorites, and the Hittites, and the Per'izzites, and the Canaanites, the Hivites, and the Jeb'usites, and I blot them out, [24] you shall not bow down to their gods, nor serve them, nor do according to their works, but you shall utterly overthrow them and break their pillars in pieces. [25] You shall serve the LORD your God, and I[n] will bless your bread and your water; and I will take sickness away from the midst of you. [26] None shall cast her young or be barren in your land; I will fulfil the number of your days. [27] I will send my terror before you, and will throw into confusion all

n Gk Vg: Heb *he*

23.10–19: A cultic calendar (34.18–26; Lev.23.1–44; Dt.16.1–17). **10–11:** See Lev.25.2–7. **12:** Here the observance of the sabbath is based upon humanitarian concern (compare 20.11). **14–17:** This law reflects the practice of making a pilgrimage to the central sanctuary of the tribal confederacy (1 Sam.1.3,21). **15:** *Empty-handed,* i.e. without a gift of the first fruits of the barley harvest. **16:** The *feast of harvest,* i.e. the feast of weeks (or pentecost, see Lev.23.15–21 n.) which was celebrated at the time of the wheat harvest (June). The third feast, *the feast of ingathering,* or feast of booths, was celebrated *at the end of the year* (autumn), according to the old agricultural calendar (see 12.2 n.), when fruit, grapes, and olives were harvested. **17:** According to ancient practice, men were the chief participants in the cult (34.23; see 10.7–11 n.). **18–19:** 34.25–26. The prohibition against seething a kid in its mother's milk (Dt.14.21) is a protest against a Canaanite method of preparing a sacrifice.

23.20–33: **The conclusion to the Covenant Code** (beginning 20.22). **20–21:** The *angel* is the

the people against whom you shall come, and I will make all your enemies turn their backs to you. 28 And I will send hornets before you, which shall drive out Hivite, Canaanite, and Hittite from before you. 29 I will not drive them out from before you in one year, lest the land become desolate and the wild beasts multiply against you. 30 Little by little I will drive them out from before you, until you are increased and possess the land. 31 And I will set your bounds from the Red Sea to the sea of the Philistines, and from the wilderness to the Euphra'tes; for I will deliver the inhabitants of the land into your hand, and you shall drive them out before you. 32 You shall make no covenant with them or with their gods. 33 They shall not dwell in your land, lest they make you sin against me; for if you serve their gods, it will surely be a snare to you."

24 And he said to Moses, "Come up to the LORD, you and Aaron, Nadab, and Abi'hu, and seventy of the elders of Israel, and worship afar off. 2 Moses alone shall come near to the LORD; but the others shall not come near, and the people shall not come up with him."

3 Moses came and told the people all the words of the LORD and all the ordinances; and all the people answered

with one voice, and said, "All the words which the LORD has spoken we will do." 4 And Moses wrote all the words of the LORD. And he rose early in the morning, and built an altar at the foot of the mountain, and twelve pillars, according to the twelve tribes of Israel. 5 And he sent young men of the people of Israel, who offered burnt offerings and sacrificed peace offerings of oxen to the LORD. 6 And Moses took half of the blood and put it in basins, and half of the blood he threw against the altar. 7 Then he took the book of the covenant, and read it in the hearing of the people; and they said, "All that the LORD has spoken we will do, and we will be obedient." 8 And Moses took the blood and threw it upon the people, and said, "Behold the blood of the covenant which the LORD has made with you in accordance with all these words."

9 Then Moses and Aaron, Nadab, and Abi'hu, and seventy of the elders of Israel went up, 10 and they saw the God of Israel; and there was under his feet as it were a pavement of sapphire stone, like the very heaven for clearness. 11 And he did not lay his hand on the chief men of the people of Israel; they beheld God, and ate and drank.

12 The LORD said to Moses, "Come up to me on the mountain, and wait

---

LORD himself (14.19; see Gen.16.7 n.). On *the name*, see Gen.32.27 n. **27.28:** Here the language of "holy war" is used. *Terror*, Gen.35.5 n. The term *hornets* apparently is used figuratively to portray the panic aroused in holy war (Dt.7.20; Jos.24.12 n.).

24.1–18: The ceremony of covenant ratification. 1–2: This tradition is continued in vv. 9–11. *Moses alone*, an indication of Moses' special role as covenant mediator (19.9; 20.19). **3–8:** The first version of the covenant ceremony stresses the people's participation (19.10–15). **3:** *The words*, i.e. the Decalogue; *the ordinances*, i.e. the laws of the Covenant Code (see 21.1 n.). **4:** The participation of all the people is symbolized by *twelve pillars*, one for each tribe. **5:** On the types of sacrifice, see Lev. chs. 1 and 3. **6–8:** The ritual dramatizes the uniting of the two parties: the LORD, whose presence is represented by the altar, and the people. Compare the ancient covenant ceremony found in Gen. ch. 15. **7:** *The book of the covenant* (Jos.24.25–26) apparently contained the covenant laws, here tacitly identified with *the words* and *the ordinances* (v. 3). **8:** *The blood of the covenant* (compare Mt.26.28; 1 Cor.11.25) reflects the ancient view that blood was efficacious in establishing community between God and man (see Lev.1.5 n.). **9–11:** The second version of the covenant ceremony (continuing vv. 1–2). **9:** The people did not take part but were represented by the seventy *elders* or *chief men*. Moses, the covenant mediator, was accompanied by the priestly family, Aaron, Nadab, and Abihu (6.14–25; Lev. 10.1–3). **10:** The leaders did not see God directly; they saw only the lower part of his heavenly throne-room–the sapphire pavement (the firmament) above which the LORD was enthroned (compare Is.6.1; Ezek.1.1,26–28). **11:** Unharmed by divine holiness (see 3.6 n.), the leaders

there; and I will give you the tables of stone, with the law and the commandment, which I have written for their instruction." ¹³ So Moses rose with his servant Joshua, and Moses went up into the mountain of God. ¹⁴ And he said to the elders, "Tarry here for us, until we come to you again; and, behold, Aaron and Hur are with you; whoever has a cause, let him go to them."

15 Then Moses went up on the mountain, and the cloud covered the mountain. ¹⁶ The glory of the LORD settled on Mount Sinai, and the cloud covered it six days; and on the seventh day he called to Moses out of the midst of the cloud. ¹⁷ Now the appearance of the glory of the LORD was like a devouring fire on the top of the mountain in the sight of the people of Israel. ¹⁸ And Moses entered the cloud, and went up on the mountain. And Moses was on the mountain forty days and forty nights.

25 The LORD said to Moses, ² "Speak to the people of Israel, that they take for me an offering; from every man whose heart makes him willing you shall receive the offering for me. ³ And this is the offering which you shall receive from them: gold, silver, and bronze, ⁴ blue and purple and scarlet stuff and

fine twined linen, goats' hair, ⁵ tanned rams' skins, goatskins, acacia wood, ⁶ oil for the lamps, spices for the anointing oil and for the fragrant incense, ⁷ onyx stones, and stones for setting, for the ephod and for the breastpiece. ⁸ And let them make me a sanctuary, that I may dwell in their midst. ⁹ According to all that I show you concerning the pattern of the tabernacle, and of all its furniture, so you shall make it.

10 "They shall make an ark of acacia wood; two cubits and a half shall be its length, a cubit and a half its breadth, and a cubit and a half its height. ¹¹ And you shall overlay it with pure gold, within and without shall you overlay it, and you shall make upon it a molding of gold round about. ¹² And you shall cast four rings of gold for it and put them on its four feet, two rings on the one side of it, and two rings on the other side of it. ¹³ You shall make poles of acacia wood, and overlay them with gold. ¹⁴ And you shall put the poles into the rings on the sides of the ark, to carry the ark by them. ¹⁵ The poles shall remain in the rings of the ark; they shall not be taken from it. ¹⁶ And you shall put into the ark the testimony which I shall give you. ¹⁷ Then you shall make a mercy seat*ᵒ*

o Or *cover*

partook of the covenant meal (18.12). **12–14:** A separate tradition about the gift of *the tables of stone* on which the Decalogue was written (32.15; 34.28; Dt.9.9,11,15). **14:** 18.16. This verse sets the stage for the episode of ch. 32. *Hur,* see 17.10 n. **15–18:** This theophany introduces the priestly material of chs. 25–31, which apparently has replaced the early tradition about Moses making the ark and putting the tables of law in it (Dt.10.1–5). *The glory,* see 16.6–7 n.
25.1–40: The ark, the table, and the lampstand. 1–9: The request for a free-will offering for making the tabernacle and its equipment (35.4–29). **7:** *The ephod* and *the breastplate,* 28.6–12, 13–30. **8:** *A sanctuary,* i.e. a tabernacle, will be the sign that God, the heavenly LORD, is present among his people. **10–22:** Specifications for the ark. In the following sections, the priestly writer moves from the center to the periphery; i.e. he begins with the most important item, the ark, and moves outward to the court. Comparable to ancient Arabic palladia, the ark was a portable wooden chest which served to guide Israel in wandering (Num.10.33), to lead in war (Num. 10.35–36), and to be a medium for oracles (1 Sam. ch. 3). It was regarded as a throne-seat above which the LORD was invisibly enthroned (1 Sam.4.4; 2 Sam.6.2; 2 Kg.19.15). In contrast to the tent of meeting (33.7–11), it signified the divine nearness. Constructed by Moses himself, according to tradition (Dt.10.3), it was stationed at Shiloh during the days of the tribal confederacy (1 Sam. chs. 3–6) and was eventually brought by David to Jerusalem (2 Sam. ch. 6). **10:** The dimensions are about 45 × 27 × 27 inches. **16:** *The testimony,* i.e. the tables of law (24.12). Hence the chest is called "the ark of the testimony" (v. 22) in view of its chief contents. **17:** The *mercy seat* (Lev.16.2,13–15) was the cover of the ark. As the footstool of the LORD's

of pure gold; two cubits and a half shall be its length, and a cubit and a half its breadth. [18] And you shall make two cherubim of gold; of hammered work shall you make them, on the two ends of the mercy seat. [19] Make one cherub on the one end, and one cherub on the other end; of one piece with the mercy seat shall you make the cherubim on its two ends. [20] The cherubim shall spread out their wings above, overshadowing the mercy seat with their wings, their faces one to another; toward the mercy seat shall the faces of the cherubim be. [21] And you shall put the mercy seat on the top of the ark; and in the ark you shall put the testimony that I shall give you. [22] There I will meet with you, and from above the mercy seat, from between the two cherubim that are upon the ark of the testimony, I will speak with you of all that I will give you in commandment for the people of Israel.

23 "And you shall make a table of acacia wood; two cubits shall be its length, a cubit its breadth, and a cubit and a half its height. [24] You shall overlay it with pure gold, and make a molding of gold around it. [25] And you shall make around it a frame a handbreadth wide, and a molding of gold around the frame. [26] And you shall make for it four rings of gold, and fasten the rings to the four corners at its four legs. [27] Close to the frame the rings shall lie, as holders for the poles to carry the table. [28] You shall make the poles of acacia wood, and overlay them with gold, and the table shall be carried with these. [29] And you shall make

its plates and dishes for incense, and its flagons and bowls with which to pour libations; of pure gold you shall make them. [30] And you shall set the bread of the Presence on the table before me always.

31 "And you shall make a lampstand of pure gold. The base and the shaft of the lampstand shall be made of hammered work; its cups, its capitals, and its flowers shall be of one piece with it; [32] and there shall be six branches going out of its sides, three branches of the lampstand out of one side of it and three branches of the lampstand out of the other side of it; [33] three cups made like almonds, each with capital and flower, on one branch, and three cups made like almonds, each with capital and flower, on the other branch—so for the six branches going out of the lampstand; [34] and on the lampstand itself four cups made like almonds, with their capitals and flowers, [35] and a capital of one piece with it under each pair of the six branches going out from the lampstand. [36] Their capitals and their branches shall be of one piece with it, the whole of it one piece of hammered work of pure gold. [37] And you shall make the seven lamps for it; and the lamps shall be set up so as to give light upon the space in front of it. [38] Its snuffers and their trays shall be of pure gold. [39] Of a talent of pure gold shall it be made, with all these utensils. [40] And see that you make them after the pattern for them, which is being shown you on the mountain.

26 "Moreover you shall make the tabernacle with ten curtains

---

throne (1 Chr.28.2; Ps.132.7), it was regarded as the place where the LORD meets the priestly representative of the people (v. 22). **18–20:** In antiquity cherubim (see Gen.3.24 n.) were adornments of a throne. **23–30:** The table for the holy bread and the sacred vessels (1 Kg.7.48). **30:** The *bread of the Presence* or "holy bread" (1 Sam.21.4,6) was bread placed before God as a sacrificial offering (Num.4.7; Lev.24.5–9; 1 Chr.9.32; Mt.12.4). **31–40:** The seven-branched golden candlestick was to illumine the interior of the holy place (30.7–8; 1 Kg.7.49). **40:** Ancients believed that earthly temples and their cultic equipment were made according to the *pattern* or prototype of heavenly models (v. 9; 26.30; 27.8).

26.1–37: The pattern of the tabernacle. This account blends the ancient tradition of the tent of meeting (33.7–11; Num.11.16–17,24–30) and the later view of the structure and adornments of Solomon's temple (1 Kg. ch. 6; Ezek. chs. 40–43). Hence it is called "the tabernacle of the tent of meeting" (39.32; 40.6,29). **1–6:** The interior was to consist of ten richly decorated cur-

of fine twined linen and blue and purple and scarlet stuff; with cherubim skilfully worked shall you make them. [2] The length of each curtain shall be twenty-eight cubits, and the breadth of each curtain four cubits; all the curtains shall have one measure. [3] Five curtains shall be coupled to one another; and the other five curtains shall be coupled to one another. [4] And you shall make loops of blue on the edge of the outmost curtain in the first set; and likewise you shall make loops on the edge of the outmost curtain in the second set. [5] Fifty loops you shall make on the one curtain, and fifty loops you shall make on the edge of the curtain that is in the second set; the loops shall be opposite one another. [6] And you shall make fifty clasps of gold, and couple the curtains one to the other with the clasps, that the tabernacle may be one whole.

7 "You shall also make curtains of goats' hair for a tent over the tabernacle; eleven curtains shall you make. [8] The length of each curtain shall be thirty cubits, and the breadth of each curtain four cubits; the eleven curtains shall have the same measure. [9] And you shall couple five curtains by themselves, and six curtains by themselves, and the sixth curtain you shall double over at the front of the tent. [10] And you shall make fifty loops on the edge of the curtain that is outmost in one set, and fifty loops on the edge of the curtain which is outmost in the second set.

11 "And you shall make fifty clasps of bronze, and put the clasps into the loops, and couple the tent together that it may be one whole. [12] And the part that remains of the curtains of the tent, the half curtain that remains, shall hang over the back of the tabernacle. [13] And the cubit on the one side, and the cubit on the other side, of what remains in the length of the curtains of the tent shall hang over the sides of the tabernacle, on this side and that side, to cover it. [14] And you shall make for the tent a covering of tanned rams' skins and goatskins.

15 "And you shall make upright frames for the tabernacle of acacia wood. [16] Ten cubits shall be the length of a frame, and a cubit and a half the breadth of each frame. [17] There shall be two tenons in each frame, for fitting together; so shall you do for all the frames of the tabernacle. [18] You shall make the frames for the tabernacle: twenty frames for the south side; [19] and forty bases of silver you shall make under the twenty frames, two bases under one frame for its two tenons, and two bases under another frame for its two tenons; [20] and for the second side of the tabernacle, on the north side twenty frames, [21] and their forty bases of silver, two bases under one frame, and two bases under another frame; [22] and for the rear of the tabernacle westward you shall make six frames. [23] And you shall make two frames for corners of the tabernacle in the rear; [24] they shall be separate beneath, but joined at the top, at the first ring; thus shall it be with both of them; they shall form the two corners. [25] And there shall be eight frames, with their bases of silver, sixteen bases; two bases under one frame, and two bases under another frame.

26 "And you shall make bars of acacia wood, five for the frames of the one side of the tabernacle, [27] and five bars for the frames of the other side of the tabernacle, and five bars for the frames of the side of the tabernacle at the rear westward. [28] The middle bar, halfway up the frames, shall pass

---

tains (compare 1 Kg.6.29). **7–14:** The oldest phase of the priestly tradition recalls the ancient tent made of goat's hair (v. 7) and reddened ram's skins (v. 14), like the ancient, Arabic red-leather shrines which were also supported on desert acacia wood. The ancient tradition concerning the tent is combined with the design of Solomon's temple, with the result that the tent is conceived as a covering for the tabernacle, i.e. *a tent over the tabernacle* (v. 7; 39.33; 40.19). **15–30:** The wooden framework is about 45 × 15 × 15 ft (1 Kg.6.2).

through from end to end. 29 You shall overlay the frames with gold, and shall make their rings of gold for holders for the bars; and you shall overlay the bars with gold. 30 And you shall erect the tabernacle according to the plan for it which has been shown you on the mountain.

31 "And you shall make a veil of blue and purple and scarlet stuff and fine twined linen; in skilled work shall it be made, with cherubim; 32 and you shall hang it upon four pillars of acacia overlaid with gold, with hooks of gold, upon four bases of silver. 33 And you shall hang the veil from the clasps, and bring the ark of the testimony in thither within the veil; and the veil shall separate for you the holy place from the most holy. 34 You shall put the mercy seat upon the ark of the testimony in the most holy place. 35 And you shall set the table outside the veil, and the lampstand on the south side of the tabernacle opposite the table; and you shall put the table on the north side.

36 "And you shall make a screen for the door of the tent, of blue and purple and scarlet stuff and fine twined linen, embroidered with needlework. 37 And you shall make for the screen five pillars of acacia, and overlay them with gold; their hooks shall be of gold, and you shall cast five bases of bronze for them.

27 "You shall make the altar of acacia wood, five cubits long and five cubits broad; the altar shall be square, and its height shall be three cubits. 2 And you shall make horns for it on its four corners; its horns shall be of one piece with it, and you shall overlay it with bronze. 3 You shall make pots for it to receive its ashes, and shovels and basins and forks and fire-pans; all its utensils you shall make of bronze. 4 You shall also make for it a grating, a network of bronze; and upon the net you shall make four bronze rings at its four corners. 5 And you shall set it under the ledge of the altar so that the net shall extend half-way down the altar. 6 And you shall make poles for the altar, poles of acacia wood, and overlay them with bronze; 7 and the poles shall be put through the rings, so that the poles shall be upon the two sides of the altar, when it is carried. 8 You shall make it hollow, with boards; as it has been shown you on the mountain, so shall it be made.

9 "You shall make the court of the tabernacle. On the south side the court shall have hangings of fine twined linen a hundred cubits long for one side; 10 their pillars shall be twenty and their bases twenty, of bronze, but the hooks of the pillars and their fillets shall be of silver. 11 And likewise for its length on the north side there shall be hangings a hundred cubits long, their pillars twenty and their bases twenty, of bronze, but the hooks of the pillars and their fillets shall be of silver. 12 And for the breadth of the court on the west side there shall be hangings for fifty cubits, with ten pillars and ten bases. 13 The breadth of the court on the front to the east shall be fifty cubits. 14 The hangings for the one side of the gate shall be fifteen cubits, with three pillars and three bases. 15 On the other side the hangings shall be fifteen cubits, with three pillars and three bases. 16 For the gate of the court there shall be a screen twenty cubits long, of blue and purple and scarlet stuff and fine twined linen, embroidered with needlework; it shall have four pillars and with them four bases. 17 All the pillars around the court shall be filleted with silver; their hooks shall be of

---

31–34: The *most holy place* (holy of holies) was to be separated from the *holy place* (sanctuary) by a rich veil, as in Solomon's temple.

27.1–21: The altar and the court. From the tabernacle, the writer turns to the surrounding sacred area. **1–8:** The central object in the court was the altar of burnt offering, where the main sacrificial services took place. In comparison with the crude altar of 20.25, this altar, overlaid with bronze (1 Kg.8.64), indicates a considerable amount of Canaanite influence. **9–19:** *The court of the tabernacle* was a sacred enclosure (150 × 75 feet), a common feature of

silver, and their bases of bronze. ¹⁸ The length of the court shall be a hundred cubits, the breadth fifty, and the height five cubits, with hangings of fine twined linen and bases of bronze. ¹⁹ All the utensils of the tabernacle for every use, and all its pegs and all the pegs of the court, shall be of bronze.

20 "And you shall command the people of Israel that they bring to you pure beaten olive oil for the light, that a lamp may be set up to burn continually. ²¹ In the tent of meeting, outside the veil which is before the testimony, Aaron and his sons shall tend it from evening to morning before the LORD. It shall be a statute for ever to be observed throughout their generations by the people of Israel.

28 "Then bring near to you Aaron your brother, and his sons with him, from among the people of Israel, to serve me as priests—Aaron and Aaron's sons, Nadab and Abi'hu, Elea'zar and Ith'amar. ² And you shall make holy garments for Aaron your brother, for glory and for beauty. ³ And you shall speak to all who have ability, whom I have endowed with an able mind, that they make Aaron's garments to consecrate him for my priesthood. ⁴ These are the garments which they shall make: a breastpiece, an ephod, a robe, a coat of checker work, a turban, and a girdle; they shall make holy garments for Aaron your brother and his sons to serve me as priests.

5 "They shall receive gold, blue and purple and scarlet stuff, and fine twined linen. ⁶ And they shall make the ephod of gold, of blue and purple and scarlet stuff, and of fine twined linen, skilfully worked. ⁷ It shall have two shoulder-pieces attached to its two edges, that it may be joined together. ⁸ And the skilfully woven band upon it, to gird it on, shall be of the same workmanship and materials, of gold, blue and purple and scarlet stuff, and fine twined linen. ⁹ And you shall take two onyx stones, and engrave on them the names of the sons of Israel, ¹⁰ six of their names on the one stone, and the names of the remaining six on the other stone, in the order of their birth. ¹¹ As a jeweler engraves signets, so shall you engrave the two stones with the names of the sons of Israel; you shall enclose them in settings of gold filigree. ¹² And you shall set the two stones upon the shoulder-pieces of the ephod, as stones of remembrance for the sons of Israel; and Aaron shall bear their names before the LORD upon his two shoulders for remembrance. ¹³ And you shall make settings of gold filigree, ¹⁴ and two chains of pure gold, twisted like cords; and you shall attach the corded chains to the settings.

15 "And you shall make a breastpiece of judgment, in skilled work; like the work of the ephod you shall make it; of gold, blue and purple and scarlet stuff, and fine twined linen shall you make it. ¹⁶ It shall be square and double, a span its length and a span its breadth. ¹⁷ And you shall set in it four rows of stones. A row of sardius, topaz, and carbuncle shall be the first row; ¹⁸ and the second row an emerald,

ancient temple plans. **20–21:** The lamp (25.31–37; Lev.24.1–3) was to burn continually as a sign of God's presence. *The testimony*, see 16.33–34 n.

28.1–43: Priestly vestments. 1–5: Early in Israelite history the tribe of Levi became a priestly class (Gen.49.5–7; Num.1.47–54). Apparently Levites first exercised their priestly office at Kadesh (Dt.33.8–10). Those of Aaron's line (Ex.6.14–25; compare Num.8.5–26; Dt.18.1 n.) are here designated to officiate at the altar of the central shrine (i.e. the tabernacle and later the Jerusalem temple). **6–12:** The *ephod* harks back to early cultic practice at the central sanctuary of Shiloh (1 Sam.2.18–19,28; 14.3). Sometimes scorned as an idolatrous object, perhaps a garment for an idol (Jg.8.27; 17.5; 18.4), it is usually thought of as a linen apron worn by a priest (2 Sam.6.14–15) and used in connection with the sacred lot (see v. 30). The engraved stones on each shoulder-piece (vv. 9–12) symbolize the priest's intercessory function on behalf of the twelve tribes (v. 29). **15–30:** Hanging from the shoulder-pieces was *the breastpiece of judgment*, a pouch which contained the sacred lots, *Urim and Thummim* (v. 30). The priestly

a sapphire, and a diamond; [19] and the third row a jacinth, an agate, and an amethyst; [20] and the fourth row a beryl, an onyx, and a jasper; they shall be set in gold filigree. [21] There shall be twelve stones with their names according to the names of the sons of Israel; they shall be like signets, each engraved with its name, for the twelve tribes. [22] And you shall make for the breastpiece twisted chains like cords, of pure gold; [23] and you shall make for the breastpiece two rings of gold, and put the two rings on the two edges of the breastpiece. [24] And you shall put the two cords of gold in the two rings at the edges of the breastpiece; [25] the two ends of the two cords you shall attach to the two settings of filigree, and so attach it in front to the shoulder-pieces of the ephod. [26] And you shall make two rings of gold, and put them at the two ends of the breastpiece, on its inside edge next to the ephod. [27] And you shall make two rings of gold, and attach them in front to the lower part of the two shoulder-pieces of the ephod, at its joining above the skilfully woven band of the ephod. [28] And they shall bind the breastpiece by its rings to the rings of the ephod with a lace of blue, that it may lie upon the skilfully woven band of the ephod, and that the breastpiece shall not come loose from the ephod. [29] So Aaron shall bear the names of the sons of Israel in the breastpiece of judgment upon his heart, when he goes into the holy place, to bring them to continual remembrance before the LORD. [30] And in the breastpiece of judgment you shall put the Urim and the Thummim, and they shall be upon Aaron's heart, when he goes in before the LORD; thus Aaron shall bear the judgment of the people of Israel upon his heart before the LORD continually.

[31] "And you shall make the robe of the ephod all of blue. [32] It shall have in it an opening for the head, with a woven binding around the opening, like the opening in a garment,*p* that it may not be torn. [33] On its skirts you shall make pomegranates of blue and purple and scarlet stuff, around its skirts, with bells of gold between them, [34] a golden bell and a pomegranate, a golden bell and a pomegranate, round about on the skirts of the robe. [35] And it shall be upon Aaron when he ministers, and its sound shall be heard when he goes into the holy place before the LORD, and when he comes out, lest he die.

[36] "And you shall make a plate of pure gold, and engrave on it, like the engraving of a signet, 'Holy to the LORD.' [37] And you shall fasten it on the turban by a lace of blue; it shall be on the front of the turban. [38] It shall be upon Aaron's forehead, and Aaron shall take upon himself any guilt incurred in the holy offering which the people of Israel hallow as their holy gifts; it shall always be upon his forehead, that they may be accepted before the LORD.

[39] "And you shall weave the coat in checker work of fine linen, and you shall make a turban of fine linen, and you shall make a girdle embroidered with needlework.

[40] "And for Aaron's sons you shall make coats and girdles and caps; you shall make them for glory and beauty. [41] And you shall put them upon Aaron your brother, and upon his sons with him, and shall anoint them and ordain them and consecrate them, that they may serve me as priests. [42] And you shall make for them linen breeches to cover their naked flesh; from the loins to the thighs they shall reach; [43] and they shall be upon Aaron, and

p The Hebrew word is of uncertain meaning

lot was used to obtain an oracular decision (Lev.8.8; Num.27.21; Dt.33.8; 1 Sam.14.41–42; 23.6–13). **31–34:** A short garment, the blue *robe of the ephod*, was worn under the ephod. The bells were once thought to protect the priest from demonic attack, *lest he die* when he enters the holy place (v. 35). **36–38:** The head piece, *a plate of pure gold* fastened to a turban, symbolizes the regal splendor of the priest (Ezek.21.26; Zech.3.5). **39:** Underneath the blue robe the priest wore a coat or long tunic with sleeves, gathered at the waist with a sash.

upon his sons, when they go into the tent of meeting, or when they come near the altar to minister in the holy place; lest they bring guilt upon themselves and die. This shall be a perpetual statute for him and for his descendants after him.

29 "Now this is what you shall do to them to consecrate them, that they may serve me as priests. Take one young bull and two rams without blemish, [2] and unleavened bread, unleavened cakes mixed with oil, and unleavened wafers spread with oil. You shall make them of fine wheat flour. [3] And you shall put them in one basket and bring them in the basket, and bring the bull and the two rams. [4] You shall bring Aaron and his sons to the door of the tent of meeting, and wash them with water. [5] And you shall take the garments, and put on Aaron the coat and the robe of the ephod, and the ephod, and the breastpiece, and gird him with the skilfully woven band of the ephod; [6] and you shall set the turban on his head, and put the holy crown upon the turban. [7] And you shall take the anointing oil, and pour it on his head and anoint him. [8] Then you shall bring his sons, and put coats on them, [9] and you shall gird them with girdles*q* and bind caps on them; and the priesthood shall be theirs by a perpetual statute. Thus you shall ordain Aaron and his sons.

10 "Then you shall bring the bull before the tent of meeting. Aaron and his sons shall lay their hands upon the head of the bull, [11] and you shall kill the bull before the LORD, at the door of the tent of meeting, [12] and shall take part of the blood of the bull and put it upon the horns of the altar with your finger, and the rest of*r* the blood you shall pour out at the base of the altar. [13] And you shall take all the fat that covers the entrails, and the appendage of the liver, and the two kidneys with the fat that is on them, and burn them upon the altar. [14] But the flesh of the bull, and its skin, and its dung, you shall burn with fire outside the camp; it is a sin offering.

15 "Then you shall take one of the rams, and Aaron and his sons shall lay their hands upon the head of the ram, [16] and you shall slaughter the ram, and shall take its blood and throw it against the altar round about. [17] Then you shall cut the ram into pieces, and wash its entrails and its legs, and put them with its pieces and its head, [18] and burn the whole ram upon the altar; it is a burnt offering to the LORD; it is a pleasing odor, an offering by fire to the LORD.

19 "You shall take the other ram; and Aaron and his sons shall lay their hands upon the head of the ram, [20] and you shall kill the ram, and take part of its blood and put it upon the tip of the right ear of Aaron and upon the tips of the right ears of his sons, and upon the thumbs of their right hands, and upon the great toes of their right feet, and throw the rest of the blood against the altar round about. [21] Then you shall take part of the blood that is on the altar, and of the anointing oil, and sprinkle it upon Aaron and his garments, and upon his sons and his sons' garments with him; and he and his gar-

q Gk: Heb *girdles, Aaron and his sons*   *r* Heb *all*

29.1–46: The service for the ordination of the priests. See Lev. ch. 8 where these directions are carried out. **1–9:** The anointing of the high priest (Lev.16.32; Ps.133.2) follows the ancient rite of anointing the king's head with oil, thus making him "the LORD's anointed" (1 Sam.24.6; Ps.2.2). Priestly tradition traces the line of the high priesthood from Aaron, to whom the priestly office belongs *by a perpetual statute* (v. 9b). **10–14:** The sin offering for the priests (Lev.4.1–12). **10:** The laying on of hands signifies identification with the sacrificial victim. **12:** The horns of the altar (27.2) were its most sacred parts (1 Kg.1.50; Am.3.14). On the efficacy of blood for the expiation of sin, see Lev.1.5 n. **15–18:** One of the rams (v. 1), as distinguished from the ram of ordination (v. 22), was for *burnt offering* (Lev. ch. 1). *Pleasing odor*, see Lev. 1.9 n. **19–34:** The installation sacrifice was essentially a peace offering (Lev. ch. 3). **20:** Touching the blood upon the ears, hands, and feet consecrates the whole person for the office. **24:** Putting

ments shall be holy, and his sons and his sons' garments with him.

22 "You shall also take the fat of the ram, and the fat tail, and the fat that covers the entrails, and the appendage of the liver, and the two kidneys with the fat that is on them, and the right thigh (for it is a ram of ordination), 23 and one loaf of bread, and one cake of bread with oil, and one wafer, out of the basket of unleavened bread that is before the LORD; 24 and you shall put all these in the hands of Aaron and in the hands of his sons, and wave them for a wave offering before the LORD. 25 Then you shall take them from their hands, and burn them on the altar in addition to the burnt offering, as a pleasing odor before the LORD; it is an offering by fire to the LORD.

26 "And you shall take the breast of the ram of Aaron's ordination and wave it for a wave offering before the LORD; and it shall be your portion. 27 And you shall consecrate the breast of the wave offering, and the thigh of the priests' portion, which is waved, and which is offered from the ram of ordination, since it is for Aaron and for his sons. 28 It shall be for Aaron and his sons as a perpetual due from the people of Israel, for it is the priests' portion to be offered by the people of Israel from their peace offerings; it is their offering to the LORD.

29 "The holy garments of Aaron shall be for his sons after him, to be anointed in them and ordained in them. 30 The son who is priest in his place shall wear them seven days, when he comes into the tent of meeting to minister in the holy place.

31 "You shall take the ram of ordination, and boil its flesh in a holy place; 32 and Aaron and his sons shall eat the flesh of the ram and the bread that is in the basket, at the door of the tent of meeting. 33 They shall eat those things with which atonement was made, to ordain and consecrate them, but an outsider shall not eat of them, because they are holy. 34 And if any of the flesh for the ordination, or of the bread, remain until the morning, then you shall burn the remainder with fire; it shall not be eaten, because it is holy.

35 "Thus you shall do to Aaron and to his sons, according to all that I have commanded you; through seven days shall you ordain them, 36 and every day you shall offer a bull as a sin offering for atonement. Also you shall offer a sin offering for the altar, when you make atonement for it, and shall anoint it, to consecrate it. 37 Seven days you shall make atonement for the altar, and consecrate it, and the altar shall be most holy; whatever touches the altar shall become holy.

38 "Now this is what you shall offer upon the altar: two lambs a year old day by day continually. 39 One lamb you shall offer in the morning, and the other lamb you shall offer in the evening; 40 and with the first lamb a tenth measure of fine flour mingled with a fourth of a hin of beaten oil, and a fourth of a hin of wine for a libation. 41 And the other lamb you shall offer in the evening, and shall offer with it a cereal offering and its libation, as in the morning, for a pleasing odor, an offering by fire to the LORD. 42 It shall be a continual burnt offering through-

---

these things in the hands of the priests signified that they were authorized to receive their portions of the offerings (1 Sam.2.12–17). To "fill the hands" (literal Hebrew) was an old expression for investment with priestly prerogatives (Jg.17.5; 1 Kg.13.33). The *wave offering* (vv. 26–28; Lev.7.29–36) refers to the act of moving the sacrifice toward and away from the altar, to symbolize presenting the gift to God and receiving it back as a portion. **31–34:** Further instructions for the ordination peace offering. *An outsider*, i.e. a layman. **35–37:** The seven day ordination ceremony. Owing to the efficacy of blood (v. 12), the sin offering is for *atonement*, i.e. it produces a "covering" for sin and sanctifies the priest. The offering is also said to make atonement for the altar, i.e. to cleanse and consecrate it with blood (Ezek.43.18–27). In a deeper sense atonement actualizes divine forgiveness and reconciliation (32.30–32). **38–42:** The daily burnt offering, compare Num.28.3–8; Ezek.46.13–15. *Tenth measure*, a tenth of an ephah, see Num.

out your generations at the door of the tent of meeting before the LORD, where I will meet with you, to speak there to you. ⁴³ There I will meet with the people of Israel, and it shall be sanctified by my glory; ⁴⁴ I will consecrate the tent of meeting and the altar; Aaron also and his sons I will consecrate, to serve me as priests. ⁴⁵ And I will dwell among the people of Israel, and will be their God. ⁴⁶ And they shall know that I am the LORD their God, who brought them forth out of the land of Egypt that I might dwell among them; I am the LORD their God.

30 "You shall make an altar to burn incense upon; of acacia wood shall you make it. ² A cubit shall be its length, and a cubit its breadth; it shall be square, and two cubits shall be its height; its horns shall be of one piece with it. ³ And you shall overlay it with pure gold, its top and its sides round about and its horns; and you shall make for it a molding of gold round about. ⁴ And two golden rings shall you make for it; under its molding on two opposite sides of it shall you make them, and they shall be holders for poles with which to carry it. ⁵ You shall make the poles of acacia wood, and overlay them with gold. ⁶ And you shall put it before the veil that is by the ark of the testimony, before the mercy seat that is over the testimony, where I will meet with you. ⁷ And Aaron shall burn fragrant incense on it; every morning when he dresses the lamps he shall burn it, ⁸ and when Aaron sets up the lamps in the evening, he shall burn it, a per-

petual incense before the LORD throughout your generations. ⁹ You shall offer no unholy incense thereon, nor burnt offering, nor cereal offering; and you shall pour no libation thereon. ¹⁰ Aaron shall make atonement upon its horns once a year; with the blood of the sin offering of atonement he shall make atonement for it once in the year throughout your generations; it is most holy to the LORD."

11 The LORD said to Moses, ¹² "When you take the census of the people of Israel, then each shall give a ransom for himself to the LORD when you number them, that there be no plague among them when you number them. ¹³ Each who is numbered in the census shall give this: half a shekel according to the shekel of the sanctuary (the shekel is twenty gerahs), half a shekel as an offering to the LORD. ¹⁴ Every one who is numbered in the census, from twenty years old and upward, shall give the LORD's offering. ¹⁵ The rich shall not give more, and the poor shall not give less, than the half shekel, when you give the LORD's offering to make atonement for yourselves. ¹⁶ And you shall take the atonement money from the people of Israel, and shall appoint it for the service of the tent of meeting; that it may bring the people of Israel to remembrance before the LORD, so as to make atonement for yourselves."

17 The LORD said to Moses, ¹⁸ "You shall also make a laver of bronze, with its base of bronze, for washing. And you shall put it between the tent of meeting and the altar, and you shall

15.2–10. **43–46:** God's meeting with his people. **43:** *It*, the door of the tent of meeting (v. 42). *Glory*, see 16.7 n. **45:** See 6.7 n.; 25.8; 40.34.

30.1–31.18: Other priestly matters. 1–10: The burning of incense was an ancient cultic practice (Is.1.13), probably taken over from the Canaanites. **10:** On atonement for the altar see 29.36–37. *Once in the year*, i.e. on the day of atonement (Lev. ch. 16). **11–16:** The tax for the support of the sanctuary. **11–12:** The census, reported in Num. ch. 1, was originally for military purposes. Fearing that God's wrath would be manifested against a census (2 Sam. ch. 24), the people paid a fee (compare 2 Chr.24.6,9; Mt.17.24–27) as a *ransom* or *atonement* (v. 16). **13:** *The shekel of the sanctuary* (Lev.5.15; 27.25; Num.3.47; 18.16; Ezek.45.12) based on the older Phoenician or Hebrew measurement, was heavier than the Babylonian shekel used in post-exilic times. Here it is explained that the sanctuary tax is to be paid in the older weight. **17–21:** The laver of bronze (1 Kg.7.38) was for ritual ablutions. **34–38:** The formula

put water in it, [19] with which Aaron and his sons shall wash their hands and their feet. [20] When they go into the tent of meeting, or when they come near the altar to minister, to burn an offering by fire to the LORD, they shall wash with water, lest they die. [21] They shall wash their hands and their feet, lest they die: it shall be a statute for ever to them, even to him and to his descendants throughout their generations."

22 Moreover, the LORD said to Moses, [23] "Take the finest spices: of liquid myrrh five hundred shekels, and of sweet-smelling cinnamon half as much, that is, two hundred and fifty, and of aromatic cane two hundred and fifty, [24] and of cassia five hundred, according to the shekel of the sanctuary, and of olive oil a hin; [25] and you shall make of these a sacred anointing oil blended as by the perfumer; a holy anointing oil it shall be. [26] And you shall anoint with it the tent of meeting and the ark of the testimony, [27] and the table and all its utensils, and the lampstand and its utensils, and the altar of incense, [28] and the altar of burnt offering with all its utensils and the laver and its base; [29] you shall consecrate them, that they may be most holy; whatever touches them will become holy. [30] And you shall anoint Aaron and his sons, and consecrate them, that they may serve me as priests. [31] And you shall say to the people of Israel, 'This shall be my holy anointing oil throughout your generations. [32] It shall not be poured upon the bodies of ordinary men, and you shall make no other like it in composition; it is holy, and it shall be holy to you. [33] Whoever compounds any like it or whoever puts any of it on an outsider shall be cut off from his people.' "

34 And the LORD said to Moses, "Take sweet spices, stacte, and onycha, and galbanum, sweet spices with pure frankincense (of each shall there be an equal part), [35] and make an incense blended as by the perfumer, seasoned with salt, pure and holy; [36] and you shall beat some of it very small, and put part of it before the testimony in the tent of meeting where I shall meet with you; it shall be for you most holy. [37] And the incense which you shall make according to its composition, you shall not make for yourselves; it shall be for you holy to the LORD. [38] Whoever makes any like it to use as perfume shall be cut off from his people."

31 The LORD said to Moses, [2] "See, I have called by name Bez'alel the son of Uri, son of Hur, of the tribe of Judah: [3] and I have filled him with the Spirit of God, with ability and intelligence, with knowledge and all craftsmanship, [4] to devise artistic designs, to work in gold, silver, and bronze, [5] in cutting stones for setting, and in carving wood, for work in every craft. [6] And behold, I have appointed with him Oho'liab, the son of Ahis'amach, of the tribe of Dan; and I have given to all able men ability, that they may make all that I have commanded you: [7] the tent of meeting, and the ark of the testimony, and the mercy seat that is thereon, and all the furnishings of the tent, [8] the table and its utensils, and the pure lampstand with all its utensils, and the altar of incense, [9] and the altar of burnt offering with all its utensils, and the laver and its base, [10] and the finely worked garments, the holy garments for Aaron the priest and the garments of his sons, for their service as priests, [11] and the anointing oil and the fragrant incense for the holy place. According to all that I have commanded you they shall do."

12 And the LORD said to Moses, [13] "Say to the people of Israel, 'You shall keep my sabbaths, for this is a sign between me and you throughout

for the incense, as for the holy oil (vv. 22–25), was a priestly secret. *Stacte*, an oil of myrrh. *Onycha*, a spice from a mollusk found in the Red Sea. *Galbanum*, an aromatic resin from Asiatic plants. *Frankincense*, a fragment gum resin from certain trees. **31.1–11:** The appointment of craftsmen. *Bezalel*, 1 Chr.2.18–20. *Oholiab* is otherwise unknown. **12–17:** The sabbath,

---

your generations, that you may know that I, the LORD, sanctify you. 14 You shall keep the sabbath, because it is holy for you; every one who profanes it shall be put to death; whoever does any work on it, that soul shall be cut off from among his people. 15 Six days shall work be done, but the seventh day is a sabbath of solemn rest, holy to the LORD; whoever does any work on the sabbath day shall be put to death. 16 Therefore the people of Israel shall keep the sabbath, observing the sabbath throughout their generations, as a perpetual covenant. 17 It is a sign for ever between me and the people of Israel that in six days the LORD made heaven and earth, and on the seventh day he rested, and was refreshed.' "

18 And he gave to Moses, when he had made an end of speaking with him upon Mount Sinai, the two tables of the testimony, tables of stone, written with the finger of God.

32 When the people saw that Moses delayed to come down from the mountain, the people gathered themselves together to Aaron, and said to him, "Up, make us gods, who shall go before us; as for this Moses, the man who brought us up out of the land of Egypt, we do not know what has become of him." 2 And Aaron said to them, "Take off the rings of gold which are in the ears of your wives, your sons, and your daughters, and bring them to me." 3 So all the people took off the rings of gold which were in their ears, and brought them to Aaron. 4 And he received the gold at their hand, and fashioned it with a graving tool, and made a molten calf; and they said, "These are your gods, O Israel, who brought you up out of the land of Egypt!" 5 When Aaron saw this, he built an altar before it; and Aaron made proclamation and said, "Tomorrow shall be a feast to the LORD." 6 And they rose up early on the morrow, and offered burnt offerings and brought peace offerings; and the people sat down to eat and drink, and rose up to play.

7 And the LORD said to Moses, "Go down; for your people, whom you brought up out of the land of Egypt, have corrupted themselves; 8 they have turned aside quickly out of the way which I commanded them; they have made for themselves a molten calf, and have worshiped it and sacrificed to it, and said, 'These are your gods, O Israel, who brought you up out of the land of Egypt!' " 9 And the LORD said to Moses, "I have seen this people, and behold, it is a stiff-necked people; 10 now therefore let me alone, that my wrath may burn hot against them and I may consume them; but of you I will make a great nation."

11 But Moses besought the LORD his God, and said, "O LORD, why does thy wrath burn hot against thy people, whom thou hast brought forth out of the land of Egypt with great power and with a mighty hand? 12 Why should the Egyptians say, 'With evil intent did he bring them forth, to slay them in the mountains, and to consume them from the face of the earth'? Turn from thy fierce wrath, and repent of this evil against thy people. 13 Remember Abraham, Isaac, and Israel,

---

anticipated by priestly tradition in 16.22–30, is here formally instituted at Sinai. **18:** A transitional verse which resumes the narrative from 24.18. The inserted block of priestly tradition (chs. 25–31) was supposedly delivered to Moses on Mount Sinai.

32.1–35: The breaking of the covenant. During Moses' absence the rebellious people chose Aaron as their leader and worshiped a golden bull. **1:** Moses stayed on the mountain top forty days and forty nights, a round number for an indefinitely long time (1 Kg.19.8; Mt.4.2). *Gods who shall go before us,* i.e visible symbols of the divine presence as in pagan idolatry (see 20.4–6 n.). **2–3:** On the golden earrings, see Gen.35.4 n. The *calf,* or young bull, was a symbol of fertility in the nature-religions of the ancient Near East (compare 1 Kg.12.28; Hos.8.5). **6:** The eating and drinking accompanied *the feast to the LORD,* a dedication of the new cultic symbol (2 Sam.6.17–19). **7–14:** Moses' first intercession (Num.14.13–19). **14:** *The*

thy servants, to whom thou didst swear by thine own self, and didst say to them, 'I will multiply your descendants as the stars of heaven, and all this land that I have promised I will give to your descendants, and they shall inherit it for ever.' " 14 And the LORD repented of the evil which he thought to do to his people.

15 And Moses turned, and went down from the mountain with the two tables of the testimony in his hands, tables that were written on both sides; on the one side and on the other were they written. 16 And the tables were the work of God, and the writing was the writing of God, graven upon the tables. 17 When Joshua heard the noise of the people as they shouted, he said to Moses, "There is a noise of war in the camp." 18 But he said, "It is not the sound of shouting for victory, or the sound of the cry of defeat, but the sound of singing that I hear." 19 And as soon as he came near the camp and saw the calf and the dancing, Moses' anger burned hot, and he threw the tables out of his hands and broke them at the foot of the mountain. 20 And he took the calf which they had made, and burnt it with fire, and ground it to powder, and scattered it upon the water, and made the people of Israel drink it.

21 And Moses said to Aaron, "What did this people do to you that you have brought a great sin upon them?" 22 And Aaron said, "Let not the anger of my lord burn hot; you know the people, that they are set on evil. 23 For they said to me, 'Make us gods, who shall go before us; as for this Moses, the man who brought us up out of the land of Egypt, we do not know what has become of him.' 24 And I said to them, 'Let any who have gold take it off'; so they gave it to me, and I threw it into the fire, and there came out this calf."

25 And when Moses saw that the people had broken loose (for Aaron had let them break loose, to their shame among their enemies), 26 then Moses stood in the gate of the camp, and said, "Who is on the LORD's side? Come to me." And all the sons of Levi gathered themselves together to him. 27 And he said to them, "Thus says the LORD God of Israel, 'Put every man his sword on his side, and go to and fro from gate to gate throughout the camp, and slay every man his brother, and every man his companion, and every man his neighbor.' " 28 And the sons of Levi did according to the word of Moses; and there fell of the people that day about three thousand men. 29 And Moses said, "Today you have ordained yourselves[s] for the service of the LORD, each one at the cost of his son and of his brother, that he may bestow a blessing upon you this day."

30 On the morrow Moses said to the people, "You have sinned a great sin. And now I will go up to the LORD; perhaps I can make atonement for your sin." 31 So Moses returned to the LORD and said, "Alas, this people have sinned a great sin; they have made for themselves gods of gold. 32 But now, if thou wilt forgive their sin—and if not,

s Gk Vg See Tg: Heb *ordain yourselves*

LORD *repented*, i.e. revised his course of action–not capriciously but in a manner consistent with his steadfast purpose (Am.7.3,6). **15:** *Tables of the testimony*, see 25.16 n. **19:** The breaking of the tables symbolized that the covenant relationship had been broken. **20:** Moses subjected the people to a trial by ordeal (Num.5.16–28). Those who suffered ill effects from drinking the water and pulverized metal were regarded as guilty and fell in a plague (v. 35). **21–24:** The rebuke of Aaron (see Num. ch. 12) stands in contrast to his priestly prestige and intercessory role as described in chs. 25–31. **24:** Aaron tries to disclaim responsibility by saying that he did not make the calf: it emerged from the fire by itself. **25–29:** A separate tradition about how the Levites (see 28.1–5 n.) were consecrated to the priesthood (compare Num.25.10–13). Instead of being consecrated by a ritual ceremony (ch. 29), the Levites *ordained themselves* by their *zeal*, that is, their passionate loyalty to the LORD (1 Kg.19.10; 2 Kg.10.16) despite social or family bonds. **30–35:** Moses' second intercession. **30:** *Make atonement*, i.e. obtain forgiveness

blot me, I pray thee, out of thy book which thou hast written." [33] But the LORD said to Moses, "Whoever has sinned against me, him will I blot out of my book. [34] But now go, lead the people to the place of which I have spoken to you; behold, my angel shall go before you. Nevertheless, in the day when I visit, I will visit their sin upon them."

35 And the LORD sent a plague upon the people, because they made the calf which Aaron made.

33 The LORD said to Moses, "Depart, go up hence, you and the people whom you have brought up out of the land of Egypt, to the land of which I swore to Abraham, Isaac, and Jacob, saying, 'To your descendants I will give it.' [2] And I will send an angel before you, and I will drive out the Canaanites, the Amorites, the Hittites, the Per'izzites, the Hivites, and the Jeb'usites. [3] Go up to a land flowing with milk and honey; but I will not go up among you, lest I consume you in the way, for you are a stiff-necked people."

4 When the people heard these evil tidings, they mourned; and no man put on his ornaments. [5] For the LORD had said to Moses, "Say to the people of Israel, 'You are a stiff-necked people; if for a single moment I should go up among you, I would consume you.

So now put off your ornaments from you, that I may know what to do with you.' " [6] Therefore the people of Israel stripped themselves of their ornaments, from Mount Horeb onward.

7 Now Moses used to take the tent and pitch it outside the camp, far off from the camp; and he called it the tent of meeting. And every one who sought the LORD would go out to the tent of meeting, which was outside the camp. [8] Whenever Moses went out to the tent, all the people rose up, and every man stood at his tent door, and looked after Moses, until he had gone into the tent. [9] When Moses entered the tent, the pillar of cloud would descend and stand at the door of the tent, and the LORD would speak with Moses. [10] And when all the people saw the pillar of cloud standing at the door of the tent, all the people would rise up and worship, every man at his tent door. [11] Thus the LORD used to speak to Moses face to face, as a man speaks to his friend. When Moses turned again into the camp, his servant Joshua the son of Nun, a young man, did not depart from the tent.

12 Moses said to the LORD, "See, thou sayest to me, 'Bring up this people'; but thou hast not let me know whom thou wilt send with me. Yet thou hast said, 'I know you by name, and you have also found favor in my sight.'

(v. 32). **32:** *Thy book* is the register of the members of the theocratic community (Ps.69.28; Is.4.3; Dan.12.1; Mal.3.16). **34:** On the *angel*, see Gen.16.7 n.; Ex.23.20.

33.1–23: The LORD's guidance. Moses seeks assurance that the LORD will accompany the people, despite their sin. **1–6:** By sending his angel or alter ego (32.34), the LORD will not forsake his people. He will not, however, accompany the sinful people himself, lest his holiness consume them. **4–6:** The people removed their ornaments as a sign of mourning. **7–11:** An old tradition about the tent of meeting. **7:** *The tent* was portable, like ancient Arabic tent-shrines (see 26.7–14 n.). Unlike the priestly tabernacle which was centrally located (25.8; Num.2.2), the tent was pitched *far off from the camp*. Originally the tent was perhaps both a place of tribal assembly and an oracle-place, both ideas being implied in the term *meeting*. However, it was chiefly a tent of revelation to Moses (Num.11.16–17,24–30; 12.1–8; Dt.31.14–15; compare Ex.29.42–46). *Sought the LORD*, i.e. for oracular decisions (18.15–16). **8–9:** While the ark symbolized the nearness and presence of the LORD (see 25.10–22 n.), the tent signified the LORD's distance and transcendence; hence he used to *descend* from time to time to meet with Moses. In priestly tradition the two views are combined by saying that the ark was placed within the tent of testimony (30.36; Num.9.15; 17.7–8). **11:** Moses' mediatorial role (19.9; 20.19) is indicated by the fact that the LORD used to speak to him *face to face, as a man speaks to his friend* (Num.12.7–8; Dt.34.10–12). Here Joshua, rather than Aaron the priest, is the custodian of the tent. **12–16:** Moses' intercession. **14:** *My presence* (literally, "face"), perhaps

[13] Now therefore, I pray thee, if I have found favor in thy sight, show me now thy ways, that I may know thee and find favor in thy sight. Consider too that this nation is thy people." [14] And he said, "My presence will go with you, and I will give you rest." [15] And he said to him, "If thy presence will not go with me, do not carry us up from here. [16] For how shall it be known that I have found favor in thy sight, I and thy people? Is it not in thy going with us, so that we are distinct, I and thy people, from all other people that are upon the face of the earth?"

[17] And the LORD said to Moses, "This very thing that you have spoken I will do; for you have found favor in my sight, and I know you by name." [18] Moses said, "I pray thee, show me thy glory." [19] And he said, "I will make all my goodness pass before you, and will proclaim before you my name 'The LORD'; and I will be gracious to whom I will be gracious, and will show mercy on whom I will show mercy. [20] But," he said, "you cannot see my face; for man shall not see me and live." [21] And the LORD said, "Behold, there is a place by me where you shall stand upon the rock; [22] and while my glory passes by I will put you in a cleft of the rock, and I will cover you with my hand until I have passed by; [23] then I will take away my hand,

and you shall see my back; but my face shall not be seen."

34 The LORD said to Moses, "Cut two tables of stone like the first; and I will write upon the tables the words that were on the first tables, which you broke. [2] Be ready in the morning, and come up in the morning to Mount Sinai, and present yourself there to me on the top of the mountain. [3] No man shall come up with you, and let no man be seen throughout all the mountain; let no flocks or herds feed before that mountain." [4] So Moses cut two tables of stone like the first; and he rose early in the morning and went up on Mount Sinai, as the LORD had commanded him, and took in his hand two tables of stone. [5] And the LORD descended in the cloud and stood with him there, and proclaimed the name of the LORD. [6] The LORD passed before him, and proclaimed, "The LORD, the LORD, a God merciful and gracious, slow to anger, and abounding in steadfast love and faithfulness, [7] keeping steadfast love for thousands, forgiving iniquity and transgression and sin, but who will by no means clear the guilty, visiting the iniquity of the fathers upon the children and the children's children, to the third and the fourth generation." [8] And Moses made haste to bow his head toward the earth, and worshiped.

---

a reference to the ark. Enthroned on the ark, the LORD goes before his people and gives them *rest* (Num.10.33). **16:** Israel is a unique people because it undertakes a special historical pilgrimage with the LORD as leader (Num.23.9). **17–23:** These verses anticipate the theophany of 34.5–9. **18:** Having asked that God show his *ways* (v. 13) or form of historical action, Moses now asks for more: that he show his *glory*, i.e. the visible radiance and majesty of the Godhead (see 16.7 n.). **19:** The proclamation of the divine name, the LORD (Yahweh; see 3.14 n.), was tantamount to a disclosure of the character or being of God (see Gen.32.27 n.). Divine freedom is emphasized; the LORD acts as he wills to act (compare Rom.9.15). His action, however, is not capricious but is the expression of his *goodness* (34.6–7). **22:** On the cave or *cleft of the rock*, see 1 Kg.19.9–18. **23:** Although employing bold anthropomorphisms (the LORD's *hand* and *back*), the story stresses that God remains hidden (v. 20) even when he manifests his presence.

34.1–35: The renewal of the covenant, symbolized by the rewriting of the commandments. **1–4:** The second tables were to contain *the words that were on the first tables* (24.12–14; compare Dt.10.1–5). However, the rewriting of the commandments gives the narrator the opportunity to introduce a cultic set of laws (vv. 12–26). **5–9:** The theophany is anticipated in 33.17–23. **6–7:** Passing by or before Moses (33.22 n.; compare 1 Kg.19.11–12), the LORD disclosed that he is the God of *steadfast love* (see Gen.24.12 n.), though this does not exclude judgment upon sin. This summary, echoed in various places in the Old Testament (Num.14.18; Neh.9.17,31;

⁹ And he said, "If now I have found favor in thy sight, O Lord, let the Lord, I pray thee, go in the midst of us, although it is a stiff-necked people; and pardon our iniquity and our sin, and take us for thy inheritance."

10 And he said, "Behold, I make a covenant. Before all your people I will do marvels, such as have not been wrought in all the earth or in any nation; and all the people among whom you are shall see the work of the LORD; for it is a terrible thing that I will do with you.

11 "Observe what I command you this day. Behold, I will drive out before you the Amorites, the Canaanites, the Hittites, the Per'izzites, the Hivites, and the Jeb'usites. ¹² Take heed to yourself, lest you make a covenant with the inhabitants of the land whither you go, lest it become a snare in the midst of you. ¹³ You shall tear down their altars, and break their pillars, and cut down their Ashe'rim ¹⁴ (for you shall worship no other god, for the LORD, whose name is Jealous, is a jealous God), ¹⁵ lest you make a covenant with the inhabitants of the land, and when they play the harlot after their gods and sacrifice to their gods and one invites you, you eat of his sacrifice, ¹⁶ and you take of their daughters for your sons, and their daughters play the harlot after their gods and make your sons play the harlot after their gods.

17 "You shall make for yourself no molten gods.

18 "The feast of unleavened bread you shall keep. Seven days you shall eat unleavened bread, as I commanded you, at the time appointed in the month Abib; for in the month Abib you came out from Egypt. ¹⁹ All that opens the womb is mine, all your male^x cattle, the firstlings of cow and sheep. ²⁰ The firstling of an ass you shall redeem with a lamb, or if you will not redeem it you shall break its neck. All the first-born of your sons you shall redeem. And none shall appear before me empty.

21 "Six days you shall work, but on the seventh day you shall rest; in plowing time and in harvest you shall rest. ²² And you shall observe the feast of weeks, the first fruits of wheat harvest, and the feast of ingathering at the year's end. ²³ Three times in the year shall all your males appear before the LORD God, the God of Israel. ²⁴ For I will cast out nations before you, and enlarge your borders; neither shall any man desire your land, when you go up to appear before the LORD your God three times in the year.

25 "You shall not offer the blood of my sacrifice with leaven; neither shall the sacrifice of the feast of the passover be left until the morning. ²⁶ The first of the first fruits of your ground you shall bring to the house of the LORD your God. You shall not boil a kid in its mother's milk."

27 And the LORD said to Moses, "Write these words; in accordance with these words I have made a covenant with you and with Israel." ²⁸ And he

x Gk Theodotion Vg Tg: Heb uncertain

Ps.103.8; Jer.32.18; Jon.4.2), is probably an old cultic confession. **10–28:** This is apparently another tradition about the making of a covenant (v. 10), parallel to that of chs. 19–24. In the present context, however, it is understood as a renewal of the covenant after it was broken by the people (ch. 32). **11–16:** Intolerance of pagan forms of worship was motivated by fear of the seductive power of idolatry (see 23.24). **13:** The *pillars* were upright stones which stood near Baal shrines; the *Asherim* (sacred poles) symbolized Asherah, the mother goddess of Canaanite religion (Jg.2.13). **14:** Religious exclusivism is derived from the fundamental conviction of Mosaic faith; the exclusive claim of Israel's God upon his people's loyalty (20.3). The LORD's *name* (or character) is *Jealous*, i.e. he will tolerate no rivals for Israel's devotion (20.5; Dt.4.24). **18–24:** A cultic calendar. The laws concerning the three annual feasts (vv. 18,22–23) are paralleled in 23.14–17. On the redemption of the first-born (vv. 19–20), see 13.13 n. **24:** The property will be protected while the men are on pilgrimage to the central sanctuary.

was there with the LORD forty days and forty nights; he neither ate bread nor drank water. And he wrote upon the tables the words of the covenant, the ten commandments.*

29 When Moses came down from Mount Sinai, with the two tables of the testimony in his hand as he came down from the mountain, Moses did not know that the skin of his face shone because he had been talking with God. 30 And when Aaron and all the people of Israel saw Moses, behold, the skin of his face shone, and they were afraid to come near him. 31 But Moses called to them; and Aaron and all the leaders of the congregation returned to him, and Moses talked with them. 32 And afterward all the people of Israel came near, and he gave them in commandment all that the LORD had spoken with him in Mount Sinai. 33 And when Moses had finished speaking with them, he put a veil on his face; 34 but whenever Moses went in before the LORD to speak with him, he took the veil off, until he came out; and when he came out, and told the people of Israel what he was commanded, 35 the people of Israel saw the face of Moses, that the skin of Moses' face shone; and Moses would put the veil upon his face again, until he went in to speak with him.

35 Moses assembled all the congregation of the people of Israel, and said to them, "These are the things which the LORD has commanded you to do. 2 Six days shall work be done, but on the seventh day you shall have a holy sabbath of solemn rest to the LORD; whoever does any work on it shall be put to death; 3 you shall kindle no fire in all your habitations on the sabbath day."

4 Moses said to all the congregation of the people of Israel, "This is the thing which the LORD has commanded. 5 Take from among you an offering to the LORD; whoever is of a generous heart, let him bring the LORD's offering: gold, silver, and bronze; 6 blue and purple and scarlet stuff and fine twined linen; goats' hair, 7 tanned rams' skins, and goatskins; acacia wood, 8 oil for the light, spices for the anointing oil and for the fragrant incense, 9 and onyx stones and stones for setting, for the ephod and for the breastpiece.

10 "And let every able man among you come and make all that the LORD has commanded: the tabernacle, 11 its tent and its covering, its hooks and its frames, its bars, its pillars, and its bases; 12 the ark with its poles, the mercy seat, and the veil of the screen; 13 the table with its poles and all its utensils, and the bread of the Presence; 14 the lampstand also for the light, with its utensils and its lamps, and the oil for the light; 15 and the altar of incense, with its poles, and the anointing oil and the fragrant incense, and the screen for the door, at the door of the tabernacle; 16 the altar of burnt offering, with its grating of bronze, its poles, and all its utensils, the laver and its base; 17 the hangings of the court, its pillars and its bases, and the screen for the gate of the court; 18 the pegs of the tabernacle and the pegs of the court, and their cords; 19 the finely wrought garments for ministering in the holy place, the holy garments for

t Heb *words*

25–26: 23.18–19. **27–28:** Moses' special role as covenant mediator (see 19.9 n.) is shown by the fact that the covenant is made with him and, through him, with Israel. *These words,* a reference to the preceding cultic laws. Some have attempted to arrange these into a decalogue (compare v. 28b). Probably, however, the editor has blended together two covenant traditions: one based on the decalogue and the other on this set of ritual laws. **29–35:** According to priestly tradition, the radiant glory of the LORD so transfigured Moses' face (compare Mt.17.1–7) that he had to wear a veil (2 Cor.3.7–18).

   Chs. 35–40: The establishment of the cult. This priestly section shows how the instructions given to Moses in chs. 25–31 were carried out. **35.1–3:** See 31.12–17. The sabbath law is placed first so as to restrict work on the tabernacle. **4–29:** An expansion of 25.1–9.

Aaron the priest, and the garments of his sons, for their service as priests." 20 Then all the congregation of the people of Israel departed from the presence of Moses. ²¹ And they came, every one whose heart stirred him, and every one whose spirit moved him, and brought the LORD's offering to be used for the tent of meeting, and for all its service, and for the holy garments. ²² So they came, both men and women; all who were of a willing heart brought brooches and earrings and signet rings and armlets, all sorts of gold objects, every man dedicating an offering of gold to the LORD. ²³ And every man with whom was found blue or purple or scarlet stuff or fine linen or goats' hair or tanned rams' skins or goatskins, brought them. ²⁴ Every one who could make an offering of silver or bronze brought it as the LORD's offering; and every man with whom was found acacia wood of any use in the work, brought it. ²⁵ And all women who had ability spun with their hands, and brought what they had spun in blue and purple and scarlet stuff and fine twined linen; ²⁶ all the women whose hearts were moved with ability spun the goats' hair. ²⁷ And the leaders brought onyx stones and stones to be set, for the ephod and for the breastpiece, ²⁸ and spices and oil for the light, and for the anointing oil, and for the fragrant incense. ²⁹ All the men and women, the people of Israel, whose heart moved them to bring anything for the work which the LORD had commanded by Moses to be done, brought it as their freewill offering to the LORD.

30 And Moses said to the people of Israel, "See, the LORD has called by name Bez'alel the son of Uri, son of Hur, of the tribe of Judah; ³¹ and he has filled him with the Spirit of God, with ability, with intelligence, with knowledge, and with all craftsmanship, ³² to devise artistic designs, to work in gold and silver and bronze, ³³ in cutting stones for setting, and in carving wood, for work in every skilled craft. ³⁴ And he has inspired him to teach, both him and Oho'liab the son of Ahis'amach of the tribe of Dan. ³⁵ He has filled them with ability to do every sort of work done by a craftsman or by a designer or by an embroiderer in blue and purple and scarlet stuff and fine twined linen, or by a weaver—by any sort of workman or skilled designer. ¹ Bez'alel and **36** Oho'liab and every able man in whom the LORD has put ability and intelligence to know how to do any work in the construction of the sanctuary shall work in accordance with all that the LORD has commanded."

2 And Moses called Bez'alel and Oho'liab and every able man in whose mind the LORD had put ability, every one whose heart stirred him up to come to do the work; ³ and they received from Moses all the freewill offering which the people of Israel had brought for doing the work on the sanctuary. They still kept bringing him freewill offerings every morning, ⁴ so that all the able men who were doing every sort of task on the sanctuary came, each from the task that he was doing, ⁵ and said to Moses, "The people bring much more than enough for doing the work which the LORD has commanded us to do." ⁶ So Moses gave command, and word was proclaimed throughout the camp, "Let neither man nor woman do anything more for the offering for the sanctuary." So the people were restrained from bringing; ⁷ for the stuff they had was sufficient to do all the work, and more.

8 And all the able men among the workmen made the tabernacle with ten curtains; they were made of fine twined linen and blue and purple and scarlet stuff, with cherubim skilfully worked. ⁹ The length of each curtain was twenty-eight cubits, and the breadth of each curtain four cubits; all the curtains had the same measure.

35.30–36.7: See 31.1–11. **36.8–38**: See 26.1–37. **37.1–9**: See 25.10–22.

10 And he coupled five curtains to one another, and the other five curtains he coupled to one another. ¹¹ And he made loops of blue on the edge of the outmost curtain of the first set; likewise he made them on the edge of the outmost curtain of the second set; ¹² he made fifty loops on the one curtain, and he made fifty loops on the edge of the curtain that was in the second set; the loops were opposite one another. ¹³ And he made fifty clasps of gold, and coupled the curtains one to the other with clasps; so the tabernacle was one whole.

14 He also made curtains of goats' hair for a tent over the tabernacle; he made eleven curtains. ¹⁵ The length of each curtain was thirty cubits, and the breadth of each curtain four cubits; the eleven curtains had the same measure. ¹⁶ He coupled five curtains by themselves, and six curtains by themselves. ¹⁷ And he made fifty loops on the edge of the outmost curtain of the one set, and fifty loops on the edge of the other connecting curtain. ¹⁸ And he made fifty clasps of bronze to couple the tent together that it might be one whole. ¹⁹ And he made for the tent a covering of tanned rams' skins and goatskins.

20 Then he made the upright frames for the tabernacle of acacia wood. ²¹ Ten cubits was the length of a frame, and a cubit and a half the breadth of each frame. ²² Each frame had two tenons, for fitting together; he did this for all the frames of the tabernacle. ²³ The frames for the tabernacle he made thus: twenty frames for the south side; ²⁴ and he made forty bases of silver under the twenty frames, two bases under one frame for its two tenons, and two bases under another frame for its two tenons. ²⁵ And for the second side of the tabernacle, on the north side, he made twenty frames ²⁶ and their forty bases of silver, two bases under one frame and two bases under another frame. ²⁷ And for the rear of the tabernacle westward he made six frames. ²⁸ And he

made two frames for corners of the tabernacle in the rear. ²⁹ And they were separate beneath, but joined at the top, at the first ring; he made two of them thus, for the two corners. ³⁰ There were eight frames with their bases of silver: sixteen bases, under every frame two bases.

31 And he made bars of acacia wood, five for the frames of the one side of the tabernacle, ³² and five bars for the frames of the other side of the tabernacle, and five bars for the frames of the tabernacle at the rear westward. ³³ And he made the middle bar to pass through from end to end halfway up the frames. ³⁴ And he overlaid the frames with gold, and made their rings of gold for holders for the bars, and overlaid the bars with gold.

35 And he made the veil of blue and purple and scarlet stuff and fine twined linen; with cherubim skilfully worked he made it. ³⁶ And for it he made four pillars of acacia, and overlaid them with gold; their hooks were of gold, and he cast for them four bases of silver. ³⁷ He also made a screen for the door of the tent, of blue and purple and scarlet stuff and fine twined linen, embroidered with needlework; ³⁸ and its five pillars with their hooks. He overlaid their capitals, and their fillets were of gold, but their five bases were of bronze.

37 Bez'alel made the ark of acacia wood; two cubits and a half was its length, a cubit and a half its breadth, and a cubit and a half its height. ² And he overlaid it with pure gold within and without, and made a molding of gold around it. ³ And he cast for it four rings of gold for its four corners, two rings on its one side and two rings on its other side. ⁴ And he made poles of acacia wood, and overlaid them with gold, ⁵ and put the poles into the rings on the sides of the ark, to carry the ark. ⁶ And he made a mercy seat of pure gold; two cubits and a half was its length, and a cubit and a half its breadth. ⁷ And he made two cherubim of hammered gold; on

the two ends of the mercy seat he made them, [8] one cherub on the one end, and one cherub on the other end; of one piece with the mercy seat he made the cherubim on its two ends. [9] The cherubim spread out their wings above, overshadowing the mercy seat with their wings, with their faces one to another; toward the mercy seat were the faces of the cherubim.

10 He also made the table of acacia wood; two cubits was its length, a cubit its breadth, and a cubit and a half its height; [11] and he overlaid it with pure gold, and made a molding of gold around it. [12] And he made around it a frame a handbreadth wide, and made a molding of gold around the frame. [13] He cast for it four rings of gold, and fastened the rings to the four corners at its four legs. [14] Close to the frame were the rings, as holders for the poles to carry the table. [15] He made the poles of acacia wood to carry the table, and overlaid them with gold. [16] And he made the vessels of pure gold which were to be upon the table, its plates and dishes for incense, and its bowls and flagons with which to pour libations.

17 He also made the lampstand of pure gold. The base and the shaft of the lampstand were made of hammered work; its cups, its capitals, and its flowers were of one piece with it. [18] And there were six branches going out of its sides, three branches of the lampstand out of one side of it and three branches of the lampstand out of the other side of it; [19] three cups made like almonds, each with capital and flower on one branch, and three cups made like almonds, each with capital and flower, on the other branch —so for the six branches going out of the lampstand. [20] And on the lampstand itself were four cups made like almonds, with their capitals and flowers, [21] and a capital of one piece with it under each pair of the six branches

going out of it. [22] Their capitals and their branches were of one piece with it; the whole of it was one piece of hammered work of pure gold. [23] And he made its seven lamps and its snuffers and its trays of pure gold. [24] He made it and all its utensils of a talent of pure gold.

25 He made the altar of incense of acacia wood; its length was a cubit, and its breadth was a cubit; it was square, and two cubits was its height; its horns were of one piece with it. [26] He overlaid it with pure gold, its top, and its sides round about, and its horns; and he made a molding of gold round about it, [27] and made two rings of gold on it under its molding, on two opposite sides of it, as holders for the poles with which to carry it. [28] And he made the poles of acacia wood, and overlaid them with gold.

29 He made the holy anointing oil also, and the pure fragrant incense, blended as by the perfumer.

38 He made the altar of burnt offering also of acacia wood; five cubits was its length, and five cubits its breadth; it was square, and three cubits was its height. [2] He made horns for it on its four corners; its horns were of one piece with it, and he overlaid it with bronze. [3] And he made all the utensils of the altar, the pots, the shovels, the basins, the forks, and the firepans: all its utensils he made of bronze. [4] And he made for the altar a grating, a network of bronze, under its ledge, extending halfway down. [5] He cast four rings on the four corners of the bronze grating as holders for the poles; [6] he made the poles of acacia wood, and overlaid them with bronze. [7] And he put the poles through the rings on the sides of the altar, to carry it with them; he made it hollow, with boards.

8 And he made the laver of bronze and its base of bronze, from the mirrors of the ministering women who

---

37.10–16: See 25.23–30. **17–24:** See 25.31–40. **25–28:** See 30.1–10. **29:** See 30.22–38. **38.1–7:** See 27.1–8. **8:** See 30.17–21.

ministered at the door of the tent of meeting.

9 And he made the court; for the south side the hangings of the court were of fine twined linen, a hundred cubits; [10] their pillars were twenty and their bases twenty, of bronze, but the hooks of the pillars and their fillets were of silver. [11] And for the north side a hundred cubits, their pillars twenty, their bases twenty, of bronze, but the hooks of the pillars and their fillets were of silver. [12] And for the west side were hangings of fifty cubits, their pillars ten, and their sockets ten; the hooks of the pillars and their fillets were of silver. [13] And for the front to the east, fifty cubits. [14] The hangings for one side of the gate were fifteen cubits, with three pillars and three bases. [15] And so for the other side; on this hand and that hand by the gate of the court were hangings of fifteen cubits, with three pillars and three bases. [16] All the hangings round about the court were of fine twined linen. [17] And the bases for the pillars were of bronze, but the hooks of the pillars and their fillets were of silver; the overlaying of their capitals was also of silver, and all the pillars of the court were filleted with silver. [18] And the screen for the gate of the court was embroidered with needlework in blue and purple and scarlet stuff and fine twined linen; it was twenty cubits long and five cubits high in its breadth, corresponding to the hangings of the court. [19] And their pillars were four; their four bases were of bronze, their hooks of silver, and the overlaying of their capitals and their fillets of silver. [20] And all the pegs for the tabernacle and for the court round about were of bronze.

21 This is the sum of the things for the tabernacle, the tabernacle of the testimony, as they were counted at the commandment of Moses, for the work of the Levites under the direction of Ith'amar the son of Aaron the priest. [22] Bez'alel the son of Uri, son of Hur, of the tribe of Judah, made all that the LORD commanded Moses; [23] and with him was Oho'liab the son of Ahis'amach, of the tribe of Dan, a craftsman and designer and embroiderer in blue and purple and scarlet stuff and fine twined linen.

24 All the gold that was used for the work, in all the construction of the sanctuary, the gold from the offering, was twenty-nine talents and seven hundred and thirty shekels, by the shekel of the sanctuary. [25] And the silver from those of the congregation who were numbered was a hundred talents and a thousand seven hundred and seventy-five shekels, by the shekel of the sanctuary: [26] a beka a head (that is, half a shekel, by the shekel of the sanctuary), for every one who was numbered in the census, from twenty years old and upward, for six hundred and three thousand, five hundred and fifty men. [27] The hundred talents of silver were for casting the bases of the sanctuary, and the bases of the veil; a hundred bases for the hundred talents, a talent for a base. [28] And of the thousand seven hundred and seventy-five shekels he made hooks for the pillars, and overlaid their capitals and made fillets for them. [29] And the bronze that was contributed was seventy talents, and two thousand and four hundred shekels; [30] with it he made the bases for the door of the tent of meeting, the bronze altar and the bronze grating for it and all the utensils of the altar, [31] the bases round about the court, and the bases of the gate of the court, all the pegs of the tabernacle, and all the pegs round about the court.

9–20: See 27.9–19. **21–31:** This is a supplement which presupposes the appointment of Ithamar as head of the Levites (Num. ch. 3; 4.33) and the Israelite census (Num. ch. 1). **21:** *The tabernacle of the testimony*, a phrase indicating that the sanctuary contained the ark and ten commandments. **24–26:** The silver tax is computed at the rate set forth in 30.11–16 and with the figures of the later census in mind (see Num.1.17–46 n.), the result being that the figures are

39 And of the blue and purple and scarlet stuff they made finely wrought garments, for ministering in the holy place; they made the holy garments for Aaron; as the LORD had commanded Moses.

2 And he made the ephod of gold, blue and purple and scarlet stuff, and fine twined linen. 3 And gold leaf was hammered out and cut into threads to work into the blue and purple and the scarlet stuff, and into the fine twined linen, in skilled design. 4 They made for the ephod shoulder-pieces, joined to it at its two edges. 5 And the skilfully woven band upon it, to gird it on, was of the same materials and workmanship, of gold, blue and purple and scarlet stuff, and fine twined linen; as the LORD had commanded Moses.

6 The onyx stones were prepared, enclosed in settings of gold filigree and engraved like the engravings of a signet, according to the names of the sons of Israel. 7 And he set them on the shoulder-pieces of the ephod, to be stones of remembrance for the sons of Israel; as the LORD had commanded Moses.

8 He made the breastpiece, in skilled work, like the work of the ephod, of gold, blue and purple and scarlet stuff, and fine twined linen. 9 It was square; the breastpiece was made double, a span its length and a span its breadth when doubled. 10 And they set in it four rows of stones. A row of sardius, topaz, and carbuncle was the first row; 11 and the second row, an emerald, a sapphire, and a diamond; 12 and the third row, a jacinth, an agate, and an amethyst; 13 and the fourth row, a beryl, an onyx, and a jasper; they were enclosed in settings of gold filigree. 14 There were twelve stones with their names according to the names of the sons of Israel; they were like signets, each engraved with its name, for the twelve tribes. 15 And they made on the breastpiece twisted chains like cords, of pure gold; 16 and they made two settings of gold filigree and two gold rings, and put the two rings on the two edges of the breastpiece; 17 and they put the two cords of gold in the two rings at the edges of the breastpiece. 18 Two ends of the two cords they had attached to the two settings of filigree; thus they attached it in front to the shoulder-pieces of the ephod. 19 Then they made two rings of gold, and put them at the two ends of the breastpiece, on its inside edge next to the ephod. 20 And they made two rings of gold, and attached them in front to the lower part of the two shoulder-pieces of the ephod, at its joining above the skilfully woven band of the ephod. 21 And they bound the breastpiece by its rings to the rings of the ephod with a lace of blue, so that it should lie upon the skilfully woven band of the ephod, and that the breastpiece should not come loose from the ephod; as the LORD had commanded Moses.

22 He also made the robe of the ephod woven all of blue; 23 and the opening of the robe in it was like the opening in a garment, with a binding around the opening, that it might not be torn. 24 On the skirts of the robe they made pomegranates of blue and purple and scarlet stuff and fine twined linen. 25 They also made bells of pure gold, and put the bells between the pomegranates upon the skirts of the robe round about, between the pomegranates; 26 a bell and a pomegranate, a bell and a pomegranate round about upon the skirts of the robe for ministering; as the LORD had commanded Moses.

27 They also made the coats, woven of fine linen, for Aaron and his sons, 28 and the turban of fine linen, and the caps of fine linen, and the linen breeches of fine twined linen, 29 and the girdle of fine twined linen and of blue and purple and scarlet stuff, embroidered with needlework; as the LORD had commanded Moses.

highly exaggerated. **39.1–31**: See 28.1–43.

30 And they made the plate of the holy crown of pure gold, and wrote upon it an inscription, like the engraving of a signet, "Holy to the LORD." [31] And they tied to it a lace of blue, to fasten it on the turban above; as the LORD had commanded Moses.

32 Thus all the work of the tabernacle of the tent of meeting was finished; and the people of Israel had done according to all that the LORD had commanded Moses; so had they done. [33] And they brought the tabernacle to Moses, the tent and all its utensils, its hooks, its frames, its bars, its pillars, and its bases; [34] the covering of tanned rams' skins and goatskins, and the veil of the screen; [35] the ark of the testimony with its poles and the mercy seat; [36] the table with all its utensils, and the bread of the Presence; [37] the lampstand of pure gold and its lamps with the lamps set and all its utensils, and the oil for the light; [38] the golden altar, the anointing oil and the fragrant incense, and the screen for the door of the tent; [39] the bronze altar, and its grating of bronze, its poles, and all its utensils; the laver and its base; [40] the hangings of the court, its pillars, and its bases, and the screen for the gate of the court, its cords, and its pegs; and all the utensils for the service of the tabernacle, for the tent of meeting; [41] the finely worked garments for ministering in the holy place, the holy garments for Aaron the priest, and the garments of his sons to serve as priests. [42] According to all that the LORD had commanded Moses, so the people of Israel had done all the work. [43] And Moses saw all the work, and behold, they had done it; as the LORD had commanded, so had they done it. And Moses blessed them.

40 The LORD said to Moses, [2] "On the first day of the first month you shall erect the tabernacle of the tent of meeting. [3] And you shall put in it the ark of the testimony, and you shall screen the ark with the veil. [4] And you shall bring in the table, and set its arrangements in order; and you shall bring in the lampstand, and set up its lamps. [5] And you shall put the golden altar for incense before the ark of the testimony, and set up the screen for the door of the tabernacle. [6] You shall set the altar of burnt offering before the door of the tabernacle of the tent of meeting, [7] and place the laver between the tent of meeting and the altar, and put water in it. [8] And you shall set up the court round about, and hang up the screen for the gate of the court. [9] Then you shall take the anointing oil, and anoint the tabernacle and all that is in it, and consecrate it and all its furniture; and it shall become holy. [10] You shall also anoint the altar of burnt offering and all its utensils, and consecrate the altar; and the altar shall be most holy. [11] You shall also anoint the laver and its base, and consecrate it. [12] Then you shall bring Aaron and his sons to the door of the tent of meeting, and shall wash them with water, [13] and put upon Aaron the holy garments, and you shall anoint him and consecrate him, that he may serve me as priest. [14] You shall bring his sons also and put coats on them, [15] and anoint them, as you anointed their father, that they may serve me as priests: and their anointing shall admit them to a perpetual priesthood throughout their generations."

16 Thus did Moses; according to all that the LORD commanded him, so he did. [17] And in the first month in the second year, on the first day of the month, the tabernacle was erected. [18] Moses erected the tabernacle; he laid its bases, and set up its frames, and put in its poles, and raised up its pillars; [19] and he spread the tent

---

39.32–43: Completion of the work of *the tabernacle of the tent of meeting*. On the blending of the tabernacle and tent traditions (vv. 33,40), compare 26.7–14. **40.1–33:** The erection and furnishing of the tabernacle according to previous instructions. **9–15:** See 30.26–30. **17:** According to priestly chronology, the workers erected the tabernacle nine months after the arrival at Sinai (19.1).

over the tabernacle, and put the covering of the tent over it, as the LORD had commanded Moses. [20] And he took the testimony and put it into the ark, and put the poles on the ark, and set the mercy seat above on the ark; [21] and he brought the ark into the tabernacle, and set up the veil of the screen, and screened the ark of the testimony; as the LORD had commanded Moses. [22] And he put the table in the tent of meeting, on the north side of the tabernacle, outside the veil, [23] and set the bread in order on it before the LORD; as the LORD had commanded Moses. [24] And he put the lampstand in the tent of meeting, opposite the table on the south side of the tabernacle, [25] and set up the lamps before the LORD; as the LORD had commanded Moses. [26] And he put the golden altar in the tent of meeting before the veil, [27] and burnt fragrant incense upon it; as the LORD had commanded Moses. [28] And he put in place the screen for the door of the tabernacle. [29] And he set the altar of burnt offering at the door of the tabernacle of the tent of meeting, and offered upon it the burnt offering and the cereal offering; as the LORD had commanded Moses. [30] And he set the laver between the tent of meeting and the altar, and put water in it for washing, [31] with which Moses and Aaron and his sons washed their hands and their feet; [32] when they went into the tent of meeting, and when they approached the altar, they washed; as the LORD commanded Moses. [33] And he erected the court round the tabernacle and the altar, and set up the screen of the gate of the court. So Moses finished the work.

34 Then the cloud covered the tent of meeting, and the glory of the LORD filled the tabernacle. [35] And Moses was not able to enter the tent of meeting, because the cloud abode upon it, and the glory of the LORD filled the tabernacle. [36] Throughout all their journeys, whenever the cloud was taken up from over the tabernacle, the people of Israel would go onward; [37] but if the cloud was not taken up, then they did not go onward till the day that it was taken up. [38] For throughout all their journeys the cloud of the LORD was upon the tabernacle by day, and fire was in it by night, in the sight of all the house of Israel.

40.34–38: These concluding verses hark back to 25.8 (see 29.43–46). *The cloud* and *the glory* are signs of God's tabernacling presence (see 16.6–7 n.). **35:** 1 Kg.8.10–11; Is.6.3,4. **36–38:** The ancient symbols of the pillar of cloud by day and the pillar of fire by night (13.21–22) are connected with the tabernacle on the view that it was a portable sanctuary which accompanied Israel on its journey (see Num.9.15–23).

LEVITICUS

Leviticus is pre-eminently a book of worship. The English title, derived from the Greek and Latin versions of the Hebrew Bible, refers to the Levitical priests who were set apart to minister at the sanctuary. The book falls into six parts: (1) laws dealing with sacrifices (chs. 1–7); (2) the consecration of the priests to their office (chs. 8–10); (3) laws setting forth the distinction between clean and unclean (chs. 11–15); (4) the ceremony for the annual day of atonement (ch. 16); (5) laws to govern Israel's life as a holy people (chs. 17–26); (6) an appendix on religious vows (ch. 27).

Although this section of the Pentateuch has become a separate "book," actually it is a continuation of the priestly tradition at the end of the book of Exodus (chs. 25–31; 35–40). Moreover, the same tradition extends without interruption through the first ten chapters of Numbers. It is generally agreed that this priestly material in its present form comes from a relatively late period (see Introduction to Pentateuch). The compiler, however, has relied upon independent source materials, such as the so-called Holiness Code (chs. 17–26), and upon numerous traditions which reach back to ancient times.

Through the various rituals and laws there breathes the conviction that the holy God tabernacles in the midst of his people during their historical pilgrimage (Ex.40.34–38). The nearness of God not only accentuates the people's sense of sin but prompts them to turn to him in sacrificial services of worship. For, according to the priestly witness, God has provided the means of atonement and forgiveness whereby the community is restored to wholeness and is reconciled to him.

THE LORD CALLED MOSES, AND spoke to him from the tent of meeting, saying, 2 "Speak to the people of Israel, and say to them, When any man of you brings an offering to the LORD, you shall bring your offering of cattle from the herd or from the flock.

3 "If his offering is a burnt offering from the herd, he shall offer a male without blemish; he shall offer it at the door of the tent of meeting, that he may be accepted before the LORD; 4 he shall lay his hand upon the head of the burnt offering, and it shall be accepted for him to make atonement for him. 5 Then he shall kill the bull before the LORD; and Aaron's sons the priests shall present the blood, and throw the blood round about against the altar that is at the door of the tent of meeting. 6 And he shall flay the burnt offering and cut it into pieces; 7 and the sons of Aaron the priest shall put fire on the altar, and lay wood in order upon the fire; 8 and Aaron's sons the priests shall lay the pieces, the head, and the fat, in order upon the wood that is on the fire upon the altar; 9 but its entrails

---

1.1–17: Burnt offerings. 1: In the priestly view the laws of Leviticus were delivered to Moses from *the tent of meeting* or tabernacle (Ex.25.22; 26.1–37) during the wilderness sojourn (7.37–38; Ex.40.16–38). 2: The sacrifices dealt with in this chapter are regarded as offerings or gifts to God out of the worshiper's substance. 3–9: A sacrifice from the herd. 3: The burnt offering, the chief daily offering (6.9), was one in which the whole animal was burnt on the altar as an act of praise and adoration. *At the door,* i.e. at the great altar in the court (Ex. 38; 40.6). 4: The worshiper symbolically identifies himself with his sacrifice (see Ex.29.10 n.). According to the ancient notion of substitutionary sacrifice, the animal sacrifice makes *atonement* for him or "puts a cover" over his sin (see Ex.29.35–37 n.). 5: Blood, the seat of the mystery of life (17.11; Dt.12.23; Gen.9.4), was held to be peculiarly sacred to God. Therefore, on the principle of the sacrifice of life for life, the shedding of blood was efficacious in forgiving sin and reconciling man to God. The act of throwing the blood against the altar symbolizes God's participation in the atonement ceremony (see Ex.24.6–8 n.). On *Aaron's sons the priests,* see Ex.28.1–5 n.

and its legs he shall wash with water. And the priest shall burn the whole on the altar, as a burnt offering, an offering by fire, a pleasing odor to the LORD.

10 "If his gift for a burnt offering is from the flock, from the sheep or goats, he shall offer a male without blemish; ¹¹ and he shall kill it on the north side of the altar before the LORD, and Aaron's sons the priests shall throw its blood against the altar round about. ¹² And he shall cut it into pieces, with its head and its fat, and the priest shall lay them in order upon the wood that is on the fire upon the altar; ¹³ but the entrails and the legs he shall wash with water. And the priest shall offer the whole, and burn it on the altar; it is a burnt offering, an offering by fire, a pleasing odor to the LORD.

14 "If his offering to the LORD is a burnt offering of birds, then he shall bring his offering of turtledoves or of young pigeons. ¹⁵ And the priest shall bring it to the altar and wring off its head, and burn it on the altar; and its blood shall be drained out on the side of the altar; ¹⁶ and he shall take away its crop with the feathers, and cast it beside the altar on the east side, in the place for ashes; ¹⁷ he shall tear it by its wings, but shall not divide it asunder. And the priest shall burn it on the altar, upon the wood that is on the fire; it is a burnt offering, an offering by fire, a pleasing odor to the LORD.

2 "When any one brings a cereal offering as an offering to the LORD, his offering shall be of fine flour; he shall pour oil upon it, and put frankin-cense on it, ² and bring it to Aaron's sons the priests. And he shall take from it a handful of the fine flour and oil, with all of its frankincense; and the priest shall burn this as its memorial portion upon the altar, an offering by fire, a pleasing odor to the LORD. ³ And what is left of the cereal offering shall be for Aaron and his sons; it is a most holy part of the offerings by fire to the LORD.

4 "When you bring a cereal offering baked in the oven as an offering, it shall be unleavened cakes of fine flour mixed with oil, or unleavened wafers spread with oil. ⁵ And if your offering is a cereal offering baked on a griddle, it shall be of fine flour unleavened, mixed with oil; ⁶ you shall break it in pieces, and pour oil on it; it is a cereal offering. ⁷ And if your offering is a cereal offering cooked in a pan, it shall be made of fine flour with oil. ⁸ And you shall bring the cereal offering that is made of these things to the LORD; and when it is presented to the priest, he shall bring it to the altar. ⁹ And the priest shall take from the cereal offering its memorial portion and burn this on the altar, an offering by fire, a pleasing odor to the LORD. ¹⁰ And what is left of the cereal offering shall be for Aaron and his sons; it is a most holy part of the offerings by fire to the LORD.

11 "No cereal offering which you bring to the LORD shall be made with leaven; for you shall burn no leaven nor any honey as an offering by fire to the LORD. ¹² As an offering of first fruits

---

9: *A pleasing odor*, a traditional expression for an offering acceptable to God (see Gen.8.20–22 n.; compare Eph.5.2). 10–13: A sacrifice from the flock. 14–17: The offering to be made by poor people who cannot afford a sacrifice from the herd or flock.

2.1–16: Cereal offerings. 1: As Abel's offering was from the flock, so Cain's was a typical cereal offering from "the fruit of the ground" (Gen.4.3–5). Both types were expressions of gratitude and praise. Cereal offerings often accompanied an animal sacrifice (7.11–14; 8.26; 9.4; Num.15.1–10). *Oil*, i.e. olive oil. *Frankincense*, Ex.30.34. 2–3: Part of the offering is a *memorial portion*, i.e. it memorializes the worshiper before God. The unburned remainder is *most holy* because, being consecrated to God, only the priests could eat it. In Israel it was not believed that sacrifices satisfied the physical needs of the Deity, as in pagan religions. Rather, sacrifice supported the priests (see Ex.29.24 n.; 1 Sam.2.13–17), who, in eating their portion, identified themselves with the worshiper in his approach to God. 11: Honey was forbidden because, like leaven (see Ex.12.15 n.), it was associated with foods that ferment.

you may bring them to the LORD, but they shall not be offered on the altar for a pleasing odor. ¹³ You shall season all your cereal offerings with salt; you shall not let the salt of the covenant with your God be lacking from your cereal offering; with all your offerings you shall offer salt.

14 "If you offer a cereal offering of first fruits to the LORD, you shall offer for the cereal offering of your first fruits crushed new grain from fresh ears, parched with fire. ¹⁵ And you shall put oil upon it, and lay frankincense on it; it is a cereal offering. ¹⁶ And the priest shall burn as its memorial portion part of the crushed grain and of the oil with all of its frankincense; it is an offering by fire to the LORD.

3 "If a man's offering is a sacrifice of peace offering, if he offers an animal from the herd, male or female, he shall offer it without blemish before the LORD. ² And he shall lay his hand upon the head of his offering and kill it at the door of the tent of meeting; and Aaron's sons the priests shall throw the blood against the altar round about. ³ And from the sacrifice of the peace offering, as an offering by fire to the LORD, he shall offer the fat covering the entrails and all the fat that is on the entrails, ⁴ and the two kidneys with the fat that is on them at the loins, and the appendage of the liver which he shall take away with the kidneys. ⁵ Then Aaron's sons shall burn it on the altar upon the burnt offering, which is upon the wood on the fire; it is an offering by fire, a pleasing odor to the LORD.

6 "If his offering for a sacrifice of peace offering to the LORD is an animal from the flock, male or female, he shall offer it without blemish. ⁷ If he offers a lamb for his offering, then he shall offer it before the LORD, ⁸ laying his hand upon the head of his offering and killing it before the tent of meeting; and Aaron's sons shall throw its blood against the altar round about. ⁹ Then from the sacrifice of the peace offering as an offering by fire to the LORD he shall offer its fat, the fat tail entire, taking it away close by the backbone, and the fat that covers the entrails, and all the fat that is on the entrails, ¹⁰ and the two kidneys with the fat that is on them at the loins, and the appendage of the liver which he shall take away with the kidneys. ¹¹ And the priest shall burn it on the altar as food offered by fire to the LORD.

12 "If his offering is a goat, then he shall offer it before the LORD, ¹³ and lay his hand upon its head, and kill it before the tent of meeting; and the sons of Aaron shall throw its blood against the altar round about. ¹⁴ Then he shall offer from it, as his offering for an offering by fire to the LORD, the fat covering the entrails, and all the fat that is on the entrails, ¹⁵ and the two kidneys with the fat that is on them at the loins, and the appendage of the liver which he shall take away with the kidneys. ¹⁶ And the priest shall burn them on the altar as food offered by fire for a pleasing odor. All fat is the LORD's. ¹⁷ It shall be a perpetual statute throughout your generations, in all your dwelling places, that you eat neither fat nor blood."

12: *First fruits* (vv. 14–16; see Ex.23.19; 34.26). **13**: *Salt of the covenant* (Num.18.19; 2 Chr.13.5) reflects the oriental practice of making a covenant by eating a meal seasoned with salt. Here salt symbolizes the covenant relation upon which the whole sacrificial system rests.

3.1–17: Peace offerings. While the burnt offering was a sacrifice of praise (ch. 1), the peace offering, also an ancient type of sacrifice (Ex.24.5; Dt.12.7,18; 1 Sam.9.11–14,22–24), was a covenant meal in which the worshiper was sacramentally related to the LORD and to fellow-Israelites. **1–5:** Sacrifice from the herd (1.3–9). In this case only certain parts (suet, kidneys) are burned; the rest is consumed by priests and people in a communion meal. **6–17:** Sacrifice from the flock (compare 1.10–13). **16:** Fat, like blood, was held to be God's portion of the sacrifice (7.22–27; Ex.23.18).

4.1–5.13: The sin offering. This is a sacrifice of repentance for sin which has broken man's

4 And the LORD said to Moses, [2] "Say to the people of Israel, If any one sins unwittingly in any of the things which the LORD has commanded not to be done, and does any one of them, [3] if it is the anointed priest who sins, thus bringing guilt on the people, then let him offer for the sin which he has committed a young bull without blemish to the LORD for a sin offering. [4] He shall bring the bull to the door of the tent of meeting before the LORD, and lay his hand on the head of the bull, and kill the bull before the LORD. [5] And the anointed priest shall take some of the blood of the bull and bring it to the tent of meeting; [6] and the priest shall dip his finger in the blood and sprinkle part of the blood seven times before the LORD in front of the veil of the sanctuary. [7] And the priest shall put some of the blood on the horns of the altar of fragrant incense before the LORD which is in the tent of meeting, and the rest of the blood of the bull he shall pour out at the base of the altar of burnt offering which is at the door of the tent of meeting. [8] And all the fat of the bull of the sin offering he shall take from it, the fat that covers the entrails and all the fat that is on the entrails, [9] and the two kidneys with the fat that is on them at the loins, and the appendage of the liver which he shall take away with the kidneys [10] (just as these are taken from the ox of the sacrifice of the peace offerings), and the priest shall burn them upon the altar of burnt offering. [11] But the skin of the bull and all its flesh, with its head, its legs, its entrails, and its dung, [12] the whole bull he shall carry forth outside the camp to a clean place, where the ashes are poured out, and shall burn it on a fire of wood; where the ashes are poured out it shall be burned.

13 "If the whole congregation of Israel commits a sin unwittingly and the thing is hidden from the eyes of the assembly, and they do any one of the things which the LORD has commanded not to be done and are guilty; [14] when the sin which they have committed becomes known, the assembly shall offer a young bull for a sin offering and bring it before the tent of meeting; [15] and the elders of the congregation shall lay their hands upon the head of the bull before the LORD, and the bull shall be killed before the LORD. [16] Then the anointed priest shall bring some of the blood of the bull to the tent of meeting, [17] and the priest shall dip his finger in the blood and sprinkle it seven times before the LORD in front of the veil. [18] And he shall put some of the blood on the horns of the altar which is in the tent of meeting before the LORD; and the rest of the blood he shall pour out at the base of the altar of burnt offering which is at the door of the tent of meeting. [19] And all its fat he shall take from it and burn upon the altar. [20] Thus shall he do with the bull; as he did with the bull of the sin offering, so shall he do with this; and the priest shall make atonement for them, and they shall be forgiven. [21] And he shall carry forth the bull outside the camp, and burn it as he burned the first bull; it is the sin offering for the assembly.

22 "When a ruler sins, doing unwittingly any one of all the things which the LORD his God has commanded not to be done, and is guilty,

relation to God and has endangered the welfare of the community. **2**: The sacrifice is efficacious only for one who sins *unwittingly*, i.e. who inadvertently offends God's holiness. The sacrifice must be accompanied by confession (5.5). Priestly tradition provides no expiation for sin committed deliberately (see Num.15.30 n.; Heb.5.2 n.). **3–12**: Offering for the high priest (compare Ex.29.10–14). **4**: Compare 1.3–4. **6**: *The veil of the sanctuary*, see Ex.26.31–33 n. **7**: *The altar of fragrant incense* was inside the tabernacle (Ex.30.1–10). **8–12**: Only the sacred, vital parts are to be sacrificed; the remainder, being contaminated by the sin of him who laid his hands upon it (v. 4), must be burned outside the camp. **13–21**: Offering for the whole congregation (compare Num.15.22–26). **15**: *The elders* are the representatives of the people. **20**: *Make atonement*

23 if the sin which he has committed is made known to him, he shall bring as his offering a goat, a male without blemish, 24 and shall lay his hand upon the head of the goat, and kill it in the place where they kill the burnt offering before the LORD; it is a sin offering. 25 Then the priest shall take some of the blood of the sin offering with his finger and put it on the horns of the altar of burnt offering, and pour out the rest of its blood at the base of the altar of burnt offering. 26 And all its fat he shall burn on the altar, like the fat of the sacrifice of peace offerings; so the priest shall make atonement for him for his sin, and he shall be forgiven.

27 "If any one of the common people sins unwittingly in doing any one of the things which the LORD has commanded not to be done, and is guilty, 28 when the sin which he has committed is made known to him he shall bring for his offering a goat, a female without blemish, for his sin which he has committed. 29 And he shall lay his hand on the head of the sin offering, and kill the sin offering in the place of burnt offering. 30 And the priest shall take some of its blood with his finger and put it on the horns of the altar of burnt offering, and pour out the rest of its blood at the base of the altar. 81 And all its fat he shall remove, as the fat is removed from the peace offerings, and the priest shall burn it upon the altar for a pleasing odor to the LORD; and the priest shall make atonement for him, and he shall be forgiven.

32 "If he brings a lamb as his offering for a sin offering, he shall bring a female without blemish, 33 and lay his hand upon the head of the sin offering, and kill it for a sin offering in the place where they kill the burnt offering. 34 Then the priest shall take some

of the blood of the sin offering with his finger and put it on the horns of the altar of burnt offering, and pour out the rest of its blood at the base of the altar. 35 And all its fat he shall remove as the fat of the lamb is removed from the sacrifice of peace offerings, and the priest shall burn it on the altar, upon the offerings by fire to the LORD; and the priest shall make atonement for him for the sin which he has committed, and he shall be forgiven.

5 "If any one sins in that he hears a public adjuration to testify and though he is a witness, whether he has seen or come to know the matter, yet does not speak, he shall bear his iniquity. 2 Or if any one touches an unclean thing, whether the carcass of an unclean beast or a carcass of unclean cattle or a carcass of unclean swarming things, and it is hidden from him, and he has become unclean, he shall be guilty. 3 Or if he touches human uncleanness, of whatever sort the uncleanness may be with which one becomes unclean, and it is hidden from him, when he comes to know it he shall be guilty. 4 Or if any one utters with his lips a rash oath to do evil or to do good, any sort of rash oath that men swear, and it is hidden from him, when he comes to know it he shall in any of these be guilty. 5 When a man is guilty in any of these, he shall confess the sin he has committed, 6 and he shall bring his guilt offering to the LORD for the sin which he has committed, a female from the flock, a lamb or a goat, for a sin offering; and the priest shall make atonement for him for his sin.

7 "But if he cannot afford a lamb, then he shall bring, as his guilt offering to the LORD for the sin which he has committed, two turtledoves or two

---

(vv. 26,31,35), see 1.4 n. **22–26:** Offering for a ruler. **27–35:** Offering for an ordinary person. **5.1–4:** Cases which require a sin offering. **1:** The refusal to testify as a witness could lead to a miscarriage of justice. *Bear his iniquity*, i.e. take the consequences of sin. **2–3:** For laws about uncleanness, see chs. 11–15; Num.19.11–13. **5:** Confession of sin must precede the rite, for sacrifice is not a magical means of atonement. **6:** Here and in v. 7 *guilt offering* refers to the sin offering (vv. 8,9,11,12). **7–13:** A supplement to 4.27–35, which covers the case of a poor man who cannot afford a more costly animal (compare 1.14–15).

young pigeons, one for a sin offering and the other for a burnt offering. [8] He shall bring them to the priest, who shall offer first the one for the sin offering; he shall wring its head from its neck, but shall not sever it, [9] and he shall sprinkle some of the blood of the sin offering on the side of the altar, while the rest of the blood shall be drained out at the base of the altar; it is a sin offering. [10] Then he shall offer the second for a burnt offering according to the ordinance; and the priest shall make atonement for him for the sin which he has committed, and he shall be forgiven.

11 "But if he cannot afford two turtledoves or two young pigeons, then he shall bring, as his offering for the sin which he has committed, a tenth of an ephah of fine flour for a sin offering; he shall put no oil upon it, and shall put no frankincense on it, for it is a sin offering. [12] And he shall bring it to the priest, and the priest shall take a handful of it as its memorial portion and burn this on the altar, upon the offerings by fire to the LORD; it is a sin offering. [13] Thus the priest shall make atonement for him for the sin which he has committed in any one of these things, and he shall be forgiven. And the remainder shall be for the priest, as in the cereal offering."

14 The LORD said to Moses, [15] "If any one commits a breach of faith and sins unwittingly in any of the holy things of the LORD, he shall bring, as his guilt offering to the LORD, a ram without blemish out of the flock, valued by you in shekels of silver, according to the shekel of the sanctuary; it is a guilt offering. [16] He shall also make restitution for what he has done amiss in the holy thing, and shall add a fifth

to it and give it to the priest; and the priest shall make atonement for him with the ram of the guilt offering, and he shall be forgiven.

17 "If any one sins, doing any of the things which the LORD has commanded not to be done, though he does not know it, yet he is guilty and shall bear his iniquity. [18] He shall bring to the priest a ram without blemish out of the flock, valued by you at the price for a guilt offering, and the priest shall make atonement for him for the error which he committed unwittingly, and he shall be forgiven. [19] It is a guilt offering; he is guilty before the LORD."

6 [a] The LORD said to Moses, [2] "If any one sins and commits a breach of faith against the LORD by deceiving his neighbor in a matter of deposit or security, or through robbery, or if he has oppressed his neighbor [3] or has found what was lost and lied about it, swearing falsely–in any of all the things which men do and sin therein, [4] when one has sinned and become guilty, he shall restore what he took by robbery, or what he got by oppression, or the deposit which was committed to him, or the lost thing which he found, [5] or anything about which he has sworn falsely; he shall restore it in full, and shall add a fifth to it, and give it to him to whom it belongs, on the day of his guilt offering. [6] And he shall bring to the priest his guilt offering to the LORD, a ram without blemish out of the flock, valued by you at the price for a guilt offering; [7] and the priest shall make atonement for him before the LORD, and he shall be forgiven for any of the things which one may do and thereby become guilty."

8[b] The LORD said to Moses,

a Ch 5.20 in Heb   *b* Ch 6.1 in Heb

5.14–6.7: The guilt offering. This type of offering is prescribed for offenses against God and fellow-men which require that restitution accompany the sacrifice. **15–16:** These verses deal with the withholding of the LORD's *holy things,* i.e. the offerings and tithes that are due him. On *the shekel of the sanctuary,* see Ex.30.13 n. **17–19:** The case of unwitting disobedience is similar to cases requiring a sin offering (4.27–35; compare 7.7). **6.1–7:** Cases involving damage against another person (compare Ex.22.7–15). This law is supplemented by the legislation in Num.5.5–10.

6.8–7.38: Instructions to priests concerning sacrifices. 9–13: A supplement to 1.3–17. **9:** The

9 "Command Aaron and his sons, saying, This is the law of the burnt offering. The burnt offering shall be on the hearth upon the altar all night until the morning, and the fire of the altar shall be kept burning on it. 10 And the priest shall put on his linen garment, and put his linen breeches upon his body, and he shall take up the ashes to which the fire has consumed the burnt offering on the altar, and put them beside the altar. 11 Then he shall put off his garments, and put on other garments, and carry forth the ashes outside the camp to a clean place. 12 The fire on the altar shall be kept burning on it, it shall not go out; the priest shall burn wood on it every morning, and he shall lay the burnt offering in order upon it, and shall burn on it the fat of the peace offerings. 13 Fire shall be kept burning upon the altar continually; it shall not go out.

14 "And this is the law of the cereal offering. The sons of Aaron shall offer it before the LORD, in front of the altar. 15 And one shall take from it a handful of the fine flour of the cereal offering with its oil and all the frankincense which is on the cereal offering, and burn this as its memorial portion on the altar, a pleasing odor to the LORD. 16 And the rest of it Aaron and his sons shall eat; it shall be eaten unleavened in a holy place; in the court of the tent of meeting they shall eat it. 17 It shall not be baked with leaven. I have given it as their portion of my offerings by fire; it is a thing most holy, like the sin offering and the guilt offering. 18 Every male among the children of Aaron may eat of it, as decreed for ever throughout your generations, from the LORD's offerings by

fire; whoever touches them shall become holy."

19 The LORD said to Moses, 20 "This is the offering which Aaron and his sons shall offer to the LORD on the day when he is anointed: a tenth of an ephah of fine flour as a regular cereal offering, half of it in the morning and half in the evening. 21 It shall be made with oil on a griddle; you shall bring it well mixed, in baked^c pieces like a cereal offering, and offer it for a pleasing odor to the LORD. 22 The priest from among Aaron's sons, who is anointed to succeed him, shall offer it to the LORD as decreed for ever; the whole of it shall be burned. 23 Every cereal offering of a priest shall be wholly burned; it shall not be eaten."

24 The LORD said to Moses, 25 "Say to Aaron and his sons, This is the law of the sin offering. In the place where the burnt offering is killed shall the sin offering be killed before the LORD; it is most holy. 26 The priest who offers it for sin shall eat it; in a holy place it shall be eaten, in the court of the tent of meeting. 27 Whatever^d touches its flesh shall be holy; and when any of its blood is sprinkled on a garment, you shall wash that on which it was sprinkled in a holy place. 28 And the earthen vessel in which it is boiled shall be broken; but if it is boiled in a bronze vessel, that shall be scoured, and rinsed in water. 29 Every male among the priests may eat of it; it is most holy. 30 But no sin offering shall be eaten from which any blood is brought into the tent of meeting to make atonement in the holy place; it shall be burned with fire.

c Meaning of Heb is uncertain
d Or Whoever

ever-burning fire on the altar (vv. 12–13) symbolizes Israel's perpetual service of the LORD. The burnt offering was sacrificed in the morning and evening according to Ex.29.38–42; Num. 28.3–8 (but compare the pre-exilic practice reflected in 2 Kg.16.15). **10:** For the priestly dress, see Ex.28.40–43. **14–18:** Supplement to ch. 2. **17:** *A thing most holy,* see 5.15–16 n. **18:** Since the priests eat their portion in the holy place in a state of ritual purity (v. 16), holiness can be transferred to anyone who touches them (see Ex.19.12 n.). **19–23:** Supplement to the law concerning the ordination of priests (Ex. ch. 29). **24–30:** Supplement to 4.1–5.13. **27–28:** These verses reflect the ancient view of holiness as something transferable by contact (v. 18). Holiness can be scoured off a bronze vessel; but an earthen vessel, because it is absorbent, must be

7 "This is the law of the guilt offering. It is most holy; [2] in the place where they kill the burnt offering they shall kill the guilt offering, and its blood shall be thrown on the altar round about. [3] And all its fat shall be offered, the fat tail, the fat that covers the entrails, [4] the two kidneys with the fat that is on them at the loins, and the appendage of the liver which he shall take away with the kidneys; [5] the priest shall burn them on the altar as an offering by fire to the LORD; it is a guilt offering. [6] Every male among the priests may eat of it; it shall be eaten in a holy place; it is most holy. [7] The guilt offering is like the sin offering, there is one law for them; the priest who makes atonement with it shall have it. [8] And the priest who offers any man's burnt offering shall have for himself the skin of the burnt offering which he has offered. [9] And every cereal offering baked in the oven and all that is prepared on a pan or a griddle shall belong to the priest who offers it. [10] And every cereal offering, mixed with oil or dry, shall be for all the sons of Aaron, one as well as another.

11 "And this is the law of the sacrifice of peace offerings which one may offer to the LORD. [12] If he offers it for a thanksgiving, then he shall offer with the thank offering unleavened cakes mixed with oil, unleavened wafers spread with oil, and cakes of fine flour well mixed with oil. [13] With the sacrifice of his peace offerings for thanksgiving he shall bring his offering with cakes of leavened bread. [14] And of such he shall offer one cake from each offering, as an offering to the LORD; it shall belong to the priest who throws the blood of the peace offerings. [15] And the flesh of the sacrifice of his peace offerings for thanksgiving shall be eaten on the day of his offering; he shall not leave any of it until the morning. [16] But if the sacrifice of his offering is a votive offering or a freewill offering, it shall be eaten on the day that he offers his sacrifice, and on the morrow what remains of it shall be eaten, [17] but what remains of the flesh of the sacrifice on the third day shall be burned with fire. [18] If any of the flesh of the sacrifice of his peace offering is eaten on the third day, he who offers it shall not be accepted, neither shall it be credited to him; it shall be an abomination, and he who eats of it shall bear his iniquity.

19 "Flesh that touches any unclean thing shall not be eaten; it shall be burned with fire. All who are clean may eat flesh, [20] but the person who eats of the flesh of the sacrifice of the LORD's peace offerings while an uncleanness is on him, that person shall be cut off from his people. [21] And if any one touches an unclean thing, whether the uncleanness of man or an unclean beast or any unclean abomination, and then eats of the flesh of the sacrifice of the LORD's peace offerings, that person shall be cut off from his people."

22 The LORD said to Moses, [23] "Say to the people of Israel, You shall eat no fat, of ox, or sheep, or goat. [24] The fat of an animal that dies of itself, and the fat of one that is torn by beasts, may be put to any other use, but on no account shall you eat it. [25] For every person who eats of the fat of an animal of which an offering by fire is made to the LORD shall be cut off from his people. [26] Moreover you shall eat no blood whatever, whether of fowl or of animal, in any of your dwellings. [27] Whoever eats any blood, that person shall be cut off from his people."

28 The LORD said to Moses, [29] "Say to the people of Israel, He that offers the sacrifice of his peace offerings to the

---

destroyed. **7.1–10:** Supplement to 5.14–6.7. **11–36:** Supplement to 3.1–17. **12–14:** The peace offering may be accompanied by a cereal offering (see 2.1 n.) for a thanksgiving. **16:** *Votive offering,* see ch. 27. **18:** *Bear his iniquity,* see 5.1 n. **19:** *Any unclean thing,* see ch. 11. **20:** Conditions of personal uncleanness are described in chs. 12–15. *Cut off from his people,* a reference to the death penalty. **23:** 3.16. **24:** See Ex.22.31 n. **26–27:** On this prohibition, see 1.5 n. **28–36:**

LORD shall bring his offering to the LORD; from the sacrifice of his peace offerings ³⁰ he shall bring with his own hands the offerings by fire to the LORD; he shall bring the fat with the breast, that the breast may be waved as a wave offering before the LORD. ³¹ The priest shall burn the fat on the altar, but the breast shall be for Aaron and his sons. ³² And the right thigh you shall give to the priest as an offering from the sacrifice of your peace offerings; ³³ he among the sons of Aaron who offers the blood of the peace offerings and the fat shall have the right thigh for a portion. ³⁴ For the breast that is waved and the thigh that is offered I have taken from the people of Israel, out of the sacrifices of their peace offerings, and have given them to Aaron the priest and to his sons, as a perpetual due from the people of Israel. ³⁵ This is the portion of Aaron and of his sons from the offerings made by fire to the LORD, consecrated to them on the day they were presented to serve as priests of the LORD; ³⁶ the LORD commanded this to be given them by the people of Israel, on the day that they were anointed; it is a perpetual due throughout their generations."

37 This is the law of the burnt offering, of the cereal offering, of the sin offering, of the guilt offering, of the consecration, and of the peace offerings, ³⁸ which the LORD commanded Moses on Mount Sinai, on the day that he commanded the people of Israel to bring their offerings to the LORD, in the wilderness of Sinai.

8 The LORD said to Moses, ² "Take Aaron and his sons with him, and the garments, and the anointing oil, and the bull of the sin offering, and the two rams, and the basket of unleavened bread; ³ and assemble all the congregation at the door of the tent of meeting." ⁴ And Moses did as the LORD commanded him; and the congregation was assembled at the door of the tent of meeting.

5 And Moses said to the congregation, "This is the thing which the LORD has commanded to be done." ⁶ And Moses brought Aaron and his sons, and washed them with water. ⁷ And he put on him the coat, and girded him with the girdle, and clothed him with the robe, and put the ephod upon him, and girded him with the skilfully woven band of the ephod, binding it to him therewith. ⁸ And he placed the breastpiece on him, and in the breastpiece he put the Urim and the Thummim. ⁹ And he set the turban upon his head, and on the turban, in front, he set the golden plate, the holy crown, as the LORD commanded Moses.

10 Then Moses took the anointing oil, and anointed the tabernacle and all that was in it, and consecrated them. ¹¹ And he sprinkled some of it on the altar seven times, and anointed the altar and all its utensils, and the laver and its base, to consecrate them. ¹² And he poured some of the anointing oil on Aaron's head, and anointed him, to consecrate him. ¹³ And Moses brought Aaron's sons, and clothed them with coats, and girded them with girdles, and bound caps on them, as the LORD commanded Moses.

14 Then he brought the bull of the sin offering; and Aaron and his sons laid their hands upon the head of the bull of the sin offering. ¹⁵ And Moses killed it, and took the blood, and with his finger put it on the horns of the altar round about, and purified the altar, and poured out the blood at the base of the altar, and consecrated it, to

The priests' portion of the peace offering. **30:** On the *wave offering*, see Ex.29.24 n. **34:** *A perpetual due*, see 2.2–3 n.

8.1–36: The ordination of the priests (based on Ex. ch. 29). **2:** On the relation of the Aaronic order to the Levites as a whole, see Num.3.5–10 n. **5–9:** Ex.29.4–6. The priestly regalia is described in Ex. ch. 28. **10–13:** The ceremony of anointment (Ex.29.7–9). On the anointing of tabernacle and furnishings, see Ex.30.26–30; 40.9–15. **14–17:** Compare Ex.29.10–14; the ceremony began with a special sin offering for the priests (4.1–12). **15:** On atonement for the altar,

make atonement for it. [16] And he took all the fat that was on the entrails, and the appendage of the liver, and the two kidneys with their fat, and Moses burned them on the altar. [17] But the bull, and its skin, and its flesh, and its dung, he burned with fire outside the camp, as the LORD commanded Moses.

18 Then he presented the ram of the burnt offering; and Aaron and his sons laid their hands on the head of the ram. [19] And Moses killed it, and threw the blood upon the altar round about. [20] And when the ram was cut into pieces, Moses burned the head and the pieces and the fat. [21] And when the entrails and the legs were washed with water, Moses burned the whole ram on the altar, as a burnt offering, a pleasing odor, an offering by fire to the LORD, as the LORD commanded Moses.

22 Then he presented the other ram, the ram of ordination; and Aaron and his sons laid their hands on the head of the ram. [23] And Moses killed it, and took some of its blood and put it on the tip of Aaron's right ear and on the thumb of his right hand and on the great toe of his right foot. [24] And Aaron's sons were brought, and Moses put some of the blood on the tips of their right ears and on the thumbs of their right hands and on the great toes of their right feet; and Moses threw the blood upon the altar round about. [25] Then he took the fat, and the fat tail, and all the fat that was on the entrails, and the appendage of the liver, and the two kidneys with their fat, and the right thigh; [26] and out of the basket of unleavened bread which was before the LORD he took one unleavened cake, and one cake of bread with oil, and one wafer, and placed them on the fat and on the right thigh; [27] and

he put all these in the hands of Aaron and in the hands of his sons, and waved them as a wave offering before the LORD. [28] Then Moses took them from their hands, and burned them on the altar with the burnt offering, as an ordination offering, a pleasing odor, an offering by fire to the LORD. [29] And Moses took the breast, and waved it for a wave offering before the LORD; it was Moses' portion of the ram of ordination, as the LORD commanded Moses.

30 Then Moses took some of the anointing oil and of the blood which was on the altar, and sprinkled it upon Aaron and his garments, and also upon his sons and his sons' garments; so he consecrated Aaron and his garments, and his sons and his sons' garments with him.

31 And Moses said to Aaron and his sons, "Boil the flesh at the door of the tent of meeting, and there eat it and the bread that is in the basket of ordination offerings, as I commanded, saying, 'Aaron and his sons shall eat it'; [32] and what remains of the flesh and the bread you shall burn with fire. [33] And you shall not go out from the door of the tent of meeting for seven days, until the days of your ordination are completed, for it will take seven days to ordain you. [34] As has been done today, the LORD has commanded to be done to make atonement for you. [35] At the door of the tent of meeting you shall remain day and night for seven days, performing what the LORD has charged, lest you die; for so I am commanded." [36] And Aaron and his sons did all the things which the LORD commanded by Moses.

9 On the eighth day Moses called Aaron and his sons and the elders of Israel; [2] and he said to Aaron, "Take

see Ex.29.35–37 n. **18–21:** The second ordination sacrifice was a burnt offering (1.10–13; Ex.29.15–17). **22–35:** Compare Ex.29.19–37. The climax of the service was the sacrifice of *the ram of ordination*, i.e. a peace offering or communion meal (vv. 31–35). **26:** The peace offering was accompanied by a cereal offering (7.12–14). **27–28:** In this case the wave offering (see Ex.29.24 n.) did not go to the priests, as in the usual peace offering (7.28–36), but to Moses the officiating priest.

9.1–24: The commencement of Aaron's high priesthood. 1: *The eighth day*, i.e. at the end of

a bull calf for a sin offering, and a ram for a burnt offering, both without blemish, and offer them before the LORD. ³ And say to the people of Israel, 'Take a male goat for a sin offering, and a calf and a lamb, both a year old without blemish, for a burnt offering, ⁴ and an ox and a ram for peace offerings, to sacrifice before the LORD, and a cereal offering mixed with oil; for today the LORD will appear to you.' " ⁵ And they brought what Moses commanded before the tent of meeting; and all the congregation drew near and stood before the LORD. ⁶ And Moses said, "This is the thing which the LORD commanded you to do; and the glory of the LORD will appear to you." ⁷ Then Moses said to Aaron, "Draw near to the altar, and offer your sin offering and your burnt offering, and make atonement for yourself and for the people; and bring the offering of the people, and make atonement for them; as the LORD has commanded."

8 So Aaron drew near to the altar, and killed the calf of the sin offering, which was for himself. ⁹ And the sons of Aaron presented the blood to him, and he dipped his finger in the blood and put it on the horns of the altar, and poured out the blood at the base of the altar; ¹⁰ but the fat and the kidneys and the appendage of the liver from the sin offering he burned upon the altar, as the LORD commanded Moses. ¹¹ The flesh and the skin he burned with fire outside the camp.

12 And he killed the burnt offering; and Aaron's sons delivered to him the blood, and he threw it on the altar round about. ¹³ And they delivered the burnt offering to him, piece by piece, and the head; and he burned them upon the altar. ¹⁴ And he washed the entrails and the legs, and burned them with the burnt offering on the altar.

15 Then he presented the people's offering, and took the goat of the sin offering which was for the people, and killed it, and offered it for sin, like the first sin offering. ¹⁶ And he presented the burnt offering, and offered it according to the ordinance. ¹⁷ And he presented the cereal offering, and filled his hand from it, and burned it upon the altar, besides the burnt offering of the morning.

18 He killed the ox also and the ram, the sacrifice of peace offerings for the people; and Aaron's sons delivered to him the blood, which he threw upon the altar round about, ¹⁹ and the fat of the ox and of the ram, the fat tail, and that which covers the entrails, and the kidneys, and the appendage of the liver; ²⁰ and they put the fat upon the breasts, and he burned the fat upon the altar, ²¹ but the breasts and the right thigh Aaron waved for a wave offering before the LORD; as Moses commanded.

22 Then Aaron lifted up his hands toward the people and blessed them; and he came down from offering the sin offering and the burnt offering and the peace offerings. ²³ And Moses and Aaron went into the tent of meeting; and when they came out they blessed the people, and the glory of the LORD appeared to all the people. ²⁴ And fire came forth from before the LORD and consumed the burnt offering and the fat upon the altar; and when all the people saw it, they shouted, and fell on their faces.

10 Now Nadab and Abi′hu, the sons of Aaron, each took his censer, and put fire in it, and laid incense on

---

the seven day ordination ceremony (8.33). **2–7:** Preparations for an assembly of the whole congregation for worship. **8–14:** Aaron offered a sin offering (4.1–12) and a burnt offering (1.3–13) to make atonement for himself. **15–21:** The people's sin offering, burnt and cereal offering, and peace offering were presented according to the ordinances of chs. 1–7. **22:** *He came down*, i.e. from the steps leading up to the great altar (Ezek.43.17). **24:** Jg.6.21.

10.1–20: The fate of Nadab and Abihu. Two of Aaron's sons were destroyed for their sin in making an unauthorized offering before the LORD. **1:** *Unholy fire* refers to incense which was offered in presumptuous defiance of the rules of the theocratic community (Ex.30.34–38;

it, and offered unholy fire before the LORD, such as he had not commanded them. [2] And fire came forth from the presence of the LORD and devoured them, and they died before the LORD. [3] Then Moses said to Aaron, "This is what the LORD has said, 'I will show myself holy among those who are near me, and before all the people I will be glorified.'" And Aaron held his peace.

4 And Moses called Mish'a-el and Elza'phan, the sons of Uz'ziel the uncle of Aaron, and said to them, "Draw near, carry your brethren from before the sanctuary out of the camp." [5] So they drew near, and carried them in their coats out of the camp, as Moses had said. [6] And Moses said to Aaron and to Elea'zar and Ith'amar, his sons, "Do not let the hair of your heads hang loose, and do not rend your clothes, lest you die, and lest wrath come upon all the congregation; but your brethren, the whole house of Israel, may bewail the burning which the LORD has kindled. [7] And do not go out from the door of the tent of meeting, lest you die; for the anointing oil of the LORD is upon you." And they did according to the word of Moses.

8 And the LORD spoke to Aaron, saying, [9] "Drink no wine nor strong drink, you nor your sons with you, when you go into the tent of meeting, lest you die; it shall be a statute for ever throughout your generations. [10] You are to distinguish between the holy and the common, and between the unclean and the clean; [11] and you are to teach the people of Israel all the statutes which the LORD has spoken to them by Moses."

12 And Moses said to Aaron and to Elea'zar and Ith'amar, his sons who were left, "Take the cereal offering that remains of the offerings by fire to the LORD, and eat it unleavened beside the altar, for it is most holy; [13] you shall eat it in a holy place, because it is your due and your sons' due, from the offerings by fire to the LORD; for so I am commanded. [14] But the breast that is waved and the thigh that is offered you shall eat in any clean place, you and your sons and your daughters with you; for they are given as your due and your sons' due, from the sacrifices of the peace offerings of the people of Israel. [15] The thigh that is offered and the breast that is waved they shall bring with the offerings by fire of the fat, to wave for a wave offering before the LORD, and it shall be yours, and your sons' with you, as a due for ever; as the LORD has commanded."

16 Now Moses diligently inquired about the goat of the sin offering, and behold, it was burned! And he was angry with Elea'zar and Ith'amar, the sons of Aaron who were left, saying, [17] "Why have you not eaten the sin offering in the place of the sanctuary, since it is a thing most holy and has been given to you that you may bear the iniquity of the congregation, to make atonement for them before the LORD? [18] Behold, its blood was not brought into the inner part of the sanctuary. You certainly ought to have eaten it in the sanctuary, as I commanded." [19] And Aaron said to Moses, "Behold, today they have offered their sin offering and their burnt offering before the LORD; and yet such things as these have befallen me! If I had eaten the sin offering today, would it have

---

Num. ch. 16). **2**: See 9.24 n. **3**: *Those who are near me*, i.e. the priests who have access to the holy place. The story explains why the priestly line was traced through Aaron's third son, Eleazar (Ex.6.23–25). **4**: *Mishael* and *Elzaphan*, cousins of Moses (Ex.6.22). **5**: *Their coats*, i.e. priestly tunics (Ex.28.4,39–40). **6**: Aaron and his sons must abstain from signs of mourning, i.e. rending the garments and letting the hair hang loose. The reason is that they are still in a state of ritual purity (v. 7; see 21.10–12). **9**: Ezek.44.21. **10–11**: See chs. 11–15. **12–15**: 7.28–36. The cereal offering (v. 12) accompanied the peace offering (7.11–14). **16–20**: When Aaron and his sons offered their first sin offering after Nadab and Abihu were struck down during the performance of their priestly duties, they failed to eat their rightful portion (see 2.2–3 n.; 6.26), fearing that the LORD was not disposed to accept their atonement for the people.

been acceptable in the sight of the LORD?" 20 And when Moses heard that, he was content.

|| And the LORD said to Moses and Aaron, 2 "Say to the people of Israel, These are the living things which you may eat among all the beasts that are on the earth. 3 Whatever parts the hoof and is cloven-footed and chews the cud, among the animals, you may eat. 4 Nevertheless among those that chew the cud or part the hoof, you shall not eat these: The camel, because it chews the cud but does not part the hoof, is unclean to you. 5 And the rock badger, because it chews the cud but does not part the hoof, is unclean to you. 6 And the hare, because it chews the cud but does not part the hoof, is unclean to you. 7 And the swine, because it parts the hoof and is cloven-footed but does not chew the cud, is unclean to you. 8 Of their flesh you shall not eat, and their carcasses you shall not touch; they are unclean to you.

9 "These you may eat, of all that are in the waters. Everything in the waters that has fins and scales, whether in the seas or in the rivers, you may eat. 10 But anything in the seas or the rivers that has not fins and scales, of the swarming creatures in the waters and of the living creatures that are in the waters, is an abomination to you. 11 They shall remain an abomination to you; of their flesh you shall not eat, and their carcasses you shall have in abomination. 12 Everything in the waters that has not fins and scales is an abomination to you.

13 "And these you shall have in abomination among the birds, they shall not be eaten, they are an abomination: the eagle, the vulture, the os-

prey, 14 the kite, the falcon according to its kind, 15 every raven according to its kind, 16 the ostrich, the nighthawk, the sea gull, the hawk according to its kind, 17 the owl, the cormorant, the ibis, 18 the water hen, the pelican, the carrion vulture, 19 the stork, the heron according to its kind, the hoopoe, and the bat.

20 "All winged insects that go upon all fours are an abomination to you. 21 Yet among the winged insects that go on all fours you may eat those which have legs above their feet, with which to leap on the earth. 22 Of them you may eat: the locust according to its kind, the bald locust according to its kind, the cricket according to its kind, and the grasshopper according to its kind. 23 But all other winged insects which have four feet are an abomination to you.

24 "And by these you shall become unclean; whoever touches their carcass shall be unclean until the evening, 25 and whoever carries any part of their carcass shall wash his clothes and be unclean until the evening. 26 Every animal which parts the hoof but is not cloven-footed or does not chew the cud is unclean to you; every one who touches them shall be unclean. 27 And all that go on their paws, among the animals that go on all fours, are unclean to you; whoever touches their carcass shall be unclean until the evening, 28 and he who carries their carcass shall wash his clothes and be unclean until the evening; they are unclean to you.

29 "And these are unclean to you among the swarming things that swarm upon the earth: the weasel, the mouse, the great lizard according to its kind, 30 the gecko, the land crocodile, the

---

11.1–47: Clean and unclean animals (Dt. 14.3–20). The laws of chs. 11–15 come after the ordination tradition (chs. 8–10) because one of the tasks of the priests was to make a distinction between clean and unclean (10.10). This distinction is not based merely on sanitary or hygienic considerations, in the modern sense that "cleanliness is next to godliness." That which is unclean is ritually impure and therefore the opposite of holy. **5–6:** Strictly, these animals do not chew the cud but only appear to. **7:** *The swine* came to be regarded as the animal that was particularly unclean (1 Macc.1.47). **24–38:** An unclean animal, when dead, transmits uncleanness at the touch but it may be safely handled while alive. Further, the contagion of unclean-

lizard, the sand lizard, and the chameleon. ³¹ These are unclean to you among all that swarm; whoever touches them when they are dead shall be unclean until the evening. ³² And anything upon which any of them falls when they are dead shall be unclean, whether it is an article of wood or a garment or a skin or a sack, any vessel that is used for any purpose; it must be put into water, and it shall be unclean until the evening; then it shall be clean. ³³ And if any of them falls into any earthen vessel, all that is in it shall be unclean, and you shall break it. ³⁴ Any food in it which may be eaten, upon which water may come, shall be unclean; and all drink which may be drunk from every such vessel shall be unclean. ³⁵ And everything upon which any part of their carcass falls shall be unclean; whether oven or stove, it shall be broken in pieces; they are unclean, and shall be unclean to you. ³⁶ Nevertheless a spring or a cistern holding water shall be clean; but whatever touches their carcass shall be unclean. ³⁷ And if any part of their carcass falls upon any seed for sowing that is to be sown, it is clean; ³⁸ but if water is put on the seed and any part of their carcass falls on it, it is unclean to you.

39 "And if any animal of which you may eat dies, he who touches its carcass shall be unclean until the evening, ⁴⁰ and he who eats of its carcass shall wash his clothes and be unclean until the evening; he also who carries the carcass shall wash his clothes and be unclean until the evening.

41 "Every swarming thing that swarms upon the earth is an abomination; it shall not be eaten. ⁴² Whatever goes on its belly, and whatever goes on all fours, or whatever has many feet, all the swarming things that swarm upon the earth, you shall not eat; for they are an abomination. ⁴³ You shall not make yourselves abominable with any swarming thing that swarms; and you shall not defile yourselves with them, lest you become unclean. ⁴⁴ For I am the LORD your God; consecrate yourselves therefore, and be holy, for I am holy. You shall not defile yourselves with any swarming thing that crawls upon the earth. ⁴⁵ For I am the LORD who brought you up out of the land of Egypt, to be your God; you shall therefore be holy, for I am holy."

46 This is the law pertaining to beast and bird and every living creature that moves through the waters and every creature that swarms upon the earth, ⁴⁷ to make a distinction between the unclean and the clean and between the living creature that may be eaten and the living creature that may not be eaten.

12 The LORD said to Moses, ² "Say to the people of Israel, If a woman conceives, and bears a male child, then she shall be unclean seven days; as at the time of her menstruation, she shall be unclean. ³ And on the eighth day the flesh of his foreskin shall be circumcised. ⁴ Then she shall continue for thirty-three days in the blood of her purifying; she shall not touch any hallowed thing, nor come into the sanctuary, until the days of her purifying are completed. ⁵ But if she bears a female child, then she shall be unclean two weeks, as in her menstruation; and she shall continue in the blood of her purifying for sixty-six days.

6 "And when the days of her purifying are completed, whether for a son or for a daughter, she shall bring to

ness, like that of its opposite, holiness (6.27–28), affects objects, vessels, etc. **44–45:** The basis for these laws is not irrational taboo but the covenant relationship, which sets Israel apart for the service of God (Ex.19.3–6). As a holy and consecrated people (Ex.22.31), Israelites must avoid all impurity in order that the holy God may tabernacle in their midst (15.31; 18.1–5; 20.22–26; 26.11–12).
12.1–8: Purification of a woman after childbirth. 2: This law does not imply that sex is evil–a view completely foreign to Israel's thought; rather, the woman becomes unclean because of

the priest at the door of the tent of meeting a lamb a year old for a burnt offering, and a young pigeon or a turtle-dove for a sin offering, [7] and he shall offer it before the LORD, and make atonement for her; then she shall be clean from the flow of her blood. This is the law for her who bears a child, either male or female. [8] And if she cannot afford a lamb, then she shall take two turtledoves or two young pigeons, one for a burnt offering and the other for a sin offering; and the priest shall make atonement for her, and she shall be clean."

13 The LORD said to Moses and Aaron, [2] "When a man has on the skin of his body a swelling or an eruption or a spot, and it turns into a leprous disease on the skin of his body, then he shall be brought to Aaron the priest or to one of his sons the priests, [3] and the priest shall ex-amine the diseased spot on the skin of his body; and if the hair in the diseased spot has turned white and the disease appears to be deeper than the skin of his body, it is a leprous disease; when the priest has examined him he shall pronounce him unclean. [4] But if the spot is white in the skin of his body, and appears no deeper than the skin, and the hair in it has not turned white, the priest shall shut up the diseased person for seven days; [5] and the priest shall examine him on the seventh day, and if in his eyes the disease is checked and the disease has not spread in the skin, then the priest shall shut him up seven days more; [6] and the priest shall examine him again on the seventh day, and if the diseased spot is dim and the disease has not spread in the skin, then the priest shall pronounce him

clean; it is only an eruption; and he shall wash his clothes, and be clean. [7] But if the eruption spreads in the skin, after he has shown himself to the priest for his cleansing, he shall appear again before the priest; [8] and the priest shall make an examination, and if the eruption has spread in the skin, then the priest shall pronounce him unclean; it is leprosy.

9 "When a man is afflicted with leprosy, he shall be brought to the priest; [10] and the priest shall make an examination, and if there is a white swelling in the skin, which has turned the hair white, and there is quick raw flesh in the swelling, [11] it is a chronic leprosy in the skin of his body, and the priest shall pronounce him unclean; he shall not shut him up, for he is un-clean. [12] And if the leprosy breaks out in the skin, so that the leprosy covers all the skin of the diseased person from head to foot, so far as the priest can see, [13] then the priest shall make an examination, and if the leprosy has covered all his body, he shall pro-nounce him clean of the disease; it has all turned white, and he is clean. [14] But when raw flesh appears on him, he shall be unclean. [15] And the priest shall examine the raw flesh, and pronounce him unclean; raw flesh is unclean, for it is leprosy. [16] But if the raw flesh turns again and is changed to white, then he shall come to the priest, [17] and the priest shall examine him, and if the disease has turned white, then the priest shall pronounce the diseased per-son clean; he is clean.

18 "And when there is in the skin of one's body a boil that has healed, [19] and in the place of the boil there comes a white swelling or a reddish-

her bodily discharge (v. 7; see 15.16–18 n.). **6:** The *sin offering* is prescribed for inadvertent sin (4.27–35). **8:** See 5.7–13 n.; Lk.2.24.

13.1–59: The diagnosis of leprosy. In this chapter and the next, the word translated "leprosy" is a generic term which includes various skin diseases (including what is called leprosy today), as well as blemishes affecting garments and buildings. **1–8:** A suspicious skin eruption. Tuber-cular leprosy begins with reddish patches and progresses into nodules and deformities; anes-thetic leprosy paralyzes the nerves so that the limbs are numb and eventually lifeless. Whatever type is in mind, the law emphasizes observation so that the disease may be detected in its early stages. **9–17:** In the case of *chronic leprosy*, quarantine for further examination (v. 11) is

white spot, then it shall be shown to the priest; [20] and the priest shall make an examination, and if it appears deeper than the skin and its hair has turned white, then the priest shall pronounce him unclean; it is the disease of leprosy, it has broken out in the boil. [21] But if the priest examines it, and the hair on it is not white and it is not deeper than the skin, but is dim, then the priest shall shut him up seven days; [22] and if it spreads in the skin, then the priest shall pronounce him unclean; it is diseased. [23] But if the spot remains in one place and does not spread, it is the scar of the boil; and the priest shall pronounce him clean.

24 "Or, when the body has a burn on its skin and the raw flesh of the burn becomes a spot, reddish-white or white, [25] the priest shall examine it, and if the hair in the spot has turned white and it appears deeper than the skin, then it is leprosy; it has broken out in the burn, and the priest shall pronounce him unclean; it is a leprous disease. [26] But if the priest examines it, and the hair in the spot is not white and it is no deeper than the skin, but is dim, the priest shall shut him up seven days, [27] and the priest shall examine him the seventh day; if it is spreading in the skin, then the priest shall pronounce him unclean; it is a leprous disease. [28] But if the spot remains in one place and does not spread in the skin, but is dim, it is a swelling from the burn, and the priest shall pronounce him clean; for it is the scar of the burn.

29 "When a man or woman has a disease on the head or the beard, [30] the priest shall examine the disease; and if it appears deeper than the skin, and the hair in it is yellow and thin, then the priest shall pronounce him unclean; it is an itch, a leprosy of the head or the beard. [31] And if the priest examines the itching disease, and it appears no deeper than the skin and there is no black hair in it, then the priest shall shut up the person with the itching disease for seven days, [32] and on the seventh day the priest shall examine the disease; and if the itch has not spread, and there is in it no yellow hair, and the itch appears to be no deeper than the skin, [33] then he shall shave himself, but the itch he shall not shave; and the priest shall shut up the person with the itching disease for seven days more; [34] and on the seventh day the priest shall examine the itch, and if the itch has not spread in the skin and it appears to be no deeper than the skin, then the priest shall pronounce him clean; and he shall wash his clothes, and be clean. [35] But if the itch spreads in the skin after his cleansing, [36] then the priest shall examine him, and if the itch has spread in the skin, the priest need not seek for the yellow hair; he is unclean. [37] But if in his eyes the itch is checked, and black hair has grown in it, the itch is healed, he is clean; and the priest shall pronounce him clean.

38 "When a man or a woman has spots on the skin of the body, white spots, [39] the priest shall make an examination, and if the spots on the skin of the body are of a dull white, it is tetter that has broken out in the skin; he is clean.

40 "If a man's hair has fallen from his head, he is bald but he is clean. [41] And if a man's hair has fallen from his forehead and temples, he has baldness of the forehead but he is clean. [42] But if there is on the bald head or the bald forehead a reddish-white diseased spot, it is leprosy breaking out on his bald head or his bald forehead. [43] Then the priest shall examine him, and if the diseased swelling is reddish-white on his bald head or on his bald forehead, like the appearance of

---

pointless. **18–23:** A boil in which leprosy may break out. **24–28:** A burn which may be infected with leprosy. **29–37:** An itching disease, perhaps ringworm. **38–39:** A vesicular skin disease. **40–44:** Falling hair, unless accompanied by other symptoms, is not necessarily a sign of leprosy.

leprosy in the skin of the body, [44] he is a leprous man, he is unclean; the priest must pronounce him unclean; his disease is on his head.

45 "The leper who has the disease shall wear torn clothes and let the hair of his head hang loose, and he shall cover his upper lip and cry, 'Unclean, unclean.' [46] He shall remain unclean as long as he has the disease; he is unclean; he shall dwell alone in a habitation outside the camp.

47 "When there is a leprous disease in a garment, whether a woolen or a linen garment, [48] in warp or woof of linen or wool, or in a skin or in anything made of skin, [49] if the disease shows greenish or reddish in the garment, whether in warp or woof or in skin or in anything made of skin, it is a leprous disease and shall be shown to the priest. [50] And the priest shall examine the disease, and shut up that which has the disease for seven days; [51] then he shall examine the disease on the seventh day. If the disease has spread in the garment, in warp or woof, or in the skin, whatever be the use of the skin, the disease is a malignant leprosy; it is unclean. [52] And he shall burn the garment, whether diseased in warp or woof, woolen or linen, or anything of skin, for it is a malignant leprosy; it shall be burned in the fire.

53 "And if the priest examines, and the disease has not spread in the garment in warp or woof or in anything of skin, [54] then the priest shall command that they wash the thing in which is the disease, and he shall shut it up seven days more; [55] and the priest shall examine the diseased thing after it has been washed. And if the diseased spot has not changed color, though the disease has not spread, it is unclean; you shall burn it in the fire, whether the leprous spot is on the back or on the front.

56 "But if the priest examines, and the disease is dim after it is washed, he shall tear the spot out of the garment or the skin or the warp or woof; [57] then if it appears again in the garment, in warp or woof, or in anything of skin, it is spreading; you shall burn with fire that in which is the disease. [58] But the garment, warp or woof, or anything of skin from which the disease departs when you have washed it, shall then be washed a second time, and be clean."

59 This is the law for a leprous disease in a garment of wool or linen, either in warp or woof, or in anything of skin, to decide whether it is clean or unclean.

14 The LORD said to Moses, [2] "This shall be the law of the leper for the day of his cleansing. He shall be brought to the priest; [3] and the priest shall go out of the camp, and the priest shall make an examination. Then, if the leprous disease is healed in the leper, [4] the priest shall command them to take for him who is to be cleansed two living clean birds and cedarwood and scarlet stuff and hyssop; [5] and the priest shall command them to kill one of the birds in an earthen vessel over running water. [6] He shall take the living bird with the cedarwood and the scarlet stuff and the hyssop, and dip them and the living bird in the blood of the bird that was killed over the running water; [7] and he shall sprinkle it seven times upon him who is to be cleansed of leprosy; then he shall pronounce him clean, and shall let the living bird go into the open field. [8] And he who is to be cleansed shall wash his clothes, and shave off all his hair, and bathe himself in water, and

---

45–46: If truly a leper, the man must appear like a mourner (10.6) and must go into isolation (Job 2.7–8). The judgment that he is *unclean* is based upon the belief that, being ritually impure (see ch. 11 n.), his defilement could be transmitted to others. Even after a leper was cured he was not "clean" until he had been ritually purified (ch. 14). **47–59:** *Leprous disease in a garment* refers to mold or mildew.

14.1–32: The cleansing of leprosy. 2: Mk.1.44. **4–8:** This ceremony has archaic elements which elude explanation. **4:** *Hyssop,* see Ex.12.22 n. **7:** Perhaps the freeing of the living bird

he shall be clean; and after that he shall come into the camp, but shall dwell outside his tent seven days. ⁹ And on the seventh day he shall shave all his hair off his head; he shall shave off his beard and his eyebrows, all his hair. Then he shall wash his clothes, and bathe his body in water, and he shall be clean.

10 "And on the eighth day he shall take two male lambs without blemish, and one ewe lamb a year old without blemish, and a cereal offering of three tenths of an ephah of fine flour mixed with oil, and one log of oil. ¹¹ And the priest who cleanses him shall set the man who is to be cleansed and these things before the LORD, at the door of the tent of meeting. ¹² And the priest shall take one of the male lambs, and offer it for a guilt offering, along with the log of oil, and wave them for a wave offering before the LORD; ¹³ and he shall kill the lamb in the place where they kill the sin offering and the burnt offering, in the holy place; for the guilt offering, like the sin offering, belongs to the priest; it is most holy. ¹⁴ The priest shall take some of the blood of the guilt offering, and the priest shall put it on the tip of the right ear of him who is to be cleansed, and on the thumb of his right hand, and on the great toe of his right foot. ¹⁵ Then the priest shall take some of the log of oil, and pour it into the palm of his own left hand, ¹⁶ and dip his right finger in the oil that is in his left hand, and sprinkle some oil with his finger seven times before the LORD. ¹⁷ And some of the oil that remains in his hand the priest shall put on the tip of the right ear of him who is to be cleansed, and on the thumb of his right hand, and on the great toe of his right foot, upon the blood of the guilt offering; ¹⁸ and the rest of the oil that is in the priest's hand he

shall put on the head of him who is to be cleansed. Then the priest shall make atonement for him before the LORD. ¹⁹ The priest shall offer the sin offering, to make atonement for him who is to be cleansed from his uncleanness. And afterward he shall kill the burnt offering; ²⁰ and the priest shall offer the burnt offering and the cereal offering on the altar. Thus the priest shall make atonement for him, and he shall be clean.

21 "But if he is poor and cannot afford so much, then he shall take one male lamb for a guilt offering to be waved, to make atonement for him, and a tenth of an ephah of fine flour mixed with oil for a cereal offering, and a log of oil; ²² also two turtledoves or two young pigeons, such as he can afford; the one shall be a sin offering and the other a burnt offering. ²³ And on the eighth day he shall bring them for his cleansing to the priest, to the door of the tent of meeting, before the LORD; ²⁴ and the priest shall take the lamb of the guilt offering, and the log of oil, and the priest shall wave them for a wave offering before the LORD. ²⁵ And he shall kill the lamb of the guilt offering; and the priest shall take some of the blood of the guilt offering, and put it on the tip of the right ear of him who is to be cleansed, and on the thumb of his right hand, and on the great toe of his right foot. ²⁶ And the priest shall pour some of the oil into the palm of his own left hand; ²⁷ and shall sprinkle with his right finger some of the oil that is in his left hand seven times before the LORD; ²⁸ and the priest shall put some of the oil that is in his hand on the tip of the right ear of him who is to be cleansed, and on the thumb of his right hand, and the great toe of his right foot, in the place where the blood of the guilt offering was put; ²⁹ and the rest of the oil that

---

symbolizes the carrying away of the leper's uncleanness. **8:** On the ritual washing of garments, see 16.23–24; Ex.19.10. **10–20:** The offering of appropriate sacrifices. **12:** In this case the guilt offering, like the sin offering (v. 19; 5.1–6), is prescribed for an inadvertent offence. *Wave offering*, see Ex.29.24 n. **21–32:** See 5.7–13 n.

is in the priest's hand he shall put on the head of him who is to be cleansed, to make atonement for him before the LORD. [30] And he shall offer, of the turtledoves or young pigeons such as he can afford, [31] one[x] for a sin offering and the other for a burnt offering, along with a cereal offering; and the priest shall make atonement before the LORD for him who is being cleansed. [32] This is the law for him in whom is a leprous disease, who cannot afford the offerings for his cleansing."

33 The LORD said to Moses and Aaron, [34] "When you come into the land of Canaan, which I give you for a possession, and I put a leprous disease in a house in the land of your possession, [35] then he who owns the house shall come and tell the priest, 'There seems to me to be some sort of disease in my house.' [36] Then the priest shall command that they empty the house before the priest goes to examine the disease, lest all that is in the house be declared unclean; and afterward the priest shall go in to see the house. [37] And he shall examine the disease; and if the disease is in the walls of the house with greenish or reddish spots, and if it appears to be deeper than the surface, [38] then the priest shall go out of the house to the door of the house, and shut up the house seven days. [39] And the priest shall come again on the seventh day, and look; and if the disease has spread in the walls of the house, [40] then the priest shall command that they take out the stones in which is the disease and throw them into an unclean place outside the city; [41] and he shall cause the inside of the house to be scraped round about, and the plaster that they scrape off they shall pour into an unclean place outside the city; [42] then they shall take other stones and put them in the place of those stones, and he shall take other plaster and plaster the house.

43 "If the disease breaks out again in the house, after he has taken out the stones and scraped the house and plastered it, [44] then the priest shall go and look; and if the disease has spread in the house, it is a malignant leprosy in the house; it is unclean. [45] And he shall break down the house, its stones and timber and all the plaster of the house; and he shall carry them forth out of the city to an unclean place. [46] Moreover he who enters the house while it is shut up shall be unclean until the evening; [47] and he who lies down in the house shall wash his clothes; and he who eats in the house shall wash his clothes.

48 "But if the priest comes and makes an examination, and the disease has not spread in the house after the house was plastered, then the priest shall pronounce the house clean, for the disease is healed. [49] And for the cleansing of the house he shall take two small birds, with cedarwood and scarlet stuff and hyssop, [50] and shall kill one of the birds in an earthen vessel over running water, [51] and shall take the cedarwood and the hyssop and the scarlet stuff, along with the living bird, and dip them in the blood of the bird that was killed and in the running water, and sprinkle the house seven times. [52] Thus he shall cleanse the house with the blood of the bird, and with the running water, and with the living bird, and with the cedarwood and hyssop and scarlet stuff; [53] and he shall let the living bird go out of the city into the open field; so he shall make atonement for the house, and it shall be clean."

54 This is the law for any leprous disease: for an itch, [55] for leprosy in a garment or in a house, [56] and for a swelling or an eruption or a spot, [57] to show when it is unclean and when it is clean. This is the law for leprosy.

x Gk Syr: Heb *afford*, [31] *such as he can afford, one*

33–57: Leprosy in houses. The "disease" appears to be mold or rot.

15 The LORD said to Moses and Aaron, [2] "Say to the people of Israel, When any man has a discharge from his body, his discharge is unclean. [3] And this is the law of his uncleanness for a discharge: whether his body runs with his discharge, or his body is stopped from discharge, it is uncleanness in him. [4] Every bed on which he who has the discharge lies shall be unclean; and everything on which he sits shall be unclean. [5] And any one who touches his bed shall wash his clothes, and bathe himself in water, and be unclean until the evening. [6] And whoever sits on anything on which he who has the discharge has sat shall wash his clothes, and bathe himself in water, and be unclean until the evening. [7] And whoever touches the body of him who has the discharge shall wash his clothes, and bathe himself in water, and be unclean until the evening. [8] And if he who has the discharge spits on one who is clean, then he shall wash his clothes, and bathe himself in water, and be unclean until the evening. [9] And any saddle on which he who has the discharge rides shall be unclean. [10] And whoever touches anything that was under him shall be unclean until the evening; and he who carries such a thing shall wash his clothes, and bathe himself in water, and be unclean until the evening. [11] Any one whom he that has the discharge touches without having rinsed his hands in water shall wash his clothes, and bathe himself in water, and be unclean until the evening. [12] And the earthen vessel which he who has the discharge touches shall be broken; and every vessel of wood shall be rinsed in water.

13 "And when he who has a discharge is cleansed of his discharge, then he shall count for himself seven days for his cleansing, and wash his clothes; and he shall bathe his body in running water, and shall be clean. [14] And on the eighth day he shall take two turtledoves or two young pigeons, and come before the LORD to the door of the tent of meeting, and give them to the priest; [15] and the priest shall offer them, one for a sin offering and the other for a burnt offering; and the priest shall make atonement for him before the LORD for his discharge.

16 "And if a man has an emission of semen, he shall bathe his whole body in water, and be unclean until the evening. [17] And every garment and every skin on which the semen comes shall be washed with water, and be unclean until the evening. [18] If a man lies with a woman and has an emission of semen, both of them shall bathe themselves in water, and be unclean until the evening.

19 "When a woman has a discharge of blood which is her regular discharge from her body, she shall be in her impurity for seven days, and whoever touches her shall be unclean until the evening. [20] And everything upon which she lies during her impurity shall be unclean; everything also upon which she sits shall be unclean. [21] And whoever touches her bed shall wash his clothes, and bathe himself in water, and be unclean until the evening. [22] And whoever touches anything upon which she sits shall wash his clothes, and bathe himself in water, and be unclean until the evening; [23] whether it is the bed or anything upon which she sits, when he touches it he shall be unclean until the evening. [24] And if any man lies with her, and her impurity is on him, he shall be unclean seven days; and every bed on which he lies shall be unclean.

15.1–32: Bodily discharges. Various bodily emissions, it was believed, produced ritual uncleanness which defiled the holy tabernacle in the midst of the people (v. 31). **3–12:** An unclean person contaminates anything or anyone he touches (11.24–38). **13–15:** The prescribed sacrifices to make atonement for uncleanness. On the sin offering, see 4.2 n. **16–18:** It is not suggested that such secretions are evil or that sex is taboo. On holy occasions, such as worship (Ex.19.15) or the conduct of holy war (1 Sam.21.4–6), sexual abstinence was required. **19–30:** See ch. 12.

25 "If a woman has a discharge of blood for many days, not at the time of her impurity, or if she has a discharge beyond the time of her impurity, all the days of the discharge she shall continue in uncleanness; as in the days of her impurity, she shall be unclean. 26 Every bed on which she lies, all the days of her discharge, shall be to her as the bed of her impurity; and everything on which she sits shall be unclean, as in the uncleanness of her impurity. 27 And whoever touches these things shall be unclean, and shall wash his clothes, and bathe himself in water, and be unclean until the evening. 28 But if she is cleansed of her discharge, she shall count for herself seven days, and after that she shall be clean. 29 And on the eighth day she shall take two turtledoves or two young pigeons, and bring them to the priest, to the door of the tent of meeting. 30 And the priest shall offer one for a sin offering and the other for a burnt offering; and the priest shall make atonement for her before the LORD for her unclean discharge.

31 "Thus you shall keep the people of Israel separate from their uncleanness, lest they die in their uncleanness by defiling my tabernacle that is in their midst."

32 This is the law for him who has a discharge and for him who has an emission of semen, becoming unclean thereby; 33 also for her who is sick with her impurity; that is, for any one, male or female, who has a discharge, and for the man who lies with a woman who is unclean.

16 The LORD spoke to Moses, after the death of the two sons of Aaron, when they drew near before the LORD and died; 2 and the LORD said to Moses, "Tell Aaron your brother not to come at all times into the holy place within the veil, before the mercy seat which is upon the ark, lest he die; for I will appear in the cloud upon the mercy seat. 3 But thus shall Aaron come into the holy place: with a young bull for a sin offering and a ram for a burnt offering. 4 He shall put on the holy linen coat, and shall have the linen breeches on his body, be girded with the linen girdle, and wear the linen turban; these are the holy garments. He shall bathe his body in water, and then put them on. 5 And he shall take from the congregation of the people of Israel two male goats for a sin offering, and one ram for a burnt offering.

6 "And Aaron shall offer the bull as a sin offering for himself, and shall make atonement for himself and for his house. 7 Then he shall take the two goats, and set them before the LORD at the door of the tent of meeting; 8 and Aaron shall cast lots upon the two goats, one lot for the LORD and the other lot for Aza'zel. 9 And Aaron shall present the goat on which the lot fell for the LORD, and offer it as a sin offering; 10 but the goat on which the lot fell for Aza'zel shall be presented alive before the LORD to make atonement over it, that it may be sent away into the wilderness to Aza'zel.

11 "Aaron shall present the bull as a sin offering for himself, and shall make atonement for himself and for

---

31: The people of Israel must be holy, for the LORD whose tabernacle is in their midst is holy (compare 19.2; see 11.44–45 n.).

16.1–34: The ritual for the day of atonement. Priestly tradition has preserved an ancient ritual, which has been elaborated during years of cultic usage, as shown by the composite character of this chapter. **1–5:** Preparatory instructions. **1:** After the block of laws on uncleanness (chs. 11–15), the account resumes from ch. 10. **2:** The high priest is to go into *the holy place within the veil* (Ex.26.31–35) only once a year to make atonement for priests and people (vv. 30,34). *The mercy seat,* see Ex.25.17 n. *The cloud,* see Ex.40.34–38 n. **4:** Compare Ex. ch. 28. **6–10:** A short version of the ritual for the day of atonement. Two goats are chosen to bear symbolically the sins of the people. The one chosen *for the LORD* is to be sacrificed as a sin offering (v. 15); the other is to be driven into the wilderness *to Azazel,* an evil spirit or desert demon (10.4; compare Lev.17.7; Is.34.14). **11–28:** A more elaborate version of the ritual. The high

his house; he shall kill the bull as a sin offering for himself. [12] And he shall take a censer full of coals of fire from the altar before the LORD, and two handfuls of sweet incense beaten small; and he shall bring it within the veil [13] and put the incense on the fire before the LORD, that the cloud of the incense may cover the mercy seat which is upon the testimony, lest he die; [14] and he shall take some of the blood of the bull, and sprinkle it with his finger on the front of the mercy seat, and before the mercy seat he shall sprinkle the blood with his finger seven times.

15 "Then he shall kill the goat of the sin offering which is for the people, and bring its blood within the veil, and do with its blood as he did with the blood of the bull, sprinkling it upon the mercy seat and before the mercy seat; [16] thus he shall make atonement for the holy place, because of the uncleannesses of the people of Israel, and because of their transgressions, all their sins; and so he shall do for the tent of meeting, which abides with them in the midst of their uncleannesses. [17] There shall be no man in the tent of meeting when he enters to make atonement in the holy place until he comes out and has made atonement for himself and for his house and for all the assembly of Israel. [18] Then he shall go out to the altar which is before the LORD and make atonement for it, and shall take some of the blood of the bull and of the blood of the goat, and put it on the horns of the altar round about. [19] And he shall sprinkle some of the blood upon it with his finger seven times, and cleanse it and hallow it from the uncleannesses of the people of Israel.

20 "And when he has made an end of atoning for the holy place and the tent of meeting and the altar, he shall present the live goat; [21] and Aaron shall lay both his hands upon the head of the live goat, and confess over him all the iniquities of the people of Israel, and all their transgressions, all their sins; and he shall put them upon the head of the goat, and send him away into the wilderness by the hand of a man who is in readiness. [22] The goat shall bear all their iniquities upon him to a solitary land; and he shall let the goat go in the wilderness.

23 "Then Aaron shall come into the tent of meeting, and shall put off the linen garments which he put on when he went into the holy place, and shall leave them there; [24] and he shall bathe his body in water in a holy place, and put on his garments, and come forth, and offer his burnt offering and the burnt offering of the people, and make atonement for himself and for the people. [25] And the fat of the sin offering he shall burn upon the altar. [26] And he who lets the goat go to Aza'zel shall wash his clothes and bathe his body in water, and afterward he may come into the camp. [27] And the bull for the sin offering and the goat for the sin offering, whose blood was brought in to make atonement in the holy place, shall be carried forth outside the camp; their skin and their flesh and their dung shall be burned with fire. [28] And he who burns them shall wash his clothes and bathe his body in water, and afterward he may come into the camp.

29 "And it shall be a statute to you

---

priest enters the Holy of Holies once to make atonement for the priests (vv. 11–14) and once for the people (vv. 15–22). **13:** The cloud of incense is to cover the mercy seat in order to protect the priest from beholding God (Ex.33.20). **16–19:** The high priest is to make atonement for the tabernacle and altar (Ex.29.35–37) because of the people's sins and uncleannesses. Priestly theology is deeply concerned about the presence of the holy God in the midst of a sinful people. **20–22:** This ritual symbolizes the transfer of the people's sins to the animal which then carries the sins off into the wilderness (see Heb.9.1–10.18 n.). **23–28:** Contact with holiness, like contact with its opposite, uncleanness, requires ceremonial change of garments and ritual ablutions. The ceremony concludes with a burnt offering for priest and people. **29–34:** A statutory requirement that the day of atonement shall be observed annually as *a sabbath of solemn rest.*

for ever that in the seventh month, on the tenth day of the month, you shall afflict yourselves, and shall do no work, either the native or the stranger who sojourns among you; [30] for on this day shall atonement be made for you, to cleanse you; from all your sins you shall be clean before the LORD. [31] It is a sabbath of solemn rest to you, and you shall afflict yourselves; it is a statute for ever. [32] And the priest who is anointed and consecrated as priest in his father's place shall make atonement, wearing the holy linen garments; [33] he shall make atonement for the sanctuary, and he shall make atonement for the tent of meeting and for the altar, and he shall make atonement for the priests and for all the people of the assembly. [34] And this shall be an everlasting statute for you, that atonement may be made for the people of Israel once in the year because of all their sins." And Moses did as the LORD commanded him.

17 And the LORD said to Moses, [2] "Say to Aaron and his sons, and to all the people of Israel, This is the thing which the LORD has commanded. [3] If any man of the house of Israel kills an ox or a lamb or a goat in the camp, or kills it outside the camp, [4] and does not bring it to the door of the tent of meeting, to offer it as a gift to the LORD before the tabernacle of the LORD, bloodguilt shall be imputed to that man; he has shed blood; and that man shall be cut off from among his people. [5] This is to the end that the people of Israel may bring their sacrifices which they slay in the open field, that they may bring them to the LORD, to the priest at the door of the tent of meeting, and slay them as sacrifices of peace offerings to the

LORD; [6] and the priest shall sprinkle the blood on the altar of the LORD at the door of the tent of meeting, and burn the fat for a pleasing odor to the LORD. [7] So they shall no more slay their sacrifices for satyrs, after whom they play the harlot. This shall be a statute for ever to them throughout their generations.

8 "And you shall say to them, Any man of the house of Israel, or of the strangers that sojourn among them, who offers a burnt offering or sacrifice, [9] and does not bring it to the door of the tent of meeting, to sacrifice it to the LORD; that man shall be cut off from his people.

10 "If any man of the house of Israel or of the strangers that sojourn among them eats any blood, I will set my face against that person who eats blood, and will cut him off from among his people. [11] For the life of the flesh is in the blood; and I have given it for you upon the altar to make atonement for your souls; for it is the blood that makes atonement, by reason of the life. [12] Therefore I have said to the people of Israel, No person among you shall eat blood, neither shall any stranger who sojourns among you eat blood. [13] Any man also of the people of Israel, or of the strangers that sojourn among them, who takes in hunting any beast or bird that may be eaten shall pour out its blood and cover it with dust.

14 "For the life of every creature is the blood of it;[e] therefore I have said to the people of Israel, You shall not eat the blood of any creature, for the life of every creature is its blood; whoever eats it shall be cut off. [15] And

e Gk Syr Compare Vg: Heb *for the life of all flesh, its blood is in its life*

17.1–16: Restrictions upon the slaughter of animals. Chapters 17–26 constitute a corpus of laws often called the Holiness Code because of the dominant theme: Israel must be holy as God is holy. **3–7:** The former practice of sacrifice at every legitimate place where the LORD was worshiped (Ex.20.24–25) is modified by this old tradition which requires that animals for food be sacrificed at the central sanctuary (Dt.12.15–28) as a peace offering (ch. 3). **4:** The reason given is that sacrifices in the open fields had been offered to *satyrs* (v. 7), i.e. demons (Is.34.14; Dt.32.17; 2 Chr.11.15). **9:** *Cut off* (v. 4), see 7.20 n. **10–14:** Prohibition against eating blood. **11:** The basis of the priestly sacrificial system (see 1.5 n.). **15:** See Ex.22.31 n.

every person that eats what dies of
itself or what is torn by beasts, whether
he is a native or a sojourner, shall wash
his clothes, and bathe himself in water,
and be unclean until the evening; then
he shall be clean. ¹⁶ But if he does not
wash them or bathe his flesh, he shall
bear his iniquity."

18 And the LORD said to Moses,
² "Say to the people of Israel, I
am the LORD your God. ³ You shall
not do as they do in the land of Egypt,
where you dwelt, and you shall not do
as they do in the land of Canaan, to
which I am bringing you. You shall not
walk in their statutes. ⁴ You shall do
my ordinances and keep my statutes
and walk in them. I am the LORD your
God. ⁵ You shall therefore keep my
statutes and my ordinances, by doing
which a man shall live: I am the LORD.

6 "None of you shall approach any
one near of kin to him to uncover
nakedness. I am the LORD. ⁷ You shall
not uncover the nakedness of your
father, which is the nakedness of your
mother; she is your mother, you shall
not uncover her nakedness. ⁸ You
shall not uncover the nakedness of your
father's wife; it is your father's nakedness. ⁹ You shall not uncover the
nakedness of your sister, the daughter
of your father or the daughter of your
mother, whether born at home or born
abroad. ¹⁰ You shall not uncover the
nakedness of your son's daughter or of
your daughter's daughter, for their
nakedness is your own nakedness.
¹¹ You shall not uncover the nakedness
of your father's wife's daughter, begotten by your father, since she is your sister. ¹² You shall not uncover the nakedness of your father's sister; she is your
father's near kinswoman. ¹³ You shall
not uncover the nakedness of your
mother's sister, for she is your mother's
near kinswoman. ¹⁴ You shall not un-

cover the nakedness of your father's
brother, that is, you shall not approach
his wife; she is your aunt. ¹⁵ You shall
not uncover the nakedness of your
daughter-in-law; she is your son's wife,
you shall not uncover her nakedness.
¹⁶ You shall not uncover the nakedness
of your brother's wife; she is your
brother's nakedness. ¹⁷ You shall not
uncover the nakedness of a woman
and of her daughter, and you shall not
take her son's daughter or her daughter's daughter to uncover her nakedness; they are your*f* near kinswomen;
it is wickedness. ¹⁸ And you shall not
take a woman as a rival wife to her
sister, uncovering her nakedness while
her sister is yet alive.

19 "You shall not approach a
woman to uncover her nakedness while
she is in her menstrual uncleanness.
²⁰ And you shall not lie carnally with
your neighbor's wife, and defile yourself with her. ²¹ You shall not give any
of your children to devote them by fire
to Molech, and so profane the name of
your God: I am the LORD. ²² You shall
not lie with a male as with a woman;
it is an abomination. ²³ And you
shall not lie with any beast and defile
yourself with it, neither shall any woman give herself to a beast to lie with
it: it is perversion.

24 "Do not defile yourselves by any
of these things, for by all these the
nations I am casting out before you
defiled themselves; ²⁵ and the land
became defiled, so that I punished its
iniquity, and the land vomited out its
inhabitants. ²⁶ But you shall keep my
statutes and my ordinances and do
none of these abominations, either the
native or the stranger who sojourns
among you ²⁷ (for all of these abominations the men of the land did, who were
before you, so that the land became de-

f Gk: Heb lacks *your*

18.1–30: Forbidden sexual relations. 1–5: As a holy people, set apart for special relation to
the LORD, Israel must not imitate the practices of other peoples (vv. 24–29; 11.44–45 n.). 6–18:
An old list of twelve sexual prohibitions (compare the twelve curses in Dt. ch. 27). 16: The
levirate marriage was an exception to this rule (see Gen.38.8 n.). 21: On the pagan rite of child
sacrifice to *Molech*, the Ammonite deity (1 Kg.11.7), see Dt.18.10 n. 26–28: Although the laws

filed); [28] lest the land vomit you out, when you defile it, as it vomited out the nation that was before you. [29] For whoever shall do any of these abominations, the persons that do them shall be cut off from among their people. [30] So keep my charge never to practice any of these abominable customs which were practiced before you, and never to defile yourselves by them: I am the LORD your God."

19 And the LORD said to Moses, [2] "Say to all the congregation of the people of Israel, You shall be holy; for I the LORD your God am holy. [3] Every one of you shall revere his mother and his father, and you shall keep my sabbaths: I am the LORD your God. [4] Do not turn to idols or make for yourselves molten gods: I am the LORD your God.

5 "When you offer a sacrifice of peace offerings to the LORD, you shall offer it so that you may be accepted. [6] It shall be eaten the same day you offer it, or on the morrow; and anything left over until the third day shall be burned with fire. [7] If it is eaten at all on the third day, it is an abomination; it will not be accepted, [8] and every one who eats it shall bear his iniquity, because he has profaned a holy thing of the LORD; and that person shall be cut off from his people.

9 "When you reap the harvest of your land, you shall not reap your field to its very border, neither shall you gather the gleanings after your harvest. [10] And you shall not strip your vineyard bare, neither shall you gather the fallen grapes of your vineyard; you

shall leave them for the poor and for the sojourner: I am the LORD your God.

11 "You shall not steal, nor deal falsely, nor lie to one another. [12] And you shall not swear by my name falsely, and so profane the name of your God: I am the LORD.

13 "You shall not oppress your neighbor or rob him. The wages of a hired servant shall not remain with you all night until the morning. [14] You shall not curse the deaf or put a stumbling block before the blind, but you shall fear your God: I am the LORD.

15 "You shall do no injustice in judgment; you shall not be partial to the poor or defer to the great, but in righteousness shall you judge your neighbor. [16] You shall not go up and down as a slanderer among your people, and you shall not stand forth against the life[g] of your neighbor: I am the LORD.

17 "You shall not hate your brother in your heart, but you shall reason with your neighbor, lest you bear sin because of him. [18] You shall not take vengeance or bear any grudge against the sons of your own people, but you shall love your neighbor as yourself: I am the LORD.

19 "You shall keep my statutes. You shall not let your cattle breed with a different kind; you shall not sow your field with two kinds of seed; nor shall there come upon you a garment of cloth made of two kinds of stuff.

20 "If a man lies carnally with a woman who is a slave, betrothed to an-

g Heb *blood*

---

of Leviticus are placed in the ancient setting of Mount Sinai, this passage clearly presupposes a time after the conquest of Canaan (vv. 25,27).
19.1–37: The life of holiness. This chapter represents a fine blending of cultic requirements and ethical obligations, as expressed classically in the Ten Commandments (see vv. 9–10,13–16). **2:** The keynote of the chapter and of the so-called Holiness Code. The God who brought Israel out of Egypt (v. 36) has separated his people for a special covenant with him (18.1–5; 20.26; 22.31–33). Israel's holiness, therefore, is derived from the nation's being related to the holy God, not from any intrinsic quality of the people. **5–8:** See ch. 3. **17–18:** Previous ethical injunctions come to a climax in this law, the source of the "second" commandment quoted in the New Testament (Mk.12.31). *Neighbor* here means a fellow-Israelite (Dt.15.3 n.); however, the law to *love your neighbor as yourself* is extended to include the sojourner in vv. 33–34. **19:** See Dt.22.9–11 n. **20–22:** The reason for this legal clemency is that the slave-woman is regarded

other man and not yet ransomed or given her freedom, an inquiry shall be held. They shall not be put to death, because she was not free; 21 but he shall bring a guilt offering for himself to the LORD, to the door of the tent of meeting, a ram for a guilt offering. 22 And the priest shall make atonement for him with the ram of the guilt offering before the LORD for his sin which he has committed; and the sin which he has committed shall be forgiven him.

23 "When you come into the land and plant all kinds of trees for food, then you shall count their fruit as forbidden;*h* three years it shall be forbidden to you, it must not be eaten. 24 And in the fourth year all their fruit shall be holy, an offering of praise to the LORD. 25 But in the fifth year you may eat of their fruit, that they may yield more richly for you: I am the LORD your God.

26 "You shall not eat any flesh with the blood in it. You shall not practice augury or witchcraft. 27 You shall not round off the hair on your temples or mar the edges of your beard. 28 You shall not make any cuttings in your flesh on account of the dead or tattoo any marks upon you: I am the LORD.

29 "Do not profane your daughter by making her a harlot, lest the land fall into harlotry and the land become full of wickedness. 30 You shall keep my sabbaths and reverence my sanctuary: I am the LORD.

31 "Do not turn to mediums or wizards; do not seek them out, to be defiled by them: I am the LORD your God.

32 "You shall rise up before the hoary head, and honor the face of an old man, and you shall fear your God: I am the LORD.

33 "When a stranger sojourns with you in your land, you shall not do him wrong. 34 The stranger who sojourns with you shall be to you as the native among you, and you shall love him as yourself; for you were strangers in the land of Egypt: I am the LORD your God.

35 "You shall do no wrong in judgment, in measures of length or weight or quantity. 36 You shall have just balances, just weights, a just ephah, and a just hin: I am the LORD your God, who brought you out of the land of Egypt. 37 And you shall observe all my statutes and all my ordinances, and do them: I am the LORD."

20 The LORD said to Moses, 2 "Say to the people of Israel, Any man of the people of Israel, or of the strangers that sojourn in Israel, who gives any of his children to Molech shall be put to death; the people of the land shall stone him with stones. 3 I myself will set my face against that man, and will cut him off from among his people, because he has given one of his children to Molech, defiling my sanctuary and profaning my holy name. 4 And if the people of the land do at all hide their eyes from that man, when he gives one of his children to Molech, and do not put him to death, 5 then I will set my face against that man and against his family, and will cut them off from among their people, him and all who follow him in playing the harlot after Molech.

6 "If a person turns to mediums and wizards, playing the harlot after them, I will set my face against that person,

h Heb *their uncircumcision*

---

as another man's property, i.e. his concubine (Ex.21.7–11). **23–25:** This law may reflect the ancient custom of propitiating the fertility powers of the soil, although here the practice is redefined in terms of Israel's faith. **26–31:** Most of the laws in this section are protests against the practices of other peoples: magic and witchcraft (v. 26), heathen mourning customs (vv. 27–28; see 21.5 n.), sacred prostitution (v. 29), and necromancy (v. 31; 1 Sam. ch. 28; 2 Kg. 21.6; 23.24).

20.1–27: Penalties for violating the rules of the theocratic community. The severity of punishment is based on the conviction that Israel is to be a holy people, separated from others by its manner of life and worship (vv. 7–8,22–26). **2–5:** On Molech worship, see 18.21 n.

and will cut him off from among his people. ⁷ Consecrate yourselves therefore, and be holy; for I am the LORD your God. ⁸ Keep my statutes, and do them; I am the LORD who sanctify you. ⁹ For every one who curses his father or his mother shall be put to death; he has cursed his father or his mother, his blood is upon him.

10 "If a man commits adultery with the wife of*ⁱ* his neighbor, both the adulterer and the adulteress shall be put to death. ¹¹ The man who lies with his father's wife has uncovered his father's nakedness; both of them shall be put to death, their blood is upon them. ¹² If a man lies with his daughter-in-law, both of them shall be put to death; they have committed incest, their blood is upon them. ¹³ If a man lies with a male as with a woman, both of them have committed an abomination; they shall be put to death, their blood is upon them. ¹⁴ If a man takes a wife and her mother also, it is wickedness; they shall be burned with fire, both he and they, that there may be no wickedness among you. ¹⁵ If a man lies with a beast, he shall be put to death; and you shall kill the beast. ¹⁶ If a woman approaches any beast and lies with it, you shall kill the woman and the beast; they shall be put to death, their blood is upon them.

17 "If a man takes his sister, a daughter of his father or a daughter of his mother, and sees her nakedness, and she sees his nakedness, it is a shameful thing, and they shall be cut off in the sight of the children of their people; he has uncovered his sister's nakedness, he shall bear his iniquity. ¹⁸ If a man lies with a woman having her sickness, and uncovers her nakedness, he has made naked her fountain,

and she has uncovered the fountain of her blood; both of them shall be cut off from among their people. ¹⁹ You shall not uncover the nakedness of your mother's sister or of your father's sister, for that is to make naked one's near kin; they shall bear their iniquity. ²⁰ If a man lies with his uncle's wife, he has uncovered his uncle's nakedness; they shall bear their sin, they shall die childless. ²¹ If a man takes his brother's wife, it is impurity; he has uncovered his brother's nakedness, they shall be childless.

22 "You shall therefore keep all my statutes and all my ordinances, and do them; that the land where I am bringing you to dwell may not vomit you out. ²³ And you shall not walk in the customs of the nation which I am casting out before you; for they did all these things, and therefore I abhorred them. ²⁴ But I have said to you, 'You shall inherit their land, and I will give it to you to possess, a land flowing with milk and honey.' I am the LORD your God, who have separated you from the peoples. ²⁵ You shall therefore make a distinction between the clean beast and the unclean, and between the unclean bird and the clean; you shall not make yourselves abominable by beast or by bird or by anything with which the ground teems, which I have set apart for you to hold unclean. ²⁶ You shall be holy to me; for I the LORD am holy, and have separated you from the peoples, that you should be mine.

27 "A man or a woman who is a medium or a wizard shall be put to death; they shall be stoned with stones, their blood shall be upon them."

21 And the LORD said to Moses, "Speak to the priests, the sons of

ⁱ Heb repeats *if a man commits adultery with the wife of*

9: See Ex.21.17 n. 10–21: The death penalty is prescribed for the sexual offenses dealt with in ch. 18. 22–24: This appeal is similar to the conclusion of the Covenant Code (Ex.23.23–33) and to the exhortations of Deuteronomy. 25: See ch. 11. 26: See 19.2 n. Much of the material in this chapter duplicates laws found elsewhere in the Holiness Code (e.g. chs. 18 and 19), indicating that the editor has compiled various independent traditions. 27: See 19.31. *Put to death*, compare 1 Sam.28.9.

21.1–24: Instructions to the priests. Behavior of the priests is governed by the fact that they have a special status: they are *holy to their God* (v. 6), i.e. separated for a special divine service.

Aaron, and say to them that none of them shall defile himself for the dead among his people, [2] except for his nearest of kin, his mother, his father, his son, his daughter, his brother, [3] or his virgin sister (who is near to him because she has had no husband; for her he may defile himself). [4] He shall not defile himself as a husband among his people and so profane himself. [5] They shall not make tonsures upon their heads, nor shave off the edges of their beards, nor make any cuttings in their flesh. [6] They shall be holy to their God, and not profane the name of their God; for they offer the offerings by fire to the LORD, the bread of their God; therefore they shall be holy. [7] They shall not marry a harlot or a woman who has been defiled; neither shall they marry a woman divorced from her husband; for the priest is holy to his God. [8] You shall consecrate him, for he offers the bread of your God; he shall be holy to you; for I the LORD, who sanctify you, am holy. [9] And the daughter of any priest, if she profanes herself by playing the harlot, profanes her father; she shall be burned with fire.

10 "The priest who is chief among his brethren, upon whose head the anointing oil is poured, and who has been consecrated to wear the garments, shall not let the hair of his head hang loose, nor rend his clothes; [11] he shall not go in to any dead body, nor defile himself, even for his father or for his mother; [12] neither shall he go out of the sanctuary, nor profane the sanctuary of his God; for the consecration of the anointing oil of his God is upon him: I am the LORD. [13] And he shall take a wife in her virginity. [14] A widow, or one divorced, or a woman who has been defiled, or a harlot, these he shall not marry; but he shall take to wife a virgin of his own people, [15] that he may not profane his children among his people; for I am the LORD who sanctify him."

16 And the LORD said to Moses, [17] "Say to Aaron, None of your descendants throughout their generations who has a blemish may approach to offer the bread of his God. [18] For no one who has a blemish shall draw near, a man blind or lame, or one who has a mutilated face or a limb too long, [19] or a man who has an injured foot or an injured hand, [20] or a hunchback, or a dwarf, or a man with a defect in his sight or an itching disease or scabs or crushed testicles; [21] no man of the descendants of Aaron the priest who has a blemish shall come near to offer the LORD's offerings by fire; since he has a blemish, he shall not come near to offer the bread of his God. [22] He may eat the bread of his God, both of the most holy and of the holy things, [23] but he shall not come near the veil or approach the altar, because he has a blemish, that he may not profane my sanctuaries; for I am the LORD who sanctify them." [24] So Moses spoke to Aaron and to his sons and to all the people of Israel.

22 And the LORD said to Moses, [2] "Tell Aaron and his sons to keep away from the holy things of the people of Israel, which they dedicate to me, so that they may not profane my holy name: I am the LORD. [3] Say to them, 'If any one of all your descendants throughout your generations approaches the holy things, which the people of Israel dedicate to the LORD,

---

1–15: Rules concerning mourning and marriage. **1–3:** Mourning rites were believed to be ritually defiling, owing to association with a dead body (10.6; Ezek.24.15–18). **5:** 19.27–28. Shaving the head and bodily mutilation were common mourning customs in antiquity (Dt.14.1; Am.8.10; Is.22.12; Jer.16.6; Mic.1.16). **6:** *The bread of their God* faintly echoes the ancient notion of sacrifice as the offering of food for the deity (see 2.2–3 n.); here the language is merely traditional. **10–12:** See 10.6 n. **16–23:** Just as the sacrificial offering must be unblemished (22.17–25), so the priest who offers it must be without bodily defect. Unnatural deformity or disfigurement is frowned upon, for man's body is God's creation, made in the divine image (Gen.5.1–3). **22.1–9:** Priests may not partake of *the holy things*, i.e. the consecrated portion of the sacrifice which is their due (see 2.2–3 n.), while in a state of ritual uncleanness as defined in the laws of

while he has an uncleanness, that person shall be cut off from my presence: I am the LORD. [4] None of the line of Aaron who is a leper or suffers a discharge may eat of the holy things until he is clean. Whoever touches anything that is unclean through contact with the dead or a man who has had an emission of semen, [5] and whoever touches a creeping thing by which he may be made unclean or a man from whom he may take uncleanness, whatever his uncleanness may be— [6] the person who touches any such shall be unclean until the evening and shall not eat of the holy things unless he has bathed his body in water. [7] When the sun is down he shall be clean; and afterward he may eat of the holy things, because such are his food. [8] That which dies of itself or is torn by beasts he shall not eat, defiling himself by it: I am the LORD.' [9] They shall therefore keep my charge, lest they bear sin for it and die thereby when they profane it: I am the LORD who sanctify them.

10 "An outsider shall not eat of a holy thing. A sojourner of the priest's or a hired servant shall not eat of a holy thing; [11] but if a priest buys a slave as his property for money, the slave may eat of it; and those that are born in his house may eat of his food. [12] If a priest's daughter is married to an outsider she shall not eat of the offering of the holy things. [13] But if a priest's daughter is a widow or divorced, and has no child, and returns to her father's house, as in her youth, she may eat of her father's food; yet no outsider shall eat of it. [14] And if a man eats of a holy thing unwittingly, he shall add the fifth of its value to it, and give the holy thing to the priest. [15] The priests shall not profane the holy things of the people of Israel, which they offer to the LORD, [16] and so cause them to bear iniquity and guilt, by eating their holy things: for I am the LORD who sanctify them."

17 And the LORD said to Moses, [18] "Say to Aaron and his sons and all the people of Israel, When any one of the house of Israel or of the sojourners in Israel presents his offering, whether in payment of a vow or as a freewill offering which is offered to the LORD as a burnt offering, [19] to be accepted you shall offer a male without blemish, of the bulls or the sheep or the goats. [20] You shall not offer anything that has a blemish, for it will not be acceptable for you. [21] And when any one offers a sacrifice of peace offerings to the LORD, to fulfil a vow or as a freewill offering, from the herd or from the flock, to be accepted it must be perfect; there shall be no blemish in it. [22] Animals blind or disabled or mutilated or having a discharge or an itch or scabs, you shall not offer to the LORD or make of them an offering by fire upon the altar to the LORD. [23] A bull or a lamb which has a part too long or too short you may present for a freewill offering; but for a votive offering it cannot be accepted. [24] Any animal which has its testicles bruised or crushed or torn or cut, you shall not offer to the LORD or sacrifice within your land; [25] neither shall you offer as the bread of your God any such animals gotten from a foreigner. Since there is a blemish in them, because of their mutilation, they will not be accepted for you."

26 And the LORD said to Moses, [27] "When a bull or sheep or goat is born, it shall remain seven days with its mother; and from the eighth day on it shall be acceptable as an offering by fire to the LORD. [28] And whether the mother is a cow or a ewe, you shall not kill both her and her young in one day. [29] And when you sacrifice a sacrifice of thanksgiving to the LORD, you shall sacrifice it so that you may be accepted.

---

chs. 11–15. **10–16:** Further definition of who may eat the consecrated portions. *An outsider,* i.e. a layman outside the priest's immediate household (which included his slaves; see Ex.12.43–49 n.). **17–25:** Directions about acceptable sacrifices.

[30] It shall be eaten on the same day, you shall leave none of it until morning: I am the LORD.

31 "So you shall keep my commandments and do them: I am the LORD. [32] And you shall not profane my holy name, but I will be hallowed among the people of Israel; I am the LORD who sanctify you, [33] who brought you out of the land of Egypt to be your God: I am the LORD."

23 The LORD said to Moses, [2] "Say to the people of Israel, The appointed feasts of the LORD which you shall proclaim as holy convocations, my appointed feasts, are these. [3] Six days shall work be done; but on the seventh day is a sabbath of solemn rest, a holy convocation; you shall do no work; it is a sabbath to the LORD in all your dwellings.

4 "These are the appointed feasts of the LORD, the holy convocations, which you shall proclaim at the time appointed for them. [5] In the first month, on the fourteenth day of the month in the evening,[j] is the LORD's passover. [6] And on the fifteenth day of the same month is the feast of unleavened bread to the LORD; seven days you shall eat unleavened bread. [7] On the first day you shall have a holy convocation; you shall do no laborious work. [8] But you shall present an offering by fire to the LORD seven days; on the seventh day is a holy convocation; you shall do no laborious work."

9 And the LORD said to Moses, [10] "Say to the people of Israel, When you come into the land which I give you and reap its harvest, you shall bring the sheaf of the first fruits of your harvest to the priest; [11] and he shall wave the sheaf before the LORD, that you may find acceptance; on the morrow after the sabbath the priest shall wave it. [12] And on the day when you wave the sheaf, you shall offer a male lamb a year old without blemish as a burnt offering to the LORD. [13] And the cereal offering with it shall be two tenths of an ephah of fine flour mixed with oil, to be offered by fire to the LORD, a pleasing odor; and the drink offering with it shall be of wine, a fourth of a hin. [14] And you shall eat neither bread nor grain parched or fresh until this same day, until you have brought the offering of your God: it is a statute for ever throughout your generations in all your dwellings.

15 "And you shall count from the morrow after the sabbath, from the day that you brought the sheaf of the wave offering; seven full weeks shall they be, [16] counting fifty days to the morrow after the seventh sabbath; then you shall present a cereal offering of new grain to the LORD. [17] You shall bring from your dwellings two loaves of bread to be waved, made of two tenths of an ephah; they shall be of fine flour, they shall be baked with leaven, as first fruits to the LORD. [18] And you shall present with the bread seven lambs a year old without blemish, and one young bull, and two rams; they shall be a burnt offering to the LORD, with their cereal offering and their drink offerings, an offering by fire, a pleasing odor to the LORD. [19] And you shall offer one male goat for a sin offering, and two male lambs a year old as a sacrifice of peace offerings. [20] And the priest shall wave

j Heb *between the two evenings*

23.1–44: The sacred calendar. 2: There shall be a proclamation by trumpets (Num.10.10) to announce the appointed feasts. **3:** Ex.16.23. **4:** The calendar of sacred feasts is paralleled in Ex.23.14–17; 34.18–24; Dt.16.1–17. **5–8:** Passover and the feast of unleavened bread are treated here (as in other calendars) as two phases of one celebration (see Ex.12.14–20 n.). *The first month*, see Ex.12.2 n. **9–14:** The offering of the first fruits (Dt.26.5–10) took place the day after the concluding sabbath of the feast of unleavened bread (v. 11; compare vv. 7–8), i.e. at the beginning of the barley harvest in April. **11:** *Wave the sheaf*, see Ex.29.24 n. **15–21:** Since the festival of weeks, celebrated at the time of the wheat harvest, was held fifty days after the feast of unleavened bread, it came to be called Pentecost (based on a Greek word meaning "fifty").

them with the bread of the first fruits as a wave offering before the LORD, with the two lambs; they shall be holy to the LORD for the priest. [21] And you shall make proclamation on the same day; you shall hold a holy convocation; you shall do no laborious work: it is a statute for ever in all your dwellings throughout your generations.

22 "And when you reap the harvest of your land, you shall not reap your field to its very border, nor shall you gather the gleanings after your harvest; you shall leave them for the poor and for the stranger: I am the LORD your God."

23 And the LORD said to Moses, [24] "Say to the people of Israel, In the seventh month, on the first day of the month, you shall observe a day of solemn rest, a memorial proclaimed with blast of trumpets, a holy convocation. [25] You shall do no laborious work; and you shall present an offering by fire to the LORD."

26 And the LORD said to Moses, [27] "On the tenth day of this seventh month is the day of atonement; it shall be for you a time of holy convocation, and you shall afflict yourselves and present an offering by fire to the LORD. [28] And you shall do no work on this same day; for it is a day of atonement, to make atonement for you before the LORD your God. [29] For whoever is not afflicted on this same day shall be cut off from his people. [30] And whoever does any work on this same day, that person I will destroy from among his people. [31] You shall do no work: it is a statute for ever throughout your generations in all your dwellings. [32] It shall be to you a sabbath of solemn rest, and you shall afflict yourselves; on the ninth day of the month beginning at evening, from evening to evening shall you keep your sabbath."

33 And the LORD said to Moses, [34] "Say to the people of Israel, On the fifteenth day of this seventh month and for seven days is the feast of booths[k] to the LORD. [35] On the first day shall be a holy convocation; you shall do no laborious work. [36] Seven days you shall present offerings by fire to the LORD; on the eighth day you shall hold a holy convocation and present an offering by fire to the LORD; it is a solemn assembly; you shall do no laborious work.

37 "These are the appointed feasts of the LORD, which you shall proclaim as times of holy convocation, for presenting to the LORD offerings by fire, burnt offerings and cereal offerings, sacrifices and drink offerings, each on its proper day; [38] besides the sabbaths of the LORD, and besides your gifts, and besides all your votive offerings, and besides all your freewill offerings, which you give to the LORD.

39 "On the fifteenth day of the seventh month, when you have gathered in the produce of the land, you shall keep the feast of the LORD seven days; on the first day shall be a solemn rest, and on the eighth day shall be a solemn rest. [40] And you shall take on the first day the fruit of goodly trees, branches of palm trees, and boughs of leafy trees, and willows of the brook; and you shall rejoice before the LORD your God seven days. [41] You shall keep it as a feast to the LORD seven days in the year; it is a statute for ever throughout your generations; you shall keep it in the seventh month. [42] You shall dwell in booths for seven days; all that are native in Israel shall dwell in booths, [43] that your generations may know that I made the people of Israel dwell in booths when I brought them out of the land of Egypt: I am the LORD your God."

k Or *tabernacles*

23–25: The festival of trumpets or New Year. This falls at the beginning of *the seventh month* (September-October), according to the ecclesiastical calendar (see Ex.12.2 n.). **26–32:** The day of atonement (ch. 16) occurs during the same month. **33–36** (supplemented in vv. 39–43): The feast of booths or thanksgiving was held at the time of the autumn ingathering. **37–38:** See further Num. chs. 28 and 29 for the sacrifices to be offered at the holy convocations.
    24.1–23: Various priestly laws. **1–4:** Oil for the sanctuary lamp (Ex.27.20–21). **5–9:** The

44 Thus Moses declared to the people of Israel the appointed feasts of the LORD.

24 The LORD said to Moses, ² "Command the people of Israel to bring you pure oil from beaten olives for the lamp, that a light may be kept burning continually. ³ Outside the veil of the testimony, in the tent of meeting, Aaron shall keep it in order from evening to morning before the LORD continually; it shall be a statute for ever throughout your generations. ⁴ He shall keep the lamps in order upon the lampstand of pure gold before the LORD continually.

5 "And you shall take fine flour, and bake twelve cakes of it; two tenths of an ephah shall be in each cake. ⁶ And you shall set them in two rows, six in a row, upon the table of pure gold. ⁷ And you shall put pure frankincense with each row, that it may go with the bread as a memorial portion to be offered by fire to the LORD. ⁸ Every sabbath day Aaron shall set it in order before the LORD continually on behalf of the people of Israel as a covenant for ever. ⁹ And it shall be for Aaron and his sons, and they shall eat it in a holy place, since it is for him a most holy portion out of the offerings by fire to the LORD, a perpetual due."

10 Now an Israelite woman's son, whose father was an Egyptian, went out among the people of Israel; and the Israelite woman's son and a man of Israel quarreled in the camp, ¹¹ and the Israelite woman's son blasphemed the Name, and cursed. And they brought him to Moses. His mother's name was Shelo'mith, the daughter of Dibri, of the tribe of Dan. ¹² And they put him in custody, till the will of the LORD should be declared to them.

13 And the LORD said to Moses, ¹⁴ "Bring out of the camp him who cursed; and let all who heard him lay their hands upon his head, and let all the congregation stone him. ¹⁵ And say to the people of Israel, Whoever curses his God shall bear his sin. ¹⁶ He who blasphemes the name of the LORD shall be put to death; all the congregation shall stone him; the sojourner as well as the native, when he blasphemes the Name, shall be put to death. ¹⁷ He who kills a man shall be put to death. ¹⁸ He who kills a beast shall make it good, life for life. ¹⁹ When a man causes a disfigurement in his neighbor, as he has done it shall be done to him, ²⁰ fracture for fracture, eye for eye, tooth for tooth; as he has disfigured a man, he shall be disfigured. ²¹ He who kills a beast shall make it good; and he who kills a man shall be put to death. ²² You shall have one law for the sojourner and for the native; for I am the LORD your God." ²³ So Moses spoke to the people of Israel; and they brought him who had cursed out of the camp, and stoned him with stones. Thus the people of Israel did as the LORD commanded Moses.

25 The LORD said to Moses on Mount Sinai, ² "Say to the people of Israel, When you come into the land which I give you, the land shall keep a sabbath to the LORD. ³ Six years you shall sow your field, and six years you shall prune your vineyard, and gather in its fruits; ⁴ but in the

---

bread of the Presence, see Ex.25.23–30. **10–14:** This incident serves as a setting for the laws that follow (see v. 23). *The Name,* a substitute for the sacred name of Israel's God (see Ex. 3.14 n.). On cursing God, see Ex.20.7; 22.28. **12:** Compare Num.15.32–36. **13:** It is held that blasphemy pollutes the community. Stoning, a communal mode of execution, is the means of purifying the evil from the midst of the people (Dt.17.2–7; 21.18–21). **15–22:** An independent set of laws. **20:** For the lex talionis (the law of "an eye for an eye, and a tooth for a tooth"), see Ex.21.22–25 n.

25.1–55: The sabbatical year and the year of jubilee. These laws attempt to prevent economic exploitation by stressing that the ownership of the land is vested in God, rather than man. **2–7:** On the seventh year *the land shall keep a sabbath,* i.e. lie fallow (Ex.23.10–11). Although this custom may be rooted ultimately in appeasement of the powers of the soil (see 19.23–25 n.),

seventh year there shall be a sabbath of solemn rest for the land, a sabbath to the LORD; you shall not sow your field or prune your vineyard. [5] What grows of itself in your harvest you shall not reap, and the grapes of your undressed vine you shall not gather; it shall be a year of solemn rest for the land. [6] The sabbath of the land shall provide food for you, for yourself and for your male and female slaves and for your hired servant and the sojourner who lives with you; [7] for your cattle also and for the beasts that are in your land all its yield shall be for food.

8 "And you shall count seven weeks[l] of years, seven times seven years, so that the time of the seven weeks of years shall be to you forty-nine years. [9] Then you shall send abroad the loud trumpet on the tenth day of the seventh month; on the day of atonement you shall send abroad the trumpet throughout all your land. [10] And you shall hallow the fiftieth year, and proclaim liberty throughout the land to all its inhabitants; it shall be a jubilee for you, when each of you shall return to his property and each of you shall return to his family. [11] A jubilee shall that fiftieth year be to you; in it you shall neither sow, nor reap what grows of itself, nor gather the grapes from the undressed vines. [12] For it is a jubilee; it shall be holy to you; you shall eat what it yields out of the field.

13 "In this year of jubilee each of you shall return to his property. [14] And

if you sell to your neighbor or buy from your neighbor, you shall not wrong one another. [15] According to the number of years after the jubilee, you shall buy from your neighbor, and according to the number of years for crops he shall sell to you. [16] If the years are many you shall increase the price, and if the years are few you shall diminish the price, for it is the number of the crops that he is selling to you. [17] You shall not wrong one another, but you shall fear your God; for I am the LORD your God.

18 "Therefore you shall do my statutes, and keep my ordinances and perform them; so you will dwell in the land securely. [19] The land will yield its fruit, and you will eat your fill, and dwell in it securely. [20] And if you say, 'What shall we eat in the seventh year, if we may not sow or gather in our crop?' [21] I will command my blessing upon you in the sixth year, so that it will bring forth fruit for three years. [22] When you sow in the eighth year, you will be eating old produce; until the ninth year, when its produce comes in, you shall eat the old. [23] The land shall not be sold in perpetuity, for the land is mine; for you are strangers and sojourners with me. [24] And in all the country you possess, you shall grant a redemption of the land.

25 "If your brother becomes poor, and sells part of his property, then his next of kin shall come and redeem what his brother has sold. [26] If a man has

l Or sabbaths

here it signifies that the LORD owns the land and gives it to his people for stewardship (v. 2). **6–7:** These verses appear to modify the law by saying that, although there shall be no reaping or storing (v. 5), the crop that grows of itself can be taken (compare v. 12). Evidently it was difficult to enforce the law (see 26.34–35). It was enforced, however, in the Maccabean period (1 Macc.6.49,53). **8–24:** After seven sabbatical years, i.e. on the fiftieth year, comes the year of jubilee, named after the Hebrew word "yobhel" (ram's horn) which was blown in proclamation. **10:** Leases are to expire and every man is to return to his ancestral estate. **13–17:** Although an Israelite shall not sell his property in perpetuity (v. 23), he may lease it for farming. **15–16:** The rent is to be reckoned at the approximated value of the crops in the remaining years of the jubilee period. **14:** *Neighbor,* see 19.17–18 n. **20–22:** A law dealing with the sabbatical years that fall during the jubilee period. **23:** A statement of the theological premise of the program: Israelites are *strangers and sojourners* on land which does not belong to them by right but which the LORD has given them as an inheritance. Thus the land is not private property, to be bought and sold speculatively. Although there is no evidence that the jubilee program was ever carried out, the law opposes foreign conceptions of property which resulted in the swallow-

no one to redeem it, and then himself becomes prosperous and finds sufficient means to redeem it, [27] let him reckon the years since he sold it and pay back the overpayment to the man to whom he sold it; and he shall return to his property. [28] But if he has not sufficient means to get it back for himself, then what he sold shall remain in the hand of him who bought it until the year of jubilee; in the jubilee it shall be released, and he shall return to his property.

29 "If a man sells a dwelling house in a walled city, he may redeem it within a whole year after its sale; for a full year he shall have the right of redemption. [30] If it is not redeemed within a full year, then the house that is in the walled city shall be made sure in perpetuity to him who bought it, throughout his generations; it shall not be released in the jubilee. [31] But the houses of the villages which have no wall around them shall be reckoned with the fields of the country; they may be redeemed, and they shall be released in the jubilee. [32] Nevertheless the cities of the Levites, the houses in the cities of their possession, the Levites may redeem at any time. [33] And if one of the Levites does not exercise[m] his right of redemption, then the house that was sold in a city of their possession shall be released in the jubilee; for the houses in the cities of the Levites are their possession among the people of Israel. [34] But the fields of common land belonging to their cities may not be sold; for that is their perpetual possession.

35 "And if your brother becomes poor, and cannot maintain himself with you, you shall maintain him; as a stranger and a sojourner he shall live with you. [36] Take no interest from him or increase, but fear your God; that your brother may live beside you. [37] You shall not lend him your money at interest, nor give him your food for profit. [38] I am the LORD your God, who brought you forth out of the land of Egypt to give you the land of Canaan, and to be your God.

39 "And if your brother becomes poor beside you, and sells himself to you, you shall not make him serve as a slave: [40] he shall be with you as a hired servant and as a sojourner. He shall serve with you until the year of the jubilee; [41] then he shall go out from you, he and his children with him, and go back to his own family, and return to the possession of his fathers. [42] For they are my servants, whom I brought forth out of the land of Egypt; they shall not be sold as slaves. [43] You shall not rule over him with harshness, but shall fear your God. [44] As for your male and female slaves whom you may have: you may buy male and female slaves from among the nations that are round about you. [45] You may also buy from among the strangers who sojourn with you and their families that are with you, who have been born in your land; and they may be your property. [46] You may bequeath them to your sons after you, to inherit as a possession for ever; you may make slaves of them, but over your brethren the people of Israel you shall not rule, one over another, with harshness.

47 "If a stranger or sojourner with you becomes rich, and your brother beside him becomes poor and sells himself to the stranger or sojourner with you, or to a member of the stranger's family, [48] then after he is sold he may

m Compare Vg: Heb exercises

ing up of ancestral holdings (1 Kg.21.3; Is.5.8). **25–55:** Laws dealing with property and its redemption. **25–28:** Even before the year of jubilee the land may be redeemed. **25:** The *next of kin* (lit., "redeemer") is the relative who upholds the rights of a family member, e.g. by blood revenge (Num.35.12) or the redemption of property (Ru. ch. 4). **29–34:** An exception to cover the case of urban houses as distinguished from houses in villages. **32–34:** Num.35.1–8. **35–38:** See Ex.22.25 n. **39–55:** An Israelite may sell himself as a hired servant but shall never become a slave. **40:** Compare Ex.21.1–6; Dt.15.12–18. **44–46:** It is permissible, however, to make slaves of non-Israelites, since, according to the ancient way of thinking, they are outside the bound-

be redeemed; one of his brothers may redeem him, ⁴⁹ or his uncle, or his cousin may redeem him, or a near kinsman belonging to his family may redeem him; or if he grows rich he may redeem himself. ⁵⁰ He shall reckon with him who bought him from the year when he sold himself to him until the year of jubilee, and the price of his release shall be according to the number of years; the time he was with his owner shall be rated as the time of a hired servant. ⁵¹ If there are still many years, according to them he shall refund out of the price paid for him the price for his redemption. ⁵² If there remain but a few years until the year of jubilee, he shall make a reckoning with him; according to the years of service due from him he shall refund the money for his redemption. ⁵³ As a servant hired year by year shall he be with him; he shall not rule with harshness over him in your sight. ⁵⁴ And if he is not redeemed by these means, then he shall be released in the year of jubilee, he and his children with him. ⁵⁵ For to me the people of Israel are servants, they are my servants whom I brought forth out of the land of Egypt: I am the LORD your God.

26 "You shall make for yourselves no idols and erect no graven image or pillar, and you shall not set up a figured stone in your land, to bow down to them; for I am the LORD your God. ² You shall keep my sabbaths and reverence my sanctuary: I am the LORD.

3 "If you walk in my statutes and observe my commandments and do them, ⁴ then I will give you your rains in their season, and the land shall yield its increase, and the trees of the field shall yield their fruit. ⁵ And your threshing shall last to the time of vin-

tage, and the vintage shall last to the time for sowing; and you shall eat your bread to the full, and dwell in your land securely. ⁶ And I will give peace in the land, and you shall lie down, and none shall make you afraid; and I will remove evil beasts from the land, and the sword shall not go through your land. ⁷ And you shall chase your enemies, and they shall fall before you by the sword. ⁸ Five of you shall chase a hundred, and a hundred of you shall chase ten thousand; and your enemies shall fall before you by the sword. ⁹ And I will have regard for you and make you fruitful and multiply you, and will confirm my covenant with you. ¹⁰ And you shall eat old store long kept, and you shall clear out the old to make way for the new. ¹¹ And I will make my abode among you, and my soul shall not abhor you. ¹² And I will walk among you, and will be your God, and you shall be my people. ¹³ I am the LORD your God, who brought you forth out of the land of Egypt, that you should not be their slaves; and I have broken the bars of your yoke and made you walk erect.

14 "But if you will not hearken to me, and will not do all these commandments, ¹⁵ if you spurn my statutes, and if your soul abhors my ordinances, so that you will not do all my commandments, but break my covenant, ¹⁶ I will do this to you: I will appoint over you sudden terror, consumption, and fever that waste the eyes and cause life to pine away. And you shall sow your seed in vain, for your enemies shall eat it; ¹⁷ I will set my face against you, and you shall be smitten before your enemies; those who hate you shall rule over you, and you shall flee when none pursues you. ¹⁸ And if in spite of this you will not

aries of the covenant community. **48–49:** See v. 25 n. **55:** This verse gives the theological basis for the prohibition against enslaving Israelites (vv. 42–43).

26.1–46: The two ways. The Holiness Code (chs. 17–26), conceived as the LORD's address to the people through Moses (17.1–2), concludes with divine warnings and promises. See also the concluding addresses in Ex.23.20–33 and Dt. ch. 28. **1:** A prohibition against the cultic objects of Canaanite religion (see Ex.34.13 n.). **11–13:** The fundamental theme of the Holiness Code: the holy God has come to dwell in the midst of a sinful people. **12:** Ex.6.7.

hearken to me, then I will chastise you again sevenfold for your sins, [19] and I will break the pride of your power, and I will make your heavens like iron and your earth like brass; [20] and your strength shall be spent in vain, for your land shall not yield its increase, and the trees of the land shall not yield their fruit.

21 "Then if you walk contrary to me, and will not hearken to me, I will bring more plagues upon you, sevenfold as many as your sins. [22] And I will let loose the wild beasts among you, which shall rob you of your children, and destroy your cattle, and make you few in number, so that your ways shall become desolate.

23 "And if by this discipline you are not turned to me, but walk contrary to me, [24] then I also will walk contrary to you, and I myself will smite you sevenfold for your sins. [25] And I will bring a sword upon you, that shall execute vengeance for the covenant; and if you gather within your cities I will send pestilence among you, and you shall be delivered into the hand of the enemy. [26] When I break your staff of bread, ten women shall bake your bread in one oven, and shall deliver your bread again by weight; and you shall eat, and not be satisfied.

27 "And if in spite of this you will not hearken to me, but walk contrary to me, [28] then I will walk contrary to you in fury, and chastise you myself sevenfold for your sins. [29] You shall eat the flesh of your sons, and you shall eat the flesh of your daughters. [30] And I will destroy your high places, and cut down your incense altars, and cast your dead bodies upon the dead bodies of your idols; and my soul will abhor you. [31] And I will lay your cities waste, and will make your sanctuaries desolate, and I will not smell your pleasing odors. [32] And I will devastate the land, so that your enemies who settle in it shall be astonished at it. [33] And I will scatter you among the nations, and I will unsheathe the sword after you; and your land shall be a desolation, and your cities shall be a waste.

34 "Then the land shall enjoy[n] its sabbaths as long as it lies desolate, while you are in your enemies' land; then the land shall rest, and enjoy[n] its sabbaths. [35] As long as it lies desolate it shall have rest, the rest which it had not in your sabbaths when you dwelt upon it. [36] And as for those of you that are left, I will send faintness into their hearts in the lands of their enemies; the sound of a driven leaf shall put them to flight, and they shall flee as one flees from the sword, and they shall fall when none pursues. [37] They shall stumble over one another, as if to escape a sword, though none pursues; and you shall have no power to stand before your enemies. [38] And you shall perish among the nations, and the land of your enemies shall eat you up. [39] And those of you that are left shall pine away in your enemies' lands because of their iniquity; and also because of the iniquities of their fathers they shall pine away like them.

40 "But if they confess their iniquity and the iniquity of their fathers in their treachery which they committed against me, and also in walking contrary to me, [41] so that I walked contrary to them and brought them into the land of their enemies; if then their uncircumcised heart is humbled and they make amends for their iniquity; [42] then I will remember my covenant with Jacob, and I will remember my covenant with Isaac and my covenant with Abraham, and I will remember the land. [43] But the land shall be left

n Or *pay for*

26: In the time of scarcity ten women will have to bake in one oven, rather than each in her own house. **29:** Dt.28.53–57. **32–33:** These and following verses indicate familiarity with the policy of deporting conquered peoples, a policy used effectively by the Assyrians (2 Kg. ch. 17), and anticipate the conquest of Judah and the exile of the people into Babylonia in 597–587 B.C. (vv. 34,38,39,41,43–44). **34–35:** See 25.6–7 n. **41:** *Uncircumcised heart*, a heart that is sealed or unresponsive to the LORD's will (Jer.4.4).

by them, and enjoy[n] its sabbaths while it lies desolate without them; and they shall make amends for their iniquity, because they spurned my ordinances, and their soul abhorred my statutes. [44] Yet for all that, when they are in the land of their enemies, I will not spurn them, neither will I abhor them so as to destroy them utterly and break my covenant with them; for I am the LORD their God; [45] but I will for their sake remember the covenant with their forefathers, whom I brought forth out of the land of Egypt in the sight of the nations, that I might be their God: I am the LORD."

46 These are the statutes and ordinances and laws which the LORD made between him and the people of Israel on Mount Sinai by Moses.

27 The LORD said to Moses, [2] "Say to the people of Israel, When a man makes a special vow of persons to the LORD at your valuation, [3] then your valuation of a male from twenty years old up to sixty years old shall be fifty shekels of silver, according to the shekel of the sanctuary. [4] If the person is a female, your valuation shall be thirty shekels. [5] If the person is from five years old up to twenty years old, your valuation shall be for a male twenty shekels, and for a female ten shekels. [6] If the person is from a month old up to five years old, your valuation shall be for a male five shekels of silver, and for a female your valuation shall be three shekels of silver. [7] And if the person is sixty years old and upward, then your valuation for a male shall be fifteen shekels, and for a female ten shekels. [8] And if a man is too poor to pay your valuation, then he shall bring the person before the priest, and the priest shall value him; according to the ability of him who vowed the priest shall value him.

9 "If it is an animal such as men offer as an offering to the LORD, all of such that any man gives to the LORD is holy. [10] He shall not substitute anything for it or exchange it, a good for a bad, or a bad for a good; and if he makes any exchange of beast for beast, then both it and that for which it is exchanged shall be holy. [11] And if it is an unclean animal such as is not offered as an offering to the LORD, then the man shall bring the animal before the priest, [12] and the priest shall value it as either good or bad; as you, the priest, value it, so it shall be. [13] But if he wishes to redeem it, he shall add a fifth to the valuation.

14 "When a man dedicates his house to be holy to the LORD, the priest shall value it as either good or bad; as the priest values it, so it shall stand. [15] And if he who dedicates it wishes to redeem his house, he shall add a fifth of the valuation in money to it, and it shall be his.

16 "If a man dedicates to the LORD part of the land which is his by inheritance, then your valuation shall be according to the seed for it; a sowing of a homer of barley shall be valued at fifty shekels of silver. [17] If he dedicates his field from the year of jubilee, it shall stand at your full valuation; [18] but if he dedicates his field after the jubilee, then the priest shall compute the money-value for it according to the years that remain until the year of jubilee, and a deduction shall be made from your valuation. [19] And if he who dedicates the field wishes to redeem it, then he shall add a fifth of the valuation in money to it, and it shall remain his. [20] But if he does not wish to redeem the field, or if he has sold the field to another man, it shall not be redeemed any more; [21] but the field, when it is released in the jubilee, shall be holy to the LORD, as a field

n Or *pay for*

27.1–34: An appendix dealing with religious vows (compare Pss.56.12; 116.14). See further Num. ch. 30. 1–8: Persons dedicated to the LORD's service (compare 1 Sam.1.11) may be freed from the vow by the payment of a monetary substitute. 3: *The shekel of the sanctuary*, see Ex.30.13 n. 9–13: If an animal, appropriate for sacrifice, is vowed, it cannot be redeemed. 14–25: Houses and lands, vowed to the LORD, are redeemable. 17–18: On this manner of

that has been devoted; the priest shall be in possession of it. ²² If he dedicates to the LORD a field which he has bought, which is not a part of his possession by inheritance, ²³ then the priest shall compute the valuation for it up to the year of jubilee, and the man shall give the amount of the valuation on that day as a holy thing to the LORD. ²⁴ In the year of jubilee the field shall return to him from whom it was bought, to whom the land belongs as a possession by inheritance. ²⁵ Every valuation shall be according to the shekel of the sanctuary: twenty gerahs shall make a shekel.

26 "But a firstling of animals, which as a firstling belongs to the LORD, no man may dedicate; whether ox or sheep, it is the LORD's. ²⁷ And if it is an unclean animal, then he shall buy it back at your valuation, and add a fifth to it; or, if it is not redeemed, it shall be sold at your valuation.

28 "But no devoted thing that a man devotes to the LORD, of anything that he has, whether of man or beast, or of his inherited field, shall be sold or redeemed; every devoted thing is most holy to the LORD. ²⁹ No one devoted, who is to be utterly destroyed from among men, shall be ransomed; he shall be put to death.

30 "All the tithe of the land, whether of the seed of the land or of the fruit of the trees, is the LORD's; it is holy to the LORD. ³¹ If a man wishes to redeem any of his tithe, he shall add a fifth to it. ³² And all the tithe of herds and flocks, every tenth animal of all that pass under the herdsman's staff, shall be holy to the LORD. ³³ A man shall not inquire whether it is good or bad, neither shall he exchange it; and if he exchanges it, then both it and that for which it is exchanged shall be holy; it shall not be redeemed."

34 These are the commandments which the LORD commanded Moses for the people of Israel on Mount Sinai.

---

valuation, see 25.15–16. **21:** *Devoted*, i.e. set apart as belonging to the LORD. Booty taken in holy war was devoted and could not be appropriated for common use (Jos.6.19). **26:** Firstlings of clean animals cannot be dedicated since they already belong to the LORD (see Ex.13.2 n.). **28:** *Devoted thing*, see v. 21 n. **29:** Compare 1 Sam. ch. 15. **30–33:** On tithes (Mal.3.8–10). **32–33:** The words *pass under the herdsman's staff* refer to the manner of counting animals (Jer.33.13).

NUMBERS

The title of this book in the Hebrew Bible, In the Wilderness, is more fitting than Numbers, which refers merely to the opening account of the numbering of the people. Actually, the census, along with instructions for encampment and for march, belongs to the larger theme of Israel's sojourn in the wilderness (see "Survey of . . . Bible Lands," § 7). Accordingly, the book falls into the following sections: (1) Preparations for departure from Sinai (1.1–10.10); (2) the journey to Kadesh, from which point an abortive attack upon southern Canaan was made (10.11–21.13); and (3) the journey from Kadesh via Transjordan for the purpose of approaching Canaan from the east (21.14–36.13).

Of the traditional forty years in the wilderness (33.38; Am.5.25), the greatest part was spent at the oasis known as Kadesh-barnea. According to priestly chronology, one year elapsed from the Exodus to the erection of the tabernacle (Ex.40.2); the legislation of Leviticus covered one month (Num.1.1); nineteen days after the census Israel left Sinai (10.11). Moses' farewell address was given at the end of the fortieth year (Dt.1.3). With time allowed for the march from Kadesh to the plains of Moab, this means that Israel spent well over thirty-five years at Kadesh.

Many of the traditions portray Israel's murmuring, occasioned by the people's precarious existence in the wilderness. The people are pictured as faithless, rebellious, and blind to God's signs. Yet the same traditions are infused with the conviction that God was marvelously guiding, sustaining, and disciplining his people so that they might know their utter dependence upon him and thus be prepared for their historical pilgrimage.

T HE LORD SPOKE TO MOSES IN THE wilderness of Sinai, in the tent of meeting, on the first day of the second month, in the second year after they had come out of the land of Egypt, saying, ² "Take a census of all the congregation of the people of Israel, by families, by fathers' houses, according to the number of names, every male, head by head; ³ from twenty years old and upward, all in Israel who are able to go forth to war, you and Aaron shall number them, company by company. ⁴ And there shall be with you a man from each tribe, each man being the head of the house of his fathers. ⁵ And these are the names of the men who shall attend you. From Reuben, Eli'zur the son of Shed'eur; ⁶ from Simeon, Shelu'mi-el the son of Zurishad'dai; ⁷ from Judah, Nahshon the son of Ammin'adab; ⁸ from Is'sachar, Nethan'el the son of Zu'ar; ⁹ from Zeb'ulun, Eli'ab the son of Helon; ¹⁰ from the sons of Joseph, from E'phraim, Eli'shama the son of Ammi'hud, and from Manas'seh, Gama'liel the son of Pedah'zur; ¹¹ from Benjamin, Abi'dan the son of Gideo'ni; ¹² from Dan, Ahi-e'zer the son of Ammishad'dai; ¹³ from Asher, Pa'giel the son of Ochran; ¹⁴ from Gad, Eli'asaph the son of Deu'el; ¹⁵ from Naph'tali, Ahi'ra the son of Enan." ¹⁶ These were the ones chosen from the congregation, the leaders of their ancestral tribes, the heads of the clans of Israel.

17 Moses and Aaron took these men

1.1–54: Census of the tribes. Moses is commanded to number all Israelites, making an exception of the tribe of Levi. **1:** One month had elapsed since the construction of the tabernacle (Ex.40.2,17). **2–4:** See Ex.30.11–12 n. Military service was one of the chief duties involved in membership in the tribal assembly (ch. 32). Strictly, a tribe included a number of *families* or clans, and a clan included several *fathers' houses* or family groups. **5–15:** This old name-list reflects the twelve-tribe league presumably formed in Joshua's time (Jos. ch. 24). No longer a landed tribe, Levi is not mentioned here (see Ex.28.1–5 n.), but is later assigned a priestly role (vv. 47–54). The twelvefold pattern is maintained by counting the "house of Joseph" as two tribes: Manasseh and Ephraim. On the mention of Ephraim before Manasseh, see Gen.48.13–

who have been named, [18] and on the first day of the second month, they assembled the whole congregation together, who registered themselves by families, by fathers' houses, according to the number of names from twenty years old and upward, head by head, [19] as the LORD commanded Moses. So he numbered them in the wilderness of Sinai.

20 The people of Reuben, Israel's first-born, their generations, by their families, by their fathers' houses, according to the number of names, head by head, every male from twenty years old and upward, all who were able to go forth to war: [21] the number of the tribe of Reuben was forty-six thousand five hundred.

22 Of the people of Simeon, their generations, by their families, by their fathers' houses, those of them that were numbered, according to the number of names, head by head, every male from twenty years old and upward, all who were able to go forth to war: [23] the number of the tribe of Simeon was fifty-nine thousand three hundred.

24 Of the people of Gad, their generations, by their families, by their fathers' houses, according to the number of the names, from twenty years old and upward, all who were able to go forth to war: [25] the number of the tribe of Gad was forty-five thousand six hundred and fifty.

26 Of the people of Judah, their generations, by their families, by their fathers' houses, according to the number of names, from twenty years old and upward, every man able to go forth to war: [27] the number of the tribe of Judah was seventy-four thousand six hundred.

28 Of the people of Is'sachar, their generations, by their families, by their fathers' houses, according to the number of names, from twenty years old and upward, every man able to go forth to war: [29] the number of the tribe of Is'sachar was fifty-four thousand four hundred.

30 Of the people of Zeb'ulun, their generations, by their families, by their fathers' houses, according to the number of names, from twenty years old and upward, every man able to go forth to war: [31] the number of the tribe of Zeb'ulun was fifty-seven thousand four hundred.

32 Of the people of Joseph, namely, of the people of E'phraim, their generations, by their families, by their fathers' houses, according to the number of names, from twenty years old and upward, every man able to go forth to war: [33] the number of the tribe of E'phraim was forty thousand five hundred.

34 Of the people of Manas'seh, their generations, by their families, by their fathers' houses, according to the number of names, from twenty years old and upward, every man able to go forth to war: [35] the number of the tribe of Manas'seh was thirty-two thousand two hundred.

36 Of the people of Benjamin, their generations, by their families, by their fathers' houses, according to the number of names, from twenty years old and upward, every man able to go forth to war: [37] the number of the tribe of Benjamin was thirty-five thousand four hundred.

38 Of the people of Dan, their generations, by their families, by their fathers' houses, according to the num-

---

14 n. and contrast 26.28; 34.23–24. **17–46:** The census total of 603,550 (compare the slightly lower figure in 26.51) is extremely high (see Ex.12.37 n.). It has been suggested that the Hebrew word translated "thousand" (vv. 21,23, etc.) is an old term for a subsection of a tribe (31.14), based on the procedures for military muster employed by other ancient peoples, and that the original number follows "thousand" in each case, e.g. Reuben had forty-six tribal subsections with a total of five hundred men (v. 21). This reduces the total to 5,550. It is alleged that the present impossibly high figures were read back from the time of the monarchy when the military unit actually included one thousand men. In any case, priestly tradition about the numerous population (see 11.21 n.) is based on the belief that the LORD marvelously increased Abraham's

ber of names, from twenty years old and upward, every man able to go forth to war: [39] the number of the tribe of Dan was sixty-two thousand seven hundred.

40 Of the people of Asher, their generations, by their families, by their fathers' houses, according to the number of names, from twenty years old and upward, every man able to go forth to war: [41] the number of the tribe of Asher was forty-one thousand five hundred.

42 Of the people of Naph'tali, their generations, by their families, by their fathers' houses, according to the number of names, from twenty years old and upward, every man able to go forth to war: [43] the number of the tribe of Naph'tali was fifty-three thousand four hundred.

44 These are those who were numbered, whom Moses and Aaron numbered with the help of the leaders of Israel, twelve men, each representing his fathers' house. [45] So the whole number of the people of Israel, by their fathers' houses, from twenty years old and upward, every man able to go forth to war in Israel— [46] their whole number was six hundred and three thousand five hundred and fifty.

47 But the Levites were not numbered by their ancestral tribe along with them. [48] For the LORD said to Moses, [49] "Only the tribe of Levi you shall not number, and you shall not take a census of them among the people of Israel; [50] but appoint the Levites over the tabernacle of the testimony, and over all its furnishings, and over all that belongs to it; they are to carry the tabernacle and all its furnishings,

and they shall tend it, and shall encamp around the tabernacle. [51] When the tabernacle is to set out, the Levites shall take it down; and when the tabernacle is to be pitched, the Levites shall set it up. And if any one else comes near, he shall be put to death. [52] The people of Israel shall pitch their tents by their companies, every man by his own camp and every man by his own standard; [53] but the Levites shall encamp around the tabernacle of the testimony, that there may be no wrath upon the congregation of the people of Israel; and the Levites shall keep charge of the tabernacle of the testimony." [54] Thus did the people of Israel; they did according to all that the LORD commanded Moses.

2 The LORD said to Moses and Aaron, [2] "The people of Israel shall encamp each by his own standard, with the ensigns of their fathers' houses; they shall encamp facing the tent of meeting on every side. [3] Those to encamp on the east side toward the sunrise shall be of the standard of the camp of Judah by their companies, the leader of the people of Judah being Nahshon the son of Ammin'adab, [4] his host as numbered being seventy-four thousand six hundred. [5] Those to encamp next to him shall be the tribe of Is'sachar, the leader of the people of Is'sachar being Nethan'el the son of Zu'ar, [6] his host as numbered being fifty-four thousand four hundred. [7] Then the tribe of Zeb'ulun, the leader of the people of Zeb'ulun being Eli'ab the son of Helon, [8] his host as numbered being fifty-seven thousand four hundred. [9] The whole number of the camp of Judah, by their companies,

---

descendants (see Ex.1.7 n.) and miraculously supported this great people in the wilderness. **47–54:** See 3.5–10 n. **50:** *Testimony*, see Ex.16.33–34 n.

2.1–34: The arrangement of the tribes while encamped or on the march (compare 10.13–28). **2:** Perhaps with the feast of tabernacles in mind (Lev.23.33–36), the priestly writer conceives the congregation as arranged symmetrically around the tent of meeting. In the oldest tradition, the tent was not in the center but on the outside of the camp (Ex.33.7–11). **3–31:** The Levites are to encamp immediately around the tabernacle court (Ex.27.9–19), to protect and transport the sacred shrine (v. 17; 1.47–54). Farther out the twelve tribes are to encamp, three on each side. The arrangement expresses the idea of the tabernacling presence of the LORD in the midst of his people (Ex.25.8). **3–4:** Judah is assigned the favored position, on the east of the

is a hundred and eighty-six thousand four hundred. They shall set out first on the march.

10 "On the south side shall be the standard of the camp of Reuben by their companies, the leader of the people of Reuben being Eli'zur the son of Shed'eur, ¹¹ his host as numbered being forty-six thousand five hundred. ¹² And those to encamp next to him shall be the tribe of Simeon, the leader of the people of Simeon being Shelu'-mi-el the son of Zurishad'dai, ¹³ his host as numbered being fifty-nine thousand three hundred. ¹⁴ Then the tribe of Gad, the leader of the people of Gad being Eli'asaph the son of Reu'el, ¹⁵ his host as numbered being forty-five thousand six hundred and fifty. ¹⁶ The whole number of the camp of Reuben, by their companies, is a hundred and fifty-one thousand four hundred and fifty. They shall set out second.

17 "Then the tent of meeting shall set out, with the camp of the Levites in the midst of the camps; as they encamp, so shall they set out, each in position, standard by standard.

18 "On the west side shall be the standard of the camp of E'phraim by their companies, the leader of the people of E'phraim being Eli'shama the son of Ammi'hud, ¹⁹ his host as numbered being forty thousand five hundred. ²⁰ And next to him shall be the tribe of Manas'seh, the leader of the people of Manas'seh being Gama'liel the son of Pedah'zur, ²¹ his host as numbered being thirty-two thousand two hundred. ²² Then the tribe of Benjamin, the leader of the people of Benjamin being Abi'dan the son of Gideo'ni, ²³ his host as numbered being thirty-five thousand four hundred. ²⁴ The whole number of the camp of E'phraim, by their companies, is a hundred and eight thousand one hundred.

They shall set out third on the march.

25 "On the north side shall be the standard of the camp of Dan by their companies, the leader of the people of Dan being Ahi-e'zer the son of Ammishad'dai, ²⁶ his host as numbered being sixty-two thousand seven hundred. ²⁷ And those to encamp next to him shall be the tribe of Asher, the leader of the people of Asher being Pa'giel the son of Ochran, ²⁸ his host as numbered being forty-one thousand five hundred. ²⁹ Then the tribe of Naph'tali, the leader of the people of Naph'tali being Ahi'ra the son of Enan, ³⁰ his host as numbered being fifty-three thousand four hundred. ³¹ The whole number of the camp of Dan is a hundred and fifty-seven thousand six hundred. They shall set out last, standard by standard."

32 These are the people of Israel as numbered by their fathers' houses; all in the camps who were numbered by their companies were six hundred and three thousand five hundred and fifty. ³³ But the Levites were not numbered among the people of Israel, as the LORD commanded Moses.

34 Thus did the people of Israel. According to all that the LORD commanded Moses, so they encamped by their standards, and so they set out, every one in his family, according to his fathers' house.

3 These are the generations of Aaron and Moses at the time when the LORD spoke with Moses on Mount Sinai. ² These are the names of the sons of Aaron: Nadab the first-born, and Abi'hu, Elea'zar, and Ith'amar; ³ these are the names of the sons of Aaron, the anointed priests, whom he ordained to minister in the priest's office. ⁴ But Nadab and Abi'hu died before the LORD when they offered unholy fire before the LORD in the wilderness of Sinai; and they had no children. So

---

camp. **9:** Each division marches in assigned order, with Judah in the lead. **18–24:** On Ephraim's position of leadership, see 1.5–15 n. **17:** During the march, the Levites are to be flanked by two divisions on both the front and the rear.

3.1–51: The Levites are set apart for special service. **1–3:** Ex.6.23–25. **4:** Lev. ch. 10. **5–10:**

Elea'zar and Ith'amar served as priests in the lifetime of Aaron their father.

5 And the LORD said to Moses, 6 "Bring the tribe of Levi near, and set them before Aaron the priest, that they may minister to him. 7 They shall perform duties for him and for the whole congregation before the tent of meeting, as they minister at the tabernacle; 8 they shall have charge of all the furnishings of the tent of meeting, and attend to the duties for the people of Israel as they minister at the tabernacle. 9 And you shall give the Levites to Aaron and his sons; they are wholly given to him from among the people of Israel. 10 And you shall appoint Aaron and his sons, and they shall attend to their priesthood; but if any one else comes near, he shall be put to death."

11 And the LORD said to Moses, 12 "Behold, I have taken the Levites from among the people of Israel instead of every first-born that opens the womb among the people of Israel. The Levites shall be mine, 13 for all the first-born are mine; on the day that I slew all the first-born in the land of Egypt, I consecrated for my own all the first-born in Israel, both of man and of beast; they shall be mine: I am the LORD."

14 And the LORD said to Moses in the wilderness of Sinai, 15 "Number the sons of Levi, by fathers' houses and by families; every male from a month old and upward you shall number." 16 So Moses numbered them according to the word of the LORD, as he was commanded. 17 And these were the sons of Levi by their names:

Gershon and Kohath and Merar'i. 18 And these are the names of the sons of Gershon by their families: Libni and Shim'e-i. 19 And the sons of Kohath by their families: Amram, Izhar, Hebron, and Uz'ziel. 20 And the sons of Merar'i by their families: Mahli and Mushi. These are the families of the Levites, by their fathers' houses.

21 Of Gershon were the family of the Libnites and the family of the Shim'e-ites; these were the families of the Gershonites. 22 Their number according to the number of all the males from a month old and upward was*a* seven thousand five hundred. 23 The families of the Gershonites were to encamp behind the tabernacle on the west, 24 with Eli'asaph, the son of La'el as head of the fathers' house of the Gershonites. 25 And the charge of the sons of Gershon in the tent of meeting was to be the tabernacle, the tent with its covering, the screen for the door of the tent of meeting, 26 the hangings of the court, the screen for the door of the court which is around the tabernacle and the altar, and its cords; all the service pertaining to these.

27 Of Kohath were the family of the Amramites, and the family of the Izhar'ites, and the family of the He'-bronites, and the family of the Uz-zie'lites; these are the families of the Ko'hathites. 28 According to the number of all the males, from a month old and upward, there were eight thousand six hundred, attending to the duties of the sanctuary. 29 The families of the sons of Kohath were to encamp on the

a Heb *their number was*

Moses and Aaron both belong to the tribe of Levi. Within the larger circle of Levites, however, a distinction is made between *Aaron and his sons* and other Levites (see Ex.28.1–5 n.). Aaron's descendants exercise the chief priestly functions in the sanctuary, while the other Levites are given to the Aaronic order as priestly assistants. **11–13:** A reinterpretation of the ancient law found in Ex.13.2; 22.29b–30; 34.19–20. Instead of having to go into life-long religious service, the first-born are redeemed by a "sacrifice" (see Ex.13.13 n.), for the LORD claims the Levites in their stead (Num.8.15–19). **14–39:** 1.47–54; ch. 4. **15:** The Levitical census is not for military purposes (compare 1.2–3) but is associated with the first-born who are redeemable from the age of *one month* (vv. 40–51). **17–19:** For *the families* (clans) *of the Levites*, see Ex.6.16–19. **25–26:** 4.21–28. The Gershonites have custody over the tent covering (Ex.26.7–14), the screen for the tent door (Ex.26.36), the hangings of the court (Ex.27.9), the screen for the court door (Ex.

south side of the tabernacle, [30] with Eli-za′phan the son of Uz′ziel as head of the fathers' house of the families of the Ko′hathites. [31] And their charge was to be the ark, the table, the lampstand, the altars, the vessels of the sanctuary with which the priests minister, and the screen; all the service pertaining to these. [32] And Elea′zar the son of Aaron the priest was to be chief over the leaders of the Levites, and to have oversight of those who had charge of the sanctuary.

33 Of Merar′i were the family of the Mahlites and the family of the Mushites: these are the families of Merar′i. [34] Their number according to the number of all the males from a month old and upward was six thousand two hundred. [35] And the head of the fathers' house of the families of Merar′i was Zu′riel the son of Ab′ihail; they were to encamp on the north side of the tabernacle. [36] And the appointed charge of the sons of Merar′i was to be the frames of the tabernacle, the bars, the pillars, the bases, and all their accessories; all the service pertaining to these; [37] also the pillars of the court round about, with their bases and pegs and cords.

38 And those to encamp before the tabernacle on the east, before the tent of meeting toward the sunrise, were Moses and Aaron and his sons, having charge of the rites within the sanctuary, whatever had to be done for the people of Israel; and any one else who came near was to be put to death. [39] All who were numbered of the Levites, whom Moses and Aaron numbered at the commandment of the LORD, by families, all the males from a month old and upward, were twenty-two thousand.

40 And the LORD said to Moses, "Number all the first-born males of the people of Israel, from a month old and upward, taking their number by names. [41] And you shall take the Levites for me—I am the LORD—instead of all the first-born among the people of Israel, and the cattle of the Levites instead of all the firstlings among the cattle of the people of Israel." [42] So Moses numbered all the first-born among the people of Israel, as the LORD commanded him. [43] And all the first-born males, according to the number of names, from a month old and upward as numbered were twenty-two thousand two hundred and seventy-three.

44 And the LORD said to Moses, [45] "Take the Levites instead of all the first-born among the people of Israel, and the cattle of the Levites instead of their cattle; and the Levites shall be mine: I am the LORD. [46] And for the redemption of the two hundred and seventy-three of the first-born of the people of Israel, over and above the number of the male Levites, [47] you shall take five shekels apiece; reckoning by the shekel of the sanctuary, the shekel of twenty gerahs, you shall take them, [48] and give the money by which the excess number of them is redeemed to Aaron and his sons." [49] So Moses took the redemption money from those

---

27.16). **31–32:** 4.4–15. The Kohathites have charge of the most holy objects (4.4–20), i.e. the ark, the table for the bread of the Presence, the lampstand (Ex. ch. 25), the bronze and gold altars (Ex.27.1–8; 30.1–10), the sacred vessels (Ex.30.17–21; 31.7–11), and *the veil of the screen* (Num.4.5; Ex.26.31–35). *Eleazar,* Aaron's oldest surviving son. **36–37:** 4.29–33. The Merarites are responsible for the tabernacle framework (Ex.26.15–30) and the supports for the court (Ex.27.9–19). **38:** Aaron and his sons encamp on the east, the favored location (see 2.3–4 n.), symbolizing their priestly pre-eminence. *Any one else* (3.10), i.e. a layman. **39:** The numbers given in ch. 3 actually total 22,300. **40–51:** Another Israelite census is taken to determine the number of first-born males, in contrast to men of military age (1.2–3). **41:** See 3.11–13 n. The substitution of Levites' cattle for the people's firstlings of cattle modifies the law of the first-born even further. **43:** A tally disclosed an excess of 273 Israelite first-born over the number of Levites (but see v. 39 n.). **46–48:** Since the Levites were a ransom for Israelite males on a one to one basis, the additional males had to be redeemed by monetary payment. *The shekel of the sanctuary,* see Ex.30.13 n.

who were over and above those redeemed by the Levites; ⁵⁰ from the
first-born of the people of Israel he
took the money, one thousand three
hundred and sixty-five shekels, reckoned by the shekel of the sanctuary;
⁵¹ and Moses gave the redemption
money to Aaron and his sons, according to the word of the LORD, as the
LORD commanded Moses.

4 The LORD said to Moses and
Aaron, ² "Take a census of the
sons of Kohath from among the sons
of Levi, by their families and their
fathers' houses, ³ from thirty years old
up to fifty years old, all who can enter
the service, to do the work in the tent
of meeting. ⁴ This is the service of the
sons of Kohath in the tent of meeting:
the most holy things. ⁵ When the camp
is to set out, Aaron and his sons shall
go in and take down the veil of the
screen, and cover the ark of the testimony with it; ⁶ then they shall put on
it a covering of goatskin, and spread
over that a cloth all of blue, and shall
put in its poles. ⁷ And over the table
of the bread of the Presence they shall
spread a cloth of blue, and put upon
it the plates, the dishes for incense,
the bowls, and the flagons for the drink
offering; the continual bread also shall
be on it; ⁸ then they shall spread
over them a cloth of scarlet, and cover
the same with a covering of goatskin,
and shall put in its poles. ⁹ And they
shall take a cloth of blue, and cover
the lampstand for the light, with its
lamps, its snuffers, its trays, and all the
vessels for oil with which it is supplied:
¹⁰ and they shall put it with all its
utensils in a covering of goatskin and
put it upon the carrying frame. ¹¹ And
over the golden altar they shall spread
a cloth of blue, and cover it with a
covering of goatskin, and shall put in

its poles; ¹² and they shall take all the
vessels of the service which are used
in the sanctuary, and put them in a
cloth of blue, and cover them with a
covering of goatskin, and put them on
the carrying frame. ¹³ And they shall
take away the ashes from the altar, and
spread a purple cloth over it; ¹⁴ and
they shall put on it all the utensils of
the altar, which are used for the service there, the firepans, the forks, the
shovels, and the basins, all the utensils
of the altar; and they shall spread upon
it a covering of goatskin, and shall put
in its poles. ¹⁵ And when Aaron and
his sons have finished covering the
sanctuary and all the furnishings of
the sanctuary, as the camp sets out,
after that the sons of Kohath shall
come to carry these, but they must not
touch the holy things, lest they die.
These are the things of the tent of meeting which the sons of Kohath are to
carry.

16 "And Elea′zar the son of Aaron
the priest shall have charge of the oil
for the light, the fragrant incense, the
continual cereal offering, and the
anointing oil, with the oversight of all
the tabernacle and all that is in it, of
the sanctuary and its vessels."

17 The LORD said to Moses and
Aaron, ¹⁸ "Let not the tribe of the
families of the Ko′hathites be destroyed
from among the Levites; ¹⁹ but deal
thus with them, that they may live and
not die when they come near to the
most holy things: Aaron and his sons
shall go in and appoint them each to
his task and to his burden, ²⁰ but they
shall not go in to look upon the holy
things even for a moment, lest they
die."

21 The LORD said to Moses,
²² "Take a census of the sons of Gershon also, by their families and their

---

4.1–49: Another Levitical census. 2–3: This census, in contrast with 3.15, is to determine the
number of Levites of the age required for the priestly duties (compare 8.23–25) which are
defined in vv. 4–33. **4–20:** The Kohathites have a special distinction among the Levites, for they
have charge of *the most holy things* and are therefore under the immediate supervision of
Eleazar (see 3.31–32 n.). **5:** *The veil of the screen*, Ex.26.31–35. **7:** *The continual bread*, i.e. the
bread of the Presence which is continually on the table (Ex.25.30). **15–20:** The precautions taken
by Aaron and his sons are explained by the fact that the Kohathites must not see or touch the

fathers' houses; [23] from thirty years old up to fifty years old, you shall number them, all who can enter for service, to do the work in the tent of meeting. [24] This is the service of the families of the Gershonites, in serving and bearing burdens: [25] they shall carry the curtains of the tabernacle, and the tent of meeting with its covering, and the covering of goatskin that is on top of it, and the screen for the door of the tent of meeting, [26] and the hangings of the court, and the screen for the entrance of the gate of the court which is around the tabernacle and the altar, and their cords, and all the equipment for their service; and they shall do all that needs to be done with regard to them. [27] All the service of the sons of the Gershonites shall be at the command of Aaron and his sons, in all that they are to carry, and in all that they have to do; and you shall assign to their charge all that they are to carry. [28] This is the service of the families of the sons of the Gershonites in the tent of meeting, and their work is to be under the oversight of Ith'amar the son of Aaron the priest.

29 "As for the sons of Merar'i, you shall number them by their families and their fathers' houses; [30] from thirty years old up to fifty years old, you shall number them, every one that can enter the service, to do the work of the tent of meeting. [31] And this is what they are charged to carry, as the whole of their service in the tent of meeting: the frames of the tabernacle, with its bars, pillars, and bases, [32] and the pillars of the court round about with their bases, pegs, and cords, with all their equipment and all their accessories; and you shall assign by name the objects which they are required to carry. [33] This is the service of the families of the sons of Merar'i, the whole of their service in the tent of meeting, under the hand of Ith'amar the son of Aaron the priest."

34 And Moses and Aaron and the leaders of the congregation numbered the sons of the Ko'hathites, by their families and their fathers' houses, [35] from thirty years old up to fifty years old, every one that could enter the service, for work in the tent of meeting; [36] and their number by families was two thousand seven hundred and fifty. [37] This was the number of the families of the Ko'hathites, all who served in the tent of meeting, whom Moses and Aaron numbered according to the commandment of the LORD by Moses.

38 The number of the sons of Gershon, by their families and their fathers' houses, [39] from thirty years old up to fifty years old, every one that could enter the service for work in the tent of meeting– [40] their number by their families and their fathers' houses was two thousand six hundred and thirty. [41] This was the number of the families of the sons of Gershon, all who served in the tent of meeting, whom Moses and Aaron numbered according to the commandment of the LORD.

42 The number of the families of the sons of Merar'i, by their families and their fathers' houses, [43] from thirty years old up to fifty years old, every one that could enter the service, for work in the tent of meeting– [44] their number by families was three thousand two hundred. [45] These are those who were numbered of the families of the sons of Merar'i, whom Moses and Aaron numbered according to the commandment of the LORD by Moses.

46 All those who were numbered of the Levites, whom Moses and Aaron and the leaders of Israel numbered, by their families and their fathers' houses, [47] from thirty years old up to fifty years old, every one that could enter to do the work of service and the work of bearing burdens in the tent of meeting, [48] those who were numbered of them were eight thousand five hundred and eighty. [49] According to the

holy objects, lest divine holiness destroy them (compare 1 Sam. ch. 5–6; 2 Sam.6.6–11). **21–28:** For the responsibility of the Gershonites, see 3.25–26. **29–33:** 3.36–37. **48:** Compare the number of male Levites in 3.39.

commandment of the LORD through Moses they were appointed, each to his task of serving or carrying; thus they were numbered by him, as the LORD commanded Moses.

5 The LORD said to Moses, 2 "Command the people of Israel that they put out of the camp every leper, and every one having a discharge, and every one that is unclean through contact with the dead; 3 you shall put out both male and female, putting them outside the camp, that they may not defile their camp, in the midst of which I dwell." 4 And the people of Israel did so, and drove them outside the camp; as the LORD said to Moses, so the people of Israel did.

5 And the LORD said to Moses, 6 "Say to the people of Israel, When a man or woman commits any of the sins that men commit by breaking faith with the LORD, and that person is guilty, 7 he shall confess his sin which he has committed; and he shall make full restitution for his wrong, adding a fifth to it, and giving it to him to whom he did the wrong. 8 But if the man has no kinsman to whom restitution may be made for the wrong, the restitution for wrong shall go to the LORD for the priest, in addition to the ram of atonement with which atonement is made for him. 9 And every offering, all the holy things of the people of Israel, which they bring to the priest, shall be his; 10 and every man's holy things shall be his; whatever any man gives to the priest shall be his."

11 And the LORD said to Moses, 12 "Say to the people of Israel, If any man's wife goes astray and acts unfaithfully against him, 13 if a man lies with her carnally, and it is hidden from the eyes of her husband, and she is undetected though she has defiled herself, and there is no witness against her, since she was not taken in the act; 14 and if the spirit of jealousy comes upon him, and he is jealous of his wife who has defiled herself; or if the spirit of jealousy comes upon him, and he is jealous of his wife, though she has not defiled herself; 15 then the man shall bring his wife to the priest, and bring the offering required of her, a tenth of an ephah of barley meal; he shall pour no oil upon it and put no frankincense on it, for it is a cereal offering of jealousy, a cereal offering of remembrance, bringing iniquity to remembrance.

16 "And the priest shall bring her near, and set her before the LORD; 17 and the priest shall take holy water in an earthen vessel, and take some of the dust that is on the floor of the tabernacle and put it into the water. 18 And the priest shall set the woman before the LORD, and unbind the hair of the woman's head, and place in her hands the cereal offering of remembrance, which is the cereal offering of jealousy. And in his hand the priest shall have the water of bitterness that brings the curse. 19 Then the priest shall make her take an oath, saying, 'If no man has lain with you, and if you have not turned aside to uncleanness, while you were under your husband's authority, be free from this water of bitterness that brings the curse. 20 But if you have gone astray, though you are under your husband's authority, and if you have defiled yourself, and some man other than your husband has lain with you, 21 then' (let the priest make the woman take

5.1–6.21: Various instructions to the people. 1–4: The sanctity of the tabernacle is the reason for excluding unclean people, such as lepers (Lev.13.46), those having a bodily discharge (Lev. ch. 15), or those defiled by contact with the dead (Lev.21.1–12). **5–10:** This case law, supplemental to Lev.6.1–7 (Ex.22.7–15), deals with a situation in which there is no *kinsman* (see Lev.25.25 n.). **11–31:** Another case law, dealing with a woman suspected of adultery. **13–14:** This old law deals with a case not covered elsewhere (e.g. Lev.20.10): no witness can testify *since she was not taken in the act*. **15:** The *cereal offering* (Lev. ch. 2) *of jealousy* is intended to bring the case directly to God. **16–28:** A trial by ordeal, a common practice among ancient peoples. **16:** *Before the LORD*, i.e. to the sanctuary (Ex.22.9). **19–22:** The oath of execra-

the oath of the curse, and say to the woman) 'the LORD make you an execration and an oath among your people, when the LORD makes your thigh fall away and your body swell; ²² may this water that brings the curse pass into your bowels and make your body swell and your thigh fall away.' And the woman shall say, 'Amen, Amen.'

23 "Then the priest shall write these curses in a book, and wash them off into the water of bitterness; ²⁴ and he shall make the woman drink the water of bitterness that brings the curse, and the water that brings the curse shall enter into her and cause bitter pain. ²⁵ And the priest shall take the cereal offering of jealousy out of the woman's hand, and shall wave the cereal offering before the LORD and bring it to the altar; ²⁶ and the priest shall take a handful of the cereal offering, as its memorial portion, and burn it upon the altar, and afterward shall make the woman drink the water. ²⁷ And when he has made her drink the water, then, if she has defiled herself and has acted unfaithfully against her husband, the water that brings the curse shall enter into her and cause bitter pain, and her body shall swell, and her thigh shall fall away, and the woman shall become an execration among her people. ²⁸ But if the woman has not defiled herself and is clean, then she shall be free and shall conceive children.

29 "This is the law in cases of jealousy, when a wife, though under her husband's authority, goes astray and defiles herself, ³⁰ or when the spirit of jealousy comes upon a man and he is jealous of his wife; then he shall set the woman before the LORD, and the priest shall execute upon her all this law. ³¹ The man shall be free from iniquity, but the woman shall bear her iniquity."

6 And the LORD said to Moses, ² "Say to the people of Israel, When either a man or a woman makes a special vow, the vow of a Nazirite,^b to separate himself to the LORD, ³ he shall separate himself from wine and strong drink; he shall drink no vinegar made from wine or strong drink, and shall not drink any juice of grapes or eat grapes, fresh or dried. ⁴ All the days of his separation^c he shall eat nothing that is produced by the grapevine, not even the seeds or the skins.

5 "All the days of his vow of separation no razor shall come upon his head; until the time is completed for which he separates himself to the LORD, he shall be holy; he shall let the locks of hair of his head grow long.

6 "All the days that he separates himself to the LORD he shall not go near a dead body. ⁷ Neither for his father nor for his mother, nor for brother or sister, if they die, shall he make himself unclean; because his separation to God is upon his head. ⁸ All the days of his separation he is holy to the LORD.

9 "And if any man dies very suddenly beside him, and he defiles his consecrated head, then he shall shave his head on the day of his cleansing; on the seventh day he shall shave it. ¹⁰ On the eighth day he shall bring two turtledoves or two young pigeons to the priest to the door of the tent of

b That is *one separated* or *one consecrated*
c Or *Naziriteship*

---

tion, compare Ex.22.10–11. **23–28:** The oath is followed by the drinking of *the water of bitterness that brings the curse* (v. 18). It was believed that if a person were guilty this potion would have effects which would signify the LORD's verdict of judgment (Ex.32.20,35). **26:** *Memorial portion*, see Lev.2.2–3 n. **6.1–21:** The vow of a Nazirite. **2:** A Nazirite is a holy person who has taken the vow to *separate himself to the LORD* (Jg.13.5; 1 Sam.1.11; Am.2.11–12). **3–5:** Abstinence from the fruit of the vine (Jer. ch. 35; compare Lk.1.15), as well as from vinegar made from soured intoxicants, dramatizes Israel's separation from Canaanite culture (compare Gen. 9.21). For this restriction, as well as the law that *no razor shall come upon his head*, see the Samson story (especially Jg.13.4–5). **6–7:** Compare Lev.21.1–12. **9–12:** Accidental contact with a corpse defiles his *consecrated head*, i.e. the long locks which evidence his holy separation

meeting, [11] and the priest shall offer one for a sin offering and the other for a burnt offering, and make atonement for him, because he sinned by reason of the dead body. And he shall consecrate his head that same day, [12] and separate himself to the LORD for the days of his separation, and bring a male lamb a year old for a guilt offering; but the former time shall be void, because his separation was defiled.

13 "And this is the law for the Nazirite, when the time of his separation has been completed: he shall be brought to the door of the tent of meeting, [14] and he shall offer his gift to the LORD, one male lamb a year old without blemish for a burnt offering, and one ewe lamb a year old without blemish as a sin offering, and one ram without blemish as a peace offering, [15] and a basket of unleavened bread, cakes of fine flour mixed with oil, and unleavened wafers spread with oil, and their cereal offering and their drink offerings. [16] And the priest shall present them before the LORD and offer his sin offering and his burnt offering, [17] and he shall offer the ram as a sacrifice of peace offering to the LORD, with the basket of unleavened bread; the priest shall offer also its cereal offering and its drink offering. [18] And the Nazirite shall shave his consecrated head at the door of the tent of meeting, and shall take the hair from his consecrated head and put it on the fire which is under the sacrifice of the peace offering. [19] And the priest shall take the shoulder of the ram, when it is boiled, and one unleavened cake out of the basket, and one unleavened wafer, and shall put them upon the hands of the Nazirite, after he has shaven the hair of his consecration, [20] and the priest shall wave them for a wave offering before the LORD; they are a holy portion for the priest, together with the breast that is waved and the thigh that is offered; and after that the Nazirite may drink wine.

21 "This is the law for the Nazirite who takes a vow. His offering to the LORD shall be according to his vow as a Nazirite, apart from what else he can afford; in accordance with the vow which he takes, so shall he do according to the law for his separation as a Nazirite."

22 The LORD said to Moses, [23] "Say to Aaron and his sons, Thus you shall bless the people of Israel: you shall say to them,
[24] The LORD bless you and keep you:
[25] The LORD make his face to shine
upon you, and be gracious to you:
[26] The LORD lift up his countenance
upon you, and give you peace.
27 "So shall they put my name upon the people of Israel, and I will bless them."

7 On the day when Moses had finished setting up the tabernacle, and had anointed and consecrated it with all its furnishings, and had anointed and consecrated the altar with all its utensils, [2] the leaders of Israel, heads of their fathers' houses, the leaders of the tribes, who were over those who were numbered, [3] offered and brought their offerings before the

---

(v. 7b), so that he must start the vow over again. **13–20:** The law for terminating the vow. **14–17:** For the kinds of sacrifice, see Lev. chs. 1–7. **18:** Hair offerings were not uncommon in ancient religion. **20:** *Wave offering*, see Ex.29.24 n. **22–27:** The Aaronic benediction. This blessing was undoubtedly used in the temple services at Jerusalem. **25:** *Make his face shine upon you*, signifies divine favor (Pss.31.16; 80.3,7,19), as does also the expression *lift up his countenance* (Pss.4.6; 44.3; 89.15). **26:** *Peace*, i.e. well-being, welfare, including peace with God in the covenant relationship. **27:** On the meaning of the *name*, see Gen.32.27 n.

7.1–89: Offerings from the tribal leaders for the service of the tabernacle and the dedication of the altar. **1:** The date suddenly shifts back to Ex.40.17 (compare Num.1.1), showing that a new block of tradition begins here. **2–9:** The leaders present wagons for transporting the tabernacle equipment, although the Kohathites, for the sake of precaution, had to carry the *holy things* on the shoulder (4.1–15).

LORD, six covered wagons and twelve oxen, a wagon for every two of the leaders, and for each one an ox; they offered them before the tabernacle. 4 Then the LORD said to Moses, 5 "Accept these from them, that they may be used in doing the service of the tent of meeting, and give them to the Levites, to each man according to his service." 6 So Moses took the wagons and the oxen, and gave them to the Levites. 7 Two wagons and four oxen he gave to the sons of Gershon, according to their service; 8 and four wagons and eight oxen he gave to the sons of Merar'i, according to their service, under the direction of Ith'amar the son of Aaron the priest. 9 But to the sons of Kohath he gave none, because they were charged with the care of the holy things which had to be carried on the shoulder. 10 And the leaders offered offerings for the dedication of the altar on the day it was anointed; and the leaders offered their offering before the altar. 11 And the LORD said to Moses, "They shall offer their offerings, one leader each day, for the dedication of the altar."

12 He who offered his offering the first day was Nahshon the son of Ammin'adab, of the tribe of Judah; 13 and his offering was one silver plate whose weight was a hundred and thirty shekels, one silver basin of seventy shekels, according to the shekel of the sanctuary, both of them full of fine flour mixed with oil for a cereal offering; 14 one golden dish of ten shekels, full of incense; 15 one young bull, one ram, one male lamb a year old, for a burnt offering; 16 one male goat for a sin offering; 17 and for the sacrifice of peace offerings, two oxen, five rams, five male goats, and five male lambs a year old. This was the offering of Nahshon the son of Ammin'adab.

18 On the second day Nethan'el the son of Zu'ar, the leader of Is'sachar, made an offering; 19 he offered for his offering one silver plate, whose weight was a hundred and thirty shekels, one silver basin of seventy shekels, according to the shekel of the sanctuary, both of them full of fine flour mixed with oil for a cereal offering; 20 one golden dish of ten shekels, full of incense; 21 one young bull, one ram, one male lamb a year old, for a burnt offering; 22 one male goat for a sin offering; 23 and for the sacrifice of peace offerings, two oxen, five rams, five male goats, and five male lambs a year old. This was the offering of Nethan'el the son of Zu'ar.

24 On the third day Eli'ab the son of Helon, the leader of the men of Zeb'ulun: 25 his offering was one silver plate, whose weight was a hundred and thirty shekels, one silver basin of seventy shekels, according to the shekel of the sanctuary, both of them full of fine flour mixed with oil for a cereal offering; 26 one golden dish of ten shekels, full of incense; 27 one young bull, one ram, one male lamb a year old, for a burnt offering; 28 one male goat for a sin offering; 29 and for the sacrifice of peace offerings, two oxen, five rams, five male goats, and five male lambs a year old. This was the offering of Eli'ab the son of Helon.

30 On the fourth day Eli'zur the son of Shed'eur, the leader of the men of Reuben: 31 his offering was one silver plate whose weight was a hundred and thirty shekels, one silver basin of seventy shekels, according to the shekel of the sanctuary, both of them full of fine flour mixed with oil for a cereal offering; 32 one golden dish of ten shekels, full of incense; 33 one young bull, one ram, one male lamb a year old, for a burnt offering; 34 one male goat for a sin offering; 35 and for the sacrifice of peace offerings, two oxen, five rams, five male goats, and five male lambs a year old. This was the offering of Eli'zur the son of Shed'eur.

36 On the fifth day Shelu'mi-el the son of Zurishad'dai, the leader of the men of Simeon: 37 his offering was one silver plate, whose weight was a hundred and thirty shekels, one silver basin of seventy shekels, according to the shekel of the sanctuary, both of

them full of fine flour mixed with oil for a cereal offering; 38 one golden dish of ten shekels, full of incense; 39 one young bull, one ram, one male lamb a year old, for a burnt offering; 40 one male goat for a sin offering; 41 and for the sacrifice of peace offerings, two oxen, five rams, five male goats, and five male lambs a year old. This was the offering of Shelu'mi-el the son of Zurishad'dai.

42 On the sixth day Eli'asaph the son of Deu'el, the leader of the men of Gad: 43 his offering was one silver plate, whose weight was a hundred and thirty shekels, one silver basin of seventy shekels, according to the shekel of the sanctuary, both of them full of fine flour mixed with oil for a cereal offering; 44 one golden dish of ten shekels, full of incense; 45 one young bull, one ram, one male lamb a year old, for a burnt offering; 46 one male goat for a sin offering; 47 and for the sacrifice of peace offerings, two oxen, five rams, five male goats, and five male lambs a year old. This was the offering of Eli'asaph the son of Deu'el.

48 On the seventh day Eli'shama the son of Ammi'hud, the leader of the men of E'phraim: 49 his offering was one silver plate, whose weight was a hundred and thirty shekels, one silver basin of seventy shekels, according to the shekel of the sanctuary, both of them full of fine flour mixed with oil for a cereal offering; 50 one golden dish of ten shekels, full of incense; 51 one young bull, one ram, one male lamb a year old, for a burnt offering; 52 one male goat for a sin offering; 53 and for the sacrifice of peace offerings, two oxen, five rams, five male goats, and five male lambs a year old. This was the offering of Eli'shama the son of Ammi'hud.

54 On the eighth day Gama'liel the son of Pedah'zur, the leader of the men of Manas'seh: 55 his offering was one silver plate, whose weight was a hundred and thirty shekels, one silver basin of seventy shekels, according to the shekel of the sanctuary, both of

them full of fine flour mixed with oil for a cereal offering; 56 one golden dish of ten shekels, full of incense; 57 one young bull, one ram, one male lamb a year old, for a burnt offering; 58 one male goat for a sin offering; 59 and for the sacrifice of peace offerings, two oxen, five rams, five male goats, and five male lambs a year old. This was the offering of Gama'liel the son of Pedah'zur.

60 On the ninth day Abi'dan the son of Gideo'ni, the leader of the men of Benjamin: 61 his offering was one silver plate, whose weight was a hundred and thirty shekels, one silver basin of seventy shekels, according to the shekel of the sanctuary, both of them full of fine flour mixed with oil for a cereal offering; 62 one golden dish of ten shekels, full of incense; 63 one young bull, one ram, one male lamb a year old, for a burnt offering; 64 one male goat for a sin offering; 65 and for the sacrifice of peace offerings, two oxen, five rams, five male goats, and five male lambs a year old. This was the offering of Abi'dan the son of Gideo'ni.

66 On the tenth day Ahie'zer the son of Ammishad'dai, the leader of the men of Dan: 67 his offering was one silver plate, whose weight was a hundred and thirty shekels, one silver basin of seventy shekels, according to the shekel of the sanctuary, both of them full of fine flour mixed with oil for a cereal offering; 68 one golden dish of ten shekels, full of incense; 69 one young bull, one ram, one male lamb a year old, for a burnt offering; 70 one male goat for a sin offering; 71 and for the sacrifice of peace offerings, two oxen, five rams, five male goats, and five male lambs a year old. This was the offering of Ahie'zer the son of Ammishad'dai.

72 On the eleventh day Pa'giel the son of Ochran, the leader of the men of Asher: 73 his offering was one silver plate, whose weight was a hundred and thirty shekels, one silver basin of seventy shekels, according to the shekel

of the sanctuary, both of them full of fine flour mixed with oil for a cereal offering; ⁷⁴ one golden dish of ten shekels, full of incense; ⁷⁵ one young bull, one ram, one male lamb a year old, for a burnt offering; ⁷⁶ one male goat for a sin offering; ⁷⁷ and for the sacrifice of peace offerings, two oxen, five rams, five male goats, and five male lambs a year old. This was the offering of Pa′giel the son of Ochran.

78 On the twelfth day Ahi′ra the son of Enan, the leader of the men of Naph′tali: ⁷⁹ his offering was one silver plate, whose weight was a hundred and thirty shekels, one silver basin of seventy shekels, according to the shekel of the sanctuary, both of them full of fine flour mixed with oil for a cereal offering; ⁸⁰ one golden dish of ten shekels, full of incense; ⁸¹ one young bull, one ram, one male lamb a year old, for a burnt offering; ⁸² one male goat for a sin offering; ⁸³ and for the sacrifice of peace offerings, two oxen, five rams, five male goats, and five male lambs a year old. This was the offering of Ahi′ra the son of Enan.

84 This was the dedication offering for the altar, on the day when it was anointed, from the leaders of Israel: twelve silver plates, twelve silver basins, twelve golden dishes, ⁸⁵ each silver plate weighing a hundred and thirty shekels and each basin seventy, all the silver of the vessels two thousand four hundred shekels according to the shekel of the sanctuary, ⁸⁶ the twelve golden dishes, full of incense, weighing ten shekels apiece according to the shekel of the sanctuary, all the gold of the dishes being a hundred and twenty shekels; ⁸⁷ all the cattle for the burnt offering twelve bulls, twelve

rams, twelve male lambs a year old, with their cereal offering; and twelve male goats for a sin offering; ⁸⁸ and all the cattle for the sacrifice of peace offerings twenty-four bulls, the rams sixty, the male goats sixty, the male lambs a year old sixty. This was the dedication offering for the altar, after it was anointed.

89 And when Moses went into the tent of meeting to speak with the LORD, he heard the voice speaking to him from above the mercy seat that was upon the ark of the testimony, from between the two cherubim; and it spoke to him.

8 Now the LORD said to Moses, ² "Say to Aaron, When you set up the lamps, the seven lamps shall give light in front of the lampstand." ³ And Aaron did so; he set up its lamps to give light in front of the lampstand, as the LORD commanded Moses. ⁴ And this was the workmanship of the lampstand, hammered work of gold; from its base to its flowers, it was hammered work; according to the pattern which the LORD had shown Moses, so he made the lampstand.

5 And the LORD said to Moses, ⁶ "Take the Levites from among the people of Israel, and cleanse them. ⁷ And thus you shall do to them, to cleanse them: sprinkle the water of expiation upon them, and let them go with a razor over all their body, and wash their clothes and cleanse themselves. ⁸ Then let them take a young bull and its cereal offering of fine flour mixed with oil, and you shall take another young bull for a sin offering. ⁹ And you shall present the Levites before the tent of meeting, and assemble the whole congregation of the people of Israel. ¹⁰ When you present the

---

12–83: The tribal names are taken from the old list found in 1.5–15 (compare 10.14–27). The dedication offering presented on successive days was the same. **85:** *The shekel of the sanctuary*, see Ex.30.13 n. **89:** Ex. 25.22.

8.1–26: The consecration of the Levites. 1–4: Ex.25.31–40; 27.20–21; Lev.24.2–4. The lighting of the lamps is the prerogative of the Aaronic priests. **4:** *The pattern*, see Ex.25.9. **5–22:** The Levites are to be consecrated for their office by a special purification ceremony (compare the ordination of the Aaronic priests, Lev. ch. 8). **7:** *The water of expiation* (compare Ezek.36.25) refers to ceremonial cleansing. Shaving the hair and washing garments were rites of purification.

Levites before the LORD, the people of Israel shall lay their hands upon the Levites, ¹¹ and Aaron shall offer the Levites before the LORD as a wave offering from the people of Israel, that it may be theirs to do the service of the LORD. ¹² Then the Levites shall lay their hands upon the heads of the bulls; and you shall offer the one for a sin offering and the other for a burnt offering to the LORD, to make atonement for the Levites. ¹³ And you shall cause the Levites to attend Aaron and his sons, and shall offer them as a wave offering to the LORD.

14 "Thus you shall separate the Levites from among the people of Israel, and the Levites shall be mine. ¹⁵ And after that the Levites shall go in to do service at the tent of meeting, when you have cleansed them and offered them as a wave offering. ¹⁶ For they are wholly given to me from among the people of Israel; instead of all that open the womb, the first-born of all the people of Israel, I have taken them for myself. ¹⁷ For all the first-born among the people of Israel are mine, both of man and of beast; on the day that I slew all the first-born in the land of Egypt I consecrated them for myself, ¹⁸ and I have taken the Levites instead of all the first-born among the people of Israel. ¹⁹ And I have given the Levites as a gift to Aaron and his sons from among the people of Israel, to do the service for the people of Israel at the tent of meeting, and to make atonement for the people of Israel, that there may be no plague among the people of Israel in case the people of Israel should come near the sanctuary."

20 Thus did Moses and Aaron and all the congregation of the people of Israel to the Levites; according to all that the LORD commanded Moses concerning the Levites, the people of Israel did to them. ²¹ And the Levites purified themselves from sin, and washed their clothes; and Aaron offered them as a wave offering before the LORD, and Aaron made atonement for them to cleanse them. ²² And after that the Levites went in to do their service in the tent of meeting in attendance upon Aaron and his sons; as the LORD had commanded Moses concerning the Levites, so they did to them.

23 And the LORD said to Moses, ²⁴ "This is what pertains to the Levites: from twenty-five years old and upward they shall go in to perform the work in the service of the tent of meeting; ²⁵ and from the age of fifty years they shall withdraw from the work of the service and serve no more, ²⁶ but minister to their brethren in the tent of meeting, to keep the charge, and they shall do no service. Thus shall you do to the Levites in assigning their duties."

9 And the LORD spoke to Moses in the wilderness of Sinai, in the first month of the second year after they had come out of the land of Egypt, saying, ² "Let the people of Israel keep the passover at its appointed time. ³ On the fourteenth day of this month, in the evening, you shall keep it at its appointed time; according to all its statutes and all its ordinances you shall keep it." ⁴ So Moses told the people of Israel that they should keep the passover. ⁵ And they kept the passover in the first month, on the fourteenth day of the month, in the evening, in the wilderness of Sinai; according to all that the LORD commanded Moses, so the people of Israel did. ⁶ And there were certain men who were unclean through touching the dead body of a

---

10–11: By the laying on of hands (Lev.1.4) the people identify themselves with the Levites who are "sacrificed" instead of their first-born (vv. 16–17; 3.13). *Wave offering* is used symbolically to indicate that the Levites belong to Aaron and his sons just as the waved sacrifice belongs to the priests (see Ex.29.24 n.). **12:** *Make atonement*, see Ex.29.35–37 n. **16–19:** 3.5–13. The Levites, by their position in the camp (1.52–53; 3.38), shielded the people from the dreadful effects of holiness, which could cause a *plague* or other calamity (1 Sam. chs. 5–6). **24:** 4.3.

9.1–10.10: Other events and instructions. 1–14: Supplement to the laws concerning the passover. **1:** Here, as in 7.1, the month is that of Ex.40.17 rather than the date assumed for chs. 1–6.

man, so that they could not keep the passover on that day; and they came before Moses and Aaron on that day; 7 and those men said to him, "We are unclean through touching the dead body of a man; why are we kept from offering the LORD's offering at its appointed time among the people of Israel?" 8 And Moses said to them, "Wait, that I may hear what the LORD will command concerning you."

9 The LORD said to Moses, 10 "Say to the people of Israel, If any man of you or of your descendants is unclean through touching a dead body, or is afar off on a journey, he shall still keep the passover to the LORD. 11 In the second month on the fourteenth day in the evening they shall keep it; they shall eat it with unleavened bread and bitter herbs. 12 They shall leave none of it until the morning, nor break a bone of it; according to all the statute for the passover they shall keep it. 13 But the man who is clean and is not on a journey, yet refrains from keeping the passover, that person shall be cut off from his people, because he did not offer the LORD's offering at its appointed time; that man shall bear his sin. 14 And if a stranger sojourns among you, and will keep the passover to the LORD, according to the statute of the passover and according to its ordinance, so shall he do; you shall have one statute, both for the sojourner and for the native."

15 On the day that the tabernacle was set up, the cloud covered the tabernacle, the tent of the testimony; and at evening it was over the tabernacle like the appearance of fire until morning. 16 So it was continually; the cloud covered it by day,*d* and the appearance of fire by night. 17 And whenever the cloud was taken up from over the tent,

after that the people of Israel set out; and in the place where the cloud settled down, there the people of Israel encamped. 18 At the command of the LORD the people of Israel set out, and at the command of the LORD they encamped; as long as the cloud rested over the tabernacle, they remained in camp. 19 Even when the cloud continued over the tabernacle many days, the people of Israel kept the charge of the LORD, and did not set out. 20 Sometimes the cloud was a few days over the tabernacle, and according to the command of the LORD they remained in camp; then according to the command of the LORD they set out. 21 And sometimes the cloud remained from evening until morning; and when the cloud was taken up in the morning, they set out, or if it continued for a day and a night, when the cloud was taken up they set out. 22 Whether it was two days, or a month, or a longer time, that the cloud continued over the tabernacle, abiding there, the people of Israel remained in camp and did not set out; but when it was taken up they set out. 23 At the command of the LORD they encamped, and at the command of the LORD they set out; they kept the charge of the LORD, at the command of the LORD by Moses.

10 The LORD said to Moses, 2 "Make two silver trumpets; of hammered work you shall make them; and you shall use them for summoning the congregation, and for breaking camp. 3 And when both are blown, all the congregation shall gather themselves to you at the entrance of the tent of meeting. 4 But if they blow only one, then the leaders, the heads of the tribes of Israel, shall gather themselves

d Gk Syr Vg: Heb lacks *by day*

2–4: Ex.12.1–13,21–27. 6–7: On uncleanness through touching a corpse, see Lev.21.1–12. 8: This verse shows that Israel's law was not fixed and unchangeable, but developed as the people faced new situations (15.23). 9: The case of one who is *afar off on a journey* apparently presupposes settlement in Canaan and goes beyond the case at hand (v. 7). 11: In these cases, the passover may be kept one month late. 13: *Cut off*, see Lev.7.20 n. 15–23: On the fiery cloud, see Ex.14.24; 40.34–38 n. These verses (compare 14.14) presuppose Israel's march, rather than the sojourn at Sinai and thus anticipate 10.11–13. 15: Ex.40.34–38. 10.1–10: Sounding the trumpets.

to you. 5 When you blow an alarm, the camps that are on the east side shall set out. 6 And when you blow an alarm the second time, the camps that are on the south side shall set out. An alarm is to be blown whenever they are to set out. 7 But when the assembly is to be gathered together, you shall blow, but you shall not sound an alarm. 8 And the sons of Aaron, the priests, shall blow the trumpets. The trumpets shall be to you for a perpetual statute throughout your generations. 9 And when you go to war in your land against the adversary who oppresses you, then you shall sound an alarm with the trumpets, that you may be remembered before the LORD your God, and you shall be saved from your enemies. 10 On the day of your gladness also, and at your appointed feasts, and at the beginnings of your months, you shall blow the trumpets over your burnt offerings and over the sacrifices of your peace offerings; they shall serve you for remembrance before your God: I am the LORD your God."

11 In the second year, in the second month, on the twentieth day of the month, the cloud was taken up from over the tabernacle of the testimony, 12 and the people of Israel set out by stages from the wilderness of Sinai; and the cloud settled down in the wilderness of Paran. 13 They set out for the first time at the command of the LORD by Moses. 14 The standard of the camp of the men of Judah set out first by their companies; and over their host was Nahshon the son of Ammin′adab. 15 And over the host of the tribe of the men of Is′sachar was Nethan′el the son of Zu′ar. 16 And over the host of the tribe of the men of Zeb′ulun was Eli′ab the son of Helon.

17 And when the tabernacle was taken down, the sons of Gershon and the sons of Merar′i, who carried the tabernacle, set out. 18 And the standard of the camp of Reuben set out by their companies; and over their host was Eli′zur the son of Shed′eur. 19 And over the host of the tribe of the men of Simeon was Shelu′mi-el the son of Zurishad′dai. 20 And over the host of the tribe of the men of Gad was Eli′-asaph the son of Deu′el.

21 Then the Ko′hathites set out, carrying the holy things, and the tabernacle was set up before their arrival. 22 And the standard of the camp of the men of E′phraim set out by their companies; and over their host was Eli′shama the son of Ammi′hud. 23 And over the host of the tribe of the men of Manas′seh was Gama′liel the son of Pedah′zur. 24 And over the host of the tribe of the men of Benjamin was Abi′dan the son of Gideo′ni.

25 Then the standard of the camp of the men of Dan, acting as the rear guard of all the camps, set out by their companies; and over their host was Ahie′zer the son of Ammishad′dai. 26 And over the host of the tribe of the men of Asher was Pa′giel the son of Ochran. 27 And over the host of the tribe of the men of Naph′tali was Ahi′ra the son of Enan. 28 This was the order of march of the people of Israel according to their hosts, when they set out.

29 And Moses said to Hobab the son of Reu′el the Mid′ianite, Moses' father-in-law, "We are setting out for the place of which the LORD said, 'I will give it to you'; come with us, and we will do you good; for the LORD has

---

5–7: An *alarm* was a military call (v. 9; Am.3.6), as distinguished from the trumpet which proclaims assembly (Lev. ch. 23, especially v. 24). 10: *The beginnings of your months,* see 28.11–15 n.

10.11–36: Israel on the march. The people departed from Sinai with signs of the LORD's accompanying presence. 11: The date was eleven months after the arrival at Sinai (Ex.19.1) or nineteen days after the census (Num.1.1). 12: *By stages,* see ch. 33. 13–28: On the order of march and Levitical tasks, see chs. 2–3. 29–36: Here old literary traditions reappear after a long, unbroken sequence of priestly material (Ex. chs. 35–40; Lev.; Num.1.1–10.28). 29: *Hobab,* otherwise known as Jethro (Ex.2.18 n.), was leader of the Kenites, a Midianite clan who were

promised good to Israel." ³⁰ But he said to him, "I will not go; I will depart to my own land and to my kindred." ³¹ And he said, "Do not leave us, I pray you, for you know how we are to encamp in the wilderness, and you will serve as eyes for us. ³² And if you go with us, whatever good the LORD will do to us, the same will we do to you."

33 So they set out from the mount of the LORD three days' journey; and the ark of the covenant of the LORD went before them three days' journey, to seek out a resting place for them. ³⁴ And the cloud of the LORD was over them by day, whenever they set out from the camp.

35 And whenever the ark set out, Moses said, "Arise, O LORD, and let thy enemies be scattered; and let them that hate thee flee before thee." ³⁶ And when it rested, he said, "Return, O LORD, to the ten thousand thousands of Israel."

And the people complained in the hearing of the LORD about their misfortunes; and when the LORD heard it, his anger was kindled, and the fire of the LORD burned among them, and consumed some outlying parts of the camp. ² Then the people cried to Moses; and Moses prayed to the LORD, and the fire abated. ³ So the name of that place was called Tab'erah,ᵉ because the fire of the LORD burned among them.

4 Now the rabble that was among them had a strong craving; and the people of Israel also wept again, and said, "O that we had meat to eat! ⁵ We remember the fish we ate in Egypt for nothing, the cucumbers, the melons, the leeks, the onions, and the garlic; ⁶ but now our strength is dried up, and there is nothing at all but this manna to look at."

7 Now the manna was like coriander seed, and its appearance like that of bdellium. ⁸ The people went about and gathered it, and ground it in mills or beat it in mortars, and boiled it in pots, and made cakes of it; and the taste of it was like the taste of cakes baked with oil. ⁹ When the dew fell upon the camp in the night, the manna fell with it.

10 Moses heard the people weeping throughout their families, every man at the door of his tent; and the anger of the LORD blazed hotly, and Moses was displeased. ¹¹ Moses said to the LORD, "Why hast thou dealt ill with thy servant? And why have I not found favor in thy sight, that thou dost lay the burden of all this people upon me? ¹² Did I conceive all this people? Did I bring them forth, that thou shouldst say to me, 'Carry them in your bosom, as a nurse carries the sucking child, to the land which thou didst swear to give their fathers?' ¹³ Where am I to get meat to give to all this people? For they weep before me and say, 'Give us meat, that we may eat.' ¹⁴ I am not able to carry all this people alone, the burden is too heavy for me. ¹⁵ If thou wilt deal thus with me, kill me at once, if I find favor in thy sight, that I may not see my wretchedness."

e That is *Burning*

---

allies during Israel's early history (Ex. ch. 18; Jg.1.16; 4.11; 5.24). **33–36:** Ancient tradition about the ark (see Ex.25.10–22 n.). **33:** This verse should not be interpreted to mean that the ark went ahead *three days' journey;* rather, it *went before* them (compare v. 21) during this duration of journey from Sinai. **35–36:** The ancient "song to the ark" is based on the conviction that the ark was the LORD's throne, upon which he was seated invisibly as holy war was waged against his enemies (Jos. chs. 3–4; 1 Sam.4.3–22; compare Ps.24.7–10).

11.1–35: Israel's murmuring in the wilderness. 1: See Ex.15.24 n. The *fire of the LORD* may refer to some natural phenomenon like lightning which was interpreted as God's consuming holiness (compare Lev.10.2). **4–15:** Not satisfied with the manna, the people craved seasoned meat dishes such as they had enjoyed in Egypt (Ex.16.3). **4:** *Rabble,* see Ex.12.38 n. *Wept again,* see Ex.16.2–3. **7–9:** *The manna,* see Ex.16.14–21,31. *Bdellium,* a resinous gum. **11–15:** In this chapter two motifs have been woven together: one dealing with the miraculous provision of desert food, the other dealing with Moses' heavy responsibilities as leader (vv. 11–12,14–17, 24–30). **11–12:** On Moses' impatience, see Ex.17.2–4. **14:** *The burden is too heavy,* see Ex.18.17–

16 And the LORD said to Moses, "Gather for me seventy men of the elders of Israel, whom you know to be the elders of the people and officers over them; and bring them to the tent of meeting, and let them take their stand there with you. [17] And I will come down and talk with you there; and I will take some of the spirit which is upon you and put it upon them; and they shall bear the burden of the people with you, that you may not bear it yourself alone. [18] And say to the people, 'Consecrate yourselves for tomorrow, and you shall eat meat; for you have wept in the hearing of the LORD, saying, "Who will give us meat to eat? For it was well with us in Egypt." Therefore the LORD will give you meat, and you shall eat. [19] You shall not eat one day, or two days, or five days, or ten days, or twenty days, [20] but a whole month, until it comes out at your nostrils and becomes loathsome to you, because you have rejected the LORD who is among you, and have wept before him, saying, "Why did we come forth out of Egypt?" ' " [21] But Moses said, "The people among whom I am number six hundred thousand on foot; and thou hast said, 'I will give them meat, that they may eat a whole month!' [22] Shall flocks and herds be slaughtered for them, to suffice them? Or shall all the fish of the sea be gathered together for them, to suffice them?" [23] And the LORD said to Moses, "Is the LORD's hand shortened? Now you shall see whether my word will come true for you or not."

24 So Moses went out and told the people the words of the LORD; and he gathered seventy men of the elders of the people, and placed them round about the tent. [25] Then the LORD came down in the cloud and spoke to him, and took some of the spirit that was upon him and put it upon the seventy elders; and when the spirit rested upon them, they prophesied. But they did so no more.

26 Now two men remained in the camp, one named Eldad, and the other named Medad, and the spirit rested upon them; they were among those registered, but they had not gone out to the tent, and so they prophesied in the camp. [27] And a young man ran and told Moses, "Eldad and Medad are prophesying in the camp." [28] And Joshua the son of Nun, the minister of Moses, one of his chosen men, said, "My lord Moses, forbid them." [29] But Moses said to him, "Are you jealous for my sake? Would that all the LORD's people were prophets, that the LORD would put his spirit upon them!" [30] And Moses and the elders of Israel returned to the camp.

31 And there went forth a wind from the LORD, and it brought quails from the sea, and let them fall beside the camp, about a day's journey on this side and a day's journey on the other side, round about the camp, and about two cubits above the face of the earth.

---

18. **16–17** (also **24–25**): Moses' burden was lightened by investing seventy elders with power to assist him (Ex.18.21–23; see Dt.1.9–18). This account presupposes the old tradition about the *tent of meeting* (Ex.33.7–11). **17**: Moses is regarded as a charismatic leader, endowed with the divine spirit (compare 24.2; Jg.11.29). The transfer of a portion of the spirit to the elders (2 Kg.2.9–10) indicates that the latter are subordinate to Moses, who stands in a close relation to God (Ex.33.11). **18–23**: Continuation of the food tradition. **21**: Ex.12.37. The story stresses the LORD's miraculous power to support an extremely large population in the wilderness. **25**: *They prophesied*, because the divine spirit was put upon them. Such ecstatic prophecy, familiar in Israel's early prophetic movement (1 Sam.10.6,10–13; 1 Kg.22.6,10–12), probably shows Canaanite influence. **26–30**: Two other elders received the gift of prophecy even though they stayed in the camp. **26**: Here it is assumed that the tent of meeting was outside the camp (Ex.33.7; see Num.2.2 n.). *Registered*, i.e. enrolled as representatives of the community. **31–35**: Continuation of vv. 18–23. **31–35**: Like the manna, the quails (Ex.16.13) are a natural phenomenon of the desert. They migrate over the region in great numbers and, when exhausted, are easily caught. **31**: *A wind from the LORD* (compare Ex.14.21) brought the quails from *the sea*, the Gulf of Aqabah. **33**: A sickness which resulted from eating quail is interpreted as divine

³² And the people rose all that day, and all night, and all the next day, and gathered the quails; he who gathered least gathered ten homers; and they spread them out for themselves all around the camp. ³³ While the meat was yet between their teeth, before it was consumed, the anger of the LORD was kindled against the people, and the LORD smote the people with a very great plague. ³⁴ Therefore the name of that place was called Kib'roth-hatta'-avah,ᶠ because there they buried the people who had the craving. ³⁵ From Kib'roth-hatta'avah the people journeyed to Haze'roth; and they remained at Haze'roth.

12 Miriam and Aaron spoke against Moses because of the Cushite woman whom he had married, for he had married a Cushite woman; ² and they said, "Has the LORD indeed spoken only through Moses? Has he not spoken through us also?" And the LORD heard it. ³ Now the man Moses was very meek, more than all men that were on the face of the earth. ⁴ And suddenly the LORD said to Moses and to Aaron and Miriam, "Come out, you three, to the tent of meeting." And the three of them came out. ⁵ And the LORD came down in a pillar of cloud, and stood at the door of the tent, and called Aaron and Miriam; and they both came forward. ⁶ And he said, "Hear my words: If there is a prophet among you, I the LORD make myself known to him in a vision, I speak with him in a dream. ⁷ Not so with my

servant Moses; he is entrusted with all my house. ⁸ With him I speak mouth to mouth, clearly, and not in dark speech; and he beholds the form of the LORD. Why then were you not afraid to speak against my servant Moses?"

9 And the anger of the LORD was kindled against them, and he departed; ¹⁰ and when the cloud removed from over the tent, behold, Miriam was leprous, as white as snow. And Aaron turned towards Miriam, and behold, she was leprous. ¹¹ And Aaron said to Moses, "Oh, my lord, do notᵍ punish us because we have done foolishly and have sinned. ¹² Let her not be as one dead, of whom the flesh is half consumed when he comes out of his mother's womb." ¹³ And Moses cried to the LORD, "Heal her, O God, I beseech thee." ¹⁴ But the LORD said to Moses, "If her father had but spit in her face, should she not be shamed seven days? Let her be shut up outside the camp seven days, and after that she may be brought in again." ¹⁵ So Miriam was shut up outside the camp seven days; and the people did not set out on the march till Miriam was brought in again. ¹⁶ After that the people set out from Haze'roth, and encamped in the wilderness of Paran.

13 The LORD said to Moses, ² "Send men to spy out the land of Canaan, which I give to the people of Israel; from each tribe of their fathers shall you send a man, every one a

f That is *Graves of craving*
g Heb *lay not sin upon us*

judgment upon the people's faithlessness. A *plague* was an act of God; see Lev.26.21; Dt. 28.27; 1 Sam.4.8.

12.1–16: The punishment of Miriam for challenging Moses' unique relation to God. **1:** Moses had married Zipporah, a Midianite (Ex.2.21). The term *Cushite* apparently includes Midianites and other Arabic peoples (Hab.3.7). **2:** The question is directed against Moses' position as covenant mediator and leader of the people (Ex.19.9; 33.11). Miriam was also recognized as a spiritual leader (Ex.15.20; Mic.6.4). **3:** *Meek*, i.e. humble before God (Ex.3.11). This verse is an age-old stumbling-block to the belief that Moses wrote the whole Pentateuch. **4:** See 11.26 n. **6–8:** The LORD normally communicates with prophets indirectly through dreams or visions (see Dt.13.1 n.); but with Moses he speaks directly (see Ex.33.11 n.). The *form of the LORD*, compare Ex.33.17–23. **14:** See 5.2–3; Lev.13.1–8. The punishment cannot be less than the defilement of being spat upon by her father, the sign of a curse (Dt.25.9). **16:** The early traditions in 10.29–12.15 assume that Israel had not yet reached Paran (10.12).

13.1–33: The reconnaissance of the land. Twelve scouts brought back a majority report that formidable obstacles stood in the way of taking Canaan. **1–16:** Priestly tradition gives the

leader among them." [3] So Moses sent them from the wilderness of Paran, according to the command of the LORD, all of them men who were heads of the people of Israel. [4] And these were their names: From the tribe of Reuben, Sham'mu-a the son of Zaccur; [5] from the tribe of Simeon, Shaphat the son of Hori; [6] from the tribe of Judah, Caleb the son of Jephun'neh; [7] from the tribe of Is'sachar, Igal the son of Joseph; [8] from the tribe of E'phraim, Hoshe'a the son of Nun; [9] from the tribe of Benjamin, Palti the son of Raphu; [10] from the tribe of Zeb'ulun, Gad'diel the son of Sodi; [11] from the tribe of Joseph (that is from the tribe of Manas'seh), Gaddi the son of Susi; [12] from the tribe of Dan, Am'miel the son of Gemal'li; [13] from the tribe of Asher, Sethur the son of Michael; [14] from the tribe of Naph'tali, Nahbi the son of Vophsi; [15] from the tribe of Gad, Geu'el the son of Machi. [16] These were the names of the men whom Moses sent to spy out the land. And Moses called Hoshe'a the son of Nun Joshua.

17 Moses sent them to spy out the land of Canaan, and said to them, "Go up into the Negeb yonder, and go up into the hill country, [18] and see what the land is, and whether the people who dwell in it are strong or weak, whether they are few or many, [19] and whether the land that they dwell in is good or bad, and whether the cities that they dwell in are camps or strongholds, [20] and whether the land is rich or poor, and whether there is wood in it or not. Be of good courage, and bring some of the fruit of the land." Now the time was the season of the first ripe grapes.

21 So they went up and spied out the land from the wilderness of Zin to Rehob, near the entrance of Hamath. [22] They went up into the Negeb, and came to Hebron; and Ahi'man, She'shai, and Talmai, the descendants of Anak, were there. (Hebron was built seven years before Zo'an in Egypt.) [23] And they came to the Valley of Eshcol, and cut down from there a branch with a single cluster of grapes, and they carried it on a pole between two of them; they brought also some pomegranates and figs. [24] That place was called the Valley of Eshcol,[h] because of the cluster which the men of Israel cut down from there.

25 At the end of forty days they returned from spying out the land. [26] And they came to Moses and Aaron and to all the congregation of the people of Israel in the wilderness of Paran, at Kadesh; they brought back word to them and to all the congregation, and showed them the fruit of the land. [27] And they told him, "We came to the land to which you sent us; it flows with milk and honey, and this is its fruit. [28] Yet the people who dwell in the land are strong, and the cities are fortified and very large; and besides, we saw the descendants of Anak there. [29] The Amal'ekites dwell in the land of the Negeb; the Hittites, the Jeb'usites, and the Amorites dwell in the hill country; and the Canaanites dwell by the sea, and along the Jordan."

30 But Caleb quieted the people

h That is *Cluster*

---

names of the spies. The leaders are not the same as those of 1.5–15. **8:** *Hoshea*, an alternate form of Joshua (v. 16). **21:** This priestly comment supposes that the spies surveyed the whole of Canaan from the area of Kadesh (see v. 26 n.) to Rehob (2 Sam.10.6) near Laish or Dan. *The entrance to Hamath*, see 34.1–12 n. **22:** The mixed population of Canaan included the tribes descended from Anak, regarded as an unusually tall people (vv. 32–33). An archaeological comment dates the history of Hebron in relation to the founding of Zoan or Tanis, rebuilt as the Hyksos capital about 1700 B.C. (see Ex.1.11 n.). **23:** *The Valley of Eshcol* was in the vicinity of Hebron, a famous grape-producing area. **26:** *Kadesh* (-barnea), an oasis on the border between the wilderness of Paran and the wilderness of Zin. The traditions found in 10.11–21.3 deal with this oasis (see Ex.17.7 n.), where Israel spent most of the forty year sojourn in the wilderness (see Introduction). **27:** *Milk and honey*, see Ex.3.8 n. **29:** *Amalekites*, see Ex.17.8 n. For the pre-Israelite inhabitants, see Ex.3.8. **33:** *Nephilim*, see Gen.6.4 n.

before Moses, and said, "Let us go up at once, and occupy it; for we are well able to overcome it." ³¹ Then the men who had gone up with him said, "We are not able to go up against the people; for they are stronger than we." ³² So they brought to the people of Israel an evil report of the land which they had spied out, saying, "The land, through which we have gone, to spy it out, is a land that devours its inhabitants; and all the people that we saw in it are men of great stature. ³³ And there we saw the Nephilim (the sons of Anak, who come from the Nephilim); and we seemed to ourselves like grasshoppers, and so we seemed to them."

14 Then all the congregation raised a loud cry; and the people wept that night. ² And all the people of Israel murmured against Moses and Aaron; the whole congregation said to them, "Would that we had died in the land of Egypt! Or would that we had died in this wilderness! ³ Why does the LORD bring us into this land, to fall by the sword? Our wives and our little ones will become a prey; would it not be better for us to go back to Egypt?"

4 And they said to one another, "Let us choose a captain, and go back to Egypt." ⁵ Then Moses and Aaron fell on their faces before all the assembly of the congregation of the people of Israel. ⁶ And Joshua the son of Nun and Caleb the son of Jephun'neh, who were among those who had spied out the land, rent their clothes, ⁷ and said to all the congregation of the people of Israel, "The land, which we passed through to spy it out, is an exceedingly good land. ⁸ If the LORD delights in us, he will bring us into this land and give it to us, a land which flows with milk and honey. ⁹ Only, do not rebel against the LORD; and do not fear the people of the land, for they are bread for us; their protection is removed from them, and the LORD is with us; do not fear them." ¹⁰ But all the congregation said to stone them with stones.

Then the glory of the LORD appeared at the tent of meeting to all the people of Israel. ¹¹ And the LORD said to Moses, "How long will this people despise me? And how long will they not believe in me, in spite of all the signs which I have wrought among them? ¹² I will strike them with the pestilence and disinherit them, and I will make of you a nation greater and mightier than they."

13 But Moses said to the LORD, "Then the Egyptians will hear of it, for thou didst bring up this people in thy might from among them, ¹⁴ and they will tell the inhabitants of this land. They have heard that thou, O LORD, art in the midst of this people; for thou, O LORD, art seen face to face, and thy cloud stands over them and thou goest before them, in a pillar of cloud by day and in a pillar of fire by night. ¹⁵ Now if thou dost kill this people as one man, then the nations who have heard thy fame will say, ¹⁶ 'Because the LORD was not able to bring this people into the land which he swore to give to them, therefore he has slain them in the wilderness.' ¹⁷ And now, I pray thee, let the power of the LORD be great as thou hast promised, saying, ¹⁸ 'The LORD is slow to anger, and abounding in steadfast love, forgiving iniquity and transgression, but he will by no means clear the guilty, visiting the iniquity of fathers upon children, upon the third and upon the fourth generation.' ¹⁹ Pardon the iniquity of this people, I pray thee, according to the greatness

---

14.1–45: Decision to attack. The Israelites attempted a foolhardy attack on Canaan from the south and were repulsed. **1–4:** See Ex.16.3 n. **5–6:** According to priestly tradition, Joshua sided with Caleb in appraising the situation (compare 13.30). **10:** On the LORD's *glory*, see Ex.16.6–7 n. **11:** The *signs* (see Ex.3.11–12 n.) were ambiguous evidences, not proofs of God's presence. **12:** Ex.32.9–10. **13–19:** In his intercession, Moses again appeals to the LORD's honor and gracious ways (Ex.32.11–13). **15–16:** Other nations, owing to limitations of understanding, will conclude that the LORD does not have the power of deity (Dt.32.26–27). In the ancient world a god was judged by whether he had the power to act (1 Kg.18.20–40). **18:** A quotation from

of thy steadfast love, and according as thou hast forgiven this people, from Egypt even until now."

20 Then the LORD said, "I have pardoned, according to your word; 21 but truly, as I live, and as all the earth shall be filled with the glory of the LORD, 22 none of the men who have seen my glory and my signs which I wrought in Egypt and in the wilderness, and yet have put me to the proof these ten times and have not hearkened to my voice, 23 shall see the land which I swore to give to their fathers; and none of those who despised me shall see it. 24 But my servant Caleb, because he has a different spirit and has followed me fully, I will bring into the land into which he went, and his descendants shall possess it. 25 Now, since the Amal'ekites and the Canaanites dwell in the valleys, turn tomorrow and set out for the wilderness by the way to the Red Sea."

26 And the LORD said to Moses and to Aaron, 27 "How long shall this wicked congregation murmur against me? I have heard the murmurings of the people of Israel, which they murmur against me. 28 Say to them, 'As I live,' says the LORD, 'what you have said in my hearing I will do to you: 29 your dead bodies shall fall in this wilderness; and of all your number, numbered from twenty years old and upward, who have murmured against me, 30 not one shall come into the land where I swore that I would make you dwell, except Caleb the son of Jephun'neh and Joshua the son of Nun. 31 But your little ones, who you said would become a prey, I will bring in, and they shall know the land which you have despised. 32 But as for you, your dead bodies shall fall in this wilderness.

33 And your children shall be shepherds in the wilderness forty years, and shall suffer for your faithlessness, until the last of your dead bodies lies in the wilderness. 34 According to the number of the days in which you spied out the land, forty days, for every day a year, you shall bear your iniquity, forty years, and you shall know my displeasure.' 35 I, the LORD, have spoken; surely this will I do to all this wicked congregation that are gathered together against me: in this wilderness they shall come to a full end, and there they shall die."

36 And the men whom Moses sent to spy out the land, and who returned and made all the congregation to murmur against him by bringing up an evil report against the land, 37 the men who brought up an evil report of the land, died by plague before the LORD. 38 But Joshua the son of Nun and Caleb the son of Jephun'neh remained alive, of those men who went to spy out the land.

39 And Moses told these words to all the people of Israel, and the people mourned greatly. 40 And they rose early in the morning, and went up to the heights of the hill country, saying, "See, we are here, we will go up to the place which the LORD has promised; for we have sinned." 41 But Moses said, "Why now are you transgressing the command of the LORD, for that will not succeed? 42 Do not go up lest you be struck down before your enemies, for the LORD is not among you. 43 For there the Amal'ekites and the Canaanites are before you, and you shall fall by the sword; because you have turned back from following the LORD, the LORD will not be with you." 44 But they presumed to go up to the heights

an old liturgical summary (Ex.34.5–8). **20:** On the LORD's repentance, see Ex.32.14 n. **22–23:** Since divine mercy does not exclude divine judgment (v. 18b), the verdict is that none of the present rebellious generation will enter Canaan. **24:** Caleb is excepted in view of 13.30. Joshua is not mentioned because the account of his siding with Caleb (vv. 5–6,26–38) comes from another tradition. **26–38:** This priestly tradition interprets the forty years in the wilderness as a time of divine judgment. **29:** *Twenty years*, the age for beginning military service (1.3). **39–45:** These verses preserve the memory of an abortive attempt to penetrate Canaan from the south. **42:** The failure is interpreted by the words *the LORD is not among you*, i.e. the ark did not go

of the hill country, although neither the ark of the covenant of the LORD, nor Moses, departed out of the camp. [45] Then the Amal'ekites and the Canaanites who dwelt in that hill country came down, and defeated them and pursued them, even to Hormah.

15 The LORD said to Moses, [2] "Say to the people of Israel, When you come into the land you are to inhabit, which I give you, [3] and you offer to the LORD from the herd or from the flock an offering by fire or a burnt offering or a sacrifice, to fulfil a vow or as a freewill offering or at your appointed feasts, to make a pleasing odor to the LORD, [4] then he who brings his offering shall offer to the LORD a cereal offering of a tenth of an ephah of fine flour, mixed with a fourth of a hin of oil; [5] and wine for the drink offering, a fourth of a hin, you shall prepare with the burnt offering, or for the sacrifice, for each lamb. [6] Or for a ram, you shall prepare for a cereal offering two tenths of an ephah of fine flour mixed with a third of a hin of oil; [7] and for the drink offering you shall offer a third of a hin of wine, a pleasing odor to the LORD. [8] And when you prepare a bull for a burnt offering, or for a sacrifice, to fulfil a vow, or for peace offerings to the LORD, [9] then one shall offer with the bull a cereal offering of three tenths of an ephah of fine flour, mixed with half a hin of oil, [10] and you shall offer for the drink offering half a hin of wine, as an offering by fire, a pleasing odor to the LORD.

11 "Thus it shall be done for each bull or ram, or for each of the male lambs or the kids. [12] According to the number that you prepare, so shall you do with every one according to their number. [13] All who are native shall do these things in this way, in offering an offering by fire, a pleasing odor to the LORD. [14] And if a stranger is sojourning with you, or any one is among you throughout your generations, and he wishes to offer an offering by fire, a pleasing odor to the LORD, he shall do as you do. [15] For the assembly, there shall be one statute for you and for the stranger who sojourns with you, a perpetual statute throughout your generations; as you are, so shall the sojourner be before the LORD. [16] One law and one ordinance shall be for you and for the stranger who sojourns with you."

17 The LORD said to Moses, [18] "Say to the people of Israel, When you come into the land to which I bring you [19] and when you eat of the food of the land, you shall present an offering to the LORD. [20] Of the first of your coarse meal you shall present a cake as an offering; as an offering from the threshing floor, so shall you present it. [21] Of the first of your coarse meal you shall give to the LORD an offering throughout your generations.

22 "But if you err, and do not observe all these commandments which the LORD has spoken to Moses, [23] all that the LORD has commanded you by Moses, from the day that the LORD gave commandment, and onward throughout your generations, [24] then if it was done unwittingly without the knowledge of the congregation, all the congregation shall offer one young bull for a burnt offering, a pleasing odor to the LORD, with its cereal offering and its drink offering, according to the ordinance, and one male goat for a sin offering. [25] And the priest shall make atonement for all the congregation of

with them into battle (v. 44). **45:** The bitterness of this and other battles is the basis of the ancient vow against the Amalekites (Ex.17.8–16).

   15.1–41: Cultic regulations. The narrative is interrupted to introduce priestly matters (chs. 15–19) and thereby to continue the main line of priestly tradition (see 10.29–36 n.). **1–16:** This law supplements the legislation of Leviticus by prescribing the cereal (Lev. ch. 2) and drink offerings that are to accompany a burnt offering (Lev. ch. 1) or peace offering (Lev. ch. 3). **3:** *A pleasing odor*, see Lev.1.9 n. **16:** See Ex.12.43–49 n. **17–21:** An offering of the first fruits (Lev.23.9–14). **22–31:** A supplement to Lev. ch. 4. **23:** Mosaic law includes the original commandments and supplementary laws, thus indicating the development of law as new situations

the people of Israel, and they shall be forgiven; because it was an error, and they have brought their offering, an offering by fire to the LORD, and their sin offering before the LORD, for their error. [26] And all the congregation of the people of Israel shall be forgiven, and the stranger who sojourns among them, because the whole population was involved in the error.

27 "If one person sins unwittingly, he shall offer a female goat a year old for a sin offering. [28] And the priest shall make atonement before the LORD for the person who commits an error, when he sins unwittingly, to make atonement for him; and he shall be forgiven. [29] You shall have one law for him who does anything unwittingly, for him who is native among the people of Israel, and for the stranger who sojourns among them. [30] But the person who does anything with a high hand, whether he is native or a sojourner, reviles the LORD, and that person shall be cut off from among his people. [31] Because he has despised the word of the LORD, and has broken his commandment, that person shall be utterly cut off; his iniquity shall be upon him."

32 While the people of Israel were in the wilderness, they found a man gathering sticks on the sabbath day. [33] And those who found him gathering sticks brought him to Moses and Aaron, and to all the congregation. [34] They put him in custody, because it had not been made plain what should be done to him. [35] And the LORD said to Moses, "The man shall be put to death; all the congregation shall stone him with stones outside the camp." [36] And all the congregation brought him outside the camp, and stoned him to death with stones, as the LORD commanded Moses.

37 The LORD said to Moses, [38] "Speak to the people of Israel, and bid them to make tassels on the corners of their garments throughout their generations, and to put upon the tassel of each corner a cord of blue; [39] and it shall be to you a tassel to look upon and remember all the commandments of the LORD, to do them, not to follow after your own heart and your own eyes, which you are inclined to go after wantonly. [40] So you shall remember and do all my commandments, and be holy to your God. [41] I am the LORD your God, who brought you out of the land of Egypt, to be your God: I am the LORD your God."

16 Now Korah the son of Izhar, son of Kohath, son of Levi, and Dathan and Abi'ram the sons of Eli'ab, and On the son of Peleth, sons of Reuben, [2] took men; and they rose up before Moses, with a number of the people of Israel, two hundred and fifty leaders of the congregation, chosen from the assembly, well-known men; [3] and they assembled themselves together against Moses and against Aaron, and said to them, "You have gone too far! For all the congregation are holy, every one of them, and the LORD is among them; why then do you exalt yourselves above the assembly of the LORD?" [4] When Moses heard it, he fell on his face; [5] and he said to Korah and all his company, "In the morning

---

were faced (see 9.8 n.). **25:** *Make atonement*, see Lev.1.4 n. **30:** Sin *with a high hand*, in contrast to sin committed inadvertently or in ignorance (vv. 25,26,27), is that which is done deliberately or defiantly (Ps.19.12–13). For such sin there is no atonement in priestly legislation. *Cut off*, see Lev.7.20 n. **32–36:** The death penalty had already been prescribed for violating the sabbath (Ex.31.14–15; 35.2). The man was put in custody until, by divine oracle, it was determined whether his action actually came under the law (see Lev.24.12). **37–41:** The ancient custom of wearing tassels is reinterpreted as a reminder of God's law.

16.1–50: Revolts against Moses. These stories preserve the memory of struggles which threatened the community during the sojourn at Kadesh. **3–11:** The rebellion led by Korah, of Levitical descent (v. 1a; Ex.6.21). Supported by other Levites (vv. 7,8,10), he challenged the subordination of some. Levites to the Aaronite order (3.5–10; 8.5–22) and sought full priestly status (vv. 9–10,40). **5:** A divine sign will determine who shall *come near* to the LORD, i.e. to

the LORD will show who is his, and who is holy, and will cause him to come near to him; him whom he will choose he will cause to come near to him. ⁶ Do this: take censers, Korah and all his company; ⁷ put fire in them and put incense upon them before the LORD tomorrow, and the man whom the LORD chooses shall be the holy one. You have gone too far, sons of Levi!" ⁸ And Moses said to Korah, "Hear now, you sons of Levi: ⁹ is it too small a thing for you that the God of Israel has separated you from the congregation of Israel, to bring you near to himself, to do service in the tabernacle of the LORD, and to stand before the congregation to minister to them; ¹⁰ and that he has brought you near him, and all your brethren the sons of Levi with you? And would you seek the priesthood also? ¹¹ Therefore it is against the LORD that you and all your company have gathered together; what is Aaron that you murmur against him?"

12 And Moses sent to call Dathan and Abi′ram the sons of Eli′ab; and they said, "We will not come up. ¹³ Is it a small thing that you have brought us up out of a land flowing with milk and honey, to kill us in the wilderness, that you must also make yourself a prince over us? ¹⁴ Moreover you have not brought us into a land flowing with milk and honey, nor given us inheritance of fields and vineyards. Will you put out the eyes of these men? We will not come up."

15 And Moses was very angry, and said to the LORD, "Do not respect their offering. I have not taken one ass from them, and I have not harmed one of them." ¹⁶ And Moses said to Korah, "Be present, you and all your company, before the LORD, you and they, and Aaron, tomorrow; ¹⁷ and let every one of you take his censer, and put incense upon it, and every one of you bring before the LORD his censer, two hundred and fifty censers; you also, and Aaron, each his censer." ¹⁸ So every man took his censer, and they put fire in them and laid incense upon them, and they stood at the entrance of the tent of meeting with Moses and Aaron. ¹⁹ Then Korah assembled all the congregation against them at the entrance of the tent of meeting. And the glory of the LORD appeared to all the congregation.

20 And the LORD said to Moses and to Aaron, ²¹ "Separate yourselves from among this congregation, that I may consume them in a moment." ²² And they fell on their faces, and said, "O God, the God of the spirits of all flesh, shall one man sin, and wilt thou be angry with all the congregation?" ²³ And the LORD said to Moses, ²⁴ "Say to the congregation, Get away from about the dwelling of Korah, Dathan, and Abi′ram."

25 Then Moses rose and went to Dathan and Abi′ram; and the elders of Israel followed him. ²⁶ And he said to the congregation, "Depart, I pray you, from the tents of these wicked men, and touch nothing of theirs, lest you be swept away with all their sins." ²⁷ So they got away from about the dwelling of Korah, Dathan, and Abi′ram; and Dathan and Abi′ram came out and stood at the door of their tents, together with their wives, their sons, and their little ones. ²⁸ And Moses said, "Hereby you shall know that the LORD has sent me to do all these works, and that it has not been of my own accord. ²⁹ If these men die the common death of all men, or if they are visited by the fate of all men, then the LORD has not sent me. ³⁰ But if the LORD creates something

the altar. **6–7:** Compare Lev.10.1–3. **12–15:** According to an older literary tradition, a civil revolt was led by laymen of the tribe of Reuben who were dissatisfied with Moses' leadership (vv. 1b–2). **13:** Here Egypt, in contrast to the wilderness, is *a land flowing with milk and honey* (see Ex.3.8 n.). **14:** *Put out the eyes,* i.e. blind with deceit. **16–24:** Continuation of the Korah story (vv. 3–11). **19:** Apparently the Levites' revolt had popular support. **24:** An editorial revision which combines the two revolts. **25–34:** A continuation of the story of the lay revolt (vv. 12–15). **27a:** See v. 24 n. **30:** *Sheol,* see Gen.37.35 n. **31–33:** These verses express the ancient

new, and the ground opens its mouth, and swallows them up, with all that belongs to them, and they go down alive into Sheol, then you shall know that these men have despised the LORD."

31 And as he finished speaking all these words, the ground under them split asunder; [32] and the earth opened its mouth and swallowed them up, with their households and all the men that belonged to Korah and all their goods. [33] So they and all that belonged to them went down alive into Sheol; and the earth closed over them, and they perished from the midst of the assembly. [34] And all Israel that were round about them fled at their cry; for they said, "Lest the earth swallow us up!" [35] And fire came forth from the LORD, and consumed the two hundred and fifty men offering the incense.

36[i] Then the LORD said to Moses, [37] "Tell Elea'zar the son of Aaron the priest to take up the censers out of the blaze; then scatter the fire far and wide. For they are holy, [38] the censers of these men who have sinned at the cost of their lives; so let them be made into hammered plates as a covering for the altar, for they offered them before the LORD; therefore they are holy. Thus they shall be a sign to the people of Israel." [39] So Elea'zar the priest took the bronze censers, which those who were burned had offered; and they were hammered out as a covering for the altar, [40] to be a reminder to the people of Israel, so that no one who is not a priest, who is not of the descendants of Aaron, should draw near to burn incense before the LORD, lest he become as Korah and as his company— as the LORD said to Elea'zar through Moses.

41 But on the morrow all the congregation of the people of Israel murmured against Moses and against Aaron, saying, "You have killed the people of the LORD." [42] And when the congregation had assembled against Moses and against Aaron, they turned toward the tent of meeting; and behold, the cloud covered it, and the glory of the LORD appeared. [43] And Moses and Aaron came to the front of the tent of meeting, [44] and the LORD said to Moses, [45] "Get away from the midst of this congregation, that I may consume them in a moment." And they fell on their faces. [46] And Moses said to Aaron, "Take your censer, and put fire therein from off the altar, and lay incense on it, and carry it quickly to the congregation, and make atonement for them; for wrath has gone forth from the LORD, the plague has begun." [47] So Aaron took it as Moses said, and ran into the midst of the assembly; and behold, the plague had already begun among the people; and he put on the incense, and made atonement for the people. [48] And he stood between the dead and the living; and the plague was stopped. [49] Now those who died by the plague were fourteen thousand seven hundred, besides those who died in the affair of Korah. [50] And Aaron returned to Moses at the entrance of the tent of meeting, when the plague was stopped.

17 The LORD said to Moses, [2] "Speak to the people of Israel, and get from them rods, one for each fathers' house, from all their leaders according to their fathers' houses, twelve rods. Write each man's name upon his rod, [3] and write Aaron's name upon the rod of Levi. For there shall be

i Ch 17.1 in Heb *j* Ch 17.16 in Heb

---

conception of corporate guilt which involves a man's whole family (Jos.7.22–26). **32:** *All the men that belonged to Korah,* see v. 24 n. **35–40:** Continuation of the Korah story (vv. 16–24). **35:** The two hundred and fifty men were Levites, sons of Korah (vv. 2b,17). **37–38:** On the bronze covering for the altar, see Ex.27.2. **40:** This verse states the purpose of the Korah story: to uphold the prerogatives of the Aaronite priesthood. **43:** *Cloud . . . glory,* see Ex.40.34–38 n.

17.1–13: Aaron's budding rod demonstrates the special status of the tribe of Levi, of whom he is the leader. **2:** *Fathers' house,* here means "tribe" (see 1.2–4 n.). The rod or staff was a symbol of tribal authority. **3:** On Aaron's Levitical descent, see Ex.6.14–25. **4:** *The testimony,*

one rod for the head of each fathers' house. [4] Then you shall deposit them in the tent of meeting before the testimony, where I meet with you. [5] And the rod of the man whom I choose shall sprout; thus I will make to cease from me the murmurings of the people of Israel, which they murmur against you." [6] Moses spoke to the people of Israel; and all their leaders gave him rods, one for each leader, according to their fathers' houses, twelve rods; and the rod of Aaron was among their rods. [7] And Moses deposited the rods before the LORD in the tent of the testimony.

8 And on the morrow Moses went into the tent of the testimony; and behold, the rod of Aaron for the house of Levi had sprouted and put forth buds, and produced blossoms, and it bore ripe almonds. [9] Then Moses brought out all the rods from before the LORD to all the people of Israel; and they looked, and each man took his rod. [10] And the LORD said to Moses, "Put back the rod of Aaron before the testimony, to be kept as a sign for the rebels, that you may make an end of their murmurings against me, lest they die." [11] Thus did Moses; as the LORD commanded him, so he did.

12 And the people of Israel said to Moses, "Behold, we perish, we are undone, we are all undone. [13] Every one who comes near, who comes near to the tabernacle of the LORD, shall die. Are we all to perish?"

18 So the LORD said to Aaron, "You and your sons and your fathers' house with you shall bear iniquity in connection with the sanctuary; and you and your sons with you shall bear iniquity in connection with your priesthood. [2] And with you bring your brethren also, the tribe of Levi, the tribe of your father, that they may join you, and minister to you while you and your sons with you are before the tent of the testimony. [3] They shall attend you and attend to all duties of the tent; but shall not come near to the vessels of the sanctuary or to the altar, lest they, and you, die. [4] They shall join you, and attend to the tent of meeting, for all the service of the tent; and no one else shall come near you. [5] And you shall attend to the duties of the sanctuary and the duties of the altar, that there be wrath no more upon the people of Israel. [6] And behold, I have taken your brethren the Levites from among the people of Israel; they are a gift to you, given to the LORD, to do the service of the tent of meeting. [7] And you and your sons with you shall attend to your priesthood for all that concerns the altar and that is within the veil; and you shall serve. I give your priesthood as a gift,[k] and any one else who comes near shall be put to death."

8 Then the LORD said to Aaron, "And behold, I have given you whatever is kept of the offerings made to me, all the consecrated things of the people of Israel; I have given them to you as a portion, and to your sons as a perpetual due. [9] This shall be yours of the most holy things, reserved from the fire; every offering of theirs, every cereal offering of theirs and every sin offering of theirs and every guilt offering of theirs, which they render to me, shall be most holy to you and to your sons. [10] In a most holy place shall you eat of it; every male may eat of it; it is holy to you. [11] This also is yours, the offering of their gift, all the wave of-

k Heb *service of gift*

see Ex.16.33–34 n. **5:** The people's murmurings, related in 16.41–50. **8:** Folk traditions of other peoples contain stories of blossoming rods, clubs, or spears. The sign signifies the LORD's choice of Aaron (v. 5) as leader of the whole priestly tribe of Levi. **10:** See Ex.25.16 n.

18.1–32: The responsibility of Aaronic priests and other Levites. This chapter comes naturally after the preceding one and gives the answer to the people's question in 17.13. **1:** *Bear iniquity*, i.e. bear the consequences for any cultic impropriety (Ex.28.38). All Levites are responsible for the sanctuary; only Aaron's sons are responsible for the priesthood (v. 7), because they minister at the altar and guard the purity of the sanctuary. **2–6:** Other Levites are assistants to the Aaronic order (3.5–10; 8.5–22). **7:** *Within the veil*, or in the Holy of Holies. **8–20:** Since the

ferings of the people of Israel; I have given them to you, and to your sons and daughters with you, as a perpetual due; every one who is clean in your house may eat of it. [12] All the best of the oil, and all the best of the wine and of the grain, the first fruits of what they give to the LORD, I give to you. [13] The first ripe fruits of all that is in their land, which they bring to the LORD, shall be yours; every one who is clean in your house may eat of it. [14] Every devoted thing in Israel shall be yours. [15] Everything that opens the womb of all flesh, whether man or beast, which they offer to the LORD, shall be yours; nevertheless the first-born of man you shall redeem, and the firstling of unclean beasts you shall redeem. [16] And their redemption price (at a month old you shall redeem them) you shall fix at five shekels in silver, according to the shekel of the sanctuary, which is twenty gerahs. [17] But the firstling of a cow, or the firstling of a sheep, or the firstling of a goat, you shall not redeem; they are holy. You shall sprinkle their blood upon the altar, and shall burn their fat as an offering by fire, a pleasing odor to the LORD; [18] but their flesh shall be yours, as the breast that is waved and as the right thigh are yours. [19] All the holy offerings which the people of Israel present to the LORD I give to you, and to your sons and daughters with you, as a perpetual due; it is a covenant of salt for ever before the LORD for you and for your offspring with you." [20] And the LORD said to Aaron, "You shall have no inheritance in their land, neither shall you have any portion among them; I am your portion and your inheritance among the people of Israel.

[21] "To the Levites I have given every tithe in Israel for an inheritance, in return for their service which they serve, their service in the tent of meeting. [22] And henceforth the people of Israel shall not come near the tent of meeting, lest they bear sin and die. [23] But the Levites shall do the service of the tent of meeting, and they shall bear their iniquity; it shall be a perpetual statute throughout your generations; and among the people of Israel they shall have no inheritance. [24] For the tithe of the people of Israel, which they present as an offering to the LORD, I have given to the Levites for an inheritance; therefore I have said of them that they shall have no inheritance among the people of Israel."

[25] And the LORD said to Moses, [26] "Moreover you shall say to the Levites, 'When you take from the people of Israel the tithe which I have given you from them for your inheritance, then you shall present an offering from it to the LORD, a tithe of the tithe. [27] And your offering shall be reckoned to you as though it were the grain of the threshing floor, and as the fulness of the wine press. [28] So shall you also present an offering to the LORD from all your tithes, which you receive from the people of Israel; and from it you shall give the LORD's offering to Aaron the priest. [29] Out of all the gifts to you, you shall present every offering due to the LORD, from all the best of them, giving the hallowed part from them.' [30] Therefore you shall say to them, 'When you have offered from it the best of it, then the rest shall be reckoned to the Levites as produce of the threshing floor, and as produce of the wine press; [31] and you may eat it in any place, you and your households;

---

tribe of Levi has no land inheritance, the Aaronic priests are to be supported from the offerings (v. 20; see Lev.2.2–3 n.). **9–10:** A definition of *the most holy things* which belong only to the Aaronic priests. For the types of sacrifice, see Lev. chs. 1–7. **11–19:** The priest and his family may eat the *holy things*, i.e. the *wave offerings* (e.g. of peace offerings, Lev.7.28–36), offerings of the *first fruits* (Num.15.17–21), or every *devoted thing*, such as the first-born of clean animals (Lev.27.26–27). **14–18:** Ex.13.11–13; 34.19–20. **19:** *A covenant of salt*, see Lev. 2.13 n. **21–24:** The rest of the Levites receive all tithes as their due (Lev.27.30–33). **25–32:** The assistant Levites are to pay a *tithe of the tithe* to the Aaronic priests.

for it is your reward in return for your service in the tent of meeting. [32] And you shall bear no sin by reason of it, when you have offered the best of it. And you shall not profane the holy things of the people of Israel, lest you die.' "

19 Now the LORD said to Moses and to Aaron, [2] "This is the statute of the law which the LORD has commanded: Tell the people of Israel to bring you a red heifer without defect, in which there is no blemish, and upon which a yoke has never come. [3] And you shall give her to Elea'zar the priest, and she shall be taken outside the camp and slaughtered before him; [4] and Elea'zar the priest shall take some of her blood with his finger, and sprinkle some of her blood toward the front of the tent of meeting seven times. [5] And the heifer shall be burned in his sight; her skin, her flesh, and her blood, with her dung, shall be burned; [6] and the priest shall take cedarwood and hyssop and scarlet stuff, and cast them into the midst of the burning of the heifer. [7] Then the priest shall wash his clothes and bathe his body in water, and afterwards he shall come into the camp; and the priest shall be unclean until evening. [8] He who burns the heifer shall wash his clothes in water and bathe his body in water, and shall be unclean until evening. [9] And a man who is clean shall gather up the ashes of the heifer, and deposit them outside the camp in a clean place; and they shall be kept for the congregation of the people of Israel for the water for impurity, for the removal of sin. [10] And he who gathers the ashes of the heifer shall wash his clothes, and be unclean until evening. And this shall be to the people of Israel, and to the stranger who sojourns among them, a perpetual statute.

11 "He who touches the dead body of any person shall be unclean seven days; [12] he shall cleanse himself with the water on the third day and on the seventh day, and so be clean; but if he does not cleanse himself on the third day and on the seventh day, he will not become clean. [13] Whoever touches a dead person, the body of any man who has died, and does not cleanse himself, defiles the tabernacle of the LORD, and that person shall be cut off from Israel; because the water for impurity was not thrown upon him, he shall be unclean; his uncleanness is still on him.

14 "This is the law when a man dies in a tent: every one who comes into the tent, and every one who is in the tent, shall be unclean seven days. [15] And every open vessel, which has no cover fastened upon it, is unclean. [16] Whoever in the open field touches one who is slain with a sword, or a dead body, or a bone of a man, or a grave, shall be unclean seven days. [17] For the unclean they shall take some ashes of the burnt sin offering, and running water shall be added in a vessel; [18] then a clean person shall take hyssop, and dip it in the water, and sprinkle it upon the tent, and upon all the furnishings, and upon the persons who were there, and upon him who touched the bone, or the slain, or the dead, or the grave; [19] and the clean person shall sprinkle upon the unclean on the third day and on the seventh day; thus on the seventh day he shall cleanse him, and he shall wash his clothes and bathe himself in water, and at evening he shall be clean. 20 "But the man who is unclean and

---

19.1–22: Rites for purifying a person who is defiled by a corpse. 1–10: The purpose of this ancient rite is to prepare ceremonially the ashes used in the *water for impurity* (vv. 9,12–13). **4:** The sacred number, the sacred blood, and the sacred tent of meeting combine to make the rite efficacious. **6:** Compare Lev.14.4. **11–22:** The ceremonial cleansing. **11:** On defilement by the dead, see Lev.21.1–12. **12:** *The water*, referred to in v. 9. **13:** The defilement was not only dangerous to the individual but to the community, owing to the holiness of the tabernacle. **14–16:** Uncleanness, like the stench of death, could contaminate a tent or even enter an open vessel. **17:** *Some ashes*, see v. 9. *Hyssop*, see Ex.12.22 n.

does not cleanse himself, that person shall be cut off from the midst of the assembly, since he has defiled the sanctuary of the LORD; because the water for impurity has not been thrown upon him, he is unclean. ²¹ And it shall be a perpetual statute for them. He who sprinkles the water for impurity shall wash his clothes; and he who touches the water for impurity shall be unclean until evening. ²² And whatever the unclean person touches shall be unclean; and any one who touches it shall be unclean until evening."

20 And the people of Israel, the whole congregation, came into the wilderness of Zin in the first month, and the people stayed in Kadesh; and Miriam died there, and was buried there.

2 Now there was no water for the congregation; and they assembled themselves together against Moses and against Aaron. ³ And the people contended with Moses, and said, "Would that we had died when our brethren died before the LORD! ⁴ Why have you brought the assembly of the LORD into this wilderness, that we should die here, both we and our cattle? ⁵ And why have you made us come up out of Egypt, to bring us to this evil place? It is no place for grain, or figs, or vines, or pomegranates; and there is no water to drink." ⁶ Then Moses and Aaron went from the presence of the assembly to the door of the tent of meeting, and fell on their faces. And the glory of the LORD appeared to them, ⁷ and the LORD said to Moses, ⁸ "Take the rod, and assemble the congregation, you and Aaron your brother, and tell the rock before their eyes to yield its water; so you shall bring water out of the rock for them; so you shall give drink to the congregation and their cattle." ⁹ And Moses took the rod from before the LORD, as he commanded him.

10 And Moses and Aaron gathered the assembly together before the rock, and he said to them, "Hear now, you rebels; shall we bring forth water for you out of this rock?" ¹¹ And Moses lifted up his hand and struck the rock with his rod twice; and water came forth abundantly, and the congregation drank, and their cattle. ¹² And the LORD said to Moses and Aaron, "Because you did not believe in me, to sanctify me in the eyes of the people of Israel, therefore you shall not bring this assembly into the land which I have given them." ¹³ These are the waters of Mer′ibah,¹ where the people of Israel contended with the LORD, and he showed himself holy among them.

14 Moses sent messengers from Kadesh to the king of Edom, "Thus says your brother Israel: You know all the adversity that has befallen us: ¹⁵ how our fathers went down to Egypt, and we dwelt in Egypt a long time; and the Egyptians dealt harshly with us and our fathers; ¹⁶ and when we cried to the LORD, he heard our voice, and sent an angel and brought us forth out of Egypt; and here we are in Kadesh, a city on the edge of your territory. ¹⁷ Now let us pass through your land. We will not pass through field or vineyard, neither will we drink water from a well; we will go along the King's Highway, we will not turn aside to the right

l That is Contention

20.1–29: Departure from Kadesh. Having failed to enter Canaan from the south (chs. 13–14), Israel planned to detour through Transjordan in order to attack Canaan from the east. **1:** A summary which condenses Israel's long sojourn at Kadesh (see 13.26 n.). The year of *the first month* has dropped out. The whole generation, condemned to wander in the wilderness for about forty years (14.20–35), passed away. **2–13:** The Meribah incident is paralleled in Ex.17.1–7. **3:** *Our brethren*, i.e. Dathan and Abiram (ch. 16). **12:** Although the preceding narrative is silent about Moses' disbelief, it is implied that he failed to interpret the giving of water as a sign from the LORD (Dt.32.50–52). **13:** See Ex.17.7 n. **14–21:** The request for passage through Edom. **14:** *Your brother*, Gen.25.24–26. By the thirteenth century B.C. Edom, one of the "Hebrew" groups (see Gen.10.21–31 n.), had developed a non-hereditary monarchy (Gen.36.31–39). **16:** *Angel*, see Ex.23.20–21 n. **17:** *The King's Highway* was the main Transjordanian route from

hand or to the left, until we have passed through your territory." ¹⁸ But Edom said to him, "You shall not pass through, lest I come out with the sword against you." ¹⁹ And the people of Israel said to him, "We will go up by the highway; and if we drink of your water, I and my cattle, then I will pay for it; let me only pass through on foot, nothing more." ²⁰ But he said, "You shall not pass through." And Edom came out against them with many men, and with a strong force. ²¹ Thus Edom refused to give Israel passage through his territory; so Israel turned away from him.

22 And they journeyed from Kadesh, and the people of Israel, the whole congregation, came to Mount Hor. ²³ And the LORD said to Moses and Aaron at Mount Hor, on the border of the land of Edom, ²⁴ "Aaron shall be gathered to his people; for he shall not enter the land which I have given to the people of Israel, because you rebelled against my command at the waters of Mer′ibah. ²⁵ Take Aaron and Elea′zar his son, and bring them up to Mount Hor; ²⁶ and strip Aaron of his garments, and put them upon Elea′zar his son; and Aaron shall be gathered to his people, and shall die there." ²⁷ Moses did as the LORD commanded; and they went up Mount Hor in the sight of all the congregation. ²⁸ And Moses stripped Aaron of his garments, and put them upon Elea′zar his son; and Aaron died there on the top of the mountain. Then Moses and Elea′zar came down from the mountain. ²⁹ And when all the congregation saw that Aaron was dead, all the house of Israel wept for Aaron thirty days.

21 When the Canaanite, the king of Arad, who dwelt in the Negeb, heard that Israel was coming by the way of Atharim, he fought against Israel, and took some of them captive. ² And Israel vowed a vow to the LORD, and said, "If thou wilt indeed give this people into my hand, then I will utterly destroy their cities." ³ And the LORD hearkened to the voice of Israel, and gave over the Canaanites; and they utterly destroyed them and their cities; so the name of the place was called Hormah.*ᵐ*

4 From Mount Hor they set out by the way to the Red Sea, to go around the land of Edom; and the people became impatient on the way. ⁵ And the people spoke against God and against Moses, "Why have you brought us up out of Egypt to die in the wilderness? For there is no food and no water, and we loathe this worthless food." ⁶ Then the LORD sent fiery serpents among the people, and they bit the people, so that many people of Israel died. ⁷ And the people came to Moses, and said, "We have sinned, for we have spoken against the LORD and against you; pray to the LORD, that he take away the serpents from us." So Moses prayed for the people. ⁸ And the LORD said to Moses, "Make a fiery serpent, and set it on a pole; and every one who is bitten, when he sees it, shall live." ⁹ So Moses made a bronze serpent, and set it on a pole; and if a serpent bit any man, he would look at the bronze serpent and live.

m Heb *Destruction*

Ezion-geber on the Gulf of Aqabah to Syria. **22–29:** The death of Aaron. **24:** See 20.12 n. *Gathered to his people*, Gen.25.8. **26:** *Garments*, i.e. of the high priest (Ex. ch. 28; Lev.8.7–9).

21.1–35: Events along the way. 1–3: Another account of the battle of Hormah (14.39–45; compare Jg.1.16–17). **1:** *The way of Atharim*, probably the name of a pass. **2–3:** A vow to wage holy war (see Ex.17.14 n.). This is apparently another tradition of an attempt to penetrate Canaan from the south; note that the people marched north from Kadesh. **4–9:** The serpent scourge. **4:** Leaving Mount Hor (20.27), the people turned south toward the Red Sea (Gulf of Aqabah), i.e. toward Ezion-geber (33.35; Dt.2.1–8). **5:** See Ex.16.3 n. **6:** An attack by *fiery serpents* or poisonous snakes was interpreted as divine judgment upon the people's rebellion. **8–9:** These verses echo serpent magic, as practiced, e.g. in ancient Egypt. The *bronze serpent* (Nehushtan) was an object of popular worship during the Israelite monarchy (2 Kg.18.4).

10 And the people of Israel set out, and encamped in Oboth. [11] And they set out from Oboth, and encamped at I'ye-ab'arim, in the wilderness which is opposite Moab, toward the sunrise. [12] From there they set out, and encamped in the Valley of Zered. [13] From there they set out, and encamped on the other side of the Arnon, which is in the wilderness, that extends from the boundary of the Amorites; for the Arnon is the boundary of Moab, between Moab and the Amorites. [14] Wherefore it is said in the Book of the Wars of the LORD,

"Waheb in Suphah,
and the valleys of the Arnon,
[15] and the slope of the valleys
that extends to the seat of Ar,
and leans to the border of Moab."

16 And from there they continued to Beer;[n] that is the well of which the LORD said to Moses, "Gather the people together, and I will give them water." [17] Then Israel sang this song:

"Spring up, O well!–Sing to it!–
[18] the well which the princes dug,
which the nobles of the people delved,
with the scepter and with their staves."

And from the wilderness they went on to Mat'tanah, [19] and from Mat'tanah to Nahal'iel, and from Nahal'iel to Bamoth, [20] and from Bamoth to the valley lying in the region of Moab by the top of Pisgah which looks down upon the desert.[o]

21 Then Israel sent messengers to Sihon king of the Amorites, saying, [22] "Let me pass through your land; we will not turn aside into field or vineyard; we will not drink the water of a well; we will go by the King's Highway, until we have passed through your territory." [23] But Sihon would not allow Israel to pass through his territory. He gathered all his men together, and went out against Israel to the wilderness, and came to Jahaz, and fought against Israel. [24] And Israel slew him with the edge of the sword, and took possession of his land from the Arnon to the Jabbok, as far as to the Ammonites; for Jazer was the boundary of the Ammonites.[p] [25] And Israel took all these cities, and Israel settled in all the cities of the Amorites, in Heshbon, and in all its villages. [26] For Heshbon was the city of Sihon the king of the Amorites, who had fought against the former king of Moab and taken all his land out of his hand, as far as the Arnon. [27] Therefore the ballad singers say,

"Come to Heshbon, let it be built,
let the city of Sihon be established.
[28] For fire went forth from Heshbon,
flame from the city of Sihon.
It devoured Ar of Moab,
the lords of the heights of the Arnon.
[29] Woe to you, O Moab!
You are undone, O people of Chemosh!
He has made his sons fugitives,
and his daughters captives,
to an Amorite king, Sihon.
[30] So their posterity perished from Heshbon,[q] as far as Dibon,
and we laid waste until fire spread to Med'eba."[r]

31 Thus Israel dwelt in the land of the Amorites. [32] And Moses sent to spy out Jazer; and they took its villages,

n That is *Well*   o Or *Jeshimon*
p Gk: Heb *the boundary of the Ammonites was strong*
q Gk: Heb *we have shot at them. Heshbon has perished*
r Compare Sam and Gk: Heb *we have laid waste to Nophah which to Medeba*

10–20: The itinerary of the march (see ch. 33; Dt. ch. 2). **14–15:** A quotation from an ancient poetic collection, *the Book of the Wars of the LORD* (compare Jos.10.13; 2 Sam.1.18). *Ar*, a chief city of Moab (v. 28). **16–18:** The "Song of the Well," another ancient poetic fragment, is quoted here because water was miraculously provided along the way. **21–32:** The defeat of the petty kingdom of the Amorites just north of Moab. **22:** The request (compare 20.14–21) was made at the boundary river, Arnon (v. 13). **27:** An ancient taunt song, quoted to show that Sihon had captured former Moabite territory, including the city of Heshbon. **29:** *Chemosh*, god of the Moabites. **33–35:** *Bashan*, a petty kingdom north of the Jabbok river. *Og*, Dt.3.1–7.

and dispossessed the Amorites that were there. ³³ Then they turned and went up by the way to Bashan; and Og the king of Bashan came out against them, he and all his people, to battle at Ed're-i. ³⁴ But the LORD said to Moses, "Do not fear him; for I have given him into your hand, and all his people, and his land; and you shall do to him as you did to Sihon king of the Amorites, who dwelt at Heshbon." ³⁵ So they slew him, and his sons, and all his people, until there was not one survivor left to him; and they possessed his land.

22 Then the people of Israel set out, and encamped in the plains of Moab beyond the Jordan at Jericho. ² And Balak the son of Zippor saw all that Israel had done to the Amorites. ³ And Moab was in great dread of the people, because they were many; Moab was overcome with fear of the people of Israel. ⁴ And Moab said to the elders of Mid'ian, "This horde will now lick up all that is round about us, as the ox licks up the grass of the field." So Balak the son of Zippor, who was king of Moab at that time, ⁵ sent messengers to Balaam the son of Be'or at Pethor, which is near the River, in the land of Amaw to call him, saying, "Behold, a people has come out of Egypt; they cover the face of the earth, and they are dwelling opposite me. ⁶ Come now, curse this people for me, since they are too mighty for me; perhaps I shall be able to defeat them and drive them from the land; for I know that he whom you bless is blessed, and he whom you curse is cursed."

7 So the elders of Moab and the elders of Mid'ian departed with the fees for divination in their hand; and they came to Balaam, and gave him Balak's message. ⁸ And he said to them, "Lodge here this night, and I will bring back word to you, as the Lord speaks to me"; so the princes of Moab stayed with Balaam. ⁹ And God came to Balaam and said, "Who are these men with you?" ¹⁰ And Balaam said to God, "Balak the son of Zippor, king of Moab, has sent to me, saying, ¹¹ 'Behold, a people has come out of Egypt, and it covers the face of the earth; now come, curse them for me; perhaps I shall be able to fight against them and drive them out.'" ¹² God said to Balaam, "You shall not go with them; you shall not curse the people, for they are blessed." ¹³ So Balaam rose in the morning, and said to the princes of Balak, "Go to your own land; for the LORD has refused to let me go with you." ¹⁴ So the princes of Moab rose and went to Balak, and said, "Balaam refuses to come with us."

15 Once again Balak sent princes, more in number and more honorable than they. ¹⁶ And they came to Balaam and said to him, "Thus says Balak the son of Zippor: 'Let nothing hinder you from coming to me; ¹⁷ for I will surely do you great honor, and whatever you say to me I will do; come, curse this people for me.'" ¹⁸ But Balaam answered and said to the servants of Balak, "Though Balak were to give me his house full of silver and gold, I could not go beyond the command of the LORD my God, to do less or more. ¹⁹ Pray, now, tarry here this night also, that I may know what more the LORD will say to me." ²⁰ And God came to Balaam at night and said to him, "If the men have come to call you, rise, go with them; but only what I bid you, that shall you do."

21 So Balaam rose in the morning,

22.1–40: Balak and Balaam. Fearful of the triumphant Israelites, the Moabite king invited a Mesopotamian diviner to put a curse on the invaders. **4:** On Moab's league with Midian, see ch. 31. **5–20:** Balak's two missions to obtain the services of Balaam who was in *Pethor*, located south of Carchemish *near the River* (Euphrates). In antiquity Babylonia was famed for the art of divination. **6:** On the power of the curse, see Gen.27.4 n. **8:** Throughout chs. 22–24 the conviction is expressed that a foreign priest-diviner, though not a member of the covenant community, was obedient to the LORD's will and that nothing could prevent the fulfilment of the divine purpose for Israel. **13:** It is implied that the LORD spoke to him in a dream (vv.

and saddled his ass, and went with the princes of Moab. ²² But God's anger was kindled because he went; and the angel of the LORD took his stand in the way as his adversary. Now he was riding on the ass, and his two servants were with him. ²³ And the ass saw the angel of the LORD standing in the road, with a drawn sword in his hand; and the ass turned aside out of the road, and went into the field; and Balaam struck the ass, to turn her into the road. ²⁴ Then the angel of the LORD stood in a narrow path between the vineyards, with a wall on either side. ²⁵ And when the ass saw the angel of the LORD, she pushed against the wall, and pressed Balaam's foot against the wall; so he struck her again. ²⁶ Then the angel of the LORD went ahead, and stood in a narrow place, where there was no way to turn either to the right or to the left. ²⁷ When the ass saw the angel of the LORD, she lay down under Balaam; and Balaam's anger was kindled, and he struck the ass with his staff. ²⁸ Then the LORD opened the mouth of the ass, and she said to Balaam, "What have I done to you, that you have struck me these three times?" ²⁹ And Balaam said to the ass, "Because you have made sport of me. I wish I had a sword in my hand, for then I would kill you." ³⁰ And the ass said to Balaam, "Am I not your ass, upon which you have ridden all your life long to this day? Was I ever accustomed to do so to you?" And he said, "No."

³¹ Then the LORD opened the eyes of Balaam, and he saw the angel of the LORD standing in the way, with his drawn sword in his hand; and he bowed his head, and fell on his face. ³² And the angel of the LORD said to him, "Why have you struck your ass these three times? Behold, I have come forth to withstand you, because your way is perverse before me; ³³ and the ass saw me, and turned aside before me these three times. If she had not turned aside from me, surely just now I would have slain you and let her live." ³⁴ Then Balaam said to the angel of the LORD, "I have sinned, for I did not know that thou didst stand in the road against me. Now therefore, if it is evil in thy sight, I will go back again." ³⁵ And the angel of the LORD said to Balaam, "Go with the men; but only the word which I bid you, that shall you speak." So Balaam went on with the princes of Balak.

³⁶ When Balak heard that Balaam had come, he went out to meet him at the city of Moab, on the boundary formed by the Arnon, at the extremity of the boundary. ³⁷ And Balak said to Balaam, "Did I not send to you to call you? Why did you not come to me? Am I not able to honor you?" ³⁸ Balaam said to Balak, "Lo, I have come to you! Have I now any power at all to speak anything? The word that God puts in my mouth, that must I speak." ³⁹ Then Balaam went with Balak, and they came to Kir'iath-hu'zoth. ⁴⁰ And Balak sacrificed oxen and sheep, and sent to Balaam and to the princes who were with him.

⁴¹ And on the morrow Balak took Balaam and brought him up to Bamoth-ba'al; and from there he saw the nearest of the people. **23** ¹ And Balaam said to Balak, "Build for me here seven altars, and provide for me here seven bulls and seven rams." ² Balak did as Balaam had said; and Balak and Balaam offered on each altar a bull and a ram. ³ And Balaam said to Balak, "Stand beside your burnt offering, and I will

8,19–20). **21–35:** The folk-story of Balaam's ass, which reflects oriental humor, is apparently another tradition. **22:** Note the contrast between this verse and the previous permission for Balaam to go (vv. 15–20). *The angel of the LORD,* see Gen.16.7 n. **23:** Jos.5.13. **34–35:** The incident serves to remind Balaam that he must speak only what the LORD bids him (compare 1 Kg.22.14), regardless of gifts or honors (v. 38).

22.41–24.25: The four oracles of Balaam, probably dating in their present form from the early Israelite monarchy (24.17–19). **23.1–6:** Babylonian diviners resorted to this kind of sacrificial

go; perhaps the LORD will come to meet me; and whatever he shows me I will tell you." And he went to a bare height. ⁴ And God met Balaam; and Balaam said to him, "I have prepared the seven altars, and I have offered upon each altar a bull and a ram." ⁵ And the LORD put a word in Balaam's mouth, and said, "Return to Balak, and thus you shall speak." ⁶ And he returned to him, and lo, he and all the princes of Moab were standing beside his burnt offering. ⁷ And Balaam took up his discourse, and said,

"From Aram Balak has brought me,
    the king of Moab from the eastern
        mountains:
'Come, curse Jacob for me,
    and come, denounce Israel!'
⁸ How can I curse whom God has not
    cursed?
How can I denounce whom the
    LORD has not denounced?
⁹ For from the top of the mountains
    I see him,
from the hills I behold him;
lo, a people dwelling alone,
    and not reckoning itself among the
        nations!
¹⁰ Who can count the dust of Jacob,
    or number the fourth part^s of
        Israel?
Let me die the death of the
        righteous,
    and let my end be like his!"

11 And Balak said to Balaam, "What have you done to me? I took you to curse my enemies, and behold, you have done nothing but bless them." ¹² And he answered, "Must I not take heed to speak what the LORD puts in my mouth?"

13 And Balak said to him, "Come with me to another place, from which you may see them; you shall see only the nearest of them, and shall not see them all; then curse them for me from there." ¹⁴ And he took him to the field of Zophim, to the top of Pisgah, and built seven altars, and offered a bull and a ram on each altar. ¹⁵ Balaam said to Balak, "Stand here beside your burnt offering, while I meet the LORD yonder." ¹⁶ And the LORD met Balaam, and put a word in his mouth, and said, "Return to Balak, and thus shall you speak." ¹⁷ And he came to him, and, lo, he was standing beside his burnt offering, and the princes of Moab with him. And Balak said to him, "What has the LORD spoken?" ¹⁸ And Balaam took up his discourse, and said,

"Rise, Balak, and hear;
    hearken to me, O son of Zippor:
¹⁹ God is not man, that he should lie,
    or a son of man, that he should
        repent.
Has he said, and will he not do it?
    Or has he spoken, and will he not
        fulfil it?
²⁰ Behold, I received a command to
        bless:
    he has blessed, and I cannot
        revoke it.
²¹ He has not beheld misfortune in
        Jacob;
    nor has he seen trouble in Israel.
The LORD their God is with them,
    and the shout of a king is among
        them.
²² God brings them out of Egypt;
    they have as it were the horns of
        the wild ox.
²³ For there is no enchantment against
        Jacob,
    no divination against Israel;

s Or *dust clouds*

ceremony to obtain an omen. **7-10:** The first oracle. **7:** *Aram*, i.e. "Aram of the Two Rivers" or Mesopotamia (Gen.24.10). **9:** Israel is not a nation like other nations (compare 1 Sam.8.4–22) but a people set apart for a special destiny. **10:** Balaam prays that, by not cursing God's people, he may come to the end of his days as a righteous man. **11-12:** See 22.20. The narrative is written with a touch of humor. **13:** Not wishing to defy God, Balak supposes that the oracle may be different if Balaam views the people from another perspective. *Pisgah*, see Dt.34.1 n. **18-24:** The second oracle. **19:** God's purpose is consistent; he is not characterized by human deceit and caprice (for another meaning of *repent*, see Ex.32.14 n.). *Son of man*, i.e. a human being (Ps.8.4). **21:** *The shout*, Israel's acclamation of the LORD as King. **22:** *The horns of the*

now it shall be said of Jacob and
    Israel,
    'What has God wrought!'
24 Behold, a people! As a lioness it
    rises up
    and as a lion it lifts itself;
it does not lie down till it devours the
    prey,
and drinks the blood of the slain."

25 And Balak said to Balaam,
"Neither curse them at all, nor bless
them at all." 26 But Balaam answered
Balak, "Did I not tell you, 'All that the
LORD says, that I must do'?" 27 And
Balak said to Balaam, "Come now, I
will take you to another place; perhaps
it will please God that you may curse
them for me from there." 28 So Balak
took Balaam to the top of Pe'or, that
overlooks the desert.*t* 29 And Balaam
said to Balak, "Build for me here seven
altars, and provide for me here seven
bulls and seven rams." 30 And Balak
did as Balaam had said, and offered
a bull and a ram on each altar.

24 When Balaam saw that it
pleased the LORD to bless Israel,
he did not go, as at other times, to
look for omens, but set his face toward
the wilderness. 2 And Balaam lifted up
his eyes, and saw Israel encamping
tribe by tribe. And the Spirit of God
came upon him, 3 and he took up his
discourse, and said,

    "The oracle of Balaam the son of
    Be'or,
    the oracle of the man whose eye
      is opened,*u*
4 the oracle of him who hears the
    words of God,
    who sees the vision of the
      Almighty,
    falling down, but having his eyes
      uncovered:
5 how fair are your tents, O Jacob,

    your encampments, O Israel!
6 Like valleys that stretch afar,
    like gardens beside a river,
    like aloes that the LORD has planted,
    like cedar trees beside the waters.
7 Water shall flow from his buckets,
    and his seed shall be in many
      waters,
    his king shall be higher than Agag,
    and his kingdom shall be exalted.
8 God brings him out of Egypt;
    he has as it were the horns of the
      wild ox,
    he shall eat up the nations his
      adversaries,
    and shall break their bones in
      pieces,
    and pierce them through with his
      arrows.
9 He couched, he lay down like a lion,
    and like a lioness; who will rouse
      him up?
    Blessed be every one who blesses
      you,
    and cursed be every one who
      curses you."

10 And Balak's anger was kindled
against Balaam, and he struck his
hands together; and Balak said to
Balaam, "I called you to curse my
enemies, and behold, you have blessed
them these three times. 11 Therefore
now flee to your place; I said, 'I will certainly honor you,' but the LORD has
held you back from honor." 12 And
Balaam said to Balak, "Did I not tell
your messengers whom you sent to me,
13 'If Balak should give me his house
full of silver and gold, I would not be
able to go beyond the word of the
LORD, to do either good or bad of my
own will; what the LORD speaks, that
will I speak'? 14 And now, behold, I
am going to my people; come, I will

t Or *Jeshimon*   *u* Or *closed* or *perfect*

---

wild ox, a symbol of brute strength. **23:** Since Israel's God cannot be coerced by magical tech-
niques, divination is ineffective in altering Israel's destiny. **28:** *Peor*, see 25.3 n. **24.1:** Balaam
begins to abandon his technique of divination. **3–9:** The third oracle. **3–4:** These verses suggest
the ecstasy during which the oracle came. **7:** Secure and prosperous, Israel's *seed shall be in
many waters* (an allusion to the subterranean ocean; see Gen.49.25 n.). *His king shall be higher
than Agag*, a traditional name for the king of Amalek (1 Sam.15.8). **9b:** Gen.12.3. **10:** Striking
the hands together was a gesture of anger and reproach (Job 27.23). **14:** Balaam not only defies
Balak's command to get out but gives his last oracle without the preparatory rites of divination

let you know what this people will do
to your people in the latter days."
15 And he took up his discourse, and
said,
"The oracle of Balaam the son of
Be'or,
  the oracle of the man whose eye
    is opened,[v]
16 the oracle of him who hears the
    words of God,
  and knows the knowledge of the
    Most High,
who sees the vision of the Almighty,
  falling down, but having his eyes
    uncovered:
17 I see him, but not now;
  I behold him, but not nigh:
a star shall come forth out of Jacob,
  and a scepter shall rise out of
    Israel;
it shall crush the forehead[w] of Moab,
  and break down all the sons of
    Sheth.
18 Edom shall be dispossessed,
  Se'ir also, his enemies, shall be
    dispossessed,
  while Israel does valiantly.
19 By Jacob shall dominion be
    exercised,
  and the survivors of cities be
    destroyed!"
20 Then he looked on Am'alek,
and took up his discourse, and said,
"Am'alek was the first of the nations,
but in the end he shall come to
    destruction."
21 And he looked on the Ken'ite,
and took up his discourse, and said,
"Enduring is your dwelling place,
  and your nest is set in the rock;

22 nevertheless Kain shall be wasted.
  How long shall Asshur take you
    away captive?"
23 And he took up his discourse,
and said,
"Alas, who shall live when God does
    this?
24 But ships shall come from Kittim
  and shall afflict Asshur and Eber;
  and he also shall come to
    destruction."
25 Then Balaam rose, and went
back to his place; and Balak also went
his way.

25 While Israel dwelt in Shittim
the people began to play the
harlot with the daughters of Moab.
2 These invited the people to the sacrifices of their gods, and the people ate,
and bowed down to their gods. 3 So
Israel yoked himself to Ba'al of Pe'or.
And the anger of the LORD was kindled
against Israel; 4 and the LORD said to
Moses, "Take all the chiefs of the people, and hang them in the sun before
the LORD, that the fierce anger of the
LORD may turn away from Israel."
5 And Moses said to the judges of
Israel, "Every one of you slay his men
who have yoked themselves to Ba'al of
Pe'or."
6 And behold, one of the people of
Israel came and brought a Mid'ianite
woman to his family, in the sight of
Moses and in the sight of the whole
congregation of the people of Israel,
while they were weeping at the door of
the tent of meeting. 7 When Phin'ehas
the son of Elea'zar, son of Aaron the

v Or *closed* or *perfect*   w Heb *corners* (of the head)

(23.1–6; 24.1 n.). **15–19:** The fourth oracle. **17–19:** What he sees is *not now* but in the future:
Israel will be victorious over Moab and Edom, a prophecy which was realized in the time of
David (2 Sam.8.2,13–14). *A star, a scepter*, these royal symbols fit a leader like David whose
empire embraced the promised land (see Gen.49.10 n.). **18:** *Seir*, a synonym for Edom. **20–24:**
Supplementary oracles. **20:** Ex.17.14–16. **21–24:** The meaning of these verses is obscure, owing
to the uncertainty of the names.
  25.1–12: Incidents of apostasy in Moab. The protest against intermarriage with foreign
peoples was based on the fear of the corruption of Israel's faith (Dt.7.1–5). **1:** *Shittim* (Abel-
shittim), opposite Jericho. *Play the harlot*, compare Hos.2.5–13. **2:** The Moabite women lured
Israelites into idolatrous rites. *Ate*, a reference to a sacred meal in connection with the sacrifices
(compare Ex.32.6). **3:** *Baal*, the Canaanite god of storm and fertility who was worshiped at the
cult center of Peor or Beth-peor (23.28; Dt.3.29). **4:** The execution of the *chiefs* was an expiation
for the people, according to the ancient conception of corporate guilt (compare 2 Sam.21.1–6).
5: *Judges*, Ex.18.25–26. **6–18:** Phinehas' zeal (compare Ex.32.25–29). **6:** The story assumes an

priest, saw it, he rose and left the congregation, and took a spear in his hand [8] and went after the man of Israel into the inner room, and pierced both of them, the man of Israel and the woman, through her body. Thus the plague was stayed from the people of Israel. [9] Nevertheless those that died by the plague were twenty-four thousand.

10 And the LORD said to Moses, [11] "Phin'ehas the son of Elea'zar, son of Aaron the priest, has turned back my wrath from the people of Israel, in that he was jealous with my jealousy among them, so that I did not consume the people of Israel in my jealousy. [12] Therefore say, 'Behold, I give to him my covenant of peace; [13] and it shall be to him, and to his descendants after him, the covenant of a perpetual priesthood, because he was jealous for his God, and made atonement for the people of Israel.'"

14 The name of the slain man of Israel, who was slain with the Mid'ianite woman, was Zimri the son of Salu, head of a fathers' house belonging to the Simeonites. [15] And the name of the Mid'ianite woman who was slain was Cozbi the daughter of Zur, who was the head of the people of a fathers' house in Mid'ian.

16 And the LORD said to Moses, [17] "Harass the Mid'ianites, and smite them; [18] for they have harassed you with their wiles, with which they beguiled you in the matter of Pe'or, and in the matter of Cozbi, the daughter of the prince of Mid'ian, their sister, who was slain on the day of the plague on account of Pe'or."

26 After the plague the LORD said to Moses and to Elea'zar the son of Aaron, the priest, [2] "Take a census of all the congregation of the people of Israel, from twenty years old and upward, by their fathers' houses, all in Israel who are able to go forth to war." [3] And Moses and Elea'zar the priest spoke with them in the plains of Moab by the Jordan at Jericho, saying, [4] "Take a census of the people,[x] from twenty years old and upward," as the LORD commanded Moses. The people of Israel, who came forth out of the land of Egypt, were:

5 Reuben, the first-born of Israel; the sons of Reuben: of Hanoch, the family of the Ha'nochites; of Pallu, the family of the Pal'luites; [6] of Hezron, the family of the Hez'ronites; of Carmi, the family of the Carmites. [7] These are the families of the Reubenites; and their number was forty-three thousand seven hundred and thirty. [8] And the sons of Pallu: Eli'ab. [9] The sons of Eli'ab: Nem'uel, Dathan, and Abi'ram. These are the Dathan and Abi'ram, chosen from the congregation, who contended against Moses and Aaron in the company of Korah, when they contended against the LORD, [10] and the earth opened its mouth and swallowed them up together with Korah, when that company died, when the fire devoured two hundred and fifty men; and they became a warning. [11] Notwithstanding, the sons of Korah did not die.

12 The sons of Simeon according to their families: of Nem'uel, the family of the Nem'uelites; of Jamin, the family of the Ja'minites; of Jachin, the family of the Ja'chinites; [13] of Zerah, the family of the Zer'ahites; of Sha'ul, the family of the Sha'ulites. [14] These are the families of the Simeonites, twenty-two thousand two hundred.

x Supplying *take a census of the people* Compare verse 2

attempt to seduce Israelites into intermarriage with Midianites, with the result that divine judgment came in the form of a plague (v. 9). In 31.16 Balaam is blamed for this incident. **11:** *Jealous*, or zealous (see Ex.34.14 n.; 1 Kg.19.10). **12:** A *covenant of peace* (Ezek.34.25; 37.26) is one of welfare and well-being, based on right relation with God and harmonious relations in the community. **13:** The Aaronic line, traced through Phinehas (Ex.6.25), is guaranteed *a perpetual priesthood*. **16–18:** See ch. 31.

26.1–65: A second census is taken to ascertain the strength of the tribes and to allot the land. **5–50:** See 1.5–15 n. **9–11:** See ch. 16. **12–14:** Simeon suffered the greatest loss during the wilder-

15 The sons of Gad according to their families: of Zephon, the family of the Ze'phonites; of Haggi, the family of the Haggites; of Shuni, the family of the Shunites; 16 of Ozni, the family of the Oznites; of Eri, the family of the Erites; 17 of Ar'od, the family of the Ar'odites; of Are'li, the family of the Are'lites. 18 These are the families of the sons of Gad according to their number, forty thousand five hundred.

19 The sons of Judah were Er and Onan; and Er and Onan died in the land of Canaan. 20 And the sons of Judah according to their families were: of Shelah, the family of the Shela'nites; of Perez, the family of the Per'ezites; of Zerah, the family of the Zer'ahites. 21 And the sons of Perez were: of Hezron, the family of the Hez'ronites; of Hamul, the family of the Hamu'lites. 22 These are the families of Judah according to their number, seventy-six thousand five hundred.

23 The sons of Is'sachar according to their families: of Tola, the family of the To'laites; of Puvah, the family of the Punites; 24 of Jashub, the family of the Jash'ubites; of Shimron, the family of the Shim'ronites. 25 These are the families of Is'sachar according to their number, sixty-four thousand three hundred.

26 The sons of Zeb'ulun, according to their families: of Sered, the family of the Ser'edites; of Elon, the family of the E'lonites; of Jahleel, the family of the Jah'leelites. 27 These are the families of the Zeb'ulunites according to their number, sixty thousand five hundred.

28 The sons of Joseph according to their families: Manas'seh and E'phraim. 29 The sons of Manas'seh: of Machir, the family of the Ma'chirites; and Machir was the father of Gilead; of Gilead, the family of the Gileadites. 30 These are the sons of Gilead: of Ie'zer, the family of the Ie'zerites; of Helek, the family of the He'lekites;

31 and of As'riel, the family of the As'rielites; and of Shechem, the family of the She'chemites; 32 and of Shemi'da, the family of the Shemi'daites; and of Hepher, the family of the He'pherites. 33 Now Zeloph'ehad the son of Hepher had no sons, but daughters: and the names of the daughters of Zeloph'ehad were Mahlah, Noah, Hoglah, Milcah, and Tirzah. 34 These are the families of Manas'seh; and their number was fifty-two thousand seven hundred.

35 These are the sons of E'phraim according to their families: of Shuthe'lah, the family of the Shuthe'lahites; of Becher, the family of the Bech'erites; of Tahan, the family of the Ta'hanites. 36 And these are the sons of Shuthe'lah: of Eran, the family of the E'ranites. 37 These are the families of the sons of E'phraim according to their number, thirty-two thousand five hundred. These are the sons of Joseph according to their families.

38 The sons of Benjamin according to their families: of Bela, the family of the Be'la-ites; of Ashbel, the family of the Ash'belites; of Ahi'ram, the family of the Ahi'ramites; 39 of Shephu'pham, the family of the Shu'phamites; of Hupham, the family of the Hu'phamites. 40 And the sons of Bela were Ard and Na'aman: of Ard, the family of the Ard'ites; of Na'aman, the family of the Na'amites. 41 These are the sons of Benjamin according to their families; and their number was forty-five thousand six hundred.

42 These are the sons of Dan according to their families: of Shuham, the family of the Shu'hamites. These are the families of Dan according to their families. 43 All the families of the Shu'hamites, according to their number, were sixty-four thousand four hundred.

44 The sons of Asher according to their families: of Imnah, the family of the Imnites; of Ishvi, the family of the Ishvites; of Beri'ah, the family of the

ness sojourn (compare 1.23; see Gen.49.5–7 n.). 28: Manasseh's priority over Ephraim (compare 1.10) points to a very old historical situation (Gen.48.13–22) and suggests that this list is

Beri'ites. ⁴⁵ Of the sons of Beri'ah: of Heber, the family of the He'berites; of Mal'chi-el, the family of the Mal'chi-elites. ⁴⁶ And the name of the daughter of Asher was Serah. ⁴⁷ These are the families of the sons of Asher according to their number, fifty-three thousand four hundred.

48 The sons of Naph'tali according to their families: of Jahzeel, the family of the Jah'zeelites; of Guni, the family of the Gunites; ⁴⁹ of Jezer, the family of the Je'zerites; of Shillem, the family of the Shil'lemites. ⁵⁰ These are the families of Naph'tali according to their families; and their number was forty-five thousand four hundred.

51 This was the number of the people of Israel, six hundred and one thousand seven hundred and thirty.

52 The LORD said to Moses: ⁵³ "To these the land shall be divided for inheritance according to the number of names. ⁵⁴ To a large tribe you shall give a large inheritance, and to a small tribe you shall give a small inheritance; every tribe shall be given its inheritance according to its numbers. ⁵⁵ But the land shall be divided by lot; according to the names of the tribes of their fathers they shall inherit. ⁵⁶ Their inheritance shall be divided according to lot between the larger and the smaller."

57 These are the Levites as numbered according to their families: of Gershon, the family of the Gershonites; of Kohath, the family of the Ko'hathites; of Merar'i, the family of the Merar'ites. ⁵⁸ These are the families of Levi: the family of the Libnites, the family of the He'bronites, the family of the Mahlites, the family of the Mushites, the family of the Ko'rahites. And Kohath was the father of Amram. ⁵⁹ The name of Amram's wife was Joch'ebed the daughter of Levi, who

was born to Levi in Egypt; and she bore to Amram Aaron and Moses and Miriam their sister. ⁶⁰ And to Aaron were born Nadab, Abi'hu, Elea'zar and Ith'amar. ⁶¹ But Nadab and Abi'hu died when they offered unholy fire before the LORD. ⁶² And those numbered of them were twenty-three thousand, every male from a month old and upward; for they were not numbered among the people of Israel, because there was no inheritance given to them among the people of Israel.

63 These were those numbered by Moses and Elea'zar the priest, who numbered the people of Israel in the plains of Moab by the Jordan at Jericho. ⁶⁴ But among these there was not a man of those numbered by Moses and Aaron the priest, who had numbered the people of Israel in the wilderness of Sinai. ⁶⁵ For the LORD had said of them, "They shall die in the wilderness." There was not left a man of them, except Caleb the son of Jephun'neh and Joshua the son of Nun.

27 Then drew near the daughters of Zeloph'ehad the son of Hepher, son of Gilead, son of Machir, son of Manas'seh, from the families of Manas'seh the son of Joseph. The names of his daughters were: Mahlah, Noah, Hoglah, Milcah, and Tirzah. ² And they stood before Moses, and before Elea'zar the priest, and before the leaders and all the congregation, at the door of the tent of meeting, saying, ³ "Our father died in the wilderness; he was not among the company of those who gathered themselves together against the LORD in the company of Korah, but died for his own sin; and he had no sons. ⁴ Why should the name of our father be taken away from his family, because he had no

---

older than that of ch. 1. **51**: See 1.17–46 n. The priestly writer emphasizes God's marvelous power to sustain his people despite the almost complete change of population (vv. 63–65). **52–56**: The census provided a basis for allotting land after the conquest. **57–62**: The Levites, the landless tribe, are numbered separately. **61**: See Lev. ch. 10.

27.1–11: Inheritance of property by women. 1: 26.33. **2–4**: In Israel a family inheritance was to remain in the family (36.7; 1 Kg.21.3), thereby perpetuating the ancestral name. The request of the daughters of Zelophehad was unusual in that, according to ancient law, normally women

son? Give to us a possession among our father's brethren."

5 Moses brought their case before the LORD. ⁶ And the LORD said to Moses, ⁷ "The daughters of Zeloph'-ehad are right; you shall give them possession of an inheritance among their father's brethren and cause the inheritance of their father to pass to them. ⁸ And you shall say to the people of Israel, 'If a man dies, and has no son, then you shall cause his inheritance to pass to his daughter. ⁹ And if he has no daughter, then you shall give his inheritance to his brothers. ¹⁰ And if he has no brothers, then you shall give his inheritance to his father's brothers. ¹¹ And if his father has no brothers, then you shall give his inheritance to his kinsman that is next to him of his family, and he shall possess it. And it shall be to the people of Israel a statute and ordinance, as the LORD commanded Moses.' "

12 The LORD said to Moses, "Go up into this mountain of Ab'arim, and see the land which I have given to the people of Israel. ¹³ And when you have seen it, you also shall be gathered to your people, as your brother Aaron was gathered, ¹⁴ because you rebelled against my word in the wilderness of Zin during the strife of the congregation, to sanctify me at the waters before their eyes." (These are the waters of Mer'ibah of Kadesh in the wilderness of Zin.) ¹⁵ Moses said to the LORD, ¹⁶ "Let the LORD, the God of the spirits of all flesh, appoint a man over the congregation, ¹⁷ who shall go out before them and come in before them, who shall lead them out and bring them in; that the congregation of the LORD may not be as sheep which have no

shepherd." ¹⁸ And the LORD said to Moses, "Take Joshua the son of Nun, a man in whom is the spirit, and lay your hand upon him; ¹⁹ cause him to stand before Elea'zar the priest and all the congregation, and you shall commission him in their sight. ²⁰ You shall invest him with some of your authority, that all the congregation of the people of Israel may obey. ²¹ And he shall stand before Elea'zar the priest, who shall inquire for him by the judgment of the Urim before the LORD; at his word they shall go out, and at his word they shall come in, both he and all the people of Israel with him, the whole congregation." ²² And Moses did as the LORD commanded him; he took Joshua and caused him to stand before Elea'zar the priest and the whole congregation, ²³ and he laid his hands upon him, and commissioned him as the LORD directed through Moses.

28 The LORD said to Moses, ² "Command the people of Israel, and say to them, 'My offering, my food for my offerings by fire, my pleasing odor, you shall take heed to offer to me in its due season.' ³ And you shall say to them, This is the offering by fire which you shall offer to the LORD: two male lambs a year old without blemish, day by day, as a continual offering. ⁴ The one lamb you shall offer in the morning, and the other lamb you shall offer in the evening; ⁵ also a tenth of an ephah of fine flour for a cereal offering, mixed with a fourth of a hin of beaten oil. ⁶ It is a continual burnt offering, which was ordained at Mount Sinai for a pleasing odor, an offering by fire to the LORD. ⁷ Its drink offering shall be a fourth of a hin for each lamb; in the holy place

---

did not inherit property. **5–11:** Another example of how law developed as unprecedented situations were faced (see 9.8 n.). Compare also ch. 36.

27.12–23: Joshua commissioned to succeed Moses (Dt.31.14–15,23). **12:** *Abarim*, a hilly region in which Mount Nebo, the scene of Moses' death, was located (Dt. ch. 34). **13:** 20.22–29. **14:** 20.12–13. *Meribah*, see Ex.17.7 n. **18–20:** Like Moses, Joshua was held to be a charismatic leader, *a man in whom is the spirit* (11.17; 24.2). **21:** *Urim*, see Ex.28.15–30 n. At Joshua's word, given in obedience to the sacred oracle, the people shall *go out* to battle and *come in* the camp (v. 17; Dt.3.28).

28.1–29.40: Offerings for various occasions. 2: *My food . . . my pleasing odor*, see Lev.1.9 n.

you shall pour out a drink offering of strong drink to the LORD. [8] The other lamb you shall offer in the evening; like the cereal offering of the morning, and like its drink offering, you shall offer it as an offering by fire, a pleasing odor to the LORD.

9 "On the sabbath day two male lambs a year old without blemish, and two tenths of an ephah of fine flour for a cereal offering, mixed with oil, and its drink offering: [10] this is the burnt offering of every sabbath, besides the continual burnt offering and its drink offering.

11 "At the beginnings of your months you shall offer a burnt offering to the LORD: two young bulls, one ram, seven male lambs a year old without blemish; [12] also three tenths of an ephah of fine flour for a cereal offering, mixed with oil, for each bull; and two tenths of fine flour for a cereal offering, mixed with oil, for the one ram; [13] and a tenth of fine flour mixed with oil as a cereal offering for every lamb; for a burnt offering of pleasing odor, an offering by fire to the LORD. [14] Their drink offerings shall be half a hin of wine for a bull, a third of a hin for a ram, and a fourth of a hin for a lamb; this is the burnt offering of each month throughout the months of the year. [15] Also one male goat for a sin offering to the LORD; it shall be offered besides the continual burnt offering and its drink offering.

16 "On the fourteenth day of the first month is the LORD's passover. [17] And on the fifteenth day of this month is a feast; seven days shall unleavened bread be eaten. [18] On the first day there shall be a holy convocation: you shall do no laborious work, [19] but offer an offering by fire, a burnt offering to the LORD: two young bulls, one ram, and seven male lambs a year old; see that they are

without blemish; [20] also their cereal offering of fine flour mixed with oil; three tenths of an ephah shall you offer for a bull, and two tenths for a ram; [21] a tenth shall you offer for each of the seven lambs; [22] also one male goat for a sin offering, to make atonement for you. [23] You shall offer these besides the burnt offering of the morning, which is for a continual burnt offering. [24] In the same way you shall offer daily, for seven days, the food of an offering by fire, a pleasing odor to the LORD; it shall be offered besides the continual burnt offering and its drink offering. [25] And on the seventh day you shall have a holy convocation; you shall do no laborious work.

26 "On the day of the first fruits, when you offer a cereal offering of new grain to the LORD at your feast of weeks, you shall have a holy convocation; you shall do no laborious work, [27] but offer a burnt offering, a pleasing odor to the LORD: two young bulls, one ram, seven male lambs a year old; [28] also their cereal offering of fine flour mixed with oil, three tenths of an ephah for each bull, two tenths for one ram, [29] a tenth for each of the seven lambs; [30] with one male goat, to make atonement for you. [31] Besides the continual burnt offering and its cereal offering, you shall offer them and their drink offering. See that they are without blemish.

29 "On the first day of the seventh month you shall have a holy convocation; you shall do no laborious work. It is a day for you to blow the trumpets, [2] and you shall offer a burnt offering, a pleasing odor to the LORD: one young bull, one ram, seven male lambs a year old without blemish; [3] also their cereal offering of fine flour mixed with oil, three tenths of an ephah for the bull, two tenths for the ram, [4] and one tenth for each of the seven

and 21.6 n. **3–8**: The daily sacrifice (Ex.29.38–42). **9–10**: The sabbath offering is mentioned only here in the Pentateuch. **11–15**: Since the year was based on a lunar calendar, a festival was held at each new moon (10.10; 1 Sam.20.5; Is.1.14; Am.8.5). **16–25**: Unleavened bread (Ex.12.1–27; Lev.23.5–8). **26–31**: Pentecost (Ex.23.16; 34.22; Lev.23.15–21). **29.1–6**: New Year (Lev.23.

lambs; [5] with one male goat for a sin offering, to make atonement for you; [6] besides the burnt offering of the new moon, and its cereal offering, and the continual burnt offering and its cereal offering, and their drink offering, according to the ordinance for them, a pleasing odor, an offering by fire to the LORD.

7 "On the tenth day of this seventh month you shall have a holy convocation, and afflict yourselves; you shall do no work, [8] but you shall offer a burnt offering to the LORD, a pleasing odor: one young bull, one ram, seven male lambs a year old; they shall be to you without blemish; [9] and their cereal offering of fine flour mixed with oil, three tenths of an ephah for the bull, two tenths for the one ram, [10] a tenth for each of the seven lambs: [11] also one male goat for a sin offering, besides the sin offering of atonement, and the continual burnt offering and its cereal offering, and their drink offerings.

12 "On the fifteenth day of the seventh month you shall have a holy convocation; you shall do no laborious work, and you shall keep a feast to the LORD seven days; [13] and you shall offer a burnt offering, an offering by fire, a pleasing odor to the LORD, thirteen young bulls, two rams, fourteen male lambs a year old; they shall be without blemish; [14] and their cereal offering of fine flour mixed with oil, three tenths of an ephah for each of the thirteen bulls, two tenths for each of the two rams, [15] and a tenth for each of the fourteen lambs; [16] also one male goat for a sin offering, besides the continual burnt offering, its cereal offering and its drink offering.

17 "On the second day twelve young bulls, two rams, fourteen male lambs a year old without blemish, [18] with the cereal offering and the drink offerings for the bulls, for the rams, and for the lambs, by number, according to the ordinance; [19] also

one male goat for a sin offering, besides the continual burnt offering and its cereal offering, and their drink offerings.

20 "On the third day eleven bulls, two rams, fourteen male lambs a year old without blemish, [21] with the cereal offering and the drink offerings for the bulls, for the rams, and for the lambs, by number, according to the ordinance; [22] also one male goat for a sin offering, besides the continual burnt offering and its cereal offering and its drink offering.

23 "On the fourth day ten bulls, two rams, fourteen male lambs a year old without blemish, [24] with the cereal offering and the drink offerings for the bulls, for the rams, and for the lambs, by number, according to the ordinance; [25] also one male goat for a sin offering, besides the continual burnt offering, its cereal offering and its drink offering.

26 "On the fifth day nine bulls, two rams, fourteen male lambs a year old without blemish, [27] with the cereal offering and the drink offerings for the bulls, for the rams, and for the lambs, by number, according to the ordinance; [28] also one male goat for a sin offering; besides the continual burnt offering and its cereal offering and its drink offering.

29 "On the sixth day eight bulls, two rams, fourteen male lambs a year old without blemish, [30] with the cereal offering and the drink offerings for the bulls, for the rams, and for the lambs, by number, according to the ordinance; [31] also one male goat for a sin offering; besides the continual burnt offering, its cereal offering, and its drink offerings.

32 "On the seventh day seven bulls, two rams, fourteen male lambs a year old without blemish, [33] with the cereal offering and the drink offerings for the bulls, for the rams, and for the lambs, by number, according to the ordinance;

23–25). **7–11:** Day of atonement (Lev.16.29–34; 23.26–32). **12–38:** The offering for the feast of booths (Lev.23.33–36) exceeds that of any other convocation.

34 also one male goat for a sin offering; besides the continual burnt offering, its cereal offering, and its drink offering.

35 "On the eighth day you shall have a solemn assembly: you shall do no laborious work, 36 but you shall offer a burnt offering, an offering by fire, a pleasing odor to the LORD: one bull, one ram, seven male lambs a year old without blemish, 37 and the cereal offering and the drink offerings for the bull, for the ram, and for the lambs, by number, according to the ordinance; 38 also one male goat for a sin offering; besides the continual burnt offering and its cereal offering and its drink offering.

39 "These you shall offer to the LORD at your appointed feasts, in addition to your votive offerings and your freewill offerings, for your burnt offerings, and for your cereal offerings, and for your drink offerings, and for your peace offerings."

40ʸ And Moses told the people of Israel everything just as the LORD had commanded Moses.

30 Moses said to the heads of the tribes of the people of Israel, "This is what the LORD has commanded. 2 When a man vows a vow to the LORD, or swears an oath to bind himself by a pledge, he shall not break his word; he shall do according to all that proceeds out of his mouth. 3 Or when a woman vows a vow to the LORD, and binds herself by a pledge, while within her father's house, in her youth, 4 and her father hears of her vow and of her pledge by which she has bound herself, and says nothing to her; then all her vows shall stand, and every pledge by which she has bound herself shall stand. 5 But if her father expresses disapproval to her on the day that he hears of it, no vow of hers, no pledge by which she has bound

herself, shall stand; and the LORD will forgive her, because her father opposed her. 6 And if she is married to a husband, while under her vows or any thoughtless utterance of her lips by which she has bound herself, 7 and her husband hears of it, and says nothing to her on the day that he hears; then her vows shall stand, and her pledges by which she has bound herself shall stand. 8 But if, on the day that her husband comes to hear of it, he expresses disapproval, then he shall make void her vow which was on her, and the thoughtless utterance of her lips, by which she bound herself; and the LORD will forgive her. 9 But any vow of a widow or of a divorced woman, anything by which she has bound herself, shall stand against her. 10 And if she vowed in her husband's house, or bound herself by a pledge with an oath, 11 and her husband heard of it, and said nothing to her, and did not oppose her; then all her vows shall stand, and every pledge by which she bound herself shall stand. 12 But if her husband makes them null and void on the day that he hears them, then whatever proceeds out of her lips concerning her vows, or concerning her pledge of herself, shall not stand: her husband has made them void, and the LORD will forgive her. 13 Any vow and any binding oath to afflict herself, her husband may establish, or her husband may make void. 14 But if her husband says nothing to her from day to day, then he establishes all her vows, or all her pledges, that are upon her; he has established them, because he said nothing to her on the day that he heard of them. 15 But if he makes them null and void after he has heard of them, then he shall bear her iniquity."

16 These are the statutes which

ʸ Ch 30.1 in Heb

30.1–16: On vows made by women. 2: Vows made by men (Gen.28.20–22; Jg.11.30–31) are absolutely binding (compare Lev. ch. 27; Dt.23.21–23). **3–15:** These cases reflect a society in which woman was subordinate to the man of the family. He could nullify her vow if he felt that it was rash or thoughtless. **9:** The exception is a vow made by a woman when widowed or divorced. **13:** *Afflict herself*, i.e. by a vow of abstinence or discipline.

the LORD commanded Moses, as between a man and his wife, and between a father and his daughter, while in her youth, within her father's house.

31 The LORD said to Moses, 2 "Avenge the people of Israel on the Mid'ianites; afterward you shall be gathered to your people." 3 And Moses said to the people, "Arm men from among you for the war, that they may go against Mid'ian, to execute the LORD'S vengeance on Mid'ian. 4 You shall send a thousand from each of the tribes of Israel to the war." 5 So there were provided, out of the thousands of Israel, a thousand from each tribe, twelve thousand armed for war. 6 And Moses sent them to the war, a thousand from each tribe, together with Phin'ehas the son of Elea'zar the priest, with the vessels of the sanctuary and the trumpets for the alarm in his hand. 7 They warred against Mid'ian, as the LORD commanded Moses, and slew every male. 8 They slew the kings of Mid'ian with the rest of their slain, Evi, Rekem, Zur, Hur, and Reba, the five kings of Mid'ian; and they also slew Balaam the son of Be'or with the sword. 9 And the people of Israel took captive the women of Mid'ian and their little ones; and they took as booty all their cattle, their flocks, and all their goods. 10 All their cities in the places where they dwelt, and all their encampments, they burned with fire, 11 and took all the spoil and all the booty, both of man and of beast. 12 Then they brought the captives and the booty and the spoil to Moses, and to Elea'zar the priest, and

to the congregation of the people of Israel, at the camp on the plains of Moab by the Jordan at Jericho.

13 Moses, and Elea'zar the priest, and all the leaders of the congregation, went forth to meet them outside the camp. 14 And Moses was angry with the officers of the army, the commanders of thousands and the commanders of hundreds, who had come from service in the war. 15 Moses said to them, "Have you let all the women live? 16 Behold, these caused the people of Israel, by the counsel of Balaam, to act treacherously against the LORD in the matter of Pe'or, and so the plague came among the congregation of the LORD. 17 Now therefore, kill every male among the little ones, and kill every woman who has known man by lying with him. 18 But all the young girls who have not known man by lying with him, keep alive for yourselves. 19 Encamp outside the camp seven days; whoever of you has killed any person, and whoever has touched any slain, purify yourselves and your captives on the third day and on the seventh day. 20 You shall purify every garment, every article of skin, all work of goats' hair, and every article of wood."

21 And Elea'zar the priest said to the men of war who had gone to battle: "This is the statute of the law which the LORD has commanded Moses: 22 only the gold, the silver, the bronze, the iron, the tin, and the lead, 23 everything that can stand the fire, you shall pass through the fire, and it shall be clean. Nevertheless it shall also be

---

31.1–54: Holy war against Midian. The reason for this war was the corrupting influence of Midianites at Peor (25.16–18). **3:** *The LORD's vengeance,* i.e. holy war in which the enemy was placed under the sacrificial ban (Ex.17.8–16). **6:** Phinehas was sent instead of Eleazar, for the high priest, more than other priests, had to avoid contact with the dead (Lev.21.10–15). Strangely, no mention is made of the ark going into battle. **8:** In contrast to early tradition which portrayed Balaam as an advocate for Israel (chs. 22–24), this priestly tradition holds him responsible for the apostasy at Peor (v. 16). **7:** Despite this annihilation, the Midianites were a formidable foe in a later period (Jg. ch. 6). **9–12:** According to the ideology of holy war, the enemy was offered as a sacrifice to the LORD (1 Sam. ch. 15). **19–24:** A major concern of the story is the removal of uncleanness through contact with the dead. See ch. 19 for the procedure for ceremonial purification. **20:** These articles could absorb uncleanness (Lev.11.24–38). **22–23:** Non-absorbent articles had to be subjected to fire as well as to *the water of impurity*

purified with the water of impurity; and whatever cannot stand the fire, you shall pass through the water. 24 You must wash your clothes on the seventh day, and you shall be clean; and afterward you shall come into the camp."

25 The LORD said to Moses, 26 "Take the count of the booty that was taken, both of man and of beast, you and Elea'zar the priest and the heads of the fathers' houses of the congregation; 27 and divide the booty into two parts, between the warriors who went out to battle and all the congregation. 28 And levy for the LORD a tribute from the men of war who went out to battle, one out of five hundred, of the persons and of the oxen and of the asses and of the flocks; 29 take it from their half, and give it to Elea'zar the priest as an offering to the LORD. 30 And from the people of Israel's half you shall take one drawn out of every fifty, of the persons, of the oxen, of the asses, and of the flocks, of all the cattle, and give them to the Levites who have charge of the tabernacle of the LORD." 31 And Moses and Elea'zar the priest did as the LORD commanded Moses.

32 Now the booty remaining of the spoil that the men of war took was: six hundred and seventy-five thousand sheep, 33 seventy-two thousand cattle, 34 sixty-one thousand asses, 35 and thirty-two thousand persons in all, women who had not known man by lying with him. 36 And the half, the portion of those who had gone out to war, was in number three hundred and thirty-seven thousand five hundred sheep, 37 and the LORD's tribute of sheep was six hundred and seventy-five. 38 The cattle were thirty-six thousand, of which the LORD's tribute was seventy-two. 39 The asses were thirty

thousand five hundred, of which the LORD's tribute was sixty-one. 40 The persons were sixteen thousand, of which the LORD's tribute was thirty-two persons. 41 And Moses gave the tribute, which was the offering for the LORD, to Elea'zar the priest, as the LORD commanded Moses.

42 From the people of Israel's half, which Moses separated from that of the men who had gone to war– 43 now the congregation's half was three hundred and thirty-seven thousand five hundred sheep, 44 thirty-six thousand cattle, 45 and thirty thousand five hundred asses, 46 and sixteen thousand persons– 47 from the people of Israel's half Moses took one of every fifty, both of persons and of beasts, and gave them to the Levites who had charge of the tabernacle of the LORD; as the LORD commanded Moses.

48 Then the officers who were over the thousands of the army, the captains of thousands and the captains of hundreds, came near to Moses, 49 and said to Moses, "Your servants have counted the men of war who are under our command, and there is not a man missing from us. 50 And we have brought the LORD's offering, what each man found, articles of gold, armlets and bracelets, signet rings, earrings, and beads, to make atonement for ourselves before the LORD." 51 And Moses and Elea'zar the priest received from them the gold, all wrought articles. 52 And all the gold of the offering that they offered to the LORD, from the commanders of thousands and the commanders of hundreds, was sixteen thousand seven hundred and fifty shekels. 53 (The men of war had taken booty, every man for himself.) 54 And Moses and Elea'zar the priest received the gold from the commanders of thousands and of hundreds, and brought it

---

(19.9). **25–30:** The law for the distribution of booty. **27:** 1 Sam.30.24–25. **28–30:** The warriors were to contribute one-fifth of one per cent from their half of the booty to the high priest; this offering was regarded as *the LORD's tribute* (vv. 32–41). The people were to give two per cent from their half to the Levites (vv. 42–47). **50:** *Make atonement* (see Lev.1.4 n.), i.e. on account of ritual defilement by the dead.

into the tent of meeting, as a memorial for the people of Israel before the LORD.

32 Now the sons of Reuben and the sons of Gad had a very great multitude of cattle; and they saw the land of Jazer and the land of Gilead, and behold, the place was a place for cattle. ² So the sons of Gad and the sons of Reuben came and said to Moses and to Elea′zar the priest and to the leaders of the congregation, ³ "At′aroth, Dibon, Jazer, Nimrah, Heshbon, Elea′leh, Sebam, Nebo, and Be′on, ⁴ the land which the LORD smote before the congregation of Israel, is a land for cattle; and your servants have cattle." ⁵ And they said, "If we have found favor in your sight, let this land be given to your servants for a possession; do not take us across the Jordan."

6 But Moses said to the sons of Gad and to the sons of Reuben, "Shall your brethren go to the war while you sit here? ⁷ Why will you discourage the heart of the people of Israel from going over into the land which the LORD has given them? ⁸ Thus did your fathers, when I sent them from Ka′desh-bar′-nea to see the land. ⁹ For when they went up to the Valley of Eshcol, and saw the land, they discouraged the heart of the people of Israel from going into the land which the LORD had given them. ¹⁰ And the LORD's anger was kindled on that day, and he swore, saying, ¹¹ 'Surely none of the men who came up out of Egypt, from twenty years old and upward, shall see the land which I swore to give to Abraham, to Isaac, and to Jacob, because they have not wholly followed me; ¹² none except Caleb the son of Jephun′neh the Ken′izzite and Joshua the son of Nun, for they have wholly followed the LORD.' ¹³ And the LORD's anger was kindled against Israel, and he made

them wander in the wilderness forty years, until all the generation that had done evil in the sight of the LORD was consumed. ¹⁴ And behold, you have risen in your fathers' stead, a brood of sinful men, to increase still more the fierce anger of the LORD against Israel! ¹⁵ For if you turn away from following him, he will again abandon them in the wilderness; and you will destroy all this people."

16 Then they came near to him, and said, "We will build sheepfolds here for our flocks, and cities for our little ones, ¹⁷ but we will take up arms, ready to go before the people of Israel, until we have brought them to their place; and our little ones shall live in the fortified cities because of the inhabitants of the land. ¹⁸ We will not return to our homes until the people of Israel have inherited each his inheritance. ¹⁹ For we will not inherit with them on the other side of the Jordan and beyond; because our inheritance has come to us on this side of the Jordan to the east." ²⁰ So Moses said to them, "If you will do this, if you will take up arms to go before the LORD for the war, ²¹ and every armed man of you will pass over the Jordan before the LORD, until he has driven out his enemies from before him ²² and the land is subdued before the LORD; then after that you shall return and be free of obligation to the LORD and to Israel; and this land shall be your possession before the LORD. ²³ But if you will not do so, behold, you have sinned against the LORD; and be sure your sin will find you out. ²⁴ Build cities for your little ones, and folds for your sheep; and do what you have promised." ²⁵ And the sons of Gad and the sons of Reuben said to Moses, "Your servants will do as my lord commands. ²⁶ Our little ones, our wives, our flocks, and all our cattle,

---

32.1–42: The allotment of land in Transjordan to Reuben, Gad, and Manasseh, on the condition that they help the other tribes in the battle for Canaan (Dt.3.12–22; Jos.13.8–32). **1:** *Jazer,* on the boundary of Ammon (21.24). **6:** Compare Jg.5.16–17. **8–13:** A summary of chs. 13–14. **20–23:** This is conceived as a holy war which imposed a sacred obligation upon all the tribal

shall remain there in the cities of Gilead; [27] but your servants will pass over, every man who is armed for war, before the LORD to battle, as my lord orders."

28 So Moses gave command concerning them to Elea'zar the priest, and to Joshua the son of Nun, and to the heads of the fathers' houses of the tribes of the people of Israel. [29] And Moses said to them, "If the sons of Gad and the sons of Reuben, every man who is armed to battle before the LORD, will pass with you over the Jordan and the land shall be subdued before you, then you shall give them the land of Gilead for a possession; [30] but if they will not pass over with you armed, they shall have possessions among you in the land of Canaan." [31] And the sons of Gad and the sons of Reuben answered, "As the LORD has said to your servants, so we will do. [32] We will pass over armed before the LORD into the land of Canaan, and the possession of our inheritance shall remain with us beyond the Jordan."

33 And Moses gave to them, to the sons of Gad and to the sons of Reuben and to the half-tribe of Manas'seh the son of Joseph, the kingdom of Sihon king of the Amorites and the kingdom of Og king of Bashan, the land and its cities with their territories, the cities of the land throughout the country. [34] And the sons of Gad built Dibon, At'aroth, Aro'er, [35] At'roth-sho'phan, Jazer, Jog'behah, [36] Beth-nim'rah and Beth-har'an, fortified cities, and folds for sheep. [37] And the sons of Reuben built Heshbon, Elea'leh, Kiriatha'im, [38] Nebo, and Ba'al-me'on (their names to be changed), and Sibmah; and they

gave other names to the cities which they built. [39] And the sons of Machir the son of Manas'seh went to Gilead and took it, and dispossessed the Amorites who were in it. [40] And Moses gave Gilead to Machir the son of Manas'seh, and he settled in it. [41] And Ja'ir the son of Manas'seh went and took their villages, and called them Hav'-voth-ja'ir.[z] [42] And Nobah went and took Kenath and its villages, and called it Nobah, after his own name.

33 These are the stages of the people of Israel, when they went forth out of the land of Egypt by their hosts under the leadership of Moses and Aaron. [2] Moses wrote down their starting places, stage by stage, by command of the LORD; and these are their stages according to their starting places. [3] They set out from Ram'eses in the first month, on the fifteenth day of the first month; on the day after the passover the people of Israel went out triumphantly in the sight of all the Egyptians, [4] while the Egyptians were burying all their first-born, whom the LORD had struck down among them; upon their gods also the LORD executed judgments.

5 So the people of Israel set out from Ram'eses, and encamped at Succoth. [6] And they set out from Succoth, and encamped at Etham, which is on the edge of the wilderness. [7] And they set out from Etham, and turned back to Pi-hahi'roth, which is east of Ba'-al-ze'phon; and they encamped before Migdol. [8] And they set out from before Hahi'roth, and passed through the midst of the sea into the wilderness, and they went a three days' journey in the wilderness of Etham, and

z That is *the villages of Jair*

confederacy (Dt.33.21). **33:** *The half-tribe of Manasseh,* i.e. the part that located east of the Jordan as distinguished from the part that settled in the region around Shechem (Jos.17.1–3). **34–36:** Gad's territory included part of the kingdom of Sihon (21.24), i.e. from Heshbon northward into Gilead (Jos.13.24–28). **37–38:** Reuben's territory extended from Heshbon south to the Arnon, the frontier of Moab (Jos.13.15–23). **39–42:** Machir (26.29; see Gen.50.23 n.) received the territory of King Og (21.33), which included the rest of Gilead and all of Bashan (Jos.13.29–31). **41:** *Havvoth-jair,* 1 Kg.4.13.

33.1–49: **Israel's itinerary** from Egypt to the border of Canaan. **5–15:** From the land of Goshen to Sinai (Ex.12.37–19.2). **8:** *Etham,* otherwise designated as Shur (Ex.15.22). **16–36:**

encamped at Marah. ⁹ And they set out from Marah, and came to Elim; at Elim there were twelve springs of water and seventy palm trees, and they encamped there. ¹⁰ And they set out from Elim, and encamped by the Red Sea. ¹¹ And they set out from the Red Sea, and encamped in the wilderness of Sin. ¹² And they set out from the wilderness of Sin, and encamped at Dophkah. ¹³ And they set out from Dophkah, and encamped at Alush. ¹⁴ And they set out from Alush, and encamped at Reph'idim, where there was no water for the people to drink. ¹⁵ And they set out from Reph'idim, and encamped in the wilderness of Sinai. ¹⁶ And they set out from the wilderness of Sinai, and encamped at Kib'roth-hatta'avah. ¹⁷ And they set out from Kib'roth-hatta'avah, and encamped at Haze'roth. ¹⁸ And they set out from Haze'roth, and encamped at Rithmah. ¹⁹ And they set out from Rithmah, and encamped at Rim'mon-per'ez. ²⁰ And they set out from Rim'-mon-per'ez, and encamped at Libnah. ²¹ And they set out from Libnah, and encamped at Rissah. ²² And they set out from Rissah, and encamped at Kehela'thah. ²³ And they set out from Kehela'thah, and encamped at Mount Shepher. ²⁴ And they set out from Mount Shepher, and encamped at Hara'dah. ²⁵ And they set out from Hara'dah, and encamped at Makhe'-loth. ²⁶ And they set out from Makhe'-loth, and encamped at Tahath. ²⁷ And they set out from Tahath, and encamped at Terah. ²⁸ And they set out from Terah, and encamped at Mithkah. ²⁹ And they set out from Mithkah, and encamped at Hashmo'nah. ³⁰ And they set out from Hashmo'nah, and encamped at Mose'roth. ³¹ And they set out from Mose'roth, and encamped at Bene-ja'akan. ³² And they set out from Bene-ja'akan, and encamped at Hor-haggid'gad. ³³ And they set out from

Hor-haggid'gad, and encamped at Jot'bathah. ³⁴ And they set out from Jot'bathah, and encamped at Abro'-nah. ³⁵ And they set out from Abro'-nah, and encamped at E'zion-ge'ber. ³⁶ And they set out from E'zion-ge'-ber, and encamped in the wilderness of Zin (that is, Kadesh). ³⁷ And they set out from Kadesh, and encamped at Mount Hor, on the edge of the land of Edom.

38 And Aaron the priest went up Mount Hor at the command of the LORD, and died there, in the fortieth year after the people of Israel had come out of the land of Egypt, on the first day of the fifth month. ³⁹ And Aaron was a hundred and twenty-three years old when he died on Mount Hor.

40 And the Canaanite, the king of Arad, who dwelt in the Negeb in the land of Canaan, heard of the coming of the people of Israel.

41 And they set out from Mount Hor, and encamped at Zalmo'nah. ⁴² And they set out from Zalmo'nah, and encamped at Punon. ⁴³ And they set out from Punon, and encamped at Oboth. ⁴⁴ And they set out from Oboth, and encamped at I'ye-ab'arim, in the territory of Moab. ⁴⁵ And they set out from I'yim, and encamped at Dibon-gad. ⁴⁶ And they set out from Dibon-gad, and encamped at Al'mon-diblatha'im. ⁴⁷ And they set out from Al'mon-diblatha'im, and encamped in the mountains of Ab'arim, before Nebo. ⁴⁸ And they set out from the mountains of Ab'arim, and encamped in the plains of Moab by the Jordan at Jericho; ⁴⁹ they encamped by the Jordan from Beth-jes'himoth as far as Abel-shittim in the plains of Moab.

50 And the LORD said to Moses in the plains of Moab by the Jordan at Jericho, ⁵¹ "Say to the people of Israel, When you pass over the Jordan into the land of Canaan, ⁵² then you shall drive out all the inhabitants of the

---

From Sinai to Kadesh-barnea (Num.10.11–20.1). **37–49:** From Kadesh to the plains of Moab (20.22–22.1). The details of this phase of the itinerary, including the journey to Ezion-geber (v. 35), are not clear. **50–56:** Ex.23.23–33; Lev. ch. 26.

land from before you, and destroy all their figured stones, and destroy all their molten images, and demolish all their high places; [53] and you shall take possession of the land and settle in it, for I have given the land to you to possess it. [54] You shall inherit the land by lot according to your families; to a large tribe you shall give a large inheritance, and to a small tribe you shall give a small inheritance; wherever the lot falls to any man, that shall be his; according to the tribes of your fathers you shall inherit. [55] But if you do not drive out the inhabitants of the land from before you, then those of them whom you let remain shall be as pricks in your eyes and thorns in your sides, and they shall trouble you in the land where you dwell. [56] And I will do to you as I thought to do to them."

34 The LORD said to Moses, [2] "Command the people of Israel, and say to them, When you enter the land of Canaan (this is the land that shall fall to you for an inheritance, the land of Canaan in its full extent), [3] your south side shall be from the wilderness of Zin along the side of Edom, and your southern boundary shall be from the end of the Salt Sea on the east; [4] and your boundary shall turn south of the ascent of Akrab'bim, and cross to Zin, and its end shall be south of Ka'desh-bar'nea; then it shall go on to Ha'zar-ad'dar, and pass along to Azmon; [5] and the boundary shall turn from Azmon to the Brook of Egypt, and its termination shall be at the sea.

6 "For the western boundary, you shall have the Great Sea and its[a] coast; this shall be your western boundary.

7 "This shall be your northern boundary: from the Great Sea you shall mark out your line to Mount Hor; [8] from Mount Hor you shall mark it out to the entrance of Hamath, and the end of the boundary shall be at Zedad; [9] then the boundary shall extend to Ziphron, and its end shall be at Ha'zar-e'nan; this shall be your northern boundary.

10 "You shall mark out your eastern boundary from Ha'zar-e'nan to Shepham; [11] and the boundary shall go down from Shepham to Riblah on the east side of A'in; and the boundary shall go down, and reach to the shoulder of the sea of Chin'nereth on the east; [12] and the boundary shall go down to the Jordan, and its end shall be at the Salt Sea. This shall be your land with its boundaries all round."

13 Moses commanded the people of Israel, saying, "This is the land which you shall inherit by lot, which the LORD has commanded to give to the nine tribes and to the half-tribe; [14] for the tribe of the sons of Reuben by fathers' houses and the tribe of the sons of Gad by their fathers' houses have received their inheritance, and also the half-tribe of Manas'seh; [15] the two tribes and the half-tribe have received their inheritance beyond the Jordan at Jericho eastward, toward the sunrise."

16 The LORD said to Moses, [17] "These are the names of the men who shall divide the land to you for inheritance: Elea'zar the priest and Joshua the son of Nun. [18] You shall take one leader of every tribe, to divide the land for inheritance. [19] These are the names of the men: Of the tribe of Judah, Caleb the son of Jephun'neh. [20] Of the tribe of the sons

a Syr: Heb lacks *its*

34.1–29: Ideal boundaries of the Promised Land (compare Jos. chs. 13–19; Ezek.47.13–20). **1–12:** The extent of the land, south to north, is essentially from *the brook of Egypt* (v. 5) to *the entrance of Hamath* (v. 8), near Riblah. Israel's territory did not extend so far north until the time of David (2 Sam.8.3–14; 1 Kg.8.65). Probably the tradition has visualized the past in the light of David, the "star" who arose out of Jacob (see 24.17–19 n.) to conquer the last of the opposing forces, thereby establishing in Israel's possession *the land of Canaan in its full extent* (v. 2). **14–15:** Jericho is said to be east, presupposing a standpoint within Canaan rather than in Transjordan.

of Simeon, Shemu'el the son of Ammi'-hud. 21 Of the tribe of Benjamin, Eli'dad the son of Chislon. 22 Of the tribe of the sons of Dan a leader, Bukki the son of Jogli. 23 Of the sons of Joseph: of the tribe of the sons of Manas'seh a leader, Han'niel the son of Ephod. 24 And of the tribe of the sons of E'phraim a leader, Kemu'el the son of Shiphtan. 25 Of the tribe of the sons of Zeb'ulun a leader, Eli-za'phan the son of Parnach. 26 Of the tribe of the sons of Is'sachar a leader, Pal'tiel the son of Azzan. 27 And of the tribe of the sons of Asher a leader, Ahi'hud the son of Shelo'mi. 28 Of the tribe of the sons of Naph'tali a leader, Pe-dah'el the son of Ammi'hud. 29 These are the men whom the LORD commanded to divide the inheritance for the people of Israel in the land of Canaan."

35 The LORD said to Moses in the plains of Moab by the Jordan at Jericho, 2 "Command the people of Israel, that they give to the Levites, from the inheritance of their posession, cities to dwell in; and you shall give to the Levites pasture lands round about the cities. 3 The cities shall be theirs to dwell in, and their pasture lands shall be for their cattle and for their livestock and for all their beasts. 4 The pasture lands of the cities, which you shall give to the Levites, shall reach from the wall of the city outward a thousand cubits all round. 5 And you shall measure, outside the city, for the east side two thousand cubits, and for the south side two thousand cubits, and for the west side two thousand cubits, and for the north side two thousand cubits, the city being in the middle; this shall belong to them as pasture land for their cities. 6 The cities

which you give to the Levites shall be the six cities of refuge, where you shall permit the manslayer to flee, and in addition to them you shall give forty-two cities. 7 All the cities which you give to the Levites shall be forty-eight, with their pasture lands. 8 And as for the cities which you shall give from the possession of the people of Israel, from the larger tribes you shall take many, and from the smaller tribes you shall take few; each, in proportion to the inheritance which it inherits, shall give of its cities to the Levites."

9 And the LORD said to Moses, 10 "Say to the people of Israel, When you cross the Jordan into the land of Canaan, 11 then you shall select cities to be cities of refuge for you, that the manslayer who kills any person without intent may flee there. 12 The cities shall be for you a refuge from the avenger, that the manslayer may not die until he stands before the congregation for judgment. 13 And the cities which you give shall be your six cities of refuge. 14 You shall give three cities beyond the Jordan, and three cities in the land of Canaan, to be cities of refuge. 15 These six cities shall be for refuge for the people of Israel, and for the stranger and for the sojourner among them, that any one who kills any person without intent may flee there.

16 "But if he struck him down with an instrument of iron, so that he died, he is a murderer; the murderer shall be put to death. 17 And if he struck him down with a stone in the hand, by which a man may die, and he died, he is a murderer; the murderer shall be put to death. 18 Or if he struck him down with a weapon of wood in the hand, by which a man

35.1–34: Plans for Levitical cities and cities of refuge. 1–8: Special cities were allotted because the Levites were not entitled to a tribal inheritance (Lev.25.32–34; Jos. ch. 21; 1 Chr.6.54–81). **9–15:** The six cities of refuge (Dt.4.41–43; 19.1–13; Jos. ch. 20) represent an attempt to restrain the tribal law of blood revenge so that a manslayer might receive a trial (v. 12). Early legislation stipulated that a man might seek asylum from the *avenger* or kinsman (Lev.25.25 n.), whose duty was to uphold family rights by killing the murderer or one of his relatives (see Ex.21.12–14 n.). **16–34:** This case law distinguishes between murder and manslaughter. As a concession to ancient blood revenge, the tribunal lets the avenger exercise his role if the killing

may die, and he died, he is a murderer; the murderer shall be put to death. [19] The avenger of blood shall himself put the murderer to death; when he meets him, he shall put him to death. [20] And if he stabbed him from hatred, or hurled at him, lying in wait, so that he died, [21] or in enmity struck him down with his hand, so that he died, then he who struck the blow shall be put to death; he is a murderer; the avenger of blood shall put the murderer to death, when he meets him.

22 "But if he stabbed him suddenly without enmity, or hurled anything on him without lying in wait, [23] or used a stone, by which a man may die, and without seeing him cast it upon him, so that he died, though he was not his enemy, and did not seek his harm; [24] then the congregation shall judge between the manslayer and the avenger of blood, in accordance with these ordinances; [25] and the congregation shall rescue the manslayer from the hand of the avenger of blood, and the congregation shall restore him to his city of refuge, to which he had fled, and he shall live in it until the death of the high priest who was anointed with the holy oil. [26] But if the manslayer shall at any time go beyond the bounds of his city of refuge to which he fled, [27] and the avenger of blood finds him outside the bounds of his city of refuge, and the avenger of blood slays the manslayer, he shall not be guilty of blood. [28] For the man must remain in his city of refuge until the death of the high priest; but after the death of the high priest the manslayer may return to the land of his possession.

29 "And these things shall be for a statute and ordinance to you throughout your generations in all your dwellings. [30] If any one kills a person, the murderer shall be put to death on the evidence of witnesses; but no person shall be put to death on the testimony of one witness. [31] Moreover you shall accept no ransom for the life of a murderer, who is guilty of death; but he shall be put to death. [32] And you shall accept no ransom for him who has fled to his city of refuge, that he may return to dwell in the land before the death of the high priest. [33] You shall not thus pollute the land in which you live; for blood pollutes the land, and no expiation can be made for the land, for the blood that is shed in it, except by the blood of him who shed it. [34] You shall not defile the land in which you live, in the midst of which I dwell; for I the LORD dwell in the midst of the people of Israel."

36 The heads of the fathers' houses of the families of the sons of Gilead the son of Machir, son of Manas'seh, of the fathers' houses of the sons of Joseph, came near and spoke before Moses and before the leaders, the heads of the fathers' houses of the people of Israel; [2] they said, "The LORD commanded my lord to give the land for inheritance by lot to the people of Israel; and my lord was commanded by the LORD to give the inheritance of Zeloph'ehad our brother to his daughters. [3] But if they are married to any of the sons of the other tribes of the people of Israel then their inheritance will be taken from the inheritance of our fathers, and added to the inheritance of the tribe to which they belong; so it will be taken away from the lot of our inheritance. [4] And when the jubilee of the people of Israel comes, then their inheritance will be added to the inheritance of the tribe to which they belong; and their inheritance will be taken from the inheritance of the tribe of our fathers."

---

was premeditated (vv. 19,21). **33–34:** Murder is a heinous offense because *blood pollutes the land* (Gen.4.10–11) in the midst of which the LORD dwells. Therefore only the blood of the murderer can expiate the crime (Dt.19.10,13).

36.1–12: Tribal property must be maintained intact. This law supplements 27.1–11 by stipulating that a woman who is allowed to inherit property must marry within her tribe. **1:** 26.28–34. **4:** On the jubilee year, see Lev.25.8–55. **6:** The law prevents tribal intermarriage only when

5 And Moses commanded the people of Israel according to the word of the LORD, saying, "The tribe of the sons of Joseph is right. 6 This is what the LORD commands concerning the daughters of Zeloph'ehad, 'Let them marry whom they think best; only, they shall marry within the family of the tribe of their father. 7 The inheritance of the people of Israel shall not be transferred from one tribe to another; for every one of the people of Israel shall cleave to the inheritance of the tribe of his fathers. 8 And every daughter who possesses an inheritance in any tribe of the people of Israel shall be wife to one of the family of the tribe of her father, so that every one of the people of Israel may possess the inheritance of his fathers. 9 So no inherit-

ance shall be transferred from one tribe to another; for each of the tribes of the people of Israel shall cleave to its own inheritance.' "

10 The daughters of Zeloph'ehad did as the LORD commanded Moses; 11 for Mahlah, Tirzah, Hoglah, Milcah, and Noah, the daughters of Zeloph'ehad, were married to sons of their father's brothers. 12 They were married into the families of the sons of Manas'seh the son of Joseph, and their inheritance remained in the tribe of the family of their father.

13 These are the commandments and the ordinances which the LORD commanded by Moses to the people of Israel in the plains of Moab by the Jordan at Jericho.

the woman is an heiress. **13:** A concluding statement covering all the laws given in Moab (22.1–36.12).

DEUTERONOMY

The basic theme of Deuteronomy, meaning the "second law," is the renewal of the covenant. Here the legal tradition of the book of Exodus (for example, the Decalogue or the Covenant Code) is not just repeated; it is reinterpreted in contemporary terms, so that the promises and demands of the covenant were brought near to every worshiping Israelite.

At the end of the book of Numbers Israel is encamped in the plains of Moab, prepared for an attack upon Canaan from the east. Deuteronomy is essentially Moses' farewell address to the people in which he rehearses the mighty acts of the Lord, solemnly warns of the temptations of the new ways of Canaan, and pleads for loyalty to and love of God as the condition for life in the promised land.

Actually Deuteronomy contains not one address by Moses, but three. The first is found in 1.6 to 4.40; the second in chs. 5–28; and the third in chs. 29 and 30. The remaining chapters (31–34) pick up the story where it was left at the end of Numbers (see Introduction to Pentateuch).

A distinctive teaching of Deuteronomy is that the worship of the LORD is to be centralized in one place, so that the paganism of local shrines may be eliminated (ch. 12). When Deuteronomy was published, the Jerusalem temple was regarded as the central sanctuary. Indeed, Deuteronomy was probably the "book of the law" which prompted Josiah's sweeping religious reform in 621 B.C. (2 Kg. chs. 22–23) and led to the revision of the history found in Joshua, Judges, Samuel, and Kings. Although Deuteronomy rests upon ancient tradition, fundamentally it is a rediscovery and reinterpretation of Mosaic teaching in the light of later historical understanding.

THESE ARE THE WORDS THAT MOSES spoke to all Israel beyond the Jordan in the wilderness, in the Arabah over against Suph, between Paran and Tophel, Laban, Haze′roth, and Di′-zahab. ² It is eleven days' journey from Horeb by the way of Mount Se′-ir to Ka′desh-bar′nea. ³ And in the fortieth year, on the first day of the eleventh month, Moses spoke to the people of Israel according to all that the LORD had given him in commandment to them, ⁴ after he had defeated Sihon the king of the Amorites, who lived in Heshbon, and Og the king of Bashan, who lived in Ash′taroth and in Ed′re-i. ⁵ Beyond the Jordan, in the land of Moab, Moses undertook to explain this law, saying, ⁶ "The LORD our God said to us in Horeb, 'You have stayed long enough at this mountain; ⁷ turn and take your journey, and go to the hill country of the Amorites, and to all their neighbors in the Arabah, in the hill country and in the lowland, and in the Negeb, and by the seacoast, the land of the Canaanites, and Lebanon, as far as the great river, the river Euphra′tes. ⁸ Behold, I have set the land before you; go in and take possession of the land which the LORD swore to your fathers, to Abraham, to Isaac, and to Jacob, to give to them and to their descendants after them.'

9 "At that time I said to you, 'I am not able alone to bear you; ¹⁰ the LORD your God has multiplied you, and behold, you are this day as the stars of

---

1.1–3.29: Historical review. Moses rehearses events since the departure from Sinai (Horeb) to show how the LORD marvelously guided his people in the wilderness. 1–5: Introduction to the first address (1.6–4.40), which was given *beyond the Jordan*, i.e. in the plains of Moab (Num.33.48; 36.13). 1–2: The places mentioned refer to the wilderness journey. 3: *Fortieth year*, counting from the Exodus (Ex.19.1; 40.17). 4: Num.21.21–35. 7: *Amorites, Canaanites*, see Num.13.29 n. The Israelite empire extended ideally to the Euphrates (Gen.15.18), the northern limit of David's conquests (2 Sam.8.3). 9–18: In this composite account (compare

heaven for multitude. [11] May the LORD, the God of your fathers, make you a thousand times as many as you are, and bless you, as he has promised you! [12] How can I bear alone the weight and burden of you and your strife? [13] Choose wise, understanding, and experienced men, according to your tribes, and I will appoint them as your heads.' [14] And you answered me, 'The thing that you have spoken is good for us to do.' [15] So I took the heads of your tribes, wise and experienced men, and set them as heads over you, commanders of thousands, commanders of hundreds, commanders of fifties, commanders of tens, and officers, throughout your tribes. [16] And I charged your judges at that time, 'Hear the cases between your brethren, and judge righteously between a man and his brother or the alien that is with him. [17] You shall not be partial in judgment; you shall hear the small and the great alike; you shall not be afraid of the face of man, for the judgment is God's; and the case that is too hard for you, you shall bring to me, and I will hear it.' [18] And I commanded you at that time all the things that you should do.

[19] "And we set out from Horeb, and went through all that great and terrible wilderness which you saw, on the way to the hill country of the Amorites, as the LORD our God commanded us; and we came to Ka'deshbar'nea. [20] And I said to you, 'You have come to the hill country of the Amorites, which the LORD our God gives us. [21] Behold, the LORD your God has set the land before you; go up, take possession, as the LORD, the God of your fathers, has told you; do not fear or be dismayed.' [22] Then all of you came near me, and said, 'Let us send men before us, that they may explore the land for us, and bring us word again of the way by which we must go up and the cities into which we shall come.' [23] The thing seemed good to me, and I took twelve men of you, one man for each tribe; [24] and they turned and went up into the hill country, and came to the Valley of Eshcol and spied it out. [25] And they took in their hands some of the fruit of the land and brought it down to us, and brought us word again, and said, 'It is a good land which the LORD our God gives us.'

[26] "Yet you would not go up, but rebelled against the command of the LORD your God; [27] and you murmured in your tents, and said, 'Because the LORD hated us he has brought us forth out of the land of Egypt, to give us into the hand of the Amorites, to destroy us. [28] Whither are we going up? Our brethren have made our hearts melt, saying, "The people are greater and taller than we; the cities are great and fortified up to heaven; and moreover we have seen the sons of the Anakim there." ' [29] Then I said to you, 'Do not be in dread or afraid of them. [30] The LORD your God who goes before you will himself fight for you, just as he did for you in Egypt before your eyes, [31] and in the wilderness, where you have seen how the LORD your God bore you, as a man bears his son, in all the way that you went until you came to this place.' [32] Yet in spite of this word you did not believe the LORD your God, [33] who went before you in the way to seek you out a place to pitch your tents, in fire by night, to show you by what way you should go, and in the cloud by day.

[34] "And the LORD heard your words, and was angered, and he swore, [35] 'Not one of these men of this evil generation shall see the good land which I swore to give to your fathers,

---

vv. 9–12 with Num.11.14–17 and vv. 13–17 with Ex.18.13–27) there is no reference to Jethro's initiative to lighten Moses' burden. **11**: *The God of your fathers*, see Gen.26.24 n. **19–46**: From Horeb to Kadesh: a summary of the spies' reconnaissance of the land (Num. ch. 13), the people's murmuring doubt about the LORD's inability to fulfil his promise (Num.14.1–38), and the abortive attempt to penetrate Canaan from the south (Num.14.39–45; compare 21.1–3). **28**: *Anakim*, see Num.13.22,33 n. **30**: Ex.14.14. **33**: *Fire . . . cloud*, see Ex.13.21–22 n. **37**: Here

[36] except Caleb the son of Jephun'neh; he shall see it, and to him and to his children I will give the land upon which he has trodden, because he has wholly followed the LORD!' [37] The LORD was angry with me also on your account, and said, 'You also shall not go in there; [38] Joshua the son of Nun, who stands before you, he shall enter; encourage him, for he shall cause Israel to inherit it. [39] Moreover your little ones, who you said would become a prey, and your children, who this day have no knowledge of good or evil, shall go in there, and to them I will give it, and they shall possess it. [40] But as for you, turn, and journey into the wilderness in the direction of the Red Sea.'

41 "Then you answered me, 'We have sinned against the LORD; we will go up and fight, just as the LORD our God commanded us.' And every man of you girded on his weapons of war, and thought it easy to go up into the hill country. [42] And the LORD said to me, 'Say to them, Do not go up or fight, for I am not in the midst of you; lest you be defeated before your enemies.' [43] So I spoke to you, and you would not hearken; but you rebelled against the command of the LORD, and were presumptuous and went up into the hill country. [44] Then the Amorites who lived in that hill country came out against you and chased you as bees do and beat you down in Se'ir as far as Hormah. [45] And you returned and wept before the LORD; but the LORD did not hearken to your voice or give ear to you. [46] So you remained at Kadesh many days, the days that you remained there.

2 "Then we turned, and journeyed into the wilderness in the direction of the Red Sea, as the LORD told me; and for many days we went about Mount Se'ir. [2] Then the LORD said to me, [3] 'You have been going about this mountain country long enough; turn northward. [4] And command the people, You are about to pass through the territory of your brethren the sons of Esau, who live in Se'ir; and they will be afraid of you. So take good heed; [5] do not contend with them; for I will not give you any of their land, no, not so much as for the sole of the foot to tread on, because I have given Mount Se'ir to Esau as a possession. [6] You shall purchase food from them for money, that you may eat; and you shall also buy water of them for money, that you may drink. [7] For the LORD your God has blessed you in all the work of your hands; he knows your going through this great wilderness; these forty years the LORD your God has been with you; you have lacked nothing.' [8] So we went on, away from our brethren the sons of Esau who live in Se'ir, away from the Arabah road from Elath and E'zi-on-ge'ber.

"And we turned and went in the direction of the wilderness of Moab. [9] And the LORD said to me, 'Do not harass Moab or contend with them in battle, for I will not give you any of their land for a possession, because I have given Ar to the sons of Lot for a possession.' [10] (The Emim formerly lived there, a people great and many, and tall as the Anakim; [11] like the Anakim they are also known as Reph'aim, but the Moabites call them Emim. [12] The Horites also lived in Se'ir formerly, but the sons of Esau dispossessed them, and destroyed them from before them, and settled in their stead; as Israel did to the land of their possession, which the LORD gave to them.) [13] 'Now rise up, and go over the

---

Moses is not punished for his own sin (Num.20.10–13; 27.12–23), but vicariously bears the divine wrath on Israel's account. **2.1–25:** The circuit via Transjordan. **1–8a:** Num.20.14–21. From Kadesh Israel turned south through the Arabah to the Gulf of Aqabah in order to go around Edom (Num.21.4; compare 33.37–49). **4:** *Sons of Esau*, Gen.36.1. **8b–25:** Num.21.4–20. Turning along the brook Zered (boundary of Edom), Israel detoured via the Moabite wilderness toward the Amorite kingdom of Sihon. **9:** Moab and Ammon (v. 19) were traditionally related through Lot (Gen.19.36–38). **10–11:** *Emim, Rephaim* (compare v. 20; 3.11–13), names

brook Zered.' So we went over the brook Zered. ¹⁴ And the time from our leaving Ka′desh-bar′nea until we crossed the brook Zered was thirty-eight years, until the entire generation, that is, the men of war, had perished from the camp, as the LORD had sworn to them. ¹⁵ For indeed the hand of the LORD was against them, to destroy them from the camp, until they had perished.

16 "So when all the men of war had perished and were dead from among the people, ¹⁷ the LORD said to me, ¹⁸ 'This day you are to pass over the boundary of Moab at Ar; ¹⁹ and when you approach the frontier of the sons of Ammon, do not harass them or contend with them, for I will not give you any of the land of the sons of Ammon as a possession, because I have given it to the sons of Lot for a possession.' ²⁰ (That also is known as a land of Reph′aim; Reph′aim formerly lived there, but the Ammonites call them Zamzum′mim, ²¹ a people great and many, and tall as the Anakim; but the LORD destroyed them before them; and they dispossessed them, and settled in their stead; ²² as he did for the sons of Esau, who live in Se′ir, when he destroyed the Horites before them, and they dispossessed them, and settled in their stead even to this day. ²³ As for the Avvim, who lived in villages as far as Gaza, the Caph′torim, who came from Caphtor, destroyed them and settled in their stead.) ²⁴ 'Rise up, take your journey, and go over the valley of the Arnon; behold, I have given into your hand Sihon the Amorite, king of Heshbon, and his land; begin to take possession, and contend with him in battle. ²⁵ This day I will begin to put the dread and fear of you upon the peoples that are under the whole heaven, who shall hear the report of you and shall tremble and be in anguish because of you.'

26 "So I sent messengers from the wilderness of Ked′emoth to Sihon the king of Heshbon, with words of peace, saying, ²⁷ 'Let me pass through your land; I will go only by the road, I will turn aside neither to the right nor to the left. ²⁸ You shall sell me food for money, that I may eat, and give me water for money, that I may drink; only let me pass through on foot, ²⁹ as the sons of Esau who live in Se′ir and the Moabites who live in Ar did for me, until I go over the Jordan into the land which the LORD our God gives to us.' ³⁰ But Sihon the king of Heshbon would not let us pass by him; for the LORD your God hardened his spirit and made his heart obstinate, that he might give him into your hand, as at this day. ³¹ And the LORD said to me, 'Behold, I have begun to give Sihon and his land over to you; begin to take possession, that you may occupy his land.' ³² Then Sihon came out against us, he and all his people, to battle at Jahaz. ³³ And the LORD our God gave him over to us; and we defeated him and his sons and all his people. ³⁴ And we captured all his cities at that time and utterly destroyed every city, men, women, and children; we left none remaining; ³⁵ only the cattle we took as spoil for ourselves, with the booty of the cities which we captured. ³⁶ From Aro′er, which is on the edge of the valley of the Arnon, and from the city that is in the valley, as far as Gilead, there was not a city too high for us; the LORD our God gave all into our hands. ³⁷ Only to the land of the sons of Ammon you did not draw near, that is, to all the banks of the river Jabbok and the cities of the hill country, and wherever the LORD our God forbade us.

3 "Then we turned and went up the way to Bashan; and Og the king of Bashan came out against us, he and all his people, to battle at Ed′re-i. ² But

---

which reflect the legend that the aborigines were giants. *Horites*, see Gen.36.20 n. **23**: *Caphtor*, i.e. Crete. This verse refers to the conquest of the coastal plain by "sea-peoples" shortly after 1200 B.C. (see Gen.10.2–5 n.). **26–37**: The victory over Sihon (Num.21.21–32), whose capital was at Heshbon. **30**: See Ex.4.21 n. **37**: The river Jabbok makes a wide bend south and thus forms the western border of Ammon (3.16). **3.1–11**: The victory over Bashan (Num.21.33–35).

the LORD said to me, 'Do not fear him; for I have given him and all his people and his land into your hand; and you shall do to him as you did to Sihon the king of the Amorites, who dwelt at Heshbon.' ³ So the LORD our God gave into our hand Og also, the king of Bashan, and all his people; and we smote him until no survivor was left to him. ⁴ And we took all his cities at that time —there was not a city which we did not take from them—sixty cities, the whole region of Argob, the kingdom of Og in Bashan. ⁵ All these were cities fortified with high walls, gates, and bars, besides very many unwalled villages. ⁶ And we utterly destroyed them, as we did to Sihon the king of Heshbon, destroying every city, men, women, and children. ⁷ But all the cattle and the spoil of the cities we took as our booty. ⁸ So we took the land at that time out of the hand of the two kings of the Amorites who were beyond the Jordan, from the valley of the Arnon to Mount Hermon ⁹ (the Sido'nians call Hermon Si'rion, while the Amorites call it Senir), ¹⁰ all the cities of the tableland and all Gilead and all Bashan, as far as Sal'ecah and Ed're-i, cities of the kingdom of Og in Bashan. ¹¹ (For only Og the king of Bashan was left of the remnant of the Reph'aim; behold, his bedstead was a bedstead of iron; is it not in Rabbah of the Ammonites? Nine cubits was its length, and four cubits its breadth, according to the common cubit.ᵃ)

12 "When we took possession of this land at that time, I gave to the Reubenites and the Gadites the territory beginning at Aro'er, which is on the edge of the valley of the Arnon, and half the hill country of Gilead with its cities; ¹³ the rest of Gilead, and all Bashan, the kingdom of Og, that is,

all the region of Argob, I gave to the half-tribe of Manas'seh. (The whole of that Bashan is called the land of Reph'-aim. ¹⁴ Ja'ir the Manas'site took all the region of Argob, that is, Bashan, as far as the border of the Gesh'urites and the Ma-ac'athites, and called the villages after his own name, Hav'voth-ja'ir, as it is to this day.) ¹⁵ To Machir I gave Gilead, ¹⁶ and to the Reubenites and the Gadites I gave the territory from Gilead as far as the valley of the Arnon, with the middle of the valley as a boundary, as far over as the river Jabbok, the boundary of the Ammonites; ¹⁷ the Arabah also, with the Jordan as the boundary, from Chin'nereth as far as the sea of the Arabah, the Salt Sea, under the slopes of Pisgah on the east.

18 "And I commanded you at that time, saying, 'The LORD your God has given you this land to possess; all your men of valor shall pass over armed before your brethren the people of Israel. ¹⁹ But your wives, your little ones, and your cattle (I know that you have many cattle) shall remain in the cities which I have given you, ²⁰ until the LORD gives rest to your brethren, as to you, and they also occupy the land which the LORD your God gives them beyond the Jordan; then you shall return every man to his possession which I have given you.' ²¹ And I commanded Joshua at that time, 'Your eyes have seen all that the LORD your God has done to these two kings; so will the LORD do to all the kingdoms into which you are going over. ²² You shall not fear them; for it is the LORD your God who fights for you.'

23 "And I besought the LORD at that time, saying, ²⁴ 'O Lord GOD, thou hast only begun to show thy servant thy greatness and thy mighty hand; for

a Heb *cubit of a man*

1: *Edrei*, on extreme south border of *Bashan*. **11:** The oversized bed of Og, one of the legendary Rephaim (2.10–11), was a "museum piece" in Rabbah, a city on the Ammonite border. **12–22:** The allotment of tribal territories in Transjordan (Num. ch. 32; Jos. ch. 13). **14:** Num.32.41. **17:** The territory included the eastern part of the Jordan Valley or Arabah. **22:** The whole story of the Exodus, wilderness journey, and invasion of Canaan is governed by the convictions of holy war: the LORD fights for his people; faith is response to his active leadership (20.1–20). **23–29:** Num.27.12–23. **24:** In contrast to the gods of pagan nature religions, the God of Israel

what god is there in heaven or on earth who can do such works and mighty acts as thine? ²⁵ Let me go over, I pray, and see the good land beyond the Jordan, that goodly hill country, and Lebanon.' ²⁶ But the LORD was angry with me on your account, and would not hearken to me; and the LORD said to me, 'Let it suffice you; speak no more to me of this matter. ²⁷ Go up to the top of Pisgah, and lift up your eyes westward and northward and southward and eastward, and behold it with your eyes; for you shall not go over this Jordan. ²⁸ But charge Joshua, and encourage and strengthen him; for he shall go over at the head of this people, and he shall put them in possession of the land which you shall see.' ²⁹ So we remained in the valley opposite Beth-pe′or.

4 "And now, O Israel, give heed to the statutes and the ordinances which I teach you, and do them; that you may live, and go in and take possession of the land which the LORD, the God of your fathers, gives you. ² You shall not add to the word which I command you, nor take from it; that you may keep the commandments of the LORD your God which I command you. ³ Your eyes have seen what the LORD did at Ba′al-pe′or; for the LORD your God destroyed from among you all the men who followed the Ba′al of Pe′or; ⁴ but you who held fast to the LORD your God are all alive this day. ⁵ Behold, I have taught you statutes and ordinances, as the LORD my God commanded me, that you should do them in the land which you are entering to take possession of it. ⁶ Keep them and do them; for that will be your wisdom and your understanding in the sight of the peoples, who, when they hear all

these statutes, will say, 'Surely this great nation is a wise and understanding people.' ⁷ For what great nation is there that has a god so near to it as the LORD our God is to us, whenever we call upon him? ⁸ And what great nation is there, that has statutes and ordinances so righteous as all this law which I set before you this day?

9 "Only take heed, and keep your soul diligently, lest you forget the things which your eyes have seen, and lest they depart from your heart all the days of your life; make them known to your children and your children's children– ¹⁰ how on the day that you stood before the LORD your God at Horeb, the LORD said to me, 'Gather the people to me, that I may let them hear my words, so that they may learn to fear me all the days that they live upon the earth, and that they may teach their children so.' ¹¹ And you came near and stood at the foot of the mountain, while the mountain burned with fire to the heart of heaven, wrapped in darkness, cloud, and gloom. ¹² Then the LORD spoke to you out of the midst of the fire; you heard the sound of words, but saw no form; there was only a voice. ¹³ And he declared to you his covenant, which he commanded you to perform, that is, the ten commandments;ᵇ and he wrote them upon two tables of stone. ¹⁴ And the LORD commanded me at that time to teach you statutes and ordinances, that you might do them in the land which you are going over to possess.

15 "Therefore take good heed to yourselves. Since you saw no form on the day that the LORD spoke to you at Horeb out of the midst of the fire, ¹⁶ beware lest you act corruptly by

b Heb *words*

---

is unique, for his *mighty acts* testify that he is the LORD of history. **26:** On Moses' vicarious suffering, see 1.37 n. **27:** Mount *Pisgah*, see 34.1 n.

4.1–40: Conclusion to the first address. The preceding recital of what the LORD had done for his people is the basis of Moses' appeal for faithful obedience. **1–8:** The incident of Peor (Num. 25.1–9) teaches that obedience of God's law is the condition for life in Canaan and a testimony to the wisdom which the LORD graciously gives his people. **9–14:** The revelation at Sinai-Horeb (Ex. chs. 19–20) should be a constant reminder to *fear*, i.e. reverence, the LORD. **12:** At Horeb Israel heard the LORD's voice but *saw no form*–a warning against idolatry and image worship

making a graven image for yourselves, in the form of any figure, the likeness of male or female, 17 the likeness of any beast that is on the earth, the likeness of any winged bird that flies in the air, 18 the likeness of anything that creeps on the ground, the likeness of any fish that is in the water under the earth. 19 And beware lest you lift up your eyes to heaven, and when you see the sun and the moon and the stars, all the host of heaven, you be drawn away and worship them and serve them, things which the Lord your God has allotted to all the peoples under the whole heaven. 20 But the Lord has taken you, and brought you forth out of the iron furnace, out of Egypt, to be a people of his own possession, as at this day. 21 Furthermore the Lord was angry with me on your account, and he swore that I should not cross the Jordan, and that I should not enter the good land which the Lord your God gives you for an inheritance. 22 For I must die in this land, I must not go over the Jordan; but you shall go over and take possession of that good land. 23 Take heed to yourselves, lest you forget the covenant of the Lord your God, which he made with you, and make a graven image in the form of anything which the Lord your God has forbidden you. 24 For the Lord your God is a devouring fire, a jealous God.

25 "When you beget children and children's children, and have grown old in the land, if you act corruptly by making a graven image in the form of anything, and by doing what is evil in the sight of the Lord your God, so as to provoke him to anger, 26 I call heaven and earth to witness against you this day, that you will soon utterly perish from the land which you are going over the Jordan to possess; you will not live long upon it, but will be utterly destroyed. 27 And the Lord will scatter you among the peoples, and you will be left few in number among the nations where the Lord will drive you. 28 And there you will serve gods of wood and stone, the work of men's hands, that neither see, nor hear, nor eat, nor smell. 29 But from there you will seek the Lord your God, and you will find him, if you search after him with all your heart and with all your soul. 30 When you are in tribulation, and all these things come upon you in the latter days, you will return to the Lord your God and obey his voice, 31 for the Lord your God is a merciful God; he will not fail you or destroy you or forget the covenant with your fathers which he swore to them.

32 "For ask now of the days that are past, which were before you, since the day that God created man upon the earth, and ask from one end of heaven to the other, whether such a great thing as this has ever happened or was ever heard of. 33 Did any people ever hear the voice of a god speaking out of the midst of the fire, as you have heard, and still live? 34 Or has any god ever attempted to go and take a nation for himself from the midst of another nation, by trials, by signs, by wonders, and by war, by a mighty hand and an outstretched arm, and by great terrors, according to all that the Lord your God did for you in Egypt before your eyes? 35 To you it was shown, that you might know that the Lord is God; there is no other besides him. 36 Out of heaven he let you hear his voice, that he might discipline you; and

---

(vv. 15–18). **15–40:** The great exhortation. **16–18:** In pagan religions, gods were represented in both human and animal form. The imageless worship of the invisible God was a fundamental tenet of Mosaic faith (Ex.20.4). Here it is grounded in the covenant (v. 23) and made by the Lord of history and creation (v. 32). **24:** *A jealous God,* see Ex.34.14 n. **27–29:** These verses allude to the exile of conquered populations, a policy used effectively by Assyrians and Babylonians. **31:** Divine wrath is a temporary reaction to specific situations; God is fundamentally and unchangeably *a merciful God* (Ex.34.6–7). **33:** Ex.20.18–26; 33.20. **34–36:** The Lord's mighty deeds in history, by which he chose and constituted Israel as his people, have demonstrated his sole deity: *there is no other beside him* (see Ex.20.3 n.). **36:** *Discipline you,* Ex.20.20.

on earth he let you see his great fire, and you heard his words out of the midst of the fire. [37] And because he loved your fathers and chose their descendants after them, and brought you out of Egypt with his own presence, by his great power, [38] driving out before you nations greater and mightier than yourselves, to bring you in, to give you their land for an inheritance, as at this day; [39] know therefore this day, and lay it to your heart, that the LORD is God in heaven above and on the earth beneath; there is no other. [40] Therefore you shall keep his statutes and his commandments, which I command you this day, that it may go well with you, and with your children after you, and that you may prolong your days in the land which the LORD your God gives you for ever."

41 Then Moses set apart three cities in the east beyond the Jordan, [42] that the manslayer might flee there, who kills his neighbor unintentionally, without being at enmity with him in time past, and that by fleeing to one of these cities he might save his life: [43] Bezer in the wilderness on the tableland for the Reubenites, and Ramoth in Gilead for the Gadites, and Golan in Bashan for the Manas'sites.

44 This is the law which Moses set before the children of Israel; [45] these are the testimonies, the statutes, and the ordinances, which Moses spoke to the children of Israel when they came out of Egypt, [46] beyond the Jordan in the valley opposite Beth-pe'or, in the land of Sihon the king of the Amorites, who lived at Heshbon, whom Moses and the children of Israel defeated when they came out of Egypt. [47] And they took possession of his land and the land of Og the king of Bashan, the two kings of the Amorites, who lived to the east beyond the Jordan; [48] from Aro'er, which is on the edge of the valley of the Arnon, as far as Mount Si'rion[c] (that is, Hermon), [49] together with all the Arabah on the east side of the Jordan as far as the Sea of the Arabah, under the slopes of Pisgah.

5 And Moses summoned all Israel, and said to them, "Hear, O Israel, the statutes and the ordinances which I speak in your hearing this day, and you shall learn them and be careful to do them. [2] The LORD our God made a covenant with us in Horeb. [3] Not with our fathers did the LORD make this covenant, but with us, who are all of us here alive this day. [4] The LORD spoke with you face to face at the mountain, out of the midst of the fire, [5] while I stood between the LORD and you at that time, to declare to you the word of the LORD; for you were afraid because of the fire, and you did not go up into the mountain. He said:

6 " 'I am the LORD your God, who brought you out of the land of Egypt, out of the house of bondage.

7 " 'You shall have no other gods before[d] me.

8 " 'You shall not make for yourself a graven image, or any likeness of anything that is in heaven above, or that is on the earth beneath, or that is in the water under the earth; [9] you shall not bow down to them or serve them; for I the LORD your God am a jealous God, visiting the iniquity of the fathers upon the children to the third and fourth generation of those who

c Syr: Heb *Sion*   d Or *besides*

37: A new element is added to the theological tradition: the LORD's election of Israel was based upon his love. Israel's obedience, therefore, should be motivated by a responding love (6.4–5). *Presence*, Ex.33.14. **41–43:** An appendix dealing with cities of refuge (see ch. 19).

4.44–26.19 (and ch. 28): Moses' second address. 4.44–49: Introduction. 5.1–33: The giving of the law at Sinai. 1: *Hear*, a frequently repeated verb, indicating that Deuteronomy is a sermon which interprets Israel's covenant responsibilities. **2–3:** The making of the covenant (Ex. ch. 24) was not just a past ceremony involving another generation but it is a contemporary covenant *with us, who are all of us here alive this day* (see Ex.13.8 n.). The language may reflect a liturgy in which the covenant was periodically recalled and renewed (26.16–19; 31.10–11). **6–21:** This version of the Decalogue differs only slightly from that in Ex.20.2–17.

hate me, [10] but showing steadfast love to thousands of those who love me and keep my commandments.

11 " 'You shall not take the name of the LORD your God in vain: for the LORD will not hold him guiltless who takes his name in vain.

12 " 'Observe the sabbath day, to keep it holy, as the LORD your God commanded you. [13] Six days you shall labor, and do all your work; [14] but the seventh day is a sabbath to the LORD your God; in it you shall not do any work, you, or your son, or your daughter, or your manservant, or your maidservant, or your ox, or your ass, or any of your cattle, or the sojourner who is within your gates, that your manservant and your maidservant may rest as well as you. [15] You shall remember that you were a servant in the land of Egypt, and the LORD your God brought you out thence with a mighty hand and an outstretched arm; therefore the LORD your God commanded you to keep the sabbath day.

16 " 'Honor your father and your mother, as the LORD your God commanded you; that your days may be prolonged, and that it may go well with you, in the land which the LORD your God gives you.

17 " 'You shall not kill.

18 " 'Neither shall you commit adultery.

19 " 'Neither shall you steal.

20 " 'Neither shall you bear false witness against your neighbor.

21 " 'Neither shall you covet your neighbor's wife; and you shall not desire your neighbor's house, his field, or his manservant, or his maidservant, his ox, or his ass, or anything that is your neighbor's.'

22 "These words the LORD spoke to all your assembly at the mountain out of the midst of the fire, the cloud, and the thick darkness, with a loud voice;

and he added no more. And he wrote them upon two tables of stone, and gave them to me. [23] And when you heard the voice out of the midst of the darkness, while the mountain was burning with fire, you came near to me, all the heads of your tribes, and your elders; [24] and you said, 'Behold, the LORD our God has shown us his glory and greatness, and we have heard his voice out of the midst of the fire; we have this day seen God speak with man and man still live. [25] Now therefore why should we die? For this great fire will consume us; if we hear the voice of the LORD our God any more, we shall die. [26] For who is there of all flesh, that has heard the voice of the living God speaking out of the midst of fire, as we have, and has still lived? [27] Go near, and hear all that the LORD our God will say; and speak to us all that the LORD our God will speak to you; and we will hear and do it.'

28 "And the LORD heard your words, when you spoke to me; and the LORD said to me, 'I have heard the words of this people, which they have spoken to you; they have rightly said all that they have spoken. [29] Oh that they had such a mind as this always, to fear me and to keep all my commandments, that it might go well with them and with their children for ever! [30] Go and say to them, "Return to your tents." [31] But you, stand here by me, and I will tell you all the commandment and the statutes and the ordinances which you shall teach them, that they may do them in the land which I give them to possess.' [32] You shall be careful to do therefore as the LORD your God has commanded you; you shall not turn aside to the right hand or to the left. [33] You shall walk in all the way which the LORD your God has commanded you, that you may live, and that it may go well with you, and that

---

22–23: While the Decalogue was given directly to the people (vv. 4–5; compare 4.10–13), the rest of the laws were mediated to the people through Moses (v. 31; 4.14). **23–27:** 4.33; Ex.20.18–21. **31:** Moses is no mere legislator but is a teacher or expositor of God's will (1.5). Hence the *statutes and the ordinances* (chs. 12–26; compare Ex.20.23–23.19) are expressed in a sermonic appeal to do God's will in the concrete situations of life.

you may live long in the land which you shall possess.

6 "Now this is the commandment, the statutes and the ordinances which the LORD your God commanded me to teach you, that you may do them in the land to which you are going over, to possess it; [2] that you may fear the LORD your God, you and your son and your son's son, by keeping all his statutes and his commandments, which I command you, all the days of your life; and that your days may be prolonged. [3] Hear therefore, O Israel, and be careful to do them; that it may go well with you, and that you may multiply greatly, as the LORD, the God of your fathers, has promised you, in a land flowing with milk and honey.

4 "Hear, O Israel: The LORD our God is one LORD;*e* [5] and you shall love the LORD your God with all your heart, and with all your soul, and with all your might. [6] And these words which I command you this day shall be upon your heart; [7] and you shall teach them diligently to your children, and shall talk of them when you sit in your house, and when you walk by the way, and when you lie down, and when you rise. [8] And you shall bind them as a sign upon your hand, and they shall be as frontlets between your eyes. [9] And you shall write them on the doorposts of your house and on your gates.

10 "And when the LORD your God brings you into the land which he swore to your fathers, to Abraham, to Isaac, and to Jacob, to give you, with great and goodly cities, which you did not build, [11] and houses full of all good things, which you did not fill, and cisterns hewn out, which you did not hew, and vineyards and olive trees, which you did not plant, and when you eat and are full, [12] then take heed lest you forget the LORD, who brought you out of the land of Egypt, out of the house of bondage. [13] You shall fear the LORD your God; you shall serve him, and swear by his name. [14] You shall not go after other gods, of the gods of the peoples who are round about you; [15] for the LORD your God in the midst of you is a jealous God; lest the anger of the LORD your God be kindled against you, and he destroy you from off the face of the earth.

16 "You shall not put the LORD your God to the test, as you tested him at Massah. [17] You shall diligently keep the commandments of the LORD your God, and his testimonies, and his statutes, which he has commanded you. [18] And you shall do what is right and good in the sight of the LORD, that it may go well with you, and that you may go in and take possession of the good land which the LORD swore to give to your fathers [19] by thrusting out all your enemies from before you, as the LORD has promised.

20 "When your son asks you in time to come, 'What is the meaning of the testimonies and the statutes and the ordinances which the LORD our God has commanded you?' [21] then you

e Or *the* LORD *our God, the* LORD *is one*
Or *the* LORD *is our God, the* LORD *is one*
Or *the* LORD *is our God, the* LORD *alone*

6.1–25: The meaning of the first commandment. 1: In this chapter Moses deals with *the commandment;* in a later section he explains *the statutes* and *the ordinances* (see 5.31 n.). **3:** A characteristic Deuteronomic note: reverent obedience will result in divine blessings of long life, fruitfulness, and welfare (5.33; 6.18–19). Thus the promise made to the fathers will be fulfilled (Gen.12.1–7; Ex.3.16–17). *Milk and honey*, see Ex.3.8 n. **4–9:** In Jewish tradition these verses are known as the Shema, from the first word in the Hebrew ("shema'"), which means *"Hear."* **4–5:** The great commandment (Mk.12.29–30) is essentially a restatement of the first command-ment of the Decalogue in positive form. There are not many gods but *one LORD* who is sovereign and unique; thus Israel is to have only one loyalty. *Heart* (mind, will), *soul* (self, vital being), *might* express the idea of loving God (see 4.37 n.) with the full measure of one's devotion. **8–9:** Putting this law on the hand, forehead, and doorpost (compare Ex.13.9) signifies that it is to be *upon your heart* (v. 6), i.e. constantly thought about and acted upon. **10–19:** See ch. 8. **13:** The love of God is blended with fear, i.e. reverence before God's holy majesty (4.9–15). **15:** Divine jealousy is associated with divine wrath (4.24; Jos.24.19–20); both are expressions of the

shall say to your son, 'We were Pharaoh's slaves in Egypt; and the LORD brought us out of Egypt with a mighty hand; [22] and the LORD showed signs and wonders, great and grievous, against Egypt and against Pharaoh and all his household, before our eyes; [23] and he brought us out from there, that he might bring us in and give us the land which he swore to give to our fathers. [24] And the LORD commanded us to do all these statutes, to fear the LORD our God, for our good always, that he might preserve us alive, as at this day. [25] And it will be righteousness for us, if we are careful to do all this commandment before the LORD our God, as he has commanded us.'

7 "When the LORD your God brings you into the land which you are entering to take possession of it, and clears away many nations before you, the Hittites, the Gir'gashites, the Amorites, the Canaanites, the Per'izzites, the Hivites, and the Jeb'usites, seven nations greater and mightier than yourselves, [2] and when the LORD your God gives them over to you, and you defeat them; then you must utterly destroy them; you shall make no covenant with them, and show no mercy to them. [3] You shall not make marriages with them, giving your daughters to their sons or taking their daughters for your sons. [4] For they would turn away your sons from following me, to serve other gods; then the anger of the LORD would be kindled against you, and he would destroy you quickly. [5] But thus shall you deal with them: you shall break

down their altars, and dash in pieces their pillars, and hew down their Ashe'rim, and burn their graven images with fire.

6 "For you are a people holy to the LORD your God; the LORD your God has chosen you to be a people for his own possession, out of all the peoples that are on the face of the earth. [7] It was not because you were more in number than any other people that the LORD set his love upon you and chose you, for you were the fewest of all peoples; [8] but it is because the LORD loves you, and is keeping the oath which he swore to your fathers, that the LORD has brought you out with a mighty hand, and redeemed you from the house of bondage, from the hand of Pharaoh king of Egypt. [9] Know therefore that the LORD your God is God, the faithful God who keeps covenant and steadfast love with those who love him and keep his commandments, to a thousand generations, [10] and requites to their face those who hate him, by destroying them; he will not be slack with him who hates him, he will requite him to his face. [11] You shall therefore be careful to do the commandment, and the statutes, and the ordinances, which I command you this day.

12 "And because you hearken to these ordinances, and keep and do them, the LORD your God will keep with you the covenant and the steadfast love which he swore to your fathers to keep; [13] he will love you, bless you, and multiply you; he will also bless the fruit of your body and the fruit of

LORD's holiness which will not tolerate idolatry. **16:** See Ex.17.2–7; compare Mt.4.7. **20–25:** Compare v. 7; Ex.13.14–16. Children are to be taught the marvelous story of God's redeeming acts which is the background and basis of the law. **21–23:** See 26.5–10 n.

7.1–26: Life in Canaan. Having dealt with the heart of the law (the Decalogue and the great commandment; chs. 5–6), Moses now interprets what it means to be God's people in the new land. **1–5:** This holy war is based on the fear of the corrupting influence of Canaanite culture (v. 16; Ex.23.23–33; 34.11–16). **1:** On the pre-Israelite peoples, see Gen.10.15–20. **2:** *Utterly destroy*, see Jos.6.17 n. **5:** *Pillars, Asherim* (see Ex.34.13 n.). **6–16:** An uncompromising attitude toward the nations is required because Israel is *a people holy to the LORD* (Ex.19.5–6), i.e. a people separated for a special service to God (see Lev. 19.2 n.); therefore Israel is not to be a nation like other nations (Num.23.9; 1 Sam.8.4–22). **7–8:** The election of Israel is not based upon her greatness or goodness (9.4–6) but upon the LORD's gracious love and his faithfulness to the promise made to the patriarchs. **9–10:** Ex.34.6–7. *Covenant*, see Gen.17.2 n. *Steadfast love*, see Gen.24.12 n. **12–14:** The blessings of fertility do not come from the nature gods of

your ground, your grain and your wine and your oil, the increase of your cattle and the young of your flock, in the land which he swore to your fathers to give you. [14] You shall be blessed above all peoples; there shall not be male or female barren among you, or among your cattle. [15] And the LORD will take away from you all sickness; and none of the evil diseases of Egypt, which you knew, will he inflict upon you, but he will lay them upon all who hate you. [16] And you shall destroy all the peoples that the LORD your God will give over to you, your eye shall not pity them; neither shall you serve their gods, for that would be a snare to you.

17 "If you say in your heart, 'These nations are greater than I; how can I dispossess them?' [18] you shall not be afraid of them, but you shall remember what the LORD your God did to Pharaoh and to all Egypt, [19] the great trials which your eyes saw, the signs, the wonders, the mighty hand, and the outstretched arm, by which the LORD your God brought you out; so will the LORD your God do to all the peoples of whom you are afraid. [20] Moreover the LORD your God will send hornets among them, until those who are left and hide themselves from you are destroyed. [21] You shall not be in dread of them; for the LORD your God is in the midst of you, a great and terrible God. [22] The LORD your God will clear away these nations before you little by little; you may not make an end of them at once,[f] lest the wild beasts grow too numerous for you. [23] But the LORD your God will give them over to you, and throw them into great confusion, until they are de-

stroyed. [24] And he will give their kings into your hand, and you shall make their name perish from under heaven; not a man shall be able to stand against you, until you have destroyed them. [25] The graven images of their gods you shall burn with fire; you shall not covet the silver or the gold that is on them, or take it for yourselves, lest you be ensnared by it; for it is an abomination to the LORD your God. [26] And you shall not bring an abominable thing into your house, and become accursed like it; you shall utterly detest and abhor it; for it is an accursed thing.

8 "All the commandment which I command you this day you shall be careful to do, that you may live and multiply, and go in and possess the land which the LORD swore to give to your fathers. [2] And you shall remember all the way which the LORD your God has led you these forty years in the wilderness, that he might humble you, testing you to know what was in your heart, whether you would keep his commandments, or not. [3] And he humbled you and let you hunger and fed you with manna, which you did not know, nor did your fathers know; that he might make you know that man does not live by bread alone, but that man lives by everything that proceeds out of the mouth of the LORD. [4] Your clothing did not wear out upon you, and your foot did not swell, these forty years. [5] Know then in your heart that, as a man disciplines his son, the LORD your God disciplines you. [6] So you shall keep the commandments of the LORD your God, by walking in his ways and by fearing him. [7] For the

f Or *quickly*

Canaan but are bestowed by Israel's God, the LORD of history (Hos. ch. 2). **15:** *Evil diseases*, a reference to the plagues of Egypt. **17–26:** Israel should not fear mighty nations, for, according to the Israelite concept of holy war, *the LORD your God is in the midst of you* (20.1–4). These verses echo ideas found in Ex.23.20–33. **20:** *Hornets*, see Ex.23.27–28 n.; Jos.24.12. **22:** Ex. 23.29–30.

8.1–20: The temptation to pride and self-sufficiency. Moses warns the people that success in Canaan will tempt them to forget the wilderness lesson of complete dependence upon God's mercies. **1–10:** An appeal to Israel's memory: in the wilderness God cared for his people daily (Ex.12.37–17.16; Num. chs. 11–14). **3:** *Manna*, see Ex. ch. 16; Num.11.7,8. **5:** Suffering is here interpreted as discipline, analogous to a father's correction of his son (Hos. ch. 11; Heb.12.3–

LORD your God is bringing you into a good land, a land of brooks of water, of fountains and springs, flowing forth in valleys and hills, [8] a land of wheat and barley, of vines and fig trees and pomegranates, a land of olive trees and honey, [9] a land in which you will eat bread without scarcity, in which you will lack nothing, a land whose stones are iron, and out of whose hills you can dig copper. [10] And you shall eat and be full, and you shall bless the LORD your God for the good land he has given you.

11 "Take heed lest you forget the LORD your God, by not keeping his commandments and his ordinances and his statutes, which I command you this day: [12] lest, when you have eaten and are full, and have built goodly houses and live in them, [13] and when your herds and flocks multiply, and your silver and gold is multiplied, and all that you have is multiplied, [14] then your heart be lifted up, and you forget the LORD your God, who brought you out of the land of Egypt, out of the house of bondage, [15] who led you through the great and terrible wilderness, with its fiery serpents and scorpions and thirsty ground where there was no water, who brought you water out of the flinty rock, [16] who fed you in the wilderness with manna which your fathers did not know, that he might humble you and test you, to do you good in the end. [17] Beware lest you say in your heart, 'My power and the might of my hand have gotten me this wealth.' [18] You shall remember the LORD your God, for it is he who gives you power to get wealth; that he may confirm his covenant which he swore to your fathers, as at this day. [19] And if you forget the LORD your God and go after other gods and serve them and

worship them, I solemnly warn you this day that you shall surely perish. [20] Like the nations that the LORD makes to perish before you, so shall you perish, because you would not obey the voice of the LORD your God.

9 "Hear, O Israel; you are to pass over the Jordan this day, to go in to dispossess nations greater and mightier than yourselves, cities great and fortified up to heaven, [2] a people great and tall, the sons of the Anakim, whom you know, and of whom you have heard it said, 'Who can stand before the sons of Anak?' [3] Know therefore this day that he who goes over before you as a devouring fire is the LORD your God; he will destroy them and subdue them before you; so you shall drive them out, and make them perish quickly, as the LORD has promised you.

4 "Do not say in your heart, after the LORD your God has thrust them out before you, 'It is because of my righteousness that the LORD has brought me in to possess this land'; whereas it is because of the wickedness of these nations that the LORD is driving them out before you. [5] Not because of your righteousness or the uprightness of your heart are you going in to possess their land; but because of the wickedness of these nations the LORD your God is driving them out from before you, and that he may confirm the word which the LORD swore to your fathers, to Abraham, to Isaac, and to Jacob.

6 "Know therefore, that the LORD your God is not giving you this good land to possess because of your righteousness; for you are a stubborn people. [7] Remember and do not forget how you provoked the LORD your God to wrath in the wilderness; from the day you came out of the land of Egypt,

---

11). The purpose of God is to humble Israel's pride and to test the quality of faith. **11–20:** The peril of prosperity. **15:** *Fiery serpents*, Num.21.6–9. *Water out of the flinty rock*, Num.20.2–13.

9.1–10.11: The temptation to self-righteousness. God does not give the land to his people as a reward for righteousness, for in the wilderness they proved to be a rebellious people. **2:** See Num.13.22 n. **4–5:** Victory will be given in the holy war because (negatively) Canaan has been corrupted by pagan religions and because (positively) the LORD is faithful to his promise. **6–24:** The historical record shows that Israel has been rebellious ever since the Exodus (Ezek.

until you came to this place, you have been rebellious against the LORD. [8] Even at Horeb you provoked the LORD to wrath, and the LORD was so angry with you that he was ready to destroy you. [9] When I went up the mountain to receive the tables of stone, the tables of the covenant which the LORD made with you, I remained on the mountain forty days and forty nights; I neither ate bread nor drank water. [10] And the LORD gave me the two tables of stone written with the finger of God; and on them were all the words which the LORD had spoken with you on the mountain out of the midst of the fire on the day of the assembly. [11] And at the end of forty days and forty nights the LORD gave me the two tables of stone, the tables of the covenant. [12] Then the LORD said to me, 'Arise, go down quickly from here; for your people whom you have brought from Egypt have acted corruptly; they have turned aside quickly out of the way which I commanded them; they have made themselves a molten image.'

13 "Furthermore the LORD said to me, 'I have seen this people, and behold, it is a stubborn people; [14] let me alone, that I may destroy them and blot out their name from under heaven; and I will make of you a nation mightier and greater than they.' [15] So I turned and came down from the mountain, and the mountain was burning with fire; and the two tables of the covenant were in my two hands. [16] And I looked, and behold, you had sinned against the LORD your God; you had made yourselves a molten calf; you had turned aside quickly from the way which the LORD had commanded you. [17] So I took hold of the two tables, and cast them out of my two hands, and broke them before your eyes. [18] Then I lay prostrate before the LORD as before, forty days and forty nights; I neither ate bread nor drank

water, because of all the sin which you had committed, in doing what was evil in the sight of the LORD, to provoke him to anger. [19] For I was afraid of the anger and hot displeasure which the LORD bore against you, so that he was ready to destroy you. But the LORD hearkened to me that time also. [20] And the LORD was so angry with Aaron that he was ready to destroy him; and I prayed for Aaron also at the same time. [21] Then I took the sinful thing, the calf which you had made, and burned it with fire and crushed it, grinding it very small, until it was as fine as dust; and I threw the dust of it into the brook that descended out of the mountain.

22 "At Tab'erah also, and at Massah, and at Kib'roth-hatta'avah, you provoked the LORD to wrath. [23] And when the LORD sent you from Ka'desh-bar'nea, saying, 'Go up and take possession of the land which I have given you,' then you rebelled against the commandment of the LORD your God, and did not believe him or obey his voice. [24] You have been rebellious against the LORD from the day that I knew you.

25 "So I lay prostrate before the LORD for these forty days and forty nights, because the LORD had said he would destroy you. [26] And I prayed to the LORD, 'O Lord GOD, destroy not thy people and thy heritage, whom thou hast redeemed through thy greatness, whom thou hast brought out of Egypt with a mighty hand. [27] Remember thy servants, Abraham, Isaac, and Jacob; do not regard the stubbornness of this people, or their wickedness, or their sin, [28] lest the land from which thou didst bring us say, "Because the LORD was not able to bring them into the land which he promised them, and because he hated them, he has brought them out to slay them in the wilderness." [29] For they are thy people and thy heritage, whom thou didst bring

20.5–8). **8–10**: Ex.24.12–18; 31.18. **11–21**: Ex. ch. 32. **22**: Num.11.1–3; Ex.17.1–7; and Num. 11.31–34. **23**: Num. chs. 13–14. **25–29**: A paraphrase of Ex.32.11–14. In Deuteronomy Moses is portrayed as the ideal prophet (34.10–12) who intercedes for the people and who bears their

out by thy great power and by thy outstretched arm.'

10 "At that time the Lord said to me, 'Hew two tables of stone like the first, and come up to me on the mountain, and make an ark of wood. [2] And I will write on the tables the words that were on the first tables which you broke, and you shall put them in the ark.' [3] So I made an ark of acacia wood, and hewed two tables of stone like the first, and went up the mountain with the two tables in my hand. [4] And he wrote on the tables, as at the first writing, the ten commandments[g] which the Lord had spoken to you on the mountain out of the midst of the fire on the day of the assembly; and the Lord gave them to me. [5] Then I turned and came down from the mountain, and put the tables in the ark which I had made; and there they are, as the Lord commanded me.

6 (The people of Israel journeyed from Be-er'oth Bene-ja'akan[h] to Mose'rah. There Aaron died, and there he was buried; and his son Elea'zar ministered as priest in his stead. [7] From there they journeyed to Gud'godah, and from Gud'godah to Jot'bathah, a land with brooks of water. [8] At that time the Lord set apart the tribe of Levi to carry the ark of the covenant of the Lord, to stand before the Lord to minister to him and to bless in his name, to this day. [9] Therefore Levi has no portion or inheritance with his brothers; the Lord is his inheritance, as the Lord your God said to him.)

10 "I stayed on the mountain, as at the first time, forty days and forty nights, and the Lord hearkened to me that time also; the Lord was unwilling to destroy you. [11] And the Lord said to me, 'Arise, go on your journey at the head of the people, that they may go in and possess the land, which I swore to their fathers to give them.'

12 "And now, Israel, what does the Lord your God require of you, but to fear the Lord your God, to walk in all his ways, to love him, to serve the Lord your God with all your heart and with all your soul, [13] and to keep the commandments and statutes of the Lord, which I command you this day for your good? [14] Behold, to the Lord your God belong heaven and the heaven of heavens, the earth with all that is in it; [15] yet the Lord set his heart in love upon your fathers and chose their descendants after them, you above all peoples, as at this day. [16] Circumcise therefore the foreskin of your heart, and be no longer stubborn. [17] For the Lord your God is God of gods and Lord of lords, the great, the mighty, and the terrible God, who is not partial and takes no bribe. [18] He executes justice for the fatherless and the widow, and loves the sojourner, giving him food and clothing. [19] Love the sojourner therefore; for you were sojourners in the land of Egypt. [20] You shall fear the Lord your God; you shall serve him and cleave to him, and by his name you shall swear. [21] He is your praise; he

g Heb *words*   h Or *the wells of the Bene-jaakan*

sins (1.37; compare Is. ch. 53). **10.1–11:** The second ascent of the mountain (Ex.34.1–4,27–28). **1–3:** These verses rest on an ancient tradition that Moses made the ark and put the stone tablets in it (1 Kg.8.9; see Ex.24.15–18 n.). **6–9:** An editorial insertion which in vv. 6–7 apparently quotes from a wilderness itinerary (compare Num.33.30–38). **6:** Num.20.22–29. **8:** Ex.32.25–59. The Levites' role is to bear the ark (Num.4.4–15), to *minister*, i.e. conduct the sacrificial services (Num. ch. 18), and to *bless* (Num.6.22–27).

10.12–11.32. What the Lord requires. This section is the climax and conclusion of the historical review found in ch. 8 and 9.1–10.11. **12:** God's gracious dealings form the background and presupposition of his requirements (compare Mic.6.1–8). **16:** *Circumcise the . . . heart* means to open the mind, to direct the will toward God (see Lev.26.41 n.). **17–18:** God's justice is disclosed in his impartiality and in his defense of the legally helpless. *The sojourner*, who resided within the covenant community without tribal status, was in danger of exploitation. **19:** Ex.22.21; 23.9; Lev.19.34. This verse implies the second great commandment of Lev.

is your God, who has done for you these great and terrible things which your eyes have seen. 22 Your fathers went down to Egypt seventy persons; and now the LORD your God has made you as the stars of heaven for multitude.

11 "You shall therefore love the LORD your God, and keep his charge, his statutes, his ordinances, and his commandments always. 2 And consider this day (since I am not speaking to your children who have not known or seen it), consider the discipline[i] of the LORD your God, his greatness, his mighty hand and his outstretched arm, 3 his signs and his deeds which he did in Egypt to Pharaoh the king of Egypt and to all his land; 4 and what he did to the army of Egypt, to their horses and to their chariots; how he made the water of the Red Sea overflow them as they pursued after you, and how the LORD has destroyed them to this day; 5 and what he did to you in the wilderness, until you came to this place; 6 and what he did to Dathan and Abi'ram the sons of Eli'ab, son of Reuben; how the earth opened its mouth and swallowed them up, with their households, their tents, and every living thing that followed them, in the midst of all Israel; 7 for your eyes have seen all the great work of the LORD which he did.

8 "You shall therefore keep all the commandment which I command you this day, that you may be strong, and go in and take possession of the land which you are going over to possess, 9 and that you may live long in the land which the LORD swore to your fathers to give to them and to their descendants, a land flowing with milk

and honey. 10 For the land which you are entering to take possession of it is not like the land of Egypt, from which you have come, where you sowed your seed and watered it with your feet, like a garden of vegetables; 11 but the land which you are going over to possess is a land of hills and valleys, which drinks water by the rain from heaven, 12 a land which the LORD your God cares for; the eyes of the LORD your God are always upon it, from the beginning of the year to the end of the year.

13 "And if you will obey my commandments which I command you this day, to love the LORD your God, and to serve him with all your heart and with all your soul, 14 he[j] will give the rain for your land in its season, the early rain and the later rain, that you may gather in your grain and your wine and your oil. 15 And he[j] will give grass in your fields for your cattle, and you shall eat and be full. 16 Take heed lest your heart be deceived, and you turn aside and serve other gods and worship them, 17 and the anger of the LORD be kindled against you, and he shut up the heavens, so that there be no rain, and the land yield no fruit, and you perish quickly off the good land which the LORD gives you.

18 "You shall therefore lay up these words of mine in your heart and in your soul; and you shall bind them as a sign upon your hand, and they shall be as frontlets between your eyes. 19 And you shall teach them to your children, talking of them when you are sitting in your house, and when you are walking by the way, and when you lie down,

i Or *instruction*　　*j* Sam Gk Vg: Heb *I*

19.17–18. **22:** *Seventy persons*, Ex.1.5. **11.1–26:** Loyalty to the covenant is the condition for life in Canaan. **2:** The words *this day* appear frequently in Deuteronomy to emphasize the contemporaneity of the covenant demands and promises (see 5.2–3 n.). *Discipline*, see 8.5 n. **6:** The address follows the early tradition of Num. ch. 16 concerning the revolt of Dathan and Abiram; note the silence about Korah's rebellion (Num.16.3–11). **10–12:** The Nile valley must be irrigated through human effort; Palestine, however, is dependent upon seasonal rainfall. This difference is mentioned to show Israel's dependence upon the LORD, who gives and withholds rain (Am.4.7–9). **14:** The *early rain* comes at the end of the summer drought (October-November); the *later rain* comes in the spring (March-April). **16–17:** See 7.12–14 n. **18–21:** 6.6–9. **24:** The territory is described in terms of the ideal limits of David's empire (see 1.7 n.).

and when you rise. [20] And you shall write them upon the doorposts of your house and upon your gates, [21] that your days and the days of your children may be multiplied in the land which the LORD swore to your fathers to give them, as long as the heavens are above the earth. [22] For if you will be careful to do all this commandment which I command you to do, loving the LORD your God, walking in all his ways, and cleaving to him, [23] then the LORD will drive out all these nations before you, and you will dispossess nations greater and mightier than yourselves. [24] Every place on which the sole of your foot treads shall be yours; your territory shall be from the wilderness and Lebanon and from the River, the river Euphra'tes, to the western sea. [25] No man shall be able to stand against you; the LORD your God will lay the fear of you and the dread of you upon all the land that you shall tread, as he promised you.

26 "Behold, I set before you this day a blessing and a curse: [27] the blessing, if you obey the commandments of the LORD your God, which I command you this day, [28] and the curse, if you do not obey the commandments of the LORD your God, but turn aside from the way which I command you this day, to go after other gods which you have not known. [29] And when the LORD your God brings you into the land which you are entering to take possession of it, you shall set the blessing on Mount Ger'izim and the curse on Mount Ebal. [30] Are they not beyond the Jordan, west of the road, toward the going down of the sun, in the land of the Canaanites who live in the Arabah, over against Gilgal, beside the oak^k of Moreh? [31] For you are to pass over the Jordan to go in to take possession of the land which the LORD your God gives you; and when you possess it and live in it, [32] you shall be careful to do all the statutes and the ordinances which I set before you this day.

12 "These are the statutes and ordinances which you shall be careful to do in the land which the LORD, the God of your fathers, has given you to possess, all the days that you live upon the earth. [2] You shall surely destroy all the places where the nations whom you shall dispossess served their gods, upon the high mountains and upon the hills and under every green tree; [3] you shall tear down their altars, and dash in pieces their pillars, and burn their Ashe'rim with fire; you shall hew down the graven images of their gods, and destroy their name out of that place. [4] You shall not do so to the LORD your God. [5] But you shall seek the place which the LORD your God will choose out of all your tribes to put his name and make his habitation there; thither you shall go, [6] and thither you shall bring your burnt offerings and your sacrifices, your tithes

k Gk Syr: See Gen 12.6. Heb *oaks* or *terebinths*

The western sea, the Mediterranean. **26–32:** The two ways (see ch. 28; 30.15–20). **26:** *Blessing . . . curse*, an echo of an ancient ceremony of covenant renewal inaugurated at Shechem (v. 29; see ch. 27). The people stand in a time of solemn decision, facing the alternatives of divine blessing or divine judgment. **29–30:** See ch. 27. *The oak of Moreh* was near Shechem (see Gen.12.6 n.).

12.1–31: The centralization of worship. Israel is to worship the LORD at the central sanctuary of his choice and to make sacrifices only at this place. **1:** Here begins the exposition of *the statutes and the ordinances* (see 5.31 n.) found in chs. 12–26. **3:** See Ex.34.13 n. **4:** The following law concerning the centralization of worship is intended to guard Israel from the paganism which flourished in local shrines (vv. 29–31). **5–7:** During the period of the tribal confederacy pilgrimages were made to Shiloh (Jos.18.1; 1 Sam.1.3–28), and under the leadership of David Jerusalem became the central sanctuary of Israel (2 Sam. ch. 6). During this whole period pilgrimages to the sanctuary did not preclude sacrificing at any altar in the land (Gen.12.7; 1 Sam.10.8; 1 Kg.3.2,4). The present stringent law, providing for only one place for sacrificial worship, was the basis of the great reform carried out by King Josiah (2 Kg. chs. 22–23). **5:** Although the LORD's dwelling place is in heaven (1 Kg.8.27–30), his *name* (see Gen.32.27 n.),

and the offering that you present, your votive offerings, your freewill offerings, and the firstlings of your herd and of your flock; ⁷ and there you shall eat before the LORD your God, and you shall rejoice, you and your households, in all that you undertake, in which the LORD your God has blessed you. ⁸ You shall not do according to all that we are doing here this day, every man doing whatever is right in his own eyes; ⁹ for you have not as yet come to the rest and to the inheritance which the LORD your God gives you. ¹⁰ But when you go over the Jordan, and live in the land which the LORD your God gives you to inherit, and when he gives you rest from all your enemies round about, so that you live in safety, ¹¹ then to the place which the LORD your God will choose, to make his name dwell there, thither you shall bring all that I command you: your burnt offerings and your sacrifices, your tithes and the offering that you present, and all your votive offerings which you vow to the LORD. ¹² And you shall rejoice before the LORD your God, you and your sons and your daughters, your menservants and your maidservants, and the Levite that is within your towns, since he has no portion or inheritance with you. ¹³ Take heed that you do not offer your burnt offerings at every place that you see; ¹⁴ but at the place which the LORD will choose in one of your tribes, there you shall offer your burnt offerings, and there you shall do all that I am commanding you.

15 "However, you may slaughter and eat flesh within any of your towns, as much as you desire, according to the blessing of the LORD your God which he has given you; the unclean and the clean may eat of it, as of the gazelle and as of the hart. ¹⁶ Only you shall not eat the blood; you shall pour it out upon the earth like water. ¹⁷ You may not eat within your towns the tithe of your grain or of your wine or of your oil, or the firstlings of your herd or of your flock, or any of your votive offerings which you vow, or your freewill offerings, or the offering that you present; ¹⁸ but you shall eat them before the LORD your God in the place which the LORD your God will choose, you and your son and your daughter, your manservant and your maidservant, and the Levite who is within your towns; and you shall rejoice before the LORD your God in all that you undertake. ¹⁹ Take heed that you do not forsake the Levite as long as you live in your land.

20 "When the LORD your God enlarges your territory, as he has promised you, and you say, 'I will eat flesh,' because you crave flesh, you may eat as much flesh as you desire. ²¹ If the place which the LORD your God will choose to put his name there is too far from you, then you may kill any of your herd or your flock, which the LORD has given you, as I have commanded you; and you may eat within your towns as much as you desire. ²² Just as the gazelle or the hart is eaten, so you may eat of it; the unclean and the clean alike may eat of it. ²³ Only be sure that you do not eat the blood; for the blood is the life, and you shall not eat the life with the flesh.

---

in which his person or nature is manifest, represents him in the sanctuary, and in this sense he makes his *habitation* there (v. 11). **6:** For the types of sacrifice, see Lev. chs. 1–7. *Votive offerings*, Lev. ch. 27; Num. ch. 30. **7:** *Eat before the LORD* refers to certain offerings which must be eaten at the sanctuary, such as the tithe (14.22–28) or the peace offering (Lev. ch. 3). **12:** *The Levite*, see 18.1 n. **15–28:** Now that sacrifice is made only at the central sanctuary, a distinction is drawn between sacrifice and slaughter of animals for food, thus modifying earlier legislation (Lev.17.1–9). **15–16:** When eating slaughtered meat in a town, it is not necessary to observe the laws of ceremonial cleanness (Lev.7.19–21), for slaughtered meat may be considered in the same category as game (e.g. gazelle or deer). However, the ancient prohibition against eating blood must be maintained (vv. 23–24; see Gen.9.3–4; Lev.17.10–11). **17–18:** *Holy things* (v. 26) which belong by right, or by dedication, to the LORD must be eaten at the central

24 You shall not eat it; you shall pour it out upon the earth like water. 25 You shall not eat it; that all may go well with you and with your children after you, when you do what is right in the sight of the LORD. 26 But the holy things which are due from you, and your votive offerings, you shall take, and you shall go to the place which the LORD will choose, 27 and offer your burnt offerings, the flesh and the blood, on the altar of the LORD your God; the blood of your sacrifices shall be poured out on the altar of the LORD your God, but the flesh you may eat. 28 Be careful to heed all these words which I command you, that it may go well with you and with your children after you for ever, when you do what is good and right in the sight of the LORD your God.

29 "When the LORD your God cuts off before you the nations whom you go in to dispossess, and you dispossess them and dwell in their land, 30 take heed that you be not ensnared to follow them, after they have been destroyed before you, and that you do not inquire about their gods, saying, 'How did these nations serve their gods?–that I also may do likewise.' 31 You shall not do so to the LORD your God; for every abominable thing which the LORD hates they have done for their gods; for they even burn their sons and their daughters in the fire to their gods.

32*l* "Everything that I command you you shall be careful to do; you shall not add to it or take from it.

13 "If a prophet arises among you, or a dreamer of dreams, and gives you a sign or a wonder, 2 and the

sign or wonder which he tells you comes to pass, and if he says, 'Let us go after other gods,' which you have not known, 'and let us serve them,' 3 you shall not listen to the words of that prophet or to that dreamer of dreams; for the LORD your God is testing you, to know whether you love the LORD your God with all your heart and with all your soul. 4 You shall walk after the LORD your God and fear him, and keep his commandments and obey his voice, and you shall serve him and cleave to him. 5 But that prophet or that dreamer of dreams shall be put to death, because he has taught rebellion against the LORD your God, who brought you out of the land of Egypt and redeemed you out of the house of bondage, to make you leave the way in which the LORD your God commanded you to walk. So you shall purge the evil from the midst of you.

6 "If your brother, the son of your mother, or your son, or your daughter, or the wife of your bosom, or your friend who is as your own soul, entices you secretly, saying, 'Let us go and serve other gods,' which neither you nor your fathers have known, 7 some of the gods of the peoples that are round about you, whether near you or far off from you, from the one end of the earth to the other, 8 you shall not yield to him or listen to him, nor shall your eye pity him, nor shall you spare him, nor shall you conceal him; 9 but you shall kill him; your hand shall be first against him to put him to death, and afterwards the hand of all the people. 10 You shall stone him to death

l Ch 13.1 in Heb

---

sanctuary. **31:** *Every abominable thing*, e.g. sacred prostitution (23.17–18) and ordeal by fire (see 18.10 n.).

12.32–13.18: Warning against idolatry. Subversives who entice their fellow men into the worship of other gods must be eliminated from the covenant community. **13.1–5:** The false prophet (Jer.23.9–32; Ezek. ch. 13). **1:** Dreams were regarded as a medium of divine communication to a prophet (Num.12.6; 22.20; 1 Sam.3.15; 28.6; Jer.23.25). This law makes it clear that a *sign or wonder* (see Ex.3.11–12 n.) is not in itself a proof that God has spoken, for God may give false prophets power to perform wonders in order to test the people's faith (compare 8.2). A miracle is not significant unless it prompts faith in the God whom Israel has *known* (vv. 6,13) in her historical experience. **5:** The punishment is severe because idolatry contaminates the health or holiness of the community. **6–11:** The same punishment applies to close friends or

with stones, because he sought to draw you away from the LORD your God, who brought you out of the land of Egypt, out of the house of bondage. [11] And all Israel shall hear, and fear, and never again do any such wickedness as this among you.

12 "If you hear in one of your cities, which the LORD your God gives you to dwell there, [13] that certain base fellows have gone out among you and have drawn away the inhabitants of the city, saying, 'Let us go and serve other gods,' which you have not known, [14] then you shall inquire and make search and ask diligently; and behold, if it be true and certain that such an abominable thing has been done among you, [15] you shall surely put the inhabitants of that city to the sword, destroying it utterly, all who are in it and its cattle, with the edge of the sword. [16] You shall gather all its spoil into the midst of its open square, and burn the city and all its spoil with fire, as a whole burnt offering to the LORD your God; it shall be a heap for ever, it shall not be built again. [17] None of the devoted things shall cleave to your hand; that the LORD may turn from the fierceness of his anger, and show you mercy, and have compassion on you, and multiply you, as he swore to your fathers, [18] if you obey the voice of the LORD your God, keeping all his commandments which I command you this day, and doing what is right in the sight of the LORD your God.

14 "You are the sons of the LORD your God; you shall not cut yourselves or make any baldness on your foreheads for the dead. [2] For you are a people holy to the LORD your God, and the LORD has chosen you to be a people for his own possession, out of all the peoples that are on the face of the earth.

3 "You shall not eat any abominable thing. [4] These are the animals you may eat: the ox, the sheep, the goat, [5] the hart, the gazelle, the roebuck, the wild goat, the ibex, the antelope, and the mountain-sheep. [6] Every animal that parts the hoof and has the hoof cloven in two, and chews the cud, among the animals, you may eat. [7] Yet of those that chew the cud or have the hoof cloven you shall not eat these: the camel, the hare, and the rock badger, because they chew the cud but do not part the hoof, are unclean for you. [8] And the swine, because it parts the hoof but does not chew the cud, is unclean for you. Their flesh you shall not eat, and their carcasses you shall not touch.

9 "Of all that are in the waters you may eat these: whatever has fins and scales you may eat. [10] And whatever does not have fins and scales you shall not eat; it is unclean for you.

11 "You may eat all clean birds. [12] But these are the ones which you shall not eat: the eagle, the vulture, the osprey, [13] the buzzard, the kite, after their kinds; [14] every raven after its kind; [15] the ostrich, the nighthawk, the sea gull, the hawk, after their kinds; [16] the little owl and the great owl, the water hen [17] and the pelican, the carrion vulture and the cormorant, [18] the stork, the heron, after their kinds; the hoopoe and the bat. [19] And all winged insects are unclean for you; they shall not be eaten. [20] All clean winged things you may eat.

21 "You shall not eat anything that

---

family members who entice one into idolatry. **10:** Stoning is prescribed because this is a communal mode of purging the evil which threatens the community (17.2–7). **12–18:** When a city has turned to idolatry, it must be put under the sacrificial ban and consumed as *a whole burnt offering*. **17:** *The devoted things* (see Lev.27.21 n., 28–29), such as people, cattle, spoil, are holy, for they belong to the LORD's sacrifice (20.10–18).

14.1–15.23: The conduct of a holy people (see Lev.19.2 n.). In this section old laws are reinterpreted to enforce the contemporaneity of God's covenant demands. **1:** Prohibition against pagan mourning customs (see Lev.19.28; 21.5). **3–21:** Clean animals that are permitted for food (Lev.11.2–23). **21:** On the first law cited, see Ex.22.31 n. and the regulation for slaughter

dies of itself; you may give it to the alien who is within your towns, that he may eat it, or you may sell it to a foreigner; for you are a people holy to the LORD your God.

"You shall not boil a kid in its mother's milk.

22 "You shall tithe all the yield of your seed, which comes forth from the field year by year. ²³ And before the LORD your God, in the place which he will choose, to make his name dwell there, you shall eat the tithe of your grain, of your wine, and of your oil, and the firstlings of your herd and flock; that you may learn to fear the LORD your God always. ²⁴ And if the way is too long for you, so that you are not able to bring the tithe, when the LORD your God blesses you, because the place is too far from you, which the LORD your God chooses, to set his name there, ²⁵ then you shall turn it into money, and bind up the money in your hand, and go to the place which the LORD your God chooses, ²⁶ and spend the money for whatever you desire, oxen, or sheep, or wine or strong drink, whatever your appetite craves; and you shall eat there before the LORD your God and rejoice, you and your household. ²⁷ And you shall not forsake the Levite who is within your towns, for he has no portion or inheritance with you.

28 "At the end of every three years you shall bring forth all the tithe of your produce in the same year, and lay it up within your towns; ²⁹ and the Levite, because he has no portion or inheritance with you, and the sojourner, the fatherless, and the widow, who are within your towns, shall come and eat and be filled; that the LORD your God may bless you in all the work of your hands that you do.

15 "At the end of every seven years you shall grant a release. ² And this is the manner of the release: every creditor shall release what he has lent to his neighbor; he shall not exact it of his neighbor, his brother, because the LORD'S release has been proclaimed. ³ Of a foreigner you may exact it; but whatever of yours is with your brother your hand shall release. ⁴ But there will be no poor among you (for the LORD will bless you in the land which the LORD your God gives you for an inheritance to possess), ⁵ if only you will obey the voice of the LORD your God, being careful to do all this commandment which I command you this day. ⁶ For the LORD your God will bless you, as he promised you, and you shall lend to many nations, but you shall not borrow; and you shall rule over many nations, but they shall not rule over you.

7 "If there is among you a poor man, one of your brethren, in any of your towns within your land which the LORD your God gives you, you shall not harden your heart or shut your hand against your poor brother, ⁸ but you shall open your hand to him, and lend him sufficient for his need, whatever it may be. ⁹ Take heed lest there be a base thought in your heart, and you say, 'The seventh year, the year of release is near,' and your eye be hostile to your poor brother, and you give him nothing, and he cry to the LORD against you, and it be sin in you. ¹⁰ You shall

in Dt.12.15–28. On the second law, see Ex.23.18–19 n. **22–29:** Israel is steward of the land which belongs to the LORD; therefore, tithes of produce must be offered annually at the harvest festival (16.9–12). **24–26:** This is a special Deuteronomic provision, arising out of centralization of worship. **27–29:** It was impractical for all Levites to serve at the central sanctuary; therefore special consideration was to be given to the town Levites (see 18.1 n.; 26.12–15). This law modifies the previous provision that an annual tithe be brought to the sanctuary for support of the Levites (Num.18.21–32). **15.1–11:** The year of release. In Ex.23.10–11 the sabbatical year is for the sake of the poor; in Lev.25.1–7 it is a fallow year for the sake of the land. Here the sabbatical year, like the jubilee year (Lev.25.8–55), is a time for remission of debts. **3:** The law does not apply to a *foreigner* who visits for business (v. 6). A *brother* or *neighbor* (v. 2) is a fellow member of the covenant community (see Lev.19.17–18 n.). **11:** If God's will were fully

give to him freely, and your heart shall not be grudging when you give to him; because for this the LORD your God will bless you in all your work and in all that you undertake. ¹¹ For the poor will never cease out of the land; therefore I command you, You shall open wide your hand to your brother, to the needy and to the poor, in the land.

12 "If your brother, a Hebrew man, or a Hebrew woman, is sold to you, he shall serve you six years, and in the seventh year you shall let him go free from you. ¹³ And when you let him go free from you, you shall not let him go empty-handed; ¹⁴ you shall furnish him liberally out of your flock, out of your threshing floor, and out of your wine press; as the LORD your God has blessed you, you shall give to him. ¹⁵ You shall remember that you were a slave in the land of Egypt, and the LORD your God redeemed you; therefore I command you this today. ¹⁶ But if he says to you, 'I will not go out from you,' because he loves you and your household, since he fares well with you, ¹⁷ then you shall take an awl, and thrust it through his ear into the door, and he shall be your bondman for ever. And to your bondwoman you shall do likewise. ¹⁸ It shall not seem hard to you, when you let him go free from you; for at half the cost of a hired servant he has served you six years. So the LORD your God will bless you in all that you do.

19 "All the firstling males that are born of your herd and flock you shall consecrate to the LORD your God; you shall do no work with the firstling of your herd, nor shear the firstling of your flock. ²⁰ You shall eat it, you and your household, before the LORD your God year by year at the place which the LORD will choose. ²¹ But if it has any blemish, if it is lame or blind, or has any serious blemish whatever, you shall not sacrifice it to the LORD your God. ²² You shall eat it within your towns; the unclean and the clean alike may eat it, as though it were a gazelle or a hart. ²³ Only you shall not eat its blood; you shall pour it out on the ground like water.

16 "Observe the month of Abib, and keep the passover to the LORD your God; for in the month of Abib the LORD your God brought you out of Egypt by night. ² And you shall offer the passover sacrifice to the LORD your God, from the flock or the herd, at the place which the LORD will choose, to make his name dwell there. ³ You shall eat no leavened bread with it; seven days you shall eat it with unleavened bread, the bread of affliction –for you came out of the land of Egypt in hurried flight–that all the days of your life you may remember the day when you came out of the land of Egypt. ⁴ No leaven shall be seen with you in all your territory for seven days; nor shall any of the flesh which you sacrifice on the evening of the first day remain all night until morning. ⁵ You may not offer the passover sacrifice within any of your towns which the LORD your God gives you; ⁶ but at the place which the LORD your God will choose, to make his name dwell in it,

---

obeyed, there would be no poverty (vv. 3–5); but until that time comes *the poor will never cease* (compare Jn.12.8) and the law must remain in force. **12–18:** The law on Hebrew servitude (Ex.21.2–11). **13–15:** An expansion, showing Deuteronomy's ethical fervor (compare Lev. 25.42–43). **17:** Unlike the older law, male and female slaves are put on the same level. **18:** Obeying the law should be easy (compare Jer.34.8–16; Neh.5.5). **19–23:** The old law on the sacrifice of firstlings (see Ex.13.2 n.) is adapted to the requirement of the central sanctuary (12.15–28).

16.1–17: A festal calendar (Ex.23.14–17; 34.18–24; Lev. ch. 23; Num. chs. 28–29). **1–8:** The feast of the passover and unleavened bread (Ex.12.1–27; 13.3–10; 23.15,18; 34.18,25; Lev. 23.5–8; Num.28.16–25). On the relation between these festivals, see Ex.12.14–20 n. Here the passover must be eaten at the central sanctuary, rather than in the towns according to previous custom. **1:** *Abib*, see Ex.13.4 n. **9–12:** The feast of weeks (Ex.23.16; 34.22; Lev.23.15–16; Num.

there you shall offer the passover sacrifice, in the evening at the going down of the sun, at the time you came out of Egypt. ⁷ And you shall boil it and eat it at the place which the Lord your God will choose; and in the morning you shall turn and go to your tents. ⁸ For six days you shall eat unleavened bread; and on the seventh day there shall be a solemn assembly to the Lord your God; you shall do no work on it.

9 "You shall count seven weeks; begin to count the seven weeks from the time you first put the sickle to the standing grain. ¹⁰ Then you shall keep the feast of weeks to the Lord your God with the tribute of a freewill offering from your hand, which you shall give as the Lord your God blesses you; ¹¹ and you shall rejoice before the Lord your God, you and your son and your daughter, your manservant and your maidservant, the Levite who is within your towns, the sojourner, the fatherless, and the widow who are among you, at the place which the Lord your God will choose, to make his name dwell there. ¹² You shall remember that you were a slave in Egypt; and you shall be careful to observe these statutes.

13 "You shall keep the feast of booths seven days, when you make your ingathering from your threshing floor and your wine press; ¹⁴ you shall rejoice in your feast, you and your son and your daughter, your manservant and your maidservant, the Levite, the sojourner, the fatherless, and the widow who are within your towns. ¹⁵ For seven days you shall keep the feast to the Lord your God at the place which the Lord will choose; because

the Lord your God will bless you in all your produce and in all the work of your hands, so that you will be altogether joyful.

16 "Three times a year all your males shall appear before the Lord your God at the place which he will choose: at the feast of unleavened bread, at the feast of weeks, and at the feast of booths. They shall not appear before the Lord empty-handed; ¹⁷ every man shall give as he is able, according to the blessing of the Lord your God which he has given you.

18 "You shall appoint judges and officers in all your towns which the Lord your God gives you, according to your tribes; and they shall judge the people with righteous judgment. ¹⁹ You shall not pervert justice; you shall not show partiality; and you shall not take a bribe, for a bribe blinds the eyes of the wise and subverts the cause of the righteous. ²⁰ Justice, and only justice, you shall follow, that you may live and inherit the land which the Lord your God gives you.

21 "You shall not plant any tree as an Ashe′rah beside the altar of the Lord your God which you shall make, ²² And you shall not set up a pillar, which the Lord your God hates.

17 "You shall not sacrifice to the Lord your God an ox or a sheep in which is a blemish, any defect whatever; for that is an abomination to the Lord your God.

2 "If there is found among you, within any of your towns which the Lord your God gives you, a man or woman who does what is evil in the sight of the Lord your God, in transgressing his covenant, ³ and has gone and served other gods and worshiped

28.26), a harvest festival held in June (in the New Testament Pentecost, Acts 2.1; 20.16; 1 Cor. 16.8). **13–15:** The feast of booths, in King James Version "tabernacles" (Ex.23.16; 34.22; Lev.23.33–43), the autumn thanksgiving festival. **16–17:** Summary of the pilgrimage festivals (Ex.23.17; 34.23).
16.18–17.20: Laws dealing with justice and religion. 18–20: The administration of justice. This law reflects a developed society in which responsibility for legal administration was delegated to appointed officials in every town. **18:** *Judges and officers,* 1.13–17. **19:** Ex.23.6–8. **21–22:** Prohibition against Canaanite cultic installations (7.5; see Ex.34.13 n.). **17.1:** An unblemished sacrifice is frequently required in cultic laws (15.21; Lev.22.17–25). **2–7:** The

them, or the sun or the moon or any of the host of heaven, which I have forbidden, ⁴ and it is told you and you hear of it; then you shall inquire diligently, and if it is true and certain that such an abominable thing has been done in Israel, ⁵ then you shall bring forth to your gates that man or woman who has done this evil thing, and you shall stone that man or woman to death with stones. ⁶ On the evidence of two witnesses or of three witnesses he that is to die shall be put to death; a person shall not be put to death on the evidence of one witness. ⁷ The hand of the witnesses shall be first against him to put him to death, and afterward the hand of all the people. So you shall purge the evil from the midst of you.

8 "If any case arises requiring decision between one kind of homicide and another, one kind of legal right and another, or one kind of assault and another, any case within your towns which is too difficult for you, then you shall arise and go up to the place which the LORD your God will choose, ⁹ and coming to the Levitical priests, and to the judge who is in office in those days, you shall consult them, and they shall declare to you the decision. ¹⁰ Then you shall do according to what they declare to you from that place which the LORD will choose; and you shall be careful to do according to all that they direct you; ¹¹ according to the instructions which they give you, and according to the decision which they pronounce to you, you shall do; you shall not turn aside from the verdict which they declare to you, either to the right hand or to the left. ¹² The man who acts presumptuously, by not obeying the priest who stands to minister there before the LORD your God, or the judge, that man shall die; so you shall purge the evil from Israel. ¹³ And all the people shall hear, and fear, and not act presumptuously again.

14 "When you come to the land which the LORD your God gives you, and you possess it and dwell in it, and then say, 'I will set a king over me, like all the nations that are round about me'; ¹⁵ you may indeed set as king over you him whom the LORD your God will choose. One from among your brethren you shall set as king over you; you may not put a foreigner over you, who is not your brother. ¹⁶ Only he must not multiply horses for himself, or cause the people to return to Egypt in order to multiply horses, since the LORD has said to you, 'You shall never return that way again.' ¹⁷ And he shall not multiply wives for himself, lest his heart turn away; nor shall he greatly multiply for himself silver and gold.

18 "And when he sits on the throne of his kingdom, he shall write for himself in a book a copy of this law, from that which is in charge of the Levitical priests; ¹⁹ and it shall be with him, and he shall read in it all the days of his life, that he may learn to fear the LORD his God, by keeping all the words of this law and these statutes, and doing

---

penalty for idolatry is the same as for enticement to idolatry (ch. 13). **3:** See 4.19. **6:** 19.15; Num.35.30. **8–13:** A supreme tribunal is to adjudicate cases which are too difficult for local judges (16.18). Older legislation had dealt with premeditated and unpremeditated *homicide* (Ex.21.12–14), bodily *assaults* (Ex.21.18–27), and other legal rights, and had provided that cases of doubt should be brought "before God" (Ex.22.9; compare 18.15–16; 33.7). Here the old legal practice is adapted to the law of the central sanctuary. **9:** *The Levitical priests* are those who function in the sanctuary in distinction from town Levites (see 18.1 n.). *The judge,* perhaps the lay chief justice (19.17). One of the priests (see v. 12) was the ecclesiastical chief justice. The tribunal set up by Jehoshaphat was composed of lay and clerical judges (2 Chr.19.5–11). **14–20:** Restrictions upon the Israelite king. **14–15:** In the view of the Israelite tribal confederacy, presumably formed at Shechem (Jos. ch. 24), kingship was alien to the theocracy (Jg.8.22–23). Israel's monarchy represented an attempt to be *like all the nations,* whose kings claimed absolute power (1 Sam.8.4–22). **16–18:** These verses allude to "the ways of the king" (compare 1 Sam.8.10–18) exemplified by Solomon, e.g. his trade in horses (1 Kg.10.26–29). **18:** *This law,* i.e. the law of Deuteronomy, which was kept in the custody of Levitical priests at the sanc-

them; ²⁰ that his heart may not be lifted up above his brethren, and that he may not turn aside from the commandment, either to the right hand or to the left; so that he may continue long in his kingdom, he and his children, in Israel.

18 "The Levitical priests, that is, all the tribe of Levi, shall have no portion or inheritance with Israel; they shall eat the offerings by fire to the LORD, and his rightful dues. ² They shall have no inheritance among their brethren; the LORD is their inheritance, as he promised them. ³ And this shall be the priests' due from the people, from those offering a sacrifice, whether it be ox or sheep: they shall give to the priest the shoulder and the two cheeks and the stomach. ⁴ The first fruits of your grain, of your wine and of your oil, and the first of the fleece of your sheep, you shall give him. ⁵ For the LORD your God has chosen him out of all your tribes, to stand and minister in the name of the LORD, him and his sons for ever.

6 "And if a Levite comes from any of your towns out of all Israel, where he lives–and he may come when he desires–to the place which the LORD will choose, ⁷ then he may minister in the name of the LORD his God, like all his fellow-Levites who stand to minister there before the LORD. ⁸ They shall have equal portions to eat, besides what

he receives from the sale of his patrimony.ᵐ

9 "When you come into the land which the LORD your God gives you, you shall not learn to follow the abominable practices of those nations. ¹⁰ There shall not be found among you any one who burns his son or his daughter as an offering,ⁿ any one who practices divination, a soothsayer, or an augur, or a sorcerer, ¹¹ or a charmer, or a medium, or a wizard, or a necromancer. ¹² For whoever does these things is an abomination to the LORD; and because of these abominable practices the LORD your God is driving them out before you. ¹³ You shall be blameless before the LORD your God. ¹⁴ For these nations, which you are about to dispossess, give heed to soothsayers and to diviners; but as for you, the LORD your God has not allowed you so to do.

15 "The LORD your God will raise up for you a prophet like me from among you, from your brethren–him you shall heed– ¹⁶ just as you desired of the LORD your God at Horeb on the day of the assembly, when you said, 'Let me not hear again the voice of the LORD my God, or see this great fire any more, lest I die.' ¹⁷ And the LORD said to me, 'They have rightly said all that they have spoken. ¹⁸ I will raise

m Heb obscure
n Heb *makes his son or his daughter pass through the fire*

---

tuary (2 Kg.22.8). **19–20:** The king, elected from among his brethren (v. 15), is subject to God's law, like any other citizen. Compare the admonitions to the "prince" (the future kings of the restored line of David) in Ezek.45.7–9.

18.1–22: The proper worship of God. 1–8: Rights of the Levitical priests. **1:** This law applies to *all the tribe of Levi* (see Ex.28.1–5 n.), i.e. Levites who officiated at the central sanctuary ("the priests, the sons of Levi," 21.5) and those who functioned as teaching priests in the towns (12.18–19; 14.27,29). Thus Deuteronomy adds a further qualification to priestly legislation which had distinguished only between Aaronic Levites who officiated at the altar and other Levites who were assistants in the sanctuary (see Num. ch. 18). **2:** As a landless tribe, Levites are entitled to support from the sacrifices, i.e. to receive portions of the *offerings by fire* (see Lev.2.2–3 n.) and of the first fruits. **3–4:** Lev.6.14–18; 7.28–36; Num.18.8–19. **6–8:** Town Levites, whose former role was changed by the centralization of worship, may take part in the services at the central sanctuary. This provision, however, proved impracticable in Josiah's time (2 Kg.23.8–9). **9–14:** Prohibition against pagan superstition and magic. **10:** The meaning of the first practice is uncertain but probably refers to an ordeal of passing through the fire (see note *n*) as a test of devotion to Molech, the god of Ammon (12.31). This pagan rite is frequently mentioned in the Old Testament(Lev. 18.21; 2 Kg.16.3; 21.6; Jer.7.31; 19.5; 32.35, etc.). **15–22:** Israelites are not to resort to pagan divination (see the foregoing law), for the LORD

up for them a prophet like you from among their brethren; and I will put my words in his mouth, and he shall speak to them all that I command him. ¹⁹ And whoever will not give heed to my words which he shall speak in my name, I myself will require it of him. ²⁰ But the prophet who presumes to speak a word in my name which I have not commanded him to speak, or who speaks in the name of other gods, that same prophet shall die.' ²¹ And if you say in your heart, 'How may we know the word which the LORD has not spoken?'– ²² when a prophet speaks in the name of the LORD, if the word does not come to pass or come true, that is a word which the LORD has not spoken; the prophet has spoken it presumptuously, you need not be afraid of him.

19 "When the LORD your God cuts off the nations whose land the LORD your God gives you, and you dispossess them and dwell in their cities and in their houses, ² you shall set apart three cities for you in the land which the LORD your God gives you to possess. ³ You shall prepare the roads, and divide into three parts the area of the land which the LORD your God gives you as a possession, so that any manslayer can flee to them.

4 "This is the provision for the manslayer, who by fleeing there may save his life. If any one kills his neighbor unintentionally without having been at enmity with him in time past– ⁵ as when a man goes into the forest with his neighbor to cut wood, and his hand swings the axe to cut down a tree, and the head slips from the handle and strikes his neighbor so that he dies–

he may flee to one of these cities and save his life; ⁶ lest the avenger of blood in hot anger pursue the manslayer and overtake him, because the way is long, and wound him mortally, though the man did not deserve to die, since he was not at enmity with his neighbor in time past. ⁷ Therefore I command you, You shall set apart three cities. ⁸ And if the LORD your God enlarges your border, as he has sworn to your fathers, and gives you all the land which he promised to give to your fathers– ⁹ provided you are careful to keep all this commandment, which I command you this day, by loving the LORD your God and by walking ever in his ways–then you shall add three other cities to these three, ¹⁰ lest innocent blood be shed in your land which the LORD your God gives you for an inheritance, and so the guilt of bloodshed be upon you.

11 "But if any man hates his neighbor, and lies in wait for him, and attacks him, and wounds him mortally so that he dies, and the man flees into one of these cities, ¹² then the elders of his city shall send and fetch him from there, and hand him over to the avenger of blood, so that he may die. ¹³ Your eye shall not pity him, but you shall purge the guilt of innocent blood*ᵒ* from Israel, so that it may be well with you.

14 "In the inheritance which you will hold in the land that the LORD your God gives you to possess, you shall not remove your neighbor's landmark, which the men of old have set.

15 "A single witness shall not prevail against a man for any crime or for any wrong in connection with any

o Or *the blood of the innocent*

---

will raise up a prophetic spokesman to reveal his will. **15:** *Like me,* Moses is regarded as the fountainhead of prophecy and the prototype of the true prophet (34.10–11). **16–17:** 5.23–31. **20–22:** The test of the true prophet (13.1–5) is that his prophecy will be brought to fulfilment according to God's purpose (1 Kg.22.26–28; Jer. ch. 28).

19.1–21: The administration of justice. 1–13: Cities of refuge are to be established to limit the ancient tribal law of blood revenge (Num. ch. 35). **1–2:** Three cities are to be set apart in Canaan, besides the three in Transjordan (4.41–43). **4–6 (11–13):** Num.35.16–28. **8–10:** Num. ch. 35 and Jos. ch. 20 provide for only six cities. **14:** This verse preserves an ancient law prohibiting the removal of a *landmark,* i.e. property boundary-stone (Is.5.8; Hos.5.10; Pr.22.28). **15–21:** The evidence of witnesses. **15:** 17.6; Num.35.30. **16:** Malicious witnessing is prohibited in the

offense that he has committed; only on the evidence of two witnesses, or of three witnesses, shall a charge be sustained. ¹⁶ If a malicious witness rises against any man to accuse him of wrongdoing, ¹⁷ then both parties to the dispute shall appear before the LORD, before the priests and the judges who are in office in those days; ¹⁸ the judges shall inquire diligently, and if the witness is a false witness and has accused his brother falsely, ¹⁹ then you shall do to him as he had meant to do to his brother; so you shall purge the evil from the midst of you. ²⁰ And the rest shall hear, and fear, and shall never again commit any such evil among you. ²¹ Your eye shall not pity; it shall be life for life, eye for eye, tooth for tooth, hand for hand, foot for foot.

20 "When you go forth to war against your enemies, and see horses and chariots and an army larger than your own, you shall not be afraid of them; for the LORD your God is with you, who brought you up out of the land of Egypt. ² And when you draw near to the battle, the priest shall come forward and speak to the people, ³ and shall say to them, 'Hear, O Israel, you draw near this day to battle against your enemies: let not your heart faint; do not fear, or tremble, or be in dread of them; ⁴ for the LORD your God is he that goes with you, to fight for you against your enemies, to give you the victory.' ⁵ Then the officers shall speak to the people, saying, 'What man is there that has built a new house and

has not dedicated it? Let him go back to his house, lest he die in the battle and another man dedicate it. ⁶ And what man is there that has planted a vineyard and has not enjoyed its fruit? Let him go back to his house, lest he die in the battle and another man enjoy its fruit. ⁷ And what man is there that has betrothed a wife and has not taken her? Let him go back to his house, lest he die in the battle and another man take her.' ⁸ And the officers shall speak further to the people, and say, 'What man is there that is fearful and fainthearted? Let him go back to his house, lest the heart of his fellows melt as his heart.' ⁹ And when the officers have made an end of speaking to the people, then commanders shall be appointed at the head of the people.

10 "When you draw near to a city to fight against it, offer terms of peace to it. ¹¹ And if its answer to you is peace and it opens to you, then all the people who are found in it shall do forced labor for you and shall serve you. ¹² But if it makes no peace with you, but makes war against you, then you shall besiege it; ¹³ and when the LORD your God gives it into your hand you shall put all its males to the sword, ¹⁴ but the women and the little ones, the cattle, and everything else in the city, all its spoil, you shall take as booty for yourselves; and you shall enjoy the spoil of your enemies, which the LORD your God has given you. ¹⁵ Thus you shall do to all the cities which are very far from you, which are not cities of the nations here. ¹⁶ But in the cities of

---

Decalogue (Ex.20.16; compare 23.1; Lev.19.16). **17:** The case must come *before the LORD*, i.e. to the supreme tribunal (17.8–13). **21:** *Life for life*, the lex talionis is quoted to emphasize that the judges shall determine a penalty appropriate to the crime (see Ex.21.22–25 n.).

20.1–20: Rules for waging holy war. The conception of holy war, rooted in ancient wilderness experiences, provides the basis for the Deuteronomic understanding of the conquest (2.33–35; 3.3–7,18–22; 7.1–5; 11.22–25). **1–4:** The premise is that holy war is not a human enterprise, like the wars fought by kings with trained soldiers and impressive *horses and chariots*, but is an action in which the LORD himself is engaged and in which his people respond with fanatical devotion (Jg. ch. 5). **4:** Ex.14.14,25. **6:** The fruit of a vineyard could not be *enjoyed* (or, put to common use) until the fifth year (Lev.19.23–25). **7:** 24.5 **8:** Holy war is waged with selected warriors. The size of the army is not important, and above all the *fearful* and *fainthearted* must be sifted out (Jg.7.2–3). **10–15:** In war against a non-Palestinian city, booty may be taken (see Num. ch. 31). **15–18:** A Palestinian city, however, must be utterly destroyed, i.e. put under the sacrificial ban, lest the inhabitants corrupt Israel's faith (9.1–6). Since the condemned city is a

these peoples that the LORD your God gives you for an inheritance, you shall save alive nothing that breathes, [17] but you shall utterly destroy them, the Hittites and the Amorites, the Canaanites and the Per'izzites, the Hivites and the Jeb'usites, as the LORD your God has commanded; [18] that they may not teach you to do according to all their abominable practices which they have done in the service of their gods, and so to sin against the LORD your God.

19 "When you besiege a city for a long time, making war against it in order to take it, you shall not destroy its trees by wielding an axe against them; for you may eat of them, but you shall not cut them down. Are the trees in the field men that they should be besieged by you? [20] Only the trees which you know are not trees for food you may destroy and cut down that you may build siegeworks against the city that makes war with you, until it falls.

21 "If in the land which the LORD your God gives you to possess, any one is found slain, lying in the open country, and it is not known who killed him, [2] then your elders and your judges shall come forth, and they shall measure the distance to the cities which are around him that is slain; [3] and the elders of the city which is nearest to the slain man shall take a heifer which has never been worked and which has not pulled in the yoke. [4] And the elders of that city shall bring the heifer down to a valley with running water, which is neither plowed nor sown, and shall break the heifer's neck there in the valley. [5] And the priests the sons of Levi shall come forward, for the LORD your God has chosen them to minister to him and to bless in the name of the LORD, and by their word every dispute and every assault shall be settled. [6] And all the elders of that city nearest to the slain man shall wash their hands over the heifer whose neck was broken in the valley; [7] and they shall testify, 'Our hands did not shed this blood, neither did our eyes see it shed. [8] Forgive, O LORD, thy people Israel, whom thou hast redeemed, and set not the guilt of innocent blood in the midst of thy people Israel; but let the guilt of blood be forgiven them.' [9] So you shall purge the guilt of innocent blood from your midst, when you do what is right in the sight of the LORD.

10 "When you go forth to war against your enemies, and the LORD your God gives them into your hands, and you take them captive, [11] and see among the captives a beautiful woman, and you have desire for her and would take her for yourself as wife, [12] then you shall bring her home to your house, and she shall shave her head and pare her nails. [13] And she shall put off her captive's garb, and shall remain in your house and bewail her father and her mother a full month; after that you may go in to her, and be her husband, and she shall be your wife. [14] Then, if you have no delight in her, you shall let her go where she will; but you shall not sell her for money, you shall not

---

holy sacrifice to the LORD (compare 13.12–18), no booty can be taken (Jos. ch. 7). **19–20:** This stipulation limits wanton destruction of natural resources which, unlike the city and its booty, are gifts from the LORD.

21.1–23.14: Miscellaneous laws. 1–9: A law for the expiation of murder when the slayer is unknown. This ancient rite rests on the belief that bloodshed pollutes the land (v. 8–9; 19.10,13) and that it is the responsibility of the community to seek atonement for the crime. **2:** *The elders* (see v. 20 n.) represent the adjacent cities; the *judges* are apparently the Levites from the supreme tribunal of the sanctuary (v. 5; compare 17.8–13). **3–4:** The ritual is in some respects similar to that of Num.19.2–10 (compare Lev.14.4–7). In this case, the victim is a substitutionary sacrifice for the guilty party (see Lev.1.4 n.). **5:** *The priests, the sons of Levi*, i.e. the Levitical priests from the central sanctuary rather than the town Levites (see 18.1 n.). **6–8:** The elders, representing the people, absolve themselves by the symbolic washing of hands and by taking a solemn oath. **10–14:** A supplement to the law on holy war against a non-Palestinian

treat her as a slave, since you have humiliated her.

15 "If a man has two wives, the one loved and the other disliked, and they have borne him children, both the loved and the disliked, and if the first-born son is hers that is disliked, ¹⁶ then on the day when he assigns his possessions as an inheritance to his sons, he may not treat the son of the loved as the first-born in preference to the son of the disliked, who is the first-born, ¹⁷ but he shall acknowledge the first-born, the son of the disliked, by giving him a double portion of all that he has, for he is the first issue of his strength; the right of the first-born is his.

18 "If a man has a stubborn and rebellious son, who will not obey the voice of his father or the voice of his mother, and, though they chastise him, will not give heed to them, ¹⁹ then his father and his mother shall take hold of him and bring him out to the elders of his city at the gate of the place where he lives, ²⁰ and they shall say to the elders of his city, 'This our son is stubborn and rebellious, he will not obey our voice; he is a glutton and a drunkard.' ²¹ Then all the men of the city shall stone him to death with stones; so you shall purge the evil from your midst; and all Israel shall hear, and fear.

22 "And if a man has committed a crime punishable by death and he is put to death, and you hang him on a tree, ²³ his body shall not remain all night upon the tree, but you shall

bury him the same day, for a hanged man is accursed by God; you shall not defile your land which the LORD your God gives you for an inheritance.

22 "You shall not see your brother's ox or his sheep go astray, and withhold your help*ᵖ* from them; you shall take them back to your brother. ² And if he is not near you, or if you do not know him, you shall bring it home to your house, and it shall be with you until your brother seeks it; then you shall restore it to him. ³ And so you shall do with his ass; so you shall do with his garment; so you shall do with any lost thing of your brother's, which he loses and you find; you may not withhold your help. ⁴ You shall not see your brother's ass or his ox fallen down by the way, and withhold your help*ᵖ* from them; you shall help him to lift them up again.

5 "A woman shall not wear anything that pertains to a man, nor shall a man put on a woman's garment; for whoever does these things is an abomination to the LORD your God.

6 "If you chance to come upon a bird's nest, in any tree or on the ground, with young ones or eggs and the mother sitting upon the young or upon the eggs, you shall not take the mother with the young; ⁷ you shall let the mother go, but the young you may take to yourself; that it may go well with you, and that you may live long.

8 "When you build a new house, you shall make a parapet for your roof,

p Heb *hide yourself*

city (20.10–15) that deals with treatment of female captives (compare Num.31.18). **15–20:** Two old case laws dealing with family affairs. **15–17:** In antiquity it was believed that the right of the first-born was inalienable (Gen.25.29–34). This law puts that right above family rivalry or preference. **18–21:** Like other ancient family laws (Ex.21.15,17; Lev.20.9; compare Dt.27.16), this law is severe. It is designed to protect the family, the basic social unit of Israelite society. **19–20:** *The elders* sat at the city gate (Ru.4.1–12) where they acted as a judicial council in legal matters. This case is an application of the fifth commandment (Ex.20.12). **22–23:** Hanging (impaling) a criminal on a tree after execution was regarded as the greatest disgrace (Jos.8.29; 10.26–27; 2 Sam.4.12). Only criminals who were regarded as accursed were subjected to this ignominy. **22.1–4:** This law is similar to Ex.23.4–5 but is recast in terms of the Deuteronomic conception of brotherly love. A *brother* is not necessarily one who is near or even known (v. 2), but is any fellow-Israelite who needs help. **5:** The distinction between the sexes is based on God's creation and should not be violated in any way as, for instance, in the simulated changes of sex in pagan religions. **6:** Man should exercise a reverent concern for God's creatures (compare 20.19–20; 25.4), taking only what he needs for his livelihood. **8:** This safety law was de-

that you may not bring the guilt of blood upon your house, if any one fall from it.

9 "You shall not sow your vineyard with two kinds of seed, lest the whole yield be forfeited to the sanctuary,[q] the crop which you have sown and the yield of the vineyard. [10] You shall not plow with an ox and an ass together. [11] You shall not wear a mingled stuff, wool and linen together.

12 "You shall make yourself tassels on the four corners of your cloak with which you cover yourself.

13 "If any man takes a wife, and goes in to her, and then spurns her, [14] and charges her with shameful conduct, and brings an evil name upon her, saying, 'I took this woman, and when I came near her, I did not find in her the tokens of virginity,' [15] then the father of the young woman and her mother shall take and bring out the tokens of her virginity to the elders of the city in the gate; [16] and the father of the young woman shall say to the elders, 'I gave my daughter to this man to wife, and he spurns her; [17] and lo, he has made shameful charges against her, saying, "I did not find in your daughter the tokens of virginity." And yet these are the tokens of my daughter's virginity.' And they shall spread the garment before the elders of the city. [18] Then the elders of that city shall take the man and whip him; [19] and they shall fine him a hundred shekels of silver, and give them to the father of the young woman, because he has brought an evil name upon a virgin of Israel; and she shall be his wife; he may not put her away all his days. [20] But if the thing is true, that the tokens of virginity were not found in the young woman,

[21] then they shall bring out the young woman to the door of her father's house, and the men of her city shall stone her to death with stones, because she has wrought folly in Israel by playing the harlot in her father's house; so you shall purge the evil from the midst of you.

22 "If a man is found lying with the wife of another man, both of them shall die, the man who lay with the woman, and the woman; so you shall purge the evil from Israel.

23 "If there is a betrothed virgin, and a man meets her in the city and lies with her, [24] then you shall bring them both out to the gate of that city, and you shall stone them to death with stones, the young woman because she did not cry for help though she was in the city, and the man because he violated his neighbor's wife; so you shall purge the evil from the midst of you.

25 "But if in the open country a man meets a young woman who is betrothed, and the man seizes her and lies with her, then only the man who lay with her shall die. [26] But to the young woman you shall do nothing; in the young woman there is no offense punishable by death, for this case is like that of a man attacking and murdering his neighbor; [27] because he came upon her in the open country, and though the betrothed young woman cried for help there was no one to rescue her.

28 "If a man meets a virgin who is not betrothed, and seizes her and lies with her, and they are found, [29] then the man who lay with her shall give to the father of the young woman fifty shekels of silver, and she shall be his

q Heb *become holy*

signed for ancient flat-roofed houses. **9–11:** The mixing of kinds was believed to be a violation of the differences which God has ordained (v. 5; Lev.19.19). **12:** Num.15.37–41. **13–30:** Laws governing sexual relations. These laws (also 21.15–21), written in the casuistic (case-law) style of some laws in the Covenant Code (Ex.21.1–22.17; see Ex.21.1 n.), are apparently quoted from an older source, since they show no trace of Deuteronomic style. **13–21:** The proof of virginity. **15:** On *the elders*, see 21.19–20 n. **21:** On the expression *wrought folly in Israel*, see Gen.34.7 n. **22–27:** Adultery, a violation of the seventh commandment, was punishable by death (Lev.18.20; 20.10). Intercourse with a betrothed virgin is considered as adultery because the woman is already, in effect, another man's wife. **28–29:** The money payment to be given to the father is

wife, because he has violated her; he may not put her away all his days.

30*r* "A man shall not take his father's wife, nor shall he uncover her who is his father's.*s*

23 "He whose testicles are crushed or whose male member is cut off shall not enter the assembly of the LORD.

2 "No bastard shall enter the assembly of the LORD; even to the tenth generation none of his descendants shall enter the assembly of the LORD.

3 "No Ammonite or Moabite shall enter the assembly of the LORD; even to the tenth generation none belonging to them shall enter the assembly of the LORD for ever; 4 because they did not meet you with bread and with water on the way, when you came forth out of Egypt, and because they hired against you Balaam the son of Be'or from Pethor of Mesopota'mia, to curse you. 5 Nevertheless the LORD your God would not hearken to Balaam; but the LORD your God turned the curse into a blessing for you, because the LORD your God loved you. 6 You shall not seek their peace or their prosperity all your days for ever.

7 "You shall not abhor an E'domite, for he is your brother; you shall not abhor an Egyptian, because you were a sojourner in his land. 8 The children of the third generation that are born to them may enter the assembly of the LORD.

9 "When you go forth against your enemies and are in camp, then you shall keep yourself from every evil thing.

10 "If there is among you any man who is not clean by reason of what chances to him by night, then he shall go outside the camp, he shall not come within the camp; 11 but when evening comes on, he shall bathe himself in water, and when the sun is down, he may come within the camp.

12 "You shall have a place outside the camp and you shall go out to it; 13 and you shall have a stick with your weapons; and when you sit down outside, you shall dig a hole with it, and turn back and cover up your excrement. 14 Because the LORD your God walks in the midst of your camp, to save you and to give up your enemies before you, therefore your camp must be holy, that he may not see anything indecent among you, and turn away from you.

15 "You shall not give up to his master a slave who has escaped from his master to you; 16 he shall dwell with you, in your midst, in the place which he shall choose within one of your towns, where it pleases him best; you shall not oppress him.

17 "There shall be no cult prostitute of the daughters of Israel, neither shall there be a cult prostitute of the sons of Israel. 18 You shall not bring the hire of a harlot, or the wages of a dog,*t* into the house of the LORD your God in payment for any vow; for both of these

r Ch 23.1 in Heb
s Heb *uncover his father's skirt*
t Or *sodomite*

---

the marriage present (Ex.22.16–17). **30:** *Father's wife*, i.e. stepmother (27.20; Lev.18.8; 20.11). **23.1–8:** Exclusions from the assembly of the LORD (33.5; Jg.20.2). **1–2:** Only those who are unblemished can "present themselves before God" (Jos.24.1). This excludes eunuchs (compare Lev.21.17–23), who in ancient pagan religions were temple priests, and perhaps also excludes children born of incestuous union (Lev.18.6–18). **3–6:** 2.9–25. The account in Num. chs. 21–22 does not mention Ammonite hostility against Israel. **7:** Gen.25.24–26; 36.1. **9–14:** A supplement to the rules for holy war (see ch. 20). Ceremonial cleanness is demanded because *the* LORD *your God walks in the midst of your camp.* **10–11:** Lev.15.16–17. **12–14:** The camp must be clean not just in the sense of being sanitary but in the sense of being *holy* (see Lev.11.1–47 n.).

23.15–25.19: Laws dealing with humanitarian and religious obligations. 23.15–16: In contrast with this humane law, the Code of Hammurabi decreed death as the penalty for sheltering a fugitive slave. **17–18:** A strict prohibition against sacred prostitution (see Gen.38.15 n.). *Dog*, a term of reproach for a male cultic prostitute. **19–20:** See Ex.22.25 n.; Lev.25.35–38; Dt.15.1–11. Loans within Israel, as distinguished from loans to outsiders, were usually occa-

are an abomination to the LORD your God.

19 "You shall not lend upon interest to your brother, interest on money, interest on victuals, interest on anything that is lent for interest. [20] To a foreigner you may lend upon interest, but to your brother you shall not lend upon interest; that the LORD your God may bless you in all that you undertake in the land which you are entering to take possession of it.

21 "When you make a vow to the LORD your God, you shall not be slack to pay it; for the LORD your God will surely require it of you, and it would be sin in you. [22] But if you refrain from vowing, it shall be no sin in you. [23] You shall be careful to perform what has passed your lips, for you have voluntarily vowed to the LORD your God what you have promised with your mouth.

24 "When you go into your neighbor's vineyard, you may eat your fill of grapes, as many as you wish, but you shall not put any in your vessel. [25] When you go into your neighbor's standing grain, you may pluck the ears with your hand, but you shall not put a sickle to your neighbor's standing grain.

24 "When a man takes a wife and marries her, if then she finds no favor in his eyes because he has found some indecency in her, and he writes her a bill of divorce and puts it in her hand and sends her out of his house, and she departs out of his house, [2] and if she goes and becomes another man's wife, [3] and the latter husband dislikes her and writes her a bill of divorce and puts it in her hand and sends her out

of his house, or if the latter husband dies, who took her to be his wife, [4] then her former husband, who sent her away, may not take her again to be his wife, after she has been defiled; for that is an abomination before the LORD, and you shall not bring guilt upon the land which the LORD your God gives you for an inheritance.

5 "When a man is newly married, he shall not go out with the army or be charged with any business; he shall be free at home one year, to be happy with his wife whom he has taken.

6 "No man shall take a mill or an upper millstone in pledge; for he would be taking a life in pledge.

7 "If a man is found stealing one of his brethren, the people of Israel, and if he treats him as a slave or sells him, then that thief shall die; so you shall purge the evil from the midst of you.

8 "Take heed, in an attack of leprosy, to be very careful to do according to all that the Levitical priests shall direct you; as I commanded them, so you shall be careful to do. [9] Remember what the LORD your God did to Miriam on the way as you came forth out of Egypt.

10 "When you make your neighbor a loan of any sort, you shall not go into his house to fetch his pledge. [11] You shall stand outside, and the man to whom you make the loan shall bring the pledge out to you. [12] And if he is a poor man, you shall not sleep in his pledge; [13] when the sun goes down, you shall restore to him the pledge that he may sleep in his cloak and bless you; and it shall be righteousness to you before the LORD your God.

---

sioned by financial desperation and therefore became means of oppressing a fellow-Israelite. **21–23:** See Lev. ch. 27. **24–25:** A neighbor's good-will should not be presumed upon to the point of stealing from his harvest. **24.1–4:** An old case law dealing with remarriage after divorce. Initiative for divorce rested with the husband, who, however, could not act without following a legal procedure, including the formulation of a *bill of divorce* (Jer.3.8), stating the grounds. **5:** Another of the rules for holy war (20.1–20; 21.10–14; 23.9–14). **6:** A limitation upon the creditor. Since daily life depends upon bread, the mill cannot be taken as security for a loan (vv. 10–13). **7:** Ex.21.16. **8–9:** See Lev. chs. 13–14. *Remember . . . Miriam* (Num.12.10–15). **10–13:** See Ex.22.26 n. (compare Am.2.8; Pr.22.27). **13:** *Righteousness*, see Gen.6.9 n. **14–15:** Lev.19.13. Israel's humanitarianism is based on the conviction that the LORD is the vindicator

14 "You shall not oppress a hired servant who is poor and needy, whether he is one of your brethren or one of the sojourners who are in your land within your towns; 15 you shall give him his hire on the day he earns it, before the sun goes down (for he is poor, and sets his heart upon it); lest he cry against you to the LORD, and it be sin in you.

16 "The fathers shall not be put to death for the children, nor shall the children be put to death for the fathers; every man shall be put to death for his own sin.

17 "You shall not pervert the justice due to the sojourner or to the fatherless, or take a widow's garment in pledge; 18 but you shall remember that you were a slave in Egypt and the LORD your God redeemed you from there; therefore I command you to do this.

19 "When you reap your harvest in your field, and have forgotten a sheaf in the field, you shall not go back to get it; it shall be for the sojourner, the fatherless, and the widow; that the LORD your God may bless you in all the work of your hands. 20 When you beat your olive trees, you shall not go over the boughs again; it shall be for the sojourner, the fatherless, and the widow. 21 When you gather the grapes of your vineyard, you shall not glean it afterward; it shall be for the sojourner, the fatherless, and the widow. 22 You shall remember that you were a slave in the land of Egypt; therefore I command you to do this.

25 "If there is a dispute between men, and they come into court, and the judges decide between them, acquitting the innocent and condemning the guilty, 2 then if the guilty man deserves to be beaten, the judge shall cause him to lie down and be beaten in his presence with a number of stripes in proportion to his offense. 3 Forty stripes may be given him, but not more; lest, if one should go on to beat him with more stripes than these, your brother be degraded in your sight.

4 "You shall not muzzle an ox when it treads out the grain.

5 "If brothers dwell together, and one of them dies and has no son, the wife of the dead shall not be married outside the family to a stranger; her husband's brother shall go in to her, and take her as his wife, and perform the duty of a husband's brother to her. 6 And the first son whom she bears shall succeed to the name of his brother who is dead, that his name may not be blotted out of Israel. 7 And if the man does not wish to take his brother's wife, then his brother's wife shall go up to the gate to the elders, and say, 'My husband's brother refuses to perpetuate his brother's name in Israel; he will not perform the duty of a husband's brother to me.' 8 Then the elders of his city shall call him, and speak to him: and if he persists, saying, 'I do not wish to take her,' 9 then his brother's wife shall go up to him in the presence of the elders, and pull his sandal off his foot, and spit in his face; and she shall answer and say, 'So shall it be done to the man who does not build up his brother's house.' 10 And the name of his house*u* shall be called in Israel,

u Heb *its name*

---

of the weak and helpless. **16:** This law modifies the ancient belief that guilt affected a whole social group, especially the family (Num.16.31–33; Jos.7.24–25; 2 Sam.21.1–9). Although Deuteronomy does not reject the solidarity of the community in guilt (21.1–9; compare 13.12–18), it puts in the foreground the principle of individual responsibility (Jer.31.29; Ezek. ch. 18). See 2 Kg.14.6 for the application of this law. **17–18:** 15.15. **19–22:** Lev.19.9–10; 23.22. **25.1–3:** An old case law which imposes judicial restrictions on corporal punishment. *The judges*, 16.18. **4:** A law in the humane spirit of 22.6–7. **5–10:** An old case law on levirate marriage (see Gen. 38.8 n.). **6:** Since a man's name, according to ancient thought, was the bearer of his person, a father lived on in his son (Gen.48.15–16). **7:** As in the case of Tamar (Gen. ch. 38), the wife had the obligation to see that *the duty of a husband's brother* (or levir) was performed. **9–10:** For the symbolic action of removing the sandal, in a more complicated levirate marriage

The house of him that had his sandal pulled off.

11 "When men fight with one another, and the wife of the one draws near to rescue her husband from the hand of him who is beating him, and puts out her hand and seizes him by the private parts, 12 then you shall cut off her hand; your eye shall have no pity.

13 "You shall not have in your bag two kinds of weights, a large and a small. 14 You shall not have in your house two kinds of measures, a large and a small. 15 A full and just weight you shall have, a full and just measure you shall have; that your days may be prolonged in the land which the LORD your God gives you. 16 For all who do such things, all who act dishonestly, are an abomination to the LORD your God.

17 "Remember what Am'alek did to you on the way as you came out of Egypt, 18 how he attacked you on the way, when you were faint and weary, and cut off at your rear all who lagged behind you; and he did not fear God. 19 Therefore when the LORD your God has given you rest from all your enemies round about, in the land which the LORD your God gives you for an inheritance to possess, you shall blot out the remembrance of Am'alek from under heaven; you shall not forget.

26 "When you come into the land which the LORD your God gives you for an inheritance, and have taken possession of it, and live in it, 2 you shall take some of the first of all the fruit of the ground, which you harvest from your land that the LORD your God gives you, and you shall put it in a basket, and you shall go to the place which the LORD your God will choose, to make his name to dwell there. 3 And you shall go to the priest who is in office at that time, and say to him, 'I declare this day to the LORD your God that I have come into the land which the LORD swore to our fathers to give us.' 4 Then the priest shall take the basket from your hand, and set it down before the altar of the LORD your God.

5 "And you shall make response before the LORD your God, 'A wandering Aramean was my father; and he went down into Egypt and sojourned there, few in number; and there he became a nation, great, mighty, and populous. 6 And the Egyptians treated us harshly, and afflicted us, and laid upon us hard bondage. 7 Then we cried to the LORD the God of our fathers, and the LORD heard our voice, and saw our affliction, our toil, and our oppression; 8 and the LORD brought us out of Egypt with a mighty hand and an outstretched arm, with great terror, with signs and wonders; 9 and he brought us into this place and gave us this land, a land flowing with milk and honey. 10 And behold, now I bring the first of the fruit of the ground, which thou, O LORD, hast given me.' And you shall set it down before the LORD your God, and worship before the LORD your God; 11 and you shall rejoice in all the good which the LORD your God has given to you and to your house, you, and the Levite, and the sojourner who is among you.

12 "When you have finished paying all the tithe of your produce in the

---

situation, see Ru.4.7 n. **11–12:** This exceptionally severe law is based on the belief that the sexual organ, the spring of fertility, should not be blemished (23.1). **13–16:** Compare Lev.19.35–36. **17–19:** Holy war against Amalek (Ex.17.8–15).

26.1–19: Concluding liturgies and exhortation. This chapter anticipates the climax and conclusion of Moses' main address (ch. 28). **1–11:** A liturgy for the presentation of the first fruits at the central sanctuary. **2–3:** The occasion is the harvest pilgrimage festival, the feast of weeks (16.9–12), when the worshiper gives thanks for the LORD's gift of the land and for his bounteous blessing. **5–10:** An ancient creedal recital of the LORD's mighty acts as manifested primarily in the Exodus and the conquest of Canaan. **5:** *A wandering Aramean*, a reference to Jacob's semi-nomadic life. **12–15:** A liturgy for *the year of tithing*. The worshiper testifies that he has set aside *the sacred portion* (or tithe) in his home town according to the ordinance of 14.28–29.

third year, which is the year of tithing, giving it to the Levite, the sojourner, the fatherless, and the widow, that they may eat within your towns and be filled, [13] then you shall say before the LORD your God, 'I have removed the sacred portion out of my house, and moreover I have given it to the Levite, the sojourner, the fatherless, and the widow, according to all thy commandment which thou hast commanded me; I have not transgressed any of thy commandments, neither have I forgotten them; [14] I have not eaten of the tithe while I was mourning, or removed any of it while I was unclean, or offered any of it to the dead; I have obeyed the voice of the LORD my God, I have done according to all that thou hast commanded me. [15] Look down from thy holy habitation, from heaven, and bless thy people Israel and the ground which thou hast given us, as thou didst swear to our fathers, a land flowing with milk and honey.'

16 "This day the LORD your God commands you to do these statutes and ordinances; you shall therefore be careful to do them with all your heart and with all your soul. [17] You have declared this day concerning the LORD that he is your God, and that you will walk in his ways, and keep his statutes and his commandments and his ordinances, and will obey his voice; [18] and the LORD has declared this day concerning you that you are a people for his own possession, as he has promised you, and that you are to keep all his commandments, [19] that he will set you high above all nations that he has made, in praise and in fame and in honor, and that you shall be a people holy to the LORD your God, as he has spoken."

27 Now Moses and the elders of Israel commanded the people, saying, "Keep all the commandment which I command you this day. [2] And on the day you pass over the Jordan to the land which the LORD your God gives you, you shall set up large stones, and plaster them with plaster; [3] and you shall write upon them all the words of this law, when you pass over to enter the land which the LORD your God gives you, a land flowing with milk and honey, as the LORD, the God of your fathers, has promised you. [4] And when you have passed over the Jordan, you shall set up these stones, concerning which I command you this day, on Mount Ebal, and you shall plaster them with plaster. [5] And there you shall build an altar to the LORD your God, an altar of stones; you shall lift up no iron tool upon them. [6] You shall build an altar to the LORD your God of unhewn[v] stones; and you shall offer burnt offerings on it to the LORD your God; [7] and you shall sacrifice peace offerings, and shall eat there; and you shall rejoice before the LORD your God. [8] And you shall write upon the stones all the words of this law very plainly."

9 And Moses and the Levitical

v Heb whole

13: *Before the LORD*, at the central sanctuary. 14: He confesses that he has not defiled the holy offering by touching it in a state of ritual uncleanness while mourning (Num.19.11–16) or by bringing it to a tomb as a funerary offering. 16–19: This exhortation concludes the exposition of the *statutes* and *ordinances* contained in chs. 12–26. The language here may echo a ceremony of covenant renewal at the central sanctuary when the law was publicly read and the covenant relation between the LORD and Israel was renewed (see 31.10–11 n.). *This day* the LORD has stated his covenant demands (v. 16), *this day* the people have declared that he alone is their God (v. 17), and *this day* the LORD has reaffirmed that Israel is his chosen people (vv. 18–19).

27.1–26: The Shechem ceremony. A cultic ceremony is to be inaugurated which will solemnly dramatize Israel's covenant responsibilities (11.26–32). 1: Here Moses is referred to in the third person. This chapter stands independently and interrupts Moses' address (chs. 5–26 and ch. 28). 4: *Mount Ebal* and Mount Gerizim (vv. 12,13) overlook the city of Shechem (see Gen.12.6 n.). Contrary to the law of ch. 12, an altar of unhewn stones (Ex.20.25) is to be set up at a place other than the central sanctuary, an evidence of the antiquity and independence of this tradition. 7: *Eat . . . rejoice*, a reference to the communion meal in connection with the *peace offer-*

priests said to all Israel, "Keep silence and hear, O Israel: this day you have become the people of the LORD your God. ¹⁰ You shall therefore obey the voice of the LORD your God, keeping his commandments and his statutes, which I command you this day."

11 And Moses charged the people the same day, saying, ¹² "When you have passed over the Jordan, these shall stand upon Mount Ger'izim to bless the people: Simeon, Levi, Judah, Is'sachar, Joseph, and Benjamin. ¹³ And these shall stand upon Mount Ebal for the curse: Reuben, Gad, Asher, Zeb'ulun, Dan, and Naph'tali. ¹⁴ And the Levites shall declare to all the men of Israel with a loud voice:

15 " 'Cursed be the man who makes a graven or molten image, an abomination to the LORD, a thing made by the hands of a craftsman, and sets it up in secret.' And all the people shall answer and say, 'Amen.'

16 " 'Cursed be he who dishonors his father or his mother.' And all the people shall say, 'Amen.'

17 " 'Cursed be he who removes his neighbor's landmark.' And all the people shall say, 'Amen.'

18 " 'Cursed be he who misleads a blind man on the road.' And all the people shall say, 'Amen.'

19 " 'Cursed be he who perverts the justice due to the sojourner, the fatherless, and the widow.' And all the people shall say, 'Amen.'

20 " 'Cursed be he who lies with his father's wife, because he has uncov-

ered her who is his father's.'ʷ And all the people shall say, 'Amen.'

21 " 'Cursed be he who lies with any kind of beast.' And all the people shall say, 'Amen.'

22 " 'Cursed be he who lies with his sister, whether the daughter of his father or the daughter of his mother.' And all the people shall say, 'Amen.'

23 " 'Cursed be he who lies with his mother-in-law.' And all the people shall say, 'Amen.'

24 " 'Cursed be he who slays his neighbor in secret.' And all the people shall say, 'Amen.'

25 " 'Cursed be he who takes a bribe to slay an innocent person.' And all the people shall say, 'Amen.'

26 " 'Cursed be he who does not confirm the words of this law by doing them.' And all the people shall say, 'Amen.'

28 "And if you obey the voice of the LORD your God, being careful to do all his commandments which I command you this day, the LORD your God will set you high above all the nations of the earth. ² And all these blessings shall come upon you and overtake you, if you obey the voice of the LORD your God. ³ Blessed shall you be in the city, and blessed shall you be in the field. ⁴ Blessed shall be the fruit of your body, and the fruit of your ground, and the fruit of your beasts, the increase of your cattle, and the young of your flock. ⁵ Blessed shall be your basket and your knead-

w Heb *uncovered his father's skirt*

---

ings (see Lev. ch. 3). **11–13:** These verses deal with an ancient ceremony at Shechem, instituted at the command of Moses according to Jos.8.30–35. The antiquity of the tribal list is seen in the facts that Levi is listed as a tribe (Gen.49.5–7) and that the division of the house of Joseph into Manasseh and Ephraim has not yet occurred (Gen.49.22–26). **15–26:** The ritual of the blessing (v. 12; 28.3–6) is not preserved in this fragmentary record; only the ceremony of the curse is given (v. 13). The presiding Levites read a curse and in response the congregation says *Amen*, i.e. in full knowledge of the divine disapproval expressed in the twelve curses (corresponding to the twelve tribes), the people solemnly take upon themselves the covenant responsibilities (Jer.11.3). The twelve curses are very old laws which, with the exception of the last two, are paralleled in other codes of the Pentateuch.

28.1–68: The conclusion of Moses' second address. Moses calls the people to decision by announcing the blessings which accompany obedience and the curses which fall upon disobedience. **1:** Continuation from 26.16–19. **3–6:** These six blessings, formulated in short, emphatic style, were perhaps part of the old covenant ceremony preserved in fragmentary form in 27.11–

ing-trough. [6] Blessed shall you be when you come in, and blessed shall you be when you go out.

7 "The LORD will cause your enemies who rise against you to be defeated before you; they shall come out against you one way, and flee before you seven ways. [8] The LORD will command the blessing upon you in your barns, and in all that you undertake; and he will bless you in the land which the LORD your God gives you. [9] The LORD will establish you as a people holy to himself, as he has sworn to you, if you keep the commandments of the LORD your God, and walk in his ways. [10] And all the peoples of the earth shall see that you are called by the name of the LORD; and they shall be afraid of you. [11] And the LORD will make you abound in prosperity, in the fruit of your body, and in the fruit of your cattle, and in the fruit of your ground, within the land which the LORD swore to your fathers to give you. [12] The LORD will open to you his good treasury the heavens, to give the rain of your land in its season and to bless all the work of your hands; and you shall lend to many nations, but you shall not borrow. [13] And the LORD will make you the head, and not the tail; and you shall tend upward only, and not downward; if you obey the commandments of the LORD your God, which I command you this day, being careful to do them, [14] and if you do not turn aside from any of the words which I command you this day, to the right hand or to the left, to go after other gods to serve them.

15 "But if you will not obey the voice of the LORD your God or be careful to do all his commandments and his statutes which I command you this day, then all these curses shall come upon you and overtake you. [16] Cursed shall you be in the city, and cursed shall you be in the field. [17] Cursed shall be your basket and your kneading-trough. [18] Cursed shall be the fruit of your body, and the fruit of your ground, the increase of your cattle, and the young of your flock. [19] Cursed shall you be when you come in, and cursed shall you be when you go out.

20 "The LORD will send upon you curses, confusion, and frustration, in all that you undertake to do, until you are destroyed and perish quickly, on account of the evil of your doings, because you have forsaken me. [21] The LORD will make the pestilence cleave to you until he has consumed you off the land which you are entering to take possession of it. [22] The LORD will smite you with consumption, and with fever, inflammation, and fiery heat, and with drought,[x] and with blasting, and with mildew; they shall pursue you until you perish. [23] And the heavens over your head shall be brass, and the earth under you shall be iron. [24] The LORD will make the rain of your land powder and dust; from heaven it shall come down upon you until you are destroyed.

25 "The LORD will cause you to be defeated before your enemies; you shall go out one way against them, and flee seven ways before them; and you shall be a horror to all the kingdoms of the earth. [26] And your dead body shall be food for all birds of the air, and for the beasts of the earth; and there shall be no one to frighten them away. [27] The LORD will smite you with the boils of Egypt, and with the ulcers and the scurvy and the itch, of which you cannot be healed. [28] The LORD will smite you with madness and blindness and confusion of mind; [29] and you shall grope at noonday, as the blind grope in darkness, and you shall not prosper in your ways; and you

x Another reading is *sword*

26. **7–14:** A commentary on the meaning of the blessings. **16–19:** These six curses, parallel to the six blessings, likewise echo the old Shechem ceremony. **20–46:** A commentary on the curses. Perhaps it was the reading of this chapter which had a profound effect upon King Josiah (2 Kg.22.11–13). **27:** A reference to the Egyptian plagues. **30:** 20.5–7. **36–37:** Conquest by a

shall be only oppressed and robbed continually, and there shall be no one to help you. ³⁰ You shall betroth a wife, and another man shall lie with her; you shall build a house, and you shall not dwell in it; you shall plant a vineyard, and you shall not use the fruit of it. ³¹ Your ox shall be slain before your eyes, and you shall not eat of it; your ass shall be violently taken away before your face, and shall not be restored to you; your sheep shall be given to your enemies, and there shall be no one to help you. ³² Your sons and your daughters shall be given to another people, while your eyes look on and fail with longing for them all the day; and it shall not be in the power of your hand to prevent it. ³³ A nation which you have not known shall eat up the fruit of your ground and of all your labors; and you shall be only oppressed and crushed continually; ³⁴ so that you shall be driven mad by the sight which your eyes shall see. ³⁵ The LORD will smite you on the knees and on the legs with grievous boils of which you cannot be healed, from the sole of your foot to the crown of your head.

36 "The LORD will bring you, and your king whom you set over you, to a nation that neither you nor your fathers have known; and there you shall serve other gods, of wood and stone. ³⁷ And you shall become a horror, a proverb, and a byword, among all the peoples where the LORD will lead you away. ³⁸ You shall carry much seed into the field, and shall gather little in; for the locust shall consume it. ³⁹ You shall plant vineyards and dress them, but you shall neither drink of the wine nor gather the grapes; for the worm shall eat them. ⁴⁰ You shall have olive trees throughout all your territory, but you shall not anoint yourself with the oil; for your olives shall drop off. ⁴¹ You shall beget sons and daughters, but they shall not be yours; for they shall go into captivity. ⁴² All your trees and the fruit of your ground the locust shall possess. ⁴³ The sojourner who is among you shall mount above you higher and higher; and you shall come down lower and lower. ⁴⁴ He shall lend to you, and you shall not lend to him; he shall be the head, and you shall be the tail. ⁴⁵ All these curses shall come upon you and pursue you and overtake you, till you are destroyed, because you did not obey the voice of the LORD your God, to keep his commandments and his statutes which he commanded you. ⁴⁶ They shall be upon you as a sign and a wonder, and upon your descendants for ever.

47 "Because you did not serve the LORD your God with joyfulness and gladness of heart, by reason of the abundance of all things, ⁴⁸ therefore you shall serve your enemies whom the LORD will send against you, in hunger and thirst, in nakedness, and in want of all things; and he will put a yoke of iron upon your neck, until he has destroyed you. ⁴⁹ The LORD will bring a nation against you from afar, from the end of the earth, as swift as the eagle flies, a nation whose language you do not understand, ⁵⁰ a nation of stern countenance, who shall not regard the person of the old or show favor to the young, ⁵¹ and shall eat the offspring of your cattle and the fruit of your ground, until you are destroyed; who also shall not leave you grain, wine, or oil, the increase of your cattle or the young of your flock, until they have caused you to perish. ⁵² They shall besiege you in all your towns, until your high and fortified walls, in which you trusted, come down throughout all your land; and they shall besiege you in all your towns throughout all your land, which the LORD your God has given you. ⁵³ And you shall eat

strange *nation* was experienced in 721 B.C. when the Assyrians destroyed the Northern Kingdom and deported its population into *captivity* (v. 41). **47–68:** A further expansion of the meaning of the curses. These verses apparently reflect the tragedy which befell Judah when the Babylonians laid siege to fortified cities (v. 52), conquered Jerusalem, and between 597 and 587 B.C.

the offspring of your own body, the flesh of your sons and daughters, whom the LORD your God has given you, in the siege and in the distress with which your enemies shall distress you. [54] The man who is the most tender and delicately bred among you will grudge food to his brother, to the wife of his bosom, and to the last of the children who remain to him; [55] so that he will not give to any of them any of the flesh of his children whom he is eating, because he has nothing left him, in the siege and in the distress with which your enemy shall distress you in all your towns. [56] The most tender and delicately bred woman among you, who would not venture to set the sole of her foot upon the ground because she is so delicate and tender, will grudge to the husband of her bosom, to her son and to her daughter, [57] her afterbirth that comes out from between her feet and her children whom she bears, because she will eat them secretly, for want of all things, in the siege and in the distress with which your enemy shall distress you in your towns.

58 "If you are not careful to do all the words of this law which are written in this book, that you may fear this glorious and awful name, the LORD your God, [59] then the LORD will bring on you and your offspring extraordinary afflictions, afflictions severe and lasting, and sicknesses grievous and lasting. [60] And he will bring upon you again all the diseases of Egypt, which you were afraid of; and they shall cleave to you. [61] Every sickness also, and every affliction which is not recorded in the book of this law, the LORD will bring upon you, until you are destroyed. [62] Whereas you were as the stars of heaven for multitude, you shall be left few in number; because you did not obey the voice

of the LORD your God. [63] And as the LORD took delight in doing you good and multiplying you, so the LORD will take delight in bringing ruin upon you and destroying you; and you shall be plucked off the land which you are entering to take possession of it. [64] And the LORD will scatter you among all peoples, from one end of the earth to the other; and there you shall serve other gods, of wood and stone, which neither you nor your fathers have known. [65] And among these nations you shall find no ease, and there shall be no rest for the sole of your foot; but the LORD will give you there a trembling heart, and failing eyes, and a languishing soul; [66] your life shall hang in doubt before you; night and day you shall be in dread, and have no assurance of your life. [67] In the morning you shall say, 'Would it were evening!' and at evening you shall say, 'Would it were morning!' because of the dread which your heart shall fear, and the sights which your eyes shall see. [68] And the LORD will bring you back in ships to Egypt, a journey which I promised that you should never make again; and there you shall offer yourselves for sale to your enemies as male and female slaves, but no man will buy you."

29 [y] These are the words of the covenant which the LORD commanded Moses to make with the people of Israel in the land of Moab, besides the covenant which he had made with them at Horeb.

2[z] And Moses summoned all Israel and said to them: "You have seen all that the LORD did before your eyes in the land of Egypt, to Pharaoh and to all his servants and to all his land, [3] the great trials which your eyes saw, the signs, and those great wonders; [4] but to this day the LORD has not given

y Ch 28.69 in Heb   *z* Ch 29.1 in Heb

led many people into captivity. **53–57**: Lev.26.29. **68**: The disaster is interpreted as a return to Egyptian bondage, more pathetic than the former bondage.

    29.1–30.20: Moses' third address. In this supplement Moses again exhorts Israel to renew the covenant and warns of the disastrous consequences of disobedience. **1**: *The covenant* in Moab is not the original covenant but a renewal of it. **2–9**: As in the other addresses, the covenant is

you a mind to understand, or eyes to see, or ears to hear. [5] I have led you forty years in the wilderness; your clothes have not worn out upon you, and your sandals have not worn off your feet; [6] you have not eaten bread, and you have not drunk wine or strong drink; that you may know that I am the LORD your God. [7] And when you came to this place, Sihon the king of Heshbon and Og the king of Bashan came out against us to battle, but we defeated them; [8] we took their land, and gave it for an inheritance to the Reubenites, the Gadites, and the half-tribe of the Manas'sites. [9] Therefore be careful to do the words of this covenant, that you may prosper*a* in all that you do.

10 "You stand this day all of you before the LORD your God; the heads of your tribes,*b* your elders, and your officers, all the men of Israel, [11] your little ones, your wives, and the sojourner who is in your camp, both he who hews your wood and he who draws your water, [12] that you may enter into the sworn covenant of the LORD your God, which the LORD your God makes with you this day; [13] that he may establish you this day as his people, and that he may be your God, as he promised you, and as he swore to your fathers, to Abraham, to Isaac, and to Jacob. [14] Nor is it with you only that I make this sworn covenant, [15] but with him who is not here with us this day as well as with him who stands here with us this day before the LORD our God.

16 "You know how we dwelt in the land of Egypt, and how we came through the midst of the nations through which you passed; [17] and you have seen their detestable things, their idols of wood and stone, of silver and gold, which were among them. [18] Beware lest there be among you a man

or woman or family or tribe, whose heart turns away this day from the LORD our God to go and serve the gods of those nations; lest there be among you a root bearing poisonous and bitter fruit, [19] one who, when he hears the words of this sworn covenant, blesses himself in his heart, saying, 'I shall be safe, though I walk in the stubbornness of my heart.' This would lead to the sweeping away of moist and dry alike. [20] The LORD would not pardon him, but rather the anger of the LORD and his jealousy would smoke against that man, and the curses written in this book would settle upon him, and the LORD would blot out his name from under heaven. [21] And the LORD would single him out from all the tribes of Israel for calamity, in accordance with all the curses of the covenant written in this book of the law. [22] And the generation to come, your children who rise up after you, and the foreigner who comes from a far land, would say, when they see the afflictions of that land and the sicknesses with which the LORD has made it sick— [23] the whole land brimstone and salt, and a burntout waste, unsown, and growing nothing, where no grass can sprout, an overthrow like that of Sodom and Gomor'rah, Admah and Zeboi'im, which the LORD overthrew in his anger and wrath— [24] yea, all the nations would say, 'Why has the LORD done thus to this land? What means the heat of this great anger?' [25] Then men would say, 'It is because they forsook the covenant of the LORD, the God of their fathers, which he made with them when he brought them out of the land of Egypt, [26] and went and served other gods and worshiped them, gods whom they had not known and whom he had not allotted to them; [27] therefore the

a Or *deal wisely*
b Gk Syr: Heb *your heads, your tribes*

---

based on a recital of the LORD's mighty acts (compare Ex.19.3–6; Jos.24.2–13). **10–14:** See 26.16–19 n. **14:** On the contemporaneity of the covenant, see 5.2–3 n. **18–19:** The community is responsible for rooting out the infectious poison of idolatry lest the *moist* (fertile and whole-some) people be swept away with the *dry* (ch. 13). **20:** *Jealousy*, see Ex.34.14 n. **23:** See Gen. ch.

anger of the LORD was kindled against this land, bringing upon it all the curses written in this book; ²⁸ and the LORD uprooted them from their land in anger and fury and great wrath, and cast them into another land, as at this day.'

29 "The secret things belong to the LORD our God; but the things that are revealed belong to us and to our children for ever, that we may do all the words of this law.

30 "And when all these things come upon you, the blessing and the curse, which I have set before you, and you call them to mind among all the nations where the LORD your God has driven you, ² and return to the LORD your God, you and your children, and obey his voice in all that I command you this day, with all your heart and with all your soul; ³ then the LORD your God will restore your fortunes, and have compassion upon you, and he will gather you again from all the peoples where the LORD your God has scattered you. ⁴ If your outcasts are in the uttermost parts of heaven, from there the LORD your God will gather you, and from there he will fetch you; ⁵ and the LORD your God will bring you into the land which your fathers possessed, that you may possess it; and he will make you more prosperous and numerous than your fathers. ⁶ And the LORD your God will circumcise your heart and the heart of your offspring, so that you will love the LORD your God with all your heart and with all your soul, that you may live. ⁷ And the LORD your God will put all these curses upon your foes and enemies who persecuted you. ⁸ And you shall again obey the voice of the LORD, and keep all his commandments which I command you this day. ⁹ The LORD your God will make you abundantly prosperous in all the work of your hand, in the fruit of your body, and in the fruit of your cattle, and in the fruit of your ground; for the LORD will again take delight in prospering you, as he took delight in your fathers, ¹⁰ if you obey the voice of the LORD your God, to keep his commandments and his statutes which are written in this book of the law, if you turn to the LORD your God with all your heart and with all your soul.

11 "For this commandment which I command you this day is not too hard for you, neither is it far off. ¹² It is not in heaven, that you should say, 'Who will go up for us to heaven, and bring it to us, that we may hear it and do it?' ¹³ Neither is it beyond the sea, that you should say, 'Who will go over the sea for us, and bring it to us, that we may hear it and do it?' ¹⁴ But the word is very near you; it is in your mouth and in your heart, so that you can do it.

15 "See, I have set before you this day life and good, death and evil. ¹⁶ If you obey the commandments of the LORD your God^c which I command you this day, by loving the LORD your God, by walking in his ways, and by keeping his commandments and his statutes and his ordinances, then you shall live and multiply, and the LORD your God will bless you in the land which you are entering to take possession of it. ¹⁷ But if your heart turns away, and you will not hear, but are drawn away to worship other gods and serve them, ¹⁸ I declare to you this day,

c Gk: Heb lacks *If you obey the commandments of the* LORD *your God*

---

19. **29:** *The secret things* refer to the divine wisdom beyond man's ken; *the revealed things* are the teachings set forth in Deuteronomy. **30.1–10:** This passage presupposes that Israel is already in exile and anticipates the time when the LORD will restore his people. **2:** *Return to the* LORD, that is, repent–an act which involves turning away from unworthy loyalties and turning the heart (see 6.4–5 n.) to God (v. 10). **6:** God himself will work the inner change which makes it possible to fulfil the law of love. On circumcision of the heart, see 10.16 n. **9:** 28.3–6. **11–14:** The covenant demand is not beyond man's reach or understanding but has been graciously revealed (29.29) and, in the service of covenant renewal (29.1), *the word is very near you*. **15–20:** The two ways, between which Israel must decide. Such a challenge formed a climactic moment

that you shall perish; you shall not live long in the land which you are going over the Jordan to enter and possess. [19] I call heaven and earth to witness against you this day, that I have set before you life and death, blessing and curse; therefore choose life, that you and your descendants may live, [20] loving the LORD your God, obeying his voice, and cleaving to him; for that means life to you and length of days, that you may dwell in the land which the LORD swore to your fathers, to Abraham, to Isaac, and to Jacob, to give them."

31 So Moses continued to speak these words to all Israel. [2] And he said to them, "I am a hundred and twenty years old this day; I am no longer able to go out and come in. The LORD has said to me, 'You shall not go over this Jordan.' [3] The LORD your God himself will go over before you; he will destroy these nations before you, so that you shall dispossess them; and Joshua will go over at your head, as the LORD has spoken. [4] And the LORD will do to them as he did to Sihon and Og, the kings of the Amorites, and to their land, when he destroyed them. [5] And the LORD will give them over to you, and you shall do to them according to all the commandment which I have commanded you. [6] Be strong and of good courage, do not fear or be in dread of them: for it is the LORD your God who goes with you; he will not fail you or forsake you."

7 Then Moses summoned Joshua, and said to him in the sight of all Israel, "Be strong and of good courage; for you shall go with this people into the land which the LORD has sworn to their fathers to give them; and you shall put them in possession of it. [8] It is the LORD who goes before you; he will be with you, he will not fail you or forsake you; do not fear or be dismayed."

9 And Moses wrote this law, and gave it to the priests the sons of Levi, who carried the ark of the covenant of the LORD, and to all the elders of Israel. [10] And Moses commanded them, "At the end of every seven years, at the set time of the year of release, at the feast of booths, [11] when all Israel comes to appear before the LORD your God at the place which he will choose, you shall read this law before all Israel in their hearing. [12] Assemble the people, men, women, and little ones, and the sojourner within your towns, that they may hear and learn to fear the LORD your God, and be careful to do all the words of this law, [13] and that their children, who have not known it, may hear and learn to fear the LORD your God, as long as you live in the land which you are going over the Jordan to possess."

14 And the LORD said to Moses, "Behold, the days approach when you must die; call Joshua, and present yourselves in the tent of meeting, that I may commission him." And Moses and Joshua went and presented themselves in the tent of meeting. [15] And the LORD appeared in the tent in a pillar of cloud; and the pillar of cloud stood by the door of the tent.

16 And the LORD said to Moses, "Behold, you are about to sleep with your fathers; then this people will rise and play the harlot after the strange

---

in ancient ceremonies of covenant renewal (26.16–27.26; Jos.24.14–15). **20:** *Life* is not the mere extension of days. It is loving, obeying, and cleaving to the LORD instead of pursuing the ways of idolatry.

31.1–29: Concluding events of Moses' life. 1–8: Moses' final charge to Joshua and the people. **2–3:** Compare 1.37–38; 3.18–28. **7–8:** Jos.1.1–9. **9–13:** A covenant ceremony, to be held every seven years, is instituted. **9:** The belief is expressed that the whole Deuteronomic law was written by Moses. **10–11:** Every *year of release* or sabbatical year (15.1–11) the Deuteronomic law is to be read at the central sanctuary during the feast of booths (16.13–15). On this occasion a ceremony of covenant renewal is presumably to take place. **14–23:** The commissioning of Joshua (Num.27.12–23). **14–15:** These verses connect with the old literary tradition in Ex. 33.7–11. **16–22:** Moses is commanded to write a song which will confront the people as *a*

gods of the land, where they go to be among them, and they will forsake me and break my covenant which I have made with them. ¹⁷ Then my anger will be kindled against them in that day, and I will forsake them and hide my face from them, and they will be devoured; and many evils and troubles will come upon them, so that they will say in that day, 'Have not these evils come upon us because our God is not among us?' ¹⁸ And I will surely hide my face in that day on account of all the evil which they have done, because they have turned to other gods. ¹⁹ Now therefore write this song, and teach it to the people of Israel; put it in their mouths, that this song may be a witness for me against the people of Israel. ²⁰ For when I have brought them into the land flowing with milk and honey, which I swore to give to their fathers, and they have eaten and are full and grown fat, they will turn to other gods and serve them, and despise me and break my covenant. ²¹ And when many evils and troubles have come upon them, this song shall confront them as a witness (for it will live unforgotten in the mouths of their descendants); for I know the purposes which they are already forming, before I have brought them into the land that I swore to give." ²² So Moses wrote this song the same day, and taught it to the people of Israel.

23 And the LORD commissioned Joshua the son of Nun and said, "Be strong and of good courage; for you shall bring the children of Israel into the land which I swore to give them: I will be with you."

24 When Moses had finished writing the words of this law in a book, to the very end, ²⁵ Moses commanded the Levites who carried the ark of the covenant of the LORD, ²⁶ "Take this book of the law, and put it by the side of the ark of the covenant of the LORD your God, that it may be there for a witness against you. ²⁷ For I know how rebellious and stubborn you are; behold, while I am yet alive with you, today you have been rebellious against the LORD; how much more after my death! ²⁸ Assemble to me all the elders of your tribes, and your officers, that I may speak these words in their ears and call heaven and earth to witness against them. ²⁹ For I know that after my death you will surely act corruptly, and turn aside from the way which I have commanded you; and in the days to come evil will befall you, because you will do what is evil in the sight of the LORD, provoking him to anger through the work of your hands."

30 Then Moses spoke the words of this song until they were finished, in the ears of all the assembly of Israel:

32 "Give ear, O heavens, and I will speak;
and let the earth hear the words
of my mouth.
² May my teaching drop as the rain,
my speech distil as the dew,
as the gentle rain upon the tender
grass,
and as the showers upon the
herb.
³ For I will proclaim the name of the
LORD.
Ascribe greatness to our God!

⁴ "The Rock, his work is perfect;
for all his ways are justice.
A God of faithfulness and without
iniquity,
just and right is he.
⁵ They have dealt corruptly with him,
they are no longer his children
because of their blemish;

---

witness when they turn to other gods. The song is found in ch. 32. **23:** Continuation of vv. 14–15. **24–27:** These verses resume the thought of vv. 9–13. **26:** *This book of the law*, i.e. Deuteronomy. **28–29:** *These words*, probably a reference to the following Song of Moses, not to the book of law. **31.30–32.47: The Song of Moses.** This psalm, which contrasts God's faithfulness with Israel's faithlessness, contains elements of a "covenant lawsuit" or legal controversy (Mic.6.1–8; Jer. 2.1–13). Probably it dates from the early monarchy. **1–3:** Introductory appeal (compare Is.1.2; Mic.1.2). **4–6:** The integrity of God's ways is contrasted to the perversity of Israel. *Rock*, an

they are a perverse and crooked
generation.
⁶ Do you thus requite the LORD,
you foolish and senseless
people?
Is not he your father, who created
you,
who made you and established
you?
⁷ Remember the days of old,
consider the years of many
generations;
ask your father, and he will show
you;
your elders, and they will tell
you.
⁸ When the Most High gave to the
nations their inheritance,
when he separated the sons of
men,
he fixed the bounds of the peoples
according to the number of the
sons of God.ᵈ
⁹ For the LORD's portion is his people,
Jacob his allotted heritage.
¹⁰ "He found him in a desert land,
and in the howling waste of the
wilderness;
he encircled him, he cared for him,
he kept him as the apple of his
eye.
¹¹ Like an eagle that stirs up its nest,
that flutters over its young,
spreading out its wings, catching
them,
bearing them on its pinions,
¹² the LORD alone did lead him,
and there was no foreign god
with him.
¹³ He made him ride on the high places
of the earth,
and he ate the produce of the
field;
and he made him suck honey out
of the rock,

and oil out of the flinty rock.
¹⁴ Curds from the herd, and milk from
the flock,
with fat of lambs and rams,
herds of Bashan and goats,
with the finest of the wheat—
and of the blood of the grape you
drank wine.

¹⁵ "But Jesh'urun waxed fat, and
kicked;
you waxed fat, you grew thick,
you became sleek;
then he forsook God who made
him,
and scoffed at the Rock of his
salvation.
¹⁶ They stirred him to jealousy with
strange gods;
with abominable practices they
provoked him to anger.
¹⁷ They sacrificed to demons which
were no gods,
to gods they had never known,
to new gods that had come in of
late,
whom your fathers had never
dreaded.
¹⁸ You were unmindful of the Rock
that begotᵉ you,
and you forgot the God who
gave you birth.

¹⁹ "The LORD saw it, and spurned
them,
because of the provocation of his
sons and his daughters.
²⁰ And he said, 'I will hide my face
from them,
I will see what their end will be,
for they are a perverse generation,
children in whom is no
faithfulness.
²¹ They have stirred me to jealousy
with what is no god;

d Compare Gk: Heb *Israel*   e Or *bore*

ancient epithet for God (vv. 15,18), suggesting stability and dependability. **7–14:** A recital of
the LORD's saving deeds in *the days of old*. **8:** *The sons of God*, the divine beings who belong to
the heavenly court (see Gen.1.26 n.). To these heavenly beings the LORD delegated authority
to govern other nations, but he chose Israel for himself. **11–12:** Ex.19.4. **15–18:** Israel's rebellious forgetfulness of the LORD. **15:** Like a well-fed animal, Israel rebelled against his master.
Jeshurun ("the Upright One"), a term applied ironically to Israel (33.5,26). **16:** *Jealousy*, see
Ex.34.14 n. **17:** *Demons*, a reference to the gods of Canaan (Ps.106.37–38), who are actually

they have provoked me with
their idols.
So I will stir them to jealousy with
those who are no people;
I will provoke them with a
foolish nation.
22 For a fire is kindled by my anger,
and it burns to the depths of
Sheol,
devours the earth and its increase,
and sets on fire the foundations
of the mountains.

23 " 'And I will heap evils upon them;
I will spend my arrows upon
them;
24 they shall be wasted with hunger,
and devoured with burning heat
and poisonous pestilence;
and I will send the teeth of beasts
against them,
with venom of crawling things
of the dust.
25 In the open the sword shall bereave,
and in the chambers shall be
terror,
destroying both young man and
virgin,
the sucking child with the man
of gray hairs.
26 I would have said, "I will scatter
them afar,
I will make the remembrance of
them cease from among men,"
27 had I not feared provocation by the
enemy,
lest their adversaries should
judge amiss,
lest they should say, "Our hand is
triumphant,
the LORD has not wrought all
this." '

28 "For they are a nation void of
counsel,
and there is no understanding in
them.
29 If they were wise, they would
understand this,
they would discern their latter
end!
30 How should one chase a thousand,
and two put ten thousand to
flight,
unless their Rock had sold them,
and the LORD had given them up?
31 For their rock is not as our Rock,
even our enemies themselves
being judges.
32 For their vine comes from the vine
of Sodom,
and from the fields of
Gomor'rah;
their grapes are grapes of poison,
their clusters are bitter;
33 their wine is the poison of serpents,
and the cruel venom of asps.

34 "Is not this laid up in store with me,
sealed up in my treasuries?
35 Vengeance is mine, and
recompense,
for the time when their foot shall
slip;
for the day of their calamity is at
hand,
and their doom comes swiftly.
36 For the LORD will vindicate his
people
and have compassion on his
servants,
when he sees that their power is
gone,
and there is none remaining, bond
or free.

---

no gods. **19–27:** The LORD's righteous indignation. **21:** *No people*, a word-play on *no god.* **22:**
The poet envisions the foundations of the earth crumbling under the fire of divine wrath.
According to ancient belief, the *foundations of the mountains* which supported the firmament
were sunk in the subterranean ocean (Ps.46.2–3). *Sheol*, see Gen.37.35 n. **28–33:** The corruption of the nations. In vv. 28–29 *they* apparently refers to Israel and in vv. 31–33 *their* refers to
the enemies. Israel cannot perceive that disaster has befallen them because *their Rock* abandoned
them. *The rock* (god) of the enemies (vv. 37–38), however, cannot be compared to Israel's
God. **32:** *Their vine* (i.e. of the enemies) is likened to the proverbial fruit of Sodom and Gomorrah: outwardly beautiful but inwardly worthless. **34–43:** Because of the corruption of the nations
the LORD will finally overthrow the wicked nations and vindicate his people. **34:** *This*, the
nations' corruption (vv. 32–33). **35:** *Vengeance* means both judgment upon the oppressor and

³⁷ Then he will say, 'Where are their
　　gods,
　　the rock in which they took
　　　refuge,
³⁸ who ate the fat of their sacrifices,
　　and drank the wine of their drink
　　　offering?
　Let them rise up and help you,
　　let them be your protection!

³⁹ " 'See now that I, even I, am he,
　　and there is no god beside me;
　I kill and I make alive;
　　I wound and I heal;
　　and there is none that can deliver
　　　out of my hand.
⁴⁰ For I lift up my hand to heaven,
　　and swear, As I live for ever,
⁴¹ if I whet my glittering sword,*f*
　　and my hand takes hold on
　　　judgment,
　I will take vengeance on my
　　　adversaries,
　　and will requite those who hate
　　　me.
⁴² I will make my arrows drunk with
　　　blood,
　　and my sword shall devour flesh—
　with the blood of the slain and the
　　captives,
　　from the long-haired heads of the
　　　enemy.'

⁴³ "Praise his people, O you nations;
　　for he avenges the blood of his
　　　servants,
　　and takes vengeance on his
　　　adversaries,
　　and makes expiation for the land
　　　of his people."*g*
44 Moses came and recited all the
words of this song in the hearing of the
people, he and Joshua*h* the son of
Nun. ⁴⁵ And when Moses had finished speaking all these words to all
Israel, ⁴⁶ he said to them, "Lay to
heart all the words which I enjoin upon
you this day, that you may command
them to your children, that they may
be careful to do all the words of this
law. ⁴⁷ For it is no trifle for you, but
it is your life, and thereby you shall
live long in the land which you are
going over the Jordan to possess."

48 And the LORD said to Moses that
very day, ⁴⁹ "Ascend this mountain of
the Ab′arim, Mount Nebo, which is in
the land of Moab, opposite Jericho; and
view the land of Canaan, which I
give to the people of Israel for a possession; ⁵⁰ and die on the mountain
which you ascend, and be gathered to
your people, as Aaron your brother
died in Mount Hor and was gathered
to his people; ⁵¹ because you broke
faith with me in the midst of the people
of Israel at the waters of Mer′i-bath-
ka′desh, in the wilderness of Zin; because you did not revere me as holy
in the midst of the people of Israel.
⁵² For you shall see the land before
you; but you shall not go there, into
the land which I give to the people of
Israel."

33 This is the blessing with which
Moses the man of God blessed
the children of Israel before his death.
² He said,
　"The LORD came from Sinai,
　　and dawned from Se′ir upon us;*i*
　he shone forth from Mount Paran,

f Heb *the lightning of my sword*
g Gk Vg: Heb *his land his people*
h Gk Syr Vg: Heb *Hoshea*
i Gk Syr Vg: Heb *them*

---

vindication of the oppressed (v. 36). *Their foot . . . their doom*, the reference is to Israel's enemies.
37–38: See v. 17 n. **39:** *Kill . . . make alive*, i.e. God is sovereign in all things according to the
poet's faith (Ex.4.11 n.; Is.45.5–7). **43:** *Makes expiation*, cleanses or purges the land and its
people of guilt. **44–47:** The conclusion of 31.16–29. **48–52:** Moses is commanded to ascend
Mount Nebo (Num.20.10–13; 27.12–14).
　33.1–29: The blessing of Moses. Before going to his death, Moses gives his final blessing to
the Israelite tribes (see introduction to the blessing of Jacob, Gen. ch. 49). **1:** On death-bed
blessings, see Gen.27.4 n. This poem assumes that the tribes are already settled in Palestine
rather than looking forward to the settlement. In its present form it probably comes from the
early period of the monarchy, though it may reflect slightly earlier tribal circumstances. Simeon,
for example, is not mentioned, perhaps because the tribe had already disappeared (Gen.49.5–7).

he came from the ten thousands of
    holy ones,
  with flaming fire*j* at his right
    hand.
3 Yea, he loved his people;*k*
  all those consecrated to him were
    in his*x* hand;
 so they followed*j* in thy steps,
  receiving direction from thee,
4 when Moses commanded us a law,
  as a possession for the assembly
    of Jacob.
5 Thus the LORD became king in
    Jesh'urun,
  when the heads of the people were
    gathered,
  all the tribes of Israel together.

6 "Let Reuben live, and not die,
  nor let his men be few."

7 And this he said of Judah:
 "Hear, O LORD, the voice of Judah,
  and bring him in to his people.
 With thy hands contend*l* for him,
  and be a help against his
    adversaries."

8 And of Levi he said,
 "Give to Levi*m* thy Thummim,
  and thy Urim to thy godly one,
 whom thou didst test at Massah,
  with whom thou didst strive at the
    waters of Mer'ibah;
9 who said of his father and mother,
  'I regard them not';
 he disowned his brothers,
  and ignored his children.
 For they observed thy word,
  and kept thy covenant.
10 They shall teach Jacob thy
    ordinances,

  and Israel thy law;
 they shall put incense before thee,
  and whole burnt offering upon thy
    altar.
11 Bless, O LORD, his substance,
  and accept the work of his hands;
 crush the loins of his adversaries,
  of those that hate him, that they
    rise not again."

12 Of Benjamin he said,
 "The beloved of the LORD,
  he dwells in safety by him;
 he encompasses him all the day long,
  and makes his dwelling between
    his shoulders."

13 And of Joseph he said,
 "Blessed by the LORD be his land,
  with the choicest gifts of heaven
    above,*n*
 and of the deep that couches
    beneath,
14 with the choicest fruits of the sun,
  and the rich yield of the months,
15 with the finest produce of the ancient
    mountains,
 and the abundance of the
    everlasting hills,
16 with the best gifts of the earth and
    its fulness,
 and the favor of him that dwelt
    in the bush.
 Let these come upon the head of
    Joseph,
 and upon the crown of the head
    of him that is prince among his
    brothers.

j The meaning of the Hebrew word is uncertain
k Gk: Heb *peoples*   *x* Heb *thy*
l Cn: Heb *with his hands he contended*
m Gk: Heb lacks *Give to Levi*
n Two Heb Mss and Tg: Heb *with the dew*

2–5: Introductory praise of the LORD, who revealed himself *from Sinai* and formed Israel as his people. **5:** *Jeshurun,* see 32.15 n. The LORD was proclaimed king in the *assembly,* the gathering of the tribes and the chiefs of the tribal confederacy (Jos.24.1; Jg.20.2). **6:** Reuben, who once had the leadership of the first-born (see Gen.49.3–4 n.), is apparently threatened with extinction, owing to military pressures in Transjordan. **7:** It is desired that Judah, in sore trouble because of an adversary (perhaps the Philistines), should be helped by other tribes. **8–11:** Levi, once a war-like tribe (Gen.49.5–7), is to receive the prerogatives of priesthood, namely teaching and officiating at the altar. **8:** *Urim* and *Thummim,* see Ex.28.15–30 n. Apparently the Levitical priesthood originated at Kadesh, i.e. *Massah* and *Meribah* (Ex.17.1–7; Num.20.2–13). **9:** On Levi's zealous covenant loyalty see Ex.32.25–29. **13–17:** The wish is that *Joseph* may be blessed with the bounties of nature and with invincible military strength (compare Gen.49.25–26). **16:** *Dwelt in the bush* is rendered by some, "tented on Sinai"–a reference to the LORD's revela-

¹⁷ His firstling bull has majesty,
     and his horns are the horns of a
         wild ox;
     with them he shall push the peoples,
         all of them, to the ends of the
         earth;
     such are the ten thousands of
         E'phraim,
     and such are the thousands of
         Manas'seh."

¹⁸ And of Zeb'ulun he said,
     "Rejoice, Zeb'ulun, in your going
         out;
     and Is'sachar, in your tents.
¹⁹ They shall call peoples to their
         mountain;
     there they offer right sacrifices;
     for they suck the affluence of the
         seas
     and the hidden treasures of the
         sand."

²⁰ And of Gad he said,
     "Blessed be he who enlarges Gad!
     Gad couches like a lion,
     he tears the arm, and the crown
         of the head.
²¹ He chose the best of the land for
         himself,
     for there a commander's portion
         was reserved;
     and he came to the heads of the
         people,
     with Israel he executed the
         commands
     and just decrees of the LORD."

²² And of Dan he said,
     "Dan is a lion's whelp,
     that leaps forth from Bashan."

²³ And of Naph'tali he said,

"O Naph'tali, satisfied with favor,
     and full of the blessing of the
     LORD,
     possess the lake and the south."

²⁴ And of Asher he said,
     "Blessed above sons be Asher;
     let him be the favorite of his
         brothers,
     and let him dip his foot in oil.
²⁵ Your bars shall be iron and bronze;
     and as your days, so shall your
         strength be.

²⁶ "There is none like God, O
         Jesh'urun,
     who rides through the heavens to
         your help,
     and in his majesty through the
         skies.
²⁷ The eternal God is your dwelling
         place,
     and underneath are the everlasting
         arms.
And he thrust out the enemy before
         you,
     and said, Destroy.
²⁸ So Israel dwelt in safety,
     the fountain of Jacob alone,
     in a land of grain and wine;
     yea, his heavens drop down dew.
²⁹ Happy are you, O Israel! Who is
         like you,
     a people saved by the LORD,
     the shield of your help,
     and the sword of your triumph!
     Your enemies shall come fawning
         to you;
     and you shall tread upon their
         high places."

34 And Moses went up from the plains of Moab to Mount Nebo, to the top of Pisgah, which is opposite

---

tion there (Ex.3.1–6). *Prince*, at the time of the poem Joseph enjoyed even greater prestige than Judah (v. 7). **17:** *Ephraim and Manasseh*, the two tribes that composed "the house of Joseph" (see Gen.48.13–14 n.). **18–19:** *Zebulun* and *Issachar* will enjoy great affluence owing to the resources of the Mediterranean and Sea of Galilee (Gen.49.13). **20–21:** *Gad* occupied the best tableland in Transjordan but aided the other tribes in the conquest of Canaan (see Num. ch. 32). **22:** *Dan*, vigorous as *a lion's whelp*, has already migrated from its former position north of Judah to the base of Mount Hermon (Jg. ch. 18). **23:** *Naphtali* is to possess *the lake* (Sea of Galilee). **24–25:** *Asher*, located below Phoenicia, is to be strong and prosperous. **26–29:** An ascription of praise to the LORD who has given Israel victory and security in the bounteous land. **26:** *Jeshurun*, 32.15. **27:** God is a place of refuge and, like a parent, his *everlasting arms* support his children.

Jericho. And the Lord showed him all the land, Gilead as far as Dan, ² all Naph'tali, the land of E'phraim and Manas'seh, all the land of Judah as far as the Western Sea, ³ the Negeb, and the Plain, that is, the valley of Jericho the city of palm trees, as far as Zo'ar. ⁴ And the Lord said to him, "This is the land of which I swore to Abraham, to Isaac, and to Jacob, 'I will give it to your descendants.' I have let you see it with your eyes, but you shall not go over there." ⁵ So Moses the servant of the Lord died there in the land of Moab, according to the word of the Lord, ⁶ and he buried him in the valley in the land of Moab opposite Beth-pe'or; but no man knows the place of his burial to this day. ⁷ Moses was a hundred and twenty years old when he died; his eye was not dim, nor

his natural force abated. ⁸ And the people of Israel wept for Moses in the plains of Moab thirty days; then the days of weeping and mourning for Moses were ended.

9 And Joshua the son of Nun was full of the spirit of wisdom, for Moses had laid his hands upon him; so the people of Israel obeyed him, and did as the Lord had commanded Moses. ¹⁰ And there has not arisen a prophet since in Israel like Moses, whom the Lord knew face to face, ¹¹ none like him for all the signs and the wonders which the Lord sent him to do in the land of Egypt, to Pharaoh and to all his servants and to all his land, ¹² and for all the mighty power and all the great and terrible deeds which Moses wrought in the sight of all Israel.

34.1–12: The death of Moses. This chapter resumes the story from the end of Numbers, after Moses' "Deuteronomic" addresses to Israel. **1:** Two traditions about the place of Moses' death are included here: *Mount Nebo* is in Transjordan east of Jericho; *Mount Pisgah* is a peak in the same range, slightly west. **2–3:** From this lofty height Moses looks northward to the Sea of Galilee (area of Dan and Naphtali), to the Western Sea (Mediterranean), south to the Negeb (southern wilderness of Judah) and the Jordan valley as far south as *Zoar* (once located at the end of the Dead Sea; Gen.14.2). **6:** *He* (i.e. the Lord) secretly buried Moses. **9:** Compare Num. 27.18–23. **10–11:** For the judgment that Moses was the greatest of Israel's prophets, see 18.15–22; Num.12.6–8; compare 11.24–30; Hos.12.13.

THE BOOK OF JOSHUA

After long years of wandering in the desert, permission came at last for the Israelites to conquer the Promised Land. The story of Joshua is the story of the conquest. Like most tales of battles, it is not a pleasant one, and many have felt–no doubt rightly–that the God of Joshua is infinitely remote from the God of Jesus. In this book Israel's God appears as a purely nationalistic deity, a God of Battles whose power is chiefly manifested in the prosecution of Holy War, which the Deuteronomist authorizes and regulates in Dt. ch. 20.

The story opens with the passage of the Jordan River and the bloody sack of Jericho (chs. 1–6); it then tells how the Hebrew armies moved from the Jordan Valley up into the highlands to capture Ai (chs. 7–8) and, through a humorous deception, to become unwilling allies of the Gibeonites (ch. 9). This led to a great battle with the chieftains of five other Canaanite cities and the conquest of the South (ch. 10). A final engagement in the north resulted in the complete destruction of Canaanite power in Palestine (ch. 11). Following a brief summary of Joshua's triumphs (ch. 12), the book describes the division of the land among the several tribes (chs. 13–23) and how Israel entered into a covenant to serve for ever the God whose might had been so awesomely demonstrated (ch. 24).

Although his victories were many, the character of Joshua remains a shadowy one, and evidence in the book of Judges has led many to suspect that the original conquest of Palestine was neither so comprehensive nor so decisive as is here represented. For later generations of Hebrews, as for the modern reader, the chief value of the book is less historical than theological, in the witness it bears to Israel's faith in a God who intends to establish his kingly rule upon earth, who has clearly exhibited his power to do so, and who summons his people to share the triumph of his kingdom by accepting the covenant which he offers them. The book is pervaded by the style and philosophy of Deuteronomy; see Introd. to Dt.

A FTER THE DEATH OF MOSES THE servant of the LORD, the LORD said to Joshua the son of Nun, Moses' minister, 2 "Moses my servant is dead; now therefore arise, go over this Jordan, you and all this people, into the land which I am giving to them, to the people of Israel. 3 Every place that the sole of your foot will tread upon I have given to you, as I promised to Moses. 4 From the wilderness and this Lebanon as far as the great river, the river Euphra'tes, all the land of the Hittites to the Great Sea toward the going down of the sun shall be your territory. 5 No man shall be able to stand before you all the days of your life; as I was with Moses, so I will be with you; I will not fail you or forsake you. 6 Be strong and of good courage; for you shall cause this people to inherit the land which I swore to their fathers to give them. 7 Only be strong and very courageous, being careful to do according to all the law which Moses my servant commanded you; turn not from it to the right hand or to the left, that you may have good success wherever you go. 8 This book of the law shall not depart out of your mouth, but you shall meditate on it day and night, that you may be careful to do according to all that is written in it; for then you shall make your way prosperous, and then you shall have good success. 9 Have I not commanded you? Be strong and of good courage; be not frightened, neither be dismayed; for

1.1–9: The LORD commands Joshua to conquer the land. The death of Moses provided the signal for beginning the invasion, since he had been forbidden to lead it himself (Num.20.12). The generation which had participated in the Exodus forty years before was now dead. 2: The *Jordan* was the natural eastern boundary of Canaan. 4: The limits of the Promised Land were: *the wilderness* (desert) to the south and east; the *Lebanon* mountains to the northwest; *the land of the Hittites* in northern Syria (once part of the Hittite empire); and to the west, *the Great Sea*–the Mediterranean. 8: *This book of the law* means the legal provisions of the Book of Deuteronomy.

the LORD your God is with you wherever you go."

10 Then Joshua commanded the officers of the people, 11 "Pass through the camp, and command the people, 'Prepare your provisions; for within three days you are to pass over this Jordan, to go in to take possession of the land which the LORD your God gives you to possess.' "

12 And to the Reubenites, the Gadites, and the half-tribe of Manas'-seh Joshua said, 13 "Remember the word which Moses the servant of the LORD commanded you, saying, 'The LORD your God is providing you a place of rest, and will give you this land.' 14 Your wives, your little ones, and your cattle shall remain in the land which Moses gave you beyond the Jordan; but all the men of valor among you shall pass over armed before your brethren and shall help them, 15 until the LORD gives rest to your brethren as well as to you, and they also take possession of the land which the LORD your God is giving them; then you shall return to the land of your possession, and shall possess it, the land which Moses the servant of the LORD gave you beyond the Jordan toward the sunrise." 16 And they answered Joshua, "All that you have commanded us we will do, and wherever you send us we will go. 17 Just as we obeyed Moses in all things, so we will obey you; only may the LORD your God be with you, as he was with Moses! 18 Whoever rebels against your commandment and disobeys your words, whatever

you command him, shall be put to death. Only be strong and of good courage."

2 And Joshua the son of Nun sent two men secretly from Shittim as spies, saying, "Go, view the land, especially Jericho." And they went, and came into the house of a harlot whose name was Rahab, and lodged there. 2 And it was told the king of Jericho, "Behold, certain men of Israel have come here tonight to search out the land." 3 Then the king of Jericho sent to Rahab, saying, "Bring forth the men that have come to you, who entered your house; for they have come to search out all the land." 4 But the woman had taken the two men and hidden them; and she said, "True, men came to me, but I did not know where they came from; 5 and when the gate was to be closed, at dark, the men went out; where the men went I do not know; pursue them quickly, for you will overtake them." 6 But she had brought them up to the roof, and hid them with the stalks of flax which she had laid in order on the roof. 7 So the men pursued after them on the way to the Jordan as far as the fords; and as soon as the pursuers had gone out, the gate was shut.

8 Before they lay down, she came up to them on the roof, 9 and said to the men, "I know that the LORD has given you the land, and that the fear of you has fallen upon us, and that all the inhabitants of the land melt away before you. 10 For we have heard how the LORD dried up the water of the

---

1.10–18: Joshua's address to the people. Joshua instructed the nation, including the Transjordanian tribes, to prepare for the invasion. **14:** *Beyond the Jordan* refers to the region east of the Jordan to which these tribes had been assigned (Num. ch. 32). **15:** After they had helped the other tribes conquer the land west of the Jordan, the two and a half tribes were to be permitted to return to their own allotted territory, *which Moses the servant of the LORD gave* them.

2.1–24: Joshua's spies at Jericho. The men whom Joshua sent to reconnoiter the situation found a friendly reception in the house of Rahab, to whom they promise safety when the city is taken. In Heb.11.31 Rahab is counted as one of the heroes of faith. **1:** *Shittim* was the site of the Israelite camp east of Jordan (Num.33.49). *Jericho*, the largest settlement in the lower Jordan valley, was the gateway to western Palestine. Archaeological excavation has thus far failed to disclose any certain remains of the city of Joshua's time. The fact that Rahab was known to be *a harlot*, accustomed to visits from strange men, would make the spies' presence less conspicuous.

Red Sea before you when you came out of Egypt, and what you did to the two kings of the Amorites that were beyond the Jordan, to Sihon and Og, whom you utterly destroyed. 11 And as soon as we heard it, our hearts melted, and there was no courage left in any man, because of you; for the LORD your God is he who is God in heaven above and on earth beneath. 12 Now then, swear to me by the LORD that as I have dealt kindly with you, you also will deal kindly with my father's house, and give me a sure sign, 13 and save alive my father and mother, my brothers and sisters, and all who belong to them, and deliver our lives from death." 14 And the men said to her, "Our life for yours! If you do not tell this business of ours, then we will deal kindly and faithfully with you when the LORD gives us the land."

15 Then she let them down by a rope through the window, for her house was built into the city wall, so that she dwelt in the wall. 16 And she said to them, "Go into the hills, lest the pursuers meet you; and hide yourselves there three days, until the pursuers have returned; then afterward you may go your way." 17 The men said to her, "We will be guiltless with respect to this oath of yours which you have made us swear. 18 Behold, when we come into the land, you shall bind this scarlet cord in the window through which you let us down; and you shall gather into your house your father and mother, your brothers, and all your father's household. 19 If any one goes out of the doors of your house into the street, his blood shall be upon his head, and we shall be guiltless; but if a hand is laid upon any one who is with you in the house, his blood shall be on our head. 20 But if you tell this business of ours, then we shall be guiltless

with respect to your oath which you have made us swear." 21 And she said, "According to your words, so be it." Then she sent them away, and they departed; and she bound the scarlet cord in the window.

22 They departed, and went into the hills, and remained there three days, until the pursuers returned; for the pursuers had made search all along the way and found nothing. 23 Then the two men came down again from the hills, and passed over and came to Joshua the son of Nun; and they told him all that had befallen them. 24 And they said to Joshua, "Truly the LORD has given all the land into our hands; and moreover all the inhabitants of the land are fainthearted because of us."

3 Early in the morning Joshua rose and set out from Shittim, with all the people of Israel; and they came to the Jordan, and lodged there before they passed over. 2 At the end of three days the officers went through the camp 3 and commanded the people, "When you see the ark of the covenant of the LORD your God being carried by the Levitical priests, then you shall set out from your place and follow it, 4 that you may know the way you shall go, for you have not passed this way before. Yet there shall be a space between you and it, a distance of about two thousand cubits; do not come near it." 5 And Joshua said to the people, "Sanctify yourselves; for tomorrow the LORD will do wonders among you." 6 And Joshua said to the priests, "Take up the ark of the covenant, and pass on before the people." And they took up the ark of the covenant, and went before the people.

7 And the LORD said to Joshua, "This day I will begin to exalt you in the sight of all Israel, that they may know that, as I was with Moses, so I will be with you. 8 And you shall com-

---

3.1–17: The miraculous crossing of the Jordan. The waters of the river, swollen by spring floods, are held back to permit the passage of the Israelites. **3:** *The ark* was the special token of the presence of the LORD (Yahweh), and in early days frequently accompanied the Israelite armies into battle (compare Num.10.35–36; 1 Sam.4.6–9). **4:** *Two thousand cubits*, about three thousand feet. **5:** To *sanctify yourselves* is to perform a ritual purification, as one might before

mand the priests who bear the ark of the covenant, 'When you come to the brink of the waters of the Jordan, you shall stand still in the Jordan.' " 9 And Joshua said to the people of Israel, "Come hither, and hear the words of the LORD your God." 10 And Joshua said, "Hereby you shall know that the living God is among you, and that he will without fail drive out from before you the Canaanites, the Hittites, the Hivites, the Per'izzites, the Gir'gashites, the Amorites, and the Jeb'usites. 11 Behold, the ark of the covenant of the Lord of all the earth is to pass over before you into the Jordan. 12 Now therefore take twelve men from the tribes of Israel, from each tribe a man. 13 And when the soles of the feet of the priests who bear the ark of the LORD, the Lord of all the earth, shall rest in the waters of the Jordan, the waters of the Jordan shall be stopped from flowing, and the waters coming down from above shall stand in one heap."

14 So, when the people set out from their tents, to pass over the Jordan with the priests bearing the ark of the covenant before the people, 15 and when those who bore the ark had come to the Jordan, and the feet of the priests bearing the ark were dipped in the brink of the water (the Jordan overflows all its banks throughout the time of harvest), 16 the waters coming down from above stood and rose up in a heap far off, at Adam, the city that is beside Zar'ethan, and those flowing down toward the sea of the Arabah, the Salt Sea, were wholly cut off; and the peo-

ple passed over opposite Jericho. 17 And while all Israel were passing over on dry ground, the priests who bore the ark of the covenant of the LORD stood on dry ground in the midst of the Jordan, until all the nation finished passing over the Jordan.

4 When all the nation had finished passing over the Jordan, the LORD said to Joshua, 2 "Take twelve men from the people, from each tribe a man, 3 and command them, 'Take twelve stones from here out of the midst of the Jordan, from the very place where the priests' feet stood, and carry them over with you, and lay them down in the place where you lodge tonight.' " 4 Then Joshua called the twelve men from the people of Israel, whom he had appointed, a man from each tribe; 5 and Joshua said to them, "Pass on before the ark of the LORD your God into the midst of the Jordan, and take up each of you a stone upon his shoulder, according to the number of the tribes of the people of Israel, 6 that this may be a sign among you, when your children ask in time to come, 'What do those stones mean to you?' 7 Then you shall tell them that the waters of the Jordan were cut off before the ark of the covenant of the LORD; when it passed over the Jordan, the waters of the Jordan were cut off. So these stones shall be to the people of Israel a memorial for ever."

8 And the men of Israel did as Joshua commanded, and took up twelve stones out of the midst of the Jordan, according to the number of the tribes of the people of Israel, as the

---

a religious ceremony. **10:** *Canaanites, Hittites,* etc., are names given somewhat indiscriminately here to the pre-Israelite population of Palestine. In many parts of the Old Testament the terms Canaanite and Amorite are used in the stricter sense as alternative names for the original people of the land, the other names being used for particular clans (such as the Jebusites, 15.63) or for local enclaves of different ethnic stock (such as the Hittites). **16:** *Adam,* where the waters stopped, perhaps because of a landslide, was about eighteen miles north of Jericho; *Zarethan* some twelve miles farther up. *The Salt Sea* is the Dead Sea. It is appropriately called this, since its waters are twenty-five per cent mineral; its surface is 1292 ft. below sea level.

4.1–5.1: A monument commemorating the passage of the river. Due to the fusion of two different original accounts, the present story tells of the setting up of two sets of twelve memorial stones, one in the bed of the river, the other at Gilgal. **4.3:** This verse evidently belongs to the Gilgal narrative, which is continued in vv. 8 and 20. **4,5,6,7,9:** These verses tell of a monument

LORD told Joshua; and they carried them over with them to the place where they lodged, and laid them down there. ⁹ And Joshua set up twelve stones in the midst of the Jordan, in the place where the feet of the priests bearing the ark of the covenant had stood; and they are there to this day. ¹⁰ For the priests who bore the ark stood in the midst of the Jordan, until everything was finished that the LORD commanded Joshua to tell the people, according to all that Moses had commanded Joshua.

The people passed over in haste; ¹¹ and when all the people had finished passing over, the ark of the LORD and the priests passed over before the people. ¹² The sons of Reuben and the sons of Gad and the half-tribe of Manas'seh passed over armed before the people of Israel, as Moses had bidden them; ¹³ about forty thousand ready armed for war passed over before the LORD for battle, to the plains of Jericho. ¹⁴ On that day the LORD exalted Joshua in the sight of all Israel; and they stood in awe of him, as they had stood in awe of Moses, all the days of his life.

15 And the LORD said to Joshua, ¹⁶ "Command the priests who bear the ark of the testimony to come up out of the Jordan." ¹⁷ Joshua therefore commanded the priests, "Come up out of the Jordan." ¹⁸ And when the priests bearing the ark of the covenant of the LORD came up from the midst of the Jordan, and the soles of the priests' feet were lifted up on dry ground, the waters of the Jordan returned to their place and overflowed all its banks, as before.

19 The people came up out of the Jordan on the tenth day of the first month, and they encamped in Gilgal on the east border of Jericho. ²⁰ And those twelve stones, which they took out of the Jordan, Joshua set up in Gilgal. ²¹ And he said to the people of Israel, "When your children ask their fathers in time to come, 'What do these stones mean?' ²² then you shall let your children know, 'Israel passed over this Jordan on dry ground.' ²³ For the LORD your God dried up the waters of the Jordan for you until you passed over, as the LORD your God did to the Red Sea, which he dried up for us until we passed over, ²⁴ so that all the peoples of the earth may know that the hand of the LORD is mighty; that you may fear the LORD your God for ever."

5 When all the kings of the Amorites that were beyond the Jordan to the west, and all the kings of the Canaanites that were by the sea, heard that the LORD had dried up the waters of the Jordan for the people of Israel until they had crossed over, their heart melted, and there was no longer any spirit in them, because of the people of Israel.

2 At that time the LORD said to Joshua, "Make flint knives and circumcise the people of Israel again the second time." ³ So Joshua made flint knives, and circumcised the people of Israel at Gibeath-haaraloth.ᵃ ⁴ And this is the reason why Joshua circumcised them: all the males of the people

ᵃ That is *the hill of the foreskins*

---

set up in the river bed, still visible in the author's day. **12:** The Transjordanian tribes were the first to cross. **19:** *The first month* was Abib (March-April), later called Nisan. *Gilgal*, the precise location of which is uncertain but obviously close to Jericho, became an important Hebrew sanctuary. Here Saul, the first king of Israel, was later crowned (1 Sam.11.15) and David, the second king, was reconciled with his rebellious subjects (2 Sam.19.15,40).

5.2–12: Israel at Gilgal. The Israelites of the new generation, who had not taken part in the Exodus, are circumcised at Gilgal, where they then set up their camp. Circumcision was a means of admission into full membership in the community, and, at least in later times, was regarded as one of the chief tokens of God's covenant relationship with his people (Gen.17.9–14). **3:** The use of flint knives is merely an example of the conservatism natural to religious ceremonies; the Israelites were familiar with the use of metal. *Gibeath-haaraloth*, meaning "the hill of the foreskins," was evidently a well-known site near Gilgal.

who came out of Egypt, all the men of war, had died on the way in the wilderness after they had come out of Egypt. 5 Though all the people who came out had been circumcised, yet all the people that were born on the way in the wilderness after they had come out of Egypt had not been circumcised. 6 For the people of Israel walked forty years in the wilderness, till all the nation, the men of war that came forth out of Egypt, perished, because they did not hearken to the voice of the LORD; to them the LORD swore that he would not let them see the land which the LORD had sworn to their fathers to give us, a land flowing with milk and honey. 7 So it was their children, whom he raised up in their stead, that Joshua circumcised; for they were uncircumcised, because they had not been circumcised on the way.

8 When the circumcising of all the nation was done, they remained in their places in the camp till they were healed. 9 And the LORD said to Joshua, "This day I have rolled away the reproach of Egypt from you." And so the name of that place is called Gilgal*b* to this day.

10 While the people of Israel were encamped in Gilgal they kept the passover on the fourteenth day of the month at evening in the plains of Jericho. 11 And on the morrow after the passover, on that very day, they ate of the produce of the land, unleavened cakes and parched grain. 12 And the manna ceased on the morrow, when they ate of the produce of the land; and the people of Israel had manna no more, but ate of the fruit of the land of Canaan that year.

13 When Joshua was by Jericho, he lifted up his eyes and looked, and behold, a man stood before him with his drawn sword in his hand; and Joshua went to him and said to him, "Are you for us, or for our adversaries?" 14 And he said, "No; but as commander of the army of the LORD I have now come." And Joshua fell on his face to the earth, and worshiped, and said to him, "What does my lord bid his servant?" 15 And the commander of the LORD's army said to Joshua, "Put off your shoes from your feet; for the place where you stand is holy." And Joshua did so.

6 Now Jericho was shut up from within and from without because of the people of Israel; none went out, and none came in. 2 And the LORD said to Joshua, "See, I have given into your hand Jericho, with its king and mighty men of valor. 3 You shall march around the city, all the men of war going around the city once. Thus shall you do for six days. 4 And seven priests shall bear seven trumpets of rams' horns before the ark; and on the seventh day you shall march around the city seven times, the priests blowing the trumpets. 5 And when they make a long blast with the ram's horn, as soon as you hear the sound of the trumpet, then all the people shall shout with a great shout; and the wall of the city will fall down flat, and the people shall go up every man straight before him." 6 So Joshua the son of Nun called the priests and said to them, "Take up the ark of the covenant, and let seven priests bear seven trumpets of rams' horns before the ark of the LORD." 7 And he said to the people, "Go forward; march around the city, and let

b From Heb *galal* to roll

9: The Hebrew verb meaning *rolled away* is from the same root as Gilgal, but the etymology is far-fetched; the true meaning of Gilgal is "circle [of stones]."

5.13–15: Joshua's encounter with the angelic commander. While reconnoitering Jericho before the siege, Joshua met the commander of the LORD's heavenly armies (compare Num.22.22; 2 Kg.6.17). The end of the story seems to be lost; some command is expected after v. 15 (compare Ex.3.5–12).

6.1–14: The beginning of the siege of Jericho. In obedience to divine instructions, the Israelites marched around the city once a day for six days, with some of the priests carrying the ark and others blowing on trumpets. **4:** The sacred number *seven* occurs repeatedly in this chapter.

the armed men pass on before the ark of the LORD."

8 And as Joshua had commanded the people, the seven priests bearing the seven trumpets of rams' horns before the LORD went forward, blowing the trumpets, with the ark of the covenant of the LORD following them. ⁹ And the armed men went before the priests who blew the trumpets, and the rear guard came after the ark, while the trumpets blew continually. ¹⁰ But Joshua commanded the people, "You shall not shout or let your voice be heard, neither shall any word go out of your mouth, until the day I bid you shout; then you shall shout." ¹¹ So he caused the ark of the LORD to compass the city, going about it once; and they came into the camp, and spent the night in the camp.

12 Then Joshua rose early in the morning, and the priests took up the ark of the LORD. ¹³ And the seven priests bearing the seven trumpets of rams' horns before the ark of the LORD passed on, blowing the trumpets continually; and the armed men went before them, and the rear guard came after the ark of the LORD, while the trumpets blew continually. ¹⁴ And the second day they marched around the city once, and returned into the camp. So they did for six days.

15 On the seventh day they rose early at the dawn of day, and marched around the city in the same manner seven times: it was only on that day that they marched around the city seven times. ¹⁶ And at the seventh time, when the priests had blown the trumpets, Joshua said to the people, "Shout; for the LORD has given you the city. ¹⁷ And the city and all that is within it shall be devoted to the LORD

for destruction; only Rahab the harlot and all who are with her in her house shall live, because she hid the messengers that we sent. ¹⁸ But you, keep yourselves from the things devoted to destruction, lest when you have devoted them you take any of the devoted things and make the camp of Israel a thing for destruction, and bring trouble upon it. ¹⁹ But all silver and gold, and vessels of bronze and iron, are sacred to the LORD; they shall go into the treasury of the LORD." ²⁰ So the people shouted, and the trumpets were blown. As soon as the people heard the sound of the trumpet, the people raised a great shout, and the wall fell down flat, so that the people went up into the city, every man straight before him, and they took the city. ²¹ Then they utterly destroyed all in the city, both men and women, young and old, oxen, sheep, and asses, with the edge of the sword.

22 And Joshua said to the two men who had spied out the land, "Go into the harlot's house, and bring out from it the woman, and all who belong to her, as you swore to her." ²³ So the young men who had been spies went in, and brought out Rahab, and her father and mother and brothers and all who belonged to her; and they brought all her kindred, and set them outside the camp of Israel. ²⁴ And they burned the city with fire, and all within it; only the silver and gold, and the vessels of bronze and of iron, they put into the treasury of the house of the LORD. ²⁵ But Rahab the harlot, and her father's household, and all who belonged to her, Joshua saved alive; and she dwelt in Israel to this day, because she hid the messengers whom Joshua sent to spy out Jericho.

26 Joshua laid an oath upon them

6.15–27: The fall of the city. When, on the seventh day, the procession makes a seven-fold circuit of the town, the shout of the Israelite army is enough to overthrow the walls. **17:** *Devoted . . . for destruction* is a technical term meaning that the city and all that is in it is to be offered as a holocaust to the LORD; the taking of booty is strictly forbidden (compare Dt.20.16; 1 Sam. 15.3). **21:** *Utterly destroyed* translates the same technical term discussed in v. 17. **24:** *The house of the LORD* is an obvious anachronism since the temple did not exist and had not even been projected in the time of Joshua. **25:** *To this day* indicates that Rahab's descendants still lived in Jericho in the writer's time. The phrase is a fixed formula in tales which are told to explain

at that time, saying, "Cursed before the LORD be the man that rises up and rebuilds this city, Jericho.

At the cost of his first-born shall he
    lay its foundation,
and at the cost of his youngest son
    shall he set up its gates."

27 So the LORD was with Joshua; and his fame was in all the land.

7 But the people of Israel broke faith in regard to the devoted things; for Achan the son of Carmi, son of Zabdi, son of Zerah, of the tribe of Judah, took some of the devoted things; and the anger of the LORD burned against the people of Israel.

2 Joshua sent men from Jericho to Ai, which is near Beth-a′ven, east of Bethel, and said to them, "Go up and spy out the land." And the men went up and spied out Ai. ³ And they returned to Joshua, and said to him, "Let not all the people go up, but let about two or three thousand men go up and attack Ai; do not make the whole people toil up there, for they are but few." ⁴ So about three thousand went up there from the people; and they fled before the men of Ai, ⁵ and the men of Ai killed about thirty-six men of them, and chased them before the gate as far as Sheb′arim, and slew them at the descent. And the hearts of the people melted, and became as water.

6 Then Joshua rent his clothes, and fell to the earth upon his face before the ark of the LORD until the evening, he and the elders of Israel; and they put dust upon their heads. ⁷ And Joshua said, "Alas, O Lord GOD, why hast thou brought this people over the Jordan at all, to give us into the hands of the Amorites, to destroy us? Would that we had been content to dwell beyond the Jordan! ⁸ O Lord, what can I say, when Israel has turned their backs before their enemies! ⁹ For the Canaanites and all the inhabitants of the land will hear of it, and will surround us, and cut off our name from the earth; and what wilt thou do for thy great name?"

10 The LORD said to Joshua, "Arise, why have you thus fallen upon your face? ¹¹ Israel has sinned; they have transgressed my covenant which I commanded them; they have taken some of the devoted things; they have stolen, and lied, and put them among their own stuff. ¹² Therefore the people of Israel cannot stand before their enemies; they turn their backs before their enemies, because they have become a thing for destruction. I will be with you no more, unless you destroy the devoted things from among you. ¹³ Up, sanctify the people, and say, 'Sanctify yourselves for tomorrow; for thus says the LORD, God of Israel, "There are devoted things in the midst of you, O Israel; you cannot stand before your enemies, until you take away the devoted things from among you." ¹⁴ In the morning therefore you shall be brought near by your tribes; and the tribe which the LORD takes shall come near by families; and the family which the LORD takes shall come near by households; and the household which the LORD takes shall come near man by man. ¹⁵ And he who is taken with the devoted things shall be burned with fire, he and all

curious facts, names, and institutions of later days (compare 4.9; 7.26; 8.28; 9.27). **26:** The fulfilment of the curse is recorded in 1 Kg.16.34.

7.1–5: Frustration at Ai. Because one man violated the oath of destruction at Jericho, Israel lost the first battle for Ai. **1:** This verse anticipates vv. 6–21. **2:** Ai was high on the mountain ridge northwest of Jericho. The words *which is near Beth-aven* should be omitted, since "Beth-aven" ("House of Wickedness") is merely a deliberate, mocking distortion of the following name, *Bethel*. Many scholars hold that this story is not really an account of the battle for Ai, but for Bethel, since otherwise the book of Joshua contains no account of the capture of this important site (compare, however, Jg.1.22–26). **3:** The spies reported the place to be so weak that a small force could take it.

7.6–26: The discovery and punishment of the criminal. 11: The ancient unitary view of society caused the entire group to be blamed for the sin of one of its members. **14:** *The LORD takes,*

that he has, because he has transgressed the covenant of the LORD, and because he has done a shameful thing in Israel.' "

16 So Joshua rose early in the morning, and brought Israel near tribe by tribe, and the tribe of Judah was taken; 17 and he brought near the families of Judah, and the family of the Zer'ahites was taken; and he brought near the family of the Zer'ahites man by man, and Zabdi was taken; 18 and he brought near his household man by man, and Achan the son of Carmi, son of Zabdi, son of Zerah, of the tribe of Judah, was taken. 19 Then Joshua said to Achan, "My son, give glory to the LORD God of Israel, and render praise to him; and tell me now what you have done; do not hide it from me." 20 And Achan answered Joshua, "Of a truth I have sinned against the LORD God of Israel, and this is what I did: 21 when I saw among the spoil a beautiful mantle from Shinar, and two hundred shekels of silver, and a bar of gold weighing fifty shekels, then I coveted them, and took them; and behold, they are hidden in the earth inside my tent, with the silver underneath."

22 So Joshua sent messengers, and they ran to the tent; and behold, it was hidden in his tent with the silver underneath. 23 And they took them out of the tent and brought them to Joshua and all the people of Israel; and they laid them down before the LORD. 24 And Joshua and all Israel with him took Achan the son of Zerah, and the silver and the mantle and the bar of gold, and his sons and daughters, and his oxen and asses and sheep, and his tent, and all that he had; and they brought them up to the Valley of Achor. 25 And Joshua said, "Why

did you bring trouble on us? The LORD brings trouble on you today." And all Israel stoned him with stones; they burned them with fire, and stoned them with stones. 26 And they raised over him a great heap of stones that remains to this day; then the LORD turned from his burning anger. Therefore to this day the name of that place is called the Valley of Achor.*c*

8 And the LORD said to Joshua, "Do not fear or be dismayed; take all the fighting men with you, and arise, go up to Ai; see, I have given into your hand the king of Ai, and his people, his city, and his land; 2 and you shall do to Ai and its king as you did to Jericho and its king; only its spoil and its cattle you shall take as booty for yourselves; lay an ambush against the city, behind it."

3 So Joshua arose, and all the fighting men, to go up to Ai; and Joshua chose thirty thousand mighty men of valor, and sent them forth by night. 4 And he commanded them, "Behold, you shall lie in ambush against the city, behind it; do not go very far from the city, but hold yourselves all in readiness; 5 and I, and all the people who are with me, will approach the city. And when they come out against us, as before, we shall flee before them; 6 and they will come out after us, till we have drawn them away from the city; for they will say, 'They are fleeing from us, as before.' So we will flee from them; 7 then you shall rise up from the ambush, and seize the city; for the LORD your God will give it into your hand. 8 And when you have taken the city, you shall set the city on fire, doing as the LORD has bidden; see, I have commanded you." 9 So Joshua sent them

c That is *Trouble*

by the casting of lots. **24–25:** The unitary conception of society required that all the members of Achan's family group, human and animal, be purged from Israel (see Dan.6.24 n.). **25:** The Hebrew word *trouble* is from the same root as the proper name Achor (compare Hos.2.15). See the last sentence of v. 26.

8.1–29: Victory at Ai. Israel, now cleansed of Achan's guilt, easily captures and destroys Ai, by a clever strategem. **4–8:** The plan of battle. **9–23:** These verses tell how the ambush was placed and the ruse successfully carried out. **9:** *Bethel*, the modern Beitin, later one of the chief shrines of the Northern Kingdom (1 Kg.12.28–30), is about one and one-quarter miles

forth; and they went to the place of ambush, and lay between Bethel and Ai, to the west of Ai; but Joshua spent that night among the people.

10 And Joshua arose early in the morning and mustered the people, and went up, with the elders of Israel, before the people to Ai. 11 And all the fighting men who were with him went up, and drew near before the city, and encamped on the north side of Ai, with a ravine between them and Ai. 12 And he took about five thousand men, and set them in ambush between Bethel and Ai, to the west of the city. 13 So they stationed the forces, the main encampment which was north of the city and its rear guard west of the city. But Joshua spent that night in the valley. 14 And when the king of Ai saw this he and all his people, the men of the city, made haste and went out early to the descent*d* toward the Arabah to meet Israel in battle; but he did not know that there was an ambush against him behind the city. 15 And Joshua and all Israel made a pretense of being beaten before them, and fled in the direction of the wilderness. 16 So all the people who were in the city were called together to pursue them, and as they pursued Joshua they were drawn away from the city. 17 There was not a man left in Ai or Bethel, who did not go out after Israel; they left the city open, and pursued Israel.

18 Then the LORD said to Joshua, "Stretch out the javelin that is in your hand toward Ai; for I will give it into your hand." And Joshua stretched out the javelin that was in his hand toward the city. 19 And the ambush rose quickly out of their place, and as soon as he had stretched out his hand, they ran and entered the city and took it; and they made haste to set the city on fire. 20 So when the men of Ai looked back, behold, the smoke of the city went up to heaven; and they had no power to flee this way or that, for the people that fled to the wilderness turned back upon the pursuers. 21 And when Joshua and all Israel saw that the ambush had taken the city, and that the smoke of the city went up, then they turned back and smote the men of Ai. 22 And the others came forth from the city against them; so they were in the midst of Israel, some on this side, and some on that side; and Israel smote them, until there was left none that survived or escaped. 23 But the king of Ai they took alive, and brought him to Joshua.

24 When Israel had finished slaughtering all the inhabitants of Ai in the open wilderness where they pursued them and all of them to the very last had fallen by the edge of the sword, all Israel returned to Ai, and smote it with the edge of the sword. 25 And all who fell that day, both men and women, were twelve thousand, all the people of Ai. 26 For Joshua did not draw back his hand, with which he stretched out the javelin, until he had utterly destroyed all the inhabitants of Ai. 27 Only the cattle and the spoil of that city Israel took as their booty, according to the word of the LORD which he commanded Joshua. 28 So Joshua burned Ai, and made it for ever a heap of ruins, as it is to this day. 29 And he hanged the king of Ai on a tree until evening; and at the going down of the sun Joshua commanded, and they took his body down from the tree, and cast it at the entrance of the gate of the city, and raised over it a great heap of stones, which stands there to this day.

30 Then Joshua built an altar in

d Cn: Heb *appointed time*

---

northwest of Ai. **18:** To *stretch out the javelin* is obviously a symbolic gesture (compare Ex. 17.8–13; 2 Kg.13.15–19). **26:** *Utterly destroyed,* see 6.17 n. **28:** Since the word *Ai* itself means "ruin," the original name of the city must have been something different. Archaeological excavation has shown that Ai (modern et-Tell) was destroyed about one thousand years before the time of Joshua, so it is probable that the story originally had reference to the capture of another site nearby, possibly Bethel. **29:** *A great heap of stones,* an historical "monument" pointed out in the writer's day (compare 4.9; 7.26; Jg. 6.24; 1 Sam.6.18).

Mount Ebal to the LORD, the God of Israel, ³¹ as Moses the servant of the LORD had commanded the people of Israel, as it is written in the book of the law of Moses, "an altar of unhewn stones, upon which no man has lifted an iron tool"; and they offered on it burnt offerings to the LORD, and sacrificed peace offerings. ³² And there, in the presence of the people of Israel, he wrote upon the stones a copy of the law of Moses, which he had written. ³³ And all Israel, sojourner as well as homeborn, with their elders and officers and their judges, stood on opposite sides of the ark before the Levitical priests who carried the ark of the covenant of the LORD, half of them in front of Mount Ger'izim and half of them in front of Mount Ebal, as Moses the servant of the LORD had commanded at the first, that they should bless the people of Israel. ³⁴ And afterward he read all the words of the law, the blessing and the curse, according to all that is written in the book of the law. ³⁵ There was not a word of all that Moses commanded which Joshua did not read before all the assembly of Israel, and the women, and the little ones, and the sojourners who lived among them.

9 When all the kings who were beyond the Jordan in the hill country and in the lowland all along the coast of the Great Sea toward Lebanon, the Hittites, the Amorites, the Canaanites, the Per'izzites, the Hivites, and the Jeb'usites, heard of this, ² they gathered together with one accord to fight Joshua and Israel.

3 But when the inhabitants of Gibeon heard what Joshua had done to Jericho and to Ai, ⁴ they on their part acted with cunning, and went and made ready provisions, and took worn-out sacks upon their asses, and wineskins, worn-out and torn and mended, ⁵ with worn-out, patched sandals on their feet, and worn-out clothes; and all their provisions were dry and moldy. ⁶ And they went to Joshua in the camp at Gilgal, and said to him and to the men of Israel, "We have come from a far country; so now make a covenant with us." ⁷ But the men of Israel said to the Hivites, "Perhaps you live among us; then how can we make a covenant with you?" ⁸ They said to Joshua, "We are your servants." And Joshua said to them, "Who are you? And where do you come from?" ⁹ They said to him, "From a very far country your servants have come, because of the name of the LORD your God; for we have heard a report of him, and all that he did in Egypt, ¹⁰ and all that he did to the two kings of the Amorites who were beyond the Jordan, Sihon the king of Heshbon, and Og king of Bashan, who dwelt in Ash'taroth. ¹¹ And our elders and all the inhabitants of our country said to us, 'Take provisions in your hand for the journey, and go to meet them, and say to them, "We are your servants; come now, make a covenant with us." ' ¹² Here is our bread; it was still warm when we took it from our houses as our food for the journey, on the day we set forth to come to you, but now, behold, it is dry and moldy; ¹³ these wineskins were new when we filled them, and behold, they are burst; and these garments and shoes of ours are worn out from the very long journey."

8.30–35: The altar on Mt. Ebal. Joshua carries out the command given to Moses in Dt. 27.4–5 (compare 11.29–30) to build an altar and set up a copy of the law. Since this section interrupts the narrative of the conquest (note how naturally 8.29 connects with 9.3), it is probably not original here. **30:** *Mount Ebal* is one of the twin mountains (Gerizim being the other) which flank the pass of Shechem in central Palestine, about twenty miles due north of Ai. **33:** *As Moses . . . had commanded* (compare Dt.27.11–12).

9.1–27: The stratagem of the Gibeonites. To avoid the fate of Jericho and Ai, the men of Gibeon trick the Israelites into making an alliance with them by pretending to come from a long distance. **3:** *Gibeon* is the modern El-Jib, about seven miles southwest of Ai. **6:** According to the law in Dt.20.15–16, Israel was permitted to make peace only with those who lived in *a*

[14] So the men partook of their provisions, and did not ask direction from the LORD. [15] And Joshua made peace with them, and made a covenant with them, to let them live; and the leaders of the congregation swore to them.

16 At the end of three days after they had made a covenant with them, they heard that they were their neighbors, and that they dwelt among them. [17] And the people of Israel set out and reached their cities on the third day. Now their cities were Gibeon, Chephi′rah, Be-er′oth, and Kir′iath-je′arim. [18] But the people of Israel did not kill them, because the leaders of the congregation had sworn to them by the LORD, the God of Israel. Then all the congregation murmured against the leaders. [19] But all the leaders said to all the congregation, "We have sworn to them by the LORD, the God of Israel, and now we may not touch them. [20] This we will do to them, and let them live, lest wrath be upon us, because of the oath which we swore to them." [21] And the leaders said to them, "Let them live." So they became hewers of wood and drawers of water for all the congregation, as the leaders had said of them.

22 Joshua summoned them, and he said to them, "Why did you deceive us, saying, 'We are very far from you,' when you dwell among us? [23] Now therefore you are cursed, and some of you shall always be slaves, hewers of wood and drawers of water for the house of my God." [24] They answered Joshua, "Because it was told to your servants for a certainty that the LORD your God had commanded his servant Moses to give you all the land, and to destroy all the inhabitants of the land from before you; so we feared greatly for our lives because of you, and did this thing. [25] And now, behold, we are in your hand: do as it seems good and right in your sight to do to us." [26] So he did to them, and delivered them out of the hand of the people of Israel; and they did not kill them. [27] But Joshua made them that day hewers of wood and drawers of water for the congregation and for the altar of the LORD, to continue to this day, in the place which he should choose.

10 When Ado′ni-ze′dek king of Jerusalem heard how Joshua had taken Ai, and had utterly destroyed it, doing to Ai and its king as he had done to Jericho and its king, and how the inhabitants of Gibeon had made peace with Israel and were among them, [2] he[x] feared greatly, because Gibeon was a great city, like one of the royal cities, and because it was greater than Ai, and all its men were mighty. [3] So Ado′ni-ze′dek king of Jerusalem sent to Hoham king of Hebron, to Piram king of Jarmuth, to Japhi′a king of Lachish, and to Debir king of Eglon, saying, [4] "Come up to me, and help me, and let us smite Gibeon; for it has made peace with Joshua and with the people of Israel." [5] Then the five kings of the Amorites, the king of Jerusalem, the king of Hebron, the king of Jarmuth, the king of Lachish, and the king of Eglon, gathered their forces,

x Heb *they*

---

far country; close neighbors were to be exterminated. **20:** An *oath* once taken, even in error, could not safely be broken. **27:** *To this day* indicates that a group of Gibeonites performed these menial services at the temple in the writer's own time. *The place which he should choose* is a conventional circumlocution for "Jerusalem" in Deuteronomy (e.g. 12.5,11,14,18) and the historical books (Joshua-Kings) which are related to it. The "nethinim" of later times (see Ezra 8.17 note *k*) were mostly foreigners who, like the Gibeonites, had come into the hands of the Hebrews usually as captives in war, and had been dedicated as temple servants (Ezra 8.20).

10.1–27: Israel's victory over the five kings. Joshua comes to the rescue of his new allies, the Gibeonites, when they are attacked by a coalition of five powerful Amorite cities. **1–5:** The loss of three important cities, two by conquest and one by capitulation, forced the Canaanite rulers to take the Israelite invasion seriously and unite to discourage any tendency toward defeatism. **3:** *Hebron* is the most important city in the south of Palestine; the other three places are a con-

and went up with all their armies and encamped against Gibeon, and made war against it.

6 And the men of Gibeon sent to Joshua at the camp in Gilgal, saying, "Do not relax your hand from your servants; come up to us quickly, and save us, and help us; for all the kings of the Amorites that dwell in the hill country are gathered against us." 7 So Joshua went up from Gilgal, he and all the people of war with him, and all the mighty men of valor. 8 And the LORD said to Joshua, "Do not fear them, for I have given them into your hands; there shall not a man of them stand before you." 9 So Joshua came upon them suddenly, having marched up all night from Gilgal. 10 And the LORD threw them into a panic before Israel, who slew them with a great slaughter at Gibeon, and chased them by the way of the ascent of Beth-hor'on, and smote them as far as Aze'-kah and Makke'dah. 11 And as they fled before Israel, while they were going down the ascent of Beth-hor'on, the LORD threw down great stones from heaven upon them as far as Aze'kah, and they died; there were more who died because of the hail-stones than the men of Israel killed with the sword.

12 Then spoke Joshua to the LORD in the day when the LORD gave the Amorites over to the men of Israel; and he said in the sight of Israel,

"Sun, stand thou still at Gibeon,
    and thou Moon in the valley of
    Ai'jalon."
13 And the sun stood still, and the
    moon stayed,
    until the nation took vengeance on
    their enemies.
Is this not written in the Book of

Jashar? The sun stayed in the midst of heaven, and did not hasten to go down for about a whole day. 14 There has been no day like it before or since, when the LORD hearkened to the voice of a man; for the LORD fought for Israel.

15 Then Joshua returned, and all Israel with him, to the camp at Gilgal.

16 These five kings fled, and hid themselves in the cave at Makke'dah. 17 And it was told Joshua, "The five kings have been found, hidden in the cave at Makke'dah." 18 And Joshua said, "Roll great stones against the mouth of the cave, and set men by it to guard them; 19 but do not stay there yourselves, pursue your enemies, fall upon their rear, do not let them enter their cities; for the LORD your God has given them into your hand." 20 When Joshua and the men of Israel had finished slaying them with a very great slaughter, until they were wiped out, and when the remnant which remained of them had entered into the fortified cities, 21 all the people returned safe to Joshua in the camp at Makke'dah; not a man moved his tongue against any of the people of Israel.

22 Then Joshua said, "Open the mouth of the cave, and bring those five kings out to me from the cave." 23 And they did so, and brought those five kings out to him from the cave, the king of Jerusalem, the king of Hebron, the king of Jarmuth, the king of Lachish, and the king of Eglon. 24 And when they brought those kings out to Joshua, Joshua summoned all the men of Israel, and said to the chiefs of the men of war who had gone with him, "Come near, put your feet upon the necks of these kings." Then they came

siderable distance to the southwest of Jerusalem. **10:** The two towns of Upper and Lower *Beth-horon* controlled the pass to the coastal plain west of Gibeon. **11:** *There were more who died because of the hailstones . . .* is a characteristic expression of the writer's belief that Israel's victories were miracles accomplished by the LORD's intervention rather than by the people's skill in warfare. The Book of Joshua views the entire conquest as a miracle rather than a military achievement. **13:** *The Book of Jashar* was an ancient collection, now lost, of Hebrew poetry (compare 2 Sam.1.18). The statement that *the sun stayed* is a prosaic literalizing of the poetic imagery of the preceding lines. **16–27:** The fugitive kings are captured, humiliated, and

near, and put their feet on their necks. [25] And Joshua said to them, "Do not be afraid or dismayed; be strong and of good courage; for thus the LORD will do to all your enemies against whom you fight." [26] And afterward Joshua smote them and put them to death, and he hung them on five trees. And they hung upon the trees until evening; [27] but at the time of the going down of the sun, Joshua commanded, and they took them down from the trees, and threw them into the cave where they had hidden themselves, and they set great stones against the mouth of the cave, which remain to this very day.

28 And Joshua took Makke′dah on that day, and smote it and its king with the edge of the sword; he utterly destroyed every person in it, he left none remaining; and he did to the king of Makke′dah as he had done to the king of Jericho.

29 Then Joshua passed on from Makke′dah, and all Israel with him, to Libnah, and fought against Libnah; [30] and the LORD gave it also and its king into the hand of Israel; and he smote it with the edge of the sword, and every person in it; he left none remaining in it; and he did to its king as he had done to the king of Jericho.

31 And Joshua passed on from Libnah, and all Israel with him, to Lachish, and laid siege to it, and assaulted it: [32] and the LORD gave Lachish into the hand of Israel, and he took it on the second day, and smote it with the edge of the sword, and every person in it, as he had done to Libnah.

33 Then Horam king of Gezer came up to help Lachish; and Joshua smote him and his people, until he left none remaining.

34 And Joshua passed on with all Israel from Lachish to Eglon; and they laid siege to it, and assaulted it; [35] and they took it on that day, and smote it with the edge of the sword; and every person in it he utterly destroyed that day, as he had done to Lachish.

36 Then Joshua went up with all Israel from Eglon to Hebron; and they assaulted it, [37] and took it, and smote it with the edge of the sword, and its king and its towns, and every person in it; he left none remaining, as he had done to Eglon, and utterly destroyed it with every person in it.

38 Then Joshua, with all Israel, turned back to Debir and assaulted it, [39] and he took it with its king and all its towns; and they smote them with the edge of the sword, and utterly destroyed every person in it; he left none remaining; as he had done to Hebron and to Libnah and its king, so he did to Debir and to its king.

40 So Joshua defeated the whole land, the hill country and the Negeb and the lowland and the slopes, and all their kings; he left none remaining, but utterly destroyed all that breathed, as the LORD God of Israel commanded. [41] And Joshua defeated them from Ka′desh-bar′nea to Gaza, and all the country of Goshen, as far as Gibeon. [42] And Joshua took all these kings and their land at one time, because the LORD God of Israel fought for Israel. [43] Then Joshua returned, and all Israel with him, to the camp at Gilgal.

11 When Jabin king of Hazor heard of this, he sent to Jobab king of Madon, and to the king of Shimron, and to the king of Ach′shaph, [2] and to the kings who were in the northern hill country, and in the Ara-

---

killed. **27:** The phrase *to this very day* shows that the story served to explain a heap of stones visible in the writer's own time.

10.28–43: Summary of Joshua's conquests in the south. After the defeat of the five kings Israel had no difficulty in subjugating the whole of southern Palestine. **40–42:** The completeness of the victory.

11.1–23: Israel's victory over the kings of the north. When the northern Canaanite rulers, aroused by the report of Israel's victories in the south, unite to oppose her, they are overwhelmingly defeated. **1:** *Hazor* was one of the largest cities of Galilee. Excavations have impressively demonstrated its importance in antiquity and confirmed the fact that it was cap-

bah south of Chin'neroth, and in the lowland, and in Naphoth-dor on the west, [3] to the Canaanites in the east and the west, the Amorites, the Hittites, the Per'izzites, and the Jeb'usites in the hill country, and the Hivites under Hermon in the land of Mizpah. [4] And they came out, with all their troops, a great host, in number like the sand that is upon the seashore, with very many horses and chariots. [5] And all these kings joined their forces, and came and encamped together at the waters of Merom, to fight with Israel.

6 And the LORD said to Joshua, "Do not be afraid of them, for tomorrow at this time I will give over all of them, slain, to Israel; you shall hamstring their horses, and burn their chariots with fire." [7] So Joshua came suddenly upon them with all his people of war, by the waters of Merom, and fell upon them. [8] And the LORD gave them into the hand of Israel, who smote them and chased them as far as Great Sidon and Mis'rephoth-ma'im, and eastward as far as the valley of Mizpeh; and they smote them, until they left none remaining. [9] And Joshua did to them as the LORD bade him; he hamstrung their horses, and burned their chariots with fire.

10 And Joshua turned back at that time, and took Hazor, and smote its king with the sword; for Hazor formerly was the head of all those kingdoms. [11] And they put to the sword all who were in it, utterly destroying them; there was none left that breathed, and he burned Hazor with fire. [12] And all the cities of those kings, and all their kings, Joshua took, and smote them with the edge of the sword, utterly destroying them, as Moses the servant of the LORD had commanded. [13] But none of the cities that stood on mounds

did Israel burn, except Hazor only; that Joshua burned. [14] And all the spoil of these cities and the cattle, the people of Israel took for their booty; but every man they smote with the edge of the sword, until they had destroyed them, and they did not leave any that breathed. [15] As the LORD had commanded Moses his servant, so Moses commanded Joshua, and so Joshua did; he left nothing undone of all that the LORD had commanded Moses.

16 So Joshua took all that land, the hill country and all the Negeb and all the land of Goshen and the lowland and the Arabah and the hill country of Israel and its lowland [17] from Mount Halak, that rises toward Se'ir, as far as Ba'al-gad in the valley of Lebanon below Mount Hermon. And he took all their kings, and smote them, and put them to death. [18] Joshua made war a long time with all those kings. [19] There was not a city that made peace with the people of Israel, except the Hivites, the inhabitants of Gibeon; they took all in battle. [20] For it was the LORD'S doing to harden their hearts that they should come against Israel in battle, in order that they should be utterly destroyed, and should receive no mercy but be exterminated, as the LORD commanded Moses.

21 And Joshua came at that time, and wiped out the Anakim from the hill country, from Hebron, from Debir, from Anab, and from all the hill country of Judah, and from all the hill country of Israel; Joshua utterly destroyed them with their cities. [22] There was none of the Anakim left in the land of the people of Israel; only in Gaza, in Gath, and in Ashdod, did some remain. [23] So Joshua took the whole land, according to all that the LORD had spoken to Moses; and Joshua gave it for an in-

tured at about the time indicated in this narrative. **2:** The *Arabah* is the Jordan Valley; *Chinneroth* is the ancient name for the Sea of Galilee. **5:** *The waters of Merom* are identified by many with a brook which flows from Merom (modern Meiron) into the Sea of Galilee on the northwest. **8:** *Sidon* is the great Phoenician seaport to the north of Palestine. **16–20:** With victory in the north, the conquest of the land is now complete. **21:** *The Anakim* were reputed to be a race of giants (compare 13.12; Dt.2.10,11). **23:** Nothing now remained but to divide the land among the various tribes.

heritance to Israel according to their tribal allotments. And the land had rest from war.

12 Now these are the kings of the land, whom the people of Israel defeated, and took possession of their land beyond the Jordan toward the sunrising, from the valley of the Arnon to Mount Hermon, with all the Arabah eastward: [2] Sihon king of the Amorites who dwelt at Heshbon, and ruled from Aro'er, which is on the edge of the valley of the Arnon, and from the middle of the valley as far as the river Jabbok, the boundary of the Ammonites, that is, half of Gilead, [3] and the Arabah to the Sea of Chin'neroth eastward, and in the direction of Beth-jesh'imoth, to the sea of the Arabah, the Salt Sea, southward to the foot of the slopes of Pisgah; [4] and Og[e] king of Bashan, one of the remnant of the Reph'aim, who dwelt at Ash'taroth and at Ed're-i [5] and ruled over Mount Hermon and Sal'ecah and all Bashan to the boundary of the Gesh'urites and the Ma-ac'athites, and over half of Gilead to the boundary of Sihon king of Heshbon. [6] Moses, the servant of the LORD, and the people of Israel defeated them; and Moses the servant of the LORD gave their land for a possession to the Reubenites and the Gadites and the half-tribe of Manas'seh.

7 And these are the kings of the land whom Joshua and the people of Israel defeated on the west side of the Jordan, from Ba'al-gad in the valley of Lebanon to Mount Halak, that rises toward Se'ir (and Joshua gave their land to the tribes of Israel as a possession according to their allotments, [8] in the hill country, in the lowland, in the Arabah, in the slopes, in the wilderness, and in the Negeb, the land of the Hittites, the Amorites, the Canaanites, the Per'izzites, the Hivites, and the Jeb'usites): [9] the king of Jericho, one; the king of Ai, which is beside Bethel, one; [10] the king of Jerusalem, one; the king of Hebron, one; [11] the king of Jarmuth, one; the king of Lachish, one; [12] the king of Eglon, one; the king of Gezer, one; [13] the king of Debir, one; the king of Geder, one; [14] the king of Hormah, one; the king of Arad, one; [15] the king of Libnah, one; the king of Adullam, one; [16] the king of Makke'dah, one; the king of Bethel, one; [17] the king of Tap'puah, one; the king of Hepher, one; [18] the king of Aphek, one; the king of Lashar'on, one; [19] the king of Madon, one; the king of Hazor, one; [20] the king of Shim'ron-me'ron, one; the king of Ach'shaph, one; [21] the king of Ta'anach, one; the king of Megid'do, one; [22] the king of Kedesh, one; the king of Jok'ne-am in Carmel, one; [23] the king of Dor in Naphath-dor, one; the king of Goi'im in Galilee,[f] one; [24] the king of Tirzah, one: in all, thirty-one kings.

13 Now Joshua was old and advanced in years; and the LORD said to him, "You are old and advanced in years, and there remains yet very much land to be possessed. [2] This is the land that yet remains: all the regions of the Philistines, and all those of the Gesh'urites [3] (from the Shihor, which is east of Egypt, northward to the boundary of Ekron, it is reckoned as Canaanite; there are five rulers of the Philistines, those of Gaza, Ashdod, Ash'kelon, Gath, and Ekron), and those of the Avvim, [4] in the south, all the land of the Canaanites, and Me-ar'ah which belongs to the Sido'nians, to Aphek, to the boundary of the Amorites, [5] and the land of the Geb'alites, and all Lebanon, toward the sunrising, from Ba'al-gad below Mount Hermon to the entrance of Hamath, [6] all the inhabitants of the hill country from Leb-

e Gk: Heb *the boundary of Og*   *f* Gk: Heb *Gilgal*

12.1–24: Summary of Israel's victories. 1–6: Moses' exploits in Transjordan. These events are related in Num.21.21–35. **7–24:** Joshua's conquests in the territory west of the Jordan. Many of these names were not mentioned previously. The "kings" were merely local chieftains.

    13.1–33: The beginning of the distribution of the land. Chapters 13–21 are entirely concerned with this subject. **2–7:** These are territories as yet unconquered, most of them (except for the

anon to Mis'rephoth-ma'im, even all the Sido'nians. I will myself drive them out from before the people of Israel; only allot the land to Israel for an inheritance, as I have commanded you. [7] Now therefore divide this land for an inheritance to the nine tribes and half the tribe of Manas'seh."

8 With the other half of the tribe of Manas'seh[g] the Reubenites and the Gadites received their inheritance, which Moses gave them, beyond the Jordan eastward, as Moses the servant of the LORD gave them: [9] from Aro'er, which is on the edge of the valley of the Arnon, and the city that is in the middle of the valley, and all the tableland of Med'eba as far as Dibon; [10] and all the cities of Sihon king of the Amorites, who reigned in Heshbon, as far as the boundary of the Ammonites; [11] and Gilead, and the region of the Gesh'urites and Ma-ac'athites, and all Mount Hermon, and all Bashan to Sal'ecah; [12] all the kingdom of Og in Bashan, who reigned in Ash'taroth and in Ed're-i (he alone was left of the remnant of the Reph'aim); these Moses had defeated and driven out. [13] Yet the people of Israel did not drive out the Gesh'urites or the Ma-ac'athites; but Geshur and Ma'acath dwell in the midst of Israel to this day.

14 To the tribe of Levi alone Moses gave no inheritance; the offerings by fire to the LORD God of Israel are their inheritance, as he said to him.

15 And Moses gave an inheritance to the tribe of the Reubenites according to their families. [16] So their territory was from Aro'er, which is on the edge of the valley of the Arnon, and the city that is in the middle of the valley, and all the tableland by Med'eba; [17] with Heshbon, and all its cities that are in the tableland; Dibon, and Ba'-moth-ba'al, and Beth-ba'al-me'on, [18] and Jahaz, and Ked'emoth, and Meph'a-ath, [19] and Kir'iatha'im, and Sibmah, and Zer'eth-sha'har on the hill of the valley, [20] and Beth-pe'or, and the slopes of Pisgah, and Beth-jesh'imoth, [21] that is, all the cities of the tableland, and all the kingdom of Sihon king of the Amorites, who reigned in Heshbon, whom Moses defeated with the leaders of Mid'ian, Evi and Rekem and Zur and Hur and Reba, the princes of Sihon, who dwelt in the land. [22] Balaam also, the son of Be'or, the soothsayer, the people of Israel killed with the sword among the rest of their slain. [23] And the border of the people of Reuben was the Jordan as a boundary. This was the inheritance of the Reubenites, according to their families with their cities and villages.

24 And Moses gave an inheritance also to the tribe of the Gadites, according to their families. [25] Their territory was Jazer, and all the cities of Gilead, and half the land of the Ammonites, to Aro'er, which is east of Rabbah, [26] and from Heshbon to Ra'math-miz'peh and Bet'onim, and from Mahana'im to the territory of Debir,[h] [27] and in the valley Beth-ha'ram, Beth-nim'rah, Succoth, and Zaphon, the rest of the kingdom of Sihon king of Heshbon, having the Jordan as a boundary, to the lower end of the Sea of Chin'nereth, eastward beyond the Jordan. [28] This is the inheritance of the Gadites according to their families, with their cities and villages.

29 And Moses gave an inheritance to the half-tribe of Manas'seh; it was allotted to the half-tribe of the Manas'sites according to their families. [30] Their region extended from Mahana'im, through all Bashan, the whole

g Cn: Heb *With it*   h Gk Syr Vg: Heb *Lidebir*

Philistine cities) lying outside Palestine proper. **8–32:** The land east of the Jordan is allotted to Reuben, Gad, and half of Manasseh. **12:** *The Rephaim*, like the Anakim of 11.21, were regarded as an aboriginal race of giants (Dt.3.11). **13:** The statement that *the people of Israel did not drive out the Geshurites* . . . is the first of a series of passages in this book and in Judges, derived from an ancient source, which indicate that the conquest was less thoroughgoing than the later editor of the book as a whole would have his readers understand (15.63; 16.10; 17.12–13; Jg.1.19,21,27–35). **33:** On *Levi*, see ch. 21.

kingdom of Og king of Bashan, and all the towns of Ja'ir, which are in Bashan, sixty cities, ³¹ and half Gilead, and Ash'taroth, and Ed're-i, the cities of the kingdom of Og in Bashan; these were allotted to the people of Machir the son of Manas'seh for the half of the Machirites according to their families.

32 These are the inheritances which Moses distributed in the plains of Moab, beyond the Jordan east of Jericho. ³³ But to the tribe of Levi Moses gave no inheritance; the LORD God of Israel is their inheritance, as he said to them.

14 And these are the inheritances which the people of Israel received in the land of Canaan, which Elea'zar the priest, and Joshua the son of Nun, and the heads of the fathers' houses of the tribes of the people of Israel distributed to them. ² Their inheritance was by lot, as the LORD had commanded Moses for the nine and one-half tribes. ³ For Moses had given an inheritance to the two and one-half tribes beyond the Jordan; but to the Levites he gave no inheritance among them. ⁴ For the people of Joseph were two tribes, Manas'seh and E'phraim; and no portion was given to the Levites in the land, but only cities to dwell in, with their pasture lands for their cattle and their substance. ⁵ The people of Israel did as the LORD commanded Moses; they allotted the land.

6 Then the people of Judah came to Joshua at Gilgal; and Caleb the son of Jephun'neh the Ken'izzite said to him, "You know what the LORD said to Moses the man of God in Ka'desh-bar'nea concerning you and me. ⁷ I was forty years old when Moses the servant of the LORD sent me from Ka'-desh-bar'nea to spy out the land; and I brought him word again as it was in my heart. ⁸ But my brethren who went up with me made the heart of the people melt; yet I wholly followed the LORD my God. ⁹ And Moses swore on that day, saying, 'Surely the land on which your foot has trodden shall be an inheritance for you and your children for ever, because you have wholly followed the LORD my God.' ¹⁰ And now, behold, the LORD has kept me alive, as he said, these forty-five years since the time that the LORD spoke this word to Moses, while Israel walked in the wilderness; and now, lo, I am this day eighty-five years old. ¹¹ I am still as strong to this day as I was in the day that Moses sent me; my strength now is as my strength was then, for war, and for going and coming. ¹² So now give me this hill country of which the LORD spoke on that day; for you heard on that day how the Anakim were there, with great fortified cities: it may be that the LORD will be with me, and I shall drive them out as the LORD said."

13 Then Joshua blessed him; and he gave Hebron to Caleb the son of Jephun'neh for an inheritance. ¹⁴ So Hebron became the inheritance of Caleb the son of Jephun'neh the Ken'-izzite to this day, because he wholly followed the LORD, the God of Israel. ¹⁵ Now the name of Hebron formerly was Kir'iath-ar'ba;ⁱ this Arba was the greatest man among the Anakim. And the land had rest from war.

15 The lot for the tribe of the people of Judah according to their families reached southward to the boundary of Edom, to the wilderness of Zin at the farthest south. ² And their south boundary ran from the end of the Salt Sea, from the bay that faces southward; ³ it goes out southward of the

i That is The city of Arba

14.1–5: General introduction to the allotment of land in western Palestine.

14.6–15: Hebron assigned to Caleb. Caleb now claims the reward which Moses had promised him (Num.14.24) for his faithfulness (Num.13.30) and receives Hebron as a permanent possession.

15.1–63: The territory assigned to Judah. 1–12: The boundaries of Judah described: vv. 2–4, from the Dead Sea to the Mediterranean on the south; vv. 5–11, the Dead Sea on the east; and from the north end of the Dead Sea to the Mediterranean on the north; v. 12, the Mediterranean

ascent of Akrab'bim, passes along to Zin, and goes up south of Ka'desh-bar'nea, along by Hezron, up to Addar, turns about to Karka, ⁴ passes along to Azmon, goes out by the Brook of Egypt, and comes to its end at the sea. This shall be your south boundary. ⁵ And the east boundary is the Salt Sea, to the mouth of the Jordan. And the boundary on the north side runs from the bay of the sea at the mouth of the Jordan; ⁶ and the boundary goes up to Beth-hoglah, and passes along north of Beth-arabah; and the boundary goes up to the stone of Bohan the son of Reuben; ⁷ and the boundary goes up to Debir from the Valley of Achor, and so northward, turning toward Gilgal, which is opposite the ascent of Adum'mim, which is on the south side of the valley; and the boundary passes along to the waters of En-she'mesh, and ends at En-ro'gel; ⁸ then the boundary goes up by the valley of the son of Hinnom at the southern shoulder of the Jeb'usite (that is, Jerusalem); and the boundary goes up to the top of the mountain that lies over against the valley of Hinnom, on the west, at the northern end of the valley of Reph'aim; ⁹ then the boundary extends from the top of the mountain to the spring of the Waters of Nephto'ah, and from there to the cities of Mount Ephron; then the boundary bends round to Ba'alah (that is, Kir'iath-je'-arim); ¹⁰ and the boundary circles west of Ba'alah to Mount Se'ir, passes along to the northern shoulder of Mount Je'arim (that is, Ches'alon), and goes down to Beth-she'mesh, and passes along by Timnah; ¹¹ the boundary goes out to the shoulder of the hill north of Ekron, then the boundary bends round to Shik'keron, and passes along to Mount Ba'alah, and goes out to Jabneel; then the boundary comes to an end at the sea. ¹² And the west boundary was the Great Sea with its coast-line. This is the boundary round about the people of Judah according to their families.

13 According to the commandment of the LORD to Joshua, he gave to Caleb the son of Jephun'neh a portion among the people of Judah, Kir'iath-ar'ba, that is, Hebron (Arba was the father of Anak). ¹⁴ And Caleb drove out from there the three sons of Anak, She'shai and Ahi'man and Talmai, the descendants of Anak. ¹⁵ And he went up from there against the inhabitants of Debir; now the name of Debir formerly was Kir'iath-se'pher. ¹⁶ And Caleb said, "Whoever smites Kir'iath-se'pher, and takes it, to him will I give Achsah my daughter as wife." ¹⁷ And Oth'ni-el the son of Kenaz, the brother of Caleb, took it; and he gave him Achsah his daughter as wife. ¹⁸ When she came to him, she urged him to ask her father for a field; and she alighted from her ass, and Caleb said to her, "What do you wish?" ¹⁹ She said to him, "Give me a present; since you have set me in the land of the Negeb, give me also springs of water." And Caleb gave her the upper springs and the lower springs.

20 This is the inheritance of the tribe of the people of Judah according to their families. ²¹ The cities belonging to the tribe of the people of Judah in the extreme South, toward the boundary of Edom, were Kabzeel, Eder, Jagur, ²² Kinah, Dimo'nah, Ada'dah, ²³ Kedesh, Hazor, Ithnan, ²⁴ Ziph, Telem, Be-a'loth, ²⁵ Ha'zor-hadat'tah, Ker'i-oth-hezron (that is, Hazor), ²⁶ Amam, Shema, Mola'dah, ²⁷ Ha'zar-gad'dah, Heshmon, Beth-pel'et, ²⁸ Hazar-shu'al, Beer-sheba, Biziothi'ah, ²⁹ Ba'alah, I'im, Ezem, ³⁰ Elto'lad, Chesil, Hormah, ³¹ Ziklag, Madman'nah, Sansan'nah, ³² Leba'oth, Shilhim, A'in, and Rimmon: in all, twenty-nine cities, with their villages.

---

on the west. **13–19:** More information about Caleb (compare 14.6–15). **14–19:** These verses are almost identical with Jg.1.11–15. **20–63:** A list of Judah's towns by districts. Many scholars believe that this list was taken from an official register of the subdivisions of the Kingdom of Judah, perhaps in the time of Josiah.

33 And in the lowland, Eshta'ol, Zorah, Ashnah, ³⁴ Zano'ah, En-gan'-nim, Tap'puah, Enam, ³⁵ Jarmuth, Adullam, Socoh, Aze'kah, ³⁶ Sha-ara'im, Aditha'im, Gede'rah, Gede-rotha'im: fourteen cities with their villages.

37 Zenan, Hadash'ah, Mig'dal-gad, ³⁸ Di'lean, Mizpeh, Jok'theel, ³⁹ La-chish, Bozkath, Eglon, ⁴⁰ Cabbon, Lahmam, Chitlish, ⁴¹ Gede'roth, Beth-da'gon, Na'amah, and Makke'dah: sixteen cities with their villages.

42 Libnah, Ether, Ashan, ⁴³ Iph-tah, Ashnah, Nezib, ⁴⁴ Kei'lah, Achzib, and Mare'shah: nine cities with their villages.

45 Ekron, with its towns and its villages; ⁴⁶ from Ekron to the sea, all that were by the side of Ashdod, with their villages.

47 Ashdod, its towns and its villages; Gaza, its towns and its villages; to the Brook of Egypt, and the Great Sea with its coast-line.

48 And in the hill country, Shamir, Jattir, Socoh, ⁴⁹ Dannah, Kir'iath-san'-nah (that is, Debir), ⁵⁰ Anab, Esh'-temoh, Anim, ⁵¹ Goshen, Holon, and Giloh: eleven cities with their villages.

52 Arab, Dumah, Eshan, ⁵³ Janim, Beth-tap'puah, Aphe'kah, ⁵⁴ Hum-tah, Kir'iath-ar'ba (that is, Hebron), and Zi'or: nine cities with their villages.

55 Ma'on, Carmel, Ziph, Juttah, ⁵⁶ Jezreel, Jok'de-am, Zano'ah, ⁵⁷ Kain, Gib'e-ah, and Timnah: ten cities with their villages.

58 Halhul, Beth-zur, Gedor, ⁵⁹ Ma'-arath, Beth-anoth, and El'tekon: six cities with their villages.

60 Kir'iath-ba'al (that is, Kir'iath-je'arim), and Rabbah: two cities with their villages.

61 In the wilderness, Beth-arabah, Middin, Seca'cah, ⁶² Nibshan, the City of Salt, and En-ge'di: six cities with their villages.

63 But the Jeb'usites, the inhabit-ants of Jerusalem, the people of Judah could not drive out; so the Jeb'usites dwell with the people of Judah at Jeru-salem to this day.

16 The allotment of the descend-ants of Joseph went from the Jordan by Jericho, east of the waters of Jericho, into the wilderness, going up from Jericho into the hill country to Bethel; ² then going from Bethel to Luz, it passes along to At'aroth, the territory of the Archites; ³ then it goes down westward to the territory of the Japh'letites, as far as the territory of Lower Beth-hor'on, then to Gezer, and it ends at the sea.

4 The people of Joseph, Manas'-seh and E'phraim, received their in-heritance.

5 The territory of the E'phraimites by their families was as follows: the boundary of their inheritance on the east was At'aroth-ad'dar as far as Upper Beth-hor'on, ⁶ and the bound-ary goes thence to the sea; on the north is Mich-me'thath; then on the east the boundary turns round toward Ta'anath-shi'loh, and passes along beyond it on the east to Jan-o'ah, ⁷ then it goes down from Jan-o'ah to At'aroth and to Na'arah, and touches Jericho, end-ing at the Jordan. ⁸ From Tap'puah the boundary goes westward to the brook Kanah, and ends at the sea. Such is the inheritance of the tribe of the E'phraimites by their families, ⁹ together with the towns which were set apart for the E'phraimites within the inheritance of the Manas'sites, all those towns with their villages. ¹⁰ How-ever they did not drive out the Ca-naanites that dwelt in Gezer: so the Ca-naanites have dwelt in the midst of E'phraim to this day but have become slaves to do forced labor.

17 Then allotment was made to the tribe of Manas'seh, for he was the first-born of Joseph. To Machir the first-born of Manas'seh, the father

---

16.1–17.18: The territory assigned to the Joseph tribes. The two tribes of Ephraim and Manasseh are allotted the central highlands. **1–4:** The southern boundary ran roughly from Jericho to the Mediterranean. **5–10:** Delimitation of the boundary of Ephraim. **10:** This verse is very similar to Jg.1.29. **17.1–6:** Arrangements for the clans of Manasseh. **2:** *The rest of the*

of Gilead, were allotted Gilead and Bashan, because he was a man of war. [2] And allotments were made to the rest of the tribe of Manas'seh, by their families, Abi-e'zer, Helek, As'ri-el, Shechem, Hepher, and Shemi'da; these were the male descendants of Manas'seh the son of Joseph, by their families.

3 Now Zeloph'ehad the son of Hepher, son of Gilead, son of Machir, son of Manas'seh, had no sons, but only daughters; and these are the names of his daughters: Mahlah, Noah, Hoglah, Milcah, and Tirzah. [4] They came before Elea'zar the priest and Joshua the son of Nun and the leaders, and said, "The LORD commanded Moses to give us an inheritance along with our brethren." So according to the commandment of the LORD he gave them an inheritance among the brethren of their father. [5] Thus there fell to Manas'seh ten portions, besides the land of Gilead and Bashan, which is on the other side of the Jordan; [6] because the daughters of Manas'seh received an inheritance along with his sons. The land of Gilead was allotted to the rest of the Manas'sites.

7 The territory of Manas'seh reached from Asher to Mich-me'thath, which is east of Shechem; then the boundary goes along southward to the inhabitants of En-tap'puah. [8] The land of Tap'puah belonged to Manas'seh, but the town of Tap'puah on the boundary of Manas'seh belonged to the sons of E'phraim. [9] Then the boundary went down to the brook Kanah. The cities here, to the south of the brook, among the cities of Manas'seh, belong to E'phraim. Then the boundary of Manas'seh goes on the north side of the brook and ends at the sea; [10] the land to the south being E'phraim's and that to the north being Manas'seh's, with the sea forming its boundary; on the north

Asher is reached, and on the east Is'sachar. [11] Also in Is'sachar and in Asher Manas'seh had Beth-she'an and its villages, and Ibleam and its villages, and the inhabitants of Dor and its villages, and the inhabitants of En-dor and its villages, and the inhabitants of Ta'anach and its villages, and the inhabitants of Megid'do and its villages; the third is Naphath.[j] [12] Yet the sons of Manas'seh could not take possession of those cities; but the Canaanites persisted in dwelling in that land. [13] But when the people of Israel grew strong, they put the Canaanites to forced labor, and did not utterly drive them out.

14 And the tribe of Joseph spoke to Joshua, saying, "Why have you given me but one lot and one portion as an inheritance, although I am a numerous people, since hitherto the LORD has blessed me?" [15] And Joshua said to them, "If you are a numerous people, go up to the forest, and there clear ground for yourselves in the land of the Per'izzites and the Reph'aim, since the hill country of E'phraim is too narrow for you." [16] The tribe of Joseph said, "The hill country is not enough for us; yet all the Canaanites who dwell in the plain have chariots of iron, both those in Beth-she'an and its villages and those in the Valley of Jezreel." [17] Then Joshua said to the house of Joseph, to E'phraim and Manas'seh, "You are a numerous people, and have great power; you shall not have one lot only, [18] but the hill country shall be yours, for though it is a forest, you shall clear it and possess it to its farthest borders; for you shall drive out the Canaanites, though they have chariots of iron, and though they are strong."

18 Then the whole congregation of the people of Israel assembled at Shiloh, and set up the tent of meet-

[j] Heb obscure

---

tribe, those who had not already settled east of the Jordan (13.29-31). **7-13:** Delimitation of the boundary of Manasseh. **11-13:** These verses are closely parallel to Jg.1.27-28. **14-18:** The Joseph tribes demand and receive a double portion.

18.1-19.51: The territory assigned to the other tribes. 1-10: General introduction. **1:** *Shiloh*, in the central highlands, was the principal Israelite sanctuary in early days (Jg.18.31; 1 Sam.

ing there; the land lay subdued before them.

2 There remained among the people of Israel seven tribes whose inheritance had not yet been apportioned. ³ So Joshua said to the people of Israel, "How long will you be slack to go in and take possession of the land, which the LORD, the God of your fathers, has given you? ⁴ Provide three men from each tribe, and I will send them out that they may set out and go up and down the land, writing a description of it with a view to their inheritances, and then come to me. ⁵ They shall divide it into seven portions, Judah continuing in his territory on the south, and the house of Joseph in their territory on the north. ⁶ And you shall describe the land in seven divisions and bring the description here to me; and I will cast lots for you here before the LORD our God. ⁷ The Levites have no portion among you, for the priesthood of the LORD is their heritage; and Gad and Reuben and half the tribe of Manas'-seh have received their inheritance beyond the Jordan eastward, which Moses the servant of the LORD gave them."

8 So the men started on their way; and Joshua charged those who went to write the description of the land, saying, "Go up and down and write a description of the land, and come again to me; and I will cast lots for you here before the LORD in Shiloh." ⁹ So the men went and passed up and down in the land and set down in a book a description of it by towns in seven divisions; then they came to Joshua in the camp at Shiloh, ¹⁰ and Joshua cast lots for them in Shiloh before the LORD; and there Joshua apportioned the land to the people of Israel, to each his portion.

11 The lot of the tribe of Benjamin according to its families came up, and the territory allotted to it fell between the tribe of Judah and the tribe of Joseph. ¹² On the north side their boundary began at the Jordan; then the boundary goes up to the shoulder north of Jericho, then up through the hill country westward; and it ends at the wilderness of Beth-a'ven. ¹³ From there the boundary passes along southward in the direction of Luz, to the shoulder of Luz (the same is Bethel), then the boundary goes down to At'-aroth-ad'dar, upon the mountain that lies south of Lower Beth-hor'on. ¹⁴ Then the boundary goes in another direction, turning on the western side southward from the mountain that lies to the south, opposite Beth-hor'on, and it ends at Kir'iath-ba'al (that is, Kir'iath-je'arim), a city belonging to the tribe of Judah. This forms the western side. ¹⁵ And the southern side begins at the outskirts of Kir'iath-je'arim; and the boundary goes from there to Ephron,ᵏ to the spring of the Waters of Nephto'ah; ¹⁶ then the boundary goes down to the border of the mountain that overlooks the valley of the son of Hinnom, which is at the north end of the valley of Reph'aim; and it then goes down the valley of Hinnom, south of the shoulder of the Jeb'usites, and downward to En-rogel; ¹⁷ then it bends in a northerly direction going on to En-she'mesh, and thence goes to Geli'loth, which is opposite the ascent of Adum'mim; then it goes down to the Stone of Bohan the son of Reuben; ¹⁸ and passing on to the north of the shoulder of Beth-ara-bahˡ it goes down to the Arabah; ¹⁹ then the boundary passes on to the north of the shoulder of Beth-hoglah; and the boundary ends at the northern bay of the Salt Sea, at the south end of the Jordan: this is the southern border. ²⁰ The Jordan forms its boundary on the eastern side. This is the inheritance of the tribe of Benjamin, according to its families, boundary by boundary round about.

21 Now the cities of the tribe of

k Cn See 15.9. Heb *westward*
l Gk: Heb *to the shoulder over against the Arabah*

4.3–4). **11–28:** The territory of Benjamin. **19.1–9:** The territory of Simeon, located within

Benjamin according to their families were Jericho, Beth-hoglah, Emek-ke′ziz, ²² Beth-arabah, Zemara′im, Bethel, ²³ Avvim, Parah, Ophrah, ²⁴ Che′pharam′moni, Ophni, Geba–twelve cities with their villages: ²⁵ Gibeon, Ramah, Be-er′oth, ²⁶ Mizpeh, Chephi′rah, Mozah, ²⁷ Rekem, Irpeel, Tar′alah, ²⁸ Zela, Ha-eleph, Jebus*ᵐ* (that is, Jerusalem), Gib′e-ah*ⁿ* and Kir′iath-je′arim*ᵒ*–fourteen cities with their villages. This is the inheritance of the tribe of Benjamin according to its families.

19 The second lot came out for Simeon, for the tribe of Simeon, according to its families; and its inheritance was in the midst of the inheritance of the tribe of Judah. ² And it had for its inheritance Beer-sheba, Sheba, Mola′dah, ³ Hazar-shu′al, Balah, Ezem, ⁴ Elto′lad, Bethul, Hormah, ⁵ Ziklag, Beth-mar′caboth, Ha′zar-su′sah, ⁶ Beth-leba′oth, and Sharu′hen–thirteen cities with their villages; ⁷ En-rimmon, Ether, and Ashan–four cities with their villages; ⁸ together with all the villages round about these cities as far as Ba′alath-beer, Ramah of the Negeb. This was the inheritance of the tribe of Simeon according to its families. ⁹ The inheritance of the tribe of Simeon formed part of the territory of Judah; because the portion of the tribe of Judah was too large for them, the tribe of Simeon obtained an inheritance in the midst of their inheritance.

10 The third lot came up for the tribe of Zeb′ulun, according to its families. And the territory of its inheritance reached as far as Sarid; ¹¹ then its boundary goes up westward, and on to Mar′eal, and touches Dab′besheth, then the brook which is east of Jok′ne-am; ¹² from Sarid it goes in the other direction eastward toward the sunrise to the boundary of Chis′loth-ta′bor; thence it goes to Dab′erath, then up to Japhi′a; ¹³ from there it passes along on the east toward the sunrise to Gath-hepher, to Eth-kazin, and going

on to Rimmon it bends toward Ne′ah; ¹⁴ then on the north the boundary turns about to Han′nathon, and it ends at the valley of Iph′tahel; ¹⁵ and Kattath, Nahal′al, Shimron, I′dalah, and Bethlehem–twelve cities with their villages. ¹⁶ This is the inheritance of the tribe of Zeb′ulun, according to its families–these cities with their villages.

17 The fourth lot came out for Is′sachar, for the tribe of Is′sachar, according to its families. ¹⁸ Its territory included Jezreel, Chesul′loth, Shunem, ¹⁹ Haph′ara-im, Shion, Ana′harath, ²⁰ Rabbith, Kish′ion, Ebez, ²¹ Remeth, En-gan′nim, En-had′dah, Beth-paz′zez; ²² the boundary also touches Tabor, Shahazu′mah, and Beth-she′mesh, and its boundary ends at the Jordan–sixteen cities with their villages. ²³ This is the inheritance of the tribe of Is′sachar, according to its families–the cities with their villages.

24 The fifth lot came out for the tribe of Asher according to its families. ²⁵ Its territory included Helkath, Hali, Beten, Ach′shaph, ²⁶ Allam′melech, Amad, and Mishal; on the west it touches Carmel and Shihor-lib′nath, ²⁷ then it turns eastward, it goes to Beth-dagon, and touches Zeb′ulun and the valley of Iph′tahel northward to Beth-emek and Nei′el; then it continues in the north to Cabul, ²⁸ Ebron, Rehob, Hammon, Kanah, as far as Sidon the Great; ²⁹ then the boundary turns to Ramah, reaching to the fortified city of Tyre; then the boundary turns to Hosah, and it ends at the sea; Mahalab,*ᵖ* Achzib, ³⁰ Ummah, Aphek and Rehob–twenty-two cities with their villages. ³¹ This is the inheritance of the tribe of Asher according to its families–these cities with their villages.

32 The sixth lot came out for the tribe of Naph′tali, for the tribe of

m Gk Syr Vg: Heb *the Jebusite*   *n* Heb *Gibeath*
o Gk: Heb *Kiriath*
p Cn Compare Gk: Heb *Mehebel*

Judah (v. 9). **10–48:** The territory of the Galilee tribes. **10–16:** Zebulun. **17–23:** Issachar. **24–31:** Asher. **32–39:** Naphtali. **40–48:** Dan. **47:** Dan never actually subjugated these lands in the

Naph'tali, according to its families.
33 And its boundary ran from Heleph, from the oak in Za-anan'nim, and Ad'ami-nekeb, and Jabneel, as far as Lakkum; and it ended at the Jordan; 34 then the boundary turns westward to Az'noth-tabor, and goes from there to Hukkok, touching Zeb'ulun at the south, and Asher on the west, and Judah on the east at the Jordan. 35 The fortified cities are Ziddim, Zer, Hammath, Rakkath, Chin'nereth, 36 Ad'-amah, Ramah, Hazor, 37 Kedesh, Ed'-re-i, En-ha'zor, 38 Yiron, Mig'dal-el, Horem, Beth-anath, and Beth-she'-mesh–nineteen cities with their villages. 39 This is the inheritance of the tribe of Naph'tali according to its families–the cities with their villages.

40 The seventh lot came out for the tribe of Dan, according to its families. 41 And the territory of its inheritance included Zorah, Esh'ta-ol, Ir-she'mesh, 42 Sha-alab'bin, Ai'jalon, Ithlah, 43 Elon, Timnah, Ekron, 44 El'tekeh, Gib'bethon, Ba'alath, 45 Jehud, Bene-be'rak, Gath-rim'mon, 46 and Me-jar'kon and Rakkon with the territory over against Joppa. 47 When the territory of the Danites was lost to them, the Danites went up and fought against Leshem, and after capturing it and putting it to the sword they took possession of it and settled in it, calling Leshem, Dan, after the name of Dan their ancestor. 48 This is the inheritance of the tribe of Dan, according to their families–these cities with their villages.

49 When they had finished distributing the several territories of the land as inheritances, the people of Israel gave an inheritance among them to Joshua the son of Nun. 50 By command of the LORD they gave him the city which he asked, Tim'nath-se'rah in the hill country of E'phraim; and he rebuilt the city, and settled in it.

51 These are the inheritances which Elea'zar the priest and Joshua the son of Nun and the heads of the fathers' houses of the tribes of the people of Israel distributed by lot at Shiloh before the LORD, at the door of the tent of meeting. So they finished dividing the land.

20 Then the LORD said to Joshua, 2 "Say to the people of Israel, 'Appoint the cities of refuge, of which I spoke to you through Moses, 3 that the manslayer who kills any person without intent or unwittingly may flee there; they shall be for you a refuge from the avenger of blood. 4 He shall flee to one of these cities and shall stand at the entrance of the gate of the city, and explain his case to the elders of that city; then they shall take him into the city, and give him a place, and he shall remain with them. 5 And if the avenger of blood pursues him, they shall not give up the slayer into his hand; because he killed his neighbor unwittingly, having had no enmity against him in times past. 6 And he shall remain in that city until he has stood before the congregation for judgment, until the death of him who is high priest at the time: then the slayer may go again to his own town and his own home, to the town from which he fled.' "

7 So they set apart Kedesh in Galilee

---

south (vv. 41–46), but was soon forced to emigrate north to the region of *Leshem* (Laish, Jg. 18.27). **49–51:** Conclusion of the distribution of land to the tribes.

20.1–9: Cities of refuge appointed (in accordance with the law of Dt.19.1–13) to which an accused murderer might flee until his case was adjudicated. **3:** *The avenger of blood* was the deceased man's nearest relative, who had the obligation of avenging his death. The word translated "avenger" is the same as that translated "next of kin" in Ru.3.9 and other passages, and "redeemer" in still others (e.g. Pr.23.11). The underlying concept of a near kinsman with certain rights and duties is the same. **4:** *The gate of the city* was the place where the council of *the elders* (the older members of the community who were responsible for its welfare) met and where business was normally transacted (Ru.4.1). The gate was not merely an opening in the city wall, but an enclosed structure sometimes containing several rooms and more than one story.

in the hill country of Naph'tali, and Shechem in the hill country of E'phraim, and Kir'iath-ar'ba (that is, Hebron) in the hill country of Judah. [8] And beyond the Jordan east of Jericho, they appointed Bezer in the wilderness on the tableland, from the tribe of Reuben, and Ramoth in Gilead, from the tribe of Gad, and Golan in Bashan, from the tribe of Manas'seh. [9] These were the cities designated for all the people of Israel, and for the stranger sojourning among them, that any one who killed a person without intent could flee there, so that he might not die by the hand of the avenger of blood, till he stood before the congregation.

21 Then the heads of the fathers' houses of the Levites came to Elea'zar the priest and to Joshua the son of Nun and to the heads of the fathers' houses of the tribes of the people of Israel; [2] and they said to them at Shiloh in the land of Canaan, "The LORD commanded through Moses that we be given cities to dwell in, along with their pasture lands for our cattle." [3] So by command of the LORD the people of Israel gave to the Levites the following cities and pasture lands out of their inheritance.

4 The lot came out for the families of the Ko'hathites. So those Levites who were descendants of Aaron the priest received by lot from the tribes of Judah, Simeon, and Benjamin, thirteen cities.

5 And the rest of the Ko'hathites received by lot from the families of the tribe of E'phraim, from the tribe of Dan and the half-tribe of Manas'seh, ten cities.

6 The Gersonites received by lot from the families of the tribe of Is'sachar, from the tribe of Asher, from the tribe of Naph'tali, and from the half-tribe of Manas'seh in Bashan, thirteen cities.

7 The Merar'ites according to their families received from the tribe of Reuben, the tribe of Gad, and the tribe of Zeb'ulun, twelve cities.

8 These cities and their pasture lands the people of Israel gave by lot to the Levites, as the LORD had commanded through Moses.

9 Out of the tribe of Judah and the tribe of Simeon they gave the following cities mentioned by name, [10] which went to the descendants of Aaron, one of the families of the Ko'hathites who belonged to the Levites; since the lot fell to them first. [11] They gave them Kir'iath-ar'ba (Arba being the father of Anak), that is Hebron, in the hill country of Judah, along with the pasture lands round about it. [12] But the fields of the city and its villages had been given to Caleb the son of Jephun'neh as his possession.

13 And to the descendants of Aaron the priest they gave Hebron, the city of refuge for the slayer, with its pasture lands, Libnah with its pasture lands, [14] Jattir with its pasture lands, Eshtemo'a with its pasture lands, [15] Holon with its pasture lands, Debir with its pasture lands, [16] A'in with its pasture lands, Juttah with its pasture lands, Beth-she'mesh with its pasture lands—nine cities out of these two tribes; [17] then out of the tribe of Benjamin, Gibeon with its pasture lands, Geba with its pasture lands, [18] An'athoth with its pasture lands, and Almon with its pasture lands—four cities. [19] The cities of the descendants of Aaron, the priests, were in all thirteen cities with their pasture lands.

20 As to the rest of the Ko'hathites belonging to the Ko'hathite families of the Levites, the cities allotted to them were out of the tribe of E'phraim. [21] To them were given Shechem, the city of refuge for the slayer, with its pasture lands in the hill country of E'phraim, Gezer with its pasture lands, [22] Kib'za-im with its pasture lands, Beth-hor'on with its pasture lands—four

---

21.1–42: **The cities assigned to the tribe of Levi,** which, because of its religious functions, did not receive an allotment of territory like the others (compare 13.14,33).

cities; 23 and out of the tribe of Dan, El'teke with its pasture lands, Gib'bethon with its pasture lands, 24 Ai'jalon with its pasture lands, Gath-rim'mon with its pasture lands–four cities; 25 and out of the half-tribe of Manas'seh, Ta'anach with its pasture lands, and Gath-rim'mon with its pasture lands–two cities. 26 The cities of the families of the rest of the Ko'-hathites were ten in all with their pasture lands.

27 And to the Gershonites, one of the families of the Levites, were given out of the half-tribe of Manas'-seh, Golan in Bashan with its pasture lands, the city of refuge for the slayer, and Be-esh'terah with its pasture lands –two cities; 28 and out of the tribe of Is'sachar, Ki'shion with its pasture lands, Dab'erath with its pasture lands, 29 Jarmuth with its pasture lands, En-gan'nim with its pasture lands–four cities; 30 and out of the tribe of Asher, Mishal with its pasture lands, Abdon with its pasture lands, 31 Hel-kath with its pasture lands, and Rehob with its pasture lands–four cities; 32 and out of the tribe of Naph'tali, Kedesh in Galilee with its pasture lands, the city of refuge for the slayer, Ham'moth-dor with its pasture lands, and Kartan with its pasture lands–three cities. 33 The cities of the several families of the Gershonites were in all thirteen cities with their pasture lands.

34 And to the rest of the Levites, the Merar'ite families, were given out of the tribe of Zeb'ulun, Jok'ne-am with its pasture lands, Kartah with its pasture lands, 35 Dimnah with its pasture lands, Na'halal with its pasture lands–four cities; 36 and out of the tribe of Reuben, Bezer with its pasture lands, Jahaz with its pasture lands, 37 Ked'-emoth with its pasture lands, and Meph'a-ath with its pasture lands–four cities; 38 and out of the tribe of Gad, Ramoth in Gilead with its pasture lands, the city of refuge for the slayer,

Mahana'im with its pasture lands, 39 Heshbon with its pasture lands, Ja-zer with its pasture lands–four cities in all. 40 As for the cities of the several Merar'ite families, that is, the remain-der of the families of the Levites, those allotted to them were in all twelve cities.

41 The cities of the Levites in the midst of the possession of the people of Israel were in all forty-eight cities with their pasture lands. 42 These cities had each its pasture lands round about it; so it was with all these cities.

43 Thus the LORD gave to Israel all the land which he swore to give to their fathers; and having taken pos-session of it, they settled there. 44 And the LORD gave them rest on every side just as he had sworn to their fathers; not one of all their enemies had with-stood them, for the LORD had given all their enemies into their hands. 45 Not one of all the good promises which the LORD had made to the house of Israel had failed; all came to pass.

22 Then Joshua summoned the Reubenites, and the Gadites, and the half-tribe of Manas'seh, 2 and said to them, "You have kept all that Moses the servant of the LORD com-manded you, and have obeyed my voice in all that I have commanded you; 3 you have not forsaken your brethren these many days, down to this day, but have been careful to keep the charge of the LORD your God. 4 And now the LORD your God has given rest to your brethren, as he prom-ised them; therefore turn and go to your home in the land where your posses-sion lies, which Moses the servant of the LORD gave you on the other side of the Jordan. 5 Take good care to ob-serve the commandment and the law which Moses the servant of the LORD commanded you, to love the LORD your God, and to walk in all his ways, and to keep his commandments, and to cleave to him, and to serve him

---

21.43–22.34: The Transjordanian tribes return. The conquest of western Palestine now com-plete (21.43–45), the two and one-half tribes are set free to go back to their own lands east of

with all your heart and with all your soul." ⁶ So Joshua blessed them, and sent them away; and they went to their homes.

7 Now to the one half of the tribe of Manas'seh Moses had given a possession in Bashan; but to the other half Joshua had given a possession beside their brethren in the land west of the Jordan. And when Joshua sent them away to their homes and blessed them, ⁸ he said to them, "Go back to your homes with much wealth, and with very many cattle, with silver, gold, bronze, and iron, and with much clothing; divide the spoil of your enemies with your brethren." ⁹ So the Reubenites and the Gadites and the half-tribe of Manas'seh returned home, parting from the people of Israel at Shiloh, which is in the land of Canaan, to go to the land of Gilead, their own land of which they had possessed themselves by command of the LORD through Moses.

10 And when they came to the region about the Jordan, that lies in the land of Canaan, the Reubenites and the Gadites and the half-tribe of Manas'seh built there an altar by the Jordan, an altar of great size. ¹¹ And the people of Israel heard say, "Behold, the Reubenites and the Gadites and the half-tribe of Manas'seh have built an altar at the frontier of the land of Canaan, in the region about the Jordan, on the side that belongs to the people of Israel." ¹² And when the people of Israel heard of it, the whole assembly of the people of Israel gathered at Shiloh, to make war against them.

13 Then the people of Israel sent to the Reubenites and the Gadites and the half-tribe of Manas'seh, in the land of Gilead, Phin'ehas the son of Elea'zar the priest, ¹⁴ and with him ten chiefs, one from each of the tribal

families of Israel, every one of them the head of a family among the clans of Israel. ¹⁵ And they came to the Reubenites, the Gadites, and the half-tribe of Manas'seh, in the land of Gilead, and they said to them, ¹⁶ "Thus says the whole congregation of the LORD, 'What is this treachery which you have committed against the God of Israel in turning away this day from following the LORD, by building yourselves an altar this day in rebellion against the LORD? ¹⁷ Have we not had enough of the sin at Pe'or from which even yet we have not cleansed ourselves, and for which there came a plague upon the congregation of the LORD, ¹⁸ that you must turn away this day from following the LORD? And if you rebel against the LORD today he will be angry with the whole congregation of Israel tomorrow. ¹⁹ But now, if your land is unclean, pass over into the LORD's land where the LORD's tabernacle stands, and take for yourselves a possession among us; only do not rebel against the LORD, or make us as rebels by building yourselves an altar other than the altar of the LORD our God. ²⁰ Did not Achan the son of Zerah break faith in the matter of the devoted things, and wrath fell upon all the congregation of Israel? And he did not perish alone for his iniquity.' "

21 Then the Reubenites, the Gadites, and the half-tribe of Manas'seh said in answer to the heads of the families of Israel, ²² "The Mighty One, God, the LORD! The Mighty One, God, the LORD! He knows; and let Israel itself know! If it was in rebellion or in breach of faith toward the LORD, spare us not today ²³ for building an altar to turn away from following the LORD; or if we did so to offer burnt offerings or cereal offerings or peace offerings on it, may the LORD himself

---

the Jordan (1.12–18). **22.10:** *The land of Canaan* is, strictly, the land west of the Jordan. **12:** Holding strictly to the Deuteronomic law which forbade the offering of sacrifice anywhere except in the one central sanctuary (Dt.12.13,14), the other tribes apparently interpret the building of the altar as an act of disloyalty to Israel and its God, and therefore prepare *to make war against them.* **17:** *The sin at Peor,* Num.25.3–5. **20:** *Achan,* 7.1. **26–27:** It was not a real altar, but merely a memorial, *a witness.*

take vengeance. ²⁴ Nay, but we did it from fear that in time to come your children might say to our children, 'What have you to do with the LORD, the God of Israel? ²⁵ For the LORD has made the Jordan a boundary between us and you, you Reubenites and Gadites; you have no portion in the LORD.' So your children might make our children cease to worship the LORD. ²⁶ Therefore we said, 'Let us now build an altar, not for burnt offering, nor for sacrifice, ²⁷ but to be a witness between us and you, and between the generations after us, that we do perform the service of the LORD in his presence with our burnt offerings and sacrifices and peace offerings; lest your children say to our children in time to come, "You have no portion in the LORD." ' ²⁸ And we thought, If this should be said to us or to our descendants in time to come, we should say, 'Behold the copy of the altar of the LORD, which our fathers made, not for burnt offerings, nor for sacrifice, but to be a witness between us and you.' ²⁹ Far be it from us that we should rebel against the LORD, and turn away this day from following the LORD by building an altar for burnt offering, cereal offering, or sacrifice, other than the altar of the LORD our God that stands before his tabernacle!"

30 When Phin'ehas the priest and the chiefs of the congregation, the heads of the families of Israel who were with him, heard the words that the Reubenites and the Gadites and the Manas'sites spoke, it pleased them well. ³¹ And Phin'ehas the son of Elea'zar the priest said to the Reubenites and the Gadites and the Manas'sites, "Today we know that the LORD is in the midst of us, because you have not committed this treachery against the LORD; now you have saved the people of Israel from the hand of the LORD."

32 Then Phin'ehas the son of Elea'zar the priest, and the chiefs, returned from the Reubenites and the Gadites in the land of Gilead to the land of Ca-naan, to the people of Israel, and brought back word to them. ³³ And the report pleased the people of Israel; and the people of Israel blessed God and spoke no more of making war against them, to destroy the land where the Reubenites and the Gadites were settled. ³⁴ The Reubenites and the Gadites called the altar Witness; "For," said they, "it is a witness between us that the LORD is God."

23 A long time afterward, when the LORD had given rest to Israel from all their enemies round about, and Joshua was old and well advanced in years, ² Joshua summoned all Israel, their elders and heads, their judges and officers, and said to them, "I am now old and well advanced in years; ³ and you have seen all that the LORD your God has done to all these nations for your sake, for it is the LORD your God who has fought for you. ⁴ Behold, I have allotted to you as an inheritance for your tribes those nations that remain, along with all the nations that I have already cut off, from the Jordan to the Great Sea in the west. ⁵ The LORD your God will push them back before you, and drive them out of your sight; and you shall possess their land, as the LORD your God promised you. ⁶ Therefore be very steadfast to keep and do all that is written in the book of the law of Moses, turning aside from it neither to the right hand nor to the left, ⁷ that you may not be mixed with these nations left here among you, or make mention of the names of their gods, or swear by them, or serve them, or bow down yourselves to them, ⁸ but cleave to the LORD your God as you have done to this day. ⁹ For the LORD has driven out before you great and strong nations; and as for you, no man has been able to withstand you to this day. ¹⁰ One man of you puts to flight a thousand, since it is the LORD your God who fights for you, as he promised you. ¹¹ Take good heed to yourselves, there-

---

23.1–16: Joshua's farewell admonitions.

fore, to love the LORD your God. ¹² For if you turn back, and join the remnant of these nations left here among you, and make marriages with them, so that you marry their women and they yours, ¹³ know assuredly that the LORD your God will not continue to drive out these nations before you; but they shall be a snare and a trap for you, a scourge on your sides, and thorns in your eyes, till you perish from off this good land which the LORD your God has given you.

14 "And now I am about to go the way of all the earth, and you know in your hearts and souls, all of you, that not one thing has failed of all the good things which the LORD your God promised concerning you; all have come to pass for you, not one of them has failed. ¹⁵ But just as all the good things which the LORD your God promised concerning you have been fulfilled for you, so the LORD will bring upon you all the evil things, until he have destroyed you from off this good land which the LORD your God has given you, ¹⁶ if you transgress the covenant of the LORD your God, which he commanded you, and go and serve other gods and bow down to them. Then the anger of the LORD will be kindled against you, and you shall perish quickly from off the good land which he has given to you."

24 Then Joshua gathered all the tribes of Israel to Shechem, and summoned the elders, the heads, the judges, and the officers of Israel; and they presented themselves before God. ² And Joshua said to all the people, "Thus says the LORD, the God of Israel, 'Your fathers lived of old beyond the Euphra'tes, Terah, the father of Abraham and of Nahor; and they served other gods. ³ Then I took your father Abraham from beyond the River and led him through all the land of Canaan, and made his offspring many.

I gave him Isaac; ⁴ and to Isaac I gave Jacob and Esau. And I gave Esau the hill country of Se'ir to possess, but Jacob and his children went down to Egypt. ⁵ And I sent Moses and Aaron, and I plagued Egypt with what I did in the midst of it; and afterwards I brought you out. ⁶ Then I brought your fathers out of Egypt, and you came to the sea; and the Egyptians pursued your fathers with chariots and horsemen to the Red Sea. ⁷ And when they cried to the LORD, he put darkness between you and the Egyptians, and made the sea come upon them and cover them; and your eyes saw what I did to Egypt; and you lived in the wilderness a long time. ⁸ Then I brought you to the land of the Amorites, who lived on the other side of the Jordan; they fought with you, and I gave them into your hand, and you took possession of their land, and I destroyed them before you. ⁹ Then Balak the son of Zippor, king of Moab, arose and fought against Israel; and he sent and invited Balaam the son of Be'or to curse you, ¹⁰ but I would not listen to Balaam; therefore he blessed you; so I delivered you out of his hand. ¹¹ And you went over the Jordan and came to Jericho, and the men of Jericho fought against you, and also the Amorites, the Per'izzites, the Canaanites, the Hittites, the Gir'gashites, the Hivites, and the Jeb'usites; and I gave them into your hand. ¹² And I sent the hornet before you, which drove them out before you, the two kings of the Amorites; it was not by your sword or by your bow. ¹³ I gave you a land on which you had not labored, and cities which you had not built, and you dwell therein; you eat the fruit of vineyards and oliveyards which you did not plant.'

14 "Now therefore fear the LORD, and serve him in sincerity and in faithfulness; put away the gods which your

---

24.1–28: The covenant at Shechem. The generation which had conquered Palestine now takes upon itself a covenant with the LORD similar to that which their fathers had entered into at Sinai (Ex.24.7–18; 34.27–28; compare Jos.8.30–35). **1:** *Shechem*, see 8.30 n. **12:** The term *hornet* is used metaphorically, possibly referring to the panic which befell the inhabitants (2.11;

fathers served beyond the River, and in Egypt, and serve the LORD. ¹⁵ And if you be unwilling to serve the LORD, choose this day whom you will serve, whether the gods your fathers served in the region beyond the River, or the gods of the Amorites in whose land you dwell; but as for me and my house, we will serve the LORD."

16 Then the people answered, "Far be it from us that we should forsake the LORD, to serve other gods; ¹⁷ for it is the LORD our God who brought us and our fathers up from the land of Egypt, out of the house of bondage, and who did those great signs in our sight, and preserved us in all the way that we went, and among all the peoples through whom we passed; ¹⁸ and the LORD drove out before us all the peoples, the Amorites who lived in the land; therefore we also will serve the LORD, for he is our God."

19 But Joshua said to the people, "You cannot serve the LORD; for he is a holy God; he is a jealous God; he will not forgive your transgressions or your sins. ²⁰ If you forsake the LORD and serve foreign gods, then he will turn and do you harm, and consume you, after having done you good." ²¹ And the people said to Joshua, "Nay; but we will serve the LORD." ²² Then Joshua said to the people, "You are witnesses against yourselves that you have chosen the LORD, to serve him." And they said, "We are witnesses." ²³ He said, "Then put away the foreign gods which are among you, and incline your heart to the LORD, the God of Israel." ²⁴ And the people said to Joshua, "The LORD our God we will serve, and his voice we will obey."

²⁵ So Joshua made a covenant with the people that day, and made statutes and ordinances for them at Shechem. ²⁶ And Joshua wrote these words in the book of the law of God; and he took a great stone, and set it up there under the oak in the sanctuary of the LORD. ²⁷ And Joshua said to all the people, "Behold, this stone shall be a witness against us; for it has heard all the words of the LORD which he spoke to us; therefore it shall be a witness against you, lest you deal falsely with your God." ²⁸ So Joshua sent the people away, every man to his inheritance.

29 After these things Joshua the son of Nun, the servant of the LORD, died, being a hundred and ten years old. ³⁰ And they buried him in his own inheritance at Tim'nath-se'rah, which is in the hill country of E'phraim, north of the mountain of Ga'ash.

31 And Israel served the LORD all the days of Joshua, and all the days of the elders who outlived Joshua and had known all the work which the LORD did for Israel.

32 The bones of Joseph which the people of Israel brought up from Egypt were buried at Shechem, in the portion of ground which Jacob bought from the sons of Hamor the father of Shechem for a hundred pieces of money;*q* it became an inheritance of the descendants of Joseph.

33 And Elea'zar the son of Aaron died; and they buried him at Gib'e-ah, the town of Phin'ehas his son, which had been given him in the hill country of E'phraim.

q Heb *qesitah*

10.1–2; Dt.2.25). **25:** The Canaanite god worshiped at Shechem was called Baal-, or El-Berith, "god of the covenant" (Jg.9.4,46). The city thus had covenant associations for the Canaanites as well as the Israelites. **26:** Sacred trees are frequently connected with ancient sanctuaries (Gen.12.6; 13.18; 35.4,8; Jg.9.6), as are stone pillars (Gen.28.18; Ex.24.4; Jg.9.6). **29–31:** The death and burial of Joshua. **30:** *Timnath-serah*, see 19.49–50. **32–33:** The burial of Joseph and Eleazar. **32:** *Brought up from Egypt*, Ex.13.19. *Which Jacob bought*, Gen.33.19. Some scholars think the story in this chapter reflects an annual ceremony in which the covenant between the LORD and his people was renewed.

THE BOOK OF JUDGES

Despite the optimistic report in the book of Joshua that Israel conquered Palestine in a brief series of campaigns under a single leader, it is evident from the book of Judges that the process was not quite so simple. Chapter 1 says plainly that many parts of the country were never subjugated, while the rest of the book is largely an account of battles which had to be fought through several generations before the land was securely in Israel's hands. The enthralling tales the book contains are traditions preserved by various tribes about the exploits of their particular heroes—the "judges" of whom the title speaks. An editor has given the tales a factitious unity by making all the judges national, instead of tribal leaders and by providing for all the events a moral and theological interpretation.

The book opens (1.1–2.5) with an account of the conquest of Canaan which is roughly parallel to that in the book of Joshua; then follows the main body of the work which, after a moralizing introduction (2.6–3.6), relates the adventures of the individual judges: Othniel (3.7–11); Ehud (3.12–30); Shamgar (3.31); Deborah (chs. 4–5); Gideon (chs. 6–8) and his infamous son, Abimelech (ch. 9); two minor judges (10.1–5); Jephthah (10.6–12.7); three more minor judges (12.8–15); and Samson (chs. 13–16). It concludes with an appendix containing tales about the migration of Dan (chs. 17–18) and the sins of the Benjaminites (chs. 19–21). While the final editor of the book was undoubtedly concerned to preserve intact these colorful stories of his people's early life in the Promised Land, he was even more concerned with the moral lesson which, with single-minded diligence, he endeavors to extract from them—the lesson that loyalty to God is the first requisite for national success and disloyalty a guarantee of disaster. In its present form the book is a set of illustrative variations on this theme, a theme which appears in classical form in the hortatory sections of Deuteronomy, and especially in Dt. ch. 28.

AFTER THE DEATH OF JOSHUA THE people of Israel inquired of the LORD, "Who shall go up first for us against the Canaanites, to fight against them?" ² The LORD said, "Judah shall go up; behold, I have given the land into his hand." ³ And Judah said to Simeon his brother, "Come up with me into the territory allotted to me, that we may fight against the Canaanites; and I likewise will go with you into the territory allotted to you." So Simeon went with him. ⁴ Then Judah went up and the LORD gave the Canaanites and the Per'izzites into their hand; and they defeated ten thousand of them at Bezek. ⁵ They came upon Ado'ni-be'zek at Bezek, and fought against him, and defeated the Canaanites and the Per'izzites. ⁶ Ado'ni-be'zek fled; but they pursued him, and caught him, and cut off his thumbs and his great toes. ⁷ And Ado'ni-be'zek said, "Seventy kings with their thumbs and their great toes cut off used to pick up scraps under my table; as I have done, so God has requited me." And they brought him to Jerusalem, and he died there.

8 And the men of Judah fought against Jerusalem, and took it, and smote it with the edge of the sword, and set the city on fire. ⁹ And afterward the men of Judah went down to fight against the Canaanites who dwelt in the hill country, in the Negeb, and in the lowland. ¹⁰ And Judah went against the Canaanites who dwelt in

1.1–2.5: **Israel's incomplete conquest of the land.** This seems to be an older account of the Israelite invasion than the one in Joshua. 1–21: The conquests of Judah (compare Jos. ch. 15). 1: The words *after the death of Joshua* contradict the general tenor of the following narrative and are probably an editor's harmonizing note. They *inquired of the LORD* by consulting the sacred lots. 3: The tribe of *Simeon* plays no significant role in the later history of Israel. Not mentioned in the Song of Deborah (5.2–31), it was probably entirely absorbed by Judah at an early day. 4: The location of *Bezek* is uncertain. 8: Jerusalem was not actually captured until the time of David (2 Sam.5.6–7). 10: Hebron was the most important city of southern

Hebron (now the name of Hebron was formerly Kir'iath-ar'ba); and they defeated She'shai and Ahi'man and Talmai. 11 From there they went against the inhabitants of Debir. The name of Debir was formerly Kir'iath-se'pher. 12 And Caleb said, "He who attacks Kir'iath-se'pher and takes it, I will give him Achsah my daughter as wife." 13 And Oth'ni-el the son of Kenaz, Caleb's younger brother, took it; and he gave him Achsah his daughter as wife. 14 When she came to him, she urged him to ask her father for a field; and she alighted from her ass, and Caleb said to her, "What do you wish?" 15 She said to him, "Give me a present; since you have set me in the land of the Negeb, give me also springs of water." And Caleb gave her the upper springs and the lower springs.

16 And the descendants of the Ken'-ite, Moses' father-in-law, went up with the people of Judah from the city of palms into the wilderness of Judah, which lies in the Negeb near Arad; and they went and settled with the people. 17 And Judah went with Simeon his brother, and they defeated the Canaanites who inhabited Zephath, and utterly destroyed it. So the name of the city was called Hormah. 18 Judah also took Gaza with its territory, and Ash'kelon with its territory, and Ekron with its territory. 19 And the LORD was with Judah, and he took possession of the hill country, but he could not drive out the inhabitants of the plain, because they had chariots of iron. 20 And Hebron was given to Caleb, as Moses had said; and he drove out from it the three sons of Anak. 21 But the people of Benjamin did not drive out the Jeb'usites who

dwelt in Jerusalem; so the Jeb'usites have dwelt with the people of Benjamin in Jerusalem to this day.

22 The house of Joseph also went up against Bethel; and the LORD was with them. 23 And the house of Joseph sent to spy out Bethel. (Now the name of the city was formerly Luz.) 24 And the spies saw a man coming out of the city, and they said to him, "Pray, show us the way into the city, and we will deal kindly with you." 25 And he showed them the way into the city; and they smote the city with the edge of the sword, but they let the man and all his family go. 26 And the man went to the land of the Hittites and built a city, and called its name Luz; that is its name to this day.

27 Manas'seh did not drive out the inhabitants of Beth-she'an and its villages, or Ta'anach and its villages, or the inhabitants of Dor and its villages, or the inhabitants of Ibleam and its villages, or the inhabitants of Megid'-do and its villages; but the Canaanites persisted in dwelling in that land. 28 When Israel grew strong, they put the Canaanites to forced labor, but did not utterly drive them out.

29 And E'phraim did not drive out the Canaanites who dwelt in Gezer; but the Canaanites dwelt in Gezer among them.

30 Zeb'ulun did not drive out the inhabitants of Kitron, or the inhabitants of Na'halol; but the Canaanites dwelt among them, and became subject to forced labor.

31 Asher did not drive out the inhabitants of Acco, or the inhabitants of Sidon, or of Ahlab, or of Achzib, or of Helbah, or of Aphik, or of Rehob; 32 but the Asherites dwelt among the Canaanites, the inhabitants of the

Palestine; its capture is also reported in Jos.10.36–37. According to v. 20 and Jos.14.13–15 it was given to the clan of Caleb. **11–15:** This story is found almost verbatim in Jos.15.13–19. **11:** *Debir* is probably the modern Tell Beit Mirsim, southwest of Hebron. **16:** The Kenites were a nomadic tribe closely allied to the Hebrews. *The city of palms* was either Jericho (as in 3.13) or a city of the Negeb. **18:** *Gaza . . . Ashkelon . . . Ekron* were three of the five cities of the Philistine confederation (see 14.19 n.). The account of their capture is almost certainly unhistorical; the Greek Old Testament (the Septuagint) says specifically that Judah "did not" take them. **22–29:** The conquests of the Joseph tribes (compare Jos. chs. 16–17). **30–36:** The

land; for they did not drive them out.

33 Naph'tali did not drive out the inhabitants of Beth-she'mesh, or the inhabitants of Beth-anath, but dwelt among the Canaanites, the inhabitants of the land; nevertheless the inhabitants of Beth-she'mesh and of Beth-anath became subject to forced labor for them.

34 The Amorites pressed the Danites back into the hill country, for they did not allow them to come down to the plain; 35 the Amorites persisted in dwelling in Har-heres, in Ai'jalon, and in Sha-al'bim, but the hand of the house of Joseph rested heavily upon them, and they became subject to forced labor. 36 And the border of the Amorites ran from the ascent of Akrab'bim, from Sela and upward.

2 Now the angel of the LORD went up from Gilgal to Bochim. And he said, "I brought you up from Egypt, and brought you into the land which I swore to give to your fathers. I said, 'I will never break my covenant with you, 2 and you shall make no covenant with the inhabitants of this land; you shall break down their altars.' But you have not obeyed my command. What is this you have done? 3 So now I say, I will not drive them out before you; but they shall become adversaries*a* to you, and their gods shall be a snare to you." 4 When the angel of the LORD spoke these words to all the people of Israel, the people lifted up their voices and wept. 5 And they called the name of that place Bochim;*b* and they sacrificed there to the LORD.

6 When Joshua dismissed the people, the people of Israel went each to his inheritance to take possession of the land. 7 And the people served the LORD all the days of Joshua, and all the days of the elders who outlived Joshua, who had seen all the great work which the LORD had done for Israel. 8 And Joshua the son of Nun, the servant of the LORD, died at the age of one hundred and ten years. 9 And they buried him within the bounds of his inheritance in Tim'nath-he'res, in the hill country of E'phraim, north of the mountain of Ga'ash. 10 And all that generation also were gathered to their fathers; and there arose another generation after them, who did not know the LORD or the work which he had done for Israel.

11 And the people of Israel did what was evil in the sight of the LORD and served the Ba'als; 12 and they forsook the LORD, the God of their fathers, who had brought them out of the land of Egypt; they went after other gods, from among the gods of the peoples who were round about them, and bowed down to them; and they provoked the LORD to anger. 13 They forsook the LORD, and served the Ba'als and the Ash'taroth. 14 So the anger of the LORD was kindled against Israel, and he gave them over to plunderers, who plundered them; and he sold them into the power of their enemies round about, so that they could no longer withstand their enemies. 15 Whenever they marched out, the hand of the LORD was against them for evil, as the LORD had warned, and as the LORD had sworn to them; and they were in sore straits.

16 Then the LORD raised up judges,

a Vg Old Latin Compare Gk: Heb *sides*
b That is *Weepers*

---

conquests of the Galilee tribes (Jos.18–19). The emphasis in this section (as in vv. 19,21 and 27–29) is on the incompleteness of the result. **2.1–5:** The moral reason for Israel's relative failure. **1:** *The angel of the LORD* is God in his self-manifestation, as the following words clearly show. *Bochim* is probably Bethel; the word means literally "weepers" (vv. 4–5).

2.6–3.6: Moralizing introduction to the book. An editor explains that the whole history of these times is to be understood in terms of constantly recurring cycles of national apostasy, enslavement, repentance, and deliverance (vv. 16–20). He wishes his readers to understand that the history he is to relate teaches the lesson that Israel was prosperous and free only when she was loyal to her God. **8:** Joshua's death is related also in Jos.24.29–31. **13:** *Baals and the Ashtaroth* were the male and female gods of the Canaanites. **16:** The *judges* of this book

who saved them out of the power of those who plundered them. [17] And yet they did not listen to their judges; for they played the harlot after other gods and bowed down to them; they soon turned aside from the way in which their fathers had walked, who had obeyed the commandments of the LORD, and they did not do so. [18] Whenever the LORD raised up judges for them, the LORD was with the judge, and he saved them from the hand of their enemies all the days of the judge; for the LORD was moved to pity by their groaning because of those who afflicted and oppressed them. [19] But whenever the judge died, they turned back and behaved worse than their fathers, going after other gods, serving them and bowing down to them; they did not drop any of their practices or their stubborn ways. [20] So the anger of the LORD was kindled against Israel; and he said, "Because this people have transgressed my covenant which I commanded their fathers, and have not obeyed my voice, [21] I will not henceforth drive out before them any of the nations that Joshua left when he died, [22] that by them I may test Israel, whether they will take care to walk in the way of the LORD as their fathers did, or not." [23] So the LORD left those nations, not driving them out at once, and he did not give them into the power of Joshua.

3 Now these are the nations which the LORD left, to test Israel by them, that is, all in Israel who had no experience of any war in Canaan; [2] it was only that the generations of the people of Israel might know war, that he might teach war to such at least as had not known it before. [3] These are the nations: the five lords of the Philis-tines, and all the Canaanites, and the Sido'nians, and the Hivites who dwelt on Mount Lebanon, from Mount Ba'al-her'mon as far as the entrance of Hamath. [4] They were for the test-ing of Israel, to know whether Israel would obey the commandments of the LORD, which he commanded their fathers by Moses. [5] So the people of Israel dwelt among the Canaanites, the Hittites, the Amorites, the Per'izzites, the Hivites, and the Jeb'usites; [6] and they took their daughters to themselves for wives, and their own daughters they gave to their sons; and they served their gods.

7 And the people of Israel did what was evil in the sight of the LORD, for-getting the LORD their God, and serv-ing the Ba'als and the Ashe'roth. [8] Therefore the anger of the LORD was kindled against Israel, and he sold them into the hand of Cu'shan-risha-tha'im king of Mesopota'mia; and the people of Israel served Cu'shan-risha-tha'im eight years. [9] But when the peo-ple of Israel cried to the LORD, the LORD raised up a deliverer for the peo-ple of Israel, who delivered them, Oth'ni-el the son of Kenaz, Caleb's younger brother. [10] The Spirit of the LORD came upon him, and he judged Israel; he went out to war, and the LORD gave Cu'shan-rishatha'im king of Mes-opota'mia into his hand; and his hand prevailed over Cu'shan-rishatha'im. [11] So the land had rest forty years. Then Oth'ni-el the son of Kenaz died.

12 And the people of Israel again did what was evil in the sight of the LORD; and the LORD strengthened Eglon the king of Moab against Israel, because they had done what was evil in the sight of the LORD. [13] He gath-ered to himself the Ammonites and the

---

were military heroes who, for their services, were entrusted with the powers of government during their own lifetime.

3.7–11: Othniel. The story is a vague one; Othniel's true place seems to be in 1.12,13. **8:** *Cushan-rishathaim* is unknown elsewhere. **10:** *The Spirit of the LORD came upon him,* a divinely inspired wrath may be suggested here; compare 11.29. **11:** A type of editorial formula which occurs repeatedly in the book (e.g. v. 30; 5.31).

3.12–30: Ehud. The people, chiefly the tribe of Benjamin, when enslaved by the Moabites, were delivered by a Benjaminite hero. **12:** *Moab,* the country immediately east of the Dead

Amal'ekites, and went and defeated Israel; and they took possession of the city of palms. ¹⁴ And the people of Israel served Eglon the king of Moab eighteen years.

15 But when the people of Israel cried to the LORD, the LORD raised up for them a deliverer, Ehud, the son of Gera, the Benjaminite, a left-handed man. The people of Israel sent tribute by him to Eglon the king of Moab. ¹⁶ And Ehud made for himself a sword with two edges, a cubit in length; and he girded it on his right thigh under his clothes. ¹⁷ And he presented the tribute to Eglon king of Moab. Now Eglon was a very fat man. ¹⁸ And when Ehud had finished presenting the tribute, he sent away the people that carried the tribute. ¹⁹ But he himself turned back at the sculptured stones near Gilgal, and said, "I have a secret message for you, O king." And he commanded, "Silence." And all his attendants went out from his presence. ²⁰ And Ehud came to him, as he was sitting alone in his cool roof chamber. And Ehud said, "I have a message from God for you." And he arose from his seat. ²¹ And Ehud reached with his left hand, took the sword from his right thigh, and thrust it into his belly; ²² and the hilt also went in after the blade, and the fat closed over the blade, for he did not draw the sword out of his belly; and the dirt came out. ²³ Then Ehud went out into the vestibule,ᶜ and closed the doors of the roof chamber upon him, and locked them.

24 When he had gone, the servants came; and when they saw that the doors of the roof chamber were locked, they thought, "He is only relieving himself in the closet of the cool chamber." ²⁵ And they waited till they were ut-

terly at a loss; but when he still did not open the doors of the roof chamber, they took the key and opened them; and there lay their lord dead on the floor.

26 Ehud escaped while they delayed, and passed beyond the sculptured stones, and escaped to Se-i'rah. ²⁷ When he arrived, he sounded the trumpet in the hill country of E'phraim; and the people of Israel went down with him from the hill country, having him at their head. ²⁸ And he said to them, "Follow after me; for the LORD has given your enemies the Moabites into your hand." So they went down after him, and seized the fords of the Jordan against the Moabites, and allowed not a man to pass over. ²⁹ And they killed at that time about ten thousand of the Moabites, all strong, able-bodied men; not a man escaped. ³⁰ So Moab was subdued that day under the hand of Israel. And the land had rest for eighty years.

31 After him was Shamgar the son of Anath, who killed six hundred of the Philistines with an oxgoad; and he too delivered Israel.

4 And the people of Israel again did what was evil in the sight of the LORD, after Ehud died. ² And the LORD sold them into the hand of Jabin king of Canaan, who reigned in Hazor; the commander of his army was Sis'era, who dwelt in Haro'sheth-ha-goiim. ³ Then the people of Israel cried to the LORD for help; for he had nine hundred chariots of iron, and oppressed the people of Israel cruelly for twenty years.

4 Now Deb'orah, a prophetess, the wife of Lapp'idoth, was judging Israel at that time. ⁵ She used to sit under the palm of Deb'orah between

ᶜ The meaning of the Hebrew word is unknown

Sea. **13:** *The city of palms,* Jericho. **19:** *Stones near Gilgal,* compare Jos.4.20. **31:** *Shamgar,* a fragment of a story. *The Philistines,* see 13.1 n.

4.1–5.31: Deborah. The story of Deborah and Barak's victories over the Canaanites of the North is told in two versions, one in prose (ch. 4), the other in poetry (ch. 5). **4.2:** King *Jabin* plays a similar role in Jos.11.1. *Hazor* was one of the most important Canaanite cities of Galilee (see Jos.11.1 n.). **3:** The *chariots of iron* gave the Canaanites a great advantage over the Hebrews who were as yet unfamiliar with the art of working in iron (Jos.17.16; 1 Sam.13.19–22). **4:** *Judging* means "ruling." **6:** *Mount Tabor* is in Galilee north of the plain of Esdraelon. **7:** *The*

Ramah and Bethel in the hill country of E'phraim; and the people of Israel came up to her for judgment. [6] She sent and summoned Barak the son of Abin'o-am from Kedesh in Naph'tali, and said to him, "The LORD, the God of Israel, commands you, 'Go, gather your men at Mount Tabor, taking ten thousand from the tribe of Naph'tali and the tribe of Zeb'ulun. [7] And I will draw out Sis'era, the general of Jabin's army, to meet you by the river Kishon with his chariots and his troops; and I will give him into your hand.'" [8] Barak said to her, "If you will go with me, I will go; but if you will not go with me, I will not go." [9] And she said, "I will surely go with you; nevertheless, the road on which you are going will not lead to your glory, for the LORD will sell Sis'era into the hand of a woman." Then Deb'orah arose, and went with Barak to Kedesh. [10] And Barak summoned Zeb'ulun and Naph'tali to Kedesh; and ten thousand men went up at his heels; and Deb'orah went up with him.

11 Now Heber the Ken'ite had separated from the Ken'ites, the descendants of Hobab the father-in-law of Moses, and had pitched his tent as far away as the oak in Za-anan'nim, which is near Kedesh.

12 When Sis'era was told that Barak the son of Abin'o-am had gone up to Mount Tabor, [13] Sis'era called out all his chariots, nine hundred chariots of iron, and all the men who were with him, from Haro'sheth-ha-goiim to the river Kishon. [14] And Deb'orah said to Barak, "Up! For this is the day in which the LORD has given Sis'era into your hand. Does not the LORD go out before you?" So Barak went down from Mount Tabor with ten thousand men following him. [15] And the LORD routed Sis'era and all his chariots and all his army before Barak at the edge of the sword; and Sis'era alighted from his chariot and fled away on foot. [16] And Barak pursued the chariots and the army to Haro'sheth-ha-goiim, and all the army of Sis'era fell by the edge of the sword; not a man was left.

17 But Sis'era fled away on foot to the tent of Ja'el, the wife of Heber the Ken'ite; for there was peace between Jabin the king of Hazor and the house of Heber the Ken'ite. [18] And Ja'el came out to meet Sis'era, and said to him, "Turn aside, my lord, turn aside to me; have no fear." So he turned aside to her into the tent, and she covered him with a rug. [19] And he said to her, "Pray, give me a little water to drink; for I am thirsty." So she opened a skin of milk and gave him a drink and covered him. [20] And he said to her, "Stand at the door of the tent, and if any man comes and asks you, 'Is any one here?' say, No." [21] But Ja'el the wife of Heber took a tent peg, and took a hammer in her hand, and went softly to him and drove the peg into his temple, till it went down into the ground, as he was lying fast asleep from weariness. So he died. [22] And behold, as Barak pursued Sis'era, Ja'el went out to meet him, and said to him, "Come, and I will show you the man whom you are seeking." So he went in to her tent; and there lay Sis'era dead, with the tent peg in his temple.

23 So on that day God subdued Jabin the king of Canaan before the people of Israel. [24] And the hand of the people of Israel bore harder and harder on Jabin the king of Canaan, until they destroyed Jabin king of Canaan.

5 Then sang Deb'orah and Barak the son of Abin'o-am on that day: [2] "That the leaders took the lead in Israel,
    that the people offered themselves willingly,

---

river Kishon is a small stream which flows westward through the plain of Esdraelon, north of Mount Carmel. **10:** *Zebulun and Naphtali* were two of the Galilean tribes (1.30,33). **11:** *The Kenites,* see 1.16 n. **5.1:** *Sang Deborah.* Verse 7 shows the song was composed about Deborah, not by her. This so-called "Song of Deborah" is the oldest remaining considerable fragment of Hebrew literature. The Hebrew text is, unfortunately, so corrupt in some places as to be almost

bless*d* the Lord!

3 "Hear, O kings; give ear, O princes;
  to the Lord I will sing,
  I will make melody to the
    Lord, the God of Israel.

4 "Lord, when thou didst go forth
    from Se'ir,
  when thou didst march from the
    region of Edom,
  the earth trembled,
    and the heavens dropped,
    yea, the clouds dropped water.
5 The mountains quaked before the
    Lord,
  yon Sinai before the Lord, the
    God of Israel.

6 "In the days of Shamgar, son of
    Anath,
  in the days of Ja'el, caravans
    ceased
  and travelers kept to the byways.
7 The peasantry ceased in Israel, they
    ceased
  until you arose, Deb'orah,
    arose as a mother in Israel.
8 When new gods were chosen,
    then war was in the gates.
  Was shield or spear to be seen
    among forty thousand in Israel?
9 My heart goes out to the
    commanders of Israel
  who offered themselves willingly
    among the people.
  Bless the Lord.

10 "Tell of it, you who ride on tawny
    asses,
  you who sit on rich carpets*e*
  and you who walk by the way.
11 To the sound of musicians*e* at the
    watering places,
  there they repeat the triumphs of
    the Lord,
  the triumphs of his peasantry in
    Israel.

"Then down to the gates marched

the people of the Lord.

12 "Awake, awake, Deb'orah!
    Awake, awake, utter a song!
  Arise, Barak, lead away your
    captives,
  O son of Abin'o-am.
13 Then down marched the remnant
    of the noble;
  the people of the Lord marched
    down for him*f* against the
    mighty.
14 From E'phraim they set out thither*x*
    into the valley,*g*
  following you, Benjamin, with
    your kinsmen;
  from Machir marched down the
    commanders,
  and from Zeb'ulun those who bear
    the marshal's staff;
15 the princes of Is'sachar came with
    Deb'orah,
  and Is'sachar faithful to Barak;
  into the valley they rushed forth
    at his heels.
  Among the clans of Reuben
    there were great searchings of
    heart.
16 Why did you tarry among the
    sheepfolds,
  to hear the piping for the flocks?
  Among the clans of Reuben
    there were great searchings of
    heart.
17 Gilead stayed beyond the Jordan;
    and Dan, why did he abide with
    the ships?
  Asher sat still at the coast of the sea,
    settling down by his landings.
18 Zeb'ulun is a people that jeoparded
    their lives to the death;
  Naph'tali too, on the heights of
    the field.

19 "The kings came, they fought;
    then fought the kings of Canaan,

d Or *You who offered yourselves willingly among the
  people, bless*
e The meaning of the Hebrew word is uncertain
f Gk: Heb *me*
x Cn: Heb *From Ephraim their root*
g Gk: Heb *in Amalek*

unintelligible. **4:** From *Seir . . . Edom.* The Lord is pictured coming from the region southeast
of the Dead Sea to help his people. **6:** That the *caravans ceased* is a detail pointing to the near
anarchy of the times. **15–17:** The far away tribes *Reuben . . . Gilead* (Gad) *. . . Dan . . . Asher*

at Ta'anach, by the waters of
  Megid'do;
they got no spoils of silver.
²⁰ From heaven fought the stars,
  from their courses they fought
  against Sis'era.
²¹ The torrent Kishon swept them
  away,
  the onrushing torrent, the
  torrent Kishon.
  March on, my soul, with might!

²² "Then loud beat the horses' hoofs
  with the galloping, galloping of
  his steeds.

²³ "Curse Meroz, says the angel of the
  LORD,
  curse bitterly its inhabitants,
because they came not to the help
  of the LORD,
  to the help of the LORD against the
  mighty.

²⁴ "Most blessed of women be Ja'el,
  the wife of Heber the Ken'ite,
  of tent-dwelling women most
  blessed.
²⁵ He asked water and she gave him
  milk,
  she brought him curds in a lordly
  bowl.
²⁶ She put her hand to the tent peg
  and her right hand to the
  workmen's mallet;
she struck Sis'era a blow,
  she crushed his head,
  she shattered and pierced his
  temple.
²⁷ He sank, he fell,
  he lay still at her feet;
at her feet he sank, he fell;
  where he sank, there he fell
  dead.

²⁸ "Out of the window she peered,
  the mother of Sis'era gazed^h
  through the lattice:
'Why is his chariot so long in
  coming?
  Why tarry the hoofbeats of his
  chariots?'
²⁹ Her wisest ladies make answer,
  nay, she gives answer to herself,
³⁰ 'Are they not finding and dividing
  the spoil?–
  A maiden or two for every man;
spoil of dyed stuffs for Sis'era,
  spoil of dyed stuffs embroidered,
  two pieces of dyed work
  embroidered for my neck
  as spoil?'

³¹ "So perish all thine enemies,
  O LORD!
  But thy friends be like the sun as
  he rises in his might."

And the land had rest for forty years.

6 The people of Israel did what was evil in the sight of the LORD; and the LORD gave them into the hand of Mid'ian seven years. ² And the hand of Mid'ian prevailed over Israel; and because of Mid'ian the people of Israel made for themselves the dens which are in the mountains, and the caves and the strongholds. ³ For whenever the Israelites put in seed the Mid'ianites and the Amal'ekites and the people of the East would come up and attack them; ⁴ they would encamp against them and destroy the produce of the land, as far as the neighborhood of Gaza, and leave no sustenance in Israel, and no sheep or ox or ass. ⁵ For they would come up with their cattle and their tents, coming like locusts for

h Gk Compare Tg: Heb *exclaimed*

took no part in the battle. Judah, Simeon, and Levi are not even mentioned. **19:** *Taanach . . . Megiddo* were two important fortresses guarding the northern approaches to the passes through Mount Carmel. **21:** The flooding waters of the Kishon bogged down the Canaanite chariots. **23:** *Meroz* was apparently a nearby Israelite village which refused to take part in the battle. **24–27:** In 4.17–22 *Jael* kills Sisera while he is asleep; here he is struck down while standing. **28–31:** The ancient bard masterfully concludes the account of Sisera's defeat with an impressionistic glimpse of his anxious mother waiting for his return.

6.1–8.35: Gideon. A hero of the tribe of Manasseh drives out the invading Midianites. **6.1–6:** Israel's plight. **3:** *The Midianites . . . the people of the East* were nomadic raiders, like

number; both they and their camels could not be counted; so that they wasted the land as they came in. [6] And Israel was brought very low because of Mid'ian; and the people of Israel cried for help to the LORD.

7 When the people of Israel cried to the LORD on account of the Mid'-ianites, [8] the LORD sent a prophet to the people of Israel; and he said to them, "Thus says the LORD, the God of Israel: I led you up from Egypt, and brought you out of the house of bondage; [9] and I delivered you from the hand of the Egyptians, and from the hand of all who oppressed you, and drove them out before you, and gave you their land; [10] and I said to you, 'I am the LORD your God; you shall not pay reverence to the gods of the Amorites, in whose land you dwell.' But you have not given heed to my voice."

11 Now the angel of the LORD came and sat under the oak at Ophrah, which belonged to Jo'ash the Abiez'-rite, as his son Gideon was beating out wheat in the wine press, to hide it from the Mid'ianites. [12] And the angel of the LORD appeared to him and said to him, "The LORD is with you, you mighty man of valor." [13] And Gideon said to him, "Pray, sir, if the LORD is with us, why then has all this befallen us? And where are all his wonderful deeds which our fathers recounted to us, saying, 'Did not the LORD bring us up from Egypt?' But now the LORD has cast us off, and given us into the hand of Mid'ian." [14] And the LORD turned to him and said, "Go in this might of yours and deliver Israel from the hand of Mid'ian; do not I send you?" [15] And he said to him, "Pray, Lord, how can I deliver Israel? Behold, my clan is the weakest in Manas'seh, and I am the least in my family." [16] And the LORD said to him, "But I will be with you, and you shall smite the Mid'ianites as one man." [17] And he said to him, "If now I have found favor with thee, then show me a sign that it is thou who speakest with me. [18] Do not depart from here, I pray thee, until I come to thee, and bring out my present, and set it before thee." And he said, "I will stay till you return."

19 So Gideon went into his house and prepared a kid, and unleavened cakes from an ephah of flour; the meat he put in a basket, and the broth he put in a pot, and brought them to him under the oak and presented them. [20] And the angel of God said to him, "Take the meat and the unleavened cakes, and put them on this rock, and pour the broth over them." And he did so. [21] Then the angel of the LORD reached out the tip of the staff that was in his hand, and touched the meat and the unleavened cakes; and there sprang up fire from the rock and consumed the flesh and the unleavened cakes; and the angel of the LORD vanished from his sight. [22] Then Gideon perceived that he was the angel of the LORD; and Gideon said, "Alas, O Lord GOD! For now I have seen the angel of the LORD face to face." [23] But the LORD said to him, "Peace be to you; do not fear, you shall not die." [24] Then Gideon built an altar there to the LORD, and called it, The LORD is peace. To this day it still stands at Ophrah, which belongs to the Abiez'rites.

25 That night the LORD said to him, "Take your father's bull, the second bull seven years old, and pull down the altar of Ba'al which your father has, and cut down the Ashe'rah that is beside it; [26] and build an altar to the LORD your God on the top of the stronghold here, with stones laid in due order; then take the second bull, and offer it as a burnt offering with the wood of the Ashe'rah which you shall cut down." [27] So Gideon took ten men

---

the Hebrews of an earlier day and the Arab bedouins of a later. **7–24:** In response to the people's cry for help, Gideon is called to save them. **11:** *The angel of the LORD*, see 2.1 n. An *Abiezrite* was a member of the small (v. 15) Manassite clan of Abiezer. He was *beating out wheat in the wine press* instead of doing it in the usual exposed position on a hill top. **25–32:** Gideon destroys the altar of Baal. **25:** *The Asherah* was probably a wooden pole representing a goddess. **32:** The

of his servants, and did as the LORD had told him; but because he was too afraid of his family and the men of the town to do it by day, he did it by night. 28 When the men of the town rose early in the morning, behold, the altar of Ba'al was broken down, and the Ashe'rah beside it was cut down, and the second bull was offered upon the altar which had been built. 29 And they said to one another, "Who has done this thing?" And after they had made search and inquired, they said, "Gideon the son of Jo'ash has done this thing." 30 Then the men of the town said to Jo'ash, "Bring out your son, that he may die, for he has pulled down the altar of Ba'al and cut down the Ashe'rah beside it." 31 But Jo'ash said to all who were arrayed against him, "Will you contend for Ba'al? Or will you defend his cause? Whoever contends for him shall be put to death by morning. If he is a god, let him contend for himself, because his altar has been pulled down." 32 Therefore on that day he was called Jerubba'al, that is to say, "Let Ba'al contend against him," because he pulled down his altar.

33 Then all the Mid'ianites and the Amal'ekites and the people of the East came together, and crossing the Jordan they encamped in the Valley of Jezreel. 34 But the Spirit of the LORD took possession of Gideon; and he sounded the trumpet, and the Abiez'-rites were called out to follow him. 35 And he sent messengers throughout all Manas'seh; and they too were called out to follow him. And he sent messengers to Asher, Zeb'ulun, and Naph'tali; and they went up to meet them.

36 Then Gideon said to God, "If thou wilt deliver Israel by my hand, as thou hast said, 37 behold, I am laying a fleece of wool on the threshing floor; if there is dew on the fleece alone, and it is dry on all the ground, then I shall know that thou wilt deliver Israel by my hand, as thou hast said." 38 And it was so. When he rose early next morning and squeezed the fleece, he wrung enough dew from the fleece to fill a bowl with water. 39 Then Gideon said to God, "Let not thy anger burn against me, let me speak but this once; pray, let me make trial only this once with the fleece; pray, let it be dry only on the fleece, and on all the ground let there be dew." 40 And God did so that night; for it was dry on the fleece only, and on all the ground there was dew.

7 Then Jerubba'al (that is, Gideon) and all the people who were with him rose early and encamped beside the spring of Harod; and the camp of Mid'ian was north of them, by the hill of Moreh, in the valley.

2 The LORD said to Gideon, "The people with you are too many for me to give the Mid'ianites into their hand, lest Israel vaunt themselves against me, saying, 'My own hand has delivered me.' 3 Now therefore proclaim in the ears of the people, saying, 'Whoever is fearful and trembling, let him return home.'" And Gideon tested them;*i* twenty-two thousand returned, and ten thousand remained.

4 And the LORD said to Gideon, "The people are still too many; take them down to the water and I will test them for you there; and he of whom I say to you, 'This man shall go with

i Cn: Heb *and depart from Mount Gilead*

explanation given of the name *Jerubbaal* is not the natural one; the bearer of such a name was certainly a worshiper of Baal, not an antagonist. Numerous other difficulties and inconsistencies in the Gideon stories are evidence that accounts from several different sources have been imperfectly fused. The whole "Jerubbaal" incident (vv. 25–32) is unrelated either to what precedes or what follows. **33–40:** He prepares to attack the Midianites. **33:** *The Valley of Jezreel*, the eastern end of the valley of Esdraelon, in the north of Palestine. **34:** *The Spirit of the LORD*, see 3.10 n. **7.1–23:** Gideon puts the Midianites to flight. **4–7:** The test, described in somewhat confusing fashion in these verses, is merely an arbitrary device for reducing the number of Gideon's warriors in order to enhance the miraculous character of the deliverance which follows. No

you,' shall go with you; and any of whom I say to you, 'This man shall not go with you,' shall not go." ⁵ So he brought the people down to the water; and the LORD said to Gideon, "Every one that laps the water with his tongue, as a dog laps, you shall set by himself; likewise every one that kneels down to drink." ⁶ And the number of those that lapped, putting their hands to their mouths, was three hundred men; but all the rest of the people knelt down to drink water. ⁷ And the LORD said to Gideon, "With the three hundred men that lapped I will deliver you, and give the Mid'ianites into your hand; and let all the others go every man to his home." ⁸ So he took the jars of the people from their hands,ʲ and their trumpets; and he sent all the rest of Israel every man to his tent, but retained the three hundred men; and the camp of Mid'ian was below him in the valley.

9 That same night the LORD said to him, "Arise, go down against the camp; for I have given it into your hand. ¹⁰ But if you fear to go down, go down to the camp with Purah your servant; ¹¹ and you shall hear what they say, and afterward your hands shall be strengthened to go down against the camp." Then he went down with Purah his servant to the outposts of the armed men that were in the camp. ¹² And the Mid'ianites and the Amal'ekites and all the people of the East lay along the valley like locusts for multitude; and their camels were without number, as the sand which is upon the seashore for multitude. ¹³ When Gideon came, behold, a man was telling a dream to his comrade; and he said, "Behold, I dreamed a dream; and lo, a cake of barley bread tumbled into the camp of Mid'ian, and came to the tent, and struck it so that it fell, and turned it upside down, so that the tent lay flat." ¹⁴ And his comrade answered, "This is no other than the

sword of Gideon the son of Jo'ash, a man of Israel; into his hand God has given Mid'ian and all the host."

15 When Gideon heard the telling of the dream and its interpretation, he worshiped; and he returned to the camp of Israel, and said, "Arise; for the LORD has given the host of Mid'-ian into your hand." ¹⁶ And he divided the three hundred men into three companies, and put trumpets into the hands of all of them and empty jars, with torches inside the jars. ¹⁷ And he said to them, "Look at me, and do likewise; when I come to the outskirts of the camp, do as I do. ¹⁸ When I blow the trumpet, I and all who are with me, then blow the trumpets also on every side of all the camp, and shout, 'For the LORD and for Gideon.' "

19 So Gideon and the hundred men who were with him came to the outskirts of the camp at the beginning of the middle watch, when they had just set the watch; and they blew the trumpets and smashed the jars that were in their hands. ²⁰ And the three companies blew the trumpets and broke the jars, holding in their left hands the torches, and in their right hands the trumpets to blow; and they cried, "A sword for the LORD and for Gideon!" ²¹ They stood every man in his place round about the camp, and all the army ran; they cried out and fled. ²² When they blew the three hundred trumpets, the LORD set every man's sword against his fellow and against all the army; and the army fled as far as Beth-shit'tah toward Zer'erah,ᵏ as far as the border of A'bel-meho'lah, by Tabbath. ²³ And the men of Israel were called out from Naph'tali and from Asher and from all Manas'seh, and they pursued after Mid'ian.

24 And Gideon sent messengers throughout all the hill country of

ʲ Cn: Heb *the people took provisions in their hands*
ᵏ Another reading is *Zeredah*

---

principle of discrimination, such as would separate the brave from the cowardly or the watchful from the careless, is involved. **13:** *Barley bread* represents the Israelite farmers; *the tent*, the nomadic Midianites. **7.24–8.3:** Oreb and Zeeb, the Midianite chieftains, are captured and

E'phraim, saying, "Come down against the Mid'ianites and seize the waters against them, as far as Beth-bar'ah, and also the Jordan." So all the men of E'phraim were called out, and they seized the waters as far as Beth-bar'ah, and also the Jordan. ²⁵ And they took the two princes of Mid'ian, Oreb and Zeeb; they killed Oreb at the rock of Oreb, and Zeeb they killed at the wine press of Zeeb, as they pursued Mid'ian; and they brought the heads of Oreb and Zeeb to Gideon beyond the Jordan.

8 And the men of E'phraim said to him, "What is this that you have done to us, not to call us when you went to fight with Mid'ian?" And they upbraided him violently. ² And he said to them, "What have I done now in comparison with you? Is not the gleaning of the grapes of E'phraim better than the vintage of Abi-e'zer? ³ God has given into your hands the princes of Mid'ian, Oreb and Zeeb; what have I been able to do in comparison with you?" Then their anger against him was abated, when he had said this.

4 And Gideon came to the Jordan and passed over, he and the three hundred men who were with him, faint yet pursuing. ⁵ So he said to the men of Succoth, "Pray, give loaves of bread to the people who follow me; for they are faint, and I am pursuing after Zebah and Zalmun'na, the kings of Mid'ian." ⁶ And the officials of Succoth said, "Are Zebah and Zalmun'na already in your hand, that we should give bread to your army?" ⁷ And Gideon said, "Well then, when the LORD has given Zebah and Zalmun'na into my hand, I will flail your flesh with the thorns of the wilderness and with

briers." ⁸ And from there he went up to Penu'el, and spoke to them in the same way; and the men of Penu'el answered him as the men of Succoth had answered. ⁹ And he said to the men of Penu'el, "When I come again in peace, I will break down this tower."

10 Now Zebah and Zalmun'na were in Karkor with their army, about fifteen thousand men, all who were left of all the army of the people of the East; for there had fallen a hundred and twenty thousand men who drew the sword. ¹¹ And Gideon went up by the caravan route east of Nobah and Jog'behah, and attacked the army; for the army was off its guard. ¹² And Zebah and Zalmun'na fled; and he pursued them and took the two kings of Mid'ian, Zebah and Zalmun'na, and he threw all the army into a panic.

13 Then Gideon the son of Jo'ash returned from the battle by the ascent of Heres. ¹⁴ And he caught a young man of Succoth, and questioned him; and he wrote down for him the officials and elders of Succoth, seventy-seven men. ¹⁵ And he came to the men of Succoth, and said, "Behold Zebah and Zalmun'na, about whom you taunted me, saying, 'Are Zebah and Zalmun'na already in your hand, that we should give bread to your men who are faint?' " ¹⁶ And he took the elders of the city and he took thorns of the wilderness and briers and with them taught the men of Succoth. ¹⁷ And he broke down the tower of Penu'el, and slew the men of the city.

18 Then he said to Zebah and Zalmun'na, "Where are the men whom you slew at Tabor?" They answered, "As you are, so were they, every one

---

executed by the tribe of Ephraim. **8.2–3:** Gideon appeases the anger of the Ephraimites at not being summoned sooner by telling them that their final accomplishment (*the gleaning of the grapes*) was greater than the whole previous *vintage of Abiezer*. **4–17:** Gideon continues to pursue the Midianites eastward and kills their chieftains Zebah and Zalmunna. This sounds like a parallel version of the events described in 7.24–8.3 (in the earlier passage the pursuit and capture of the Midianite princes, Oreb and Zeeb; here the pursuit and capture of the Midianite kings, Zebah and Zalmunna). **5:** *Succoth* and the other places mentioned in this section are all east of the Jordan. **18–19:** These verses indicate that Gideon's motives were not merely religious or patriotic, but personal. The original beginning of the story must have recorded the death of Gideon's brothers at the hands of the Midianites and his resolve, as their next of kin, to avenge

of them; they resembled the sons of a king." ¹⁹ And he said, "They were my brothers, the sons of my mother; as the LORD lives, if you had saved them alive, I would not slay you." ²⁰ And he said to Jether his first-born, "Rise, and slay them." But the youth did not draw his sword; for he was afraid, because he was still a youth. ²¹ Then Zebah and Zalmun'na said, "Rise yourself, and fall upon us; for as the man is, so is his strength." And Gideon arose and slew Zebah and Zalmun'na; and he took the crescents that were on the necks of their camels.

22 Then the men of Israel said to Gideon, "Rule over us, you and your son and your grandson also; for you have delivered us out of the hand of Mid'ian." ²³ Gideon said to them, "I will not rule over you, and my son will not rule over you; the LORD will rule over you." ²⁴ And Gideon said to them, "Let me make a request of you; give me every man of you the earrings of his spoil." (For they had golden earrings, because they were Ish'maelites.) ²⁵ And they answered, "We will willingly give them." And they spread a garment, and every man cast in it the earrings of his spoil. ²⁶ And the weight of the golden earrings that he requested was one thousand seven hundred shekels of gold; besides the crescents and the pendants and the purple garments worn by the kings of Mid'ian, and besides the collars that were about the necks of their camels. ²⁷ And Gideon made an ephod of it and put it in his city, in Ophrah; and all Israel played the harlot after it there, and it became a snare to Gideon and to his family. ²⁸ So Mid'ian was subdued before the people of Israel,

and they lifted up their heads no more. And the land had rest forty years in the days of Gideon.

29 Jerubba'al the son of Jo'ash went and dwelt in his own house. ³⁰ Now Gideon had seventy sons, his own offspring, for he had many wives. ³¹ And his concubine who was in Shechem also bore him a son, and he called his name Abim'elech. ³² And Gideon the son of Jo'ash died in a good old age, and was buried in the tomb of Jo'ash his father, at Ophrah of the Abiez'rites.

33 As soon as Gideon died, the people of Israel turned again and played the harlot after the Ba'als, and made Ba'al-be'rith their god. ³⁴ And the people of Israel did not remember the LORD their God, who had rescued them from the hand of all their enemies on every side; ³⁵ and they did not show kindness to the family of Jerrubba'al (that is, Gideon) in return for all the good that he had done to Israel.

9 Now Abim'elech the son of Jerubba'al went to Shechem to his mother's kinsmen and said to them and to the whole clan of his mother's family, ² "Say in the ears of all the citizens of Shechem, 'Which is better for you, that all seventy of the sons of Jerubba'al rule over you, or that one rule over you?' Remember also that I am your bone and your flesh." ³ And his mother's kinsmen spoke all these words on his behalf in the ears of all the men of Shechem; and their hearts inclined to follow Abim'elech, for they said, "He is our brother." ⁴ And they gave him seventy pieces of silver out of the house of Ba'al-be'rith with which Abim'elech hired worthless and

---

them (compare Jos.20.3). **22–23:** Gideon refuses an offer of hereditary kingship. **24–28:** He makes an ephod (probably some kind of image) out of the spoil of the Midianites. **29–32:** Gideon's family and his death. **33–35:** Israel's renewed apostasy.

9.1–57: Abimelech. Gideon's half-Canaanite son comes to a disastrous end when he tries to make himself king. **1–6:** Abimelech becomes king. **1:** *Jerubbaal,* see 6.32 n. *Shechem,* the most important city and sanctuary in north central Palestine. It guarded the important east and west highway which passed between Mount Ebal and Mount Gerizim. **4:** *Baal-berith,* "the lord of the covenant," was the god of Shechem. It is perhaps significant that the Israelites entered into a covenant with the LORD at Shechem (Jos.24.1–27), where there is this evidence of Canaanite

reckless fellows, who followed him. [5] And he went to his father's house at Ophrah, and slew his brothers the sons of Jerubba'al, seventy men, upon one stone; but Jotham the youngest son of Jerubba'al was left, for he hid himself. [6] And all the citizens of Shechem came together, and all Beth-millo, and they went and made Abim'elech king, by the oak of the pillar at Shechem.

[7] When it was told to Jotham, he went and stood on the top of Mount Ger'izim, and cried aloud and said to them, "Listen to me, you men of Shechem, that God may listen to you. [8] The trees once went forth to anoint a king over them; and they said to the olive tree, 'Reign over us.' [9] But the olive tree said to them, 'Shall I leave my fatness, by which gods and men are honored, and go to sway over the trees?' [10] And the trees said to the fig tree, 'Come you, and reign over us.' [11] But the fig tree said to them, 'Shall I leave my sweetness and my good fruit, and go to sway over the trees?' [12] And the trees said to the vine, 'Come you, and reign over us.' [13] But the vine said to them, 'Shall I leave my wine which cheers gods and men, and go to sway over the trees?' [14] Then all the trees said to the bramble, 'Come you, and reign over us.' [15] And the bramble said to the trees, 'If in good faith you are anointing me king over you, then come and take refuge in my shade; but if not, let fire come out of the bramble and devour the cedars of Lebanon.'

[16] "Now therefore, if you acted in good faith and honor when you made Abim'elech king, and if you have dealt well with Jerubba'al and his house, and have done to him as his deeds deserved– [17] for my father fought for you, and risked his life, and rescued you from the hand of Mid'ian; [18] and you have risen up against my father's house this day, and have slain his sons, seventy men on one stone, and have made Abim'elech, the son of his maidservant, king over the citizens of Shechem, because he is your kinsman– [19] if you then have acted in good faith and honor with Jerubba'al and with his house this day, then rejoice in Abim'elech, and let him also rejoice in you; [20] but if not, let fire come out from Abim'elech, and devour the citizens of Shechem, and Beth-millo; and let fire come out from the citizens of Shechem, and from Beth-millo, and devour Abim'elech." [21] And Jotham ran away and fled, and went to Beer and dwelt there, for fear of Abim'elech his brother.

[22] Abim'elech ruled over Israel three years. [23] And God sent an evil spirit between Abim'elech and the men of Shechem; and the men of Shechem dealt treacherously with Abim'elech; [24] that the violence done to the seventy sons of Jerubba'al might come and their blood be laid upon Abim'elech their brother, who slew them, and upon the men of Shechem, who strengthened his hands to slay his brothers. [25] And the men of Shechem put men in ambush against him on the mountain tops, and they robbed all who passed by them along that way; and it was told Abim'elech.

[26] And Ga'al the son of Ebed moved into Shechem with his kinsmen; and the men of Shechem put confidence in him. [27] And they went out into the field, and gathered the grapes from their vineyards and trod them, and held festival, and went into the house of their god, and ate and drank and reviled Abim'elech. [28] And Ga'al the son of Ebed said, "Who is Abim'elech, and who are we of Shechem, that we should serve him? Did not the son of Jerubba'al and Zebul his officer serve the men of Hamor the father of Shechem? Why then should we serve him? [29] Would that this people were under my hand! then I would remove Abim'-

---

cultic associations with covenant ideology (see Jos.24.25 n.). **6:** *The oak of the pillar*, see Jos. 24.26. **7–21:** Jotham denounces Abimelech. **7:** *Mount Gerizim*, the mountain south of Shechem (see Dt.11.29). **8:** *The olive tree* is the noblest tree, while the bramble (v. 14) is a useless shrub. **22–25:** A quarrel breaks out between Abimelech and the Shechemites. **26–49:** Abimelech crushes

[306]

elech, I would say[l] to Abim'elech, 'Increase your army, and come out.' "

30 When Zebul the ruler of the city heard the words of Ga'al the son of Ebed, his anger was kindled. [31] And he sent messengers to Abim'elech at Aru'mah,[m] saying, "Behold, Ga'al the son of Ebed and his kinsmen have come to Shechem, and they are stirring up[n] the city against you. [32] Now therefore, go by night, you and the men that are with you, and lie in wait in the fields. [33] Then in the morning, as soon as the sun is up, rise early and rush upon the city; and when he and the men that are with him come out against you, you may do to them as occasion offers."

34 And Abim'elech and all the men that were with him rose up by night, and laid wait against Shechem in four companies. [35] And Ga'al the son of Ebed went out and stood in the entrance of the gate of the city; and Abim'elech and the men that were with him rose from the ambush. [36] And when Ga'al saw the men, he said to Zebul, "Look, men are coming down from the mountain tops!" And Zebul said to him, "You see the shadow of the mountains as if they were men." [37] Ga'al spoke again and said, "Look, men are coming down from the center of the land, and one company is coming from the direction of the Diviners' Oak." [38] Then Zebul said to him, "Where is your mouth now, you who said, 'Who is Abim'elech, that we should serve him?' Are not these the men whom you despised? Go out now and fight with them." [39] And Ga'al went out at the head of the men of Shechem, and fought with Abim'elech. [40] And Abim'elech chased him, and he fled before him; and many fell wounded, up to the entrance of the gate. [41] And Abim'elech dwelt at Aru'mah; and Zebul drove out Ga'al and his kinsmen, so that they could not live on at Shechem.

42 On the following day the men went out into the fields. And Abim'elech was told. [43] He took his men and divided them into three companies, and laid wait in the fields; and he looked and saw the men coming out of the city, and he rose against them and slew them. [44] Abim'elech and the company[o] that was with him rushed forward and stood at the entrance of the gate of the city, while the two companies rushed upon all who were in the fields and slew them. [45] And Abim'elech fought against the city all that day; he took the city, and killed the people that were in it; and he razed the city and sowed it with salt.

46 When all the people of the Tower of Shechem heard of it, they entered the stronghold of the house of El-be'rith. [47] Abim'elech was told that all the people of the Tower of Shechem were gathered together. [48] And Abim'elech went up to Mount Zalmon, he and all the men that were with him; and Abim'elech took an axe in his hand, and cut down a bundle of brushwood, and took it up and laid it on his shoulder. And he said to the men that were with him, "What you have seen me do, make haste to do, as I have done." [49] So every one of the people cut down his bundle and following Abimelech put it against the stronghold, and they set the stronghold on fire over them, so that all the people of the Tower of Shechem also died, about a thousand men and women.

50 Then Abim'elech went to Thebez, and encamped against Thebez, and took it. [51] But there was a strong tower within the city, and all the people of the city fled to it, all the men and women, and shut themselves in; and they went to the roof of the tower. [52] And Abim'elech came to the tower, and fought against it, and drew near to the door of the tower to burn it with fire. [53] And a certain

l Gk: Heb *and he said*
m Cn See 9.41. Heb *Tormah*   *n* Cn: Heb *besieging*
o Vg and some Mss of Gk: Heb *companies*

Gaal's rebellion. **28:** Abimelech lived at Arumah (vv. 31,41) and governed Shechem by a deputy, *Zebul*. **50–57:** Abimelech killed at Thebez.

woman threw an upper millstone upon Abim'elech's head, and crushed his skull. [54] Then he called hastily to the young man his armor-bearer, and said to him, "Draw your sword and kill me, lest men say of me, 'A woman killed him.' " And his young man thrust him through, and he died. [55] And when the men of Israel saw that Abim'elech was dead, they departed every man to his home. [56] Thus God requited the crime of Abim'elech, which he committed against his father in killing his seventy brothers; [57] and God also made all the wickedness of the men of Shechem fall back upon their heads, and upon them came the curse of Jotham the son of Jerubba'al.

10 After Abim'elech there arose to deliver Israel Tola the son of Pu'ah, son of Dodo, a man of Is'sachar; and he lived at Shamir in the hill country of E'phraim. [2] And he judged Israel twenty-three years. Then he died, and was buried at Shamir.

3 After him arose Ja'ir the Gileadite, who judged Israel twenty-two years. [4] And he had thirty sons who rode on thirty asses; and they had thirty cities, called Hav'voth-ja'ir to this day, which are in the land of Gilead. [5] And Ja'ir died, and was buried in Kamon.

6 And the people of Israel again did what was evil in the sight of the LORD, and served the Ba'als and the Ash'-taroth, the gods of Syria, the gods of Sidon, the gods of Moab, the gods of the Ammonites, and the gods of the Philistines; and they forsook the LORD, and did not serve him. [7] And the anger of the LORD was kindled against Israel,

and he sold them into the hand of the Philistines and into the hand of the Ammonites, [8] and they crushed and oppressed the children of Israel that year. For eighteen years they oppressed all the people of Israel that were beyond the Jordan in the land of the Amorites, which is in Gilead. [9] And the Ammonites crossed the Jordan to fight also against Judah and against Benjamin and against the house of E'phraim; so that Israel was sorely distressed.

10 And the people of Israel cried to the LORD, saying, "We have sinned against thee, because we have forsaken our God and have served the Ba'als." [11] And the LORD said to the people of Israel, "Did I not deliver you from the Egyptians and from the Amorites, from the Ammonites and from the Philistines? [12] The Sido'nians also, and the Amal'ekites, and the Ma'onites, oppressed you; and you cried to me, and I delivered you out of their hand. [13] Yet you have forsaken me and served other gods; therefore I will deliver you no more. [14] Go and cry to the gods whom you have chosen; let them deliver you in the time of your distress." [15] And the people of Israel said to the LORD, "We have sinned; do to us whatever seems good to thee; only deliver us, we pray thee, this day." [16] So they put away the foreign gods from among them and served the LORD; and he became indignant over the misery of Israel.

17 Then the Ammonites were called to arms, and they encamped in Gilead; and the people of Israel came together, and they encamped at Mizpah. [18] And

---

10.1–5: Two minor judges. The role played by the so-called "minor judges" who are listed here and in 12.8–15 is one of the puzzles of the book, since they were apparently not leaders in war. It has been plausibly suggested that they were the civil heads of the Israelite confederacy, charged with the custody of traditional law, and therefore "judges" in the strict sense of the term. The word would then later have been extended loosely to military heroes of the same period.

10.6–12.7: Jephthah. A Transjordanian hero saves his people from the Ammonites. **10.6–16:** General introduction. **10.17–11.11:** Jephthah, whose disfavor with his own family had forced him to take up a Robin Hood-like existence as head of an outlaw gang, is recalled from exile to lead his people against their Ammonite oppressors. **10.17:** *The Ammonites* were a central Transjordanian people who had Rabbath-Ammon (the modern Amman) as their capital.

the people, the leaders of Gilead, said one to another, "Who is the man that will begin to fight against the Ammonites? He shall be head over all the inhabitants of Gilead."

Now Jephthah the Gileadite was a mighty warrior, but he was the son of a harlot. Gilead was the father of Jephthah. ² And Gilead's wife also bore him sons; and when his wife's sons grew up, they thrust Jephthah out, and said to him, "You shall not inherit in our father's house; for you are the son of another woman." ³ Then Jephthah fled from his brothers, and dwelt in the land of Tob; and worthless fellows collected round Jephthah, and went raiding with him.

4 After a time the Ammonites made war against Israel. ⁵ And when the Ammonites made war against Israel, the elders of Gilead went to bring Jephthah from the land of Tob; ⁶ and they said to Jephthah, "Come and be our leader, that we may fight with the Ammonites." ⁷ But Jephthah said to the elders of Gilead, "Did you not hate me, and drive me out of my father's house? Why have you come to me now when you are in trouble?" ⁸ And the elders of Gilead said to Jephthah, "That is why we have turned to you now, that you may go with us and fight with the Ammonites, and be our head over all the inhabitants of Gilead." ⁹ Jephthah said to the elders of Gilead, "If you bring me home again to fight with the Ammonites, and the LORD gives them over to me, I will be your head." ¹⁰ And the elders of Gilead said to Jephthah, "The LORD will be witness between us; we will surely do as you say." ¹¹ So Jephthah went with the elders of Gilead, and the people made him head and leader over them; and Jephthah spoke all his words before the LORD at Mizpah.

12 Then Jephthah sent messengers to the king of the Ammonites and said, "What have you against me, that you have come to me to fight against my land?" ¹³ And the king of the Ammonites answered the messengers of Jephthah, "Because Israel on coming from Egypt took away my land, from the Arnon to the Jabbok and to the Jordan; now therefore restore it peaceably." ¹⁴ And Jephthah sent messengers again to the king of the Ammonites ¹⁵ and said to him, "Thus says Jephthah: Israel did not take away the land of Moab or the land of the Ammonites, ¹⁶ but when they came up from Egypt, Israel went through the wilderness to the Red Sea and came to Kadesh. ¹⁷ Israel then sent messengers to the king of Edom, saying, 'Let us pass, we pray, through your land'; but the king of Edom would not listen. And they sent also to the king of Moab, but he would not consent. So Israel remained at Kadesh. ¹⁸ Then they journeyed through the wilderness, and went around the land of Edom and the land of Moab, and arrived on the east side of the land of Moab, and camped on the other side of the Arnon; but they did not enter the territory of Moab, for the Arnon was the boundary of Moab. ¹⁹ Israel then sent messengers to Sihon king of the Amorites, king of Heshbon; and Israel said to him, 'Let us pass, we pray, through your land to our country.' ²⁰ But Sihon did not trust Israel to pass through his territory; so Sihon gathered all his people together, and encamped at Jahaz, and fought with Israel. ²¹ And the LORD, the God of Israel, gave Sihon and all his people into the hand of Israel, and they defeated them; so Israel took possession of all the land of the Amorites, who inhabited that country. ²² And they took possession of all the territory of the Amorites from the Arnon to the Jabbok and from the wilderness to the Jordan. ²³ So then the LORD, the God of Israel, dispos-

---

Gilead was the northern part of Transjordan. **11.1:** There is some confusion here because Gilead is properly the name of a district, not a person. **5:** A Hebrew community was governed by a council of the older men, *the elders.* **12–28:** Jephthah negotiates in vain with the king of Ammon. **17:** Num.20.14–21. **19–23:** Num.21.21–32. **24:** The argument is that a nation has a right to

sessed the Amorites from before his people Israel; and are you to take possession of them? ²⁴ Will you not possess what Chemosh your god gives you to possess? And all that the LORD our God has dispossessed before us, we will possess. ²⁵ Now are you any better than Balak the son of Zippor, king of Moab? Did he ever strive against Israel, or did he ever go to war with them? ²⁶ While Israel dwelt in Heshbon and its villages, and in Aro'er and its villages, and in all the cities that are on the banks of the Arnon, three hundred years, why did you not recover them within that time? ²⁷ I therefore have not sinned against you, and you do me wrong by making war on me; the LORD, the Judge, decide this day between the people of Israel and the people of Ammon." ²⁸ But the king of the Ammonites did not heed the message of Jephthah which he sent to him.

29 Then the Spirit of the LORD came upon Jephthah, and he passed through Gilead and Manas'seh, and passed on to Mizpah of Gilead, and from Mizpah of Gilead he passed on to the Ammonites. ³⁰ And Jephthah made a vow to the LORD, and said, "If thou wilt give the Ammonites into my hand, ³¹ then whoever comes forth from the doors of my house to meet me, when I return victorious from the Ammonites, shall be the LORD's, and I will offer him up for a burnt offering." ³² So Jephthah crossed over to the Ammonites to fight against them; and the LORD gave them into his hand. ³³ And he smote them from Aro'er to the neighborhood of Minnith, twenty cities, and as far as Abel-keramim,

with a very great slaughter. So the Ammonites were subdued before the people of Israel.

34 Then Jephthah came to his home at Mizpah; and behold, his daughter came out to meet him with timbrels and with dances; she was his only child; beside her he had neither son nor daughter. ³⁵ And when he saw her, he rent his clothes, and said, "Alas, my daughter! you have brought me very low, and you have become the cause of great trouble to me; for I have opened my mouth to the LORD, and I cannot take back my vow." ³⁶ And she said to him, "My father, if you have opened your mouth to the LORD, do to me according to what has gone forth from your mouth, now that the LORD has avenged you on your enemies, on the Ammonites." ³⁷ And she said to her father, "Let this thing be done for me; let me alone two months, that I may go and wander*p* on the mountains, and bewail my virginity, I and my companions." ³⁸ And he said, "Go." And he sent her away for two months; and she departed, she and her companions, and bewailed her virginity upon the mountains. ³⁹ And at the end of two months, she returned to her father, who did with her according to his vow which he had made. She had never known a man. And it became a custom in Israel ⁴⁰ that the daughters of Israel went year by year to lament the daughter of Jephthah the Gileadite four days in the year.

12 The men of E'phraim were called to arms, and they crossed to Zaphon and said to Jephthah, "Why

p Cn: Heb *go down*

---

keep that which its god gives to it in war. Curiously, however, Chemosh was the god of the Moabites, not the Ammonites, whose chief god was called Milcom (or Molech; 1 Kg.11.5,7). **25:** *Balak*, see Num. chs. 22–24. **29–33:** Jephthah defeats the Ammonites by means of a vow. **29:** *The Spirit of the LORD*, see 3.10 n.; 6.34. **31:** He takes the extreme step of vowing a human sacrifice (compare 2 Kg.3.27). While human sacrifice was viewed with abhorrence by the Hebrews throughout most of their later history, there is some evidence (as here) that it was practiced in early times, and there were occasional relapses even at a relatively late date (2 Kg. 21.6). **34–40:** Jephthah fulfils his vow by sacrificing his only daughter. **37:** Because a Hebrew woman could suffer no greater disgrace than to die childless, Jephthah's daughter asks time to *bewail* her *virginity*. **12.1–7:** Jephthah punishes the quarrelsome Ephraimites. **1:** The tribe of Ephraim, located west of the Jordan, exhibited a similar contentious spirit in the Gideon story

did you cross over to fight against the Ammonites, and did not call us to go with you? We will burn your house over you with fire." [2] And Jephthah said to them, "I and my people had a great feud with the Ammonites; and when I called you, you did not deliver me from their hand. [3] And when I saw that you would not deliver me, I took my life in my hand, and crossed over against the Ammonites, and the LORD gave them into my hand; why then have you come up to me this day, to fight against me?" [4] Then Jephthah gathered all the men of Gilead and fought with E'phraim; and the men of Gilead smote E'phraim, because they said, "You are fugitives of E'phraim, you Gileadites, in the midst of E'phraim and Manas'seh." [5] And the Gileadites took the fords of the Jordan against the E'phraimites. And when any of the fugitives of E'phraim said, "Let me go over," the men of Gilead said to him, "Are you an E'phraimite?" When he said, "No," [6] they said to him, "Then say Shibboleth," and he said, "Sibboleth," for he could not pronounce it right; then they seized him and slew him at the fords of the Jordan. And there fell at that time forty-two thousand of the E'phraimites.

[7] Jephthah judged Israel six years. Then Jephthah the Gileadite died, and was buried in his city in Gilead.*q*

[8] After him Ibzan of Bethlehem judged Israel. [9] He had thirty sons; and thirty daughters he gave in marriage outside his clan, and thirty daughters he brought in from outside for his sons. And he judged Israel seven years. [10] Then Ibzan died, and was buried at Bethlehem.

[11] After him Elon the Zeb'ulunite judged Israel; and he judged Israel ten years. [12] Then Elon the Zeb'-ulunite died, and was buried at Ai'-jalon in the land of Zeb'ulun.

[13] After him Abdon the son of Hillel the Pira'thonite judged Israel. [14] He had forty sons and thirty grandsons, who rode on seventy asses; and he judged Israel eight years. [15] Then Abdon the son of Hillel the Pira'thonite died, and was buried at Pira'thon in the land of E'phraim, in the hill country of the Amal'ekites.

13 And the people of Israel again did what was evil in the sight of the LORD; and the LORD gave them into the hand of the Philistines for forty years.

2 And there was a certain man of Zorah, of the tribe of the Danites, whose name was Mano'ah; and his wife was barren and had no children. [3] And the angel of the LORD appeared to the woman and said to her, "Behold, you are barren and have no children; but you shall conceive and bear a son. [4] Therefore beware, and drink no wine or strong drink, and eat nothing unclean, [5] for lo, you shall conceive and bear a son. No razor shall come upon

q Gk: Heb *in the cities of Gilead*

(8.1). **3:** Jephthah, unlike Gideon (8.2–3), decided to fight fire with fire instead of gentle words. **4:** The meaning of the second part of this verse is not clear. **5:** The Ephraimites tried to slip back to their own country west of the Jordan by *the fords*. **6:** The Ephraimites spoke a slightly different dialect of Hebrew and could easily be recognized by their inability to pronounce the "sh" sound in "shibboleth," meaning "ear [head] of grain."

12.8–15: Three more minor judges. See 10.1–5 n.

13.1–16.31: Samson. Although a legendary hero of the tribe of Dan and frequently engaged in fighting with the Philistines, Samson does not really fit the pattern of the judges since his conflicts are almost entirely personal rather than tribal or national. **13.1–25:** Samson's birth. **1:** *The Philistines* were a non-Semitic people, possibly from Crete, who settled on the coastal plain of Palestine about the same time the Hebrews were entering the land from the east. **2:** *The Danites* were at this period situated in the southwest, near the Philistine plain; later, because of the pressure from the aggressive and expanding Philistine nation, they were forced to move to the north (ch. 18). The Samson stories have considerable historical value in that they illustrate the conditions of life in this uncomfortable situation and the kind of pressures which eventually made the migration necessary. *Barren,* see 11.37 n. **3:** *The angel of the LORD,* see

his head, for the boy shall be a Nazirite to God from birth; and he shall begin to deliver Israel from the hand of the Philistines." [6] Then the woman came and told her husband, "A man of God came to me, and his countenance was like the countenance of the angel of God, very terrible; I did not ask him whence he was, and he did not tell me his name; [7] but he said to me, 'Behold, you shall conceive and bear a son; so then drink no wine or strong drink, and eat nothing unclean, for the boy shall be a Nazirite to God from birth to the day of his death.' "

8 Then Mano'ah entreated the LORD, and said, "O, LORD, I pray thee, let the man of God whom thou didst send come again to us, and teach us what we are to do with the boy that will be born." [9] And God listened to the voice of Mano'ah, and the angel of God came again to the woman as she sat in the field; but Mano'ah her husband was not with her. [10] And the woman ran in haste and told her husband, "Behold, the man who came to me the other day has appeared to me." [11] And Mano'ah arose and went after his wife, and came to the man and said to him, "Are you the man who spoke to this woman?" And he said, "I am." [12] And Mano'ah said, "Now when your words come true, what is to be the boy's manner of life, and what is he to do?" [13] And the angel of the LORD said to Mano'ah, "Of all that I said to the woman let her beware. [14] She may not eat of anything that comes from the vine, neither let her drink wine or strong drink, or eat any unclean thing; all that I commanded her let her observe."

15 Mano'ah said to the angel of the LORD, "Pray, let us detain you, and pre-pare a kid for you." [16] And the angel of the LORD said to Mano'ah, "If you detain me, I will not eat of your food; but if you make ready a burnt offering, then offer it to the LORD." (For Mano'ah did not know that he was the angel of the LORD.) [17] And Mano'ah said to the angel of the LORD, "What is your name, so that, when your words come true, we may honor you?" [18] And the angel of the LORD said to him, "Why do you ask my name, seeing it is wonderful?" [19] So Mano'ah took the kid with the cereal offering, and offered it upon the rock to the LORD, to him who works[r] wonders.[s] [20] And when the flame went up toward heaven from the altar, the angel of the LORD ascended in the flame of the altar while Mano'ah and his wife looked on; and they fell on their faces to the ground.

21 The angel of the LORD appeared no more to Mano'ah and to his wife. Then Mano'ah knew that he was the angel of the LORD. [22] And Mano'ah said to his wife, "We shall surely die, for we have seen God." [23] But his wife said to him, "If the LORD had meant to kill us, he would not have accepted a burnt offering and a cereal offering at our hands, or shown us all these things, or now announced to us such things as these." [24] And the woman bore a son, and called his name Samson; and the boy grew, and the LORD blessed him. [25] And the Spirit of the LORD began to stir him in Ma'haneh-dan, between Zorah and Esh'ta-ol.

14 Samson went down to Timnah, and at Timnah he saw one of the daughters of the Philistines. [2] Then he came up, and told his father and

r Gk Vg: Heb *and working*
s Heb *wonders, while Manoah and his wife looked on*

2.1 n. **5:** A *Nazirite* was one consecrated to God by the taking of these special vows; in early Israel the vows were for life, in later times (as in the law of Num.6.1–21) only temporary. It is only in this chapter and in 16.17 that Samson is designated a Nazirite. **14:** Even the eating of grapes was forbidden, since they were the chief symbol of the culture and religion of the Canaanites (Num.6.4–5). **17:** The knowledge of a god's *name* was necessary in order that he might be reached again when desired (compare Gen.32.29). **18:** *Wonderful*, incommunicable. **25:** *The Spirit of the LORD*, see 3.10 n. (and 14.6,19).

14.1–20: Samson's brief marriage to a Philistine woman. 3: *Uncircumcised*, the Philistines,

mother, "I saw one of the daughters of the Philistines at Timnah; now get her for me as my wife." 3 But his father and mother said to him, "Is there not a woman among the daughters of your kinsmen, or among all our people, that you must go to take a wife from the uncircumcised Philistines?" But Samson said to his father, "Get her for me; for she pleases me well."

4 His father and mother did not know that it was from the LORD; for he was seeking an occasion against the Philistines. At that time the Philistines had dominion over Israel.

5 Then Samson went down with his father and mother to Timnah, and he came to the vineyards of Timnah. And behold, a young lion roared against him; 6 and the Spirit of the LORD came mightily upon him, and he tore the lion asunder as one tears a kid; and he had nothing in his hand. But he did not tell his father or his mother what he had done. 7 Then he went down and talked with the woman; and she pleased Samson well. 8 And after a while he returned to take her; and he turned aside to see the carcass of the lion, and behold, there was a swarm of bees in the body of the lion, and honey. 9 He scraped it out into his hands, and went on, eating as he went; and he came to his father and mother, and gave some to them, and they ate. But he did not tell them that he had taken the honey from the carcass of the lion.

10 And his father went down to the woman, and Samson made a feast there; for so the young men used to do. 11 And when the people saw him, they brought thirty companions to be with him. 12 And Samson said to them, "Let me now put a riddle to you; if you can tell me what it is, within the seven days of the feast, and find it out, then I will give you thirty linen garments and thirty festal garments; 13 but if you cannot tell me what it is, then you shall give me thirty linen garments and thirty festal garments." And they said to him, "Put your riddle, that we may hear it." 14 And he said to them,

"Out of the eater came something
    to eat.
Out of the strong came something
    sweet."

And they could not in three days tell what the riddle was.

15 On the fourth*t* day they said to Samson's wife, "Entice your husband to tell us what the riddle is, lest we burn you and your father's house with fire. Have you invited us here to impoverish us?" 16 And Samson's wife wept before him, and said, "You only hate me, you do not love me; you have put a riddle to my countrymen, and you have not told me what it is." And he said to her, "Behold, I have not told my father nor my mother, and shall I tell you?" 17 She wept before him the seven days that their feast lasted; and on the seventh day he told her, because she pressed him hard. Then she told the riddle to her countrymen. 18 And the men of the city said to him on the seventh day before the sun went down,

"What is sweeter than honey?
What is stronger than a lion?"

And he said to them,

"If you had not plowed with my
    heifer,
you would not have found out my
    riddle."

19 And the Spirit of the LORD came mightily upon him, and he went down

t Gk Syr: Heb *seventh*

---

unlike the Hebrews and most of their neighbors, did not practice circumcision. **4:** *Had dominion over Israel*, the Philistine wars were a major preoccupation in the following period of Israelite history; at the beginning the Philistines had the advantage because of their higher level of material culture (1 Sam.13.19). **6:** Crude and primitive as this passage is, it is of great importance as showing that the experience underlying the Biblical conception of *the Spirit of the* LORD (see 3.10 n.) is that of a tremendous accession of power beyond the normal capabilities of man. In later times the idea became that of moral and spiritual rather than merely physical power (Ps.51.11; Ezek.36.26–27; 1 Cor.2.4). **10:** It was evidently customary in the days of the judges for the bridegroom to provide the marriage *feast.* **14:** *They could not . . . tell what the*

to Ash'kelon and killed thirty men of the town, and took their spoil and gave the festal garments to those who had told the riddle. In hot anger he went back to his father's house. ²⁰ And Samson's wife was given to his companion, who had been his best man.

15 After a while, at the time of wheat harvest, Samson went to visit his wife with a kid; and he said, "I will go in to my wife in the chamber." But her father would not allow him to go in. ² And her father said, "I really thought that you utterly hated her; so I gave her to your companion. Is not her younger sister fairer than she? Pray take her instead." ³ And Samson said to them, "This time I shall be blameless in regard to the Philistines, when I do them mischief." ⁴ So Samson went and caught three hundred foxes, and took torches; and he turned them tail to tail, and put a torch between each pair of tails. ⁵ And when he had set fire to the torches, he let the foxes go into the standing grain of the Philistines, and burned up the shocks and the standing grain, as well as the olive orchards. ⁶ Then the Philistines said, "Who has done this?" And they said, "Samson, the son-in-law of the Timnite, because he has taken his wife and given her to his companion." And the Philistines came up, and burned her and her father with fire. ⁷ And Samson said to them, "If this is what you do, I swear I will be avenged upon you, and after that I will quit." ⁸ And he smote them hip and thigh with great slaughter; and he went down and stayed in the cleft of the rock of Etam.

9 Then the Philistines came up and encamped in Judah, and made a raid on Lehi. ¹⁰ And the men of Judah said, "Why have you come up against us?" They said, "We have come up to bind Samson, to do to him as he did to us." ¹¹ Then three thousand men of Judah went down to the cleft of the rock of Etam, and said to Samson, "Do you not know that the Philistines are rulers over us? What then is this that you have done to us?" And he said to them, "As they did to me, so have I done to them." ¹² And they said to him, "We have come down to bind you, that we may give you into the hands of the Philistines." And Samson said to them, "Swear to me that you will not fall upon me yourselves." ¹³ They said to him, "No; we will only bind you and give you into their hands; we will not kill you." So they bound him with two new ropes, and brought him up from the rock.

14 When he came to Lehi, the Philistines came shouting to meet him; and the Spirit of the LORD came mightily upon him, and the ropes which were on his arms became as flax that has caught fire, and his bonds melted off his hands. ¹⁵ And he found a fresh jawbone of an ass, and put out his hand and seized it, and with it he slew a thousand men. ¹⁶ And Samson said,

"With the jawbone of an ass,
  heaps upon heaps,
 with the jawbone of an ass
  have I slain a thousand men."

¹⁷ When he had finished speaking, he threw away the jawbone out of his hand; and that place was called Ra'-math-le'hi.*ᵘ*

u That is The hill of the jawbone

---

riddle was, because it was insoluble without the key! **19:** *Ashkelon* was one of the five principal Philistine cities, the Philistines being not a unified state, but a confederation of five cities. The other members were Ekron, Ashdod, Gaza, and Gath.

15.1–8: Samson's revenge for the loss of his wife. 1: The marriage which Samson believed himself to have contracted was of an ancient type in which the husband came only from time to time *to visit his wife*, who continued to live with her parents. *A kid* was perhaps the usual gift for sexual intimacy (Gen.38.17). **8:** *Hip and thigh* is a proverbial expression of which the original significance has been lost.

15.9–20: Samson's further vengeance. When the Philistines attempt to capture him, Samson kills a thousand of them with an improvised weapon. **9:** *Lehi* in Hebrew means jawbone (vv. 15–16). **16:** Like the riddle in v. 14 this couplet involves a pun, the Hebrew words for *ass* and

18 And he was very thirsty, and he called on the LORD and said, "Thou hast granted this great deliverance by the hand of thy servant; and shall I now die of thirst, and fall into the hands of the uncircumcised?" ¹⁹ And God split open the hollow place that is at Lehi, and there came water from it; and when he drank, his spirit returned, and he revived. Therefore the name of it was called En-hakkor'e;ᵛ it is at Lehi to this day. ²⁰ And he judged Israel in the days of the Philistines twenty years.

16 Samson went to Gaza, and there he saw a harlot, and he went in to her. ² The Gazites were told, "Samson has come here," and they surrounded the place and lay in wait for him all night at the gate of the city. They kept quiet all night, saying, "Let us wait till the light of the morning; then we will kill him." ³ But Samson lay till midnight, and at midnight he arose and took hold of the doors of the gate of the city and the two posts, and pulled them up, bar and all, and put them on his shoulders and carried them to the top of the hill that is before Hebron.

4 After this he loved a woman in the valley of Sorek, whose name was Deli'lah. ⁵ And the lords of the Philistines came to her and said to her, "Entice him, and see wherein his great strength lies, and by what means we may overpower him, that we may bind him to subdue him; and we will each give you eleven hundred pieces of silver." ⁶ And Deli'lah said to Samson, "Please tell me wherein your great strength lies, and how you might be bound, that one could subdue you." ⁷ And Samson said to her, "If they bind me with seven fresh bowstrings which

have not been dried, then I shall become weak, and be like any other man." ⁸ Then the lords of the Philistines brought her seven fresh bowstrings which had not been dried, and she bound him with them. ⁹ Now she had men lying in wait in an inner chamber. And she said to him, "The Philistines are upon you, Samson!" But he snapped the bowstrings, as a string of tow snaps when it touches the fire. So the secret of his strength was not known.

10 And Deli'lah said to Samson, "Behold, you have mocked me, and told me lies; please tell me how you might be bound." ¹¹ And he said to her, "If they bind me with new ropes that have not been used, then I shall become weak, and be like any other man." ¹² So Deli'lah took new ropes and bound him with them, and said to him, "The Philistines are upon you, Samson!" And the men lying in wait were in an inner chamber. But he snapped the ropes off his arms like a thread.

13 And Deli'lah said to Samson, "Until now you have mocked me, and told me lies; tell me how you might be bound." And he said to her, "If you weave the seven locks of my head with the web and make it tight with the pin, then I shall become weak, and be like any other man." ¹⁴ So while he slept, Deli'lah took the seven locks of his head and wove them into the web.ʷ And she made them tight with the pin, and said to him, "The Philistines are upon you, Samson!" But he awoke from his sleep, and pulled away the pin, the loom, and the web.

15 And she said to him, "How can

ᵛ That is *The spring of him who called*
ʷ Compare Gk: Heb lacks *and make it tight . . . into the web*

---

heap(s) being identical. **18–19:** A story explaining the place name En-hakkore, literally "the spring of him who called."

16.1–3: Samson eludes the Philistines at Gaza. 1: *Gaza* was another city of the Philistine pentapolis or five-city confederation (1.18 n.; 14.19). Samson's relations with the *harlot* are typical of his character and the morals of his day. **3:** *Hebron*, nearly forty miles east of *Gaza*.

16.4–22: Delilah's betrayal of Samson. His third adventure with a Philistine woman brings Samson to a tragic end. **4:** *The valley of Sorek* led into the north end of the Philistine plain. **13:** *The web* and *the pin* were parts of a loom.

you say, 'I love you,' when your heart is not with me? You have mocked me these three times, and you have not told me wherein your great strength lies." [16] And when she pressed him hard with her words day after day, and urged him, his soul was vexed to death. [17] And he told her all his mind, and said to her, "A razor has never come upon my head; for I have been a Nazirite to God from my mother's womb. If I be shaved, then my strength will leave me, and I shall become weak, and be like any other man."

18 When Deli'lah saw that he had told her all his mind, she sent and called the lords of the Philistines, saying, "Come up this once, for he has told me all his mind." Then the lords of the Philistines came up to her, and brought the money in their hands. [19] She made him sleep upon her knees; and she called a man, and had him shave off the seven locks of his head. Then she began to torment him, and his strength left him. [20] And she said, "The Philistines are upon you, Samson!" And he awoke from his sleep, and said, "I will go out as at other times, and shake myself free." And he did not know that the LORD had left him. [21] And the Philistines seized him and gouged out his eyes, and brought him down to Gaza, and bound him with bronze fetters; and he ground at the mill in the prison. [22] But the hair of his head began to grow again after it had been shaved.

23 Now the lords of the Philistines gathered to offer a great sacrifice to Dagon their god, and to rejoice; for they said, "Our god has given Samson our enemy into our hand." [24] And when the people saw him, they praised their god; for they said, "Our god has given our enemy into our hand, the ravager of our country, who has slain many of us." [25] And when their hearts were merry, they said, "Call Samson, that he make sport for us." So they called Samson out of the prison, and he made sport before them. They made him stand between the pillars; [26] and Samson said to the lad who held him by the hand, "Let me feel the pillars on which the house rests, that I may lean against them." [27] Now the house was full of men and women; all the lords of the Philistines were there, and on the roof there were about three thousand men and women, who looked on while Samson made sport.

28 Then Samson called to the LORD and said, "O Lord GOD, remember me, I pray thee, and strengthen me, I pray thee, only this once, O God, that I may be avenged upon the Philistines for one of my two eyes." [29] And Samson grasped the two middle pillars upon which the house rested, and he leaned his weight upon them, his right hand on the one and his left hand on the other. [30] And Samson said, "Let me die with the Philistines." Then he bowed with all his might; and the house fell upon the lords and upon all the people that were in it. So the dead whom he slew at his death were more than those whom he had slain during his life. [31] Then his brothers and all his family came down and took him and brought him up and buried him between Zorah and Esh'ta-ol in the tomb of Mano'ah his father. He had judged Israel twenty years.

17 There was a man of the hill country of E'phraim, whose name was Micah. [2] And he said to his

---

17: The story that Samson was a *Nazirite* (ch. 13) seems to be a late attempt to make Samson respectable; none of his exploits show him as a religious enthusiast. The motif of the unshorn hair is probably derived from mythology rather than high religion. The name Samson is connected with the Hebrew word for "sun"; some scholars believe the stories originally go back to pre-Hebrew sources in which the hair represented the sun's rays, i.e. its strength.

16.23–31: Samson's final act of vengeance. 23: *Dagon* was an ancient Semitic deity whose cult had been adopted by the Philistines after their settlement in the land (see 1 Sam.5.2 n.). **28:** The expression *for one of my two eyes* shows that to the end Samson's motives were personal rather than religious or national.

mother, "The eleven hundred pieces of silver which were taken from you, about which you uttered a curse, and also spoke it in my ears, behold, the silver is with me; I took it." And his mother said, "Blessed be my son by the LORD." ³ And he restored the eleven hundred pieces of silver to his mother; and his mother said, "I consecrate the silver to the LORD from my hand for my son, to make a graven image and a molten image; now therefore I will restore it to you." ⁴ So when he restored the money to his mother, his mother took two hundred pieces of silver, and gave it to the silversmith, who made it into a graven image and a molten image; and it was in the house of Micah. ⁵ And the man Micah had a shrine, and he made an ephod and teraphim, and installed one of his sons, who became his priest. ⁶ In those days there was no king in Israel; every man did what was right in his own eyes.

7 Now there was a young man of Bethlehem in Judah, of the family of Judah, who was a Levite; and he sojourned there. ⁸ And the man departed from the town of Bethlehem in Judah, to live where he could find a place; and as he journeyed, he came to the hill country of E'phraim to the house of Micah. ⁹ And Micah said to him, "From where do you come?" And he said to him, "I am a Levite of Bethlehem in Judah, and I am going to sojourn where I may find a place." ¹⁰ And Micah said to him, "Stay with

me, and be to me a father and a priest, and I will give you ten pieces of silver a year, and a suit of apparel, and your living."ʷ ¹¹ And the Levite was content to dwell with the man; and the young man became to him like one of his sons. ¹² And Micah installed the Levite, and the young man became his priest, and was in the house of Micah. ¹³ Then Micah said, "Now I know that the LORD will prosper me, because I have a Levite as priest."

18 In those days there was no king in Israel. And in those days the tribe of the Danites was seeking for itself an inheritance to dwell in; for until then no inheritance among the tribes of Israel had fallen to them. ² So the Danites sent five able men from the whole number of their tribe, from Zorah and from Esh'ta-ol, to spy out the land and to explore it; and they said to them, "Go and explore the land." And they came to the hill country of E'phraim, to the house of Micah, and lodged there. ³ When they were by the house of Micah, they recognized the voice of the young Levite; and they turned aside and said to him, "Who brought you here? What are you doing in this place? What is your business here?" ⁴ And he said to them, "Thus and thus has Micah dealt with me: he has hired me, and I have become his priest." ⁵ And they said to him, "Inquire of God, we pray thee, that we may know whether the journey on which we are setting out

w Heb *living, and the Levite went*

17.1–6: The shrine of Micah. The two tales which occupy chs. 17–21 are not concerned with "judges" although they relate to the same period. This one (chs. 17–18) begins with the story of a certain Micah whose mother expiated his theft of a large sum of silver from her by erecting a family shrine containing silver images. The fully matured religion of Israel forbade the use of graven and molten images (Ex.20.4,23; 34.17), but there were evidently circles in early times, such as those in this story, where such laws were unknown. **5:** *An ephod and teraphim* were cult objects (8.27; 2 Kg.23.24) perhaps used for divination (Ezek.21.21). **6:** This verse, like 21.25, expresses the feeling of a later editor that such things were possible only because of the near anarchy of the times.

17.7–13: Micah obtains a Levite for his family chaplain. The story shows that the Levites at this time enjoyed a certain prestige even though others could act as priests when necessary. **7:** *Bethlehem,* a city in Judah five miles south of Jerusalem, and later the birthplace of David.

18.1–31: The migration of the tribe of Dan. In the early days of the judges Dan was located in the southwest (Jos.19.40–46; Jg.1.34; 13.2), but the pressure of the Philistines forced them to move to the far north. **1–10:** Spies locate a favorable place to settle. **5:** To *inquire of God* is to

will succeed." [6] And the priest said to them, "Go in peace. The journey on which you go is under the eye of the LORD."

7 Then the five men departed, and came to La'ish, and saw the people who were there, how they dwelt in security, after the manner of the Sido'-nians, quiet and unsuspecting, lack-ing[x] nothing that is in the earth, and possessing wealth, and how they were far from the Sido'nians and had no dealings with any one. [8] And when they came to their brethren at Zorah and Esh'ta-ol, their brethren said to them, "What do you report?" [9] They said, "Arise, and let us go up against them; for we have seen the land, and behold, it is very fertile. And will you do nothing? Do not be slow to go, and enter in and possess the land. [10] When you go, you will come to an unsuspect-ing people. The land is broad; yea, God has given it into your hands, a place where there is no lack of any-thing that is in the earth."

11 And six hundred men of the tribe of Dan, armed with weapons of war, set forth from Zorah and Esh'ta-ol, [12] and went up and encamped at Kir'-iath-je'arim in Judah. On this account that place is called Ma'haneh-dan[y] to this day; behold, it is west of Kir'-iath-je'arim. [13] And they passed on from there to the hill country of E'phraim, and came to the house of Micah.

14 Then the five men who had gone to spy out the country of La'ish said to their brethren, "Do you know that in these houses there are an ephod, teraphim, a graven image, and a molten image? Now therefore consider what you will do." [15] And they turned aside thither, and came to the house of the young Levite, at the home of Micah, and asked him of his welfare. [16] Now

the six hundred men of the Danites, armed with their weapons of war, stood by the entrance of the gate; [17] and the five men who had gone to spy out the land went up, and entered and took the graven image, the ephod, the teraphim, and the molten image, while the priest stood by the entrance of the gate with the six hundred men armed with weapons of war. [18] And when these went into Micah's house and took the graven image, the ephod, the teraphim, and the molten image, the priest said to them, "What are you do-ing?" [19] And they said to him, "Keep quiet, put your hand upon your mouth, and come with us, and be to us a father and a priest. Is it better for you to be priest to the house of one man, or to be priest to a tribe and family in Israel?" [20] And the priest's heart was glad; he took the ephod, and the teraphim, and the graven image, and went in the midst of the people.

21 So they turned and departed, putting the little ones and the cattle and the goods in front of them. [22] When they were a good way from the home of Micah, the men who were in the houses near Micah's house were called out, and they overtook the Danites. [23] And they shouted to the Danites, who turned round and said to Micah, "What ails you that you come with such a company?" [24] And he said, "You take my gods which I made, and the priest, and go away, and what have I left? How then do you ask me, 'What ails you?'" [25] And the Danites said to him, "Do not let your voice be heard among us, lest angry fellows fall upon you, and you lose your life with the lives of your household." [26] Then the Danites went their way; and when Micah saw that they were

x Cn Compare 18.10. The Hebrew text is uncertain
y That is *Camp of Dan*

consult the sacred oracle, probably by the casting of lots. The original function of the priest-hood seems to have been the determination of God's will through consulting an oracle. Later this function in a somewhat different form was adopted by the prophets, and the priests took over the responsibility for offering sacrifices and exercising other functions in the cult. **7:** *Laish*, near the sources of the Jordan, was allied with the Phoenicians (*the Sidonians*), who were, however, very far away. **11–26:** Dan emigrates and, on the way, steals Micah's priest

too strong for him, he turned and went back to his home.

27 And taking what Micah had made, and the priest who belonged to him, the Danites came to La'ish, to a people quiet and unsuspecting, and smote them with the edge of the sword, and burned the city with fire. [28] And there was no deliverer because it was far from Sidon, and they had no dealings with any one. It was in the valley which belongs to Beth-rehob. And they rebuilt the city, and dwelt in it. [29] And they named the city Dan, after the name of Dan their ancestor, who was born to Israel; but the name of the city was La'ish at the first. [30] And the Danites set up the graven image for themselves; and Jonathan the son of Gershom, son of Moses,[z] and his sons were priests to the tribe of the Danites until the day of the captivity of the land. [31] So they set up Micah's graven image which he made, as long as the house of God was at Shiloh.

19 In those days, when there was no king in Israel, a certain Levite was sojourning in the remote parts of the hill country of E'phraim, who took to himself a concubine from Bethlehem in Judah. [2] And his concubine became angry with[a] him, and she went away from him to her father's house at Bethlehem in Judah, and was there some four months. [3] Then her husband arose and went after her, to speak kindly to her and bring her back. He had with him his servant and a couple of asses. And he came[b] to her father's house; and when the girl's father saw him, he came with joy to meet him. [4] And his father-in-law, the girl's father, made him stay, and he remained with him three days; so they ate and drank, and lodged there. [5] And on the fourth day they arose

early in the morning, and he prepared to go; but the girl's father said to his son-in-law, "Strengthen your heart with a morsel of bread, and after that you may go." [6] So the two men sat and ate and drank together; and the girl's father said to the man, "Be pleased to spend the night, and let your heart be merry." [7] And when the man rose up to go, his father-in-law urged him, till he lodged there again. [8] And on the fifth day he arose early in the morning to depart; and the girl's father said, "Strengthen your heart, and tarry until the day declines." So they ate, both of them. [9] And when the man and his concubine and his servant rose up to depart, his father-in-law, the girl's father, said to him, "Behold, now the day has waned toward evening; pray tarry all night. Behold, the day draws to its close; lodge here and let your heart be merry; and tomorrow you shall arise early in the morning for your journey, and go home."

10 But the man would not spend the night; he rose up and departed, and arrived opposite Jebus (that is, Jerusalem). He had with him a couple of saddled asses, and his concubine was with him. [11] When they were near Jebus, the day was far spent, and the servant said to his master, "Come now, let us turn aside to this city of the Jeb'usites, and spend the night in it." [12] And his master said to him, "We will not turn aside into the city of foreigners, who do not belong to the people of Israel; but we will pass on to Gib'e-ah." [13] And he said to his servant, "Come and let us draw near to one of these places, and spend the night at Gib'e-ah or at Ramah." [14] So they passed on and went their way; and the

z Another reading is *Manasseh*
a Gk Old Latin: Heb *played the harlot against*
b Gk: Heb *she brought him*

---

and images. **27–31:** Dan captures Laish and settles there. **30:** The shrine of Dan was one of the two great shrines of the later northern kingdom (1 Kg.12.29).

19.1–30: The appalling crime of the Benjaminites. 1–9: An Ephraimite Levite goes to Bethlehem to bring back his concubine. *Ephraim* is at the center of the country; *Bethlehem* a little south of Jerusalem. **10–21:** On the return journey they are hospitably received by an aged fellow-countryman living in Gibeah. **12:** Jerusalem was still occupied by foreigners, the Canaanite clan called the Jebusites (2 Sam.5.6). *Gibeah*, a short distance north of Jerusalem, was later

sun went down on them near Gib'e-ah, which belongs to Benjamin, [15] and they turned aside there, to go in and spend the night at Gib'e-ah. And he went in and sat down in the open square of the city; for no man took them into his house to spend the night.

16 And behold, an old man was coming from his work in the field at evening; the man was from the hill country of E'phraim, and he was sojourning in Gib'e-ah; the men of the place were Benjaminites. [17] And he lifted up his eyes, and saw the wayfarer in the open square of the city; and the old man said, "Where are you going? and whence do you come?" [18] And he said to him, "We are passing from Bethlehem in Judah to the remote parts of the hill country of E'phraim, from which I come. I went to Bethlehem in Judah; and I am going to my home;[c] and nobody takes me into his house. [19] We have straw and provender for our asses, with bread and wine for me and your maidservant and the young man with your servants; there is no lack of anything." [20] And the old man said, "Peace be to you; I will care for all your wants; only, do not spend the night in the square." [21] So he brought him into his house, and gave the asses provender; and they washed their feet, and ate and drank.

22 As they were making their hearts merry, behold, the men of the city, base fellows, beset the house round about, beating on the door; and they said to the old man, the master of the house, "Bring out the man who came into your house, that we may know him." [23] And the man, the master of the house, went out to them and said to them, "No, my brethren, do not act so wickedly; seeing that this man has come into my house, do not do this vile thing. [24] Behold, here are my

virgin daughter and his concubine; let me bring them out now. Ravish them and do with them what seems good to you; but against this man do not do so vile a thing." [25] But the men would not listen to him. So the man seized his concubine, and put her out to them; and they knew her, and abused her all night until the morning. And as the dawn began to break, they let her go. [26] And as morning appeared, the woman came and fell down at the door of the man's house where her master was, till it was light.

27 And her master rose up in the morning, and when he opened the doors of the house and went out to go on his way, behold, there was his concubine lying at the door of the house, with her hands on the threshold. [28] He said to her, "Get up, let us be going." But there was no answer. Then he put her upon the ass; and the man rose up and went away to his home. [29] And when he entered his house, he took a knife, and laying hold of his concubine he divided her, limb by limb, into twelve pieces, and sent her throughout all the territory of Israel. [30] And all who saw it said, "Such a thing has never happened or been seen from the day that the people of Israel came up out of the land of Egypt until this day; consider it, take counsel, and speak."

20 Then all the people of Israel came out, from Dan to Beersheba, including the land of Gilead, and the congregation assembled as one man to the LORD at Mizpah. [2] And the chiefs of all the people, of all the tribes of Israel, presented themselves in the assembly of the people of God, four hundred thousand men on foot that drew the sword. [3] (Now the Benjaminites heard that the people of Israel had gone up to Mizpah.) And the people of Israel said, "Tell us,

c Gk Compare 19.29. Heb *to the house of the* LORD

---

the home of Saul (1 Sam.10.26). **22–26:** The Benjaminites ravish the concubine until she dies. Such behavior was supposed to be typical of the Canaanites (Gen.19.4–9), but abhorrent to the Hebrews. **27–30:** The Levite summons the other tribes to avenge the crime. **29:** In 1 Sam. 11.7 Saul calls up the tribes of Israel in strikingly similar fashion.

20.1–48: The punishment of Benjamin. 1–11: The tribes assemble to take counsel. **1:** *Mizpah,*

how was this wickedness brought to pass?" [4] And the Levite, the husband of the woman who was murdered, answered and said, "I came to Gib'e-ah that belongs to Benjamin, I and my concubine, to spend the night. [5] And the men of Gib'e-ah rose against me, and beset the house round about me by night; they meant to kill me, and they ravished my concubine, and she is dead. [6] And I took my concubine and cut her in pieces, and sent her throughout all the country of the inheritance of Israel; for they have committed abomination and wantonness in Israel. [7] Behold, you people of Israel, all of you, give your advice and counsel here."

8 And all the people arose as one man, saying, "We will not any of us go to his tent, and none of us will return to his house. [9] But now this is what we will do to Gib'e-ah: we will go up against it by lot, [10] and we will take ten men of a hundred throughout all the tribes of Israel, and a hundred of a thousand, and a thousand of ten thousand, to bring provisions for the people, that when they come they may requite Gib'e-ah of Benjamin, for all the wanton crime which they have committed in Israel." [11] So all the men of Israel gathered against the city, united as one man.

12 And the tribes of Israel sent men through all the tribe of Benjamin, saying, "What wickedness is this that has taken place among you? [13] Now therefore give up the men, the base fellows in Gib'e-ah, that we may put them to death, and put away evil from Israel." But the Benjaminites would not listen to the voice of their brethren, the people of Israel. [14] And the Benjaminites came together out of the cities to Gib'e-ah, to go out to battle against the people of Israel. [15] And the Ben-

jaminites mustered out of their cities on that day twenty-six thousand men that drew the sword, besides the inhabitants of Gib'e-ah, who mustered seven hundred picked men. [16] Among all these were seven hundred picked men who were left-handed; every one could sling a stone at a hair, and not miss. [17] And the men of Israel, apart from Benjamin, mustered four hundred thousand men that drew sword; all these were men of war.

18 The people of Israel arose and went up to Bethel, and inquired of God, "Which of us shall go up first to battle against the Benjaminites?" And the LORD said, "Judah shall go up first."

19 Then the people of Israel rose in the morning, and encamped against Gib'e-ah. [20] And the men of Israel went out to battle against Benjamin; and the men of Israel drew up the battle line against them at Gib'e-ah. [21] The Benjaminites came out of Gib'e-ah, and felled to the ground on that day twenty-two thousand men of the Israelites. [22] But the people, the men of Israel, took courage, and again formed the battle line in the same place where they had formed it on the first day. [23] And the people of Israel went up and wept before the LORD until the evening; and they inquired of the LORD, "Shall we again draw near to battle against our brethren the Benjaminites?" And the LORD said, "Go up against them."

24 So the people of Israel came near against the Benjaminites the second day. [25] And Benjamin went against them out of Gib'e-ah the second day, and felled to the ground eighteen thousand men of the people of Israel; all these were men who drew the sword. [26] Then all the people of Israel, the whole army, went up and came to Bethel and wept; they sat there before

a city on the northern boundary of Benjamin. **12–36:** After two initial defeats, the tribes defeat the Benjaminites by a ruse. **17:** Such numbers as *four hundred thousand* in this chapter are vastly exaggerated. **18:** *Bethel*, an important sacred place in the stories of the patriarchs (Gen. 12.8; 28.11–19) and later one of the two principal sanctuaries of the northern kingdom (1 Kg. 12.29), was just a few miles northeast of Mizpah (v. 1). On the phrase *inquired of God*, see 18.5. **23:** *Wept before the LORD*, Dt.1.45; 2 Kg.22.19; Jl.2.15–17.

the LORD, and fasted that day until evening, and offered burnt offerings and peace offerings before the LORD. ²⁷ And the people of Israel inquired of the LORD (for the ark of the covenant of God was there in those days, ²⁸ and Phin'ehas the son of Elea'zar, son of Aaron, ministered before it in those days), saying, "Shall we yet again go out to battle against our brethren the Benjaminites, or shall we cease?" And the LORD said, "Go up; for tomorrow I will give them into your hand."

29 So Israel set men in ambush round about Gib'e-ah. ³⁰ And the people of Israel went up against the Benjaminites on the third day, and set themselves in array against Gib'e-ah, as at other times. ³¹ And the Benjaminites went out against the people, and were drawn away from the city; and as at other times they began to smite and kill some of the people, in the highways, one of which goes up to Bethel and the other to Gib'e-ah, and in the open country, about thirty men of Israel. ³² And the Benjaminites said, "They are routed before us, as at the first." But the men of Israel said, "Let us flee, and draw them away from the city to the highways." ³³ And all the men of Israel rose up out of their place, and set themselves in array at Ba'al-ta'mar; and the men of Israel who were in ambush rushed out of their place west^d of Geba. ³⁴ And there came against Gib'e-ah ten thousand picked men out of all Israel, and the battle was hard; but the Benjaminites did not know that disaster was close upon them. ³⁵ And the LORD defeated Benjamin before Israel; and the men of Israel destroyed twenty-five thousand one hundred men of Benjamin that day; all these were men who drew the sword. ³⁶ So the Benjaminites saw that they were defeated.

The men of Israel gave ground to Benjamin, because they trusted to the men in ambush whom they had set against Gib'e-ah. ³⁷ And the men in ambush made haste and rushed upon Gib'e-ah; the men in ambush moved out and smote all the city with the edge of the sword. ³⁸ Now the appointed signal between the men of Israel and the men in ambush was that when they made a great cloud of smoke rise up out of the city ³⁹ the men of Israel should turn in battle. Now Benjamin had begun to smite and kill about thirty men of Israel; they said, "Surely they are smitten down before us, as in the first battle." ⁴⁰ But when the signal began to rise out of the city in a column of smoke, the Benjaminites looked behind them; and behold, the whole of the city went up in smoke to heaven. ⁴¹ Then the men of Israel turned, and the men of Benjamin were dismayed, for they saw that disaster was close upon them. ⁴² Therefore they turned their backs before the men of Israel in the direction of the wilderness; but the battle overtook them, and those who came out of the cities destroyed them in the midst of them. ⁴³ Cutting down^e the Benjaminites, they pursued them and trod them down from Nohah^f as far as opposite Gib'e-ah on the east. ⁴⁴ Eighteen thousand men of Benjamin fell, all of them men of valor. ⁴⁵ And they turned and fled toward the wilderness to the rock of Rimmon; five thousand men of them were cut down in the highways, and they were pursued hard to Gidom, and two thousand men of them were slain. ⁴⁶ So all who fell that day of Benjamin were twenty-five thousand men that drew the sword, all of them men of valor. ⁴⁷ But six hundred men turned and fled toward the wilderness to the rock of Rimmon, and abode at the rock of Rimmon four months. ⁴⁸ And the men of Israel turned back against the Benjaminites, and smote them with the edge of the sword, men

d Gk Vg: Heb *in the plain*
e Gk: Heb *surrounding*
f Gk: Heb *(at their) resting place*

36–48: A further account of the ambush and subsequent victory. This section seems to contain a different version of the Israelites' stratagem.

and beasts and all that they found. And all the towns which they found they set on fire.

21 Now the men of Israel had sworn at Mizpah, "No one of us shall give his daughter in marriage to Benjamin." 2 And the people came to Bethel, and sat there till evening before God, and they lifted up their voices and wept bitterly. 3 And they said, "O LORD, the God of Israel, why has this come to pass in Israel, that there should be today one tribe lacking in Israel?" 4 And on the morrow the people rose early, and built there an altar, and offered burnt offerings and peace offerings. 5 And the people of Israel said, "Which of all the tribes of Israel did not come up in the assembly to the LORD?" For they had taken a great oath concerning him who did not come up to the LORD to Mizpah, saying, "He shall be put to death." 6 And the people of Israel had compassion for Benjamin their brother, and said, "One tribe is cut off from Israel this day. 7 What shall we do for wives for those who are left, since we have sworn by the LORD that we will not give them any of our daughters for wives?"

8 And they said, "What one is there of the tribes of Israel that did not come up to the LORD to Mizpah?" And behold, no one had come to the camp from Ja'besh-gil'ead, to the assembly. 9 For when the people were mustered, behold, not one of the inhabitants of Ja'besh-gil'ead was there. 10 So the congregation sent thither twelve thousand of their bravest men, and commanded them, "Go and smite the inhabitants of Ja'besh-gil'ead with the edge of the sword; also the women and the little ones. 11 This is what you shall do; every male and every woman that has lain with a male you shall utterly destroy." 12 And they found among the inhabitants of Ja'besh-gil'ead four hundred young virgins who had not known man by lying with him; and they brought them to the camp at Shiloh, which is in the land of Canaan.

13 Then the whole congregation sent word to the Benjaminites who were at the rock of Rimmon, and proclaimed peace to them. 14 And Benjamin returned at that time; and they gave them the women whom they had saved alive of the women of Ja'besh-gil'ead; but they did not suffice for them. 15 And the people had compassion on Benjamin because the LORD had made a breach in the tribes of Israel.

16 Then the elders of the congregation said, "What shall we do for wives for those who are left, since the women are destroyed out of Benjamin?" 17 And they said, "There must be an inheritance for the survivors of Benjamin, that a tribe be not blotted out from Israel. 18 Yet we cannot give them wives of our daughters." For the people of Israel had sworn, "Cursed be he who gives a wife to Benjamin." 19 So they said, "Behold, there is the yearly feast of the LORD at Shiloh, which is north of Bethel, on the east of the highway that goes up from Bethel to Shechem, and south of Lebo'nah." 20 And they commanded the Benjaminites, saying, "Go and lie in wait in the vineyards, 21 and watch; if the daughters of Shiloh come out to dance in the dances, then come out of the vineyards and seize each man his wife from the daughters of Shiloh, and go to the land of Benjamin. 22 And when their fathers or their brothers come to complain to us, we will say to them, 'Grant them graciously to us; because we did not take for each man of them

---

21.1–25: Two devices to secure wives for the Benjaminites. With swift change of heart, the tribes realize that Benjamin is on the verge of extinction and take measures to find wives for the remaining men. **1–15:** They exterminate most of the inhabitants of Jabesh-Gilead, east of the Jordan, for disloyalty to the common enterprise, but save four hundred girls as wives for the Benjaminites. **16–25:** The remaining Benjaminite men are granted permission to snatch wives for themselves from the dancers in the annual vintage festival at Shiloh. For the Shiloh festival, see 1 Sam.1.3,21.

his wife in battle, neither did you give them to them, else you would now be guilty.' " 23 And the Benjaminites did so, and took their wives, according to their number, from the dancers whom they carried off; then they went and returned to their inheritance, and re-built the towns, and dwelt in them.

24 And the people of Israel departed from there at that time, every man to his tribe and family, and they went out from there every man to his inherit-ance.

25 In those days there was no king in Israel; every man did what was right in his own eyes.

THE BOOK OF RUTH

The quiet, idyllic mood of the book of Ruth and the charm of its gentle heroine have given it a special appeal to many generations of readers. Although the story is ostensibly set in the days of the Judges, it has nothing in common with the sanguinary tales of inter-national and inter-tribal warfare narrated in the preceding book. Since the woman Ruth is a Moabitess, not an Israelite, the effect of the book, if not its purpose, is to create a sym-pathetic feeling toward foreigners who put themselves under the protection of Israel's God. For this reason many have supposed it to be a post-exilic composition, based on an older tale, intended to counteract the harsh decrees of Ezra and Nehemiah which required Hebrew men to divorce their foreign wives and marry only within the covenant community (Ezra 10.1–5; Neh.13.23–27).

Israel after the Exile developed tendencies in two quite opposite directions: on the one hand a major tendency to draw within herself and emphasize the exclusiveness of her elec-tion as God's chosen people, and on the other hand a broad and liberal one which sought to make of her "a blessing in the midst of the earth" (Is.19.24), "a light to the nations" (Is.49.6). Among the noblest monuments of this latter tendency are the books of Jonah and Ruth. The opening verses of our story tell of Ruth's marriage to a Hebrew man and how, on his death, she chose to return to Judah with her mother-in-law to share the fortunes of her husband's people rather than remain in the relative security of her native land (ch. 1). There her loyalty and kindliness won her the love of Boaz (2.1–4.12), and through her marriage to him she became the great-grandmother of David the king (4.13–22).

I N THE DAYS WHEN THE JUDGES ruled there was a famine in the land, and a certain man of Bethlehem in Judah went to sojourn in the country of Moab, he and his wife and his two sons. ² The name of the man was Elim'elech and the name of his wife Na'omi, and the names of his two sons were Mahlon and Chil'ion; they were Eph'rathites from Bethlehem in Judah. They went into the country of Moab and remained there. ³ But Elim'elech, the husband of Na'omi, died, and she was left with her two sons. ⁴ These took Moabite wives; the name of the one was Orpah and the name of the other Ruth. They lived there about ten years; ⁵ and both Mahlon and Chil'ion died, so that the woman was bereft of her two sons and her husband.

6 Then she started with her daugh-ters-in-law to return from the country of Moab, for she had heard in the country of Moab that the LORD had visited his people and given them food. ⁷ So she set out from the place where she was, with her two daughters-in-law, and they went on the way to return to the land of Judah. ⁸ But Na'omi said to her two daughters-in-law, "Go, re-turn each of you to her mother's house. May the LORD deal kindly with you, as you have dealt with the dead and with me. ⁹ The LORD grant that you may find a home, each of you in the house of her husband!" Then she kissed them, and they lifted up their voices and wept. ¹⁰ And they said to her, "No, we will return with you to your people." ¹¹ But Na'omi said, "Turn back, my daughters, why will you go with me? Have I yet sons in my

1.1–22: Ruth's courageous decision. 1–5: Naomi, a Hebrew woman who, with her family, had settled in Moab, loses through death both her husband and her two sons. One of the sons was the husband of Ruth, the other the husband of Orpah, both Moabite women. 1: *Bethlehem*, the later birthplace of David (and Jesus). *Moab*, the country directly east of the Dead Sea. The Moabites were often regarded as particular enemies of the Israelites (Dt.23.3). 6–18: Ruth deliberately chooses to go to Judah and become a member of her mother-in-law's people. 19–22: They arrive in Bethlehem.

womb that they may become your husbands? ¹² Turn back, my daughters, go your way, for I am too old to have a husband. If I should say I have hope, even if I should have a husband this night and should bear sons, ¹³ would you therefore wait till they were grown? Would you therefore refrain from marrying? No, my daughters, for it is exceedingly bitter to me for your sake that the hand of the LORD has gone forth against me." ¹⁴ Then they lifted up their voices and wept again; and Orpah kissed her mother-in-law, but Ruth clung to her.

15 And she said, "See, your sister-in-law has gone back to her people and to her gods; return after your sister-in-law." ¹⁶ But Ruth said, "Entreat me not to leave you or to return from following you; for where you go I will go, and where you lodge I will lodge; your people shall be my people, and your God my God; ¹⁷ where you die I will die, and there will I be buried. May the LORD do so to me and more also if even death parts me from you." ¹⁸ And when Na'omi saw that she was determined to go with her, she said no more.

19 So the two of them went on until they came to Bethlehem. And when they came to Bethlehem, the whole town was stirred because of them; and the women said, "Is this Na'omi?" ²⁰ She said to them, "Do not call me Na'omi,*a* call me Mara,*b* for the Almighty has dealt very bitterly with me. ²¹ I went away full, and the LORD has brought me back empty. Why call me Na'omi, when the LORD has afflicted*c* me and the Almighty has brought calamity upon me?"

22 So Na'omi returned, and Ruth the Moabitess her daughter-in-law with her, who returned from the country of Moab. And they came to Bethlehem at the beginning of barley harvest.

2 Now Na'omi had a kinsman of her husband's, a man of wealth, of the family of Elim'elech, whose name was Bo'az. ² And Ruth the Moabitess said to Na'omi, "Let me go to the field, and glean among the ears of grain after him in whose sight I shall find favor." And she said to her, "Go, my daughter." ³ So she set forth and went and gleaned in the field after the reapers; and she happened to come to the part of the field belonging to Bo'az, who was of the family of Elim'elech. ⁴ And behold, Bo'az came from Bethlehem; and he said to the reapers, "The LORD be with you!" And they answered, "The LORD bless you." ⁵ Then Bo'az said to his servant who was in charge of the reapers, "Whose maiden is this?" ⁶ And the servant who was in charge of the reapers answered, "It is the Moabite maiden, who came back with Na'omi from the country of Moab. ⁷ She said, 'Pray, let me glean and gather among the sheaves after the reapers.' So she came, and she has continued from early morning until now, without resting even for a moment."*d*

8 Then Bo'az said to Ruth, "Now, listen, my daughter, do not go to glean in another field or leave this one, but keep close to my maidens. ⁹ Let your eyes be upon the field which they are reaping, and go after them. Have I not charged the young men not to molest you? And when you are thirsty, go to the vessels and drink what the young men have drawn." ¹⁰ Then she fell on her face, bowing to the ground, and said to him, "Why have I found favor in your eyes, that you should take notice of me, when I am a foreigner?" ¹¹ But Bo'az answered her, "All that you have done for your mother-in-law

a That is *Pleasant*   *b* That is *Bitter*
c Gk Syr Vg: Heb *testified against*
d Compare Gk Vg: the meaning of the Hebrew text is uncertain

2.1–23: Ruth in the field of Boaz. 1–3: While gleaning, Ruth happens to come to the part owned by Boaz. **2:** Hebrew law allowed the poor to *glean* the fields, i.e. to pick up what was left after the reapers had passed (Lev.19.9–10). **4–23:** She attracts the kindly attention of Boaz. **15–16:** He authorizes a little generous cheating on her behalf.

since the death of your husband has been fully told me, and how you left your father and mother and your native land and came to a people that you did not know before. [12] The LORD recompense you for what you have done, and a full reward be given you by the LORD, the God of Israel, under whose wings you have come to take refuge!" [13] Then she said, "You are most gracious to me, my lord, for you have comforted me and spoken kindly to your maidservant, though I am not one of your maidservants."

14 And at mealtime Bo'az said to her, "Come here, and eat some bread, and dip your morsel in the wine." So she sat beside the reapers, and he passed to her parched grain; and she ate until she was satisfied, and she had some left over. [15] When she rose to glean, Bo'az instructed his young men, saying, "Let her glean even among the sheaves, and do not reproach her. [16] And also pull out some from the bundles for her, and leave it for her to glean, and do not rebuke her."

17 So she gleaned in the field until evening; then she beat out what she had gleaned, and it was about an ephah of barley. [18] And she took it up and went into the city; she showed her mother-in-law what she had gleaned, and she also brought out and gave her what food she had left over after being satisfied. [19] And her mother-in-law said to her, "Where did you glean today? And where have you worked? Blessed be the man who took notice of you." So she told her mother-in-law with whom she had worked, and said, "The man's name with whom I worked today is Bo'az." [20] And Na'-omi said to her daughter-in-law, "Blessed be he by the LORD, whose kindness has not forsaken the living or the dead!" Na'omi also said to her, "The man is a relative of ours, one of

our nearest kin." [21] And Ruth the Moabitess said, "Besides, he said to me, 'You shall keep close by my servants, till they have finished all my harvest.'" [22] And Na'omi said to Ruth, her daughter-in-law, "It is well, my daughter, that you go out with his maidens, lest in another field you be molested." [23] So she kept close to the maidens of Bo'az, gleaning until the end of the barley and wheat harvests; and she lived with her mother-in-law.

3 Then Na'omi her mother-in-law said to her, "My daughter, should I not seek a home for you, that it may be well with you? [2] Now is not Bo'az our kinsman, with whose maidens you were? See, he is winnowing barley tonight at the threshing floor. [3] Wash therefore and anoint yourself, and put on your best clothes and go down to the threshing floor; but do not make yourself known to the man until he has finished eating and drinking. [4] But when he lies down, observe the place where he lies; then, go and uncover his feet and lie down; and he will tell you what to do." [5] And she replied, "All that you say I will do."

6 So she went down to the threshing floor and did just as her mother-in-law had told her. [7] And when Bo'az had eaten and drunk, and his heart was merry, he went to lie down at the end of the heap of grain. Then she came softly, and uncovered his feet, and lay down. [8] At midnight the man was startled, and turned over, and behold, a woman lay at his feet! [9] He said, "Who are you?" And she answered, "I am Ruth, your maidservant; spread your skirt over your maidservant, for you are next of kin." [10] And he said, "May you be blessed by the LORD, my daughter; you have made this last kindness greater than the first, in that you have not gone after young

---

3.1–4.12: **Ruth becomes engaged to Boaz. 3.1–5:** Naomi instructs her how to show her love for Boaz. **6–18:** She carries out Naomi's instructions and wins the assent of Boaz. **9:** *Spread your skirt over your maidservant* means to take her for wife. The *next of kin* had the right and obligation to protect the property and honor of his kinsman and to maintain his family line

men, whether poor or rich. [11] And now, my daughter, do not fear, I will do for you all that you ask, for all my fellow townsmen know that you are a woman of worth. [12] And now it is true that I am a near kinsman, yet there is a kinsman nearer than I. [13] Remain this night, and in the morning, if he will do the part of the next of kin for you, well; let him do it; but if he is not willing to do the part of the next of kin for you, then, as the LORD lives, I will do the part of the next of kin for you. Lie down until the morning."

14 So she lay at his feet until the morning, but arose before one could recognize another; and he said, "Let it not be known that the woman came to the threshing floor." [15] And he said, "Bring the mantle you are wearing and hold it out." So she held it, and he measured out six measures of barley, and laid it upon her; then she went into the city. [16] And when she came to her mother-in-law, she said, "How did you fare, my daughter?" Then she told her all that the man had done for her, [17] saying, "These six measures of barley he gave to me, for he said, 'You must not go back empty-handed to your mother-in-law.'" [18] She replied, "Wait, my daughter, until you learn how the matter turns out, for the man will not rest, but will settle the matter today."

4 And Bo'az went up to the gate and sat down there; and behold, the next of kin, of whom Bo'az had spoken, came by. So Bo'az said, "Turn aside, friend; sit down here"; and he turned aside and sat down. [2] And he took ten men of the elders of the city, and said, "Sit down here"; so they sat down.

[3] Then he said to the next of kin, "Na'omi, who has come back from the country of Moab, is selling the parcel of land which belonged to our kinsman Elim'elech. [4] So I thought I would tell you of it, and say, Buy it in the presence of those sitting here, and in the presence of the elders of my people. If you will redeem it, redeem it; but if you will not, tell me, that I may know, for there is no one besides you to redeem it, and I come after you." And he said, "I will redeem it." [5] Then Bo'az said, "The day you buy the field from the hand of Na'omi, you are also buying Ruth[e] the Moabitess, the widow of the dead, in order to restore the name of the dead to his inheritance." [6] Then the next of kin said, "I cannot redeem it for myself, lest I impair my own inheritance. Take my right of redemption yourself, for I cannot redeem it."

7 Now this was the custom in former times in Israel concerning redeeming and exchanging: to confirm a transaction, the one drew off his sandal and gave it to the other, and this was the manner of attesting in Israel. [8] So when the next of kin said to Bo'az, "Buy it for yourself," he drew off his sandal. [9] Then Bo'az said to the elders and all the people, "You are witnesses this day that I have bought from the hand of Na'omi all that belonged to Elim'elech and all that belonged to Chil'ion and to Mahlon. [10] Also Ruth the Moabitess, the widow of Mahlon, I have bought to be my wife, to perpetuate the name of the dead in his inheritance, that the name of the dead may not be cut off from among his brethren and from the gate

e Old Latin Vg: Heb *of Naomi and from Ruth*

(Lev.25.25; Dt.25.5–6; see also Jos.20.3 n.). **12:** The nearest of kin had first rights with respect to the wife and any property which might be involved. **4.1–6:** The nearer kinsman renounces his rights. **1:** *The gate* of the city was the normal place for transacting business (see Jos.20.4 n.). **5:** Boaz tells his rival that he cannot legally acquire the property without also marrying Ruth. **6:** The kinsman refuses to accept the property under these conditions, because to raise up a son in the name of another would confuse the whole question of the inheritance of the estate. **7:** The custom here attested is somewhat different from that prescribed in Dt.25.7–10, either because the situation is more complicated than the one envisaged there or because the passages represent different stages in the development of Hebrew law. **7–12:** Boaz lays formal claim both to the property in question and to Ruth. **12:** *Perez . . . Tamar . . . Judah*, Gen. ch. 38.

of his native place; you are witnesses this day." [11] Then all the people who were at the gate, and the elders, said, "We are witnesses. May the LORD make the woman, who is coming into your house, like Rachel and Leah, who together built up the house of Israel. May you prosper in Eph'rathah and be renowned in Bethlehem; [12] and may your house be like the house of Perez, whom Tamar bore to Judah, because of the children that the LORD will give you by this young woman."

13 So Bo'az took Ruth and she became his wife; and he went in to her, and the LORD gave her conception, and she bore a son. [14] Then the women said to Na'omi, "Blessed be the LORD, who has not left you this day without next of kin; and may his name be renowned in Israel! [15] He shall be to you a restorer of life and a nourisher of your old age; for your daughter-in-law who loves you, who is more to you than seven sons, has borne him." [16] Then Na'omi took the child and laid him in her bosom, and became his nurse. [17] And the women of the neighborhood gave him a name, saying, "A son has been born to Na'omi." They named him Obed; he was the father of Jesse, the father of David.

18 Now these are the descendants of Perez: Perez was the father of Hezron, [19] Hezron of Ram, Ram of Ammin'adab, [20] Ammin'adab of Nahshon, Nahshon of Salmon, [21] Salmon of Bo'az, Bo'az of Obed, [22] Obed of Jesse, and Jesse of David.

4.13–22: Ruth the ancestress of David. **18**: *The descendants of Perez*, compare Mt.1.3–6.

THE FIRST BOOK OF

SAMUEL

The two books of Samuel were originally one in Hebrew. There are three principal characters in the two books: Samuel, Saul, and David. The story of Samuel is confined to 1 Samuel, as is also the story of Saul, except for the report of his death at the beginning of 2 Samuel. The story of David begins midway in 1 Samuel (ch. 16), continues through 2 Samuel, and is completed in the second chapter of 1 Kings.

There are two main literary strands of thought interwoven in 1 Samuel; they are usually referred to as the Early Source and the Late Source. The Late Source, with which the book begins, is basically an interpretation of the life of Samuel, beginning with his birth in ch. 1 and ending with his death in ch. 25. The leading ideas of this source are (1) that Samuel was the judge and true ruler of Israel under God (see 7.7–17); (2) that the choosing of a king was really a mistake (see 8.10–22; 12.19); (3) that the personal failure of such figures as Eli and his sons and Saul was punishment for their sins (see 2.25; 13.13–14); (4) that David, in spite of his being a king, was a man who merited God's favor (see 13.14; 16.13; 24.16–21). This source was compiled in the latter days of the monarchy (750–650 B.C.).

The Early Source, most of which was probably written by a single individual during the reign of Solomon, is of such remarkable historical and literary quality that its author deserves the title "the father of history"–a title usually given to the Greek historian Herodotus, who lived five hundred years later. As is the case with so many of the Biblical writings, the identity of the author of this unusual document is unknown, though Abiathar (1 Sam.22.20–23; 1 Kg.2.26) and Ahimaaz (2 Sam.18.19–32) have been mentioned as candidates for the honor. In the Early Source the establishment of the kingship is regarded as a divinely or-dained blessing and the salvation of the nation. Samuel is a less important figure, a modest prophet, not a ruler in his own right. Saul is a noble but tragic figure. David is the real hero, but a very human hero, who does both noble and ignoble deeds, the latter being in no way disguised by the author. Second Samuel is made up almost entirely of the Early Source, and it could very well have been called "the book of David."

The final editing of the books of Samuel took place in the post-exilic period. Much of the work of putting the books into their present form was done by the Deuteronomic school of theologians (which was also largely responsible for the compilation and editing of Deuter-onomy, Joshua, Judges, and Kings), whose ideas were similar to those reflected in the Late Source. They probably rewrote 1 Sam. ch. 12 and contributed 2 Sam. ch. 8. Still other editors added 1 Sam.2.1–10,27–36; 2 Sam. ch. 7; ch. 22; 23.1–7. Each of the differing interpreta-tions of the monarchy has its value; taken together, they enable us to understand well how God protected his people and established them as a community that was ultimately reli-gious rather than merely national (see "Survey of . . . Bible Lands." §§ 8–9).

THERE WAS A CERTAIN MAN OF Ramatha'im-zo'phim of the hill country of E'phraim, whose name was Elka'nah the son of Jero'ham, son of Eli'hu, son of Tohu, son of Zuph, an E'phraimite. 2 He had two wives; the name of the one was Hannah, and the name of the other Penin'nah. And

1.1–28: The birth and consecration of Samuel. The story of a formerly barren woman who bears unusual offspring late in life as a special favor from God appears several times in the Bible. Besides Hannah, note Sarah (Gen.17.16–19), Rebekah (Gen.25.21–26), Rachel (Gen.29. 31; 30.22–24), the mother of Samson (Jg.13.2–5), and Elizabeth (Lk.1.5–17). The unusual birth was thought to be symbolic of the importance of the person in later life. **1:** The Greek version begins thus: "There was a certain man of Ramah, a Zuphite of the hill country . . ."; comparison with v. 19 shows that Ramah was probably the familiar name of the place. **2:** *Two wives*, bigamy was not common in Old Testament times, but was allowed (Dt.21.15–17).

Penin'nah had children, but Hannah had no children.

3 Now this man used to go up year by year from his city to worship and to sacrifice to the LORD of hosts at Shiloh, where the two sons of Eli, Hophni and Phin'ehas, were priests of the LORD. ⁴ On the day when Elka'-nah sacrificed, he would give portions to Penin'nah his wife and to all her sons and daughters; ⁵ and, although*ᵃ* he loved Hannah, he would give Hannah only one portion, because the LORD had closed her womb. ⁶ And her rival used to provoke her sorely, to irritate her, because the LORD had closed her womb. ⁷ So it went on year by year; as often as she went up to the house of the LORD, she used to provoke her. Therefore Hannah wept and would not eat. ⁸ And Elka'nah, her husband, said to her, "Hannah, why do you weep? And why do you not eat? And why is your heart sad? Am I not more to you than ten sons?"

9 After they had eaten and drunk in Shiloh, Hannah rose. Now Eli the priest was sitting on the seat beside the doorpost of the temple of the LORD. ¹⁰ She was deeply distressed and prayed to the LORD, and wept bitterly. ¹¹ And she vowed a vow and said, "O LORD of hosts, if thou wilt indeed look on the affliction of thy maidservant, and remember me, and not forget thy maidservant, but wilt give to thy maidservant a son, then I will give him to the LORD all the days of his life, and no razor shall touch his head." 12 As she continued praying before the LORD, Eli observed her mouth.

¹³ Hannah was speaking in her heart; only her lips moved, and her voice was not heard; therefore Eli took her to be a drunken woman. ¹⁴ And Eli said to her, "How long will you be drunken? Put away your wine from you." ¹⁵ But Hannah answered, "No, my lord, I am a woman sorely troubled; I have drunk neither wine nor strong drink, but I have been pouring out my soul before the LORD. ¹⁶ Do not regard your maidservant as a base woman, for all along I have been speaking out of my great anxiety and vexation." ¹⁷ Then Eli answered, "Go in peace, and the God of Israel grant your petition which you have made to him." ¹⁸ And she said, "Let your maidservant find favor in your eyes." Then the woman went her way and ate, and her countenance was no longer sad.

19 They rose early in the morning and worshiped before the LORD; then they went back to their house at Ramah. And Elka'nah knew Hannah his wife, and the LORD remembered her; ²⁰ and in due time Hannah conceived and bore a son, and she called his name Samuel, for she said, "I have asked him of the LORD."

21 And the man Elka'nah and all his house went up to offer to the LORD the yearly sacrifice, and to pay his vow. ²² But Hannah did not go up, for she said to her husband, "As soon as the child is weaned, I will bring him, that he may appear in the presence of the LORD, and abide there for ever." ²³ Elka'nah her husband said to her, "Do what seems best to you, wait until

a Gk: Heb obscure

3: The original meaning of the expression LORD *of hosts* is "LORD of armies" or "God of battles," referring to God's leadership of his people in war. There was an important shrine at *Shiloh* in the days before the monarchy (Jos.18.1; Jg.21.19; Jer.7.12; Ps.78.60). We should read (with the Greek version), "Eli and his two sons"; it is evident from later verses that Eli had not retired. **9–18:** Hannah went to the temple and prayed for a son, promising to consecrate him to God's service if her prayer was granted. **19–28:** The prayer was answered and the promise fulfilled. The Hebrew word for *asked* in v. 20 seems to be a play on the meaning of the name "Saul" rather than *Samuel*, which probably means "name of God," suggesting the boy's close affinity with God. There may be some confusion between Saul and Samuel here; but the word *asked* in Hebrew also means "borrowed," so perhaps this word should be connected with the word *lent* in v. 28; Hannah had begged or borrowed (same word in Hebrew) her son from God, so she *lent* him back to God, by whose grace he had been granted (see 2.20).

you have weaned him; only, may the LORD establish his word." So the woman remained and nursed her son, until she weaned him. 24 And when she had weaned him, she took him up with her, along with a three-year-old bull,*b* an ephah of flour, and a skin of wine; and she brought him to the house of the LORD at Shiloh; and the child was young. 25 Then they slew the bull, and they brought the child to Eli. 26 And she said, "Oh, my lord! As you live, my lord, I am the woman who was standing here in your presence, praying to the LORD. 27 For this child I prayed; and the LORD has granted me my petition which I made to him. 28 Therefore I have lent him to the LORD; as long as he lives, he is lent to the LORD."

And they*x* worshiped the LORD there.

2 Hannah also prayed and said,
   "My heart exults in the LORD;
     my strength is exalted in the LORD.
My mouth derides my enemies,
   because I rejoice in thy salvation.

2 "There is none holy like the LORD,
   there is none besides thee;
   there is no rock like our God.
3 Talk no more so very proudly,
   let not arrogance come from your
     mouth;

for the LORD is a God of knowledge,
   and by him actions are weighed.
4 The bows of the mighty are broken,
   but the feeble gird on strength.
5 Those who were full have hired
   themselves out for bread,
but those who were hungry have
   ceased to hunger.
The barren has borne seven,
   but she who has many children
     is forlorn.
6 The LORD kills and brings to life;
   he brings down to Sheol and
     raises up.
7 The LORD makes poor and makes
     rich;
   he brings low, he also exalts.
8 He raises up the poor from the dust;
   he lifts the needy from the ash
     heap,
to make them sit with princes
   and inherit a seat of honor.
For the pillars of the earth are the
     LORD'S,
   and on them he has set the world.

9 "He will guard the feet of his
     faithful ones;
but the wicked shall be cut off in
     darkness;
for not by might shall a man
     prevail.
10 The adversaries of the LORD shall

b Gk Syr: Heb three bulls   x Heb he

2.1–10: The song of Hannah. It was the custom of Biblical editors to insert poems into prose books to increase artistic and religious appeal. The poems may be older or later than the contexts into which they are inserted. In this case the poem seems to be considerably later. It is really a psalm of national thanksgiving, and has a certain appropriateness at this point; but perhaps its greatest claim to fame is that it became the model for Mary's song of thanksgiving (the Magnificat) in the New Testament (Lk.1.46–55). **1:** *My strength*, literally "my horn," the figure of an animal tossing its head. The *I* of this psalm, as of many others, is the nation as well as the individual worshiper. The group and the individual are often identified in the Bible in a way strange to modern thinking. **2:** *Rock*, 2 Sam.22.2–3; Pss.18.2; 28.1; 62.2,6; etc. **3:** The enemies of Israel are addressed. **4:** The reversal of fortune for the downtrodden and oppressed (also vv. 5,8); compare Ps.113.7–9. **5:** *The barren has borne seven*, this line probably suggested the insertion of the poem at this place. *Seven* is merely symbolic of a sizable family; Hannah seems not to have had more than six children (see v. 21). **6–7:** God controls all of life. *Brings to life* probably refers to birth rather than to resurrection from the dead; likewise the next line probably refers to deep trouble or desperate injuries and recovery from them. *Sheol*, the place of the dead under the earth, like Hades among the Greeks (Is.14.9–21); but the term is sometimes used of conditions near death (Pss.86.13; 88.3–7). **8:** *Pillars of the earth;* the earth was conceived of as a platform resting on great pillars. **9:** The idea that the good would prosper and the wicked suffer ill fortune in this world was widespread in the post-exilic period (see Pr.3.9–10; 5.22–23); the books of Job and Ecclesiastes are a protest against this view of life.

be broken to pieces;
against them he will thunder in
heaven.
The LORD will judge the ends of the
earth;
he will give strength to his king,
and exalt the power of his
anointed."

11 Then Elka'nah went home to Ramah. And the boy ministered to the LORD, in the presence of Eli the priest.

12 Now the sons of Eli were worthless men; they had no regard for the LORD. [13] The custom of the priests with the people was that when any man offered sacrifice, the priest's servant would come, while the meat was boiling, with a three-pronged fork in his hand, [14] and he would thrust it into the pan, or kettle, or caldron, or pot; all that the fork brought up the priest would take for himself.[c] So they did at Shiloh to all the Israelites who came there. [15] Moreover, before the fat was burned, the priest's servant would come and say to the man who was sacrificing, "Give meat for the priest to roast; for he will not accept boiled meat from you, but raw." [16] And if the man said to him, "Let them burn the fat first, and then take as much as you wish," he would say, "No, you must give it now; and if not, I will take it by force." [17] Thus the sin of the young men was very great in the sight of the LORD; for the men treated the offering of the LORD with contempt.

18 Samuel was ministering before the LORD, a boy girded with a linen ephod. [19] And his mother used to make for him a little robe and take it to him each year, when she went up with her husband to offer the yearly sacrifice. [20] Then Eli would bless Elka'nah and his wife, and say, "The LORD give you children by this woman for the loan which she lent to[d] the LORD"; so then they would return to their home.

21 And the LORD visited Hannah, and she conceived and bore three sons and two daughters. And the boy Samuel grew in the presence of the LORD.

22 Now Eli was very old, and he heard all that his sons were doing to all Israel, and how they lay with the women who served at the entrance to the tent of meeting. [23] And he said to them, "Why do you do such things? For I hear of your evil dealings from all the people. [24] No, my sons; it is no good report that I hear the people of the LORD spreading abroad. [25] If a man sins against a man, God will mediate for him; but if a man sins against the LORD, who can intercede for him?" But they would not listen to the voice of their father; for it was the will of the LORD to slay them.

26 Now the boy Samuel continued to grow both in stature and in favor with the LORD and with men.

27 And there came a man of God to Eli, and said to him, "Thus the LORD

c Gk Syr Vg: Heb *with it*
d Or *for the petition which she asked of*

10: For God as the final judge of all, see Ps.98.9. *His king* and *his anointed* could refer to the historical monarchy, but more probably they look forward to the new David, the ideal king of the future (see 10.1 n.).

2.12–26: The sons of Eli. The Late Source continues at this point. The evil conduct of the sons of Eli contrasts with the growing spirituality of Samuel (vv. 21,26 and ch. 3). **18:** The *linen ephod* was a light ceremonial garment covering only the front of the body (2 Sam.6.14); it is sometimes referred to as an apron. Later the priests wore a more elaborate ephod (Ex.28.5–14). **20:** See 1.19–28 n. **22:** The *tent of meeting* seems to be an error here, for the sanctuary at Shiloh was a building, not a tent. Perhaps there is some confusion with Ex.38.8. **25:** *It was the will of the LORD to slay them* is a theological way of saying that they were incorrigible, and therefore God had to punish them.

2.27–36: The condemnation of the house of Eli. This is an interruption of the Late Source by the insertion of a prose passage designed to justify the exclusion of Abiathar and his descendants from the priesthood in favor of Zadok and his descendants (1 Kg.2.27,35; see 3.11–14 n.).

[333]

has said, 'I revealed[e] myself to the house of your father when they were in Egypt subject to the house of Pharaoh. 28 And I chose him out of all the tribes of Israel to be my priest, to go up to my altar, to burn incense, to wear an ephod before me; and I gave to the house of your father all my offerings by fire from the people of Israel. 29 Why then look with greedy eye at[f] my sacrifices and my offerings which I commanded, and honor your sons above me by fattening yourselves upon the choicest parts of every offering of my people Israel?' 30 Therefore the LORD the God of Israel declares: 'I promised that your house and the house of your father should go in and out before me for ever'; but now the LORD declares: 'Far be it from me; for those who honor me I will honor, and those who despise me shall be lightly esteemed. 31 Behold, the days are coming, when I will cut off your strength and the strength of your father's house, so that there will not be an old man in your house. 32 Then in distress you will look with envious eye on all the prosperity which shall be bestowed upon Israel; and there shall not be an old man in your house for ever. 33 The man of you whom I shall not cut off from my altar shall be spared to weep out his[g] eyes and grieve his[g] heart; and all the increase of your house shall die by the sword of men.[h] 34 And this which shall befall your two sons, Hophni and Phin'ehas, shall be the sign to you: both of them shall die on the same day. 35 And I will raise up for myself a faith-ful priest, who shall do according to what is in my heart and in my mind; and I will build him a sure house, and he shall go in and out before my anointed for ever. 36 And every one who is left in your house shall come to implore him for a piece of silver or a loaf of bread, and shall say, "Put me, I pray you, in one of the priest's places, that I may eat a morsel of bread." ' "

3 Now the boy Samuel was ministering to the LORD under Eli. And the word of the LORD was rare in those days; there was no frequent vision. 2 At that time Eli, whose eyesight had begun to grow dim, so that he could not see, was lying down in his own place; 3 the lamp of God had not yet gone out, and Samuel was lying down within the temple of the LORD, where the ark of God was. 4 Then the LORD called, "Samuel! Samuel!"[i] and he said, "Here I am!" 5 and ran to Eli, and said, "Here I am, for you called me." But he said, "I did not call; lie down again." So he went and lay down. 6 And the LORD called again, "Samuel!" And Samuel arose and went to Eli, and said, "Here I am, for you called me." But he said, "I did not call, my son; lie down again." 7 Now Samuel did not yet know the LORD, and the word of the LORD had not yet been revealed to him. 8 And the LORD called Samuel again the third time. And he arose and went to Eli, and said, "Here I am, for you called me." Then Eli per-

e Gk Tg: Heb *Did I reveal*
f Or *treat with scorn* Gk: Heb *kick at*
g Gk: Heb *your* h Gk: Heb *die as men*
i Gk See 3.10: Heb *the LORD called Samuel*

Eli was an ancestor of Abiathar, according to the writer of this passage, and the sins of the fathers (Eli and his sons) were visited upon the children (Dt.5.9). 27: *Your father* refers to Aaron. 28: *An ephod*, see v. 18 n. 33: *The man* is Abiathar, the only one to escape at Nob (1 Sam.22.18–23; 1 Kg.2.26–27). 35: The *faithful priest* is Zadok (2 Sam.8.17; 15.24; 1 Kg.1.8; 2.35). *My anointed* refers to the king, real or ideal (see v. 10 n.).

3.1–4.1a: **God's first revelation to Samuel.** The continuation of the Late Source from 2.26. According to Jewish tradition Samuel was twelve years old at this time, the age of Jesus when he discoursed in the temple at Jerusalem (Lk.2.40–52). These beautiful stories of the birth and childhood of Samuel were in the mind of Luke as he began the writing of his Gospel (see 2.1–10 n.). 1: *Word* and *vision* here are essentially the same thing–a revelation from God. 3: *The lamp of God* burned all night (Ex.27.21); hence the time was just before dawn. The *lamp* was near *the ark of God*, the portable shrine or chest symbolizing the presence and power of the Deity. Its early form was simple, but in later conception it became highly ornate (Ex.25.10–22; 37.1–9). The simple early form plays an important part in the story that follows in the next section.

ceived that the LORD was calling the boy. [9] Therefore Eli said to Samuel, "Go, lie down; and if he calls you, you shall say, 'Speak, LORD, for thy servant hears.'" So Samuel went and lay down in his place.

10 And the LORD came and stood forth, calling as at other times, "Samuel! Samuel!" And Samuel said, "Speak, for thy servant hears." [11] Then the LORD said to Samuel, "Behold, I am about to do a thing in Israel, at which the two ears of every one that hears it will tingle. [12] On that day I will fulfil against Eli all that I have spoken concerning his house, from beginning to end. [13] And I tell him that I am about to punish his house for ever, for the iniquity which he knew, because his sons were blaspheming God,[j] and he did not restrain them. [14] Therefore I swear to the house of Eli that the iniquity of Eli's house shall not be expiated by sacrifice or offering for ever."

15 Samuel lay until morning; then he opened the doors of the house of the LORD. And Samuel was afraid to tell the vision to Eli. [16] But Eli called Samuel and said, "Samuel, my son." And he said, "Here I am." [17] And Eli said, "What was it that he told you? Do not hide it from me. May God do so to you and more also, if you hide anything from me of all that he told you." [18] So Samuel told him everything and hid nothing from him. And he said, "It is the LORD; let him do what seems good to him."

19 And Samuel grew, and the LORD was with him and let none of his words fall to the ground. [20] And all Israel from Dan to Beer-sheba knew that Samuel was established as a prophet of the LORD. [21] And the LORD appeared again at Shiloh, for the LORD revealed himself to Samuel at Shiloh by the word of the LORD. [1] And the word of Samuel came to all Israel.

4 Now Israel went out to battle against the Philistines; they encamped at Ebene'zer, and the Philistines encamped at Aphek. [2] The Philistines drew up in line against Israel, and when the battle spread, Israel was defeated by the Philistines, who slew about four thousand men on the field of battle. [3] And when the troops came to the camp, the elders of Israel said, "Why has the LORD put us to rout today before the Philistines? Let us bring the ark of the covenant of the LORD here from Shiloh, that he may come among us and save us from the power of our enemies." [4] So the people sent to Shiloh, and brought from there the ark of the covenant of the LORD of hosts, who is enthroned on the cherubim; and the two sons of Eli, Hophni and Phin'ehas, were there with the ark of the covenant of God.

5 When the ark of the covenant of

[j] Another reading is *for themselves*

11–14: These verses may have suggested the insertion of 2.27–36 above. It was necessary that God's first revelation to Samuel should be a tragic one. God must chasten as well as offer salvation. **4.1a:** *Word* here probably means "reputation"; Samuel became known and trusted throughout all the land as a man who spoke for God.

4.1b–7.2: The beginning of the war with the Philistines. The great body of literary material known as the Early Source begins here (see Introduction). The first sentence of this section of the Greek version tells us that *the Philistines* took the lead in the war by mustering their forces against the Israelites. For the origin of the Philistines, see Jg.13.1 n.; Am.9.7 n. At the time this story begins (about 1050 B.C.) the Philistines apparently had decided that they were strong enough to attack the Israelites and perhaps to take over the whole land. Thus begins for the Israelites a life-and-death struggle. Samuel is not mentioned in this section; one might almost say that *the ark*, rather than any person, is here the center of the author's attention.

4.1b–22: The defeat of Israel and capture of the ark. The strategy of the Philistines was to drive up the coast, then down the plain of Esdraelon to the Jordan river, thus cutting communication between the parts of Israel north and south of the plain. By the end of 1 Samuel this strategy had succeeded, though in the meantime there were attempts to penetrate Israelite territory farther south. **3–4:** *Ark of the covenant*, see 3.3 n. *The LORD of hosts*, see 1.3 n. *Who is enthroned on the cherubim*, 2 Sam.6.2; 2 Kg.19.15; Pss.80.1; 99.1; etc. *Cherubim*, see Gen.

the LORD came into the camp, all Israel gave a mighty shout, so that the earth resounded. [6] And when the Philistines heard the noise of the shouting, they said, "What does this great shouting in the camp of the Hebrews mean?" And when they learned that the ark of the LORD had come to the camp, [7] the Philistines were afraid; for they said, "A god has come into the camp." And they said, "Woe to us! For nothing like this has happened before. [8] Woe to us! Who can deliver us from the power of these mighty gods? These are the gods who smote the Egyptians with every sort of plague in the wilderness. [9] Take courage, and acquit yourselves like men, O Philistines, lest you become slaves to the Hebrews as they have been to you; acquit yourselves like men and fight."

10 So the Philistines fought, and Israel was defeated, and they fled, every man to his home; and there was a very great slaughter, for there fell of Israel thirty thousand foot soldiers. [11] And the ark of God was captured; and the two sons of Eli, Hophni and Phin'ehas, were slain.

12 A man of Benjamin ran from the battle line, and came to Shiloh the same day, with his clothes rent and with earth upon his head. [13] When he arrived, Eli was sitting upon his seat by the road watching, for his heart trembled for the ark of God. And when the man came into the city and told the news, all the city cried out. [14] When Eli heard the sound of the outcry, he said, "What is this uproar?" Then the man hastened and came and told Eli. [15] Now Eli was ninety-eight years old and his eyes were set, so that he could not see. [16] And the man said to Eli, "I am he who has come from the battle; I fled from the battle today." And he said, "How did it go, my son?" [17] He who brought the tidings answered and said, "Israel has fled before the Philistines, and there has also been a great slaughter among the people; your two sons also, Hophni and Phin'ehas, are dead, and the ark of God has been captured." [18] When he mentioned the ark of God, Eli fell over backward from his seat by the side of the gate; and his neck was broken and he died, for he was an old man, and heavy. He had judged Israel forty years.

19 Now his daughter-in-law, the wife of Phin'ehas, was with child, about to give birth. And when she heard the tidings that the ark of God was captured, and that her father-in-law and her husband were dead, she bowed and gave birth; for her pains came upon her. [20] And about the time of her death the women attending her said to her, "Fear not, for you have borne a son." But she did not answer or give heed. [21] And she named the

---

3.24 n. In Phoenicia the king was sometimes represented as sitting on a throne supported by cherubim; the translators here suggest that the LORD God of Israel is similarly *enthroned*. Another interpretation is that God "dwells in the cherubim." There is no necessary implication that cherubim formed a part of this early, simple ark.

4.5–11: The loss of the ark. 6: The word *Hebrews* in the earlier parts of the Old Testament is nearly always used by non-Israelites as a term of contempt (compare Gen.39.14; 43.32); the Israelites seldom use it of themselves. Only later could Jonah and Paul say proudly, "I am a Hebrew" (Jon.1.9; Phil.3.5). **7,8:** The plural expression *gods* would seem to imply that the Philistines had no conception of how the Israelites worshiped only one God (but compare 5.7,8,10,11). Since the plagues occurred in Egypt, either the phrase "in the wilderness" was added by mistake, or the author is making sport of the ignorance of the Philistines. **10:** Most ancient documents, Biblical and non-Biblical, are less exact with regard to numbers than are modern writings.

4.12–18: The death of Eli. 13: *By the road;* the reading of the Greek version, "by the gate" (presumably the door of the temple), is preferable (1.9). **18:** *He had judged Israel forty years,* added by the Deuteronomic editor on the assumption that practically every prominent man in those days was a judge of all Israel (Jg.16.31). **19–22:** The birth of Ichabod. The name *Ichabod* means "no glory" or "alas for the glory!" Many names in the Bible describe the circumstances

child Ich'abod, saying, "The glory has departed from Israel!" because the ark of God had been captured and because of her father-in-law and her husband. ²² And she said, "The glory has departed from Israel, for the ark of God has been captured."

5 When the Philistines captured the ark of God, they carried it from Ebene'zer to Ashdod; ² then the Philistines took the ark of God and brought it into the house of Dagon and set it up beside Dagon. ³ And when the people of Ashdod rose early the next day, behold, Dagon had fallen face downward on the ground before the ark of the LORD. So they took Dagon and put him back in his place. ⁴ But when they rose early on the next morning, behold, Dagon had fallen face downward on the ground before the ark of the LORD, and the head of Dagon and both his hands were lying cut off upon the threshold; only the trunk of Dagon was left to him. ⁵ This is why the priests of Dagon and all who enter the house of Dagon do not tread on the threshold of Dagon in Ashdod to this day.

6 The hand of the LORD was heavy upon the people of Ashdod, and he terrified and afflicted them with tumors, both Ashdod and its territory. ⁷ And when the men of Ashdod saw how things were, they said, "The ark of the God of Israel must not remain with us;

for his hand is heavy upon us and upon Dagon our god." ⁸ So they sent and gathered together all the lords of the Philistines, and said, "What shall we do with the ark of the God of Israel?" They answered, "Let the ark of the God of Israel be brought around to Gath." So they brought the ark of the God of Israel there. ⁹ But after they had brought it around, the hand of the LORD was against the city, causing a very great panic, and he afflicted the men of the city, both young and old, so that tumors broke out upon them. ¹⁰ So they sent the ark of God to Ekron. But when the ark of God came to Ekron, the people of Ekron cried out, "They have brought around to us the ark of the God of Israel to slay us and our people." ¹¹ They sent therefore and gathered together all the lords of the Philistines, and said, "Send away the ark of the God of Israel, and let it return to its own place, that it may not slay us and our people." For there was a deathly panic throughout the whole city. The hand of God was very heavy there; ¹² the men who did not die were stricken with tumors, and the cry of the city went up to heaven.

6 The ark of the LORD was in the country of the Philistines seven months. ² And the Philistines called for the priests and the diviners and said, "What shall we do with the ark of the LORD? Tell us with what we shall send

---

surrounding the bearer's birth or give an omen; compare the naming of Cain (Gen.4.1), Isaac ("laugh," Gen.21.3,6), the children of Jacob (Gen.30.6–24), Moses ("draw out," Ex.2.10), and Jesus ("save," Mt.1.21).

5.1–12: The ark troubles the Philistines. It is obvious that the early Israelites must have taken much delight in this primitive story of the power of the symbol of their God. **1:** *Ashdod* was one of the five principal Philistine towns (pentapolis), along with Ashkelon, Ekron, Gath, and Gaza (Jg.14.19 n.). **2:** *House* here means temple. *Dagon*, the principal deity of the Philistines (Jg.16.23), appears to have been borrowed, at least in name, from some of the surrounding Semitic peoples. The root meaning of the word was formerly thought to be "fish" (the Philistines being near the sea), but is now considered to be "grain." Hence Dagon is reckoned among the "fertility" deities that have to do with agricultural productivity. **5:** Leaping over *the threshold* was a common practice in primitive religions (Zeph.1.9), the doorsill being regarded with superstitious awe (compare the modern custom of carrying a bride over the threshold). The origins of the custom are very ancient, hence the explanation given here can hardly be correct. **6,9,12:** These *tumors* are generally considered to have been the swellings of the bubonic plague. **7,8,10,11:** The Philistines appear to understand that Israel has but one God.

6.1–7.2: The voluntary return of the ark. The Philistines, attributing the plague to the presence of the ark, make arrangements to return it to its former owners. **3:** The Philistines wish to make

it to its place." ³ They said, "If you send away the ark of the God of Israel, do not send it empty, but by all means return him a guilt offering. Then you will be healed, and it will be known to you why his hand does not turn away from you." ⁴ And they said, "What is the guilt offering that we shall return to him?" They answered, "Five golden tumors and five golden mice, according to the number of the lords of the Philistines; for the same plague was upon all of you and upon your lords. ⁵ So you must make images of your tumors and images of your mice that ravage the land, and give glory to the God of Israel; perhaps he will lighten his hand from off you and your gods and your land. ⁶ Why should you harden your hearts as the Egyptians and Pharaoh hardened their hearts? After he had made sport of them, did not they let the people go, and they departed? ⁷ Now then, take and prepare a new cart and two milch cows upon which there has never come a yoke, and yoke the cows to the cart, but take their calves home, away from them. ⁸ And take the ark of the LORD and place it on the cart, and put in a box at its side the figures of gold, which you are returning to him as a guilt offering. Then send it off, and let it go its way. ⁹ And watch; if it goes up on the way to its own land, to Beth-she'mesh, then it is he who has done us this great harm; but if not, then we shall know that it is not his hand that struck us, it happened to us by chance."

10 The men did so, and took two milch cows and yoked them to the cart, and shut up their calves at home.

¹¹ And they put the ark of the LORD on the cart, and the box with the golden mice and the images of their tumors. ¹² And the cows went straight in the direction of Beth-she'mesh along one highway, lowing as they went; they turned neither to the right nor to the left, and the lords of the Philistines went after them as far as the border of Beth-she'mesh. ¹³ Now the people of Beth-she'mesh were reaping their wheat harvest in the valley; and when they lifted up their eyes and saw the ark, they rejoiced to see it. ¹⁴ The cart came into the field of Joshua of Beth-she'mesh, and stopped there. A great stone was there; and they split up the wood of the cart and offered the cows as a burnt offering to the LORD. ¹⁵ And the Levites took down the ark of the LORD and the box that was beside it, in which were the golden figures, and set them upon the great stone; and the men of Beth-she'mesh offered burnt offerings and sacrificed sacrifices on that day to the LORD. ¹⁶ And when the five lords of the Philistines saw it, they returned that day to Ekron.

17 These are the golden tumors, which the Philistines returned as a guilt offering to the LORD: one for Ashdod, one for Gaza, one for Ash'kelon, one for Gath, one for Ekron; ¹⁸ also the golden mice, according to the number of all the cities of the Philistines belonging to the five lords, both fortified cities and unwalled villages. The great stone, beside which they set down the ark of the LORD, is a witness to this day in the field of Joshua of Beth-she'mesh.

19 And he slew some of the men of

---

a guilt offering, to appease the God of Israel, who (so they thought) was angry. **4,5:** *Five golden tumors and five golden mice* were prepared. We learn from the Greek version (5.6 and 6.1) that the plague was accompanied by swarms of mice. Bubonic plague is usually spread by a flea carried by rats. The Philistines may have been correct in connecting the disease with these "mice" (probably rats). By sending away images of the troublesome objects they hoped, by a process of sympathetic magic, to be rid of the troubles themselves; and they hoped that *the God of Israel* would be pleased by their generosity in making the images of gold. **6:** To *harden your hearts* means to "make your minds stubborn" (Ex.8.19,32). **9:** *Beth-shemesh* was probably the nearest important Israelite town to Ekron, where the ark was prior to its return. **15:** This verse was inserted by a priestly editor to make the procedure conform to later requirements. The Levites did not begin to function as priestly assistants until later times. **17:** See 5.1 n.

Beth-she'mesh, because they looked into the ark of the LORD; he slew seventy men of them,[k] and the people mourned because the LORD had made a great slaughter among the people. [20] Then the men of Beth-she'mesh said, "Who is able to stand before the LORD, this holy God? And to whom shall he go up away from us?" [21] So they sent messengers to the inhabitants of Kir'iath-je'arim, saying, "The Philistines have returned the ark of the LORD.

7 Come down and take it up to you." [1] And the men of Kir'iath-je'arim came and took up the ark of the LORD, and brought it to the house of Abin'adab on the hill; and they consecrated his son, Elea'zar, to have charge of the ark of the LORD. [2] From the day that the ark was lodged at Kir'iath-je'arim, a long time passed, some twenty years, and all the house of Israel lamented after the LORD.

3 Then Samuel said to all the house of Israel, "If you are returning to the LORD with all your heart, then put away the foreign gods and the Ash'taroth from among you, and direct your heart to the LORD, and serve him only, and he will deliver you out of the hand of the Philistines." [4] So Israel put away the Ba'als and the Ash'taroth, and they served the LORD only.

5 Then Samuel said, "Gather all Israel at Mizpah, and I will pray to the LORD for you." [6] So they gathered at Mizpah, and drew water and poured it out before the LORD, and fasted on that day, and said there, "We have sinned against the LORD." And Samuel judged the people of Israel at Mizpah. [7] Now when the Philistines heard that the people of Israel had gathered at Mizpah, the lords of the Philistines went up against Israel. And when the people of Israel heard of it they were afraid of the Philistines. [8] And the people of Israel said to Samuel, "Do not cease to cry to the LORD our God for us, that he may save us from the hand of the Philistines." [9] So Samuel took a sucking lamb and offered it as a whole burnt offering to the LORD; and Samuel cried to the LORD for Israel, and the LORD answered him. [10] As Samuel was offering up the burnt offering, the Philistines drew near to attack Israel; but the LORD thundered with a mighty voice that day against the Philistines and threw them into confusion; and they were routed before Israel. [11] And the men of Israel went out of Mizpah and pursued the Philistines, and smote them, as far as below Beth-car.

12 Then Samuel took a stone and set it up between Mizpah and Jesha'nah,[l] and called its name Ebene'zer;[m] for he said, "Hitherto the LORD has helped us." [13] So the Philistines were

k Cn: Heb *of the people seventy men, fifty thousand men*
l Gk Syr: Heb *Shen*　　*m* That is *Stone of help*

19: The ungrammatical addition of the phrase "fifty thousand men" (see note *k*) shows how easily exaggerations could occur (see 4.10 n.). **21:** The ark was taken to *Kiriath-jearim* probably because Shiloh had been destroyed in the meantime (Jer.7.12–14; 26.6–9). **7.2:** The expression *lamented after the LORD* seems to mean, in the light of what follows, "implored the LORD for help."

7.3–17: Samuel as judge of all Israel. *Samuel* immediately comes to the fore, as the Late Source resumes. **3–4:** Probably added by the Deuteronomic editor, who felt that the worship of false gods was always the chief sin of his people (Jg.2.11–15; 3.7; 10.6; 13.1; etc.). *The Baals and the Ashtaroth* (plural of Ashtoreth, the Hebrew word for Astarte, goddess of fertility and profane love) were the principal deities of the Canaanites, often worshiped also by the Israelites when they departed from the true faith. **5:** Continuation of v. 2. **6:** Libations of *water* were unusual (wine was used generally), but to people with a desert background water would be sufficiently precious. **9:** *A whole burnt offering*, one that is entirely consumed (Ex.29.18; Lev.8.21; Dt.13.16; 33.10). Most burnt offerings were of this type; the use of the word *whole* emphasizes the importance of the occasion. **10:** It is characteristic of the Late Source (and similar literary material) that battles are often won or lost by miraculous divine intervention. **13–14:** These verses are probably by the Deuteronomic editor, for they are more extreme in their glorification of Samuel than even the Late Source. If Samuel had won the war in this

subdued and did not again enter the territory of Israel. And the hand of the LORD was against the Philistines all the days of Samuel. [14] The cities which the Philistines had taken from Israel were restored to Israel, from Ekron to Gath; and Israel rescued their territory from the hand of the Philistines. There was peace also between Israel and the Amorites.

15 Samuel judged Israel all the days of his life. [16] And he went on a circuit year by year to Bethel, Gilgal, and Mizpah; and he judged Israel in all these places. [17] Then he would come back to Ramah, for his home was there, and there also he administered justice to Israel. And he built there an altar to the LORD.

8 When Samuel became old, he made his sons judges over Israel. [2] The name of his first-born son was Jo'el, and the name of his second, Abi'jah; they were judges in Beer-sheba. [3] Yet his sons did not walk in his ways, but turned aside after gain; they took bribes and perverted justice.

4 Then all the elders of Israel gathered together and came to Samuel at Ramah, [5] and said to him, "Behold, you are old and your sons do not walk in your ways; now appoint for us a king to govern us like all the nations." [6] But the thing displeased Samuel when they said, "Give us a king to govern us." And Samuel prayed to the LORD. [7] And the LORD said to Samuel, "Hearken to the voice of the people in all that they say to you; for they have not rejected you, but they have rejected

me from being king over them. [8] According to all the deeds which they have done to me,[n] from the day I brought them up out of Egypt even to this day, forsaking me and serving other gods, so they are also doing to you. [9] Now then, hearken to their voice; only, you shall solemnly warn them, and show them the ways of the king who shall reign over them."

10 So Samuel told all the words of the LORD to the people who were asking a king from him. [11] He said, "These will be the ways of the king who will reign over you: he will take your sons and appoint them to his chariots and to be his horsemen, and to run before his chariots; [12] and he will appoint for himself commanders of thousands and commanders of fifties, and some to plow his ground and to reap his harvest, and to make his implements of war and the equipment of his chariots. [13] He will take your daughters to be perfumers and cooks and bakers. [14] He will take the best of your fields and vineyards and olive orchards and give them to his servants. [15] He will take the tenth of your grain and of your vineyards and give it to his officers and to his servants. [16] He will take your menservants and maidservants, and the best of your cattle[o] and your asses, and put them to his work. [17] He will take the tenth of your flocks, and you shall be his slaves. [18] And in that day you will cry out because of your king, whom you have

n Gk: Heb lacks *to me*
o Gk: Heb *young men*

---

fashion, there would have been no occasion at all for the rise of Saul and the other events that followed. Most of the other potential enemies of Israel besides the Philistines could be classified as *Amorites*. The final sentence of v. 14 makes Samuel's success as a temporal ruler complete. But he was not really a "judge" or military hero like those in the Book of Judges; he was more like a circuit judge in the ordinary sense of the word (compare vv. 16–17).

8.1–22: The people request a king. A continuation of the Late Source, showing the antimonarchical tendency (see Introduction and 7.13–14 n.). Samuel dislikes the request, but after seeking God's will, he finds that he must yield, even though God himself feels offended. At God's behest Samuel delivers a severe lecture on the evils of kingship before yielding (vv. 9–18; compare Dt.17.14–20). The evils described here and in the Deuteronomy passage seem to be mainly those of the reign of Solomon, and it is probable that the resentment against the monarchy arose at this time and never ceased, becoming a part of the thought of many of the prophets and of the Deuteronomic writers.

chosen for yourselves; but the LORD will not answer you in that day."

19 But the people refused to listen to the voice of Samuel; and they said, "No! but we will have a king over us, 20 that we also may be like all the nations, and that our king may govern us and go out before us and fight our battles." 21 And when Samuel had heard all the words of the people, he repeated them in the ears of the LORD. 22 And the LORD said to Samuel, "Hearken to their voice, and make them a king." Samuel then said to the men of Israel, "Go every man to his city."

9 There was a man of Benjamin whose name was Kish, the son of Abi'el, son of Zeror, son of Beco'rath, son of Aphi'ah, a Benjaminite, a man of wealth; 2 and he had a son whose name was Saul, a handsome young man. There was not a man among the people of Israel more handsome than he; from his shoulders upward he was taller than any of the people.

3 Now the asses of Kish, Saul's father, were lost. So Kish said to Saul his son, "Take one of the servants with you, and arise, go and look for the asses." 4 And they^p passed through the hill country of E'phraim and passed through the land of Shal'ishah, but they did not find them. And they passed through the land of Sha'alim, but they were not there. Then they passed through the land of Benjamin, but did not find them.

5 When they came to the land of Zuph, Saul said to his servant who was with him, "Come, let us go back, lest my father cease to care about the asses and become anxious about us." 6 But he said to him, "Behold, there is a man of God in this city, and he is a man that is held in honor; all that he says comes true. Let us go there; perhaps he can tell us about the journey on which we have set out." 7 Then Saul said to his servant, "But if we go, what can we bring the man? For the bread in our sacks is gone, and there is no present to bring to the man of God. What have we?" 8 The servant answered Saul again, "Here, I have with me the fourth part of a shekel of silver, and I will give it to the man of God, to tell us our way." 9 (Formerly in Israel, when a man went to inquire of God, he said, "Come, let us go to the seer"; for he who is now called a prophet was formerly called a seer.) 10 And Saul said to his servant, "Well said; come, let us go." So they went to the city where the man of God was.

11 As they went up the hill to the city, they met young maidens coming out to draw water, and said to them, "Is the seer here?" 12 They answered, "He is; behold, he is just ahead of you. Make haste; he has come just now to the city, because the people have a sacrifice today on the high place. 13 As soon as you enter the city, you will find him, before he goes up to the

p Gk Vg: Heb *he*

9.1–10.16: The secret choice of Saul. From the Early Source. Samuel appears here in the Early Source for the first time. He is not the judge or ruler of all Israel (7.5), but a more modest figure, a local *man of God* (9.6), a highly respected *seer* (9.11), that is, a clairvoyant (9.20; 10.2), and possibly a circuit judge, as depicted in the Late Source (7.16–17; compare 9.12). Most noteworthy in this section is the idea that the kingship is a splendid thing, a blessing from God voluntarily bestowed, and not a concession to the improper desires of the people (9.16; 10.1). Samuel himself seems immensely pleased with the idea of the kingship and his part in creating it (9.19–24), in contrast to his attitude in ch. 8. In other words, the Early Source is just as clearly pro-monarchical as the Late Source is anti-monarchical. It will soon appear also that the Early Source is friendly to Saul, whereas the Late Source is just the opposite. **9.2:** *Young man* here means "man in the prime of life," for Saul had grown children. **6:** *This city* may be Ramah (7.17). **7:** Saul appears not to have heard of Samuel; contrast 4.1a and 7.15. **8:** There was no coinage in those days; *the fourth part of a shekel* was merely a bit of silver of a certain weight (about one-eighth oz., worth about ten cents now, but much more then). **9:** A note by an editor, inserted after the word *seer* had gone out of use. **11–14:** The *city* was apparently a small walled town, lying on the side of a hill, with only one gate; the spring was below, *the high*

high place to eat; for the people will not eat till he comes, since he must bless the sacrifice; afterward those eat who are invited. Now go up, for you will meet him immediately." ¹⁴ So they went up to the city. As they were entering the city, they saw Samuel coming out toward them on his way up to the high place.

15 Now the day before Saul came, the LORD had revealed to Samuel: ¹⁶ "Tomorrow about this time I will send to you a man from the land of Benjamin, and you shall anoint him to be prince over my people Israel. He shall save my people from the hand of the Philistines; for I have seen the affliction of*q* my people, because their cry has come to me." ¹⁷ When Samuel saw Saul, the LORD told him, "Here is the man of whom I spoke to you! He it is who shall rule over my people." ¹⁸ Then Saul approached Samuel in the gate, and said, "Tell me where is the house of the seer?" ¹⁹ Samuel answered Saul, "I am the seer; go up before me to the high place, for today you shall eat with me, and in the morning I will let you go and will tell you all that is on your mind. ²⁰ As for your asses that were lost three days ago, do not set your mind on them, for they have been found. And for whom is all that is desirable in Israel? Is it not for you and for all your father's house?" ²¹ Saul answered, "Am I not a Benjaminite, from the least of the tribes of Israel? And is not my family the humblest of all the families of the tribe of Benjamin? Why then have you spoken to me in this way?"

22 Then Samuel took Saul and his servant and brought them into the hall and gave them a place at the head of those who had been invited, who were about thirty persons. ²³ And Samuel said to the cook, "Bring the portion I gave you, of which I said to you, 'Put it aside.'" ²⁴ So the cook took up the leg and the upper portion*r* and set them before Saul; and Samuel said, "Seë, what was kept is set before you. Eat; because it was kept for you until the hour appointed, that you might eat with the guests."*s*

So Saul ate with Samuel that day. ²⁵ And when they came down from the high place into the city, a bed was spread for Saul*t* upon the roof, and he lay down to sleep. ²⁶ Then at the break of dawn*u* Samuel called to Saul upon the roof, "Up, that I may send you on your way." So Saul arose, and both he and Samuel went out into the street.

27 As they were going down to the outskirts of the city, Samuel said to Saul, "Tell the servant to pass on before us, and when he has passed on stop here yourself for a while, that I may make known to you the word of God."

10 Then Samuel took a vial of oil and poured it on his head, and kissed him and said, "Has not the LORD anointed you to be prince over his people Israel? And you shall reign over the people of the LORD and you will save them from the hand of their enemies round about. And this shall be the sign to you that the LORD has anointed you to be prince*w* over his heritage. ² When you depart from me today you will meet two men by

q Gk: Heb lacks *the affliction of*   *r* Heb obscure
s Cn: Heb *saying, I have invited the people*
t Gk: Heb *and he spoke with Saul*
u Gk: Heb *and they arose early and at break of dawn*
w Gk: Heb lacks *over his people Israel? And you shall . . . to be prince*

---

place above. Samuel presided over the sacrificial meal as a sort of priest. Later, pagan practices developed at the high place shrines, and they were ordered to be destroyed (Dt.12.2–3; 2 Kg. 23.8–9). **19:** Perhaps Saul had been brooding over the oppression by the Philistines. **25:** Roofs in that part of the world were flat, with protecting parapets, as they still are. Hence they were and are well adapted for sleeping during the summer months, when no rain falls. **10.1:** The unguent used in anointing kings was olive oil. Though priests (Ex.29.7) and prophets (1 Kg. 19.16) were sometimes anointed, the ceremony was more relevant to the kingship, so that the king came to be called "the LORD's anointed" (16.6; 24.6), or simply "the anointed one." This title was applied to the ideal future king in the form "Messiah" in Hebrew, "Christos" in Greek (see Mt.1.16 n.). **2:** This site of *Rachel's tomb* is in Benjamin, north of Jerusalem

Rachel's tomb in the territory of Benjamin at Zelzah, and they will say to you, 'The asses which you went to seek are found, and now your father has ceased to care about the asses and is anxious about you, saying, "What shall I do about my son?" ' ³ Then you shall go on from there further and come to the oak of Tabor; three men going up to God at Bethel will meet you there, one carrying three kids, another carrying three loaves of bread, and another carrying a skin of wine. ⁴ And they will greet you and give you two loaves of bread, which you shall accept from their hand. ⁵ After that you shall come to Gib′e-ath-elo′him,ˣ where there is a garrison of the Philistines; and there, as you come to the city, you will meet a band of prophets coming down from the high place with harp, tambourine, flute, and lyre before them, prophesying. ⁶ Then the spirit of the LORD will come mightily upon you, and you shall prophesy with them and be turned into another man. ⁷ Now when these signs meet you, do whatever your hand finds to do, for God is with you. ⁸ And you shall go down before me to Gilgal; and behold, I am coming to you to offer burnt offerings and to sacrifice peace offerings. Seven days you shall wait, until I come to you and show you what you shall do."

9 When he turned his back to leave Samuel, God gave him another heart; and all these signs came to pass that day. ¹⁰ When they came to Gib′e-ah,ᶻ behold, a band of prophets met him; and the spirit of God came mightily

upon him, and he prophesied among them. ¹¹ And when all who knew him before saw how he prophesied with the prophets, the people said to one another, "What has come over the son of Kish? Is Saul also among the prophets?" ¹² And a man of the place answered, "And who is their father?" Therefore it became a proverb, "Is Saul also among the prophets?" ¹³ When he had finished prophesying, he came to the high place.

14 Saul's uncle said to him and to his servant, "Where did you go?" And he said, "To seek the asses; and when we saw they were not to be found, we went to Samuel." ¹⁵ And Saul's uncle said, "Pray, tell me what Samuel said to you." ¹⁶ And Saul said to his uncle, "He told us plainly that the asses had been found." But about the matter of the kingdom, of which Samuel had spoken, he did not tell him anything.

17 Now Samuel called the people together to the LORD at Mizpah; ¹⁸ and he said to the people of Israel, "Thus says the LORD, the God of Israel, 'I brought up Israel out of Egypt, and I delivered you from the hand of the Egyptians and from the hand of all the kingdoms that were oppressing you.' ¹⁹ But you have this day rejected your God, who saves you from all your calamities and your distresses; and you have said, 'No! but set a king over us.' Now therefore present yourselves before the LORD by your tribes and by your thousands."

20 Then Samuel brought all the

x Or *the hill of God*   *z* Or *the hill*

(Jer.31.15). Another tradition locates it south of Jerusalem near Bethlehem, at the site shown to tourists today (Gen.35.16; 48.7; Mt.2.16–18). **3**: *Going up to God* means "going up to offer sacrifice." **5**: The mention of the *garrison* (or prefect) *of the Philistines* is a reminder of the task that lay before Saul. **6**: To *prophesy . . . and be turned into another man* means here to dance ecstatically and be out of one's head, in the fashion of the so-called ecstatic prophecy of those days (19.23–24). This was to be a sort of initiatory religious experience for the new king. **9**: *God gave him another heart*, that is, made a new man of him. **11**: The change in Saul began to be noticed. **12**: The phrase, *And who is their father?*, is unintelligible and interrupts the sequence of thought, which is that people begin to suspect that Saul had a mission. **13**: *Came to the high place* is probably a textual error for "came home."

10.17–27: Saul chosen king by lot. Resumption of Late Source. We see again the anti-monarchical tendency of the Late Source. Samuel proceeds reluctantly (see v. 19), in contrast to 9.19–24. The story told here follows naturally upon ch. 8, and has the same point of view.

tribes of Israel near, and the tribe of Benjamin was taken by lot. ²¹ He brought the tribe of Benjamin near by its families, and the family of the Matrites was taken by lot; finally he brought the family of the Matrites near man by man,ᵃ and Saul the son of Kish was taken by lot. But when they sought him, he could not be found. ²² So they inquired again of the LORD, "Did the man come hither?"ᵇ and the LORD said, "Behold, he has hidden himself among the baggage." ²³ Then they ran and fetched him from there; and when he stood among the people, he was taller than any of the people from his shoulders upward. ²⁴ And Samuel said to all the people, "Do you see him whom the LORD has chosen? There is none like him among all the people." And all the people shouted, "Long live the king!"

25 Then Samuel told the people the rights and duties of the kingship; and he wrote them in a book and laid it up before the LORD. Then Samuel sent all the people away, each one to his home. ²⁶ Saul also went to his home at Gib′e-ah, and with him went men of valor whose hearts God had touched. ²⁷ But some worthless fellows said, "How can this man save us?" And they despised him, and brought him no present. But he held his peace.

11 Then Nahash the Ammonite went up and besieged Ja′besh-gil′ead; and all the men of Jabesh said to Nahash, "Make a treaty with us, and we will serve you." ² But Nahash the Ammonite said to them, "On this condition I will make a treaty with you,

that I gouge out all your right eyes, and thus put disgrace upon all Israel." ³ The elders of Jabesh said to him, "Give us seven days respite that we may send messengers through all the territory of Israel. Then, if there is no one to save us, we will give ourselves up to you." ⁴ When the messengers came to Gib′e-ah of Saul, they reported the matter in the ears of the people; and all the people wept aloud.

5 Now Saul was coming from the field behind the oxen; and Saul said, "What ails the people, that they are weeping?" So they told him the tidings of the men of Jabesh. ⁶ And the spirit of God came mightily upon Saul when he heard these words, and his anger was greatly kindled. ⁷ He took a yoke of oxen, and cut them in pieces and sent them throughout all the territory of Israel by the hand of messengers, saying, "Whoever does not come out after Saul and Samuel, so shall it be done to his oxen!" Then the dread of the LORD fell upon the people, and they came out as one man. ⁸ When he mustered them at Bezek, the men of Israel were three hundred thousand, and the men of Judah thirty thousand. ⁹ And they said to the messengers who had come, "Thus shall you say to the men of Ja′besh-gil′ead: 'Tomorrow, by the time the sun is hot, you shall have deliverance.'" When the messengers came and told the men of Jabesh, they were glad. ¹⁰ Therefore the men of Jabesh said, "Tomorrow we will give ourselves up to you, and you may do

a Gk: Heb lacks *finally . . . man by man*
b Gk: Heb *Is there yet a man to come hither?*

21: The clan of the *Matrites* is not mentioned elsewhere. **21–22:** These verses seem to reflect on Saul unfavorably. **25:** This verse may be an editorial preparation for ch. 12. The mention of *a book* is designed to show Samuel as a man of letters as well as priest, prophet, and judge. We know nothing more of this book. **26–27:** These verses, which also may be editorial, reflect both favorable and unfavorable opinion about Saul.

11.1–15: Saul proves himself able to lead in battle and is publicly made king. This chapter, from the Early Source, logically follows 10.16, portraying the opportunity for which Saul had been advised to be ready (10.1). The Ammonites to the east (Gen.19.38; Num.21.24; Dt.2.37; Jg.10.9) were not so dangerous to national security as the Philistines, but a victory over them would show Saul capable of meeting the stronger enemy on the west, and also free Israel from having to fight on two fronts. **1:** *Jabesh-gilead*, an Israelite town east of the Jordan. **7:** Sending around the *pieces* of a sacrifice was a call to war (Jg.19.29). **8:** *Bezek* was between Shechem and

to us whatever seems good to you." [11] And on the morrow Saul put the people in three companies; and they came into the midst of the camp in the morning watch, and cut down the Ammonites until the heat of the day; and those who survived were scattered, so that no two of them were left together.

12 Then the people said to Samuel, "Who is it that said, 'Shall Saul reign over us?' Bring the men, that we may put them to death." [13] But Saul said, "Not a man shall be put to death this day, for today the LORD has wrought deliverance in Israel." [14] Then Samuel said to the people, "Come, let us go to Gilgal and there renew the kingdom." [15] So all the people went to Gilgal, and there they made Saul king before the LORD in Gilgal. There they sacrificed peace offerings before the LORD, and there Saul and all the men of Israel rejoiced greatly.

12 And Samuel said to all Israel, "Behold, I have hearkened to your voice in all that you have said to me, and have made a king over you. [2] And now, behold, the king walks before you; and I am old and gray, and behold, my sons are with you; and I have walked before you from my youth until this day. [3] Here I am; testify against me before the LORD and before his anointed. Whose ox have I taken? Or whose ass have I taken? Or whom have I defrauded? Whom have I oppressed? Or from whose hand have I taken a bribe to blind my eyes with it? Testify against me[c] and I will restore it to you." [4] They said, "You have not de-

frauded us or oppressed us or taken anything from any man's hand." [5] And he said to them, "The LORD is witness against you, and his anointed is witness this day, that you have not found anything in my hand." And they said, "He is witness."

6 And Samuel said to the people, "The LORD is witness,[d] who appointed Moses and Aaron and brought your fathers up out of the land of Egypt. [7] Now therefore stand still, that I may plead with you before the LORD concerning all the saving deeds of the LORD which he performed for you and for your fathers. [8] When Jacob went into Egypt and the Egyptians oppressed them,[e] then your fathers cried to the LORD and the LORD sent Moses and Aaron, who brought forth your fathers out of Egypt, and made them dwell in this place. [9] But they forgot the LORD their God; and he sold them into the hand of Sis'era, commander of the army of Jabin king of[f] Hazor, and into the hand of the Philistines, and into the hand of the king of Moab; and they fought against them. [10] And they cried to the LORD, and said, 'We have sinned, because we have forsaken the LORD, and have served the Ba'als and the Ash'taroth; but now deliver us out of the hand of our enemies, and we will serve thee.' [11] And the LORD sent Jerubba'al and Barak,[g] and Jephthah, and Samuel, and delivered you out of the hand of your enemies on every side; and you dwelt

c Gk: Heb lacks *Testify against me*
d Gk: Heb lacks *is witness*
e Gk: Heb lacks *and the Egyptians oppressed them*
f Gk: Heb lacks *Jabin king of*
g Gk Syr: Heb *Bedan*

Beth-shan. On the numbers see 4.10 n. **11**: Their day began at sundown, hence *on the morrow* would mean "that evening" in our reckoning. Apparently the Israelites marched all night to attack by surprise in the morning. **14**: Probably editorial, for, according to the Early Source, Saul's kingship had not previously been publicly proclaimed.

12.1–25: Samuel's farewell address. Late Source with Deuteronomic editing. This chapter logically follows 10.17–27 (compare ch. 8), though there are certain adjustments to ch. 11 (compare 12.12). Most ancient historical documents, Biblical and non-Biblical alike, contain speeches written at a time later than the events of the narrative, but regarded as appropriate to the occasion. This chapter is an excellent example of such literary material. **2**: The misconduct of the sons is not mentioned here (compare 8.3). **2,5**: The expression *his anointed* refers to the king (see 10.1 n.). **9,10,11**: Note the similarity to the Deuteronomic framework of the Book of Judges; e.g. Jg.4.2–3. *The Baals and the Ashtaroth*, see 7.3–4 n. In v. 11 *Samuel* is listed as the

in safety. [12] And when you saw that Nahash the king of the Ammonites came against you, you said to me, 'No, but a king shall reign over us,' when the LORD your God was your king. [13] And now behold the king whom you have chosen, for whom you have asked; behold, the LORD has set a king over you. [14] If you will fear the LORD and serve him and hearken to his voice and not rebel against the commandment of the LORD, and if both you and the king who reigns over you will follow the LORD your God, it will be well; [15] but if you will not hearken to the voice of the LORD, but rebel against the commandment of the LORD, then the hand of the LORD will be against you and your king.[h] [16] Now therefore stand still and see this great thing, which the LORD will do before your eyes. [17] Is it not wheat harvest today? I will call upon the LORD, that he may send thunder and rain; and you shall know and see that your wickedness is great, which you have done in the sight of the LORD, in asking for yourselves a king." [18] So Samuel called upon the LORD, and the LORD sent thunder and rain that day; and all the people greatly feared the LORD and Samuel.

19 And all the people said to Samuel, "Pray for your servants to the LORD your God, that we may not die; for we have added to all our sins this evil, to ask for ourselves a king." [20] And Samuel said to the people, "Fear not; you have done all this evil, yet do not turn aside from following the LORD, but serve the LORD with all your heart; [21] and do not turn aside after[i] vain

things which cannot profit or save, for they are vain. [22] For the LORD will not cast away his people, for his great name's sake, because it has pleased the LORD to make you a people for himself. [23] Moreover as for me, far be it from me that I should sin against the LORD by ceasing to pray for you; and I will instruct you in the good and the right way. [24] Only fear the LORD, and serve him faithfully with all your heart; for consider what great things he has done for you. [25] But if you still do wickedly, you shall be swept away, both you and your king."

13 Saul was . . .[j] years old when he began to reign; and he reigned . . .and two[k] years over Israel.

2 Saul chose three thousand men of Israel; two thousand were with Saul in Michmash and the hill country of Bethel, and a thousand were with Jonathan in Gib'e-ah of Benjamin; the rest of the people he sent home, every man to his tent. [3] Jonathan defeated the garrison of the Philistines which was at Geba; and the Philistines heard of it. And Saul blew the trumpet throughout all the land, saying, "Let the Hebrews hear." [4] And all Israel heard it said that Saul had defeated the garrison of the Philistines, and also that Israel had become odious to the Philistines. And the people were called out to join Saul at Gilgal.

5 And the Philistines mustered to fight with Israel, thirty thousand chariots, and six thousand horsemen, and

h Gk: Heb *fathers*
i Gk Syr Tg Vg: Heb *because after*
j The number is lacking in Heb
k *Two* is not the entire number. Something has dropped out.

---

last of the judges, the idea being that as long as he was alive no king was necessary. **14,15,24,25:** This philosophy of divine retribution is more fully developed in Dt. ch. 28 and Jg.2.11–23. **16–19:** The author wishes to show that Samuel was still in greater favor with God than was the king. *Rain* during the *wheat harvest* would be like "snow in summer" (Pr.26.1). This harvest took place in early summer, when no rain could be expected until autumn. Thus it is a miracle, the *thunder* making it more impressive. The miracle story is the writer's way of making a theological point. If one accepts the Biblical writers in their own time and in their own ways of thinking, the message of no Biblical writer need be lost.

13.1–7a: Saul begins the war with the Philistines. The Early Source. Saul's son Jonathan made the first move. **1:** Saul's age at this time is not known. Some suppose that he reigned twelve years, others put the figure at twenty-two (see note *k*). **5:** *Beth-aven*, probably an alternative name for Bethel. **7:** *Fords of the Jordan*, see Jg.12.5. *Gad and Gilead*, east of the Jordan.

troops like the sand on the seashore in multitude; they came up and encamped in Michmash, to the east of Beth-a'ven. 6 When the men of Israel saw that they were in straits (for the people were hard pressed), the people hid themselves in caves and in holes and in rocks and in tombs and in cisterns, 7 or crossed the fords of the Jordan*l* to the land of Gad and Gilead. Saul was still at Gilgal, and all the people followed him trembling.

8 He waited seven days, the time appointed by Samuel; but Samuel did not come to Gilgal, and the people were scattering from him. 9 So Saul said, "Bring the burnt offering here to me, and the peace offerings." And he offered the burnt offering. 10 As soon as he had finished offering the burnt offering, behold, Samuel came; and Saul went out to meet him and salute him. 11 Samuel said, "What have you done?" And Saul said, "When I saw that the people were scattering from me, and that you did not come within the days appointed, and that the Philistines had mustered at Michmash, 12 I said, 'Now the Philistines will come down upon me at Gilgal, and I have not entreated the favor of the LORD'; so I forced myself, and offered the burnt offering." 13 And Samuel said to Saul, "You have done foolishly; you have not kept the commandment of the LORD your God, which he commanded you; for now the LORD would have established your kingdom over Israel for ever. 14 But now your king-dom shall not continue; the LORD has sought out a man after his own heart; and the LORD has appointed him to be prince over his people, because you have not kept what the LORD commanded you." 15 And Samuel arose, and went up from Gilgal to Gib'e-ah of Benjamin.

And Saul numbered the people who were present with him, about six hundred men. 16 And Saul, and Jonathan his son, and the people who were present with them, stayed in Geba of Benjamin; but the Philistines encamped in Michmash. 17 And raiders came out of the camp of the Philistines in three companies; one company turned toward Ophrah, to the land of Shu'al, 18 another company turned toward Beth-hor'on, and another company turned toward the border that looks down upon the valley of Zebo'im toward the wilderness.

19 Now there was no smith to be found throughout all the land of Israel; for the Philistines said, "Lest the Hebrews make themselves swords or spears"; 20 but every one of the Israelites went down to the Philistines to sharpen his plowshare, his mattock, his axe, or his sickle;*m* 21 and the charge was a pim for the plowshares and for the mattocks, and a third of a shekel for sharpening the axes and for setting the goads.*n* 22 So on the day of the battle there was neither sword nor spear found in the hand of any

l Cn: Heb *Hebrews crossed the Jordan*
m Gk: Heb *plowshare*
n The Heb of this verse is obscure

13.7b–15a: Saul's ritual sin and rejection by God. This passage is an interruption of the Early Source by a writer even more hostile to Saul than the Late Source (see ch. 15 for the Late Source's version of the rejection). The thought is that the king had no right to exercise priestly functions, or at least Saul had no such right. Contrast the very different view of the Early Source in 14.31–35, where Saul definitely assists in priestly functions. Later David (2 Sam.6.12–19; 24.25) and Solomon (1 Kg.3.15) also exercised such functions. The *man after his* [God's] *own heart* (v. 14) is David. **8:** *The time appointed by Samuel,* see 10.8. No reason for Samuel's delay is given.

13.15b–14.52: Continuation of the Philistine War. The Early Source. **15b:** The words, *And Saul numbered the people . . . ,* follow directly on the words *to the land of Gad and Gilead* in v. 7a. The Israelites had scattered and only *six hundred* fighting men (a realistic estimate) remained with Saul. **19–22:** These verses are by an editor who conceived the situation to be worse than it really was. The age of iron was just beginning in Palestine; the Philistines were superior to the Israelites in material culture, but the latter overcame the deficiency and eventually won the war. A *shekel* (about eleven and one-half grams) of silver would be worth about fifty cents;

of the people with Saul and Jonathan;
but Saul and Jonathan his son had
them. 23 And the garrison of the Philistines went out to the pass of Michmash.

14 One day Jonathan the son of
Saul said to the young man who
bore his armor, "Come, let us go over
to the Philistine garrison on yonder
side." But he did not tell his father.
2 Saul was staying in the outskirts of
Gib′e-ah under the pomegranate tree
which is at Migron; the people who
were with him were about six hundred
men, 3 and Ahi′jah the son of Ahi′tub,
Ich′abod's brother, son of Phin′ehas,
son of Eli, the priest of the LORD in
Shiloh, wearing an ephod. And the people did not know that Jonathan had
gone. 4 In the pass,[o] by which Jonathan sought to go over to the Philistine
garrison, there was a rocky crag on the
one side and a rocky crag on the other
side; the name of the one was Bozez,
and the name of the other Seneh. 5 The
one crag rose on the north in front
of Michmash, and the other on the
south in front of Geba.

6 And Jonathan said to the young
man who bore his armor, "Come, let us
go over to the garrison of these uncircumcised; it may be that the LORD will
work for us; for nothing can hinder
the LORD from saving by many or by
few." 7 And his armor-bearer said to
him, "Do all that your mind inclines
to;[p] behold, I am with you, as is your
mind so is mine."[q] 8 Then said Jonathan, "Behold, we will cross over to
the men, and we will show ourselves
to them. 9 If they say to us, 'Wait until
we come to you,' then we will stand
still in our place, and we will not go
up to them. 10 But if they say, 'Come
up to us,' then we will go up; for the
LORD has given them into our hand.
And this shall be the sign to us." 11 So
both of them showed themselves to the
garrison of the Philistines; and the
Philistines said, "Look, Hebrews are
coming out of the holes where they
have hid themselves." 12 And the men
of the garrison hailed Jonathan and his
armor-bearer, and said, "Come up to
us, and we will show you a thing."
And Jonathan said to his armor-bearer,
"Come up after me; for the LORD has
given them into the hand of Israel."
13 Then Jonathan climbed up on his
hands and feet, and his armor-bearer
after him. And they fell before Jonathan, and his armor-bearer killed them
after him; 14 and that first slaughter,
which Jonathan and his armor-bearer
made, was of about twenty men within
as it were half a furrow's length in an
acre[r] of land. 15 And there was a
panic in the camp, in the field, and
among all the people; the garrison and
even the raiders trembled; the earth
quaked; and it became a very great
panic.

16 And the watchmen of Saul in
Gib′e-ah of Benjamin looked; and behold, the multitude was surging
hither and thither.[s] 17 Then Saul said
to the people who were with him,
"Number and see who has gone from
us." And when they had numbered, behold, Jonathan and his armor-bearer
were not there. 18 And Saul said to
Ahi′jah, "Bring hither the ark of God."
For the ark of God went at that time

o Heb *between the passes*
p Gk: Heb *Do all that is in your mind. Turn*
q Gk: Heb lacks *so is mine* *r* Heb *yoke*
s Gk: Heb *they went and thither*

---

the *pim* was two-thirds of a shekel. With v. 22 compare Jg.5.8. **14.1–5:** Jonathan again takes the lead in forcing the fighting. **3:** *Wearing an ephod,* translate "carrying an ephod," for this was not the *linen ephod* of 2.18, but a box containing Urim and Thummim, the sacred objects for determining the divine will by lot (v. 41; see Ex.28.30 n.). **6–15:** Jonathan's bravery leads to victory. *Uncircumcised* (v. 6) and *Hebrews* (v. 11) are used as uncomplimentary terms (see 4.6 n.). The Israelites, along with the other Semitic peoples to the east, such as the Amorites, Ammonites, Moabites, and Edomites, practiced circumcision (see Jer.9.25 n.). The non-Semitic Philistines, coming from the west (see 4.1b n.), had no such custom. **11:** *Hebrews,* see 4.6 n. **16–23:** Saul capitalizes on the advantage gained by Jonathan. **18:** Instead of *the ark of God,* the Greek version reads "the ephod" (compare ephod vv. 3,41). **19:** *Withdraw your hand,* the

with the people of Israel. [19] And while Saul was talking to the priest, the tumult in the camp of the Philistines increased more and more; and Saul said to the priest, "Withdraw your hand." [20] Then Saul and all the people who were with him rallied and went into the battle; and behold, every man's sword was against his fellow, and there was very great confusion. [21] Now the Hebrews who had been with the Philistines before that time and who had gone up with them into the camp, even they also turned to be with[t] the Israelites who were with Saul and Jonathan. [22] Likewise, when all the men of Israel who had hid themselves in the hill country of E'phraim heard that the Philistines were fleeing, they too followed hard after them in the battle. [23] So the LORD delivered Israel that day; and the battle passed beyond Beth-a'ven.

24 And the men of Israel were distressed that day; for Saul laid an oath on the people, saying, "Cursed be the man who eats food until it is evening and I am avenged on my enemies." So none of the people tasted food. [25] And all the people[u] came into the forest; and there was honey on the ground. [26] And when the people entered the forest, behold, the honey was dropping, but no man put his hand to his mouth; for the people feared the oath. [27] But Jonathan had not heard his father charge the people with the oath; so he put forth the tip of the staff that was in his hand, and dipped it in the honeycomb, and put his hand to his mouth; and his eyes became bright. [28] Then one of the people said, "Your father strictly charged the people with an oath, saying, 'Cursed be the man who eats food this day.'" And the people were faint. [29] Then Jonathan said, "My father has troubled the land; see how my eyes have become bright, because I tasted a little of this honey. [30] How much better if the people had eaten freely today of the spoil of their enemies which they found; for now the slaughter among the Philistines has not been great."

31 They struck down the Philistines that day from Michmash to Ai'jalon. And the people were very faint; [32] the people flew upon the spoil, and took sheep and oxen and calves, and slew them on the ground; and the people ate them with the blood. [33] Then they told Saul, "Behold, the people are sinning against the LORD, by eating with the blood." And he said, "You have dealt treacherously; roll a great stone to me here."[v] [34] And Saul said, "Disperse yourselves among the people, and say to them, 'Let every man bring his ox or his sheep, and slay them here, and eat; and do not sin against the LORD by eating with the blood.'" So every one of the people brought his ox with him that night, and slew them there. [35] And Saul built an altar to the LORD; it was the first altar that he built to the LORD.

36 Then Saul said, "Let us go down after the Philistines by night and despoil them until the morning light; let us not leave a man of them." And they said, "Do whatever seems good to you." But the priest said, "Let us draw near hither to God." [37] And Saul inquired of God, "Shall I go down after the Philistines? Wilt thou give them into the hand of Israel?" But he did not answer him that day. [38] And Saul said, "Come hither, all you leaders of the people; and know and see how this sin has arisen today. [39] For as the

---

t Gk Syr Vg Tg: Heb *round about, they also, to be with*
u Heb *land* *v* Gk: Heb *this day*

---

priest had begun the casting of the Urim and Thummim. **21:** *Hebrews* and *Israelites* are not necessarily identical peoples here. Perhaps we can say that not all Hebrews were Israelites, since the former was the broader term. **24–30:** Fasting was supposed to be pleasing to God. Saul hoped thus to further his cause, but he was remiss in not seeing that Jonathan was informed. **31–35:** Saul rather than the priests seems to have been in charge of the religious rites (contrast the attitude of the Late Source, 13.7b–15a). The law against partaking of the blood appears in Lev.19.26; Dt.12.16. **36–37:** Saul wanted to press his advantage, but the priest sensed that

LORD lives who saves Israel, though it be in Jonathan my son, he shall surely die." But there was not a man among all the people that answered him. ⁴⁰ Then he said to all Israel, "You shall be on one side, and I and Jonathan my son will be on the other side." And the people said to Saul, "Do what seems good to you." ⁴¹ Therefore Saul said, "O LORD God of Israel, why hast thou not answered thy servant this day? If this guilt is in me or in Jonathan my son, O LORD, God of Israel, give Urim; but if this guilt is in thy people Israel,ʷ give Thummim." And Jonathan and Saul were taken, but the people escaped. ⁴² Then Saul said, "Cast the lot between me and my son Jonathan." And Jonathan was taken.

43 Then Saul said to Jonathan, "Tell me what you have done." And Jonathan told him, "I tasted a little honey with the tip of the staff that was in my hand; here I am, I will die." ⁴⁴ And Saul said, "God do so to me and more also; you shall surely die, Jonathan." ⁴⁵ Then the people said to Saul, "Shall Jonathan die, who has wrought this great victory in Israel? Far from it! As the LORD lives, there shall not one hair of his head fall to the ground; for he has wrought with God this day." So the people ransomed Jonathan, that he did not die. ⁴⁶ Then Saul went up from pursuing the Philistines; and the Philistines went to their own place.

47 When Saul had taken the king-ship over Israel, he fought against all his enemies on every side, against Moab, against the Ammonites, against Edom, against the kings of Zobah, and against the Philistines; wherever he turned he put them to the worse. ⁴⁸ And he did valiantly, and smote the Amal'ekites, and delivered Israel out of the hands of those who plundered them.

49 Now the sons of Saul were Jonathan, Ishvi, and Mal'chishu'a; and the names of his two daughters were these: the name of the first-born was Merab, and the name of the younger Michal; ⁵⁰ and the name of Saul's wife was Ahin'o-am the daughter of Ahim'a-az. And the name of the commander of his army was Abner the son of Ner, Saul's uncle; ⁵¹ Kish was the father of Saul, and Ner the father of Abner was the son of Abi'el.

52 There was hard fighting against the Philistines all the days of Saul; and when Saul saw any strong man, or any valiant man, he attached him to himself.

15 And Samuel said to Saul, "The LORD sent me to anoint you king over his people Israel; now therefore hearken to the words of the LORD. ² Thus says the LORD of hosts, 'I will punish what Am'alek did to Israel in opposing them on the way, when they came up out of Egypt. ³ Now go and smite Am'alek, and utterly destroy all

ʷ Vg Compare Gk: Heb *Saul said to the* LORD, *the God of Israel*

something was wrong and suggested use of the sacred lots, *Urim* and *Thummim*. **43–46:** Presumably the ransom took the form of the substitution of an animal (Gen.22.13; Ex.13.13; 34.20). Verse 46 shows this point to be the end of a phase of the war. **47–48,49–51,52:** A series of three editorial notes, summarizing the public and private situation of Saul at this time. Observe how favorably Saul is presented, especially in the first note (vv. 47–48). Verse 52 prepares for the resumption of the Early Source at 16.14.

15.1–35: Another story of Saul's rejection. The Late Source. Compare this section with 13.7b–15a and contrast with the preceding section. Samuel, not Saul, is the leading figure once more. Though Saul is king, and wins a military victory, he is depicted as a moral and religious reprobate, unworthy of the position he holds. **2:** *Amalek* (or the Amalekites) is the name of a people traditionally descended from Esau (Gen.36.12). They were a wandering tribe from southern Canaan or northern Sinai which had been constantly troublesome to the Israelites (Dt. 25.17–19; Ex.17.7–13; Jg.6.33). **3:** This verse seems to pick up the curse recorded in Dt.25.19. *Utterly destroy* means "put under the ban" or "destroy in the name of religion" (Dt.20.16–18). Both the Israelites and their neighbors attempted at times this type of holy war, but usually without complete success. The *Amalekites* are still numerous and troublesome to David in

that they have; do not spare them, but kill both man and woman, infant and suckling, ox and sheep, camel and ass.'"

4 So Saul summoned the people, and numbered them in Tela'im, two hundred thousand men on foot, and ten thousand men of Judah. ⁵ And Saul came to the city of Am'alek, and lay in wait in the valley. ⁶ And Saul said to the Ken'ites, "Go, depart, go down from among the Amal'ekites, lest I destroy you with them; for you showed kindness to all the people of Israel when they came up out of Egypt." So the Ken'ites departed from among the Amal'ekites. ⁷ And Saul defeated the Amal'ekites, from Hav'ilah as far as Shur, which is east of Egypt. ⁸ And he took Agag the king of the Amal'-ekites alive, and utterly destroyed all the people with the edge of the sword. ⁹ But Saul and the people spared Agag, and the best of the sheep and of the oxen and of the fatlings, and the lambs, and all that was good, and would not utterly destroy them; all that was despised and worthless they utterly destroyed.

10 The word of the LORD came to Samuel: ¹¹ "I repent that I have made Saul king; for he has turned back from following me, and has not performed my commandments." And Samuel was angry; and he cried to the LORD all night. ¹² And Samuel rose early to meet Saul in the morning; and it was told Samuel, "Saul came to Carmel, and behold, he set up a monument for himself and turned, and passed on, and went down to Gilgal." ¹³ And Samuel came to Saul, and Saul said to him, "Blessed be you to the LORD; I have performed the commandment of the LORD." ¹⁴ And Samuel said, "What then is this bleating of the sheep in my ears, and the lowing of the oxen which I hear?" ¹⁵ Saul said, "They have brought them from the Amal'ekites; for the people spared the best of the sheep and of the oxen, to sacrifice to the LORD your God; and the rest we have utterly destroyed." ¹⁶ Then Samuel said to Saul, "Stop! I will tell you what the LORD said to me this night." And he said to him, "Say on."

17 And Samuel said, "Though you are little in your own eyes, are you not the head of the tribes of Israel? The LORD anointed you king over Israel. ¹⁸ And the LORD sent you on a mission, and said, 'Go, utterly destroy the sinners, the Amal'ekites, and fight against them until they are consumed.' ¹⁹ Why then did you not obey the voice of the LORD? Why did you swoop on the spoil, and do what was evil in the sight of the LORD?" ²⁰ And Saul said to Samuel, "I have obeyed the voice of the LORD, I have gone on the mission on which the LORD sent me, I have brought Agag the king of Am'-alek, and I have utterly destroyed the Amal'ekites. ²¹ But the people took of the spoil, sheep and oxen, the best of the things devoted to destruction, to sacrifice to the LORD your God in Gilgal." ²² And Samuel said,

"Has the LORD as great delight in
    burnt offerings and sacrifices,
    as in obeying the voice of the
        LORD?
Behold, to obey is better than
    sacrifice,
    and to hearken than the fat of
        rams.
²³ For rebellion is as the sin of
    divination,
    and stubbornness is as iniquity
        and idolatry.
Because you have rejected the word
    of the LORD,
    he has also rejected you from
        being king."
24 And Saul said to Samuel, "I have sinned; for I have transgressed the commandment of the LORD and your words, because I feared the people and

ch. 30. **4:** Exaggerated numbers are characteristic of many ancient documents. **5–7:** *The Kenites* were a clan partly with the Midianites and partly with the Amalekites. Moses' father-in-law seems to have belonged to this group (Jg.1.16; 4.11). The tradition of *kindness* referred to here appears in Num.10.29–32. **22:** *To obey is better than sacrifice;* compare Hos.6.6. **23:** On *the*

obeyed their voice. ²⁵ Now therefore, I pray, pardon my sin, and return with me, that I may worship the LORD." ²⁶ And Samuel said to Saul, "I will not return with you; for you have rejected the word of the LORD, and the LORD has rejected you from being king over Israel." ²⁷ As Samuel turned to go away, Saul laid hold upon the skirt of his robe, and it tore. ²⁸ And Samuel said to him, "The LORD has torn the kingdom of Israel from you this day, and has given it to a neighbor of yours, who is better than you. ²⁹ And also the Glory of Israel will not lie or repent; for he is not a man, that he should repent." ³⁰ Then he said, "I have sinned; yet honor me now before the elders of my people and before Israel, and return with me, that I may worship the LORD your God." ³¹ So Samuel turned back after Saul; and Saul worshiped the LORD.

32 Then Samuel said, "Bring here to me Agag the king of the Amal'-ekites." And Agag came to him cheerfully. Agag said, "Surely the bitterness of death is past." ³³ And Samuel said, "As your sword has made women childless, so shall your mother be childless among women." And Samuel hewed Agag in pieces before the LORD in Gilgal.

34 Then Samuel went to Ramah; and Saul went up to his house in Gib'e-ah of Saul. ³⁵ And Samuel did not see Saul again until the day of his death, but Samuel grieved over Saul. And the LORD repented that he had made Saul king over Israel.

16 The LORD said to Samuel, "How long will you grieve over Saul, seeing I have rejected him from being king over Israel? Fill your horn with oil, and go; I will send you to Jesse the Bethlehemite, for I have provided for myself a king among his sons." ² And Samuel said, "How can I go? If Saul hears it, he will kill me." And the LORD said, "Take a heifer with you, and say, 'I have come to sacrifice to the LORD.' ³ And invite Jesse to the sacrifice, and I will show you what you shall do; and you shall anoint for me him whom I name to you." ⁴ Samuel did what the LORD commanded, and came to Bethlehem. The elders of the city came to meet him trembling, and said, "Do you come peaceably?" ⁵ And he said, "Peaceably; I have come to sacrifice to the LORD; consecrate yourselves, and come with me to the sacrifice." And he consecrated Jesse and his sons, and invited them to the sacrifice.

6 When they came, he looked on Eli'ab and thought, "Surely the LORD's anointed is before him." ⁷ But the LORD said to Samuel, "Do not look on his appearance or on the height of his stature, because I have rejected him; for the LORD sees not as man sees; man looks on the outward appearance, but the LORD looks on the heart." ⁸ Then Jesse called Abin'adab, and made him pass before Samuel. And he said, "Neither has the LORD chosen this one." ⁹ Then Jesse made Shammah pass by. And he said, "Neither has the LORD chosen this one." ¹⁰ And Jesse made seven of his sons pass before Samuel. And Samuel said to Jesse, "The LORD has not chosen these." ¹¹ And Samuel said to Jesse, "Are all your sons here?" And he said, "There remains yet the youngest, but behold, he is keeping the sheep." And Samuel said to Jesse, "Send and fetch him; for we will not sit down till he

---

sin of divination see Dt.18.9–14. **28:** The *neighbor* is David. **35:** There is a slight discrepancy between this verse and 19.24, though both are sometimes assigned to the Late Source.

    16.1–13: Sequel to ch. 15–the anointing of David. This continuation of the Late Source may be a counterpart to the anointing of Saul (see 10.1 n.). The phrase *in the midst of his brothers* (v. 13) seems to be inconsistent with the attitude of the brothers in the next chapter (see 17.28), which is also usually assigned to the Late Source. It must be remembered, however, that not all modern writings are perfectly consistent with themselves. The Late Source is probably the product of a number of writers, all of whom had the same general point of view without attempting to be consistent in every detail. **5:** Consecration perhaps involved the ceremony of ritual

comes here." [12] And he sent, and brought him in. Now he was ruddy, and had beautiful eyes, and was handsome. And the LORD said, "Arise, anoint him; for this is he." [13] Then Samuel took the horn of oil, and anointed him in the midst of his brothers; and the Spirit of the LORD came mightily upon David from that day forward. And Samuel rose up, and went to Ramah.

14 Now the Spirit of the LORD departed from Saul, and an evil spirit from the LORD tormented him. [15] And Saul's servants said to him, "Behold now, an evil spirit from God is tormenting you. [16] Let our lord now command your servants, who are before you, to seek out a man who is skilful in playing the lyre; and when the evil spirit from God is upon you, he will play it, and you will be well." [17] So Saul said to his servants, "Provide for me a man who can play well, and bring him to me." [18] One of the young men answered, "Behold, I have seen a son of Jesse the Bethlehemite, who is skilful in playing, a man of valor, a man of war, prudent in speech, and a man of good presence; and the LORD is with him." [19] Therefore Saul sent messengers to Jesse, and said, "Send me David your son, who is with the sheep." [20] And Jesse took an ass laden with bread, and a skin of wine and a kid, and sent them by David his son to Saul. [21] And David came to Saul, and entered his service. And Saul loved him greatly, and he became his armor-bearer. [22] And Saul sent to Jesse, saying, "Let David remain in my service, for he has found favor in my sight." [23] And whenever the evil spirit from God was upon Saul, David took the lyre and played it with his hand; so Saul was refreshed, and was well, and the evil spirit departed from him.

17 Now the Philistines gathered their armies for battle; and they were gathered at Socoh, which belongs to Judah, and encamped between Socoh and Aze'kah, in E'phes-dam'mim. [2] And Saul and the men of Israel were gathered, and encamped in the valley of Elah, and drew up in line of battle against the Philistines. [3] And the Philistines stood on the mountain on the one side, and Israel stood on the mountain on the other side, with a valley between them. [4] And there came out from the camp of the Philistines a champion named Goliath, of Gath, whose height was six cubits and a span. [5] He had a helmet of bronze on his head, and he was armed with a coat of mail, and the weight of the coat was five thousand shekels of bronze. [6] And he had greaves of bronze upon his legs, and a javelin of bronze slung between his shoulders. [7] And the shaft of his spear was like a weaver's beam, and his spear's head weighed six hundred shekels of iron; and his shield-bearer went before him. [8] He stood and shouted to the ranks of Israel, "Why have you come out to draw up for battle? Am I not a Philistine, and are you

---

washing. **12:** The word *ruddy* (compare 17.42) is sometimes taken to mean that David was red-haired, but the reference is to his complexion (compare S. of S.5.10,11).

   16.14–23: David wins a position at the court of Saul. This is a story from the Early Source of how Saul became acquainted with David. It also marks the beginning of the story of Saul's sufferings from mental illness, attributed in ancient times to *an evil spirit* (v. 14; compare Lk. 11.24–26). **21–22:** Note the good relations between Saul and David.

   17.1–58: David kills Goliath. A problem arises because according to vv. 55–58 Saul does not know David (16.21–23). Some would put the whole chapter in the Late Source. Others point to 21.9 (Early Source) and attribute all of ch. 17 to the Early Source. Both sources may have had the story and parts of both may have been combined here. According to this solution, the Early Source, continuing 16.14–23, is found in 17.1–11,32–40,42–48a,49,51–54; the Late Source, continuing 16.1–13, is seen in 17.12–31,41,48b,50,55–58, continued by 18.1–5. **4:** According to 2 Sam.21.19, *Goliath of Gath* was slain at a later time by Elhanan, one of David's warriors. It may be supposed that this name became erroneously attached to David's victim, whose name was unknown (1 Chr.20.5). *Six cubits and a span*, about ten feet. **5:** *Five thousand*

not servants of Saul? Choose a man for yourselves, and let him come down to me. [9] If he is able to fight with me and kill me, then we will be your servants; but if I prevail against him and kill him, then you shall be our servants and serve us." [10] And the Philistine said, "I defy the ranks of Israel this day; give me a man, that we may fight together." [11] When Saul and all Israel heard these words of the Philistine, they were dismayed and greatly afraid.

12 Now David was the son of an Eph'rathite of Bethlehem in Judah, named Jesse, who had eight sons. In the days of Saul the man was already old and advanced in years.[x] [13] The three eldest sons of Jesse had followed Saul to the battle; and the names of his three sons who went to the battle were Eli'ab the first-born, and next to him Abin'adab, and the third Shammah. [14] David was the youngest; the three eldest followed Saul, [15] but David went back and forth from Saul to feed his father's sheep at Bethlehem. [16] For forty days the Philistine came forward and took his stand, morning and evening.

17 And Jesse said to David his son, "Take for your brothers an ephah of this parched grain, and these ten loaves, and carry them quickly to the camp to your brothers; [18] also take these ten cheeses to the commander of their thousand. See how your brothers fare, and bring some token from them."

19 Now Saul, and they, and all the men of Israel, were in the valley of Elah, fighting with the Philistines. [20] And David rose early in the morning, and left the sheep with a keeper, and took the provisions, and went, as Jesse had commanded him; and he came to the encampment as the host was going forth to the battle line, shouting the war cry. [21] And Israel and the Philistines drew up for battle, army against

army. [22] And David left the things in charge of the keeper of the baggage, and ran to the ranks, and went and greeted his brothers. [23] As he talked with them, behold, the champion, the Philistine of Gath, Goliath by name, came up out of the ranks of the Philistines, and spoke the same words as before. And David heard him.

24 All the men of Israel, when they saw the man, fled from him, and were much afraid. [25] And the men of Israel said, "Have you seen this man who has come up? Surely he has come up to defy Israel; and the man who kills him, the king will enrich with great riches, and will give him his daughter, and make his father's house free in Israel." [26] And David said to the men who stood by him, "What shall be done for the man who kills this Philistine, and takes away the reproach from Israel? For who is this uncircumcised Philistine, that he should defy the armies of the living God?" [27] And the people answered him in the same way, "So shall it be done to the man who kills him."

28 Now Eli'ab his eldest brother heard when he spoke to the men; and Eli'ab's anger was kindled against David, and he said, "Why have you come down? And with whom have you left those few sheep in the wilderness? I know your presumption, and the evil of your heart; for you have come down to see the battle." [29] And David said, "What have I done now? Was it not but a word?" [30] And he turned away from him toward another, and spoke in the same way; and the people answered him again as before.

31 When the words which David spoke were heard, they repeated them before Saul; and he sent for him. [32] And David said to Saul, "Let no man's heart fail because of him; your servant will go and fight with this Philis-

x Gk Syr: Heb *among men*

---

shekels, about one hundred and fifty lbs. **7**: *Six hundred shekels*, about nineteen lbs. **12**: The abrupt break in the narrative at this point probably marks insertion of material from the Late Source. **32–40**: These verses naturally continue v. 11. Saul knows David well, in conformity

tine." [33] And Saul said to David, "You are not able to go against this Philistine to fight with him; for you are but a youth, and he has been a man of war from his youth." [34] But David said to Saul, "Your servant used to keep sheep for his father; and when there came a lion, or a bear, and took a lamb from the flock, [35] I went after him and smote him and delivered it out of his mouth; and if he arose against me, I caught him by his beard, and smote him and killed him. [36] Your servant has killed both lions and bears; and this uncircumcised Philistine shall be like one of them, seeing he has defied the armies of the living God." [37] And David said, "The LORD who delivered me from the paw of the lion and from the paw of the bear, will deliver me from the hand of this Philistine." And Saul said to David, "Go, and the LORD be with you!" [38] Then Saul clothed David with his armor; he put a helmet of bronze on his head, and clothed him with a coat of mail. [39] And David girded his sword over his armor, and he tried in vain to go, for he was not used to them. Then David said to Saul, "I cannot go with these; for I am not used to them." And David put them off. [40] Then he took his staff in his hand, and chose five smooth stones from the brook, and put them in his shepherd's bag or wallet; his sling was in his hand, and he drew near to the Philistine.

41 And the Philistine came on and drew near to David, with his shield-bearer in front of him. [42] And when the Philistine looked, and saw David, he disdained him; for he was but a youth, ruddy and comely in appearance. [43] And the Philistine said to David, "Am I a dog, that you come to me with sticks?" And the Philistine cursed David by his gods. [44] The Philistine said to David, "Come to me, and I will give your flesh to the birds of the air and to the beasts of the field." [45] Then David said to the Philistine,

"You come to me with a sword and with a spear and with a javelin; but I come to you in the name of the LORD of hosts, the God of the armies of Israel, whom you have defied. [46] This day the LORD will deliver you into my hand, and I will strike you down, and cut off your head; and I will give the dead bodies of the host of the Philistines this day to the birds of the air and to the wild beasts of the earth; that all the earth may know that there is a God in Israel, [47] and that all this assembly may know that the LORD saves not with sword and spear; for the battle is the LORD's and he will give you into our hand."

48 When the Philistine arose and came and drew near to meet David, David ran quickly toward the battle line to meet the Philistine. [49] And David put his hand in his bag and took out a stone, and slung it, and struck the Philistine on his forehead; the stone sank into his forehead, and he fell on his face to the ground.

50 So David prevailed over the Philistine with a sling and with a stone, and struck the Philistine, and killed him; there was no sword in the hand of David. [51] Then David ran and stood over the Philistine, and took his sword and drew it out of its sheath, and killed him, and cut off his head with it. When the Philistines saw that their champion was dead, they fled. [52] And the men of Israel and Judah rose with a shout and pursued the Philistines as far as Gath[y] and the gates of Ekron, so that the wounded Philistines fell on the way from Sha-ara'im as far as Gath and Ekron. [53] And the Israelites came back from chasing the Philistines, and they plundered their camp. [54] And David took the head of the Philistine and brought it to Jerusalem; but he put his armor in his tent.

55 When Saul saw David go forth against the Philistine, he said to Abner,

y Gk: Heb *Gai*

with 16.14–23. **55–58**: Note how completely unknown David is to Saul, in contrast to vv. 32–40, but in entire consistency with 16.1–13.

the commander of the army, "Abner, whose son is this youth?" And Abner said, "As your soul lives, O king, I cannot tell." [56] And the king said, "Inquire whose son the stripling is." [57] And as David returned from the slaughter of the Philistine, Abner took him, and brought him before Saul with the head of the Philistine in his hand. [58] And Saul said to him, "Whose son are you, young man?" And David answered, "I am the son of your servant Jesse the Bethlehemite."

18 When he had finished speaking to Saul, the soul of Jonathan was knit to the soul of David, and Jonathan loved him as his own soul. [2] And Saul took him that day, and would not let him return to his father's house. [3] Then Jonathan made a covenant with David, because he loved him as his own soul. [4] And Jonathan stripped himself of the robe that was upon him, and gave it to David, and his armor, and even his sword and his bow and his girdle. [5] And David went out and was successful wherever Saul sent him; so that Saul set him over the men of war. And this was good in the sight of all the people and also in the sight of Saul's servants.

6 As they were coming home, when David returned from slaying the Philistine, the women came out of all the cities of Israel, singing and dancing, to meet King Saul, with timbrels, with songs of joy, and with instruments[z] of music. [7] And the women sang to one another as they made merry,

"Saul has slain his thousands,
and David his ten thousands."

[8] And Saul was very angry, and this saying displeased him; he said, "They have ascribed to David ten thousands, and to me they have ascribed thou-

sands; and what more can he have but the kingdom?" [9] And Saul eyed David from that day on.

10 And on the morrow an evil spirit from God rushed upon Saul, and he raved within his house, while David was playing the lyre, as he did day by day. Saul had his spear in his hand; [11] and Saul cast the spear, for he thought, "I will pin David to the wall." But David evaded him twice.

12 Saul was afraid of David, because the LORD was with him but had departed from Saul. [13] So Saul removed him from his presence, and made him a commander of a thousand; and he went out and came in before the people. [14] And David had success in all his undertakings; for the LORD was with him. [15] And when Saul saw that he had great success, he stood in awe of him. [16] But all Israel and Judah loved David; for he went out and came in before them.

17 Then Saul said to David, "Here is my elder daughter Merab; I will give her to you for a wife; only be valiant for me and fight the LORD's battles." For Saul thought, "Let not my hand be upon him, but let the hand of the Philistines be upon him." [18] And David said to Saul, "Who am I, and who are my kinsfolk, my father's family in Israel, that I should be son-in-law to the king?" [19] But at the time when Merab, Saul's daughter, should have been given to David, she was given to A'driel the Meho'lathite for a wife.

20 Now Saul's daughter Michal loved David; and they told Saul, and the thing pleased him. [21] Saul thought, "Let me give her to him, that she may be a snare for him, and that the hand of the Philistines may be against him."

z Or *triangles,* or *three-stringed instruments*

18.1–30: Saul becomes jealous of David. Sources: vv. 1–5, Late Source, a continuation of ch. 17; vv. 6–9, probably Early Source; vv. 10–11, Late Source or editorial anticipation of 19.8–10; vv. 12–16, could be Early Source, except for the words *Because the LORD was with him but had departed from Saul;* vv. 17–19, probably Late Source; vv. 20–29, Early Source (omitting *a second time* in v. 21); v. 30, editorial. **1–3:** A deep friendship arose between David and Jonathan. **6–9:** Saul's first anger at David. **10–11:** This incident seems to come too soon here. **17–19:** This incident of *Merab* is lacking in some Greek texts. **25:** The *marriage present* is regarded by some as a gift to the bride's family, by others as a "price" paid for the bride.

Therefore Saul said to David a second time,[a] "You shall now be my son-in-law." [22] And Saul commanded his servants, "Speak to David in private and say, 'Behold, the king has delight in you, and all his servants love you; now then become the king's son-in-law.' " [23] And Saul's servants spoke those words in the ears of David. And David said, "Does it seem to you a little thing to become the king's son-in-law, seeing that I am a poor man and of no repute?" [24] And the servants of Saul told him, "Thus and so did David speak." [25] Then Saul said, "Thus shall you say to David, 'The king desires no marriage present except a hundred foreskins of the Philistines, that he may be avenged of the king's enemies.' " Now Saul thought to make David fall by the hand of the Philistines. [26] And when his servants told David these words, it pleased David well to be the king's son-in-law. Before the time had expired, [27] David arose and went, along with his men, and killed two hundred of the Philistines; and David brought their foreskins, which were given in full number to the king, that he might become the king's son-in-law. And Saul gave him his daughter Michal for a wife. [28] But when Saul saw and knew that the LORD was with David, and that all Israel[b] loved him, [29] Saul was still more afraid of David. So Saul was David's enemy continually.

[30] Then the princes of the Philistines came out to battle, and as often as they came out David had more success than all the servants of Saul; so that his name was highly esteemed.

19 And Saul spoke to Jonathan his son and to all his servants, that they should kill David. But Jonathan, Saul's son, delighted much in David. [2] And Jonathan told David, "Saul my father seeks to kill you; therefore take heed to yourself in the morning, stay in a secret place and hide yourself; [3] and I will go out and stand beside my father in the field where you are, and I will speak to my father about you; and if I learn anything I will tell you." [4] And Jonathan spoke well of David to Saul his father, and said to him, "Let not the king sin against his servant David; because he has not sinned against you, and because his deeds have been of good service to you; [5] for he took his life in his hand and he slew the Philistine, and the LORD wrought a great victory for all Israel. You saw it, and rejoiced; why then will you sin against innocent blood by killing David without cause?" [6] And Saul hearkened to the voice of Jonathan; Saul swore, "As the LORD lives, he shall not be put to death." [7] And Jonathan called David, and Jonathan showed him all these things. And Jonathan brought David to Saul, and he was in his presence as before.

8 And there was war again; and David went out and fought with the Philistines, and made a great slaughter among them, so that they fled before him. [9] Then an evil spirit from the LORD came upon Saul, as he sat in his house with his spear in his hand; and David was playing the lyre. [10] And Saul sought to pin David to the wall with the spear; but he eluded Saul, so that he struck the spear into the wall. And David fled, and escaped.

11 That night Saul[x] sent messengers to David's house to watch him, that he might kill him in the morning. But Michal, David's wife, told him, "If you do not save your life tonight, tomorrow you will be killed." [12] So Michal let David down through the window; and he fled away and

a Heb *by two*
b Gk: Heb *Michal, Saul's daughter*
x Gk Old Latin: Heb *escaped that night.* [11]*And Saul*

Probably the custom combined both elements. **27:** Only one hundred *foreskins* were required (v. 25); this story is to show David's superior prowess.

19.1–10: Saul seeks David's life. Late Source. **6–7:** Jonathan succeeds in restraining his father temporarily. **8–10:** Compare 18.10–11. The incident is in place here.

19.11–17: David forced to flee. Early Source. This incident follows naturally upon the marriage in 18.20–29. David seems to be unaware of the danger (compare the preceding vv. in the

escaped. ¹³ Michal took an image*ᶜ* and laid it on the bed and put a pillow*ᵈ* of goats' hair at its head, and covered it with the clothes. ¹⁴ And when Saul sent messengers to take David, she said, "He is sick." ¹⁵ Then Saul sent the messengers to see David, saying, "Bring him up to me in the bed, that I may kill him." ¹⁶ And when the messengers came in, behold, the image*ᶜ* was in the bed, with the pillow*ᵈ* of goats' hair at its head. ¹⁷ Saul said to Michal, "Why have you deceived me thus, and let my enemy go, so that he has escaped?" And Michal answered Saul, "He said to me, 'Let me go; why should I kill you?' "

18 Now David fled and escaped, and he came to Samuel at Ramah, and told him all that Saul had done to him. And he and Samuel went and dwelt at Nai'oth. ¹⁹ And it was told Saul, "Behold, David is at Nai'oth in Ramah." ²⁰ Then Saul sent messengers to take David; and when they saw the company of the prophets prophesying, and Samuel standing as head over them, the Spirit of God came upon the messengers of Saul, and they also prophesied. ²¹ When it was told Saul, he sent other messengers, and they also prophesied. And Saul sent messengers again the third time, and they also prophesied. ²² Then he himself went to Ramah, and came to the great well that is in Secu; and he asked, "Where are Samuel and David?" And one said, "Behold, they are at Nai'oth in Ramah." ²³ And he went from*ᶠ* there to Nai'oth in Ramah; and

the Spirit of God came upon him also, and as he went he prophesied, until he came to Nai'oth in Ramah. ²⁴ And he too stripped off his clothes, and he too prophesied before Samuel, and lay naked all that day and all that night. Hence it is said, "Is Saul also among the prophets?"

20 Then David fled from Nai'oth in Ramah, and came and said before Jonathan, "What have I done? What is my guilt? And what is my sin before your father, that he seeks my life?" ² And he said to him, "Far from it! You shall not die. Behold, my father does nothing either great or small without disclosing it to me; and why should my father hide this from me? It is not so." ³ But David replied,*ᵍ* "Your father knows well that I have found favor in your eyes; and he thinks, 'Let not Jonathan know this, lest he be grieved.' But truly, as the LORD lives and as your soul lives, there is but a step between me and death." ⁴ Then said Jonathan to David, "Whatever you say, I will do for you." ⁵ David said to Jonathan, "Behold, tomorrow is the new moon, and I should not fail to sit at table with the king; but let me go, that I may hide myself in the field till the third day at evening. ⁶ If your father misses me at all, then say, 'David earnestly asked leave of me to run to Bethlehem his city; for there is a yearly sacrifice there for all the family.' ⁷ If he says, 'Good!' it will be well with your servant; but if he is

c Heb *teraphim*
d The meaning of the Hebrew word is uncertain
f Gk: Heb lacks *from*   *g* Gk: Heb *swore again*

Late Source) until Michal tells him. **13:** *Image*, see Gen.31.19 n.; Jg.17.5. The nature of the *image* and *pillow* here is obscure.

19.18–24: Saul's ecstatic behavior. Probably an independent story belonging to neither of our sources. The Early Source has its own version of this matter (10.10–12), and the Late Source says that Samuel never saw Saul again (15.35). The nature of this *prophesying* (v. 20) as ecstatic dancing or whirling must be kept in mind (see 10.6 n.). The names *Secu* and *Naioth in Ramah* (v. 22) seem to indicate locations within the town of Ramah.

20.1–42: An independent tradition of the break between Saul and David, incompatible with all three sections of ch. 19. David is represented as still a member of the king's household and Jonathan seems unaware of Saul's hatred of David. The break between Saul and David was so significant that many different stories about it were told. **1:** The first part of this verse is an editorial attempt to join it to ch. 19. Actually, according to what follows, David had not yet left the court of Saul. **5:** *The new moon* was a festival day, when all members of the household

angry, then know that evil is determined by him. [8] Therefore deal kindly with your servant, for you have brought your servant into a sacred covenant[h] with you. But if there is guilt in me, slay me yourself; for why should you bring me to your father?" [9] And Jonathan said, "Far be it from you! If I knew that it was determined by my father that evil should come upon you, would I not tell you?" [10] Then said David to Jonathan, "Who will tell me if your father answers you roughly?" [11] And Jonathan said to David, "Come, let us go out into the field." So they both went out into the field.

[12] And Jonathan said to David, "The LORD, the God of Israel, be witness![i] When I have sounded my father, about this time tomorrow, or the third day, behold, if he is well disposed toward David, shall I not then send and disclose it to you? [13] But should it please my father to do you harm, the LORD do so to Jonathan, and more also, if I do not disclose it to you, and send you away, that you may go in safety. May the LORD be with you, as he has been with my father. [14] If I am still alive, show me the loyal love of the LORD, that I may not die;[j] [15] and do not cut off your loyalty from my house for ever. When the LORD cuts off every one of the enemies of David from the face of the earth, [16] let not the name of Jonathan be cut off from the house of David.[k] And may the LORD take vengeance on David's enemies." [17] And Jonathan made David swear again by his love for him; for he loved him as he loved his own soul.

[18] Then Jonathan said to him, "Tomorrow is the new moon; and you will be missed, because your seat will be empty. [19] And on the third day you will be greatly missed;[l] then go to the place where you hid yourself when the matter was in hand, and remain beside yonder stone heap.[m] [20] And I will shoot three arrows to the side of it, as though I shot at a mark. [21] And behold, I will send the lad, saying, 'Go, find the arrows.' If I say to the lad, 'Look, the arrows are on this side of you, take them,' then you are to come, for, as the LORD lives, it is safe for you and there is no danger. [22] But if I say to the youth, 'Look, the arrows are beyond you,' then go; for the LORD has sent you away. [23] And as for the matter of which you and I have spoken, behold, the LORD is between you and me for ever."

[24] So David hid himself in the field; and when the new moon came, the king sat down to eat food. [25] The king sat upon his seat, as at other times, upon the seat by the wall; Jonathan sat opposite,[n] and Abner sat by Saul's side, but David's place was empty.

[26] Yet Saul did not say anything that day; for he thought, "Something has befallen him; he is not clean, surely he is not clean." [27] But on the second day, the morrow after the new moon, David's place was empty. And Saul said to Jonathan his son, "Why has not the son of Jesse come to the meal, either yesterday or today?" [28] Jonathan answered Saul, "David earnestly asked leave of me to go to Bethlehem; [29] he said, 'Let me go; for our family holds a sacrifice in the city, and my brother has commanded me to be there. So now, if I have found favor in your eyes, let me get away, and see my brothers.' For this reason he has not come to the king's table."

[30] Then Saul's anger was kindled against Jonathan, and he said to him, "You son of a perverse, rebellious woman, do I not know that you have

h Heb *a covenant of the* LORD
i Heb lacks *be witness*   j Heb uncertain
k Gk: Heb *earth, and Jonathan made a covenant with the house of David*   l Gk: Heb *go down quickly*
m Gk: Heb *the stone Ezel*
n Cn See Gk: Heb *stood up*

---

were supposed to eat together. **8:** *Sacred covenant* is a reference to the deep friendship of David and Jonathan. **17:** *His own soul*, meaning "his own life" or "himself." **26:** Some mishap could have caused temporary ritual uncleanness. **30:** A popular form of cursing was then, and is now, to berate a person's mother; hence the words *your mother's nakedness*, as though she

chosen the son of Jesse to your own shame, and to the shame of your mother's nakedness? [31] For as long as the son of Jesse lives upon the earth, neither you nor your kingdom shall be established. Therefore send and fetch him to me, for he shall surely die." [32] Then Jonathan answered Saul his father, "Why should he be put to death? What has he done?" [33] But Saul cast his spear at him to smite him; so Jonathan knew that his father was determined to put David to death. [34] And Jonathan rose from the table in fierce anger and ate no food the second day of the month, for he was grieved for David, because his father had disgraced him.

35 In the morning Jonathan went out into the field to the appointment with David, and with him a little lad. [36] And he said to his lad, "Run and find the arrows which I shoot." As the lad ran, he shot an arrow beyond him. [37] And when the lad came to the place of the arrow which Jonathan had shot, Jonathan called after the lad and said, "Is not the arrow beyond you?" [38] And Jonathan called after the lad, "Hurry, make haste, stay not." So Jonathan's lad gathered up the arrows, and came to his master. [39] But the lad knew nothing; only Jonathan and David knew the matter. [40] And Jonathan gave his weapons to his lad, and said to him, "Go and carry them to the city." [41] And as soon as the lad had gone, David rose from beside the stone heap*o* and fell on his face to the ground, and bowed three times; and they kissed one another, and wept with one another, until David recovered himself.*p* [42] Then Jonathan said to David, "Go in peace, forasmuch as we have sworn both of us in the name of the Lord, saying, 'The Lord shall be between me and you, and between my descendants and your descendants, for ever.'" And he rose and departed; and Jonathan went into the city.*q*

21 *r* Then came David to Nob to Ahim'elech the priest; and Ahim'elech came to meet David trembling, and said to him, "Why are you alone, and no one with you?" [2] And David said to Ahim'elech the priest, "The king has charged me with a matter, and said to me, 'Let no one know anything of the matter about which I send you, and with which I have charged you.' I have made an appointment with the young men for such and such a place. [3] Now then, what have you at hand? Give me five loaves of bread, or whatever is here." [4] And the priest answered David, "I have no common bread at hand, but there is holy bread; if only the young men have kept themselves from women." [5] And David answered the priest, "Of a truth women have been kept from us as always when I go on an expedition; the vessels of the young men are holy, even when it is a common journey; how much more today will their vessels be holy?" [6] So the priest gave him the holy bread; for there was no bread there but the bread of the Presence, which is removed from before the Lord, to be replaced by hot bread on the day it is taken away.

7 Now a certain man of the servants of Saul was there that day, detained before the Lord; his name was Do'eg the E'domite, the chief of Saul's herdsmen.

8 And David said to Ahim'elech,

o Gk: Heb *from beside the south*   *p* Or *exceeded*
q This sentence is 21.1 in Heb   *r* Ch 21.2 in Heb

---

were a prostitute or something of that sort. **33:** Compare the similar treatment of David, 18.11 and 19.10.

21.1–9: David escapes to Nob. Early Source. This incident follows directly upon 19.11–17, David's flight with the help of Michal. Note that he is *alone* (v. 1), that he avoids telling the real reason for his coming in that fashion, and claims to have a retinue (*the young men*) nearby (v. 2). **6:** On *the holy bread* or *the bread of the Presence* in later tradition, see Lev.24.5–9; on the use of this passage in the New Testament, see Mk.2.23–28. **7:** *Doeg* appears later as David's betrayer (22.9). He was *detained* to perform some sort of religious ceremony. **8:** David was not

"And have you not here a spear or a sword at hand? For I have brought neither my sword nor my weapons with me, because the king's business required haste." ⁹ And the priest said, "The sword of Goliath the Philistine, whom you killed in the valley of Elah, behold, it is here wrapped in a cloth behind the ephod; if you will take that, take it, for there is none but that here." And David said, "There is none like that; give it to me."

10 And David rose and fled that day from Saul, and went to A′chish the king of Gath. ¹¹ And the servants of A′chish said to him, "Is not this David the king of the land? Did they not sing to one another of him in dances,

'Saul has slain his thousands,
and David his ten thousands'?"

¹² And David took these words to heart, and was much afraid of A′chish the king of Gath. ¹³ So he changed his behavior before them, and feigned himself mad in their hands, and made marks on the doors of the gate, and let his spittle run down his beard. ¹⁴ Then said A′chish to his servants, "Lo, you see the man is mad; why then have you brought him to me? ¹⁵ Do I lack madmen, that you have brought this fellow to play the madman in my presence? Shall this fellow come into my house?"

22 David departed from there and escaped to the cave of Adullam; and when his brothers and all his father's house heard it, they went down there to him. ² And every one who was in distress, and every one who was in debt, and every one who was discontented, gathered to him; and he became captain over them. And there

were with him about four hundred men.

3 And David went from there to Mizpeh of Moab; and he said to the king of Moab, "Pray let my father and my mother stay*ˢ* with you, till I know what God will do for me." ⁴ And he left them with the king of Moab, and they stayed with him all the time that David was in the stronghold. ⁵ Then the prophet Gad said to David, "Do not remain in the stronghold; depart, and go into the land of Judah." So David departed, and went into the forest of Hereth.

6 Now Saul heard that David was discovered, and the men who were with him. Saul was sitting at Gib′e-ah, under the tamarisk tree on the height, with his spear in his hand, and all his servants were standing about him. ⁷ And Saul said to his servants who stood about him, "Hear now, you Benjaminites; will the son of Jesse give every one of you fields and vineyards, will he make you all commanders of thousands and commanders of hundreds, ⁸ that all of you have conspired against me? No one discloses to me when my son makes a league with the son of Jesse, none of you is sorry for me or discloses to me that my son has stirred up my servant against me, to lie in wait, as at this day." ⁹ Then answered Do′eg the E′domite, who stood by the servants of Saul, "I saw the son of Jesse coming to Nob, to Ahim′elech the son of Ahi′tub, ¹⁰ and he inquired of the Lᴏʀᴅ for him, and gave him provisions, and gave him the sword of Goliath the Philistine."

11 Then the king sent to summon

ˢ Syr Vg: Heb *come out*

only alone, but unarmed, a fact testifying to the hastiness of his flight (contrast the story of more leisurely departure in ch. 20). **9**: *The ephod* is here a box, not a linen apron (see 14.3 n.).
21.10-15: David flees to Gath. Late Source. The Early Source's version of this episode is found in ch. 27. **11**: The purpose of this version of the story may have been to show that David and Achish had nothing to do with one another, in contrast to ch. 27, where they get along very well.
22.1-23: David at Adullam; massacre of the priests of Nob. Early Source. **1**: *Adullam* was a place southwest of Bethlehem, in David's home territory, so to speak. **2**: David collects a retinue of malcontents from his native Judah. **3-5**: The locations of *Mizpeh of Moab* and *Hereth* are unknown. On *the prophet Gad* see 2 Sam.24.12. **9**: *Doeg the Edomite*, a foreigner who

Ahim'elech the priest, the son of Ahi'-tub, and all his father's house, the priests who were at Nob; and all of them came to the king. 12 And Saul said, "Hear now, son of Ahi'tub." And he answered, "Here I am, my lord." 13 And Saul said to him, "Why have you conspired against me, you and the son of Jesse, in that you have given him bread and a sword, and have inquired of God for him, so that he has risen against me, to lie in wait, as at this day?" 14 Then Ahim'elech answered the king, "And who among all your servants is so faithful as David, who is the king's son-in-law, and captain over' your bodyguard, and honored in your house? 15 Is today the first time that I have inquired of God for him? No! Let not the king impute anything to his servant or to all the house of my father; for your servant has known nothing of all this, much or little." 16 And the king said, "You shall surely die, Ahim'elech, you and all your father's house." 17 And the king said to the guard who stood about him, "Turn and kill the priests of the LORD; because their hand also is with David, and they knew that he fled, and did not disclose it to me." But the servants of the king would not put forth their hand to fall upon the priests of the LORD. 18 Then the king said to Do'eg, "You turn and fall upon the priests." And Do'eg the E'domite turned and fell upon the priests, and he killed on that day eighty-five persons who wore the linen ephod. 19 And Nob, the city of the priests, he put to the sword; both men and women,

children and sucklings, oxen, asses and sheep, he put to the sword.

20 But one of the sons of Ahim'-elech the son of Ahi'tub, named Abi'-athar, escaped and fled after David. 21 And Abi'athar told David that Saul had killed the priests of the LORD. 22 And David said to Abi'athar, "I knew on that day, when Do'eg the E'domite was there, that he would surely tell Saul. I have occasioned the death of all the persons of your father's house. 23 Stay with me, fear not; for he that seeks my life seeks your life; with me you shall be in safekeeping."

23 Now they told David, "Behold, the Philistines are fighting against Kei'lah, and are robbing the threshing floors." 2 Therefore David inquired of the LORD, "Shall I go and attack these Philistines?" And the LORD said to David, "Go and attack the Philistines and save Kei'lah." 3 But David's men said to him, "Behold, we are afraid here in Judah; how much more then if we go to Kei'lah against the armies of the Philistines?" 4 Then David inquired of the LORD again. And the LORD answered him, "Arise, go down to Kei'lah; for I will give the Philistines into your hand." 5 And David and his men went to Kei'lah, and fought with the Philistines, and brought away their cattle, and made a great slaughter among them. So David delivered the inhabitants of Kei'lah.

6 When Abi'athar the son of Ahim'-elech fled to David to Kei'lah, he came down with an ephod in his hand. 7 Now

t Gk Tg: Heb *and has turned aside to*

had attached himself to Saul and held a good position under him (21.7). **17:** The soldiers of Saul refused to commit this atrocious deed against their fellow Israelites, and Saul did not have the authority to compel them. **18:** *Doeg*, the foreigner, with loyalty to Saul but none to the Israelites, willingly did the deed. *Linen ephod*, see 2.18 n. **19:** See 15.3 n. Compare Jos. ch. 7. **20–23:** *Abiathar* was to play a very important part in the subsequent history of David. Some have even supposed that he is the author of the Early Source, writing of himself objectively in the third person (see Introduction).

23.1–13: David's relief of Keilah. Early Source. **1:** *Keilah* was a few miles south of Adullam (22.1). **3:** From this verse it is clear that *Keilah* belonged neither to *Judah* nor to *the Philistines* at that time. **6:** This verse is probably an annotation originally made in the margin of the manuscript. It fits better just before v. 4. The *ephod* here is the box containing the sacred lots, as in 21.9 (see 14.3 n.); compare vv. 9–10.

it was told Saul that David had come to Kei'lah. And Saul said, "God has given him into my hand; for he has shut himself in by entering a town that has gates and bars." [8] And Saul summoned all the people to war, to go down to Kei'lah, to besiege David and his men. [9] David knew that Saul was plotting evil against him; and he said to Abi'athar the priest, "Bring the ephod here." [10] Then said David, "O Lord, the God of Israel, thy servant has surely heard that Saul seeks to come to Kei'lah, to destroy the city on my account. [11] Will the men of Kei'lah surrender me into his hand? Will Saul come down, as thy servant has heard? O Lord, the God of Israel, I beseech thee, tell thy servant." And the Lord said, "He will come down." [12] Then said David, "Will the men of Kei'lah surrender me and my men into the hand of Saul?" And the Lord said, "They will surrender you." [13] Then David and his men, who were about six hundred, arose and departed from Kei'lah, and they went wherever they could go. When Saul was told that David had escaped from Kei'lah, he gave up the expedition. [14] And David remained in the strongholds in the wilderness, in the hill country of the Wilderness of Ziph. And Saul sought him every day, but God did not give him into his hand.

15 And David was afraid because[u] Saul had come out to seek his life. David was in the Wilderness of Ziph at Horesh. [16] And Jonathan, Saul's son, rose, and went to David at Horesh, and strengthened his hand in God. [17] And he said to him, "Fear not; for the hand of Saul my father shall not find you; you shall be king over Israel, and I shall be next to you; Saul my

father also knows this." [18] And the two of them made a covenant before the Lord; David remained at Horesh, and Jonathan went home.

19 Then the Ziphites went up to Saul at Gib'e-ah, saying, "Does not David hide among us in the strongholds at Horesh, on the hill of Hachi'-lah, which is south of Jeshi'mon? [20] Now come down, O king, according to all your heart's desire to come down; and our part shall be to surrender him into the king's hand." [21] And Saul said, "May you be blessed by the Lord; for you have had compassion on me. [22] Go, make yet more sure; know and see the place where his haunt is, and who has seen him there; for it is told me that he is very cunning. [23] See therefore, and take note of all the lurking places where he hides, and come back to me with sure information. Then I will go with you; and if he is in the land, I will search him out among all the thousands of Judah." [24] And they arose, and went to Ziph ahead of Saul.

Now David and his men were in the wilderness of Ma'on, in the Arabah to the south of Jeshi'mon. [25] And Saul and his men went to seek him. And David was told; therefore he went down to the rock which is[v] in the wilderness of Ma'on. And when Saul heard that, he pursued after David in the wilderness of Ma'on. [26] Saul went on one side of the mountain, and David and his men on the other side of the mountain; and David was making haste to get away from Saul, as Saul and his men were closing in upon David and his men to capture them, [27] when a messenger came to Saul, saying, "Make haste and come; for the Philis-

u Or *saw that*   *v* Gk: Heb *and dwelt*

23.14–24.22: David spares Saul's life. Late Source. The Early Source's version of this incident is found in ch. 26. The present passage marks the conclusion of the Late Source, except for the death of Samuel, briefly noted in 25.1 and 28.3. **14:** *Ziph* was a rocky area south of Hebron. *Every day,* in this context means "all the time" or "constantly." **19:** The names *Hachilah* and *Jeshimon,* which mean "dark" and "desolate" respectively, suggest good places for hiding. **24:** *Maon* was a little *south* of Ziph, Hachilah, and *Jeshimon* (compare Jos.15.55). *Arabah* here simply means "desert," not the depression north and south of the Dead Sea. **27–29:** In the Early Source (ch. 26) there is no interruption by *the Philistines,* nor does the scene shift to

tines have made a raid upon the land." ²⁸ So Saul returned from pursuing after David, and went against the Philistines; therefore that place was called the Rock of Escape. ^{29w} And David went up from there, and dwelt in the strongholds of En-ge′di.

24 When Saul returned from following the Philistines, he was told, "Behold, David is in the wilderness of En-ge′di." ² Then Saul took three thousand chosen men out of all Israel, and went to seek David and his men in front of the Wildgoats' Rocks. ³ And he came to the sheepfolds by the way, where there was a cave; and Saul went in to relieve himself. Now David and his men were sitting in the innermost parts of the cave. ⁴ And the men of David said to him, "Here is the day of which the LORD said to you, 'Behold, I will give your enemy into your hand, and you shall do to him as it shall seem good to you.'" Then David arose and stealthily cut off the skirt of Saul's robe. ⁵ And afterward David's heart smote him, because he had cut off Saul's skirt. ⁶ He said to his men, "The LORD forbid that I should do this thing to my lord, the LORD's anointed, to put forth my hand against him, seeing he is the LORD's anointed." ⁷ So David persuaded his men with these words, and did not permit them to attack Saul. And Saul rose up and left the cave, and went upon his way.

⁸ Afterward David also arose, and went out of the cave, and called after Saul, "My lord the king!" And when Saul looked behind him, David bowed with his face to the earth, and did obeisance. ⁹ And David said to Saul, "Why do you listen to the words of men who say, 'Behold, David seeks your hurt'? ¹⁰ Lo, this day your eyes

have seen how the LORD gave you today into my hand in the cave; and some bade me kill you, but I^x spared you. I said, 'I will not put forth my hand against my lord; for he is the LORD's anointed.' ¹¹ See, my father, see the skirt of your robe in my hand; for by the fact that I cut off the skirt of your robe, and did not kill you, you may know and see that there is no wrong or treason in my hands. I have not sinned against you, though you hunt my life to take it. ¹² May the LORD judge between me and you, may the LORD avenge me upon you; but my hand shall not be against you. ¹³ As the proverb of the ancients says, 'Out of the wicked comes forth wickedness'; but my hand shall not be against you. ¹⁴ After whom has the king of Israel come out? After whom do you pursue? After a dead dog! After a flea! ¹⁵ May the LORD therefore be judge, and give sentence between me and you, and see to it, and plead my cause, and deliver me from your hand."

16 When David had finished speaking these words to Saul, Saul said, "Is this your voice, my son David?" And Saul lifted up his voice and wept. ¹⁷ He said to David, "You are more righteous than I; for you have repaid me good, whereas I have repaid you evil. ¹⁸ And you have declared this day how you have dealt well with me, in that you did not kill me when the LORD put me into your hands. ¹⁹ For if a man finds his enemy, will he let him go away safe? So may the LORD reward you with good for what you have done to me this day. ²⁰ And now, behold, I know that you shall surely be king, and that the kingdom of Israel shall be established in your hand. ²¹ Swear to me therefore by the LORD

w Ch 24.1 in Heb   *x* Gk Syr Tg: Heb *you*

En-gedi, on the west shore of the Dead Sea. **24.2:** *Wildgoats' Rocks* is most descriptive of the character of the terrain. **4b–5:** *Then David arose . . .* ; this belongs after v. 7a, *. . . to attack Saul.* **14:** Dogs were held in low esteem in those days; *a dead dog* would be less than nothing (2 Sam.9.8; 16.9). **20–21:** The Late Source comes to a close with Saul practically in tears, handing the kingdom to David (compare what Jonathan says in 23.17). In the Early Source (26.22) nothing is said about David's becoming king, a question that did not arise until after the death of Saul.

that you will not cut off my descendants after me, and that you will not destroy my name out of my father's house." ²² And David swore this to Saul. Then Saul went home; but David and his men went up to the stronghold.

25 Now Samuel died; and all Israel assembled and mourned for him, and they buried him in his house at Ramah.

Then David rose and went down to the wilderness of Paran. ² And there was a man in Ma'on, whose business was in Carmel. The man was very rich; he had three thousand sheep and a thousand goats. He was shearing his sheep in Carmel. ³ Now the name of the man was Nabal, and the name of his wife Ab'igail. The woman was of good understanding and beautiful, but the man was churlish and ill-behaved; he was a Calebite. ⁴ David heard in the wilderness that Nabal was shearing his sheep. ⁵ So David sent ten young men; and David said to the young men, "Go up to Carmel, and go to Nabal, and greet him in my name. ⁶ And thus you shall salute him: 'Peace be to you, and peace be to your house, and peace be to all that you have. ⁷ I hear that you have shearers; now your shepherds have been with us, and we did them no harm, and they missed nothing, all the time they were in Carmel. ⁸ Ask your young men, and they will tell you. Therefore let my young men find favor in your eyes; for we come on a feast day. Pray, give whatever you have at hand to your servants and to your son David.' "

9 When David's young men came, they said all this to Nabal in the name of David; and then they waited. ¹⁰ And Nabal answered David's servants, "Who is David? Who is the son of Jesse? There are many servants nowadays who are breaking away from their masters. ¹¹ Shall I take my bread and my water and my meat that I have killed for my shearers, and give it to men who come from I do not know where?" ¹² So David's young men turned away, and came back and told him all this. ¹³ And David said to his men, "Every man gird on his sword!" And every man of them girded on his sword; David also girded on his sword; and about four hundred men went up after David, while two hundred remained with the baggage.

14 But one of the young men told Ab'igail, Nabal's wife, "Behold, David sent messengers out of the wilderness to salute our master; and he railed at them. ¹⁵ Yet the men were very good to us, and we suffered no harm, and we did not miss anything when we were in the fields, as long as we went with them; ¹⁶ they were a wall to us both by night and by day, all the while we were with them keeping the sheep. ¹⁷ Now therefore know this and consider what you should do; for evil is determined against our master and against all his house, and he is so ill-natured that one cannot speak to him."

18 Then Ab'igail made haste, and took two hundred loaves, and two skins of wine, and five sheep ready dressed, and five measures of parched grain, and a hundred clusters of raisins, and two hundred cakes of figs, and laid them on asses. ¹⁹ And she said to her young men, "Go on before me; behold, I come after you." But she did not tell

---

25.1a: The death of Samuel. The notation of an editor, or the conclusion of the Late Source; repeated in 28.3a. The brevity of the obituary is surprising.

25.1b–44: David, Nabal, and Abigail. Early Source. The story of how David obtained his second wife. **1b:** *The wilderness of Paran* is so far to the south that it could hardly have had any connection with the movements of David at this time; the Greek version reads "the wilderness of Maon," and some modern translations follow this reading. **2:** This *Carmel* lay between Ziph and Maon (see 23.14 n. and 24 n.); it must not be confused with the famous Mount Carmel to the north near the seacoast. **3:** The *Calebite* clan had not yet been absorbed by the tribes of Judah (Jos.15.13–19; Jg.1.12–15). **11:** *Water*, the Greek version reads "wine," no doubt correctly (compare vv. 18 and 36). **16:** David and his men were outlaws, but of the

her husband Nabal. [20] And as she rode on the ass, and came down under cover of the mountain, behold, David and his men came down toward her; and she met them. [21] Now David had said, "Surely in vain have I guarded all that this fellow has in the wilderness, so that nothing was missed of all that belonged to him; and he has returned me evil for good. [22] God do so to David[y] and more also, if by morning I leave so much as one male of all who belong to him."

23 When Ab'igail saw David, she made haste, and alighted from the ass, and fell before David on her face, and bowed to the ground. [24] She fell at his feet and said, "Upon me alone, my lord, be the guilt; pray let your handmaid speak in your ears, and hear the words of your handmaid. [25] Let not my lord regard this ill-natured fellow, Nabal; for as his name is, so is he; Nabal[z] is his name, and folly is with him; but I your handmaid did not see the young men of my lord, whom you sent. [26] Now then, my lord, as the LORD lives, and as your soul lives, seeing the LORD has restrained you from bloodguilt, and from taking vengeance with your own hand, now then let your enemies and those who seek to do evil to my lord be as Nabal. [27] And now let this present which your servant has brought to my lord be given to the young men who follow my lord. [28] Pray forgive the trespass of your handmaid; for the LORD will certainly make my lord a sure house, because my lord is fighting the battles of the LORD; and evil shall not be found in you so long as you live. [29] If men rise up to pursue you and to seek your life, the life of my lord shall be bound in the bundle of the living in the care of the LORD your God; and the lives of

your enemies he shall sling out as from the hollow of a sling. [30] And when the LORD has done to my lord according to all the good that he has spoken concerning you, and has appointed you prince over Israel, [31] my lord shall have no cause of grief, or pangs of conscience, for having shed blood without cause or for my lord taking vengeance himself. And when the LORD has dealt well with my lord, then remember your handmaid."

32 And David said to Ab'igail, "Blessed be the LORD, the God of Israel, who sent you this day to meet me! [33] Blessed be your discretion, and blessed be you, who have kept me this day from bloodguilt and from avenging myself with my own hand! [34] For as surely as the LORD the God of Israel lives, who has restrained me from hurting you, unless you had made haste and come to meet me, truly by morning there had not been left to Nabal so much as one male." [35] Then David received from her hand what she had brought him; and he said to her, "Go up in peace to your house; see, I have hearkened to your voice, and I have granted your petition."

36 And Ab'igail came to Nabal; and, lo, he was holding a feast in his house, like the feast of a king. And Nabal's heart was merry within him, for he was very drunk; so she told him nothing at all until the morning light. [37] And in the morning, when the wine had gone out of Nabal, his wife told him these things, and his heart died within him, and he became as a stone. [38] And about ten days later the LORD smote Nabal; and he died.

39 When David heard that Nabal was dead, he said, "Blessed be the LORD

y Gk Compare Syr: Heb *the enemies of David*
z That is *fool*

"Robin Hood" type, even acting as a police force at times (compare v. 21). **26:** The oath, *as the LORD lives, and as your soul lives*, may be translated more simply thus: "by the life of the LORD and by your own life." The word *soul* here has nothing to do with the life after death. **29:** *The bundle of the living* is the precious package of those for whom the LORD cares. **30:** The writer anticipates the future events in crediting Abigail with knowing that David was going to be king of Israel. **37:** Perhaps a stroke or a heart attack. **38:** In Biblical theology life and death

who has avenged the insult I received at the hand of Nabal, and has kept back his servant from evil; the LORD has returned the evil-doing of Nabal upon his own head." Then David sent and wooed Ab'igail, to make her his wife. ⁴⁰ And when the servants of David came to Ab'igail at Carmel, they said to her, "David has sent us to you to take you to him as his wife." ⁴¹ And she rose and bowed with her face to the ground, and said, "Behold, your handmaid is a servant to wash the feet of the servants of my lord." ⁴² And Ab'igail made haste and rose and mounted on an ass, and her five maidens attended her; she went after the messengers of David, and became his wife.

43 David also took Ahin'o-am of Jezreel; and both of them became his wives. ⁴⁴ Saul had given Michal his daughter, David's wife, to Palti the son of La'ish, who was of Gallim.

26 Then the Ziphites came to Saul at Gib'e-ah, saying, "Is not David hiding himself on the hill of Hachi'lah, which is on the east of Jeshi'mon?" ² So Saul arose and went down to the wilderness of Ziph, with three thousand chosen men of Israel, to seek David in the wilderness of Ziph. ³ And Saul encamped on the hill of Hachi'lah, which is beside the road on the east of Jeshi'mon. But David remained in the wilderness; and when he saw that Saul came after him into the wilderness, ⁴ David sent out spies, and learned of a certainty that Saul had come. ⁵ Then David rose and came to the place where Saul had encamped;

and David saw the place where Saul lay, with Abner the son of Ner, the commander of his army; Saul was lying within the encampment, while the army was encamped around him.

6 Then David said to Ahim'elech the Hittite, and to Jo'ab's brother Abi'-shai the son of Zeru'iah, "Who will go down with me into the camp to Saul?" And Abi'shai said, "I will go down with you." ⁷ So David and Abi'shai went to the army by night; and there lay Saul sleeping within the encampment, with his spear stuck in the ground at his head; and Abner and the army lay around him. ⁸ Then said Abi'shai to David, "God has given your enemy into your hand this day; now therefore let me pin him to the earth with one stroke of the spear, and I will not strike him twice." ⁹ But David said to Abi'shai, "Do not destroy him; for who can put forth his hand against the LORD's anointed, and be guiltless?" ¹⁰ And David said, "As the LORD lives, the LORD will smite him; or his day shall come to die; or he shall go down into battle and perish. ¹¹ The LORD forbid that I should put forth my hand against the LORD's anointed; but take now the spear that is at his head, and the jar of water, and let us go." ¹² So David took the spear and the jar of water from Saul's head; and they went away. No man saw it, or knew it, nor did any awake; for they were all asleep, because a deep sleep from the LORD had fallen upon them.

13 Then David went over to the other side, and stood afar off on the top of the mountain, with a great space

---

are in the hands of God. **41:** Note the formal obsequiousness of Abigail's words. **43–44:** David lost one wife and gained two more. By marrying Abigail, David consolidated his position with the powerful Calebite clan. *Ahinoam* was also a woman of the southern area; compare Jos.15.56 for the location of this *Jezreel* (not to be confused with the Plain of Esdraelon). These marriages were a great help to David politically.

26.1–25: David spares Saul's life. Early Source. See 23.14–24.22 for the Late Source's version of this incident. **5–6:** *Abner, Joab,* and *Abishai* were destined to play important parts in the history of David's reign in 2 Samuel. *Ahimelech the Hittite* is not to be confused with Ahimelech the priest in ch. 21. Hittites had settled in the country in earlier times (Gen.23.7; Jos.1.4), coming from the north. The few who remained in the time of David joined with the Israelites, adopting Hebrew names (as Uriah the Hittite, 2 Sam.11.3). **9:** *The LORD's anointed,* see 10.1 n. **13–16:** Even today the Arabs in the wilder parts of the country shout across great

between them; [14] and David called to the army, and to Abner the son of Ner, saying, "Will you not answer, Abner?" Then Abner answered, "Who are you that calls to the king?" [15] And David said to Abner, "Are you not a man? Who is like you in Israel? Why then have you not kept watch over your lord the king? For one of the people came in to destroy the king your lord. [16] This thing that you have done is not good. As the LORD lives, you deserve to die, because you have not kept watch over your lord, the LORD's anointed. And now see where the king's spear is, and the jar of water that was at his head."

17 Saul recognized David's voice, and said, "Is this your voice, my son David?" And David said, "It is my voice, my lord, O king." [18] And he said, "Why does my lord pursue after his servant? For what have I done? What guilt is on my hands? [19] Now therefore let my lord the king hear the words of his servant. If it is the LORD who has stirred you up against me, may he accept an offering; but if it is men, may they be cursed before the LORD, for they have driven me out this day that I should have no share in the heritage of the LORD, saying, 'Go, serve other gods.' [20] Now therefore, let not my blood fall to the earth away from the presence of the LORD; for the king of Israel has come out to seek my life,[a] like one who hunts a partridge in the mountains."

21 Then Saul said, "I have done wrong; return, my son David, for I will no more do you harm, because my life was precious in your eyes this day; be-

hold, I have played the fool, and have erred exceedingly." [22] And David made answer, "Here is the spear, O king! Let one of the young men come over and fetch it. [23] The LORD rewards every man for his righteousness and his faithfulness; for the LORD gave you into my hand today, and I would not put forth my hand against the LORD's anointed. [24] Behold, as your life was precious this day in my sight, so may my life be precious in the sight of the LORD, and may he deliver me out of all tribulation." [25] Then Saul said to David, "Blessed be you, my son David! You will do many things and will succeed in them." So David went his way, and Saul returned to his place.

27 And David said in his heart, "I shall now perish one day by the hand of Saul; there is nothing better for me than that I should escape to the land of the Philistines; then Saul will despair of seeking me any longer within the borders of Israel, and I shall escape out of his hand." [2] So David arose and went over, he and the six hundred men who were with him, to A'chish the son of Ma'och, king of Gath. [3] And David dwelt with A'chish at Gath, he and his men, every man with his household, and David with his two wives, Ahin'o-am of Jezreel, and Ab'igail of Carmel, Nabal's widow. [4] And when it was told Saul that David had fled to Gath, he sought for him no more.

5 Then David said to A'chish, "If I have found favor in your eyes, let a place be given me in one of the

a Gk: Heb *a flea* (as in 24.14)

---

distances in this manner. **17:** See 24.16. **21–24:** The meeting ends on a note of reconciliation, but, to judge from the opening words of the next chapter, David trusted Saul not at all.

27.1–28.2: David becomes a vassal of the Philistines. Early Source. If David really became loyal to the Philistines, then he was a traitor to his own people; if he was not loyal to the Philistines, then he was a deceiver–so the dilemma is posed. In 27.10–12 he seems to be deceiving the Philistines, yet in 29.8 he seems to affirm his loyalty to Achish. Actually, the situation developed in such a way that he did not have to make a public choice (ch. 29); of his real state of mind there is no record. Perhaps he himself was uncertain, and waited for God's guidance. From the standpoint of Biblical theology, it was God's will that he should return and become king of Judah first, and then of all Israel. **2:** David went to *Gath*, the very place from which Goliath was reputed to have come (17.4). **3:** Hope of better conditions for their wives and children was one of the reasons why David and his men took this step. **5–7:** These verses

country towns, that I may dwell there; for why should your servant dwell in the royal city with you?" 6 So that day A'chish gave him Ziklag; therefore Ziklag has belonged to the kings of Judah to this day. 7 And the number of the days that David dwelt in the country of the Philistines was a year and four months.

8 Now David and his men went up, and made raids upon the Gesh'urites, the Gir'zites, and the Amal'ekites; for these were the inhabitants of the land from of old, as far as Shur, to the land of Egypt. 9 And David smote the land, and left neither man nor woman alive, but took away the sheep, the oxen, the asses, the camels, and the garments, and came back to A'chish. 10 When A'chish asked, "Against whom*b* have you made a raid today?" David would say, "Against the Negeb of Judah," or "Against the Negeb of the Jerah'-meelites," or, "Against the Negeb of the Ken'ites." 11 And David saved neither man nor woman alive, to bring tidings to Gath, thinking, "Lest they should tell about us, and say, 'So David has done.'" Such was his custom all the while he dwelt in the country of the Philistines. 12 And A'chish trusted David, thinking, "He has made himself utterly abhorred by his people Israel; therefore he shall be my servant always."

28 In those days the Philistines gathered their forces for war, to fight against Israel. And A'chish said to David, "Understand that you and your men are to go out with me in the army." 2 David said to A'chish, "Very well, you shall know what your servant can do." And A'chish said to David, "Very well, I will make you my bodyguard for life."

3 Now Samuel had died, and all Israel had mourned for him and buried him in Ramah, his own city. And Saul had put the mediums and the wizards out of the land. 4 The Philistines assembled, and came and encamped at Shunem; and Saul gathered all Israel, and they encamped at Gilbo'a. 5 When Saul saw the army of the Philistines, he was afraid, and his heart trembled greatly. 6 And when Saul inquired of the LORD, the LORD did not answer him, either by dreams, or by Urim, or by prophets. 7 Then Saul said to his servants, "Seek out for me a woman who is a medium, that I may go to her and inquire of her." And his servants said to him, "Behold, there is a medium at Endor."

8 So Saul disguised himself and put on other garments, and went, he and two men with him; and they came to the woman by night. And he said, "Divine for me by a spirit, and bring up for me whomever I shall name to you." 9 The woman said to him, "Surely you know what Saul has done, how he has cut off the mediums and the wizards from the land. Why then are you laying a snare for my life to bring about my death?" 10 But Saul swore to her by the LORD, "As the

b Gk Vg: Heb lacks *whom*

should come after v. 12. *Ziklag* was located somewhere near the border between the territory of the Philistines and Judah. **8–12:** David actually raided more distant and hostile peoples, such as *the Geshurites, the Girzites, and the Amalekites* (ch. 15), while pretending that he had attacked his own or friendly peoples, such as *Judah, the Jerahmeelites,* or *the Kenites* (30.26–31), who lived in the *Negeb* (southern Palestine). **28.1–2:** Achish is convinced of David's loyalty to the Philistines.

28.3–25: Saul consults the spirit of Samuel through the witch (medium) of Endor. Early Source. This passage interrupts the sequence between 28.2 and 29.1, and belongs after ch. 30, the scene being laid at Gilboa (v. 4) and nearby Endor (v. 7) on the night before the battle. **3:** The first part of the verse is a doublet of 25.1 and the second part is an anticipatory explanation of v. 9. **4:** The Philistines are now in Shunem opposite Gilboa; they had started at Aphek (29.1), and then moved to Jezreel (29.11) before reaching their present position. **6:** The ordinary means of finding God's will had failed Saul. On *Urim* ("and Thummim" understood) see 14.3 n. and 14.42. **9:** Necromancy (consultation of the dead) continued to be practiced from time to time (Is.8.19; 2 Kg.21.6) and was finally forbidden by written law (Dt.18.10–11; Lev.

LORD lives, no punishment shall come upon you for this thing." ¹¹ Then the woman said, "Whom shall I bring up for you?" He said, "Bring up Samuel for me." ¹² When the woman saw Samuel, she cried out with a loud voice; and the woman said to Saul, "Why have you deceived me? You are Saul." ¹³ The king said to her, "Have no fear; what do you see?" And the woman said to Saul, "I see a god coming up out of the earth." ¹⁴ He said to her, "What is his appearance?" And she said, "An old man is coming up; and he is wrapped in a robe." And Saul knew that it was Samuel, and he bowed with his face to the ground, and did obeisance.

15 Then Samuel said to Saul, "Why have you disturbed me by bringing me up?" Saul answered, "I am in great distress; for the Philistines are warring against me, and God has turned away from me and answers me no more, either by prophets or by dreams; therefore I have summoned you to tell me what I shall do." ¹⁶ And Samuel said, "Why then do you ask me, since the LORD has turned from you and become your enemy? ¹⁷ The LORD has done to you as he spoke by me; for the LORD has torn the kingdom out of your hand, and given it to your neighbor, David. ¹⁸ Because you did not obey the voice of the LORD, and did not carry out his fierce wrath against Am′alek, therefore the LORD has done this thing to you this day. ¹⁹ Moreover the LORD will give Israel also with you into the hand of

the Philistines; and tomorrow you and your sons shall be with me; the LORD will give the army of Israel also into the hand of the Philistines."

20 Then Saul fell at once full length upon the ground, filled with fear because of the words of Samuel; and there was no strength in him, for he had eaten nothing all day and all night. ²¹ And the woman came to Saul, and when she saw that he was terrified, she said to him, "Behold, your handmaid has hearkened to you; I have taken my life in my hand, and have hearkened to what you have said to me. ²² Now therefore, you also hearken to your handmaid; let me set a morsel of bread before you; and eat, that you may have strength when you go on your way." ²³ He refused, and said, "I will not eat." But his servants, together with the woman, urged him; and he hearkened to their words. So he arose from the earth, and sat upon the bed. ²⁴ Now the woman had a fatted calf in the house, and she quickly killed it, and she took flour, and kneaded it and baked unleavened bread of it, ²⁵ and she put it before Saul and his servants; and they ate. Then they rose and went away that night.

29 Now the Philistines gathered all their forces at Aphek; and the Israelites were encamped by the fountain which is in Jezreel. ² As the lords of the Philistines were passing on by hundreds and by thousands, and David and his men were passing on in the rear with A′chish, ³ the commanders

---

19.31; 20.6,27). Apparently it was already considered evil and a threat to true religion in Saul's time, and he had made an effort to stamp it out; but under pressure he himself relapsed into former practice. **12:** *Samuel*, probably an error for "Saul." **13:** The word *god* here means a being from another world; that world was Sheol, the abode of the dead, conceived of as a great hollow place under the flat earth, hence the expression *coming up* (compare the word *up* in v. 11). **17–18:** A later editor, in the spirit of the Late Source, has added the prediction of David's kingship and a reference to the Amalek incident (compare ch. 15). **20–25:** Note the human kindness of the medium toward Saul.

29.1–11: The services of David rejected by the Philistine army. Early Source. This chapter continues 28.2. On David's attitude toward the Philistines, see 27.1–28.2 n. **1:** *The Philistines gathered . . . at Aphek*, where they had captured the ark at the beginning of the war (4.1b). *The Israelites* were at *Jezreel*, a considerable distance away in the plain of Esdraelon (Esdraelon is the Greek form of Jezreel). **3:** *Hebrews*, see 4.6 r **6:** According to the Hebrew text,

of the Philistines said, "What are these Hebrews doing here?" And A'chish said to the commanders of the Philistines, "Is not this David, the servant of Saul, king of Israel, who has been with me now for days and years, and since he deserted to me I have found no fault in him to this day." ⁴ But the commanders of the Philistines were angry with him; and the commanders of the Philistines said to him, "Send the man back, that he may return to the place to which you have assigned him; he shall not go down with us to battle, lest in the battle he become an adversary to us. For how could this fellow reconcile himself to his lord? Would it not be with the heads of the men here? ⁵ Is not this David, of whom they sing to one another in dances,

'Saul has slain his thousands,
and David his ten thousands'?"

6 Then A'chish called David and said to him, "As the LORD lives, you have been honest, and to me it seems right that you should march out and in with me in the campaign; for I have found nothing wrong in you from the day of your coming to me to this day. Nevertheless the lords do not approve of you. ⁷ So go back now; and go peaceably, that you may not displease the lords of the Philistines." ⁸ And David said to A'chish, "But what have I done? What have you found in your servant from the day I entered your service until now, that I may not go and fight against the enemies of my lord the king?" ⁹ And A'chish made answer to David, "I know that you are as blameless in my sight as an angel of God; nevertheless the commanders of the Philistines have said, 'He shall not go up with us to the battle.' ¹⁰ Now then rise early in the morning with the servants of your lord who came with you; and start early in the morning, and depart as soon as you have light." ¹¹ So David set out with his men early in the morning, to return to the land of the Philistines. But the Philistines went up to Jezreel.

30 Now when David and his men came to Ziklag on the third day, the Amal'ekites had made a raid upon the Negeb and upon Ziklag. They had overcome Ziklag, and burned it with fire, ² and taken captive the women and all*c* who were in it, both small and great; they killed no one, but carried them off, and went their way. ³ And when David and his men came to the city, they found it burned with fire, and their wives and sons and daughters taken captive. ⁴ Then David and the people who were with him raised their voices and wept, until they had no more strength to weep. ⁵ David's two wives also had been taken captive, Ahin'o-am of Jezreel, and Ab'igail the widow of Nabal of Carmel. ⁶ And David was greatly distressed; for the people spoke of stoning him, because all the people were bitter in soul, each for his sons and daughters. But David strengthened himself in the LORD his God.

7 And David said to Abi'athar the priest, the son of Ahim'elech, "Bring me the ephod." So Abi'athar brought the ephod to David. ⁸ And David inquired of the LORD, "Shall I pursue after this band? Shall I overtake them?" He answered him, "Pursue; for you shall surely overtake and shall surely rescue." ⁹ So David set out, and the six hundred men who were with him, and they came to the brook Besor, where those stayed who were left be-

c Gk: Heb lacks *and all*

Achish shows his respect for David by swearing by David's God (compare *an angel of God* in v. 9). **11:** *The Philistines* quickly marched on *Jezreel*, about seventy-five miles away, where the Israelites were encamped. The latter then moved up Mount Gilboa, where they fortified themselves in preparation for the battle; the Philistines took up positions at Shunem (28.4).
   30.1–31: An interlude: the burning of Ziklag and David's pursuit of the Amalekites. Early Source. **1:** *Ziklag* was about eighty miles south of Aphek, a long two-day march through rough terrain. **6:** The men almost revolted, and David saved himself only by an appeal in the name of God. **7:** *Abiathar*, see 22.20–23 n. *The ephod*, see 14.3 n. **9–10:** *The brook Besor*, south of

hind. [10] But David went on with the pursuit, he and four hundred men; two hundred stayed behind, who were too exhausted to cross the brook Besor.

11 They found an Egyptian in the open country, and brought him to David; and they gave him bread and he ate, they gave him water to drink, [12] and they gave him a piece of a cake of figs and two clusters of raisins. And when he had eaten, his spirit revived; for he had not eaten bread or drunk water for three days and three nights. [13] And David said to him, "To whom do you belong? And where are you from?" He said, "I am a young man of Egypt, servant to an Amal'ekite; and my master left me behind because I fell sick three days ago. [14] We had made a raid upon the Negeb of the Cher'ethites and upon that which belongs to Judah and upon the Negeb of Caleb; and we burned Ziklag with fire." [15] And David said to him, "Will you take me down to this band?" And he said, "Swear to me by God, that you will not kill me, or deliver me into the hands of my master, and I will take you down to this band."

16 And when he had taken him down, behold, they were spread abroad over all the land, eating and drinking and dancing, because of all the great spoil they had taken from the land of the Philistines and from the land of Judah. [17] And David smote them from twilight until the evening of the next day; and not a man of them escaped, except four hundred young men, who mounted camels and fled. [18] David recovered all that the Amal'ekites had taken; and David rescued his two wives. [19] Nothing was missing, whether small or great, sons or daughters, spoil or anything that had been

taken; David brought back all. [20] David also captured all the flocks and herds; and the people drove those cattle before him,[d] and said, "This is David's spoil."

21 Then David came to the two hundred men, who had been too exhausted to follow David, and who had been left at the brook Besor; and they went out to meet David and to meet the people who were with him; and when David drew near to the people he saluted them. [22] Then all the wicked and base fellows among the men who had gone with David said, "Because they did not go with us, we will not give them any of the spoil which we have recovered, except that each man may lead away his wife and children, and depart." [23] But David said, "You shall not do so, my brothers, with what the LORD has given us; he has preserved us and given into our hand the band that came against us. [24] Who would listen to you in this matter? For as his share is who goes down into the battle, so shall his share be who stays by the baggage; they shall share alike." [25] And from that day forward he made it a statute and an ordinance for Israel to this day.

26 When David came to Ziklag, he sent part of the spoil to his friends, the elders of Judah, saying, "Here is a present for you from the spoil of the enemies of the LORD"; [27] it was for those in Bethel, in Ramoth of the Negeb, in Jattir, [28] in Aro'er, in Siphmoth, in Eshtemo'a, [29] in Racal, in the cities of the Jerah'meelites, in the cities of the Ken'ites, [30] in Hormah, in Borash'an, in A'thach, [31] in Hebron, for all the places where David and his men had roamed.

d Cn: Heb *they drove before those cattle*

Ziklag. **14:** See 27.8–12 n. Some interpret the word *Cherethites* as meaning "Cretans" and so equate them with the Philistines (see 4.1b–7.2 n.; compare Ezek.25.16; Zeph.2.5). **21–24:** David was not only fairminded, but politically wise at this point; he retained everybody's support. **25:** This verse is editorial; David was not yet king of Judah, to say nothing of Israel (compare Num.31.27). **26–31:** All these places, including *Bethel* (not the familiar one farther north), were in Judah. It is little wonder that David was soon made king of Judah (2 Sam.2.4). He could now work to that end, having been freed of his Philistine entanglement.

31 Now the Philistines fought against Israel; and the men of Israel fled before the Philistines, and fell slain on Mount Gilbo'a. ² And the Philistines overtook Saul and his sons; and the Philistines slew Jonathan and Abin'adab and Mal'chishu'a, the sons of Saul. ³ The battle pressed hard upon Saul, and the archers found him; and he was badly wounded by the archers. ⁴ Then Saul said to his armor-bearer, "Draw your sword, and thrust me through with it, lest these uncircumcised come and thrust me through, and make sport of me." But his armor-bearer would not; for he feared greatly. Therefore Saul took his own sword, and fell upon it. ⁵ And when his armor-bearer saw that Saul was dead, he also fell upon his sword, and died with him. ⁶ Thus Saul died, and his three sons, and his armor-bearer, and all his men, on the same day together. ⁷ And when the men of Israel who were on the other side of the valley and those beyond the Jordan saw that the men of Israel had fled and that Saul and his sons were dead, they forsook their cities and fled; and the Philistines came and dwelt in them.

8 On the morrow, when the Philistines came to strip the slain, they found Saul and his three sons fallen on Mount Gilbo'a. ⁹ And they cut off his head, and stripped off his armor, and sent messengers throughout the land of the Philistines, to carry the good news to their idols*e* and to the people. ¹⁰ They put his armor in the temple of Ash'taroth; and they fastened his body to the wall of Beth-shan. ¹¹ But when the inhabitants of Ja'besh-gil'ead heard what the Philistines had done to Saul, ¹² all the valiant men arose, and went all night, and took the body of Saul and the bodies of his sons from the wall of Beth-shan; and they came to Jabesh and burnt them there. ¹³ And they took their bones and buried them under the tamarisk tree in Jabesh, and fasted seven days.

e Gk Compare 1 Chr 10.9: Heb *to the house of their idols*

31.1–13: The battle of Gilboa; death of Saul and his older sons. Early Source. This chapter follows the episode of Saul's séance with the medium (28.3–25). No details of the battle are given. Obviously the Israelites fortified themselves near the summit of the hill and the Philistines stormed their position successfully. **1–3:** The Israelites were totally defeated, three of Saul's sons were killed, and Saul was *badly wounded*. **4:** *These uncircumcised*, see 14.6 n. **5:** Biblical suicides are rare; compare 2 Sam.17.23; 1 Kg.16.18; Mt.27.5. **7:** The phrase *and those beyond the Jordan* seems to be in error (it is lacking in 1 Chr.10.7). There is no evidence that the Philistines occupied territory east of the Jordan. **10:** *Ashtaroth*, see 7.3–4 n. The word here probably should be singular, "Astarte." Was this *temple* in *Beth-shan*, which the Philistines apparently had occupied, or back in Philistia? The story is told somewhat differently in 1 Chr.10.10. **11–13:** The men of *Jabesh-gilead* now had opportunity to show their gratitude for what Saul had done for them (ch. 11). With the burial in Jabesh, the story of Saul in the Early Source comes to an end, except for the later return of his bones to his native territory (2 Sam.21.12–14). According to this source, Saul came to a noble but tragic end, defending his people and land to the best of his ability. To the Late Source, however, he was utterly unworthy, entirely deserving of an unhappy fate. Note the similar conclusion of 1 Chr.10.13–14. Later writers, in order to glorify David, felt it necessary to depreciate Saul. David himself had no such attitude (compare the immediate sequel, 2 Sam. ch. 1).

SAMUEL

The Second Book of Samuel relates the rule of David, first as king of Judah alone (chs. 1–4) and then as king over Judah and Israel (chs. 5–24). Chapters 9–20 are concerned particularly with the domestic and political troubles of David's reign (see "Survey of . . . Bible Lands," § 10). Chapters 21–24 are something of an appendix, consisting of two hymns (ch. 22; 23.1–7) and the account of events which are chronologically out of place here (ch. 21; 23.8–39; ch. 24). The two books of Samuel were originally one book, and problems of sources and editing of both are discussed in the Introduction to 1 Samuel.

Since so much of 2 Samuel belongs to the Early Source, this classification will be assumed in the comments unless otherwise noted. Thanks to the genius of the author of the Early Source, 2 Samuel is one of the most clearly written, most homogenous, and most easily understood of all Biblical books; this is especially true of chs. 9–20, where the author seems to be writing from direct personal knowledge. Throughout the account of David's reign there shines the conviction that Israel is the people of the Lord and that his providence is at work in their history.

AFTER THE DEATH OF SAUL, WHEN David had returned from the slaughter of the Amal'ekites, David remained two days in Ziklag; ² and on the third day, behold, a man came from Saul's camp, with his clothes rent and earth upon his head. And when he came to David, he fell to the ground and did obeisance. ³ David said to him, "Where do you come from?" And he said to him, "I have escaped from the camp of Israel." ⁴ And David said to him, "How did it go? Tell me." And he answered, "The people have fled from the battle, and many of the people also have fallen and are dead; and Saul and his son Jonathan are also dead." ⁵ Then David said to the young man who told him, "How do you know that Saul and his son Jonathan are dead?" ⁶ And the young man who told him said, "By chance I happened to be on Mount Gilbo'a; and there was Saul leaning upon his spear; and lo, the chariots and the horsemen were close upon him. ⁷ And when he looked behind him, he saw me, and called to me. And I answered, 'Here I am.' ⁸ And he said to me, 'Who are you?' I answered him, 'I am an Amal'ekite.' ⁹ And he said to me, 'Stand beside me and slay me; for anguish has seized me, and yet my life still lingers.' ¹⁰ So I stood beside him, and slew him, because I was sure that he could not live after he had fallen; and I took the crown which was on his head and the armlet which was on his arm, and I have brought them here to my lord."

11 Then David took hold of his clothes, and rent them; and so did all the men who were with him; ¹² and they mourned and wept and fasted until evening for Saul and for Jonathan his son and for the people of the Lord and for the house of Israel, because they had fallen by the sword. ¹³ And David said to the young man who told him, "Where do you come from?" And he answered, "I am the son of a sojourner, an Amal'ekite." ¹⁴ David said to him, "How is it you were not afraid to put forth your hand to destroy the Lord's anointed?"

1.1–16: David learns of the death of Saul and Jonathan. Some deny that this passage can belong to the Early Source, because it contains a different version of Saul's death from that found in 1 Sam. ch. 31. It is more likely, however, that 1 Sam. ch. 31 tells the true story and that the young Amalekite was lying in the hope of gaining favor with David. **1:** This chapter takes up where 1 Sam. ch. 30 leaves off. **13:** *Sojourner*, Hebrew "gēr," a technical term for a foreigner residing in Israel over a long period, deserving protection but not entitled to full civil rights

15 Then David called one of the young men and said, "Go, fall upon him." And he smote him so that he died. 16 And David said to him, "Your blood be upon your head; for your own mouth has testified against you, saying, 'I have slain the LORD's anointed.' "

17 And David lamented with this lamentation over Saul and Jonathan his son, 18 and he said it*a* should be taught to the people of Judah; behold, it is written in the Book of Jashar.*b* He said:

19 "Thy glory, O Israel, is slain upon
    thy high places!
    How are the mighty fallen!
20 Tell it not in Gath,
    publish it not in the streets of
        Ash'kelon;
  lest the daughters of the Philistines
      rejoice,
    lest the daughters of the
        uncircumcised exult.

21 "Ye mountains of Gilbo'a,
    let there be no dew or rain upon
        you,
    nor upsurging of the deep!*c*
  For there the shield of the mighty
      was defiled,
    the shield of Saul, not anointed
        with oil.

22 "From the blood of the slain,
    from the fat of the mighty,

the bow of Jonathan turned not
    back,
  and the sword of Saul returned not
      empty.

23 "Saul and Jonathan, beloved and
        lovely!
  In life and in death they were not
      divided;
  they were swifter than eagles,
    they were stronger than lions.

24 "Ye daughters of Israel, weep over
        Saul,
  who clothed you daintily in scarlet,
  who put ornaments of gold upon
      your apparel.

25 "How are the mighty fallen
    in the midst of the battle!

"Jonathan lies slain upon thy high
        places.
26 I am distressed for you, my brother
        Jonathan;
  very pleasant have you been to me;
    your love to me was wonderful,
    passing the love of women.

27 "How are the mighty fallen,
    and the weapons of war per-
        ished!'"

2 After this David inquired of the LORD, "Shall I go up into any of

a Gk: Heb *the Bow*   *b* Or *The upright*
c Cn: Heb *fields of offerings*

(Ex.20.10; Dt.14.29). Perhaps "resident alien" is a better translation. **14–16:** Note David's continued respect for the memory of Saul and the office he held (1 Sam.26.9,11,16,24). David of course did not know that the Amalekite was lying.

1.17–27: David's elegy over Saul and Jonathan. David is known to have played the lyre (1 Sam.16.23) and is traditionally connected with the composition of psalms (see superscriptions to Pss. 3–6 and many others). The text has been damaged by transmission through the centuries, but the original feeling and flavor remain. Note the absence of any specifically religious reference. This is simply great lyric poetry. **18:** *The Book of Jashar* was apparently a collection of poems from various sources (see Jos.10.13 n.). **20.** *Gath* and *Ashkelon* were Philistine cities. *The uncircumcised,* see 1 Sam.14.6 n. **21:** The expression *upsurging of the deep,* paralleled in a Canaanite poem, recalls Gen.7.11. David invokes the curse of drought upon Gilboa. The words *not anointed with oil* may refer to *the shield,* meaning not in proper condition for use. If the reference is to Saul, then the word *not* has been inserted by an editor who refused to acknowledge Saul as the LORD's *anointed.* One of the signs of genuineness in this poem is David's expression of affection for Saul as well as Jonathan, in contrast with the attitude of the author of the Late Source in 1 Samuel.

2.1–11. David becomes king of Judah only. 1: Probably David *inquired of the LORD* by means of the ephod and Urim and Thummim (see 1 Sam.14.3,41; 30.7–8). It should occasion no surprise that the tribe of *Judah* was able and willing to set up a separate kingdom. In the list of

the cities of Judah?" And the LORD said to him, "Go up." David said, "To which shall I go up?" And he said, "To Hebron." ² So David went up there, and his two wives also, Ahin′-o-am of Jezreel, and Ab′igail the widow of Nabal of Carmel. ³ And David brought up his men who were with him, every one with his household; and they dwelt in the towns of Hebron. ⁴ And the men of Judah came, and there they anointed David king over the house of Judah.

When they told David, "It was the men of Ja′besh-gil′ead who buried Saul," ⁵ David sent messengers to the men of Ja′besh-gil′ead, and said to them, "May you be blessed by the LORD, because you showed this loyalty to Saul your lord, and buried him! ⁶ Now may the LORD show steadfast love and faithfulness to you! And I will do good to you because you have done this thing. ⁷ Now therefore let your hands be strong, and be valiant; for Saul your lord is dead, and the house of Judah has anointed me king over them."

8 Now Abner the son of Ner, commander of Saul's army, had taken Ish-bo′sheth the son of Saul, and brought him over to Mahana′im; ⁹ and he made him king over Gilead and the Ash′-urites and Jezreel and E′phraim and Benjamin and all Israel. ¹⁰ Ish-bo′-sheth, Saul's son, was forty years old when he began to reign over Israel, and he reigned two years. But the house of Judah followed David. ¹¹ And the time that David was king in Hebron over the house of Judah was seven years and six months.

12 Abner the son of Ner, and the servants of Ish-bo′sheth the son of Saul, went out from Mahana′im to Gibeon. ¹³ And Jo′ab the son of Zeru′iah, and the servants of David, went out and met them at the pool of Gibeon; and they sat down, the one on the one side of the pool, and the other on the other side of the pool. ¹⁴ And Abner said to Jo′ab, "Let the young men arise and play before us." And Jo′ab said, "Let them arise." ¹⁵ Then they arose and passed over by number, twelve for Benjamin and Ish-bo′sheth the son of Saul, and twelve of the servants of David.

---

the tribes of Israel in Jg.5.13–18 Judah is not mentioned; it was apparently leading a separate existence. For other indications of separateness, see 3.10; 5.5; 19.8–15,40–43; 20.1–2. *Judah* might never have joined the other tribes if the Philistine danger had not arisen. **4b–7:** David showed again his respect for the memory of Saul. When he dropped the political hint in v. 7, he probably did not know that Israel had a new king (vv. 8–9), or the new king had not yet been appointed. **8:** On the relation of *Abner* to Saul, see 1 Sam.14.50–51. The original form of the name *Ish-bosheth* ("man of shame") was Ish-baal or Esh-baal ("man of the Lord," 1 Chr.8.33; 9.39). This change was sometimes made by an editor because the element "baal" in the name suggested the detested Canaanite god Baal, the rival of the LORD. For this reason, such names were later abandoned altogether. *Mahanaim* was the principal town of Gilead; the Philistines were in control of the territory west of the Jordan. **9:** At the moment Ish-bosheth was king over *Gilead* only, but was theoretically king over *all Israel.* The other places mentioned probably sent representatives. The word *Ashurites* really means "Assyrians," a manifest impossibility; probably the correct form is "Asherites." **10–11:** As so frequently in ancient works, Biblical and non-Biblical, the figures seem doubtful. *Ish-bosheth* could not have been *forty years old.* Though he is mentioned in 1 Sam.14.49 (called "Ishvi" there), he did not fight at Gilboa; therefore he was probably a minor at this time. This circumstance would explain why he was so completely under the control of Abner. If *he reigned two years* only, then *David* could hardly have reigned more than *seven years* in *Hebron.* We gain the impression from 5.6 that *David* left *Hebron* soon after the death of *Ish-bosheth.* Probably the latter reigned more than *two years* and the former less than *seven years* in Hebron.

2.12–32: War with Israel breaks out. *Gibeon* (Jos. ch. 9) was an important town about five miles northwest of Jerusalem. Apparently both sides were planning to occupy the place when their fighting men met there. Something like a tournament, the exact nature of which is not clear, was agreed upon, but this soon degenerated into a real military engagement. *Joab* was David's nephew; both Saul (v. 8) and David had appointed relatives to be their commanders-

16 And each caught his opponent by the head, and thrust his sword in his opponent's side; so they fell down together. Therefore that place was called Hel'kath-hazzu'rim,[d] which is at Gibeon. 17 And the battle was very fierce that day; and Abner and the men of Israel were beaten before the servants of David.

18 And the three sons of Zeru'iah were there, Jo'ab, Abi'shai, and As'ahel. Now As'ahel was as swift of foot as a wild gazelle; 19 and As'ahel pursued Abner, and as he went he turned neither to the right hand nor to the left from following Abner. 20 Then Abner looked behind him and said, "Is it you, As'ahel?" And he answered, "It is I." 21 Abner said to him, "Turn aside to your right hand or to your left, and seize one of the young men, and take his spoil." But As'ahel would not turn aside from following him. 22 And Abner said again to As'ahel, "Turn aside from following me; why should I smite you to the ground? How then could I lift up my face to your brother Jo'ab?" 23 But he refused to turn aside; therefore Abner smote him in the belly with the butt of his spear, so that the spear came out at his back; and he fell there, and died where he was. And all who came to the place where As'ahel had fallen and died, stood still.

24 But Jo'ab and Abi'shai pursued Abner; and as the sun was going down they came to the hill of Ammah, which lies before Gi'ah on the way to the wilderness of Gibeon. 25 And the Benjaminites gathered themselves together behind Abner, and became one band, and took their stand on the top of a hill. 26 Then Abner called to Jo'ab, "Shall the sword devour for ever? Do you not know that the end will be bitter? How long will it be before you bid your people turn from the pursuit of their brethren?" 27 And Jo'ab said, "As God lives, if you had not spoken, surely the men would have given up the pursuit of their brethren in the morning." 28 So Jo'ab blew the trumpet; and all the men stopped, and pursued Israel no more, nor did they fight any more.

29 And Abner and his men went all that night through the Arabah; they crossed the Jordan, and marching the whole forenoon they came to Mahana'im. 30 Jo'ab returned from the pursuit of Abner; and when he had gathered all the people together, there were missing of David's servants nineteen men besides As'ahel. 31 But the servants of David had slain of Benjamin three hundred and sixty of Abner's men. 32 And they took up As'ahel, and buried him in the tomb of his father, which was at Bethlehem. And Jo'ab and his men marched all night, and the day broke upon them at Hebron.

3 There was a long war between the house of Saul and the house of David; and David grew stronger and stronger, while the house of Saul became weaker and weaker.

2 And sons were born to David at Hebron: his first-born was Amnon, of Ahin'o-am of Jezreel; 3 and his second, Chil'e-ab, of Ab'igail the widow of Nabal of Carmel; and the third, Ab'salom the son of Ma'acah the daughter of Talmai king of Geshur; 4 and the fourth, Adoni'jah the son of Haggith; and the fifth, Shephati'ah

d That is *the field of sword-edges*

---

in-chief. **18:** *Zeruiah* was a sister or half sister of David (1 Chr.2.13–16). Joab and Abishai (1 Sam.26.6–9) play important parts in the history that follows. **22–23:** The killing of *Asahel* by *Abner* brought about a blood feud between *Joab* and *Abner*. **24–28:** Both commanders realized that they had gone too far and a truce was called. **29:** *The Arabah* ("the desert") here means the Jordan valley north of the Dead Sea. The term is also used of the dry depression south of the Dead Sea. **30–32:** The initial victory of David's forces was symptomatic of what was to come (see 3.1).

3.1–39: Continuation of the war with Israel. 2–5: These valuable verses were inserted by an editor interested in family statistics. **6–11: Abner quarrels with Ish-bosheth.** According to the

the son of Abi'tal; [5] and the sixth, Ith're-am, of Eglah, David's wife. These were born to David in Hebron.

6 While there was war between the house of Saul and the house of David, Abner was making himself strong in the house of Saul. [7] Now Saul had a concubine, whose name was Rizpah, the daughter of Ai'ah; and Ish-bo'-sheth said to Abner, "Why have you gone in to my father's concubine?" [8] Then Abner was very angry over the words of Ish-bo'sheth, and said, "Am I a dog's head of Judah? This day I keep showing loyalty to the house of Saul your father, to his brothers, and to his friends, and have not given you into the hand of David; and yet you charge me today with a fault concerning a woman. [9] God do so to Abner, and more also, if I do not accomplish for David what the LORD has sworn to him, [10] to transfer the kingdom from the house of Saul, and set up the throne of David over Israel and over Judah, from Dan to Beer-sheba." [11] And Ish-bo'sheth could not answer Abner another word, because he feared him.

12 And Abner sent messengers to David at Hebron,[e] saying, "To whom does the land belong? Make your covenant with me, and behold, my hand shall be with you to bring over all Israel to you." [13] And he said, "Good; I will make a covenant with you; but one thing I require of you; that is, you shall not see my face, unless you first bring Michal, Saul's daughter, when you come to see my face." [14] Then David sent messengers to Ish-bo'sheth Saul's son, saying, "Give me my wife Michal, whom I betrothed at the price of a hundred foreskins of the Philistines." [15] And Ish-bo'sheth sent, and took her from her husband Pal'ti-el the son of La'ish. [16] But her husband went with her, weeping after her all the way to Bahu'rim. Then Abner said to him, "Go, return"; and he returned.

17 And Abner conferred with the elders of Israel, saying, "For some time past you have been seeking David as king over you. [18] Now then bring it about; for the LORD has promised David, saying, 'By the hand of my servant David I will save my people Israel from the hand of the Philistines, and from the hand of all their enemies.' " [19] Abner also spoke to Benjamin; and then Abner went to tell David at Hebron all that Israel and the whole house of Benjamin thought good to do.

20 When Abner came with twenty men to David at Hebron, David made a feast for Abner and the men who were with him. [21] And Abner said to David, "I will arise and go, and will gather all Israel to my lord the king, that they may make a covenant with you, and that you may reign over all that your heart desires." So David sent Abner away; and he went in peace.

22 Just then the servants of David arrived with Jo'ab from a raid, bringing much spoil with them. But Abner was not with David at Hebron, for he had sent him away, and he had gone in peace. [23] When Jo'ab and all the army that was with him came, it was told Jo'ab, "Abner the son of Ner came to the king, and he has let him go, and he has gone in peace." [24] Then

e Gk: Heb *where he was*

---

usage of that day, a king's *concubines* were royal property that must be kept within the royal household. To aspire to have such a *concubine* (v. 7) was to aspire to the kingship, and that was treason (16.21–22; 1 Kg.2.22). The *dog*, being regarded as an unclean animal, served as a term of reproach; "a dead dog" or *a dog's head* (v. 8) were common expressions (9.8; 16.9; 1 Sam.17.43; 24.14). Evidently Abner realized that references to *Judah* and to *David* (vv. 8,9,10) would frighten *Ish-bosheth* into submission. **12–21: Abner negotiates with David.** David's demand for the return of Michal (1 Sam.18.20–27) was not due to any lack of wives, but had the political purpose of strengthening David's claim to Saul's throne as a son-in-law of the late king. **19:** It was particularly necessary to obtain the consent of Benjamin, Saul's own tribe, which was most likely to object. **22–39: The murder of Abner by Joab.** *Joab* had two motives for this murder: (a) to avenge the death of *Asahel* (2.22–23); (b) to eliminate a rival for

Jo'ab went to the king and said, "What have you done? Behold, Abner came to you; why is it that you have sent him away, so that he is gone? ²⁵ You know that Abner the son of Ner came to deceive you, and to know your going out and your coming in, and to know all that you are doing."

26 When Jo'ab came out from David's presence, he sent messengers after Abner, and they brought him back from the cistern of Sirah; but David did not know about it. ²⁷ And when Abner returned to Hebron, Jo'ab took him aside into the midst of the gate to speak with him privately, and there he smote him in the belly, so that he died, for the blood of As'ahel his brother. ²⁸ Afterward, when David heard of it, he said, "I and my kingdom are for ever guiltless before the LORD for the blood of Abner the son of Ner. ²⁹ May it fall upon the head of Jo'ab, and upon all his father's house; and may the house of Jo'ab never be without one who has a discharge, or who is leprous, or who holds a spindle, or who is slain by the sword, or who lacks bread!" ³⁰ So Jo'ab and Abi'shai his brother slew Abner, because he had killed their brother As'ahel in the battle at Gibeon.

31 Then David said to Jo'ab and to all the people who were with him, "Rend your clothes, and gird on sackcloth, and mourn before Abner." And King David followed the bier. ³² They buried Abner at Hebron; and the king lifted up his voice and wept at the grave of Abner; and all the people wept. ³³ And the king lamented for Abner, saying,

"Should Abner die as a fool dies?
³⁴ Your hands were not bound,
    your feet were not fettered;
as one falls before the wicked
    you have fallen."

And all the people wept again over him. ³⁵ Then all the people came to persuade David to eat bread while it was yet day; but David swore, saying, "God do so to me and more also, if I taste bread or anything else till the sun goes down!" ³⁶ And all the people took notice of it, and it pleased them; as everything that the king did pleased all the people. ³⁷ So all the people and all Israel understood that day that it had not been the king's will to slay Abner the son of Ner. ³⁸ And the king said to his servants, "Do you not know that a prince and a great man has fallen this day in Israel? ³⁹ And I am this day weak, though anointed king; these men the sons of Zeru'iah are too hard for me. The LORD requite the evildoer according to his wickedness!"

4 When Ish-bo'sheth, Saul's son, heard that Abner had died at Hebron, his courage failed, and all Israel was dismayed. ² Now Saul's son had two men who were captains of raiding bands; the name of the one was Ba'anah, and the name of the other Rechab, sons of Rimmon a man of Benjamin from Be-er'oth (for Be-er'oth also is reckoned to Benjamin; ³ the Be-er'othites fled to Gitta'im, and have been sojourners there to this day).

4 Jonathan, the son of Saul, had a

---

the post of commander-in-chief of David's army (19.13; 20.9–10). **28–39:** *Joab* was too powerful (v. 39) for *David* to order him executed, as had been done in the case of the Amalekite (1.15). Yet this murder greatly endangered David's position among the northern tribes. Therefore *David* did the best he could to make amends by invoking a series of curses upon *Joab* and his descendents (the *spindle* was a sign of effeminacy), by proclaiming public mourning throughout Judah, by himself taking the position of chief mourner at Abner's funeral and fasting all that day, then continuing to praise Abner thereafter. The people of Israel were convinced of David's innocence (v. 37) of the murder, though naturally any idea of making David king of Israel was put aside for the time.

4.1–12: The murder of Ish-bosheth and David's punishment of the murderers. 2–3: *Beeroth* was originally a city under Gibeonite control (Jos.9.17); but the Gibeonite *Beerothites* had *fled to Gittaim*, probably during Saul's persecution (21.1–2,5), thus making it possible for *Rimmon* and other Israelites to settle in *Beeroth*. **4:** This verse is out of place here; it belongs in

son who was crippled in his feet. He was five years old when the news about Saul and Jonathan came from Jezreel; and his nurse took him up, and fled; and, as she fled in her haste, he fell, and became lame. And his name was Mephib'osheth.

5 Now the sons of Rimmon the Be-er'othite, Rechab and Ba'anah, set out, and about the heat of the day they came to the house of Ish-bo'-sheth, as he was taking his noonday rest. ⁶ And behold, the doorkeeper of the house had been cleaning wheat, but she grew drowsy and slept; so Rechab and Ba'anah his brother slipped in.ᶠ ⁷ When they came into the house, as he lay on his bed in his bedchamber, they smote him, and slew him, and beheaded him. They took his head, and went by the way of the Arabah all night, ⁸ and brought the head of Ish-bo'sheth to David at Hebron. And they said to the king, "Here is the head of Ish-bo'sheth, the son of Saul, your enemy, who sought your life; the LORD has avenged my lord the king this day on Saul and on his offspring." ⁹ But David answered Rechab and Ba'anah his brother, the sons of Rimmon the Be-er'othite, "As the LORD lives, who has redeemed my life out of every adversity, ¹⁰ when one told me, 'Behold, Saul is dead,' and thought he was bringing good news, I seized him and slew him at Ziklag, which was the reward I gave him for his news. ¹¹ How much more, when wicked men have slain a righteous man

in his own house upon his bed, shall I not now require his blood at your hand, and destroy you from the earth?" ¹² And David commanded his young men, and they killed them, and cut off their hands and feet, and hanged them beside the pool at Hebron. But they took the head of Ish-bo'sheth, and buried it in the tomb of Abner at Hebron.

5 Then all the tribes of Israel came to David at Hebron, and said, "Behold, we are your bone and flesh. ² In times past, when Saul was king over us, it was you that led out and brought in Israel; and the LORD said to you, 'You shall be shepherd of my people Israel, and you shall be prince over Israel.' " ³ So all the elders of Israel came to the king at Hebron; and King David made a covenant with them at Hebron before the LORD, and they anointed David king over Israel. ⁴ David was thirty years old when he began to reign, and he reigned forty years. ⁵ At Hebron he reigned over Judah seven years and six months; and at Jerusalem he reigned over all Israel and Judah thirty-three years.

6 And the king and his men went to Jerusalem against the Jeb'usites, the inhabitants of the land, who said to David, "You will not come in here, but the blind and the lame will ward you off"–thinking, "David cannot come in here." ⁷ Nevertheless David took the stronghold of Zion, that is, the city of

ᶠ Gk: Heb ⁶*And hither they came into the midst of the house fetching wheat; and they smote him in the belly; and Rechab and Baanah his brother escaped*

---

or just before ch. 9. The original form of *Mephibosheth* ("he who spreads [?] shame") was Meribbaal ("he who strives for [?] the Lord," 1 Chr.8.34; 9.40). On reasons for the change, see 2.8 n. **8:** By saying *the LORD has avenged my lord*, the guilty pair try to justify what they had done. **9–12:** David continues to show respect for the family of Saul and to punish anyone seeking to harm members of that family (1.14–16; 3.28–39).

5.1–16: David becomes king of all Israel and Judah; he captures Jerusalem and makes it his capital. 1–2: These two sentences seem to be the work of an editor in the spirit of the Late Source of 1 Samuel (see Introduction to 1 Samuel). In the Early Source David was not a general in Saul's army, nor was he promised the kingship of Israel. **3:** This sentence tells the unembellished story of what was done. **4–5:** A chronological note by an editor which may be approximately correct, though David could hardly have been *thirty years old* at this time. *Forty years* is a favorite Biblical expression meaning a reasonably long time. *Israel and Judah* are kept clearly separate in the writer's mind. **6–9:** The details of how David captured *Jerusalem* or *Zion*, the last town remaining to the Canaanites (locally called *Jebusites*) are not clear (compare

David. [8] And David said on that day, "Whoever would smite the Jeb'usites, let him get up the water shaft to attack the lame and the blind, who are hated by David's soul." Therefore it is said, "The blind and the lame shall not come into the house." [9] And David dwelt in the stronghold, and called it the city of David. And David built the city round about from the Millo inward. [10] And David became greater and greater, for the LORD, the God of hosts, was with him.

11 And Hiram king of Tyre sent messengers to David, and cedar trees, also carpenters and masons who built David a house. [12] And David perceived that the LORD had established him king over Israel, and that he had exalted his kingdom for the sake of his people Israel.

13 And David took more concubines and wives from Jerusalem, after he came from Hebron; and more sons and daughters were born to David. [14] And these are the names of those who were born to him in Jerusalem: Sham'mu-a, Shobab, Nathan, Solomon, [15] Ibhar, Eli'shu-a, Nepheg, Japhi'a, [16] Eli'shama, Eli'ada, and Eliph'elet.

17 When the Philistines heard that David had been anointed king over Israel, all the Philistines went up in search of David; but David heard of it and went down to the stronghold. [18] Now the Philistines had come and spread out in the valley of Reph'aim. [19] And David inquired of the LORD, "Shall I go up against the Philistines? Wilt thou give them into my hand?" And the LORD said to David, "Go up; for I will certainly give the Philistines into your hand." [20] And David came to Ba'al-pera'zim, and David defeated them there; and he said, "The LORD has broken through[g] my enemies before me, like a bursting flood." Therefore the name of that place is called Ba'al-pera'zim.[h] [21] And the Philistines left their idols there, and David and his men carried them away.

22 And the Philistines came up yet again, and spread out in the valley of Reph'aim. [23] And when David inquired of the LORD, he said, "You shall not go up; go around to their rear, and come upon them opposite the balsam trees. [24] And when you hear the sound of marching in the tops of the balsam trees, then bestir yourself; for then the LORD has gone out before you to smite the army of the Philistines." [25] And

g Heb *paraz*   h That is *Lord of breaking through*

1 Chr.11.4–9 for a somewhat different account). The capture was important because it removed the last vestige of Canaanite power in the land, and also provided a place where David could establish a neutral capital, belonging to neither Israel nor Judah, but lying between the two. Later tradition assumed an earlier possession of the city; contrast Jg.1.8 and 1 Sam.17.54 with Jg.19.10–12. *The Millo*, see 1 Kg.9.15 n. **11:** Apparently the same *Hiram* who much later helped Solomon in the building of the temple (1 Kg.5.1–12). **13–16:** Sons of David. Editorial information similar to that in 3.2–5, though somewhat out of place, since *Solomon* at least was born later. Large harems were customary at that time (see Jg.8.30–31) and increased the prestige of the ruler. David, with at least twenty concubines and wives, was apparently never criticized on this score. It was quite otherwise with Solomon (1 Kg.11.1–4).

5.17–25: War with the Philistines. The Philistines now realized that David was steering a course that would make him an enemy, and one to be feared (1 Sam. chs. 27 and 29); and David no longer pretended to be their ally. His success as king would depend on his ability to deal with the Philistines. **17:** It is not clear which *stronghold* is meant; some think Adullam (1 Sam.22.1). **18:** *The valley of Rephaim* was probably located southwest of Jerusalem. **20:** In good oriental fashion, David made a pun on the place where his enemies were defeated (compare Gen.38.29). **21:** Formerly the Philistines had captured the sacred ark of the Israelites (1 Sam.4.11; 5.1); now the tables were turned, and the Philistines lost their *idols.* **22–25:** David defeated the Philistines again, pushing them back *from Geba*, near Jerusalem, *to Gezer*, near the border of their own territory. **24:** The rustling of the leaves *in the tops of the balsam trees* became *the sound of marching*, the signal to advance.

At this point 21.15–22 and 23.8–39 should be read; see the notes on these passages.

David did as the LORD commanded him, and smote the Philistines from Geba to Gezer.

6 David again gathered all the chosen men of Israel, thirty thousand. ² And David arose and went with all the people who were with him from Ba'ale-judah, to bring up from there the ark of God, which is called by the name of the LORD of hosts who sits enthroned on the cherubim. ³ And they carried the ark of God upon a new cart, and brought it out of the house of Abin'adab which was on the hill; and Uzzah and Ahi'o,*ⁱ* the sons of Abin'adab, were driving the new cart*ʲ* ⁴ with the ark of God; and Ahi'o*ⁱ* went before the ark. ⁵ And David and all the house of Israel were making merry before the LORD with all their might, with songs*ᵏ* and lyres and harps and tambourines and castanets and cymbals.

6 And when they came to the threshing floor of Nacon, Uzzah put out his hand to the ark of God and took hold of it, for the oxen stumbled. ⁷ And the anger of the LORD was kindled against Uzzah; and God smote him there because he put forth his hand to the ark;*ˡ* and he died there beside the ark of God. ⁸ And David was angry because the LORD had broken forth upon Uzzah; and that place is called

Pe'rez-uz'zah,*ᵐ* to this day. ⁹ And David was afraid of the LORD that day; and he said, "How can the ark of the LORD come to me?" ¹⁰ So David was not willing to take the ark of the LORD into the city of David; but David took it aside to the house of O'bed-e'dom the Gittite. ¹¹ And the ark of the LORD remained in the house of O'bed-e'dom the Gittite three months; and the LORD blessed O'bed-e'dom and all his household.

12 And it was told King David, "The LORD has blessed the household of O'bed-e'dom and all that belongs to him, because of the ark of God." So David went and brought up the ark of God from the house of O'bed-e'dom to the city of David with rejoicing; ¹³ and when those who bore the ark of the LORD had gone six paces, he sacrificed an ox and a fatling. ¹⁴ And David danced before the LORD with all his might; and David was girded with a linen ephod. ¹⁵ So David and all the house of Israel brought up the ark of the LORD with shouting, and with the sound of the horn.

16 As the ark of the LORD came

i Or *and his brother*
j Compare Gk: Heb *the new cart, and brought it out of the house of Abinadab which was on the hill*
k Gk 1 Chr 13.8: Heb *fir-trees*
l 1 Chr 13.10: Heb uncertain
m That is *The breaking forth upon Uzzah*

6.1–15: The bringing of the ark to Jerusalem. David wished to add to the prestige of Jerusalem by making it a religious, as well as a political and military center. Hence it was particularly appropriate for him to bring there the ark, the sacred object of the northern tribes, and now the symbol of the national God. **2:** *Baale-judah* is either an error or another name for Kiriath-jearim, the place where the ark was left (1 Sam.6.21–7.2). *The LORD of hosts who sits enthroned on the cherubim,* see 1 Sam.4.4 n. **5:** Some interpreters consider this verse a later embellishment, since the full orchestra seems more appropriate to the time after the temple had been built (compare 2 Chr.5.12–13; Ps.150.3–5). **6:** *Uzzah* was apparently trying to steady the ark as *the oxen stumbled.* **7:** At this point Uzzah died. Most ancient peoples attributed disaster to the anger of a deity. According to a later interpretation introduced here, Uzzah should not have touched the ark (see Num.4.15 n.). Even in these earlier times, the ark was regarded as very dangerous (1 Sam.5.11–12; 6.19). **8–9:** Was David *angry* or was he *afraid?* Probably the latter; v. 8 seems to be the work of a later editor, as is shown by the words *to this day.* **10–11:** A *Gittite* means a man from Gath, but *Obed-edom* was not necessarily from the Philistine town. Gath means "wine press," and there were several towns by that name in Israelite territory. On the other hand, this man could have been a follower of *David* from the latter's Philistine days (1 Sam.27.2–4). **12–15:** The prosperity and peace of *the household of Obed-edom* were taken as signs that God's anger in connection with the ark had ceased (v.12). Note that it was perfectly permissible for *David* to offer sacrifice (vv. 13,17; compare 1 Sam. 13.10–13); only later was this function restricted to priests. On religious dancing, see Ex.15.20 n.; 32.19; 1 Kg.18.26. On the *linen ephod,* see 1 Sam.2.18 n.

into the city of David, Michal the daughter of Saul looked out of the window, and saw King David leaping and dancing before the LORD; and she despised him in her heart. [17] And they brought in the ark of the LORD, and set it in its place, inside the tent which David had pitched for it; and David offered burnt offerings and peace offerings before the LORD. [18] And when David had finished offering the burnt offerings and the peace offerings, he blessed the people in the name of the LORD of hosts, [19] and distributed among all the people, the whole multitude of Israel, both men and women, to each a cake of bread, a portion of meat,[n] and a cake of raisins. Then all the people departed, each to his house.

20 And David returned to bless his household. But Michal the daughter of Saul came out to meet David, and said, "How the king of Israel honored himself today, uncovering himself today before the eyes of his servants' maids, as one of the vulgar fellows shamelessly uncovers himself!" [21] And David said to Michal, "It was before the LORD, who chose me above your father, and above all his house, to appoint me as prince over Israel, the people of the LORD–and I will make merry before the LORD. [22] I will make myself yet more contemptible than this, and I will be abased in your[o] eyes; but by the maids of whom you have spoken, by them I shall be held in honor." [23] And Michal the daughter of Saul had no child to the day of her death.

7 Now when the king dwelt in his house, and the LORD had given him rest from all his enemies round about, [2] the king said to Nathan the prophet, "See now, I dwell in a house of cedar, but the ark of God dwells in a tent." [3] And Nathan said to the king, "Go, do all that is in your heart; for the LORD is with you."

4 But that same night the word of the LORD came to Nathan, [5] "Go and tell my servant David, 'Thus says the LORD: Would you build me a house to dwell in? [6] I have not dwelt in a house since the day I brought up the people of Israel from Egypt to this day, but I have been moving about in a tent for my dwelling. [7] In all places where I have moved with all the people of Israel, did I speak a word with any of the judges[p] of Israel, whom I commanded to shepherd my people Israel, saying, "Why have you not built me a house of cedar?" ' [8] Now therefore thus you shall say to my servant David, 'Thus says the LORD of hosts, I took you from the pasture, from following the sheep, that you should be prince over my people Israel; [9] and I have been with you wherever you went, and have cut off all your enemies from before you; and I will make for you a great name, like the name of the great ones of the earth. [10] And I will appoint a place for my people Israel, and will plant them, that they may dwell in their own place, and be disturbed no more; and

n Vg: Heb uncertain   *o* Gk: Heb *my*
p 1 Chr 17.6: Heb *tribes*

6.16–23: **Michal's alienation.** *Michal* may have been resentful at being torn away from her husband Paltiel (3.15–16), or at the discovery that she was only one among many wives of David, or at the decline of her family's fortunes (vv. 16,20). **23:** It is not clear whether *Michal . . . had no child* because David put her away or because she was barren. Childlessness was considered a great misfortune; compare Gen.30.1; 1 Sam.1.6–11.

At this point 21.1–14 and ch. 24 should be read; see the notes on these passages.

7.1–29: David wishes to build a temple, but God wills that he establish an everlasting dynasty. This chapter is the only serious interruption of the Early Source in the entire book. Like 1 Sam. 2.27–36, it is a late theological commentary inserted into an early historical source, seeking to explain why David was not chosen to build the temple. It seems to have been based to some extent on Ps. 89 (compare Ps.132.11–12). Nathan the prophet (vv. 2,3,4,17) is used as a mouthpiece of the author, though the historical Nathan does not appear in the Early Source until 12.1. Verses 4–17 are often referred to as The Prophecy of Nathan and vv. 18–29 as The Prayer of David. In v. 6 the writer ignores the temple at Shiloh (1 Sam.1.7; 3.3).

violent men shall afflict them no more, as formerly, [11] from the time that I appointed judges over my people Israel; and I will give you rest from all your enemies. Moreover the LORD declares to you that the LORD will make you a house. [12] When your days are fulfilled and you lie down with your fathers, I will raise up your offspring after you, who shall come forth from your body, and I will establish his kingdom. [13] He shall build a house for my name, and I will establish the throne of his kingdom for ever. [14] I will be his father, and he shall be my son. When he commits iniquity, I will chasten him with the rod of men, with the stripes of the sons of men; [15] but I will not take[q] my steadfast love from him, as I took it from Saul, whom I put away from before you. [16] And your house and your kingdom shall be made sure for ever before me; your throne shall be established for ever.'" [17] In accordance with all these words, and in accordance with all this vision, Nathan spoke to David.

18 Then King David went in and sat before the LORD, and said, "Who am I, O Lord GOD, and what is my house, that thou hast brought me thus far? [19] And yet this was a small thing in thy eyes, O Lord GOD; thou hast spoken also of thy servant's house for a great while to come, and hast shown me future generations,[r] O Lord GOD! [20] And what more can David say to thee? For thou knowest thy servant, O Lord GOD! [21] Because of thy promise, and according to thy own heart, thou hast wrought all this greatness, to make thy servant know it. [22] Therefore thou art great, O LORD God; for there is none like thee, and there is no God besides thee, according to all that we have heard with our ears. [23] What other[s] nation on earth is like thy people Israel, whom God went to redeem to be his people, making himself a name, and doing for them[t] great and terrible things, by driving out[u] before his people a nation and its gods?[v] [24] And thou didst establish for thyself thy people Israel to be thy people for ever; and thou, O LORD, didst become their God. [25] And now, O LORD God, confirm for ever the word which thou hast spoken concerning thy servant and concerning his house, and do as thou hast spoken; [26] and thy name will be magnified for ever, saying, 'The LORD of hosts is God over Israel,' and the house of thy servant David will be established before thee. [27] For thou, O LORD of hosts, the God of Israel, hast made this revelation to thy servant, saying, 'I will build you a house'; therefore thy servant has found courage to pray this prayer to thee. [28] And now, O Lord GOD, thou art God, and thy words are true, and thou hast promised this good thing to thy servant; [29] now therefore may it please thee to bless the house of thy servant, that it may continue for ever before thee; for thou, O Lord GOD, hast spoken, and with thy blessing shall the house of thy servant be blessed for ever."

8 After this David defeated the Philistines and subdued them, and

q Gk Syr Vg 1 Chr 17.13: Heb *shall not depart*
r Cn: Heb *this is the law for man*
s Gk: Heb *one*
t Heb *you*
u Gk 1 Chr 17.21: Heb *for your land*
v Heb *before thy people, whom thou didst redeem for thyself from Egypt, nations and its gods*

The key to the understanding of this chapter is the play on the various meanings of the word *house;* in vv. 1–2 it means "palace"; in vv. 5,6,7,13 it means "temple"; in vv. 11,16,19, 25,26,27,29 it means "dynasty"; in v. 18 it means "family status."

Historically the dynasty of David was not everlasting. It fell in 587 (586) B.C., probably some time before our author wrote. He may have been dreaming of a literal restoration of the kingdom of David, while at the same time vaguely anticipating the Kingdom of God, the only eternal kingdom.

8.1–18: Summary of David's wars and the administration of his kingdom. This chapter was contributed by a Deuteronomic editor (see Introduction to 1 Samuel). It has been conjectured that the book once ended with this summary, the more detailed and earlier material that

David took Meth'eg-am'mah out of the hand of the Philistines.

2 And he defeated Moab, and measured them with a line, making them lie down on the ground; two lines he measured to be put to death, and one full line to be spared. And the Moabites became servants to David and brought tribute.

3 David also defeated Hadade'-zer the son of Rehob, king of Zobah, as he went to restore his power at the river Euphra'tes. 4 And David took from him a thousand and seven hundred horsemen, and twenty thousand foot soldiers; and David hamstrung all the chariot horses, but left enough for a hundred chariots. 5 And when the Syrians of Damascus came to help Hadade'zer king of Zobah, David slew twenty-two thousand men of the Syrians. 6 Then David put garrisons in Aram of Damascus; and the Syrians became servants to David and brought tribute. And the LORD gave victory to David wherever he went. 7 And David took the shields of gold which were carried by the servants of Hadade'zer, and brought them to Jerusalem. 8 And from Betah and from Bero'thai, cities of Hadade'zer, King David took very much bronze.

9 When To'i king of Hamath heard that David had defeated the whole army

of Hadade'zer, 10 To'i sent his son Joram to King David, to greet him, and to congratulate him because he had fought against Hadade'zer and defeated him; for Hadade'zer had often been at war with To'i. And Joram brought with him articles of silver, of gold, and of bronze; 11 these also King David dedicated to the LORD, together with the silver and gold which he dedicated from all the nations he subdued, 12 from Edom, Moab, the Ammonites, the Philistines, Am'alek, and from the spoil of Hadade'zer the son of Rehob, king of Zobah.

13 And David won a name for himself. When he returned, he slew eighteen thousand E'domites[w] in the Valley of Salt. 14 And he put garrisons in Edom; throughout all Edom he put garrisons, and all the E'domites became David's servants. And the LORD gave victory to David wherever he went.

15 So David reigned over all Israel; and David administered justice and equity to all his people. 16 And Jo'ab the son of Zeru'iah was over the army; and Jehosh'aphat the son of Ahi'lud was recorder; 17 and Zadok the son of Ahi'tub and Ahim'elech the son of Abi'athar were priests; and Serai'ah

w Gk: Heb *returned from smiting eighteen thousand Syrians*

---

follows having been suppressed for a time, though finally restored. The present chapter is not a mere digest of what follows, for it contains information not found elsewhere. **1:** This seems intended as a statement of the final defeat of the Philistines; compare 21.15–22 and 23.8–39 for some details. *Methegh-ammah,* 1 Chr.18.1 reads "Gath and its villages." **2:** The slaughter of two-thirds of the Moabites does not accord with the friendly relations implied by 1 Sam.22.3–4. Perhaps something happened to revive the old enmity (1 Sam.14.47). **3–8:** David defeats the Arameans (Syrians). This passage may be a partial summary of 10.6–19. *Zobah* (vv. 3,5) lay north of Damascus (vv. 5,6) and was attempting to extend its power to the *Euphrates* (v. 3). South of *Zobah,* Syria was controlled by *Damascus.* David defeated the coalition (v. 5), and thus controlled all of Syria. He kept enough *horses* for *a hundred chariots* only (v. 4). Solomon greatly expanded the use of horses and chariots (1 Kg.10.26–29). **9:** *Hamath* lay north of Zobah. David did not control this territory, but its king was friendly. **13–14:** David defeated Edom, and thus his little empire was enlarged to the south. In these campaigns the king did not always take to the field in person (11.1). *The Valley of Salt* is either the depression south of the Dead Sea, or a valley running southeast from Beer-sheba. **16–18:** Another version of this list is found in 20.23–26. *Zadok* appears here (v. 17) historically for the first time (1 Sam. 2.35). His earlier history is not known, though later his ancestry is traced back to Aaron (1 Chr. 6.3–8). *Ahimelech the son of Abiathar* should perhaps be reversed (1 Sam.22.20), though it is also possible that *Abiathar* had a son *Ahimelech* who acted in place of his aged father (1 Chr. 18.16; 24.3,6,31). **18:** *The Cherethites and Pelethites* were foreign mercenaries; probably the

was secretary; [18] and Benai'ah the son of Jehoi'ada was over[x] the Cher'ethites and the Pel'ethites; and David's sons were priests.

9 And David said, "Is there still any one left of the house of Saul, that I may show him kindness for Jonathan's sake?" [2] Now there was a servant of the house of Saul whose name was Ziba, and they called him to David; and the king said to him, "Are you Ziba?" And he said, "Your servant is he." [3] And the king said, "Is there not still some one of the house of Saul, that I may show the kindness of God to him?" Ziba said to the king, "There is still a son of Jonathan; he is crippled in his feet." [4] The king said to him, "Where is he?" And Ziba said to the king, "He is in the house of Machir the son of Am'miel, at Lo-debar." [5] Then King David sent and brought him from the house of Machir the son of Am'miel, at Lo-debar. [6] And Mephib'osheth the son of Jonathan, son of Saul, came to David, and fell on his face and did obeisance. And David said, "Mephib'osheth!" And he answered, "Behold, your servant." [7] And David said to him, "Do not fear; for I will show you kindness for the sake of your father Jona-

than, and I will restore to you all the land of Saul your father; and you shall eat at my table always." [8] And he did obeisance, and said, "What is your servant, that you should look upon a dead dog such as I?"

9 Then the king called Ziba, Saul's servant, and said to him, "All that belonged to Saul and to all his house I have given to your master's son. [10] And you and your sons and your servants shall till the land for him, and shall bring in the produce, that your master's son may have bread to eat; but Mephib'osheth your master's son shall always eat at my table." Now Ziba had fifteen sons and twenty servants. [11] Then Ziba said to the king, "According to all that my lord the king commands his servant, so will your servant do." So Mephib'osheth ate at David's[y] table, like one of the king's sons. [12] And Mephib'osheth had a young son, whose name was Mica. And all who dwelt in Ziba's house became Mephib'osheth's servants. [13] So Mephib'osheth dwelt in Jerusalem; for he ate always at the king's table. Now he was lame in both his feet.

x Syr Tg Vg 20.23; 1 Chr 18.17: Heb lacks *was over*
y Gk: Heb *my*

names are equivalent to "Cretans and Philistines" (15.18; 20.7,23; 1 Kg.1.38,44; see 1 Sam. 30.14 n.). It is entirely possible that some of *David's sons were priests*, for the restriction of the priesthood to a certain family had not yet arisen. The parallels, however, in 20.26 and 1 Chr. 18.17 have different readings.

9.1–20.26: The domestic and political troubles of David's reign. This section of the Early Source is, in view of its superb literary style and sober objectivity, the prose masterpiece of the Old Testament. The writer was obviously dealing with events of which he had personal knowledge and in which he may have participated. For the fullest appreciation the section should be read as a unit with its conclusion in 1 Kg. chs. 1–2.

9.1–13: David shows dutiful kindness to Mephibosheth. As preparation for this chapter, read 4.4 and 21.1–14 (omitting v. 7); see comments on these passages and on ch. 6 (end). **1:** The word translated *kindness* contains the idea of obligation, "kindness required by loyalty to a covenant." *David* and *Jonathan* had sworn eternal loyalty to one another (1 Sam.18.1–4; 20.14–17). *David* was probably also fearful of reaction to the execution of seven of Saul's descendants at the request of the Gibeonites (see 21.11–14 n.). The king also needed to know whether any member of the former royal family remained who might serve as a focal point of rebellion. **3:** *The kindness of God* is a stronger expression of the *kindness* of v. 1, meaning "obligation under God." **4:** *Machir* of *Lo-debar*, see 17.27. **6:** The proper form of *Mephibosheth* is Meribbaal (see 4.4 n.). **7:** Probably one reason for *fear* on the part of Mephibosheth was what had happened to two of his half brothers and five of his nephews (21.8–9). **8:** *Dead dog*, see 1 Sam.24.14 n. **13:** David must have been pained that Jonathan's son was such a pathetic cripple, and yet relieved that this scion of Saul could hardly be expected to head an insurrection. *Ziba* claimed later that Mephibosheth was disloyal (16.1–4), but the claim seems to have been false (19.24–30).

10 After this the king of the Ammonites died, and Hanun his son reigned in his stead. [2] And David said, "I will deal loyally with Hanun the son of Nahash, as his father dealt loyally with me." So David sent by his servants to console him concerning his father. And David's servants came into the land of the Ammonites. [3] But the princes of the Ammonites said to Hanun their lord, "Do you think, because David has sent comforters to you, that he is honoring your father? Has not David sent his servants to you to search the city, and to spy it out, and to overthrow it?" [4] So Hanun took David's servants, and shaved off half the beard of each, and cut off their garments in the middle, at their hips, and sent them away. [5] When it was told David, he sent to meet them, for the men were greatly ashamed. And the king said, "Remain at Jericho until your beards have grown, and then return."

6 When the Ammonites saw that they had become odious to David, the Ammonites sent and hired the Syrians of Beth-re'hob, and the Syrians of Zobah, twenty thousand foot soldiers, and the king of Ma'acah with a thousand men, and the men of Tob, twelve thousand men. [7] And when David heard of it, he sent Jo'ab and all the host of the mighty men. [8] And the Ammonites came out and drew up in battle array at the entrance of the gate; and the Syrians of Zobah and of Rehob, and the men of Tob and Ma'acah, were by themselves in the open country.

9 When Jo'ab saw that the battle was set against him both in front and in the rear, he chose some of the picked men of Israel, and arrayed them against the Syrians; [10] the rest of his men he put in the charge of Abi'shai his brother, and he arrayed them against the Ammonites. [11] And he said, "If the Syrians are too strong for me, then you shall help me; but if the Ammonites are too strong for you, then I will come and help you. [12] Be of good courage, and let us play the man for our people, and for the cities of our God; and may the LORD do what seems good to him." [13] So Jo'ab and the people who were with him drew near to battle against the Syrians; and they fled before him. [14] And when the Ammonites saw that the Syrians fled, they likewise fled before Abi'shai, and entered the city. Then Jo'ab returned from fighting against the Ammonites, and came to Jerusalem.

15 But when the Syrians saw that they had been defeated by Israel, they gathered themselves together. [16] And Hadade'zer sent, and brought out the Syrians who were beyond the Euphra'tes;[z] and they came to Helam, with Shobach the commander of the army of Hadade'zer at their head. [17] And when it was told David, he gathered all Israel together, and crossed the Jordan, and came to Helam. And the Syrians arrayed themselves against David, and fought with him. [18] And the Syrians fled before Israel; and David slew of the Syrians the men of seven hundred chariots, and forty thousand horsemen, and wounded Shobach the commander of their army, so that he died there. [19] And when all the kings who were servants of Hadade'zer saw that they had been defeated by Israel, they made peace with Israel, and became subject to them.

z Heb *river*

10.1–19: David defeats the Ammonites and Arameans (Syrians). 2: There is no record of the covenant or agreement between *David* and *Nahash* (but compare 17.27). The relations between Saul and Nahash had been hostile (1 Sam. ch. 11). **3:** Perhaps Hanun's advisers were thinking of David's treatment of the Moabites (see 8.2 n.). **4:** Mutilation of the beard, the symbol of a man's honor, and forcible indecent exposure were the worst insults imaginable in those days. **6–19:** The summary of these engagements in 8.3–8 omits mention of the part the Ammonites played in calling the Arameans (*Syrians*) into the conflict. **16:** Here *beyond the Euphrates* means "west of the Euphrates," as in 1 Kg.4.24. David now takes to the field in person, in spite of the earlier warning in 21.17 (compare 12.28). **18:** On the numbers, see 1 Sam.4.10 n.

So the Syrians feared to help the Ammonites any more.

In the spring of the year, the time when kings go forth to battle, David sent Jo'ab, and his servants with him, and all Israel; and they ravaged the Ammonites, and besieged Rabbah. But David remained at Jerusalem.

2 It happened, late one afternoon, when David arose from his couch and was walking upon the roof of the king's house, that he saw from the roof a woman bathing; and the woman was very beautiful. ³ And David sent and inquired about the woman. And one said, "Is not this Bathshe'ba, the daughter of Eli'am, the wife of Uri'ah the Hittite?" ⁴ So David sent messengers, and took her; and she came to him, and he lay with her. (Now she was purifying herself from her uncleanness.) Then she returned to her house. ⁵ And the woman conceived; and she sent and told David, "I am with child."

6 So David sent word to Jo'ab, "Send me Uri'ah the Hittite." And Jo'ab sent Uri'ah to David. ⁷ When Uri'ah came to him, David asked how Jo'ab was doing, and how the people fared, and how the war prospered. ⁸ Then David said to Uri'ah, "Go down to your house, and wash your feet." And Uri'ah went out of the king's house, and there followed him a present from the king. ⁹ But Uri'ah slept at the door of the king's house with all the servants of his lord, and did not go down to his house. ¹⁰ When they told David, "Uri'ah did not go down to his house," David said to Uri'ah, "Have you not come from a journey? Why did you not go down to your house?" ¹¹ Uri'ah said to David, "The ark and Israel and Judah dwell in booths; and my lord Jo'ab and the servants of my lord are camping in the open field; shall I then go to my house, to eat and to drink, and to lie with my wife? As you live, and as your soul lives, I will not do this thing." ¹² Then David said to Uri'ah, "Remain here today also, and tomorrow I will let you depart." So Uri'ah remained in Jerusalem that day, and the next. ¹³ And David invited him, and he ate in his presence and drank, so that he made him drunk; and in the evening he went out to lie on his couch with the servants of his lord, but he did not go down to his house.

14 In the morning David wrote a letter to Jo'ab, and sent it by the hand of Uri'ah. ¹⁵ In the letter he wrote, "Set Uri'ah in the forefront of the hardest fighting, and then draw back from him, that he may be struck down, and die." ¹⁶ And as Jo'ab was besieging the city, he assigned Uri'ah to the place where he knew there were valiant men. ¹⁷ And the men of the city came out and fought with Jo'ab; and some of the servants of David among the people fell. Uri'ah the Hittite was slain also. ¹⁸ Then Jo'ab sent and told David all the news about the fighting; ¹⁹ and he instructed the messenger, "When you have finished

---

11.1–27: Second campaign against Ammon; David wrongs Uriah. At this point the author begins his intimate portrait of the domestic and political troubles of the royal family and the court, with all their sordidness and tragic consequences. The military history serves only as a framework in which to place the personal episodes in the private and public life of the king. The amazing realism of the account could only have been achieved by a person with first-hand knowledge. By such a writer the sin of David with Bathsheba could not be omitted (as in 1 Chr. 20.1–3) or glossed over (as in 1 Sam.13.14). The consequences are so much a part of the story which follows that the cause must be clearly exhibited. Compare the superscription to Ps. 51, added by an editor, who at least recognized the facts and the need for repentance and divine mercy in such a case. **1:** *His servants*, outstanding men of the royal bodyguard (23.8–39); *all Israel*, the army in general. **3:** *Uriah the Hittite*, see 1 Sam.26.6 n. **4:** See Lev.15.19–24 for the later codification of the law on the purification from *uncleanness*. The parenthesis probably was added by an editor who wished to indicate moral *uncleanness* by a physical symbol. **8:** The invitation *wash your feet* was standard custom after a journey (Gen.18.4; 19.2; 24.32). **9–13:** Continence was required of soldiers consecrated for war by religious sanction (1 Sam.21.4–5).

telling all the news about the fighting to the king, 20 then, if the king's anger rises, and if he says to you, 'Why did you go so near the city to fight? Did you not know that they would shoot from the wall? 21 Who killed Abim'elech the son of Jerub'besheth? Did not a woman cast an upper millstone upon him from the wall, so that he died at Thebez? Why did you go so near the wall?' then you shall say, 'Your servant Uri'ah the Hittite is dead also.' "

22 So the messenger went, and came and told David all that Jo'ab had sent him to tell. 23 The messenger said to David, "The men gained an advantage over us, and came out against us in the field; but we drove them back to the entrance of the gate. 24 Then the archers shot at your servants from the wall; some of the king's servants are dead; and your servant Uri'ah the Hittite is dead also." 25 David said to the messenger, "Thus shall you say to Jo'ab, 'Do not let this matter trouble you, for the sword devours now one and now another; strengthen your attack upon the city, and overthrow it.' And encourage him."

26 When the wife of Uri'ah heard that Uri'ah her husband was dead, she made lamentation for her husband. 27 And when the mourning was over, David sent and brought her to his house, and she became his wife, and bore him a son. But the thing that David had done displeased the LORD.

12 And the LORD sent Nathan to David. He came to him, and said to him, "There were two men in a certain city, the one rich and the other poor. 2 The rich man had very many flocks and herds; 3 but the poor man had nothing but one little ewe lamb, which he had bought. And he brought it up, and it grew up with him and with his children; it used to eat of his morsel, and drink from his cup, and lie in his bosom, and it was like a daughter to him. 4 Now there came a traveler to the rich man, and he was unwilling to take one of his own flock or herd to prepare for the wayfarer who had come to him, but he took the poor man's lamb, and prepared it for the man who had come to him." 5 Then David's anger was greatly kindled against the man; and he said to Nathan, "As the LORD lives, the man who has done this deserves to die; 6 and he shall restore the lamb fourfold, because he did this thing, and because he had no pity."

7 Nathan said to David, "You are the man. Thus says the LORD, the God of Israel, 'I anointed you king over Israel, and I delivered you out of the hand of Saul; 8 and I gave you your master's house, and your master's wives into your bosom, and gave you the house of Israel and of Judah; and if this were too little, I would add to you as much more. 9 Why have you despised the word of the LORD, to do what is evil in his sight? You have smitten Uri'ah the Hittite with the sword, and have taken his wife to be your wife, and have slain him with the sword of the Ammonites. 10 Now therefore the sword shall never depart from your house, because you have despised me, and have taken the wife of Uri'ah the Hittite to be your wife.' 11 Thus says the LORD, 'Behold, I will raise up evil against you out of your own house; and I will take your wives before your eyes, and give them to your neighbor,

---

Uriah refused to violate this taboo even when David made him drunk. **21:** The name *Jerubbesheth* was originally Jerubbaal (see 2.8 n. and Jg.7.1); *besheth* is another form of the Hebrew word for "shame." **27:** Note the moral condemnation by the author in the name of God.

12.1–25: Rebuke of David by the prophet Nathan; David's repentance and the birth of Solomon. 1–6: Nathan's famous parable of the ewe lamb. The prophet showed courage, but not originality; what David had done was wrong, even according to the standards of that day. Later Nathan became an active supporter of Bathsheba (1 Kg.1.5–14). **8:** There is no other hint that David took over Saul's wives, though such was the custom (16.21–22; 1 Kg.2.17–25). **11:** The prediction of *evil . . . out of your own house* is very exact; it may have been added by an editor. The *neighbor* is presumably Absalom (16.21–22). **13–14:** According to the idea of the lex

and he shall lie with your wives in the sight of this sun. [12] For you did it secretly; but I will do this thing before all Israel, and before the sun.' " [13] David said to Nathan, "I have sinned against the LORD." And Nathan said to David, "The LORD also has put away your sin; you shall not die. [14] Nevertheless, because by this deed you have utterly scorned the LORD, [a] the child that is born to you shall die." [15] Then Nathan went to his house.

And the LORD struck the child that Uri'ah's wife bore to David, and it became sick. [16] David therefore besought God for the child; and David fasted, and went in and lay all night upon the ground. [17] And the elders of his house stood beside him, to raise him from the ground; but he would not, nor did he eat food with them. [18] On the seventh day the child died. And the servants of David feared to tell him that the child was dead; for they said, "Behold, while the child was yet alive, we spoke to him, and he did not listen to us; how then can we say to him the child is dead? He may do himself some harm." [19] But when David saw that his servants were whispering together, David perceived that the child was dead; and David said to his servants, "Is the child dead?" They said, "He is dead." [20] Then David arose from the earth, and washed, and anointed himself, and changed his clothes; and he went into the house of the LORD, and worshiped; he then went to his own house; and when he asked, they set food before him, and he ate. [21] Then his servants said to him,

"What is this thing that you have done? You fasted and wept for the child while it was alive; but when the child died, you arose and ate food." [22] He said, "While the child was still alive, I fasted and wept; for I said, 'Who knows whether the LORD will be gracious to me, that the child may live?' [23] But now he is dead; why should I fast? Can I bring him back again? I shall go to him, but he will not return to me."

24 Then David comforted his wife, Bathshe'ba, and went in to her, and lay with her; and she bore a son, and he called his name Solomon. And the LORD loved him, [25] and sent a message by Nathan the prophet; so he called his name Jedidi'ah,[b] because of the LORD.

26 Now Jo'ab fought against Rabbah of the Ammonites, and took the royal city. [27] And Jo'ab sent messengers to David, and said, "I have fought against Rabbah; moreover, I have taken the city of waters. [28] Now, then, gather the rest of the people together, and encamp against the city, and take it; lest I take the city, and it be called by my name." [29] So David gathered all the people together and went to Rabbah, and fought against it and took it. [30] And he took the crown of their king[c] from his head; the weight of it was a talent of gold, and in it was a precious stone; and it was placed on David's head. And he brought forth the spoil of the city, a very great amount. [31] And he brought forth the people who were in it, and set them to labor with

a Heb *the enemies of the* LORD
b That is *beloved of the* LORD
c Or *Milcom* See Zeph 1.5

---

talionis (law of exact retaliation, Ex.21.23–25; Lev.24.19–21; Dt.19.21) David should have died. Instead, divine judgment fell upon the child, according to the ideas of that day, as a special favor to David. The sin is *against the LORD;* it is God who sets the moral standard, not man. **23:** This verse reflects the idea of Sheol, the cavity under the earth where all the dead go (see Gen.37.35 n.; 1 Sam.2.6–7 n.), and from which there is no return (Job 7.9–10).

12.26–31: Conclusion of the campaign against Ammon. David takes the Ammonite capital. **26:** *Rabbah of the Ammonites* was the full name of the city, called more briefly Rabbath-Ammon or simply Rabbah. **27:** *The city of waters* means the place protecting the water supply. **28–29:** *Joab* was always careful to keep himself subservient to *David.* The word *people* here refers to the army. **30:** *Milcom* (see note c), the god of the Ammonites, may be the better reading (compare 1 Kg.11.5); if so, the reference is to an image of the god. *The weight* (a talent, about sixty-five lbs.) may be exaggerated.

saws and iron picks and iron axes, and made them toil at*d* the brickkilns; and thus he did to all the cities of the Ammonites. Then David and all the people returned to Jerusalem.

13 Now Ab'salom, David's son, had a beautiful sister, whose name was Tamar; and after a time Amnon, David's son, loved her. ² And Amnon was so tormented that he made himself ill because of his sister Tamar; for she was a virgin, and it seemed impossible to Amnon to do anything to her. ³ But Amnon had a friend, whose name was Jon'adab, the son of Shim'-e-ah, David's brother; and Jon'adab was a very crafty man. ⁴ And he said to him, "O son of the king, why are you so haggard morning after morning? Will you not tell me?" Amnon said to him, "I love Tamar, my brother Ab'-salom's sister." ⁵ Jon'adab said to him, "Lie down on your bed, and pretend to be ill; and when your father comes to see you, say to him, 'Let my sister Tamar come and give me bread to eat, and prepare the food in my sight, that I may see it, and eat it from her hand.'" ⁶ So Amnon lay down, and pretended to be ill; and when the king came to see him, Amnon said to the king, "Pray let my sister Tamar come and make a couple of cakes in my sight, that I may eat from her hand."

7 Then David sent home to Tamar, saying, "Go to your brother Amnon's house, and prepare food for him." ⁸ So Tamar went to her brother Amnon's house, where he was lying down. And she took dough, and kneaded it, and made cakes in his sight, and baked the cakes. ⁹ And she took the pan and emptied it out before him, but he refused to eat. And Amnon said, "Send out every one from me." So every one went out from him. ¹⁰ Then Amnon said to Tamar, "Bring the food into the chamber, that I may eat from your hand." And Tamar took the cakes she had made, and brought them into the chamber to Amnon her brother. ¹¹ But when she brought them near him to eat, he took hold of her, and said to her, "Come, lie with me, my sister." ¹² She answered him, "No, my brother, do not force me; for such a thing is not done in Israel; do not do this wanton folly. ¹³ As for me, where could I carry my shame? And as for you, you would be as one of the wanton fools in Israel. Now therefore, I pray you, speak to the king; for he will not withhold me from you." ¹⁴ But he would not listen to her; and being stronger than she, he forced her, and lay with her.

15 Then Amnon hated her with very great hatred; so that the hatred with which he hated her was greater than the love with which he had loved her. And Amnon said to her, "Arise, be gone." ¹⁶ But she said to him, "No, my brother; for this wrong in sending me away is greater than the other which you did to me"*e* But he would not listen to her. ¹⁷ He called the young man who served him and said, "Put this woman out of my presence, and bolt the door after her." ¹⁸ Now she was wearing a long robe with sleeves; for thus were the virgin daughters of the king clad of old.*f* So his servant put her

d Cn: Heb *pass through*
e Cn Compare Gk Vg: Heb *No, for this great wrong in sending me away is (worse) than the other which you did to me*   *f* Cn: Heb *clad in robes*

13.1–20.26: The story of Absalom. The ensuing events show what a later editor meant by *evil . . . out of your own house* (12.11). The actions of Absalom brought forth a series of political crises, with decisive effect on the future of the nation. The deaths of Amnon and Absalom opened the way for Solomon (12.24) to become king, though he was originally far down in the line of succession (3.2–5; 1 Kg. ch. 1).

13.1–39: Tamar raped by Amnon; Absalom has Amnon murdered and flees from the court. 1: Tamar was a full sister of Absalom, a half sister of Amnon. The latter, being the eldest son of David (3.2), would normally have succeeded David as king. Chileab, the second son (3.3), seems to have died young, leaving Absalom as the next in line of succession to the throne; this fact must be borne in mind as one considers the deeds of Absalom. **13:** At that time a man could marry his half sister, though later this practice was forbidden (Lev.18.9). **19:** On these

out, and bolted the door after her.
[19] And Tamar put ashes on her head,
and rent the long robe which she wore;
and she laid her hand on her head, and
went away, crying aloud as she went.
20 And her brother Ab'salom said
to her, "Has Amnon your brother been
with you? Now hold your peace, my
sister; he is your brother; do not take
this to heart." So Tamar dwelt, a desolate woman, in her brother Ab'salom's
house. [21] When King David heard of
all these things, he was very angry.
[22] But Ab'salom spoke to Amnon
neither good nor bad; for Ab'salom
hated Amnon, because he had forced
his sister Tamar.

23 After two full years Ab'salom
had sheepshearers at Ba'al-ha'zor,
which is near E'phraim, and Ab'salom
invited all the king's sons. [24] And Ab'-
salom came to the king, and said,
"Behold, your servant has sheepshearers; pray let the king and his servants
go with your servant." [25] But the
king said to Ab'salom, "No, my son,
let us not all go, lest we be burdensome
to you." He pressed him, but he would
not go but gave him his blessing.
[26] Then Ab'salom said, "If not, pray
let my brother Amnon go with us."
And the king said to him, "Why
should he go with you?" [27] But Ab'-
salom pressed him until he let Amnon and all the king's sons go with him.
[28] Then Ab'salom commanded his
servants, "Mark when Amnon's heart
is merry with wine, and when I say to
you, 'Strike Amnon,' then kill him.
Fear not; have I not commanded you?
Be courageous and be valiant." [29] So
the servants of Ab'salom did to Amnon
as Ab'salom had commanded. Then all
the king's sons arose, and each
mounted his mule and fled.

30 While they were on the way,
tidings came to David, "Ab'salom has
slain all the king's sons, and not one of
them is left." [31] Then the king arose,
and rent his garments, and lay on the
earth; and all his servants who were
standing by rent their garments.
[32] But Jon'adab the son of Shim'e-ah,
David's brother, said, "Let not my lord
suppose that they have killed all the
young men the king's sons, for Amnon
alone is dead, for by the command of
Ab'salom this has been determined
from the day he forced his sister Tamar. [33] Now therefore let not my lord
the king so take it to heart as to suppose that all the king's sons are dead;
for Amnon alone is dead."

34 But Ab'salom fled. And the
young man who kept the watch lifted up
his eyes, and looked, and behold, many
people were coming from the Horona'im road[g] by the side of the mountain. [35] And Jon'adab said to the king,
"Behold, the king's sons have come; as
your servant said, so it has come
about." [36] And as soon as he had
finished speaking, behold, the king's
sons came, and lifted up their voice
and wept; and the king also and all his
servants wept very bitterly.

37 But Ab'salom fled, and went to
Talmai the son of Ammi'hud, king of
Geshur. And David mourned for his
son day after day. [38] So Ab'salom
fled, and went to Geshur, and was
there three years. [39] And the spirit[h]
of the king longed to go forth to
Ab'salom; for he was comforted about
Amnon, seeing he was dead.

14 Now Jo'ab the son of Zeru'iah
perceived that the king's heart
went out to Ab'salom. [2] And Jo'ab sent

g Cn Compare Gk: Heb *the road behind him*
h Gk: Heb *David*

---

signs of grief see 15.32; 2 Kg.5.7; Est.4.1; Jer.2.37. **23–29:** Festivities at the time of sheepshear-
ing were usual (1 Sam.25.4–13). **37:** *Absalom fled* to the land of his maternal grandfather
(3.3). As an Aramean kingdom (15.8), *Geshur* was under the military control of David (8.3–8;
10.6–19).
   14.1–33: Joab brings about the return of Absalom. This incident is another manifestation of
the power and influence of *Joab*, who had a way of taking things into his own hands, though
he carefully remained subservient to David (v. 22 and 12.28). **2:** *Tekoa*, a few miles south of
Bethlehem, and thus in the home territory of David and Joab. Perhaps this helps to explain

to Teko'a, and fetched from there a wise woman, and said to her, "Pretend to be a mourner, and put on mourning garments; do not anoint yourself with oil, but behave like a woman who has been mourning many days for the dead; ³ and go to the king, and speak thus to him." So Jo'ab put the words in her mouth.

4 When the woman of Teko'a came to the king, she fell on her face to the ground, and did obeisance, and said, "Help, O king." ⁵ And the king said to her, "What is your trouble?" She answered, "Alas, I am a widow; my husband is dead. ⁶ And your handmaid had two sons, and they quarreled with one another in the field; there was no one to part them, and one struck the other and killed him. ⁷ And now the whole family has risen against your handmaid, and they say, 'Give up the man who struck his brother, that we may kill him for the life of his brother whom he slew'; and so they would destroy the heir also. Thus they would quench my coal which is left, and leave to my husband neither name nor remnant upon the face of the earth."

8 Then the king said to the woman, "Go to your house, and I will give orders concerning you." ⁹ And the woman of Teko'a said to the king, "On me be the guilt, my lord the king, and on my father's house; let the king and his throne be guiltless." ¹⁰ The king said, "If any one says anything to you, bring him to me, and he shall never touch you again." ¹¹ Then she said, "Pray let the king invoke the LORD your God, that the avenger of blood slay no more, and my son be not destroyed." He said, "As the LORD lives, not one hair of your son shall fall to the ground."

12 Then the woman said, "Pray let your handmaid speak a word to my lord the king." He said, "Speak." ¹³ And the woman said, "Why then have you planned such a thing against the people of God? For in giving this decision the king convicts himself, inasmuch as the king does not bring his banished one home again. ¹⁴ We must all die, we are like water spilt on the ground, which cannot be gathered up again; but God will not take away the life of him who devises*i* means not to keep his banished one an outcast. ¹⁵ Now I have come to say this to my lord the king because the people have made me afraid; and your handmaid thought, 'I will speak to the king; it may be that the king will perform the request of his servant. ¹⁶ For the king will hear, and deliver his servant from the hand of the man who would destroy me and my son together from the heritage of God.' ¹⁷ And your handmaid thought, 'The word of my lord the king will set me at rest'; for my lord the king is like the angel of God to discern good and evil. The LORD your God be with you!"

18 Then the king answered the woman, "Do not hide from me anything I ask you." And the woman said, "Let my lord the king speak." ¹⁹ The king said, "Is the hand of Jo'ab with you in all this?" The woman answered and said, "As surely as you live, my lord the king, one cannot turn to the right hand or to the left from anything that my lord the king has said. It was your servant Jo'ab who bade me; it was he who put all these words in the mouth of your handmaid. ²⁰ In order to change the course of affairs your servant Jo'ab did this. But my lord has wisdom like the wisdom of the angel of God to know all things that are on the earth."

21 Then the king said to Jo'ab, "Behold now, I grant this; go, bring back the young man Ab'salom." ²² And Jo'ab fell on his face to the ground, and did obeisance, and blessed the king; and Jo'ab said, "Today your servant knows that I have found favor in your

i Cn: Heb *and he devises*

---

why the king allowed the woman to speak so long and so freely with him. **7**: The use of the word *heir* by *the woman* is a good indication that Absalom was expected to succeed David as king.

sight, my lord the king, in that the king has granted the request of his servant." ²³ So Jo'ab arose and went to Geshur, and brought Ab'salom to Jerusalem. ²⁴ And the king said, "Let him dwell apart in his own house; he is not to come into my presence." So Ab'salom dwelt apart in his own house, and did not come into the king's presence.

25 Now in all Israel there was no one so much to be praised for his beauty as Ab'salom; from the sole of his foot to the crown of his head there was no blemish in him. ²⁶ And when he cut the hair of his head (for at the end of every year he used to cut it; when it was heavy on him, he cut it), he weighed the hair of his head, two hundred shekels by the king's weight. ²⁷ There were born to Ab'-salom three sons, and one daughter whose name was Tamar; she was a beautiful woman.

28 So Ab'salom dwelt two full years in Jerusalem, without coming into the king's presence. ²⁹ Then Ab'-salom sent for Jo'ab, to send him to the king; but Jo'ab would not come to him. And he sent a second time, but Jo'ab would not come. ³⁰ Then he said to his servants, "See, Jo'ab's field is next to mine, and he has barley there; go and set it on fire." So Ab'-salom's servants set the field on fire. ³¹ Then Jo'ab arose and went to Ab'-salom at his house, and said to him, "Why have your servants set my field on fire?" ³² Ab'salom answered Jo'ab,

"Behold, I sent word to you, 'Come here, that I may send you to the king, to ask, "Why have I come from Geshur? It would be better for me to be there still." Now therefore let me go into the presence of the king; and if there is guilt in me, let him kill me.'" ³³ Then Jo'ab went to the king, and told him; and he summoned Ab'salom. So he came to the king, and bowed himself on his face to the ground before the king; and the king kissed Ab'salom.

15 After this Ab'salom got himself a chariot and horses, and fifty men to run before him. ² And Ab'-salom used to rise early and stand beside the way of the gate; and when any man had a suit to come before the king for judgment, Ab'salom would call to him, and say, "From what city are you?" And when he said, "Your serv-ant is of such and such a tribe in Israel," ³ Ab'salom would say to him, "See, your claims are good and right; but there is no man deputed by the king to hear you." ⁴ Ab'salom said more-over, "Oh that I were judge in the land! Then every man with a suit or cause might come to me, and I would give him justice." ⁵ And whenever a man came near to do obeisance to him, he would put out his hand, and take hold of him, and kiss him. ⁶ Thus Ab'salom did to all of Israel who came to the king for judgment; so Ab'salom stole the hearts of the men of Israel.

7 And at the end of four*ʲ* years

ʲ Gk Syr: Heb *forty*

26: There were at least two standards of *weight* at that time, the common and the royal, or *the king's weight.* The latter was somewhat heavier; *two hundred shekels* would have been roughly five pounds. **27:** Absalom seems to have named his daughter after his ravished sister, Tamar. The information in this verse is doubtless correct; contrast 18.18. **28:** It was very likely during this period that Absalom began to plot revolt. Some have blamed David for de-laying the reconciliation too long

15.1–37: Absalom revolts and David flees from Jerusalem. Since *Absalom* was the natural heir to the throne (see 14.7 n.), it may be asked why he revolted during David's lifetime. Primo-geniture was the normal practice in Israel (2 Sam.2.8–10; Dt.21.15–17), but there were excep-tions (1 Chr.5.1–2; 26.10). David himself had established a new dynasty, and had failed to lay down a law of succession (1 Kg.1.27). Absalom, knowing that he had once been out of favor with his father, may have feared that something similar would happen again. Or perhaps, like Amnon, he simply could not wait for what he wanted so badly. **1–6:** *Chariot and horses, and fifty men,* compare 1 Kg.1.5. Absalom attacks another weakness of David's administration, the failure to establish a judiciary system, with consequent delay in the hearing of cases. David

Ab'salom said to the king, "Pray let me go and pay my vow, which I have vowed to the LORD, in Hebron. ⁸ For your servant vowed a vow while I dwelt at Geshur in Aram, saying, 'If the LORD will indeed bring me back to Jerusalem, then I will offer worship to the LORD.' " ⁹ The king said to him, "Go in peace." So he arose, and went to Hebron. ¹⁰ But Ab'salom sent secret messengers throughout all the tribes of Israel, saying, "As soon as you hear the sound of the trumpet, then say, 'Ab'salom is king at Hebron!' " ¹¹ With Ab'salom went two hundred men from Jerusalem who were invited guests, and they went in their simplicity, and knew nothing. ¹² And while Ab'salom was offering the sacrifices, he sent for*ᵏ* Ahith'opel the Gi'lonite, David's counselor, from his city Giloh. And the conspiracy grew strong, and the people with Ab'salom kept increasing.

13 And a messenger came to David, saying, "The hearts of the men of Israel have gone after Ab'salom." ¹⁴ Then David said to all his servants who were with him at Jerusalem, "Arise, and let us flee; or else there will be no cscape for us from Ab'salom; go in haste, lest he overtake us quickly, and bring down evil upon us, and smite the city with the edge of the sword." ¹⁵ And the king's servants said to the king, "Behold, your servants are ready to do whatever my lord the king decides." ¹⁶ So the king went forth, and all his household after him. And the king left ten concubines to keep the house. ¹⁷ And the king went forth, and all the people after him; and they halted at the last house. ¹⁸ And all his servants passed by him; and all the Cher'ethites, and all the Pel'-ethites, and all the six hundred Gittites who had followed him from Gath, passed on before the king.

19 Then the king said to It'tai the Gittite, "Why do you also go with us? Go back, and stay with the king; for you are a foreigner, and also an exile from*ˡ* your home. ²⁰ You came only yesterday, and shall I today make you wander about with us, seeing I go I know not where? Go back, and take your brethren with you; and may the LORD show*ᵐ* steadfast love and faithfulness to you." ²¹ But It'tai answered the king, "As the LORD lives, and as my lord the king lives, wherever my lord the king shall be, whether for death or for life, there also will your servant be." ²² And David said to It'tai, "Go then, pass on." So It'tai the Gittite passed on, with all his men and all the little ones who were with him. ²³ And all the country wept aloud as all the people passed by, and the king crossed the brook Kidron, and all the people passed on toward the wilderness.

24 And Abi'athar came up, and lo, Zadok came also, with all the Levites, bearing the ark of the covenant of God; and they set down the ark of God, until the people had all passed out of the city. ²⁵ Then the king said to

k Or *sent*
l Gk Syr Vg: Heb *to*
m Gk: Heb lacks *may the* LORD *show*

---

was better as a military leader than as a peace-time organizer. **7–12:** The conspiracy was carefully nurtured for a period of *four years.* Absalom could have worshiped in Jerusalem, but he had probably found disaffection in Hebron over the loss of status as the capital city. *Ahithophel the Gilonite* was perhaps the grandfather of Bathsheba (compare 11.3 with 23.34). If so, he may have resented David's conduct with his granddaughter in spite of the higher status which it brought to the family. **13–18:** David flees Jerusalem, perhaps feeling that he would have an advantage by fighting in the open country. He probably also suspected the loyalty of some of those around him; by leaving, he could find out who would follow him regardless of circumstances, and at the same time he could leave behind his agents to work secretly for him in the city. See the superscription to Ps. 3. *Ten concubines,* see 5.13–16 n. *Cherethites and . . . Pelethites,* see 8.18 n. *Gittites* (rather than "Gathites") is the proper form designating people *from Gath.* It is rather surprising to find so many Philistines in David's army. **23:** The weeping of *the people* indicates that *the king* retained much popular support. *The brook Kidron* marked

Zadok, "Carry the ark of God back into the city. If I find favor in the eyes of the LORD, he will bring me back and let me see both it and his habitation; [26] but if he says, 'I have no pleasure in you,' behold, here I am, let him do to me what seems good to him." [27] The king also said to Zadok the priest, "Look,[n] go back to the city in peace, you and Abi'athar,[o] with your two sons, Ahim'a-az your son, and Jonathan the son of Abi'athar. [28] See, I will wait at the fords of the wilderness, until word comes from you to inform me." [29] So Zadok and Abi'athar carried the ark of God back to Jerusalem; and they remained there.

30 But David went up the ascent of the Mount of Olives, weeping as he went, barefoot and with his head covered; and all the people who were with him covered their heads, and they went up, weeping as they went. [31] And it was told David, "Ahith'ophel is among the conspirators with Ab'salom." And David said, "O LORD, I pray thee, turn the counsel of Ahith'ophel into foolishness."

32 When David came to the summit, where God was worshiped, behold, Hushai the Archite came to meet him with his coat rent and earth upon his head. [33] David said to him, "If you go on with me, you will be a burden to me. [34] But if you return to the city, and say to Ab'salom, 'I will be your servant, O king; as I have been your father's servant in time past, so now I will be your servant,' then you will defeat for me the counsel of Ahith'ophel.

[35] Are not Zadok and Abi'athar the priests with you there? So whatever you hear from the king's house, tell it to Zadok and Abi'athar the priests. [36] Behold, their two sons are with them there, Ahim'a-az, Zadok's son, and Jonathan, Abi'athar's son; and by them you shall send to me everything you hear." [37] So Hushai, David's friend, came into the city, just as Ab'salom was entering Jerusalem.

16 When David had passed a little beyond the summit, Ziba the servant of Mephib'osheth met him, with a couple of asses saddled, bearing two hundred loaves of bread, a hundred bunches of raisins, a hundred of summer fruits, and a skin of wine. [2] And the king said to Ziba, "Why have you brought these?" Ziba answered, "The asses are for the king's household to ride on, the bread and summer fruit for the young men to eat, and the wine for those who faint in the wilderness to drink." [3] And the king said, "And where is your master's son?" Ziba said to the king, "Behold, he remains in Jerusalem; for he said, 'Today the house of Israel will give me back the kingdom of my father.'" [4] Then the king said to Ziba, "Behold, all that belonged to Mephib'osheth is now yours." And Ziba said, "I do obeisance; let me ever find favor in your sight, my lord the king."

5 When King David came to Bahu'rim, there came out a man of the family of the house of Saul, whose

____

n Gk: Heb *Are you a seer* or *Do you see?*
o Cn: Heb lacks *and Abiathar*

____

the eastern boundary of the city. **24–37**: David's leaving *the ark* in Jerusalem was a fair indication that he expected to return. It was also good diplomacy to have the loyal priests in the city (vv. 35–36). On *Zadok*, see 8.17 n. *Abiathar* and *Ahimaaz* (v. 27) have been mentioned as possible authors of the Early Source (see Introduction to 1 Samuel). *Hushai the Archite, David's friend* (i.e. "royal counselor," an official title, 1 Kg.4.5), came from an originally Canaanite group settled near Bethel (Jos.16.2). Under David's inclusive policy, various non-Israelite groups (Hittites, Philistines, Canaanites, and the like) became naturalized. These people seem to have been particularly loyal to David, perhaps partly because of his policies and personality, partly because he himself was not an Israelite (19.11–15).

16.1–23: **David in flight; Absalom takes over Jerusalem. 1–4**: *Mephibosheth*, see ch. 9 and notes there. *Ziba* was probably lying for his own advantage; see Mephibosheth's defense in 19.24–30. David, perhaps disturbed by the reference to the dynasty of Saul, here makes too hasty a decision. **5–14**: The disaffection in Judah over loss of the capital has already been noted (see 15.7–

name was Shim'e-i, the son of Gera; and as he came he cursed continually. ⁶ And he threw stones at David, and at all the servants of King David; and all the people and all the mighty men were on his right hand and on his left. ⁷ And Shim'e-i said as he cursed, "Begone, begone, you man of blood, you worthless fellow! ⁸ The LORD has avenged upon you all the blood of the house of Saul, in whose place you have reigned; and the LORD has given the kingdom into the hand of your son Ab'salom. See, your ruin is on you; for you are a man of blood."

9 Then Abi'shai the son of Zeru'iah said to the king, "Why should this dead dog curse my lord the king? Let me go over and take off his head." ¹⁰ But the king said, "What have I to do with you, you sons of Zeru'iah? If he is cursing because the LORD has said to him, 'Curse David,' who then shall say, 'Why have you done so?' " ¹¹ And David said to Abi'shai and to all his servants, "Behold, my own son seeks my life; how much more now may this Benjaminite! Let him alone, and let him curse; for the LORD has bidden him. ¹² It may be that the LORD will look upon my affliction,ᵖ and that the LORD will repay me with good for this cursing of me today." ¹³ So David and his men went on the road, while Shim'e-i went along on the hillside opposite him and cursed as he went, and threw stones at him and flung dust. ¹⁴ And the king, and all the people who were with him, arrived weary at the Jordan;ᵍ and there he refreshed himself.

15 Now Ab'salom and all the people, the men of Israel, came to Jerusalem, and Ahith'ophel with him.

¹⁶ And when Hushai the Archite, David's friend, came to Ab'salom, Hushai said to Ab'salom, "Long live the king! Long live the king!" ¹⁷ And Ab'salom said to Hushai, "Is this your loyalty to your friend? Why did you not go with your friend?" ¹⁸ And Hushai said to Ab'salom, "No; for whom the LORD and this people and all the men of Israel have chosen, his I will be, and with him I will remain. ¹⁹ And again, whom should I serve? Should it not be his son? As I have served your father, so I will serve you."

20 Then Ab'salom said to Ahith'ophel, "Give your counsel; what shall we do?" ²¹ Ahith'ophel said to Ab'salom, "Go in to your father's concubines, whom he has left to keep the house; and all Israel will hear that you have made yourself odious to your father, and the hands of all who are with you will be strengthened." ²² So they pitched a tent for Ab'salom upon the roof; and Ab'salom went in to his father's concubines in the sight of all Israel. ²³ Now in those days the counsel which Ahith'ophel gave was as if one consulted the oracleʳ of God; so was all the counsel of Ahith'ophel esteemed, both by David and by Ab'salom.

17 Moreover Ahith'ophel said to Ab'salom, "Let me choose twelve thousand men, and I will set out and pursue David tonight. ² I will come upon him while he is weary and discouraged, and throw him into a panic; and all the people who are with him will flee. I will strike down the king only, ³ and I will bring all the people back to you as a bride comes home to her husband. You seek the

p Gk Vg: Heb *iniquity*
q Gk: Heb lacks *at the Jordan*
r Heb *word*

12 n.); here we see the disaffection in Israel over loss of the ruling dynasty (v. 8). This time, however, David keeps a cool head and refuses to be pushed into a hasty judgment. For the result, see 19.16–23; compare 1 Kg.2.8–9. *This dead dog*, see 3.8 n. On the undue haste of a *son of Zeruiah* with the sword, see 3.39. **20–23:** The *concubines* were royal property; hence taking them over publicly was a sensational way of showing the people that Absalom had assumed the office and prerogatives of kingship (3.7; 15.16; 1 Kg.2.17–25).

17.1–23: Hushai frustrates the plan of Ahithophel. 1–14: The plan of Ahithophel would probably have led to success for Absalom. The plan of Hushai gave the advantage to David by

life of only one man,[s] and all the people will be at peace." [4] And the advice pleased Ab'salom and all the elders of Israel.

5 Then Ab'salom said, "Call Hushai the Archite also, and let us hear what he has to say." [6] And when Hushai came to Ab'salom, Ab'salom said to him, "Thus has Ahith'ophel spoken; shall we do as he advises? If not, you speak." [7] Then Hushai said to Ab'salom, "This time the counsel which Ahith'ophel has given is not good." [8] Hushai said moreover, "You know that your father and his men are mighty men, and that they are enraged, like a bear robbed of her cubs in the field. Besides, your father is expert in war; he will not spend the night with the people. [9] Behold, even now he has hidden himself in one of the pits, or in some other place. And when some of the people fall[t] at the first attack, whoever hears it will say, 'There has been a slaughter among the people who follow Ab'salom.' [10] Then even the valiant man, whose heart is like the heart of a lion, will utterly melt with fear; for all Israel knows that your father is a mighty man, and that those who are with him are valiant men. [11] But my counsel is that all Israel be gathered to you, from Dan to Beersheba, as the sand by the sea for multitude, and that you go to battle in person. [12] So we shall come upon him in some place where he is to be found, and we shall light upon him as the dew falls on the ground; and of him and all the men with him not one will be left. [13] If he withdraws into a city, then all Israel will bring ropes to that city, and we shall drag it into the valley, until not even a pebble is to be found there."

[14] And Ab'salom and all the men of Israel said, "The counsel of Hushai the Archite is better than the counsel of Ahith'ophel." For the LORD had ordained to defeat the good counsel of Ahith'ophel, so that the LORD might bring evil upon Ab'salom.

15 Then Hushai said to Zadok and Abi'athar the priests, "Thus and so did Ahith'ophel counsel Ab'salom and the elders of Israel; and thus and so have I counseled. [16] Now therefore send quickly and tell David, 'Do not lodge tonight at the fords of the wilderness, but by all means pass over; lest the king and all the people who are with him be swallowed up.'" [17] Now Jonathan and Ahim'a-az were waiting at En-ro'gel; a maidservant used to go and tell them, and they would go and tell King David; for they must not be seen entering the city. [18] But a lad saw them, and told Ab'salom; so both of them went away quickly, and came to the house of a man at Bahu'rim, who had a well in his courtyard; and they went down into it. [19] And the woman took and spread a covering over the well's mouth, and scattered grain upon it; and nothing was known of it. [20] When Ab'salom's servants came to the woman at the house, they said, "Where are Ahim'a-az and Jonathan?" And the woman said to them, "They have gone over the brook[u] of water." And when they had sought and could not find them, they returned to Jerusalem.

21 After they had gone, the men came up out of the well, and went and told King David. They said to

s Gk: Heb *like the return of the whole (is) the man whom you seek*
t Or *when he falls upon them*
u The meaning of the Hebrew word is uncertain

---

enabling him to collect his forces for a formal battle in which experience and skill would be decisive. Recognition of these facts led to the suicide of Ahithophel (v. 23). The last sentence of v. 14 was added by an editor who wished to remind the reader that all things are *ordained* by God. **15–22:** David is informed and crosses the Jordan. Hushai did not know which way the decision had gone; hence his recommendation to cross the river immediately. *En-rogel* is a spring near the southeast corner of Jerusalem, now called Job's Well. *Bahurim* is east of the Mt. of Olives. Only a person with intimate knowledge of the events could have written these verses. Was the author *Abiathar*, *Ahimaaz*, or someone else? See comments on 15.27 and on the next chapter. **23:** On Biblical suicides, see 1 Sam.31.5 n.

David, "Arise, and go quickly over the water; for thus and so has Ahith'ophel counseled against you." ²² Then David arose, and all the people who were with him, and they crossed the Jordan; by daybreak not one was left who had not crossed the Jordan.

23 When Ahith'ophel saw that his counsel was not followed, he saddled his ass, and went off home to his own city. And he set his house in order, and hanged himself; and he died, and was buried in the tomb of his father.

24 Then David came to Mahana'im. And Ab'salom crossed the Jordan with all the men of Israel. ²⁵ Now Ab'salom had set Ama'sa over the army instead of Jo'ab. Ama'sa was the son of a man named Ithra the Ish'maelite,ᵛ who had married Ab'igal the daughter of Nahash, sister of Zeru'iah, Jo'ab's mother. ²⁶ And Israel and Ab'salom encamped in the land of Gilead.

27 When David came to Mahana'im, Shobi the son of Nahash from Rabbah of the Ammonites, and Machir the son of Am'mi-el from Lo'debar, and Barzil'lai the Gileadite from Ro'-gelim, ²⁸ brought beds, basins, and earthen vessels, wheat, barley, meal, parched grain, beans and lentils,ʷ ²⁹ honey and curds and sheep and cheese from the herd, for David and the people with him to eat; for they said, "The people are hungry and weary and thirsty in the wilderness."

18 Then David mustered the men who were with him, and set over them commanders of thousands and commanders of hundreds. ² And David sent forth the army, one third under the command of Jo'ab, one third under the command of Abi'shai the son of Zeru'iah, Jo'ab's brother, and one third under the command of It'tai the Gittite. And the king said to the men, "I myself will also go out with you." ³ But the men said, "You shall not go out. For if we flee, they will not care about us. If half of us die, they will not care about us. But you are worth ten thousand of us;ˣ therefore it is better that you send us help from the city." ⁴ The king said to them, "Whatever seems best to you I will do." So the king stood at the side of the gate, while all the army marched out by hundreds and by thousands. ⁵ And the king ordered Jo'ab and Abi'shai and It'tai, "Deal gently for my sake with the young man Ab'salom." And all the people heard when the king gave orders to all the commanders about Ab'salom.

6 So the army went out into the field against Israel; and the battle was fought in the forest of E'phraim. ⁷ And the men of Israel were defeated there by the servants of David, and the slaughter there was great on that day, twenty thousand men. ⁸ The battle spread over the face of all the country; and the forest devoured more people that day than the sword.

ᵛ 1 Chr 2.17: Heb *Israelite*
ʷ Heb *lentils and parched grain*
ˣ Gk Vg Symmachus: Heb *for now there are ten thousand such as we*

17.24–29: David in Transjordan. *Amasa* was a cousin of Joab; both of them were nephews of David and cousins of Absalom (1 Chr.2.13–17). The *Nahash* in v. 25 (probably an error) is not the same person as the *Nahash* of v. 27. On the latter as a friend of David, see 10.2. *Shobi*, unlike his brother Hanun, was friendly to David. It has even been proposed that David had deposed Hanun after the events of ch. 10, putting *Shobi* in his place. *Machir*, see 9.4. The Aramean name of *Barzillai* shows him to have been a non-Israelite; see the comment on Hushai, 15.24–37 n.

18.1–8: The battle in the forest of Ephraim. 3–4: For an earlier agreement that David should remain out of the front line of battle, see 21.17; for an exception, see 12.28–29. **5:** In spite of Absalom's complete apostasy, David still loved him and wished that his life might be saved. **6–8:** As might have been expected, Absalom's hastily assembled forces were no match for David's standing army under skilled and experienced commanders. Great numbers of the raw recruits were driven into *the forest*, a trackless jungle, from which there was no escape. The number *twenty thousand* is an overgenerous estimate; there was no counting before or after the battle (see 12.30 n. and 1 Sam.4.10 n.).

9 And Ab'salom chanced to meet the servants of David. Ab'salom was riding upon his mule, and the mule went under the thick branches of a great oak, and his head caught fast in the oak, and he was left hanging[y] between heaven and earth, while the mule that was under him went on. [10] And a certain man saw it, and told Jo'ab, "Behold, I saw Ab'salom hanging in an oak." [11] Jo'ab said to the man who told him, "What, you saw him! Why then did you not strike him there to the ground? I would have been glad to give you ten pieces of silver and a girdle." [12] But the man said to Jo'ab, "Even if I felt in my hand the weight of a thousand pieces of silver, I would not put forth my hand against the king's son; for in our hearing the king commanded you and Abi'shai and It'tai, 'For my sake protect the young man Ab'salom.' [13] On the other hand, if I had dealt treacherously against his life[z] (and there is nothing hidden from the king), then you yourself would have stood aloof." [14] Jo'ab said, "I will not waste time like this with you." And he took three darts in his hand, and thrust them into the heart of Ab'salom, while he was still alive in the oak. [15] And ten young men, Jo'ab's armor-bearers, surrounded Ab'salom and struck him, and killed him.

16 Then Jo'ab blew the trumpet, and the troops came back from pursuing Israel; for Jo'ab restrained them. [17] And they took Ab'salom, and threw him into a great pit in the forest, and raised over him a very great heap of stones; and all Israel fled every one to his own home. [18] Now Ab'salom in his lifetime had taken and set up for himself the pillar which is in the King's Valley, for he said, "I have no son to keep my name in remembrance"; he called the pillar after his own name, and it is called Ab'salom's monument to this day.

19 Then said Ahi'ma-az the son of Zadok, "Let me run, and carry tidings to the king that the LORD has delivered him from the power of his enemies." [20] And Jo'ab said to him, "You are not to carry tidings today; you may carry tidings another day, but today you shall carry no tidings, because the king's son is dead." [21] Then Jo'ab said to the Cushite, "Go, tell the king what you have seen." The Cushite bowed before Jo'ab, and ran. [22] Then Ahi'ma-az the son of Zadok said again to Jo'ab, "Come what may, let me also run after the Cushite." And Jo'ab said, "Why will you run, my son, seeing that you will have no reward for the tidings?" [23] "Come what may," he said, "I will run." So he said to him, "Run." Then Ahi'ma-az ran by the way of the plain, and outran the Cushite.

24 Now David was sitting between the two gates; and the watchman went up to the roof of the gate by the wall, and when he lifted up his eyes and looked, he saw a man running alone. [25] And the watchman called out and

y Gk Syr Tg: Heb *was put*
z Another reading is *at the risk of my life*

18.9–18: The death of Absalom. There is a popular notion, based on 14.26, that Absalom was caught by his hair. The present text implies that his whole *head* was caught (v. 9). Joab never withheld a fatal blow when he felt that it would be to his own or David's advantage (3.27; 20.10). Verse 15 seems unnecessary and may have been added later. **16–18:** These verses show that Absalom's tomb was very different from what he had intended; he had prepared for himself a showy monument near Jerusalem. The statement about his having *no son* appears to be an error (compare 14.27). The monument commonly called "Absalom's Tomb," still standing today in the Kidron valley, is of Hellenistic or Roman date, and has no connection with the original *Absalom's monument*.

18.19–33: The grief of David. The story in these verses provides the reason why many commentators believe *Ahimaaz the son of Zadok* to be the author of the Early Source. In any case, such detailed information about the incident could have come only from *the son of Zadok*. Ahimaaz was too excited to remain behind, yet when he faced *the king* he lacked the courage

told the king. And the king said, "If he is alone, there are tidings in his mouth." And he came apace, and drew near. ²⁶ And the watchman saw another man running; and the watchman called to the gate and said, "See, another man running alone!" The king said, "He also brings tidings." ²⁷ And the watchman said, "I think the running of the foremost is like the running of Ahi′ma-az the son of Zadok." And the king said, "He is a good man, and comes with good tidings."

28 Then Ahi′ma-az cried out to the king, "All is well." And he bowed before the king with his face to the earth, and said, "Blessed be the LORD your God, who has delivered up the men who raised their hand against my lord the king." ²⁹ And the king said, "Is it well with the young man Ab′salom?" Ahi′ma-az answered, "When Jo′ab sent your servant,^b I saw a great tumult, but I do not know what it was." ³⁰ And the king said, "Turn aside, and stand here." So he turned aside, and stood still.

31 And behold, the Cushite came; and the Cushite said, "Good tidings for my lord the king! For the LORD has delivered you this day from the power of all who rose up against you." ³² The king said to the Cushite, "Is it well with the young man Ab′salom?" And the Cushite answered, "May the enemies of my lord the king, and all who rise up against you for evil, be like that young man." ^{33c} And the king was deeply moved, and went up to the chamber over the gate, and wept; and as he went, he said, "O my son Ab′-salom, my son, my son Ab′salom! Would I had died instead of you, O Ab′salom, my son, my son!"

19 It was told Jo′ab, "Behold, the king is weeping and mourning for Ab′salom." ² So the victory that day was turned into mourning for all the people; for the people heard that day, "The king is grieving for his son." ³ And the people stole into the city that day as people steal in who are ashamed when they flee in battle. ⁴ The king covered his face, and the king cried with a loud voice, "O my son Ab′salom, O Ab′salom, my son, my son!" ⁵ Then Jo′ab came into the house to the king, and said, "You have today covered with shame the faces of all your servants, who have this day saved your life, and the lives of your sons and your daughters, and the lives of your wives and your concubines, ⁶ because you love those who hate you and hate those who love you. For you have made it clear today that commanders and servants are nothing to you; for today I perceive that if Ab′salom were alive and all of us were dead today, then you would be pleased. ⁷ Now therefore arise, go out and speak kindly to your servants; for I swear by the LORD, if you do not go, not a man will stay with you this night; and this will be worse for you than all the evil that has come upon you from your youth until now." ⁸ Then the king arose, and took his seat in the gate. And the people were all told, "Behold, the king is sitting in the gate"; and all the people came before the king.

Now Israel had fled every man to his own home. ⁹ And all the people were at strife throughout all the tribes of Israel, saying, "The king delivered us from the hand of our enemies, and saved us from the hand of the Philistines; and now he has fled out of the land from Ab′salom. ¹⁰ But Ab′salom, whom we anointed over us, is dead in battle. Now therefore why do you say nothing about bringing the king back?"

b Heb *the King's servant, your servant*
c Ch 19.1 in Heb

to tell the whole story, as Joab had foreseen. **31–33:** It remained for the Ethiopian slave (*the Cushite;* compare Jer.13.23; 38.7; 39.16–18) to reveal the true state of affairs. In his personal grief, David momentarily forgot his military victory and his public duties.

19.1–43: David attempts to restore a divided and disorganized nation. 1–8a: It was only Joab who could speak realistically to the king about his royal obligations. **8b–10:** The Israelites made the first overtures to renew allegiance to David. **11–15:** *David* appeals to the Judahites

11 And King David sent this message to Zadok and Abi'athar the priests, "Say to the elders of Judah, 'Why should you be the last to bring the king back to his house, when the word of all Israel has come to the king?*d* 12 You are my kinsmen, you are my bone and my flesh; why then should you be the last to bring back the king?' 13 And say to Ama'sa, 'Are you not my bone and my flesh? God do so to me, and more also, if you are not commander of my army henceforth in place of Jo'ab.' " 14 And he swayed the heart of all the men of Judah as one man; so that they sent word to the king, "Return, both you and all your servants." 15 So the king came back to the Jordan; and Judah came to Gilgal to meet the king and to bring the king over the Jordan.

16 And Shim'e-i the son of Gera, the Benjaminite, from Bahu'rim, made haste to come down with the men of Judah to meet King David; 17 and with him were a thousand men from Benjamin. And Ziba the servant of the house of Saul, with his fifteen sons and his twenty servants, rushed down to the Jordan before the king, 18 and they crossed the ford*e* to bring over the king's household, and to do his pleasure. And Shim'e-i the son of Gera fell down before the king, as he was about to cross the Jordan, 19 and said to the king, "Let not my lord hold me guilty or remember how your servant did wrong on the day my lord the king left Jerusalem; let not the king bear it in mind. 20 For your servant knows that I have sinned; therefore, behold, I have come this day, the first of all the house of Joseph to come down to meet my lord the king." 21 Abi'shai the son of Zeru'iah answered, "Shall not Shim'e-i be put to death for this, because he cursed the LORD's anointed?" 22 But David said, "What have I to do with you, you sons of Zeru'iah, that you should this day be as an adversary to me? Shall any one be put to death in Israel this day? For do I not know that I am this day king over Israel?" 23 And the king said to Shim'e-i, "You shall not die." And the king gave him his oath.

24 And Mephib'osheth the son of Saul came down to meet the king; he had neither dressed his feet, nor trimmed his beard, nor washed his clothes, from the day the king departed until the day he came back in safety. 25 And when he came from*f* Jerusalem to meet the king, the king said to him, "Why did you not go with me, Mephib'osheth?" 26 He answered, "My lord, O king, my servant deceived me; for your servant said to him, 'Saddle an ass for me,*g* that I may ride upon it and go with the king.' For your servant is lame. 27 He has slandered your servant to my lord the king. But my lord the king is like the angel of God; do therefore what seems good to you. 28 For all my father's house were but men doomed to death before my lord the king; but you set your servant among those who eat at your table. What further right have I, then, to cry to the king?" 29 And the king said to him, "Why speak any more of your affairs? I have decided: you and Ziba shall divide the land." 30 And Mephib'osheth said to the king, "Oh, let him take it all, since my lord the king has come safely home."

31 Now Barzil'lai the Gileadite had come down from Ro'gelim; and he went on with the king to the Jordan, to escort him over the Jordan. 32 Bar-

d Gk: Heb *to the king, to his house*
e Cn: Heb *the ford crossed*   *f* Heb *to*
g Gk Syr Vg: Heb *said, I will saddle an ass for myself*

---

on the basis of tribal loyalty and by giving Joab's position to *Amasa*. On Amasa's kinship to David and Joab, see 17.24–29 n. David no doubt resented Joab's killing of Absalom (18.14) and also remembered the case of Abner (3.27–29). **16–23:** *Shimei* and *Ziba* rushed to pay homage to *David* (compare 16.1–14). *David* forgave *Shimei. House of Joseph* (v. 20), another name for the northern tribes or Israel. **24–30:** See ch. 9 and 16.1–5. David had made a hasty decision in Ziba's case against Mephibosheth. Now, confronted by both parties, *the king* seemed unable to make a firm decision, though Mephibosheth's evidences of loyalty (v. 24) and

zil'lai was a very aged man, eighty years old; and he had provided the king with food while he stayed at Mahana'im; for he was a very wealthy man. ³³ And the king said to Barzil'lai, "Come over with me, and I will provide for you with me in Jerusalem." ³⁴ But Barzil'lai said to the king, "How many years have I still to live, that I should go up with the king to Jerusalem? ³⁵ I am this day eighty years old; can I discern what is pleasant and what is not? Can your servant taste what he eats or what he drinks? Can I still listen to the voice of singing men and singing women? Why then should your servant be an added burden to my lord the king? ³⁶ Your servant will go a little way over the Jordan with the king. Why should the king recompense me with such a reward? ³⁷ Pray let your servant return, that I may die in my own city, near the grave of my father and my mother. But here is your servant Chimham; let him go over with my lord the king; and do for him whatever seems good to you." ³⁸ And the king answered, "Chimham shall go over with me, and I will do for him whatever seems good to you; and all that you desire of me I will do for you." ³⁹ Then all the people went over the Jordan, and the king went over; and the king kissed Barzil'lai and blessed him, and he returned to his own home. ⁴⁰ The king went on to Gilgal, and Chimham went on with him; all the people of Judah, and also half the people of Israel, brought the king on his way.

41 Then all the men of Israel came to the king, and said to the king, "Why have our brethren the men of Judah stolen you away, and brought the king and his household over the Jordan, and all David's men with him?" ⁴² All the men of Judah answered the men of Israel, "Because the king is near of kin to us. Why then are you angry over this matter? Have we eaten at all at the king's expense? Or has he given us any gift?" ⁴³ And the men of Israel answered the men of Judah, "We have ten shares in the king, and in David also we have more than you. Why then did you despise us? Were we not the first to speak of bringing back our king?" But the words of the men of Judah were fiercer than the words of the men of Israel.

20 Now there happened to be there a worthless fellow, whose name was Sheba, the son of Bichri, a Benjaminite; and he blew the trumpet, and said,

"We have no portion in David,
    and we have no inheritance in the son of Jesse;
    every man to his tents, O Israel!"

² So all the men of Israel withdrew from David, and followed Sheba the son of Bichri; but the men of Judah followed their king steadfastly from the Jordan to Jerusalem.

3 And David came to his house at Jerusalem; and the king took the ten concubines whom he had left to care for the house, and put them in a house under guard, and provided for them, but did not go in to them. So they were shut up until the day of their death, living as if in widowhood.

4 Then the king said to Ama'sa, "Call the men of Judah together to me within three days, and be here yourself." ⁵ So Ama'sa went to sum-

---

self-abnegation (vv. 28,30) appear genuine. **31–40a:** It is usually assumed that *Chimham* was the son of *Barzillai*, though the text does not specifically so state (compare 1 Kg.2.7). **40b:** The word *all* is something of an exaggeration, signifying that by this time Judah was solidly in favor of David, whereas Israel was hardly more than half persuaded (compare 20.2). **41–43:** The antagonism between *Israel* and *Judah* breaks out again. In the light of this passage, it can be seen that the final division of the kingdom after the death of Solomon (1 Kg.12.16–20) had its roots in an old cleavage.

    20.1–22: New revolt in Israel; Joab murders Amasa, regains his position, and quells the revolt. **1–2:** It is significant that *Sheba* came from Benjamin, the most disaffected tribe (compare 16.5,8). The war cry is repeated in 1 Kg.12.16. **3:** See 6.23 n. **4–13:** The delay of *Amasa* showed David

mon Judah; but he delayed beyond the set time which had been appointed him. ⁶ And David said to Abi'shai, "Now Sheba the son of Bichri will do us more harm than Ab'salom; take your lord's servants and pursue him, lest he get himself fortified cities, and cause us trouble."ʰ ⁷ And there went out after Abi'shai, Jo'abⁱ and the Cher'ethites and the Pel'ethites, and all the mighty men; they went out from Jerusalem to pursue Sheba the son of Bichri. ⁸ When they were at the great stone which is in Gibeon, Ama'sa came to meet them. Now Jo'ab was wearing a soldier's garment, and over it was a girdle with a sword in its sheath fastened upon his loins, and as he went forward it fell out. ⁹ And Jo'ab said to Ama'sa, "Is it well with you, my brother?" And Jo'ab took Ama'sa by the beard with his right hand to kiss him. ¹⁰ But Ama'sa did not observe the sword which was in Jo'ab's hand; so Jo'ab struck him with it in the body, and shed his bowels to the ground, without striking a second blow; and he died.

Then Jo'ab and Abi'shai his brother pursued Sheba the son of Bichri. ¹¹ And one of Jo'ab's men took his stand by Ama'sa, and said, "Whoever favors Jo'ab, and whoever is for David, let him follow Jo'ab." ¹² And Ama'sa lay wallowing in his blood in the highway. And any one who came by, seeing him, stopped;ʲ and when the man saw that all the people stopped, he carried Ama'sa out of the highway into the field, and threw a garment over him. ¹³ When he was taken out of the highway, all the peo-

ple went on after Jo'ab to pursue Sheba the son of Bichri.

14 And Sheba passed through all the tribes of Israel to Abel of Beth-ma'acah;ᵏ and all the Bichritesˡ assembled, and followed him in. ¹⁵ And all the men who were with Jo'ab came and besieged him in Abel of Beth-ma'acah; they cast up a mound against the city, and it stood against the rampart; and they were battering the wall, to throw it down. ¹⁶ Then a wise woman called from the city, "Hear! Hear! Tell Jo'ab, 'Come here, that I may speak to you.'" ¹⁷ And he came near her; and the woman said, "Are you Jo'ab?" He answered, "I am." Then she said to him, "Listen to the words of your maidservant." And he answered, "I am listening." ¹⁸ Then she said, "They were wont to say in old time, 'Let them but ask counsel at Abel'; and so they settled a matter. ¹⁹ I am one of those who are peaceable and faithful in Israel; you seek to destroy a city which is a mother in Israel; why will you swallow up the heritage of the LORD?" ²⁰ Jo'ab answered, "Far be it from me, far be it, that I should swallow up or destroy! ²¹ That is not true. But a man of the hill country of E'phraim, called Sheba the son of Bichri, has lifted up his hand against King David; give up him alone, and I will withdraw from the city." And the woman said to Jo'ab, "Behold, his head shall be thrown to you over the wall." ²² Then the woman went to all the people in her wisdom. And they cut

h Tg: Heb *snatch away our eyes*
i Cn Compare Gk: Heb *after him Joab's men*
j This clause is transposed from the end of the verse
k With 20.15: Heb *and Beth-maacah*   l Heb *Berites*

---

that the new commander was not equal to Joab; but the king was too proud to approach Joab directly. Hence he called upon Abishai, Joab's brother, knowing that Joab would soon take the initiative (note the order of names in v. 10b and the name of Joab alone in v. 13). On the *Cherethites and the Pelethites* (v. 7), see 8.18 n. **14–22:** Joab was now in complete command of the army and of the situation. Joab showed his energy and efficiency in pursuing the rebel to this remote spot. **14:** The *Bichrites* were the members of Sheba's own clan (v. 1), perhaps the only followers remaining to him. **18:** This verse is not clear in the original, but it would seem that the town had a reputation for wisdom and the settling of disputes. **19:** *A city which is a mother in Israel* means one that had dependent villages called "daughters" (compare *villages*, literally "daughters," in Num.21.25,32; Jos.15.45; Jg.11.26). **22:** The story continues in 1 Kg. chs. 1–2.
    20.23–26: A list of David's officials, added by an editor; it seems to be another version of the

off the head of Sheba the son of Bichri, and threw it out to Jo'ab. So he blew the trumpet, and they dispersed from the city, every man to his home. And Jo'ab returned to Jerusalem to the king.

23 Now Jo'ab was in command of all the army of Israel; and Benai'ah the son of Jehoi'ada was in command of the Cher'ethites and the Pel'ethites; ²⁴ and Ador'am was in charge of the forced labor; and Jehosh'aphat the son of Ahi'lud was the recorder; ²⁵ and Sheva was secretary; and Zadok and Abi'athar were priests; ²⁶ and Ira the Ja'irite was also David's priest.

21 Now there was a famine in the days of David for three years, year after year; and David sought the face of the LORD. And the LORD said, "There is bloodguilt on Saul and on his house, because he put the Gib'eonites to death." ² So the king called the Gib'eonites.ᵐ Now the Gib'eonites were not of the people of Israel, but of the remnant of the Amorites; although the people of Israel had sworn to spare them, Saul had sought to slay them in his zeal for the people of Israel and Judah. ³ And David said to the Gib'eonites, "What shall I do for you? And how shall I make expiation,

that you may bless the heritage of the LORD?" ⁴ The Gib'eonites said to him, "It is not a matter of silver or gold between us and Saul or his house; neither is it for us to put any man to death in Israel." And he said, "What do you say that I shall do for you?" ⁵ They said to the king, "The man who consumed us and planned to destroy us, so that we should have no place in all the territory of Israel, ⁶ let seven of his sons be given to us, so that we may hang them up before the LORD at Gibeon on the mountain of the LORD."ⁿ And the king said, "I will give them."

7 But the king spared Mephib'osheth, the son of Saul's son Jonathan, because of the oath of the LORD which was between them, between David and Jonathan the son of Saul. ⁸ The king took the two sons of Rizpah the daughter of Ai'ah, whom she bore to Saul, Armo'ni and Mephib'osheth; and the five sons of Meraboᵒ the daughter of Saul, whom she bore to A'dri-el the son of Barzil'lai the Meho'lathite; ⁹ and he gave them into the hands of the Gib'eonites, and they hanged them

m Heb *the Gibeonites and said to them*
n Cn Compare Gk and 21.9: Heb *at Gibeah of Saul, the chosen of the* LORD
o Two Hebrew Mss Gk: Heb *Michal*

---

similar list in 8.16–18 (see note there). Perhaps it was inserted here to emphasize that *Joab* was again in command. *Adoram* (or Adoniram) kept his position under Solomon (1 Kg.4.6). The institution of *forced labor* was one of the causes of the final division of the kingdom (1 Kg. 12.18–19). *Ira the Jairite* was from Gilead, a territory which had welcomed *David* when he was in flight before Absalom (compare Num.32.40–41).

21.1–24.25: This section is something of an appendix to 2 Samuel, included, according to one theory, when chs. 9–20 were restored (see ch. 8 n.), and causing an interruption of the main narrative. Some of the material is late, but some of it belongs to the Early Source, though it is out of order here, as will be noted below.

21.1–14: The famine and the execution of the descendants of Saul. This passage (probably with ch. 24) belongs before ch. 9 and should be read in connection with that chapter; see note at end of ch. 6. The time is the early part of David's reign. **1:** There is no record of the occasion upon which *Saul . . . put the Gibeonites to death.* Apparently Saul was highly intolerant of non-Israelite elements in his kingdom, in contrast to the inclusive policy of David (see 15.24–37 n.). *David* heard a complaint from *the Gibeonites,* which he took as the voice of God, connected with *the famine.* The notion of *blood guilt* was based on the lex talionis (see 12.13–14 n.). **2:** For the story of the original contact with *the Gibeonites,* see Jos.9.3–27. The pre-Israelite inhabitants of Palestine are sometimes called Canaanites, sometimes *Amorites.* **6:** The number *seven* was thought to have special significance. **7:** In ch. 9, which should follow the present passage, David knows nothing of Mephibosheth; hence this verse is a note added by an editor after the present passage was displaced. **8:** Only *two sons* of Saul were found; the other *five* were grandsons. On *Rizpah,* see 3.7. The *Mephibosheth* of this verse is not the same person as

on the mountain before the LORD, and the seven of them perished together. They were put to death in the first days of harvest, at the beginning of barley harvest.

10 Then Rizpah the daughter of Ai'ah took sackcloth, and spread it for herself on the rock, from the beginning of harvest until rain fell upon them from the heavens; and she did not allow the birds of the air to come upon them by day, or the beasts of the field by night. ¹¹ When David was told what Rizpah the daughter of Ai'ah, the concubine of Saul, had done, ¹² David went and took the bones of Saul and the bones of his son Jonathan from the men of Ja'besh-gil'ead, who had stolen them from the public square of Beth-shan, where the Philistines had hanged them, on the day the Philistines killed Saul on Gilbo'a; ¹³ and he brought up from there the bones of Saul and the bones of his son Jonathan; and they gathered the bones of those who were hanged. ¹⁴ And they buried the bones of Saul and his son Jonathan in the land of Benjamin in Zela, in the tomb of Kish his father; and they did all that the king commanded. And

after that God heeded supplications for the land.

15 The Philistines had war again with Israel, and David went down together with his servants, and they fought against the Philistines; and David grew weary. ¹⁶ And Ish'bi-be'nob, one of the descendants of the giants, whose spear weighed three hundred shekels of bronze, and who was girded with a new sword, thought to kill David. ¹⁷ But Abi'shai the son of Zeru'iah came to his aid, and attacked the Philistine and killed him. Then David's men adjured him, "You shall no more go out with us to battle, lest you quench the lamp of Israel."

18 After this there was again war with the Philistines at Gob; then Sib'becai the Hu'shathite slew Saph, who was one of the descendants of the giants. ¹⁹ And there was again war with the Philistines at Gob; and Elha'nan the son of Ja'areor'egim, the Bethlehemite, slew Goliath the Gittite, the shaft of whose spear was like a weaver's beam. ²⁰ And there was again war at Gath, where there was a man of great stature, who had six fingers on each hand, and six toes on

the son of Jonathan in v. 7 and ch. 9. **10:** The *beginning of the harvest* was in late April or May; rain does not fall in Palestine from that time until late autumn; hence the bodies were exposed all summer. The law of Dt.21.22–23 was not yet in effect; the long exposure (an added insult to the deceased; compare 1 Sam.31.10–13) was doubtless a part of the expiation which David was cooperating with the Gibeonites to bring about. **11–14:** The amazing vigil of Rizpah had doubtless excited much sympathy. David began to feel that the expiation had been overdone, and that it was time to do something favorable to the memory of Saul to avoid repercussions from partisans of the late king. Also, the beginning of rain had marked the end of the famine. For these reasons, the great public mass burial, including the bones of Saul and Jonathan (1 Sam.31.11–13), seemed in order. After this, the favors to Mephibosheth related in ch. 9 follow logically.

21.15–22: Exploits in the war against the Philistines. This brief fragment (probably with 23.8–39) belongs just after ch. 5, being a part of the now partially lost story of David's victory over the Philistines. The tradition that there were giants among the Philistines here comes into full view. Another reflection of this idea is in 1 Sam. ch. 17. Some have supposed that these giants were the descendants of the Anakim, who had been defeated earlier by the Israelites (see Num.13.22 n.; Dt.1.28). The stories may be in part exaggerations, growing out of the initial fear of the Philistines, a fear which lessened when the Israelites under David began to get the upper hand in the war. **16:** Compare the figure of *three hundred shekels* with that in 1 Sam.17.7. **17:** For other references to *Abishai*, see 2.18; 16.9–10; 19.21–22; 20.6–7. On the arrangement that David should stay behind, see 11.1; 12.28; 18.3–4. **19:** On the problem raised by the statement that *Elhanan . . . slew Goliath*, see 1 Sam.17.4 n. and 1 Chr.20.5 n. **22:** The preceding verses give no instance of a *giant* who *fell by the hand of David;* perhaps these words were influenced by 1 Sam. ch. 17.

each foot, twenty-four in number; and he also was descended from the giants. 21 And when he taunted Israel, Jonathan the son of Shim′e-i, David's brother, slew him. 22 These four were descended from the giants in Gath; and they fell by the hand of David and by the hand of his servants.

22 And David spoke to the LORD the words of this song on the day when the LORD delivered him from the hand of all his enemies, and from the hand of Saul. 2 He said,

"The LORD is my rock, and my
    fortress, and my deliverer,
3 my*p* God, my rock, in whom I
    take refuge,
my shield and the horn of my
    salvation,
    my stronghold and my refuge,
    my savior; thou savest me from
        violence.
4 I call upon the LORD, who is worthy
    to be praised,
and I am saved from my enemies.

5 "For the waves of death
    encompassed me,
    the torrents of perdition assailed
        me;
6 the cords of Sheol entangled me,
    the snares of death confronted
        me.

7 "In my distress I called upon the
    LORD;
    to my God I called.
From his temple he heard my voice,
    and my cry came to his ears.

8 "Then the earth reeled and rocked;
    the foundations of the heavens
        trembled
    and quaked, because he was
        angry.
9 Smoke went up from his nostrils,
    and devouring fire from his
        mouth;
    glowing coals flamed forth from
        him.

10 He bowed the heavens, and came
    down;
    thick darkness was under his feet.
11 He rode on a cherub, and flew;
    he was seen upon the wings of
    the wind.
12 He made darkness around him
    his canopy, thick clouds, a
        gathering of water.
13 Out of the brightness before him
    coals of fire flamed forth.
14 The LORD thundered from heaven,
    and the Most High uttered his
        voice.
15 And he sent out arrows, and
    scattered them;
    lightning, and routed them.
16 Then the channels of the sea were
        seen,
    the foundations of the world
        were laid bare,
    at the rebuke of the LORD,
    at the blast of the breath of his
        nostrils.

17 "He reached from on high, he took
    me,
    he drew me out of many waters.
18 He delivered me from my strong
        enemy,
    from those who hated me;
    for they were too mighty for me.
19 They came upon me in the day of
        my calamity;
    but the LORD was my stay.
20 He brought me forth into a broad
        place;
    he delivered me, because he
        delighted in me.

21 "The LORD rewarded me
    according to my righteousness;
    according to the cleanness of
        my hands he recompensed me.
22 For I have kept the ways of the
    LORD,
    and have not wickedly departed
        from my God.

p Gk Ps 18.2: Heb lacks *my*

22.1–51: A hymn of praise. It was the custom of certain Old Testament editors to insert poems into prose books for artistic and religious effect (see 1 Sam.2.1–10 n.). The present example is also preserved as Ps. 18, to which reference should be made.

23 For all his ordinances were before
me,
and from his statutes I did not turn
aside.
24 I was blameless before him,
and I kept myself from guilt.
25 Therefore the LORD has
recompensed me according to
my righteousness,
according to my cleanness in his
sight.

26 "With the loyal thou dost show
thyself loyal;
with the blameless man thou dost
show thyself blameless;
27 with the pure thou dost show
thyself pure,
and with the crooked thou dost
show thyself perverse.
28 Thou dost deliver a humble people,
but thy eyes are upon the haughty
to bring them down.
29 Yea, thou art my lamp, O LORD,
and my God lightens my darkness.
30 Yea, by thee I can crush a troop,
and by my God I can leap over a
wall.
31 This God—his way is perfect;
the promise of the LORD proves
true;
he is a shield for all those who
take refuge in him.

32 "For who is God, but the LORD?
And who is a rock, except our
God?
33 This God is my strong refuge,
and has made[r] my[s] way safe.
34 He made my[s] feet like hinds' feet,
and set me secure on the heights.
35 He trains my hands for war,
so that my arms can bend a bow
of bronze.
36 Thou hast given me the shield of
thy salvation,
and thy help[t] made me great.
37 Thou didst give a wide place for
my steps under me,
and my feet[u] did not slip;
38 I pursued my enemies and
destroyed them,

and did not turn back until they
were consumed.
39 I consumed them; I thrust them
through, so that they did not
rise;
they fell under my feet.
40 For thou didst gird me with strength
for the battle;
thou didst make my assailants
sink under me.
41 Thou didst make my enemies turn
their backs to me,
those who hated me, and I
destroyed them.
42 They looked, but there was none to
save;
they cried to the LORD, but he did
not answer them.
43 I beat them fine as the dust of the
earth,
I crushed them and stamped them
down like the mire of the
streets.

44 "Thou didst deliver me from strife
with the peoples;[v]
thou didst keep me as the head
of the nations;
people whom I had not known
served me.
45 Foreigners came cringing to me;
as soon as they heard of me, they
obeyed me.
46 Foreigners lost heart,
and came trembling[w] out of their
fastnesses.

47 "The LORD lives; and blessed be my
rock,
and exalted be my God, the rock
of my salvation,
48 the God who gave me vengeance
and brought down peoples under
me,
49 who brought me out from my
enemies;
thou didst exalt me above my
adversaries,

r Ps 18.32: Heb *set free*
s Another reading is *his*
t Or *gentleness*
u Heb *ankles*
v Gk: Heb *from strife with my people*
w Ps 18.45: Heb *girded themselves*

thou didst deliver me from men of
violence.

50 "For this I will extol thee, O LORD,
    among the nations,
    and sing praises to thy name.
51 Great triumphs he gives^x to his
    king,
    and shows steadfast love to his
    anointed,
    to David, and his descendants for
    ever."

23 Now these are the last words of
   David:
The oracle of David, the son of
    Jesse,
    the oracle of the man who was
    raised on high,
the anointed of the God of Jacob,
    the sweet psalmist of Israel:^{y}

2 "The Spirit of the LORD speaks by
    me,
    his word is upon my tongue.
3 The God of Israel has spoken,
    the Rock of Israel has said to
    me:
When one rules justly over men,
    ruling in the fear of God,
4 he dawns on them like the morning
    light,
    like the sun shining forth upon a
    cloudless morning,
    like rain^z that makes grass to
    sprout from the earth.
5 Yea, does not my house stand so with
    God?
For he has made with me an
    everlasting covenant,

ordered in all things and secure.
For will he not cause to prosper
    all my help and my desire?
6 But godless men^a are all like thorns
    that are thrown away;
    for they cannot be taken with the
    hand;
7 but the man who touches them
    arms himself with iron and the
    shaft of a spear,
    and they are utterly consumed
    with fire."^{b}
8 These are the names of the mighty
men whom David had: Josheb-basshe'-
beth a Tah-che'monite; he was chief
of the three;^{c} he wielded his spear^d
against eight hundred whom he slew
at one time.
9 And next to him among the three
mighty men was Elea'zar the son of
Dodo, son of Aho'hi. He was with
David when they defied the Philistines
who were gathered there for battle, and
the men of Israel withdrew. 10 He rose
and struck down the Philistines until
his hand was weary, and his hand
cleaved to the sword; and the LORD
wrought a great victory that day; and
the men returned after him only to strip
the slain.
11 And next to him was Shammah,
the son of Agee the Har'arite. The
Philistines gathered together at Lehi,
where there was a plot of ground full
of lentils; and the men fled from the
Philistines. 12 But he took his stand
in the midst of the plot, and defended

x Another reading is *He is a tower of salvation*
y Or *the favorite of the songs of Israel*
z Heb *from rain*   a Heb *worthlessness*
b Heb *fire in the sitting*   c Or *captains*
d 1 Chr 11.11: Heb obscure

23.1–7: Another hymn of praise, represented as *the last words of David* (see Gen.48.21–49.2 and Dt.33.1). This psalm is a late composition in the style of Ps. 1 and Pr.4.10–19, with an introduction suggestive of the oracles of Balaam (Num.24.3–4,15–16). The theme of the perpetuity of the *house* (dynasty) *of David* (v. 5) has already appeared in ch. 7 (see the concluding note there). *The anointed of the God of Jacob,* see 1 Sam.2.10 n. and 10.1 n. On the tradition of David as *the sweet psalmist,* see Introduction to the Psalms. The text of the last two verses is very corrupt, so that the exact meaning is not certain. It is also not certain whether the poem is complete as it stands or is only a fragment.

23.8–39: Other exploits in the war against the Philistines, with a roster of warriors. This passage is a continuation of 21.15–22. It is also preserved in 1 Chr.11.11–47 at a more logical place in the narrative, but with some variation in the names and details. Here there are two orders of heroes, the order of *the three* (v. 8) and the order of *the thirty* (v. 18). **8–11:** *Josheb-basshebeth a Tahchemonite* is an error of a copyist; 1 Chr.11.11 has *Jashobeam a Hachmonite.* It has been

it, and slew the Philistines; and the LORD wrought a great victory.

13 And three of the thirty chief men went down, and came about harvest time to David at the cave of Adullam, when a band of Philistines was encamped in the valley of Reph'-aim. 14 David was then in the stronghold; and the garrison of the Philistines was then at Bethlehem. 15 And David said longingly, "O that some one would give me water to drink from the well of Bethlehem which is by the gate!" 16 Then the three mighty men broke through the camp of the Philistines, and drew water out of the well of Bethlehem which was by the gate, and took and brought it to David. But he would not drink of it; he poured it out to the LORD, 17 and said, "Far be it from me, O LORD, that I should do this. Shall I drink the blood of the men who went at the risk of their lives?" Therefore he would not drink it. These things did the three mighty men.

18 Now Abi'shai, the brother of Jo'ab, the son of Zeru'iah, was chief of the thirty.[e] And he wielded his spear against three hundred men and slew them, and won a name beside the three. 19 He was the most renowned of the thirty,[f] and became their commander; but he did not attain to the three.

20 And Benai'ah the son of Jehoi'-ada was a valiant man[g] of Kabzeel, a doer of great deeds; he smote two ariels[h] of Moab. He also went down and slew a lion in a pit on a day when snow had fallen. 21 And he slew an Egyptian, a handsome man. The Egyptian had a spear in his hand; but Benai'ah went down to him with a staff, and snatched the spear out of the Egyptian's hand, and slew him with his own spear. 22 These things did Benai'ah the son of Jehoi'ada, and won a name beside the three mighty men. 23 He was renowned among the thirty, but he did not attain to the three. And David set him over his bodyguard.

24 As'ahel the brother of Jo'ab was one of the thirty; Elha'nan the son of Dodo of Bethlehem, 25 Shammah of Harod, Eli'ka of Harod, 26 Helez the Paltite, Ira the son of Ikkesh of Teko'a, 27 Abi-e'zer of An'athoth, Mebun'nai the Hu'shathite, 28 Zalmon the Aho'hite, Ma'harai of Netoph'ah, 29 Heleb the son of Ba'anah of Netoph'ah, It'tai the son of Ri'bai of Gib'e-ah of the Benjaminites, 30 Benai'ah of Pira'thon, Hid'dai of the brooks of Ga'ash, 31 Abi-al'bon the Ar'bathite, Az'maveth of Bahu'rim, 32 Eli'ahba of Sha-al'bon, the sons of Jashen, Jonathan, 33 Shammah the Har'arite, Ahi'am the son of Sharar the Har'arite, 34 Eliph'elet the son of Ahas'bai of Ma'acah, Eli'am the son of Ahith'ophel of Gilo, 35 Hezro[i] of Carmel, Pa'arai the Arbite, 36 Igal the son of Nathan of Zobah, Bani the Gadite, 37 Zelek the Ammonite, Na'-harai of Be-er'oth, the armor-bearer of

e Two Hebrew Mss Syr: MT *three*
f 1 Chr 11.25: Heb *Was he the most renowned of the three?*   g Another reading is *the son of Ish-hai*
h The meaning of the word *ariel* is unknown
i Another reading is *Hezrai*

---

proposed that the man's original name was Ishbaal (see 2.8 n. and 11.21 n.). **13–17:** This story is slightly misplaced, since it concerns *three of the thirty*, not *the three* of the preceding verses. *The thirty* are introduced in v. 18. The last sentence of v. 17 belongs after v. 12. **18–23:** On *Abishai*, see 2.18; 10.10; 16.9–10; 18.2; 19.21–22; 20.6. On *Benaiah*, see 8.18; 20.23. On the *bodyguard*, see 8.18 n. *Joab* is not listed here; he had a special status as commander-in-chief (20.23). **24–39:** There is some confusion in the list, and more than *thirty* names occur. Doubtless the number was not intended to be exact. **24:** *Asahel the brother of Joab* was killed while David was king of Judah only (2.23); either this name was included on an honorary basis, or the organization of *the thirty* arose in the early days of David's kingship. On Elhanan, see 21.19 n. **33:** *Shammah the Hararite* seems to be repeated from v. 11. **39:** The inclusion of *Uriah the Hittite* is noteworthy (compare 11.15–17); he certainly deserved the honor. The number *thirty-seven*, added by an editor, seems to be intended to include all the names mentioned in vv. 8–39, though they total only thirty-six. It has been suggested that Joab, as commander-in-chief, was included in the reckoning.

Jo'ab the son of Zeru'iah, [38] Ira the Ithrite, Gareb the Ithrite, [39] Uri'ah the Hittite: thirty-seven in all.

24 Again the anger of the LORD was kindled against Israel, and he incited David against them, saying, "Go, number Israel and Judah." [2] So the king said to Jo'ab and the commanders of the army,[j] who were with him, "Go through all the tribes of Israel, from Dan to Beer-sheba, and number the people, that I may know the number of the people." [3] But Jo'ab said to the king, "May the LORD your God add to the people a hundred times as many as they are, while the eyes of my lord the king still see it; but why does my lord the king delight in this thing?" [4] But the king's word prevailed against Jo'ab and the commanders of the army. So Jo'ab and the commanders of the army went out from the presence of the king to number the people of Israel. [5] They crossed the Jordan, and began from Aro'er,[k] and from the city that is in the middle of the valley, toward Gad and on to Jazer. [6] Then they came to Gilead, and to Kadesh in the land of the Hittites;[l] and they came to Dan, and from Dan[m] they went around to Sidon, [7] and came to the fortress of Tyre and to all the cities of the Hivites and Canaanites; and they went out to the Negeb of Judah at Beer-sheba. [8] So when they had gone through all the land, they came to Jerusalem at the end of nine months and twenty days. [9] And Jo'ab gave the

sum of the numbering of the people to the king: in Israel there were eight hundred thousand valiant men who drew the sword, and the men of Judah were five hundred thousand.

10 But David's heart smote him after he had numbered the people. And David said to the LORD, "I have sinned greatly in what I have done. But now, O LORD, I pray thee, take away the iniquity of thy servant; for I have done very foolishly." [11] And when David arose in the morning, the word of the LORD came to the prophet Gad, David's seer, saying, [12] "Go and say to David, 'Thus says the LORD, Three things I offer[n] you; choose one of them, that I may do it to you.'" [13] So Gad came to David and told him, and said to him, "Shall three[o] years of famine come to you in your land? Or will you flee three months before your foes while they pursue you? Or shall there be three days' pestilence in your land? Now consider, and decide what answer I shall return to him who sent me." [14] Then David said to Gad, "I am in great distress; let us fall into the hand of the LORD, for his mercy is great; but let me not fall into the hand of man."

15 So the LORD sent a pestilence upon Israel from the morning until the appointed time; and there died of the

j 1 Chr 21.2 Gk: Heb *to Joab the commander of the army*
k Gk: Heb *encamped in Aroer*
l Gk: Heb *to the land of Tahtim-hodshi*
m Cn Compare Gk: Heb *they came to Dan-jaan and*
n Or *hold over*   *o* 1 Chr 21.12 Gk: Heb *seven*

24.1–25: The census, the plague, and the building of the altar. This passage, along with 21.1–14, belongs before ch. 9. Like 21.1–14, it reflects the belief that natural calamity is caused by the wrath of God against human sin, and that this wrath must be appeased before the calamity can be stopped (compare Lk.13.1–4; Rom.1.18–23). **1:** 1 Chr.21.1 substitutes "Satan" for *the LORD* in this verse, a significant theological change. Some have wondered why it should have been considered sinful to *number Israel and Judah.* The reason must have been that taking a census was deemed an infringement upon the prerogatives of their God, the sole arbiter of the destinies of the nation and its people. **3:** Joab expressed the popular fear in the matter, but he had to yield and oversee the counting in person (v. 4). **5–7:** Those who took the census began at *Aroer* (Dt.2.36; Jos.13.9) on the east side of the Dead Sea, went north to the limits of the country, then returned on the west side to *Beersheba.* If *Kadesh, Sidon,* and *Tyre* were included, the census must have been taken after David's Syrian campaigns (8.3–12; 10.15–19); but these cities were not truly in Israel or Judah, even when under the control of David. **9:** The numbers here given are round numbers and incredibly high (1,300,000 fighting men alone); see 1 Sam. 4.10 n. **10–14:** We might say today that "David had an uneasy conscience" (v. 10). Most of vv. 11–14 is secondary; compare the appearance of *Gad* in another editorial passage, 1 Sam.22.5.

people from Dan to Beer-sheba seventy thousand men. [16] And when the angel stretched forth his hand toward Jerusalem to destroy it, the LORD repented of the evil, and said to the angel who was working destruction among the people, "It is enough; now stay your hand." And the angel of the LORD was by the threshing floor of Arau'nah the Jeb'usite. [17] Then David spoke to the LORD when he saw the angel who was smiting the people, and said, "Lo, I have sinned, and I have done wickedly; but these sheep, what have they done? Let thy hand, I pray thee, be against me and against my father's house."

18 And Gad came that day to David, and said to him, "Go up, rear an altar to the LORD on the threshing floor of Arau'nah the Jeb'usite." [19] So David went up at Gad's word, as the LORD commanded. [20] And when Arau'nah looked down, he saw the king and his servants coming on toward him; and Arau'nah went forth, and did obeisance to the king with his face to the ground. [21] And Arau'nah said, "Why has my lord the king come to his servant?" David said, "To buy the threshing floor of you, in order to build an altar to the LORD, that the plague may be averted from the people." [22] Then Arau'nah said to David, "Let my lord the king take and offer up what seems good to him; here are the oxen for the burnt offering, and the threshing sledges and the yokes of the oxen for the wood. [23] All this, O king, Arau'nah gives to the king." And Arau'nah said to the king, "The LORD your God accept you." [24] But the king said to Arau'nah, "No, but I will buy it of you for a price; I will not offer burnt offerings to the LORD my God which cost me nothing." So David bought the threshing floor and the oxen for fifty shekels of silver. [25] And David built there an altar to the LORD, and offered burnt offerings and peace offerings. So the LORD heeded supplications for the land, and the plague was averted from Israel.

16: *The angel* here is not specifically the angel of death, but simply a "messenger" (the original meaning of the word *angel*) of the LORD doing the LORD's will. **17:** The people are like innocent sheep led to slaughter; David feels that the evil should fall upon him. **18–25:** *The threshing floor of Araunah the Jebusite* later became the site of Solomon's temple (1 Chr.22.1; 2 Chr.3.1). The acquisition of this holy place, the building of an altar, and a sacrifice there were regarded as sufficient expiation to avert the plague from Israel (v. 25). *Fifty shekels of silver* would be worth about twenty dollars (see 1 Sam.9.8 n.).

THE FIRST BOOK OF THE

KINGS

The two books of Kings, like those of Samuel, were originally one. This book, or pair of books, is a continuation of the book, or books, of Samuel, thus giving a consecutive history from the time of the Judges to the Exile (see "Survey of . . . Bible Lands," §§ 8–12). The literary structure of Kings, however, is somewhat different from that of Samuel, where there are two main sources with a small amount of Deuteronomic editing. The structure of Kings is more like that of the book of Judges, where various sources are collected and inserted into a Deuteronomic "framework" (see Introduction to Judges). Some of these sources are as follows: conclusion of the Early Source of Samuel (1 Kg. chs. 1–2; see 2 Sam.20.22 n.); "the Book of the Acts of Solomon" (1 Kg.11.41); "the Book of the Chronicles of the Kings of Israel" (mentioned in 1 Kg.14.19 and in sixteen other places); "the Book of the Chronicles of the Kings of Judah" (mentioned in 1 Kg.14.29 and in fourteen other places; these books were official annals, not to be confused with the Biblical books of Chronicles); stories of Kings and prophets from both Israel and Judah, notably Jeroboam I, Ahab, Hezekiah, Elijah, and Elisha; archives of the temple, especially from the times of Solomon and Josiah.

From these and similar sources two Deuteronomic author-editors compiled the present books of Kings. The first Deuteronomist carried the story to a point either just before or just after the death of Josiah in 609 B.C. This writer judged every king on the basis of religious loyalty, with David as the standard. His theme is that national success depends on obedience to the national God, as set forth in Deuteronomy. Cardinal sins are worship in the "high places" outside of Jerusalem and idolatry. Every king of the northern kingdom (Israel) failed to meet the standard, and hence that kingdom fell because of the judgment of God as carried out by the Assyrians.

The second Deuteronomist wrote about 550 B.C., during the Babylonian Exile. By that time Judah also had fallen, and so could not be considered superior to Israel. Again national apostasy had brought divine judgment and punishment, this time at the hands of the Chaldeans. So reasoned the second Deuteronomist, who added that part of the story concerned with events after the reign of Josiah, and inserted comments of his own in earlier sections of the narrative. The interpretation as well as the history has its value; it is still true that gross national sin, and folly among leaders, will bring national ruin, even at the hands of an unjust conqueror.

First Kings begins with the enthronement of Solomon and the death of David (chs. 1–2), and recounts the reign of Solomon (chs. 3–11) and the kings of the Divided Monarchy through the reigns of Ahab of Israel and Jehoshaphat of Judah (chs. 12–22).

Now KING DAVID WAS OLD AND advanced in years; and although they covered him with clothes, he could not get warm. ²Therefore his servants said to him, "Let a young maiden be sought for my lord the king, and let her wait upon the king, and be his nurse; let her lie in your bosom, that my lord the king may be warm." ³So they sought for a beautiful maiden throughout all the territory of Israel, and found Ab′ishag the Shu′nammite, and brought her to the king. ⁴The maiden was very beautiful; and she became the king's nurse and ministered to him; but the king knew her not.

5 Now Adoni′jah the son of Haggith exalted himself, saying, "I will be king"; and he prepared for himself chariots and horsemen, and fifty men

---

1.1–53: The struggle for the succession and Solomon's attainment of the kingship. This chapter continues the Early Source of Samuel, left off at 2 Sam.20.22. A number of years had intervened and *now King David was old and advanced in years* (v. 1). **3:** *Abishag the Shunammite,* i.e. from Shunem in the plain of Esdraelon near Mount Gilboa (1 Sam.28.4). **4:** *The king knew her not,* i.e. did not have marital relations with her. **5–10:** *Adonijah,* as David's eldest living son (Chileab

to run before him. ⁶ His father had never at any time displeased him by asking, "Why have you done thus and so?" He was also a very handsome man; and he was born next after Ab'salom. ⁷ He conferred with Jo'ab the son of Zeru'iah and with Abi'athar the priest; and they followed Adoni'jah and helped him. ⁸ But Zadok the priest, and Benai'ah the son of Jehoi'ada, and Nathan the prophet, and Shim'e-i, and Re'i, and David's mighty men were not with Adoni'jah.

9 Adoni'jah sacrificed sheep, oxen, and fatlings by the Serpent's Stone, which is beside En-ro'gel, and he invited all his brothers, the king's sons, and all the royal officials of Judah, ¹⁰ but he did not invite Nathan the prophet or Benai'ah or the mighty men or Solomon his brother.

11 Then Nathan said to Bathshe'ba the mother of Solomon, "Have you not heard that Adoni'jah the son of Haggith has become king and David our lord does not know it? ¹² Now therefore come, let me give you counsel, that you may save your own life and the life of your son Solomon. ¹³ Go in at once to King David, and say to him, 'Did you not, my lord the king, swear to your maidservant, saying, "Solomon your son shall reign after me, and he shall sit upon my throne"? Why then is Adoni'jah king?' ¹⁴ Then while you are still speaking with the king, I also will come in after you and confirm your words."

15 So Bathshe'ba went to the king into his chamber (now the king was very old, and Ab'ishag the Shu'nammite was ministering to the king). ¹⁶ Bathshe'ba bowed and did obeisance to the king, and the king said,

"What do you desire?" ¹⁷ She said to him, "My lord, you swore to your maidservant by the LORD your God, saying, 'Solomon your son shall reign after me, and he shall sit upon my throne.' ¹⁸ And now, behold, Adoni'jah is king, although you, my lord the king, do not know it. ¹⁹ He has sacrificed oxen, fatlings, and sheep in abundance, and has invited all the sons of the king, Abi'athar the priest, and Jo'ab the commander of the army; but Solomon your servant he has not invited. ²⁰ And now, my lord the king, the eyes of all Israel are upon you, to tell them who shall sit on the throne of my lord the king after him. ²¹ Otherwise it will come to pass, when my lord the king sleeps with his fathers, that I and my son Solomon will be counted offenders."

22 While she was still speaking with the king, Nathan the prophet came in. ²³ And they told the king, "Here is Nathan the prophet." And when he came in before the king, he bowed before the king, with his face to the ground. ²⁴ And Nathan said, "My lord the king, have you said, 'Adoni'jah shall reign after me, and he shall sit upon my throne'? ²⁵ For he has gone down this day, and has sacrificed oxen, fatlings, and sheep in abundance, and has invited all the king's sons, Jo'ab the commander*a* of the army, and Abi'athar the priest; and behold, they are eating and drinking before him, and saying, 'Long live King Adoni'jah!' ²⁶ But me, your servant, and Zadok the priest, and Benai'ah the son of Jehoi'ada, and your servant Solomon, he has not invited. ²⁷ Has this thing been brought about by my

a Gk: Heb *commanders*

seems to have died young, 2 Sam.3.3–4), naturally assumed that he would succeed his father. This seems to have been taken for granted also by the older followers of David, such as *Joab* and *Abiathar* (1 Sam.22.20–23; 2 Sam.2.13). Apparently, however, there was no strict law of primogeniture at that time (compare v. 20), and hence the younger followers of David, such as *Zadok* (2 Sam.8.17), *Benaiah* (2 Sam.8.18), and *Nathan* (2 Sam.12.1) were plotting to install Solomon in spite of his disadvantage in age. The group favoring Solomon had the advantage of including David's bodyguard of mighty men. **9:** *En-rogel*, now known as Job's Well, a source of water southeast of the city, was considered a sacred place, appropriate for affairs of this kind (2 Sam.17.17). **11–27:** It is surprising to find Nathan, who once so eloquently denounced

lord the king and you have not told your servants who should sit on the throne of my lord the king after him?" 28 Then King David answered, "Call Bathshe′ba to me." So she came into the king's presence, and stood before the king. ²⁹ And the king swore, saying, "As the LORD lives, who has redeemed my soul out of every adversity, ³⁰ as I swore to you by the LORD, the God of Israel, saying, 'Solomon your son shall reign after me, and he shall sit upon my throne in my stead'; even so will I do this day." ³¹ Then Bathshe′ba bowed with her face to the ground, and did obeisance to the king, and said, "May my lord King David live for ever!"

32 King David said, "Call to me Zadok the priest, Nathan the prophet, and Benai′ah the son of Jehoi′ada." So they came before the king. ³³ And the king said to them, "Take with you the servants of your lord, and cause Solomon my son to ride on my own mule, and bring him down to Gihon; ³⁴ and let Zadok the priest and Nathan the prophet there anoint him king over Israel; then blow the trumpet, and say, 'Long live King Solomon!' ³⁵ You shall then come up after him, and he shall come and sit upon my throne; for he shall be king in my stead; and I have appointed him to be ruler over Israel and over Judah." ³⁶ And Benai′ah the son of Jehoi′ada answered the king, "Amen! May the LORD, the God of my lord the king, say so. ³⁷ As the LORD has been with my lord the king, even so may he be with Solomon, and make his throne greater than the throne of my lord King David."

38 So Zadok the priest, Nathan the prophet, and Benai′ah the son of Jehoi′ada, and the Cher′ethites and the Pel′ethites, went down and caused Solomon to ride on King David's mule, and brought him to Gihon. ³⁹ There Zadok the priest took the horn of oil from the tent, and anointed Solomon. Then they blew the trumpet; and all the people said, "Long live King Solomon!" ⁴⁰ And all the people went up after him, playing on pipes, and rejoicing with great joy, so that the earth was split by their noise.

41 Adoni′jah and all the guests who were with him heard it as they finished feasting. And when Jo′ab heard the sound of the trumpet, he said, "What does this uproar in the city mean?" ⁴² While he was still speaking, behold, Jonathan the son of Abi′athar the priest came; and Adoni′jah said, "Come in, for you are a worthy man and bring good news." ⁴³ Jonathan answered Adoni′jah, "No, for our lord King David has made Solomon king; ⁴⁴ and the king has sent with him Zadok the priest, Nathan the prophet, and Benai′ah the son of Jehoi′ada, and the Cher′ethites and the Pel′ethites; and they have caused him to ride on the king's mule; ⁴⁵ and Zadok the priest and Nathan the prophet have anointed him king at Gihon; and they have gone up from there rejoicing, so that the city is in an uproar. This is the noise that you have heard. ⁴⁶ Solomon sits upon the royal throne. ⁴⁷ Moreover the king's servants came to congratulate our lord King David, saying, 'Your God make the name of Solomon more famous than yours, and make his throne greater than your throne.' And the king bowed himself upon the bed. ⁴⁸ And the king also said, 'Blessed be

David for his affair with Bathsheba (2 Sam.12.1–15), now on Bathsheba's side. **28–31**: Bathsheba had apparently gone out while Nathan was speaking. **32–37**: When Bathsheba came back, Nathan left and hence had to be recalled. **33**: *Gihon*, now called the Virgin's Fountain or Mary's Spring, is a short distance north of En-rogel (v. 9), out of sight of the latter because of a curve in the valley (Kidron) in which they lie, but well within earshot (compare v. 41). Gihon for long was the principal source of water for the city of Jerusalem (2 Chr.32.30), and hence was a place of special significance. **38–40**: *Cherethites* and *Pelethites*, see 1 Sam.30.14 n.; 2 Sam.8.18; 15.18. On the ceremony of anointing, see 1 Sam.10.1 n. **41–48**: *Jonathan the son of Abiathar*, see 2 Sam.15.27,36; 17.17–21. **49–53**: *The horns of the altar* were projections re-

the LORD, the God of Israel, who has granted one of my offspring[b] to sit on my throne this day, my own eyes seeing it.' " 49 Then all the guests of Adoni'jah trembled, and rose, and each went his own way. 50 And Adoni'jah feared Solomon; and he arose, and went, and caught hold of the horns of the altar. 51 And it was told Solomon, "Behold, Adoni'jah fears King Solomon; for, lo, he has laid hold of the horns of the altar, saying, 'Let King Solomon swear to me first that he will not slay his servant with the sword.' " 52 And Solomon said, "If he prove to be a worthy man, not one of his hairs shall fall to the earth; but if wickedness is found in him, he shall die." 53 So King Solomon sent, and they brought him down from the altar. And he came and did obeisance to King Solomon; and Solomon said to him, "Go to your house."

2 When David's time to die drew near, he charged Solomon his son, saying, 2 "I am about to go the way of all the earth. Be strong, and show yourself a man, 3 and keep the charge of the LORD your God, walking in his ways and keeping his statutes, his commandments, his ordinances, and his testimonies, as it is written in the law of Moses, that you may prosper in all that you do and wherever you turn; 4 that the LORD may establish his word which he spoke concerning me, saying, 'If your sons take heed to their way, to walk before me in faithfulness with all their heart and with all their soul, there shall not fail you a man on the throne of Israel.'

5 "Moreover you know also what Jo'ab the son of Zeru'iah did to me, how he dealt with the two commanders of the armies of Israel, Abner the son of Ner, and Ama'sa the son of Jether, whom he murdered, avenging[c] in time of peace blood which had been shed in war, and putting innocent blood[d] upon the girdle about my[e] loins, and upon the sandals on my[e] feet. 6 Act therefore according to your wisdom, but do not let his gray head go down to Sheol in peace. 7 But deal loyally with the sons of Barzil'lai the Gileadite, and let them be among those who eat at your table; for with such loyalty they met me when I fled from Ab'-salom your brother. 8 And there is also with you Shim'e-i the son of Gera, the Benjaminite from Bahu'rim, who cursed me with a grievous curse on the day when I went to Mahana'im; but when he came down to meet me at the Jordan, I swore to him by the LORD, saying, 'I will not put you to death with the sword.' 9 Now therefore hold him not guiltless, for you are a wise man; you will know what you ought to do to him, and you shall bring his gray head down with blood to Sheol."

10 Then David slept with his fathers, and was buried in the city of David. 11 And the time that David reigned over Israel was forty years; he reigned seven years in Hebron, and thirty-three years in Jerusalem. 12 So Solomon sat upon the throne of David his father; and his kingdom was firmly established.

b Gk: Heb *one*   c Gk: Heb *placing*
d Gk: Heb *blood of war*   e Gk: Heb *his*

sembling horns at the four corners of an altar (Ex.29.12; 30.10; Lev.4.7; Ps.118.27). An altar was sacred, so that a person touching it was not supposed to be slain; but the taboo was not always honored (Ex.21.14; 1 Kg.2.28–34). **2.1–46: The death of David and the elimination of men dangerous to the reign of Solomon. 1–4:** The first example in the book of the editorial work of the first Deuteronomist (see Introduction). Solomon is warned that he must follow *the law of Moses* (i.e. the Deuteronomic law) or national ruin will result. See the Introduction to Deuteronomy and compare Dt.4.40,44–45; 5.1; 11.1–17; 17.14–20. **5–9:** When *Joab* (2 Sam.3.27; 20.10) and *Shimei* (2 Sam.16.5–14; 19.18–23) committed the offenses referred to here, David was in such precarious political situations that he did not dare have these men put to death. On the friendship of Barzillai, see 2 Sam.17.27–29; 19.31–39. **13–25:** An excuse is found to eliminate Adonijah. The members of

13 Then Adoni'jah the son of Haggith came to Bathshe'ba the mother of Solomon. And she said, "Do you come peaceably?" He said, "Peaceably." ¹⁴ Then he said, "I have something to say to you." She said, "Say on." ¹⁵ He said, "You know that the kingdom was mine, and that all Israel fully expected me to reign; however the kingdom has turned about and become my brother's, for it was his from the LORD. ¹⁶ And now I have one request to make of you; do not refuse me." She said to him, "Say on." ¹⁷ And he said, "Pray ask King Solomon–he will not refuse you–to give me Ab'ishag the Shu'- nammite as my wife." ¹⁸ Bathshe'ba said, "Very well; I will speak for you to the king."

19 So Bathshe'ba went to King Solomon, to speak to him on behalf of Adoni'jah. And the king rose to meet her, and bowed down to her; then he sat on his throne, and had a seat brought for the king's mother; and she sat on his right. ²⁰ Then she said, "I have one small request to make of you; do not refuse me." And the king said to her, "Make your request, my mother; for I will not refuse you." ²¹ She said, "Let Ab'ishag the Shu'nammite be given to Adoni'jah your brother as his wife." ²² King Solomon answered his mother, "And why do you ask Ab'- ishag the Shu'nammite for Adoni'jah? Ask for him the kingdom also; for he is my elder brother, and on his side are Abi'athar*f* the priest and Jo'ab the son of Zeru'iah." ²³ Then King Solomon swore by the LORD, saying, "God do so to me and more also if this word does not cost Adoni'jah his life! ²⁴ Now therefore as the LORD lives, who has established me, and placed me on the throne of David my father, and who has made me a house, as he promised, Adoni'jah shall be put to death this day." ²⁵ So King Solomon sent Benai'ah the son of Jehoi'ada; and he struck him down, and he died.

26 And to Abi'athar the priest the king said, "Go to An'athoth, to your estate; for you deserve death. But I will not at this time put you to death, because you bore the ark of the Lord GOD before David my father, and because you shared in all the affliction of my father." ²⁷ So Solomon expelled Abi'athar from being priest to the LORD, thus fulfilling the word of the LORD which he had spoken concerning the house of Eli in Shiloh.

28 When the news came to Jo'ab –for Jo'ab had supported Adoni'jah although he had not supported Ab'- salom–Jo'ab fled to the tent of the LORD and caught hold of the horns of the altar. ²⁹ And when it was told King Solomon, "Jo'ab has fled to the tent of the LORD, and behold, he is beside the altar," Solomon sent Benai'ah the son of Jehoi'ada, saying, "Go, strike him down." ³⁰ So Benai'ah came to the tent of the LORD, and said to him, "The king commands, 'Come forth.'" But he said, "No, I will die here." Then Benai'ah brought the king word again, saying, "Thus said Jo'ab, and thus he answered me." ³¹ The king replied to him, "Do as he has said, strike him down and bury him; and thus take away from me and from my father's house the guilt for the blood which Jo'ab shed without cause. ³² The LORD will bring back his bloody deeds upon his own head, because, without the knowledge of my father David, he attacked and slew with the sword two men more righteous and better than himself, Abner the

f Gk Syr Vg: Heb *and for him and for Abiathar*

the king's harem were considered royal property, to be passed on to the next king (compare v. 22). *Adonijah* made himself vulnerable by his request (2 Sam.3.6–11; 16.21–22). **26–27:** Since *Abiathar* was a priest, and hence a sacrosanct personality, Solomon could not execute him. Therefore the king did what he could, banishing Abiathar to his ancestral home. Some have theorized that the banished priest composed what we now call the Early Source of Samuel (see Introduction to 1 Samuel). **27:** An editorial addition reminiscent of 1 Sam.2.27–36. **28–35:** *Solomon* had orders from *David* to do away with *Joab*, and he proceeds quickly to carry out

son of Ner, commander of the army of Israel, and Ama'sa the son of Jether, commander of the army of Judah. ³³ So shall their blood come back upon the head of Jo'ab and upon the head of his descendants for ever; but to David, and to his descendants, and to his house, and to his throne, there shall be peace from the LORD for evermore." ³⁴ Then Benai'ah the son of Jehoi'ada went up, and struck him down and killed him; and he was buried in his own house in the wilderness. ³⁵ The king put Benai'ah the son of Jehoi'ada over the army in place of Jo'ab, and the king put Zadok the priest in the place of Abi'athar.

36 Then the king sent and summoned Shim'e-i, and said to him, "Build yourself a house in Jerusalem, and dwell there, and do not go forth from there to any place whatever. ³⁷ For on the day you go forth, and cross the brook Kidron, know for certain that you shall die; your blood shall be upon your own head." ³⁸ And Shim'e-i said to the king, "What you say is good; as my lord the king has said, so will your servant do." So Shim'e-i dwelt in Jerusalem many days.

39 But it happened at the end of three years that two of Shim'e-i's slaves ran away to Achish, son of Ma'acah, king of Gath. And when it was told Shim'e-i, "Behold, your slaves are in Gath," ⁴⁰ Shim'e-i arose and saddled an ass, and went to Gath to Achish, to seek his slaves; Shim'e-i went and brought his slaves from Gath. ⁴¹ And when Solomon was told that

Shim'e-i had gone from Jerusalem to Gath and returned, ⁴² the king sent and summoned Shim'e-i, and said to him, "Did I not make you swear by the LORD, and solemnly admonish you, saying, 'Know for certain that on the day you go forth and go to any place whatever, you shall die'? And you said to me, 'What you say is good; I obey.' ⁴³ Why then have you not kept your oath to the LORD and the commandment with which I charged you?" ⁴⁴ The king also said to Shim'e-i, "You know in your own heart all the evil that you did to David my father; so the LORD will bring back your evil upon your own head. ⁴⁵ But King Solomon shall be blessed, and the throne of David shall be established before the LORD for ever." ⁴⁶ Then the king commanded Benai'ah the son of Jehoi'ada; and he went out and struck him down, and he died.

So the kingdom was established in the hand of Solomon.

3 Solomon made a marriage alliance with Pharaoh king of Egypt; he took Pharaoh's daughter, and brought her into the city of David, until he had finished building his own house and the house of the LORD and the wall around Jerusalem. ² The people were sacrificing at the high places, however, because no house had yet been built for the name of the LORD.

3 Solomon loved the LORD, walking in the statutes of David his father; only, he sacrificed and burnt incense at the high places. ⁴ And the king went to Gibeon to sacrifice there, for that was the great high place; Solomon used

---

the orders (see 1.49–53 n.). The ever ready *Benaiah* becomes the new commander. **36–46:** *Shimei* had not joined the party of Adonijah (1.8); hence *Solomon* by agreement placed him in protective custody instead of executing him. *Shimei*, however, violated the agreement, and Benaiah had the welcome task of performing another execution.

3.1–28: Solomon in a dream prays for wisdom, and receives it; he exercises it in judgment. A new section now begins, based on "the Book of the Acts of Solomon" (see 11.41 and Introduction). One might say that the story begins with wisdom (ch. 3), but ends with folly (ch. 11). **1–2:** The identity of the pharaoh whose daughter Solomon married is uncertain. Verse 2 is Deuteronomic and apologetic, since to worship anywhere except at the temple was contrary to the editor's principles (Dt.12.1–14). Worship at *the high places* (hilltop shrines) was not outlawed until the time of Josiah (2 Kg.23.8). Solomon himself worshiped at *the great high place* at *Gibeon* (v. 4). **3–15:** On the story of how *Gibeon* became a part of the community of Israel,

to offer a thousand burnt offerings upon that altar. 5 At Gibeon the LORD appeared to Solomon in a dream by night; and God said, "Ask what I shall give you." 6 And Solomon said, "Thou hast shown great and steadfast love to thy servant David my father, because he walked before thee in faithfulness, in righteousness, and in uprightness of heart toward thee; and thou hast kept for him this great and steadfast love, and hast given him a son to sit on his throne this day. 7 And now, O LORD my God, thou hast made thy servant king in place of David my father, although I am but a little child; I do not know how to go out or come in. 8 And thy servant is in the midst of thy people whom thou hast chosen, a great people, that cannot be numbered or counted for multitude. 9 Give thy servant therefore an understanding mind to govern thy people, that I may discern between good and evil; for who is able to govern this thy great people?"

10 It pleased the Lord that Solomon had asked this. 11 And God said to him, "Because you have asked this, and have not asked for yourself long life or riches or the life of your enemies, but have asked for yourself understanding to discern what is right, 12 behold, I now do according to your word. Behold, I give you a wise and discerning mind, so that none like you has been before you and none like you shall arise after you. 13 I give you also what you have not asked, both riches and honor, so that no other king shall compare with you, all your days. 14 And if you will walk in my ways, keeping my statutes and my commandments, as your father David walked, then I will lengthen your days."

15 And Solomon awoke, and behold, it was a dream. Then he came to Jerusalem, and stood before the ark of the covenant of the LORD, and offered up burnt offerings and peace offerings, and made a feast for all his servants.

16 Then two harlots came to the king, and stood before him. 17 The one woman said, "Oh, my lord, this woman and I dwell in the same house; and I gave birth to a child while she was in the house. 18 Then on the third day after I was delivered, this woman also gave birth; and we were alone; there was no one else with us in the house, only we two were in the house. 19 And this woman's son died in the night, because she lay on it. 20 And she arose at midnight, and took my son from beside me, while your maidservant slept, and laid it in her bosom, and laid her dead son in my bosom. 21 When I rose in the morning to nurse my child, behold, it was dead; but when I looked at it closely in the morning, behold, it was not the child that I had borne." 22 But the other woman said, "No, the living child is mine, and the dead child is yours." The first said, "No, the dead child is yours, and the living child is mine." Thus they spoke before the king.

23 Then the king said, "The one says, 'This is my son that is alive, and your son is dead'; and the other says, 'No; but your son is dead, and my son is the living one.'" 24 And the king said, "Bring me a sword." So a sword was brought before the king. 25 And the king said, "Divide the living child in two, and give half to the one, and half to the other." 26 Then the woman whose son was alive said to the king, because her heart yearned for her son, "Oh, my lord, give her the living child, and by no means slay it." But the other said, "It shall be neither mine nor yours; divide it." 27 Then the king answered and said, "Give the living child to the first woman, and by no means slay it; she is its mother." 28 And all Israel heard of the judg-

see Jos. ch. 9; compare 2 Sam.21.2. **7:** The expression *but a little child* denotes humility; Solomon was probably about twenty years old. **14:** See v. 6. **15:** See 2 Sam.6.17–18. **16–28:** This is the most famous of the stories of Solomon's wisdom. Solomon was at his best in matters such as this, rather than in the larger affairs of statecraft.

ment which the king had rendered; and they stood in awe of the king, because they perceived that the wisdom of God was in him, to render justice.

4 King Solomon was king over all Israel, ² and these were his high officials: Azari′ah the son of Zadok was the priest; ³ Elihor′eph and Ahi′- jah the sons of Shisha were secretaries; Jehosh′aphat the son of Ahi′- lud was recorder; ⁴ Benai′ah the son of Jehoi′ada was in command of the army; Zadok and Abi′athar were priests; ⁵ Azari′ah the son of Nathan was over the officers; Zabud the son of Nathan was priest and king's friend; ⁶ Ahi′shar was in charge of the palace; and Adoni′ram the son of Abda was in charge of the forced labor.

7 Solomon had twelve officers over all Israel, who provided food for the king and his household; each man had to make provision for one month in the year. ⁸ These were their names: Ben-hur, in the hill country of E′phraim; ⁹ Ben-deker, in Makaz, Sha-al′bim, Beth-she′mesh, and E′lonbeth-ha′nan; ¹⁰ Ben-hesed, in Arub′both (to him belonged Socoh and all the land of Hepher); ¹¹ Ben-abin′adab, in all Naphath-dor (he had Taphath the daughter of Solomon as his wife); ¹² Ba′ana the son of Ahi′lud, in Ta′- anach, Megid′do, and all Beth-she′an which is beside Zarethan below Jezreel, and from Beth-she′an to A′bel-meho′lah, as far as the other side of Jok′meam; ¹³ Ben-geber, in Ra′- moth-gil′ead (he had the villages of Ja′ir the son of Manas′seh, which are in Gilead, and he had the region of Argob, which is in Bashan, sixty great cities with walls and bronze bars); ¹⁴ Ahin′adab the son of Iddo, in Mahana′im; ¹⁵ Ahi′ma-az, in Naph′- tali (he had taken Bas′emath the daughter of Solomon as his wife); ¹⁶ Ba′ana the son of Hushai, in Asher and Bealoth; ¹⁷ Jehosh′aphat the son of Paru′ah, in Is′sachar; ¹⁸ Shim′e-i the son of Ela, in Benjamin; ¹⁹ Geber the son of Uri, in the land of Gilead, the country of Sihon king of the Amorites and of Og king of Bashan. And there was one officer in the land of Judah.

20 Judah and Israel were as many as the sand by the sea; they ate and drank and were happy. ²¹ᵍ Solomon ruled over all the kingdoms from the Euphra′tes to the land of the Philistines and to the border of Egypt; they brought tribute and served Solomon all the days of his life.

22 Solomon's provision for one day was thirty cors of fine flour, and sixty cors of meal, ²³ ten fat oxen, and twenty pasture-fed cattle, a hundred sheep, besides harts, gazelles, roebucks, and fatted fowl. ²⁴ For he had dominion over all the region west of the Euphra′tes from Tiphsah to Gaza, over all the kings west of the Euphra′tes; and he had peace on all sides round about him. ²⁵ And Judah and Israel dwelt in safety, from Dan even to Beer-sheba, every man under his vine and under his fig tree, all the days of Solomon. ²⁶ Solomon also had forty thousand stalls of horses for his chariots, and twelve thousand horsemen. ²⁷ And those officers supplied provisions for King Solomon, and for all who came to King Solomon's table, each one in his month; they let nothing be lacking.

g Ch 5.1 in Heb

4.1–28: Solomon's organization of his kingdom. 1–6: This list of high officials from the court records is now somewhat disordered. *Azariah the son of Zadok* was probably not *the priest* (v. 2); that honor belonged to (another ?) Zadok (2.35) alone, *Abiathar* (v. 4) having been deposed (2.27). 7–19: Solomon's new administrative districts did not conform to the old tribal boundaries. Possibly this was one of the reasons for the revolt at the end of Solomon's reign, especially since Judah (v. 19) seems to have been exempt from the taxation mentioned in v. 7. 20–21: In the end, things turned out not to be so *happy*. Also, during Solomon's reign, the empire stretching *from the Euphrates . . . to the border of Egypt* began to fall away. Compare ch. 11. 22–28: Solomon's . . . *stalls of horses for his chariots* (v. 26; compare 10.26–29) may have been similar to those of the time of Ahab found in the excavations at Megiddo.

²⁸ Barley also and straw for the horses and swift steeds they brought to the place where it was required, each according to his charge.

29 And God gave Solomon wisdom and understanding beyond measure, and largeness of mind like the sand on the seashore, ³⁰ so that Solomon's wisdom surpassed the wisdom of all the people of the east, and all the wisdom of Egypt. ³¹ For he was wiser than all other men, wiser than Ethan the Ez'rahite, and Heman, Calcol, and Darda, the sons of Mahol; and his fame was in all the nations round about. ³² He also uttered three thousand proverbs; and his songs were a thousand and five. ³³ He spoke of trees, from the cedar that is in Lebanon to the hyssop that grows out of the wall; he spoke also of beasts, and of birds, and of reptiles, and of fish. ³⁴ And men came from all peoples to hear the wisdom of Solomon, and from all the kings of the earth, who had heard of his wisdom.

5 ʰ Now Hiram king of Tyre sent his servants to Solomon, when he heard that they had anointed him king in place of his father; for Hiram always loved David. ² And Solomon sent word to Hiram, ³ "You know that David my father could not build a house for the name of the LORD his God because of the warfare with which his enemies surrounded him, until the LORD put them under the soles of his feet. ⁴ But now the LORD my God has given me rest on every side; there is neither adversary nor misfortune. ⁵ And so I purpose to build a house for the name of the LORD my God, as the LORD said to David my father, 'Your son, whom I will set upon your throne in your place, shall build the house for my name.' ⁶ Now therefore command that cedars of Lebanon be cut for me; and my servants will join your servants, and I will pay you for your servants such wages as you set; for you know that there is no one among us who knows how to cut timber like the Sido'nians."

7 When Hiram heard the words of Solomon, he rejoiced greatly, and said, "Blessed be the LORD this day, who has given to David a wise son to be over this great people." ⁸ And Hiram sent to Solomon, saying, "I have heard the message which you have sent to me; I am ready to do all you desire in the matter of cedar and cypress timber. ⁹ My servants shall bring it down to the sea from Lebanon; and I will make it into rafts to go by sea to the place you direct, and I will have them broken up there, and you shall receive it; and you shall meet my wishes by providing food for my household." ¹⁰ So Hiram supplied Solomon with all the timber of cedar and cypress that he desired, ¹¹ while Solomon gave Hiram twenty thousand cors of wheat as food for his household, and twenty thousandⁱ cors of beaten oil. Solomon gave this to Hiram year by year. ¹² And the LORD gave Solomon wis-

h Ch 5.15 in Heb   *i* Gk: Heb *twenty*

4.29–34: Further remarks on Solomon's wisdom. In the Biblical tradition, wisdom became Solomonic, just as laws were Mosaic, and psalms Davidic (compare Pr.1.1; Ec.1.1,12). **31:** On *Ethan* and *Heman*, compare the titles of Pss. 88 and 89. **32:** On Solomon's reputation as a maker of *proverbs*, see Pr.1.1. With regard to the attribution of *songs* to Solomon, compare Pss. 72; 127; and S. of S.1.1. The number *a thousand and five* suggests *The Thousand and One Nights* of Arabic literature or the number of Solomon's wives and concubines (11.3).

5.1–18: Preparations for the building of the temple. 1–6: On the friendship of *Hiram king of Tyre* with David, see 2 Sam.5.11–12. *The Sidonians* (v. 6), a term used here for all the people later called Phoenicians. From their two chief cities, Tyre and Sidon, they carried on a vast maritime enterprise, two of their chief articles of commerce being cedar wood and purple dye. About a century after the time of Solomon they established their most famous colony, Carthage in North Africa. **11:** *Twenty thousand cors of wheat*, estimated to equal 125,000 bushels; *twenty thousand cors* of liquid would equal over a million gallons, according to some computations. *Beaten oil*, oil extracted from olives by beating, considered the best method for quality produc-

dom, as he promised him; and there was peace between Hiram and Solomon; and the two of them made a treaty.

13 King Solomon raised a levy of forced labor out of all Israel; and the levy numbered thirty thousand men. [14] And he sent them to Lebanon, ten thousand a month in relays; they would be a month in Lebanon and two months at home; Adoni'ram was in charge of the levy. [15] Solomon also had seventy thousand burden-bearers and eighty thousand hewers of stone in the hill country, [16] besides Solomon's three thousand three hundred chief officers who were over the work, who had charge of the people who carried on the work. [17] At the king's command, they quarried out great, costly stones in order to lay the foundation of the house with dressed stones. [18] So Solomon's builders and Hiram's builders and the men of Gebal did the hewing and prepared the timber and the stone to build the house.

6 In the four hundred and eightieth year after the people of Israel came out of the land of Egypt, in the fourth year of Solomon's reign over Israel, in the month of Ziv, which is the second month, he began to build the house of the LORD. [2] The house which King Solomon built for the LORD was sixty cubits long, twenty cubits wide, and thirty cubits high. [3] The vestibule in front of the nave of the house was twenty cubits long, equal to the width of the house, and ten cubits deep in front of the house. [4] And he made for the house windows with recessed frames. [5] He also built a structure against the wall of the house, running round the walls of the house, both the nave and the inner sanctuary; and he made side chambers all around. [6] The lowest story[j] was five cubits broad, the middle one was six cubits broad, and the third was seven cubits broad; for around the outside of the house he made offsets on the wall in order that the supporting beams should not be inserted into the walls of the house.

7 When the house was built, it was with stone prepared at the quarry; so that neither hammer nor axe nor any tool of iron was heard in the temple, while it was being built.

8 The entrance for the lowest[k] story was on the south side of the house; and one went up by stairs to the middle story, and from the middle story to the third. [9] So he built the house, and finished it; and he made the ceiling of the house of beams and planks of cedar. [10] He built the structure against the whole house, each story[l] five cubits high, and it was joined to the house with timbers of cedar.

11 Now the word of the LORD came to Solomon, [12] "Concerning this house which you are building, if you will walk in my statutes and obey my ordinances and keep all my commandments and walk in them, then I will establish my word with you, which I

j Gk: Heb *structure*
k Gk Tg: Heb *middle*
l Heb lacks *each story*

tion. **13–18:** One of the causes of the later disruption of the kingdom was *forced labor* (12.4). *Adoniram*, also called Adoram and Hadoram (2 Sam.20.24; 2 Chr.10.18); compare 4.6; 12.18. *Gebal*, called Byblos by the Greeks, famous for its trade in Egyptian papyrus, the ancient form of paper. From the Greek name our word "Bible" is indirectly derived.
6.1–38: The building of the temple. 1: An editorial expansion of v. 37. *The fourth year of Solomon's reign* would be approximately 960 B.C. *The four hundred and eightieth year* before this (1440 B.C.) is now considered too early as a date for the Exodus. *The month of Ziv* came in the spring (April–May). **2–6:** The *cubit*, approximately eighteen inches. Thus the temple had a rectangular floor plan of about 90 × 30 ft., was about 45 ft. high. There were three rooms: *the vestibule* or entrance hall, about 30 ft. wide and 10 ft. deep; *the nave* or main room, about 60 ft. long (v. 17); and *the inner sanctuary* or holy of holies, a perfect cube of about 30 ft. (v. 20). *Side chambers* surrounded the *nave and the inner sanctuary*, but not the vestibule. **7:** There is no reason to doubt that the *stone was prepared at the quarry*, though a later editor has exaggerated the silence of the building operations. **8–10:** A further description of the side chambers.

spoke to David your father. [13] And I will dwell among the children of Israel, and will not forsake my people Israel."

14 So Solomon built the house, and finished it. [15] He lined the walls of the house on the inside with boards of cedar; from the floor of the house to the rafters[m] of the ceiling, he covered them on the inside with wood; and he covered the floor of the house with boards of cypress. [16] He built twenty cubits of the rear of the house with boards of cedar from the floor to the rafters,[m] and he built this within as an inner sanctuary, as the most holy place. [17] The house, that is, the nave in front of the inner sanctuary, was forty cubits long. [18] The cedar within the house was carved in the form of gourds and open flowers; all was cedar, no stone was seen. [19] The inner sanctuary he prepared in the innermost part of the house, to set there the ark of the covenant of the LORD. [20] The inner sanctuary[n] was twenty cubits long, twenty cubits wide, and twenty cubits high; and he overlaid it with pure gold. He also made[o] an altar of cedar. [21] And Solomon overlaid the inside of the house with pure gold, and he drew chains of gold across, in front of the inner sanctuary, and overlaid it with gold. [22] And he overlaid the whole house with gold, until all the house was finished. Also the whole altar that belonged to the inner sanctuary he overlaid with gold.

23 In the inner sanctuary he made two cherubim of olivewood, each ten cubits high. [24] Five cubits was the length of one wing of the cherub, and five cubits the length of the other wing of the cherub; it was ten cubits from the tip of one wing to the tip of the other. [25] The other cherub also measured ten cubits; both cherubim had the same measure and the same form. [26] The height of one cherub was ten cubits, and so was that of the other cherub.

[27] He put the cherubim in the innermost part of the house; and the wings of the cherubim were spread out so that a wing of one touched the one wall, and a wing of the other cherub touched the other wall; their other wings touched each other in the middle of the house. [28] And he overlaid the cherubim with gold.

29 He carved all the walls of the house round about with carved figures of cherubim and palm trees and open flowers, in the inner and outer rooms. [30] The floor of the house he overlaid with gold in the inner and outer rooms.

31 For the entrance to the inner sanctuary he made doors of olivewood; the lintel and the doorposts formed a pentagon.[p] [32] He covered the two doors of olivewood with carvings of cherubim, palm trees, and open flowers; he overlaid them with gold, and spread gold upon the cherubim and upon the palm trees.

33 So also he made for the entrance to the nave doorposts of olivewood, in the form of a square, [34] and two doors of cypress wood; the two leaves of the one door were folding, and the two leaves of the other door were folding. [35] On them he carved cherubim and palm trees and open flowers; and he overlaid them with gold evenly applied upon the carved work. [36] He built the inner court with three courses of hewn stone and one course of cedar beams.

37 In the fourth year the foundation of the house of the LORD was laid, in the month of Ziv. [38] And in the eleventh year, in the month of Bul, which is the eighth month, the house was finished in all its parts, and according to all its specifications. He was seven years in building it.

m Gk: Heb *walls*
n Vg: Heb *and before the inner sanctuary*
o Gk: Heb *covered*
p Heb obscure

14–22: No doubt the decorations of the temple were artistically intricate; the amount of gold, however, has probably been somewhat exaggerated. On *the ark of the covenant,* see 1 Sam.3.3 n. **23–28:** On *the cherubim,* see 1 Sam.4.4 n. **37–38:** See v. 1 n. *The month of Bul* was in the autumn (October-November).

7 Solomon was building his own house thirteen years, and he finished his entire house.

2 He built the House of the Forest of Lebanon; its length was a hundred cubits, and its breadth fifty cubits, and its height thirty cubits, and it was built upon three*q* rows of cedar pillars, with cedar beams upon the pillars. 3 And it was covered with cedar above the chambers that were upon the forty-five pillars, fifteen in each row. 4 There were window frames in three rows, and window opposite window in three tiers. 5 All the doorways and windows*r* had square frames, and window was opposite window in three tiers.

6 And he made the Hall of Pillars; its length was fifty cubits, and its breadth thirty cubits; there was a porch in front with pillars, and a canopy before them.

7 And he made the Hall of the Throne where he was to pronounce judgment, even the Hall of Judgment; it was finished with cedar from floor to rafters.*s*

8 His own house where he was to dwell, in the other court back of the hall, was of like workmanship. Solomon also made a house like this hall for Pharaoh's daughter whom he had taken in marriage.

9 All these were made of costly stones, hewn according to measure, sawed with saws, back and front, even from the foundation to the coping, and from the court of the house of the LORD*t* to the great court. 10 The foundation was of costly stones, huge stones, stones of eight and ten cubits. 11 And above were costly stones, hewn according to measurement, and cedar. 12 The great court had three courses of hewn stone round about,

and a course of cedar beams; so had the inner court of the house of the LORD, and the vestibule of the house.

13 And King Solomon sent and brought Hiram from Tyre. 14 He was the son of a widow of the tribe of Naph′tali, and his father was a man of Tyre, a worker in bronze; and he was full of wisdom, understanding, and skill, for making any work in bronze. He came to King Solomon, and did all his work.

15 He cast two pillars of bronze. Eighteen cubits was the height of one pillar, and a line of twelve cubits measured its circumference; it was hollow, and its thickness was four fingers; the second pillar was the same.*u* 16 He also made two capitals of molten bronze, to set upon the tops of the pillars; the height of the one capital was five cubits, and the height of the other capital was five cubits. 17 Then he made two*v* nets of checker work with wreaths of chain work for the capitals upon the tops of the pillars; a net*w* for the one capital, and a net*w* for the other capital. 18 Likewise he made pomegranates;*x* in two rows round about upon the one network, to cover the capital that was upon the top of the pillar; and he did the same with the other capital. 19 Now the capitals that were upon the tops of the pillars in the vestibule were of lily-work, four cubits. 20 The capitals were upon the two pillars and also above the rounded projection which was beside the network; there were two hundred pomegranates, in two

q Gk: Heb *four*   r Gk: Heb *posts*
s Syr Vg: Heb *floor*
t With 7.12: Heb *from the outside*
u Tg Syr Compare Gk and Jer 52.21: Heb *and a line of twelve cubits measured the circumference of the second pillar*
v Gk: Heb lacks *he made two*   w Gk: Heb *seven*
x With 2 Mss Compare Gk: Heb *pillars*

7.1–51: Details of Solomon's building operations. 1: See 3.1. The palace and administrative complex took *thirteen years* to build, the temple only seven (6.38); compare 9.10. **6–12:** Details of the palace and administrative complex lying immediately south of the temple. **13–14:** The artisan *Hiram of Tyre* is not to be confused with the king of the same name; compare 2 Chr. 2.13, where the name is given as Huram-abi. **15–22:** In front of the vestibule were set up the two great free-standing *pillars of bronze* called *Jachin* and *Boaz*. The names mean something like "God establishes" and "He comes with power." The pillars themselves doubtless had a symbolic significance (e.g. "trees of life") which now eludes us. On their role at ceremonial occasions,

rows round about; and so with the other capital. ²¹ He set up the pillars at the vestibule of the temple; he set up the pillar on the south and called its name Jachin; and he set up the pillar on the north and called its name Bo'az. ²² And upon the tops of the pillars was lily-work. Thus the work of the pillars was finished.

23 Then he made the molten sea; it was round, ten cubits from brim to brim, and five cubits high, and a line of thirty cubits measured its circumference. ²⁴ Under its brim were gourds, for thirty^y cubits, compassing the sea round about; the gourds were in two rows, cast with it when it was cast. ²⁵ It stood upon twelve oxen, three facing north, three facing west, three facing south, and three facing east; the sea was set upon them, and all their hinder parts were inward. ²⁶ Its thickness was a handbreadth; and its brim was made like the brim of a cup, like the flower of a lily; it held two thousand baths.

27 He also made the ten stands of bronze; each stand was four cubits long, four cubits wide, and three cubits high. ²⁸ This was the construction of the stands: they had panels, and the panels were set in the frames ²⁹ and on the panels that were set in the frames were lions, oxen, and cherubim. Upon the frames, both above and below the lions and oxen, there were wreaths of beveled work. ³⁰ Moreover each stand had four bronze wheels and axles of bronze; and at the four corners were supports for a laver. The supports were cast, with wreaths at the side of each. ³¹ Its opening was within a crown which projected upward one cubit; its opening was round, as a

pedestal is made, a cubit and a half deep. At its opening there were carvings; and its panels were square, not round. ³² And the four wheels were underneath the panels; the axles of the wheels were of one piece with the stands; and the height of a wheel was a cubit and a half. ³³ The wheels were made like a chariot wheel; their axles, their rims, their spokes, and their hubs, were all cast. ³⁴ There were four supports at the four corners of each stand; the supports were of one piece with the stands. ³⁵ And on the top of the stand there was a round band half a cubit high; and on the top of the stand its stays and its panels were of one piece with it. ³⁶ And on the surfaces of its stays and on its panels, he carved cherubim, lions, and palm trees, according to the space of each, with wreaths round about. ³⁷ After this manner he made the ten stands; all of them were cast alike, of the same measure and the same form.

38 And he made ten lavers of bronze; each laver held forty baths, each laver measured four cubits, and there was a laver for each of the ten stands. ³⁹ And he set the stands, five on the south side of the house, and five on the north side of the house; and he set the sea on the southeast corner of the house.

40 Hiram also made the pots, the shovels, and the basins. So Hiram finished all the work that he did for King Solomon on the house of the LORD: ⁴¹ the two pillars, the two bowls of the capitals that were on the tops of the pillars, and the two networks to cover the two bowls of capitals that were on the tops of the

y Heb ten

---

see 2 Kg.11.14; 23.3. **23–26:** *The molten sea* was a huge bowl or tank supported on *twelve oxen.* Its capacity was *two thousand baths* (the bath was a liquid measure equal to about six gallons). According to 2 Chr.4.6 the purpose *was for the priests to wash in,* though it is difficult to imagine just how the ablutions were accomplished, since the rim of the tank was some ten feet above the pavement. As with the pillars, there may have been also a symbolic significance (such as "life-giving water"; compare the artificial lakes near Egyptian temples). The *twelve oxen* were really couchant bulls, symbols of fertility and power in many religions of the ancient Near East. Their arrangement according to the four points of the compass suggested universal dominion. **27–39:** *The ten stands,* highly ornamented bronze wagons on each of which was mounted

pillars; ⁴²and the four hundred pomegranates for the two networks, two rows of pomegranates for each network, to cover the two bowls of the capitals that were upon the pillars; ⁴³the ten stands, and the ten lavers upon the stands; ⁴⁴and the one sea, and the twelve oxen underneath the sea.

45 Now the pots, the shovels, and the basins, all these vessels in the house of the LORD, which Hiram made for King Solomon, were of burnished bronze. ⁴⁶In the plain of the Jordan the king cast them, in the clay ground between Succoth and Zarethan. ⁴⁷And Solomon left all the vessels unweighed, because there were so many of them; the weight of the bronze was not found out.

48 So Solomon made all the vessels that were in the house of the LORD: the golden altar, the golden table for the bread of the Presence, ⁴⁹the lampstands of pure gold, five on the south side and five on the north, before the inner sanctuary; the flowers, lamps, and the tongs, of gold; ⁵⁰The cups, snuffers, basins, dishes for incense, and firepans, of pure gold; and the sockets of gold, for the doors of the innermost part of the house, the most holy place, and for the doors of the nave of the temple.

51 Thus all the work that King Solomon did on the house of the LORD was finished. And Solomon brought in the things which David his father had dedicated, the silver, the gold, and the vessels, and stored them in the treasuries of the house of the LORD.

8 Then Solomon assembled the elders of Israel and all the heads of the tribes, the leaders of the fathers' houses of the people of Israel, before King Solomon in Jerusalem, to bring up the ark of the covenant of the LORD out of the city of David, which is Zion. ²And all the men of Israel assembled to King Solomon at the feast in the month Eth'anim, which is the seventh month. ³And all the elders of Israel came, and the priests took up the ark. ⁴And they brought up the ark of the LORD, the tent of meeting, and all the holy vessels that were in the tent; the priests and the Levites brought them up. ⁵And King Solomon and all the congregation of Israel, who had assembled before him, were with him before the ark, sacrificing so many sheep and oxen that they could not be counted or numbered. ⁶Then the priests brought the ark of the covenant of the LORD to its place, in the inner sanctuary of the house, in the most holy place, underneath the wings of the cherubim. ⁷For the cherubim spread out their wings over the place of the ark, so that the cherubim made a covering above the ark and its poles. ⁸And the poles were so long that the ends of the poles were seen from the holy place before the inner sanctuary; but they could not be seen from outside; and they are there to this day. ⁹There was nothing in the ark except the two tables of stone which Moses put there at Horeb, where the LORD made a covenant with the people of Israel, when they came out of the land of Egypt.

one of the *ten lavers* or wash basins. **48–50:** In *the nave* were *the golden altar* for incense, the *table for the bread of the Presence* (or showbread, see Lev.24.5–9), and the ten *lampstands*, plus smaller objects. The *lampstands* were simple, each being a rod resting on a base, with a small bowl at the top for oil and wick; not to be confused with the lampstand described in Ex.25.31–40.

8.1–66: The dedication of the temple. 1–11: Bringing *the ark of the covenant* into the temple (2 Sam.6.12–15). *The city of David*, or *Zion*, was south of the temple area, in the southeastern part of the city. *The month Ethanim* or Tishri occurred in the autumn (September-October). The dedication of the temple was, therefore, postponed for eleven months (6.38), in order to make it a part of the autumnal new-year festival, the religious high point of the year. **7:** *The cherubim*, see 6.23–28. The ark was carried by *the poles* (v. 8); the writer here is the first Deuteronomist (see Introduction), of a time before the destruction of the temple, as is seen from the

10 And when the priests came out of the holy place, a cloud filled the house of the LORD, 11 so that the priests could not stand to minister because of the cloud; for the glory of the LORD filled the house of the LORD.

12 Then Solomon said,
"The LORD has set the sun in the heavens,
but[z] has said that he would dwell in thick darkness.
13 I have built thee an exalted house, a place for thee to dwell in for ever."

14 Then the king faced about, and blessed all the assembly of Israel, while all the assembly of Israel stood. 15 And he said, "Blessed be the LORD, the God of Israel, who with his hand has fulfilled what he promised with his mouth to David my father, saying, 16 'Since the day that I brought my people Israel out of Egypt, I chose no city in all the tribes of Israel in which to build a house, that my name might be there; but I chose David to be over my people Israel.' 17 Now it was in the heart of David my father to build a house for the name of the LORD, the God of Israel. 18 But the LORD said to David my father, 'Whereas it was in your heart to build a house for my name, you did well that it was in your heart; 19 nevertheless you shall not build the house, but your son who shall be born to you shall build the house for my name.' 20 Now the LORD has fulfilled his promise which he made; for I have risen in the place of David my father, and sit on the throne of Israel, as the LORD promised, and I have built the house for the name of the LORD, the God of Israel. 21 And there I have provided a place for the ark, in which is the covenant of the LORD which he made with our fathers, when he brought them out of the land of Egypt."

22 Then Solomon stood before the altar of the LORD in the presence of all the assembly of Israel, and spread forth his hands toward heaven; 23 and said, "O LORD, God of Israel, there is no God like thee, in heaven above or on earth beneath, keeping covenant and showing steadfast love to thy servants who walk before thee with all their heart; 24 who hast kept with thy servant David my father what thou didst declare to him; yea, thou didst speak with thy mouth, and with thy hand hast fulfilled it this day. 25 Now therefore, O LORD, God of Israel, keep with thy servant David my father what thou hast promised him, saying, 'There shall never fail you a man before me to sit upon the throne of Israel, if only your sons take heed to their way, to walk before me as you have walked before me.' 26 Now therefore, O God of Israel, let thy word be confirmed, which thou hast spoken to thy servant David my father.

27 "But will God indeed dwell on the earth? Behold, heaven and the highest heaven cannot contain thee; how much less this house which I have built! 28 Yet have regard to the prayer of thy servant and to his supplication, O LORD my God, hearkening to the cry and to the prayer which thy servant prays before thee this day; 29 that thy eyes may be open night and day toward this house, the place of which thou hast said, 'My name shall be there,' that thou mayest hearken to the prayer which thy servant offers toward this place. 30 And hearken thou to the supplication of thy servant and of thy people Israel, when they pray toward this place; yea, hear thou in heaven thy dwelling place; and when thou hearest, forgive.

31 "If a man sins against his neigh-

z Gk: Heb lacks *has set the sun in the heavens, but*

---

words *they are there to this day.* **12–21:** Solomon's address to the people. The writer here is the first Deuteronomist; it is impossible to tell how much of this comes from Solomon and how much from the later writer. The *thick darkness* (v. 12) refers to the fact that the inner sanctuary had no windows, being in total darkness except when the door was opened on rare occasions. According to the Greek version, the poetic prologue (vv. 12–13) was taken from the Book of Jashar (see Jos.10.13 n.). **22–40:** Solomon's prayer of dedication. This prayer, entirely in the

bor and is made to take an oath, and comes and swears his oath before thine altar in this house, 32 then hear thou in heaven, and act, and judge thy servants, condemning the guilty by bringing his conduct upon his own head, and vindicating the righteous by rewarding him according to his righteousness.

33 "When thy people Israel are defeated before the enemy because they have sinned against thee, if they turn again to thee, and acknowledge thy name, and pray and make supplication to thee in this house; 34 then hear thou in heaven, and forgive the sin of thy people Israel, and bring them again to the land which thou gavest to their fathers.

35 "When heaven is shut up and there is no rain because they have sinned against thee, if they pray toward this place, and acknowledge thy name, and turn from their sin, when thou dost afflict them, 36 then hear thou in heaven, and forgive the sin of thy servants, thy people Israel, when thou dost teach them the good way in which they should walk; and grant rain upon thy land, which thou hast given to thy people as an inheritance.

37 "If there is famine in the land, if there is pestilence or blight or mildew or locust or caterpillar; if their enemy besieges them in any*a* of their cities; whatever plague, whatever sickness there is; 38 whatever prayer, whatever supplication is made by any man or by all thy people Israel, each knowing the affliction of his own heart and stretching out his hands toward this house; 39 then hear thou in heaven thy dwelling place, and forgive, and act, and render to each whose heart thou knowest, according to all his ways (for thou, thou only, knowest the hearts of all the children of men); 40 that they may fear thee all the days

that they live in the land which thou gavest to our fathers.

41 "Likewise when a foreigner, who is not of thy people Israel, comes from a far country for thy name's sake 42 (for they shall hear of thy great name, and thy mighty hand, and of thy outstretched arm), when he comes and prays toward this house, 43 hear thou in heaven thy dwelling place, and do according to all for which the foreigner calls to thee; in order that all the peoples of the earth may know thy name and fear thee, as do thy people Israel, and that they may know that this house which I have built is called by thy name.

44 "If thy people go out to battle against their enemy, by whatever way thou shalt send them, and they pray to the LORD toward the city which thou hast chosen and the house which I have built for thy name, 45 then hear thou in heaven their prayer and their supplication, and maintain their cause.

46 "If they sin against thee–for there is no man who does not sin–and thou art angry with them, and dost give them to an enemy, so that they are carried away captive to the land of the enemy, far off or near; 47 yet if they lay it to heart in the land to which they have been carried captive, and repent, and make supplication to thee in the land of their captors, saying, 'We have sinned, and have acted perversely and wickedly'; 48 if they repent with all their mind and with all their heart in the land of their enemies, who carried them captive, and pray to thee toward their land, which thou gavest to their fathers, the city which thou hast chosen, and the house which I have built for thy name; 49 then hear thou in heaven thy dwelling place their prayer and their supplication, and maintain their cause 50 and forgive thy people who have

a Gk Syr: Heb *the land*

---

spirit of the book of Deuteronomy, was composed mostly by the first Deuteronomist. The phrase *and bring them again to the land which thou gavest to their fathers* (v. 34) was added during the Exile, probably by the second Deuteronomist. **41–53:** An expansion of the prayer by the second Deuteronomist. The many references to being *carried away captive to the land*

sinned against thee, and all their transgressions which they have committed against thee; and grant them compassion in the sight of those who carried them captive, that they may have compassion on them ⁵¹ (for they are thy people, and thy heritage, which thou didst bring out of Egypt, from the midst of the iron furnace). ⁵² Let thy eyes be open to the supplication of thy servant, and to the supplication of thy people Israel, giving ear to them whenever they call to thee. ⁵³ For thou didst separate them from among all the peoples of the earth, to be thy heritage, as thou didst declare through Moses, thy servant, when thou didst bring our fathers out of Egypt, O Lord GOD."

54 Now as Solomon finished offering all this prayer and supplication to the LORD, he arose from before the altar of the LORD, where he had knelt with hands outstretched toward heaven; ⁵⁵ and he stood, and blessed all the assembly of Israel with a loud voice, saying, ⁵⁶ "Blessed be the LORD who has given rest to his people Israel, according to all that he promised; not one word has failed of all his good promise, which he uttered by Moses his servant. ⁵⁷ The LORD our God be with us, as he was with our fathers; may he not leave us or forsake us; ⁵⁸ that he may incline our hearts to him, to walk in all his ways, and to keep his commandments, his statutes, and his ordinances, which he commanded our fathers. ⁵⁹ Let these words of mine, wherewith I have made supplication before the LORD, be near to the LORD our God day and night, and may he maintain the cause of his servant, and the cause of his people Israel, as each day requires; ⁶⁰ that all the peoples of the earth may know that the LORD is God; there is no other. ⁶¹ Let your heart therefore be wholly

true to the LORD our God, walking in his statutes and keeping his commandments, as at this day."

62 Then the king, and all Israel with him, offered sacrifice before the LORD. ⁶³ Solomon offered as peace offerings to the LORD twenty-two thousand oxen and a hundred and twenty thousand sheep. So the king and all the people of Israel dedicated the house of the LORD. ⁶⁴ The same day the king consecrated the middle of the court that was before the house of the LORD; for there he offered the burnt offering and the cereal offering and the fat pieces of the peace offerings, because the bronze altar that was before the LORD was too small to receive the burnt offering and the cereal offering and the fat pieces of the peace offerings.

65 So Solomon held the feast at that time, and all Israel with him, a great assembly, from the entrance of Hamath to the Brook of Egypt, before the LORD our God, seven days.ᵇ ⁶⁶ On the eighth day he sent the people away; and they blessed the king, and went to their homes joyful and glad of heart for all the goodness that the LORD had shown to David his servant and to Israel his people.

9 When Solomon had finished building the house of the LORD and the king's house and all that Solomon desired to build, ² the LORD appeared to Solomon a second time, as he had appeared to him at Gibeon. ³ And the LORD said to him, "I have heard your prayer and your supplication, which you have made before me; I have consecrated this house which you have built, and put my name there for ever; my eyes and my heart will be there for all time.⁴ And as for you, if you will walk before me, as David your father walked, with integrity of heart and

b Gk: Heb *seven days and seven days, fourteen days*

---

of the enemy, especially in vv. 46–53, should be noticed. **62–66:** This is the natural conclusion of the chapter by the first Deuteronomist. In v. 64 *the bronze altar* in front of the temple is specifically mentioned for the first time, though it is alluded to in vv. 22 and 54.
9.1–9: Solomon's vision. A thoroughly Deuteronomic composition, probably by the second Deuteronomist, who lived after the temple had *become a heap of ruins* (v. 8), and could point out the sinfulness that had led to national ruin (see Introduction).

uprightness, doing according to all that I have commanded you, and keeping my statutes and my ordinances, [5] then I will establish your royal throne over Israel for ever, as I promised David your father, saying, 'There shall not fail you a man upon the throne of Israel.' [6] But if you turn aside from following me, you or your children, and do not keep my commandments and my statutes which I have set before you, but go and serve other gods and worship them,[7] then I will cut off Israel from the land which I have given them; and the house which I have consecrated for my name I will cast out of my sight; and Israel will become a proverb and a byword among all peoples. [8] And this house will become a heap of ruins;[c] every one passing by it will be astonished, and will hiss; and they will say, 'Why has the LORD done thus to this land and to this house?' [9] Then they will say, 'Because they forsook the LORD their God who brought their fathers out of the land of Egypt, and laid hold on other gods, and worshiped them and served them; therefore the LORD has brought all this evil upon them.' "

10 At the end of twenty years, in which Solomon had built the two houses, the house of the LORD and the king's house, [11] and Hiram king of Tyre had supplied Solomon with cedar and cypress timber and gold, as much as he desired, King Solomon gave to Hiram twenty cities in the land of Galilee. [12] But when Hiram came from Tyre to see the cities which Solomon had given him, they did not please him. [13] Therefore he said, "What kind of cities are these which you have given me, my brother?" So they are called the land of Cabul to this day. [14] Hiram had sent to the king one hundred and twenty talents of gold.

15 And this is the account of the forced labor which King Solomon levied to build the house of the LORD and his own house and the Millo and the wall of Jerusalem and Hazor and Megid'do and Gezer [16] (Pharaoh king of Egypt had gone up and captured Gezer and burnt it with fire, and had slain the Canaanites who dwelt in the city, and had given it as dowry to his daughter, Solomon's wife; [17] so Solomon rebuilt Gezer) and Lower Beth-hor'on [18] and Ba'alath and Tamar in the wilderness, in the land of Judah,[d] [19] and all the store-cities that Solomon had, and the cities for his chariots, and the cities for his horsemen, and whatever Solomon desired to build in Jerusalem, in Lebanon, and in all the land of his dominion. [20] All the people who were left of the Amorites, the Hittites, the Per'izzites, the Hivites, and the Jeb'usites, who were not of the people of Israel– [21] their descendants who were left after them in the land, whom the people of Israel were unable to destroy utterly–these Solomon made a forced levy of slaves, and so they are to this day. [22] But of the people of Israel Solomon made no slaves; they were the soldiers, they were his officials, his commanders, his captains, his chariot commanders and his horsemen.

23 These were the chief officers who were over Solomon's work: five hundred and fifty, who had charge of the people who carried on the work.

24 But Pharaoh's daughter went up from the city of David to her own house which Solomon had built for her; then he built the Millo.

c Syr Old Latin: Heb *high*   d Heb lacks *of Judah*

9.10–14: An interlude; a story told to explain the origin of a name. The meaning of *Cabul* is not known; "like nothing" is as good a conjecture as any. On the historical side, Hiram's supplying of timber is irrelevant; Solomon had paid for that (5.11). It would seem that Solomon was in financial difficulties and was forced to cede *twenty cities* to Hiram for a cash consideration (the value of a gold talent has been roughly estimated at thirty thousand dollars).

9.15–22: The forced levy (see 5.13). *The Millo* (also v. 24; 2 Sam.5.9) is usually interpreted as an earthwork south of the temple area; the word probably means "a filling." Verse 22 seems to be contradicted by 5.13 and 12.4. **23–28: Miscellaneous details. 24:** Compare v. 16 and 3.1.

25 Three times a year Solomon used to offer up burnt offerings and peace offerings upon the altar which he built to the LORD, burning incense[e] before the LORD. So he finished the house.

26 King Solomon built a fleet of ships at E′zion-ge′ber, which is near Eloth on the shore of the Red Sea, in the land of Edom.[27] And Hiram sent with the fleet his servants, seamen who were familiar with the sea, together with the servants of Solomon; [28] and they went to Ophir, and brought from there gold, to the amount of four hundred and twenty talents; and they brought it to King Solomon.

10 Now when the queen of Sheba heard of the fame of Solomon concerning the name of the LORD, she came to test him with hard questions. [2] She came to Jerusalem with a very great retinue, with camels bearing spices, and very much gold, and precious stones; and when she came to Solomon, she told him all that was on her mind. [3] And Solomon answered all her questions; there was nothing hidden from the king which he could not explain to her. [4] And when the queen of Sheba had seen all the wisdom of Solomon, the house that he had built, [5] the food of his table, the seating of his officials, and the attendance of his servants, their clothing, his cupbearers, and his burnt offerings which he offered at the house of the LORD, there was no more spirit in her.

6 And she said to the king, "The report was true which I heard in my own land of your affairs and of your wisdom, [7] but I did not believe the reports until I came and my own eyes had seen it; and, behold, the half was not told me; your wisdom and prosperity surpass the report which I heard. [8] Happy are your wives![f] Happy are these your servants, who continually stand before you and hear your wisdom! [9] Blessed be the LORD your God, who has delighted in you and set you on the throne of Israel! Because the LORD loved Israel for ever, he has made you king, that you may execute justice and righteousness." [10] Then she gave the king a hundred and twenty talents of gold, and a very great quantity of spices, and precious stones; never again came such an abundance of spices as these which the queen of Sheba gave to King Solomon.

11 Moreover the fleet of Hiram, which brought gold from Ophir, brought from Ophir a very great amount of almug wood and precious stones. [12] And the king made of the almug wood supports for the house of the LORD, and for the king's house, lyres also and harps for the singers; no such almug wood has come or been seen, to this day.

13 And King Solomon gave to the queen of Sheba all that she desired, whatever she asked besides what was given her by the bounty of King Solomon. So she turned and went back to her own land, with her servants.

14 Now the weight of gold that came to Solomon in one year was six

e Gk: Heb *burning incense with it which*
f Gk Syr: Heb *men*

25: In those early days the king still exercised priestly functions. 26–28: *Red Sea* here refers to the Gulf of Aqabah. The location of *Ophir* is unknown; it may have been in southern Arabia (compare 10.11 and Gen.10.29). Excavations at Ezion-geber have disclosed the refineries in which copper from the Arabah mines was smelted.

10.1–29: The visit of the queen of Sheba; Solomon's wealth and business enterprises. 1–5: *Sheba* is usually considered to have been located in southwest Arabia, modern Yemen. Some, however, think that this queen came from a colony of Sheba in northern Arabia, where a number of queens are known to have ruled. Practical wisdom, proverbial sayings, and contests of wits were characteristic of the Biblical world; compare 4.29–34 and the Old Testament books of "wisdom," such as Job and Proverbs. The word for *spirit* (v. 5) can be translated "breath"– the queen was breathless with amazement. 10: On the value of *talents of gold*, see 9.14 n. 11–12: An interlude, related to 9.26–28. *Almug wood* is now often called sandalwood. 13: The Ethiopians (Abyssinians) have a tradition according to which *all that she desired* included an heir, who later became king of Ethiopia, thus establishing the true dynasty of David for that country.

[431]

hundred and sixty-six talents of gold, [15] besides that which came from the traders and from the traffic of the merchants, and from all the kings of Arabia and from the governors of the land. [16] King Solomon made two hundred large shields of beaten gold; six hundred shekels of gold went into each shield. [17] And he made three hundred shields of beaten gold; three minas of gold went into each shield; and the king put them in the House of the Forest of Lebanon. [18] The king also made a great ivory throne, and overlaid it with the finest gold. [19] The throne had six steps, and at the back of the throne was a calf's head, and on each side of the seat were arm rests and two lions standing beside the arm rests, [20] while twelve lions stood there, one on each end of a step on the six steps. The like of it was never made in any kingdom. [21] All King Solomon's drinking vessels were of gold, and all the vessels of the House of the Forest of Lebanon were of pure gold; none were of silver, it was not considered as anything in the days of Solomon. [22] For the king had a fleet of ships of Tarshish at sea with the fleet of Hiram. Once every three years the fleet of ships of Tarshish used to come bringing gold, silver, ivory, apes, and peacocks.[g]

23 Thus King Solomon excelled all the kings of the earth in riches and in wisdom. [24] And the whole earth sought the presence of Solomon to hear his wisdom, which God had put into his mind. [25] Every one of them brought his present, articles of silver and gold, garments, myrrh, spices, horses, and mules, so much year by year.

26 And Solomon gathered together chariots and horsemen; he had fourteen hundred chariots and twelve thousand horsemen, whom he stationed in the chariot cities and with the king in Jerusalem. [27] And the king made silver as common in Jerusalem as stone, and he made cedar as plentiful as the sycamore of the Shephe'lah. [28] And Solomon's import of horses was from Egypt and Ku'e, and the king's traders received them from Ku'e at a price. [29] A chariot could be imported from Egypt for six hundred shekels of silver, and a horse for a hundred and fifty; and so through the king's traders they were exported to all the kings of the Hittites and the kings of Syria.

Now King Solomon loved many foreign women: the daughter of Pharaoh, and Moabite, Ammonite, E'domite, Sido'nian, and Hittite women, [2] from the nations concerning which the LORD had said to the people of Israel, "You shall not enter into marriage with them, neither shall they with you, for surely they will turn away your heart after their gods"; Solomon clung to these in love. [3] He had seven hundred wives, princesses, and three hundred concubines; and his wives turned away his heart. [4] For when Solomon was old his wives turned away his heart after other gods; and his heart was not wholly true to the LORD his God, as was the heart of David his father. [5] For Solomon went after Ash'toreth the goddess of the Sido'nians, and after Milcom the abomination of the Ammonites. [6] So Solomon did what was evil in the sight of the LORD, and did not wholly follow the LORD, as David his father had done. [7] Then Solo-

g Or *baboons*

16–17: If there were fifty shekels in a mina (Ezek.45.12), the smaller shields weighed one hundred and fifty shekels. **22:** *Ships of Tarshish*, i.e. ships capable of making long voyages; compare vv. 11–12; 9.26–28; Is.23.1. **26–29:** These verses describe Solomon's very large commerce in *horses* and *chariots*. *Kue* was Cilicia, in southeast Asia Minor. *The kings of the Hittites* ruled small principalities in northern *Syria*.

11.1–43: The dark side of Solomon's reign. The second Deuteronomist, who was less friendly to Judah, may have contributed heavily to this chapter. In any case, the writers knew the tragedies that followed (vv. 12–13) and sought to probe their causes. In this connection, Dt. 17.14–20, from the same school of writers, should be carefully considered. **1–13:** Judgment on Solomon. Compare Dt.7.1–4. On *Ashtoreth*, see 1 Sam.7.3–4 n. On the *high place*, see 3.1–2 n.

mon built a high place for Chemosh the abomination of Moab, and for Molech the abomination of the Ammonites, on the mountain east of Jerusalem. ⁸ And so he did for all his foreign wives, who burned incense and sacrificed to their gods.

9 And the LORD was angry with Solomon, because his heart had turned away from the LORD, the God of Israel, who had appeared to him twice, ¹⁰ and had commanded him concerning this thing, that he should not go after other gods; but he did not keep what the LORD commanded. ¹¹ Therefore the LORD said to Solomon, "Since this has been your mind and you have not kept my covenant and my statutes which I have commanded you, I will surely tear the kingdom from you and will give it to your servant.¹² Yet for the sake of David your father I will not do it in your days, but I will tear it out of the hand of your son. ¹³ However I will not tear away all the kingdom; but I will give one tribe to your son, for the sake of David my servant and for the sake of Jerusalem which I have chosen."

14 And the LORD raised up an adversary against Solomon, Hadad the E'domite; he was of the royal house in Edom.¹⁵ For when David was in Edom, and Jo'ab the commander of the army went up to bury the slain, he slew every male in Edom ¹⁶ (for Jo'ab and all Israel remained there six months, until he had cut off every male in Edom); ¹⁷ but Hadad fled to Egypt, together with certain E'domites of his father's servants, Hadad being yet a little child. ¹⁸ They set out from Mid'ian and came to Paran, and took men with them from Paran and came to Egypt, to Pharaoh king of Egypt, who gave him a house, and assigned him an allowance of food, and gave him land. ¹⁹ And Hadad found great favor in the sight of Pharaoh, so that he gave him in marriage the sister of his own wife, the sister of Tah'penes the queen. ²⁰ And the sister of Tah'penes bore him Genu'bath his son, whom Tah'penes weaned in Pharaoh's house; and Genu'bath was in Pharaoh's house among the sons of Pharaoh. ²¹ But when Hadad heard in Egypt that David slept with his fathers and that Jo'ab the commander of the army was dead, Hadad said to Pharaoh, "Let me depart, that I may go to my own country." ²² But Pharaoh said to him, "What have you lacked with me that you are now seeking to go to your own country?" And he said to him, "Only let me go."

23 God also raised up as an adversary to him, Rezon the son of Eli'ada, who had fled from his master Hadade'zer king of Zobah. ²⁴ And he gathered men about him and became leader of a marauding band, after the slaughter by David; and they went to Damascus, and dwelt there, and made him king in Damascus. ²⁵ He was an adversary of Israel all the days of Solomon, doing mischief as Hadad did; and he abhorred Israel, and reigned over Syria.

26 Jerobo'am the son of Nebat, an E'phraimite of Zer'edah, a servant of Solomon, whose mother's name was Zeru'ah, a widow, also lifted up his hand against the king. ²⁷ And this was the reason why he lifted up his hand against the king. Solomon built the Millo, and closed up the breach of the city of David his father. ²⁸ The man Jerobo'am was very able, and when Solomon saw that the young man was

14–40: Adversaries of Solomon. **14–22**: Hadad the Edomite. **15**: *David* had conquered *Edom* (*every male* is of course an exaggeration). Near the beginning of Solomon's reign (v. 21), *Hadad the Edomite* revolted rather successfully (v. 25). **23–25**: Rezon of Syria. On David's conquest of *Hadadezer king of Zobah* and of the Syrians (Arameans) of *Damascus*, see 2 Sam. 8.3–6; 10.15–19. *Rezon* set up a new kingdom in *Damascus* and defied Solomon. Thus the empire of *David* began to melt away under Solomon. **26–40**: Jeroboam of Israel. The greatest danger, namely internal revolt, came from *Jeroboam the son of Nebat*. The prophet Ahijah the Shilonite (of Shiloh) expected that *Jeroboam* would be more loyal to *the God of Israel* than

industrious he gave him charge over all the forced labor of the house of Joseph. ²⁹ And at that time, when Jerobo'am went out of Jerusalem, the prophet Ahi'jah the Shi'lonite found him on the road. Now Ahi'jah had clad himself with a new garment; and the two of them were alone in the open country. ³⁰ Then Ahi'jah laid hold of the new garment that was on him, and tore it into twelve pieces. ³¹ And he said to Jerobo'am, "Take for yourself ten pieces; for thus says the LORD, the God of Israel, 'Behold, I am about to tear the kingdom from the hand of Solomon, and will give you ten tribes ³² (but he shall have one tribe, for the sake of my servant David and for the sake of Jerusalem, the city which I have chosen out of all the tribes of Israel), ³³ because he has[h] forsaken me, and worshiped Ash'toreth the goddess of the Sido'nians, Chemosh the god of Moab, and Milcom the god of the Ammonites, and has[h] not walked in my ways, doing what is right in my sight and keeping my statutes and my ordinances, as David his father did. ³⁴ Nevertheless I will not take the whole kingdom out of his hand; but I will make him ruler all the days of his life, for the sake of David my servant whom I chose, who kept my commandments and my statutes; ³⁵ but I will take the kingdom out of his son's hand, and will give it to you, ten tribes. ³⁶ Yet to his son I will give one tribe, that David my servant may always have a lamp before me in Jerusalem, the city where I have chosen to put my name. ³⁷ And I will take you, and you shall reign over all that your soul desires, and you shall be king over Israel. ³⁸ And if you will hearken to all that I command you, and will walk in my ways, and do what is right in my

eyes by keeping my statutes and my commandments, as David my servant did, I will be with you, and will build you a sure house, as I built for David, and I will give Israel to you. ³⁹ And I will for this afflict the descendants of David, but not for ever.' " ⁴⁰ Solomon sought therefore to kill Jerobo'am; but Jerobo'am arose, and fled into Egypt, to Shishak king of Egypt, and was in Egypt until the death of Solomon.

41 Now the rest of the acts of Solomon, and all that he did, and his wisdom, are they not written in the book of the acts of Solomon? ⁴² And the time that Solomon reigned in Jerusalem over all Israel was forty years. ⁴³ And Solomon slept with his fathers, and was buried in the city of David his father; and Rehobo'am his son reigned in his stead.

12 Rehobo'am went to Shechem, for all Israel had come to Shechem to make him king. ² And when Jerobo'am the son of Nebat heard of it (for he was still in Egypt, whither he had fled from King Solomon), then Jerobo'am returned from[i] Egypt. ³ And they sent and called him; and Jerobo'am and all the assembly of Israel came and said to Rehobo'am, ⁴ "Your father made our yoke heavy. Now therefore lighten the hard service of your father and his heavy yoke upon us, and we will serve you." ⁵ He said to them, "Depart for three days, then come again to me." So the people went away.

6 Then King Rehobo'am took counsel with the old men, who had stood before Solomon his father while he was yet alive, saying, "How do you advise me to answer this people?" ⁷ And they said to him, "If you will be a servant to this people today and serve them,

h Gk Syr Vg: Heb *they have*
i Gk Vg Compare 2 Chr 10.2: Heb *dwelt in*

Solomon had been. *The lamp* (v. 36) was a symbol of the permanence of the Davidic dynasty (2 Sam.21.17). *Shishak king of Egypt* was probably the less friendly successor of the pharaoh whose daughter was married to *Solomon* (3.1). **41–43:** Conclusion. On *the book of the acts of Solomon*, see the Introduction. The figure *forty years* is an approximation; compare the same figure for David in 2.11.

12.1–33: The kingdom divided; Jeroboam's idolatry. 1–5: *Shechem* was at that time the chief town of the northern tribes (Jos.24.1,32), where *Rehoboam* needed to be confirmed as *king* in

and speak good words to them when you answer them, then they will be your servants for ever." [8] But he forsook the counsel which the old men gave him, and took counsel with the young men who had grown up with him and stood before him. [9] And he said to them, "What do you advise that we answer this people who have said to me, 'Lighten the yoke that your father put upon us'?" [10] And the young men who had grown up with him said to him, "Thus shall you speak to this people who said to you, 'Your father made our yoke heavy, but do you lighten it for us'; thus shall you say to them, 'My little finger is thicker than my father's loins. [11] And now, whereas my father laid upon you a heavy yoke, I will add to your yoke. My father chastised you with whips, but I will chastise you with scorpions.'"

12 So Jerobo'am and all the people came to Rehobo'am the third day, as the king said, "Come to me again the third day." [13] And the king answered the people harshly, and forsaking the counsel which the old men had given him, [14] he spoke to them according to the counsel of the young men, saying, "My father made your yoke heavy, but I will add to your yoke; my father chastised you with whips, but I will chastise you with scorpions." [15] So the king did not hearken to the people; for it was a turn of affairs brought about by the LORD that he might fulfil his word, which the LORD spoke by Ahi'jah the Shi'lonite to Jerobo'am the son of Nebat.

16 And when all Israel saw that the king did not hearken to them, the people answered the king,

"What portion have we in David?
We have no inheritance in the son of Jesse.
To your tents, O Israel!
Look now to your own house, David."

So Israel departed to their tents. [17] But Rehobo'am reigned over the people of Israel who dwelt in the cities of Judah. [18] Then King Rehobo'am sent Ador'am, who was taskmaster over the forced labor, and all Israel stoned him to death with stones. And King Rehobo'am made haste to mount his chariot, to flee to Jerusalem. [19] So Israel has been in rebellion against the house of David to this day. [20] And when all Israel heard that Jerobo'am had returned, they sent and called him to the assembly and made him king over all Israel. There was none that followed the house of David, but the tribe of Judah only.

21 When Rehobo'am came to Jerusalem, he assembled all the house of Judah, and the tribe of Benjamin, a hundred and eighty thousand chosen warriors, to fight against the house of Israel, to restore the kingdom to Rehobo'am the son of Solomon. [22] But the word of God came to Shemai'ah the man of God: [23] "Say to Rehobo'am the son of Solomon, king of Judah, and to all the house of Judah and Benjamin, and to the rest of the people, [24] 'Thus says the LORD, You shall not go up or fight against your kinsmen the people of Israel. Return every man to his home, for this thing is from me.'" So they hearkened to the word of the LORD, and went home again, according to the word of the LORD.

25 Then Jerobo'am built Shechem

---

order to hold the allegiance of these tribes. **11:** The word *scorpions* designates here stinging whips, much more cruel than ordinary *whips*. **12–15:** *Rehoboam* takes the tragically wrong advice of *the young men*. The reason for the attitude of the writer in v. 15 is given in 11.33. **16:** On the readiness of the northern tribes to withdraw from Judah, compare 2 Sam.20.1, where even the wording is similar. **17–20:** Certain Israelites remained in *Judah;* and when *Rehoboam* attempted to enforce his oppressive policy in the north, *Jeroboam* was promptly made *king over all Israel. Judah only* remained under *Rehoboam.* **21–24:** According to these verses, the prophetic party of *Judah*, represented by *Shemaiah*, favored the division, hoping that the north would be more loyal to the LORD (see 11.26–40 n.). *Benjamin* in vv. 21,23 is editorial, to support the idea that there were exactly ten tribes in the north and two in the south. Actually, Benjamin may

in the hill country of E′phraim, and dwelt there; and he went out from there and built Penu′el. ²⁶ And Jerobo′am said in his heart, "Now the kingdom will turn back to the house of David; ²⁷ if this people go up to offer sacrifices in the house of the LORD at Jerusalem, then the heart of this people will turn again to their lord, to Rehobo′am king of Judah, and they will kill me and return to Rehobo′am king of Judah." ²⁸ So the king took counsel, and made two calves of gold. And he said to the people, "You have gone up to Jerusalem long enough. Behold your gods, O Israel, who brought you up out of the land of Egypt." ²⁹ And he set one in Bethel, and the other he put in Dan. ³⁰ And this thing became a sin, for the people went to the one at Bethel and to the other as far as Dan.*j* ³¹ He also made houses on high places, and appointed priests from among all the people, who were not of the Levites. ³² And Jerobo′am appointed a feast on the fifteenth day of the eighth month like the feast that was in Judah, and he offered sacrifices upon the altar; so he did in Bethel, sacrificing to the calves that he had made. And he placed in Bethel the priests of the high places that he had made. ³³ He went up to the altar which he had made in Bethel on the fifteenth day in the eighth month, in the month which he had devised of his own heart; and he ordained a feast for the people of Israel, and went up to the altar to burn incense.

13 And behold, a man of God came out of Judah by the word of the LORD to Bethel. Jerobo′am was standing by the altar to burn incense. ² And the man cried against the altar by the word of the LORD, and said, "O altar, altar, thus says the LORD: 'Behold, a son shall be born to the house of David, Josi′ah by name; and he shall sacrifice upon you the priests of the high places who burn incense upon you, and men's bones shall be burned upon you.' " ³ And he gave a sign the same day, saying, "This is the sign that the LORD has spoken: 'Behold, the altar shall be torn down, and the ashes that are upon it shall be poured out.' " ⁴ And when the king heard the saying of the man of God, which he cried against the altar at Bethel, Jerobo′am stretched out his hand from the altar, saying, "Lay hold of him." And his hand, which he stretched out against him, dried up, so that he could not draw it back to himself. ⁵ The altar also was torn down, and the ashes poured out from the altar, according to the sign which the man of God had given by the word of the LORD. ⁶ And the king said to the man of God, "Entreat now the favor of the LORD your God, and pray for me, that my hand may be restored to me." And the man of God entreated the LORD; and the king's hand was restored to him, and became as it was before. ⁷ And the king said to the man of God, "Come home with me, and refresh yourself, and I will give you a reward." ⁸ And the man of God said to

j Gk: Heb *went to the one as far as Dan*

---

have been split in the division. **25–33:** *Jeroboam* straightway led his people into worse apostasy than that of the south. *Jeroboam* intended the *two calves of gold* (really bulls) to represent the LORD (*gods* in v. 28 should probably be "God"); according to the Deuteronomic writer, this was very wrong, since the bull was also the symbol of Baal, and all images were forbidden (see 7.23–26 n.; Dt.5.8–9). Jeroboam also had a political purpose in attempting to keep his people from going to Jerusalem.

13.1–34: The prophets turn against Jeroboam. This chapter continues the condemnation of Jeroboam begun in ch. 12. To *eat bread or drink water* (vv. 9,22) in Israel would have implied approval of what was happening there. There are two definite indications of date in the story: the territory of Israel was not called *Samaria* (v. 32) until after that kingdom fell in 721 B.C. (2 Kg.17.24); Josiah (v. 2) died in 609 B.C., near the time when the first Deuteronomist wrote (see Introduction). The writer of about 600 B.C. is trying to evaluate the conditions existing about three hundred years before his time.

the king, "If you give me half your house, I will not go in with you. And I will not eat bread or drink water in this place; ⁹ for so was it commanded me by the word of the LORD, saying, 'You shall neither eat bread, nor drink water, nor return by the way that you came.'" ¹⁰ So he went another way, and did not return by the way that he came to Bethel.

11 Now there dwelt an old prophet in Bethel. And his sons[k] came and told him all that the man of God had done that day in Bethel; the words also which he had spoken to the king, they told to their father. ¹² And their father said to them, "Which way did he go?" And his sons showed him the way which the man of God who came from Judah had gone. ¹³ And he said to his sons, "Saddle the ass for me." So they saddled the ass for him and he mounted it. ¹⁴ And he went after the man of God, and found him sitting under an oak; and he said to him, "Are you the man of God who came from Judah?" And he said, "I am." ¹⁵ Then he said to him, "Come home with me and eat bread." ¹⁶ And he said, "I may not return with you, or go in with you; neither will I eat bread nor drink water with you in this place; ¹⁷ for it was said to me by the word of the LORD, 'You shall neither eat bread nor drink water there, nor return by the way that you came.'" ¹⁸ And he said to him, "I also am a prophet as you are, and an angel spoke to me by the word of the LORD, saying, 'Bring him back with you into your house that he may eat bread and drink water.'" But he lied to him. ¹⁹ So he went back with him, and ate bread in his house, and drank water.

20 And as they sat at the table, the word of the LORD came to the prophet who had brought him back; ²¹ and he cried to the man of God who came from Judah, "Thus says the LORD, 'Because you have disobeyed the word of the LORD, and have not kept the commandment which the LORD your God commanded you, ²² but have come

back, and have eaten bread and drunk water in the place of which he said to you, "Eat no bread, and drink no water"; your body shall not come to the tomb of your fathers.'" ²³ And after he had eaten bread and drunk, he saddled the ass for the prophet whom he had brought back. ²⁴ And as he went away a lion met him on the road and killed him. And his body was thrown in the road, and the ass stood beside it; the lion also stood beside the body. ²⁵ And behold, men passed by, and saw the body thrown in the road, and the lion standing by the body. And they came and told it in the city where the old prophet dwelt.

26 And when the prophet who had brought him back from the way heard of it, he said, "It is the man of God, who disobeyed the word of the LORD; therefore the LORD has given him to the lion, which has torn him and slain him, according to the word which the LORD spoke to him." ²⁷ And he said to his sons, "Saddle the ass for me." And they saddled it. ²⁸ And he went and found his body thrown in the road, and the ass and the lion standing beside the body. The lion had not eaten the body or torn the ass. ²⁹ And the prophet took up the body of the man of God and laid it upon the ass, and brought it back to the city,[l] to mourn and to bury him. ³⁰ And he laid the body in his own grave; and they mourned over him, saying, "Alas, my brother!" ³¹ And after he had buried him, he said to his sons, "When I die, bury me in the grave in which the man of God is buried; lay my bones beside his bones. ³² For the saying which he cried by the word of the LORD against the altar in Bethel, and against all the houses of the high places which are in the cities of Sama′ria, shall surely come to pass."

33 After this thing Jerobo′am did not turn from his evil way, but made priests for the high places again from among all the people; any who

k Gk Syr Vg: Heb *son*
l Gk: Heb *he came to the city of the old prophet*

[437]

would, he consecrated to be priests of the high places. ³⁴ And this thing became sin to the house of Jerobo'am, so as to cut it off and to destroy it from the face of the earth.

14 At that time Abi'jah the son of Jerobo'am fell sick. ² And Jerobo'am said to his wife, "Arise, and disguise yourself, that it be not known that you are the wife of Jerobo'am, and go to Shiloh; behold, Ahi'jah the prophet is there, who said of me that I should be king over this people. ³ Take with you ten loaves, some cakes, and a jar of honey, and go to him; he will tell you what shall happen to the child."

4 Jerobo'am's wife did so; she arose, and went to Shiloh, and came to the house of Ahi'jah. Now Ahi'jah could not see, for his eyes were dim because of his age. ⁵ And the LORD said to Ahi'jah, "Behold, the wife of Jerobo'am is coming to inquire of you concerning her son; for he is sick. Thus and thus shall you say to her."

When she came, she pretended to be another woman. ⁶ But when Ahi'jah heard the sound of her feet, as she came in at the door, he said, "Come in, wife of Jerobo'am; why do you pretend to be another? For I am charged with heavy tidings for you. ⁷ Go, tell Jerobo'am, 'Thus says the LORD, the God of Israel: "Because I exalted you from among the people, and made you leader over my people Israel, ⁸ and tore the kingdom away from the house of David and gave it to you; and yet you have not been like my servant David, who kept my commandments, and followed me with all his heart, doing only that which was right in my eyes, ⁹ but you have done evil above all that were before you and have gone and made for yourself other gods, and molten images, provoking me to anger, and have cast me behind your back; ¹⁰ therefore behold, I will bring evil upon the house of Jerobo'am, and will cut off from Jerobo'am every male, both bond and free in Israel, and will utterly consume the house of Jerobo'am, as a man burns up dung until it is all gone. ¹¹ Any one belonging to Jerobo'am who dies in the city the dogs shall eat; and any one who dies in the open country the birds of the air shall eat; for the LORD has spoken it."'
¹² Arise therefore, go to your house. When your feet enter the city, the child shall die. ¹³ And all Israel shall mourn for him, and bury him; for he only of Jerobo'am shall come to the grave, because in him there is found something pleasing to the LORD, the God of Israel, in the house of Jerobo'am. ¹⁴ Moreover the LORD will raise up for himself a king over Israel, who shall cut off the house of Jerobo'am today. And henceforth*ᵐ* ¹⁵ the LORD will smite Israel, as a reed is shaken in the water, and root up Israel out of this good land which he gave to their fathers, and scatter them beyond the Euphra'tes, because they have made their Ashe'rim, provoking the LORD to anger. ¹⁶ And he will give Israel up because of the sins of Jerobo'am, which he sinned and which he made Israel to sin."

17 Then Jerobo'am's wife arose, and departed, and came to Tirzah. And as she came to the threshold of the house, the child died. ¹⁸ And all Israel buried him and mourned for

m Heb obscure

14.1–31: Conclusion of the reigns of Jeroboam and Rehoboam. From this point to the downfall of the northern kingdom (2 Kg.17.6), the writer skillfully weaves back and forth from one kingdom to the other in order to tell the story of both kingdoms as nearly continuously as possible. **1–16:** *Ahijah,* who had encouraged *Jeroboam* to revolt in the first place (11.29–31), now also turns against the king in bitter disappointment. The writer of about 600 B.C. knew how short-lived was the *house* (dynasty) *of Jeroboam* (15.25–30) and how the whole northern kingdom fell in 721 B.C. (v. 15), and he is attempting to explain these somber events in terms of religious apostasy (vv. 9,16). **15:** *Asherim* were wooden poles, symbols of the Canaanite fertility goddess Asherah, who is mentioned about forty times in the Old Testament as a temptation to the Israelites. **17:** *Tirzah* was *Jeroboam's* place of residence after Shechem (12.25), thus becom-

him, according to the word of the LORD, which he spoke by his servant Ahi'jah the prophet. [19] Now the rest of the acts of Jerobo'am, how he warred and how he reigned, behold, they are written in the Book of the Chronicles of the Kings of Israel. [20] And the time that Jerobo'am reigned was twenty-two years; and he slept with his fathers, and Nadab his son reigned in his stead.

21 Now Rehobo'am the son of Solomon reigned in Judah. Rehobo'am was forty-one years old when he began to reign, and he reigned seventeen years in Jerusalem, the city which the LORD had chosen out of all the tribes of Israel, to put his name there. His mother's name was Na'amah the Ammonitess. [22] And Judah did what was evil in the sight of the LORD, and they provoked him to jealousy with their sins which they committed, more than all that their fathers had done. [23] For they also built for themselves high places, and pillars, and Ashe'rim on every high hill and under every green tree; [24] and there were also male cult prostitutes in the land. They did according to all the abominations of the nations which the LORD drove out before the people of Israel.

25 In the fifth year of King Rehobo'am, Shishak king of Egypt came up against Jerusalem; [26] he took away the treasures of the house of the LORD and the treasures of the king's house; he took away everything. He also took away all the shields of gold which Solomon had made; [27] and King Rehobo'am made in their stead shields of bronze, and committed them to the hands of the officers of the guard, who kept the door of the king's house. [28] And as often as the king went into the house of the LORD, the guard bore them and brought them back to the guardroom.

29 Now the rest of the acts of Rehobo'am, and all that he did, are they not written in the Book of the Chronicles of the Kings of Judah? [30] And there was war between Rehobo'am and Jerobo'am continually. [31] And Rehobo'am slept with his fathers and was buried with his fathers in the city of David. His mother's name was Na'amah the Ammonitess. And Abi'jam his son reigned in his stead.

15 Now in the eighteenth year of King Jerobo'am the son of Nebat, Abi'jam began to reign over Judah. [2] He reigned for three years in Jerusalem. His mother's name was Ma'acah the daughter of Abish'alom. [3] And he walked in all the sins which his father did before him; and his heart was not wholly true to the LORD his God, as the heart of David his father. [4] Nevertheless for David's sake the LORD his God gave him a lamp in Jerusalem, setting up his son after him, and establishing Jerusalem; [5] because David did what was right in the eyes of the LORD, and did not turn aside from anything that he commanded him all the days of his life, except in the matter of Uri'ah the Hittite. [6] Now there was war between Rehobo'am and Jerobo'am all the days of his life. [7] The rest of the acts of Abi'jam, and all that he did, are they not written in the Book of the Chronicles of the Kings of Judah? And there was war between Abi'jam and Jerobo'am. [8] And Abi'jam slept with his fathers; and they buried him in the city of David. And Asa his son reigned in his stead.

9 In the twentieth year of Jerobo'am king of Israel Asa began to reign over Judah, [10] and he reigned forty-one years in Jerusalem. His mother's name was Ma'acah the daughter of Abish'alom. [11] And Asa did what was right in the eyes of the LORD, as David his

ing the capital of Israel (15.33) until Samaria was built (16.24). **21–31:** The reign of Rehoboam. Judah at this time did no better than Israel, according to the writer (vv. 22–24). According to Egyptian sources, *Shishak* (v. 25) also invaded Israel; a fragment of his stela has been found in the excavations at Megiddo.

15.1–8: Abijam of Judah was little better than his father. Verse 6 is out of place; compare 14.30. **9–24: Asa of Judah.** This king is credited with reforms and given a fairly clean bill of

father had done. ¹² He put away the male cult prostitutes out of the land, and removed all the idols that his fathers had made. ¹³ He also removed Ma'acah his mother from being queen mother because she had an abominable image made for Ashe'rah; and Asa cut down her image and burned it at the brook Kidron. ¹⁴ But the high places were not taken away. Nevertheless the heart of Asa was wholly true to the LORD all his days. ¹⁵ And he brought into the house of the LORD the votive gifts of his father and his own votive gifts, silver, and gold, and vessels.

16 And there was war between Asa and Ba'asha king of Israel all their days. ¹⁷ Ba'asha king of Israel went up against Judah, and built Ramah, that he might permit no one to go out or come in to Asa king of Judah. ¹⁸ Then Asa took all the silver and the gold that were left in the treasures of the house of the LORD and the treasures of the king's house, and gave them into the hands of his servants; and King Asa sent them to Ben-ha'dad the son of Tabrim'mon, the son of He'zi-on, king of Syria, who dwelt in Damascus, saying, ¹⁹ "Let there be a league between me and you, as between my father and your father: behold, I am sending to you a present of silver and gold; go, break your league with Ba'asha king of Israel, that he may withdraw from me." ²⁰ And Ben-ha'dad hearkened to King Asa, and sent the commanders of his armies against the cities of Israel, and conquered Ijon, Dan, A'bel-bethma'acah, and all Chin'neroth, with all the land of Naph'tali. ²¹ And when Ba'asha heard of it, he stopped building Ramah, and he dwelt in Tirzah. ²² Then King Asa made a proclamation to all Judah, none was exempt, and they carried away the stones of Ramah and its timber, with which

Ba'asha had been building; and with them King Asa built Geba of Benjamin and Mizpah. ²³ Now the rest of all the acts of Asa, all his might, and all that he did, and the cities which he built, are they not written in the Book of the Chronicles of the Kings of Judah? But in his old age he was diseased in his feet. ²⁴ And Asa slept with his fathers, and was buried with his fathers in the city of David his father; and Jehosh'aphat his son reigned in his stead.

25 Nadab the son of Jerobo'am began to reign over Israel in the second year of Asa king of Judah; and he reigned over Israel two years. ²⁶ He did what was evil in the sight of the LORD, and walked in the way of his father, and in his sin which he made Israel to sin.

27 Ba'asha the son of Ahi'jah, of the house of Is'sachar, conspired against him; and Ba'asha struck him down at Gib'bethon, which belonged to the Philistines; for Nadab and all Israel were laying siege to Gib'bethon. ²⁸ So Ba'asha killed him in the third year of Asa king of Judah, and reigned in his stead. ²⁹ And as soon as he was king, he killed all the house of Jerobo'am; he left to the house of Jerobo'am not one that breathed, until he had destroyed it, according to the word of the LORD which he spoke by his servant Ahi'jah the Shi'lonite; ³⁰ it was for the sins of Jerobo'am which he sinned and which he made Israel to sin, and because of the anger to which he provoked the LORD, the God of Israel.

31 Now the rest of the acts of Nadab, and all that he did, are they not written in the Book of the Chronicles of the Kings of Israel? ³² And there was war between Asa and Ba'-asha king of Israel all their days.

33 In the third year of Asa king of

---

religious health. **13:** *Asherah*, see 14.15 n. **18–22:** Asa carried on continual war with Israel, and bribed *Ben-hadad . . . king of Syria* to change sides, thus tipping the balance in favor of Judah. **25–32:** **Nadab of Israel** and his assassination. Here begins a series of assassinations of kings of Israel, interpreted by the writer as a just judgment against the northern kingdom (vv. 29–30); see 14.1–16 n.

Judah, Ba'asha the son of Ahi'jah began to reign over all Israel at Tirzah, and reigned twenty-four years. ³⁴ He did what was evil in the sight of the LORD, and walked in the way of Jerobo'am and in his sin which he made Israel to sin.

16 And the word of the LORD came to Jehu the son of Hana'ni against Ba'asha, saying, ² "Since I exalted you out of the dust and made you leader over my people Israel, and you have walked in the way of Jerobo'am, and have made my people Israel to sin, provoking me to anger with their sins, ³ behold, I will utterly sweep away Ba'asha and his house, and I will make your house like the house of Jerobo'am the son of Nebat. ⁴ Any one belonging to Ba'asha who dies in the city the dogs shall eat; and any one of his who dies in the field the birds of the air shall eat."

5 Now the rest of the acts of Ba'asha, and what he did, and his might, are they not written in the Book of the Chronicles of the Kings of Israel? ⁶ And Ba'asha slept with his fathers, and was buried at Tirzah; and Elah his son reigned in his stead. ⁷ Moreover the word of the LORD came by the prophet Jehu the son of Hana'ni against Ba'asha and his house, both because of all the evil that he did in the sight of the LORD, provoking him to anger with the work of his hands, in being like the house of Jerobo'am, and also because he destroyed it.

8 In the twenty-sixth year of Asa king of Judah, Elah the son of Ba'asha began to reign over Israel in Tirzah, and reigned two years. ⁹ But his servant Zimri, commander of half his chariots, conspired against him. When he was at Tirzah, drinking himself drunk in the house of Arza, who was over the household in Tirzah, ¹⁰ Zimri came in and struck him down and killed him, in the twenty-seventh year of Asa king of Judah, and reigned in his stead.

11 When he began to reign, as soon as he had seated himself on his throne, he killed all the house of Ba'asha; he did not leave him a single male of his kinsmen or his friends. ¹² Thus Zimri destroyed all the house of Ba'asha, according to the word of the LORD, which he spoke against Ba'asha by Jehu the prophet, ¹³ for all the sins of Ba'asha and the sins of Elah his son which they sinned, and which they made Israel to sin, provoking the LORD God of Israel to anger with their idols. ¹⁴ Now the rest of the acts of Elah, and all that he did, are they not written in the Book of the Chronicles of the Kings of Israel?

15 In the twenty-seventh year of Asa king of Judah, Zimri reigned seven days in Tirzah. Now the troops were encamped against Gib'bethon, which belonged to the Philistines, ¹⁶ and the troops who were encamped heard it said, "Zimri has conspired, and he has killed the king"; therefore all Israel made Omri, the commander of the army, king over Israel that day in the camp. ¹⁷ So Omri went up from Gib'bethon, and all Israel with him, and they besieged Tirzah. ¹⁸ And when Zimri saw that the city was taken, he went into the citadel of the king's house, and burned the king's house over him with fire, and died, ¹⁹ because of his sins which he committed, doing evil in the sight of the LORD, walking in the way of Jerobo'am, and for his sin which he committed, making Israel to sin. ²⁰ Now the rest of the acts of Zimri, and the conspiracy which he made, are they not written in the Book of the Chronicles of the Kings of Israel?

21 Then the people of Israel were divided into two parts; half of the people followed Tibni the son of Ginath, to make him king, and half followed

---

15.33–16.7: Baasha of Israel. A new prophet, *Jehu the son of Hanani*, takes up the theme of condemnation already made familiar by Ahijah the Shilonite. **16.8–14: Elah of Israel** and his assassination by *Zimri*. Note the now familiar evaluation in v. 13. **15–20: Zimri of Israel** is attacked by *Omri* and commits suicide. **21–28: Omri of Israel.** Omri was an able and important

Omri. ²² But the people who followed Omri overcame the people who followed Tibni the son of Ginath; so Tibni died, and Omri became king. ²³ In the thirty-first year of Asa king of Judah, Omri began to reign over Israel, and reigned for twelve years; six years he reigned in Tirzah. ²⁴ He bought the hill of Sama'ria from Shemer for two talents of silver; and he fortified the hill, and called the name of the city which he built, Sama'ria, after the name of Shemer, the owner of the hill.

25 Omri did what was evil in the sight of the LORD, and did more evil than all who were before him. ²⁶ For he walked in all the way of Jerobo'am the son of Nebat, and in the sins which he made Israel to sin, provoking the LORD, the God of Israel, to anger by their idols. ²⁷ Now the rest of the acts of Omri which he did, and the might that he showed, are they not written in the Book of the Chronicles of the Kings of Israel? ²⁸ And Omri slept with his fathers, and was buried in Sama'ria; and Ahab his son reigned in his stead.

29 In the thirty-eighth year of Asa king of Judah, Ahab the son of Omri began to reign over Israel, and Ahab the son of Omri reigned over Israel in Sama'ria twenty-two years. ³⁰ And Ahab the son of Omri did evil in the sight of the LORD more than all that were before him. ³¹ And as if it had been a light thing for him to walk in the sins of Jerobo'am the son of Nebat, he took for wife Jez'ebel the daughter of Ethba'al king of the Sido'-nians, and went and served Ba'al, and worshiped him. ³² He erected an altar for Ba'al in the house of Ba'al, which he built in Sama'ria. ³³ And Ahab made an Ashe'rah. Ahab did more to provoke the LORD, the God of Israel, to anger than all the kings of Israel who were before him. ³⁴ In his days Hi'el of Bethel built Jericho; he laid its foundation at the cost of Abi'ram his first-born, and set up its gates at the cost of his youngest son Segub, according to the word of the LORD, which he spoke by Joshua the son of Nun.

17 Now Eli'jah the Tishbite, of Tishbeⁿ in Gilead, said to Ahab, "As the LORD the God of Israel lives, before whom I stand, there shall be neither dew nor rain these years, except by my word." ² And the word of the LORD came to him, ³ "Depart from here and turn eastward, and hide yourself by the brook Cherith, that is east

n Gk: Heb *of the settlers*

---

king, as we know from extra-Biblical sources. The Moabite Stone tells us that he subjugated Moab, and the Assyrian records refer to Israel as "the land of the house of Omri" long after Omri's descendants had ceased to rule. The Deuteronomic writer, interested chiefly in religious matters, lists among the accomplishments of Omri only the founding of Samaria as the new capital. Otherwise, the king is roundly condemned, no doubt chiefly because he married his son Ahab to Jezebel, the daughter of the king of the neighboring Phoenicians (*Sidonians*). This was good political policy, but it turned out to be religiously disastrous.

16.29–34: Introduction to the reign of Ahab in Israel. This reign is treated in great detail (17.1–22.40) because of the religious crisis that ensued. *The Sidonians*, see 5.1–6 n. *Asherah*, see 14.15 n. **34:** The bodies of the children were buried under the foundations to bring good luck to the building project. Such practices were regarded as abominable by the Deuteronomists; hence the curse in Jos.6.26. The last clause of v. 34 was added to bring the account into conformity with the passage in Joshua.

17.1–24: The beginning of the story of Elijah. 1 Kg. ch. 17 to 2 Kg. ch. 10 is mostly a detailed account of affairs in the northern kingdom, featuring the prophets Elijah and Elisha, the reign of Ahab, and the destruction of the dynasty of Omri. These stories are based on good northern source material, brought to Judah by refugees from Israel. It must be remembered that all final redaction was done in Judah, and therefore we are fortunate in having this northern material. The element of the miraculous in the stories must be accepted as an integral part of the writer's method. The ancients did not have the concept of the uniformity of nature. **1–7:** The story opens abruptly, leading some to believe that the beginning, with a proper introduction of Elijah, has been lost. **1:** The Canaanite (or Phoenician) god Baal (16.31–32) was held by his worshipers to be the one who controlled the *rain*. Elijah intended to show that

of the Jordan. ⁴ You shall drink from the brook, and I have commanded the ravens to feed you there." ⁵ So he went and did according to the word of the LORD; he went and dwelt by the brook Cherith that is east of the Jordan. ⁶ And the ravens brought him bread and meat in the morning, and bread and meat in the evening; and he drank from the brook. ⁷ And after a while the brook dried up, because there was no rain in the land.

8 Then the word of the LORD came to him, ⁹ "Arise, go to Zar′ephath, which belongs to Sidon, and dwell there. Behold, I have commanded a widow there to feed you." ¹⁰ So he arose and went to Zar′ephath; and when he came to the gate of the city, behold, a widow was there gathering sticks; and he called to her and said, "Bring me a little water in a vessel, that I may drink." ¹¹ And as she was going to bring it, he called to her and said, "Bring me a morsel of bread in your hand." ¹² And she said, "As the LORD your God lives, I have nothing baked, only a handful of meal in a jar, and a little oil in a cruse; and now, I am gathering a couple of sticks, that I may go in and prepare it for myself and my son, that we may eat it, and die." ¹³ And Eli′jah said to her, "Fear not; go and do as you have said; but first make me a little cake of it and bring it to me, and afterward make for yourself and your son. ¹⁴ For thus says the LORD the God of Israel, 'The jar of meal shall not be spent, and the cruse of oil shall not fail, until the day that the LORD sends rain upon the earth.'" ¹⁵ And she went and did as Eli′jah said; and she, and he, and her

household ate for many days. ¹⁶ The jar of meal was not spent, neither did the cruse of oil fail, according to the word of the LORD which he spoke by Eli′jah.

17 After this the son of the woman, the mistress of the house, became ill; and his illness was so severe that there was no breath left in him. ¹⁸ And she said to Eli′jah, "What have you against me, O man of God? You have come to me to bring my sin to remembrance, and to cause the death of my son!" ¹⁹ And he said to her, "Give me your son." And he took him from her bosom, and carried him up into the upper chamber, where he lodged, and laid him upon his own bed. ²⁰ And he cried to the LORD, "O LORD my God, hast thou brought calamity even upon the widow with whom I sojourn, by slaying her son?" ²¹ Then he stretched himself upon the child three times, and cried to the LORD, "O LORD my God, let this child's soul come into him again." ²² And the LORD hearkened to the voice of Eli′jah; and the soul of the child came into him again, and he revived. ²³ And Eli′jah took the child, and brought him down from the upper chamber into the house, and delivered him to his mother; and Eli′jah said, "See, your son lives." ²⁴ And the woman said to Eli′jah, "Now I know that you are a man of God, and that the word of the LORD in your mouth is truth."

18 After many days the word of the LORD came to Eli′jah, in the third year, saying, "Go, show yourself to Ahab; and I will send rain upon the earth." ² So Eli′jah went to show himself to Ahab. Now the famine was

his God, *the LORD the God of Israel*, was the one who really controlled the *rain*. 3: The words *east of the Jordan* (also v. 5) probably refer to territory outside of Ahab's jurisdiction. Ahab had been eagerly seeking to apprehend the prophet in order to find some reconciliation with him to end the drought (18.10). 8–16: *Zarephath*, on the Phoenician coast, was definitely in territory beyond the control of Ahab. 17–24: Some have argued that the child was not really dead, and hence that no miracle was involved. This is beside the point. The writer meant to portray a powerful God and a worthy prophet (compare 2 Kg.4.32–37; Acts 20.9–12).

18.1–46: The contest on Mount Carmel. 1–6: The drought is about to end. The question is, Which God withholds and sends the rain: Yahweh (the LORD) or the great Baal, called Baal of the Heavens by his followers? The very name of *Elijah*, meaning "Yah [short form of Yahweh,

severe in Sama'ria. ³ And Ahab called Obadi'ah, who was over the household. (Now Obadi'ah revered the LORD greatly; ⁴ and when Jez'ebel cut off the prophets of the LORD, Obadi'ah took a hundred prophets and hid them by fifties in a cave, and fed them with bread and water.) ⁵ And Ahab said to Obadi'ah, "Go through the land to all the springs of water and to all the valleys; perhaps we may find grass and save the horses and mules alive, and not lose some of the animals." ⁶ So they divided the land between them to pass through it; Ahab went in one direction by himself, and Obadi'ah went in another direction by himself.

7 And as Obadi'ah was on the way, behold, Eli'jah met him; and Obadi'ah recognized him, and fell on his face, and said, "Is it you, my lord Eli'jah?" ⁸ And he answered him, "It is I. Go, tell your lord, 'Behold, Eli'jah is here.' " ⁹ And he said, "Wherein have I sinned, that you would give your servant into the hand of Ahab, to kill me? ¹⁰ As the LORD your God lives, there is no nation or kingdom whither my lord has not sent to seek you; and when they would say, 'He is not here,' he would take an oath of the kingdom or nation, that they had not found you. ¹¹ And now you say, 'Go, tell your lord, "Behold, Eli'jah is here." ' ¹² And as soon as I have gone from you, the Spirit of the LORD will carry you whither I know not; and so, when I come and tell Ahab and he cannot find you, he will kill me, although I your servant have revered the LORD from my youth. ¹³ Has it not been told my lord what I did when Jez'ebel killed the prophets of the LORD, how I hid a hundred men of the LORD's prophets by fifties in a cave, and fed them with bread and water? ¹⁴ And

now you say, 'Go, tell your lord, "Behold, Eli'jah is here" '; and he will kill me." ¹⁵ And Eli'jah said, "As the LORD of hosts lives, before whom I stand, I will surely show myself to him today." ¹⁶ So Obadi'ah went to meet Ahab, and told him; and Ahab went to meet Eli'jah.

17 When Ahab saw Eli'jah, Ahab said to him, "Is it you, you troubler of Israel?" ¹⁸ And he answered, "I have not troubled Israel; but you have, and your father's house, because you have forsaken the commandments of the LORD and followed the Ba'als. ¹⁹ Now therefore send and gather all Israel to me at Mount Carmel, and the four hundred and fifty prophets of Ba'al and the four hundred prophets of Ashe'rah, who eat at Jez'ebel's table."

20 So Ahab sent to all the people of Israel, and gathered the prophets together at Mount Carmel. ²¹ And Eli'jah came near to all the people, and said, "How long will you go limping with two different opinions? If the LORD is God, follow him; but if Ba'al, then follow him." And the people did not answer him a word. ²² Then Eli'jah said to the people, "I, even I only, am left a prophet of the LORD; but Ba'al's prophets are four hundred and fifty men. ²³ Let two bulls be given to us; and let them choose one bull for themselves, and cut it in pieces and lay it on the wood, but put no fire to it; and I will prepare the other bull and lay it on the wood, and put no fire to it. ²⁴ And you call on the name of your god and I will call on the name of the LORD; and the God who answers by fire, he is God." And all the people answered, "It is well spoken." ²⁵ Then Eli'jah said to the prophets of Ba'al, "Choose for yourselves one bull and prepare it first, for you are many; and

---

the LORD] is God," proclaims his faith. *Obadiah* means "Servant of Yahweh." *Jezebel* has been persecuting *the prophets of the LORD* (Yahweh). **7–16:** *Ahab* has been hunting *Elijah* everywhere, but now the prophet volunteers to meet the king (see 17.1–7 n.). **17–19:** *Elijah* is quick to point out that the fault lies with *Ahab* in not recognizing the LORD as the supreme God, and in allowing his wife *Jezebel* to propagate her religion in Israel. *Asherah,* one of the consorts of *Baal* (see 14.15 n.). *The Baals* were the local versions of the great sky-god, *Baal;* thus there was one *Baal,* but also many *Baals.* **20–29:** The contest begins; the Baal worshipers test their god

call on the name of your god, but put no fire to it." [26] And they took the bull which was given them, and they prepared it, and called on the name of Ba'al from morning until noon, saying, "O Ba'al, answer us!" But there was no voice, and no one answered. And they limped about the altar which they had made. [27] And at noon Eli'jah mocked them, saying, "Cry aloud, for he is a god; either he is musing, or he has gone aside, or he is on a journey, or perhaps he is asleep and must be awakened." [28] And they cried aloud, and cut themselves after their custom with swords and lances, until the blood gushed out upon them. [29] And as midday passed, they raved on until the time of the offering of the oblation, but there was no voice; no one answered, no one heeded.

30 Then Eli'jah said to all the people, "Come near to me"; and all the people came near to him. And he repaired the altar of the LORD that had been thrown down; [31] Eli'jah took twelve stones, according to the number of the tribes of the sons of Jacob, to whom the word of the LORD came, saying, "Israel shall be your name"; [32] and with the stones he built an altar in the name of the LORD. And he made a trench about the altar, as great as would contain two measures of seed. [33] And he put the wood in order, and cut the bull in pieces and laid it on the wood. And he said, "Fill four jars with water, and pour it on the burnt offering, and on the wood." [34] And he said, "Do it a second time"; and they did it a second time. And he said, "Do it

a third time"; and they did it a third time. [35] And the water ran round about the altar, and filled the trench also with water.

36 And at the time of the offering of the oblation, Eli'jah the prophet came near and said, "O LORD, God of Abraham, Isaac, and Israel, let it be known this day that thou art God in Israel, and that I am thy servant, and that I have done all these things at thy word. [37] Answer me, O LORD, answer me, that this people may know that thou, O LORD, art God, and that thou hast turned their hearts back." [38] Then the fire of the LORD fell, and consumed the burnt offering, and the wood, and the stones, and the dust, and licked up the water that was in the trench. [39] And when all the people saw it, they fell on their faces; and they said, "The LORD, he is God; the LORD, he is God." [40] And Eli'jah said to them, "Seize the prophets of Ba'al; let not one of them escape." And they seized them; and Eli'jah brought them down to the brook Kishon, and killed them there.

41 And Eli'jah said to Ahab, "Go up, eat and drink; for there is a sound of the rushing of rain." [42] So Ahab went up to eat and to drink. And Eli'jah went up to the top of Carmel; and he bowed himself down upon the earth, and put his face between his knees. [43] And he said to his servant, "Go up now, look toward the sea." And he went up and looked, and said, "There is nothing." And he said, "Go again seven times." [44] And at the seventh time he said, "Behold, a little cloud like a man's hand is rising

first. **26:** *They limped about the altar*, i.e. they performed a kind of limping dance, bending first one knee and then the other. This form of ritual is well known from a number of sources (compare Ps.26.6–7). **27:** One of the sharpest satires on paganism ever penned. *He has gone aside* is probably a euphemism for attending to natural needs. **28:** Ritualistic gashing of one's self was fairly common (compare Dt.14.1; Lev.19.28; Hos.7.14; Jer.16.6; 41.5; 47.5). **29:** *The time of the offering of the oblation* was 3 p.m. (compare 2 Kg.16.15; Acts 3.1). **30–35:** Verses 31–32a are an editorial insertion based on Gen.35.10. **38:** Some wish to rationalize *the fire of the LORD* by calling it lightning preceding the rain; but it must be borne in mind that the ancient writer intended to describe a miracle. **40:** The slaughter of *the prophets of Baal* is sometimes interpreted as a vast human sacrifice to the LORD. The people of the time and the (slightly later) writer saw the struggle between Baal and the LORD as one of life and death. **41–46:** *Eat and drink*, i.e. break the fast which was in effect during the religious ceremonies. The end of the drought was supposed to be final proof that the LORD, not Baal, ruled the heavens, and con-

out of the sea." And he said, "Go up, say to Ahab, 'Prepare your chariot and go down, lest the rain stop you.' " ⁴⁵ And in a little while the heavens grew black with clouds and wind, and there was a great rain. And Ahab rode and went to Jezreel. ⁴⁶ And the hand of the LORD was on Eli′jah; and he girded up his loins and ran before Ahab to the entrance of Jezreel.

19 Ahab told Jez′ebel all that Eli′jah had done, and how he had slain all the prophets with the sword. ² Then Jez′ebel sent a messenger to Eli′jah, saying, "So may the gods do to me, and more also, if I do not make your life as the life of one of them by this time tomorrow." ³ Then he was afraid, and he arose and went for his life, and came to Beer-sheba, which belongs to Judah, and left his servant there.

4 But he himself went a day's journey into the wilderness, and came and sat down under a broom tree; and he asked that he might die, saying, "It is enough; now, O LORD, take away my life; for I am no better than my fathers." ⁵ And he lay down and slept under a broom tree; and behold, an angel touched him, and said to him, "Arise and eat." ⁶ And he looked, and behold, there was at his head a cake baked on hot stones and a jar of water. And he ate and drank, and lay down again. ⁷ And the angel of the LORD came again a second time, and touched him, and said, "Arise and eat, else the journey will be too great for you."

⁸ And he arose, and ate and drank, and went in the strength of that food forty days and forty nights to Horeb the mount of God.

9 And there he came to a cave, and lodged there; and behold, the word of the LORD came to him, and he said to him, "What are you doing here, Eli′jah?" ¹⁰ He said, "I have been very jealous for the LORD, the God of hosts; for the people of Israel have forsaken thy covenant, thrown down thy altars, and slain thy prophets with the sword; and I, even I only, am left; and they seek my life, to take it away." ¹¹ And he said, "Go forth, and stand upon the mount before the LORD." And behold, the LORD passed by, and a great and strong wind rent the mountains, and broke in pieces the rocks before the LORD, but the LORD was not in the wind; and after the wind an earthquake, but the LORD was not in the earthquake; ¹² and after the earthquake a fire, but the LORD was not in the fire; and after the fire a still small voice. ¹³ And when Eli′jah heard it, he wrapped his face in his mantle and went out and stood at the entrance of the cave. And behold, there came a voice to him, and said, "What are you doing here, Eli′jah?" ¹⁴ He said, "I have been very jealous for the LORD, the God of hosts; for the people of Israel have forsaken thy covenant, thrown down thy altars, and slain thy prophets with the sword; and I, even I only, am left; and they seek my life, to take it away." ¹⁵ And the LORD said

---

trolled the destinies of the Israelites. The town of *Jezreel*, near Mount Gilboa (1 Sam.29.1; 31.1), was used by *Ahab* as a second place of residence (21.1), the primary capital being Samaria (16.24; 20.43; 21.1). *Elijah* ran seventeen miles (a feasible feat for a man of the desert) before the *chariot* of *Ahab*, in a high state of excitement, to herald what he considered a complete victory over the forces of Baal.

19.1–18: The revelation to Elijah on Mount Horeb. 1–3: The power of *Jezebel* very quickly turned the tables, and Elijah *was afraid*. Suddenly, it seems, he is at *Beer-sheba*, one hundred and thirty miles south of Jezreel (see 17.8–16 n.), well within *Judah*. **4–8:** By miraculous divine help, the prophet arrived at *Horeb*, the place where the LORD revealed the law to Moses, according to northern (Israelite) tradition–called Sinai in the southern (Judahite) literature. The round number, *forty days*, simply indicates a great distance (compare Ex.34.28). The traditional site of Mount Horeb, probably not intended here, is some two hundred miles to the south. **9–18:** Compare Ex.33.17–23. **12:** The *still small voice* was a voice demanding the slaughter of all enemies of the LORD. Elijah was willing to oblige, for he was "very zealous" (a better translation than *very jealous* in v. 14). **15:** The *wilderness of Damascus*, the Syrian Desert. **18:** The

to him, "Go, return on your way to the wilderness of Damascus; and when you arrive, you shall anoint Haz′ael to be king over Syria; ¹⁶ and Jehu the son of Nimshi you shall anoint to be king over Israel; and Eli′sha the son of Shaphat of A′bel-meho′lah you shall anoint to be prophet in your place. ¹⁷ And him who escapes from the sword of Haz′ael shall Jehu slay; and him who escapes from the sword of Jehu shall Eli′sha slay. ¹⁸ Yet I will leave seven thousand in Israel, all the knees that have not bowed to Ba′al, and every mouth that has not kissed him."

19 So he departed from there, and found Eli′sha the son of Shaphat, who was plowing, with twelve yoke of oxen before him, and he was with the twelfth. Eli′jah passed by him and cast his mantle upon him. ²⁰ And he left the oxen, and ran after Eli′jah, and said, "Let me kiss my father and my mother, and then I will follow you." And he said to him, "Go back again; for what have I done to you?" ²¹ And he returned from following him, and took the yoke of oxen, and slew them, and boiled their flesh with the yokes of the oxen, and gave it to the people, and they ate. Then he arose and went after Eli′jah, and ministered to him.

20 Ben-ha′dad the king of Syria gathered all his army together; thirty-two kings were with him, and horses and chariots; and he went up and besieged Sama′ria, and fought against it. ² And he sent messengers into the city to Ahab king of Israel, and said to him, "Thus says Ben-ha′dad: ³ 'Your silver and your gold are mine; your fairest wives and children also are mine.' " ⁴ And the king of Israel answered, "As you say, my lord, O king, I am yours, and all that I have." ⁵ The messengers came again, and said, "Thus says Ben-ha′dad: 'I sent to you, saying, "Deliver to me your silver and your gold, your wives and your children"; ⁶ nevertheless I will send my servants to you tomorrow about this time, and they shall search your house and the houses of your servants, and lay hands on whatever pleases them,ᵒ and take it away.' "

7 Then the king of Israel called all the elders of the land, and said, "Mark, now, and see how this man is seeking trouble; for he sent to me for my wives and my children, and for my silver and my gold, and I did not refuse him." ⁸ And all the elders and all the people said to him, "Do not heed or consent." ⁹ So he said to the messengers of Ben-ha′dad, "Tell my lord the king, 'All that you first demanded of your servant I will do; but this thing I cannot do.' " And the messengers departed and brought him word again. ¹⁰ Ben-ha′dad sent to him and said, "The gods do so to me, and more also, if the dust of Sama′ria shall suffice for handfuls for all the people who follow me." ¹¹ And the king of Israel an-

o Gk Syr Vg: Heb *you*

words *seven thousand* express the idea of the righteous remnant, which appears again in Am.5.15; Is.10.20; 11.11. *Kissed* the Baal image, see Hos.13.2.

19.19-21: The call of Elisha. *Elijah* returns from Horeb and proceeds to carry out first the third command of the "still small voice." He did not actually "anoint" *Elisha* (v. 16), but *cast his mantle upon him.* The end of v. 20 means, "Go, and return to me, for I have done something very important to you." For similar extemporaneous sacrifices (v. 21), compare 1 Sam. 6.14; 2 Sam.24.22-25. It was *Elisha,* not *Elijah,* who carried out the first and second injunctions of the "voice" (2 Kg.8.13; 9.1-3).

20.1-43: Ahab's wars with Syria; prophetic opposition to his policy. Verses 1-34 come from a source favorable to *Ahab,* in sharp contrast to vv. 35-43 and to chs. 17-19 and ch. 21; Elijah and Elisha disappear for a moment. *Ahab* appears as an able and popular ruler; his *people* stand by him in adversity (v. 8), and the prophets of the LORD support him (vv. 13-14,22); to a defeated enemy he shows noble generosity (vv. 32,34). **1-6:** *Kings* here no doubt means, as often in the Bible, petty rulers of small independent towns. The second demand (v. 6) was more drastic even than the first (v. 3), amounting to the privilege of unlimited looting. **11:** Ahab quotes a proverb to the effect that as long as there is a battle to be fought, one should not boast; the

swered, "Tell him, 'Let not him that girds on his armor boast himself as he that puts it off.' " [12] When Ben-ha'dad heard this message as he was drinking with the kings in the booths, he said to his men, "Take your positions." And they took their positions against the city.

13 And behold, a prophet came near to Ahab king of Israel and said, "Thus says the LORD, Have you seen all this great multitude? Behold, I will give it into your hand this day; and you shall know that I am the LORD." [14] And Ahab said, "By whom?" He said, "Thus says the LORD, By the servants of the governors of the districts." Then he said, "Who shall begin the battle?" He answered, "You." [15] Then he mustered the servants of the governors of the districts, and they were two hundred and thirty-two; and after them he mustered all the people of Israel, seven thousand.

16 And they went out at noon, while Ben-ha'dad was drinking himself drunk in the booths, he and the thirty-two kings who helped him. [17] The servants of the governors of the districts went out first. And Ben-ha'dad sent out scouts, and they reported to him, "Men are coming out from Sama'ria." [18] He said, "If they have come out for peace, take them alive; or if they have come out for war, take them alive."

19 So these went out of the city, the servants of the governors of the districts, and the army which followed them. [20] And each killed his man; the Syrians fled and Israel pursued them, but Ben-ha'dad king of Syria escaped on a horse with horsemen. [21] And the king of Israel went out, and captured[p] the horses and chariots, and killed the Syrians with a great slaughter.

22 Then the prophet came near to the king of Israel, and said to him, "Come, strengthen yourself, and consider well what you have to do; for in the spring the king of Syria will come up against you."

23 And the servants of the king of Syria said to him, "Their gods are gods of the hills, and so they were stronger than we; but let us fight against them in the plain, and surely we shall be stronger than they. [24] And do this: remove the kings, each from his post, and put commanders in their places; [25] and muster an army like the army that you have lost, horse for horse, and chariot for chariot; then we will fight against them in the plain, and surely we shall be stronger than they." And he hearkened to their voice, and did so.

26 In the spring Ben-ha'dad mustered the Syrians, and went up to Aphek, to fight against Israel. [27] And the people of Israel were mustered, and were provisioned, and went against them; the people of Israel encamped before them like two little flocks of goats, but the Syrians filled the country. [28] And a man of God came near and said to the king of Israel, "Thus says the LORD, 'Because the Syrians have said, "The LORD is a god of the hills but he is not a god of the valleys," therefore I will give all this great multitude into your hand, and you shall know that I am the LORD.' " [29] And they encamped opposite one another seven days. Then on the seventh day the battle was joined; and the people of Israel smote of the Syrians a hundred thousand foot soldiers in one day. [30] And the rest fled into the city of Aphek; and the wall fell upon twenty-seven thousand men that were left.

Ben-ha'dad also fled, and entered an inner chamber in the city. [31] And his servants said to him, "Behold now, we have heard that the kings of the house of Israel are merciful kings; let us put sackcloth on our loins and ropes upon our heads, and go out to

p Gk: Heb *smote*

---

battle may go either way. **24:** *The kings* were figureheads, the *commanders* experienced military men. **29:** The figure *hundred thousand foot soldiers* is not to be taken numerically; the meaning

the king of Israel; perhaps he will spare your life." ³² So they girded sackcloth on their loins, and put ropes on their heads, and went to the king of Israel and said, "Your servant Ben-ha′dad says, 'Pray, let me live.' " And he said, "Does he still live? He is my brother." ³³ Now the men were watching for an omen, and they quickly took it up from him and said, "Yes, your brother Ben-ha′dad." Then he said, "Go and bring him." Then Ben-ha′dad came forth to him; and he caused him to come up into the chariot. ³⁴ And Ben-ha′dad said to him, "The cities which my father took from your father I will restore; and you may establish bazaars for yourself in Damascus, as my father did in Sama′ria." And Ahab said, "I will let you go on these terms." So he made a covenant with him and let him go.

35 And a certain man of the sons of the prophets said to his fellow at the command of the LORD, "Strike me, I pray." But the man refused to strike him. ³⁶ Then he said to him, "Because you have not obeyed the voice of the LORD, behold, as soon as you have gone from me, a lion shall kill you." And as soon as he had departed from him, a lion met him and killed him. ³⁷ Then he found another man, and said, "Strike me, I pray." And the man struck him, smiting and wounding him. ³⁸ So the prophet departed, and waited for the king by the way, disguising himself with a bandage over his eyes. ³⁹ And as the king passed, he cried to the king and said, "Your servant went out into the midst of the battle; and behold, a soldier turned and brought a man to me, and said, 'Keep this man; if by any means he be miss-

ing, your life shall be for his life, or else you shall pay a talent of silver.' ⁴⁰ And as your servant was busy here and there, he was gone." The king of Israel said to him, "So shall your judgment be; you yourself have decided it." ⁴¹Then he made haste to take the bandage away from his eyes; and the king of Israel recognized him as one of the prophets. ⁴² And he said to him, "Thus says the LORD, 'Because you have let go out of your hand the man whom I had devoted to destruction, therefore your life shall go for his life, and your people for his people.' " ⁴³ And the king of Israel went to his house resentful and sullen, and came to Sama′ria.

21 Now Naboth the Jezreelite had a vineyard in Jezreel, beside the palace of Ahab king of Sama′ria. ² And after this Ahab said to Naboth, "Give me your vineyard, that I may have it for a vegetable garden, because it is near my house; and I will give you a better vineyard for it; or, if it seems good to you, I will give you its value in money." ³ But Naboth said to Ahab, "The LORD forbid that I should give you the inheritance of my fathers." ⁴ And Ahab went into his house vexed and sullen because of what Naboth the Jezreelite had said to him; for he had said, "I will not give you the inheritance of my fathers." And he lay down on his bed, and turned away his face, and would eat no food.

5 But Jez′ebel his wife came to him, and said to him, "Why is your spirit so vexed that you eat no food?" ⁶ And he said to her, "Because I spoke to Naboth the Jezreelite, and said to him, 'Give me your vineyard for money; or else, if it please you, I will give you an-

---

is "a large number." **35–43:** The change of tone in this section from another source should be noted. Ahab is violently criticized for what seems a noble act in v. 34. **39:** *A talent of silver*, roughly fifteen hundred dollars, would have been an enormous fine in those days. **42:** On the ban or "herem," a practice whereby something or someone is *devoted to destruction* as a religious act, see Jos.6.17 n.; 1 Sam.15.3 n.

21.1–29: Naboth's vineyard. In this chapter Elijah and the source concerned with him return. **1–4:** *Naboth* could not give up "*the inheritance of my fathers*" because by well established legal and religious custom, ancestral property must remain in the family in perpetuity (Lev.25.10, 13–17,23–24,34). *Ahab* was *vexed and sullen* because he knew that *Naboth* was legally and religiously right. **5–7:** *Jezebel* had no real respect for the laws and religion of Israel. **8–14:** For

other vineyard for it'; and he answered, 'I will not give you my vineyard.' " [7] And Jez'ebel his wife said to him, "Do you now govern Israel? Arise, and eat bread, and let your heart be cheerful; I will give you the vineyard of Naboth the Jezreelite."

8 So she wrote letters in Ahab's name and sealed them with his seal, and she sent the letters to the elders and the nobles who dwelt with Naboth in his city. [9] And she wrote in the letters, "Proclaim a fast, and set Naboth on high among the people; [10] and set two base fellows opposite him, and let them bring a charge against him, saying, 'You have cursed God and the king.' Then take him out, and stone him to death." [11] And the men of his city, the elders and the nobles who dwelt in his city, did as Jez'ebel had sent word to them. As it was written in the letters which she had sent to them, [12] they proclaimed a fast, and set Naboth on high among the people. [13] And the two base fellows came in and sat opposite him; and the base fellows brought a charge against Naboth, in the presence of the people, saying, "Naboth cursed God and the king." So they took him outside the city, and stoned him to death with stones. [14] Then they sent to Jez'ebel, saying, "Naboth has been stoned; he is dead."

15 As soon as Jez'ebel heard that Naboth had been stoned and was dead, Jez'ebel said to Ahab, "Arise, take possession of the vineyard of Naboth the Jezreelite, which he refused to give you for money; for Naboth is not alive, but dead." [16] And as soon as Ahab heard that Naboth was dead, Ahab arose to go down to the vineyard of Naboth the Jezreelite, to take possession of it.

17 Then the word of the LORD came to Eli'jah the Tishbite, saying, [18] "Arise, go down to meet Ahab king of Israel, who is in Sama'ria; behold, he is in the vineyard of Naboth, where he has gone to take possession. [19] And you shall say to him, 'Thus says the LORD, "Have you killed, and also taken possession?" ' And you shall say to him, 'Thus says the LORD: "In the place where dogs licked up the blood of Naboth shall dogs lick your own blood." ' "

20 Ahab said to Eli'jah, "Have you found me, O my enemy?" He answered, "I have found you, because you have sold yourself to do what is evil in the sight of the LORD. [21] Behold, I will bring evil upon you; I will utterly sweep you away, and will cut off from Ahab every male, bond or free, in Israel; [22] and I will make your house like the house of Jerobo'am the son of Nebat, and like the house of Ba'asha the son of Ahi'jah, for the anger to which you have provoked me, and because you have made Israel to sin. [23] And of Jez'ebel the LORD also said, 'The dogs shall eat Jez'ebel within the bounds of Jezreel.' [24] Any one belonging to Ahab who dies in the city the dogs shall eat; and any one of his who dies in the open country the birds of the air shall eat."

25 (There was none who sold himself to do what was evil in the sight of the LORD like Ahab, whom Jez'ebel his wife incited. [26] He did very abominably in going after idols, as the Amorites had done, whom the LORD cast out before the people of Israel.)

27 And when Ahab heard those words, he rent his clothes, and put sackcloth upon his flesh, and fasted and lay in sackcloth, and went about

---

a fast as part of the solemn assembly when a serious problem was to be considered, see Jg.20.26; 1 Sam.7.6; 14.24. To *set Naboth on high* probably means that he, as a prominent citizen, was to preside. *Two* witnesses and *death* by stoning, see Dt.17.5–6; 19.15. *Naboth cursed God and the king,* compare Ex.22.28; Lev.24.10–16. **22–24:** Probably an expansion of Elijah's speech by the Deuteronomic editor (compare 13.33–34; 14.10–11; 16.1–4; 2 Kg.9.35–36). **25–26:** The evaluation by the Deuteronomic editor, breaking the connection between vv. 24 and 27. *Amorites,* see 2 Sam.21.2 n. **29:** This verse, in the light of what happened, appraises the situation more realistically than vv. 21 and 24; it was perhaps added by the second Deuteronomist.

dejectedly. ²⁸ And the word of the LORD came to Eli′jah the Tishbite, saying, ²⁹ "Have you seen how Ahab has humbled himself before me? Because he has humbled himself before me, I will not bring the evil in his days; but in his son's days I will bring the evil upon his house."

22 For three years Syria and Israel continued without war. ² But in the third year Jehosh′aphat the king of Judah came down to the king of Israel. ³ And the king of Israel said to his servants, "Do you know that Ramoth-gilead belongs to us, and we keep quiet and do not take it out of the hand of the king of Syria?" ⁴ And he said to Jehosh′aphat, "Will you go with me to battle at Ramoth-gilead?" And Jehosh′aphat said to the king of Israel, "I am as you are, my people as your people, my horses as your horses."

5 And Jehosh′aphat said to the king of Israel, "Inquire first for the word of the LORD." ⁶ Then the king of Israel gathered the prophets together, about four hundred men, and said to them, "Shall I go to battle against Ramoth-gilead, or shall I forbear?" And they said, "Go up; for the Lord will give it into the hand of the king." ⁷ But Jehosh′aphat said, "Is there not here another prophet of the LORD of whom we may inquire?" ⁸ And the king of Israel said to Jehosh′aphat, "There is yet one man by whom we may inquire of the LORD, Micai′ah the son of Imlah; but I hate him, for he never prophesies good concerning me, but evil." And Jehosh′aphat said, "Let not the king say so." ⁹ Then the king of Israel summoned an officer and said,

"Bring quickly Micai′ah the son of Imlah." ¹⁰ Now the king of Israel and Jehosh′aphat the king of Judah were sitting on their thrones, arrayed in their robes, at the threshing floor at the entrance of the gate of Sama′ria; and all the prophets were prophesying before them. ¹¹ And Zedeki′ah the son of Chena′anah made for himself horns of iron, and said, "Thus says the LORD, 'With these you shall push the Syrians until they are destroyed.' " ¹² And all the prophets prophesied so, and said, "Go up to Ramoth-gilead and triumph; the LORD will give it into the hand of the king."

13 And the messenger who went to summon Micai′ah said to him, "Behold, the words of the prophets with one accord are favorable to the king; let your word be like the word of one of them, and speak favorably." ¹⁴ But Micai′ah said, "As the LORD lives, what the LORD says to me, that I will speak." ¹⁵ And when he had come to the king, the king said to him, "Micai′ah, shall we go to Ramoth-gilead to battle, or shall we forbear?" And he answered him, "Go up and triumph; the LORD will give it into the hand of the king." ¹⁶ But the king said to him, "How many times shall I adjure you that you speak to me nothing but the truth in the name of the LORD?" ¹⁷ And he said, "I saw all Israel scattered upon the mountains, as sheep that have no shepherd; and the LORD said, 'These have no master; let each return to his home in peace.' " ¹⁸ And the king of Israel said to Jehosh′aphat, "Did I not tell you that he would not prophesy good concerning me, but

22.1–53: Ahab dies in battle; reign of Jehoshaphat in Judah; accession of Ahaziah in Israel. Verses 1–40 resume the story of the Syrian (Aramean) wars from ch. 20. **1–4:** During the *three years* of peace between themselves, *Syria and Israel* had formed a military alliance and had successfully fought, together with other allies, against the invading Assyrians at Qarqar (853 B.C.), thus preserving both kingdoms. Ahab now formed an alliance with *Jehoshaphat*, marrying his daughter Athaliah to the son of *the king of Judah* (2 Kg.8.18,26); for he had quarreled with *the king of Syria* over the possession of the town of *Ramoth-gilead*, east of the Jordan (4.13; Dt.4.43). **5–12:** The need to *inquire* of one's god before a battle was widely felt in ancient times (1 Sam.23.2). In this source *the prophets* of the LORD are mostly on the side of Ahab (compare 20.13,28). Yet there is one *prophet of the LORD*, not Elijah, but *Micaiah,* who appears only here and is hostile. *Horns of iron*, compare Dt.33.17; Zech.1.18–21. **15:** *Micaiah* mimics the "yes

evil?" ¹⁹ And Micai'ah said, "Therefore hear the word of the LORD: I saw
the LORD sitting on his throne, and all
the host of heaven standing beside him
on his right hand and on his left; ²⁰ and
the LORD said, 'Who will entice Ahab,
that he may go up and fall at Ramoth-
gilead?' And one said one thing, and
another said another. ²¹ Then a spirit
came forward and stood before the
LORD, saying, 'I will entice him.'
²² And the LORD said to him, 'By
what means?' And he said, 'I will go
forth, and will be a lying spirit in the
mouth of all his prophets.' And he said,
'You are to entice him, and you shall
succeed; go forth and do so.' ²³ Now
therefore behold, the LORD has put a
lying spirit in the mouth of all these
your prophets; the LORD has spoken
evil concerning you."

24 Then Zedeki'ah the son of
Chena'anah came near and struck
Micai'ah on the cheek, and said, "How
did the Spirit of the LORD go from me
to speak to you?" ²⁵ And Micai'ah
said, "Behold, you shall see on that
day when you go into an inner chamber to hide yourself." ²⁶ And the king
of Israel said, "Seize Micai'ah, and
take him back to Amon the governor
of the city and to Jo'ash the king's son;
²⁷ and say, 'Thus says the king, "Put
this fellow in prison, and feed him with
scant fare of bread and water, until I
come in peace." ' " ²⁸ And Micai'ah
said, "If you return in peace, the LORD
has not spoken by me." And he said,
"Hear, all you peoples!"

29 So the king of Israel and Jehosh'-
aphat the king of Judah went up to
Ramoth-gilead. ³⁰ And the king of Israel said to Jehosh'aphat, "I will disguise myself and go into battle, but you
wear your robes." And the king of Israel disguised himself and went into
battle. ³¹ Now the king of Syria had
commanded the thirty-two captains of
his chariots, "Fight with neither small
nor great, but only with the king of
Israel." ³² And when the captains of
the chariots saw Jehosh'aphat, they
said, "It is surely the king of Israel."
So they turned to fight against him;
and Jehosh'aphat cried out. ³³ And
when the captains of the chariots saw
that it was not the king of Israel, they
turned back from pursuing him. ³⁴ But
a certain man drew his bow at a venture, and struck the king of Israel between the scale armor and the breastplate; therefore he said to the driver of
his chariot, "Turn about, and carry me
out of the battle, for I am wounded."
³⁵ And the battle grew hot that day,
and the king was propped up in his
chariot facing the Syrians, until at evening he died; and the blood of the
wound flowed into the bottom of the
chariot. ³⁶ And about sunset a cry
went through the army, "Every man
to his city, and every man to his country!"

37 So the king died, and was
brought to Sama'ria; and they buried
the king in Sama'ria. ³⁸ And they
washed the chariot by the pool of
Sama'ria, and the dogs licked up his
blood, and the harlots washed themselves in it, according to the word of
the LORD which he had spoken.
³⁹ Now the rest of the acts of Ahab,
and all that he did, and the ivory house
which he built, and all the cities that
he built, are they not written in the
Book of the Chronicles of the Kings of

men" of *the king.* **19–23:** The celestial scene portrayed here is unique in the earlier literature of
Israel. The *lying spirit,* here still under the control of the LORD, later developed into the figure
of Satan (compare Zech.3.1–2; Job chs. 1–2). **26:** Ahab put the prisoner in charge of *the king's
son* (one of his own sons) for maximum security. **27–28:** *In peace,* i.e. "victorious." **30:** The
disguise shows that Ahab was fearful that Micaiah might be right. **31:** *Thirty-two captains,*
compare 20.1,24. **38:** This verse is editorial, with reference to 21.19, though Naboth died in
Jezreel. The addition of *the harlots* symbolizes the fertility cult, a prominent feature of the Baal
religion that included sacred prostitution. **39:** *The ivory house,* a palace in Samaria, decorated
with carved ivory inlay and containing furniture so decorated. Some of these decorative in-
lays have been found in the archaeological excavation at Samaria (compare 10.22; Am.3.15;

Israel? ⁴⁰ So Ahab slept with his fathers; and Ahazi'ah his son reigned in his stead.

41 Jehosh'aphat the son of Asa began to reign over Judah in the fourth year of Ahab king of Israel. ⁴² Jehosh'aphat was thirty-five years old when he began to reign, and he reigned twenty-five years in Jerusalem. His mother's name was Azu'bah the daughter of Shilhi. ⁴³ He walked in all the way of Asa his father; he did not turn aside from it, doing what was right in the sight of the LORD; yet the high places were not taken away, and the people still sacrificed and burned incense on the high places. ⁴⁴ Jehosh'aphat also made peace with the king of Israel.

45 Now the rest of the acts of Jehosh'aphat, and his might that he showed, and how he warred, are they not written in the Book of the Chronicles of the Kings of Judah? ⁴⁶ And the remnant of the male cult prostitutes who remained in the days of his father Asa, he exterminated from the land.

47 There was no king in Edom; a deputy was king. ⁴⁸ Jehosh'aphat made ships of Tarshish to go to Ophir for gold; but they did not go, for the ships were wrecked at E'zion-ge'-ber. ⁴⁹ Then Ahazi'ah the son of Ahab said to Jehosh'aphat, "Let my servants go with your servants in the ships," but Jehosh'aphat was not willing. ⁵⁰ And Jehosh'aphat slept with his fathers, and was buried with his fathers in the city of David his father; and Jeho'ram his son reigned in his stead.

51 Ahazi'ah the son of Ahab began to reign over Israel in Sama'ria in the seventeenth year of Jehosh'aphat king of Judah, and he reigned two years over Israel. ⁵² He did what was evil in the sight of the LORD, and walked in the way of his father, and in the way of his mother, and in the way of Jerobo'am the son of Nebat, who made Israel to sin. ⁵³ He served Ba'al and worshiped him, and provoked the LORD, the God of Israel, to anger in every way that his father had done.

6.4; Ps.45.8). **41–46:** *Jehoshaphat* of *Judah* is credited with certain reforms and given qualified approval by the Deuteronomic editor, as was his father *Asa* (15.9–14). **47–50:** Jehoshaphat controlled Edom (2 Chr. ch. 20), and wished to imitate Solomon in maritime operations (compare 9.26–28; 10.22). *Ships of Tarshish,* see 10.22 n. **48–49:** For a different version, see 2 Chr. 20.35–37. **51–53:** *Ahaziah* is condemned by the Deuteronomic editor, as are all the kings of *Israel.* The account of his reign is continued immediately in 2 Kg. ch. 1.

THE SECOND BOOK OF THE

KINGS

Since 1 and 2 Kings are really one book, the problems and sources common to both are discussed in the Introduction to 1 Kings. Second Kings continues the story of the Hebrew monarchies. Chapters 1–17 describe the period from the reigns of Ahaziah of Israel and Jehoshaphat of Judah until the fall of Samaria and the end of the kingdom of Israel in 721 B.C. Chapters 18–25 relate the story of the kingdom of Judah from the fall of the kingdom of Israel to the fall of Judah with the capture and destruction of Jerusalem by Nebuchadnezzar in 586 B.C., ending with a brief account of the governorship of Gedaliah and the elevation of King Jehoiachin in exile. The book thus covers the period from the middle of the ninth century to near the middle of the sixth century (see "Survey of . . . Bible Lands," § 12). The fall of both Israel and Judah is interpreted in terms of the judgment of the Lord.

AFTER THE DEATH OF AHAB, MOAB rebelled against Israel.

2 Now Ahazi′ah fell through the lattice in his upper chamber in Sama′ria, and lay sick; so he sent messengers, telling them, "Go, inquire of Ba′al-ze′bub, the god of Ekron, whether I shall recover from this sickness." 3 But the angel of the LORD said to Eli′jah the Tishbite, "Arise, go up to meet the messengers of the king of Sama′ria, and say to them, 'Is it because there is no God in Israel that you are going to inquire of Ba′al-ze′bub, the god of Ekron?' 4 Now therefore thus says the LORD, 'You shall not come down from the bed to which you have gone, but you shall surely die.'" So Eli′jah went.

5 The messengers returned, to the king, and he said to them, "Why have you returned?" 6 And they said to him, "There came a man to meet us, and said to us, 'Go back to the king who sent you, and say to him, Thus says the LORD, Is it because there is no God in Israel that you are sending to inquire of Ba′al-ze′bub, the god of Ekron? Therefore you shall not come down

from the bed to which you have gone, but shall surely die.'" 7 He said to them, "What kind of man was he who came to meet you and told you these things?" 8 They answered him, "He wore a garment of haircloth, with a girdle of leather about his loins." And he said, "It is Eli′jah the Tishbite."

9 Then the king sent to him a captain of fifty men with his fifty. He went up to Eli′jah, who was sitting on the top of a hill, and said to him, "O man of God, the king says, 'Come down.'" 10 But Eli′jah answered the captain of fifty, "If I am a man of God, let fire come down from heaven and consume you and your fifty." Then fire came down from heaven, and consumed him and his fifty.

11 Again the king sent to him another captain of fifty men with his fifty. And he went up[a] and said to him, "O man of God, this is the king's order, 'Come down quickly!'" 12 But Eli′jah answered them, "If I am a man of God, let fire come down from heaven and consume you and your fifty." Then the fire of God came down from

a Gk Compare verses 9, 13: Heb *answered*

1.1–18: The reappearance of Elijah, the death of Ahaziah, and the accession of Jehoram of Israel. 1: This information is probably out of place here (compare 3.5). **2–5:** *The lattice,* some sort of protective fence or grating, in this case failed to perform its function. *Baal-zebub* means "lord of flies"; it is a mocking distortion of Baal-zebul, meaning either "lord of the divine abode," or "Baal the Prince," one of the names and manifestations of the great Baal, the rival of the God of Israel (see 1 Kg.18.1–6 n.,17–19 n.). Later, the name of this pagan deity became a synonym for Satan in Jewish theology (Mt.10.25; 12.24; Mk.3.22; Lk.11.15–19). If Ahaziah was a son of Jezebel, it is not surprising that he preferred Baal to the LORD. **9–16:** As before

heaven and consumed him and his fifty.

13 Again the king sent the captain of a third fifty with his fifty. And the third captain of fifty went up, and came and fell on his knees before Eli'jah, and entreated him, "O man of God, I pray you, let my life, and the life of these fifty servants of yours, be precious in your sight. [14] Lo, fire came down from heaven, and consumed the two former captains of fifty men with their fifties; but now let my life be precious in your sight." [15] Then the angel of the LORD said to Eli'jah, "Go down with him; do not be afraid of him." So he arose and went down with him to the king, [16] and said to him, "Thus says the LORD, 'Because you have sent messengers to inquire of Ba'al-ze'bub, the god of Ekron,–is it because there is no God in Israel to inquire of his word?–therefore you shall not come down from the bed to which you have gone, but you shall surely die.' "

17 So he died according to the word of the LORD which Eli'jah had spoken. Jeho'ram, his brother,[b] became king in his stead in the second year of Jeho'ram the son of Jehosh'aphat, king of Judah, because Ahazi'ah had no son. [18] Now the rest of the acts of Ahazi'ah which he did, are they not written in the Book of the Chronicles of the Kings of Israel?

2 Now when the LORD was about to take Eli'jah up to heaven by a whirlwind, Eli'jah and Eli'sha were on their way from Gilgal. [2] And Eli'jah said to Eli'sha, "Tarry here, I pray you; for the LORD has sent me as far as Bethel." But Eli'sha said, "As the LORD lives, and as you yourself live, I

will not leave you." So they went down to Bethel. [3] And the sons of the prophets who were in Bethel came out to Eli'sha, and said to him, "Do you know that today the LORD will take away your master from over you?" And he said, "Yes, I know it; hold your peace."

4 Eli'jah said to him, "Eli'sha, tarry here, I pray you; for the LORD has sent me to Jericho." But he said, "As the LORD lives, and as you yourself live, I will not leave you." So they came to Jericho. [5] The sons of the prophets who were at Jericho drew near to Eli'sha, and said to him, "Do you know that today the LORD will take away your master from over you?" And he answered, "Yes, I know it; hold your peace."

6 Then Eli'jah said to him, "Tarry here, I pray you; for the LORD has sent me to the Jordan." But he said, "As the LORD lives, and as you yourself live, I will not leave you." So the two of them went on. [7] Fifty men of the sons of the prophets also went, and stood at some distance from them, as they both were standing by the Jordan. [8] Then Eli'jah took his mantle, and rolled it up, and struck the water, and the water was parted to the one side and to the other, till the two of them could go over on dry ground.

9 When they had crossed, Eli'jah said to Eli'sha, "Ask what I shall do for you, before I am taken from you." And Eli'sha said, "I pray you, let me inherit a double share of your spirit." [10] And he said, "You have asked a hard thing; yet, if you see me as I am being taken from you, it shall be so for you; but if you do not see me, it

b Gk Syr: Heb lacks his brother

(1 Kg.18.38), the power of God acting through Elijah is symbolized by fire. **17:** *Jehoram*, son of Ahab and king of Israel, must not be confused with his brother-in-law, *Jehoram the son of Jehoshaphat, king of Judah* (8.18,26).

2.1–25: Elijah, taken up to heaven, is succeeded by Elisha. As always, the power and greatness of Elijah are expressed by the ancient writer in terms of legend and miracle. According to Biblical tradition, only two men, Enoch (Gen.5.24) and Elijah, were worthy to be taken up by God without having to die. **1–2:** This *Gilgal* was north of *Bethel*. **3:** The expression *the sons of the prophets* refers not to physical relationship, but means "members of the prophetic order"; see 1 Sam.10.5. **11:** The *chariot of fire and horses of fire* continue the symbolism of fire (see

shall not be so." [11] And as they still went on and talked, behold, a chariot of fire and horses of fire separated the two of them. And Eli'jah went up by a whirlwind into heaven. [12] And Eli'sha saw it and he cried, "My father, my father! the chariots of Israel and its horsemen!" And he saw him no more.

Then he took hold of his own clothes and rent them in two pieces. [13] And he took up the mantle of Eli'jah that had fallen from him, and went back and stood on the bank of the Jordan. [14] Then he took the mantle of Eli'jah that had fallen from him, and struck the water, saying, "Where is the LORD, the God of Eli'jah?" And when he had struck the water, the water was parted to the one side and to the other; and Eli'sha went over.

[15] Now when the sons of the prophets who were at Jericho saw him over against them, they said, "The spirit of Eli'jah rests on Eli'sha." And they came to meet him, and bowed to the ground before him. [16] And they said to him, "Behold now, there are with your servants fifty strong men; pray, let them go, and seek your master; it may be that the Spirit of the LORD has caught him up and cast him upon some mountain or into some valley." And he said, "You shall not send." [17] But when they urged him till he was ashamed, he said, "Send." They sent therefore fifty men; and for three days they sought him but did not find him. [18] And they came back to him, while he tarried at Jericho, and he said to them, "Did I not say to you, Do not go?"

19 Now the men of the city said to Eli'sha, "Behold, the situation of this city is pleasant, as my lord sees; but the water is bad, and the land is unfruitful." [20] He said, "Bring me a new bowl, and put salt in it." So they brought it to him. [21] Then he went to the spring of water and threw salt in it, and said, "Thus says the LORD, I have made this water wholesome; henceforth neither death nor miscarriage shall come from it." [22] So the water has been wholesome to this day, according to the word which Eli'sha spoke.

23 He went up from there to Bethel; and while he was going up on the way, some small boys came out of the city and jeered at him, saying, "Go up, you baldhead! Go up, you baldhead!" [24] And he turned around, and when he saw them, he cursed them in the name of the LORD. And two she-bears came out of the woods and tore forty-two of the boys. [25] From there he went on to Mount Carmel, and thence he returned to Sama'ria.

3 In the eighteenth year of Jehosh'aphat king of Judah, Jeho'ram the son of Ahab became king over Israel in Sama'ria, and he reigned twelve years. [2] He did what was evil in the sight of the LORD, though not like his father and mother, for he put away the pillar of Ba'al which his father had made. [3] Nevertheless he clung to the sin of Jerobo'am the son of Nebat, which he made Israel to sin; he did not depart from it.

4 Now Mesha king of Moab was a sheep breeder; and he had to deliver annually[c] to the king of Israel a hundred thousand lambs, and the wool of

c **Tg: Heb lacks** *annually*

1.9–16 n.). **12:** Elisha means that Elijah was more important and more powerful than *chariots* and *horsemen;* in 13.14 Elisha receives the same compliment. *Father* as the title of a man of religion is a very old usage (Jg.17.10). **13–14:** See 1 Kg.19.19. **15:** Elisha is acknowledged leader by *the sons of the prophets.* **19–22:** The God-given power of Elisha is attested by a miracle. Today, the finest spring in Jericho is sometimes called Elisha's Fountain. **23–25:** Not all ancient writers, to say nothing of modern, would have told a story like this to inculcate respect for a prophet. Mt.19.13–15; Mk.10.13–16; Lk.18.15–17 provide a better guide to Biblical teaching on how to treat children. On *forty-two* as a number of ill-omen, compare 10.14; Rev.11.2; 13.5.

    3.1–27: The war with Moab. 1–3: *In the eighteenth year of Jehoshaphat* does not agree with 1.17 ("second year of Jehoram . . . of Judah"). The data come from two irreconcilable chrono-

a hundred thousand rams. ⁵ But when Ahab died, the king of Moab rebelled against the king of Israel. ⁶ So King Jeho'ram marched out of Sama'ria at that time and mustered all Israel. ⁷ And he went and sent word to Jehosh'aphat king of Judah, "The king of Moab has rebelled against me; will you go with me to battle against Moab?" And he said, "I will go; I am as you are, my people as your people, my horses as your horses." ⁸ Then he said, "By which way shall we march?" Jeho'ram answered, "By the way of the wilderness of Edom."

9 So the king of Israel went with the king of Judah and the king of Edom. And when they had made a circuitous march of seven days, there was no water for the army or for the beasts which followed them. ¹⁰ Then the king of Israel said, "Alas! The LORD has called these three kings to give them into the hand of Moab." ¹¹ And Jehosh'aphat said, "Is there no prophet of the LORD here, through whom we may inquire of the LORD?" Then one of the king of Israel's servants answered, "Eli'sha the son of Shaphat is here, who poured water on the hands of Eli'jah." ¹² And Jehosh'aphat said, "The word of the LORD is with him." So the king of Israel and Jehosh'aphat and the king of Edom went down to him.

13 And Eli'sha said to the king of Israel, "What have I to do with you? Go to the prophets of your father and the prophets of your mother." But the king of Israel said to him, "No; it is

the LORD who has called these three kings to give them into the hand of Moab." ¹⁴ And Eli'sha said, "As the LORD of hosts lives, whom I serve, were it not that I have regard for Jehosh'aphat the king of Judah, I would neither look at you, nor see you. ¹⁵ But now bring me a minstrel." And when the minstrel played, the power of the LORD came upon him. ¹⁶ And he said, "Thus says the LORD, 'I will make this dry stream-bed full of pools.' ¹⁷ For thus says the LORD, 'You shall not see wind or rain, but that streambed shall be filled with water, so that you shall drink, you, your cattle, and your beasts.' ¹⁸ This is a light thing in the sight of the LORD; he will also give the Moabites into your hand, ¹⁹ and you shall conquer every fortified city, and every choice city, and shall fell every good tree, and stop up all springs of water, and ruin every good piece of land with stones." ²⁰ The next morning, about the time of offering the sacrifice, behold, water came from the direction of Edom, till the country was filled with water.

21 When all the Moabites heard that the kings had come up to fight against them, all who were able to put on armor, from the youngest to the oldest, were called out, and were drawn up at the frontier. ²² And when they rose early in the morning, and the sun shone upon the water, the Moabites saw the water opposite them as red as blood. ²³ And they said, "This is blood; the kings have surely fought together, and slain one another.

---

logical systems. **4–8:** The famous "Moabite Stone," discovered in 1868 and now in the Louvre, gives an account of the war from the standpoint of *Mesha king of Moab*. In naming *King Jehoram*, the author disregards the brief reign of Ahaziah (vv. 5–6; compare 1 Kg.22.40). The naming of *Jehoshaphat king of Judah* is based on the synchronism in v. 1, not that in 1.17. It was necessary for *the king of Israel* to get the co-operation of the *king of Judah* in order to march through the territory west of the Dead Sea on the way to *the wilderness of Edom*. **9–12:** The plan was to strike *Moab* from the south through *Edom*. At that time the *king of Edom* was a vassal of *the king of Judah*, not a king in his own right (1 Kg.22.47). *Poured water on the hands of Elijah* (when he washed), i.e. *Elisha* had waited on his mentor like a servant. **13–20:** The phrase *the prophets of your mother* (prophets of Baal) indicates that Jehoram was a son of Jezebel. **15:** The *minstrel* was used to induce a trance, out of which the prophet could give his oracle (1 Sam.10.5–6; 19.20–24). **16:** The *dry stream-bed* is thought to have been "the brook Zered" (Dt.2.13). **22:** *Red as blood*, colored by the red sandstone of Edom (see Gen.25.30

Now then, Moab, to the spoil!" [24] But when they came to the camp of Israel, the Israelites rose and attacked the Moabites, till they fled before them; and they went forward, slaughtering the Moabites as they went.[d] [25] And they overthrew the cities, and on every good piece of land every man threw a stone, until it was covered; they stopped every spring of water, and felled all the good trees; till only its stones were left in Kir-har'eseth, and the slingers surrounded and conquered it. [26] When the king of Moab saw that the battle was going against him, he took with him seven hundred swordsmen to break through, opposite the king of Edom; but they could not. [27] Then he took his eldest son who was to reign in his stead, and offered him for a burnt offering upon the wall. And there came great wrath upon Israel; and they withdrew from him and returned to their own land.

4 Now the wife of one of the sons of the prophets cried to Eli'sha, "Your servant my husband is dead; and you know that your servant feared the LORD, but the creditor has come to take my two children to be his slaves." [2] And Eli'sha said to her, "What shall I do for you? Tell me; what have you in the house?" And she said, "Your maidservant has nothing in the house, except a jar of oil." [3] Then he said, "Go outside, borrow vessels of all your neighbors, empty vessels and not too few. [4] Then go in, and shut the door upon yourself and your sons, and pour into all these vessels; and when one is full, set it aside." [5] So she went from him and shut the door upon herself and her sons; and as she poured they brought the vessels to her. [6] When the vessels were full, she said to her son, "Bring me another vessel." And he said to her, "There is not another." Then the oil stopped flowing. [7] She came and told the man of God, and he said, "Go, sell the oil and pay your debts, and you and your sons can live on the rest."

8 One day Eli'sha went on to Shunem, where a wealthy woman lived, who urged him to eat some food. So whenever he passed that way, he would turn in there to eat food. [9] And she said to her husband, "Behold now, I perceive that this is a holy man of God, who is continually passing our way. [10] Let us make a small roof chamber with walls, and put there for him a bed, a table, a chair, and a lamp, so that whenever he comes to us, he can go in there."

11 One day he came there, and he turned into the chamber and rested there. [12] And he said to Geha'zi his servant, "Call this Shu'nammite."

[d] Gk: Heb uncertain

---

note s). **27:** Human sacrifice, common in many ancient religions, was not unknown among the people of Israel and Judah (Ex.22.29–30; Jg.11.30–31,39; 1 Kg.16.34), though they learned that it was wrong (Gen.22.12; Ex.34.20; Dt.18.10). *The king of Moab* in his terrible extremity made the supreme sacrifice of *his eldest son*, and the forces of Israel were so impressed and so filled with fear of the *great wrath* of Chemosh, the god of Moab, that they gave up the victory that lay within their grasp and hastily *returned to their own land.* Two later kings of Judah, with less excuse, revived the horrible practice there (16.3; 21.6).

4.1–8.6: An interlude on the miracles of Elisha. See 2.19–22 n. In ancient times, miracle stories were considered to be one of the best ways of portraying the importance of a religious leader. We are fortunate in having preserved for us this fine collection of prophetic lore (see 1 Kg. ch. 17 n.). Two differences from Elijah should be noted: *Elisha* belonged to and worked with *the sons of the prophets* (members of the prophetic order living in communities); he was often in the company of the king and the army (compare ch. 3).

4.1–7: The jar of oil. This story is a parallel to Elijah's miracle in 1 Kg.17.14–16. Taking *children* as *slaves* for debt was legal in Israel (Ex.21.7). Later, in Judah, the practice was modified somewhat (Dt.15.12–18; Lev.25.39–46), at least in theory (compare Jer.34.8–16).

4.8–37: The son restored to life. The first part of this story (vv. 8–17) exhibits the favorite theme of the birth of a child late in life to a hitherto barren woman (see 1 Sam. ch. 1 n.). The second part of the story (vv. 18–37) parallels the account of Elijah's resuscitation of a child

When he had called her, she stood before him. ¹³ And he said to him, "Say now to her, See, you have taken all this trouble for us; what is to be done for you? Would you have a word spoken on your behalf to the king or to the commander of the army?" She answered, "I dwell among my own people." ¹⁴ And he said, "What then is to be done for her?" Geha'zi answered, "Well, she has no son, and her husband is old." ¹⁵ He said, "Call her." And when he had called her, she stood in the doorway. ¹⁶ And he said, "At this season, when the time comes round, you shall embrace a son." And she said, "No, my lord, O man of God; do not lie to your maidservant." ¹⁷ But the woman conceived, and she bore a son about that time the following spring, as Eli'sha had said to her.

18 When the child had grown, he went out one day to his father among the reapers. ¹⁹ And he said to his father, "Oh, my head, my head!" The father said to his servant, "Carry him to his mother." ²⁰ And when he had lifted him, and brought him to his mother, the child sat on her lap till noon, and then he died. ²¹ And she went up and laid him on the bed of the man of God, and shut the door upon him, and went out. ²² Then she called to her husband, and said, "Send me one of the servants and one of the asses, that I may quickly go to the man of God, and come back again." ²³ And he said, "Why will you go to him today? It is neither new moon nor sabbath." She said, "It will be well." ²⁴ Then she saddled the ass, and she said to her servant, "Urge the beast on; do not slacken the pace for me unless I tell you." ²⁵ So she set out, and came to the man of God at Mount Carmel.

When the man of God saw her coming, he said to Geha'zi his servant, "Look, yonder is the Shu'nammite; ²⁶ run at once to meet her, and say to her, Is it well with you? Is it well with your husband? Is it well with the child?" And she answered, "It is well." ²⁷ And when she came to the mountain to the man of God, she caught hold of his feet. And Geha'zi came to thrust her away. But the man of God said, "Let her alone, for she is in bitter distress; and the LORD has hidden it from me, and has not told me." ²⁸ Then she said, "Did I ask my lord for a son? Did I not say, Do not deceive me?" ²⁹ He said to Geha'zi, "Gird up your loins, and take my staff in your hand, and go. If you meet any one, do not salute him; and if any one salutes you, do not reply; and lay my staff upon the face of the child." ³⁰ Then the mother of the child said, "As the LORD lives, and as you yourself live, I will not leave you." So he arose and followed her. ³¹ Geha'zi went on ahead and laid the staff upon the face of the child, but there was no sound or sign of life. Therefore he returned to meet him, and told him, "The child has not awaked."

32 When Eli'sha came into the house, he saw the child lying dead on his bed. ³³ So he went in and shut the door upon the two of them, and prayed to the LORD. ³⁴ Then he went up and lay upon the child, putting his mouth upon his mouth, his eyes upon his eyes, and his hands upon his hands; and as he stretched himself upon him, the flesh of the child became warm. ³⁵ Then he got up again, and walked once to and fro in the house, and went up, and stretched himself upon him; the child sneezed seven times, and the child opened his eyes. ³⁶ Then he summoned Geha'zi and said, "Call this Shu'nammite." So he called her. And when she came to him, he said, "Take up your son." ³⁷ She came and fell at his feet, bowing to the ground; then she took up her son and went out.

38 And Eli'sha came again to Gilgal when there was a famine in the

---

in 1 Kg.17.17–24. **23:** *It is neither new moon nor sabbath;* it was considered more propitious to visit holy men on holy days.

land. And as the sons of the prophets were sitting before him, he said to his servant, "Set on the great pot, and boil pottage for the sons of the prophets." 39 One of them went out into the field to gather herbs, and found a wild vine and gathered from it his lap full of wild gourds, and came and cut them up into the pot of pottage, not knowing what they were. 40 And they poured out for the men to eat. But while they were eating of the pottage, they cried out, "O man of God, there is death in the pot!" And they could not eat it. 41 He said, "Then bring meal." And he threw it into the pot, and said, "Pour out for the men, that they may eat." And there was no harm in the pot.

42 A man came from Ba'al-shal'-ishah, bringing the man of God bread of the first fruits, twenty loaves of barley, and fresh ears of grain in his sack. And Eli'sha said, "Give to the men, that they may eat." 43 But his servant said, "How am I to set this before a hundred men?" So he repeated, "Give them to the men, that they may eat, for thus says the LORD, 'They shall eat and have some left.'" 44 So he set it before them. And they ate, and had some left, according to the word of the LORD.

5 Na'aman, commander of the army of the king of Syria, was a great man with his master and in high favor, because by him the LORD had given victory to Syria. He was a mighty man of valor, but he was a leper. 2 Now the Syrians on one of their raids had carried off a little maid from the land of Israel, and she waited on Na'aman's wife. 3 She said to her mistress, "Would that my lord were with the prophet who is in Sama'ria! He would cure him of his leprosy." 4 So Na'-aman went in and told his lord, "Thus

and so spoke the maiden from the land of Israel." 5 And the king of Syria said, "Go now, and I will send a letter to the king of Israel."

So he went, taking with him ten talents of silver, six thousand shekels of gold, and ten festal garments. 6 And he brought the letter to the king of Israel, which read, "When this letter reaches you, know that I have sent to you Na'aman my servant, that you may cure him of his leprosy." 7 And when the king of Israel read the letter, he rent his clothes and said, "Am I God, to kill and to make alive, that this man sends word to me to cure a man of his leprosy? Only consider, and see how he is seeking a quarrel with me."

8 But when Eli'sha the man of God heard that the king of Israel had rent his clothes, he sent to the king, saying, "Why have you rent your clothes? Let him come now to me, that he may know that there is a prophet in Israel." 9 So Na'aman came with his horses and chariots, and halted at the door of Eli'sha's house. 10 And Eli'-sha sent a messenger to him, saying, "Go and wash in the Jordan seven times, and your flesh shall be restored, and you shall be clean." 11 But Na'aman was angry, and went away, saying, "Behold, I thought that he would surely come out to me, and stand, and call on the name of the LORD his God, and wave his hand over the place, and cure the leper. 12 Are not Aba'na[e] and Pharpar, the rivers of Damascus, better than all the waters of Israel? Could I not wash in them, and be clean?" So he turned and went away in a rage. 13 But his servants came near and said to him, "My father, if the prophet had commanded you to do some great thing, would you not

e Another reading is *Amana*

4.38–41: The spoiled pottage. Compare 2.19–22. **42–44: The twenty loaves.** The most striking parallels to this miracle are to be found in the New Testament, Mt.14.13–21; 15.32–38.

5.1–27: The curing of the leprosy of Naaman. 1–7: Neither the name of *the king of Syria* nor that of *the king of Israel* is mentioned. The story assumes that the Syrians held the upper hand at this time. The value of *ten talents of silver*, plus *six thousand shekels of gold*, has been estimated to be as high as $80,000. **14:** For another description of the disease of leprosy, compare Lev.

have done it? How much rather, then, when he says to you, 'Wash, and be clean'?" ¹⁴ So he went down and dipped himself seven times in the Jordan, according to the word of the man of God; and his flesh was restored like the flesh of a little child, and he was clean.

15 Then he returned to the man of God, he and all his company, and he came and stood before him; and he said, "Behold, I know that there is no God in all the earth but in Israel; so accept now a present from your servant." ¹⁶ But he said, "As the LORD lives, whom I serve, I will receive none." And he urged him to take it, but he refused. ¹⁷ Then Na'aman said, "If not, I pray you, let there be given to your servant two mules' burden of earth; for henceforth your servant will not offer burnt offering or sacrifice to any god but the LORD. ¹⁸ In this matter may the LORD pardon your servant: when my master goes into the house of Rimmon to worship there, leaning on my arm, and I bow myself in the house of Rimmon, when I bow myself in the house of Rimmon, the LORD pardon your servant in this matter." ¹⁹ He said to him, "Go in peace."

But when Na'aman had gone from him a short distance, ²⁰ Geha'zi, the servant of Eli'sha the man of God, said, "See, my master has spared this Na'aman the Syrian, in not accepting from his hand what he brought. As the LORD lives, I will run after him, and get something from him." ²¹ So Geha'zi followed Na'aman. And when Na'aman saw some one running after him, he alighted from the chariot to meet him, and said, "Is all well?" ²² And he said, "All is well. My mas-ter has sent me to say, 'There have just now come to me from the hill country of E'phraim two young men of the sons of the prophets; pray, give them a talent of silver and two festal gar-ments.' " ²³ And Na'aman said, "Be pleased to accept two talents." And he urged him, and tied up two talents of silver in two bags, with two festal garments, and laid them upon two of his servants; and they carried them before Geha'zi. ²⁴ And when he came to the hill, he took them from their hand, and put them in the house; and he sent the men away, and they de-parted. ²⁵ He went in, and stood be-fore his master, and Eli'sha said to him, "Where have you been, Geha'zi?" And he said, "Your servant went no-where." ²⁶ But he said to him, "Did I not go with you in spirit when the man turned from his chariot to meet you? Was it a time to accept money and garments, olive orchards and vine-yards, sheep and oxen, menservants and maidservants? ²⁷ Therefore the leprosy of Na'aman shall cleave to you, and to your descendants for ever." So he went out from his presence a leper, as white as snow.

6 Now the sons of the prophets said to Eli'sha, "See, the place where we dwell under your charge is too small for us. ² Let us go to the Jordan and each of us get there a log, and let us make a place for us to dwell there." And he answered, "Go." ³ Then one of them said, "Be pleased to go with your servants." And he answered, "I will go." ⁴ So he went with them. And when they came to the Jordan, they cut down trees. ⁵ But as one was fell-ing a log, his axe head fell into the water; and he cried out, "Alas, my

ch. 13. The New Testament has a number of examples of the healing of this disease (Mt.8.2–3; Mk.1.40–42; Lk.5.12–13; compare Mt.11.5; Lk.7.22). **15–19a**: *Naaman* would have preferred to worship the LORD alone thenceforth if that would have been possible. He asked to take home *two mules' burden of earth* from Israel, the idea being that a god could not be worshiped apart from his own land. If he should bow down to *Rimmon* (another name for Hadad, the chief god of Syria), it would only be because he was forced to do so. **26**: Elisha caught the cul-prit by extrasensory perception (*in spirit*). This trait comes out more strongly in the next chapter. **27**: For another case of *leprosy* as punishment, compare 15.4–5.

6.1–7: The iron axe head. See 4.1–8.6 n.

master! It was borrowed." ⁶ Then the man of God said, "Where did it fall?" When he showed him the place, he cut off a stick, and threw it in there, and made the iron float. ⁷ And he said, "Take it up." So he reached out his hand and took it.

8 Once when the king of Syria was warring against Israel, he took counsel with his servants, saying, "At such and such a place shall be my camp." ⁹ But the man of God sent word to the king of Israel, "Beware that you do not pass this place, for the Syrians are going down there." ¹⁰ And the king of Israel sent to the place of which the man of God told him. Thus he used to warn him, so that he saved himself there more than once or twice.

11 And the mind of the king of Syria was greatly troubled because of this thing; and he called his servants and said to them, "Will you not show me who of us is for the king of Israel?" ¹² And one of his servants said, "None, my lord, O king; but Eli'sha, the prophet who is in Israel, tells the king of Israel the words that you speak in your bedchamber." ¹³ And he said, "Go and see where he is, that I may send and seize him." It was told him, "Behold, he is in Dothan." ¹⁴ So he sent there horses and chariots and a great army; and they came by night, and surrounded the city.

15 When the servant of the man of God rose early in the morning and went out, behold, an army with horses and chariots was round about the city. And the servant said, "Alas, my master! What shall we do?" ¹⁶ He said, "Fear not, for those who are with us are more than those who are with

them." ¹⁷ Then Eli'sha prayed, and said, "O LORD, I pray thee, open his eyes that he may see." So the LORD opened the eyes of the young man, and he saw; and behold, the mountain was full of horses and chariots of fire round about Eli'sha. ¹⁸ And when the Syrians came down against him, Eli'sha prayed to the LORD, and said, "Strike this people, I pray thee, with blindness." So he struck them with blindness in accordance with the prayer of Eli'sha. ¹⁹ And Eli'sha said to them, "This is not the way, and this is not the city; follow me, and I will bring you to the man whom you seek." And he led them to Sama'ria.

20 As soon as they entered Sama'ria, Eli'sha said, "O LORD, open the eyes of these men, that they may see." So the LORD opened their eyes, and they saw; and lo, they were in the midst of Sama'ria. ²¹ When the king of Israel saw them he said to Eli'sha, "My father, shall I slay them? Shall I slay them?" ²² He answered, "You shall not slay them. Would you slay those whom you have taken captive with your sword and with your bow? Set bread and water before them, that they may eat and drink and go to their master." ²³ So he prepared for them a great feast; and when they had eaten and drunk, he sent them away, and they went to their master. And the Syrians came no more on raids into the land of Israel.

24 Afterward Ben-ha'dad king of Syria mustered his entire army, and went up, and besieged Sama'ria. ²⁵ And there was a great famine in Sama'ria, as they besieged it, until an ass's head was sold for eighty shekels

6.8–23: The Syrian army blinded and captured. As in 5.1–7 neither *the king of Syria* nor *the king of Israel* is named. Verses 8–14 portray Elisha's extraordinary skill in the use of extrasensory perception. **10:** The meaning is that the *king of Israel sent* someone else to investigate. *Dothan* (v. 14) was about ten miles north of *Samaria* (v. 19). **17:** The *horses and chariots of fire* remind one of the stories about Elijah (2.11; 1 Kg.18.38). **23:** *The Syrians* were either so pleased by the hospitality of the king or so frightened by the power of the prophet that they gave up the war momentarily.

6.24–7.20: Ben-hadad's siege of Samaria repulsed by divine intervention. 24: The mention of the name of the *king of Syria* does not establish the chronology, since there were probably two Ben-hadads during these times, and the name of the king of Israel is not mentioned. **25:** These

of silver, and the fourth part of a kab of dove's dung for five shekels of silver. ²⁶ Now as the king of Israel was passing by upon the wall, a woman cried out to him, saying, "Help, my lord, O king!" ²⁷ And he said, "If the LORD will not help you, whence shall I help you? From the threshing floor, or from the wine press?" ²⁸ And the king asked her, "What is your trouble?" She answered, "This woman said to me, 'Give your son, that we may eat him today, and we will eat my son tomorrow.' ²⁹ So we boiled my son, and ate him. And on the next day I said to her, 'Give your son, that we may eat him'; but she has hidden her son." ³⁰ When the king heard the words of the woman he rent his clothes–now he was passing by upon the wall–and the people looked, and behold, he had sackcloth beneath upon his body– ³¹ and he said, "May God do so to me, and more also, if the head of Eli′sha the son of Shaphat remains on his shoulders today."

32 Eli′sha was sitting in his house, and the elders were sitting with him. Now the king had dispatched a man from his presence; but before the messenger arrived Eli′sha said to the elders, "Do you see how this murderer has sent to take off my head? Look, when the messenger comes, shut the door, and hold the door fast against him. Is not the sound of his master's feet behind him?" ³³ And while he was still speaking with them, the king* came down to him and said, "This trouble is from the LORD! Why should I wait for the LORD any longer?"

7 ¹ But Eli′sha said, "Hear the word of the LORD: thus says the LORD, Tomorrow about this time a measure of fine meal shall be sold for a shekel, and two measures of barley for a shekel, at the gate of Sama′ria." ² Then the captain on whose hand the king leaned said to the man of God, "If the LORD himself should make windows in heaven, could this thing be?" But he said, "You shall see it with your own eyes, but you shall not eat of it."

3 Now there were four men who were lepers at the entrance to the gate; and they said to one another, "Why do we sit here till we die? ⁴ If we say, 'Let us enter the city,' the famine is in the city, and we shall die there; and if we sit here, we die also. So now come, let us go over to the camp of the Syrians; if they spare our lives we shall live, and if they kill us we shall but die." ⁵ So they arose at twilight to go to the camp of the Syrians; but when they came to the edge of the camp of the Syrians, behold, there was no one there. ⁶ For the Lord had made the army of the Syrians hear the sound of chariots, and of horses, the sound of a great army, so that they said to one another, "Behold, the king of Israel has hired against us the kings of the Hittites and the kings of Egypt to come upon us." ⁷ So they fled away in the twilight and forsook their tents, their horses, and their asses, leaving the camp as it was, and fled for their lives. ⁸ And when these lepers came to the edge of the camp, they went into a tent, and ate and drank, and they carried off silver and gold and clothing, and went and hid them; then they came back, and entered another tent, and carried off things from it, and went and hid them.

9 Then they said to one another, "We are not doing right. This day is a day of good news; if we are silent and wait until the morning light,

f See 7.2: Heb *messenger*

---

prices were enormously high. A *shekel* was roughly fifty cents, *a kab* about a quart. **28–29:** See Dt.28.54–57; Lam.2.20; 4.10; Ezek.5.10. **31:** For some unknown reason, the king blamed *Elisha*, although in vv. 8–23 king and prophet were on the best of terms. **6.32–7.2:** Elisha predicted a quick reversal of fortune; a *captain* doubted and his doom was predicted by the prophet. **3–8:** The lepers do not seem to be overly ill from their disease. It is the LORD alone who routs the enemy; no fighting is recorded. The word here translated *Egypt* probably refers to a small country to the north, in the same general area as *the Hittites* (likewise in 1 Kg.10.28–29).

punishment will overtake us; now therefore come, let us go and tell the king's household." [10] So they came and called to the gatekeepers of the city, and told them, "We came to the camp of the Syrians, and behold, there was no one to be seen or heard there, nothing but the horses tied, and the asses tied, and the tents as they were." [11] Then the gatekeepers called out, and it was told within the king's household. [12] And the king rose in the night, and said to his servants, "I will tell you what the Syrians have prepared against us. They know that we are hungry; therefore they have gone out of the camp to hide themselves in the open country, thinking, 'When they come out of the city, we shall take them alive and get into the city.' " [13] And one of his servants said, "Let some men take five of the remaining horses, seeing that those who are left here will fare like the whole multitude of Israel that have already perished; let us send and see." [14] So they took two mounted men, and the king sent them after the army of the Syrians, saying, "Go and see." [15] So they went after them as far as the Jordan; and, lo, all the way was littered with garments and equipment which the Syrians had thrown away in their haste. And the messengers returned, and told the king.

16 Then the people went out, and plundered the camp of the Syrians. So a measure of fine meal was sold for a shekel, and two measures of barley for a shekel, according to the word of the LORD. [17] Now the king had appointed the captain on whose hand he leaned to have charge of the gate; and the people trod upon him in the gate, so that he died, as the man of God had said when the king came down to him. [18] For when the man of God had said to the king, "Two measures of barley shall be sold for a shekel, and a measure of fine meal for a shekel, about this time tomorrow in the gate of Sama'ria," [19] the captain had answered the man of God, "If the LORD himself should make windows in heaven, could such a thing be?" And he had said, "You shall see it with your own eyes, but you shall not eat of it." [20] And so it happened to him, for the people trod upon him in the gate and he died.

8 Now Eli'sha had said to the woman whose son he had restored to life, "Arise, and depart with your household, and sojourn wherever you can; for the LORD has called for a famine, and it will come upon the land for seven years." [2] So the woman arose, and did according to the word of the man of God; she went with her household and sojourned in the land of the Philistines seven years. [3] And at the end of the seven years, when the woman returned from the land of the Philistines, she went forth to appeal to the king for her house and her land. [4] Now the king was talking with Geha'zi the servant of the man of God, saying, "Tell me all the great things that Eli'sha has done." [5] And while he was telling the king how Eli'sha had restored the dead to life, behold, the woman whose son he had restored to life appealed to the king for her house and her land. And Geha'zi said, "My lord, O king, here is the woman, and here is her son whom Eli'sha restored to life." [6] And when the king asked the woman, she told him. So the king appointed an official for her, saying, "Restore all that was hers, together with all the produce of the fields from the day that she left the land until now."

7 Now Eli'sha came to Damascus. Ben-ha'dad the king of Syria was sick;

8.1–6: **Elisha again helps the woman whose child he had saved.** This section is a continuation of 4.8–37. 1–2: Isaac also went to *the land of the Philistines* to avoid *a famine* (Gen.26.1); compare Gen.12.10, where the place of refuge is Egypt. Drought and famine were common (4.38; 1 Kg.17.1). 3: Apparently the caretakers were trying to usurp the property. 4: The leprosy of *Gehazi* (5.27) is ignored here. Perhaps it was a mild case (7.3,8), or perhaps the tradition from which this story comes knew nothing of it.

and when it was told him, "The man of God has come here," [8] the king said to Haz'ael, "Take a present with you and go to meet the man of God, and inquire of the LORD through him, saying, 'Shall I recover from this sickness?'" [9] So Haz'ael went to meet him, and took a present with him, all kinds of goods of Damascus, forty camel loads. When he came and stood before him, he said, "Your son Benha'dad king of Syria has sent me to you, saying, 'Shall I recover from this sickness?'" [10] And Eli'sha said to him, "Go, say to him, 'You shall certainly recover'; but the LORD has shown me that he shall certainly die." [11] And he fixed his gaze and stared at him, until he was ashamed. And the man of God wept. [12] And Haz'ael said, "Why does my lord weep?" He answered, "Because I know the evil that you will do to the people of Israel; you will set on fire their fortresses, and you will slay their young men with the sword, and dash in pieces their little ones, and rip up their women with child." [13] And Haz'ael said, "What is your servant, who is but a dog, that he should do this great thing?" Eli'sha answered, "The LORD has shown me that you are to be king over Syria." [14] Then he departed from Eli'sha, and came to his master, who said to him, "What did Eli'sha say to you?" And he answered, "He told me that you would certainly recover." [15] But on the morrow he took the coverlet and dipped it in water and spread it over

his face, till he died. And Haz'ael became king in his stead.

16 In the fifth year of Joram the son of Ahab, king of Israel,[g] Jeho'ram the son of Jehosh'aphat, king of Judah, began to reign. [17] He was thirty-two years old when he became king, and he reigned eight years in Jerusalem. [18] And he walked in the way of the kings of Israel, as the house of Ahab had done, for the daughter of Ahab was his wife. And he did what was evil in the sight of the LORD. [19] Yet the LORD would not destroy Judah, for the sake of David his servant, since he promised to give a lamp to him and to his sons for ever.

20 In his days Edom revolted from the rule of Judah, and set up a king of their own. [21] Then Joram passed over to Za'ir with all his chariots, and rose by night, and he and his chariot commanders smote the E'domites who had surrounded him; but his army fled home. [22] So Edom revolted from the rule of Judah to this day. Then Libnah revolted at the same time. [23] Now the rest of the acts of Joram, and all that he did, are they not written in the Book of the Chronicles of the Kings of Judah? [24] So Joram slept with his fathers, and was buried with his fathers in the city of David; and Ahazi'ah his son reigned in his stead.

25 In the twelfth year of Joram the son of Ahab, king of Israel, Ahazi'ah the son of Jeho'ram, king of Judah, began to reign. [26] Ahazi'ah was twenty-

g Gk Syr: Heb *Israel, Jehoshaphat being king of Judah*

8.7–15: Elisha foments revolution in Syria. Elijah was able to carry out only one (the third) of the three commands of the "still small voice" at Horeb (1 Kg.19.15–16). *Elisha* now proceeds to carry out the first command of the "voice." The idea behind this is that Israel needed to be punished for its sins, and that Hazael was divinely ordained to do this work. The prophet was sorrowful over this doleful necessity (vv. 11–12), but nevertheless felt that God's will must be done (compare Hos.13.16).

8.16–24: The reign of Jehoram (Joram) of Judah. 16: This synchronism with *Joram* (Jehoram) *of Israel* agrees with that in 3.1, not with that in 1.17 (see 3.1–3 n.). **18:** See 1 Kg.22.1–4 n. The adverse moral evaluation of the Deuteronomist is probably owing to the marriage. **19:** On the *lamp* as a symbol of the permanence of the Davidic dynasty, see 2 Sam.21.17; 1 Kg.11.36; 15.4. **20:** See 3.9–12 n.

8.25–29: The reign of Ahaziah of Judah. This *Ahaziah* must not be confused with his uncle, Ahaziah of Israel (1.2–18; 1 Kg.22.40,51–53). His relationship to *the house of Ahab* was enough to condemn him in the eyes of the editor. The term *son-in-law* (v. 27) would apply more accurately to Ahaziah's father. Ahaziah himself was actually related by blood *to the house of Ahab*.

two years old when he began to reign, and he reigned one year in Jerusalem. His mother's name was Athali'ah; she was a granddaughter of Omri king of Israel. 27 He also walked in the way of the house of Ahab, and did what was evil in the sight of the LORD, as the house of Ahab had done, for he was son-in-law to the house of Ahab.

28 He went with Joram the son of Ahab to make war against Haz'ael king of Syria at Ramoth-gilead, where the Syrians wounded Joram. 29 And King Joram returned to be healed in Jezreel of the wounds which the Syrians had given him at Ramah, when he fought against Haz'ael king of Syria. And Ahazi'ah the son of Jeho'ram king of Judah went down to see Joram the son of Ahab in Jezreel, because he was sick.

9 Then Eli'sha the prophet called one of the sons of the prophets and said to him, "Gird up your loins, and take this flask of oil in your hand, and go to Ramoth-gilead. 2 And when you arrive, look there for Jehu the son of Jehosh'aphat, son of Nimshi; and go in and bid him rise from among his fellows, and lead him to an inner chamber. 3 Then take the flask of oil, and pour it on his head, and say, 'Thus says the LORD, I anoint you king over Israel.' Then open the door and flee; do not tarry."

4 So the young man, the prophet,[h] went to Ramoth-gilead. 5 And when he came, behold, the commanders of the army were in council; and he said, "I have an errand to you, O commander." And Jehu said, "To which of us all?" And he said, "To you, O commander." 6 So he arose, and went into the house; and the young man poured the oil on his head, saying to him, "Thus says the LORD the God of Israel, I anoint you king over the people of the LORD, over Israel. 7 And you shall strike down the house of Ahab your master, that I may avenge on Jez'ebel the blood of my servants the prophets, and the blood of all the servants of the LORD. 8 For the whole house of Ahab shall perish; and I will cut off from Ahab every male, bond or free, in Israel. 9 And I will make the house of Ahab like the house of Jerobo'am the son of Nebat, and like the house of Ba'asha the son of Ahi'jah. 10 And the dogs shall eat Jez'ebel in the territory of Jezreel, and none shall bury her." Then he opened the door, and fled.

11 When Jehu came out to the servants of his master, they said to him, "Is all well? Why did this mad fellow come to you?" And he said to them, "You know the fellow and his talk." 12 And they said, "That is not true; tell us now." And he said, "Thus and so he spoke to me, saying, 'Thus says the LORD, I anoint you king over Israel.'" 13 Then in haste every man of them took his garment, and put it under him on the bare[i] steps, and they blew the trumpet, and proclaimed, "Jehu is king."

14 Thus Jehu the son of Jehosh'aphat the son of Nimshi conspired against Joram. (Now Joram with all Israel had been on guard at Ramoth-gilead against Haz'ael king of Syria; 15 but King Joram had returned to be healed in Jezreel of the wounds which the Syrians had given him, when he fought with Haz'ael king of Syria.) So Jehu said, "If this is your mind, then let no one slip out of the city to go and tell the news in Jezreel." 16 Then Jehu mounted his chariot, and went to Jezreel, for Joram lay there. And Ahazi'ah king of Judah had come down to visit Joram.

h Gk Syr: Heb *the young man, the young man, the prophet*
i The meaning of the Hebrew word is uncertain

Ramoth-gilead, see 1 Kg.22.29–36. Like *Ahab*, *Joram* sought help from the *king of Judah*. The visit of *Ahaziah* to *Joram* set the stage for the catastrophic events of the next chapter. (*Ramah* is the same as Ramoth-gilead.)

9.1–37: Elisha foments the revolution of Jehu; assassination of Joram, Ahaziah, and Jezebel. Elisha now proceeds to carry out the second and only unfulfilled command of the "still small voice" at Horeb (see 8.7–15 n.). **16:** Compare 8.29. *Jezreel*, see 1 Kg.18.41–46 n. **26:** Compare

17 Now the watchman was standing on the tower in Jezreel, and he spied the company of Jehu as he came, and said, "I see a company." And Joram said, "Take a horseman, and send to meet them, and let him say, 'Is it peace?'" ¹⁸ So a man on horseback went to meet him, and said, "Thus says the king, 'Is it peace?'" And Jehu said, "What have you to do with peace? Turn round and ride behind me." And the watchman reported, saying, "The messenger reached them, but he is not coming back." ¹⁹ Then he sent out a second horseman, who came to them, and said, "Thus the king has said, 'Is it peace?'" And Jehu answered, "What have you to do with peace? Turn round and ride behind me." ²⁰ Again the watchman reported, "He reached them, but he is not coming back. And the driving is like the driving of Jehu the son of Nimshi; for he drives furiously."

21 Joram said, "Make ready." And they made ready his chariot. Then Joram king of Israel and Ahazi'ah king of Judah set out, each in his chariot, and went to meet Jehu, and met him at the property of Naboth the Jezreelite. ²² And when Joram saw Jehu, he said, "Is it peace, Jehu?" He answered, "What peace can there be, so long as the harlotries and the sorceries of your mother Jez'ebel are so many?" ²³ Then Joram reined about and fled, saying to Ahazi'ah, "Treachery, O Ahazi'ah!" ²⁴ And Jehu drew his bow with his full strength, and shot Joram between the shoulders, so that the arrow pierced his heart, and he sank in his chariot. ²⁵ Jehu said to Bidkar his aide, "Take him up, and cast him on the plot of ground belonging to Naboth the Jezreelite; for remember, when you and I rode side by side behind Ahab his father, how the LORD uttered this oracle against him: ²⁶ 'As surely as I saw yesterday the blood of Naboth and the blood of his sons—says the LORD—I will requite you on this plot of ground.' Now therefore take him up and cast him on the plot of ground, in accordance with the word of the LORD."

27 When Ahazi'ah the king of Judah saw this, he fled in the direction of Beth-haggan. And Jehu pursued him, and said, "Shoot him also"; and they shot him*ʲ* in the chariot at the ascent of Gur, which is by Ibleam. And he fled to Megid'do, and died there. ²⁸ His servants carried him in a chariot to Jerusalem, and buried him in his tomb with his fathers in the city of David.

29 In the eleventh year of Joram the son of Ahab, Ahazi'ah began to reign over Judah.

30 When Jehu came to Jezreel, Jez'ebel heard of it; and she painted her eyes, and adorned her head, and looked out of the window. ³¹ And as Jehu entered the gate, she said, "Is it peace, you Zimri, murderer of your master?" ³² And he lifted up his face to the window, and said, "Who is on my side? Who?" Two or three eunuchs looked out at him. ³³ He said, "Throw her down." So they threw her down; and some of her blood spattered on the wall and on the horses, and they trampled on her. ³⁴ Then he went in and ate and drank; and he said, "See now to this cursed woman, and bury her; for she is a king's daughter." ³⁵ But when they went to bury her, they found no more of her than the skull and the feet and the palms of her hands. ³⁶ When they came back and told him, he said, "This is the word of the LORD, which he spoke by his servant Eli'jah the Tishbite, 'In the territory of Jezreel the dogs shall eat the flesh of Jez'ebel; ³⁷ and the corpse of Jez'ebel shall be as dung upon the face of the field in the territory of Jezreel, so that no one can say, This is Jez'ebel.'"

j Syr Vg Compare Gk: Heb lacks *and they shot him*

1 Kg.21.17–19,28–29. **29:** This verse may be a correction of 8.25. **31:** *Zimri* was infamous for his brutal assassinations (1 Kg.16.8–12). **37:** The editor adds this verse to the oracle in 1 Kg. 21.23.

10 Now Ahab had seventy sons in Sama'ria. So Jehu wrote letters, and sent them to Sama'ria, to the rulers of the city,[k] to the elders, and to the guardians of the sons of Ahab, saying, 2 "Now then, as soon as this letter comes to you, seeing your master's sons are with you, and there are with you chariots and horses, fortified cities also, and weapons, 3 select the best and fittest of your master's sons and set him on his father's throne, and fight for your master's house." 4 But they were exceedingly afraid, and said, "Behold, the two kings could not stand before him; how then can we stand?" 5 So he who was over the palace, and he who was over the city, together with the elders and the guardians, sent to Jehu, saying, "We are your servants, and we will do all that you bid us. We will not make any one king; do whatever is good in your eyes." 6 Then he wrote to them a second letter, saying, "If you are on my side, and if you are ready to obey me, take the heads of your master's sons, and come to me at Jezreel tomorrow at this time." Now the king's sons, seventy persons, were with the great men of the city, who were bringing them up. 7 And when the letter came to them, they took the king's sons, and slew them, seventy persons, and put their heads in baskets, and sent them to him at Jezreel. 8 When the messenger came and told him, "They have brought the heads of the king's sons," he said, "Lay them in two heaps at the entrance of the gate until the morning." 9 Then in the morning, when he went out, he stood, and said to all the people, "You are innocent. It was I who conspired against my master, and slew him; but who struck down all these? 10 Know then that there shall

fall to the earth nothing of the word of the LORD, which the LORD spoke concerning the house of Ahab; for the LORD has done what he said by his servant Eli'jah." 11 So Jehu slew all that remained of the house of Ahab in Jezreel, all his great men, and his familiar friends, and his priests, until he left him none remaining.

12 Then he set out and went to Sama'ria. On the way, when he was at Beth-eked of the Shepherds, 13 Jehu met the kinsmen of Ahazi'ah king of Judah, and he said, "Who are you?" And they answered, "We are the kinsmen of Ahazi'ah, and we came down to visit the royal princes and the sons of the queen mother." 14 He said, "Take them alive." And they took them alive, and slew them at the pit of Beth-eked, forty-two persons, and he spared none of them.

15 And when he departed from there, he met Jehon'adab the son of Rechab coming to meet him; and he greeted him, and said to him, "Is your heart true to my heart as mine is to yours?"[l] And Jehon'adab answered, "It is." Jehu said,[m] "If it is, give me your hand." So he gave him his hand. And Jehu took him up with him into the chariot. 16 And he said, "Come with me, and see my zeal for the LORD." So he[n] had him ride in his chariot. 17 And when he came to Sama'ria, he slew all that remained to Ahab in Sama'ria, till he had wiped them out, according to the word of the LORD which he spoke to Eli'jah.

18 Then Jehu assembled all the people, and said to them, "Ahab served

k Gk Vg: Heb *Jezreel*
l Gk: Heb *Is it right with your heart, as my heart is with your heart?*
m Gk: Heb lacks *Jehu said*
n Gk Syr Tg: Heb *they*

10.1–36: Continuation of the purge; massacre of the princes of Israel, the princes of Judah, and the worshipers of Baal; decline of the power of Israel. **1:** *Seventy sons* probably includes grandsons (compare, however, Jg.8.30; 9.5; 12.13). **10–11:** Compare 1 Kg.21.21. **15:** *Jehonadab* (or Jonadab) *the son of Rechab* was the leader of that group, called the Rechabites, which fiercely maintained the old desert way of life, believing that only thus could they properly worship the LORD (1 Chr.2.55; Jer. ch. 35). The Nazirites were of similar type, though they practiced as individuals (Jg.13.4–5; Am.2.11–12; Num.6.1–21). **18–27:** In slaughtering *the prophets of Baal*, with *his priests* and *worshipers*, Jehu was following in the footsteps of Elijah (compare

Ba'al a little; but Jehu will serve him much. ¹⁹ Now therefore call to me all the prophets of Ba'al, all his worshipers and all his priests; let none be missing, for I have a great sacrifice to offer to Ba'al; whoever is missing shall not live." But Jehu did it with cunning in order to destroy the worshipers of Ba'al. ²⁰ And Jehu ordered, "Sanctify a solemn assembly for Ba'al." So they proclaimed it. ²¹ And Jehu sent throughout all Israel; and all the worshipers of Ba'al came, so that there was not a man left who did not come. And they entered the house of Ba'al, and the house of Ba'al was filled from one end to the other. ²² He said to him who was in charge of the wardrobe, "Bring out the vestments for all the worshipers of Ba'al." So he brought out the vestments for them. ²³ Then Jehu went into the house of Ba'al with Jehon'adab the son of Rechab; and he said to the worshipers of Ba'al, "Search, and see that there is no servant of the LORD here among you, but only the worshipers of Ba'al." ²⁴ Then he⁰ went in to offer sacrifices and burnt offerings.

Now Jehu had stationed eighty men outside, and said, "The man who allows any of those whom I give into your hands to escape shall forfeit his life." ²⁵ So as soon as he had made an end of offering the burnt offering, Jehu said to the guard and to the officers, "Go in and slay them; let not a man escape." So when they put them to the sword, the guard and the officers cast them out and went into the inner roomᵖ of the house of Ba'al ²⁶ and they brought out the pillar that was in the house of Ba'al, and burned it. ²⁷ And they demolished the pillar of Ba'al, and demol-

ished the house of Ba'al, and made it a latrine to this day.

28 Thus Jehu wiped out Ba'al from Israel. ²⁹ But Jehu did not turn aside from the sins of Jerobo'am the son of Nebat, which he made Israel to sin, the golden calves that were in Bethel, and in Dan. ³⁰ And the LORD said to Jehu, "Because you have done well in carrying out what is right in my eyes, and have done to the house of Ahab according to all that was in my heart, your sons of the fourth generation shall sit on the throne of Israel." ³¹ But Jehu was not careful to walk in the law of the LORD the God of Israel with all his heart; he did not turn from the sins of Jerobo'am, which he made Israel to sin.

32 In those days the LORD began to cut off parts of Israel. Haz'ael defeated them throughout the territory of Israel: ³³ from the Jordan eastward, all the land of Gilead, the Gadites, and the Reubenites, and the Manas'sites, from Aro'er, which is by the valley of the Arnon, that is, Gilead and Bashan. ³⁴ Now the rest of the acts of Jehu, and all that he did, and all his might, are they not written in the Book of the Chronicles of the Kings of Israel? ³⁵ So Jehu slept with his fathers, and they buried him in Sama'ria. And Jeho'ahaz his son reigned in his stead. ³⁶ The time that Jehu reigned over Israel in Sama'ria was twenty-eight years.

11 Now when Athali'ah the mother of Ahazi'ah saw that her son was dead, she arose and destroyed all the royal family. ² But Jehosh'eba, the daughter of King Joram, sister of

o Gk Compare verse 25: Heb *they*
p Cn: Heb *city*

---

v. 25 with 1 Kg.18.40). **28–31:** The verses belong to the "framework" (see Introduction to 1 Kings). A later prophet condemns this butchery by Jehu (Hos.1.4–5). **32–36:** On the successes of *Hazael* against *the territory of Israel*, see the prediction in 8.12. After the death of so many leaders, the defensive position of Israel was naturally weakened. It was probably during this time that Moab, south of the Arnon, also attacked Israel again and won final freedom from vassalage, as related on the Moabite Stone (see 3.4–8 n.).

11.1–20: The usurpation of Athaliah in Judah, the revolt against her, and the coronation of Joash (Jehoash). Jehu's attempt to eliminate the family of Ahab and the worship of Baal from Israel resulted in the temporary seizure of the throne of Judah by one who was both a descendant of Ahab and a worshiper of Baal (v. 18). **2–3:** *Jehosheba* was not a daughter of Atha-

Ahazi'ah, took Jo'ash the son of Ahazi'ah, and stole him away from among the king's sons who were about to be slain, and she put^q him and his nurse in a bedchamber. Thus she^r hid him from Athali'ah, so that he was not slain; ^{3} and he remained with her six years, hid in the house of the LORD, while Athali'ah reigned over the land.

4 But in the seventh year Jehoi'ada sent and brought the captains of the Carites and of the guards, and had them come to him in the house of the LORD; and he made a covenant with them and put them under oath in the house of the LORD, and he showed them the king's son. ^{5} And he commanded them, "This is the thing that you shall do: one third of you, those who come off duty on the sabbath and guard the king's house ^{6} (another third being at the gate Sur and a third at the gate behind the guards), shall guard the palace; ^{7} and the two divisions of you, which come on duty in force on the sabbath and guard the house of the LORD,^{s} ^{8} shall surround the king, each with his weapons in his hand; and whoever approaches the ranks is to be slain. Be with the king when he goes out and when he comes in."

9 The captains did according to all that Jehoi'ada the priest commanded, and each brought his men who were to go off duty on the sabbath, with those who were to come on duty on the sabbath, and came to Jehoi'ada the priest. ^{10} And the priest delivered to the captains the spears and shields that had been King David's, which were in the house of the LORD; ^{11} and the guards stood, every man with his weapons in his hand, from the south side of the house to the north side of the house, around the altar and the

house.^{t} ^{12} Then he brought out the king's son, and put the crown upon him, and gave him the testimony; and they proclaimed him king, and anointed him; and they clapped their hands, and said, "Long live the king!"

13 When Athali'ah heard the noise of the guard and of the people, she went into the house of the LORD to the people; ^{14} and when she looked, there was the king standing by the pillar, according to the custom, and the captains and the trumpeters beside the king, and all the people of the land rejoicing and blowing trumpets. And Athali'ah rent her clothes, and cried, "Treason! Treason!" ^{15} Then Jehoi'ada the priest commanded the captains who were set over the army, "Bring her out between the ranks; and slay with the sword any one who follows her." For the priest said, "Let her not be slain in the house of the LORD." ^{16} So they laid hands on her; and she went through the horses' entrance to the king's house, and there she was slain.

17 And Jehoi'ada made a convenant between the LORD and the king and people, that they should be the LORD's people; and also between the king and the people. ^{18} Then all the people of the land went to the house of Ba'al, and tore it down; his altars and his images they broke in pieces, and they slew Mattan the priest of Ba'al before the altars. And the priest posted watchmen over the house of the LORD. ^{19} And he took the captains, the Carites, the guards, and all the people of the land; and they brought the king down from the house of the LORD, marching through the gate of the guards

q With 2 Chr 22.11: Heb lacks *and she put*
r Gk Syr Vg Compare 2 Chr 22.11: Heb *they*
s Heb *the* LORD *to the king*
t Heb *the house to the king*

liah; hence she was only a half *sister of Ahaziah.* According to 2 Chr.22.11 she was the wife of Jehoiada the priest (vv. 4,9). *Joash* (Jehoash, 12.1) was the grandson of *Athaliah* as well as of *King Joram;* but while he was *hid in the house of the LORD,* he was taught the ways of the LORD. 4: The revolt was led by Jehoiada, the priest of the LORD (v. 9). *The Carites* were mercenaries; the word may be only an error for Cherethites (see 1 Sam.30.14 n.; 2 Sam.8.16–18 n.). 12: The word *testimony* may refer to a book or document; or it may be an error for "armlet," a royal symbol in 2 Sam.1.10. 14: *The pillar* (before the temple), see 1 Kg.7.15–22 n. *The people of the land* were the common people, who had remained loyal to the LORD.

to the king's house. And he took his seat on the throne of the kings. 20 So all the people of the land rejoiced; and the city was quiet after Athali'ah had been slain with the sword at the king's house.

21[u] Jeho'ash was seven years old when he began to reign.

12 In the seventh year of Jehu Jeho'-ash began to reign, and he reigned forty years in Jerusalem. His mother's name was Zib'iah of Beer-sheba. 2 And Jeho'ash did what was right in the eyes of the LORD all his days, because Jehoi'ada the priest instructed him. 3 Nevertheless the high places were not taken away; the people continued to sacrifice and burn incense on the high places.

4 Jeho'ash said to the priests, "All the money of the holy things which is brought into the house of the LORD, the money for which each man is assessed –the money from the assessment of persons–and the money which a man's heart prompts him to bring into the house of the LORD, 5 let the priests take, each from his acquaintance; and let them repair the house wherever any need of repairs is discovered." 6 But by the twenty-third year of King Jeho'-ash the priests had made no repairs on the house. 7 Therefore King Jeho'ash summoned Jehoi'ada the priest and the other priests and said to them, "Why are you not repairing the house? Now therefore take no more money from your acquaintances, but hand it over for the repair of the house." 8 So the priests agreed that they should take no more money from the people, and that they should not repair the house.

9 Then Jehoi'ada the priest took a chest, and bored a hole in the lid of it, and set it beside the altar on the right side as one entered the house of the LORD; and the priests who guarded the threshold put in it all the money that was brought into the house of the LORD. 10 And whenever they saw that there was much money in the chest, the king's secretary and the high priest came up and they counted and tied up in bags the money that was found in the house of the LORD. 11 Then they would give the money that was weighed out into the hands of the workmen who had the oversight of the house of the LORD; and they paid it out to the carpenters and the builders who worked upon the house of the LORD, 12 and to the masons and the stonecutters, as well as to buy timber and quarried stone for making repairs on the house of the LORD, and for any outlay upon the re-pairs of the house. 13 But there were not made for the house of the LORD basins of silver, snuffers, bowls, trum-pets, or any vessels of gold, or of silver, from the money that was brought into the house of the LORD, 14 for that was given to the workmen who were repairing the house of the LORD with it. 15 And they did not ask an account-ing from the men into whose hand they delivered the money to pay out to the workmen, for they dealt honestly. 16 The money from the guilt offerings and the money from the sin offerings was not brought into the house of the LORD; it belonged to the priests.

17 At that time Haz'ael king of Syria went up and fought against Gath, and took it. But when Haz'ael set his face to go up against Jerusalem, 18 Jeho'ash king of Judah took all the votive gifts that Jehosh'aphat and Je-

u Ch 12.1 in Heb

12.1–21: Reign of Jehoash of Judah; difficulties with repairs to the temple; attack by the Syrians; assassination of Jehoash. 1–3: During the childhood of the king, *Jehoiada the priest instructed him,* being no doubt the real power behind the throne. **4–8:** According to the early source reflected in these verses, the controversy over the repair of the temple was the fault of the priests rather than of the king. The identity of the *acquaintances* (vv. 5,7) is not clear. **9–16:** A new method of collection resulted in enough funds for repairs, but not enough for replacement of the valuable furnishings probably lost during Athaliah's regime (2 Chr.24.7). *Jehoiada* might properly be called "chief priest," but the term *high priest* is post-exilic and here editorial. For a story about apostasy on the part of Joash, and his assassination of Jehoiada's

ho'ram and Ahazi'ah, his fathers, the kings of Judah, had dedicated, and his own votive gifts, and all the gold that was found in the treasuries of the house of the LORD and of the king's house, and sent these to Haz'ael king of Syria. Then Haz'ael went away from Jerusalem.

19 Now the rest of the acts of Jo'-ash, and all that he did, are they not written in the Book of the Chronicles of the Kings of Judah? 20 His servants arose and made a conspiracy, and slew Jo'ash in the house of Millo, on the way that goes down to Silla. 21 It was Jo'zacar the son of Shim'e-ath and Jeho'zabad the son of Shomer, his serv-ants, who struck him down, so that he died. And they buried him with his fathers in the city of David, and Am-azi'ah his son reigned in his stead.

13 In the twenty-third year of Jo'-ash the son of Ahazi'ah, king of Judah, Jeho'ahaz the son of Jehu be-gan to reign over Israel in Sama'ria, and he reigned seventeen years. 2 He did what was evil in the sight of the LORD, and followed the sins of Jero-bo'am the son of Nebat, which he made Israel to sin; he did not depart from them. 3 And the anger of the LORD was kindled against Israel, and he gave them continually into the hand of Haz'-ael king of Syria and into the hand of Ben-ha'dad the son of Haz'ael. 4 Then Jeho'ahaz besought the LORD, and the LORD hearkened to him; for he saw the oppression of Israel, how the king of Syria oppressed them. 5 (Therefore the LORD gave Israel a savior, so that they escaped from the hand of the Syrians; and the people of Israel dwelt in their homes as formerly. 6 Never-theless they did not depart from the sins of the house of Jerobo'am, which he made Israel to sin, but walked^v

in them; and the Ashe'rah also re-mained in Sama'ria.) 7 For there was not left to Jeho'ahaz an army of more than fifty horsemen and ten chariots and ten thousand footmen; for the king of Syria had destroyed them and made them like the dust at threshing. 8 Now the rest of the acts of Jeho'ahaz and all that he did, and his might, are they not written in the Book of the Chron-icles of the Kings of Israel? 9 So Jeho'-ahaz slept with his fathers, and they buried him in Sama'ria; and Jo'ash his son reigned in his stead.

10 In the thirty-seventh year of Jo'-ash king of Judah Jeho'ash the son of Jeho'ahaz began to reign over Israel in Sama'ria, and he reigned sixteen years. 11 He also did what was evil in the sight of the LORD; he did not de-part from all the sins of Jerobo'am the son of Nebat, which he made Israel to sin, but he walked in them. 12 Now the rest of the acts of Jo'ash, and all that he did, and the might with which he fought against Amazi'ah king of Judah, are they not written in the Book of the Chronicles of the Kings of Israel? 13 So Jo'ash slept with his fathers, and Jerobo'am sat upon his throne; and Jo'ash was buried in Sama'ria with the kings of Israel.

14 Now when Eli'sha had fallen sick with the illness of which he was to die, Jo'ash king of Israel went down to him, and wept before him, crying, "My father, my father! The chariots of Israel and its horsemen!" 15 And Eli'sha said to him, "Take a bow and arrows"; so he took a bow and arrows. 16 Then he said to the king of Israel, "Draw the bow"; and he drew it. And Eli'sha laid his hands upon the king's hands. 17 And he said, "Open the window eastward"; and he opened it. Then

v Gk Syr Tg Vg: Heb *he walked*

---

son, see 2 Chr.24.17–22. **19–21:** According to 2 Chr.24.23–27, *Joash* (Jehoash) was defeated and assassinated because of his apostasy. In the end he turned out to be a true grandson of Athaliah (see 11.2–3 n.).
    13.1–25: The reigns of Jehoahaz and Jehoash of Israel; the death of Elisha. **3:** Compare 8.12. **4–5:** Compare the "framework" of Judges (see Introduction to Judges). **6:** *The Asherah*, here a symbol of the goddess (see 1 Kg.14.15 n.; 18.17–19 n.). **13:** This Jeroboam is Jeroboam II, to be distinguished from Jeroboam I mentioned in v. 11. **14:** Note the friendly relations between

Eli'sha said, "Shoot"; and he shot. And he said, "The LORD's arrow of victory, the arrow of victory over Syria! For you shall fight the Syrians in Aphek until you have made an end of them." [18] And he said, "Take the arrows"; and he took them. And he said to the king of Israel, "Strike the ground with them"; and he struck three times, and stopped. [19] Then the man of God was angry with him, and said, "You should have struck five or six times; then you would have struck down Syria until you had made an end of it, but now you will strike down Syria only three times."

20 So Eli'sha died, and they buried him. Now bands of Moabites used to invade the land in the spring of the year. [21] And as a man was being buried, lo, a marauding band was seen and the man was cast into the grave of Eli'sha; and as soon as the man touched the bones of Eli'sha, he revived, and stood on his feet.

22 Now Haz'ael king of Syria oppressed Israel all the days of Jeho'ahaz. [23] But the LORD was gracious to them and had compassion on them, and he turned toward them, because of his covenant with Abraham, Isaac, and Jacob, and would not destroy them; nor has he cast them from his presence until now.

24 When Haz'ael king of Syria died, Ben-ha'dad his son became king in his stead. [25] Then Jeho'ash the son of Jeho'ahaz took again from Ben-ha'dad the son of Haz'ael the cities which he had taken from Jeho'ahaz his father in war. Three times Jo'ash defeated him and recovered the cities of Israel.

14 In the second year of Jo'ash the son of Jo'ahaz, king of Israel, Amazi'ah the son of Jo'ash, king of Judah, began to reign. [2] He was twenty-five years old when he began to reign, and he reigned twenty-nine years in Jerusalem. His mother's name was Jeho-ad'din of Jerusalem. [3] And he did what was right in the eyes of the LORD, yet not like David his father; he did in all things as Jo'ash his father had done. [4] But the high places were not removed; the people still sacrificed and burned incense on the high places. [5] And as soon as the royal power was firmly in his hand he killed his servants who had slain the king his father. [6] But he did not put to death the children of the murderers; according to what is written in the book of the law of Moses, where the LORD commanded, "The fathers shall not be put to death for the children, or the children be put to death for the fathers; but every man shall die for his own sin."

7 He killed ten thousand E'domites in the Valley of Salt and took Sela by storm, and called it Jok'the-el, which is its name to this day.

8 Then Amazi'ah sent messengers to Jeho'ash the son of Jeho'ahaz, son of Jehu, king of Israel, saying, "Come, let us look one another in the face." [9] And Jeho'ash king of Israel sent word to Amazi'ah king of Judah, "A thistle on Lebanon sent to a cedar on Leb-

---

the prophet and the grandson of Jehu; on the words of Joash, see 2.12 n. **18:** The striking *three times* refers to the three victories in v. 25. **20–21:** On the miracle, see 4.1–8.6 n. **23:** A theological anticipation of vv. 24–25, added by an editor who, though friendly to Israel, yet knew that in the end the kingdom had fallen. **24–25:** This *Ben-hadad* (also in v. 3) is the third of that name, possibly the fourth, mentioned in these pages (compare 1 Kg.15.18–21; 20.1; 2 Kg.6.24; 8.7).

14.1–22: Warfare between Amaziah of Judah and Jehoash of Israel. 1: The reigns of *Joash* (Jehoash) *of Israel* and *Joash* (Jehoash) *of Judah* overlapped by about two years. Compare the earlier overlapping and more nearly coincident reigns of the two brothers-in-law, Joram (Jehoram) of Israel and Joram (Jehoram) of Judah (see 1.17; 8.16,25–exhibiting two different chronological systems; see p. 1532). **6:** *The law,* Dt.24.16; compare Jer.31.29–30; Ezek.18.2–4, 20; earlier theory and practice may be seen from Ex.20.5; Dt.5.9–10; Jos.7.24–25; 1 Kg.21.21. **7:** *The Valley of Salt,* probably the depression south of the Dead Sea. On the relations between Judah and the *Edomites,* compare 8.20–22. **8–10:** See Jg.9.8–15. The analogy in the fable here should not be pressed in every detail. In general, the idea is that a miserable little *thistle* tried

anon, saying, 'Give your daughter to my son for a wife'; and a wild beast of Lebanon passed by and trampled down the thistle. ¹⁰ You have indeed smitten Edom, and your heart has lifted you up. Be content with your glory, and stay at home; for why should you provoke trouble so that you fall, you and Judah with you?"

11 But Amazi'ah would not listen. So Jeho'ash king of Israel went up, and he and Amazi'ah king of Judah faced one another in battle at Beth-she'mesh, which belongs to Judah. ¹² And Judah was defeated by Israel, and every man fled to his home. ¹³ And Jeho'ash king of Israel captured Amazi'ah king of Judah, the son of Jeho'ash, son of Ahazi'ah, at Beth-she'mesh, and came to Jerusalem, and broke down the wall of Jerusalem for four hundred cubits, from the E'phraim Gate to the Corner Gate. ¹⁴ And he seized all the gold and silver, and all the vessels that were found in the house of the LORD and in the treasuries of the king's house, also hostages, and he returned to Sama'ria.

15 Now the rest of the acts of Jeho'-ash which he did, and his might, and how he fought with Amazi'ah king of Judah, are they not written in the Book of the Chronicles of the Kings of Israel? ¹⁶ And Jeho'ash slept with his fathers, and was buried in Sama'ria with the kings of Israel; and Jerobo'am his son reigned in his stead.

17 Amazi'ah the son of Jo'ash, king of Judah, lived fifteen years after the death of Jeho'ash son of Jeho'ahaz, king of Israel. ¹⁸ Now the rest of the deeds of Amazi'ah, are they not written in the Book of the Chronicles of the Kings of Judah? ¹⁹ And they made a conspiracy against him in Jerusalem, and he fled to Lachish. But they sent after him to Lachish, and slew him there. ²⁰ And they brought him upon horses; and he was buried in Jerusalem with his fathers in the city of David. ²¹ And all the people of Judah took Azari'ah, who was sixteen years old, and made him king instead of his father Amazi'ah. ²² He built Elath and restored it to Judah, after the king slept with his fathers.

23 In the fifteenth year of Amazi'ah the son of Jo'ash, king of Judah, Jerobo'am the son of Jo'ash, king of Israel, began to reign in Sama'ria, and he reigned forty-one years. ²⁴ And he did what was evil in the sight of the LORD; he did not depart from all the sins of Jerobo'am the son of Nebat, which he made Israel to sin. ²⁵ He restored the border of Israel from the entrance of Hamath as far as the Sea of the Arabah, according to the word of the LORD, the God of Israel, which he spoke by his servant Jonah the son of Amit'tai, the prophet, who was from Gath-he'pher. ²⁶ For the LORD saw that the affliction of Israel was very bitter, for there was none left, bond or free, and there was none to help Israel. ²⁷ But the LORD had not said that he would blot out the name of Israel from under heaven, so he saved them by

---

to make itself equal to a *cedar*, and was badly *trampled* for its trouble. *Jehoash* was both *cedar* and *wild beast*. **13**: *Four hundred cubits*, about two hundred yards. *The Ephraim Gate* would naturally be in the north wall. *The Corner Gate* was probably near the northwest angle of the wall. **14**: Compare 12.18. Apparently the captured king (v. 13) was released and *hostages* were taken instead. **15-16**: These verses duplicate 13.12–13. **19**: Perhaps Amaziah was assassinated by those resentful of the punishment he had meted out to his father's assassins (v. 5). **21**: *Azariah*, also called Uzziah (2 Chr.26.1). **22**: The restoration of Elath as a seaport of Judah was possible because Edom had again been subdued (v. 7; see 8.20–22; 1 Kg.9.26–28; 22.47–50).

14.23–29: The reign of Jeroboam II was long and prosperous. **25**: Jeroboam is here said to have ruled from the Dead Sea (*Sea of the Arabah*) as far north as Solomon's limit (1 Kg.8.65). His prophetic supporter was *Jonah the son of Amittai*, whose name was long afterwards given to the hero of the Book of Jonah (see Introduction to Jonah and Jon.1.1). **26–27**: These verses show sympathy for Israel; perhaps they were written by the second Deuteronomist (see Introduction to 1 Kings and contrast v. 24). Contrast the attitudes of Amos (Am.7.11) and Hosea (Hos.1.4–5; 10.7,15; 13.16), who prophesied during the reign of *Jeroboam* (see Introductions

the hand of Jerobo'am the son of Jo'ash.

28 Now the rest of the acts of Jerobo'am, and all that he did, and his might, how he fought, and how he recovered for Israel Damascus and Hamath, which had belonged to Judah, are they not written in the Book of the Chronicles of the Kings of Israel? ²⁹ And Jerobo'am slept with his fathers, the kings of Israel, and Zechari'ah his son reigned in his stead.

15 In the twenty-seventh year of Jerobo'am king of Israel Azari'ah the son of Amazi'ah, king of Judah, began to reign. ² He was sixteen years old when he began to reign, and he reigned fifty-two years in Jerusalem. His mother's name was Jecoli'ah of Jerusalem. ³ And he did what was right in the eyes of the LORD, according to all that his father Amazi'ah had done. ⁴ Nevertheless the high places were not taken away; the people still sacrificed and burned incense on the high places. ⁵ And the LORD smote the king, so that he was a leper to the day of his death, and he dwelt in a separate house. And Jotham the king's son was over the household, governing the people of the land. ⁶ Now the rest of the acts of Azari'ah, and all that he did, are they not written in the Book of the Chronicles of the Kings of Judah? ⁷ And Azari'ah slept with his fathers, and they buried him with his fathers in the city of David, and Jotham his son reigned in his stead.

8 In the thirty-eighth year of Azari'ah king of Judah Zechari'ah the son

of Jerobo'am reigned over Israel in Sama'ria six months. ⁹ And he did what was evil in the sight of the LORD, as his fathers had done. He did not depart from the sins of Jerobo'am the son of Nebat, which he made Israel to sin. ¹⁰ Shallum the son of Jabesh conspired against him, and struck him down at Ibleam,ʷ and killed him, and reigned in his stead. ¹¹ Now the rest of the deeds of Zechari'ah, behold, they are written in the Book of the Chronicles of the Kings of Israel. ¹² (This was the promise of the LORD which he gave to Jehu, "Your sons shall sit upon the throne of Israel to the fourth generation." And so it came to pass.)

13 Shallum the son of Jabesh began to reign in the thirty-ninth year of Uzzi'ah king of Judah, and he reigned one month in Sama'ria. ¹⁴ Then Men'-ahem the son of Gadi came up from Tirzah and came to Sama'ria, and he struck down Shallum the son of Jabesh in Sama'ria and slew him, and reigned in his stead. ¹⁵ Now the rest of the deeds of Shallum, and the conspiracy which he made, behold, they are written in the Book of the Chronicles of the Kings of Israel. ¹⁶ At that time Men'-ahem sacked Tappuahˣ and all who were in it and its territory from Tirzah on; because they did not open it to him, therefore he sacked it, and he ripped up all the women in it who were with child.

17 In the thirty-ninth year of Azari'ah king of Judah Men'ahem the son

w Gk Compare 9.27: Heb *before the people*
x Compare Gk: Heb *Tiphsah*

to Amos and Hosea). **28:** This verse has been badly damaged in transmission; we should read something like this: "how he fought with Damascus and how he averted the wrath of the LORD from Israel . . ."

15.1–7: The reign of Azariah (Uzziah) in Judah. The reign of *Azariah* (called Uzziah in vv. 13,30,32,34, and elsewhere) was long and prosperous, like that of *Jeroboam* II in Israel (see 14.23–24 and additional data in 2 Chr.26.6–15). **5:** Because *the king* became *a leper*, his son *Jotham* acted as regent (*was over the household*) during the latter years of the reign. **7:** On his death see Is.6.1. A limestone inscription found at Jerusalem bears the inscription: "Hither were brought the bones of Uzziah, King of Judah: not to be opened" (date 1st cent. A.D.).

15.8–31: The reigns of Zechariah, Shallum, Menahem, Pekahiah, and Pekah in Israel. 8–12: *Zechariah* was the last of the dynasty of *Jehu* (v. 12; compare 10.30). His assassination began a series of revolts and counter-revolts like those preceding the reign of Omri (1 Kg. ch. 16). **13–16:** *Shallum* was quickly murdered by *Menahem*. On the custom of disemboweling pregnant women, see 8.12; Hos.13.16; Am.1.13. **17–22:** Menahem's reign. Israel, tottering internally,

of Gadi began to reign over Israel, and he reigned ten years in Sama'ria. ¹⁸ And he did what was evil in the sight of the LORD; he did not depart all his days from all the sins of Jerobo'am the son of Nebat, which he made Israel to sin. ¹⁹ Pul the king of Assyria came against the land; and Men'ahem gave Pul a thousand talents of silver, that he might help him to confirm his hold of the royal power. ²⁰ Men'ahem exacted the money from Israel, that is, from all the wealthy men, fifty shekels of silver from every man, to give to the king of Assyria. So the king of Assyria turned back, and did not stay there in the land. ²¹ Now the rest of the deeds of Men'ahem, and all that he did, are they not written in the Book of the Chronicles of the Kings of Israel? ²² And Men'ahem slept with his fathers, and Pekahi'ah his son reigned in his stead.

23 In the fiftieth year of Azari'ah king of Judah Pekahi'ah the son of Men'ahem began to reign over Israel in Sama'ria, and he reigned two years. ²⁴ And he did what was evil in the sight of the LORD; he did not turn away from the sins of Jerobo'am the son of Nebat, which he made Israel to sin. ²⁵ And Pekah the son of Remali'ah, his captain, conspired against him with fifty men of the Gileadites, and slew him in Sama'ria, in the citadel of the king's house;^y he slew him, and reigned in his stead. ²⁶ Now the rest of the

deeds of Pekahi'ah, and all that he did, behold, they are written in the Book of the Chronicles of the Kings of Israel.

27 In the fifty-second year of Azari'ah king of Judah Pekah the son of Remali'ah began to reign over Israel in Sama'ria, and reigned twenty years. ²⁸ And he did what was evil in the sight of the LORD; he did not depart from the sins of Jerobo'am the son of Nebat, which he made Israel to sin.

29 In the days of Pekah king of Israel Tig'lath-pile'ser king of Assyria came and captured I'jon, A'bel-beth-ma'acah, Jan-o'ah, Kedesh, Hazor, Gilead, and Galilee, all the land of Naph'tali; and he carried the people captive to Assyria. ³⁰ Then Hoshe'a the son of Elah made a conspiracy against Pekah the son of Remali'ah, and struck him down, and slew him, and reigned in his stead, in the twentieth year of Jotham the son of Uzzi'ah. ³¹ Now the rest of the acts of Pekah, and all that he did, behold, they are written in the Book of the Chronicles of the Kings of Israel.

32 In the second year of Pekah the son of Remali'ah, king of Israel, Jotham the son of Uzzi'ah, king of Judah, began to reign. ³³ He was twenty-five years old when he began to reign, and he reigned sixteen years in Jerusalem. His mother's name was Jeru'sha the daughter of Zadok.

^y Heb adds *Argob and Arieh*, which probably belong to the list of places in verse 29

was an easy prey to outside attack by a reviving Assyria. **19–20:** *Pul* was another name of Tiglath-pileser III, *king of Assyria*. Menahem was forced to pay a huge sum to be allowed to hold his throne (roughly, a silver talent is fifteen hundred dollars; a talent contains 3000 shekels; hence 60,000 *wealthy men* were each taxed *fifty shekels of silver*, about twenty-five dollars). The time was 738 B.C. Israel was henceforth a vassal state. **23–26:** Pekahiah's reign. **27–31:** Pekah's reign. **27:** The total of *twenty years* is much too long for the reign of Pekah (see 14.1 n.). **29:** A somewhat garbled list, containing first the names of certain towns, followed by three names of larger areas: *Gilead, and Galilee, all the land of Naphtali.* Two or three lists may have been combined. In any case, all the names belong to the northern part of the country, which was ravaged by Tiglath-pileser in his campaigns of 733–732 B.C., when he punished Pekah for anti-Assyrian plotting (v. 37; 16.5,7–8) and also put an end to the kingdom of Syria (Aram) by capturing Damascus (16.9). We notice the beginning of Israelite deportation in this verse (compare 17.6). **30:** Tiglath-pileser in his own "Annals" claims to have had a hand in the overthrow of Pekah by Hoshea. Thus Hoshea began with a pro-Assyrian policy.

15.32–38: The reign of Jotham in Judah. For further details of his reign, see 2 Chr.27.1–9. **37:** The idea of this attack was to force Judah to join a coalition against Assyria (see v. 29 n. and 16.5–9).

[34] And he did what was right in the eyes of the LORD, according to all that his father Uzzi′ah had done. [35] Nevertheless the high places were not removed; the people still sacrificed and burned incense on the high places. He built the upper gate of the house of the LORD. [36] Now the rest of the acts of Jotham, and all that he did, are they not written in the Book of the Chronicles of the Kings of Judah? [37] In those days the LORD began to send Rezin the king of Syria and Pekah the son of Remali′ah against Judah. [38] Jotham slept with his fathers, and was buried with his fathers in the city of David his father; and Ahaz his son reigned in his stead.

16 In the seventeenth year of Pekah the son of Remali′ah, Ahaz the son of Jotham, king of Judah, began to reign. [2] Ahaz was twenty years old when he began to reign, and he reigned sixteen years in Jerusalem. And he did not do what was right in the eyes of the LORD his God, as his father David had done, [3] but he walked in the way of the kings of Israel. He even burned his son as an offering,[z] according to the abominable practices of the nations whom the LORD drove out before the people of Israel. [4] And he sacrificed and burned incense on the high places, and on the hills, and under every green tree.

5 Then Rezin king of Syria and Pekah the son of Remali′ah, king of Israel, came up to wage war on Jerusalem, and they besieged Ahaz but could not conquer him. [6] At that time[a] the king of Edom[b] recovered Elath for Edom,[b] and drove the men of Judah from Elath; and the E′domites came to Elath, where they dwell to this day. [7] So Ahaz sent messengers to Tig′lath-pile′-ser king of Assyria, saying, "I am your servant and your son. Come up, and rescue me from the hand of the king of Syria and from the hand of the king of Israel, who are attacking me." [8] Ahaz also took the silver and gold that was found in the house of the LORD and in the treasures of the king's house, and sent a present to the king of Assyria. [9] And the king of Assyria hearkened to him; the king of Assyria marched up against Damascus, and took it, carrying its people captive to Kir, and he killed Rezin.

10 When King Ahaz went to Damascus to meet Tig′lath-pile′ser king of Assyria, he saw the altar that was at Damascus. And King Ahaz sent to Uri′ah the priest a model of the altar, and its pattern, exact in all its details. [11] And Uri′ah the priest built the altar; in accordance with all that King Ahaz had sent from Damascus, so Uri′ah the priest made it, before King Ahaz arrived from Damascus. [12] And when the king came from Damascus, the king viewed the altar. Then the king drew near to the altar, and went up on it, [13] and burned his burnt offering and his cereal offering, and poured his drink offering, and threw the blood of his peace offerings upon the altar. [14] And the bronze altar which was be-

z Or *made his son to pass through the fire*   a Heb *At that time Rezin*   b Heb *Aram* (Syria)

16.1–20: The reign of Ahaz in Judah. 1–4: *Ahaz* is condemned as unusually bad by the Deuteronomic editor in comparison with other kings of Judah. Worst of all, he revived the barbarous custom of human sacrifice (see 3.27 n.). **5:** See 15.37 n.; compare also Is.7.1–17; 8.1–8a. **6:** *Edom* took advantage of the situation to throw off the control of Judah (see 14.22 n.). **7–9:** *Ahaz* disregarded the advice of Isaiah (Is.7.4,16–17; 8.4–8a) and called on *Tiglath-pileser* for help, sending an enormous gift. *The king of Assyria,* glad to be paid for what he had intended to do anyhow, took Damascus and devastated Israel (see 15.29 n.). *Kir* was the place in Mesopotamia from which some of the Arameans (Syrians) had come originally (Am.1.5; 9.7). **10–16:** *Ahaz went to Damascus* to pay homage to his overlord, *the king of Assyria;* while there he saw an altar, probably of Assyrian type, which he liked. He had this altar duplicated and placed before the temple in Jerusalem. Ahaz was probably thus paying his respects to a foreign religion, though the matter is not absolutely certain. *Urijah the priest* is probably the same person as the Uriah of Is.8.2, and hence could hardly have been wholly disloyal to the

fore the LORD he removed from the front of the house, from the place between his altar and the house of the LORD, and put it on the north side of his altar. ¹⁵ And King Ahaz commanded Uri'ah the priest, saying, "Upon the great altar burn the morning burnt offering, and the evening cereal offering, and the king's burnt offering, and his cereal offering, with the burnt offering of all the people of the land, and their cereal offering, and their drink offering; and throw upon it all the blood of the burnt offering, and all the blood of the sacrifice; but the bronze altar shall be for me to inquire by." ¹⁶ Uri'ah the priest did all this, as King Ahaz commanded.

17 And King Ahaz cut off the frames of the stands, and removed the laver from them, and he took down the sea from off the bronze oxen that were under it, and put it upon a pediment of stone. ¹⁸ And the covered way for the sabbath which had been built inside the palace, and the outer entrance for the king he removed from*c* the house of the LORD, because of the king of Assyria. ¹⁹ Now the rest of the acts of Ahaz which he did, are they not written in the Book of the Chronicles of the Kings of Judah? ²⁰ And Ahaz slept with his fathers, and was buried with his fathers in the city of David; and Hezeki'ah his son reigned in his stead.

17 In the twelfth year of Ahaz king of Judah Hoshe'a the son of Elah began to reign in Sama'ria over Israel, and he reigned nine years. ² And he did what was evil in the sight of the LORD, yet not as the kings of Israel who were before him. ³ Against him came up Shalmane'ser king of Assyria; and Hoshe'a became his vassal, and paid him tribute. ⁴ But the king of Assyria found treachery in Hoshe'a; for he had sent messengers to So, king of Egypt, and offered no tribute to the king of Assyria, as he had done year by year; therefore the king of Assyria shut him up, and bound him in prison. ⁵ Then the king of Assyria invaded all the land and came to Sama'ria, and for three years he besieged it. ⁶ In the ninth year of Hoshe'a the king of Assyria captured Sama'ria, and he carried the Israelites away to Assyria, and placed them in Halah, and on the Habor, the river of Gozan, and in the cities of the Medes.

7 And this was so, because the people of Israel had sinned against the LORD their God, who had brought them up out of the land of Egypt from under the hand of Pharaoh king of Egypt, and had feared other gods ⁸ and walked in the customs of the nations whom the LORD drove out before the people of Israel, and in the customs which the kings of Israel had introduced.*d* ⁹ And the people of Israel did secretly against the LORD their God things that were not right. They built for themselves high places at all their

c Cn: Heb *turned to*   *d* Heb obscure

LORD. **17–18:** It was necessary for Ahaz to dismantle some of the costly bronze equipment of the temple in order to pay the heavy tribute to Assyria. *The stands*, see 1 Kg.7.27–37. *The sea* and *the bronze oxen that were under it*, 1 Kg.7.23–26. The words *the covered way for the sabbath* represent a Hebrew phrase of uncertain meaning. Another interpretation is "the foundation of the seat."

17.1–41: The end of Israel, with reasons for the catastrophe; the origin of the Samaritans. 1: *In the twelfth year of Ahaz* is probably an erroneous synchronism (compare 15.30; see p. 1533). **2:** Perhaps the writer treated *Hoshea* more gently because of his tragic position as the last king of Israel. **3:** This was *Shalmaneser* V (727–722 B.C.). **4–5:** See 15.30 n. *Hoshea* now foolishly and disastrously plotted with Egypt (compare Hos.7.11); he left the capital, perhaps to plead for mercy, but was imprisoned; the siege of *Samaria* continued *for three years.* **6:** In the meantime Shalmaneser died and was succeeded by Sargon II (Is.20.1), who captured the city and deported, according to his own records, 27,290 inhabitants to faraway places. Thus ended for all time the kingdom of Israel (721 B.C.). **7–18:** These verses are the most important in the entire book (1 and 2 Kg.) for the understanding of the theological and ethical viewpoint of the first Deuteronomist (see Introduction to 1 Kings). The Israelites were considered sinners in the

towns, from watchtower to fortified city; ¹⁰ they set up for themselves pillars and Ashe'rim on every high hill and under every green tree; ¹¹ and there they burned incense on all the high places, as the nations did whom the LORD carried away before them. And they did wicked things, provoking the LORD to anger, ¹² and they served idols, of which the LORD had said to them, "You shall not do this." ¹³ Yet the LORD warned Israel and Judah by every prophet and every seer, saying, "Turn from your evil ways and keep my commandments and my statutes, in accordance with all the law which I commanded your fathers, and which I sent to you by my servants the prophets." ¹⁴ But they would not listen, but were stubborn, as their fathers had been, who did not believe in the LORD their God. ¹⁵ They despised his statutes, and his covenant that he made with their fathers, and the warnings which he gave them. They went after false idols, and became false, and they followed the nations that were round about them, concerning whom the LORD had commanded them that they should not do like them. ¹⁶ And they forsook all the commandments of the LORD their God, and made for themselves molten images of two calves; and they made an Ashe'rah, and worshiped all the host of heaven, and served Ba'al. ¹⁷ And they burned their sons and their daughters as offerings,ᵉ and used divination and sorcery, and sold themselves to do evil in the sight of the LORD, provoking him to anger. ¹⁸ Therefore the LORD was very angry with Israel, and removed them out of his sight; none was left but the tribe of Judah only.

19 Judah also did not keep the commandments of the LORD their God, but walked in the customs which Israel had introduced. ²⁰ And the LORD rejected all the descendants of Israel, and afflicted them, and gave them into the hand of spoilers, until he had cast them out of his sight.

21 When he had torn Israel from the house of David they made Jerobo'am the son of Nebat king. And Jerobo'am drove Israel from following the LORD and made them commit great sin. ²² The people of Israel walked in all the sins which Jerobo'am did; they did not depart from them, ²³ until the LORD removed Israel out of his sight, as he had spoken by all his servants the prophets. So Israel was exiled from their own land to Assyria until this day.

24 And the king of Assyria brought people from Babylon, Cuthah, Avva, Hamath, and Sephar-va'im, and placed them in the cities of Sama'ria instead of the people of Israel; and they took possession of Sama'ria, and dwelt in its cities. ²⁵ And at the beginning of their dwelling there, they did not fear the LORD; therefore the LORD sent lions among them, which killed some of them. ²⁶ So the king of Assyria was told, "The nations which you have carried away and placed in the cities of Sama'ria do not know the law of the god of the land; therefore he has sent lions among them, and behold, they are killing them, because they do not know the law of the god of the land." ²⁷ Then the king of Assyria commanded, "Send there one of the priests whom you carried away thence; and

ᵉ Or *made their sons and their daughters pass through the fire*

---

hands of an angry God (v. 18). Israel, not Assyria, was blamed. Playing politics with Egypt and Assyria was of no avail. Israel could have been saved by a proper attitude toward God and internal religious reform, but the warnings of the prophets were disregarded (vv. 13–14). *Asherim* (v. 10) and *Asherah* (v. 16), see 1 Kg.14.15 n.; 18.17–19 n. On the worship of the heavenly bodies (*host of heaven*, v. 16), see 21.5; 23.4–5. **17:** Human sacrifice, see 3.27 n. **19–20:** By a later writer, probably the second Deuteronomist, who knew the fate of the southern kingdom. **21–23:** A concluding summary of vv. 7–18. **24–28:** Sargon's own record confirms v. 24 thus: "[The cities] I set up again and made more populous than before. People from lands which I had taken I settled there." Later Assyrian kings continued this policy. The land was no

let him*f* go and dwell there, and teach them the law of the god of the land."
²⁸ So one of the priests whom they had carried away from Sama'ria came and dwelt in Bethel, and taught them how they should fear the LORD.

29 But every nation still made gods of its own, and put them in the shrines of the high places which the Samaritans had made, every nation in the cities in which they dwelt; ³⁰ the men of Babylon made Suc'coth-be'noth, the men of Cuth made Nergal, the men of Hamath made Ashi'ma, ³¹ and the Av'vites made Nibhaz and Tartak; and the Sephar'vites burned their children in the fire to Adram'melech and Anam'melech, the gods of Sepharva'im. ³² They also feared the LORD, and appointed from among themselves all sorts of people as priests of the high places, who sacrificed for them in the shrines of the high places. ³³ So they feared the LORD but also served their own gods, after the manner of the nations from among whom they had been carried away. ³⁴ To this day they do according to the former manner.

They do not fear the LORD, and they do not follow the statutes or the ordi-nances or the law or the commandment which the LORD commanded the children of Jacob, whom he named Israel. ³⁵ The LORD made a covenant with them, and commanded them, "You shall not fear other gods or bow yourselves to them or serve them or sacrifice to them; ³⁶ but you shall fear the LORD, who brought you out of the land of Egypt with great power and with an outstretched arm; you shall bow yourselves to him, and to him you shall sacrifice. ³⁷ And the statutes and the ordinances and the law and the commandment which he wrote for you, you shall always be careful to do. You shall not fear other gods, ³⁸ and you shall not forget the covenant that I have made with you. You shall not fear other gods, ³⁹ but you shall fear the LORD your God, and he will deliver you out of the hand of all your enemies." ⁴⁰ However they would not listen, but they did according to their former manner.

41 So these nations feared the LORD, and also served their graven images; their children likewise, and their children's children—as their fathers did, so they do to this day.

f Syr Vg: Heb *them*

longer called Israel, but *Samaria* (v. 24). The peoples were *Samaritans* (v. 29), not Israelites. **29–34a:** Thus it came about that the worship of the LORD became contaminated by various foreign cults. *To this day* (v. 34a) presumably means the time of the first Deuteronomist, a century after the fall of Israel; *the former manner* refers to their pagan religions practiced before they were brought to Samaria. **34b–40:** An addition by a late Deuteronomic editor (neither the first nor the second Deuteronomist) who wished to make it plain that the Samaritans were not to be credited with any proper worship of the LORD whatever—they were to be considered beyond the pale of religiously proper persons. This Jewish attitude toward the Samaritans continued into New Testament times (Ezra 4.1–3; Lk.10.33; 17.16–18; Jn.4.9; 8.48). **41:** This verse summarizes vv. 29–34a.
18.1–20.21: The reign of Hezekiah. *Hezekiah* was almost as highly favored by the Deuteronomic writer (18.5) as Josiah (23.25). For this reason, perhaps, a comparatively large amount of space is allotted to Hezekiah's reign. The reign was also significant because of political events such as the attack of *Sennacherib* (18.13), and because of the activities of *the prophet Isaiah* (19.2). These three chapters present many exegetical problems, but the main outlines of the story seem to be clear: Hezekiah revolted against Assyria (18.7) and Judah was severely punished (701 B.C.). Sennacherib himself reported that forty-six of the fortified cities and "countless small villages" were taken, while Hezekiah was shut up in Jerusalem "like a bird in a cage" (compare Is.1.7–8). Jerusalem escaped capture only by the payment of a huge sum for indemnity (18 13–16). Judah was forced to remain a subservient vassal of Assyria. Some scholars believe that Sennacherib attacked again several years later and was repulsed; solid proof of this view (called "the two-campaign theory") is lacking. 18.13–20.19 is repeated in Is. chs. 36–39 with certain omissions and additions. For additional comments see notes there.

18 In the third year of Hoshe'a son of Elah, king of Israel, Hezeki'ah the son of Ahaz, king of Judah, began to reign. ² He was twenty-five years old when he began to reign, and he reigned twenty-nine years in Jerusalem. His mother's name was Abi the daughter of Zechari'ah. ³ And he did what was right in the eyes of the LORD, according to all that David his father had done. ⁴ He removed the high places, and broke the pillars, and cut down the Ashe'rah. And he broke in pieces the bronze serpent that Moses had made, for until those days the people of Israel had burned incense to it; it was called Nehush'tan. ⁵ He trusted in the LORD the God of Israel; so that there was none like him among all the kings of Judah after him, nor among those who were before him. ⁶ For he held fast to the LORD; he did not depart from following him, but kept the commandments which the LORD commanded Moses. ⁷ And the LORD was with him; wherever he went forth, he prospered. He rebelled against the king of Assyria, and would not serve him. ⁸ He smote the Philistines as far as Gaza and its territory, from watchtower to fortified city.

9 In the fourth year of King Hezeki'ah, which was the seventh year of Hoshe'a son of Elah, king of Israel, Shalmane'ser king of Assyria came up against Sama'ria and besieged it ¹⁰ and at the end of three years he took it. In the sixth year of Hezeki'ah, which was the ninth year of Hoshe'a king of Israel, Sama'ria was taken. ¹¹ The king of Assyria carried the Israelites away to Assyria, and put them in Halah, and on the Habor, the river of Gozan, and in the cities of the Medes, ¹² because they did not obey the voice of the LORD their God but transgressed his covenant, even all that Moses the servant of the LORD commanded; they neither listened nor obeyed.

13 In the fourteenth year of King Hezeki'ah Sennach'erib king of Assyria came up against all the fortified cities of Judah and took them. ¹⁴ And Hezeki'ah king of Judah sent to the king of Assyria at Lachish, saying, "I have done wrong; withdraw from me; whatever you impose on me I will bear." And the king of Assyria required of Hezeki'ah king of Judah three hundred talents of silver and thirty talents of gold. ¹⁵ And Hezeki'ah gave him all the silver that was found in the house of the LORD, and in the treasuries of the king's house. ¹⁶ At that time Hezeki'ah stripped the gold from the doors of the temple of the LORD, and from the doorposts which Hezeki'ah king of Judah had overlaid and gave it to the king of Assyria. ¹⁷ And the king of Assyria sent the Tartan, the Rab'saris, and the Rab'shakeh with a great army from Lachish to King Hezeki'ah at Jerusalem. And they went up and came to Jerusalem. When they arrived, they came and stood by the conduit of the upper pool, which is on the highway to the Fuller's Field. ¹⁸ And when they called for the king, there came out to them Eli'akim the son of Hilki'ah, who was over the household, and Shebnah the secretary,

---

18.1–12: The accession of Hezekiah, his reforms. 1: *In the third year of Hoshea* is probably too early. The Deuteronomic author wishes to place the fall of Samaria during the reign of Hezekiah (vv. 9–10), but modern chronologists tend to place this catastrophe in the reign of Ahaz, in conformity with v. 13 (fourteenth yr. of Hezekiah = about 701 B.C., first yr. = about 715 B.C.). **4:** *Asherah*, see 1 Kg.14.15 n. *The bronze serpent*, see Num.21.6–9; this object doubtless had pagan associations, since the serpent was one of the symbols of the Baal religion. **9–12:** The fall of Samaria; largely a repetition of 17.5–6.

   18.13–37: The attack of Sennacherib. See Is. ch. 36. These verses present the basic elements of the historical incident. Verses 14–16 are lacking from the account in Is. ch. 36. **17–36:** If this narrative belongs to the first (and only historically certain) attack of Sennacherib, it should come before v. 14. Otherwise, it may be referred to the hypothetical second campaign some twelve or thirteen years later. **17–18:** Three Assyrian officials, *the Tartan, the Rabsaris, and*

and Jo'ah the son of Asaph, the recorder.

19 And the Rab'shakeh said to them, "Say to Hezeki'ah, 'Thus says the great king, the king of Assyria: On what do you rest this confidence of yours? ²⁰ Do you think that mere words are strategy and power for war? On whom do you now rely, that you have rebelled against me? ²¹ Behold, you are relying now on Egypt, that broken reed of a staff, which will pierce the hand of any man who leans on it. Such is Pharaoh king of Egypt to all who rely on him. ²² But if you say to me, "We rely on the LORD our God," is it not he whose high places and altars Hezeki'ah has removed, saying to Judah and to Jerusalem, "You shall worship before this altar in Jerusalem"? ²³ Come now, make a wager with my master the king of Assyria: I will give you two thousand horses, if you are able on your part to set riders upon them. ²⁴ How then can you repulse a single captain among the least of my master's servants, when you rely on Egypt for chariots and for horsemen? ²⁵ Moreover, is it without the LORD that I have come up against this place to destroy it? The LORD said to me, Go up against this land, and destroy it.' "

26 Then Eli'akim the son of Hilki'ah, and Shebnah, and Jo'ah, said to the Rab'shakeh, "Pray, speak to your servants in the Aramaic language, for we understand it; do not speak to us in the language of Judah within the hearing of the people who are on the wall." ²⁷ But the Rab'shakeh said to them, "Has my master sent me to speak these words to your master and to you, and not to the men sitting on the wall, who are doomed with you to eat their own dung and to drink their own urine?"

28 Then the Rab'shakeh stood and called out in a loud voice in the language of Judah: "Hear the word of the great king, the king of Assyria! ²⁹ Thus says the king: 'Do not let Hezeki'ah deceive you, for he will not be able to deliver you out of my hand. ³⁰ Do not let Hezeki'ah make you to rely on the LORD by saying, The LORD will surely deliver us, and this city will not be given into the hand of the king of Assyria.' ³¹ Do not listen to Hezeki'ah; for thus says the king of Assyria: 'Make your peace with me and come out to me; then every one of you will eat of his own vine, and every one of his own fig tree, and every one of you will drink the water of his own cistern; ³² until I come and take you away to a land like your own land, a land of grain and wine, a land of bread and vineyards, a land of olive trees and honey, that you may live, and not die. And do not listen to Hezeki'ah when he misleads you by saying, The LORD will deliver us. ³³ Has any of the gods of the nations ever delivered his land out of the hand of the king of Assyria? ³⁴ Where are the gods of Hamath and Arpad? Where are the gods of Sepharva'im, Hena, and Ivvah? Have they delivered Sama'ria out of my hand? ³⁵ Who among all the gods of the countries have delivered their countries out of my hand, that the LORD should deliver Jerusalem out of my hand?' "

36 But the people were silent and answered him not a word, for the king's command was, "Do not answer him." ³⁷ Then Eli'akim the son of Hilki'ah, who was over the household, and Shebna the secretary, and Jo'ah the son of Asaph, the recorder, came to Hezeki'ah with their clothes rent, and told him the words of the Rab'shakeh.

19 When King Hezeki'ah heard it, he rent his clothes, and covered himself with sackcloth, and went into

---

the Rabshakeh confer with three Judahite officials. **26:** After the Exile *the Aramaic language* (the language of Syria) came into common use among the Jews of Palestine (see Neh.8.7–8 n.), and thus was the medium in which Jesus proclaimed the Christian gospel; *the language of Judah* here means what is now called Hebrew, which was largely superseded by Aramaic.
19.1–37: Hezekiah consults Isaiah. See Is. ch. 37. Sennacherib departs without capturing

the house of the LORD. ² And he sent Eli′akim, who was over the household, and Shebna the secretary, and the senior priests, covered with sackcloth, to the prophet Isaiah the son of Amoz. ³ They said to him, "Thus says Hezeki′ah, This day is a day of distress, of rebuke, and of disgrace; children have come to the birth, and there is no strength to bring them forth. ⁴ It may be that the LORD your God heard all the words of the Rab′shakeh, whom his master the king of Assyria has sent to mock the living God, and will rebuke the words which the LORD your God has heard; therefore lift up your prayer for the remnant that is left." ⁵ When the servants of King Hezeki′ah came to Isaiah, ⁶ Isaiah said to them, "Say to your master, 'Thus says the LORD: Do not be afraid because of the words that you have heard, with which the servants of the king of Assyria have reviled me. ⁷ Behold, I will put a spirit in him, so that he shall hear a rumor and return to his own land; and I will cause him to fall by the sword in his own land.' "

8 The Rab′shakeh returned, and found the king of Assyria fighting against Libnah; for he heard that the king had left Lachish. ⁹ And when the king heard concerning Tirha′kah king of Ethiopia, "Behold, he has set out to fight against you," he sent messengers again to Hezeki′ah, saying, ¹⁰ "Thus shall you speak to Hezeki′ah king of Judah: 'Do not let your God on whom you rely deceive you by promising that Jerusalem will not be given into the hand of the king of Assyria. ¹¹ Behold, you have heard what the kings of Assyria have done to all lands, destroying them utterly. And shall you be delivered? ¹² Have the gods of the nations delivered them, the nations which my fathers destroyed, Gozan, Haran, Rezeph, and the people of Eden who were in Tel-assar? ¹³ Where is the king of Hamath, the king of Arpad, the king of the city of Sepharva′im, the king of Hena, or the king of Ivvah?' "

14 Hezeki′ah received the letter from the hand of the messengers, and read it; and Hezeki′ah went up to the house of the LORD, and spread it before the LORD. ¹⁵ And Hezeki′ah prayed before the LORD, and said: "O LORD the God of Israel, who art enthroned above the cherubim, thou art the God, thou alone, of all the kingdoms of the earth; thou hast made heaven and earth. ¹⁶ Incline thy ear, O LORD, and hear; open thy eyes, O LORD, and see; and hear the words of Sennach′erib, which he has sent to mock the living God. ¹⁷ Of a truth, O LORD, the kings of Assyria have laid waste the nations and their lands, ¹⁸ and have cast their gods into the fire; for they were no gods, but the work of men's hands, wood and stone; therefore they were destroyed. ¹⁹ So now, O LORD our God, save us, I beseech thee, from his hand, that all the kingdoms of the earth may know that thou, O LORD, art God alone."

20 Then Isaiah the son of Amoz sent to Hezeki′ah, saying, "Thus says the LORD, the God of Israel: Your prayer to me about Sennach′erib king of Assyria I have heard. ²¹ This is the word that the LORD has spoken concerning him:

"She despises you, she scorns you—
the virgin daughter of Zion;

Jerusalem and is assassinated by his sons. Legend and history seem to be interwoven here. In neither campaign (if there were two) did Judah really win a victory; Jerusalem merely escaped capture. It is questionable whether *the prophet Isaiah* predicted the assassination of Sennacherib (v. 7), uttered a taunt song or ode of derision against the Assyrian king (vv. 20–28), or proclaimed the inviolability of the city (v. 34). Tradition tended to turn an escape into a victory. **9:** *Tirhakah king of Ethiopia* did not become king or pharaoh of Egypt until 690 or 688 B.C.; hence some have regarded mention of this name as proof of a second campaign (see 18.17–36 n.). Others regard the name as an error, or point out that *Tirhakah* was a general long before he became king. **20–28:** For similar anti-Assyrian material, also attributed to *Isaiah*, compare Is.10.12–19; 14.24–27. **21:** *Daughter of Zion* and *daughter of Jerusalem*, read "daughter Zion"

she wags her head behind you–
the daughter of Jerusalem.

22 "Whom have you mocked and
reviled?
Against whom have you raised
your voice
and haughtily lifted your eyes?
Against the Holy One of Israel!
23 By your messengers you have
mocked the Lord,
and you have said, 'With my many
chariots
I have gone up the heights of the
mountains,
to the far recesses of Lebanon;
I felled its tallest cedars,
its choicest cypresses;
I entered its farthest retreat,
its densest forest.
24 I dug wells
and drank foreign waters,
and I dried up with the sole of my
foot
all the streams of Egypt.'
25 "Have you not heard
that I determined it long ago?
I planned from days of old
what now I bring to pass,
that you should turn fortified cities
into heaps of ruins,
26 while their inhabitants, shorn of
strength,
are dismayed and confounded,
and have become like plants of the
field,
and like tender grass,
like grass on the housetops;
blighted before it is grown?

27 "But I know your sitting down
and your going out and coming in,
and your raging against me.
28 Because you have raged against me
and your arrogance has come into
my ears,
I will put my hook in your nose
and my bit in your mouth,
and I will turn you back on the way
by which you came.

29 "And this shall be the sign for
you: this year you shall eat what
grows of itself, and in the second
year what springs of the same; then in
the third year sow, and reap, and plant
vineyards, and eat their fruit. 30 And
the surviving remnant of the house of
Judah shall again take root downward,
and bear fruit upward; 31 for out of
Jerusalem shall go forth a remnant, and
out of Mount Zion a band of survivors.
The zeal of the LORD will do this.

32 "Therefore thus says the LORD
concerning the king of Assyria, He
shall not come into this city or shoot an
arrow there, or come before it with a
shield or cast up a siege mound against
it. 33 By the way that he came, by the
same he shall return, and he shall not
come into this city, says the LORD.
34 For I will defend this city to save
it, for my own sake and for the sake
of my servant David."

35 And that night the angel of the
LORD went forth, and slew a hundred
and eighty-five thousand in the camp
of the Assyrians; and when men arose
early in the morning, behold, these
were all dead bodies. 36 Then Sen-

---

and "daughter Jerusalem," terms of endearment. **29–31:** These verses, though not very clear,
seem to be more modestly realistic than the rest of the chapter in expecting only *a remnant*
and *a band of survivors* to carry forward the work of the LORD. **32–34:** Contrast these verses
with the preceding. It has been claimed, on the basis of this passage and the parallel in Is.37.33–
35, that Isaiah taught the doctrine of "the inviolability of Zion," i.e. that Jerusalem could
never be taken (compare 20.6). Many interpreters doubt this claim, with very good reason.
35: Does this miracle story have a basis in fact? Some call attention to the statement in Herodotus (*Hist.*, II.141) that *the Assyrians* suffered a defeat on the borders of Egypt because their
bowstrings and other leather equipment were chewed by a sudden onslaught of field mice.
Mice may be carriers of the plague (see 1 Sam.6.4–5 n.). **37:** The murder did not take place
until the year 681, twenty years after the first (and only?) campaign against Jerusalem, and
at least eight years after the hypothetical second campaign. The god *Nisroch* has not been
identified with certainty. *Ararat* is Armenia (compare Gen.8.4).

nach'erib king of Assyria departed, and went home, and dwelt at Nin'eveh. [37] And as he was worshiping in the house of Nisroch his god, Adram'melech and Share'zer, his sons, slew him with the sword, and escaped into the land of Ar'arat. And Esarhad'don his son reigned in his stead.

20 In those days Hezeki'ah became sick and was at the point of death. And Isaiah the prophet the son of Amoz came to him, and said to him, "Thus says the LORD, 'Set your house in order; for you shall die, you shall not recover.'" [2] Then Hezeki'ah turned his face to the wall, and prayed to the LORD, saying, [3] "Remember now, O LORD, I beseech thee, how I have walked before thee in faithfulness and with a whole heart, and have done what is good in thy sight." And Hezeki'ah wept bitterly. [4] And before Isaiah had gone out of the middle court, the word of the LORD came to him: [5] "Turn back, and say to Hezeki'ah the prince of my people, Thus says the LORD, the God of David your father: I have heard your prayer, I have seen your tears; behold, I will heal you; on the third day you shall go up to the house of the LORD. [6] And I will add fifteen years to your life. I will deliver you and this city out of the hand of the king of Assyria, and I will defend this city for my own sake and for my servant David's sake." [7] And Isaiah said, "Bring a cake of figs. And let them take and lay it on the boil, that he may recover."

8 And Hezeki'ah said to Isaiah, "What shall be the sign that the LORD will heal me, and that I shall go up to the house of the LORD on the third day?" [9] And Isaiah said, "This is the sign to you from the LORD, that the LORD will do the thing that he has promised: shall the shadow go forward ten steps, or go back ten steps?" [10] And Hezeki'ah answered, "It is an easy thing for the shadow to lengthen ten steps; rather let the shadow go back ten steps." [11] And Isaiah the prophet cried to the LORD; and he brought the shadow back ten steps, by which the sun[g] had declined on the dial of Ahaz.

12 At that time Mero'dach-bal'adan the son of Bal'adan, king of Babylon, sent envoys with letters and a present to Hezeki'ah; for he heard that Hezeki'ah had been sick. [13] And Hezeki'ah welcomed them, and he showed them all his treasure house, the silver, the gold, the spices, the precious oil, his armory, all that was found in his storehouses; there was nothing in his house or in all his realm that Hezeki'ah did not show them. [14] Then Isaiah the prophet came to King Hezeki'ah, and said to him, "What did these men say? And whence did they come to you?" And Hezeki'ah said, "They have come from a far country, from Babylon." [15] He said, "What have they seen in your house?" And Hezeki'ah answered, "They have seen all that is in my house; there is nothing in my storehouses that I did not show them."

16 Then Isaiah said to Hezeki'ah, "Hear the word of the LORD: [17] Behold, the days are coming, when all

g Syr See Is 38.8 and Tg: Heb lacks *the sun*

20.1–11: Hezekiah's illness and recovery. See Is. ch. 38. **1**: *In those days* is only a vague indication of time. Actually, this chapter (except for vv. 20–21) is out of order, for both stories in it belong before the attack of Sennacherib in 701 B.C. (compare v. 6; Merodach-baladan ruled in Babylon, 722–710 B.C. and 703–702). **7**: The use of *a cake of figs* as a poultice was widespread in Bible times. **8–10**: Compare Jos.10.12–13 and 1 Kg. ch. 17 n. Though it is really the earth which moves, we sophisticated moderns still say, "The sun rises."

20.12–19: Merodach-baladan's embassy. See Is. 39.1–8. The Babylonian name of *Merodach-baladan* was Marduk-apaliddina. This mission was a part of the plotting against Assyria to which *Isaiah* was opposed and which led to the disastrous attack of 701 B.C., discussed above (18.7,21; Is.7.17; 8.7–8; 20.1–6; 31.1–3). **16–19**: Babylon and Egypt were both plotting; Isaiah was a neutralist, opposed to both; he was equally opposed to an alliance with Assyria (see 16.7–9 n.); but after Judah became an Assyrian vassal, he advocated loyalty to the obligation.

that is in your house, and that which your fathers have stored up till this day, shall be carried to Babylon; nothing shall be left, says the LORD. [18] And some of your own sons, who are born to you, shall be taken away; and they shall be eunuchs in the palace of the king of Babylon." [19] Then said Hezeki'ah to Isaiah, "The word of the LORD which you have spoken is good." For he thought, "Why not, if there will be peace and security in my days?"

20 The rest of the deeds of Hezeki'ah, and all his might, and how he made the pool and the conduit and brought water into the city, are they not written in the Book of the Chronicles of the Kings of Judah? [21] And Hezeki'ah slept with his fathers; and Manas'seh his son reigned in his stead.

21 Manas'seh was twelve years old when he began to reign, and he reigned fifty-five years in Jerusalem. His mother's name was Heph'zibah. [2] And he did what was evil in the sight of the LORD, according to the abominable practices of the nations whom the LORD drove out before the people of Israel. [3] For he rebuilt the high places which Hezeki'ah his father had destroyed; and he erected altars for Ba'al, and made an Ashe'rah, as Ahab king of Israel had done, and worshiped all the host of heaven, and served them. [4] And he built altars in the house of the LORD, of which the LORD had said, "In Jerusalem will I put my name." [5] And he built altars for all the host of heaven in the two courts of the house of the LORD. [6] And he burned his son as an offering, and practiced soothsaying and augury, and dealt with mediums and with wizards. He did much evil in the sight of the LORD, provoking him to anger. [7] And the graven image of Ashe'rah that he had made he set in the house of which the LORD said to David and to Solomon his son, "In this house, and in Jerusalem, which I have chosen out of all the tribes of Israel, I will put my name for ever; [8] and I will not cause the feet of Israel to wander any more out of the land which I gave to their fathers, if only they will be careful to do according to all that I have commanded them, and according to all the law that my servant Moses commanded them." [9] But they did not listen, and Manas'seh seduced them to do more evil than the nations had done whom the LORD destroyed before the people of Israel.

10 And the LORD said by his servants the prophets, [11] "Because Manas'seh king of Judah has committed these abominations, and has done things more wicked than all that the Amorites did, who were before him, and has made Judah also to sin with his idols; [12] therefore thus says the LORD, the God of Israel, Behold, I am bringing upon Jerusalem and Judah such evil that the ears of every one

---

The point of these verses, that Isaiah rebuked Hezekiah, and warned against the danger of invasion, would seem to be correct; the anachronistic reference to the Babylonian captivity, which took place more than a century later, was introduced by a careless post-exilic editor. It was Assyria not Babylon that punished Hezekiah.

20.20–21: Deuteronomic conclusion to the reign of Hezekiah, with an additional note about *the pool and the conduit*, improvements in the water supply of Jerusalem in preparation for possible attack (compare Is.22.8b–11). This conduit, with an identifying inscription, has been found and is now popularly called Hezekiah's Tunnel, or the Siloam Tunnel (compare 2 Chr. 32.30). It runs from Gihon (see 1 Kg.1.33 n.), which was outside the city wall, to the Pool of Siloam, which was inside the wall. Extending 1700 feet through solid rock, this tunnel was a remarkable engineering achievement in its time.

21.1–26: The wicked reigns of Manasseh and Amon. According to the Deuteronomists, this was the worst period of apostasy in Judah. Any good done by Hezekiah was quickly undone by Manasseh, who probably reigned longer than any other king of Israel or Judah, though the figure of *fifty-five years* appears to be exaggerated (see p. 1533). For a somewhat different interpretation, see 2 Chr. ch. 33. **3:** *Asherah,* see 1 Kg.14.15 n. Child sacrifice, see 3.27 n. **7–9:** Compare Dt.12.5,29–31; 17.3; 18.9–14. **10–15:** This section is from the second Deuteronomist,

who hears of it will tingle. ¹³ And I will stretch over Jerusalem the measuring line of Sama′ria, and the plummet of the house of Ahab; and I will wipe Jerusalem as one wipes a dish, wiping it and turning it upside down. ¹⁴ And I will cast off the remnant of my heritage, and give them into the hand of their enemies, and they shall become a prey and a spoil to all their enemies, ¹⁵ because they have done what is evil in my sight and have provoked me to anger, since the day their fathers came out of Egypt, even to this day.''

16 Moreover Manas′seh shed very much innocent blood, till he had filled Jerusalem from one end to another, besides the sin which he made Judah to sin so that they did what was evil in the sight of the LORD.

17 Now the rest of the acts of Manas′seh, and all that he did, and the sin that he committed, are they not written in the Book of the Chronicles of the Kings of Judah? ¹⁸ And Manas′seh slept with his fathers, and was buried in the garden of his house, in the garden of Uzza; and Amon his son reigned in his stead.

19 Amon was twenty-two years old when he began to reign, and he reigned two years in Jerusalem. His mother's name was Meshul′lemeth the daughter of Haruz of Jotbah. ²⁰ And he did what was evil in the sight of the LORD, as Manas′seh his father had done. ²¹ He walked in all the way in which his father walked, and served the idols that his father served, and worshiped them; ²² he forsook the LORD, the God of his fathers, and did not walk in the way of the LORD. ²³ And the servants of Amon conspired against

him, and killed the king in his house. ²⁴ But the people of the land slew all those who had conspired against King Amon, and the people of the land made Josi′ah his son king in his stead. ²⁵ Now the rest of the acts of Amon which he did, are they not written in the Book of the Chronicles of the Kings of Judah? ²⁶ And he was buried in his tomb in the garden of Uzza; and Josi′ah his son reigned in his stead.

22 Josi′ah was eight years old when he began to reign, and he reigned thirty-one years in Jerusalem. His mother's name was Jedi′dah the daughter of Adai′ah of Bozkath. ² And he did what was right in the eyes of the LORD, and walked in all the way of David his father, and he did not turn aside to the right hand or to the left.

3 In the eighteenth year of King Josi′ah, the king sent Shaphan the son of Azali′ah, son of Meshul′lam, the secretary, to the house of the LORD, saying, ⁴ "Go up to Hilki′ah the high priest, that he may reckon the amount of the money which has been brought into the house of the LORD, which the keepers of the threshold have collected from the people; ⁵ and let it be given into the hand of the workmen who have the oversight of the house of the LORD; and let them give it to the workmen who are at the house of the LORD, repairing the house, ⁶ that is, to the carpenters, and to the builders, and to the masons, as well as for buying timber and quarried stone to repair the house. ⁷ But no accounting shall be asked from them for the money which is delivered into their hand, for they deal honestly.''

---

writing after the fall of *Jerusalem* in 587–6 B.C. and during the Babylonian captivity (see Introduction to 1 Kings). This writer blames the fall of Jerusalem and Judah on the apostasy of Manasseh. *Amorites*, see 2 Sam.21.2 n. *The measuring line . . . and the plummet*, see Is.34.11; Lam.2.8; Am.7.7–9. **16:** *Manasseh* actually persecuted the followers of the LORD, practically driving them underground. **19–26:** A popular reaction and revolt set in, ending in the assassination of Amon early in his reign, and the accession of Josiah.

22.1–20: The beginning of the reign of Josiah; the repairing of the temple and the finding of the book of the law. 1–2: *Josiah* is the favorite king of the Deuteronomists because of his reforms (see ch. 23). **3–7:** *The eighteenth year of King Josiah*, 621 B.C. On the collection of *money* (unminted metal) to repair the temple, compare 12.4–16. **8–10:** This *book of the law*, really a scroll,

8 And Hilki′ah the high priest said to Shaphan the secretary, "I have found the book of the law in the house of the LORD." And Hilki′ah gave the book to Shaphan, and he read it. ⁹ And Shaphan the secretary came to the king, and reported to the king, "Your servants have emptied out the money that was found in the house, and have delivered it into the hand of the workmen who have the oversight of the house of the LORD." ¹⁰ Then Shaphan the secretary told the king, "Hilki′ah the priest has given me a book." And Shaphan read it before the king.

11 And when the king heard the words of the book of the law, he rent his clothes. ¹² And the king commanded Hilki′ah the priest, and Ahi′kam the son of Shaphan, and Achbor the son of Micai′ah, and Shaphan the secretary, and Asai′ah the king's servant, saying, ¹³ "Go, inquire of the LORD for me, and for the people, and for all Judah, concerning the words of this book that has been found; for great is the wrath of the LORD that is kindled against us, because our fathers have not obeyed the words of this book, to do according to all that is written concerning us."

14 So Hilki′ah the priest, and Ahi′kam, and Achbor, and Shaphan, and Asai′ah went to Huldah the prophetess, the wife of Shallum the son of Tikvah, son of Harhas, keeper of the wardrobe (now she dwelt in Jerusalem in the Second Quarter); and they talked with her. ¹⁵ And she said to them,

"Thus says the LORD, the God of Israel: 'Tell the man who sent you to me, ¹⁶ Thus says the LORD, Behold, I will bring evil upon this place and upon its inhabitants, all the words of the book which the king of Judah has read. ¹⁷ Because they have forsaken me and have burned incense to other gods, that they might provoke me to anger with all the work of their hands, therefore my wrath will be kindled against this place, and it will not be quenched. ¹⁸ But as to the king of Judah, who sent you to inquire of the LORD, thus shall you say to him, Thus says the LORD, the God of Israel: Regarding the words which you have heard, ¹⁹ because your heart was penitent, and you humbled yourself before the LORD, when you heard how I spoke against this place, and against its inhabitants, that they should become a desolation and a curse, and you have rent your clothes and wept before me, I also have heard you, says the LORD. ²⁰ Therefore, behold, I will gather you to your fathers, and you shall be gathered to your grave in peace, and your eyes shall not see all the evil which I will bring upon this place.' " And they brought back word to the king.

23 Then the king sent, and all the elders of Judah and Jerusalem were gathered to him. ² And the king went up to the house of the LORD, and with him all the men of Judah and all the inhabitants of Jerusalem, and the priests and the prophets, all the people, both small and great; and he read in their hearing all the words of the

---

was apparently found in a collection box (12.9) or in some rubbish about to be removed from the temple. It is also possible that *Hilkiah* had known about it and brought it forth intentionally at this time. The scroll almost certainly contained the earliest form of our present book of Deuteronomy (see Introduction to Deuteronomy), as subsequent references in this and the following chapter will show. **11–13:** The consternation of *the king* and his reference to *the wrath of the LORD* suggest that the scroll contained such words as those of Dt.6.13–15 and 28.15–24. To *inquire of the LORD* in an emergency by consulting a prophet was common practice (see 1 Kg.22.5–12 n.). **16–17:** These words seem so threatening that they may have been rewritten by the second Deuteronomist after the fall of Jerusalem. **20:** This sounds original; Huldah could not have known that Josiah would die a violent death on the field of battle.

23.1–30: The reforms and death of Josiah. 1–3: The adoption of this program not only meant a religious reform, but also a declaration of political independence from Assyria, which was now in its last days as a great power (Nineveh fell in 612 B.C.). **2:** *The book of the covenant*, contrast 22.8,11. The idea of *the covenant*, or agreement, between the LORD and his people is

book of the covenant which had been found in the house of the LORD. [3] And the king stood by the pillar and made a covenant before the LORD, to walk after the LORD and to keep his commandments and his testimonies and his statutes, with all his heart and all his soul, to perform the words of this covenant that were written in this book; and all the people joined in the covenant.

4 And the king commanded Hilki'ah, the high priest, and the priests of the second order, and the keepers of the threshold, to bring out of the temple of the LORD all the vessels made for Ba'al, for Ashe'rah, and for all the host of heaven; he burned them outside Jerusalem in the fields of the Kidron, and carried their ashes to Bethel. [5] And he deposed the idolatrous priests whom the kings of Judah had ordained to burn incense in the high places at the cities of Judah and round about Jerusalem; those also who burned incense to Ba'al, to the sun, and the moon, and the constellations, and all the host of the heavens. [6] And he brought out the Ashe'rah from the house of the LORD, outside Jerusalem, to the brook Kidron, and burned it at the brook Kidron, and beat it to dust and cast the dust of it upon the graves of the common people. [7] And he broke down the houses of the male cult prostitutes which were in the house of the LORD, where the women wove hangings for the Ashe'rah. [8] And he brought all the priests out of the cities of Judah, and defiled the high places where the priests had burned incense, from Geba to Beer-sheba; and he broke down the high places of the gates that were at the entrance of the gate of Joshua the governor of the city, which were on one's left at the gate of the city. [9] However, the priests of the high

places did not come up to the altar of the LORD in Jerusalem, but they ate unleavened bread among their brethren. [10] And he defiled To'pheth, which is in the valley of the sons of Hinnom, that no one might burn his son or his daughter as an offering to Molech. [11] And he removed the horses that the kings of Judah had dedicated to the sun, at the entrance to the house of the LORD, by the chamber of Nathan-melech the chamberlain, which was in the precincts;[h] and he burned the chariots of the sun with fire.[12] And the altars on the roof of the upper chamber of Ahaz, which the kings of Judah had made, and the altars which Manas'seh had made in the two courts of the house of the LORD, he pulled down and broke in pieces,[i] and cast the dust of them into the brook Kidron. [13] And the king defiled the high places that were east of Jerusalem, to the south of the mount of corruption, which Solomon the king of Israel had built for Ash'toreth the abomination of the Sido'nians, and for Chemosh the abomination of Moab, and for Milcom the abomination of the Ammonites. [14] And he broke in pieces the pillars, and cut down the Ashe'rim, and filled their places with the bones of men.

15 Moreover the altar at Bethel, the high place erected by Jerobo'am the son of Nebat, who made Israel to sin, that altar with the high place he pulled down and he broke in pieces its stones,[j] crushing them to dust; also he burned the Ashe'rah. [16] And as Josi'ah turned, he saw the tombs there on the mount; and he sent and took the bones out of the tombs, and burned them upon the altar, and defiled it, according to the word of the LORD which the

h The meaning of the Hebrew word is uncertain
i Heb *pieces from there*
j Gk: Heb *he burned the high place*

---

one of the most important elements in Old Testament religion (see Ex.24.7–8; Dt.29.1; Jer. 11.3–4; 30.22 and many other similar passages). *The pillar*, see 11.14; 1 Kg.7.15–22 n. **4–14:** Josiah tried valiantly to get rid of the pagan cults in accordance with Dt.15.19–18.22. He even attempted to abolish all worship of the LORD outside of the temple in Jerusalem (at *the high places*, .v. 8, compare Dt. ch. 12). The consequently unemployed local priests (called Levites in Deuteronomy) were supposed to join the temple staff in Jerusalem (Dt.18.6–8), but this

man of God proclaimed, who had predicted these things. ¹⁷ Then he said, "What is yonder monument that I see?" And the men of the city told him, "It is the tomb of the man of God who came from Judah and predicted these things which you have done against the altar at Bethel." ¹⁸ And he said, "Let him be; let no man move his bones." So they let his bones alone, with the bones of the prophet who came out of Sama′ria. ¹⁹ And all the shrines also of the high places that were in the cities of Sama′ria, which kings of Israel had made, provoking the LORD to anger, Josi′ah removed; he did to them according to all that he had done at Bethel. ²⁰ And he slew all the priests of the high places who were there, upon the altars, and burned the bones of men upon them. Then he returned to Jerusalem.

21 And the king commanded all the people, "Keep the passover to the LORD your God, as it is written in this book of the covenant." ²² For no such passover had been kept since the days of the judges who judged Israel, or during all the days of the kings of Israel or of the kings of Judah; ²³ but in the eighteenth year of King Josi′ah this passover was kept to the LORD in Jerusalem.

24 Moreover Josi′ah put away the mediums and the wizards and the teraphim and the idols and all the abominations that were seen in the land of Judah and in Jerusalem, that he might establish the words of the law which were written in the book that Hilki′ah

the priest found in the house of the LORD. ²⁵ Before him there was no king like him, who turned to the LORD with all his heart and with all his soul and with all his might, according to all the law of Moses; nor did any like him arise after him.

26 Still the LORD did not turn from the fierceness of his great wrath, by which his anger was kindled against Judah, because of all the provocations with which Manas′seh had provoked him. ²⁷ And the LORD said, "I will remove Judah also out of my sight, as I have removed Israel, and I will cast off this city which I have chosen, Jerusalem, and the house of which I said, My name shall be there."

28 Now the rest of the acts of Josi′ah, and all that he did, are they not written in the Book of the Chronicles of the Kings of Judah? ²⁹ In his days Pharaoh Neco king of Egypt went up to the king of Assyria to the river Euphra′tes. King Josi′ah went to meet him; and Pharaoh Neco slew him at Megid′do, when he saw him. ³⁰ And his servants carried him dead in a chariot from Megid′do, and brought him to Jerusalem, and buried him in his own tomb. And the people of the land took Jeho′ahaz the son of Josi′ah, and anointed him, and made him king in his father's stead.

31 Jeho′ahaz was twenty-three years old when he began to reign, and he reigned three months in Jerusalem. His mother's name was Hamu′tal the daughter of Jeremiah of Libnah. ³² And he did what was evil in the

---

arrangement did not succeed (v. 9). **17–18:** See 1 Kg. ch. 13 (and notes there). *Samaria* is probably an error for Bethel (compare 1 Kg.13.11,31). **21–23:** The great *passover,* the climax of the reform. **24–25:** Opinion differs as to whether the first Deuteronomist ended his account just before or just after the death of Josiah in 609 B.C. The last clause of v. 25 is from the second Deuteronomist. Compare the evaluation of Hezekiah in 18.5. **26–27:** These verses are definitely from the second Deuteronomist (see 21.10–15 n.). **28–30:** If the first Deuteronomist ended his work with the death of Josiah (609 B.C.), these verses are his. Compare the fuller account of Josiah's death in 2 Chr.35.20–24. Nineveh had fallen in 612 before the Medes and Chaldeans, but Assyria was still fighting; Egypt was the ally of Assyria, hence *Pharaoh Neco king of Egypt went up to the king of Assyria* to help him. Josiah, now in revolt against Assyria, felt it necessary to oppose Neco. Josiah lost his life, and Judah became a vassal of Egypt.

23.31–37: The reign of Jehoahaz and the beginning of the reign of Jehoiakim. The people's choice for king (v. 30) was *Jehoahaz* or Shallum (1 Chr.3.15; Jer.22.11), a younger son of Josiah;

sight of the LORD, according to all that his fathers had done. [33] And Pharaoh Neco put him in bonds at Riblah in the land of Hamath, that he might not reign in Jerusalem, and laid upon the land a tribute of a hundred talents of silver and a talent of gold. [34] And Pharaoh Neco made Eli'akim the son of Josi'ah king in the place of Josi'ah his father, and changed his name to Jehoi'akim. But he took Jeho'ahaz away; and he came to Egypt, and died there. [35] And Jehoi'akim gave the silver and the gold to Pharaoh, but he taxed the land to give the money according to the command of Pharaoh. He exacted the silver and the gold of the people of the land, from every one according to his assessment, to give it to Pharaoh Neco.

36 Jehoi'akim was twenty-five years old when he began to reign, and he reigned eleven years in Jerusalem. His mother's name was Zebi'dah the daughter of Pedai'ah of Rumah. [37] And he did what was evil in the sight of the LORD, according to all that his fathers had done.

24 In his days Nebuchadnez'zar king of Babylon came up, and Jehoi'akim became his servant three years; then he turned and rebelled against him. [2] And the LORD sent against him bands of the Chalde'ans, and bands of the Syrians, and bands of the Moabites, and bands of the Ammonites, and sent them against Judah to destroy it, according to the word of the LORD which he spoke by his servants the prophets. [3] Surely this came

upon Judah at the command of the LORD, to remove them out of his sight, for the sins of Manas'seh, according to all that he had done, [4] and also for the innocent blood that he had shed; for he filled Jerusalem with innocent blood, and the LORD would not pardon. [5] Now the rest of the deeds of Jehoi'akim, and all that he did, are they not written in the Book of the Chronicles of the Kings of Judah? [6] So Jehoi'akim slept with his fathers, and Jehoi'achin his son reigned in his stead. [7] And the king of Egypt did not come again out of his land, for the king of Babylon had taken all that belonged to the king of Egypt from the Brook of Egypt to the river Euphra'tes.

8 Jehoi'achin was eighteen years old when he became king, and he reigned three months in Jerusalem. His mother's name was Nehush'ta the daughter of Elna'than of Jerusalem. [9] And he did what was evil in the sight of the LORD, according to all that his father had done.

10 At that time the servants of Nebuchadnez'zar king of Babylon came up to Jerusalem, and the city was besieged. [11] And Nebuchadnez'zar king of Babylon came to the city, while his servants were besieging it; [12] and Jehoi'achin the king of Judah gave himself up to the king of Babylon, himself, and his mother, and his servants, and his princes, and his palace officials. The king of Babylon took him prisoner in the eighth year of his reign, [13] and carried off all the treasures of the house of the LORD, and the

---

but *Pharaoh Neco* was now master. He deposed *Jehoahaz*, levied heavy *tribute*, and made *Eliakim*, an older son, king, changing his name to *Jehoiakim* as a symbol of his vassalage.

24.1–17: The first fall of Jerusalem and the first deportation (reigns of Jehoiakim and Jehoiachin). 1–7: Verse 7 should really come first. The Chaldeans (the Neo-Babylonians) defeated the Assyrians and Egyptians at the battle of Carchemish in 605 B.C. (Jer.46.2). This event removed Egyptian control of Judah, which thereupon came under the dominance of the Chaldeans, but revolted after *three years* (v. 1). Verses 3–4 are the comment of the second Deuteronomist. **8:** Jehoiakim died (598 B.C.) before he could be punished, and his young son Jehoiachin (also called Jeconiah, 1 Chr.3.16, and Coniah, Jer.22.24) took the tottering throne. **10–17:** Jehoiachin almost immediately surrendered to *Nebuchadnezzar* (more correct form, Nebuchadrezzar, Jer.21.2 and frequently in Jeremiah), on March 16, 597 B.C., in the seventh (Jer.52.28) year of Nebuchadrezzar, as related in the Babylonian records. According to v. 14, *ten thousand captives* were deported; according to v. 16, eight thousand; Jer.52.28 says 3,023, which perhaps does not count women and children, or perhaps it is a more accurate figure. Tablets found in Babylon

treasures of the king's house, and cut in pieces all the vessels of gold in the temple of the LORD, which Solomon king of Israel had made, as the LORD had foretold. ¹⁴ He carried away all Jerusalem, and all the princes, and all the mighty men of valor, ten thousand captives, and all the craftsmen and the smiths; none remained, except the poorest people of the land. ¹⁵ And he carried away Jehoi'achin to Babylon; the king's mother, the king's wives, his officials, and the chief men of the land, he took into captivity from Jerusalem to Babylon. ¹⁶ And the king of Babylon brought captive to Babylon all the men of valor, seven thousand, and the craftsmen and the smiths, one thousand, all of them strong and fit for war. ¹⁷ And the king of Babylon made Mattani'ah, Jehoi'achin's uncle, king in his stead, and changed his name to Zedeki'ah.

18 Zedeki'ah was twenty-one years old when he became king, and he reigned eleven years in Jerusalem. His mother's name was Hamu'tal the daughter of Jeremiah of Libnah. ¹⁹ And he did what was evil in the sight of the LORD, according to all that Jehoi'akim had done. ²⁰ For because of the anger of the LORD it came to the point in Jerusalem and Judah that he cast them out from his presence.

And Zedeki'ah rebelled against the king of Babylon. ¹ And in the ninth year of his reign, in the tenth month, on the tenth day of the month, Nebuchadnez'zar king of Babylon came with all his army against

Jerusalem, and laid siege to it; and they built siegeworks against it round about. ² So the city was besieged till the eleventh year of King Zedeki'ah. ³ On the ninth day of the fourth month the famine was so severe in the city that there was no food for the people of the land. ⁴ Then a breach was made in the city; the king with all the men of war fled^k by night by the way of the gate between the two walls, by the king's garden, though the Chalde'ans were around the city. And they went in the direction of the Arabah. ⁵ But the army of the Chalde'ans pursued the king, and overtook him in the plains of Jericho; and all his army was scattered from him. ⁶ Then they captured the king, and brought him up to the king of Babylon at Riblah, who passed sentence upon him. ⁷ They slew the sons of Zedeki'ah before his eyes, and put out the eyes of Zedeki'ah, and bound him in fetters, and took him to Babylon.

8 In the fifth month, on the seventh day of the month—which was the nineteenth year of King Nebuchadnez'zar, king of Babylon—Nebu'zarad'an, the captain of the bodyguard, a servant of the king of Babylon, came to Jerusalem. ⁹ And he burned the house of the LORD, and the king's house and all the houses of Jerusalem; every great house he burned down. ¹⁰ And all the army of the Chalde'ans, who were with the captain of the guard, broke down the walls around Jerusalem. ¹¹ And

k Gk Compare Jer 39.4; 52.7: Heb lacks *the king* and *fled*

make reference to Jehoiachin and five sons (compare 1 Chr.3.17–18). His uncle *Mattaniah*, another son of Josiah (1 Chr.3.15), was made *king in his stead*, and given a new name, *Zedekiah*, as a token of vassalage (see 23.31–37 n.).

24.18–25.21: The reign of Zedekiah; second fall of Jerusalem and its destruction; the second deportation. This section is repeated in Jer. ch. 52 with certain changes; 25.1–12 is found in Jer.39.1–10 with changes; compare the parallel in 2 Chr.36.11–21. **24.18:** More information about Zedekiah is found in Jer. chs. 21; 24; 27; 29; 32; 37; 38; Ezek.17.11–21. **24.20b–25.7:** The sad story hastens to its woeful conclusion. In spite of his oath of allegiance (2 Chr.36.13; Ezek.17.13), *Zedekiah* began to plot with Egypt and other nations against the Chaldeans (Jer. 27.3–7; Ezek.17.15), and *rebelled against the king of Babylon*. Jerusalem was besieged, and after terrible privation (25.3; Dt.28.52–57; Lam.4.10), fell in *the eleventh year of King Zedekiah*, 587 or 586 B.C. The king was tortured and carried *to Babylon*, where he died (Jer.52.11). **25.8–12:** The temple, the palace, *and all the houses of Jerusalem* were *burned*, and the walls were broken down. A second deportation was carried out (see 24.10–17 n.), the number taken being only 832,

the rest of the people who were left in the city and the deserters who had deserted to the king of Babylon, together with the rest of the multitude, Nebu'zarad'an the captain of the guard carried into exile. [12] But the captain of the guard left some of the poorest of the land to be vinedressers and plowmen.

13 And the pillars of bronze that were in the house of the LORD, and the stands and the bronze sea that were in the house of the LORD, the Chalde'ans broke in pieces, and carried the bronze to Babylon. [14] And they took away the pots, and the shovels, and the snuffers, and the dishes for incense and all the vessels of bronze used in the temple service, [15] the firepans also, and the bowls. What was of gold the captain of the guard took away as gold, and what was of silver, as silver. [16] As for the two pillars, the one sea, and the stands, which Solomon had made for the house of the LORD, the bronze of all these vessels was beyond weight. [17] The height of the one pillar was eighteen cubits, and upon it was a capital of bronze; the height of the capital was three cubits; a network and pomegranates, all of bronze, were upon the capital round about. And the second pillar had the like, with the network.

18 And the captain of the guard took Serai'ah the chief priest, and Zephani'ah the second priest, and the three keepers of the threshold; [19] and from the city he took an officer who had been in command of the men of war, and five men of the king's council who were found in the city; and the secretary of the commander of the army who mustered the people of the land; and sixty men of the people of the land who were found in the city. [20] And Nebu'zarad'an the captain of the guard took them, and brought them to the king of Babylon at Riblah. [21] And the king of Babylon smote them, and put them to death at Riblah in the land of Hamath. So Judah was taken into exile out of its land.

22 And over the people who remained in the land of Judah, whom Nebuchadnez'zar king of Babylon had left, he appointed Gedali'ah the son of Ahi'kam, son of Shaphan, governor. [23] Now when all the captains of the forces in the open country[l] and their men heard that the king of Babylon had appointed Gedali'ah governor, they came with their men to Gedali'ah at Mizpah, namely, Ish'mael the son of Nethani'ah, and Joha'nan the son of Kare'ah, and Serai'ah the son of Tanhu'meth the Netoph'athite, and Jaazani'ah the son of the Ma-ac'athite. [24] And Gedali'ah swore to them and their men, saying, "Do not be afraid because of the Chalde'an officials; dwell in the land, and serve the king of Babylon, and it shall be well with you." [25] But in the seventh month, Ish'mael the son of Nethani'ah, son of Eli'shama, of the royal family, came with ten men, and attacked and killed Gedali'ah and the Jews and the Chalde'ans who were with him at

l With Jer 40.7: Heb lacks *in the open country*

according to Jer.52.29. **13–17:** All the valuable equipment of the temple was carried to Babylon. **18–21:** All remaining leaders were executed. **22–26:** This section does not appear in Jer. ch. 52; there is, however, an expanded account in Jer.40.7–41.18. In Jer.40.6 and chs. 42–43, the prophet is brought into the story. It is a cause for amazement that Jeremiah is not mentioned even once in 2 Kings, whereas the book of Jeremiah contains a wealth of additional information about the last days of Judah.

25.22–26: The governorship of Gedaliah. 22–24: The abolition of the monarchy and the appointment of *Gedaliah* as a native governor under Chaldean control should have meant peace and stability for Judah. Gedaliah's father, *Ahikam*, had been a trusted adviser of Josiah (22.12) and a friend of Jeremiah (Jer.26.24). *Gedaliah* himself was well disposed toward the prophet (Jer.39.14; 40.6), and enjoyed the confidence of his fellow citizens (Jer.40.11–12). **25–26:** The dastardly assassination of this good man by *Ishmael*, a member of the deposed *royal family*, brought about utter chaos and ruin (Jer.40.13–41.18); see the evaluation of the situation by the Deuteronomic editor of the book of Jeremiah in Jer.44.1–14.

Mizpah. ²⁶ Then all the people, both small and great, and the captains of the forces arose, and went to Egypt; for they were afraid of the Chalde′ans.

27 And in the thirty-seventh year of the exile of Jehoi′achin king of Judah, in the twelfth month, on the twenty-seventh day of the month, Evil-mero′dach king of Babylon, in the year that he began to reign, graciously freed Jehoi′achin king of Judah from prison; ²⁸ and he spoke kindly to him, and gave him a seat above the seats of the kings who were with him in Babylon. ²⁹ So Jehoi′achin put off his prison garments. And every day of his life he dined regularly at the king's table; ³⁰ and for his allowance, a regular allowance was given him by the king, every day a portion, as long as he lived.

25.27–30: Jehoiachin in exile. Also found in Jer.52.31–34. From about 560 B.C., shortly before he finished the book in about 550 (see Introduction to 1 Kings), the second Deuteronomist received this report that Jehoiachin was still safe, and was enjoying favored treatment by *the king of Babylon.* The report has been partially confirmed by archaeological researches. The writer may have used this information to end his book with a note of modest hope, as though to say (in spite of 24.9): the Davidic dynasty has not been snuffed out.

CHRONICLES

In the Hebrew Bible 1 and 2 Chronicles were originally a single book, as were 1 and 2 Samuel and also 1 and 2 Kings (see p. 330). The two books of Chronicles are now usually considered to have been part of a larger work which included the books of Ezra and Nehemiah (see Introduction to Ezra).

The purpose of 1 and 2 Chronicles, like that of 1 and 2 Kings, is theological and idealistic. There is practically no attempt to present history as we understand the word. The Chronicler wishes to advocate a certain pattern of religious life for his own day, and to indicate what a proper kingdom of his people under God would be like. He does this by describing the reigns of David and Solomon in particular, not as they actually had been, but as they ought to have been. David, especially, is highly idealized, and becomes the real founder of the temple and its ritual. A primary interest of the Chronicler is in the staff of the post-exilic temple, the organization of the priests, Levites, musicians, custodians, and others. Because of his manifest concern with Levites and singers in particular, it has been conjectured that the Chronicler was both a Levite and a singer.

The sources used by the Chronicler are mainly the books of Samuel and Kings, which are often quoted verbatim though never mentioned by name. Likewise utilized are parts of Genesis, Exodus, Numbers, Joshua, and Ruth. In addition, about sixteen titles of other sources are mentioned, such as "the Book of the Kings of Israel and Judah," "the Chronicles of Samuel the Seer," "the Chronicles of Nathan the Prophet," "the Commentary on the Book of Kings," and the like. It is probable that all of these titles refer to parts of a single book, now lost. Though in a few instances the Chronicler seems to have had better information than that incorporated in other canonical books, most of the changes and additions came from the writer's strong sense of what ought to have been as a pattern for conduct in his own time and in the future.

If Ezra-Nehemiah are a part of the Chronicler's work, our books cannot be dated before about 400 B.C. Some scholars date them as late as 250 B.C., well into the Greek period. Since the evidences of Greek influence are few, it is well to adopt an intermediate date of 350–300 B.C.

Chapters 1–9 of 1 Chronicles present a series of genealogies. The Chronicler, or the final editor of his book, wished to make it clear that he was dealing with the true Chosen People. Chapters 10–29 are the Chronicler's account of David as a great monarch and the founder of the temple and its ritual.

ADAM, SETH, ENOSH; ² KENAN, Ma-hal'alel, Jared; ³ Enoch, Methu'selah, Lamech; ⁴ Noah, Shem, Ham, and Japheth.

5 The sons of Japheth: Gomer, Magog, Madai, Javan, Tubal, Meshech, and Tiras. ⁶ The sons of Gomer: Ash'kenaz, Diphath, and Togar'mah. ⁷ The sons of Javan: Eli'-shah, Tarshish, Kittim, and Ro'danim.

8 The sons of Ham: Cush, Egypt, Put, and Canaan. ⁹ The sons of Cush: Seba, Hav'ilah, Sabta, Ra'ama, and Sab'teca. The sons of Ra'amah: Sheba and Dedan. ¹⁰ Cush was the father of Nimrod; he began to be a mighty one in the earth.

11 Egypt was the father of Ludim,

1.1–54: The place of Abraham and his descendants among the nations of mankind. 1–4: Summary of Gen. ch. 5. 5–7: The sons of Japheth, or the Japhethites, were in general the ancestors of those people whom today we call Indo-Europeans; for example, *Javan* (lit., Ionia) refers to the Greeks (compare Gen.10.2–4). 8–16: Today the term "Hamitic" is restricted largely to the peoples and languages of ancient Egypt; the Canaanites (*Canaan*) and *the Amorites* are now classified as Semites, and the Hittites (*Heth*) are sometimes classified among the Indo-Europeans. *Cush* sometimes refers to Ethiopia (v. 8), sometimes to a location in Mesopotamia (v. 10).

An'amim, Le'habim, Naph-tu'him, 12 Pathru'sim, Caslu'him (whence came the Philis'tines), and Caph'-torim.

13 Canaan was the father of Sidon his first-born, and Heth, 14 and the Jeb'usites, the Am'orites, the Gir'-gashites, 15 the Hivites, the Arkites, the Sinites, 16 the Ar'vadites, the Zem'arites, and the Ha'mathites.

17 The sons of Shem: Elam, As-shur, Arpach'shad, Lud, Aram, Uz, Hul, Gether, and Meshech. 18 Ar-pach'shad was the father of Shelah; and Shelah was the father of Eber. 19 To Eber were born two sons: the name of the one was Peleg (for in his days the earth was divided), and the name of his brother Joktan. 20 Joktan was the father of Almo'dad, Sheleph, Hazarma'veth, Jerah, 21 Hador'am, Uzal, Diklah, 22 Ebal, Abim'a-el, Sheba, 23 Ophir, Hav'ilah, and Jobab; all these were the sons of Joktan.

24 Shem, Arpach'shad, Shelah; 25 Eber, Peleg, Re'u; 26 Serug, Nahor, Terah; 27 Abram, that is, Abraham.

28 The sons of Abraham: Isaac and Ish'mael. 29 These are their gene-alogies: the first-born of Ish'mael, Ne-ba'ioth; and Kedar, Adbeel, Mibsam, 30 Mishma, Dumah, Massa, Hadad, Tema, 31 Jetur, Naphish, and Ked'-emah. These are the sons of Ish'mael. 32 The sons of Ketu'rah, Abraham's concubine: she bore Zimran, Jokshan, Medan, Mid'ian, Ishbak, and Shu'ah. The sons of Jokshan: Sheba and Dedan. 33 The sons of Mid'ian: Ephah, Epher, Hanoch, Abida, and Elda'ah. All these were the descend-ants of Ketu'rah.

34 Abraham was the father of Isaac. The sons of Isaac: Esau and Israel. 35 The sons of Esau: Eli'phaz, Reu'el, Je'ush, Jalam, and Korah. 36 The sons of Eli'phaz: Teman, Omar, Zephi, Gatam, Kenaz, Timna, and Am'alek. 37 The sons of Reu'el: Nahath, Zerah, Shammah, and Mizzah.

38 The sons of Se'ir: Lotan, Sho-bal, Zib'eon, Anah, Dishon, Ezer, and Dishan. 39 The sons of Lotan: Hori and Homam; and Lotan's sister was Timna. 40 The sons of Shobal: Al'ian, Man'ahath, Ebal, Shephi, and Onam. The sons of Zib'eon: Ai'ah and Anah. 41 The sons of Anah: Dishon. The sons of Dishon: Hamran, Eshban, Ithran, and Cheran. 42 The sons of Ezer: Bilhan, Za'avan, and Ja'akan. The sons of Dishan: Uz and Aran.

43 These are the kings who reigned in the land of Edom before any king reigned over the Israelites: Bela the son of Be'or, the name of whose city was Din'habah. 44 When Bela died, Jobab the son of Zerah of Bozrah reigned in his stead. 45 When Jobab died, Husham of the land of the Te'manites reigned in his stead. 46 When Husham died, Hadad the son of Bedad, who defeated Mid'ian in the country of Moab, reigned in his stead; and the name of his city was Avith. 47 When Hadad died, Samlah of Mas-re'kah reigned in his stead. 48 When Samlah died, Sha'ul of Reho'both on the Euphra'tes reigned in his stead. 49 When Sha'ul died, Ba'al-ha'nan, the son of Achbor, reigned in his stead. 50 When Ba'al-ha'nan died, Hadad reigned in his stead; and the name of his city was Pa'i, and his wife's name Mehet'abel the daughter of Matred,

---

Compare Gen.10.6–20. **17–27**: *The sons of Shem*, or the Semites. The Hebrews (*Eber*) belonged to this group, and from it emerged *Abram* or *Abraham*. Such modern terms as "Hamitic" and "Semitic" have linguistic, rather than racial, connotations. Ancient classifications (such as *sons of Shem*) were based more on considerations of geography and cultural (not racial) affinity. Verses 17–23 are condensed from Gen.10.21–31, vv. 24–27 from Gen.11.10–26. **28–33**: From *Abraham* sprang both *Isaac*, the progenitor of the Edomites and Israelites (v. 34), and *Ishmael*, the progenitor of the Arabs (compare Gen.25.1–4,12–18). **34–37**: The Chronicler does not use the personal name Jacob at all, but only the community term, *Israel*. *Esau* (Edom) is given special attention as the brother of *Israel*. **38–42**: *Seir* is another name for Edom (Gen.36.8, 20–30). **43–54**: *The kings . . . of Edom*, compare Gen.36.31–43.

the daughter of Me′zahab. ⁵¹ And Hadad died.

The chiefs of Edom were: chiefs Timna, Al′iah, Jetheth, ⁵² Oholiba′-mah, Elah, Pinon, ⁵³ Kenaz, Teman, Mibzar, ⁵⁴ Mag′di-el, and Iram; these are the chiefs of Edom.

2 These are the sons of Israel: Reuben, Simeon, Levi, Judah, Is′sachar, Zeb′ulun, ² Dan, Joseph, Benjamin, Naph′tali, Gad, and Asher. ³ The sons of Judah: Er, Onan, and Shelah; these three Bath-shu′a the Canaanitess bore to him. Now Er, Judah's firstborn, was wicked in the sight of the LORD, and he slew him. ⁴ His daughter-in-law Tamar also bore him Perez and Zerah. Judah had five sons in all.

5 The sons of Perez: Hezron and Hamul. ⁶ The sons of Zerah: Zimri, Ethan, Heman, Calcol, and Dara, five in all. ⁷ The sons of Carmi: Achar, the troubler of Israel, who transgressed in the matter of the devoted thing; ⁸ and Ethan's son was Azari′ah.

9 The sons of Hezron, that were born to him: Jerah′meel, Ram, and Chelu′bai. ¹⁰ Ram was the father of Ammin′adab, and Ammin′adab was the father of Nahshon, prince of the sons of Judah. ¹¹ Nahshon was the father of Salma, Salma of Bo′az, ¹² Bo′az of Obed, Obed of Jesse. ¹³ Jesse was the father of Eli′ab his first-born, Abin′adab the second, Shim′ea the third, ¹⁴ Nethan′el the fourth, Raddai the fifth, ¹⁵ Ozem the sixth, David the seventh; ¹⁶ and their sisters were Zeru′iah and Ab′igail. The sons of Zeru′iah: Abi′shai, Jo′ab, and As′ahel, three. ¹⁷ Ab′igail bore Ama′sa, and the father of Ama′sa was Jether the Ish′maelite.

18 Caleb the son of Hezron had children by his wife Azu′bah, and by Jer′ioth; and these were her sons: Jesher, Shobab, and Ardon. ¹⁹ When Azu′bah died, Caleb married Ephrath, who bore him Hur. ²⁰ Hur was the father of Uri, and Uri was the father of Bez′alel.

21 Afterward Hezron went in to the daughter of Machir the father of Gilead, whom he married when he was sixty years old; and she bore him Segub; ²² and Segub was the father of Ja′ir, who had twenty-three cities in the land of Gilead. ²³ But Geshur and Aram took from them Havvoth-ja′ir, Kenath and its villages, sixty towns. All these were descendants of Machir, the father of Gilead. ²⁴ After the death of Hezron, Caleb went in to Eph′-rathah,ᵃ the wife of Hezron his father, and she bore him Ashhur, the father of Teko′a.

25 The sons of Jerah′meel, the firstborn of Hezron: Ram, his first-born, Bunah, Oren, Ozem, and Ahi′jah. ²⁶ Jerah′meel also had another wife, whose name was At′arah; she was the mother of Onam. ²⁷ The sons of Ram, the first-born of Jerah′meel: Ma′az, Jamin, and Eker. ²⁸ The sons of Onam: Sham′mai and Jada. The sons of Sham′mai: Nadab and Abi′shur. ²⁹ The name of Abi′shur's wife was Ab′ihail, and she bore him Ahban and Molid. ³⁰ The sons of Nadab: Seled and Ap′pa-im; and Seled died childless. ³¹ The sons of Ap′pa-im: Ishi. The sons of Ishi: Sheshan. The sons of Sheshan: Ahlai. ³² The sons of Jada, Sham′mai's brother: Jether and Jonathan; and Jether died childless. ³³ The sons of Jonathan: Peleth and Zaza. These were the descendants of Jerah′-meel. ³⁴ Now Sheshan had no sons, only daughters; but Sheshan had an Egyptian slave, whose name was Jarha. ³⁵ So Sheshan gave his daughter in marriage to Jarha his slave; and she bore him Attai. ³⁶ Attai was the father of Nathan and Nathan of Zabad. ³⁷ Zabad was the father of Ephlal, and Ephlal of Obed. ³⁸ Obed was the father of Jehu, and Jehu of Azari′ah. ³⁹ Azari′ah was the father of Helez, and Helez of Ele-a′sah. ⁴⁰ Ele-a′sah was the father of Sismai, and Sismai of Shallum. ⁴¹ Shallum was the father of Jeka-

ᵃ Gk Vg: Heb *in Caleb Ephrathah*

2.1–55: Descendants of Judah. The chief sources are Gen. chs. 35; 38; 46; Num. 1.7; 32.41–42; Jos. chs. 7; 14; 15; Ru. 4.18–22; 1 Sam. 27.10.

mi'ah, and Jekami'ah of Eli'shama.

42 The sons of Caleb the brother of Jerah'meel: Mare'shah[b] his firstborn, who was the father of Ziph. The sons of Mare'shah: Hebron.[c] 43 The sons of Hebron: Korah, Tap'puah, Rekem, and Shema. 44 Shema was the father of Raham, the father of Jor'ke-am; and Rekem was the father of Sham'mai. 45 The son of Sham'mai: Ma'on; and Ma'on was the father of Bethzur. 46 Ephah also, Caleb's concubine, bore Haran, Moza, and Gazez; and Haran was the father of Gazez. 47 The sons of Jah'dai: Regem, Jotham, Geshan, Pelet, Ephah, and Sha'aph. 48 Ma'acah, Caleb's concubine, bore Sheber and Tir'hanah. 49 She also bore Sha'aph the father of Madman'nah, Sheva the father of Machbe'nah and the father of Gib'e-a; and the daughter of Caleb was Achsah. 50 These were the descendants of Caleb.

The sons[d] of Hur the first-born of Eph'rathah: Shobal the father of Kir'iath-je'arim, 51 Salma, the father of Bethlehem, and Hareph the father of Beth-gader. 52 Shobal the father of Kir'iath-je'arim had other sons: Haro'eh, half of the Menu'-hoth. 53 And the families of Kir'iath-je'arim: the Ithrites, the Puthites, the Shu'mathites, and the Mish'ra-ites; from these came the Zo'rathites and the Esh'taolites. 54 The sons of Salma: Bethlehem, the Netoph'athites, At'roth-beth-jo'ab, and half of the Man'aha'thites, the Zorites. 55 The families also of the scribes that dwelt at Jabez: the Ti'rathites, the Shim'e-athites, and the Su'cathites. These are the Ken'ites who came from Hammath, the father of the house of Rechab.

3 These are the sons of David that were born to him in Hebron: the first-born Amnon, by Ahin'o-am the Jezreelitess; the second Daniel, by Ab'igail the Car'melitess, 2 the third Ab'salom, whose mother was Ma'acah, the daughter of Talmai, king of Geshur; the fourth Adoni'jah, whose mother was Haggith; 3 the fifth Shephati'ah, by Abi'tal; the sixth Ith'ream, by his wife Eglah; 4 six were born to him in Hebron, where he reigned for seven years and six months. And he reigned thirty-three years in Jerusalem. 5 These were born to him in Jerusalem: Shim'e-a, Shobab, Nathan, and Solomon, four by Bath-shu'a, the daughter of Am'mi-el; 6 then Ibhar, Eli'shama, Eliph'elet, 7 Nogah, Nepheg, Japhi'a, 8 Eli'shama, Eli'ada, and Eliph'elet, nine. 9 All these were David's sons, besides the sons of the concubines; and Tamar was their sister.

10 The descendants of Solomon: Rehobo'am, Abi'jah his son, Asa his son, Jehosh'aphat his son, 11 Joram his son, Ahazi'ah his son, Jo'ash his son, 12 Amazi'ah his son, Azari'ah his son, Jotham his son, 13 Ahaz his son, Hezeki'ah his son, Manas'seh his son, 14 Amon his son, Josi'ah his son. 15 The sons of Josi'ah: Joha'nan the first-born, the second Jehoi'akim, the third Zedeki'ah, the fourth Shallum. 16 The descendants of Jehoi'akim: Jeconi'ah his son, Zedeki'ah his son; 17 and the sons of Jeconi'ah, the captive: Sheal'tiel his son, 18 Malchi'ram, Pedai'ah, Shenaz'zar, Jekami'ah, Hosh'ama, and Nedabi'ah; 19 and the sons of Pedai'ah: Zerub'babel and Shim'e-i; and the sons of Zerub'babel: Meshul'lam and Hanani'ah, and Shelo'mith was their sister; 20 and Hashu'bah, Ohel, Berechi'ah, Hasadi'ah, Ju'shab-he'sed, five. 21 The sons of Hanani'ah: Pelati'ah and Jeshai'ah, his son[e] Rephai'ah, his son[e] Arnan, his son[e] Obadi'ah, his son[e] Shecani'ah. 22 The sons of Shecani'ah: Shemai'ah. And the sons of Shemai'ah: Hattush,

b Gk: Heb *Mesha*
c Heb *the father of Hebron*   d Gk Vg: Heb *son*
e Gk Compare Syr Vg: Heb *sons of*

3.1–24: The descendants of David are traced down to the Chronicler's own time. These were very important people, even though the dynasty of David had not been restored (compare 2 Sam.3.2–5; 5.13–16; 13.1). Non-biblical sources were also utilized.

Igal, Bari'ah, Neari'ah, and Shaphat, six. ²³ The sons of Neari'ah: Eli-o-e'-nai, Hizki'ah, and Azri'kam, three. ²⁴ The sons of Eli-o-e'nai: Hod'avi'ah, Eli'ashib, Pelai'ah, Akkub, Joha'nan, Delai'ah, and Ana'ni, seven.

4 The sons of Judah: Perez, Hezron, Carmi, Hur, and Shobal. ² Re-ai'-ah the son of Shobal was the father of Jahath, and Jahath was the father of Ahu'mai and Lahad. These were the families of the Zo'rathites. ³ These were the sons*f* of Etam: Jezreel, Ishma, and Idbash; and the name of their sister was Hazzelelpo'ni, ⁴ and Penu'el was the father of Gedor, and Ezer the father of Hushah. These were the sons of Hur, the first-born of Eph'rathah, the father of Bethlehem. ⁵ Ashhur, the father of Teko'a, had two wives, Helah and Na'arah; ⁶ Na'-arah bore him Ahuz'zam, Hepher, Te'meni, and Ha-ahash'tari. These were the sons of Na'arah. ⁷ The sons of Helah: Zereth, Izhar, and Ethnan. ⁸ Koz was the father of Anub, Zobe'-bah, and the families of Ahar'hel the son of Harum. ⁹ Jabez was more honorable than his brothers; and his mother called his name Jabez, saying, "Because I bore him in pain." ¹⁰ Jabez called on the God of Israel, saying, "Oh that thou wouldst bless me and enlarge my border, and that thy hand might be with me, and that thou wouldst keep me from harm so that it might not hurt me!" And God granted what he asked. ¹¹ Chelub, the brother of Shuhah, was the father of Mehir, who was the father of Eshton. ¹² Eshton was the father of Bethra'-pha, Pase'ah, and Tehin'nah the father of Irna'hash. These are the men of Recah. ¹³ The sons of Kenaz: Oth'-ni-el and Serai'ah; and the sons of Oth'ni-el: Hathath and Meo'nothai.*g* ¹⁴ Meo'nothai was the father of Ophrah; and Serai'ah was the father of Jo'ab the father of Ge-har'ashim,*h* so-

called because they were craftsmen. ¹⁵ The sons of Caleb the son of Jephun'neh: Iru, Elah, and Na'am; and the sons of Elah: Kenaz. ¹⁶ The sons of Jehal'lelel: Ziph, Ziphah, Tir'-i-a, and As'arel. ¹⁷ The sons of Ezrah: Jether, Mered, Epher, and Jalon. These are the sons of Bith'i-ah, the daughter of Pharaoh, whom Mered married;*i* and she conceived and bore*j* Miriam, Sham'mai, and Ishbah, the father of Eshtemo'a. ¹⁸ And his Jewish wife bore Jered the father of Gedor, Heber the father of Soco, and Jeku'thiel the father of Zano'ah. ¹⁹ The sons of the wife of Hodi'ah, the sister of Naham, were the fathers of Kei'lah the Garmite and Eshtemo'a the Ma-ac'athite. ²⁰ The sons of Shimon: Amnon, Rinnah, Ben-ha'-nan, and Tilon. The sons of Ishi: Zoheth and Ben-zo'heth. ²¹ The sons of Shelah the son of Judah: Er the father of Lecah, La'adah the father of Mare'shah, and the families of the house of linen workers at Beth-ashbe'a; ²² and Jokim, and the men of Co-ze'ba, and Jo'ash, and Saraph, who ruled in Moab and returned to Le-hem*k* (now the records*l* are ancient). ²³ These were the potters and inhabitants of Neta'im and Gede'rah; they dwelt there with the king for his work.

24 The sons of Simeon: Nem'uel, Jamin, Jarib, Zerah, Sha'ul; ²⁵ Shallum was his son, Mibsam his son, Mishma his son. ²⁶ The sons of Mishma: Ham'mu-el his son, Zac'cur his son, Shim'e-i his son. ²⁷ Shim'e-i had sixteen sons and six daughters; but his brothers had not many children, nor did all their family multiply like the men of Judah. ²⁸ They dwelt in

f Gk Compare Vg: Heb *father*
g Gk Vg: Heb lacks *Meonothai*
h That is *Valley of craftsmen*
i The clause: *These are . . . married* is transposed from verse 18
j Heb lacks *and bore*
k Vg Compare Gk: Heb *and Jashubi-lahem*
l Or *matters*

4.1–43: The descendants of Judah and Simeon. The writer takes a genealogical excursion into the early days of the tribes of Judah and Simeon (compare Jos. chs. 15 and 19). These two tribes were closely related (Gen.29.33,35), and Simeon was finally absorbed into Judah and lost its identity (note its absence in Dt. ch. 33).

Beer-sheba, Mola'dah, Ha'zar-shu'al, ²⁹ Bilhah, Ezem, Tolad, ³⁰ Bethu'el, Hormah, Ziklag, ³¹ Beth-mar'caboth, Ha'zar-su'sim, Beth-biri, and Shaara'im. These were their cities until David reigned. ³² And their villages were Etam, A'in, Rimmon, Tochen, and Ashan, five cities, ³³ along with all their villages which were round about these cities as far as Ba'al. These were their settlements, and they kept a genealogical record.

³⁴ Mesho'bab, Jamlech, Joshah the son of Amazi'ah, ³⁵ Jo'el, Jehu the son of Joshibi'ah, son of Serai'ah, son of As'i-el, ³⁶ Eli-o-e'nai, Ja-ako'-bah, Jeshohai'ah, Asai'ah, Ad'i-el, Jesim'iel, Benai'ah, ³⁷ Ziza the son of Shiphi, son of Allon, son of Jedai'-ah, son of Shimri, son of Shemai'ah — ³⁸ these mentioned by name were princes in their families, and their fathers' houses increased greatly. ³⁹ They journeyed to the entrance of Gedor, to the east side of the valley, to seek pasture for their flocks, ⁴⁰ where they found rich, good pasture, and the land was very broad, quiet, and peaceful; for the former inhabitants there belonged to Ham. ⁴¹ These, registered by name, came in the days of Hezeki'ah, king of Judah, and destroyed their tents and the Me-u'nim who were found there, and exterminated them to this day, and settled in their place, because there was pasture there for their flocks. ⁴² And some of them, five hundred men of the Simeonites, went to Mount Se'ir, having as their leaders Pelati'ah, Ne-ari'ah, Rephai'ah, and Uz'ziel, the sons of Ishi; ⁴³ and they destroyed the remnant of the Amal'-ekites that had escaped, and they have dwelt there to this day.

5 The sons of Reuben the first-born of Israel (for he was the first-born; but because he polluted his father's couch, his birthright was given to the sons of Joseph the son of Israel, so that he is not enrolled in the genealogy according to the birthright; ² though Judah became strong among his brothers and a prince was from him, yet the birthright belonged to Joseph), ³ the sons of Reuben, the first-born of Israel: Hanoch, Pallu, Hezron, and Carmi. ⁴ The sons of Jo'el: Shemai'ah his son, Gog his son, Shim'e-i his son, ⁵ Micah his son, Re-ai'ah his son, Ba'al his son, ⁶ Be-er'ah his son, whom Til'gath-pilne'ser king of Assyria carried away into exile; he was a chieftain of the Reubenites. ⁷ And his kinsmen by their families, when the genealogy of their generations was reckoned: the chief, Je-i'el, and Zechari'ah, ⁸ and Bela the son of Azaz, son of Shema, son of Jo'el, who dwelt in Aro'er, as far as Nebo and Ba'al-me'on. ⁹ He also dwelt to the east as far as the entrance of the desert this side of the Euphra'tes, because their cattle had multiplied in the land of Gilead. ¹⁰ And in the days of Saul they made war on the Hagrites, who fell by their hand; and they dwelt in their tents throughout all the region east of Gilead.

11 The sons of Gad dwelt over against them in the land of Bashan as far as Sal'ecah: ¹² Jo'el the chief, Shapham the second, Ja'nai, and Shaphat in Bashan. ¹³ And their kinsmen according to their fathers' houses: Michael, Meshul'lam, Sheba, Jo'rai, Jacan, Zi'a, and Eber, seven. ¹⁴ These were the sons of Ab'ihail the son of Huri, son of Jaro'ah, son of Gilead, son of Michael, son of Jeshish'ai, son of Jahdo, son of Buz; ¹⁵ Ahi the son of Ab'di-el, son of Guni, was chief in their fathers' houses; ¹⁶ and they dwelt in

---

5.1–26: **The descendants of Reuben, Gad, and the half-tribe of Manasseh,** the tribes located east of the Jordan. 1–10: *Reuben* was traditionally connected with *Judah* (Gen.29.32,35), but by remaining east of the Jordan lost power and influence (Gen.35.22; Dt.33.6). The Joseph tribes (*sons of Joseph*) became dominant (Gen.49.22–26; Dt.33.13–17), yet from *Judah* sprang *a prince*, David, the greatest figure of the past, and the prototype of the Messiah to come. 11–17: *Gad* was just north of Reuben and seems to have been stronger and more important

Gilead, in Bashan and in its towns, and in all the pasture lands of Sharon to their limits. [17] All of these were enrolled by genealogies in the days of Jotham king of Judah, and in the days of Jerobo'am king of Israel.

18 The Reubenites, the Gadites, and the half-tribe of Manas'seh had valiant men, who carried shield and sword, and drew the bow, expert in war, forty-four thousand seven hundred and sixty, ready for service. [19] They made war upon the Hagrites, Jetur, Naphish, and Nodab; [20] and when they received help against them, the Hagrites and all who were with them were given into their hands, for they cried to God in the battle, and he granted their entreaty because they trusted in him. [21] They carried off their livestock: fifty thousand of their camels, two hundred and fifty thousand sheep, two thousand asses, and a hundred thousand men alive. [22] For many fell slain, because the war was of God. And they dwelt in their place until the exile.

23 The members of the half-tribe of Manas'seh dwelt in the land; they were very numerous from Bashan to Ba'al-her'mon, Senir, and Mount Hermon. [24] These were the heads of their fathers' houses: Epher,[m] Ishi, Eli'el, Az'ri-el, Jeremiah, Hodavi'ah, and Jah'di-el, mighty warriors, famous men, heads of their fathers' houses. [25] But they transgressed against the God of their fathers, and played the harlot after the gods of the peoples of the land, whom God had destroyed before them. [26] So the God of Israel

stirred up the spirit of Pul king of Assyria, the spirit of Til'gath-pilne'ser king of Assyria, and he carried them away, namely, the Reubenites, the Gadites, and the half-tribe of Manas'-seh, and brought them to Halah, Habor, Hara, and the river Gozan, to this day.

6 [n] The sons of Levi: Gershom, Kohath, and Merar'i. [2] The sons of Kohath: Amram, Izhar, Hebron, and Uz'ziel. [3] The children of Amram: Aaron, Moses, and Miriam. The sons of Aaron: Nadab, Abi'hu, Elea'zar, and Ith'amar. [4] Elea'zar was the father of Phin'ehas, Phin'ehas of Abishu'a, [5] Abishu'a of Bukki, Bukki of Uzzi, [6] Uzzi of Zerahi'ah, Zerahi'ah of Merai'oth, [7] Merai'oth of Amari'ah, Amari'ah of Ahi'tub, [8] Ahi'tub of Zadok, Zadok of Ahim'a-az, [9] Ahim'-a-az of Azari'ah, Azari'ah of Joha'nan, [10] and Joha'nan of Azari'ah (it was he who served as priest in the house that Solomon built in Jerusalem). [11] Azari'ah was the father of Amari'ah, Amari'ah of Ahi'tub, [12] Ahi'tub of Zadok, Zadok of Shallum, [13] Shallum of Hilki'ah, Hilki'ah of Azari'ah, [14] Azari'ah of Serai'ah, Serai'ah of Jehoz'-adak; [15] and Jehoz'adak went into exile when the LORD sent Judah and Jerusalem into exile by the hand of Nebuchadnez'zar.

16[o] The sons of Levi: Gershom, Kohath, and Merar'i. [17] And these are the names of the sons of Gershom: Libni and Shim'e-i. [18] The sons of Kohath: Amram, Izhar, Hebron, and

m Gk Vg: Heb *and Epher*
n Ch 5.27 in Heb   *o* Ch 6.1 in Heb

(Dt.33.20–21). **18–22:** In this story of the wars of the Transjordanian tribes with their neighbors, we see the tendency to express the greatness of God's people in terms of military might, with figures somewhat exaggerated. **23–26:** To the north of Gad was the *half-tribe of Manasseh*, i.e. the part of Manasseh that remained east of the Jordan (Num.32.33–42). All these tribes were carried into exile by the Assyrians, according to the tradition utilized in these verses (compare 2 Kg.15.29).

   6.1–81: The lineage of the Levites. 1–5: The Levites were an ancient warlike tribe (Gen. 49.5–7) that became a priestly caste (Dt.33.8–10; Jg.17.9–13; 18.19). The line running through Zadok (v. 8; compare 2 Sam.8.17) produced the chief priests, which are here traced down to the Exile (compare Gen.46.11; Ex.6.18–19; Num.26.59–60). **16–48:** Other Levites, not of the privileged priestly family, performed auxiliary duties in the temple, such as singing (*the service of song*, v. 31). *David* is credited with instituting the musical service of the temple as it existed

Uz'ziel. 19 The sons of Merar'i: Mahli and Mushi. These are the families of the Levites according to their fathers. 20 Of Gershom: Libni his son, Jahath his son, Zimmah his son, 21 Jo'ah his son, Iddo his son, Zerah his son, Jeath'erai his son. 22 The sons of Kohath: Ammin'adab his son, Korah his son, Assir his son, 23 Elka'nah his son, Ebi'-asaph his son, Assir his son, 24 Tahath his son, Uri'el his son, Uzzi'ah his son, and Sha'ul his son. 25 The sons of Elka'-nah: Ama'sai and Ahi'moth, 26 Elka'-nah his son, Zophai his son, Nahath his son, 27 Eli'ab his son, Jero'ham his son, Elka'nah his son. 28 The sons of Samuel: Jo'el*p* his first-born, the second Abi'jah.*q* 29 The sons of Merar'i: Mahli, Libni his son, Shim'e-i his son, Uzzah his son, 30 Shim'e-a his son, Haggi'ah his son, and Asai'ah his son.

31 These are the men whom David put in charge of the service of song in the house of the LORD, after the ark rested there. 32 They ministered with song before the tabernacle of the tent of meeting, until Solomon had built the house of the LORD in Jerusalem; and they performed their service in due order. 33 These are the men who served and their sons. Of the sons of the Ko'hathites: Heman the singer the son of Jo'el, son of Samuel, 34 son of Elka'nah, son of Jero'ham, son of Eli'el, son of To'ah, 35 son of Zuph, son of Elka'nah, son of Mahath, son of Ama'sai, 36 son of Elka'nah, son of Jo'el, son of Azari'ah, son of Zephani'ah, 37 son of Tahath, son of Assir, son of Ebi'asaph, son of Korah, 38 son of Izhar, son of Kohath, son of Levi, son of Israel; 39 and his brother Asaph, who stood on his right hand, namely, Asaph the son of Berechi'ah, son of Shim'e-a, 40 son of Michael,

son of Ba-ase'iah, son of Malchi'jah, 41 son of Ethni, son of Zerah, son of Adai'ah, 42 son of Ethan, son of Zimmah, son of Shim'e-i, 43 son of Jahath, son of Gershom, son of Levi. 44 On the left hand were their brethren the sons of Merar'i: Ethan the son of Kishi, son of Abdi, son of Malluch, 45 son of Hashabi'ah, son of Amazi'ah, son of Hilki'ah, 46 son of Amzi, son of Bani, son of Shemer, 47 son of Mahli, son of Mushi, son of Merar'i, son of Levi; 48 and their brethren the Levites were appointed for all the service of the tabernacle of the house of God.

49 But Aaron and his sons made offerings upon the altar of burnt offering and upon the altar of incense for all the work of the most holy place, and to make atonement for Israel, according to all that Moses the servant of God had commanded. 50 These are the sons of Aaron: Elea'zar his son, Phin'ehas his son, Abishu'a his son, 51 Bukki his son, Uzzi his son, Zerahi'ah his son, 52 Merai'oth his son, Amari'ah his son, Ahi'tub his son, 53 Zadok his son, Ahim'a-az his son.

54 These are their dwelling places according to their settlements within their borders: to the sons of Aaron of the families of Ko'hathites, for theirs was the lot, 55 to them they gave Hebron in the land of Judah and its surrounding pasture lands, 56 but the fields of the city and its villages they gave to Caleb the son of Jephun'neh. 57 To the sons of Aaron they gave the cities of refuge: Hebron, Libnah with its pasture lands, Jattir, Eshtemo'a with its pasture lands, 58 Hilen with its pasture lands, Debir with its pasture lands, 59 Ashan with its pasture lands,

p Gk Syr Compare verse 33 and 1 Sam 8.2: Heb lacks *Joel*
q Heb *and Abijah*

---

in the Chronicler's own day, somewhat as Moses is credited with all the laws in Deuteronomy. Prominent family names associated with these singers were *Heman* (v. 33), *Korah* (v. 37), *Asaph* (v. 39), and *Ethan* (v. 44); see the titles to Pss. 73–83; 88–89. The Chronicler himself probably belonged to one of these groups. **49–53:** To be a priest in the Chronicler's time it was necessary to be a descendant of Aaron; to be a high priest, one had to be a descendant of Zadok. **54–81:** Territory allotted to Levitical clans before the Levites had become a priestly cast supported by other Israelites and thus needing no land (Num.26.62). The main source is Jos. ch. 21.

and Beth-she′mesh with its pasture lands; ⁶⁰ and from the tribe of Benjamin, Geba with its pasture lands, Al′emeth with its pasture lands, and An′athoth with its pasture lands. All their cities throughout their families were thirteen.

61 To the rest of the Ko′hathites were given by lot out of the family of the tribe, out of the half-tribe, the half of Manas′seh, ten cities. ⁶² To the Gershomites according to their families were allotted thirteen cities out of the tribes of Is′sachar, Asher, Naph′tali, and Manas′seh in Bashan. ⁶³ To the Merar′ites according to their families were allotted twelve cities out of the tribes of Reuben, Gad, and Zeb′ulun. ⁶⁴ So the people of Israel gave the Levites the cities with their pasture lands. ⁶⁵ They also gave them by lot out of the tribes of Judah, Simeon, and Benjamin these cities which are mentioned by name.

66 And some of the families of the sons of Kohath had cities of their territory out of the tribe of E′phraim. ⁶⁷ They were given the cities of refuge: Shechem with its pasture lands in the hill country of E′phraim, Gezer with its pasture lands, ⁶⁸ Jok′me-am with its pasture lands, Beth-hor′on with its pasture lands, ⁶⁹ Ai′jalon with its pasture lands, Gath-rim′mon with its pasture lands, ⁷⁰ and out of the half-tribe of Manas′seh, Aner with its pasture lands, and Bil′e-am with its pasture lands, for the rest of the families of the Ko′hathites.

71 To the Gershomites were given out of the half-tribe of Manas′seh: Golan in Bashan with its pasture lands and Ash′taroth with its pasture lands; ⁷² and out of the tribe of Is′sachar: Kedesh with its pasture lands, Dab′erath with its pasture lands, ⁷³ Ramoth with its pasture lands, and Anem with its pasture lands; ⁷⁴ out of the tribe of Asher: Mashal with its pasture lands, Abdon with its pasture lands, ⁷⁵ Hukok with its pasture lands, and Rehob with its pasture lands; ⁷⁶ and out of the tribe of Naph′tali: Kedesh in Galilee with its pasture lands, Ham′mon with its pasture lands, and Kiriatha′im with its pasture lands. ⁷⁷ To the rest of the Merar′ites were allotted out of the tribe of Zeb′ulun: Rim′mono with its pasture lands, Tabor with its pasture lands, ⁷⁸ and beyond the Jordan at Jericho, on the east side of the Jordan, out of the tribe of Reuben: Bezer in the steppe with its pasture lands, Jahzah with its pasture lands, ⁷⁹ Ked′emoth with its pasture lands, and Meph′a-ath with its pasture lands; ⁸⁰ and out of the tribe of Gad: Ramoth in Gilead with its pasture lands, Mahana′im with its pasture lands, ⁸¹ Heshbon with its pasture lands, and Jazer with its pasture lands.

7 The sonsʳ of Is′sachar: Tola, Pu′ah, Jashub, and Shimron, four. ² The sons of Tola: Uzzi, Rephai′ah, Je′ri-el, Jah′mai, Ibsam, and Shem′uel, heads of their fathers' houses, namely of Tola, mighty warriors of their generations, their number in the days of David being twenty-two thousand six hundred. ³ The sons of Uzzi: Izrahi′ah. And the sons of Izrahi′ah: Michael, Obadi′ah, Jo′el, and Isshi′ah, five, all of them chief men; ⁴ and along with them, by their generations, according to their fathers' houses, were units of the army for war, thirty-six thousand, for they had many wives and sons. ⁵ Their kinsmen belonging to all the families of Is′sachar were in all eighty-seven thousand mighty warriors, enrolled by genealogy.

6 The sons of Benjamin: Bela,

ʳ Syr Compare Vg: Heb *and to the sons*

7.1–40: **Descendants of Issachar, Benjamin, Naphtali, Ephraim, and Asher.** A swift genealogical glance at the northern tribes, which were perhaps of interest to the writer mainly because they served David (v. 2). 6: *Benjamin*, which appears again in the next chapter, may have been confused with Zebulun, which strangely fails to appear here in its proper place (compare Gen.46. 17–27; Num.26.23–50; much non-canonical material is also used).

Becher, and Jedi'a-el, three. ⁷ The sons of Bela: Ezbon, Uzzi, Uz'-ziel, Jer'imoth, and Iri, five, heads of fathers' houses, mighty warriors; and their enrollment by genealogies was twenty-two thousand and thirty-four. ⁸ The sons of Becher: Zemi'rah, Jo'-ash, Elie'zer, Eli-o-e'nai, Omri, Jer'-emoth, Abi'jah, An'athoth, and Al'-emeth. All these were the sons of Becher; ⁹ and their enrollment by genealogies, according to their generations, as heads of their fathers' houses, mighty warriors, was twenty thousand two hundred. ¹⁰ The sons of Jedi'a-el: Bilhan. And the sons of Bilhan: Je'ush, Benjamin, Ehud, Chena'anah, Zethan, Tarshish, and Ahish'ahar. ¹¹ All these were the sons of Jedi'a-el according to the heads of their fathers' houses, mighty warriors, seventeen thousand and two hundred, ready for service in war. ¹² And Shuppim and Huppim were the sons of Ir, Hushim the sons of Aher.

13 The sons of Naph'tali: Jah'zi-el, Guni, Jezer, and Shallum, the offspring of Bilhah.

14 The sons of Manas'seh: As'ri-el, whom his Aramean concubine bore; she bore Machir the father of Gilead. ¹⁵ And Machir took a wife for Huppim and for Shuppim. The name of his sister was Ma'acah. And the name of the second was Zeloph'ehad; and Zeloph'ehad had daughters. ¹⁶ And Ma'acah the wife of Machir bore a son, and she called his name Peresh; and the name of his brother was Sheresh; and his sons were Ulam and Rakem. ¹⁷ The sons of Ulam: Bedan. These were the sons of Gilead the son of Machir, son of Manas'seh. ¹⁸ And his sister Hammo'lecheth bore Ishhod, Abi-e'zer, and Mahlah. ¹⁹ The sons of Shemi'da were Ahi'an, Shechem, Likhi, and Ani'am.

20 The sons of E'phraim: Shuthe'-lah, and Bered his son, Tahath his son, Ele-a'dah his son, Tahath his son, ²¹ Zabad his son, Shuthe'lah his son, and Ezer and E'le-ad, whom the men of Gath who were born in the land slew, because they came down to raid their cattle. ²² And E'phraim their father mourned many days, and his brothers came to comfort him. ²³ And E'phraim went in to his wife, and she conceived and bore a son; and he called his name Beri'ah, because evil had befallen his house. ²⁴ His daughter was She'erah, who built both Lower and Upper Beth-hor'on, and Uz'-zen-she'erah. ²⁵ Rephah was his son, Resheph his son, Telah his son, Tahan his son, ²⁶ Ladan his son, Ammi'hud his son, Eli'shama his son, ²⁷ Nun his son, Joshua his son. ²⁸ Their possessions and settlements were Bethel and its towns, and eastward Na'aran, and westward Gezer and its towns, Shechem and its towns, and Ayyah and its towns; ²⁹ also along the borders of the Manas'sites, Beth-she'an and its towns, Ta'anach and its towns, Megid'do and its towns, Dor and its towns. In these dwelt the sons of Joseph the son of Israel.

30 The sons of Asher: Imnah, Ishvah, Ishvi, Beri'ah, and their sister Serah. ³¹ The sons of Beri'ah: Heber and Mal'chi-el, who was the father of Bir'zaith. ³² Heber was the father of Japhlet, Shomer, Hotham, and their sister Shu'a. ³³ The sons of Japhlet: Pasach, Bimhal, and Ashvath. These are the sons of Japhlet. ³⁴ The sons of Shemer his brother: Rohgah, Jehub'-bah, and Aram. ³⁵ The sons of Helem his brother: Zophah, Imna, Shelesh, and Amal. ³⁶ The sons of Zophah: Su'ah, Har'nepher, Shu'al, Beri, Imrah, ³⁷ Bezer, Hod, Shamma, Shilshah, Ithran, and Be-e'ra. ³⁸ The sons of Jether: Jephun'neh, Pispa, and Ara. ³⁹ The sons of Ulla: Arah, Han'niel, and Rizi'a. ⁴⁰ All of these were men of Asher, heads of fathers' houses, approved, mighty warriors, chief of the princes. Their number enrolled by genealogies, for service in war, was twenty-six thousand men.

8 Benjamin was the father of Bela his first-born, Ashbel the second, Ahar'ah the third, ² Nohah the fourth,

[504]

and Rapha the fifth. ³ And Bela had sons: Addar, Gera, Abi'hud, ⁴ Abishu'a, Na'aman, Aho'ah, ⁵ Gera, Shephu'phan, and Huram. ⁶ These are the sons of Ehud (they were heads of fathers' houses of the inhabitants of Geba, and they were carried into exile to Mana'hath): ⁷ Na'aman,ˢ Ahi'jah, and Gera, that is, Heglam,ᵗ who was the father of Uzza and Ahi'hud. ⁸ And Shahara'im had sons in the country of Moab after he had sent away Hushim and Ba'ara his wives. ⁹ He had sons by Hodesh his wife: Jobab, Zib'i-a, Mesha, Malcam, ¹⁰ Je'uz, Sachi'a, and Mirmah. These were his sons, heads of fathers' houses. ¹¹ He also had sons by Hushim: Abi'tub and Elpa'al. ¹² The sons of Elpa'al: Eber, Misham, and Shemed, who built Ono and Lod with its towns, ¹³ and Beri'ah and Shema (they were heads of fathers' houses of the inhabitants of Ai'jalon, who put to flight the inhabitants of Gath); ¹⁴ and Ahi'o, Shashak, and Jer'emoth. ¹⁵ Zebadi'ah, Arad, Eder, ¹⁶ Michael, Ishpah, and Joha were sons of Beri'ah. ¹⁷ Zebadi'ah, Meshul'lam, Hizki, Heber, ¹⁸ Ish'-merai, Izli'ah, and Jobab were the sons of Elpa'al. ¹⁹ Jakim, Zichri, Zabdi, ²⁰ Eli-e'nai, Zil'lethai, Eli'el, ²¹ Adai'ah, Berai'ah, and Shimrath were the sons of Shim'e-i. ²² Ishpan, Eber, Eli'el, ²³ Abdon, Zichri, Hanan, ²⁴ Hanani'ah, Elam, Anthothi'jah, ²⁵ Iphdei'ah, and Penu'el were the sons of Shashak. ²⁶ Sham'sherai, Shehari'ah, Athali'ah, ²⁷ Ja-areshi'ah, Eli'jah, and Zichri were the sons of Jero'ham. ²⁸ These were the heads of fathers' houses, according to their

generations, chief men. These dwelt in Jerusalem.

29 Je-i'elᵘ the father of Gibeon dwelt in Gibeon, and the name of his wife was Ma'acah. ³⁰ His first-born son: Abdon, then Zur, Kish, Ba'al, Nadab, ³¹ Gedor, Ahi'o, Zecher, ³² and Mikloth (he was the father of Shim'e-ah). Now these also dwelt opposite their kinsmen in Jerusalem, with their kinsmen. ³³ Ner was the father of Kish, Kish of Saul, Saul of Jonathan, Mal'chishu'a, Abin'adab, and Esh-ba'al; ³⁴ and the son of Jonathan was Mer'ib-ba'al; and Mer'ib-ba'al was the father of Micah. ³⁵ The sons of Micah: Pithon, Melech, Tare'a, and Ahaz. ³⁶ Ahaz was the father of Jeho'addah; and Jeho'addah was the father of Al'-emeth, Az'maveth, and Zimri; Zimri was the father of Moza. ³⁷ Moza was the father of Bin'e-a; Raphah was his son, Ele-a'sah his son, Azel his son. ³⁸ Azel had six sons, and these are their names: Azri'kam, Bo'cheru, Ish'mael, She-ari'ah, Obadi'ah, and Hanan. All these were the sons of Azel. ³⁹ The sons of Eshek his brother: Ulam his first-born, Je'ush the second, and Eliph'-elet the third. ⁴⁰ The sons of Ulam were men who were mighty warriors, bowmen, having many sons and grandsons, one hundred and fifty. All these were Benjaminites.

9 So all Israel was enrolled by genealogies; and these are written in the Book of the Kings of Israel. And Judah was taken into exile in Babylon because of their unfaithfulness. ² Now the first to dwell again in their

s Heb *and Naaman*
t Or *he carried them into exile*
u Compare 9.35: Heb lacks *Jeiel*

8.1–40: The descendants of Benjamin. *Benjamin* was given special treatment because *Jerusalem* (v. 28) belonged traditionally to this tribe (Jos.18.28), and perhaps because from it came *Saul* (v. 33), who, though disliked by the Chronicler (10.13–14), was nevertheless the first king of Israel and the predecessor of David. Verse 28 is usually taken to mean that there were numerous Benjaminites in Jerusalem in the Chronicler's own time. **33–34:** The names *Eshbaal* and *Merib-baal* are correctly transmitted (see 2 Sam.2.8 n. and 4.4 n.).

9.1–44: The genealogies of families in Jerusalem after the Exile. 1: *The Book of the Kings of Israel* is not to be confused with the canonical books of Kings (see Introduction). When the northern kingdom fell, the southern kingdom appropriated the name *Israel* (Mic.1.13–15; 2.7; 3.1,9–10). For a further comment on *their unfaithfulness*, see 2 Chr.36.11–21. **2–16:** These verses have an inexact parallel in Neh.11.3–19, though it is not claimed there that *people of . . .*

possessions in their cities were Israel, the priests, the Levites, and the temple servants. ³ And some of the people of Judah, Benjamin, E′phraim, and Manas′seh dwelt in Jerusalem: ⁴ Uthai the son of Ammi′hud, son of Omri, son of Imri, son of Bani, from the sons of Perez the son of Judah. ⁵ And of the Shi′lonites: Asai′ah the first-born, and his sons. ⁶ Of the sons of Zerah: Jeu′el and their kinsmen, six hundred and ninety. ⁷ Of the Benjaminites: Sallu the son of Meshul′lam, son of Hodavi′ah, son of Hassenu′ah, ⁸ Ibne′iah the son of Jero′ham, Elah the son of Uzzi, son of Michri, and Meshul′lam the son of Shephati′ah, son of Reu′el, son of Ibni′jah; ⁹ and their kinsmen according to their generations, nine hundred and fifty-six. All these were heads of fathers' houses according to their fathers' houses.

10 Of the priests: Jedai′ah, Jehoi′arib, Jachin, ¹¹ and Azari′ah the son of Hilki′ah, son of Meshul′lam, son of Zadok, son of Merai′oth, son of Ahi′tub, the chief officer of the house of God; ¹² and Adai′ah the son of Jero′ham, son of Pashhur, son of Malchi′jah, and Ma′asai the son of Ad′i-el, son of Jah′zerah, son of Meshul′lam, son of Meshil′lemith, son of Immer; ¹³ besides their kinsmen, heads of their fathers' houses, one thousand seven hundred and sixty, very able men for the work of the service of the house of God.

14 Of the Levites: Shemai′ah the son of Hasshub, son of Azri′kam, son of Hashabi′ah, of the sons of Merar′i; ¹⁵ and Bakbak′kar, Heresh, Galal, and Mattani′ah the son of Mica, son of Zichri, son of Asaph; ¹⁶ and Obadi′ah the son of Shemai′ah, son of Galal, son of Jedu′thun, and Berechi′ah the son of Asa, son of Elka′nah, who dwelt in the villages of the Netoph′athites.

17 The gatekeepers were: Shallum, Akkub, Talmon, Ahi′man, and their kinsmen (Shallum being the chief), ¹⁸ stationed hitherto in the king's gate on the east side. These were the gatekeepers of the camp of the Levites. ¹⁹ Shallum the son of Ko′re, son of Ebi′asaph, son of Korah, and his kinsmen of his fathers' house, the Ko′rahites, were in charge of the work of the service, keepers of the thresholds of the tent, as their fathers had been in charge of the camp of the LORD, keepers of the entrance. ²⁰ And Phin′ehas the son of Elea′zar was the ruler over them in time past; the LORD was with him. ²¹ Zechari′ah the son of Meshelemi′ah was gatekeeper at the entrance of the tent of meeting. ²² All these, who were chosen as gatekeepers at the thresholds, were two hundred and twelve. They were enrolled by genealogies in their villages. David and Samuel the seer established them in their office of trust. ²³ So they and their sons were in charge of the gates of the house of the LORD, that is, the house of the tent, as guards. ²⁴ The gatekeepers were on the four sides, east, west, north, and south; ²⁵ and their kinsmen who were in their villages were obliged to come in every seven days, from time to time, to be with these; ²⁶ for the four chief gatekeepers, who were Levites, were in charge of the chambers and the treasures of the house of God. ²⁷ And they lodged round about the house of God; for upon them lay the duty of watching, and they had charge of opening it every morning.

28 Some of them had charge of the utensils of service, for they were required to count them when they were

---

Ephraim and Manasseh dwelt in Jerusalem. In earlier times people of these tribes did not live in Jerusalem, but in the Chronicler's time representatives of "all Israel" (the post-exilic Jews) did live there. **17–34:** In these paragraphs is developed the idea that *David* established (with the help of *Samuel*) all the arrangements of the temple and its services which were carried on into post-exilic times. Since David did not actually accomplish the building of the temple, he must perforce have utilized *the tent of meeting* (or "tabernacle"), the portable shrine that preceded

brought in and taken out. ²⁹ Others of them were appointed over the furniture, and over all the holy utensils, also over the fine flour, the wine, the oil, the incense, and the spices. ³⁰ Others, of the sons of the priests, prepared the mixing of the spices, ³¹ and Mattithi′ah, one of the Levites, the firstborn of Shallum the Ko′rahite, was in charge of making the flat cakes. ³² Also some of their kinsmen of the Ko′hathites had charge of the showbread, to prepare it every sabbath.

33 Now these are the singers, the heads of fathers' houses of the Levites, dwelling in the chambers of the temple free from other service, for they were on duty day and night. ³⁴ These were heads of fathers' houses of the Levites, according to their generations, leaders, who lived in Jerusalem.

35 In Gibeon dwelt the father of Gibeon, Je-i′el, and the name of his wife was Ma′acah, ³⁶ and his firstborn son Abdon, then Zur, Kish, Ba′al, Ner, Nadab, ³⁷ Gedor, Ahi′o, Zechari′ah, and Mikloth; ³⁸ and Mikloth was the father of Shim′e-am; and these also dwelt opposite their kinsmen in Jerusalem, with their kinsmen. ³⁹ Ner was the father of Kish, Kish of Saul, Saul of Jonathan, Mal′chishu′a, Abin′adab, and Eshba′al; ⁴⁰ and the son of Jonathan was Mer′ib-ba′al; and Mer′ib-ba′al was the father of Micah. ⁴¹ The sons of Micah: Pithon, Melech, Tahr′e-a, and Ahaz;ᵛ ⁴² and Ahaz was the father of Jarah, and Jarah of Al′emeth, Az′maveth, and Zimri; and Zimri was the father of Moza. ⁴³ Moza was the father of Bin′e-a; and Rephai′-ah was his son, Ele-a′sah his son, Azel his son. ⁴⁴ Azel had six sons and these are their names: Azri′kam, Bo′cheru, Ish′mael, She-ari′ah, Obadi′ah, and Hanan; these were the sons of Azel.

10 Now the Philistines fought against Israel; and the men of Israel fled before the Philistines, and fell slain on Mount Gilbo′a. ² And the Philistines overtook Saul and his sons; and the Philistines slew Jonathan and Abin′adab and Mal′chishu′a, the sons of Saul. ³ The battle pressed hard upon Saul, and the archers found him; and he was wounded by the archers. ⁴ Then Saul said to his armor-bearer, "Draw your sword, and thrust me through with it, lest these uncircumcised come and make sport of me." But his armor-bearer would not; for he feared greatly. Therefore Saul took his own sword, and fell upon it. ⁵ And when his armor-bearer saw that Saul was dead, he also fell upon his sword, and died. ⁶ Thus Saul died; he and his three sons and all his house died together. ⁷ And when all the men of Israel who were in the valley saw that the armyʷ had fled and that Saul and his sons were dead, they forsook their cities and fled; and the Philistines came and dwelt in them.

8 On the morrow, when the Philistines came to strip the slain, they found Saul and his sons fallen on Mount Gilbo′a. ⁹ And they stripped him and took his head and his armor, and sent messengers throughout the land of the Philistines, to carry the good news to their idols and to the people. ¹⁰ And they put his armor in the temple of their gods, and fastened his head in the temple of Dagon. ¹¹ But when all Ja′-besh-gil′ead heard all that the Philistines had done to Saul, ¹² all the valiant men arose, and took away the body of Saul and the bodies of his sons, and brought them to Jabesh. And they buried their bones under the oak in Jabesh, and fasted seven days.

13 So Saul died for his unfaithful-

v Compare 8.35: Heb lacks and Ahaz   w Heb they

the temple. **35–44:** The genealogy of the family of Saul is repeated here from 8.29–38 in anticipation of the next chapter.

    10.1–14: Saul, the unfaithful predecessor of David. 1–12: These verses follow closely their source, 1 Sam.31.1–13, except in v. 10. Compare also v. 12 in the two passages. In spite of his dislike of Saul, the Chronicler hesitated to relate the disgraceful exposure of the bodies. **13–14:** The Chronicler brings *Saul* into his story mainly in contrast with *David* to the greater glory of the latter (see 1 Sam.31.10–13 n.). *Medium*, 1 Sam.28.3–25.

ness; he was unfaithful to the LORD in that he did not keep the command of the LORD, and also consulted a medium, seeking guidance, [14] and did not seek guidance from the LORD. Therefore the LORD slew him, and turned the kingdom over to David the son of Jesse.

Then all Israel gathered together to David at Hebron, and said, "Behold, we are your bone and flesh. [2] In times past, even when Saul was king, it was you that led out and brought in Israel; and the LORD your God said to you, 'You shall be shepherd of my people Israel, and you shall be prince over my people Israel.' " [3] So all the elders of Israel came to the king at Hebron; and David made a covenant with them at Hebron before the LORD, and they anointed David king over Israel, according to the word of the LORD by Samuel.

4 And David and all Israel went to Jerusalem, that is Jebus, where the Jeb'usites were, the inhabitants of the land. [5] The inhabitants of Jebus said to David, "You will not come in here." Nevertheless David took the stronghold of Zion, that is, the city of David. [6] David said, "Whoever shall smite the Jeb'usites first shall be chief and commander." And Jo'ab the son of Zeru'iah went up first, so he became chief. [7] And David dwelt in the stronghold; therefore it was called the city of David. [8] And he built the city round about from the Millo in complete circuit; and Jo'ab repaired the rest of the city. [9] And David became greater and greater, for the LORD of hosts was with him.

10 Now these are the chiefs of David's mighty men, who gave him strong support in his kingdom, together with all Israel, to make him king, ac-

cording to the word of the LORD concerning Israel. [11] This is an account of David's mighty men: Jasho'be-am, a Hach'monite, was chief of the three;[x] he wielded his spear against three hundred whom he slew at one time.

12 And next to him among the three mighty men was Elea'zar the son of Dodo, the Aho'hite. [13] He was with David at Pas-dam'mim when the Philistines were gathered there for battle. There was a plot of ground full of barley, and the men fled from the Philistines. [14] But he[y] took his[y] stand in the midst of the plot, and defended it, and slew the Philistines; and the LORD saved them by a great victory.

15 Three of the thirty chief men went down to the rock to David at the cave of Adullam, when the army of Philistines was encamped in the valley of Reph'aim. [16] David was then in the stronghold; and the garrison of the Philistines was then at Bethlehem. [17] And David said longingly, "O that some one would give me water to drink from the well of Bethlehem which is by the gate!" [18] Then the three mighty men broke through the camp of the Philistines, and drew water out of the well of Bethlehem which was by the gate, and took and brought it to David. But David would not drink of it; he poured it out to the LORD, [19] and said, "Far be it from me before my God that I should do this. Shall I drink the lifeblood of these men? For at the risk of their lives they brought it." Therefore he would not drink it. These things did the three mighty men.

20 Now Abi'shai, the brother of Jo'ab, was chief of the thirty.[z] And he wielded his spear against three hundred men and slew them, and won a

x Compare 2 Sam 23.8: Heb *thirty* or *captains*
y Compare 2 Sam 23.12: Heb *they . . . their*
z Syr: Heb *three*

11.1–47: The accession of David, the capture of Jerusalem, and a list of David's mighty warriors. 1–3: Omitting all the problems and troubles of 2 Sam. chs. 1–4, the Chronicler sees *David* quickly and easily anointed king over all *Israel*. The source is 2 Sam.5.1–3, except the last phrase, which is condensed from 1 Sam.16.1–13. 4–9: The source is 2 Sam.5.6–10. The additional information on *Joab* presented here is generally considered to be historical (see 2 Sam.5.6–9 n.). 10–47: The main source of this list is 2 Sam.23.8–39, though additional names of unknown origin are also present.

name beside the three. ²¹ He was the most renowned*a* of the thirty,*z* and became their commander; but he did not attain to the three.

22 And Benai'ah the son of Jehoi'-ada was a valiant man*b* of Kabzeel, a doer of great deeds; he smote two ariels*c* of Moab. He also went down and slew a lion in a pit on a day when snow had fallen. ²³ And he slew an Egyptian, a man of great stature, five cubits tall. The Egyptian had in his hand a spear like a weaver's beam; but Benai'ah went down to him with a staff, and snatched the spear out of the Egyptian's hand, and slew him with his own spear. ²⁴ These things did Benai'ah the son of Jehoi'ada, and won a name beside the three mighty men. ²⁵ He was renowned among the thirty, but he did not attain to the three. And David set him over his bodyguard.

26 The mighty men of the armies were As'ahel the brother of Jo'ab, Elha'nan the son of Dodo of Bethlehem, ²⁷ Shammoth of Harod,*d* Helez the Pel'onite, ²⁸ Ira the son of Ikkesh of Teko'a, Abi-e'zer of An'athoth, ²⁹ Sib'becai the Hu'shathite, I'lai the Aho'hite, ³⁰ Ma'harai of Netoph'ah, Heled the son of Ba'anah of Netoph'ah, ³¹ Ithai the son of Ribai of Gib'e-ah of the Benjaminites, Benai'ah of Pira'-thon, ³² Hurai of the brooks of Ga'ash, Abi'el the Ar'bathite, ³³ Az'maveth of Baha'rum, Eli'ahba of Sha-al'bon, ³⁴ Hashem*e* the Gi'zonite, Jonathan the son of Shagee the Har'arite, ³⁵ Ahi'am the son of Sachar the Har'-arite, Eli'phal the son of Ur, ³⁶ Hepher the Meche'rathite, Ahi'jah the Pel'-onite, ³⁷ Hezro of Carmel, Na'arai the son of Ezbai, ³⁸ Jo'el the brother of Nathan, Mibhar the son of Hagri, ³⁹ Zelek the Ammonite, Na'harai of Be-er'oth, the armor-bearer of Jo'ab the son of Zeru'iah, ⁴⁰ Ira the Ithrite, Gareb the Ithrite, ⁴¹ Uri'ah the Hittite, Zabad the son of Ahlai, ⁴² Ad'ina

the son of Shiza the Reubenite, a leader of the Reubenites, and thirty with him, ⁴³ Hanan the son of Ma'acah, and Josh'aphat the Mithnite, ⁴⁴ Uzzi'a the Ash'terathite, Shama and Je-i'el the sons of Hotham the Aro'erite, ⁴⁵ Jedi'a-el the son of Shimri, and Joha his brother, the Tizite, ⁴⁶ Eli'el the Ma'havite, and Jer'ibai, and Joshavi'ah, the sons of El'na-am, and Ithmah the Mo'abite, ⁴⁷ Eli'el, and Obed, and Ja-asi'el the Mezo'ba-ite.

12 Now these are the men who came to David at Ziklag, while he could not move about freely because of Saul the son of Kish; and they were among the mighty men who helped him in war. ² They were bowmen, and could shoot arrows and sling stones with either the right or the left hand; they were Benjaminites, Saul's kinsmen. ³ The chief was Ahi-e'zer, then Jo'ash, both sons of Shema'ah of Gib'e-ah; also Je'zi-el and Pelet the sons of Az'maveth; Ber'acah, Jehu of An'athoth, ⁴ Ishma'iah of Gibeon, a mighty man among the thirty and a leader over the thirty; Jeremiah,*f* Jaha'-ziel, Joha'nan, Joz'abad of Gede'rah, ⁵ Elu'zai,*g* Jer'imoth, Beali'ah, Shemari'ah, Shephati'ah the Har'uphite; ⁶ Elka'nah, Isshi'ah, Az'arel, Jo-e'zer, and Jasho'be-am, the Ko'rahites; ⁷ and Jo-e'lah and Zebadi'ah, the sons of Jero'-ham of Gedor.

8 From the Gadites there went over to David at the stronghold in the wilderness mighty and experienced warriors, expert with shield and spear, whose faces were like the faces of lions, and who were swift as gazelles upon the mountains: ⁹ Ezer the chief, Obadi'ah second, Eli'ab third, ¹⁰ Mishman'-nah fourth, Jeremiah fifth, ¹¹ Attai

z Syr: Heb *three*
a Compare 2 Sam 23.19: Heb *more renowned among the two*
b Syr: Heb *the son of a valiant man*
c The meaning of the word *ariel* is unknown
d Compare 2 Sam 23.25: Heb *the Harorite*
e Compare Gk and 2 Sam 23.32: Heb *the sons of Hashem*
f Heb verse 5　g Heb verse 6

12.1–40: David's ability to attract men of valor. A description of David's army. David is linked to the past by historical allusions, yet he is also the prototype of the ideal future king or Messiah. **1–7:** Compare v. 1 with 1 Sam.27.5–12; v. 2 with Jg.3.15 and 20.15–16; v. 4 with 2 Sam.23.18–19. **8–15:** Compare 1 Sam.26.1–3 and Dt.33.20–21. These *Gadites*, like *David*

sixth, Eli'el seventh, 12 Joha'nan eighth, Elza'bad ninth, 13 Jeremiah tenth, Mach'bannai eleventh. 14 These Gadites were officers of the army, the lesser over a hundred and the greater over a thousand. 15 These are the men who crossed the Jordan in the first month, when it was overflowing all its banks, and put to flight all those in the valleys, to the east and to the west.

16 And some of the men of Benjamin and Judah came to the stronghold to David. 17 David went out to meet them and said to them, "If you have come to me in friendship to help me, my heart will be knit to you; but if to betray me to my adversaries, although there is no wrong in my hands, then may the God of our fathers see and rebuke you." 18 Then the Spirit came upon Ama'sai, chief of the thirty, and he said,

"We are yours, O David;
  and with you, O son of Jesse!
Peace, peace to you,
  and peace to your helpers!
For your God helps you."

Then David received them, and made them officers of his troops.

19 Some of the men of Manas'seh deserted to David when he came with the Philistines for the battle against Saul. (Yet he did not help them, for the rulers of the Philistines took counsel and sent him away, saying, "At peril to our heads he will desert to his master Saul.") 20 As he went to Ziklag these men of Manas'seh deserted to him: Adnah, Joz'abad, Jedi'a-el, Michael, Joz'abad, Eli'hu, and Zil'lethai, chiefs of thousands in Manas'seh. 21 They helped David against the band of raiders;*h* for they were all mighty men of valor, and were commanders in the army. 22 For from day to day

men kept coming to David to help him, until there was a great army, like an army of God.

23 These are the numbers of the divisions of the armed troops, who came to David in Hebron, to turn the kingdom of Saul over to him, according to the word of the LORD. 24 The men of Judah bearing shield and spear were six thousand eight hundred armed troops. 25 Of the Simeonites, mighty men of valor for war, seven thousand one hundred. 26 Of the Levites four thousand six hundred. 27 The prince Jehoi'ada, of the house of Aaron, and with him three thousand seven hundred. 28 Zadok, a young man mighty in valor, and twenty-two commanders from his own father's house. 29 Of the Benjaminites, the kinsmen of Saul, three thousand, of whom the majority had hitherto kept their allegiance to the house of Saul. 30 Of the E'phraimites twenty thousand eight hundred, mighty men of valor, famous men in their fathers' houses. 31 Of the half-tribe of Manas'seh eighteen thousand, who were expressly named to come and make David king. 32 Of Is'sachar men who had understanding of the times, to know what Israel ought to do, two hundred chiefs, and all their kinsmen under their command. 33 Of Zeb'ulun fifty thousand seasoned troops, equipped for battle with all the weapons of war, to help David*i* with singleness of purpose. 34 Of Naph'tali a thousand commanders with whom were thirty-seven thousand men armed with shield and spear. 35 Of the Danites twenty-eight thousand six hundred men equipped for battle. 36 Of Asher forty thousand seasoned troops ready for battle. 37 Of the Reubenites and Gadites and the half-tribe

h Or *as officers of his troops*
i Gk: Heb lacks *David*

himself, are here highly idealized. They are as much soldiers of the future as of the past. **19–22:** The Chronicler's revised version of 1 Sam. chs. 29–30. That *Manasseh deserted to David* in this manner is not historically attested. But in the ideal future, all the tribes, northern as well as southern, would flock to the new David to form *a great army, like an army of God.* **23–37:** The writer now returns to the enthronement scene of 11.1–3. The total number of fighting men listed here is fantastic, historically speaking; but in the new age of the new David, things will

of Manas'seh from beyond the Jordan, one hundred and twenty thousand men armed with all the weapons of war.

38 All these, men of war, arrayed in battle order, came to Hebron with full intent to make David king over all Israel; likewise all the rest of Israel were of a single mind to make David king. ³⁹ And they were there with David for three days, eating and drinking, for their brethren had made preparation for them. ⁴⁰ And also their neighbors, from as far as Is'sachar and Zeb'ulun and Naph'tali, came bringing food on asses and on camels and on mules and on oxen, abundant provisions of meal, cakes of figs, clusters of raisins, and wine and oil, oxen and sheep, for there was joy in Israel.

13 David consulted with the commanders of thousands and of hundreds, with every leader. ² And David said to all the assembly of Israel, "If it seems good to you, and if it is the will of the LORD our God, let us send abroad to our brethren who remain in all the land of Israel, and with them to the priests and Levites in the cities that have pasture lands, that they may come together to us. ³ Then let us bring again the ark of our God to us; for we neglected it in the days of Saul." ⁴ All the assembly agreed to do so, for the thing was right in the eyes of all the people.

5 So David assembled all Israel from the Shihor of Egypt to the entrance of Hamath, to bring the ark of God from Kir'iath-je'arim. ⁶ And David and all Israel went up to Ba'-

alah, that is, to Kir'iath-je'arim which belongs to Judah, to bring up from there the ark of God, which is called by the name of the LORD who sits enthroned above the cherubim. ⁷ And they carried the ark of God upon a new cart, from the house of Abin'adab, and Uzzah and Ahi'o*ʲ* were driving the cart. ⁸ And David and all Israel were making merry before God with all their might, with song and lyres and harps and tambourines and cymbals and trumpets.

9 And when they came to the threshing floor of Chidon, Uzzah put out his hand to hold the ark, for the oxen stumbled. ¹⁰ And the anger of the LORD was kindled against Uzzah; and he smote him because he put forth his hand to the ark; and he died there before God. ¹¹ And David was angry because the LORD had broken forth upon Uzzah; and that place is called Pe'rez-uz'za*ᵏ* to this day. ¹² And David was afraid of God that day; and he said, "How can I bring the ark of God home to me?" ¹³ So David did not take the ark home into the city of David, but took it aside to the house of O'bed-e'dom the Gittite. ¹⁴ And the ark of God remained with the household of O'bed-e'dom in his house three months; and the LORD blessed the household of O'bed-e'dom and all that he had.

14 And Hiram king of Tyre sent messengers to David, and cedar trees, also masons and carpenters to

j Or *and his brother*
k That is *The breaking forth upon Uzzah*

---

be different. **38–40:** In line with the interpretation suggested in the preceding notes, there is in these verses a kind of Messianic banquet (compare Is.25.6–8; Jl.3.18; Mt.26.29; Mk.14.25).
13.1–14: David's concern to bring the ark to Jerusalem. The Chronicler partly reverses the order of 2 Samuel, placing his version of 2 Sam.6.2–11, which is the source of the present chapter, ahead of his treatment of 2 Sam.5.11–25 (in ch. 14). 2 Sam.6.12–19 is then utilized in 15.25–16.3. The purpose of this rearrangement is probably to show the new David's primary concern with ecclesiastical rather than military matters, in spite of his skill in the latter (compare 14.17). **1–4:** In the times of the historical *David*, the distinction between *priests* and *Levites* did not exist. **5:** *The Shihor of Egypt*, the eastern branch of the Nile delta; *the entrance* of *Hamath* was in Syria. *The cherubim*, see 1 Sam.4.4 n.
14.1–17: David's family and his defeat of the Philistines. The source is 2 Sam.5.11–25. The Chronicler adds v. 17 to make his new *David* (see 12.23–37 n.) a military figure feared throughout the world.

build a house for him. ² And David perceived that the LORD had established him king over Israel, and that his kingdom was highly exalted for the sake of his people Israel.

3 And David took more wives in Jerusalem, and David begot more sons and daughters. ⁴ These are the names of the children whom he had in Jerusalem: Shammu'a, Shobab, Nathan, Solomon, ⁵ Ibhar, Eli'shu-a, El'pelet, ⁶ Nogah, Nepheg, Japhi'a, ⁷ Eli'shama, Beeli'ada, and Eliph'elet.

8 When the Philistines heard that David had been anointed king over all Israel, all the Philistines went up in search of David; and David heard of it and went out against them. ⁹ Now the Philistines had come and made a raid in the valley of Reph'aim. ¹⁰ And David inquired of God, "Shall I go up against the Philistines? Wilt thou give them into my hand?" And the LORD said to him, "Go up, and I will give them into your hand." ¹¹ And he went up to Ba'al-pera'zim, and David defeated them there; and David said, "God has broken through*l* my enemies by my hand, like a bursting flood." Therefore the name of that place is called Ba'al-pera'zim.*m* ¹² And they left their gods there, and David gave command, and they were burned.

13 And the Philistines yet again made a raid in the valley. ¹⁴ And when David again inquired of God, God said to him, "You shall not go up after them; go around and come upon them opposite the balsam trees. ¹⁵ And when you hear the sound of marching in the tops of the balsam trees, then go out to battle; for God has gone out before you to smite the army of the Philistines." ¹⁶ And David did as God commanded him, and they smote the Philistine army from Gibeon to Gezer. ¹⁷ And the fame of David went out into all lands, and the LORD brought the fear of him upon all nations.

15 David built houses for himself in the city of David; and he prepared a place for the ark of God, and pitched a tent for it. ² Then David said, "No one but the Levites may carry the ark of God, for the LORD chose them to carry the ark of the LORD and to minister to him for ever." ³ And David assembled all Israel at Jerusalem, to bring up the ark of the LORD to its place, which he had prepared for it. ⁴ And David gathered together the sons of Aaron and the Levites: ⁵ of the sons of Kohath, Uri'el the chief, with a hundred and twenty of his brethren; ⁶ of the sons of Merar'i, Asai'ah the chief, with two hundred and twenty of his brethren; ⁷ of the sons of Gershom, Jo'el the chief, with a hundred and thirty of his brethren; ⁸ of the sons of Eli-za'phan, Shemai'ah the chief, with two hundred of his brethren; ⁹ of the sons of Hebron, Eli'el the chief, with eighty of his brethren; ¹⁰ of the sons of Uz'ziel, Ammin'adab the chief, with a hundred and twelve of his brethren. ¹¹ Then David summoned the priests Zadok and Abi'athar, and the Levites Uri'el, Asai'ah, Jo'el, Shemai'ah, Eli'el, and Ammin'adab, ¹² and said to them, "You are the heads of the fathers' houses of the Levites; sanctify yourselves, you and your brethren, so that you may bring up the ark of the LORD, the God of Israel, to the place that I have prepared for it. ¹³ Because you did not carry it the first time,*n* the LORD our God broke forth upon us, because we did not care for it in the way that is ordained." ¹⁴ So the priests and the Levites sanctified themselves to bring up the ark of the LORD, the God of Israel. ¹⁵ And the Levites carried the ark of God upon their shoulders with the poles, as Moses had commanded according to the word of the LORD.

l Heb *paraz*
m That is *Lord of breaking through*
n The meaning of the Hebrew word is uncertain

15.1–29: The ark is brought to Jerusalem. The Chronicler returns to his interest in the new David as an ecclesiastical figure (see ch. 13 n.). **1–15:** Note the emphasis on the Levites, who did not exist as a special class in the time of the historical *David;* they are not even mentioned in 2 Sam. ch. 6. **16–24:** The musical arrangements here set forth were largely drawn from the

16 David also commanded the chiefs of the Levites to appoint their brethren as the singers who should play loudly on musical instruments, on harps and lyres and cymbals, to raise sounds of joy. ¹⁷ So the Levites appointed Heman the son of Jo'el; and of his brethren Asaph the son of Berechi'ah; and of the sons of Merar'i, their brethren, Ethan the son of Kusha'-iah; ¹⁸ and with them their brethren of the second order, Zechari'ah, Ja-a'-ziel, Shemi'ramoth, Jehi'el, Unni, Eli'ab, Benai'ah, Ma-asei'ah, Mattithi'-ah, Eliph'elehu, and Miknei'ah, and the gatekeepers O'bed-e'dom and Je-i'el. ¹⁹ The singers, Heman, Asaph, and Ethan, were to sound bronze cymbals; ²⁰ Zechari'ah, A'zi-el, Shemi'ramoth, Jehi'el, Unni, Eli'ab, Ma-asei'ah, and Benai'ah were to play harps according to Al'amoth; ²¹ but Mattithi'ah, Eliph'elehu, Miknei'ah, O'bed-e'dom, Je-i'el, and Azazi'ah were to lead with lyres according to the Shem'inith. ²² Chenani'ah, leader of the Levites in music, should direct the music, for he understood it. ²³ Berechi'ah and Elka'nah were to be gatekeepers for the ark. ²⁴ Shebani'ah, Josh'aphat, Nethan'el, Ama'sai, Zechari'ah, Benai'ah, and Elie'zer, the priests, should blow the trumpets before the ark of God. O'bed-e'dom and Jehi'ah also were to be gatekeepers for the ark.

25 So David and the elders of Israel, and the commanders of thousands, went to bring up the ark of the covenant of the LORD from the house of O'bed-e'dom with rejoicing. ²⁶ And because God helped the Levites who were carrying the ark of the covenant of the LORD, they sacrificed seven bulls and seven rams. ²⁷ David was clothed with a robe of fine linen, as also were all the Levites who were carrying the ark, and the singers, and Chenani'ah the leader of the music of the singers; and David wore a linen ephod. ²⁸ So all Israel brought up the ark of the covenant of the LORD with shouting, to the sound of the horn, trumpets, and cymbals, and made loud music on harps and lyres.

29 And as the ark of the covenant of the LORD came to the city of David, Michal the daughter of Saul looked out of the window, and saw King David dancing and making merry; and she despised him in her heart.

16 And they brought in the ark of God, and set it inside the tent which David had pitched for it; and they offered burnt offerings and peace offerings before God. ² And when David had finished offering the burnt offerings and the peace offerings, he blessed the people in the name of the LORD, ³ and distributed to all Israel, both men and women, to each a loaf of bread, a portion of meat,ᵒ and a cake of raisins.

4 Moreover he appointed certain of the Levites as ministers before the ark of the LORD, to invoke, to thank, and to praise the LORD, the God of Israel. ⁵ Asaph was the chief, and second to him were Zechari'ah, Je-i'el, Shemi'-ramoth, Jehi'el, Mattithi'ah, Eli'ab, Benai'ah, O'bed-e'dom, and Je-i'el, who were to play harps and lyres; Asaph was to sound the cymbals, ⁶ and Benai'ah and Jaha'ziel the priests were to blow trumpets continually, before the ark of the covenant of God.

7 Then on that day David first appointed that thanksgiving be sung to the LORD by Asaph and his brethren.

o Compare Gk Syr Vg: Heb uncertain

---

practice in the Chronicler's own day. These names had become traditional in the musical guild. *Sheminith* (v. 21), a musical term; the exact meaning is unknown. **25–28**: Based upon 2 Sam. 6.12–15, with the addition of Levites, singers, more musical instruments, and more clothing on the person of *David* (see 1 Sam.2.18 n.). **29**: A close approximation of 2 Sam.6.16.

16.1–43: A service of dedication, and further ecclesiastical arrangements. A continuation of ch. 15. **1–3**: Compare 2 Sam.6.17–19 as source. All reference to 2 Sam.6.20–23 is omitted. The new David would not be guilty of indecent exposure (see 15.25–28 n.) or of unseemly disputes with members of his harem. **8–36**: A composite psalm inserted for artistic effect, probably by

[8] O give thanks to the LORD, call on
his name,
make known his deeds among the
peoples!
[9] Sing to him, sing praises to him,
tell of all his wonderful works!
[10] Glory in his holy name;
let the hearts of those who seek the
LORD rejoice!
[11] Seek the LORD and his strength,
seek his presence continually!
[12] Remember the wonderful works that
he has done,
the wonders he wrought, the
judgments he uttered,
[13] O offspring of Abraham his servant,
sons of Jacob, his chosen ones!

[14] He is the LORD our God;
his judgments are in all the earth.
[15] He is mindful of his covenant for
ever,
of the word that he commanded,
for a thousand generations,
[16] the covenant which he made with
Abraham,
his sworn promise to Isaac,
[17] which he confirmed as a statute to
Jacob,
as an everlasting covenant to
Israel,
[18] saying, "To you I will give the land
of Canaan,
as your portion for an
inheritance."

[19] When they were few in number,
and of little account, and
sojourners in it,
[20] wandering from nation to nation,
from one kingdom to another
people,
[21] he allowed no one to oppress them;
he rebuked kings on their account,
[22] saying, "Touch not my anointed
ones,
do my prophets no harm!"

[23] Sing to the LORD, all the earth!
Tell of his salvation from day to
day.

[24] Declare his glory among the nations,
his marvelous works among all
the peoples!
[25] For great is the LORD, and greatly
to be praised,
and he is to be held in awe above
all gods.
[26] For all the gods of the peoples are
idols;
but the LORD made the heavens.
[27] Honor and majesty are before him;
strength and joy are in his place.

[28] Ascribe to the LORD, O families of
the peoples,
ascribe to the LORD glory and
strength!
[29] Ascribe to the LORD the glory due
his name;
bring an offering, and come before
him!
Worship the LORD in holy array;
[30] tremble before him, all the earth;
yea, the world stands firm, never
to be moved.
[31] Let the heavens be glad, and let the
earth rejoice,
and let them say among the
nations, "The LORD reigns!"
[32] Let the sea roar, and all that fills it,
let the field exult, and everything
in it!
[33] Then shall the trees of the wood
sing for joy
before the LORD, for he comes to
judge the earth.
[34] O give thanks to the LORD, for he
is good;
for his steadfast love endures for
ever!

[35] Say also:
"Deliver us, O God of our salvation,
and gather and save us from
among the nations,
that we may give thanks to thy holy
name,
and glory in thy praise.
[36] Blessed be the LORD, the God of
Israel,
from everlasting to everlasting!"

an editor (see 1 Sam.2.1–10 n.; 2 Sam. ch. 22 n.; 23.1–7 n.). The sources of the present compo-

Then all the people said "Amen!" and praised the LORD.

37 So David left Asaph and his brethren there before the ark of the covenant of the LORD to minister continually before the ark as each day required, 38 and also O'bed-e'dom and his*p* sixty-eight brethren; while O'bed-e'dom, the son of Jedu'thun, and Hosah were to be gatekeepers. 39 And he left Zadok the priest and his brethren the priests before the tabernacle of the LORD in the high place that was at Gibeon, 40 to offer burnt offerings to the LORD upon the altar of burnt offering continually morning and evening, according to all that is written in the law of the LORD which he commanded Israel. 41 With them were Heman and Jedu'thun, and the rest of those chosen and expressly named to give thanks to the LORD, for his steadfast love endures for ever. 42 Heman and Jedu'thun had trumpets and cymbals for the music and instruments for sacred song. The sons of Jedu'thun were appointed to the gate.

43 Then all the people departed each to his house, and David went home to bless his household.

17 Now when David dwelt in his house, David said to Nathan the prophet, "Behold, I dwell in a house of cedar, but the ark of the covenant of the LORD is under a tent." 2 And Nathan said to David, "Do all that is in your heart, for God is with you."

3 But that same night the word of the LORD came to Nathan, 4 "Go and tell my servant David, 'Thus says the LORD: You shall not build me a house to dwell in. 5 For I have not dwelt in a house since the day I led up Israel to this day, but I have gone from tent to tent and from dwelling to dwelling. 6 In all places where I have moved with all Israel, did I speak a word with any of the judges of Israel, whom I commanded to shepherd my people, saying, "Why have you not built me a house of cedar?" ' 7 Now therefore thus shall you say to my servant David, 'Thus says the LORD of hosts, I took you from the pasture, from following the sheep, that you should be prince over my people Israel; 8 and I have been with you wherever you went, and have cut off all your enemies from before you; and I will make for you a name, like the name of the great ones of the earth. 9 And I will appoint a place for my people Israel, and will plant them, that they may dwell in their own place, and be disturbed no more; and violent men shall waste them no more, as formerly, 10 from the time that I appointed judges over my people Israel; and I will subdue all your enemies. Moreover I declare to you that the LORD will build you a house. 11 When your days are fulfilled to go to be with your fathers, I will raise up your offspring after you, one of your own sons, and I will establish his kingdom. 12 He shall build a house for me, and I will establish his throne for ever. 13 I will be his father, and he shall be my son; I will not take my steadfast love from him, as I took it from him who was before you, 14 but I will confirm him in my house and in my kingdom for ever and his throne shall be established for ever.' " 15 In accordance with all these words, and in accordance with all this vision, Nathan spoke to David.

16 Then King David went in and sat before the LORD, and said, "Who am I, O LORD God, and what is my house, that thou hast brought me thus far? 17 And this was a small thing in thy eyes, O God; thou hast also spoken of thy servant's house for a great while to come, and hast shown

p Heb their

sition are Ps.105.1–15 (vv. 8–22); Ps.96.1–13 (vv. 23–33); Ps.106.1,47–48 (vv. 34–36). **37–42:** A continuation of vv. 4–6; similar to 15.1–24. **43:** Taken from 2 Sam.6.19b–20a; a continuation of v. 3.

    17.1–27: Why David himself did not build the temple. This chapter follows closely its source, 2 Sam. ch. 7.

me future generations,[q] O LORD God! [18] And what more can David say to thee for honoring thy servant? For thou knowest thy servant. [19] For thy servant's sake, O LORD, and according to thy own heart, thou hast wrought all this greatness, in making known all these great things. [20] There is none like thee, O LORD, and there is no God besides thee, according to all that we have heard with our ears. [21] What other[r] nation on earth is like thy people Israel, whom God went to redeem to be his people, making for thyself a name for great and terrible things, in driving out nations before thy people whom thou didst redeem from Egypt? [22] And thou didst make thy people Israel to be thy people for ever; and thou, O LORD, didst become their God. [23] And now, O LORD, let the word which thou hast spoken concerning thy servant and concerning his house be established for ever, and do as thou hast spoken; [24] and thy name will be established and magnified for ever, saying, 'The LORD of hosts, the God of Israel, is Israel's God,' and the house of thy servant David will be established before thee. [25] For thou, my God, hast revealed to thy servant that thou wilt build a house for him; therefore thy servant has found courage to pray before thee. [26] And now, O LORD, thou art God, and thou hast promised this good thing to thy servant; [27] now therefore may it please thee to bless the house of thy servant, that it may continue for ever before thee; for what thou, O LORD, hast blessed is blessed for ever."

18 After this David defeated the Philistines and subdued them, and he took Gath and its villages out of the hand of the Philistines.

2 And he defeated Moab, and the Mo'abites became servants to David and brought tribute.

3 David also defeated Hadade'zer king of Zobah, toward Hamath, as he went to set up his monument[s] at the river Euphra'tes. [4] And David took from him a thousand chariots, seven thousand horsemen, and twenty thousand foot soldiers; and David hamstrung all the chariot horses, but left enough for a hundred chariots. [5] And when the Syrians of Damascus came to help Hadade'zer king of Zobah, David slew twenty-two thousand men of the Syrians. [6] Then David put garrisons[t] in Syria of Damascus; and the Syrians became servants to David, and brought tribute. And the LORD gave victory to David wherever he went. [7] And David took the shields of gold which were carried by the servants of Hadade'zer, and brought them to Jerusalem. [8] And from Tibhath and from Cun, cities of Hadade'zer, David took very much bronze; with it Solomon made the bronze sea and the pillars and the vessels of bronze.

9 When To'u king of Hamath heard that David had defeated the whole army of Hadade'zer, king of Zobah, [10] he sent his son Hador'am to King David, to greet him, and to congratulate him because he had fought against Hadade'zer and defeated him; for Hadade'zer had often been at war with To'u. And he sent all sorts of articles of gold, of silver, and of bronze; [11] these also King David dedicated to the LORD, together with the silver and gold which he had carried off from all the nations, from Edom, Moab, the Ammonites, the Philistines, and Am'-alek.

12 And Abi'shai, the son of Zeru'iah, slew eighteen thousand E'domites in the Valley of Salt. [13] And he put garrisons in Edom; and all the E'domites became David's servants. And the LORD gave victory to David wherever he went.

q Cn: Heb uncertain
r Gk Vg: Heb *one*   s Heb *hand*
t Gk Vg 2 Sam 8.6 Compare Syr: Heb lacks *garrisons*

18.1–17: David's further military prowess. This chapter and the two following resume the theme of ch. 14 (see note there). The idealized *David* was both a great military leader and a noble founder of religious institutions. **1–13:** *David defeats the Philistines, Moabites, Syrians*

14 So David reigned over all Israel; and he administered justice and equity to all his people. [15] And Jo'ab the son of Zeru'iah was over the army; and Jehosh'aphat the son of Ahi'lud was recorder; [16] and Zadok the son of Ahi'tub and Ahim'elech the son of Abi'athar were priests; and Shavsha was secretary; [17] and Benai'ah the son of Jehoi'ada was over the Cher'ethites and the Pel'ethites; and David's sons were the chief officials in the service of the king.

19 Now after this Nahash the king of the Ammonites died, and his son reigned in his stead. [2] And David said, "I will deal loyally with Hanun the son of Nahash, for his father dealt loyally with me." So David sent messengers to console him concerning his father. And David's servants came to Hanun in the land of the Ammonites, to console him. [3] But the princes of the Ammonites said to Hanun, "Do you think, because David has sent comforters to you, that he is honoring your father? Have not his servants come to you to search and to overthrow and to spy out the land?" [4] So Hanun took David's servants, and shaved them, and cut off their garments in the middle, at their hips, and sent them away; [5] and they departed. When David was told concerning the men, he sent to meet them, for the men were greatly ashamed. And the king said, "Remain at Jericho until your beards have grown, and then return."

6 When the Ammonites saw that they had made themselves odious to David, Hanun and the Ammonites sent a thousand talents of silver to hire chariots and horsemen from Mesopota'mia, from Aram-ma'acah, and from Zobah. [7] They hired thirty-two thousand chariots and the king of Ma'acah with his army, who came and encamped before Med'eba. And the Ammonites were mustered from their cities and came to battle. [8] When David heard of it, he sent Jo'ab and all the army of the mighty men. [9] And the Ammonites came out and drew up in battle array at the entrance of the city, and the kings who had come were by themselves in the open country.

10 When Jo'ab saw that the battle was set against him both in front and in the rear, he chose some of the picked men of Israel, and arrayed them against the Syrians; [11] the rest of his men he put in the charge of Abi'shai his brother, and they were arrayed against the Ammonites. [12] And he said, "If the Syrians are too strong for me, then you shall help me; but if the Ammonites are too strong for you, then I will help you. [13] Be of good courage, and let us play the man for our people, and for the cities of our God; and may the Lord do what seems good to him." [14] So Jo'ab and the people who were with him drew near before the Syrians for battle; and they fled before him. [15] And when the Ammonites saw that the Syrians fled, they likewise fled before Abi'shai, Jo'ab's brother, and entered the city. Then Jo'ab came to Jerusalem.

16 But when the Syrians saw that they had been defeated by Israel, they sent messengers and brought out the Syrians who were beyond the Euphra'tes, with Shophach the commander of the army of Hadade'zer at their head. [17] And when it was told David, he gathered all Israel together, and crossed the Jordan, and came to them, and drew up his forces against them. And when David set the battle in array against the Syrians, they fought with him. [18] And the Syrians

(Arameans), and *Edomites.* 2 Sam.8.1–14 is the source. **14–17:** The source is 2 Sam.8.15–18. **17:** *David's sons* are changed from priests (see 2 Sam.8.18 n.) to *chief officials,* for the Chronicler believed only descendants of Aaron could be priests.

19.1–19: David defeats the Ammonites and their Syrian (Aramean) allies. The Chronicler omits 2 Sam. ch. 9, having already declared (10.6) that the whole house of Saul had disappeared. The theme of David's military prowess is continued, the source being 2 Sam. ch. 10 with a few changes.

fled before Israel; and David slew of the Syrians the men of seven thousand chariots, and forty thousand foot soldiers, and killed also Shophach the commander of their army. ¹⁹ And when the servants of Hadade'zer saw that they had been defeated by Israel, they made peace with David, and became subject to him. So the Syrians were not willing to help the Ammonites any more.

20 In the spring of the year, the time when kings go forth to battle, Jo'ab led out the army, and ravaged the country of the Ammonites, and came and besieged Rabbah. But David remained at Jerusalem. And Jo'ab smote Rabbah, and overthrew it. ² And David took the crown of their king*u* from his head; he found that it weighed a talent of gold, and in it was a precious stone; and it was placed on David's head. And he brought forth the spoil of the city, a very great amount. ³ And he brought forth the people who were in it, and set them to labor*v* with saws and iron picks and axes;*w* and thus David did to all the cities of the Ammonites. Then David and all the people returned to Jerusalem.

4 And after this there arose war with the Philistines at Gezer; then Sib'becai the Hu'shathite slew Sip'pai, who was one of the descendants of the giants; and the Philistines were subdued. ⁵ And there was again war with the Philistines; and Elha'nan the son of Ja'ir slew Lahmi the brother of Goliath the Gittite, the shaft of whose spear was like a weaver's beam. ⁶ And there was again war at Gath, where there was a man of great stature, who had six fingers on each hand, and six toes on each foot, twenty-four in number; and he also was descended from the giants. ⁷ And when he taunted Israel, Jonathan the son of Shim'e-a, David's brother, slew him. ⁸ These were descended from the giants in Gath; and they fell by the hand of David and by the hand of his servants.

21 Satan stood up against Israel, and incited David to number Israel. ² So David said to Jo'ab and the commanders of the army, "Go, number Israel, from Beer-sheba to Dan, and bring me a report, that I may know their number." ³ But Jo'ab said, "May the LORD add to his people a hundred times as many as they are! Are they not, my lord the king, all of

u Or *Milcom* See 1 Kg 11.5
v Compare 2 Sam 12.31: Heb *he sawed*
w Compare 2 Sam 12.31: Heb *saws*

20.1–8: The conquest of Ammon; further wars with the Philistines. 1: The first two sentences of this verse come from 2 Sam.11.1; to get the last sentence the Chronicler turned to 2 Sam.12.26, thus eliminating the story of David's adultery with Bathsheba, his murder of her husband, and the prophet's rebuke of the king for his conduct. The omission is perfectly in order, since the Chronicler was not writing history, and the new David in the new age would certainly not be guilty of such conduct, nor would a prophet have occasion to rebuke him. **2–3:** The source is 2 Sam.12.30–31 (see 2 Sam.12.30 n.). **4–8:** The writer now jumps to 2 Sam.21.18–22 for source material, thus eliminating a whole series of discreditable incidents: the violent and immoral conduct of David's sons, Absalom's rebellion, David's flight and weak sentimentality, the disaffection of the northern tribes, Joab's control over David, the execution of more of Saul's descendants. **5:** The addition of the words *Lahmi the brother of* would seem to be for the purpose of resolving the conflict between 1 Sam. ch. 17 and 2 Sam.21.19 as to who killed Goliath (see 1 Sam.17.4 n.).

21.1–22.1: The census, the plague, and the acquisition of a site for the sanctuary. This story, based upon 2 Sam. ch. 24, though not altogether to the credit of David, was used by the Chronicler as the introduction to the next section of his book because the outcome of the trouble in the story was the fixing of the temple site, and the Chronicler from here on is concerned with David as the real founder of the temple. **1:** *Satan* replaces "the anger of the LORD" of 2 Sam. 24.1. During the more than five hundred years since the writing of the earlier account, a considerable theological change had taken place. In the thinking of Biblical men, God came to be considered as doing only good; and the figure of Satan (the word means "adversary") was developed to account for evil and misfortune (compare Rev.12.9). For earlier conceptions of

them my lord's servants? Why then should my lord require this? Why should he bring guilt upon Israel?" ⁴ But the king's word prevailed against Jo'ab. So Jo'ab departed and went throughout all Israel, and came back to Jerusalem. ⁵ And Jo'ab gave the sum of the numbering of the people to David. In all Israel there were one million one hundred thousand men who drew the sword, and in Judah four hundred and seventy thousand who drew the sword. ⁶ But he did not include Levi and Benjamin in the numbering, for the king's command was abhorrent to Jo'ab.

7 But God was displeased with this thing, and he smote Israel. ⁸ And David said to God, "I have sinned greatly in that I have done this thing. But now, I pray thee, take away the iniquity of thy servant; for I have done very foolishly." ⁹ And the LORD spoke to Gad, David's seer, saying, ¹⁰ "Go and say to David, 'Thus says the LORD, Three things I offer you; choose one of them, that I may do it to you.'" ¹¹ So Gad came to David and said to him, "Thus says the LORD, 'Take which you will: ¹² either three years of famine; or three months of devastation by your foes, while the sword of your enemies overtakes you; or else three days of the sword of the LORD, pestilence upon the land, and the angel of the LORD destroying throughout all the territory of Israel.' Now decide what answer I shall return to him who sent me." ¹³ Then David said to Gad, "I am in great distress; let me fall into the hand of the LORD, for his mercy is very great; but let me not fall into the hand of man."

14 So the LORD sent a pestilence upon Israel; and there fell seventy thousand men of Israel. ¹⁵ And God sent the angel to Jerusalem to destroy it; but when he was about to destroy it, the LORD saw, and he repented of the evil; and he said to the destroying angel, "It is enough; now stay your hand." And the angel of the LORD was standing by the threshing floor of Ornan the Jeb'usite. ¹⁶ And David lifted his eyes and saw the angel of the LORD standing between earth and heaven, and in his hand a drawn sword stretched out over Jerusalem. Then David and the elders, clothed in sackcloth, fell upon their faces. ¹⁷ And David said to God, "Was it not I who gave command to number the people? It is I who have sinned and done very wickedly. But these sheep, what have they done? Let thy hand, I pray thee, O LORD my God, be against me and against my father's house; but let not the plague be upon thy people."

18 Then the angel of the LORD commanded Gad to say to David that David should go up and rear an altar to the LORD on the threshing floor of Ornan the Jeb'usite. ¹⁹ So David went up at Gad's word, which he had spoken in the name of the LORD. ²⁰ Now Ornan was threshing wheat; he turned and saw the angel, and his four sons who were with him hid themselves. ²¹ As David came to Ornan, Ornan looked and saw David and went forth from the threshing floor, and did obeisance to David with his face to the ground. ²² And David said to Ornan, "Give me the site of the threshing floor that I may build on it an altar to the LORD—give it to me at its full price—that the plague may be averted from the people." ²³ Then Ornan said to David, "Take it; and let my lord the king do what seems good to him; see, I give the oxen for burnt offerings, and the threshing sledges for the wood, and the wheat for a cereal offering. I give it all." ²⁴ But King David said to Ornan, "No, but I will buy it for the full price; I will not take for the LORD what is yours, nor offer burnt offerings which cost me nothing." ²⁵ So David

Satan, see 1 Kg.22.19–22; Zech.3.1–2; Job 1.6–2.10. **5:** The numbers are somewhat different in 2 Sam.24.9. **6:** *Levi*, compare Num.1.47–49. **15:** *Ornan*, Araunah in 2 Sam.24.16–24. **20:** The *four sons* do not appear in 2 Sam.24.19–20. **25:** The modest price of fifty shekels of silver (see 2 Sam.24.18–25 n.) is here raised to the very large sum of *six hundred shekels of gold*, perhaps

paid Ornan six hundred shekels of gold by weight for the site. ²⁶ And David built there an altar to the LORD and presented burnt offerings and peace offerings, and called upon the LORD, and he answered him with fire from heaven upon the altar of burnt offering. ²⁷ Then the LORD commanded the angel; and he put his sword back into its sheath.

28 At that time, when David saw that the LORD had answered him at the threshing floor of Ornan the Jeb'-usite, he made his sacrifices there. ²⁹ For the tabernacle of the LORD, which Moses had made in the wilderness, and the altar of burnt offering were at that time in the high place at Gibeon; ³⁰ but David could not go before it to inquire of God, for he was afraid of the sword of the angel of the LORD. ¹ Then David said, "Here

22 shall be the house of the LORD God and here the altar of burnt offering for Israel."

2 David commanded to gather together the aliens who were in the land of Israel, and he set stonecutters to prepare dressed stones for building the house of God. ³ David also provided great stores of iron for nails for the doors of the gates and for clamps, as well as bronze in quantities beyond weighing, ⁴ and cedar timbers without number; for the Sido'nians and Tyrians brought great quantities of cedar to David. ⁵ For David said, "Solomon my son is young and inexperienced, and the house that is to be

built for the LORD must be exceedingly magnificent, of fame and glory throughout all lands; I will therefore make preparation for it." So David provided materials in great quantity before his death.

6 Then he called for Solomon his son, and charged him to build a house for the LORD, the God of Israel. ⁷ David said to Solomon, "My son, I had it in my heart to build a house to the name of the LORD my God. ⁸ But the word of the LORD came to me, saying, 'You have shed much blood and have waged great wars; you shall not build a house to my name, because you have shed so much blood before me upon the earth. ⁹ Behold, a son shall be born to you; he shall be a man of peace. I will give him peace from all his enemies round about; for his name shall be Solomon, and I will give peace and quiet to Israel in his days. ¹⁰ He shall build a house for my name. He shall be my son, and I will be his father, and I will establish his royal throne in Israel for ever.' ¹¹ Now, my son, the LORD be with you, so that you may succeed in building the house of the LORD your God, as he has spoken concerning you. ¹² Only, may the LORD grant you discretion and understanding, that when he gives you charge over Israel you may keep the law of the LORD your God. ¹³ Then you will prosper if you are careful to observe the statutes and the ordinances which the LORD commanded Moses for Israel. Be strong, and of good courage. Fear not;

---

the equivalent of ten thousand dollars. The author is telling his readers that no price was too great for this precious site. **26:** The *fire from heaven* is lacking in the original account; it is a symbol of God's strong approval (compare 1 Kg.18.36–39). **28–30:** These verses, not in 2 Sam. ch. 24, are designed to show that there is now only one true place of sacrifice. **22.1:** A continuation of the preceding verses. The source, 2 Sam. ch. 24, identified the site as that of *the altar*, but said nothing about *the house of the LORD God*.

22.2–19: David makes preparations for the construction of the temple. According to the earlier record, David may have thought of building a temple (1 Kg.5.2–6), but it was Solomon who made and executed the plans, with the aid of Hiram of Tyre (1 Kg. chs. 5–7). The Chronicler regarded the temple as Judaism's greatest institution, and the new David as his nation's most important human figure. This figure and this institution must, therefore, be brought together. **2:** The reference to forced labor of *aliens* only may be based on 1 Kg.9.22, which overlooks 1 Kg.5.13; 11.28; 12.4. **3–5:** See 1 Kg. ch. 5, where this preparatory activity is credited to Solomon. **6–12:** Compare 1 Kg.8.17–21. **8:** *Blood and . . . wars*, compare 1 Kg.5.3. **13:** Compare

be not dismayed. ¹⁴ With great pains I have provided for the house of the LORD a hundred thousand talents of gold, a million talents of silver, and bronze and iron beyond weighing, for there is so much of it; timber and stone too I have provided. To these you must add. ¹⁵ You have an abundance of workmen: stonecutters, masons, carpenters, and all kinds of craftsmen without number, skilled in working ¹⁶ gold, silver, bronze, and iron. Arise and be doing! The LORD be with you!"

17 David also commanded all the leaders of Israel to help Solomon his son, saying, ¹⁸ "Is not the LORD your God with you? And has he not given you peace on every side? For he has delivered the inhabitants of the land into my hand; and the land is subdued before the LORD and his people. ¹⁹ Now set your mind and heart to seek the LORD your God. Arise and build the sanctuary of the LORD God, so that the ark of the covenant of the LORD and the holy vessels of God may be brought into a house built for the name of the LORD."

23 When David was old and full of days, he made Solomon his son king over Israel.

2 David assembled all the leaders of Israel and the priests and the Levites. ³ The Levites, thirty years old and upward, were numbered, and the total was thirty-eight thousand men. ⁴ "Twenty-four thousand of these," David said, "shall have charge of the work in the house of the LORD, six thousand shall be officers and judges, ⁵ four thousand gatekeepers, and four

thousand shall offer praises to the LORD with the instruments which I have made for praise." ⁶ And David organized them in divisions corresponding to the sons of Levi: Gershom, Kohath, and Merar'i.

7 The sons of Gershomˣ were Ladan and Shim'e-i. ⁸ The sons of Ladan: Jehi'el the chief, and Zetham, and Jo'el, three. ⁹ The sons of Shim'-e-i: Shelo'moth, Ha'zi-el, and Haran, three. These were the heads of the fathers' houses of Ladan. ¹⁰ And the sons of Shim'e-i: Jahath, Zina, and Je'ush, and Beri'ah. These four were the sons of Shim'e-i. ¹¹ Jahath was the chief, and Zizah the second; but Je'ush and Beri'ah had not many sons, therefore they became a father's house in one reckoning.

12 The sons of Kohath: Amram, Izhar, Hebron, and Uz'ziel, four. ¹³ The sons of Amram: Aaron and Moses. Aaron was set apart to consecrate the most holy things, that he and his sons for ever should burn incense before the LORD, and minister to him and pronounce blessings in his name for ever. ¹⁴ But the sons of Moses the man of God were named among the tribe of Levi. ¹⁵ The sons of Moses: Gershom and Elie'zer. ¹⁶ The sons of Gershom: Sheb'uel the chief. ¹⁷ The sons of Elie'zer: Rehabi'ah the chief; Elie'zer had no other sons, but the sons of Rehabi'ah were very many. ¹⁸ The sons of Izhar: Shelo'mith the chief. ¹⁹ The sons of Hebron: Jeri'ah the chief, Amari'ah the second, Jaha'ziel the third, and

x Vg Compare Gk Syr: Heb *to the Gershonite*

---

1 Kg.2.2. **14:** The amount of *gold* and *silver* is fantastically large (value estimated at five billion dollars). It is not to be taken literally, but as a figure of speech expressing the inestimable preciousness of the temple as a religious institution. Compare the more modest figures in 1 Kg.9.14,28; 10.10,14.

23.1–32: David organizes the Levites and assigns them their duties. In the time of the historical David there was no special class of Levites (see notes on ch. 6). But to the Chronicler and in his time, more than five hundred years later, they were very important (see Introduction); hence they must be brought into relationship with David. **1:** This single verse moves swiftly all the way from 1 Kg.1.1 to 1 Kg.2.1. **2–6:** On the use of men *thirty years old and upward*, compare Num.4.3; this was apparently older practice (but see Num.8.24). When more elaborate ritual required more men, the age for beginning service was apparently lowered to *twenty years*, as in vv. 24,27. On *the instruments*, see ch. 26, and compare Am.6.5. **7–21:** These

Jekame'am the fourth. ²⁰ The sons of Uz'ziel: Micah the chief and Isshi'ah the second. 21 The sons of Merar'i: Mahli and Mushi. The sons of Mahli: Elea'zar and Kish. ²² Elea'zar died having no sons, but only daughters; their kinsmen, the sons of Kish, married them. ²³ The sons of Mushi: Mahli, Eder, and Jer'emoth, three.

24 These were the sons of Levi by their fathers' houses, the heads of fathers' houses as they were registered according to the number of the names of the individuals from twenty years old and upward who were to do the work for the service of the house of the LORD. ²⁵ For David said, "The LORD, the God of Israel, has given peace to his people; and he dwells in Jerusalem for ever. ²⁶ And so the Levites no longer need to carry the tabernacle or any of the things for its service"– ²⁷ for by the last words of David these were the number of the Levites from twenty years old and upward– ²⁸ "but their duty shall be to assist the sons of Aaron for the service of the house of the LORD, having the care of the courts and the chambers, the cleansing of all that is holy, and any work for the service of the house of God; ²⁹ to assist also with the showbread, the flour for the cereal offering, the wafers of unleavened bread, the baked offering, the offering mixed with oil, and all measures of quantity or size. ³⁰ And they shall stand every morning, thanking and praising the LORD, and likewise at evening, ³¹ and whenever burnt offerings are offered to the LORD on sabbaths, new moons, and feast days, according to the number required of them, continually before the LORD. ³² Thus they shall

keep charge of the tent of meeting and the sanctuary, and shall attend the sons of Aaron, their brethren, for the service of the house of the LORD."

24 The divisions of the sons of Aaron were these. The sons of Aaron: Nadab, Abi'hu, Elea'zar, and Ith'amar. ² But Nadab and Abi'hu died before their father, and had no children, so Elea'zar and Ith'amar became the priests. ³ With the help of Zadok of the sons of Elea'zar, and Ahim'elech of the sons of Ith'amar, David organized them according to the appointed duties in their service. ⁴ Since more chief men were found among the sons of Elea'zar than among the sons of Ith'amar, they organized them under sixteen heads of fathers' houses of the sons of Elea'zar, and eight of the sons of Ith'amar. ⁵ They organized them by lot, all alike, for there were officers of the sanctuary and officers of God among both the sons of Elea'zar and the sons of Ith'amar. ⁶ And the scribe Shemai'ah the son of Nethan'el, a Levite, recorded them in the presence of the king, and the princes, and Zadok the priest, and Ahim'elech the son of Abi'athar, and the heads of the fathers' houses of the priests and of the Levites; one father's house being chosen for Elea'zar and one chosen for Ith'amar.

7 The first lot fell to Jehoi'arib, the second to Jedai'ah, ⁸ the third to Harim, the fourth to Se-o'rim, ⁹ the fifth to Malchi'jah, the sixth to Mij'-amin, ¹⁰ the seventh to Hakkoz, the eighth to Abi'jah, ¹¹ the ninth to Jeshua, the tenth to Shecani'ah, ¹² the eleventh to Eli'ashib, the twelfth to Jakim, ¹³ the thirteenth to Huppah, the fourteenth to Jesheb'e-ab, ¹⁴ the fifteenth to Bilgah, the sixteenth to Im-

---

verses were probably inspired by Num. chs. 3; 4; 8, at least in part. **24–32:** The new duties of *the Levites* are here more carefully defined.

24.1–31: David organizes the priests. David organized not only the Levites (ch. 23), but also the priests. Thus the highest ecclesiastical activity stemmed from the new David. **1–6:** See Num.3.2–4. **3:** *Zadok . . . and Ahimelech*, this should read "Zadok . . . and Abiathar"; compare vv. 6,31; 18.16; see also 2 Sam.8.16–18 n. **4:** The priests, at least in theory, were organized into twenty-four groups or divisions. **7–19:** A detailed exposition of the twenty-four divisions as they were or should have been in the Chronicler's own day. On the division of Abijah, see

mer, [15] the seventeenth to Hezir, the eighteenth to Hap'pizzez, [16] the nineteenth to Pethahi'ah, the twentieth to Jehez'kel, [17] the twenty-first to Jachin, the twenty-second to Gamul, [18] the twenty-third to Delai'ah, the twenty-fourth to Ma-azi'ah. [19] These had as their appointed duty in their service to come into the house of the LORD according to the procedure established for them by Aaron their father, as the LORD God of Israel had commanded him.

20 And of the rest of the sons of Levi: of the sons of Amram, Shu'-ba-el; of the sons of Shu'ba-el, Jehde'-iah. [21] Of Rehabi'ah: of the sons of Rehabi'ah, Isshi'ah the chief. [22] Of the Iz'harites, Shelo'moth; of the sons of Shelo'moth, Jahath. [23] The sons of Hebron:*y* Jeri'ah the chief,*z* Amari'ah the second, Jaha'ziel the third, Jekame'am the fourth. [24] The sons of Uz'-ziel, Micah; of the sons of Micah, Shamir. [25] The brother of Micah, Isshi'ah; of the sons of Isshi'ah, Zechari'ah. [26] The sons of Merar'i: Mahli and Mushi. The sons of Ja-azi'ah: Beno. [27] The sons of Merar'i: of Ja-azi'ah, Beno, Shoham, Zaccur, and Ibri. [28] Of Mahli: Elea'zar, who had no sons. [29] Of Kish, the sons of Kish: Jerah'meel. [30] The sons of Mushi: Mahli, Eder, and Jer'imoth. These were the sons of the Levites according to their fathers' houses. [31] These also, the head of each father's house and his younger brother alike, cast lots, just as their brethren the sons of Aaron, in the presence of King David, Zadok, Ahim'elech, and the heads of fathers' houses of the priests and of the Levites.

25 David and the chiefs of the service also set apart for the service certain of the sons of Asaph, and of Heman, and of Jedu'thun, who should prophesy with lyres, with harps, and with cymbals. The list of those who did the work and of their duties was: [2] Of the sons of Asaph: Zaccur, Joseph, Nethani'ah, and Ashare'lah, sons of Asaph, under the direction of Asaph, who prophesied under the direction of the king. [3] Of Jedu'thun, the sons of Jedu'thun: Gedali'ah, Zeri, Jeshai'ah, Shim'e-i,*a* Hashabi'ah, and Mattithi'ah, six, under the direction of their father Jedu'thun, who prophesied with the lyre in thanksgiving and praise to the LORD. [4] Of Heman, the sons of Heman: Bukki'ah, Mattani'ah, Uz'ziel, Shebu'el, and Jer'imoth, Hanani'ah, Hana'ni, Eli'athah, Giddal'ti, and Romam'ti-e'zer, Joshbekash'ah, Mallo'-thi, Hothir, Maha'zi-oth. [5] All these were the sons of Heman the king's seer, according to the promise of God to exalt him; for God had given Heman fourteen sons and three daughters. [6] They were all under the direction of their father in the music in the house of the LORD with cymbals, harps, and lyres for the service of the house of God. Asaph, Jedu'thun, and Heman were under the order of the king. [7] The number of them along with their brethren, who were trained in singing to the LORD, all who were skilful, was two hundred and eighty-eight. [8] And they cast lots for their duties, small and great, teacher and pupil alike.

9 The first lot fell for Asaph to Joseph; the second to Gedali'ah, to him and his brethren and his sons, twelve; [10] the third to Zaccur, his sons and his brethren, twelve; [11] the

y See 23.19: Heb lacks *Hebron*
z See 23.19: Heb lacks *the chief*
a One Ms: Gk: Heb lacks *Shimei*

Lk.1.5. **20–31:** A supplementary list of Levites, having some names in common with 23.7–23.
25.1–31: David organizes the musicians. 1–8: Corresponding to the twenty-four divisions of priests (ch. 24) are projected twenty-four divisions of musicians, arranged under three great names, Asaph, Heman, and Jeduthun (compare 6.31–48; 15.16–24; 16.4–7,37–42; 23.5). Here Jeduthun takes the place of Ethan in some of the other lists. According to 23.5 the total number of musicians was thought to be four thousand but here (v. 7) only *two hundred and eighty-eight* (24 × 12) are considered. For a more primitive use of music by a *seer* (v. 5) to aid him to *prophesy* (v. 1), see 2 Kg.3.15; compare 1 Sam.10.5. **4:** Hananiah . . . *Mahazioth*, these nine names seem artificially formed, for when put together and translated they suggest a series

fourth to Izri, his sons and his brethren, twelve; [12] the fifth to Nethani'ah, his sons and his brethren, twelve; [13] the sixth to Bukki'ah, his sons and his brethren, twelve; [14] the seventh to Jeshare'lah, his sons and his brethren, twelve; [15] the eighth to Jeshai'ah, his sons and his brethren, twelve; [16] the ninth to Mattani'ah, his sons and his brethren, twelve; [17] the tenth to Shim'-e-i, his sons and his brethren, twelve; [18] the eleventh to Az'arel, his sons and his brethren, twelve; [19] the twelfth to Hashabi'ah, his sons and his brethren, twelve; [20] to the thirteenth, Shu'ba-el, his sons and his brethren, twelve; [21] to the fourteenth, Mattithi'ah, his sons and his brethren, twelve; [22] to the fifteenth, to Jer'emoth, his sons and his brethren, twelve; [23] to the sixteenth, to Hanani'ah, his sons and his brethren, twelve; [24] to the seventeenth, to Joshbekash'ah, his sons and his brethren, twelve; [25] to the eighteenth, to Hana'ni, his sons and his brethren, twelve; [26] to the nineteenth, to Mallo'-thi, his sons and his brethren, twelve; [27] to the twentieth, to Eli'athah, his sons and his brethren, twelve; [28] to the twenty-first, to Hothir, his sons and his brethren, twelve; [29] to the twenty-second, to Giddal'ti, his sons and his brethren, twelve; [30] to the twenty-third, to Maha'zi-oth, his sons and his brethren, twelve; [31] to the twenty-fourth, to Romam'ti-e'zer, his sons and his brethren, twelve.

26 As for the divisions of the gatekeepers: of the Ko'rahites, Meshelemi'ah the son of Ko're, of the sons of Asaph. [2] And Meshelemi'ah had sons: Zechari'ah the first-born, Jedi'a-el the second, Zebadi'ah the third, Jath'ni-el the fourth, [3] Elam the fifth, Jehoha'nan the sixth, Eli-e-ho-e'-nai the seventh. [4] And O'bed-e'dom had sons: Shemai'ah the first-born, Jehoz'abad the second, Jo'ah the third, Sachar the fourth, Nethan'el the fifth, [5] Am'mi-el the sixth, Is'sachar the seventh, Pe-ul'lethai the eighth; for God blessed him. [6] Also to his son Shemai'ah were sons born who were rulers in their fathers' houses, for they were men of great ability. [7] The sons of Shemai'ah: Othni, Reph'a-el, Obed, and Elza'bad, whose brethren were able men, Eli'hu and Semachi'ah. [8] All these were of the sons of O'bed-e'dom with their sons and brethren, able men qualified for the service; sixty-two of O'bed-e'dom. [9] And Meshelemi'ah had sons and brethren, able men, eighteen. [10] And Hosah, of the sons of Merar'i, had sons: Shimri the chief (for though he was not the first-born, his father made him chief), [11] Hilki'ah the second, Tebali'ah the third, Zechari'ah the fourth: all the sons and brethren of Hosah were thirteen.

12 These divisions of the gatekeepers, corresponding to their chief men, had duties, just as their brethren did, ministering in the house of the LORD; [13] and they cast lots by fathers' houses, small and great alike, for their gates. [14] The lot for the east fell to Shelemi'-ah. They cast lots also for his son Zechari'ah, a shrewd counselor, and his lot came out for the north. [15] O'bed-e'dom's came out for the south, and to his sons was allotted the storehouse. [16] For Shuppim and Hosah it came out for the west, at the gate of Shal'lecheth on the road that goes up.

of phrases often used in prayer: "Be gracious, O LORD, be gracious to me; thou art my God, whom I magnify and exalt, my help when in trouble; I have fulfilled (or spoken), he has increased visions." **9–31:** This is a highly artificial alternating arrangement of the names of vv. 2–4.

26.1–32: Organization of the gatekeepers, treasurers, and other functionaries. The Chronicler concludes his presentation of the organization of the Levites in the service of the temple (compare 9.17–27; 15.23–24; 16.37–42; Ps.84.10). **1–11:** It is obvious from such names as *Korahites* (6.37), *Asaph* (6.39), and *Obed-edom* (15.21) that the gatekeepers were considered to be closely related to the musicians. All told there were four thousand (23.5), though only ninety-three (62 + 18 + 13, vv. 8,9,11) are considered here. **12–19:** Here the Chronicler forgets entirely his historical pose and describes the temple as it is in his time, mentioning the four sides on the *east*,

Watch corresponded to watch. [17] On the east there were six each day,[b] on the north four each day, on the south four each day, as well as two and two at the storehouse; [18] and for the parbar[c] on the west there were four at the road and two at the parbar. [19] These were the divisions of the gate-keepers among the Ko'rahites and the sons of Merar'i.

20 And of the Levites, Ahi'jah had charge of the treasuries of the house of God and the treasuries of the dedicated gifts. [21] The sons of Ladan, the sons of the Gershonites belonging to Ladan, the heads of the fathers' houses belonging to Ladan the Gershonite: Jehi'eli.[d]

22 The sons of Jehi'eli, Zetham and Jo'el his brother, were in charge of the treasuries of the house of the LORD. [23] Of the Am'ramites, the Iz'harites, the He'bronites, and the Uzzie'lites— [24] and Sheb'uel the son of Gershom, son of Moses, was chief officer in charge of the treasuries. [25] His brethren: from Elie'zer were his son Rehabi'ah, and his son Jeshai'ah, and his son Joram, and his son Zichri, and his son Shelo'moth. [26] This Shelo'moth and his brethren were in charge of all the treasuries of the dedicated gifts which David the king, and the heads of the fathers' houses, and the officers of the thousands and the hundreds, and the commanders of the army, had dedicated. [27] From spoil won in battles they dedicated gifts for the maintenance of the house of the LORD. [28] Also all that Samuel the seer, and Saul the son of Kish, and Abner the son of Ner, and Jo'ab the son of Zeru'iah had dedicated—all dedicated gifts were in the care of Shelo'moth[e] and his brethren.

29 Of the Iz'harites, Chenani'ah and his sons were appointed to outside duties for Israel, as officers and judges. [30] Of the He'bronites, Hashabi'ah and his brethren, one thousand seven hundred men of ability, had the oversight of Israel westward of the Jordan for all the work of the LORD and for the service of the king. [31] Of the He'-bronites, Jeri'jah was chief of the He'-bronites of whatever genealogy or fathers' houses. (In the fortieth year of David's reign search was made and men of great ability among them were found at Jazer in Gilead.) [32] King David appointed him and his brethren, two thousand seven hundred men of ability, heads of fathers' houses, to have the oversight of the Reubenites, the Gadites, and the half-tribe of the Manas'sites for everything pertaining to God and for the affairs of the king.

27 This is the list of the people of Israel, the heads of fathers' houses, the commanders of thousands and hundreds, and their officers who served the king in all matters concerning the divisions that came and went, month after month throughout the year, each division numbering twenty-four thousand.

2 Jasho'beam the son of Zab'di-el was in charge of the first division in the first month; in his division were twenty-four thousand. [3] He was a descendant of Perez, and was chief of all the commanders of the army for the first month. [4] Dodai the Aho'hite[f] was in charge of the division of the second month; in his division were twenty-four thousand. [5] The third

b Gk: Heb *Levites*
c The meaning of the word *parbar* is unknown
d The Hebrew text of verse 21 is confused
e Heb *Shelomith*
f Gk: Heb *Ahohite and his division and Mikloth the chief officer*

---

north, south, and west; also the gates (v. 13), even giving the name of one (v. 16). **26:** Compare Num.31.48–54. **29–32:** Those appointed to outside duties were to look after the interests of the religious establishment in all the rest of the idealized nation.

27.1–34: David organizes military and civil affairs. The arbitrary numerical schemes already applied to the clergy (23.4–5; 24.4; 25.9–31) are extended to the military and other groups. **1:** The total number of the king's bodyguard, 288,000 (12 × 24,000) is historically unrealistic, but entirely in line with the Chronicler's dream of a marvelous future kingdom (see 22.14 n.) and contrast the modest figure in 2 Sam.15.18). **2–4:** Compare 11.11–12; 2 Sam.23.8–9. **5:**

commander, for the third month, was Benai'ah, the son of Jehoi'ada the priest, as chief; in his division were twenty-four thousand. [6] This is the Benai'ah who was a mighty man of the thirty and in command of the thirty; Ammiz'abad his son was in charge of his division.[g] [7] As'ahel the brother of Jo'ab was fourth, for the fourth month, and his son Zebadi'ah after him; in his division were twenty-four thousand. [8] The fifth commander, for the fifth month, was Shamhuth, the Iz'rahite; in his division were twenty-four thousand. [9] Sixth, for the sixth month, was Ira, the son of Ikkesh the Teko'ite; in his division were twenty-four thousand. [10] Seventh, for the seventh month, was Helez the Pel'onite, of the sons of E'phraim; in his division were twenty-four thousand. [11] Eighth, for the eighth month, was Sib'becai the Hu'shathite, of the Ze'-rahites; in his division were twenty-four thousand. [12] Ninth, for the ninth month, was Abi-e'zer of An'athoth, a Benjaminite; in his division were twenty-four thousand. [13] Tenth, for the tenth month, was Ma'harai of Ne-toph'ah, of the Ze'rahites; in his division were twenty-four thousand. [14] Eleventh, for the eleventh month, was Benai'ah of Pira'thon, of the sons of E'phraim; in his division were twenty-four thousand. [15] Twelfth, for the twelfth month, was Heldai the Netoph'athite, of Oth'ni-el; in his division were twenty-four thousand.

16 Over the tribes of Israel, for the Reubenites Elie'zer the son of Zichri was chief officer; for the Simeonites, Shephati'ah the son of Ma'acah; [17] for Levi, Hashabi'ah the son of Kem'uel; for Aaron, Zadok; [18] for Judah, Eli'-hu, one of David's brothers; for Is'-sachar, Omri the son of Michael; [19] for Zeb'ulun, Ishma'iah the son of Obadi'ah; for Naph'tali, Jer'emoth the son of Az'riel; [20] for the E'phraim-ites, Hoshe'a the son of Azazi'ah; for the half-tribe of Manas'seh, Jo'el the son of Pedai'ah; [21] for the half-tribe of Manas'seh in Gilead, Iddo the son of Zechari'ah; for Benjamin, Ja-a'si-el the son of Abner; [22] for Dan, Az'arel the son of Jero'ham. These were the leaders of the tribes of Israel. [23] David did not number those below twenty years of age, for the Lord had promised to make Israel as many as the stars of heaven. [24] Jo'ab the son of Zeru'iah began to number, but did not finish; yet wrath came upon Israel for this, and the number was not entered in the chronicles of King David.

25 Over the king's treasuries was Az'maveth the son of Ad'i-el; and over the treasuries in the country, in the cities, in the villages and in the towers, was Jonathan the son of Uzzi'-ah; [26] and over those who did the work of the field for tilling the soil was Ezri the son of Chelub; [27] and over the vineyards was Shim'e-i the Ra'-mathite; and over the produce of the vineyards for the wine cellars was Zabdi the Shiphmite. [28] Over the olive and sycamore trees in the Shephe'-lah was Ba'al-ha'nan the Gede'rite; and over the stores of oil was Jo'-ash. [29] Over the herds that pastured in Sharon was Shitrai the Shar'onite; over the herds in the valleys was Shaphat the son of Adlai. [30] Over the camels was Obil the Ish'maelite; and over the she-asses was Jehde'iah the Meron'othite. Over the flocks was Jaziz the Hagrite. [31] All these were stewards of King David's property.

32 Jonathan, David's uncle, was a counselor, being a man of understanding and a scribe; he and Jehi'el the son of Hach'moni attended the king's sons. [33] Ahith'ophel was the king's counselor, and Hushai the Archite was the

g Gk Vg: Heb *was his division*

Compare 11.22; 2 Sam.23.20–23. **7**: *Asahel* was killed early in his career (2 Sam.2.18–23); hence *his son Zebadiah* had to take his place. **16–22**: The traditional tribal divisions, obsolete in the Chronicler's day, are regarded as important in dreams of future restoration. **23–24**: Two references to the census of ch. 21. **23**: Compare 22.17. **32–34**: No *Jonathan* who was David's uncle is known elsewhere; perhaps the name here is reminiscent of Saul's son (1 Sam.18.1–4).

king's friend. [34] Ahith'ophel was succeeded by Jehoi'ada the son of Benai'ah, and Abi'athar. Jo'ab was commander of the king's army.

28 David assembled at Jerusalem all the officials of Israel, the officials of the tribes, the officers of the divisions that served the king, the commanders of thousands, the commanders of hundreds, the stewards of all the property and cattle of the king and his sons, together with the palace officials, the mighty men, and all the seasoned warriors. [2] Then King David rose to his feet and said: "Hear me, my brethren and my people. I had it in my heart to build a house of rest for the ark of the covenant of the LORD, and for the footstool of our God; and I made preparations for building. [3] But God said to me, 'You may not build a house for my name, for you are a warrior and have shed blood.' [4] Yet the LORD God of Israel chose me from all my father's house to be king over Israel for ever; for he chose Judah as leader, and in the house of Judah my father's house, and among my father's sons he took pleasure in me to make me king over all Israel. [5] And of all my sons (for the LORD has given me many sons) he has chosen Solomon my son to sit upon the throne of the kingdom of the LORD over Israel. [6] He said to me, 'It is Solomon your son who shall build my house and my courts, for I have chosen him to be my son, and I will be his father. [7] I will establish his kingdom for ever if he continues resolute in keeping my commandments and my ordinances, as he is today.' [8] Now therefore in the sight of all Israel, the assembly of the LORD, and in the hearing of our God, observe and seek out all the commandments of the LORD your God; that you may possess this good land, and leave it for an inheritance to your children after you for ever.

9 "And you, Solomon my son, know the God of your father, and serve him with a whole heart and with a willing mind; for the LORD searches all hearts, and understands every plan and thought. If you seek him, he will be found by you; but if you forsake him, he will cast you off for ever. [10] Take heed now, for the LORD has chosen you to build a house for the sanctuary; be strong, and do it."

11 Then David gave Solomon his son the plan of the vestibule of the temple, and of its houses, its treasuries, its upper rooms, and its inner chambers, and of the room for the mercy seat; [12] and the plan of all that he had in mind for the courts of the house of the LORD, all the surrounding chambers, the treasuries of the house of God, and the treasuries for dedicated gifts; [13] for the divisions of the priests and of the Levites, and all the work of the service in the house of the LORD; for all the vessels for the service in the house of the LORD, [14] the weight of gold for all golden vessels for each service, the weight of silver vessels for each service, [15] the weight of the golden lampstands and their lamps, the weight of gold for each lampstand and its lamps, the weight of silver for a lampstand and its lamps, according to the use of each lampstand in the service, [16] the weight of gold for each table for the showbread, the silver for the

---

This *Jehiel* is otherwise unknown. *Ahithophel* (2 Sam.15.31; 16.23; 17.23) and *Hushai the Archite* (2 Sam.15.32–37; 16.16–19; 17.5–16) were well-known historical characters. *Jehoiada the son of Benaiah*, the reverse of the names in v. 5; probably correct, as boys were often named after their grandfathers. *Abiathar* is doubtless the priest (compare 1 Sam.22.20–23). *Joab*, see 2 Sam. 2.12–17 n.

28.1–21: David transmits the final plans for the temple to Solomon. 1–8: Compare 22.2–19 and 23.1, where the new David's resolve to name Solomon his successor and to turn the temple plans over to him is already set forth (see 22.2–19 n.). Here a great assembly is called to carry out the resolve. **2:** Compare Ps. 132. **3:** See 22.6–12 n. **6–8:** Compare 17.11–14; 22.9–10; Dt.4.5. **9–10:** Compare Dt.4.25–31. **11–19:** The Chronicler must make his point that David is much greater than Solomon, and that all these things were done in accordance with the divine will.

silver tables, [17] and pure gold for the forks, the basins, and the cups; for the golden bowls and the weight of each; for the silver bowls and the weight of each; [18] for the altar of incense made of refined gold, and its weight; also his plan for the golden chariot of the cherubim that spread their wings and covered the ark of the covenant of the LORD. [19] All this he made clear by the writing from the hand of the LORD concerning it,[h] all the work to be done according to the plan.

20 Then David said to Solomon his son, "Be strong and of good courage, and do it. Fear not, be not dismayed; for the LORD God, even my God, is with you. He will not fail you or forsake you, until all the work for the service of the house of the LORD is finished. [21] And behold the divisions of the priests and the Levites for all the service of the house of God; and with you in all the work will be every willing man who has skill for any kind of service; also the officers and all the people will be wholly at your command."

29 And David the king said to all the assembly, "Solomon my son, whom alone God has chosen, is young and inexperienced, and the work is great; for the palace will not be for man but for the LORD God. [2] So I have provided for the house of my God, so far as I was able, the gold for the things of gold, the silver for the things of silver, and the bronze for the things of bronze, the iron for the things of iron, and wood for the things of wood, besides great quantities of onyx and stones for setting, antimony, colored stones, all sorts of precious stones, and marble. [3] Moreover, in addition to all that I have provided for the holy house,

I have a treasure of my own of gold and silver, and because of my devotion to the house of my God I give it to the house of my God: [4] three thousand talents of gold, of the gold of Ophir, and seven thousand talents of refined silver, for overlaying the walls of the house, [5] and for all the work to be done by craftsmen, gold for the things of gold and silver for the things of silver. Who then will offer willingly, consecrating himself today to the LORD?"

6 Then the heads of fathers' houses made their freewill offerings, as did also the leaders of the tribes, the commanders of thousands and of hundreds, and the officers over the king's work. [7] They gave for the service of the house of God five thousand talents and ten thousand darics of gold, ten thousand talents of silver, eighteen thousand talents of bronze, and a hundred thousand talents of iron. [8] And whoever had precious stones gave them to the treasury of the house of the LORD, in the care of Jehi'el the Gershonite. [9] Then the people rejoiced because these had given willingly, for with a whole heart they had offered freely to the LORD; David the king also rejoiced greatly.

10 Therefore David blessed the LORD in the presence of all the assembly; and David said: "Blessed art thou, O LORD, the God of Israel our father, for ever and ever. [11] Thine, O LORD, is the greatness, and the power, and the glory, and the victory, and the majesty; for all that is in the heavens and in the earth is thine; thine is the kingdom, O LORD, and thou art exalted as head above all. [12] Both riches and

h Cn: Heb *upon me*

The golden chariot may have been suggested by Ps.18.10 and Ezek.1.4–21. **19:** David is said to have received plans for the temple in much the same way as Moses traditionally received plans for the tabernacle (Ex. ch. 25). It is not clear whether *the writing* is thought of as done by David or the LORD (compare Ex.24.4,12; 31.18; 34.1,27–28; Dt.5.22).
29.1–30: The investiture of Solomon and the death of David. 1: The word *palace* is probably an error for "house," meaning the temple. **2–5:** Compare 22.14–16. **6–9:** The call for a freewill offering again follows the tradition of Moses (see 28.19 n.; compare Ex.25.1–9; 35.4–29). *Darics* were originally coins of Persian origin; compare Ezra 8.27. **10–19:** David's prayer of farewell, a beautiful composition of the Chronicler, reflecting the best theology of his time

honor come from thee, and thou rulest over all. In thy hand are power and might; and in thy hand it is to make great and to give strength to all. [13] And now we thank thee, our God, and praise thy glorious name.

14 "But who am I, and what is my people, that we should be able thus to offer willingly? For all things come from thee, and of thy own have we given thee. [15] For we are strangers before thee, and sojourners, as all our fathers were; our days on the earth are like a shadow, and there is no abiding.[i] [16] O LORD our God, all this abundance that we have provided for building thee a house for thy holy name comes from thy hand and is all thy own. [17] I know, my God, that thou triest the heart, and hast pleasure in uprightness; in the uprightness of my heart I have freely offered all these things, and now I have seen thy people, who are present here, offering freely and joyously to thee. [18] O LORD, the God of Abraham, Isaac, and Israel, our fathers, keep for ever such purposes and thoughts in the hearts of thy people, and direct their hearts toward thee. [19] Grant to Solomon my son that with a whole heart he may keep thy commandments, thy testimonies, and thy statutes, performing all, and that he may build the palace for which I have made provision."

20 Then David said to all the assembly, "Bless the LORD your God." And all the assembly blessed the LORD, the God of their fathers, and bowed their heads, and worshiped the LORD, and did obeisance to the king. [21] And they performed sacrifices to the LORD, and on the next day offered burnt offerings to the LORD, a thousand bulls, a thousand rams, and a thousand lambs, with their drink offerings, and sacrifices in abundance for all Israel; [22] and they ate and drank before the LORD on that day with great gladness.

And they made Solomon the son of David king the second time, and they anointed him as prince for the LORD, and Zadok as priest. [23] Then Solomon sat on the throne of the LORD as king instead of David his father; and he prospered, and all Israel obeyed him. [24] All the leaders and the mighty men, and also all the sons of King David, pledged their allegiance to King Solomon. [25] And the LORD gave Solomon great repute in the sight of all Israel, and bestowed upon him such royal majesty as had not been on any king before him in Israel.

26 Thus David the son of Jesse reigned over all Israel. [27] The time that he reigned over Israel was forty years; he reigned seven years in Hebron, and thirty-three years in Jerusalem. [28] Then he died in a good old age, full of days, riches, and honor; and Solomon his son reigned in his stead. [29] Now the acts of King David, from first to last, are written in the Chronicles of Samuel the seer, and in the Chronicles of Nathan the prophet, and in the Chronicles of Gad the seer, [30] with accounts of all his rule and his might and of the circumstances that came upon him and upon Israel, and upon all the kingdoms of the countries.

i Gk Vg: Heb *hope*

(probably fourth century B.C.); there is as yet no hint of a blissful after-life (see 1 Kg.8.12–21 n., 22–40 n.). **19:** *Palace*, see v. 1 n. **22:** The phrase *the second time* is used in reference to 23.1. The scene here is a kind of ratification of what David had already done because God had determined it (v. 1). Note the part played by *Zadok* in 1 Kg. ch. 1. **23:** The equivalent of this verse in the earlier account (1 Kg.2.12) comes after the death of David. **27:** See 1 Kg.2.11. **28:** Compare the adulatory quality of this verse with 1 Kg.2.10. **29–30:** On the nature of these sources, see the Introduction. The phrase *the kingdoms of the countries* refers to the surrounding peoples with which David came into contact, such as the Philistines, the Arameans, the Ammonites, the Moabites, and the Edomites.

CHRONICLES

The general character and problems of 2 Chronicles are discussed in the Introduction to 1 Chronicles, for 1 and 2 Chronicles were originally a single book. Taking up the story of the monarchy where 1 Chronicles leaves off, chs. 1 to 9 of 2 Chronicles present the reign of Solomon from the viewpoint of the Chronicler; his Solomon is an ideal figure, second only to David in importance. The greater part of the book, chs. 10–36, is the Chronicler's account of the period of the Divided Monarchy, Judah and Israel (see "Survey of . . . Bible Lands," §§ 11–12). He writes as little as possible about the northern kingdom (Israel), since to him it did not represent the true Israel and hence was not really important. His hostility toward the northern kingdom is sometimes attributed to hatred of the Samaritans. The Chronicler was at the same time aware of the grave apostasy of the southern kingdom (Judah). Accepting the Deuteronomic view that national calamity is the result of national sin, he found sufficient reason for the disaster that overtook Judah. He interpreted the past as a warning for his own time and for the future.

SOLOMON THE SON OF DAVID ESTABlished himself in his kingdom, and the LORD his God was with him and made him exceedingly great.

2 Solomon spoke to all Israel, to the commanders of thousands and of hundreds, to the judges, and to all the leaders in all Israel, the heads of fathers' houses. ³ And Solomon, and all the assembly with him, went to the high place that was at Gibeon; for the tent of meeting of God, which Moses the servant of the LORD had made, in the wilderness, was there. ⁴ (But David had brought up the ark of God from Kir′iath-je′arim to the place that David had prepared for it, for he had pitched a tent for it in Jerusalem.) ⁵ Moreover the bronze altar that Bez′alel the son of Uri, son of Hur, had made, was there before the tabernacle of the LORD. And Solomon and the assembly sought the LORD. ⁶ And Solomon went up there to the bronze altar before the LORD, which was at the tent of meeting, and offer-

ed a thousand burnt offerings upon it.

7 In that night God appeared to Solomon, and said to him, "Ask what I shall give you." ⁸ And Solomon said to God, "Thou hast shown great and steadfast love to David my father, and hast made me king in his stead. ⁹ O LORD God, let thy promise to David my father be now fulfilled, for thou hast made me king over a people as many as the dust of the earth. ¹⁰ Give me now wisdom and knowledge to go out and come in before this people, for who can rule this thy people, that is so great?" ¹¹ God answered Solomon, "Because this was in your heart, and you have not asked possessions, wealth, honor, or the life of those who hate you, and have not even asked long life, but have asked wisdom and knowledge for yourself that you may rule my people over whom I have made you king, ¹² wisdom and knowledge are granted to you. I will also give you riches, possessions, and honor, such as none of the kings had who were before you,

---

1.1–17: Solomon receives wisdom. 2–6: Our author passes over the machinations and murders of 1 Kg. chs. 1–2, also the marriage alliance with Egypt of 1 Kg.3.1–2, and begins his account of Solomon with a religious act, the visit to the high place at Gibeon. The ark of the covenant is introduced into the story (contrast 1 Kg.3.3–15) to make less objectionable a visit to a high place (compare 1 Kg.3.3; 2 Kg.23.5; 1 Chr.21.29). *Bezazel* and *the bronze altar*, compare Ex. 27.1–2; 31.1; 1 Chr.2.20. **7–13:** This episode, very creditable to Solomon, is here abridged from 1 Kg.3.3–15; the statement that it was a dream has been removed. Also removed is the story of the judgment between the two harlots (1 Kg.3.16–28). **9:** *People as many as the dust of the earth*, compare 1 Kg.4.20. **14–17:** This section is taken from 1 Kg.10.26–29.

and none after you shall have the like."
[13] So Solomon came from[a] the high
place at Gibeon, from before the tent
of meeting, to Jerusalem. And he
reigned over Israel.

14 Solomon gathered together chariots and horsemen; he had fourteen
hundred chariots and twelve thousand
horsemen, whom he stationed in the
chariot cities and with the king in
Jerusalem. [15] And the king made silver and gold as common in Jerusalem
as stone, and he made cedar as plentiful as the sycamore of the Shephe'-
lah. [16] And Solomon's import of
horses was from Egypt and Ku'e, and
the king's traders received them from
Ku'e for a price. [17] They imported a
chariot from Egypt for six hundred
shekels of silver, and a horse for a
hundred and fifty; likewise through
them these were exported to all the
kings of the Hittites and the kings of
Syria.

2[b] Now Solomon purposed to build
a temple for the name of the
LORD, and a royal palace for himself.
[2c] And Solomon assigned seventy
thousand men to bear burdens and
eighty thousand to quarry in the hill
country, and three thousand six hundred to oversee them. [3] And Solomon
sent word to Huram the king of Tyre:
"As you dealt with David my father and
sent him cedar to build himself a house
to dwell in, so deal with me. [4] Behold, I
am about to build a house for the name
of the LORD my God and dedicate it to
him for the burning of incense of sweet
spices before him, and for the continual offering of the showbread, and
for burnt offerings morning and evening, on the sabbaths and the new
moons and the appointed feasts of the
LORD our God, as ordained for ever
for Israel. [5] The house which I am to
build will be great, for our God is
greater than all gods. [6] But who is able
to build him a house, since heaven,

even highest heaven, cannot contain
him? Who am I to build a house for
him, except as a place to burn incense
before him? [7] So now send me a
man skilled to work in gold, silver,
bronze, and iron, and in purple, crimson, and blue fabrics, trained also in
engraving, to be with the skilled workers who are with me in Judah and Jerusalem, whom David my father provided. [8] Send me also cedar, cypress,
and algum timber from Lebanon, for I
know that your servants know how to
cut timber in Lebanon. And my servants will be with your servants, [9] to
prepare timber for me in abundance,
for the house I am to build will be
great and wonderful. [10] I will give for
your servants, the hewers who cut timber, twenty thousand cors of crushed
wheat, twenty thousand cors of barley,
twenty thousand baths of wine, and
twenty thousand baths of oil."

11 Then Huram the king of Tyre
answered in a letter which he sent to
Solomon, "Because the LORD loves his
people he has made you king over
them." [12] Huram also said, "Blessed
be the LORD God of Israel, who made
heaven and earth, who has given King
David a wise son, endued with discretion and understanding, who will
build a temple for the LORD, and a
royal palace for himself.

13 "Now I have sent a skilled man,
endued with understanding, Huram-
abi, [14] the son of a woman of the
daughters of Dan, and his father was a
man of Tyre. He is trained to work
in gold, silver, bronze, iron, stone, and
wood, and in purple, blue, and crimson fabrics and fine linen, and to do
all sorts of engraving and execute any
design that may be assigned him, with
your craftsmen, the craftsmen of my
lord, David your father. [15] Now
therefore the wheat and barley, oil

a Gk Vg: Heb *to*
b Ch 1.18 in Heb
c Ch 2.1 in Heb

2.1–18: Solomon prepares to build the temple. 1–10: This is a rewritten version of 1 Kg.5.1–6,
11; note *Huram* instead of Hiram as the name of *the king of Tyre.* **11–12:** Expanded from
1 Kg.5.7, where the *letter* does not appear. **13–16:** *Huram-abi,* see 1 Kg.7.13–14 n. Here his
mother is from *Dan,* in 1 Kg.7.14 from the tribe of Naphtali (compare Ex.31.1–5). *Joppa* is not

and wine, of which my lord has spoken, let him send to his servants; [16] and we will cut whatever timber you need from Lebanon, and bring it to you in rafts by sea to Joppa, so that you may take it up to Jerusalem."

17 Then Solomon took a census of all the aliens who were in the land of Israel, after the census of them which David his father had taken; and there were found a hundred and fifty-three thousand six hundred. [18] Seventy thousand of them he assigned to bear burdens, eighty thousand to quarry in the hill country, and three thousand six hundred as overseers to make the people work.

3 Then Solomon began to build the house of the LORD in Jerusalem on Mount Mori'ah, where the LORD had appeared to David his father, at the place that David had appointed, on the threshing floor of Ornan the Jeb'usite. [2] He began to build in the second month of the fourth year of his reign. [3] These are Solomon's measurements[d] for building the house of God: the length, in cubits of the old standard, was sixty cubits, and the breadth twenty cubits. [4] The vestibule in front of the nave of the house was twenty cubits long, equal to the width of the house;[e] and its height was a hundred and twenty cubits. He overlaid it on the inside with pure gold. [5] The nave he lined with cypress, and covered it with fine gold, and made palms and chains on it. [6] He adorned the house with settings of precious stones. The gold was gold of Parva'im. [7] So he lined the house with gold–its beams, its thresholds, its walls, and its doors; and he carved cherubim on the walls.

8 And he made the most holy place; its length, corresponding to the breadth of the house, was twenty cubits, and its breadth was twenty cubits; he overlaid it with six hundred talents of fine gold. [9] The weight of the nails was one shekel[f] to fifty shekels of gold. And he overlaid the upper chambers with gold.

10 In the most holy place he made two cherubim of wood[g] and overlaid[h] them with gold. [11] The wings of the cherubim together extended twenty cubits: one wing of the one, of five cubits, touched the wall of the house, and its other wing, of five cubits, touched the wing of the other cherub; [12] and of this cherub, one wing, of five cubits, touched the wall of the house, and the other wing, also of five cubits, was joined to the wing of the first cherub. [13] The wings of these cherubim extended twenty cubits; the cherubim[i] stood on their feet, facing the nave. [14] And he made the veil of blue and purple and crimson fabrics

d Syr: Heb *foundations*   *e* 1 Kg 6.3: Heb uncertain
f Compare Gk: Heb lacks *one shekel*
g Gk: Heb uncertain
h Heb *they overlaid*   *i* Heb *they*

---

mentioned in 1 Kg.5.9. **17–18:** In the new Israel of the Chronicler (see Introduction to 1 Chronicles) *aliens* must of course perform the forced labor, though the historical arrangement was quite otherwise (compare 1 Kg.5.13–18, especially v. 13; also 1 Kg.9.22; 12.4).

3.1–17: Details of the building. This is a condensed and rewritten version of 1 Kg. ch. 6 and 1 Kg.7.15–22 (see notes there). **1:** The name *Moriah* appears only here and in Gen.22.2, where another location is probably to be understood. *Ornan the Jebusite*, in 2 Sam.24.16 "Araunah" (compare 1 Chr.21.15). **3:** *Cubits*, see 1 Kg.6.2–6 n. The *cubits of the old standard* were larger, being about twenty inches in length. **4:** In 1 Kg.6.2 the height of the main part of the building is given as "thirty cubits"; here the measurement *hundred and twenty cubits*, given as the height of *the vestibule*, is either a textual error or a typical exaggeration of the Chronicler to emphasize the impressiveness of the ideal temple. **6:** The location of *Parvaim* is unknown; it may be Arabia (see Ophir, 1 Kg.9.28 n.). **8–9:** Compare 1 Kg.6.19–22, where much *gold* is already in evidence; but *six hundred talents* (about 40,000 lbs.) stands here only and fairly staggers the imagination, which is perhaps what the Chronicler intended to do in his zeal to make the ideal temple impressive. **10–14:** Abridged from 1 Kg.6.23–28. *Cherubim*, see 1 Sam.4.4 n. The desciption of *the veil* before *the most holy place* (the inner room at the rear of the temple, sometimes called the "holy of holies") is drawn from a similar feature of the tabernacle (Ex.26.31). The historical temple of Solomon had doors at this point (1 Kg.6.31). At the time of the Chron-

and fine linen, and worked cherubim on it.

15 In front of the house he made two pillars thirty-five cubits high, with a capital of five cubits on the top of each. [16] He made chains like a necklace[j] and put them on the tops of the pillars; and he made a hundred pomegranates, and put them on the chains. [17] He set up the pillars in front of the temple, one on the south, the other on the north; that on the south he called Jachin, and that on the north Bo'az.

4 He made an altar of bronze, twenty cubits long, and twenty cubits wide, and ten cubits high. [2] Then he made the molten sea; it was round, ten cubits from brim to brim, and five cubits high, and a line of thirty cubits measured its circumference. [3] Under it were figures of gourds,[k] for thirty[l] cubits, compassing the sea round about; the gourds[k] were in two rows, cast with it when it was cast. [4] It stood upon twelve oxen, three facing north, three facing west, three facing south, and three facing east; the sea was set upon them, and all their hinder parts were inward. [5] Its thickness was a handbreadth; and its brim was made like the brim of a cup, like the flower of a lily; it held over three thousand baths. [6] He also made ten lavers in which to wash, and set five on the south side, and five on the north side. In these they were to rinse off what was used for the burnt offering, and the sea was for the priests to wash in.

7 And he made ten golden lampstands as prescribed, and set them in the temple, five on the south side and five on the north. [8] He also made ten tables, and placed them in the temple, five on the south side and five on north. And he made a hundred basins of gold. [9] He made the court of the priests, and the great court, and doors for the court, and overlaid their doors with bronze; [10] and he set the sea at the southeast corner of the house.

11 Huram also made the pots, the shovels, and the basins. So Huram finished the work that he did for King Solomon on the house of God: [12] the two pillars, the bowls, and the two capitals on the top of the pillars; and the two networks to cover the two bowls of the capitals that were on the top of the pillars; [13] and the four hundred pomegranates for the two networks, two rows of pomegranates for each network, to cover the two bowls of the capitals that were upon the pillars. [14] He made the stands also, and the lavers upon the stands, [15] and the one sea, and the twelve oxen underneath it. [16] The pots, the shovels, the forks, and all the equipment for these Huram-abi made of burnished bronze for King Solomon for the house of the LORD. [17] In the plain of the Jordan the king cast them, in the clay ground between Succoth and Zer'edah. [18] Solomon made all these things in great quantities, so that the weight of the bronze was not ascertained.

19 So Solomon made all the things that were in the house of God: the golden altar, the tables for the bread of the Presence, [20] the lampstands and their lamps of pure gold to burn before the inner sanctuary, as prescribed; [21] the flowers, the lamps, and the tongs, of purest gold; [22] the snuffers, basins, dishes for incense, and firepans, of pure gold; and the sockets[m] of the temple, for the inner doors to the most holy place and for the doors of the nave of the temple were of gold.

j Cn: Heb *in the inner sanctuary*
k 1 Kg 7.24: Heb *oxen*
l Compare verse 2: Heb *ten*
m 1 Kg 7.50: Heb *the door of the house*

icler there may have been a veil, as there was in New Testament times (Mt.27.51; Mk.15.38; Lk.23.45). **15–17:** *Two pillars . . . called Jachin and . . . Boaz,* see 1 Kg.7.15–22 n.

4.1–22: The temple equipment. This chapter is taken mainly from 1 Kg.7.23–51, omitting vv. 27–37. **1:** The *altar of bronze* is not mentioned in 1 Kg. ch. 7, but it appears in 1 Kg.8.64 and 2 Kg.16.14. **5–6:** On the idea *that the sea was for the priests to wash in,* see 1 Kg.7.23–26 n. (which has the more correct figure of "two thousand" rather than *three thousand baths*).

5 Thus all the work that Solomon did for the house of the LORD was finished. And Solomon brought in the things which David his father had dedicated, and stored the silver, the gold, and all the vessels in the treasuries of the house of God.

2 Then Solomon assembled the elders of Israel and all the heads of the tribes, the leaders of the fathers' houses of the people of Israel, in Jerusalem, to bring up the ark of the covenant of the LORD out of the city of David, which is Zion. 3 And all the men of Israel assembled before the king at the feast which is in the seventh month. 4 And all the elders of Israel came, and the Levites took up the ark. 5 And they brought up the ark, the tent of meeting, and all the holy vessels that were in the tent; the priests and the Levites brought them up. 6 And King Solomon and all the congregation of Israel, who had assembled before him, were before the ark, sacrificing so many sheep and oxen that they could not be counted or numbered. 7 So the priests brought the ark of the covenant of the LORD to its place, in the inner sanctuary of the house, in the most holy place, underneath the wings of the cherubim. 8 For the cherubim spread out their wings over the place of the ark, so that the cherubim made a covering above the ark and its poles. 9 And the poles were so long that the ends of the poles were seen from the holy place before the inner sanctuary; but they could not be seen from outside; and they are there to this day.

10 There was nothing in the ark except the two tables which Moses put there at Horeb, where the LORD made a covenant with the people of Israel, when they came out of Egypt. 11 Now when the priests came out of the holy place (for all the priests who were present had sanctified themselves, without regard to their divisions; 12 and all the Levitical singers, Asaph, Heman, and Jedu'thun, their sons and kinsmen, arrayed in fine linen, with cymbals, harps, and lyres, stood east of the altar with a hundred and twenty priests who were trumpeters; 13 and it was the duty of the trumpeters and singers to make themselves heard in unison in praise and thanksgiving to the LORD), and when the song was raised, with trumpets and cymbals and other musical instruments, in praise to the LORD,

"For he is good,
   for his steadfast love endures for
      ever,"

the house, the house of the LORD, was filled with a cloud, 14 so that the priests could not stand to minister because of the cloud; for the glory of the LORD filled the house of God.

6 Then Solomon said,
   "The LORD has said that he would
      dwell in thick darkness.
2 I have built thee an exalted house,
   a place for thee to dwell in for
      ever."
3 Then the king faced about, and blessed all the assembly of Israel, while all the assembly of Israel stood. 4 And he said, "Blessed be the LORD,

---

5.1–14: Bringing the ark of the covenant into the temple. This is drawn mainly from 1 Kg.8.1–11, with the insertion of a section on the priests and the Levitical singers (vv. 11b–13a), in which the Chronicler was particularly interested (see Introduction to 1 Chronicles); compare 1 Chr. chs. 25–26. **4:** *The Levites* are substituted for "the priests" of the source (1 Kg.8.3).

6.1–42: Solomon's address to the people and his prayer of dedication. This whole chapter, with the exception of vv. 13 and 41–42, is taken with little change from 1 Kg.8.12–52 (see the notes there). Verses 4–11 are the address to the people and vv. 12–42 the prayer of dedication. The *bronze platform* of v. 13, added by the Chronicler, provides a proper place for *Solomon* to kneel; the regular place of prayer before the altar was sacred to the priests, according to usage at the time of the Chronicler. Verses 41–42, adapted from Ps.132.8–10, provide a fitting conclusion, showing the idealized Solomon to be a very devout and holy man, yet reminding the reader that *David* is, after all, the more important figure; *do not turn away the face of* means "do not reject"; *thy anointed one* is king Solomon himself.

the God of Israel, who with his hand has fulfilled what he promised with his mouth to David my father, saying, [5] 'Since the day that I brought my people out of the land of Egypt, I chose no city in all the tribes of Israel in which to build a house, that my name might be there, and I chose no man as prince over my people Israel; [6] but I have chosen Jerusalem that my name may be there and I have chosen David to be over my people Israel.' [7] Now it was in the heart of David my father to build a house for the name of the LORD, the God of Israel. [8] But the LORD said to David my father, 'Whereas it was in your heart to build a house for my name, you did well that it was in your heart; [9] nevertheless you shall not build the house, but your son who shall be born to you shall build the house for my name.' [10] Now the LORD has fulfilled his promise which he made; for I have risen in the place of David my father, and sit on the throne of Israel, as the LORD promised, and I have built the house for the name of the LORD, the God of Israel. [11] And there I have set the ark, in which is the covenant of the LORD which he made with the people of Israel."

12 Then Solomon stood before the altar of the LORD in the presence of all the assembly of Israel, and spread forth his hands. [13] Solomon had made a bronze platform five cubits long, five cubits wide, and three cubits high, and had set it in the court; and he stood upon it. Then he knelt upon his knees in the presence of all the assembly of Israel, and spread forth his hands toward heaven; [14] and said, "O LORD, God of Israel, there is no God like thee, in heaven or on earth, keeping covenant and showing steadfast love to thy servants who walk before thee with all their heart; [15] who hast kept with thy servant David my father what thou didst declare to him; yea, thou didst speak with thy mouth, and with thy hand hast fulfilled it this day. [16] Now therefore, O LORD, God of Israel, keep with thy servant David my father what thou hast promised him, saying, 'There shall never fail you a man before me to sit upon the throne of Israel, if only your sons take heed to their way, to walk in my law as you have walked before me.' [17] Now therefore, O LORD, God of Israel, let thy word be confirmed, which thou hast spoken to thy servant David.

18 "But will God dwell indeed with man on the earth? Behold, heaven and the highest heaven cannot contain thee; how much less this house which I have built! [19] Yet have regard to the prayer of thy servant and to his supplication, O LORD my God, hearkening to the cry and to the prayer which thy servant prays before thee; [20] that thy eyes may be open day and night toward this house, the place where thou hast promised to set thy name, that thou mayest hearken to the prayer which thy servant offers toward this place. [21] And hearken thou to the supplications of thy servant and of thy people Israel, when they pray toward this place; yea, hear thou from heaven thy dwelling place; and when thou hearest, forgive.

22 "If a man sins against his neighbor and is made to take an oath, and comes and swears his oath before thy altar in this house, [23] then hear thou from heaven, and act, and judge thy servants, requiting the guilty by bringing his conduct upon his own head, and vindicating the righteous by rewarding him according to his righteousness.

24 "If thy people Israel are defeated before the enemy because they have sinned against thee, when they turn again and acknowledge thy name, and pray and make supplication to thee in this house, [25] then hear thou from heaven, and forgive the sin of thy people Israel, and bring them again to the land which thou gavest to them and to their fathers.

26 "When heaven is shut up and there is no rain because they have sinned against thee, if they pray toward this place, and acknowledge thy name,

and turn from their sin, when thou dost afflict them, [27] then hear thou in heaven, and forgive the sin of thy servants, thy people Israel, when thou dost teach them the good way[n] in which they should walk; and grant rain upon thy land, which thou hast given to thy people as an inheritance.

28 "If there is famine in the land, if there is pestilence or blight or mildew or locust or caterpillar; if their enemies besiege them in any of their cities; whatever plague, whatever sickness there is; [29] whatever prayer, whatever supplication is made by any man or by all thy people Israel, each knowing his own affliction, and his own sorrow and stretching out his hands toward this house; [30] then hear thou from heaven thy dwelling place, and forgive, and render to each whose heart thou knowest, according to all his ways (for thou, thou only, knowest the hearts of the children of men); [31] that they may fear thee and walk in thy ways all the days that they live in the land which thou gavest to our fathers.

32 "Likewise when a foreigner, who is not of thy people Israel, comes from a far country for the sake of thy great name, and thy mighty hand, and thy outstretched arm, when he comes and prays toward this house, [33] hear thou from heaven thy dwelling place, and do according to all for which the foreigner calls to thee; in order that all the peoples of the earth may know thy name and fear thee, as do thy people Israel, and that they may know that this house which I have built is called by thy name.

34 "If thy people go out to battle against their enemies, by whatever way thou shalt send them, and they pray to thee toward this city which thou hast chosen and the house which I have built for thy name, [35] then hear thou from heaven their prayer and their supplication, and maintain their cause.

36 "If they sin against thee–for there is no man who does not sin–and thou art angry with them, and dost give them to an enemy, so that they are carried away captive to a land far or near; [37] yet if they lay it to heart in the land to which they have been carried captive, and repent, and make supplication to thee in the land of their captivity, saying, 'We have sinned, and have acted perversely and wickedly'; [38] if they repent with all their mind and with all their heart in the land of their captivity, to which they were carried captive, and pray toward their land, which thou gavest to their fathers, the city which thou hast chosen, and the house which I have built for thy name, [39] then hear thou from heaven thy dwelling place their prayer and their supplications, and maintain their cause and forgive thy people who have sinned against thee. [40] Now, O my God, let thy eyes be open and thy ears attentive to a prayer of this place.

[41] "And now arise, O LORD God, and
    go to thy resting place,
  thou and the ark of thy might.
Let thy priests, O LORD God, be
    clothed with salvation,
  and let thy saints rejoice in thy
    goodness.
[42] O LORD God, do not turn away the
    face of thy anointed one!
Remember thy steadfast love for
    David thy servant."

7 When Solomon had ended his prayer, fire came down from heaven and consumed the burnt offering and the sacrifices, and the glory of the LORD filled the temple. [2] And the priests could not enter the house of the LORD, because the glory of the LORD filled the LORD's house. [3] When all the children of Israel saw the fire come down and the glory of the LORD

n Gk Syr Vg: Heb *toward the good way*

7.1–22: The consecration of the sanctuary and the divine admonition. 1: *Fire . . . from heaven* (not in 1 Kg.8.54), see 1 Chr. 21.26 n. and compare Lev.9.24. 2: *The glory of the LORD*, compare 5.14 and see 1 Kg.8.11. 3: The Chronicler added the obeisance of the people. For the liturgical

upon the temple, they bowed down with their faces to the earth on the pavement, and worshiped and gave thanks to the Lord, saying,

"For he is good,
   for his steadfast love endures for ever."

4 Then the king and all the people offered sacrifice before the Lord. 5 King Solomon offered as a sacrifice twenty-two thousand oxen and a hundred and twenty thousand sheep. So the king and all the people dedicated the house of God. 6 The priests stood at their posts; the Levites also, with the instruments for music to the Lord which King David had made for giving thanks to the Lord–for his steadfast love endures for ever–whenever David offered praises by their ministry; opposite them the priests sounded trumpets; and all Israel stood.

7 And Solomon consecrated the middle of the court that was before the house of the Lord; for there he offered the burnt offering and the fat of the peace offerings, because the bronze altar Solomon had made could not hold the burnt offering and the cereal offering and the fat.

8 At that time Solomon held the feast for seven days, and all Israel with him, a very great congregation, from the entrance of Hamath to the Brook of Egypt. 9 And on the eighth day they held a solemn assembly; for they had kept the dedication of the altar seven days and the feast seven days. 10 On the twenty-third day of the seventh month he sent the people away to their homes, joyful and glad of heart for the goodness that the Lord had shown to David and to Solomon and to Israel his people.

11 Thus Solomon finished the house of the Lord and the king's house; all

that Solomon had planned to do in the house of the Lord and in his own house he successfully accomplished. 12 Then the Lord appeared to Solomon in the night and said to him: "I have heard your prayer, and have chosen this place for myself as a house of sacrifice. 13 When I shut up the heavens so that there is no rain, or command the locust to devour the land, or send pestilence among my people, 14 if my people who are called by my name humble themselves, and pray and seek my face, and turn from their wicked ways, then I will hear from heaven, and will forgive their sin and heal their land. 15 Now my eyes will be open and my ears attentive to the prayer that is made in this place. 16 For now I have chosen and consecrated this house that my name may be there for ever; my eyes and my heart will be there for all time. 17 And as for you, if you walk before me, as David your father walked, doing according to all that I have commanded you and keeping my statutes and my ordinances, 18 then I will establish your royal throne, as I covenanted with David your father, saying, 'There shall not fail you a man to rule Israel.'

19 "But if you*o* turn aside and forsake my statutes and my commandments which I have set before you, and go and serve other gods and worship them, 20 then I will pluck you*p* up from the land which I have given you;*p* and this house, which I have consecrated for my name, I will cast out of my sight, and will make it a proverb and a byword among all peoples. 21 And at this house, which is exalted, every one passing by will be astonished, and say, 'Why has the Lord done thus to this land and to this

o The word *you* is plural here   *p* Heb *them*

words, see 5.13; Ps.136.1. **4–5**: Compare 1 Kg.8.62–63, the source. **6**: Compare 5.11–13, also 1 Chr. ch. 25; the Levitical musicians did not exist in Solomon's day. **7–8**: Compare 1 Kg.8.64– 65, the source. **9–10**: The source, 1 Kg.8.66, has been drastically changed. The people are not sent away *on the eighth day*, but are kept on for another occasion, *a solemn assembly*, until *the twenty-third day* (compare Lev.23.36; Num.29.35–38; Neh.8.18). **11–22**: This section, the divine admonition, is taken from 1 Kg.9.1–9, with little change except that vv. 13–15 were inserted to give a slightly more hopeful tone (compare 6.26–27,37–39).

house?' ²² Then they will say, 'Because they forsook the LORD the God of their fathers who brought them out of the land of Egypt, and laid hold on other gods, and worshiped them and served them; therefore he has brought all this evil upon them.' "

8 At the end of twenty years, in which Solomon had built the house of the LORD and his own house, ² Solomon rebuilt the cities which Huram had given to him, and settled the people of Israel in them.

3 And Solomon went to Ha′math-zo′bah, and took it. ⁴ He built Tadmor in the wilderness and all the store-cities which he built in Hamath. ⁵ He also built Upper Beth-hor′on and Lower Beth-hor′on, fortified cities with walls, gates, and bars, ⁶ and Ba′alath, and all the store-cities that Solomon had, and all the cities for his chariots, and the cities for his horsemen, and whatever Solomon desired to build in Jerusalem, in Lebanon, and in all the land of his dominion. ⁷ All the people who were left of the Hittites, the Amorites, the Per′izzites, the Hivites, and the Jeb′usites, who were not of Israel, ⁸ from their descendants who were left after them in the land, whom the people of Israel had not destroyed —these Solomon made a forced levy and so they are to this day. ⁹ But of the people of Israel Solomon made no slaves for his work; they were soldiers, and his officers, the commanders of his chariots, and his horsemen. ¹⁰ And these were the chief officers of King Solomon, two hundred and fifty, who exercised authority over the people.

11 Solomon brought Pharaoh's daughter up from the city of David to the house which he had built for her, for he said, "My wife shall not live in the house of David king of Israel, for the places to which the ark of the LORD has come are holy."

12 Then Solomon offered up burnt offerings to the LORD upon the altar of the LORD which he had built before the vestibule, ¹³ as the duty of each day required, offering according to the commandment of Moses for the sabbaths, the new moons, and the three annual feasts—the feast of unleavened bread, the feast of weeks, and the feast of tabernacles. ¹⁴ According to the ordinance of David his father, he appointed the divisions of the priests for their service, and the Levites for their offices of praise and ministry before the priests as the duty of each day required, and the gatekeepers in their divisions for the several gates; for so David the man of God had commanded. ¹⁵ And they did not turn aside from what the king had commanded the priests and Levites concerning any matter and concerning treasuries.

16 Thus was accomplished all the work of Solomon from*q* the day the foundation of the house of the LORD was laid until it was finished. So the house of the LORD was completed.

17 Then Solomon went to E′zion-ge′ber and Eloth on the shore of the sea, in the land of Edom. ¹⁸ And Huram

q Gk Syr Vg: Heb *to*

8.1–18: Various activities of Solomon. This chapter is based on 1 Kg.9.10–28. **2:** In 1 Kg. 9.10–14 *Solomon* ceded *the cities* to Hiram (here called *Huram*) to raise needed money; but here the cities go to Solomon. **3:** This campaign is otherwise unknown; it is perhaps an adaptation of 1 Chr.18.3. **4:** *Tadmor* is Palmyra, the great city of the Syrian desert, which could hardly be intended here; 1 Kg.9.18 reads "Tamar," a small place in southern Judah (Ezek.47.19; 48.28). **7–10:** These verses follow 1 Kg.9.20–23 closely, except that in v. 10 a smaller number is given; usually the numbers of the Chronicler are larger (see 1 Chr.27.1 n.). **11:** Compare 1 Kg.3.1; 7.8; 9.24. The reason given for moving the residence of the woman is an addition by the Chronicler (compare Ezek.44.9). **12–15:** These verses are an expansion of 1 Kg.9.25 to bring these acts of Solomon in line with the ideas of the Chronicler. In v. 12 it is made clear that Solomon remained outside the sanctuary *before the vestibule;* only the priests could go inside (see 1 Kg.9.25 n.). **16:** Added by the Chronicler. **17–18:** Taken with a few changes from 1 Kg. 9.26–28 (see notes there.)

sent him by his servants ships and servants familiar with the sea, and they went to Ophir together with the servants of Solomon, and fetched from there four hundred and fifty talents of gold and brought it to King Solomon.

9 Now when the queen of Sheba heard of the fame of Solomon she came to Jerusalem to test him with hard questions, having a very great retinue and camels bearing spices and very much gold and precious stones. When she came to Solomon, she told him all that was on her mind. [2] And Solomon answered all her questions; there was nothing hidden from Solomon which he could not explain to her. [3] And when the queen of Sheba had seen the wisdom of Solomon, the house that he had built, [4] the food of his table, the seating of his officials, and the attendance of his servants, and their clothing, his cupbearers, and their clothing, and his burnt offerings which he offered at the house of the LORD, there was no more spirit in her.

[5] And she said to the king, "The report was true which I heard in my own land of your affairs and of your wisdom, [6] but I did not believe the[r] reports until I came and my own eyes had seen it; and behold, half the greatness of your wisdom was not told me; you surpass the report which I heard. [7] Happy are your wives![s] Happy are these your servants, who continually stand before you and hear your wisdom! [8] Blessed be the LORD your God, who has delighted in you and set you on his throne as king for the LORD your God! Because your God loved Israel and would establish them for ever, he has made you king over them, that you may execute justice and righteousness." [9] Then she gave the king a hundred and twenty talents of gold, and a very great quantity of spices, and precious stones: there were no spices such as those which the queen of Sheba gave to King Solomon.

[10] Moreover the servants of Huram and the servants of Solomon, who brought gold from Ophir, brought algum wood and precious stones. [11] And the king made of the algum wood steps[t] for the house of the LORD and for the king's house, lyres also and harps for the singers; there never was seen the like of them before in the land of Judah.

[12] And King Solomon gave to the queen of Sheba all that she desired, whatever she asked besides what she had brought to the king. So she turned and went back to her own land, with her servants.

[13] Now the weight of gold that came to Solomon in one year was six hundred and sixty-six talents of gold, [14] besides that which the traders and merchants brought; and all the kings of Arabia and the governors of the land brought gold and silver to Solomon. [15] King Solomon made two hundred large shields of beaten gold; six hundred shekels of beaten gold went into each shield. [16] And he made three hundred shields of beaten gold; three hundred shekels of gold went into each shield; and the king put them in the House of the Forest of Lebanon. [17] The king also made a great ivory throne, and overlaid it with pure gold. [18] The throne had six steps and a footstool of gold, which were attached to the throne, and on each side of the seat were arm rests and two lions standing beside the arm rests, [19] while twelve lions stood there, one on each end of a step on the six steps. The like of it was never made in any kingdom. [20] All King Solomon's drinking vessels were of gold, and all the vessels of the House of the Forest of Lebanon were of pure gold; silver was not considered as anything in the days of Solomon. [21] For the king's ships went to Tarshish with the servants of Huram;

r Heb *their*
s Gk Compare 1 Kg 10.8: Heb *men*
t Gk Vg: The meaning of the Hebrew word is uncertain

9.1–31: The visit of the queen of Sheba; Solomon's wealth and grandeur; his death. 1–12: Taken with little change from 1 Kg.10.1–13 (see notes there). **13–28:** From 1 Kg.10.14–28a

once every three years the ships of Tarshish used to come bringing gold, silver, ivory, apes, and peacocks.*x*

22 Thus King Solomon excelled all the kings of the earth in riches and in wisdom. 23 And all the kings of the earth sought the presence of Solomon to hear his wisdom, which God had put into his mind. 24 Every one of them brought his present, articles of silver and of gold, garments, myrrh, spices, horses, and mules, so much year by year. 25 And Solomon had four thousand stalls for horses and chariots, and twelve thousand horsemen, whom he stationed in the chariot cities and with the king in Jerusalem. 26 And he ruled over all the kings from the Euphra'tes to the land of the Philistines, and to the border of Egypt. 27 And the king made silver as common in Jerusalem as stone, and cedar as plentiful as the sycamore of the Shephe'lah. 28 And horses were imported for Solomon from Egypt and from all lands.

29 Now the rest of the acts of Solomon, from first to last, are they not written in the history of Nathan the prophet, and in the prophecy of Ahi'jah the Shi'lonite, and in the visions of Iddo the seer concerning Jerobo'am the son of Nebat? 30 Solomon reigned in Jerusalem over all Israel forty years. 31 And Solomon slept with his fathers, and was buried in the city of David his father; and Rehobo'am his son reigned in his stead.

10 Rehobo'am went to Shechem, for all Israel had come to Shechem to make him king. 2 And when Jerobo'am the son of Nebat heard of it (for he was in Egypt, whither he had fled from King Solomon), then Jerobo'am returned from Egypt. 3 And they sent and called him; and Jerobo'am and all Israel came and said to Rehobo'am, 4 "Your father made our yoke heavy. Now therefore lighten the hard service of your father and his heavy yoke upon us, and we will serve you." 5 He said to them, "Come to me again in three days." So the people went away.

6 Then King Rehobo'am took counsel with the old men, who had stood before Solomon his father while he was yet alive, saying, "How do you advise me to answer this people?" 7 And they said to him, "If you will be kind to this people and please them, and speak good words to them, then they will be your servants for ever." 8 But he forsook the counsel which the old men gave him, and took counsel with the young men who had grown up with him and stood before him. 9 And he said to them, "What do you advise that we answer this people who have said to me, 'Lighten the yoke that your father put upon us'?" 10 And the young men who had grown up with him said to him, "Thus shall you speak to the people who said to you, 'Your father made our yoke heavy, but do you lighten it for us'; thus shall you say to them, 'My little finger is thicker than my father's loins. 11 And now, whereas my father laid upon you a heavy yoke, I will add to your yoke. My father chastised you with whips, but I will chastise you with scorpions.' "

12 So Jerobo'am and all the people came to Rehobo'am the third day, as the king said, "Come to me again the third day." 13 And the king answered them harshly, and forsaking the counsel of the old men, 14 King Rehobo'am spoke to them according to the counsel of the young men, saying, "My father made your yoke heavy, but I will add to it; my father chastised you with whips, but I will chastise you with scorpions." 15 So the

x Or *baboons*

---

with a few changes. With vv. 25–28, compare 1.14–17; 1 Kg.4.21,26. **29–31:** Taken with changes from 1 Kg.11.41–43, omitting all unfavorable aspects of Solomon's reign presented in 1 Kg. 11.1–40 (see notes there). On the books mentioned in v. 29, see Introduction to 1 Chronicles.

10.1–19: The division of the kingdom. This chapter reproduces almost exactly 1 Kg.12.1–19, in spite of the fact that the account reflects little credit on *Rehoboam;* 1 Kg.12.20, which reveals the weakness of Judah, is omitted.

king did not hearken to the people; for it was a turn of affairs brought about by God that the LORD might fulfil his word, which he spoke by Ahi′jah the Shi′lonite to Jerobo′am the son of Nebat.

16 And when all Israel saw that the king did not hearken to them, the people answered the king,

"What portion have we in David?
  We have no inheritance in the son
    of Jesse.
Each of you to your tents, O Israel!
Look now to your own house,
    David."

So all Israel departed to their tents. [17] But Rehobo′am reigned over the people of Israel who dwelt in the cities of Judah. [18] Then King Rehobo′am sent Hador′am, who was taskmaster over the forced labor, and the people of Israel stoned him to death with stones. And King Rehobo′am made haste to mount his chariot, to flee to Jerusalem. [19] So Israel has been in rebellion against the house of David to this day.

When Rehobo′am came to Jerusalem, he assembled the house of Judah, and Benjamin, a hundred and eighty thousand chosen warriors, to fight against Israel, to restore the kingdom to Rehobo′am. [2] But the word of the LORD came to Shemai′ah the man of God: [3] "Say to Rehobo′am the son of Solomon king of Judah, and to all Israel in Judah and Benjamin, [4] 'Thus says the LORD, You shall not go up or fight against your brethren. Return every man to his home, for this thing is from me.' " So they hearkened to the word of the LORD, and returned and did not go against Jerobo′am.

5 Rehobo′am dwelt in Jerusalem, and he built cities for defense in Judah. [6] He built Bethlehem, Etam, Teko′a, [7] Beth-zur, Soco, Adullam, [8] Gath, Mare′shah, Ziph, [9] Adora′im, Lachish, Aze′kah, [10] Zorah, Ai′jalon, and Hebron, fortified cities which are in Judah and in Benjamin. [11] He made the fortresses strong, and put commanders in them, and stores of food, oil, and wine. [12] And he put shields and spears in all the cities, and made them very strong. So he held Judah and Benjamin.

13 And the priests and the Levites that were in all Israel resorted to him from all places where they lived. [14] For the Levites left their common lands and their holdings and came to Judah and Jerusalem, because Jerobo′am and his sons cast them out from serving as priests of the LORD, [15] and he appointed his own priests for the high places, and for the satyrs, and for the calves which he had made. [16] And those who had set their hearts to seek the LORD God of Israel came after them from all the tribes of Israel to Jerusalem to sacrifice to the LORD, the God of their fathers. [17] They strengthened the kingdom of Judah, and for three years they made Rehobo′am the son of Solomon secure, for they walked for three years in the way of David and Solomon.

18 Rehobo′am took as wife Ma′- halath the daughter of Jer′imoth the

---

11.1–23: The beginning of the reign of Rehoboam. 1–4: These verses follow closely 1 Kg.12.21–24, in spite of a tendency in favor of the northern kingdom. The phrase *all Israel in Judah and Benjamin*, lacking in 1 Kg.12.23, is intended to make clear that the southern kingdom was the true Israel. In the older sources, "all Israel" means the northern tribes only (compare 2 Sam. 2.9; 1 Kg.12.18,20). After the fall of the northern kingdom, this name was gradually assumed by Judah. **5–12:** These verses, which have no parallel in 1 Kings, are added for the purpose of showing the strength of Judah; they are probably based on a good source. **10,12:** *Benjamin*, see 1 Kg.12.21–24 n. **13–17:** These verses, also without parallel in 1 Kings, are designed to show that the northern kingdom (*all Israel*, v. 13; see vv. 1–4 n.) was faithless to the LORD; hence *the priests and Levites* flocked to the south. Other good people also came, and things went well *for three years*. **18–23:** In 1 Kg. ch. 11, Solomon is reproached for having a multitude of *wives and concubines*. The Chronicler omits this section of his source. Here, in an account from an otherwise unknown source, he transfers some of the onus to *Rehoboam*.

son of David, and of Ab'ihail the daughter of Eli'ab the son of Jesse; [19] and she bore him sons, Je'ush, Shemari'ah, and Zaham. [20] After her he took Ma'acah the daughter of Ab'salom, who bore him Abi'jah, Attai, Ziza, and Shelo'mith. [21] Rehobo'am loved Ma'acah the daughter of Ab'salom above all his wives and concubines (he took eighteen wives and sixty concubines, and had twenty-eight sons and sixty daughters); [22] and Rehobo'am appointed Abi'jah the son of Ma'acah as chief prince among his brothers, for he intended to make him king. [23] And he dealt wisely, and distributed some of his sons through all the districts of Judah and Benjamin, in all the fortified cities; and he gave them abundant provisions, and procured wives for them.[u]

12 When the rule of Rehobo'am was established and was strong, he forsook the law of the LORD, and all Israel with him. [2] In the fifth year of King Rehobo'am, because they had been unfaithful to the LORD, Shishak king of Egypt came up against Jerusalem [3] with twelve hundred chariots and sixty thousand horsemen. And the people were without number who came with him from Egypt—Libyans, Suk'ki-im, and Ethiopians. [4] And he took the fortified cities of Judah and came as far as Jerusalem. [5] Then Shemai'ah the prophet came to Rehobo'am and to the princes of Judah, who had gathered at Jerusalem because of Shishak, and said to them, "Thus says the LORD, 'You abandoned me, so I have abandoned you to the hand of Shishak.'" [6] Then the princes of Israel and the king humbled themselves and said, "The LORD is righteous." [7] When the LORD saw that they humbled themselves, the word of the LORD came to Shemai'ah: "They have humbled themselves; I will not destroy them, but

I will grant them some deliverance, and my wrath shall not be poured out upon Jerusalem by the hand of Shishak. [8] Nevertheless they shall be servants to him, that they may know my service and the service of the kingdoms of the countries."

9 So Shishak king of Egypt came up against Jerusalem; he took away the treasures of the house of the LORD and the treasures of the king's house; he took away everything. He also took away the shields of gold which Solomon had made; [10] and King Rehobo'am made in their stead shields of bronze, and committed them to the hands of the officers of the guard, who kept the door of the king's house. [11] And as often as the king went into the house of the LORD, the guard came and bore them, and brought them back to the guardroom. [12] And when he humbled himself the wrath of the LORD turned from him, so as not to make a complete destruction; moreover, conditions were good in Judah.

13 So King Rehobo'am established himself in Jerusalem and reigned. Rehobo'am was forty-one years old when he began to reign, and he reigned seventeen years in Jerusalem, the city which the LORD had chosen out of all the tribes of Israel to put his name there. His mother's name was Na'amah the Ammonitess. [14] And he did evil, for he did not set his heart to seek the LORD.

15 Now the acts of Rehobo'am, from first to last, are they not written in the chronicles of Shemai'ah the prophet and of Iddo the seer?[v] There were continual wars between Rehobo'am and Jerobo'am. [16] And Rehobo'am slept with his fathers, and was buried in the city of David; and Abi'jah his son reigned in his stead.

u Cn: Heb *sought a multitude of wives*
v Heb *seer, to enroll oneself*

12.1–16: Rehoboam's sin; his punishment and death. The source is 1 Kg.14.21–31, with expansions to show that Shishak's invasion was the direct result of the apostasy of *Rehoboam* and *all Israel* (meaning Judah; compare v. 6 and see 11.1–4 n.). *Complete destruction* was averted by repentance (vv. 7,12). See 1 Kg.14.21–31 n.

13 In the eighteenth year of King Jerobo'am Abi'jah began to reign over Judah. ² He reigned for three years in Jerusalem. His mother's name was Micai'ah the daughter of U'riel of Gib'e-ah.

Now there was war between Abi'jah and Jerobo'am. ³ Abi'jah went out to battle having an army of valiant men of war, four hundred thousand picked men; and Jerobo'am drew up his line of battle against him with eight hundred thousand picked mighty warriors. ⁴ Then Abi'jah stood up on Mount Zemara'im which is in the hill country of E'phraim, and said, "Hear me, O Jerobo'am and all Israel! ⁵ Ought you not to know that the LORD God of Israel gave the kingship over Israel for ever to David and his sons by a covenant of salt? ⁶ Yet Jerobo'am the son of Nebat, a servant of Solomon the son of David, rose up and rebelled against his lord; ⁷ and certain worthless scoundrels gathered about him and defied Rehobo'am the son of Solomon, when Rehobo'am was young and irresolute and could not withstand them.

8 "And now you think to withstand the kingdom of the LORD in the hand of the sons of David, because you are a great multitude and have with you the golden calves which Jerobo'am made you for gods. ⁹ Have you not driven out the priests of the LORD, the sons of Aaron, and the Levites, and made priests for yourselves like the peoples of other lands? Whoever comes to consecrate himself with a young bull or seven rams becomes a priest of what are no gods. ¹⁰ But as for us, the LORD is our God, and we have not forsaken him. We have priests ministering to the LORD who are sons of Aaron, and Levites for their service. ¹¹ They offer to the LORD every morning and every evening burnt offerings and incense of sweet spices, set out the showbread on the table of pure gold, and care for the golden lampstand that its lamps may burn every evening; for we keep the charge of the LORD our God, but you have forsaken him. ¹² Behold, God is with us at our head, and his priests with their battle trumpets to sound the call to battle against you. O sons of Israel, do not fight against the LORD, the God of your fathers; for you cannot succeed."

13 Jerobo'am had sent an ambush around to come on them from behind; thus his troopsʷ were in front of Judah, and the ambush was behind them. ¹⁴ And when Judah looked, behold, the battle was before and behind them; and they cried to the LORD, and the priests blew the trumpets. ¹⁵ Then the men of Judah raised the battle shout. And when the men of Judah shouted, God defeated Jerobo'am and all Israel before Abi'jah and Judah. ¹⁶ The men of Israel fled before Judah, and God gave them into their hand. ¹⁷ Abi'jah and his people slew them with a great slaughter; so there fell slain of Israel five hundred thousand picked men. ¹⁸ Thus the men of Israel were subdued at that time, and the men of Judah prevailed, because they relied upon the LORD, the God of their fathers. ¹⁹ And Abi'jah pursued Jerobo'am, and took cities from him, Bethel with its villages and Jesha'nah with its villages and Ephronˣ with its villages. ²⁰ Jerobo'am did not recover his power in the days of Abi'jah; and the LORD smote him, and he died. ²¹ But Abi'jah grew mighty. And he took fourteen wives, and had twenty-two sons and sixteen daughters. ²² The rest of the acts of Abi'jah, his ways

w Heb *they*
x Another reading is *Ephrain*

13.1–22: The reign of Abijah; his great victory over the north. Verses 1–2 parallel 1 Kg.15.1–2, with slight differences in names; v. 22 may be compared with 1 Kg.15.7a. Except for these parallels, the chapter is apparently a free composition of the Chronicler, developed from 1 Kg.15.7b. The theme is not really a war between north and south, or Israel and Judah (note the exaggerated numbers); rather it is the perpetual conflict between apostasy and true worship in all times.

and his sayings, are written in the story of the prophet Iddo.

14 ʸ So Abi′jah slept with his fathers, and they buried him in the city of David; and Asa his son reigned in his stead. In his days the land had rest for ten years. ²ᶻ And Asa did what was good and right in the eyes of the LORD his God. ³ He took away the foreign altars and the high places, and broke down the pillars and hewed down the Ashe′rim, ⁴ and commanded Judah to seek the LORD, the God of their fathers, and to keep the law and the commandment. ⁵ He also took out of all the cities of Judah the high places and the incense altars. And the kingdom had rest under him. ⁶ He built fortified cities in Judah, for the land had rest. He had no war in those years, for the LORD gave him peace. ⁷ And he said to Judah, "Let us build these cities, and surround them with walls and towers, gates and bars; the land is still ours, because we have sought the LORD our God; we have sought him, and he has given us peace on every side." So they built and prospered. ⁸ And Asa had an army of three hundred thousand from Judah, armed with bucklers and spears, and two hundred and eighty thousand men from Benjamin, that carried shields and drew bows; all these were mighty men of valor.

9 Zerah the Ethiopian came out against them with an army of a million men and three hundred chariots, and came as far as Mare′shah. ¹⁰ And Asa went out to meet him, and they drew up their lines of battle in the valley of Zeph′athah at Mare′shah. ¹¹ And Asa cried to the LORD his God,

"O LORD, there is none like thee to help, between the mighty and the weak. Help us, O LORD our God, for we rely on thee, and in thy name we have come against this multitude. O LORD, thou art our God; let not man prevail against thee." ¹² So the LORD defeated the Ethiopians before Asa and before Judah, and the Ethiopians fled. ¹³ Asa and the people that were with him pursued them as far as Gerar, and the Ethiopians fell until none remained alive; for they were broken before the LORD and his army. The men of Judahᵃ carried away very much booty. ¹⁴ And they smote all the cities round about Gerar, for the fear of the LORD was upon them. They plundered all the cities, for there was much plunder in them. ¹⁵ And they smote the tents of those who had cattle,ᵇ and carried away sheep in abundance and camels. Then they returned to Jerusalem.

15 The Spirit of God came upon Azari′ah the son of Oded, ² and he went out to meet Asa, and said to him, "Hear me, Asa, and all Judah and Benjamin: The LORD is with you, while you are with him. If you seek him, he will be found by you, but if you forsake him, he will forsake you. ³ For a long time Israel was without the true God, and without a teaching priest, and without law; ⁴ but when in their distress they turned to the LORD, the God of Israel, and sought him, he was found by them. ⁵ In those times there was no peace to him who went out or to him who came in, for great

ʸ Ch 13.23 in Heb   ᶻ Ch 14.1 in Heb
ᵃ Heb *they*   ᵇ Heb obscure

14.1–15: The beginning of the reign of Asa, and his great victory over the Ethiopians. In 1 Kings only a relatively brief passage (1 Kg.15.9–24) deals with Asa; here the story is expanded to three chapters (chs. 14; 15; 16). Asa is presented by the Chronicler as a man like David, great on the field of battle and diligent in religious reform. In the end, his religious loyalty flagged, and he had to be suitably punished. **1–5:** Roughly parallel to 1 Kg.15.8–14. **6–8:** Added by the Chronicler from another source (compare 1 Kg.15.23; Jer.41.9). **9–15:** This is another legendary battle, like that of ch. 13, to show the power of the LORD. There is no hint of it elsewhere in the Bible. *The Ethiopian* may mean "the Egyptian" (see 2 Kg.19.9 n.) or "the Arabian," but no king named *Zerah* is otherwise known.
15.1–19: Asa's reform. 1–5: In this passage, which has no parallel, Asa is pictured as a great reformer, like Hezekiah and Josiah at a later date. The prophet *Azariah the son of Oded* is not

disturbances afflicted all the inhabitants of the lands. [6] They were broken in pieces, nation against nation and city against city, for God troubled them with every sort of distress. [7] But you, take courage! Do not let your hands be weak, for your work shall be rewarded."

8 When Asa heard these words, the prophecy of Azari'ah the son of Oded,[c] he took courage, and put away the abominable idols from all the land of Judah and Benjamin and from the cities which he had taken in the hill country of E'phraim, and he repaired the altar of the LORD that was in front of the vestibule of the house of the LORD.[d] [9] And he gathered all Judah and Benjamin, and those from E'phraim, Manas'seh, and Simeon who were sojourning with them, for great numbers had deserted to him from Israel when they saw that the LORD his God was with him. [10] They were gathered at Jerusalem in the third month of the fifteenth year of the reign of Asa. [11] They sacrificed to the LORD on that day, from the spoil which they had brought, seven hundred oxen and seven thousand sheep. [12] And they entered into a covenant to seek the LORD, the God of their fathers, with all their heart and with all their soul; [13] and that whoever would not seek the LORD, the God of Israel, should be put to death, whether young or old, man or woman. [14] They took oath to the LORD with a loud voice, and with shouting, and with trumpets, and with horns. [15] And all Judah rejoiced over the oath; for they had sworn with all their heart, and had sought him with their whole desire, and he was found by them, and the LORD gave them rest round about.

16 Even Ma'acah, his mother, King Asa removed from being queen mother because she had made an abominable image for Ashe'rah. Asa cut down her image, crushed it, and burned it at the brook Kidron. [17] But the high places were not taken out of Israel. Nevertheless the heart of Asa was blameless all his days. [18] And he brought into the house of God the votive gifts of his father and his own votive gifts, silver, and gold, and vessels. [19] And there was no more war until the thirty-fifth year of the reign of Asa.

16 In the thirty-sixth year of the reign of Asa, Ba'asha king of Israel went up against Judah, and built Ramah, that he might permit no one to go out or come in to Asa king of Judah. [2] Then Asa took silver and gold from the treasures of the house of the LORD and the king's house, and sent them to Ben-ha'dad king of Syria, who dwelt in Damascus, saying, [3] "Let there be a league between me and you, as between my father and your father; behold, I am sending to you silver and gold; go, break your league with Ba'asha king of Israel, that he may withdraw from me." [4] And Ben-ha'dad hearkened to King Asa, and sent the commanders of his armies against the cities of Israel, and they conquered I'jon, Dan, A'bel-ma'im, and all the store-cities of Naph'tali. [5] And when Ba'asha heard of it, he stopped building Ramah, and let his work cease. [6] Then King Asa took all Judah, and they carried away the stones of Ramah and its timber, with which Ba'asha had been building, and with them he built Geba and Mizpah.

7 At that time Hana'ni the seer came to Asa king of Judah, and said to him, "Because you relied on the king of Syria, and did not rely on the LORD your God, the army of the king of Syria has escaped you. [8] Were not the Ethiopians and the Libyans a huge

c Compare Syr Vg: Heb *the prophecy, Oded the prophet*
d Heb *the vestibule of the LORD*

mentioned elsewhere. **16–19:** For a parallel, see 1 Kg.15.13–15, which suggested Asa as a reformer. **16:** *Asherah,* see 1 Kg.14.15 n.
 16.1–14: The war with Baasha; Asa's apostasy, punishment, and death. 1–6: Except for the date, these verses follow closely 1 Kg.15.17–22. **7–10:** This rebuke by the prophet and the unrepentant attitude of Asa were introduced here by the Chronicler to explain the later illness

army with exceedingly many chariots and horsemen? Yet because you relied on the LORD, he gave them into your hand. ⁹ For the eyes of the LORD run to and fro throughout the whole earth, to show his might in behalf of those whose heart is blameless toward him. You have done foolishly in this; for from now on you will have wars." ¹⁰ Then Asa was angry with the seer, and put him in the stocks, in prison, for he was in a rage with him because of this. And Asa inflicted cruelties upon some of the people at the same time.

11 The acts of Asa, from first to last, are written in the Book of the Kings of Judah and Israel. ¹² In the thirty-ninth year of his reign Asa was diseased in his feet, and his disease became severe; yet even in his disease he did not seek the LORD, but sought help from physicians. ¹³ And Asa slept with his fathers, dying in the forty-first year of his reign. ¹⁴ They buried him in the tomb which he had hewn out for himself in the city of David. They laid him on a bier which had been filled with various kinds of spices prepared by the perfumer's art; and they made a very great fire in his honor.

17 Jehosh′aphat his son reigned in his stead, and strengthened himself against Israel. ² He placed forces in all the fortified cities of Judah, and set garrisons in the land of Judah, and in the cities of E′phraim which Asa his father had taken. ³ The LORD was with Jehosh′aphat, because he walked in the earlier ways of his father;ᵉ he did not seek the

Ba′als, ⁴ but sought the God of his father and walked in his commandments, and not according to the ways of Israel. ⁵ Therefore the LORD established the kingdom in his hand; and all Judah brought tribute to Jehosh′aphat; and he had great riches and honor. ⁶ His heart was courageous in the ways of the LORD; and furthermore he took the high places and the Ashe′rim out of Judah.

7 In the third year of his reign he sent his princes, Ben-hail, Obadi′ah, Zechari′ah, Nethan′el, and Micai′ah, to teach in the cities of Judah; ⁸ and with them the Levites, Shemai′ah, Nethani′ah, Zebadi′ah, As′ahel, Shemi′ramoth, Jehon′athan, Adoni′jah, Tobi′jah, and Tobadoni′jah; and with these Levites, the priests Eli′shama and Jeho′ram. ⁹ And they taught in Judah, having the book of the law of the LORD with them; they went about through all the cities of Judah and taught among the people.

10 And the fear of the LORD fell upon all the kingdoms of the lands that were round about Judah, and they made no war against Jehosh′aphat. ¹¹ Some of the Philistines brought Jehosh′aphat presents, and silver for tribute; and the Arabs also brought him seven thousand seven hundred rams and seven thousand seven hundred he-goats. ¹² And Jehosh′aphat grew steadily greater. He built in Judah fortresses and store-cities, ¹³ and he had great stores in the cities of Judah. He had soldiers, mighty men of valor,

e Another reading is *his father David*

---

of the king (v. 12). **11–14:** 1 Kg.15.23–24a has been expanded by emphasis on the culpability of Asa and the grandeur of his funeral, in spite of his sin.

17.1–19: The initially good and prosperous reign of Jehoshaphat. Chapters 17–20 are taken up with the reign of this king, exhibiting, as also in the case of Asa (see 14.1–14 n.), a considerable expansion of the source material (found in 1 Kg.15.24b; 22.1–35a,41–49). Jehoshaphat is represented as a ruler who did mostly good things, for which he was rewarded, but also some bad things, for which he was punished. **1–6:** With the exception of v. 1a (1 Kg.15.24b), this comes largely from sources now lost or is the author's creation. **6:** This contradicts 20.33 and 1 Kg. 22.43. *The Asherim*, see 1 Kg.14.15 n. **7–9:** No parallel. Here the Chronicler has the king send out a delegation of five princes, nine Levites, and two priests for religious education *among the people*. The preponderance of Levites is significant for the Chronicler's ideology. *The book of the law*, compare 2 Kg.22.8–13; Dt.17.18–20. **10–19:** Without parallel. The king was not only a man of religion, but also a man of military might. Since he is represented as having an

in Jerusalem. [14] This was the muster of them by fathers' houses: Of Judah, the commanders of thousands: Adnah the commander, with three hundred thousand mighty men of valor, [15] and next to him Jehoha'nan the commander, with two hundred and eighty thousand, [16] and next to him Amasi'ah the son of Zichri, a volunteer for the service of the LORD, with two hundred thousand mighty men of valor. [17] Of Benjamin: Eli'ada, a mighty man of valor, with two hundred thousand men armed with bow and shield, [18] and next to him Jeho'zabad with a hundred and eighty thousand armed for war. [19] These were in the service of the king, besides those whom the king had placed in the fortified cities throughout all Judah.

18 Now Jehosh'aphat had great riches and honor; and he made a marriage alliance with Ahab. [2] After some years he went down to Ahab in Sama'ria. And Ahab killed an abundance of sheep and oxen for him and for the people who were with him, and induced him to go up against Ramoth-gilead. [3] Ahab king of Israel said to Jehosh'aphat king of Judah, "Will you go with me to Ramoth-gilead?" He answered him, "I am as you are, my people as your people. We will be with you in the war."

4 And Jehosh'aphat said to the king of Israel, "Inquire first for the word of the LORD." [5] Then the king of Israel gathered the prophets together, four hundred men, and said to them, "Shall we go to battle against Ramoth-gilead, or shall I forbear?" And they said, "Go up; for God will give it into the hand of the king." [6] But Jehosh'aphat said, "Is there not here another prophet of the LORD of whom we may inquire?" [7] And the king of Israel said

to Jehosh'aphat, "There is yet one man by whom we may inquire of the LORD, Micai'ah the son of Imlah; but I hate him, for he never prophesies good concerning me, but always evil." And Jehosh'aphat said, "Let not the king say so." [8] Then the king of Israel summoned an officer and said, "Bring quickly Micai'ah the son of Imlah." [9] Now the king of Israel and Jehosh'aphat the king of Judah were sitting on their thrones, arrayed in their robes; and they were sitting at the threshing floor at the entrance of the gate of Sama'ria; and all the prophets were prophesying before them. [10] And Zedeki'ah the son of Chena'anah made for himself horns of iron, and said, "Thus says the LORD, 'With these you shall push the Syrians until they are destroyed.'" [11] And all the prophets prophesied so, and said, "Go up to Ramoth-gilead and triumph; the LORD will give it into the hand of the king."

12 And the messenger who went to summon Micai'ah said to him, "Behold, the words of the prophets with one accord are favorable to the king; let your word be like the word of one of them, and speak favorably." [13] But Micai'ah said, "As the LORD lives, what my God says, that I will speak." [14] And when he had come to the king, the king said to him, "Micai'ah, shall we go to Ramoth-gilead to battle, or shall I forbear?" And he answered, "Go up and triumph; they will be given into your hand." [15] But the king said to him, "How many times shall I adjure you that you speak to me nothing but the truth in the name of the LORD?" [16] And he said, "I saw all Israel scattered upon the mountains, as sheep that have no shepherd; and the LORD said, 'These have no master; let each return to his home in peace.'"

army of 1,160,000 men, it is understandable that *the fear of the LORD fell upon all the kingdoms of the lands that were round about*. This is hardly the historical Jehoshaphat.

18.1–34: Jehoshaphat's ill-fated alliance with Ahab. With the exception of vv. 1–2, this chapter is taken almost verbatim from 1 Kg.22.1–35a. It constitutes by far the largest body of material from the northern kingdom used by the Chronicler. It was inserted here probably because it reflects upon Ahab and prepares for the rebuke of Jehoshaphat in the next chapter (see 1 Kg. ch. 22 n.). **1**: Compare 2 Kg.8.18,25–27. **2**: An expansion of 1 Kg.22.2.

¹⁷ And the king of Israel said to Jehosh'aphat, "Did I not tell you that he would not prophesy good concerning me, but evil?" ¹⁸ And Micai'ah said, "Therefore hear the word of the LORD: I saw the LORD sitting on his throne, and all the host of heaven standing on his right hand and on his left; ¹⁹ and the LORD said, 'Who will entice Ahab the king of Israel, that he may go up and fall at Ramoth-gilead?' And one said one thing, and another said another. ²⁰ Then a spirit came forward and stood before the LORD, saying, 'I will entice him.' And the LORD said to him, 'By what means?' ²¹ And he said, 'I will go forth, and will be a lying spirit in the mouth of all his prophets.' And he said, 'You are to entice him, and you shall succeed; go forth and do so.' ²² Now therefore behold, the LORD has put a lying spirit in the mouth of these your prophets; the LORD has spoken evil concerning you."

23 Then Zedeki'ah the son of Chena'anah came near and struck Micai'ah on the cheek, and said, "Which way did the Spirit of the LORD go from me to speak to you?" ²⁴ And Micai'ah said, "Behold, you shall see on that day when you go into an inner chamber to hide yourself." ²⁵ And the king of Israel said, "Seize Micai'ah, and take him back to Amon the governor of the city and to Jo'ash the king's son; ²⁶ and say, 'Thus says the king, Put this fellow in prison, and feed him with scant fare of bread and water, until I return in peace.'" ²⁷ And Micai'ah said, "If you return in peace, the LORD has not spoken by me." And he said, "Hear, all you peoples!"

28 So the king of Israel and Jehosh'aphat the king of Judah went up to Ramoth-gilead. ²⁹ And the king of Israel said to Jehosh'aphat, "I will disguise myself and go into battle, but you wear your robes." And the king of Israel disguised himself; and they went into battle. ³⁰ Now the king of Syria had commanded the captains of his chariots, "Fight with neither small nor great, but only with the king of Israel." ³¹ And when the captains of the chariots saw Jehosh'aphat, they said, "It is the king of Israel." So they turned to fight against him; and Jehosh'aphat cried out, and the LORD helped him. God drew them away from him, ³² for when the captains of the chariots saw that it was not the king of Israel, they turned back from pursuing him. ³³ But a certain man drew his bow at a venture, and struck the king of Israel between the scale armor and the breastplate; therefore he said to the driver of his chariot, "Turn about, and carry me out of the battle, for I am wounded." ³⁴ And the battle grew hot that day, and the king of Israel propped himself up in his chariot facing the Syrians until evening; then at sunset he died.

19 Jehosh'aphat the king of Judah returned in safety to his house in Jerusalem. ² But Jehu the son of Hana'ni the seer went out to meet him, and said to King Jehosh'aphat, "Should you help the wicked and love those who hate the LORD? Because of this, wrath has gone out against you from the LORD. ³ Nevertheless some good is found in you, for you destroyed the Ashe'rahs out of the land, and have set your heart to seek God."

4 Jehosh'aphat dwelt at Jerusalem; and he went out again among the people, from Beer-sheba to the hill country of E'phraim, and brought them back to the LORD, the God of their fathers. ⁵ He appointed judges in the land in all the fortified cities of Judah, city by city, ⁶ and said to the

---

19.1–11: Jehoshaphat, having been rebuked by a prophet, rules wisely. 1–3: These verses were composed by the Chronicler, who felt it necessary to protest against the entanglement with Ahab. The real *Jehu the son of Hanani* prophesied nearly fifty years earlier (compare 1 Kg.16.1). This may be the same man, or an imaginary person of the same name; compare the "Hanani" of 16.7. *The Asherahs*, see 1 Kg.14.15 n. 4–7: No parallel in 1 Kings. The idea of the appointment of *judges* by this king may have been suggested to the Chronicler by the name *Jehoshaphat*,

judges, "Consider what you do, for you judge not for man but for the LORD; he is with you in giving judgment. ⁷ Now then, let the fear of the LORD be upon you; take heed what you do, for there is no perversion of justice with the LORD our God, or partiality, or taking bribes."

8 Moreover in Jerusalem Jehosh'-aphat appointed certain Levites and priests and heads of families of Israel, to give judgment for the LORD and to decide disputed cases. They had their seat at Jerusalem. ⁹ And he charged them: "Thus you shall do in the fear of the LORD, in faithfulness, and with your whole heart: ¹⁰ whenever a case comes to you from your brethren who live in their cities, concerning bloodshed, law or commandment, statutes or ordinances, then you shall instruct them, that they may not incur guilt before the LORD and wrath may not come upon you and your brethren. Thus you shall do, and you will not incur guilt. ¹¹ And behold, Amari'ah the chief priest is over you in all matters of the LORD; and Zebadi'ah the son of Ish'-mael, the governor of the house of Judah, in all the king's matters; and the Levites will serve you as officers. Deal courageously, and may the LORD be with the upright!"

20 After this the Moabites and Ammonites, and with them some of the Me-u'nites,ʲ came against Jehosh'aphat for battle. ² Some men came and told Jehosh'aphat, "A great multitude is coming against you from Edom,ᵍ from beyond the sea; and, behold, they are in Haz'azon-ta'mar" (that is, En-ge'di). ³ Then Jehosh'-aphat feared, and set himself to seek the LORD, and proclaimed a fast

throughout all Judah. ⁴ And Judah assembled to seek help from the LORD; from all the cities of Judah they came to seek the LORD.

5 And Jehosh'aphat stood in the assembly of Judah and Jerusalem, in the house of the LORD, before the new court, ⁶ and said, "O LORD, God of our fathers, art thou not God in heaven? Dost thou not rule over all the kingdoms of the nations? In thy hand are power and might, so that none is able to withstand thee. ⁷ Didst thou not, O our God, drive out the inhabitants of this land before thy people Israel, and give it for ever to the descendants of Abraham thy friend? ⁸ And they have dwelt in it, and have built thee in it a sanctuary for thy name, saying, ⁹ 'If evil comes upon us, the sword, judgment,ʰ or pestilence, or famine, we will stand before this house, and before thee, for thy name is in this house, and cry to thee in our affliction, and thou wilt hear and save.' ¹⁰ And now behold, the men of Ammon and Moab and Mount Se'ir, whom thou wouldest not let Israel invade when they came from the land of Egypt, and whom they avoided and did not destroy— ¹¹ behold, they reward us by coming to drive us out of thy possession, which thou hast given us to inherit. ¹² O our God, wilt thou not execute judgment upon them? For we are powerless against this great multitude that is coming against us. We do not know what to do, but our eyes are upon thee."

13 Meanwhile all the men of Judah stood before the LORD, with their little ones, their wives, and their children. ¹⁴ And the Spirit of the LORD came

ʲ Compare 26.7: Heb *Ammonites*
ᵍ One Ms: Heb *Aram* (Syria)
ʰ Or *the sword of judgment*

which means "the LORD judges." Compare Dt.1.16–17; 16.18. **8:** Here *Israel* means Judah, the true Israel in the eyes of the Chronicler (see 11.1–4 n.). **11:** Note the prominence of *the Levites*, who did not exist as a separate class in the time of the historical *Jehoshaphat* (see 1 Chr. 6.1–5 n.; 13.1–4 n.). Compare the procedure of judges in Dt.17.8–13.

20.1–37: The great victory over enemies of the true faith; Jehoshaphat's final mistake and consequent punishment. The Chronicler, having established the character of Jehoshaphat as a righteous king, attributes to him a victory of faith even greater than those of Abijah (ch. 13) and Asa (ch. 14). The story is often called a parable. There is only a faint parallel in 2 Kg.3.4–27. **5:** *The new court* was a feature of the temple of the Chronicler's time. **6:** This highly developed

upon Jaha'ziel the son of Zechari'ah, son of Benai'ah, son of Je-i'el, son of Mattani'ah, a Levite of the sons of Asaph, in the midst of the assembly. [15] And he said, "Hearken, all Judah and inhabitants of Jerusalem, and King Jehosh'aphat: Thus says the LORD to you, 'Fear not, and be not dismayed at this great multitude; for the battle is not yours but God's. [16] Tomorrow go down against them; behold, they will come up by the ascent of Ziz; you will find them at the end of the valley, east of the wilderness of Jeru'el. [17] You will not need to fight in this battle; take your position, stand still, and see the victory of the LORD on your behalf, O Judah and Jerusalem.' Fear not, and be not dismayed; tomorrow go out against them, and the LORD will be with you."

18 Then Jehosh'aphat bowed his head with his face to the ground, and all Judah and the inhabitants of Jerusalem fell down before the LORD, worshiping the LORD. [19] And the Levites, of the Ko'hathites and the Kor'ahites, stood up to praise the LORD, the God of Israel, with a very loud voice.

20 And they rose early in the morning and went out into the wilderness of Teko'a; and as they went out, Jehosh'aphat stood and said, "Hear me, Judah and inhabitants of Jerusalem! Believe in the LORD your God, and you will be established; believe his prophets, and you will succeed." [21] And when he had taken counsel with the people, he appointed those who were to sing to the LORD and praise him in holy array, as they went before the army, and say,

"Give thanks to the LORD,
    for his steadfast love endures for
      ever."

[22] And when they began to sing and praise, the LORD set an ambush against

the men of Ammon, Moab, and Mount Se'ir, who had come against Judah, so that they were routed. [23] For the men of Ammon and Moab rose against the inhabitants of Mount Se'ir, destroying them utterly, and when they had made an end of the inhabitants of Se'ir, they all helped to destroy one another.

24 When Judah came to the watchtower of the wilderness, they looked toward the multitude; and behold, they were dead bodies lying on the ground; none had escaped. [25] When Jehosh'aphat and his people came to take the spoil from them, they found cattle[i] in great numbers, goods, clothing, and precious things, which they took for themselves until they could carry no more. They were three days in taking the spoil, it was so much. [26] On the fourth day they assembled in the Valley of Bera'cah,[j] for there they blessed the LORD; therefore the name of that place has been called the Valley of Bera'cah to this day. [27] Then they returned, every man of Judah and Jerusalem, and Jehosh'aphat at their head, returning to Jerusalem with joy, for the LORD had made them rejoice over their enemies. [28] They came to Jerusalem, with harps and lyres and trumpets, to the house of the LORD. [29] And the fear of God came on all the kingdoms of the countries when they heard that the LORD had fought against the enemies of Israel. [30] So the realm of Jehosh'aphat was quiet, for his God gave him rest round about.

31 Thus Jehosh'aphat reigned over Judah. He was thirty-five years old when he began to reign, and he reigned twenty-five years in Jerusalem. His mother's name was Azu'bah the daughter of Shilhi. [32] He walked in the way of Asa his father and did not turn aside from it; he did what was right in the sight of the LORD. [33] The high

i Gk: Heb *among them*   *j* That is *Blessing*

monotheism was characteristic of the theology of the Chronicler's time (compare 6.14). **14:** *A Levite* takes the lead in prophecy. **17:** In battles of this kind, God's people do *not need to fight* (compare 13.15; 14.12; Ezek.38.17–23). Jehoshaphat's army of 1,160,000 (see 17.10–19 n.) was unnecessary. **18–23:** The singing of *the Levites* seems to have been the decisive human factor in this victory (compare Jg.7.22). **24–30:** Compare Ezek. ch. 39. **31–33:** Compare the

places, however, were not taken away; the people had not yet set their hearts upon the God of their fathers.

34 Now the rest of the acts of Jehosh'aphat, from first to last, are written in the chronicles of Jehu the son of Hana'ni, which are recorded in the Book of the Kings of Israel.

35 After this Jehosh'aphat king of Judah joined with Ahazi'ah king of Israel, who did wickedly. 36 He joined him in building ships to go to Tarshish, and they built the ships in E'zion-ge'-ber. 37 Then Elie'zer the son of Dodav'ahu of Mare'shah prophesied against Jehosh'aphat, saying, "Because you have joined with Ahazi'ah, the LORD will destroy what you have made." And the ships were wrecked and were not able to go to Tarshish.

21 Jehosh'aphat slept with his fathers, and was buried with his fathers in the city of David; and Jeho'ram his son reigned in his stead. 2 He had brothers, the sons of Jehosh'aphat: Azari'ah, Jehi'el, Zechari'ah, Azari'ah, Michael, and Shephati'ah; all these were the sons of Jehosh'aphat king of Judah. 3 Their father gave them great gifts, of silver, gold, and valuable possessions, together with fortified cities in Judah; but he gave the kingdom to Jeho'ram, because he was the firstborn. 4 When Jeho'ram had ascended the throne of his father and was established, he slew all his brothers with the sword, and also some of the princes of Israel. 5 Jeho'ram was thirty-two years old when he became king, and he reigned eight years in Jerusalem. 6 And he walked in the way of the kings of Israel, as the house of Ahab had done;

for the daughter of Ahab was his wife. And he did what was evil in the sight of the LORD. 7 Yet the LORD would not destroy the house of David, because of the covenant which he had made with David, and since he had promised to give a lamp to him and to his sons for ever.

8 In his days Edom revolted from the rule of Judah, and set up a king of their own. 9 Then Jeho'ram passed over with his commanders and all his chariots, and he rose by night and smote the E'domites who had surrounded him and his chariot commanders. 10 So Edom revolted from the rule of Judah to this day. At that time Libnah also revolted from his rule, because he had forsaken the LORD, the God of his fathers.

11 Moreover he made high places in the hill country of Judah, and led the inhabitants of Jerusalem into unfaithfulness, and made Judah go astray. 12 And a letter came to him from Eli'jah the prophet, saying, "Thus says the LORD, the God of David your father, 'Because you have not walked in the ways of Jehosh'aphat your father, or in the ways of Asa king of Judah, 13 but have walked in the way of the kings of Israel, and have led Judah and the inhabitants of Jerusalem into unfaithfulness, as the house of Ahab led Israel into unfaithfulness, and also you have killed your brothers, of your father's house, who were better than yourself; 14 behold, the LORD will bring a great plague on your people, your children, your wives, and all your possessions, 15 and you yourself will have a severe sickness with a dis-

---

source, 1 Kg.22.41–43. **34**: The parallel is 1 Kg.22.45, with a difference in the name of the book. *Israel* here means Judah (see 11.1–4 n.). **35–37**: The parallel is 1 Kg.22.44,48–49, drastically rewritten to show that the loss of the ships was due to improper association with *Ahaziah*.

21.1–20: Jehoram's wicked reign and his punishment. *Jehoram* is already given a bad reputation in 2 Kg.8.18; the Chronicler makes him worse and increases his punishments. **1**: The source is 1 Kg.22.50. **2–4**: These verses, which have no known source, are probably based on historically correct information (compare 11.22–23; Jg.9.1–6). **5–7**: Taken with changes from 2 Kgs.8.17–19. **8–10**: Taken from 2 Kg.8.20–22, with the addition of the last clause giving the Chronicler's explanation why *Jehoram* was having this trouble. **11–15**: The *letter . . . from Elijah the prophet* is a creation of the Chronicler. The question as to whether Elijah was still living at this time is pointless. Though the Chronicler avoided for the most part the use of names and incidents from the northern kingdom, he knew of the reputation of Elijah as a mighty

ease of your bowels, until your bowels come out because of the disease, day by day.' "

16 And the LORD stirred up against Jeho'ram the anger of the Philistines and of the Arabs who are near the Ethiopians; [17] and they came up against Judah, and invaded it, and carried away all the possessions they found that belonged to the king's house, and also his sons and his wives, so that no son was left to him except Jeho'ahaz, his youngest son.

18 And after all this the LORD smote him in his bowels with an incurable disease. [19] In course of time, at the end of two years, his bowels came out because of the disease, and he died in great agony. His people made no fire in his honor, like the fires made for his fathers. [20] He was thirty-two years old when he began to reign, and he reigned eight years in Jerusalem; and he departed with no one's regret. They buried him in the city of David, but not in the tombs of the kings.

22 And the inhabitants of Jerusalem made Ahazi'ah his youngest son king in his stead; for the band of men that came with the Arabs to the camp had slain all the older sons. So Ahazi'ah the son of Jeho'ram king of Judah reigned. [2] Ahazi'ah was forty-two years old when he began to reign, and he reigned one year in Jerusalem. His mother's name was Athali'ah, the granddaughter of Omri. [3] He also walked in the ways of the house of Ahab, for his mother was his counselor in doing wickedly. [4] He did what was evil in the sight of the LORD, as the house of Ahab had done; for after the

death of his father they were his counselors, to his undoing. [5] He even followed their counsel, and went with Jeho'ram the son of Ahab king of Israel to make war against Haz'ael king of Syria at Ramoth-gilead. And the Syrians wounded Joram, [6] and he returned to be healed in Jezreel of the wounds which he had received at Ramah, when he fought against Haz'-ael king of Syria. And Ahazi'ah the son of Jeho'ram king of Judah went down to see Joram the son of Ahab in Jezreel, because he was sick.

7 But it was ordained by God that the downfall of Ahazi'ah should come about through his going to visit Joram. For when he came there he went out with Jeho'ram to meet Jehu the son of Nimshi, whom the LORD had anointed to destroy the house of Ahab. [8] And when Jehu was executing judgment upon the house of Ahab, he met the princes of Judah and the sons of Ahazi'ah's brothers, who attended Ahazi'ah, and he killed them. [9] He searched for Ahazi'ah, and he was captured while hiding in Sama'ria, and he was brought to Jehu and put to death. They buried him, for they said, "He is the grandson of Jehosh'aphat, who sought the LORD with all his heart." And the house of Ahazi'ah had no one able to rule the kingdom.

10 Now when Athali'ah the mother of Ahazi'ah saw that her son was dead, she arose and destroyed all the royal family of the house of Judah. [11] But Jeho-shab'e-ath, the daughter of the king, took Jo'ash the son of Ahazi'ah, and stole him away from among the king's sons who were about to be slain,

---

man to rebuke kings in the name of the LORD, and used him accordingly to give more point to the rebuke of Jehoram. **16–17:** More military punishment; not found in 2 Kings. *Arabs who are near the Ethiopians,* see 14.9–15 n. **18–19:** Personal punishment, to fulfill the prophecy in v. 15. **20:** The same as v. 5, with typical additions (compare 2 Kg.8.24a).

22.1–12: The brief but wicked reign of Ahaziah; his punishment; the usurpation of Athaliah. **1–6:** This is a slightly rewritten version of 2 Kg.8.24b–29, with the guilt of Ahaziah heightened. **2:** *Forty-two* is an error for "twenty-two"; compare 2 Kg.8.26. **7:** A theological interpretation of v. 6 and of 2 Kg.9.21. **8–9:** Drawn from 2 Kg.9.27–28, but somewhat rewritten to make the end of Ahaziah less honorable, and to prepare for what follows. **10–12:** 2 Kg.11.1–3 with slight changes.

and she put him and his nurse in a bed-chamber. Thus Jeho-shab'e-ath, the daughter of King Jeho'ram and wife of Jehoi'ada the priest, because she was a sister of Ahazi'ah, hid him from Athali'ah, so that she did not slay him; 12 and he remained with them six years, hid in the house of God, while Athali'ah reigned over the land.

23 But in the seventh year Jehoi'ada took courage, and entered into a compact with the commanders of hundreds, Azari'ah the son of Jero'ham, Ish'mael the son of Jehoha'nan, Azari'ah the son of Obed, Ma-asei'ah the son of Adai'ah, and Elisha'phat the son of Zichri. 2 And they went about through Judah and gathered the Levites from all the cities of Judah, and the heads of fathers' houses of Israel, and they came to Jerusalem. 3 And all the assembly made a covenant with the king in the house of God. And Jehoi'-ada¹ said to them, "Behold, the king's son! Let him reign, as the LORD spoke concerning the sons of David. 4 This is the thing that you shall do: of you priests and Levites who come off duty on the sabbath, one third shall be gatekeepers, 5 and one third shall be at the king's house and one third at the Gate of the Foundation; and all the people shall be in the courts of the house of the LORD. 6 Let no one enter the house of the LORD except the priests and ministering Levites; they may enter, for they are holy, but all the people shall keep the charge of the LORD. 7 The Levites shall surround the king, each with his weapons in his hand; and whoever enters the house shall be slain. Be with the king when he comes in, and when he goes out."

8 The Levites and all Judah did according to all that Jehoi'ada the priest commanded. They each brought his men, who were to go off duty on the sabbath, with those who were to come on duty on the sabbath; for Jehoi'ada the priest did not dismiss the divisions. 9 And Jehoi'ada the priest delivered to the captains the spears and the large and small shields that had been King David's, which were in the house of God; 10 and he set all the people as a guard for the king, every man with his weapon in his hand, from the south side of the house to the north side of the house, around the altar and the house. 11 Then he brought out the king's son, and put the crown upon him, and gave him the testimony; and they proclaimed him king, and Jehoi'ada and his sons anointed him; and they said, "Long live the king."

12 When Athali'ah heard the noise of the people running and praising the king, she went into the house of the LORD to the people; 13 and when she looked, there was the king standing by his pillar at the entrance, and the captains and the trumpeters beside the king, and all the people of the land rejoicing and blowing trumpets, and the singers with their musical instruments leading in the celebration. And Athali'ah rent her clothes, and cried, "Treason! Treason!" 14 Then Jehoi'ada the priest brought out the captains who were set over the army, saying to them, "Bring her out between the ranks; any one who follows her is to be slain with the sword." For the priest said, "Do not slay her in the house of the LORD." 15 So they laid hands on her; and she went into the entrance of the horse gate of the king's house, and they slew her there.

16 And Jehoi'ada made a covenant between himself and all the people and the king that they should be the LORD's people. 17 Then all the people went to the house of Ba'al, and tore it

1 Heb *he*

23.1–21: The revolt against Athaliah; her punishment by death and the enthronement of Joash. Taken from 2 Kg.11.4–20, with certain characteristic changes and additions with a view to making the revolt the work of the Levites and singers rather than of the military; see vv. 2–3,6, 18–19, added by the Chronicler; in v. 19, even *the gatekeepers* have a share (compare 1 Chr. ch. 26). In v. 13 the insertion of *the singers with their musical instruments leading in the celebration* changes drastically the tense military atmosphere of 2 Kg. ch. 11.

down; his altars and his images they broke in pieces, and they slew Mattan the priest of Ba'al before the altars. ¹⁸ And Jehoi'ada posted watchmen for the house of the LORD under the direction of the Levitical priests and the Levites whom David had organized to be in charge of the house of the LORD, to offer burnt offerings to the LORD, as it is written in the law of Moses, with rejoicing and with singing, according to the order of David. ¹⁹ He stationed the gatekeepers at the gates of the house of the LORD so that no one should enter who was in any way unclean. ²⁰ And he took the captains, the nobles, the governors of the people, and all the people of the land; and they brought the king down from the house of the LORD, marching through the upper gate to the king's house. And they set the king upon the royal throne. ²¹ So all the people of the land rejoiced; and the city was quiet, after Athali'ah had been slain with the sword.

24 Jo'ash was seven years old when he began to reign, and he reigned forty years in Jerusalem; his mother's name was Zib'iah of Beer-sheba. ² And Jo'ash did what was right in the eyes of the LORD all the days of Jehoi'ada the priest. ³ Jehoi'ada got for him two wives, and he had sons and daughters.

4 After this Jo'ash decided to restore the house of the LORD. ⁵ And he gathered the priests and the Levites, and said to them, "Go out to the cities of Judah, and gather from all Israel money to repair the house of your God from year to year; and see that you hasten the matter." But the Levites did not hasten it. ⁶ So the king summoned Jehoi'ada the chief, and said to him, "Why have you not required the Levites to bring in from Judah and

Jerusalem the tax levied by Moses, the servant of the LORD, on*m* the congregation of Israel for the tent of testimony?" ⁷ For the sons of Athali'ah, that wicked woman, had broken into the house of God; and had also used all the dedicated things of the house of the LORD for the Ba'als.

8 So the king commanded, and they made a chest, and set it outside the gate of the house of the LORD. ⁹ And proclamation was made throughout Judah and Jerusalem, to bring in for the LORD the tax that Moses the servant of God laid upon Israel in the wilderness. ¹⁰ And all the princes and all the people rejoiced and brought their tax and dropped it into the chest until they had finished. ¹¹ And whenever the chest was brought to the king's officers by the Levites, when they saw that there was much money in it, the king's secretary and the officer of the chief priest would come and empty the chest and take it and return it to its place. Thus they did day after day, and collected money in abundance. ¹² And the king and Jehoi'ada gave it to those who had charge of the work of the house of the LORD, and they hired masons and carpenters to restore the house of the LORD, and also workers in iron and bronze to repair the house of the LORD. ¹³ So those who were engaged in the work labored, and the repairing went forward in their hands, and they restored the house of God to its proper condition and strengthened it. ¹⁴ And when they had finished, they brought the rest of the money before the king and Jehoi'ada, and with it were made utensils for the house of the LORD, both for the service and for the burnt offerings, and dishes for incense, and vessels of gold and silver. And they

m Compare Vg: Heb *and*

24.1–27: The good beginning of Joash; his later apostasy and consequent punishment. Based upon 2 Kg. ch. 12. Joash is depicted by the Chronicler as being considerably worse than he appears to be in 2 Kings, probably because he was a grandson of Athaliah (see 2 Kg.12.19–21 n.). Such treatment also provides an explanation of Joash's military misfortune and his assassination, both unexplained in 2 Kings. **1–3:** 2 Kg.12.3 is omitted and v. 3 here is added. **4–7:** Rewritten to give *the Levites* a greater share, even in the delaying tactics (v. 5). Verse 7 is an added observation, doubtless correct. **8–14:** See 2 Kg.12.9–16 n. **15–22:** This story, not attested else-

offered burnt offerings in the house of the LORD continually all the days of Jehoi'ada.

15 But Jehoi'ada grew old and full of days, and died; he was a hundred and thirty years old at his death. 16 And they buried him in the city of David among the kings, because he had done good in Israel, and toward God and his house.

17 Now after the death of Jehoi'ada the princes of Judah came and did obeisance to the king; then the king hearkened to them. 18 And they forsook the house of the LORD, the God of their fathers, and served the Ashe'rim and the idols. And wrath came upon Judah and Jerusalem for this their guilt. 19 Yet he sent prophets among them to bring them back to the LORD; these testified against them, but they would not give heed.

20 Then the Spirit of God took possession of[n] Zechari'ah the son of Jehoi'ada the priest; and he stood above the people, and said to them, "Thus says God, 'Why do you transgress the commandments of the LORD, so that you cannot prosper? Because you have forsaken the LORD, he has forsaken you.'" 21 But they conspired against him, and by command of the king they stoned him with stones in the court of the house of the LORD. 22 Thus Jo'ash the king did not remember the kindness which Jehoi'ada, Zechari'ah's father, had shown him, but killed his son. And when he was dying, he said, "May the LORD see and avenge!"

23 At the end of the year the army of the Syrians came up against Jo'ash. They came to Judah and Jerusalem, and destroyed all the princes of the people from among the people, and sent all their spoil to the king of Damascus. 24 Though the army of the Syrians had come with few men, the LORD delivered into their hand a very great army, because they had forsaken the LORD, the God of their fathers. Thus they executed judgment on Jo'ash.

25 When they had departed from him, leaving him severely wounded, his servants conspired against him because of the blood of the son[o] of Jehoi'ada the priest, and slew him on his bed. So he died; and they buried him in the city of David, but they did not bury him in the tombs of the kings. 26 Those who conspired against him were Zabad the son of Shim'e-ath the Ammonitess, and Jeho'zabad the son of Shimrith the Moabitess. 27 Accounts of his sons, and of the many oracles against him, and of the rebuilding[p] of the house of God are written in the Commentary on the Book of the Kings. And Amazi'ah his son reigned in his stead.

25 Amazi'ah was twenty-five years old when he began to reign, and he reigned twenty-nine years in Jerusalem. His mother's name was Jeho-ad'dan of Jerusalem. 2 And he did what was right in the eyes of the LORD, yet not with a blameless heart. 3 And as soon as the royal power was firmly in his hand he killed his servants who had slain the king his father. 4 But he did not put their children to death, according to what is written in the law, in the book of Moses, where the LORD commanded, "The fathers shall not be put to death for the children, or the children be put to death for the fathers; but every man shall die for his own sin."

5 Then Amazi'ah assembled the men of Judah, and set them by fathers' houses under commanders of thou-

n Heb *clothed itself with*
o Gk Vg: Heb *sons*   p Heb *founding*

where, prepares for what follows. Compare Lk.11.51. **23–24:** A drastically rewritten form of 2 Kg.12.17–18. **25–27:** A reinterpretation of 2 Kg.12.19–21. *The Commentary on the Book of the Kings* can no more be identified than can other such works referred to by the Chronicler (see Introduction to 1 Chronicles).
  25.1–28: Amaziah acts wrongfully and suffers punishment. Based upon 2 Kg.14.2–14,17–20. **1–4:** Not essentially different from 2 Kg.14.2–6. **5–13:** An expansion of a single verse, 2 Kg.14.7. *Amaziah* did wrong in hiring troops from the northern kingdom; even while winning a victory

sands and of hundreds for all Judah and Benjamin. He mustered those twenty years old and upward, and found that they were three hundred thousand picked men, fit for war, able to handle spear and shield. [6] He hired also a hundred thousand mighty men of valor from Israel for a hundred talents of silver. [7] But a man of God came to him and said, "O king, do not let the army of Israel go with you, for the LORD is not with Israel, with all these E′phraimites. [8] But if you suppose that in this way you will be strong for war,[q] God will cast you down before the enemy; for God has power to help or to cast down." [9] And Amazi′ah said to the man of God, "But what shall we do about the hundred talents which I have given to the army of Israel?" The man of God answered, "The LORD is able to give you much more than this." [10] Then Amazi′ah discharged the army that had come to him from E′phraim, to go home again. And they became very angry with Judah, and returned home in fierce anger. [11] But Amazi′ah took courage, and led out his people, and went to the Valley of Salt and smote ten thousand men of Se′ir. [12] The men of Judah captured another ten thousand alive, and took them to the top of a rock and threw them down from the top of the rock; and they were all dashed to pieces. [13] But the men of the army whom Amazi′ah sent back, not letting them go with him to battle, fell upon the cities of Judah, from Sama′ria to Beth-hor′on, and killed three thousand people in them, and took much spoil.

14 After Amazi′ah came from the slaughter of the E′domites, he brought the gods of the men of Se′ir, and set them up as his gods, and worshiped them, making offerings to them. [15] Therefore the LORD was angry with Amazi′ah and sent to him a prophet, who said to him, "Why have you resorted to the gods of a people, which did not deliver their own people from your hand?" [16] But as he was speaking the king said to him, "Have we made you a royal counselor? Stop! Why should you be put to death?" So the prophet stopped, but said, "I know that God has determined to destroy you, because you have done this and have not listened to my counsel."

17 Then Amazi′ah king of Judah took counsel and sent to Jo′ash the son of Jeho′ahaz, son of Jehu, king of Israel, saying, "Come, let us look one another in the face." [18] And Jo′ash the king of Israel sent word to Amazi′ah king of Judah, "A thistle on Lebanon sent to a cedar on Lebanon, saying, 'Give your daughter to my son for a wife'; and a wild beast of Lebanon passed by and trampled down the thistle. [19] You say, 'See, I have smitten Edom,' and your heart has lifted you up in boastfulness. But now stay at home; why should you provoke trouble so that you fall, you and Judah with you?"

20 But Amazi′ah would not listen; for it was of God, in order that he might give them into the hand of their enemies, because they had sought the gods of Edom. [21] So Jo′ash king of Israel went up; and he and Amazi′ah king of Judah faced one another in battle at Beth-she′mesh, which belongs to Judah. [22] And Judah was defeated by Israel, and every man fled to his home. [23] And Jo′ash king of Israel captured Amazi′ah king of Judah, the son of Jo′ash, son of Ahazi′ah, at Beth-she′mesh, and brought him to Jerusalem, and broke down the wall of Jerusalem for four hundred cubits, from the E′phraim Gate to the Corner Gate. [24] And he seized all the gold and silver, and all the vessels that were found in the house of God, and O′bed-

q Gk: Heb *But if you go, act, be strong for the battle*

over Edom, he was punished for his indiscretion (v. 13). *Samaria* and *Beth-horon* were not among the *cities of Judah;* there is some confusion here. **14–16:** These verses, not found in 2 Kings, are the Chronicler's way of explaining what follows. **17–19:** See note on the parallel, 2 Kg.14.8–10. **20–24:** Similar to 2 Kg.14.11–14, except for the theological explanation in v. 20b.

e'dom with them; he seized also the treasuries of the king's house, and hostages, and he returned to Sama'ria.

25 Amazi'ah the son of Jo'ash king of Judah lived fifteen years after the death of Jo'ash the son of Jeho'ahaz, king of Israel. 26 Now the rest of the deeds of Amazi'ah, from first to last, are they not written in the Book of the Kings of Judah and Israel? 27 From the time when he turned away from the LORD they made a conspiracy against him in Jerusalem, and he fled to Lachish. But they sent after him to Lachish, and slew him there. 28 And they brought him upon horses; and he was buried with his fathers in the city of David.

26 And all the people of Judah took Uzzi'ah, who was sixteen years old, and made him king instead of his father Amazi'ah. 2 He built Eloth and restored it to Judah, after the king slept with his fathers. 3 Uzzi'ah was sixteen years old when he began to reign, and he reigned fifty-two years in Jerusalem. His mother's name was Jecoli'ah of Jerusalem. 4 And he did what was right in the eyes of the LORD, according to all that his father Amazi'ah had done. 5 He set himself to seek God in the days of Zechari'ah, who instructed him in the fear of God; and as long as he sought the LORD, God made him prosper.

6 He went out and made war against the Philistines, and broke down the wall of Gath and the wall of Jabneh and the wall of Ashdod; and he built cities in the territory of Ashdod and elsewhere among the Philistines. 7 God helped him against the Philistines, and against the Arabs that dwelt in Gurba'al, and against the Me-u'-nites. 8 The Ammonites paid tribute to Uzzi'ah, and his fame spread even to the border of Egypt, for he became very strong. 9 Moreover Uzzi'ah built towers in Jerusalem at the Corner Gate and at the Valley Gate and at the Angle, and fortified them. 10 And he built towers in the wilderness, and hewed out many cisterns, for he had large herds, both in the Shephe'lah and in the plain, and he had farmers and vinedressers in the hills and in the fertile lands, for he loved the soil. 11 Moreover Uzzi'ah had an army of soldiers, fit for war, in divisions according to the numbers in the muster made by Je-i'el the secretary and Ma-asei'ah the officer, under the direction of Hanani'ah, one of the king's commanders. 12 The whole number of the heads of fathers' houses of mighty men of valor was two thousand six hundred. 13 Under their command was an army of three hundred and seven thousand five hundred, who could make war with mighty power, to help the king against the enemy. 14 And Uzzi'ah prepared for all the army shields, spears, helmets, coats of mail, bows, and stones for slinging. 15 In Jerusalem he made engines, invented by skilful men, to be on the towers and the corners, to shoot arrows and great stones. And his fame spread far, for he was marvelously helped, till he was strong.

16 But when he was strong he grew proud, to his destruction. For he was false to the LORD his God, and entered the temple of the LORD to burn incense on the altar of incense. 17 But Azari'ah the priest went in after him, with eighty priests of the LORD who were men of valor; 18 and they withstood King Uzzi'ah, and said to him, "It is

---

25–28: Much the same as 2 Kg.14.17–20, except for the explanatory phrase *From the time when he turned away from the LORD* (v. 27).

26.1–23: Uzziah's good beginning and consequent prosperity; his subsequent sin and consequent punishment. The brief parallel is found in 2 Kg.14.21–22; 15.2–3,5–7. The reign of Uzziah (called also Azariah in 2 Kings) was a long one (v. 3), and the account is greatly expanded here. **1–4:** Compare 2 Kg.14.21–22; 15.2–3. **5:** Added by the Chronicler. This Zechariah is otherwise unknown; he served the same function as Jehoiada in 24.2. **6–15:** Without parallel in 2 Kings, but there is here valuable historical material from an unknown source. **16–20:** A free composition of the Chronicler to explain the leprosy of Uzziah and to warn that in the new,

not for you, Uzzi'ah, to burn incense to the LORD, but for the priests the sons of Aaron, who are consecrated to burn incense. Go out of the sanctuary; for you have done wrong, and it will bring you no honor from the LORD God." ¹⁹ Then Uzzi'ah was angry. Now he had a censer in his hand to burn incense, and when he became angry with the priests leprosy broke out on his forehead, in the presence of the priests in the house of the LORD, by the altar of incense. ²⁰ And Azari'ah the chief priest, and all the priests, looked at him, and behold, he was leprous in his forehead! And they thrust him out quickly, and he himself hastened to go out, because the LORD had smitten him. ²¹ And King Uzzi'ah was a leper to the day of his death, and being a leper dwelt in a separate house, for he was excluded from the house of the LORD. And Jotham his son was over the king's household, governing the people of the land.

22 Now the rest of the acts of Uzzi'ah, from first to last, Isaiah the prophet the son of Amoz wrote. ²³ And Uzzi'ah slept with his fathers, and they buried him with his fathers in the burial field which belonged to the kings, for they said, "He is a leper." And Jotham his son reigned in his stead.

27 Jotham was twenty-five years old when he began to reign, and he reigned sixteen years in Jerusalem. His mother's name was Jeru'shah the daughter of Zadok. ² And he did what was right in the eyes of the LORD according to all that his father

Uzzi'ah had done—only he did not invade the temple of the LORD. But the people still followed corrupt practices. ³ He built the upper gate of the house of the LORD, and did much building on the wall of Ophel. ⁴ Moreover he built cities in the hill country of Judah, and forts and towers on the wooded hills. ⁵ He fought with the king of the Ammonites and prevailed against them. And the Ammonites gave him that year a hundred talents of silver, and ten thousand cors of wheat and ten thousand of barley. The Ammonites paid him the same amount in the second and the third years. ⁶ So Jotham became mighty, because he ordered his ways before the LORD his God. ⁷ Now the rest of the acts of Jotham, and all his wars, and his ways, behold, they are written in the Book of the Kings of Israel and Judah. ⁸ He was twenty-five years old when he began to reign, and he reigned sixteen years in Jerusalem. ⁹ And Jotham slept with his fathers, and they buried him in the city of David; and Ahaz his son reigned in his stead.

28 Ahaz was twenty years old when he began to reign, and he reigned sixteen years in Jerusalem. And he did not do what was right in the eyes of the LORD, like his father David, ² but walked in the ways of the kings of Israel. He even made molten images for the Ba'als; ³ and he burned incense in the valley of the son of Hinnom, and burned his sons as an offering, according to the abominable practices of the nations whom the LORD drove out before the people of

---

ideal kingdom the king is not to assume priestly prerogatives. **21–23:** Parallel to 2 Kg.15.5–7, with the change of the name of a book in v. 22.

27.1–9: Jotham's goodness and consequent prosperity. This short chapter parallels 2 Kg.15.33–38, with a few significant changes. Jotham is represented by the Chronicler as a totally good and hence completely prosperous king. Verse 2b was added to show that the king was ritually correct; v. 2c to show that faults came from the people, not the king. Verses 4–6 were added to show the good king's military might. 2 Kg.15.37 was omitted because the Chronicler wished to present the reign of the idealized Jotham as being without any troubles whatever.

28.1–27: The enormous iniquity of Ahaz and the appropriate punishments which he received. Based upon 2 Kg. ch. 16 with drastic rewriting to intensify the unfavorable portrait already present in the source. To the Chronicler, the wholly good reign of Jotham was followed by the wholly bad reign of Ahaz. **1–4:** Not greatly changed from the source, 2 Kg.16.2–4. **5–15:** A

Israel. ⁴ And he sacrificed and burned incense on the high places, and on the hills, and under every green tree.

5 Therefore the LORD his God gave him into the hand of the king of Syria, who defeated him and took captive a great number of his people and brought them to Damascus. He was also given into the hand of the king of Israel, who defeated him with great slaughter. ⁶ For Pekah the son of Remali′ah slew a hundred and twenty thousand in Judah in one day, all of them men of valor, because they had forsaken the LORD, the God of their fathers. ⁷ And Zichri, a mighty man of E′phraim, slew Ma-asei′ah the king's son and Azri′kam the commander of the palace and Elka′nah the next in authority to the king.

8 The men of Israel took captive two hundred thousand of their kinsfolk, women, sons, and daughters; they also took much spoil from them and brought the spoil to Sama′ria. ⁹ But a prophet of the LORD was there, whose name was Oded; and he went out to meet the army that came to Sama′ria, and said to them, "Behold, because the LORD, the God of your fathers, was angry with Judah, he gave them into your hand, but you have slain them in a rage which has reached up to heaven. ¹⁰ And now you intend to subjugate the people of Judah and Jerusalem, male and female, as your slaves. Have you not sins of your own against the LORD your God? ¹¹ Now hear me, and send back the captives from your kinsfolk whom you have taken, for the fierce wrath of the LORD is upon you." ¹² Certain chiefs also of the men of E′phraim, Azari′ah the son of Joha′nan, Berechi′ah the son of Meshil′lemoth, Jehizki′ah the son of Shallum, and Ama′sa the son of Had-lai, stood up against those who were coming from the war, ¹³ and said to them, "You shall not bring the cap-

tives in here, for you propose to bring upon us guilt against the LORD in addition to our present sins and guilt. For our guilt is already great, and there is fierce wrath against Israel." ¹⁴ So the armed men left the captives and the spoil before the princes and all the assembly. ¹⁵ And the men who have been mentioned by name rose and took the captives, and with the spoil they clothed all that were naked among them; they clothed them, gave them sandals, provided them with food and drink, and anointed them; and carrying all the feeble among them on asses, they brought them to their kinsfolk at Jericho, the city of palm trees. Then they returned to Sama′ria.

16 At that time King Ahaz sent to the king*ʳ* of Assyria for help. ¹⁷ For the E′domites had again invaded and defeated Judah, and carried away captives. ¹⁸ And the Philistines had made raids on the cities in the Shephe′-lah and the Negeb of Judah, and had taken Beth-she′mesh, Ai′jalon, Gede′-roth, Soco with its villages, Timnah with its villages, and Gimzo with its villages; and they settled there. ¹⁹ For the LORD brought Judah low because of Ahaz king of Israel, for he had dealt wantonly in Judah and had been faithless to the LORD. ²⁰ So Til′-gath-pilne′ser king of Assyria came against him, and afflicted him instead of strengthening him. ²¹ For Ahaz took from the house of the LORD and the house of the king and of the princes, and gave tribute to the king of Assyria; but it did not help him.

22 In the time of his distress he became yet more faithless to the LORD— this same King Ahaz. ²³ For he sacrificed to the gods of Damascus which had defeated him, and said, "Because the gods of the kings of Syria helped them, I will sacrifice to them that they may help me." But they were the ruin

ʳ Gk Syr Vg Compare 2 Kg 16.7: Heb *kings*

drastic rewriting and expansion of 2 Kg.16.5–6. Both *Syria* and *Israel* defeat *Judah* with tremendous slaughter, signalizing God's retributive justice. At the same time, the wicked northern kingdom is not allowed to retain any advantage from its punitive victory (vv. 8–15). **16–25:** Somewhat briefer than the source, 2 Kg.16.7–18. The aim of the writer is to show that Ahaz did

of him, and of all Israel. [24] And Ahaz gathered together the vessels of the house of God and cut in pieces the vessels of the house of God, and he shut up the doors of the house of the LORD; and he made himself altars in every corner of Jerusalem. [25] In every city of Judah he made high places to burn incense to other gods, provoking to anger the LORD, the God of his fathers. [26] Now the rest of his acts and all his ways, from first to last, behold, they are written in the Book of the Kings of Judah and Israel. [27] And Ahaz slept with his fathers, and they buried him in the city, in Jerusalem, for they did not bring him into the tombs of the kings of Israel. And Hezeki'ah his son reigned in his stead.

29 Hezeki'ah began to reign when he was twenty-five years old, and he reigned twenty-nine years in Jerusalem. His mother's name was Abi'jah the daughter of Zechari'ah. [2] And he did what was right in the eyes of the LORD, according to all that David his father had done.

3 In the first year of his reign, in the first month, he opened the doors of the house of the LORD, and repaired them. [4] He brought in the priests and the Levites, and assembled them in the square on the east, [5] and said to them, "Hear me, Levites! Now sanctify yourselves, and sanctify the house of the LORD, the God of your fathers, and carry out the filth from the holy place. [6] For our fathers have been unfaithful and have done what was evil in the sight of the LORD our God; they have forsaken him, and have turned away their faces from the habitation of the LORD, and turned their backs. [7] They also shut the doors of the vestibule and put out the lamps, and have not burned incense or offered burnt offerings in the holy place to the God of Israel. [8] Therefore the wrath of the LORD came on Judah and Jerusalem, and he has made them an object of horror, of astonishment, and of hissing, as you see with your own eyes. [9] For lo, our fathers have fallen by the sword and our sons and our daughters and our wives are in captivity for this. [10] Now it is in my heart to make a covenant with the LORD, the God of Israel, that his fierce anger may turn away from us. [11] My sons, do not now be negligent, for the LORD has chosen you to stand in his presence, to minister to him, and to be his ministers and burn incense to him."

12 Then the Levites arose, Mahath the son of Ama'sai, and Jo'el the son of Azari'ah, of the sons of the Ko'hathites; and of the sons of Merar'i, Kish the son of Abdi, and Azari'ah the son of Jehal'lelel; and of the Gershonites, Jo'ah the son of Zimmah, and Eden the son of Jo'ah; [13] and of the sons of Eli-za'phan, Shimri and Jeu'el; and of the sons of Asaph, Zechari'ah and Mattani'ah; [14] and of the sons of Heman, Jehu el and Shim'e-i; and of the sons of Jedu'thun, Shemai'ah and Uz'ziel. [15] They gathered their brethren, and sanctified themselves, and went in as the king had commanded, by the words of the LORD, to cleanse the house of the LORD. [16] The priests went into the inner part of the house of the LORD to

---

not profit even temporarily from his unholy alliance with the Assyrians. **26–27:** Rewritten from 2 Kg.16.19–20. Verse 27 contradicts 2 Kg.16.20 with regard to the burial of the king; the evil Ahaz could not be buried in a royal tomb (compare 21.20; 24.25; 26.23).

29.1–36: Hezekiah begins his good reign by cleansing the temple. Second Kings considers Hezekiah an important and on the whole a good king; three chapters (chs. 18–20) are devoted to him. The Chronicler makes him a reformer like the later Josiah, and devotes four chapters to him (chs. 29–32). **1–2:** Taken with little change from 2 Kg.18.2–3. **3–11:** In 28.24 the Chronicler had said that Ahaz closed down the temple entirely (in contrast to 2 Kg.16.10–16). Thus the way was prepared for the present passage, with its theme of reform carried out by *priests and Levites*–a favorite subject with the Chronicler. There is only the slightest affinity with 2 Kg.18.4–6. Verses 6–9 suggest liturgical confession during the Babylonian captivity (compare Zech.1.1–6). **12–19:** Continuation of the reform; no parallel; the Chronicler presents an ideal

cleanse it, and they brought out all the uncleanness that they found in the temple of the LORD into the court of the house of the LORD; and the Levites took it and carried it out to the brook Kidron. ¹⁷ They began to sanctify on the first day of the first month, and on the eighth day of the month they came to the vestibule of the LORD; then for eight days they sanctified the house of the LORD, and on the sixteenth day of the first month they finished. ¹⁸ Then they went in to Hezeki′ah the king and said, "We have cleansed all the house of the LORD, the altar of burnt offering and all its utensils, and the table for the showbread and all its utensils. ¹⁹ All the utensils which King Ahaz discarded in his reign when he was faithless, we have made ready and sanctified; and behold, they are before the altar of the LORD."

20 Then Hezeki′ah the king rose early and gathered the officials of the city, and went up to the house of the LORD. ²¹ And they brought seven bulls, seven rams, seven lambs, and seven he-goats for a sin offering for the kingdom and for the sanctuary and for Judah. And he commanded the priests the sons of Aaron to offer them on the altar of the LORD. ²² So they killed the bulls, and the priests received the blood and threw it against the altar; and they killed the rams and their blood was thrown against the altar; and they killed the lambs and their blood was thrown against the altar. ²³ Then the he-goats for the sin offering were brought to the king and the assembly, and they laid their hands upon them, ²⁴ and the priests killed them and made a sin offering with their blood on the altar, to make atonement for all Israel. For the king commanded that the burnt offering and the sin offering should be made for all Israel.

25 And he stationed the Levites in the house of the LORD with cymbals, harps, and lyres, according to the commandment of David and of Gad the king's seer and of Nathan the prophet; for the commandment was from the LORD through his prophets. ²⁶ The Levites stood with the instruments of David, and the priests with the trumpets. ²⁷ Then Hezeki′ah commanded that the burnt offering be offered on the altar. And when the burnt offering began, the song to the LORD began also, and the trumpets, accompanied by the instruments of David king of Israel. ²⁸ The whole assembly worshiped, and the singers sang, and the trumpeters sounded; all this continued until the burnt offering was finished. ²⁹ When the offering was finished, the king and all who were present with him bowed themselves and worshiped. ³⁰ And Hezeki′ah the king and the princes commanded the Levites to sing praises to the LORD with the words of David and of Asaph the seer. And they sang praises with gladness, and they bowed down and worshiped.

31 Then Hezeki′ah said, "You have now consecrated yourselves to the LORD; come near, bring sacrifices and thank offerings to the house of the LORD." And the assembly brought sacrifices and thank offerings; and all who were of a willing heart brought burnt offerings. ³² The number of the burnt offerings which the assembly brought was seventy bulls, a hundred rams, and two hundred lambs; all these were for a burnt offering to the LORD. ³³ And the consecrated offerings were six hundred bulls and three thousand sheep. ³⁴ But the priests were too few and could not flay all the burnt offerings, so until other priests had sanctified themselves their brethren the Levites helped them, until the work was finished—for the Levites were more upright in heart than the priests in sanctifying themselves. ³⁵ Besides the great number of burnt offerings there

reform with emphasis on *the Levites*. **20–24**: The ideal sacrifice of rededication. **25–30**: Note the great importance of the Levitical musicians (see Introduction to 1 Chronicles and compare 1 Chr. ch. 25). **31–36**: To the Chronicler, *the Levites were more upright in heart than the priests.*

was the fat of the peace offerings, and there were the libations for the burnt offerings. Thus the service of the house of the LORD was restored. [36] And Hezeki'ah and all the people rejoiced because of what God had done for the people; for the thing came about suddenly.

30 Hezeki'ah sent to all Israel and Judah, and wrote letters also to E'phraim and Manas'seh, that they should come to the house of the LORD at Jerusalem, to keep the passover to the LORD the God of Israel. [2] For the king and his princes and all the assembly in Jerusalem had taken counsel to keep the passover in the second month– [3] for they could not keep it in its time because the priests had not sanctified themselves in sufficient number, nor had the people assembled in Jerusalem– [4] and the plan seemed right to the king and all the assembly. [5] So they decreed to make a proclamation throughout all Israel, from Beer-sheba to Dan, that the people should come and keep the passover to the LORD the God of Israel, at Jerusalem; for they had not kept it in great numbers as prescribed. [6] So couriers went throughout all Israel and Judah with letters from the king and his princes, as the king had commanded, saying, "O people of Israel, return to the LORD, the God of Abraham, Isaac, and Israel, that he may turn again to the remnant of you who have escaped from the hand of the kings of Assyria. [7] Do not be like your fathers and your brethren, who were faithless to the LORD God of their fathers, so that he made them a desolation, as you see. [8] Do not now be stiff-necked as your fathers were, but yield yourselves to the LORD, and come to his sanctuary, which he has sanctified for ever, and serve the LORD your God, that his fierce anger may turn away from you. [9] For if you

return to the LORD, your brethren and your children will find compassion with their captors, and return to this land. For the LORD your God is gracious and merciful, and will not turn away his face from you, if you return to him."

10 So the couriers went from city to city through the country of E'phraim and Manas'seh, and as far as Zeb'ulun; but they laughed them to scorn, and mocked them. [11] Only a few men of Asher, of Manas'seh, and of Zeb'ulun humbled themselves and came to Jerusalem. [12] The hand of God was also upon Judah to give them one heart to do what the king and the princes commanded by the word of the LORD.

13 And many people came together in Jerusalem to keep the feast of unleavened bread in the second month, a very great assembly. [14] They set to work and removed the altars that were in Jerusalem, and all the altars for burning incense they took away and threw into the Kidron valley. [15] And they killed the passover lamb on the fourteenth day of the second month. And the priests and the Levites were put to shame, so that they sanctified themselves, and brought burnt offerings into the house of the LORD. [16] They took their accustomed posts according to the law of Moses the man of God; the priests sprinkled the blood which they received from the hand of the Levites. [17] For there were many in the assembly who had not sanctified themselves; therefore the Levites had to kill the passover lamb for every one who was not clean, to make it holy to the LORD. [18] For a multitude of the people, many of them from E'phraim, Manas'seh, Is'sachar, and Zeb'ulun, had not cleansed themselves, yet they ate the passover otherwise than as prescribed. For Hezeki'ah had prayed for them, saying, "The

---

30.1–27: Hezekiah's great passover festival. There is no hint of this in 2 Kings. It seems to be a kind of parallel to or preparation for Josiah's great passover in ch. 35. Included is the prophetic hope of the return of the northern tribes to their former loyalty to Jerusalem (compare Ezek.37.15–23). The tolerant laxity of vv. 17–19 is in contrast to the usual attitude of this writer.

good LORD pardon every one [19] who sets his heart to seek God, the LORD the God of his fathers, even though not according to the sanctuary's rules of cleanness." [20] And the LORD heard Hezeki'ah, and healed the people. [21] And the people of Israel that were present at Jerusalem kept the feast of unleavened bread seven days with great gladness; and the Levites and the priests praised the LORD day by day, singing with all their might[s] to the LORD. [22] And Hezeki'ah spoke encouragingly to all the Levites who showed good skill in the service of the LORD. So the people ate the food of the festival for seven days, sacrificing peace offerings and giving thanks to the LORD the God of their fathers.

23 Then the whole assembly agreed together to keep the feast for another seven days; so they kept it for another seven days with gladness. [24] For Hezeki'ah king of Judah gave the assembly a thousand bulls and seven thousand sheep for offerings, and the princes gave the assembly a thousand bulls and ten thousand sheep. And the priests sanctified themselves in great numbers. [25] The whole assembly of Judah, and the priests and the Levites, and the whole assembly that came out of Israel, and the sojourners who came out of the land of Israel, and the sojourners who dwelt in Judah, rejoiced. [26] So there was great joy in Jerusalem, for since the time of Solomon the son of David king of Israel there had been nothing like this in Jerusalem. [27] Then the priests and the Levites arose and blessed the people, and their voice was heard, and their prayer came to his holy habitation in heaven.

31 Now when all this was finished, all Israel who were present went out to the cities of Judah and broke in

pieces the pillars and hewed down the Ashe'rim and broke down the high places and the altars throughout all Judah and Benjamin, and in E'phraim and Manas'seh, until they had destroyed them all. Then all the people of Israel returned to their cities, every man to his possession.

2 And Hezeki'ah appointed the divisions of the priests and of the Levites, division by division, each according to his service, the priests and the Levites, for burnt offerings and peace offerings, to minister in the gates of the camp of the LORD and to give thanks and praise. [3] The contribution of the king from his own possessions was for the burnt offerings: the burnt offerings of morning and evening, and the burnt offerings for the sabbaths, the new moons, and the appointed feasts, as it is written in the law of the LORD. [4] And he commanded the people who lived in Jerusalem to give the portion due to the priests and the Levites, that they might give themselves to the law of the LORD. [5] As soon as the command was spread abroad, the people of Israel gave in abundance the first fruits of grain, wine, oil, honey, and of all the produce of the field; and they brought in abundantly the tithe of everything. [6] And the people of Israel and Judah who lived in the cities of Judah also brought in the tithe of cattle and sheep, and the dedicated things[t] which had been consecrated to the LORD their God, and laid them in heaps. [7] In the third month they began to pile up the heaps, and finished them in the seventh month. [8] When Hezeki'ah and the princes came and saw the heaps, they blessed the LORD and his people Israel. [9] And Hezeki'ah questioned the priests and the Levites

s Compare 1 Chr 13.8: Heb *with instruments of might*
t Heb *the tithe of the dedicated things*

31.1–21: Hezekiah's reform and his re-establishment of the priests and Levites. 1: Similar to 2 Kg.18.4 (see note there), except that here the reforming activity is extended to the territory of the former northern kingdom. Some regard this latter as historically correct, pointing out that the northern kingdom had fallen, and claiming that the Assyrians did not exercise strict control. There is also the possibility that we have here the hope of reunion referred to in ch. 30 (see notes there). **2–10:** As David established *the divisions of the priests and of the Levites*, so Heze-

about the heaps. ¹⁰ Azari'ah the chief priest, who was of the house of Zadok, answered him, "Since they began to bring the contributions into the house of the LORD we have eaten and had enough and have plenty left; for the LORD has blessed his people, so that we have this great store left."

11 Then Hezeki'ah commanded them to prepare chambers in the house of the LORD; and they prepared them. ¹² And they faithfully brought in the contributions, the tithes and the dedicated things. The chief officer in charge of them was Conani'ah the Levite, with Shim'e-i his brother as second; ¹³ while Jehi'el, Azazi'ah, Nahath, As'ahel, Jer'imoth, Jo'zabad, Eli'el, Ismachi'ah, Mahath, and Benai'ah were overseers assisting Conani'ah and Shim'e-i his brother, by the appointment of Hezeki'ah the king and Azari'ah the chief officer of the house of God. ¹⁴ And Ko're the son of Imnah the Levite, keeper of the east gate, was over the freewill offerings to God, to apportion the contribution reserved for the LORD and the most holy offerings. ¹⁵ Eden, Mini'-amin, Jeshua, Shemai'ah, Amari'ah, and Shecani'ah were faithfully assisting him in the cities of the priests, to distribute the portions to their brethren, old and young alike, by divisions, ¹⁶ except those enrolled by genealogy, males from three years old and upwards, all who entered the house of the LORD as the duty of each day required, for their service according to their offices, by their divisions. ¹⁷ The enrollment of the priests was according to their fathers' houses; that of the Levites from twenty years old and upwards was according to their offices, by their divisions. ¹⁸ The priests were enrolled with all their little children, their wives, their sons, and their daughters, the whole multitude; for they were faithful in keeping themselves holy. ¹⁹ And for the sons of Aaron, the priests, who were in the fields of common land belonging to their cities, there were men in the several cities who were designated by name to distribute portions to every male among the priests and to every one among the Levites who was enrolled.

20 Thus Hezeki'ah did throughout all Judah; and he did what was good and right and faithful before the LORD his God. ²¹ And every work that he undertook in the service of the house of God and in accordance with the law and the commandments, seeking his God, he did with all his heart, and prospered.

32 After these things and these acts of faithfulness Sennach'-erib king of Assyria came and invaded Judah and encamped against the fortified cities, thinking to win them for himself. ² And when Hezeki'ah saw that Sennach'erib had come and intended to fight against Jerusalem, ³ he planned with his officers and his mighty men to stop the water of the springs that were outside the city; and they helped him. ⁴ A great many people were gathered, and they stopped all the springs and the brook that flowed through the land, saying, "Why should the kings of Assyria come and find much water?" ⁵ He set to work resolutely and built up all the wall that was broken down, and raised towers upon it,ᵘ and outside it he built another wall; and he strengthened the Millo in the city of David. He also made weapons and shields in abundance. ⁶ And he set combat commanders over the people, and gathered them together to him in the square at the gate of the city and spoke encouragingly to them, saying, ⁷ "Be strong and of good courage. Do not be afraid or dismayed before the king of Assyria and all the horde that is with

ᵘ Vg: Heb *and raised upon the towers*

---

kiah re-established them, and saw that they were provided for. **11–21**: Compare 1 Chr.23.7–23.
32.1–33: The invasion of Sennacherib and the end of Hezekiah's reign. Based upon 2 Kg. 18.13–20.21, with much omission and some addition. **1**: From 2 Kg.18.13, with the change of "and took them" to *thinking to win them for himself*. **2–8**: These preparations for the siege were

him; for there is one greater with us than with him. [8] With him is an arm of flesh; but with us is the LORD our God, to help us and to fight our battles." And the people took confidence from the words of Hezeki'ah king of Judah.

9 After this Sennach'erib king of Assyria, who was besieging Lachish with all his forces, sent his servants to Jerusalem to Hezeki'ah king of Judah and to all the people of Judah that were in Jerusalem, saying, [10] "Thus says Sennach'erib king of Assyria, 'On what are you relying, that you stand siege in Jerusalem? [11] Is not Hezeki'ah misleading you, that he may give you over to die by famine and by thirst, when he tells you, "The LORD our God will deliver us from the hand of the king of Assyria"? [12] Has not this same Hezeki'ah taken away his high places and his altars and commanded Judah and Jerusalem, "Before one altar you shall worship, and upon it you shall burn your sacrifices"? [13] Do you not know what I and my fathers have done to all the peoples of other lands? Were the gods of the nations of those lands at all able to deliver their lands out of my hand? [14] Who among all the gods of those nations which my fathers utterly destroyed was able to deliver his people from my hand, that your God should be able to deliver you from my hand? [15] Now therefore do not let Hezeki'ah deceive you or mislead you in this fashion, and do not believe him, for no god of any nation or kingdom has been able to deliver his people from my hand or from the hand of my fathers. How much less will your God deliver you out of my hand!' "

16 And his servants said still more against the Lord GOD and against his servant Hezeki'ah. [17] And he wrote letters to cast contempt on the LORD the God of Israel and to speak against him, saying, "Like the gods of the nations of the lands who have not delivered their people from my hands, so the God of Hezeki'ah will not deliver his people from my hand." [18] And they shouted it with a loud voice in the language of Judah to the people of Jerusalem who were upon the wall, to frighten and terrify them, in order that they might take the city. [19] And they spoke of the God of Jerusalem as they spoke of the gods of the peoples of the earth, which are the work of men's hands.

20 Then Hezeki'ah the king and Isaiah the prophet, the son of Amoz, prayed because of this and cried to heaven. [21] And the LORD sent an angel, who cut off all the mighty warriors and commanders and officers in the camp of the king of Assyria. So he returned with shame of face to his own land. And when he came into the house of his god, some of his own sons struck him down there with the sword. [22] So the LORD saved Hezeki'ah and the inhabitants of Jerusalem from the hand of Sennach'erib king of Assyria and from the hand of all his enemies; and he gave them rest on every side. [23] And many brought gifts to the LORD to Jerusalem and precious things to Hezeki'ah king of Judah, so that he was exalted in the sight of all nations from that time onward.

24 In those days Hezeki'ah became sick and was at the point of death, and he prayed to the LORD; and he answered him and gave him a sign. [25] But Hezeki'ah did not make return according to the benefit done to him, for his heart was proud. Therefore wrath came upon him and Judah and Jerusalem. [26] But Hezeki'ah humbled himself for the pride of his heart, both he and the inhabitants of Jerusalem, so that the wrath of the LORD did not come upon them in the days of Hezeki'ah.

27 And Hezeki'ah had very great

added by the Chronicler from a source now lost. **9–19:** A greatly condensed version of 2 Kg. 18.17–35. **20:** This single sentence is a condensation of the long passage, 2 Kg.19.1–34. **21:** The Chronicler's version of 2 Kg.19.35–37. **22–23:** The Chronicler's comments on the preceding part of the chapter. **24–26:** A condensation of 2 Kg.20.1–19 (Is. chs. 38–39), showing that

riches and honor; and he made for himself treasuries for silver, for gold, for precious stones, for spices, for shields, and for all kinds of costly vessels; 28 storehouses also for the yield of grain, wine, and oil; and stalls for all kinds of cattle, and sheepfolds. 29 He likewise provided cities for himself, and flocks and herds in abundance; for God had given him very great possessions. 30 This same Hezeki'ah closed the upper outlet of the waters of Gihon and directed them down to the west side of the city of David. And Hezeki'ah prospered in all his works. 31 And so in the matter of the envoys of the princes of Babylon, who had been sent to him to inquire about the sign that had been done in the land, God left him to himself, in order to try him and to know all that was in his heart.

32 Now the rest of the acts of Hezeki'ah, and his good deeds, behold, they are written in the vision of Isaiah the prophet the son of Amoz, in the Book of the Kings of Judah and Israel. 33 And Hezeki'ah slept with his fathers, and they buried him in the ascent of the tombs of the sons of David; and all Judah and the inhabitants of Jerusalem did him honor at his death. And Manas'seh his son reigned in his stead.

33 Manas'seh was twelve years old when he began to reign, and he reigned fifty-five years in Jerusalem. 2 He did what was evil in the sight of the LORD, according to the abominable practices of the nations whom the LORD drove out before the

people of Israel. 3 For he rebuilt the high places which his father Hezeki'ah had broken down, and erected altars to the Ba'als, and made Ashe'rahs, and worshiped all the host of heaven, and served them. 4 And he built altars in the house of the LORD, of which the LORD had said, "In Jerusalem shall my name be for ever." 5 And he built altars for all the host of heaven in the two courts of the house of the LORD. 6 And he burned his sons as an offering in the valley of the son of Hinnom, and practiced soothsaying and augury and sorcery, and dealt with mediums and with wizards. He did much evil in the sight of the LORD, provoking him to anger. 7 And the image of the idol which he had made he set in the house of God, of which God said to David and to Solomon his son, "In this house, and in Jerusalem, which I have chosen out of all the tribes of Israel, I will put my name for ever; 8 and I will no more remove the foot of Israel from the land which I appointed for your fathers, if only they will be careful to do all that I have commanded them, all the law, the statutes, and the ordinances given through Moses." 9 Manas'seh seduced Judah and the inhabitants of Jerusalem, so that they did more evil than the nations whom the LORD destroyed before the people of Israel.

10 The LORD spoke to Manas'seh and to his people, but they gave no heed. 11 Therefore the LORD brought upon them the commanders of the army of the king of Assyria, who took Manas'seh with hooks and bound him

---

Hezekiah was very good, but not quite perfect. **27–29:** Compare 2 Kg.20.13. **30:** Compare vv. 3–4 and see 2 Kg.20.20–21 n. **31:** Further comment on 2 Kg.20.12–19. **32–33:** Slightly expanded from 2 Kg.20.20–21. The reference to *the vision of Isaiah the prophet* is not necessarily to the canonical book of this prophet, which does, however, contain material on Hezekiah (Is. chs. 36–39; compare Is.1.1).

33.1–25: The bad beginning of Manasseh; his punishment and repentance; the evil reign of Amon. This chapter is unusual in that it presents a king of Judah, Manasseh, as less evil than he appears in 2 Kings. Perhaps the Chronicler could not believe that Manasseh was wholly bad, since he reigned longer than any other king of Israel or Judah. **1–9:** These verses follow closely their source, 2 Kg.21.1–9. **10–13:** There is no hint of Manasseh's captivity and release in 2 Kings, though his name appears in Assyrian inscriptions as a vassal of Esarhaddon and Ashurbanipal, sometimes under suspicion. Thus the Babylonian captivity of Manasseh is historically

with fetters of bronze and brought him to Babylon. [12] And when he was in distress he entreated the favor of the LORD his God and humbled himself greatly before the God of his fathers. [13] He prayed to him, and God received his entreaty and heard his supplication and brought him again to Jerusalem into his kingdom. Then Manas'seh knew that the LORD was God.

14 Afterwards he built an outer wall for the city of David west of Gihon, in the valley, and for the entrance into the Fish Gate, and carried it round Ophel, and raised it to a very great height; he also put commanders of the army in all the fortified cities in Judah. [15] And he took away the foreign gods and the idol from the house of the LORD, and all the altars that he had built on the mountain of the house of the LORD and in Jerusalem, and he threw them outside of the city. [16] He also restored the altar of the LORD and offered upon it sacrifices of peace offerings and of thanksgiving; and he commanded Judah to serve the LORD the God of Israel. [17] Nevertheless the people still sacrificed at the high places, but only to the LORD their God.

18 Now the rest of the acts of Manas'seh, and his prayer to his God, and the words of the seers who spoke to him in the name of the LORD the God of Israel, behold, they are in the Chronicles of the Kings of Israel. [19] And his prayer, and how God received his entreaty, and all his sin and his faithlessness, and the sites on which he built high places and set up the Ashe'rim and the images, before

he humbled himself, behold, they are written in the Chronicles of the Seers.[v] [20] So Manas'seh slept with his fathers, and they buried him in his house; and Amon his son reigned in his stead.

21 Amon was twenty-two years old when he began to reign, and he reigned two years in Jerusalem. [22] He did what was evil in the sight of the LORD, as Manas'seh his father had done. Amon sacrificed to all the images that Manas'seh his father had made, and served them. [23] And he did not humble himself before the LORD, as Manas'seh his father had humbled himself, but this Amon incurred guilt more and more. [24] And his servants conspired against him and killed him in his house. [25] But the people of the land slew all those who had conspired against King Amon; and the people of the land made Josi'ah his son king in his stead.

34 Josi'ah was eight years old when he began to reign, and he reigned thirty-one years in Jerusalem. [2] He did what was right in the eyes of the LORD, and walked in the ways of David his father; and he did not turn aside to the right or to the left. [3] For in the eighth year of his reign, while he was yet a boy, he began to seek the God of David his father; and in the twelfth year he began to purge Judah and Jerusalem of the high places, the Ashe'rim, and the graven and the molten images. [4] And they broke down the altars of the Ba'als in his presence; and he hewed down the incense altars which stood above them; and he broke in pieces the Ashe'rim and the graven

v One Ms: Gk: Heb of Hozai

possible, though the Chronicler uses it here as divine punishment to bring the sinning king to repentance. This repentance is somewhat doubtful in view of 2 Kg.21.10–17. **14–17:** None of these verses, except the last, has any parallel. Verse 17 shows that the reform fell short of perfection; compare 2 Kg.21.16, which is much stronger in condemnation. **18–20:** These verses are a new version of 2 Kg.21.17–18 in the light of the Chronicler's own interpretation of the reign of Manasseh. **21–25:** From 2 Kg.21.19–24, and in agreement with the source in the low evaluation of Amon; v. 23 has been rewritten to conform to the new evaluation of Manasseh.

34.1–33: The good reign of Josiah; his reforms and the finding of the book of the law. The Chronicler pictures Josiah as the great reformer, the best king since David and Solomon, and the last good king. 2 Kg.22.1–23.30 is in basic agreement on the character and importance of Josiah. **3–7:** These verses transfer the great reform from a time after the finding of the book of

and the molten images, and he made dust of them and strewed it over the graves of those who had sacrificed to them. [5] He also burned the bones of the priests on their altars, and purged Judah and Jerusalem. [6] And in the cities of Manas'seh, E'phraim, and Simeon, and as far as Naph'tali, in their ruins[w] round about, [7] he broke down the altars, and beat the Ashe'rim and the images into powder, and hewed down all the incense altars throughout all the land of Israel. Then he returned to Jerusalem.

8 Now in the eighteenth year of his reign, when he had purged the land and the house, he sent Shaphan the son of Azali'ah, and Ma-asei'ah the governor of the city, and Jo'ah the son of Jo'ahaz, the recorder, to repair the house of the LORD his God. [9] They came to Hilki'ah the high priest and delivered the money that had been brought into the house of God, which the Levites, the keepers of the threshold, had collected from Manas'seh and E'phraim and from all the remnant of Israel and from all Judah and Benjamin and from the inhabitants of Jerusalem. [10] They delivered it to the workmen who had the oversight of the house of the LORD; and the workmen who were working in the house of the LORD gave it for repairing and restoring the house. [11] They gave it to the carpenters and the builders to buy quarried stone, and timber for binders and beams for the buildings which the kings of Judah had let go to ruin. [12] And the men did the work faithfully. Over them were set Jahath and Obadi'ah the Levites, of the sons of Merar'i, and Zechari'ah and Meshul'lam, of the sons of the Ko'hathites, to have oversight. The Levites, all who were skilful with instruments of music, [13] were over the burden bearers and directed all who did work in every kind of service; and some of the Levites were scribes, and officials, and gatekeepers.

14 While they were bringing out the money that had been brought into the house of the LORD, Hilki'ah the priest found the book of the law of the LORD given through Moses. [15] Then Hilki'ah said to Shaphan the secretary, "I have found the book of the law in the house of the LORD"; and Hilki'ah gave the book to Shaphan. [16] Shaphan brought the book to the king, and further reported to the king, "All that was committed to your servants they are doing. [17] They have emptied out the money that was found in the house of the LORD and have delivered it into the hand of the overseers and the workmen." [18] Then Shaphan the secretary told the king, "Hilki'ah the priest has given me a book." And Shaphan read it before the king.

19 When the king heard the words of the law he rent his clothes. [20] And the king commanded Hilki'ah, Ahi'-kam the son of Shaphan, Abdon the son of Micah, Shaphan the secretary, and Asai'ah the king's servant, saying, [21] "Go, inquire of the LORD for me and for those who are left in Israel and in Judah, concerning the words of the book that has been found; for great is the wrath of the LORD that is poured out on us, because our fathers have not kept the word of the LORD, to do according to all that is written in this book."

22 So Hilki'ah and those whom the king had sent[x] went to Huldah the prophetess, the wife of Shallum the son of Tokhath, son of Hasrah, keeper of the wardrobe (now she dwelt in Jerusalem in the Second Quarter) and spoke to her to that effect. [23] And she said to them, "Thus says the LORD, the God of Israel: 'Tell the man who sent

w Heb uncertain   x Syr Vg: Heb lacks *had sent*

the law to a time near the beginning of Josiah's reign (compare 2 Kg.23.4–20). *The Asherim*, see 1 Kg.14.15 n. **8–13:** The repair of the temple. This paragraph follows 2 Kg.22.3–7, but with more attention to the Levites, the musicians, and the help from the territory of the former northern kingdom. **14–18:** The finding of the book of the law. This account is not essentially different from its source, 2 Kg.22.8–10 (see note there). **19–28:** Very similar to its source, 2 Kg.

you to me, ²⁴ Thus says the LORD, Behold, I will bring evil upon this place and upon its inhabitants, all the curses that are written in the book which was read before the king of Judah. ²⁵ Because they have forsaken me and have burned incense to other gods, that they might provoke me to anger with all the works of their hands, therefore my wrath will be poured out upon this place and will not be quenched. ²⁶ But to the king of Judah, who sent you to inquire of the LORD, thus shall you say to him, Thus says the LORD, the God of Israel: Regarding the words which you have heard, ²⁷ because your heart was penitent and you humbled yourself before God when you heard his words against this place and its inhabitants, and you have humbled yourself before me, and have rent your clothes and wept before me, I also have heard you, says the LORD. ²⁸ Behold, I will gather you to your fathers, and you shall be gathered to your grave in peace, and your eyes shall not see all the evil which I will bring upon this place and its inhabitants.' " And they brought back word to the king.

29 Then the king sent and gathered together all the elders of Judah and Jerusalem. ³⁰ And the king went up to the house of the LORD, with all the men of Judah and the inhabitants of Jerusalem and the priests and the Levites, all the people both great and small; and he read in their hearing all the words of the book of the covenant which had been found in the house of the LORD. ³¹ And the king stood in his place and made a covenant before the LORD, to walk after the LORD and to keep his commandments and his testimonies and his statutes, with all his heart and all his soul, to perform the words of the covenant that were written in this book. ³² Then he made all who were present in Jerusalem and in Benjamin stand to it. And the inhabitants of Jerusalem did according to the covenant of God, the God of their fathers. ³³ And Josi′ah took away all the abominations from all the territory that belonged to the people of Israel, and made all who were in Israel serve the LORD their God. All his days they did not turn away from following the LORD the God of their fathers.

35 Josi′ah kept a passover to the LORD in Jerusalem; and they killed the passover lamb on the fourteenth day of the first month. ² He appointed the priests to their offices and encouraged them in the service of the house of the LORD. ³ And he said to the Levites who taught all Israel and who were holy to the LORD, "Put the holy ark in the house which Solomon the son of David, king of Israel, built; you need no longer carry it upon your shoulders. Now serve the LORD your God and his people Israel. ⁴ Prepare yourselves according to your fathers' houses by your divisions, following the directions of David king of Israel and the directions of Solomon his son. ⁵ And stand in the holy place according to the groupings of the fathers' houses of your brethren the lay people, and let there be for each a part of a father's house of the Levites.ʸ ⁶ And kill the passover lamb, and sanctify yourselves, and prepare for your brethren, to do according to the word of the LORD by Moses."

7 Then Josi′ah contributed to the lay people, as passover offerings for all that were present, lambs and kids from the flock to the number of thirty

ʸ Heb obscure

22.11–20 (see notes there). **29–33**: Expanded from 2 Kg.23.1–3. **30**: *The Levites* are substituted for "the prophets." **32**: *Benjamin* is added; the word *stand* means "adhere." **33**: A kind of summary of 2 Kg.23.4–20.

35.1–27: Josiah's great passover celebration; his tragic mistake and consequent death. **1–6**: 2 Kg.23.21–23 tells us that Josiah kept the greatest passover of any up to his time, but gives no details. The Chronicler seizes the opportunity to describe in detail what he regarded as the most important festival, as it was kept in his time, or as it ought to be kept in the future. Verse 4 refers to 1 Chr. chs. 24–26. **7–9**: Compare 1 Chr.29.6–9. **10–15**: A prominent place is given to

thousand, and three thousand bulls; these were from the king's possessions. [8] And his princes contributed willingly to the people, to the priests, and to the Levites. Hilki'ah, Zechari'ah, and Jehi'el, the chief officers of the house of God, gave to the priests for the passover offerings two thousand six hundred lambs and kids and three hundred bulls. [9] Conani'ah also, and Shemai'ah and Nethan'el his brothers, and Hashabi'ah and Je-i'el and Jo'zabad, the chiefs of the Levites, gave to the Levites for the passover offerings five thousand lambs and kids and five hundred bulls.

10 When the service had been prepared for, the priests stood in their place, and the Levites in their divisions according to the king's command. [11] And they killed the passover lamb, and the priests sprinkled the blood which they received from them while the Levites flayed the victims. [12] And they set aside the burnt offerings that they might distribute them according to the groupings of the fathers' houses of the lay people, to offer to the LORD, as it is written in the book of Moses. And so they did with the bulls. [13] And they roasted the passover lamb with fire according to the ordinance; and they boiled the holy offerings in pots, in caldrons, and in pans, and carried them quickly to all the lay people. [14] And afterward they prepared for themselves and for the priests, because the priests the sons of Aaron were busied in offering the burnt offerings and the fat parts until night; so the Levites prepared for themselves and for the priests the sons of Aaron. [15] The singers, the sons of Asaph, were in their place according to the command of David, and Asaph, and Heman, and Jedu'thun the king's seer; and the gatekeepers were at each gate; they did not need to depart from their service, for their brethren the Levites prepared for them.

16 So all the service of the LORD was prepared that day, to keep the passover and to offer burnt offerings on the altar of the LORD, according to the command of King Josi'ah. [17] And the people of Israel who were present kept the passover at that time, and the feast of unleavened bread seven days. [18] No passover like it had been kept in Israel since the days of Samuel the prophet; none of the kings of Israel had kept such a passover as was kept by Josi'ah, and the priests and the Levites, and all Judah and Israel who were present, and the inhabitants of Jerusalem. [19] In the eighteenth year of the reign of Josi'ah this passover was kept.

20 After all this, when Josi'ah had prepared the temple, Neco king of Egypt went up to fight at Car'chemish on the Euphra'tes and Josi'ah went out against him. [21] But he sent envoys to him, saying, "What have we to do with each other, king of Judah? I am not coming against you this day, but against the house with which I am at war; and God has commanded me to make haste. Cease opposing God, who is with me, lest he destroy you." [22] Nevertheless Josi'ah would not turn away from him, but disguised himself in order to fight with him. He did not listen to the words of Neco from the mouth of God, but joined battle in the plain of Megid'do. [23] And the archers shot King Josi'ah; and the king said to his servants, "Take me away, for I am badly wounded." [24] So his servants took him out of the chariot and carried him in his second chariot and brought him to Jerusalem. And he died, and was buried in the tombs of his fathers. All Judah and Jerusalem mourned for

---

the Levites and *the singers* (see Introduction to 1 Chronicles). **16–19:** Compare 2 Kg.23.22–23. **20–24:** A greatly expanded version of 2 Kg.23.29–30; some of the added details are doubtless historically correct. The most characteristic touch of the Chronicler is in describing *the words of Neco* as coming *from the mouth of God* (v. 22). Only thus could a man who believed every misfortune a direct punishment from God explain the untimely death of the otherwise righteous Josiah. **25:** Strangely enough *Jeremiah* the prophet is not mentioned in 2 Kings. The Chronicler

Josi'ah. [25] Jeremiah also uttered a lament for Josi'ah; and all the singing men and singing women have spoken of Josi'ah in their laments to this day. They made these an ordinance in Israel; behold, they are written in the Laments. [26] Now the rest of the acts of Josi'ah, and his good deeds according to what is written in the law of the LORD, [27] and his acts, first and last, behold, they are written in the Book of the Kings of Israel and Judah.

36 The people of the land took Jeho'ahaz the son of Josi'ah and made him king in his father's stead in Jerusalem. [2] Jeho'ahaz was twenty-three years old when he began to reign; and he reigned three months in Jerusalem. [3] Then the king of Egypt deposed him in Jerusalem and laid upon the land a tribute of a hundred talents of silver and a talent of gold. [4] And the king of Egypt made Eli'akim his brother king over Judah and Jerusalem, and changed his name to Jehoi'akim; but Neco took Jeho'ahaz his brother and carried him to Egypt.

5 Jehoi'akim was twenty-five years old when he began to reign, and he reigned eleven years in Jerusalem. He did what was evil in the sight of the LORD his God. [6] Against him came up Nebuchadnez'zar king of Babylon, and bound him in fetters to take him to Babylon. [7] Nebuchadnez'zar also carried part of the vessels of the house of the LORD to Babylon and put them in his palace in Babylon. [8] Now the

rest of the acts of Jehoi'akim, and the abominations which he did, and what was found against him, behold, they are written in the Book of the Kings of Israel and Judah; and Jehoi'achin his son reigned in his stead.

9 Jehoi'achin was eight years old when he began to reign, and he reigned three months and ten days in Jerusalem. He did what was evil in the sight of the LORD. [10] In the spring of the year King Nebuchadnez'zar sent and brought him to Babylon, with the precious vessels of the house of the LORD, and made his brother Zedeki'ah king over Judah and Jerusalem.

11 Zedeki'ah was twenty-one years old when he began to reign, and he reigned eleven years in Jerusalem. [12] He did what was evil in the sight of the LORD his God. He did not humble himself before Jeremiah the prophet, who spoke from the mouth of the LORD. [13] He also rebelled against King Nebuchadnez'zar, who had made him swear by God; he stiffened his neck and hardened his heart against turning to the LORD, the God of Israel. [14] All the leading priests and the people likewise were exceedingly unfaithful, following all the abominations of the nations; and they polluted the house of the LORD which he had hallowed in Jerusalem.

15 The LORD, the God of their fathers, sent persistently to them by his messengers, because he had compassion on his people and on his dwell-

---

here makes good the omission (compare Jer.1.2; 3.6; 22.10,15). *The Laments* mentioned here are not to be confused with the canonical book of Lamentations. **26–27**: A characteristic expansion of 2 Kg.23.28.

36.1–23: The last agonies of the doomed nation. The goodness of David, Solomon, Asa, Hezekiah, and Josiah was not sufficient, and the apostate nation was doomed (compare 34.24–28). The source is 2 Kg.23.30b–25.21, with some condensation and much rewriting near the end. **1–4**: The ill-fated reign of Jehoahaz, taken with slight condensation from 2 Kg.23.30b–34. **5–8**: Much abridged from 2 Kg.23.36–24.6. In v. 6 Jehoiakim seems to be taken *to Babylon*, contrary to the source, 2 Kg.24.6 (compare Dan.1.1–2). Verse 7 is added, anticipating v. 10 (compare Dan.1.2). **9–10**: The story of *Jehoiachin* is drastically abridged from 2 Kg.24.8–17. The correct age in v. 9 is not *eight years*, but eighteen years (compare 2 Kg.24.8). Tablets from Babylonia disclose that by 592 B.C. he had five sons. **11–13**: Based on 2 Kg.24.18–20, but with certain changes, such as the dropping of the names of the king's mother and grandfather, the introduction of *Jeremiah the prophet* (see 35.25 n. and compare Jer. chs. 37–39), and the mention of the king's oath (compare Ezek.17.16). **14**: There is no parallel to this in 2 Kings, where the blame is laid chiefly on the king (compare Jer. ch. 7; Ezek. ch. 8). The Chronicler does not

ing place; [16] but they kept mocking the messengers of God, despising his words, and scoffing at his prophets, till the wrath of the LORD rose against his people, till there was no remedy.

17 Therefore he brought up against them the king of the Chalde'ans, who slew their young men with the sword in the house of their sanctuary, and had no compassion on young man or virgin, old man or aged; he gave them all into his hand. [18] And all the vessels of the house of God, great and small, and the treasures of the house of the LORD, and the treasures of the king and of his princes, all these he brought to Babylon. [19] And they burned the house of God, and broke down the wall of Jerusalem, and burned all its palaces with fire, and destroyed all its precious vessels. [20] He took into exile in Babylon those who had escaped from the sword, and they became servants to him and to his sons until the establishment of the kingdom of Persia, [21] to fulfil the word of the LORD by the mouth of Jeremiah, until the land had enjoyed its sabbaths. All the days that it lay desolate it kept sabbath, to fulfil seventy years.

22 Now in the first year of Cyrus king of Persia, that the word of the LORD by the mouth of Jeremiah might be accomplished, the LORD stirred up the spirit of Cyrus king of Persia so that he made a proclamation throughout all his kingdom and also put it in writing: [23] "Thus says Cyrus king of Persia, 'The LORD, the God of heaven, has given me all the kingdoms of the earth, and he has charged me to build him a house at Jerusalem, which is in Judah. Whoever is among you of all his people, may the LORD his God be with him. Let him go up.'"

---

include the Levites and musicians in his condemnation. **15–16:** The Chronicler is fond of the theme of the unheeded prophet (compare 12.5–8; 15.1–8; 19.1–3; 21.12–15; 25.7–9,15–17; Jer.26.20–24; 29.16–20; 35.14–15). **17–21:** A condensation of 2 Kg.25.1–21, with additional references to *the establishment of the kingdom of Persia* (compare v. 22), the prophecies of *Jeremiah* (compare Jer.25.11–12; 29.10), and the *sabbaths* (sabbatical years; compare Lev. 25.1–7; 26.27–39). **22–23:** This note of hope is reproduced here from what immediately follows, Ezra 1.1–3, where it more properly belongs. In the work of this author, 1 and 2 Chronicles portray the downfall, Ezra and Nehemiah the restoration of God's people. In the present arrangement of the Hebrew Old Testament, 2 Chronicles is the last book; apparently an editor added these verses so that the Old Testament would not end on a note of doom (compare 2 Kg.25.27–30 and see note there).

THE BOOK OF EZRA

Anciently several books circulated under the name of Ezra, not only our Ezra and Nehemiah as a single book, but others now preserved in the Apocrypha and Pseudepigrapha. Our Ezra-Nehemiah is by the Chronicler (see Introduction to 1 Chronicles), prepared as a supplement to Chronicles on the basis of Hebrew and Aramaic documents, memoirs of Nehemiah, a memorial of Ezra, genealogies, and archives. Chronicles ends with the destruction of Jerusalem and the carrying away of treasure and captives. This supplement, the first verses of which appear also at the end of Chronicles, was written to tell how some returned from captivity and labored at restoring religion at a restored temple in a refortified Jerusalem (see "Survey of . . . Bible Lands," § 13). Among the exiles, religion, their strong bond of unity, had developed; whereas among those who remained and had mingled largely with the local and incoming peoples, religion had declined. During the exile religious interest had concentrated particularly on the laws associated with the name of Moses, and had fostered that exclusiveness which became so characteristic of Judaism. Thus the returned exiles were concerned not only with reconstruction of altar, temple, and city, but with social and religious problems, freeing the community of foreign elements, and establishing religious practice in stricter conformity to their understanding of Mosaic law. To the Chronicler the returned exiles were a godly remnant with a religious mission.

There seem to have been four stages of the return: (1) a return under Cyrus (about 538 B.C.) led by Sheshbazzar, who commenced rebuilding the temple but, under local opposition, had to leave it unfinished; (2) a return under Darius I (521–485) led by Zerubbabel and Jeshua, who also encountered opposition but, with encouragement from the prophets Haggai and Zechariah, completed the temple; (3) a group led by Nehemiah who came twice under Artaxerxes I (464–423) to build the walls of Jerusalem, still against opposition from the local groups, and to attempt to establish purity of community and worship; (4) a return under Artaxerxes II (404–358) led by Ezra, who brought a codification of the Mosaic law, and found a community which had again backslidden. An alternate solution of difficult textual problems places Ezra's return under Artaxerxes I, before Nehemiah. See 7.7 n. Neh.2.1–20 n.

The text of the Chronicler's supplement has been dislocated in transmission, some of the Nehemiah material appearing in Ezra, and Ezra material in Nehemiah, so that it no longer reads chronologically. Often the order is better preserved in the apocryphal book I Esdras. The books of Ezra and Nehemiah are more intelligible if read in the order Ezra ch. 1; 2.1–70 (Neh.7.6–73a); 3.1–4.6; 4.24–6.22; 4.7–23; Neh.1.1–7.5; chs. 11–13; 9.38–10.39; Ezra chs. 7–10; Neh.8.1–9.37. An editor about 300 B.C., faced with this textual confusion, endeavored to ease it by supplying connecting sentences and by insertions, such as the name of Nehemiah in Neh.8.9 and Ezra in Neh.12.26,36.

I N THE FIRST YEAR OF CYRUS KING OF Persia, that the word of the LORD by the mouth of Jeremiah might be accomplished, the LORD stirred up the spirit of Cyrus king of Persia so that he made a proclamation throughout all his kingdom and also put it in writing:

2 "Thus says Cyrus king of Persia: The LORD, the God of heaven, has given me all the kingdoms of the earth, and he has charged me to build him a house at Jerusalem, which is in Judah. ³ Whoever is among you of all his people, may his God be with him, and let him go up to Jerusalem, which is in Judah, and rebuild the house of the LORD, the God of Israel–he is the God who is in Jerusalem; ⁴ and let each survivor, in whatever place he sojourns, be assisted by the men of his place with silver and gold, with goods

---

1.1–4: Cyrus' decree. His *first year* at Babylon was 538 B.C., and his proclamation seemed the fulfilment of Jer.29.10 (2 Chr.36.21) under divine direction (Is.44.28; 45.1–3). **2–3:** In his inscriptions Cyrus shows interest in restoring temples. To him the LORD is the local deity of Jerusalem (6.12), whose temple was destroyed in 586 B.C. by Nebuchadnezzar (5.12).

and with beasts, besides freewill offerings for the house of God which is in Jerusalem."

5 Then rose up the heads of the fathers' houses of Judah and Benjamin, and the priests and the Levites, every one whose spirit God had stirred to go up to rebuild the house of the LORD which is in Jerusalem; 6 and all who were about them aided them with vessels of silver, with gold, with goods, with beasts, and with costly wares, besides all that was freely offered. 7 Cyrus the king also brought out the vessels of the house of the LORD which Nebuchadnez'zar had carried away from Jerusalem and placed in the house of his gods. 8 Cyrus king of Persia brought these out in charge of Mith'redath the treasurer, who counted them out to Shesh-baz'zar the prince of Judah. 9 And this was the number of them: a thousand*a* basins of gold, a thousand basins of silver, twenty-nine censers, 10 thirty bowls of gold, two thousand*b* four hundred and ten bowls of silver, and a thousand other vessels; 11 all the vessels of gold and of silver were five thousand four hundred and sixty-nine.*c* All these did Shesh-baz'zar bring up, when the exiles were brought up from Babylonia to Jerusalem.

2 Now these were the people of the province who came up out of the captivity of those exiles whom Nebuchadnez'zar the king of Babylon had carried captive to Babylonia; they returned to Jerusalem and Judah, each to his own town. 2 They came with Zerub'babel, Jeshua, Nehemi'ah, Serai'ah, Re-el-ai'ah, Mor'decai, Bilshan, Mispar, Bigva'i, Rehum, and Ba'anah.

The number of the men of the people of Israel: 3 the sons of Parosh, two thousand one hundred and seventy-two. 4 The sons of Shephati'ah,

three hundred and seventy-two. 5 The sons of Arah, seven hundred and seventy-five. 6 The sons of Pa'hath-moab, namely the sons of Jeshua and Jo'ab, two thousand eight hundred and twelve. 7 The sons of Elam, one thousand two hundred and fifty-four. 8 The sons of Zattu, nine hundred and forty-five. 9 The sons of Zac'cai, seven hundred and sixty. 10 The sons of Bani, six hundred and forty-two. 11 The sons of Be'bai, six hundred and twenty-three. 12 The sons of Azgad, one thousand two hundred and twenty-two. 13 The sons of Adoni'kam, six hundred and sixty-six. 14 The sons of Bigva'i, two thousand and fifty-six. 15 The sons of Adin, four hundred and fifty-four. 16 The sons of Ater, namely of Hezeki'ah, ninety-eight. 17 The sons of Be'zai, three hundred and twenty-three. 18 The sons of Jorah, one hundred and twelve. 19 The sons of Hashum, two hundred and twenty-three. 20 The sons of Gibbar, ninety-five. 21 The sons of Bethlehem, one hundred and twenty-three. 22 The men of Neto'phah, fifty-six. 23 The men of An'athoth, one hundred and twenty-eight. 24 The sons of Az'maveth, forty-two. 25 The sons of Kir'iathar'im, Chephi'rah, and Be-er'oth, seven hundred and forty-three. 26 The sons of Ramah and Geba, six hundred and twenty-one. 27 The men of Michmas, one hundred and twenty-two. 28 The men of Bethel and Ai, two hundred and twenty-three. 29 The sons of Nebo, fifty-two. 30 The sons of Magbish, one hundred and fifty-six. 31 The sons of the other Elam, one thousand two hundred and fifty-four. 32 The sons of Harim, three hundred and twenty. 33 The sons of Lod, Hadid, and Ono, seven hundred and twenty-five. 34 The sons of Jeri-

a 1 Esdras 2.13: Heb *thirty*
b 1 Esdras 2.13: Heb *of a second sort*
c 1 Esdras 2.14: Heb *five thousand four hundred*

1.5–11: Gifts for refurnishing the temple, including the return of the *vessels* taken by *Nebuchadnezzar* (2 Kg.25.14–16). **8:** *Mithredath* (Mithridates) was temple *treasurer. Sheshbazzar* is the Babylonian name of a Jewish court official. **9–11:** These numbers vary in different texts and are uncertain.

2.1–70: A census of the first return (= Neh.7.6–73a), covering five groups: leaders, laymen, temple officials, those of dubious genealogy, servants, and animals. *Sons of* and *men of* are

cho, three hundred and forty-five. [35] The sons of Sena'ah, three thousand six hundred and thirty.

36 The priests: the sons of Jedai'ah, of the house of Jeshua, nine hundred and seventy-three. [37] The sons of Immer, one thousand and fifty-two. [38] The sons of Pashhur, one thousand two hundred and forty-seven. [39] The sons of Harim, one thousand and seventeen.

40 The Levites: the sons of Jeshua and Kad'mi-el, of the sons of Hodavi'ah, seventy-four. [41] The singers: the sons of Asaph, one hundred and twenty-eight. [42] The sons of the gatekeepers: the sons of Shallum, the sons of Ater, the sons of Talmon, the sons of Akkub, the sons of Hati'ta, and the sons of Sho'bai, in all one hundred and thirty-nine.

43 The temple servants:[d] the sons of Ziha, the sons of Hasu'pha, the sons of Tabba'oth, [44] the sons of Keros, the sons of Si'aha, the sons of Padon, [45] the sons of Leba'nah, the sons of Hag'-abah, the sons of Akkub, [46] the sons of Hagab, the sons of Shamlai, the sons of Hanan, [47] the sons of Giddel, the sons of Gahar, the sons of Re-ai'ah, [48] the sons of Rezin, the sons of Neko'da, the sons of Gazzam, [49] the sons of Uzza, the sons of Pase'ah, the sons of Besai, [50] the sons of Asnah, the sons of Me-u'-nim, the sons of Nephi'sim, [51] the sons of Bakbuk, the sons of Haku'pha, the sons of Harhur, [52] the sons of Bazluth, the sons of Mehi'da, the sons of Harsha, [53] the sons of Barkos, the sons of Sis'era, the sons of Temah, [54] the sons of Nezi'ah, and the sons of Hati'pha.

55 The sons of Solomon's servants: the sons of So'tai, the sons of Hasso'-phereth, the sons of Peru'da, [56] the sons of Ja'alah, the sons of Darkon, the sons of Giddel, [57] the sons of Shephati'ah, the sons of Hattil, the sons of Po'chereth-hazzeba'im, and the sons of Ami.

58 All the temple servants[d] and the sons of Solomon's servants were three hundred and ninety-two.

59 The following were those who came up from Tel-me'lah, Tel-har'sha, Cherub, Addan, and Immer, though they could not prove their fathers' houses or their descent, whether they belonged to Israel: [60] the sons of Delai'ah, the sons of Tobi'ah, and the sons of Neko'da, six hundred and fifty-two. [61] Also, of the sons of the priests: the sons of Habai'ah, the sons of Hakkoz, and the sons of Barzil'lai (who had taken a wife from the daughters of Barzil'lai the Gileadite, and was called by their name). [62] These sought their registration among those enrolled in the genealogies, but they were not found there, and so they were excluded from the priesthood as unclean; [63] the governor told them that they were not to partake of the most holy food, until there should be a priest to consult Urim and Thummim.

64 The whole assembly together was forty-two thousand three hundred and sixty, [65] besides their menservants and maidservants, of whom there were seven thousand three hundred and thirty-seven; and they had two hundred male and female singers. [66] Their horses were seven hundred and thirty-six, their mules were two hundred and forty-five, [67] their camels were four hundred and thirty-five, and their asses were six thousand seven hundred and twenty.

68 Some of the heads of families, when they came to the house of the LORD which is in Jerusalem, made freewill offerings for the house of God, to erect it on its site; [69] according to their ability they gave to the treasury of the work sixty-one thousand darics of

d Heb *nethinim*

---

equivalent phrases. **36–39:** There are only four priestly groups as against twenty-four in 1 Chr. ch. 24. **43,58:** *The temple servants* are the Nethinim (lit., "those given" [to the temple]; see 1 Chr. 9.2; Jos.9.27 n.), many of whose names are non-Jewish. **63:** The *governor* is Sheshbazzar. *Urim and Thummim* are the sacred lots (1 Sam.14.41; Dt.33.8). **64:** This total exceeds the numbers of the various groups; it doubtless includes others unmentioned. **69:** A *daric* was a Persian gold

gold, five thousand minas of silver, and one hundred priests' garments.

70 The priests, the Levites, and some of the people lived in Jerusalem and its vicinity;*e* and the singers, the gatekeepers, and the temple servants lived in their towns, and all Israel in their towns.

3 When the seventh month came, and the sons of Israel were in the towns, the people gathered as one man to Jerusalem. ² Then arose Jeshua the son of Jo′zadak, with his fellow priests, and Zerub′babel the son of She-al′ti-el with his kinsmen, and they built the altar of the God of Israel, to offer burnt offerings upon it, as it is written in the law of Moses the man of God. ³ They set the altar in its place, for fear was upon them because of the peoples of the lands, and they offered burnt offerings upon it to the LORD, burnt offerings morning and evening. ⁴ And they kept the feast of booths, as it is written, and offered the daily burnt offerings by number according to the ordinance, as each day required, ⁵ and after that the continual burnt offerings, the offerings at the new moon and at all the appointed feasts of the LORD, and the offerings of every one who made a freewill offering to the LORD. ⁶ From the first day of the seventh month they began to offer burnt offerings to the LORD. But the foundation of the temple of the LORD was not yet laid. ⁷ So they gave money to the masons and the carpenters, and food, drink, and oil to the Sido′nians and the Tyrians to bring cedar trees from Lebanon to the sea,

to Joppa, according to the grant which they had from Cyrus king of Persia.

8 Now in the second year of their coming to the house of God at Jerusalem, in the second month, Zerub′babel the son of She-al′ti-el and Jeshua the son of Jo′zadak made a beginning, together with the rest of their brethren, the priests and the Levites and all who had come to Jerusalem from the captivity. They appointed the Levites, from twenty years old and upward, to have the oversight of the work of the house of the LORD. ⁹ And Jeshua with his sons and his kinsmen, and Kad′mi-el and his sons, the sons of Judah, together took the oversight of the workmen in the house of God, along with the sons of Hen′adad and the Levites, their sons and kinsmen.

10 And when the builders laid the foundation of the temple of the LORD, the priests in their vestments came forward with trumpets, and the Levites, the sons of Asaph, with cymbals, to praise the LORD, according to the directions of David king of Israel; ¹¹ and they sang responsively, praising and giving thanks to the LORD,

"For he is good,
    for his steadfast love endures for
    ever toward Israel."

And all the people shouted with a great shout, when they praised the LORD, because the foundation of the house of the LORD was laid. ¹² But many of the priests and Levites and heads of fathers' houses, old men who

e 1 Esdras 5.46: Heb lacks *lived in Jerusalem and its vicinity*

---

coin, a *mina* a Mesopotamian weight for precious metals. The amount differs from that mentioned in Neh.7.70–72.

3.1–13: Rebuilding the temple. This had commenced under Sheshbazzar (5.14–16) but stopped, and recommenced now under Zerubbabel and Jeshua, leaders of the second return, who *built the altar* as center for the temple cultus. The *seventh month* would be Tishri (September-October) of 520 B.C., in the second year of Darius I (Hag.2.1–4). **2:** *The law of Moses* is not our Pentateuch, but the body of laws associated with Moses' name. Once the altar was *set*, the religious life with *morning and evening* sacrifice, annual feasts such as *booths* (tabernacles), etc., could be recommenced, and then the temple built. **7:** Compare Solomon's preparations in 2 Chr.2.1–11. Minted *money* was known in the Persian period, though payment in kind was more common. **10–11:** The laying of the foundation was celebrated with music and praise. For the directions of David see 2 Chr.29.25–30.

had seen the first house, wept with a loud voice when they saw the foundation of this house being laid, though many shouted aloud for joy; [13] so that the people could not distinguish the sound of the joyful shout from the sound of the people's weeping, for the people shouted with a great shout, and the sound was heard afar.

4 Now when the adversaries of Judah and Benjamin heard that the returned exiles were building a temple to the Lord, the God of Israel, [2] they approached Zerub'babel and the heads of fathers' houses and said to them, "Let us build with you; for we worship your God as you do, and we have been sacrificing to him ever since the days of E'sar-had'don king of Assyria who brought us here." [3] But Zerub'babel, Jeshua, and the rest of the heads of fathers' houses in Israel said to them, "You have nothing to do with us in building a house to our God; but we alone will build to the Lord, the God of Israel, as King Cyrus the king of Persia has commanded us."

4 Then the people of the land discouraged the people of Judah, and made them afraid to build, [5] and hired counselors against them to frustrate their purpose, all the days of Cyrus king of Persia, even until the reign of Darius king of Persia.

6 And in the reign of Ahasu-e'rus, in the beginning of his reign, they wrote an accusation against the inhabitants of Judah and Jerusalem.

7 And in the days of Ar-ta-xerx'es, Bishlam and Mith'redath and Tab'eel and the rest of their associates wrote to Ar-ta-xerx'es king of Persia; the letter was written in Aramaic and translated.*f* [8] Rehum the commander and Shim'shai the scribe wrote a letter against Jerusalem to Ar-ta-xerx'es the king as follows— [9] then wrote Rehum the commander, Shim'shai the scribe, and the rest of their associates, the judges, the governors, the officials, the Persians, the men of Erech, the Babylonians, the men of Susa, that is, the Elamites, [10] and the rest of the nations whom the great and noble Osnap'par deported and settled in the cities of Sama'ria and in the rest of the province Beyond the River, and now [11] this is a copy of the letter that they sent—"To Ar-ta-xerx'es the king: Your servants, the men of the province Beyond the River, send greeting. And now [12] be it known to the king that the Jews who came up from you to us have gone to Jerusalem. They are rebuilding that rebellious and wicked city; they are finishing the walls and repairing the foundations. [13] Now be it known to the king that, if this city is rebuilt and the walls finished, they will not pay tribute, custom, or toll, and the royal revenue will be impaired. [14] Now because we eat the salt of the palace and it is not fitting for us to witness the king's dishonor, therefore we send and inform the king, [15] in order that search may be made in the book of the records of your fathers. You will find in the book of the records and learn that this city is a rebellious

f Heb adds *in Aramaic*, indicating that 4.8–6.18 is in Aramaic. Another interpretation is *The letter was written in the Aramaic script and set forth in the Aramaic language*

4.1–6: Opposition to the rebuilding of the temple. The rejoicing alerted neighboring mixed groups who claimed fellowship in religion (2 Kg.17.24–28). *Esarhaddon* settled groups there in 676 B.C. **3:** The phrase *we alone* evidences the exclusiveness which turned these neighbors into *adversaries*. **5:** The *counselors* would plead their case at court. *Cyrus* died in 529 B.C. *Darius* reigned 521–485. *Ahasuerus* Xerxes I, reigned 485–464.

4.7–23. Opposition to the rebuilding of the city. A misplaced section belonging probably between Ezra ch. 10 and Neh. ch. 1, but inserted here as dealing also with opposition to rebuilding. Artaxerxes reigned 464–423 B.C. The Aramaic letter to him is from his local officials, authorized by the *commander*, and written by the *scribe*. **10:** *Osnappar* apparently means Assurbanipal (668–630 B.C.). *Beyond the river* denotes the Syro-Palestinian region west of the Euphrates. **13:** The revenues expected by the Persian treasury were the provincial *tribute*, the *custom* levies for provincial expenses, and *toll* for upkeep of the roads. **15:** For such books of

city, hurtful to kings and provinces, and that sedition was stirred up in it from of old. That was why this city was laid waste. [16] We make known to the king that, if this city is rebuilt and its walls finished, you will then have no possession in the province Beyond the River."

17 The king sent an answer: "To Rehum the commander and Shim'-shai the scribe and the rest of their associates who live in Sama'ria and in the rest of the province Beyond the River, greeting. And now [18] the letter which you sent to us has been plainly read before me. [19] And I made a decree, and search has been made, and it has been found that this city from of old has risen against kings, and that rebellion and sedition have been made in it. [20] And mighty kings have been over Jerusalem, who ruled over the whole province Beyond the River, to whom tribute, custom, and toll were paid. [21] Therefore make a decree that these men be made to cease, and that this city be not rebuilt, until a decree is made by me. [22] And take care not to be slack in this matter; why should damage grow to the hurt of the king?"

23 Then, when the copy of King Ar-ta-xerx'es' letter was read before Rehum and Shim'shai the scribe and their associates, they went in haste to the Jews at Jerusalem and by force and power made them cease. [24] Then the work on the house of God which is in Jerusalem stopped; and it ceased until the second year of the reign of Darius king of Persia.

5 Now the prophets, Haggai and Zechari'ah the son of Iddo, prophesied to the Jews who were in Judah and Jerusalem, in the name of the God of Israel who was over them. [2] Then Zerub'babel the son of She-al'ti-el and Jeshua the son of Jo'zadak arose

and began to rebuild the house of God which is in Jerusalem; and with them were the prophets of God, helping them.

3 At the same time Tat'tenai the governor of the province Beyond the River and She'thar-boz'enai and their associates came to them and spoke to them thus, "Who gave you a decree to build this house and to finish this structure?" [4] They[g] also asked them this, "What are the names of the men who are building this building?" [5] But the eye of their God was upon the elders of the Jews, and they did not stop them till a report should reach Darius and then answer be returned by letter concerning it.

6 The copy of the letter which Tat'-tenai the governor of the province Beyond the River and She'thar-boz'-enai and his associates the governors who were in the province Beyond the River sent to Darius the king; [7] they sent him a report, in which was written as follows: "To Darius the king, all peace. [8] Be it known to the king that we went to the province of Judah, to the house of the great God. It is being built with huge stones, and timber is laid in the walls; this work goes on diligently and prospers in their hands. [9] Then we asked those elders and spoke to them thus, 'Who gave you a decree to build this house and to finish this structure?' [10] We also asked them their names, for your information, that we might write down the names of the men at their head. [11] And this was their reply to us: 'We are the servants of the God of heaven and earth, and we are rebuilding the house that was built many years ago, which a great king of Israel built and finished. [12] But because our fathers had angered the God of heaven, he gave them into the

g Gk Syr: Aramaic *We*

---

records see Est.2.23; 6.1; Mal.3.16. *Laid waste*, see 2 Kg.24.13–15. **23.** *Made them cease*. This situation introduces Neh. ch. 1

4.24–6.22. The rebuilding continued. Verse 24 follows naturally on v. 5, taking us back to the reign of Darius, in whose second year the prophets Haggai and Zechariah encouraged the building (Hag.1.1–4; 2.1–4; Zech.4.9; 6.15). **5.3:** *Tattenai* appears in cuneiform tablets as governor of the province *Beyond the River.* **11:** The *great king* was Solomon. **14:** *The temple*

hand of Nebuchadnez'zar king of Babylon, the Chalde'an, who destroyed this
house and carried away the people to
Babylonia. ¹³ However in the first
year of Cyrus king of Babylon, Cyrus
the king made a decree that this house
of God should be rebuilt. ¹⁴ And the
gold and silver vessels of the house of
God, which Nebuchadnez'zar had
taken out of the temple that was in
Jerusalem and brought into the temple
of Babylon, these Cyrus the king took
out of the temple of Babylon, and they
were delivered to one whose name was
Shesh-baz'zar, whom he had made
governor; ¹⁵ and he said to him, "Take
these vessels, go and put them in the
temple which is in Jerusalem, and
let the house of God be rebuilt on its
site." ¹⁶ Then this Shesh-baz'zar came
and laid the foundations of the house of
God which is in Jerusalem; and from
that time until now it has been in
building, and it is not yet finished.'
¹⁷ Therefore, if it seem good to the
king, let search be made in the royal
archives there in Babylon, to see
whether a decree was issued by Cyrus
the king for the rebuilding of this house
of God in Jerusalem. And let the king
send us his pleasure in this matter."

6 Then Darius the king made a
decree, and search was made in
Babylonia, in the house of the archives
where the documents were stored.
² And in Ecbat'ana, the capital which
is in the province of Media, a scroll
was found on which this was written:
"A record. ³ In the first year of Cyrus
the king, Cyrus the king issued a
decree: Concerning the house of God
at Jerusalem, let the house be rebuilt, the place where sacrifices are
offered and burnt offerings are brought;
its height shall be sixty cubits and its
breadth sixty cubits, ⁴ with three
courses of great stones and one course
of timber; let the cost be paid from

the royal treasury. ⁵ And also let the
gold and silver vessels of the house of
God, which Nebuchadnez'zar took out
of the temple that is in Jerusalem and
brought to Babylon, be restored and
brought back to the temple which is in
Jerusalem, each to its place; you shall
put them in the house of God.

6 "Now therefore, Tat'tenai, governor of the province Beyond the River,
She'thar-boz'enai, and your associates
the governors who are in the province
Beyond the River, keep away; ⁷ let the
work on this house of God alone; let
the governor of the Jews and the elders
of the Jews rebuild this house of God
on its site. ⁸ Moreover I make a decree
regarding what you shall do for these
elders of the Jews for the rebuilding of
this house of God; the cost is to be paid
to these men in full and without delay from the royal revenue, the tribute
of the province from Beyond the River.
⁹ And whatever is needed—young
bulls, rams, or sheep for burnt offerings to the God of heaven, wheat, salt,
wine, or oil, as the priests at Jerusalem
require—let that be given to them day
by day without fail, ¹⁰ that they may
offer pleasing sacrifices to the God of
heaven, and pray for the life of the
king and his sons. ¹¹ Also I make a
decree that if any one alters this edict,
a beam shall be pulled out of his house,
and he shall be impaled upon it, and
his house shall be made a dunghill.
¹² May the God who has caused his
name to dwell there overthrow any
king or people that shall put forth a
hand to alter this, or to destroy this
house of God which is in Jerusalem. I
Darius make a decree; let it be done
with all diligence."

13 Then, according to the word sent
by Darius the king, Tat'tenai, the
governor of the province Beyond the
River, She'thar-boz'enai. and their associates did with all diligence what

---

of Babylon would be that of Marduk. **17:** *Royal archives,* the *king's treasury* of 7.20; compare
6.1. **6.2:** *Ecbatana* was the king's summer residence. **7:** *Governor* probably means Zerubbabel
(see Hag.2.21). **9:** Provision is made for the burnt offering (Lev. ch. 1), meal offering, (Lev.2.1–
13), and drink offering (Lev.23.13). **11:** The punishment for interference was impalement, on
which see Est.2.23; 9.14; Herodotus, *Hist.* III, 159. To make a house a dunghill was the limit

Darius the king had ordered. ¹⁴ And the elders of the Jews built and prospered, through the prophesying of Haggai the prophet and Zechari'ah the son of Iddo. They finished their building by command of the God of Israel and by decree of Cyrus and Darius and Ar-ta-xerx'es king of Persia; ¹⁵ and this house was finished on the third day of the month of Adar, in the sixth year of the reign of Darius the king.

16 And the people of Israel, the priests and the Levites, and the rest of the returned exiles, celebrated the dedication of this house of God with joy. ¹⁷ They offered at the dedication of this house of God one hundred bulls, two hundred rams, four hundred lambs, and as a sin offering for all Israel twelve he-goats, according to the number of the tribes of Israel. ¹⁸ And they set the priests in their divisions and the Levites in their courses, for the service of God at Jerusalem, as it is written in the book of Moses.

19 On the fourteenth day of the first month the returned exiles kept the passover. ²⁰ For the priests and the Levites had purified themselves together; all of them were clean. So they killed the passover lamb for all the returned exiles, for their fellow priests, and for themselves; ²¹ it was eaten by the people of Israel who had returned from exile, and also by every one who had joined them and separated himself from the pollutions of the peoples of the land to worship the LORD, the God of Israel. ²² And they kept the feast of unleavened bread seven days

with joy; for the LORD had made them joyful, and had turned the heart of the king of Assyria to them, so that he aided them in the work of the house of God, the God of Israel.

7 Now after this, in the reign of Ar-ta-xerx'es king of Persia, Ezra the son of Serai'ah, son of Azari'ah, son of Hilki'ah, ² son of Shallum, son of Zadok, son of Ahi'tub, ³ son of Amari'ah, son of Azari'ah, son of Merai'oth, ⁴ son of Zerahi'ah, son of Uzzi, son of Bukki, ⁵ son of Abi'shu-a, son of Phin'ehas, son of Elea'zar, son of Aaron the chief priest– ⁶ this Ezra went up from Babylonia. He was a scribe skilled in the law of Moses which the LORD the God of Israel had given; and the king granted him all that he asked, for the hand of the LORD his God was upon him.

7 And there went up also to Jerusalem, in the seventh year of Ar-ta-xerx'es the king, some of the people of Israel, and some of the priests and Levites, the singers and gatekeepers, and the temple servants. ⁸ And he came to Jerusalem in the fifth month, which was in the seventh year of the king; ⁹ for on the first day of the first month he began* to go up from Babylonia, and on the first day of the fifth month he came to Jerusalem, for the good hand of his God was upon him. ¹⁰ For Ezra had set his heart to study the law of the LORD, and to do it, and to teach his statutes and ordinances in Israel.

11 This is a copy of the letter which King Ar-ta-xerx'es gave to Ezra the

h Vg See Syr: Heb *that was the foundation of the going up*

---

of contempt (2 Kg.10.27; Dan.2.5). **15:** *Adar,* the twelfth month (March-April). *The sixth year . . . of Darius,* 516 B.C.; therefore *Artaxerxes* in v. 14 is a scribal interpolation on the ground of 4.7. **16–18:** There was a dedication of the new temple as Solomon had dedicated his (1 Kg.8.5, 63), and only then could *priests and Levites* take up their *courses.* No such division of courses is contained in the Pentateuch. **19–22:** Now also the feasts (e.g. *the passover* and then *unleavened bread;* Dt.16.1–8), could be celebrated by officiants ritually *clean.* **22:** *King of Assyria,* perhaps because Persia now ruled the former Assyria.

7.1–10.16: The history of Ezra. This chronologically belongs after the story in Neh. chs. 1–7, and is continued in Neh. chs. 8–10. Almost one hundred and twenty years have elapsed when, under *Artaxerxes* II (404–358 B.C.), Ezra, with royal authority, led to Jerusalem another group comprising the same classes as the earlier group. Ezra's primary interest was in the code of the law. **7:** *Seventh year of Artaxerxes* II, 398 B.C. (of Artaxerxes I, 458 B.C. See Introd.).

priest, the scribe, learned in matters of the commandments of the Lord and his statutes for Israel: [12] "Ar-ta-xerx'es, king of kings, to Ezra the priest, the scribe of the law of the God of heaven.[x] And now [13] I make a decree that any one of the people of Israel or their priests or Levites in my kingdom, who freely offers to go to Jerusalem, may go with you. [14] For you are sent by the king and his seven counselors to make inquiries about Judah and Jerusalem according to the law of your God, which is in your hand, [15] and also to convey the silver and gold which the king and his counselors have freely offered to the God of Israel, whose dwelling is in Jerusalem, [16] with all the silver and gold which you shall find in the whole province of Babylonia, and with the freewill offerings of the people and the priests, vowed willingly for the house of their God which is in Jerusalem. [17] With this money, then, you shall with all diligence buy bulls, rams, and lambs, with their cereal offerings and their drink offerings, and you shall offer them upon the altar of the house of your God which is in Jerusalem. [18] Whatever seems good to you and your brethren to do with the rest of the silver and gold, you may do, according to the will of your God. [19] The vessels that have been given you for the service of the house of your God, you shall deliver before the God of Jerusalem. [20] And whatever else is required for the house of your God, which you have occasion to provide, you may provide it out of the king's treasury.

21 "And I, Ar-ta-xerx'es the king, make a decree to all the treasurers in the province Beyond the River: Whatever Ezra the priest, the scribe of the law of the God of heaven, requires of you, be it done with all diligence, [22] up to a hundred talents of silver, a hundred cors of wheat, a hundred baths of wine, a hundred baths of oil, and salt without prescribing how much. [23] Whatever is commanded by the God of heaven, let it be done in full for the house of the God of heaven, lest his wrath be against the realm of the king and his sons. [24] We also notify you that it shall not be lawful to impose tribute, custom, or toll upon any one of the priests, the Levites, the singers, the doorkeepers, the temple servants, or other servants of this house of God.

25 "And you, Ezra, according to the wisdom of your God which is in your hand, appoint magistrates and judges who may judge all the people in the province Beyond the River, all such as know the laws of your God; and those who do not know them, you shall teach. [26] Whoever will not obey the law of your God and the law of the king, let judgment be strictly executed upon him, whether for death or for banishment or for confiscation of his goods or for imprisonment."

27 Blessed be the Lord, the God of our fathers, who put such a thing as this into the heart of the king, to beautify the house of the Lord which is in Jerusalem, [28] and who extended to me his steadfast love before the king and his counselors, and before all the king's mighty officers. I took courage, for the hand of the Lord my God was upon me, and I gathered leading men from Israel to go up with me.

8 These are the heads of their fathers' houses, and this is the genealogy of those who went up with me from Babylonia, in the reign of Ar-ta-xerx'es the king: [2] Of the sons of Phin'ehas, Gershom. Of the sons of Ith'amar, Daniel. Of the sons of David, Hattush, [3] of the sons of Shecani'ah. Of the sons of Parosh, Zechari'ah, with whom were registered one hundred

[x] Aram adds a word of uncertain meaning

7.12–26: The *king's letter* is in Aramaic. **14:** For the *seven counselors* see Est.1.14; Herodotus, *Hist.* III, 84. **20:** The *king's treasury* must mean the provincial treasure house, see v. 21. **22:** For the equivalent of the *talent, cor,* and *bath,* see pp. 1530–1531. **24:** Temple functionaries are exempted from taxation. **25:** The *wisdom* of Ezra is that of the new law book of v. 14, which he was empowered to enforce through *magistrates and judges,* with four types of penalty.

and fifty men. ⁴ Of the sons of Pa'-hath-mo'ab, Eli-e-ho-e'nai the son of Zerahi'ah, and with him two hundred men. ⁵ Of the sons of Zattu,ⁱ Shecani'-ah the son of Jaha'ziel, and with him three hundred men. ⁶ Of the sons of Adin, Ebed the son of Jonathan, and with him fifty men. ⁷ Of the sons of Elam, Jeshai'ah the son of Athali'ah, and with him seventy men. ⁸ Of the sons of Shephati'ah, Zebadi'ah the son of Michael, and with him eighty men. ⁹ Of the sons of Jo'ab, Obadi'ah the son of Jehi'el, and with him two hundred and eighteen men. ¹⁰ Of the sons of Bani,ʲ Shelo'mith the son of Josi-phi'ah, and with him a hundred and sixty men. ¹¹ Of the sons of Be'bai, Zechari'ah, the son of Be'bai, and with him twenty-eight men. ¹² Of the sons of Azgad, Joha'nan the son of Hak'-katan, and with him a hundred and ten men. ¹³ Of the sons of Adoni'kam, those who came later, their names being Eliph'elet, Jeu'el, and Shemai'-ah, and with them sixty men. ¹⁴ Of the sons of Bigva'i, Uthai and Zaccur, and with them seventy men.

15 I gathered them to the river that runs to Aha'va, and there we encamped three days. As I reviewed the people and the priests, I found there none of the sons of Levi. ¹⁶ Then I sent for Elie'zer, Ar'i-el, Shemai'ah, Elna'-than, Jarib, Elna'than, Nathan, Zechari'ah, and Meshul'lam, leading men, and for Joi'arib and Elna'than, who were men of insight, ¹⁷ and sent them to Iddo, the leading man at the place Casiphi'a, telling them what to say to Iddo and his brethren the temple servantsᵏ at the place Casiphi'a, namely, to send us ministers for the house of our God. ¹⁸ And by the good hand of our God upon us, they brought us a man of discretion, of the sons of Mahli the son of Levi, son of Israel, namely Sherebi'ah with his sons and kinsmen,

eighteen; ¹⁹ also Hashabi'ah and with him Jeshai'ah of the sons of Merar'i, with his kinsmen and their sons, twenty; ²⁰ besides two hundred and twenty of the temple servants, whom David and his officials had set apart to attend the Levites. These were all mentioned by name.

21 Then I proclaimed a fast there, at the river Aha'va, that we might humble ourselves before our God, to seek from him a straight way for ourselves, our children, and all our goods. ²² For I was ashamed to ask the king for a band of soldiers and horsemen to protect us against the enemy on our way; since we had told the king, "The hand of our God is for good upon all that seek him, and the power of his wrath is against all that forsake him." ²³ So we fasted and besought our God for this, and he listened to our entreaty.

24 Then I set apart twelve of the leading priests: Sherebi'ah, Hashabi'ah, and ten of their kinsmen with them. ²⁵ And I weighed out to them the silver and the gold and the vessels, the offering for the house of our God which the king and his counselors and his lords and all Israel there present had offered; ²⁶ I weighed out into their hand six hundred and fifty talents of silver, and silver vessels worth a hundred talents, and a hundred talents of gold, ²⁷ twenty bowls of gold worth a thousand darics, and two vessels of fine bright bronze as precious as gold. ²⁸ And I said to them, "You are holy to the LORD, and the vessels are holy; and the silver and the gold are a free-will offering to the LORD, the God of your fathers. ²⁹ Guard them and keep them until you weigh them before the chief priests and the Levites and the heads of fathers' houses in Israel at Jerusalem, within the chambers of the

ⁱ Gk 1 Esdras 8.32: Heb lacks *of Zattu*
ʲ Gk 1 Esdras 8.36: Heb lacks *Bani*
ᵏ Heb *nethinim*

8.1–14: A list of priestly and lay clans who returned with Ezra. 15: The location of *Ahava* is unknown, but *the river* was doubtless a tributary of the Euphrates. The dearth of Levites parallels that of 2.40. **17:** *Casiphia* is unidentified. **21,23:** For preparatory fasting see Est.4.16; 2 Chr.20.3; Jer.36.9. **28:** Only *holy* persons should handle *holy* things. **29:** The *chambers* were the temple store-houses (10.6; Neh.10.37; 13.4–7).

house of the LORD." [30] So the priests and the Levites took over the weight of the silver and the gold and the vessels, to bring them to Jerusalem, to the house of our God.

[31] Then we departed from the river Aha'va on the twelfth day of the first month, to go to Jerusalem; the hand of our God was upon us, and he delivered us from the hand of the enemy and from ambushes by the way. [32] We came to Jerusalem, and there we remained three days. [33] On the fourth day, within the house of our God, the silver and the gold and the vessels were weighed into the hands of Mer'emoth the priest, son of Uri'ah, and with him was Elea'zar the son of Phin'ehas, and with them were the Levites, Jo'zabad the son of Jeshua and No-adi'ah the son of Bin'nui. [34] The whole was counted and weighed, and the weight of everything was recorded.

[35] At that time those who had come from captivity, the returned exiles, offered burnt offerings to the God of Israel, twelve bulls for all Israel, ninety-six rams, seventy-seven lambs, and as a sin offering twelve he-goats; all this was a burnt offering to the LORD. [36] They also delivered the king's commissions to the king's satraps and to the governors of the province Beyond the River; and they aided the people and the house of God.

9 After these things had been done, the officials approached me and said, "The people of Israel and the priests and the Levites have not separated themselves from the peoples of the lands with their abominations, from the Canaanites, the Hittites, the Per'izzites, the Jeb'usites, the Ammonites, the Moabites, the Egyptians, and the Amorites. [2] For they have taken some of their daughters to be wives for themselves and for their sons; so that the holy race has mixed itself with the peoples of the lands. And in this faithlessness the hand of the officials and chief men has been foremost." [3] When I heard this, I rent my garments and my mantle, and pulled hair from my head and beard, and sat appalled. [4] Then all who trembled at the words of the God of Israel, because of the faithlessness of the returned exiles, gathered round me while I sat appalled until the evening sacrifice. [5] And at the evening sacrifice I rose from my fasting, with my garments and my mantle rent, and fell upon my knees and spread out my hands to the LORD my God, [6] saying:

"O my God, I am ashamed and blush to lift my face to thee, my God, for our iniquities have risen higher than our heads, and our guilt has mounted up to the heavens. [7] From the days of our fathers to this day we have been in great guilt; and for our iniquities we, our kings, and our priests have been given into the hand of the kings of the lands, to the sword, to captivity, to plundering, and to utter shame, as at this day. [8] But now for a brief moment favor has been shown by the LORD our God, to leave us a remnant, and to give us a secure hold[l] within his holy place, that our God may brighten our eyes and grant us a little reviving in our bondage. [9] For we are bondmen; yet our God has not forsaken us in our bondage, but has extended to us his steadfast love before the kings of Persia, to grant us some reviving to set up the house of our God,

l Heb *nail* or *tent-pin*

9.1–15: The problem of mixed marriages. The older codes had not specially discouraged intermarriages, but experience during the exile, which had developed the principle of exclusiveness, made this contamination of the *holy race* a major problem for those who returned under Zerubbabel (4.3; 6.21), under Nehemiah (Neh.10.28–30; 13.3,23–30), and now under Ezra, who found priests, Levites, and chief officials involved therein. **1.** This list of peoples is only a formula (Dt.7.1; Neh.13.23). **2:** *Holy race*, because as dedicated to God they were separated (Ex.19.5,6; Is.62.12).

9.5–15: Ezra's confession. 7: *As at this day*, for they were still subject to Persia (v. 9). **8:** *Remnant*, see vv. 13–15; Zech.8.12; Is.28.5. **9:** *Kings*, i.e. Cyrus, Darius, Xerxes, and Artaxerxes.

to repair its ruins, and to give us protection[m] in Judea and Jerusalem.

10 "And now, O our God, what shall we say after this? For we have forsaken thy commandments, [11] which thou didst command by thy servants the prophets, saying, 'The land which you are entering, to take possession of it, is a land unclean with the pollutions of the peoples of the lands, with their abominations which have filled it from end to end with their uncleanness. [12] Therefore give not your daughters to their sons, neither take their daughters for your sons, and never seek their peace or prosperity, that you may be strong, and eat the good of the land, and leave it for an inheritance to your children for ever.' [13] And after all that has come upon us for our evil deeds and for our great guilt, seeing that thou, our God, hast punished us less than our iniquities deserved and hast given us such a remnant as this, [14] shall we break thy commandments again and intermarry with the peoples who practice these abominations? Wouldst thou not be angry with us till thou wouldst consume us, so that there should be no remnant, nor any to escape? [15] O LORD the God of Israel, thou art just, for we are left a remnant that has escaped, as at this day. Behold, we are before thee in our guilt, for none can stand before thee because of this."

10 While Ezra prayed and made confession, weeping and casting himself down before the house of God, a very great assembly of men, women, and children, gathered to him out of Israel; for the people wept bitterly. [2] And Shecani′ah the son of Jehi′el, of the sons of Elam, addressed Ezra: "We have broken faith with our God and have married foreign women from the peoples of the land, but even

now there is hope for Israel in spite of this. [3] Therefore let us make a covenant with our God to put away all these wives and their children, according to the counsel of my lord and of those who tremble at the commandment of our God; and let it be done according to the law. [4] Arise, for it is your task, and we are with you; be strong and do it." [5] Then Ezra arose and made the leading priests and Levites and all Israel take oath that they would do as had been said. So they took the oath.

6 Then Ezra withdrew from before the house of God, and went to the chamber of Jehoha′nan the son of Eli′ashib, where he spent the night,[n] neither eating bread nor drinking water; for he was mourning over the faithlessness of the exiles. [7] And a proclamation was made throughout Judah and Jerusalem to all the returned exiles that they should assemble at Jerusalem, [8] and that if any one did not come within three days, by order of the officials and the elders all his property should be forfeited, and he himself banned from the congregation of the exiles.

9 Then all the men of Judah and Benjamin assembled at Jerusalem within the three days; it was the ninth month, on the twentieth day of the month. And all the people sat in the open square before the house of God, trembling because of this matter and because of the heavy rain. [10] And Ezra the priest stood up and said to them, "You have trespassed and married foreign women, and so increased the guilt of Israel. [11] Now then make confession to the LORD the God of your fathers, and do his will; separate yourselves from the peoples

m Heb *a wall*
n 1 Esdras 9.2: Heb *where he went*

11–12: No such passage occurs in extant prophetic writings, but see Lev.18.24–30 and Dt.7.3.
   10.1–43: Repentance of the people and divorce of gentile wives. 2: No extant law required divorce in such cases, so *Shechaniah* proposes a way out, a *hope* by a *covenant*, suggesting by the words he uses for *married* and *foreign women* that these had not been true marriages. **3:** *The law* would be that of Dt.7.3. **4:** *It is your task*, for the covenant *oath* must be administered by Ezra. **6:** *Jehohanan* was grandson of Eliashib the high priest, and became himself high priest under Darius II. **9:** *Heavy rain* is usual in Chislev, *the ninth month* (November-December); so

of the land and from the foreign wives."
[12] Then all the assembly answered with a loud voice, "It is so; we must do as you have said. [13] But the people are many, and it is a time of heavy rain; we cannot stand in the open. Nor is this a work for one day or for two; for we have greatly transgressed in this matter. [14] Let our officials stand for the whole assembly; let all in our cities who have taken foreign wives come at appointed times, and with them the elders and judges of every city, till the fierce wrath of our God over this matter be averted from us." [15] Only Jonathan the son of As'ahel and Jahzei'ah the son of Tikvah opposed this, and Meshul'lam and Shab'-bethai the Levite supported them.

16 Then the returned exiles did so. Ezra the priest selected men,[o] heads of fathers' houses, according to their fathers' houses, each of them designated by name. On the first day of the tenth month they sat down to examine the matter; [17] and by the first day of the first month they had come to the end of all the men who had married foreign women.

18 Of the sons of the priests who had married foreign women were found Ma-asei'ah, Elie'zer, Jarib, and Gedaii'ah, of the sons of Jeshua the son of Jo'zadak and his brethren. [19] They pledged themselves to put away their wives, and their guilt offering was a ram of the flock for their guilt. [20] Of the sons of Immer: Hana'ni and Zebadi'ah. [21] Of the sons of Harim: Ma-asei'ah, Eli'jah, Shemai'ah, Jehi'el, and Uzzi'ah. [22] Of the sons of Pashhur: Eli-o-e'nai, Ma-asei'ah, Ish'mael, Nethan'el, Jo'zabad, and Ela'sah.

23 Of the Levites: Jo'zabad, Shim'-e-i, Kelai'ah (that is, Keli'ta), Petha-hi'ah, Judah, and Elie'zer. [24] Of the singers: Eli'ashib. Of the gatekeepers: Shallum, Telem, and Uri. 25 And of Israel: of the sons of Parosh: Rami'ah, Izzi'ah, Malchi'jah, Mi'jamin, Elea'zar, Hashabi'ah,[p] and Benai'ah. [26] Of the sons of Elam: Mattani'ah, Zechari'ah, Jehi'el, Abdi, Jer'emoth, and Eli'jah. [27] Of the sons of Zattu: Eli-o-e'nai, Eli'ashib, Mattani'ah, Jer'emoth, Zabad, and Azi'-za. [28] Of the sons of Be'bai were Jehoha'nan, Hanani'ah, Zab'bai, and Ath'lai. [29] Of the sons of Bani were Meshul'lam, Malluch, Adai'ah, Jashub, She'al, and Jer'emoth. [30] Of the sons of Pa'hath-mo'ab: Adna, Chelal, Benai'ah, Ma-asei'ah, Mattani'ah, Bez'alel, Bin'nui, and Manas'seh. [31] Of the sons of Harim: Elie'zer, Isshi'jah, Malchi'jah, Shemai'ah, Shim'e-on, [32] Benjamin, Malluch, and Shemari'ah. [33] Of the sons of Hashum: Matte'nai, Mat'tattah, Zabad, Eliph'elet, Jer'emai, Manas'seh, and Shim'e-i. [34] Of the sons of Bani: Ma-ada'i, Amram, Uel, [35] Benai'ah, Bedei'ah, Chel'uhi, [36] Vani'ah, Mer'emoth, Eli'-ashib, [37] Mattani'ah, Matte'nai, Ja'asu. [38] Of the sons of Bin'nui:[q] Shim'e-i, [39] Shelemi'ah, Nathan, Adai'ah, [40] Machnad'ebai, Shashai, Sha'rai, [41] Az'arel, Shelemi'ah, Shemari'ah, [42] Shallum, Amari'ah, and Joseph. [43] Of the sons of Nebo: Je-i'el, Matti-thi'ah, Zabad, Zebi'na, Jaddai, Jo'el, and Benai'ah. [44] All these had married foreign women, and they put them away with their children.[r]

o 1 Esdras 9.16: Syr: Heb *and there were selected Ezra, etc.*
p 1 Esdras 9.26: Gk: Heb *Malchijah*
q Gk: Heb *Bani, Binnui*
r 1 Esdras 9.36: Heb obscure

the assembly asks for local enforcement of the covenant. **16–17:** The work commenced in Tebet (*the tenth month*, December-January) and was completed in Nisan (*the first month*, March-April). **18–43:** Lists, which were probably derived from official archives. **19:** The *guilt offering* signified that the wrong had been righted.

THE BOOK OF NEHEMIAH

Since the books of Ezra and Nehemiah are really one book, prepared as a supplement to 1 and 2 Chronicles, and since parts of Nehemiah are apparently misplaced and belong in Ezra, problems of origin, structure, and historical background are discussed in the Introduction to Ezra. It is sufficient to say here that the book which we call Nehemiah relates the return of Nehemiah for two periods of governorship over Judah during the reign of Artaxerxes I (426–424 B.C.). The first return was in 445/444. Nehemiah rebuilt the walls of Jerusalem and instituted social and religious reforms. An outstanding aspect of Nehemiah's religious life was his dependence on God and his frequent prayers to him (1.4–10; 2.18; 4.4,20; 5.9,19; 6.14; 13.14,31).

THE WORDS OF NEHEMI'AH THE son of Hacali'ah.

Now it happened in the month of Chislev, in the twentieth year, as I was in Susa the capital, ² that Hana'ni, one of my brethren, came with certain men out of Judah; and I asked them concerning the Jews that survived, who had escaped exile, and concerning Jerusalem. ³ And they said to me, "The survivors there in the province who escaped exile are in great trouble and shame; the wall of Jerusalem is broken down, and its gates are destroyed by fire."

4 When I heard these words I sat down and wept, and mourned for days; and I continued fasting and praying before the God of heaven. ⁵ And I said, "O LORD God of heaven, the great and terrible God who keeps covenant and steadfast love with those who love him and keep his commandments; ⁶ let thy ear be attentive, and thy eyes open, to hear the prayer of thy servant which I now pray before thee day and night for the people of Israel thy servants, confessing the sins of the people of Israel, which we have sinned against thee. Yea, I and my father's house have sinned. ⁷ We have acted very corruptly against thee, and have not kept the commandments, the statutes, and the ordinances which thou didst command thy servant Moses. ⁸ Remember the word which thou didst command thy servant Moses, saying, 'If you are unfaithful, I will scatter you among the peoples; ⁹ but if you return to me and keep my commandments and do them, though your dispersed be under the farthest skies, I will gather them thence and bring them to the place which I have chosen, to make my name dwell there.' ¹⁰ They are thy servants and thy people, whom thou hast redeemed by thy great power and by thy strong hand. ¹¹ O Lord, let thy ear be attentive to the prayer of thy servant, and to the prayer of thy servants who delight to fear thy name; and give success to thy servant today, and grant him mercy in the sight of this man."

Now I was cupbearer to the king.

2 In the month of Nisan, in the twentieth year of King Ar-ta-xerx'es, when wine was before him, I took up the wine and gave it to the king. Now I had not been sad in his presence. ² And the king said to me, "Why is your face sad, seeing you are not sick? This is nothing else but sadness of the heart." Then I was very

much afraid. [3] I said to the king, "Let the king live for ever! Why should not my face be sad, when the city, the place of my fathers' sepulchres, lies waste, and its gates have been destroyed by fire?" [4] Then the king said to me, "For what do you make request?" So I prayed to the God of heaven. [5] And I said to the king, "If it pleases the king, and if your servant has found favor in your sight, that you send me to Judah, to the city of my fathers' sepulchres, that I may rebuild it." [6] And the king said to me (the queen sitting beside him), "How long will you be gone, and when will you return?" So it pleased the king to send me; and I set him a time. [7] And I said to the king, "If it pleases the king, let letters be given me to the governors of the province Beyond the River, that they may let me pass through until I come to Judah; [8] and a letter to Asaph, the keeper of the king's forest, that he may give me timber to make beams for the gates of the fortress of the temple, and for the wall of the city, and for the house which I shall occupy." And the king granted me what I asked, for the good hand of my God was upon me.

9 Then I came to the governors of the province Beyond the River, and gave them the king's letters. Now the king had sent with me officers of the army and horsemen. [10] But when Sanbal'lat the Hor'onite and Tobi'ah the servant, the Ammonite, heard this, it displeased them greatly that some one had come to seek the welfare of the children of Israel.

11 So I came to Jerusalem and was there three days. [12] Then I arose in the night, I and a few men with me; and I told no one what my God had put into my heart to do for Jerusalem. There was no beast with me but the beast on which I rode. [13] I went out by night by the Valley Gate to the Jackal's Well and to the Dung Gate, and I inspected the walls of Jerusalem which were broken down and its gates which had been destroyed by fire. [14] Then I went on to the Fountain Gate and to the King's Pool; but there was no place for the beast that was under me to pass. [15] Then I went up in the night by the valley and inspected the wall; and I turned back and entered by the Valley Gate, and so · returned. [16] And the officials did not know where I had gone or what I was doing; and I had not yet told the Jews, the priests, the nobles, the officials, and the rest that were to do the work.

17 Then I said to them, "You see the trouble we are in, how Jerusalem lies in ruins with its gates burned. Come, let us build the wall of Jerusalem, that we may no longer suffer disgrace." [18] And I told them of the hand of my God which had been upon me for good, and also of the words which the king had spoken to me. And they said, "Let us rise up and build." So they strengthened their hands for the good work. [19] But when Sanbal'lat the Hor'onite and Tobi'ah the servant, the Ammonite, and Geshem the Arab heard of it, they derided us and despised us and said, "What is this thing that you are doing? Are you rebelling against the king?" [20] Then I replied to them, "The God of heaven will make us prosper, and we his servants will arise and build; but you have no portion or right or memorial in Jerusalem."

a polite understatement, for his plan was to restore the walls, (vv. 8,12–15). **6:** *Queen*, the word perhaps here means only "harem woman." **8:** *Fortress*, see 7.2; 1 Macc.13.52; Acts 21.37. **10:** As local leaders had hindered the work under Zerubbabel (Ezra 4.3–24), so they try again. *Sanballat* is mentioned in the Elephantine papyri as governor of Samaria. Tobiah was apparently an Ammonite official in Persian service. **12–16:** A secret inspection of the ruined walls by night, making a complete circuit of the walls, beginning and ending at the *Valley Gate*. **19:** His enemies suspect the building of the wall was a prelude to rebellion. *Geshem* (6.6) was king of Kedar. **20:** Non-Jews have no *portion*, i.e. property, no *right*, i.e. authority, no *memorial*, i.e. remembrance in the community.

3 Then Eli′ashib the high priest rose up with his brethren the priests and they built the Sheep Gate. They consecrated it and set its doors; they consecrated it as far as the Tower of the Hundred, as far as the Tower of Hanan′el. ² And next to him the men of Jericho built. And next to them*a* Zaccur the son of Imri built.

3 And the sons of Hassena′ah built the Fish Gate; they laid its beams and set its doors, its bolts, and its bars. ⁴ And next to them Mer′emoth the son of Uri′ah, son of Hakkoz repaired. And next to them Meshul′lam the son of Berechi′ah, son of Meshez′-abel repaired. And next to them Zadok the son of Ba′ana repaired. ⁵ And next to them the Teko′ites repaired; but their nobles did not put their necks to the work of their Lord.*b*

6 And Joi′ada the son of Pase′ah and Meshul′lam the son of Besodei′ah repaired the Old Gate; they laid its beams and set its doors, its bolts, and its bars. ⁷ And next to them repaired Melati′ah the Gib′eonite and Jadon the Mero′nothite, the men of Gibeon and of Mizpah, who were under the jurisdiction of the governor of the province Beyond the River. ⁸ Next to them Uz′-ziel the son of Harhai′ah, goldsmiths, repaired. Next to him Hanani′ah, one of the perfumers, repaired; and they restored*c* Jerusalem as far as the Broad Wall. ⁹ Next to them Rephai′ah the son of Hur, ruler of half the district of*d* Jerusalem, repaired. ¹⁰ Next to them Jedai′ah the son of Haru′maph repaired opposite his house; and next to him Hattush the son of Hashabnei′ah repaired. ¹¹ Malchi′jah the son of Harim and Hasshub the son of Pa′hathmo′ab repaired another section and the Tower of the Ovens. ¹² Next to him Shallum the son of Hallo′hesh, ruler of half the district of*d* Jerusalem, repaired, he and his daughters.

13 Hanun and the inhabitants of Zano′ah repaired the Valley Gate; they rebuilt it and set its doors, its bolts, and its bars, and repaired a thousand cubits of the wall, as far as the Dung Gate.

14 Malchi′jah the son of Rechab, ruler of the district of*d* Beth-hacche′-rem, repaired the Dung Gate; he rebuilt it and set its doors, its bolts, and its bars.

15 And Shallum the son of Colho′-zeh, ruler of the district of*d* Mizpah, repaired the Fountain Gate; he rebuilt it and covered it and set its doors, its bolts, and its bars; and he built the wall of the Pool of Shelah of the king's garden, as far as the stairs that go down from the City of David. ¹⁶ After him Nehemi′ah the son of Azbuk, ruler of half the district of*d* Beth-zur, repaired to a point opposite the sepulchres of David, to the artificial pool, and to the house of the mighty men. ¹⁷ After him the Levites repaired: Rehum the son of Bani; next to him Hashabi′ah, ruler of half the district of*d* Kei′lah, repaired for his district. ¹⁸ After him their brethren repaired: Bav′vai the son of Hen′adad, ruler of half the district of*d* Kei′lah; ¹⁹ next to him Ezer the son of Jeshua, ruler of Mizpah, repaired another section opposite the ascent to the armory at the Angle. ²⁰ After him Baruch the son of Zab′bai repaired another section from the Angle to the door of the house of Eli′ashib the high priest. ²¹ After him Mer′emoth the son of Uri′ah, son of Hakkoz repaired another section from the door of the house of Eli′ashib to the end of the house of Eli′ashib. ²² After him the priests, the men of the Plain, repaired. ²³ After them Benjamin and Hasshub repaired opposite their house. After

a Heb *him* *b* Or *lords* *c* Or *abandoned*
d Or *foreman of half the portion assigned to*

3.1–32: Work on the wall. 1: *Eliashib* (12.22; 13.4) was grandson of that Jeshua who worked with Zerubbabel (12.10), and grandfather of the later high priest Jehohanan. **5:** *The Tekoites* (Am.1.1) were not supported by their upper class families. **15:** *City of David*, the old Jebusite town on the hill (2 Sam.5.6–9). **16:** *Sepulchres of David*, 2 Chr.32.33. The *house of the mighty men* was the barracks.

them Azari'ah the son of Ma-asei'ah, son of Anani'ah repaired beside his own house. [24] After him Bin'nui the son of Hen'adad repaired another section, from the house of Azari'ah to the Angle [25] and to the corner. Palal the son of Uzai repaired opposite the Angle and the tower projecting from the upper house of the king at the court of the guard. After him Pedai'ah the son of Parosh [26] and the temple servants living[e] on Ophel repaired to a point opposite the Water Gate on the east and the projecting tower. [27] After him the Teko'ites repaired another section opposite the great projecting tower as far as the wall of Ophel.

28 Above the Horse Gate the priests repaired, each one opposite his own house. [29] After them Zadok the son of Immer repaired opposite his own house. After him Shemai'ah the son of Shecani'ah, the keeper of the East Gate, repaired. [30] After him Hanani'ah the son of Shelemi'ah and Hanun the sixth son of Zalaph repaired another section. After him Meshul'lam the son of Berechi'ah repaired opposite his chamber. [31] After him Malchi'jah, one of the goldsmiths, repaired as far as the house of the temple servants and of the merchants, opposite the Muster Gate,[f] and to the upper chamber of the corner. [32] And between the upper chamber of the corner and the Sheep Gate the goldsmiths and the merchants repaired.

4 [g] Now when Sanbal'lat heard that we were building the wall, he was angry and greatly enraged, and he ridiculed the Jews. [2] And he said in the presence of his brethren and of the army of Sama'ria, "What are these feeble Jews doing? Will they restore things? Will they sacrifice? Will they finish up in a day? Will they revive the stones out of the heaps of rubbish, and burned ones at that?" [3] Tobi'ah the Ammonite was by him, and he said,

"Yes, what they are building–if a fox goes up on it he will break down their stone wall!" [4] Hear, O our God, for we are despised; turn back their taunt upon their own heads, and give them up to be plundered in a land where they are captives. [5] Do not cover their guilt, and let not their sin be blotted out from thy sight; for they have provoked thee to anger before the builders.

6 So we built the wall; and all the wall was joined together to half its height. For the people had a mind to work.

[7h] But when Sanbal'lat and Tobi'ah and the Arabs and the Ammonites and the Ash'dodites heard that the repairing of the walls of Jerusalem was going forward and that the breaches were beginning to be closed, they were very angry; [8] and they all plotted together to come and fight against Jerusalem and to cause confusion in it. [9] And we prayed to our God, and set a guard as a protection against them day and night.

10 But Judah said, "The strength of the burden-bearers is failing, and there is much rubbish; we are not able to work on the wall." [11] And our enemies said, "They will not know or see till we come into the midst of them and kill them and stop the work." [12] When the Jews who lived by them came they said to us ten times, "From all the places where they live[i] they will come up against us."[i] [13] So in the lowest parts of the space behind the wall, in open places, I stationed the people according to their families, with their swords, their spears, and their bows. [14] And I looked, and arose, and said to the nobles and to the officials and to the rest of the people, "Do not be afraid of them. Remember the Lord, who is great and terrible, and

e Cn: Heb *were living*   f Or *Hammiphkad Gate*
g Ch 3.33 in Heb   h Ch 4.1 in Heb
i Cn: Heb *you return*
j Compare Gk Syr: Heb uncertain

4.1–7.5: Troubles for the builders. 4.1–9: Trouble from Sanballat and his associates. **4–5:** Words of ill omen must be countered by words of ill omen. **10–14:** To trouble from without

fight for your brethren, your sons, your daughters, your wives, and your homes."

15 When our enemies heard that it was known to us and that God had frustrated their plan, we all returned to the wall, each to his work. [16] From that day on, half of my servants worked on construction, and half held the spears, shields, bows, and coats of mail; and the leaders stood behind all the house of Judah, [17] who were building on the wall. Those who carried burdens were laden in such a way that each with one hand labored on the work and with the other held his weapon. [18] And each of the builders had his sword girded at his side while he built. The man who sounded the trumpet was beside me. [19] And I said to the nobles and to the officials and to the rest of the people, "The work is great and widely spread, and we are separated on the wall, far from one another. [20] In the place where you hear the sound of the trumpet, rally to us there. Our God will fight for us."

21 So we labored at the work, and half of them held the spears from the break of dawn till the stars came out. [22] I also said to the people at that time, "Let every man and his servant pass the night within Jerusalem, that they may be a guard for us by night and may labor by day." [23] So neither I nor my brethren nor my servants nor the men of the guard who followed me, none of us took off our clothes; each kept his weapon in his hand.*k*

5 Now there arose a great outcry of the people and of their wives against their Jewish brethren. [2] For there were those who said, "With our sons and our daughters, we are many; let us get grain, that we may eat and keep alive." [3] There were also those who said, "We are mortgaging our fields,

our vineyards, and our houses to get grain because of the famine." [4] And there were those who said, "We have borrowed money for the king's tax upon our fields and our vineyards. [5] Now our flesh is as the flesh of our brethren, our children are as their children; yet we are forcing our sons and our daughters to be slaves, and some of our daughters have already been enslaved; but it is not in our power to help it, for other men have our fields and our vineyards."

6 I was very angry when I heard their outcry and these words. [7] I took counsel with myself, and I brought charges against the nobles and the officials. I said to them, "You are exacting interest, each from his brother." And I held a great assembly against them, [8] and said to them, "We, as far as we are able, have bought back our Jewish brethren who have been sold to the nations; but you even sell your brethren that they may be sold to us!" They were silent, and could not find a word to say. [9] So I said, "The thing that you are doing is not good. Ought you not to walk in the fear of our God to prevent the taunts of the nations our enemies? [10] Moreover I and my brethren and my servants are lending them money and grain. Let us leave off this interest. [11] Return to them this very day their fields, their vineyards, their olive orchards, and their houses, and the hundredth of money, grain, wine, and oil which you have been exacting of them." [12] Then they said, "We will restore these and require nothing from them. We will do as you say." And I called the priests, and took an oath of them to do as they had promised. [13] I also shook out my lap and said, "So may God shake out every man from his house and from

k Cn: Heb *each his weapon the water*

was added trouble from within. **16:** By *my servants* he would mean his personal, better armed, bodyguard. **21:** Night work was hardly possible in those days. **5.1–13:** Economic ills. Concentration on the walls had led to economic crisis. **3:** *Mortgaging*, i.e. giving as security. **4:** *The king's tax* was the tribute due to Persia. **7–10:** It was legal to take *interest* from non-Jews but not from fellow Jews (Dt.23.20), so the crime was that Jewish leaders had been taking advantage of their brethren in economic troubles. **11:** The *hundredth* represents one per cent monthly. **13:**

[590]

his labor who does not perform this promise. So may he be shaken out and emptied." And all the assembly said "Amen" and praised the LORD. And the people did as they had promised.

14 Moreover from the time that I was appointed to be their governor in the land of Judah, from the twentieth year to the thirty-second year of Ar-ta-xerx'es the king, twelve years, neither I nor my brethren ate the food allowance of the governor. [15] The former governors who were before me laid heavy burdens upon the people, and took from them food and wine, besides forty shekels of silver. Even their servants lorded it over the people. But I did not do so, because of the fear of God. [16] I also held to the work on this wall, and acquired no land; and all my servants were gathered there for the work. [17] Moreover there were at my table a hundred and fifty men, Jews and officials, besides those who came to us from the nations which were about us. [18] Now that which was prepared for one day was one ox and six choice sheep; fowls likewise were prepared for me, and every ten days skins of wine in abundance; yet with all this I did not demand the food allowance of the governor, because the servitude was heavy upon this people. [19] Remember for my good, O my God, all that I have done for this people.

6 Now when it was reported to Sanbal'lat and Tobi'ah and to Geshem the Arab and to the rest of our enemies that I had built the wall and that there was no breach left in it (although up to that time I had not set up the doors in the gates), [2] Sanbal'lat and Geshem sent to me, saying, "Come and let us meet together in one of the villages in the plain of Ono." But they intended to do me harm. [3] And

I sent messengers to them, saying, "I am doing a great work and I cannot come down. Why should the work stop while I leave it and come down to you?" [4] And they sent to me four times in this way and I answered them in the same manner. [5] In the same way Sanbal'lat for the fifth time sent his servant to me with an open letter in his hand. [6] In it was written, "It is reported among the nations, and Geshem[l] also says it, that you and the Jews intend to rebel; that is why you are building the wall; and you wish to become their king, according to this report. [7] And you have also set up prophets to proclaim concerning you in Jerusalem, 'There is a king in Judah.' And now it will be reported to the king according to these words. So now come, and let us take counsel together." [8] Then I sent to him, saying, "No such things as you say have been done, for you are inventing them out of your own mind." [9] For they all wanted to frighten us, thinking, "Their hands will drop from the work, and it will not be done." But now, O God, strengthen thou my hands.

10 Now when I went into the house of Shemai'ah the son of Delai'ah, son of Mehet'abel, who was shut up, he said, "Let us meet together in the house of God, within the temple, and let us close the doors of the temple; for they are coming to kill you, at night they are coming to kill you." [11] But I said, "Should such a man as I flee? And what man such as I could go into the temple and live?[m] I will not go in." [12] And I understood, and saw that God had not sent him, but he had pronounced the prophecy against me because Tobi'ah and Sanbal'lat had hired him. [13] For this purpose he was hired, that I should be afraid and act

l Heb *Gashmu*
m Or *would go into the temple to save his life*

Lap refers to that part of the outer garment which served as a pocket. **14–19:** Nehemiah's apologia for his *twelve years* as *governor*. **15:** *Forty shekels*, about twenty-five dollars. **6.1–19:** Finishing the wall, in spite of plots. **2:** They try to lure Nehemiah to *Ono* near Lydda to *harm* him. **5–7:** Failing this, they try to frighten him by threatening to report him to the king, mentioning *prophets* because they were known as fomenters of rebellion (Jer.28.1–4). **10:** *Shemaiah*

in this way and sin, and so they could give me an evil name, in order to taunt me. [14] Remember Tobi′ah and Sanbal′lat, O my God, according to these things that they did, and also the prophetess No-adi′ah and the rest of the prophets who wanted to make me afraid.

15 So the wall was finished on the twenty-fifth day of the month Elul, in fifty-two days. [16] And when all our enemies heard of it, all the nations round about us were afraid[n] and fell greatly in their own esteem; for they perceived that this work had been accomplished with the help of our God. [17] Moreover in those days the nobles of Judah sent many letters to Tobi′ah, and Tobi′ah's letters came to them. [18] For many in Judah were bound by oath to him, because he was the son-in-law of Shecani′ah the son of Arah: and his son Jehoha′nan had taken the daughter of Meshul′lam the son of Berechi′ah as his wife. [19] Also they spoke of his good deeds in my presence, and reported my words to him. And Tobi′ah sent letters to make me afraid.

7 Now when the wall had been built and I had set up the doors, and the gatekeepers, the singers, and the Levites had been appointed, [2] I gave my brother Hana′ni and Hanani′ah the governor of the castle charge over Jerusalem, for he was a more faithful and God-fearing man than many. [3] And I said to them, "Let not the gates of Jerusalem be opened until the sun is hot; and while they are still standing guard[o] let them shut and bar the doors. Appoint guards from among the inhabitants of Jerusalem, each to his station and each opposite his own house." [4] The city was wide and large, but the people within it were few and no houses had been built.

5 Then God put it into my mind to assemble the nobles and the officials and the people to be enrolled by genealogy. And I found the book of the genealogy of those who came up at the first, and I found written in it:

6 These were the people of the province who came up out of the captivity of those exiles whom Nebuchadnez′zar the king of Babylon had carried into exile; they returned to Jerusalem and Judah, each to his town. [7] They came with Zerub′babel, Jeshua, Nehemi′ah, Azari′ah, Raami′ah, Naham′ani, Mor′decai, Bilshan, Mis′pereth, Bigva′i, Nehum, Ba′anah.

The number of the men of the people of Israel: [8] the sons of Parosh, two thousand a hundred and seventy-two. [9] The sons of Shephati′ah, three hundred and seventy-two. [10] The sons of Arah, six hundred and fifty-two. [11] The sons of Pa′hath-mo′ab, namely the sons of Jeshua and Jo′ab, two thousand eight hundred and eighteen. [12] The sons of Elam, a thousand two hundred and fifty-four. [13] The sons of Zattu, eight hundred and forty-five. [14] The sons of Zac′cai, seven hundred and sixty. [15] The sons of Bin′nui, six hundred and forty-eight. [16] The sons of Be′bai, six hundred and twenty-eight. [17] The sons of Azgad, two thousand three hundred and twenty-two. [18] The sons of Adoni′kam, six hundred and sixty-seven. [19] The sons of Bigva′i, two thousand and sixty-seven. [20] The sons of Adin, six hundred and fifty-five. [21] The sons of Ater, namely of Hezeki′ah, ninety-eight. [22] The sons of Hashum, three hundred and twenty-eight. [23] The sons of

n Another reading is *saw*　　o Heb obscure

is the enemy within the camp. That prophets could be *hired* illustrates Zech.13.2–6. **15:** *Elul* was the sixth month (August-September). **7.1–5:** Setting up the guards. **2:** *Hanani*, see 1.2. *The castle* is the fortress (2.8). **3:** *The gates* are to be open from sunrise to sunset. At v. 5a the memoirs of Nehemiah break off to be picked up again after chapter 10. Verse 5b is a transition verse to introduce the genealogies of vv. 6–73a which parallel Ezra 2.1–70.
7.6–73: A census of the first return. See Ezra 2.1–70 n. **73b:** A connecting verse based on Ezra 3.1.

Be'zai, three hundred and twenty-four. ²⁴ The sons of Hariph, a hundred and twelve. ²⁵ The sons of Gibeon, ninety-five. ²⁶ The men of Bethlehem and Neto'phah, a hundred and eighty-eight. ²⁷ The men of An'athoth, a hundred and twenty-eight. ²⁸ The men of Beth-az'maveth, forty-two. ²⁹ The men of Kir'iath-je'arim, Chephi'rah, and Be-er'oth, seven hundred and forty-three. ³⁰ The men of Ramah and Geba, six hundred and twenty-one. ³¹ The men of Michmas, a hundred and twenty-two. ³² The men of Bethel and Ai, a hundred and twenty-three. ³³ The men of the other Nebo, fifty-two. ³⁴ The sons of the other Elam, a thousand two hundred and fifty-four. ³⁵ The sons of Harim, three hundred and twenty. ³⁶ The sons of Jericho, three hundred and forty-five. ³⁷ The sons of Lod, Hadid, and Ono, seven hundred and twenty-one. ³⁸ The sons of Sena'ah, three thousand nine hundred and thirty.

39 The priests: the sons of Jedai'ah, namely the house of Jeshua, nine hundred and seventy-three. ⁴⁰ The sons of Immer, a thousand and fifty-two. ⁴¹ The sons of Pashhur, a thousand two hundred and forty-seven. ⁴² The sons of Harim, a thousand and seventeen.

43 The Levites: the sons of Jeshua, namely of Kad'mi-el of the sons of Ho'devah, seventy-four. ⁴⁴ The singers: the sons of Asaph, a hundred and forty-eight. ⁴⁵ The gatekeepers: the sons of Shallum, the sons of Ater, the sons of Talmon, the sons of Akkub, the sons of Hati'ta, the sons of Sho'bai, a hundred and thirty-eight.

46 The temple servants:^p the sons of Ziha, the sons of Hasu'pha, the sons of Tabba'oth, ⁴⁷ the sons of Keros, the sons of Si'a, the sons of Padon, ⁴⁸ the sons of Leba'na, the sons of Hag'aba, the sons of Shalmai, ⁴⁹ the sons of Hanan, the sons of Giddel, the sons of Gahar, ⁵⁰ the sons of Re-ai'ah, the sons of Rezin, the sons of Neko'da, ⁵¹ the sons of Gazzam, the sons of Uzza, the sons of Pase'ah, ⁵² the sons

of Besai, the sons of Me-u'nim, the sons of Nephush'esim, ⁵³ the sons of Bakbuk, the sons of Haku'pha, the sons of Harhur, ⁵⁴ the sons of Bazlith, the sons of Mehi'da, the sons of Harsha, ⁵⁵ the sons of Barkos, the sons of Sis'-era, the sons of Temah, ⁵⁶ the sons of Nezi'ah, the sons of Hati'pha.

57 The sons of Solomon's servants: the sons of So'tai, the sons of So'-phereth, the sons of Peri'da, ⁵⁸ the sons of Ja'ala, the sons of Darkon, the sons of Giddel, ⁵⁹ the sons of Shepha-ti'ah, the sons of Hattil, the sons of Po'-chereth-hazzeba'im, the sons of Amon.

60 All the temple servants and the sons of Solomon's servants were three hundred and ninety-two.

61 The following were those who came up from Tel-me'lah, Tel-har'-sha, Cherub, Addon, and Immer, but they could not prove their fathers' houses nor their descent, whether they belonged to Israel: ⁶² the sons of De-lai'ah, the sons of Tobi'ah, the sons of Neko'da, six hundred and forty-two. ⁶³ Also, of the priests: the sons of Hobai'ah, the sons of Hakkoz, the sons of Barzil'lai (who had taken a wife of the daughters of Barzil'lai the Gilead-ite and was called by their name). ⁶⁴ These sought their registration among those enrolled in the genealo-gies, but it was not found there, so they were excluded from the priesthood as unclean; ⁶⁵ the governor told them that they were not to partake of the most holy food, until a priest with Urim and Thummim should arise.

66 The whole assembly together was forty-two thousand three hundred and sixty, ⁶⁷ besides their menservants and maidservants, of whom there were seven thousand three hundred and thirty-seven; and they had two hundred and forty-five singers, male and female. ⁶⁸ Their horses were seven hundred and thirty-six, their mules two hundred and forty-five,^q ⁶⁹ their camels four hundred and thirty-five,

p Heb nethinim
q Ezra 2.66 and the margins of some Hebrew Mss: Heb lacks *their horses . . . forty-five*

and their asses six thousand seven hundred and twenty.

70 Now some of the heads of fathers' houses gave to the work. The governor gave to the treasury a thousand darics of gold, fifty basins, five hundred and thirty priests' garments. [71] And some of the heads of fathers' houses gave into the treasury of the work twenty thousand darics of gold and two thousand two hundred minas of silver. [72] And what the rest of the people gave was twenty thousand darics of gold, two thousand minas of silver, and sixty-seven priests' garments.

73 So the priests, the Levites, the gatekeepers, the singers, some of the people, the temple servants, and all Israel, lived in their towns.

And when the seventh month had come, the children of Israel were in their towns. [1] And all the people gathered as one man into the square before the Water Gate; and they told Ezra the scribe to bring the book of the law of Moses which the LORD had given to Israel. [2] And Ezra the priest brought the law before the assembly, both men and women and all who could hear with understanding, on the first day of the seventh month. [3] And he read from it facing the square before the Water Gate from early morning until midday, in the presence of the men and the women and those who could understand; and the ears of all the people were attentive to the book of the law. [4] And Ezra the scribe stood on a wooden pulpit which they had made for the purpose; and beside him stood Mattithi'ah, Shema, Anai'ah, Uri'ah, Hilki'ah, and Ma-asei'ah on his right hand; and Pedai'ah, Mish'a-el, Malchi'jah, Hashum, Hashbad'danah, Zechari'ah, and Meshul'-

lam on his left hand. [5] And Ezra opened the book in the sight of all the people, for he was above all the people; and when he opened it all the people stood. [6] And Ezra blessed the LORD, the great God; and all the people answered, "Amen, Amen," lifting up their hands; and they bowed their heads and worshiped the LORD with their faces to the ground. [7] Also Jeshua, Bani, Sherebi'ah, Jamin, Akkub, Shab'bethai, Hodi'ah, Ma-asei'ah, Keli'ta, Azari'ah, Jo'zabad, Hanan, Pelai'ah, the Levites,[r] helped the people to understand the law, while the people remained in their places. [8] And they read from the book, from the law of God, clearly;[s] and they gave the sense, so that the people understood the reading.

9 And Nehemi'ah, who was the governor, and Ezra the priest and scribe, and the Levites who taught the people said to all the people, "This day is holy to the LORD your God; do not mourn or weep." For all the people wept when they heard the words of the law. [10] Then he said to them, "Go your way, eat the fat and drink sweet wine and send portions to him for whom nothing is prepared; for this day is holy to our Lord; and do not be grieved, for the joy of the LORD is your strength." [11] So the Levites stilled all the people, saying, "Be quiet, for this day is holy; do not be grieved." [12] And all the people went their way to eat and drink and to send portions and to make great rejoicing, because they had understood the words that were declared to them.

13 On the second day the heads of fathers' houses of all the people, with the priests and the Levites, came to-

r 1 Esdras 9.48 Vg: Heb *and the Levites*
s Or *with interpretation*

8.1–9.37: Continuation of the Ezra story. 8.1–12: Reading the book of the law. 1: *The Water Gate* is doubtless that of 3.26. For Ezra's *book of law* see Ezra 7.6,10,14. The citations from it in vv. 14,15 (and Ezra 9.11,12) are not in our Pentateuch. **2:** *The seventh month* was Tishri (September-October), the *first day* of which was a day of convocation (Num.29.1). **4:** *Pulpit*, lit. "tower." **7–8:** Since the *book* was in Hebrew, it was interpreted to the people in the more familiar Aramaic. The name *Nehemiah* in v. 9 is a scribal insertion. **10–12:** A feast is appointed to celebrate the event.

gether to Ezra the scribe in order to study the words of the law. [14] And they found it written in the law that the LORD had commanded by Moses that the people of Israel should dwell in booths during the feast of the seventh month, [15] and that they should publish and proclaim in all their towns and in Jerusalem, "Go out to the hills and bring branches of olive, wild olive, myrtle, palm, and other leafy trees to make booths, as it is written." [16] So the people went out and brought them and made booths for themselves, each on his roof, and in their courts and in the courts of the house of God, and in the square at the Water Gate and in the square at the Gate of E'phraim. [17] And all the assembly of those who had returned from the captivity made booths and dwelt in the booths; for from the days of Jeshua the son of Nun to that day the people of Israel had not done so. And there was very great rejoicing. [18] And day by day, from the first day to the last day, he read from the book of the law of God. They kept the feast seven days; and on the eighth day there was a solemn assembly, according to the ordinance.

9 Now on the twenty-fourth day of this month the people of Israel were assembled with fasting and in sackcloth, and with earth upon their heads. [2] And the Israelites separated themselves from all foreigners, and stood and confessed their sins and the iniquities of their fathers. [3] And they stood up in their place and read from the book of the law of the LORD their God for a fourth of the day; for another fourth of it they made confession and worshiped the LORD their God. [4] Upon the stairs of the Levites stood Jeshua, Bani, Kad'mi-el,

Shebani'ah, Bunni, Sherebi'ah, Bani, and Chena'ni; and they cried with a loud voice to the LORD their God. [5] Then the Levites, Jeshua, Kad'mi-el, Bani, Hashabnei'ah, Sherebi'ah, Hodi'ah, Shebani'ah, and Pethahi'ah, said, "Stand up and bless the LORD your God from everlasting to everlasting. Blessed be thy glorious name which is exalted above all blessing and praise."

6 And Ezra said:[t] "Thou art the LORD, thou alone; thou hast made heaven, the heaven of heavens, with all their host, the earth and all that is on it, the seas and all that is in them; and thou preservest all of them; and the host of heaven worships thee. [7] Thou art the LORD, the God who didst choose Abram and bring him forth out of Ur of the Chalde'ans and give him the name Abraham; [8] and thou didst find his heart faithful before thee, and didst make with him the covenant to give to his descendants the land of the Canaanite, the Hittite, the Amorite, the Per'izzite, the Jeb'usite, and the Gir'gashite; and thou hast fulfilled thy promise, for thou art righteous.

9 "And thou didst see the affliction of our fathers in Egypt and hear their cry at the Red Sea, [10] and didst perform signs and wonders against Pharaoh and all his servants and all the people of his land, for thou knewest that they acted insolently against our fathers; and thou didst get thee a name, as it is to this day. [11] And thou didst divide the sea before them, so that they went through the midst of the sea on dry land; and thou didst cast their pursuers into the depths, as a stone into mighty waters. [12] By a pillar of cloud

t Gk: Heb lacks and Ezra said

8.13–18: Celebration of the feast of booths. Reading *the law* made them aware that this month of Tishri (September-October) was the time for the feast of *booths*, the Mosaic regulations for which are in Lev.23.33–43. **15:** *The hills* must mean the hilly country around Jerusalem. **16:** The *booths* were apparently both domestic and communal. **17:** *Jeshua the son of Nun* may be meant to refer to that Jeshua who worked with Zerubbabel.

9.1–37: The great confession. 1–5: The setting. **2:** The confession was something in which non-Jews might not participate. **3:** They *read,* i.e. they listened to the reading. **4:** *The stairs* possibly belonged to the pulpit of 8.4. **6–37:** Ezra's confession and complaint.

thou didst lead them in the day, and by a pillar of fire in the night to light for them the way in which they should go. [13] Thou didst come down upon Mount Sinai, and speak with them from heaven and give them right ordinances and true laws, good statutes and commandments, [14] and thou didst make known to them thy holy sabbath and command them commandments and statutes and a law by Moses thy servant. [15] Thou didst give them bread from heaven for their hunger and bring forth water for them from the rock for their thirst, and thou didst tell them to go in to possess the land which thou hadst sworn to give them.

16 "But they and our fathers acted presumptuously and stiffened their neck and did not obey thy commandments; [17] they refused to obey, and were not mindful of the wonders which thou didst perform among them; but they stiffened their neck and appointed a leader to return to their bondage in Egypt. But thou art a God ready to forgive, gracious and merciful, slow to anger and abounding in steadfast love, and didst not forsake them. [18] Even when they had made for themselves a molten calf and said, 'This is your God who brought you up out of Egypt,' and had committed great blasphemies, [19] thou in thy great mercies didst not forsake them in the wilderness; the pillar of cloud which led them in the way did not depart from them by day, nor the pillar of fire by night which lighted for them the way by which they should go. [20] Thou gavest thy good Spirit to instruct them, and didst not withhold thy manna from their mouth, and gavest them water for their thirst. [21] Forty years didst thou sustain them in the wilderness, and they lacked nothing; their clothes did not wear out and their feet did not swell. [22] And thou didst give them kingdoms and peoples, and didst allot to them every corner; so they took possession of the land of Sihon king of Heshbon and the land of Og king of Bashan. [23] Thou didst multiply their descendants as the stars of heaven, and thou didst bring them into the land which thou hadst told their fathers to enter and possess. [24] So the descendants went in and possessed the land, and thou didst subdue before them the inhabitants of the land, the Canaanites, and didst give them into their hands, with their kings and the peoples of the land, that they might do with them as they would. [25] And they captured fortified cities and a rich land, and took possession of houses full of all good things, cisterns hewn out, vineyards, olive orchards and fruit trees in abundance; so they ate, and were filled and became fat, and delighted themselves in thy great goodness.

26 "Nevertheless they were disobedient and rebelled against thee and cast thy law behind their back and killed thy prophets, who had warned them in order to turn them back to thee, and they committed great blasphemies. [27] Therefore thou didst give them into the hand of their enemies, who made them suffer; and in the time of their suffering they cried to thee and thou didst hear them from heaven; and according to thy great mercies thou didst give them saviors who saved them from the hand of their enemies. [28] But after they had rest they did evil again before thee, and thou didst abandon them to the hand of their enemies, so that they had dominion over them; yet when they turned and cried to thee thou didst hear from heaven, and many times thou didst deliver them according to thy mercies. [29] And thou didst warn them in order to turn them back to thy law. Yet they acted presumptuously and did not obey thy commandments, but sinned against thy ordinances, by the observ-

---

17: Num.14.4 says only that they suggested appointing such a leader. **20a:** *Gavest thy good Spirit*, perhaps a reference to the appointment of elders (Num.11.17–29). **27:** The *saviors* here are the judges (Jg.2.16). **30:** *By thy Spirit*, see Zech.7.12; 2 Chr.24.20.

ance of which a man shall live, and turned a stubborn shoulder and stiffened their neck and would not obey. [30] Many years thou didst bear with them, and didst warn them by thy Spirit through thy prophets; yet they would not give ear. Therefore thou didst give them into the hand of the peoples of the lands. [31] Nevertheless in thy great mercies thou didst not make an end of them or forsake them; for thou art a gracious and merciful God.

32 "Now therefore, our God, the great and mighty and terrible God, who keepest covenant and steadfast love, let not all the hardship seem little to thee that has come upon us, upon our kings, our princes, our priests, our prophets, our fathers, and all thy people, since the time of the kings of Assyria until this day. [33] Yet thou hast been just in all that has come upon us, for thou hast dealt faithfully and we have acted wickedly; [34] our kings, our princes, our priests, and our fathers have not kept thy law or heeded thy commandments and thy warnings which thou didst give them. [35] They did not serve thee in their kingdom, and in thy great goodness which thou gavest them, and in the large and rich land which thou didst set before them; and they did not turn from their wicked works. [36] Behold, we are slaves this day; in the land that thou gavest to our fathers to enjoy its fruit and its good gifts, behold, we are slaves. [37] And its rich yield goes to the kings whom thou hast set over us because of our sins; they have power also over our bodies and over our cattle at their pleasure, and we are in great distress."

38[u] Because of all this we make a firm covenant and write it, and our princes, our Levites, and our priests set their seal to it.

10[v] Those who set their seal are Nehemi′ah the governor, the son of Hacali′ah, Zedeki′ah, [2] Serai′ah, Azari′ah, Jeremiah, [3] Pashhur, Amari′ah, Malchi′jah, [4] Hattush, Shebani′ah, Malluch, [5] Harim, Mer′emoth, Obadi′ah, [6] Daniel, Gin′nethon, Baruch, [7] Meshul′lam, Abi′jah, Mi′jamin, [8] Ma-azi′ah, Bil′gai, Shemai′ah; these are the priests. [9] And the Levites: Jeshua the son of Azani′ah, Bin′nui of the sons of Hen′adad, Kad′mi-el; [10] and their brethren, Shebani′ah, Hodi′ah, Keli′ta, Pelai′ah, Hanan, [11] Mica, Rehob, Hashabi′ah, [12] Zaccur, Sherebi′ah, Shebani′ah, [13] Hodi′ah, Bani, Beni′nu. [14] The chiefs of the people: Parosh, Pa′hath-mo′ab, Elam, Zattu, Bani, [15] Bunni, Azgad, Be′bai, [16] Adoni′jah, Bigva′i, Adin, [17] Ater, Hezeki′ah, Azzur, [18] Hodi′ah, Hashum, Be′zai, [19] Hariph, An′athoth, Ne′bai, [20] Mag′piash, Meshul′lam, Hezir, [21] Meshez′abel, Zadok, Jad′du-a, [22] Pelati′ah, Hanan, Anai′ah, [23] Hoshe′a, Hanani′ah, Hasshub, [24] Hallo′hesh, Pi′lha, Shobek, [25] Rehum, Hashab′nah, Ma-asei′ah, [26] Ahi′ah, Hanan, Anan, [27] Malluch, Harim, Ba′anah.

28 The rest of the people, the priests, the Levites, the gatekeepers, the singers, the temple servants, and all who have separated themselves from the peoples of the lands to the law of God, their wives, their sons, their daughters, all who have knowledge and understanding, [29] join with their brethren, their nobles, and enter into a curse and an oath to walk in God's law which was given by Moses the servant of God, and to observe and do all the commandments of the LORD our Lord and his ordinances and his statutes. [30] We will not give our daughters to the peoples of the land or take their daughters for our sons; [31] and if

u Ch 10.1 in Heb   *v* Ch 10.2 in Heb

9.38–10.39: The covenant to support God's house; a document belonging to the Nehemiah story. **9.38:** *Because of all this* refers to chapter 13. **10.28:** *Separated themselves*, see 9.2; 13.3; and Ezra 6.21. **31:** *Sabbath day*, see 13.15–18. *A holy day* was treated as a sabbath. For the *seventh year* see Ex.23.10, and for the *debt*, Dt.15.1–3. **32:** The temple tax was voluntary;

the peoples of the land bring in wares or any grain on the sabbath day to sell, we will not buy from them on the sabbath or on a holy day; and we will forego the crops of the seventh year and the exaction of every debt.

32 We also lay upon ourselves the obligation to charge ourselves yearly with the third part of a shekel for the service of the house of our God: 33 for the showbread, the continual cereal offering, the continual burnt offering, the sabbaths, the new moons, the appointed feasts, the holy things, and the sin offerings to make atonement for Israel, and for all the work of the house of our God. 34 We have likewise cast lots, the priests, the Levites, and the people, for the wood offering, to bring it into the house of our God, according to our fathers' houses, at times appointed, year by year, to burn upon the altar of the LORD our God, as it is written in the law. 35 We obligate ourselves to bring the first fruits of our ground and the first fruits of all fruit of every tree, year by year, to the house of the LORD; 36 also to bring to the house of our God, to the priests who minister in the house of our God, the first-born of our sons and of our cattle, as it is written in the law, and the firstlings of our herds and of our flocks; 37 and to bring the first of our coarse meal, and our contributions, the fruit of every tree, the wine and the oil, to the priests, to the chambers of the house of our God; and to bring to the Levites the tithes from our ground, for it is the Levites who collect the tithes in all our rural towns. 38 And the priest, the son of Aaron, shall be with the Levites when the Levites receive the tithes; and the Levites shall bring up the tithe of the tithes to the house of our God, to the chambers, to the storehouse. 39 For the people of Israel

and the sons of Levi shall bring the contribution of grain, wine, and oil to the chambers, where are the vessels of the sanctuary, and the priests that minister and the gatekeepers and the singers. We will not neglect the house of our God.

Now the leaders of the people lived in Jerusalem; and the rest of the people cast lots to bring one out of ten to live in Jerusalem the holy city, while nine tenths remained in the other towns. 2 And the people blessed all the men who willingly offered to live in Jerusalem.

3 These are the chiefs of the province who lived in Jerusalem; but in the towns of Judah every one lived on his property in their towns: Israel, the priests, the Levites, the temple servants, and the descendants of Solomon's servants. 4 And in Jerusalem lived certain of the sons of Judah and of the sons of Benjamin. Of the sons of Judah: Athai'ah the son of Uzzi'ah, son of Zechari'ah, son of Amari'ah, son of Shephati'ah, son of Mahal'alel, of the sons of Perez; 5 and Ma-asei'ah the son of Baruch, son of Col-ho'zeh, son of Hazai'ah, son of Adai'ah, son of Joi'arib, son of Zechari'ah, son of the Shi'lonite. 6 All the sons of Perez who lived in Jerusalem were four hundred and sixty-eight valiant men.

7 And these are the sons of Benjamin: Sallu the son of Meshul'lam, son of Jo'ed, son of Pedai'ah, son of Kolai'ah, son of Ma-asei'ah, son of I'thi-el, son of Jeshai'ah. 8 And after him Gabba'i, Salla'i, nine hundred and twenty-eight. 9 Jo'el the son of Zichri was their overseer; and Judah the son of Hassen'u-ah was second over the city.

10 Of the priests: Jedai'ah the son of Joi'arib, Jachin, 11 Serai'ah the son of Hilki'ah, son of Meshul'lam, son of

---

later it became an obligatory half-shekel tax (Ex.30.13; Mt.17.24). **34:** Casting *lots* was a recognized procedure (11.1; 1 Chr.25.8; 1 Sam.14.40–45; Acts 1.23–26). *The wood offering* was for the altar fires (13.31; Lev.6.12). **35–36:** The law on *first fruits*, Ex.22.29; 23.19; Num.18.15–18. **37:** *Tithes*, see Lev.27.30; Num.18.25–32. *The chambers* were the temple store-rooms (13.13; Ezra 8.29; 10.6).
  11.1–13.31: Continuation of Nehemiah's memoirs, picking up from 7.5a. **11.1–36: A census**

Zadok, son of Merai'oth, son of Ahi'-
tub, ruler of the house of God, ¹² and
their brethren who did the work of the
house, eight hundred and twenty-two;
and Adai'ah the son of Jero'ham, son
of Pelali'ah, son of Amzi, son of Zechari'ah, son of Pashhur, son of Malchi'-
jah, ¹³ and his brethren, heads of
fathers' houses, two hundred and forty-
two; and Amash'sai, the son of
Az'arel, son of Ah'zai, son of Meshil'-
lemoth, son of Immer, ¹⁴ and their
brethren, mighty men of valor, a
hundred and twenty-eight; their overseer was Zab'diel the son of Hagge-
do'lim.

15 And of the Levites: Shemai'ah
the son of Hasshub, son of Azri'-
kam, son of Hashabi'ah, son of
Bunni; ¹⁶ and Shab'bethai and Jo'zabad, of the chiefs of the Levites, who
were over the outside work of the
house of God; ¹⁷ and Mattani'ah the
son of Mica, son of Zabdi, son of
Asaph, who was the leader to begin
the thanksgiving in prayer, and Bakbuki'ah, the second among his brethren; and Abda the son of Sham'mua,
son of Galal, son of Jedu'thun. ¹⁸ All
the Levites in the holy city were two
hundred and eighty-four.

19 The gatekeepers, Akkub, Talmon and their brethren, who kept
watch at the gates, were a hundred and
seventy-two. ²⁰ And the rest of Israel,
and of the priests and the Levites,
were in all the towns of Judah, every
one in his inheritance. ²¹ But the temple servants lived on Ophel; and Ziha
and Gishpa were over the temple servants.

22 The overseer of the Levites in
Jerusalem was Uzzi the son of Bani,
son of Hashabi'ah, son of Mattani'ah,
son of Mica, of the sons of Asaph, the
singers, over the work of the house
of God. ²³ For there was a command
from the king concerning them, and a
settled provision for the singers, as

every day required. ²⁴ And Pethahi'ah
the son of Meshez'abel, of the sons of
Zerah the son of Judah, was at the
king's hand in all matters concerning
the people.

25 And as for the villages, with
their fields, some of the people of
Judah lived in Kir'iath-ar'ba and its
villages, and in Dibon and its villages,
and in Jekab'zeel and its villages,
²⁶ and in Jeshua and in Mola'dah and
Beth-pelet, ²⁷ in Ha'zar-shu'al, in
Beer-sheba and its villages, ²⁸ in Ziklag, in Meco'nah and its villages, ²⁹ in
En-rim'mon, in Zorah, in Jarmuth,
³⁰ Zano'ah, Adullam, and their villages, Lachish and its fields, and Aze'-
kah and its villages. So they encamped
from Beer-sheba to the valley of Hinnom. ³¹ The people of Benjamin also
lived from Geba onward, at Michmash, Ai'ja, Bethel and its villages,
³² An'athoth, Nob, Anani'ah, ³³ Hazor, Ramah, Git'taim, ³⁴ Hadid, Zebo'im, Nebal'lat, ³⁵ Lod, and Ono, the
valley of craftsmen. ³⁶ And certain
divisions of the Levites in Judah were
joined to Benjamin.

12 These are the priests and the
Levites who came up with Ze-
rub'babel the son of She-al'ti-el, and
Jeshua: Serai'ah, Jeremiah, Ezra,
² Amari'ah, Malluch, Hattush, ³ Shecani'ah, Rehum, Mer'emoth, ⁴ Iddo,
Gin'nethoi, Abi'jah, ⁵ Mi'jamin, Ma-
adi'ah, Bilgah, ⁶ Shemai'ah, Joi'arib,
Jedai'ah, ⁷ Sallu, Amok, Hilki'ah,
Jedai'ah. These were the chiefs of the
priests and of their brethren in the days
of Jeshua.

8 And the Levites: Jeshua, Bin'-
nui, Kad'mi-el, Sherebi'ah, Judah,
and Mattani'ah, who with his brethren was in charge of the songs of
thanksgiving. ⁹ And Bakbuki'ah and
Unno their brethren stood opposite
them in the service. ¹⁰ And Jeshua
was the father of Joi'akim, Joi'akim
the father of Eli'ashib, Eli'ashib the

list. 9,14,22: There was an overseer over each group. 24: *At the king's hand*, i.e. he was one of
the Persian monarch's famous "eyes" reporting on Judean affairs. 25–36: Census of the village
distribution. 12.1–26: An appendix to the census lists, see Ezra 2.36–40. Verses 9 and 24 suggest

father of Joi'ada, ¹¹ Joi'ada the father of Jonathan, and Jonathan the father of Jad'du-a.

12 And in the days of Joi'akim were priests, heads of fathers' houses: of Serai'ah, Merai'ah; of Jeremiah, Hanani'ah; ¹³ of Ezra, Meshul'lam; of Amari'ah, Jehoha'nan; ¹⁴ of Mal'luchi, Jonathan; of Shebani'ah, Joseph; ¹⁵ of Harim, Adna; of Merai'oth, Hel'kai; ¹⁶ of Iddo, Zechari'ah; of Gin'nethon, Meshul'lam; ¹⁷ of Abi'jah, Zichri; of Mini'amin, of Moadi'ah, Pil'tai; ¹⁸ of Bilgah, Sham'mu-a; of Shemai'ah, Jehon'athan; ¹⁹ of Joi'arib, Matte'nai; of Jedai'ah, Uzzi; ²⁰ of Sal'lai, Kal'lai; of Amok, Eber; ²¹ of Hilki'ah, Hashabi'ah; of Jedai'ah, Nethan'el.

22 As for the Levites, in the days of Eli'ashib, Joi'ada, Joha'nan, and Jad'du-a, there were recorded the heads of fathers' houses; also the priests until the reign of Darius the Persian. ²³ The sons of Levi, heads of fathers' houses, were written in the Book of the Chronicles until the days of Joha'nan the son of Eli'ashib. ²⁴ And the chiefs of the Levites: Hashabi'ah, Sherebi'ah, and Jeshua the son of Kad'mi-el, with their brethren over against them, to praise and to give thanks, according to the commandment of David the man of God, watch corresponding to watch. ²⁵ Mattani'ah, Bakbuki'ah, Obadi'ah, Meshul'lam, Talmon, and Akkub were gatekeepers standing guard at the storehouses of the gates. ²⁶ These were in the days of Joi'akim the son of Jeshua son of Jo'zadak, and in the days of Nehemi'ah the governor and of Ezra the priest the scribe.

27 And at the dedication of the wall of Jerusalem they sought the Levites in all their places, to bring them to Jerusalem to celebrate the dedication with gladness, with thanksgivings and with singing, with cymbals, harps, and lyres. ²⁸ And the sons of the singers gathered together from the circuit round Jerusalem and from the villages of the Netoph'athites; ²⁹ also from Beth-gilgal and from the region of Geba and Az'maveth; for the singers had built for themselves villages around Jerusalem. ³⁰ And the priests and the Levites purified themselves; and they purified the people and the gates and the wall.

31 Then I brought up the princes of Judah upon the wall, and appointed two great companies which gave thanks and went in procession. One went to the right upon the wall to the Dung Gate; ³² and after them went Hoshai'ah and half of the princes of Judah, ³³ and Azari'ah, Ezra, Meshul'lam, ³⁴ Judah, Benjamin, Shemai'ah, and Jeremiah, ³⁵ and certain of the priests' sons with trumpets: Zechari'ah the son of Jonathan, son of Shemai'ah, son of Mattani'ah, son of Micai'ah, son of Zaccur, son of Asaph; ³⁶ and his kinsmen, Shemai'ah, Az'arel, Mil'alai, Gil'alai, Ma'ai, Nethan'el, Judah, and Hana'ni, with the musical instruments of David the man of God; and Ezra the scribe went before them. ³⁷ At the Fountain Gate they went up straight before them by the stairs of the city of David, at the ascent of the wall, above the house of David, to the Water Gate on the east.

38 The other company of those who gave thanks went to the left, and I followed them with half of the people, upon the wall, above the Tower of the Ovens, to the Broad Wall, ³⁹ and above the Gate of E'phraim, and by the Old Gate, and by the Fish Gate and the Tower of Hanan'el and the Tower of the Hundred, to the Sheep Gate; and they came to a halt at the

antiphonal singing. **23**: This does not necessarily mean our book of Chronicles. **26**: The phrase *Ezra the priest the scribe* is an editorial insertion.

12.27–43: The dedication of the walls, with music, purification, procession, and sacrifice. **28**: Men from Netophath, southwest of Jerusalem (1 Chr.9.16; Ezra 2.22). **31**: *Two companies,* for they marched in opposite directions and met at the temple. **36**: They used the same kinds of instruments which tradition said belonged to David's time. The reference to Ezra here and in

Gate of the Guard. [40] So both companies of those who gave thanks stood in the house of God, and I and half of the officials with me; [41] and the priests Eli'akim, Ma-asei'ah, Mini'amin, Micai'ah, Eli-o-e'nai, Zechari'ah, and Hanani'ah, with trumpets; [42] and Ma-asei'ah, Shemai'ah, Elea'zar, Uzzi, Jehoha'nan, Malchi'jah, Elam, and Ezer. And the singers sang with Jezrahi'ah as their leader. [43] And they offered great sacrifices that day and rejoiced, for God had made them rejoice with great joy; the women and children also rejoiced. And the joy of Jerusalem was heard afar off.

44 On that day men were appointed over the chambers for the stores, the contributions, the first fruits, and the tithes, to gather into them the portions required by the law for the priests and for the Levites according to the fields of the towns; for Judah rejoiced over the priests and the Levites who ministered. [45] And they performed the service of their God and the service of purification, as did the singers and the gatekeepers, according to the command of David and his son Solomon. [46] For in the days of David and Asaph of old there was a chief of the singers, and there were songs of praise and thanksgiving to God. [47] And all Israel in the days of Zerub'babel and in the days of Nehemi'ah gave the daily portions for the singers and the gatekeepers; and they set apart that which was for the Levites; and the Levites set apart that which was for the sons of Aaron.

13 On that day they read from the book of Moses in the hearing of the people; and in it was found written that no Ammonite or Moabite should ever enter the assembly of God; [2] for they did not meet the children of Israel with bread and water, but hired Balaam against them to curse them— yet our God turned the curse into a blessing. [3] When the people heard the law, they separated from Israel all those of foreign descent.

4 Now before this, Eli'ashib the priest, who was appointed over the chambers of the house of our God, and who was connected with Tobi'ah, [5] prepared for Tobi'ah a large chamber where they had previously put the cereal offering, the frankincense, the vessels, and the tithes of grain, wine, and oil, which were given by commandment to the Levites, singers, and gatekeepers, and the contributions for the priests. [6] While this was taking place I was not in Jerusalem, for in the thirty-second year of Ar-ta-xerx'es king of Babylon I went to the king. And after some time I asked leave of the king [7] and came to Jerusalem, and I then discovered the evil that Eli'ashib had done for Tobi'ah, preparing for him a chamber in the courts of the house of God. [8] And I was very angry, and I threw all the household furniture of Tobi'ah out of the chamber. [9] Then I gave orders and they cleansed the chambers; and I brought back thither the vessels of the house of God, with the cereal offering and the frankincense.

10 I also found out that the portions of the Levites had not been given to them; so that the Levites and the singers, who did the work, had fled each to his field. [11] So I remonstrated with the officials and said, "Why is the house of God forsaken?" And I gath-

---

v. 33 is an editorial insertion. **43:** *Great sacrifices,* see Ezra 6.17. **44–47: Arrangements for temple revenues. 45:** See 2 Chr.8.14, referring back to 1 Chr. chs. 23–26.

   13.1–30: Nehemiah's second administration. Verses 1–3 are introductory to connect with 8.18. **1:** *Written,* compare Dt.23.3–5. **2:** *Balaam,* see Num. chs. 22–24. **4–9:** The ejection of *Tobiah* an Ammonite (2.10). **4:** *Eliashib* is the high priest of 3.1,20; 12.22; Ezra 10.6, and who was connected by marriage with Sanballat (v. 28); in defiance of the law against Ammonites (v. 1), he had allotted Tobiah a temple *chamber.* **6:** Artaxerxes' *thirty-second year,* 433 B.C. (5.14); as he died in 423 the *some time* falls between those two years. **9:** That he *gave orders* proves that his return was with royal authority. **10–14:** Restoration of tithes to the temple staff.

ered them together and set them in their stations. [12] Then all Judah brought the tithe of the grain, wine, and oil into the storehouses. [13] And I appointed as treasurers over the storehouses Shelemi'ah the priest, Zadok the scribe, and Pedai'ah of the Levites, and as their assistant Hanan the son of Zaccur, son of Mattani'ah, for they were counted faithful; and their duty was to distribute to their brethren. [14] Remember me, O my God, concerning this, and wipe not out my good deeds that I have done for the house of my God and for his service.

15 In those days I saw in Judah men treading wine presses on the sabbath, and bringing in heaps of grain and loading them on asses; and also wine, grapes, figs, and all kinds of burdens, which they brought into Jerusalem on the sabbath day; and I warned them on the day when they sold food. [16] Men of Tyre also, who lived in the city, brought in fish and all kinds of wares and sold them on the sabbath to the people of Judah, and in Jerusalem. [17] Then I remonstrated with the nobles of Judah and said to them, "What is this evil thing which you are doing, profaning the sabbath day? [18] Did not your fathers act in this way, and did not our God bring all this evil on us and on this city? Yet you bring more wrath upon Israel by profaning the sabbath."

19 When it began to be dark at the gates of Jerusalem before the sabbath, I commanded that the doors should be shut and gave orders that they should not be opened until after the sabbath. And I set some of my servants over the gates, that no burden might be brought in on the sabbath day. [20] Then the merchants and sellers of all kinds of wares lodged outside Jerusalem once or twice. [21] But I warned them and said to them, "Why do you lodge before the wall? If you

do so again I will lay hands on you." From that time on they did not come on the sabbath. [22] And I commanded the Levites that they should purify themselves and come and guard the gates, to keep the sabbath day holy. Remember this also in my favor, O my God, and spare me according to the greatness of thy steadfast love.

23 In those days also I saw the Jews who had married women of Ashdod, Ammon, and Moab; [24] and half of their children spoke the language of Ashdod, and they could not speak the language of Judah, but the language of each people. [25] And I contended with them and cursed them and beat some of them and pulled out their hair; and I made them take oath in the name of God, saying, "You shall not give your daughters to their sons, or take their daughters for your sons or for yourselves. [26] Did not Solomon king of Israel sin on account of such women? Among the many nations there was no king like him, and he was beloved by his God, and God made him king over all Israel; nevertheless foreign women made even him to sin. [27] Shall we then listen to you and do all this great evil and act treacherously against our God by marrying foreign women?"

28 And one of the sons of Jehoi'ada, the son of Eli'ashib the high priest, was the son-in-law of Sanbal'lat the Hor'onite; therefore I chased him from me. [29] Remember them, O my God, because they have defiled the priesthood and the covenant of the priesthood and the Levites.

30 Thus I cleansed them from everything foreign, and I established the duties of the priests and Levites, each in his work; [31] and I provided for the wood offering, at appointed times, and for the first fruits. Remember me, O my God, for good.

14: *Wipe not out,* see 4.5. **15–22:** Instances of sabbath breaking. **19–20:** Shutting the gates prevented produce from entering the city, a restriction which merchants sought to nullify by trading *outside* the walls. **23–30:** The problem of mixed marriages (10.30; Ezra 9.1–2; 10.2). **25:** Such physical violence is common in Oriental history. **26:** *Solomon,* 1 Kg.11.1–8.

THE BOOK OF ESTHER

In the Hebrew Bible, Esther comes last of the five rolls (megillōth) which are read at the great festivals of the Jewish year. It is the roll for Purim, a secular feast celebrating deliverance from a subtly planned anti-Semitic pogrom. Its reception into Scripture was long disputed by the Rabbis, for it contains no reference to the most precious things in Jewish religion and does not even mention the name of God. In the Greek Bible, it has its place among the historical books, and has been lengthened by the addition of passages intended to make it a more religious book. Our English Bible includes these, "The Additions to the Book of Esther," among the Apocrypha.

Some have thought the book was written in Maccabean times to celebrate Jewish triumph over the Seleucids (see "Survey of . . . Bible Lands," § 15), but it is probably earlier and seems to have been written as propaganda for the observance in Palestine of a festival, brought home by Jews from the Dispersion, which they called Purim and celebrated on the 14th or 15th of Adar (in February–March). It is not history, but a legend, set back early in the Persian period, intended to explain the origin and significance of Purim. Though embellished with numerous fictional devices, it may well rest on an historical account of some local deliverance of the Jews in Persia, for there is external evidence of a certain Marduka holding an official post at Susa under Xerxes I.

N THE DAYS OF AHASU-E′RUS, THE Ahasu-e′rus who reigned from India to Ethiopia over one hundred and twenty-seven provinces, [2] in those days when King Ahasu-e′rus sat on his royal throne in Susa the capital, [3] in the third year of his reign he gave a banquet for all his princes and servants, the army chiefs[a] of Persia and Media and the nobles and governors of the provinces being before him, [4] while he showed the riches of his royal glory and the splendor and pomp of his majesty for many days, a hundred and eighty days. [5] And when these days were completed, the king gave for all the people present in Susa the capital, both great and small, a banquet lasting for seven days, in the court of the garden of the king's palace. [6] There were white cotton curtains and blue hangings caught up with cords of fine linen and purple to silver rings[b] and marble pillars, and also couches of gold and silver on a mosaic pavement of porphyry, marble, mother-of-pearl and precious stones. [7] Drinks were served in golden goblets, goblets of different kinds, and the royal wine was lavished according to the bounty of the king. [8] And drinking was according to the law, no one was compelled; for the king had given orders to all the officials of his palace to do as every man desired. [9] Queen Vashti also gave a banquet for the women in the palace which belonged to King Ahasu-e′rus.

10 On the seventh day, when the heart of the king was merry with wine, he commanded Mehu′man, Biztha, Harbo′na, Bigtha and Abag′tha, Zethar and Carkas, the seven eunuchs who served King Ahasu-e′rus as chamberlains, [11] to bring Queen Vashti before the king with her royal crown, in order to show the peoples and the princes her beauty; for she was fair to

a Heb the army   b Or rods

1.1–9: Ahasuerus' feast. *Ahasuerus* (Ezra 4.6; Dan.9.1) is Xerxes I (485–464 B.C.), whose Persian empire, from *India*, i.e. the Indus valley, to *Ethiopia*, the modern Nubia, included some twenty satrapies (Herodotus, *Hist*. III, 89), subdivided into *provinces*. 2: Persepolis was his capital; Susa, a citadel (*capital*) in Elam, was his winter residence. 3: Greek writers mention fabulous feasts given by Persian kings. 5: Excavations at *Susa* have uncovered such a *court*. 9: *Vashti* is an Elamitish name, perhaps of a royal concubine, for Xerxes' *queen* was Amestris, a Persian (Herodotus, *Hist*. VII, 61).

1.10–2.4: Vashti's fall. The names here, as elsewhere in this book, are attempts to reproduce Persian names. 11: *Crown* indicates that she was to appear in royal attire. 13: *Wise men*, prob-

behold. [12] But Queen Vashti refused to come at the king's command conveyed by the eunuchs. At this the king was enraged, and his anger burned within him.

13 Then the king said to the wise men who knew the times–for this was the king's procedure toward all who were versed in law and judgment, [14] the men next to him being Carshe'na, Shethar, Adma'tha, Tarshish, Meres, Marse'na, and Memu'can, the seven princes of Persia and Media, who saw the king's face, and sat first in the kingdom–: [15] "According to the law, what is to be done to Queen Vashti, because she has not performed the command of King Ahasu-e'rus conveyed by the eunuchs?" [16] Then Memu'can said in presence of the king and the princes, "Not only to the king has Queen Vashti done wrong, but also to all the princes and all the peoples who are in all the provinces of King Ahasue'rus. [17] For this deed of the queen will be made known to all women, causing them to look with contempt upon their husbands, since they will say, 'King Ahasu-e'rus commanded Queen Vashti to be brought before him, and she did not come.' [18] This very day the ladies of Persia and Media who have heard of the queen's behavior will be telling it to all the king's princes, and there will be contempt and wrath in plenty. [19] If it please the king, let a royal order go forth from him, and let it be written among the laws of the Persians and the Medes so that it may not be altered, that Vashti is to come no more before King Ahasu-e'rus; and let the king give her royal position to another who is better than she.

[20] So when the decree made by the king is proclaimed throughout all his kingdom, vast as it is, all women will give honor to their husbands, high and low." [21] This advice pleased the king and the princes, and the king did as Memu'can proposed; [22] he sent letters to all the royal provinces, to every province in its own script and to every people in its own language, that every man be lord in his own house and speak according to the language of his people.

2 After these things, when the anger of King Ahasu-e'rus had abated, he remembered Vashti and what she had done and what had been decreed against her. [2] Then the king's servants who attended him said, "Let beautiful young virgins be sought out for the king. [3] And let the king appoint officers in all the provinces of his kingdom to gather all the beautiful young virgins to the harem in Susa the capital, under custody of Hegai the king's eunuch who is in charge of the women; let their ointments be given them. [4] And let the maiden who pleases the king be queen instead of Vashti." This pleased the king, and he did so.

5 Now there was a Jew in Susa the capital whose name was Mor'decai, the son of Ja'ir, son of Shim'e-i, son of Kish, a Benjaminite, [6] who had been carried away from Jerusalem among the captives carried away with Jeconi'ah king of Judah, whom Nebuchadnez'zar king of Babylon had carried away. [7] He had brought up Hadas'sah, that is Esther, the daughter of his uncle, for she had neither father nor mother; the maiden was beautiful and lovely, and when her father and her

---

ably his seven privy counselors (Ezra 7.14; Herodotus, *Hist*. III, 31,84). **19:** This belief in the immutability of Medo-Persian law appears in 8.8; Dan.6.8. **22:** Aramaic was normally used for such official correspondence; so here, as in 3.12 and 8.9, there is rhetorical exaggeration. **2.2:** *Servants*, i.e. his pages, not his counselors. **3,9:** *Harem*, lit. "house of women"; *ointments* means cosmetics.

    2.5–23: Mordecai and Esther. They were cousins with names derived from the deities Marduk and Ishtar, who also were cousins. That, like Saul, he was a Benjaminite, is emphasized to prepare readers for the enmity of Haman, an Amalekite of the Agag family, Saul's enemy (see 3.1–15 n.). **6:** *Jeconiah* is Jehoiachin (2 Kg.24.6); so Mordecai was about one hundred and twenty years old. **7:** He was her foster-father (Is.49.23). **10:** Esther's concealment of her race

mother died, Mor'decai adopted her as his own daughter. [8] So when the king's order and his edict were proclaimed, and when many maidens were gathered in Susa the capital in custody of Hegai, Esther also was taken into the king's palace and put in custody of Hegai who had charge of the women. [9] And the maiden pleased him and won his favor; and he quickly provided her with her ointments and her portion of food, and with seven chosen maids from the king's palace, and advanced her and her maids to the best place in the harem. [10] Esther had not made known her people or kindred, for Mor'decai had charged her not to make it known. [11] And every day Mor'decai walked in front of the court of the harem, to learn how Esther was and how she fared.

12 Now when the turn came for each maiden to go in to King Ahasu-e'rus, after being twelve months under the regulations for the women, since this was the regular period of their beautifying, six months with oil of myrrh and six months with spices and ointments for women— [13] when the maiden went in to the king in this way she was given whatever she desired to take with her from the harem to the king's palace. [14] In the evening she went, and in the morning she came back to the second harem in custody of Sha-ash'gaz the king's eunuch who was in charge of the concubines; she did not go in to the king again, unless the king delighted in her and she was summoned by name.

15 When the turn came for Esther the daughter of Ab'ihail the uncle of Mor'decai, who had adopted her as his own daughter, to go in to the king,

she asked for nothing except what Hegai the king's eunuch, who had charge of the women, advised. Now Esther found favor in the eyes of all who saw her. [16] And when Esther was taken to King Ahasu-e'rus into his royal palace in the tenth month, which is the month of Tebeth, in the seventh year of his reign, [17] the king loved Esther more than all the women, and she found grace and favor in his sight more than all the virgins, so that he set the royal crown on her head and made her queen instead of Vashti. [18] Then the king gave a great banquet to all his princes and servants; it was Esther's banquet. He also granted a remission of taxes[c] to the provinces, and gave gifts with royal liberality.

19 When the virgins were gathered together the second time, Mor'decai was sitting at the king's gate. [20] Now Esther had not made known her kindred or her people, as Mor'decai had charged her; for Esther obeyed Mor'decai just as when she was brought up by him. [21] And in those days, as Mor'decai was sitting at the king's gate, Bigthan and Teresh, two of the king's eunuchs, who guarded the threshold, became angry and sought to lay hands on King Ahasu-e'rus. [22] And this came to the knowledge of Mor'decai, and he told it to Queen Esther, and Esther told the king in the name of Mor'decai. [23] When the affair was investigated and found to be so, the men were both hanged on the gallows. And it was recorded in the Book of the Chronicles in the presence of the king.

3 After these things King Ahasu-e'rus promoted Haman the Ag'agite, the son of Hammeda'tha, and ad-

c Or a holiday

---

is a necessary literary device (v. 20). **11:** Mordecai's closeness to the *harem* suggests that he was a minor official, perhaps a eunuch gatekeeper (vv. 19,21; 6.10). **12:** *Their beautifying*, apparently by massage. **16:** *Tebeth* (December-January), as all the month-names in this book, is a Babylonian name. **18:** This *banquet* being a wedding feast, the king favors his subjects with largesse. **21:** *The threshold*, that of the bed-chamber. Xerxes actually fell victim to such a conspiracy of bed-chamber servants, as have other Oriental potentates. **23:** *On the gallows*, lit. "on a tree," i.e. impalement, the normal form of punishment in Persia for political offenders. *Chronicles*, such records kept by court scribes in Persia are mentioned by Greek writers.

3.1–15: Haman and Mordecai. For the Benjaminite-Agagite enmity see 1 Sam.15.7–9.

vanced him and set his seat above all the princes who were with him. ² And all the king's servants who were at the king's gate bowed down and did obeisance to Haman; for the king had so commanded concerning him. But Mor'decai did not bow down or do obeisance. ³ Then the king's servants who were at the king's gate said to Mor'decai, "Why do you transgress the king's command?" ⁴ And when they spoke to him day after day and he would not listen to them, they told Haman, in order to see whether Mor'decai's words would avail; for he had told them that he was a Jew. ⁵ And when Haman saw that Mor'decai did not bow down or do obeisance to him, Haman was filled with fury. ⁶ But he disdained to lay hands on Mor'decai alone. So, as they had made known to him the people of Mor'decai, Haman sought to destroy all the Jews, the people of Mor'decai, throughout the whole kingdom of Ahasu-e'rus.

7 In the first month, which is the month of Nisan, in the twelfth year of King Ahasu-e'rus, they cast Pur, that is the lot, before Haman day after day; and they cast it month after month till the twelfth month, which is the month of Adar. ⁸ Then Haman said to King Ahasu-e'rus, "There is a certain people scattered abroad and dispersed among the peoples in all the provinces of your kingdom; their laws are different from those of every other people, and they do not keep the king's laws, so that it is not for the king's profit to tolerate them. ⁹ If it please the king, let it be decreed that they be destroyed, and I will pay ten thousand talents of silver into the hands of those who have charge of the king's business, that they may put it into the king's treasuries." ¹⁰ So the king took his signet ring from his hand and gave it to Haman the Ag'agite, the son of Hammeda'tha, the enemy of the Jews. ¹¹ And the king said to Haman, "The money is given to you, the people also, to do with them as it seems good to you."

12 Then the king's secretaries were summoned on the thirteenth day of the first month, and an edict, according to all that Haman commanded, was written to the king's satraps and to the governors over all the provinces and to the princes of all the peoples, to every province in its own script and every people in its own language; it was written in the name of King Ahasu-e'rus and sealed with the king's ring. ¹³ Letters were sent by couriers to all the king's provinces, to destroy, to slay, and to annihilate all Jews, young and old, women and children, in one day, the thirteenth day of the twelfth month, which is the month of Adar, and to plunder their goods. ¹⁴ A copy of the document was to be issued as a decree in every province by proclamation to all the peoples to be ready for that day. ¹⁵ The couriers went in haste by order of the king, and the decree was issued in Susa the capital. And the king and Haman sat down to drink; but the city of Susa was perplexed.

4 When Mor'decai learned all that had been done, Mor'decai rent his clothes and put on sackcloth and ashes, and went out into the midst of the city, wailing with a loud and bitter cry;

Haman was *advanced* to be grand vizier, to whom lower officials must make obeisance, an honor which Mordecai as a Benjaminite would not pay an Agagite (see 2.5–23 n.; 9.16 n.). **6**: Haman's indignation naturally suggested a pogrom of *all the Jews*. **7**: *Pur* is an Akkadian word for lot, and casting lots was not irreligious (1 Sam.14.42; Acts 1.26; Herodotus, *Hist.* III, 128). The lot was to decide an appropriate date for the pogrom. **9**: To clinch his argument Haman offers a bribe of about $18,000,000. **10**: *His ring* was his signet ring which gave validity to documents (8.2,8; Gen.41.42). **11**: The king refuses the bribe but authorizes the pogrom. **13**: The *couriers* carrying the *edict* were the famous post service organized by Cyrus. The apocryphal Additions to the Book of Esther give the text of the documents. **14**: The *copy* was the local public distribution of the *edict*.

4.1–17: The appeal to Esther. 1: These are traditional Oriental manifestations of grief and

2 he went up to the entrance of the king's gate, for no one might enter the king's gate clothed with sackcloth. 3 And in every province, wherever the king's command and his decree came, there was great mourning among the Jews, with fasting and weeping and lamenting, and most of them lay in sackcloth and ashes.

4 When Esther's maids and her eunuchs came and told her, the queen was deeply distressed; she sent garments to clothe Mor'decai, so that he might take off his sackcloth, but he would not accept them. 5 Then Esther called for Hathach, one of the king's eunuchs, who had been appointed to attend her, and ordered him to go to Mor'decai to learn what this was and why it was. 6 Hathach went out to Mor'decai in the open square of the city in front of the king's gate, 7 and Mor'decai told him all that had happened to him, and the exact sum of money that Haman had promised to pay into the king's treasuries for the destruction of the Jews. 8 Mor'decai also gave him a copy of the written decree issued in Susa for their destruction, that he might show it to Esther and explain it to her and charge her to go to the king to make supplication to him and entreat him for her people. 9 And Hathach went and told Esther what Mor'decai had said. 10 Then Esther spoke to Hathach and gave him a message for Mor'decai, saying, 11 "All the king's servants and the people of the king's provinces know that if any man or woman goes to the king inside the inner court without being called, there is but one law; all alike are to be put to death, except the one to whom the king holds out the golden scepter that he may live. And I have not been called to come in to the king these thirty days." 12 And they told Mor'decai what Esther had said. 13 Then Mor'decai told them to return answer to Esther, "Think not that in the king's palace you will escape any more than all the other Jews. 14 For if you keep silence at such a time as this, relief and deliverance will rise for the Jews from another quarter, but you and your father's house will perish. And who knows whether you have not come to the kingdom for such a time as this?" 15 Then Esther told them to reply to Mor'decai, 16 "Go, gather all the Jews to be found in Susa, and hold a fast on my behalf, and neither eat nor drink for three days, night or day. I and my maids will also fast as you do. Then I will go to the king, though it is against the law; and if I perish, I perish." 17 Mor'decai then went away and did everything as Esther had ordered him.

5 On the third day Esther put on her royal robes and stood in the inner court of the king's palace, opposite the king's hall. The king was sitting on his royal throne inside the palace opposite the entrance to the palace; 2 and when the king saw Queen Esther standing in the court, she found favor in his sight and he held out to Esther the golden scepter that was in his hand. Then Esther approached and touched the top of the scepter. 3 And the king said to her, "What is it, Queen Esther? What is your request? It shall be given you, even to the half of my kingdom." 4 And Esther said, "If it please the king, let the king and Haman come this day to a dinner that I have prepared for the king." 5 Then said the king,

---

mourning, which render one ritually unclean, so Mordecai (v. 2) could not *enter the king's gate.*
11: Interdiction to enter without being summoned was a security precaution. **14:** *From another quarter* probably refers to Divine providence. The apocryphal Additions to the Book of Esther insert here the prayers of Esther and Mordecai.

    5.1–8: Esther before the king. 1: By appearing unbidden she had violated custom; so she *stood* at the *inner court* to await the monarch's reaction. **3,6:** *The half of my kingdom* (7.2) is a customary hyperbole (compare Mk.6.23). **4,8:** No subtle reason need be sought for the first and second *dinner,* nor for Haman's being the only guest; these are but literary embellishments needful to the story.

"Bring Haman quickly, that we may do as Esther desires." So the king and Haman came to the dinner that Esther had prepared. [6] And as they were drinking wine, the king said to Esther, "What is your petition? It shall be granted you. And what is your request? Even to the half of my kingdom, it shall be fulfilled." [7] But Esther said, "My petition and my request is: [8] If I have found favor in the sight of the king, and if it please the king to grant my petition and fulfil my request, let the king and Haman come tomorrow[d] to the dinner which I will prepare for them, and tomorrow I will do as the king has said."

9 And Haman went out that day joyful and glad of heart. But when Haman saw Mor'decai in the king's gate, that he neither rose nor trembled before him, he was filled with wrath against Mor'decai. [10] Nevertheless Haman restrained himself, and went home; and he sent and fetched his friends and his wife Zeresh. [11] And Haman recounted to them the splendor of his riches, the number of his sons, all the promotions with which the king had honored him, and how he had advanced him above the princes and the servants of the king. [12] And Haman added, "Even Queen Esther let no one come with the king to the banquet she prepared but myself. And tomorrow also I am invited by her together with the king. [13] Yet all this does me no good, so long as I see Mor'decai the Jew sitting at the king's gate." [14] Then his wife Zeresh and all his friends said to him, "Let a gallows fifty cubits high be made, and in the morning tell the king to have Mor'decai hanged upon it; then go merrily with the king to the dinner." This counsel pleased Haman, and he had the gallows made.

6 On that night the king could not sleep; and he gave orders to bring the book of memorable deeds, the chronicles, and they were read before the king. [2] And it was found written how Mor'decai had told about Bigthana and Teresh, two of the king's eunuchs, who guarded the threshold, and who had sought to lay hands upon King Ahasu-e'rus. [3] And the king said, "What honor or dignity has been bestowed on Mor'decai for this?" The king's servants who attended him said, "Nothing has been done for him." [4] And the king said, "Who is in the court?" Now Haman had just entered the outer court of the king's palace to speak to the king about having Mor'decai hanged on the gallows that he had prepared for him. [5] So the king's servants told him, "Haman is there, standing in the court." And the king said, "Let him come in." [6] So Haman came in, and the king said to him, "What shall be done to the man whom the king delights to honor?" And Haman said to himself, "Whom would the king delight to honor more than me?" [7] and Haman said to the king, "For the man whom the king delights to honor, [8] let royal robes be brought, which the king has worn, and the horse which the king has ridden, and on whose head a royal crown is set; [9] and let the robes and the horse be handed over to one of the king's most noble princes; let him[e] array the man

d Gk: Heb lacks *tomorrow*   *e* Heb *them*

5.9–14: **Haman's exaltation and chagrin. 10:** Haman's boasting before *his friends* is characteristically Oriental. They are the *wise men* of 6.13. **14:** *Gallows*, see 2.23 n. The *fifty cubits*, i.e. eighty-three feet, is hyperbole for literary effect. Haman could prepare this, but only the monarch could condemn men.

    6.1–14: Mordecai's triumph. The sleeplessness of kings is a common motif in Oriental tales. It and the numerous coincidences which here accumulate are literary devices. **3:** Herodotus (*Hist.* VIII, 85,90) records how Persian monarchs kept records of notable services rendered. **4:** The inquiry, *Who is in the court?* merely means, What official is currently in attendance? Haman's eagerness drove him to early attendance, and his superior rank gave him precedence. **8:** The bestowal of *robes* of honor was common in ancient times (Gen.41.42; 1 Sam.18.4), and is still practiced. The *royal crown* here was an ornament for the horse, such as is pictured on

whom the king delights to honor, and let him[e] conduct the man on horseback through the open square of the city, proclaiming before him: 'Thus shall it be done to the man whom the king delights to honor.'" [10] Then the king said to Haman, "Make haste, take the robes and the horse, as you have said, and do so to Mor'decai the Jew who sits at the king's gate. Leave out nothing that you have mentioned." [11] So Haman took the robes and the horse, and he arrayed Mor'decai and made him ride through the open square of the city, proclaiming, "Thus shall it be done to the man whom the king delights to honor."

12 Then Mor'decai returned to the king's gate. But Haman hurried to his house, mourning and with his head covered. [13] And Haman told his wife Zeresh and all his friends everything that had befallen him. Then his wise men and his wife Zeresh said to him, "If Mor'decai, before whom you have begun to fall, is of the Jewish people, you will not prevail against him but will surely fall before him."

14 While they were yet talking with him, the king's eunuchs arrived and brought Haman in haste to the banquet that Esther had prepared.

7 So the king and Haman went in to feast with Queen Esther. [2] And on the second day, as they were drinking wine, the king again said to Esther, "What is your petition, Queen Esther? It shall be granted you. And what is your request? Even to the half of my kingdom, it shall be fulfilled." [3] Then Queen Esther answered, "If I have found favor in your sight, O king, and

if it please the king, let my life be given me at my petition, and my people at my request. [4] For we are sold, I and my people, to be destroyed, to be slain, and to be annihilated. If we had been sold merely as slaves, men and women, I would have held my peace; for our affliction is not to be compared with the loss to the king." [5] Then King Ahasue'rus said to Queen Esther, "Who is he, and where is he, that would presume to do this?" [6] And Esther said, "A foe and enemy! This wicked Haman!" Then Haman was in terror before the king and the queen. [7] And the king rose from the feast in wrath and went into the palace garden; but Haman stayed to beg his life from Queen Esther, for he saw that evil was determined against him by the king. [8] And the king returned from the palace garden to the place where they were drinking wine, as Haman was falling on the couch where Esther was; and the king said, "Will he even assault the queen in my presence, in my own house?" As the words left the mouth of the king, they covered Haman's face. [9] Then said Harbo'na, one of the eunuchs in attendance on the king, "Moreover, the gallows which Haman has prepared for Mor'decai, whose word saved the king, is standing in Haman's house, fifty cubits high." [10] And the king said, "Hang him on that." So they hanged Haman on the gallows which he had prepared for Mor'decai. Then the anger of the king abated.

8 On that day King Ahasu-e'rus gave to Queen Esther the house of

e Heb *them*

---

monuments. **12:** *Mourning*, i.e. weeping with chagrin. To cover the head was a sign of grief (2 Sam.15.30; Jer.14.4). **14:** It was an Oriental custom for guests to be brought to an entertainment (Lk.14.17).

7.1–10: Haman's fall. 4: *We are* (have been) *sold* is a reference to Haman's bribe. Had Haman planned to sell the Jews into slavery to enrich the royal treasury, Esther would not have intervened; but planned destruction changes the situation. **6:** *Enemy* is used to recall the ancient enmity of Agag and the Amalekites (see 3.1–15 n.). **8:** *Falling* as a suppliant at someone's feet was a common custom (8.3; 1 Sam.25.23,24; 2 Kg.4.27; Mk.7.25). That they covered the face of one doomed indicates a Greco-Roman custom rather than Persian. **9:** It was inevitable that some servant would think of this "poetic justice."

8.1–17: The rise of Mordecai and the revocation of the edict. 1: Herodotus (*Hist.* III, 129)

Haman, the enemy of the Jews. And Mor'decai came before the king, for Esther had told what he was to her; [2] and the king took off his signet ring, which he had taken from Haman, and gave it to Mor'decai. And Esther set Mor'decai over the house of Haman.

3 Then Esther spoke again to the king; she fell at his feet and besought him with tears to avert the evil design of Haman the Ag'agite and the plot which he had devised against the Jews. [4] And the king held out the golden scepter to Esther, [5] and Esther rose and stood before the king. And she said, "If it please the king, and if I have found favor in his sight, and if the thing seem right before the king, and I be pleasing in his eyes, let an order be written to revoke the letters devised by Haman the Ag'agite, the son of Hammeda'tha, which he wrote to destroy the Jews who are in all the provinces of the king. [6] For how can I endure to see the calamity that is coming to my people? Or how can I endure to see the destruction of my kindred?" [7] Then King Ahasu-e'rus said to Queen Esther and to Mor'decai the Jew, "Behold, I have given Esther the house of Haman, and they have hanged him on the gallows, because he would lay hands on the Jews. [8] And you may write as you please with regard to the Jews, in the name of the king, and seal it with the king's ring; for an edict written in the name of the king and sealed with the king's ring cannot be revoked."

9 The king's secretaries were summoned at that time, in the third month, which is the month of Sivan, on the twenty-third day; and an edict was written according to all that Mor'decai commanded concerning the Jews to the satraps and the governors and the princes of the provinces from India to Ethiopia, a hundred and twenty-seven provinces, to every province in its own script and to every people in its own language, and also to the Jews in their script and their language. [10] The writing was in the name of King Ahasu-e'rus and sealed with the king's ring, and letters were sent by mounted couriers riding on swift horses that were used in the king's service, bred from the royal stud. [11] By these the king allowed the Jews who were in every city to gather and defend their lives, to destroy, to slay, and to annihilate any armed force of any people or province that might attack them, with their children and women, and to plunder their goods, [12] upon one day throughout all the provinces of King Ahasu-e'rus, on the thirteenth day of the twelfth month, which is the month of Adar. [13] A copy of what was written was to be issued as a decree in every province, and by proclamation to all peoples, and the Jews were to be ready on that day to avenge themselves upon their enemies. [14] So the couriers, mounted on their swift horses that were used in the king's service, rode out in haste, urged by the king's command; and the decree was issued in Susa the capital.

15 Then Mor'decai went out from the presence of the king in royal robes of blue and white, with a great golden crown and a mantle of fine linen and purple, while the city of Susa shouted and rejoiced. [16] The Jews had light and gladness and joy and honor. [17] And in every province and in every city, wherever the king's command and

---

mentions the property of criminals being confiscated. The transference of the signet ring indicates promotion of Mordecai as grand vizier. **5:** Esther subtly suggests that the edict was not really his but *devised by Haman.* **8:** The king rejects this subterfuge, accepts the responsibility, but neutralizes the edict by new instructions. **10:** Greek writers mention the *horses* of the Persian postal system. **12:** The date is carefully given, for it is important for the Purim festival. After v. 12 the apocryphal Additions to the Book of Esther insert the text of the king's letter. **15:** Mordecai appears in his state robes, *crown* here being the viziral turban. **17:** *A feast and a holiday* contrast with the fasting and lamentation of 4.3. The improbability of many Persians becoming proselytes leads some to translate the verb as "joined themselves to," i.e. took the part of the Jews (9.27).

his edict came, there was gladness and joy among the Jews, a feast and a holiday. And many from the peoples of the country declared themselves Jews, for the fear of the Jews had fallen upon them.

9 Now in the twelfth month, which is the month of Adar, on the thirteenth day of the same, when the king's command and edict were about to be executed, on the very day when the enemies of the Jews hoped to get the mastery over them, but which had been changed to a day when the Jews should get the mastery over their foes, ² the Jews gathered in their cities throughout all the provinces of King Ahasu-e'rus to lay hands on such as sought their hurt. And no one could make a stand against them, for the fear of them had fallen upon all peoples. ³ All the princes of the provinces and the satraps and the governors and the royal officials also helped the Jews, for the fear of Mor'decai had fallen upon them. ⁴ For Mor'decai was great in the king's house, and his fame spread throughout all the provinces; for the man Mor'decai grew more and more powerful. ⁵ So the Jews smote all their enemies with the sword, slaughtering, and destroying them, and did as they pleased to those who hated them. ⁶ In Susa the capital itself the Jews slew and destroyed five hundred men, ⁷ and also slew Par-shan-da'tha and Dalphon and Aspa'tha ⁸ and Pora'-tha and Ada'lia and Arida'tha ⁹ and Parmash'ta and Ar'isai and Ar'idai and Vaiza'tha, ¹⁰ the ten sons of Haman the son of Hammeda'tha, the enemy of the Jews; but they laid no hand on the plunder.

11 That very day the number of those slain in Susa the capital was reported to the king. ¹² And the king said to Queen Esther, "In Susa the capital the Jews have slain five hundred men and also the ten sons of Haman. What then have they done in the rest of the king's provinces! Now what is your petition? It shall be granted you. And what further is your request? It shall be fulfilled." ¹³ And Esther said, "If it please the king, let the Jews who are in Susa be allowed tomorrow also to do according to this day's edict. And let the ten sons of Haman be hanged on the gallows." ¹⁴ So the king commanded this to be done; a decree was issued in Susa, and the ten sons of Haman were hanged. ¹⁵ The Jews who were in Susa gathered also on the fourteenth day of the month of Adar and they slew three hundred men in Susa; but they laid no hands on the plunder.

16 Now the other Jews who were in the king's provinces also gathered to defend their lives, and got relief from their enemies, and slew seventy-five thousand of those who hated them; but they laid no hands on the plunder. ¹⁷ This was on the thirteenth day of the month of Adar, and on the fourteenth day they rested and made that a day of feasting and gladness. ¹⁸ But the Jews who were in Susa gathered on the thirteenth day and on the fourteenth, and rested on the fifteenth day, making that a day of feasting and gladness. ¹⁹ Therefore the Jews of the villages, who live in the open towns, hold the fourteenth day of the month of Adar as a day for gladness and feasting and holiday-making, and a day on which they send choice portions to one another.

20 And Mor'decai recorded these things, and sent letters to all the Jews

---

9.1–32: Destruction of the enemies and inauguration of the feast of Purim. 1: The important date is again given (compare 8.12). **3–5:** *The royal officials*, anxious to please the new vizier, *helped the Jews.* **7:** The names of Haman's sons, represented as Persian names, are written peculiarly in the Hebrew text, favoring cryptic interpretations. **15:** The second day's slaughter is probably a device to explain why the city Jews had a two-day Purim celebration but the country Jews only one. **16:** The emphasis here, as in vv. 10,15, that the Jews did not *plunder* seems a reminder of the Agag story, where they plundered to their own hurt (1 Sam.15.9). **19,22:** *Choice portions*, i.e. dainties, gifts of food-stuffs (Neh.8.10). **20–32:** The official institu-

who were in all the provinces of King Ahasu-e′rus, both near and far, ²¹ enjoining them that they should keep the fourteenth day of the month Adar and also the fifteenth day of the same, year by year, ²² as the days on which the Jews got relief from their enemies, and as the month that had been turned for them from sorrow into gladness and from mourning into a holiday; that they should make them days of feasting and gladness, days for sending choice portions to one another and gifts to the poor.

23 So the Jews undertook to do as they had begun, and as Mor′decai had written to them. ²⁴ For Haman the Ag′agite, the son of Hammeda′tha, the enemy of all the Jews, had plotted against the Jews to destroy them, and had cast Pur, that is the lot, to crush and destroy them; ²⁵ but when Esther came before the king, he gave orders in writing that his wicked plot which he had devised against the Jews should come upon his own head, and that he and his sons should be hanged on the gallows. ²⁶ Therefore they called these days Purim, after the term Pur. And therefore, because of all that was written in this letter, and of what they had faced in this matter, and of what had befallen them, ²⁷ the Jews ordained and took it upon themselves and their descendants and all who joined them, that without fail they would keep these two days according to what was written and at the time appointed every year, ²⁸ that these days should be re-

membered and kept throughout every generation, in every family, province, and city, and that these days of Purim should never fall into disuse among the Jews, nor should the commemoration of these days cease among their descendants.

29 Then Queen Esther, the daughter of Ab′ihail, and Mor′decai the Jew gave full written authority, confirming this second letter about Purim. ³⁰ Letters were sent to all the Jews, to the hundred and twenty-seven provinces of the kingdom of Ahasu-e′rus, in words of peace and truth, ³¹ that these days of Purim should be observed at their appointed seasons, as Mor′decai the Jew and Queen Esther enjoined upon the Jews, and as they had laid down for themselves and for their descendants, with regard to their fasts and their lamenting. ³² The command of Queen Esther fixed these practices of Purim, and it was recorded in writing.

10 King Ahasu-e′rus laid tribute on the land and on the coastlands of the sea. ² And all the acts of his power and might, and the full account of the high honor of Mor′decai, to which the king advanced him, are they not written in the Book of the Chronicles of the kings of Media and Persia? ³ For Mor′decai the Jew was next in rank to King Ahasu-e′rus, and he was great among the Jews and popular with the multitude of his brethren, for he sought the welfare of his people and spoke peace to all his people.

---

tion of Purim (an addition to the book from a different source). Mordecai as vizier takes the initiative; Esther with queenly authority confirms the arrangements, so Mordecai writes to the Jewish communities and Esther follows with a letter. This emphasis on the *written* word is doubtless intended to legalize a festival not mentioned in the Torah.

10.1–3: Conclusion. A paragraph on the continued greatness of Xerxes and fame of Mordecai. After 10.3 the apocryphal Additions to the Book of Esther append Mordecai's soliloquy.

THE BOOK OF JOB

The book of Job does not attempt to explain the mystery of suffering or to "justify the ways of God with men." It aims at probing the depths of faith in spite of suffering. The ancient folktale of a patient Job (1.1–2.13; 42.7–17; Jas. 5.11) circulated orally among oriental sages in the second millennium B.C. and was probably written down in Hebrew at the time of David and Solomon or a century later (about 1000–800 B.C.). An anonymous poet of the Exile sixth century B.C. used it as a setting for the discussion between an impatient Job and his three friends (3.1–31.40) and the Lord's discourses from the whirlwind (38.1–42.6). A later poet contributed Elihu's speeches (32.1–37.24).

The storyteller asked, "Does [man] fear God for nought?" (1.9). The poet echoed the question, "What is the Almighty, that we should serve him? And what profit do we get if we pray to him?" (21.15). Unlike the hero of the folktale who is rewarded materially for his virtues, the Job of the poem demands justice, and his final challenge shows that he regards religion and morality as man's claim for happiness (29.1–31.40). Job renounces his defiance only after the Lord asks, "Will you condemn me that you may be justified?" (40.8). Job is satisfied without self-vindication by an experience of immediate communion with God, not unlike that of the great prophets: "Now my eye sees thee" (42.5).

In the poetic language of the book, God is at work in the universe, even "to bring rain on a land where no man is" (38.26), and he is aware of evil (personified by the monsters Behemoth and Leviathan, 40.15–41.34). At the same time, he cares for Job so fully that he reveals himself personally to him and shares with him the vision of his cosmic responsibilities. A God who confesses his burdens to man is a God who is profoundly involved in the destiny of man. He is not an impassive force. In the presence of holiness and creative love, virtuous man surrenders his pride in adoration. In his own way the poet conveyed a view of sin which transcends morality, the awareness of which is possible only in the context of faith.

HERE WAS A MAN IN THE LAND OF Uz, whose name was Job; and that man was blameless and upright, one who feared God, and turned away from evil. ² There were born to him seven sons and three daughters. ³ He had seven thousand sheep, three thousand camels, five hundred yoke of oxen, and five hundred she-asses, and very many servants; so that this man was the greatest of all the people of the east. ⁴ His sons used to go and hold a feast in the house of each on his day; and they would send and invite their three sisters to eat and drink with them. ⁵ And when the days of the feast had run their course, Job would send and sanctify them, and he would rise early in the morning and offer burnt offerings according to the number of them all; for Job said, "It may be that my sons have sinned, and cursed God in their hearts." Thus Job did continually.

6 Now there was a day when the sons of God came to present themselves before the LORD, and Satan[a] also came among them. ⁷ The LORD said to Satan, "Whence have you come?" Satan answered the LORD, "From going to and fro on the earth, and from walking up and down on it." ⁸ And the LORD said to Satan, "Have you considered my servant Job, that there is none like him on the earth, a blameless and upright man, who fears God and turns away from evil?" ⁹ Then Satan answered the LORD, "Does Job fear God for nought? ¹⁰ Hast thou not put a hedge about him and his house and all

a Heb the adversary

1.1–2.13: The prologue. A blameless man is deprived of wealth, posterity, and health, but keeps his faith in God. 1: *The land of Uz* is probably Edom, although some locate it in north Transjordan. The name *Job* may mean "hostile" or "penitent." *Blameless,* i.e. healthy, whole, and socially responsible. 6–8: *Satan* (see note *a*; Zech.3.1 n.) is *among the sons of God.* He is not yet the demonic personification of later Judaism (compare 1 Chr.21.1) and Christianity.

that he has, on every side? Thou hast blessed the work of his hands, and his possessions have increased in the land. 11 But put forth thy hand now, and touch all that he has, and he will curse thee to thy face." 12 And the LORD said to Satan, "Behold, all that he has is in your power; only upon himself do not put forth your hand." So Satan went forth from the presence of the LORD.

13 Now there was a day when his sons and daughters were eating and drinking wine in their eldest brother's house; 14 and there came a messenger to Job, and said, "The oxen were plowing and the asses feeding beside them; 15 and the Sabe'ans fell upon them and took them, and slew the servants with the edge of the sword; and I alone have escaped to tell you." 16 While he was yet speaking, there came another, and said, "The fire of God fell from heaven and burned up the sheep and the servants, and consumed them; and I alone have escaped to tell you." 17 While he was yet speaking, there came another, and said, "The Chalde'ans formed three companies, and made a raid upon the camels and took them, and slew the servants with the edge of the sword; and I alone have escaped to tell you." 18 While he was yet speaking, there came another, and said, "Your sons and daughters were eating and drinking wine in their eldest brother's house; 19 and behold, a great wind came across the wilderness, and struck the four corners of the house, and it fell upon the young people, and they are dead; and I alone have escaped to tell you."

20 Then Job arose, and rent his robe, and shaved his head, and fell upon the ground, and worshiped. 21 And he said, "Naked I came from my mother's womb, and naked shall I return; the LORD gave, and the LORD has taken away; blessed be the name of the LORD."

22 In all this Job did not sin or charge God with wrong.

2 Again there was a day when the sons of God came to present themselves before the LORD, and Satan also came among them to present himself before the LORD. 2 And the LORD said to Satan, "Whence have you come?" Satan answered the LORD, "From going to and fro on the earth, and from walking up and down on it." 3 And the LORD said to Satan, "Have you considered my servant Job, that there is none like him on the earth, a blameless and upright man, who fears God and turns away from evil? He still holds fast his integrity, although you moved me against him, to destroy him without cause." 4 Then Satan answered the LORD, "Skin for skin! All that a man has he will give for his life. 5 But put forth thy hand now, and touch his bone and his flesh, and he will curse thee to thy face." 6 And the LORD said to Satan, "Behold, he is in your power; only spare his life."

7 So Satan went forth from the presence of the LORD, and afflicted Job with loathsome sores from the sole of his foot to the crown of his head. 8 And he took a potsherd with which to scrape himself, and sat among the ashes.

9 Then his wife said to him, "Do you still hold fast your integrity? Curse God, and die." 10 But he said to her, "You speak as one of the foolish women would speak. Shall we receive good at the hand of God, and shall

---

15: *Sabeans*, nomads from Arabia. 17: *Chaldeans*, originally from southern Mesopotamia. The folk-teller respects archaic and local color. 21: *Naked shall I return*, Hebrew adds "there," suggesting correspondence between *mother's womb* and "mother earth." Although a foreigner, Job uses the covenant-name, Yahweh (the LORD); this is an indication of early date. In the poem, the sacred name Yahweh is never used by the speakers (except in 12.9, a proverbial quotation). 22: The Deity is not accused of capricious malevolence. 2.4: *Skin for skin*, a hide for a hide, a proverb probably used by tradesmen. 7: *Loathsome sores*, not necessarily leprosy (Hansen's disease) but a skin ailment, one of many in the Near East. 9: *Curse God, and die*, Job's wife still believed in his *integrity* (see 4.6 n.) but wished to shorten his torture. 10: *Foolish*

we not receive evil?" In all this Job did
not sin with his lips.

11 Now when Job's three friends
heard of all this evil that had come
upon him, they came each from his
own place, Eli′phaz the Te′manite,
Bildad the Shuhite, and Zophar the
Na′amathite. They made an appointment together to come to condole with
him and comfort him. 12 And when
they saw him from afar, they did not
recognize him; and they raised their
voices and wept; and they rent their
robes and sprinkled dust upon their
heads toward heaven. 13 And they sat
with him on the ground seven days
and seven nights, and no one spoke a
word to him, for they saw that his
suffering was very great.

3 After this Job opened his mouth
and cursed the day of his birth.
2 And Job said:
3 "Let the day perish wherein I was
　　born,
　and the night which said,
　　'A man-child is conceived.'
4 Let that day be darkness!
　May God above not seek it,
　　nor light shine upon it.
5 Let gloom and deep darkness claim
　　it.
　Let clouds dwell upon it;
　let the blackness of the day
　　terrify it.
6 That night—let thick darkness seize
　　it!
　let it not rejoice among the days
　　of the year,
　let it not come into the number of
　　the months.
7 Yea, let that night be barren;
　let no joyful cry be heard[b] in it.
8 Let those curse it who curse the day,
　who are skilled to rouse up
　　Leviathan.
9 Let the stars of its dawn be dark;

　let it hope for light, but have none,
　　nor see the eyelids of the morning;
10 because it did not shut the doors of
　　my mother's womb,
　nor hide trouble from my eyes.

11 "Why did I not die at birth,
　come forth from the womb and
　　expire?
12 Why did the knees receive me?
　Or why the breasts, that I should
　　suck?
13 For then I should have lain down
　　and been quiet;
　I should have slept; then I should
　　have been at rest,
14 with kings and counselors of the
　　earth
　who rebuilt ruins for themselves,
15 or with princes who had gold,
　who filled their houses with silver.
16 Or why was I not as a hidden
　　untimely birth,
　as infants that never see the light?
17 There the wicked cease from
　　troubling,
　and there the weary are at rest.
18 There the prisoners are at ease
　　together;
　they hear not the voice of the
　　taskmaster.
19 The small and the great are there,
　and the slave is free from his
　　master.

20 "Why is light given to him that is in
　　misery,
　and life to the bitter in soul,
21 who long for death, but it comes not,
　and dig for it more than for hid
　　treasures;
22 who rejoice exceedingly,
　and are glad, when they find the
　　grave?
23 Why is light given to a man whose
　　way is hid,

b Heb *come*

women, i.e. those who do not believe in divine intervention into human affairs (see Ps.14.1 n.).
11: The friends of Job came from northwest Arabia.
　3.1–26: Job's soliloquy. 8: Those *who are skilled to rouse Leviathan* are magicians, astrologers,
and calendar-makers who were believed to produce as well as announce eclipses. *Leviathan,*
the sea monster (7.12), like Rahab (9.13; 26.12; Is.51.9), threatens to engulf the created order
and the succession of days and nights, especially during eclipses of the sun or moon. 14: *Ruins,*

whom God has hedged in?
24 For my sighing comes as[c] my bread,
and my groanings are poured out
like water.
25 For the thing that I fear comes upon
me,
and what I dread befalls me.
26 I am not at ease, nor am I quiet;
I have no rest; but trouble comes."

4 Then Eli′phaz the Te′manite answered:
2 "If one ventures a word with you,
will you be offended?
Yet who can keep from speaking?
3 Behold, you have instructed many,
and you have strengthened the
weak hands.
4 Your words have upheld him who
was stumbling,
and you have made firm the feeble
knees.
5 But now it has come to you, and you
are impatient;
it touches you, and you are
dismayed.
6 Is not your fear of God your
confidence,
and the integrity of your ways
your hope?
7 "Think now, who that was innocent
ever perished?
Or where were the upright cut
off?
8 As I have seen, those who plow
iniquity
and sow trouble reap the same.
9 By the breath of God they perish,
and by the blast of his anger they
are consumed.
10 The roar of the lion, the voice of the
fierce lion,

the teeth of the young lions, are
broken.
11 The strong lion perishes for lack of
prey,
and the whelps of the lioness are
scattered.

12 "Now a word was brought to me
stealthily,
my ear received the whisper of it.
13 Amid thoughts from visions of the
night,
when deep sleep falls on men,
14 dread came upon me, and
trembling,
which made all my bones shake.
15 A spirit glided past my face;
the hair of my flesh stood up.
16 It stood still,
but I could not discern its
appearance.
A form was before my eyes;
there was silence, then I heard a
voice:
17 'Can mortal man be righteous
before[d] God?
Can a man be pure before[d] his
Maker?
18 Even in his servants he puts no trust,
and his angels he charges with
error;
19 how much more those who dwell in
houses of clay,
whose foundation is in the dust,
who are crushed before the moth.
20 Between morning and evening they
are destroyed;
they perish for ever without any
regarding it.
21 If their tent-cord is plucked up
within them,

c Heb *before*   d Or *more than*

---

probably pyramids. The thought of a happy afterlife is not Hebraic but Egyptian. **23:** *God,*
Hebrew Eloah, a name which stresses the terrible aspect of the Deity, whose omnipotence is
never doubted by Job. Job's dilemma is directly related to his theological view that God is the
cause of both good and evil (disaster, calamities, etc.); see 2.10; Is.45.7; Am.3.6.
    4.1–5.27: First discourse of Eliphaz. 1–4: The opening words are courteous. The poet insists
on the sincerity of Job's comforters. **6:** Job's *integrity* (Hebrew word related to "blameless"
in 1.1; see 2.9 n.) is not yet questioned. **7:** The dogma of individual, this-worldly retribution is
upheld. **12–16:** Eliphaz appeals to a supranatural, almost prophetic, source of authority. He
does not speak in the name of tradition or experience, as wise men generally do. **17:** Surely no
mortal man is *righteous before God,* and Job should adopt an attitude of humility instead of
rebelling against the divine will. **21:** The word translated *tent-cord* has two separate meanings;

do they not die, and that without wisdom?"

5 "Call now; is there any one who will answer you?
To which of the holy ones will you turn?
² Surely vexation kills the fool, and jealousy slays the simple.
³ I have seen the fool taking root, but suddenly I cursed his dwelling.
⁴ His sons are far from safety, they are crushed in the gate, and there is no one to deliver them.
⁵ His harvest the hungry eat, and he takes it even out of thorns;*e* and the thirsty*f* pant after his*g* wealth.
⁶ For affliction does not come from the dust, nor does trouble sprout from the ground;
⁷ but man is born to trouble as the sparks fly upward.

⁸ "As for me, I would seek God, and to God would I commit my cause;
⁹ who does great things and unsearchable, marvelous things without number:
¹⁰ he gives rain upon the earth and sends waters upon the fields;
¹¹ he sets on high those who are lowly, and those who mourn are lifted to safety.
¹² He frustrates the devices of the crafty, so that their hands achieve no success.
¹³ He takes the wise in their own craftiness; and the schemes of the wily are brought to a quick end.
¹⁴ They meet with darkness in the daytime,

and grope at noonday as in the night.
¹⁵ But he saves the fatherless from their mouth,*h* the needy from the hand of the mighty.
¹⁶ So the poor have hope, and injustice shuts her mouth.

¹⁷ "Behold, happy is the man whom God reproves; therefore despise not the chastening of the Almighty.
¹⁸ For he wounds, but he binds up; he smites, but his hands heal.
¹⁹ He will deliver you from six troubles; in seven there shall no evil touch you.
²⁰ In famine he will redeem you from death, and in war from the power of the sword.
²¹ You shall be hid from the scourge of the tongue, and shall not fear destruction when it comes.
²² At destruction and famine you shall laugh, and shall not fear the beasts of the earth.
²³ For you shall be in league with the stones of the field, and the beasts of the field shall be at peace with you.
²⁴ You shall know that your tent is safe, and you shall inspect your fold and miss nothing.
²⁵ You shall know also that your descendants shall be many, and your offspring as the grass of the earth.

e Heb obscure
f Aquila Symmachus Syr Vg: Heb *snare*
g Heb *their*
h Cn: Heb uncertain

here it should be translated "pre-eminence" or "excellency"; men's pre-eminence or excellency is of no avail. They have only an illusion of *wisdom*. **5.1**: *The holy ones*, divine beings (see 15.15; Ex.15.11 n.; Ps.82.1 n.); members of the heavenly court cannot be intercessors. Eliphaz suspects, perhaps, that Job has attempted to justify himself by invoking other gods. **8**: *I would*, that is, were I in Job's place; if Job would only turn from his arrogance, his present misery would be ended. **17–27**: Suffering must be accepted as *the chastening of the Almighty*. The poet refers to the doctrine of *musar* (chastening or correction), which is characteristic of Jewish orthodoxy.

26 You shall come to your grave in ripe
   old age,
   as a shock of grain comes up to
   the threshing floor in its season.
27 Lo, this we have searched out; it is
   true.
   Hear, and know it for your
   good."*i*

6 Then Job answered:
2 "O that my vexation were
   weighed,
   and all my calamity laid in the
   balances!
3 For then it would be heavier than
   the sand of the sea;
   therefore my words have been
   rash.
4 For the arrows of the Almighty are
   in me;
   my spirit drinks their poison;
   the terrors of God are arrayed
   against me.
5 Does the wild ass bray when he has
   grass,
   or the ox low over his fodder?
6 Can that which is tasteless be eaten
   without salt,
   or is there any taste in the slime
   of the purslane?*j*
7 My appetite refuses to touch them;
   they are as food that is loathsome
   to me.*k*

8 "O that I might have my request,
   and that God would grant my
   desire;
9 that it would please God to crush
   me,
   that he would let loose his hand
   and cut me off!
10 This would be my consolation;
   I would even exult*l* in pain
   unsparing;

for I have not denied the words of
   the Holy One.
11 What is my strength, that I should
   wait?
   And what is my end, that I should
   be patient?
12 Is my strength the strength of stones,
   or is my flesh bronze?
13 In truth I have no help in me,
   and any resource is driven from
   me.

14 "He who withholds*m* kindness from
   a friend
   forsakes the fear of the Almighty.
15 My brethren are treacherous as a
   torrent-bed,
   as freshets that pass away,
16 which are dark with ice,
   and where the snow hides itself.
17 In time of heat they disappear;
   when it is hot, they vanish from
   their place.
18 The caravans turn aside from their
   course;
   they go up into the waste, and
   perish.
19 The caravans of Tema look,
   the travelers of Sheba hope.
20 They are disappointed because they
   were confident;
   they come thither and are
   confounded.
21 Such you have now become to
   me;*n*
   you see my calamity, and are
   afraid.
22 Have I said, 'Make me a gift'?
   Or, 'From your wealth offer a
   bribe for me'?

i Heb *for yourself*
j The meaning of the Hebrew word is uncertain
k Heb obscure
l The meaning of the Hebrew word is uncertain
m Syr Vg Compare Tg: Heb obscure
n Cn Compare Gk Syr: Heb obscure

6.1–7.21: Reply of Job. The orthodox explanation cannot be valid in Job's case, for his
calamity exceeds all ordinary misfortunes. **6:** *Slime of the purslane,* an insipid and repulsive food.
Purslane is a potherb. **8–11:** The Egyptian theme of desire for an early death reappears (see
ch. 3). Moreover Job fears that, if his days (and hence, his tortures) are prolonged, he may deny
the words of the Holy One (v. 10). The poet suggests thereby the complexity of the hero's personality; Job is an unwilling blasphemer. **14:** The test of true religion lies in human compassion
for others. Another rendering is: "A man should show kindness to a man in despair, even to
one who forsakes the fear of the Almighty." Some commentators suggest that the verse is a
marginal note made by a scribe. **15–20:** Friendship fails precisely when it is needed. **24:** Job is

²³ Or, 'Deliver me from the adversary's
   hand' ?
   Or, 'Ransom me from the hand of
   oppressors' ?

²⁴ "Teach me, and I will be silent;
   make me understand how I have
   erred.
²⁵ How forceful are honest words!
   But what does reproof from you
   reprove?
²⁶ Do you think that you can reprove
   words,
   when the speech of a despairing
   man is wind?
²⁷ You would even cast lots over the
   fatherless,
   and bargain over your friend.

²⁸ "But now, be pleased to look at me;
   for I will not lie to your face.
²⁹ Turn, I pray, let no wrong be done.
   Turn now, my vindication is at
   stake.
³⁰ Is there any wrong on my tongue?
   Cannot my taste discern calamity?

7 "Has not man a hard service upon
   earth,
   and are not his days like the days
   of a hireling?
² Like a slave who longs for the
   shadow,
   and like a hireling who looks for
   his wages,
³ so I am allotted months of emptiness,
   and nights of misery are
   apportioned to me.
⁴ When I lie down I say, 'When shall
   I arise?'
   But the night is long,
   and I am full of tossing till the
   dawn.

⁵ My flesh is clothed with worms and
   dirt;
   my skin hardens, then breaks out
   afresh.
⁶ My days are swifter than a weaver's
   shuttle,
   and come to their end without
   hope.

⁷ "Remember that my life is a breath;
   my eye will never again see
   good.
⁸ The eye of him who sees me will
   behold me no more;
   while thy eyes are upon me, I shall
   be gone.
⁹ As the cloud fades and vanishes,
   so he who goes down to Sheol does
   not come up;
¹⁰ he returns no more to his house,
   nor does his place know him any
   more.

¹¹ "Therefore I will not restrain my
   mouth;
   I will speak in the anguish of my
   spirit;
   I will complain in the bitterness of
   my soul.
¹² Am I the sea, or a sea monster,
   that thou settest a guard over me?
¹³ When I say, 'My bed will comfort
   me,
   my couch will ease my complaint,'
¹⁴ then thou dost scare me with dreams
   and terrify me with visions,
¹⁵ so that I would choose strangling
   and death rather than my bones.
¹⁶ I loathe my life; I would not live for
   ever.
   Let me alone, for my days are a
   breath.

---

willing to admit that he has *erred*, if only convincing evidence is brought forward. **30:** His conscience, however, is able to *discern* the right of his case. **7.1–6:** The life of mortal man in general is comparable to that of *a slave who longs for the shadow;* moreover, its transient nature is the source of new anguish. **7–21:** A prayer. It is at the moment of despair that man begins to pray. **7–9:** *Remember that my life is a breath.* Job appeals to divine compassion with the implied mockery that God will act when it will be too late. Job has heard of foreign speculations on the descent of men and gods to the underworld, only to deny any return from there. **12:** *Am I the sea, or a sea monster?* Again the hero alludes to the personification of evil (see 3.8 n.) in a context of sarcastic humor. Job compares himself in jest to the primeval forces which in Semitic polytheism threaten the security of the inhabited earth. His pain and his destitution are likened to the watch or *guard* which Marduk posted around the conquered dragon in the Babylonian

17 What is man, that thou dost make so
much of him,
and that thou dost set thy mind
upon him,
18 dost visit him every morning,
and test him every moment?
19 How long wilt thou not look away
from me,
nor let me alone till I swallow my
spittle?
20 If I sin, what do I do to thee, thou
watcher of men?
Why hast thou made me thy mark?
Why have I become a burden to
thee?
21 Why dost thou not pardon my
transgression
and take away my iniquity?
For now I shall lie in the earth;
thou wilt seek me, but I shall not
be."

8 Then Bildad the Shuhite answered:
2 "How long will you say these
things,
and the words of your mouth be a
great wind?
3 Does God pervert justice?
Or does the Almighty pervert the
right?
4 If your children have sinned against
him,
he has delivered them into the
power of their transgression.
5 If you will seek God
and make supplication to the
Almighty,
6 if you are pure and upright,
surely then he will rouse himself
for you

and reward you with a rightful
habitation.
7 And though your beginning was
small,
your latter days will be very great.

8 "For inquire, I pray you, of bygone
ages,
and consider what the fathers
have found;
9 for we are but of yesterday, and
know nothing,
for our days on earth are a shadow.
10 Will they not teach you, and tell you,
and utter words out of their
understanding?

11 "Can papyrus grow where there is
no marsh?
Can reeds flourish where there is
no water?
12 While yet in flower and not cut
down,
they wither before any other plant.
13 Such are the paths of all who forget
God;
the hope of the godless man shall
perish.
14 His confidence breaks in sunder,
and his trust is a spider's web.*o*
15 He leans against his house, but it does
not stand;
he lays hold of it, but it does not
endure.
16 He thrives before the sun,
and his shoots spread over his
garden.
17 His roots twine about the stone-
heap;
he lives among the rocks.*p*

o Heb *house*   *p* Gk Vg: Heb uncertain

---

poem on creation. **17–18:** A parody of Ps. 8. While the psalmist praised the creator who assigns
to insignificant and mortal man a place of pre-eminence in nature, Job ironically prefers to
receive minimal attention (see also Ps.144.3–4). **20:** Human sin cannot justify God's hostility
to man. **21:** *Thou wilt seek me*, i.e. thou wilt grope in the darkness after me, *but I shall not be.*
Job threatens the Almighty with his own non-being! He at once reaffirms his former trust in a
loving God and sarcastically implies the frustration of that love.
    8.1–22: First discourse of Bildad. The second friend dispenses with oriental etiquette. **3–4:** In
order to uphold the dogma of divine *justice*, he implies that Job suffers for the sin of his *children*,
whose *transgression* has *the power* to destroy the collective personality of the clan to which they
belonged. **5–7:** In a flagrant disregard of logic, Bildad advises the sufferer to *make supplication*,
literally, "to implore grace," and immediately proceeds to defend a moralistic view of salvation
as a reward for purity and uprightness (see vv. 11–22). His sources of authority are proverbs
gathered from *bygone ages* (v. 8; see vv. 11,20,22).

18 If he is destroyed from his place,
　then it will deny him, saying, 'I
　have never seen you.'
19 Behold, this is the joy of his way;
　and out of the earth others will
　spring.

20 "Behold, God will not reject a
　　blameless man,
　　nor take the hand of evildoers.
21 He will yet fill your mouth with
　　laughter,
　　and your lips with shouting.
22 Those who hate you will be clothed
　　with shame,
　　and the tent of the wicked will be
　　no more."

9 Then Job answered:
　2 "Truly I know that it is so:
　but how can a man be just before
　　God?
3 If one wished to contend with him,
　one could not answer him once in
　　a thousand times.
4 He is wise in heart, and mighty in
　　strength
　—who has hardened himself against
　　him, and succeeded?—
5 he who removes mountains, and
　　they know it not,
　when he overturns them in his
　　anger;
6 who shakes the earth out of its place,
　and its pillars tremble;
7 who commands the sun, and it does
　　not rise;
　who seals up the stars;
8 who alone stretched out the heavens,
　and trampled the waves of the
　　sea;*q*
9 who made the Bear and Orion,
　the Plei'ades and the chambers of
　　the south;
10 who does great things beyond
　　understanding,
　and marvelous things without
　　number.

11 Lo, he passes by me, and I see him
　　not;
　he moves on, but I do not perceive
　　him.
12 Behold, he snatches away; who can
　　hinder him?
　Who will say to him, 'What doest
　　thou'?

13 "God will not turn back his anger;
　beneath him bowed the helpers of
　　Rahab.
14 How then can I answer him,
　choosing my words with him?
15 Though I am innocent, I cannot
　　answer him;
　I must appeal for mercy to my
　　accuser.*r*
16 If I summoned him and he answered
　　me,
　I would not believe that he was
　　listening to my voice.
17 For he crushes me with a tempest,
　and multiplies my wounds without
　　cause;
18 he will not let me get my breath,
　but fills me with bitterness.
19 If it is a contest of strength, behold
　　him!
　If it is a matter of justice, who can
　　summon him?*s*
20 Though I am innocent, my own
　　mouth would condemn me;
　though I am blameless, he would
　　prove me perverse.
21 I am blameless; I regard not myself;
　I loathe my life.
22 It is all one; therefore I say,
　he destroys both the blameless and
　　the wicked.
23 When disaster brings sudden death,
　he mocks at the calamity*t* of the
　　innocent.
24 The earth is given into the hand of
　　the wicked;

q Or *trampled the back of the sea dragon*
r Or *for my right*
s Compare Gk: Heb *me*. The text of the verse is
uncertain
t The meaning of the Hebrew word is uncertain

9.1–10.22: Reply of Job. Following the principle of delayed reaction, Job replies not to
Bildad, who has just spoken, but to Eliphaz (compare 9.2 with 4.17). **9.3–29:** In a contest of
strength the Creator has the advantage. There is no human or divine judge of God (who is
implicitly compared to a thief or kidnapper; v. 12), a thought which anticipates the theme of
the mediator (see vv. 33–35). **23:** God is compared to an irresponsible person who *mocks.*

he covers the faces of its judges—
if it is not he, who then is it?

25 "My days are swifter than a runner;
they flee away, they see no good.
26 They go by like skiffs of reed,
like an eagle swooping on the
prey.
27 If I say, 'I will forget my complaint,
I will put off my sad countenance,
and be of good cheer,'
28 I become afraid of all my suffering,
for I know thou wilt not hold me
innocent.
29 I shall be condemned;
why then do I labor in vain?
30 If I wash myself with snow,
and cleanse my hands with lye,
31 yet thou wilt plunge me into a pit,
and my own clothes will abhor
me.
32 For he is not a man, as I am, that I
might answer him,
that we should come to trial
together.
33 There is no*u* umpire between us,
who might lay his hand upon us
both.
34 Let him take his rod away from me,
and let not dread of him terrify me.
35 Then I would speak without fear of
him,
for I am not so in myself.

10 "I loathe my life;
I will give free utterance to my
complaint;
I will speak in the bitterness of my
soul.
2 I will say to God, Do not condemn
me;
let me know why thou dost
contend against me.
3 Does it seem good to thee to oppress,
to despise the work of thy hands
and favor the designs of the
wicked?
4 Hast thou eyes of flesh?

Dost thou see as man sees?
5 Are thy days as the days of man,
or thy years as man's years,
6 that thou dost seek out my iniquity
and search for my sin,
7 although thou knowest that I am not
guilty,
and there is none to deliver out of
thy hand?
8 Thy hands fashioned and made me;
and now thou dost turn about and
destroy me.*v*
9 Remember that thou hast made me
of clay;*w*
and wilt thou turn me to dust
again?
10 Didst thou not pour me out like milk
and curdle me like cheese?
11 Thou didst clothe me with skin and
flesh,
and knit me together with bones
and sinews.
12 Thou has granted me life and
steadfast love;
and thy care has preserved my
spirit.
13 Yet these things thou didst hide in
thy heart;
I know that this was thy purpose.
14 If I sin, thou dost mark me,
and dost not acquit me of my
iniquity.
15 If I am wicked, woe to me!
If I am righteous, I cannot lift up
my head,
for I am filled with disgrace
and look upon my affliction.
16 And if I lift myself up,*x* thou dost
hunt me like a lion,
and again work wonders against
me;
17 thou dost renew thy witnesses
against me,
and increase thy vexation toward
me;

u Another reading is *Would that there were*
v Cn Compare Gk Syr: Heb *made me together round
about and thou dost destroy me*
w Gk: Heb *like clay*   *x* Syr: Heb *he lifts himself up*

30–31: Man's willingness to wash himself cannot prevent God from throwing him back into
the mud. **33:** *There is no umpire between us,* not merely an umpire who decides, but a conciliator,
a go-between, an intermediary, a mediator, since such a being *would lay his hand upon us both.*
10.1–22: Although God is remote, the hero obstinately and tenderly addresses him in prayer.
8–12: He appeals to the love of an artist for his handiwork (compare Ps.139.14–18). **18–19:**

thou dost bring fresh hosts against
me.[y]

18 "Why didst thou bring me forth from
the womb?
Would that I had died before any
eye had seen me,
19 and were as though I had not been,
carried from the womb to the
grave.
20 Are not the days of my life few?[z]
Let me alone, that I may find a
little comfort[a]
21 before I go whence I shall not return,
to the land of gloom and deep
darkness,
22 the land of gloom[b] and chaos,
where light is as darkness."

Then Zophar the Na'amathite answered:
2 "Should a multitude of words go
unanswered,
and a man full of talk be
vindicated?
3 Should your babble silence men,
and when you mock, shall no one
shame you?
4 For you say, 'My doctrine is pure,
and I am clean in God's eyes.'
5 But oh, that God would speak,
and open his lips to you,
6 and that he would tell you the secrets
of wisdom!
For he is manifold in
understanding.[c]
Know then that God exacts of you
less than your guilt deserves.

7 "Can you find out the deep things of
God?
Can you find out the limit of the
Almighty?
8 It is higher than heaven[d] —what can
you do?

Deeper than Sheol—what can you
know?
9 Its measure is longer than the earth,
and broader than the sea.
10 If he passes through, and imprisons,
and calls to judgment, who can
hinder him?
11 For he knows worthless men;
when he sees iniquity, will he not
consider it?
12 But a stupid man will get
understanding,
when a wild ass's colt is born a
man.

13 "If you set your heart aright,
you will stretch out your hands
toward him.
14 If iniquity is in your hand, put it far
away,
and let not wickedness dwell in
your tents.
15 Surely then you will lift up your face
without blemish;
you will be secure, and will not
fear.
16 You will forget your misery;
you will remember it as waters
that have passed away.
17 And your life will be brighter than
the noonday;
its darkness will be like the
morning.
18 And you will have confidence,
because there is hope;
you will be protected[e] and take
your rest in safety.
19 You will lie down, and none will
make you afraid;
many will entreat your favor.
20 But the eyes of the wicked will fail;

y Cn Compare Gk: Heb *changes and a host are with me*
z Cn Compare Gk Syr: Heb *Are not my days few? Let
him cease*　　a Heb *brighten up*
b Heb *gloom as darkness, deep darkness*
c Heb obscure　　d Heb *The heights of heaven*
e Or *you will look around*

The sufferer is attracted by the theme of non-being. **20–22:** At the same time he laments the
proximity and the inevitability of death.

11.1–20: First discourse of Zophar. The third friend cannot restrain his theological passion.
4: It is not quite true that Job has claimed purity of *doctrine*. **6:** At last the direct charge is made:
the sufferer is told that he deserves his misery as a penalty for his *guilt*. The poet indicates a
development of thought among the three friends up to this point; afterwards the arguments are
merely repeated in various forms. Bildad is quite wrong in charging Job with ethical crimes, but
he is right in stressing man's finitude in the face of God's infinity (v. 7), another illustration of
the poet's skill at showing the complexity of truth mixed with error in the minds of the friends.

all way of escape will be lost to
them,
and their hope is to breathe their
last.”

12 Then Job answered:
2 “No doubt you are the people,
and wisdom will die with you.
3 But I have understanding as well as
you;
I am not inferior to you.
Who does not know such things as
these?
4 I am a laughingstock to my friends;
I, who called upon God and he
answered me,
a just and blameless man, am a
laughingstock.
5 In the thought of one who is at ease
there is contempt for
misfortune;
it is ready for those whose feet slip.
6 The tents of robbers are at peace,
and those who provoke God are
secure,
who bring their god in their hand.*f*

7 “But ask the beasts, and they will
teach you;
the birds of the air, and they will
tell you;
8 or the plants of the earth,*g* and they
will teach you;
and the fish of the sea will declare
to you.
9 Who among all these does not know
that the hand of the LORD has done
this?
10 In his hand is the life of every living
thing
and the breath of all mankind.
11 Does not the ear try words
as the palate tastes food?
12 Wisdom is with the aged,
and understanding in length of
days.

13 “With God*h* are wisdom and might;
he has counsel and understanding.
14 If he tears down, none can rebuild;
if he shuts a man in, none can
open.
15 If he withholds the waters, they dry
up;
if he sends them out, they
overwhelm the land.
16 With him are strength and wisdom;
the deceived and the deceiver are
his.
17 He leads counselors away stripped,
and judges he makes fools.
18 He looses the bonds of kings,
and binds a waistcloth on their
loins.
19 He leads priests away stripped,
and overthrows the mighty.
20 He deprives of speech those who are
trusted,
and takes away the discernment
of the elders.
21 He pours contempt on princes,
and looses the belt of the strong.
22 He uncovers the deeps out of
darkness,
and brings deep darkness to light.
23 He makes nations great, and he
destroys them:
he enlarges nations, and leads
them away.
24 He takes away understanding from
the chiefs of the people of the
earth,
and makes them wander in a
pathless waste.
25 They grope in the dark without light;
and he makes them stagger like a
drunken man.

13 “Lo, my eye has seen all this,
my ear has heard and understood
it.

f Hebrew uncertain
g Or *speak to the earth*
h Heb *him*

12.1–14.22: Reply of Job. 12.2–3: The sick man replies with heavy sarcasm. **4:** *And he
answered me;* the Hebrew, with a change of vowels, may be read, “that he might answer me”;
or better, translate “and he oppressed me.” **6:** *Who bring their god in their hand.* Job seems to
discern that there can be a spiritual form of idolatry, whenever man makes his own power the
object of his ultimate concern. **7–25:** Divine omnipotence knows neither obstacle nor law.
13.1–12: In spite of God's lawlessness, the friends who are *worthless physicians* (v. 4) will not

² What you know, I also know;
     I am not inferior to you.
³ But I would speak to the Almighty,
     and I desire to argue my case with
     God.
⁴ As for you, you whitewash with lies;
     worthless physicians are you all.
⁵ Oh that you would keep silent,
     and it would be your wisdom!
⁶ Hear now my reasoning,
     and listen to the pleadings of my
     lips.
⁷ Will you speak falsely for God,
     and speak deceitfully for him?
⁸ Will you show partiality toward him,
     will you plead the case for God?
⁹ Will it be well with you when he
     searches you out?
     Or can you deceive him, as one
     deceives a man?
¹⁰ He will surely rebuke you
     if in secret you show partiality.
¹¹ Will not his majesty terrify you,
     and the dread of him fall upon
     you?
¹² Your maxims are proverbs of ashes,
     your defenses are defenses of clay.

¹³ "Let me have silence, and I will
     speak,
     and let come on me what may.
¹⁴ I will take*ⁱ* my flesh in my teeth,
     and put my life in my hand.
¹⁵ Behold, he will slay me; I have no
     hope;
     yet I will defend my ways to his
     face.
¹⁶ This will be my salvation,
     that a godless man shall not come
     before him.
¹⁷ Listen carefully to my words,

and let my declaration be in your
     ears.
¹⁸ Behold, I have prepared my case;
     I know that I shall be vindicated.
¹⁹ Who is there that will contend with
     me?
     For then I would be silent and die.
²⁰ Only grant two things to me,
     then I will not hide myself from
     thy face:
²¹ withdraw thy hand far from me,
     and let not dread of thee terrify
     me.
²² Then call, and I will answer;
     or let me speak, and do thou reply
     to me.
²³ How many are my iniquities and my
     sins?
     Make me know my transgression
     and my sin.
²⁴ Why dost thou hide thy face,
     and count me as thy enemy?
²⁵ Wilt thou frighten a driven leaf
     and pursue dry chaff?
²⁶ For thou writest bitter things against
     me,
     and makest me inherit the
     iniquities of my youth.
²⁷ Thou puttest my feet in the stocks,
     and watchest all my paths;
     thou settest a bound to the soles of
     my feet.
²⁸ Man*ʲ* wastes away like a rotten thing,
     like a garment that is moth-eaten.

14 "Man that is born of a woman
     is of few days, and full of trouble.
² He comes forth like a flower, and
     withers;

i Gk: Heb *Why should I take?*
j Heb *He*

---

escape the Deity's rebuke (v. 10). **15:** *I have no hope*, the time-honored rendering, "yet will I trust in him," is based on a pious note in the margin of the manuscripts. The negative in the Hebrew text is supported by the context, which suggests a mood of defiance, not of selfless devotion. Job no longer claims that he is blameless; however, he discovers in the depth of his despair that his passionate desire to see God, his would-be slayer, is evidence of his inward purity, for *no godless* man would ever dare to *come before* God (v. 16). **23:** Job is willing to learn from God whether his *iniquities*, his *sins*, and his *transgressions* are the cause of his misery. **24:** The prayer remains unanswered, and God continues to *hide* his *face*, even to count Job an *enemy*. **26:** In his search for an explanation of his pain, the hero acknowledges *the iniquities of his youth*, but he implies that the enormity of his fate is disproportionate. **14.1–22:** One of the great poems in all literature. **1:** *Man that is born of a woman* . . . , as in 7.1, the poet is concerned with the human condition in general. No implication is to be drawn from this verse on the

he flees like a shadow, and
  continues not.
3 And dost thou open thy eyes upon
    such a one
    and bring him[k] into judgment with
    thee?
4 Who can bring a clean thing out of an
    unclean?
    There is not one.
5 Since his days are determined,
    and the number of his months is
    with thee,
    and thou hast appointed his
    bounds that he cannot pass,
6 look away from him, and desist,[l]
    that he may enjoy, like a hireling,
    his day.

7 "For there is hope for a tree,
    if it be cut down, that it will sprout
    again,
    and that its shoots will not cease.
8 Though its root grow old in the earth,
    and its stump die in the ground,
9 yet at the scent of water it will bud
    and put forth branches like a
    young plant.
10 But man dies, and is laid low;
    man breathes his last, and where
    is he?
11 As waters fail from a lake,
    and a river wastes away and dries
    up,
12 so man lies down and rises not
    again;
    till the heavens are no more he
    will not awake,
    or be roused out of his sleep.
13 Oh that thou wouldest hide me in
    Sheol,
    that thou wouldest conceal me
    until thy wrath be past,
    that thou wouldest appoint me a
    set time, and remember me!
14 If a man die, shall he live again?

All the days of my service I would
  wait,
  till my release should come.
15 Thou wouldest call, and I would
    answer thee;
    thou wouldest long for the work of
    thy hands.
16 For then thou wouldest number my
    steps,
    thou wouldest not keep watch over
    my sin;
17 my transgression would be sealed up
    in a bag,
    and thou wouldest cover over my
    iniquity.

18 "But the mountain falls and
    crumbles away,
    and the rock is removed from its
    place;
19 the waters wear away the stones;
    the torrents wash away the soil of
    the earth;
    so thou destroyest the hope of
    man.
20 Thou prevailest for ever against him,
    and he passes;
    thou changest his countenance,
    and sendest him away.
21 His sons come to honor, and he does
    not know it;
    they are brought low, and he
    perceives it not.
22 He feels only the pain of his own
    body,
    and he mourns only for himself."

15 Then Eli'phaz the Te'manite an-
    swered:
2 "Should a wise man answer with
    windy knowledge,
    and fill himself with the east wind?
3 Should he argue in unprofitable talk,

k Gk Syr Vg: Heb *me*
l Cn: Heb *that he may desist*

---

responsibility of womanhood for transmitting impurity to children, which is the lot of all men and women (see v. 4). **16**: *For then thou wouldst number my steps*, translate, "Now thou numberest my steps"; the phrase implies malevolence. Perhaps v. 16a contrasts the present horror with the hope of v. 16b. **17**: Read, "My transgression is sealed up in a bag and thou sewest up my iniquity."

   15.1–35: Second discourse of Eliphaz. A second round of discussion now begins. **2–3**: This time the speaker dispenses completely with soothing formulas of introduction (contrast 4.1–4). Job's remonstrances do not befit *a wise man*. **4**: The insecurity of traditional opinion faces the

or in words with which he can do
no good?
4 But you are doing away with the fear
of God,
and hindering meditation before
God.
5 For your iniquity teaches your
mouth,
and you choose the tongue of the
crafty.
6 Your own mouth condemns you, and
not I;
your own lips testify against you.

7 "Are you the first man that was born?
Or were you brought forth before
the hills?
8 Have you listened in the council of
God?
And do you limit wisdom to
yourself?
9 What do you know that we do not
know?
What do you understand that is not
clear to us?
10 Both the gray-haired and the aged
are among us,
older than your father.
11 Are the consolations of God too
small for you,
or the word that deals gently with
you?
12 Why does your heart carry you away,
and why do your eyes flash,
13 that you turn your spirit against God,
and let such words go out of your
mouth?
14 What is man, that he can be clean?
Or he that is born of a woman,
that he can be righteous?
15 Behold, God puts no trust in his holy
ones,
and the heavens are not clean in
his sight;

16 how much less one who is
abominable and corrupt,
a man who drinks iniquity like
water!

17 "I will show you, hear me;
and what I have seen I will
declare
18 (what wise men have told,
and their fathers have not hidden,
19 to whom alone the land was given,
and no stranger passed among
them).
20 The wicked man writhes in pain all
his days,
through all the years that are laid
up for the ruthless.
21 Terrifying sounds are in his ears;
in prosperity the destroyer will
come upon him.
22 He does not believe that he will
return out of darkness,
and he is destined for the sword.
23 He wanders abroad for bread,
saying, 'Where is it?'
He knows that a day of darkness
is ready at his hand;
24 distress and anguish terrify him;
they prevail against him, like a
king prepared for battle.
25 Because he has stretched forth his
hand against God,
and bids defiance to the
Almighty,
26 running stubbornly against him
with a thick-bossed shield;
27 because he has covered his face with
his fat,
and gathered fat upon his loins,
28 and has lived in desolate cities,
in houses which no man should
inhabit,
which were destined to become
heaps of ruins;

courage of non-conformism. Moffatt translates, "You undermine religion." **7**: *Are you the first man that was born?* Eliphaz perceives that Job the heretic is also Job the Titan, a rebel against God. The sufferer speaks the language of the *crafty* (like the serpent in Gen.3.1). Borrowing the Semitic myth of the Primeval Man who existed before the creation of the earth, Eliphaz sees quite clearly that Job, through the intensity of his grief, forgets the limitations of his humanity. Like Adam (Gen.3.5), Job wishes to be similar to God, setting up himself as judge of his Creator. Like personified Wisdom (Pr.8.25b), he thinks that he was *brought forth before the hills*. **11**: Eliphaz commits the same crime of which he accuses the hero, since he calls his own words *the consolations of God*. **14-16**: The traditionalist repeats himself (compare 4.17–19).

29 he will not be rich, and his wealth
    will not endure,
  nor will he strike root in the
    earth;*m*
30 he will not escape from darkness;
  the flame will dry up his shoots,
  and his blossom*n* will be swept
    away*o* by the wind.
31 Let him not trust in emptiness,
    deceiving himself;
  for emptiness will be his
    recompense.
32 It will be paid in full before his time,
  and his branch will not be green.
33 He will shake off his unripe grape,
    like the vine,
  and cast off his blossom, like the
    olive tree.
34 For the company of the godless is
    barren,
  and fire consumes the tents of
    bribery.
35 They conceive mischief and bring
    forth evil
  and their heart prepares deceit."

16 Then Job answered:
2 "I have heard many such things;
  miserable comforters are you all.
3 Shall windy words have an end?
  Or what provokes you that you
    answer?
4 I also could speak as you do,
  if you were in my place;
  I could join words together against
    you,
  and shake my head at you.
5 I could strengthen you with my
    mouth,
  and the solace of my lips would
    assuage your pain.

6 "If I speak, my pain is not assuaged,
  and if I forbear, how much of it
    leaves me?
7 Surely now God has worn me out;
  he has*p* made desolate all my
    company.
8 And he has*p* shriveled me up,

which is a witness against me;
  and my leanness has risen up against
    me,
  it testifies to my face.
9 He has torn me in his wrath, and
    hated me;
  he has gnashed his teeth at me;
  my adversary sharpens his eyes
    against me.
10 Men have gaped at me with their
    mouth,
  they have struck me insolently
    upon the cheek,
  they mass themselves together
    against me.
11 God gives me up to the ungodly,
  and casts me into the hands of the
    wicked.
12 I was at ease, and he broke me
    asunder;
  he seized me by the neck and
    dashed me to pieces;
  he set me up as his target,
13   his archers surround me.
  He slashes open my kidneys, and
    does not spare;
  he pours out my gall on the
    ground.
14 He breaks me with breach upon
    breach;
  he runs upon me like a warrior.
15 I have sewed sackcloth upon my
    skin,
  and have laid my strength in the
    dust.
16 My face is red with weeping,
  and on my eyelids is deep
    darkness;
17 although there is no violence in my
    hands,
  and my prayer is pure.

18 "O earth, cover not my blood,
  and let my cry find no resting
    place.
19 Even now, behold, my witness is in
    heaven,

m Vg: Heb obscure   *n* Gk: Heb *mouth*
o Cn: Heb *will depart*   *p* Heb *thou hast*

16.1–17.16: Reply of Job. 16.1–17: In the face of God's continuing hostility (vv. 6–16), Job reaffirms his innocence (v. 17). **18:** His "murder" must be avenged; personified *earth* is invited to assist in the avenging (compare Gen.4.10–11). **18–22:** Some believe that Job appeals from God the slayer to God the heavenly *witness.* Such a view, however, is syntactically difficult,

and he that vouches for me is on high.

²⁰ My friends scorn me;
my eye pours out tears to God,
²¹ that he would maintain the right of a man with God,
like*q* that of a man with his neighbor.
²² For when a few years have come I shall go the way whence I shall not return.

17 My spirit is broken, my days are extinct,
the grave is ready for me.
² Surely there are mockers about me, and my eye dwells on their provocation.

³ "Lay down a pledge for me with thyself;
who is there that will give surety for me?
⁴ Since thou hast closed their minds to understanding,
therefore thou wilt not let them triumph.
⁵ He who informs against his friends to get a share of their property,
the eyes of his children will fail.

⁶ "He has made me a byword of the peoples,
and I am one before whom men spit.
⁷ My eye has grown dim from grief, and all my members are like a shadow.
⁸ Upright men are appalled at this, and the innocent stirs himself up against the godless.
⁹ Yet the righteous holds to his way, and he that has clean hands grows stronger and stronger.
¹⁰ But you, come on again, all of you, and I shall not find a wise man among you.

¹¹ My days are past, my plans are broken off,
the desires of my heart.
¹² They make night into day;
'The light,' they say, 'is near to the darkness.'*r*
¹³ If I look for Sheol as my house, if I spread my couch in darkness,
¹⁴ if I say to the pit, 'You are my father,'
and to the worm, 'My mother,' or 'My sister,'
¹⁵ where then is my hope?
Who will see my hope?
¹⁶ Will it go down to the bars of Sheol?
Shall we descend together into the dust?"

18 Then Bildad the Shuhite answered:
² "How long will you hunt for words?
Consider, and then we will speak.
³ Why are we counted as cattle?
Why are we stupid in your sight?
⁴ You who tear yourself in your anger, shall the earth be forsaken for you,
or the rock be removed out of its place?

⁵ "Yea, the light of the wicked is put out,
and the flame of his fire does not shine.
⁶ The light is dark in his tent, and his lamp above him is put out.
⁷ His strong steps are shortened and his own schemes throw him down.
⁸ For he is cast into a net by his own feet,
and he walks on a pitfall.
⁹ A trap seizes him by the heel, a snare lays hold of him.
¹⁰ A rope is hid for him in the ground, a trap for him in the path.

q Syr Vg Tg: Heb *and*   *r* Heb obscure

since the same witness is expected to *maintain the right of a man with God* (v. 21). In all probability the poet remembers the earlier theme of the mediator (9.33–35). As his thought progresses, Job is led to abandon that dream and to substitute for it a present certainty. **17.1–10:** Job's fate has made him *a byword;* he criticizes his friends, who have failed him. **6:** Compare Ps.69.11. *Spit,* see 30.10. **11–16:** Job turns again to the thought of his death.
  18.1–21: Second discourse of Bildad. 2–4: *Counted as beasts,* perhaps a reference to Job's words in 12.7. *Rock be removed,* compare 14.18. **5–21:** The ungodly man receives through his

11 Terrors frighten him on every side,
  and chase him at his heels.
12 His strength is hunger-bitten,
  and calamity is ready for his
  stumbling.
13 By disease his skin is consumed,[s]
  the first-born of death consumes
  his limbs.
14 He is torn from the tent in which he
  trusted,
  and is brought to the king of
  terrors.
15 In his tent dwells that which is none
  of his;
  brimstone is scattered upon his
  habitation.
16 His roots dry up beneath,
  and his branches wither above.
17 His memory perishes from the earth,
  and he has no name in the street.
18 He is thrust from light into darkness,
  and driven out of the world.
19 He has no offspring or descendant
  among his people,
  and no survivor where he used to
  live.
20 They of the west are appalled at his
  day,
  and horror seizes them of the east.
21 Surely such are the dwellings of the
  ungodly,
  such is the place of him who
  knows not God."

19 Then Job answered:
2 "How long will you torment me,
  and break me in pieces with
  words?
3 These ten times you have cast
  reproach upon me;
  are you not ashamed to wrong me?
4 And even if it be true that I have
  erred,
  my error remains with myself.

5 If indeed you magnify yourselves
  against me,
  and make my humiliation an
  argument against me,
6 know then that God has put me in
  the wrong,
  and closed his net about me.
7 Behold, I cry out, 'Violence!' but I
  am not answered;
  I call aloud, but there is no justice.
8 He has walled up my way, so that I
  cannot pass,
  and he has set darkness upon my
  paths.
9 He has stripped from me my glory,
  and taken the crown from my
  head.
10 He breaks me down on every side,
  and I am gone,
  and my hope has he pulled up like
  a tree.
11 He has kindled his wrath against me,
  and counts me as his adversary.
12 His troops come on together;
  they have cast up siegeworks[t]
  against me,
  and encamp round about my tent.

13 "He has put my brethren far from
  me,
  and my acquaintances are wholly
  estranged from me.
14 My kinsfolk and my close friends
  have failed me;
15 the guests in my house have
  forgotten me;
  my maidservants count me as a
  stranger;
  I have become an alien in their
  eyes.
16 I call to my servant, but he gives me
  no answer;

s Cn: Heb *it consumes the limbs of his skin*
t Heb *their way*

disease, which is *the first-born of death*, a foretaste of his ultimate fate, when he will be brought
before *the king of terrors* (v. 14). Job has spoken of a witness who will vouch for him after his
demise (16.19), but he has no *offspring, descendant*, or *survivor* (v. 19). **20:** Only the memory of
his crimes will remain for ever as an example of horror among peoples of *west* and *east*.
19.1–29: Reply of Job. The sufferer discerns that he is now completely isolated. **2–6:** His
friends do not understand. **4:** *Even if it be true that I have erred* (see 6.24 n.), *my error remains
with myself*, my words may have been in error, but they concern only myself and do not constitute an offense against God or man. **7–12:** God's enmity has lowered Job below the dignity
of man (v. 9; compare 7.17). **13–19:** Society has likewise expelled Job from its ranks, even his

I must beseech him with my
  mouth.
¹⁷ I am repulsive to my wife,
  loathsome to the sons of my own
  mother.
¹⁸ Even young children despise me;
  when I rise they talk against me.
¹⁹ All my intimate friends abhor me,
  and those whom I loved have
  turned against me.
²⁰ My bones cleave to my skin and to
  my flesh,
  and I have escaped by the skin of
  my teeth.
²¹ Have pity on me, have pity on me, O
  you my friends,
  for the hand of God has touched
  me!
²² Why do you, like God, pursue me?
  Why are you not satisfied with my
  flesh?

²³ "Oh that my words were written!
  Oh that they were inscribed in a
  book!
²⁴ Oh that with an iron pen and lead
  they were graven in the rock for
  ever!
²⁵ For I know that my Redeemer[u]
  lives,
  and at last he will stand upon the
  earth;[v]

²⁶ and after my skin has been thus
  destroyed,
  then from[w] my flesh I shall see
  God,[x]
²⁷ whom I shall see on my side,[y]
  and my eyes shall behold, and not
  another.
  My heart faints within me!
²⁸ If you say, 'How we will pursue him!'
  and, 'The root of the matter is
  found in him';
²⁹ be afraid of the sword,
  for wrath brings the punishment of
  the sword,
  that you may know there is a
  judgment."

20 Then Zophar the Na'amathite
  answered:
² "Therefore my thoughts answer me,
  because of my haste within me.
³ I hear censure which insults me,
  and out of my understanding a
  spirit answers me.
⁴ Do you not know this from of old,
  since man was placed upon earth,
⁵ that the exulting of the wicked is
  short,
  and the joy of the godless but for
  a moment?

u Or *Vindicator*   *v* Or *dust*   *w* Or *without*
x The meaning of this verse is uncertain
y Or *for myself*

most intimate circle of household, family, and friends. **20:** *I have escaped with the skin of my teeth*, an expression of proverbial origin which has received many different interpretations, all of which are hypothetical. **21–22:** *Have pity on me, O you my friends*, a pathetic appeal which stresses Job's total solitariness. **23–24:** He therefore wishes that his *words were written* so that he may be vindicated by posterity. *In a book*, on a copper scroll, which will resist the ravages of time. *In the rock*, as some inscriptions engraved on a cliff in Lebanon by military conquerors of many centuries. **25:** *My Redeemer*, translate, *my Vindicator* (see note *u*), one who will avenge my honor after my murder has been committed. The avenger (2 Sam.14.11) is usually the next-of-kin and the heir (Lev.25.25; Dt.25.5–10; Ru.2.20). Though God is often called "redeemer" (Ex.6.6; Ps.103.4), it is not likely that Job's "Vindicator" should be identified with the divine Being. The Vindicator *at last will stand upon the earth;* the sufferer has already called for a mediator between God and man (9.33–35) and for a witness who will defend man before God (16.19–21); he hopes to obtain through the Vindicator an audience with God himself (v. 26). In his utmost destitution, rejected by friends, deprived of heirs, attacked by God, uncertain of future fame, Job's faith leaps for a moment to the certainty that after death his most cherished wish will be fulfilled. **26–27:** *From my flesh*, Job insists that he will *see God*. The Hebrew of v. 26 is corrupt, perhaps as the result of an accident or of scribal polemics against the later Jewish belief in the resurrection of the flesh. Whether or not Job expresses here a new faith in life beyond death, he no longer asks for a recognition of his innocence. The vision of God will be sufficient (42.5–6).
  20.1–29: Second discourse of Zophar. 2: *Therefore my thoughts answer*, the Hebrew noun implies disturbing and anxious reflections, and the line means, "My disquieting thoughts cause me to answer." *Haste*, i.e. agitation. Job's obstinacy is matched by his theological vigor. For a

⁶ Though his height mount up to the
   heavens,
   and his head reach to the clouds,
⁷ he will perish for ever like his own
   dung;
   those who have seen him will say,
   'Where is he?'
⁸ He will fly away like a dream, and
   not be found;
   he will be chased away like a vision
   of the night.
⁹ The eye which saw him will see him
   no more,
   nor will his place any more behold
   him.
¹⁰ His children will seek the favor of the
   poor,
   and his hands will give back his
   wealth.
¹¹ His bones are full of youthful vigor,
   but it will lie down with him in the
   dust.

¹² "Though wickedness is sweet in his
   mouth,
   though he hides it under his
   tongue,
¹³ though he is loath to let it go,
   and holds it in his mouth,
¹⁴ yet his food is turned in his stomach;
   it is the gall of asps within him.
¹⁵ He swallows down riches and vomits
   them up again;
   God casts them out of his belly.
¹⁶ He will suck the poison of asps;
   the tongue of a viper will kill him.
¹⁷ He will not look upon the rivers,
   the streams flowing with honey and
   curds.
¹⁸ He will give back the fruit of his toil,
   and will not swallow it down;
   from the profit of his trading
   he will get no enjoyment.
¹⁹ For he has crushed and abandoned
   the poor,
   he has seized a house which he did
   not build.

²⁰ "Because his greed knew no rest,
   he will not save anything in
   which he delights.
²¹ There was nothing left after he had
   eaten;
   therefore his prosperity will not
   endure.
²² In the fulness of his sufficiency he
   will be in straits;
   all the force of misery will come
   upon him.
²³ To fill his belly to the full
   Godᶻ will send his fierce anger
   into him,
   and rain it upon him as his food.ᵃ
²⁴ He will flee from an iron weapon;
   a bronze arrow will strike him
   through.
²⁵ It is drawn forth and comes out of
   his body,
   the glittering point comes out of
   his gall;
   terrors come upon him.
²⁶ Utter darkness is laid up for his
   treasures;
   a fire not blown upon will devour
   him;
   what is left in his tent will be
   consumed.
²⁷ The heavens will reveal his iniquity,
   and the earth will rise up against
   him.
²⁸ The possessions of his house will be
   carried away,
   dragged off in the day of God'sᵇ
   wrath.
²⁹ This is the wicked man's portion
   from God,
   the heritage decreed for him by
   God."

21 Then Job answered:
² "Listen carefully to my words,
   and let this be your consolation.
³ Bear with me, and I will speak,
   and after I have spoken, mock on.

z Heb *he*   *a* Cn: Heb *in his flesh*   *b* Heb *his*

---

moment Zophar is shaken out of his static certainty, but he soon reaffirms the thesis of individual retribution (vv. 4–29).
  21.1–34: Reply of Job. In a bold display of wordly skepticism, the sufferer retorts that the wicked usually remain unpunished (vv. 7–13) though they repudiated God (vv. 14–18), and that belief in hereditary guilt (collective responsibility) is immoral (vv. 19–26), as is also the honor-

⁴ As for me, is my complaint against
    man?
    Why should I not be impatient?
⁵ Look at me, and be appalled,
    and lay your hand upon your
    mouth.
⁶ When I think of it I am dismayed,
    and shuddering seizes my flesh.
⁷ Why do the wicked live,
    reach old age, and grow mighty
    in power?
⁸ Their children are established in
    their presence,
    and their offspring before their
    eyes.
⁹ Their houses are safe from fear,
    and no rod of God is upon them.
¹⁰ Their bull breeds without fail;
    their cow calves, and does not cast
    her calf.
¹¹ They send forth their little ones like
    a flock,
    and their children dance.
¹² They sing to the tambourine and the
    lyre,
    and rejoice to the sound of the
    pipe.
¹³ They spend their days in prosperity,
    and in peace they go down to
    Sheol.
¹⁴ They say to God, 'Depart from us!
    We do not desire the knowledge
    of thy ways.
¹⁵ What is the Almighty, that we
    should serve him?
    And what profit do we get if we
    pray to him?'
¹⁶ Behold, is not their prosperity in
    their hand?
    The counsel of the wicked is far
    from me.

¹⁷ "How often is it that the lamp of the
    wicked is put out?
    That their calamity comes upon
    them?
    That God^c distributes pains in his
    anger?
¹⁸ That they are like straw before the
    wind,

and like chaff that the storm
    carries away?
¹⁹ You say, 'God stores up their
    iniquity for their sons.'
    Let him recompense it to
    themselves, that they may
    know it.
²⁰ Let their own eyes see their
    destruction,
    and let them drink of the wrath of
    the Almighty.
²¹ For what do they care for their
    houses after them,
    when the number of their months
    is cut off?
²² Will any teach God knowledge,
    seeing that he judges those that are
    on high?
²³ One dies in full prosperity,
    being wholly at ease and secure,
²⁴ his body^d full of fat
    and the marrow of his bones moist.
²⁵ Another dies in bitterness of soul,
    never having tasted of good.
²⁶ They lie down alike in the dust,
    and the worms cover them.

²⁷ "Behold, I know your thoughts,
    and your schemes to wrong me.
²⁸ For you say, 'Where is the house of
    the prince?
    Where is the tent in which the
    wicked dwelt?'
²⁹ Have you not asked those who travel
    the roads,
    and do you not accept their
    testimony
³⁰ that the wicked man is spared in the
    day of calamity,
    that he is rescued in the day of
    wrath?
³¹ Who declares his way to his face,
    and who requites him for what he
    has done?
³² When he is borne to the grave,
    watch is kept over his tomb.
³³ The clods of the valley are sweet to
    him;

c Heb *he*
d The meaning of the Hebrew word is uncertain

able funeral of the wicked (vv. 27–34). **15:** The wicked agree with the thesis brought forward by
Satan in the prologue (1.9).

all men follow after him,
and those who go before him are
innumerable.
34 How then will you comfort me with
empty nothings?
There is nothing left of your
answers but falsehood."

22 Then Eli′phaz the Te′manite
answered:
2 "Can a man be profitable to God?
Surely he who is wise is profitable
to himself.
3 Is it any pleasure to the Almighty if
you are righteous,
or is it gain to him if you make
your ways blameless?
4 Is it for your fear of him that he
reproves you,
and enters into judgment with you?
5 Is not your wickedness great?
There is no end to your iniquities.
6 For you have exacted pledges of your
brothers for nothing,
and stripped the naked of their
clothing.
7 You have given no water to the weary
to drink,
and you have withheld bread from
the hungry.
8 The man with power possessed the
land,
and the favored man dwelt in it.
9 You have sent widows away empty,
and the arms of the fatherless were
crushed.
10 Therefore snares are round about
you,
and sudden terror overwhelms
you;
11 your light is darkened, so that*e* you
cannot see,
and a flood of water covers you.

12 "Is not God high in the heavens?
See the highest stars, how lofty
they are!
13 Therefore you say, 'What does God
know?
Can he judge through the deep
darkness?
14 Thick clouds enwrap him, so that he
does not see,
and he walks on the vault of
heaven.'
15 Will you keep to the old way
which wicked men have trod?
16 They were snatched away before
their time;
their foundation was washed away.
17 They said to God, 'Depart from us,'
and 'What can the Almighty do to
us?'*f*
18 Yet he filled their houses with good
things–
but the counsel of the wicked is far
from me.
19 The righteous see it and are glad;
the innocent laugh them to scorn,
20 saying, 'Surely our adversaries are
cut off,
and what they left the fire has
consumed.'

21 "Agree with God, and be at peace;
thereby good will come to you.
22 Receive instruction from his mouth,
and lay up his words in your heart.
23 If you return to the Almighty and
humble yourself,*g*
if you remove unrighteousness far
from your tents,
24 if you lay gold in the dust,
and gold of Ophir among the
stones of the torrent bed,

e Cn Compare Gk: Heb *or darkness*
f Gk Syr: Heb *them*
g Gk: Heb *you will be built up*

22.1–30: Third discourse of Eliphaz. 2: In his role as the self-appointed upholder of a lofty form of theism, Eliphaz stretches a truth to the absurd. Surely God does not need man (the word suggests a strong, vigorous man) or even a wise man. The renowned teacher, Eliphaz, admits that even a member of his own profession is not *profitable to God!* At the same time, religion is profitable to man. **3:** Job's righteousness would not give any *pleasure to the Almighty.* The friend implies a doctrine of an impassive deity, which is quite contrary to Biblical thought (Hos. ch. 9; Is.62.5; Lk.15.7). **17–18:** These words are almost identical with those of Job in 21.14–16; perhaps Eliphaz is quoting in order to rebuke. **18:** *From me,* read with the Greek version, "from him."

25 and if the Almighty is your gold,
  and your precious silver;
26 then you will delight yourself in the
    Almighty,
  and lift up your face to God.
27 You will make your prayer to him,
    and he will hear you;
  and you will pay your vows.
28 You will decide on a matter, and it
    will be established for you,
  and light will shine on your ways.
29 For God abases the proud,[h]
  but he saves the lowly.
30 He delivers the innocent man;[i]
  you will be delivered through the
  cleanness of your hands."

23 Then Job answered:
2 "Today also my complaint is
    bitter,[j]
  his[k] hand is heavy in spite of my
  groaning.
3 Oh, that I knew where I might find
    him,
  that I might come even to his seat!
4 I would lay my case before him
  and fill my mouth with arguments.
5 I would learn what he would answer
    me,
  and understand what he would
  say to me.
6 Would he contend with me in the
    greatness of his power?
  No; he would give heed to me.
7 There an upright man could reason
    with him,
  and I should be acquitted for ever
  by my judge.

8 "Behold, I go forward, but he is not
    there;

and backward, but I cannot
  perceive him;
9 on the left hand I seek him,[l] but I
  cannot behold him;
  I[m] turn to the right hand, but I
  cannot see him.
10 But he knows the way that I take;
  when he has tried me, I shall
  come forth as gold.
11 My foot has held fast to his steps;
  I have kept his way and have not
  turned aside.
12 I have not departed from the
    commandment of his lips;
  I have treasured in[n] my bosom
  the words of his mouth.
13 But he is unchangeable and who
    can turn him?
  What he desires, that he does.
14 For he will complete what he
    appoints for me;
  and many such things are in his
  mind.
15 Therefore I am terrified at his
    presence;
  when I consider, I am in dread of
  him.
16 God has made my heart faint;
  the Almighty has terrified me;
17 for I am[o] hemmed in by darkness,
  and thick darkness covers my
  face.[p]

24 "Why are not times of judgment
    kept by the Almighty,
  and why do those who know him
  never see his days?

h Cn: Heb *when they abased you said, Proud*
i Gk Syr Vg: Heb *him that is not innocent*
j Syr Vg Tg: Heb *rebellious*   k Gk Syr: Heb *my*
l Compare Syr: Heb *on the left hand when he works*
m Syr Vg: Heb *he*   n Gk Vg: Heb *from*
o With one Ms: Heb *am not*   p Vg: Heb *from my face*

23.1–24.17: Reply of Job. A new search for God's presence. **2:** *Today,* this suggests that the discussion extended over a long period of time. Retain the Hebrew "rebellious" (note *j*); Job is aware of his revolt. **3–7:** For the absent God or the God who hides himself, see Ps.22.1–5; Is.45.15. Job seeks to obtain from the elusive judge an audience and a recognition of his virtue. **7:** *I should be acquitted for ever by my judge,* read with the Greek version, "I should recover my right for ever." **8–17:** Job looks for God. **13:** *He is unchangeable,* literally, "he is in one," which may mean, as paraphrased in the Greek, "he has decided." There is no reference to his immutability. **17:** Perhaps render, "For I did not keep quiet in spite of the [coming] darkness," or, "I am not overwhelmed by darkness," since the terror of God is worse than the proximity of death (vv. 15–16). **24.1–17:** God pays no heed to prayer. **1.** The Hebrew is obscure; probably read, "Why are not times [i.e. events] kept hidden from the Almighty, since those who know him never see his days [i.e. of judgment]?" If God were not omniscient, the problem of evil would

2 Men remove landmarks;
    they seize flocks and pasture
      them.
3 They drive away the ass of the
    fatherless;
    they take the widow's ox for a
      pledge.
4 They thrust the poor off the road;
    the poor of the earth all hide
      themselves.
5 Behold, like wild asses in the desert
    they go forth to their toil,
    seeking prey in the wilderness
      as food*q* for their children.
6 They gather their*r* fodder in the field
    and they glean the vineyard of
      the wicked man.
7 They lie all night naked, without
    clothing,
    and have no covering in the cold.
8 They are wet with the rain of the
    mountains,
    and cling to the rock for want of
      shelter.
9 (There are those who snatch the
    fatherless child from the
      breast,
    and take in pledge the infant of
      the poor.)
10 They go about naked, without
    clothing;
    hungry, they carry the sheaves;
11 among the olive rows of the
    wicked*s* they make oil;
    they tread the wine presses, but
      suffer thirst.
12 From out of the city the dying
    groan,
    and the soul of the wounded
      cries for help;
    yet God pays no attention to their
      prayer.
13 "There are those who rebel against
    the light,

who are not acquainted with its
    ways,
    and do not stay in its paths.
14 The murderer rises in the dark,*t*
    that he may kill the poor and
      needy;
    and in the night he is as a thief.
15 The eye of the adulterer also waits
    for the twilight,
    saying, 'No eye will see me';
    and he disguises his face.
16 In the dark they dig through houses;
    by day they shut themselves up;
    they do not know the light.
17 For deep darkness is morning to all
    of them;
    for they are friends with the
      terrors of deep darkness.

18 "You say, 'They are swiftly carried
    away upon the face of the
      waters;
    their portion is cursed in the land;
    no treader turns toward their
      vineyards.
19 Drought and heat snatch away the
    snow waters;
    so does Sheol those who have
      sinned.
20 The squares of the town*u* forget
    them;
    their name*v* is no longer
      remembered;
    so wickedness is broken like a
      tree.'

21 "They feed on the barren childless
    woman,
    and do no good to the widow.
22 Yet God*w* prolongs the life of the
    mighty by his power;
    they rise up when they despair of
      life.

q Heb *food to him*   *r* Heb *his*
s Heb *their olive rows*   *t* Cn: Heb *at the light*
u Cn: Heb obscure   *v* Cn: Heb *a worm*   *w* Heb *he*

not be a stumbling-block to men of faith. **12:** *The wounded*, perhaps read with the Greek version, "the little children."

    24.18–25: Third discourse of Zophar (?). A fragment of what was probably the original third discourse of the third friend, now transferred to the mouth of Job by a pious editor who softened the hero's blasphemous arrogance (see also 27.13–23). This poetic section develops the dogma of individual retribution; God's justice may be delayed (v. 22), but it never fails (vv. 23–25). The RSV inserts the words, *You say* (v. 18), to indicate that these lines are a quotation of the friend's views made by Job.

23 He gives them security, and they
    are supported;
  and his eyes are upon their ways.
24 They are exalted a little while, and
    then are gone;
  they wither and fade like the
    mallow;[x]
  they are cut off like the heads of
    grain.
25 If it is not so, who will prove me a
    liar,
  and show that there is nothing in
    what I say?"

25 Then Bildad the Shuhite an-
    swered:
2 "Dominion and fear are with God;[y]
  he makes peace in his high
    heaven.
3 Is there any number to his armies?
  Upon whom does his light not
    arise?
4 How then can man be righteous
    before God?
  How can he who is born of
    woman be clean?
5 Behold, even the moon is not bright
  and the stars are not clean in his
    sight;
6 how much less man, who is a
    maggot,
  and the son of man, who is a
    worm!"

26 Then Job answered:
2 "How you have helped him
  who has no power!

How you have saved the arm that
  has no strength!
3 How you have counseled him who
    has no wisdom,
  and plentifully declared sound
    knowledge!
4 With whose help have you uttered
    words,
  and whose spirit has come forth
    from you?
5 The shades below tremble,
  the waters and their inhabitants.
6 Sheol is naked before God,
  and Abaddon has no covering.
7 He stretches out the north over
    the void,
  and hangs the earth upon nothing.
8 He binds up the waters in his thick
    clouds,
  and the cloud is not rent under
    them.
9 He covers the face of the moon,[z]
  and spreads over it his cloud.
10 He has described a circle upon the
    face of the waters
  at the boundary between light
    and darkness.
11 The pillars of heaven tremble,
  and are astounded at his rebuke.
12 By his power he stilled the sea;
  by his understanding he smote
    Rahab.
13 By his wind the heavens were made
    fair;
  his hand pierced the fleeing
    serpent.

x Gk: Heb *all*   *y* Heb *him*   *z* Or *his throne*

25.1–6: Third discourse of Bildad. The theme of man's uncleanness and abasement, already developed by Eliphaz (4.17–21; 15.14–16) and Zophar (11.5–12), to which Job has subscribed (9.2–12; 12.9–25; 14.4) without using it for self-accusation.

26.1–4: Reply of Job. The sufferer again uses heavy sarcasm. He implies that Bildad, however lofty the monotheism of the wise men may be on the surface, has communed with evil spirits.

26.5–14: Continuation of Bildad's third discourse (?). While the theme of divine omnipotence is not impossible in the mouth of Job, it has been ignored by the hero in the third round of discussion and is replaced by the theme of divine indifference. Moreover, this section is unrelated to its immediate context (vv. 2–4 and 27.2), while its ideas fit closely with those which have just been enunciated by Bildad. After referring to heaven and earth (25.2–6), the poet normally turns to *Sheol*. Job had hoped to be hidden in the underworld (14.13), but he cannot escape, even there, the reach of God (an idea common to wisdom literature, 12.22; Ps.139.7; Pr.15.11; see Am.9.2. **6:** *Abaddon,* a name of Sheol, meaning "[place of] destruction" (Ps.88.11; Pr.15.11; Rev.9.11). **7:** *Over the void . . . upon nothing,* the poet stresses the completeness of the creative act, an anticipation of the later doctrine of creation "ex nihilo" (from nothing). Pagan mythology with its dualistic cosmogony has influenced the poet's allusions to a cosmic fight (vv.10–13), but it is now absorbed in a completely monistic theology.

¹⁴ Lo, these are but the outskirts of
  his ways;
    and how small a whisper do we
    hear of him!
  But the thunder of his power who
  can understand?"

27 And Job again took up his discourse, and said:
² "As God lives, who has taken away
  my right,
    and the Almighty, who has made
    my soul bitter;
³ as long as my breath is in me,
    and the spirit of God is in my
    nostrils;
⁴ my lips will not speak falsehood,
    and my tongue will not utter
    deceit.
⁵ Far be it from me to say that you
  are right;
    till I die I will not put away my
    integrity from me.
⁶ I hold fast my righteousness, and
  will not let it go;
    my heart does not reproach me
    for any of my days.

⁷ "Let my enemy be as the wicked,
    and let him that rises up against
    me be as the unrighteous.
⁸ For what is the hope of the godless
  when God cuts him off,
    when God takes away his life?
⁹ Will God hear his cry,
    when trouble comes upon him?
¹⁰ Will he take delight in the Almighty?
  Will he call upon God at all times?
¹¹ I will teach you concerning the
  hand of God;
    what is with the Almighty I will
    not conceal.
¹² Behold, all of you have seen it
  yourselves;
    why then have you become
    altogether vain?

¹³ "This is the portion of a wicked man
  with God,
    and the heritage which oppressors
    receive from the Almighty:
¹⁴ If his children are multiplied, it is for
  the sword;
    and his offspring have not enough
    to eat.
¹⁵ Those who survive him the
  pestilence buries,
    and their widows make no
    lamentation.
¹⁶ Though he heap up silver like dust,
    and pile up clothing like clay;
¹⁷ he may pile it up, but the just will
  wear it,
    and the innocent will divide the
    silver.
¹⁸ The house which he builds is like a
  spider's web,ᵃ
    like a booth which a watchman
    makes.
¹⁹ He goes to bed rich, but will do so
  no more;ᵇ
    he opens his eyes, and his wealth
    is gone.
²⁰ Terrors overtake him like a flood;
    in the night a whirlwind carries
    him off.
²¹ The east wind lifts him up and he is
  gone;
    it sweeps him out of his place.
²² Itᶜ hurls at him without pity;
    he flees from itsᵈ power in
    headlong flight.
²³ Itᶜ claps itsᵈ hands at him,
    and hisses at him from itsᵈ place.

28 "Surely there is a mine for
silver,
    and a place for gold which they
    refine.
² Iron is taken out of the earth,

---

a Cn Compare Gk Syr: Heb *He builds his house like the moth*
b Gk Compare Syr: Heb *shall not be gathered*
c Or *he* (that is God)   d Or *his*

27.1–12: Job's reply. Job again maintains his innocence and affirms his sincerity.

27.13–23: Continuation of third discourse of Zophar (?), see 24.18–25 n. A traditional picture of the destiny of the wicked and of his sons. After vv. 11–12 one would expect a new expression of defiance; therefore this section probably represents a fragment of the third speech of the third friend, now placed on the hero's lips.

28.1–28: Hymn on the inaccessibility of wisdom. Wisdom is not at the disposal of man but remains the prerogative of God (see refrains in vv. 12–13,20–21). As Bildad had praised divine

and copper is smelted from the ore.

³ Men put an end to darkness,
and search out to the farthest
bound
the ore in gloom and deep
darkness.
⁴ They open shafts in a valley away
from where men live;
they are forgotten by travelers,
they hang afar from men, they
swing to and fro.
⁵ As for the earth, out of it comes
bread;
but underneath it is turned up as
by fire.
⁶ Its stones are the place of sapphires,ᵉ
and it has dust of gold.

⁷ "That path no bird of prey knows,
and the falcon's eye has not seen
it.
⁸ The proud beasts have not trodden
it;
the lion has not passed over it.

⁹ "Man puts his hand to the flinty
rock,
and overturns mountains by the
roots.
¹⁰ He cuts out channels in the rocks,
and his eye sees every precious
thing.
¹¹ He binds up the streams so that they
do not trickle,
and the thing that is hid he brings
forth to light.

¹² "But where shall wisdom be found?
And where is the place of
understanding?
¹³ Man does not know the way to it,ᶠ
and it is not found in the land of
the living.
¹⁴ The deep says, 'It is not in me,'

and the sea says, 'It is not with me.'
¹⁵ It cannot be gotten for gold,
and silver cannot be weighed as
its price.
¹⁶ It cannot be valued in the gold of
Ophir,
in precious onyx or sapphire.ᵍ
¹⁷ Gold and glass cannot equal it,
nor can it be exchanged for jewels
of fine gold.
¹⁸ No mention shall be made of coral
or of crystal;
the price of wisdom is above
pearls.
¹⁹ The topaz of Ethiopia cannot
compare with it,
nor can it be valued in pure gold.

²⁰ "Whence then comes wisdom?
And where is the place of
understanding?
²¹ It is hid from the eyes of all living,
and concealed from the birds of
the air.
²² Abaddon and Death say,
'We have heard a rumor of it
with our ears.'

²³ "God understands the way to it,
and he knows its place.
²⁴ For he looks to the ends of the earth,
and sees everything under the
heavens.
²⁵ When he gave to the wind its weight,
and meted out the waters by
measure;
²⁶ when he made a decree for the rain,
and a way for the lightning of the
thunder;
²⁷ then he saw it and declared it;
he established it, and searched it
out.
²⁸ And he said to man,

ᵉ Or *lapis lazuli*
ᶠ Gk: Heb *its price*
ᵍ Or *lapis lazuli*

power in heaven, earth, and Sheol (25.2–6; 26.5–14), the poet searches every part of the universe in order to discover divine wisdom. **1–22:** Human technology is powerless in the realm of divine knowledge. **2–6:** Allusions to Egyptian mines, probably in the Sinaitic peninsula. **14:** The forces of *the deep* and of *the sea* were deified by ancient man, who worshiped them in an effort to secure their favor and his safety. **23–27:** Wisdom is the exclusive property of God (Pr.8.22–31). **28:** The orthodox motto of the Jewish sages after the Babylonian exile; it reveals an entirely different concept of wisdom from that implied in the body of the poem. Here, wisdom is accessible to man and identified with piety (*the fear of the Lord*) and morality (*to depart from evil*).

'Behold, the fear of the Lord, that is wisdom;
and to depart from evil is understanding' "

29 And Job again took up his discourse, and said:

2 "Oh, that I were as in the months of old,
as in the days when God watched over me;
3 when his lamp shone upon my head,
and by his light I walked through darkness;
4 as I was in my autumn days,
when the friendship of God was upon my tent;
5 when the Almighty was yet with me,
when my children were about me;
6 when my steps were washed with milk,
and the rock poured out for me streams of oil!
7 When I went out to the gate of the city,
when I prepared my seat in the square,
8 the young men saw me and withdrew,
and the aged rose and stood;
9 the princes refrained from talking,
and laid their hand on their mouth;
10 the voice of the nobles was hushed,
and their tongue cleaved to the roof of their mouth.
11 When the ear heard, it called me blessed,
and when the eye saw, it approved;
12 because I delivered the poor who cried,
and the fatherless who had none to help him.
13 The blessing of him who was about to perish came upon me,
and I caused the widow's heart to sing for joy.

14 I put on righteousness, and it clothed me;
my justice was like a robe and a turban.
15 I was eyes to the blind,
and feet to the lame.
16 I was a father to the poor,
and I searched out the cause of him whom I did not know.
17 I broke the fangs of the unrighteous,
and made him drop his prey from his teeth.
18 Then I thought, 'I shall die in my nest,
and I shall multiply my days as the sand,
19 my roots spread out to the waters,
with the dew all night on my branches,
20 my glory fresh with me,
and my bow ever new in my hand.'

21 "Men listened to me, and waited,
and kept silence for my counsel.
22 After I spoke they did not speak again,
and my word dropped upon them.
23 They waited for me as for the rain;
and they opened their mouths as for the spring rain.
24 I smiled on them when they had no confidence;
and the light of my countenance they did not cast down.
25 I chose their way, and sat as chief,
and I dwelt like a king among his troops,
like one who comforts mourners.

30 "But now they make sport of me,
men who are younger than I,
whose fathers I would have disdained
to set with the dogs of my flock.

29.1–31.40: The final defense of Job. Contrasting his happy past (ch. 29) with the present distress (ch. 30), the sufferer delivers his final plea or oath of clearance (ch. 31). **29.4:** *In my autumn days,* literally, "in the days of fruit gathering," perhaps meaning, in the days of the full powers of his adulthood, rather than a reference to old age. The traditional picture of Job as an old man is not supported by the many incidental references to his vigorous maturity. The sufferer's agony is made the more cruel by the circumstance that he was stricken at the height of his physical and intellectual powers (v. 20). **18:** *As the sand,* with different vowels the Hebrew

2 What could I gain from the strength
of their hands,
men whose vigor is gone?
3 Through want and hard hunger
they gnaw the dry and desolate
ground;[h]
4 they pick mallow and the leaves of
bushes,
and to warm themselves the roots
of the broom.
5 They are driven out from among
men;
they shout after them as after a
thief.
6 In the gullies of the torrents they
must dwell,
in holes of the earth and of the
rocks.
7 Among the bushes they bray;
under the nettles they huddle
together.
8 A senseless, a disreputable brood,
they have been whipped out of the
land.

9 "And now I have become their song,
I am a byword to them.
10 They abhor me, they keep aloof from
me;
they do not hesitate to spit at the
sight of me.
11 Because God has loosed my cord
and humbled me,
they have cast off restraint in my
presence.
12 On my right hand the rabble rise,
they drive me[i] forth,
they cast up against me their ways
of destruction.
13 They break up my path,
they promote my calamity;
no one restrains[j] them.
14 As through[k] a wide breach they
come;
amid the crash they roll on.
15 Terrors are turned upon me;
my honor is pursued as by the
wind,
and my prosperity has passed
away like a cloud.

16 "And now my soul is poured out
within me;
days of affliction have taken hold
of me.
17 The night racks my bones,
and the pain that gnaws me takes
no rest.
18 With violence it seizes my garment;[l]
it binds me about like the collar of
my tunic.
19 God has cast me into the mire,
and I have become like dust and
ashes.
20 I cry to thee and thou dost not answer
me;
I stand, and thou dost not[m] heed me.
21 Thou hast turned cruel to me;
with the might of thy hand thou
dost persecute me.
22 Thou liftest me up on the wind,
thou makest me ride on it,
and thou tossest me about in the
roar of the storm.
23 Yea, I know that thou wilt bring me
to death,
and to the house appointed for all
living.

24 "Yet does not one in a heap of ruins
stretch out his hand,
and in his disaster cry for help?[n]
25 Did not I weep for him whose day
was hard?
Was not my soul grieved for the
poor?
26 But when I looked for good, evil
came;
and when I waited for light,
darkness came.
27 My heart is in turmoil, and is never
still;
days of affliction come to meet me.
28 I go about blackened, but not by the
sun;
I stand up in the assembly, and
cry for help.
29 I am a brother of jackals,
and a companion of ostriches.

h Heb *ground yesterday waste*   i Heb *my feet*
j Cn: Heb *helps*   k Cn: Heb *like*
l Gk: Heb *my garment is disfigured*
m One Heb Ms and Vg: Heb lacks *not*
n Cn: Heb obscure

can be read, "as the phoenix" (note *nest* in preceding line).

30 My skin turns black and falls from
me,
and my bones burn with heat.
31 My lyre is turned to mourning,
and my pipe to the voice of those
who weep.

31 "I have made a covenant with my
eyes;
how then could I look upon a
virgin?
2 What would be my portion from
God above,
and my heritage from the
Almighty on high?
3 Does not calamity befall the
unrighteous,
and disaster the workers of
iniquity?
4 Does not he see my ways,
and number all my steps?

5 "If I have walked with falsehood,
and my foot has hastened to
deceit;
6 (Let me be weighed in a just balance,
and let God know my integrity!)
7 if my step has turned aside from
the way,
and my heart has gone after my
eyes,
and if any spot has cleaved to my
hands;
8 then let me sow, and another eat;
and let what grows for me be
rooted out.

9 "If my heart has been enticed to a
woman,
and I have lain in wait at my
neighbor's door;
10 then let my wife grind for another,
and let others bow down upon
her.
11 For that would be a heinous crime;

that would be an iniquity to be
punished by the judges;
12 for that would be a fire which
consumes unto Abaddon,
and it would burn to the root all
my increase.

13 "If I have rejected the cause of my
manservant or my maidservant,
when they brought a complaint
against me;
14 what then shall I do when God
rises up?
When he makes inquiry, what
shall I answer him?
15 Did not he who made me in the
womb make him?
And did not one fashion us in the
womb?

16 "If I have withheld anything that the
poor desired,
or have caused the eyes of the
widow to fail,
17 or have eaten my morsel alone,
and the fatherless has not eaten
of it
18 (for from his youth I reared him
as a father,
and from his mother's womb I
guided him*);
19 if I have seen any one perish for lack
of clothing,
or a poor man without covering;
20 if his loins have not blessed me,
and if he was not warmed with the
fleece of my sheep;
21 if I have raised my hand against the
fatherless,
because I saw help in the gate;
22 then let my shoulder blade fall from
my shoulder,
and let my arm be broken from
its socket.

o Cn: Heb *for from my youth he grew up to me as a
father, and from my mother's womb I guided her*

31.1–34,38–40: To convince God and men of his innocence, Job reviews his past behavior
in the form of sixteen oaths, covering various aspects of religious and moral misdeeds. The
poet offers by implication the evidence of a refined ethical consciousness (which has parallels with the Egyptian Book of the Dead, ch. 125). 1: *A covenant with my eyes* implies a
mature form of introspective awareness. *Look upon a virgin*, Job knows the psychology of
covetousness (Mt.5.28). 13–15: Slaves have rights, established by the Creator for all men.
16–23: A nomadic sense of social responsibility for the total community. 24–28: Job is con-

23 For I was in terror of calamity from God,
and I could not have faced his majesty.

24 "If I have made gold my trust,
or called fine gold my confidence;
25 if I have rejoiced because my wealth was great,
or because my hand had gotten much;
26 if I have looked at the sun*p* when it shone,
or the moon moving in splendor,
27 and my heart has been secretly enticed,
and my mouth has kissed my hand;
28 this also would be an iniquity to be punished by the judges,
for I should have been false to God above.

29 "If I have rejoiced at the ruin of him that hated me,
or exulted when evil overtook him
30 (I have not let my mouth sin
by asking for his life with a curse);
31 if the men of my tent have not said,
'Who is there that has not been filled with his meat?'
32 (the sojourner has not lodged in the street;
I have opened my doors to the wayfarer);
33 if I have concealed my transgressions from men,*q*
by hiding my iniquity in my bosom,

34 because I stood in great fear of the multitude,
and the contempt of families terrified me,
so that I kept silence, and did not go out of doors—
35 Oh, that I had one to hear me!
(Here is my signature! let the Almighty answer me!)
Oh, that I had the indictment written by my adversary!
36 Surely I would carry it on my shoulder;
I would bind it on me as a crown;
37 I would give him an account of all my steps;
like a prince I would approach him.

38 "If my land has cried out against me,
and its furrows have wept together;
39 if I have eaten its yield without payment,
and caused the death of its owners;
40 let thorns grow instead of wheat,
and foul weeds instead of barley."

The words of Job are ended.

32 So these three men ceased to answer Job, because he was righteous in his own eyes. 2 Then Eli'hu the son of Bar'achel the Buzite, of the family of Ram, became angry. He was angry at Job because he justified himself rather than God; 3 he was angry also at Job's three friends be-

---

p Heb *the light*   *q* Cn: Heb *like men* or *like Adam*

scious of the spiritual deterioration behind the worship of idols. **26–27:** Nature worship (compare 2 Kg.21.3–5; Jer.44.17–18; Ezek.8.16) is condemned, because it gives man the illusion of being the master of his destiny (v. 28). *My mouth has kissed my hand,* a form of idolatrous worship (compare 1 Kg.19.18). **33:** *I have concealed my transgression from men;* read with note *q,* "like Adam." The poet is haunted by the relevance of the story of the garden of Eden (Gen.3.10). **35–37:** The thought which has dominated the speeches of Job has been his intense desire to see God. The ultimate challenge is hurled at the Deity, but not in a spirit of surrender and humility. *Here is my signature!* Literally, "my taw" (*taw,* the last letter of the Hebrew alphabet, was then in the shape of an X). Job does not fear any *indictment;* he would use it as a symbol of honor (v. 36). **37:** *Like a prince I would approach him,* not as a servant, in the manner of oriental monarchs presenting themselves before their gods and goddesses, but as a noble, unbowed, unshattered hero. Job's self-confidence remains unshaken. **38–40:** A last protest, asserting Job's freedom from corruption of the fields; it may be a subtle allusion to the curse on the soil (compare Gen.3.17–18).

32.1–37.24: Discourses of Elihu. Most commentators believe that these chapters, with their peculiar language (containing many Aramaic words) and different style (the new speaker seems to quote Job's speeches and even the yet-undelivered discourse of the LORD), belong to a

cause they had found no answer, although they had declared Job to be in the wrong. 4 Now Eli′hu had waited to speak to Job because they were older than he. 5 And when Eli′hu saw that there was no answer in the mouth of these three men, he became angry.

6 And Eli′hu the son of Bar′achel the Buzite answered:

"I am young in years,
and you are aged;
therefore I was timid and afraid
to declare my opinion to you.
7 I said, 'Let days speak,
and many years teach wisdom.'
8 But it is the spirit in a man,
the breath of the Almighty, that
makes him understand.
9 It is not the old′ that are wise,
nor the aged that understand what
is right.
10 Therefore I say, 'Listen to me;
let me also declare my opinion.'

11 "Behold, I waited for your words,
I listened for your wise sayings,
while you searched out what to
say.
12 I gave you my attention,
and, behold, there was none that
confuted Job,
or that answered his words,
among you.
13 Beware lest you say, 'We have
found wisdom;

God may vanquish him, not man.'
14 He has not directed his words
against me,
and I will not answer him with
your speeches.

15 "They are discomfited, they answer
no more;
they have not a word to say.
16 And shall I wait, because they do
not speak,
because they stand there, and
answer no more?
17 I also will give my answer;
I also will declare my opinion.
18 For I am full of words,
the spirit within me constrains me.
19 Behold, my heart is like wine that
has no vent;
like new wineskins, it is ready to
burst.
20 I must speak, that I may find relief;
I must open my lips and answer.
21 I will not show partiality to any
person
or use flattery toward any man.
22 For I do not know how to flatter,
else would my Maker soon put an
end to me.

33 "But now, hear my speech, O
Job,
and listen to all my words.
2 Behold, I open my mouth;

r Gk Syr Vg: Heb *many*

---

later hand than that of the poet. In addition to these internal differences, Job's final challenge (31.35–37) calls for the immediate manifestation of God. Likewise, the epilogue (42.7–17) ignores Elihu, which may indicate that he did not belong to the original cast of characters. Nevertheless, this section of the book presents with genuine depth a series of new ideas: the revelatory function of suffering, the stern nature of the love of God, and a hint of salvation by faith. And Elihu's speeches serve to prepare dramatically, psychologically, and theologically for the intervention of the LORD. **32.1–6: Prose introductions.** The repetitions indicate the long process of literary transmission. **2:** The name *Elihu* means, "My God is he," perhaps a symbolic name here (it also occurs in 1 Sam.1.1; 1 Chr.12.20). *Buzite* suggests that Elihu was an Aramean living not far from Edom, for Buz in Gen.22.21 is a brother of Uz (see Job 1.1 n.) and an Aramean (compare Gen.11.26–32), and in Jer.25.23 it is a place name in Edom. **2:** *He justified himself rather than God,* Elihu quite correctly estimates the situation. Job has risen for the defense of man, not God. **3:** There is some evidence that the statement, *they had declared Job to be in the wrong,* originally read, "they had condemned God," an offensive phrase which the scribes corrected in the manuscripts. The silence of the friends after Job's final oath amounts to their assent. **6–22:** Poetic introduction. Spirit, not age, is the source of wisdom. Elihu offers revealed knowledge (v. 8) rather than the voice of human experience and tradition. The ludicrous boastfulness of his introductory remarks may have been introduced as a comical element, to relieve tragic tension.

the tongue in my mouth speaks.
3 My words declare the uprightness
of my heart,
and what my lips know they speak
sincerely.
4 The spirit of God has made me,
and the breath of the Almighty
gives me life.
5 Answer me, if you can;
set your words in order before me;
take your stand.
6 Behold, I am toward God as you are;
I too was formed from a piece of
clay.
7 Behold, no fear of me need terrify
you;
my pressure will not be heavy
upon you.

8 "Surely, you have spoken in my
hearing,
and I have heard the sound of
your words.
9 You say, 'I am clean, without
transgression;
I am pure, and there is no iniquity
in me.
10 Behold, he finds occasions against
me,
he counts me as his enemy;
11 he puts my feet in the stocks,
and watches all my paths.'

12 "Behold, in this you are not right. I
will answer you.
God is greater than man.
13 Why do you contend against him,
saying, 'He will answer none of
my*s* words'?
14 For God speaks in one way,
and in two, though man does not
perceive it.
15 In a dream, in a vision of the night,
when deep sleep falls upon men,

while they slumber on their beds,
16 then he opens the ears of men,
and terrifies them with warnings,
17 that he may turn man aside from his
deed,
and cut off*t* pride from man;
18 he keeps back his soul from the Pit,
his life from perishing by the
sword.

19 "Man is also chastened with pain
upon his bed,
and with continual strife in his
bones;
20 so that his life loathes bread,
and his appetite dainty food.
21 His flesh is so wasted away that it
cannot be seen;
and his bones which were not seen
stick out.
22 His soul draws near the Pit,
and his life to those who bring
death.
23 If there be for him an angel,
a mediator, one of the thousand,
to declare to man what is right for
him;
24 and he is gracious to him, and says,
'Deliver him from going down into
the Pit,
I have found a ransom;
25 let his flesh become fresh with
youth;
let him return to the days of his
youthful vigor';
26 then man prays to God, and he
accepts him,
he comes into his presence with
joy.
He recounts*u* to men his salvation,
27 and he sings before men, and says:

s Compare Gk: Heb *his*
t Cn: Heb *hide*
u Cn: Heb *returns*

33.1–33: First poem of Elihu. 6: The obscure Hebrew of the first line seems to mean, "Behold I am your equal, not God!" **23–28:** Grace is given man, not bought or forced by him. Suffering prepares man to receive the self-disclosure of God. If there is *an angel, a mediator* (rather, "an intercessor"), who would also *declare to man what is right for him,* then God would *be gracious to him* (v. 24a). Here is a whole theology of salvation by grace in miniature. Man does not save himself by an achievement of his will. The intercessor offers on his behalf *a ransom* (v. 24c). Only as a result of this mediation will man be able to pray to God and to come *into his presence with joy* (v. 26). Afterwards he will testify to other men, for repentance and awareness of sin are not the cause but the result of God's goodness (vv. 27–28).

'I sinned, and perverted what was
    right,
    and it was not requited to me.
28 He has redeemed my soul from going
    down into the Pit,
    and my life shall see the light.'

29 "Behold, God does all these things,
    twice, three times, with a man,
30 to bring back his soul from the Pit,
    that he may see the light of life.*v*
31 Give heed, O Job, listen to me;
    be silent, and I will speak.
32 If you have anything to say, answer
    me;
    speak, for I desire to justify you.
33 If not, listen to me;
    be silent, and I will teach you
    wisdom."

34 Then Eli'hu said:
2 "Hear my words, you wise
    men,
    and give ear to me, you who know;
3 for the ear tests words
    as the palate tastes food.
4 Let us choose what is right;
    let us determine among ourselves
    what is good.
5 For Job has said, 'I am innocent,
    and God has taken away my
    right;
6 in spite of my right I am counted a
    liar;
    my wound is incurable, though I
    am without transgression.'
7 What man is like Job,
    who drinks up scoffing like water,
8 who goes in company with evildoers
    and walks with wicked men?
9 For he has said, 'It profits a man
    nothing
    that he should take delight in God.'

10 "Therefore, hear me, you men of
    understanding,
    far be it from God that he should
    do wickedness,
    and from the Almighty that he
    should do wrong.

11 For according to the work of a man
    he will requite him,
    and according to his ways he will
    make it befall him.
12 Of a truth, God will not do wickedly,
    and the Almighty will not pervert
    justice.
13 Who gave him charge over the earth
    and who laid on him*w* the whole
    world?
14 If he should take back his spirit*x* to
    himself,
    and gather to himself his breath,
15 all flesh would perish together,
    and man would return to dust.
16 "If you have understanding, hear
    this;
    listen to what I say.
17 Shall one who hates justice govern?
    Will you condemn him who is
    righteous and mighty,
18 who says to a king, 'Worthless one,'
    and to nobles, 'Wicked man';
19 who shows no partiality to princes,
    nor regards the rich more than the
    poor,
    for they are all the work of his
    hands?
20 In a moment they die;
    at midnight the people are shaken
    and pass away,
    and the mighty are taken away by
    no human hand.

21 "For his eyes are upon the ways of a
    man,
    and he sees all his steps.
22 There is no gloom or deep darkness
    where evildoers may hide
    themselves.
23 For he has not appointed a time*y* for
    any man
    to go before God in judgment.
24 He shatters the mighty without
    investigation,
    and sets others in their place.
25 Thus, knowing their works,

v Syr: Heb *to be lighted with the light of life*
w Heb lacks *on him*
x Heb *his heart his spirit*
y Cn: Heb *yet*

34.1–37: Second poem of Elihu. The ways of God are ultimately just; there is neither evil nor partiality in him. **37:** Job's sin is one of theological arrogance.

he overturns them in the night, and
they are crushed.
26 He strikes them for their wickedness
in the sight of men,
27 because they turned aside from
following him,
and had no regard for any of his
ways,
28 so that they caused the cry of the
poor to come to him,
and he heard the cry of the
afflicted–
29 When he is quiet, who can condemn?
When he hides his face, who can
behold him,
whether it be a nation or a man?–
30 that a godless man should not reign,
that he should not ensnare the
people.

31 "For has any one said to God,
'I have borne chastisement; I will
not offend any more;
32 teach me what I do not see;
if I have done iniquity, I will do it
no more'?
33 Will he then make requital to suit
you,
because you reject it?
For you must choose, and not I;
therefore declare what you know.z
34 Men of understanding will say to me,
and the wise man who hears me
will say:
35 'Job speaks without knowledge,
his words are without insight.'
36 Would that Job were tried to the end,
because he answers like wicked
men.
37 For he adds rebellion to his sin;
he claps his hands among us,
and multiplies his words against
God."

35 And Eli'hu said:
2 "Do you think this to be just?
Do you say, 'It is my right before
God,'
3 that you ask, 'What advantage
have I?

How am I better off than if I had
sinned?'
4 I will answer you
and your friends with you.
5 Look at the heavens, and see;
and behold the clouds, which are
higher than you.
6 If you have sinned, what do you
accomplish against him?
And if your transgressions are
multiplied, what do you do to
him?
7 If you are righteous, what do you
give to him;
or what does he receive from your
hand?
8 Your wickedness concerns a man
like yourself,
and your righteousness a son of
man.

9 "Because of the multitude of
oppressions people cry out;
they call for help because of the
arm of the mighty.
10 But none says, 'Where is God my
Maker,
who gives songs in the night,
11 who teaches us more than the beasts
of the earth,
and makes us wiser than the birds
of the air?'
12 There they cry out, but he does not
answer,
because of the pride of evil men.
13 Surely God does not hear an empty
cry,
nor does the Almighty regard it.
14 How much less when you say that
you do not see him,
that the case is before him, and
you are waiting for him!
15 And now, because his anger does
not punish,
and he does not greatly heed
transgression,a
16 Job opens his mouth in empty talk,

z The Hebrew of verses 29–33 is obscure
a Theodotion Symmachus Compare Vg: The meaning
of the Hebrew word is uncertain

35.1–16: Third poem of Elihu. God is independent of man (vv. 5–8), but his gifts of *songs in
the night* (v. 10) show the emptiness of man's haste in judging divine behavior.

he multiplies words without
knowledge."

36 And Eli′hu continued, and said:
2 "Bear with me a little, and I
   will show you,
for I have yet something to say on
   God's behalf.
3 I will fetch my knowledge from afar,
   and ascribe righteousness to my
   Maker.
4 For truly my words are not false;
   one who is perfect in knowledge is
   with you.

5 "Behold, God is mighty, and does
   not despise any;
he is mighty in strength of
   understanding.
6 He does not keep the wicked alive,
   but gives the afflicted their right.
7 He does not withdraw his eyes from
   the righteous,
but with kings upon the throne
he sets them for ever, and they are
   exalted.
8 And if they are bound in fetters
   and caught in the cords of
   affliction,
9 then he declares to them their work
   and their transgressions, that they
   are behaving arrogantly.
10 He opens their ears to instruction,
   and commands that they return
   from iniquity.
11 If they hearken and serve him,
   they complete their days in
   prosperity,
   and their years in pleasantness.
12 But if they do not hearken, they
   perish by the sword,
   and die without knowledge.

13 "The godless in heart cherish anger;
   they do not cry for help when he
   binds them.
14 They die in youth,

and their life ends in shame.[b]
15 He delivers the afflicted by their
   affliction,
   and opens their ear by adversity.
16 He also allured you out of distress
   into a broad place where there was
   no cramping,
   and what was set on your table was
   full of fatness.

17 "But you are full of the judgment on
   the wicked;
   judgment and justice seize you.
18 Beware lest wrath entice you into
   scoffing;
   and let not the greatness of the
   ransom turn you aside.
19 Will your cry avail to keep you from
   distress,
   or all the force of your strength?
20 Do not long for the night,
   when peoples are cut off in their
   place.
21 Take heed, do not turn to iniquity,
   for this you have chosen rather
   than affliction.
22 Behold, God is exalted in his power;
   who is a teacher like him?
23 Who has prescribed for him his way,
   or who can say, 'Thou hast done
   wrong'?

24 "Remember to extol his work,
   of which men have sung.
25 All men have looked on it;
   man beholds it from afar.
26 Behold, God is great, and we know
   him not;
   the number of his years is
   unsearchable.
27 For he draws up the drops of water,
   he[c] distils his mist in rain
28 which the skies pour down,
   and drop upon man abundantly.

b Heb *among the cult prostitutes*
c Cn: Heb *they distil*

36.1–25: **Fourth poem of Elihu.** Since affliction always has a purpose (vv. 5–15), let Job
beware, and instead of moaning over his fate, may he contemplate the hidden mercy of the
upholder of nature and give praise as he participates in the work of God (vv. 16–25).
36.26–37.22: **Fifth poem of Elihu.** Although without the usual introduction, this may be
taken as a separate poem of Elihu. The sovereign ruler of nature, his purpose and his benevolence appeared in the majestic unfolding of the seasons, autumn (vv. 26–33), winter (37.1–13)

²⁹ Can any one understand the
        spreading of the clouds,
    the thunderings of his pavilion?
³⁰ Behold, he scatters his lightning
        about him,
    and covers the roots of the sea.
³¹ For by these he judges peoples;
    he gives food in abundance.
³² He covers his hands with the
        lightning,
    and commands it to strike the
        mark.
³³ Its crashing declares concerning him,
    who is jealous with anger against
        iniquity.

37 "At this also my heart trembles,
    and leaps out of its place.
² Hearken to the thunder of his voice
    and the rumbling that comes from
        his mouth.
³ Under the whole heaven he lets it go,
    and his lightning to the corners of
        the earth.
⁴ After it his voice roars;
    he thunders with his majestic
        voice
    and he does not restrain the
        lightnings^d when his voice is
        heard.
⁵ God thunders wondrously with his
        voice;
    he does great things which we
        cannot comprehend.
⁶ For to the snow he says, 'Fall on the
        earth';
    and to the shower and the rain,^e
        'Be strong.'
⁷ He seals up the hand of every man,
    that all men may know his work.^f
⁸ Then the beasts go into their lairs,
    and remain in their dens.
⁹ From its chamber comes the
        whirlwind,
    and cold from the scattering winds.
¹⁰ By the breath of God ice is given,
    and the broad waters are frozen
        fast.
¹¹ He loads the thick cloud with
        moisture;

    the clouds scatter his lightning.
¹² They turn round and round by his
        guidance,
    to accomplish all that he
        commands them
    on the face of the habitable world.
¹³ Whether for correction, or for his
        land,
    or for love, he causes it to happen.

¹⁴ "Hear this, O Job;
    stop and consider the wondrous
        works of God.
¹⁵ Do you know how God lays his
        command upon them,
    and causes the lightning of his
        cloud to shine?
¹⁶ Do you know the balancings of the
        clouds,
    the wondrous works of him who is
        perfect in knowledge,
¹⁷ you whose garments are hot
    when the earth is still because of
        the south wind?
¹⁸ Can you, like him, spread out the
        skies,
    hard as a molten mirror?
¹⁹ Teach us what we shall say to him;
    we cannot draw up our case
        because of darkness.
²⁰ Shall it be told him that I would
        speak?
    Did a man ever wish that he would
        be swallowed up?

²¹ "And now men cannot look on the
        light
    when it is bright in the skies,
    when the wind has passed and
        cleared them.
²² Out of the north comes golden
        splendor;
    God is clothed with terrible
        majesty.
²³ The Almighty—we cannot find him;
    he is great in power and justice,

d Heb *them*
e Cn Compare Syr: Heb *shower of rain and shower of rains*
f Vg Compare Syr Tg: Heb *that all men whom he has made may know it*

and summer (vv. 14–22); a sequence which points to an autumnal calendar, with the new year's
festival in the fall.
    37.23–24: Final admonition of Elihu. Let Job recognize that although God is far beyond

and abundant righteousness he
will not violate.
24 Therefore men fear him;
he does not regard any who are
wise in their own conceit."

38 Then the LORD answered Job
out of the whirlwind:
2 "Who is this that darkens counsel
by words without knowledge?
3 Gird up your loins like a man,
I will question you, and you shall
declare to me.

4 "Where were you when I laid the
foundation of the earth?
Tell me, if you have
understanding.
5 Who determined its measurements
—surely you know!
Or who stretched the line upon it?
6 On what were its bases sunk,
or who laid its cornerstone,
7 when the morning stars sang
together,
and all the sons of God shouted
for joy?

8 "Or who shut in the sea with doors,
when it burst forth from the womb;
9 when I made clouds its garment,
and thick darkness its swaddling
band,
10 and prescribed bounds for it,
and set bars and doors,
11 and said, 'Thus far shall you come,
and no farther,
and here shall your proud waves
be stayed'?

12 "Have you commanded the morning
since your days began,
and caused the dawn to know its
place,
13 that it might take hold of the skirts
of the earth,
and the wicked be shaken out of
it?
14 It is changed like clay under the seal,
and it is dyed[g] like a garment.
15 From the wicked their light is
withheld,
and their uplifted arm is broken.

16 "Have you entered into the springs
of the sea,
or walked in the recesses of the
deep?
17 Have the gates of death been
revealed to you,
or have you seen the gates of deep
darkness?
18 Have you comprehended the
expanse of the earth?
Declare, if you know all this.

19 "Where is the way to the dwelling
of light,
and where is the place of
darkness,
20 that you may take it to its territory
and that you may discern the paths
to its home?
21 You know, for you were born then,
and the number of your days is
great!

22 "Have you entered the storehouses
of the snow,
or have you seen the storehouses
of the hail,
23 which I have reserved for the time of
trouble,

g Cn: Heb *they stand forth*

---

man's knowledge or imagination, *abundant righteousness he will not violate.* Human wisdom
cannot be a substitute for the fear of God.
   38.1–42.6: The voice from the whirlwind. Many commentators used to consider these chapters to be editorial additions. Contemporary scholarship points out their linguistic and literary
homogeneity with the main body of the poem.
   38.1–40.5: First discourse of the LORD. 38.1: *The whirlwind,* a frequent setting of theophanies,
i.e. divine appearances (Nah.1.3; Zech.9.14; Pss.18.7–15; 50.3; Ezek.1.4; Hab. ch. 3). **2–3:**
Like a man. Throughout the discussion Job has asked why misfortune happened to him, a man.
The Deity now offers such a man the right to challenge the divine rule. **4–7:** The creator of the
earth. There is here no trace of a dualistic cosmogony with a cosmic fight (compare 3.8 n.;
7.12 n.; 26.10–13). **8–11:** The creator of the sea. **12–15:** The creator of time. **16–38:** The master
of the deep, light and darkness, snow, hail, and lightning, constellations, clouds and mist.

for the day of battle and war?
²⁴ What is the way to the place where
the light is distributed,
or where the east wind is scattered
upon the earth?

²⁵ "Who has cleft a channel for the
torrents of rain,
and a way for the thunderbolt,
²⁶ to bring rain on a land where no man
is,
on the desert in which there is no
man;
²⁷ to satisfy the waste and desolate land,
and to make the ground put forth
grass?

²⁸ "Has the rain a father,
or who has begotten the drops of
dew?
²⁹ From whose womb did the ice come
forth,
and who has given birth to the
hoarfrost of heaven?
³⁰ The waters become hard like stone,
and the face of the deep is frozen.

³¹ "Can you bind the chains of the
Plei′ades,
or loose the cords of Orion?
³² Can you lead forth the Maz′zaroth
in their season,
or can you guide the Bear with its
children?
³³ Do you know the ordinances of the
heavens?
Can you establish their rule on the
earth?

³⁴ "Can you lift up your voice to the
clouds,
that a flood of waters may cover
you?
³⁵ Can you send forth lightnings, that
they may go
and say to you, 'Here we are'?
³⁶ Who has put wisdom in the clouds,ʰ
or given understanding to the
mists?ʰ
³⁷ Who can number the clouds by
wisdom?

Or who can tilt the waterskins of
the heavens,
³⁸ when the dust runs into a mass
and the clods cleave fast together?

³⁹ "Can you hunt the prey for the lion,
or satisfy the appetite of the young
lions,
⁴⁰ when they crouch in their dens,
or lie in wait in their covert?
⁴¹ Who provides for the raven its prey,
when its young ones cry to God,
and wander about for lack of food?

39 "Do you know when the
mountain goats bring forth?
Do you observe the calving of the
hinds?
² Can you number the months that
they fulfil,
and do you know the time when
they bring forth,
³ when they crouch, bring forth their
offspring,
and are delivered of their young?
⁴ Their young ones become strong,
they grow up in the open;
they go forth, and do not return
to them.

⁵ "Who has let the wild ass go free?
Who has loosed the bonds of the
swift ass,
⁶ to whom I have given the steppe for
his home,
and the salt land for his dwelling
place?
⁷ He scorns the tumult of the city;
he hears not the shouts of the
driver.
⁸ He ranges the mountains as his
pasture,
and he searches after every green
thing.

⁹ "Is the wild ox willing to serve you?
Will he spend the night at your
crib?
¹⁰ Can you bind him in the furrow
with ropes,

ʰ The meaning of the Hebrew word is uncertain

38.39–39.30: The protector of animals.

or will he harrow the valleys after
  you?
11 Will you depend on him because his
  strength is great,
  and will you leave to him your
  labor?
12 Do you have faith in him that he will
  return,
  and bring your grain to your
  threshing floor?[i]

13 "The wings of the ostrich wave
  proudly;
  but are they the pinions and
  plumage of love?[j]
14 For she leaves her eggs to the earth,
  and lets them be warmed on the
  ground,
15 forgetting that a foot may crush
  them,
  and that the wild beast may
  trample them.
16 She deals cruelly with her young, as
  if they were not hers;
  though her labor be in vain, yet
  she has no fear;
17 because God has made her forget
  wisdom,
  and given her no share in
  understanding.
18 When she rouses herself to flee,[k]
  she laughs at the horse and his
  rider.

19 "Do you give the horse his might?
  Do you clothe his neck with
  strength?[l]
20 Do you make him leap like the
  locust?
  His majestic snorting is terrible.
21 He paws[m] in the valley, and exults
  in his strength;
  he goes out to meet the weapons.
22 He laughs at fear, and is not
  dismayed;
  he does not turn back from the
  sword.
23 Upon him rattle the quiver,
  the flashing spear and the javelin.

24 With fierceness and rage he swallows
  the ground;
  he cannot stand still at the sound of
  the trumpet.
25 When the trumpet sounds, he says
  'Aha!'
  He smells the battle from afar,
  the thunder of the captains, and
  the shouting.

26 "Is it by your wisdom that the hawk
  soars,
  and spreads his wings toward the
  south?
27 Is it at your command that the eagle
  mounts up
  and makes his nest on high?
28 On the rock he dwells and makes
  his home
  in the fastness of the rocky crag.
29 Thence he spies out the prey;
  his eyes behold it afar off.
30 His young ones suck up blood;
  and where the slain are, there is
  he."

40 And the LORD said to Job:
  2 "Shall a faultfinder contend
  with the Almighty?
  He who argues with God, let him
  answer it."

3 Then Job answered the LORD:
4 "Behold, I am of small account;
  what shall I answer thee?
  I lay my hand on my mouth.
5 I have spoken once, and I will not
  answer;
  twice, but I will proceed no
  further."

6 Then the LORD answered Job out of
  the whirlwind:
7 "Gird up your loins like a man;
  I will question you, and you
  declare to me.

i Heb *your grain and your threshing floor*
j Heb obscure   *k* Heb obscure
l Tg: The meaning of the Hebrew word is obscure
m Gk Syr Vg: Heb *they dig*

40.1–5: Job refuses the challenge to fight. **1:** *Shall a faultfinder contend with the Almighty?*
Read, with some ancient versions, "Will he who disputes with the Almighty yield?" The
Deity never condemns Job for moral faults but clearly implies that he has been guilty of theo-
logical insolence.

8 Will you even put me in the wrong?
Will you condemn me that you may be justified?
9 Have you an arm like God,
and can you thunder with a voice like his?

10 "Deck yourself with majesty and dignity;
clothe yourself with glory and splendor.
11 Pour forth the overflowings of your anger,
and look on every one that is proud, and abase him.
12 Look on every one that is proud, and bring him low;
and tread down the wicked where they stand.
13 Hide them all in the dust together;
bind their faces in the world below.[n]
14 Then will I also acknowledge to you,
that your own right hand can give you victory.

15 "Behold, Be′hemoth,[o]
which I made as I made you;
he eats grass like an ox.
16 Behold, his strength in his loins,
and his power in the muscles of his belly.
17 He makes his tail stiff like a cedar;
the sinews of his thighs are knit together.
18 His bones are tubes of bronze,
his limbs like bars of iron.

19 "He is the first of the works[p] of God;
let him who made him bring near his sword!
20 For the mountains yield food for him
where all the wild beasts play.
21 Under the lotus plants he lies,
in the covert of the reeds and in the marsh.
22 For his shade the lotus trees cover him;
the willows of the brook surround him.
23 Behold, if the river is turbulent he is not frightened;
he is confident though Jordan rushes against his mouth.
24 Can one take him with hooks,[q]
or pierce his nose with a snare?

41 [r] "Can you draw out Levi′athan[s] with a fishhook,
or press down his tongue with a cord?
2 Can you put a rope in his nose,
or pierce his jaw with a hook?
3 Will he make many supplications to you?
Will he speak to you soft words?
4 Will he make a covenant with you
to take him for your servant for ever?
5 Will you play with him as with a bird,
or will you put him on leash for your maidens?
6 Will traders bargain over him?
Will they divide him up among the merchants?
7 Can you fill his skin with harpoons,
or his head with fishing spears?
8 Lay hands on him;
think of the battle; you will not do it again!

n Heb *hidden place* *o* Or *the hippopotamus* *p* Heb *ways* *q* Cn: Heb *in his eyes* *r* Ch 40.25 in Heb *s* Or *the crocodile*

40.6–41.34: Second discourse of the LORD. 40.6–9: The divine challenge of man is renewed, apparently because Job is only silenced but not convinced. **8:** *Will you condemn me that you may be justified?* The poet indicates here the central theme of the work. Self-righteousness leads man to condemn God. **15–24:** This portrait of *Behemoth* (like that of Leviathan, 41.1–34) may have received literary amplification, but it plays an integral part of the poet's purpose: the creating God is in control of all forces of evil, despite appearances to the contrary. **15:** The primeval monster (compare v. 19) is not a mere hippopotamus, but a mythical symbol. *Which I made as I made you,* the mystery of evil is not dissolved, but the divine sway embraces all. **41.1–34:** *Leviathan,* not an ordinary crocodile, but the sea-monster (3.8; 26.13; Ps.74.14), which was associated with chaos. Like the psalmist (Ps.104.26), the poet shows that it is only a plaything in the eyes of God.

9*t* Behold, the hope of a man is
    disappointed;
    he is laid low even at the sight of
      him.
10 No one is so fierce that he dares to
    stir him up.
    Who then is he that can stand
      before me?
11 Who has given to me,*u* that I should
    repay him?
    Whatever is under the whole
      heaven is mine.

12 "I will not keep silence concerning
    his limbs,
    or his mighty strength, or his
      goodly frame.
13 Who can strip off his outer garment?
    Who can penetrate his double
      coat of mail?*v*
14 Who can open the doors of his face?
    Round about his teeth is terror.
15 His back*w* is made of rows of shields,
    shut up closely as with a seal.
16 One is so near to another
    that no air can come between
      them.
17 They are joined one to another;
    they clasp each other and cannot
      be separated.
18 His sneezings flash forth light,
    and his eyes are like the eyelids of
      the dawn.
19 Out of his mouth go flaming torches;
    sparks of fire leap forth.
20 Out of his nostrils comes forth
    smoke,
    as from a boiling pot and burning
      rushes.
21 His breath kindles coals,
    and a flame comes forth from his
      mouth.
22 In his neck abides strength,
    and terror dances before him.
23 The folds of his flesh cleave
    together,
    firmly cast upon him and
      immovable.
24 His heart is hard as a stone,

    hard as the nether millstone.
25 When he raises himself up the
    mighty*x* are afraid;
    at the crashing they are beside
      themselves.
26 Though the sword reaches him, it
    does not avail;
    nor the spear, the dart, or the
      javelin.
27 He counts iron as straw,
    and bronze as rotten wood.
28 The arrow cannot make him flee;
    for him slingstones are turned to
      stubble.
29 Clubs are counted as stubble;
    he laughs at the rattle of javelins.
30 His underparts are like sharp
    potsherds;
    he spreads himself like a threshing
      sledge on the mire.
31 He makes the deep boil like a pot;
    he makes the sea like a pot of
      ointment.
32 Behind him he leaves a shining wake;
    one would think the deep to be
      hoary.
33 Upon earth there is not his like,
    a creature without fear.
34 He beholds everything that is high;
    he is king over all the sons of
      pride."

42 Then Job answered the Lord:
2 "I know that thou canst do all
      things,
    and that no purpose of thine can
      be thwarted.
3 'Who is this that hides counsel
    without knowledge?'
    Therefore I have uttered what I did
      not understand,
    things too wonderful for me, which
      I did not know.
4 'Hear, and I will speak;
    I will question you, and you
      declare to me.'

t Ch 41.1 in Heb
u The meaning of the Hebrew is uncertain
v Gk: Heb *bridle*
w Cn Compare Gk Vg: Heb *pride*   *x* Or *gods*

42.1–6: The answer of Job. Having contemplated divine activity, the sufferer now knows
the purposefulness of God (v. 2). **3a:** A quotation from 38.2; Job acknowledges his finitude.
4: An echo of the divine questioning (40.7), preparing for the confession of the following lines.
5: The contrast between belief through tradition and faith through prophetic vision. God has

⁵ I had heard of thee by the hearing of
  the ear,
but now my eye sees thee;
⁶ therefore I despise myself,
  and repent in dust and ashes."

7 After the LORD had spoken these
words to Job, the LORD said to Eli′-
phaz the Te′manite: "My wrath is
kindled against you and against your
two friends; for you have not spoken
of me what is right, as my servant
Job has. ⁸ Now therefore take seven
bulls and seven rams, and go to my
servant Job, and offer up for yourselves a burnt offering; and my servant
Job shall pray for you, for I will accept his prayer not to deal with you according to your folly; for you have not
spoken of me what is right, as my servant Job has." ⁹ So Eli′phaz the Te′-
manite and Bildad the Shuhite and
Zophar the Na′amathite went and did
what the LORD had told them; and the
LORD accepted Job's prayer.

10 And the LORD restored the fortunes of Job, when he had prayed for
his friends; and the LORD gave Job
twice as much as he had before.
¹¹ Then came to him all his brothers
and sisters and all who had known him
before, and ate bread with him in his
house; and they showed him sympathy
and comforted him for all the evil that
the LORD had brought upon him; and
each of them gave him a piece of
money*y* and a ring of gold. ¹² And
the LORD blessed the latter days of Job
more than his beginning; and he had
fourteen thousand sheep, six thousand camels, a thousand yoke of oxen,
and a thousand she-asses. ¹³ He had
also seven sons and three daughters.
¹⁴ And he called the name of the
first Jemi′mah; and the name of the
second Kezi′ah; and the name of
the third Ker′en-hap′puch. ¹⁵ And in
all the land there were no women so
fair as Job's daughters; and their father
gave them inheritance among their
brothers. ¹⁶ And after this Job lived
a hundred and forty years, and saw
his sons, and his sons' sons, four generations. ¹⁷ And Job died, an old man,
and full of days.

y Heb *qesitah*

---

not justified Job, but he has come to him personally; the upholder of the universe cares for a
lonely man so deeply that he offers him the fulness of his communion. Job is not vindicated but
he has obtained far more than a recognition of his innocence: he has been accepted by the
ever-present master-worker, and intimacy with the Creator makes vindication superfluous.
The philosophical problem is not solved, but it is transfigured by the theological reality of the
divine-human rapport. **6**: *I despise myself;* the Hebrew verb is obscure, but is probably related
to a root meaning "to melt into nothing." *I repent,* the Hebrew verb used here is not the usual
one for repentance of sins, but a word expressing the utmost grief and self-depreciation. Such
an experience follows rather than precedes the vision of God.

42.7–17: The epilogue. The style, language, and situation of the folktale (1.1–2.13) reappear
abruptly (see Introduction). **8**: *Burnt offering,* sacrificial ritual, absent from the poem, is a characteristic of the archaic story (1.5). **10**: Job's restoration follows not his repentance but his
intercession on behalf of his friends (v. 8). Intercessory power is a feature which is in accord
with the figure of the ancient legend (Ezek.14.14,20). **10–17**: Job receives a double restitution,
although no healing of his disease is explicitly mentioned. **11**: *A piece of money,* a qesitah (see
note *y* and Gen.33.19; Jos.24.32). **14**: The names of Job's new daughters have a flavor of
folklore: *Jemimah,* Dove; *Keziah,* Cinnamon; *Keren-happuch,* Horn of eye-shadow. **15b**: An exceptional procedure (contrast Num.27.1–11). **16–17**: A patriarchal theme (Gen.25.8; 35.29;
50.23; see also Ps.128.6; Pr.17.6; 1 Chr.29.28).

THE PSALMS

The living spirit of any religion shines through most clearly in its hymns. The Psalter is the hymnal of ancient Israel, compiled from older collections of lyrics for use in the temple of Zerubbabel (Ezra 5.2; Hag.1.14). Most of the psalms were probably composed to accompany acts of worship in the temple and may be classified as follows: *Hymns* (acts of praise suitable for any occasion and including the sub-types *Enthronement Hymns*, celebrating the Lord's kingship, and *Songs of Zion*, expressing devotion to the Holy City); *Laments* (in which an individual seeks deliverance from illness or false accusation, or the nation asks for help in time of distress); *Songs of Trust* (in which an individual expresses his confidence in God's readiness to help); *Thanksgivings* (in which an individual expresses his gratitude for deliverance); *Sacred History* (in which the nation recounts the story of God's dealings with it); *Royal Psalms* (designed to be used for occasions such as a coronation or royal wedding); *Wisdom Psalms* (which are meditations on life and the ways of God); and *Liturgies* (which are often of mixed type and were composed for some special cultic or historical occasion. One presumed cultic occasion is an annual ceremony for renewing the covenant). In imitation of the Pentateuch the Psalter is divided into five books (see 41.13 n.)

The titles or superscriptions of the psalms contain a variety of items. They frequently include musical directions, such as "To the choirmaster: with stringed instruments" (Pss. 4; 6; etc.). The meaning of a number of technical terms is no longer definitely known; for example, Shiggaion (Ps. 7), Miktam (Pss. 16; 56–60), Maskil (Pss. 42; 44; 52–55; etc.), Sheminith (Pss. 6; 12), Gittith (Pss. 8; 81; 84), Muth-Labben (Ps. 9), Alamoth (Ps. 46), Mahalath (Ps. 53), Mahalath Leannoth (Ps. 88), Shushan-Eduth (Ps. 60). The first three may refer to types of psalms, and the rest, preceded by "According to," may be the names of tunes, as also The Hind of the Dawn (Ps. 22), Lilies (Pss. 45; 69), The Dove on the Far-off Terebinths (Ps. 56), and Do Not Destroy (Pss. 57–59; 75). References to the Sons of Korah (Pss. 42; 44–49; 84; etc.), Jeduthun (Pss. 39; 62; 77), Asaph (Pss. 50; 73–83), Heman (Ps. 88), and Ethan (Ps. 89) point to the work of professional Levitical musicians (1 Chr.15.16–22; Neh.12.41–46). Song of Ascents (Pss. 120–134) may mean "pilgrim song," that is, of ascent to Jerusalem. The ascription of nearly half of the psalms to David is testimony to the regard in which the great singer of Israel was held (2 Sam.23.1). For the significance of the frequently recurring word, "Selah," see 3.2 n.

The book of Psalms reflects many aspects of the religious experience of Israel. Its intrinsic spiritual depth and beauty have made it from earliest times a treasury of resources for public and private devotion.

BOOK I

Blessed is the man
who walks not in the counsel of
  the wicked,
nor stands in the way of sinners,
  nor sits in the seat of scoffers;
² but his delight is in the law of the
  LORD,
and on his law he meditates day
  and night.
³ He is like a tree
planted by streams of water,
that yields its fruit in its season,
and its leaf does not wither.
In all that he does, he prospers.

⁴ The wicked are not so,
but are like chaff which the wind
  drives away.
⁵ Therefore the wicked will not stand
  in the judgment,
nor sinners in the congregation of
  the righteous;

Ps. 1: The contrasting fate of the righteous and the wicked (a wisdom psalm). Compare Jer.17.5–8. **1–3:** The prosperity of the righteous. **1:** *Blessed* is the conventional translation of a Hebrew expression meaning literally "O how happy . . . !" **2:** Compare Ps. 119. **4–6:** The disastrous end of the wicked. **4:** In threshing, the crushed sheaves were tossed into the air, where the wind blew away the lighter *chaff*.

⁶ for the LORD knows the way of the
　　righteous,
　　but the way of the wicked will
　　perish.

2 Why do the nations conspire,
　　and the peoples plot in vain?
² The kings of the earth set
　　themselves,
　　and the rulers take counsel
　　together,
　　against the LORD and his
　　anointed, saying,
³ "Let us burst their bonds asunder,
　　and cast their cords from us."

⁴ He who sits in the heavens laughs;
　　the LORD has them in derision.
⁵ Then he will speak to them in his
　　wrath,
　　and terrify them in his fury, saying,
⁶ "I have set my king
　　on Zion, my holy hill."

⁷ I will tell of the decree of the LORD:
　　He said to me, "You are my son,
　　today I have begotten you.
⁸ Ask of me, and I will make the
　　nations your heritage,
　　and the ends of the earth your
　　possession.
⁹ You shall break them with a rod of
　　iron,
　　and dash them in pieces like a
　　potter's vessel."

¹⁰ Now therefore, O kings, be wise;
　　be warned, O rulers of the earth.
¹¹ Serve the LORD with fear,
　　with trembling ¹² kiss his feet,*a*

lest he be angry, and you perish in
　　the way;
　　for his wrath is quickly kindled.

Blessed are all who take refuge in
　　him.

A Psalm of David, when he fled from
　　Absalom his son.

3 O LORD, how many are my foes!
　　Many are rising against me;
² many are saying of me,
　　there is no help for him in God.
　　　　　　　　　　　　　　Selah

³ But thou, O LORD, art a shield about
　　me,
　　my glory, and the lifter of my head.
⁴ I cry aloud to the LORD,
　　and he answers me from his holy
　　hill.　　　　　　　　　　*Selah*

⁵ I lie down and sleep;
　　I wake again, for the LORD
　　sustains me.
⁶ I am not afraid of ten thousands of
　　people
　　who have set themselves against
　　me round about.

⁷ Arise, O LORD!
　　Deliver me, O my God!
　　For thou dost smite all my enemies
　　on the cheek,
　　thou dost break the teeth of the
　　wicked.

a Cn: The Hebrew of 11b and 12a is uncertain

Ps. 2: The LORD gives universal dominion to his king (a royal psalm, composed for a coronation). **1–3:** Israel's subject peoples plot rebellion against the new king. **2:** The word *anointed*
in Hebrew is literally "messiah," one of the titles of an Israelite king; after the extinction of the
Hebrew monarchy, this became a name for the ideal king of a future, hoped-for restoration, and
the psalm was reinterpreted accordingly (compare Acts 4.25–29). **4–9:** The newly enthroned
king quotes God's promise of universal rule. **7:** *You are my son . . . begotten you,* a formula of
adoption whereby the king became God's son (compare 2 Sam.7.14; Ps.89.26–27; also Acts
13.33). **10–12:** Rebellious rulers are warned to submit.
　　Ps. 3: Prayer for deliverance from personal enemies (a lament). **1–2:** The psalmist's complaint.
2: *Selah* is a liturgical direction; it may indicate that there should be an instrumental interlude
at this point in the singing of the psalm. **3–4:** Expression of trust, a regular element in psalms
which are laments. **5–6:** It is perhaps after having spent the night in the temple that the psalmist
receives assurance that the LORD is still on his side. **7–8:** Concluding prayer for the psalmist
and the nation.

8 Deliverance belongs to the LORD;
  thy blessing be upon thy people!
                    Selah

To the choirmaster: with stringed
instruments. A Psalm of David.

4 Answer me when I call, O God of
  my right!
  Thou hast given me room when I
  was in distress.
  Be gracious to me, and hear my
  prayer.

2 O men, how long shall my honor
  suffer shame?
  How long will you love vain words,
  and seek after lies?   *Selah*
3 But know that the LORD has set
  apart the godly for himself;
  the LORD hears when I call to him.

4 Be angry, but sin not;
  commune with your own hearts on
  your beds, and be silent. *Selah*
5 Offer right sacrifices,
  and put your trust in the LORD.

6 There are many who say, "O that we
  might see some good!
  Lift up the light of thy
  countenance upon us, O
  LORD!"
7 Thou hast put more joy in my heart
  than they have when their grain
  and wine abound.

8 In peace I will both lie down and
  sleep;
  for thou alone, O LORD, makest
  me dwell in safety.

To the choirmaster: for the flutes. A
Psalm of David.

5 Give ear to my words, O LORD;
  give heed to my groaning.
2 Hearken to the sound of my cry,
  my King and my God,
  for to thee do I pray.
3 O LORD, in the morning thou dost
  hear my voice;
  in the morning I prepare a
  sacrifice for thee, and
  watch.

4 For thou art not a God who delights
  in wickedness;
  evil may not sojourn with thee.
5 The boastful may not stand before
  thy eyes;
  thou hatest all evildoers.
6 Thou destroyest those who speak
  lies;
  the LORD abhors bloodthirsty and
  deceitful men.

7 But I through the abundance of thy
  steadfast love
  will enter thy house,
  I will worship toward thy holy
  temple
  in the fear of thee.
8 Lead me, O LORD, in thy
  righteousness
  because of my enemies;
  make thy way straight before me.

9 For there is no truth in their mouth;
  their heart is destruction,
  their throat is an open sepulchre,
  they flatter with their tongue.
10 Make them bear their guilt, O God;
  let them fall by their own
  counsels;

Ps. 4: Prayer for deliverance from personal enemies (a lament). **1**: Cry for help. **2–4**: The psalmist rebukes those who falsely accuse him of wrong-doing. The charge is probably a formal accusation to which the accused replies by publicly protesting his innocence (compare 26.4–7). **2,4**: *Selah*, see 3.2 n. **5–8**: He is assured of the LORD's help. The ceremony in which this psalm was used evidently included sacrifice (v. 5) and possibly spending the night in the temple (v. 8; compare 3.5).

Ps. 5: Prayer for deliverance from personal enemies (a lament). **1–2**: Cry for help. **3–7**: Expression of trust (compare 3.3–4). **3**: *In the morning . . . a sacrifice* probably refers to a ceremony at the end of a night's vigil (compare 3.5; 4.8). **8–12**: Concluding prayer. **9–10**: See 4.2–4 n.

because of their many transgressions
　　cast them out,
　for they have rebelled against
　　thee.

11 But let all who take refuge in thee
　　rejoice,
　let them ever sing for joy;
　and do thou defend them,
　　that those who love thy name may
　　exult in thee.
12 For thou dost bless the righteous,
　　O LORD;
　thou dost cover him with favor as
　　with a shield.

To the choirmaster: with stringed instruments; according to The Sheminith.
　　　　A Psalm of David.

6　O LORD, rebuke me not in thy
　　anger,
　nor chasten me in thy wrath.
2 Be gracious to me, O LORD, for I
　　am languishing;
　O LORD, heal me, for my bones
　　are troubled.
3 My soul also is sorely troubled.
　But thou, O LORD—how long?

4 Turn, O LORD, save my life;
　deliver me for the sake of thy
　　steadfast love.
5 For in death there is no
　　remembrance of thee;
　in Sheol who can give thee praise?

6 I am weary with my moaning;
　every night I flood my bed with
　　tears;
　I drench my couch with my
　　weeping.

7 My eye wastes away because of
　　grief,
　it grows weak because of all my
　　foes.

8 Depart from me, all you workers of
　　evil;
　for the LORD has heard the sound
　　of my weeping.
9 The LORD has heard my
　　supplication;
　the LORD accepts my prayer.
10 All my enemies shall be ashamed and
　　sorely troubled;
　they shall turn back, and be put to
　　shame in a moment.

A Shiggaion of David, which he sang to
　　the LORD concerning Cush a
　　　　Benjaminite.

7　O LORD my God, in thee do I take
　　refuge;
　save me from all my pursuers, and
　　deliver me,
2 lest like a lion they rend me,
　dragging me away, with none to
　　rescue.

3 O LORD my God, if I have done this,
　　if there is wrong in my hands,
4 if I have requited my friend with evil
　　or plundered my enemy without
　　cause,
5 let the enemy pursue me and
　　overtake me,
　and let him trample my life to the
　　ground,
　and lay my soul in the dust.　*Selah*

6 Arise, O LORD, in thy anger,
　lift thyself up against the fury of
　　my enemies;

Ps. 6: Prayer for healing from severe illness (a lament). In the church liturgy this is the first
of seven Penitential Psalms (6; 32; 38; 51; 102; 130; 143). **1–5:** Cry for help. **5:** *Sheol*, the place
of the dead, where men retain only the faintest semblance of life (compare 88.5–6; Job 3.13–19;
see Gen.37.35 n.). **6–7:** The psalmist's weakened condition. **8–10:** He receives assurance that
his prayer is heard. **8:** He blames his enemies for his illness, perhaps believing that they have
put a curse upon him (compare 102.3–8).
　Ps. 7: Prayer for deliverance from personal enemies (a lament). **1–2:** Cry for help. **3–5:** Protestation of innocence (see 4.2–4 n.). **3:** *This*, the specific crime of which the psalmist was
accused. **5:** *Selah*, see 3.2 n. **6–9:** Prayer for God's intervention in his trial.

awake, O my God;[b] thou hast
    appointed a judgment.
[7] Let the assembly of the peoples be
    gathered about thee;
    and over it take thy seat[c] on high.
[8] The LORD judges the peoples;
    judge me, O LORD, according to
      my righteousness
    and according to the integrity that
      is in me.

[9] O let the evil of the wicked come to
    an end,
    but establish thou the righteous,
thou who triest the minds and hearts,
    thou righteous God.
[10] My shield is with God,
    who saves the upright in heart.
[11] God is a righteous judge,
    and a God who has indignation
      every day.

[12] If a man[d] does not repent, God[d]
    will whet his sword;
    he has bent and strung his bow;
[13] he has prepared his deadly weapons,
    making his arrows fiery shafts.
[14] Behold, the wicked man conceives
    evil,
    and is pregnant with mischief,
    and brings forth lies.
[15] He makes a pit, digging it out,
    and falls into the hole which he
      has made.
[16] His mischief returns upon his own
    head,
    and on his own pate his violence
      descends.

[17] I will give to the LORD the thanks
    due to his righteousness,
    and I will sing praise to the name
    of the LORD, the Most High.

To the choirmaster: according to The
Gittith. A Psalm of David.

8 O LORD, our Lord,
    how majestic is thy name in all
      the earth!

Thou whose glory above the heavens
    is chanted
[2]   by the mouth of babes and
      infants,
thou hast founded a bulwark
    because of thy foes,
    to still the enemy and the avenger.

[3] When I look at thy heavens, the
    work of thy fingers,
    the moon and the stars which thou
      hast established;
[4] what is man that thou art mindful of
    him,
    and the son of man that thou dost
      care for him?

[5] Yet thou hast made him little less
    than God,
    and dost crown him with glory
      and honor.
[6] Thou hast given him dominion over
    the works of thy hands;
    thou hast put all things under his
      feet,
[7] all sheep and oxen,
    and also the beasts of the field,
[8] the birds of the air, and the fish of
    the sea,
    whatever passes along the paths of
      the sea.

[9] O LORD, our Lord,
    how majestic is thy name in all
      the earth!

b Or *for me*   *c* Cn: Heb *return*   *d* Heb *he*

10–16: Expression of trust in God's righteous dealing (compare 3.3–4). **17:** The psalmist promises to give formal thanks to God, probably by offering a thanksgiving sacrifice (compare 66.13–15).

    Ps. 8: Hymn celebrating God's glory and man's God-given dignity. 1–4: The glory of God as manifest in the night sky and in the songs of children. **4:** See 144.3–4; Job 7.17–18 n. *Son of man* means "individual man." **5–8:** God has given man a share in his own dignity by conferring on him dominion over the rest of creation (Gen.1.26). **9:** The opening verse repeated as a refrain.

    Pss. 9–10: Prayer for deliverance from personal enemies (lament). This composition, which

To the choirmaster: according to
Muth-labben. A Psalm of David.

9 I will give thanks to the LORD with
my whole heart;
I will tell of all thy wonderful
deeds.
² I will be glad and exult in thee,
I will sing praise to thy name, O
Most High.

³ When my enemies turned back,
they stumbled and perished
before thee.
⁴ For thou hast maintained my just
cause;
thou hast sat on the throne giving
righteous judgment.

⁵ Thou hast rebuked the nations, thou
hast destroyed the wicked;
thou hast blotted out their name
for ever and ever.
⁶ The enemy have vanished in
everlasting ruins;
their cities thou hast rooted out;
the very memory of them has
perished.

⁷ But the LORD sits enthroned for
ever,
he has established his throne for
judgment;
⁸ and he judges the world with
righteousness,
he judges the peoples with equity.

⁹ The LORD is a stronghold for the
oppressed,
a stronghold in times of trouble.
¹⁰ And those who know thy name put
their trust in thee,
for thou, O LORD, hast not
forsaken those who seek thee.

¹¹ Sing praises to the LORD, who
dwells in Zion!

Tell among the peoples his deeds!
¹² For he who avenges blood is
mindful of them;
he does not forget the cry of the
afflicted.

¹³ Be gracious to me, O LORD!
Behold what I suffer from those
who hate me,
O thou who liftest me up from the
gates of death,
¹⁴ that I may recount all thy praises,
that in the gates of the daughter
of Zion
I may rejoice in thy deliverance.

¹⁵ The nations have sunk in the pit
which they made;
in the net which they hid has their
own foot been caught.
¹⁶ The LORD has made himself known,
he has executed judgment;
the wicked are snared in the work
of their own hands.
Higgaion. Selah

¹⁷ The wicked shall depart to Sheol,
all the nations that forget God.

¹⁸ For the needy shall not always be
forgotten,
and the hope of the poor shall not
perish for ever.

¹⁹ Arise, O LORD! Let not man prevail;
let the nations be judged before
thee!
²⁰ Put them in fear, O LORD!
Let the nations know that they are
but men! *Selah*

10 Why dost thou stand afar off,
O LORD?
Why dost thou hide thyself in
times of trouble?
² In arrogance the wicked hotly
pursue the poor;

is printed as a single psalm in the Septuagint, is constructed on the acrostic principle, every
second verse beginning with a different successive letter of the Hebrew alphabet, a circumstance which helps to account for the seeming lack of logical sequence. **1–2:** A vow in anticipation of deliverance (see 7.17 n.). **3–12:** Expression of confidence, based on God's previous just
dealings (compare 3.3–4). **13–14:** The psalmist's situation. **15–18:** Renewed expression of
confidence. **15:** *The nations*, the psalmist's enemies. **16:** The meaning of *Higgaion* is unknown.
Selah, see 3.2 n. **17:** *Sheol*, see 6.5 n. **9.19–10.15:** Prayer that God may intervene against the

let them be caught in the schemes
which they have devised.

3 For the wicked boasts of the desires
of his heart,
and the man greedy for gain
curses and renounces the
LORD.
4 In the pride of his countenance the
wicked does not seek him;
all his thoughts are, "There is no
God."

5 His ways prosper at all times;
thy judgments are on high, out of
his sight;
as for all his foes, he puffs at
them.
6 He thinks in his heart, "I shall not
be moved;
throughout all generations I shall
not meet adversity."

7 His mouth is filled with cursing and
deceit and oppression;
under his tongue are mischief and
iniquity.
8 He sits in ambush in the villages;
in hiding places he murders the
innocent.

His eyes stealthily watch for the
hapless,
9   he lurks in secret like a lion in his
covert;
he lurks that he may seize the poor,
he seizes the poor when he draws
him into his net.

10 The hapless is crushed, sinks down,
and falls by his might.
11 He thinks in his heart, "God has
forgotten,
he has hidden his face, he will
never see it."

12 Arise, O LORD; O God, lift up thy
hand;

forget not the afflicted.
13 Why does the wicked renounce
God,
and say in his heart, "Thou wilt
not call to account"?

14 Thou dost see; yea, thou dost note
trouble and vexation,
that thou mayst take it into thy
hands;
the hapless commits himself to thee;
thou hast been the helper of the
fatherless.

15 Break thou the arm of the wicked
and evildoer;
seek out his wickedness till thou
find none.
16 The LORD is king for ever and ever;
the nations shall perish from his
land.

17 O LORD, thou wilt hear the desire of
the meek;
thou wilt strengthen their heart,
thou wilt incline thy ear
18 to do justice to the fatherless and
the oppressed,
so that man who is of the earth
may strike terror no more.

To the choirmaster. Of David.

11 In the LORD I take refuge;
how can you say to me,
"Flee like a bird to the
mountains;*e*
2 for lo, the wicked bend the bow,
they have fitted their arrow to the
string,
to shoot in the dark at the upright
in heart;
3 if the foundations are destroyed,
what can the righteous do"?

e Gk Syr Jerome Tg: Heb *flee to your mountain, O bird*

---

wicked. **10.3–11:** The greedy, haughty, irreligious, and tyrannical spirit of the psalmist's enemies.
4: They are not atheists, but they deny that God is concerned with moral retribution (compare
v. 11 and 94.7). **16–18:** Concluding expression of confidence.
    Ps. 11: Confidence in God's concern for justice. This type of psalm (the song of trust) probably developed as an expansion of the expression of trust which is a common feature of the
laments (see 3.3–4 n.; compare 5.3–7; 7.10–16; 9.3–12). **1–3:** The psalmist rebukes those who

⁴ The LORD is in his holy temple,
  the LORD's throne is in heaven;
  his eyes behold, his eyelids test,
    the children of men.
⁵ The LORD tests the righteous and
    the wicked,
  and his soul hates him that loves
    violence.
⁶ On the wicked he will rain coals of
    fire and brimstone;
  a scorching wind shall be the
    portion of their cup.
⁷ For the LORD is righteous, he loves
    righteous deeds;
  the upright shall behold his
    face.

To the choirmaster: according to The
Sheminith. A Psalm of David.

12 Help, LORD; for there is no
    longer any that is godly;
  for the faithful have vanished
    from among the sons of men.
² Every one utters lies to his
    neighbor;
  with flattering lips and a double
    heart they speak.

³ May the LORD cut off all flattering
    lips,
  the tongue that makes great boasts,
⁴ those who say, "With our tongue we
    will prevail,
  our lips are with us; who is our
    master?"

⁵ "Because the poor are despoiled,
    because the needy groan,
  I will now arise," says the LORD;
  "I will place him in the safety for
    which he longs."

⁶ The promises of the LORD are
    promises that are pure,
  silver refined in a furnace on the
    ground,
  purified seven times.

⁷ Do thou, O LORD, protect us,
  guard us ever from this
    generation.
⁸ On every side the wicked prowl,
  as vileness is exalted among the
    sons of men.

To the choirmaster. A Psalm of David.

13 How long, O LORD? Wilt thou
    forget me for ever?
  How long wilt thou hide thy
    face from me?
² How long must I bear pain*f* in my
    soul,
  and have sorrow in my heart all
    the day?
  How long shall my enemy be exalted
    over me?

³ Consider and answer me, O LORD
    my God;
  lighten my eyes, lest I sleep the
    sleep of death;
⁴ lest my enemy say, "I have
    prevailed over him";
  lest my foes rejoice because I am
    shaken.

⁵ But I have trusted in thy steadfast
    love;
  my heart shall rejoice in thy
    salvation.
⁶ I will sing to the LORD,
  because he has dealt bountifully
    with me.

f Syr: Heb *hold counsels*

---

tell him that his only safety lies in flight from his enemies. **4–7:** He will stand his ground and depend on God for his vindication. **6:** *Brimstone*, sulphur (Gen.19.24). *Cup*, Is.51.17; see Lk. 22.42 n.

  Ps. 12: Prayer for deliverance from personal enemies (a lament). **1–4:** Cry for help. The psalmist's trials are characteristic of the faithlessness of the times. **5:** Perhaps spoken by a priest or temple prophet as a formal act of assurance to the suppliant. **6–8:** The choir (which is perhaps implied in the use of *us*) commends reliance on the promise just made and prays that it may soon be carried out.

  Ps. 13: Prayer for deliverance from personal enemies (a lament). **1–2:** The psalmist's complaint is given special emotional force by the four-fold "How long?" **3–4:** Prayer for help (see 4.2–4 n.). *Lighten my eyes*, compare 38.10. **5:** Expression of trust (compare 3.3–4). **6:** The vow (see 7.17 n.).

To the choirmaster. Of David.

14
The fool says in his heart,
"There is no God."
They are corrupt, they do
abominable deeds,
there is none that does good.

2 The LORD looks down from heaven
upon the children of men,
to see if there are any that act
wisely,
that seek after God.

3 They have all gone astray, they are
all alike corrupt;
there is none that does good,
no, not one.

4 Have they no knowledge, all the
evildoers
who eat up my people as they eat
bread,
and do not call upon the LORD?

5 There they shall be in great terror,
for God is with the generation of
the righteous.
6 You would confound the plans of
the poor,
but the LORD is his refuge.

7 O that deliverance for Israel would
come out of Zion!
When the LORD restores the
fortunes of his people,
Jacob shall rejoice, Israel shall be
glad.

A Psalm of David.

15
O LORD, who shall sojourn in
thy tent?
Who shall dwell on thy holy hill?

2 He who walks blamelessly, and does
what is right,
and speaks truth from his heart;
3 who does not slander with his
tongue,
and does no evil to his friend,
nor takes up a reproach against
his neighbor;
4 in whose eyes a reprobate is
despised,
but who honors those who fear
the LORD;
who swears to his own hurt and does
not change;
5 who does not put out his money at
interest,
and does not take a bribe against
the innocent.

He who does these things shall never
be moved.

A Miktam of David.

16
Preserve me, O God, for in thee
I take refuge.
2 I say to the LORD, "Thou art my
Lord;
I have no good apart from thee."*g*

3 As for the saints in the land, they are
the noble,
in whom is all my delight.

g Jerome Tg: The meaning of the Hebrew is uncertain

Ps. 14: Condemnation of a cynical and unrighteous age. This psalm (which is almost identical with Ps. 53) seems to be a variation on the typical lament, the psalmist generalizing his personal troubles as characteristic of an evil generation (compare 12.1–4). **1–3:** The corruption of the age. **1:** *The fool,* not a silly man, but one who is utterly corrupt in his moral character (compare 2 Sam.13.13; Pr.10.23). *There is no God,* see 10.4 n. **4–6:** A threat to the evil-doers, having the force of a curse. *Eat up my people,* compare Mic.3.2–3. **7:** A yearning for better times.

Ps. 15: A liturgy for admission to the temple. 1: The question: Who shall be admitted to the worshiping congregation? **2–5:** The answer: Only those who have the requisite moral qualities. **5:** The prohibition of *interest* (Ex.22.25; Lev.25.35–37) has reference to charitable loans made for the relief of distress rather than to the purely business type of loan which became common in a later commercial age.

Ps. 16: An act of personal faith in God's power to save (a song of trust; see Ps. 11 n.). **1:** Prayer for deliverance from trouble. **2–8:** The psalmist bases his appeal upon his own past

⁴ Those who choose another god
  multiply their sorrows;*ʰ*
  their libations of blood I will not
  pour out
  or take their names upon my lips.

⁵ The LORD is my chosen portion and
  my cup;
  thou holdest my lot.
⁶ The lines have fallen for me in
  pleasant places;
  yea, I have a goodly heritage.

⁷ I bless the LORD who gives me
  counsel;
  in the night also my heart instructs
  me.
⁸ I keep the LORD always before me;
  because he is at my right hand, I
  shall not be moved.

⁹ Therefore my heart is glad, and my
  soul rejoices;
  my body also dwells secure.
¹⁰ For thou dost not give me up to
  Sheol,
  or let thy godly one see the Pit.

¹¹ Thou dost show me the path of life;
  in thy presence there is fulness of
  joy,
  in thy right hand are pleasures for
  evermore.

A Prayer of David.

17 Hear a just cause, O LORD;
  attend to my cry!
  Give ear to my prayer from lips
  free of deceit!
² From thee let my vindication come!
  Let thy eyes see the right!

³ If thou triest my heart, if thou visitest
  me by night,
  if thou testest me, thou wilt find no
  wickedness in me;
  my mouth does not transgress.
⁴ With regard to the works of men, by
  the word of thy lips
  I have avoided the ways of the
  violent.
⁵ My steps have held fast to thy paths,
  my feet have not slipped.

⁶ I call upon thee, for thou wilt answer
  me, O God;
  incline thy ear to me, hear my
  words.
⁷ Wondrously show thy steadfast love,
  O savior of those who seek
  refuge
  from their adversaries at thy right
  hand.

⁸ Keep me as the apple of the eye;
  hide me in the shadow of thy
  wings,
⁹ from the wicked who despoil me,
  my deadly enemies who surround
  me.

¹⁰ They close their hearts to pity;
  with their mouths they speak
  arrogantly.
¹¹ They track me down; now they
  surround me;
  they set their eyes to cast me to
  the ground.
¹² They are like a lion eager to tear,
  as a young lion lurking in
  ambush.

¹³ Arise, O LORD! confront them,
  overthrow them!
  Deliver my life from the wicked
  by thy sword,

h Cn: The meaning of the Hebrew is uncertain

---

devotion to God and to the community of the faithful. **3:** *Saints*, literally, "holy ones." **9–11:** He has complete confidence that God will not permit him to perish. **10:** *Sheol*, see 6.5 n.; *the Pit* is a synonym. *Godly one* means "devout adherent." **11:** He will survive his ordeal and through God's help enjoy life's pleasures again.

   Ps. 17: Prayer for deliverance from personal enemies (a lament). **1:** Cry for vindication against false accusers (compare vv. 9–12). **3–5:** Protestation of innocence (see 4.2–4 n.). **3:** *By night*, see 3.5–6 n. **6–14:** The psalmist's prayer renewed. **8:** *Apple of the eye*, the pupil, the most precious part (Zech.2.8). **10–12:** Description of the accusers. **15:** Expression of confidence (see 3.3–4 n.). *When I awake*, compare v. 3.

14 from men by thy hand, O LORD,
   from men whose portion in life is
   of the world.
May their belly be filled with what
   thou hast stored up for them;
may their children have more than
   enough;
may they leave something over to
   their babes.

15 As for me, I shall behold thy face in
   righteousness;
when I awake, I shall be satisfied
   with beholding thy form.

To the choirmaster. A Psalm of David
the servant of the LORD, who addressed
the words of this song to the LORD on
the day when the LORD delivered him
from the hand of all his enemies, and
from the hand of Saul. He said:

18 I love thee, O LORD, my strength.
    2 The LORD is my rock, and my
    fortress, and my deliverer,
my God, my rock, in whom I take
   refuge,
my shield, and the horn of my
   salvation, my stronghold.
3 I call upon the LORD, who is worthy
   to be praised,
and I am saved from my enemies.

4 The cords of death encompassed me,
   the torrents of perdition assailed
   me;
5 the cords of Sheol entangled me,
   the snares of death confronted me.

6 In my distress I called upon the
   LORD;
to my God I cried for help.
From his temple he heard my voice,
   and my cry to him reached his ears.

7 Then the earth reeled and rocked;
   the foundations also of the
    mountains trembled
and quaked, because he was
   angry.
8 Smoke went up from his nostrils,
   and devouring fire from his
    mouth;
glowing coals flamed forth from
   him.
9 He bowed the heavens, and came
   down;
thick darkness was under his feet.
10 He rode on a cherub, and flew;
   he came swiftly upon the wings of
   the wind.
11 He made darkness his covering
   around him,
his canopy thick clouds dark with
   water.
12 Out of the brightness before him
   there broke through his clouds
hailstones and coals of fire.
13 The LORD also thundered in the
   heavens,
and the Most High uttered his
   voice,
hailstones and coals of fire.
14 And he sent out his arrows, and
   scattered them;
he flashed forth lightnings, and
   routed them.
15 Then the channels of the sea were
   seen,
and the foundations of the world
   were laid bare,
at thy rebuke, O LORD,
   at the blast of the breath of thy
   nostrils.

16 He reached from on high, he took
   me,
he drew me out of many waters.
17 He delivered me from my strong
   enemy,

Ps. 18: A king gives thanks for a victory in battle (a royal thanksgiving). This psalm is also found in 2 Sam. ch. 22. **1–3:** Confession of faith in God's readiness to help. **4–6:** Metaphorical description of the psalmist's difficulties; for the actual situation see vv. 37–45. Narration of the troubles from which the worshiper has been saved is a regular feature of the thanksgiving psalms. **7–19:** God's intervention in the battle. The imagery associates the LORD's appearance with the phenomena of a thunderstorm (compare Jg.5.4–5; Ps.29.3–9). **8:** *Glowing coals*, the lightning. **10:** *Cherub*, probably a personification of the storm cloud (see Ezek.1.5 n.; Pss.68.33; 104.3). **13:** *His voice*, the thunder, as in Ps. 29. **15:** *The breath of thy nostrils*, the storm wind.

and from those who hated me;
for they were too mighty for me.
¹⁸ They came upon me in the day of
my calamity;
but the LORD was my stay.
¹⁹ He brought me forth into a broad
place;
he delivered me, because he
delighted in me.

²⁰ The LORD rewarded me according
to my righteousness;
according to the cleanness of my
hands he recompensed me.
²¹ For I have kept the ways of the
LORD,
and have not wickedly departed
from my God.
²² For all his ordinances were before
me,
and his statutes I did not put
away from me.
²³ I was blameless before him,
and I kept myself from guilt.
²⁴ Therefore the LORD has
recompensed me according to
my righteousness,
according to the cleanness of my
hands in his sight.

²⁵ With the loyal thou dost show
thyself loyal;
with the blameless man thou dost
show thyself blameless;
²⁶ with the pure thou dost show
thyself pure;
and with the crooked thou dost
show thyself perverse.
²⁷ For thou dost deliver a humble
people;
but the haughty eyes thou dost
bring down.
²⁸ Yea, thou dost light my lamp;
the LORD my God lightens my
darkness.
²⁹ Yea, by thee I can crush a troop;
and by my God I can leap over a
wall.
³⁰ This God–his way is perfect;

the promise of the LORD proves
true;
he is a shield for all those who take
refuge in him.

³¹ For who is God, but the LORD?
And who is a rock, except our
God?–
³² the God who girded me with
strength,
and made my way safe.
³³ He made my feet like hinds' feet,
and set me secure on the heights.
³⁴ He trains my hands for war,
so that my arms can bend a bow
of bronze.
³⁵ Thou hast given me the shield of thy
salvation,
and thy right hand supported me,
and thy help*ⁱ* made me great.
³⁶ Thou didst give a wide place for my
steps under me,
and my feet did not slip.
³⁷ I pursued my enemies and overtook
them;
and did not turn back till they
were consumed.
³⁸ I thrust them through, so that they
were not able to rise;
they fell under my feet.
³⁹ For thou didst gird me with strength
for the battle;
thou didst make my assailants
sink under me.
⁴⁰ Thou didst make my enemies turn
their backs to me,
and those who hated me I
destroyed.
⁴¹ They cried for help, but there was
none to save,
they cried to the LORD, but he did
not answer them.
⁴² I beat them fine as dust before the
wind;
I cast them out like the mire of the
streets.
⁴³ Thou didst deliver me from strife
with the peoples;*ʲ*

i Or *gentleness*   *j* Gk Tg: Heb *people*

20–27: The king attributes the LORD's favor toward him to his own previous loyalty to God
and his keeping the commandments. **28–30:** An exuberant outburst of confidence in what he
can accomplish with God's help. **31–42:** A more prosaic account of the battle and the subse-

thou didst make me the head of
the nations;
people whom I had not known
served me.
⁴⁴ As soon as they heard of me they
obeyed me;
foreigners came cringing to me.
⁴⁵ Foreigners lost heart,
and came trembling out of their
fastnesses.

⁴⁶ The LORD lives; and blessed be my
rock,
and exalted be the God of my
salvation,
⁴⁷ the God who gave me vengeance
and subdued peoples under me;
⁴⁸ who delivered me from my enemies;
yea, thou didst exalt me above my
adversaries;
thou didst deliver me from men of
violence.

⁴⁹ For this I will extol thee, O LORD,
among the nations,
and sing praises to thy name.
⁵⁰ Great triumphs he gives to his king,
and shows steadfast love to his
anointed,
to David and his descendants for
ever.

To the choirmaster. A Psalm of David.

19 The heavens are telling the glory
of God;
and the firmament proclaims his
handiwork.
² Day to day pours forth speech,

and night to night declares
knowledge.
³ There is no speech, nor are there
words;
their voice is not heard;
⁴ yet their voice[k] goes out through all
the earth,
and their words to the end of the
world.

In them he has set a tent for the sun,
⁵ which comes forth like a bridegroom
leaving his chamber,
and like a strong man runs its
course with joy.
⁶ Its rising is from the end of the
heavens,
and its circuit to the end of them;
and there is nothing hid from its
heat.

⁷ The law of the LORD is perfect,
reviving the soul;
the testimony of the LORD is sure,
making wise the simple;
⁸ the precepts of the LORD are right,
rejoicing the heart;
the commandment of the LORD is
pure,
enlightening the eyes;
⁹ the fear of the LORD is clean,
enduring for ever;
the ordinances of the LORD are true,
and righteous altogether.
¹⁰ More to be desired are they than
gold,
even much fine gold;
sweeter also than honey
and drippings of the honeycomb.

k Gk Jerome Compare Syr: Heb *line*

---

quent victory (compare vv. 17–19). **43–45:** The king became ruler of an empire at peace. **46–50:**
Concluding hymn of praise and thanksgiving. **50:** This verse establishes the identity of the
psalmist as a king of the Davidic dynasty. *His anointed,* see Ps.2.2 n. At least the nucleus of this
psalm may go back to David.
    Ps. 19: Hymn to God as creator of nature and giver of the law. 1–6: The glory of God is
manifested in the phenomena of the heavens and particularly in the might of the sun. **1–4a:** The
sky and the successive days and nights are personified as members of a choir ceaselessly singing
God's praises. **3:** *There is no speech* . . . i.e. they cannot be heard by human ears. **4b–6:** The
skies provide a track along which the sun, like an athlete, runs his daily course. **7–14:** Probably
a later writer added these verses praising the revelation of God's will in the Mosaic law in order
to counterbalance what seemed to him the almost pagan emphasis upon the revelation of God
in nature (vv. 1–6). **7–9:** Six synonyms are used to describe the law (compare Ps. 119). **9:** *Fear,*
many scholars emend to "word" (see 119.11). **10:** Observance of the law is a joy, not a burden.

11 Moreover by them is thy servant
    warned;
  in keeping them there is great
    reward.
12 But who can discern his errors?
  Clear thou me from hidden
    faults.
13 Keep back thy servant also from
    presumptuous sins;
  let them not have dominion over
    me!
  Then I shall be blameless,
  and innocent of great
    transgression.

14 Let the words of my mouth and the
    meditation of my heart
  be acceptable in thy sight,
  O LORD, my rock and my
    redeemer.

To the choirmaster. A Psalm of David.

20 The LORD answer you in the day
    of trouble!
  The name of the God of Jacob
    protect you!
2 May he send you help from the
    sanctuary,
  and give you support from Zion!
3 May he remember all your offerings,
  and regard with favor your burnt
    sacrifices! *Selah*

4 May he grant you your heart's
    desire,
  and fulfil all your plans!
5 May we shout for joy over your
    victory,
  and in the name of our God
    set up our banners!

May the LORD fulfil all your
    petitions!

6 Now I know that the LORD will help
    his anointed;
  he will answer him from his holy
    heaven
  with mighty victories by his right
    hand.
7 Some boast of chariots, and some of
    horses;
  but we boast of the name of the
    LORD our God.
8 They will collapse and fall;
  but we shall rise and stand
    upright.

9 Give victory to the king, O LORD;
  answer us when we call.*1*

To the choirmaster. A Psalm of David.

21 In thy strength the king rejoices,
    O LORD;
  and in thy help how greatly he
    exults!
2 Thou hast given him his heart's
    desire,
  and hast not withheld the request
    of his lips. *Selah*
3 For thou dost meet him with
    goodly blessings;
  thou dost set a crown of fine gold
    upon his head.
4 He asked life of thee; thou gavest it
    to him,
  length of days for ever and ever.
5 His glory is great through thy help;
  splendor and majesty thou dost
    bestow upon him.

1 Gk: Heb *give victory, O* LORD, *let the King answer us
when we call*

12–13: The poet asks to be delivered from either accidental or deliberate violations of the commandments. **14:** He prays that his hymn may be pleasing to God.
  Ps. 20: Prayer for the king's victory in battle. This psalm was probably composed to accompany a sacrifice offered before the battle was begun (v. 3; compare 1 Sam.13.8–15a). **1–5:** The prayer sung at the altar, or while approaching it. **3:** *Selah,* see 3.2 n. **5:** Between v. 5 and v. 6 some liturgical action evidently occurred, probably the proclamation of an oracle of victory by a priest or temple prophet (see 12.5 n.; compare also 21.8–12), which then inspired the expression of confidence in vv. 6–8. **6:** *Anointed,* see 2.2 n. **9:** Concluding exclamatory prayer.
  Ps. 21: Thanksgiving after the king's victory in battle. This psalm is intentionally paired with Ps. 20. **1–7:** God is praised for having answered the king's prayer. **2:** *Selah,* see 3.2 n.

⁶ Yea, thou dost make him most
    blessed for ever;
  thou dost make him glad with the
    joy of thy presence.
⁷ For the king trusts in the LORD;
  and through the steadfast love of
    the Most High he shall not be
    moved.

⁸ Your hand will find out all your
    enemies;
  your right hand will find out those
    who hate you.
⁹ You will make them as a blazing
    oven
  when you appear.
The LORD will swallow them up in
    his wrath;
  and fire will consume them.
¹⁰ You will destroy their offspring
    from the earth,
  and their children from among the
    sons of men.
¹¹ If they plan evil against you,
  if they devise mischief, they will
    not succeed.
¹² For you will put them to flight;
  you will aim at their faces with
    your bows.

¹³ Be exalted, O LORD, in thy strength!
  We will sing and praise thy power.

To the choirmaster: according to The
Hind of the Dawn. A Psalm of David.

22 My God, my God, why hast
    thou forsaken me?
Why art thou so far from helping
  me, from the words of my
  groaning?
² O my God, I cry by day, but thou
  dost not answer;

and by night, but find no rest.

³ Yet thou art holy,
  enthroned on the praises of Israel.
⁴ In thee our fathers trusted;
  they trusted, and thou didst
    deliver them.
⁵ To thee they cried, and were saved;
  in thee they trusted, and were not
    disappointed.

⁶ But I am a worm, and no man;
  scorned by men, and despised
    by the people.
⁷ All who see me mock at me,
  they make mouths at me, they wag
    their heads;
⁸ "He committed his cause to the
    LORD; let him deliver him,
  let him rescue him, for he delights
    in him!"

⁹ Yet thou art he who took me from
    the womb;
  thou didst keep me safe upon my
    mother's breasts.
¹⁰ Upon thee was I cast from my birth,
  and since my mother bore me thou
    hast been my God.
¹¹ Be not far from me,
  for trouble is near
  and there is none to help.

¹² Many bulls encompass me,
  strong bulls of Bashan surround
    me;
¹³ they open wide their mouths at
    me,
  like a ravening and roaring lion.

¹⁴ I am poured out like water,
  and all my bones are out of joint;
my heart is like wax,
  it is melted within my breast;

8–12: An oracle promising a succession of victories, addressed to the king by a priest or temple prophet (compare 20.5 n.). **13:** Concluding exclamation of praise.
    Ps. 22: Prayer for deliverance from mortal illness (a lament). **1–2:** Cry for help. **1:** Quoted by Jesus on the cross (Mk.15.34). **3:** God has helped his people in time past. **6–8:** The psalmist's misery is aggravated by the mockery of those who regard his illness as proof that God has forsaken him. **9–11:** God's help in former times inspires him to pray that it may continue in the present. **12–18:** Description of his condition. **12–13:** His detractors behave like savage animals (see also v. 16, although the meaning of the third line is obscure; and vv. 20–21). *Bulls of Bashan,* Am.4.1. **14–15,17–18:** A vivid account of the poet's fever and resulting weakness.

¹⁵ my strength is dried up like a
 potsherd,
 and my tongue cleaves to my
  jaws;
 thou dost lay me in the dust of
  death.

¹⁶ Yea, dogs are round about me;
 a company of evildoers encircle
  me;
 they have pierced^{*m*} my hands
  and feet–
¹⁷ I can count all my bones–
 they stare and gloat over me;
¹⁸ they divide my garments among
 them,
 and for my raiment they cast lots.

¹⁹ But thou, O LORD, be not far off!
 O thou my help, hasten to my
  aid!
²⁰ Deliver my soul from the sword,
 my life^{*n*} from the power of the
  dog!
²¹ Save me from the mouth of the lion,
 my afflicted soul^{*o*} from the horns
  of the wild oxen!

²² I will tell of thy name to my
 brethren;
 in the midst of the congregation
  I will praise thee:
²³ You who fear the LORD, praise him!
 all you sons of Jacob, glorify him,
 and stand in awe of him, all you
  sons of Israel!
²⁴ For he has not despised or abhorred
 the affliction of the afflicted;
 and he has not hid his face from
  him,
 but has heard, when he cried to
  him.

²⁵ From thee comes my praise in the
 great congregation;

 my vows I will pay before those
  who fear him.
²⁶ The afflicted^{*p*} shall eat and be
 satisfied;
 those who seek him shall praise
  the LORD!
 May your hearts live for ever!

²⁷ All the ends of the earth shall
 remember
 and turn to the LORD;
 and all the families of the nations
  shall worship before him.^{*q*}
²⁸ For dominion belongs to the
 LORD,
 and he rules over the nations.

²⁹ Yea, to him^{*r*} shall all the proud of
 the earth bow down;
 before him shall bow all who go
  down to the dust,
 and he who cannot keep himself
  alive.
³⁰ Posterity shall serve him;
 men shall tell of the Lord to the
  coming generation,
³¹ and proclaim his deliverance to a
 people yet unborn,
 that he has wrought it.

A Psalm of David.

23 The LORD is my shepherd, I
 shall not want;
² he makes me lie down in green
  pastures.
He leads me beside still waters;^{*s*}
³ he restores my soul.^{*t*}

m Gk Syr Jerome: Heb *like a lion*
n Heb *my only one*
o Gk Syr: Heb *thou hast answered me*
p Or *poor*
q Gk Syr Jerome: Heb *thee*
r Cn: Heb *they have eaten and*
s Heb *the waters of rest*
t Or *life*

16: *Dogs,* enemies (compare *lion, wild oxen,* v. 21). **18:** He is so nearly dead that his neighbors and relatives have already begun to divide his property. **19–21:** Prayer for healing and for deliverance from slanderers. **22–31:** If he recovers, he vows to offer a formal thanksgiving *in the midst of the congregation,* the temple (see 7.17 n.). **22:** The vow (compare v. 25). **23–31:** The hymn which will then be sung. **Ps. 23: An expression of confidence in God's protection** (a song of trust; see Ps. 11 n.). **1–4:** The LORD is compared to a shepherd. **3:** *Soul* means vitality, life. *Paths of righteousness,* or

He leads me in paths of
  righteousness*u*
for his name's sake.

4 Even though I walk through the
    valley of the shadow of death,*v*
  I fear no evil;
for thou art with me;
  thy rod and thy staff,
  they comfort me.

5 Thou preparest a table before me
    in the presence of my enemies;
  thou anointest my head with oil,
  my cup overflows.
6 Surely*w* goodness and mercy*x* shall
    follow me
  all the days of my life;
and I shall dwell in the house of the
    LORD
  for ever.*y*

A Psalm of David.

24 The earth is the LORD's and the
    fulness thereof,
  the world and those who dwell
    therein;
2 for he has founded it upon the seas,
    and established it upon the rivers.

3 Who shall ascend the hill of the
    LORD?
  And who shall stand in his holy
    place?
4 He who has clean hands and a pure
    heart,

who does not lift up his soul to
    what is false,
  and does not swear deceitfully.
5 He will receive blessing from the
    LORD,
  and vindication from the God of
    his salvation.
6 Such is the generation of those who
    seek him,
  who seek the face of the God of
    Jacob.*z*   *Selah*

7 Lift up your heads, O gates!
    and be lifted up, O ancient doors!
  that the King of glory may come
    in.
8 Who is the King of glory?
    The LORD, strong and mighty,
  the LORD, mighty in battle!
9 Lift up your heads, O gates!
    and be lifted up,*a* O ancient
      doors!
  that the King of glory may come
    in.
10 Who is this King of glory?
    The LORD of hosts,
  he is the King of glory!   *Selah*

A Psalm of David.

25 To thee, O LORD, I lift up my
    soul.
2 O my God, in thee I trust,
    let me not be put to shame;
  let not my enemies exult over me.

u Or *right paths*   v Or *the valley of deep darkness*
w Or *Only*   x Or *kindness*
y Or *as long as I live*
z Gk Syr: Heb *thy face, O Jacob*
a Gk Syr Jerome Tg Compare verse 7: Heb *lift up*

"of rightness," that is, right paths (see note *u*), which suits the context better. 4: *Shadow of death* is the reading of the scribes, but "deep darkness" (see note *v*) is the better rendering; compare 44.19; 107.10; Job 3.5; Is.9.2; etc., where the same Hebrew expression occurs. 5–6: The LORD is compared to a gracious host. 6: *Dwell in the house of the LORD* means to worship in the temple (compare 27.4). *For ever*, Hebrew "for length of days," meaning "as long as I live" (see note *y* and 27.4).

Ps. 24: A liturgy on entering the sanctuary, probably used in connection with a procession of the ark. 1–6: Perhaps sung by a choir within the temple gates. 1–2: Acknowledgment of the LORD as the creator. 3: The question: Who shall be admitted to the temple? (compare Ps. 15). 4–6: The answer: Only those who have the requisite moral qualities. 6: *Selah*, see 3.2 n. 7–10: The choir outside the gates, presumably accompanied by the ark, now requests to be admitted. 7: *Heads*, lintels. 8–10: *The King of glory . . .* , means the God of Israel, whose presence was associated with the ark (Num.10.35–36).

Ps. 25: Prayer for deliverance from personal enemies (a lament). In acrostic form (compare Pss. 9–10 n.), every successive verse beginning with another letter of the Hebrew alphabet. This

³ Yea, let none that wait for thee be
  put to shame;
  let them be ashamed who are
  wantonly treacherous.

⁴ Make me to know thy ways, O LORD;
  teach me thy paths.
⁵ Lead me in thy truth, and teach me,
  for thou art the God of my
  salvation;
  for thee I wait all the day long.

⁶ Be mindful of thy mercy, O LORD,
  and of thy steadfast love,
  for they have been from of old.
⁷ Remember not the sins of my youth,
  or my transgressions;
  according to thy steadfast love
  remember me,
  for thy goodness' sake, O LORD!

⁸ Good and upright is the LORD;
  therefore he instructs sinners in
  the way.
⁹ He leads the humble in what is right,
  and teaches the humble his way.
¹⁰ All the paths of the LORD are
  steadfast love and faithfulness,
  for those who keep his covenant
  and his testimonies.

¹¹ For thy name's sake, O LORD,
  pardon my guilt, for it is great.
¹² Who is the man that fears the LORD?
  Him will he instruct in the way
  that he should choose.
¹³ He himself shall abide in
  prosperity,
  and his children shall possess the
  land.
¹⁴ The friendship of the LORD is for
  those who fear him,
  and he makes known to them his
  covenant.
¹⁵ My eyes are ever toward the LORD,

for he will pluck my feet out of the
  net.

¹⁶ Turn thou to me, and be gracious to
  me;
  for I am lonely and afflicted.
¹⁷ Relieve the troubles of my heart,
  and bring me*ᵇ* out of my
  distresses.
¹⁸ Consider my affliction and my
  trouble,
  and forgive all my sins.

¹⁹ Consider how many are my foes,
  and with what violent hatred they
  hate me.
²⁰ Oh guard my life, and deliver me;
  let me not be put to shame, for I
  take refuge in thee.
²¹ May integrity and uprightness
  preserve me,
  for I wait for thee.

²² Redeem Israel, O God,
  out of all his troubles.

A Psalm of David.

26 Vindicate me, O LORD,
  for I have walked in my
  integrity,
  and I have trusted in the LORD
  without wavering.
² Prove me, O LORD, and try me;
  test my heart and my mind.
³ For thy steadfast love is before my
  eyes,
  and I walk in faithfulness to
  thee.*ᶜ*

⁴ I do not sit with false men,
  nor do I consort with dissemblers;

b Or The troubles of my heart are enlarged; bring me
c Or in thy faithfulness

artificial pattern accounts for the absence of any clear, logical structure, although the psalm has most of the elements of the typical lament: cry for help (vv. 1–3), the psalmist's situation (vv. 18–19), protestation of innocence (v. 21), expression of trust (vv. 8–15), prayer for vindication (vv. 16–20). **13:** *Possess the land*, see 37.9,11,29; compare Dt.11.8–9. **22:** Probably a liturgical addition adapting an individual prayer to congregational use.
  Ps. 26: Prayer for deliverance from personal enemies (a lament). **1–3:** Cry for vindication against an unjust charge (compare 1 Kg.8.31–32). **4–7:** Protestation of innocence (compare

⁵ I hate the company of evildoers,
     and I will not sit with the wicked.

⁶ I wash my hands in innocence,
     and go about thy altar, O LORD,
⁷ singing aloud a song of thanksgiving,
     and telling all thy wondrous
        deeds.

⁸ O LORD, I love the habitation of thy
        house,
     and the place where thy glory
        dwells.
⁹ Sweep me not away with sinners,
     nor my life with bloodthirsty men,
¹⁰ men in whose hands are evil devices,
     and whose right hands are full of
        bribes.

¹¹ But as for me, I walk in my integrity;
     redeem me, and be gracious to me.
¹² My foot stands on level ground;
     in the great congregation I will
        bless the LORD.

A Psalm of David.

27   The LORD is my light and my
        salvation;
    whom shall I fear?
The LORD is the stronghold*d* of my
        life;
    of whom shall I be afraid?

² When evildoers assail me,
    uttering slanders against me,*e*
my adversaries and foes,
    they shall stumble and fall.

³ Though a host encamp against me,
    my heart shall not fear;
though war arise against me,
    yet I will be confident.

⁴ One thing have I asked of the LORD,
     that will I seek after;
that I may dwell in the house of the
     LORD
all the days of my life,
to behold the beauty of the LORD,
     and to inquire in his temple.

⁵ For he will hide me in his shelter
    in the day of trouble;
he will conceal me under the cover
     of his tent,
he will set me high upon a rock.

⁶ And now my head shall be lifted up
    above my enemies round about
     me;
and I will offer in his tent
    sacrifices with shouts of joy;
I will sing and make melody to the
    LORD.

⁷ Hear, O LORD, when I cry aloud,
     be gracious to me and answer me!
⁸ Thou hast said, "Seek ye my face."
    My heart says to thee,
"Thy face, LORD, do I seek."
⁹   Hide not thy face from me.

Turn not thy servant away in anger,
    thou who hast been my help.
Cast me not off, forsake me not,
    O God of my salvation!
¹⁰ For my father and my mother have
     forsaken me,
    but the LORD will take me up.

¹¹ Teach me thy way, O LORD;
    and lead me on a level path
    because of my enemies.
¹² Give me not up to the will of my
     adversaries;
for false witnesses have risen
     against me,
and they breathe out violence.

d Or *refuge*   *e* Heb *to eat up my flesh*

4.2–4). **6–7:** The protest is dramatized in a liturgical ceremony. *Wash my hands in innocence,* compare Dt.21.6–8; Ps.51.7. **8–11:** Prayer for help. *Thy glory dwells,* Is.4.5; Ezek.43.4–5. **12:** The vow (see 7.17 n.).
    Ps. 27: An act of devotion and a prayer for deliverance. 1–6: Song of trust (see Ps. 11 n.). **4:** *Dwell in the house of the LORD,* see 23.6 n. As with most of the psalms, the author is probably a temple functionary, a Levite. **6:** *Tent,* poetic name for the temple. **7–14:** A lament. **7–9:** Cry for help. **10–12:** The psalmist's situation. **13–14:** Expression of confidence. *In the land of the living,* i.e. "during my life."

13 I believe that I shall see the
  goodness of the LORD
  in the land of the living!
14 Wait for the LORD;
  be strong, and let your heart take
    courage;
  yea, wait for the LORD!

A Psalm of David.

28 To thee, O LORD, I call;
  my rock, be not deaf to me,
lest, if thou be silent to me,
  I become like those who go down
    to the Pit.
2 Hear the voice of my supplication,
  as I cry to thee for help,
as I lift up my hands
  toward thy most holy sanctuary.*f*

3 Take me not off with the wicked,
  with those who are workers of
    evil,
who speak peace with their
    neighbors,
  while mischief is in their hearts.
4 Requite them according to their
    work,
  and according to the evil of their
    deeds;
requite them according to the work
    of their hands;
  render them their due reward.
5 Because they do not regard the works
    of the LORD,
  or the work of his hands,
he will break them down and build
    them up no more.

6 Blessed be the LORD!
  for he has heard the voice of my
    supplications.
7 The LORD is my strength and my
    shield;

in him my heart trusts;
  so I am helped, and my heart exults,
  and with my song I give thanks to
    him.

8 The LORD is the strength of his
    people,
  he is the saving refuge of his
    anointed.
9 O save thy people, and bless thy
    heritage;
  be thou their shepherd, and carry
    them for ever.

A Psalm of David.

29 Ascribe to the LORD, O
  heavenly beings,*g*
ascribe to the LORD glory and
    strength.
2 Ascribe to the LORD the glory of his
    name;
  worship the LORD in holy array.

3 The voice of the LORD is upon the
    waters;
  the God of glory thunders,
  the LORD, upon many waters.
4 The voice of the LORD is powerful,
  the voice of the LORD is full of
    majesty.

5 The voice of the LORD breaks the
    cedars,
  the LORD breaks the cedars of
    Lebanon.
6 He makes Lebanon to skip like a
    calf,
  and Si'rion like a young wild ox.

7 The voice of the LORD flashes forth
  flames of fire.

f Heb *thy innermost sanctuary*
g Heb *sons of gods*

Ps. 28: Prayer for deliverance from personal enemies (a lament). 1–5: Cry for vindication
(compare 26.1–3). 1: *The Pit,* i.e. Sheol (see 6.5 n.). 6–7: After v. 5, a priest or temple prophet
probably delivered an oracle of assurance (compare 12.5 n.), to which these verses are the
psalmist's grateful response. 8–9: See 25.22 n. 8: *Anointed,* see 2.2 n. 9: *Shepherd,* Is.40.11.
  Ps. 29: Hymn to the God of the storm. 1–2: Call to worship. 3–9: The LORD's manifestation
in the thunderstorm. 3: *The voice of the LORD,* the thunder. *The waters,* the Mediterranean, but
with mythological overtones. 5: *Lebanon,* the principal mountains of Syria. 6: *Sirion,* Mount
Hermon. 7: *Flames of fire,* the lightning. 8: *Kadesh,* probably the Kadesh of the wilderness

8 The voice of the LORD shakes the
  wilderness,
  the LORD shakes the wilderness of
  Kadesh.

9 The voice of the LORD makes the
  oaks to whirl,*h*
  and strips the forests bare;
  and in his temple all cry, "Glory!"

10 The LORD sits enthroned over the
   flood;
   the LORD sits enthroned as king
   for ever.
11 May the LORD give strength to his
   people!
   May the LORD bless his people
   with peace!

A Psalm of David. A Song at the
dedication of the Temple.

30 I will extol thee, O LORD, for
   thou hast drawn me up,
   and hast not let my foes rejoice
   over me.
2 O LORD my God, I cried to thee for
  help,
  and thou hast healed me.
3 O LORD, thou hast brought up my
  soul from Sheol,
  restored me to life from among
  those gone down to the Pit.*i*

4 Sing praises to the LORD, O you his
  saints,
  and give thanks to his holy name.
5 For his anger is but for a moment,
  and his favor is for a lifetime.
  Weeping may tarry for the night,
  but joy comes with the morning.

6 As for me, I said in my prosperity,
  "I shall never be moved."
7 By thy favor, O LORD,
  thou hadst established me as a
  strong mountain;
  thou didst hide thy face,
  I was dismayed.

8 To thee, O LORD, I cried;
  and to the LORD I made
  supplication:
9 "What profit is there in my death,
  if I go down to the Pit?
  Will the dust praise thee?
  Will it tell of thy faithfulness?
10 Hear, O LORD, and be gracious to me!
   O LORD, be thou my helper!"

11 Thou hast turned for me my
   mourning into dancing;
   thou hast loosed my sackcloth
   and girded me with gladness,
12 that my soul*j* may praise thee and
   not be silent.
   O LORD my God, I will give thanks
   to thee for ever.

To the choirmaster. A Psalm of David.

31 In thee, O LORD, do I seek refuge;
   let me never be put to shame;
   in thy righteousness deliver me!
2 Incline thy ear to me,
  rescue me speedily!
  Be thou a rock of refuge for me,
  a strong fortress to save me!

3 Yea, thou art my rock and my
  fortress;

h Or *makes the hinds to calve*
i Or *that I should not go down to the Pit*
j Heb *that glory*

wanderings (Num.20.1). **10–11:** Above the tumult of the storm, the LORD reigns in majestic
peace.
  Ps. 30: Thanksgiving for healing. 1–3: God is praised for the psalmist's recovery. The psalm
was probably sung in fulfilment of a vow (see 7.17 n.). **3:** *Sheol . . . the Pit*, see 28.1 n. **4–5:** The
congregation is invited to join in his thanksgiving. **4:** *Saints*, devout adherents (see 16.10 n.,
same Hebrew word). **6–12:** The narrative of his experience (see 18.4–6 n.): Before his illness he
had felt perfectly secure (vv. 6–7); when illness came, he turned to God in prayer (vv. 8–10),
and God answered him (vv. 11–12).
  Ps. 31: Prayer for deliverance from personal enemies (a lament). Verses 1–8 and 9–24 are
parallel in form, both containing the principal elements of a lament. **1–8:** Cry for help (vv. 1–5),

for thy name's sake lead me and
guide me,
4 take me out of the net which is hidden
for me,
for thou art my refuge.
5 Into thy hand I commit my spirit;
thou hast redeemed me, O LORD,
faithful God.

6 Thou hatest[k] those who pay regard
to vain idols;
but I trust in the LORD.
7 I will rejoice and be glad for thy
steadfast love,
because thou hast seen my
affliction,
thou hast taken heed of my
adversities,
8 and hast not delivered me into the
hand of the enemy;
thou hast set my feet in a broad
place.

9 Be gracious to me, O LORD, for I am
in distress;
my eye is wasted from grief,
my soul and my body also.
10 For my life is spent with sorrow,
and my years with sighing;
my strength fails because of my
misery,[l]
and my bones waste away.

11 I am the scorn of all my adversaries,
a horror[m] to my neighbors,
an object of dread to my
acquaintances;
those who see me in the street flee
from me.
12 I have passed out of mind like one
who is dead;
I have become like a broken
vessel.
13 Yea, I hear the whispering of many—
terror on every side!—
as they scheme together against me,
as they plot to take my life.

14 But I trust in thee, O LORD,
I say, "Thou art my God."
15 My times are in thy hand;
deliver me from the hand of my
enemies and persecutors!
16 Let thy face shine on thy servant;
save me in thy steadfast love!
17 Let me not be put to shame, O
LORD,
for I call on thee;
let the wicked be put to shame,
let them go dumbfounded to Sheol.
18 Let the lying lips be dumb,
which speak insolently against the
righteous
in pride and contempt.

19 O how abundant is thy goodness,
which thou hast laid up for those
who fear thee,
and wrought for those who take
refuge in thee,
in the sight of the sons of men!
20 In the covert of thy presence thou
hidest them
from the plots of men;
thou holdest them safe under thy
shelter
from the strife of tongues.

21 Blessed be the LORD,
for he has wondrously shown his
steadfast love to me
when I was beset as in a besieged
city.
22 I had said in my alarm,
"I am driven far[n] from thy sight."
But thou didst hear my
supplications,
when I cried to thee for help.

23 Love the LORD, all you his saints!
The LORD preserves the faithful,
but abundantly requites him who
acts haughtily.

k With one Heb Ms Gk Syr Jerome: Heb *I hate*
l Gk Syr: Heb *iniquity*
m Cn: Heb *exceedingly*
n Another reading is *cut off*

the psalmist's situation (v. 4), expression of confidence (v. 5), protestation of innocence (v. 6), grateful recognition of God's help (vv. 7–8; perhaps this followed an oracle of assurance; see 12.5 n.). **9–24:** Cry for help (v. 9), the psalmist's situation (vv. 10–13), expression of confidence (vv. 14,19–20), prayer for vindication (vv. 15–18), grateful recognition of God's help (vv. 21–24). **12:** *Broken vessel,* compare Ec.12.6. **13:** Jer.20.10. **23:** See 30.4 n.

24 Be strong, and let your heart take
   courage,
all you who wait for the LORD!

A Psalm of David. A Maskil.

32 Blessed is he whose
   transgression is forgiven,
whose sin is covered.
2 Blessed is the man to whom the
   LORD imputes no iniquity,
and in whose spirit there is no
   deceit.

3 When I declared not my sin, my
   body wasted away
through my groaning all day long.
4 For day and night thy hand was
   heavy upon me;
my strength was dried up*o* as by
   the heat of summer.   *Selah*

5 I acknowledged my sin to thee,
   and I did not hide my iniquity;
I said, "I will confess my
   transgressions to the LORD";
then thou didst forgive the guilt
   of my sin.   *Selah*

6 Therefore let every one who is godly
   offer prayer to thee;
at a time of distress,*p* in the rush of
   great waters,
they shall not reach him.
7 Thou art a hiding place for me,
   thou preservest me from trouble;
thou dost encompass me with
   deliverance.*q*   *Selah*

8 I will instruct you and teach you
   the way you should go;
I will counsel you with my eye
   upon you.
9 Be not like a horse or a mule,
   without understanding,

which must be curbed with bit
   and bridle,
else it will not keep with you.

10 Many are the pangs of the wicked;
   but steadfast love surrounds him
who trusts in the LORD.
11 Be glad in the LORD, and rejoice, O
   righteous,
and shout for joy, all you upright
   in heart!

33 Rejoice in the LORD, O you
   righteous!
Praise befits the upright.
2 Praise the LORD with the lyre,
   make melody to him with the
   harp of ten strings!
3 Sing to him a new song,
   play skillfully on the strings, with
   loud shouts.

4 For the word of the LORD is upright;
   and all his work is done in
   faithfulness.
5 He loves righteousness and justice;
   the earth is full of the steadfast
   love of the LORD.

6 By the word of the LORD the
   heavens were made,
and all their host by the breath of
   his mouth.
7 He gathered the waters of the sea as
   in a bottle;
he put the deeps in storehouses.

8 Let all the earth fear the LORD,
   let all the inhabitants of the world
   stand in awe of him!
9 For he spoke, and it came to be;
   he commanded, and it stood
   forth.

o Heb obscure
p Cn: Heb *at a time of finding only*
q Cn: Heb *shouts of deliverance*

Ps. 32: Thanksgiving for healing. 1–2: God is praised for the psalmist's recovery. **1:** *Blessed*,
see 1.1 n. Since disease was commonly regarded as punishment for sin, healing is evidence that
the *transgression is forgiven*. **3–5:** The psalmist's experience (see 18.4–6 n.). **4:** *Selah*, see 3.2 n.
5: Healing came only after he acknowledged himself to be a sinner. **6–11:** The psalmist commends to the congregation similar faith in God (vv. 6–7,10) and obedience to God's will (vv.
8–9).
   Ps. 33: Hymn to God as creator and lord of history. 1–3: Call to worship. **4–5:** The character
of Israel's God. **6–9:** The LORD as creator. The emphasis upon the divine word in vv. 6 and 9

¹⁰ The Lord brings the counsel of the
nations to nought;
he frustrates the plans of the
peoples.
¹¹ The counsel of the Lord stands for
ever,
the thoughts of his heart to all
generations.
¹² Blessed is the nation whose God is
the Lord,
the people whom he has chosen
as his heritage!

¹³ The Lord looks down from heaven,
he sees all the sons of men;
¹⁴ from where he sits enthroned he
looks forth
on all the inhabitants of the earth,
¹⁵ he who fashions the hearts of them
all,
and observes all their deeds.
¹⁶ A king is not saved by his great
army;
a warrior is not delivered by his
great strength.
¹⁷ The war horse is a vain hope for
victory,
and by its great might it cannot
save.

¹⁸ Behold, the eye of the Lord is on
those who fear him,
on those who hope in his steadfast
love,
¹⁹ that he may deliver their soul from
death,
and keep them alive in famine.

²⁰ Our soul waits for the Lord;
he is our help and shield.
²¹ Yea, our heart is glad in him,
because we trust in his holy name.
²² Let thy steadfast love, O Lord, be
upon us,
even as we hope in thee.

A Psalm of David, when he feigned
madness before Abimelech, so that he
drove him out, and he went away.

34 I will bless the Lord at all times;
his praise shall continually
be in my mouth.
² My soul makes its boast in the Lord;
let the afflicted hear and be glad.
³ O magnify the Lord with me,
and let us exalt his name together!

⁴ I sought the Lord, and he answered
me,
and delivered me from all my
fears.
⁵ Look to him, and be radiant;
so your*ʳ* faces shall never be
ashamed.
⁶ This poor man cried, and the Lord
heard him,
and saved him out of all his
troubles.
⁷ The angel of the Lord encamps
around those who fear him, and
delivers them.
⁸ O taste and see that the Lord is
good!
Happy is the man who takes refuge
in him!
⁹ O fear the Lord, you his saints,
for those who fear him have no
want!
¹⁰ The young lions suffer want and
hunger;
but those who seek the Lord lack
no good thing.

¹¹ Come, O sons, listen to me,
I will teach you the fear of the
Lord.
¹² What man is there who desires life,
and covets many days, that he
may enjoy good?

ʳ Gk Syr Jerome: Heb *their*

---

reflects Gen.1.3–31. **10–19:** The Lord rules over the destinies of nations. **20–22:** Israel puts her
complete trust in him.
   Ps. 34: Thanksgiving for deliverance from trouble. Like Pss. 9–10 and 25, this psalm is an
alphabetical acrostic. **1–3:** A brief hymn of praise. **4–6:** The narrative of the psalmist's experience (see 18.4–6 n.; compare 30.6–12; 32.3–5). **7–22:** He commends to the congregation the
same kind of faith in God, and assures them that the Lord will never be found wanting (compare 32.6–11). The style is that of the teachers of wisdom (compare Pss. 1 and 37; also v. 11
with Pr.1.8; 2.1). **9:** *Saints,* see 16.3 n. **12–14:** 1 Pet.3.10–12. **20:** Jn.19.36.

¹³ Keep your tongue from evil,
   and your lips from speaking
      deceit.
¹⁴ Depart from evil, and do good;
   seek peace, and pursue it.

¹⁵ The eyes of the LORD are toward the
      righteous,
   and his ears toward their cry.
¹⁶ The face of the LORD is against
      evildoers,
   to cut off the remembrance of
      them from the earth.
¹⁷ When the righteous cry for help, the
      LORD hears,
   and delivers them out of all their
      troubles.
¹⁸ The LORD is near to the
      brokenhearted,
   and saves the crushed in spirit.

¹⁹ Many are the afflictions of the
      righteous;
   but the LORD delivers him out of
      them all.
²⁰ He keeps all his bones;
   not one of them is broken.
²¹ Evil shall slay the wicked;
   and those who hate the righteous
      will be condemned.
²² The LORD redeems the life of his
      servants;
   none of those who take refuge in
      him will be condemned.

A Psalm of David.

35 Contend, O LORD, with those
   who contend with me;
   fight against those who fight
      against me!
² Take hold of shield and buckler,
   and rise for my help!
³ Draw the spear and javelin
   against my pursuers!
Say to my soul,

"I am your deliverance!"

⁴ Let them be put to shame and
      dishonor
   who seek after my life!
   Let them be turned back and
      confounded
   who devise evil against me!
⁵ Let them be like chaff before the
      wind,
   with the angel of the LORD
      driving them on!
⁶ Let their way be dark and slippery,
   with the angel of the LORD
      pursuing them!

⁷ For without cause they hid their net
      for me;
   without cause they dug a pitˢ for
      my life.
⁸ Let ruin come upon them unawares!
   And let the net which they hid
      ensnare them;
   let them fall therein to ruin!

⁹ Then my soul shall rejoice in the
      LORD,
   exulting in his deliverance.
¹⁰ All my bones shall say,
   "O LORD, who is like thee,
   thou who deliverest the weak
      from him who is too strong for
         him,
   the weak and needy from him who
      despoils him?"

¹¹ Malicious witnesses rise up;
   they ask me of things that I know
      not.
¹² They requite me evil for good;
   my soul is forlorn.
¹³ But I, when they were sick—
   I wore sackcloth,
   I afflicted myself with fasting.
   I prayed with head bowedᵗ on my
      bosom,

ˢ The word *pit* is transposed from the preceding line
ᵗ Or *My prayer turned back*

Ps. 35: Prayer for deliverance from personal enemies (a lament). As in Ps. 31, the elements of
the lament occur more than once, so that vv. 1–10, 11–18, and 19–28 can be treated as separate
units. **1–10:** The first lament. **1–6:** Cry for vindication and vengeance. **7:** The psalmist's situation. **8:** Prayer for vengeance renewed. **9–10:** The vow (see 7.17 n.). **11–18:** The second lament.
11–16: The psalmist's situation; his innocence. As in some other laments, it is not clear whether
the psalmist's principal trouble arises from his enemies or from a sickness of which they have

14 as though I grieved for my friend
    or my brother;
   I went about as one who laments
    his mother,
    bowed down and in mourning.

15 But at my stumbling they gathered
    in glee,
    they gathered together against me;
   cripples whom I knew not
    slandered me without ceasing;
16 they impiously mocked more and
    more,*u*
    gnashing at me with their teeth.

17 How long, O LORD, wilt thou look
    on?
   Rescue me from their ravages,
    my life from the lions!
18 Then I will thank thee in the great
    congregation;
   in the mighty throng I will praise
    thee.

19 Let not those rejoice over me
   who are wrongfully my foes,
and let not those wink the eye
   who hate me without cause.
20 For they do not speak peace,
   but against those who are quiet in
    the land
   they conceive words of deceit.
21 They open wide their mouths
    against me;
   they say, "Aha, Aha!
   our eyes have seen it!"

22 Thou hast seen, O LORD; be not
    silent!
   O Lord, be not far from me!
23 Bestir thyself, and awake for my
    right,
   for my cause, my God and my
    Lord!
24 Vindicate me, O LORD, my God,
   according to thy righteousness;

and let them not rejoice over me!
25 Let them not say to themselves,
   "Aha, we have our heart's desire!"
Let them not say, "We have
    swallowed him up."

26 Let them be put to shame and
    confusion altogether
who rejoice at my calamity!
Let them be clothed with shame and
    dishonor
who magnify themselves against
    me!

27 Let those who desire my vindication
   shout for joy and be glad,
   and say evermore,
"Great is the LORD,
   who delights in the welfare of his
    servant!"
28 Then my tongue shall tell of thy
    righteousness
   and of thy praise all the day long.

To the choirmaster. A Psalm of David,
   the servant of the LORD.

36 Transgression speaks to the
   wicked
  deep in his heart;
there is no fear of God
  before his eyes.
2 For he flatters himself in his own
    eyes
  that his iniquity cannot be found
   out and hated.
3 The words of his mouth are mischief
   and deceit;
  he has ceased to act wisely and do
   good.
4 He plots mischief while on his bed;
  he sets himself in a way that is not
   good;
  he spurns not evil.

u Cn Compare Gk: Heb *like the profanest of mockers of
a cake*

---

taken advantage. **17:** Cry for help. **18:** The vow (see 7.17 n.). **19–29:** The third lament. **19:** Cry
for help. **20–21:** The psalmist's situation. **22–27:** Prayer for vindication. **28:** The vow (compare v. 18).
    Ps. 36: A psalm of mixed type: vv. 1–4 are in the type of a wisdom psalm; vv. 5–9, a hymn;
vv. 10–12, a prayer in the style of a lament. Since the last section seems to determine the character of the whole, the psalm should probably be classified as a liturgy of lament. **1–4:** The
character of the wicked man. **1:** The wicked man is inspired by *transgression* just as a prophet

5 Thy steadfast love, O LORD, extends
    to the heavens,
  thy faithfulness to the clouds.
6 Thy righteousness is like the
    mountains of God,
  thy judgments are like the great
    deep;
  man and beast thou savest, O
    LORD.

7 How precious is thy steadfast love,
    O God!
  The children of men take refuge
    in the shadow of thy wings.
8 They feast on the abundance of thy
    house,
  and thou givest them drink from
    the river of thy delights.
9 For with thee is the fountain of life;
  in thy light do we see light.

10 O continue thy steadfast love to
    those who know thee,
  and thy salvation to the upright of
    heart!
11 Let not the foot of arrogance come
    upon me,
  nor the hand of the wicked drive
    me away.
12 There the evildoers lie prostrate,
  they are thrust down, unable to
    rise.

A Psalm of David.

37 Fret not yourself because of the
    wicked,
  be not envious of wrongdoers!
2 For they will soon fade like the
    grass,
  and wither like the green herb.

3 Trust in the LORD, and do good;

so you will dwell in the land, and
  enjoy security.
4 Take delight in the LORD,
  and he will give you the desires of
    your heart.

5 Commit your way to the LORD;
  trust in him, and he will act.
6 He will bring forth your vindication
    as the light,
  and your right as the noonday.

7 Be still before the LORD, and wait
    patiently for him;
  fret not yourself over him who
    prospers in his way,
  over the man who carries out evil
    devices!

8 Refrain from anger, and forsake
    wrath!
  Fret not yourself; it tends only to
    evil.
9 For the wicked shall be cut off;
  but those who wait for the LORD
    shall possess the land.

10 Yet a little while, and the wicked will
    be no more;
  though you look well at his place,
    he will not be there.
11 But the meek shall possess the land,
  and delight themselves in
    abundant prosperity.

12 The wicked plots against the
    righteous,
  and gnashes his teeth at him;
13 but the LORD laughs at the wicked,
  for he sees that his day is coming.
14 The wicked draw the sword and
    bend their bows,
  to bring down the poor and needy,

---

is inspired by the Spirit of God. **5–9:** The character of God, who is a source of blessing to the righteous and provides them with a refuge. *Fountain of life,* compare Jer.2.13. **10–11:** Prayer for deliverance. **12:** Assurance of having been heard.

    Ps. 37. The certainty of retribution for the wicked (a wisdom psalm). The argument is directed to those discouraged by the injustices which apparently dominate the world. The acrostic form of the psalm (see Pss. 9–10 n.) explains the lack of a clear outline or logical progression of thought. **3:** *The land,* Palestine (vv. 9,11,22,29; compare Dt.11.8–32). **10:** The heart of the argument: Do not be impatient! Retribution will come soon, even though it is not evident now (compare vv. 35–36). **11:** Compare Mt.5.5.

to slay those who walk uprightly;
15 their sword shall enter their own
heart,
and their bows shall be broken.

16 Better is a little that the righteous
has
than the abundance of many
wicked.
17 For the arms of the wicked shall be
broken;
but the Lord upholds the
righteous.

18 The Lord knows the days of the
blameless,
and their heritage will abide for
ever;
19 they are not put to shame in evil
times,
in the days of famine they have
abundance.

20 But the wicked perish;
the enemies of the Lord are like
the glory of the pastures,
they vanish–like smoke they
vanish away.

21 The wicked borrows, and cannot
pay back,
but the righteous is generous and
gives;
22 for those blessed by the Lord shall
possess the land,
but those cursed by him shall be
cut off.

23 The steps of a man are from the
Lord,
and he establishes him in whose
way he delights;
24 though he fall, he shall not be cast
headlong,
for the Lord is the stay of his
hand.

25 I have been young, and now am old;
yet I have not seen the righteous
forsaken

or his children begging bread.
26 He is ever giving liberally and
lending,
and his children become a
blessing.

27 Depart from evil, and do good;
so shall you abide for ever.
28 For the Lord loves justice;
he will not forsake his saints.

The righteous shall be preserved for
ever,
but the children of the wicked
shall be cut off.
29 The righteous shall possess the land,
and dwell upon it for ever.

30 The mouth of the righteous utters
wisdom,
and his tongue speaks justice.
31 The law of his God is in his heart;
his steps do not slip.

32 The wicked watches the righteous,
and seeks to slay him.
33 The Lord will not abandon him to
his power,
or let him be condemned when he
is brought to trial.

34 Wait for the Lord, and keep to his
way,
and he will exalt you to possess
the land;
you will look on the destruction
of the wicked.

35 I have seen a wicked man
overbearing,
and towering like a cedar of
Lebanon.[v]
36 Again I[w] passed by, and, lo, he was
no more;
though I sought him, he could not
be found.

37 Mark the blameless man, and
behold the upright,

v Gk: Heb obscure   *w* Gk Syr Jerome: Heb *he*

25: Compare Job 4.7. **28:** *Saints*, see 30.4 n. **34:** Not querulous anxiety, but patient waiting for
the Lord to act (compare v. 9; 38.15; 62.1,5; 130.5; Is.40.31).

for there is posterity for the man
of peace.
38 But transgressors shall be altogether
destroyed;
the posterity of the wicked shall
be cut off.

39 The salvation of the righteous is
from the LORD;
he is their refuge in the time of
trouble.
40 The LORD helps them and delivers
them;
he delivers them from the wicked,
and saves them,
because they take refuge in him.

A Psalm of David, for the
memorial offering.

38 O LORD, rebuke me not in
thy anger,
nor chasten me in thy wrath!
2 For thy arrows have sunk into me,
and thy hand has come down on
me.

3 There is no soundness in my flesh
because of thy indignation;
there is no health in my bones
because of my sin.
4 For my iniquities have gone over
my head;
they weigh like a burden too
heavy for me.

5 My wounds grow foul and fester
because of my foolishness,
6 I am utterly bowed down and
prostrate;
all the day I go about mourning.
7 For my loins are filled with burning,

and there is no soundness in my
flesh.
8 I am utterly spent and crushed;
I groan because of the tumult of
my heart.

9 Lord, all my longing is known to
thee,
my sighing is not hidden from
thee.
10 My heart throbs, my strength fails
me;
and the light of my eyes–it also
has gone from me.
11 My friends and companions stand
aloof from my plague,
and my kinsmen stand afar off.

12 Those who seek my life lay their
snares,
those who seek my hurt speak of
ruin,
and meditate treachery all the
day long.

13 But I am like a deaf man, I do not
hear,
like a dumb man who does not
open his mouth.
14 Yea, I am like a man who does not
hear,
and in whose mouth are no
rebukes.

15 But for thee, O LORD, do I wait;
it is thou, O LORD my God, who
wilt answer.
16 For I pray, "Only let them not
rejoice over me,
who boast against me when my
foot slips!"
17 For I am ready to fall,
and my pain is ever with me.

Ps. 38: Prayer for healing in sickness (a lament). The psalmist's main concern is with some
grave disease, but he is also troubled by enemies who are taking advantage of it. Their attack
was made more plausible by the common belief that illness was a punishment for sin and
therefore an indication that God was against the sick man (compare Ps. 22). Title: *Memorial
offering*, Lev.2.1–10; compare Lev.24.7. **1:** Cry for help. **2–20:** The psalmist's situation. **2:**
Thy arrows, Job 6.4; 16.12,13. **3–10:** His disease. **3–4:** He acknowledges that the disease must
be a deserved punishment for some sin he has committed, perhaps unwittingly (compare v. 18).
11: His former friends avoid him as one forsaken by God. **12:** His enemies are circulating lies
about him (compare vv. 19–20). **13–16:** But he is not really fretful; he is waiting for God to

[18] I confess my iniquity,
   I am sorry for my sin.
[19] Those who are my foes without
   cause[x] are mighty,
   and many are those who hate me
    wrongfully.
[20] Those who render me evil for good
   are my adversaries because I
   follow after good.

[21] Do not forsake me, O LORD!
   O my God, be not far from me!
[22] Make haste to help me,
   O Lord, my salvation!

To the choirmaster: to Jeduthun.
A Psalm of David.

39 I said, "I will guard my ways,
   that I may not sin with my
   tongue;
I will bridle[y] my mouth,
   so long as the wicked are in my
   presence."
[2] I was dumb and silent,
   I held my peace to no avail;
my distress grew worse,
[3]   my heart became hot within me.
As I mused, the fire burned;
   then I spoke with my tongue:

[4] "LORD, let me know my end,
   and what is the measure of my
   days;
   let me know how fleeting my life
   is!
[5] Behold, thou hast made my days a
   few handbreadths,
   and my lifetime is as nothing in
   thy sight.

Surely every man stands as a mere
   breath!   *Selah*
[6]   Surely man goes about as a
   shadow!
Surely for nought are they in
   turmoil;
   man heaps up, and knows not
   who will gather!

[7] "And now, Lord, for what do I
   wait?
   My hope is in thee.
[8] Deliver me from all my
   transgressions.
   Make me not the scorn of the
   fool!
[9] I am dumb, I do not open my
   mouth;
   for it is thou who hast done it.
[10] Remove thy stroke from me;
   I am spent by the blows[z] of thy
   hand.
[11] When thou dost chasten man
   with rebukes for sin,
   thou dost consume like a moth what
   is dear to him;
   surely every man is a mere breath!
      Selah

[12] "Hear my prayer, O LORD,
   and give ear to my cry;
   hold not thy peace at my tears!
For I am thy passing guest,
   a sojourner, like all my
   fathers.
[13] Look away from me, that I may
   know gladness,
   before I depart and be no
   more!"

x Cn: Heb *living*
y Heb *muzzle*
z Heb *hostility*

act (compare 37.34). **18:** By confessing that he is a sinner, he hopes to be forgiven and healed (compare 32.3–5). **21–22:** Cry for help.
   Ps. 39: Prayer for healing in sickness (a lament). **1–3:** During his severe illness, which has almost shaken his faith in God's good-will, the psalmist has not made any public complaint because he did not wish to give encouragement to *the wicked* (i.e. the skeptical), who denied God's concern for justice and goodness (compare 10.4 and Ps.14). But now he can contain himself no longer; he must cry out, if only to God in private. **4–6:** He knows that all human life is short. **5:** *Selah*, see 3.2 n. *Handbreadths*, a measure of about 3 inches (four fingers); compare Ezek.40.5; 43.13. **7–13:** Prayer for healing. **8:** *Deliver . . . from . . . transgressions*, i.e. heal the disease which they have caused (compare 32.1). **12–13:** He knows that, in any case, he has not long to live, but hopes for at least one more respite, however brief.

To the choirmaster. A Psalm
of David.

40 I waited patiently for the Lord;
he inclined to me and heard
my cry.
2 He drew me up from the desolate
pit,*a*
out of the miry bog,
and set my feet upon a rock,
making my steps secure.
3 He put a new song in my mouth,
a song of praise to our God.
Many will see and fear,
and put their trust in the Lord.

4 Blessed is the man who makes
the Lord his trust,
who does not turn to the proud,
to those who go astray after false
gods!
5 Thou hast multiplied, O Lord my
God,
thy wondrous deeds and thy
thoughts toward us;
none can compare with thee!
Were I to proclaim and tell of them,
they would be more than can be
numbered.

6 Sacrifice and offering thou dost not
desire;
but thou hast given me an open
ear.*b*
Burnt offering and sin offering
thou hast not required.
7 Then I said, "Lo, I come;
in the roll of the book it is written
of me;
8 I delight to do thy will, O my God;
thy law is within my heart."

9 I have told the glad news of
deliverance

in the great congregation;
lo, I have not restrained my lips,
as thou knowest, O Lord.
10 I have not hid thy saving help
within my heart,
I have spoken of thy faithfulness
and thy salvation;
I have not concealed thy steadfast
love and thy faithfulness
from the great congregation.

11 Do not thou, O Lord, withhold
thy mercy from me,
let thy steadfast love and thy
faithfulness
ever preserve me!
12 For evils have encompassed me
without number;
my iniquities have overtaken me,
till I cannot see;
they are more than the hairs of my
head;
my heart fails me.

13 Be pleased, O Lord, to deliver me!
O Lord, make haste to help me!
14 Let them be put to shame and
confusion altogether
who seek to snatch away my life;
let them be turned back and brought
to dishonor
who desire my hurt!
15 Let them be appalled because of
their shame
who say to me, "Aha, Aha!"

16 But may all who seek thee
rejoice and be glad in thee;
may those who love thy salvation
say continually, "Great is the
Lord!"
17 As for me, I am poor and needy;

a Cn: Heb *pit of tumult*
b Heb *ears thou hast dug for me*

Ps. 40: Thanksgiving for deliverance from trouble, together with a prayer for help. A composite psalm: vv. 1–11 are a thanksgiving; vv. 12–17, a lament. Perhaps two originally independent units have been combined into a liturgy. **1–3:** The psalmist's experience (compare 18.4–6). The nature of his trouble is not specified. **4–10:** Fulfilment of his vow (see 7.17 n. and 22.22–31 n.). **6–8:** Rather than offer a formal sacrifice of thanksgiving, he pledges himself to do God's will. Quoted in Heb.10.5–7. **6:** Compare 50.8–13; 51.16,17; Am.5.21–24; Hos.6.6. **7:** *Roll of the book,* compare 56.8; 139.16. **9:** Compare 22.22. **11:** Prayer for continuing help. **12–17:** A lament. **12:** The psalmist's situation. **13–17:** Prayer for deliverance. This passage is almost identical with Ps. 70.

but the Lord takes thought for
   me.
Thou art my help and my deliverer;
   do not tarry, O my God!

To the choirmaster. A Psalm
   of David.

41 Blessed is he who considers the
   poor!*c*
   The LORD delivers him in the day
    of trouble;
2 the LORD protects him and keeps him
   alive;
   he is called blessed in the land;
   thou dost not give him up to the
    will of his enemies.
3 The LORD sustains him on his
   sickbed;
   in his illness thou healest all his
   infirmities.*d*

4 As for me, I said, "O LORD, be
   gracious to me;
   heal me, for I have sinned against
   thee!"
5 My enemies say of me in malice:
   "When will he die, and his name
   perish?"
6 And when one comes to see me, he
   utters empty words,
   while his heart gathers mischief;
   when he goes out, he tells it
   abroad.
7 All who hate me whisper together
   about me;
   they imagine the worst for me.

8 They say, "A deadly thing has
   fastened upon him;
   he will not rise again from where
   he lies."

9 Even my bosom friend in whom I
   trusted,
   who ate of my bread, has lifted
   his heel against me.
10 But do thou, O LORD, be gracious to
   me,
   and raise me up, that I may
   requite them!

11 By this I know that thou art pleased
   with me,
   in that my enemy has not
   triumphed over me.
12 But thou hast upheld me because
   of my integrity,
   and set me in thy presence for
   ever.

13 Blessed be the LORD, the God of
   Israel,
   from everlasting to everlasting!
   Amen and Amen.

BOOK II

To the choirmaster. A Maskil
   of the Sons of Korah.

42 As a hart longs
   for flowing streams,
so longs my soul
   for thee, O God.
2 My soul thirsts for God,
   for the living God.
When shall I come and behold
   the face of God?
3 My tears have been my food
   day and night,
while men say to me continually,
   "Where is your God?"

c Or *weak*   *d* Heb *thou changest all his bed*

Ps. 41: Prayer for healing from sickness (a lament). **1–3:** Act of faith, in the style of the
wisdom writers (compare Ps. 1). **4–9:** The psalmist's situation: he is mortally ill and his enemies
are glad of it; even one of his best friends has turned against him. **10–12:** Prayer for deliverance.
13: A doxology (no part of the psalm) marking the end of the first of the five books into which
the Psalter was divided in imitation of the Pentateuch (compare 72.18–20; 89.52; 106.48).
   Pss. 42–43: Prayer for healing in preparation for a pilgrimage (a lament). These two psalms
are a single lyric consisting of three stanzas with a refrain (42.5,11; 43.5). The author, who lives
in the far north of Palestine near Mount Hermon and the sources of the Jordan (42.6–7), has
been prevented by illness (42.10) from making his accustomed pilgrimage to Jerusalem (42.4;
43.3–4). **42.1–4:** The psalmist's love for the temple and for God's presence there. **3:** Men

⁴ These things I remember,
    as I pour out my soul:
how I went with the throng,
    and led them in procession to the
       house of God,
with glad shouts and songs of
       thanksgiving,
a multitude keeping festival.
⁵ Why are you cast down, O my soul,
    and why are you disquieted
       within me?
Hope in God; for I shall again praise
       him,
    my help ⁶ and my God.

My soul is cast down within me,
    therefore I remember thee
from the land of Jordan and of
       Hermon,
    from Mount Mizar.
⁷ Deep calls to deep
    at the thunder of thy cataracts;
all thy waves and thy billows
    have gone over me.
⁸ By day the LORD commands his
       steadfast love;
    and at night his song is with me,
a prayer to the God of my life.

⁹ I say to God, my rock:
    "Why hast thou forgotten me?
Why go I mourning
    because of the oppression of the
       enemy?"
¹⁰ As with a deadly wound in my body,
    my adversaries taunt me,
while they say to me continually,
    "Where is your God?"

¹¹ Why are you cast down, O my soul,
    and why are you disquieted within
       me?
Hope in God; for I shall again
       praise him,
    my help and my God.

43 Vindicate me, O God, and
      defend my cause
against an ungodly people;
from deceitful and unjust men
    deliver me!
² For thou art the God in whom I take
       refuge;
    why hast thou cast me off?
Why go I mourning
    because of the oppression of the
       enemy?

³ Oh send out thy light and thy truth;
    let them lead me,
let them bring me to thy holy hill
    and to thy dwelling!
⁴ Then I will go to the altar of God,
    to God my exceeding joy;
and I will praise thee with the lyre,
    O God, my God.

⁵ Why are you cast down, O my soul,
    and why are you disquieted
       within me?
Hope in God; for I shall again praise
       him,
    my help and my God.

To the choirmaster. A Maskil of the
       Sons of Korah.

44 We have heard with our ears,
      O God,
our fathers have told us,
what deeds thou didst perform in
       their days,
    in the days of old:
² thou with thy own hand didst drive
       out the nations,
    but them thou didst plant;
thou didst afflict the peoples,
    but them thou didst set free;
³ for not by their own sword did they
       win the land,
    nor did their own arm give them
       victory;

regard his sickness as evidence that God has forsaken him (compare 22.6–8). **42.5–10:** His present situation: he is sick and far from the temple. **6:** *Mount Mizar*, probably near Mount *Hermon*, but exact location is unknown. **43.1–4:** Prayer that, by the healing of his disease, he may be vindicated as a righteous man and enabled to go to Jerusalem.
    Ps. 44: Prayer for deliverance from national enemies (a group lament). Israel has suffered a humiliating defeat at the hand of some unnamed foreign nation. **1–8:** God is reminded of the victories he had given Israel in previous times, from the days of the conquest onward. **3:** Dt.8.17;

but thy right hand, and thy arm,
and the light of thy countenance;
for thou didst delight in them.

4 Thou art my King and my God,
who ordainest*e* victories for
Jacob.
5 Through thee we push down our
foes;
through thy name we tread down
our assailants.
6 For not in my bow do I trust,
nor can my sword save me.
7 But thou hast saved us from our
foes,
and hast put to confusion those
who hate us.
8 In God we have boasted continually,
and we will give thanks to thy
name for ever.　　　*Selah*

9 Yet thou hast cast us off and abased
us,
and hast not gone out with our
armies.
10 Thou hast made us turn back from
the foe;
and our enemies have gotten
spoil.
11 Thou hast made us like sheep for
slaughter,
and hast scattered us among the
nations.
12 Thou hast sold thy people for a
trifle,
demanding no high price for
them.

13 Thou hast made us the taunt of our
neighbors,
the derision and scorn of those
about us.
14 Thou hast made us a byword among
the nations,
a laughingstock*f* among the
peoples.

15 All day long my disgrace is before
me,
and shame has covered my face,
16 at the words of the taunters and
revilers,
at the sight of the enemy and the
avenger.

17 All this has come upon us,
though we have not forgotten thee,
or been false to thy covenant.
18 Our heart has not turned back,
nor have our steps departed from
thy way,
19 that thou shouldst have broken us in
the place of jackals,
and covered us with deep
darkness.

20 If we had forgotten the name of our
God,
or spread forth our hands to a
strange god,
21 would not God discover this?
For he knows the secrets of the
heart.
22 Nay, for thy sake we are slain all the
day long,
and accounted as sheep for the
slaughter.

23 Rouse thyself! Why sleepest thou, O
Lord?
Awake! Do not cast us off for ever!
24 Why dost thou hide thy face?
Why dost thou forget our affliction
and oppression?
25 For our soul is bowed down to the
dust;
our body cleaves to the ground.
26 Rise up, come to our help!
Deliver us for the sake of thy
steadfast love!

e Gk Syr: Heb *Thou art my King, O God; ordain*
f Heb *a shaking of the head*

Jg.7.2. **8:** *Selah*, see 3.2 n. **9–16:** Now God has allowed Israel to be defeated and shamed. **11:**
Thou . . . hast scattered us among the nations seems appropriate only to the period after the
Babylonian Exile, a circumstance which helps to date the poem. Some have put it as late as the
Maccabean Age (second century B.C.). **17–22:** Defeat has not been the result of sin or apostasy,
but of unshaken loyalty to the God of Israel. **23–26:** Cry for help (compare 78.65; Is 51.9).
The language emphasizes the strong emotions of the speaker.

To the choirmaster: according to
Lilies. A Maskil of the Sons of
   Korah; a love song.

45 My heart overflows with a
goodly theme;
I address my verses to the king;
my tongue is like the pen of a
   ready scribe.

2 You are the fairest of the sons of
   men;
grace is poured upon your lips;
therefore God has blessed you for
   ever.
3 Gird your sword upon your thigh, O
   mighty one,
in your glory and majesty!

4 In your majesty ride forth
   victoriously
for the cause of truth and to
   defend[g] the right;
let your right hand teach you
   dread deeds!
5 Your arrows are sharp
in the heart of the king's enemies;
the peoples fall under you.

6 Your divine throne[h] endures for
   ever and ever.
Your royal scepter is a scepter of
   equity;
7   you love righteousness and hate
   wickedness.
Therefore God, your God, has
   anointed you
with the oil of gladness above your
   fellows;
8   your robes are all fragrant with
   myrrh and aloes and cassia.
From ivory palaces stringed
   instruments make you glad;

9   daughters of kings are among
   your ladies of honor;
at your right hand stands the
   queen in gold of Ophir.

10 Hear, O daughter, consider, and
   incline your ear;
forget your people and your
   father's house;
11   and the king will desire your
   beauty.
Since he is your lord, bow to him;
12   the people[i] of Tyre will sue your
   favor with gifts,
the richest of the people 13 with all
   kinds of wealth.

The princess is decked in her
   chamber with gold-woven
   robes;[j]
14   in many-colored robes she is led
   to the king,
with her virgin companions, her
   escort,[k] in her train.
15 With joy and gladness they are led
   along
as they enter the palace of the
   king.

16 Instead of your fathers shall be your
   sons;
you will make them princes in all
   the earth.
17 I will cause your name to be
   celebrated in all generations;
therefore the peoples will praise
   you for ever and ever.

g Cn: Heb *and the meekness of*
h Or *Your throne is a throne of God,* or *Thy throne, O
  God*
i Heb *daughter*
j Or *people. All glorious is the princess within, gold em-
  broidery is her clothing*
k Heb *those brought to you*

Ps. 45: An ode for a royal wedding. 1: Introduction. The author identifies himself as a professional writer (*a ready scribe*), presumably a court poet. **2–9:** He addresses the king in flattering language. **6:** *Your divine throne* is more naturally translated (as in note h), *your throne, O
God,* and is so quoted in Heb.1.8. **8:** The mention of *ivory palaces* (1 Kg.22.39; Am.3.15) shows
that the bridegroom was a king of the kingdom of Israel. **10–13a:** The queen, probably a
Phoenician (note the mention of *Tyre* in v. 12), is instructed to forget her own ancestry and be
loyal to her husband. **13b–15:** The wedding procession. **16–17:** The poet promises the king
(the pronouns, in Hebrew, are masculine) successful progeny and literary immortality.

To the choirmaster. A Psalm of
the Sons of Korah. According
to Alamoth. A Song.

46 God is our refuge and strength,
a very present*l* help in trouble.
2 Therefore we will not fear though
the earth should change,
though the mountains shake in the
heart of the sea;
3 though its waters roar and foam,
though the mountains tremble
with its tumult. *Selah*

4 There is a river whose streams make
glad the city of God,
the holy habitation of the Most
High.
5 God is in the midst of her, she shall
not be moved;
God will help her right early.
6 The nations rage, the kingdoms
totter;
he utters his voice, the earth melts.
7 The LORD of hosts is with us;
the God of Jacob is our refuge.*m*
Selah

8 Come, behold the works of the LORD,
how he has wrought desolations in
the earth.
9 He makes wars cease to the end of
the earth;
he breaks the bow, and shatters
the spear,
he burns the chariots with fire!
10 "Be still, and know that I am God.
I am exalted among the nations,
I am exalted in the earth!"

11 The LORD of hosts is with us;
the God of Jacob is our refuge.*m*
Selah

To the choirmaster. A Psalm of
the Sons of Korah.

47 Clap your hands, all peoples!
Shout to God with loud
songs of joy!
2 For the LORD, the Most High, is
terrible,
a great king over all the earth.
3 He subdued peoples under us,
and nations under our feet.
4 He chose our heritage for us,
the pride of Jacob whom he loves.
Selah

5 God has gone up with a shout,
the LORD with the sound of a
trumpet.
6 Sing praises to God, sing praises!
Sing praises to our King, sing
praises!
7 For God is the king of all the earth;
sing praises with a psalm!*n*

8 God reigns over the nations;
God sits on his holy throne.
9 The princes of the peoples gather
as the people of the God of
Abraham.
For the shields of the earth belong to
God;
he is highly exalted!

l Or *well proved*
m Or *fortress*
n Heb *Maskil*

Ps. 46: A song of Zion celebrating God's ultimate victory over the nations. **1–3:** God will preserve his people even during the cosmic tumults of the latter days (compare Jl.3.16). **1:** This verse inspired Luther's hymn, "A Mighty Fortress." **3:** *Selah*, see 3.2 n. **4–7:** Jerusalem, God's dwelling place on earth, will stand secure. This emphasis upon the Holy City leads to the classification of this and some other psalms as "songs of Zion" (for the term, see 137.3). **4:** *A river*, compare Is.33.21; Ezek.47.1–12; Zech.14.8; Rev.22.1–2. **7:** A refrain (compare v. 11); it has probably dropped out by accident after v. 3. **8–11:** The establishment of God's kingdom will bring peace to the earth (compare Is.2.4).

Ps. 47: A hymn celebrating God's enthronement as king of all nations. **1–4:** Summons to all the world to praise the God of Israel as king. **4:** *Selah*, see 3.2 n. **5–9:** These words were evidently composed to accompany a religious ceremony, probably connected with the ark, which dramatized the LORD's kingship (compare 24.7–10 and 68.17–18). **7:** The word translated "psalm" is Maskil; see Introduction. **8:** *Throne*, Is.6.1. **9:** *Shields*, rulers (compare 89.18 n.).

A Song. A Psalm of the Sons of Korah.

48 Great is the LORD and greatly
to be praised
in the city of our God!
His holy mountain, ² beautiful in
elevation,
is the joy of all the earth,
Mount Zion, in the far north,
the city of the great King.
³ Within her citadels God
has shown himself a sure defense.

⁴ For lo, the kings assembled,
they came on together.
⁵ As soon as they saw it, they were
astounded,
they were in panic, they took to
flight;
⁶ trembling took hold of them there,
anguish as of a woman in travail.
⁷ By the east wind thou didst shatter
the ships of Tarshish.
⁸ As we have heard, so have we seen
in the city of the LORD of hosts,
in the city of our God,
which God establishes for ever.
Selah

⁹ We have thought on thy steadfast
love, O God,
in the midst of thy temple.
¹⁰ As thy name, O God,
so thy praise reaches to the ends of
the earth.
Thy right hand is filled with victory;
¹¹ let Mount Zion be glad!
Let the daughters of Judah rejoice
because of thy judgments!

¹² Walk about Zion, go round about
her,
number her towers,

¹³ consider well her ramparts,
go through her citadels;
that you may tell the next generation
¹⁴ that this is God,
our God for ever and ever.
He will be our guide for ever.

To the choirmaster. A Psalm of
the Sons of Korah.

49 Hear this, all peoples!
Give ear, all inhabitants of
the world,
² both low and high,
rich and poor together!
³ My mouth shall speak wisdom;
the meditation of my heart shall
be understanding.
⁴ I will incline my ear to a proverb;
I will solve my riddle to the music
of the lyre.

⁵ Why should I fear in times of
trouble,
when the iniquity of my
persecutors surrounds me,
⁶ men who trust in their wealth
and boast of the abundance of
their riches?
⁷ Truly no man can ransom himself,^o
or give to God the price of his life,
⁸ for the ransom of his^p life is costly,
and can never suffice,
⁹ that he should continue to live on
for ever,
and never see the Pit.

¹⁰ Yea, he shall see that even the wise
die,

o Another reading is *no man can ransom his brother*
p Gk: Heb *their*

Ps. 48: **A song celebrating the beauty and security of Zion. 1–3:** The LORD is praised as the God of Jerusalem. **2:** Mount Zion, one of the hills upon which Jerusalem is built. *In the far north,* a curious phrase which apparently identifies the Israelite holy mountain with the Canaanite mountain of the gods (called Zaphon or "North" in the Ras Shamra tablets). **4–8:** When, in the last days, the heathen unite to attack God's city, they will be routed (compare Ezek. chs. 38–39; Zech. chs. 12; 14; Rev.20.9–10). **7:** *Ships of Tarshish,* see 1 Kg.10.22 n. **8:** *Selah,* see 3.2 n. **9–11:** All of this causes anticipatory rejoicing in the ceremonies of the temple. **12–14:** Call for a procession about the city walls (Ps.24.7–10).

Ps. 49: **Meditation on the transience of life and wealth** (a wisdom psalm). **1:** The poet summons his audience. **5–6:** The theme: Why should one be afraid of wealthy, powerful men? **7–12:** No man has power over the disposition of his own life, nor can he take his wealth with

the fool and the stupid alike must
   perish
and leave their wealth to others.
¹¹ Their graves*q* are their homes for
   ever,
   their dwelling places to all
      generations,
   though they named lands their
      own.
¹² Man cannot abide in his pomp,
   he is like the beasts that perish.

¹³ This is the fate of those who have
   foolish confidence,
   the end of those*r* who are pleased
      with their portion.   *Selah*
¹⁴ Like sheep they are appointed for
   Sheol;
   Death shall be their shepherd;
   straight to the grave they descend,*s*
   and their form shall waste away;
   Sheol shall be their home.*t*
¹⁵ But God will ransom my soul from
   the power of Sheol,
   for he will receive me.   *Selah*

¹⁶ Be not afraid when one becomes
   rich,
   when the glory*u* of his house
      increases.
¹⁷ For when he dies he will carry
   nothing away;
   his glory*u* will not go down after
   him.
¹⁸ Though, while he lives, he counts
   himself happy,
   and though a man gets praise
      when he does well for himself,
¹⁹ he will go to the generation of his
   fathers,
   who will never more see the
      light.
²⁰ Man cannot abide in his pomp,
   he is like the beasts that
      perish.

A Psalm of Asaph.

50 The Mighty One, God the
     Lord,
speaks and summons the earth
from the rising of the sun to its
   setting.
² Out of Zion, the perfection of
   beauty,
   God shines forth.

³ Our God comes, he does not keep
   silence,
   before him is a devouring fire,
   round about him a mighty tempest.
⁴ He calls to the heavens above
   and to the earth, that he may judge
      his people:
⁵ "Gather to me my faithful ones,
   who made a covenant with me by
      sacrifice!"
⁶ The heavens declare his
   righteousness,
   for God himself is judge!   *Selah*

⁷ "Hear, O my people, and I will
   speak,
   O Israel, I will testify against you.
   I am God, your God.
⁸ I do not reprove you for your
   sacrifices;
   your burnt offerings are
      continually before me.
⁹ I will accept no bull from your house,
   nor he-goat from your folds.
¹⁰ For every beast of the forest is mine,
   the cattle on a thousand hills.
¹¹ I know all the birds of the air,*v*
   and all that moves in the field is
      mine.

¹² "If I were hungry, I would not tell
   you;

q Gk Syr Compare Tg: Heb *their inward* (thought)
r Tg: Heb *after them*
s Cn: Heb *the upright shall have dominion over them in
  the morning*   *t* Heb uncertain
u Or *wealth*   *v* Gk Syr Tg: Heb *mountains*

him. **9**: *The Pit*, Sheol (see 6.5 n.). **12**: A refrain; compare v. 20. **13–14**: Death is the end, even
for the arrogant. **13**: *Selah*, see 3.2 n. **15**: This might express the psalmist's assurance of his own
immortality, but is perhaps better understood merely as confidence that he will be delivered
from present trouble (89.48; Hos.13.14). **16–20**: He instructs his audience therefore not to be
afraid of the wealthy.
    Ps. 50: A liturgy of divine judgment. 1–6: God coming to judge his people. **3**: Compare 18.8;
Hab.3.4. **6**: *Selah*, see 3.2 n. **7–23**: The Lord's arraignment of the nation. **8–13**: They have

for the world and all that is in it is mine.
13 Do I eat the flesh of bulls,
or drink the blood of goats?
14 Offer to God a sacrifice of thanksgiving,ʷ
and pay your vows to the Most High;
15 and call upon me in the day of trouble;
I will deliver you, and you shall glorify me."

16 But to the wicked God says:
"What right have you to recite my statutes,
or take my covenant on your lips?
17 For you hate discipline,
and you cast my words behind you.
18 If you see a thief, you are a friend of his;
and you keep company with adulterers.

19 "You give your mouth free rein for evil,
and your tongue frames deceit.
20 You sit and speak against your brother;
you slander your own mother's son.
21 These things you have done and I have been silent;
you thought that I was one like yourself.
But now I rebuke you, and lay the charge before you.

22 "Mark this, then, you who forget God,
lest I rend, and there be none to deliver!

23 He who brings thanksgiving as his sacrifice honors me;
to him who orders his way aright
I will show the salvation of God!"

To the choirmaster. A Psalm of David, when Nathan the prophet came to him, after he had gone in to Bathsheba.

51 Have mercy on me, O God,
according to thy steadfast love;
according to thy abundant mercy blot out my transgressions.
2 Wash me thoroughly from my iniquity,
and cleanse me from my sin!

3 For I know my transgressions,
and my sin is ever before me.
4 Against thee, thee only, have I sinned,
and done that which is evil in thy sight,
so that thou art justified in thy sentence
and blameless in thy judgment.
5 Behold, I was brought forth in iniquity,
and in sin did my mother conceive me.

6 Behold, thou desirest truth in the inward being;
therefore teach me wisdom in my secret heart.
7 Purge me with hyssop, and I shall be clean;
wash me, and I shall be whiter than snow.
8 Fillˣ me with joy and gladness;

w Or *make thanksgiving your sacrifice to God*
x Syr: Heb *Make to hear*

brought sacrifices in abundance, but this is not what God wants (see 40.6 n.). **14–15**: His demand is rather for thanksgiving and prayer. **16–21**: They have violated God's law by tolerating evil (v. 18) and indulging in slander (vv. 19–20). **16**: The first line is probably an editorial addition, modifying the poet's sweeping judgment on the nation as a whole. **22–23**: Concluding warning.
    Ps. 51: Prayer for healing and moral renewal (a lament). **1–2**: Prayer for deliverance. Although v. 8 makes it clear that the psalmist's problem is one of illness, the main emphasis is upon restoration to moral, rather than merely physical, health. **3–5**: Confession of the psalmist that his nature has been sinful even from the moment of conception. **6–12**: Renewed prayer for deliverance. **7**: Purging with hyssop is a reference to some ceremony of sprinkling (Ex.12.22;

let the bones which thou hast
broken rejoice.
[9] Hide thy face from my sins,
and blot out all my iniquities.

[10] Create in me a clean heart, O God,
and put a new and right[y] spirit
within me.
[11] Cast me not away from thy presence,
and take not thy holy Spirit from
me.
[12] Restore to me the joy of thy
salvation,
and uphold me with a willing spirit.

[13] Then I will teach transgressors thy
ways,
and sinners will return to thee.
[14] Deliver me from bloodguiltiness,[z] O
God,
thou God of my salvation,
and my tongue will sing aloud of
thy deliverance.

[15] O Lord, open thou my lips,
and my mouth shall show forth
thy praise.
[16] For thou hast no delight in sacrifice;
were I to give a burnt offering,
thou wouldst not be pleased.
[17] The sacrifice acceptable to God[a] is
a broken spirit;
a broken and contrite heart, O
God, thou wilt not despise.

[18] Do good to Zion in thy good
pleasure;
rebuild the walls of Jerusalem,
[19] then wilt thou delight in right
sacrifices,
in burnt offerings and whole burnt
offerings;
then bulls will be offered on thy
altar.

To the choirmaster. A Maskil of
David, when Doeg, the Edomite,
came and told Saul, "David has come
to the house of Ahimelech."

52 Why do you boast, O mighty
man,
of mischief done against the
godly?[b]
All the day [2] you are plotting
destruction.
Your tongue is like a sharp razor,
you worker of treachery.
[3] You love evil more than good,
and lying more than speaking the
truth. *Selah*
[4] You love all words that devour,
O deceitful tongue.

[5] But God will break you down for
ever;
he will snatch and tear you from
your tent;
he will uproot you from the land of
the living. *Selah*
[6] The righteous shall see, and fear,
and shall laugh at him, saying,
[7] "See the man who would not make
God his refuge,
but trusted in the abundance of his
riches,
and sought refuge in his wealth!"[c]

[8] But I am like a green olive tree
in the house of God.
I trust in the steadfast love of God
for ever and ever.
[9] I will thank thee for ever,
because thou hast done it.
I will proclaim[d] thy name, for it is
good,
in the presence of the godly.

y Or *steadfast*   z Or *death*
a Or *My sacrifice, O God*
b Cn Compare Syr: Heb *the kindness of God*
c Syr Tg: Heb *his destruction*   d Cn: Heb *wait for*

Lev.14.51), but in a purely metaphorical sense. **13–17:** The vow (see 7.17 n.) is to instruct others
and to praise and serve God rather than to offer a sacrifice (see 40.6 n.). **14:** *Bloodguiltiness*,
"death" (see note z) seems to give better sense. **18–19:** A later addition, designed to modify the
anti-sacrificial spirit of the preceding verses and to adapt the psalm to liturgical use.
  Ps. 52: God's imminent judgment against a tyrant (a lament). Prayer for deliverance in
the form of a denunciation of the psalmist's enemy. **1–4:** Character of the psalmist's enemy.
3: *Selah*, see 3.2 n. **5–7:** Retribution is about to befall his enemy. **8:** The psalmist is confident of his own deliverance (compare 1.3). **9:** The vow (see 7.17 n.). *Godly*, see 16.10 n.

To the choirmaster: according to Mahalath. A Maskil of David.

53 The fool says in his heart,
"There is no God."
They are corrupt, doing abominable iniquity;
there is none that does good.

2 God looks down from heaven
upon the sons of men
to see if there are any that are wise,
that seek after God.

3 They have all fallen away;
they are all alike depraved;
there is none that does good,
no, not one.

4 Have those who work evil no understanding,
who eat up my people as they eat bread,
and do not call upon God?

5 There they are, in great terror,
in terror such as has not been!
For God will scatter the bones of the ungodly;[e]
they will be put to shame,[f] for God has rejected them.

6 O that deliverance for Israel would come from Zion!
When God restores the fortunes of his people,
Jacob will rejoice and Israel be glad.

To the choirmaster: with stringed instruments. A Maskil of David, when the Ziphites went and told Saul, "David is in hiding among us."

54 Save me, O God, by thy name,
and vindicate me by thy might.

2 Hear my prayer, O God;
give ear to the words of my mouth.

3 For insolent[g] men have risen against me,
ruthless men seek my life;
they do not set God before them.
Selah

4 Behold, God is my helper;
the Lord is the upholder[h] of my life.
5 He will requite my enemies with evil;
in thy faithfulness put an end to them.

6 With a freewill offering I will sacrifice to thee;
I will give thanks to thy name, O LORD, for it is good.
7 For thou hast delivered me from every trouble,
and my eye has looked in triumph on my enemies.

To the choirmaster: with stringed instruments. A Maskil of David.

55 Give ear to my prayer, O God;
and hide not thyself from my supplication!
2 Attend to me, and answer me;
I am overcome by my trouble.
I am distraught 3 by the noise of the enemy,
because of the oppression of the wicked.
For they bring[i] trouble upon me,
and in anger they cherish enmity against me.

4 My heart is in anguish within me,

e Cn Compare Gk Syr: Heb *him who encamps against you*
f Gk: Heb *you will put to shame*
g Another reading is *strangers*
h Gk Syr Jerome: Heb *of* or *with those who uphold*
i Cn Compare Gk: Heb *they cause to totter*

Ps. 53: Condemnation of a cynical and unrighteous age. This Psalm is almost identical with Ps. 14, except for the alteration of the divine name Yahweh (the LORD) to Elohim (God).

Ps. 54: Prayer for deliverance from personal enemies (a lament). **1:** Cry for help. **3:** The psalmist's situation. *Selah*, see 3.2 n. **4–5:** Expression of trust. **6–7:** The vow (see 7.17 n.). **6:** *Freewill offering*, Num.15.3.

Ps. 55: Prayer for deliverance from personal enemies (a lament). **1–2:** Cry for help. **3–14:**

the terrors of death have fallen
　upon me.
5 Fear and trembling come upon me,
　and horror overwhelms me.
6 And I say, "O that I had wings like
　　a dove!
　I would fly away and be at rest;
7 yea, I would wander afar,
　I would lodge in the wilderness,
　　　　　　　　Selah
8 I would haste to find me a shelter
　from the raging wind and
　　tempest."

9 Destroy their plans,*j* O Lord,
　confuse their tongues;
　for I see violence and strife in the
　　city.
10 Day and night they go around it
　on its walls;
　and mischief and trouble are within
　　it,
11 　ruin is in its midst;
　oppression and fraud
　　do not depart from its market
　　place.

12 It is not an enemy who taunts me—
　then I could bear it;
　it is not an adversary who deals
　　insolently with me—
　　then I could hide from him.
13 But it is you, my equal,
　my companion, my familiar friend.
14 We used to hold sweet converse
　　together;
　within God's house we walked in
　　fellowship.
15 Let death*k* come upon them;
　let them go down to Sheol alive;
　let them go away in terror into
　　their graves.*l*

16 But I call upon God;
　and the LORD will save me.
17 Evening and morning and at noon
　I utter my complaint and moan,

and he will hear my voice.
18 He will deliver my soul in safety
　from the battle that I wage,
　for many are arrayed against me.
19 God will give ear, and humble
　　them,
　he who is enthroned from of old;
　because they keep no law,*m*
　and do not fear God.　　*Selah*

20 My companion stretched out his
　　hand against his friends,
　he violated his covenant.
21 His speech was smoother than
　　butter,
　yet war was in his heart;
　his words were softer than oil,
　yet they were drawn swords.

22 Cast your burden*n* on the LORD,
　and he will sustain you;
　he will never permit
　the righteous to be moved.

23 But thou, O God, wilt cast them
　　down
　into the lowest pit;
　men of blood and treachery
　shall not live out half their days.
　But I will trust in thee.

To the choirmaster: according to The
Dove on Far-off Terebinths. A Miktam
of David, when the Philistines seized
　　him in Gath.

5 6 Be gracious to me, O God, for
　　men trample upon me;
　all day long foemen oppress me;
2 my enemies trample upon me all
　　day long,
　for many fight against me proudly.
3 When I am afraid,
　I put my trust in thee.

j Tg: Heb lacks *their plans*　*k* Or *desolations*
l Cn: Heb *evils are in their habitation, in their midst*
m Or *do not change*　*n* Or *what he has given you*

The psalmist's situation. His chief enemy is a former friend (vv. 12–14,20–21). **7**: *Selah*, see
3.2 n. **15**: He curses his enemies. The violence of the language is probably an attempt to counteract the effect of a curse he believes they have put upon him (compare Ps. 58). *To Sheol alive*,
compare Num.16.30. **16–19**: Expression of trust. **20–23**: Complaint (vv. 20–21); confidence
(vv. 22–23).
　Ps. 56: Prayer for deliverance from personal enemies (a lament). **1–2,5–6ab**: The psalmist's

⁴ In God, whose word I praise,
in God I trust without a fear.
What can flesh do to me?

⁵ All day long they seek to injure my
cause;
all their thoughts are against me
for evil.
⁶ They band themselves together,
they lurk,
they watch my steps.
As they have waited for my life,
⁷ so recompenseᵒ them for their
crime;
in wrath cast down the peoples, O
God!

⁸ Thou hast kept count of my tossings;
put thou my tears in thy bottle!
Are they not in thy book?
⁹ Then my enemies will be turned
back
in the day when I call.
This I know, thatᵖ God is for me.
¹⁰ In God, whose word I praise,
in the LORD, whose word I praise,
¹¹ in God I trust without a fear.
What can man do to me?

¹² My vows to thee I must perform, O
God;
I will render thank offerings to
thee.
¹³ For thou hast delivered my soul
from death,
yea, my feet from falling,
that I may walk before God
in the light of life.

To the choirmaster: according to Do
Not Destroy. A Miktam of David, when
he fled from Saul, in the cave.

57 Be merciful to me, O God, be
merciful to me,

for in thee my soul takes refuge;
in the shadow of thy wings I will take
refuge,
till the storms of destruction pass
by.
² I cry to God Most High,
to God who fulfils his purpose for
me.
³ He will send from heaven and save
me,
he will put to shame those who
trample upon me. Selah
God will send forth his steadfast
love and his faithfulness!

⁴ I lie in the midst of lions
that greedily devourq the sons of
men;
their teeth are spears and arrows,
their tongues sharp swords.

⁵ Be exalted, O God, above the
heavens!
Let thy glory be over all the earth!

⁶ They set a net for my steps;
my soul was bowed down.
They dug a pit in my way,
but they have fallen into it
themselves. Selah

⁷ My heart is steadfast, O God,
my heart is steadfast!
I will sing and make melody!
⁸ Awake, my soul!
Awake, O harp and lyre!
I will awake the dawn!
⁹ I will give thanks to thee, O Lord,
among the peoples;
I will sing praises to thee among
the nations.
¹⁰ For thy steadfast love is great to
the heavens,
thy faithfulness to the clouds.

o Cn: Heb *deliver*
p Or *because*
q Cn: Heb *are aflame*

situation. **3–4,8–11:** Expression of trust. **6c–7:** Prayer for vindication. **7:** *The peoples*, a metaphor for the psalmist's enemies. **8:** *Thy book*, 40.7. **12–13:** The vow (see 7.17 n.).
Ps. 57: Prayer for deliverance from personal enemies (a lament). **1:** Cry for help. **2–3:** Expression of trust. **3:** *Selah*, see 3.2 n. **4–6:** The psalmist's situation, his prayer and certainty of being heard. **5:** A refrain (compare v. 11). **7–11:** The customary vow (see 7.17 n.) in the form of a thanksgiving sung in anticipation of deliverance (compare 22.22–31). These verses are practically identical with 108.1–5.

11 Be exalted, O God, above the
　　heavens!
　　Let thy glory be over all the earth!

To the choirmaster: according to Do
Not Destroy. A Miktam of David.

58 Do you indeed decree what is
　　right, you gods?*s*
　　Do you judge the sons of men
　　　uprightly?
2 Nay, in your hearts you devise
　　　wrongs;
　　your hands deal out violence on
　　　earth.

3 The wicked go astray from the
　　womb,
　　they err from their birth, speaking
　　　lies.
4 They have venom like the venom of a
　　serpent,
　　like the deaf adder that stops its
　　　ear,
5 so that it does not hear the voice of
　　charmers
　　or of the cunning enchanter.

6 O God, break the teeth in their
　　mouths;
　　tear out the fangs of the young
　　　lions, O LORD!
7 Let them vanish like water that runs
　　away;
　　like grass let them be trodden
　　　down and wither.*t*
8 Let them be like the snail which
　　dissolves into slime,
　　like the untimely birth that never
　　　sees the sun.
9 Sooner than your pots can feel the
　　heat of thorns,
　　whether green or ablaze, may he
　　　sweep them away!

10 The righteous will rejoice when he
　　sees the vengeance;
　　he will bathe his feet in the blood
　　　of the wicked.
11 Men will say, "Surely there is a
　　reward for the righteous;
　　surely there is a God who judges
　　　on earth."

To the choirmaster: according to Do
Not Destroy. A Miktam of David, when
Saul sent men to watch his house in
　　order to kill him.

59 Deliver me from my enemies,
　　O my God,
　　protect me from those who rise
　　　up against me,
2 deliver me from those who work
　　evil,
　　and save me from bloodthirsty
　　　men.

3 For, lo, they lie in wait for my life;
　　fierce men band themselves
　　　against me.
　　For no transgression or sin of mine,
　　　O LORD,
4 　for no fault of mine, they run and
　　make ready.

　　Rouse thyself, come to my help, and
　　　see!
5 　Thou, LORD God of hosts, art
　　God of Israel.
　　Awake to punish all the nations;
　　spare none of those who
　　　treacherously plot evil.　　*Selah*

6 Each evening they come back,
　　howling like dogs
　　and prowling about the city.
7 There they are, bellowing with their
　　mouths,

s Or *mighty lords*　　*t* Cn: Heb uncertain

Ps. 58: Curse upon enemies (a lament). The violent language is probably to be explained as
a curse which the psalmist utters to counteract the effect of a curse he believes his enemies have
placed upon him (compare Ps.109.17–19). **1–5:** The character of his enemies. It is unclear
whether they are heathen *gods* or "mighty lords" (note *s*); the translation of v. 1 is uncertain
(compare 82.1). **6–9:** The curse. **10–11:** Deliverance is certain.
　　Ps. 59: Prayer for deliverance from personal enemies (a lament). **1–2:** Cry for help. **3–7:** The
psalmist's situation (and prayer, vv. 4b–5). **5:** *Nations,* see 56.7 n. *Selah,* see 3.2 n.

and snarling with[u] their lips—
for "Who," they think, "will hear
    us?"

8 But thou, O LORD, dost laugh at
    them;
    thou dost hold all the nations in
       derision.
9 O my Strength, I will sing praises to
    thee;[v]
    for thou, O God, art my fortress.
10 My God in his steadfast love will
    meet me;
    my God will let me look in
       triumph on my enemies.

11 Slay them not, lest my people forget;
    make them totter by thy power,
       and bring them down,
    O Lord, our shield!
12 For the sin of their mouths, the
       words of their lips,
    let them be trapped in their pride.
    For the cursing and lies which they
       utter,
13   consume them in wrath,
    consume them till they are no
       more,
    that men may know that God rules
       over Jacob
    to the ends of the earth.   *Selah*

14 Each evening they come back,
    howling like dogs
    and prowling about the city.
15 They roam about for food,
    and growl if they do not get their
       fill.

16 But I will sing of thy might;
    I will sing aloud of thy steadfast
       love in the morning.
    For thou hast been to me a fortress
    and a refuge in the day of my
       distress.
17 O my Strength, I will sing praises to
    thee,

for thou, O God, art my fortress,
    the God who shows me steadfast
       love.

To the choirmaster: according to Shushan Eduth. A Miktam of David; for
instruction; when he strove with Aram-
naharaim and with Aram-zobah, and
when Joab on his return killed twelve
thousand of Edom in the Valley of Salt.

60 O God, thou hast rejected us,
    broken our defenses;
    thou hast been angry; oh, restore
       us.
2 Thou hast made the land to quake,
    thou hast rent it open;
    repair its breaches, for it totters.
3 Thou hast made thy people suffer
    hard things;
    thou hast given us wine to drink
       that made us reel.

4 Thou hast set up a banner for those
    who fear thee,
    to rally to it from the bow.[w]
                     Selah
5 That thy beloved may be delivered,
    give victory by thy right hand
       and answer us!

6 God has spoken in his sanctuary:[x]
    "With exultation I will divide up
       Shechem
    and portion out the Vale of
       Succoth.
7 Gilead is mine; Manas'seh is mine;
    E'phraim is my helmet;
    Judah is my scepter.
8 Moab is my washbasin;
    upon Edom I cast my shoe;
    over Philistia I shout in triumph."

u Cn: Heb *swords in*
v Syr: Heb *I will watch for thee*
w Gk Syr Jerome: Heb *truth*
x Or *by his holiness*

8–10: Expression of trust. **11–15:** Appeal for vengeance. **12:** *Cursing,* see Ps. 58 n. **16–17:**
The vow (see 7.17 n.).
     Ps. 60: Prayer for deliverance from national enemies (a group lament). **1–3:** The people's
situation. They have suffered a humiliating defeat, probably by the Edomites (see v. 9). **4–5:**
Prayer for deliverance. **4:** *Selah,* see 3.2 n. **5:** *Thy beloved,* either the nation or its king. **6–8:**
The answer prayed for in v. 5–a divine oracle, probably delivered by a priest or temple prophet.
The places referred to are either Hebrew territories or parts of the one-time Hebrew empire

⁹ Who will bring me to the fortified
    city?
  Who will lead me to Edom?
¹⁰ Hast thou not rejected us, O God?
    Thou dost not go forth, O God,
      with our armies.
¹¹ O grant us help against the foe,
    for vain is the help of man!
¹² With God we shall do valiantly;
    it is he who will tread down our
      foes.

To the choirmaster: with stringed
instruments. A Psalm of David.

61 Hear my cry, O God,
    listen to my prayer;
² from the end of the earth I call to
    thee,
  when my heart is faint.

Lead thou me
  to the rock that is higher than I;
³ for thou art my refuge,
  a strong tower against the enemy.

⁴ Let me dwell in thy tent for ever!
  Oh to be safe under the shelter of
    thy wings!   *Selah*
⁵ For thou, O God, hast heard my
    vows,
  thou hast given me the heritage of
    those who fear thy name.

⁶ Prolong the life of the king;
  may his years endure to all
    generations!
⁷ May he be enthroned for ever before
    God;
  bid steadfast love and faithfulness
    watch over him!

⁸ So will I ever sing praises to thy
    name,

as I pay my vows day after day.

To the choirmaster: according to
Jeduthun. A Psalm of David.

62 For God alone my soul waits in
    silence;
  from him comes my salvation.
² He only is my rock and my salvation,
  my fortress; I shall not be greatly
    moved.

³ How long will you set upon a man
  to shatter him, all of you,
  like a leaning wall, a tottering
    fence?
⁴ They only plan to thrust him down
    from his eminence.
  They take pleasure in falsehood.
  They bless with their mouths,
  but inwardly they curse.   *Selah*

⁵ For God alone my soul waits in
    silence,
  for my hope is from him.
⁶ He only is my rock and my salvation,
  my fortress; I shall not be shaken.
⁷ On God rests my deliverance and
    my honor;
  my mighty rock, my refuge is God.

⁸ Trust in him at all times, O people;
  pour out your heart before him;
  God is a refuge for us.   *Selah*

⁹ Men of low estate are but a breath,
    men of high estate are a delusion;
  in the balances they go up;
    they are together lighter than a
      breath.
¹⁰ Put no confidence in extortion,
    set no vain hopes on robbery;
  if riches increase, set not your
    heart on them.

---

under the United Monarchy. The God of Israel lays claim to them all. **9–12:** Prayer for victory.
9: *Me,* probably the king. *The fortified city,* perhaps Sela, Edom's capital.
  Ps. 61: Prayer for protection (a lament). **1–2:** Cry for help. **2:** *From the end of the earth* seems
to show that the psalmist did not live in Palestine. **3–5:** Expression of trust. **4:** *Thy tent,* see
27.6 n. The psalmist is perhaps preparing to make a pilgrimage. *Selah,* see 3.2 n. **6–7:** Prayer
for the king, the guarantor of safety for pilgrims and others. **8:** The vow (see 7.17 n.).
  Ps. 62: Confidence in God's protection (a song of trust; see Ps. 11 n.). **1–2,5–7:** God is the
psalmist's only help. **3–4:** The psalmist's situation: he is cursed by enemies. **8–12:** He instructs
his compatriots to trust in God also.

11 Once God has spoken;
twice have I heard this:
that power belongs to God;
12 and that to thee, O Lord, belongs
steadfast love.
For thou dost requite a man
according to his work.

A Psalm of David, when he was in the
Wilderness of Judah.

63 O God, thou art my God, I seek
thee,
my soul thirsts for thee;
my flesh faints for thee,
as in a dry and weary land where
no water is.
2 So I have looked upon thee in the
sanctuary,
beholding thy power and glory.
3 Because thy steadfast love is better
than life,
my lips will praise thee.
4 So I will bless thee as long as I live;
I will lift up my hands and call on
thy name.

5 My soul is feasted as with marrow
and fat,
and my mouth praises thee with
joyful lips,
6 when I think of thee upon my bed,
and meditate on thee in the
watches of the night;
7 for thou hast been my help,
and in the shadow of thy wings I
sing for joy.
8 My soul clings to thee;
thy right hand upholds me.

9 But those who seek to destroy my
life
shall go down into the depths of
the earth;
10 they shall be given over to the power
of the sword,

they shall be prey for jackals.
11 But the king shall rejoice in God;
all who swear by him shall glory;
for the mouths of liars will be
stopped.

To the choirmaster. A Psalm of David.

64 Hear my voice, O God, in my
complaint;
preserve my life from dread of the
enemy,
2 hide me from the secret plots of the
wicked,
from the scheming of evildoers,
3 who whet their tongues like swords,
who aim bitter words like arrows,
4 shooting from ambush at the
blameless,
shooting at him suddenly and
without fear.
5 They hold fast to their evil purpose;
they talk of laying snares secretly,
thinking, "Who can see us?*y*
6 Who can search out our crimes?*z*
We have thought out a cunningly
conceived plot."
For the inward mind and heart of
a man are deep!

7 But God will shoot his arrow at
them;
they will be wounded suddenly.
8 Because of their tongue he will bring
them to ruin;*a*
all who see them will wag their
heads.
9 Then all men will fear;
they will tell what God has
wrought,
and ponder what he has done.

10 Let the righteous rejoice in the LORD,

y Syr: Heb *them*
z Cn: Heb *they search out crimes*
a Cn: Heb *They will bring him to ruin, their tongue being
against them*

Ps. 63: Prayer for deliverance from personal enemies (a lament; though this psalm may also
be classified as a song of trust, see vv. 9–10). The psalmist's almost mystical delight in God's
presence nearly obscures his sense of need for personal security (compare 73.23–28). **1**: Compare
42.1–2. **6**: See 3.5–6 n. The night was divided into three *watches*. **11**: *The king*, see 61.6–7 n.
Ps. 64: Prayer for deliverance from personal enemies (a lament). **1–2**: Cry for help. **3–6**:
The psalmist's situation. **3**: *Bitter words*, perhaps magical curses (compare Ps. 58 n.). **7–9**:
Expression of confidence. **10**: Concluding prayer.

and take refuge in him!
Let all the upright in heart glory!

To the choirmaster. A Psalm of David.
A Song.

65 Praise is due to thee,
    O God, in Zion;
    and to thee shall vows be performed,
2   O thou who hearest prayer!
    To thee shall all flesh come
3   on account of sins.
    When our transgressions prevail over
      us,[b]
    thou dost forgive them.
4 Blessed is he whom thou dost choose
    and bring near,
    to dwell in thy courts!
    We shall be satisfied with the
      goodness of thy house,
    thy holy temple!

5 By dread deeds thou dost answer us
    with deliverance,
    O God of our salvation,
    who art the hope of all the ends of the
      earth,
    and of the farthest seas;
6 who by thy strength hast established
    the mountains,
    being girded with might;
7 who dost still the roaring of the seas,
    the roaring of their waves,
    the tumult of the peoples;
8 so that those who dwell at earth's
    farthest bounds
    are afraid at thy signs;
    thou makest the outgoings of the
      morning and the evening
    to shout for joy.

9 Thou visitest the earth and waterest
    it,
    thou greatly enrichest it;
    the river of God is full of water;
    thou providest their grain,
    for so thou hast prepared it.

10 Thou waterest its furrows
    abundantly,
    settling its ridges,
    softening it with showers,
    and blessing its growth.
11 Thou crownest the year with thy
    bounty;
    the tracks of thy chariot drip with
      fatness.
12 The pastures of the wilderness drip,
    the hills gird themselves with joy,
13 the meadows clothe themselves with
    flocks,
    the valleys deck themselves with
      grain,
    they shout and sing together for
      joy.

To the choirmaster. A Song. A Psalm.

66 Make a joyful noise to God, all
    the earth;
2   sing the glory of his name;
    give to him glorious praise!
3 Say to God, "How terrible are thy
    deeds!
    So great is thy power that thy
      enemies cringe before thee.
4 All the earth worships thee;
    they sing praises to thee,
    sing praises to thy name."   *Selah*

5 Come and see what God has done:
    he is terrible in his deeds among
      men.
6 He turned the sea into dry land;
    men passed through the river on
      foot.
    There did we rejoice in him,
7   who rules by his might for ever,
    whose eyes keep watch on the
      nations—
    let not the rebellious exalt
      themselves.   *Selah*

8 Bless our God, O peoples,

b Gk: Heb me

Ps. 65: Thanksgiving for a good harvest. 1–5: It is good to gather at the temple to sing God's praises. **6–8:** It was he who created the world. **9–13:** And it is he who makes the earth fertile. **9:** 104.13. *River of God*, see Ps.46.4 n.

    Ps. 66: Liturgy of praise and thanksgiving. 1–12: Hymn in praise of God's might and his care for his people. **4:** *Selah*, see 3.2 n. **13–20:** An individual presents a thanksgiving sacrifice in

let the sound of his praise be
    heard,
9 who has kept us among the living,
    and has not let our feet slip.
10 For thou, O God, hast tested us;
    thou hast tried us as silver is tried.
11 Thou didst bring us into the net;
    thou didst lay affliction on our
      loins;
12 thou didst let men ride over our
    heads;
    we went through fire and through
      water;
    yet thou hast brought us forth to a
      spacious place.*c*

13 I will come into thy house with
    burnt offerings;
    I will pay thee my vows,
14 that which my lips uttered
    and my mouth promised when I
      was in trouble.
15 I will offer to thee burnt offerings of
    fatlings,
    with the smoke of the sacrifice of
      rams;
    I will make an offering of bulls and
      goats.   *Selah*

16 Come and hear, all you who fear
    God,
    and I will tell what he has done for
      me.
17 I cried aloud to him,
    and he was extolled with my
      tongue.
18 If I had cherished iniquity in my
    heart,
    the Lord would not have listened.
19 But truly God has listened;
    he has given heed to the voice of
      my prayer.

20 Blessed be God,
    because he has not rejected my
      prayer

or removed his steadfast love from
    me!

To the choirmaster: with stringed
instruments. A Psalm. A Song.

67 May God be gracious to us and
    bless us
    and make his face to shine upon us,
                       Selah
2 that thy way may be known upon
    earth,
    thy saving power among all
      nations.
3 Let the peoples praise thee, O God;
    let all the peoples praise thee!

4 Let the nations be glad and sing for
    joy,
    for thou dost judge the peoples
      with equity
    and guide the nations upon earth.
                       Selah
5 Let the peoples praise thee, O God;
    let all the peoples praise thee!

6 The earth has yielded its increase;
    God, our God, has blessed us.
7 God has blessed us;
    let all the ends of the earth fear
      him!

To the choirmaster. A Psalm of David.
A Song.

68 Let God arise, let his enemies
    be scattered;
    let those who hate him flee before
      him!
2 As smoke is driven away, so drive
    them away;
    as wax melts before fire,

c Cn Compare Gk Syr Jerome Tg: Heb *saturation*

---

fulfilment of a vow (7.17). **13–15:** Announcement of the worshiper's purpose. **16–19:** The story
of his experience (see 18.4–6 n.). **20:** Concluding act of praise.
    Ps. 67: Thanksgiving for a good harvest (see v. 6). **1–2:** Prayer that the blessing may con-
tinue (compare Num.6.25). *Selah*, see 3.2 n. **3–5:** May other nations know that Israel's God is
Lord of all! **6–7:** The occasion of the psalm.
    Ps. 68: Liturgy for a festival celebration in the temple. This is the most difficult of the psalms
to interpret, and there is no general agreement either as to its meaning as a whole or in many of
its details. Some scholars regard it as merely a collection of unrelated fragments. **1–3:** Prayer

let the wicked perish before God!
3 But let the righteous be joyful;
    let them exult before God;
    let them be jubilant with joy!

4 Sing to God, sing praises to his
        name;
    lift up a song to him who rides
        upon the clouds;*d*
    his name is the LORD, exult before
        him!

5 Father of the fatherless and
        protector of widows
    is God in his holy habitation.
6 God gives the desolate a home to
        dwell in;
    he leads out the prisoners to
        prosperity;
    but the rebellious dwell in a
        parched land.

7 O God, when thou didst go forth
        before thy people,
    when thou didst march through
        the wilderness,   *Selah*
8 the earth quaked, the heavens
        poured down rain,
    at the presence of God;
    yon Sinai quaked at the presence
        of God,
    the God of Israel.
9 Rain in abundance, O God, thou
        didst shed abroad;
    thou didst restore thy heritage as
        it languished;
10 thy flock found a dwelling in it;
    in thy goodness, O God, thou didst
        provide for the needy.

11 The Lord gives the command;
    great is the host of those who bore
        the tidings:
12 "The kings of the armies, they
        flee, they flee!"
    The women at home divide the spoil,

13 though they stay among the
        sheepfolds—
    the wings of a dove covered with
        silver,
    its pinions with green gold.
14 When the Almighty scattered kings
        there,
    snow fell on Zalmon.

15 O mighty mountain, mountain of
        Bashan;
    O many-peaked mountain,
        mountain of Bashan!
16 Why look you with envy, O
        many-peaked mountain,
    at the mount which God desired
        for his abode,
    yea, where the LORD will dwell
        for ever?

17 With mighty chariotry, twice ten
        thousand,
    thousands upon thousands,
    the Lord came from Sinai into the
        holy place.*e*
18 Thou didst ascend the high mount,
    leading captives in thy train,
    and receiving gifts among men,
    even among the rebellious, that the
        LORD God may dwell there.

19 Blessed be the Lord,
    who daily bears us up;
    God is our salvation.   *Selah*
20 Our God is a God of salvation;
    and to God, the Lord, belongs
        escape from death.

21 But God will shatter the heads of his
        enemies,
    the hairy crown of him who walks
        in his guilty ways.
22 The Lord said,

d Or *cast up a highway for him who rides through the deserts*
e Cn: Heb *The Lord among them Sinai in the holy place*

---

for God to manifest himself in battle (compare v. 1 with Num.10.35). **4–6**: Praise to God as helper of the helpless. **7–10**: God's care for his people in time past (compare vv. 7–8 with Jg.5.4–5). **7**: *Selah*, see 3.2 n. **11–14**: Announcement of a great victory. **13**: *The wings of a dove . . . ,* presumably describes some treasure found among the spoil. **14**: An incident otherwise unknown. **15–16**: Praise of the mount of God (Zion). **15**: *Bashan,* a region east of the Sea of Galilee. **17–18**: God ascends his throne in the temple (compare 47.5). **19–20**: Praise of the God who daily delivers his people. **21**: Expression of certainty that God will give victory to his

"I will bring them back from
    Bashan,
I will bring them back from the
    depths of the sea,
23 that you may bathe*f* your feet in
    blood,
    that the tongues of your dogs may
        have their portion from the
        foe."

24 Thy solemn processions are seen,*g*
    O God,
    the processions of my God, my
        King, into the sanctuary–
25 the singers in front, the minstrels
    last,
    between them maidens playing
        timbrels:
26 "Bless God in the great
    congregation,
    the LORD, O you who are of
        Israel's fountain!"
27 There is Benjamin, the least of them,
    in the lead,
    the princes of Judah in their
        throng,
    the princes of Zeb'ulun, the
        princes of Naph'tali.

28 Summon thy might, O God;
    show thy strength, O God, thou
        who hast wrought for us.
29 Because of thy temple at Jerusalem
    kings bear gifts to thee.
30 Rebuke the beasts that dwell among
    the reeds,
    the herd of bulls with the calves of
        the peoples.
    Trample*h* under foot those who lust
        after tribute;
    scatter the peoples who delight in
        war.*i*
31 Let bronze be brought from
    Egypt;
    let Ethiopia hasten to stretch out
        her hands to God.

32 Sing to God, O kingdoms of the
    earth;
    sing praises to the Lord,   *Selah*
33 to him who rides in the heavens, the
    ancient heavens;
    lo, he sends forth his voice, his
        mighty voice.
34 Ascribe power to God,
    whose majesty is over Israel,
    and his power is in the skies.
35 Terrible is God in his*j* sanctuary,
    the God of Israel,
    he gives power and strength to his
        people.

Blessed be God!

To the choirmaster: according to Lilies.
    A Psalm of David.

69 Save me, O God!
    For the waters have come
    up to my neck.
2 I sink in deep mire,
    where there is no foothold;
    I have come into deep waters,
    and the flood sweeps over me.
3 I am weary with my crying;
    my throat is parched.
My eyes grow dim
    with waiting for my God.

4 More in number than the hairs of my
    head
    are those who hate me without
        cause;
    mighty are those who would destroy
        me,
    those who attack me with lies.
What I did not steal
    must I now restore?
5 O God, thou knowest my folly;
    the wrongs I have done are not
        hidden from thee.

---

f Gk Syr Tg: Heb *shatter*
g Or *have been seen*   *h* Cn: Heb *trampling*
i The Hebrew of verse 30 is obscure
j Gk: Heb *from thy*

---

people. **24–27**: A procession enters the temple (see 24.7–10 n.). **27**: The reason for the mention
of just these four tribes–the first two from the south, the other two from Galilee–is uncertain.
Benjamin was the tribe of Saul; Judah, of David. **28–31**: Prayer for victory against Egypt
(*the beasts . . . among the reeds*, v. 30). **32–35**: Hymn to the God of heaven. **33**: 18.10–13.
    Ps. 69: Prayer for deliverance from personal enemies (a lament). **1–4**: Cry for help. The
language in vv. 2–3 is metaphorical. **5**: Confession of sin (compare 32.3–5; 51.3–5). **6**: The prayer

⁶ Let not those who hope in thee be
    put to shame through me,
O Lord GOD of hosts;
let not those who seek thee be
    brought to dishonor through
    me,
O God of Israel.
⁷ For it is for thy sake that I have
    borne reproach,
    that shame has covered my face.
⁸ I have become a stranger to my
    brethren,
    an alien to my mother's sons.

⁹ For zeal for thy house has consumed
    me,
    and the insults of those who insult
    thee have fallen on me.
¹⁰ When I humbled^k my soul with
    fasting,
    it became my reproach.
¹¹ When I made sackcloth my clothing,
    I became a byword to them.
¹² I am the talk of those who sit in
    the gate,
    and the drunkards make songs
    about me.

¹³ But as for me, my prayer is to thee,
    O LORD.
    At an acceptable time, O God,
    in the abundance of thy steadfast
    love answer me.
    With thy faithful help ¹⁴ rescue me
    from sinking in the mire;
    let me be delivered from my
    enemies
    and from the deep waters.
¹⁵ Let not the flood sweep over me,
    or the deep swallow me up,
    or the pit close its mouth over me.

¹⁶ Answer me, O LORD, for thy
    steadfast love is good;
    according to thy abundant mercy,
    turn to me.
¹⁷ Hide not thy face from thy servant;

for I am in distress, make haste to
    answer me.
¹⁸ Draw near to me, redeem me,
    set me free because of my
    enemies!

¹⁹ Thou knowest my reproach,
    and my shame and my dishonor;
    my foes are all known to thee.
²⁰ Insults have broken my heart,
    so that I am in despair.
    I looked for pity, but there was none;
    and for comforters, but I found
    none.
²¹ They gave me poison for food,
    and for my thirst they gave me
    vinegar to drink.

²² Let their own table before them
    become a snare;
    let their sacrificial feasts^l be a
    trap.
²³ Let their eyes be darkened, so that
    they cannot see;
    and make their loins tremble
    continually.
²⁴ Pour out thy indignation upon them,
    and let thy burning anger overtake
    them.
²⁵ May their camp be a desolation,
    let no one dwell in their tents.
²⁶ For they persecute him whom thou
    hast smitten,
    and him^m whom thou hast
    wounded, they afflict still more.^{n}
²⁷ Add to them punishment upon
    punishment;
    may they have no acquittal from
    thee.
²⁸ Let them be blotted out of the book
    of the living;
    let them not be enrolled among
    the righteous.

k Gk Syr: Heb *I wept with fasting my soul* or *I made my
    soul mourn with fasting*
l Tg: Heb *for security*
m One Ms Tg Compare Syr: Heb *those*
n Gk Syr: Heb *recount the pain of*

continued. **7–21:** The psalmist's situation. He may have been, like Haggai and Zechariah, a
zealot for the rebuilding of the temple after the Exile (compare v. 9 with vv. 35–36; see also
Ezra.4.1–5,23–24; 5.2–3), and thus have aroused opposition. **9:** Quoted in Jn.2.17. **13–18:** His
deep emotions force him to interrupt the narrative with a prayer. **21:** Quoted in all the gospels
(Mt.27.34,48; Mk.15.36; Lk.23.36; Jn.19.29). **22–28:** Curse upon his enemies (see Ps. 58 n.).
25: Quoted in Acts 1.20. **29:** Exclamatory prayer. **30–36:** Thanksgiving for a favorable answer.

²⁹ But I am afflicted and in pain;
     let thy salvation, O God, set me
          on high!

³⁰ I will praise the name of God with a
          song;
     I will magnify him with
          thanksgiving.
³¹ This will please the LORD more than
          an ox
     or a bull with horns and hoofs.
³² Let the oppressed see it and be glad;
     you who seek God, let your hearts
          revive.
³³ For the LORD hears the needy,
     and does not despise his own that
          are in bonds.

³⁴ Let heaven and earth praise him,
     the seas and everything that moves
          therein.
³⁵ For God will save Zion
     and rebuild the cities of Judah;
     and his servants shall dwell° there
          and possess it;
³⁶   the children of his servants shall
          inherit it,
     and those who love his name shall
          dwell in it.

To the choirmaster. A Psalm of David,
     for the memorial offering.

70 Be pleased, O God, to deliver
     me!
     O LORD, make haste to help me!
² Let them be put to shame and
          confusion
     who seek my life!
     Let them be turned back and brought
          to dishonor
     who desire my hurt!

³ Let them be appalled because of
          their shame
     who say, "Aha, Aha!"

⁴ May all who seek thee
     rejoice and be glad in thee!
     May those who love thy salvation
     say evermore, "God is great!"
⁵ But I am poor and needy;
     hasten to me, O God!
     Thou art my help and my deliverer;
     O LORD, do not tarry!

71 In thee, O LORD, do I take
     refuge;
     let me never be put to shame!
² In thy righteousness deliver me and
          rescue me;
     incline thy ear to me, and save
          me!
³ Be thou to me a rock of refuge,
     a strong fortress,ᵖ to save me,
     for thou art my rock and my
          fortress.

⁴ Rescue me, O my God, from the
          hand of the wicked,
     from the grasp of the unjust and
          cruel man.
⁵ For thou, O Lord, art my hope,
     my trust, O LORD, from my
          youth.
⁶ Upon thee I have leaned from my
          birth;
     thou art he who took me from my
          mother's womb.
     My praise is continually of thee.

⁷ I have been as a portent to many;
     but thou art my strong refuge.
⁸ My mouth is filled with thy praise,
     and with thy glory all the day.

o Syr: Heb *and they shall dwell*
p Gk Compare 31.3: Heb *to come continually thou hast
commanded*

A priest or temple prophet may have delivered an oracle of assurance between v. 29 and v. 30
(see 12.5 n. and 20.5 n.). **30–31:** Like the authors of Pss. 40 (vv. 6–8); 50 (vv. 8–13); and 51
(vv. 16–17), the psalmist prefers to offer a hymn of thanksgiving. **35–36:** If these verses are not
a later addition, they show the psalm to be post-exilic (compare 51.18–19).
     Ps. 70: Prayer for deliverance from personal enemies (a lament). This psalm is practically
identical with 40.13–17.
     Ps. 71: An old man's prayer for deliverance from personal enemies (a lament). **1–8:** Cry for
help, mingled with expressions of trust. **5–6:** In all his previous life, God has never failed him.

9 Do not cast me off in the time of old
    age;
    forsake me not when my strength
      is spent.
10 For my enemies speak concerning
    me,
    those who watch for my life
      consult together,
11 and say, "God has forsaken him;
    pursue and seize him,
    for there is none to deliver him."

12 O God, be not far from me;
    O my God, make haste to help me!
13 May my accusers be put to shame
    and consumed;
    with scorn and disgrace may they
      be covered
    who seek my hurt.
14 But I will hope continually,
    and will praise thee yet more and
      more.
15 My mouth will tell of thy righteous
    acts,
    of thy deeds of salvation all the
      day,
    for their number is past my
      knowledge.
16 With the mighty deeds of the Lord
    GOD I will come,
    I will praise thy righteousness,
      thine alone.

17 O God, from my youth thou hast
    taught me,
    and I still proclaim thy wondrous
      deeds.
18 So even to old age and gray hairs,
    O God, do not forsake me,
    till I proclaim thy might
    to all the generations to come.*q*
Thy power 19 and thy righteousness,
    O God,
    reach the high heavens.

Thou who hast done great things,

O God, who is like thee?
20 Thou who hast made me see many
    sore troubles
    wilt revive me again;
from the depths of the earth
    thou wilt bring me up again.
21 Thou wilt increase my honor,
    and comfort me again.

22 I will also praise thee with the harp
    for thy faithfulness, O my God;
    I will sing praises to thee with the
      lyre,
    O Holy One of Israel.
23 My lips will shout for joy,
    when I sing praises to thee;
    my soul also, which thou hast
      rescued.
24 And my tongue will talk of thy
    righteous help
    all the day long,
    for they have been put to shame and
      disgraced
    who sought to do me hurt.

A Psalm of Solomon.

72 Give the king thy justice, O
    God,
    and thy righteousness to the royal
      son!
2 May he judge thy people with
    righteousness,
    and thy poor with justice!
3 Let the mountains bear prosperity
    for the people,
    and the hills, in righteousness!
4 May he defend the cause of the poor
    of the people,
    give deliverance to the needy,
    and crush the oppressor!

5 May he live*r* while the sun endures,

q Gk Compare Syr: Heb *to a generation, to all that come*
r Gk: Heb *may they fear thee*

9–11: The psalmist's situation: he has violent enemies and his age is a disadvantage to him
(compare v. 18). **12–13:** Prayer for vindication. **14–24:** The vow (see 7.17 n.). If the prayer is
answered, he will use his musical talents (v. 22) to celebrate God's saving acts (vv. 15–16) so
that future generations will know of them (v. 18). **20:** *From the depths of the earth*, compare
9.13; 30.3.
    Ps. 72: Prayer for God's blessing on the king. The occasion for the psalm may have been a
coronation or its annual commemoration. **1–4:** The king is to be the guarantor of justice for the

and as long as the moon,
throughout all generations!
6 May he be like rain that falls on the
mown grass,
like showers that water the earth!
7 In his days may righteousness
flourish,
and peace abound, till the moon
be no more!

8 May he have dominion from sea to
sea,
and from the River to the ends of
the earth!
9 May his foes*s* bow down before him,
and his enemies lick the dust!
10 May the kings of Tarshish and of the
isles
render him tribute,
may the kings of Sheba and Seba
bring gifts!
11 May all kings fall down before him,
all nations serve him!

12 For he delivers the needy when he
calls,
the poor and him who has no
helper.
13 He has pity on the weak and the
needy,
and saves the lives of the needy.
14 From oppression and violence he
redeems their life;
and precious is their blood in his
sight.

15 Long may he live,
may gold of Sheba be given to him!
May prayer be made for him
continually,

and blessings invoked for him all
the day!
16 May there be abundance of grain in
the land;
on the tops of the mountains may
it wave;
may its fruit be like Lebanon;
and may men blossom forth from the
cities
like the grass of the field!
17 May his name endure for ever,
his fame continue as long as the
sun!
May men bless themselves by him,
all nations call him blessed!

18 Blessed be the LORD, the God of
Israel,
who alone does wondrous things.
19 Blessed be his glorious name for
ever;
may his glory fill the whole earth!
Amen and Amen!

20 The prayers of David, the son of
Jesse, are ended.

BOOK III

A Psalm of Asaph.

73 Truly God is good to the
upright,
to those who are pure in heart.*t*
2 But as for me, my feet had almost
stumbled,

s Cn: Heb *those who dwell in the wilderness*
t Or *Truly God is good to Israel, to those who are pure in*
heart

helpless (vv. 12–15). **5–6:** These verses suggest the supernatural aura which surrounded the person of the king in the thought of the ancient Near East (even in Israel he could be called "God's son," see 2.7). The health, fertility, and success of the nation were bound up inextricably in those of its monarch. **7:** *Righteousness* and *peace*, as frequently elsewhere, mean "right conditions" and "prosperity." **8–11:** The king's ideal universal empire. These verses suggested the ascription of the psalm to Solomon. **8:** *The River*, the Euphrates (1 Kg.4.21). **10:** *Tarshish*, in the western Mediterranean. *Sheba and Seba*, in south Arabia. **12–14:** The character of the king. **15–17:** The prayer concluded. **18–19:** A doxology (no part of the psalm) marking the end of Book II of the Psalter (see 41.13 n.). **20:** An editorial colophon to one of the collections of psalms now included in the Psalter.

Ps. 73: Meditation on the justice of God (a wisdom psalm). The problem is the same as that of the book of Job: How can one reconcile the belief that God is just with the apparent inequities in his government of the world? (compare Ps. 37). **1:** Both a confession of faith and a

my steps had well nigh slipped.
³ For I was envious of the arrogant,
  when I saw the prosperity of the
  wicked.

⁴ For they have no pangs;
  their bodies are sound and sleek.
⁵ They are not in trouble as other men
  are;
  they are not stricken like other
  men.
⁶ Therefore pride is their necklace;
  violence covers them as a
  garment.
⁷ Their eyes swell out with fatness,
  their hearts overflow with follies.
⁸ They scoff and speak with malice;
  loftily they threaten oppression.
⁹ They set their mouths against the
  heavens,
  and their tongue struts through the
  earth.

¹⁰ Therefore the people turn and praise
  them;ᵘ
  and find no fault in them.ᵛ
¹¹ And they say, "How can God know?
  Is there knowledge in the Most
  High?"
¹² Behold, these are the wicked;
  always at ease, they increase in
  riches.
¹³ All in vain have I kept my heart
  clean
  and washed my hands in
  innocence.
¹⁴ For all the day long I have been
  stricken,
  and chastened every morning.

¹⁵ If I had said, "I will speak thus,"

I would have been untrue to the
  generation of thy children.
¹⁶ But when I thought how to
  understand this,
  it seemed to me a wearisome task,
¹⁷ until I went into the sanctuary of
  God;
  then I perceived their end.
¹⁸ Truly thou dost set them in slippery
  places;
  thou dost make them fall to ruin.
¹⁹ How they are destroyed in a
  moment,
  swept away utterly by terrors!
²⁰ They areʷ like a dream when one
  awakes,
  on awaking you despise their
  phantoms.

²¹ When my soul was embittered,
  when I was pricked in heart,
²² I was stupid and ignorant,
  I was like a beast toward thee.
²³ Nevertheless I am continually with
  thee;
  thou dost hold my right hand.
²⁴ Thou dost guide me with thy
  counsel,
  and afterward thou wilt receive
  me to glory.ˣ
²⁵ Whom have I in heaven but thee?
  And there is nothing upon earth
  that I desire besides thee.
²⁶ My flesh and my heart may fail,
  but God is the strengthʸ of my
  heart and my portion for ever.

²⁷ For lo, those who are far from thee
  shall perish;

u Cn: Heb *his people return hither*
v Cn: Heb *abundant waters are drained by them*
w Cn: Heb *Lord* x Or *honor* y Heb *rock*

thesis to be debated. **2–16:** The psalmist's experience and the grounds for his doubt. **2:** He had nearly lost his faith. **3–12:** Cynical, wicked men seemed to grow fat on their crimes (in sharp contradiction of such promises as Ps.1.4–6 or Dt.28.15–19; compare Job ch. 21). **11:** Their indifference to morality was grounded in a skeptical attitude toward God (10.4; 14.1). **13–16:** The psalmist's immediate, impulsive reaction. **13:** If wickedness is not punished, why be good? **14:** His efforts to be righteous brought him only suffering. **15:** This is what he was tempted to say, but had refrained from doing so because of the effect it might have on others (39.1). **16:** He found no answer to the problem in his private cogitations. **17–28:** It was only when he went to the temple to seek God's help that a satisfying answer came to him. **17–22:** First of all, he saw that the prosperity of the wicked is only temporary (compare Ps. 37). **21–22:** His previous attitude had been foolish and obtuse. **23–28:** In the second place, and far more importantly, he now realized that the righteous man has something the wicked man could never enjoy, however prosperous he might become: a sense of the nearness of God (compare Ps. 63; also 27.4).

thou dost put an end to those who
are false to thee.
28 But for me it is good to be near God;
I have made the Lord GOD my
refuge,
that I may tell of all thy works.

A Maskil of Asaph.

74 O God, why dost thou cast us off
for ever?
Why does thy anger smoke against
the sheep of thy pasture?
2 Remember thy congregation, which
thou hast gotten of old,
which thou hast redeemed to be
the tribe of thy heritage!
Remember Mount Zion, where
thou hast dwelt.
3 Direct thy steps to the perpetual
ruins;
the enemy has destroyed
everything in the sanctuary!

4 Thy foes have roared in the midst of
thy holy place;
they set up their own signs for
signs.
5 At the upper entrance they hacked
the wooden trellis with axes.z
6 And then all its carved wood
they broke down with hatchets
and hammers.
7 They set thy sanctuary on fire;
to the ground they desecrated the
dwelling place of thy name.
8 They said to themselves, "We will
utterly subdue them";
they burned all the meeting places
of God in the land.

9 We do not see our signs;
there is no longer any prophet,
and there is none among us who
knows how long.
10 How long, O God, is the foe to scoff?
Is the enemy to revile thy name
for ever?
11 Why dost thou hold back thy hand,
why dost thou keep thy right hand
ina thy bosom?

12 Yet God my King is from of old,
working salvation in the midst of
the earth.
13 Thou didst divide the sea by thy
might;
thou didst break the heads of the
dragons on the waters.
14 Thou didst crush the heads of
Leviathan,
thou didst give him as foodb for
the creatures of the wilderness.
15 Thou didst cleave open springs and
brooks;
thou didst dry up ever-flowing
streams.
16 Thine is the day, thine also the night;
thou hast established the
luminaries and the sun.
17 Thou hast fixed all the bounds of
the earth;
thou hast made summer and
winter.

18 Remember this, O LORD,
how the enemy scoffs,
and an impious people reviles thy
name.

z Cn Compare Gk Syr: Heb uncertain
a Cn: Heb *consume thy right hand from*
b Heb *food for the people*

Ps. 74: **Prayer for deliverance from national enemies** (a group lament; compare Ps. 44).
1–3: Cry for help. **4–11:** The foe has devastated and burned the temple. If it were not for the
statement in v. 9 that there is no longer any prophet, it would be natural to take the situation as
being that of the conquest by the Babylonians in 587 B.C., but at that time, as evidenced by the
activity of Jeremiah and Ezekiel, the prophetic movement was at its height. Consequently the
situation must be some otherwise unknown event of the post-exilic period (compare Is.64.11).
Some have connected it with the Maccabean age. **4:** *Signs*, perhaps military standards. **12–17:**
A hymn-like interlude, celebrating God as the creator. The allusion in vv. 13–15 is to one of the
popular accounts of creation in which God was said to have subdued the monster of chaos
(Leviathan or Rahab), a personification of the restless waters of the sea, before beginning his
constructive activity (compare 89.10; Job 3.8 n.; 26.12–13; Is.27.1; 51.9). **18–23:** Prayer for
deliverance. **19:** *Thy dove*, Israel.

19 Do not deliver the soul of thy dove
    to the wild beasts;
  do not forget the life of thy poor
    for ever.

20 Have regard for thy*c* covenant;
  for the dark places of the land
    are full of the habitations of
      violence.
21 Let not the downtrodden be put to
    shame;
  let the poor and needy praise thy
    name.

22 Arise, O God, plead thy cause;
  remember how the impious scoff
    at thee all the day!
23 Do not forget the clamor of thy foes,
  the uproar of thy adversaries
    which goes up continually!

To the choirmaster: according
  to Do Not Destroy. A Psalm
  of Asaph. A Song.

75 We give thanks to thee, O God;
  we give thanks;
  we call on thy name and recount*d*
    thy wondrous deeds.

2 At the set time which I appoint
  I will judge with equity.
3 When the earth totters, and all its
    inhabitants,
  it is I who keep steady its pillars.
           Selah
4 I say to the boastful, "Do not boast,"
  and to the wicked, "Do not lift up
    your horn;
5 do not lift up your horn on high,
  or speak with insolent neck."

6 For not from the east or from the
    west
  and not from the wilderness comes
    lifting up;
7 but it is God who executes
    judgment,
  putting down one and lifting up
    another.
8 For in the hand of the LORD there is
    a cup,
  with foaming wine, well mixed;
  and he will pour a draught from it,
  and all the wicked of the earth
    shall drain it down to the dregs.

9 But I will rejoice*e* for ever,
  I will sing praises to the God of
    Jacob.
10 All the horns of the wicked he*f* will
    cut off,
  but the horns of the righteous
    shall be exalted.

To the choirmaster: with stringed
  instruments. A Psalm of Asaph.
    A Song.

76 In Judah God is known,
  his name is great in Israel.
2 His abode has been established in
    Salem,
  his dwelling place in Zion.
3 There he broke the flashing arrows,
  the shield, the sword, and the
    weapons of war.   *Selah*

4 Glorious art thou, more majestic
  than the everlasting mountains.*g*

c Gk Syr: Heb *the*
d Syr Compare Gk: Heb *and near is thy name. They recount*
e Gk: Heb *declare*   *f* Heb *I*
g Gk: Heb *the mountains of prey*

Ps. 75: National thanksgiving for God's mighty acts. 1: The verse shows that the basic theme is Israel's corporate (*we*) thankfulness, perhaps for a victory in battle. **2–5:** A divine oracle prophesying judgment for the wicked, probably spoken by a priest or temple prophet. **3:** *Selah*, see 3.2 n. **4–5:** *Horn*, symbol of strength and power. **6–8:** A warning to all that the God of Israel controls the destinies of nations. **8:** *Cup*, see Is.51.22–23; Jer.25.15; Lk.22.42 n. **9–10:** An individual, perhaps the king (see 60.9 n.) brings the thanksgiving liturgy to a conclusion in an act of praise and faith.
    Ps. 76: A song of Zion celebrating God's ultimate victory over the nations (compare Ps. 46). **1–3:** Announcement of God's victory. **2:** *Salem*, a poetical name for Jerusalem (compare Gen.14.18). **3:** Although the verb is past, the reference is almost certainly to the great eschatological conflict of the latter days (see 48.4–8 n.; 46.6,9). *Selah*, see 3.2 n. **4–9:** Hymn to the

⁵ The stouthearted were stripped of
  their spoil;
  they sank into sleep;
all the men of war
  were unable to use their hands.
⁶ At thy rebuke, O God of Jacob,
  both rider and horse lay stunned.

⁷ But thou, terrible art thou!
  Who can stand before thee
  when once thy anger is roused?
⁸ From the heavens thou didst utter
    judgment;
  the earth feared and was still,
⁹ when God arose to establish
    judgment
  to save all the oppressed of the
    earth.   *Selah*

¹⁰ Surely the wrath of men shall praise
    thee;
  the residue of wrath thou wilt gird
    upon thee.
¹¹ Make your vows to the LORD your
    God, and perform them;
  let all around him bring gifts
  to him who is to be feared,
¹² who cuts off the spirit of princes,
  who is terrible to the kings of the
    earth.

To the choirmaster: according to
Jeduthun. A Psalm of Asaph.

77 I cry aloud to God,
  aloud to God, that he may
  hear me.
² In the day of my trouble I seek the
    Lord;
  in the night my hand is stretched
    out without wearying;
  my soul refuses to be comforted.

³ I think of God, and I moan;
  I meditate, and my spirit
  faints.   *Selah*

⁴ Thou dost hold my eyelids from
    closing;
  I am so troubled that I cannot
    speak.
⁵ I consider the days of old,
  I remember the years long ago.
⁶ I commune[h] with my heart in the
    night;
  I meditate and search my spirit:[i]
⁷ "Will the Lord spurn for ever,
  and never again be favorable?
⁸ Has his steadfast love for ever
    ceased?
  Are his promises at an end for all
    time?
⁹ Has God forgotten to be gracious?
  Has he in anger shut up his
  compassion?"   *Selah*
¹⁰ And I say, "It is my grief
  that the right hand of the Most
  High has changed."

¹¹ I will call to mind the deeds of the
    LORD;
  yea, I will remember thy wonders
    of old.
¹² I will meditate on all thy work,
  and muse on thy mighty deeds.
¹³ Thy way, O God, is holy.
  What god is great like our God?
¹⁴ Thou art the God who workest
    wonders,
  who hast manifested thy might
    among the peoples.
¹⁵ Thou didst with thy arm redeem thy
    people,
  the sons of Jacob and Joseph.   *Selah*

¹⁶ When the waters saw thee, O God,
  when the waters saw thee, they
    were afraid,
  yea, the deep trembled.
¹⁷ The clouds poured out water;

h Gk Syr: Heb *my music*
i Syr Jerome: Heb *my spirit searches*

---

victorious God of Israel. **10:** God turns even men's evil intentions to his own good purposes.
11–12: The congregation is exhorted to join in worshiping him.
    Ps. 77: Prayer for deliverance from personal trouble (a lament). **1–6:** The psalmist's miserable
situation. He does not specify the nature of his difficulty. **3:** *Selah*, see 3.2 n. **7–10:** His agony is
so intense that he is tempted to question God's justice and love. **11–15:** To encourage himself,
he recalls God's mighty works in the past. **16–20:** He quotes a fragment of an ancient hymn
praising God for his work in creation (vv. 16–19) and in the history of Israel (v. 20).

the skies gave forth thunder;
thy arrows flashed on every side.
¹⁸ The crash of thy thunder was in the
whirlwind;
thy lightnings lighted up the world;
the earth trembled and shook.
¹⁹ Thy way was through the sea,
thy path through the great waters;
yet thy footprints were unseen.
²⁰ Thou didst lead thy people like a
flock
by the hand of Moses and Aaron.

A Maskil of Asaph.

78 Give ear, O my people, to my
teaching;
incline your ears to the words of
my mouth!
² I will open my mouth in a parable;
I will utter dark sayings from of
old,
³ things that we have heard and
known,
that our fathers have told us.
⁴ We will not hide them from their
children,
but tell to the coming generation
the glorious deeds of the LORD, and
his might,
and the wonders which he has
wrought.

⁵ He established a testimony in Jacob,
and appointed a law in Israel,
which he commanded our fathers
to teach to their children;
⁶ that the next generation might know
them,
the children yet unborn,
and arise and tell them to their
children,

⁷ so that they should set their
hope in God,
and not forget the works of God,
but keep his commandments;
⁸ and that they should not be like
their fathers,
a stubborn and rebellious
generation,
a generation whose heart was not
steadfast,
whose spirit was not faithful to
God.

⁹ The E'phraimites, armed with[j] the
bow,
turned back on the day of battle.
¹⁰ They did not keep God's covenant,
but refused to walk according to
his law.
¹¹ They forgot what he had done,
and the miracles that he had
shown them.
¹² In the sight of their fathers he
wrought marvels
in the land of Egypt, in the fields
of Zo'an.
¹³ He divided the sea and let them pass
through it,
and made the waters stand like a
heap.
¹⁴ In the daytime he led them with a
cloud,
and all the night with a fiery light.
¹⁵ He cleft rocks in the wilderness,
and gave them drink abundantly
as from the deep.
¹⁶ He made streams come out of the
rock,
and caused waters to flow down
like rivers.

¹⁷ Yet they sinned still more against
him,

j Heb *armed with shooting*

Ps. 78: The story of God's great deeds and his people's faithlessness. One of a group of psalms
(105; 106; 135; 136), composed for use at the major festivals, which simply recite the history of
God's dealings with Israel. This psalm emphasizes the disobedience and ingratitude of the
people, especially noting the defection of the Ephraimites (vv. 9–11) which led God to reject
them in favor of Judah (vv. 67–69). **1–4:** The poet addresses the congregation in the style of the
wisdom writers (compare 49.1–4). **2:** Quoted in Mt.13.35. **5–8:** The giving of the law. **6:** Dt.6.7.
9–11: It is uncertain what incident is referred to. **12–53:** God's miraculous care for his people
during the Exodus and the wilderness wanderings, a review of events in Exodus and Numbers,
vv. 17–20 and 32–41 being interludes which describe the characteristic faithlessness of Israel.
12: *Zoan*, a royal Egyptian store city, is identical with the Raamses of Ex.1.11. **15–16:** Ex.17.6;

rebelling against the Most High in
the desert.

18 They tested God in their heart
by demanding the food they
craved.

19 They spoke against God, saying,
"Can God spread a table in the
wilderness?

20 He smote the rock so that water
gushed out
and streams overflowed.
Can he also give bread,
or provide meat for his people?"

21 Therefore, when the LORD heard, he
was full of wrath;
a fire was kindled against Jacob,
his anger mounted against Israel;

22 because they had no faith in God,
and did not trust his saving power.

23 Yet he commanded the skies above,
and opened the doors of heaven;

24 and he rained down upon them
manna to eat,
and gave them the grain of
heaven.

25 Man ate of the bread of the angels;
he sent them food in abundance.

26 He caused the east wind to blow in
the heavens,
and by his power he led out the
south wind;

27 he rained flesh upon them like dust,
winged birds like the sand of the
seas;

28 he let them fall in the midst of their
camp,
all around their habitations.

29 And they ate and were well filled,
for he gave them what they craved.

30 But before they had sated their
craving,
while the food was still in their
mouths,

31 the anger of God rose against them
and he slew the strongest of them,
and laid low the picked men of
Israel.

32 In spite of all this they still sinned;

despite his wonders they did not
believe.

33 So he made their days vanish like a
breath,
and their years in terror.

34 When he slew them, they sought
for him;
they repented and sought God
earnestly.

35 They remembered that God was
their rock,
the Most High God their
redeemer.

36 But they flattered him with their
mouths;
they lied to him with their tongues.

37 Their heart was not steadfast
toward him;
they were not true to his
covenant.

38 Yet he, being compassionate,
forgave their iniquity,
and did not destroy them;
he restrained his anger often,
and did not stir up all his wrath.

39 He remembered that they were but
flesh,
a wind that passes and comes not
again.

40 How often they rebelled against him
in the wilderness
and grieved him in the desert!

41 They tested him again and again,
and provoked the Holy One of
Israel.

42 They did not keep in mind his
power,
or the day when he redeemed
them from the foe;

43 when he wrought his signs in Egypt,
and his miracles in the fields of
Zo'an.

44 He turned their rivers to blood,
so that they could not drink of
their streams.

45 He sent among them swarms of
flies, which devoured them,
and frogs, which destroyed them.

46 He gave their crops to the
caterpillar,

Num.20.10–13. **21–31**: Ex. ch. 16; Num. ch. 11. **24**: Quoted in Jn.6.31. **25**: The manna is
fancifully interpreted as *the bread of the angels*. **44–51**: The plagues, Ex. chs. 7–12. **51**: *Ham,* a

and the fruit of their labor to the
  locust.
⁴⁷ He destroyed their vines with hail,
  and their sycamores with frost.
⁴⁸ He gave over their cattle to the hail,
  and their flocks to thunderbolts.
⁴⁹ He let loose on them his fierce
  anger,
  wrath, indignation, and distress,
  a company of destroying angels.
⁵⁰ He made a path for his anger;
  he did not spare them from death,
  but gave their lives over to the
  plague.
⁵¹ He smote all the first-born in Egypt,
  the first issue of their strength in
  the tents of Ham.
⁵² Then he led forth his people like
  sheep,
  and guided them in the wilderness
  like a flock.
⁵³ He led them in safety, so that they
  were not afraid;
  but the sea overwhelmed their
  enemies.
⁵⁴ And he brought them to his holy
  land,
  to the mountain which his right
  hand had won.
⁵⁵ He drove out nations before them;
  he apportioned them for a
  possession
  and settled the tribes of Israel in
  their tents.

⁵⁶ Yet they tested and rebelled against
  the Most High God,
  and did not observe his
  testimonies,
⁵⁷ but turned away and acted
  treacherously like their fathers;
  they twisted like a deceitful bow.
⁵⁸ For they provoked him to anger
  with their high places;
  they moved him to jealousy with

their graven images.
⁵⁹ When God heard, he was full of
  wrath,
  and he utterly rejected Israel.
⁶⁰ He forsook his dwelling at Shiloh,
  the tent where he dwelt among
  men,
⁶¹ and delivered his power to captivity,
  his glory to the hand of the foe.
⁶² He gave his people over to the
  sword,
  and vented his wrath on his
  heritage.
⁶³ Fire devoured their young men,
  and their maidens had no
  marriage song.
⁶⁴ Their priests fell by the sword,
  and their widows made no
  lamentation.
⁶⁵ Then the Lord awoke as from sleep,
  like a strong man shouting
  because of wine.
⁶⁶ And he put his adversaries to rout;
  he put them to everlasting shame.

⁶⁷ He rejected the tent of Joseph,
  he did not choose the tribe of
  E′phraim;
⁶⁸ but he chose the tribe of Judah,
  Mount Zion, which he loves.
⁶⁹ He built his sanctuary like the high
  heavens,
  like the earth, which he has
  founded for ever.
⁷⁰ He chose David his servant,
  and took him from the
  sheepfolds;
⁷¹ from tending the ewes that had
  young he brought him
  to be the shepherd of Jacob his
  people,
  of Israel his inheritance.
⁷² With upright heart he tended them,
  and guided them with skilful
  hand.

---

poetic synonym for Egypt (Gen.10.6). **54–64:** God's care for his people during the conquest and in the days of the Judges; their continued faithlessness. **55:** *Nations*, Dt.7.1. **60–64:** The destruction of the temple at *Shiloh* is mentioned elsewhere only in Jer.7.12–14 and 26.6; the period was that of the events related in 1 Sam.4.1–7.2. **65–66:** Victories over the Philistines in the time of Saul and David. **67–72:** The building of the temple and the establishment of the Davidic dynasty. The passage reflects the tension between North and South which led to the division of the nation into Judah and Israel (Ephraim) and the eventual schism between Jews and Samaritans.

A Psalm of Asaph.

79 O God, the heathen have come
into thy inheritance;
they have defiled thy holy temple;
they have laid Jerusalem in ruins.
² They have given the bodies of thy
servants
to the birds of the air for food,
the flesh of thy saints to the beasts
of the earth.
³ They have poured out their blood
like water
round about Jerusalem,
and there was none to bury them.
⁴ We have become a taunt to our
neighbors,
mocked and derided by those
round about us.

⁵ How long, O LORD? Wilt thou be
angry for ever?
Will thy jealous wrath burn like
fire?
⁶ Pour out thy anger on the nations
that do not know thee,
and on the kingdoms
that do not call on thy name!
⁷ For they have devoured Jacob,
and laid waste his habitation.

⁸ Do not remember against us the
iniquities of our forefathers;
let thy compassion come speedily
to meet us,
for we are brought very low.
⁹ Help us, O God of our salvation,
for the glory of thy name;
deliver us, and forgive our sins,
for thy name's sake!
¹⁰ Why should the nations say,
"Where is their God?"
Let the avenging of the outpoured
blood of thy servants
be known among the nations
before our eyes!

¹¹ Let the groans of the prisoners come
before thee;
according to thy great power
preserve those doomed to die!
¹² Return sevenfold into the bosom of
our neighbors
the taunts with which they have
taunted thee, O Lord!
¹³ Then we thy people, the flock of thy
pasture,
will give thanks to thee for ever;
from generation to generation we
will recount thy praise.

To the choirmaster: according to Lilies.
A Testimony of Asaph. A Psalm.

80 Give ear, O Shepherd of Israel,
thou who leadest Joseph like a
flock!
Thou who art enthroned upon the
cherubim, shine forth
²   before E′phraim and Benjamin
and Manas′seh!
Stir up thy might,
and come to save us!

³ Restore us, O God;
let thy face shine, that we may be
saved!

⁴ O LORD God of hosts,
how long wilt thou be angry with
thy people's prayers?
⁵ Thou hast fed them with the bread
of tears,
and given them tears to drink in
full measure.
⁶ Thou dost make us the scorn*ᵏ* of
our neighbors;
and our enemies laugh among
themselves.

⁷ Restore us, O God of hosts;

k Syr: Heb *strife*

Ps. 79: Prayer for deliverance from national enemies (a group lament). The occasion is probably the same as that of Ps. 74 (see 74.4–11 n.). **1–4:** The people's situation: they are defeated and persecuted. **2:** *Saints,* see 30.4 n. **5–12:** Prayer for deliverance and vengeance. **13:** The vow (see 7.17 n.).

Ps. 80: Prayer for deliverance from national enemies (a group lament). **1–3:** Cry for help. The tribes mentioned show that the psalm is a product of the northern kingdom, Israel (compare 78.67–68). **1:** *Cherubim,* see 1 Sam.4.4. **3:** A refrain (see vv. 7,19). **8–13:** Israel as a vine,

let thy face shine, that we may be
saved!

8 Thou didst bring a vine out of
Egypt;
thou didst drive out the nations
and plant it.
9 Thou didst clear the ground for it;
it took deep root and filled the
land.
10 The mountains were covered with
its shade,
the mighty cedars with its
branches;
11 it sent out its branches to the sea,
and its shoots to the River.
12 Why then hast thou broken down
its walls,
so that all who pass along the
way pluck its fruit?
13 The boar from the forest ravages it,
and all that move in the field feed
on it.

14 Turn again, O God of hosts!
Look down from heaven, and see;
have regard for this vine,
15   the stock which thy right hand
planted.*l*
16 They have burned it with fire, they
have cut it down;
may they perish at the rebuke of
thy countenance!
17 But let thy hand be upon the man of
thy right hand,
the son of man whom thou hast
made strong for thyself!
18 Then we will never turn back from
thee;
give us life, and we will call on
thy name!
19 Restore us, O LORD God of hosts!
let thy face shine, that we may be
saved!

To the choirmaster: according to The
Gittith. A Psalm of Asaph.

81 Sing aloud to God our strength;
shout for joy to the God of
Jacob!
2 Raise a song, sound the timbrel,
the sweet lyre with the harp.
3 Blow the trumpet at the new moon,
at the full moon, on our feast day.
4 For it is a statute for Israel,
an ordinance of the God of Jacob.
5 He made it a decree in Joseph,
when he went out over*m* the land
of Egypt.

I hear a voice I had not known:
6 "I relieved your*n* shoulder of the
burden;
your*n* hands were freed from the
basket.
7 In distress you called, and I
delivered you;
I answered you in the secret place
of thunder;
I tested you at the waters of
Mer'ibah.   *Selah*
8 Hear, O my people, while I
admonish you!
O Israel, if you would but listen
to me!
9 There shall be no strange god among
you;
you shall not bow down to a
foreign god.
10 I am the LORD your God,
who brought you up out of the
land of Egypt.
Open your mouth wide, and I will
fill it.

11 "But my people did not listen to my
voice;

l Heb *planted and upon the son whom thou hast reared for
thyself*
m Or *against*   *n* Heb *his*

---

once carefully tended, but now forsaken (compare Is.5.1–7). **8**: *Nations,* see 78.55 n. **11**: *The
River,* the Euphrates (1 Kg.4.21). **14–19**: Prayer for deliverance. **17**: *Man* and *son of man* are
personifications of Israel.
    Ps. 81: Liturgy for a festival. 1–5a: Hymn-like summons to worship. **3:** *Feast day,* probably
feast of booths (Dt.16.13–15). **5b–16:** A priest or temple prophet delivers a divine oracle in
which God reminds his people of what he has done for them in the past (vv.6–7); his demand
for their loyalty (vv. 8–10) and their disobedience to it (vv. 11–12); their future prosperity
depends on their willingness now to change their ways (vv. 13–16; compare 95.7b–11). **7:** *The
secret place of thunder,* Sinai. *Meribah,* Ex.17.7; Num.20.13. *Selah,* see 3.2 n.

Israel would have none of me.
12 So I gave them over to their
　　stubborn hearts,
　to follow their own counsels.
13 O that my people would listen to me,
　that Israel would walk in my
　　ways!
14 I would soon subdue their enemies,
　and turn my hand against their
　　foes.
15 Those who hate the LORD would
　cringe toward him,
　and their fate would last for ever.
16 I would feed you*o* with the finest of
　the wheat,
　and with honey from the rock I
　would satisfy you."

A Psalm of Asaph.

82 God has taken his place in the
　　divine council;
　in the midst of the gods he holds
　　judgment:
2 "How long will you judge unjustly
　and show partiality to the wicked?
　　　　　　　　　　　　　Selah
3 Give justice to the weak and the
　　fatherless;
　maintain the right of the afflicted
　and the destitute.
4 Rescue the weak and the needy;
　deliver them from the hand of the
　wicked."

5 They have neither knowledge nor
　understanding,
　they walk about in darkness;
　all the foundations of the earth are
　shaken.

6 I say, "You are gods,

sons of the Most High, all of you;
7 nevertheless, you shall die like men,
　and fall like any prince."*p*

8 Arise, O God, judge the earth;
　for to thee belong all the nations!

A Song. A Psalm of Asaph.

83 O God, do not keep silence;
　　do not hold thy peace or be
　　still, O God!
2 For lo, thy enemies are in tumult;
　those who hate thee have raised
　their heads.
3 They lay crafty plans against thy
　people;
　they consult together against thy
　protected ones.
4 They say, "Come, let us wipe them
　out as a nation;
　let the name of Israel be
　remembered no more!"
5 Yea, they conspire with one accord;
　against thee they make a
　covenant–
6 the tents of Edom and the
　Ish'maelites,
　Moab and the Hagrites,
7 Gebal and Ammon and Am'alek,
　Philistia with the inhabitants of
　Tyre;
8 Assyria also has joined them;
　they are the strong arm of the
　children of Lot.　　　　　*Selah*

9 Do to them as thou didst to Mid'ian,
　as to Sis'era and Jabin at the
　river Kishon,
10 who were destroyed at En-dor,

o Cn Compare verse 16b: Heb *he would feed him*
p Or *fall as one man, O princes*

Ps. 82: Liturgy of the LORD'S judgment on pagan gods. 1: Making use of a conception, common to the ancient Near East, that the world is ruled by a council of gods (89.5–7), the poet (presumably a priest or temple prophet) sees, in a vision, the God of Israel standing up in the midst of the council and pronouncing judgment upon all the other members. **2–7:** Because they govern the earth unjustly, they shall all perish like mere human beings (Ezek.28.9). **2:** *Selah*, see 3.2 n. **6:** Quoted in Jn.10.34. **8:** A prayer that the poet's vision may be realized.
　　Ps. 83: Prayer for deliverance from national enemies (a lament). **1:** Cry for help. **2–8:** Israel's perilous situation, attacked by a powerful group of foreign allies. **6–7:** These are Israel's near neighbors. **8:** *Children* (sons) *of Lot*, Moab and Edom (Gen.19.36–38; Dt.2.9). *Selah*, see 3.2 n. **9–18:** Prayer for victory. **9–11:** Gideon's decisive victory over Midian is recorded in Jg. chs.

who became dung for the ground.
¹¹ Make their nobles like Oreb and
Zeeb,
all their princes like Zebah and
Zalmun'na,
¹² who said, "Let us take possession for
ourselves
of the pastures of God."

¹³ O my God, make them like
whirling dust,*q*
like chaff before the wind.
¹⁴ As fire consumes the forest,
as the flame sets the mountains
ablaze,
¹⁵ so do thou pursue them with thy
tempest
and terrify them with thy
hurricane!
¹⁶ Fill their faces with shame,
that they may seek thy name, O
LORD.
¹⁷ Let them be put to shame and
dismayed for ever;
let them perish in disgrace.
¹⁸ Let them know that thou alone,
whose name is the LORD,
art the Most High over all the
earth.

To the choirmaster: according to The
Gittith. A Psalm of the Sons of Korah.

84 How lovely is thy dwelling
place,
O LORD of hosts!
² My soul longs, yea, faints
for the courts of the LORD;
my heart and flesh sing for joy
to the living God.

³ Even the sparrow finds a home,
and the swallow a nest for herself,

where she may lay her young,
at thy altars, O LORD of hosts,
my King and my God.
⁴ Blessed are those who dwell in thy
house,
ever singing thy praise!   *Selah*

⁵ Blessed are the men whose strength
is in thee,
in whose heart are the highways
to Zion.*r*
⁶ As they go through the valley of
Baca
they make it a place of
springs;
the early rain also covers it with
pools.
⁷ They go from strength to strength;
the God of gods will be seen in
Zion.

⁸ O LORD God of hosts, hear my
prayer;
give ear, O God of Jacob!   *Selah*
⁹ Behold our shield, O God;
look upon the face of thine
anointed!

¹⁰ For a day in thy courts is better
than a thousand elsewhere.
I would rather be a doorkeeper in
the house of my God
than dwell in the tents of
wickedness.
¹¹ For the LORD God is a sun and
shield;
he bestows favor and honor.
No good thing does the LORD
withhold
from those who walk uprightly.
¹² O LORD of hosts,
blessed is the man who trusts in
thee!

q Or *a tumbleweed*
r Heb lacks *to Zion*

6–8; the defeat of *Sisera and Jabin* by Deborah and Barak in Jg. chs. 4–5. *Oreb and Zeeb,*
Jg.7.25. *Zebah and Zalmunna,* Jg.8.21.
   Ps. 84: Song praising Zion as the longed-for goal of the pilgrim. 1–2: Praise for the temple.
3–4: Envy of the birds and servitors who live there. **4:** *Selah,* see 3.2 n. **5–7:** The joys of the
pilgrimage. **6:** *Baca,* some unknown, desolate place through which the pilgrims must go. **8–9:**
Prayer for the king (see 61.6–7 n.). **9:** *Anointed,* see 2.2 n. **10–12:** The superiority of life in the
temple to life anywhere else.

To the choirmaster. A Psalm of the
Sons of Korah.

85 LORD, thou wast favorable to
thy land;
thou didst restore the fortunes of
Jacob.
2 Thou didst forgive the iniquity of
thy people;
thou didst pardon all their sin.
Selah
3 Thou didst withdraw all thy wrath;
thou didst turn from thy hot anger.

4 Restore us again, O God of our
salvation,
and put away thy indignation
toward us!
5 Wilt thou be angry with us for ever?
Wilt thou prolong thy anger to all
generations?
6 Wilt thou not revive us again,
that thy people may rejoice in
thee?
7 Show us thy steadfast love, O LORD,
and grant us thy salvation.

8 Let me hear what God the LORD will
speak,
for he will speak peace to his
people,
to his saints, to those who turn to
him in their hearts.*s*
9 Surely his salvation is at hand for
those who fear him,
that glory may dwell in our land.

10 Steadfast love and faithfulness will
meet;
righteousness and peace will kiss
each other.
11 Faithfulness will spring up from the
ground,
and righteousness will look down
from the sky.
12 Yea, the LORD will give what is good,
and our land will yield its increase.

13 Righteousness will go before him,
and make his footsteps a way.

A Prayer of David.

86 Incline thy ear, O LORD, and
answer me,
for I am poor and needy.
2 Preserve my life, for I am godly;
save thy servant who trusts in
thee.
Thou art my God; 3 be gracious
to me, O Lord,
for to thee do I cry all the day.
4 Gladden the soul of thy servant,
for to thee, O Lord, do I lift up my
soul.
5 For thou, O Lord, art good and
forgiving,
abounding in steadfast love to all
who call on thee.
6 Give ear, O LORD, to my prayer;
hearken to my cry of supplication.
7 In the day of my trouble I call on
thee,
for thou dost answer me.

8 There is none like thee among the
gods, O Lord,
nor are there any works like thine.
9 All the nations thou hast made shall
come
and bow down before thee, O
Lord,
and shall glorify thy name.
10 For thou art great and doest
wondrous things,
thou alone art God.
11 Teach me thy way, O LORD,
that I may walk in thy truth;
unite my heart to fear thy name.
12 I give thanks to thee, O Lord my
God, with my whole heart,
and I will glorify thy name for
ever.

s Gk: Heb *but let them not turn back to folly*

Ps. 85: Prayer for deliverance from national adversity (a group lament). **1–3:** God's favor
toward his people in time past. **4–7:** Prayer that God's favor may be manifested again in their
present difficulties (perhaps poor crops; compare v. 12). **8–13:** A priest or temple prophet
delivers an oracle of assurance. **8:** *Saints*, see 30.4 n.
Ps. 86: Prayer for deliverance from personal enemies (a lament). **1–7:** Cry for help. **8–10:**
God is praised for his power. **11:** Prayer for guidance. **12–13:** Thanksgiving, spoken in confident

13 For great is thy steadfast love
    toward me;
  thou hast delivered my soul from
    the depths of Sheol.

14 O God, insolent men have risen up
    against me;
  a band of ruthless men seek my
    life,
  and they do not set thee before
    them.
15 But thou, O Lord, art a God
    merciful and gracious,
  slow to anger and abounding in
    steadfast love and faithfulness.
16 Turn to me and take pity on me;
  give thy strength to thy servant,
  and save the son of thy handmaid.
17 Show me a sign of thy favor,
  that those who hate me may see
    and be put to shame
  because thou, Lord, hast helped
    me and comforted me.

A Psalm of the Sons of Korah. A Song.

87 On the holy mount stands the
    city he founded;
2   the Lord loves the gates of Zion
  more than all the dwelling places
    of Jacob.
3 Glorious things are spoken of you,
  O city of God.   *Selah*

4 Among those who know me I
    mention Rahab and Babylon;
  behold, Philistia and Tyre, with
    Ethiopia–
  "This one was born there," they
    say.

5 And of Zion it shall be said,
  "This one and that one were born
    in her";
  for the Most High himself will
    establish her.
6 The Lord records as he registers the
    peoples,
  "This one was born there."   *Selah*

7 Singers and dancers alike say,
  "All my springs are in you."

A Song. A Psalm of the Sons of Korah.
To the choirmaster: according to
Mahalath Leannoth. A Maskil of
Heman the Ezrahite.

88 O Lord, my God, I call for
    help[t] by day;

  I cry out in the night before thee.
2 Let my prayer come before thee,
  incline thy ear to my cry!

3 For my soul is full of troubles,
  and my life draws near to Sheol.
4 I am reckoned among those who go
    down to the Pit;
  I am a man who has no strength,
5 like one forsaken among the dead,
  like the slain that lie in the grave,
  like those whom thou dost
    remember no more,
  for they are cut off from thy hand.
6 Thou hast put me in the depths of
    the Pit,
  in the regions dark and deep.
7 Thy wrath lies heavy upon me,
  and thou dost overwhelm me
  with all thy waves.   *Selah*

t Cn: Heb O Lord, *God of my salvation*

anticipation of deliverance. **13:** *Sheol*, the abode of the dead. The psalmist is sure God will not permit him to die. **14:** His prayer is for preservation from ruthless enemies. **15–17:** He returns to the mood of supplication. **16:** *Son of thy handmaid*, synonymous with *thy servant*.

Ps. 87: Song praising Zion as the mother of believers everywhere. The text of this psalm is damaged and disarranged. **1–3:** The glory of Zion (Jerusalem). **3:** This verse provided the theme for Augustine's *City of God* and was the inspiration of a popular hymn. *Selah*, see 3.2 n. **4:** God's people, the citizens of Zion, are found in every country. *Rahab*, a poetical name for Egypt. **5:** The roll of Zion's citizens is a long and proud one. **6:** As God keeps the census records of the world, he notes with special pleasure the citizens of Zion. **7:** This verse seems to be only a fragment. *Springs*, sources of welfare.

Ps. 88: Desperate prayer for healing in sickness (a lament). **1–2:** Cry for help. **3–9:** The psalmist's situation, probably one of lifelong illness (compare v. 15). **3–4:** *Sheol . . . the Pit*, see 6.5 n. **5–6:** A classic description of Sheol (compare vv. 10–12; Job 10.21–22; Is.38.18–19). **7:** *Selah*,

8 Thou hast caused my companions
 to shun me;
 thou hast made me a thing of
 horror to them.
 I am shut in so that I cannot escape;
9 my eye grows dim through sorrow.
 Every day I call upon thee, O LORD;
 I spread out my hands to thee.
10 Dost thou work wonders for the
 dead?
 Do the shades rise up to praise
 thee?   *Selah*
11 Is thy steadfast love declared in the
 grave,
 or thy faithfulness in Abaddon?
12 Are thy wonders known in the
 darkness,
 or thy saving help in the land of
 forgetfulness?

13 But I, O LORD, cry to thee;
 in the morning my prayer comes
 before thee.
14 O LORD, why dost thou cast me off?
 Why dost thou hide thy face from
 me?
15 Afflicted and close to death from my
 youth up,
 I suffer thy terrors; I am helpless.*u*
16 Thy wrath has swept over me;
 thy dread assaults destroy me.
17 They surround me like a flood all
 day long;
 they close in upon me together.
18 Thou hast caused lover and friend
 to shun me;
 my companions are in darkness.

A Maskil of Ethan the Ezrahite.

89 I will sing of thy steadfast love,
 O LORD,*v* for ever;
 with my mouth I will proclaim
 thy faithfulness to all
 generations.
2 For thy steadfast love was
 established for ever,

thy faithfulness is firm as the
 heavens.
3 Thou hast said, "I have made a
 covenant with my chosen one,
 I have sworn to David my servant:
4 'I will establish your descendants for
 ever,
 and build your throne for all
 generations.' "   *Selah*

5 Let the heavens praise thy wonders,
 O LORD,
 thy faithfulness in the assembly of
 the holy ones!
6 For who in the skies can be
 compared to the LORD?
 Who among the heavenly
 beings*w* is like the LORD,
7 a God feared in the council of the
 holy ones,
 great and terrible*x* above all that
 are round about him?
8 O LORD God of hosts,
 who is mighty as thou art, O
 LORD,
 with thy faithfulness round about
 thee?
9 Thou dost rule the raging of the sea;
 when its waves rise, thou stillest
 them.
10 Thou didst crush Rahab like a carcass,
 thou didst scatter thy enemies with
 thy mighty arm.
11 The heavens are thine, the earth also
 is thine;
 the world and all that is in it, thou
 hast founded them.
12 The north and the south, thou hast
 created them;
 Tabor and Hermon joyously
 praise thy name.
13 Thou hast a mighty arm;
 strong is thy hand, high thy right
 hand.

u The meaning of the Hebrew word is uncertain
v Gk: Heb *the steadfast love of the* LORD
w Or *sons of gods*
x Gk Syr: Heb *greatly terrible*

see 3.2 n. **10–18:** Prayer for deliverance, notable for the absence of even a spark of hopefulness.
11: *Abaddon,* see Job 26.6 n.
 Ps. 89: A king prays for deliverance from his enemies. 1–18: Hymn extolling God's power and
faithfulness. **3–4:** His covenant with David recalled (compare vv. 19–37; 2 Sam.7.16). **4:** *Selah,*
see 3.2 n. **5–7:** See 82.1 n. **10:** *Rahab,* see 74.12–17 n. **12:** *Tabor,* a mountain in the north of

14 Righteousness and justice are the
foundation of thy throne;
steadfast love and faithfulness go
before thee.
15 Blessed are the people who know
the festal shout,
who walk, O LORD, in the light of
thy countenance,
16 who exult in thy name all the day,
and extol^y thy righteousness.
17 For thou art the glory of their
strength;
by thy favor our horn is exalted.
18 For our shield belongs to the LORD,
our king to the Holy One of Israel.

19 Of old thou didst speak in a vision
to thy faithful one, and say:
"I have set the crown^z upon one
who is mighty,
I have exalted one chosen from
the people.
20 I have found David, my servant;
with my holy oil I have anointed
him;
21 so that my hand shall ever abide
with him,
my arm also shall strengthen him.
22 The enemy shall not outwit him,
the wicked shall not humble him.
23 I will crush his foes before him
and strike down those who hate
him.
24 My faithfulness and my steadfast
love shall be with him,
and in my name shall his horn be
exalted.
25 I will set his hand on the sea
and his right hand on the rivers.
26 He shall cry to me, 'Thou art my
Father,
my God, and the Rock of my
salvation.'
27 And I will make him the first-born,
the highest of the kings of the
earth.
28 My steadfast love I will keep for him
for ever,

and my covenant will stand firm
for him.
29 I will establish his line for ever
and his throne as the days of the
heavens.
30 If his children forsake my law
and do not walk according to my
ordinances,
31 if they violate my statutes
and do not keep my
commandments,
32 then I will punish their transgression
with the rod
and their iniquity with scourges;
33 but I will not remove from him my
steadfast love,
or be false to my faithfulness.
34 I will not violate my covenant,
or alter the word that went forth
from my lips.
35 Once for all I have sworn by my
holiness;
I will not lie to David.
36 His line shall endure for ever,
his throne as long as the sun
before me.
37 Like the moon it shall be established
for ever;
it shall stand firm while the skies
endure."^a   *Selah*

38 But now thou hast cast off and
rejected,
thou art full of wrath against thy
anointed.
39 Thou hast renounced the covenant
with thy servant;
thou hast defiled his crown in the
dust.
40 Thou hast breached all his walls;
thou hast laid his strongholds in
ruins.
41 All that pass by despoil him;
he has become the scorn of his
neighbors.
42 Thou hast exalted the right hand of
his foes;

y Cn: Heb *are exalted in*   *z* Cn: Heb *help*
a Cn: Heb *the witness in the skies is sure*

Palestine. *Hermon*, the highest mountain of Syria. **17**: *Horn*, see 75.4–5 n. **18**: *Shield*, the king
(see 47.9 n.). **19–37**: The terms of the unalterable covenant which God had once established
with the Davidic dynasty. **19**: *Faithful one*, David (compare vv. 3–4); alternatively, Nathan
(see 2 Sam. 7.4). **27**: *The first-born*, compare 2.7. **38–45**: The king has been defeated in battle
(v. 43), and it seems that God has forsaken the covenant. **38**: *Anointed* (see v. 20; 2.2. n.).

thou hast made all his enemies
rejoice.
⁴³ Yea, thou hast turned back the edge
of his sword,
and thou hast not made him stand
in battle.
⁴⁴ Thou hast removed the scepter from
his hand,[b]
and cast his throne to the
ground.
⁴⁵ Thou hast cut short the days of his
youth;
thou hast covered him with shame.
Selah

⁴⁶ How long, O LORD? Wilt thou hide
thyself for ever?
How long will thy wrath burn like
fire?
⁴⁷ Remember, O Lord,[c] what the
measure of life is,
for what vanity thou hast created
all the sons of men!
⁴⁸ What man can live and never see
death?
Who can deliver his soul from the
power of Sheol?   *Selah*

⁴⁹ Lord, where is thy steadfast love of
old,
which by thy faithfulness thou
didst swear to David?
⁵⁰ Remember, O Lord, how thy
servant is scorned;
how I bear in my bosom the
insults[d] of the peoples,
⁵¹ with which thy enemies taunt, O
LORD,
with which they mock the
footsteps of thy anointed.

⁵² Blessed be the LORD for ever!
Amen and Amen.

BOOK IV

A Prayer of Moses, the man of God.

90 Lord, thou hast been our
dwelling place[e]
in all generations.
² Before the mountains were brought
forth,
or ever thou hadst formed the
earth and the world,
from everlasting to everlasting
thou art God.

³ Thou turnest man back to the dust,
and sayest, "Turn back, O children
of men!"
⁴ For a thousand years in thy sight
are but as yesterday when it is
past,
or as a watch in the night.

⁵ Thou dost sweep men away; they are
like a dream,
like grass which is renewed in the
morning:
⁶ in the morning it flourishes and is
renewed;
in the evening it fades and
withers.

⁷ For we are consumed by thy anger;
by thy wrath we are overwhelmed.
⁸ Thou hast set our iniquities before
thee,
our secret sins in the light of thy
countenance.

⁹ For all our days pass away under thy
wrath,
our years come to an end[f] like a
sigh.
¹⁰ The years of our life are threescore
and ten,

b Cn: Heb *removed his cleanness*   *c* Cn: Heb *I*
d Cn: Heb *all of many*   *e* Another reading is *refuge*
f Syr: Heb *we bring our years to an end*

46–51: Prayer that God will remember his promises and give victory to David's descendant.
48: *Sheol*, see 6.5 n.; 49.15. **52:** A doxology (no part of the psalm) marking the end of Book III
of the Psalter (see 41.13 n.).
   Ps. 90: Prayer for deliverance from national adversity (a group lament). **1–6:** Hymn-like
introduction declaring God's eternity and man's transience (compare Is.40.6–8). **4:** *Watch*, see
63.6 n. **7–10:** Brevity and sorrow of human existence. **11–12:** Prayer that men may learn wisdom
from considering this. **13–17:** Prayer that Israel may be delivered from her difficulties.

or even by reason of strength
fourscore;
yet their span[g] is but toil and
trouble;
they are soon gone, and we fly
away.

11 Who considers the power of thy
anger,
and thy wrath according to the
fear of thee?
12 So teach us to number our days
that we may get a heart of
wisdom.

13 Return, O Lord! How long?
Have pity on thy servants!
14 Satisfy us in the morning with thy
steadfast love,
that we may rejoice and be glad
all our days.
15 Make us glad as many days as thou
hast afflicted us,
and as many years as we have
seen evil.
16 Let thy work be manifest to thy
servants,
and thy glorious power to their
children.
17 Let the favor of the Lord our God
be upon us,
and establish thou the work of our
hands upon us,
yea, the work of our hands
establish thou it.

91 He who dwells in the shelter of
the Most High,
who abides in the shadow of the
Almighty,
2 will say to the Lord, "My refuge and
my fortress;
my God, in whom I trust."
3 For he will deliver you from the
snare of the fowler
and from the deadly pestilence;
4 he will cover you with his pinions,

and under his wings you will find
refuge;
his faithfulness is a shield and
buckler.
5 You will not fear the terror of the
night,
nor the arrow that flies by day,
6 nor the pestilence that stalks in
darkness,
nor the destruction that wastes at
noonday.

7 A thousand may fall at your side,
ten thousand at your right hand;
but it will not come near you.
8 You will only look with your eyes
and see the recompense of the
wicked.

9 Because you have made the Lord
your refuge,[h]
the Most High your habitation,
10 no evil shall befall you,
no scourge come near your tent.

11 For he will give his angels charge of
you
to guard you in all your ways.
12 On their hands they will bear you up,
lest you dash your foot against
a stone.
13 You will tread on the lion and the
adder,
the young lion and the serpent you
will trample under foot.

14 Because he cleaves to me in love,
I will deliver him;
I will protect him, because he
knows my name.
15 When he calls to me, I will answer
him;
I will be with him in trouble,
I will rescue him and honor him.
16 With long life I will satisfy him,
and show him my salvation.

g Cn Compare Gk Syr Jerome Tg: Heb *pride*
h Cn: Heb *Because thou,* Lord, *art my refuge; you have made*

Ps. 91: Meditation on God as the protector of the faithful (a wisdom psalm). **1–13:** Those who trust in the Lord need have no fear of any peril (121.2–8). Some of the dangers mentioned are human foes; others are demonic forces. **11–12:** Quoted in Mt.4.6; Lk.4.10–11. **14–16:** A divine oracle of assurance, probably spoken by a priest or temple prophet.

A Psalm. A Song for the Sabbath.

92 It is good to give thanks to the LORD,
    to sing praises to thy name, O
      Most High;
2 to declare thy steadfast love in the
      morning,
    and thy faithfulness by night,
3 to the music of the lute and the harp,
    to the melody of the lyre.
4 For thou, O LORD, hast made me
      glad by thy work;
    at the works of thy hands I sing
      for joy.

5 How great are thy works, O LORD!
    Thy thoughts are very deep!
6 The dull man cannot know,
    the stupid cannot understand this:
7 that, though the wicked sprout like
      grass
    and all evildoers flourish,
    they are doomed to destruction for
      ever,
8   but thou, O LORD, art on high for
      ever.
9 For, lo, thy enemies, O LORD,
    for, lo, thy enemies shall perish;
    all evildoers shall be scattered.

10 But thou hast exalted my horn like
      that of the wild ox;
    thou hast poured over me*i* fresh
      oil.
11 My eyes have seen the downfall of
      my enemies,
    my ears have heard the doom of
      my evil assailants.

12 The righteous flourish like the palm
      tree,
    and grow like a cedar in
      Lebanon.
13 They are planted in the house of the
      LORD,
    they flourish in the courts of our
      God.
14 They still bring forth fruit in old age,
    they are ever full of sap and green,
15 to show that the LORD is upright;
    he is my rock, and there is no
      unrighteousness in him.

93 The LORD reigns; he is robed in
    majesty;
    the LORD is robed, he is girded
      with strength.
    Yea, the world is established; it shall
      never be moved;
2   thy throne is established from of
      old;
    thou art from everlasting.

3 The floods have lifted up, O LORD,
    the floods have lifted up their
      voice,
    the floods lift up their roaring.
4 Mightier than the thunders of many
      waters,
    mightier than the waves*j* of the
      sea,
    the LORD on high is mighty!

5 Thy decrees are very sure;
    holiness befits thy house,
    O LORD, for evermore.

i Syr: Heb uncertain
j Cn: Heb *mighty the waves*

Ps. 92: Thanksgiving after deliverance from personal enemies. 1–3: Hymn-like introduction·
2: *Morning . . . night*, compare the morning and evening sacrifices (Ex.29.38–42). **4**: The occasion (described more explicitly in vv. 10–11) is a desire to give thanks for an answer to the psalmist's prayer for help. **5–9**: The mystery and power of God. **10–11**: The psalmist exults in his vindication. *Horn*, see 75.4–5 n. **12–15**: The rewards of righteousness (1.1–3). **13**: Compare 52.8.

Ps. 93: Hymn extolling God as king. This psalm begins a collection of hymns (Pss. 93; 95–99) dealing with the kingly rule of the God of Israel. They were apparently composed for use in connection with some feast, perhaps the feast of booths, when the theme of God's kingship (or "kingdom") was especially emphasized. Compare Ps. 47, which is closely related. **1–2**: The theme is stated. **3–4**: God's rule is based upon his control over the powers of chaos, symbolized by the waters of the sea (74.12–17; 104.7–9; Job 38.8–11). **5**: God is praised because his law offers dependable guidance and his temple is holy.

94 O LORD, thou God of vengeance,
thou God of vengeance, shine forth!

2 Rise up, O judge of the earth;
render to the proud their deserts!

3 O LORD, how long shall the wicked,
how long shall the wicked exult?

4 They pour out their arrogant words,
they boast, all the evildoers.

5 They crush thy people, O LORD,
and afflict thy heritage.

6 They slay the widow and the sojourner,
and murder the fatherless;

7 and they say, "The LORD does not see;
the God of Jacob does not perceive."

8 Understand, O dullest of the people!
Fools, when will you be wise?

9 He who planted the ear, does he not hear?
He who formed the eye, does he not see?

10 He who chastens the nations, does he not chastise?
He who teaches men knowledge,

11 the LORD, knows the thoughts of man,
that they are but a breath.

12 Blessed is the man whom thou dost chasten, O LORD,
and whom thou dost teach out of thy law

13 to give him respite from days of trouble,
until a pit is dug for the wicked.

14 For the LORD will not forsake his people;
he will not abandon his heritage;

15 for justice will return to the righteous,
and all the upright in heart will follow it.

16 Who rises up for me against the wicked?
Who stands up for me against evildoers?

17 If the LORD had not been my help,
my soul would soon have dwelt in the land of silence.

18 When I thought, "My foot slips,"
thy steadfast love, O LORD, held me up.

19 When the cares of my heart are many,
thy consolations cheer my soul.

20 Can wicked rulers be allied with thee,
who frame mischief by statute?

21 They band together against the life of the righteous,
and condemn the innocent to death.

22 But the LORD has become my stronghold,
and my God the rock of my refuge.

23 He will bring back on them their iniquity
and wipe them out for their wickedness;
the LORD our God will wipe them out.

95 O come, let us sing to the LORD;

Ps. 94: **A prayer for deliverance from evil men** (a lament). Although this seems to be originally the prayer of an individual (note vv. 16–23), the enemies are described in such general and indefinite terms (vv. 4–7,20–21) that it was easily adapted to congregational use. **1–3:** Cry for help. **4–7:** The psalmist's situation. He sees his own misfortunes as typical of the corruption of his age (compare 10.2–11; Ps. 14). **8–15:** In the style of the wisdom writers, he appeals to the congregation to understand the ways of the LORD. **16:** Prayer for deliverance in the form of a rhetorical question. **17–23:** An expression of confidence, perhaps in response to an oracle of assurance delivered after v. 16 (see 12.5 n.). **17:** *Land of silence*, Sheol (compare 115.17). **20–21:** The psalmist's enemies were persons in high official position in the state.

Ps. 95: **A liturgy of God's kingship.** This brief outline of a service opens with a hymn celebrating God's kingship (vv. 1–7a; see Ps. 93 n.) and closes with an oracle, delivered by a priest or temple prophet, warning the congregation against disobeying God's laws (vv. 7b–11; com-

let us make a joyful noise to the
   rock of our salvation!
2 Let us come into his presence with
   thanksgiving;
   let us make a joyful noise to him
     with songs of praise!
3 For the LORD is a great God,
   and a great King above all gods.
4 In his hand are the depths of the
   earth;
   the heights of the mountains are
   his also.
5 The sea is his, for he made it;
   for his hands formed the dry land.

6 O come, let us worship and bow
   down,
   let us kneel before the LORD, our
   Maker!
7 For he is our God,
   and we are the people of his
   pasture,
   and the sheep of his hand.

O that today you would hearken to
   his voice!
8   Harden not your hearts, as at
   Mer′ibah,
   as on the day at Massah in the
   wilderness,
9 when your fathers tested me,
   and put me to the proof, though
   they had seen my work.
10 For forty years I loathed that
   generation
   and said, "They are a people who
   err in heart,
   and they do not regard my ways."
11 Therefore I swore in my anger
   that they should not enter my rest.

96 O sing to the LORD a new song;
   sing to the LORD, all the earth!

2 Sing to the LORD, bless his name;
   tell of his salvation from day to
   day.
3 Declare his glory among the nations,
   his marvelous works among all
   the peoples!
4 For great is the LORD, and greatly
   to be praised;
   he is to be feared above all gods.
5 For all the gods of the peoples are
   idols;
   but the LORD made the heavens.
6 Honor and majesty are before him;
   strength and beauty are in his
   sanctuary.

7 Ascribe to the LORD, O families of
   the peoples,
   ascribe to the LORD glory and
   strength!
8 Ascribe to the LORD the glory due
   his name;
   bring an offering, and come into
   his courts!
9 Worship the LORD in holy array;
   tremble before him, all the
   earth!

10 Say among the nations, "The LORD
   reigns!
   Yea, the world is established, it
   shall never be moved;
   he will judge the peoples with
   equity."
11 Let the heavens be glad, and let the
   earth rejoice;
   let the sea roar, and all that fills it;
12   let the field exult, and everything
   in it!
   Then shall all the trees of the wood
   sing for joy
13   before the LORD, for he comes,
   for he comes to judge the earth.

pare 81.6–16). **1–2:** Summons to worship. **3–5:** God's rule based upon the fact that he created
the world. **6–7a:** Renewed summons to worship. **7b–11:** Prophetic warning against disobedience.
Quoted in Heb.3.7–11; 4.3–11. The declaration that worship without obedience is displeasing
to God is a cardinal principle of Old Testament religion (Pss. 15; 24.3–6; see 40.6 n.). **8:** *Meribah . . . Massah,* Ex.17.1–7; Num.20.1–13; compare 106.32–33. **10–11:** Num.14.33. *My rest,* the
Promised Land.
    Ps. 96: Hymn celebrating God's kingship. 1–3: Summons to worship. **4–6:** The LORD is the
powerful creator; all other gods are only powerless images (115.3–8). **7–13:** Summons to all
nations and to the physical universe to join in his praise. **9:** *Holy array* means ceremonial
garments. **10:** The kingship of the God of Israel. **13:** Compare Ps.98.4–9.

He will judge the world with
  righteousness,
and the peoples with his truth.

97 The Lord reigns; let the earth
    rejoice;
  let the many coastlands be glad!
2 Clouds and thick darkness are
    round about him;
  righteousness and justice are the
    foundation of his throne.
3 Fire goes before him,
  and burns up his adversaries
    round about.
4 His lightnings lighten the world;
  the earth sees and trembles.
5 The mountains melt like wax before
    the Lord,
  before the Lord of all the earth.

6 The heavens proclaim his
    righteousness;
  and all the peoples behold his
    glory.
7 All worshipers of images are put to
    shame,
  who make their boast in
    worthless idols;
  all gods bow down before him.
8 Zion hears and is glad,
  and the daughters of Judah
    rejoice,
  because of thy judgments, O God.
9 For thou, O Lord, art most high
    over all the earth;
  thou art exalted far above all gods.

10 The Lord loves those who hate
    evil;*k*
  he preserves the lives of his saints;
  he delivers them from the hand of
    the wicked.
11 Light dawns*l* for the righteous,

and joy for the upright in heart.
12 Rejoice in the Lord, O you
    righteous,
  and give thanks to his holy name!

A Psalm.

98 O sing to the Lord a new song,
    for he has done marvelous
    things!
  His right hand and his holy arm
    have gotten him victory.
2 The Lord has made known his
    victory,
  he has revealed his vindication
    in the sight of the nations.
3 He has remembered his steadfast
    love and faithfulness
    to the house of Israel.
  All the ends of the earth have seen
    the victory of our God.

4 Make a joyful noise to the Lord, all
    the earth;
  break forth into joyous song and
    sing praises!
5 Sing praises to the Lord with the
    lyre,
  with the lyre and the sound of
    melody!
6 With trumpets and the sound of the
    horn
  make a joyful noise before the
    King, the Lord!

7 Let the sea roar, and all that fills it;
  the world and those who dwell in
    it!
8 Let the floods clap their hands;
  let the hills sing for joy together

k Cn: Heb *You who love the* Lord *hate evil*
l Gk Syr Jerome: Heb *is sown*

Ps. 97: **Hymn celebrating God's kingship. 1:** Summons to worship the Lord as king. **2–6:**
The manifestation of the Lord (18.7–15; 50.1–3). **7:** Idolaters will realize their folly (96.5).
8–9: Israel's faith will be vindicated. **10–11:** Expression of confidence in the Lord's justice.
10: *Saints,* see 30.4 n. **12:** Renewed call to worship.
  Ps. 98: **Hymn proclaiming the future establishment of God's kingship on the earth. 1:** Summons
to worship. **2–3:** The Lord's triumph over all the powers that oppose him. Although the verbs
are past tense, the reference is to a future event (compare 76.3; also Pss. 46; 47; 48.4–8). **4–9:**
Summons to all nations and to the physical universe to join in God's praise (96.7–13). The
language in this and other of the "kingship" psalms is strikingly similar to that of many passages in Is. chs. 40–55 (e.g. 44.23; 52.10; 55.12).

[9] before the LORD, for he comes
    to judge the earth.
He will judge the world with
    righteousness,
and the peoples with equity.

99 The LORD reigns; let the
    peoples tremble!
He sits enthroned upon the
    cherubim; let the earth
    quake!
[2] The LORD is great in Zion;
    he is exalted over all the peoples.
[3] Let them praise thy great and
    terrible name!
    Holy is he!
[4] Mighty King,[m] lover of justice,
    thou hast established equity;
thou hast executed justice
    and righteousness in Jacob.
[5] Extol the LORD our God;
    worship at his footstool!
    Holy is he!

[6] Moses and Aaron were among his
    priests,
    Samuel also was among those
    who called on his name.
    They cried to the LORD, and he
    answered them.
[7] He spoke to them in the pillar of
    cloud;
    they kept his testimonies,
    and the statutes that he gave them.

[8] O LORD our God, thou didst answer
    them;
    thou wast a forgiving God to
    them,
    but an avenger of their
    wrongdoings.
[9] Extol the LORD our God,
    and worship at his holy mountain;
    for the LORD our God is holy!

A Psalm for the thank offering.

100 Make a joyful noise to the
    LORD, all the lands![n]
[2]   Serve the LORD with gladness!
    Come into his presence with
    singing!

[3] Know that the LORD is God!
    It is he that made us, and we are
    his;[o]
    we are his people, and the sheep
    of his pasture.

[4] Enter his gates with thanksgiving,
    and his courts with praise!
    Give thanks to him, bless his
    name!

[5] For the LORD is good;
    his steadfast love endures for ever,
    and his faithfulness to all
    generations.

A Psalm of David.

101 I will sing of loyalty and of
    justice;
    to thee, O LORD, I will sing.
[2] I will give heed to the way that is
    blameless.
    Oh when wilt thou come to me?

I will walk with integrity of heart
    within my house;
[3] I will not set before my eyes
    anything that is base.

I hate the work of those who fall
    away;
    it shall not cleave to me.
[4] Perverseness of heart shall be far
    from me;

m Cn: Heb *and the king's strength*
n Heb *land* or *earth*
o Another reading is *and not we ourselves*

Ps. 99: Hymn celebrating God's kingship. 1–3: The LORD God of Israel is the ruler of the earth. **3:** *Holy is he!* is the refrain (see v. 5 and v. 9). **4–5:** God's concern for justice. **6–9:** His fidelity toward his people.

Ps. 100: Hymn calling on all nations to praise the LORD. While this psalm does not refer specifically to God as king, its mood is similar to that of the preceding "kingship" psalms (see Ps. 93 n.) and it may be taken as a doxology for the collection.

Ps. 101: A king pledges himself to rule justly. This psalm may have been used as part of a coronation ceremony.

I will know nothing of evil.

⁵ Him who slanders his neighbor
    secretly
    I will destroy.
The man of haughty looks and
    arrogant heart
    I will not endure.

⁶ I will look with favor on the faithful
    in the land,
that they may dwell with me;
he who walks in the way that is
    blameless
    shall minister to me.

⁷ No man who practices deceit
    shall dwell in my house;
no man who utters lies
    shall continue in my presence.

⁸ Morning by morning I will destroy
    all the wicked in the land,
cutting off all the evildoers
    from the city of the LORD.

A prayer of one afflicted, when he is
faint and pours out his complaint
before the LORD.

102 Hear my prayer, O LORD;
    let my cry come to thee!
² Do not hide thy face from me
    in the day of my distress!
Incline thy ear to me;
    answer me speedily in the day
      when I call!

³ For my days pass away like smoke,
    and my bones burn like a furnace.
⁴ My heart is smitten like grass, and
    withered;
    I forget to eat my bread.
⁵ Because of my loud groaning
    my bones cleave to my flesh.
⁶ I am like a vulture*ᵖ* of the
    wilderness,
    like an owl of the waste places;

⁷ I lie awake,
    I am like a lonely bird on the
    housetop.
⁸ All the day my enemies taunt me,
    those who deride me use my name
    for a curse.
⁹ For I eat ashes like bread,
    and mingle tears with my drink,
¹⁰ because of thy indignation and
    anger;
for thou hast taken me up and
    thrown me away.
¹¹ My days are like an evening
    shadow;
    I wither away like grass.

¹² But thou, O LORD, art enthroned
    for ever;
thy name endures to all
    generations.
¹³ Thou wilt arise and have pity on
    Zion;
it is the time to favor her;
    the appointed time has come.
¹⁴ For thy servants hold her stones
    dear,
    and have pity on her dust.
¹⁵ The nations will fear the name of the
    LORD,
and all the kings of the earth thy
    glory.
¹⁶ For the LORD will build up Zion,
    he will appear in his glory;
¹⁷ he will regard the prayer of the
    destitute,
and will not despise their
    supplication.

¹⁸ Let this be recorded for a generation
    to come,
so that a people yet unborn may
    praise the LORD:
¹⁹ that he looked down from his holy
    height,
from heaven the LORD looked at
    the earth,
²⁰ to hear the groans of the prisoners,
    to set free those who were doomed
    to die;

p The meaning of the Hebrew word is uncertain

Ps. 102: Prayer for healing in sickness (a lament). **1–2:** Cry for help. **3–11** (and **23**): The psalmist's situation. His pain torments him and his enemies regard him as forsaken by God. **12–22:** He offers a hymn of praise to God; the words are perhaps quoted from a familiar song

21 that men may declare in Zion the
    name of the LORD,
    and in Jerusalem his praise,
22 when peoples gather together,
    and kingdoms, to worship the
    LORD.

23 He has broken my strength in
    mid-course;
    he has shortened my days.
24 "O my God," I say, "take me not
    hence
    in the midst of my days,
thou whose years endure
    throughout all generations!"

25 Of old thou didst lay the foundation
    of the earth,
    and the heavens are the work of
    thy hands.
26 They will perish, but thou dost
    endure;
    they will all wear out like a
    garment.
Thou changest them like raiment,
    and they pass away;
27   but thou art the same, and thy
    years have no end.
28 The children of thy servants shall
    dwell secure;
    their posterity shall be established
    before thee.

A Psalm of David.

103 Bless the LORD, O my soul;
    and all that is within me,
    bless his holy name!
2 Bless the LORD, O my soul,
    and forget not all his benefits,
3 who forgives all your iniquity,

who heals all your diseases,
4 who redeems your life from the Pit,
    who crowns you with steadfast
    love and mercy,
5 who satisfies you with good as long
    as you live*q*
so that your youth is renewed
    like the eagle's.

6 The LORD works vindication
    and justice for all who are
    oppressed.
7 He made known his ways to Moses,
    his acts to the people of Israel.
8 The LORD is merciful and gracious,
    slow to anger and abounding in
    steadfast love.
9 He will not always chide,
    nor will he keep his anger for
    ever.
10 He does not deal with us according
    to our sins,
    nor requite us according to our
    iniquities.
11 For as the heavens are high above
    the earth,
    so great is his steadfast love
    toward those who fear him;
12 as far as the east is from the west,
    so far does he remove our
    transgressions from us.
13 As a father pities his children,
    so the LORD pities those who fear
    him.
14 For he knows our frame;
    he remembers that we are dust.

15 As for man, his days are like grass;
    he flourishes like a flower of the
    field;

q Heb uncertain

---

of Zion anticipating the future glory of Jerusalem. **24**: His prayer. **25–28**: He concludes by again singing a fragment of a hymn, this time one in praise of God's eternity. **25–27**: Quoted in Heb.1.10–12. **27**: *Thou art the same,* literally, "Thou art he," compare Is.43.10,13,25.

    Ps. 103: Thanksgiving for recovery from sickness. This might be classified as a hymn, but vv. 1–5 suggest that the words, though general, are intended to express the emotion of a particular individual on a specific occasion. **1–5**: The psalmist summons his whole being to praise God for what he has done; v. 3 and v. 4a show that he refers to physical healing. **3**: *Forgives all your iniquity,* see 32.1 n. *The Pit,* see 16.10 n. *Your,* the psalmist is addressing his soul (i.e. his self). **5**: *Like the eagle's,* the vigor of the eagle was proverbial (Is.40.31). **6–18**: The being of God, in his justice, love, and eternity, compared with the frail and transient nature of man. **15**: Compare Is.40.6–8.

16 for the wind passes over it, and it is
    gone,
  and its place knows it no more.
17 But the steadfast love of the Lord is
    from everlasting to everlasting
    upon those who fear him,
  and his righteousness to children's
    children,
18 to those who keep his covenant
  and remember to do his
    commandments.

19 The Lord has established his
    throne in the heavens,
  and his kingdom rules over all.
20 Bless the Lord, O you his angels,
    you mighty ones who do his word,
    hearkening to the voice of his
    word!
21 Bless the Lord, all his hosts,
    his ministers that do his will!
22 Bless the Lord, all his works,
    in all places of his dominion.
  Bless the Lord, O my soul!

104

Bless the Lord, O my soul!
O Lord my God, thou art
very great!
Thou art clothed with honor and
    majesty,
2 who coverest thyself with light as
    with a garment,
  who hast stretched out the heavens
    like a tent,
3 who hast laid the beams of thy
    chambers on the waters,
  who makest the clouds thy chariot,
  who ridest on the wings of the
    wind,
4 who makest the winds thy
    messengers,
  fire and flame thy ministers.

5 Thou didst set the earth on its
    foundations,
  so that it should never be shaken.

6 Thou didst cover it with the deep
    as with a garment;
  the waters stood above the
    mountains.
7 At thy rebuke they fled;
    at the sound of thy thunder they
    took to flight.
8 The mountains rose, the valleys
    sank down
  to the place which thou didst
    appoint for them.
9 Thou didst set a bound which they
    should not pass,
  so that they might not again cover
    the earth.

10 Thou makest springs gush forth in
    the valleys;
  they flow between the hills,
11 they give drink to every beast of the
    field;
  the wild asses quench their thirst.
12 By them the birds of the air have
    their habitation;
  they sing among the branches.
13 From thy lofty abode thou waterest
    the mountains;
  the earth is satisfied with the fruit
    of thy work.

14 Thou dost cause the grass to grow
    for the cattle,
  and plants for man to cultivate,*r*
  that he may bring forth food from
    the earth,
15 and wine to gladden the heart of
    man,
  oil to make his face shine,
  and bread to strengthen man's
    heart.
16 The trees of the Lord are watered
    abundantly,
  the cedars of Lebanon which he
    planted.
17 In them the birds build their nests;

r Or fodder for the animals that serve man

19–22: Conclusion, with a hymn-like summons to all created things to join their voices with that of the psalmist.
    Ps. 104: Hymn to God the creator. 1: Address. The first line was probably added in imitation of the preceding psalm (compare also v. 35) **2–4:** The creation of the heavens. The account is much more mythological than that of Gen. ch. 1. **2:** *Light,* compare Gen.1.3; 1 Tim.6.16. **3:** See 18.10 n. **4:** Quoted in Heb.1.7. **5–9:** The creation of the earth. **7–9:** God's victory over the waters, the symbol of chaos (see 93.3–4 n.). **10–18:** God's continuing care for the earth and

the stork has her home in the fir
trees.
¹⁸ The high mountains are for the wild
goats;
the rocks are a refuge for the
badgers.
¹⁹ Thou hast made the moon to mark
the seasons;
the sun knows its time for setting.
²⁰ Thou makest darkness, and it is
night,
when all the beasts of the forest
creep forth.
²¹ The young lions roar for their prey,
seeking their food from God.
²² When the sun rises, they get them
away
and lie down in their dens.
²³ Man goes forth to his work
and to his labor until the evening.

²⁴ O LORD, how manifold are thy
works!
In wisdom hast thou made them
all;
the earth is full of thy creatures.
²⁵ Yonder is the sea, great and wide,
which teems with things
innumerable,
living things both small and great.
²⁶ There go the ships,
and Leviathan which thou didst
form to sport in it.

²⁷ These all look to thee,
to give them their food in due
season.
²⁸ When thou givest to them, they
gather it up;
when thou openest thy hand, they

are filled with good things.
²⁹ When thou hidest thy face, they
are dismayed;
when thou takest away their
breath, they die
and return to their dust.
³⁰ When thou sendest forth thy Spirit,*
they are created;
and thou renewest the face of the
ground.

³¹ May the glory of the LORD endure
for ever,
may the LORD rejoice in his
works,
³² who looks on the earth and it
trembles,
who touches the mountains and
they smoke!
³³ I will sing to the LORD as long as I
live;
I will sing praise to my God
while I have being.
³⁴ May my meditation be pleasing to
him,
for I rejoice in the LORD.
³⁵ Let sinners be consumed from the
earth,
and let the wicked be no more!
Bless the LORD, O my soul!
Praise the LORD!

105 O give thanks to the LORD,
call on his name,
make known his deeds among the
peoples!
² Sing to him, sing praises to him,
tell of all his wonderful works!
³ Glory in his holy name;

s Or breath

its inhabitants, animal and human. **19:** God's careful demarcation of the limits of months and days. **24:** The poet's exclamation of praise and admiration. **25–26:** The wonders of the sea. **26:** The monster *Leviathan* (see 74.12–17 n.) has become, for this author, merely a harmless, sportive creature of God. **27–30:** All living things depend on God at every moment for their existence. **31:** Concluding act of praise. **35:** The psalmist prays for the restoration of the original, intended harmony of creation. Ancient Hebrew man tended to use the personal and concrete words (*sinners . . . wicked*) where we should use the impersonal and abstract ("sin," "wickedness"). *Praise the LORD!* (Hebrew "Hallelujah!") belongs to the beginning of the following psalm (see 105 n.).

    Ps. 105: The story of God's great deeds on behalf of his people (compare Ps. 78). This psalm, now paired with Ps. 106, was composed for use at one of the major festivals and consists of a recital of the basic events which created the nation of Israel; its mood is one of grateful recollection. Both 105 and 106 at some point in their history were provided with the ritual shout "Hallelujah!" (*Praise the LORD!*) at the beginning and end (see 104.35 n). **1–6:** Hymn-like

let the hearts of those who seek
  the LORD rejoice!
4 Seek the LORD and his strength,
  seek his presence continually!
5 Remember the wonderful works
  that he has done,
  his miracles, and the judgments
  he uttered,
6 O offspring of Abraham his servant,
  sons of Jacob, his chosen ones!

7 He is the LORD our God;
  his judgments are in all the earth.
8 He is mindful of his covenant for
  ever,
  of the word that he commanded,
  for a thousand generations,
9 the covenant which he made with
  Abraham,
  his sworn promise to Isaac,
10 which he confirmed to Jacob as a
  statute,
  to Israel as an everlasting
  covenant,
11 saying, "To you I will give the land
  of Canaan
  as your portion for an
  inheritance."

12 When they were few in number,
  of little account, and sojourners in
  it,
13 wandering from nation to nation,
  from one kingdom to another
  people,
14 he allowed no one to oppress them;
  he rebuked kings on their
  account,
15 saying, "Touch not my anointed
  ones,
  do my prophets no harm!"

16 When he summoned a famine on
  the land,
  and broke every staff of bread,
17 he had sent a man ahead of them,
  Joseph, who was sold as a slave.

18 His feet were hurt with fetters,
  his neck was put in a collar of
  iron;
19 until what he had said came to pass
  the word of the LORD tested him.
20 The king sent and released him,
  the ruler of the peoples set him
  free;
21 he made him lord of his house,
  and ruler of all his possessions,
22 to instruct*t* his princes at his
  pleasure,
  and to teach his elders wisdom.

23 Then Israel came to Egypt;
  Jacob sojourned in the land of
  Ham.
24 And the LORD made his people
  very fruitful,
  and made them stronger than
  their foes.
25 He turned their hearts to hate his
  people,
  to deal craftily with his servants.

26 He sent Moses his servant,
  and Aaron whom he had chosen.
27 They wrought his signs among
  them,
  and miracles in the land of Ham.
28 He sent darkness, and made the
  land dark;
  they rebelled*u* against his words.
29 He turned their waters into blood,
  and caused their fish to die.
30 Their land swarmed with frogs,
  even in the chambers of their
  kings.
31 He spoke, and there came swarms
  of flies,
  and gnats throughout their
  country.
32 He gave them hail for rain,
  and lightning that flashed through
  their land.

t Gk Syr Jerome: Heb *to bind*
u Cn Compare Gk Syr: Heb *they did not rebel*

introduction summoning the congregation to praise and thanksgiving. **7–11:** The psalmist's
theme: God's faithfulness to his covenant with Israel's ancestors (Gen.15.18–21; 17.1–8; 26.1–5;
28.10–15). **12–41:** The narrative. **12–15:** The story of the patriarchs. **14:** *Rebuked kings*, Gen.
12.17; 20.3. **15:** Only here are the patriarchs given the title *anointed ones*, presumably because
they are called *prophets* (compare Gen.20.7; 1 Kg.19.16). **16–22:** The story of Joseph (Gen.
chs. 37; 39–50). **23–38:** The story of the Exodus (Ex.1.1–15.21). **27:** *Ham*, see 78.51 n.

³³ He smote their vines and fig trees,
and shattered the trees of their
country.
³⁴ He spoke, and the locusts came,
and young locusts without
number;
³⁵ which devoured all the vegetation
in their land,
and ate up the fruit of their
ground.
³⁶ He smote all the first-born in their
land,
the first issue of all their strength.

³⁷ Then he led forth Israel with silver
and gold,
and there was none among his
tribes who stumbled.
³⁸ Egypt was glad when they departed,
for dread of them had fallen upon
it.
³⁹ He spread a cloud for a covering,
and fire to give light by night.
⁴⁰ They asked, and he brought quails,
and gave them bread from
heaven in abundance.
⁴¹ He opened the rock, and water
gushed forth;
it flowed through the desert like
a river.
⁴² For he remembered his holy
promise,
and Abraham his servant.

⁴³ So he led forth his people with joy,
his chosen ones with singing.
⁴⁴ And he gave them the lands of the
nations;
and they took possession of the
fruit of the peoples' toil,

⁴⁵ to the end that they should keep his
statutes,
and observe his laws.
Praise the LORD!

106 Praise the LORD!
O give thanks to the LORD,
for he is good;
for his steadfast love endures for
ever!
² Who can utter the mighty doings
of the LORD,
or show forth all his praise?
³ Blessed are they who observe
justice,
who do righteousness at all times!

⁴ Remember me, O LORD, when thou
showest favor to thy people;
help me when thou deliverest
them;
⁵ that I may see the prosperity of thy
chosen ones,
that I may rejoice in the gladness
of thy nation,
that I may glory with thy
heritage.

⁶ Both we and our fathers have
sinned;
we have committed iniquity, we
have done wickedly.
⁷ Our fathers, when they were in
Egypt,
did not consider thy wonderful
works;
they did not remember the
abundance of thy steadfast love,
but rebelled against the Most
High[v] at the Red Sea.

v Cn Compare 78.17, 56: Heb *at the sea*

39–42: Incidents from the wilderness wanderings (Ex.13.21–22; 16.13–15; 17.6). It is remarkable that no mention is made of the giving of the Law or any of the other events at Sinai (Ex. 19.1–Num. 10.10). **43–45:** Return of the theme: God fulfilled his part in the covenant by giving Israel the land of Canaan. **45:** Israel must be faithful to her part of the covenant by obeying God's laws (95.7b–11).
    Ps. 106: The story of God's great deeds, with confession of sin and prayer for help. In contrast to Ps. 105, the mood of this psalm is a somber one, stress being laid on the perversity and obtuseness of the people. **1–2:** Call to praise the LORD. **3:** The need for right-doing on the part of his worshipers (105.45). **4–5:** The psalmist prays that he may share in Israel's blessings when God restores prosperity to her (compare v. 47). **6:** The theme: Whatever God has done, Israel has always been unfaithful (vv. 7,13–14,19,21,24–25,28–29,32,34–39,43); nevertheless he has constantly forgiven her disobedience and shown mercy (vv. 8,15,23,30,44–46). This thought encourages the psalmist to offer the prayer in v. 47. **7–46:** The narrative. **7–12:** The story of

8 Yet he saved them for his name's
    sake,
  that he might make known his
    mighty power.
9 He rebuked the Red Sea, and it
    became dry;
  and he led them through the deep
    as through a desert.
10 So he saved them from the hand
    of the foe,
  and delivered them from the
    power of the enemy.
11 And the waters covered their
    adversaries;
  not one of them was left.
12 Then they believed his words;
  they sang his praise.

13 But they soon forgot his works;
  they did not wait for his counsel.
14 But they had a wanton craving in
    the wilderness,
  and put God to the test in the
    desert;
15 he gave them what they asked,
  but sent a wasting disease among
    them.

16 When men in the camp were jealous
    of Moses
  and Aaron, the holy one of the
    LORD,
17 the earth opened and swallowed up
    Dathan,
  and covered the company of
    Abi'ram.
18 Fire also broke out in their company;
  the flame burned up the wicked.

19 They made a calf in Horeb
  and worshiped a molten image.
20 They exchanged the glory of God
  for the image of an ox that eats
    grass.
21 They forgot God, their Savior,
  who had done great things in
    Egypt,
22 wondrous works in the land of Ham,

  and terrible things by the Red
    Sea.
23 Therefore he said he would destroy
    them—
  had not Moses, his chosen one,
  stood in the breach before him,
  to turn away his wrath from
    destroying them.

24 Then they despised the pleasant
    land,
  having no faith in his promise.
25 They murmured in their tents,
  and did not obey the voice of the
    LORD.
26 Therefore he raised his hand and
    swore to them
  that he would make them fall in
    the wilderness,
27 and would disperse^w their
    descendants among the nations,
  scattering them over the lands.

28 Then they attached themselves to
    the Ba'al of Pe'or,
  and ate sacrifices offered to the
    dead;
29 they provoked the LORD to anger
    with their doings,
  and a plague broke out among
    them.
30 Then Phin'ehas stood up and
    interposed,
  and the plague was stayed.
31 And that has been reckoned to
    him as righteousness
  from generation to generation for
    ever.

32 They angered him at the waters of
    Mer'ibah,
  and it went ill with Moses on
    their account;
33 for they made his spirit bitter,
  and he spoke words that were
    rash.

w Syr Compare Ezek 20.23: Heb *cause to fall*

---

the Exodus (105.23–38). **13–33**: Incidents in the wilderness wanderings and at Sinai. **13–15**:
The manna and quails (Num.11.4–6,31–35). **16–18**: Dathan and Abiram's rebellion (Num. ch.
16). **19–23**: The golden *calf* (Ex. ch. 32). **19**: *Horeb*, alternative name for Mount Sinai. **24–27**:
The refusal to enter Canaan (Num.14.1–35). **28–31**: Apostasy to *the Baal of Peor* (Num.25.1–13).
32–33: *The waters of Meribah*, Num.20.2–13 (compare Ex.17.1–7). **34–39**: Israel's apostasies in

34 They did not destroy the peoples,
as the LORD commanded them,
35 but they mingled with the nations
and learned to do as they did.
36 They served their idols,
which became a snare to them.
37 They sacrificed their sons
and their daughters to the
demons;
38 they poured out innocent blood,
the blood of their sons and
daughters,
whom they sacrificed to the idols of
Canaan;
and the land was polluted with
blood.
39 Thus they became unclean by their
acts,
and played the harlot in their
doings.

40 Then the anger of the LORD was
kindled against his people,
and he abhorred his heritage;
41 he gave them into the hand of the
nations,
so that those who hated them
ruled over them.
42 Their enemies oppressed them,
and they were brought into
subjection under their power.
43 Many times he delivered them,
but they were rebellious in their
purposes,
and were brought low through
their iniquity.
44 Nevertheless he regarded their
distress,
when he heard their cry.
45 He remembered for their sake his
covenant,
and relented according to the
abundance of his steadfast love.
46 He caused them to be pitied

by all those who held them
captive.

47 Save us, O LORD our God,
and gather us from among the
nations,
that we may give thanks to thy holy
name
and glory in thy praise.

48 Blessed be the LORD, the God of
Israel,
from everlasting to everlasting!
And let all the people say, "Amen!"
Praise the LORD!

BOOK V

107 O give thanks to the LORD, for
he is good;
for his steadfast love endures for
ever!
2 Let the redeemed of the LORD say so,
whom he has redeemed from
trouble
3 and gathered in from the lands,
from the east and from the west,
from the north and from the south.

4 Some wandered in desert wastes,
finding no way to a city to dwell in;
5 hungry and thirsty,
their soul fainted within them.
6 Then they cried to the LORD in
their trouble,
and he delivered them from their
distress;
7 he led them by a straight way,
till they reached a city to dwell
in.
8 Let them thank the LORD for his
steadfast love,

the days of the judges (Jg.2.11–19). **47:** Prayer that Israel may be delivered in her present distress. *Gather us from among the nations* suggests that the psalm, in its present form at least, dates from after the Babylonian exile. **48:** A doxology (no original part of the psalm) marking the end of Book IV of the Psalter (see 41.13 n.). *Praise the LORD!* has been illogically attached to this verse rather than the preceding verse (see n. at beginning of Ps. 105).
   Ps. 107: A group thanksgiving for pilgrims. This psalm was perhaps sung by groups of pilgrims who came to Jerusalem to celebrate one of the feasts, offering thanks for escape from various dangers. **1–3:** Call for everyone to give thanks. **4–9:** Thanksgiving of those who traveled across the desert. **8–9:** A refrain (see vv. 15–16,21–22,31–32), appropriately varied for each

for his wonderful works to the
sons of men!
⁹ For he satisfies him who is thirsty,
and the hungry he fills with good
things.

¹⁰ Some sat in darkness and in gloom,
prisoners in affliction and in irons,
¹¹ for they had rebelled against the
words of God,
and spurned the counsel of the
Most High.
¹² Their hearts were bowed down with
hard labor;
they fell down, with none to help.
¹³ Then they cried to the LORD in their
trouble,
and he delivered them from their
distress;
¹⁴ he brought them out of darkness
and gloom,
and broke their bonds asunder.
¹⁵ Let them thank the LORD for his
steadfast love,
for his wonderful works to the
sons of men!
¹⁶ For he shatters the doors of bronze,
and cuts in two the bars of iron.

¹⁷ Some were sickˣ through their
sinful ways,
and because of their iniquities
suffered affliction;
¹⁸ they loathed any kind of food,
and they drew near to the gates
of death.
¹⁹ Then they cried to the LORD in
their trouble,
and he delivered them from their
distress;
²⁰ he sent forth his word, and healed
them,
and delivered them from
destruction.
²¹ Let them thank the LORD for his
steadfast love,
for his wonderful works to the
sons of men!

²² And let them offer sacrifices of
thanksgiving,
and tell of his deeds in songs of
joy!

²³ Some went down to the sea in ships,
doing business on the great
waters;
²⁴ they saw the deeds of the LORD,
his wondrous works in the deep.
²⁵ For he commanded, and raised the
stormy wind,
which lifted up the waves of the
sea.
²⁶ They mounted up to heaven, they
went down to the depths;
their courage melted away in
their evil plight;
²⁷ they reeled and staggered like
drunken men,
and were at their wits' end.
²⁸ Then they cried to the LORD in their
trouble,
and he delivered them from their
distress;
²⁹ he made the storm be still,
and the waves of the sea were
hushed.
³⁰ Then they were glad because they
had quiet,
and he brought them to their
desired haven.
³¹ Let them thank the LORD for his
steadfast love,
for his wonderful works to the
sons of men!
³² Let them extol him in the
congregation of the people,
and praise him in the assembly of
the elders.

³³ He turns rivers into a desert,
springs of water into thirsty
ground,
³⁴ a fruitful land into a salty waste,
because of the wickedness of its
inhabitants.

x Cn: Heb *fools*

occasion. **10–16:** Thanksgiving of those who had been freed from prison. **17–22:** Thanksgiving
of those healed from sickness. **22:** *Sacrifices of thanksgiving*, see 7.17 n. **23–32:** Thanksgiving
of those who had traveled by sea. **33–43:** Part of a hymn praising God for his bounty; it was
probably not originally composed to go with the preceding verses, but nevertheless provides a
suitable unison conclusion for the thanksgiving liturgy.

35 He turns a desert into pools of water,
   a parched land into springs of
      water.
36 And there he lets the hungry dwell,
   and they establish a city to live in;
37 they sow fields, and plant vineyards,
   and get a fruitful yield.
38 By his blessing they multiply
      greatly;
   and he does not let their cattle
      decrease.

39 When they are diminished and
      brought low
   through oppression, trouble, and
      sorrow,
40 he pours contempt upon princes
   and makes them wander in
      trackless wastes;
41 but he raises up the needy out of
      affliction,
   and makes their families like
      flocks.
42 The upright see it and are glad;
   and all wickedness stops its
      mouth.
43 Whoever is wise, let him give heed
   to these things;
   let men consider the steadfast
      love of the LORD.

A Song. A Psalm of David.

108 My heart is steadfast, O God,
      my heart is steadfast!
   I will sing and make melody!
   Awake, my soul!
2 Awake, O harp and lyre!
   I will awake the dawn!
3 I will give thanks to thee, O LORD,
      among the peoples,
   I will sing praises to thee among
      the nations.
4 For thy steadfast love is great above
      the heavens,

thy faithfulness reaches to the
   clouds.

5 Be exalted, O God, above the
   heavens!
   Let thy glory be over all the
      earth!
6 That thy beloved may be delivered,
   give help by thy right hand, and
      answer me!

7 God has promised in his sanctuary:*y*
   "With exultation I will divide up
      Shechem,
   and portion out the Vale of
      Succoth.
8 Gilead is mine; Manas'seh is mine;
   E'phraim is my helmet;
   Judah my scepter.
9 Moab is my washbasin;
   upon Edom I cast my shoe;
   over Philistia I shout in triumph."

10 Who will bring me to the fortified
      city?
   Who will lead me to Edom?
11 Hast thou not rejected us, O God?
   Thou dost not go forth, O God,
      with our armies.
12 O grant us help against the foe,
   for vain is the help of man!
13 With God we shall do valiantly;
   it is he who will tread down our
      foes.

To the choirmaster. A Psalm of David.

109 Be not silent, O God of my
      praise!
2 For wicked and deceitful mouths
   are opened against me,
   speaking against me with lying
      tongues.
3 They beset me with words of hate,
   and attack me without cause.

y Or *by his holiness*

Ps. 108: A liturgy of prayer for victory over national enemies. This liturgy is entirely composed of portions of two other psalms. Verses 1–5 are practically identical with 57.7–11; vv. 6–13, with 60.5–12. For details of interpretation see those psalms.

Ps. 109: Prayer for deliverance from personal enemies (a lament). **1**: Cry for help. **2–5**: The psalmist's situation. He has been cursed and falsely accused of crime (compare vv. 22–25).

⁴ In return for my love they accuse
　　me,
　　even as I make prayer for them.*z*
⁵ So they reward me evil for good,
　　and hatred for my love.

⁶ Appoint a wicked man against him;
　　let an accuser bring him to trial.*a*
⁷ When he is tried, let him come forth
　　guilty;
　　let his prayer be counted as sin!
⁸ May his days be few;
　　may another seize his goods!
⁹ May his children be fatherless,
　　and his wife a widow!
¹⁰ May his children wander about
　　and beg;
　　may they be driven out of*b* the
　　ruins they inhabit!
¹¹ May the creditor seize all that he
　　has;
　　may strangers plunder the fruits
　　of his toil!
¹² Let there be none to extend
　　kindness to him,
　　nor any to pity his fatherless
　　children!
¹³ May his posterity be cut off;
　　may his name be blotted out in
　　the second generation!
¹⁴ May the iniquity of his fathers be
　　remembered before the Lord,
　　and let not the sin of his mother
　　be blotted out!
¹⁵ Let them be before the Lord
　　continually;
　　and may his*c* memory be cut
　　off from the earth!
¹⁶ For he did not remember to show
　　kindness,
　　but pursued the poor and needy
　　and the brokenhearted to their
　　death.
¹⁷ He loved to curse; let curses come
　　on him!
　　He did not like blessing; may it
　　be far from him!

¹⁸ He clothed himself with cursing as
　　his coat,
　　may it soak into his body like
　　water,
　　like oil into his bones!
¹⁹ May it be like a garment which he
　　wraps round him,
　　like a belt with which he daily
　　girds himself!

²⁰ May this be the reward of my
　　accusers from the Lord,
　　of those who speak evil against
　　my life!
²¹ But thou, O God my Lord,
　　deal on my behalf for thy name's
　　sake;
　　because thy steadfast love is
　　good, deliver me!
²² For I am poor and needy,
　　and my heart is stricken within
　　me.
²³ I am gone, like a shadow at evening;
　　I am shaken off like a locust.
²⁴ My knees are weak through fasting;
　　my body has become gaunt.
²⁵ I am an object of scorn to my
　　accusers;
　　when they see me, they wag their
　　heads.

²⁶ Help me, O Lord my God!
　　Save me according to thy
　　steadfast love!
²⁷ Let them know that this is thy hand;
　　thou, O Lord, hast done it!
²⁸ Let them curse, but do thou bless!
　　Let my assailants be put to
　　shame;*d* may thy servant be
　　glad!
²⁹ May my accusers be clothed with
　　dishonor;
　　may they be wrapped in their
　　own shame as in a mantle!

z Syr: Heb *I prayer*
a Heb *stand at his right hand*
b Gk: Heb *and seek*
c Gk: Heb *their*
d Gk: Heb *they have arisen and have been put to shame*

4–5: In view of the temper of vv. 6–19, it is important to note that he believed love for others to
be the proper attitude and was accustomed to pray for them. **6–19:** The curse. It is clear that the
purpose of the violent and repellent language of this section is to provide a counter-curse which
will be effective against the black-magic curses of the psalmist's enemies (note vv. 17–19).
Compare Ps. 58. **8:** The second line is quoted in Acts 1.20, though translated differently. **20–29:**
Prayer for deliverance. The poet does not share the popular, primitive belief that his curse

³⁰ With my mouth I will give great
    thanks to the LORD;
  I will praise him in the midst of
    the throng.
³¹ For he stands at the right hand of
    the needy,
  to save him from those who
    condemn him to death.

A Psalm of David.

110 The LORD says to my lord:
      "Sit at my right hand,
  till I make your enemies your
    footstool."

² The LORD sends forth from Zion
    your mighty scepter.
  Rule in the midst of your foes!
³ Your people will offer themselves
    freely
  on the day you lead your host
    upon the holy mountains.ᵉ
  From the womb of the morning
  like dew your youthᶠ will come
    to you.
⁴ The LORD has sworn
  and will not change his mind,
  "You are a priest for ever
    after the order of Melchiz′edek."

⁵ The Lord is at your right hand;
  he will shatter kings on the day
    of his wrath.
⁶ He will execute judgment among
    the nations,

filling them with corpses;
  he will shatter chiefsᵍ
    over the wide earth.
⁷ He will drink from the brook by
    the way;
  therefore he will lift up his head.

111 Praise the LORD.
      I will give thanks to the LORD
    with my whole heart,
  in the company of the upright, in
    the congregation.
² Great are the works of the LORD,
    studied by all who have pleasure
    in them.
³ Full of honor and majesty is his
    work,
  and his righteousness endures for
    ever.
⁴ He has caused his wonderful works
    to be remembered;
  the LORD is gracious and merciful.
⁵ He provides food for those who
    fear him;
  he is ever mindful of his
    covenant.
⁶ He has shown his people the power
    of his works,
  in giving them the heritage of the
    nations.
⁷ The works of his hands are faithful
    and just;
  all his precepts are trustworthy,
⁸ they are established for ever and
    ever,

e Another reading is *in holy array*
f Cn: Heb *the dew of your youth*
g Or *the head*

would be automatically efficacious apart from the personal intervention of God. **30–31:** His
vow (see 7.17 n.).
  Ps. 110: The LORD promises victory to his king (a royal psalm, probably composed for a
coronation; compare Ps. 2). The Hebrew text is unusually corrupt and the interpretation of many
details extremely difficult. **1:** The king (*my lord*) is invited by Israel's God (*the LORD*) to ascend
the throne. This verse is quoted frequently in the New Testament (e.g. Mt.22.44; Acts 2.34;
1 Cor.15.25; Eph.1.20; Heb.1.3,13), where the later Jewish belief that it was composed by
David in honor of the Messiah is naturally assumed to be correct. **2–7:** The new king, who also
bears the dignity of priesthood, will thoroughly defeat his enemies. **3:** The meaning of the
second sentence can no longer be recovered with certainty. **4:** Like all early Israelite kings, the
new king will have the privileges of a priest (compare 2 Sam.8.18; 1 Kg.3.4). In this respect he
will be like Melchizedek, the ancient Canaanite priest-king of Jerusalem (Gen.14.18). **7:** The
meaning is not clear. The verse may be only a fragment.
  Ps. 111: Hymn of praise to the LORD for his great deeds, especially for his fidelity to the
covenant. An acrostic psalm, every line beginning with a successive letter of the alphabet. **1:**
Like the two following psalms, it begins with the ritual cry, *Praise the LORD!* (Hallelujah!); see
104.35 n. **10:** Job 28.28; Pr.1.7.

to be performed with faithfulness
and uprightness.
9 He sent redemption to his people;
he has commanded his covenant
for ever.
Holy and terrible is his name!
10 The fear of the LORD is the
beginning of wisdom;
a good understanding have all
those who practice it.
His praise endures for ever!

112 Praise the LORD.
Blessed is the man who fears
the LORD,
who greatly delights in his
commandments!
2 His descendants will be mighty in
the land;
the generation of the upright will
be blessed.
3 Wealth and riches are in his house;
and his righteousness endures for
ever.
4 Light rises in the darkness for the
upright;
the LORD[h] is gracious, merciful,
and righteous.
5 It is well with the man who deals
generously and lends,
who conducts his affairs with
justice.
6 For the righteous will never be
moved;
he will be remembered for ever.
7 He is not afraid of evil tidings;
his heart is firm, trusting in the
LORD.
8 His heart is steady, he will not be
afraid,
until he sees his desire on his
adversaries.

9 He has distributed freely, he has
given to the poor;
his righteousness endures for
ever;
his horn is exalted in honor.
10 The wicked man sees it and is
angry;
he gnashes his teeth and melts
away;
the desire of the wicked man
comes to nought.

113 Praise the LORD!
Praise, O servants of the LORD,
praise the name of the LORD!

2 Blessed be the name of the LORD
from this time forth and for
evermore!
3 From the rising of the sun to its
setting
the name of the LORD is to be
praised!
4 The LORD is high above all nations,
and his glory above the heavens!

5 Who is like the LORD our God,
who is seated on high,
6 who looks far down
upon the heavens and the earth?
7 He raises the poor from the dust,
and lifts the needy from the ash
heap,
8 to make them sit with princes,
with the princes of his people.
9 He gives the barren woman a home,
making her the joyous mother of
children.
Praise the LORD!

114 When Israel went forth from
Egypt,

h Gk: Heb lacks *the* LORD

Ps. 112: The contrasting fate of the righteous and the wicked (a wisdom psalm). An acrostic like Ps. 111, and similar in theme to Ps. 1. It is, however, more concerned with the rewards of righteousness (vv. 1–9) than the punishment of ungodliness (v. 10). **1:** *Praise the LORD,* see 111.1 n. *Blessed,* see 1.1 n. **9:** Quoted in part in 2 Cor.9.9. *Horn,* see 75.4–5 n.

Ps. 113: Hymn celebrating the LORD as helper of the humble. Another "Hallelujah!" psalm (see 111.1 n.). In Jewish liturgical tradition, Pss. 113–118 constitute the so-called "Egyptian Hallel," used in connection with the great festivals. At the Passover, Pss. 113–114 are sung before the meal; 115–118 afterwards (compare Mt.26.30). **1:** Summons to worship. **2–4:** Choral response. **5–9:** Though the LORD is gloriously exalted, he cares for the needy (1 Sam.2.4–8; Lk.1.48–53).

Ps. 114: Hymn in praise of God's great work in creating the nation. Although its form is unusual, vv. 7–8 show this psalm should be classified as a hymn (see Ps. 113 n.). **1–2:** The events

the house of Jacob from a people
of strange language,
2 Judah became his sanctuary,
Israel his dominion.

3 The sea looked and fled,
Jordan turned back.
4 The mountains skipped like rams,
the hills like lambs.

5 What ails you, O sea, that you flee?
O Jordan, that you turn back?
6 O mountains, that you skip like
rams?
O hills, like lambs?

7 Tremble, O earth, at the presence
of the Lord,
at the presence of the God of
Jacob,
8 who turns the rock into a pool of
water,
the flint into a spring of water.

115 Not to us, O Lord, not to us,
but to thy name give glory,
for the sake of thy steadfast love
and thy faithfulness!
2 Why should the nations say,
"Where is their God?"

3 Our God is in the heavens;
he does whatever he pleases.
4 Their idols are silver and gold,
the work of men's hands.
5 They have mouths, but do not
speak;
eyes, but do not see.
6 They have ears, but do not hear;
noses, but do not smell.
7 They have hands, but do not feel;
feet, but do not walk;

and they do not make a sound in
their throat.
8 Those who make them are like
them;
so are all who trust in them.

9 O Israel, trust in the Lord!
He is their help and their shield.
10 O house of Aaron, put your trust in
the Lord!
He is their help and their shield.
11 You who fear the Lord, trust in
the Lord!
He is their help and their shield.

12 The Lord has been mindful of us;
he will bless us;
he will bless the house of Israel;
he will bless the house of Aaron;
13 he will bless those who fear the
Lord,
both small and great.

14 May the Lord give you increase,
you and your children!
15 May you be blessed by the Lord,
who made heaven and earth!

16 The heavens are the Lord's heavens,
but the earth he has given to the
sons of men.
17 The dead do not praise the Lord,
nor do any that go down into
silence.
18 But we will bless the Lord
from this time forth and for
evermore.
Praise the Lord!

116 I love the Lord, because he
has heard
my voice and my supplications.

of the Exodus recalled. **3–6:** The remarkable natural phenomena which accompanied Israel's crossing of the Red Sea and the Jordan. The past events of vv. 3–4 become contemporary in vv. 5–6. **7–8:** The physical world summoned to worship the Lord. *Who turns the rock into a pool*, Ex.17.6; Num.20.11.
    Ps. 115: Liturgy contrasting the Lord's power with the impotence of heathen gods. Perhaps sung antiphonally as follows: **1–2:** A choir ascribes glory to God alone. **3–8:** A soloist proclaims that God is omnipotent; idols have no life at all. **9–11:** The choir therefore asks Israel to trust in the Lord. **10:** *House of Aaron*, the priests. **12–13:** The congregation confidently responds. **14–15:** A priest pronounces a blessing. **16–18:** Concluding hymn of praise. **17:** In early Israel it was believed that the dead in Sheol (*silence*) were separated from God (88.5–6). **18:** *Praise the Lord!* Hallelujah! (see Ps. 113 n.).
    Ps. 116: Thanksgiving for healing. 1–2: Address to the congregation. **3–11:** The psalmist's

2 Because he inclined his ear to me,
  therefore I will call on him as
  long as I live.
3 The snares of death encompassed
  me;
  the pangs of Sheol laid hold on
  me;
  I suffered distress and anguish.
4 Then I called on the name of the
  LORD:
  "O LORD, I beseech thee, save
  my life!"

5 Gracious is the LORD, and
  righteous;
  our God is merciful.
6 The LORD preserves the simple;
  when I was brought low, he saved
  me.
7 Return, O my soul, to your rest;
  for the LORD has dealt
  bountifully with you.

8 For thou hast delivered my soul
  from death,
  my eyes from tears,
  my feet from stumbling;
9 I walk before the LORD
  in the land of the living.
10 I kept my faith, even when I said,
  "I am greatly afflicted";
11 I said in my consternation,
  "Men are all a vain hope."

12 What shall I render to the LORD
  for all his bounty to me?
13 I will lift up the cup of salvation
  and call on the name of the LORD,
14 I will pay my vows to the LORD
  in the presence of all his people.

15 Precious in the sight of the LORD
  is the death of his saints.
16 O LORD, I am thy servant;
  I am thy servant, the son of thy
  handmaid.
  Thou hast loosed my bonds.
17 I will offer to thee the sacrifice of
  thanksgiving
  and call on the name of the LORD.
18 I will pay my vows to the LORD
  in the presence of all his people,
19 in the courts of the house of the
  LORD,
  in your midst, O Jerusalem.
  Praise the LORD!

117 Praise the LORD, all nations!
  Extol him, all peoples!
2 For great is his steadfast love
  toward us;
  and the faithfulness of the LORD
  endures for ever.
  Praise the LORD!

118 O give thanks to the LORD, for
  he is good;
  his steadfast love endures for
  ever!

2 Let Israel say,
  "His steadfast love endures for
  ever."
3 Let the house of Aaron say,
  "His steadfast love endures for
  ever."
4 Let those who fear the LORD say,
  "His steadfast love endures for
  ever."

5 Out of my distress I called on the
  LORD;

experience (see 18.4–6 n.). **3:** His illness. *Sheol*, see 6.5 n. **5–8:** Strong emotion leads the psalmist to address God directly in describing the answer to his prayer (v. 8). **9:** Now he has recovered. **10–11:** Even when most profoundly depressed, he had trusted in God rather than men. **12–19:** The fulfilment of his vow (see 7.17 n.). **13:** He offers a libation (Ex.29.40). **15:** *Precious . . . is the death* means that such a death is rarely allowed to happen. *Saints*, see 30.4 n. **16:** See 86.16 n. **19:** *Praise the LORD!* Hallelujah! (see Ps. 113 n.).

Ps. 117: Doxology. 1. *Praise the LORD!* Hallelujah! (see Ps. 113 n.). **2:** *Praise the LORD!* properly belongs to the following psalm.

Ps. 118: Thanksgiving for deliverance in battle. The last of the "Egyptian Hallel" psalms (see Ps. 113 n.). While it is difficult to be sure whether the language of vv. 10–14 is literal or figurative, it is tenable that the speaker is a king who has come to the temple to offer thanks for a victory. **1–4:** Summons to thanksgiving. **2–4:** *Let Israel say*, etc. These are probably actual directions to various groups in the congregation. **3:** *House of Aaron*, see 115.10 n. **5–18:** The

[747]

the LORD answered me and set
me free.
6 With the LORD on my side I do not
fear.
What can man do to me?
7 The LORD is on my side to help me;
I shall look in triumph on those
who hate me.
8 It is better to take refuge in the LORD
than to put confidence in man.
9 It is better to take refuge in the LORD
than to put confidence in princes.

10 All nations surrounded me;
in the name of the LORD I cut
them off!
11 They surrounded me, surrounded
me on every side;
in the name of the LORD I cut
them off!
12 They surrounded me like bees,
they blazed*i* like a fire of thorns;
in the name of the LORD I cut
them off!
13 I was pushed hard,*j* so that I was
falling,
but the LORD helped me.
14 The LORD is my strength and my
song;
he has become my salvation.

15 Hark, glad songs of victory
in the tents of the righteous:
"The right hand of the LORD does
valiantly,
16   the right hand of the LORD is
exalted,
the right hand of the LORD does
valiantly!"
17 I shall not die, but I shall live,
and recount the deeds of the
LORD.

18 The LORD has chastened me sorely,
but he has not given me over to
death.

19 Open to me the gates of
righteousness,
that I may enter through them
and give thanks to the LORD.

20 This is the gate of the LORD;
the righteous shall enter through
it.

21 I thank thee that thou hast
answered me
and hast become my salvation.
22 The stone which the builders
rejected
has become the head of the
corner.
23 This is the LORD's doing;
it is marvelous in our eyes.
24 This is the day which the LORD has
made;
let us rejoice and be glad in it.
25 Save us, we beseech thee, O LORD!
O LORD, we beseech thee, give
us success!

26 Blessed be he who enters in the name
of the LORD!
We bless you from the house of
the LORD
27 The LORD is God,
and he has given us light.
Bind the festal procession with
branches,
up to the horns of the altar!

28 Thou art my God, and I will give
thanks to thee;

i Gk: Heb *were extinguished*
j Gk Syr Jerome: Heb *thou didst push me hard*

---

psalmist's experience (see 18.4–6 n.). **6:** Quoted in Heb.13.6. **10–13:** The desperateness of his situation. **14–18:** God gave him the victory. **19:** He asks to be admitted at the temple gates. The preceding ceremony evidently took place outside. **20:** A voice from within replies that only the qualified may enter (compare Ps. 15 and 24.3–6). **21–22:** He answers that God had borne witness to his character by delivering him (18.20–24) when others had given him up. **22–23:** Frequently quoted in the New Testament (e.g. Mt.21.42; Acts 4.11; 1 Pet.2.7). **23–25:** The choir joyously acknowledges what God has done. **25:** *Save us*, in Hebrew, is "Hoshianna" (Hosanna). This verse and the following are alluded to in Mt.21.9 and parallel passages. **26–27:** The suppliant is admitted with a choral blessing. (The second sentence of v. 27 is perhaps a liturgical direction.) **28:** He makes his act of thanksgiving. **29:** The choir begins a hymn of praise (compare Ps. 136).

thou art my God, I will extol thee.

²⁹ O give thanks to the LORD, for he
is good;
for his steadfast love endures for
ever!

119 Blessed are those whose way is
blameless,
who walk in the law of the LORD!
² Blessed are those who keep his
testimonies,
who seek him with their whole
heart,
³ who also do no wrong,
but walk in his ways!
⁴ Thou hast commanded thy precepts
to be kept diligently.
⁵ O that my ways may be steadfast
in keeping thy statutes!
⁶ Then I shall not be put to shame,
having my eyes fixed on all thy
commandments.
⁷ I will praise thee with an upright
heart,
when I learn thy righteous
ordinances.
⁸ I will observe thy statutes;
O forsake me not utterly!

⁹ How can a young man keep his way
pure?
By guarding it according to thy
word.
¹⁰ With my whole heart I seek thee;
let me not wander from thy
commandments!
¹¹ I have laid up thy word in my heart,
that I might not sin against thee.
¹² Blessed be thou, O LORD;
teach me thy statutes!
¹³ With my lips I declare
all the ordinances of thy mouth.

¹⁴ In the way of thy testimonies I
delight
as much as in all riches.
¹⁵ I will meditate on thy precepts,
and fix my eyes on thy ways.
¹⁶ I will delight in thy statutes;
I will not forget thy word.

¹⁷ Deal bountifully with thy servant,
that I may live and observe thy
word.
¹⁸ Open my eyes, that I may behold
wondrous things out of thy law.
¹⁹ I am a sojourner on earth;
hide not thy commandments
from me!
²⁰ My soul is consumed with longing
for thy ordinances at all times.
²¹ Thou dost rebuke the insolent,
accursed ones,
who wander from thy
commandments;
²² take away from me their scorn and
contempt,
for I have kept thy testimonies.
²³ Even though princes sit plotting
against me,
thy servant will meditate on thy
statutes.
²⁴ Thy testimonies are my delight,
they are my counselors.

²⁵ My soul cleaves to the dust;
revive me according to thy word!
²⁶ When I told of my ways, thou didst
answer me;
teach me thy statutes!
²⁷ Make me understand the way of
thy precepts,
and I will meditate on thy
wondrous works.
²⁸ My soul melts away for sorrow;
strengthen me according to thy
word!

Ps. 119: Meditation on the law of God. The length of this psalm is the result of its unusual, and highly artificial, structure. It is an alphabetical acrostic (compare Pss. 9–10; 25; 34; 37; 111; 112; 145) in which each stanza consists of eight lines all beginning with the same Hebrew letter. In addition almost every line contains the word "law" or a synonym (e.g. "testimonies," "ways," "precepts"; compare Ps.19.7–14). The predominant mood of lament suggests that it may have been composed as a prayer for deliverance from trouble, though the language may be merely imitative and the whole a purely literary exercise in honor of the written law. It is a very late composition. **1–8,9–16:** Prayer for help in observing the law. **1:** *Blessed*, see 1.1 n. **17–24:** Prayer for deliverance from enemies. **25–32:** Declaration of fidelity to the law. **33–40:** Prayer

29 Put false ways far from me;
    and graciously teach me thy law!
30 I have chosen the way of
    faithfulness,
    I set thy ordinances before me.
31 I cleave to thy testimonies,
    O LORD;
    let me not be put to shame!
32 I will run in the way of thy
    commandments
    when thou enlargest my
    understanding!

33 Teach me, O LORD, the way of thy
    statutes;
    and I will keep it to the end.
34 Give me understanding, that I may
    keep thy law
    and observe it with my whole
    heart.
35 Lead me in the path of thy
    commandments,
    for I delight in it.
36 Incline my heart to thy testimonies,
    and not to gain!
37 Turn my eyes from looking at
    vanities;
    and give me life in thy ways.
38 Confirm to thy servant thy promise,
    which is for those who fear thee.
39 Turn away the reproach which I
    dread;
    for thy ordinances are good.
40 Behold, I long for thy precepts;
    in thy righteousness give me life!

41 Let thy steadfast love come to me,
    O LORD,
    thy salvation according to thy
    promise;
42 then shall I have an answer for those
    who taunt me,
    for I trust in thy word.
43 And take not the word of truth
    utterly out of my mouth,
    for my hope is in thy ordinances.
44 I will keep thy law continually,
    for ever and ever;
45 and I shall walk at liberty,
    for I have sought thy precepts.

46 I will also speak of thy testimonies
    before kings,
    and shall not be put to shame;
47 for I find my delight in thy
    commandments,
    which I love.
48 I revere thy commandments, which
    I love,
    and I will meditate on thy statutes.

49 Remember thy word to thy servant,
    in which thou hast made me hope.
50 This is my comfort in my affliction
    that thy promise gives me life.
51 Godless men utterly deride me,
    but I do not turn away from thy
    law.
52 When I think of thy ordinances
    from of old,
    I take comfort, O LORD.
53 Hot indignation seizes me because
    of the wicked,
    who forsake thy law.
54 Thy statutes have been my songs
    in the house of my pilgrimage.
55 I remember thy name in the night,
    O LORD,
    and keep thy law.
56 This blessing has fallen to me,
    that I have kept thy precepts.

57 The LORD is my portion;
    I promise to keep thy words.
58 I entreat thy favor with all my
    heart;
    be gracious to me according to thy
    promise.
59 When I think of thy ways,
    I turn my feet to thy testimonies;
60 I hasten and do not delay
    to keep thy commandments.
61 Though the cords of the wicked
    ensnare me,
    I do not forget thy law.
62 At midnight I rise to praise thee,
    because of thy righteous
    ordinances.
63 I am a companion of all who fear
    thee,
    of those who keep thy precepts.

to understand the law. **41–48**: Prayer for an answer to taunters. **49–56**: Expression of confidence during persecution. **57–64**: Declaration of devotion to God. **65–72**: Recognition of the

⁶⁴ The earth, O LORD, is full of thy
steadfast love;
  teach me thy statutes!

⁶⁵ Thou hast dealt well with thy
servant,
  O LORD, according to thy word.
⁶⁶ Teach me good judgment and
knowledge,
  for I believe in thy
  commandments.
⁶⁷ Before I was afflicted I went astray;
  but now I keep thy word.
⁶⁸ Thou art good and doest good;
  teach me thy statutes.
⁶⁹ The godless besmear me with lies,
  but with my whole heart I keep
  thy precepts;
⁷⁰ their heart is gross like fat,
  but I delight in thy law.
⁷¹ It is good for me that I was afflicted,
  that I might learn thy statutes.
⁷² The law of thy mouth is better to
me
  than thousands of gold and silver
  pieces.

⁷³ Thy hands have made and fashioned
me;
  give me understanding that I
  may learn thy commandments.
⁷⁴ Those who fear thee shall see me
and rejoice,
  because I have hoped in thy
  word.
⁷⁵ I know, O LORD, that thy
judgments are right,
  and that in faithfulness thou hast
  afflicted me.
⁷⁶ Let thy steadfast love be ready to
comfort me
  according to thy promise to thy
  servant.
⁷⁷ Let thy mercy come to me, that I
may live;
  for thy law is my delight.
⁷⁸ Let the godless be put to shame,
  because they have subverted me
  with guile;
  as for me, I will meditate on thy
  precepts.

⁷⁹ Let those who fear thee turn to me,
  that they may know thy
  testimonies.
⁸⁰ May my heart be blameless in thy
statutes,
  that I may not be put to shame!

⁸¹ My soul languishes for thy salvation;
  I hope in thy word.
⁸² My eyes fail with watching for thy
promise;
  I ask, "When wilt thou comfort
  me?"
⁸³ For I have become like a wineskin
in the smoke,
  yet I have not forgotten thy
  statutes.
⁸⁴ How long must thy servant endure?
  When wilt thou judge those who
  persecute me?
⁸⁵ Godless men have dug pitfalls for
me,
  men who do not conform to thy
  law.
⁸⁶ All thy commandments are sure;
  they persecute me with falsehood;
  help me!
⁸⁷ They have almost made an end of
me on earth;
  but I have not forsaken thy
  precepts.
⁸⁸ In thy steadfast love spare my life,
  that I may keep the testimonies
  of thy mouth.

⁸⁹ For ever, O LORD, thy word
  is firmly fixed in the heavens.
⁹⁰ Thy faithfulness endures to all
generations;
  thou hast established the earth,
  and it stands fast.
⁹¹ By thy appointment they stand this
day;
  for all things are thy servants.
⁹² If thy law had not been my delight,
  I should have perished in my
  affliction.
⁹³ I will never forget thy precepts;
  for by them thou hast given me
  life.
⁹⁴ I am thine, save me;

disciplinary value of suffering. **73–80**: Acknowledgment of the justice of God's ways, and prayer for help. **81–88**: Plea for deliverance from enemies. **89–96**: Faith in God's word. **97–104**:

for I have sought thy precepts.
⁹⁵ The wicked lie in wait to destroy me;
  but I consider thy testimonies.
⁹⁶ I have seen a limit to all perfection,
  but thy commandment is
    exceedingly broad.

⁹⁷ Oh, how I love thy law!
  It is my meditation all the day.
⁹⁸ Thy commandment makes me wiser
    than my enemies,
  for it is ever with me.
⁹⁹ I have more understanding than all
    my teachers,
  for thy testimonies are my
    meditation.
¹⁰⁰ I understand more than the aged,
  for I keep thy precepts.
¹⁰¹ I hold back my feet from every
    evil way,
  in order to keep thy word.
¹⁰² I do not turn aside from thy
    ordinances,
  for thou hast taught me.
¹⁰³ How sweet are thy words to my
    taste,
  sweeter than honey to my mouth!
¹⁰⁴ Through thy precepts I get
    understanding;
  therefore I hate every false way.

¹⁰⁵ Thy word is a lamp to my feet
  and a light to my path.
¹⁰⁶ I have sworn an oath and
    confirmed it,
  to observe thy righteous
    ordinances.
¹⁰⁷ I am sorely afflicted;
  give me life, O LORD, according
    to thy word!
¹⁰⁸ Accept my offerings of praise, O
    LORD,
  and teach me thy ordinances.
¹⁰⁹ I hold my life in my hand
    continually,
  but I do not forget thy law.
¹¹⁰ The wicked have laid a snare for me,
  but I do not stray from thy
    precepts.
¹¹¹ Thy testimonies are my heritage
    for ever;

yea, they are the joy of my heart.
¹¹² I incline my heart to perform
    thy statutes
  for ever, to the end.

¹¹³ I hate double-minded men,
  but I love thy law.
¹¹⁴ Thou art my hiding place and my
    shield;
  I hope in thy word.
¹¹⁵ Depart from me, you evildoers,
  that I may keep the
    commandments of my God.
¹¹⁶ Uphold me according to thy
    promise, that I may live,
  and let me not be put to shame in
    my hope!
¹¹⁷ Hold me up, that I may be safe
  and have regard for thy statutes
    continually!
¹¹⁸ Thou dost spurn all who go astray
    from thy statutes;
  yea, their cunning is in vain.
¹¹⁹ All the wicked of the earth thou
    dost count as dross;
  therefore I love thy testimonies.
¹²⁰ My flesh trembles for fear of thee,
  and I am afraid of thy judgments.

¹²¹ I have done what is just and right;
  do not leave me to my oppressors.
¹²² Be surety for thy servant for good;
  let not the godless oppress me.
¹²³ My eyes fail with watching for thy
    salvation,
  and for the fulfilment of thy
    righteous promise.
¹²⁴ Deal with thy servant according to
    thy steadfast love,
  and teach me thy statutes.
¹²⁵ I am thy servant; give me
    understanding,
  that I may know thy testimonies!
¹²⁶ It is time for the LORD to act,
  for thy law has been broken.
¹²⁷ Therefore I love thy
    commandments
  above gold, above fine gold.
¹²⁸ Therefore I direct my steps by all
    thy precepts;[k]

k Gk Jerome: Heb uncertain

The beauty and sweetness of the law. **105–112:** Prayer for help. **113–120:** Expression of confidence and prayers for deliverance. **121–128:** Declaration of juridical innocence and loyalty

I hate every false way.

129 Thy testimonies are wonderful;
therefore my soul keeps them.
130 The unfolding of thy words gives
light;
it imparts understanding to the
simple.
131 With open mouth I pant,
because I long for thy
commandments.
132 Turn to me and be gracious to me,
as is thy wont toward those who
love thy name.
133 Keep steady my steps according to
thy promise,
and let no iniquity get dominion
over me.
134 Redeem me from man's
oppression,
that I may keep thy precepts.
135 Make thy face shine upon thy
servant,
and teach me thy statutes.
136 My eyes shed streams of tears,
because men do not keep thy law.

137 Righteous art thou, O LORD,
and right are thy judgments.
138 Thou hast appointed thy
testimonies in righteousness
and in all faithfulness.
139 My zeal consumes me,
because my foes forget thy words.
140 Thy promise is well tried,
and thy servant loves it.
141 I am small and despised,
yet I do not forget thy precepts.
142 Thy righteousness is righteous for
ever,
and thy law is true.
143 Trouble and anguish have come
upon me,
but thy commandments are my
delight.
144 Thy testimonies are righteous for
ever;
give me understanding that I may
live.

145 With my whole heart I cry; answer
me, O LORD!
I will keep thy statutes.
146 I cry to thee; save me,
that I may observe thy
testimonies.
147 I rise before dawn and cry for help;
I hope in thy words.
148 My eyes are awake before the
watches of the night,
that I may meditate upon thy
promise.
149 Hear my voice in thy steadfast
love;
O LORD, in thy justice preserve
my life.
150 They draw near who persecute me
with evil purpose;
they are far from thy law.
151 But thou art near, O LORD,
and all thy commandments are
true.
152 Long have I known from thy
testimonies
that thou hast founded them for
ever.

153 Look on my affliction and deliver
me,
for I do not forget thy law.
154 Plead my cause and redeem me;
give me life according to thy
promise!
155 Salvation is far from the wicked,
for they do not seek thy statutes.
156 Great is thy mercy, O LORD;
give me life according to thy
justice.
157 Many are my persecutors and my
adversaries,
but I do not swerve from thy
testimonies.
158 I look at the faithless with disgust,
because they do not keep thy
commands.
159 Consider how I love thy precepts!
Preserve my life according to thy
steadfast love.
160 The sum of thy word is truth;

---

to the law. **129–136:** Praise of the law and prayer for deliverance from enemies. **137–144:**
Acknowledgment of God's justice. **145–152:** Passionate cry to be saved from persecution.
153–160: Prayer for the preservation of the psalmist's life.

and every one of thy righteous
  ordinances endures for ever.

161 Princes persecute me without cause,
  but my heart stands in awe of thy
    words.
162 I rejoice at thy word
  like one who finds great spoil.
163 I hate and abhor falsehood,
  but I love thy law.
164 Seven times a day I praise thee
  for thy righteous ordinances.
165 Great peace have those who love
    thy law;
  nothing can make them stumble.
166 I hope for thy salvation, O LORD,
  and I do thy commandments.
167 My soul keeps thy testimonies;
  I love them exceedingly.
168 I keep thy precepts and testimonies,
  for all my ways are before thee.

169 Let my cry come before thee, O
    LORD;
  give me understanding
    according to thy word!
170 Let my supplication come before
    thee;
  deliver me according to thy word.
171 My lips will pour forth praise
  that thou dost teach me thy
    statutes.
172 My tongue will sing of thy word,
  for all thy commandments are
    right.
173 Let thy hand be ready to help me,
  for I have chosen thy precepts.
174 I long for thy salvation, O LORD,
  and thy law is my delight.
175 Let me live, that I may praise thee,
  and let thy ordinances help me.
176 I have gone astray like a lost sheep;
    seek thy servant,
  for I do not forget thy
    commandments.

A Song of Ascents.

120 In my distress I cry to the
      LORD,
  that he may answer me:
2 "Deliver me, O LORD,
  from lying lips,
  from a deceitful tongue."

3 What shall be given to you?
  And what more shall be done to
    you,
  you deceitful tongue?
4 A warrior's sharp arrows,
  with glowing coals of the broom
    tree!

5 Woe is me, that I sojourn in
    Meshech,
  that I dwell among the tents of
    Kedar!
6 Too long have I had my dwelling
  among those who hate peace.
7 I am for peace;
  but when I speak,
  they are for war!

A Song of Ascents.

121 I lift up my eyes to the hills.
      From whence does my help
    come?
2 My help comes from the LORD,
  who made heaven and earth.

3 He will not let your foot be moved,
  he who keeps you will not slumber.
4 Behold, he who keeps Israel
  will neither slumber nor sleep.

5 The LORD is your keeper;
  the LORD is your shade
  on your right hand.

161-168: His piety contrasted with the unjust actions of his persecutors. 169-176: If delivered,
he vows to sing the praise of God's law.
  Ps. 120: An exile's prayer for deliverance from enemies (a lament). **4:** *The broom tree* produces
a specially hot, long-burning fire. **5:** *Meshech . . . Kedar*, remote regions in Asia Minor and
north Arabia. The psalmist lives in such a place, far from his native soil.
  Ps. 121: A liturgy of blessing. 1: The psalmist asks a rhetorical question. *The hills* may be
the "high places" where the baals, the local fertility gods, were worshiped (2 Kg.23.5). **2-8:** A
priest answers and pronounces a blessing. **2:** Probably *my* should be emended to "your"
(compare v. 3).

⁶ The sun shall not smite you by day,
　nor the moon by night.

⁷ The LORD will keep you from all
　evil;
　he will keep your life.
⁸ The LORD will keep
　your going out and your coming in
　from this time forth and for
　evermore.

A Song of Ascents. Of David.

122 I was glad when they said to
me,
"Let us go to the house of the
LORD!"
² Our feet have been standing
within your gates, O Jerusalem!

³ Jerusalem, built as a city
which is bound firmly together,
⁴ to which the tribes go up,
the tribes of the LORD,
as was decreed for Israel,
to give thanks to the name of the
LORD.
⁵ There thrones for judgment were set,
the thrones of the house of David.

⁶ Pray for the peace of Jerusalem!
"May they prosper who love you!
⁷ Peace be within your walls,
and security within your towers!"
⁸ For my brethren and companions'
sake
I will say, "Peace be within you!"
⁹ For the sake of the house of the
LORD our God,
I will seek your good.

A Song of Ascents.

123 To thee I lift up my eyes,
O thou who art enthroned
in the heavens!

² Behold, as the eyes of servants
look to the hand of their master,
as the eyes of a maid
to the hand of her mistress,
so our eyes look to the LORD our
God,
till he have mercy upon us.

³ Have mercy upon us, O LORD, have
mercy upon us,
for we have had more than enough
of contempt.
⁴ Too long our soul has been sated
with the scorn of those who are at
ease,
the contempt of the proud.

A Song of Ascents. Of David.

124 If it had not been the LORD
who was on our side,
let Israel now say–
² if it had not been the LORD who was
on our side,
when men rose up against us,
³ then they would have swallowed us
up alive,
when their anger was kindled
against us;
⁴ then the flood would have swept us
away,
the torrent would have gone over
us;
⁵ then over us would have gone
the raging waters.

⁶ Blessed be the LORD,
who has not given us
as prey to their teeth!
⁷ We have escaped as a bird
from the snare of the fowlers;
the snare is broken,
and we have escaped!

⁸ Our help is in the name of the LORD,
who made heaven and earth.

Ps. 122: A song praising Zion as the pilgrim's goal. 1–5: Arrived in Jerusalem, a group of pilgrims admire its buildings and the unity it symbolizes. **6–9:** They pray for its continuing prosperity.

Ps. 123: Prayer for deliverance from enemies (a group lament). **1–2:** An act of humble submission to God's will. **3–4:** Prayer for help. The speakers may represent either Israel or some oppressed class or sect within it.

Ps. 124: Thanksgiving for a national deliverance. 4–5: Compare 32.6; 69.1–2,14–15.

A Song of Ascents.

125 Those who trust in the LORD
are like Mount Zion,
which cannot be moved, but abides
for ever.
2 As the mountains are round about
Jerusalem,
so the LORD is round about his
people,
from this time forth and for
evermore.
3 For the scepter of wickedness shall
not rest
upon the land allotted to the
righteous,
lest the righteous put forth
their hands to do wrong.
4 Do good, O LORD, to those who are
good,
and to those who are upright in
their hearts!
5 But those who turn aside upon their
crooked ways
the LORD will lead away with
evildoers!
Peace be in Israel!

A Song of Ascents.

126 When the LORD restored the
fortunes of Zion,[1]
we were like those who dream.
2 Then our mouth was filled with
laughter,
and our tongue with shouts of joy;
then they said among the nations,
"The LORD has done great things
for them."
3 The LORD has done great things for
us;
we are glad.

4 Restore our fortunes, O LORD,
like the watercourses in the Negeb!
5 May those who sow in tears
reap with shouts of joy!
6 He that goes forth weeping,
bearing the seed for sowing,
shall come home with shouts of joy,
bringing his sheaves with him.

A Song of Ascents. Of Solomon.

127 Unless the LORD builds the
house,
those who build it labor in vain.
Unless the LORD watches over the
city,
the watchman stays awake in vain.
2 It is in vain that you rise up early
and go late to rest,
eating the bread of anxious toil;
for[m] he gives to his beloved
sleep.

3 Lo, sons are a heritage from the
LORD,
the fruit of the womb a reward.
4 Like arrows in the hand of a warrior
are the sons of one's youth.
5 Happy is the man who has
his quiver full of them!
He shall not be put to shame
when he speaks with his enemies
in the gate.

A Song of Ascents.

128 Blessed is every one who
fears the LORD,
who walks in his ways!

1 Or *brought back those who returned to Zion*
m Another reading is *so*

Ps. 125: **Prayer for deliverance from national enemies** (a group lament). **1–3:** Expression of confidence. **4–5:** Prayer for help.
Ps. 126: **Prayer for deliverance from national misfortune. 1–3:** The joy inspired by God's favor toward his people in former times. **4–6:** Prayer that it may be granted once again. **4:** *Negeb*, the arid region to the south of Palestine.
Ps. 127: **A safe home and a large family are the LORD'S gift** (a wisdom psalm). **1–2:** Anxiety has no place in the life of the faithful (compare Mt.6.25–34). **3–5:** The gift of many stalwart sons makes a father feel secure.
Ps. 128: **A large and prosperous family is a reward for devotion to the LORD** (a wisdom psalm). **1:** *Blessed*, see 1.1 n.

2 You shall eat the fruit of the labor of
   your hands;
   you shall be happy, and it shall be
   well with you.

3 Your wife will be like a fruitful vine
   within your house;
   your children will be like olive shoots
   around your table.
4 Lo, thus shall the man be blessed
   who fears the LORD.

5 The LORD bless you from Zion!
   May you see the prosperity of
   Jerusalem
   all the days of your life!
6 May you see your children's
   children!
   Peace be upon Israel!

A Song of Ascents.

129 "Sorely have they afflicted me
   from my youth,"
   let Israel now say—
2 "Sorely have they afflicted me from
   my youth,
   yet they have not prevailed against
   me.
3 The plowers plowed upon my back;
   they made long their furrows."
4 The LORD is righteous;
   he has cut the cords of the wicked.
5 May all who hate Zion
   be put to shame and turned
   backward!
6 Let them be like the grass on the
   housetops,
   which withers before it grows up,
7 with which the reaper does not fill
   his hand
   or the binder of sheaves his bosom,
8 while those who pass by do not say,
   "The blessing of the LORD be upon
   you!

We bless you in the name of the
   LORD!"

A Song of Ascents.

130 Out of the depths I cry to thee,
   O LORD!
2 Lord, hear my voice!
   Let thy ears be attentive
   to the voice of my supplications!

3 If thou, O LORD, shouldst mark
   iniquities,
   Lord, who could stand?
4 But there is forgiveness with thee,
   that thou mayest be feared.

5 I wait for the LORD, my soul waits,
   and in his word I hope;
6 my soul waits for the LORD
   more than watchmen for the
   morning,
   more than watchmen for the
   morning.

7 O Israel, hope in the LORD!
   For with the LORD there is
   steadfast love,
   and with him is plenteous
   redemption.
8 And he will redeem Israel
   from all his iniquities.

A Song of Ascents. Of David.

131 O LORD, my heart is not lifted
   up,
   my eyes are not raised too high;
   I do not occupy myself with things
   too great and too marvelous for
   me.
2 But I have calmed and quieted my
   soul,
   like a child quieted at its mother's
   breast;

Ps. 129: Prayer for deliverance from national enemies (a group lament). **1–4:** God has preserved Israel in spite of all her suffering in the past. **5–8:** May her present enemies be destroyed!
   Ps. 130: Prayer for deliverance from personal trouble (a lament). **1–2:** Cry for help. The
psalmist's trouble is described only in general terms. **3–6:** Because it is God's nature to be
merciful, the psalmist eagerly awaits his help. **7–8:** Israel should take the same attitude in her
national difficulties.
   Ps. 131: Act of humble submission to God's will and guidance (a song of trust; see Ps. 11 n.).

like a child that is quieted is my
soul.

³ O Israel, hope in the LORD
from this time forth and for
evermore.

A Song of Ascents.

132 Remember, O LORD, in
David's favor,
all the hardships he endured;
² how he swore to the LORD
and vowed to the Mighty One of
Jacob,
³ "I will not enter my house
or get into my bed;
⁴ I will not give sleep to my eyes
or slumber to my eyelids,
⁵ until I find a place for the LORD,
a dwelling place for the Mighty
One of Jacob."

⁶ Lo, we heard of it in Eph'rathah,
we found it in the fields of Ja'ar.
⁷ "Let us go to his dwelling place;
let us worship at his footstool!"

⁸ Arise, O LORD, and go to thy resting
place,
thou and the ark of thy might.
⁹ Let thy priests be clothed with
righteousness,
and let thy saints shout for joy.
¹⁰ For thy servant David's sake
do not turn away the face of thy
anointed one.

¹¹ The LORD swore to David a sure
oath
from which he will not turn back:

"One of the sons of your body
I will set on your throne.
¹² If your sons keep my covenant
and my testimonies which I shall
teach them,
their sons also for ever
shall sit upon your throne."

¹³ For the LORD has chosen Zion;
he has desired it for his
habitation:
¹⁴ "This is my resting place for ever;
here I will dwell, for I have
desired it.
¹⁵ I will abundantly bless her
provisions;
I will satisfy her poor with bread.
¹⁶ Her priests I will clothe with
salvation,
and her saints will shout for joy.
¹⁷ There I will make a horn to sprout
for David;
I have prepared a lamp for my
anointed.
¹⁸ His enemies I will clothe with shame,
but upon himself his crown will
shed its luster."

A Song of Ascents.

133 Behold, how good and
pleasant it is
when brothers dwell in unity!
² It is like the precious oil upon the
head,
running down upon the beard,
upon the beard of Aaron,
running down on the collar of his
robes!
³ It is like the dew of Hermon,

Ps. 132: Liturgy commemorating God's choice of Zion and the Davidic dynasty. 1–5: God is reminded of David's determination to provide him a sanctuary (2 Sam.7.1–2). **6–10:** These words evidently accompanied a dramatic ceremony which re-enacted the discovery of the ark by David and the procession by which he brought it to the sanctuary (2 Sam.6.2–15). **6:** *Ephrathah*, Bethlehem, David's city. *The fields of Jaar*, Kiriath-jearim, where the ark had been kept from Samuel's time until David became king in Jerusalem (1 Sam.7.1–2; 2 Chr.1.4). **9:** *Saints*, see 30.4 n. **11–18:** A priest or temple prophet recites God's promise concerning Jerusalem and the dynasty.

Ps. 133: The joys of fraternal harmony (a wisdom psalm). **2:** *Aaron*, the ancestor and type of the priests. Anointing with consecrated *oil* was part of the ordination ceremony (Ex.29.7). **3:** *Hermon*, the chief mountain of Syria.

which falls on the mountains of
Zion!
For there the LORD has commanded
the blessing,
life for evermore.

A Song of Ascents.

134 Come, bless the LORD,
all you servants of the LORD,
who stand by night in the house of
the LORD!
2 Lift up your hands to the holy place,
and bless the LORD!

3 May the LORD bless you from Zion,
he who made heaven and earth!

135 Praise the LORD.
Praise the name of the
LORD,
give praise, O servants of the
LORD,
2 you that stand in the house of the
LORD,
in the courts of the house of our
God!
3 Praise the LORD, for the LORD is
good;
sing to his name, for he is gracious!
4 For the LORD has chosen Jacob for
himself,
Israel as his own possession.

5 For I know that the LORD is great,
and that our Lord is above all
gods.
6 Whatever the LORD pleases he does,
in heaven and on earth,
in the seas and all deeps.
7 He it is who makes the clouds rise at
the end of the earth,
who makes lightnings for the rain
and brings forth the wind from his
storehouses.

8 He it was who smote the first-born
of Egypt,
both of man and of beast;
9 who in thy midst, O Egypt,
sent signs and wonders
against Pharaoh and all his
servants;
10 who smote many nations
and slew mighty kings,
11 Sihon, king of the Amorites,
and Og, king of Bashan,
and all the kingdoms of Canaan,
12 and gave their land as a heritage,
a heritage to his people Israel.

13 Thy name, O LORD, endures for
ever,
thy renown, O LORD, throughout
all ages.
14 For the LORD will vindicate his
people,
and have compassion on his
servants.

15 The idols of the nations are silver
and gold,
the work of men's hands.
16 They have mouths, but they speak
not,
they have eyes, but they see not,
17 they have ears, but they hear not,
nor is there any breath in their
mouths.
18 Like them be those who make
them!–
yea, every one who trusts in them!

19 O house of Israel, bless the LORD!
O house of Aaron, bless the LORD!
20 O house of Levi, bless the LORD!
You that fear the LORD, bless the
LORD!
21 Blessed be the LORD from Zion,
he who dwells in Jerusalem!
Praise the LORD!

Ps. 134: A liturgy of blessing. 1–2: The priests are summoned to offer praise to the LORD.
3: They bless the congregation.

Ps. 135: Hymn praising the LORD for his mighty deeds. 1–4: Call to worship. 5–7: The LORD's
control of nature. 8–12: His work in the Exodus and the conquest of Palestine. 11: *Sihon . . . Og,*
Num.21.21–35. 13–14: A lyrical interlude. 15–18: The LORD's power contrasted with the
impotence of heathen gods (compare 115.3–8). 19–21: Concluding summons to worship. 19:
House of Aaron . . . Levi, the priests and their assistants, the Levites.

136 O give thanks to the LORD,
for he is good,
for his steadfast love endures for
ever.

2 O give thanks to the God of gods,
for his steadfast love endures for
ever.

3 O give thanks to the Lord of lords,
for his steadfast love endures for
ever;

4 to him who alone does great
wonders,
for his steadfast love endures for
ever;

5 to him who by understanding made
the heavens,
for his steadfast love endures for
ever;

6 to him who spread out the earth
upon the waters,
for his steadfast love endures for
ever;

7 to him who made the great lights,
for his steadfast love endures for
ever;

8 the sun to rule over the day,
for his steadfast love endures for
ever;

9 the moon and stars to rule over the
night,
for his steadfast love endures for
ever;

10 to him who smote the first-born of
Egypt,
for his steadfast love endures for
ever;

11 and brought Israel out from among
them,
for his steadfast love endures for
ever;

12 with a strong hand and an
outstretched arm,
for his steadfast love endures for
ever;

13 to him who divided the Red Sea in
sunder,

for his steadfast love endures for
ever;

14 and made Israel pass through the
midst of it,
for his steadfast love endures for
ever;

15 but overthrew Pharaoh and his host
in the Red Sea,
for his steadfast love endures for
ever;

16 to him who led his people through
the wilderness,
for his steadfast love endures for
ever;

17 to him who smote great kings,
for his steadfast love endures for
ever;

18 and slew famous kings,
for his steadfast love endures for
ever;

19 Sihon, king of the Amorites,
for his steadfast love endures for
ever;

20 and Og, king of Bashan,
for his steadfast love endures for
ever;

21 and gave their land as a heritage,
for his steadfast love endures for
ever;

22 a heritage to Israel his servant,
for his steadfast love endures for
ever.

23 It is he who remembered us in our
low estate,
for his steadfast love endures for
ever;

24 and rescued us from our foes,
for his steadfast love endures for
ever;

25 he who gives food to all flesh,
for his steadfast love endures for
ever.

26 O give thanks to the God of heaven,
for his steadfast love endures for
ever.

Ps. 136: Thanksgiving for the LORD'S great deeds on behalf of his people. The second half of
each verse is a congregational response. **1–3:** Summons to give thanks. **4–9:** God's work in
creation. **10–22:** His work in the history of Israel. **10–15:** The Exodus. **16:** The wilderness
wanderings. **17–22:** The conquest of Canaan. *Sihon . . . Og,* Num.21.21–35. **23–25:** Recapitulation. **26:** Concluding summons to give thanks.

137

By the waters*o* of Babylon,
    there we sat down and
    wept,
when we remembered Zion.
2 On the willows*p* there
    we hung up our lyres.
3 For there our captors
    required of us songs,
and our tormentors, mirth, saying,
    "Sing us one of the songs of
    Zion!"

4 How shall we sing the LORD'S song
    in a foreign land?
5 If I forget you, O Jerusalem,
    let my right hand wither!
6 Let my tongue cleave to the roof of
    my mouth,
if I do not remember you,
if I do not set Jerusalem
    above my highest joy!

7 Remember, O LORD, against the
    E′domites
the day of Jerusalem,
how they said, "Rase it, rase it!
    Down to its foundations!"
8 O daughter of Babylon, you
    devastator!*q*
Happy shall he be who requites
    you
with what you have done to us!
9 Happy shall he be who takes your
    little ones
and dashes them against the rock!

A Psalm of David.

138

I give thee thanks, O LORD,
    with my whole heart;
before the gods I sing thy praise;
2 I bow down toward thy holy temple
    and give thanks to thy name for thy

steadfast love and thy
    faithfulness;
for thou hast exalted above
    everything
thy name and thy word.*r*
3 On the day I called, thou didst
    answer me,
my strength of soul thou didst
    increase.*s*

4 All the kings of the earth shall praise
    thee, O LORD,
for they have heard the words of
    thy mouth;
5 and they shall sing of the ways of the
    LORD,
for great is the glory of the LORD.
6 For though the LORD is high, he
    regards the lowly;
but the haughty he knows from
    afar.

7 Though I walk in the midst of
    trouble,
thou dost preserve my life;
thou dost stretch out thy hand against
    the wrath of my enemies,
and thy right hand delivers me.
8 The LORD will fulfil his purpose for
    me;
thy steadfast love, O LORD,
    endures for ever.
Do not forsake the work of thy
    hands.

To the choirmaster. A Psalm of David.

139

O LORD, thou hast searched
    me and known me!

o Heb *streams*   *p* Or *poplars*
q Or *you who are devastated*
r Cn: Heb *thou hast exalted thy word above all thy name*
s Syr Compare Gk Tg: Heb *thou didst make me arrogant in my soul* with *strength*

Ps. 137: Prayer for vengeance on Israel's enemies (a lament). **1–6:** Lament over the holy city. **1–4:** It is difficult to sing the LORD's praise when an exile among foreigners. **1:** *Waters of Babylon,* streams or canals of the Tigris and Euphrates rivers. **3:** *Songs of Zion,* see 46.4–7 n. **5–6:** The psalmist's solemn pledge. **7–9:** Cry for revenge. **7:** *Edomites,* who helped the Babylonians sack Jerusalem in 587 (586) B.C. (Ob.10–14; 2 Kg.25.8–12). **8:** *Daughter of Babylon,* personification of the Babylonian people.

Ps. 138: Thanksgiving for deliverance from trouble. 1–2: The psalmist in the temple court to offer thanks. **3:** His experience (compare 18.37–45). **4–6:** A hymn of praise. **7–8:** An expression of faith.

Ps. 139: Prayer for deliverance from personal enemies (a lament). **1–18:** An appeal to the

2 Thou knowest when I sit down and
    when I rise up;
   thou discernest my thoughts from
    afar.
3 Thou searchest out my path and my
    lying down,
   and art acquainted with all my
    ways.
4 Even before a word is on my tongue,
   lo, O LORD, thou knowest it
    altogether.
5 Thou dost beset me behind and
    before,
   and layest thy hand upon me.
6 Such knowledge is too wonderful for
    me;
   it is high, I cannot attain it.

7 Whither shall I go from thy Spirit?
   Or whither shall I flee from thy
    presence?
8 If I ascend to heaven, thou art there!
   If I make my bed in Sheol, thou
    art there!
9 If I take the wings of the morning
   and dwell in the uttermost parts of
    the sea,
10 even there thy hand shall lead me,
   and thy right hand shall hold me.
11 If I say, "Let only darkness cover me,
   and the light about me be night,"
12 even the darkness is not dark to thee,
   the night is bright as the day;
   for darkness is as light with thee.

13 For thou didst form my inward parts,
   thou didst knit me together in my
    mother's womb.
14 I praise thee, for thou art fearful and
    wonderful.*t*
   Wonderful are thy works!
   Thou knowest me right well;
15   my frame was not hidden from
    thee,

when I was being made in
    secret,
intricately wrought in the depths of
    the earth.
16 Thy eyes beheld my unformed
    substance;
   in thy book were written, every
    one of them,
   the days that were formed for me,
   when as yet there was none of
    them.
17 How precious to me are thy thoughts,
    O God!
   How vast is the sum of them!
18 If I would count them, they are more
    than the sand.
   When I awake, I am still with
    thee.*u*

19 O that thou wouldst slay the wicked,
    O God,
   and that men of blood would
    depart from me,
20 men who maliciously defy thee,
   who lift themselves up against thee
    for evil!*v*
21 Do I not hate them that hate thee, O
    LORD?
   And do I not loathe them that rise
    up against thee?
22 I hate them with perfect
    hatred;
   I count them my enemies.
23 Search me, O God, and know my
    heart!
   Try me and know my
    thoughts!
24 And see if there be any wicked*w* way
    in me,
   and lead me in the way
    everlasting!*x*

t Cn Compare Gk Syr Jerome: Heb *fearful things I am wonderful*
u Or *were I to come to the end I would still be with thee*
v Cn: Heb uncertain
w Heb *hurtful*
x Or *the ancient way.* Compare Jer 6.16

LORD, on the basis of his omniscience and universal power, to demonstrate the psalmist's innocence and to save him (compare vv. 23–24). **1–6:** Everything the psalmist has ever done or thought is known to God. **7–12:** He could have committed no secret crimes, for God is with him everywhere. **8:** *Sheol,* see 88.5–6 n. It is a new thought that God is in Sheol as well as in heaven (see 115.17 n.). **13–16:** God formed him in the womb (poetically called *the depths of the earth*) and knew his character from his conception. **16:** *Thy book,* compare 40.7 n. **17–18:** Exclamation of wonder. **19–24:** Prayer for vindication and deliverance. **21:** The psalmist, a religious leader, does not hesitate to identify his enemies as God's enemies also.

To the choirmaster. A Psalm of David.

140 Deliver me, O LORD, from evil men;
    preserve me from violent men,
2 who plan evil things in their heart,
    and stir up wars continually.
3 They make their tongue sharp as a serpent's,
    and under their lips is the poison of vipers.   *Selah*

4 Guard me, O LORD, from the hands of the wicked;
    preserve me from violent men,
    who have planned to trip up my feet.
5 Arrogant men have hidden a trap for me,
    and with cords they have spread a net,*y*
    by the wayside they have set snares for me.   *Selah*

6 I say to the LORD, Thou art my God;
    give ear to the voice of my supplications, O LORD!
7 O LORD, my Lord, my strong deliverer,
    thou hast covered my head in the day of battle.
8 Grant not, O LORD, the desires of the wicked;
    do not further his evil plot!   *Selah*

9 Those who surround me lift up their head,*z*
    let the mischief of their lips overwhelm them!
10 Let burning coals fall upon them!
    Let them be cast into pits, no more to rise!
11 Let not the slanderer be established in the land;
    let evil hunt down the violent man speedily!

12 I know that the LORD maintains the cause of the afflicted,
    and executes justice for the needy.
13 Surely the righteous shall give thanks to thy name;
    the upright shall dwell in thy presence.

A Psalm of David.

141 I call upon thee, O LORD; make haste to me!
    Give ear to my voice, when I call to thee!
2 Let my prayer be counted as incense before thee,
    and the lifting up of my hands as an evening sacrifice!

3 Set a guard over my mouth, O LORD,
    keep watch over the door of my lips!
4 Incline not my heart to any evil,
    to busy myself with wicked deeds
in company with men who work iniquity;
    and let me not eat of their dainties!

5 Let a good man strike or rebuke me in kindness,
    but let the oil of the wicked never anoint my head;*a*
    for my prayer is continually*b*
    against their wicked deeds.
6 When they are given over to those who shall condemn them,
    then they shall learn that the word of the LORD is true.
7 As a rock which one cleaves and shatters on the land,

y Or *they have spread cords as a net*
z Cn Compare Gk: Heb *those who surround me are uplifted in head*
a Gk: Heb obscure
b Cn: Heb *for continually and my prayer*

Ps. 140: Prayer for deliverance from personal enemies (a lament). **1–2:** Cry for help. **3–5:** The psalmist's situation. **3:** The mention of *their tongue* and *lips* probably implies that they have pronounced a curse against him (compare Pss. 58 and 109). *Selah*, see 3.2 n. **6–11:** Prayer for deliverance. **7:** *Covered my head*, given protection. **12–13:** Expression of confidence.
    Ps. 141: Prayer for deliverance from personal enemies (a lament). **1–2:** Cry for help. *Evening sacrifice*, Ex.29.38–42; 1 Kg.18.36. **3–7:** He prays that he may never compromise with the wicked, whose destruction is sure. **5:** *Oil*, compare 133.2. **7:** *Sheol*, see 88.3–6 n. **8–10:** Prayer for deliverance.

so shall their bones be strewn at
the mouth of Sheol.[c]

8 But my eyes are toward thee, O
LORD God;
in thee I seek refuge; leave me
not defenseless!
9 Keep me from the trap which they
have laid for me,
and from the snares of evildoers!
10 Let the wicked together fall into their
own nets,
while I escape.

A Maskil of David, when he was in the
cave. A Prayer.

142 I cry with my voice to the
LORD,
with my voice I make supplication
to the LORD,
2 I pour out my complaint before him,
I tell my trouble before him.
3 When my spirit is faint,
thou knowest my way!

In the path where I walk
they have hidden a trap for me.
4 I look to the right and watch,[d]
but there is none who takes notice
of me;
no refuge remains to me,
no man cares for me.

5 I cry to thee, O LORD;
I say, Thou art my refuge,
my portion in the land of the
living.
6 Give heed to my cry;
for I am brought very low!

Deliver me from my persecutors;
for they are too strong for me!
7 Bring me out of prison,
that I may give thanks to thy
name!
The righteous will surround me;
for thou wilt deal bountifully with
me.

A Psalm of David.

143 Hear my prayer, O LORD;
give ear to my supplications!
In thy faithfulness answer me, in
thy righteousness!
2 Enter not into judgment with thy
servant;
for no man living is righteous
before thee.

3 For the enemy has pursued me;
he has crushed my life to the
ground;
he has made me sit in darkness
like those long dead.
4 Therefore my spirit faints within
me;
my heart within me is appalled.

5 I remember the days of old,
I meditate on all that thou hast
done;
I muse on what thy hands have
wrought.
6 I stretch out my hands to thee;
my soul thirsts for thee like a
parched land.   *Selah*

7 Make haste to answer me, O LORD!
My spirit fails!
Hide not thy face from me,
lest I be like those who go down
to the Pit.
8 Let me hear in the morning of thy
steadfast love,
for in thee I put my trust.
Teach me the way I should go,
for to thee I lift up my soul.

9 Deliver me, O LORD, from my
enemies!
I have fled to thee for refuge![e]
10 Teach me to do thy will,
for thou art my God!
Let thy good spirit lead me
on a level path!

c The Hebrew of verses 5–7 is obscure
d Or *Look to the right and watch*
e One Heb Ms Gk: Heb *to thee I have hidden*

Ps. 142: **Prayer for deliverance from personal enemies** (a lament). **1–3a:** Cry for help. **3b–4:**
The psalmist's situation. **5–7:** Prayer for deliverance.
    Ps. 143: **Prayer for deliverance from personal enemies** (a lament). **1–2:** Cry for vindication.
3–6: The psalmist's situation. **6:** *Selah*, see 3.2 n. **7–12:** Prayer for deliverance. **7:** *Pit*, see
16.10 n.

¹¹ For thy name's sake, O LORD,
　preserve my life!
　In thy righteousness bring me out
　　of trouble!
¹² And in thy steadfast love cut off my
　　enemies,
　and destroy all my adversaries,
　for I am thy servant.

A Psalm of David.

144 Blessed be the LORD, my
　rock,
who trains my hands for war,
　and my fingers for battle;
² my rockᶠ and my fortress,
　my stronghold and my deliverer,
my shield and he in whom I take
　refuge,
　who subdues the peoples under
　him.ᵍ

³ O LORD, what is man that thou dost
　regard him,
　or the son of man that thou dost
　think of him?
⁴ Man is like a breath,
　his days are like a passing shadow.

⁵ Bow thy heavens, O LORD, and
　come down!
　Touch the mountains that they
　smoke!
⁶ Flash forth the lightning and scatter
　them,
　send out thy arrows and rout them!
⁷ Stretch forth thy hand from on high,
　rescue me and deliver me from
　the many waters,
　from the hand of aliens,
⁸ whose mouths speak lies,
　and whose right hand is a right
　hand of falsehood.

⁹ I will sing a new song to thee, O
　God;

upon a ten-stringed harp I will
　play to thee,
¹⁰ who givest victory to kings,
　who rescuest David thyʰ servant.
¹¹ Rescue me from the cruel sword,
　and deliver me from the hand of
　aliens,
　whose mouths speak lies,
　and whose right hand is a right
　hand of falsehood.

¹² May our sons in their youth
　be like plants full grown,
　our daughters like corner pillars
　cut for the structure of a palace;
¹³ may our garners be full,
　providing all manner of store;
　may our sheep bring forth
　thousands
　and ten thousands in our fields;
¹⁴ may our cattle be heavy with young,
　suffering no mischance or failure
　in bearing;
　may there be no cry of distress in our
　streets!
¹⁵ Happy the people to whom such
　blessings fall!
　Happy the people whose God is
　the LORD!

A Song of Praise. Of David.

145 I will extol thee, my God and
　King,
　and bless thy name for ever and
　ever.
² Every day I will bless thee,
　and praise thy name for ever
　and ever.
³ Great is the LORD, and greatly to
　be praised,
　and his greatness is unsearchable.

ᶠ With 18.2 2 Sam 22.2: Heb *my steadfast love*
ᵍ Another reading is *my people under me*
ʰ Heb *his*

Ps. 144: A king prays for deliverance from his enemies (a royal lament). **1–2**: Praise to God
for his protecting power. **3–4**: The inadequacy of man (compare 8.4; 90.5–6; 146.3–4). **5–8**:
Prayer for victory (compare 18.6–17). **9–10**: The vow (see 7.17 n.). **12–15**: Prayer for a prosperous year, perhaps originally a separate psalm.
　Ps. 145: Hymn epitomizing the character of the God of Israel. An acrostic psalm, each new
verse beginning with the next in order of the Hebrew alphabet (see Ps. 119 n.); the verse beginning with the Hebrew letter "nun" appears as the third and fourth lines of verse 13 (see note *i*).

⁴ One generation shall laud thy works
      to another,
   and shall declare thy mighty acts.
⁵ On the glorious splendor of thy
      majesty,
   and on thy wondrous works, I will
      meditate.
⁶ Men shall proclaim the might of thy
      terrible acts,
   and I will declare thy greatness.
⁷ They shall pour forth the fame of
      thy abundant goodness,
   and shall sing aloud of thy
      righteousness.

⁸ The LORD is gracious and merciful,
   slow to anger and abounding in
      steadfast love.
⁹ The LORD is good to all,
   and his compassion is over all that
      he has made.

¹⁰ All thy works shall give thanks to
      thee, O LORD,
   and all thy saints shall bless thee!
¹¹ They shall speak of the glory of thy
      kingdom,
   and tell of thy power,
¹² to make known to the sons of men
      thy*ʰ* mighty deeds,
   and the glorious splendor of thy*ʰ*
      kingdom.
¹³ Thy kingdom is an everlasting
      kingdom,
   and thy dominion endures
      throughout all generations.

The LORD is faithful in all his words,
   and gracious in all his deeds.*ⁱ*
¹⁴ The LORD upholds all who are
      falling,
   and raises up all who are bowed
      down.
¹⁵ The eyes of all look to thee,
   and thou givest them their food in
      due season.
¹⁶ Thou openest thy hand,

thou satisfiest the desire of every
      living thing.
¹⁷ The LORD is just in all his ways,
   and kind in all his doings.
¹⁸ The LORD is near to all who call
      upon him,
   to all who call upon him in truth.
¹⁹ He fulfils the desire of all who fear
      him,
   he also hears their cry, and saves
      them.
²⁰ The LORD preserves all who love
      him;
   but all the wicked he will destroy.

²¹ My mouth will speak the praise of
      the LORD,
   and let all flesh bless his holy
      name for ever and ever.

146 Praise the LORD!
       Praise the LORD, O my soul!
² I will praise the LORD as long as I
      live;
   I will sing praises to my God while
      I have being.

³ Put not your trust in princes,
   in a son of man, in whom there is
      no help.
⁴ When his breath departs he returns
      to his earth;
   on that very day his plans perish.

⁵ Happy is he whose help is the God
      of Jacob,
   whose hope is in the LORD his God,
⁶ who made heaven and earth,
   the sea, and all that is in them;
who keeps faith for ever;
⁷   who executes justice for the
      oppressed;
   who gives food to the hungry.

The LORD sets the prisoners free;

h Heb *his*
i These two lines are supplied by one Hebrew Ms, Gk
and Syr

1–3: The psalmist's personal expression of praise. **4–7:** God's wonderful deeds. **8–9:** The love
of God (Ex.34.6; Num.14.18; etc.). **10–13a:** The kingship of God (see Ps. 93 n.). **13b–20:** God's
providential care for his creatures. **21:** Return to the personal mood of vv. 1–3.
   Ps. 146: Hymn praising God for his help. Pss. 146–150 all begin and end with "Hallelujah!"
(see Ps.111.1 n.). **1–2:** Personal expression of praise (compare 145.1–3). **3–4:** The inadequacy

8 the LORD opens the eyes of the
blind.
The LORD lifts up those who are
bowed down;
the LORD loves the righteous.
9 The LORD watches over the
sojourners,
he upholds the widow and the
fatherless;
but the way of the wicked he
brings to ruin.

10 The LORD will reign for ever,
thy God, O Zion, to all
generations.
Praise the LORD!

147 Praise the LORD!
For it is good to sing praises
to our God;
for he is gracious, and a song of
praise is seemly.
2 The LORD builds up Jerusalem;
he gathers the outcasts of Israel.
3 He heals the brokenhearted,
and binds up their wounds.
4 He determines the number of the
stars,
he gives to all of them their names.
5 Great is our LORD, and abundant in
power;
his understanding is beyond
measure.
6 The LORD lifts up the downtrodden,
he casts the wicked to the ground.

7 Sing to the LORD with thanksgiving;
make melody to our God upon
the lyre!
8 He covers the heavens with clouds,
he prepares rain for the earth,
he makes grass grow upon the
hills.
9 He gives to the beasts their food,
and to the young ravens which
cry.
10 His delight is not in the strength of
the horse,

nor his pleasure in the legs of a
man;
11 but the LORD takes pleasure in those
who fear him,
in those who hope in his steadfast
love.

12 Praise the LORD, O Jerusalem!
Praise your God, O Zion!
13 For he strengthens the bars of your
gates;
he blesses your sons within you.
14 He makes peace in your borders;
he fills you with the finest of the
wheat.
15 He sends forth his command to the
earth;
his word runs swiftly.
16 He gives snow like wool;
he scatters hoarfrost like ashes.
17 He casts forth his ice like morsels;
who can stand before his cold?
18 He sends forth his word, and melts
them;
he makes his wind blow, and the
waters flow.
19 He declares his word to Jacob,
his statutes and ordinances to
Israel.
20 He has not dealt thus with any other
nation;
they do not know his ordinances.
Praise the LORD!

148 Praise the LORD!
Praise the LORD from the
heavens,
praise him in the heights!
2 Praise him, all his angels,
praise him, all his host!

3 Praise him, sun and moon,
praise him, all you shining stars!
4 Praise him, you highest heavens,
and you waters above the
heavens!

5 Let them praise the name of the
LORD!

---

of man (compare 144.3–4). **5–9:** The LORD gives help to all who need it. **10:** Concluding ex-
pression of praise.
Ps. 147: Hymn praising God for his universal power and providential care. 4: Is.40.26. **16–18:**
Compare Job 37.9–11.
Ps. 148: Hymn calling upon all created things to praise the LORD. 1–6: All things in heaven

For he commanded and they were
created.
⁶ And he established them for ever
and ever;
he fixed their bounds which
cannot be passed.ʲ

⁷ Praise the LORD from the earth,
you sea monsters and all deeps,
⁸ fire and hail, snow and frost,
stormy wind fulfilling his
command!

⁹ Mountains and all hills,
fruit trees and all cedars!
¹⁰ Beasts and all cattle,
creeping things and flying birds!

¹¹ Kings of the earth and all peoples,
princes and all rulers of the earth!
¹² Young men and maidens together,
old men and children!

¹³ Let them praise the name of the
LORD,
for his name alone is exalted;
his glory is above earth and
heaven.
¹⁴ He has raised up a horn for his
people,
praise for all his saints,
for the people of Israel who are
near to him.
Praise the LORD!

149 Praise the LORD!
Sing to the LORD a new
song,
his praise in the assembly of the
faithful!
² Let Israel be glad in his Maker,
let the sons of Zion rejoice in their
King!
³ Let them praise his name with
dancing,

making melody to him with
timbrel and lyre!
⁴ For the LORD takes pleasure in his
people;
he adorns the humble with
victory.
⁵ Let the faithful exult in glory;
let them sing for joy on their
couches.
⁶ Let the high praises of God be in
their throats
and two-edged swords in their
hands,
⁷ to wreak vengeance on the nations
and chastisement on the peoples,
⁸ to bind their kings with chains
and their nobles with fetters of
iron,
⁹ to execute on them the judgment
written!
This is glory for all his faithful
ones.
Praise the LORD!

150 Praise the LORD!
Praise God in his sanctuary;
praise him in his mighty
firmament!
² Praise him for his mighty deeds;
praise him according to his
exceeding greatness!

³ Praise him with trumpet sound;
praise him with lute and harp!
⁴ Praise him with timbrel and dance;
praise him with strings and pipe!
⁵ Praise him with sounding cymbals;
praise him with loud clashing
cymbals!
⁶ Let everything that breathes praise
the LORD!
Praise the LORD!

ʲ Or *he set a law which cannot pass away*

---

called to praise him. **7–10:** All animals, plants, and objects on earth called to praise him.
11–14: All men summoned to join in the chorus also. **14:** *Horn*, see 75.4–5 n. *Saints*, see 30.4 n.
    Ps. 149: Hymn to accompany a festival dance. 3: *Timbrel*, an instrument resembling a tam-
bourine. **5:** *On their couches*, the meaning is uncertain; perhaps reclining on couches was part
of the festival drama. **6–9:** The dance was evidently of war-like character.
    Ps. 150: Doxology marking the end of the Psalter (compare 41.13). Verses 3–5 indicate the
nature of the instrumental accompaniment to the psalms. **1:** *Praise the LORD!* see Ps. 146 n.
3: *Lute*, a stringed instrument. **3:** *Timbrel*, see 149.3 n. **6:** The climax of the psalm and a fitting
conclusion to the book of Psalms.

THE PROVERBS

The book of Proverbs is a compendium of moral and religious instruction as given to Jewish youth by professional sages in the post-exilic period. It includes much older material from the long tradition of such training in the wisdom deemed necessary for the good life. Proverbs is the most typical example of a "wisdom" book in the Old Testament (compare Job, Ecclesiastes), with its emphasis on moral probity based on religion, its teaching that reward and punishment follow in this life, its appeal to the lessons of experience rather than to revelation, and its brief but significant exploration of the nature of wisdom and of wisdom's relation to God.

The book is a small library of teaching materials of different origins and dates. Each of its four main parts (1.1–9.18; 10.1–22.16; 22.17–24.22; and 25.1–29.27) is a separate work with its own title; the title of the first is expanded in 1.2–6 so as to serve as an introduction stating the purpose of the scholar who assembled the various materials. Five smaller pieces appear as appendixes, one (24.23–34) attached to the third main section and the remainder placed together at the end of the book.

Book I (1.1–9.18) contains ten extended discourses of admonition and warning, two poems in which Wisdom is personified (1.20–33; 8.1–36), a poetic allegory contrasting Wisdom and Folly (9.1–6,13–18), and sundry shorter admonitions and poems. This material seems to come from a teacher of the fourth or third century B.C. who assembled and edited the whole work for use in his school.

Book II (10.1–22.16) and Book IV (25.1–29.27) are separately entitled "Proverbs of Solomon," and the same heading has been used by the editor in 1.1. It is hardly a claim, still less proof, of Solomonic authorship, but rather a conventional name for pithy maxims in poetic parallel lines, and dealing with virtues and vices and their consequences. Solomon's wisdom had become legendary, though his proverbs and songs are said to have concerned phenomena of nature rather than human behavior (1 Kg.4.32–33).

Book III contains a series of exhortations resembling the "instructions" of Egyptian sages, and appears to have been modeled upon the Egyptian book of Wisdom entitled "The Instruction of Amen-em-ope," which may be older than 1000 B.C. To this is attached the first of the five appendixes, 24.23–34. The other appendixes are 30.1–9, a dialogue between a sceptic and a believer, recalling the book of Job; 30.10–33, admonitions and proverbs, chiefly of the progressive numerical type; 31.1–9, a queen mother's counsel to a young king; and 31.10–31, a portrait of the ideal wife of a prominent man.

THE PROVERBS OF SOLOMON, SON of David, king of Israel:

2 That men may know wisdom and instruction,
understand words of insight,
3 receive instruction in wise dealing,
righteousness, justice, and equity;
4 that prudence may be given to the simple,
knowledge and discretion to the youth–
5 the wise man also may hear and increase in learning,
and the man of understanding acquire skill,
6 to understand a proverb and a figure,
the words of the wise and their riddles.

1.1–9.18: Book I, prologue: Invitation to wisdom. 1.1: Title of the work, expanded from headings of Books II and IV (see Introduction). *Proverbs* include two-line maxims and also longer forms, such as parables and discourses.

1.2–6: The purpose of the teacher in assembling and editing the work is to serve the mental awakening and moral education of youth, and the further instruction of the mature. **6:** *A figure* is a metaphor, parable, or allegory such as in vv. 20–33. A *riddle* is a comparison or analogy which enforces a lesson when the hearer discerns its intention and is able to complete it (see 25.14; 26.7; 30.18–19).

7 The fear of the LORD is the
  beginning of knowledge;
  fools despise wisdom and
  instruction.

8 Hear, my son, your father's
  instruction,
  and reject not your mother's
  teaching;
9 for they are a fair garland for your
  head,
  and pendants for your neck.
10 My son, if sinners entice you,
  do not consent.
11 If they say, "Come with us, let us
  lie in wait for blood,
  let us wantonly ambush the
  innocent;
12 like Sheol let us swallow them alive
  and whole, like those who go
  down to the Pit;
13 we shall find all precious goods,
  we shall fill our houses with spoil;
14 throw in your lot among us,
  we will all have one purse"–
15 my son, do not walk in the way with
  them,
  hold back your foot from their
  paths;
16 for their feet run to evil,
  and they make haste to shed
  blood.
17 For in vain is a net spread
  in the sight of any bird;
18 but these men lie in wait for their
  own blood,
  they set an ambush for their own
  lives.
19 Such are the ways of all who get
  gain by violence;
  it takes away the life of its
  possessors.

20 Wisdom cries aloud in the street;

in the markets she raises her
  voice;
21 on the top of the walls*a* she cries
  out;
  at the entrance of the city gates
  she speaks:
22 "How long, O simple ones, will you
  love being simple?
  How long will scoffers delight in
  their scoffing
  and fools hate knowledge?
23 Give heed*b* to my reproof;
  behold, I will pour out my
  thoughts*c* to you;
  I will make my words known to
  you.
24 Because I have called and you
  refused to listen,
  have stretched out my hand and
  no one has heeded,
25 and you have ignored all my
  counsel
  and would have none of my
  reproof,
26 I also will laugh at your calamity;
  I will mock when panic strikes
  you,
27 when panic strikes you like a storm,
  and your calamity comes like a
  whirlwind,
  when distress and anguish come
  upon you.
28 Then they will call upon me, but I
  will not answer;
  they will seek me diligently but
  will not find me.
29 Because they hated knowledge
  and did not choose the fear of the
  LORD,
30 would have none of my counsel,
  and despised all my reproof,
31 therefore they shall eat the fruit of
  their way

a Heb uncertain
b Heb *Turn*
c Heb *spirit*

1.7: The theme of chs. 1–9: An attitude of reverent obedience toward God is the necessary preliminary and first stage of enlightenment.
   1.8–19: Home-training is a moral safeguard. It will protect a youth going out into the world from temptation by criminals and the ruin which falls on them. **12:** *Sheol . . . the Pit,* i.e. the grave. Sheol is a common expression for death and the place and state of the dead (see Gen. 37.35 n.). **17:** *In vain . . . any bird* is a quotation of a popular proverb affirming that the consequences of crime are too obvious to be missed.
   1.20–33: Wisdom personified as a prophetess. She denounces those who despise moral in-

and be sated with their own
devices.
³² For the simple are killed by their
turning away,
and the complacence of fools
destroys them;
³³ but he who listens to me will dwell
secure
and will be at ease, without dread
of evil."

2 My son, if you receive my words
and treasure up my commandments with you,
² making your ear attentive to wisdom
and inclining your heart to
understanding;
³ yes, if you cry out for insight
and raise your voice for
understanding,
⁴ if you seek it like silver
and search for it as for hidden
treasures;
⁵ then you will understand the fear of
the LORD
and find the knowledge of God.
⁶ For the LORD gives wisdom;
from his mouth come knowledge
and understanding;
⁷ he stores up sound wisdom for the
upright;
he is a shield to those who walk
in integrity,
⁸ guarding the paths of justice
and preserving the way of his
saints.
⁹ Then you will understand
righteousness and justice
and equity, every good path;
¹⁰ for wisdom will come into your
heart,
and knowledge will be pleasant
to your soul;
¹¹ discretion will watch over you;
understanding will guard you;

¹² delivering you from the way of evil,
from men of perverted speech,
¹³ who forsake the paths of uprightness
to walk in the ways of darkness,
¹⁴ who rejoice in doing evil
and delight in the perverseness of
evil;
¹⁵ men whose paths are crooked,
and who are devious in their ways.

¹⁶ You will be saved from the loose*d*
woman,
from the adventuress*e* with her
smooth words,
¹⁷ who forsakes the companion of her
youth
and forgets the covenant of her
God;
¹⁸ for her house sinks down to death,
and her paths to the shades;
¹⁹ none who go to her come back
nor do they regain the paths of
life.

²⁰ So you will walk in the way of good
men
and keep to the paths of the
righteous.
²¹ For the upright will inhabit the land,
and men of integrity will remain
in it;
²² but the wicked will be cut off from
the land,
and the treacherous will be rooted
out of it.

3 My son, do not forget my teaching,
but let your heart keep my
commandments;
² for length of days and years of life
and abundant welfare will they
give you.

³ Let not loyalty and faithfulness
forsake you;

d Heb *strange*   e Heb *foreign woman*

struction, and who will realize their need of wisdom when it is too late. **32:** *Turning away*,
i.e. waywardness.
   2.1–22: The fruits of the search for wisdom. The pursuit of wisdom brings understanding of
religion and morality, and its possession is an inner safeguard against bad companions and
sexual immorality. **17:** *Covenant of her God*, i.e. "her covenant before God." Marital faithfulness is a sacred obligation (Gen.2.24; Hos. ch. 2; Mt.19.6).
   3.1–12: The precepts of religion lead to physical and spiritual well-being; even misfortune
becomes the discipline of a loving Father (v. 12). Knowledge without reverence is not enough.

bind them about your neck,
write them on the tablet of your
heart.
⁴ So you will find favor and good
repute*ᶠ*
in the sight of God and man.

⁵ Trust in the LORD with all your
heart,
and do not rely on your own
insight.
⁶ In all your ways acknowledge him,
and he will make straight your
paths.
⁷ Be not wise in your own eyes;
fear the LORD, and turn away
from evil.
⁸ It will be healing to your flesh*ᵍ*
and refreshment*ʰ* to your bones.

⁹ Honor the LORD with your
substance
and with the first fruits of all
your produce;
¹⁰ then your barns will be filled with
plenty,
and your vats will be bursting
with wine.

¹¹ My son, do not despise the LORD'S
discipline
or be weary of his reproof,
¹² for the LORD reproves him whom
he loves,
as a father the son in whom he
delights.

¹³ Happy is the man who finds wisdom,
and the man who gets
understanding,
¹⁴ for the gain from it is better than
gain from silver
and its profit better than gold.

¹⁵ She is more precious than jewels,
and nothing you desire can
compare with her.
¹⁶ Long life is in her right hand;
in her left hand are riches and
honor.
¹⁷ Her ways are ways of pleasantness,
and all her paths are peace.
¹⁸ She is a tree of life to those who lay
hold of her;
those who hold her fast are called
happy.

¹⁹ The LORD by wisdom founded the
earth;
by understanding he established
the heavens;
²⁰ by his knowledge the deeps broke
forth,
and the clouds drop down the dew.

²¹ My son, keep sound wisdom and
discretion;
let them not escape from your
sight,*ⁱ*
²² and they will be life for your soul
and adornment for your neck.
²³ Then you will walk on your way
securely
and your foot will not stumble.
²⁴ If you sit down,*ʲ* you will not be
afraid;
when you lie down, your sleep will
be sweet.
²⁵ Do not be afraid of sudden panic,
or of the ruin*ᵏ* of the wicked,
when it comes;
²⁶ for the LORD will be your confidence
and will keep your foot from
being caught.

f Cn: Heb *understanding*   *g* Heb *navel*
h Or *medicine*
i Reversing the order of the clauses
j Gk: Heb *lie down*   *k* Heb *storm*

3.13–18: True wealth is not measured in material things but in the abundant life and happiness which wisdom brings. **18:** The *tree of life* was a symbol of divine life and immortality in ancient mythology and art (compare Gen.3.22; Rev.2.7); here it is a metaphor for life itself.

3.19–20: Wisdom is divine, since the created world declares the wisdom of its Creator, an important theological idea, further developed in 8.22–31. *The deeps* were the abyss of waters under the earth (Ex.20.4) from which it was believed springs and floods *broke forth* (see Gen. 7.11 n.). The word here for *clouds* means the highest clouds, the sky.

3.21–35: Wisdom gives peace of mind through confidence in God. One should always do good and not harm, for God's blessing is on the one and his curse on the other. **25:** *Ruin*, or "fury." **34:** *Scorners*, or "arrogant."

27 Do not withhold good from those
    to whom it[l] is due,
  when it is in your power to do it.

28 Do not say to your neighbor, "Go,
    and come again,
  tomorrow I will give it"–when
    you have it with you.
29 Do not plan evil against your
    neighbor
  who dwells trustingly beside you.
30 Do not contend with a man for no
    reason,
  when he has done you no harm.
31 Do not envy a man of violence
  and do not choose any of his
    ways;
32 for the perverse man is an
    abomination to the LORD,
  but the upright are in his
    confidence.
33 The LORD's curse is on the house of
    the wicked,
  but he blesses the abode of the
    righteous.
34 Toward the scorners he is scornful,
  but to the humble he shows favor.
35 The wise will inherit honor,
  but fools get[m] disgrace.

4 Hear, O sons, a father's
    instruction,
  and be attentive, that you may
    gain[n] insight;
2 for I give you good precepts:
  do not forsake my teaching.
3 When I was a son with my father,
  tender, the only one in the sight of
    my mother,
4 he taught me, and said to me,
  "Let your heart hold fast my words;
  keep my commandments, and
    live;
5 do not forget, and do not turn away
    from the words of my mouth.
  Get wisdom; get insight.[o]
6 Do not forsake her, and she will
    keep you;
  love her, and she will guard you.

7 The beginning of wisdom is this:
    Get wisdom,
  and whatever you get, get insight
8 Prize her highly,[p] and she will exalt
    you;
  she will honor you if you embrace
    her.
9 She will place on your head a fair
    garland;
  she will bestow on you a beautiful
    crown."

10 Hear, my son, and accept my words,
  that the years of your life may be
    many.
11 I have taught you the way of
    wisdom;
  I have led you in the paths of
    uprightness.
12 When you walk, your step will not
    be hampered;
  and if you run, you will not
    stumble.
13 Keep hold of instruction, do not let
    go;
  guard her, for she is your life.
14 Do not enter the path of the wicked,
  and do not walk in the way of evil
    men.
15 Avoid it; do not go on it;
  turn away from it and pass on.
16 For they cannot sleep unless they
    have done wrong;
  they are robbed of sleep unless
    they have made some one
    stumble.
17 For they eat the bread of wickedness
  and drink the wine of violence.
18 But the path of the righteous is like
    the light of dawn,
  which shines brighter and brighter
    until full day.
19 The way of the wicked is like deep
    darkness;
  they do not know over what they
    stumble.

l Heb *Do not withhold good from its owners*
m Cn: Heb *exalt*   n Heb *know*
o Reversing the order of the lines
p The meaning of the Hebrew is uncertain

4.1–9: The teacher himself was directed toward wisdom by his parents. **7:** A father gives his child the first impulse toward wisdom, and the first lesson is reverence (1.7).
    4.10–19: The pupil is admonished to profit by the lessons taught.

²⁰ My son, be attentive to my words;
   incline your ear to my sayings.
²¹ Let them not escape from your sight;
   keep them within your heart.
²² For they are life to him who finds
      them,
   and healing to all his flesh.
²³ Keep your heart with all vigilance;
   for from it flow the springs of life.
²⁴ Put away from you crooked speech,
   and put devious talk far from you.
²⁵ Let your eyes look directly forward,
   and your gaze be straight before
      you.
²⁶ Take heed to*q* the path of your feet,
   then all your ways will be sure.
²⁷ Do not swerve to the right or to the
      left;
   turn your foot away from evil.

5 My son, be attentive to my
   wisdom,
   incline your ear to my
      understanding;
² that you may keep discretion,
   and your lips may guard
      knowledge.
³ For the lips of a loose woman drip
      honey,
   and her speech*r* is smoother than
      oil;
⁴ but in the end she is bitter as
      wormwood,
   sharp as a two-edged sword.
⁵ Her feet go down to death;
   her steps follow the path to*s*
      Sheol;
⁶ she does not take heed to*t* the path
      of life;
   her ways wander, and she does
      not know it.

⁷ And now, O sons, listen to me,
   and do not depart from the words
      of my mouth.
⁸ Keep your way far from her,
   and do not go near the door of her
      house;
⁹ lest you give your honor to others

and your years to the merciless;
¹⁰ lest strangers take their fill of your
      strength,*u*
   and your labors go to the house of
      an alien;
¹¹ and at the end of your life you groan,
   when your flesh and body are
      consumed,
¹² and you say, "How I hated
      discipline,
   and my heart despised reproof!
¹³ I did not listen to the voice of my
      teachers
   or incline my ear to my instructors.
¹⁴ I was at the point of utter ruin
   in the assembled congregation."

¹⁵ Drink water from your own cistern,
   flowing water from your own well.
¹⁶ Should your springs be scattered
      abroad,
   streams of water in the streets?
¹⁷ Let them be for yourself alone,
   and not for strangers with you.
¹⁸ Let your fountain be blessed,
   and rejoice in the wife of your
      youth,
¹⁹   a lovely hind, a graceful doe.
   Let her affection fill you at all times
      with delight,
   be infatuated always with her
      love.
²⁰ Why should you be infatuated, my
      son, with a loose woman
   and embrace the bosom of an
      adventuress?
²¹ For a man's ways are before the eyes
      of the LORD,
   and he watches*v* all his paths.
²² The iniquities of the wicked ensnare
      him,
   and he is caught in the toils of his
      sin.
²³ He dies for lack of discipline,
   and because of his great folly he is
      lost.

q The meaning of the Hebrew word is uncertain
r Heb *palate*   *s* Heb *lay hold of*
t The meaning of the Hebrew word is uncertain
u Or *wealth*
v The meaning of the Hebrew word is uncertain

4.20–27: Remembered wisdom is a source of life, health, and personal integrity.
   5.1–23: Grave warnings against sexual indulgence and an exhortation to marital faithfulness.
3: *Speech*, or "mouth"; i.e. not her words but her kisses. **4**: *Wormwood*, a bitter herb.

6 My son, if you have become surety
  for your neighbor,
  have given your pledge for a
  stranger;
2 if you are snared in the utterance of
  your lips,[w]
  caught in the words of your
  mouth;
3 then do this, my son, and save
  yourself,
  for you have come into your
  neighbor's power:
  go, hasten,[x] and importune your
  neighbor.
4 Give your eyes no sleep
  and your eyelids no slumber;
5 save yourself like a gazelle from the
  hunter,[y]
  like a bird from the hand of the
  fowler.

6 Go to the ant, O sluggard;
  consider her ways, and be wise.
7 Without having any chief,
  officer or ruler,
8 she prepares her food in summer,
  and gathers her sustenance in
  harvest.
9 How long will you lie there, O
  sluggard?
  When will you arise from your
  sleep?
10 A little sleep, a little slumber,
  a little folding of the hands to
  rest,
11 and poverty will come upon you like
  a vagabond,
  and want like an armed man.

12 A worthless person, a wicked man,
  goes about with crooked speech,
13 winks with his eyes, scrapes[z] with
  his feet,

14 with perverted heart devises evil,
  continually sowing discord;
15 therefore calamity will come upon
  him suddenly;
  in a moment he will be broken
  beyond healing.

16 There are six things which the LORD
  hates,
  seven which are an abomination
  to him:
17 haughty eyes, a lying tongue,
  and hands that shed innocent
  blood,
18 a heart that devises wicked plans,
  feet that make haste to run to evil,
19 a false witness who breathes out lies,
  and a man who sows discord
  among brothers.

20 My son, keep your father's
  commandment,
  and forsake not your mother's
  teaching.
21 Bind them upon your heart always;
  tie them about your neck.
22 When you walk, they[a] will lead you;
  when you lie down, they[a] will
  watch over you;
  and when you awake, they[a] will
  talk with you.
23 For the commandment is a lamp and
  the teaching a light,
  and the reproofs of discipline are
  the way of life,
24 to preserve you from the evil
  woman,
  from the smooth tongue of the
  adventuress.

w Cn Compare Gk Syr: Heb *the words of your mouth*
x Or *humble yourself*
y Cn: Heb *hand*
z Or *taps*   a Heb *it*

6.1–19: Four short sections dealing with particular faults. **6.1–5**: A rash pledge could have disastrous consequences (see 2 Kg.4.1); one must not hesitate to grovel to obtain release. **3**: *Hasten*, preferably "humble yourself" (see note *x*) or "look disconsolate." **6–11**: The sluggard who makes no provision for future needs can learn a lesson from the ants (20.4; 30.25). Another contemptuous remark about the sluggard in 24.30–34 has the same concluding words. **12–15**: In contrast with the straightforward man (4.24–27) is the evil-minded person with his suggestive gestures. **13**: *Scrapes*, i.e. "makes signs." **16–19**: Seven bad qualities of personal character are portrayed in concrete images, in typical Hebrew manner. The progressive numerical saying (30.15–31; Am.1.3–2.8) was a rhetorical form common in Semitic poetry.

6.20–35: Further commendation of training in wisdom, with a stern warning against adultery

25 Do not desire her beauty in your
    heart,
  and do not let her capture you
    with her eyelashes;
26 for a harlot may be hired for a loaf
    of bread,*b*
  but an adulteress*c* stalks a man's
    very life.
27 Can a man carry fire in his bosom
    and his clothes not be burned?
28 Or can one walk upon hot coals
    and his feet not be scorched?
29 So is he who goes in to his neighbor's
    wife;
  none who touches her will go
    unpunished.
30 Do not men despise*d* a thief if he
    steals
  to satisfy his appetite when he is
    hungry?
31 And if he is caught, he will pay
    sevenfold;
  he will give all the goods of his
    house.
32 He who commits adultery has no
    sense;
  he who does it destroys himself.
33 Wounds and dishonor will he get,
  and his disgrace will not be wiped
    away.
34 For jealousy makes a man furious,
  and he will not spare when he
    takes revenge.
35 He will accept no compensation,
  nor be appeased though you
    multiply gifts.

7 My son, keep my words
  and treasure up my command-
    ments with you;
2 keep my commandments and live,
  keep my teachings as the apple of
    your eye;
3 bind them on your fingers,

write them on the tablet of your
    heart.
4 Say to wisdom, "You are my sister,"
  and call insight your intimate
    friend;
5 to preserve you from the loose
    woman,
  from the adventuress with her
    smooth words.

6 For at the window of my house
  I have looked out through my
    lattice,
7 and I have seen among the simple,
  I have perceived among the
    youths,
  a young man without sense,
8 passing along the street near her
    corner,
  taking the road to her house
9 in the twilight, in the evening,
  at the time of night and darkness.

10 And lo, a woman meets him,
  dressed as a harlot, wily of heart.*e*
11 She is loud and wayward,
  her feet do not stay at home;
12 now in the street, now in the market,
  and at every corner she lies in wait.
13 She seizes him and kisses him,
  and with impudent face she says
    to him:
14 "I had to offer sacrifices,
  and today I have paid my vows;
15 so now I have come out to meet you,
  to seek you eagerly, and I have
    found you.
16 I have decked my couch with
    coverings,
  colored spreads of Egyptian linen;
17 I have perfumed my bed with myrrh,

b Cn Compare Gk Syr Vg Tg: Heb *for because of a harlot*
  to a piece of bread
c Heb *a man's wife*   *d* Or *Men do not despise*
e The meaning of the Hebrew is uncertain

(see 5.1–23). **25:** *Eyelashes,* in v. 4 "eyelids," the eyes in movement. **30–31:** A statement, not a question; *a thief if he steals* because he is hungry is not despicable, yet *he will pay* a *sevenfold* penalty. But an adulterer is dishonored, and *no compensation* can atone for the wrong he has done.
    7.1–27: Wisdom as a safeguard against adultery, with some repetitions from ch. 2. **4:** Wisdom is personified as a woman, as in 1.20–33; 4.8–9; 8.1–36; 9.1–6. **14:** *Sacrifices, and . . . vows* provided the occasion for a feast with meat retained by the worshiper, since only the fat and entrails were consumed on the altar (see Lev.3.1–5 n.; 7.15; 1 Sam.9.12–13). The separation here illustrated between religion and morality is "an abomination to the LORD" (15.8; 21.3).

aloes, and cinnamon.
18 Come, let us take our fill of love till
morning;
let us delight ourselves with love.
19 For my husband is not at home;
he has gone on a long journey;
20 he took a bag of money with him;
at full moon he will come home."

21 With much seductive speech she
persuades him;
with her smooth talk she compels
him.
22 All at once he follows her,
as an ox goes to the slaughter,
or as a stag is caught fast[f]
23 till an arrow pierces its entrails;
as a bird rushes into a snare;
he does not know that it will cost
him his life.

24 And now, O sons, listen to me,
and be attentive to the words of
my mouth.
25 Let not your heart turn aside to her
ways,
do not stray into her paths;
26 for many a victim has she laid low;
yea, all her slain are a mighty
host.
27 Her house is the way to Sheol,
going down to the chambers of
death.

8 Does not wisdom call,
does not understanding raise
her voice?
2 On the heights beside the way,
in the paths she takes her stand;
3 beside the gates in front of the town,
at the entrance of the portals she
cries aloud:
4 "To you, O men, I call,
and my cry is to the sons of men.
5 O simple ones, learn prudence;
O foolish men, pay attention.
6 Hear, for I will speak noble things,

and from my lips will come what
is right;
7 for my mouth will utter truth;
wickedness is an abomination to
my lips.
8 All the words of my mouth are
righteous;
there is nothing twisted or crooked
in them.
9 They are all straight to him who
understands
and right to those who find
knowledge.
10 Take my instruction instead of silver,
and knowledge rather than choice
gold;
11 for wisdom is better than jewels,
and all that you may desire cannot
compare with her.
12 I, wisdom, dwell in prudence,[g]
and I find knowledge and
discretion.
13 The fear of the LORD is hatred of
evil.
Pride and arrogance and the way of
evil
and perverted speech I hate.
14 I have counsel and sound wisdom,
I have insight, I have strength.
15 By me kings reign,
and rulers decree what is just;
16 by me princes rule,
and nobles govern[h] the earth.
17 I love those who love me,
and those who seek me diligently
find me.
18 Riches and honor are with me,
enduring wealth and prosperity.
19 My fruit is better than gold, even
fine gold,
and my yield than choice silver.
20 I walk in the way of righteousness,
in the paths of justice,
21 endowing with wealth those who love
me,
and filling their treasuries.

f Cn Compare Gk: Heb uncertain
g Heb obscure   h Gk: Heb *all the governors of*

8.1–36: Wisdom again speaks as a prophetess (compare 1.20–33), proclaiming her worth
(vv. 6–11), her authority (vv. 12–16), her rewards (vv. 17–21), and her primacy in the creative
work of God (vv. 22–31). **12:** *Dwell in*, or "dwell with." *Find*, or "am found through" (compare
v. 35). **13:** The first line is a reader's note, not part of Wisdom's speech. **15–16:** *By me kings
reign;* a divine gift of wisdom is needed by rulers to govern well, do justice, and maintain the

22 The LORD created me at the
    beginning of his work,[i]
    the first of his acts of old.
23 Ages ago I was set up,
    at the first, before the beginning of
    the earth.
24 When there were no depths I was
    brought forth,
    when there were no springs
    abounding with water.
25 Before the mountains had been
    shaped,
    before the hills, I was brought
    forth;
26 before he had made the earth with its
    fields,[j]
    or the first of the dust[j] of the
    world.
27 When he established the heavens, I
    was there,
    when he drew a circle on the face
    of the deep,
28 when he made firm the skies above,
    when he established[j] the fountains
    of the deep,
29 when he assigned to the sea its limit,
    so that the waters might not
    transgress his command,
    when he marked out the foundations
    of the earth,
30   then I was beside him, like a
    master workman;[l]
    and I was daily his[m] delight,
    rejoicing before him always,
31 rejoicing in his inhabited world
    and delighting in the sons of men.

32 And now, my sons, listen to me:

happy are those who keep my
    ways.
33 Hear instruction and be wise,
    and do not neglect it.
34 Happy is the man who listens to me,
    watching daily at my gates,
    waiting beside my doors.
35 For he who finds me finds life
    and obtains favor from the LORD;
36 but he who misses me injures
    himself;
    all who hate me love death."

9 Wisdom has built her house,
    she has set up[n] her seven pillars.
2 She has slaughtered her beasts, she
    has mixed her wine,
    she has also set her table.
3 She has sent out her maids to call
    from the highest places in the
    town,
4 "Whoever is simple, let him turn in
    here!"
    To him who is without sense she
    says,
5 "Come, eat of my bread
    and drink of the wine I have
    mixed.
6 Leave simpleness,[o] and live,
    and walk in the way of insight."

7 He who corrects a scoffer gets
    himself abuse,
    and he who reproves a wicked
    man incurs injury.

i Heb *way*
j The meaning of the Hebrew is uncertain
l Another reading is *little child*
m Gk: Heb lacks *his*   n Gk Syr Tg: Heb *hewn*
o Gk Syr Vg Tg: Heb *simple ones*

---

right (1 Kg.3.9; Is.11.1–9). **22–31:** God's attribute of wisdom was shown in creation. This is a development of the thought in 3.19–20 towards the concept of a divine agent, "first-born of all creation," through whom "all things were made" (Col.1.15–16; Jn.1.1–3). **22:** *Created me*, or "came to possess me." Wisdom here is not a pre-existent divine being distinct from God, but an aspect or activity of God metaphorically endowed with speech. **23:** *Set up*, or "became a reality," or "was poured out" (like the Spirit, Acts 2.17). **27:** *Drew a circle*, the horizon. **28:** *Made firm the skies*, thought of as a solid dome resting on mountain pillars or the sea at the extremities of a round, flat earth (see Gen.1.6–8 n.; Job 26.10–11; Ps.104.2–3). **29:** Compare Gen.1.9; Job 38.10–11. **30:** *Master workman* and "little child" (see note *l*) are ancient guesses as to the meaning of a rare Hebrew word; alternatively, it may mean either "confident" or something like "co-ordinator" (compare Col.1.17).

    9.1–6: A poetic allegory. Wisdom, the gracious hostess, invites the unwise to her feast. **1:** *Seven pillars* supporting the roof suggest the banqueting hall of a palatial residence. Wisdom's *house* (see 8.34) is the world, and the pillars are the "pillars of heaven" (see 8.28 n.; Job 26.11).
    9.7–12: Maxims on scoffers and wise men. **7:** *A scoffer* is filled with arrogant self-assurance

8 Do not reprove a scoffer, or he will
  hate you;
  reprove a wise man, and he will
  love you.
9 Give instruction[p] to a wise man, and
  he will be still wiser;
  teach a righteous man and he will
  increase in learning.
10 The fear of the LORD is the
  beginning of wisdom,
  and the knowledge of the Holy
  One is insight.
11 For by me your days will be
  multiplied,
  and years will be added to your
  life.
12 If you are wise, you are wise for
  yourself;
  if you scoff, you alone will bear it.

13 A foolish woman is noisy;
  she is wanton[q] and knows no
  shame.[r]
14 She sits at the door of her house,
  she takes a seat on the high places
  of the town,
15 calling to those who pass by,
  who are going straight on their
  way,
16 "Whoever is simple, let him turn in
  here!"
  And to him who is without sense
  she says,
17 "Stolen water is sweet,
  and bread eaten in secret is
  pleasant."
18 But he does not know that the dead[s]
  are there,

that her guests are in the depths of
  Sheol.

10 The proverbs of Solomon.

A wise son makes a glad father,
  but a foolish son is a sorrow to
  his mother.
2 Treasures gained by wickedness do
  not profit,
  but righteousness delivers from
  death.
3 The LORD does not let the righteous
  go hungry,
  but he thwarts the craving of the
  wicked.
4 A slack hand causes poverty,
  but the hand of the diligent makes
  rich.
5 A son who gathers in summer is
  prudent,
  but a son who sleeps in harvest
  brings shame.
6 Blessings are on the head of the
  righteous,
  but the mouth of the wicked
  conceals violence.
7 The memory of the righteous is a
  blessing,
  but the name of the wicked will
  rot.
8 The wise of heart will heed
  commandments,
  but a prating fool will come to
  ruin.

p Heb lacks *instruction*
q Cn Compare Syr Vg: The meaning of the Hebrew is
  uncertain
r Gk Syr: The meaning of the Hebrew is uncertain
s Heb *shades*

and feels no need of learning or religion (21.24). **10:** The theme of 1.7 is repeated as the teacher's discourses in chs. 1–9 draw to a close. **11:** A displaced verse which fits after 8.17. **12:** *You are wise for yourself*, or, "wisdom is yours." Responsibility for his wisdom or folly rests with every man.

9.13–18: Folly, in contrast to the lady Wisdom (vv. 1–6), **is a harlot leading man to death;** she is loud-mouthed, stupid, and without shame. **17:** A popular proverb applied to adultery. **18:** 5.23; 7.26–27.

10.1–22.16: Book II, a collection of **miscellaneous maxims,** each being two lines in parallelism. By sage observations on life and behavior, vices are held up to scorn, while virtues are commended as based on common sense, intelligence and obedience to God. Punishment of vice and reward of virtue can be observed in experience. The individual maxims and observations would serve as texts for instruction in a home or school of wisdom. **10.1:** *The proverbs of Solomon,* see Introduction.

10.2: *Delivers from death,* i.e. is rewarded by long life. An early death was regarded as punishment for sin. **3:** An affirmation based more on faith than on experience.

⁹ He who walks in integrity walks
  securely,
  but he who perverts his ways will
  be found out.
¹⁰ He who winks the eye causes trouble,
  but he who boldly reproves makes
  peace.ᵗ
¹¹ The mouth of the righteous is a
  fountain of life,
  but the mouth of the wicked
  conceals violence.
¹² Hatred stirs up strife,
  but love covers all offenses.
¹³ On the lips of him who has
  understanding wisdom is found,
  but a rod is for the back of him
  who lacks sense.
¹⁴ Wise men lay up knowledge,
  but the babbling of a fool brings
  ruin near.
¹⁵ A rich man's wealth is his strong
  city;
  the poverty of the poor is their
  ruin.
¹⁶ The wage of the righteous leads to
  life,
  the gain of the wicked to sin.
¹⁷ He who heeds instruction is on the
  path to life,
  but he who rejects reproof goes
  astray.
¹⁸ He who conceals hatred has lying
  lips,
  and he who utters slander is a fool.
¹⁹ When words are many, transgression
  is not lacking,
  but he who restrains his lips is
  prudent.
²⁰ The tongue of the righteous is choice
  silver;
  the mind of the wicked is of little
  worth.
²¹ The lips of the righteous feed many,
  but fools die for lack of sense.
²² The blessing of the LORD makes
  rich,
  and he adds no sorrow with it.ᵘ
²³ It is like sport to a fool to do wrong,

but wise conduct is pleasure to a
  man of understanding.
²⁴ What the wicked dreads will come
  upon him,
  but the desire of the righteous will
  be granted.
²⁵ When the tempest passes, the wicked
  is no more,
  but the righteous is established for
  ever.
²⁶ Like vinegar to the teeth, and smoke
  to the eyes,
  so is the sluggard to those who
  send him.
²⁷ The fear of the LORD prolongs life,
  but the years of the wicked will be
  short.
²⁸ The hope of the righteous ends in
  gladness,
  but the expectation of the wicked
  comes to nought.
²⁹ The LORD is a stronghold to him
  whose way is upright,
  but destruction to evildoers.
³⁰ The righteous will never be
  removed,
  but the wicked will not dwell in
  the land.
³¹ The mouth of the righteous brings
  forth wisdom,
  but the perverse tongue will be
  cut off.
³² The lips of the righteous know what
  is acceptable,
  but the mouth of the wicked, what
  is perverse.

11 A false balance is an abomination
  to the LORD,
  but a just weight is his delight.
² When pride comes, then comes
  disgrace;
  but with the humble is wisdom.
³ The integrity of the upright guides
  them,
  but the crookedness of the
  treacherous destroys them.

t Gk: Heb *but a prating fool will come to ruin*
u Or *and toil adds nothing to it*

16: *The wage of the righteous,* or "what the righteous does." *Sin,* or "destruction," compare
Rom.6.23, which may be derived from this verse. **19:** It is better to say little than too much. **22:**
See note *u*; not painful toil but God's blessing brings wealth.
  11.1: Compare Dt.25.13–16. **6:** *Lust,* or "craving," as in 10.3.

4 Riches do not profit in the day of
  wrath,
   but righteousness delivers from
   death.
5 The righteousness of the blameless
  keeps his way straight,
   but the wicked falls by his own
   wickedness.
6 The righteousness of the upright
  delivers them,
   but the treacherous are taken
   captive by their lust.
7 When the wicked dies, his hope
  perishes,
   and the expectation of the godless
   comes to nought.
8 The righteous is delivered from
  trouble,
   and the wicked gets into it instead.
9 With his mouth the godless man
  would destroy his neighbor,
   but by knowledge the righteous are
   delivered.
10 When it goes well with the righteous,
   the city rejoices;
   and when the wicked perish there
   are shouts of gladness.
11 By the blessing of the upright a city
   is exalted,
   but it is overthrown by the mouth
   of the wicked.
12 He who belittles his neighbor lacks
   sense,
   but a man of understanding
   remains silent.
13 He who goes about as a talebearer
   reveals secrets,
   but he who is trustworthy in spirit
   keeps a thing hidden.
14 Where there is no guidance, a people
   falls;
   but in an abundance of counselors
   there is safety.
15 He who gives surety for a stranger
   will smart for it,
   but he who hates suretyship is
   secure.
16 A gracious woman gets honor,
   and violent men get riches.

17 A man who is kind benefits himself,
   but a cruel man hurts himself.
18 A wicked man earns deceptive
   wages,
   but one who sows righteousness
   gets a sure reward.
19 He who is steadfast in righteousness
   will live,
   but he who pursues evil will die.
20 Men of perverse mind are an
   abomination to the LORD,
   but those of blameless ways are
   his delight.
21 Be assured, an evil man will not go
   unpunished,
   but those who are righteous will
   be delivered.
22 Like a gold ring in a swine's snout
   is a beautiful woman without
   discretion.
23 The desire of the righteous ends only
   in good;
   the expectation of the wicked in
   wrath.
24 One man gives freely, yet grows all
   the richer;
   another withholds what he should
   give, and only suffers want.
25 A liberal man will be enriched,
   and one who waters will himself
   be watered.
26 The people curse him who holds
   back grain,
   but a blessing is on the head of
   him who sells it.
27 He who diligently seeks good seeks
   favor,
   but evil comes to him who
   searches for it.
28 He who trusts in his riches will
   wither,[v]
   but the righteous will flourish like
   a green leaf.
29 He who troubles his household will
   inherit wind,
   and the fool will be servant to the
   wise.

v Cn: Heb *fall*

13: *Secrets*, i.e. confidences. 15: *Hates suretyship*, or "is loathe to make pledges for others."
16: *Violent*, or "vigorous." 18: *Deceptive*, illusory, (1.17–19). 25: *Who waters* when water is
precious. 26: *Holds back* for higher prices. 27: *Seeks favor*, see Am.5.4,14. 30: *Of the righteous*,
or "of righteousness." *Is* (like the fruit of) *a tree of life*, 3.18; Gen.3.22.

³⁰ The fruit of the righteous is a tree of
life,
but lawlessness^w takes away lives.
³¹ If the righteous is requited on earth,
how much more the wicked and
the sinner!

12 Whoever loves discipline loves
knowledge,
but he who hates reproof is
stupid.
² A good man obtains favor from the
LORD,
but a man of evil devices he
condemns.
³ A man is not established by
wickedness,
but the root of the righteous will
never be moved.
⁴ A good wife is the crown of her
husband,
but she who brings shame is like
rottenness in his bones.
⁵ The thoughts of the righteous are
just;
the counsels of the wicked are
treacherous.
⁶ The words of the wicked lie in
wait for blood,
but the mouth of the upright
delivers men.
⁷ The wicked are overthrown and
are no more,
but the house of the righteous will
stand.
⁸ A man is commended according to
his good sense,
but one of perverse mind is
despised.
⁹ Better is a man of humble standing
who works for himself
than one who plays the great
man but lacks bread.
¹⁰ A righteous man has regard for the
life of his beast,
but the mercy of the wicked is
cruel.
¹¹ He who tills his land will have
plenty of bread,
but he who follows worthless
pursuits has no sense.

¹² The strong tower of the wicked
comes to ruin,
but the root of the righteous
stands firm.^x
¹³ An evil man is ensnared by the
transgression of his lips,
but the righteous escapes from
trouble.
¹⁴ From the fruit of his words a man
is satisfied with good,
and the work of a man's hand
comes back to him.
¹⁵ The way of a fool is right in his own
eyes,
but a wise man listens to advice.
¹⁶ The vexation of a fool is known at
once,
but the prudent man ignores an
insult.
¹⁷ He who speaks the truth gives
honest evidence,
but a false witness utters deceit.
¹⁸ There is one whose rash words are
like sword thrusts,
but the tongue of the wise brings
healing.
¹⁹ Truthful lips endure for ever,
but a lying tongue is but for a
moment.
²⁰ Deceit is in the heart of those who
devise evil,
but those who plan good have joy.
²¹ No ill befalls the righteous,
but the wicked are filled with
trouble.
²² Lying lips are an abomination to
the LORD,
but those who act faithfully are his
delight.
²³ A prudent man conceals his
knowledge,
but fools^y proclaim their folly.
²⁴ The hand of the diligent will rule,
while the slothful will be put to
forced labor.
²⁵ Anxiety in a man's heart weighs
him down,
but a good word makes him glad.

w Cn Compare Gk Syr: Heb *a wise man*
x Cn: The Hebrew of verse 12 is obscure
y Heb *the heart of fools*

12.1: There is no short-cut to knowledge. **3:** The invisible *root* holds the tree firm (Hos.14.5–
6). **6:** Bad men talk of violence but good men of rescue. **10:** What passes for *mercy* with *the*

26 A righteous man turns away from
   evil,*z*
   but the way of the wicked leads
     them astray.
27 A slothful man will not catch his
   prey,*a*
   but the diligent man will get
     precious wealth.*b*
28 In the path of righteousness is life,
   but the way of error leads to
     death.*c*

13 A wise son hears his father's
   instruction,
   but a scoffer does not listen to
     rebuke.
2 From the fruit of his mouth a good
   man eats good,
   but the desire of the treacherous
     is for violence.
3 He who guards his mouth preserves
   his life;
   he who opens wide his lips comes
     to ruin.
4 The soul of the sluggard craves, and
   gets nothing,
   while the soul of the diligent is
     richly supplied.
5 A righteous man hates falsehood,
   but a wicked man acts shamefully
     and disgracefully.
6 Righteousness guards him whose
   way is upright,
   but sin overthrows the wicked.
7 One man pretends to be rich, yet
   has nothing;
   another pretends to be poor, yet
     has great wealth.
8 The ransom of a man's life is his
   wealth,
   but a poor man has no means of
     redemption.*d*
9 The light of the righteous
   rejoices,
   but the lamp of the wicked will
     be put out.
10 By insolence the heedless make
   strife,

   but with those who take advice
     is wisdom.
11 Wealth hastily gotten*e* will dwindle,
   but he who gathers little by little
     will increase it.
12 Hope deferred makes the heart sick,
   but a desire fulfilled is a tree of
     life.
13 He who despises the word brings
   destruction on himself,
   but he who respects the
     commandment will be
     rewarded.
14 The teaching of the wise is a
   fountain of life,
   that one may avoid the snares of
     death.
15 Good sense wins favor,
   but the way of the faithless is
     their ruin.*f*
16 In everything a prudent man acts
   with knowledge,
   but a fool flaunts his folly.
17 A bad messenger plunges men into
   trouble,
   but a faithful envoy brings healing.
18 Poverty and disgrace come to him
   who ignores instruction,
   but he who heeds reproof is
     honored.
19 A desire fulfilled is sweet to the soul;
   but to turn away from evil is an
     abomination to fools.
20 He who walks with wise men
   becomes wise,
   but the companion of fools will
     suffer harm.
21 Misfortune pursues sinners,
   but prosperity rewards the
     righteous.
22 A good man leaves an inheritance
   to his children's children,

z Cn: The meaning of the Hebrew is uncertain
a Cn Compare Gk Syr: The meaning of the Hebrew is
  uncertain
b Cn: The meaning of the Hebrew is uncertain
c Cn: The meaning of the Hebrew is uncertain
d Cn: Heb *does not hear rebuke*
e Gk Vg: Heb *from vanity*
f Cn Compare Gk Syr Vg Tg: Heb *is enduring*

wicked is *cruel*. **26:** *Turns away from evil*, or "survives his trouble," in contrast to the wicked who
ends in trouble. **27a:** This means something like "the indolent is not worth his salt."
    13.2: Good words bring good results (see 12.14). **4:** *Soul*, or "desire." **9:** *Light* is a symbol of
life (1 Kg.15.4; Jn.1.4). *Rejoices*, or "burns brightly." **12:** See 3.18 n. **13:** *Word* of warning. **17:**
Healing, or "benefit." **19:** Disconnected lines from different proverbs. **23:** This may mean
"a lawsuit devours the poor man's land, and his home is swept away when there is no justice."

but the sinner's wealth is laid up
for the righteous.
²³ The fallow ground of the poor yields
much food,
but it is swept away through
injustice.
²⁴ He who spares the rod hates his son,
but he who loves him is diligent
to discipline him.
²⁵ The righteous has enough to satisfy
his appetite,
but the belly of the wicked suffers
want.

14 Wisdom*g* builds her house,
but folly with her own hands
tears it down.
² He who walks in uprightness fears
the LORD,
but he who is devious in his ways
despises him.
³ The talk of a fool is a rod for his
back,*h*
but the lips of the wise will
preserve them.
⁴ Where there are no oxen, there is
no*i* grain;
but abundant crops come by the
strength of the ox.
⁵ A faithful witness does not lie,
but a false witness breathes out
lies.
⁶ A scoffer seeks wisdom in vain,
but knowledge is easy for a man
of understanding.
⁷ Leave the presence of a fool,
for there you do not meet words
of knowledge.
⁸ The wisdom of a prudent man is to
discern his way,
but the folly of fools is deceiving.
⁹ God scorns the wicked,*j*
but the upright enjoy his favor.
¹⁰ The heart knows its own bitterness,
and no stranger shares its joy.
¹¹ The house of the wicked will be
destroyed,
but the tent of the upright will
flourish.
¹² There is a way which seems right to
a man,

but its end is the way to death.*k*
¹³ Even in laughter the heart is sad,
and the end of joy is grief.
¹⁴ A perverse man will be filled with
the fruit of his ways,
and a good man with the fruit of
his deeds.*l*
¹⁵ The simple believes everything,
but the prudent looks where he
is going.
¹⁶ A wise man is cautious and turns
away from evil,
but a fool throws off restraint and
is careless.
¹⁷ A man of quick temper acts
foolishly,
but a man of discretion is
patient.*m*
¹⁸ The simple acquire folly,
but the prudent are crowned with
knowledge.
¹⁹ The evil bow down before the good,
the wicked at the gates of the
righteous.
²⁰ The poor is disliked even by his
neighbor,
but the rich has many friends.
²¹ He who despises his neighbor is a
sinner,
but happy is he who is kind to
the poor.
²² Do they not err that devise evil?
Those who devise good meet
loyalty and faithfulness.
²³ In all toil there is profit,
but mere talk tends only to want.
²⁴ The crown of the wise is their
wisdom,*n*
but folly is the garland*o* of fools.
²⁵ A truthful witness saves lives,
but one who utters lies is a
betrayer.
²⁶ In the fear of the LORD one has
strong confidence,
and his children will have a
refuge.

g Heb *Wisdom of women*
h Cn: Heb *a rod of pride*
i Cn: Heb *a manger of*   j Cn: Heb obscure
k Heb *ways of death*   l Cn: Heb *from upon him*
m Gk: Heb *is hated*
n Cn Compare Gk: Heb *riches*   o Cn: Heb *folly*

14.1: The *house* of life. **3**: *Is a rod for*, brings a switch on. **9**: Possibly should be read, "Guilt dwells with fools, but favor among the upright." **12**: What seems a clear road leads to death.

27 The fear of the LORD is a fountain
　　of life,
　　　that one may avoid the snares of
　　　　death.
28 In a multitude of people is the glory
　　of a king,
　　　but without people a prince is
　　　　ruined.
29 He who is slow to anger has great
　　understanding,
　　　but he who has a hasty temper
　　　　exalts folly.
30 A tranquil mind gives life to the
　　flesh,
　　　but passion makes the bones rot.
31 He who oppresses a poor man
　　insults his Maker,
　　　but he who is kind to the needy
　　　　honors him.
32 The wicked is overthrown through
　　his evil-doing,
　　　but the righteous finds refuge
　　　　through his integrity.*p*
33 Wisdom abides in the mind of a
　　man of understanding,
　　　but it is not*q* known in the heart
　　　　of fools.
34 Righteousness exalts a nation,
　　　but sin is a reproach to any
　　　　people.
35 A servant who deals wisely has the
　　king's favor,
　　　but his wrath falls on one who
　　　　acts shamefully.

15 A soft answer turns away wrath,
　　　but a harsh word stirs up anger.
2 The tongue of the wise dispenses
　　knowledge,*r*
　　　but the mouths of fools pour out
　　　　folly.
3 The eyes of the LORD are in every
　　place,
　　　keeping watch on the evil and the
　　　　good.
4 A gentle tongue is a tree of life,
　　　but perverseness in it breaks the
　　　　spirit.
5 A fool despises his father's
　　instruction,

but he who heeds admonition is
　　prudent.
6 In the house of the righteous there
　　is much treasure,
　　　but trouble befalls the income of
　　　　the wicked.
7 The lips of the wise spread
　　knowledge;
　　　not so the minds of fools.
8 The sacrifice of the wicked is an
　　abomination to the LORD,
　　　but the prayer of the upright is
　　　　his delight.
9 The way of the wicked is an
　　abomination to the LORD,
　　　but he loves him who pursues
　　　　righteousness.
10 There is severe discipline for him
　　who forsakes the way;
　　　he who hates reproof will die.
11 Sheol and Abaddon lie open before
　　the LORD,
　　　how much more the hearts of men!
12 A scoffer does not like to be
　　reproved;
　　　he will not go to the wise.
13 A glad heart makes a cheerful
　　countenance,
　　　but by sorrow of heart the spirit is
　　　　broken.
14 The mind of him who has
　　understanding seeks knowledge,
　　　but the mouths of fools feed on
　　　　folly.
15 All the days of the afflicted are evil,
　　　but a cheerful heart has a
　　　　continual feast.
16 Better is a little with the fear of the
　　LORD
　　　than great treasure and trouble
　　　　with it.
17 Better is a dinner of herbs where
　　love is
　　　than a fatted ox and hatred with
　　　　it.
18 A hot-tempered man stirs up strife,

p Gk Syr: Heb *in his death*
q Gk Syr: Heb lacks *not*
r Cn: Heb *makes knowledge good*

30: A healthy mind makes a vigorous body, and vice versa. **31:** *His* (i.e. the poor man's) *Maker*.
　　15.8: *Sacrifice* and *prayer* connote worship, for which sincerity is essential (Is.1.10–17). **11:**
Sheol and Abaddon, the place and state (destruction) of the dead (see Gen.37.35 n.). **15:** *Evil*,
bad, unhappy. **16:** *Trouble*, uneasiness.

but he who is slow to anger quiets
  contention.
19 The way of a sluggard is overgrown
  with thorns,
  but the path of the upright is a
    level highway.
20 A wise son makes a glad father,
  but a foolish man despises his
    mother.
21 Folly is a joy to him who has no
  sense,
  but a man of understanding walks
    aright.
22 Without counsel plans go wrong,
  but with many advisers they
    succeed.
23 To make an apt answer is a joy to
  a man,
  and a word in season, how good
    it is!
24 The wise man's path leads upward
  to life,
  that he may avoid Sheol beneath.
25 The LORD tears down the house of
  the proud,
  but maintains the widow's
    boundaries.
26 The thoughts of the wicked are an
  abomination to the LORD,
  the words of the pure are
    pleasing to him.*s*
27 He who is greedy for unjust gain
  makes trouble for his household,
  but he who hates bribes will live.
28 The mind of the righteous ponders
  how to answer,
  but the mouth of the wicked pours
    out evil things.
29 The LORD is far from the wicked,
  but he hears the prayer of the
    righteous.
30 The light of the eyes rejoices the
  heart,
  and good news refreshes*t* the
    bones.
31 He whose ear heeds wholesome
  admonition

will abide among the wise.
32 He who ignores instruction despises
  himself,
  but he who heeds admonition gains
    understanding.
33 The fear of the LORD is instruction in
  wisdom,
  and humility goes before honor.

16 The plans of the mind belong to
  man,
  but the answer of the tongue is
    from the LORD.
2 All the ways of a man are pure in
  his own eyes,
  but the LORD weighs the spirit.
3 Commit your work to the LORD,
  and your plans will be established.
4 The LORD has made everything for
  its purpose,
  even the wicked for the day of
    trouble.
5 Every one who is arrogant is an
  abomination to the LORD;
  be assured, he will not go
    unpunished.
6 By loyalty and faithfulness iniquity
  is atoned for,
  and by the fear of the LORD a man
    avoids evil.
7 When a man's ways please the LORD,
  he makes even his enemies to be
    at peace with him.
8 Better is a little with righteousness
  than great revenues with injustice.
9 A man's mind plans his way,
  but the LORD directs his steps.
10 Inspired decisions are on the lips of
  a king;
  his mouth does not sin in
    judgment.
11 A just balance and scales are the
  LORD's;
  all the weights in the bag are his
    work.

s Cn Compare Gk: Heb *pleasant words are pure*
t Heb *makes fat*

24: *Upward,* away from Sheol, the grave. **30:** A *light* shines in *the eyes* of the messenger
with *good news.* **33:** *Instruction in,* or "the foundation of." *Humility* here means humility before
God (Mic.6.8).
  16.1: To be able to express thought in speech is a gift of God; see v. 9. **2:** *Weighs the spirit*
which moves a man. **4:** The will of God determines the doom of evil men. **6:** *Iniquity is atoned
for* by goodness which implies repentance. **10:** *Sin,* err. **11:** Commercial honesty is a divine

¹² It is an abomination to kings to do
evil,
for the throne is established by
righteousness.
¹³ Righteous lips are the delight of a
king,
and he loves him who speaks what
is right.
¹⁴ A king's wrath is a messenger of
death,
and a wise man will appease it.
¹⁵ In the light of a king's face there is
life,
and his favor is like the clouds
that bring the spring rain.
¹⁶ To get wisdom is better*u* than gold;
to get understanding is to be
chosen rather than silver.
¹⁷ The highway of the upright turns
aside from evil;
he who guards his way preserves
his life.
¹⁸ Pride goes before destruction,
and a haughty spirit before a fall.
¹⁹ It is better to be of a lowly spirit
with the poor
than to divide the spoil with the
proud.
²⁰ He who gives heed to the word will
prosper,
and happy is he who trusts in the
LORD.
²¹ The wise of heart is called a man of
discernment,
and pleasant speech increases
persuasiveness.
²² Wisdom is a fountain of life to him
who has it,
but folly is the chastisement of
fools.
²³ The mind of the wise makes his
speech judicious,
and adds persuasiveness to his
lips.
²⁴ Pleasant words are like a honeycomb,
sweetness to the soul and health
to the body.
²⁵ There is a way which seems right to
a man,
but its end is the way to death.*v*

²⁶ A worker's appetite works for him;
his mouth urges him on.
²⁷ A worthless man plots evil,
and his speech is like a scorching
fire.
²⁸ A perverse man spreads strife,
and a whisperer separates close
friends.
²⁹ A man of violence entices his
neighbor
and leads him in a way that is not
good.
³⁰ He who winks his eyes plans*w*
perverse things,
he who compresses his lips brings
evil to pass.
³¹ A hoary head is a crown of glory;
it is gained in a righteous life.
³² He who is slow to anger is better
than the mighty,
and he who rules his spirit than he
who takes a city.
³³ The lot is cast into the lap,
but the decision is wholly from the
LORD.

17 Better is a dry morsel with quiet
than a house full of feasting
with strife.
² A slave who deals wisely will rule
over a son who acts shamefully,
and will share the inheritance as
one of the brothers.
³ The crucible is for silver, and the
furnace is for gold,
and the LORD tries hearts.
⁴ An evildoer listens to wicked lips;
and a liar gives heed to a
mischievous tongue.
⁵ He who mocks the poor insults his
Maker;
he who is glad at calamity will not
go unpunished.
⁶ Grandchildren are the crown of the
aged,
and the glory of sons is their
fathers.
⁷ Fine speech is not becoming to a
fool;

u Gk Syr Vg Tg: Heb *how much better*
v Heb *ways of death*
w Gk Syr Vg Tg: Heb *to plan*

---

command (11.1; Ezek.45.10). **20:** *The word,* the commandment. **25:** 14.12. **31:** *Glory,* or
"beauty"; compare 1 Kg.3.14. **33:** The fall of *the lot* is not by chance but by God's will.

still less is false speech to a prince.

8 A bribe is like a magic stone in the
  eyes of him who gives it;
  wherever he turns he prospers.

9 He who forgives an offense seeks
  love,
  but he who repeats a matter
  alienates a friend.

10 A rebuke goes deeper into a man of
  understanding
  than a hundred blows into a fool.

11 An evil man seeks only rebellion,
  and a cruel messenger will be sent
  against him.

12 Let a man meet a she-bear robbed
  of her cubs,
  rather than a fool in his folly.

13 If a man returns evil for good,
  evil will not depart from his house.

14 The beginning of strife is like letting
  out water;
  so quit before the quarrel breaks
  out.

15 He who justifies the wicked and he
  who condemns the righteous
  are both alike an abomination to
  the LORD.

16 Why should a fool have a price in
  his hand to buy wisdom,
  when he has no mind?

17 A friend loves at all times,
  and a brother is born for
  adversity.

18 A man without sense gives a pledge,
  and becomes surety in the presence
  of his neighbor.

19 He who loves transgression loves
  strife;
  he who makes his door high seeks
  destruction.

20 A man of crooked mind does not
  prosper,
  and one with a perverse tongue
  falls into calamity.

21 A stupid son is a grief to a father;
  and the father of a fool has no joy.

22 A cheerful heart is a good medicine,

but a downcast spirit dries up the
  bones.

23 A wicked man accepts a bribe from
  the bosom
  to pervert the ways of justice.

24 A man of understanding sets his
  face toward wisdom,
  but the eyes of a fool are on the
  ends of the earth.

25 A foolish son is a grief to his father
  and bitterness to her who bore
  him.

26 To impose a fine on a righteous
  man is not good;
  to flog noble men is wrong.

27 He who restrains his words has
  knowledge,
  and he who has a cool spirit is a
  man of understanding.

28 Even a fool who keeps silent is
  considered wise;
  when he closes his lips, he is
  deemed intelligent.

18 He who is estranged[x] seeks
  pretexts[y]
  to break out against all sound
  judgment.

2 A fool takes no pleasure in
  understanding,
  but only in expressing his opinion.

3 When wickedness comes, contempt
  comes also;
  and with dishonor comes disgrace.

4 The words of a man's mouth are
  deep waters;
  the fountain of wisdom is a
  gushing stream.

5 It is not good to be partial to a
  wicked man,
  or to deprive a righteous man of
  justice.

6 A fool's lips bring strife,
  and his mouth invites a flogging.

7 A fool's mouth is his ruin,
  and his lips are a snare to himself.

x Heb *separated*
y Gk Vg: Heb *desire*

17.8: *A magic stone*, a charm to bring good luck. **9:** *Repeats*, harps on. **11:** Rebellion provokes
severity. **14:** *Letting out water* from a dam or irrigation channel is easier to start than to stop.
17: *Is born for*, to help in *adversity* is what *a brother* is for. **18:** See 6.1–5 n. **19:** *Makes his door
high*, that is, "wide open" (see Ps.24.7), hence insecure. **23:** *From the bosom*, clandestinely. **24:**
A wise man acts on principle, a fool on impulse.
18.1: Or, "An unsociable man wants to be left alone." **4:** *Deep waters*, unfathomable or

⁸ The words of a whisperer are like
　delicious morsels;
　they go down into the inner parts
　of the body.
⁹ He who is slack in his work
　is a brother to him who destroys.
¹⁰ The name of the LORD is a strong
　tower;
　the righteous man runs into it and
　is safe.
¹¹ A rich man's wealth is his strong
　city,
　and like a high wall protecting
　him.ᶻ
¹² Before destruction a man's heart is
　haughty,
　but humility goes before honor.
¹³ If one gives answer before he hears,
　it is his folly and shame.
¹⁴ A man's spirit will endure sickness;
　but a broken spirit who can bear?
¹⁵ An intelligent mind acquires
　knowledge,
　and the ear of the wise seeks
　knowledge.
¹⁶ A man's gift makes room for him
　and brings him before great men.
¹⁷ He who states his case first seems
　right,
　until the other comes and
　examines him.
¹⁸ The lot puts an end to disputes
　and decides between powerful
　contenders.
¹⁹ A brother helped is like a strong
　city,ᵃ
　but quarreling is like the bars of
　a castle.
²⁰ From the fruit of his mouth a man
　is satisfied;
　he is satisfied by the yield of his
　lips.
²¹ Death and life are in the power of
　the tongue,
　and those who love it will eat its
　fruits.
²² He who finds a wife finds a good
　thing,
　and obtains favor from the LORD.

²³ The poor use entreaties,
　but the rich answer roughly.
²⁴ There areᵇ friends who pretend to
　be friends,ᶜ
　but there is a friend who sticks
　closer than a brother.

19 Better is a poor man who walks
　in his integrity
　than a man who is perverse in
　speech, and is a fool.
² It is not good for a man to be
　without knowledge,
　and he who makes haste with his
　feet misses his way.
³ When a man's folly brings his way
　to ruin,
　his heart rages against the LORD.
⁴ Wealth brings many new friends,
　but a poor man is deserted by his
　friend.
⁵ A false witness will not go
　unpunished,
　and he who utters lies will not
　escape.
⁶ Many seek the favor of a generous
　man,
　and every one is a friend to a man
　who gives gifts.
⁷ All a poor man's brothers hate him;
　how much more do his friends go
　far from him!
He pursues them with words, but
　does not have them.ᵈ
⁸ He who gets wisdom loves himself;
　he who keeps understanding will
　prosper.
⁹ A false witness will not go
　unpunished,
　and he who utters lies will perish.
¹⁰ It is not fitting for a fool to live in
　luxury,
　much less for a slave to rule over
　princes.
¹¹ Good sense makes a man slow to
　anger,

z Or *in his imagination*
a Gk Syr Vg Tg: The meaning of the Hebrew is uncertain
b Syr Tg: Heb *A man of*
c Cn Compare Syr Vg Tg: Heb *to be broken*
d Heb uncertain

dangerous (10.19), *a gushing stream* refreshes. **8:** Slander listened to is not soon forgotten.
17: A figure from the law courts. **18:** A legal wisdom saying; compare 16.33. **19:** Or, "An
aggrieved brother is harder to overcome than a fortress." **20:** See 13.2 n. **19.7c:** When *he pursues*
them they speak angrily to him.

and it is his glory to overlook an
    offense.
12 A king's wrath is like the growling
    of a lion,
    but his favor is like dew upon the
      grass.
13 A foolish son is ruin to his father,
    and a wife's quarreling is a
      continual dripping of rain.
14 House and wealth are inherited
    from fathers,
    but a prudent wife is from the
      LORD.
15 Slothfulness casts into a deep sleep,
    and an idle person will suffer
      hunger.
16 He who keeps the commandment
    keeps his life;
    he who despises the word[e] will die.
17 He who is kind to the poor lends
    to the LORD,
    and he will repay him for his deed.
18 Discipline your son while there is
    hope;
    do not set your heart on his
      destruction.
19 A man of great wrath will pay the
    penalty;
    for if you deliver him, you will
      only have to do it again.[f]
20 Listen to advice and accept
    instruction,
    that you may gain wisdom for the
      future.
21 Many are the plans in the mind of
    a man,
    but it is the purpose of the LORD
    that will be established.
22 What is desired in a man is loyalty,
    and a poor man is better than a
      liar.
23 The fear of the LORD leads to life;
    and he who has it rests satisfied;
    he will not be visited by harm.
24 The sluggard buries his hand in the
    dish,
    and will not even bring it back to
      his mouth.
25 Strike a scoffer, and the simple will
    learn prudence;
    reprove a man of understanding,

and he will gain knowledge.
26 He who does violence to his father
    and chases away his mother
    is a son who causes shame and
      brings reproach.
27 Cease, my son, to hear instruction
    only to stray from the words of
      knowledge.
28 A worthless witness mocks at justice,
    and the mouth of the wicked
      devours iniquity.
29 Condemnation is ready for scoffers,
    and flogging for the backs of fools.

20 Wine is a mocker, strong drink
    a brawler;
    and whoever is led astray by it
    is not wise.
2 The dread wrath of a king is like
    the growling of a lion;
    he who provokes him to anger
      forfeits his life.
3 It is an honor for a man to keep aloof
    from strife;
    but every fool will be quarreling.
4 The sluggard does not plow in the
    autumn;
    he will seek at harvest and have
      nothing.
5 The purpose in a man's mind is like
    deep water,
    but a man of understanding will
      draw it out.
6 Many a man proclaims his own
    loyalty,
    but a faithful man who can find?
7 A righteous man who walks in his
    integrity–
    blessed are his sons after him!
8 A king who sits on the throne of
    judgment
    winnows all evil with his eyes.
9 Who can say, "I have made my
    heart clean;
    I am pure from my sin"?
10 Diverse weights and diverse
    measures
    are both alike an abomination to
      the LORD.
11 Even a child makes himself known
    by his acts,

e Cn Compare 13.13: Heb *his ways*   *f* Heb obscure

20.5: See 18.4 n. *Deep water*, in a well. *Draw out*, or up. **8:** *Winnows all evil*, sees through

whether what he does is pure and
right.

¹² The hearing ear and the seeing eye,
the LORD has made them both.

¹³ Love not sleep, lest you come to
poverty;
open your eyes, and you will have
plenty of bread.

¹⁴ "It is bad, it is bad," says the buyer;
but when he goes away, then he
boasts.

¹⁵ There is gold, and abundance of
costly stones;
but the lips of knowledge are a
precious jewel.

¹⁶ Take a man's garment when he has
given surety for a stranger,
and hold him in pledge when he
gives surety for foreigners.

¹⁷ Bread gained by deceit is sweet to
a man,
but afterward his mouth will be
full of gravel.

¹⁸ Plans are established by counsel;
by wise guidance wage war.

¹⁹ He who goes about gossiping
reveals secrets;
therefore do not associate with
one who speaks foolishly.

²⁰ If one curses his father or his
mother,
his lamp will be put out in utter
darkness.

²¹ An inheritance gotten hastily in the
beginning
will in the end not be blessed.

²² Do not say, "I will repay evil";
wait for the LORD, and he will help
you.

²³ Diverse weights are an abomination
to the LORD,
and false scales are not good.

²⁴ A man's steps are ordered by the
LORD;
how then can man understand his
way?

²⁵ It is a snare for a man to say
rashly, "It is holy,"

and to reflect only after making
his vows.

²⁶ A wise king winnows the wicked,
and drives the wheel over them.

²⁷ The spirit of man is the lamp of the
LORD,
searching all his innermost parts.

²⁸ Loyalty and faithfulness preserve
the king,
and his throne is upheld by
righteousness.ᵍ

²⁹ The glory of young men is their
strength,
but the beauty of old men is their
gray hair.

³⁰ Blows that wound cleanse away evil;
strokes make clean the innermost
parts.

21 The king's heart is a stream of
water in the hand of the LORD;
he turns it wherever he will.

² Every way of a man is right in his
own eyes,
but the LORD weighs the heart.

³ To do righteousness and justice
is more acceptable to the LORD
than sacrifice.

⁴ Haughty eyes and a proud heart,
the lamp of the wicked, are sin.

⁵ The plans of the diligent lead surely
to abundance,
but every one who is hasty comes
only to want.

⁶ The getting of treasures by a lying
tongue
is a fleeting vapor and a snare of
death.

⁷ The violence of the wicked will
sweep them away,
because they refuse to do what is
just.

⁸ The way of the guilty is crooked,
but the conduct of the pure is
right.

⁹ It is better to live in a corner of the
housetop

g Gk: Heb *loyalty*

claims of *evil* men. **12:** The Creator of the *ear* and *eye* himself hears and sees. **16:** Nearly identical
with 27.13. See 6.1–5 n. **20:** See 13.9 n. **22:** Rom.12.19. **25:** On vows see Lev. ch. 27. **26:** *Drives
the wheel*, requites their guilt. **27:** *The spirit of man* is the divine element in man, "the breath of
life" (Gen.2.7), his moral consciousness.

21.1: *The king* gives favors on behalf of God. **3:** Hos.6.6. **4:** For *lamp*, perhaps read "vow,"

than in a house shared with a
contentious woman.

10 The soul of the wicked desires evil;
his neighbor finds no mercy in his
eyes.

11 When a scoffer is punished, the
simple becomes wise;
when a wise man is instructed, he
gains knowledge.

12 The righteous observes the house of
the wicked;
the wicked are cast down to ruin.

13 He who closes his ear to the cry of
the poor
will himself cry out and not be
heard.

14 A gift in secret averts anger;
and a bribe in the bosom, strong
wrath.

15 When justice is done, it is a joy to
the righteous,
but dismay to evildoers.

16 A man who wanders from the way
of understanding
will rest in the assembly of the
dead.

17 He who loves pleasure will be a
poor man;
he who loves wine and oil will not
be rich.

18 The wicked is a ransom for the
righteous,
and the faithless for the upright.

19 It is better to live in a desert land
than with a contentious and
fretful woman.

20 Precious treasure remains*h* in a
wise man's dwelling,
but a foolish man devours it.

21 He who pursues righteousness and
kindness
will find life*i* and honor.

22 A wise man scales the city of the
mighty
and brings down the stronghold in
which they trust.

23 He who keeps his mouth and his
tongue
keeps himself out of trouble.

24 "Scoffer" is the name of the proud,
haughty man

who acts with arrogant pride.

25 The desire of the sluggard kills him
for his hands refuse to labor.

26 All day long the wicked covets,*j*
but the righteous gives and does
not hold back.

27 The sacrifice of the wicked is an
abomination;
how much more when he brings
it with evil intent.

28 A false witness will perish,
but the word of a man who
hears will endure.

29 A wicked man puts on a bold face,
but an upright man considers*k*
his ways.

30 No wisdom, no understanding, no
counsel,
can avail against the LORD.

31 The horse is made ready for the day
of battle,
but the victory belongs to the
LORD.

22 A good name is to be chosen
rather than great riches,
and favor is better than silver or
gold.

2 The rich and the poor meet together;
the LORD is the maker of them all.

3 A prudent man sees danger and
hides himself;
but the simple go on, and suffer for
it.

4 The reward for humility and fear of
the LORD
is riches and honor and life.

5 Thorns and snares are in the way
of the perverse;
he who guards himself will keep
far from them.

6 Train up a child in the way he should
go,
and when he is old he will not
depart from it.

7 The rich rules over the poor,
and the borrower is the slave of
the lender.

8 He who sows injustice will reap
calamity,

h Gk: Heb *and oil*   *i* Gk: Heb *life and righteousness*
j Gk: Heb *all day long he covets covetously*
k Another reading is *establishes*

compare 11.30. **18**: A *ransom*, his punishment is a warning to others. **31**: Compare Ps.20.7.
22.8: *The rod* of punishment will destroy the results of his work.

and the rod of his fury will fail.
9 He who has a bountiful eye will be
  blessed,
   for he shares his bread with the
   poor.
10 Drive out a scoffer, and strife will
   go out,
    and quarreling and abuse will
    cease.
11 He who loves purity of heart,
    and whose speech is gracious, will
    have the king as his friend.
12 The eyes of the LORD keep watch
   over knowledge,
    but he overthrows the words of the
    faithless.
13 The sluggard says, "There is a lion
   outside!
    I shall be slain in the streets!"
14 The mouth of a loose woman is a
   deep pit;
    he with whom the LORD is angry
    will fall into it.
15 Folly is bound up in the heart of a
   child,
    but the rod of discipline drives it
    far from him.
16 He who oppresses the poor to
   increase his own wealth,
    or gives to the rich, will only come
    to want.

17 Incline your ear, and hear the words
   of the wise,
    and apply your mind to my
    knowledge;
18 for it will be pleasant if you keep
   them within you,
    if all of them are ready on your
    lips.
19 That your trust may be in the LORD,
   I have made them known to you
   today, even to you.

20 Have I not written for you thirty
   sayings
    of admonition and knowledge,
21 to show you what is right and true,
    that you may give a true answer
    to those who sent you?

22 Do not rob the poor, because he is
   poor,
    or crush the afflicted at the gate;
23 for the LORD will plead their cause
    and despoil of life those who
    despoil them.
24 Make no friendship with a man
    given to anger,
    nor go with a wrathful man,
25 lest you learn his ways
    and entangle yourself in a snare.
26 Be not one of those who give pledges,
    who become surety for debts.
27 If you have nothing with which to
   pay,
    why should your bed be taken
    from under you?
28 Remove not the ancient landmark
    which your fathers have set.
29 Do you see a man skilful in his work?
    he will stand before kings;
    he will not stand before obscure
    men.

23 When you sit down to eat with
   a ruler,
    observe carefully what[l] is before
    you;
2 and put a knife to your throat
    if you are a man given to appetite.
3 Do not desire his delicacies,
    for they are deceptive food.
4 Do not toil to acquire wealth;
    be wise enough to desist.
5 When your eyes light upon it, it is
   gone;

l Or *who*

22.17–24.22: Book III, a teacher's admonitions to his pupil ("son") in training for responsibility, with introduction (22.17–21) and conclusion (24.21–22). The Egyptian "Instruction of Amen-em-ope" (see Introduction) also has thirty sections (22.20), of which ten have parallels here.
22.17: *The words of the wise*, the title of the section (compare 24.23) has been included by mistake in the first line. **21:** *Sent*, or "asked." **22:** *At the gate* of a city the elders gave judgment in disputes (Am.5.10–15). **28:** As in Amen-em-ope, vi, "Do not carry off the landmark" (compare 23.10; Dt.19.14).
23.1–2: *Observe carefully what is before you*, keep attention on what has been served you, for politeness' sake. **4–5:** Amen-em-ope, vii, "Riches . . . have made themselves wings like

for suddenly it takes to itself wings,
flying like an eagle toward heaven.
6 Do not eat the bread of a man who
is stingy;
do not desire his delicacies;
7 for he is like one who is inwardly
reckoning.*m*
"Eat and drink!" he says to you;
but his heart is not with you.
8 You will vomit up the morsels
which you have eaten,
and waste your pleasant words.
9 Do not speak in the hearing of a
fool,
for he will despise the wisdom of
your words.
10 Do not remove an ancient landmark
or enter the fields of the fatherless;
11 for their Redeemer is strong;
he will plead their cause against
you.
12 Apply your mind to instruction
and your ear to words of
knowledge.
13 Do not withhold discipline from a
child;
if you beat him with a rod, he will
not die.
14 If you beat him with the rod
you will save his life from Sheol.
15 My son, if your heart is wise,
my heart too will be glad.
16 My soul will rejoice
when your lips speak what is right.
17 Let not your heart envy sinners,
but continue in the fear of the
LORD all the day.
18 Surely there is a future,
and your hope will not be cut
off.

19 Hear, my son, and be wise,
and direct your mind in the way.
20 Be not among winebibbers,
or among gluttonous eaters of
meat;
21 for the drunkard and the glutton
will come to poverty,

and drowsiness will clothe a man
with rags.

22 Hearken to your father who begot
you,
and do not despise your mother
when she is old.
23 Buy truth, and do not sell it;
buy wisdom, instruction, and
understanding.
24 The father of the righteous will
greatly rejoice;
he who begets a wise son will be
glad in him.
25 Let your father and mother be glad,
let her who bore you rejoice.

26 My son, give me your heart,
and let your eyes observe*n* my
ways.
27 For a harlot is a deep pit;
an adventuress is a narrow well.
28 She lies in wait like a robber
and increases the faithless among
men.

29 Who has woe? Who has sorrow?
Who has strife? Who has
complaining?
Who has wounds without cause?
Who has redness of eyes?
30 Those who tarry long over wine,
those who go to try mixed wine.
31 Do not look at wine when it is red,
when it sparkles in the cup
and goes down smoothly.
32 At the last it bites like a serpent,
and stings like an adder.
33 Your eyes will see strange things,
and your mind utter perverse
things.
34 You will be like one who lies down
in the midst of the sea,
like one who lies on the top of a
mast.*o*
35 "They struck me," you will say,*p*
"but I was not hurt;

m Heb obscure   *n* Another reading is *delight in*
o Heb obscure
p Gk Syr Vg Tg: Heb lacks *you will say*

geese." **6:** Add here the second line of v. 3. **7:** *Like . . . reckoning*, or "like a hair in your throat."
18: *Surely there is*, or "then you will have." **34:** *Who lies down . . . sea*, "who is prostrated
(with seasickness) far at sea." *Who lies on the top of a mast*, or perhaps "who rolls drunkenly
(from side to side) like the top of a mast."

they beat me, but I did not feel it.
When shall I awake?
I will seek another drink."

24 Be not envious of evil men,
nor desire to be with them;
2 for their minds devise violence,
and their lips talk of mischief.

3 By wisdom a house is built,
and by understanding it is
established;
4 by knowledge the rooms are filled
with all precious and pleasant
riches.
5 A wise man is mightier than a strong
man,*q*
and a man of knowledge than he
who has strength;
6 for by wise guidance you can wage
your war,
and in abundance of counselors
there is victory.
7 Wisdom is too high for a fool;
in the gate he does not open his
mouth.

8 He who plans to do evil
will be called a mischief-maker.
9 The devising of folly is sin,
and the scoffer is an abomination
to men.

10 If you faint in the day of adversity,
your strength is small.
11 Rescue those who are being taken
away to death;
hold back those who are
stumbling to the slaughter.
12 If you say, "Behold, we did not
know this,"
does not he who weighs the
heart perceive it?
Does not he who keeps watch over
your soul know it,
and will he not requite man
according to his work?

13 My son, eat honey, for it is good,
and the drippings of the
honeycomb are sweet to
your taste.

14 Know that wisdom is such to your
soul;
if you find it, there will be a
future,
and your hope will not be cut off.

15 Lie not in wait as a wicked man
against the dwelling of the
righteous;
do not violence to his home;
16 for a righteous man falls seven
times, and rises again;
but the wicked are overthrown by
calamity.

17 Do not rejoice when your enemy
falls,
and let not your heart be glad
when he stumbles;
18 lest the LORD see it, and be
displeased,
and turn away his anger from him.

19 Fret not yourself because of
evildoers,
and be not envious of the wicked;
20 for the evil man has no future;
the lamp of the wicked will be put
out.

21 My son, fear the LORD and the king,
and do not disobey either of
them;*r*
22 for disaster from them will rise
suddenly,
and who knows the ruin that will
come from them both?

23　These also are sayings of the wise.

Partiality in judging is not good.
24 He who says to the wicked, "You
are innocent,"
will be cursed by peoples,
abhorred by nations;
25 but those who rebuke the wicked
will have delight,
and a good blessing will be upon
them.

q Gk Compare Syr Tg: Heb *is in strength*
r Gk: Heb *do not associate with those who change*

24.10: *Faint,* "weaken." **11:** A good man should intervene on behalf of victims of violence.
24.23–34: Appendix I, added to Book III. **23b–26:** A legal maxim commented on. *Kisses the*

²⁶ He who gives a right answer
  kisses the lips.

²⁷ Prepare your work outside,
  get everything ready for you in
    the field;
  and after that build your house.

²⁸ Be not a witness against your
  neighbor without cause,
  and do not deceive with your lips.
²⁹ Do not say, "I will do to him as he
  has done to me;
  I will pay the man back for what
  he has done."

³⁰ I passed by the field of a sluggard,
  by the vineyard of a man without
    sense;
³¹ and lo, it was all overgrown with
    thorns;
  the ground was covered with
    nettles,
  and its stone wall was broken
    down.
³² Then I saw and considered it;
  I looked and received instruction.
³³ A little sleep, a little slumber,
  a little folding of the hands to rest,
³⁴ and poverty will come upon you
  like a robber,
  and want like an armed man.

25 These also are proverbs of Solomon which the men of Hezeki′ah
king of Judah copied.

² It is the glory of God to conceal
  things,
  but the glory of kings is to search
  things out.
³ As the heavens for height, and the
  earth for depth,
  so the mind of kings is
  unsearchable.

⁴ Take away the dross from the silver,
  and the smith has material for a
    vessel;
⁵ take away the wicked from the
  presence of the king,
  and his throne will be established
  in righteousness.
⁶ Do not put yourself forward in the
  king's presence
  or stand in the place of the great;
⁷ for it is better to be told, "Come up
  here,"
  than to be put lower in the
  presence of the prince.

What your eyes have seen
⁸   do not hastily bring into court;
  for*s* what will you do in the end,
  when your neighbor puts you to
  shame?
⁹ Argue your case with your neighbor
  himself,
  and do not disclose another's
  secret;
¹⁰ lest he who hears you bring shame
  upon you,
  and your ill repute have no end.

¹¹ A word fitly spoken
  is like apples of gold in a setting
  of silver.
¹² Like a gold ring or an ornament of
  gold
  is a wise reprover to a listening
  ear.
¹³ Like the cold of snow in the time of
  harvest
  is a faithful messenger to those
  who send him,
  he refreshes the spirit of his
  masters.
¹⁴ Like clouds and wind without rain
  is a man who boasts of a gift he
  does not give.

s Cn: Heb *lest*

---

lips, i.e. is a true friend. **27**: Prudent preparation is the way to success. **29**: Rom.12.21. **30–34**:
6.6–11.
    25.1–29.27: Book IV, a second collection of "Proverbs of Solomon"; see Introduction.
25.1: *Men of Hezekiah*, scribes of king Hezekiah (715–687 B.C.), who sought to model himself
on Solomon (2 Chr.30.26; 32.27–29). **2–3**: The king, like God, questions men but cannot be
questioned. **7**: Lk.14.7–11. **7c–10**: A caution against rash accusations (compare Mt.18.15–17).
13: *Cold of snow*, a drink cooled with snow from Mount Hermon (compare Jer.18.14). **14**:
After the summer drought autumn rains were eagerly looked for. **15–16**: Moral instruction

15 With patience a ruler may be
   persuaded,
   and a soft tongue will break a
   bone.
16 If you have found honey, eat only
   enough for you,
   lest you be sated with it and
   vomit it.
17 Let your foot be seldom in your
   neighbor's house,
   lest he become weary of you and
   hate you.
18 A man who bears false witness
   against his neighbor
   is like a war club, or a sword, or
   a sharp arrow.
19 Trust in a faithless man in time of
   trouble
   is like a bad tooth or a foot that
   slips.
20 He who sings songs to a heavy
   heart
   is like one who takes off a garment
   on a cold day,
   and like vinegar on a wound.*t*
21 If your enemy is hungry, give him
   bread to eat;
   and if he is thirsty, give him water
   to drink;
22 for you will heap coals of fire on
   his head,
   and the LORD will reward you.
23 The north wind brings forth rain;
   and a backbiting tongue, angry
   looks.
24 It is better to live in a corner of the
   housetop
   than in a house shared with a
   contentious woman.
25 Like cold water to a thirsty soul,
   so is good news from a far
   country.
26 Like a muddied spring or a polluted
   fountain
   is a righteous man who gives way
   before the wicked.
27 It is not good to eat much honey,

   so be sparing of complimentary
   words.*u*
28 A man without self-control
   is like a city broken into and left
   without walls.

26 Like snow in summer or rain
   in harvest,
   so honor is not fitting for a fool.
2 Like a sparrow in its flitting, like a
   swallow in its flying,
   a curse that is causeless does not
   alight.
3 A whip for the horse, a bridle for
   the ass,
   and a rod for the back of fools.
4 Answer not a fool according to his
   folly,
   lest you be like him yourself.
5 Answer a fool according to his folly,
   lest he be wise in his own eyes.
6 He who sends a message by the
   hand of a fool
   cuts off his own feet and drinks
   violence.
7 Like a lame man's legs, which
   hang useless,
   is a proverb in the mouth of
   fools.
8 Like one who binds the stone in the
   sling
   is he who gives honor to a fool.
9 Like a thorn that goes up into the
   hand of a drunkard
   is a proverb in the mouth of fools.
10 Like an archer who wounds
   everybody
   is he who hires a passing fool or
   drunkard.*v*
11 Like a dog that returns to his vomit
   is a fool that repeats his folly.
12 Do you see a man who is wise in his
   own eyes?
   There is more hope for a fool than
   for him.

t Gk: Heb *lye*
u Cn Compare Gk Syr Tg: Heb *searching out their glory
is glory*
v The Hebrew text of this verse is uncertain

through figures of speech. **21–22:** *Heap coals of fire,* i.e. torture is less effective than mercy, or
the best way to take vengeance on one's enemy is to be merciful to him (Rom.12.20; Mt.5.44–45).
26: *Gives way,* or "falters."
26.1: Summer in Palestine is hot and dry. **2:** *Does not alight,* has no effect. **4–5:** *According
to his folly* in v. 4 means "in a fool's words"; in v. 5, "as a fool deserves." **6:** *Drinks violence,*
invites trouble (4.17). **8:** A stone tied in its sling is useless. **9:** Alternative translation of *thorn,*

13 The sluggard says, "There is a lion
in the road!
There is a lion in the streets!"
14 As a door turns on its hinges,
so does a sluggard on his bed.
15 The sluggard buries his hand in
the dish;
it wears him out to bring it back to
his mouth.
16 The sluggard is wiser in his own
eyes
than seven men who can answer
discreetly.
17 He who meddles in a quarrel not
his own
is like one who takes a passing dog
by the ears.
18 Like a madman who throws
firebrands,
arrows, and death,
19 is the man who deceives his neighbor
and says, "I am only joking!"
20 For lack of wood the fire goes out;
and where there is no whisperer,
quarreling ceases.
21 As charcoal to hot embers and wood
to fire,
so is a quarrelsome man for
kindling strife.
22 The words of a whisperer are like
delicious morsels;
they go down into the inner parts
of the body.
23 Like the glaze*w* covering an
earthen vessel
are smooth*x* lips with an evil
heart.
24 He who hates, dissembles with his
lips
and harbors deceit in his heart;
25 when he speaks graciously, believe
him not,
for there are seven abominations in
his heart;
26 though his hatred be covered with
guile,
his wickedness will be exposed in
the assembly.
27 He who digs a pit will fall into it,

and a stone will come back upon
him who starts it rolling.
28 A lying tongue hates its victims,
and a flattering mouth works ruin.

27 Do not boast about tomorrow,
for you do not know what a
day may bring forth.
2 Let another praise you, and not
your own mouth;
a stranger, and not your own lips.
3 A stone is heavy, and sand is
weighty,
but a fool's provocation is
heavier than both.
4 Wrath is cruel, anger is
overwhelming;
but who can stand before
jealousy?
5 Better is open rebuke
than hidden love.
6 Faithful are the wounds of a friend;
profuse are the kisses of an
enemy.
7 He who is sated loathes honey,
but to one who is hungry
everything bitter is sweet.
8 Like a bird that strays from its nest,
is a man who strays from his
home.
9 Oil and perfume make the heart
glad,
but the soul is torn by trouble.*y*
10 Your friend, and your father's
friend, do not forsake;
and do not go to your brother's
house in the day of your
calamity.
Better is a neighbor who is near
than a brother who is far away.
11 Be wise, my son, and make my
heart glad,
that I may answer him who
reproaches me.
12 A prudent man sees danger and
hides himself;
but the simple go on, and suffer
for it.

w Cn: Heb *silver of dross*   *x* Gk: Heb *burning*
y Gk: Heb *the sweetness of his friend from hearty counsel*

"pointed stick." *Goes up into*, "is taken up by." **22:** See 18.8 n. **23–26:** A folk proverb with
comments.
    27.3: *A fool's*, or "by a fool." **6:** *Faithful*, sincere. *Profuse*, false. **9b:** Alternative translation:
"so the sweetness of a friend strengthens the soul" (16.24). **10:** The third line explains the

13 Take a man's garment when he
  has given surety for a stranger,
  and hold him in pledge when he
  gives surety for foreigners.*z*
14 He who blesses his neighbor with
  a loud voice,
  rising early in the morning,
  will be counted as cursing.
15 A continual dripping on a rainy day
  and a contentious woman are alike;
16 to restrain her is to restrain the
  wind*a*
  or to grasp oil in his right hand.
17 Iron sharpens iron,
  and one man sharpens another.
18 He who tends a fig tree will eat its
  fruit,
  and he who guards his master
  will be honored.
19 As in water face answers to face,
  so the mind of man reflects the
  man.
20 Sheol and Abaddon are never
  satisfied,
  and never satisfied are the eyes of
  man.
21 The crucible is for silver, and the
  furnace is for gold,
  and a man is judged by his praise.
22 Crush a fool in a mortar with a
  pestle
  along with crushed grain,
  yet his folly will not depart from
  him.

23 Know well the condition of your
  flocks,
  and give attention to your herds;
24 for riches do not last for ever;
  and does a crown endure to all
  generations?
25 When the grass is gone, and the new
  growth appears,
  and the herbage of the mountains
  is gathered,
26 the lambs will provide your clothing,
  and the goats the price of a field;
27 there will be enough goats' milk
  for your food,

for the food of your household
  and maintenance for your
  maidens.

28 The wicked flee when no one
  pursues,
  but the righteous are bold as a
  lion.
2 When a land transgresses
  it has many rulers;
  but with men of understanding and
  knowledge
  its stability will long continue.
3 A poor man who oppresses the
  poor
  is a beating rain that leaves no
  food.
4 Those who forsake the law praise
  the wicked,
  but those who keep the law strive
  against them.
5 Evil men do not understand justice,
  but those who seek the LORD
  understand it completely.
6 Better is a poor man who walks in
  his integrity
  than a rich man who is perverse in
  his ways.
7 He who keeps the law is a wise son,
  but a companion of gluttons
  shames his father.
8 He who augments his wealth by
  interest and increase
  gathers it for him who is kind to
  the poor.
9 If one turns away his ear from
  hearing the law,
  even his prayer is an abomination.
10 He who misleads the upright into
  an evil way
  will fall into his own pit;
  but the blameless will have a
  goodly inheritance.
11 A rich man is wise in his own eyes,
  but a poor man who has
  understanding will find him out.
12 When the righteous triumph, there
  is great glory;

z Vg and 20.16: Heb *a foreign woman*
a Heb obscure

---

second. **13:** Do not hesitate to exact a pledge made rashly (see 6.1–5 n.). **20:** See 15.11 n. **21:**
Judged by his praise, tested by praise.
  28.3a: A difficult line, probably read "chieftain" for "poor man." **12:** *Glory*, delight (20.29).

but when the wicked rise, men
hide themselves.
13 He who conceals his transgressions
will not prosper,
but he who confesses and
forsakes them will obtain mercy.
14 Blessed is the man who fears the
LORD always;
but he who hardens his heart will
fall into calamity.
15 Like a roaring lion or a charging
bear
is a wicked ruler over a poor
people.
16 A ruler who lacks understanding is
a cruel oppressor;
but he who hates unjust gain will
prolong his days.
17 If a man is burdened with the
blood of another,
let him be a fugitive until death;
let no one help him.
18 He who walks in integrity will be
delivered,
but he who is perverse in his
ways will fall into a pit.*b*
19 He who tills his land will have plenty
of bread,
but he who follows worthless
pursuits will have plenty of
poverty.
20 A faithful man will abound with
blessings,
but he who hastens to be rich will
not go unpunished.
21 To show partiality is not good;
but for a piece of bread a man
will do wrong.
22 A miserly man hastens after wealth,
and does not know that want will
come upon him.
23 He who rebukes a man will
afterward find more favor
than he who flatters with his
tongue.
24 He who robs his father or his
mother
and says, "That is no
transgression,"
is the companion of a man who
destroys.

25 A greedy man stirs up strife,
but he who trusts in the LORD
will be enriched.
26 He who trusts in his own mind is a
fool;
but he who walks in wisdom will
be delivered.
27 He who gives to the poor will not
want,
but he who hides his eyes will get
many a curse.
28 When the wicked rise, men hide
themselves,
but when they perish, the
righteous increase.

29 He who is often reproved, yet
stiffens his neck
will suddenly be broken beyond
healing.
2 When the righteous are in authority,
the people rejoice;
but when the wicked rule, the
people groan.
3 He who loves wisdom makes his
father glad,
but one who keeps company with
harlots squanders his
substance.
4 By justice a king gives stability to
the land,
but one who exacts gifts ruins it.
5 A man who flatters his neighbor
spreads a net for his feet.
6 An evil man is ensnared in his
transgression,
but a righteous man sings and
rejoices.
7 A righteous man knows the rights of
the poor;
a wicked man does not
understand such knowledge.
8 Scoffers set a city aflame,
but wise men turn away wrath.
9 If a wise man has an argument with
a fool,
the fool only rages and laughs, and
there is no quiet.
10 Bloodthirsty men hate one who is
blameless,
and the wicked*c* seek his life.

b Syr: Heb *in one*   *c* Cn: Heb *upright*

29.4: *Gifts*, forced contributions. **9:** *And there is no quiet*, or, "no satisfaction." **13:** 22.2;

11 A fool gives full vent to his anger,
   but a wise man quietly holds it
   back.
12 If a ruler listens to falsehood,
   all his officials will be wicked.
13 The poor man and the oppressor
   meet together;
   the LORD gives light to the eyes
   of both.
14 If a king judges the poor with
   equity
   his throne will be established for
   ever.
15 The rod and reproof give wisdom,
   but a child left to himself brings
   shame to his mother.
16 When the wicked are in authority,
   transgression increases;
   but the righteous will look upon
   their downfall.
17 Discipline your son, and he will give
   you rest;
   he will give delight to your heart.
18 Where there is no prophecy the
   people cast off restraint,
   but blessed is he who keeps the
   law.
19 By mere words a servant is not
   disciplined,
   for though he understands, he will
   not give heed.
20 Do you see a man who is hasty in
   his words?
   There is more hope for a fool than
   for him.
21 He who pampers his servant from
   childhood,
   will in the end find him his heir.*d*
22 A man of wrath stirs up strife,
   and a man given to anger causes
   much transgression.
23 A man's pride will bring him low,
   but he who is lowly in spirit will
   obtain honor.

24 The partner of a thief hates his own
   life;
   he hears the curse, but discloses
   nothing.
25 The fear of man lays a snare,
   but he who trusts in the LORD is
   safe.
26 Many seek the favor of a ruler,
   but from the LORD a man gets
   justice.
27 An unjust man is an abomination to
   the righteous,
   but he whose way is straight is an
   abomination to the wicked.

30 The words of Agur son of Jakeh
   of Massa.*e*

   The man says to Ith'i-el,
      to Ith'i-el and Ucal:*f*
2 Surely I am too stupid to be a man.
   I have not the understanding of a
      man.
3 I have not learned wisdom,
   nor have I knowledge of the
      Holy One.
4 Who has ascended to heaven and
      come down?
   Who has gathered the wind in his
      fists?
   Who has wrapped up the waters in
      a garment?
   Who has established all the ends
      of the earth?
   What is his name, and what is his
      son's name?
   Surely you know!

5 Every word of God proves true;
   he is a shield to those who take
      refuge in him.

d The meaning of the Hebrew word is uncertain
e Or *the oracle*
f The Hebrew of this verse is obscure

Mt. 5.45. **18:** *He who keeps,* or "that people which keeps." **21:** For *his heir* read perhaps "refractory." **24:** A guilty secret is a danger.
   30.1–9: Appendix II, dialogue of a sceptic and a believer, recalling Job. **1:** *Massa,* a tribe in
Arabia in Gen.25.14; 1 Chr.1.30; but see note *e* and 31.1 note *k. Agur* is unknown and was
probably, like Job, not an Israelite. *To Ithiel . . . Ucal,* not proper names but the obscure opening of the first speech. The words may mean "There is no God and I am exhausted," or "I have
no God, yet I endure." **2–3:** Sarcasm, see Job 12.2; 26.3. **4:** *Come down,* probably to be read
"assumed dominion," since the answer to all five questions must be "God" as in Job 38.5ff.
His name . . . his son's name, a rhetorical way of asking who knows God so familiarly. **5–6:**

6 Do not add to his words,
  lest he rebuke you, and you be
  found a liar.

7 Two things I ask of thee;
  deny them not to me before I die:
8 Remove far from me falsehood and
  lying;
    give me neither poverty nor
    riches;
    feed me with the food that is
    needful for me,
9 lest I be full, and deny thee,
  and say, "Who is the LORD?"
  or lest I be poor, and steal,
  and profane the name of my God.

10 Do not slander a servant to his
   master,
     lest he curse you, and you be
     held guilty.

11 There are those who curse their
   fathers
   and do not bless their mothers.
12 There are those who are pure in
   their own eyes
   but are not cleansed of their filth.
13 There are those–how lofty are their
   eyes,
   how high their eyelids lift!
14 There are those whose teeth are
   swords,
     whose teeth are knives,
   to devour the poor from off the earth,
   the needy from among men.

15 The leech[g] has two daughters;
   "Give, give," they cry.
   Three things are never satisfied;
     four never say, "Enough":
16 Sheol, the barren womb,
   the earth ever thirsty for water,
   and the fire which never says,
   "Enough."[h]

17 The eye that mocks a father
   and scorns to obey a mother
   will be picked out by the ravens of
   the valley
   and eaten by the vultures.

18 Three things are too wonderful for
   me;
     four I do not understand:
19 the way of an eagle in the sky,
   the way of a serpent on a rock,
   the way of a ship on the high seas,
   and the way of a man with a
   maiden.

20 This is the way of an adulteress:
   she eats, and wipes her mouth,
   and says, "I have done no wrong."

21 Under three things the earth
   trembles;
     under four it cannot bear up:
22 a slave when he becomes king,
   and a fool when he is filled with
   food;
23 an unloved woman when she gets a
   husband,
   and a maid when she succeeds
   her mistress.

24 Four things on earth are small,
   but they are exceedingly wise:
25 the ants are a people not strong,
   yet they provide their food in the
   summer;
26 the badgers are a people not mighty,
   yet they make their homes in the
   rocks;
27 the locusts have no king,
   yet all of them march in rank;
28 the lizard you can take in your hands,
   yet it is in kings' palaces.

g The meaning of the Hebrew word is uncertain
h Heb obscure

The reply: God's promises are true and he will rebuke presumption (Job 40.2). **7–9:** He asks only *two* things–truth and daily food (Job 13.20; 14.1–6).
   30.10–33: Appendix III, admonitions and numerical proverbs (see 6.16–19 n.). **11–14:** Four types of sinners–the unfilial, self-satisfied, arrogant, and avaricious. **15–16:** A folk proverb, and four things which are insatiable. *Two daughters,* "Give" and "Give." **18–19:** Four wonders. **20:** *She eats and wipes her mouth,* a euphemism. **21–23:** Four intolerable situations. **24–28:** Four small creatures which can teach man lessons. **29–31:** Four examples of arrogance. *Striding before,* or "dominating."

²⁹ Three things are stately in their
  tread;
  four are stately in their stride:
³⁰ the lion, which is mightiest among
  beasts
  and does not turn back before any;
³¹ the strutting cock,ⁱ the he-goat,
  and a king striding beforeʲ his
  people.

³² If you have been foolish, exalting
  yourself,
  or if you have been devising evil,
  put your hand on your mouth.
³³ For pressing milk produces curds,
  pressing the nose produces blood,
  and pressing anger produces
  strife.

3 1 ‖ The words of Lemuel, king of
    Massa,ᵏ which his mother taught
him:

² What, my son? What, son of my
  womb?
  What, son of my vows?
³ Give not your strength to women,
  your ways to those who destroy
  kings.
⁴ It is not for kings, O Lemuel,
  it is not for kings to drink wine,
  or for rulers to desireˡ strong
  drink;
⁵ lest they drink and forget what has
  been decreed,
  and pervert the rights of all the
  afflicted.
⁶ Give strong drink to him who is
  perishing,
  and wine to those in bitter distress;
⁷ let them drink and forget their
  poverty,

and remember their misery no
  more.
⁸ Open your mouth for the dumb,
  for the rights of all who are left
  desolate.ᵐ
⁹ Open your mouth, judge righteously,
  maintain the rights of the poor
  and needy.

¹⁰ A good wife who can find?
  She is far more precious than
  jewels.
¹¹ The heart of her husband trusts in
  her,
  and he will have no lack of gain.
¹² She does him good, and not harm,
  all the days of her life.
¹³ She seeks wool and flax,
  and works with willing hands.
¹⁴ She is like the ships of the merchant,
  she brings her food from afar.
¹⁵ She rises while it is yet night
  and provides food for her
  household
  and tasks for her maidens.
¹⁶ She considers a field and buys it;
  with the fruit of her hands she
  plants a vineyard.
¹⁷ She girds her loins with strength
  and makes her arms strong.
¹⁸ She perceives that her merchandise
  is profitable.
  Her lamp does not go out at night.
¹⁹ She puts her hands to the distaff,
  and her hands hold the spindle.
²⁰ She opens her hand to the poor,
  and reaches out her hands to the
  needy.
²¹ She is not afraid of snow for her
  household,

i Gk Syr Tg Compare Vg: Heb obscure
j The meaning of the Hebrew is uncertain
k Or *King Lemuel, the oracle*   *l* Cn: Heb *where*
m Heb *are sons of passing away*

31.1–9: Appendix IV, a queen mother's counsel. 1: King *Lemuel* is unidentified; the text is possibly corrupt. *Massa*, a kingdom in N.W. Arabia, known from recently discovered inscriptions and Gen.25.14. Compare 30.1. **3–7:** The king is warned against succumbing to the wiles of women who would sap his strength (compare 2.16–19; 5.3–4), and to avoid wine and strong drink lest he rule unwisely and unjustly. Strong drink and wine have a place as an opiate for the unfortunate and poor. **8–9:** These verses recall the concern of the prophets.

31.10–31: Appendix V, an acrostic on the ideal housewife. The good wife has a status of honor in the opinion of the author of this fine bit of wisdom literature. She is more precious than jewels, trusted by her husband, wise, industrious in providing for the needs of her household even to the point of engaging in commerce, considerate of the less fortunate, and praised by her family.

for all her household are clothed
in scarlet.
²² She makes herself coverings;
her clothing is fine linen and
purple.
²³ Her husband is known in the
gates,
when he sits among the elders
of the land.
²⁴ She makes linen garments and sells
them;
she delivers girdles to the
merchant.
²⁵ Strength and dignity are her
clothing,
and she laughs at the time to
come.
²⁶ She opens her mouth with wisdom,
and the teaching of kindness is on
her tongue.

²⁷ She looks well to the ways of her
household,
and does not eat the bread of
idleness.
²⁸ Her children rise up and call her
blessed;
her husband also, and he praises
her:
²⁹ "Many women have done
excellently,
but you surpass them all."
³⁰ Charm is deceitful, and beauty is
vain,
but a woman who fears the LORD
is to be praised.
³¹ Give her of the fruit of her hands,
and let her works praise her in the
gates.

ECCLESIASTES

OR THE PREACHER

Ecclesiastes contains the reflections of a philosopher rather than a testimony of belief. The author seeks to understand by the use of reason the meaning of human existence and the good which man can find in life. He questions many of the accepted beliefs of Hebrew tradition. To him God is the inscrutable originator of the world and determiner of man's fate. As the natural world is in constant movement without real change, so man's expenditure of effort achieves nothing. All is "vanity," a breath, unsubstantial and fleeting. Man's character and accomplishments make no difference to his fate, which is the same as that of beasts. Yet, though reason leaves him baffled, the author nevertheless affirms that life with its limitations is worth living. One must face facts, accept what cannot be changed, and enjoy whatever good things God permits until death brings oblivion.

The author is described in 12.9–10 as a sage, a teacher, and a skilled writer. The literary role of Solomon is assumed only in chapters 1–2. The rationalistic tone of the book and its echoes of Greek philosophies point to a date about the third century B.C. Except for the opening statement of the theme and the concluding poem on old age, the work is without formal structure. "Ecclesiastes" is an attempted Greek translation of the author's pen-name, *Qoheleth*. This comes from the same Hebrew root as *qahal*, "assembly," and means one who conducts an assembly or school.

The inclusion in the Jewish canon of Scripture of a work so much at variance with its dominant teaching may be explained by the traditional association with Solomon, its sponsorship by influential "wise men," and the inclusion of an orthodox postscript (12.9–14) which lays down the religious position in the light of which it is to be understood.

THE WORDS OF THE PREACHER,[a] the son of David, king in Jerusalem.
2 Vanity of vanities, says the Preacher,
 vanity of vanities! All is vanity.
3 What does man gain by all the toil
 at which he toils under the sun?
4 A generation goes, and a generation comes,
 but the earth remains for ever.
5 The sun rises and the sun goes down,
 and hastens to the place where it rises.
6 The wind blows to the south,
 and goes round to the north;
round and round goes the wind,
 and on its circuits the wind returns.
7 All streams run to the sea,
 but the sea is not full;
to the place where the streams flow,
 there they flow again.

8 All things are full of weariness;
 a man cannot utter it;
the eye is not satisfied with seeing,
 nor the ear filled with hearing.
9 What has been is what will be,
 and what has been done is what will be done;
 and there is nothing new under the sun.
10 Is there a thing of which it is said,
 "See, this is new"?
It has been already,
 in the ages before us.
11 There is no remembrance of former things,
 nor will there be any remembrance
 of later things yet to happen
 among those who come after.
12 I the Preacher have been king over Israel in Jerusalem. 13 And I

a Heb *Koheleth*

1.1–3: Title and thesis. Experience is as fleeting and unsubstantial as *vanity*, "a breath."

1.4–11: Evidence for the thesis–generations pass, nature is in ceaseless motion, but nothing new results.

1.12–2.11: The fruitless search for the fruit of human effort (a) to change the world, (b) to reach understanding, (c) to possess happiness. **13:** *Unhappy business*, "sore (grievous) task."

applied my mind to seek and to search out by wisdom all that is done under heaven; it is an unhappy business that God has given to the sons of men to be busy with. [14] I have seen everything that is done under the sun; and behold, all is vanity and a striving after wind.[b]
[15] What is crooked cannot be made straight,
   and what is lacking cannot be numbered.
16 I said to myself, "I have acquired great wisdom, surpassing all who were over Jerusalem before me; and my mind has had great experience of wisdom and knowledge." [17] And I applied my mind to know wisdom and to know madness and folly. I perceived that this also is but a striving after wind.
[18] For in much wisdom is much vexation,
   and he who increases knowledge increases sorrow.

2 I said to myself, "Come now, I will make a test of pleasure; enjoy yourself." But behold, this also was vanity. [2] I said of laughter, "It is mad," and of pleasure, "What use is it?" [3] I searched with my mind how to cheer my body with wine–my mind still guiding me with wisdom–and how to lay hold on folly, till I might see what was good for the sons of men to do under heaven during the few days of their life. [4] I made great works; I built houses and planted vineyards for myself; [5] I made myself gardens and parks, and planted in them all kinds of fruit trees. [6] I made myself pools from which to water the forest of growing trees. [7] I bought male and female slaves, and had slaves who were born in my house; I had also great possessions of herds and flocks, more than any who had been before me in Jerusalem. [8] I also gathered for myself silver and gold

and the treasure of kings and provinces; I got singers, both men and women, and many concubines,[c] man's delight.
9 So I became great and surpassed all who were before me in Jerusalem; also my wisdom remained with me. [10] And whatever my eyes desired I did not keep from them; I kept my heart from no pleasure, for my heart found pleasure in all my toil, and this was my reward for all my toil. [11] Then I considered all that my hands had done and the toil I had spent in doing it, and behold, all was vanity and a striving after wind, and there was nothing to be gained under the sun.
12 So I turned to consider wisdom and madness and folly; for what can the man do who comes after the king? Only what he has already done. [13] Then I saw that wisdom excels folly as light excels darkness. [14] The wise man has his eyes in his head, but the fool walks in darkness; and yet I perceived that one fate comes to all of them. [15] Then I said to myself, "What befalls the fool will befall me also; why then have I been so very wise?" And I said to myself that this also is vanity. [16] For of the wise man as of the fool there is no enduring remembrance, seeing that in the days to come all will have been long forgotten. How the wise man dies just like the fool! [17] So I hated life, because what is done under the sun was grievous to me; for all is vanity and a striving after wind.
18 I hated all my toil in which I had toiled under the sun, seeing that I must leave it to the man who will come after me; [19] and who knows whether he will be a wise man or a fool? Yet he will be master of all for which I toiled and used my wisdom under the sun. This also is vanity. [20] So I turned about and gave my heart

b Or *a feeding on wind*. See Hos 12.1
c The meaning of the Hebrew word is uncertain

15: *Numbered*, "made up." **16:** The writer forgets that Jerusalem became Hebrew only one generation before Solomon. **17:** *Know*, "analyze." **2.4–9:** Solomon's fabulous magnificence (1 Kg. ch. 10). **10:** An absolute monarch is free to experiment. Qoheleth's great discovery was that satisfaction lies in effort even without tangible result.

   2.12–26: Mortality robs wisdom and labor of their fruits; man's sole good is present enjoy-

up to despair over all the toil of my labors under the sun, ²¹ because sometimes a man who has toiled with wisdom and knowledge and skill must leave all to be enjoyed by a man who did not toil for it. This also is vanity and a great evil. ²² What has a man from all the toil and strain with which he toils beneath the sun? ²³ For all his days are full of pain, and his work is a vexation; even in the night his mind does not rest. This also is vanity.

24 There is nothing better for a man than that he should eat and drink, and find enjoyment in his toil. This also, I saw, is from the hand of God; ²⁵ for apart from him*d* who can eat or who can have enjoyment? ²⁶ For to the man who pleases him God gives wisdom and knowledge and joy; but to the sinner he gives the work of gathering and heaping, only to give to one who pleases God. This also is vanity and a striving after wind.

3 For everything there is a season, and a time for every matter under heaven:
² a time to be born, and a time to die;
 a time to plant, and a time to pluck up what is planted;
³ a time to kill, and a time to heal;
 a time to break down, and a time to build up;
⁴ a time to weep, and a time to laugh;
 a time to mourn, and a time to dance;
⁵ a time to cast away stones, and a time to gather stones together;
 a time to embrace, and a time to refrain from embracing;
⁶ a time to seek, and a time to lose;
 a time to keep, and a time to cast away;
⁷ a time to rend, and a time to sew;
 a time to keep silence, and a time to speak;
⁸ a time to love, and a time to hate;
 a time for war, and a time for peace.
⁹ What gain has the worker from his toil?

10 I have seen the business that God has given to the sons of men to be busy with. ¹¹ He has made everything beautiful in its time; also he has put eternity into man's mind, yet so that he cannot find out what God has done from the beginning to the end. ¹² I know that there is nothing better for them than to be happy and enjoy themselves as long as they live; ¹³ also that it is God's gift to man that every one should eat and drink and take pleasure in all his toil. ¹⁴ I know that whatever God does endures for ever; nothing can be added to it, nor anything taken from it; God has made it so, in order that men should fear before him. ¹⁵ That which is, already has been; that which is to be, already has been; and God seeks what has been driven away.

16 Moreover I saw under the sun that in the place of justice, even there was wickedness, and in the place of righteousness, even there was wickedness. ¹⁷ I said in my heart, God will judge the righteous and the wicked, for he has appointed a time for every matter, and for every work. ¹⁸ I said in my heart with regard to the sons of men that God is testing them to show them that they are but beasts. ¹⁹ For the fate of the sons of men and the fate of beasts is the same; as one dies, so dies the other. They all have the same breath, and man has no advantage over the beasts; for all is vanity. ²⁰ All

d Gk Syr: Heb *apart from me*

---

ment, if God so wills. **26**: *For . . . pleases God*, a note originally made in the margin of the manuscript by a scribe, correcting the view that goodness makes no difference to man's fate.
    3.1–15: Man can neither understand nor change the predetermined pattern of his life. Everything happens at the time fixed for it. **11**: *Beautiful*, "right for." *Eternity*, what is hidden; man knows only that the succession of "times" goes on forever (3.14). **15**: *Seeks what has been driven away*, repeats what has happened before.
    3.16–22: Injustice and oppression will be judged when God decides it is the proper time; meanwhile, innocent and guilty suffer the same fate as animals. **16**: *Place of justice*, where justice should be done, in court. **19**: *Vanity*, "transience," thus revealing man's insignificance.

go to one place; all are from the dust, and all turn to dust again. 21 Who knows whether the spirit of man goes upward and the spirit of the beast goes down to the earth? 22 So I saw that there is nothing better than that a man should enjoy his work, for that is his lot; who can bring him to see what will be after him?

4 Again I saw all the oppressions that are practiced under the sun. And behold, the tears of the oppressed, and they had no one to comfort them! On the side of their oppressors there was power, and there was no one to comfort them. 2 And I thought the dead who are already dead more fortunate than the living who are still alive; 3 but better than both is he who has not yet been, and has not seen the evil deeds that are done under the sun.

4 Then I saw that all toil and all skill in work come from a man's envy of his neighbor. This also is vanity and a striving after wind.

5 The fool folds his hands, and eats his own flesh.

6 Better is a handful of quietness than two hands full of toil and a striving after wind.

7 Again, I saw vanity under the sun: 8 a person who has no one, either son or brother, yet there is no end to all his toil, and his eyes are never satisfied with riches, so that he never asks, "For whom am I toiling and depriving myself of pleasure?" This also is vanity and an unhappy business.

9 Two are better than one, because they have a good reward for their toil. 10 For if they fall, one will lift up his fellow; but woe to him who is alone when he falls and has not another to lift him up. 11 Again, if two lie together, they are warm; but how can one be warm alone? 12 And though a man might prevail against one who is alone, two will withstand him. A threefold cord is not quickly broken.

13 Better is a poor and wise youth than an old and foolish king, who will no longer take advice, 14 even though he had gone from prison to the throne or in his own kingdom had been born poor. 15 I saw all the living who move about under the sun, as well as that*f* youth, who was to stand in his place; 16 there was no end of all the people; he was over all of them. Yet those who come later will not rejoice in him. Surely this also is vanity and a striving after wind.

5 *g* Guard your steps when you go to the house of God; to draw near to listen is better than to offer the sacrifice of fools; for they do not know that they are doing evil. 2*h* Be not rash with your mouth, nor let your heart be hasty to utter a word before God, for God is in heaven, and you upon earth; therefore let your words be few.

3 For a dream comes with much business, and a fool's voice with many words.

4 When you vow a vow to God, do not delay paying it; for he has no pleasure in fools. Pay what you vow. 5 It is better that you should not vow than that you should vow and not pay. 6 Let not your mouth lead you into sin, and do not say before the messenger*i* that it was a mistake; why should God be angry at your voice, and destroy the work of your hands?

f Heb *the second*   g Ch 4.17 in Heb
h Ch 5.1 in Heb   i Or *angel*

21: Since there is no proof of man's survival after death, his only good is to enjoy life while he can.

4.1–12: Because of greed and envy, man's life is misery mitigated only by human companionship. 7–12: A miser's wealth is a poor substitute for human companionship.

4.13–16: The impermanence of fame; a king who rose from obscurity will be supplanted by one like himself whose glory in turn will pass away.

5.1–7: Advice on religious observance. Qoheleth deprecates enthusiastic but ignorant piety; the reflective man will maintain his detachment, but will pay such vows as he makes. **6:** *The messenger* who comes to collect what has been vowed. **7:** Though *dreams* and *empty words* are associated with religion by fools, the wise man will reverence God.

7 For when dreams increase, empty words grow many:*j* but do you fear God.

8 If you see in a province the poor oppressed and justice and right violently taken away, do not be amazed at the matter; for the high official is watched by a higher, and there are yet higher ones over them. ⁹ But in all, a king is an advantage to a land with cultivated fields.*k*

10 He who loves money will not be satisfied with money; nor he who loves wealth, with gain: this also is vanity.

11 When goods increase, they increase who eat them; and what gain has their owner but to see them with his eyes?

12 Sweet is the sleep of a laborer, whether he eats little or much; but the surfeit of the rich will not let him sleep.

13 There is a grievous evil which I have seen under the sun: riches were kept by their owner to his hurt, ¹⁴ and those riches were lost in a bad venture; and he is father of a son, but he has nothing in his hand. ¹⁵ As he came from his mother's womb he shall go again, naked as he came, and shall take nothing for his toil, which he may carry away in his hand. ¹⁶ This also is a grievous evil: just as he came, so shall he go; and what gain has he that he toiled for the wind, ¹⁷ and spent all his days in darkness and grief,*l* in much vexation and sickness and resentment?

18 Behold, what I have seen to be good and to be fitting is to eat and drink and find enjoyment in all the toil with which one toils under the sun the few days of his life which God has given him, for this is his lot. ¹⁹ Every man also to whom God has given wealth and possessions and power to enjoy them, and to accept his lot and find enjoyment in his toil–this is the gift of God. ²⁰ For he will not much remember the days of his life because

God keeps him occupied with joy in his heart.

6 There is an evil which I have seen under the sun, and it lies heavy upon men: ² a man to whom God gives wealth, possessions, and honor, so that he lacks nothing of all that he desires, yet God does not give him power to enjoy them, but a stranger enjoys them; this is vanity; it is a sore affliction. ³ If a man begets a hundred children, and lives many years, so that the days of his years are many, but he does not enjoy life's good things, and also has no burial, I say that an untimely birth is better off than he. ⁴ For it comes into vanity and goes into darkness, and in darkness its name is covered; ⁵ moreover it has not seen the sun or known anything; yet it finds rest rather than he. ⁶ Even though he should live a thousand years twice told, yet enjoy no good–do not all go to the one place?

7 All the toil of man is for his mouth, yet his appetite is not satisfied. ⁸ For what advantage has the wise man over the fool? And what does the poor man have who knows how to conduct himself before the living? ⁹ Better is the sight of the eyes than the wandering of desire; this also is vanity and a striving after wind.

10 Whatever has come to be has already been named, and it is known what man is, and that he is not able to dispute with one stronger than he. ¹¹ The more words, the more vanity, and what is man the better? ¹² For who knows what is good for man while he lives the few days of his vain life, which he passes like a shadow? For who can tell man what will be after him under the sun?

7 A good name is better than precious ointment;

j Or *For in a multitude of dreams there is futility, and ruin in a flood of words*
k Or *The profit of the land is among all of them; a cultivated field has a king*
l Gk: Heb *all his days also he eats in darkness*

5.8–6.9: The wise man is not disturbed by oppression, which is the responsibility of those in authority; nor does he yield to the drive of desires which can never be satisfied.

6.10–7.12: Man cannot change his lot nor foresee the future or the ultimate good. But he can experience what is relatively good, as illustrated by seven proverbs commending reflection and

and the day of death, than the day
of birth.

2 It is better to go to the house of
mourning
than to go to the house of
feasting;
for this is the end of all men,
and the living will lay it to heart.

3 Sorrow is better than laughter,
for by sadness of countenance
the heart is made glad.

4 The heart of the wise is in the
house of mourning;
but the heart of fools is in the
house of mirth.

5 It is better for a man to hear the
rebuke of the wise
than to hear the song of fools.

6 For as the crackling of thorns under
a pot,
so is the laughter of the fools;
this also is vanity.

7 Surely oppression makes the wise
man foolish,
and a bribe corrupts the mind.

8 Better is the end of a thing than its
beginning;
and the patient in spirit is better
than the proud in spirit.

9 Be not quick to anger,
for anger lodges in the bosom of
fools.

10 Say not, "Why were the former days
better than these?"
For it is not from wisdom that you
ask this.

11 Wisdom is good with an inheritance,
an advantage to those who see the
sun.

12 For the protection of wisdom is like
the protection of money;
and the advantage of knowledge
is that wisdom preserves the
life of him who has it.

13 Consider the work of God;
who can make straight what he
has made crooked?

14 In the day of prosperity be joyful,
and in the day of adversity consider;
God has made the one as well as the
other, so that man may not find out
anything that will be after him.

15 In my vain life I have seen everything; there is a righteous man who
perishes in his righteousness, and
there is a wicked man who prolongs
his life in his evil-doing. 16 Be not
righteous overmuch, and do not make
yourself overwise; why should you
destroy yourself? 17 Be not wicked
overmuch, neither be a fool; why
should you die before your time? 18 It
is good that you should take hold of
this, and from that withhold not your
hand; for he who fears God shall come
forth from them all.

19 Wisdom gives strength to the
wise man more than ten rulers that are
in a city.

20 Surely there is not a righteous
man on earth who does good and never
sins.

21 Do not give heed to all the
things that men say, lest you hear your
servant cursing you; 22 your heart
knows that many times you have yourself cursed others.

23 All this I have tested by wisdom;
I said, "I will be wise"; but it was far
from me. 24 That which is, is far off,
and deep, very deep; who can find it
out? 25 I turned my mind to know and
to search out and to seek wisdom and
the sum of things, and to know the
wickedness of folly and the foolishness which is madness. 26 And I found
more bitter than death the woman
whose heart is snares and nets, and
whose hands are fetters; he who
pleases God escapes her, but the

---

self-control. **7.1:** Reputation is never secure until death. **11–12:** A wise heir will live to enjoy his
inheritance.

7.13–21: Since man cannot change the order of the world, and righteousness brings no advantage,
the moderation of the wise man is better than folly or excessive piety. **18:** *Come forth from them
all,* having done his duty.

7.23–8.9: The meaning of existence is hidden, and few men and no women seek it; their schemes
to alter the unalterable are vain. The wise man will accommodate himself to the harsh facts of
life and its uncertainties.

sinner is taken by her. ²⁷ Behold, this is what I found, says the Preacher, adding one thing to another to find the sum, ²⁸ which my mind has sought repeatedly, but I have not found. One man among a thousand I found, but a woman among all these I have not found. ²⁹ Behold, this alone I found, that God made man upright, but they have sought out many devices.

8 Who is like the wise man?
And who knows the interpretation of a thing?
A man's wisdom makes his face shine,
and the hardness of his countenance is changed.

2 Keep[m] the king's command, and because of your sacred oath be not dismayed; ³ go from his presence, do not delay when the matter is unpleasant, for he does whatever he pleases. ⁴ For the word of the king is supreme, and who may say to him, "What are you doing?" ⁵ He who obeys a command will meet no harm, and the mind of a wise man will know the time and way. ⁶ For every matter has its time and way, although man's trouble lies heavy upon him. ⁷ For he does not know what is to be, for who can tell him how it will be? ⁸ No man has power to retain the spirit, or authority over the day of death; there is no discharge from war, nor will wickedness deliver those who are given to it. ⁹ All this I observed while applying my mind to all that is done under the sun, while man lords it over man to his hurt.

10 Then I saw the wicked buried; they used to go in and out of the holy place, and were praised in the city where they had done such things. This also is vanity. ¹¹ Because sentence against an evil deed is not executed speedily, the heart of the sons of men is fully set to do evil. ¹² Though a sinner does evil a hundred times and

prolongs his life, yet I know that it will be well with those who fear God, because they fear before him; ¹³ but it will not be well with the wicked, neither will he prolong his days like a shadow, because he does not fear before God.

14 There is a vanity which takes place on earth, that there are righteous men to whom it happens according to the deeds of the wicked, and there are wicked men to whom it happens according to the deeds of the righteous. I said that this also is vanity. ¹⁵ And I commend enjoyment, for man has no good thing under the sun but to eat and drink, and enjoy himself, for this will go with him in his toil through the days of life which God gives him under the sun.

16 When I applied my mind to know wisdom, and to see the business that is done on earth, how neither day nor night one's eyes see sleep; ¹⁷ then I saw all the work of God, that man cannot find out the work that is done under the sun. However much man may toil in seeking, he will not find it out; even though a wise man claims to know, he cannot find it out.

9 But all this I laid to heart, examining it all, how the righteous and the wise and their deeds are in the hand of God; whether it is love or hate man does not know. Everything before them is vanity,[n] ² since one fate comes to all, to the righteous and the wicked, to the good and the evil,[o] to the clean and the unclean, to him who sacrifices and him who does not sacrifice. As is the good man, so is the sinner; and he who swears is as he who shuns an oath. ³ This is an evil in all that is done under the sun, that one fate comes to all; also the hearts of men are full of evil, and madness is in

m Heb inserts an *I*
n Sy. Compare Gk: Heb *Everything before them is everything*
o Gk Syr Vg: Heb lacks *and the evil*

8.10–9.1: The failure of retribution to overtake the wicked is an anomaly one must accept; no man knows whether God will favor him or not.
9.2–12: Life is to be relished so far as God permits, since good and bad men meet inexorable

their hearts while they live, and after that they go to the dead. ⁴ But he who is joined with all the living has hope, for a living dog is better than a dead lion. ⁵ For the living know that they will die, but the dead know nothing, and they have no more reward; but the memory of them is lost. ⁶ Their love and their hate and their envy have already perished, and they have no more for ever any share in all that is done under the sun.

7 Go, eat your bread with enjoyment, and drink your wine with a merry heart; for God has already approved what you do.

8 Let your garments be always white; let not oil be lacking on your head.

9 Enjoy life with the wife whom you love, all the days of your vain life which he has given you under the sun, because that is your portion in life and in your toil at which you toil under the sun. ¹⁰ Whatever your hand finds to do, do it with your might; for there is no work or thought or knowledge or wisdom in Sheol, to which you are going.

11 Again I saw that under the sun the race is not to the swift, nor the battle to the strong, nor bread to the wise, nor riches to the intelligent, nor favor to the men of skill; but time and chance happen to them all. ¹² For man does not know his time. Like fish which are taken in an evil net, and like birds which are caught in a snare, so the sons of men are snared at an evil time, when it suddenly falls upon them.

13 I have also seen this example of wisdom under the sun, and it seemed great to me. ¹⁴ There was a little city with few men in it; and a great king came against it and besieged it, building great siegeworks against it. ¹⁵ But

there was found in it a poor wise man, and he by his wisdom delivered the city. Yet no one remembered that poor man. ¹⁶ But I say that wisdom is better than might, though the poor man's wisdom is despised, and his words are not heeded.

17 The words of the wise heard in quiet are better than the shouting of a ruler among fools. ¹⁸ Wisdom is better than weapons of war, but one sinner destroys much good.

10 Dead flies make the perfumer's ointment give off an evil odor;
so a little folly outweighs wisdom and honor.
² A wise man's heart inclines him toward the right,
but a fool's heart toward the left.
³ Even when the fool walks on the road, he lacks sense,
and he says to every one that he is a fool.
⁴ If the anger of the ruler rises against you, do not leave your place,
for deference will make amends for great offenses.

5 There is an evil which I have seen under the sun, as it were an error proceeding from the ruler: ⁶ folly is set in many high places, and the rich sit in a low place. ⁷ I have seen slaves on horses, and princes walking on foot like slaves.
⁸ He who digs a pit will fall into it;
and a serpent will bite him who breaks through a wall.
⁹ He who quarries stones is hurt by them;
and he who splits logs is endangered by them.
¹⁰ If the iron is blunt, and one does not whet the edge,
he must put forth more strength; but wisdom helps one to succeed.
¹¹ If the serpent bites before it is charmed,

---

death. The operation of fate appears to be random. **10:** *Sheol*, where the dead are, in dust and silence.
9.13–10.20: A parable and sundry maxims and observations on life and wisdom. Wisdom is better than might, but is despised and is vulnerable to folly. **18:** *Sinner*, the fool in his moral aspect. **10.2–3,12–15:** The man not directed by moral intelligence is held up to contempt. **2:** *Right* and *left* have a moral connotation, as in Mt.25.33–46. **4–6:** Wisdom is unperturbed by

there is no advantage in a
charmer.

12 The words of a wise man's mouth
win him favor,
but the lips of a fool consume
him.
13 The beginning of the words of his
mouth is foolishness,
and the end of his talk is wicked
madness.
14 A fool multiplies words,
though no man knows what is to
be,
and who can tell him what will
be after him?
15 The toil of a fool wearies him,
so that he does not know the way
to the city.

16 Woe to you, O land, when your
king is a child,
and your princes feast in the
morning!
17 Happy are you, O land, when your
king is the son of free men,
and your princes feast at the
proper time,
for strength, and not for
drunkenness!
18 Through sloth the roof sinks in,
and through indolence the house
leaks.
19 Bread is made for laughter,
and wine gladdens life,
and money answers everything.
20 Even in your thought, do not
curse the king,
nor in your bedchamber curse
the rich;
for a bird of the air will carry your
voice,
or some winged creature tell the
matter.

11 Cast your bread upon the waters,
for you will find it after many
days.
2 Give a portion to seven, or even to
eight,
for you know not what evil may
happen on earth.
3 If the clouds are full of rain,
they empty themselves on the
earth;
and if a tree falls to the south or to
the north,
in the place where the tree falls,
there it will lie.
4 He who observes the wind will not
sow;
and he who regards the clouds
will not reap.

5 As you do not know how the spirit
comes to the bones in the womb[p] of
a woman with child, so you do not
know the work of God who makes
everything.

6 In the morning sow your seed, and
at evening withhold not your hand; for
you do not know which will prosper,
this or that, or whether both alike will
be good.

7 Light is sweet, and it is pleasant
for the eyes to behold the sun.

8 For if a man lives many years,
let him rejoice in them all; but let
him remember that the days of
darkness will be many. All that comes
is vanity.

9 Rejoice, O young man, in your
youth, and let your heart cheer you in
the days of your youth; walk in the
ways of your heart and the sight of your
eyes. But know that for all these things
God will bring you into judgment.

10 Remove vexation from your

p Or *As you do not know the way of the wind, or how the
bones grow in the womb*

---

arbitrary power, and helps one to succeed and avoid danger. **19:** *Money answers everything*,
provides it all.

11.1–6: Qoheleth calls on men to act in spite of life's uncertainties, since the satisfaction of
work is in doing it (2.24). **1–2:** *Cast your bread*, "venture your livelihood" (in foreign trade?).
Give a portion to . . . eight, "diversify your risks." **3–4:** What happens will happen anyway, and
man cannot wait for certainty if he would live at all.

11.7–12.8: Youth is to be relished as the best of life, since old age and death come soon. In the
famous allegory of old age (12.1–7) the poetry rises to great heights, though the symbolism is
not everywhere clear. **11.8:** *Is vanity*, or "soon passes." **11.9c:** an editor's cautionary addition.

mind, and put away pain from your body; for youth and the dawn of life are vanity.

12 Remember also your Creator in the days of your youth, before the evil days come, and the years draw nigh, when you will say, "I have no pleasure in them"; ² before the sun and the light and the moon and the stars are darkened and the clouds return after the rain; ³ in the day when the keepers of the house tremble, and the strong men are bent, and the grinders cease because they are few, and those that look through the windows are dimmed, ⁴ and the doors on the street are shut; when the sound of the grinding is low, and one rises up at the voice of a bird, and all the daughters of song are brought low; ⁵ they are afraid also of what is high, and terrors are in the way; the almond tree blossoms, the grasshopper drags itself along*q* and desire fails; because man goes to his eternal home, and the mourners go about the streets; ⁶ before the silver cord is snapped,*r* or the golden bowl is broken, or the pitcher is broken at

the fountain, or the wheel broken at the cistern, ⁷ and the dust returns to the earth as it was, and the spirit returns to God who gave it. ⁸ Vanity of vanities, says the Preacher; all is vanity.

9 Besides being wise, the Preacher also taught the people knowledge, weighing and studying and arranging proverbs with great care. ¹⁰ The Preacher sought to find pleasing words, and uprightly he wrote words of truth.

11 The sayings of the wise are like goads, and like nails firmly fixed are the collected sayings which are given by one Shepherd. ¹² My son, beware of anything beyond these. Of making many books there is no end, and much study is a weariness of the flesh.

13 The end of the matter; all has been heard. Fear God, and keep his commandments; for this is the whole duty of man.*s* ¹⁴ For God will bring every deed into judgment, with*t* every secret thing, whether good or evil.

q Or *is a burden*
r Syr Vg Compare Gk: Heb *is removed*
s Or *the duty of all men*
t Or *into the judgment on*

10: *Vanity*, "quickly passing." **12.1:** *Remember your Creator* seems unlikely counsel on the lips of Qoheleth; a very similar Hebrew word meaning "your grave" suits the context. **2–4:** Symbols of decrepitude. *Daughters of song*, "songsters." **5:** *Almond tree blossoms* are white, a figure suggesting the color of the hair of the aged. *The grasshopper drags itself along*, perhaps a figure for the stiff-legged gait of the aged. **6:** Two metaphors: the lamp which falls and goes out, and the water of life that fails. *Wheel*, better, "cup."

12.9–12: Biographical appendix by a disciple of the Shepherd, "teacher." **13–14: Cautionary footnote** by an orthodox editor: when *all has been heard* do not let yourself be turned away from belief and obedience.

THE SONG OF SOLOMON

This book is a collection of about twenty-five lyric poems or fragments of poems of human love and courtship such as would be sung appropriately at weddings (Jer.33.11). The poetry is graceful, sensuous, and replete with erotic imagery and allusions to the ancient myth of the love of a god and a goddess on which the fertility of nature was thought to depend. There is no clear literary structure, but the pronouns imply that the speakers are a bridegroom, bride and chorus. Its unity is that of subject matter, style, and possibly of authorship. It is anonymous, since the addition of Solomon's name to the title has no support beyond the tradition that he was the composer of many proverbs and songs (1 Kg.4.32).

The Song has no overt religious content corresponding to that of the other books of the Bible, and can be so interpreted only by assuming that a mystical symbolism is involved in its highly figurative language. Its inclusion in the Old Testament is to be explained from the prophetic figure of the LORD as the "husband" of his people (Hos.2.16–19). In Christian tradition it has been interpreted as an allegory of the love of Christ for his bride, the church (Rev.21.2,9), or as symbolizing the intimate experience of divine love in the individual soul.

In its present written form the Song dates from about the third century B.C., but its material is much more ancient. Symbols and motifs derived from early mythology are still recognizable, but their original reference has been forgotten and they have become part of the special language of human love and courtship. It should be noted that the translation is sometimes uncertain because many words employed in these poems are rare in Biblical Hebrew.

THE SONG OF SONGS, WHICH IS Solomon's.

2 O that you[a] would kiss me with the
    kisses of your[b] mouth!
For your love is better than wine,
3   your anointing oils are fragrant,
your name is oil poured out;
    therefore the maidens love you.
4 Draw me after you, let us make
    haste.
The king has brought me into his
    chambers.
We will exult and rejoice in you;
we will extol your love more than
    wine;
rightly do they love you.

5 I am very dark, but comely,
    O daughters of Jerusalem,
like the tents of Kedar,
    like the curtains of Solomon.

6 Do not gaze at me because I am
    swarthy,
because the sun has scorched me.
My mother's sons were angry with
    me,
they made me keeper of the
    vineyards;
but, my own vineyard I have not
    kept!
7 Tell me, you whom my soul loves,
    where you pasture your flock,
    where you make it lie down at
    noon;
for why should I be like one who
    wanders[c]
beside the flocks of your
    companions?

8 If you do not know,
    O fairest among women,

a Heb he   b Heb his
c Gk Syr Vg: Heb is veiled

1.1: Title. *Song of songs* is a superlative, like "Holy of holies." *Which is Solomon's,* i.e. either "about Solomon," because he is named in 3.9,11 as the king being wed, or "by Solomon," a late addition based on 1 Kg.4.32.

1.2–4: The maiden longs for her lover. 3: *Your name,* or "you." **4:** *The king,* i.e. the bridegroom. *Has brought me,* the maiden anticipates. *We,* the maiden's companions, a chorus.

1.5–6: The maiden boasts of her rustic beauty, dark as *the tents of Kedar,* sumptuous as *the curtains of Solomon.*

1.7–8: The maiden asks where her lover is, and is answered by the chorus.

follow in the tracks of the flock,
and pasture your kids
beside the shepherds' tents.

⁹ I compare you, my love,
to a mare of Pharaoh's chariots.
¹⁰ Your cheeks are comely with
ornaments,
your neck with strings of jewels.
¹¹ We will make you ornaments of
gold,
studded with silver.

¹² While the king was on his couch,
my nard gave forth its fragrance.
¹³ My beloved is to me a bag of myrrh,
that lies between my breasts.
¹⁴ My beloved is to me a cluster of
henna blossoms
in the vineyards of En-ge′di.

¹⁵ Behold, you are beautiful, my love;
behold, you are beautiful;
your eyes are doves.
¹⁶ Behold, you are beautiful, my
beloved,
truly lovely.
Our couch is green;
¹⁷   the beams of our house are cedar,
our rafters*d* are pine.

2 I am a rose*e* of Sharon,
a lily of the valleys.

² As a lily among brambles,
so is my love among maidens.

³ As an apple tree among the trees
of the wood,
so is my beloved among young
men.
With great delight I sat in his shadow,
and his fruit was sweet to my taste.

⁴ He brought me to the banqueting
house,
and his banner over me was love.
⁵ Sustain me with raisins,
refresh me with apples;
for I am sick with love.
⁶ O that his left hand were under my
head,
and that his right hand embraced
me!
⁷ I adjure you, O daughters of
Jerusalem,
by the gazelles or the hinds of the
field,
that you stir not up nor awaken
love
until it please.

⁸ The voice of my beloved!
Behold, he comes,
leaping upon the mountains,
bounding over the hills.
⁹ My beloved is like a gazelle,
or a young stag.
Behold, there he stands
behind our wall,
gazing in at the windows,
looking through the lattice.
¹⁰ My beloved speaks and says to me:
"Arise, my love, my fair one,
and come away;
¹¹ for lo, the winter is past,
the rain is over and gone.
¹² The flowers appear on the earth,
the time of singing has come,
and the voice of the turtledove
is heard in our land.
¹³ The fig tree puts forth its figs,
and the vines are in blossom;
they give forth fragrance.
Arise, my love, my fair one,
and come away.

d The meaning of the Hebrew word is uncertain
e Heb *crocus*

1.9–11: The youth praises the bejewelled maiden.
1.12–17: The lovers' dialogue, as they lie together in the open air. *Beloved*, originally an epithet of the fertility god, here simply a term of endearment. In Is.5.1 it is applied to the LORD.
14: *En-gedi*, a fertile oasis by the Dead Sea.
2.1–4: A second dialogue of the lovers. **1**: *Rose*, more correctly "crocus." *Sharon*, the rich coastal plain south of Carmel. **4**: *His banner over me;* translation uncertain; perhaps read, "he gazed on me with love."
2.5–7: The maiden's longing for love when the time is ripe.
2.8–14: The lover comes in the spring to summon his bride. **8**: *Voice*, or sound of his approach. **11**: *Winter*, the rainy season. **14**: *Clefts* . . . *covert*, figures of the bride's home.

¹⁴ O my dove, in the clefts of the rock,
  in the covert of the cliff,
let me see your face,
let me hear your voice,
for your voice is sweet,
and your face is comely.
¹⁵ Catch us the foxes,
  the little foxes,
that spoil the vineyards,
for our vineyards are in blossom."

¹⁶ My beloved is mine and I am his,
  he pastures his flock among the
    lilies.
¹⁷ Until the day breathes
  and the shadows flee,
turn, my beloved, be like a gazelle,
or a young stag upon rugged*f*
  mountains.

3 Upon my bed by night
  I sought him whom my soul
    loves;
I sought him, but found him not;
  I called him, but he gave no
    answer.*g*
² "I will rise now and go about the
    city,
  in the streets and in the squares;
I will seek him whom my soul loves."
  I sought him, but found him not.
³ The watchmen found me,
  as they went about in the city.
"Have you seen him whom my soul
    loves?"
⁴ Scarcely had I passed them,
  when I found him whom my soul
    loves.
I held him, and would not let him go
  until I had brought him into my
    mother's house,
  and into the chamber of her that
    conceived me.
⁵ I adjure you, O daughters of
    Jerusalem,

by the gazelles or the hinds of the
    field,
that you stir not up nor awaken love
  until it please.

⁶ What is that coming up from the
    wilderness,
  like a column of smoke,
perfumed with myrrh and
    frankincense,
  with all the fragrant powders of
    the merchant?
⁷ Behold, it is the litter of Solomon!
  About it are sixty mighty men
  of the mighty men of Israel,
⁸ all girt with swords
  and expert in war,
each with his sword at his thigh,
  against alarms by night.
⁹ King Solomon made himself a
    palanquin
  from the wood of Lebanon.
¹⁰ He made its posts of silver,
  its back of gold, its seat of purple;
it was lovingly wrought within*h*
  by the daughters of Jerusalem.
¹¹ Go forth, O daughters of Zion,
  and behold King Solomon,
with the crown with which his
    mother crowned him
  on the day of his wedding,
  on the day of the gladness of his
    heart.

4 Behold, you are beautiful, my love,
  behold, you are beautiful!
Your eyes are doves
  behind your veil.
Your hair is like a flock of goats,
  moving down the slopes of
    Gilead.
² Your teeth are like a flock of shorn
    ewes

f The meaning of the Hebrew word is unknown
g Gk: Heb lacks this line
h The meaning of the Hebrew is uncertain

2.15: Apparently an allusion to what would spoil the luxuriance of love; an isolated fragment.
2.16–17: *The maiden delights in her lover's presence. Until the day breathes,* the breeze of evening.
3.1–5: *The maiden dreams of searching for her lover.*
3.6–11: *A wedding procession of the bridegroom,* in the guise of *Solomon.* **10:** Alternative translation of the third line: "Its interior was wrought in leather."
4.1–7: *The bridegroom describes the charms of the maiden.* **6:** *Mountain . . . hill,* her breasts.

that have come up from the
washing,
all of which bear twins,
and not one among them is
bereaved.
³ Your lips are like a scarlet thread,
and your mouth is lovely.
Your cheeks are like halves of a
pomegranate
behind your veil.
⁴ Your neck is like the tower of David,
built for an arsenal,*
whereon hang a thousand bucklers,
all of them shields of warriors.
⁵ Your two breasts are like two fawns,
twins of a gazelle,
that feed among the lilies.
⁶ Until the day breathes
and the shadows flee,
I will hie me to the mountain of
myrrh
and the hill of frankincense.
⁷ You are all fair, my love;
there is no flaw in you.
⁸ Come with me from Lebanon, my
bride;
come with me from Lebanon.
Depart*ʲ* from the peak of Ama′na,
from the peak of Senir and
Hermon,
from the dens of lions,
from the mountains of leopards.

⁹ You have ravished my heart, my
sister, my bride,
you have ravished my heart with
a glance of your eyes,
with one jewel of your necklace.
¹⁰ How sweet is your love, my sister,
my bride!
how much better is your love than
wine,
and the fragrance of your oils than
any spice!
¹¹ Your lips distil nectar, my bride;
honey and milk are under your
tongue;

the scent of your garments is like
the scent of Lebanon.
¹² A garden locked is my sister, my
bride,
a garden locked, a fountain sealed.
¹³ Your shoots are an orchard of
pomegranates
with all choicest fruits,
henna with nard,
¹⁴ nard and saffron, calamus and
cinnamon,
with all trees of frankincense,
myrrh and aloes,
with all chief spices—
¹⁵ a garden fountain, a well of living
water,
and flowing streams from
Lebanon.

¹⁶ Awake, O north wind,
and come, O south wind!
Blow upon my garden,
let its fragrance be wafted abroad.
Let my beloved come to his garden,
and eat its choicest fruits.

5 I come to my garden, my sister, my
bride,
I gather my myrrh with my spice,
I eat my honeycomb with my
honey,
I drink my wine with my milk.

Eat, O friends, and drink:
drink deeply, O lovers!

² I slept, but my heart was awake.
Hark! my beloved is knocking.
"Open to me, my sister, my love,
my dove, my perfect one;
for my head is wet with dew,
my locks with the drops of the
night."
³ I had put off my garment,
how could I put it on?

i The meaning of the Hebrew word is uncertain
j Or *Look*

4.8–15: The lover bids the maiden accompany him, and praises her love. 8: These were the
mountain dwellings of the Syrian goddess. **12:** *Locked* against any other lover. This verse
should follow v. 4.
    4.16–5.1: Invitation and response. 5.1: *Drink deeply, O lovers,* or "Be intoxicated with love."
    5.2–6.3: The maiden's fruitless search for her lover. A dream like that in 3.1–5, but with a
different conclusion.

I had bathed my feet,
how could I soil them?
4 My beloved put his hand to the
latch,
and my heart was thrilled within
me.
5 I arose to open to my beloved,
and my hands dripped with myrrh,
my fingers with liquid myrrh,
upon the handles of the bolt.
6 I opened to my beloved,
but my beloved had turned and
gone.
My soul failed me when he spoke.
I sought him, but found him not;
I called him, but he gave no
answer.
7 The watchmen found me,
as they went about in the city;
they beat me, they wounded me,
they took away my mantle,
those watchmen of the walls.
8 I adjure you, O daughters of
Jerusalem,
if you find my beloved,
that you tell him
I am sick with love.

9 What is your beloved more than
another beloved,
O fairest among women?
What is your beloved more than
another beloved,
that you thus adjure us?

10 My beloved is all radiant and ruddy,
distinguished among ten
thousand.
11 His head is the finest gold;
his locks are wavy,
black as a raven.
12 His eyes are like doves
beside springs of water,
bathed in milk,
fitly set.[k]
13 His cheeks are like beds of spices,
yielding fragrance.
His lips are lilies,
distilling liquid myrrh.

14 His arms are rounded gold,
set with jewels.
His body is ivory work,[l]
encrusted with sapphires.[m]
15 His legs are alabaster columns,
set upon bases of gold.
His appearance is like Lebanon,
choice as the cedars.
16 His speech is most sweet,
and he is altogether desirable.
This is my beloved and this is my
friend,
O daughters of Jerusalem.

6 Whither has your beloved gone,
O fairest among women?
Whither has your beloved turned,
that we may seek him with you?

2 My beloved has gone down to his
garden,
to the beds of spices,
to pasture his flock in the gardens,
and to gather lilies.
3 I am my beloved's and my beloved
is mine;
he pastures his flock among the
lilies.

4 You are beautiful as Tirzah, my
love,
comely as Jerusalem,
terrible as an army with banners.
5 Turn away your eyes from me,
for they disturb me—
Your hair is like a flock of goats,
moving down the slopes of Gilead.
6 Your teeth are like a flock of ewes,
that have come up from the
washing,
all of them bear twins,
not one among them is bereaved.
7 Your cheeks are like halves of a
pomegranate
behind your veil.
8 There are sixty queens and eighty
concubines,
and maidens without number.

k The meaning of the Hebrew is uncertain
l The meaning of the Hebrew word is uncertain
m Heb *lapis lazuli*

6.4–10: The groom praises the bride's beauty. 4: *Tirzah,* "the pleasant," once capital of Israel (1 Kg.15.21). *Terrible . . . banners,* or "awe-inspiring as banners." **8–9:** There may be *sixty queens,* etc., but *my perfect one* is the *only one.*

9 My dove, my perfect one, is only
   one,
  the darling of her mother,
  flawless to her that bore her.
The maidens saw her and called her
   happy;
  the queens and concubines also,
  and they praised her.
10 "Who is this that looks forth like
   the dawn,
  fair as the moon, bright as the sun,
  terrible as an army with banners?"

11 I went down to the nut orchard,
  to look at the blossoms of the
   valley,
to see whether the vines had budded,
  whether the pomegranates were
  in bloom.
12 Before I was aware, my fancy set me
  in a chariot beside my prince.*n*

13 *o* Return, return, O Shu'lammite,
  return, return, that we may look
  upon you.

Why should you look upon the
   Shu'lammite,
  as upon a dance before two
   armies?*p*

7 How graceful are your feet in
   sandals,
  O queenly maiden!
Your rounded thighs are like jewels,
  the work of a master hand.
2 Your navel is a rounded bowl
  that never lacks mixed wine.
Your belly is a heap of wheat,
  encircled with lilies.
3 Your two breasts are like two fawns,
  twins of a gazelle.
4 Your neck is like an ivory tower.
Your eyes are pools in Heshbon,
  by the gate of Bath-rab'bim.
Your nose is like a tower of
   Lebanon,
  overlooking Damascus.

5 Your head crowns you like Carmel,
  and your flowing locks are like
   purple;
  a king is held captive in the
   tresses.*q*

6 How fair and pleasant you are,
  O loved one, delectable maiden!*r*
7 You are stately*s* as a palm tree,
  and your breasts are like its
   clusters.
8 I say I will climb the palm tree
  and lay hold of its branches.
Oh, may your breasts be like
   clusters of the vine,
  and the scent of your breath like
   apples,
9 and your kisses*t* like the best wine
  that goes down*u* smoothly,
  gliding over lips and teeth.*v*

10 I am my beloved's,
  and his desire is for me.
11 Come, my beloved,
  let us go forth into the fields,
  and lodge in the villages;
12 let us go out early to the vineyards,
  and see whether the vines have
   budded,
  whether the grape blossoms have
   opened
  and the pomegranates are in
   bloom.
There I will give you my love.
13 The mandrakes give forth fragrance,
  and over our doors are all choice
   fruits,
  new as well as old,
  which I have laid up for you, O
   my beloved.

8 O that you were like a brother to
   me,
  that nursed at my mother's
   breast!

n Cn: The meaning of the Hebrew is uncertain
o Ch 7.1 in Heb   *p* Or *dance of Mahanaim*
q The meaning of the Hebrew word is uncertain
r Syr: Heb *in delights*   *s* Heb *This your stature is*
t Heb *palate*   *u* Heb *down for my lover*
v Gk Syr Vg: Heb *lips of sleepers*

6.11–12: The maiden visits the garden.
   6.13–7.9: The maiden called on to dance, and her charms arouse the lover's desire. **6.13:** *Shulammite*, the meaning of the word is doubtful; it may perhaps mean "bride of Solomon."
   7.10–13: The maiden invites her lover to come with her into the fields and promises to give him her love.

If I met you outside, I would kiss
you,
and none would despise me.
2 I would lead you and bring you
into the house of my mother,
and into the chamber of her that
conceived me.[w]
I would give you spiced wine to
drink,
the juice of my pomegranates.
3 O that his left hand were under
my head,
and that his right hand embraced
me!
4 I adjure you, O daughters of
Jerusalem,
that you stir not up nor awaken
love
until it please.

5 Who is that coming up from the
wilderness,
leaning upon her beloved?

Under the apple tree I awakened
you.
There your mother was in travail
with you,
there she who bore you was in
travail.

6 Set me as a seal upon your heart,
as a seal upon your arm;
for love is strong as death,
jealousy is cruel as the
grave.
Its flashes are flashes of fire,
a most vehement flame.
7 Many waters cannot quench love,
neither can floods drown it.
If a man offered for love

all the wealth of his house,
it would be utterly scorned.

8 We have a little sister,
and she has no breasts.
What shall we do for our sister,
on the day when she is spoken
for?
9 If she is a wall,
we will build upon her a
battlement of silver;
but if she is a door,
we will enclose her with boards of
cedar.
10 I was a wall,
and my breasts were like towers;
then I was in his eyes
as one who brings[x] peace.

11 Solomon had a vineyard at
Ba′al-ha′mon;
he let out the vineyard to keepers;
each one was to bring for its fruit
a thousand pieces of silver.
12 My vineyard, my very own, is for
myself;
you, O Solomon, may have the
thousand,
and the keepers of the fruit two
hundred.

13 O you who dwell in the gardens,
my companions are listening for
your voice;
let me hear it.

14 Make haste, my beloved,
and be like a gazelle
or a young stag
upon the mountains of spices.

w Gk Syr: Heb *mother; she* (or *you*) *will teach me*
x Or *finds*

8.1–4: The maiden wishes to marry her lover. 1: *Brother*, husband; compare "my sister, my bride" in 4.9.
8.5–7: The lovers return, the maiden imploring her lover to be faithful.
8.8–12: The maiden boasts of her previous chastity.
8.13–14: The lover calls and the maiden answers.

THE BOOK OF ISAIAH

The prophet Isaiah, the son of Amoz, proclaimed his message to Judah and Jerusalem between 742 and 687 B.C., that critical period in which the Northern Kingdom was annexed to the Assyrian empire (2 Kg. ch. 17) while Judah lived uneasily in its shadow as a tributary (2 Chr.28.21). Nothing is known about the early life of the prophet, although it has been conjectured from certain aspects of his message and from Is.6.1–8 that he may have been a priest.

Only chs. 1–39 can be assigned to Isaiah's time; it is generally accepted that chs. 40–66 come from the time of Cyrus of Persia (539 B.C.) and later, as shown by the differences in historical background, literary style, and theological emphases. Isaiah I (chs. 1–39) begins with Isaiah's memoirs (1.1–12.6); it continues with oracles against foreign and domestic enemies (13.1–23.18), followed by the "Isaiah Apocalypse" (24.1–27.13). Oracles generally concerned with Judah's intrigue with Egypt, its implications and consequences (28.1–32.20), are followed by a short collection of post-exilic eschatological oracles (33.1–35.10). An historical appendix (36.1–39.8) completes the pre-exilic section, in which there are other additions and some rearranging of oracles by post-exilic editors.

In the tradition of Amos, Hosea, and Micah, contemporaries whose work he seems to know, Isaiah attacks social injustice as that which is most indicative of Judah's tenuous relationship with God. He exhorts his hearers to place their confidence in their omnipotent God and to lead public and private lives which manifest this. Thus justice and righteousness, teaching and word, and assurance of divine blessing upon the faithful and punishment upon the faithless are recurrent themes in his message from the Holy One of Israel to a proud and stubborn people.

Chapters 40–66, commonly called Second Isaiah (or Second and Third Isaiah), originated immediately before the fall of Babylon (October 29, 539 B.C.) to the armies of Cyrus, king of Persia, and during the generation following. The anonymous author of the first bipartite section (chs. 40–55 [40–48; 49–55]) exults in joyful anticipation of exiled Judah's restoration to Palestine, for which Cyrus is God's precipitating agent (44.28). Second Isaiah emphasizes the significance of historical events in God's plan, a plan which extends from creation to redemption—and beyond. Blindness to God's way is a cardinal sin in Second Isaiah. The author's interest in cosmogony was unique up to his time; it is used to emphasize the concept of God as exclusive creator and lord of all, whose ultimate glorious manifestation will be accompanied by a new creation.

This eschatological hope is shared with the author, or authors, of the second bipartite section (chs. 56–66 [56–59 and 63–66; 60–62]). The contents of this section (sometimes called Third Isaiah) suggest a date between 530 and 510 B.C., perhaps contemporary with Haggai and Zechariah (520–518); chapters 60–62 may be later. Other concepts are also shared. Jacob and Israel have primarily religious, albeit national, significance. God's concern for the exiles in chs. 40–55 is paralleled by his comforting assurance to Zion's afflicted in chs. 56–66. But the direct "I–thou" relationship of Second Isaiah gives way to a more transcendent concept. In chs. 56–66 one is confronted by the sobering realities of life in the restored community. The Servant-motif vanishes, and there is growing emphasis on cultic matters.

Together these theologically significant sections present a moving vision of the assured hope of God's people in a world whose times are in God's hands. God's message to his responsible people is heard today as his covenant community, the church, redeemed by God through Jesus the Suffering Servant incarnate, proclaims to the world, "Arise, shine; for your light has come" (60.1).

THE VISION OF ISAIAH THE SON OF Amoz, which he saw concerning Judah and Jerusalem in the days of Uzzi′ah, Jotham, Ahaz, and Hezeki′ah, kings of Judah.

2 Hear, O heavens, and give ear, O earth;
for the LORD has spoken:
"Sons have I reared and brought up,
but they have rebelled against me.
3 The ox knows its owner,
and the ass its master's crib;
but Israel does not know,
my people does not understand."

4 Ah, sinful nation,
a people laden with iniquity,
offspring of evildoers,
sons who deal corruptly!
They have forsaken the LORD,
they have despised the Holy One of Israel,
they are utterly estranged.

5 Why will you still be smitten,
that you continue to rebel?
The whole head is sick,
and the whole heart faint.
6 From the sole of the foot even to the head,
there is no soundness in it,
but bruises and sores
and bleeding wounds;
they are not pressed out, or bound up,
or softened with oil.

7 Your country lies desolate,
your cities are burned with fire;
in your very presence
aliens devour your land;
it is desolate, as overthrown by aliens.
8 And the daughter of Zion is left
like a booth in a vineyard,
like a lodge in a cucumber field,
like a besieged city.

9 If the LORD of hosts
had not left us a few survivors,
we should have been like Sodom,
and become like Gomor′rah.

10 Hear the word of the LORD,
you rulers of Sodom!
Give ear to the teaching of our God,
you people of Gomor′rah!
11 "What to me is the multitude of your sacrifices?
says the LORD;
I have had enough of burnt offerings of rams
and the fat of fed beasts;
I do not delight in the blood of bulls,
or of lambs, or of he-goats.

12 "When you come to appear before me,
who requires of you
this trampling of my courts?
13 Bring no more vain offerings;
incense is an abomination to me.
New moon and sabbath and the calling of assemblies–
I cannot endure iniquity and solemn assembly.

1.1–5.24: Oracles against rebellious Judah. 1.1: Superscription. *Vision of Isaiah* (6.1–13; Jer. ch. 1; Ezek. chs. 1–3) identifies Is. chs. 1–39 as God's message to Judah through the prophet. The name *Isaiah* means "The LORD [Yahweh] gives salvation." The latter part of the verse beginning with "in the days of" may be an editorial expansion.

1.2–31: First series of oracles, serving as a kind of prologue. **2–3:** Poetic exhortation reminiscent of God's address to the heavenly host in 40.1–2. *Sons* compare Jer.3.19–22. The Biblical word *know* implies a profound, identifying comprehension of the right relationship with God; it is a recurring prophetic theme (Jer.1.5; Hos.2.20; 4.1,6; 5.4). **4–9:** An appeal to a people heedless of the significance of Judah's devastation by Tiglath-Pileser III (734–733 B.C.) or Sennacherib (701 B.C.; 36.1) and Jerusalem's isolation (*daughter of Zion*, see Jer.4.29–31 n.). **4:** Note the poetic parallelism: *nation, people; offspring, sons.* The expression, *Holy One of Israel* (5.19,24; 10.20; 12.6; 17.7; 29.19; 30.11,12,15; 37.23), emphasizes God's unapproachable separateness, which he has bridged by his gracious election of Israel as his people (Hos.8.1; Jer.3.20). **10–20:** God's pronouncement concerning Judah's religious superficiality (Am.5.21–24; Jer.6.20). Judah may repent and return (Jer.7.5–7); the alternative is destruction (Jer.7.22–34). **10:** *Teaching,* the Hebrew word is "torah," which is frequently translated "law." On *Sodom* and

14 Your new moons and your appointed
      feasts
    my soul hates;
    they have become a burden to me,
    I am weary of bearing them.
15 When you spread forth your hands,
    I will hide my eyes from you;
    even though you make many prayers,
    I will not listen;
    your hands are full of blood.
16 Wash yourselves; make yourselves
      clean;
    remove the evil of your doings
    from before my eyes;
    cease to do evil,
17   learn to do good;
    seek justice,
      correct oppression;
    defend the fatherless,
      plead for the widow.

18 "Come now, let us reason together,
    says the LORD:
    though your sins are like scarlet,
      they shall be as white as snow;
    though they are red like crimson,
      they shall become like wool.
19 If you are willing and obedient,
    you shall eat the good of the land;
20 But if you refuse and rebel,
    you shall be devoured by the
      sword;
    for the mouth of the LORD has
      spoken."

21 How the faithful city
    has become a harlot,
    she that was full of justice!
    Righteousness lodged in her,
    but now murderers.
22 Your silver has become dross,
    your wine mixed with water.

23 Your princes are rebels
    and companions of thieves.
    Every one loves a bribe
    and runs after gifts.
    They do not defend the fatherless,
    and the widow's cause does not
      come to them.

24 Therefore the Lord says,
    the LORD of hosts,
    the Mighty One of Israel:
    "Ah, I will vent my wrath on my
      enemies,
    and avenge myself on my foes.
25 I will turn my hand against you
    and will smelt away your dross as
      with lye
    and remove all your alloy.
26 And I will restore your judges as at
      the first,
    and your counselors as at the
      beginning.
    Afterward you shall be called the
      city of righteousness,
    the faithful city."

27 Zion shall be redeemed by justice,
    and those in her who repent, by
      righteousness.
28 But rebels and sinners shall be
      destroyed together,
    and those who forsake the LORD
      shall be consumed.
29 For you shall be ashamed of the
      oaks
    in which you delighted;
    and you shall blush for the gardens
    which you have chosen.
30 For you shall be like an oak
    whose leaf withers,
    and like a garden without water.
31 And the strong shall become tow,
    and his work a spark,

Gomorrah see Gen.18.16–19.28; Jer.23.14; Ezek.16.46–58. **14:** *My soul*, a Hebrew idiom which
in this context means "I" (compare Lev.26.11,30). *Burden*, see Jer.23.33–40. **16–17:** Compare
Ex.22.21,22; Am.5.6–7. **18:** *Reason*, as one argues a case before a judge (Job 23.7). *White* for
holiness (Rev.19.8); *scarlet* for wickedness (garments of Babylon, Rev.17.4). **21–23:** Lamentation over Jerusalem. **21:** *Harlot*, Jer.3.6–10; Ezek. chs. 16 and 23. *Justice* and *righteousness*
express Isaiah's ideal for the people of God. **24:** *Mighty one of Israel* recalls Israel's patriarchal
traditions (49.26; Gen.49.24; Ps.132.2,5). **25:** *As with lye*, or "thoroughly." **26:** Isaiah frequently
uses symbolic names (7.14; 8.1; 9.6; see also Jer.33.16; Ezek.48.35 n.). There will be a new
creation; compare Am.9.11; Rev.3.12; 21.1–4. **29–31:** An allegory on Judah's faithlessness
based on one of Isaiah's rare references to pagan religious practices; compare 57.5; Jer.2.27;
Ezek.6.1–14.

and both of them shall burn together,
with none to quench them.

2 The word which Isaiah the son of
Amoz saw concerning Judah and
Jerusalem.

2 It shall come to pass in the latter days
that the mountain of the house of
the LORD
shall be established as the highest of
the mountains,
and shall be raised above the hills;
and all the nations shall flow to it,
3   and many peoples shall come,
and say:
"Come, let us go up to the mountain
of the LORD,
to the house of the God of Jacob;
that he may teach us his ways
and that we may walk in his
paths."
For out of Zion shall go forth the law,
and the word of the LORD from
Jerusalem.
4 He shall judge between the nations,
and shall decide for many
peoples;
and they shall beat their swords into
plowshares,
and their spears into pruning
hooks;
nation shall not lift up sword against
nation,
neither shall they learn war any
more.

5 O house of Jacob,
come, let us walk
in the light of the LORD.

6 For thou hast rejected thy people,

the house of Jacob,
because they are full of diviners*a*
from the east
and of soothsayers like the
Philistines,
and they strike hands with
foreigners.
7 Their land is filled with silver and
gold,
and there is no end to their
treasures;
their land is filled with horses,
and there is no end to their
chariots.
8 Their land is filled with idols;
they bow down to the work of their
hands,
to what their own fingers have
made.
9 So man is humbled,
and men are brought low—
forgive them not!
10 Enter into the rock,
and hide in the dust
from before the terror of the LORD,
and from the glory of his majesty.
11 The haughty looks of man shall be
brought low,
and the pride of men shall be
humbled;
and the LORD alone will be exalted
in that day.

12 For the LORD of hosts has a day
against all that is proud and lofty,
against all that is lifted up and
high;*b*
13 against all the cedars of Lebanon,
lofty and lifted up;

a Cn: Heb lacks *of diviners*
b Cn Compare Gk: Heb *low*

2.1: Second superscription, perhaps for chs. 2–4. *Word* connotes "message" (Jer.7.1; 11.1).
2–5: The new age, involving the elevation of Zion, the acknowledgment of the nations, and the
age of peace. This oracle (vv. 2–4) is also found in Mic.4.1–4. **3:** *Law,* i.e. "teaching" (1.10),
which is more suitable to the thought of the passage. **4:** The age of peace will follow the judgment of the LORD (compare 5.25; 30.27–28). **5:** Compare v. 3, paraphrased in Mic.4.5.
2.6–22: The day of the LORD. This is probably to be taken as three stanzas, vv. 6–11,12–17,
18–22. The first two have a similar conclusion (compare vv. 11,17), and it is suggested that the
third ended similarly, for the present v. 22 is missing in the Septuagint and is grammatically
corrupt. **6–11:** Judgment on idolatry. **6:** *Diviners* were forbidden in Israel (Ex.22.18; Lev.20.27;
Dt.18.10–11; compare 8.19; 1 Sam.28.8–25; Ezek.13.9). The situation fits Uzziah's reign
(2 Kg.15.1–7; 2 Chr. ch. 26). **7:** Judah's prosperity (Dt.17.16–17; 1 Kg.10.14–29). **11:** *In that
day,* the day of the LORD, in which God judges his enemies and manifests his glory, is a recurring
prophetic theme (13.6; Am.5.18–20; Jer.17.16–18; Ezek.30.3; Jl.1.15). **12–17:** Pride and punish-

and against all the oaks of
    Bashan;
14 against all the high mountains,
    and against all the lofty hills;
15 against every high tower,
    and against every fortified wall;
16 against all the ships of Tarshish,
    and against all the beautiful craft.
17 And the haughtiness of man shall
    be humbled,
  and the pride of men shall be
    brought low;
  and the LORD alone will be exalted
    in that day.
18 And the idols shall utterly pass
    away.
19 And men shall enter the caves of
    the rocks
  and the holes of the ground,
from before the terror of the LORD,
  and from the glory of his majesty,
  when he rises to terrify the earth.

20 In that day men will cast forth
    their idols of silver and their idols
    of gold,
  which they made for themselves to
    worship,
  to the moles and to the bats,
21 to enter the caverns of the rocks
  and the clefts of the cliffs,
from before the terror of the LORD,
  and from the glory of his majesty,
  when he rises to terrify the earth.
22 Turn away from man
  in whose nostrils is breath,
  for of what account is he?

3 For, behold, the Lord, the LORD
   of hosts,
  is taking away from Jerusalem and
    from Judah
stay and staff,
  the whole stay of bread,
  and the whole stay of water;

2 the mighty man and the soldier,
  the judge and the prophet,
  the diviner and the elder,
3 the captain of fifty
  and the man of rank,
the counselor and the skilful
  magician
  and the expert in charms.
4 And I will make boys their princes,
  and babes shall rule over them.
5 And the people will oppress one
    another,
  every man his fellow
  and every man his neighbor;
the youth will be insolent to the
  elder,
  and the base fellow to the
  honorable.

6 When a man takes hold of his
    brother
  in the house of his father, saying:
"You have a mantle;
  you shall be our leader,
and this heap of ruins
  shall be under your rule";
7 in that day he will speak out, saying:
"I will not be a healer;
  in my house there is neither bread
  nor mantle;
you shall not make me
  leader of the people."
8 For Jerusalem has stumbled,
  and Judah has fallen;
because their speech and their deeds
  are against the LORD,
  defying his glorious presence.

9 Their partiality witnesses against
    them;
  they proclaim their sin like Sodom,
  they do not hide it.
Woe to them!
  For they have brought evil upon
  themselves.

---

ment. **13:** *Lebanon, Bashan,* Ezek.27.5–6; Jer.22.20. **16:** *Ships of Tarshish,* the phrase may mean
"refinery fleet" (see 1 Kg.10.22 n.; Jer.10.9 n.). **18–22:** Judgment on idolatry. **19:** The innumerable *caves* in Palestine's limestone hills are age-old places of refuge.

   3.1–15: Anarchy in Jerusalem. 1–7: Without key men, society breaks down. **1:** *Stay and
staff,* everything which supports life, including food and drink (economic resources), and
perhaps also the functionaries in vv. 2–3. **2–3:** Offices deemed necessary for the continuity and
stability of the state. **4:** The inexperienced and naïve will rule. **5–6:** Civil unrest will become
open violence. **8–12:** A commentary on vv. 1–7. Judah's brazen sinfulness and rejection of

10 Tell the righteous that it shall be
  well with them,
 for they shall eat the fruit of their
  deeds.
11 Woe to the wicked! It shall be ill
  with him,
 for what his hands have done shall
  be done to him.
12 My people–children are their
  oppressors,
 and women rule over them.
 O my people, your leaders mislead
  you,
 and confuse the course of your
  paths.

13 The LORD has taken his place to
  contend,
 he stands to judge his people.*d*
14 The LORD enters into judgment
  with the elders and princes of his
  people:
 "It is you who have devoured the
  vineyard,
 the spoil of the poor is in your
  houses.
15 What do you mean by crushing my
  people,
 by grinding the face of the poor?"
 says the Lord GOD of hosts.

16 The LORD said:
 Because the daughters of Zion are
  haughty
 and walk with outstretched necks,
 glancing wantonly with their eyes,
 mincing along as they go,
 tinkling with their feet;
17 the Lord will smite with a scab
 the heads of the daughters of Zion,
 and the LORD will lay bare their
  secret parts.

18 In that day the Lord will take
away the finery of the anklets, the
headbands, and the crescents; 19 the
pendants, the bracelets, and the scarfs;
20 the headdresses, the armlets, the
sashes, the perfume boxes, and the
amulets; 21 the signet rings and nose
rings; 22 the festal robes, the mantles,
the cloaks, and the handbags; 23 the
garments of gauze, the linen garments,
the turbans, and the veils.
24 Instead of perfume there will be
  rottenness;
 and instead of a girdle, a rope;
 and instead of well-set hair,
  baldness;
 and instead of a rich robe, a
  girding of sackcloth;
 instead of beauty, shame.*e*
25 Your men shall fall by the sword
 and your mighty men in battle.
26 And her gates shall lament and
  mourn;
 ravaged, she shall sit upon the
  ground.

4 And seven women shall take hold
of one man in that day, saying,
"We will eat our own bread and wear
our own clothes, only let us be called
by your name; take away our reproach."

2 In that day the branch of the LORD
shall be beautiful and glorious, and
the fruit of the land shall be the pride
and glory of the survivors of Israel.
3 And he who is left in Zion and remains in Jerusalem will be called
holy, every one who has been recorded
for life in Jerusalem, 4 when the Lord
shall have washed away the filth of the
daughters of Zion and cleansed the
bloodstains of Jerusalem from its midst
by a spirit of judgment and by a spirit
of burning. 5 Then the LORD will cre-

d Gk Syr: Heb *judge peoples*
e One ancient Ms: Heb lacks *shame*

God's leadership has ruined the people. **13–15:** God will judge the corrupt judges. *Elders*,
primary administrators of justice (Ex.19.7; Jos.20.4; Dt.21.19–21). *Princes*, royal appointees
(1 Kg.4.2; 2 Kg.10.1; Jer.34.19). *Vineyard*, see 5.1–7.
 3.16–4.1: The humiliation of Jerusalem's women (Am.4.1–3). **18–24:** Detailed expansion of
v. 17. **3.25–4.1:** War's decimation of the male population forces the women to resort to desperate
measures to preserve themselves and their self-respect. *Our reproach* summarizes 3.16–4.1.
 4.2–6: Jerusalem's restoration. 2: *Branch*, the righteous remnant (3.10; compare the Messiah
as Branch in 11.1; Jer.23.5); *fruit of the land*, a "return to paradise." **3:** *Recorded for life*, com-

ate over the whole site of Mount Zion and over her assemblies a cloud by day, and smoke and the shining of a flaming fire by night; for over all the glory there will be a canopy and a pavilion. [6] It will be for a shade by day from the heat, and for a refuge and a shelter from the storm and rain.

5 Let me sing for my beloved
a love song concerning his
   vineyard:
My beloved had a vineyard
   on a very fertile hill.
[2] He digged it and cleared it of stones,
   and planted it with choice vines;
he built a watchtower in the midst of
   it,
   and hewed out a wine vat in it;
and he looked for it to yield grapes,
   but it yielded wild grapes.

[3] And now, O inhabitants of
   Jerusalem
   and men of Judah,
judge, I pray you, between me
   and my vineyard.
[4] What more was there to do for my
   vineyard,
   that I have not done in it?
When I looked for it to yield grapes,
   why did it yield wild grapes?

[5] And now I will tell you
   what I will do to my vineyard.
I will remove its hedge,
   and it shall be devoured;
I will break down its wall,
   and it shall be trampled down.

[6] I will make it a waste;
   it shall not be pruned or hoed,
   and briers and thorns shall grow
   up;
I will also command the clouds
   that they rain no rain upon it.

[7] For the vineyard of the LORD of hosts
   is the house of Israel,
   and the men of Judah
   are his pleasant planting;
and he looked for justice,
   but behold, bloodshed;
for righteousness,
   but behold, a cry!

[8] Woe to those who join house to
   house,
   who add field to field,
until there is no more room,
   and you are made to dwell alone
   in the midst of the land.
[9] The LORD of hosts has sworn in my
   hearing:
"Surely many houses shall be
   desolate,
   large and beautiful houses,
   without inhabitant.
[10] For ten acres of vineyard shall yield
   but one bath,
   and a homer of seed shall yield
   but an ephah."

[11] Woe to those who rise early in the
   morning,
   that they may run after strong
   drink,
who tarry late into the evening
   till wine inflames them!

---

pare Ex.32.32; Mal.3.16; Dan.12.1; Rev.20.12,15. **5**: *Smoke and flaming fire*, the signs of God's presence among his people at the Exodus (Ex.13.21–22; 40.34–38).

   5.1–7: Song of the vineyard (Hos.10.1; Jer.2.21; Ezek.19.10–14), an allegory. This unique didactic poem may have been composed for a celebration of the feast of tabernacles during Jotham's reign, the prophet imitating a vintage festival song. **1a:** Introduction to the poem. **2:** *Choice vines*, the Hebrew word ("soreq") means either red grapes, or grapes native to the valley of Sorek, west of Jerusalem. **3–4:** Judah's only possible answer would be judgment against the vineyard. Judah is asked to pass judgment on herself, much as Nathan through a parable had David pass judgment on himself (2 Sam.12.1–12). **7:** *Justice*, the faithful application of God's will to daily living. *Righteousness*, the living, dynamic relationship between man and God wherein man is spiritually and morally acceptable to God (1.27; 9.7; 16.5; 28.17). Righteousness and justice are naturally coupled (1.21) and grow out of the covenant relationship, the existence of which is assumed (Ex. chs. 19–20). *A cry*, from the oppressed.

   5.8–23: Six reproaches (vv. 8,11,18,20,21,22; perhaps 10.1–4 is a seventh). Compare Am.5.7, 18; 6.1; Jer.22.13. **8–10:** Against covetousness (Mic.2.1–5,8–9; Ex.20.17). *Bath, ephah*, 6.07

12 They have lyre and harp,
timbrel and flute and wine at their
feasts;
but they do not regard the deeds of
the LORD,
or see the work of his hands.

13 Therefore my people go into exile
for want of knowledge;
their honored men are dying of
hunger,
and their multitude is parched with
thirst.
14 Therefore Sheol has enlarged its
appetite
and opened its mouth beyond
measure,
and the nobility of Jerusalem*f* and
her multitude go down,
her throng and he who exults in
her.
15 Man is bowed down, and men are
brought low,
and the eyes of the haughty are
humbled.
16 But the LORD of hosts is exalted in
justice,
and the Holy God shows
himself holy in righteousness.
17 Then shall the lambs graze as in
their pasture,
fatlings and kids*g* shall feed among
the ruins.

18 Woe to those who draw iniquity
with cords of falsehood,
who draw sin as with cart ropes,
19 who say: "Let him make haste,
let him speed his work
that we may see it;
let the purpose of the Holy One of
Israel draw near,
and let it come, that we may know
it!"
20 Woe to those who call evil good
and good evil,

who put darkness for light
and light for darkness,
who put bitter for sweet
and sweet for bitter!
21 Woe to those who are wise in their
own eyes,
and shrewd in their own sight!
22 Woe to those who are heroes at
drinking wine,
and valiant men in mixing strong
drink,
23 who acquit the guilty for a bribe,
and deprive the innocent of his
right!

24 Therefore, as the tongue of fire
devours the stubble,
and as dry grass sinks down in the
flame,
so their root will be as rottenness,
and their blossom go up like dust;
for they have rejected the law of the
LORD of hosts,
and have despised the word of
the Holy One of Israel.
25 Therefore the anger of the LORD
was kindled against his people,
and he stretched out his hand
against them and smote them,
and the mountains quaked;
and their corpses were as refuse
in the midst of the streets.
For all this his anger is not turned
away
and his hand is stretched out still.

26 He will raise a signal for a nation
afar off,
and whistle for it from the ends of
the earth;
and lo, swiftly, speedily it comes!
27 None is weary, none stumbles,
none slumbers or sleeps,
not a waistcloth is loose,
not a sandal-thong broken;

f Heb *her nobility*   *g* Cn Compare Gk: Heb *aliens*

gallons; *homer*, 6.5 bushels (see Ezek.45.11 n.). **11–12**: Against carousing (Am.6.4–6). **13–17**: *Knowledge*, 1.3. The severity of Judah's punishment will require the enlargement of *Sheol* (the underworld, 14.9–18). **16**: In all he does, God is just and right. **18–19**: Against mocking God. **20**: Against moral depravity (32.5; Pr.17.15). **21**: Against conceit. **22–23**: Against bravado and bribery. **24b–30**: These verses should probably follow 10.4 (see 9.8–10.4 n.). *Law*, here also in the sense of "teaching" (see 1.10 n.). The Assyrians (*a nation afar off*; Jer.5.15, referring to Babylon) will be the executors of God's judgment.

²⁸ their arrows are sharp,
  all their bows bent,
their horses' hoofs seem like flint,
  and their wheels like the
    whirlwind.
²⁹ Their roaring is like a lion,
  like young lions they roar;
they growl and seize their prey,
  they carry it off, and none can
    rescue.
³⁰ They will growl over it on that day,
  like the roaring of the sea.
And if one look to the land,
  behold, darkness and distress;
and the light is darkened by its
  clouds.

6 In the year that King Uzzi'ah died I saw the Lord sitting upon a throne, high and lifted up; and his train filled the temple. ² Above him stood the seraphim; each had six wings: with two he covered his face, and with two he covered his feet, and with two he flew. ³ And one called to another and said:

"Holy, holy, holy is the LORD of
  hosts;
the whole earth is full of his glory."

⁴ And the foundations of the thresholds shook at the voice of him who called, and the house was filled with smoke. ⁵ And I said: "Woe is me! For I am lost; for I am a man of unclean lips, and I dwell in the midst of a people of unclean lips; for my eyes have seen the King, the LORD of hosts!"

6 Then flew one of the seraphim to me, having in his hand a burning coal which he had taken with tongs from the altar. ⁷ And he touched my mouth,

and said: "Behold, this has touched your lips; your guilt is taken away, and your sin forgiven." ⁸ And I heard the voice of the Lord saying, "Whom shall I send, and who will go for us?" Then I said, "Here am I! Send me." ⁹ And he said, "Go, and say to this people:

'Hear and hear, but do not
  understand;
see and see, but do not perceive.'
¹⁰ Make the heart of this people fat,
  and their ears heavy,
  and shut their eyes;
lest they see with their eyes,
  and hear with their ears,
and understand with their hearts,
  and turn and be healed."

¹¹ Then I said, "How long, O Lord?"
And he said:

"Until cities lie waste
  without inhabitant,
and houses without men,
  and the land is utterly desolate,
¹² and the LORD removes men far
    away,
  and the forsaken places are many
    in the midst of the land.
¹³ And though a tenth remain in it,
  it will be burned again,
like a terebinth or an oak,
  whose stump remains standing
    when it is felled."
The holy seed is its stump.

7 In the days of Ahaz the son of Jotham, son of Uzzi'ah, king of Judah, Rezin the king of Syria and Pekah the son of Remali'ah the king of Israel came up to Jerusalem to wage war against it, but they could not conquer it. ² When the house of David

---

6.1–13: The call of Isaiah. God's appearance is described in the setting of the Jerusalem temple (compare the description of the enthroned deity in 1 Kg.22.19–23; Ezek.1.4–2.1). **1:** *Year*, 742 B.C. *Throne*, ark of the covenant. **2:** *Seraphim*, possibly griffin-like creatures; compare the cherubim, also associated with the glory of the Lord (Ezek. ch. 1). **3:** Thrice-*holy* for emphasis (Jer.7.4). **5:** Before the holy God, sinful man cannot stand (Ex.33.18–20). **6–8:** Cleansed by God's forgiving act, Isaiah may now speak for God. **9–12:** Compare Jer.1.10,13–19. Verses 9b–10 are quoted in Mt.13.10–15; compare Mk.4.12; Lk.8.10; Jn.12.39–41; Acts 28.26–27. **13:** The last part of the verse is obscure and textually corrupt and perhaps should be restored to read, ". . . . like the terebinth [of the goddess] and the oak of Asherah, cast out with the pillar of the high places," that is, like the destroyed furnishings of a pagan high place.

7.1–8.15: Isaiah and the Syro-Ephraimite War (734–733 B.C.). For the historical background see 2 Kg.16.1–20. **1–9: Sign of Shear-jashub. 2:** The continuation of the Davidic monarchy was

was told, "Syria is in league with E'-phraim," his heart and the heart of his people shook as the trees of the forest shake before the wind.

3 And the Lord said to Isaiah, "Go forth to meet Ahaz, you and She'-ar-jash'ub[h] your son, at the end of the conduit of the upper pool on the highway to the Fuller's Field, [4] and say to him, 'Take heed, be quiet, do not fear, and do not let your heart be faint because of these two smoldering stumps of firebrands, at the fierce anger of Rezin and Syria and the son of Remali'ah. [5] Because Syria, with E'phraim and the son of Remali'ah, has devised evil against you, saying, [6] "Let us go up against Judah and terrify it, and let us conquer it for ourselves, and set up the son of Ta'be-el as king in the midst of it," [7] thus says the Lord God:

It shall not stand,
   and it shall not come to pass.
[8] For the head of Syria is Damascus,
   and the head of Damascus is
      Rezin.
(Within sixty-five years E'phraim will be broken to pieces so that it will no longer be a people.)
[9] And the head of E'phraim is
      Sama'ria,
   and the head of Sama'ria is the
      son of Remali'ah.
If you will not believe,
   surely you shall not be
      established.'"

10 Again the Lord spoke to Ahaz, [11] "Ask a sign of the Lord your God; let it be deep as Sheol or high as heaven." [12] But Ahaz said, "I will not ask, and I will not put the Lord to the test." [13] And he said, "Hear then, O house of David! Is it too little for you to weary men, that you weary my God also? [14] Therefore the Lord himself will give you a sign. Behold, a young woman[i] shall conceive and bear[j] a son, and shall call his name Imman'u-el.[k] [15] He shall eat curds and honey when he knows how to refuse the evil and choose the good. [16] For before the child knows how to refuse the evil and choose the good, the land before whose two kings you are in dread will be deserted. [17] The Lord will bring upon you and upon your people and upon your father's house such days as have not come since the day that E'phraim departed from Judah–the king of Assyria."

18 In that day the Lord will whistle for the fly which is at the sources of the streams of Egypt, and for the bee which is in the land of Assyria. [19] And they will all come and settle in the steep ravines, and in the clefts of the rocks, and on all the thornbushes, and on all the pastures.

20 In that day the Lord will shave with a razor which is hired beyond the River–with the king of Assyria–the head and the hair of the feet, and it will sweep away the beard also.

21 In that day a man will keep alive a young cow and two sheep; [22] and because of the abundance of milk which they give, he will eat curds; for every one that is left in the land will eat curds and honey.

23 In that day every place where there used to be a thousand vines, worth a thousand shekels of silver, will become briers and thorns. [24] With bow and arrows men will come there,

h That is *A remnant shall return*   i Or *virgin*
j Or *is with child and shall bear*
k That is *God is with us*

---

threatened (see v. 6). **3:** *Shear-jashub*, "A remnant shall return"; assuming the worst eventuality, God's promise to David (2 Sam.7.8–16) will be preserved in the remnant (10.20–23). *Upper pool*, reservoir south of the Pool of Siloam. **5:** *Son of Tabeel*, perhaps a prince of Judah whose mother came from Tabeel, a region of northern Transjordan. **8–9a:** The text and meaning are unclear. **7.10–17: Sign of Immanuel. 13:** This expresses Isaiah's impatience. **14:** The sign is *Immanuel*, "God with us"; a second (compare vv. 3–9) assurance to the frightened, wavering Ahaz. *Young woman*, Hebrew *'almah*, feminine of *'elem*, young man (1 Sam.17.56; 20.22); the word appears in Gen.24.43; Ex.2.8; Ps.68.25, and elsewhere, where it is translated "young woman," "girl," "maiden." **15:** *Curds, honey*, simple foods suggesting difficult times; *good and evil*, age of moral discrimination. **18–25:** Four threats amplifying v. 17. **20:** *Feet*, see Ex.4.25 n.

for all the land will be briers and thorns; 25 and as for all the hills which used to be hoed with a hoe, you will not come there for fear of briers and thorns; but they will become a place where cattle are let loose and where sheep tread.

8 Then the LORD said to me, "Take a large tablet and write upon it in common characters, 'Belonging to Ma'her-shal'al-hash-baz.' "*l* 2 And I got reliable witnesses, Uri'ah the priest and Zechari'ah the son of Jeberechi'ah, to attest for me. 3 And I went to the prophetess, and she conceived and bore a son. Then the LORD said to me, "Call his name Ma'her-shal'al-hash-baz; 4 for before the child knows how to cry 'My father' or 'My mother,' the wealth of Damascus and the spoil of Sama'ria will be carried away before the king of Assyria."

5 The LORD spoke to me again: 6 "Because this people have refused the waters of Shilo'ah that flow gently, and melt in fear before*m* Rezin and the son of Remali'ah; 7 therefore, behold, the Lord is bringing up against them the waters of the River, mighty and many, the king of Assyria and all his glory; and it will rise over all its channels and go over all its banks; 8 and it will sweep on into Judah, it will overflow and pass on, reaching even to the neck; and its outspread wings will fill the breadth of your land, O Imman'u-el."

9 Be broken, you peoples, and be dismayed;
    give ear, all you far countries;
gird yourselves and be dismayed;
gird yourselves and be dismayed.
10 Take counsel together, but it will come to nought;
    speak a word, but it will not stand, for God is with us.*x*

11 For the LORD spoke thus to me with his strong hand upon me, and warned me not to walk in the way of this people, saying: 12 "Do not call conspiracy all that this people call conspiracy, and do not fear what they fear, nor be in dread. 13 But the LORD of hosts, him you shall regard as holy; let him be your fear, and let him be your dread. 14 And he will become a sanctuary, and a stone of offense, and a rock of stumbling to both houses of Israel, a trap and a snare to the inhabitants of Jerusalem. 15 And many shall stumble thereon; they shall fall and be broken; they shall be snared and taken."

16 Bind up the testimony, seal the teaching among my disciples. 17 I will wait for the LORD, who is hiding his face from the house of Jacob, and I will hope in him. 18 Behold, I and the children whom the LORD has given me are signs and portents in Israel from the LORD of hosts, who dwells on Mount Zion. 19 And when they say to you, "Consult the mediums and the wizards who chirp and mutter," should not a people consult their God? Should they consult the dead on behalf of the living? 20 To the teaching and to the testimony! Surely for this word which they speak there is no dawn. 21 They will pass through the land,*n* greatly distressed and hungry; and when they are hungry, they will be enraged and

l That is *The spoil speeds, the prey hastes*
m Cn: Heb *rejoices in*
x Heb *immanu el*   *n* Heb *it*

8.1–4: The sign of Maher-shalal-hash-baz, "The spoil speeds, the prey hastes"; Isaiah's third assurance to Ahaz. **1:** *Tablet,* of wood. **2:** *Uriah,* 2 Kg.16.10–16. *Zechariah,* perhaps Ahaz's father-in-law (2 Kg.18.2). **3:** *Prophetess,* Isaiah's wife. **5–8:** Oracle of Shiloah and the Euphrates; Judah also is included in Assyria's sweep. *Shiloah,* a conduit flanking Ophel from the spring Gihon (see 1 Kg.1.33 n.) to the reservoir (7.3), is contrasted with the *River,* the great Euphrates. Ahaz's mighty ally, Assyria, will inundate tiny Judah, God's people. **9–10:** God is with his people (see 7.14 n.) to deliver them (Ps. 46, esp. vv. 7,11).
    8.11–22: The testimony and the teaching. 11–15: "Man proposes–God disposes" (Pr.16.9). **16:** *Bind, seal,* as one binds and seals a scroll (Jer.32.10). **18:** *Signs,* 7.3; 7.14; 8.1. **19–20:** Condemnation of superstition (2.6). For necromancy (consultation of the dead), see 1 Sam.28.7

will curse[o] their king and their God,
and turn their faces upward; [22] and
they will look to the earth, but behold, distress and darkness, the gloom
of anguish; and they will be thrust into
thick darkness.

9[p] But there will be no gloom for
her that was in anguish. In the
former time he brought into contempt
the land of Zeb'ulun and the land of
Naph'tali, but in the latter time he will
make glorious the way of the sea, the
land beyond the Jordan, Galilee of the
nations.

[2q] The people who walked in darkness
  have seen a great light;
  those who dwelt in a land of deep
    darkness,
  on them has light shined.
[3] Thou hast multiplied the nation,
  thou hast increased its joy;
  they rejoice before thee
  as with joy at the harvest,
  as men rejoice when they divide
    the spoil.
[4] For the yoke of his burden,
  and the staff for his shoulder,
  the rod of his oppressor,
  thou hast broken as on the day of
    Mid'ian.
[5] For every boot of the tramping
    warrior in battle tumult
  and every garment rolled in blood
  will be burned as fuel for the fire.
[6] For to us a child is born,
  to us a son is given;
  and the government will be upon
    his shoulder,
  and his name will be called
  "Wonderful Counselor, Mighty God,

Everlasting Father, Prince of
  Peace."
[7] Of the increase of his government
    and of peace
  there will be no end,
  upon the throne of David, and over
    his kingdom,
  to establish it, and to uphold it
  with justice and with righteousness
  from this time forth and for
    evermore.
The zeal of the LORD of hosts will do
  this.

[8] The Lord has sent a word against
    Jacob,
  and it will light upon Israel;
[9] and all the people will know,
  E'phraim and the inhabitants of
    Sama'ria,
  who say in pride and in arrogance
    of heart:
[10] "The bricks have fallen,
  but we will build with dressed
    stones;
  the sycamores have been cut down,
  but we will put cedars in their
    place."
[11] So the LORD raises adversaries[r]
    against them,
  and stirs up their enemies.
[12] The Syrians on the east and the
    Philistines on the west
  devour Israel with open mouth.
  For all this his anger is not turned
    away
  and his hand is stretched out still.

o Or *curse by*
p Ch 8.23 in Heb
q Ch 9.1 in Heb
r Cn: Heb *the adversaries of Rezin*

---

n. **9.1**: Transitional verse from doom to promise. *Zebulun, Naphtali,* and *Issachar* constituted later *Galilee. Way of the sea,* the highway from Damascus to the sea, probable route of the Assyrian invasion in 733–732 B.C. (2 Kg.15.29).
9.2–7: The messianic king (compare 11.1–9). Filled with borrowed phrases referring to the Davidic monarchy, this passage may have originally celebrated the accession of a Judean king, perhaps Hezekiah; in its present context it describes the coming Messiah as the ideal king. **4:** *Midian,* Jg.7.15–25. **6:** *Government,* symbol of authority. *Mighty God,* divine in might. *Everlasting Father,* continuing fatherly love and care. *Prince of Peace,* the king who brings peace and prosperity. The king represents the best qualities of Israel's heroes (Ezek.37.25).
9.8–10.4: Ephraim's judgment an object lesson for Judah (five stanzas, including 5.24b–30; with the same refrain, 9.12,17,21; 10.4; 5.25; compare Jer.3.6–10; Ezek.16.44–58). **8–12:** Punishment for pride and unrepented wickedness. **8:** *Word,* more than a statement; it includes the potential and fact of accomplishment (55.10–11; Jer.23.18–20). **10:** *Bricks, sycamore,* for ordinary houses; *dressed stone, cedar* for palaces (Jer.22.7,23). **13–17:** Corrupt leaders misled

¹³ The people did not turn to him who
   smote them,
   nor seek the LORD of hosts.
¹⁴ So the LORD cut off from Israel
   head and tail,
   palm branch and reed in one day–
¹⁵ the elder and honored man is the
   head,
   and the prophet who teaches lies
   is the tail;
¹⁶ for those who lead this people lead
   them astray,
   and those who are led by them
   are swallowed up.
¹⁷ Therefore the Lord does not
   rejoice over their young men,
   and has no compassion on their
   fatherless and widows;
for every one is godless and an
   evildoer,
   and every mouth speaks folly.
For all this his anger is not turned
   away
   and his hand is stretched out still.

¹⁸ For wickedness burns like a fire,
   it consumes briers and
   thorns;
it kindles the thickets of the forest,
   and they roll upward in a column
   of smoke.
¹⁹ Through the wrath of the LORD of
   hosts
   the land is burned,
   and the people are like fuel for the
   fire;
   no man spares his brother.
²⁰ They snatch on the right, but are
   still hungry,
   and they devour on the left, but
   are not satisfied;
   each devours his neighbor's*ˢ* flesh,
²¹ Manas'seh E'phraim, and
   E'phraim Manas'seh,
   and together they are against
   Judah.

For all this his anger is not turned
   away
   and his hand is stretched out still.

1O Woe to those who decree
   iniquitous decrees,
   and the writers who keep writing
   oppression,
² to turn aside the needy from justice
   and to rob the poor of my people
   of their right,
   that widows may be their spoil,
   and that they may make the
   fatherless their prey!
³ What will you do on the day of
   punishment,
   in the storm which will come
   from afar?
To whom will you flee for help,
   and where will you leave your
   wealth?
⁴ Nothing remains but to crouch
   among the prisoners
   or fall among the slain.
For all this his anger is not turned
   away
   and his hand is stretched out still.

⁵ Ah, Assyria, the rod of my anger,
   the staff of my fury!*ᵗ*
⁶ Against a godless nation I send him,
   and against the people of my
   wrath I command him,
to take spoil and seize plunder,
   and to tread them down like the
   mire of the streets.
⁷ But he does not so intend,
   and his mind does not so think;
but it is in his mind to destroy,
   and to cut off nations not a few;
⁸ for he says:
   "Are not my commanders all kings?
⁹ Is not Calno like Car'chemish?
   Is not Hamath like Arpad?

s Tg Compare Gk: Heb *the flesh of his arm*
t Heb *a staff it is in their hand my fury*

their people (Jer.6.14). **18–21:** Moral decay consumes like a forest fire (Hos.7.6); civil war
breaks out (2 Kg.15.23–31; 16.5). **20:** *His neighbor's flesh;* the Hebrew consonantal text may be
read "the flesh of his offspring" (on cannibalism, see Jer.19.9). Some treat this passage as a
proverb. **10.1–4:** Justice is miscarried (3.13–15; Jer.8.8).
   10.5–19: Woe, O Assyria! Unaware that he was serving as God's instrument, powerful
Assyria was doomed by his pride to destruction (Jer.25.8–14; 50.23). **9:** In northern Syria,
Tiglath-Pileser III captured *Calno* (742 B.C.), *Carchemish, Hamath* (738), *Arpad* (741), southern

  Is not Sama'ria like Damascus?
[10] As my hand has reached to the
    kingdoms of the idols
  whose graven images were greater
    than those of Jerusalem and
    Sama'ria,
[11] shall I not do to Jerusalem and her
    idols
  as I have done to Sama'ria and
    her images?''

12 When the Lord has finished all his work on Mount Zion and on Jerusalem he[u] will punish the arrogant boasting of the king of Assyria and his haughty pride. [13] For he says:
  "By the strength of my hand I have
    done it,
  and by my wisdom, for I have
    understanding;
  I have removed the boundaries of
    peoples,
  and have plundered their
    treasures;
  like a bull I have brought down
    those who sat on thrones.
[14] My hand has found like a nest
    the wealth of the peoples;
  and as men gather eggs that have
    been forsaken
  so I have gathered all the earth;
  and there was none that moved a
    wing,
  or opened the mouth, or chirped.''

[15] Shall the axe vaunt itself over him
    who hews with it,
  or the saw magnify itself against
    him who wields it?
  As if a rod should wield him who
    lifts it,

  or as if a staff should lift him who
    is not wood!
[16] Therefore the Lord, the LORD of
    hosts,
  will send wasting sickness among
    his stout warriors,
  and under his glory a burning will
    be kindled,
  like the burning of fire.
[17] The light of Israel will become a
    fire,
  and his Holy One a flame;
  and it will burn and devour
    his thorns and briers in one day.
[18] The glory of his forest and of his
    fruitful land
  the LORD will destroy, both soul
    and body,
  and it will be as when a sick man
    wastes away.
[19] The remnant of the trees of his
    forest will be so few
  that a child can write them down.

20 In that day the remnant of Israel and the survivors of the house of Jacob will no more lean upon him that smote them, but will lean upon the LORD, the Holy One of Israel, in truth. [21] A remnant will return, the remnant of Jacob, to the mighty God. [22] For though your people Israel be as the sand of the sea, only a remnant of them will return. Destruction is decreed, overflowing with righteousness. [23] For the Lord, the LORD of hosts, will make a full end, as decreed, in the midst of all the earth.

24 Therefore thus says the Lord, the LORD of hosts: "O my people,

u Heb *I*

Syria, *Damascus* (732). Menahem of Israel paid him tribute (2 Kg.15.19–20). **10–11:** To Assyria, the LORD was another idol. **12:** Prose summation of vv. 5–11,13–19. **13–14:** Assyria's boast. *Removed boundaries,* to discourage rebellion, Assyria transplanted subject peoples. **15:** Rhetorical question recalling v. 5 (45.9). **16–19:** Light of Israel, God's majestic glory (2.10; 29.6; Ezek.1.26–28). God will ravage Assyria like a forest fire.

    10.20–23: Only a remnant will return. 21: *A remnant will return,* in Hebrew this is the same as the name of Isaiah's son Shear-jashub; in 7.3–4 it stands in an oracle of encouragement, but here in an oracle of doom. **22:** *Sand of the sea* recalls God's oath to the patriarchs (Gen.22.17; compare Rom.9.27). In Isaiah (4.2–3; 6.13; 7.3; 28.5–6; 37.4; 37.31–32; compare Mic.4.7; 5.2–9; Zeph.2.7) *remnant* refers to those remaining after Judah's punishment, from whom a great people will arise. During the Exile the remnant was the deported people (Ezek.6.8–10; Jer.23.3; 31.7), whom God would bring back and make great. After the Exile Jewish faithlessness evoked again the pre-exilic concept (Zech.8.11; Hag.1.12; Zech.14.2).

who dwell in Zion, be not afraid of the Assyrians when they smite with the rod and lift up their staff against you as the Egyptians did. ²⁵ For in a very little while my indignation will come to an end, and my anger will be directed to their destruction. ²⁶ And the LORD of hosts will wield against them a scourge, as when he smote Mid'ian at the rock of Oreb; and his rod will be over the sea, and he will lift it as he did in Egypt. ²⁷ And in that day his burden will depart from your shoulder, and his yoke will be destroyed from your neck."

He has gone up from Rimmon,^v
²⁸ he has come to Ai'ath;
he has passed through Migron,
at Michmash he stores his
baggage;
²⁹ they have crossed over the pass,
at Geba they lodge for the night;
Ramah trembles,
Gib'e-ah of Saul has fled.
³⁰ Cry aloud, O daughter of Gallim!
Hearken, O La'ishah!
Answer her, O An'athoth!
³¹ Madme'nah is in flight,
the inhabitants of Gebim flee for
safety.
³² This very day he will halt at Nob,
he will shake his fist
at the mount of the daughter of
Zion,
the hill of Jerusalem.

³³ Behold, the Lord, the LORD of hosts
will lop the boughs with terrifying
power;
the great in height will be hewn
down,
and the lofty will be brought low.
³⁴ He will cut down the thickets of the
forest with an axe,
and Lebanon with its majestic
trees^w will fall.

11 There shall come forth a shoot
from the stump of Jesse,
and a branch shall grow out of his
roots.
² And the Spirit of the LORD shall
rest upon him,
the spirit of wisdom and
understanding,
the spirit of counsel and might,
the spirit of knowledge and the
fear of the LORD.
³ And his delight shall be in the fear
of the LORD.

He shall not judge by what his
eyes see,
or decide by what his ears hear;
⁴ but with righteousness he shall
judge the poor,
and decide with equity for the
meek of the earth;
and he shall smite the earth with the
rod of his mouth,
and with the breath of his lips he
shall slay the wicked.
⁵ Righteousness shall be the girdle of
his waist,
and faithfulness the girdle of his
loins.

⁶ The wolf shall dwell with the lamb,
and the leopard shall lie down
with the kid,
and the calf and the lion and the
fatling together,

---

v Cn: Heb *and his yoke from your neck, and a yoke will be destroyed because of fatness*
w Cn Compare Gk Vg: Heb *with a majestic one*

10.24–27c: Oracle of promise. *Oreb*, Jg.7.25; *rod*, Ex.14.16.

10.27d–32: The approach of the Assyrians. The invader (Tiglath-Pileser III or Sennacherib, 1.4–9 n.) approached from the north toward the outskirts of Jerusalem (Jer.6.1–3). This may be a "traditional" description of the northern invasion route; for a southern route, see Mic.1.10–15. **33–34:** The LORD, the forester, will cut down Assyria.

11.1–9: The messianic king (compare 9.2–7). For the occasion of the original oracle, see 9.2–7 n. **1–3a:** The Messiah will manifest the characteristics of Israel's great men. **1:** *Jesse*, David's father (1 Sam.16.1–20). **2:** To these six "Gifts of the Spirit" the Septuagint adds "piety." **3b–5:** Wisdom and justice (5.7) were traditionally associated in the ideal king (1 Kg. ch. 3; Ps. 72). **6–8:** His reign will be "paradise regained"; the disorder of nature will be restored to its pristine harmony (Ezek.47.1–12). **9:** *My holy mountain*, 65.25; Ezek.20.40.

and a little child shall lead them.
7 The cow and the bear shall feed;
    their young shall lie down together;
    and the lion shall eat straw like
      the ox.
8 The sucking child shall play over
      the hole of the asp,
    and the weaned child shall put his
      hand on the adder's den.
9 They shall not hurt or destroy
    in all my holy mountain;
  for the earth shall be full of the
      knowledge of the LORD
    as the waters cover the sea.

10 In that day the root of Jesse shall
stand as an ensign to the peoples; him
shall the nations seek, and his dwellings shall be glorious.
11 In that day the Lord will extend
his hand yet a second time to recover
the remnant which is left of his people,
from Assyria, from Egypt, from Pathros, from Ethiopia, from Elam, from
Shinar, from Hamath, and from the
coastlands of the sea.
12 He will raise an ensign for the
      nations,
    and will assemble the outcasts of
      Israel,
  and gather the dispersed of Judah
    from the four corners of the earth.
13 The jealousy of E'phraim shall
      depart,
    and those who harass Judah shall
      be cut off;
E'phraim shall not be jealous of
      Judah,
  and Judah shall not harass
      E'phraim.
14 But they shall swoop down upon the
      shoulder of the Philistines in
      the west,
  and together they shall plunder

the people of the east.
They shall put forth their hand
    against Edom and Moab,
  and the Ammonites shall obey
    them.
15 And the LORD will utterly destroy
    the tongue of the sea of Egypt;
  and will wave his hand over the River
    with his scorching wind,
  and smite it into seven channels
    that men may cross dryshod.
16 And there will be a highway from
    Assyria
  for the remnant which is left of
    his people,
as there was for Israel
  when they came up from the land
    of Egypt.

12 You will say in that day:
  "I will give thanks to thee, O
      LORD,
  for though thou wast angry with
      me,
thy anger turned away,
  and thou didst comfort me.

2 "Behold, God is my salvation;
  I will trust, and will not be afraid;
  for the LORD GOD is my strength and
    my song,
  and he has become my salvation."

3 With joy you will draw water from
the wells of salvation. 4 And you will
say in that day:
"Give thanks to the LORD,
  call upon his name;
make known his deeds among the
    nations,
  proclaim that his name is exalted.

5 "Sing praises to the LORD, for he has
    done gloriously;

11.10–16: The messianic age. 10: *Root* is a person, not the dynasty (v. 1). **11–16:** Restored and reunited Israel takes vengeance against her oppressors. The terminology and mood of vv. 11–16 indicate a post-exilic date. **11:** *Pathros*, Upper Egypt; *Shinar*, Babylonia; *coastlands*, Aegean seacoast and islands. **12:** *Ensign*, here a standard, not a person (v. 10). **15:** *The tongue of the sea*, the Red Sea (Ex. ch. 14), *River*, Euphrates.

12.1–6: Two songs conclude Section I of the book of Isaiah. (a) **1–3:** Song of deliverance (compare Ps. 116). **1a** and **4a** are liturgical rubrics. **2b:** Ex.15.2; Ps.118.14. (b) **4–6:** Song of thanksgiving. *Shout and sing for joy*, compare Zeph.3.14. *In your midst*, God in his temple. *Holy One*, see 1.4.

let this be known[x] in all the earth.
⁶ Shout, and sing for joy, O inhabitant
    of Zion,
  for great in your midst is the Holy
    One of Israel."

13 The oracle concerning Babylon
   which Isaiah the son of Amoz
saw.
² On a bare hill raise a signal,
    cry aloud to them;
  wave the hand for them to enter
    the gates of the nobles.
³ I myself have commanded my
      consecrated ones,
  have summoned my mighty men
    to execute my anger,
  my proudly exulting ones.

⁴ Hark, a tumult on the mountains
    as of a great multitude!
  Hark, an uproar of kingdoms,
    of nations gathering together!
  The LORD of hosts is mustering
    a host for battle.
⁵ They come from a distant land,
    from the end of the heavens,
  the LORD and the weapons of his
      indignation,
  to destroy the whole earth.

⁶ Wail, for the day of the LORD is
    near;
  as destruction from the Almighty
    it will come!
⁷ Therefore all hands will be feeble,
    and every man's heart will melt,
⁸ and they will be dismayed.
  Pangs and agony will seize them;
    they will be in anguish like a
      woman in travail.
  They will look aghast at one another;
    their faces will be aflame.

⁹ Behold, the day of the LORD comes,
    cruel, with wrath and fierce anger,
  to make the earth a desolation
    and to destroy its sinners from it.
¹⁰ For the stars of the heavens and
      their constellations
  will not give their light;
  the sun will be dark at its rising
    and the moon will not shed its
      light.
¹¹ I will punish the world for its evil,
    and the wicked for their iniquity;
  I will put an end to the pride of the
      arrogant,
    and lay low the haughtiness of the
      ruthless.
¹² I will make men more rare than fine
      gold,
    and mankind than the gold of
      Ophir.
¹³ Therefore I will make the heavens
      tremble,
    and the earth will be shaken out
      of its place,
  at the wrath of the LORD of hosts
    in the day of his fierce anger.
¹⁴ And like a hunted gazelle,
    or like sheep with none to gather
      them,
  every man will turn to his own
      people,
    and every man will flee to his own
      land.
¹⁵ Whoever is found will be thrust
      through,
    and whoever is caught will fall by
      the sword.
¹⁶ Their infants will be dashed in
      pieces
    before their eyes;
  their houses will be plundered
    and their wives ravished.

x Or *this is made known*

13.1–23.18. Oracles against foreign nations (compare Jer. chs. 46–51; Ezek. chs. 25–32); each
is introduced by the word "oracle."
   13.1–22: Oracle against Babylon. This is obviously subsequent to Isaiah, when Babylon,
whose power is here assumed, superseded Assyria; vv. 17–22 suggest a time after Nebuchadrezzar's death in 562 B.C. **2:** *Gates of the nobles*, perhaps the name of one of Babylon's city gates
(Jer.19.2). **3:** *My consecrated ones*, perhaps Persian soldiers serving God's purposes (10.5–6;
45.1–4). **5:** *Distant land*, perhaps Persia. *The whole earth*, the Babylonian empire. **6–16:** The
cataclysmic fall of Babylon, attended by portents in the heavens and civil disorder, is seen as
the *day of the LORD* (compare 2.11). Before the Exile, the day of the LORD marked the punishment of Israel (Am.8.9–10; Jer.30.5–7); after the Exile, it referred to the punishment of Israel's

17 Behold, I am stirring up the Medes
　　against them,
　who have no regard for silver
　　and do not delight in gold.
18 Their bows will slaughter the
　　young men;
　they will have no mercy on the
　　fruit of the womb;
　their eyes will not pity children.
19 And Babylon, the glory of
　　kingdoms,
　the splendor and pride of the
　　Chalde′ans,
　will be like Sodom and Gomor′rah
　　when God overthrew them.
20 It will never be inhabited
　　or dwelt in for all generations;
　no Arab will pitch his tent there,
　　no shepherds will make their flocks
　　lie down there.
21 But wild beasts will lie down there,
　　and its houses will be full of
　　howling creatures;
　there ostriches will dwell,
　　and there satyrs will dance.
22 Hyenas will cry in its towers,
　　and jackals in the pleasant
　　palaces;
　its time is close at hand
　　and its days will not be prolonged.

14 The LORD will have compas-
　sion on Jacob and will again
choose Israel, and will set them in
their own land, and aliens will join
them and will cleave to the house of
Jacob. 2 And the peoples will take them
and bring them to their place, and the
house of Israel will possess them in the
LORD's land as male and female slaves;
they will take captive those who were

their captors, and rule over those who
oppressed them.
3 When the LORD has given you rest
from your pain and turmoil and the
hard service with which you were made
to serve, 4 you will take up this taunt
against the king of Babylon:
　"How the oppressor has ceased,
　　the insolent fury^y ceased!
5 The LORD has broken the staff of the
　　wicked,
　the scepter of rulers,
6 that smote the peoples in wrath
　　with unceasing blows,
　that ruled the nations in anger
　　with unrelenting persecution.
7 The whole earth is at rest and quiet;
　　they break forth into singing.
8 The cypresses rejoice at you,
　　the cedars of Lebanon, saying,
　'Since you were laid low,
　　no hewer comes up against us.'
9 Sheol beneath is stirred up
　　to meet you when you come,
　it rouses the shades to greet you,
　　all who were leaders of the earth;
　it raises from their thrones
　　all who were kings of the nations.
10 All of them will speak
　　and say to you:
　'You too have become as weak as
　　we!
　You have become like us!'
11 Your pomp is brought down to
　　Sheol,
　　the sound of your harps;
　maggots are the bed beneath you,
　　and worms are your covering.

12 "How you are fallen from heaven,

y One ancient Ms Compare Gk Syr Vg: The meaning of
the Hebrew word is uncertain

---

oppressors, and was again a day of hope for Israel (Am.5.18). **17–19:** *Medes*, people northwest
of Persia who earlier were Babylon's allies against Assyria. **20–22:** Busy Babylon will become
a wasteland inhabited only by animals (Jer.50.35–40). *Satyr*, goat demon (34.14; Lev. 17.7).
　14.1–2: The return from Exile. *Aliens*, proselytes to Judaism, referred to in post-exilic prophecy (Zech.8.20–22). **3–23: "How are the mighty fallen!"** A dirge against a tyrant; the tyrant
may be a king (Nebuchadrezzar?), a nation (Babylon?), or a power (Persia?) whose fall would
precede Judah's restoration. **3–4a:** Prose introduction. **4b–8:** After the tyrant's fall, peace
settles over the oppressed peoples. **8:** Assyrian and Babylonian kings used great quantities of
cedars for their palaces. **9–11:** The tyrant joins earlier rulers in *Sheol* (see 5.14–17 n.; Ezek.
32.17–22). **12–15:** From aspirations for divinity (compare Gen.11.4–8), he falls to the anonymity
of Sheol. Canaanite mythological background is reflected in *Day Star* and *Dawn* (Hebrew
"Helal" and "Shahar," names of deities), *mount of assembly* (of the gods, and located at Jebel

O Day Star, son of Dawn!
How you are cut down to the ground,
you who laid the nations low!
[13] You said in your heart,
'I will ascend to heaven;
above the stars of God
I will set my throne on high;
I will sit on the mount of assembly
in the far north;
[14] I will ascend above the heights of
the clouds,
I will make myself like the Most
High.'
[15] But you are brought down to Sheol,
to the depths of the Pit.
[16] Those who see you will stare at you,
and ponder over you:
'Is this the man who made the earth
tremble,
who shook kingdoms,
[17] who made the world like a desert
and overthrew its cities,
who did not let his prisoners go
home?'
[18] All the kings of the nations lie in
glory,
each in his own tomb;
[19] but you are cast out, away from
your sepulchre,
like a loathed untimely birth,[z]
clothed with the slain, those pierced
by the sword,
who go down to the stones of the
Pit,
like a dead body trodden under
foot.
[20] You will not be joined with them
in burial,
because you have destroyed your
land,
you have slain your people.

"May the descendants of evildoers
nevermore be named!

[21] Prepare slaughter for his sons
because of the guilt of their
fathers,
lest they rise and possess the earth,
and fill the face of the world with
cities."

[22] "I will rise up against them,"
says the LORD of hosts, "and will cut
off from Babylon name and remnant,
offspring and posterity, says the LORD.
[23] And I will make it a possession of
the hedgehog, and pools of water, and
I will sweep it with the broom of destruction, says the LORD of hosts."

[24] The LORD of hosts has sworn:
"As I have planned,
so shall it be,
and as I have purposed,
so shall it stand,
[25] that I will break the Assyrian in
my land,
and upon my mountains trample
him under foot;
and his yoke shall depart from
them,
and his burden from their
shoulder."
[26] This is the purpose that is purposed
concerning the whole earth;
and this is the hand that is stretched
out
over all the nations.
[27] For the LORD of hosts has purposed,
and who will annul it?
His hand is stretched out,
and who will turn it back?

[28] In the year that King Ahaz died
came this oracle:
[29] "Rejoice not, O Philistia, all of you,
that the rod which smote you is
broken,

z Cn Compare Tg Symmachus: Heb *a loathed branch*

'Aqra, north of Ugarit), and *Most High*, a title also applied to Baal Shamaim (Lord of Heaven).
15: *The Pit*, an alternative designation of the underworld (Ezek.31.15–18). **16–19**: He will have
no greatness in death. *Untimely birth*, the stillborn received the same fate as other forms of violent
death (Ezek.32.17–21). **20–21**: Ignominy and hatred are his fate and heritage. **22–23**: Prose
conclusion.
14.24–27: Against Assyria (17.12–14; 30.27–33; 37.22–29); no power on earth can prevent
God from accomplishing his purposes. **28–32**: Against Philistia (715 B.C.; Jer. ch. 47; Am.1.6–8).
Though momentarily it appears that Philistia is secure, the foe *out of the north* (Jer.1.13–15)
will shortly destroy her, too.

for from the serpent's root will come
  forth an adder,
  and its fruit will be a flying
  serpent.
30 And the first-born of the poor will
  feed,
  and the needy lie down in safety;
  but I will kill your root with famine,
  and your remnant I*a* will slay.
31 Wail, O gate; cry, O city;
  melt in fear, O Philistia, all of you!
  For smoke comes out of the north,
  and there is no straggler in his
  ranks."

32 What will one answer the messengers
  of the nation?
  "The LORD has founded Zion,
  and in her the afflicted of his
  people find refuge."

15 An oracle concerning Moab.
  Because Ar is laid waste in a
  night
  Moab is undone;
  because Kir is laid waste in a night
  Moab is undone.
2 The daughter of Dibon*b* has gone
  up
  to the high places to weep;
  over Nebo and over Med'eba
  Moab wails.
  On every head is baldness,
  every beard is shorn;
3 in the streets they gird on sackcloth;
  on the housetops and in the
  squares
  every one wails and melts in tears.
4 Heshbon and Ele-a'leh cry out,
  their voice is heard as far as Jahaz;
  therefore the armed men of Moab
  cry aloud;
  his soul trembles.
5 My heart cries out for Moab;
  his fugitives flee to Zo'ar,
  to Eg'lath-shelish'iyah.
  For at the ascent of Luhith
  they go up weeping;
  on the road to Horona'im

they raise a cry of destruction;
6 the waters of Nimrim
  are a desolation;
  the grass is withered, the new
  growth fails,
  the verdure is no more.
7 Therefore the abundance they have
  gained
  and what they have laid up
  they carry away
  over the Brook of the Willows.
8 For a cry has gone
  round the land of Moab;
  the wailing reaches to Egla'im,
  the wailing reaches to Beer-e'lim.
9 For the waters of Dibon*c* are full of
  blood;
  yet I will bring upon Dibon*c*
  even more,
  a lion for those of Moab who
  escape,
  for the remnant of the land.

16 They have sent lambs
  to the ruler of the land,
  from Sela, by way of the desert,
  to the mount of the daughter of
  Zion.
2 Like fluttering birds,
  like scattered nestlings,
  so are the daughters of Moab
  at the fords of the Arnon.
3 "Give counsel,
  grant justice;
  make your shade like night
  at the height of noon;
  hide the outcasts,
  betray not the fugitive;
4 let the outcasts of Moab
  sojourn among you;
  be a refuge to them
  from the destroyer.
  When the oppressor is no more,
  and destruction has ceased,
  and he who tramples under foot
  has vanished from the land,

a One ancient Ms Vg: Heb *he*
b Cn: Heb *the house and Dibon*
c One ancient Ms Vg Compare Syr: Heb *Dimon*

15.1–16.14: Against Moab (Ezek.25.8–11; Am.2.1–3). This oracle and Jer. ch. 48 are two recensions of the same elegy over once despised Moab (Gen.19.30–37) lying prostrate under the invader's (probably Assyria) heel (vv. 1–9). **16.1–5:** Moabite refugees, appealing to the mercies of the crown, seek sanctuary in Judah; since the thought seems out of place here, the passage

⁵ then a throne will be established
   in steadfast love
and on it will sit in faithfulness
   in the tent of David
one who judges and seeks justice
   and is swift to do righteousness."

⁶ We have heard of the pride of
   Moab,
   how proud he was;
of his arrogance, his pride, and his
   insolence–
   his boasts are false.
⁷ Therefore let Moab wail,
   let every one wail for Moab.
Mourn, utterly stricken,
   for the raisin-cakes of
   Kir-har′eseth.

⁸ For the fields of Heshbon languish,
   and the vine of Sibmah;
the lords of the nations
   have struck down its branches,
which reached to Jazer
   and strayed to the desert;
its shoots spread abroad
   and passed over the sea.
⁹ Therefore I weep with the weeping
   of Jazer
   for the vine of Sibmah;
I drench you with my tears,
   O Heshbon and Ele-a′leh;
for upon your fruit and your harvest
   the battle shout has fallen.
¹⁰ And joy and gladness are taken
   away
   from the fruitful field;
and in the vineyards no songs are
   sung,
   no shouts are raised;
no treader treads out wine in the
   presses;
   the vintage shout is hushed.*d*
¹¹ Therefore my soul moans like a
   lyre for Moab,
   and my heart for Kir-he′res.

12 And when Moab presents himself, when he wearies himself upon the
high place, when he comes to his sanctuary to pray, he will not prevail.
13 This is the word which the LORD
spoke concerning Moab in the past.
¹⁴ But now the LORD says, "In three
years, like the years of a hireling, the
glory of Moab will be brought into contempt, in spite of all his great multitude, and those who survive will be very
few and feeble."

17 An oracle concerning Damascus.
   Behold, Damascus will cease to
     be a city,
   and will become a heap of ruins.
² Her cities will be deserted for
     ever;*e*
   they will be for flocks,
   which will lie down, and none will
     make them afraid.
³ The fortress will disappear from
     E′phraim,
   and the kingdom from Damascus;
and the remnant of Syria will be
   like the glory of the children of
     Israel,
        says the LORD of hosts.

⁴ And in that day
   the glory of Jacob will be brought
     low,
   and the fat of his flesh will grow
     lean.
⁵ And it shall be as when the reaper
     gathers standing grain
   and his arm harvests the ears,
and as when one gleans the ears of
     grain
   in the Valley of Reph′aim.
⁶ Gleanings will be left in it,
   as when an olive tree is beaten–
   two or three berries

d Gk: Heb *I have hushed*
e Cn Compare Gk: Heb *the cities of Aroer are deserted*

---

may be an insertion. *Lambs,* a gift; compare earlier tribute Moab paid Judah (2 Kg.3.4). **6–12:**
A description of the disaster, especially the destruction of the vineyards (parallel, Jer.48.29–33).
Kir-hareseth and *Kir-heres,* the same as Kir, 15.1. **13–14:** In a short time, despite intervening
prosperity, Moab will again be devastated.
    17.1–6: Against the Syro-Ephraimite alliance (about 734 B.C.–see 2 Kg.16.1–20 n.; Is.7.1–8.4).
Two stanzas (1–3,4–6) reaffirm the ultimate defeat of *Damascus* and *Ephraim. The glory of . . .
Israel* refers to Samaria; *Rephaim,* valley northwest of Jerusalem (2 Sam.5.18).

in the top of the highest bough,
four or five
on the branches of a fruit tree,
says the LORD God of Israel.

7 In that day men will regard their
Maker, and their eyes will look to the
Holy One of Israel; 8 they will not
have regard for the altars, the work of
their hands, and they will not look to
what their own fingers have made,
either the Ashe'rim or the altars of
incense.

9 In that day their strong cities will
be like the deserted places of the Hivites and the Amorites,*f* which they
deserted because of the children of
Israel, and there will be desolation.

10 For you have forgotten the God of
your salvation,
and have not remembered the
Rock of your refuge;
therefore, though you plant pleasant
plants
and set out slips of an alien god,
11 though you make them grow on the
day that you plant them,
and make them blossom in the
morning that you sow;
yet the harvest will flee away
in a day of grief and incurable
pain.

12 Ah, the thunder of many peoples,
they thunder like the thundering
of the sea!
Ah, the roar of nations,
they roar like the roaring of
mighty waters!
13 The nations roar like the roaring of
many waters,
but he will rebuke them, and
they will flee far away,

chased like chaff on the mountains
before the wind
and whirling dust before the storm.
14 At evening time, behold, terror!
Before morning, they are no more!
This is the portion of those who
despoil us,
and the lot of those who plunder
us.

18 Ah, land of whirring wings
which is beyond the rivers of
Ethiopia;
2 which sends ambassadors by the
Nile,
in vessels of papyrus upon the
waters!
Go, you swift messengers,
to a nation, tall and smooth,
to a people feared near and far,
a nation mighty and conquering,
whose land the rivers divide.

3 All you inhabitants of the world,
you who dwell on the earth,
when a signal is raised on the
mountains, look!
When a trumpet is blown, hear!
4 For thus the LORD said to me:
"I will quietly look from my dwelling
like clear heat in sunshine,
like a cloud of dew in the heat of
harvest."
5 For before the harvest, when the
blossom is over,
and the flower becomes a ripening
grape,
he will cut off the shoots with
pruning hooks,
and the spreading branches he
will hew away.
6 They shall all of them be left

f Cn Compare Gk: Heb *the wood and the highest bough*

17.7–11: **Against idolatry.** 7–8: Eventually man will return to God (1.29–31). *Asherim*, cult images of Asherah, e.g. sacred wooden poles (6.13 n.). 9–11: Those who forsake God for idols will be displaced as Israel displaced the *Hivites* and *Amorites*, original inhabitants of Palestine (Dt.7.1). *Plants, slips*, plants dedicated to Tammuz (compare Ezek.8.14–18). 12–14: The appearance of a potentially destructive storm (perhaps Assyria's onslaught of 701 B.C.) is dispelled by God who defends his people.
18.1–20.6: **Concerning Egypt.** 18.1–7: **Against Egypt.** The occasion may be Egypt's invitation to participate in an anti-Assyrian plot, about 714 B.C. Using the figure of harvest, Isaiah cautions that since God determines the course of events man must wait. When ready, God will signal the beginning of revolt. *Land the rivers divide*, Egypt divided by the Nile.

to the birds of prey of the
    mountains
and to the beasts of the earth.
And the birds of prey will summer
    upon them,
    and all the beasts of the earth will
        winter upon them.

7 At that time gifts will be brought
to the LORD of hosts
from a people tall and smooth,
    from a people feared near and far,
a nation mighty and conquering,
    whose land the rivers divide,
to Mount Zion, the place of the name
of the LORD of hosts.

19 An oracle concerning Egypt.
    Behold, the LORD is riding on a
    swift cloud
    and comes to Egypt;
and the idols of Egypt will tremble
    at his presence,
    and the heart of the Egyptians
        will melt within them.
2 And I will stir up Egyptians against
    Egyptians,
    and they will fight, every man
        against his brother
    and every man against his
        neighbor,
    city against city, kingdom against
        kingdom;
3 and the spirit of the Egyptians within
        them will be emptied out,
    and I will confound their plans;
and they will consult the idols and
        the sorcerers,
    and the mediums and the wizards;
4 and I will give over the Egyptians
    into the hand of a hard master;
and a fierce king will rule over them,
    says the Lord, the LORD of hosts.

5 And the waters of the Nile will be
    dried up,

and the river will be parched and
    dry;
6 and its canals will become foul,
    and the branches of Egypt's Nile
        will diminish and dry up,
    reeds and rushes will rot away.
7 There will be bare places by the Nile,
    on the brink of the Nile,
and all that is sown by the Nile will
    dry up,
    be driven away, and be no more.
8 The fishermen will mourn and
    lament,
    all who cast hook in the Nile;
and they will languish
    who spread nets upon the water.
9 The workers in combed flax will
        be in despair,
    and the weavers of white cotton.
10 Those who are the pillars of the
        land will be crushed,
    and all who work for hire will
        be grieved.

11 The princes of Zo'an are utterly
        foolish;
    the wise counselors of Pharaoh
        give stupid counsel.
How can you say to Pharaoh,
    "I am a son of the wise,
    a son of ancient kings"?
12 Where then are your wise men?
    Let them tell you and make
        known
    what the LORD of hosts has
        purposed against Egypt.
13 The princes of Zo'an have become
        fools,
    and the princes of Memphis are
        deluded;
those who are the cornerstones of
        her tribes
    have led Egypt astray.
14 The LORD has mingled within her
        a spirit of confusion;
    and they have made Egypt stagger
        in all her doings

19.1–15: Against Egypt (compare Ezek. chs. 29–32). 1–4: God's judgment is seen in civil turbulence, perhaps that which came with the transition to the Twenty-fifth (Ethiopian) Dynasty,
begun about 714 B.C. by Piankhi (the *hard master* of v. 4; it may also refer to Assyria). 5–10:
The Nile, Egypt's lifeline, will dry up, destroying her economy. Man has no control over natural
catastrophes. 11–15: Isaiah taunts Egypt; if she, with her vaunted wisdom, can devise schemes
effecting national destinies, how could she have overlooked God's plan for herself? For *Zoan*

as a drunken man staggers in his vomit.

15 And there will be nothing for Egypt which head or tail, palm branch or reed, may do.

16 In that day the Egyptians will be like women, and tremble with fear before the hand which the LORD of hosts shakes over them. 17 And the land of Judah will become a terror to the Egyptians; every one to whom it is mentioned will fear because of the purpose which the LORD of hosts has purposed against them.

18 In that day there will be five cities in the land of Egypt which speak the language of Canaan and swear allegiance to the LORD of hosts. One of these will be called the City of the Sun.

19 In that day there will be an altar to the LORD in the midst of the land of Egypt, and a pillar to the LORD at its border. 20 It will be a sign and a witness to the LORD of hosts in the land of Egypt; when they cry to the LORD because of oppressors he will send them a savior, and will defend and deliver them. 21 And the LORD will make himself known to the Egyptians; and the Egyptians will know the LORD in that day and worship with sacrifice and burnt offering, and they will make vows to the LORD and perform them. 22 And the LORD will smite Egypt, smiting and healing, and they will return to the LORD, and he will heed their supplications and heal them.

23 In that day there will be a highway from Egypt to Assyria, and the Assyrian will come into Egypt, and the Egyptian into Assyria, and the Egyptians will worship with the Assyrians.

24 In that day Israel will be the third with Egypt and Assyria, a blessing in the midst of the earth, 25 whom the LORD of hosts has blessed, saying, "Blessed be Egypt my people, and Assyria the work of my hands, and Israel my heritage."

20 In the year that the commander in chief, who was sent by Sargon the king of Assyria, came to Ashdod and fought against it and took it,– 2 at that time the LORD had spoken by Isaiah the son of Amoz, saying, "Go, and loose the sackcloth from your loins and take off your shoes from your feet," and he had done so, walking naked and barefoot– 3 the LORD said, "As my servant Isaiah has walked naked and barefoot for three years as a sign and a portent against Egypt and Ethiopia, 4 so shall the king of Assyria lead away the Egyptians captives and the Ethiopians exiles, both the young and the old, naked and barefoot, with buttocks uncovered, to the shame of Egypt. 5 Then they shall be dismayed and confounded because of Ethiopia their hope and of Egypt their boast. 6 And the inhabitants of this coastland will say in that day, 'Behold, this is what has happened to those in whom we hoped and to whom we fled for help to be delivered from the king of Assyria! And we, how shall we escape?' "

21 The oracle concerning the wilderness of the sea.

---

and Memphis see Ezek.30.13–19 n. *Palm* and *reed* represent rulers and the ruled (9.14). **16–25:** *Conversion of Egypt and Assyria* (five paragraphs, each beginning with *In that day*). **16–17:** A later nationalistic paragraph emphasizing Judah's (and God's) eventual overthrow of Egypt (v. 12). **18:** *Language of Canaan,* Jewish settlements in Egypt from the early sixth century on are known (Jer.44.1). *City of the sun,* identification uncertain (compare Jer.43.13); there were temples to the LORD at Elephantine and Leontopolis in Egypt. **19–22:** Egyptian proselytes will be treated as Israel, with punishment and mercy (*smiting* and *healing*). **23,24–25:** Israel will become the mediator and blessing for the nations (Gen.12.3).

　　20.1–6: Against Egypt. Egypt failed to defend a co-conspirator, *Ashdod,* against Sargon's devastating attack, 711 B.C. Isaiah, naked like a prisoner, warns Egypt of its approaching captivity. **2:** Apparently *sackcloth* was customarily worn by prophets (2 Kg.1.8; Zech.13.4–6).
　　21.1–10: Against Babylon (13.1).**1:** Perhaps emend to read, "Words like whirlwinds sweeping

As whirlwinds in the Negeb sweep
  on,
  it comes from the desert,
  from a terrible land.
2 A stern vision is told to me;
  the plunderer plunders,
  and the destroyer destroys.
Go up, O Elam,
  lay siege, O Media;
all the sighing she has caused
  I bring to an end.
3 Therefore my loins are filled with
    anguish;
  pangs have seized me,
  like the pangs of a woman in
    travail;
I am bowed down so that I cannot
    hear,
  I am dismayed so that I cannot
    see.
4 My mind reels, horror has appalled
    me;
  the twilight I longed for
  has been turned for me into
    trembling.
5 They prepare the table,
  they spread the rugs,
  they eat, they drink.
Arise, O princes,
  oil the shield!
6 For thus the Lord said to me:
"Go, set a watchman,
  let him announce what he sees.
7 When he sees riders, horsemen in
    pairs,
  riders on asses, riders on camels,
let him listen diligently,
  very diligently."
8 Then he who saw[g] cried:
"Upon a watchtower I stand, O
    Lord,
  continually by day,
and at my post I am stationed
  whole nights.

9 And, behold, here come riders,
  horsemen in pairs!"
And he answered,
  "Fallen, fallen is Babylon;
  and all the images of her gods
  he has shattered to the ground."
10 O my threshed and winnowed one,
  what I have heard from the LORD
    of hosts,
  the God of Israel, I announce to
    you.

11 The oracle concerning Dumah.
  One is calling to me from Se'ir,
  "Watchman, what of the night?
  Watchman, what of the night?"
12 The watchman says:
  "Morning comes, and also the night.
  If you will inquire, inquire;
  come back again."

13 The oracle concerning Arabia.
  In the thickets in Arabia you will
    lodge,
  O caravans of De'danites.
14 To the thirsty bring water,
  meet the fugitive with bread,
  O inhabitants of the land of
    Tema.
15 For they have fled from the swords,
  from the drawn sword,
  from the bent bow,
  and from the press of battle.

16 For thus the Lord said to me,
"Within a year, according to the years
of a hireling, all the glory of Kedar will
come to an end; 17 and the remainder
of the archers of the mighty men of the
sons of Kedar will be few; for the
LORD, the God of Israel, has spoken."

22 The oracle concerning the valley of vision.

g One ancient Ms: Heb *a lion*

---

through the Negeb, coming from the desert . . ." *Negeb,* southern Palestine. **2–5:** Prepare for
the attack! *Elam,* Jer.49.34–39. *Media* aided Persia against Babylon (13.17–19). *Oil the shield,*
to preserve the leather's suppleness. **6–10:** The prophet (*a watchman;* Ezek.3.17) awaits the news
of Babylon's fall (Jer.51.33; Rev.18.2). **9:** *Ground,* underworld (see Jer.17.12,13 n.).
 21.11–12: Concerning Edom, who shared Ashdod's fate (20.1). The prophet suggests a time
of deliverance (*morning*) followed by renewed oppression (*night*). *Dumah,* a town in Arabia;
the word also means "silence" and here may be a symbolic name for Edom (*Seir,* Gen.32.3).
 21.13–17: Concerning Arabia. *Dedan* in northern Arabia (Ezek.25.13); *Tema* an oasis in
northwestern Arabia (Jer.25.23); *Kedar* in northern Arabia, apparently the aggressor (Jer.49.28).

What do you mean that you have
  gone up,
all of you, to the housetops,
2 you who are full of shoutings,
  tumultuous city, exultant town?
Your slain are not slain with the
  sword
  or dead in battle.
3 All your rulers have fled together,
  without the bow they were
    captured.
All of you who were found were
    captured,
  though they had fled far away.*h*
4 Therefore I said:
  "Look away from me,
  let me weep bitter tears;
  do not labor to comfort me
    for the destruction of the daughter
    of my people."

5 For the Lord GOD of hosts has a day
  of tumult and trampling and
    confusion
  in the valley of vision,
  a battering down of walls
    and a shouting to the mountains.
6 And Elam bore the quiver
  with chariots and horsemen,*i*
  and Kir uncovered the shield.
7 Your choicest valleys were full of
    chariots,
  and the horsemen took their stand
    at the gates.
8 He has taken away the covering of
    Judah.

In that day you looked to the
weapons of the House of the Forest,

9 and you saw that the breaches of
the city of David were many, and you
collected the waters of the lower pool,
10 and you counted the houses of Jerusalem, and you broke down the houses
to fortify the wall. 11 You made a reservoir between the two walls for the
water of the old pool. But you did not
look to him who did it, or have regard
for him who planned it long ago.

12 In that day the Lord GOD of hosts
    called to weeping and
      mourning,
  to baldness and girding with
      sackcloth;
13 and behold, joy and gladness,
    slaying oxen and killing sheep,
    eating flesh and drinking wine.
  "Let us eat and drink,
    for tomorrow we die."
14 The LORD of hosts has revealed
      himself in my ears:
  "Surely this iniquity will not be
      forgiven you
    till you die."
  says the Lord GOD of hosts.

15 Thus says the Lord GOD of
hosts, "Come, go to this steward, to
Shebna, who is over the household,
and say to him: 16 What have you to
do here and whom have you here, that
you have hewn here a tomb for yourself, you who hew a tomb on the
height, and carve a habitation for
yourself in the rock? 17 Behold, the
LORD will hurl you away violently, O

h Gk Syr Vg: Heb *from far away*
i The Hebrew of this line is obscure

22.1–14: Warning to Jerusalem of approaching destruction. The occasion may have been
Sargon's expedition of 711 B.C. (20.1), which by-passed Judah, or the period of civil strife in
Assyria following Sargon's death (705 B.C.). **1**: *Valley of vision*, the title is taken from v. 5 and
the reference perhaps to the valley of Hinnom (compare Jer.7.30–34; 32.35). **4**: *Daughter of
my people*, Jerusalem. **5–8a**: The *day* of the Lord GOD is described as a day of invasion (2.11;
13.6). *Elam* (21.2) and *Kir* (identification uncertain), mercenaries in Assyria's army. *Choicest
valleys*, such as Valley of Rephaim and the King's Valley (17.5; 2 Sam.18.18). **8b–11**: Military
preparedness does not replace faithfulness to God. *House*, the royal palace (Jer.22.13–14).
The city of David was the oldest (southeastern) section of Jerusalem (2 Sam.5.7). *Collected the
waters* may refer to the excavation of Hezekiah's tunnel (2 Kg.20.20; 2 Chr.32.3–5). **12–14**:
The words of the revelers are turned against them (5.11–12).

22.15–25: Against Shebna (Jer.20.1–6). Hezekiah's major-domo apparently arrogated
improper status to himself, and may have been an instigator in the anti-Assyrian plot preceding
711 B.C. (18.1–7 n.). Verses 24–25 suggest that Eliakim (36.3), a welcome replacement, failed to
fulfil expectations.

you strong man. He will seize firm hold on you, [18] and whirl you round and round, and throw you like a ball into a wide land; there you shall die, and there shall be your splendid chariots, you shame of your master's house. [19] I will thrust you from your office, and you will be cast down from your station. [20] In that day I will call my servant Eli'akim the son of Hilki'ah, [21] and I will clothe him with your robe, and will bind your girdle on him, and will commit your authority to his hand; and he shall be a father to the inhabitants of Jerusalem and to the house of Judah. [22] And I will place on his shoulder the key of the house of David; he shall open, and none shall shut; and he shall shut, and none shall open. [23] And I will fasten him like a peg in a sure place, and he will become a throne of honor to his father's house. [24] And they will hang on him the whole weight of his father's house, the offspring and issue, every small vessel, from the cups to all the flagons. [25] In that day, says the LORD of hosts, the peg that was fastened in a sure place will give way; and it will be cut down and fall, and the burden that was upon it will be cut off, for the LORD has spoken."

23

The oracle concerning Tyre.
Wail, O ships of Tarshish,
for Tyre is laid waste, without
house or haven!
From the land of Cyprus
it is revealed to them.
[2] Be still, O inhabitants of the coast,
O merchants of Sidon;
your messengers passed over the sea[j]
[3]   and were on many waters;
your revenue was the grain of
Shihor,
the harvest of the Nile;
you were the merchant of the
nations.

[4] Be ashamed, O Sidon, for the sea
has spoken,
the stronghold of the sea, saying:
"I have neither travailed nor given
birth,
I have neither reared young men
nor brought up virgins."
[5] When the report comes to Egypt,
they will be in anguish over the
report about Tyre.
[6] Pass over to Tarshish,
wail, O inhabitants of the coast!
[7] Is this your exultant city
whose origin is from days of old,
whose feet carried her
to settle afar?
[8] Who has purposed this
against Tyre, the bestower of
crowns,
whose merchants were princes,
whose traders were the honored of
the earth?
[9] The LORD of hosts has purposed it,
to defile the pride of all glory,
to dishonor all the honored of the
earth.
[10] Overflow your land like the Nile,
O daughter of Tarshish;
there is no restraint any more.
[11] He has stretched out his hand over
the sea,
he has shaken the kingdoms;
the LORD has given command
concerning Canaan
to destroy its strongholds.
[12] And he said:
"You will no more exult,
O oppressed virgin daughter of
Sidon;
arise, pass over to Cyprus,
even there you will have no rest."

13 Behold the land of the Chalde'ans! This is the people; it was not Assyria. They destined Tyre for wild beasts. They erected their siege towers,

j One ancient Ms: Heb *who passed over the sea, they replenished you*

23.1–18: The oracle concerning Sidon (vv. 1–4,12–14) is combined with a later one against Tyre (vv. 5–11,15–18). **1a:** Superscription for the chapter. **1b–c:** *Tarshish,* see Jer.10.9 n. There were Phoenician colonies in *Cyprus.* **3:** *Shihor,* the "waters of Horus," near Zoan. **4:** Ruined Sidon is barren like the sea without sailors (*young men*). **5–11:** Fallen Tyre's commercial empire

they razed her palaces, they made her a ruin.*k*
14 Wail, O ships of Tarshish,
for your stronghold is laid waste.
15 In that day Tyre will be forgotten for seventy years, like the days of one king. At the end of seventy years, it will happen to Tyre as in the song of the harlot:
16 "Take a harp,
go about the city,
O forgotten harlot!
Make sweet melody,
sing many songs,
that you may be remembered."
17 At the end of seventy years, the LORD will visit Tyre, and she will return to her hire, and will play the harlot with all the kingdoms of the world upon the face of the earth. 18 Her merchandise and her hire will be dedicated to the LORD; it will not be stored or hoarded, but her merchandise will supply abundant food and fine clothing for those who dwell before the LORD.

24 Behold, the LORD will lay waste the earth and make it desolate, and he will twist its surface and scatter its inhabitants.
2 And it shall be, as with the people, so with the priest;
as with the slave, so with his master;
as with the maid, so with her mistress;
as with the buyer, so with the seller;
as with the lender, so with the borrower;
as with the creditor, so with the debtor.
3 The earth shall be utterly laid waste and utterly despoiled;
for the LORD has spoken this word.

4 The earth mourns and withers,
the world languishes and withers;
the heavens languish together with the earth.
5 The earth lies polluted
under its inhabitants;
for they have transgressed the laws,
violated the statutes,
broken the everlasting covenant.
6 Therefore a curse devours the earth,
and its inhabitants suffer for their guilt;
therefore the inhabitants of the earth are scorched,
and few men are left.
7 The wine mourns,
the vine languishes,
all the merry-hearted sigh.
8 The mirth of the timbrels is stilled,
the noise of the jubilant has ceased,
the mirth of the lyre is stilled.
9 No more do they drink wine with singing;
strong drink is bitter to those who drink it.

k The Hebrew of this verse is obscure

reacts with alarm. With this section compare Ezek. ch. 26; 27.1–9,25–36; ch. 28. **15–18:** A very late addition (perhaps third century); compare the restoration in the late oracles in Jer.48.47; 49.6,39. *Seventy years*, Jer.25.11. **17:** *Play the harlot*, do anything for gain. **18:** Even these sordid treasures will finally be dedicated to God (18.7; 45.14).

Chs. 24–27: The "Isaiah Apocalypse." These chapters, unrelated to their context, are frequently called the "Isaiah Apocalypse" because of their use of eschatological themes found in later apocalyptic writings (universal judgment, eschatological banquet, heavenly signs, and the like). One may regard the section as a transitional form between traditional prophetic and apocalyptic materials, dating between 540 and 425 B.C. The chapters contain a variety of types of materials, e.g. eschatological prophecy in four sections (24.1–6,16b–23; 25.6–10a; 26.20–27.1), four apocalyptic poems of deliverance (24.7–16a; 25.1–5; 26.1–6; 27.2–11), oracles of doom and triumph (26.20–27.1; 27.12–13; compare 25.10b–12), and a processional and an apocalyptic psalm (26.1–6; 27.2–11).

24.1–6: Universal judgment (compare vv. 16b–23). A picture of total destruction; compare the flood of Noah. **1:** *Twist*, by *earthquake*. **2:** Expansion of Hos.4.9. **3:** *This word*, vv. 1–2. **5:** *Laws . . . statutes . . . covenants*, Is.42.22–25. *Everlasting covenant*, perhaps a reference to the promise to Noah (Gen.9.1–17; compare Is.54.9); in any case, not the Mosaic covenant.
24.7–16a: Deliverance after destruction. 7–12: Happiness of the vintage festivals is stilled.

10 The city of chaos is broken down,
    every house is shut up so that none
    can enter.
11 There is an outcry in the streets for
    lack of wine;
    all joy has reached its eventide;
    the gladness of the earth is
    banished.
12 Desolation is left in the city,
    the gates are battered into ruins.
13 For thus it shall be in the midst of
    the earth
    among the nations,
as when an olive tree is beaten,
as at the gleaning when the
    vintage is done.

14 They lift up their voices, they sing
    for joy;
    over the majesty of the LORD they
    shout from the west.
15 Therefore in the east give glory to
    the LORD;
    in the coastlands of the sea, to the
    name of the LORD, the God of
    Israel.
16 From the ends of the earth we hear
    songs of praise,
    of glory to the Righteous One.
But I say, "I pine away,
I pine away. Woe is me!
For the treacherous deal
    treacherously,
    the treacherous deal very
    treacherously."

17 Terror, and the pit, and the snare
    are upon you, O inhabitant of the
    earth!
18 He who flees at the sound of the
    terror
    shall fall into the pit;

and he who climbs out of the pit
    shall be caught in the snare.
For the windows of heaven are
    opened,
    and the foundations of the earth
    tremble.
19 The earth is utterly broken,
    the earth is rent asunder,
    the earth is violently shaken.
20 The earth staggers like a drunken
    man,
    it sways like a hut;
its transgression lies heavy upon it,
and it falls, and will not rise again.

21 On that day the LORD will punish
    the host of heaven, in heaven,
    and the kings of the earth, on the
    earth.
22 They will be gathered together
    as prisoners in a pit;
they will be shut up in a prison,
    and after many days they will be
    punished.
23 Then the moon will be confounded,
    and the sun ashamed;
for the LORD of hosts will reign
    on Mount Zion and in Jerusalem
and before his elders he will manifest
    his glory.

25 O LORD, thou art my God;
    I will exalt thee, I will praise
    thy name;
for thou hast done wonderful things,
    plans formed of old, faithful and
    sure.
2 For thou hast made the city a heap,
    the fortified city a ruin;
the palace of aliens is a city no more,
    it will never be rebuilt.
3 Therefore strong peoples will glorify
    thee;

10: *City of chaos*, not Jerusalem (26.1–6); perhaps Babylon, destroyed by Xerxes I (485 B.C.), or it may refer to the universal destruction of vv. 1–6. **13–16a:** The coming triumph. *It*, the scattered Jewish remnant (19.24; Ezek.38.12), which praises God for saving and vindicating Israel, *the righteous one.*

  24.16b–23: Universal judgment. **16b–18b:** This continues vv. 1–6. **17–18b:** This appears in Jer.48.43–44. **18c–23:** Reflection of Canaanite and Babylonian mythological background. *Windows of heaven*, source of downpours (Gen.7.11). **21–22:** *Host of heaven*, rebellious astral deities (Zeph.1.5; Jer.19.13) imprisoned in the *pit* (Is.14.15; Rev.20.1–3). *Many days*, compare Rev.20.3,7. **23:** *Moon . . . confounded, sun . . . ashamed* after losing their divine status (Jer.8.2; Dt.17.3). *Elders*, as with Moses (Ex.24.9–11,12–16; compare Rev.4.4,10–11).

  25.1–5: Psalm of thanksgiving (compare Ps. 145). **2:** Identity of *the city* uncertain. **4:** *Poor,*

cities of ruthless nations will fear
thee.
⁴ For thou hast been a stronghold to
the poor,
a stronghold to the needy in his
distress,
a shelter from the storm and a
shade from the heat;
for the blast of the ruthless is like a
storm against a wall,
⁵ like heat in a dry place.
Thou dost subdue the noise of the
aliens;
as heat by the shade of a cloud,
so the song of the ruthless is stilled.

6 On this mountain the LORD of
hosts will make for all peoples a feast of
fat things, a feast of wine on the lees, of
fat things full of marrow, of wine on
the lees well refined. ⁷ And he will destroy on this mountain the covering that
is cast over all peoples, the veil that is
spread over all nations. ⁸ He will swallow up death for ever, and the Lord
GOD will wipe away tears from all faces,
and the reproach of his people he will
take away from all the earth; for the
LORD has spoken.
9 It will be said on that day, "Lo,
this is our God; we have waited for
him, that he might save us. This is the
LORD; we have waited for him; let us
be glad and rejoice in his salvation."
10 For the hand of the LORD will
rest on this mountain, and Moab shall
be trodden down in his place, as straw
is trodden down in a dung-pit. ¹¹ And
he will spread out his hands in the midst
of it as a swimmer spreads his hands
out to swim; but the LORD will lay low

his pride together with the skill*l* of his
hands. ¹² And the high fortifications of
his walls he will bring down, lay low,
and cast to the ground, even to the dust.

26 In that day this song will be
sung in the land of Judah:
"We have a strong city;
he sets up salvation
as walls and bulwarks.
² Open the gates,
that the righteous nation which
keeps faith
may enter in.
³ Thou dost keep him in perfect peace,
whose mind is stayed on thee,
because he trusts in thee.
⁴ Trust in the LORD for ever,
for the LORD GOD
is an everlasting rock.
⁵ For he has brought low
the inhabitants of the height,
the lofty city.
He lays it low, lays it low to the
ground,
casts it to the dust.
⁶ The foot tramples it,
the feet of the poor,
the steps of the needy."

⁷ The way of the righteous is level;
thou*m* dost make smooth the path
of the righteous.
⁸ In the path of thy judgments,
O LORD, we wait for thee;
thy memorial name
is the desire of our soul.
⁹ My soul yearns for thee in the night,
my spirit within me earnestly seeks
thee.

l The meaning of the Hebrew word is uncertain
m Cn Compare Gk: Heb *thou (that art) upright*

the helpless (perhaps Jews) contrasted with *strong peoples* (v. 3). **6–10a: Third eschatological section.** **6:** *This mountain*, Zion. Cultic *feast*, (1 Sam.9.13), later a part of the Messianic expecta-tion (Lk.14.15–24). **7–8:** *Destroy . . . covering . . . veil* (of mourning, or perhaps ignorance), *swallow up death*, phrases reminiscent of Canaanite mythology. **25.10b–12: Oracle of doom.** **10b:** The mention of *Moab* is unexpected; possibly only symbolic, or emend to read "the enemy."
26.1–6: Song of victory (24.7–16a; 25.1–5), a processional psalm, sung on entering Jerusalem, the *strong city* (v. 1; compare Ps.24.7–10), celebrating God's victory (*salvation*) over the enemies of Judah, the *righteous nation*. **5:** *Low . . . height*, a familiar antithesis: the proud are abased, the humble exalted (Ps.147.6; Lk.1.52).
26.7–19: Apocalyptic psalm. 7: Proverb of confidence in God's help (Ps.9.19; 18.25–27; 34.21–22). **8:** Compare Rev.22.20. God's chastisements are designed to benefit those chastized.

For when thy judgments are in the
earth,
the inhabitants of the world learn
righteousness.
10 If favor is shown to the wicked,
he does not learn righteousness;
in the land of uprightness he deals
perversely
and does not see the majesty of the
LORD.
11 O LORD, thy hand is lifted up,
but they see it not.
Let them see thy zeal for thy people,
and be ashamed.
Let the fire for thy adversaries
consume them.
12 O LORD, thou wilt ordain peace for
us,
thou hast wrought for us all our
works.
13 O LORD our God,
other lords besides thee have ruled
over us,
but thy name alone we
acknowledge.
14 They are dead, they will not live;
they are shades, they will not arise;
to that end thou hast visited them
with destruction
and wiped out all remembrance of
them.
15 But thou hast increased the nation,
O LORD,
thou hast increased the nation;
thou art glorified;
thou hast enlarged all the borders
of the land.

16 O LORD, in distress they sought thee,
they poured out a prayer[n]
when thy chastening was upon
them.
17 Like a woman with child,

who writhes and cries out in her
pangs,
when she is near her time,
so were we because of thee, O LORD;
18 we were with child, we writhed,
we have as it were brought forth
wind.
We have wrought no deliverance in
the earth,
and the inhabitants of the world
have not fallen.
19 Thy dead shall live, their bodies[o]
shall rise.
O dwellers in the dust, awake and
sing for joy!
For thy dew is a dew of light,
and on the land of the shades thou
wilt let it fall.

20 Come, my people, enter your
chambers,
and shut your doors behind you;
hide yourselves for a little while
until the wrath is past.
21 For behold, the LORD is coming forth
out of his place
to punish the inhabitants of the
earth for their iniquity,
and the earth will disclose the blood
shed upon her,
and will no more cover her slain.

27 In that day the LORD with his
hard and great and strong
sword will punish Leviathan the fleeing serpent, Leviathan the twisting
serpent, and he will slay the dragon that
is in the sea.

2 In that day:
"A pleasant vineyard, sing of it!

n Heb uncertain
o Cn Compare Syr Tg: Heb *my body*

10–14: In good times or bad the wicked fail to note God's guiding hand, but God and the
righteous will ultimately defeat them. **14:** Compare v. 19. **16–19:** Without God, the people
were in agony and helpless before their oppressors. Though as dead, they will be raised up by
God, whose *light* will illumine the gloom of despair.
   26.20–27.1: Fourth eschatological section, following logically the preceding petition, returns
to the theme of judgment, and prepares for the return of the exiles referred to in 27.12–13.
20–21: The people should await God's victory. **27.1:** *Leviathan,* Canaanite mythological sea
monster; *dragon,* Hebrew "tannin," another sea monster (compare Ps.74.13–14). Here *Leviathan*
may refer to Assyria and Babylonia and *the dragon,* Egypt (vv. 12–13; Ezek.29.3; Rev.12.7–12).
   27.2–11: Fourth apocalyptic poem of deliverance. 2–5: God's vineyard; compare 5.1–7, where

3 I, the LORD, am its keeper;
    every moment I water it.
Lest any one harm it,
    I guard it night and day;
4 I have no wrath.
Would that I had thorns and briers
    to battle!
I would set out against them,
I would burn them up together.
5 Or let them lay hold of my
    protection,
    let them make peace with me,
    let them make peace with me."

6 In days to come*q* Jacob shall take
    root,
    Israel shall blossom and put forth
    shoots,
    and fill the whole world with fruit.

7 Has he smitten them as he smote
    those who smote them?
Or have they been slain as their
    slayers were slain?
8 Measure by measure,*r* by exile thou
    didst contend with them;
    he removed them with his fierce
    blast in the day of the east wind.
9 Therefore by this the guilt of Jacob
    will be expiated,
    and this will be the full fruit of the
    removal of his sin:
    when he makes all the stones of the
    altars
    like chalkstones crushed to pieces,
    no Ashe'rim or incense altars will
    remain standing.
10 For the fortified city is solitary,
    a habitation deserted and
    forsaken, like the wilderness;
    there the calf grazes,

there he lies down, and strips its
    branches.
11 When its boughs are dry, they are
    broken;
    women come and make a fire of
    them.
For this is a people without
    discernment;
therefore he who made them will
    not have compassion on them,
he that formed them will show
    them no favor.

12 In that day from the river Euphra'tes to the Brook of Egypt the
LORD will thresh out the grain, and you
will be gathered one by one, O people
of Israel. 13 And in that day a great
trumpet will be blown, and those who
were lost in the land of Assyria and
those who were driven out to the land
of Egypt will come and worship the
LORD on the holy mountain at Jerusalem.

28 Woe to the proud crown of the
    drunkards of E'phraim,
    and to the fading flower of its
    glorious beauty,
    which is on the head of the rich
    valley of those overcome with
    wine!
2 Behold, the Lord has one who is
    mighty and strong;
    like a storm of hail, a destroying
    tempest,
    like a storm of mighty, overflowing
    waters,
    he will cast down to the earth with
    violence.

q Heb *Those to come*
r Compare Syr Vg Tg: The meaning of the Hebrew word
is unknown

---

the same figure is used in another sense. **7–11:** Israel (*Jacob*) will be blessed after all semblance
of idolatry has been removed. The enemy will be vanquished, his *city* destroyed (vv. 10–11;
24.10; 26.5).
    27.12–13: Concluding oracle of doom and triumph. 12: The figure of an eschatological harvest
symbolizes the separation of the wicked from the righteous (Jl.3.13; Mt.13.39; Rev.14.15–16).
Brook of Egypt, Wadi el-'Arish, fifty miles southwest of Gaza. **13:** *The great trumpet*, which
summoned Israel for solemn convocations (Num.10.2–10; Jl.2.15), will signal the final assembly
of God's elect (Mt.24.31; 1 Th.4.16).
    28.1–35.10: Oracles concerning Judah and Ephraim. 28.1–13: Against religious leaders. 1–4:
An oracle concerning *Ephraim* (Samaria), pronounced before Assyria's onslaught (2 Kg.17.5)
and introducing the longer (and later) oracle concerning *Judah* (for the occasion see 22.1–14 n.).
1: *Crown*, walls of Samaria (Am.3.9,15). **4:** *First-ripe fig*, just as quickly will Samaria be con-

³ The proud crown of the drunkards
  of E′phraim
  will be trodden under foot;
⁴ and the fading flower of its glorious
  beauty,
  which is on the head of the rich
  valley,
  will be like a first-ripe fig before the
  summer:
  when a man sees it, he eats it up
  as soon as it is in his hand.

⁵ In that day the LORD of hosts will
  be a crown of glory,
  and a diadem of beauty, to the
  remnant of his people;
⁶ and a spirit of justice to him who
  sits in judgment,
  and strength to those who turn
  back the battle at the gate.

⁷ These also reel with wine
  and stagger with strong drink;
  the priest and the prophet reel with
  strong drink,
  they are confused with wine,
  they stagger with strong drink;
  they err in vision,
  they stumble in giving judgment.
⁸ For all tables are full of vomit,
  no place is without filthiness.

⁹ "Whom will he teach knowledge,
  and to whom will he explain the
  message?
  Those who are weaned from the
  milk,
  those taken from the breast?
¹⁰ For it is precept upon precept,
  precept upon precept,
  line upon line, line upon line,
  here a little, there a little."

¹¹ Nay, but by men of strange lips

and with an alien tongue
  the LORD will speak to this people,
¹² to whom he has said,
  "This is rest;
  give rest to the weary;
  and this is repose";
  yet they would not hear.
¹³ Therefore the word of the LORD
  will be to them
  precept upon precept, precept upon
  precept,
  line upon line, line upon line,
  here a little, there a little;
  that they may go, and fall backward,
  and be broken, and snared, and
  taken.

¹⁴ Therefore hear the word of the
  LORD, you scoffers,
  who rule this people in Jerusalem!
¹⁵ Because you have said, "We have
  made a covenant with death,
  and with Sheol we have an
  agreement;
  when the overwhelming scourge
  passes through
  it will not come to us;
  for we have made lies our refuge,
  and in falsehood we have taken
  shelter";
¹⁶ therefore thus says the Lord GOD,
  "Behold, I am laying in Zion for a
  foundation
  a stone, a tested stone,
  a precious cornerstone, of a sure
  foundation:
  'He who believes will not be in
  haste.'
¹⁷ And I will make justice the line,
  and righteousness the plummet;
  and hail will sweep away the refuge
  of lies,
  and waters will overwhelm the
  shelter."

---

sumed. **5–6:** A later interpolation; here *crown* is God's blessing of the remnant. **7–10:** This section continues vv. 1–4, but is directed against Judah. The unrestrained hedonism of Samaria was paralleled in Judah, whose intemperate religious leaders were incapable of responsible guidance (Jer.13.12–14). *Priest* and *prophet*, presumably Isaiah's opponents (Jer.26.7–9), resented (compare vv. 9–10) Isaiah's condescending attitude. *Tables*, for sacrificial feast (1 Sam. 9.12–13). **11–13:** If the people reject Isaiah, others (the Assyrians) will address them (Jer.5.15).
    28.14–22: Against civil leaders. **14–15:** The *scoffers* have forsaken God, their only defender, for other gods. **16–17a:** The symbolic name of the foundation stone (v. 16d; 1.26) proclaims salvation for those who trust God. *Justice* and *righteousness* (1.21; 5.16) will characterize the

18 Then your covenant with death will
  be annulled,
  and your agreement with Sheol
  will not stand;
when the overwhelming scourge
  passes through
you will be beaten down by it.
19 As often as it passes through it will
  take you;
  for morning by morning it will pass
  through,
  by day and by night;
and it will be sheer terror to
  understand the message.
20 For the bed is too short to stretch
  oneself on it,
  and the covering too narrow to
  wrap oneself in it.
21 For the LORD will rise up as on
  Mount Pera′zim,
  he will be wroth as in the valley
  of Gibeon;
to do his deed–strange is his deed!
  and to work his work–alien is his
  work!
22 Now therefore do not scoff,
  lest your bonds be made strong;
for I have heard a decree of
  destruction
  from the Lord GOD of hosts upon
  the whole land.

23 Give ear, and hear my voice;
  hearken, and hear my speech.
24 Does he who plows for sowing plow
  continually?
  does he continually open and
  harrow his ground?
25 When he has leveled its surface,
  does he not scatter dill, sow
  cummin,
and put in wheat in rows
  and barley in its proper place,
  and spelt as the border?

26 For he is instructed aright;
  his God teaches him.

27 Dill is not threshed with a threshing
  sledge,
  nor is a cart wheel rolled over
  cummin;
but dill is beaten out with a stick,
  and cummin with a rod.
28 Does one crush bread grain?
  No, he does not thresh it for ever;
when he drives his cart wheel over it
  with his horses, he does not crush
  it.
29 This also comes from the LORD of
  hosts;
  he is wonderful in counsel,
  and excellent in wisdom.

29 Ho Ariel, Ariel,
  the city where David
  encamped!
Add year to year;
  let the feasts run their round.
2 Yet I will distress Ariel,
  and there shall be moaning and
  lamentation,
  and she shall be to me like an Ariel.
3 And I will encamp against you
  round about,
  and will besiege you with towers
  and I will raise siegeworks against
  you.
4 Then deep from the earth you shall
  speak,
  from low in the dust your words
  shall come;
your voice shall come from the
  ground like the voice of a ghost,
  and your speech shall whisper out
  of the dust.

5 But the multitude of your foes*s* shall
  be like small dust,

s Cn: Heb *strangers*

---

new Jerusalem. **17b–22:** The faithless will be destroyed by the storm of God's wrath. **20:** A proverb describing an irremediable situation. **21:** *Perazim,* 2 Sam.5.17–21.

28.23–29: Parable of the farmer, patterned on contemporary wisdom literature. God, like the farmer, conducts his affairs according to plan (compare vv. 16–17a). **25:** *Spelt,* less valuable than wheat. **27:** *Dill* and *cummin,* spices, too soft to thresh with a sledge.

29.1–8: Judah's eventual restoration. 1: *Ariel,* meaning "mountain of God" or "hero," an allusion to Jerusalem. **2:** *Like an Ariel,* meaning "underworld" or "shade," a second meaning of Ariel (from the Babylonian word "Arallu," used here in a word-play to describe Jerusalem's degradation.

and the multitude of the ruthless
like passing chaff.
And in an instant, suddenly,
6 you will be visited by the LORD
of hosts
with thunder and with earthquake
and great noise,
with whirlwind and tempest, and
the flame of a devouring fire.
7 And the multitude of all the nations
that fight against Ariel,
all that fight against her and her
stronghold and distress her,
shall be like a dream, a vision of
the night.
8 As when a hungry man dreams he
is eating
and awakes with his hunger not
satisfied,
or as when a thirsty man dreams he
is drinking
and awakes faint, with his thirst
not quenched,
so shall the multitude of all the
nations be
that fight against Mount Zion.

9 Stupefy yourselves and be in a
stupor,
blind yourselves and be blind!
Be drunk, but not with wine;
stagger, but not with strong drink!
10 For the LORD has poured out upon
you
a spirit of deep sleep,
and has closed your eyes, the
prophets,
and covered your heads, the seers.
11 And the vision of all this has
become to you like the words of a book
that is sealed. When men give it to one
who can read, saying, "Read this," he
says, "I cannot, for it is sealed." 12 And
when they give the book to one who

cannot read, saying, "Read this," he
says, "I cannot read."

13 And the Lord said:
"Because this people draw near with
their mouth
and honor me with their lips,
while their hearts are far from me,
and their fear of me is a commandment of men learned by rote;
14 therefore, behold, I will again
do marvelous things with this
people,
wonderful and marvelous;
and the wisdom of their wise men
shall perish,
and the discernment of their
discerning men shall be hid."

15 Woe to those who hide deep from the
LORD their counsel,
whose deeds are in the dark,
and who say, "Who sees us? Who
knows us?"
16 You turn things upside down!
Shall the potter be regarded as the
clay;
that the thing made should say of
its maker,
"He did not make me";
or the thing formed say of him who
formed it,
"He has no understanding"?

17 Is it not yet a very little while
until Lebanon shall be turned into
a fruitful field,
and the fruitful field shall be
regarded as a forest?
18 In that day the deaf shall hear
the words of a book,
and out of their gloom and darkness
the eyes of the blind shall see.
19 The meek shall obtain fresh joy in
the LORD,

29.9-24: Spiritual insensibility; miscellaneous oracles. 9-12: An independent section, related in thought to vv. 1-8 and 13-14. 9-10: As drunkards, Jerusalem's leaders are incapable of moral discrimination. 11-12: Explanatory later prose addition. *Book*, a scroll (Jer.32.9-15). 13-14: A new relationship with God, based on a positive response to his acts (Ex.19.4-6), will replace Judah's superficial traditionalism (ironically called *wisdom* and *discernment;* compare 1 Cor. 1.19). 15-16: Judah's leaders have usurped God's prerogatives by plotting against Assyria (45.9; Jer.18.1-6; Rom.9.20-21; Mt.10.24). 17-24: Two later stanzas based on materials from chs. 40-66 and reflecting that period. 17-21: Israel's suffering will soon be completed (35.1-2; 41.17). 19: *Holy one of Israel*, see 1.4 n.; 41.14,16,20, and elsewhere. 22-24: Abraham's God will

and the poor among men shall
exult in the Holy One of Israel.
20 For the ruthless shall come to
nought and the scoffer cease,
and all who watch to do evil shall
be cut off,
21 who by a word make a man out to
be an offender,
and lay a snare for him who
reproves in the gate,
and with an empty plea turn aside
him who is in the right.

22 Therefore thus says the LORD,
who redeemed Abraham, concerning
the house of Jacob:
"Jacob shall no more be ashamed,
no more shall his face grow pale.
23 For when he sees his children,
the work of my hands, in his midst,
they will sanctify my name;
they will sanctify the Holy One of
Jacob,
and will stand in awe of the God
of Israel.
24 And those who err in spirit will
come to understanding,
and those who murmur will accept
instruction."

30 "Woe to the rebellious
children," says the LORD,
"who carry out a plan, but not mine;
and who make a league, but not of
my spirit,
that they may add sin to sin;
2 who set out to go down to Egypt,
without asking for my counsel,
to take refuge in the protection of
Pharaoh,
and to seek shelter in the shadow
of Egypt!

3 Therefore shall the protection of
Pharaoh turn to your shame,
and the shelter in the shadow of
Egypt to your humiliation.
4 For though his officials are at Zo'an
and his envoys reach Ha'nes,
5 every one comes to shame
through a people that cannot profit
them,
that brings neither help nor profit,
but shame and disgrace."

6 An oracle on the beasts of the
Negeb.
Through a land of trouble and
anguish,
from where come the lioness and
the lion,
the viper and the flying serpent,
they carry their riches on the backs
of asses,
and their treasures on the humps
of camels,
to a people that cannot profit them.
7 For Egypt's help is worthless and
empty,
therefore I have called her
"Rahab who sits still."

8 And now, go, write it before them
on a tablet,
and inscribe it in a book,
that it may be for the time to come
as a witness for ever.
9 For they are a rebellious people,
lying sons,
sons who will not hear
the instruction of the LORD;
10 who say to the seers, "See not";
and to the prophets, "Prophesy not
to us what is right;
speak to us smooth things,

restore repentant Israel, who will accept God's instruction (Ezek.36.22–32). Compare the references to *Abraham* in 41.8; 51.2. This kind of reference is later than Isaiah's time.
30.1–7: Concerning the embassy sent to Egypt (about 703 B.C.) soliciting support against Assyria, *a plan* which Isaiah considered rebellion against God (28.14–22; 29.15–16). **1–5:** Since the pact is against God's wishes, it will fail. *Zoan*, see Ezek.30.13–19 n.; *Hanes* (Anusis), fifty miles south of Memphis. **6a:** Obscure, perhaps emend to read, "They carry, through the heat of the Negeb, . . ." **7b:** Obscure, perhaps emend to read, "Rahab, who shall be destroyed." *Rahab*, a mythological sea dragon vanquished in cosmic combat (26.20–27.1; Job 26.12).
30.8–17: Judah's connivance with Egypt against Assyria. **8–11:** Isaiah is to preserve his oracles in writing in preparation for their ultimate fulfilment (8.16–18). *Tablet*, see 8.1 n. *Book*, 29.11 n. *Lying sons*, those who deny their sonship (1.2–4). *Instruction*, Hebrew "torah," see 1.10 n.

prophesy illusions,
11 leave the way, turn aside from the
    path,
  let us hear no more of the Holy
    One of Israel."
12 Therefore thus says the Holy One
    of Israel,
  "Because you despise this word,
  and trust in oppression and
    perverseness,
  and rely on them;
13 therefore this iniquity shall be to you
  like a break in a high wall, bulging
    out, and about to collapse,
  whose crash comes suddenly, in an
    instant;
14 and its breaking is like that of a
    potter's vessel
  which is smashed so ruthlessly
that among its fragments not a sherd
    is found
  with which to take fire from the
    hearth,
  or to dip up water out of the
    cistern."

15 For thus said the Lord GOD, the Holy
    One of Israel,
  "In returning and rest you shall be
    saved;
  in quietness and in trust shall be
    your strength."
And you would not, 16 but you said,
  "No! We will speed upon horses,"
  therefore you shall speed away;
and, "We will ride upon swift
    steeds,"
  therefore your pursuers shall be
    swift.
17 A thousand shall flee at the threat of
    one,
  at the threat of five you shall flee,
  till you are left

like a flagstaff on the top of a
    mountain,
  like a signal on a hill.

18 Therefore the LORD waits to be
    gracious to you;
  therefore he exalts himself to show
    mercy to you.
For the LORD is a God of justice;
  blessed are all those who wait for
    him.
19 Yea, O people in Zion who dwell
at Jerusalem; you shall weep no more.
He will surely be gracious to you at the
sound of your cry; when he hears it,
he will answer you. 20 And though
the Lord give you the bread of adversity and the water of affliction, yet your
Teacher will not hide himself any more,
but your eyes shall see your Teacher.
21 And your ears shall hear a word
behind you, saying, "This is the way,
walk in it," when you turn to the right
or when you turn to the left. 22 Then
you will defile your silver-covered
graven images and your gold-plated
molten images. You will scatter them as
unclean things; you will say to them,
"Begone!"
23 And he will give rain for the seed
with which you sow the ground, and
grain, the produce of the ground,
which will be rich and plenteous. In
that day your cattle will graze in large
pastures; 24 and the oxen and the asses
that till the ground will eat salted provender, which has been winnowed with
shovel and fork. 25 And upon every
lofty mountain and every high hill
there will be brooks running with water,
in the day of the great slaughter, when
the towers fall. 26 Moreover the light
of the moon will be as the light of the

Smooth things, pleasant, though false (Jer.28.8–9). **12–14:** Sentence of judgment; this should probably follow vv. 15–17, since *this word* (v. 12b) is recorded in v. 15. Judah's perverseness is a basic flaw which, under pressure, will burst and all will be lost. **15–17:** Instead of demonstrating victorious faith, Judah seeks more tangible military devices, but these will be no source of strength (7.3–9; 10.20–21).
    30.18–26: Hope for the afflicted. A later (perhaps Exilic) addition. Judah is not condemned for faithlessness, but encouraged to have patience under trial. Verses 19–26 are a commentary on v. 18 and include familiar, though later, imagery (Jer.31.10–14; Ezek.34.25–30). **20:** *Teacher*, with some Hebrew manuscripts, but probably to be read "teachers," i.e. prophets. **24:** *Salted provender*, some kind of silage.

sun, and the light of the sun will be sevenfold, as the light of seven days, in the day when the LORD binds up the hurt of his people, and heals the wounds inflicted by his blow.

[27] Behold, the name of the LORD comes
  from far,
    burning with his anger, and in
    thick rising smoke;
  his lips are full of indignation,
    and his tongue is like a devouring
    fire;
[28] his breath is like an overflowing
  stream
    that reaches up to the neck;
  to sift the nations with the sieve of
  destruction,
    and to place on the jaws of the
    peoples a bridle that leads
    astray

29 You shall have a song as in the night when a holy feast is kept; and gladness of heart, as when one sets out to the sound of the flute to go to the mountain of the LORD, to the Rock of Israel. [30] And the LORD will cause his majestic voice to be heard and the descending blow of his arm to be seen, in furious anger and a flame of devouring fire, with a cloudburst and tempest and hailstones. [31] The Assyrians will be terror-stricken at the voice of the LORD, when he smites with his rod. [32] And every stroke of the staff of punishment which the LORD lays upon them will be to the sound of timbrels and lyres; battling with brandished arm he will fight with them. [33] For a burning place[t] has long been prepared; yea, for the king[u] it is made ready, its pyre made deep and wide, with fire and wood in abundance; the breath of the LORD, like a stream of brimstone, kindles it.

3 1 Woe to those who go down to
      Egypt for help
    and rely on horses,
  who trust in chariots because they
    are many
    and in horsemen because they are
    very strong,
  but do not look to the Holy One of
    Israel
    or consult the LORD!
[2] And yet he is wise and brings
    disaster,
    he does not call back his words,
  but will arise against the house of
    the evildoers,
    and against the helpers of those
    who work iniquity.
[3] The Egyptians are men, and not God;
    and their horses are flesh, and not
    spirit.
  When the LORD stretches out his
    hand,
    the helper will stumble, and he
    who is helped will fall,
  and they will all perish together.

[4] For thus the LORD said to me,
  As a lion or a young lion growls over
    his prey,
    and when a band of shepherds is
    called forth against him
  is not terrified by their shouting
    or daunted at their noise,
  so the LORD of hosts will come down
    to fight upon Mount Zion and
    upon its hill.
[5] Like birds hovering, so the LORD
    of hosts
    will protect Jerusalem;
  he will protect and deliver it,
    he will spare and rescue it.

6 Turn to him from whom you[v] have deeply revolted, O people of Is-

t Or *Topheth*   *u* Or *Molech*   *v* Heb *they*

30.27–33: Oracle against Assyria (about 701 B.C.; see chs. 36–37). The text is combined with a song of deliverance, and the probable original order is: vv. 27–28,30–32a,33,25de,29,32b. **27–28,30:** Like an approaching thunderstorm, God's fury will burst over Judah's enemies. **33:** *Burning place*, Topheth (see 2 Kg.23.10 n.). *For the king*, i.e. Molech (see Lev.18.21 n.).

31.1–3: Against Egypt (see 30.1–7). **1:** Judah's limited treasury precluded extensive military expenditures; her terrain was unfavorable for Egyptian chariots. **3:** Perhaps a reference to the crossing of the Red Sea (Ex.14.26–31).

31.4–9: Against Sennacherib (29.1–8; 37.21–25). **4–5:** God will defend Jerusalem. **6–7:** A

rael. ⁷ For in that day every one shall cast away his idols of silver and his idols of gold, which your hands have sinfully made for you.

⁸ "And the Assyrian shall fall by a
    sword, not of man;
and a sword, not of man, shall
    devour him;
and he shall flee from the sword,
    and his young men shall be put
    to forced labor.
⁹ His rock shall pass away in terror,
    and his officers desert the standard
    in panic,"
says the LORD, whose fire is in Zion,
    and whose furnace is in Jerusalem.

32 Behold, a king will reign in
    righteousness,
    and princes will rule in justice.
² Each will be like a hiding place from
    the wind,
    a covert from the tempest,
like streams of water in a dry place,
    like the shade of a great rock in
    a weary land.
³ Then the eyes of those who see will
    not be closed,
    and the ears of those who hear
    will hearken.
⁴ The mind of the rash will have
    good judgment,
    and the tongue of the stammerers
    will speak readily and distinctly.
⁵ The fool will no more be called
    noble,
    nor the knave said to be
    honorable.
⁶ For the fool speaks folly,
    and his mind plots iniquity:
to practice ungodliness,

to utter error concerning the LORD,
to leave the craving of the hungry
    unsatisfied,
and to deprive the thirsty of drink.
⁷ The knaveries of the knave are evil;
    he devises wicked devices
to ruin the poor with lying words,
    even when the plea of the needy
    is right.
⁸ But he who is noble devises noble
    things,
    and by noble things he stands.

⁹ Rise up, you women who are at ease,
    hear my voice;
you complacent daughters, give
    ear to my speech.
¹⁰ In little more than a year
    you will shudder, you complacent
    women;
for the vintage will fail,
    the fruit harvest will not come.
¹¹ Tremble, you women who are at
    ease,
    shudder, you complacent ones;
strip, and make yourselves bare,
    and gird sackcloth upon your loins.
¹² Beat upon your breasts for the
    pleasant fields,
    for the fruitful vine,
¹³ for the soil of my people
    growing up in thorns and briers;
yea, for all the joyous houses
    in the joyful city.
¹⁴ For the palace will be forsaken,
    the populous city deserted;
the hill and the watchtower
    will become dens for ever,
a joy of wild asses,
    a pasture of flocks;
¹⁵ until the Spirit is poured upon us
    from on high,

---

later addition (compare 2.20). **8–9:** God's *sword* will destroy Assyria (Ezek. ch. 21). *Fire, furnace*, a reference to the temple altar.

    32.1–8: The coming age of justice (possibly a later addition). Patterned on wisdom literature (28.23–29), this non-messianic oracle describes Judah's coming rulers as men of integrity, patience and high-mindedness (Pr.8.15–21). Fools will no longer receive attention (compare Pr.15.2,7,14, etc.).

    32.9–14: Against the complacency of Judah's women (3.16–4.1) who now celebrate vintage festival but in another year will bemoan Judah's desolation. **11–12a:** Typical signs of mourning (Jer.4.7–8; 16.1–9).

    32.15–20: The age of the Spirit (11.2) **will see the transformation of all creation.** The outpouring of the Spirit will produce a condition wherein man may enjoy true happiness (compare Jer.31.31–34). The section was probably added later (see 29.17–24).

and the wilderness becomes a
　　fruitful field,
and the fruitful field is deemed
　　a forest.
16 Then justice will dwell in the
　　wilderness,
　　and righteousness abide in the
　　　fruitful field.
17 And the effect of righteousness will
　　be peace,
　　and the result of righteousness,
　　　quietness and trust for ever.
18 My people will abide in a peaceful
　　habitation,
　　in secure dwellings, and in quiet
　　　resting places.
19 And the forest will utterly go down,^w
　　and the city will be utterly laid low.
20 Happy are you who sow beside all
　　waters,
　　who let the feet of the ox and the
　　　ass range free.

33 Woe to you, destroyer,
　　who yourself have not been
　　destroyed;
you treacherous one,
　　with whom none has dealt
　　　treacherously!
When you have ceased to destroy,
　　you will be destroyed;
and when you have made an end
　　of dealing treacherously,
　　you will be dealt with
　　　treacherously.

2 O Lord, be gracious to us; we wait
　　for thee.
　　Be our arm every morning,
　　our salvation in the time of trouble.
3 At the thunderous noise peoples
　　flee,
　　at the lifting up of thyself nations
　　are scattered;
4 and spoil is gathered as the
　　caterpillar gathers;

as locusts leap, men leap upon it.

5 The Lord is exalted, for he dwells
　　on high;
　　he will fill Zion with justice and
　　righteousness;
6 and he will be the stability of your
　　times,
　　abundance of salvation, wisdom,
　　and knowledge;
　　the fear of the Lord is his
　　treasure.

7 Behold, the valiant ones^y cry
　　without;
　　the envoys of peace weep bitterly.
8 The highways lie waste,
　　the wayfaring man ceases.
Covenants are broken,
　　witnesses^z are despised,
　　there is no regard for man.
9 The land mourns and languishes;
　　Lebanon is confounded and
　　withers away;
Sharon is like a desert;
　　and Bashan and Carmel shake off
　　their leaves.

10 "Now I will arise," says the Lord,
　　"now I will lift myself up;
　　now I will be exalted.
11 You conceive chaff, you bring forth
　　stubble;
　　your breath is a fire that will
　　consume you.
12 And the peoples will be as if burned
　　to lime,
　　like thorns cut down, that are
　　burned in the fire."

13 Hear, you who are far off, what I
　　have done;
　　and you who are near,
　　acknowledge my might.

w Cn: Heb *And it will hail when the forest comes down*
y The meaning of the Hebrew word is uncertain
z One ancient Ms: Heb *cities*

33.1–24: A prophetic liturgy, an independent post-exilic addition, consisting of entreaties
and oracles (compare Pss. 85; 46), perhaps used in the temple service, led by a prophet (Jer.14.2;
18.20). 1–6: First section. 1: A prophetic reproach; *destroyer*, used of Babylon in 21.2, here
unidentified. 2: A congregational prayer. *Our arm*, source of strength. 3–6: Promise of God's
victory and restoration of Zion. 7–16: Second section. 7–9: A congregational lament. The
conditions (insecurity, distrust) are as critical as if normally forested and fruitful regions became
barren. 10–13: God commands the nations to acknowledge his might.

14 The sinners in Zion are afraid;
    trembling has seized the godless:
"Who among us can dwell with the
    devouring fire?
Who among us can dwell with
    everlasting burnings?"
15 He who walks righteously and speaks
    uprightly,
who despises the gain of
    oppressions,
who shakes his hands, lest they hold
    a bribe,
who stops his ears from hearing of
    bloodshed
and shuts his eyes from looking
    upon evil,
16 he will dwell on the heights;
his place of defense will be the
    fortresses of rocks;
his bread will be given him, his
    water will be sure.

17 Your eyes will see the king in his
    beauty;
they will behold a land that
    stretches afar.
18 Your mind will muse on the terror:
"Where is he who counted, where
    is he who weighed the tribute?
Where is he who counted the
    towers?"
19 You will see no more the insolent
    people,
the people of an obscure speech
    which you cannot comprehend,
stammering in a tongue which you
    cannot understand.
20 Look upon Zion, the city of our
    appointed feasts!
Your eyes will see Jerusalem,
a quiet habitation, an immovable
    tent,
whose stakes will never be plucked
    up,
nor will any of its cords be broken.
21 But there the LORD in majesty will
    be for us

a place of broad rivers and
    streams,
where no galley with oars can go,
    nor stately ship can pass.
22 For the LORD is our judge, the LORD
    is our ruler,
the LORD is our king; he will save
    us.

23 Your tackle hangs loose;
it cannot hold the mast firm in
    its place,
or keep the sail spread out.

Then prey and spoil in abundance
    will be divided;
even the lame will take the prey.
24 And no inhabitant will say, "I am
    sick";
the people who dwell there will be
    forgiven their iniquity.

34 Draw near, O nations, to hear,
    and hearken, O peoples!
Let the earth listen, and all that fills
    it;
the world, and all that comes from
    it.
2 For the LORD is enraged against all
    the nations,
and furious against all their host,
he has doomed them, has given
    them over for slaughter.
3 Their slain shall be cast out,
and the stench of their corpses
    shall rise;
the mountains shall flow with their
    blood.
4 All the host of heaven shall rot away,
    and the skies roll up like a scroll.
All their host shall fall,
as leaves fall from the vine,
like leaves falling from the fig
    tree.

5 For my sword has drunk its fill in
    the heavens;

14–16: God's wrath will destroy both *the sinners in Zion* and Zion's external enemies. **15–16:** See Ps. 15 and 24.3–5. **17–24:** Third section. **17–20:** The unpleasant past (28.11–13) will become a memory in the peaceful reign of the Messianic king. **21–24:** The land will be amply watered (Ezek.47.1–12), not for war fleets but to satisfy the people's needs.

   34.1–17. The terrible end of God's enemies. Compare Ezek. chs. 38–39. **4:** For the destruction and fall of *the host of heaven*, synonymous with God's earthly enemies, see 24.21. **5:** The de-

behold, it descends for judgment
    upon Edom,
upon the people I have doomed.
⁶ The LORD has a sword; it is sated
    with blood,
it is gorged with fat,
    with the blood of lambs and goats,
    with the fat of the kidneys of
        rams.
For the LORD has a sacrifice in
        Bozrah,
    a great slaughter in the land of
        Edom.
⁷ Wild oxen shall fall with them,
    and young steers with the mighty
        bulls.
Their land shall be soaked with
        blood,
    and their soil made rich with fat.

⁸ For the LORD has a day of
        vengeance,
    a year of recompense for the cause
        of Zion.
⁹ And the streams of Edom*a* shall be
    turned into pitch,
    and her soil into brimstone;
    her land shall become burning
        pitch.
¹⁰ Night and day it shall not be
        quenched;
    its smoke shall go up for ever.
From generation to generation it
        shall lie waste;
    none shall pass through it for ever
        and ever.
¹¹ But the hawk and the porcupine
        shall possess it,
    the owl and the raven shall dwell
        in it.
He shall stretch the line of confusion
        over it,
    and the plummet of chaos over*b*
        its nobles.

¹² They shall name it No Kingdom
        There,
    and all its princes shall be nothing.

¹³ Thorns shall grow over its
        strongholds,
    nettles and thistles in its fortresses.
It shall be the haunt of jackals,
    an abode for ostriches.
¹⁴ And wild beasts shall meet with
        hyenas,
    the satyr shall cry to his fellow;
yea, there shall the night hag alight,
    and find for herself a resting place.

¹⁵ There shall the owl nest and lay
    and hatch and gather her young
        in her shadow;
yea, there shall the kites be gathered,
    each one with her mate.
¹⁶ Seek and read from the book of the
        LORD:
    Not one of these shall be missing;
    none shall be without her mate.
For the mouth of the LORD has
        commanded,
    and his Spirit has gathered them.
¹⁷ He has cast the lot for them,
    his hand has portioned it out to
        them with the line;
they shall possess it for ever,
    from generation to generation
        they shall dwell in it.

35 The wilderness and the dry
        land shall be glad,
    the desert shall rejoice and
        blossom;
like the crocus ² it shall blossom
        abundantly,
    and rejoice with joy and singing.
The glory of Lebanon shall be given
        to it,

a Heb *her streams*
b Heb lacks *over*

struction of Edom (see Jer.49.7–22) illustrates the fate of all of God's enemies, as in Ob.15–16. For the *sword* of the LORD, see Ezek. ch. 21. *Sacrifice*, compare Ezek.39.17–20. The animals named are those usually sacrificed. **8:** *Day*, see 13.6; 27.2. **9–17:** Aftermath of God's assault. **9–10:** Edom suffers the punishment of Sodom and Gomorrah (13.19; Gen.19.24). **11:** Her desolation will be as the primordial chaos (Jer.4.23–28). **12:** *No Kingdom There*, a mocking name suggesting the end of all who oppose God. **13–15:** *Night hag*, the storm demon Lilith, found in abandoned places, and wild animals (13.19–22) haunt her ruins. **16:** *The book of the LORD*, compare 4.3.

35.1–10: Zion restored. With 34.1–17 this probably belonged originally to chs. 40–66.

the majesty of Carmel and Sharon.
They shall see the glory of the LORD,
the majesty of our God.

3 Strengthen the weak hands,
   and make firm the feeble knees.
4 Say to those who are of a fearful
      heart,
   "Be strong, fear not!
Behold, your God
   will come with vengeance,
with the recompense of God.
   He will come and save you."

5 Then the eyes of the blind shall be
      opened,
   and the ears of the deaf unstopped;
6 then shall the lame man leap like
      a hart,
   and the tongue of the dumb sing
      for joy.
For waters shall break forth in the
      wilderness,
   and streams in the desert;
7 the burning sand shall become a
      pool,
   and the thirsty ground springs of
      water;
the haunt of jackals shall become
      a swamp,*c*
   the grass shall become reeds and
      rushes.

8 And a highway shall be there,
   and it shall be called the Holy
      Way;
the unclean shall not pass over it,*d*
   and fools shall not err therein.
9 No lion shall be there,
   nor shall any ravenous beast come
      up on it;
they shall not be found there,
   but the redeemed shall walk there.
10 And the ransomed of the LORD shall
      return,
   and come to Zion with singing;

everlasting joy shall be upon their
      heads;
   they shall obtain joy and gladness,
   and sorrow and sighing shall flee
      away.

36 In the fourteenth year of King
Hezeki'ah, Sennach'erib king of
Assyria came up against all the fortified
cities of Judah and took them. 2 And
the king of Assyria sent the Rab'shakeh
from Lachish to King Hezeki'ah at Jerusalem, with a great army. And he
stood by the conduit of the upper pool
on the highway to the Fuller's Field.
3 And there came out to him Eli'akim
the son of Hilki'ah, who was over the
household, and Shebna the secretary,
and Jo'ah the son of Asaph, the recorder.

4 And the Rab'shakeh said to them,
"Say to Hezeki'ah, 'Thus says the great
king, the king of Assyria: On what do
you rest this confidence of yours? 5 Do
you think that mere words are strategy
and power for war? On whom do you
now rely, that you have rebelled
against me? 6 Behold, you are relying
on Egypt, that broken reed of a staff,
which will pierce the hand of any man
who leans on it. Such is Pharaoh king of
Egypt to all who rely on him. 7 But if
you say to me, "We rely on the LORD
our God," is it not he whose high places
and altars Hezeki'ah has removed, saying to Judah and to Jerusalem, "You
shall worship before this altar"? 8 Come
now, make a wager with my master the
king of Assyria: I will give you two
thousand horses, if you are able on your
part to set riders upon them. 9 How
then can you repulse a single captain
among the least of my master's servants, when you rely on Egypt for chari-

c Cn: Heb *in the haunt of jackals is her resting place*
d Heb *it and he is for them a wayfarer*

1–6a: All creation will see God's glory; the helpless exiles (*feeble knees* of exhausted prisoners;
blind; dumb) will receive new courage and hope. 8–10: On *the Holy Way*, through a land like
paradise (11.6–9), they will *come to Zion* to sing the praises of God, their deliverer.
   36.1–39.8: Historical appendix, duplicated in 2 Kg.18.13–20.19, except for 38.9–20. 36.1–22:
The attack of Sennacherib (701 B.C.), see 2 Kg.18.13–27. 1: *All the fortified cities*, forty-six
according to Sennacherib's account. 2: *Rabshakeh*, Assyrian title meaning "chief steward."
3: *Eliakim, Shebna*, compare 22.15–25. 6: Compare 31.1–3; Ezek.29.6. 7: A reference to Heze-

ots and for horsemen? [10] Moreover, is it without the LORD that I have come up against this land to destroy it? The LORD said to me, Go up against this land, and destroy it.' "

11 Then Eli′akim, Shebna, and Jo′ah said to the Rab′shakeh, "Pray, speak to your servants in Aramaic, for we understand it; do not speak to us in the language of Judah within the hearing of the people who are on the wall." [12] But the Rab′shakeh said, "Has my master sent me to speak these words to your master and to you, and not to the men sitting on the wall, who are doomed with you to eat their own dung and drink their own urine?"

13 Then the Rab′shakeh stood and called out in a loud voice in the language of Judah: "Hear the words of the great king, the king of Assyria! [14] Thus says the king: 'Do not let Hezeki′ah deceive you, for he will not be able to deliver you. [15] Do not let Hezeki′ah make you rely on the LORD by saying, "The LORD will surely deliver us; this city will not be given into the hand of the king of Assyria." [16] Do not listen to Hezeki′ah; for thus says the king of Assyria: Make your peace with me and come out to me; then every one of you will eat of his own vine, and every one of his own fig tree, and every one of you will drink the water of his own cistern; [17] until I come and take you away to a land like your own land, a land of grain and wine, a land of bread and vineyards. [18] Beware lest Hezeki′ah mislead you by saying, "The LORD will deliver us." Has any of the gods of the nations delivered his land out of the hand of the king of Assyria? [19] Where are the gods of Hamath and Arpad? Where are the gods of Sepharva′im? Have they delivered Sama′ria

out of my hand? [20] Who among all the gods of these countries have delivered their countries out of my hand, that the LORD should deliver Jerusalem out of my hand?' "

21 But they were silent and answered him not a word, for the king's command was, "Do not answer him." [22] Then Eli′akim the son of Hilki′ah, who was over the household, and Shebna the secretary, and Jo′ah the son of Asaph, the recorder, came to Hezeki′ah with their clothes rent, and told him the words of the Rab′shakeh.

37 When King Hezeki′ah heard it, he rent his clothes, and covered himself with sackcloth, and went into the house of the LORD. [2] And he sent Eli′akim, who was over the household, and Shebna the secretary, and the senior priests, clothed with sackcloth, to the prophet Isaiah the son of Amoz. [3] They said to him, "Thus says Hezeki′ah, 'This day is a day of distress, of rebuke, and of disgrace; children have come to the birth, and there is no strength to bring them forth.[4] It may be that the LORD your God heard the words of the Rab′shakeh, whom his master the king of Assyria has sent to mock the living God, and will rebuke the words which the LORD your God has heard; therefore lift up your prayer for the remnant that is left.' "

5 When the servants of King Hezeki′ah came to Isaiah, [6] Isaiah said to them, "Say to your master, 'Thus says the LORD: Do not be afraid because of the words that you have heard, with which the servants of the king of Assyria have reviled me. [7] Behold, I will put a spirit in him, so that he shall hear a rumor, and return to his own land; and I will make him fall by the sword in his own land.' "

---

kiah's reform, 2 Kg.18.4. **11:** *Aramaic* was the current diplomatic language. **12:** The results of the projected siege. **13–20:** A speech intended to demoralize Jerusalem's defenders. **19:** *Hamath, Arpad,* see 10.9 n.; *Sepharvaim* (Sibraim, Ezek.47.16), a town between Hamath and Damascus, near Homs; *Samaria,* now an Assyrian province (2 Kg.17.5–6,24).

    37.1–35: Hezekiah consults Isaiah. See 2 Kg. ch. 19. **1:** *Clothes rent, sackcloth,* signs of mourning and despair (15.3; J1.2.12). For recourse to the temple in national crises, see Neh. ch. 9; Jl.1.13–14. **2:** The embassy to Isaiah recalls the consultation of prophets by earlier kings (1 Kg.22.8–28; 2 Kg.1.9–17; 3.11–27). **5–7:** Isaiah's reply reassures Hezekiah. *Rumor* of internal

8 The Rab'shakeh returned, and found the king of Assyria fighting against Libnah; for he had heard that the king had left Lachish. ⁹ Now the king heard concerning Tirha'kah king of Ethiopia, "He has set out to fight against you." And when he heard it, he sent messengers to Hezeki'ah, saying, ¹⁰ "Thus shall you speak to Hezeki'ah king of Judah: 'Do not let your God on whom you rely deceive you by promising that Jerusalem will not be given into the hand of the king of Assyria. ¹¹ Behold, you have heard what the kings of Assyria have done to all lands, destroying them utterly. And shall you be delivered? ¹² Have the gods of the nations delivered them, the nations which my fathers destroyed, Gozan, Haran, Rezeph, and the people of Eden who were in Tel-assar? ¹³ Where is the king of Hamath, the king of Arpad, the king of the city of Sepharva'im, the king of Hena, or the king of Ivvah?' "

14 Hezeki'ah received the letter from the hand of the messengers, and read it; and Hezeki'ah went up to the house of the LORD, and spread it before the LORD. ¹⁵ And Hezeki'ah prayed to the LORD: ¹⁶ "O LORD of hosts, God of Israel, who art enthroned above the cherubim, thou art the God, thou alone, of all the kingdoms of the earth; thou hast made heaven and earth. ¹⁷ Incline thy ear, O LORD, and hear; open thy eyes, O LORD, and see; and hear all the words of Sennach'-erib, which he has sent to mock the living God. ¹⁸ Of a truth, O LORD, the kings of Assyria have laid waste all the nations and their lands, ¹⁹ and have cast their gods into the fire; for they were no gods, but the work of men's hands, wood and stone; therefore they were destroyed. ²⁰ So now, O LORD our God, save us from his hand, that all the kingdoms of the earth may know that thou alone art the LORD."

21 Then Isaiah the son of Amoz sent to Hezeki'ah, saying, "Thus says the LORD, the God of Israel: Because you have prayed to me concerning Sennach'erib king of Assyria, ²² this is the word that the LORD has spoken concerning him:

'She despises you, she scorns you–
    the virgin daughter of Zion;
she wags her head behind you–
    the daughter of Jerusalem.

²³ 'Whom have you mocked and
    reviled?
    Against whom have you raised
      your voice
and haughtily lifted your eyes?
    Against the Holy One of Israel!
²⁴ By your servants you have mocked
    the Lord,
and you have said, With my many
    chariots
I have gone up the heights of the
    mountains,
    to the far recesses of Lebanon;
I felled its tallest cedars,
    its choicest cypresses;
I came to its remotest height,
    its densest forest.
²⁵ I dug wells
    and drank waters,
and I dried up with the sole of my
    foot
    all the streams of Egypt.

²⁶ 'Have you not heard
    that I determined it long ago?
I planned from days of old
    what now I bring to pass,

---

problems at home. **8–20:** Sennacherib's second challenge to Hezekiah (about 688–687 B.C., perhaps at the time of a later attack on Jerusalem). **8:** *Libnah*, ten miles north of Lachish. **9:** *Tirhakah*, 2 Kg.19.9. **12:** Places in Mesopotamia: *Gozan*, on west tributary of Khabur River, east of Haran; *Haran*, on upper Balikh River (Gen.11.27–32); *Rezeph*, between Nineveh and northern Khabur; *Eden*, Bit Adini, on middle Euphrates (Ezek.27.23); *Telassar*, on middle Euphrates. **14:** *Letter*, i.e. scroll. **16:** *Enthroned* . . ., temple imagery (1 Kg.8.6–7; Ezek.1.4–28). **17–20:** This recalls Sennacherib's claim, vv. 11–13; *no gods*, Jer.10.1–16. **21:** See vv. 33–35. **22–29:** Isaiah's challenge to Sennacherib (10.5–19). **22–29:** Isaiah taunts Sennacherib, reminding him that he has defied God, who has determined history's course and will frustrate Senna-

that you should make fortified cities
   crash into heaps of ruins,
²⁷ while their inhabitants, shorn of
   strength,
   are dismayed and confounded,
and have become like plants of the
   field
and like tender grass,
like grass on the housetops,
   blighted*e* before it is grown.

²⁸ 'I know your sitting down
   and your going out and coming in,
   and your raging against me.
²⁹ Because you have raged against me
   and your arrogance has come to
     my ears,
I will put my hook in your nose
   and my bit in your mouth,
and I will turn you back on the way
   by which you came.'

30 "And this shall be the sign for
you: this year eat what grows of itself,
and in the second year what springs of
the same; then in the third year sow
and reap, and plant vineyards, and eat
their fruit. ³¹ And the surviving remnant of the house of Judah shall again
take root downward, and bear fruit
upward; ³² for out of Jerusalem shall
go forth a remnant, and out of Mount
Zion a band of survivors. The zeal of
the LORD of hosts will accomplish this.

33 "Therefore thus says the LORD
concerning the king of Assyria: He
shall not come into this city, or shoot
an arrow there, or come before it with
a shield, or cast up a siege mound
against it. ³⁴ By the way that he came,
by the same he shall return, and he shall
not come into this city, says the LORD.
³⁵ For I will defend this city to save it,

for my own sake and for the sake of
my servant David."

36 And the angel of the LORD went
forth, and slew a hundred and eighty-
five thousand in the camp of the Assyrians; and when men arose early in
the morning, behold, these were all
dead bodies. ³⁷ Then Sennach'erib king
of Assyria departed, and went home
and dwelt at Nin'eveh. ³⁸ And as he
was worshiping in the house of Nisroch
his god, Adram'melech and Share'zer,
his sons, slew him with the sword, and
escaped into the land of Ar'arat. And
E'sar-had'don his son reigned in his
stead.

38 In those days Hezeki'ah became sick and was at the point
of death. And Isaiah the prophet the
son of Amoz came to him, and said to
him, "Thus says the LORD: Set your
house in order; for you shall die, you
shall not recover." ² Then Hezeki'ah
turned his face to the wall, and prayed
to the LORD, ³ and said, "Remember
now, O LORD, I beseech thee, how I
have walked before thee in faithfulness
and with a whole heart, and have done
what is good in thy sight." And Hezeki'ah wept bitterly. ⁴ Then the word of
the LORD came to Isaiah: ⁵ "Go and
say to Hezeki'ah, Thus says the LORD,
the God of David your father: I have
heard your prayer, I have seen your
tears; behold, I will add fifteen years to
your life. ⁶ I will deliver you and this
city out of the hand of the king of Assyria, and defend this city.

7 "This is the sign to you from the
LORD, that the LORD will do this thing
that he has promised: ⁸ Behold, I will
make the shadow cast by the declining

e With 2 Kg 19.26: Heb *field*

---

cherib's plans. **27–28:** Read with the Dead Sea Scroll of Isaiah, ". . . housetops which is parched
by the east wind; your rising and your sitting down I know . . ." **30–32:** A second assurance to
Hezekiah (see vv. 5–7), of which the sign will be a return to normal conditions by the third
year. These verses belong between v. 35 and v. 36. *Remnant*, see 10.22 n. **33–35:** A third word of
assurance to Hezekiah (compare v. 21). Verse 35 recalls Nathan's words to David (2 Sam.
7.12–17).
    37.36–38: Devastation of Sennacherib's army. 36: *Angel*, a figure and explanation for a
plague (Ex.12.29; 2 Sam.24.15–17).
    38.1–22: Hezekiah's illness and recovery. See 2 Kg. ch. 20. **3:** The form of Hezekiah's prayer

sun on the dial of Ahaz turn back ten steps." So the sun turned back on the dial the ten steps by which it had declined.[f]

9 A writing of Hezeki'ah king of Judah, after he had been sick and had recovered from his sickness:
[10] I said, In the noontide of my days
   I must depart;
I am consigned to the gates of Sheol
   for the rest of my years.
[11] I said, I shall not see the LORD
   in the land of the living;
I shall look upon man no more
   among the inhabitants of the
     world.
[12] My dwelling is plucked up and
     removed from me
   like a shepherd's tent;
like a weaver I have rolled up my
   life;
   he cuts me off from the loom;
from day to night thou dost bring
   me to an end;[g]
[13]   I cry for help[h] until morning;
like a lion he breaks all my bones;
   from day to night thou dost bring
   me to an end.[g]

[14] Like a swallow or a crane[i] I clamor,
   I moan like a dove.
My eyes are weary with looking
   upward.
   O Lord, I am oppressed; be thou
   my security!
[15] But what can I say? For he has
     spoken to me,
   and he himself has done it.
All my sleep has fled[j]
   because of the bitterness of my
     soul.

[16] O Lord, by these things men live,
   and in all these is the life of my
     spirit.[k]
Oh, restore me to health and make
   me live!
[17] Lo, it was for my welfare
   that I had great bitterness;
but thou hast held back[l] my life
   from the pit of destruction,
for thou hast cast all my sins
   behind thy back.
[18] For Sheol cannot thank thee,
   death cannot praise thee;
those who go down to the pit cannot
   hope
   for thy faithfulness.
[19] The living, the living, he thanks thee,
   as I do this day;
the father makes known to the
   children
   thy faithfulness.

[20] The LORD will save me,
   and we will sing to stringed
     instruments[m]
all the days of our life,
   at the house of the LORD.

21 Now Isaiah had said, "Let them take a cake of figs, and apply it to the boil, that he may recover." [22] Hezeki'ah also had said, "What is the sign that I shall go up to the house of the LORD?"

39 At that time Mer'odach-bal'-adan the son of Bal'adan, king of Babylon, sent envoys with letters

f The Hebrew of this verse is obscure
g Heb uncertain   h Cn: Heb obscure
i Heb uncertain
j Cn Compare Syr: Heb *I will walk slowly all my years*
k Heb uncertain
l Cn Compare Gk Vg: Heb *loved*
m Heb *my stringed instruments*

for recovery is found in the Psalms (compare Ps. 6). **8:** *Dial*, literally "stairs" or "steps." Following the text of one ancient Hebrew manuscript (among the Dead Sea Scrolls) one may translate: " '. . . Behold, I shall turn back the shadow of the steps down which the sun has moved on the steps of the roof chamber of Ahaz your father. I will cause the sun to move backwards ten steps.' And the sun moved back ten steps on the steps down which the shadow had descended." **9–20:** This song, traditionally ascribed to Hezekiah, is a liturgical thanksgiving for use when presenting in the temple a thank-offering for personal deliverance (Ps. 32; 1 Sam.2.1–10; Jon.2.2–9). **9:** *Writing*, Hebrew "miktab," read "Miktam," as in Pss. 56–60. **16ab:** Corrupted text; emend to read, "O LORD, with thee are the days of my life, thine alone is the life of my spirit." **17:** God's saving power is shown in recovery from illness and forgiveness of sins (Lk.5.17–26). **21–22:** These verses belong between vv. 6–7.
39.1–8: Merodach-baladan's embassy. See 2 Kg.20.12–19. **2:** The tribute paid Sennacherib

and a present to Hezeki'ah, for he heard that he had been sick and had recovered. ² And Hezeki'ah welcomed them; and he showed them his treasure house, the silver, the gold, the spices, the precious oil, his whole armory, all that was found in his storehouses. There was nothing in his house or in all his realm that Hezeki'ah did not show them. ³ Then Isaiah the prophet came to King Hezeki'ah, and said to him, "What did these men say? And whence did they come to you?" Hezeki'ah said, "They have come to me from a far country, from Babylon." ⁴ He said, "What have they seen in your house?" Hezeki'ah answered, "They have seen all that is in my house; there is nothing in my storehouses that I did not show them."

5 Then Isaiah said to Hezeki'ah, "Hear the word of the LORD of hosts: ⁶ Behold, the days are coming, when all that is in your house, and that which your fathers have stored up till this day, shall be carried to Babylon; nothing shall be left, says the LORD. ⁷ And some of your own sons, who are born to you, shall be taken away; and they shall be eunuchs in the palace of the king of Babylon." ⁸ Then said Hezeki'ah to Isaiah, "The word of the LORD which you have spoken is good." For he thought, "There will be peace and security in my days."

40 Comfort, comfort my people, says your God.
² Speak tenderly to Jerusalem,

and cry to her
that her warfare*ⁿ* is ended,
that her iniquity is pardoned,
that she has received from the LORD's hand
double for all her sins.

³ A voice cries:
"In the wilderness prepare the way of the LORD,
make straight in the desert a highway for our God.
⁴ Every valley shall be lifted up,
and every mountain and hill be made low;
the uneven ground shall become level,
and the rough places a plain.
⁵ And the glory of the LORD shall be revealed,
and all flesh shall see it together,
for the mouth of the LORD has spoken."

⁶ A voice says, "Cry!"
And I said, "What shall I cry?"
All flesh is grass,
and all its beauty is like the flower of the field.
⁷ The grass withers, the flower fades,
when the breath of the LORD blows upon it;
surely the people is grass.
⁸ The grass withers, the flower fades;
but the word of our God will stand for ever.

⁹ Get you up to a high mountain,

n Or *time of service*

(701 B.C.) depleted Hezekiah's treasury (2 Kg.18.14–16), much of which had been derived from Arabian trade (2 Chr.32.27–29). **3–4:** Isaiah suspected intrigue with the Babylonian revolutionary. **5–7:** The description fits the events of 597 B.C.; see 2 Kg.24.10–17. **8:** With this postponement of punishment, compare 1 Kg.21.27–29.

Chapters 40–55: Book of the Consolation of Israel. 40.1–11: The prophet is called to announce God's coming. The background scene is the council of heaven, from which the voices come. **1–2:** Introduction. *Comfort,* for the Exile is nearly over (for similar repetitions, see 51.9; 52.1; 57.14). *My people . . . your God,* covenant words (Ex.19.4–6; Jer.11.5). *Her warfare,* meaning "her time of service" (the Exile). *Double* may reflect Ex.22.7–8, or suggest that God exacted more from his people than was to be expected. **3–5:** Quoted in Lk.3.4–6; see also Mt.3.3; Mk.1.3; Jn.1.23. *The way of the LORD* (common figure in II Isaiah; 42.16; 43.16,19; 48.17; 49.11; 51.10), who comes to restore his people (35.1–10). *The glory of the LORD* shall return (Ezek.1.28; 10.18–19; 43.1–5). **6–8:** The *voice* of God's herald proclaims the immutability of God's word (9.8; 55.8–11) in contrast to all living things. Quoted in 1 Pet.1.24–25. **6a:** Compare Jer.1.4–8. **6b:** See 51.12 n. **7:** *Breath,* wind (Jer.4.11).

O Zion, herald of good tidings;*o*
lift up your voice with strength,
O Jerusalem, herald of good
tidings,*p*
lift it up, fear not;
say to the cities of Judah,
"Behold your God!"
¹⁰ Behold, the Lord GOD comes with
might,
and his arm rules for him;
behold, his reward is with him,
and his recompense before him.
¹¹ He will feed his flock like a
shepherd,
he will gather the lambs in his
arms,
he will carry them in his bosom,
and gently lead those that are with
young.

¹² Who has measured the waters in the
hollow of his hand
and marked off the heavens with
a span,
enclosed the dust of the earth in a
measure
and weighed the mountains in
scales
and the hills in a balance?
¹³ Who has directed the Spirit of the
LORD,
or as his counselor has instructed
him?
¹⁴ Whom did he consult for his
enlightenment,
and who taught him the path of
justice,
and taught him knowledge,
and showed him the way of
understanding?
¹⁵ Behold, the nations are like a drop
from a bucket,
and are accounted as the dust on
the scales;
behold, he takes up the isles like
fine dust.

¹⁶ Lebanon would not suffice for fuel,
nor are its beasts enough for a
burnt offering.
¹⁷ All the nations are as nothing
before him,
they are accounted by him as less
than nothing and emptiness.

¹⁸ To whom then will you liken God,
or what likeness compare with
him?
¹⁹ The idol! a workman casts it,
and a goldsmith overlays it with
gold,
and casts for it silver chains.
²⁰ He who is impoverished*q* chooses
for an offering
wood that will not rot;
he seeks out a skilful craftsman
to set up an image that will not
move.

²¹ Have you not known? Have you not
heard?
Has it not been told you from the
beginning?
Have you not understood from the
foundations of the earth?
²² It is he who sits above the circle of
the earth,
and its inhabitants are like
grasshoppers;
who stretches out the heavens like a
curtain,
and spreads them like a tent to
dwell in;
²³ who brings princes to nought,
and makes the rulers of the earth
as nothing.

²⁴ Scarcely are they planted, scarcely
sown,
scarcely has their stem taken root
in the earth,

o Or *O herald of good tidings to Zion*
p Or *O herald of good tidings to Jerusalem*
q Heb uncertain

9–11: "*Behold, your God*" who comes in celestial grandeur, yet is compassionate (Ezek. ch. 34). See Acts 10.36; Rom. 10.15; Rev.22.7. *Jerusalem*, used for Judah over thirty times in chs. 40–55. *Arm*, symbol of power (33.2; 48.14; 51.5,9; 52.10; 53.1).

40.12–31: Creator of the universe. 12: *Waters* (seas), *heavens, earth*–the world's three divisions. **13–14:** God is the source of all knowledge and wisdom (Pr.8.22–31; Job 38.2–39.30). **15–17:** Before him all nations must bow. **18–20:** Idols cannot be compared with him (see 42.17; 45.16,20; Jer.10.1–16). **21–24:** God, the creator, is also Lord of history (44.24–28; 51.9–10).

when he blows upon them, and they
    wither,
  and the tempest carries them off
    like stubble.

25 To whom then will you compare me,
    that I should be like him? says the
    Holy One.
26 Lift up your eyes on high and see:
    who created these?
He who brings out their host by
    number,
  calling them all by name;
by the greatness of his might,
  and because he is strong in power
    not one is missing.

27 Why do you say, O Jacob,
    and speak, O Israel,
"My way is hid from the LORD,
  and my right is disregarded by my
    God"?
28 Have you not known? Have you not
    heard?
The LORD is the everlasting God,
  the Creator of the ends of the
    earth.
He does not faint or grow weary,
  his understanding is unsearchable.
29 He gives power to the faint,
  and to him who has no might he
    increases strength.
30 Even youths shall faint and be
    weary,
  and young men shall fall
    exhausted;
31 but they who wait for the LORD
    shall renew their strength,
  they shall mount up with wings
    like eagles,
  they shall run and not be weary,
    they shall walk and not faint.

41 Listen to me in silence, O
    coastlands;
  let the peoples renew their
    strength;
let them approach, then let them
    speak;
  let us together draw near for
    judgment.

2 Who stirred up one from the east
  whom victory meets at every step?
He gives up nations before him,
  so that he tramples kings under
    foot;
he makes them like dust with his
    sword,
  like driven stubble with his bow.
3 He pursues them and passes on
    safely,
  by paths his feet have not trod.
4 Who has performed and done this,
  calling the generations from the
    beginning?
I, the LORD, the first,
  and with the last; I am He.

5 The coastlands have seen and are
    afraid,
  the ends of the earth tremble;
  they have drawn near and come.
6 Every one helps his neighbor,
  and says to his brother, "Take
    courage!"
7 The craftsman encourages the
    goldsmith,
  and he who smooths with the
    hammer him who strikes the
    anvil,
saying of the soldering, "It is good";
  and they fasten it with nails so
    that it cannot be moved.

Circle, tent, the vault of heaven (Pr.8.27; Job 22.14). **25–27**: God is incomparable (vv. 18–20) and omniscient. *Created* (Gen.1.1), a word used more often by Second Isaiah than by other Old Testament writers (v. 28; 41.20; 42.5; 43.7,15; 45.7,8,12,18; 54.16). **26**: *Host* of heaven (3.1). **28–31**: The omnipotent God is concerned for man. **31**: *Wait* expresses confidence that God will not desert his people; a common concept from this period on (49.23; Ps.25.3; 33.20).
    41.1–42.4: The trial of the nations. 1: The background scene is the law court (a recurrent theme in chs. 41–46; 48). The historical background is the victories of Cyrus of Persia. *Coastlands*, Mediterranean lands and islands (frequent in Second Isaiah, 40.15; 42.4; 49.1; 51.5). **2–4**: *One from the east*, Cyrus. The God of history is calling Cyrus. *Victory*, the Hebrew term implies God's approval. *First . . . last*, 43.10; 44.6; Rev.22.13. **5–7**: The nations are as powerless as their gods (40.19–22). **8–10**: *Israel, my servant* (Jer.30.10; 46.27–28), though punished for

⁸ But you, Israel, my servant,
Jacob, whom I have chosen,
the offspring of Abraham, my
friend;
⁹ you whom I took from the ends of
the earth,
and called from its farthest
corners,
saying to you, "You are my servant,
I have chosen you and not cast
you off";
¹⁰ fear not, for I am with you,
be not dismayed, for I am your
God;
I will strengthen you, I will help you,
I will uphold you with my
victorious right hand.

¹¹ Behold, all who are incensed against
you
shall be put to shame and
confounded;
those who strive against you
shall be as nothing and shall
perish.
¹² You shall seek those who contend
with you,
but you shall not find them;
those who war against you
shall be as nothing at all.
¹³ For I, the LORD your God,
hold your right hand;
it is I who say to you, "Fear not,
I will help you."

¹⁴ Fear not, you worm Jacob,
you men of Israel!
I will help you, says the LORD;
your Redeemer is the Holy One
of Israel.
¹⁵ Behold, I will make of you a
threshing sledge,
new, sharp, and having teeth;
you shall thresh the mountains and
crush them,

and you shall make the hills like
chaff;
¹⁶ you shall winnow them and the wind
shall carry them away,
and the tempest shall scatter them.
And you shall rejoice in the LORD;
in the Holy One of Israel you
shall glory.

¹⁷ When the poor and needy seek
water,
and there is none,
and their tongue is parched with
thirst,
I the LORD will answer them,
I the God of Israel will not forsake
them.
¹⁸ I will open rivers on the bare heights,
and fountains in the midst of the
valleys;
I will make the wilderness a pool of
water,
and the dry land springs of water.
¹⁹ I will put in the wilderness the cedar,
the acacia, the myrtle, and the
olive;
I will set in the desert the cypress,
the plane and the pine together;
²⁰ that men may see and know,
may consider and understand
together,
that the hand of the LORD has done
this,
the Holy One of Israel has created
it.

²¹ Set forth your case, says the LORD;
bring your proofs, says the King
of Jacob.
²² Let them bring them, and tell us
what is to happen.
Tell us the former things, what they
are,
that we may consider them,
that we may know their outcome;

---

faithlessness, will now be restored (44.1–5; 45.4; 48.10). There is a different emphasis on "servant" in the Servant Songs (see 42.1). **11–13:** The nations are judged. **14–16:** With God's help Israel can thresh the mountains into dust. *Redeemer*, the Hebrew term elsewhere may refer to the blood avenger (e.g. Num.35.19), but here it describes the avenger of the oppressed and liberator of the LORD's people (43.14; 44.6; 47.4). **17–20:** A rhapsody on God as Lord of nature (55.13; Ezek.47.12). *Holy One*, v. 16; 40.25; 1.4. **21–24:** The pagan nations are challenged to prove the validity of their claims and their gods. *Former things* (46.9) have a present significance. The nations have no defense. Verses 23–24 contain the first explicit statement against the very

or declare to us the things to come.
23 Tell us what is to come hereafter,
   that we may know that you are
    gods;
do good, or do harm,
   that we may be dismayed and
    terrified.
24 Behold, you are nothing,
   and your work is nought;
an abomination is he who chooses
   you.

25 I stirred up one from the north, and
   he has come,
from the rising of the sun, and he
   shall call on my name;
he shall trample[r] on rulers as on
   mortar,
as the potter treads clay.
26 Who declared it from the beginning,
   that we might know,
and beforetime, that we might
   say, "He is right"?
There was none who declared it,
   none who proclaimed,
   none who heard your words.
27 I first have declared it to Zion,[s]
   and I give to Jerusalem a herald
   of good tidings.
28 But when I look there is no one;
   among these there is no counselor
   who, when I ask, gives an answer.
29 Behold, they are all a delusion;
   their works are nothing;
   their molten images are empty
   wind.

42 Behold my servant, whom I
   uphold,
my chosen, in whom my soul
   delights;

I have put my Spirit upon him,
   he will bring forth justice to the
    nations.
2 He will not cry or lift up his voice,
   or make it heard in the street;
3 a bruised reed he will not break,
   and a dimly burning wick he will
    not quench;
he will faithfully bring forth
   justice.
4 He will not fail[t] or be discouraged[u]
   till he has established justice in
    the earth;
and the coastlands wait for his
   law.

5 Thus says God, the LORD,
   who created the heavens and
    stretched them out,
who spread forth the earth and
   what comes from it,
who gives breath to the people upon
   it
   and spirit to those who walk in it:
6 "I am the LORD, I have called you
   in righteousness,
I have taken you by the hand and
   kept you;
I have given you as a covenant to
   the people,
   a light to the nations,
7   to open the eyes that are blind,
to bring out the prisoners from the
   dungeon,
from the prison those who sit in
   darkness.
8 I am the LORD, that is my name;
   my glory I give to no other,
   nor my praise to graven images.

r Cn: Heb *come*
s Cn: Heb *first to Zion, Behold, behold them*
t Or *burn dimly*   *u* Or *bruised*

---

existence of the gods of other nations (43.8–13). **25–29:** Second (compare vv. 11–13) judgment against the nations. *From the north . . . the rising of the sun*, from Persia to the northeast (the first phrase earlier referred to Assyria [14.31], and Babylonia [Jer.6.22]). **29:** Compare v. 24; 40.18–20.

   42.1–4: The first Servant Song (49.1–6; 50.4–11; 52.13–53.12). Scholars hold differing views of the identity of the Servant in these Songs. The position taken here is that the Servant is the nation; others regard him as an individual, and some as both. **The mission of the Servant.** The Servant is Israel (*my chosen;* not Cyrus) who will, with all patience (v. 3–4a), bring God's teaching (*law*, 1.10) and restore *justice* (5.16) to the nations. *Spirit*, 11.2. See Mt.12.18–21.

   42.5–17: God's glorious victory. 5: God is creator of all (40.21–22) and source of life (Gen. 2.7; Acts 17.24–25). **6–9:** God illumines history. **6–7:** He has called Israel, his covenant people, to bring *light* to the nations groping in the darkness of ignorance (60.1–3; Lk.2.30–32; Acts 13.47; 26.23). **8:** *LORD*, Yahweh, the only God (41.23–24; Dt.4.23–24). **10–13:** Song of victory

⁹ Behold, the former things have come
    to pass,
    and new things I now declare;
before they spring forth
    I tell you of them."

¹⁰ Sing to the LORD a new song,
    his praise from the end of the
      earth!
Let the sea roar*ᵛ* and all that fills it,
    the coastlands and their
      inhabitants.
¹¹ Let the desert and its cities lift up
    their voice,
    the villages that Kedar inhabits;
let the inhabitants of Sela sing for
    joy,
    let them shout from the top of the
      mountains.
¹² Let them give glory to the LORD,
    and declare his praise in the
      coastlands.
¹³ The LORD goes forth like a mighty
    man,
    like a man of war he stirs up his
      fury;
he cries out, he shouts aloud,
    he shows himself mighty against
      his foes.

¹⁴ For a long time I have held my peace,
    I have kept still and restrained
      myself;
now I will cry out like a woman in
    travail,
    I will gasp and pant.
¹⁵ I will lay waste mountains and hills,
    and dry up all their herbage;
I will turn the rivers into islands,
    and dry up the pools.
¹⁶ And I will lead the blind
    in a way that they know not,
in paths that they have not known
    I will guide them.

I will turn the darkness before them
    into light,
    the rough places into level ground.
These are the things I will do,
    and I will not forsake them.
¹⁷ They shall be turned back and
      utterly put to shame,
    who trust in graven images,
who say to molten images,
    "You are our gods."

¹⁸ Hear, you deaf;
    and look, you blind, that you may
      see!
¹⁹ Who is blind but my servant,
    or deaf as my messenger whom I
      send?
Who is blind as my dedicated one,
    or blind as the servant of the
      LORD?
²⁰ He sees*ʷ* many things, but does not
      observe them;
    his ears are open, but he does not
      hear.
²¹ The LORD was pleased, for his
      righteousness' sake,
    to magnify his law and make it
      glorious.
²² But this is a people robbed and
      plundered,
    they are all of them trapped in
      holes
    and hidden in prisons;
they have become a prey with none
    to rescue,
    a spoil with none to say,
    "Restore!"
²³ Who among you will give ear to this,
    will attend and listen for the time
      to come?
²⁴ Who gave up Jacob to the spoiler,
    and Israel to the robbers?
Was it not the LORD, against whom
    we have sinned,

v Cn Compare Ps 96.11; 98.7: Heb *Those who go down to
the sea*   *w* Heb *you see*

(Pss. 93; 96; 149). *Kedar* (Jer.49.28–29) and *Sela* (see Jer.49.20) represent remote and isolated
places; all the world praises God, the victorious warrior (Ex.15.1–18; Jg.5.2–5). **14–17:** God's
intervention in history. *Long time,* from creation (v. 5) to redemption (vv. 14–16). **15:** Jer.4.23–
28. **16:** *Blind,* (vv. 6–7) recalling God's leading Israel safely through the wilderness (41.17–20;
Ex.13.21–22).
    42.18–43.7: Israel, the blind and deaf servant. 18–25: Israel's judgment. **19–21:** *Blindness*
to God's will and way is, for Second Isaiah, Israel's chief sin (compare 6.9–10). *Law,* better,
"teaching," or "revelation" (1.10) concerning the LORD. **23–25:** God has punished Israel for

in whose ways they would not
　walk,
and whose law they would not
　obey?
25 So he poured upon him the heat of
　his anger
and the might of battle;
it set him on fire round about, but he
　did not understand;
it burned him, but he did not take
　it to heart.

43 But now thus says the LORD,
　he who created you, O Jacob,
he who formed you, O Israel:
"Fear not, for I have redeemed
　you;
I have called you by name, you
　are mine.
2 When you pass through the waters
　I will be with you;
and through the rivers, they shall
　not overwhelm you;
when you walk through fire you shall
　not be burned,
and the flame shall not consume
　you.
3 For I am the LORD your God,
　the Holy One of Israel, your
　Savior.
I give Egypt as your ransom,
　Ethiopia and Seba in exchange
　for you.
4 Because you are precious in my
　eyes,
and honored, and I love you,
I give men in return for you,
　peoples in exchange for your life.
5 Fear not, for I am with you;
I will bring your offspring from
　the east,
and from the west I will gather
　you;
6 I will say to the north, Give up,

and to the south, Do not withhold;
bring my sons from afar
and my daughters from the end of
　the earth,
7 every one who is called by my name,
　whom I created for my glory,
　whom I formed and made."

8 Bring forth the people who are blind,
　yet have eyes,
who are deaf, yet have ears!
9 Let all the nations gather together,
　and let the peoples assemble.
Who among them can declare this,
　and show us the former things?
Let them bring their witnesses to
　justify them,
and let them hear and say, It is
　true.
10 "You are my witnesses," says the
　LORD,
"and my servant whom I have
　chosen,
that you may know and believe me
　and understand that I am He.
Before me no god was formed,
　nor shall there be any after me.
11 I, I am the LORD,
　and besides me there is no savior.
12 I declared and saved and
　proclaimed,
when there was no strange god
　among you;
and you are my witnesses," says
　the LORD.
13 "I am God, and also henceforth I
　am He;
there is none who can deliver from
　my hand;
I work and who can hinder it?"

14 Thus says the LORD,
　your Redeemer, the Holy One of
　Israel:

---

its sins. **43.1–7:** Israel's redemption (41.8–13). **1–3b:** God is Israel's creator (44.2,21,24) and redeemer (41.14; 48.17; 49.7). *By name,* Israel is God's unique possession (45.3–4; Ex.19.5; 33.17). Through all dangers, God is with his people (Ps.66.12). **3c–7:** God's ransom of Israel includes the nations of Africa (Egypt and Ethiopia) and Arabia (Seba), all of which Cyrus was expected to conquer.

43.8–13: The servant Israel is the LORD'S witness. 8: Israel is capable of conversion. **9:** Who can defend the nations' claims for their gods? **11–13:** Besides God there is and will be no other god (41.23–24; 48.5).

43.14–44.5: The redemption and restoration of Israel. 14–15: The apposition of *Redeemer*

"For your sake I will send to
  Babylon
and break down all the bars,
and the shouting of the Chalde′ans
  will be turned to lamentations.*x*
15 I am the LORD, your Holy One,
  the Creator of Israel, your King."
16 Thus says the LORD,
  who makes a way in the sea,
  a path in the mighty waters,
17 who brings forth chariot and horse,
  army and warrior;
they lie down, they cannot rise,
  they are extinguished, quenched
  like a wick:
18 "Remember not the former things,
  nor consider the things of old.
19 Behold, I am doing a new thing;
  now it springs forth, do you not
  perceive it?
I will make a way in the wilderness
  and rivers in the desert.
20 The wild beasts will honor me,
  the jackals and the ostriches;
for I give water in the wilderness,
  rivers in the desert,
to give drink to my chosen people,
21   the people whom I formed for
  myself
that they might declare my praise.

22 "Yet you did not call upon me, O
  Jacob;
but you have been weary of me, O
  Israel!
23 You have not brought me your sheep
  for burnt offerings,
  or honored me with your sacrifices.
I have not burdened you with
  offerings,
  or wearied you with frankincense.

24 You have not bought me sweet cane
  with money,
  or satisfied me with the fat of your
  sacrifices.
But you have burdened me with your
  sins,
  you have wearied me with your
  iniquities.

25 "I, I am He
  who blots out your transgressions
  for my own sake,
  and I will not remember your sins.
26 Put me in remembrance, let us argue
  together;
  set forth your case, that you may
  be proved right.
27 Your first father sinned,
  and your mediators transgressed
  against me.
28 Therefore I profaned the princes of
  the sanctuary,
  I delivered Jacob to utter
  destruction
  and Israel to reviling.

44 "But now hear, O Jacob my
  servant,
Israel whom I have chosen!
2 Thus says the LORD who made you,
  who formed you from the womb
  and will help you:
Fear not, O Jacob my servant,
  Jeshu′run whom I have chosen.
3 For I will pour water on the thirsty
  land,
  and streams on the dry ground;
I will pour my Spirit upon your
  descendants,
  and my blessing on your offspring.

x Heb obscure

(v. 1; 54.5; 59.20; Jer.50.34) and *Holy One* (41.14; 47.4; 48.17) is noteworthy. Second Isaiah
refers to God as Redeemer more often than do other Old Testament writers. God redeems Israel
not for its merits but because of his covenant relationship with Israel. Other nations have kings,
but God is Israel's *king* (1 Sam.8.4–9). **16–17:** Allusion to the passage through the Red Sea
(Ex.14–15). The "new (and greater) Exodus" is an important theme in Second Isaiah (41.17–20;
42.16; compare Ex.14–15). **18–19:** *New thing,* the return of Israel to Palestine. *A way in the
wilderness.* This theme (40.3) is a part of the Exodus story (vv. 16–17). **20–21:** *Water in the
wilderness,* see Ex.17.1–7. **22–24:** Israel has ignored and offended God. *Sweet cane,* Ex.30.23;
Jer.6.20. **25–28:** The imagery of a lawcourt (41.1); God shows himself gracious, yet just. *First
father,* Jacob (Gen. ch. 27; Hos.12.2–4). *Mediators,* perhaps other patriarchal figures or prophets
(1 Kg.13.11–32). **44.1–2:** *Jeshurun* (Dt.32.15; 33.5,26), a poetic name of endearment for Israel;
it may mean "dearest upright one." **3–4:** Israel, like the world of nature, will be transformed.

4 They shall spring up like grass amid
    waters,*y*
    like willows by flowing streams.
5 This one will say, 'I am the LORD's,'
    another will call himself by the
      name of Jacob,
and another will write on his hand,
    'The LORD's,'
    and surname himself by the name
      of Israel."

6 Thus says the LORD, the King of
    Israel
    and his Redeemer, the LORD of
      hosts:
"I am the first and I am the last;
    besides me there is no god.
7 Who is like me? Let him proclaim it,
    let him declare and set it forth
      before me.
Who has announced from of old the
    things to come?*z*
Let them tell us*a* what is yet to be.
8 Fear not, nor be afraid;
    have I not told you from of old and
      declared it?
    And you are my witnesses!
Is there a God besides me?
    There is no Rock; I know not any."

9 All who make idols are nothing,
and the things they delight in do not
profit; their witnesses neither see nor
know, that they may be put to shame.
10 Who fashions a god or casts an image, that is profitable for nothing?
11 Behold, all his fellows shall be put
to shame, and the craftsmen are but
men; let them all assemble, let them
stand forth, they shall be terrified, they
shall be put to shame together.
12 The ironsmith fashions it*b* and
works it over the coals; he shapes it
with hammers, and forges it with his
strong arm; he becomes hungry and his
strength fails, he drinks no water and is
faint. 13 The carpenter stretches a line,
he marks it out with a pencil; he fashions it with planes, and marks it with a
compass; he shapes it into the figure of
a man, with the beauty of a man, to
dwell in a house. 14 He cuts down
cedars; or he chooses a holm tree or an
oak and lets it grow strong among the
trees of the forest; he plants a cedar and
the rain nourishes it. 15 Then it becomes
fuel for a man; he takes a part of it and
warms himself, he kindles a fire and
bakes bread; also he makes a god and
worships it, he makes it a graven image
and falls down before it. 16 Half of it
he burns in the fire; over the half he eats
flesh, he roasts meat and is satisfied;
also he warms himself and says, "Aha,
I am warm, I have seen the fire!"
17 And the rest of it he makes into a
god, his idol; and falls down to it and
worships it; he prays to it and says,
"Deliver me, for thou art my god!"

18 They know not, nor do they discern; for he has shut their eyes, so that
they cannot see, and their minds, so that
they cannot understand. 19 No one considers, nor is there knowledge or discernment to say, "Half of it I burned
in the fire, I also baked bread on its
coals, I roasted flesh and have eaten;
and shall I make the residue of it an
abomination? Shall I fall down before a block of wood?" 20 He feeds on
ashes; a deluded mind has led him
astray, and he cannot deliver himself
or say, "Is there not a lie in my right
hand?"

y Gk Compare Tg: Heb *They shall spring up in among*
  grass
z Cn: Heb *from my placing an eternal people and things*
  to come
a Tg: Heb *them*
b Cn: Heb *an axe*

God's *Spirit* brings new life. **5:** All people will identify themselves with Israel and Israel's God.
Write on the hand, compare Dt.6.8. **6–8:** God's uniqueness (compare vv. 21–23). **6:** Note the
apposition of *Redeemer* (43.14; 60.16) and *LORD of hosts* (first of several references in Second
Isaiah; 45.13; 47.4). *First . . . last*, 41.4; Rev.1.8,17; 2.8; 22.13. **7:** Perhaps a reference to God's
promises to the patriarchs (Gen.12.1–3). **8:** *Rock*, 17.10; Ps.18.2.
    44.9–20: Satire against idolatry (interpolated here perhaps in view of vv. 8b and 21; compare
40.18–20; 41.6–7). **9–11:** An idol is not a god but an image. **13–14:** It is made by human craftsmen. **14–20:** The same tree is used for fuel and for carving a god; but Israel does not note this
ridiculous inconsistency.

21 Remember these things, O Jacob,
  and Israel, for you are my servant;
I formed you, you are my servant;
  O Israel, you will not be forgotten
    by me.
22 I have swept away your
    transgressions like a cloud,
  and your sins like mist;
return to me, for I have redeemed
  you.

23 Sing, O heavens, for the LORD has
    done it;
  shout, O depths of the earth;
break forth into singing, O
    mountains,
  O forest, and every tree in it!
For the LORD has redeemed Jacob,
  and will be glorified in Israel.

24 Thus says the LORD, your Redeemer,
    who formed you from the womb:
"I am the LORD, who made all things,
  who stretched out the heavens
    alone,
  who spread out the earth–Who
    was with me?*c*–
25 who frustrates the omens of liars,
  and makes fools of diviners;
who turns wise men back,
  and makes their knowledge
    foolish;
26 who confirms the word of his
    servant,
  and performs the counsel of his
    messengers;
who says of Jerusalem, 'She shall be
  inhabited,'
and of the cities of Judah, 'They
  shall be built,
and I will raise up their ruins';
27 who says to the deep, 'Be dry,
  I will dry up your rivers';

28 who says of Cyrus, 'He is my
    shepherd,
  and he shall fulfil all my purpose';
saying of Jerusalem, 'She shall be
    built,'
  and of the temple, 'Your
    foundation shall be laid.' "

45 Thus says the LORD to his
    anointed, to Cyrus,
  whose right hand I have grasped,
to subdue nations before him
  and ungird the loins of kings,
to open doors before him
  that gates may not be closed:
2 "I will go before you
  and level the mountains,*d*
I will break in pieces the doors of
    bronze
  and cut asunder the bars of iron,
3 I will give you the treasures of
    darkness
  and the hoards in secret places,
that you may know that it is I, the
    LORD,
  the God of Israel, who call you by
    your name.
4 For the sake of my servant Jacob,
  and Israel my chosen,
I call you by your name,
  I surname you, though you do not
    know me.
5 I am the LORD, and there is no other,
  besides me there is no God;
I gird you, though you do not
    know me,
6 that men may know, from the rising
    of the sun
  and from the west, that there is
    none besides me;
I am the LORD, and there is no
    other.

c Another reading is who spread out the earth by myself
d One ancient Ms Gk: Heb the swellings

44.21–23: Israel is forgiven and redeemed. (A continuation of vv. 6–8.) 22: Like the morning sun, God, the Redeemer (41.14; 63.9), removes the sin which beclouds Israel. 23: Let all creation praise the LORD! (Compare Jer.51.48; Rev.12.12; 18.20).
  44.24–45.13: The commission of Cyrus. 24–28: An historical-prophetic prologue summarizing the preceding poems, and coming to a climax in God's designating *Cyrus* to be his *shepherd* (term for king, Jer.23.4). 45.1–7: Charge to Cyrus, God's *anointed* (i.e. messiah), is universal in scope, just as Israel's mission is to all nations. 1: The only Old Testament passage in which "messiah" refers to a non-Israelite. 2–3: God has commissioned Cyrus and will assist him in accomplishing his mission (40.4). 4: *My servant . . . my chosen*, 41.8; 42.1; 44.1; 49.3,5,6. 5–7: Cyrus is unaware of his charge from God, who alone determines history's course and will

7 I form light and create darkness,
  I make weal and create woe,
  I am the LORD, who do all these
    things.

8 "Shower, O heavens, from above,
  and let the skies rain down
    righteousness;
  let the earth open, that salvation
    may sprout forth,*e*
  and let it cause righteousness to
    spring up also;
  I the LORD have created it.

9 "Woe to him who strives with his
    Maker,
  an earthen vessel with the potter!*f*
  Does the clay say to him who
    fashions it, 'What are you
    making'?
  or 'Your work has no handles'?
10 Woe to him who says to a father,
  'What are you begetting?'
  or to a woman, 'With what are you
    in travail?' "
11 Thus says the LORD,
  the Holy One of Israel, and his
    Maker:
  "Will you question me*g* about my
    children,
  or command me concerning the
    work of my hands?
12 I made the earth,
  and created man upon it;
  it was my hands that stretched out
    the heavens,
  and I commanded all their host.
13 I have aroused him in righteousness,
  and I will make straight all his
    ways;
  he shall build my city
  and set my exiles free,
  not for price or reward,"
  says the LORD of hosts.

14 Thus says the LORD:
  "The wealth of Egypt and the
    merchandise of Ethiopia,
  and the Sabe′ans, men of stature,
  shall come over to you and be yours,
    they shall follow you;
  they shall come over in chains and
    bow down to you.
  They will make supplication to you,
    saying:
  'God is with you only, and there
    is no other,
  no god besides him.' "
15 Truly, thou art a God who hidest
    thyself,
  O God of Israel, the Savior.
16 All of them are put to shame and
    confounded,
  the makers of idols go in
    confusion together.
17 But Israel is saved by the LORD
  with everlasting salvation;
  you shall not be put to shame or
    confounded
  to all eternity.

18 For thus says the LORD,
  who created the heavens
    (he is God!),
  who formed the earth and made it
    (he established it;
  he did not create it a chaos,
    he formed it to be inhabited!) :
  "I am the LORD, and there is no
    other.
19 I did not speak in secret,
  in a land of darkness;
  I did not say to the offspring of
    Jacob,
  'Seek me in chaos.'
  I the LORD speak the truth,

e One ancient Ms: Heb *that they may bring forth salvation*
f Cn: Heb *potsherds* or *potters*
g Cn: Heb *Ask me of things to come*

reveal his uniqueness (44.6–8) to all. **8:** A song exulting in the extension of salvation to all. **9–13:** The sovereign power of God. **9–10:** This is the only invective in Second Isaiah; it is directed against those questioning the propriety of Cyrus's messiahship (29.16). **9:** Rom.9.20. **11:** *Children, . . . the work of my hands*, the Gentiles. As Lord of creation and history, God's action should be unquestioned. **12:** 40.12–31; 44.24.

45.14–25: The conversion of the nations (2.2–4; 42.1–4; 55.3–5; Jer.16.19–21). **14–15:** The nations' wealth will pour into Israel; they will acknowledge Israel's God. Earlier the nations listed here served as Israel's ransom (43.3). **14:** 1 Cor.14.25. **16–17:** Idol-makers are condemned (44.9–20), but Israel is saved. **18–19:** The Creator has revealed himself to Israel. *Chaos*, the state

I declare what is right.

20 "Assemble yourselves and come,
draw near together,
you survivors of the nations!
They have no knowledge
who carry about their wooden
idols,
and keep on praying to a god
that cannot save.
21 Declare and present your case;
let them take counsel together!
Who told this long ago?
Who declared it of old?
Was it not I, the LORD?
And there is no other god besides
me,
a righteous God and a Savior;
there is none besides me.

22 "Turn to me and be saved,
all the ends of the earth!
For I am God, and there is no
other.
23 By myself I have sworn,
from my mouth has gone forth in
righteousness
a word that shall not return:
'To me every knee shall bow,
every tongue shall swear.'

24 "Only in the LORD, it shall be said
of me,
are righteousness and strength;
to him shall come and be ashamed,
all who were incensed against
him.
25 In the LORD all the offspring of
Israel
shall triumph and glory."

46 Bel bows down, Nebo stoops,
their idols are on beasts and
cattle;
these things you carry are loaded

as burdens on weary beasts.
2 They stoop, they bow down together,
they cannot save the burden,
but themselves go into captivity.

3 "Hearken to me, O house of Jacob,
all the remnant of the house of
Israel,
who have been borne by me from
your birth,
carried from the womb;
4 even to your old age I am He,
and to gray hairs I will carry you.
I have made, and I will bear;
I will carry and will save.

5 "To whom will you liken me and
make me equal,
and compare me, that we may be
alike?
6 Those who lavish gold from the
purse,
and weigh out silver in the scales,
hire a goldsmith, and he makes it
into a god;
then they fall down and worship!
7 They lift it upon their shoulders,
they carry it,
they set it in its place, and it
stands there;
it cannot move from its place.
If one cries to it, it does not answer
or save him from his trouble.

8 "Remember this and consider,
recall it to mind, you
transgressors,
9 remember the former things of
old;
for I am God, and there is no other;
I am God, and there is none like
me,
10 declaring the end from the beginning
and from ancient times things not
yet done,
saying, 'My counsel shall stand,

of the world before creation (Gen.1.2). **20–21:** The nations' gods are powerless (44.8; Acts 15.18). **22–25:** Let all nations bow before God and sing his praises! **23:** Compare Rom.14.11; Phil. 2.10–11.

46.1–13: The LORD supports Israel. 1–4: *Bel*, chief god of Babylon, Bel-Marduk; *Nebo*, the Babylonian god Nabu, son of Marduk (Jer.39.3). The gods must be borne and are incapable of protecting their devotees (37.12–13), but God bears (44.2) and protects his devotees. **5–7:** 40.18–20. **7:** Perhaps a reference to New Year's festival processions in Babylon (45.20). **8–11:** 45.9–13. **8:** *This*, Israel's history (44.21). **9:** 41.22–29; 42.8–9.

[880]

and I will accomplish all my
   purpose,'
11 calling a bird of prey from the east,
   the man of my counsel from a far
   country.
  I have spoken, and I will bring it to
   pass;
  I have purposed, and I will do it.

12 "Hearken to me, you stubborn of
   heart,
  you who are far from deliverance:
13 I bring near my deliverance, it is not
   far off,
  and my salvation will not tarry;
  I will put salvation in Zion,
   for Israel my glory."

47 Come down and sit in the dust,
   O virgin daughter of Babylon;
sit on the ground without a throne,
  O daughter of the Chalde'ans!
For you shall no more be called
  tender and delicate.
2 Take the millstones and grind meal,
  put off your veil,
strip off your robe, uncover your
   legs,
  pass through the rivers.
3 Your nakedness shall be uncovered,
  and your shame shall be seen.
I will take vengeance,
  and I will spare no man.
4 Our Redeemer–the LORD of hosts is
   his name–
is the Holy One of Israel.

5 Sit in silence, and go into darkness,
  O daughter of the Chalde'ans;
for you shall no more be called
  the mistress of kingdoms.
6 I was angry with my people,
  I profaned my heritage;
I gave them into your hand,
  you showed them no mercy;

on the aged you made your yoke
  exceedingly heavy.
7 You said, "I shall be mistress for
   ever,"
so that you did not lay these things
  to heart
  or remember their end.

8 Now therefore hear this, you lover
  of pleasures,
who sit securely,
who say in your heart,
  "I am, and there is no one besides
   me;
I shall not sit as a widow
  or know the loss of children":
9 These two things shall come to you
  in a moment, in one day;
the loss of children and widowhood
  shall come upon you in full
   measure,
in spite of your many sorceries
  and the great power of your
   enchantments.

10 You felt secure in your wickedness,
  you said, "No one sees me";
your wisdom and your knowledge
  led you astray,
and you said in your heart,
  "I am, and there is no one besides
   me."
11 But evil shall come upon you,
  for which you cannot atone;
disaster shall fall upon you,
  which you will not be able to
   expiate;
and ruin shall come on you suddenly,
  of which you know nothing.

12 Stand fast in your enchantments
  and your many sorceries,
  with which you have labored from
   your youth;
perhaps you may be able to succeed,

11: *Bird of prey,* a reference to Cyrus (41.2; 44.28). **12–13:** Only God can save; unbelievers
take note!
    47.1–15: Lamentation over Babylon. 1–4: God strips Babylon of her royalty. **1:** *Virgin
daughter,* unconquered (used of Jerusalem, 37.22; Israel, Jer.31.4; Egypt, Jer.46.11). **2:** *Grind
meal,* do the work of slaves. **3:** Hos.2.9–12; Jer.13.20–27; Nah.3.5. **5–7:** Babylon's pride condemned. She wrongly attributed her strength to herself; it came from God (Jer.27.6–7; 25.12–
14). **8–9:** Babylon's sense of security is illusory. **8:** *I am . . . ,* an arrogant presumption of divinity
(42.8; 44.6). **9:** Jer.10.17–22; 15.5–9; Rev.18.8. **10–11:** *Wisdom* and *knowledge* (e.g. divination,

perhaps you may inspire terror.

13 You are wearied with your many
    counsels;
let them stand forth and save you,
those who divide the heavens,
    who gaze at the stars,
who at the new moons predict
    what[h] shall befall you.

14 Behold, they are like stubble,
    the fire consumes them;
they cannot deliver themselves
    from the power of the flame.
No coal for warming oneself is this,
    no fire to sit before!
15 Such to you are those with whom
    you have labored,
who have trafficked with you from
    your youth;
they wander about each in his own
    direction;
there is no one to save you.

48 Hear this, O house of Jacob,
    who are called by the name of
    Israel,
and who came forth from the loins[i]
    of Judah;
who swear by the name of the LORD,
    and confess the God of Israel,
    but not in truth or right.
2 For they call themselves after the
    holy city,
and stay themselves on the God of
    Israel;
the LORD of hosts is his name.

3 "The former things I declared of old,
    they went forth from my mouth
    and I made them known;
then suddenly I did them and they
    came to pass.

4 Because I know that you are
    obstinate,
and your neck is an iron sinew
and your forehead brass,
5 I declared them to you from of old,
    before they came to pass I
    announced them to you,
lest you should say, 'My idol did
    them,
my graven image and my molten
    image commanded them.'

6 "You have heard; now see all this;
    and will you not declare it?
From this time forth I make you
    hear new things,
hidden things which you have not
    known.
7 They are created now, not long ago;
    before today you have never
    heard of them,
lest you should say, 'Behold, I
    knew them.'
8 You have never heard, you have
    never known,
from of old your ear has not been
    opened.
For I knew that you would deal very
    treacherously,
and that from birth you were called
    a rebel.

9 "For my name's sake I defer my
    anger,
for the sake of my praise I restrain
    it for you,
that I may not cut you off.
10 Behold, I have refined you, but not
    like[j] silver;
I have tried you in the furnace of
    affliction.

h Gk Syr Compare Vg: Heb *from what*
i Cn: Heb *waters*   *j* Cn: Heb *with*

astrology, magic; vv. 12–13) fail to reveal her approaching fall (*you know nothing*). **14–15:** Like stubble in a fire, so Babylon will be consumed; both vassals and allies will desert her (Jer.2.33–37; 4.29–31).

48.1–22: Hear and see. This chapter summarizes the first section of Second Isaiah, which it concludes. It emphasizes the control of God over history and his action within it. **1–2:** The close relationship between God and his undeserving people (*not in truth or right*). **3–5:** God's prophets announced future events to preclude Israel's wrongly ascribing them to other forces (*idol; molten image*). *Former things*, 41.22–29; 43.9–12; 45.21. Israel's obstinacy is frequently deplored (Ex.32.9; Dt.9.13; Jer.5.5; 7.26). **6–8:** *New things*, Israel's deliverance by Cyrus (43.18–19). God's goodness is renewed daily, but Israel's unfaithfulness is almost axiomatic (Ezek.2.6–8; Dt.32.5). **9–10:** The glory of God is the purpose of Israel's salvation (Ezek.20.22).

11 For my own sake, for my own sake,
   I do it,
  for how should my name[k] be
    profaned?
  My glory I will not give to another.

12 "Hearken to me, O Jacob,
  and Israel, whom I called!
  I am He, I am the first,
  and I am the last.
13 My hand laid the foundation of the
   earth,
  and my right hand spread out the
   heavens;
  when I call to them,
  they stand forth together.

14 "Assemble, all of you, and hear!
  Who among them has declared
   these things?
  The Lord loves him;
  he shall perform his purpose on
   Babylon,
  and his arm shall be against the
   Chalde'ans.
15 I, even I, have spoken and called
   him,
  I have brought him, and he will
   prosper in his way.
16 Draw near to me, hear this:
  from the beginning I have not
   spoken in secret,
  from the time it came to be I have
   been there."
  And now the Lord God has sent me
   and his Spirit.

17 Thus says the Lord,
  your Redeemer, the Holy One of
   Israel:
  "I am the Lord your God,
  who teaches you to profit,
  who leads you in the way you
   should go.

18 O that you had hearkened to my
   commandments!
  Then your peace would have been
   like a river,
  and your righteousness like the
   waves of the sea;
19 your offspring would have been like
   the sand,
  and your descendants like its
   grains;
  their name would never be cut off
   or destroyed from before me."

20 Go forth from Babylon, flee from
   Chalde'a,
  declare this with a shout of joy,
   proclaim it,
  send it forth to the end of the earth;
  say, "The Lord has redeemed his
   servant Jacob!"
21 They thirsted not when he led
   them through the deserts;
  he made water flow for them from
   the rock;
  he cleft the rock and the water
   gushed out.
22 "There is no peace," says the
  Lord, "for the wicked."

49 Listen to me, O coastlands,
  and hearken, you peoples
  from afar.
  The Lord called me from the womb,
  from the body of my mother he
   named my name.
2 He made my mouth like a sharp
   sword,
  in the shadow of his hand he
   hid me;
  he made me a polished arrow,
  in his quiver he hid me away.
3 And he said to me, "You are my
   servant,

k Gk Old Latin: Heb lacks *my name*

Furnace, the Exile; earlier used to refer to the Egyptian bondage (Dt.4.20; Jer.11.4). **12–13:**
I am He . . . the first . . . the last, emphasizing God's oneness, uniqueness, and eternity (43.10;
44.6; Rev.1.17; 2.8; 22.13). **14–15:** *You*, Israel; *them*, idols; *him*, Cyrus. **16:** *It*, the creation.
17: *Teaches* and *leads*, description of God's historic relationship with Israel (55.12; Ex.13.18;
Dt.29.5; Ps.27.11). **18–19:** Ps.81.13–16. *Peace* in the Biblical sense is the state of physical and
spiritual well-being within the covenant relationship. *Sand*, Gen.22.17. **20–22:** The prophet
sees Israel's deliverance as the Exodus (Ex.17.1–7; 22.19). **22:** 57.21.
    49.1–6: The second Servant Song (see 42.1–4 n.). **1–3:** The servant (Israel) speaks. **1:** *Listen*,
41.1. *Called . . . my name*, Jer.1.5; Gal.1.15. **2:** *Sharp sword*, Eph.6.17; Heb.4.12. **3–4:** In serving

Israel, in whom I will be
  glorified.”
⁴ But I said, “I have labored in vain,
  I have spent my strength for
    nothing and vanity;
  yet surely my right is with the LORD,
  and my recompense with my
    God.”

⁵ And now the LORD says,
  who formed me from the womb
    to be his servant,
  to bring Jacob back to him,
  and that Israel might be gathered
    to him,
  for I am honored in the eyes of the
    LORD,
  and my God has become my
    strength–
⁶ he says:
  “It is too light a thing that you
    should be my servant
  to raise up the tribes of Jacob
  and to restore the preserved of
    Israel;
  I will give you as a light to the
    nations,
  that my salvation may reach to
    the end of the earth.”

⁷ Thus says the LORD,
  the Redeemer of Israel and his
    Holy One,
  to one deeply despised, abhorred by
    the nations,
  the servant of rulers:
  “Kings shall see and arise;
  princes, and they shall prostrate
    themselves;
  because of the LORD, who is faithful,
  the Holy One of Israel, who has
    chosen you.”

⁸ Thus says the LORD:
  “In a time of favor I have answered
    you,

in a day of salvation I have
    helped you;
  I have kept you and given you
    as a covenant to the people,
  to establish the land,
  to apportion the desolate
    heritages;
⁹ saying to the prisoners, ‘Come forth,’
  to those who are in darkness,
    ‘Appear.’
  They shall feed along the ways,
  on all bare heights shall be their
    pasture;
¹⁰ they shall not hunger or thirst,
  neither scorching wind nor sun
    shall smite them,
  for he who has pity on them will
    lead them,
  and by springs of water will guide
    them.
¹¹ And I will make all my mountains
    a way,
  and my highways shall be raised
    up.
¹² Lo, these shall come from afar,
  and lo, these from the north and
    from the west,
  and these from the land of
    Syene.”¹
¹³ Sing for joy, O heavens, and exult,
    O earth;
  break forth, O mountains, into
    singing!
  For the LORD has comforted his
    people,
  and will have compassion on his
    afflicted.

¹⁴ But Zion said, “The LORD has
    forsaken me,
  my Lord has forgotten me.”
¹⁵ “Can a woman forget her sucking
    child,
  that she should have no

l Cn: Heb Sinim

God, Israel will be glorified. Though his ministry appears futile, his reward is in God (1 Kg.19.4–18; Jer.15.15–21). **5–6:** The life and mission of old and new Israel are contrasted (compare Acts 13.47; 26.23). *Light,* 42.6.
  49.7–26: Return and restoration. 7: The Servant of the nations is served by them (some take this verse with vv. 1–6). God’s historic faithfulness is Israel’s assurance. **8–9b:** Though in bondage as in Egypt (48.10), they will be released and restored (compare 2 Cor.6.2). **9c–11:** The imagery of the Exodus (48.20–22) is combined with that of Israel’s deliverance (40.3–4,11). **12:** *Syene,* see Ezek.29.10 n. **13:** Hymn praising God, the Comforter (44.23). **14–16:** God pro-

compassion on the son of her
womb?
Even these may forget,
yet I will not forget you.
¹⁶ Behold, I have graven you on the
palms of my hands;
your walls are continually before
me.
¹⁷ Your builders outstrip your
destroyers,
and those who laid you waste go
forth from you.
¹⁸ Lift up your eyes round about and
see;
they all gather, they come to you.
As I live, says the LORD,
you shall put them all on as an
ornament,
you shall bind them on as a bride
does.

¹⁹ "Surely your waste and your
desolate places
and your devastated land–
surely now you will be too narrow
for your inhabitants,
and those who swallowed you up
will be far away.
²⁰ The children born in the time of
your bereavement
will yet say in your ears:
'The place is too narrow for me;
make room for me to dwell in.'
²¹ Then you will say in your heart:
'Who has borne me these?
I was bereaved and barren,
exiled and put away,
but who has brought up these?
Behold, I was left alone;
whence then have these come?' "

²² Thus says the Lord GOD:
"Behold, I will lift up my hand to
the nations,
and raise my signal to the peoples;

and they shall bring your sons in
their bosom,
and your daughters shall be
carried on their shoulders.
²³ Kings shall be your foster fathers,
and their queens your nursing
mothers.
With their faces to the ground they
shall bow down to you,
and lick the dust of your feet.
Then you will know that I am the
LORD;
those who wait for me shall not be
put to shame."

²⁴ Can the prey be taken from the
mighty,
or the captives of a tyrant*ᵐ* be
rescued?
²⁵ Surely, thus says the LORD:
"Even the captives of the mighty
shall be taken,
and the prey of the tyrant be
rescued,
for I will contend with those who
contend with you,
and I will save your children.
²⁶ I will make your oppressors eat their
own flesh,
and they shall be drunk with their
own blood as with wine.
Then all flesh shall know
that I am the LORD your Savior,
and your Redeemer, the Mighty
One of Jacob."

50 Thus says the LORD:
"Where is your mother's bill
of divorce,
with which I put her away?
Or which of my creditors is it
to whom I have sold you?
Behold, for your iniquities you were
sold,

m One ancient Ms Syr Vg: Heb righteous man

---

tests his love for Israel (Hos.2.14–23; Jer.31.20). *Graven you*, as a tattoo. **18:** As if studded with
jewels (28.1,3,5), ruined Jerusalem will be repopulated. **20–21:** She (Zion) who had no hope for
children will have more inhabitants than room for them (Jer.31.15–17). *Children*, those born
during the Exile. **22–23:** A *signal* (fire, 30.17; Jer.6.1) announces, not an invasion (5.26; 13.2;
18.3), but the beginning of Judah's restoration (11.10,12; 62.10). Those who oppress God's
people will become their servants. **24–26:** God will free helpless captive Israel (9.20). All the
earth will acknowledge Israel's God (1.24; 60.16).
50.1–3: Covenant, faithfulness, and judgment. 1: Exiled Israel is neither divorced (Dt.24.1–4)

and for your transgressions your
　　mother was put away.
2 Why, when I came, was there no
　　man?
　　When I called, was there no one
　　　to answer?
　Is my hand shortened, that it
　　cannot redeem?
　　Or have I no power to deliver?
　Behold, by my rebuke I dry up the
　　sea,
　I make the rivers a desert;
　their fish stink for lack of water,
　　and die of thirst.
3 I clothe the heavens with blackness,
　　and make sackcloth their
　　　covering."

4 The Lord GOD has given me
　　the tongue of those who are
　　　taught,
　that I may know how to sustain with
　　a word
　him that is weary.
　Morning by morning he wakens,
　he wakens my ear
　to hear as those who are taught.
5 The Lord GOD has opened my ear,
　　and I was not rebellious,
　I turned not backward.
6 I gave my back to the smiters,
　　and my cheeks to those who
　　　pulled out the beard;
　I hid not my face
　from shame and spitting.

7 For the Lord GOD helps me;
　　therefore I have not been
　　　confounded;
　therefore I have set my face like a
　　flint,

and I know that I shall not be put
　to shame;
8 he who vindicates me is near.
　Who will contend with me?
　Let us stand up together.
　Who is my adversary?
　Let him come near to me.
9 Behold, the Lord GOD helps me;
　who will declare me guilty?
　Behold, all of them will wear out like
　　a garment;
　the moth will eat them up.

10 Who among you fears the LORD
　　and obeys the voice of his servant,
　who walks in darkness
　　and has no light,
　yet trusts in the name of the LORD
　　and relies upon his God?
11 Behold, all you who kindle a fire,
　　who set brands alight![n]
　Walk by the light of your fire,
　　and by the brands which you have
　　　kindled!
　This shall you have from my hand:
　　you shall lie down in torment.

51 "Hearken to me, you who pursue
　deliverance,
　　you who seek the LORD;
　look to the rock from which you were
　　hewn,
　　and to the quarry from which you
　　　were digged.
2 Look to Abraham your father
　　and to Sarah who bore you;
　for when he was but one I called him,
　　and I blessed him and made him
　　　many.
3 For the LORD will comfort Zion;

n Syr: Heb *gird yourselves with brands*

---

nor irretrievably sold into slavery (52.3; Ex.21.7) but punished for her unfaithfulness (Hos.2.4–9;
Jer. ch. 3; Ezek. ch. 16). **2–3:** When God appeared in his mighty acts or spoke through his
prophets, no one responded.
　　50.4–11: The third Servant Song (see 42.1–4 n.). **4–6:** Taught by God (Jer.1.4–10), the Servant
conscientiously brings God's comfort to his fellow Israelites (the *weary*) who treat him despicably
(52.13–53.12). Here the prophet may be identifying himself with the Servant (Jer.11.18; compare
Lk.2.32; Acts 13.47; 26.23). **7–9:** Using law court terminology, the Servant expresses unshakable
confidence that God will vindicate him (Jer.1.18–19; 17.17–18; Ezek.3.7–11; Rom.8.33).
10–11: God leads his Servant safely through the darkness of his faithless people's rejection;
they who walk by their own lights will be punished.
　　51.1–16: Salvation for Abraham's children. 1–8: Past revelation and future salvation. **1–3:**
As with his promises to Abraham (Gen.12.1–3), God will fulfil his promised salvation of Zion
(49.20–21). **1:** *Rock, quarry,* symbols of Israel's solidarity. **2:** The only reference to *Sarah* in

he will comfort all her waste
places,
and will make her wilderness like
Eden,
her desert like the garden of the
LORD;
joy and gladness will be found in her,
thanksgiving and the voice of song.

4 "Listen to me, my people,
and give ear to me, my nation;
for a law will go forth from me,
and my justice for a light to the
peoples.
5 My deliverance draws near speedily,
my salvation has gone forth,
and my arms will rule the peoples;
the coastlands wait for me,
and for my arm they hope.
6 Lift up your eyes to the heavens,
and look at the earth beneath;
for the heavens will vanish like
smoke,
the earth will wear out like a
garment,
and they who dwell in it will die
like gnats;*o*
but my salvation will be for ever,
and my deliverance will never be
ended.

7 "Hearken to me, you who know
righteousness,
the people in whose heart is my
law;
fear not the reproach of men,
and be not dismayed at their
revilings.
8 For the moth will eat them up like
a garment,
and the worm will eat them like
wool;
but my deliverance will be for ever,

and my salvation to all
generations."

9 Awake, awake, put on strength,
O arm of the LORD;
awake, as in days of old,
the generations of long ago.
Was it not thou that didst cut Rahab
in pieces,
that didst pierce the dragon?
10 Was it not thou that didst dry up the
sea,
the waters of the great deep;
that didst make the depths of the
sea a way
for the redeemed to pass over?
11 And the ransomed of the LORD
shall return,
and come to Zion with singing;
everlasting joy shall be upon their
heads;
they shall obtain joy and gladness,
and sorrow and sighing shall flee
away.

12 "I, I am he that comforts you;
who are you that you are afraid
of man who dies,
of the son of man who is made
like grass,
13 and have forgotten the LORD, your
Maker,
who stretched out the heavens
and laid the foundations of the
earth,
and fear continually all the day
because of the fury of the
oppressor,
when he sets himself to destroy?
And where is the fury of the
oppressor?
14 He who is bowed down shall
speedily be released;

o Or in like manner

the Old Testament outside of Genesis. **3:** *Eden, garden of the LORD;* the symbolism of creation appears often in Biblical pictures of the new age. The end-time will be a return to the ideal conditions in Eden (see Ezek.36.35; 47.1–12). **4–6:** Salvation is imminent. **4:** *Law* (revealed teaching, 1.10) and *justice* (42.4) recall First Isaiah (1.21; 5.7). **5:** *Arms,* 40.10. **6:** Mt.24.35. **9–16:** Prayer of lament and assuring answer (for pattern of vv. 1–8,9–16, compare 26.8–14, 16–21; 49.14–23,24–26; Jer.15.10,15–21). **9–11:** Plea for God's intervention, using the Hebrew version of the primeval combat between God and chaos-monsters (*Rahab,* 30.7; *dragon* [Hebrew, "tannin"], 27.1; Ezek.29.3; *sea* [Hebrew, "yam"], Job 38.8; *deep* [Hebrew, "tehom"], Ezek.26.19; Job 38.16). **12–14:** What mortal man can compete with the omnipotent and eternal God (Ps.

he shall not die and go down to
the Pit,
neither shall his bread fail.
15 For I am the LORD your God,
who stirs up the sea so that its
waves roar–
the LORD of hosts is his name.
16 And I have put my words in your
mouth,
and hid you in the shadow of my
hand,
stretching out^p the heavens
and laying the foundations of
the earth,
and saying to Zion, 'You are my
people.' "

17 Rouse yourself, rouse yourself,
stand up, O Jerusalem,
you who have drunk at the hand of
the LORD
the cup of his wrath,
who have drunk to the dregs
the bowl of staggering.
18 There is none to guide her
among all the sons she has borne;
there is none to take her by the hand
among all the sons she has
brought up.
19 These two things have befallen
you–
who will condole with you?–
devastation and destruction, famine
and sword;
who will comfort you?^q
20 Your sons have fainted,
they lie at the head of every
street
like an antelope in a net;
they are full of the wrath of the
LORD,
the rebuke of your God.

21 Therefore hear this, you who are
afflicted,

who are drunk, but not with wine:
22 Thus says your Lord, the LORD,
your God who pleads the cause of
his people:
"Behold, I have taken from your
hand
the cup of staggering;
the bowl of my wrath
you shall drink no more;
23 and I will put it into the hand of your
tormentors,
who have said to you,
'Bow down, that we may pass
over';
and you have made your back like
the ground
and like the street for them to pass
over."

52 Awake, awake,
put on your strength, O Zion;
put on your beautiful garments,
O Jerusalem, the holy city;
for there shall no more come into
you
the uncircumcised and the
unclean.
2 Shake yourself from the dust, arise,
O captive^r Jerusalem;
loose the bonds from your neck,
O captive daughter of Zion.

3 For thus says the LORD: "You
were sold for nothing, and you shall be
redeemed without money. 4 For thus
says the Lord GOD: My people went
down at the first into Egypt to sojourn
there, and the Assyrian oppressed
them for nothing. 5 Now therefore
what have I here, says the LORD, seeing that my people are taken away
for nothing? Their rulers wail, says the
LORD, and continually all the day my

p Syr: Heb *plant*
q One ancient Ms Gk Syr Vg: Heb *how may I comfort you*
r Cn: Heb *sit*

90.5)? *Bowed down,* as a prisoner. *Pit,* Sheol (14.9–11). **15–16:** *Your God . . . my people* re-
emphasizes the covenant relationship (40.1). **15:** Jer.31.35.
   51.17–52.12: God's kingship. 17–20: Jerusalem has drunk deeply of *the cup of* God's *wrath*
(Jer.25.15–31) and lies exhausted, depopulated, and destroyed. **21–23:** But now her oppressors
will drink of it (41.1–42.4; 45.20–25). **52.1–2:** Jerusalem is bidden to arise (51.17). *Uncircumcised and unclean* refers to foreigners (33.19) and ritually unclean Jews. **3–6:** A prose interpolation. *Name* is more than appellation; it involves the person himself (compare Ex.20.7). God will
not allow himself to be contemned by his people's oppressors: Egypt (Ezek.29.9), Assyria

name is despised. ⁶ Therefore my
people shall know my name; therefore in that day they shall know that it
is I who speak; here am I."

⁷ How beautiful upon the mountains
  are the feet of him who brings
    good tidings,
  who publishes peace, who brings
    good tidings of good,
  who publishes salvation,
  who says to Zion, "Your God
    reigns."
⁸ Hark, your watchmen lift up their
    voice,
  together they sing for joy;
for eye to eye they see
  the return of the LORD to Zion.
⁹ Break forth together into singing,
  you waste places of Jerusalem;
for the LORD has comforted his
    people,
  he has redeemed Jerusalem.
¹⁰ The LORD has bared his holy arm
    before the eyes of all the nations;
  and all the ends of the earth shall
    see
  the salvation of our God.

¹¹ Depart, depart, go out thence,
    touch no unclean thing;
  go out from the midst of her, purify
    yourselves,
  you who bear the vessels of the
    LORD.
¹² For you shall not go out in haste,
    and you shall not go in flight,
  for the LORD will go before you,
  and the God of Israel will be your
    rear guard.

¹³ Behold, my servant shall prosper,
  he shall be exalted and lifted up,

  and shall be very high.
¹⁴ As many were astonished at him*ˢ*–
    his appearance was so marred,
    beyond human semblance,
  and his form beyond that of the
    sons of men–
¹⁵ so shall he startle*ᵗ* many nations;
    kings shall shut their mouths
    because of him;
  for that which has not been told them
    they shall see,
  and that which they have not
    heard they shall understand.

53 Who has believed what we
   have heard?
  And to whom has the arm of the
    LORD been revealed?
² For he grew up before him like a
    young plant,
  and like a root out of dry ground;
  he had no form or comeliness that
    we should look at him,
  and no beauty that we should
    desire him.
³ He was despised and rejected*ᵘ* by
    men;
  a man of sorrows,*ᵛ* and acquainted
    with grief;*ʷ*
  and as one from whom men hide
    their faces
  he was despised, and we esteemed
    him not.

⁴ Surely he has borne our griefs*ˣ*
  and carried our sorrows;*ʸ*
  yet we esteemed him stricken,
  smitten by God, and afflicted.
⁵ But he was wounded for our
    transgressions,

s Syr Tg: Heb you
t The meaning of the Hebrew word is uncertain
u Or forsaken   v Or pains   w Or sickness
x Or sicknesses   y Or pains

(10.7–11), Babylon (Jer.50.29). **7–8:** Tensely, all creation awaits word of God's decisive victory
(Ps.125.2; 2 Sam.18.25–27; Nah.1.15; Rom.10.15). The *watchmen* see the victor returning
(40.5). **11–12:** Ritually clean, people and priests return home in peace (Ex.13.21–22).
    52.13–53.12: The fourth Servant Song (see 42.1–4 n.). **52.13–15:** God will exalt his brutally
disfigured Servant (Israel) to the numbed astonishment of the world's rulers (49.7,23). **15:**
Rom.15.21. **53.1–3:** A lament (40.12; 50.8–10). The Servant's background and appearance
(52.14) are undistinguished; his person, rejected. **1:** Jn.12.38. **2:** *Young plant*, compare 11.1;
root, 11.10, compare Jer.23.5; these are sometimes considered Messianic allusions. **3:** Like a
leper, he suffers painful loneliness and rejection by the community (Job 19.13–19). **4–6:** By the
Servant's vicarious suffering, he restores all people to God (Mt.8.17; 1 Pet.2.24–25). *Whole,*

he was bruised for our iniquities;
upon him was the chastisement that
    made us whole,
and with his stripes we are healed.
6 All we like sheep have gone astray;
    we have turned every one to his
    own way;
and the LORD has laid on him
    the iniquity of us all.

7 He was oppressed, and he was
    afflicted,
    yet he opened not his mouth;
like a lamb that is led to the
    slaughter,
    and like a sheep that before its
    shearers is dumb,
so he opened not his mouth.
8 By oppression and judgment he was
    taken away;
    and as for his generation, who
    considered
that he was cut off out of the land
    of the living,
    stricken for the transgression of
    my people?
9 And they made his grave with the
    wicked
    and with a rich man in his death,
although he had done no violence,
    and there was no deceit in his
    mouth.

10 Yet it was the will of the LORD to
    bruise him;
    he has put him to grief;z
when he makes himselfa an offering
    for sin,
    he shall see his offspring, he shall
    prolong his days;
the will of the LORD shall prosper
    in his hand;
11   he shall see the fruit of the travail
    of his soul and be satisfied;

by his knowledge shall the righteous
    one, my servant,
    make many to be accounted
    righteous;
and he shall bear their iniquities.
12 Therefore I will divide him a portion
    with the great,
    and he shall divide the spoil with
    the strong;
because he poured out his soul to
    death,
    and was numbered with the
    transgressors;
yet he bore the sin of many,
    and made intercession for the
    transgressors.

54 "Sing, O barren one, who did
    not bear;
break forth into singing and cry
    aloud,
    you who have not been in travail!
For the children of the desolate one
    will be more
    than the children of her that is
    married, says the LORD.
2 Enlarge the place of your tent,
    and let the curtains of your
    habitations be stretched out;
hold not back, lengthen your cords
    and strengthen your stakes.
3 For you will spread abroad to the
    right and to the left,
    and your descendants will possess
    the nations
and will people the desolate cities.

4 "Fear not, for you will not be
    ashamed;
be not confounded, for you will
    not be put to shame;
for you will forget the shame of your
    youth,

z Heb *made him sick*
a Vg: Heb *thou makest his soul*

---

general well-being ("peace," 48.18). **7–9:** Unlike Jeremiah (11.18–12.6) or Job, the Servant suffers silently. He is unjustly condemned (compare Lk.22.37), executed, and ignominiously buried (compare Mt.27.57–60). See Acts 8.32–33. **9b:** Some emend to read, "and his tomb with evildoers" (others read "with demons [satyrs]"). **10–12:** The Servant's suffering manifests God's judgment (against sin) and mercy (upon sinful man). Israel, Abraham's "child," brings blessings to many. The poem describes the purpose of God's people, the covenant community.

    54.1–17: Song of assurance to Israel. 1–3: 49.14–21. **1:** *Barren*, exilic Zion, deserted by God, her "husband" (Ezek. ch. 16); *married*, pre-exilic Zion (62.4; Gal.4.27). **4–8:** God, the faithful husband. **4:** *Shame . . . youth*, pre-exilic infidelity; *widowhood*, the Exile. **6:** God will not irrev-

and the reproach of your
　　widowhood you will remember
　　no more.
⁵ For your Maker is your husband,
　　the LORD of hosts is his name;
and the Holy One of Israel is your
　　Redeemer,
　　the God of the whole earth he is
　　called.
⁶ For the LORD has called you
　　like a wife forsaken and grieved
　　in spirit,
like a wife of youth when she is cast
　　off,
　　says your God.
⁷ For a brief moment I forsook you,
　　but with great compassion I will
　　gather you.
⁸ In overflowing wrath for a moment
　　I hid my face from you,
but with everlasting love I will have
　　compassion on you,
　　says the LORD, your Redeemer.

⁹ "For this is like the days of Noah
　　to me:
　　as I swore that the waters of
　　Noah
　　should no more go over the earth,
so I have sworn that I will not be
　　angry with you
　　and will not rebuke you.
¹⁰ For the mountains may depart
　　and the hills be removed,
but my steadfast love shall not
　　depart from you,
　　and my covenant of peace shall
　　not be removed,
says the LORD, who has
　　compassion on you.

¹¹ "O afflicted one, storm-tossed, and
　　not comforted,
　　behold, I will set your stones in
　　antimony,

and lay your foundations with
　　sapphires.*b*
¹² I will make your pinnacles of agate,
　　your gates of carbuncles,
　　and all your wall of precious
　　stones.
¹³ All your sons shall be taught by the
　　LORD,
　　and great shall be the prosperity
　　of your sons.
¹⁴ In righteousness you shall be
　　established;
　　you shall be far from oppression,
　　for you shall not fear;
　　and from terror, for it shall not
　　come near you.
¹⁵ If any one stirs up strife,
　　it is not from me;
whoever stirs up strife with you
　　shall fall because of you.
¹⁶ Behold, I have created the smith
　　who blows the fire of coals,
　　and produces a weapon for its
　　purpose.
I have also created the ravager to
　　destroy;
¹⁷ 　no weapon that is fashioned
　　against you shall prosper,
　　and you shall confute every
　　tongue that rises against
　　you in judgment.
This is the heritage of the servants
　　of the LORD
　　and their vindication from me,
　　says the LORD."

55 "Ho, every one who thirsts,
　　come to the waters;
and he who has no money,
　　come, buy and eat!
Come, buy wine and milk
　　without money and without
　　price.

b Or *lapis lazuli*

ocably reject his "wife" (Hos.2.19; 11.8–9). **7:** Reconciliation is imminent (Ps.27.10; 2 Cor.
4.17–18). **8:** God's *everlasting love* for his people (43.4; Jer.31.3; a parent's love, 49.14–16;
Jer.31.20; a husband's love, Jer.2.2; Ezek.16.8) is unmerited and unwavering ly faithful. **9–10:**
The everlasting covenant (Jer.32.40). **9:** Gen.8.21–22; 9.11–17. **10:** Jer.31.35–36; Mk.13.31;
covenant of peace, 48.18; Ezek.34.25. **11–14:** New Jerusalem (*afflicted one*, compare 51.21) is
Paradise restored (Ezek.28.13–19; Jn.6.45; Rev.21.19). **15:** Commentary on v. 14. **17:** No one
can assault God's *servants* with impunity (65.13–15).
　　55.1–13: A hymn of joy and triumph, celebrating the approaching consummation of Israel's
restoration. This concludes the first section of Second Isaiah. **1–2:** Reminiscent of wisdom's

2 Why do you spend your money for
  that which is not bread,
and your labor for that which
  does not satisfy?
Hearken diligently to me, and eat
  what is good,
and delight yourselves in fatness.
3 Incline your ear, and come to me;
  hear, that your soul may live;
and I will make with you an
  everlasting covenant,
my steadfast, sure love for David.
4 Behold, I made him a witness to
  the peoples,
a leader and commander for the
  peoples.
5 Behold, you shall call nations that
  you know not,
and nations that knew you not
  shall run to you,
because of the LORD your God, and
  of the Holy One of Israel,
for he has glorified you.

6 "Seek the LORD while he may be
  found,
call upon him while he is near;
7 let the wicked forsake his way,
  and the unrighteous man his
  thoughts;
let him return to the LORD, that he
  may have mercy on him,
and to our God, for he will
  abundantly pardon.
8 For my thoughts are not your
  thoughts,
neither are your ways my ways,
  says the LORD.
9 For as the heavens are higher than
  the earth,
so are my ways higher than your
  ways
and my thoughts than your
  thoughts.

10 "For as the rain and the snow come
  down from heaven,
and return not thither but water
  the earth,
making it bring forth and sprout,
  giving seed to the sower and bread
  to the eater,
11 so shall my word be that goes forth
  from my mouth;
it shall not return to me empty,
but it shall accomplish that which I
  purpose,
and prosper in the thing for which
  I sent it.

12 "For you shall go out in joy,
  and be led forth in peace;
the mountains and the hills before
  you
shall break forth into singing,
  and all the trees of the field shall
  clap their hands.
13 Instead of the thorn shall come up
  the cypress;
instead of the brier shall come up
  the myrtle;
and it shall be to the LORD for a
  memorial,
for an everlasting sign which shall
  not be cut off."

56 Thus says the LORD:
  "Keep justice, and do
  righteousness,
for soon my salvation will come,
  and my deliverance be revealed.
2 Blessed is the man who does this,
  and the son of man who holds it
  fast,
who keeps the sabbath, not profaning
  it,
and keeps his hand from doing
  any evil."

---

invitation to a banquet (Pr.9.3–6; compare Jn.7.37); God's grace cannot be purchased. **3–5:** God's promise to David (2 Sam.7.4–17) continues in the *everlasting covenant* (54.9–10; Jer. 33.19–26; compare Jer.31.31–34). Emphasis is on Israel's messianism, not Davidic messianism. **6–9:** A call to repentance (Jer.29.12–14; Mt.3.2) and trust in God's inscrutable grace (Ps.103.11; Rom.11.33–36). **10–11:** As *rain* causes germination and ultimately provides sustenance, so does God's word (see 9.8). **12–13:** The new Exodus (compare 43.16–21; 49.9–11) into an Eden-like land (see 51.3 n.; 41.18,19; 44.3–4).
    56.1–66.24: Miscellaneous post-restoration oracles (after 538 B.C.; see Introduction, p. 822). **56.1–8:** A blessing on all who keep the sabbath (compare 58.13–14; Jer.17.19–27). **2:** *Blessed*

³ Let not the foreigner who has joined
    himself to the Lord say,
"The Lord will surely separate
    me from his people";
and let not the eunuch say,
"Behold, I am a dry tree."
⁴ For thus says the Lord:
"To the eunuchs who keep my
    sabbaths,
who choose the things that please
    me
and hold fast my covenant,
⁵ I will give in my house and within
    my walls
a monument and a name
better than sons and daughters;
I will give them an everlasting name
which shall not be cut off.

⁶ "And the foreigners who join
    themselves to the Lord,
to minister to him, to love the
    name of the Lord,
and to be his servants,
every one who keeps the sabbath,
    and does not profane it,
and holds fast my covenant–
⁷ these I will bring to my holy
    mountain,
and make them joyful in my
    house of prayer;
their burnt offerings and their
    sacrifices
will be accepted on my altar;
for my house shall be called a house
    of prayer
for all peoples.
⁸ Thus says the Lord God,
    who gathers the outcasts of Israel,
I will gather yet others to him
    besides those already gathered."*c*

⁹ All you beasts of the field, come to
    devour–

all you beasts in the forest.
¹⁰ His watchmen are blind,
    they are all without knowledge;
they are all dumb dogs,
    they cannot bark;
dreaming, lying down,
    loving to slumber.
¹¹ The dogs have a mighty appetite;
    they never have enough.
The shepherds also have no
    understanding;
they have all turned to their own
    way,
each to his own gain, one and all.
¹² "Come," they say, "let us*d* get wine,
    let us fill ourselves with strong
    drink;
and tomorrow will be like this day,
    great beyond measure."

57 The righteous man perishes,
    and no one lays it to heart;
devout men are taken away,
    while no one understands.
For the righteous man is taken away
    from calamity,
²   he enters into peace;
they rest in their beds
    who walk in their uprightness.
³ But you, draw near hither,
    sons of the sorceress,
offspring of the adulterer and the
    harlot.
⁴ Of whom are you making sport?
    Against whom do you open your
    mouth wide
and put out your tongue?
Are you not children of
    transgression,
the offspring of deceit,
⁵ you who burn with lust among the
    oaks,

c Heb *his gathered ones*
d One ancient Ms Syr Vg Tg: Heb *me*

---

is the man, compare Ps.1.1; Jer.17.7; Mt.5.2–12. **3**: *Foreigner*, the reference is to the proselyte
(see v. 6). **4–5**: God himself will honor faithful *eunuchs*. **6–7**: Faithful proselytes will present
acceptable sacrifices; *house of prayer*, Mk.11.17; *for all people*, 60.1–14. **8**: God's community
includes Israel and proselytes.
    56.9–12: Against corrupt leaders. **9**: *Beasts*, nations (Jer.12.8–9; Ezek.39.17). **10**: *Watchmen*,
prophets (Ezek.3.17; 33.7). **11**: *Shepherds*, rulers (Ezek.34.1; Zech.11.4–17).
    57.1–13: Against idolatry. **1–2**: The *righteous* die unnoticed by their hedonistic religious
leaders. *Beds*, graves. **3–4**: *You*, i.e. Jerusalem's apostates ("illegitimate children") who abuse
the righteous ("legitimate children"; Jer.3.1–20; Ezek.16.1–63). **5–6**: The old fertility cults

under every green tree;
who slay your children in the valleys,
under the clefts of the rocks?
⁶ Among the smooth stones of the
valley is your portion;
they, they, are your lot;
to them you have poured out a drink
offering,
you have brought a cereal offering.
Shall I be appeased for these
things?
⁷ Upon a high and lofty mountain
you have set your bed,
and thither you went up to offer
sacrifice.
⁸ Behind the door and the doorpost
you have set up your symbol;
for, deserting me, you have
uncovered your bed,
you have gone up to it,
you have made it wide;
and you have made a bargain for
yourself with them,
you have loved their bed,
you have looked on nakedness.*e*
⁹ You journeyed to Molech*f* with oil
and multiplied your perfumes;
you sent your envoys far off,
and sent down even to Sheol.
¹⁰ You were wearied with the length of
your way,
but you did not say, "It is hopeless";
you found new life for your strength,
and so you were not faint.

¹¹ Whom did you dread and fear,
so that you lied,
and did not remember me,
did not give me a thought?
Have I not held my peace, even for
a long time,
and so you do not fear me?
¹² I will tell of your righteousness and
your doings,

but they will not help you.
¹³ When you cry out, let your collection
of idols deliver you!
The wind will carry them off,
a breath will take them away.
But he who takes refuge in me shall
possess the land,
and shall inherit my holy
mountain.

¹⁴ And it shall be said,
"Build up, build up, prepare the
way,
remove every obstruction from
my people's way."
¹⁵ For thus says the high and lofty One
who inhabits eternity, whose
name is Holy:
"I dwell in the high and holy place,
and also with him who is of a
contrite and humble spirit,
to revive the spirit of the humble,
and to revive the heart of the
contrite.
¹⁶ For I will not contend for ever,
nor will I always be angry;
for from me proceeds the spirit,
and I have made the breath of
life.
¹⁷ Because of the iniquity of his
covetousness I was angry,
I smote him, I hid my face and
was angry;
but he went on backsliding in the
way of his own heart.
¹⁸ I have seen his ways, but I will
heal him;
I will lead him and requite him
with comfort,
creating for his mourners the fruit
of the lips.
¹⁹ Peace, peace, to the far and to the
near, says the LORD;

e The meaning of the Hebrew is uncertain
f Or *the king*

---

persist. *Oak*, see 6.13 n.; *slay your children*, Jer.19.5; *portion*, *lot*, the gods of the valleys (v. 6), mountains (v. 7), house (v. 8), and other shrines (vv. 9–10), rather than the true God (Jer.10.16). **7–8**: Sexual immorality was characteristic of these cults. **9–10**: *Molech*, see Jer.7.31 n.; *to Sheol*, to the gods of the underworld (14.9–11). All such practices are futile (Jer.2.25). **11–13**: God rebukes the idolators (42.8); their gods are impotent (42.17; Jer.2.20–28).

57.14–21: Poem of consolation. 14: Compare 40.1–4. **15:** God is both distant and near (Jn.1.1–18). **16–21:** God's justifiable wrath is not unending. **17:** Israel continued to sin despite repeated punishments. **18:** Yet the LORD will heal him, by an act of grace. *Mourners*, a reference to those who repent. **19–21:** Israel will have peace, but the wicked will not (48.18; Eph.2.17).

and I will heal him.
20 But the wicked are like the tossing
    sea;
for it cannot rest,
    and its waters toss up mire and
        dirt.
21 There is no peace, says my God,
    for the wicked."

58 "Cry aloud, spare not,
    lift up your voice like a
        trumpet;
declare to my people their
    transgression,
to the house of Jacob their sins.
2 Yet they seek me daily,
    and delight to know my ways,
as if they were a nation that did
    righteousness
    and did not forsake the ordinance
        of their God;
they ask of me righteous judgments,
    they delight to draw near to God.
3 'Why have we fasted, and thou seest
        it not?
Why have we humbled ourselves,
    and thou takest no knowledge
        of it?'
Behold, in the day of your fast you
    seek your own pleasure,*g*
and oppress all your workers.
4 Behold, you fast only to quarrel and
        to fight
    and to hit with wicked fist.
Fasting like yours this day
    will not make your voice to be
        heard on high.
5 Is such the fast that I choose,
    a day for a man to humble
        himself?
Is it to bow down his head like a rush,
    and to spread sackcloth and ashes
        under him?
Will you call this a fast,
    and a day acceptable to the LORD?

6 "Is not this the fast that I choose:
    to loose the bonds of wickedness,
    to undo the thongs of the yoke,
to let the oppressed go free,
    and to break every yoke?
7 Is it not to share your bread with
        the hungry,
    and bring the homeless poor into
        your house;
when you see the naked, to cover
        him,
    and not to hide yourself from
        your own flesh?
8 Then shall your light break forth
        like the dawn,
    and your healing shall spring up
        speedily;
your righteousness shall go before
        you,
    the glory of the LORD shall be
        your rear guard.
9 Then you shall call, and the LORD
        will answer;
    you shall cry, and he will say,
        Here I am.

"If you take away from the midst
        of you the yoke,
    the pointing of the finger, and
        speaking wickedness,
10 if you pour yourself out for the
        hungry
    and satisfy the desire of the
        afflicted,
then shall your light rise in the
        darkness
    and your gloom be as the
        noonday.
11 And the LORD will guide you
        continually,
    and satisfy your desire with good
        things,*h*
    and make your bones strong;

g Or *pursue your own business*
h The meaning of the Hebrew word is uncertain

58.1–14: The LORD **does not desire fasting, but kindness and justice;** compare Mic.6.6–8;
Jas.1.27. **1–5:** Proper motivation is necessary for the acceptance of fasting. **1:** *Trumpet*, the
trumpet was used to announce a fast day (Jl.2.15; compare Ezek.33.3). **3:** *Day of your fast*,
Lev.23.26–32; Jer.36.9. **5:** *Sackcloth*, worn by mourners (Ezek.7.18), by prisoners (3.24), and
by prophets (20.2). **6–9b:** One's relationship to his fellows reveals one's relationship to God
(Lk.10.25–37). When appropriate "fruits" are present (social justice, mercy, sharing; Lk.3.8),
God will hear (1.10–20; Mt.25.34–40). *Light*, 42.6–7; *rear guard*, 52.12. **9c–12:** God will give his
people strength (66.14), abundance (Jer.31.12) and auspicious circumstances for reconstruction

and you shall be like a watered
garden,
like a spring of water,
whose waters fail not.
¹² And your ancient ruins shall be
rebuilt;
you shall raise up the foundations
of many generations;
you shall be called the repairer of
the breach,
the restorer of streets to dwell in.

¹³ "If you turn back your foot from
the sabbath,
from doing your pleasure*i* on
my holy day,
and call the sabbath a delight
and the holy day of the LORD
honorable;
if you honor it, not going your own
ways,
or seeking your own pleasure,*j*
or talking idly;
¹⁴ then you shall take delight in the
LORD,
and I will make you ride upon the
heights of the earth;
I will feed you with the heritage of
Jacob your father,
for the mouth of the LORD has
spoken."

59 Behold, the LORD's hand is
not shortened, that it cannot
save,
or his ear dull, that it cannot hear;
² but your iniquities have made a
separation
between you and your God,
and your sins have hid his face from
you
so that he does not hear.
³ For your hands are defiled with
blood
and your fingers with iniquity;

your lips have spoken lies,
your tongue mutters wickedness.
⁴ No one enters suit justly,
no one goes to law honestly;
they rely on empty pleas, they
speak lies,
they conceive mischief and bring
forth iniquity.
⁵ They hatch adders' eggs,
they weave the spider's web;
he who eats their eggs dies,
and from one which is crushed a
viper is hatched.
⁶ Their webs will not serve as clothing;
men will not cover themselves
with what they make.
Their works are works of iniquity,
and deeds of violence are in their
hands.
⁷ Their feet run to evil,
and they make haste to shed
innocent blood;
their thoughts are thoughts of
iniquity,
desolation and destruction are in
their highways.
⁸ The way of peace they know not,
and there is no justice in their
paths;
they have made their roads crooked,
no one who goes in them knows
peace.

⁹ Therefore justice is far from us,
and righteousness does not
overtake us;
we look for light, and behold,
darkness,
and for brightness, but we walk
in gloom.
¹⁰ We grope for the wall like the blind,
we grope like those who have no
eyes;

i Or *business*
j Or *pursuing your own business*

(44.26; 61.4). *Point the finger*, gesture of contempt (Pr.6.13). **13–14:** Strict observance of *the sabbath* was increasingly emphasized in post-exilic Judaism (56.2; Mt.12.1–8).
59.1–21: Call to national repentance. 1–4: God is not impotent or deaf; Judah's transgressions have broken the covenant (50.1–2). The people are totally given over to wickedness; injustice and dishonesty are rampant (Rom.3.10–18). **5–8:** Graphic continuation of vv. 3–4. The whole community is contaminated (Mt.23.13–36). Synonyms of "ways" in vv. 7–8 (Rom.3.15–17) describe the blind alleys down which Judah is going. **9–11:** Consequently, Judah gropes in the darkness of social and spiritual depravity (13.10; 50.10–11), fear, and foreboding (38.14).

we stumble at noon as in the
  twilignt,
  among those in full vigor we are
    like dead men.
11 We all growl like bears,
  we moan and moan like doves;
  we look for justice, but there is none;
    for salvation, but it is far from us.
12 For our transgressions are
    multiplied before thee,
  and our sins testify against us;
  for our transgressions are with us,
  and we know our iniquities:
13 transgressing, and denying the
    LORD,
  and turning away from following
    our God,
  speaking oppression and revolt,
    conceiving and uttering from the
    heart lying words.
14 Justice is turned back,
  and righteousness stands afar off;
  for truth has fallen in the public
    squares,
  and uprightness cannot enter.
15 Truth is lacking,
  and he who departs from evil
    makes himself a prey.

The LORD saw it, and it displeased
    him
  that there was no justice.
16 He saw that there was no man,
  and wondered that there was
    no one to intervene;
  then his own arm brought him
    victory,
  and his righteousness upheld him.
17 He put on righteousness as a
    breastplate,
  and a helmet of salvation upon
    his head;
  he put on garments of vengeance for
    clothing,

and wrapped himself in fury as a
  mantle.
18 According to their deeds, so will he
  repay,
  wrath to his adversaries, requital
    to his enemies;
  to the coastlands he will render
    requital.
19 So they shall fear the name of the
    LORD from the west,
  and his glory from the rising of
    the sun;
  for he will come like a rushing
    stream,
  which the wind of the LORD
    drives.

20 "And he will come to Zion as
    Redeemer,
  to those in Jacob who turn from
    transgression, says the LORD.
21 "And as for me, this is my covenant
with them, says the LORD: my spirit
which is upon you, and my words
which I have put in your mouth,
shall not depart out of your mouth, or
out of the mouth of your children, or
out of the mouth of your children's
children, says the LORD, from this time
forth and for evermore."

60 Arise, shine; for your light
  has come,
  and the glory of the LORD has
    risen upon you.
2 For behold, darkness shall cover the
  earth,
  and thick darkness the peoples;
  but the LORD will arise upon you,
  and his glory will be seen upon
    you.
3 And nations shall come to your
    light,

12–15b: The community confesses the magnitude of its offenses: rebellion (*transgressing*),
faithlessness (*denying*), disobedience (*turning away*); its integrity is wholly corrupted. **15c–17:**
With no human helper available, God himself intervened with every means at his command
(42.13; compare Eph.6.14–17). **18–20:** God brings judgment upon all his enemies with irresistible fury and might (30.27–28) to redeem repentant *Zion* (Jerusalem; compare Rom.11.26).
21: A prose oracle assuring Judah of the abiding presence of God's *spirit* and *words* (44.3–5).
    60.1–62.12: Poems on the glory of Jerusalem and of God's people, reminiscent of chapters
40–55. **60.1–22: Jerusalem's glorious restoration. 1–3:** Fallen Zion bidden to *arise, shine*
(42.6–7), and reflect *the glory of the LORD* (6.3; Ezek.1.4–28; 10.4), which will attract all nations

and kings to the brightness of your rising.

4 Lift up your eyes round about, and see;
  they all gather together, they come to you;
  your sons shall come from far,
  and your daughters shall be carried in the arms.
5 Then you shall see and be radiant,
  your heart shall thrill and rejoice;*k*
  because the abundance of the sea shall be turned to you,
  the wealth of the nations shall come to you.
6 A multitude of camels shall cover you,
  the young camels of Mid′ian and Ephah;
  all those from Sheba shall come.
  They shall bring gold and frankincense,
  and shall proclaim the praise of the LORD.
7 All the flocks of Kedar shall be gathered to you,
  the rams of Nebai′oth shall minister to you;
  they shall come up with acceptance on my altar,
  and I will glorify my glorious house.

8 Who are these that fly like a cloud,
  and like doves to their windows?
9 For the coastlands shall wait for me,
  the ships of Tarshish first,
  to bring your sons from far,
  their silver and gold with them,
  for the name of the LORD your God,
  and for the Holy One of Israel,
  because he has glorified you.

10 Foreigners shall build up your walls,
  and their kings shall minister to you;
  for in my wrath I smote you,
  but in my favor I have had mercy on you.
11 Your gates shall be open continually;
  day and night they shall not be shut;
  that men may bring to you the wealth of the nations,
  with their kings led in procession.
12 For the nation and kingdom that will not serve you shall perish;
  those nations shall be utterly laid waste.
13 The glory of Lebanon shall come to you,
  the cypress, the plane, and the pine,
  to beautify the place of my sanctuary;
  and I will make the place of my feet glorious.
14 The sons of those who oppressed you
  shall come bending low to you;
  and all who despised you
  shall bow down at your feet;
  they shall call you the City of the LORD,
  the Zion of the Holy One of Israel.

15 Whereas you have been forsaken and hated,
  with no one passing through,
  I will make you majestic for ever,
  a joy from age to age.
16 You shall suck the milk of nations,
  you shall suck the breast of kings;
  and you shall know that I, the LORD,
  am your Savior

k Heb *be enlarged*

(66.18). **4–5**: Risen Zion welcomes her children home (49.18ab, 22de); her poverty is replaced by wealth (45.14; 61.6). **6–7**: Arabia's riches are brought by camel caravan. *Midian* (see Ex. 2.15 n.), *Ephah,* Arab tribes east of Gulf of Aqabah; *Sheba* (Gen.10.7); *Kedar* (21.16); *Nebaioth,* an Arab tribe (Gen.25.13). **8–9**: Some returning exiles (*sons*) and wealth from the west arrive by ship (v. 8). *Tarshish* (see Jer.10.9 n.). **10–11**: Destroyed by foreigners (Jer.52.13–16), the new Jerusalem will be built by foreigners (compare Rev.21.24–27). **13–14**: As before (1 Kg.5.8–10) wood from *Lebanon* (41.19) and wealth from the nations will build the temple and holy *City* (35.1–10; 49.26). **15–16**: Once forsaken (54.6–7), Zion will be exalted (1.24; Ezek.16.1–63).

and your Redeemer, the Mighty
One of Jacob.

17 Instead of bronze I will bring gold,
and instead of iron I will bring
silver;
instead of wood, bronze,
instead of stones, iron.
I will make your overseers peace
and your taskmasters
righteousness.
18 Violence shall no more be heard
in your land,
devastation or destruction within
your borders;
you shall call your walls Salvation,
and your gates Praise.

19 The sun shall be no more
your light by day,
nor for brightness shall the moon
give light to you by night;*l*
but the LORD will be your everlasting
light,
and your God will be your glory.
20 Your sun shall no more go down,
nor your moon withdraw itself;
for the LORD will be your
everlasting light,
and your days of mourning shall
be ended.
21 Your people shall all be righteous;
they shall possess the land for
ever,
the shoot of my planting, the work
of my hands,
that I might be glorified.
22 The least one shall become a clan,
and the smallest one a mighty
nation;
I am the LORD;
in its time I will hasten it.

61 The Spirit of the Lord GOD is
upon me,

because the LORD has anointed me
to bring good tidings to the
afflicted;*m*
he has sent me to bind up the
brokenhearted,
to proclaim liberty to the captives,
and the opening of the prison*n*
to those who are bound;
2 to proclaim the year of the LORD's
favor,
and the day of vengeance of our
God;
to comfort all who mourn;
3 to grant to those who mourn in
Zion—
to give them a garland instead of
ashes,
the oil of gladness instead of
mourning,
the mantle of praise instead of a
faint spirit;
that they may be called oaks of
righteousness,
the planting of the LORD, that he
may be glorified.
4 They shall build up the ancient
ruins,
they shall raise up the former
devastations;
they shall repair the ruined cities,
the devastations of many
generations.

5 Aliens shall stand and feed your
flocks,
foreigners shall be your
plowmen and vinedressers;
6 but you shall be called the priests
of the LORD,
men shall speak of you as the
ministers of our God;
you shall eat the wealth of the
nations,

l One ancient Ms Gk Old Latin Tg: Heb lacks *by night*
m Or *poor*
n Or *the opening of the eyes:* Heb *the opening*

17–18: The new Jerusalem will surpass Solomon's city in beauty and tranquillity. **19–20:** God's
glory will perpetually illumine the joyful city (35.10; Rev.21.4). **21–22:** In the divinely restored
city, God will be glorified (9.7; 54.1–2).

61.1–11: The mission to Zion. This poem recalls the Servant Songs of chs. 42–53, especially
50.4–11. **1–3:** Lk.4.16–20; compare Mt.11.5; Lk.7.22. God sends his prophet to bring encouragement to the exiled and oppressed; he will make them mighty oaks (60.21; Jer.17.8). *Spirit*
is strongly emphasized in exilic and post-exilic writings (42.1; 59.21; Ezek.2.2). **2:** *Vengeance,*
better, "rescue." **4–5:** 60.10–11. **6–7:** *Priests* (Ex.19.6). *Double portion,* for double punishment

and in their riches you shall glory.

7 Instead of your shame you shall
      have a double portion,
      instead of dishonor you*o* shall
      rejoice in your*p* lot;
    therefore in your*p* land you*o* shall
      possess a double portion;
      yours*q* shall be everlasting joy.

8 For I the LORD love justice,
      I hate robbery and wrong;*r*
    I will faithfully give them their
      recompense,
    and I will make an everlasting
      covenant with them.
9 Their descendants shall be known
      among the nations,
    and their offspring in the midst of
      the peoples;
    all who see them shall acknowledge
      them,
    that they are a people whom the
      LORD has blessed.

10 I will greatly rejoice in the LORD,
      my soul shall exult in my God;
    for he has clothed me with the
      garments of salvation,
      he has covered me with the robe of
      righteousness,
    as a bridegroom decks himself with a
      garland,
    and as a bride adorns herself with
      her jewels.
11 For as the earth brings forth its
      shoots,
    and as a garden causes what is
      sown in it to spring up,
    so the Lord GOD will cause
      righteousness and praise
    to spring forth before all the
      nations.

62 For Zion's sake I will not
      keep silent,

and for Jerusalem's sake I will not
      rest,
    until her vindication goes forth as
      brightness,
    and her salvation as a burning
      torch.
2 The nations shall see your
      vindication,
    and all the kings your glory;
    and you shall be called by a new
      name
    which the mouth of the LORD will
      give.
3 You shall be a crown of beauty in
      the hand of the LORD,
    and a royal diadem in the hand
      of your God.
4 You shall no more be termed
      Forsaken,*s*
    and your land shall no more be
      termed Desolate;*t*
    but you shall be called My delight
      is in her,*u*
    and your land Married;*v*
    for the LORD delights in you,
    and your land shall be married.
5 For as a young man marries a
      virgin,
    so shall your sons marry you,
    and as the bridegroom rejoices over
      the bride,
    so shall your God rejoice over
      you.

6 Upon your walls, O Jerusalem,
      I have set watchmen;
    all the day and all the night
      they shall never be silent.
    You who put the LORD in
      remembrance,
      take no rest,
7 and give him no rest

o Heb *they*   p Heb *their*
q Heb *theirs*   r Or *robbery with a burnt offering*
s Heb *Azubah*   t Heb *Shemamah*
u Heb *Hephzibah* v Heb *Beulah*

(40.2). **8–9**: In Judah, all nations will see God's faithfulness and his blessing. *Justice*, 5.7,16.
Everlasting covenant, 54.9–10. **10–11**: The prophet identifies himself with Zion and rejoices in
her salvation (compare vv. 1–3), which is as certain as the earth's producing vegetation.
      62.1–12: The glory of God's people. 1–3: The prophet continues to proclaim Zion's approach-
ing vindication. *New name* denotes a change in status (1.26; Jer.33.16; Ezek.48.35; compare
Abram, Abraham, Gen.17.5 notes *x* and *y*). *Crown of beauty* (28.1–6). **4–5:** New status, new
names. *Your sons*, read (with a slight emendation), "your Builder." **6–9:** *Watchmen*, probably
prophets (52.8; Ezek. ch. 33), to remind Jerusalem of her imminent salvation, the certainty of

until he establishes Jerusalem
and makes it a praise in the earth.
8 The LORD has sworn by his right
hand
and by his mighty arm:
"I will not again give your grain
to be food for your enemies,
and foreigners shall not drink your
wine
for which you have labored;
9 but those who garner it shall eat it
and praise the LORD,
and those who gather it shall drink it
in the courts of my sanctuary."

10 Go through, go through the gates,
prepare the way for the people;
build up, build up the highway,
clear it of stones,
lift up an ensign over the peoples.
11 Behold, the LORD has proclaimed
to the end of the earth:
Say to the daughter of Zion,
"Behold, your salvation comes;
behold, his reward is with him,
and his recompense before him."
12 And they shall be called The holy
people,
The redeemed of the LORD;
and you shall be called Sought out,
a city not forsaken.

63 Who is this that comes from
Edom,
in crimsoned garments from
Bozrah,
he that is glorious in his apparel,
marching in the greatness of his
strength?

"It is I, announcing vindication,
mighty to save."

2 Why is thy apparel red,
and thy garments like his that
treads in the wine press?

3 "I have trodden the wine press
alone,
and from the peoples no one
was with me;
I trod them in my anger
and trampled them in my wrath;
their lifeblood is sprinkled upon my
garments,
and I have stained all my raiment.
4 For the day of vengeance was in my
heart,
and my year of redemption*w* has
come.
5 I looked, but there was no one to
help;
I was appalled, but there was no
one to uphold;
so my own arm brought me victory,
and my wrath upheld me.
6 I trod down the peoples in my anger,
I made them drunk in my wrath,
and I poured out their lifeblood
on the earth."

7 I will recount the steadfast love of
the LORD,
the praises of the LORD,
according to all that the LORD has
granted us,
and the great goodness to the
house of Israel
which he has granted them
according to his mercy,
according to the abundance of his
steadfast love.
8 For he said, Surely they are my
people,

w Or the year of my redeemed

---

which the LORD's oath (vv. 8–9) underscores. *Right hand* (Ex.15.6,12). *Mighty arm* (40.10; Dt.7.19). *Foreigners*, invaders, as the Babylonians, and encroachers, as the Edomites (Ob.13). **10–12:** A summary of the eschatological hopes described in chs. 60–62. **10b:** 49.22. **11b:** 40.10.

63.1–6: Poem on divine vengeance. 1: The prophet (watchman; see 62.6 n.) challenges him who approaches. *Edom, Bozrah,* symbolic of God's opponents (34.5–7). **2–3:** Compare Jl.3.13; Rev.14.19–20. **4–6:** *Day of vengeance* and *year of redemption* are synchronous. *Drunk,* see Jer.25.15–29; Zech.12.2.

63.7–64.12: Psalm of intercession. 7–14: Historical prologue recalling Israel's deliverance from Egypt. Israel is called (v. 8; Ex.4.22–23; 19.3–6), protected (v. 9a; Ex.12.1–32), exalted (v. 9b; Ezek. ch. 16), delivered (vv. 11–12; Ex.14.9–15.21; Jer.15.1), and safely led through Sinai into Canaan (vv. 13–14). Israel's rebellion necessitated God's opposing them (Jer.5.20–29). **7:** *Steadfast love* expresses God's continuing covenant loyalty despite Israel's faithlessness.

sons who will not deal falsely;
and he became their Savior.
⁹ In all their affliction he was
afflicted,ˣ
and the angel of his presence
saved them;
in his love and in his pity he
redeemed them;
he lifted them up and carried
them all the days of old.

¹⁰ But they rebelled
and grieved his holy Spirit;
therefore he turned to be their
enemy,
and himself fought against them.
¹¹ Then he remembered the days of
old,
of Moses his servant.
Where is he who brought up out of
the sea
the shepherds of his flock?
Where is he who put in the midst of
them
his holy Spirit,
¹² who caused his glorious arm
to go at the right hand of Moses,
who divided the waters before them
to make for himself an everlasting
name,
¹³ who led them through the depths?
Like a horse in the desert,
they did not stumble.
¹⁴ Like cattle that go down into the
valley,
the Spirit of the LORD gave them
rest.
So thou didst lead thy people,
to make for thyself a glorious
name.

¹⁵ Look down from heaven and see,
from thy holy and glorious
habitation.
Where are thy zeal and thy might?
The yearning of thy heart and
thy compassion

are withheld from me.
¹⁶ For thou art our Father,
though Abraham does not know
us
and Israel does not acknowledge
us;
thou, O LORD, art our Father,
our Redeemer from of old is thy
name.
¹⁷ O LORD, why dost thou make us err
from thy ways
and harden our heart, so that we
fear thee not?
Return for the sake of thy servants,
the tribes of thy heritage.
¹⁸ Thy holy people possessed thy
sanctuary a little while;
our adversaries have trodden it
down.
¹⁹ We have become like those over
whom thou hast never ruled,
like those who are not called by
thy name.

64 O that thou wouldst rend
the heavens and come down,
that the mountains might quake
at thy presence—
²ʸ as when fire kindles brushwood
and the fire causes water to boil—
to make thy name known to thy
adversaries,
and that the nations might tremble
at thy presence!
³ When thou didst terrible things
which we looked not for,
thou camest down, the mountains
quaked at thy presence.
⁴ From of old no one has heard
or perceived by the ear,
no eye has seen a God besides thee,
who works for those who wait for
him.
⁵ Thou meetest him that joyfully
works righteousness,

---

x Another reading is *he did not afflict*
y Ch 64.1 in Heb

15–16: The prophet therefore hopefully petitions God, whose immortality is contrasted with the mortality of Israel's patriarchs (*Abraham, Israel* [Jacob]). **17–19:** Israel's sinfulness begets sinfulness. The prophet begs God to deliver his forsaken people from their sins and to restore their ruined sanctuary. **64.1–5b:** A prayer that God should reveal himself in power as in days of old (Ex.19.16–18; Jg.5.4–5; Hab.3.3–15). Man cannot approach God (Gen.11.1–9; Ex. 33.17–23), but God comes to man (Ex.19–20). **5c–7:** The prophet, in behalf of his people, con-

those that remember thee in thy
ways.
Behold, thou wast angry, and we
sinned;
in our sins we have been a long
time, and shall we be saved?*z*
⁶ We have all become like one who
is unclean,
and all our righteous deeds are
like a polluted garment.
We all fade like a leaf,
and our iniquities, like the wind,
take us away.
⁷ There is no one that calls upon thy
name,
that bestirs himself to take hold
of thee;
for thou hast hid thy face from us,
and hast delivered*a* us into the
hand of our iniquities.

⁸ Yet, O Lᴏʀᴅ, thou art our Father;
we are the clay, and thou art our
potter;
we are all the work of thy hand.
⁹ Be not exceedingly angry, O Lᴏʀᴅ,
and remember not iniquity for
ever.
Behold, consider, we are all thy
people.
¹⁰ Thy holy cities have become a
wilderness,
Zion has become a wilderness,
Jerusalem a desolation.
¹¹ Our holy and beautiful house,
where our fathers praised thee,
has been burned by fire,
and all our pleasant places have
become ruins.
¹² Wilt thou restrain thyself at these
things, O Lᴏʀᴅ?
Wilt thou keep silent, and afflict
us sorely?

65 I was ready to be sought by
those who did not ask for me;
I was ready to be found by those
who did not seek me.
I said, "Here am I, here am I,"
to a nation that did not call on my
name.
² I spread out my hands all the day
to a rebellious people,
who walk in a way that is not good,
following their own devices;
³ a people who provoke me
to my face continually,
sacrificing in gardens
and burning incense upon bricks;
⁴ who sit in tombs,
and spend the night in secret
places;
who eat swine's flesh,
and broth of abominable things
is in their vessels;
⁵ who say, "Keep to yourself,
do not come near me, for I am set
apart from you."
These are a smoke in my nostrils,
a fire that burns all the day.
⁶ Behold, it is written before me:
"I will not keep silent, but I will
repay,
yea, I will repay into their bosom
⁷ their*b* iniquities and their*b*
fathers' iniquities together,
says the Lᴏʀᴅ;
because they burned incense upon
the mountains
and reviled me upon the hills,
I will measure into their bosom
payment for their former doings."

⁸ Thus says the Lᴏʀᴅ:

z Hebrew obscure
a Gk Syr Old Latin Tg: Heb *melted*
b Gk Syr: Heb *your*

fesses their sin and hopelessness. **8–12:** In his final petition he pleads that the Lᴏʀᴅ relent his anger and have compassion on desolate Jerusalem and the destroyed temple. **10:** *Thy holy cities*, the cities are the Lᴏʀᴅ's, for the Promised Land is his. **12:** *Wilt thou keep silent . . .* ? compare Ps.79.5; 85.5–7.
    65.1–25: God's answer. 1–2: Not God, but the people were silent. *Spread out my hands*, in a gesture of invitation (Rom.10.20–21). **3:** *Sacrificing in gardens*, an allusion to nature-cult practices. *Burning incense* was peculiarly associated with pagan worship, although also a part of Israelite worship (Jer.1.16). **4:** *Sit in tombs*, for divination, to consult the dead (29.4). *Spend the night in secret places*, in a shrine to receive visions (compare 1 Kg.3.4–15). To *eat swine's flesh* was forbidden (Dt.14.8). **5:** *I am set apart*, sanctified by some idolatrous rite. **6–7:** God has

[903]

"As the wine is found in the
cluster,
and they say, 'Do not destroy it,
for there is a blessing in it,'
so I will do for my servants' sake,
and not destroy them all.
⁹ I will bring forth descendants from
Jacob,
and from Judah inheritors of my
mountains;
my chosen shall inherit it,
and my servants shall dwell there.
¹⁰ Sharon shall become a pasture for
flocks,
and the Valley of Achor a place for
herds to lie down,
for my people who have sought
me.
¹¹ But you who forsake the LORD,
who forget my holy mountain,
who set a table for Fortune
and fill cups of mixed wine for
Destiny;
¹² I will destine you to the sword,
and all of you shall bow down to
the slaughter;
because, when I called, you did not
answer,
when I spoke, you did not listen,
but you did what was evil in my eyes,
and chose what I did not delight
in."

¹³ Therefore thus says the Lord GOD:
"Behold, my servants shall eat,
but you shall be hungry;
behold, my servants shall drink,
but you shall be thirsty;
behold, my servants shall rejoice,
but you shall be put to shame;
¹⁴ behold, my servants shall sing for
gladness of heart,
but you shall cry out for pain of
heart,
and shall wail for anguish of spirit.

¹⁵ You shall leave your name to my
chosen for a curse,
and the Lord GOD will slay you;
but his servants he will call by a
different name.
¹⁶ So that he who blesses himself in
the land
shall bless himself by the God of
truth,
and he who takes an oath in the land
shall swear by the God of truth;
because the former troubles are
forgotten
and are hid from my eyes.

¹⁷ "For behold, I create new heavens
and a new earth;
and the former things shall not be
remembered
or come into mind.
¹⁸ But be glad and rejoice for ever
in that which I create;
for behold, I create Jerusalem a
rejoicing,
and her people a joy.
¹⁹ I will rejoice in Jerusalem,
and be glad in my people;
no more shall be heard in it the
sound of weeping
and the cry of distress.
²⁰ No more shall there be in it
an infant that lives but a few
days,
or an old man who does not fill
out his days,
for the child shall die a hundred
years old,
and the sinner a hundred years old
shall be accursed.
²¹ They shall build houses and inhabit
them;
they shall plant vineyards and eat
their fruit.
²² They shall not build and another
inhabit;

they shall not plant and another
  eat;
for like the days of a tree shall the
  days of my people be,
and my chosen shall long enjoy the
  work of their hands.
23 They shall not labor in vain,
  or bear children for calamity;*c*
for they shall be the offspring of the
  blessed of the LORD,
and their children with them.
24 Before they call I will answer,
  while they are yet speaking I will
    hear.
25 The wolf and the lamb shall feed
  together,
  the lion shall eat straw like the ox;
  and dust shall be the serpent's
    food.
They shall not hurt or destroy
  in all my holy mountain,
    says the LORD."

66 Thus says the LORD:
  "Heaven is my throne
and the earth is my footstool;
what is the house which you would
  build for me,
  and what is the place of my rest?
2 All these things my hand has made,
  and so all these things are mine,*d*
    says the LORD.
But this is the man to whom I will
  look,
  he that is humble and contrite in
    spirit,
  and trembles at my word.

3 "He who slaughters an ox is like
  him who kills a man;
  he who sacrifices a lamb, like him

who breaks a dog's neck;
he who presents a cereal offering,
  like him who offers swine's
    blood;
he who makes a memorial offering
  of frankincense, like him who
  blesses an idol.
These have chosen their own ways,
  and their soul delights in their
    abominations;
4 I also will choose affliction for them,
  and bring their fears upon them;
because, when I called, no one
    answered,
  when I spoke they did not listen;
but they did what was evil in my
    eyes,
  and chose that in which I did not
    delight."

5 Hear the word of the LORD,
  you who tremble at his word:
"Your brethren who hate you
  and cast you out for my name's
    sake
have said, 'Let the LORD be glorified,
  that we may see your joy';
  but it is they who shall be put to
    shame.

6 "Hark, an uproar from the city!
  A voice from the temple!
The voice of the LORD,
  rendering recompense to his
    enemies!

7 "Before she was in labor
  she gave birth;
before her pain came upon her
  she was delivered of a son.

c Or *sudden terror*   *d* Gk Syr: Heb *came to be*

misfortune (Jer.15.8). **24–25:** In the new Jerusalem restored, all will be at peace (11.6–9). *My holy mountain*, see 11.9 n.; compare 27.13; 56.7; Jl.3.17.
  66.1–24: Concluding oracles. 1–6: On temple worship. **1–2:** A house made of created materials cannot contain the Creator and Lord of heaven and earth (compare 1 Kg.8.27), nor do mere acts suffice for devout humility (1.10–20). **3–4:** These verses are perhaps best taken as the continuation of the thought in vv. 1–2. The insertion of the word "like" (not in the Hebrew) interprets one possible meaning of these verses. In accord with another interpretation read: "He who slaughters an ox, he who kills a man . . . ; these have chosen their own ways . . ." The first part of each line describes normally acceptable practice, the second what is not. The "Canaanitish" practices of sacrificing humans (*kills a man*), dogs (*breaks a dog's neck*), and swine (*offers swine's blood*) are abominations. **5–6:** Vindication for true believers. God has returned to his temple (Ezek.43.1–5). **7–16:** On Jerusalem's restoration. **7–9:** Jerusalem's rebirth is a

8 Who has heard such a thing?
  Who has seen such things?
Shall a land be born in one day?
  Shall a nation be brought forth in
    one moment?
For as soon as Zion was in labor
  she brought forth her sons.
9 Shall I bring to the birth and not
    cause to bring forth?
  says the LORD;
shall I, who cause to bring forth, shut
    the womb?
  says your God.

10 "Rejoice with Jerusalem, and be
    glad for her,
  all you who love her;
rejoice with her in joy,
  all you who mourn over her;
11 that you may suck and be satisfied
    with her consoling breasts;
that you may drink deeply with
    delight
  from the abundance of her glory."

12 For thus says the LORD:
"Behold, I will extend prosperity to
    her like a river,
  and the wealth of the nations like
    an overflowing stream;
and you shall suck, you shall be
    carried upon her hip,
  and dandled upon her knees.
13 As one whom his mother comforts,
  so I will comfort you;
you shall be comforted in
    Jerusalem.
14 You shall see, and your heart shall
    rejoice;
  your bones shall flourish like the
    grass;
and it shall be known that the hand
  of the LORD is with his
    servants,

and his indignation is against his
    enemies.

15 "For behold, the LORD will come in
    fire,
  and his chariots like the
    stormwind,
to render his anger in fury,
  and his rebuke with flames of fire.
16 For by fire will the LORD execute
    judgment,
  and by his sword, upon all flesh;
  and those slain by the LORD shall
    be many.

17 "Those who sanctify and purify themselves to go into the gardens, following one in the midst, eating swine's flesh and the abomination and mice, shall come to an end together, says the LORD.

18 "For I know[e] their works and their thoughts, and I am[f] coming to gather all nations and tongues; and they shall come and shall see my glory, 19 and I will set a sign among them. And from them I will send survivors to the nations, to Tarshish, Put,[g] and Lud, who draw the bow, to Tubal and Javan, to the coastlands afar off, that have not heard my fame or seen my glory; and they shall declare my glory among the nations. 20 And they shall bring all your brethren from all the nations as an offering to the LORD, upon horses, and in chariots, and in litters, and upon mules, and upon dromedaries, to my holy mountain Jerusalem, says the LORD, just as the Israelites bring their cereal offering in a clean vessel to the house of the LORD. 21 And

e Gk Syr: Heb lacks *know*
f Gk Syr Vg Tg: Heb *it is*
g Gk: Heb *Pul*

divinely wrought miracle. **10–11:** Restored "Mother" Jerusalem can provide abundantly for all (49.17–21). **12–14:** Continuation of the vision of Jerusalem's prosperity and comfort. **15–16:** With *fire* (29.6; 64.11) and *sword* (31.8; Ezek. ch. 21), God will destroy his enemies. **17:** Compare vv. 3–4. *In the midst*, perhaps in a pagan procession. **18–24:** The return of Israel and the fate of the wicked. **18–21:** God will reveal his glory to the nations. They with Israel will assemble in Jerusalem, some Gentiles even becoming priests. **22–23:** A magnificent climax: God's people, like the new creation, will endure forever (Jer.31.34–36) and a mighty chorus of praises will ceaselessly rise to God's throne. **24:** Final reminder of the eternal punishment of the wicked.

some of them also I will take for priests
and for Levites, says the LORD.

22 "For as the new heavens and the new
　　earth
　which I will make
　shall remain before me, says the
　　LORD;
　so shall your descendants and
　　your name remain.
23 From new moon to new moon,

and from sabbath to sabbath,
all flesh shall come to worship before
　me,
says the LORD.

24 "And they shall go forth and look
on the dead bodies of the men that
have rebelled against me; for their
worm shall not die, their fire shall not
be quenched, and they shall be an
abhorrence to all flesh."

THE BOOK OF JEREMIAH

Jeremiah was a descendant of the priest Abiathar, who was banished by Solomon to Anathoth (1 Kg.2.26,27; compare 1 Sam.3.10–14). His ministry began in 627 B.C. and ended sometime after 580, probably in Egypt.

The book bearing his name consists essentially of a collection of oracles against Judah and Jerusalem which he dictated to his aide Baruch (1.4–6.30, from the time of Josiah; 7.1–20.18, from the time of Jehoiakim; 21.1–25.14, from the time of Zedekiah), Baruch's memoirs (chs. 26–35; 36–45), and a group of oracles against foreign nations (25.15–38; chs. 46–51), together with an introduction (1.1–3) and an historical appendix (ch. 52). Some other materials were added when the book was edited sometime after 560 B.C. In general a chronological order is followed in the two main sections of the book (1.4–25.14; chs. 26–45), but because of the editing, some materials are now misplaced.

The present Hebrew text differs from the Greek version (the Septuagint) in both content and order. The Septuagint omits several passages (e.g. 33.14–26) and combines the oracles against the foreign nations into a single section following 25.14, though in a different order.

Jeremiah is much concerned with rewards and punishment, the recompense for good and evil, faithfulness and disobedience (see ch. 35). He criticized Judah for its worship of gods other than the LORD, with all the attendant evils in cult and daily life. God's covenant people must return to him. The judgment must come, but the ominous future (later, the unhappy present) would be replaced by a new and more enduring relationship with God.

THE WORDS OF JEREMIAH, THE SON of Hilki'ah, of the priests who were in An'athoth in the land of Benjamin, [2] to whom the word of the LORD came in the days of Josi'ah the son of Amon, king of Judah, in the thirteenth year of his reign. [3] It came also in the days of Jehoi'akim the son of Josi'ah, king of Judah, and until the end of the eleventh year of Zedeki'ah, the son of Josi'ah, king of Judah, until the captivity of Jerusalem in the fifth month.

4 Now the word of the LORD came to me saying,
[5] "Before I formed you in the womb
  I knew you,
and before you were born I
  consecrated you;
I appointed you a prophet to the
  nations."
[6] Then I said, "Ah, Lord GOD! Behold, I do not know how to speak, for I am only a youth." [7] But the LORD said to me,
"Do not say, 'I am only a youth';
for to all to whom I send you you
  shall go,
and whatever I command you you
  shall speak.
[8] Be not afraid of them,
for I am with you to deliver you,
  says the LORD."
[9] Then the LORD put forth his hand and touched my mouth; and the LORD said to me,
"Behold, I have put my words in
  your mouth.
[10] See, I have set you this day over
  nations and over kingdoms,
to pluck up and to break down,
to destroy and to overthrow,
to build and to plant."

1.1–3 Superscription. 1: *Words*, i.e. "history." The name *Jeremiah* means "The LORD [Yahweh] exalts." *Priests . . . in Anathoth*, see Introduction. Anathoth is located at modern Ras Kharrubeh about two miles northeast of Jerusalem. 2: *Thirteenth year of Josiah*, 627 B.C. 3: *Eleventh year of Zedekiah*, 587 B.C.

1.4–19: Jeremiah's call and related visions. 4: *Word of the LORD*, characteristic expression in Jeremiah, perhaps emphasizing that his message is God's word. 5: *Knew*, in the Biblical sense, a profound and intimate knowledge. *To the nations*, Assyria, Babylonia, Egypt, Judah. 6–8: God's support will supplement Jeremiah's inexperience (*youth*). 9: Compare 15.19; Mt.10.19–20. 10: God's word is a dynamic and vital force, not a static and symbolic figure (Is.55.10–11).

11 And the word of the LORD came to me, saying, "Jeremiah, what do you see?" And I said, "I see a rod of almond."*a* 12 Then the LORD said to me, "You have seen well, for I am watching*b* over my word to perform it."

13 The word of the LORD came to me a second time, saying, "What do you see?" And I said, "I see a boiling pot, facing away from the north." 14 Then the LORD said to me, "Out of the north evil shall break forth upon all the inhabitants of the land. 15 For, lo, I am calling all the tribes of the kingdoms of the north, says the LORD; and they shall come and every one shall set his throne at the entrance of the gates of Jerusalem, against all its walls round about, and against all the cities of Judah. 16 And I will utter my judgments against them, for all their wickedness in forsaking me; they have burned incense to other gods, and worshiped the works of their own hands. 17 But you, gird up your loins; arise, and say to them everything that I command you. Do not be dismayed by them, lest I dismay you before them. 18 And I, behold, I make you this day a fortified city, an iron pillar, and bronze walls, against the whole land, against the kings of Judah, its princes, its priests, and the people of the land. 19 They will fight against you; but they shall not prevail against you, for I am with you, says the LORD, to deliver you."

2 The word of the LORD came to me, saying, 2 "Go and proclaim in the hearing of Jerusalem, Thus says the LORD,

I remember the devotion of your youth,

your love as a bride,
how you followed me in the
　　wilderness,
in a land not sown.
3 Israel was holy to the LORD,
　　the first fruits of his harvest.
All who ate of it became guilty;
　　evil came upon them,
　　　　　　says the LORD."

4 Hear the word of the LORD, O house of Jacob, and all the families of the house of Israel. 5 Thus says the LORD:
"What wrong did your fathers find in
　　me
　　that they went far from me,
and went after worthlessness, and
　　became worthless?
6 They did not say, 'Where is the
　　LORD
　　who brought us up from the land
　　　　of Egypt,
who led us in the wilderness,
　　in a land of deserts and pits,
in a land of drought and deep
　　darkness,
　　in a land that none passes through,
　　where no man dwells?'
7 And I brought you into a plentiful
　　land
　　to enjoy its fruits and its good
　　　　things.
But when you came in you defiled
　　my land,
　　and made my heritage an
　　　　abomination.
8 The priests did not say, 'Where is
　　the LORD?'
　　Those who handle the law did not
　　　　know me;
the rulers*c* transgressed against me;

a Heb *shaqed*　　b Heb *shoqed*　　c Heb *shepherds*

11–12: Play on words (see notes *a* and *b*) to encourage the hesitant young prophet in the face of certain opposition. **13–14:** *Facing away from the north*, the meaning of the Hebrew is uncertain; this translation implies that the pot was spilling its hot contents toward the south, symbolizing the trouble which would come from the north. Another view is that the draft on the fire came from the north. Invaders into Palestine often came from *the north*. **17–19:** An expansion of the thought in vv. 4–8.
　　2.1–37: The apostasy of Israel. 1–3: God defended *his bride* (comparing the Sinai covenant with the marriage vow, see Hos.2.16) against all attempts to violate her (Amalekites, Canaanites, Philistines, etc.). **4–9:** God remained unwaveringly faithful, despite Israel's rebellion. **8:** *Priests* and *law* suggest a time during Josiah's reform. After Josiah's death, Jeremiah attacked

the prophets prophesied by Ba'al,
and went after things that do not
  profit.

9 "Therefore I still contend with you,
                    says the LORD,
and with your children's children
  I will contend.
10 For cross to the coasts of Cyprus
    and see,
  or send to Kedar and examine with
    care;
  see if there has been such a thing.
11 Has a nation changed its gods,
  even though they are no gods?
But my people have changed their
    glory
  for that which does not profit.
12 Be appalled, O heavens, at this,
  be shocked, be utterly desolate,
                    says the LORD,
13 for my people have committed two
    evils:
  they have forsaken me,
the fountain of living waters,
  and hewed out cisterns for
    themselves,
broken cisterns,
  that can hold no water.

14 "Is Israel a slave? Is he a homeborn
    servant?
  Why then has he become a prey?
15 The lions have roared against him,
  they have roared loudly.
They have made his land a waste;
  his cities are in ruins, without
    inhabitant.
16 Moreover, the men of Memphis and
    Tah'panhes
  have broken the crown of your
    head.

17 Have you not brought this upon
    yourself
  by forsaking the LORD your God,
    when he led you in the way?
18 And now what do you gain by going
    to Egypt,
  to drink the waters of the Nile?
Or what do you gain by going to
    Assyria,
  to drink the waters of the
    Euphra'tes?
19 Your wickedness will chasten you,
  and your apostasy will reprove
    you.
Know and see that it is evil and
    bitter
  for you to forsake the LORD your
    God;
  the fear of me is not in you,
            says the Lord GOD of hosts.

20 "For long ago you broke your yoke
    and burst your bonds;
  and you said, 'I will not serve.'
Yea, upon every high hill
  and under every green tree
  you bowed down as a harlot.
21 Yet I planted you a choice vine,
  wholly of pure seed.
How then have you turned
    degenerate
  and become a wild vine?
22 Though you wash yourself with lye
  and use much soap,
  the stain of your guilt is still
    before me,
                    says the Lord GOD.
23 How can you say, 'I am not defiled,
  I have not gone after the
    Ba'als'?
Look at your way in the valley;
  know what you have done—

---

the prophets primarily (ch. 23). **10–13:** The LORD calls (upon the heavenly assembly [?]; compare Is.1.2; Mic.6.1) to witness the folly unprecedented (8.4) in both West (*Cyprus*) and East
(*Kedar*) of a people who forsake the *fountain of living waters* (Jn.4.10–15; 7.38) for the stagnant
water at the bottom of a leaky *cistern*. **14–19:** Israel has forsaken her covenant birthright of
responsible freedom to become a slave of Assyria (*the lions*) and Egypt (*Memphis*, the capital
of northern Egypt, fourteen miles south of Cairo) bringing disgrace (with v. 16b compare
Is.3.17; 7.20) upon themselves. **16,18:** Compare v. 36. **20–28:** Unfaithful Israel is compared to
a stubborn ox, to a wild vine (Is.5.1–7; Hos.10.1) germinating from good seed but now in-
explicably and irremediably worthless, to a nymphomaniacal prostitute (Hos.4.13) who rest-
lessly seeks satisfaction from anyone and yet denies her guilt in spite of evidence (such as human
sacrifice *in the valley*), and to a thief who is remorseful only when confronted by evidence of his

a restive young camel interlacing her
    tracks,
²⁴ a wild ass used to the wilderness,
    in her heat sniffing the wind!
    Who can restrain her lust?
None who seek her need weary
    themselves;
    in her month they will find her.
²⁵ Keep your feet from going unshod
    and your throat from thirst.
But you said, 'It is hopeless,
    for I have loved strangers,
    and after them I will go.'

²⁶ "As a thief is shamed when caught,
    so the house of Israel shall be
    shamed:
they, their kings, their princes,
    their priests, and their prophets,
²⁷ who say to a tree, 'You are my
    father,'
    and to a stone, 'You gave me
    birth.'
For they have turned their back to
    me,
    and not their face.
But in the time of their trouble they
    say,
    'Arise and save us!'
²⁸ But where are your gods
    that you made for yourself?
Let them arise, if they can save you,
    in your time of trouble;
for as many as your cities
    are your gods, O Judah.

²⁹ "Why do you complain against me?
    You have all rebelled against me,
        says the LORD.
³⁰ In vain have I smitten your children,
    they took no correction;
your own sword devoured your
    prophets
    like a ravening lion.
³¹ And you, O generation, heed the
    word of the LORD.

Have I been a wilderness to Israel,
    or a land of thick darkness?
Why then do my people say, 'We are
    free,
    we will come no more to thee'?
³² Can a maiden forget her
    ornaments,
    or a bride her attire?
Yet my people have forgotten me
    days without number.

³³ "How well you direct your course
    to seek lovers!
So that even to wicked women
    you have taught your ways.
³⁴ Also on your skirts is found
    the lifeblood of guiltless poor;
you did not find them breaking in.
    Yet in spite of all these things
³⁵ you say, 'I am innocent;
    surely his anger has turned from
    me.'
Behold, I will bring you to judgment
    for saying, 'I have not sinned.'
³⁶ How lightly you gad about,
    changing your way!
You shall be put to shame by Egypt
    as you were put to shame by
    Assyria.
³⁷ From it too you will come away
    with your hands upon your head,
for the LORD has rejected those in
    whom you trust,
    and you will not prosper by them.

3 "If^d a man divorces his wife
    and she goes from him
and becomes another man's wife,
    will he return to her?
Would not that land be greatly
    polluted?
You have played the harlot with
    many lovers;
    and would you return to me?
        says the LORD.

d Gk Syr: Heb *Saying, If*

wrong-doing (such as the *tree* or Asherah and the *stone* or sacred pillar, both cult furnishings).
Let their gods now rescue Israel in her time of need! **29–31:** Israel rejected God's correction
and leadership, even killing his prophets (1 Kg.19.10; 2 Kg.21.16). **32:** See vv. 2–3. **33–37:**
Undeniable evidence accuses her. In shame and sorrow (*hands upon your head*), abandoned by
her lovers (*Egypt* and *Assyria*), faithless Israel will stand alone and condemned before God.
    3.1–4.4: Exhortations to repent. 3.1–5: Judah's sin surpasses anything envisioned by the law
(Dt.24.1–4). Though there is a drought in the land (14.1–6) she does not abandon her indiscriminate harlotry (2.20); she can expect no re-acceptance (contrast vv. 6–13). **1:** *Land,* the

² Lift up your eyes to the bare heights,
    and see!
Where have you not been lain
    with?
By the waysides you have sat
    awaiting lovers
like an Arab in the wilderness.
You have polluted the land
    with your vile harlotry.
³ Therefore the showers have been
    withheld,
and the spring rain has not come;
yet you have a harlot's brow,
    you refuse to be ashamed.
⁴ Have you not just now called to me,
    'My father, thou art the friend of
    my youth—
⁵ will he be angry for ever,
    will he be indignant to the end?'
Behold, you have spoken,
    but you have done all the evil
    that you could."

6 The LORD said to me in the days of King Josi'ah: "Have you seen what she did, that faithless one, Israel, how she went up on every high hill and under every green tree, and there played the harlot? ⁷ And I thought, 'After she has done all this she will return to me'; but she did not return, and her false sister Judah saw it. ⁸ She saw that for all the adulteries of that faithless one, Israel, I had sent her away with a decree of divorce; yet her false sister Judah did not fear, but she too went and played the harlot. ⁹ Because harlotry was so light to her, she polluted the land, committing adultery with stone and tree. ¹⁰ Yet for all this her false sister Judah did not return to me with her whole heart, but in pretense, says the LORD."

11 And the LORD said to me, "Faithless Israel has shown herself less

guilty than false Judah. ¹² Go, and proclaim these words toward the north, and say,
'Return, faithless Israel,
               says the LORD.
I will not look on you in anger,
    for I am merciful,
               says the LORD;
I will not be angry for ever.
¹³ Only acknowledge your guilt,
    that you rebelled against the LORD
    your God
and scattered your favors among
    strangers under every green
    tree,
and that you have not obeyed my
    voice,
               says the LORD.
¹⁴ Return, O faithless children,
               says the LORD;
for I am your master;
I will take you, one from a city and
    two from a family,
and I will bring you to Zion.

15 " 'And I will give you shepherds after my own heart, who will feed you with knowledge and understanding. ¹⁶ And when you have multiplied and increased in the land, in those days, says the LORD, they shall no more say, "The ark of the covenant of the LORD." It shall not come to mind, or be remembered, or missed; it shall not be made again. ¹⁷ At that time Jerusalem shall be called the throne of the LORD, and all nations shall gather to it, to the presence of the LORD in Jerusalem, and they shall no more stubbornly follow their own evil heart. ¹⁸ In those days the house of Judah shall join the house of Israel, and together they shall come from the land of the north to the land that I gave your fathers for a heritage.
¹⁹ " 'I thought
how I would set you among my
    sons,

Septuagint reads "woman." **6–14:** The return of Israel. This oracle, although by Jeremiah (some scholars disagree), is intrusive here. Compare chs. 30–31; Ezek. chs. 16; 23. Because of her unheeding unfaithfulness (Hos.2.20) God sent Israel into exile (with a *decree of divorce*, Dt. 24.1–4), but Judah's guilt is worse; she failed to learn from Israel's experience. Somewhat inconsistent with vv. 1–5, Israel is invited to repent and return. **15–18:** Return from exile and reunion of Israel and Judah under faithful rulers. This oracle is probably later than the rest of the section. **15:** *Shepherds*, rulers. **16–17:** Jerusalem will replace the *ark* as the symbol of

and give you a pleasant land,
  a heritage most beauteous of all
   nations.
And I thought you would call me,
   My Father,
  and would not turn from
   following me.
²⁰ Surely, as a faithless wife leaves her
   husband,
  so have you been faithless to me,
   O house of Israel,
              says the LORD.' "

²¹ A voice on the bare heights is heard,
   the weeping and pleading of
   Israel's sons,
  because they have perverted their
   way,
   they have forgotten the LORD
   their God.
²² "Return, O faithless sons,
   I will heal your faithlessness."
  "Behold, we come to thee;
   for thou art the LORD our God.
²³ Truly the hills are a delusion,
   the orgies on the mountains.
  Truly in the LORD our God
   is the salvation of Israel.

24 "But from our youth the shameful thing has devoured all for which
our fathers labored, their flocks and
their herds, their sons and their daughters. ²⁵ Let us lie down in our shame,
and let our dishonor cover us; for we
have sinned against the LORD our
God, we and our fathers, from our
youth even to this day; and we have
not obeyed the voice of the LORD our
God."

4 "If you return, O Israel,
              says the LORD,
  to me you should return.

If you remove your abominations
  from my presence,
  and do not waver,
² and if you swear, 'As the LORD lives,'
  in truth, in justice, and in
   uprightness,
  then nations shall bless themselves
   in him,
  and in him shall they glory."
3 For thus says the LORD to the men
of Judah and to the inhabitants of
Jerusalem:
  "Break up your fallow ground,
   and sow not among thorns.
⁴ Circumcise yourselves to the LORD,
   remove the foreskin of your
   hearts,
  O men of Judah and inhabitants
   of Jerusalem;
  lest my wrath go forth like fire,
   and burn with none to quench it,
  because of the evil of your
   doings."

5 Declare in Judah, and proclaim in
Jerusalem, and say,
  "Blow the trumpet through the land;
   cry aloud and say,
  'Assemble, and let us go
   into the fortified cities!'
⁶ Raise a standard toward Zion,
   flee for safety, stay not,
  for I bring evil from the north,
   and great destruction.
⁷ A lion has gone up from his thicket,
   a destroyer of nations has set out;
  he has gone forth from his place
  to make your land a waste;
   your cities will be ruins
   without inhabitant.
⁸ For this gird you with sackcloth,
   lament and wail;
  for the fierce anger of the LORD

---

the *throne of God* (14.21; 17.12). **19–20:** These verses continue vv. 1–5. Contrary to custom
(Num.27.1–8) God would have made "his daughter" Judah his heir, but her faithlessness
renders this impossible. **3.21–4.4:** From the *heights*, sites of futile idolatry, come cries of profound repentance (vv. 12–14) and resolve to return to God (Hos.14.2–3). The conditions of
repentance are removal of pagan shrines, recognition of God's exclusive claim by swearing in
his name only (4.2b), and cleansing of hearts. **3–4:** Compare 9.26; Hos.10.12; Rom.2.25–29.
   4.5–31: The foe from the north, a recurring theme of Jeremiah (1.13–14; 5.15–17; 6.1–5; etc.).
5–12: Sound the alarm! Muster for the defense (6.1–8)! Like a beast of prey, the foe approaches
(5.6)! Courage will fail the leaders of the people who have ignored all warnings of impending
doom (6.13–15; 14.13–16; 23.16–17). God's judgment will sweep over the land like the *hot*

has not turned back from us."

9 "In that day, says the LORD, courage shall fail both king and princes; the priests shall be appalled and the prophets astounded." 10 Then I said, "Ah, Lord GOD, surely thou hast utterly deceived this people and Jerusalem, saying, 'It shall be well with you'; whereas the sword has reached their very life."

11 At that time it will be said to this people and to Jerusalem, "A hot wind from the bare heights in the desert toward the daughter of my people, not to winnow or cleanse, 12 a wind too full for this comes for me. Now it is I who speak in judgment upon them."
13 Behold, he comes up like clouds,
    his chariots like the whirlwind;
his horses are swifter than eagles—
    woe to us, for we are ruined!
14 O Jerusalem, wash your heart from
    wickedness,
    that you may be saved.
How long shall your evil thoughts
    lodge within you?
15 For a voice declares from Dan
    and proclaims evil from Mount
      E'phraim.
16 Warn the nations that he is coming;
    announce to Jerusalem,
"Besiegers come from a distant land;
    they shout against the cities of
      Judah.
17 Like keepers of a field are they
    against her round about,
    because she has rebelled against
      me,
               says the LORD.
18 Your ways and your doings
    have brought this upon you.
This is your doom, and it is bitter;
    it has reached your very heart."

19 My anguish, my anguish! I writhe
    in pain!
Oh, the walls of my heart!
My heart is beating wildly;
    I cannot keep silent;
for I hear the sound of the trumpet,
    the alarm of war.
20 Disaster follows hard on disaster,
    the whole land is laid waste.
Suddenly my tents are destroyed,
    my curtains in a moment.
21 How long must I see the standard,
    and hear the sound of the
      trumpet?
22 "For my people are foolish,
    they know me not;
they are stupid children,
    they have no understanding.
They are skilled in doing evil,
    but how to do good they know
      not."

23 I looked on the earth, and lo, it
    was waste and void;
and to the heavens, and they had
    no light.
24 I looked on the mountains, and lo,
    they were quaking,
and all the hills moved to and fro.
25 I looked, and lo, there was no man,
    and all the birds of the air had
      fled.
26 I looked, and lo, the fruitful land
    was a desert,
and all its cities were laid in ruins
    before the LORD, before his fierce
      anger.
27 For thus says the LORD, "The whole land shall be a desolation; yet I will not make a full end.
28 For this the earth shall mourn,
    and the heavens above be black;
for I have spoken, I have purposed;
    I have not relented nor will I turn
      back."

---

desert wind (the sirocco), desiccating everything before it (18.17). **13–18:** Swiftly, like the eagle and the stormwind, the chariotry and cavalry of the enemy approach. Communiqués trace this advance from *Dan* (8.16), through *Mount Ephraim* (central Palestine), *Benjamin* (6.1) into Judah's heartland. **19–22:** Though the people are foolish and stupid (5.2–3), the prophet laments the sudden disaster which has destroyed his beloved land like the striking of a tent (10.19–21). **23–28:** In a vision, the prophet sees the terrifying results of God's irrevocable judgment (7.16; 15.1–4). As if struck by a mighty nuclear bomb, the earth has been returned to its primeval state: waste and void (Gen.1.2). **29–31:** Like a rejected prostitute (3.2–3), like a woman

29 At the noise of horseman and archer
    every city takes to flight;
  they enter thickets; they climb among
      rocks;
    all the cities are forsaken,
    and no man dwells in them.
30 And you, O desolate one,
  what do you mean that you dress in
      scarlet,
    that you deck yourself with
      ornaments of gold,
    that you enlarge your eyes with
      paint?
In vain you beautify yourself.
  Your lovers despise you;
  they seek your life.
31 For I heard a cry as of a woman in
    travail,
  anguish as of one bringing forth
    her first child,
the cry of the daughter of Zion
    gasping for breath,
  stretching out her hands,
"Woe is me! I am fainting before
  murderers."

5 Run to and fro through the
    streets of Jerusalem,
  look and take note!
Search her squares to see
  if you can find a man,
one who does justice
  and seeks truth;
  that I may pardon her.
2 Though they say, "As the LORD
    lives,"
  yet they swear falsely.
3 O LORD, do not thy eyes look for
    truth?
Thou hast smitten them,
  but they felt no anguish;
thou hast consumed them,
  but they refused to take
    correction.

They have made their faces harder
    than rock;
  they have refused to repent.
4 Then I said, "These are only the
    poor,
  they have no sense;
for they do not know the way of the
    LORD,
  the law of their God.
5 I will go to the great,
  and will speak to them;
for they know the way of the LORD,
  the law of their God."
But they all alike had broken the
    yoke,
  they had burst the bonds.

6 Therefore a lion from the forest
    shall slay them,
  a wolf from the desert shall
    destroy them.
A leopard is watching against their
    cities,
  every one who goes out of them
    shall be torn in pieces;
because their transgressions are
    many,
  their apostasies are great.

7 "How can I pardon you?
  Your children have forsaken me,
  and have sworn by those who are
    no gods.
When I fed them to the full,
  they committed adultery
  and trooped to the houses of
    harlots.
8 They were well-fed lusty stallions,
  each neighing for his neighbor's
    wife.
9 Shall I not punish them for these
    things?
              says the LORD;
  and shall I not avenge myself

---

in the anguish of childbirth, like a victim helpless before her murderer, Jerusalem, the daughter of Zion, stretches out her hands in futile appeal and suffers her death throes–alone.

5.1–6.30: The corruptions for which judgment is coming. 1–6: Jeremiah is commanded to search carefully for a faithful man (6.9–10). If one could be found, the LORD would pardon (Gen.18.23–33). He seeks among the "little people" (*poor*), but finds none–perhaps they know no better. He seeks among the privileged *great*, but there is none there either (compare Mt.19.23–25). Therefore beasts of prey will be unleashed against this wayward people (2,15; 4.7; Hab.1.8). **7–11:** God has no alternative in the face of rampant idolatry (2.11) and immorality (v. 29; 9.9).

on a nation such as this?

¹⁰ "Go up through her vine-rows and
destroy,
but make not a full end;
strip away her branches,
for they are not the LORD's.
¹¹ For the house of Israel and the house
of Judah
have been utterly faithless to me,
says the LORD.
¹² They have spoken falsely of the
LORD,
and have said, 'He will do
nothing;
no evil will come upon us,
nor shall we see sword or famine.
¹³ The prophets will become wind;
the word is not in them.
Thus shall it be done to them!' "

¹⁴ Therefore thus says the LORD, the
God of hosts:
"Because they*ᵉ* have spoken this
word,
behold, I am making my words in
your mouth a fire,
and this people wood, and the
fire shall devour them.
¹⁵ Behold, I am bringing upon you
a nation from afar, O house of
Israel,
says the LORD.
It is an enduring nation,
it is an ancient nation,
a nation whose language you do not
know,
nor can you understand what they
say.
¹⁶ Their quiver is like an open tomb,
they are all mighty men.
¹⁷ They shall eat up your harvest and
your food;

they shall eat up your sons and
your daughters;
they shall eat up your flocks and your
herds;
they shall eat up your vines and
your fig trees;
your fortified cities in which you trust
they shall destroy with the sword."

18 "But even in those days, says the
LORD, I will not make a full end of
you. ¹⁹ And when your people say,
'Why has the LORD our God done all
these things to us?' you shall say to
them, 'As you have forsaken me and
served foreign gods in your land, so
you shall serve strangers in a land
that is not yours.' "

²⁰ Declare this in the house of Jacob,
proclaim it in Judah:
²¹ "Hear this, O foolish and senseless
people,
who have eyes, but see not,
who have ears, but hear not.
²² Do you not fear me? says the LORD;
Do you not tremble before me?
I placed the sand as the bound for
the sea,
a perpetual barrier which it
cannot pass;
though the waves toss, they cannot
prevail,
though they roar, they cannot pass
over it.
²³ But this people has a stubborn and
rebellious heart;
they have turned aside and
gone away.
²⁴ They do not say in their hearts,
'Let us fear the LORD our God,
who gives the rain in its season,

e Heb *you*

The LORD's choice vineyard has grown wild and must be destroyed (2.20–21; Is.5.1–7). **12–17:**
The judgment. The prophetic words which the people had ignored as *wind* will be revealed as
the consuming *word* of God. God is not powerless (Pss.10.4; 14.1) but will bring upon them
the ravages of a vicious invader. **18–19:** A recurring comment (9.12–14; 16.10–13; 22.8–9),
modifying Jeremiah's customary warnings of total destruction (vv. 16–17; 13.13–14). **20–25:**
Judah's foolish stubbornness has closed her eyes and ears to the manifest acts of God (Pr.1.7;
Is.6.9–10; Mt.13.10–15). **22:** Perhaps a reflection of the ancient myth of a deity's conquest of
the mighty monster, the primordial sea (Job.38.8–11; Ps.104.6–9; compare Is.51.9–10). **24b:**
The seven weeks from Passover to Pentecost (Dt.16.9–10) when rain could ruin the harvest

the autumn rain and the spring
rain,
and keeps for us
the weeks appointed for the
harvest.'
25 Your iniquities have turned these
away,
and your sins have kept good from
you.
26 For wicked men are found among
my people;
they lurk like fowlers lying in
wait.*f*
They set a trap;
they catch men.
27 Like a basket full of birds,
their houses are full of treachery;
therefore they have become great
and rich,
28 they have grown fat and sleek.
They know no bounds in deeds of
wickedness;
they judge not with justice
the cause of the fatherless, to make
it prosper,
and they do not defend the rights
of the needy.
29 Shall I not punish them for these
things?
says the LORD,
and shall I not avenge myself
on a nation such as this?"

30 An appalling and horrible thing
has happened in the land:
31 the prophets prophesy falsely,
and the priests rule at their
direction;
my people love to have it so,
but what will you do when the end
comes?

6 Flee for safety, O people of
Benjamin,
from the midst of Jerusalem!
Blow the trumpet in Teko'a,

and raise a signal on
Beth-hacche'rem;
for evil looms out of the north,
and great destruction.
2 The comely and delicately bred I will
destroy,
the daughter of Zion.
3 Shepherds with their flocks shall
come against her;
they shall pitch their tents around
her,
they shall pasture, each in his
place.
4 "Prepare war against her;
up, and let us attack at noon!"
"Woe to us, for the day declines,
for the shadows of evening
lengthen!"
5 "Up, and let us attack by night,
and destroy her palaces!"

6 For thus says the LORD of hosts:
"Hew down her trees;
cast up a siege mound against
Jerusalem.
This is the city which must be
punished;
there is nothing but oppression
within her.
7 As a well keeps its water fresh,
so she keeps fresh her
wickedness;
violence and destruction are heard
within her;
sickness and wounds are ever
before me.
8 Be warned, O Jerusalem,
lest I be alienated from you;
lest I make you a desolation,
an uninhabited land."

9 Thus says the LORD of hosts:
"Glean*g* thoroughly as a vine
the remnant of Israel;

f Heb uncertain
g Cn: Heb *they shall glean*

(1 Sam.12.16–18). **26–31**: Judah must be punished (v. 9) for her tolerance of those who grow wealthy by defrauding the defenseless (Dt.24.17–18; Am.2.6–7) like fowlers catching hapless birds in nets and putting them in baskets, and especially for her hearty approval of the perversity of priest and prophet (6.13–15; 23.9–22; Mic.3.5–8). **6.1–8**: The foe approaches from the north. **1**: *Tekoa*, twelve miles south of Jerusalem; *Beth-haccherem*, modern Ramet Rahel, two miles south of Jerusalem. **3**: *Shepherds with their flocks*, kings with their armies (compare 1.15; 12.10). **4**: *Prepare*, more literally, "sanctify" (see Jl.3.9 note *f*). **9–15**: Jerusalem's obduracy.

like a grape-gatherer pass your hand
again
over its branches."
10 To whom shall I speak and give
warning,
that they may hear?
Behold, their ears are closed,[h]
they cannot listen;
behold, the word of the LORD is
to them an object of scorn,
they take no pleasure in it.
11 Therefore I am full of the wrath
of the LORD;
I am weary of holding it in.
"Pour it out upon the children in the
street,
and upon the gatherings of young
men, also;
both husband and wife shall be taken,
the old folk and the very aged.
12 Their houses shall be turned over
to others,
their fields and wives together;
for I will stretch out my hand
against the inhabitants of the
land,"
           says the LORD.
13 "For from the least to the greatest
of them,
every one is greedy for unjust
gain;
and from prophet to priest,
every one deals falsely.
14 They have healed the wound of my
people lightly,
saying, 'Peace, peace,'
when there is no peace.
15 Were they ashamed when they
committed abomination?
No, they were not at all ashamed;
they did not know how to blush.
Therefore they shall fall among
those who fall;
at the time that I punish them,
they shall be overthrown,"
           says the LORD.

16 Thus says the LORD:
"Stand by the roads, and look,
and ask for the ancient paths,
where the good way is; and walk
in it,
and find rest for your souls.
But they said, 'We will not walk in it.'
17 I set watchmen over you, saying,
'Give heed to the sound of the
trumpet!'
But they said, 'We will not give heed.'
18 Therefore hear, O nations,
and know, O congregation, what
will happen to them.
19 Hear, O earth; behold, I am
bringing evil upon this people,
the fruit of their devices,
because they have not given heed to
my words;
and as for my law, they have
rejected it.
20 To what purpose does frankincense
come to me from Sheba,
or sweet cane from a distant land?
Your burnt offerings are not
acceptable,
nor your sacrifices pleasing to me.
21 Therefore thus says the LORD:
'Behold, I will lay before this people
stumbling blocks against which
they shall stumble;
fathers and sons together,
neighbor and friend shall
perish.' "

22 Thus says the LORD:
"Behold, a people is coming from
the north country,
a great nation is stirring from the
farthest parts of the earth.
23 They lay hold on bow and spear,
they are cruel and have no mercy,
the sound of them is like the
roaring sea;
they ride upon horses,

h Heb *uncircumcised*

Jeremiah is to search meticulously for a God-fearing person (5.1), but he finds none (20.7–18;
Mic.7.1–2). God will pour out his wrath (Is.5.25; Ezek.6.14) upon the impenitent people,
especially on the leaders who promised material and spiritual well-being (*peace*) when none
was to be had (8.10–12; Ezek.13.10–11). **16–21:** Jerusalem is without excuse. God gave his
covenant and instruction (*paths, my law*) and sent his prophets (*watchmen, my words;* compare
Hos.9.8) but both were ignored. The finest and rarest offerings (*frankincense, sweet cane*) are
no substitute for faithfulness (7.21–23; Am.5.21–24). *Sheba,* southwest Arabia. **22–26:** The foe

set in array as a man for battle,
  against you, O daughter of Zion!"
²⁴ We have heard the report of it,
  our hands fall helpless;
anguish has taken hold of us,
  pain as of a woman in travail.
²⁵ Go not forth into the field,
  nor walk on the road;
for the enemy has a sword,
  terror is on every side.
²⁶ O daughter of my people, gird on
    sackcloth,
  and roll in ashes;
make mourning as for an only son,
  most bitter lamentation;
for suddenly the destroyer
  will come upon us.

²⁷ "I have made you an assayer and
    tester among my people,
  that you may know and assay
    their ways.
²⁸ They are all stubbornly rebellious,
  going about with slanders;
they are bronze and iron,
  all of them act corruptly.
²⁹ The bellows blow fiercely,
  the lead is consumed by the fire;
in vain the refining goes on,
  for the wicked are not removed.
³⁰ Refuse silver they are called,
  for the LORD has rejected them."

7 The word that came to Jeremiah
  from the LORD: ² "Stand in the
gate of the LORD's house, and proclaim
there this word, and say, Hear the
word of the LORD, all you men of Judah
who enter these gates to worship the
LORD. ³ Thus says the LORD of hosts,

the God of Israel, Amend your ways
and your doings, and I will let you dwell
in this place. ⁴ Do not trust in these
deceptive words: 'This is the temple
of the LORD, the temple of the LORD,
the temple of the LORD.'

5 "For if you truly amend your
ways and your doings, if you truly execute justice one with another, ⁶ if you
do not oppress the alien, the fatherless
or the widow, or shed innocent blood
in this place, and if you do not go after
other gods to your own hurt, ⁷ then I
will let you dwell in this place, in the
land that I gave of old to your fathers
for ever.

8 "Behold, you trust in deceptive
words to no avail. ⁹ Will you steal,
murder, commit adultery, swear falsely,
burn incense to Ba'al, and go after
other gods that you have not known,
¹⁰ and then come and stand before
me in this house, which is called by my
name, and say, 'We are delivered!'–
only to go on doing all these abominations? ¹¹ Has this house, which is
called by my name, become a den of
robbers in your eyes? Behold, I myself
have seen it, says the LORD. ¹² Go
now to my place that was in Shiloh,
where I made my name dwell at first,
and see what I did to it for the wickedness of my people Israel. ¹³ And now,
because you have done all these
things, says the LORD, and when I
spoke to you persistently you did not
listen, and when I called you, you did
not answer, ¹⁴ therefore I will do to
the house which is called by my
name, and in which you trust, and

---

from the north (4.5–8) remains unidentified (25.1–14). The approach of an invading army has,
in all ages, struck terror into the hearts of the people of the invaded land (Am.8.10; Zech.12.10).
25: *Terror on every side,* a characteristic expression of Jeremiah to describe all-encompassing
danger (20.3,10; 46.5; 49.29; Lam.2.22). **27–30:** Jeremiah, the assayer. One function of the
prophetic office was to assay the faithfulness (*silver*) of the people. Jeremiah discovers that there
is no precious metal to be found.

  7.1–15: The temple sermon (compare 26.4–6). **4:** The temple's presence was mistakenly interpreted as necessarily assuring God's protection (Is.31.4; for three-fold emphasis, compare
22.29; Is.6.3). Jeremiah disagreed (Mic.3.12); a complete moral change was required (vv. 5–6;
compare Hos.4.2; Mic.6.8). As *Shiloh* (eighteen miles north of Jerusalem), the earlier central
shrine, was destroyed (around 1050 B.C. in the days of Samuel; compare 1 Sam. chs. 4–6;
Ps.78.56–72), so also *this house,* desecrated by idolatry, will be destroyed (v. 11; compare Mt.
21.13). Immediately following this sermon, Jeremiah was arrested (see 26.8).

to the place which I gave to you and to your fathers, as I did to Shiloh. [15] And I will cast you out of my sight, as I cast out all your kinsmen, all the offspring of E'phraim.

16 "As for you, do not pray for this people, or lift up cry or prayer for them, and do not intercede with me, for I do not hear you. [17] Do you not see what they are doing in the cities of Judah and in the streets of Jerusalem? [18] The children gather wood, the fathers kindle fire, and the women knead dough, to make cakes for the queen of heaven; and they pour out drink offerings to other gods, to provoke me to anger. [19] Is it I whom they provoke? says the LORD. Is it not themselves, to their own confusion? [20] Therefore thus says the Lord GOD: Behold, my anger and my wrath will be poured out on this place, upon man and beast, upon the trees of the field and the fruit of the ground; it will burn and not be quenched."

21 Thus says the LORD of hosts, the God of Israel: "Add your burnt offerings to your sacrifices, and eat the flesh. [22] For in the day that I brought them out of the land of Egypt, I did not speak to your fathers or command them concerning burnt offerings and sacrifices. [23] But this command I gave them, 'Obey my voice, and I will be your God, and you shall be my people; and walk in all the way that I command you, that it may be well with you.' [24] But they did not obey or incline their ear, but walked in their own counsels and the stubbornness of their evil hearts, and went backward and not forward. [25] From the day that your fathers came out of the land of Egypt

to this day, I have persistently sent all my servants the prophets to them, day after day; [26] yet they did not listen to me, or incline their ear, but stiffened their neck. They did worse than their fathers.

27 "So you shall speak all these words to them, but they will not listen to you. You shall call to them, but they will not answer you. [28] And you shall say to them, 'This is the nation that did not obey the voice of the LORD their God, and did not accept discipline; truth has perished; it is cut off from their lips.

[29] Cut off your hair and cast it away;
    raise a lamentation on the bare
       heights,
for the LORD has rejected and
    forsaken
    the generation of his wrath.'

30 "For the sons of Judah have done evil in my sight, says the LORD; they have set their abominations in the house which is called by my name, to defile it. [31] And they have built the high place*i* of Topheth, which is in the valley of the son of Hinnom, to burn their sons and their daughters in the fire; which I did not command, nor did it come into my mind. [32] Therefore, behold, the days are coming, says the LORD, when it will no more be called Topheth, or the valley of the son of Hinnom, but the valley of Slaughter: for they will bury in Topheth, because there is no room elsewhere. [33] And the dead bodies of this people will be food for the birds of the air, and for the beasts of the earth; and none will frighten them away. [34] And I will make to cease

i Gk Tg: Heb *high places*

7.16–8.3: Abuses in worship. 16–20: Because of Judah's general apostasy, God forbids Jeremiah to exercise one of the functions of the prophetic office: intercession (7.16; 11.14; 15.1; compare Am.7.2,5). *Queen of heaven*, see 44.15–28 n. **21–28:** Faithfulness, not sacrifice, is required. Sacrifices are acceptable only when the right relationship exists between God and man (6.20; Ps.51.15–19). Until then, man may as well eat the flesh of the *burnt offering*, customarily incinerated (Lev. ch. 1), as well as the other offerings (Lev. ch. 3; 7.11–18). **7.29–8.3:** The fate of Judah. **29:** *Cut your hair,* a sign of mourning (16.6; Mic.1.16). **31:** The most gruesome of Israel's aberrations was the sacrifice of children (19.5; 32.35) on the burning platform (*Topheth,* 2 Kg.23.10). Strictly forbidden by God (Lev.18.21), it will eventually be recognized as murder. *Valley of the son of Hinnom,* southwest of the city joining the Kidron valley.

from the cities of Judah and from the streets of Jerusalem the voice of mirth and the voice of gladness, the voice of the bridegroom and the voice of the bride; for the land shall become a waste.

8 "At that time, says the LORD, the bones of the kings of Judah, the bones of its princes, the bones of the priests, the bones of the prophets, and the bones of the inhabitants of Jerusalem shall be brought out of their tombs; ² and they shall be spread before the sun and the moon and all the host of heaven, which they have loved and served, which they have gone after, and which they have sought and worshiped; and they shall not be gathered or buried; they shall be as dung on the surface of the ground. ³ Death shall be preferred to life by all the remnant that remains of this evil family in all the places where I have driven them, says the LORD of hosts.

4 "You shall say to them, Thus says
the LORD:
When men fall, do they not rise
again?
If one turns away, does he not
return?
5 Why then has this people turned
away
in perpetual backsliding?
They hold fast to deceit,
they refuse to return.
6 I have given heed and listened,
but they have not spoken
aright;
no man repents of his wickedness,
saying, 'What have I done?'
Every one turns to his own course,
like a horse plunging headlong
into battle.
7 Even the stork in the heavens
knows her times;

and the turtledove, swallow, and
crane^j
keep the time of their coming;
but my people know not
the ordinance of the LORD.

8 "How can you say, 'We are wise,
and the law of the LORD is with
us'?
But, behold, the false pen of the
scribes
has made it into a lie.
9 The wise men shall be put to shame,
they shall be dismayed and taken;
lo, they have rejected the word of
the LORD,
and what wisdom is in them?
10 Therefore I will give their wives to
others
and their fields to conquerors,
because from the least to the greatest
every one is greedy for unjust
gain;
from prophet to priest
every one deals falsely.
11 They have healed the wound of my
people lightly,
saying, 'Peace, peace,'
when there is no peace.
12 Were they ashamed when they
committed abomination?
No, they were not at all ashamed;
they did not know how to blush.
Therefore they shall fall among the
fallen;
when I punish them, they shall be
overthrown,
says the LORD.
13 When I would gather them, says the
LORD,
there are no grapes on the vine,
nor figs on the fig tree;
even the leaves are withered,
and what I gave them has passed
away from them."^k

_j_ The meaning of the Hebrew word is uncertain
_k_ Heb uncertain

33: Corpses as carrion were a frightful prospect for ancient man. **34:** 16.9. **8.1–2:** Jeremiah here uses biting irony.

8.4–10.25: Miscellaneous oracles. 8.4–7: Israel's incredible indifference (18.13–17). A man who falls naturally gets up; the birds follow their natural instincts; but Israel, God's people, forgets God's law. **8–9:** Word vs. law. Here Jeremiah contrasts his proclaimed *word of the* LORD with the written tradition (*law*) misinterpreted by those who administer it (*scribes;* compare 2.8). **10–12:** A doublet of 6.12–15. **13–17:** Judah, like an unfruitful *vine* or *fig tree*, will be

14 Why do we sit still?
Gather together, let us go into the
fortified cities
and perish there;
for the LORD our God has doomed
us to perish,
and has given us poisoned water
to drink,
because we have sinned against
the LORD.
15 We looked for peace, but no good
came,
for a time of healing, but behold,
terror.

16 "The snorting of their horses is
heard from Dan;
at the sound of the neighing of
their stallions
the whole land quakes.
They come and devour the land and
all that fills it,
the city and those who dwell in it.
17 For behold, I am sending among
you serpents,
adders which cannot be charmed,
and they shall bite you,"
says the LORD.

18 My grief is beyond healing,[l]
my heart is sick within me.
19 Hark, the cry of the daughter of my
people
from the length and breadth of
the land:
"Is the LORD not in Zion?
Is her King not in her?"
"Why have they provoked me to
anger with their graven images,
and with their foreign idols?"
20 "The harvest is past, the summer is
ended,
and we are not saved."

21 For the wound of the daughter of
my people is my heart wounded,
I mourn, and dismay has taken
hold on me.
22 Is there no balm in Gilead?
Is there no physician there?
Why then has the health of the
daughter of my people
not been restored?

9[m] O that my head were waters,
and my eyes a fountain of tears,
that I might weep day and night
for the slain of the daughter of
my people!
2[n] O that I had in the desert
a wayfarers' lodging place,
that I might leave my people
and go away from them!
For they are all adulterers,
a company of treacherous men.
3 They bend their tongue like a bow;
falsehood and not truth has grown
strong[o] in the land;
for they proceed from evil to evil,
and they do not know me, says the
LORD.

4 Let every one beware of his
neighbor,
and put no trust in any brother;
for every brother is a supplanter,
and every neighbor goes about as
a slanderer.
5 Every one deceives his neighbor,
and no one speaks the truth;
they have taught their tongue to
speak lies;
they commit iniquity and are too
weary to repent.[p]

l Cn Compare Gk: Heb uncertain
m Ch 8.23 in Heb   n Ch 9.1 in Heb
o Gk: Heb *and not for truth they have grown strong*
p Cn Compare Gk: Heb *your dwelling*

---

destroyed (Lk.13.7). Panic-stricken before the invader (unidentifiable here), they seek temporary defense in their fortresses but there is no defense. *Poisoned water* (cup of God's wrath, 9.15; Ps.75.8; Num. ch. 5). *Dan*, northernmost point in Israel. *Serpents* (Ec.10.11; Ps.58.4–5; Num. 21.4–9). **8.18–9.1:** Lament over Judah. It distresses Jeremiah to denounce his people. **20:** They were perhaps suffering from drought (ch. 14). *Daughter of my people*, Judah (4.11). **22:** *Balm in Gilead*, resin from the Styrax tree, produced especially in the north Transjordan region of Gilead, widely used for medicinal purposes (46.11; Gen.37.25). **9.2–9:** The complete corruption of the people is the basis for this lament, which thus differs from the preceding. Here, instead of sympathy, Jeremiah has nothing but contempt for the lying, deceiving, untrustworthy nation (11.19–23; 12.6; 20.10). A remote stopping place in the desert would be preferable (1 Kg.19.3–4).

⁶ Heaping oppression upon
oppression, and deceit upon
deceit,
they refuse to know me, says the
Lord.

⁷ Therefore thus says the Lord of
hosts:
"Behold, I will refine them and test
them,
for what else can I do, because
of my people?
⁸ Their tongue is a deadly arrow;
it speaks deceitfully;
with his mouth each speaks
peaceably to his neighbor,
but in his heart he plans an
ambush for him.
⁹ Shall I not punish them for these
things? says the Lord;
and shall I not avenge myself
on a nation such as this?

¹⁰ "Take up*q* weeping and wailing for
the mountains,
and a lamentation for the pastures
of the wilderness,
because they are laid waste so that
no one passes through,
and the lowing of cattle is not
heard;
both the birds of the air and the
beasts
have fled and are gone.
¹¹ I will make Jerusalem a heap of
ruins,
a lair of jackals;
and I will make the cities of Judah
a desolation,
without inhabitant."

12 Who is the man so wise that he
can understand this? To whom has the
mouth of the Lord spoken, that he
may declare it? Why is the land ruined
and laid waste like a wilderness, so that
no one passes through? ¹³ And the
Lord says: "Because they have forsaken my law which I set before them,
and have not obeyed my voice, or
walked in accord with it, ¹⁴ but have
stubbornly followed their own hearts
and have gone after the Ba'als, as their
fathers taught them. ¹⁵ Therefore thus
says the Lord of hosts, the God of Israel: Behold, I will feed this people
with wormwood, and give them poisonous water to drink. ¹⁶ I will scatter
them among the nations whom neither
they nor their fathers have known; and
I will send the sword after them, until
I have consumed them."

¹⁷ Thus says the Lord of hosts:
"Consider, and call for the mourning
women to come;
send for the skilful women to
come;
¹⁸ let them make haste and raise a
wailing over us,
that our eyes may run down with
tears,
and our eyelids gush with water.
¹⁹ For a sound of wailing is heard from
Zion:
'How we are ruined!
We are utterly shamed,
because we have left the land,
because they have cast down our
dwellings.' "

²⁰ Hear, O women, the word of the
Lord,
and let your ear receive the word
of his mouth;
teach to your daughters a lament,
and each to her neighbor a dirge.
²¹ For death has come up into our
windows,
it has entered our palaces,
cutting off the children from the
streets
and the young men from the
squares.
²² Speak, "Thus says the Lord:

q Gk Syr: Heb *I will take up*

9: 5.9. **10–22:** Lamentation over Zion. **13–16:** A composite commentary on Jeremiah's oracle in vv. 10–12,17–22 (compare 5.18–19). *Poisonous water,* 8.14; 23.15; Ezek.23.31–34. Baal worship was man's fabrication, not God's revelation. **10–12,17–22:** The stillness of death shrouds the ruined land (7.34); only the howl of jackals breaks the silence. As customary in the ancient world, professional *mourning women* are hired to bewail the fate of Zion. **21:** The verse reflects

'The dead bodies of men shall fall
  like dung upon the open field,
like sheaves after the reaper,
  and none shall gather them.' "

23 Thus says the LORD: "Let not
the wise man glory in his wisdom, let
not the mighty man glory in his might,
let not the rich man glory in his riches;
24 but let him who glories glory in this,
that he understands and knows me,
that I am the LORD who practice
steadfast love, justice, and righteousness in the earth; for in these things
I delight, says the LORD."
25 "Behold, the days are coming,
says the LORD, when I will punish
all those who are circumcised but yet
uncircumcised– 26 Egypt, Judah,
Edom, the sons of Ammon, Moab,
and all who dwell in the desert that
cut the corners of their hair; for all
these nations are uncircumcised, and
all the house of Israel is uncircumcised in heart."

10 Hear the word which the LORD
speaks to you, O house of Israel.
2 Thus says the LORD:
"Learn not the way of the nations,
  nor be dismayed at the signs of
    the heavens
  because the nations are dismayed
    at them,
3 for the customs of the peoples are
    false.
A tree from the forest is cut down,
  and worked with an axe by the
    hands of a craftsman.
4 Men deck it with silver and gold;
  they fasten it with hammer and
    nails
so that it cannot move.

5 Their idols*r* are like scarecrows in
  a cucumber field,
  and they cannot speak;
they have to be carried,
  for they cannot walk.
Be not afraid of them,
  for they cannot do evil,
  neither is it in them to do good."

6 There is none like thee, O LORD;
  thou art great, and thy name is
    great in might.
7 Who would not fear thee, O King
  of the nations?
For this is thy due;
  for among all the wise ones of the
    nations
  and in all their kingdoms
  there is none like thee.
8 They are both stupid and foolish;
  the instruction of idols is but
    wood!
9 Beaten silver is brought from
    Tarshish,
  and gold from Uphaz.
They are the work of the craftsman
  and of the hands of the
    goldsmith;
  their clothing is violet and purple;
  they are all the work of skilled
    men.
10 But the LORD is the true God;
  he is the living God and the
    everlasting King.
At his wrath the earth quakes,
  and the nations cannot endure his
    indignation.

11 Thus shall you say to them:
"The gods who did not make the heavens and the earth shall perish from
the earth and from under the
heavens."*s*

r Heb *They*   *s* This verse is in Aramaic

the figure of speech of a Canaanite mythological allusion to the god of death. **23–24:** True
glory (1 Cor.1.31). Man's common goals are nothing (1 Kg.3.10–12) compared with the knowledge of God. **25–26:** Though physically circumcised, her neighbors will share with faithless
Israel the lot of those not in right relationship with God (Dt.10.16; Rom.2.25–29). *Those who . . .
cut . . . their hair,* Arab tribes (25.23). **10.1–16:** God and the idols. This passage is a later elaboration of a now lost oracle by Jeremiah (compare Is.44.9–20; Ps.115.3–8), if it is to be ascribed
at all to him. **2:** *Signs of the heavens* (eclipses, comets, astrological observations) are meaningless. **4:** *Men deck it with silver and gold,* compare the description of making an idol in Is.40.18–
20; 41.6–7. **5:** *They have to be carried,* this theme is effectively presented in Is.46.1–7. *Cucumber
field,* Is.1.8. **9:** *Tarshish,* Sardinia, or Tartessus in southern Spain. *Uphaz,* unknown. **11:** An

12 It is he who made the earth by his
    power,
  who established the world by his
    wisdom,
  and by his understanding
    stretched out the heavens.
13 When he utters his voice there is a
    tumult of waters in the
    heavens,
  and he makes the mist rise from
    the ends of the earth.
  He makes lightnings for the rain,
    and he brings forth the wind from
    his storehouses.
14 Every man is stupid and without
    knowledge;
  every goldsmith is put to shame
    by his idols;
  for his images are false,
    and there is no breath in them.
15 They are worthless, a work of
    delusion;
  at the time of their punishment
    they shall perish.
16 Not like these is he who is the
    portion of Jacob,
  for he is the one who formed all
    things,
  and Israel is the tribe of his
    inheritance;
  the LORD of hosts is his name.

17 Gather up your bundle from the
    ground,
  O you who dwell under siege!
18 For thus says the LORD:
  "Behold, I am slinging out the
    inhabitants of the land
    at this time,
  and I will bring distress on them,
    that they may feel it."

19 Woe is me because of my hurt!
  My wound is grievous.

But I said, "Truly this is an affliction,
    and I must bear it."
20 My tent is destroyed,
    and all my cords are broken;
  my children have gone from me,
    and they are not;
  there is no one to spread my tent
    again,
  and to set up my curtains.
21 For the shepherds are stupid,
    and do not inquire of the LORD;
  therefore they have not prospered,
    and all their flock is scattered.

22 Hark, a rumor! Behold, it comes!—
    a great commotion out of the
    north country
  to make the cities of Judah a
    desolation,
    a lair of jackals.

23 I know, O LORD, that the way of
    man is not in himself,
  that it is not in man who walks
    to direct his steps.
24 Correct me, O LORD, but in just
    measure;
  not in thy anger, lest thou bring
    me to nothing.

25 Pour out thy wrath upon the nations
    that know thee not,
  and upon the peoples that call not
    on thy name;
  for they have devoured Jacob;
    they have devoured him and
    consumed him,
  and have laid waste his
    habitation.

11 The word that came to Jeremiah
    from the LORD: 2 "Hear the words
of this covenant, and speak to the men
of Judah and the inhabitants of Jeru-

Aramaic gloss (unique in Jeremiah) from about the fifth century B.C. **12–16:** He alone (*the portion of Jacob;* Lam.3.24) is worthy of worship (51.15–19). **17–22:** Prepare to leave! Related to but later than 9.10–22, this passage describes a siege (perhaps in 597 B.C.) which will not be lifted. In Exile, mother Zion will lose her children (Is.49.14–23; 54.1–3) because of the stupidity of Judah's rulers (*shepherds*). God's role in political events is not to be overlooked. **22b:** 9.11. **23–25:** Prayer of Jeremiah. While Judah is guilty and deserves punishment (Pr.20.24; compare Rom.1.18–23), God is asked to be merciful and not destroy Judah (Am.7.2–6; Ps.6.1). **25:** A later addition, reflecting the sixth century desolation of Judah as an accomplished fact (as in Ps.79.6–7).

salem. ³ You shall say to them, Thus says the LORD, the God of Israel: Cursed be the man who does not heed the words of this covenant ⁴ which I commanded your fathers when I brought them out of the land of Egypt, from the iron furnace, saying, Listen to my voice, and do all that I command you. So shall you be my people, and I will be your God, ⁵ that I may perform the oath which I swore to your fathers, to give them a land flowing with milk and honey, as at this day." Then I answered, "So be it, LORD."

6 And the LORD said to me, "Proclaim all these words in the cities of Judah, and in the streets of Jerusalem: Hear the words of this covenant and do them. ⁷ For I solemnly warned your fathers when I brought them up out of the land of Egypt, warning them persistently, even to this day, saying, Obey my voice. ⁸ Yet they did not obey or incline their ear, but every one walked in the stubbornness of his evil heart. Therefore I brought upon them all the words of this covenant, which I commanded them to do, but they did not."

9 Again the LORD said to me, "There is revolt among the men of Judah and the inhabitants of Jerusalem. ¹⁰ They have turned back to the iniquities of their forefathers, who refused to hear my words; they have gone after other gods to serve them; the house of Israel and the house of Judah have broken my covenant which I made with their fathers. ¹¹ Therefore, thus says the LORD, Behold, I am bringing evil upon them which they cannot escape; though they cry to me, I will not listen to them. ¹² Then the cities of Judah and the inhabitants of Jerusalem will go and cry to the gods to whom they burn incense, but they cannot save them in the time of their trouble. ¹³ For your gods have become as many as your cities, O Judah; and as many as the streets of Jerusalem are the altars you have set up to shame, altars to burn incense to Ba'al.

14 "Therefore do not pray for this people, or lift up a cry or prayer on their behalf, for I will not listen when they call to me in the time of their trouble. ¹⁵ What right has my beloved in my house, when she has done vile deeds? Can vows*t* and sacrificial flesh avert your doom? Can you then exult? ¹⁶ The LORD once called you, 'A green olive tree, fair with goodly fruit'; but with the roar of a great tempest he will set fire to it, and its branches will be consumed. ¹⁷ The LORD of hosts, who planted you, has pronounced evil against you, because of the evil which the house of Israel and the house of Judah have done, provoking me to anger by burning incense to Ba'al."

18 The LORD made it known to me and
    I knew;
    then thou didst show me their evil
      deeds.
19 But I was like a gentle lamb
    led to the slaughter.
I did not know it was against me
    they devised schemes, saying,

t Gk: Heb *many*

11.1–17: Jeremiah and the covenant. Jeremiah undoubtedly strongly supported Josiah's effort to eradicate practices of foreign worship (2 Kg. chs. 22–23) and to return to the provisions of the Mosaic covenant (v. 3, *this covenant;* v. 10, *my covenant*). Prophetic preaching was based upon the covenant relationship with God. Whether this somewhat re-edited speech is contemporary with Josiah's reform (627 B.C.) or is in retrospect (after 609) cannot be determined. Typically Deuteronomic is the word *command* used of the covenant (Dt.4.13; 6.17; etc.); note also other familiar Deuteronomic phrases: v. 3, Dt.27.26; v. 4, Dt.4.20; v. 5, Dt.7.12–13; v. 8, Dt.29.19. *Iron furnace*, Dt.4.20; 1 Kg.8.51; Is.48.10. Intercession for the apostate people is useless (14.11–12), as are also their rituals. **16:** Symbolic of Judah's destruction is the incineration of the *green olive trees* in the temple area (Ps.52.8).

    11.18–12.6: Jeremiah's first personal lament. A plot against the life of Jeremiah (11.18,19; 12.6; 11.20; 12.3b are perhaps to be transposed in this order). The first of Jeremiah's six personal

"Let us destroy the tree with its
    fruit,
  let us cut him off from the land
    of the living,
  that his name be remembered no
    more."
20 But, O LORD of hosts, who judgest
    righteously,
  who triest the heart and the mind,
  let me see thy vengeance upon them,
  for to thee have I committed my
    cause.

21 Therefore thus says the LORD
concerning the men of An'athoth, who
seek your life, and say, "Do not prophesy in the name of the LORD, or you
will die by our hand"– 22 therefore thus
says the LORD of hosts: "Behold, I
will punish them; the young men shall
die by the sword; their sons and their
daughters shall die by famine; 23 and
none of them shall be left. For I will
bring evil upon the men of An'athoth,
the year of their punishment."

12 Righteous art thou, O LORD,
  when I complain to thee;
  yet I would plead my case before
    thee.
Why does the way of the wicked
    prosper?
Why do all who are treacherous
    thrive?
2 Thou plantest them, and they take
    root;
  they grow and bring forth fruit;
  thou art near in their mouth
  and far from their heart.
3 But thou, O LORD, knowest me;
  thou seest me, and triest my mind
    toward thee.

Pull them out like sheep for the
    slaughter,
and set them apart for the day of
    slaughter.
4 How long will the land mourn,
  and the grass of every field wither?
For the wickedness of those who
    dwell in it
  the beasts and the birds are swept
    away,
  because men said, "He will not see
    our latter end."

5 "If you have raced with men on
    foot, and they have wearied
    you,
  how will you compete with horses?
And if in a safe land you fall down,
  how will you do in the jungle of
    the Jordan?
6 For even your brothers and the
    house of your father,
  even they have dealt
    treacherously with you;
  they are in full cry after you;
believe them not,
  though they speak fair words to
    you."

7 "I have forsaken my house,
  I have abandoned my heritage;
  I have given the beloved of my soul
  into the hands of her enemies.
8 My heritage has become to me
  like a lion in the forest,
  she has lifted up her voice against
    me;
  therefore I hate her.
9 Is my heritage to me like a speckled
    bird of prey?

---

laments; the others are 15.10–21; 17.14–18; 18.18–23; 20.7–13; 20.14–18. He learns that he is
the unwitting object (*gentle lamb;* compare Is.53.7) of an assassination plot, and prays the
omniscient God for protection (17.10; Ps. 26). **21–23:** The origin of the grievance against
Jeremiah may be his identification of certain fellow citizens with false prophets and priests. In
his characteristic phraseology (5.12; 18.21; 19.15; 23.12) their end is foretold. **12.1,2,4b,3a,4a,5:**
Against the background of the law court, Jeremiah questions the then nearly universal idea
that the wicked always suffer and the righteous always prosper. The wicked, ostensibly faithful,
prosper (Job. ch. 21; Ps. 73). After Jeremiah's assertion of integrity (Ps.139.23–24), God, by
two proverbs, informs him that the present is but a preparation for a more demanding future.
Jungle of the Jordan, the thickets, abode of wild animals, in the gorge of the Jordan (49.19).
    12.7–13: God's lament. Using several figures (*beloved of my soul,* 11.15; *lion; speckled bird;
vineyard,* 5.10; Is.5.1–7), God laments the necessary ravaging of Judah (*my house,* Hos.9.15;

Are the birds of prey against her
round about?
Go, assemble all the wild beasts;
bring them to devour.
[10] Many shepherds have destroyed my
vineyard,
they have trampled down my
portion,
they have made my pleasant portion
a desolate wilderness.
[11] They have made it a desolation;
desolate, it mourns to me.
The whole land is made desolate,
but no man lays it to heart.
[12] Upon all the bare heights in the
desert
destroyers have come;
for the sword of the LORD devours
from one end of the land to the
other;
no flesh has peace.
[13] They have sown wheat and have
reaped thorns,
they have tired themselves out
but profit nothing.
They shall be ashamed of their[u]
harvests
because of the fierce anger of the
LORD."

14 Thus says the LORD concerning all my evil neighbors who touch the heritage which I have given my people Israel to inherit: "Behold, I will pluck them up from their land, and I will pluck up the house of Judah from among them. [15] And after I have plucked them up, I will again have compassion on them, and I will bring them again each to his heritage and each to his land. [16] And it shall come to pass, if they will diligently learn the ways of my people, to swear by my name, 'As the LORD lives,' even as they taught my people to swear by Ba'al, then they shall be built up in the midst of my people. [17] But if any nation will not listen, then I will utterly pluck it up and destroy it, says the LORD."

13 Thus said the LORD to me, "Go and buy a linen waistcloth, and put it on your loins, and do not dip it in water." [2] So I bought a waistcloth according to the word of the LORD, and put it on my loins. [3] And the word of the LORD came to me a second time, [4] "Take the waistcloth which you have bought, which is upon your loins, and arise, go to the Euphra'tes, and hide it there in a cleft of the rock." [5] So I went, and hid it by the Euphra'tes, as the LORD commanded me. [6] And after many days the LORD said to me, "Arise, go to the Euphra'tes, and take from there the waistcloth which I commanded you to hide there." [7] Then I went to the Euphra'tes, and dug, and I took the waistcloth from the place where I had hidden it. And behold, the waistcloth was spoiled; it was good for nothing.

8 Then the word of the LORD came to me: [9] "Thus says the LORD: Even so will I spoil the pride of Judah and the great pride of Jerusalem. [10] This evil people, who refuse to hear my words, who stubbornly follow their own heart and have gone after other gods to serve them and worship them,

u Heb *your*

---

heritage, 1 Sam.10.1) by the Babylonian-inspired raids of 601 B.C., led by several puppet rulers (*birds of prey, shepherds*), in reprisal for Jehoiakim's short-lived revolt (2 Kg.24.1–4).

12.14–17: Judah's neighbors. If Judah's erstwhile enemies are converted (16.19–21; Ps. 87), God will spare them when Judah is restored; otherwise they will be destroyed (25.12–38). **16:** *They*, a reference to the Canaanites.

13.1–11: The story of the waistcloth. Using the figure of a linen waistcloth (v. 11; compare Ex.19.6; Lev.16.4), buried in the moist bank of the Euphrates (v. 7), Jeremiah underscores the corrupting effect of Jehoiakim's pro-Babylonian foreign policy (2.18) and the accompanying religious syncretism in Judah (2 Kg.24.1–7). The four hundred miles between Judah and the Euphrates have led some scholars to question whether Jeremiah made the journey, although the prophets sometimes took extreme measures to illustrate an oracle (compare Is.20.1–6; Ezek.4.1–17). It has been interpreted as a parable or vision.

shall be like this waistcloth, which is good for nothing. ¹¹ For as the waistcloth clings to the loins of a man, so I made the whole house of Israel and the whole house of Judah cling to me, says the LORD, that they might be for me a people, a name, a praise, and a glory, but they would not listen.

12 "You shall speak to them this word: 'Thus says the LORD, the God of Israel, "Every jar shall be filled with wine." ' And they will say to you, 'Do we not indeed know that every jar will be filled with wine?' ¹³ Then you shall say to them, 'Thus says the LORD: Behold, I will fill with drunkenness all the inhabitants of this land: the kings who sit on David's throne, the priests, the prophets, and all the inhabitants of Jerusalem. ¹⁴ And I will dash them one against another, fathers and sons together, says the LORD. I will not pity or spare or have compassion, that I should not destroy them.' "

¹⁵ Hear and give ear; be not proud,
    for the LORD has spoken.
¹⁶ Give glory to the LORD your God
    before he brings darkness,
before your feet stumble
    on the twilight mountains,
and while you look for light
    he turns it into gloom
    and makes it deep darkness.
¹⁷ But if you will not listen,
    my soul will weep in secret for
      your pride;
my eyes will weep bitterly and run
      down with tears,
because the LORD's flock has
      been taken captive.

¹⁸ Say to the king and the queen
    mother:
"Take a lowly seat,
for your beautiful crown
    has come down from your head."ᵛ
¹⁹ The cities of the Negeb are shut
    up,
    with none to open them;
all Judah is taken into exile,
    wholly taken into exile.

²⁰ "Lift up your eyes and see
    those who come from the north.
Where is the flock that was given
    you,
    your beautiful flock?
²¹ What will you say when they set
    as head over you
those whom you yourself have
    taught
    to be friends to you?
Will not pangs take hold of you,
    like those of a woman in travail?
²² And if you say in your heart,
    'Why have these things come upon
      me?'
it is for the greatness of your iniquity
    that your skirts are lifted up,
    and you suffer violence.
²³ Can the Ethiopian change his skin
    or the leopard his spots?
Then also you can do good
    who are accustomed to do evil.
²⁴ I will scatter youʷ like chaff
    driven by the wind from the
      desert.
²⁵ This is your lot,
    the portion I have measured out
      to you, says the LORD,
because you have forgotten me
    and trusted in lies.

v Gk Syr Vg: Heb obscure   *w* Heb *them*

13.12–14: The allegory of the wine jar. Jeremiah uses a proverb (v. 12a) and the figure of drunkenness (v. 13; compare 25.15–16; Ezek.23.31) to describe the divine judgment.
13.15–17: The last opportunity for repentance is offered to wayward Judah; her captivity is imminent (v. 17). **18–19:** Exile! Almost resignedly, Jeremiah notes the deposition of Jehoiachin (2 Kg.24.8,15), the Babylonian military occupation of Judah (597 B.C.), and the first deportation (Jer.52.28).
13.20–27: Jerusalem's shame. Using a common Biblical simile for judgment, the ravishing of a woman (Is.47.2; here the untrustworthy shepherdess), Jeremiah describes the approaching rape (vv. 22,26) of Jerusalem by Babylon. **20:** *North*, see 1.13–14 n.; 4.6. Her shamelessness and her shame are directly related. **23:** In her present state, she cannot change herself (Hos.5.4; Jn.8.34; compare 3.22).

26 I myself will lift up your skirts over
　　your face,
　　and your shame will be seen.
27 I have seen your abominations,
　　your adulteries and neighings,
　　your lewd harlotries,
　　on the hills in the field.
　Woe to you, O Jerusalem!
　How long will it be
　before you are made clean?"

14 The word of the LORD which
came to Jeremiah concerning the
drought:
2 "Judah mourns
　　and her gates languish;
　her people lament on the ground,
　　and the cry of Jerusalem goes up.
3 Her nobles send their servants for
　　water;
　they come to the cisterns,
　they find no water,
　they return with their vessels
　　empty;
　they are ashamed and confounded
　　and cover their heads.
4 Because of the ground which is
　　dismayed,
　since there is no rain on the land,
　the farmers are ashamed,
　they cover their heads.
5 Even the hind in the field forsakes
　　her newborn calf
　because there is no grass.
6 The wild asses stand on the bare
　　heights,
　they pant for air like jackals;
　their eyes fail
　because there is no herbage.

7 "Though our iniquities testify
　　against us,
　act, O LORD, for thy name's sake;
　for our backslidings are many,
　　we have sinned against thee.

8 O thou hope of Israel,
　　its savior in time of trouble,
　why shouldst thou be like a stranger
　　in the land,
　like a wayfarer who turns aside
　　to tarry for a night?
9 Why shouldst thou be like a man
　　confused,
　like a mighty man who cannot
　　save?
　Yet thou, O LORD, art in the midst
　　of us,
　and we are called by thy name;
　leave us not."

10 Thus says the LORD concerning this
　　people:
　"They have loved to wander thus,
　they have not restrained their feet;
　therefore the LORD does not accept
　　them,
　now he will remember their
　　iniquity
　and punish their sins."

11 The LORD said to me: "Do not
pray for the welfare of this people.
12 Though they fast, I will not hear
their cry, and though they offer burnt
offering and cereal offering, I will not
accept them; but I will consume them
by the sword, by famine, and by pestilence."

13 Then I said: "Ah, Lord GOD,
behold, the prophets say to them, 'You
shall not see the sword, nor shall you
have famine, but I will give you assured peace in this place.' " 14 And the
LORD said to me: "The prophets are
prophesying lies in my name; I did
not send them, nor did I command
them or speak to them. They are prophesying to you a lying vision, worthless divination, and the deceit of their
own minds. 15 Therefore thus says

14.1–16: Lament over catastrophic drought. 2–6: By examples drawn from city and country,
forest and wilderness, Jeremiah describes his people's plight. **7–9:** Prostrate on the ground
(v. 2), in the words of a prayer for a Day of Repentance, the people confess their sins and, as
they are his covenant people, plead with God to remember them. **10–12:** In their need, they remember God; in their prosperity, they forget him. No intercession or ritual acts will avert the
divine punishment (7.16). **13–16:** *In this place*, in the temple. Jeremiah's effort to excuse the
people's heedlessness because of misplaced reliance in the false prophets' beguiling message is
rejected. The people have made their decision–the wrong one–and will be punished.

the LORD concerning the prophets who prophesy in my name although I did not send them, and who say, 'Sword and famine shall not come on this land': By sword and famine those prophets shall be consumed. 16 And the people to whom they prophesy shall be cast out in the streets of Jerusalem, victims of famine and sword, with none to bury them–them, their wives, their sons, and their daughters. For I will pour out their wickedness upon them.

17 "You shall say to them this word:
'Let my eyes run down with tears
　　night and day,
　and let them not cease,
for the virgin daughter of my people
　is smitten with a great wound,
　with a very grievous blow.
18 If I go out into the field,
　behold, those slain by the sword!
And if I enter the city,
　behold, the diseases of famine!
For both prophet and priest ply their
　　trade through the land,
　and have no knowledge.'"

19 Hast thou utterly rejected Judah?
　Does thy soul loathe Zion?
Why hast thou smitten us
　so that there is no healing for us?
We looked for peace, but no good
　　came;
　for a time of healing, but behold,
　terror.
20 We acknowledge our wickedness,
　O LORD,
　and the iniquity of our fathers,
　for we have sinned against thee.
21 Do not spurn us, for thy name's
　　sake;
　do not dishonor thy glorious
　throne;

remember and do not break thy
　covenant with us.
22 Are there any among the false gods
　of the nations that can bring
　rain?
Or can the heavens give showers?
Art thou not he, O LORD our God?
　We set our hope on thee,
　for thou doest all these things.

15 Then the LORD said to me, "Though Moses and Samuel stood before me, yet my heart would not turn toward this people. Send them out of my sight, and let them go! 2 And when they ask you, 'Where shall we go?' you shall say to them, 'Thus says the LORD:

"Those who are for pestilence, to
　pestilence,
and those who are for the sword,
　to the sword;
those who are for famine, to famine,
　and those who are for captivity,
　to captivity."'

3 "I will appoint over them four kinds of destroyers, says the LORD: the sword to slay, the dogs to tear, and the birds of the air and the beasts of the earth to devour and destroy. 4 And I will make them a horror to all the kingdoms of the earth because of what Manas'seh the son of Hezeki'ah, king of Judah, did in Jerusalem.

5 "Who will have pity on you, O
　Jerusalem,
　or who will bemoan you?
Who will turn aside
　to ask about your welfare?
6 You have rejected me, says the
　LORD,
　you keep going backward;
so I have stretched out my hand
　against you and destroyed
　you;–

14.17–15.4: **Further lament.** 14.17–18: Here Jeremiah describes the calamity, using figures of war, drought, unburied dead, hunger, and confused spiritual leaders. 19–22: More strongly than in vv. 10–12, the people plead their case, casting themselves wholly on God's mercy. 15.1–4: If the people's greatest intercessors, *Moses* (Ex.32.11–14; Num.14.13–19; one of four references to Moses in prophetic literature [the others are Mic.6.4; Is.63.11; Mal.4.4]) and *Samuel* (1 Sam.12.17–18), were to plead for them, their sentence of total destruction would not be withdrawn (17.16–17). *Manasseh,* 2 Kg. ch. 21. 15.5–9: **Jerusalem's end.** Though the passage is later (after 597 B.C.), the preceding theme of

I am weary of relenting.
7 I have winnowed them with a
winnowing fork
in the gates of the land;
I have bereaved them, I have
destroyed my people;
they did not turn from their ways.
8 I have made their widows more in
number
than the sand of the seas;
I have brought against the mothers
of young men
a destroyer at noonday;
I have made anguish and terror
fall upon them suddenly.
9 She who bore seven has languished;
she has swooned away;
her sun went down while it was yet
day;
she has been shamed and
disgraced.
And the rest of them I will give to
the sword
before their enemies,
                    says the LORD."

10 Woe is me, my mother, that you
bore me, a man of strife and contention to the whole land! I have not lent,
nor have I borrowed, yet all of them
curse me. 11 So let it be, O LORD,[x] if
I have not entreated[y] thee for their
good, if I have not pleaded with thee
on behalf of the enemy in the time of
trouble and in the time of distress!
12 Can one break iron, iron from the
north, and bronze? 13 "Your wealth and your treasures
I will give as spoil, without price, for
all your sins, throughout all your territory. 14 I will make you serve your
enemies in a land which you do not
know, for in my anger a fire is kindled
which shall burn for ever."

15 O LORD, thou knowest;
remember me and visit me,
and take vengeance for me on
my persecutors.
In thy forbearance take me not away;
know that for thy sake I bear
reproach.
16 Thy words were found, and I ate
them,
and thy words became to me a joy
and the delight of my heart;
for I am called by thy name,
O LORD, God of hosts.
17 I did not sit in the company of
merrymakers,
nor did I rejoice;
I sat alone, because thy hand was
upon me,
for thou hadst filled me with
indignation.
18 Why is my pain unceasing,
my wound incurable,
refusing to be healed?
Wilt thou be to me like a deceitful
brook,
like waters that fail?

19 Therefore thus says the LORD:
"If you return, I will restore you,
and you shall stand before me.
If you utter what is precious, and
not what is worthless,
you shall be as my mouth.
They shall turn to you,
but you shall not turn to them.
20 And I will make you to this people
a fortified wall of bronze;
they will fight against you,
but they shall not prevail over you,
for I am with you
to save you and deliver you,
                    says the LORD.

x Gk Old Latin: Heb *the* LORD *said*
y Cn: Heb obscure

punishment by war continues. **6:** *Weary of relenting*, compare Am.7.1–9. **7:** *Winnowed them*,
a common threshing figure (see Is.21.10; 27.12; Jer.51.2; Mt.3.12; Lk.3.17). **9:** *She who bore
seven*, a sign of favor (Ru.4.15; 1 Sam.2.5). Jerusalem will be bereaved (compare Hos.9.12).

15.10–21: Jeremiah's second personal lament, see 11.18–12.6 n. **10–18:** Jeremiah points to
his ostracism and the continued rejection of the life-giving word (v. 16; Ezek.2.8–10; Jn.4.32–34).
Verses 13–14 are misplaced from 17.3–4. **15:** With the familiar phrase, *thou knowest* (Pss.40.9;
139). Jeremiah prays God for vengeance against his persecutors. **17:** The *hand* of God, often
the symbol of inspiration (Is.8.11; Ezek.3.14,22), is here a symbol of burden. **19–21:** God
applies Jeremiah's own message to himself; God promises no respite from opposition, but

21 I will deliver you out of the hand of
　　the wicked,
　　and redeem you from the grasp
　　　of the ruthless."

16 The word of the LORD came to
me: 2 "You shall not take a wife,
nor shall you have sons or daughters
in this place. 3 For thus says the LORD
concerning the sons and daughters who
are born in this place, and concerning
the mothers who bore them and the
fathers who begot them in this land:
4 They shall die of deadly diseases.
They shall not be lamented, nor shall
they be buried; they shall be as dung
on the surface of the ground. They
shall perish by the sword and by
famine, and their dead bodies shall be
food for the birds of the air and for the
beasts of the earth.

5 "For thus says the LORD: Do not
enter the house of mourning, or go to
lament, or bemoan them; for I have
taken away my peace from this people, says the LORD, my steadfast love
and mercy. 6 Both great and small
shall die in this land; they shall not be
buried, and no one shall lament for
them or cut himself or make himself
bald for them. 7 No one shall break
bread for the mourner, to comfort him
for the dead; nor shall any one give him
the cup of consolation to drink for his
father or his mother. 8 You shall not
go into the house of feasting to sit with
them, to eat and drink. 9 For thus
says the LORD of hosts, the God of Israel: Behold, I will make to cease from
this place, before your eyes and in
your days, the voice of mirth and the
voice of gladness, the voice of the
bridegroom and the voice of the bride.

10 "And when you tell this people
all these words, and they say to you,
'Why has the LORD pronounced all this
great evil against us? What is our iniquity? What is the sin that we have
committed against the LORD our God?'
11 then you shall say to them: 'Because
your fathers have forsaken me, says
the LORD, and have gone after other
gods and have served and worshiped
them, and have forsaken me and have
not kept my law, 12 and because you
have done worse than your fathers,
for behold, every one of you follows
his stubborn evil will, refusing to listen
to me; 13 therefore I will hurl you out of
this land into a land which neither you
nor your fathers have known, and there
you shall serve other gods day and
night, for I will show you no favor.'

14 "Therefore, behold, the days are
coming, says the LORD, when it shall
no longer be said, 'As the LORD lives
who brought up the people of Israel
out of the land of Egypt,' 15 but 'As
the LORD lives who brought up the
people of Israel out of the north country and out of all the countries where
he had driven them.' For I will bring
them back to their own land which I
gave to their fathers.

16 "Behold, I am sending for many
fishers, says the LORD, and they shall
catch them; and afterwards I will
send for many hunters, and they shall
hunt them from every mountain and
every hill, and out of the clefts of the
rocks. 17 For my eyes are upon all
their ways; they are not hid from me,
nor is their iniquity concealed from
my eyes. 18 And[z] I will doubly recompense their iniquity and their sin, be-

z Gk: Heb *And first*

---

promising him constant support (1.18–19), urges Jeremiah to continue as his *mouth* (Ex.4.16).
　16.1–13: Jeremiah's life, a symbol (Hos.1.2–9; Is.8.3–4). **1–9:** An illustration of 15.17. **1–4:**
In view of the impending doom, Jeremiah relinquishes hope for home and family as a sign of
the judgment (Ezek.24.15–27; 1 Cor.7.25–40). **5–7:** Israel's faithlessness has nullified God's
obligation for covenant loyalty. All symbols of mourning (*cut himself*, 41.5; *make himself bald*,
Am.8.10; Is.22.12; compare Dt.14.1) are as futile as death is comfortless. **8–9:** 25.10. **10–13:**
So Israel too will be alone (5.18–19).
　16.14–15: Israel's homecoming. Their return, accomplished by God's actions, will be celebrated as the new Exodus (the passage duplicates 23.7–8; probably an editorial inclusion here).
　16.16–18: No refuge for Israel (continues v. 13). As nothing escapes God's knowledge, so

cause they have polluted my land with the carcasses of their detestable idols, and have, filled my inheritance with their abominations.''

¹⁹ O LORD, my strength and my
  stronghold,
  my refuge in the day of trouble,
to thee shall the nations come
  from the ends of the earth and
  say:
"Our fathers have inherited nought
  but lies,
  worthless things in which there is
  no profit.
²⁰ Can man make for himself gods?
  Such are no gods!''

21 "Therefore, behold, I will make them know, this once I will make them know my power and my might, and they shall know that my name is the LORD.''

17 "The sin of Judah is written with a pen of iron; with a point of diamond it is engraved on the tablet of their heart, and on the horns of their altars, ² while their children remember their altars and their Ashe′rim, beside every green tree, and on the high hills, ³ on the mountains in the open country. Your wealth and all your treasures I will give for spoil as the price of your sin*a* throughout all your territory. ⁴ You shall loosen your hand*b* from your heritage which I gave to you, and I will make you serve your enemies in a land which you do not know, for in my anger a fire is kindled which shall burn for ever.''

⁵ Thus says the LORD:
"Cursed is the man who trusts in
  man
  and makes flesh his arm,
  whose heart turns away from the
  LORD.
⁶ He is like a shrub in the desert,
  and shall not see any good come.
He shall dwell in the parched places
  of the wilderness,
  in an uninhabited salt land.

⁷ "Blessed is the man who trusts in
  the LORD,
  whose trust is the LORD.
⁸ He is like a tree planted by water,
  that sends out its roots by the
  stream,
and does not fear when heat comes,
  for its leaves remain green,
and is not anxious in the year of
  drought,
  for it does not cease to bear fruit.''

⁹ The heart is deceitful above all
  things,
  and desperately corrupt;
  who can understand it?
¹⁰ "I the LORD search the mind
  and try the heart,
to give to every man according to his
  ways,
  according to the fruit of his
  doings.''

¹¹ Like the partridge that gathers a
  brood which she did not hatch,
so is he who gets riches but not
  by right;
  in the midst of his days they will
  leave him,

a Cn: Heb *your high places for sin*
b Cn: Heb *and in you*

---

no one will escape the Babylonians (*fishers* and *hunters;* Hab.1.14–15). **18:** Editorial duplication of v. 11.

    16.19–21: Conversion of the heathen (Is.45.20–24; Mic.4.1-4). Recognizing the vanity of their idol-worship, all nations will join in worshiping Israel's omnipotent God.

    17.1–4: Judah's sin. The practice of the Judeans indelibly and openly demonstrates their attitudes. **1:** *Pen of iron,* a diamond-tipped stylus (Job 19.24). *Horns of altar,* Ex.29.12.

    17.5–11: Proverbs. 5–8: Probable source of Ps. 1. The godless man is like a fruitless desert plant; the godly man is like a fruitful, well-watered tree (Ps.1.3; Pr.3.18). **9–10:** Only God can really understand man (Rom.7.18–19); only God can therefore properly judge man (1 Sam. 16.7; Ps.62.12). **11:** A proverb, perhaps referring to Jehoiakim (22.13; 2 Kg.23.35). **12–13:** *Throne,* the ark in the temple (Is.6.1). *Written in the earth,* assigned to the underworld (Is.4.3). *Fountain,* 2.13.

and at his end he will be a fool.

¹² A glorious throne set on high from
    the beginning
    is the place of our sanctuary.
¹³ O LORD, the hope of Israel,
    all who forsake thee shall be put
    to shame;
    those who turn away from thee[c]
    shall be written in the earth,
    for they have forsaken the LORD,
    the fountain of living water.

¹⁴ Heal me, O LORD, and I shall be
    healed;
    save me, and I shall be saved;
    for thou art my praise.
¹⁵ Behold, they say to me,
    "Where is the word of the LORD?
    Let it come!"
¹⁶ I have not pressed thee to send
    evil,
    nor have I desired the day of
    disaster,
    thou knowest;
    that which came out of my lips
    was before thy face.
¹⁷ Be not a terror to me;
    thou art my refuge in the day of
    evil.
¹⁸ Let those be put to shame who
    persecute me,
    but let me not be put to shame;
    let them be dismayed,
    but let me not be dismayed;
    bring upon them the day of evil;
    destroy them with double
    destruction!

19 Thus said the LORD to me: "Go
and stand in the Benjamin[d] Gate, by
which the kings of Judah enter and by
which they go out, and in all the gates
of Jerusalem, ²⁰ and say: 'Hear the
word of the LORD, you kings of Judah,
and all Judah, and all the inhabitants
of Jerusalem, who enter by these gates.
²¹ Thus says the LORD: Take heed for
the sake of your lives, and do not bear
a burden on the sabbath day or bring
it in by the gates of Jerusalem. ²² And
do not carry a burden out of your
houses on the sabbath or do any work,
but keep the sabbath day holy, as I
commanded your fathers. ²³ Yet they
did not listen or incline their ear, but
stiffened their neck, that they might
not hear and receive instruction.

24 " 'But if you listen to me, says the
LORD, and bring in no burden by the
gates of this city on the sabbath day,
but keep the sabbath day holy and do
no work on it, ²⁵ then there shall enter
by the gates of this city kings[e] who sit
on the throne of David, riding in chariots and on horses, they and their
princes, the men of Judah and the inhabitants of Jerusalem; and this city
shall be inhabited for ever. ²⁶ And
people shall come from the cities of
Judah and the places round about
Jerusalem, from the land of Benjamin,
from the Shephe'lah, from the hill
country, and from the Negeb, bringing
burnt offerings and sacrifices, cereal
offerings and frankincense, and bringing thank offerings to the house of the
LORD. ²⁷ But if you do not listen to
me, to keep the sabbath day holy, and
not to bear a burden and enter by the
gates of Jerusalem on the sabbath day,
then I will kindle a fire in its gates,
and it shall devour the palaces of Jerusalem and shall not be quenched.' "

c Heb *me*
d Cn: Heb *sons of people*
e Cn: Heb *kings and princes*

17.14–18: Jeremiah's third personal lament (see 11.18–12.6 n.). Sick at heart because of his
opponents' taunts, Jeremiah prays for healing (Ps.6.2–3). He does not want to see God's day
of judgment (Am.5.18; Is.2.11); but if this be the only means of vindication, let it descend in
all its fury.

17.19–27: Judah and the sabbath. Perhaps an illustration of 16.11 and an editorial expansion
of Jeremiah's oracle citing the violation of the sabbath (Ex.23.12; Neh.13.15–22; compare
Mt.12.1–8) as symptomatic of the people's general alienation from God (11.1–8; Am.8.5).
Jeremiah's position at the Benjamin Gate (location unknown) would permit all concerned to
hear. Only faithfulness would make their sacrifices acceptable (Ps.51.15–19) and preserve their
land.

18 The word that came to Jeremiah from the LORD: ² "Arise, and go down to the potter's house, and there I will let you hear my words." ³ So I went down to the potter's house, and there he was working at his wheel. ⁴ And the vessel he was making of clay was spoiled in the potter's hand, and he reworked it into another vessel, as it seemed good to the potter to do.

5 Then the word of the LORD came to me: ⁶ "O house of Israel, can I not do with you as this potter has done? says the LORD. Behold, like the clay in the potter's hand, so are you in my hand, O house of Israel. ⁷ If at any time I declare concerning a nation or a kingdom, that I will pluck up and break down and destroy it, ⁸ and if that nation, concerning which I have spoken, turns from its evil, I will repent of the evil that I intended to do to it. ⁹ And if at any time I declare concerning a nation or a kingdom that I will build and plant it, ¹⁰ and if it does evil in my sight, not listening to my voice, then I will repent of the good which I had intended to do to it. ¹¹ Now, therefore, say to the men of Judah and the inhabitants of Jerusalem: 'Thus says the LORD, Behold, I am shaping evil against you and devising a plan against you. Return, every one from his evil way, and amend your ways and your doings.' 12 "But they say, 'That is in vain! We will follow our own plans, and will every one act according to the stubbornness of his evil heart.'

13 "Therefore thus says the LORD:

Ask among the nations,
 who has heard the like of this?
The virgin Israel
 has done a very horrible thing.
¹⁴ Does the snow of Lebanon leave
 the crags of Si′rion?*f*
Do the mountain*g* waters run dry,*h*
 the cold flowing streams?
¹⁵ But my people have forgotten me,
 they burn incense to false gods;
they have stumbled*i* in their ways,
 in the ancient roads,
and have gone into bypaths,
 not the highway,
¹⁶ making their land a horror,
 a thing to be hissed at for ever.
Every one who passes by it is
 horrified
 and shakes his head.
¹⁷ Like the east wind I will scatter
 them
 before the enemy.
I will show them my back, not my
 face,
 in the day of their calamity."

18 Then they said, "Come, let us make plots against Jeremiah, for the law shall not perish from the priest, nor counsel from the wise, nor the word from the prophet. Come, let us smite him with the tongue, and let us not heed any of his words."

¹⁹ Give heed to me, O LORD,
 and hearken to my plea.*j*
²⁰ Is evil a recompense for good?

f Cn: Heb *the field*   *g* Cn: Heb *foreign*
h Cn: Heb *Are . . . plucked up?*
i Gk Syr Vg: Heb *they made them stumble*
j Gk Compare Syr Tg: Heb *my adversaries*

18.1–12: The allegory of the potter. Probably in Jerusalem's southern section, Jeremiah watched a *potter* shaping the inanimate clay. So God molds his people (Rom.9.20–24). God does not deal capriciously with them. The design for *evil* can be replaced by the design for *good*—if they repent. But they refuse.

   18.13–17: A poetic commentary on v. 12. Judah has committed the nearly incredible folly of forsaking her God (2.10,32). God will ignore them (2.27–28) and will scatter them as before the east wind (4.11; 13.24; 23.19). *Sirion*, Mount Hermon. *Mountain waters*, perhaps from the Anti-Lebanon Mountains or from Mount Hermon itself, such as the Pharpar and Abanah rivers or the sources of the Jordan.

   18.18–23: Jeremiah's fourth personal lament (see 11.18–12.6 n.). *They* (identity unknown) plot against Jeremiah because of his attacks against the leaders (2.8; 8.8). Jeremiah defends his innocence and prays to God for the merciless, total destruction of his enemies and their families. Note the assignment of the law to the priests (v. 18).

Yet they have dug a pit for my
   life.
Remember how I stood before thee
   to speak good for them,
   to turn away thy wrath from them.
21 Therefore deliver up their children
   to famine;
   give them over to the power of
     the sword,
let their wives become childless and
   widowed.
May their men meet death by
   pestilence,
their youths be slain by the
   sword in battle.
22 May a cry be heard from their
   houses,
   when thou bringest the marauder
     suddenly upon them!
For they have dug a pit to take me,
   and laid snares for my feet.
23 Yet, thou, O LORD, knowest
   all their plotting to slay me.
Forgive not their iniquity,
   nor blot out their sin from thy
     sight.
Let them be overthrown before thee;
   deal with them in the time of thine
     anger.

19 Thus said the LORD, "Go, buy a potter's earthen flask, and take some of the elders of the people and some of the senior priests, 2 and go out to the valley of the son of Hinnom at the entry of the Potsherd Gate, and proclaim there the words that I tell you. 3 You shall say, 'Hear the word of the LORD, O kings of Judah and inhabitants of Jerusalem. Thus says the LORD of hosts, the God of Israel, Behold, I am bringing such evil upon this place that the ears of every one who hears of it will tingle. 4 Because the people have forsaken me, and have profaned this place by burning incense in it to other gods whom neither they nor their fathers nor the kings of Judah have known; and because they have filled this place with the blood of innocents, 5 and have built the high places of Ba'al to burn their sons in the fire as burnt offerings to Ba'al, which I did not command or decree, nor did it come into my mind; 6 therefore, behold, days are coming, says the LORD, when this place shall no more be called Topheth, or the valley of the son of Hinnom, but the valley of Slaughter. 7 And in this place I will make void the plans of Judah and Jerusalem, and will cause their people to fall by the sword before their enemies, and by the hand of those who seek their life. I will give their dead bodies for food to the birds of the air and to the beasts of the earth. 8 And I will make this city a horror, a thing to be hissed at; every one who passes by it will be horrified and will hiss because of all its disasters. 9 And I will make them eat the flesh of their sons and their daughters, and every one shall eat the flesh of his neighbor in the siege and in the distress, with which their enemies and those who seek their life afflict them.'

10 "Then you shall break the flask in the sight of the men who go with you, 11 and shall say to them, 'Thus says the LORD of hosts: So will I break this people and this city, as one breaks a potter's vessel, so that it can never be mended. Men shall bury in Topheth because there will be no place else to bury. 12 Thus will I do to this place, says the LORD, and to its inhabitants, making this city like Topheth. 13 The houses of Jerusalem and the houses of the kings of Judah—all the houses upon whose roofs incense has been burned to all the host of heaven, and drink offerings have been poured out to

---

19.1–20.6: The public persecution of Jeremiah. 1–2: Jeremiah buys a flask and goes to the Potsherd Gate (later called the Dung Gate, Neh.2.13), taking with him some sympathizers. **3–9:** Condemnation of the people for forsaking the LORD and for worshiping idols, and worst of all, for the offering of children to Baal (7.30–32). With a play on the Hebrew words for *flask* and *make void*, Jeremiah announces the people's horrible fate, which will make them resort to cannibalism. **10–15:** The idol-worshiping city, like the flask, will be irreparably smashed; the specter of death will hover over it as over *Topheth* (see 7.31 n.). *Host of heaven*, 8.2; 2 Kg.21.3–5.

other gods–shall be defiled like the place of Topheth.' "

14 Then Jeremiah came from Topheth, where the LORD had sent him to prophesy, and he stood in the court of the LORD's house, and said to all the people: 15 "Thus says the LORD of hosts, the God of Israel, Behold, I am bringing upon this city and upon all its towns all the evil that I have pronounced against it, because they have stiffened their neck, refusing to hear my words."

20 Now Pashhur the priest, the son of Immer, who was chief officer in the house of the LORD, heard Jeremiah prophesying these things. 2 Then Pashhur beat Jeremiah the prophet, and put him in the stocks that were in the upper Benjamin Gate of the house of the LORD. 3 On the morrow, when Pashhur released Jeremiah from the stocks, Jeremiah said to him, "The LORD does not call your name Pashhur, but Terror on every side. 4 For thus says the LORD: Behold, I will make you a terror to yourself and to all your friends. They shall fall by the sword of their enemies while you look on. And I will give all Judah into the hand of the king of Babylon; he shall carry them captive to Babylon, and shall slay them with the sword. 5 Moreover, I will give all the wealth of the city, all its gains, all its prized belongings, and all the treasures of the kings of Judah into the hand of their enemies, who shall plunder them, and seize them, and carry them to Babylon. 6 And you, Pashhur, and all who dwell in your house, shall go into captivity; to Babylon you shall go; and there you shall die, and there you shall be bur-

ied, you and all your friends, to whom you have prophesied falsely."

7 O LORD, thou hast deceived me,
    and I was deceived;
thou art stronger than I,
    and thou hast prevailed.
I have become a laughingstock all
        the day;
    every one mocks me.
8 For whenever I speak, I cry out,
    I shout, "Violence and
        destruction!"
For the word of the LORD has
        become for me
    a reproach and derision all day
        long.
9 If I say, "I will not mention him,
    or speak any more in his name,"
there is in my heart as it were a
        burning fire
    shut up in my bones,
and I am weary with holding it in,
    and I cannot.
10 For I hear many whispering.
    Terror is on every side!
"Denounce him! Let us denounce
        him!"
    say all my familiar friends,
    watching for my fall.
"Perhaps he will be deceived,
    then we can overcome him,
    and take our revenge on him."
11 But the LORD is with me as a dread
        warrior;
    therefore my persecutors will
        stumble,
    they will not overcome me.
They will be greatly shamed,
    for they will not succeed.
Their eternal dishonor
    will never be forgotten.
12 O LORD of hosts, who triest the
        righteous,

20.1–6: To forestall a repetition of this frightful pronouncement, Pashhur of the temple police publicly punishes Jeremiah. On his release (v. 3) he tells Pashhur that *Terror* (6.25; Ps.31.13) will be his name and lot, for he and his family will share the fate of the doomed city (25.8–11).

20.7–13,14–18: **Jeremiah's fifth and sixth personal laments** (see 11.18–12.6 n.). 7–9: Almost blasphemously, Jeremiah accuses God of deceiving him and of exerting irresistible power over him. Regardless of its effect, Jeremiah cannot refrain from his proclamation (Am.3.8; 1 Cor. 9.16). 10–13: Though his opponents plot his fall, Jeremiah expresses confidence in God's invincible protection of those who rely on him (*the needy*); he uses excerpts from liturgical

who seest the heart and the mind,
let me see thy vengeance upon them,
for to thee have I committed my
cause.

13 Sing to the LORD;
praise the LORD!
For he has delivered the life of the
needy
from the hand of evildoers.

14 Cursed be the day
on which I was born!
The day when my mother bore me,
let it not be blessed!
15 Cursed be the man
who brought the news to my
father,
"A son is born to you,"
making him very glad.
16 Let that man be like the cities
which the LORD overthrew
without pity;
let him hear a cry in the morning
and an alarm at noon,
17 because he did not kill me in the
womb;
so my mother would have been my
grave,
and her womb for ever great.
18 Why did I come forth from the
womb
to see toil and sorrow,
and spend my days in shame?

21 This is the word which came to
Jeremiah from the LORD, when
King Zedeki'ah sent to him Pashhur
the son of Malchi'ah and Zephani'ah
the priest, the son of Ma-asei'ah, saying, 2 "Inquire of the LORD for us, for
Nebuchadrez'zar king of Babylon is
making war against us; perhaps the
LORD will deal with us according to all
his wonderful deeds, and will make him
withdraw from us."

3 Then Jeremiah said to them:
4 "Thus you shall say to Zedeki'ah,
'Thus says the LORD, the God of Israel: Behold, I will turn back the
weapons of war which are in your
hands and with which you are fighting
against the king of Babylon and
against the Chalde'ans who are besieging you outside the walls; and I will
bring them together into the midst of
this city. 5 I myself will fight against
you with outstretched hand and strong
arm, in anger, and in fury, and in
great wrath. 6 And I will smite the inhabitants of this city, both man and
beast; they shall die of a great pestilence. 7 Afterward, says the LORD, I
will give Zedeki'ah king of Judah, and
his servants, and the people in this
city who survive the pestilence, sword,
and famine, into the hand of Nebuchadrez'zar king of Babylon and into
the hand of their enemies, into the
hand of those who seek their lives.
He shall smite them with the edge of
the sword; he shall not pity them, or
spare them, or have compassion.'

8 "And to this people you shall say:
'Thus says the LORD: Behold, I set before you the way of life and the way of
death. 9 He who stays in this city shall
die by the sword, by famine, and by
pestilence; but he who goes out and
surrenders to the Chalde'ans who are
besieging you shall live and shall have
his life as a prize of war. 10 For I have
set my face against this city for evil
and not for good, says the LORD: it shall

---

hymns (compare Pss.6.9–10; 31.13; 109.30; 140.12–13). **14–18:** In this independent section,
Jeremiah curses not God but his own existence (15.10; Job ch. 3). In it one glimpses the inner
agony of God's prophet as he confronts the unheeding godlessness of his day.
**21.1–24.10: Oracles from the time of Zedekiah. 21.1–10: Oracle against Zedekiah and Jerusa-
lem. 1–7:** These verses have been regarded by some scholars as another account of the event
described in 37.1–10, although the delegation to Jeremiah is a different one (v. 1, compare
37.3) and the Chaldeans here have not yet withdrawn from the city (compare 37.5). The two
accounts have much in common (e.g. compare vv. 4,5 and 37.10). Pashhur, the son of Malchiah,
appears also in ch. 38. Zephaniah the priest was later executed at Riblah by Nebuchadrezzar
(52.24–27). **5a:** Dt.4.34; 5.15. **5b:** Dt.29.28. **8–10:** The only possibility for life is surrender; but
Jerusalem will be destroyed (38.17).

be given into the hand of the king of Babylon, and he shall burn it with fire.'
11 "And to the house of the king of Judah say, 'Hear the word of the LORD, 12 O house of David! Thus says the LORD:

" 'Execute justice in the morning,
  and deliver from the hand of the
    oppressor
  him who has been robbed,
lest my wrath go forth like fire,
  and burn with none to quench it,
because of your evil doings.' "

13 "Behold, I am against you, O
  inhabitant of the valley,
  O rock of the plain,
        says the LORD;
you who say, 'Who shall come down
  against us,
  or who shall enter our
    habitations?'
14 I will punish you according to the
  fruit of your doings,
        says the LORD;
I will kindle a fire in her forest,
  and it shall devour all that is round
    about her."

22 Thus says the LORD: "Go down to the house of the king of Judah, and speak there this word, 2 and say, 'Hear the word of the LORD, O King of Judah, who sit on the throne of David, you, and your servants, and your people who enter these gates. 3 Thus says the LORD: Do justice and righteousness, and deliver from the hand of the oppressor him who has been robbed. And do no wrong or violence to the alien, the fatherless, and the widow, nor shed innocent blood in this place. 4 For if you will indeed obey this word, then there shall enter the gates of this house kings who sit on the throne of David, riding in chariots and on horses, they, and their servants, and their people. 5 But if you will not heed these words, I swear by myself, says the LORD, that this house shall become a desolation. 6 For thus says the LORD concerning the house of the king of Judah:

" 'You are as Gilead to me,
  as the summit of Lebanon,
yet surely I will make you a desert,
  an uninhabited city.*k*
7 I will prepare destroyers against you,
  each with his weapons;
and they shall cut down your
  choicest cedars,
  and cast them into the fire.

8 " 'And many nations will pass by this city, and every man will say to his neighbor, "Why has the LORD dealt thus with this great city?" 9 And they will answer, "Because they forsook the covenant of the LORD their God, and worshiped other gods and served them." ' "

10 Weep not for him who is dead,
  nor bemoan him;
but weep bitterly for him who goes
  away,
for he shall return no more
  to see his native land.

11 For thus says the LORD concerning Shallum the son of Josi'ah, king of Judah, who reigned instead of Josi'ah his father, and who went away from this place: "He shall return here no more, 12 but in the place where

k Cn: Heb *cities*

21.11–23.8: Oracles concerning the royal house. 21.11–22.9: General oracle. 21.11–14: The king is to administer justice (1 Kg.3.9; Ps.72.1–4); if he does evil, he will incur the wrath of God. **13:** Text and meaning are unclear. **14:** *Forest* suggests royal palace (1 Kg.7.2). **22.1–5:** Expansion of 21.11–14 (compare 22.3 with 21.12). If the people repent, their destruction will be averted and the Davidic dynasty (*house*) preserved. **6–7:** Continuation of 21.14. Woodsmen (*destroyers*) with axes and saws (*weapons*) will burn the "forest" (cedarwood palace), reducing its once beautiful site to wasteland. **8–9:** A later comment (5.19; Dt.29.23–28; 1 Kg.9.8–9) referring to Jerusalem, not the palace.

22.10–30: Oracles concerning Jehoahaz, Jehoiakim, and Jehoiachin, kings of Judah. 10–12: The dead Josiah was better off than *Shallum* (personal name of Jehoahaz; 1 Chr.3.15), who in 609 B.C. was banished (*went away*) to Egypt by Neco (2 Kg.23.33–34; 2 Chr.36.1–4; Ezek.19.4).

they have carried him captive, there
shall he die, and he shall never see
this land again."

13 "Woe to him who builds his house
      by unrighteousness,
   and his upper rooms by injustice;
who makes his neighbor serve him
      for nothing,
   and does not give him his wages;
14 who says, 'I will build myself a great
      house
   with spacious upper rooms,'
and cuts out windows for it,
   paneling it with cedar,
   and painting it with vermilion.
15 Do you think you are a king
      because you compete in cedar?
Did not your father eat and drink
   and do justice and righteousness?
   Then it was well with him.
16 He judged the cause of the poor and
      needy;
   then it was well.
Is not this to know me?
   says the LORD.
17 But you have eyes and heart
      only for your dishonest gain,
   for shedding innocent blood,
      and for practicing oppression and
         violence."
18 Therefore thus says the LORD
concerning Jehoi'akim the son of
Josi'ah, king of Judah:
   "They shall not lament for him,
      saying,
   'Ah my brother!' or 'Ah sister!'
They shall not lament for him,
      saying,
   'Ah lord!' or 'Ah his majesty!'
19 With the burial of an ass he shall be
      buried,
   dragged and cast forth beyond the
      gates of Jerusalem."

20 "Go up to Lebanon, and cry out,
      and lift up your voice in Bashan;
   cry from Ab'arim,
      for all your lovers are destroyed.
21 I spoke to you in your prosperity,
      but you said, 'I will not listen.'
This has been your way from your
      youth,
   that you have not obeyed my
      voice.
22 The wind shall shepherd all your
      shepherds,
   and your lovers shall go into
      captivity;
then you will be ashamed and
      confounded
   because of all your wickedness.
23 O inhabitant of Lebanon,
      nested among the cedars,
   how you will groan¹ when pangs
      come upon you,
   pain as of a woman in travail!"

24 "As I live, says the LORD,
though Coni'ah the son of Jehoi'akim,
king of Judah, were the signet ring on
my right hand, yet I would tear you off
25 and give you into the hand of those
who seek your life, into the hand of
those of whom you are afraid, even into
the hand of Nebuchadrez'zar king of
Babylon and into the hand of the Chalde'ans. 26 I will hurl you and the mother
who bore you into another country,
where you were not born, and there
you shall die. 27 But to the land to which
they will long to return, there they shall
not return."
28 Is this man Coni'ah a despised,
      broken pot,
   a vessel no one cares for?
Why are he and his children hurled
      and cast

l Gk Vg Syr: Heb *be pitied*

13–19: Jeremiah censures Jehoiakim for irresponsibly expanding his palace (*house*) after
Egyptian styles (v. 14). Just administration, not the house, makes the king (21.11–12; Mic.3.9–
10). Jehoiakim should emulate his *father* Josiah whose death was mourned. His own death will
be accompanied by indignities because of his misdeeds (36.30; 2 Kg.24.1–5). **20–30:** From the
highest peaks lamentations will rise over the desertion of Jerusalem by her gods (*lovers;* 3.1),
the exile of her leaders (*shepherds;* 23.1), and the terror of her king (*inhabitant of Lebanon;*
compare 21.13–14) before his fate. The inexorable punishment of Jehoiachin (*Coniah*) and his
mother (13.18) is described by the symbol of authority (*signet ring;* Hag.2.23) and a *broken pot.*

into a land which they do not
know?
²⁹ O land, land, land,
hear the word of the LORD!
³⁰ Thus says the LORD:
"Write this man down as childless,
a man who shall not succeed in
his days;
for none of his offspring shall succeed
in sitting on the throne of David,
and ruling again in Judah."

23 "Woe to the shepherds who
destroy and scatter the sheep of
my pasture!" says the LORD. ² Therefore thus says the LORD, the God of
Israel, concerning the shepherds who
care for my people: "You have scattered my flock, and have driven them
away, and you have not attended to
them. Behold, I will attend to you for
your evil doings, says the LORD.
³ Then I will gather the remnant of my
flock out of all the countries where I
have driven them, and I will bring them
back to their fold, and they shall be
fruitful and multiply. ⁴ I will set shepherds over them who will care for them,
and they shall fear no more, nor be dismayed, neither shall any be missing,
says the LORD.
5 "Behold, the days are coming,
says the LORD, when I will raise up for
David a righteous Branch, and he shall
reign as king and deal wisely, and shall
execute justice and righteousness in
the land. ⁶ In his days Judah will be
saved, and Israel will dwell securely.
And this is the name by which he will
be called: 'The LORD is our righteousness.'
7 "Therefore, behold, the days are

coming, says the LORD, when men shall
no longer say, 'As the LORD lives who
brought up the people of Israel out of
the land of Egypt,' ⁸ but 'As the LORD
lives who brought up and led the descendants of the house of Israel out of
the north country and out of all the
countries where he*ᵐ* had driven them.'
Then they shall dwell in their own
land."

9 Concerning the prophets:
My heart is broken within me,
all my bones shake;
I am like a drunken man,
like a man overcome by wine,
because of the LORD
and because of his holy words.
¹⁰ For the land is full of adulterers;
because of the curse the land
mourns,
and the pastures of the
wilderness are dried up.
Their course is evil,
and their might is not right.
¹¹ "Both prophet and priest are
ungodly;
even in my house I have found
their wickedness,
says the LORD.
¹² Therefore their way shall be to them
like slippery paths in the darkness,
into which they shall be driven
and fall;
for I will bring evil upon them
in the year of their punishment,
says the LORD.
¹³ In the prophets of Sama'ria
I saw an unsavory thing:
they prophesied by Ba'al
and led my people Israel astray.

m Gk: Heb *I*

The threefold address (v. 29a; Is.6.3; Ezek.21.27) emphasizes the following oracle announcing
that no descendant of Jehoiachin shall rule Judah.

23.1–8: A messianic oracle. After reproaching Judah's rulers (*shepherds;* 22.22; Ezek. ch. 34)
for scattering Judah (his *flock*), God promises to establish a righteous member (*branch*; Is.11.1;
Zech.3.8) of David's line over a restored Israel (30.9). He will rule responsibly before God as a
king (Is.9.2–7), not as a puppet (like Zedekiah). This messianic expectation differs from the
later militant nationalism (16.14–15).

23.9–40: Oracles concerning the prophets. 9–12: In the light of God's will, Jeremiah is distraught over the moral delinquency of *priest* and *prophet,* supposedly guardians of Israel's
faith. **12:** By their own devices the prophets will be destroyed. **13–15:** In words they are worse
than the prophets of Baal in Samaria; and in deeds, worse than the people of Sodom and

14 But in the prophets of Jerusalem
     I have seen a horrible thing:
  they commit adultery and walk in
     lies;
       they strengthen the hands of
          evildoers,
     so that no one turns from his
          wickedness;
  all of them have become like Sodom
     to me,
     and its inhabitants like
       Gomor'rah."
15 Therefore thus says the LORD of
hosts concerning the prophets:
  "Behold, I will feed them with
     wormwood,
     and give them poisoned water to
       drink;
  for from the prophets of Jerusalem
     ungodliness has gone forth into all
       the land."

16 Thus says the LORD of hosts:
"Do not listen to the words of the
prophets who prophesy to you, filling
you with vain hopes; they speak visions
of their own minds, not from the mouth
of the LORD. 17 They say continually to
those who despise the word of the
LORD, 'It shall be well with you'; and to
every one who stubbornly follows his
own heart, they say, 'No evil shall
come upon you.'"

18 For who among them has stood in
     the council of the LORD
  to perceive and to hear his word,
  or who has given heed to his word
     and listened?
19 Behold, the storm of the LORD!
     Wrath has gone forth,
  a whirling tempest;
     it will burst upon the head of the
       wicked.
20 The anger of the LORD will not turn
     back

until he has executed and
     accomplished
  the intents of his mind.
  In the latter days you will
     understand it clearly.

21 "I did not send the prophets,
     yet they ran;
  I did not speak to them,
     yet they prophesied.
22 But if they had stood in my council,
     then they would have proclaimed
       my words to my people,
  and they would have turned them
     from their evil way,
  and from the evil of their doings.

23 "Am I a God at hand, says the
LORD, and not a God afar off? 24 Can
a man hide himself in secret places so
that I cannot see him? says the LORD.
Do I not fill heaven and earth? says
the LORD. 25 I have heard what the
prophets have said who prophesy lies
in my name, saying, 'I have dreamed,
I have dreamed!' 26 How long shall
there be lies[n] in the heart of the
prophets who prophesy lies, and who
prophesy the deceit of their own heart,
27 who think to make my people forget my name by their dreams which
they tell one another, even as their
fathers forgot my name for Ba'al?
28 Let the prophet who has a dream tell
the dream, but let him who has my word
speak my word faithfully. What has
straw in common with wheat? says the
LORD. 29 Is not my word like fire, says
the LORD, and like a hammer which
breaks the rock in pieces? 30 Therefore, behold, I am against the prophets,
says the LORD, who steal my words
from one another. 31 Behold, I am
against the prophets, says the LORD,
who use their tongues and say, 'Says

n Cn Compare Syr: Heb obscure

Gomorrah. **16–22:** Turning from their deeds to their message, Jeremiah reproves the prophets
for their assurance of well-being to those who flout God's word. Obviously they cannot be
God's emissaries or his spokesmen (for the divine *council*, see 1 Kg.22.19–23; Is.6.1–7; 40.1–2).
23–32: God's omnipresence precludes his being unaware of the prophets' misleading his
people by their claims of divine revelation through *dreams* (27.9; 29.8; Dt.13.3; compare 2.8b).
29: God's living word is devastating as *fire* (5.14) and shattering as a *hammer*. With biting
sarcasm (*tell the dream*, v. 28; *steal my words*, v. 30) and threefold emphasis (*behold*, vv. 30,31,32),

the LORD.' ³² Behold, I am against those who prophesy lying dreams, says the LORD, and who tell them and lead my people astray by their lies and their recklessness, when I did not send them or charge them; so they do not profit this people at all, says the LORD.

33 "When one of this people, or a prophet, or a priest asks you, 'What is the burden of the LORD?' you shall say to them, 'You are the burden,ᵒ and I will cast you off, says the LORD.' ³⁴ And as for the prophet, priest, or one of the people who says, 'The burden of the LORD,' I will punish that man and his household. ³⁵ Thus shall you say, every one to his neighbor and every one to his brother, 'What has the LORD answered?' or 'What has the LORD spoken?' ³⁶ But 'the burden of the LORD' you shall mention no more, for the burden is every man's own word, and you pervert the words of the living God, the LORD of hosts, our God. ³⁷ Thus you shall say to the prophet, 'What has the LORD answered you?' or 'What has the LORD spoken?' ³⁸ But if you say, 'The burden of the LORD,' thus says the LORD, 'Because you have said these words, "The burden of the LORD," when I sent to you, saying, "You shall not say, 'The burden of the LORD,'" ³⁹ therefore, behold, I will surely lift you up and cast you away from my presence, you and the city which I gave to you and your fathers. ⁴⁰ And I will bring upon you everlasting reproach and perpetual shame, which shall not be forgotten.' "

24 After Nebuchadrez'zar king of Babylon had taken into exile from Jerusalem Jeconi'ah the son of Jehoi'akim, king of Judah, together with the princes of Judah, the crafts-men, and the smiths, and had brought them to Babylon, the LORD showed me this vision: Behold, two baskets of figs placed before the temple of the LORD. ² One basket had very good figs, like first-ripe figs, but the other basket had very bad figs, so bad that they could not be eaten. ³ And the LORD said to me, "What do you see, Jeremiah?" I said, "Figs, the good figs very good, and the bad figs very bad, so bad that they cannot be eaten."

4 Then the word of the LORD came to me: ⁵ "Thus says the LORD, the God of Israel: Like these good figs, so I will regard as good the exiles from Judah, whom I have sent away from this place to the land of the Chalde'ans. ⁶ I will set my eyes upon them for good, and I will bring them back to this land. I will build them up, and not tear them down; I will plant them, and not uproot them. ⁷ I will give them a heart to know that I am the LORD; and they shall be my people and I will be their God, for they shall return to me with their whole heart.

8 "But thus says the LORD: Like the bad figs which are so bad they cannot be eaten, so will I treat Zedeki'ah the king of Judah, his princes, the remnant of Jerusalem who remain in this land, and those who dwell in the land of Egypt. ⁹ I will make them a horrorᵖ to all the kingdoms of the earth, to be a reproach, a byword, a taunt, and a curse in all the places where I shall drive them. ¹⁰ And I will send sword, famine, and pestilence upon them, until they shall be utterly destroyed from the land which I gave to them and their fathers."

o Gk Vg: Heb *What burden*
p Compare Gk: Heb *horror for evil*

Jeremiah proclaims God's condemnation of their pretensions. **33:** With bitter irony, Jeremiah uses a play on words. **34–40:** This is a later commentary on v. 33, which it misunderstood, concentrating on the phrase "the burden of the LORD"; it is theologically non-Jeremianic.

24.1–10: The vision of the baskets of figs. Those remaining in Palestine and Egypt (identity of these latter is unknown) after 597 B.C. (*the bad figs*) appropriated the property of those deported (*the good figs*), who were considered the objects of God's wrath (29.15–19; Ezek. 11.14–15). But the exiles will be returned (29.10–14) and will become a faithful nation. The others will be destroyed for their wilful indifference to God's chastisement.

25 The word that came to Jeremiah concerning all the people of Judah, in the fourth year of Jehoi'akim the son of Josi'ah, king of Judah (that was the first year of Nebuchadrez'zar king of Babylon), ² which Jeremiah the prophet spoke to all the people of Judah and all the inhabitants of Jerusalem: ³ "For twenty-three years, from the thirteenth year of Josi'ah the son of Amon, king of Judah, to this day, the word of the LORD has come to me, and I have spoken persistently to you, but you have not listened. ⁴ You have neither listened nor inclined your ears to hear, although the LORD persistently sent to you all his servants the prophets, ⁵ saying, 'Turn now, every one of you, from his evil way and wrong doings, and dwell upon the land which the LORD has given to you and your fathers from of old and for ever; ⁶ do not go after other gods to serve and worship them, or provoke me to anger with the work of your hands. Then I will do you no harm.' ⁷ Yet you have not listened to me, says the LORD, that you might provoke me to anger with the work of your hands to your own harm.

8 "Therefore thus says the LORD of hosts: Because you have not obeyed my words, ⁹ behold, I will send for all the tribes of the north, says the LORD, and for Nebuchadrez'zar the king of Babylon, my servant, and I will bring them against this land and its inhabitants, and against all these nations round about; I will utterly destroy them, and make them a horror, a hissing, and an everlasting reproach.*q* ¹⁰ Moreover, I will banish from them the voice of mirth and the voice of gladness, the voice of the bridegroom and the voice of the bride, the grinding of the millstones and the light of the lamp. ¹¹ This whole land shall become a ruin and a waste, and these nations shall serve the king of Babylon seventy years. ¹² Then after seventy years are completed, I will punish the king of Babylon and that nation, the land of the Chalde'ans, for their iniquity, says the LORD, making the land an everlasting waste. ¹³ I will bring upon that land all the words which I have uttered against it, everything written in this book, which Jeremiah prophesied against all the nations. ¹⁴ For many nations and great kings shall make slaves even of them; and I will recompense them according to their deeds and the work of their hands."

15 Thus the LORD, the God of Israel, said to me: "Take from my hand this cup of the wine of wrath, and make all the nations to whom I send you drink it. ¹⁶ They shall drink and stagger and be crazed because of the sword which I am sending among them."

17 So I took the cup from the LORD's hand, and made all the nations to whom the Lord sent me drink it: ¹⁸ Jerusalem and the cities of Judah, its kings and princes, to make them a desolation and a waste, a hissing and a curse, as at this day; ¹⁹ Pharaoh king of Egypt, his servants, his princes, all his people, ²⁰ and all the foreign folk among them; all the kings of the land of Uz and all the kings of the land of the Philistines (Ash'kelon, Gaza, Ekron, and the remnant of Ashdod); ²¹ Edom, Moab, and the sons of Ammon; ²² all the kings of Tyre, all the

q Gk Compare Syr: Heb *desolations*

25.1–14: Babylon, God's instrument for punishment. This conclusion to Jeremiah's memoirs (36.1–4) was written after Nebuchadrezzar's victory over Neco of Egypt at Carchemish, in June, 605 B.C. Jeremiah's warnings to Judah are near fulfilment. The foe from the north (6.1) will devastate the apostate land. All manifestations of normal daily life will disappear. No one of this faithless generation will see the restoration "seventy years" later (v. 12; compare Num. 14.20–24). Though Judah's destruction is her punishment, wanton destruction does not go unpunished; ultimately Babylon herself will succumb to her enemies.

25.15–38: The cup of wrath. 15–29: The vision originally introduced the now separated section of oracles against the nations (chs. 46–51; compare 1.5). All nations, because of their transgressions (Am.1.3–3.2), must suffer God's wrath (vv. 27–29 continue v. 16). The *cup* as a

kings of Sidon, and the kings of the coastland across the sea; 23 Dedan, Tema, Buz, and all who cut the corners of their hair; 24 all the kings of Arabia and all the kings of the mixed tribes that dwell in the desert; 25 all the kings of Zimri, all the kings of Elam, and all the kings of Media; 26 all the kings of the north, far and near, one after another, and all the kingdoms of the world which are on the face of the earth. And after them the king of Babylon*r* shall drink.

27 "Then you shall say to them, 'Thus says the LORD of hosts, the God of Israel: Drink, be drunk and vomit, fall and rise no more, because of the sword which I am sending among you.'

28 "And if they refuse to accept the cup from your hand to drink, then you shall say to them, 'Thus says the LORD of hosts: You must drink! 29 For behold, I begin to work evil at the city which is called by my name, and shall you go unpunished? You shall not go unpunished, for I am summoning a sword against all the inhabitants of the earth, says the LORD of hosts.'

30 "You, therefore, shall prophesy against them all these words, and say to them:
'The LORD will roar from on high,
and from his holy habitation
utter his voice;
he will roar mightily against his fold,
and shout, like those who tread grapes,
against all the inhabitants of the earth.
31 The clamor will resound to the ends of the earth,
for the LORD has an indictment against the nations;
he is entering into judgment with all flesh,

and the wicked he will put to the sword,
says the LORD.'

32 "Thus says the LORD of hosts:
Behold, evil is going forth
from nation to nation,
and a great tempest is stirring
from the farthest parts of the earth!

33 "And those slain by the LORD on that day shall extend from one end of the earth to the other. They shall not be lamented, or gathered, or buried; they shall be dung on the surface of the ground.

34 "Wail, you shepherds, and cry,
and roll in ashes, you lords of the flock,
for the days of your slaughter and dispersion have come,
and you shall fall like choice rams.*s*
35 No refuge will remain for the shepherds,
nor escape for the lords of the flock.
36 Hark, the cry of the shepherds,
and the wail of the lords of the flock!
For the LORD is despoiling their pasture,
37 and the peaceful folds are devastated,
because of the fierce anger of the LORD.
38 Like a lion he has left his covert,
for their land has become a waste
because of the sword of the oppressor,
and because of his fierce anger."

26 In the beginning of the reign of Jehoi′akim the son of Josi′ah,

r Heb *Sheshach*, a cipher for Babylon
s Gk: Heb *a choice vessel*

symbol of God's judgment (note its equation with *sword*, v. 29) originated perhaps with Jeremiah (8.14; Is.51.17; Ps.11.6). **26:** *Babylon* is written in the Hebrew text as "Sheshach"; this kind of cipher, in which the letters are substituted in reverse order of the Hebrew alphabet, is called "atbash" (see 51.1,41 n.). **30–31:** The judgment is described in conventional figures: roaring (Am.1.2; Ps.46.6); vintage (Is.16.9–10; 63.1–3); courtroom (12.1); sword (12.12). **32–33:** Distant foe (6.22) and heavy casualties (8.2; 16.4). **34–38:** The rulers (*shepherds, lords of the flock*) are confused and desperate. **38:** The *lion* is either God, or Nebuchadrezzar (4.7).
26.1–35.19: Events and prophecies (largely from Baruch's memoirs); predictions of restoration.

king of Judah, this word came from the LORD, 2 "Thus says the LORD: Stand in the court of the LORD's house, and speak to all the cities of Judah which come to worship in the house of the LORD all the words that I command you to speak to them; do not hold back a word. 3 It may be they will listen, and every one turn from his evil way, that I may repent of the evil which I intend to do to them because of their evil doings. 4 You shall say to them, 'Thus says the LORD: If you will not listen to me, to walk in my law which I have set before you, 5 and to heed the words of my servants the prophets whom I send to you urgently, though you have not heeded, 6 then I will make this house like Shiloh, and I will make this city a curse for all the nations of the earth.'"

7 The priests and the prophets and all the people heard Jeremiah speaking these words in the house of the LORD. 8 And when Jeremiah had finished speaking all that the LORD had commanded him to speak to all the people, then the priests and the prophets and all the people laid hold of him, saying, "You shall die! 9 Why have you prophesied in the name of the LORD, saying, 'This house shall be like Shiloh, and this city shall be desolate, without inhabitant'?" And all the people gathered about Jeremiah in the house of the LORD.

10 When the princes of Judah heard these things, they came up from the king's house to the house of the LORD and took their seat in the entry of the New Gate of the house of the LORD. 11 Then the priests and the prophets said to the princes and to all the people, "This man deserves the sentence of death, because he has prophesied against this city, as you have heard with your own ears."

12 Then Jeremiah spoke to all the princes and all the people, saying, "The LORD sent me to prophesy against this house and this city all the words you have heard. 13 Now therefore amend your ways and your doings, and obey the voice of the LORD your God, and the LORD will repent of the evil which he has pronounced against you. 14 But as for me, behold, I am in your hands. Do with me as seems good and right to you. 15 Only know for certain that if you put me to death, you will bring innocent blood upon yourselves and upon this city and its inhabitants, for in truth the LORD sent me to you to speak all these words in your ears."

16 Then the princes and all the people said to the priests and the prophets, "This man does not deserve the sentence of death, for he has spoken to us in the name of the LORD our God." 17 And certain of the elders of the land arose and spoke to all the assembled people, saying, 18 "Micah of Mo'resheth prophesied in the days of Hezeki'ah king of Judah, and said to all the people of Judah: 'Thus says the LORD of hosts,

Zion shall be plowed as a field;
Jerusalem shall become a heap of
   ruins,
and the mountain of the house a
   wooded height.'

19 Did Hezeki'ah king of Judah and all Judah put him to death? Did he not fear the LORD and entreat the favor of the LORD, and did not the LORD repent of the evil which he had pronounced against them? But we are about to bring great evil upon ourselves."

20 There was another man who

26.1–24: The temple sermon. 1–6: The sermon (7.1–15) was delivered perhaps during the Feast of Booths (September–October), 609 B.C. Baruch's summation here contains elements of ch. 7 and other sayings of Jeremiah (4.1–2; 18.7–11; 36.3). **7–19:** Jeremiah's arrest and release. Frequently criticized by Jeremiah (2.8; 5.30–31; 6.13–14), priest and prophet alike would suffer from the temple's destruction. The royal officials assemble to hear the case. Jeremiah's dignified defense wins his release; the judges base their decision on a century-old precedent set by Hezekiah (715–687 B.C.) regarding the prophet Micah. *New Gate*, perhaps the Benjamin Gate, north of the temple (20.2; 2 Kg.15.35). Avenging of *innocent blood*, Gen.4.10; 2 Sam.21.1–14;

prophesied in the name of the LORD, Uri'ah the son of Shemai'ah from Kir'-iath-je'arim. He prophesied against this city and against this land in words like those of Jeremiah. ²¹ And when King Jehoi'akim, with all his warriors and all the princes, heard his words, the king sought to put him to death; but when Uri'ah heard of it, he was afraid and fled and escaped to Egypt. ²² Then King Jehoi'akim sent to Egypt certain men, Elna'than the son of Achbor and others with him, ²³ and they fetched Uri'ah from Egypt and brought him to King Jehoi'akim, who slew him with the sword and cast his dead body into the burial place of the common people.

24 But the hand of Ahi'kam the son of Shaphan was with Jeremiah so that he was not given over to the people to be put to death.

27 In the beginning of the reign of Zedeki'ah^u the son of Josi'ah, king of Judah, this word came to Jeremiah from the LORD. ² Thus the LORD said to me: "Make yourself thongs and yoke-bars, and put them on your neck. ³ Send word^v to the king of Edom, the king of Moab, the king of the sons of Ammon, the king of Tyre, and the king of Sidon by the hand of the envoys who have come to Jerusalem to Zedeki'ah king of Judah. ⁴ Give them this charge for their masters: 'Thus says the LORD of hosts, the God of Israel: This is what you shall say to your masters: ⁵ "It is I who by my great power and my outstretched arm have made the earth, with the men

and animals that are on the earth, and I give it to whomever it seems right to me. ⁶ Now I have given all these lands into the hand of Nebuchadnez'zar, the king of Babylon, my servant, and I have given him also the beasts of the field to serve him. ⁷ All the nations shall serve him and his son and his grandson, until the time of his own land comes; then many nations and great kings shall make him their slave.

8 " ' "But if any nation or kingdom will not serve this Nebuchadnez'zar king of Babylon, and put its neck under the yoke of the king of Babylon, I will punish that nation with the sword, with famine, and with pestilence, says the LORD, until I have consumed it by his hand. ⁹ So do not listen to your prophets, your diviners, your dreamers,^w your soothsayers, or your sorcerers, who are saying to you, 'You shall not serve the king of Babylon.' ¹⁰ For it is a lie which they are prophesying to you, with the result that you will be removed far from your land, and I will drive you out, and you will perish. ¹¹ But any nation which will bring its neck under the yoke of the king of Babylon and serve him, I will leave on its own land, to till it and dwell there, says the LORD." ' "

12 To Zedeki'ah king of Judah I spoke in like manner: "Bring your necks under the yoke of the king of Babylon, and serve him and his people, and live. ¹³ Why will you and your people die by the sword, by famine, and by pestilence, as the LORD

u Another reading is Jehoiakim
v Cn: Heb send them
w Gk Syr Vg: Heb dreams

---

1 Kg. ch. 21. **20–24**: Martyrdom of Uriah. Baruch adds this story to illustrate Jeremiah's personal danger and fortunate official support (*Ahikam*, 2 Kg.22.12,14). As Egypt's vassal (2 Kg.23.34–35), Jehoiakim had no difficulty arresting Uriah (*Elnathan*, 36.12,25). His execution is unusual in the annals of Israelite prophetism (2 Chr.24.20–22; Mt.23.29–31).

27.1–28.17: The yoke of the king of Babylon. 27.1–11: The yoke of Babylon was imposed by God upon Judah and her neighbors (21.1–10; 32.3–5); thus their plans for rebellion are against God's will. The occasion for the conspiracy lay in a revolt within Nebuchadrezzar's army (December 595–January 594 B.C.) and the accession in Egypt of Psammetichus II (594). Perhaps responding to Jeremiah's warning, Zedekiah did not carry out the rebellion, and so Judah was spared during Nebuchadrezzar's punitive campaign later that year. The form "Nebuchadnezzar" occurs in Jer. chs. 27–29; elsewhere in Jer. "Nebuchadrezzar" appears. The Babylonian form is Nabu-kudurru-usur. **12–15:** Jeremiah repeats his warning: since God has not sent the prophets

has spoken concerning any nation which will not serve the king of Babylon? ¹⁴ Do not listen to the words of the prophets who are saying to you, 'You shall not serve the king of Babylon,' for it is a lie which they are prophesying to you. ¹⁵ I have not sent them, says the LORD, but they are prophesying falsely in my name, with the result that I will drive you out and you will perish, you and the prophets who are prophesying to you."

16 Then I spoke to the priests and to all this people, saying, "Thus says the LORD: Do not listen to the words of your prophets who are prophesying to you, saying, 'Behold, the vessels of the LORD's house will now shortly be brought back from Babylon,' for it is a lie which they are prophesying to you. ¹⁷ Do not listen to them; serve the king of Babylon and live. Why should this city become a desolation? ¹⁸ If they are prophets, and if the word of the LORD is with them, then let them intercede with the LORD of hosts, that the vessels which are left in the house of the LORD, in the house of the king of Judah, and in Jerusalem may not go to Babylon. ¹⁹ For thus says the LORD of hosts concerning the pillars, the sea, the stands, and the rest of the vessels which are left in this city, ²⁰ which Nebuchadnez′zar king of Babylon did not take away, when he took into exile from Jerusalem to Babylon Jeconi′ah the son of Jehoi′akim, king of Judah, and all the nobles of Judah and Jerusalem– ²¹ thus says the LORD of hosts, the God of Israel, concerning the vessels which are left in the house of the LORD, in the house of the king of Judah, and in Jerusalem: ²² They shall be carried to Babylon and remain there until the day when I give attention to them, says the LORD. Then I will bring them back and restore them to this place."

28 In that same year, at the beginning of the reign of Zedeki′ah king of Judah, in the fifth month of the fourth year, Hanani′ah the son of Azzur, the prophet from Gibeon, spoke to me in the house of the LORD, in the presence of the priests and all the people, saying, ² "Thus says the LORD of hosts, the God of Israel: I have broken the yoke of the king of Babylon. ³ Within two years I will bring back to this place all the vessels of the LORD's house, which Nebuchadnez′zar king of Babylon took away from this place and carried to Babylon. ⁴ I will also bring back to this place Jeconi′ah the son of Jehoi′akim, king of Judah, and all the exiles from Judah who went to Babylon, says the LORD, for I will break the yoke of the king of Babylon."

5 Then the prophet Jeremiah spoke to Hanani′ah the prophet in the presence of the priests and all the people who were standing in the house of the LORD; ⁶ and the prophet Jeremiah said, "Amen! May the LORD do so; may the LORD make the words which you have prophesied come true, and bring back to this place from Babylon the vessels of the house of the LORD, and all the exiles. ⁷ Yet hear now this word which I speak in your hearing and in the hearing of all the people. ⁸ The prophets who preceded you and me from ancient times prophesied war, famine, and pestilence against many countries and great kingdoms. ⁹ As for the prophet who prophesies peace, when the word of that prophet comes to pass, then it will be known that the LORD has truly sent the prophet."

10 Then the prophet Hanani′ah took the yoke-bars from the neck of Jeremiah the prophet, and broke them. ¹¹ And Hanani′ah spoke in the presence of all the people, saying, "Thus

---

who are advising Zedekiah (14.14), they are unreliable guides. **16–22:** He cautions the priests and the people against believing the baseless assurances of these prophets that the temple equipment taken as booty in 597 B.C. would be shortly returned. Instead, they should pray that what they have (Jer.52.17; 2 Kg.25.13) will not also be taken to Babylon. **28.1–17:** Jeremiah and Hananiah. In August 594 B.C., Hananiah faced Jeremiah in the temple and predicted total restoration within two years, breaking Jeremiah's yoke to emphasize his point. Jeremiah

says the LORD: Even so will I break the yoke of Nebuchadnez'zar king of Babylon from the neck of all the nations within two years." But Jeremiah the prophet went his way.

12 Sometime after the prophet Hanani'ah had broken the yoke-bars from off the neck of Jeremiah the prophet, the word of the LORD came to Jeremiah: 13 "Go, tell Hanani'ah, 'Thus says the LORD: You have broken wooden bars, but I^x will make in their place bars of iron. 14 For thus says the LORD of hosts, the God of Israel: I have put upon the neck of all these nations an iron yoke of servitude to Nebuchadnez'zar king of Babylon, and they shall serve him, for I have given to him even the beasts of the field.' " 15 And Jeremiah the prophet said to the prophet Hanani'ah, "Listen, Hanani'ah, the LORD has not sent you, and you have made this people trust in a lie. 16 Therefore thus says the LORD: 'Behold, I will remove you from the face of the earth. This very year you shall die, because you have uttered rebellion against the LORD.' "

17 In that same year, in the seventh month, the prophet Hanani'ah died.

29 These are the words of the letter which Jeremiah the prophet sent from Jerusalem to the elders^y of the exiles, and to the priests, the prophets, and all the people, whom Nebuchadnez'zar had taken into exile from Jerusalem to Babylon. 2 This was after King Jeconi'ah, and the queen mother, the eunuchs, the princes of Judah and Jerusalem, the craftsmen, and the smiths had departed from Jerusalem. 3 The letter was sent by the hand of Ela'sah the son of Shaphan and Gemari'ah the son of Hilki'ah, whom Zedeki'ah king of Judah sent to Babylon to Nebuchadnez'zar king of Babylon. It said: 4 "Thus says the LORD of hosts, the God of Israel, to all the exiles whom I have sent into exile from Jerusalem to Babylon: 5 Build houses and live in them; plant gardens and eat their produce. 6 Take wives and have sons and daughters; take wives for your sons, and give your daughters in marriage, that they may bear sons and daughters; multiply there, and do not decrease. 7 But seek the welfare of the city where I have sent you into exile, and pray to the LORD on its behalf, for in its welfare you will find your welfare. 8 For thus says the LORD of hosts, the God of Israel: Do not let your prophets and your diviners who are among you deceive you, and do not listen to the dreams which they dream,^{z} 9 for it is a lie which they are prophesying to you in my name; I did not send them, says the LORD.

10 "For thus says the LORD: When seventy years are completed for Babylon, I will visit you, and I will fulfil to you my promise and bring you back to this place. 11 For I know the plans I have for you, says the LORD, plans for welfare and not for evil, to give you a future and a hope. 12 Then you will call upon me and come and pray to me, and I will hear you. 13 You will seek me and find me; when you seek me with all your heart, 14 I will be found by you, says the LORD, and I

x Gk: Heb *you*
y Gk: Heb *the rest of the elders*
z Cn: Heb *your dreams which you cause to dream*

---

recalled that their predecessors had predicted chastisement (Dt.18.20–22; Mic.3.5–12). Because the situation was unchanged, Hananiah's promise, though attractive, seemed very doubtful. Later Jeremiah used the symbolism of an iron yoke to emphasize that the Exile would continue (27.7). *Yoke*, placed on the neck of an ox, held on by leather straps.

29.1–32: Jeremiah's letters to Babylon. 1–23: Letter to the exiles. The exiles were being misled by the same baseless assurances of speedy return as those in Palestine (ch. 27). To counter this Jeremiah sent a letter by *Elasah* (perhaps the brother of Ahikam, 26.24) and *Gemariah* (36.10) to the *elders* of the people (Ezek.8.1; 14.1). His advice was revolutionary. They were to establish homes in Babylonia and even assist in the welfare of the state. God would be with them and would ultimately restore them (*seventy years*, 25.11; 27.7). Two colleagues of Hananiah, Ahab and Zedekiah (v. 21), were condemned by Jeremiah (compare Ezek. ch. 13). He pre-

will restore your fortunes and gather you from all the nations and all the places where I have driven you, says the LORD, and I will bring you back to the place from which I sent you into exile.

15 "Because you have said, 'The LORD has raised up prophets for us in Babylon,'– 16 Thus says the LORD concerning the king who sits on the throne of David, and concerning all the people who dwell in this city, your kinsmen who did not go out with you into exile: 17 'Thus says the LORD of hosts, Behold, I am sending on them sword, famine, and pestilence, and I will make them like vile figs which are so bad they cannot be eaten. 18 I will pursue them with sword, famine, and pestilence, and will make them a horror to all the kingdoms of the earth, to be a curse, a terror, a hissing, and a reproach among all the nations where I have driven them, 19 because they did not heed my words, says the LORD, which I persistently sent to you by my servants the prophets, but you would not listen, says the LORD.'– 20 Hear the word of the LORD, all you exiles whom I sent away from Jerusalem to Babylon: 21 'Thus says the LORD of hosts, the God of Israel, concerning Ahab the son of Kola'iah and Zedeki'ah the son of Ma-asei'ah, who are prophesying a lie to you in my name: Behold, I will deliver them into the hand of Nebuchadrez'zar king of Babylon, and he shall slay them before your eyes. 22 Because of them this curse shall be used by all the exiles from Judah in Babylon: "The LORD make you like Zedeki'ah and Ahab, whom the king of Babylon roasted in the fire," 23 because they have committed folly in Israel, they

have committed adultery with their neighbors' wives, and they have spoken in my name lying words which I did not command them. I am the one who knows, and I am witness, says the LORD.' "

24 To Shemai'ah of Nehel'am you shall say: 25 "Thus says the LORD of hosts, the God of Israel: You have sent letters in your name to all the people who are in Jerusalem, and to Zephani'ah the son of Ma-asei'ah the priest, and to all the priests, saying, 26 'The LORD has made you priest instead of Jehoi'ada the priest, to have charge in the house of the LORD over every madman who prophesies, to put him in the stocks and collar. 27 Now why have you not rebuked Jeremiah of An'athoth who is prophesying to you? 28 For he has sent to us in Babylon, saying, "Your exile will be long; build houses and live in them, and plant gardens and eat their produce." ' "

29 Zephani'ah the priest read this letter in the hearing of Jeremiah the prophet. 30 Then the word of the LORD came to Jeremiah: 31 "Send to all the exiles, saying, 'Thus says the LORD concerning Shemai'ah of Nehel'am: Because Shemai'ah has prophesied to you when I did not send him, and has made you trust in a lie, 32 therefore thus says the LORD: Behold, I will punish Shemai'ah of Nehel'am and his descendants; he shall not have any one living among this people to see[a] the good that I will do to my people, says the LORD, for he has talked rebellion against the LORD.' "

30 The word that came to Jeremiah from the LORD: 2 "Thus

a Gk: Heb *and he shall not see*

---

dicted their execution; from the Babylonian point of view it would be for political subversion, not for the reason mentioned in v. 23. Verses 21–23 should follow v. 15; vv. 16–20 are an editorial comment on Jeremiah's letter. **24–32:** Jeremiah and Shemaiah. Another "colleague" of Hananiah, Shemaiah, wrote from Babylon a scathing letter to the new temple overseer (compare 20.1), Zephaniah, charging him with dereliction of duty in not arresting Jeremiah for his letter (above). Instead Zephaniah (21.1; 37.3) read the letter to his friend Jeremiah. The latter sent another letter to the exiles, condemning Shemaiah and predicting that neither he nor his descendants would see the day of restoration (20.6).

30.1–31.40: The Book of Consolation. 30.1–4: Introduction. Initially collected by Baruch,

says the LORD, the God of Israel: Write in a book all the words that I have spoken to you. ³ For behold, days are coming, says the LORD, when I will restore the fortunes of my people, Israel and Judah, says the LORD, and I will bring them back to the land which I gave to their fathers, and they shall take possession of it."

4 These are the words which the LORD spoke concerning Israel and Judah:

⁵ "Thus says the LORD:
We have heard a cry of panic,
  of terror, and no peace.
⁶ Ask now, and see,
  can a man bear a child?
Why then do I see every man
  with his hands on his loins like a
    woman in labor?
Why has every face turned pale?
⁷ Alas! that day is so great
  there is none like it;
it is a time of distress for Jacob;
  yet he shall be saved out of it.
8 "And it shall come to pass in that day, says the LORD of hosts, that I will break the yoke from off their*b* neck, and I will burst their*b* bonds, and strangers shall no more make servants of them.*c* ⁹ But they shall serve the LORD their God and David their king, whom I will raise up for them.

¹⁰ "Then fear not, O Jacob my servant,
  says the LORD,
  nor be dismayed, O Israel;
for lo, I will save you from afar,
  and your offspring from the land
    of their captivity.
Jacob shall return and have quiet
  and ease,
  and none shall make him afraid.
¹¹ For I am with you to save you,
      says the LORD;

I will make a full end of all the
  nations
  among whom I scattered you,
  but of you I will not make a full
    end.
I will chasten you in just measure,
  and I will by no means leave you
    unpunished.

¹² "For thus says the LORD:
Your hurt is incurable,
  and your wound is grievous.
¹³ There is none to uphold your cause,
  no medicine for your wound,
  no healing for you.
¹⁴ All your lovers have forgotten you;
  they care nothing for you;
for I have dealt you the blow of an
  enemy,
  the punishment of a merciless foe,
because your guilt is great,
  because your sins are flagrant.
¹⁵ Why do you cry out over your hurt?
  Your pain is incurable.
Because your guilt is great,
  because your sins are flagrant,
  I have done these things to you.
¹⁶ Therefore all who devour you shall
  be devoured,
  and all your foes, every one of
    them, shall go into captivity;
those who despoil you shall become
  a spoil,
  and all who prey on you I will
    make a prey.
¹⁷ For I will restore health to you,
  and your wounds I will heal,
       says the LORD,
because they have called you an
  outcast:
'It is Zion, for whom no one
  cares!'

b Gk Old Latin: Heb *your*
c Heb *make a servant of him*

---

most of chs. 30–31 reflect the period 622–609 B.C. (3.1–4.4). **5–9**: Oracles concerning Israel. After the travail (6.24) of God's judgment (*that day* [of the LORD], Am.5.18–20), God will break the yoke and a Davidic king will again rule Israel (23.5–6; Hos.3.5). **10–11**: *Fear not*, common phrase in God's address to man, Gen.15.1; Is.35.4; Lk.2.10. *Not make a full end*, a remnant will be left (see 4.27; 5.10,18; compare 46.27–28). **12–17**: Though ostensibly incurably wounded (8.22; 14.17) and deserted (4.30; 13.21) because of her sinfulness, Israel will be healed (Hos.14.4) and her oppressors (the notoriously cruel Assyrians) despoiled (9.25–26; 25.13–14). **18–22**: *The city* (probably Samaria) will be *rebuilt upon its mound;* it was customary in antiquity

18 "Thus says the LORD:
Behold, I will restore the fortunes of
  the tents of Jacob,
 and have compassion on his
  dwellings;
the city shall be rebuilt upon its
  mound,
 and the palace shall stand where
  it used to be.
19 Out of them shall come songs of
  thanksgiving,
 and the voices of those who make
  merry.
I will multiply them, and they
  shall not be few;
 I will make them honored, and
  they shall not be small.
20 Their children shall be as they were
  of old,
 and their congregation shall be
  established before me;
 and I will punish all who oppress
  them.
21 Their prince shall be one of
  themselves,
 their ruler shall come forth
  from their midst;
I will make him draw near, and he
  shall approach me,
 for who would dare of himself to
  approach me?
                        says the LORD.
22 And you shall be my people,
 and I will be your God."

23 Behold the storm of the LORD!
  Wrath has gone forth,
a whirling tempest;
 it will burst upon the head of the
  wicked.
24 The fierce anger of the LORD will
  not turn back
 until he has executed and
  accomplished

the intents of his mind.
In the latter days you will
  understand this.

31 "At that time, says the LORD,
  I will be the God of all the families of Israel, and they shall be my people."
2 Thus says the LORD:
"The people who survived the sword
  found grace in the wilderness;
when Israel sought for rest,
3   the LORD appeared to him[d]
    from afar.
I have loved you with an
  everlasting love;
 therefore I have continued my
  faithfulness to you.
4 Again I will build you, and you shall
  be built,
 O virgin Israel!
Again you shall adorn yourself with
  timbrels,
 and shall go forth in the dance of
  the merrymakers.
5 Again you shall plant vineyards
  upon the mountains of Sama'ria;
the planters shall plant,
 and shall enjoy the fruit.
6 For there shall be a day when
  watchmen will call
 in the hill country of E'phraim:
'Arise, and let us go up to Zion,
  to the LORD our God.'"

7 For thus says the LORD:
"Sing aloud with gladness for Jacob,
  and raise shouts for the chief of
  the nations;
proclaim, give praise, and say,
 'The LORD has saved his people,
  the remnant of Israel.'
8 Behold, I will bring them from the
  north country,

d Gk: Heb *me*

to rebuild on the leveled rubble of the preceding city, producing the present flat-topped hills, called tells. **21:** *Make him draw near* refers to the danger of approaching God (Ex.19.21; 33.20; Num.8.19). **22:** 7.23; 11.4; 24.7. **30.23–31.1:** The storm of the LORD. **30.23–24** = 23.19–20. **31.1:** This emphasizes the inclusiveness of the term *Israel;* compare 30.22. **2–6:** With a formula taken from the Exodus narrative (*found grace* [favor], Ex.33.12–17; compare Jer.23.7–8) and the emphatic historical-theological implications of *everlasting love* and *faithfulness*, God promises the joyful restoration of all Israel, including the renewal of pilgrimages to the Jerusalem temple (*Zion;* 41.5). **7–14:** Homecoming. God will assemble the dispersed in their homeland (Is.35.5–10; Ps.23.2–3). *Israel . . . Ephraim, my first-born* (Ex.4.22), as Ephraim is restored,

and gather them from the farthest
parts of the earth,
among them the blind and the lame,
the woman with child and her who
is in travail, together;
a great company, they shall
return here.
⁹ With weeping they shall come,
and with consolations*e* I will
lead them back,
I will make them walk by brooks of
water,
in a straight path in which they
shall not stumble;
for I am a father to Israel,
and E′phraim is my first-born.

¹⁰ "Hear the word of the LORD, O
nations,
and declare it in the coastlands
afar off;
say, 'He who scattered Israel will
gather him,
and will keep him as a shepherd
keeps his flock.'
¹¹ For the LORD has ransomed
Jacob,
and has redeemed him from
hands too strong for him.
¹² They shall come and sing aloud on
the height of Zion,
and they shall be radiant over the
goodness of the LORD,
over the grain, the wine, and the oil,
and over the young of the flock
and the herd;
their life shall be like a watered
garden,
and they shall languish no more.
¹³ Then shall the maidens rejoice in
the dance,
and the young men and the old
shall be merry.
I will turn their mourning into joy,
I will comfort them, and give
them gladness for sorrow.

¹⁴ I will feast the soul of the priests
with abundance,
and my people shall be satisfied
with my goodness,
says the LORD."

¹⁵ Thus says the LORD:
"A voice is heard in Ramah,
lamentation and bitter weeping.
Rachel is weeping for her
children;
she refuses to be comforted for
her children,
because they are not."

¹⁶ Thus says the LORD:
"Keep your voice from weeping,
and your eyes from tears;
for your work shall be rewarded,
says the LORD,
and they shall come back from the
land of the enemy.
¹⁷ There is hope for your future,
says the LORD,
and your children shall come
back to their own country.
¹⁸ I have heard E′phraim bemoaning,
'Thou hast chastened me, and I was
chastened,
like an untrained calf;
bring me back that I may be restored,
for thou art the LORD my God.
¹⁹ For after I had turned away I
repented;
and after I was instructed, I smote
upon my thigh;
I was ashamed, and I was
confounded,
because I bore the disgrace of my
youth.'
²⁰ Is E′phraim my dear son?
Is he my darling child?
For as often as I speak against him,
I do remember him still.
Therefore my heart yearns for him;

e Gk Compare Vg Tg: Heb *supplications*

so is all Israel (including Judah; 2.3; 3.19). **12:** Praises to God will be raised far (*coastlands*,
Ps.72.10–11; Is.41.1,5) and near for deliverance (*shepherd*, Is.40.11; *redeem*, Is.48.20). **14:**
Bountiful produce of the land will mark the new age of well-being (Is.58.11). **15–22:** *Rachel*,
mother of Joseph and Benjamin (Gen.30.22; 35.16–20; 1 Sam.10.2), laments their (the northern
tribes') exile (*Ramah*, 1 Sam.8.4). Matthew 2.18 depicts unmitigated grief, but here the verse
introduces the promise of restoration. **18:** *Ephraim* (Joseph's son, Gen.41.50–52) repents (3.22–
25; Hos.6.1–3); to prevent repeating his past errors he is admonished to note the *waymarks*

I will surely have mercy on him,
          says the LORD.

21 "Set up waymarks for yourself,
     make yourself guideposts;
   consider well the highway,
     the road by which you went.
   Return, O virgin Israel,
     return to these your cities.
22 How long will you waver,
     O faithless daughter?
   For the LORD has created a new
     thing on the earth:
   a woman protects a man."

23 Thus says the LORD of hosts, the God of Israel: "Once more they shall use these words in the land of Judah and in its cities, when I restore their fortunes:
   'The LORD bless you, O habitation
        of righteousness,
     O holy hill!'
24 And Judah and all its cities shall dwell there together, and the farmers and those who wander[f] with their flocks. 25 For I will satisfy the weary soul, and every languishing soul I will replenish."

26 Thereupon I awoke and looked, and my sleep was pleasant to me.

27 "Behold, the days are coming, says the LORD, when I will sow the house of Israel and the house of Judah with the seed of man and the seed of beast. 28 And it shall come to pass that as I have watched over them to pluck up and break down, to overthrow, destroy, and bring evil, so I will watch over them to build and to plant, says the LORD. 29 In those days they shall no longer say:
   'The fathers have eaten sour grapes,

and the children's teeth are set on edge.'
30 But every one shall die for his own sin; each man who eats sour grapes, his teeth shall be set on edge.

31 "Behold, the days are coming, says the LORD, when I will make a new covenant with the house of Israel and the house of Judah, 32 not like the covenant which I made with their fathers when I took them by the hand to bring them out of the land of Egypt, my covenant which they broke, though I was their husband, says the LORD. 33 But this is the covenant which I will make with the house of Israel after those days, says the LORD: I will put my law within them, and I will write it upon their hearts; and I will be their God, and they shall be my people. 34 And no longer shall each man teach his neighbor and each his brother, saying, 'Know the LORD,' for they shall all know me, from the least of them to the greatest, says the LORD; for I will forgive their iniquity, and I will remember their sin no more."

35 Thus says the LORD,
   who gives the sun for light by day
     and the fixed order of the moon
       and the stars for light by night,
   who stirs up the sea so that its waves
        roar—
   the LORD of hosts is his name:
36 "If this fixed order departs
     from before me, says the LORD,
   then shall the descendants of Israel
        cease
   from being a nation before me for
        ever."

f Cn Compare Syr Vg Tg: Heb *and they shall wander*

(sign-posts) leading to his punishment. **22:** *A new thing*, compare Is.43.19. *A woman protects a man*, she does not have to be protected by a man; compare Is.11.6–9 for the reversal of the usual in the new age. **23–40:** Restoration and the new covenant. The following oracles are after 587 B.C. **23–30:** As God depopulated and depleted Judah (1.10), he will also restore it (Ezek. 36.8–11) and reunite it with Israel (vv. 2–14; Is.11.11–16). **29–30:** This may reflect the contemporary problem (Dt.24.16), discussed in some detail by Ezekiel (ch. 18). **31–34:** Using the oldest expression for covenant making ("to cut a covenant") and opposing what was an increasingly limited concept of the Sinai covenant, the prophet affirms that God will *make a new covenant* (32.38–40; Heb.8.8–12; 10.16–17) inscribed in the hearts of men (17.1; Ezek.11.19; Hos.2.20). **35–37:** The seemingly eternal cycle of nature (5.22) is used to emphasize God's

37 Thus says the LORD:
"If the heavens above can be
   measured,
and the foundations of the earth
   below can be explored,
then I will cast off all the
   descendants of Israel
for all that they have done,
         says the LORD."

38 "Behold, the days are coming, says the LORD, when the city shall be rebuilt for the LORD from the tower of Han'anel to the Corner Gate. 39 And the measuring line shall go out farther, straight to the hill Gareb, and shall then turn to Go'ah. 40 The whole valley of the dead bodies and the ashes, and all the fields as far as the brook Kidron, to the corner of the Horse Gate toward the east, shall be sacred to the LORD. It shall not be uprooted or overthrown any more for ever."

32 The word that came to Jeremiah from the LORD in the tenth year of Zedeki'ah king of Judah, which was the eighteenth year of Nebuchadrez'zar. 2 At that time the army of the king of Babylon was besieging Jerusalem, and Jeremiah the prophet was shut up in the court of the guard which was in the palace of the king of Judah. 3 For Zedeki'ah king of Judah had imprisoned him, saying, "Why do you prophesy and say, 'Thus says the LORD: Behold, I am giving this city into the hand of the king of Babylon, and he shall take it; 4 Zedeki'ah king of Judah shall not escape out of the hand of the

Chalde'ans, but shall surely be given into the hand of the king of Babylon, and shall speak with him face to face and see him eye to eye; 5 and he shall take Zedeki'ah to Babylon, and there he shall remain until I visit him, says the LORD; though you fight against the Chalde'ans, you shall not succeed'?"

6 Jeremiah said, "The word of the LORD came to me: 7 Behold, Han'amel the son of Shallum your uncle will come to you and say, 'Buy my field which is at An'athoth, for the right of redemption by purchase is yours.' 8 Then Han'amel my cousin came to me in the court of the guard, in accordance with the word of the LORD, and said to me, 'Buy my field which is at An'athoth in the land of Benjamin, for the right of possession and redemption is yours; buy it for yourself.' Then I knew that this was the word of the LORD.

9 "And I bought the field at An'athoth from Han'amel my cousin, and weighed out the money to him, seventeen shekels of silver. 10 I signed the deed, sealed it, got witnesses, and weighed the money on scales. 11 Then I took the sealed deed of purchase, containing the terms and conditions, and the open copy; 12 and I gave the deed of purchase to Baruch the son of Neri'ah son of Mahsei'ah, in the presence of Han'amel my cousin, in the presence of the witnesses who signed the deed of purchase, and in the presence of all the Jews who were sitting in the court of the guard. 13 I charged Baruch in their presence, say-

assurance of Israel's continued existence (Is.44.24; 54.9–10). **38–40:** This passage, coming from after the time of Jeremiah (compare Zech.14.10–11), describes Jerusalem's four corners: northeast (*Hananel*, Neh.3.1), northwest (Corner Gate, 2 Kg.14.13), southeast and southwest (*Gareb, Goah,* both unidentified); and southern (Hinnom, 7.31–32) and eastern (Kidron, 2 Kg.23.4,6) boundaries. *Horse Gate* (southeast corner), Neh.3.28.

32.1–44: Jeremiah purchases land in Anathoth. 1–5: For background, see ch. 37 (date: early 587 B.C.). Chronologically the account should follow ch. 37. Its being placed here emphasizes the validity of the preceding oracles concerning Judah's restoration. **6–15:** To prevent the loss of family property, Jeremiah's cousin, *Hanamel,* offered to sell his land to Jeremiah (Lev.25.25–28). This is the most detailed account of a business transaction in the Bible (compare Gen.23.1–16). *Seventeen shekels* (about seven ounces) refers to weight, not coins. The official copy of the deed, written on papyrus, was rolled up and sealed; *the open copy* was for easy reference. Similar storage of deeds in earthen jars is known from Elephantine in Egypt. *Baruch,* Jeremiah's secretary, see ch. 36. Jeremiah's purchase illustrates his confidence in the future of

ing, ¹⁴ 'Thus says the LORD of hosts, the God of Israel: Take these deeds, both this sealed deed of purchase and this open deed, and put them in an earthenware vessel, that they may last for a long time. ¹⁵ For thus says the LORD of hosts, the God of Israel: Houses and fields and vineyards shall again be bought in this land.'

16 "After I had given the deed of purchase to Baruch the son of Neri'ah, I prayed to the LORD, saying: ¹⁷ 'Ah Lord GOD! It is thou who hast made the heavens and the earth by thy great power and by thy outstretched arm! Nothing is too hard for thee, ¹⁸ who showest steadfast love to thousands, but dost requite the guilt of fathers to their children after them, O great and mighty God whose name is the LORD of hosts, ¹⁹ great in counsel and mighty in deed; whose eyes are open to all the ways of men, rewarding every man according to his ways and according to the fruit of his doings; ²⁰ who hast shown signs and wonders in the land of Egypt, and to this day in Israel and among all mankind, and hast made thee a name, as at this day. ²¹ Thou didst bring thy people Israel out of the land of Egypt with signs and wonders, with a strong hand and outstretched arm, and with great terror; ²² and thou gavest them this land, which thou didst swear to their fathers to give them, a land flowing with milk and honey; ²³ and they entered and took possession of it. But they did not obey thy voice or walk in thy law; they did nothing of all thou didst command them to do. Therefore thou hast made all this evil come upon them. ²⁴ Behold, the siege mounds have come up to the city to take it, and because of

sword and famine and pestilence the city is given into the hands of the Chalde'ans who are fighting against it. What thou didst speak has come to pass, and behold, thou seest it. ²⁵ Yet thou, O Lord GOD, hast said to me, "Buy the field for money and get witnesses"– though the city is given into the hands of the Chalde'ans.' "

26 The word of the LORD came to Jeremiah: ²⁷ "Behold, I am the LORD, the God of all flesh; is anything too hard for me? ²⁸ Therefore, thus says the LORD: Behold, I am giving this city into the hands of the Chalde'ans and into the hand of Nebuchadrez'zar king of Babylon, and he shall take it. ²⁹ The Chalde'ans who are fighting against this city shall come and set this city on fire, and burn it, with the houses on whose roofs incense has been offered to Ba'al and drink offerings have been poured out to other gods, to provoke me to anger. ³⁰ For the sons of Israel and the sons of Judah have done nothing but evil in my sight from their youth; the sons of Israel have done nothing but provoke me to anger by the work of their hands, says the LORD. ³¹ This city has aroused my anger and wrath, from the day it was built to this day, so that I will remove it from my sight ³² because of all the evil of the sons of Israel and the sons of Judah which they did to provoke me to anger –their kings and their princes, their priests and their prophets, the men of Judah and the inhabitants of Jerusalem. ³³ They have turned to me their back and not their face; and though I have taught them persistently they have not listened to receive instruction. ³⁴ They set up their abominations in the house which is called by my name,

---

Judah. **16–44**: This section is probably editorial, a later expansion of the preceding theme of the future of Judah. First is a formal prayer (vv. 16–25), drawn perhaps from liturgical sources (Neh.9.6–38). After praising God's omnipotence (10.16; 27.5), his omniscience (17.10), and his wondrous deeds in Israel's behalf (11.5), Jeremiah discreetly questions the wisdom of his purchase in view of the circumstances (vv. 24–25). God's answer (vv. 26–44) summarizes Jeremiah's (and the Deuteronomic) interpretation of the contemporary critical events. After a résumé of Judah's idolatry (incense, wine and oil offered on the rooftops, 19.13; comparative sinfulness of Israel and Judah, 3.6–11; human sacrifices, 7.30–32) and her stubborn indifference to God's warnings (17.21–23), her imminent destruction (in conventional terms: sword,

to defile it. [35] They built the high places of Ba'al in the valley of the son of Hinnom, to offer up their sons and daughters to Molech, though I did not command them, nor did it enter into my mind, that they should do this abomination, to cause Judah to sin.

36 "Now therefore thus says the LORD, the God of Israel, concerning this city of which you say, 'It is given into the hand of the king of Babylon by sword, by famine, and by pestilence': [37] Behold, I will gather them from all the countries to which I drove them in my anger and my wrath and in great indignation; I will bring them back to this place, and I will make them dwell in safety. [38] And they shall be my people, and I will be their God. [39] I will give them one heart and one way, that they may fear me for ever, for their own good and the good of their children after them. [40] I will make with them an everlasting covenant, that I will not turn away from doing good to them; and I will put the fear of me in their hearts, that they may not turn from me. [41] I will rejoice in doing them good, and I will plant them in this land in faithfulness, with all my heart and all my soul.

42 "For thus says the LORD: Just as I have brought all this great evil upon this people, so I will bring upon them all the good that I promise them. [43] Fields shall be bought in this land of which you are saying, It is a desolation, without man or beast; it is given into the hands of the Chalde'ans. [44] Fields shall be bought for money, and deeds shall be signed and sealed and witnessed, in the land of Benjamin, in the places about Jerusalem, and in the cities of Judah, in the cities of the hill country, in the cities of the Shephe'-

lah, and in the cities of the Negeb; for I will restore their fortunes, says the LORD."

33 The word of the LORD came to Jeremiah a second time, while he was still shut up in the court of the guard: [2] "Thus says the LORD who made the earth,[g] the LORD who formed it to establish it—the LORD is his name: [3] Call to me and I will answer you, and will tell you great and hidden things which you have not known. [4] For thus says the LORD, the God of Israel, concerning the houses of this city and the houses of the kings of Judah which were torn down to make a defense against the siege mounds and before the sword:[h] [5] The Chalde'ans are coming in to fight[i] and to fill them with the dead bodies of men whom I shall smite in my anger and my wrath, for I have hidden my face from this city because of all their wickedness. [6] Behold, I will bring to it health and healing, and I will heal them and reveal to them abundance[j] of prosperity and security. [7] I will restore the fortunes of Judah and the fortunes of Israel, and rebuild them as they were at first. [8] I will cleanse them from all the guilt of their sin against me, and I will forgive all the guilt of their sin and rebellion against me. [9] And this city[k] shall be to me a name of joy, a praise and a glory before all the nations of the earth who shall hear of all the good that I do for them; they shall fear and tremble because of all the good and all the prosperity I provide for it.

10 "Thus says the LORD: In this place of which you say, 'It is a waste

g Gk: Heb *it*   h Heb obscure
i Cn: Heb *They are coming in to fight against the Chaldeans*
j Heb uncertain   k Heb *and it*

---

pestilence, and famine, 14.11–12; 21.7) is affirmed. The section concludes with assurances of restoration, first with reference to the new covenant (31.31–34) and then the exchange and holding of property (vv. 42–44).

33.1–26: Appendix to the Book of Consolation. 1: Editorial connection with preceding chapter. **2:** Liturgical doxology (Am.4.13; Is.45.18). **3:** Apocalyptic overtones. **4:** In siege defense measures, there was demolition of houses abutting against the wall to allow for easier troop movements (Is.22.10). **5–9:** After punishment (and repentance) will come healing (3.22; 30.17), forgiveness, and the city will be to God a joyful name (renown), *praise*, and *glory* before

without man or beast,' in the cities of Judah and the streets of Jerusalem that are desolate, without man or inhabitant or beast, there shall be heard again [11] the voice of mirth and the voice of gladness, the voice of the bridegroom and the voice of the bride, the voices of those who sing, as they bring thank offerings to the house of the LORD:

'Give thanks to the LORD of hosts,
  for the LORD is good,
  for his steadfast love endures for
    ever!'

For I will restore the fortunes of the land as at first, says the LORD.

12 "Thus says the LORD of hosts: In this place which is waste, without man or beast, and in all of its cities, there shall again be habitations of shepherds resting their flocks. [13] In the cities of the hill country, in the cities of the Shephe'lah, and in the cities of the Negeb, in the land of Benjamin, the places about Jerusalem, and in the cities of Judah, flocks shall again pass under the hands of the one who counts them, says the LORD.

14 "Behold, the days are coming, says the LORD, when I will fulfil the promise I made to the house of Israel and the house of Judah. [15] In those days and at that time I will cause a righteous Branch to spring forth for David; and he shall execute justice and righteousness in the land. [16] In those days Judah will be saved and Jerusalem will dwell securely. And this is the name by which it will be called: 'The LORD is our righteousness.'

17 "For thus says the LORD: David shall never lack a man to sit on the throne of the house of Israel, [18] and the Levitical priests shall never lack a man in my presence to offer burnt offerings, to burn cereal offerings, and to make sacrifices for ever."

19 The word of the LORD came to Jeremiah: [20] "Thus says the LORD: If you can break my covenant with the day and my covenant with the night, so that day and night will not come at their appointed time, [21] then also my covenant with David my servant may be broken, so that he shall not have a son to reign on his throne, and my covenant with the Levitical priests my ministers. [22] As the host of heaven cannot be numbered and the sands of the sea cannot be measured, so I will multiply the descendants of David my servant, and the Levitical priests who minister to me."

23 The word of the LORD came to Jeremiah: [24] "Have you not observed what these people are saying, 'The LORD has rejected the two families which he chose'? Thus they have despised my people so that they are no longer a nation in their sight. [25] Thus says the LORD: If I have not established my covenant with day and night and the ordinances of heaven and earth, [26] then I will reject the descendants of Jacob and David my servant and will not choose one of his descendants to rule over the seed of Abraham, Isaac, and Jacob. For I will restore their fortunes, and will have mercy upon them."

34 The word which came to Jeremiah from the LORD, when Nebuchadrez'zar king of Babylon and all his army and all the kingdoms of the earth under his dominion and all the peoples were fighting against Jeru-

---

all the Gentile nations (13.11; Dt.26.19). **10–11:** The silence of death (7.34) will be broken by the sounds of life (30.19) and songs of praise (Ps. 136). **12–13:** Shepherds will again find pasture in the once desolate land (31.12; Ezek.20.37). **14–26:** Commentary on 23.5–6, from the time of Haggai and Zechariah (520 B.C.); these verses are lacking in the Septuagint. **14–18:** There will be not one but a succession of Davidic rulers (2 Sam.7.16; 1 Kg.9.5). The Deuteronomic reference to *Levitical priests* is unique in Jeremiah (Dt.18.1–5). **16:** The new *name* of Jerusalem (see Is.1.26 n.). **22:** A reinterpretation of Gen.22.17–18. **23–26:** As night follows day (31.35–37; Gen.1.5; 8.22), God's promise to the patriarchs (compare Rom.4.13) and David will be kept.

34.1–7: Warning to Zedekiah. The siege of Jerusalem (January 588 B.C.) was but weeks away;

salem and all of its cities: 2 "Thus says the LORD, the God of Israel: Go and speak to Zedeki'ah king of Judah and say to him, 'Thus says the LORD: Behold, I am giving this city into the hand of the king of Babylon, and he shall burn it with fire. 3 You shall not escape from his hand, but shall surely be captured and delivered into his hand; you shall see the king of Babylon eye to eye and speak with him face to face; and you shall go to Babylon.' 4 Yet hear the word of the LORD, O Zedeki'ah king of Judah! Thus says the LORD concerning you: 'You shall not die by the sword. 5 You shall die in peace. And as spices were burned for your fathers, the former kings who were before you, so men shall burn spices for you and lament for you, saying, "Alas, lord!" ' For I have spoken the word, says the LORD."

6 Then Jeremiah the prophet spoke all these words to Zedeki'ah king of Judah, in Jerusalem, 7 when the army of the king of Babylon was fighting against Jerusalem and against all the cities of Judah that were left, Lachish and Aze'kah; for these were the only fortified cities of Judah that remained.

8 The word which came to Jeremiah from the LORD, after King Zedeki'ah had made a covenant with all the people in Jerusalem to make a proclamation of liberty to them, 9 that every one should set free his Hebrew slaves, male and female, so that no one should enslave a Jew, his brother. 10 And they obeyed, all the princes and all the people who had entered into the covenant

that every one would set free his slave, male or female, so that they would not be enslaved again; they obeyed and set them free. 11 But afterward they turned around and took back the male and female slaves they had set free, and brought them into subjection as slaves. 12 The word of the LORD came to Jeremiah from the LORD: 13 "Thus says the LORD, the God of Israel: I made a covenant with your fathers when I brought them out of the land of Egypt, out of the house of bondage, saying, 14 'At the end of six*l* years each of you must set free the fellow Hebrew who has been sold to you and has served you six years; you must set him free from your service.' But your fathers did not listen to me or incline their ears to me. 15 You recently repented and did what was right in my eyes by proclaiming liberty, each to his neighbor, and you made a covenant before me in the house which is called by my name; 16 but then you turned around and profaned my name when each of you took back his male and female slaves, whom you had set free according to their desire, and you brought them into subjection to be your slaves. 17 Therefore, thus says the LORD: You have not obeyed me by proclaiming liberty, every one to his brother and to his neighbor; behold, I proclaim to you liberty to the sword, to pestilence, and to famine, says the LORD. I will make you a horror to all the kingdoms of the earth. 18 And the men who transgressed my covenant

l Gk: Heb *seven*

only *Lachish* (twenty-three miles southwest of Jerusalem) and *Azekah* (eleven miles north of Lachish) held out. Warning Zedekiah of Jerusalem's imminent destruction and his own captivity, Jeremiah assured Zedekiah of a peaceful death and appropriate funeral rites (but compare 52.8–11).

34.8–22: Manumission of slaves and perfidy of the Jerusalemites. Probably to simplify the problem of the domestic food supply, to free more men for Jerusalem's defense, and to propitiate the LORD, Zedekiah proclaimed the manumission of all slaves. But when the Egyptian army approached (37.6–15), causing the Babylonians temporarily to lift the siege, the manumission was rescinded. **13–22:** Making reference to Ex.21.2 and Dt.15.12, Jeremiah condemned this perfidy as one more example of notorious faithlessness. He assured the people of punishment like that implied in their covenant ritual (v. 18; Gen.15.9–17); the transgressor should suffer the same fate as the slaughtered animal, a practice known from non-Biblical sources also. The use of the ancient formula "cut a covenant" is noteworthy here (in vv. 8,13,15, etc.,

and did not keep the terms of the covenant which they made before me, I will make like*m* the calf which they cut in two and passed between its parts— **19** the princes of Judah, the princes of Jerusalem, the eunuchs, the priests, and all the people of the land who passed between the parts of the calf; **20** and I will give them into the hand of their enemies and into the hand of those who seek their lives. Their dead bodies shall be food for the birds of the air and the beasts of the earth. **21** And Zedeki'ah king of Judah, and his princes I will give into the hand of their enemies and into the hand of those who seek their lives, into the hand of the army of the king of Babylon which has withdrawn from you. **22** Behold, I will command, says the Lord, and will bring them back to this city; and they will fight against it, and take it, and burn it with fire. I will make the cities of Judah a desolation without inhabitant."

35 The word which came to Jeremiah from the Lord in the days of Jehoi'akim the son of Josi'ah, king of Judah: **2** "Go to the house of the Re'chabites, and speak with them, and bring them to the house of the Lord, into one of the chambers; then offer them wine to drink." **3** So I took Ja-azani'ah the son of Jeremiah, son of Habazzini'ah, and his brothers, and all his sons, and the whole house of the Re'chabites. **4** I brought them to the house of the Lord into the chamber of the sons of Hanan the son of Igdali'ah, the man of God, which was near the chamber of the princes, above the chamber of Ma-asei'ah the son of Shal-

lum, keeper of the threshold. **5** Then I set before the Re'chabites pitchers full of wine, and cups; and I said to them, "Drink wine." **6** But they answered, "We will drink no wine, for Jon'adab the son of Rechab, our father, commanded us, 'You shall not drink wine, neither you nor your sons for ever; **7** you shall not build a house; you shall not sow seed; you shall not plant or have a vineyard; but you shall live in tents all your days, that you may live many days in the land where you sojourn.' **8** We have obeyed the voice of Jon'adab the son of Rechab, our father, in all that he commanded us, to drink no wine all our days, ourselves, our wives, our sons, or our daughters, **9** and not to build houses to dwell in. We have no vineyard or field or seed; **10** but we have lived in tents, and have obeyed and done all that Jon'adab our father commanded us. **11** But when Nebuchadrez'zar king of Babylon came up against the land, we said, 'Come, and let us go to Jerusalem for fear of the army of the Chalde'ans and the army of the Syrians.' So we are living in Jerusalem."

12 Then the word of the Lord came to Jeremiah: **13** "Thus says the Lord of hosts, the God of Israel: Go and say to the men of Judah and the inhabitants of Jerusalem, Will you not receive instruction and listen to my words? says the Lord. **14** The command which Jon'adab the son of Rechab gave to his sons, to drink no wine, has been kept; and they drink none to this day, for they have obeyed their father's command. I have spoken to you persistently, but you have not listened to

m Cn: Heb lacks *like*

"made" is literally "cut"; see 31.31 n.) rather than the Deuteronomic formula "command a covenant."

35.1–19: The symbol of the Rechabites. The Rechabites were a religious order, similar to the Nazirites (Num.6.1–21), founded by Jonadab, son of Rechab, during the reign of Jehu (842–815 b.c.). Religious fanatics, they assisted Jehu in the blood-bath accompanying the revolt against the dynasty of Omri (2 Kg.10.15–28). They held that the more sophisticated sedentary life in Canaan jeopardized the purity of the worship of the Lord. Consequently, returning to desert ways, they lived in tents, were shepherds, and abstained from wine (for symbolic, not religious reasons). Jeremiah's association with them does not imply acceptance of their position, but only the approbation of their faithfulness to their principles, in contrast to Judah's

me. ¹⁵ I have sent to you all my servants the prophets, sending them persistently, saying, 'Turn now every one of you from his evil way, and amend your doings, and do not go after other gods to serve them, and then you shall dwell in the land which I gave to you and your fathers.' But you did not incline your ear or listen to me. ¹⁶ The sons of Jon'adab the son of Rechab have kept the command which their father gave them, but this people has not obeyed me. ¹⁷ Therefore, thus says the LORD, the God of hosts, the God of Israel: Behold, I am bringing on Judah and all the inhabitants of Jerusalem all the evil that I have pronounced against them; because I have spoken to them and they have not listened, I have called to them and they have not answered."

18 But to the house of the Re'chabites Jeremiah said, "Thus says the LORD of hosts, the God of Israel: Because you have obeyed the command of Jon'adab your father, and kept all his precepts, and done all that he commanded you, ¹⁹ therefore thus says the LORD of hosts, the God of Israel: Jon'adab the son of Rechab shall never lack a man to stand before me."

36 In the fourth year of Jehoi'akim the son of Josi'ah, king of Judah, this word came to Jeremiah from the LORD: ² "Take a scroll and write on it all the words that I have spoken to you against Israel and Judah and all the nations, from the day I spoke to you, from the days of Josi'ah until today. ³ It may be that the house of Judah will hear all the evil which I intend to do to them, so that every one

may turn from his evil way, and that I may forgive their iniquity and their sin."

4 Then Jeremiah called Baruch the son of Neri'ah, and Baruch wrote upon a scroll at the dictation of Jeremiah all the words of the LORD which he had spoken to him. ⁵ And Jeremiah ordered Baruch, saying, "I am debarred from going to the house of the LORD; ⁶ so you are to go, and on a fast day in the hearing of all the people in the LORD's house you shall read the words of the LORD from the scroll which you have written at my dictation. You shall read them also in the hearing of all the men of Judah who come out of their cities. ⁷ It may be that their supplication will come before the LORD, and that every one will turn from his evil way, for great is the anger and wrath that the LORD has pronounced against this people." ⁸ And Baruch the son of Neri'ah did all that Jeremiah the prophet ordered him about reading from the scroll the words of the LORD in the LORD's house.

9 In the fifth year of Jehoi'akim the son of Josi'ah, king of Judah, in the ninth month, all the people in Jerusalem and all the people who came from the cities of Judah to Jerusalem proclaimed a fast before the LORD. ¹⁰ Then, in the hearing of all the people, Baruch read the words of Jeremiah from the scroll, in the house of the LORD, in the chamber of Gemari'ah the son of Shaphan the secretary, which was in the upper court, at the entry of the New Gate of the LORD's house.

11 When Micai'ah the son of Gemari'ah, son of Shaphan, heard all the

---

faithlessness. The occasion is probably the crisis of 601 B.C. (see 12.7–13 n.). *Maaseiah*, perhaps the father of Zephaniah (compare 21.1).

36.1–45.5: The trials and the sufferings of Jeremiah. 36.1–32: Jeremiah, Jehoiakim, and the scrolls. 1–4: In the light of portentous contemporary events (25.1–14), Jeremiah commissioned *Baruch, the son of Neriah* and brother of Seraiah (32.12; 51.59), to transcribe his oracles (*words of the* LORD) on a papyrus scroll. *Fourth year*, 605 B.C. **5–10:** For an unknown reason, Jeremiah was barred from the temple; so, on the occasion of a fast proclaimed by Jehoiakim because of Nebuchadrezzar's advance against Ashkelon (in November, 604 B.C.), he instructed Baruch to read the scroll in his stead. *Shaphan*, a friend of Jeremiah (26.24). **11–19:** Baruch was asked to re-read the scroll before an assembly of royal officials. Deeply impressed, they

words of the LORD from the scroll, [12] he went down to the king's house, into the secretary's chamber; and all the princes were sitting there: Eli'-shama the secretary, Delai'ah the son of Shemai'ah, Elna'than the son of Achbor, Gemari'ah the son of Shaphan, Zedeki'ah the son of Hanani'ah, and all the princes. [13] And Micai'ah told them all the words that he had heard, when Baruch read the scroll in the hearing of the people. [14] Then all the princes sent Jehu'di the son of Nethani'ah, son of Shelemi'ah, son of Cushi, to say to Baruch, "Take in your hand the scroll that you read in the hearing of the people, and come." So Baruch the son of Neri'ah took the scroll in his hand and came to them. [15] And they said to him, "Sit down and read it." So Baruch read it to them. [16] When they heard all the words, they turned one to another in fear; and they said to Baruch, "We must report all these words to the king." [17] Then they asked Baruch, "Tell us, how did you write all these words? Was it at his dictation?" [18] Baruch answered them, "He dictated all these words to me, while I wrote them with ink on the scroll." [19] Then the princes said to Baruch, "Go and hide, you and Jeremiah, and let no one know where you are."

20 So they went into the court to the king, having put the scroll in the chamber of Eli'shama the secretary; and they reported all the words to the king. [21] Then the king sent Jehu'di to get the scroll, and he took it from the chamber of Eli'shama the secretary; and Jehu'di read it to the king and all the princes who stood beside the king. [22] It was the ninth month, and the king was sitting in the winter house

and there was a fire burning in the brazier before him. [23] As Jehu'di read three or four columns, the king would cut them off with a penknife and throw them into the fire in the brazier, until the entire scroll was consumed in the fire that was in the brazier. [24] Yet neither the king, nor any of his servants who heard all these words, was afraid, nor did they rend their garments. [25] Even when Elna'than and Delai'ah and Gemari'ah urged the king not to burn the scroll, he would not listen to them. [26] And the king commanded Jerah'meel the king's son and Serai'ah the son of Az'ri-el and Shelemi'ah the son of Abdeel to seize Baruch the secretary and Jeremiah the prophet, but the LORD hid them.

27 Now, after the king had burned the scroll with the words which Baruch wrote at Jeremiah's dictation, the word of the LORD came to Jeremiah: [28] "Take another scroll and write on it all the former words that were in the first scroll, which Jehoi'akim the king of Judah has burned. [29] And concerning Jehoi'akim king of Judah you shall say, 'Thus says the LORD, You have burned this scroll, saying, "Why have you written in it that the king of Babylon will certainly come and destroy this land, and will cut off from it man and beast?" [30] Therefore thus says the LORD concerning Jehoi'akim king of Judah, He shall have none to sit upon the throne of David, and his dead body shall be cast out to the heat by day and the frost by night. [31] And I will punish him and his offspring and his servants for their iniquity; I will bring upon them, and upon the inhabitants of Jerusalem, and upon the men of Judah, all the evil that I have pronounced against them, but they would not hear.'"

resolved to inform Jehoiakim. Sensing the possibility of repercussions, they instructed Baruch and Jeremiah to go into hiding. **20–26:** Jehoiakim ordered the scroll brought from the court scribe's office. Despite protests from some officials, he burned it as it was read, three or four columns at a time. Irritated by its contents, Jehoiakim ordered the arrest of Jeremiah and Baruch. *Penknife*, a knife used to sharpen the point of the scribes' reed pens. **27–32:** Using the destruction of the scroll as a symbol, Jeremiah announced the ignominious death of Jehoiakim (22.18–19; 2 Kg.24.6–15) and dictated an expanded copy of the scroll (probably contained largely in chs. 1–25).

32 Then Jeremiah took another scroll and gave it to Baruch the scribe, the son of Neri'ah, who wrote on it at the dictation of Jeremiah all the words of the scroll which Jehoi'akim king of Judah had burned in the fire; and many similar words were added to them.

37 Zedeki'ah the son of Josi'ah, whom Nebuchadrez'zar king of Babylon made king in the land of Judah, reigned instead of Coni'ah the son of Jehoi'akim. ² But neither he nor his servants nor the people of the land listened to the words of the LORD which he spoke through Jeremiah the prophet.

3 King Zedeki'ah sent Jehu'cal the son of Shelemi'ah, and Zephani'ah the priest, the son of Ma-asei'ah, to Jeremiah the prophet, saying, "Pray for us to the LORD our God." ⁴ Now Jeremiah was still going in and out among the people, for he had not yet been put in prison. ⁵ The army of Pharaoh had come out of Egypt; and when the Chalde'ans who were besieging Jerusalem heard news of them, they withdrew from Jerusalem.

6 Then the word of the LORD came to Jeremiah the prophet: ⁷ "Thus says the LORD, God of Israel: Thus shall you say to the king of Judah who sent you to me to inquire of me, 'Behold, Pharaoh's army which came to help you is about to return to Egypt, to its own land. ⁸ And the Chalde'ans shall come back and fight against this city; they shall take it and burn it with fire. ⁹ Thus says the LORD, Do not deceive yourselves, saying, "The Chalde'ans will surely stay away from us," for they will not stay away. ¹⁰ For even if you should defeat the whole army

of Chalde'ans who are fighting against you, and there remained of them only wounded men, every man in his tent, they would rise up and burn this city with fire.'"

11 Now when the Chalde'an army had withdrawn from Jerusalem at the approach of Pharaoh's army, ¹² Jeremiah set out from Jerusalem to go to the land of Benjamin to receive his portion^n there among the people. ¹³ When he was at the Benjamin Gate, a sentry there named Iri'jah the son of Shelemi'ah, son of Hanani'ah, seized Jeremiah the prophet, saying, "You are deserting to the Chalde'ans." ¹⁴ And Jeremiah said, "It is false; I am not deserting to the Chalde'ans." But Iri'jah would not listen to him, and seized Jeremiah and brought him to the princes. ¹⁵ And the princes were enraged at Jeremiah, and they beat him and imprisoned him in the house of Jonathan the secretary, for it had been made a prison.

16 When Jeremiah had come to the dungeon cells, and remained there many days, ¹⁷ King Zedeki'ah sent for him, and received him. The king questioned him secretly in his house, and said, "Is there any word from the LORD?" Jeremiah said, "There is." Then he said, "You shall be delivered into the hand of the king of Babylon." ¹⁸ Jeremiah also said to King Zedeki'ah, "What wrong have I done to you or your servants or this people, that you have put me in prison? ¹⁹ Where are your prophets who prophesied to you, saying, 'The king of Babylon will not come against you and against this land'? ²⁰ Now hear, I pray you, O my lord the king: let my humble plea

n Heb obscure

37.1–38.28: Jeremiah, Zedekiah, and the siege. 37.1–2: Editorial transition from ch. 36 to 37. 3–10: Shortly after his accession (spring, 588 B.C.), an army of Pharaoh Hophra (Apries) came up from Egypt to relieve besieged Jerusalem (34.21). The inhabitants concluded that a deliverance as in the days of Hezekiah (2 Kg.19.32–37) had occurred, but Jeremiah warned them that such optimism was wholly unwarranted. 11–15: Leaving the city by the Benjamin Gate (20.2), Jeremiah was arrested on suspicion of desertion (38.18–19), perhaps based on oracles such as 21.1–10. 12: *To receive his portion;* see 32.6–15, which may suggest the occasion. 16–21: In a secret interview, Zedekiah sought reassurance for his ill-advised revolt, but in vain (21.2). He modified Jeremiah's imprisonment to house arrest, and guaranteed him a

come before you, and do not send me back to the house of Jonathan the secretary, lest I die there." ²¹ So King Zedeki′ah gave orders, and they committed Jeremiah to the court of the guard; and a loaf of bread was given him daily from the bakers' street, until all the bread of the city was gone. So Jeremiah remained in the court of the guard.

38 Now Shephati′ah the son of Mattan, Gedali′ah the son of Pashhur, Jucal the son of Shelemi′ah, and Pashhur the son of Malchi′ah heard the words that Jeremiah was saying to all the people, ² "Thus says the LORD, He who stays in this city shall die by the sword, by famine, and by pestilence; but he who goes out to the Chalde′ans shall live; he shall have his life as a prize of war, and live. ³ Thus says the LORD, This city shall surely be given into the hand of the army of the king of Babylon and be taken." ⁴ Then the princes said to the king, "Let this man be put to death, for he is weakening the hands of the soldiers who are left in this city, and the hands of all the people, by speaking such words to them. For this man is not seeking the welfare of this people, but their harm." ⁵ King Zedeki′ah said, "Behold, he is in your hands; for the king can do nothing against you." ⁶ So they took Jeremiah and cast him into the cistern of Malchi′ah, the king's son, which was in the court of the guard, letting Jeremiah down by ropes. And there was no water in the cistern, but only mire, and Jeremiah sank in the mire.

7 When E′bed-mel′ech the Ethiopian, a eunuch, who was in the king's house, heard that they had put Jeremiah into the cistern–the king was sitting in the Benjamin Gate– ⁸ E′bed-mel′ech went from the king's house and said to the king, ⁹ "My lord the king, these men have done evil in all that they did to Jeremiah the prophet by casting him into the cistern; and he will die there of hunger, for there is no bread left in the city." ¹⁰ Then the king commanded E′bed-mel′ech, the Ethiopian, "Take three men with you from here, and lift Jeremiah the prophet out of the cistern before he dies." ¹¹ So E′bed-mel′ech took the men with him and went to the house of the king, to a wardrobe of° the storehouse, and took from there old rags and worn-out clothes, which he let down to Jeremiah in the cistern by ropes. ¹² Then E′bed-mel′ech the Ethiopian said to Jeremiah, "Put the rags and clothes between your armpits and the ropes." Jeremiah did so. ¹³ Then they drew Jeremiah up with ropes and lifted him out of the cistern. And Jeremiah remained in the court of the guard.

14 King Zedeki′ah sent for Jeremiah the prophet and received him at the third entrance of the temple of the LORD. The king said to Jeremiah, "I will ask you a question; hide nothing from me." ¹⁵ Jeremiah said to Zedeki′ah, "If I tell you, will you not be sure to put me to death? And if I give you counsel, you will not listen to me." ¹⁶ Then King Zedeki′ah swore secretly to Jeremiah, "As the LORD lives, who made our souls, I will not put you to death or deliver you into the hand of these men who seek your life."

o Cn: Heb *to under*

---

minimum food ration as long as there were supplies. **38.1–13:** Jeremiah's continued insistence on surrender to Nebuchadrezzar was dangerous for Zedekiah's pro-Egyptian counselors (*Gedaliah, son of Pashhur*, 20.1; *Jucal* = Jehucal, 37.3; *Pashhur*, 21.1). They persuaded the vacillating Zedekiah that Jeremiah was subverting the war effort (there is similar phraseology in a letter written eighteen months earlier, found in the excavations at Lachish). **6:** The *cistern* was nearly dry, indicating a time shortly before Nebuchadrezzar's final assault August 587 B.C. (52.5–7). Ironically, Jeremiah was delivered from murder at the hands of his countrymen by a foreign court official (who was not necessarily a *eunuch* physically, v. 7). **14–28:** Uncertain and fearful, Zedekiah again (37.17–20) summoned Jeremiah for a private interview (location of *third entrance* is unknown). Justifiably suspicious, Jeremiah exacted an oath from Zedekiah

17 Then Jeremiah said to Zedeki'ah, "Thus says the LORD, the God of hosts, the God of Israel, If you will surrender to the princes of the king of Babylon, then your life shall be spared, and this city shall not be burned with fire, and you and your house shall live. 18 But if you do not surrender to the princes of the king of Babylon, then this city shall be given into the hand of the Chalde'ans, and they shall burn it with fire, and you shall not escape from their hand." 19 King Zedeki'ah said to Jeremiah, "I am afraid of the Jews who have deserted to the Chalde'ans, lest I be handed over to them and they abuse me." 20 Jeremiah said, "You shall not be given to them. Obey now the voice of the LORD in what I say to you, and it shall be well with you, and your life shall be spared. 21 But if you refuse to surrender, this is the vision which the LORD has shown to me: 22 Behold, all the women left in the house of the king of Judah were being led out to the princes of the king of Babylon and were saying,

'Your trusted friends have deceived
        you
    and prevailed against you;
    now that your feet are sunk in the
        mire,
    they turn away from you.'

23 All your wives and your sons shall be led out to the Chalde'ans, and you yourself shall not escape from their hand, but shall be seized by the king of Babylon; and this city shall be burned with fire."

24 Then Zedeki'ah said to Jeremiah, "Let no one know of these words and you shall not die. 25 If the princes hear that I have spoken with you and come to you and say to you, 'Tell us

what you said to the king and what the king said to you; hide nothing from us and we will not put you to death,' 26 then you shall say to them, 'I made a humble plea to the king that he would not send me back to the house of Jonathan to die there.' " 27 Then all the princes came to Jeremiah and asked him, and he answered them as the king had instructed him. So they left off speaking with him, for the conversation had not been overheard. 28 And Jeremiah remained in the court of the guard until the day that Jerusalem was taken.

39 In the ninth year of Zedeki'ah king of Judah, in the tenth month, Nebuchadrez'zar king of Babylon and all his army came against Jerusalem and besieged it; 2 in the eleventh year of Zedeki'ah, in the fourth month, on the ninth day of the month, a breach was made in the city. 3 When Jerusalem was taken,ᵖ all the princes of the king of Babylon came and sat in the middle gate: Ner'gal-share'zer, Sam'-gar-ne'bo, Sar'sechim the Rab'saris, Ner'gal-share'zer the Rabmag, with all the rest of the officers of the king of Babylon. 4 When Zedeki'ah king of Judah and all the soldiers saw them, they fled, going out of the city at night by way of the king's garden through the gate between the two walls; and they went toward the Arabah. 5 But the army of the Chalde'ans pursued them, and overtook Zedeki'ah in the plains of Jericho; and when they had taken him, they brought him up to Nebuchadrez'zar king of Babylon, at Riblah, in the land of Hamath; and he passed sentence upon him. 6 The king

ᵖ This clause has been transposed from the end of Chapter 38

---

for his safety. He repeated his counsel of "surrender and live" (20.1–16; 21.4–10; 27.1–11) and emphasized it by relating a vision depicting the capture of the royal household and the burning of Jerusalem (*in the mire* recalls Jeremiah's own recent experience, 38.6). Jeremiah assured Zedekiah of safety from Judean deserters (39.9), if he surrendered. Zedekiah characteristically hesitated, exacted a promise of secrecy from Jeremiah, and returned him to house arrest (37.21).

39.1–40.6: Jeremiah and the fall of Jerusalem. 39.1–14: Verses 1–10 summarize 52.4–16 (2 Kg.25.1–12) adding the names of Babylonian officials (v. 3). Alternative reading of v. 3: ". . . Nergal-sharezer the Simmagir, Nebushazban the chief court official, Nergal-sharezer the Rabmag . . . " Simmagir and Rabmag are titles of Babylonian officials. According to 52.6–14,

of Babylon slew the sons of Zedeki′ah at Riblah before his eyes; and the king of Babylon slew all the nobles of Judah. [7] He put out the eyes of Zedeki′ah, and bound him in fetters to take him to Babylon. [8] The Chalde′ans burned the king's house and the house of the people, and broke down the walls of Jerusalem. [9] Then Nebu′zarad′an, the captain of the guard, carried into exile to Babylon the rest of the people who were left in the city, those who had deserted to him, and the people who remained. [10] Nebu′zarad′an, the captain of the guard, left in the land of Judah some of the poor people who owned nothing, and gave them vineyards and fields at the same time.

11 Nebuchadrez′zar king of Babylon gave command concerning Jeremiah through Nebu′zarad′an, the captain of the guard, saying, [12] "Take him, look after him well and do him no harm, but deal with him as he tells you." [13] So Nebu′zarad′an the captain of the guard, Nebushaz′ban the Rab′saris, Ner′gal-share′zer the Rabmag, and all the chief officers of the king of Babylon [14] sent and took Jeremiah from the court of the guard. They entrusted him to Gedali′ah the son of Ahi′kam, son of Shaphan, that he should take him home. So he dwelt among the people.

15 The word of the LORD came to Jeremiah while he was shut up in the court of the guard: [16] "Go, and say to E′bed-mel′ech the Ethiopian, 'Thus says the LORD of hosts, the God of Israel: Behold, I will fulfil my words against this city for evil and not for good, and they shall be accomplished before you on that day. [17] But I will deliver you on that day, says the LORD, and you shall not be given into the hand of the men of whom you are afraid. [18] For I will surely save you, and you shall not fall by the sword; but you shall have your life as a prize of war, because you have put your trust in me, says the LORD.' "

40 The word that came to Jeremiah from the LORD after Nebu′zarad′an the captain of the guard had let him go from Ramah, when he took him bound in chains along with all the captives of Jerusalem and Judah who were being exiled to Babylon. [2] The captain of the guard took Jeremiah and said to him, "The LORD your God pronounced this evil against this place; [3] the LORD has brought it about, and has done as he said. Because you sinned against the LORD, and did not obey his voice, this thing has come upon you. [4] Now, behold, I release you today from the chains on your hands. If it seems good to you to come with me to Babylon, come, and I will look after you well; but if it seems wrong to you to come with me to Babylon, do not come. See, the whole land is before you; go wherever you think it good and right to go. [5] If you remain,*q* then return to Gedali′ah the son of Ahi′kam, son of Shaphan, whom the king of Babylon appointed governor of the cities of Judah, and dwell with him among the people; or go wherever you think it right to go." So the captain of the guard gave him an allowance of food and a present, and let him go. [6] Then Jeremiah went to Gedali′ah the son of Ahi′kam, at Mizpah, and dwelt with him among the people who were left in the land.

7 When all the captains of the forces in the open country and their men heard that the king of Babylon had appointed Gedali′ah the son of Ahi′-

q Syr: Heb obscure

the sack of Jerusalem (v. 8) occurred a month after its capture. **15–18:** This oracle, assuring Ebed-melech of his personal safety because of his trust in God, is a continuation of 38.13. **40.1–6:** Ramah (31.15) was a transit point for deportees. For reasons unknown, Jeremiah was allowed to choose exile or residence in Judah. Choosing the latter, he was placed in the custody of Gedaliah, the newly-appointed governor of Judah with whose family Jeremiah had long been friendly (26.24; 36.10).

40.7–41.18: The third revolt. 40.7–12: Gedaliah, a member of a prominent Judean family

kam governor in the land, and had committed to him men, women, and children, those of the poorest of the land who had not been taken into exile to Babylon, [8] they went to Gedali'ah at Mizpah–Ish'mael the son of Nethani'ah, Joha'nan the son of Kare'ah, Serai'ah the son of Tanhu'meth, the sons of Ephai the Netoph'athite, Jezani'ah the son of the Ma-ac'athite, they and their men. [9] Gedali'ah the son of Ahi'kam, son of Shaphan, swore to them and their men, saying, "Do not be afraid to serve the Chalde'ans. Dwell in the land, and serve the king of Babylon, and it shall be well with you. [10] As for me, I will dwell at Mizpah, to stand for you before the Chalde'ans who will come to us; but as for you, gather wine and summer fruits and oil, and store them in your vessels, and dwell in your cities that you have taken." [11] Likewise, when all the Jews who were in Moab and among the Ammonites and in Edom and in other lands heard that the king of Babylon had left a remnant in Judah and had appointed Gedali'ah the son of Ahi'kam, son of Shaphan, as governor over them, [12] then all the Jews returned from all the places to which they had been driven and came to the land of Judah, to Gedali'ah at Mizpah; and they gathered wine and summer fruits in great abundance.

13 Now Joha'nan the son of Kare'ah and all the leaders of the forces in the open country came to Gedali'ah at Mizpah [14] and said to him, "Do you know that Ba'alis the king of the Ammonites has sent Ish'mael the son of Nethani'ah to take your life?" But Gedali'ah the son of Ahi'kam would not believe them. [15] Then Joha'nan the son of Kare'ah spoke secretly to Gedali'ah at Mizpah, "Let me go and slay Ish'mael the son of Nethani'ah, and no one will know it. Why should he take your life, so that all the Jews who are gathered about you would be scattered, and the remnant of Judah would perish?" [16] But Gedali'ah the son of Ahi'kam said to Joha'nan the son of Kare'ah, "You shall not do this thing, for you are speaking falsely of Ish'mael."

41 In the seventh month, Ish'mael the son of Nethani'ah, son of Eli'shama, of the royal family, one of the chief officers of the king, came with ten men to Gedali'ah the son of Ahi'kam, at Mizpah. As they ate bread together there at Mizpah, [2] Ish'mael the son of Nethani'ah and the ten men with him rose up and struck down Gedali'ah the son of Ahi'kam, son of Shaphan, with the sword, and killed him, whom the king of Babylon had appointed governor in the land. [3] Ish'mael also slew all the Jews who were with Gedali'ah at Mizpah, and the Chalde'an soldiers who happened to be there.

4 On the day after the murder of Gedali'ah, before any one knew of it, [5] eighty men arrived from Shechem and Shiloh and Sama'ria, with their beards shaved and their clothes torn, and their bodies gashed, bringing cereal offerings and incense to present at the temple of the LORD. [6] And Ish'mael the son of Nethani'ah came out from Mizpah to meet them, weeping as he came. As he met them, he said to them, "Come in to Gedali'ah the son of Ahi'kam." [7] When they came into the city,

(2 Kg.22.12–14), assured his countrymen that he would represent them before the Babylonians (*Chaldeans*) and urged them to return to their fields and cities. Benjamin seems to have been largely spared (32.1–8; Neh. ch. 7) and *Mizpah* (perhaps at present-day Tell en-Nasbeh, seven miles north of Jerusalem) became the provincial capital. **40.13–41.3:** After about five prosperous years and with encouragement from Baalis of Ammon (for political reasons), Ishmael, a member of the royal family (as Gedaliah was not) and a super-patriot, plotted Gedaliah's assassination. When told of it, Gedaliah discredited the report. Probably in September 582 B.C. (52.30), Gedaliah, his entourage, and the Babylonian garrison in Mizpah, were slain. **4–10:** The next day Ishmael intercepted a group from the north on a pilgrimage to Jerusalem. Luring them into Mizpah, he slaughtered all but ten who bought their lives with *stores* of food. After

Ish'mael the son of Nethani'ah and the men with him slew them, and cast them into a cistern. [8] But there were ten men among them who said to Ish'-mael, "Do not kill us, for we have stores of wheat, barley, oil, and honey hidden in the fields." So he refrained and did not kill them with their companions.

9 Now the cistern into which Ish'-mael cast all the bodies of the men whom he had slain was the large cistern[r] which King Asa had made for defense against Ba'asha king of Israel; Ish'mael the son of Nethani'ah filled it with the slain. [10] Then Ish'-mael took captive all the rest of the people who were in Mizpah, the king's daughters and all the people who were left at Mizpah, whom Nebu'zarad'an, the captain of the guard, had committed to Gedali'ah the son of Ahi'kam. Ish'mael the son of Nethani'ah took them captive and set out to cross over to the Ammonites.

11 But when Joha'nan the son of Kare'ah and all the leaders of the forces with him heard of all the evil which Ish'mael the son of Nethani'ah had done, [12] they took all their men and went to fight against Ish'mael the son of Nethani'ah. They came upon him at the great pool which is in Gibeon. [13] And when all the people who were with Ish'mael saw Joha'nan the son of Kare'ah and all the leaders of the forces with him, they rejoiced. [14] So all the people whom Ish'mael had carried away captive from Mizpah turned about and came back, and went to Joha'nan the son of Kare'ah. [15] But Ish'mael the son of Nethani'ah escaped from Joha'nan with eight men, and went to the Ammonites. [16] Then Joha'-nan the son of Kare'ah and all the leaders of the forces with him took all the rest of the people whom Ish'mael the son of Nethani'ah had carried away captive[s] from Mizpah after he had slain Gedali'ah the son of Ahi'kam–soldiers, women, children, and eunuchs, whom Joha'nan brought back from Gibeon. [17] And they went and stayed at Geruth Chimham near Bethlehem, intending to go to Egypt [18] because of the Chalde'-ans; for they were afraid of them, because Ish'mael the son of Nethani'ah had slain Gedali'ah the son of Ahi'kam, whom the king of Babylon had made governor over the land.

42 Then all the commanders of the forces, and Joha'nan the son of Kare'ah and Azari'ah[t] the son of Ho-shai'ah, and all the people from the least to the greatest, came near [2] and said to Jeremiah the prophet, "Let our supplication come before you, and pray to the LORD your God for us, for all this remnant (for we are left but a few of many, as your eyes see us), [3] that the LORD your God may show us the way we should go, and the thing that we should do." [4] Jeremiah the prophet said to them, "I have heard you; behold, I will pray to the LORD your God according to your request, and whatever the LORD answers you I will tell you; I will keep nothing back from you." [5] Then they said to Jeremiah, "May the LORD be a true and faithful witness against us if we do not act according to all the word with which the LORD your God sends you to us. [6] Whether it is good or evil, we will obey the voice of the LORD our God to whom we are sending you, that it may

r Gk: Heb *he had slain by the hand of Gedaliah*
s Cn: Heb *whom he recovered from Ishmael*
t Gk: Heb *Jezaniah*

casting the bodies into an old cistern (1 Kg.15.22), the assassins took the remaining people in Mizpah and headed for Ammon. **11–18:** An avenging group under Johanan overtook Ishmael at Gibeon (28.1; 2 Sam.2.13). In the melee, Ishmael and eight conspirators escaped to Ammon (40.14), but their captives were freed. Fearing Babylonian reprisals Johanan's group turned toward Egypt, encamping en route at *Geruth Chimham* (perhaps "Chimham's Inn") near Bethlehem.

42.1–43.7: Flight to Egypt. 42.1–6: Jeremiah may have been one of the captives freed by Johanan (41.16). He was asked to intercede (15.11) for the group, who were uncertain what they should do and where they should go. To remain could mean reprisals from Babylon (52.30);

be well with us when we obey the voice of the LORD our God." 7 At the end of ten days the word of the LORD came to Jeremiah. 8 Then he summoned Joha'nan the son of Kare'ah and all the commanders of the forces who were with him, and all the people from the least to the greatest, 9 and said to them, "Thus says the LORD, the God of Israel, to whom you sent me to present your supplication before him: 10 If you will remain in this land, then I will build you up and not pull you down; I will plant you, and not pluck you up; for I repent of the evil which I did to you. 11 Do not fear the king of Babylon, of whom you are afraid; do not fear him, says the LORD, for I am with you, to save you and to deliver you from his hand. 12 I will grant you mercy, that he may have mercy on you and let you remain in your own land. 13 But if you say, 'We will not remain in this land,' disobeying the voice of the LORD your God 14 and saying, 'No, we will go to the land of Egypt, where we shall not see war, or hear the sound of the trumpet, or be hungry for bread, and we will dwell there,' 15 then hear the word of the LORD, O remnant of Judah. Thus says the LORD of hosts, the God of Israel: If you set your faces to enter Egypt and go to live there, 16 then the sword which you fear shall overtake you there in the land of Egypt; and the famine of which you are afraid shall follow hard after you to Egypt; and there you shall die. 17 All the men who set their faces to go to Egypt to live there shall die by the sword, by famine, and by pestilence; they shall have no remnant or survivor

from the evil which I will bring upon them. 18 "For thus says the LORD of hosts, the God of Israel: As my anger and my wrath were poured out on the inhabitants of Jerusalem, so my wrath will be poured out on you when you go to Egypt. You shall become an execration, a horror, a curse, and a taunt. You shall see this place no more. 19 The LORD has said to you, O remnant of Judah, 'Do not go to Egypt.' Know for a certainty that I have warned you this day 20 that you have gone astray at the cost of your lives. For you sent me to the LORD your God, saying, 'Pray for us to the LORD our God, and whatever the LORD our God says declare to us and we will do it.' 21 And I have this day declared it to you, but you have not obeyed the voice of the LORD your God in anything that he sent me to tell you. 22 Now therefore know for a certainty that you shall die by the sword, by famine, and by pestilence in the place where you desire to go to live."

43 When Jeremiah finished speaking to all the people all these words of the LORD their God, with which the LORD their God had sent him to them, 2 Azari'ah the son of Hoshai'ah and Joha'nan the son of Kare'ah and all the insolent men said to Jeremiah, "You are telling a lie. The LORD our God did not send you to say, 'Do not go to Egypt to live there'; 3 but Baruch the son of Neri'ah has set you against us, to deliver us into the hand of the Chalde'ans, that they may kill us or take us into exile in Babylon." 4 So Joha'nan the son of Kare'ah and

---

to flee would mean safety, though with a *de facto* admission of guilt. **7–22:** After ten days, Jeremiah brought the reply: to remain was God's will (29.1–14; 32.6–15) and they would receive God's blessing; to flee would only bring suffering upon the fugitives. **43.1–7:** Apparently the tension in the camp during the ten days that followed allowed those who favored the flight to prevail over the good intentions of those who wished to abide by Jeremiah's oracle. Jeremiah was accused of being unduly influenced by Baruch, and his oracle was not regarded as God's word. It has been suggested that 42.19–22 should come between verses 3 and 4 as Jeremiah's response to Azariah and his colleagues, since 42.19–22 may indicate that the decision had already been made to go to Egypt; Jeremiah reminded them of their earlier resolve and the danger of disobeying the LORD's will. They decided to go to Egypt, taking Jeremiah and Baruch with them, perhaps to assure themselves of the continuing availability of oracles

all the commanders of the forces and all the people did not obey the voice of the LORD, to remain in the land of Judah. ⁵ But Joha′nan the son of Kare′ah and all the commanders of the forces took all the remnant of Judah who had returned to live in the land of Judah from all the nations to which they had been driven– ⁶ the men, the women, the children, the princesses, and every person whom Nebu′zarad′an the captain of the guard had left with Gedali′ah the son of Ahi′kam, son of Shaphan; also Jeremiah the prophet and Baruch the son of Neri′ah. ⁷ And they came into the land of Egypt, for they did not obey the voice of the LORD. And they arrived at Tah′panhes.

8 Then the word of the LORD came to Jeremiah in Tah′panhes: ⁹ "Take in your hands large stones, and hide them in the mortar in the pavement which is at the entrance to Pharaoh's palace in Tah′panhes, in the sight of the men of Judah, ¹⁰ and say to them, 'Thus says the LORD of hosts, the God of Israel: Behold, I will send and take Nebuchadrez′zar the king of Babylon, my servant, and he*ᵘ* will set his throne above these stones which I have hid, and he will spread his royal canopy over them. ¹¹ He shall come and smite the land of Egypt, giving to the pestilence those who are doomed to the pestilence, to captivity those who are doomed to captivity, and to the sword those who are doomed to the sword. ¹² He*ᵛ* shall kindle a fire in the temples of the gods of Egypt; and he shall burn them and carry them

away captive; and he shall clean the land of Egypt, as a shepherd cleans his cloak of vermin; and he shall go away from there in peace. ¹³ He shall break the obelisks of Heliop′olis which is in the land of Egypt; and the temples of the gods of Egypt he shall burn with fire.' "

44 The word that came to Jeremiah concerning all the Jews that dwelt in the land of Egypt, at Migdol, at Tah′panhes, at Memphis, and in the land of Pathros, ² "Thus says the LORD of hosts, the God of Israel: You have seen all the evil that I brought upon Jerusalem and upon all the cities of Judah. Behold, this day they are a desolation, and no one dwells in them, ³ because of the wickedness which they committed, provoking me to anger, in that they went to burn incense and serve other gods that they knew not, neither they, nor you, nor your fathers. ⁴ Yet I persistently sent to you all my servants the prophets, saying, 'Oh, do not do this abominable thing that I hate!' ⁵ But they did not listen or incline their ear, to turn from their wickedness and burn no incense to other gods. ⁶ Therefore my wrath and my anger were poured forth and kindled in the cities of Judah and in the streets of Jerusalem; and they became a waste and a desolation, as at this day. ⁷ And now thus says the LORD God of hosts, the God of Israel: Why do you commit this great evil against yourselves, to cut off from you man and

u Gk Syr: Heb *I*
v Gk Syr Vg: Heb *I*

---

from God. **7**: *Tahpanhes*, Egyptian border fortress, also known as Baal-Zephon, Greek Daphne, modern Tell Defneh (2.16). **43.8–45.5**: Jeremiah in Egypt. **43.8–13**: This oracle is intended to show that Egypt is no safe refuge from Nebuchadrezzar (*my servant*, 25.9; 27.6), who led a successful raid against Amasis (Ahmosis II) in 568/567 B.C., probably some years later than this oracle (46.13–26). *Clean his cloak*, literally "delouse," illustrates Jeremiah's low opinion of Egypt. *Heliopolis* (also called On; Gen.41.45), six miles northeast of Cairo; ancient center of the worship of sungod Re (see Is.19:18 n.). *Obelisks*, monuments, slightly tapered square granite shafts, capped by a pyramidion. **44.1–14**: This oracle, addressed to the Jewish diaspora in Egypt, is an expansion of Jeremiah's warning against repeating the mistakes of their fathers in Judah and suffering the consequences (compare 42.14–18). **1**: *Migdol*, present day Tell el-Heir, east of Tahpanhes (43.7). *Memphis*, 2.16. *Pathros*, "Land of the South," upper (i.e. southern) Egypt, where perhaps there was already by this time a Jewish colony at Elephantine, known from discoveries of Aramaic

woman, infant and child, from the midst of Judah, leaving you no remnant? ⁸ Why do you provoke me to anger with the works of your hands, burning incense to other gods in the land of Egypt where you have come to live, that you may be cut off and become a curse and a taunt among all the nations of the earth? ⁹ Have you forgotten the wickedness of your fathers, the wickedness of the kings of Judah, the wickedness of their ʷ wives, your own wickedness, and the wickedness of your wives, which they committed in the land of Judah and in the streets of Jerusalem? ¹⁰ They have not humbled themselves even to this day, nor have they feared, nor walked in my law and my statutes which I set before you and before your fathers.

11 "Therefore thus says the LORD of hosts, the God of Israel: Behold, I will set my face against you for evil, to cut off all Judah. ¹² I will take the remnant of Judah who have set their faces to come to the land of Egypt to live, and they shall all be consumed; in the land of Egypt they shall fall; by the sword and by famine they shall be consumed; from the least to the greatest, they shall die by the sword and by famine; and they shall become an execration, a horror, a curse, and a taunt. ¹³ I will punish those who dwell in the land of Egypt, as I have punished Jerusalem, with the sword, with famine, and with pestilence, ¹⁴ so that none of the remnant of Judah who have come to live in the land of Egypt shall escape or survive or return to the land of Judah, to which they desire to return to dwell there; for they shall not return, except some fugitives."

15 Then all the men who knew that their wives had offered incense to other gods, and all the women who stood by, a great assembly, all the people who dwelt in Pathros in the land of Egypt, answered Jeremiah: ¹⁶ "As for the word which you have spoken to us in the name of the LORD, we will not listen to you. ¹⁷ But we will do everything that we have vowed, burn incense to the queen of heaven and pour out libations to her, as we did, both we and our fathers, our kings and our princes, in the cities of Judah and in the streets of Jerusalem; for then we had plenty of food, and prospered, and saw no evil. ¹⁸ But since we left off burning incense to the queen of heaven and pouring out libations to her, we have lacked everything and have been consumed by the sword and by famine." ¹⁹ And the women said,ˣ "When we burned incense to the queen of heaven and poured out libations to her, was it without our husbands' approval that we made cakes for her bearing her image and poured out libations to her?"

20 Then Jeremiah said to all the people, men and women, all the people who had given him this answer: ²¹ "As for the incense that you burned in the cities of Judah and in the streets of Jerusalem, you and your fathers, your kings and your princes, and the people of the land, did not the LORD remember it?ʸ Did it not come into his mind? ²² The LORD could no longer bear your evil doings and the abominations which you committed; therefore your land has become a desolation and a waste and a curse, without inhabitant, as it is this day. ²³ It is because you burned incense, and because you sinned

w Heb *his*
x Compare Syr: Heb lacks *And the women said*
y Syr: Heb *them*

---

papyri dating from the fifth century B.C. **15–28:** The refugees return to the worship of the *queen of heaven* (7.16–20), which was the Babylonian-Assyrian goddess Ishtar, goddess of the star Venus (compare the Canaanite Astarte, Greek Aphrodite, Roman Venus). First introduced, presumably, by Manasseh (2 Kg.21.1–18), suppressed by Josiah (2 Kg.23.4–14), and restored by Jehoiakim (2 Kg.23.36–24.7), the cult was especially popular among women, who had an inferior role in the cult of the LORD. Offerings included wine and star-shaped or crescent-shaped cakes or figurines bearing the *image* of the goddess. The cult persisted into the Christian centuries, and features of it were incorporated by the early Syrian church in the veneration of

against the LORD and did not obey the voice of the LORD or walk in his law and in his statutes and in his testimonies, that this evil has befallen you, as at this day."

24 Jeremiah said to all the people and all the women, "Hear the word of the LORD, all you of Judah who are in the land of Egypt, ²⁵ Thus says the LORD of hosts, the God of Israel: You and your wives have declared with your mouths, and have fulfilled it with your hands, saying, 'We will surely perform our vows that we have made, to burn incense to the queen of heaven and to pour out libations to her.' Then confirm your vows and perform your vows! ²⁶ Therefore hear the word of the LORD, all you of Judah who dwell in the land of Egypt: Behold, I have sworn by my great name, says the LORD, that my name shall no more be invoked by the mouth of any man of Judah in all the land of Egypt, saying, 'As the Lord GOD lives.' ²⁷ Behold, I am watching over them for evil and not for good; all the men of Judah who are in the land of Egypt shall be consumed by the sword and by famine, until there is an end of them. ²⁸ And those who escape the sword shall return from the land of Egypt to the land of Judah, few in number; and all the remnant of Judah, who came to the land of Egypt to live, shall know whose word will stand, mine or theirs. ²⁹ This shall be the sign to you, says the LORD, that I will punish you in this place, in order that you may know that my words will surely stand against you for evil: ³⁰ Thus says the LORD, Behold, I will give Pharaoh Hophra king of Egypt into the hand of his enemies and into the hand of those who seek his life,

as I gave Zedeki′ah king of Judah into the hand of Nebuchadrez′zar king of Babylon, who was his enemy and sought his life."

45 The word that Jeremiah the prophet spoke to Baruch the son of Neri′ah, when he wrote these words in a book at the dictation of Jeremiah, in the fourth year of Jehoi′akim the son of Josi′ah, king of Judah: ² "Thus says the LORD, the God of Israel, to you, O Baruch: ³ You said, 'Woe is me! for the LORD has added sorrow to my pain; I am weary with my groaning, and I find no rest.' ⁴ Thus shall you say to him, Thus says the LORD: Behold, what I have built I am breaking down, and what I have planted I am plucking up—that is, the whole land. ⁵ And do you seek great things for yourself? Seek them not; for, behold, I am bringing evil upon all flesh, says the LORD; but I will give you your life as a prize of war in all places to which you may go."

46 The word of the LORD which came to Jeremiah the prophet concerning the nations.

2 About Egypt. Concerning the army of Pharaoh Neco, king of Egypt, which was by the river Euphra′tes at Car′chemish and which Nebuchadrez′zar king of Babylon defeated in the fourth year of Jehoi′akim the son of Josi′ah, king of Judah:

³ "Prepare buckler and shield,
  and advance for battle!
⁴ Harness the horses;
  mount, O horsemen!
Take your stations with your
  helmets,
  polish your spears,

---

the Virgin. **29–30:** *Hophra* (Apries, 588–569 B.C.; 37.5) was assassinated by Ahmosis II (Amasis, 569–526 B.C.), a former court official, co-regent for three years, and founder of the Twenty-seventh (Libyan) Dynasty. For similar *signs*, see Is.7.11–17; Ex.3.12. **45.1–5:** Advised at the outset of the difficulties ahead (36.1–4; 1.10) and surveying the trying years now past, *Baruch* concludes his memoirs by recalling God's assurance of physical deliverance (39.15–18).

46.1–51.64: Oracles against foreign nations (compare Is. chs. 13–23; Ezek. chs. 25–32). **46.1:** Introduction (1.2; 14.1); continues 25.15–38. **2–28: Against Egypt. 2–12:** In May or June 605 B.C. Crown Prince Nebuchadrezzar of Babylon defeated Neco II of Egypt at Car-chemish, on the northern Euphrates, sixty miles west of Haran (Gen. 11.31), the last capital of

put on your coats of mail!
⁵ Why have I seen it?
They are dismayed
and have turned backward.
Their warriors are beaten down,
and have fled in haste;
they look not back—
terror on every side!
                                    says the LORD.
⁶ The swift cannot flee away,
nor the warrior escape;
in the north by the river Euphra'tes
they have stumbled and fallen.

⁷ "Who is this, rising like the Nile,
like rivers whose waters surge?
⁸ Egypt rises like the Nile,
like rivers whose waters surge.
He said, I will rise, I will cover the
earth,
I will destroy cities and their
inhabitants.
⁹ Advance, O horses,
and rage, O chariots!
Let the warriors go forth:
men of Ethiopia and Put who
handle the shield,
men of Lud, skilled in handling
the bow.
¹⁰ That day is the day of the Lord GOD
of hosts,
a day of vengeance,
to avenge himself on his foes.
The sword shall devour and be
sated,
and drink its fill of their blood.
For the Lord GOD of hosts holds a
sacrifice
in the north country by the river
Euphra'tes.
¹¹ Go up to Gilead, and take balm,
O virgin daughter of Egypt!
In vain you have used many
medicines;

there is no healing for you.
¹² The nations have heard of your
shame,
and the earth is full of your cry;
for warrior has stumbled against
warrior;
they have both fallen together."

13 The word which the LORD spoke
to Jeremiah the prophet about the
coming of Nebuchadrez'zar king of
Babylon to smite the land of Egypt:
¹⁴ "Declare in Egypt, and proclaim in
Migdol;
proclaim in Memphis and
Tah'panhes;
Say, 'Stand ready and be prepared,
for the sword shall devour round
about you.'
¹⁵ Why has Apis fled?ᶻ
Why did not your bull stand?
Because the LORD thrust him
down.
¹⁶ Your multitude stumbledᵃ and fell,
and they said one to another,
'Arise, and let us go back to our own
people
and to the land of our birth,
because of the sword of the
oppressor.'
¹⁷ Call the name of Pharaoh, king of
Egypt,
'Noisy one who lets the hour go
by.'
¹⁸ "As I live, says the King,
whose name is the LORD of hosts,
like Tabor among the mountains,
and like Carmel by the sea, shall
one come.
¹⁹ Prepare yourselves baggage for
exile,

z Gk: Heb *Why was it swept away*
a Gk: Heb *He made many stumble*

Assyria, and pursued him to the borders of Egypt. Like the Nile, Egypt was preparing to inundate the lands to the north. Instead she was grievously wounded, driven back, and humiliated
before the nations. *Put*, Cyrene. *Lud*, unidentified African country (Ezek.30.5). **13–26:**
This oracle may date from one of three occasions: (a) 605 B.C. (see above); (b) November 601,
when, according to the Babylonian Chronicle, Nebuchadrezzar and Neco fought to a stalemate
at the Egyptian border; (c) 568/567 (see 43.8–13 n.). One of the first two dates is preferable.
The poetic section refers to lower Egypt (Memphis); the prose to upper Egypt (Thebes). *Apis*,
bull-god of (southern) Egypt (Nah.3.8). *Tabor*, great mountain rising above the plain of Jezreel
(Esdraelon; Jos.19.22). *Carmel*, mountain at the end of the plain of Jezreel, projecting into the

O inhabitants of Egypt!
For Memphis shall become a waste,
a ruin, without inhabitant.

20 "A beautiful heifer is Egypt,
but a gadfly from the north has
come upon her.
21 Even her hired soldiers in her midst
are like fatted calves;
yea, they have turned and fled
together,
they did not stand;
for the day of their calamity has
come upon them,
the time of their punishment.

22 "She makes a sound like a serpent
gliding away;
for her enemies march in force,
and come against her with axes,
like those who fell trees.
23 They shall cut down her forest,
says the LORD,
though it is impenetrable,
because they are more numerous
than locusts;
they are without number.
24 The daughter of Egypt shall be put
to shame,
she shall be delivered into the
hand of a people from the
north."

25 The LORD of hosts, the God of
Israel, said: "Behold, I am bringing
punishment upon Amon of Thebes,
and Pharaoh, and Egypt and her gods
and her kings, upon Pharaoh and
those who trust in him. 26 I will deliver
them into the hand of those who seek
their life, into the hand of Nebuchadrez'zar king of Babylon and his officers. Afterward Egypt shall be inhabited as in the days of old, says the LORD.

27 "But fear not, O Jacob my servant,
nor be dismayed, O Israel;

for lo, I will save you from afar,
and your offspring from the land
of their captivity.
Jacob shall return and have quiet
and ease,
and none shall make him afraid.
28 Fear not, O Jacob my servant,
says the LORD,
for I am with you.
I will make a full end of all the
nations
to which I have driven you,
but of you I will not make a full
end.
I will chasten you in just measure,
and I will by no means leave you
unpunished."

47 The word of the LORD that
came to Jeremiah the prophet
concerning the Philistines, before
Pharaoh smote Gaza.
2 "Thus says the LORD:
Behold, waters are rising out of
the north,
and shall become an overflowing
torrent;
they shall overflow the land and all
that fills it,
the city and those who dwell in it.
Men shall cry out,
and every inhabitant of the land
shall wail.
3 At the noise of the stamping of the
hoofs of his stallions,
at the rushing of his chariots, at
the rumbling of their wheels
the fathers look not back to the
children,
so feeble are their hands,
4 because of the day that is coming to
destroy
all the Philistines,
to cut off from Tyre and Sidon
every helper that remains.
For the LORD is destroying the
Philistines,

Mediterranean (Jos.19.26). **27–28:** A doublet of 30.10–11, which here contrasts the destruction of Egypt (except 26b) and the reconstruction of all Israel.
47.1–7: Against the Philistines. Dissimilar from other oracles against the Philistines (Is.14.29–31; Ezek.25.15–17), this oracle may be associated with Nebuchadrezzar's sack of Ashkelon (vv. 5,7; 36.9). The Phoenician cities, Tyre and Sidon, were perhaps allied also with the Philis-tines (27.3). The Philistines were related to the Indo-European inhabitants of Crete (*Caphtor;*

the remnant of the coastland of
Caphtor.
5 Baldness has come upon Gaza,
Ash'kelon has perished.
O remnant of the Anakim,*b*
how long will you gash yourselves?
6 Ah, sword of the LORD!
How long till you are quiet?
Put yourself into your scabbard,
rest and be still!
7 How can it*c* be quiet,
when the LORD has given it a
charge?
Against Ash'kelon and against the
seashore
he has appointed it."

48 Concerning Moab.
Thus says the LORD of hosts,
the God of Israel:
"Woe to Nebo, for it is laid waste!
Kiriatha'im is put to shame, it is
taken;
the fortress is put to shame and
broken down;
2   the renown of Moab is no more.
In Heshbon they planned evil
against her:
'Come, let us cut her off from
being a nation!'
You also, O Madmen, shall be
brought to silence;
the sword shall pursue you.

3 "Hark! a cry from Horona'im,
'Desolation and great destruction!'
4 Moab is destroyed;
a cry is heard as far as Zo'ar.*d*
5 For at the ascent of Luhith
they go up weeping;*e*
for at the descent of Horona'im
they have heard the cry*f* of
destruction.

6 Flee! Save yourselves!
Be like a wild ass*g* in the desert!
7 For, because you trusted in your
strongholds*h* and your
treasures,
you also shall be taken;
and Chemosh shall go forth into
exile,
with his priests and his princes.
8 The destroyer shall come upon
every city,
and no city shall escape;
the valley shall perish,
and the plain shall be destroyed,
as the LORD has spoken.

9 "Give wings to Moab,
for she would fly away;
her cities shall become a desolation,
with no inhabitant in them.

10 "Cursed is he who does the work
of the LORD with slackness; and cursed
is he who keeps back his sword from
bloodshed.

11 "Moab has been at ease from his
youth
and has settled on his lees;
he has not been emptied from vessel
to vessel,
nor has he gone into exile;
so his taste remains in him,
and his scent is not changed.
12 "Therefore, behold, the days are
coming, says the LORD, when I shall
send to him tilters who will tilt him,
and empty his vessels, and break his*i*
jars in pieces. 13 Then Moab shall be

b Gk: Heb *their valley*   *c* Gk Vg: Heb *you*
d Gk: Heb *her little ones*
e Cn: Heb *weeping goes up with weeping*
f Gk Compare Is 15.5: Heb *the distress of the cry*
g Gk Aquila: Heb *like Aroer*
h Gk: Heb *works*   *i* Gk Aquila: Heb *their*

See Am.9.7 n.; 2 Sam.8.18 n. **5:** *Anakim*, Jos.11.21–22. For similar signs of lamentation, compare 16.6; 41.5.
    48.1–47: Against Moab. The original occasion for this dirge may have been the suppression of the revolt of Moab and other western states by Asshurbanipal about 650 B.C. The immediate occasion may be either the punitive raids against Judah in 601 (12.7–13) or the inconclusive plot to revolt in 594 (27.1–11)–probably the former. The dirge was apparently popular in Judah (Is.15.1–16.14). **1–10:** The advance of the enemy (perhaps Nebuchadrezzar), against which Moab is defenseless. **7:** For *Chemosh*, chief god of Moab, see Jg.11.24 n. **11–17:** Though Moab was not on the main trade-route or invasion-route, she will not escape; her heroes will quail before the enemy. **13:** Perhaps here *Bethel* is the name of a contemporary god

ashamed of Chemosh, as the house of Israel was ashamed of Bethel, their confidence.

14 "How do you say, 'We are heroes
    and mighty men of war'?
15 The destroyer of Moab and his cities
        has come up,
    and the choicest of his young men
        have gone down to slaughter,
    says the King, whose name is the
        LORD of hosts.
16 The calamity of Moab is near at
        hand
    and his affliction hastens apace.
17 Bemoan him, all you who are round
        about him,
    and all who know his name;
    say, 'How the mighty scepter is
        broken,
    the glorious staff.'

18 "Come down from your glory,
    and sit on the parched ground,
    O inhabitant of Dibon!
    For the destroyer of Moab has come
        up against you;
    he has destroyed your strongholds.
19 Stand by the way and watch,
    O inhabitant of Aro'er!
    Ask him who flees and her who
        escapes;
    say, 'What has happened?'
20 Moab is put to shame, for it is
        broken;
    wail and cry!
    Tell it by the Arnon,
    that Moab is laid waste.

21 "Judgment has come upon the tableland, upon Holon, and Jahzah, and Meph'a-ath, 22 and Dibon, and Nebo, and Beth-diblatha'im, 23 and Kiriatha'im, and Beth-ga'mul, and Beth-me'on, 24 and Ker'i-oth, and Bozrah, and all the cities of the land of Moab, far and near. 25 The horn of Moab is cut off, and his arm is broken, says the LORD.

26 "Make him drunk, because he magnified himself against the LORD; so that Moab shall wallow in his vomit, and he too shall be held in derision. 27 Was not Israel a derision to you? Was he found among thieves, that whenever you spoke of him you wagged your head?

28 "Leave the cities, and dwell in the
        rock,
    O inhabitants of Moab!
    Be like the dove that nests
        in the sides of the mouth of a
            gorge.
29 We have heard of the pride of
        Moab—
    he is very proud—
    of his loftiness, his pride, and his
        arrogance,
    and the haughtiness of his heart.
30 I know his insolence, says the LORD;
    his boasts are false,
    his deeds are false.
31 Therefore I wail for Moab;
    I cry out for all Moab;
    for the men of Kir-he'res I mourn.
32 More than for Jazer I weep for you,
    O vine of Sibmah!
    Your branches passed over the sea,
        reached as far as Jazer;*j*
    upon your summer fruits and your
        vintage
    the destroyer has fallen.
33 Gladness and joy have been taken
        away
    from the fruitful land of Moab;
    I have made the wine cease from the
        wine presses;
    no one treads them with shouts of
        joy;
    the shouting is not the shout of
        joy.

34 "Heshbon and Ele-a'leh cry out;*k* as far as Jahaz they utter their voice, from Zo'ar to Horona'im and

j Cn: Heb *the sea of Jazer*
k Cn: Heb *From the cry of Heshbon to Elealeh*

---

of Aramaic origin, not the city. **18–28:** As Moab had spitefully derided Judah, may she now choke on her own spite! The desert is no safe refuge; as the wild dove (Ezek. 7.16), she must take to the rocks. **29–39:** Moab, once so proud, is humiliated before her conqueror. As a

Eg'lath-shelish'iyah. For the waters of Nimrim also have become desolate. [35] And I will bring to an end in Moab, says the LORD, him who offers sacrifice in the high place and burns incense to his god. [36] Therefore my heart moans for Moab like a flute, and my heart moans like a flute for the men of Kir-he'res; therefore the riches they gained have perished.

37 "For every head is shaved and every beard cut off; upon all the hands are gashes, and on the loins is sackcloth. [38] On all the housetops of Moab and in the squares there is nothing but lamentation; for I have broken Moab like a vessel for which no one cares, says the LORD. [39] How it is broken! How they wail! How Moab has turned his back in shame! So Moab has become a derision and a horror to all that are round about him."

[40] For thus says the LORD:

"Behold, one shall fly swiftly like an
  eagle,
    and spread his wings against
      Moab;
[41] the cities shall be taken
    and the strongholds seized.
The heart of the warriors of Moab
    shall be in that day
  like the heart of a woman in her
      pangs;
[42] Moab shall be destroyed and be no
      longer a people,
  because he magnified himself
    against the LORD.
[43] Terror, pit, and snare
  are before you, O inhabitant of
      Moab!
                    says the LORD.
[44] He who flees from the terror
  shall fall into the pit,
  and he who climbs out of the pit

shall be caught in the snare.
For I will bring these things[l] upon
  Moab
  in the year of their punishment,
                    says the LORD.
[45] "In the shadow of Heshbon
    fugitives stop without strength;
for a fire has gone forth from
      Heshbon,
    a flame from the house of Sihon;
  it has destroyed the forehead of
      Moab,
    the crown of the sons of tumult.
[46] Woe to you, O Moab!
    The people of Chemosh is
      undone;
  for your sons have been taken
      captive,
    and your daughters into captivity.
[47] Yet I will restore the fortunes of
      Moab
  in the latter days, says the LORD."
Thus far is the judgment on Moab.

49 Concerning the Ammonites.
    Thus says the LORD:
"Has Israel no sons?
    Has he no heir?
Why then has Milcom dispossessed
      Gad,
    and his people settled in its cities?
[2] Therefore, behold, the days are
      coming,
    says the LORD,
when I will cause the battle cry to be
      heard
    against Rabbah of the Ammonites;
it shall become a desolate mound,
    and its villages shall be burned
      with fire;
then Israel shall dispossess those
    who dispossesed him,
    says the LORD.

l Gk Syr: Heb *to her*

---

broken pot is discarded, so smitten Moab is accounted worthless. **40–42:** God's judgment against Moab. **43–47:** After thoroughgoing devastation (23.12; Is.24.17–18) Moab will be restored.

49.1–6: Against Ammon. The occasion for this comparatively mild oracle may be the Ammonite raid of 601 B.C. (see 12.7–13 n.). Ammon, the northern "brother" of Moab (Gen.19.30–38), had previously occupied Transjordanian territory claimed by Israel (Jg.10.6–12.6; 2 Kg. 15.29) and was Israelite territory under David (2 Sam.12.26–31; Am.1.13–14 perhaps reflects their war for independence). Ammon too must suffer for its idolatry and violence. *Milcom,* Ammonite national god (1 Kg.11.5,33); *Rabbah,* capital of Ammon.

3 "Wail, O Heshbon, for Ai is laid
waste!
Cry, O daughters of Rabbah!
Gird yourselves with sackcloth,
lament, and run to and fro among
the hedges!
For Milcom shall go into exile,
with his priests and his princes.
4 Why do you boast of your valleys,*m*
O faithless daughter,
who trusted in her treasures, saying,
'Who will come against me?'
5 Behold, I will bring terror upon you,
says the Lord GOD of hosts,
from all who are round about you,
and you shall be driven out, every
man straight before him,
with none to gather the fugitives.
6 But afterward I will restore the
fortunes of the Ammonites, says the
LORD."

7 Concerning Edom.
Thus says the LORD of hosts:
"Is wisdom no more in Teman?
Has counsel perished from the
prudent?
Has their wisdom vanished?
8 Flee, turn back, dwell in the
depths,
O inhabitants of Dedan!
For I will bring the calamity of
Esau upon him,
the time when I punish him.
9 If grape-gatherers came to you,
would they not leave gleanings?
If thieves came by night,
would they not destroy only
enough for themselves?
10 But I have stripped Esau bare,
I have uncovered his hiding
places,
and he is not able to conceal
himself.
His children are destroyed, and his
brothers,

and his neighbors; and he is no
more.
11 Leave your fatherless children, I
will keep them alive;
and let your widows trust in me."
12 For thus says the LORD: "If
those who did not deserve to drink the
cup must drink it, will you go unpunished? You shall not go unpunished, but you must drink. 13 For
I have sworn by myself, says the
LORD, that Bozrah shall become a
horror, a taunt, a waste, and a curse;
and all her cities shall be perpetual
wastes."
14 I have heard tidings from the LORD,
and a messenger has been sent
among the nations:
"Gather yourselves together and
come against her,
and rise up for battle!"
15 For behold, I will make you small
among the nations,
despised among men.
16 The horror you inspire has deceived
you,
and the pride of your heart,
you who live in the clefts of the
rock,*n*
who hold the height of the hill.
Though you make your nest as high
as the eagle's,
I will bring you down from there,
says the LORD.
17 "Edom shall become a horror;
every one who passes by it will be horrified and will hiss because of all its
disasters. 18 As when Sodom and
Gomor'rah and their neighbor cities
were overthrown, says the LORD, no
man shall dwell there, no man shall
sojourn in her. 19 Behold, like a lion
coming up from the jungle of the Jordan against a strong sheepfold, I will

m Heb *valleys, your valley flows*
n Or *Sela*

49.7–22: Against Edom. After 587 B.C. the relationship between Israel and "brother" Edom (Dt.23.7–8) deteriorated to consistent Jewish vengefulness because of Edom's occupation of southern Judah (Lam.4.21–22; Ezek.25.12–14), an occupation caused by pressure from Arab tribes. Jeremiah and Obadiah (Ob.1–9) share an oracle (which may be original with neither) that describes the bleak future of Edom. For another possible occasion, see vv. 1–6 n. *Teman,* modern Tawilan, about three miles east of Sela (Petra). *Bozrah,* a great fortress city in northern Edom. **19–21:** Editorial revision of 50.44–46.

suddenly make them[o] run away from her; and I will appoint over her whomever I choose. For who is like me? Who will summon me? What shepherd can stand before me? [20] Therefore hear the plan which the LORD has made against Edom and the purposes which he has formed against the inhabitants of Teman: Even the little ones of the flock shall be dragged away; surely their fold shall be appalled at their fate. [21] At the sound of their fall the earth shall tremble; the sound of their cry shall be heard at the Red Sea. [22] Behold, one shall mount up and fly swiftly like an eagle, and spread his wings against Bozrah, and the heart of the warriors of Edom shall be in that day like the heart of a woman in her pangs."

[23] Concerning Damascus.
"Hamath and Arpad are
  confounded,
  for they have heard evil tidings;
they melt in fear, they are troubled
  like the sea[p]
  which cannot be quiet.
[24] Damascus has become feeble, she
  turned to flee,
  and panic seized her;
anguish and sorrows have taken
  hold of her,
  as of a woman in travail.
[25] How the famous city is forsaken,[q]
  the joyful city![r]
[26] Therefore her young men shall fall
  in her squares,
  and all her soldiers shall be
   destroyed in that day,
      says the LORD of hosts.
[27] And I will kindle a fire in the wall
  of Damascus,
  and it shall devour the strongholds
  of Ben-ha′dad."

[28] Concerning Kedar and the kingdoms of Hazor which Nebuchadrez′zar king of Babylon smote.
Thus says the LORD:
"Rise up, advance against Kedar!
  Destroy the people of the east!
[29] Their tents and their flocks shall be
  taken,
  their curtains and all their goods;
their camels shall be borne away
  from them,
  and men shall cry to them:
  'Terror on every side!'
[30] Flee, wander far away, dwell in the
  depths,
  O inhabitants of Hazor!
      says the LORD.
For Nebuchadrez′zar king of Babylon
  has made a plan against you,
  and formed a purpose against you.

[31] "Rise up, advance against a nation
   at ease,
   that dwells securely,
      says the LORD,
  that has no gates or bars,
  that dwells alone.
[32] Their camels shall become booty,
  their herds of cattle a spoil.
I will scatter to every wind
  those who cut the corners of their
   hair,
and I will bring their calamity
  from every side of them,
      says the LORD.
[33] Hazor shall become a haunt of
  jackals,
  an everlasting waste;
no man shall dwell there,
  no man shall sojourn in her."

[34] The word of the LORD that came to Jeremiah the prophet concerning

o Gk Syr: Heb *him*
p Cn: Heb *there is trouble in the sea*
q Vg: Heb *not forsaken*
r Syr Vg Tg: Heb *city of my joy*

49.23–27: Against Damascus. The occasion for this composite oracle (compare v. 27; Am.1.4) is unidentifiable. Damascus lost its independence with the capture of *Arpad* by Tiglath-Pileser III in 740 B.C., *Hamath* in 738, and Damascus in 732 (Is.10.9; 37.13). *Ben-hadad,* 1 Kg.15.18,20.
  49.28–33: Against Kedar and Hazor. In mid-winter 599/598 B.C. Nebuchadrezzar led a successful expedition against the Arab tribes in the desert east of Syria-Palestine, which may have been the occasion for this oracle (9.26; 25.23–24). These people with no fortresses, who lived in the desert expanses, would not escape attack from the wide-ranging Nebuchadrezzar.

Elam, in the beginning of the reign of Zedeki'ah king of Judah.

35 Thus says the LORD of hosts: "Behold, I will break the bow of Elam, the mainstay of their might; [36] and I will bring upon Elam the four winds from the four quarters of heaven; and I will scatter them to all those winds, and there shall be no nation to which those driven out of Elam shall not come. [37] I will terrify Elam before their enemies, and before those who seek their life; I will bring evil upon them, my fierce anger, says the LORD. I will send the sword after them, until I have consumed them; [38] and I will set my throne in Elam, and destroy their king and princes, says the LORD.

39 "But in the latter days I will restore the fortunes of Elam, says the LORD."

50 The word which the LORD spoke concerning Babylon, concerning the land of the Chalde'ans, by Jeremiah the prophet:
[2] "Declare among the nations and proclaim,
    set up a banner and proclaim,
    conceal it not, and say:
'Babylon is taken,
    Bel is put to shame,
    Mer'odach is dismayed.
Her images are put to shame,
    her idols are dismayed.'
3 "For out of the north a nation has come up against her, which shall make her land a desolation, and none shall dwell in it; both man and beast shall flee away.

4 "In those days and in that time, says the LORD, the people of Israel and the people of Judah shall come together, weeping as they come; and they shall seek the LORD their God. [5] They shall ask the way to Zion, with faces turned toward it, saying, 'Come, let us join ourselves to the LORD in an everlasting covenant which will never be forgotten.'

6 "My people have been lost sheep; their shepherds have led them astray, turning them away on the mountains; from mountain to hill they have gone, they have forgotten their fold. [7] All who found them have devoured them, and their enemies have said, 'We are not guilty, for they have sinned against the LORD, their true habitation, the LORD, the hope of their fathers.'

8 "Flee from the midst of Babylon, and go out of the land of the Chalde'- ans, and be as he-goats before the flock. [9] For behold, I am stirring up and bringing against Babylon a company of great nations, from the north country; and they shall array themselves against her; from there she shall be taken. Their arrows are like a skilled warrior who does not return empty-handed. [10] Chalde'a shall be

---

49.34–39: Against Elam. In the winter of 596 B.C. Nebuchadrezzar attacked Elam, east of Babylonia, and was apparently successful. *Zedekiah* became king in March 597, when Jehoia- chin was deposed. *Bow of Elam* reflects the prowess of Elamite archers (Is.22.6). **39:** This verse (like 46.26; 48.47; and 49.6) is probably an editorial addition.

50.1–51.64: Against Babylon. This collection of illogically arranged and sometimes redupli- cated oracles was probably not composed by Jeremiah, though materials from his oracles were used. It contains two main themes: the fall of Babylon (sometimes represented as accomplished, sometimes represented as still in the future) and the return of the exiles (compare 24.6; 29.10). The attitude toward Babylon is somewhat harsher (50.14,24) than one finds elsewhere in the book (27.6; 43.10), but is not unprecedented (e.g. 25.12–14). The oracles concerning Judah (Israel) are here marked with the letters (a) to (f). **50.1:** *By Jeremiah*, literally "by the hand of Jeremiah," an idiom found also in the superscriptions in Hag.1.1; Mal.1.1; contrast Jer.46.1; 49.34. **2–3:** The downfall of Babylon. The nation *out of the north*, patterned on Jeremiah's expression (4.6), may or may not refer to Cyrus and Persia, before whom Babylon fell in October 539 B.C. *Bel* (Baal), 51.44; Is.46.1, originally chief god of Nippur, later identified in Babylon with the great cosmic god Marduk (*Merodach*). **4–5,6–7:** (a) An apostrophe on Israel's homecoming (31.7–9) and guilt (2.20; 23.1–2). **8–16:** The residents are urged to flee before

plundered; all who plunder her shall
be sated, says the LORD.

11 "Though you rejoice, though you
    exult,
O plunderers of my heritage,
though you are wanton as a heifer
    at grass,
and neigh like stallions,
12 your mother shall be utterly shamed,
    and she who bore you shall be
    disgraced.
Lo, she shall be the last of the
    nations,
    a wilderness dry and desert.
13 Because of the wrath of the
    LORD she shall not be
    inhabited,
    but shall be an utter desolation;
every one who passes by Babylon
    shall be appalled,
    and hiss because of all her
    wounds.
14 Set yourselves in array against
    Babylon round about,
all you that bend the bow;
shoot at her, spare no arrows,
    for she has sinned against the
    LORD.
15 Raise a shout against her round
    about,
    she has surrendered;
her bulwarks have fallen,
    her walls are thrown down.
For this is the vengeance of the
    LORD:
    take vengeance on her,
    do to her as she has done.
16 Cut off from Babylon the sower,
    and the one who handles the
    sickle in time of harvest;
because of the sword of the
    oppressor,
    every one shall turn to his own
    people,

and every one shall flee to his
    own land.

17 "Israel is a hunted sheep driven
away by lions. First the king of Assyria devoured him, and now at last
Nebuchadrez'zar king of Babylon has
gnawed his bones. 18 Therefore, thus
says the LORD of hosts, the God of
Israel: Behold, I am bringing punishment on the king of Babylon and his
land, as I punished the king of Assyria. 19 I will restore Israel to his
pasture, and he shall feed on Carmel
and in Bashan, and his desire shall be
satisfied on the hills of E'phraim and
in Gilead. 20 In those days and in
that time, says the LORD, iniquity shall
be sought in Israel, and there shall be
none; and sin in Judah, and none shall
be found; for I will pardon those
whom I leave as a remnant.

21 "Go up against the land of
    Meratha'im,ˢ
    and against the inhabitants of
    Pekod.ᵗ
Slay, and utterly destroy after them,
        says the LORD,
    and do all that I have commanded
    you.
22 The noise of battle is in the land,
    and great destruction!
23 How the hammer of the whole earth
    is cut down and broken!
How Babylon has become
    a horror among the nations!
24 I set a snare for you and you were
    taken, O Babylon,
    and you did not know it;
you were found and caught,
    because you strove against the
    LORD.
25 The LORD has opened his armory,

s Or *Double Rebellion*
t Or *Punishment*

Babylon's approaching doom (13.14) and desolation (18.16). Not only is the city destroyed,
but more damaging, in a way, is the destruction of food production. **17–20:** (b) Though successively subject to Assyria and Babylonia, Israel will be restored (31.4–5; 33.8) and Babylon,
as Assyria earlier, will be destroyed (25.12). **21–32:** God's judgment against Babylon. *Mera-
thaim*, "Double Rebellion" is a play on the name of southern Babylonia, *mât marrâti*, "Land of
the Lagoons." *Pekod*, "Punishment," is a play on the name *Puqûdu*, an east Babylonian tribe
(Ezek.23.23). The writer derides Babylon as a smashed hammer and a captured bird (compare
5.26–27). He sees the destruction of the temple as an affront to God which must and will be

and brought out the weapons of
  his wrath,
for the Lord GOD of hosts has a
  work to do
in the land of the Chalde′ans.
²⁶ Come against her from every
  quarter;
  open her granaries;
pile her up like heaps of grain, and
  destroy her utterly;
  let nothing be left of her.
²⁷ Slay all her bulls,
  let them go down to the slaughter.
Woe to them, for their day has come,
  the time of their punishment.

28 "Hark! they flee and escape
from the land of Babylon, to declare
in Zion the vengeance of the LORD our
God, vengeance for his temple.

29 "Summon archers against Babylon, all those who bend the bow. Encamp round about her; let no one escape. Requite her according to her
deeds, do to her according to all that
she has done; for she has proudly defied the LORD, the Holy One of Israel.
³⁰ Therefore her young men shall fall
in her squares, and all her soldiers
shall be destroyed on that day, says
the LORD.

³¹ "Behold, I am against you, O proud
  one,
  says the Lord GOD of hosts;
for your day has come,
  the time when I will punish you.
³² The proud one shall stumble and
  fall,
  with none to raise him up,
and I will kindle a fire in his cities,
  and it will devour all that is round
  about him.

33 "Thus says the LORD of hosts:
The people of Israel are oppressed,
and the people of Judah with them;
all who took them captive have held
them fast, they refuse to let them go.
³⁴ Their Redeemer is strong; the LORD
of hosts is his name. He will surely
plead their cause, that he may give rest
to the earth, but unrest to the inhabitants of Babylon.

³⁵ "A sword upon the Chalde′ans,
  says the LORD,
and upon the inhabitants of
  Babylon,
and upon her princes and her wise
  men!
³⁶ A sword upon the diviners,
  that they may become fools!
A sword upon her warriors,
  that they may be destroyed!
³⁷ A sword upon her horses and upon
  her chariots,
and upon all the foreign troops
  in her midst,
  that they may become women!
A sword upon all her treasures,
  that they may be plundered!
³⁸ A drought upon her waters,
  that they may be dried up!
For it is a land of images,
  and they are mad over idols.

39 "Therefore wild beasts shall
dwell with hyenas in Babylon, and
ostriches shall dwell in her; she shall
be peopled no more for ever, nor inhabited for all generations. ⁴⁰ As when
God overthrew Sodom and Gomor′rah
and their neighbor cities, says the
LORD, so no man shall dwell there, and
no son of man shall sojourn in her.

⁴¹ "Behold, a people comes from the
  north;
  a mighty nation and many kings
  are stirring from the farthest parts
  of the earth.
⁴² They lay hold of bow and spear;

---

avenged (21.14; Am.2.2). **33–34:** (c) While Israel is helpless, God, her *Redeemer* (Is.47.4), will
deliver her and discomfit her oppressors. **35–37:** The oracle of the sword. **38–40:** Babylon will
lie as a desert, unproductive, and inhabited only by wild animals (Is. 34.13–14). **41–46:** Babylon,
once the foe from the north (6.22–24), now stands in dread anticipation of a foe from the north.
As Edom could not escape her punishment (49.19–21), neither can Babylon. There is no king
(*shepherd*) who can successfully defy God.

they are cruel, and have no mercy.
The sound of them is like the
   roaring of the sea;
they ride upon horses,
arrayed as a man for battle
   against you, O daughter of
   Babylon!

43 "The king of Babylon heard the
   report of them,
and his hands fell helpless;
anguish seized him,
   pain as of a woman in travail.

44 "Behold, like a lion coming up from the jungle of the Jordan against a strong sheepfold, I will suddenly make them run away from her; and I will appoint over her whomever I choose. For who is like me? Who will summon me? What shepherd can stand before me? 45 Therefore hear the plan which the LORD has made against Babylon, and the purposes which he has formed against the land of the Chalde'ans: Surely the little ones of their flock shall be dragged away; surely their fold shall be appalled at their fate. 46 At the sound of the capture of Babylon the earth shall tremble, and her cry shall be heard among the nations."

51 Thus says the LORD:
   "Behold, I will stir up the spirit
   of a destroyer
against Babylon,
against the inhabitants of
   Chalde'a;^{u}
2 and I will send to Babylon
   winnowers,
and they shall winnow her,
and they shall empty her land,
   when they come against her from
   every side
on the day of trouble.
3 Let not the archer bend his bow,

and let him not stand up in his
   coat of mail.
Spare not her young men;
   utterly destroy all her host.
4 They shall fall down slain in the
   land of the Chalde'ans,
and wounded in her streets.
5 For Israel and Judah have not
   been forsaken
by their God, the LORD of hosts;
but the land of the Chalde'ans^v is
   full of guilt
against the Holy One of Israel.

6 "Flee from the midst of Babylon,
   let every man save his life!
Be not cut off in her punishment,
   for this is the time of the LORD's
   vengeance,
   the requital he is rendering her.
7 Babylon was a golden cup in the
   LORD's hand,
   making all the earth drunken;
the nations drank of her wine,
   therefore the nations went mad.
8 Suddenly Babylon has fallen and
   been broken;
   wail for her!
Take balm for her pain;
   perhaps she may be healed.
9 We would have healed Babylon,
   but she was not healed.
Forsake her, and let us go
   each to his own country;
for her judgment has reached up to
   heaven
and has been lifted up even to the
   skies.
10 The LORD has brought forth our
   vindication;
come, let us declare in Zion
   the work of the LORD our God.

11 "Sharpen the arrows!
   Take up the shields!

u Heb *Leb-qamai*, a cipher for Chaldea
v Heb *their land*

51.1–19: God's judgment against Babylon. 1–4: As grain is winnowed, so will Babylon be cut down and winnowed (see 15.7 n.). *Chaldea* is written in the Hebrew text as "Leb-qamai," an atbash cipher (see 25.26 n.). **5–10:** (d) A note reminding Israel that while they have hope, Babylon's case is hopeless (50.33–34). Babylon was the golden cup from which the nations would drink of God's wrath (see 25.15–29 n.), but now that cup is smashed; she stands desolate (46.11; Ezek.27.27) as God delivers his people. **11–19:** Terse military commands precede the

The LORD has stirred up the spirit of the kings of the Medes, because his purpose concerning Babylon is to destroy it, for that is the vengeance of the LORD, the vengeance for his temple.

12 Set up a standard against the walls of Babylon;
make the watch strong;
set up watchmen;
prepare the ambushes;
for the LORD has both planned and done
what he spoke concerning the inhabitants of Babylon.
13 O you who dwell by many waters, rich in treasures,
your end has come,
the thread of your life is cut.
14 The LORD of hosts has sworn by himself:
Surely I will fill you with men, as many as locusts,
and they shall raise the shout of victory over you.

15 "It is he who made the earth by his power,
who established the world by his wisdom,
and by his understanding stretched out the heavens.
16 When he utters his voice there is a tumult of waters in the heavens,
and he makes the mist rise from the ends of the earth.
He makes lightnings for the rain,
and he brings forth the wind from his storehouses.
17 Every man is stupid and without knowledge;
every goldsmith is put to shame by his idols;
for his images are false,
and there is no breath in them.

18 They are worthless, a work of delusion;
at the time of their punishment they shall perish.
19 Not like these is he who is the portion of Jacob,
for he is the one who formed all things,
and Israel is the tribe of his inheritance;
the LORD of hosts is his name.

20 "You are my hammer and weapon of war:
with you I break nations in pieces;
with you I destroy kingdoms;
21 with you I break in pieces the horse and his rider;
with you I break in pieces the chariot and the charioteer;
22 with you I break in pieces man and woman;
with you I break in pieces the old man and the youth;
with you I break in pieces the young man and the maiden;
23 with you I break in pieces the shepherd and his flock;
with you I break in pieces the farmer and his team;
with you I break in pieces governors and commanders.

24 "I will requite Babylon and all the inhabitants of Chalde'a before your very eyes for all the evil that they have done in Zion, says the LORD.

25 "Behold, I am against you, O destroying mountain,
says the LORD,
which destroys the whole earth;
I will stretch out my hand against you,
and roll you down from the crags,

---

attack by the *Medes;* either a reference to Media which, lying northeast of Babylonia, participated in the overthrow of Assyria and was a threat to Babylonia during this period, or an oblique reference to Persia. The phrase *many waters* refers to the Euphrates and the network of canals around Babylon. In connection with God's judgment on Babylon, the writer appends the oracle against the idols from 10.12–16 (50.38). **20–23:** This oracle of the hammer describes Babylon as God's punitive instrument (27.6; 50.23). **24–26:** As did Assyria (Is.10.5,15), so too Babylon will fall. *Destroying mountain* may reflect the great ziggurat or temple tower of Babylon, thrusting its shrine into the heavens, and here symbolizing Babylon itself. *Burnt mountain,*

and make you a burnt mountain.
26 No stone shall be taken from you
    for a corner
and no stone for a foundation,
but you shall be a perpetual waste,
    says the LORD.

27 "Set up a standard on the earth,
    blow the trumpet among the
      nations;
prepare the nations for war against
    her,
    summon against her the
      kingdoms,
    Ar'arat, Minni, and Ash'kenaz;
appoint a marshal against her,
    bring up horses like bristling
      locusts.
28 Prepare the nations for war against
    her,
    the kings of the Medes, with their
      governors and deputies,
    and every land under their
      dominion.
29 The land trembles and writhes in
    pain,
    for the LORD's purposes against
      Babylon stand,
to make the land of Babylon a
    desolation,
    without inhabitant.
30 The warriors of Babylon have
    ceased fighting,
    they remain in their strongholds;
their strength has failed,
    they have become women;
her dwellings are on fire,
    her bars are broken.
31 One runner runs to meet another,
    and one messenger to meet
      another,
    to tell the king of Babylon
    that his city is taken on every
      side;
32 the fords have been seized,
    the bulwarks are burned with fire,
    and the soldiers are in panic.

33 For thus says the LORD of hosts, the
    God of Israel:
The daughter of Babylon is like a
    threshing floor
    at the time when it is trodden;
yet a little while
    and the time of her harvest will
      come."

34 "Nebuchadrez'zar the king
    of Babylon has devoured me,
    he has crushed me;
he has made me an empty vessel,
    he has swallowed me like a
      monster;
he has filled his belly with my
    delicacies,
    he has rinsed me out.
35 The violence done to me and to my
    kinsmen be upon Babylon,"
    let the inhabitant of Zion say.
"My blood be upon the inhabitants
    of Chalde'a,"
    let Jerusalem say.
36 Therefore thus says the LORD:
"Behold, I will plead your cause
    and take vengeance for you.
I will dry up her sea
    and make her fountain dry;
37 and Babylon shall become a heap
    of ruins,
    the haunt of jackals,
a horror and a hissing,
    without inhabitant.

38 "They shall roar together like lions;
    they shall growl like lions' whelps.
39 While they are inflamed I will
    prepare them a feast
    and make them drunk, till they
      swoon away[w]
and sleep a perpetual sleep
    and not wake, says the LORD.
40 I will bring them down like lambs
    to the slaughter,
    like rams and he-goats.

w Gk Vg: Heb *rejoice*

---

nothing useful remains (Is.33.12). **27–33:** As Babylon subdued the nations (25.15–26) so the nations will gather against Babylon. *Ararat*, ancient Urartu, modern Armenia, north of Lake Van. *Minni*, Mannaeans living south of Lake Urmia. *Ashkenaz*, the Scythians–all defeated by the Medes in the early sixth century. Desolate Babylon (4.6–7) is as barren as a threshing floor thoroughly cleaned before the harvest. **34–40:** (e) Again Jerusalem's deliverance is viewed as a mighty act of God (50.34); he will make Babylonia a desert (9.10); the once mighty lion will

41 "How Babylon[x] is taken,
   the praise of the whole earth
      seized!
How Babylon has become
   a horror among the nations!
42 The sea has come up on Babylon;
   she is covered with its tumultuous
      waves.
43 Her cities have become a horror,
   a land of drought and a desert,
a land in which no one dwells,
   and through which no son of man
      passes.
44 And I will punish Bel in Babylon,
   and take out of his mouth what
      he has swallowed.
The nations shall no longer flow to
   him;
   the wall of Babylon has fallen.

45 "Go out of the midst of her, my
      people!
   Let every man save his life
   from the fierce anger of the LORD!
46 Let not your heart faint, and be not
      fearful
   at the report heard in the land,
when a report comes in one year
   and afterward a report in another
      year,
and violence is in the land,
   and ruler is against ruler.

47 "Therefore, behold, the days are
      coming
   when I will punish the images of
      Babylon;
her whole land shall be put to shame,
   and all her slain shall fall in the
      midst of her.
48 Then the heavens and the earth,
   and all that is in them,
shall sing for joy over Babylon;
   for the destroyers shall come
      against them out of the north,
      says the LORD.

49 Babylon must fall for the slain of
      Israel,
   as for Babylon have fallen the
      slain of all the earth.

50 "You that have escaped from the
      sword,
   go, stand not still!
Remember the LORD from afar,
   and let Jerusalem come into your
      mind:
51 'We are put to shame, for we have
      heard reproach;
   dishonor has covered our face,
for aliens have come
   into the holy places of the LORD'S
      house.'

52 "Therefore, behold, the days are
      coming, says the LORD,
   when I will execute judgment
      upon her images,
and through all her land
   the wounded shall groan.
53 Though Babylon should mount up
      to heaven,
   and though she should fortify her
      strong height,
yet destroyers would come from me
   upon her,
   says the LORD.

54 "Hark! a cry from Babylon!
   The noise of great destruction
      from the land of the
      Chalde'ans!
55 For the LORD is laying Babylon
      waste,
   and stilling her mighty voice.
Their waves roar like many waters,
   the noise of their voice is raised;
56 for a destroyer has come upon her,
   upon Babylon;
her warriors are taken,
   their bows are broken in pieces;
   for the LORD is a God of recompense,

x Heb *Sheshach*, a cipher for Babylon

become drunk (25.15–16) and fall into a helpless, permanent sleep. **41–43:** Babylon (written "Sheshach," an atbash cipher; see 25.26 n.), will be inundated by the waves of her attackers (46.7–8; Is.8.7–8); when the flood recedes, she will be a trackless wasteland. **44–49:** In antiquity, the fall of a land was viewed as the defeat of its god(s) (Is.37.12). **50–58:** (f) The doubts raised by the destruction of the temple (a problem which Ezekiel also considers) should be allayed by God's assurance of certain punishment for Babylon which desecrated the holy places. This

he will surely requite.
⁵⁷ I will make drunk her princes and
    her wise men,
    her governors, her commanders,
    and her warriors;
they shall sleep a perpetual sleep
    and not wake,
    says the King, whose name is the
    LORD of hosts.

⁵⁸ "Thus says the LORD of hosts:
The broad wall of Babylon
    shall be leveled to the ground
and her high gates
    shall be burned with fire.
The peoples labor for nought,
    and the nations weary
    themselves only for fire."

59 The word which Jeremiah the
prophet commanded Serai'ah the son
of Neri'ah, son of Mahsei'ah, when he
went with Zedeki'ah king of Judah to
Babylon, in the fourth year of his reign.
Serai'ah was the quartermaster.
⁶⁰ Jeremiah wrote in a book all the
evil that should come upon Babylon,
all these words that are written concerning Babylon. ⁶¹ And Jeremiah
said to Serai'ah: "When you come to
Babylon, see that you read all these
words, ⁶² and say, 'O LORD, thou hast
said concerning this place that thou
wilt cut it off, so that nothing shall dwell
in it, neither man nor beast, and it shall
be desolate for ever.' ⁶³ When you
finish reading this book, bind a stone
to it, and cast it into the midst of the
Euphra'tes, ⁶⁴ and say, 'Thus shall
Babylon sink, to rise no more, because

of the evil that I am bringing upon
her.' "ʸ

Thus far are the words of Jeremiah.

52 Zedeki'ah was twenty-one
    years old when he became
king; and he reigned eleven years in
Jerusalem. His mother's name was
Hamu'tal the daughter of Jeremiah of
Libnah. ² And he did what was evil
in the sight of the LORD, according to
all that Jehoi'akim had done. ³ Surely
because of the anger of the LORD things
came to such a pass in Jerusalem and
Judah that he cast them out from his
presence.

And Zedeki'ah rebelled against the
king of Babylon. ⁴ And in the ninth
year of his reign, in the tenth month,
on the tenth day of the month, Nebuchadrez'zar king of Babylon came
with all his army against Jerusalem,
and they laid siege to it and built siegeworks against it round about. ⁵ So the
city was besieged till the eleventh year
of King Zedeki'ah. ⁶ On the ninth day
of the fourth month the famine was
so severe in the city, that there was no
food for the people of the land. ⁷ Then
a breach was made in the city; and all
the men of war fled and went out from
the city by night by the way of a gate
between the two walls, by the king's
garden, while the Chalde'ans were
round about the city. And they went
in the direction of the Arabah. ⁸ But
the army of the Chalde'ans pursued the
king, and overtook Zedeki'ah in the
plains of Jericho; and all his army was

ʸ Gk: Heb *upon her. And they shall weary themselves*

section is largely a composite of other verses in this collection of oracles. **59–64:** The oracles
are written in a book and taken to Babylon. Though we know of no journey of Zedekiah, he
may have gone to renew his fealty after the abortive plot of 594 B.C. (chs. 27–28) became known
to Nebuchadrezzar. *Seraiah,* brother of Baruch (32.12). **63:** By a symbolic act the oracle
against Babylon is emphasized; this oracle may have been the causative factor for the composition of 50.1–51.58. Though for a time God endowed Babylon with great power, he did so that
it might accomplish his purposes, not that it should be established as a great power forever.
   52.1–34: Historical appendix. Though largely a duplicate of 2 Kg.24.18–25.30, this historical
section, together with 39.1–10 and 40.7–43.7, provides much important complementary information (for similar historical additions, see Is. chs. 36–39). **1–3:** Reign of Zedekiah (2 Kg.24.18–20;
597–587 B.C.). For details on the contemporary religious situation, see Ezek. ch. 8. **4–27:** Siege
and fall of Jerusalem (39.1–10; 2 Kg.24.20b–25.26). **4–11:** January 588 B.C. to August 587.
The last scene enacted before Zedekiah, the rebellious vassal (37.1; Ezek.17.18–21), at Nebu-

[988]

scattered from him. ⁹ Then they captured the king, and brought him up to the king of Babylon at Riblah in the land of Hamath, and he passed sentence upon him. ¹⁰ The king of Babylon slew the sons of Zedeki'ah before his eyes, and also slew all the princes of Judah at Riblah. ¹¹ He put out the eyes of Zedeki'ah, and bound him in fetters, and the king of Babylon took him to Babylon, and put him in prison till the day of his death.

12 In the fifth month, on the tenth day of the month—which was the nineteenth year of King Nebuchadrez'zar, king of Babylon—Nebu'zarad'an the captain of the bodyguard who served the king of Babylon, entered Jerusalem. ¹³ And he burned the house of the LORD, and the king's house and all the houses of Jerusalem; every great house he burned down. ¹⁴ And all the army of the Chalde'ans, who were with the captain of the guard, broke down all the walls round about Jerusalem. ¹⁵ And Nebu'zarad'an the captain of the guard carried away captive some of the poorest of the people and the rest of the people who were left in the city and the deserters who had deserted to the king of Babylon, together with the rest of the artisans. ¹⁶ But Nebu'zarad'an the captain of the guard left some of the poorest of the land to be vinedressers and plowmen.

17 And the pillars of bronze that were in the house of the LORD, and the stands and the bronze sea that were in the house of the LORD, the Chalde'ans broke in pieces, and carried all the bronze to Babylon. ¹⁸ And they took away the pots, and the shovels, and the snuffers, and the basins, and the dishes for incense, and all the vessels of bronze used in the temple service; ¹⁹ also the small bowls, and the firepans, and the basins, and the pots, and

the lampstands, and the dishes for incense, and the bowls for libation. What was of gold the captain of the guard took away as gold, and what was of silver, as silver. ²⁰ As for the two pillars, the one sea, the twelve bronze bulls which were under the sea,ᶻ and the stands, which Solomon the king had made for the house of the LORD, the bronze of all these things was beyond weight. ²¹ As for the pillars, the height of the one pillar was eighteen cubits, its circumference was twelve cubits, and its thickness was four fingers, and it was hollow. ²² Upon it was a capital of bronze; the height of the one capital was five cubits; a network and pomegranates, all of bronze, were upon the capital round about. And the second pillar had the like, with pomegranates. ²³ There were ninety-six pomegranates on the sides; all the pomegranates were a hundred upon the network round about.

24 And the captain of the guard took Serai'ah the chief priest, and Zephani'ah the second priest, and the three keepers of the threshold; ²⁵ and from the city he took an officer who had been in command of the men of war, and seven men of the king's council, who were found in the city; and the secretary of the commander of the army who mustered the people of the land; and sixty men of the people of the land, who were found in the midst of the city. ²⁶ And Nebu'zarad'an the captain of the guard took them, and brought them to the king of Babylon at Riblah. ²⁷ And the king of Babylon smote them, and put them to death at Riblah in the land of Hamath. So Judah was carried captive out of its land.

28 This is the number of the people whom Nebuchadrez'zar carried

z Heb lacks *the sea*

chadrezzar's headquarters at *Riblah* (in the central valley northeast of Byblos) was the slaughter of his sons and court officials. Then he was blinded and taken to Babylon to die in prison. **12–16:** August 587 B.C. The reasons for the actions of Nebuzaradan, Nebuchadrezzar's field general, are unknown. **17–23:** A detailed description of the booty taken from the temple. **24–27:** 2 Kg.25.18–21. *Seraiah*, perhaps the same as in 36.26; otherwise unknown. *Zephaniah*, 21.1; 29.29. **28–30:** The three deportations listed here coincide with the surrender of Jehoiachin

away captive: in the seventh year, three thousand and twenty-three Jews; [29] in the eighteenth year of Nebuchadrez'zar he carried away captive from Jerusalem eight hundred and thirty-two persons; [30] in the twenty-third year of Nebuchadrez'zar, Nebu'zarad'an the captain of the guard carried away captive of the Jews seven hundred and forty-five persons; all the persons were four thousand and six hundred.

31 And in the thirty-seventh year of the captivity of Jehoi'achin king of Judah, in the twelfth month, on the twenty-fifth day of the month, E'vil-mer'odach king of Babylon, in the year that he became king, lifted up the head of Jehoi'achin king of Judah and brought him out of prison; [32] and he spoke kindly to him, and gave him a seat above the seats of the kings who were with him in Babylon. [33] So Jehoi'achin put off his prison garments. And every day of his life he dined regularly at the king's table; [34] as for his allowance, a regular allowance was given him by the king according to his daily need, until the day of his death as long as he lived.

(597 B.C.; 2 Kg.24.12–16), the suppression of Zedekiah's revolt (587 B.C.), and the reprisals for Gedaliah's assassination (582 B.C.; 40.7–41.18; 2 Kg.25.22–26). **31–34:** 2 Kg.25.27–30. The presence of this material proves that the editing of Jeremiah's material was later than 560 B.C. Jehoiachin's restoration may well have been viewed by his contemporaries as the beginning of Judah's restoration (23.5–6).

THE LAMENTATIONS

OF JEREMIAH

Lamentations is a small psalter of communal laments over Jerusalem, following its destruction by the Babylonians in 587 (586) B.C. These psalms have been traditionally ascribed to Jeremiah because of 2 Chr.35.25, but those laments were for the death of Josiah, not for the desolation of Jerusalem. The thought and diction are sufficiently unlike Jeremiah's to make his authorship unlikely. The first four chapters are alphabetic acrostics (with a stanza for each of the twenty-two letters of the Hebrew alphabet), and the fifth has the same number of verses as the alphabet. All were composed or adapted for public recitation on days of fasting and mourning (Jl.2.15–17; Zech.7.2–3), notably that of the ninth of Ab (August), which commemorated the disaster of 587 (586).

Chapters 1, 2, and 4 are in form dirges over the dead city. The elegy's limping 3:2 meter (three beats followed by two beats) is recognizable even in translation, together with the exclamatory "How . . ." in the opening line as an expression of grief (2 Sam.1.25, 27; Is.1.21). In ch. 3 the sadness of the desolate people and reflection upon the meaning of the disaster are voiced by an individual. Chapter 5 in its form and language recalls the liturgies for use in time of national trouble, such as Pss. 74 and 79. The common theme of all the poems is the agony of the people, the apparent desertion of Zion by her God, and the hope that God will yet restore a humbled and repentant Israel.

Lamentations may be the work of one or several authors, speaking out of the dreadful situation of the inhabitants of Jerusalem following the overthrow of the city.

How LONELY SITS THE CITY
  that was full of people!
How like a widow has she become,
  she that was great among the
    nations!
She that was a princess among the
    cities
  has become a vassal.

2 She weeps bitterly in the night,
  tears on her cheeks;
among all her lovers
  she has none to comfort her;
all her friends have dealt
    treacherously with her,
  they have become her enemies.

3 Judah has gone into exile because
    of affliction
  and hard servitude;
she dwells now among the nations,
  but finds no resting place;
her pursuers have all overtaken her
  in the midst of her distress.

4 The roads to Zion mourn,
  for none come to the appointed
    feasts;

all her gates are desolate,
  her priests groan;
her maidens have been dragged
    away,*a*
  and she herself suffers bitterly.

5 Her foes have become the head,
  her enemies prosper,
because the LORD has made her
    suffer
  for the multitude of her
    transgressions;
her children have gone away,
  captives before the foe.

6 From the daughter of Zion has
    departed
  all her majesty.
Her princes have become like harts
  that find no pasture;
they fled without strength
  before the pursuer.

7 Jerusalem remembers
  in the days of her affliction and
    bitterness*b*

a Gk Old Latin: Heb *afflicted*
b Cn: Heb *wandering*

1.1–22: Jerusalem the widow calls on men and God for pity. 6: *Daughter of Zion,* the city is

[991]

all the precious things
  that were hers from days of old.
When her people fell into the hand
    of the foe,
  and there was none to help her,
the foe gloated over her,
  mocking at her downfall.

8 Jerusalem sinned grievously,
  therefore she became filthy;
all who honored her despise her,
  for they have seen her nakedness;
yea, she herself groans,
  and turns her face away.

9 Her uncleanness was in her skirts;
  she took no thought of her doom;
therefore her fall is terrible,
  she has no comforter.
"O LORD, behold my affliction,
  for the enemy has triumphed!"

10 The enemy has stretched out his
    hands
  over all her precious things;
yea, she has seen the nations
  invade her sanctuary,
those whom thou didst forbid
  to enter thy congregation.

11 All her people groan
  as they search for bread;
they trade their treasures for food
  to revive their strength.
"Look, O LORD, and behold,
  for I am despised."

12 "Is it nothing to you,c all you who
    pass by?
  Look and see
if there is any sorrow like my sorrow
  which was brought upon me,
which the LORD inflicted
  on the day of his fierce anger.

13 "From on high he sent fire;
  into my bonesd he made it
    descend;
he spread a net for my feet;
  he turned me back;
he has left me stunned,

faint all the day long.

14 "My transgressions were bounde
    into a yoke;
  by his hand they were fastened
    together;
they were set upon my neck;
  he caused my strength to fail;
the Lord gave me into the hands
  of those whom I cannot
    withstand.

15 "The Lord flouted all my mighty
    men
  in the midst of me;
he summoned an assembly against
    me
  to crush my young men;
the Lord has trodden as in a wine
    press
  the virgin daughter of Judah.

16 "For these things I weep;
  my eyes flow with tears;
for a comforter is far from me,
  one to revive my courage;
my children are desolate,
  for the enemy has prevailed."

17 Zion stretches out her hands,
  but there is none to comfort her;
the LORD has commanded against
    Jacob
  that his neighbors should be his
    foes;
Jerusalem has become
  a filthy thing among them.

18 "The LORD is in the right,
  for I have rebelled against his
    word;
but hear, all you peoples,
  and behold my suffering;
my maidens and my young men
  have gone into captivity.

19 "I called to my lovers
  but they deceived me;
my priests and elders
  perished in the city,

c Heb uncertain d Gk: Heb *bones and*
e Cn: Heb uncertain

personified as a maiden. **8:** *Filthy,* or "a mockery." **12:** The rendering, *is it nothing to you?*
is doubtful; the sentence is probably an idiomatic exclamation of entreaty, "O that you . . . !" or
"would that I were as you!" (see v. 17).

[992]

while they sought food
  to revive their strength.

20 "Behold, O LORD, for I am in
      distress,
  my soul is in tumult,
my heart is wrung within me,
  because I have been very
    rebellious.
In the street the sword bereaves;
  in the house it is like death.

21 "Hear*f* how I groan;
  there is none to comfort me.
All my enemies have heard of my
    trouble;
  they are glad that thou hast done
    it.
Bring thou*g* the day thou hast
    announced,
  and let them be as I am.

22 "Let all their evil-doing come
      before thee;
  and deal with them
as thou hast dealt with me
  because of all my transgressions;
for my groans are many
  and my heart is faint."

2 How the Lord in his anger
    has set the daughter of Zion
      under a cloud!
He has cast down from heaven to
    earth
  the splendor of Israel;
he has not remembered his
    footstool
  in the day of his anger.

2 The Lord has destroyed without
    mercy
  all the habitations of Jacob;
in his wrath he has broken down
  the strongholds of the daughter
    of Judah;
he has brought down to the ground
    in dishonor
  the kingdom and its rulers.

3 He has cut down in fierce anger
  all the might of Israel;
he has withdrawn from them his
    right hand
  in the face of the enemy;
he has burned like a flaming fire in
    Jacob,
  consuming all around.

4 He has bent his bow like an enemy,
  with his right hand set like a foe;
and he has slain all the pride of our
    eyes
  in the tent of the daughter of Zion;
he has poured out his fury like fire.

5 The Lord has become like an
    enemy,
  he has destroyed Israel;
he has destroyed all its palaces,
  laid in ruins its strongholds;
and he has multiplied in the
    daughter of Judah
  mourning and lamentation.

6 He has broken down his booth like
    that of a garden,
  laid in ruins the place of his
    appointed feasts;
the LORD has brought to an end in
    Zion
  appointed feast and sabbath,
and in his fierce indignation has
    spurned
  king and priest.

7 The Lord has scorned his altar,
  disowned his sanctuary;
he has delivered into the hand of the
    enemy
  the walls of her palaces;
a clamor was raised in the house of
    the LORD
  as on the day of an appointed
    feast.

8 The LORD determined to lay in
    ruins

f Gk Syr: Heb *they heard*
g Syr: Heb *thou hast brought*

2.1–22: The people's agony and their cry to God for mercy. 6: *Booth,* "tabernacle," i.e., the temple. 7: *Clamor* of battle in place of the shout of acclamation in worship. 8: *Line,* a measuring line (Job 38.5).

the wall of the daughter of Zion;
he marked it off by the line;
  he restrained not his hand from
    destroying;
he caused rampart and wall to
    lament,
  they languish together.

⁹ Her gates have sunk into the
    ground;
  he has ruined and broken her
    bars;
her king and princes are among the
    nations;
  the law is no more,
and her prophets obtain
  no vision from the LORD.

¹⁰ The elders of the daughter of Zion
    sit on the ground in silence;
they have cast dust on their heads
    and put on sackcloth;
the maidens of Jerusalem
    have bowed their heads to the
      ground.

¹¹ My eyes are spent with weeping;
    my soul is in tumult;
my heart is poured out in grief*ʰ*
  because of the destruction of the
    daughter of my people,
because infants and babes faint
  in the streets of the city.

¹² They cry to their mothers,
    "Where is bread and wine?"
as they faint like wounded men
    in the streets of the city,
as their life is poured out
  on their mothers' bosom.

¹³ What can I say for you, to what
    compare you,
  O daughter of Jerusalem?
What can I liken to you, that I may
    comfort you,
  O virgin daughter of Zion?
For vast as the sea is your ruin;
  who can restore you?

¹⁴ Your prophets have seen for you
    false and deceptive visions;
they have not exposed your iniquity
    to restore your fortunes,
but have seen for you oracles
    false and misleading.

¹⁵ All who pass along the way
    clap their hands at you;
they hiss and wag their heads
    at the daughter of Jerusalem;
"Is this the city which was called
    the perfection of beauty,
  the joy of all the earth?"

¹⁶ All your enemies
    rail against you;
they hiss, they gnash their teeth,
    they cry: "We have destroyed her!
Ah, this is the day we longed for;
    now we have it; we see it!"

¹⁷ The LORD has done what he
    purposed,
  has carried out his threat;
as he ordained long ago,
  he has demolished without pity;
he has made the enemy rejoice over
    you,
  and exalted the might of your foes.

¹⁸ Cry aloud*ⁱ* to the Lord!
    O*ʲ* daughter of Zion!
Let tears stream down like a torrent
    day and night!
Give yourself no rest,
    your eyes no respite!

¹⁹ Arise, cry out in the night,
    at the beginning of the watches!
Pour out your heart like water
    before the presence of the Lord!
Lift your hands to him
    for the lives of your children,
who faint for hunger
    at the head of every street.

h Heb *to the ground*
i Cn: Heb *Their heart cried*
j Cn: Heb *O wall of*

9: *The law* or teaching given by priests (Jer.18.18; Mal.2.5–8). **14:** *Deceptive visions* of victory (Jer.23.25–27). **15:** *Clap their hands,* or "slap their hands," in derision. **17:** *His threat* to punish disobedience (see 1 Kg.9.6–9). **20:** 2 Kg.6.28–29. **22:** Am.5.18–20.

²⁰ Look, O LORD, and see!
   With whom hast thou dealt thus?
Should women eat their offspring,
   the children of their tender care?
Should priest and prophet be slain
   in the sanctuary of the Lord?

²¹ In the dust of the streets
   lie the young and the old;
my maidens and my young men
   have fallen by the sword;
in the day of thy anger thou hast
   slain them,
   slaughtering without mercy.

²² Thou didst invite as to the day of
   an appointed feast
my terrors on every side;
and on the day of the anger of the
   LORD
none escaped or survived;
   those whom I dandled and reared
my enemy destroyed.

3 I am the man who has seen
   affliction
under the rod of his wrath;
² he has driven and brought me
   into darkness without any light;
³ surely against me he turns his hand
   again and again the whole day
   long.

⁴ He has made my flesh and my skin
   waste away,
   and broken my bones;
⁵ he has besieged and enveloped me
   with bitterness and tribulation;
⁶ he has made me dwell in darkness
   like the dead of long ago.

⁷ He has walled me about so that I
   cannot escape;
   he has put heavy chains on me;
⁸ though I call and cry for help,
   he shuts out my prayer;

⁹ he has blocked my ways with hewn
   stones,
   he has made my paths crooked.

¹⁰ He is to me like a bear lying in wait,
   like a lion in hiding;
¹¹ he led me off my way and tore me
   to pieces;
   he has made me desolate;
¹² he bent his bow and set me
   as a mark for his arrow.

¹³ He drove into my heart
   the arrows of his quiver;
¹⁴ I have become the laughingstock of
   all peoples,
   the burden of their songs all day
   long.
¹⁵ He has filled me with bitterness,
   he has sated me with wormwood.

¹⁶ He has made my teeth grind on
   gravel,
   and made me cower in ashes;
¹⁷ my soul is bereft of peace,
   I have forgotten what happiness is;
¹⁸ so I say, "Gone is my glory,
   and my expectation from the
   LORD."

¹⁹ Remember my affliction and my
   bitterness,ᵏ
   the wormwood and the gall!
²⁰ My soul continually thinks of it
   and is bowed down within me.
²¹ But this I call to mind,
   and therefore I have hope:

²² The steadfast love of the LORD never
   ceases,ˡ
   his mercies never come to an end;
²³ they are new every morning;
   great is thy faithfulness.
²⁴ "The LORD is my portion," says my
   soul,

k Cn: Heb *wandering*
l Syr Tg: Heb *we are not cut off*

3.1–66: An acrostic in three parts, with three verses to each letter of the alphabet. **1–24: A psalm of personal distress and trust in God** (compare Ps. 56). The distress is expressed in terms recalling Job's complaints against God; v. 1, compare Job 9.34; v. 2, compare Job 19.8; v. 3, compare Job 7.18; v. 4, compare Job 7.5; 30.30; v. 5, compare Job 19.6,12; v. 6, compare Job 23.16–17; v. 7, compare Job 19.8; v. 8, compare Job 30.20; v. 9, compare Job 19.8; vv. 10–11, compare Job 16.9; vv. 12–13, compare Job 16.12–13; v. 14, compare Job 30.9; v. 15, compare Job 9.18; vv. 16–18, compare Job 19.10; 30.19.

"therefore I will hope in him."

²⁵ The LORD is good to those who wait
for him,
to the soul that seeks him.
²⁶ It is good that one should wait
quietly
for the salvation of the LORD.
²⁷ It is good for a man that he bear
the yoke in his youth.

²⁸ Let him sit alone in silence
when he has laid it on him;
²⁹ let him put his mouth in the dust—
there may yet be hope;
³⁰ let him give his cheek to the smiter,
and be filled with insults.

³¹ For the Lord will not
cast off for ever,
³² but, though he cause grief, he will
have compassion
according to the abundance of
his steadfast love;
³³ for he does not willingly afflict
or grieve the sons of men.

³⁴ To crush under foot
all the prisoners of the earth,
³⁵ to turn aside the right of a man
in the presence of the Most High,
³⁶ to subvert a man in his cause,
the Lord does not approve.

³⁷ Who has commanded and it came
to pass,
unless the Lord has ordained it?
³⁸ Is it not from the mouth of the Most
High
that good and evil come?
³⁹ Why should a living man complain,
a man, about the punishment of
his sins?

⁴⁰ Let us test and examine our ways,
and return to the LORD!
⁴¹ Let us lift up our hearts and hands

to God in heaven:
⁴² "We have transgressed and rebelled,
and thou hast not forgiven.

⁴³ "Thou hast wrapped thyself with
anger and pursued us,
slaying without pity;
⁴⁴ thou hast wrapped thyself with a
cloud
so that no prayer can pass through.
⁴⁵ Thou hast made us offscouring
and refuse
among the peoples.

⁴⁶ "All our enemies
rail against us;
⁴⁷ panic and pitfall have come upon us,
devastation and destruction;
⁴⁸ my eyes flow with rivers of tears
because of the destruction of the
daughter of my people.

⁴⁹ "My eyes will flow without ceasing,
without respite,
⁵⁰ until the LORD from heaven
looks down and sees;
⁵¹ my eyes cause me grief
at the fate of all the maidens of
my city.

⁵² "I have been hunted like a bird
by those who were my enemies
without cause;
⁵³ they flung me alive into the pit
and cast stones on me;
⁵⁴ water closed over my head;
I said, 'I am lost.'

⁵⁵ "I called on thy name, O LORD,
from the depths of the pit;
⁵⁶ thou didst hear my plea, 'Do not
close
thine ear to my cry for help!'ᵐ
⁵⁷ Thou didst come near when I called
on thee;
thou didst say, 'Do not fear!'

m Heb uncertain

25–51: A wise man counsels submission and penitence in acknowledgment of God's righteousness and mercy. **29**: *His mouth in the dust*, i.e. in self-abasement. **33**: *Willingly*, lit., "from his heart." **38**: *Good and evil*, compare Is.45.7; Am.3.6. **40**: *Us*, i.e. the nation Israel. **48**: See 2.11; Jer.9.1. **52–66**: An individual psalm pleading God's past mercies and praying for vindication and the requiting of the enemy (compare 5.1–22). The sentiment of v. 59 is in contrast to that of v. 39 in the previous section. **54**: Symbol of drowning, see Jon.2.3–6.

58 "Thou hast taken up my cause, O
    Lord,
    thou hast redeemed my life.
59 Thou hast seen the wrong done to
    me, O LORD;
    judge thou my cause.
60 Thou hast seen all their vengeance,
    all their devices against me.

61 "Thou hast heard their taunts, O
    LORD,
    all their devices against me.
62 The lips and thoughts of my
    assailants
    are against me all the day long.
63 Behold their sitting and their rising;
    I am the burden of their songs.

64 "Thou wilt requite them, O LORD,
    according to the work of their
    hands.
65 Thou wilt give them dullness of
    heart;
    thy curse will be on them.
66 Thou wilt pursue them in anger
    and destroy them
    from under thy heavens, O
    LORD."[n]

4 How the gold has grown dim,
    how the pure gold is changed!
    The holy stones lie scattered
    at the head of every street.

2 The precious sons of Zion,
    worth their weight in fine gold,
    how they are reckoned as earthen
    pots,
    the work of a potter's hands!

3 Even the jackals give the breast
    and suckle their young,
    but the daughter of my people has
    become cruel,
    like the ostriches in the wilderness.

4 The tongue of the nursling cleaves
    to the roof of its mouth for thirst;

the children beg for food,
    but no one gives to them.

5 Those who feasted on dainties
    perish in the streets;
    those who were brought up in purple
    lie on ash heaps.

6 For the chastisement[o] of the
    daughter of my people has been
    greater
    than the punishment[p] of Sodom,
    which was overthrown in a moment,
    no hand being laid on it.[q]

7 Her princes were purer than snow,
    whiter than milk;
    their bodies were more ruddy than
    coral,
    the beauty of their form[r] was
    like sapphire.[s]

8 Now their visage is blacker than
    soot,
    they are not recognized in the
    streets;
    their skin has shriveled upon their
    bones,
    it has become as dry as wood.

9 Happier were the victims of the
    sword
    than the victims of hunger,
    who pined away, stricken
    by want of the fruits of the field.

10 The hands of compassionate women
    have boiled their own children;
    they became their food
    in the destruction of the daughter
    of my people.

11 The LORD gave full vent to his wrath,
    he poured out his hot anger;
    and he kindled a fire in Zion,

n Syr Compare Gk Vg: Heb *the heavens of the* LORD
o Or *iniquity*   p Or *sin*   q Heb uncertain
r Heb uncertain   s Heb *lapis lazuli*

64–66: These verses recall the cries against the enemies of the persecuted righteous in the Psalms; see Pss.3.7; 17.13,14; 35.26; 59.11–13; compare Jer.11.20–23; 18.21,22.
    4.1–22: The horrors of the siege and sack of Jerusalem. 1–2: *Gold . . . holy stones*, the temple treasures; but the people are more precious to God. **3:** Jerusalem can no longer care for her children. **4–5,9–10:** See 2 Kg.25.3. **12:** See Is. chs. 36–37. **13–16:** Judah's religious leaders had

which consumed its foundations.

¹² The kings of the earth did not
    believe,
    or any of the inhabitants of the
    world,
that foe or enemy could enter
    the gates of Jerusalem.

¹³ This was for the sins of her prophets
    and the iniquities of her priests,
who shed in the midst of her
    the blood of the righteous.

¹⁴ They wandered, blind, through the
    streets,
    so defiled with blood
that none could touch
    their garments.

¹⁵ "Away! Unclean!" men cried at
    them;
    "Away! Away! Touch not!"
So they became fugitives and
    wanderers;
men said among the nations,
    "They shall stay with us no
    longer."

¹⁶ The LORD himself has scattered
    them,
    he will regard them no more;
no honor was shown to the priests,
    no favor to the elders.

¹⁷ Our eyes failed, ever watching
    vainly for help;
in our watching*t* we watched
    for a nation which could not
    save.

¹⁸ Men dogged our steps
    so that we could not walk in our
    streets;
our end drew near; our days were
    numbered;
    for our end had come.

¹⁹ Our pursuers were swifter
    than the vultures in the heavens;
they chased us on the mountains,
    they lay in wait for us in the
    wilderness.

²⁰ The breath of our nostrils, the
    LORD'S anointed,
    was taken in their pits,
he of whom we said, "Under his
    shadow
    we shall live among the nations."

²¹ Rejoice and be glad, O daughter
    of Edom,
    dweller in the land of Uz;
but to you also the cup shall pass;
    you shall become drunk and strip
    yourself bare.

²² The punishment of your iniquity,
    O daughter of Zion, is
    accomplished,
he will keep you in exile no longer;
but your iniquity, O daughter of
    Edom, he will punish,
he will uncover your sins.

5 Remember, O LORD, what has
    befallen us;
    behold, and see our disgrace!
² Our inheritance has been turned
    over to strangers,
    our homes to aliens.
³ We have become orphans,
    fatherless;
    our mothers are like widows.
⁴ We must pay for the water we drink,
    the wood we get must be bought.
⁵ With a yoke*u* on our necks we are
    hard driven;
    we are weary, we are given no rest.
⁶ We have given the hand to Egypt,
    and to Assyria, to get bread
    enough.

t Heb uncertain
u Symmachus: Heb lacks *with a yoke*

been moral lepers. **17:** *A nation which could not save*, Egypt (Jer.37.5–10). **20:** *The LORD's
anointed*, king Zedekiah (2 Kg.25.4–6). *Pits*, hunters' traps. **21–22:** Unlike chs. 1–3, which end
with a prayer for mercy and deliverance, ch. 4 ends with a vow or prophecy that *Edom* too will
suffer for her treachery to her brother Jacob (see Ob.8–14).
   5.1–22: A community psalm of lament and petition for restoration (like Pss. 44; 74; 79; 80).
1–14: The misery of Judah's people under the heel of Babylon. **8:** *Slaves rule*, important posts

⁷ Our fathers sinned, and are no more;
 and we bear their iniquities.
⁸ Slaves rule over us;
 there is none to deliver us from
 their hand.
⁹ We get our bread at the peril of
 our lives,
 because of the sword in the
 wilderness.
¹⁰ Our skin is hot as an oven
 with the burning heat of famine.
¹¹ Women are ravished in Zion,
 virgins in the towns of Judah.
¹² Princes are hung up by their hands;
 no respect is shown to the elders.
¹³ Young men are compelled to grind
 at the mill;
 and boys stagger under loads of
 wood.
¹⁴ The old men have quit the city gate,
 the young men their music.
¹⁵ The joy of our hearts has ceased;

our dancing has been turned to
 mourning.
¹⁶ The crown has fallen from our head;
 woe to us, for we have sinned!
¹⁷ For this our heart has become sick,
 for these things our eyes have
 grown dim,
¹⁸ for Mount Zion which lies desolate;
 jackals prowl over it.

¹⁹ But thou, O LORD, dost reign for
 ever;
 thy throne endures to all
 generations.
²⁰ Why dost thou forget us for ever,
 why dost thou so long forsake us?
²¹ Restore us to thyself, O LORD, that
 we may be restored!
 Renew our days as of old!
²² Or hast thou utterly rejected us?
 Art thou exceedingly angry with
 us?

---

were sometimes given to slaves of the king. **10:** *Hot as an oven*, or "burned as in an oven."
15–18: The Davidic monarchy is no more, and the temple site is desolate. **16:** *Crown*, a double
reference to the garland of the dancers and to the king's crown. **19–22:** A plea for divine remembrance and mercy (compare Pss.74.1–2; 79.5–8; 80.1–7).

THE BOOK OF EZEKIEL

Ezekiel was a priest whose ministry to his fellow exiles extended from 593 (1.2) to 563 B.C., if the enigmatic "thirtieth year" in 1.1 is taken as the thirtieth year after his call and as the date of the initial compilation of the book of Ezekiel by the prophet himself. The latest dated oracle included in the book is of the year 571 B.C. (29.17). The book of Ezekiel has the most thoroughgoing chronological notations of any of the books of the prophets, with only three dates out of order (26.1; 29.17; 33.21). The dates do not necessarily apply to all the oracles following a given date, and the chronological position of undated oracles may be ascertained from the nature of their contents. The capture and destruction of Jerusalem in 587 B.C. was a decisive factor in Ezekiel's ministry. The oracles of warning (chs. 1–24) are to be dated before the fall of Jerusalem. The oracles of hope (chs. 33–48) belong after the fall of Jerusalem. The oracles against the foreign nations (chs. 25–32) belong to the middle period of Ezekiel's ministry (587 to 585 B.C.; but 29.17–21, 571 B.C.)

The original collection was rewritten and expanded by an editor, but Ezekiel's beautiful prose and poetry may be recognized throughout the book. The text has suffered much in transmission; as a consequence, the interpretation is frequently uncertain.

As a prophet to the exiles, Ezekiel assured his hearers of the abiding presence of God among them. He constantly emphasized the LORD's role in the events of the day, so that Israel and the nations "will know that I am the LORD" (a refrain which occurs many times throughout the book). He underscored the integrity of the individual and his personal responsibility to God. To a helpless and hopeless people he brought hope of restoration to homeland and temple by their just and holy God. In Ezekiel we have an unparalleled synthesis of the terrestrial and celestial in Israel's religion, truly fitting for one whose ministry marks the transition from pre-exilic Israelite religion to post-exilic Judaism.

‖N THE THIRTIETH YEAR, IN THE fourth month, on the fifth day of the month, as I was among the exiles by the river Chebar, the heavens were opened, and I saw visions of God. ² On the fifth day of the month (it was the fifth year of the exile of King Jehoi'achin), ³ the word of the LORD came to Ezekiel the priest, the son of Buzi, in the land of the Chalde'ans by the river Chebar; and the hand of the LORD was upon him there.

4 As I looked, behold, a stormy wind came out of the north, and a great cloud, with brightness round about it, and fire flashing forth continually, and in the midst of the fire, as it were gleaming bronze. ⁵ And from the midst of it came the likeness of four living creatures. And this was their appearance: they had the form of men, ⁶ but each had four faces, and each of them had four wings. ⁷ Their legs were straight, and the soles of their feet were like the sole of a calf's foot; and they sparkled like burnished

1.1–3.27: The call of Ezekiel. 1.1–3: Superscription. *The thirtieth year*, perhaps the thirtieth year after Ezekiel's call, and if so, the date of the initial composition of the book, 563 B.C. (compare Jer.36.1–3). *Fifth day* of the *fourth month . . . , fifth year of the exile* would be July 31, 593 B.C. This is reckoned from a lunar calendar, with the year beginning in the spring. The name *Ezekiel* means "God strengthens." *Chebar*, a canal which is mentioned also in the Babylonian records, flowing southeast from its fork above Babylon, through Nippur, and rejoining the Euphrates near Erech. *Hand of the LORD* expresses Ezekiel's sense of divine compulsion (3.14,22; 8.1; 33.22; 37.1; 40.1).

1.4–28a: The throne chariot vision. Compare the imagery in 1 Kg.22.19–22; Is.6.1–9. 4: *Out of the north*, a literary figure drawn from Canaanite mythology, according to which the gods lived in the north. *Stormy wind* (1 Kg.19.11), *cloud* (Ex.19.16), and *fire* (1 Kg.19.11–12) are all elements in the theophany (manifestation) of God. 5: The *living creatures* (Rev.4.7) are cherubim, guardians of God's throne (see Ex.25.10–22; 1 Kg.6.23–28), namely winged human-

bronze. [8] Under their wings on their four sides they had human hands. And the four had their faces and their wings thus: [9] their wings touched one another; they went every one straight forward, without turning as they went. [10] As for the likeness of their faces, each had the face of a man in front;[a] the four had the face of a lion on the right side, the four had the face of an ox on the left side, and the four had the face of an eagle at the back.[b] [11] Such were their faces. And their wings were spread out above; each creature had two wings, each of which touched the wing of another, while two covered their bodies. [12] And each went straight forward; wherever the spirit would go, they went, without turning as they went. [13] In the midst of[c] the living creatures there was something that looked like burning coals of fire, like torches moving to and fro among the living creatures; and the fire was bright, and out of the fire went forth lightning. [14] And the living creatures darted to and fro, like a flash of lightning.

15 Now as I looked at the living creatures, I saw a wheel upon the earth beside the living creatures, one for each of the four of them.[d] [16] As for the appearance of the wheels and their construction: their appearance was like the gleaming of a chrysolite; and the four had the same likeness, their construction being as it were a wheel within a wheel. [17] When they went, they went in any of their four directions[e] without turning as they went. [18] The four wheels had rims and they had spokes;[f] and their rims were full of eyes round about. [19] And when the living creatures went, the wheels went beside them; and when the living creatures rose from the earth, the wheels rose. [20] Wherever the spirit would go, they went, and the wheels rose along with them; for the spirit of the living creatures was in the wheels. [21] When those went, these went; and when those stood, these stood; and when those rose from the earth, the wheels rose along with them; for the spirit of the living creatures was in the wheels.

22 Over the heads of the living creatures there was the likeness of a firmament, shining like crystal,[g] spread out above their heads. [23] And under the firmament their wings were stretched out straight, one toward another; and each creature had two wings covering its body. [24] And when they went, I heard the sound of their wings like the sound of many waters, like the thunder of the Almighty, a sound of tumult like the sound of a host; when they stood still, they let down their wings. [25] And there came a voice from above the firmament over their heads; when they stood still, they let down their wings.

26 And above the firmament over their heads there was the likeness of a throne, in appearance like sapphire;[h] and seated above the likeness of a throne was a likeness as it were of a human form. [27] And upward from what had the appearance of his loins I saw as it were gleaming bronze, like the appearance of fire enclosed round about; and downward from what had the appearance of his loins I saw as it were the appearance of fire, and there was brightness round about him.[i] [28] Like the appearance of the bow that is in the cloud on the day of rain, so was the appearance of the brightness round about.

Such was the appearance of the likeness of the glory of the LORD. And

a Cn: Heb lacks *in front*
b Cn: Heb lacks *at the back*
c Gk Old Latin: Heb *And the likeness of*
d Heb *of their faces*   e Heb *on their four sides*
f Cn: Heb uncertain
g Gk: Heb *awesome crystal*
h Heb *lapis lazuli*   i Or *it*

headed lions or oxen, symbolizing mobility, intelligence, and strength. **15–21:** *The four wheels* (compare the four faces of the creatures) symbolize omni-directional mobility. **22:** In ancient cosmology, the firmament separated the waters above the earth from the earth (Gen.1.6–8). **26–28:** Thus the LORD was enthroned above his creatures; compare the LORD enthroned above the cherubim in Ex.37.9 (on the ark); 1 Sam.4.4.

when I saw it, I fell upon my face, and I heard the voice of one speaking.

2 And he said to me, "Son of man, stand upon your feet, and I will speak with you." [2] And when he spoke to me, the Spirit entered into me and set me upon my feet; and I heard him speaking to me. [3] And he said to me, "Son of man, I send you to the people of Israel, to a nation[j] of rebels, who have rebelled against me; they and their fathers have transgressed against me to this very day. [4] The people also are impudent and stubborn: I send you to them; and you shall say to them, 'Thus says the Lord GOD.' [5] And whether they hear or refuse to hear (for they are a rebellious house) they will know that there has been a prophet among them. [6] And you, son of man, be not afraid of them, nor be afraid of their words, though briers and thorns are with you and you sit upon scorpions; be not afraid of their words, nor be dismayed at their looks, for they are a rebellious house. [7] And you shall speak my words to them, whether they hear or refuse to hear; for they are a rebellious house.

8 "But you, son of man, hear what I say to you; be not rebellious like that rebellious house; open your mouth, and eat what I give you." [9] And when I looked, behold, a hand was stretched out to me, and, lo, a written scroll was in it; [10] and he spread it before me; and it had writing on the front and on the back, and there were written on it words of lamentation and mourning 3 and woe. [1] And he said to me, "Son of man, eat what is offered to you; eat this scroll, and go, speak to the house of Israel." [2] So I opened my mouth, and he gave me the scroll to eat. [3] And he said to me, "Son of man, eat this scroll that I give you and fill your stomach with it." Then I ate it; and it was in my mouth as sweet as honey.

4 And he said to me, "Son of man, go, get you to the house of Israel, and speak with my words to them. [5] For you are not sent to a people of foreign speech and a hard language, but to the house of Israel– [6] not to many peoples of foreign speech and a hard language, whose words you cannot understand. Surely, if I sent you to such, they would listen to you. [7] But the house of Israel will not listen to you; for they are not willing to listen to me; because all the house of Israel are of a hard forehead and of a stubborn heart. [8] Behold, I have made your face hard against their faces, and your forehead hard against their foreheads. [9] Like adamant harder than flint have I made your forehead; fear them not, nor be dismayed at their looks, for they are a rebellious house." [10] Moreover he said to me, "Son of man, all my words that I shall speak to you receive in your heart, and hear with your ears. [11] And go, get you to the exiles, to your people, and say to them, 'Thus says the Lord GOD'; whether they hear or refuse to hear."

12 Then the Spirit lifted me up, and as the glory of the LORD arose[k] from its place, I heard behind me the sound of a great earthquake; [13] it was the sound of the wings of the living crea-

j Syr: Heb *nations*
k Cn: Heb *blessed be the glory of the* LORD

1.28b–3.27: The five commissions. 1.28b–2.8a: The first commission. The non-messianic term, *son of man*, occurs ninety-three times in Ezekiel; it emphasizes man's finite dependence and insignificance before God's infinite power and glory (Ps.8.4). **2.2:** *The Spirit* is synonymous with "Spirit of the LORD" (11.5; 37.1; Is.61.1). **5:** *Rebellious house,* a designation of Judah, whose apostasy was the cause of the exile (Jer.2.29; 3.13). **6–7:** Compare the LORD's encouragement of the prophet in Jer.1.6–8,16–19. **2.8b–3.3:** So that he will speak only what the LORD has written, Ezekiel must eat a papyrus *scroll* filled with words of woe (compare Jer.15.16; Zech.5.1–4; Rev.10.8–11). *Sweet,* Ps.19.10. **3.4–9:** Second commission. Ezekiel's determination to prophesy (Jer.1.18) must be stronger than Israel's refusal to hear (Am.7.10–17; Jer.20.7–18). **10–15:** Third commission. An editorial reduplication of the preceding materials, emphasizing the mission to the exiles (2.4–5). *Tel-abib* (derived from Babylonian *til abubi,* "mound of the

tures as they touched one another, and the sound of the wheels beside them, that sounded like a great earthquake. ¹⁴ The Spirit lifted me up and took me away, and I went in bitterness in the heat of my spirit, the hand of the LORD being strong upon me; ¹⁵ and I came to the exiles at Tel-abib, who dwelt by the river Chebar.*l* And I sat there overwhelmed among them seven days.

16 And at the end of seven days, the word of the LORD came to me: ¹⁷ "Son of man, I have made you a watchman for the house of Israel; whenever you hear a word from my mouth, you shall give them warning from me. ¹⁸ If I say to the wicked, 'You shall surely die,' and you give him no warning, nor speak to warn the wicked from his wicked way, in order to save his life, that wicked man shall die in his iniquity; but his blood I will require at your hand. ¹⁹ But if you warn the wicked, and he does not turn from his wickedness, or from his wicked way, he shall die in his iniquity; but you will have saved your life. ²⁰ Again, if a righteous man turns from his righteousness and commits iniquity, and I lay a stumbling block before him, he shall die; because you have not warned him, he shall die for his sin, and his righteous deeds which he has done shall not be remembered; but his blood I will require at your hand. ²¹ Nevertheless if you warn the righteous man not to sin, and he does not sin, he shall surely live, because he took warning; and you will have saved your life."

22 And the hand of the LORD was there upon me; and he said to me,

"Arise, go forth into the plain,*m* and there I will speak with you." ²³ So I arose and went forth into the plain;*m* and, lo, the glory of the LORD stood there, like the glory which I had seen by the river Chebar; and I fell on my face. ²⁴ But the Spirit entered into me, and set me upon my feet; and he spoke with me and said to me, "Go, shut yourself within your house. ²⁵ And you, O son of man, behold, cords will be placed upon you, and you shall be bound with them, so that you cannot go out among the people; ²⁶ and I will make your tongue cleave to the roof of your mouth, so that you shall be dumb and unable to reprove them; for they are a rebellious house. ²⁷ But when I speak with you, I will open your mouth, and you shall say to them, 'Thus says the Lord GOD'; he that will hear, let him hear; and he that will refuse to hear, let him refuse; for they are a re-bellious house.

4 "And you, O son of man, take a brick and lay it before you, and portray upon it a city, even Jerusalem; ² and put siegeworks against it, and build a siege wall against it, and cast up a mound against it; set camps also against it, and plant battering rams against it round about. ³ And take an iron plate, and place it as an iron wall between you and the city; and set your face toward it, and let it be in a state of siege, and press the siege against it. This is a sign for the house of Israel.

4 "Then lie upon your left side, and I will lay the punishment of the house of Israel upon you;*n* for the number of the days that you lie upon it, you

l Heb *Chebar, and to where they dwelt.* Another reading is *Chebar, and I sat where they sat*
m Or *valley*   *n* Cn: Heb *you shall lay . . . upon it*

deluge"), a Jewish settlement near Nippur, not far from the Chebar canal. **16–21**: Fourth commission. This *watchman* passage (Jer.6.17; Hos.9.8) is an application of Ezekiel's doctrine of personal responsibility (18.1–32) to the prophetic office (33.7–16). **22–27**: Fifth commission. *The plain* (valley) is the southern Tigris-Euphrates valley (37.1; Gen.11.2). Ezekiel's *dumbness* may refer to his apparent inability to speak of anything but the doom of Judah and Jerusalem for the following seven and one-half years (24.26–27; 33.21–22).

4.1–5.17: Symbolic actions describing the coming siege of Jerusalem. 4.1–3: A sun-dried *brick* (common in Babylonia) with a relief drawing of Jerusalem under siege, and *an iron plate*, a griddle, symbolizing God's role in Jerusalem's fall (Jer.21.5). **4–8**: As a symbol of the years of the punishment of Israel (exact significance unknown), the prophet is directed to lie on his

shall bear their punishment. ⁵ For I assign to you a number of days, three hundred and ninety days, equal to the number of the years of their punishment; so long shall you bear the punishment of the house of Israel. ⁶ And when you have completed these, you shall lie down a second time, but on your right side, and bear the punishment of the house of Judah; forty days I assign you, a day for each year. ⁷ And you shall set your face toward the siege of Jerusalem, with your arm bared; and you shall prophesy against the city. ⁸ And, behold, I will put cords upon you, so that you cannot turn from one side to the other, till you have completed the days of your siege.

9 "And you, take wheat and barley, beans and lentils, millet and spelt, and put them into a single vessel, and make bread of them. During the number of days that you lie upon your side, three hundred and ninety days, you shall eat it. ¹⁰ And the food which you eat shall be by weight, twenty shekels a day; once a day you shall eat it. ¹¹ And water you shall drink by measure, the sixth part of a hin; once a day you shall drink. ¹² And you shall eat it as a barley cake, baking it in their sight on human dung." ¹³ And the LORD said, "Thus shall the people of Israel eat their bread unclean, among the nations whither I will drive them." ¹⁴ Then I said, "Ah Lord GOD! behold, I have never defiled myself; from my youth up till now I have never eaten what died of itself or was torn by beasts, nor has foul flesh come into my mouth." ¹⁵ Then he said to me, "See, I will let

you have cow's dung instead of human dung, on which you may prepare your bread." ¹⁶ Moreover he said to me, "Son of man, behold, I will break the staff of bread in Jerusalem; they shall eat bread by weight and with fearfulness; and they shall drink water by measure and in dismay. ¹⁷ I will do this that they may lack bread and water, and look at one another in dismay, and waste away under their punishment.

5 "And you, O son of man, take a sharp sword; use it as a barber's razor and pass it over your head and your beard; then take balances for weighing, and divide the hair. ² A third part you shall burn in the fire in the midst of the city, when the days of the siege are completed; and a third part you shall take and strike with the sword round about the city; and a third part you shall scatter to the wind, and I will unsheathe the sword after them. ³ And you shall take from these a small number, and bind them in the skirts of your robe. ⁴ And of these again you shall take some, and cast them into the fire, and burn them in the fire; from there a fire will come forth into all the house of Israel. ⁵ Thus says the Lord GOD: This is Jerusalem; I have set her in the center of the nations, with countries round about her. ⁶ And she has wickedly rebelled against my ordinances*ᵒ* more than the nations, and against my statutes more than the countries round about her, by rejecting my ordinances and not walking in my statutes. ⁷ Therefore thus says the Lord GOD: Because you are more turbulent than the nations that are

o Or changed my ordinances into wickedness

---

left side *three-hundred ninety days*, and as a symbol of the years of the punishment of Judah to lie on his right side *forty days* (compare the forty years in the wilderness, Num.14.33; Jer.25.11–12). The actual performance of this command seems most unlikely. **9–17:** Unclean food and rationing reflect the rigors of the siege during which the people even practiced cannibalism (Jer.19.9; Lam.2.20). **9:** Mixing the grains indicates scarcity of foodstuffs, not uncleanness. **12:** *Human dung* was considered unclean (Dt.23.12–14). Dried *cow dung* was and is common fuel in the East. **14:** Compare Lev.17.10–16. **16:** *Staff of bread*, 5.16. Jerusalem's water during the siege came from cisterns and two springs, Gihon in the Kidron Valley and En-rogel to the south (2 Kg.20.20). **5.1–17:** Shorn hair as a symbol of the fate awaiting the people of Jerusalem. The *sword* is appropriately used as a *razor* to convey the idea of military defeat. **5:** *Center of the nations*, Jerusalem, the holy city, was regarded as the geographical center of the earth (see

round about you, and have not walked in my statutes or kept my ordinances, but have acted[p] according to the ordinances of the nations that are round about you; [8] therefore thus says the Lord GOD: Behold, I, even I, am against you; and I will execute judgments in the midst of you in the sight of the nations. [9] And because of all your abominations I will do with you what I have never yet done, and the like of which I will never do again. [10] Therefore fathers shall eat their sons in the midst of you, and sons shall eat their fathers; and I will execute judgments on you, and any of you who survive I will scatter to all the winds. [11] Wherefore, as I live, says the Lord GOD, surely, because you have defiled my sanctuary with all your detestable things and with all your abominations, therefore I will cut you down;[q] my eye will not spare, and I will have no pity. [12] A third part of you shall die of pestilence and be consumed with famine in the midst of you; a third part shall fall by the sword round about you; and a third part I will scatter to all the winds and will unsheathe the sword after them.

13 "Thus shall my anger spend itself, and I will vent my fury upon them and satisfy myself; and they shall know that I, the LORD, have spoken in my jealousy, when I spend my fury upon them. [14] Moreover I will make you a desolation and an object of reproach among the nations round about you and in the sight of all that pass by. [15] You shall be[r] a reproach and a taunt, a warning and a horror, to the nations round about you, when I execute judgments on you in anger and fury, and with furious chastisements— I, the LORD, have spoken— [16] when I loose against you[s] my deadly arrows

of famine, arrows for destruction, which I will loose to destroy you, and when I bring more and more famine upon you, and break your staff of bread. [17] I will send famine and wild beasts against you, and they will rob you of your children; pestilence and blood shall pass through you; and I will bring the sword upon you. I, the LORD, have spoken."

6 The word of the LORD came to me: [2] "Son of man, set your face toward the mountains of Israel, and prophesy against them, [3] and say, You mountains of Israel, hear the word of the Lord GOD! Thus says the Lord GOD to the mountains and the hills, to the ravines and the valleys: Behold, I, even I, will bring a sword upon you, and I will destroy your high places. [4] Your altars shall become desolate, and your incense altars shall be broken; and I will cast down your slain before your idols. [5] And I will lay the dead bodies of the people of Israel before their idols; and I will scatter your bones round about your altars. [6] Wherever you dwell your cities shall be waste and your high places ruined, so that your altars will be waste and ruined,[t] your idols broken and destroyed, your incense altars cut down, and your works wiped out. [7] And the slain shall fall in the midst of you, and you shall know that I am the LORD.

8 "Yet I will leave some of you alive. When you have among the nations some who escape the sword, and when you are scattered through the countries, [9] then those of you who escape will remember me among the nations where they are carried captive, when I have broken[u] their

p Another reading is *and have not acted*
q Another reading is *I will withdraw*
r Gk Syr Vg Tg: Heb *And it shall be*   s Heb *them*
t Syr Vg Tg: Heb *and be made guilty*
u Syr Vg Tg: Heb *I have been broken*

38.12, "center [literally, navel] of the earth"), as later Rome was looked upon as the navel of the earth. **14:** 36.34; compare Jer.24.9–10. **17:** 14.21.

6.1–14: Oracle against the mountains. Compare 36.1–15. The address to the mountains is figurative for the *high places*, funerary cairns used as open-air pagan sanctuaries. The cultic equipment at these sanctuaries included *incense altars* and statues or other representations (such as the oak or other trees; v. 13; Hos.4.13) of fertility goddesses such as Asherah and Anath. *Works* (v. 6) may refer to the sacred pillars or standing stones, which may have been

wanton heart which has departed from me, and blinded their eyes which turn wantonly after their idols; and they will be loathsome in their own sight for the evils which they have committed, for all their abominations. ¹⁰ And they shall know that I am the LORD; I have not said in vain that I would do this evil to them.''

11 Thus says the Lord GOD: "Clap your hands, and stamp your foot, and say, Alas! because of all the evil abominations of the house of Israel; for they shall fall by the sword, by famine, and by pestilence. ¹² He that is far off shall die of pestilence; and he that is near shall fall by the sword; and he that is left and is preserved shall die of famine. Thus I will spend my fury upon them. ¹³ And you shall know that I am the LORD, when their slain lie among their idols round about their altars, upon every high hill, on all the mountain tops, under every green tree, and under every leafy oak, wherever they offered pleasing odor to all their idols. ¹⁴ And I will stretch out my hand against them, and make the land desolate and waste, throughout all their habitations, from the wilderness to Riblah.ᵛ Then they will know that I am the LORD.''

7 The word of the LORD came to me: ² "And you, O son of man, thus says the Lord GOD to the land of Israel: An end! The end has come upon the four corners of the land. ³ Now the end is upon you, and I will let loose my anger upon you, and will judge you according to your ways; and I will punish you for all your abominations. ⁴ And my eye will not spare you, nor will I have pity; but I will punish you for your ways, while your abomina-

tions are in your midst. Then you will know that I am the LORD.

5 "Thus says the Lord GOD: Disaster after disaster! Behold, it comes. ⁶ An end has come, the end has come; it has awakened against you. Behold, it comes. ⁷ Your doomʷ has come to you, O inhabitant of the land; the time has come, the day is near, a day of tumult, and not of joyful shouting upon the mountains. ⁸ Now I will soon pour out my wrath upon you, and spend my anger against you, and judge you according to your ways; and I will punish you for all your abominations. ⁹ And my eye will not spare, nor will I have pity; I will punish you according to your ways, while your abominations are in your midst. Then you will know that I am the LORD, who smite.

10 "Behold, the day! Behold, it comes! Your doomʷ has come, in-justiceˣ has blossomed, pride has budded. ¹¹ Violence has grown up into a rod of wickedness; none of them shall remain, nor their abundance, nor their wealth; neither shall there be pre-eminence among them.ʸ ¹² The time has come, the day draws near. Let not the buyer rejoice, nor the seller mourn, for wrath is upon all their multitude. ¹³ For the seller shall not return to what he has sold, while they live. For wrathᶻ is upon all their multitude; it shall not turn back; and because of his iniquity, none can maintain his life.ᵃ

14 "They have blown the trumpet and made all ready; but none goes to battle, for my wrath is upon all their multitude. ¹⁵ The sword is without, pestilence and famine are within; he

v Another reading is *Diblah*
w The meaning of the Hebrew word is uncertain
x Or *the rod*
y The Hebrew of verse 11 is uncertain
z Cn: Heb *vision*   a Heb obscure

---

commemorative monuments (Ex.23.24; Dt.7.5). **14:** *From the wilderness to Riblah* (the wilderness of south Judah and Riblah in central Syria) was the maximum extent of Israelite territory (47.16; 1 Kg.8.65).

7.1–27: Oracles on the approaching judgment. 1–4: The theme, *the end*, is reminiscent of Am.8.2; it is the sequel to the judgments of chs. 4–6. **3:** Compare Ps.78.49. **7:** *The day* (Jl.1.15; Mal.4.1; Heb.10.25) is "the day of the LORD" (Am.5.18–20; Is.2.11,12–17). **10–23a:** As Jerusalem's end approaches, people will sell at a loss to recover what they can, and the buyers will have little prospect of retaining their purchases. The trumpet calls to the defense, but instead of battle-dress one sees only signs of mourning (Jer.16.6–9; Is.15.2). The gold and silver they had

that is in the field dies by the sword; and him that is in the city famine and pestilence devour. [16] And if any survivors escape, they will be on the mountains, like doves of the valleys, all of them moaning, every one over his iniquity. [17] All hands are feeble, and all knees weak as water. [18] They gird themselves with sackcloth, and horror covers them; shame is upon all faces, and baldness on all their heads. [19] They cast their silver into the streets, and their gold is like an unclean thing; their silver and gold are not able to deliver them in the day of the wrath of the LORD; they cannot satisfy their hunger or fill their stomachs with it. For it was the stumbling block of their iniquity. [20] Their[b] beautiful ornament they used for vainglory, and they made their abominable images and their detestable things of it; therefore I will make it an unclean thing to them. [21] And I will give it into the hands of foreigners for a prey, and to the wicked of the earth for a spoil; and they shall profane it. [22] I will turn my face from them, that they may profane my precious[c] place; robbers shall enter and profane it, [23] and make a desolation.[d]

"Because the land is full of bloody crimes and the city is full of violence, [24] I will bring the worst of the nations to take possession of their houses; I will put an end to their proud might, and their holy places shall be profaned. [25] When anguish comes, they will seek peace, but there shall be none. [26] Disaster comes upon disaster, rumor follows rumor; they seek a vision from the prophet, but the law perishes from the priest, and counsel from the elders. [27] The king mourns, the prince is wrapped in despair, and the hands

of the people of the land are palsied by terror. According to their way I will do to them, and according to their own judgments I will judge them; and they shall know that I am the LORD."

8 In the sixth year, in the sixth month, on the fifth day of the month, as I sat in my house, with the elders of Judah sitting before me, the hand of the Lord GOD fell there upon me. [2] Then I beheld, and, lo, a form that had the appearance of a man;[e] below what appeared to be his loins it was fire, and above his loins it was like the appearance of brightness, like gleaming bronze. [3] He put forth the form of a hand, and took me by a lock of my head; and the Spirit lifted me up between earth and heaven, and brought me in visions of God to Jerusalem, to the entrance of the gateway of the inner court that faces north, where was the seat of the image of jealousy, which provokes to jealousy. [4] And behold, the glory of the God of Israel was there, like the vision that I saw in the plain.

5 Then he said to me, "Son of man, lift up your eyes now in the direction of the north." So I lifted up my eyes toward the north, and behold, north of the altar gate, in the entrance, was this image of jealousy. [6] And he said to me, "Son of man, do you see what they are doing, the great abominations that the house of Israel are committing here, to drive me far from my sanctuary? But you will see still greater abominations."

7 And he brought me to the door of the court; and when I looked, behold, there was a hole in the wall. [8] Then said he to me, "Son of man, dig in the wall"; and when I dug in the wall, lo,

b Syr Symmachus: Heb *Its*   c Or *secret*
d Cn: Heb *make the chain*   e Gk: Heb *fire*

cast into idols cannot nourish the body, just as the idols themselves are useless (Jer.2.26–28; 10.1–16; Zeph.1.18) except as booty for the conqueror. **22:** *My precious place*, the temple. **23b–27:** The confusion and brutality of the invasion and siege. *Peace* recalls Jer.6.14; see also Ezek.22.28; the distraught leadership is reminiscent of Jer.4.9–10; 13.13.

8.1–11.25: The temple visions. 8.1–18: The vision of idolatry (September 17, 592 B.C.). **1–4:** The gateway to the inner court was the third gate leading north from the palace complex into the temple precincts (1 Kg.7.12; 2 Kg.20.4). The *seat . . .* was a niche for a figured slab. **7–13:** The description suggests the worship of Osiris, allegedly assuring a happy after-life; the wall-

[1007]

there was a door. ⁹ And he said to me, "Go in, and see the vile abominations that they are committing here." ¹⁰ So I went in and saw; and there, portrayed upon the wall round about, were all kinds of creeping things, and loathsome beasts, and all the idols of the house of Israel. ¹¹ And before them stood seventy men of the elders of the house of Israel, with Ja-azani'ah the son of Shaphan standing among them. Each had his censer in his hand, and the smoke of the cloud of incense went up. ¹² Then he said to me, "Son of man, have you seen what the elders of the house of Israel are doing in the dark, every man in his room*ᶠ* of pictures? For they say, 'The LORD does not see us, the LORD has forsaken the land.' " ¹³ He said also to me, "You will see still greater abominations which they commit."

14 Then he brought me to the entrance of the north gate of the house of the LORD; and behold, there sat women weeping for Tammuz. ¹⁵ Then he said to me, "Have you seen this, O son of man? You will see still greater abominations than these."

16 And he brought me into the inner court of the house of the LORD; and behold, at the door of the temple of the LORD, between the porch and the altar, were about twenty-five men, with their backs to the temple of the LORD, and their faces toward the east, worshiping the sun toward the east. ¹⁷ Then he said to me, "Have you seen this, O son of man? Is it too slight a thing for the house of Judah to commit the abominations which they commit

here, that they should fill the land with violence, and provoke me further to anger? Lo, they put the branch to their nose. ¹⁸ Therefore I will deal in wrath; my eye will not spare, nor will I have pity; and though they cry in my ears with a loud voice, I will not hear them."

9 Then he cried in my ears with a loud voice, saying, "Draw near, you executioners of the city, each with his destroying weapon in his hand." ² And lo, six men came from the direction of the upper gate, which faces north, every man with his weapon for slaughter in his hand, and with them was a man clothed in linen, with a writing case at his side. And they went in and stood beside the bronze altar.

3 Now the glory of the God of Israel had gone up from the cherubim on which it rested to the threshold of the house; and he called to the man clothed in linen, who had the writing case at his side. ⁴ And the LORD said to him, "Go through the city, through Jerusalem, and put a mark upon the foreheads of the men who sigh and groan over all the abominations that are committed in it." ⁵ And to the others he said in my hearing, "Pass through the city after him, and smite; your eye shall not spare, and you shall show no pity; ⁶ slay old men outright, young men and maidens, little children and women, but touch no one upon whom is the mark. And begin at my sanctuary." So they began with the elders who were before the house. ⁷ Then he said to them, "Defile the house, and fill the courts with the slain. Go forth." So

f Gk Syr Vg Tg: Heb *rooms*

---

paintings recall those of the Egyptian Book of the Dead. **14–15:** *Tammuz*, the Sumero-Accadian vegetation god; the weeping was for his descent into the underworld, coinciding with the annual decline of vegetation. **16–18:** This may reflect the Egyptian worship of the sun-god, who was thought to bring forth all vegetation, or the worship of Tammuz-Adonis (compare Is.17.10). The *branch*, or vine-sprout, may be a symbol in the cult rites.

9.1–11: The punishment of the guilty. 1–2: From the *north* (see 1.4 n.) came the divine *executioners* (compare the temple guards, or "watchmen," in 2 Kg.11.18, designated by the same Hebrew word) and a man clothed in linen, who functioned as the LORD's scribe, as did Nabu in the Babylonian pantheon. *Linen,* a ritually clean fabric, was worn by priests (Lev.6.10) and angels (Dan.10.5). **4:** The *mark* was the Hebrew letter "tau," made like an **x** (compare Rev.7.3–4). **6:** The *elders* are those of 8.16. **8:** *All that remains,* those remaining in Palestine after 597 B.C.

they went forth, and smote in the city. [8] And while they were smiting, and I was left alone, I fell upon my face, and cried, "Ah Lord GOD! wilt thou destroy all that remains of Israel in the outpouring of thy wrath upon Jerusalem?"

9 Then he said to me, "The guilt of the house of Israel and Judah is exceedingly great; the land is full of blood, and the city full of injustice; for they say, 'The LORD has forsaken the land, and the LORD does not see.' [10] As for me, my eye will not spare, nor will I have pity, but I will requite their deeds upon their heads."

11 And lo, the man clothed in linen, with the writing case at his side, brought back word, saying, "I have done as thou didst command me."

10 Then I looked, and behold, on the firmament that was over the heads of the cherubim there appeared above them something like a sapphire, in form resembling a throne. [2] And he said to the man clothed in linen, "Go in among the whirling wheels underneath the cherubim; fill your hands with burning coals from between the cherubim, and scatter them over the city."

And he went in before my eyes. [3] Now the cherubim were standing on the south side of the house, when the man went in; and a cloud filled the inner court. [4] And the glory of the LORD went up from the cherubim to the threshold of the house; and the house was filled with the cloud, and the court was full of the brightness of the glory of the LORD. [5] And the sound of the wings of the cherubim was heard as far as the outer court, like the voice of God Almighty when he speaks.

6 And when he commanded the man clothed in linen, "Take fire from between the whirling wheels, from between the cherubim," he went in and stood beside a wheel. [7] And a cherub stretched forth his hand from between the cherubim to the fire that was between the cherubim, and took some of it, and put it into the hands of the man clothed in linen, who took it and went out. [8] The cherubim appeared to have the form of a human hand under their wings.

9 And I looked, and behold, there were four wheels beside the cherubim, one beside each cherub; and the appearance of the wheels was like sparkling chrysolite. [10] And as for their appearance, the four had the same likeness, as if a wheel were within a wheel. [11] When they went, they went in any of their four directions[g] without turning as they went, but in whatever direction the front wheel faced the others followed without turning as they went. [12] And[h] their rims, and their spokes,[i] and the wheels were full of eyes round about–the wheels that the four of them had. [13] As for the wheels, they were called in my hearing the whirling wheels. [14] And every one had four faces: the first face was the face of the cherub, and the second face was the face of a man, and the third the face of a lion, and the fourth the face of an eagle.

15 And the cherubim mounted up. These were the living creatures that I saw by the river Chebar. [16] And when the cherubim went, the wheels went beside them; and when the cherubim lifted up their wings to mount up from the earth, the wheels did not turn from beside them. [17] When they stood still, these stood still, and when they mounted up, these mounted up with them; for the spirit of the living creatures[j] was in them.

g Heb *on their four sides*
h Gk: Heb *And their whole body and*
i Heb *spokes and their wings*   j Or *of life*

10.1–22 and 11.22–25: The LORD leaves his temple, and instructs the scribe to get coals from the fire between the cherubim (1.13) and to scatter them over the city (compare Gen.19.1–29; Rev.8.5). **3–4:** The *cloud* of *the glory of the LORD* recalls Ex.16.10; Num.10.34. The expression *the glory of the* LORD appears nineteen times in Ezekiel in the sense of the objective overpowering majesty of God, not so much as an attribute as an expression for God himself (Lev.9.23; Num.20.6). **12:** *Full of eyes*, symbolic of the all-seeing nature of God (Rev.4.8).

18 Then the glory of the LORD went forth from the threshold of the house, and stood over the cherubim. ¹⁹ And the cherubim lifted up their wings and mounted up from the earth in my sight as they went forth, with the wheels beside them; and they stood at the door of the east gate of the house of the LORD; and the glory of the God of Israel was over them.

20 These were the living creatures that I saw underneath the God of Israel by the river Chebar; and I knew that they were cherubim. ²¹ Each had four faces, and each four wings, and underneath their wings the semblance of human hands. ²² And as for the likeness of their faces, they were the very faces whose appearance I had seen by the river Chebar. They went every one straight forward.

¦¦ The Spirit lifted me up, and brought me to the east gate of the house of the LORD, which faces east. And behold, at the door of the gateway there were twenty-five men; and I saw among them Ja-azani′ah the son of Az-zur, and Pelati′ah the son of Benai′ah, princes of the people. ² And he said to me, "Son of man, these are the men who devise iniquity and who give wicked counsel in this city; ³ who say, 'The time is not near*ᵏ* to build houses; this city is the caldron, and we are the flesh.' ⁴ Therefore prophesy against them, prophesy, O son of man."

5 And the Spirit of the LORD fell upon me, and he said to me, "Say, Thus says the LORD: So you think, O house of Israel; for I know the things that come into your mind. ⁶ You have multiplied your slain in this city, and have filled its streets with the slain. ⁷ Therefore thus says the Lord GOD: Your slain whom you have laid in the midst of it, they are the flesh, and this city is the caldron; but you shall be brought forth out of the midst of it. ⁸ You have feared the sword; and I will bring the sword upon you, says the Lord GOD. ⁹ And I will bring you forth out of the midst of it, and give you into the hands of foreigners, and execute judgments upon you. ¹⁰ You shall fall by the sword; I will judge you at the border of Israel; and you shall know that I am the LORD. ¹¹ This city shall not be your caldron, nor shall you be the flesh in the midst of it; I will judge you at the border of Israel; ¹² and you shall know that I am the LORD; for you have not walked in my statutes, nor executed my ordinances, but have acted according to the ordinances of the nations that are round about you."

13 And it came to pass, while I was prophesying, that Pelati′ah the son of Benai′ah died. Then I fell down upon my face, and cried with a loud voice, and said, "Ah Lord GOD! wilt thou make a full end of the remnant of Israel?"

14 And the word of the LORD came to me: ¹⁵ "Son of man, your brethren, even your brethren, your fellow exiles,*ˡ* the whole house of Israel, all of them, are those of whom the inhabitants of Jerusalem have said, 'They have gone far from the LORD; to us this land is given for a possession.' ¹⁶ Therefore say, 'Thus says the Lord

k Or *Is not the time near . . . ?*
l Gk Syr: Heb *men of your kindred*

19: *East gate*, the main processional gate into the temple precinct (Ps.118.19–20; 24.7,9). Here God in his throne chariot paused a moment and then forsook his sanctuary, desecrated by pagan rites and superficial worship. The departure continues in 11.22–25.
   11.1–25: Judgment and promise. 1–13: These verses should follow 8.18. *Jaazaniah* and *Pelatiah* are otherwise unknown. *Wicked counsel* perhaps refers to the plot between Egypt and Zedekiah's pro-Egyptian counselors against Nebuchadrezzar (Jer.27.1–3; 37.5,7,11). Encouraged by the negotiations, they assure the populace of the city's security and urge them to continue domestic construction. Accusing the leaders of gross violence (ch. 22; Jer.34.8–16), Ezekiel tells them that the city's walls (the *cauldron;* 24.1–14) will not protect them, but they will be taken to Israel's *borders*, there to be judged (at Riblah?; Jer.52.24–27). **13:** Ezekiel added this note when these oracles were transcribed (1.1). **14–21:** This passage condemns the attitude

GOD: Though I removed them far off among the nations, and though I scattered them among the countries, yet I have been a sanctuary to them for a while[m] in the countries where they have gone.' 17 Therefore say, 'Thus says the Lord GOD: I will gather you from the peoples, and assemble you out of the countries where you have been scattered, and I will give you the land of Israel.' 18 And when they come there, they will remove from it all its detestable things and all its abominations. 19 And I will give them one[n] heart, and put a new spirit within them; I will take the stony heart out of their flesh and give them a heart of flesh, 20 that they may walk in my statutes and keep my ordinances and obey them; and they shall be my people, and I will be their God. 21 But as for those[o] whose heart goes after their detestable things and their abominations, I will requite their deeds upon their own heads, says the Lord GOD."

22 Then the cherubim lifted up their wings, with the wheels beside them; and the glory of the God of Israel was over them. 23 And the glory of the LORD went up from the midst of the city, and stood upon the mountain which is on the east side of the city. 24 And the Spirit lifted me up and brought me in the vision by the Spirit of God into Chalde′a, to the exiles. Then the vision that I had seen went up from me. 25 And I told the exiles all the things that the LORD had showed me.

12 The word of the LORD came to me: 2 "Son of man, you dwell in the midst of a rebellious house, who have eyes to see, but see not, who have ears to hear, but hear not; 3 for they are a rebellious house. Therefore, son of man, prepare for yourself an exile's baggage, and go into exile by day in their sight; you shall go like an exile from your place to another place in their sight. Perhaps they will understand, though[p] they are a rebellious house. 4 You shall bring out your baggage by day in their sight, as baggage for exile; and you shall go forth yourself at evening in their sight, as men do who must go into exile. 5 Dig through the wall in their sight, and go[q] out through it. 6 In their sight you shall lift the baggage upon your shoulder, and carry it out in the dark; you shall cover your face, that you may not see the land; for I have made you a sign for the house of Israel."

7 And I did as I was commanded. I brought out my baggage by day, as baggage for exile, and in the evening I dug through the wall with my own hands; I went forth in the dark, carrying my outfit upon my shoulder in their sight.

8 In the morning the word of the LORD came to me: 9 "Son of man, has not the house of Israel, the rebellious house, said to you, 'What are you doing?' 10 Say to them, 'Thus says the Lord GOD: This oracle concerns the prince in Jerusalem and all the house of Israel who are in it.'[r] 11 Say, 'I am a sign for you: as I have done, so shall it be done to them; they shall go into exile, into captivity.' 12 And the prince who is among them shall lift his baggage

m Or *in small measure*
n Another reading is *a new*
o Cn: Heb *To the heart of their detestable things and their abominations their heart goes*
p Or *will see that*   q Gk Syr Vg Tg: Heb *bring*
r Heb *in the midst of them*

which maintained that the exiles had borne God's punishment and their property now belonged to those who remained. Ezekiel warns them that God is with his exiled people and will restore them, while they, the presumptuous idolators, will be punished (Jer.24.1–10). *New heart*, Jer.32.37–41. **22–25**: See 10.1–22. **23**: *The mountain* to the *east* is the Mount of Olives.

12.1–20: Symbols of the Exile. 1–16: Ezekiel is commanded to symbolize by appropriate actions the collecting of whatever goods the exiles could carry (Jer.10.17) and the leaving of the city in the cool of the evening through its breached wall. *Dig through the wall* indicates a Babylonian locale in which mud-brick ("adobe") houses were common. Many scholars justifiably feel this oracle has been revised to refer to Zedekiah (the *prince*) who left Jerusalem by night,

upon his shoulder in the dark, and shall go forth; he[s] shall dig through the wall and go[t] out through it; he shall cover his face, that he may not see the land with his eyes. [13] And I will spread my net over him, and he shall be taken in my snare; and I will bring him to Babylon in the land of the Chalde'ans, yet he shall not see it; and he shall die there. [14] And I will scatter toward every wind all who are round about him, his helpers[u] and all his troops; and I will unsheathe the sword after them. [15] And they shall know that I am the LORD, when I disperse them among the nations and scatter them through the countries. [16] But I will let a few of them escape from the sword, from famine and pestilence, that they may confess all their abominations among the nations where they go, and may know that I am the LORD."

17 Moreover the word of the LORD came to me: [18] "Son of man, eat your bread with quaking, and drink water with trembling and with fearfulness; [19] and say of the people of the land, Thus says the Lord GOD concerning the inhabitants of Jerusalem in the land of Israel: They shall eat their bread with fearfulness, and drink water in dismay, because their land will be stripped of all it contains, on account of the violence of all those who dwell in it. [20] And the inhabited cities shall be laid waste, and the land shall become a desolation; and you shall know that I am the LORD."

21 And the word of the LORD came to me: [22] "Son of man, what is this proverb that you have about the land of Israel, saying, 'The days grow long, and every vision comes to nought'? [23] Tell them therefore, 'Thus says the

Lord GOD: I will put an end to this proverb, and they shall no more use it as a proverb in Israel.' But say to them, The days are at hand, and the fulfilment[v] of every vision. [24] For there shall be no more any false vision or flattering divination within the house of Israel. [25] But I the LORD will speak the word which I will speak, and it will be performed. It will no longer be delayed, but in your days, O rebellious house, I will speak the word and perform it, says the Lord GOD."

26 Again the word of the LORD came to me: [27] "Son of man, behold, they of the house of Israel say, 'The vision that he sees is for many days hence, and he prophesies of times far off.' [28] Therefore say to them, Thus says the Lord GOD: None of my words will be delayed any longer, but the word which I speak will be performed, says the Lord GOD."

13 The word of the LORD came to me: [2] "Son of man, prophesy against the prophets of Israel, prophesy[w] and say to those who prophesy out of their own minds: 'Hear the word of the LORD!' [3] Thus says the Lord GOD, Woe to the foolish prophets who follow their own spirit, and have seen nothing! [4] Your prophets have been like foxes among ruins, O Israel. [5] You have not gone up into the breaches, or built up a wall for the house of Israel, that it might stand in battle in the day of the LORD. [6] They have spoken falsehood and divined a lie; they say, 'Says the LORD,' when the LORD has not sent them, and yet they expect him to fulfil their word. [7] Have you not seen a delusive vision, and

s Gk Syr: Heb *they*   t Gk Syr Tg: Heb *bring*
u Gk Syr Tg: Heb *his help*   v Heb *word*
w Gk: Heb *who prophesy*

was captured (17.20), taken to Riblah and blinded (*may not see*, vv. 6,12; Jer.39.1–10). **14:** Seems to reflect 5.2,10,12. **15–16:** 14.21–23. **17–20:** The people's terror at the approaching invasion (4.9–11,16–17; Jer.4.19–21).

12.21–14.23: Of prophets and people. 21–28: A condemnation of the popular attitude that prophetic visions could be safely ignored (Hos.12.10; Jer.14.14–15; 23.28–29), and a correction of the impression that the fulfilment of prophecies of destruction such as those of Jeremiah was distant (Jer.5.12–13; 17.15). **27:** Compare Is.22.13; 1 Cor.15.32. **13.1–16:** Against false prophets. The absence of objective criteria (Jer.28.8–9) resulted in the perennial problem of identifying the true prophet (1 Kg. ch. 22; Mic.3.5; Is.9.15; Jer. chs. 14–15; with this passage, compare

uttered a lying divination, whenever you have said, 'Says the LORD,' although I have not spoken?"

8 Therefore thus says the Lord GOD: "Because you have uttered delusions and seen lies, therefore behold, I am against you, says the Lord GOD. ⁹ My hand will be against the prophets who see delusive visions and who give lying divinations; they shall not be in the council of my people, nor be enrolled in the register of the house of Israel, nor shall they enter the land of Israel; and you shall know that I am the Lord GOD. ¹⁰ Because, yea, because they have misled my people, saying, 'Peace,' when there is no peace; and because, when the people build a wall, these prophets daub it with whitewash; ¹¹ say to those who daub it with whitewash that it shall fall! There will be a deluge of rain,ˣ great hailstones will fall, and a stormy wind break out; ¹² and when the wall falls, will it not be said to you, 'Where is the daubing with which you daubed it?' ¹³ Therefore thus says the Lord GOD: I will make a stormy wind break out in my wrath; and there shall be a deluge of rain in my anger, and great hailstones in wrath to destroy it. ¹⁴ And I will break down the wall that you have daubed with whitewash, and bring it down to the ground, so that its foundation will be laid bare; when it falls, you shall perish in the midst of it; and you shall know that I am the LORD. ¹⁵ Thus will I spend my wrath upon the wall, and upon those who have daubed it with whitewash; and I will say to you, The wall is no more, nor those who daubed it, ¹⁶ the prophets of Israel who prophesied concerning Jerusalem and saw visions of peace for her, when there was no peace, says the Lord GOD.

17 "And you, son of man, set your face against the daughters of your people, who prophesy out of their own minds; prophesy against them ¹⁸ and say, Thus says the Lord GOD: Woe to the women who sew magic bands upon all wrists, and make veils for the heads of persons of every stature, in the hunt for souls! Will you hunt down souls belonging to my people, and keep other souls alive for your profit? ¹⁹ You have profaned me among my people for handfuls of barley and for pieces of bread, putting to death persons who should not die and keeping alive persons who should not live, by your lies to my people, who listen to lies.

20 "Wherefore thus says the Lord GOD: Behold, I am against your magic bands with which you hunt the souls,ʸ and I will tear them from your arms; and I will let the souls that you hunt go freeᶻ like birds. ²¹ Your veils also I will tear off, and deliver my people out of your hand, and they shall be no more in your hand as prey; and you shall know that I am the LORD. ²² Because you have disheartened the righteous falsely, although I have not disheartened him, and you have encouraged the wicked, that he should not turn from his wicked way to save his life; ²³ therefore you shall no more see delusive visions nor practice divination; I will deliver my people out of your hand. Then you will know that I am the LORD."

14 Then came certain of the elders of Israel to me, and sat before

x Heb *rain and you*
y Gk Syr: Heb *souls for birds*
z Cn: Heb *the souls*

Jer.23.9–32). *Divination* (Ex.28.30; 1 Sam.28.6) played practically no role among the great prophets of Israel, but was common in contemporary non-Israelite prophetism, and apparently also in Israel. The false prophets' message (Jer. chs. 28–29) was like whitewash on a mud-brick wall (12.5) which provided no protection against the storm. **9:** *Register*, Ezra ch. 2; Ex.32.32–33. **17–23:** Against prophetesses. The reference here is to sorceresses and mediums (vv. 18,20; 1 Sam.28.7–25), who were probably outside the cult of Yahweh, which provided few opportunities for participation of women (Miriam, Ex.15.20; Deborah, Jg.4.4; Huldah, 2 Kg.22.14, are widely scattered Old Testament examples; compare 1 Cor.14.34). The significance of *magic bands* and *veils* is unknown. **14.1–11:** Against idolators. Religious duplicity was so reprehensi-

me. ² And the word of the LORD came to me: ³ "Son of man, these men have taken their idols into their hearts, and set the stumbling block of their iniquity before their faces; should I let myself be inquired of at all by them? ⁴ Therefore speak to them, and say to them, Thus says the Lord GOD: Any man of the house of Israel who takes his idols into his heart and sets the stumbling block of his iniquity before his face, and yet comes to the prophet, I the LORD will answer him myself*ᵃ* because of the multitude of his idols, ⁵ that I may lay hold of the hearts of the house of Israel, who are all estranged from me through their idols.

6 "Therefore say to the house of Israel, Thus says the Lord GOD: Repent and turn away from your idols; and turn away your faces from all your abominations. ⁷ For any one of the house of Israel, or of the strangers that sojourn in Israel, who separates himself from me, taking his idols into his heart and putting the stumbling block of his iniquity before his face, and yet comes to a prophet to inquire for himself of me, I the LORD will answer him myself; ⁸ and I will set my face against that man, I will make him a sign and a byword and cut him off from the midst of my people; and you shall know that I am the LORD. ⁹ And if the prophet be deceived and speak a word, I, the LORD, have deceived that prophet, and I will stretch out my hand against him, and will destroy him from the midst of my people Israel. ¹⁰ And they shall bear their punishment–the punishment of the prophet and the punishment of the inquirer shall be alike– ¹¹ that the house of

Israel may go no more astray from me, nor defile themselves any more with all their transgressions, but that they may be my people and I may be their God, says the Lord GOD."

12 And the word of the LORD came to me: ¹³ "Son of man, when a land sins against me by acting faithlessly, and I stretch out my hand against it, and break its staff of bread and send famine upon it, and cut off from it man and beast, ¹⁴ even if these three men, Noah, Daniel, and Job, were in it, they would deliver but their own lives by their righteousness, says the Lord GOD. ¹⁵ If I cause wild beasts to pass through the land, and they ravage it, and it be made desolate, so that no man may pass through because of the beasts; ¹⁶ even if these three men were in it, as I live, says the Lord GOD, they would deliver neither sons nor daughters; they alone would be delivered, but the land would be desolate. ¹⁷ Or if I bring a sword upon that land, and say, Let a sword go through the land; and I cut off from it man and beast; ¹⁸ though these three men were in it, as I live, says the Lord GOD, they would deliver neither sons nor daughters, but they alone would be delivered. ¹⁹ Or if I send a pestilence into that land, and pour out my wrath upon it with blood, to cut off from it man and beast; ²⁰ even if Noah, Daniel, and Job were in it, as I live, says the Lord GOD, they would deliver neither son nor daughter; they would deliver but their own lives by their righteousness.

21 "For thus says the Lord GOD: How much more when I send upon Jerusalem my four sore acts of judg-

a Cn Compare Tg: Heb uncertain

---

ble to God that God himself would punish anyone guilty of it. *Idols* translates Ezekiel's characteristic term "gillulim" (literally, "dung balls"), found thirty-nine times in Ezekiel, compared with nine times in the rest of the Old Testament. *Strangers* probably refers to proselytes who were considered equal with Israelites (47.22; Lev.17.8). **12–23:** Against false hopes. One would be saved only if he were righteous; righteousness is non-transferable and non-cumulative (33.12). Noah and Job are known in the Bible for their righteousness, as is Daniel. Ezekiel's reference to Daniel (see 28.3 n.), however, suggests the Canaanite Dan'el (so spelled in Ezekiel also) rather than the Biblical Daniel. There were undoubtedly cycles of literature associated with these patriarchs of which we now know very little.

ment, sword, famine, evil beasts, and pestilence, to cut off from it man and beast! ²² Yet, if there should be left in it any survivors to lead out sons and daughters, when they come forth to you, and you see their ways and their doings, you will be consoled for the evil that I have brought upon Jerusalem, for all that I have brought upon it. ²³ They will console you, when you see their ways and their doings; and you shall know that I have not done without cause all that I have done in it, says the Lord GOD."

15 And the word of the LORD came to me: ² "Son of man, how does the wood of the vine surpass any wood, the vine branch which is among the trees of the forest? ³ Is wood taken from it to make anything? Do men take a peg from it to hang any vessel on? ⁴ Lo, it is given to the fire for fuel; when the fire has consumed both ends of it, and the middle of it is charred, is it useful for anything? ⁵ Behold, when it was whole, it was used for nothing; how much less, when the fire has consumed it and it is charred, can it ever be used for anything! ⁶ Therefore thus says the Lord GOD: Like the wood of the vine among the trees of the forest, which I have given to the fire for fuel, so will I give up the inhabitants of Jerusalem. ⁷ And I will set my face against them; though they escape from the fire, the fire shall yet consume them; and you will know that I am the LORD, when I set my face against them. ⁸ And I will make the land desolate,

because they have acted faithlessly, says the Lord GOD."

16 Again the word of the LORD came to me: ² "Son of man, make known to Jerusalem her abominations, ³ and say, Thus says the Lord GOD to Jerusalem: Your origin and your birth are of the land of the Canaanites; your father was an Amorite, and your mother a Hittite. ⁴ And as for your birth, on the day you were born your navel string was not cut, nor were you washed with water to cleanse you, nor rubbed with salt, nor swathed with bands. ⁵ No eye pitied you, to do any of these things to you out of compassion for you; but you were cast out on the open field, for you were abhorred, on the day that you were born.

6 "And when I passed by you, and saw you weltering in your blood, I said to you in your blood, 'Live, ⁷ and grow up*b* like a plant of the field.' And you grew up and became tall and arrived at full maidenhood;*c* your breasts were formed, and your hair had grown; yet you were naked and bare.

8 "When I passed by you again and looked upon you, behold, you were at the age for love; and I spread my skirt over you, and covered your nakedness: yea, I plighted my troth to you and entered into a covenant with you, says the Lord GOD, and you became mine. ⁹ Then I bathed you with

b Gk Syr: Heb *I made you a myriad*
c Cn: Heb *ornament of ornaments*

15.1–8: Allegory of the vine. Vines and vineyards are common figures (Jg.9.8–15; Is.5.1–7; Jer.2.21) but the reference to the *wood* is unique. The wood of the vine is good only when it produces satisfactorily; otherwise, even as fuel, it is practically useless. This is a figure for Judah; unproductive Judah must be destroyed (compare Jn.15.1–11).
16.1–63: The allegory of the unfaithful wife. 1–7: Jerusalem, the foundling. Ezekiel uses a folk-tale as an allegory. Jerusalem's ancestry was pagan and not related to the covenant. The *Canaanites* were the Semitic-speaking residents in Palestine before the Israelite invasion in the thirteenth century B.C., probably largely a part of the Amorite irruption into the Fertile Crescent in the early second millennium B.C. The *Hittites* were an Armenoid people living in Palestine with the Canaanites (Gen. ch. 23; Jos.3.10; compare 2 Sam.11.3). Unwanted and denied the common Palestinian amenities at birth, she, like female children in pagan antiquity, constituted a financial liability and was abandoned to die. By God's help, however, she grew into full maidenhood. **8–14:** The maiden. She was adopted (by marriage) into God's covenant (compare 2 Sam.5.6–10) and became queen, receiving lavish adornment and generous nourishment

water and washed off your blood from you, and anointed you with oil. [10] I clothed you also with embroidered cloth and shod you with leather, I swathed you in fine linen and covered you with silk. [11] And I decked you with ornaments, and put bracelets on your arms, and a chain on your neck. [12] And I put a ring on your nose, and earrings in your ears, and a beautiful crown upon your head. [13] Thus you were decked with gold and silver; and your raiment was of fine linen, and silk, and embroidered cloth; you ate fine flour and honey and oil. You grew exceedingly beautiful, and came to regal estate. [14] And your renown went forth among the nations because of your beauty, for it was perfect through the splendor which I had bestowed upon you, says the Lord GOD.

15 "But you trusted in your beauty, and played the harlot because of your renown, and lavished your harlotries on any passer-by. [16] You took some of your garments, and made for yourself gaily decked shrines, and on them played the harlot; the like has never been, nor ever shall be. [17] You also took your fair jewels of my gold and of my silver, which I had given you, and made for yourself images of men, and with them played the harlot; [18] and you took your embroidered garments to cover them, and set my oil and my incense before them. [19] Also my bread which I gave you–I fed you with fine flour and oil and honey–you set before them for a pleasing odor, says the Lord GOD.[d] [20] And you took your sons and your daughters, whom you had borne to me, and these you sacrificed to them to be devoured. Were your harlotries so small a matter [21] that you slaughtered my children

and delivered them up as an offering by fire to them? [22] And in all your abominations and your harlotries you did not remember the days of your youth, when you were naked and bare, weltering in your blood.

23 "And after all your wickedness (woe, woe to you! says the Lord GOD), [24] you built yourself a vaulted chamber, and made yourself a lofty place in every square; [25] at the head of every street you built your lofty place and prostituted your beauty, offering yourself to any passer-by, and multiplying your harlotry. [26] You also played the harlot with the Egyptians, your lustful neighbors, multiplying your harlotry, to provoke me to anger. [27] Behold, therefore, I stretched out my hand against you, and diminished your allotted portion, and delivered you to the greed of your enemies, the daughters of the Philistines, who were ashamed of your lewd behavior. [28] You played the harlot also with the Assyrians, because you were insatiable; yea, you played the harlot with them, and still you were not satisfied. [29] You multiplied your harlotry also with the trading land of Chalde′a; and even with this you were not satisfied.

30 "How lovesick is your heart, says the Lord GOD, seeing you did all these things, the deeds of a brazen harlot; [31] building your vaulted chamber at the head of every street, and making your lofty place in every square. Yet you were not like a harlot, because you scorned hire. [32] Adulterous wife, who receives strangers instead of her husband! [33] Men give gifts to all harlots; but you gave your gifts to all your lovers, bribing them to come to you from every side for your harlotries.

d Syr: Heb *and it was, says the Lord* GOD

(Jerusalem in Israel's golden age under Solomon). **15–22:** The degenerate. The word *harlotries* is used here in a double sense, referring both to the actual practice of cult prostitution and to Jerusalem's unfaithfulness (Hos.4.13–14), which became widespread in the days of Manasseh (687–642 B.C.; 2 Kg.21.1–18) and Zedekiah (ch. 8). She used her *garments* to make shrines and on them indulged in her promiscuity (Am.2.7–8). She fashioned her jewelry into idols (Jg.8.24–27) and amulets. God's gifts were used as offerings to other gods. **23–34:** Jerusalem is condemned for her religious infidelity and her proclivity toward foreign alliances–a major cause of her degeneration. But she was worse than a common prostitute who is paid for her services;

³⁴ So you were different from other women in your harlotries: none solicited you to play the harlot; and you gave hire, while no hire was given to you; therefore you were different.

35 "Wherefore, O harlot, hear the word of the LORD: ³⁶ Thus says the Lord GOD, Because your shame was laid bare and your nakedness uncovered in your harlotries with your lovers, and because of all your idols, and because of the blood of your children that you gave to them, ³⁷ therefore, behold, I will gather all your lovers, with whom you took pleasure, all those you loved and all those you loathed; I will gather them against you from every side, and will uncover your nakedness to them, that they may see all your nakedness. ³⁸ And I will judge you as women who break wedlock and shed blood are judged, and bring upon you the blood of wrath and jealousy. ³⁹ And I will give you into the hand of your lovers, and they shall throw down your vaulted chamber and break down your lofty places; they shall strip you of your clothes and take your fair jewels, and leave you naked and bare. ⁴⁰ They shall bring up a host against you, and they shall stone you and cut you to pieces with their swords. ⁴¹ And they shall burn your houses and execute judgments upon you in the sight of many women; I will make you stop playing the harlot, and you shall also give hire no more. ⁴² So will I satisfy my fury on you, and my jealousy shall depart from you; I will be calm, and will no more be angry. ⁴³ Because you have not remembered the days of your youth, but have enraged me with all these things; therefore, behold, I will requite your deeds upon your head, says the Lord GOD.

"Have you not committed lewdness in addition to all your abominations? ⁴⁴ Behold, every one who uses proverbs will use this proverb about you, 'Like mother, like daughter.' ⁴⁵ You are the daughter of your mother, who loathed her husband and her children; and you are the sister of your sisters, who loathed their husbands and their children. Your mother was a Hittite and your father an Amorite. ⁴⁶ And your elder sister is Sama'ria, who lived with her daughters to the north of you; and your younger sister, who lived to the south of you, is Sodom with her daughters. ⁴⁷ Yet you were not content to walk in their ways, or do according to their abominations; within a very little time you were more corrupt than they in all your ways. ⁴⁸ As I live, says the Lord GOD, your sister Sodom and her daughters have not done as you and your daughters have done. ⁴⁹ Behold, this was the guilt of your sister Sodom: she and her daughters had pride, surfeit of food, and prosperous ease, but did not aid the poor and needy. ⁵⁰ They were haughty, and did abominable things before me; therefore I removed them, when I saw it. ⁵¹ Sama'ria has not committed half your sins; you have committed more abominations than they, and have made your sisters appear righteous by all the abominations which you have committed. ⁵² Bear your disgrace, you also, for you have made judgment favorable to your sisters; because of your sins in which you acted more abominably than they, they are more in the right than you. So be ashamed, you also, and bear your disgrace, for you have made your sisters appear righteous.

53 "I will restore their fortunes, both the fortunes of Sodom and her daughters, and the fortunes of Sama'-

Jerusalem invited her lovers and paid them (Is.30.6; Hos. ch. 2; 8.9; Jer. chs. 2–3). **35–43:** Her lovers will turn against her and strip her. God himself will divorce her and expose her to be stoned (Dt.22.21,24). Her beauty will be destroyed and she will again find herself ignoble and ignored. **44–52:** This section expands on the preceding theme, showing Jerusalem to be so much worse than her "elder sister" *Samaria* and the "younger sister" *Sodom* (Jer.3.6–11), both of whom were destroyed, that they *appear righteous* by comparison. **53–63:** The revision of the oracle is manifest in the reference to *Edom* which occupied Judahite territory after 587 B.C.

ria and her daughters, and I will restore your own fortunes in the midst of them, [54] that you may bear your disgrace and be ashamed of all that you have done, becoming a consolation to them. [55] As for your sisters, Sodom and her daughters shall return to their former estate, and Sama'ria and her daughters shall return to their former estate; and you and your daughters shall return to your former estate. [56] Was not your sister Sodom a byword in your mouth in the day of your pride, [57] before your wickedness was uncovered? Now you have become like her[e] an object of reproach for the daughters of Edom[f] and all her neighbors, and for the daughters of the Philistines, those round about who despise you. [58] You bear the penalty of your lewdness and your abominations, says the LORD.

[59] "Yea, thus says the Lord GOD: I will deal with you as you have done, who have despised the oath in breaking the covenant, [60] yet I will remember my covenant with you in the days of your youth, and I will establish with you an everlasting covenant. [61] Then you will remember your ways, and be ashamed when I[g] take your sisters, both your elder and your younger, and give them to you as daughters, but not on account of the covenant with you. [62] I will establish my covenant with you, and you shall know that I am the LORD, [63] that you may remember and be confounded, and never open your mouth again because of your shame, when I forgive you all that you have done, says the Lord GOD."

17 The word of the LORD came to me: [2] "Son of man, propound a riddle, and speak an allegory to the house of Israel; [3] say, Thus says the Lord GOD: A great eagle with great wings and long pinions, rich in plumage of many colors, came to Lebanon and took the top of the cedar; [4] he broke off the topmost of its young twigs and carried it to a land of trade, and set it in a city of merchants. [5] Then he took of the seed of the land and planted it in fertile soil; he placed it beside abundant waters. He set it like a willow twig, [6] and it sprouted and became a low spreading vine, and its branches turned toward him, and its roots remained where it stood. So it became a vine, and brought forth branches and put forth foliage.

[7] "But there was another great eagle with great wings and much plumage; and behold, this vine bent its roots toward him, and shot forth its branches toward him that he might water it. From the bed where it was planted [8] he transplanted it[h] to good soil by abundant waters, that it might bring forth branches, and bear fruit, and become a noble vine. [9] Say, Thus says the Lord GOD: Will it thrive? Will he not pull up its roots and cut off its branches,[i] so that all its fresh sprouting leaves wither? It will not take a strong arm or many people to pull it from its roots. [10] Behold, when it is transplanted, will it thrive? Will it not utterly wither when the east wind strikes it—wither away on the bed where it grew?"

[11] Then the word of the LORD came to me: [12] "Say now to the rebellious house, Do you not know what these things mean? Tell them, Behold, the king of Babylon came to Jerusalem, and took her king and her princes and brought them to him to Babylon.

e Cn: Heb uncertain f Another reading is *Aram*
g Syr: Heb *you* h Cn: Heb *it was transplanted*
i Cn: Heb *fruit*

All three will be restored (Jer.12.14–17) and a new covenant established (Jer.31.31–34). **62:** *I will establish my covenant* (see also v. 60), this phrase is characteristic of the "P" source in the Pentateuch (see Gen.6.18; 9.9,11; 17.7,19, etc.).

17.1–21: The allegory of the eagles. Dramatis personae: *great eagle*, Nebuchadrezzar; *the top of the cedar*, house of David (Jer.22.5–6,23); *young twig*, Jehoiachin; *land of trade*, Babylonia; *city of merchants*, Babylon; *seed of the land*, Zedekiah; *another eagle*, Psammetichus II (594–588 B.C.), who engaged Zedekiah and other western states in anti-Babylonian intrigue (Jer. ch. 27). **5:** *Planted it*, i.e. made him king. **9:** Zedekiah will be unable long to resist Nebu-

13 And he took one of the seed royal and made a covenant with him, putting him under oath. (The chief men of the land he had taken away, 14 that the kingdom might be humble and not lift itself up, and that by keeping his covenant it might stand.) 15 But he rebelled against him by sending ambassadors to Egypt, that they might give him horses and a large army. Will he succeed? Can a man escape who does such things? Can he break the covenant and yet escape? 16 As I live, says the Lord GOD, surely in the place where the king dwells who made him king, whose oath he despised, and whose covenant with him he broke, in Babylon he shall die. 17 Pharaoh with his mighty army and great company will not help him in war, when mounds are cast up and siege walls built to cut off many lives. 18 Because he despised the oath and broke the covenant, because he gave his hand and yet did all these things, he shall not escape. 19 Therefore thus says the Lord GOD: As I live, surely my oath which he despised, and my covenant which he broke, I will requite upon his head. 20 I will spread my net over him, and he shall be taken in my snare, and I will bring him to Babylon and enter into judgment with him there for the treason he has committed against me. 21 And all the pick*ʲ* of his troops shall fall by the sword, and the survivors shall be scattered to every wind; and you shall know that I, the LORD, have spoken."

22 Thus says the Lord GOD: "I my-self will take a sprig from the lofty top of the cedar, and will set it out; I will break off from the topmost of its young twigs a tender one, and I myself will plant it upon a high and lofty mountain; 23 on the mountain height of Israel will I plant it, that it may bring forth boughs and bear fruit, and become a noble cedar; and under it will dwell all kinds of beasts;*ᵏ* in the shade of its branches birds of every sort will nest. 24 And all the trees of the field shall know that I the LORD bring low the high tree, and make high the low tree, dry up the green tree, and make the dry tree flourish. I the LORD have spoken, and I will do it."

18 The word of the LORD came to me again: 2 "What do you mean by repeating this proverb concerning the land of Israel, 'The fathers have eaten sour grapes, and the children's teeth are set on edge'? 3 As I live, says the Lord GOD, this proverb shall no more be used by you in Israel. 4 Behold, all souls are mine; the soul of the father as well as the soul of the son is mine: the soul that sins shall die.

5 "If a man is righteous and does what is lawful and right— 6 if he does not eat upon the mountains or lift up his eyes to the idols of the house of Israel, does not defile his neighbor's wife or approach a woman in her time of impurity, 7 does not oppress any one, but restores to the debtor his pledge, commits no robbery, gives his bread to the hungry and covers

j Another reading is *fugitives*
k Gk: Heb lacks *all kinds of beasts*

---

chadrezzar (*the east wind*), though the siege lasted nineteen months (Jer. ch. 52). **17:** *Pharaoh* has been added either through editorial revision or scribal error; read, "and not with a mighty army . . . shall he [Nebuchadrezzar] deal with him . . ." (Jer.37.3–11). Both Jeremiah and Ezekiel felt that Zedekiah should honor his oath of fealty to Nebuchadrezzar; his revolt was seen as rebellion against God's design (Jer.27.6–7).

17.22–24: Allegory of the cedar, a messianic allegory. For similar imagery, see 31.1–9; for the Messiah as a *branch* compare Jer.23.5–6; Zech.3.8; *the lofty mountain*, Mount Zion (Mic.4.1).

18.1–32: Individual responsibility. 1–4: It is human to blame someone else for one's plight; the exiles did this, blaming their fathers for their misfortunes (Jer.31.27–30), presumably based on the covenant provision in Ex.20.5. Ezekiel points out that the blame rests directly upon themselves. This discussion parallels the provision regarding three generations in Ex.20.5. **5–9:** First generation. *Eat upon the mountains*, sacred meals in pagan high places (6.1–14). The list includes moral and religious provisions; note the strong legalistic emphasis: if he is "careful

the naked with a garment, [8] does not lend at interest or take any increase, withholds his hand from iniquity, executes true justice between man and man, [9] walks in my statutes, and is careful to observe my ordinances[l]—he is righteous, he shall surely live, says the Lord GOD.

10 "If he begets a son who is a robber, a shedder of blood,[m] [11] who does none of these duties, but eats upon the mountains, defiles his neighbor's wife, [12] oppresses the poor and needy, commits robbery, does not restore the pledge, lifts up his eyes to the idols, commits abomination, [13] lends at interest, and takes increase; shall he then live? He shall not live. He has done all these abominable things; he shall surely die; his blood shall be upon himself.

14 "But if this man begets a son who sees all the sins which his father has done, and fears, and does not do likewise, [15] who does not eat upon the mountains or lift up his eyes to the idols of the house of Israel, does not defile his neighbor's wife, [16] does not wrong any one, exacts no pledge, commits no robbery, but gives his bread to the hungry and covers the naked with a garment, [17] withholds his hand from iniquity,[n] takes no interest or increase, observes my ordinances, and walks in my statutes; he shall not die for his father's iniquity; he shall surely live. [18] As for his father, because he practiced extortion, robbed his brother, and did what is not good among his people, behold, he shall die for his iniquity.

19 "Yet you say, 'Why should not the son suffer for the iniquity of the father?' When the son has done what is lawful and right, and has been careful to observe all my statutes, he shall surely live. [20] The soul that sins shall die. The son shall not suffer for the iniquity of the father, nor the father suffer for the iniquity of the son; the righteousness of the righteous shall be upon himself, and the wickedness of the wicked shall be upon himself.

21 "But if a wicked man turns away from all his sins which he has committed and keeps all my statutes and does what is lawful and right, he shall surely live; he shall not die. [22] None of the transgressions which he has committed shall be remembered against him; for the righteousness which he has done he shall live. [23] Have I any pleasure in the death of the wicked, says the Lord GOD, and not rather that he should turn from his way and live? [24] But when a righteous man turns away from his righteousness and commits iniquity and does the same abominable things that the wicked man does, shall he live? None of the righteous deeds which he has done shall be remembered; for the treachery of which he is guilty and the sin he has committed, he shall die.

25 "Yet you say, 'The way of the Lord is not just.' Hear now, O house of Israel: Is my way not just? Is it not your ways that are not just? [26] When a righteous man turns away from his righteousness and commits iniquity, he shall die for it; for the iniquity which he has committed he shall die. [27] Again, when a wicked man turns away from the wickedness he has committed and does what is lawful and right, he shall save his life. [28] Because he considered and turned away from all the transgressions which he had committed, he shall surely live, he shall not die. [29] Yet the house of Israel says, 'The way of the Lord is not just.' O house of Israel, are my ways not just? Is it not your ways that are not just?

l Gk: Heb *has kept my ordinances, to deal truly*
m Heb *blood, and he does any one of these things*
n Gk: Heb *the poor*

---

to observe my ordinances—he is righteous." **10–13:** Second generation. *Shedder of blood*, a murderer. A life opposite to that of his father is represented. **14–18:** Third generation. Again a reversal from the father's life. **19–20:** Summation: neither the righteousness nor the iniquities of a previous generation are transferable to the next. **21–24:** Within one's life the same principle of non-extension pertains. **25–29:** Objection to this principle is a misunderstanding of God's

30 "Therefore I will judge you, O house of Israel, every one according to his ways, says the Lord GOD. Repent and turn from all your transgressions, lest iniquity be your ruin.*o* 31 Cast away from you all the transgressions which you have committed against me, and get yourselves a new heart and a new spirit! Why will you die, O house of Israel? 32 For I have no pleasure in the death of any one, says the Lord GOD; so turn, and live."

19 And you, take up a lamentation for the princes of Israel, 2 and say:
What a lioness was your mother
   among lions!
She couched in the midst of young
   lions,
   rearing her whelps.
3 And she brought up one of her
   whelps;
   he became a young lion,
and he learned to catch prey;
   he devoured men.
4 The nations sounded an alarm
   against him;
   he was taken in their pit;
and they brought him with hooks
   to the land of Egypt.
5 When she saw that she was baffled,*p*
   that her hope was lost,
she took another of her whelps
   and made him a young lion.
6 He prowled among the lions;
   he became a young lion,
and he learned to catch prey;
   he devoured men.
7 And he ravaged their strongholds,*q*
   and laid waste their cities;
and the land was appalled and all
   who were in it
   at the sound of his roaring.

8 Then the nations set against him
   snares*r* on every side;
they spread their net over him;
   he was taken in their pit.
9 With hooks they put him in a cage,
   and brought him to the king of
   Babylon;
they brought him into custody,
that his voice should no more be
   heard
   upon the mountains of Israel.

10 Your mother was like a vine in a
   vineyard*s*
   transplanted by the water,
fruitful and full of branches
   by reason of abundant water.
11 Its strongest stem became
   a ruler's scepter;
   it towered aloft
   among the thick boughs;
it was seen in its height
   with the mass of its branches.
12 But the vine was plucked up in fury,
   cast down to the ground;
   the east wind dried it up;
its fruit was stripped off,
its strong stem was withered;
   the fire consumed it.
13 Now it is transplanted in the
   wilderness,
   in a dry and thirsty land.
14 And fire has gone out from its stem,
   has consumed its branches and
   fruit,
so that there remains in it no strong
   stem,
   no scepter for a ruler.

This is a lamentation, and has become a lamentation.

o Or *so that they shall not be a stumbling block of iniquity to you*   *p* Heb *had waited*
q Tg Compare Theodotion: Heb *knew his widows*
r Cn: Heb *from the provinces*
s Cn: Heb *in your blood*

justice. **30–32:** Because God is just, Israel's only hope is to repent and renew their covenant with him (v. 23; 36.24–32; Lam.3.33).
   19.1–14: Two laments. 1–9: *The lioness* is Judah (Gen.49.9; symbol of Judah in 1 Kg.10.18–20 and found on Israelite seals). The first whelp is Jehoahaz, who was taken to Egypt (Jer. 22.10–12; 2 Kg.23.30–34). Jehoiachin, the second whelp, was exiled to Babylon (Jer.22.24–30; 2 Kg.24.8–16). Each reigned only three months and accomplished little, so the description should not be pressed. **10–14:** *The vine* is Judah (Is.5.1–7; Jer.2.21). *The strongest stem* is Zedekiah (17.13) who was stripped (Jer.6.9) by *the east wind* (Nebuchadrezzar) and taken to Babylon (*transplanted;* Jer.52.1–11).

20 In the seventh year, in the fifth month, on the tenth day of the month, certain of the elders of Israel came to inquire of the LORD, and sat before me. ² And the word of the LORD came to me: ³ "Son of man, speak to the elders of Israel, and say to them, Thus says the Lord GOD, Is it to inquire of me that you come? As I live, says the Lord GOD, I will not be inquired of by you. ⁴ Will you judge them, son of man, will you judge them? Then let them know the abominations of their fathers, ⁵ and say to them, Thus says the Lord GOD: On the day when I chose Israel, I swore to the seed of the house of Jacob, making myself known to them in the land of Egypt, I swore to them, saying, I am the LORD your God. ⁶ On that day I swore to them that I would bring them out of the land of Egypt into a land that I had searched out for them, a land flowing with milk and honey, the most glorious of all lands. ⁷ And I said to them, Cast away the detestable things your eyes feast on, every one of you, and do not defile yourselves with the idols of Egypt; I am the LORD your God. ⁸ But they rebelled against me and would not listen to me; they did not every man cast away the detestable things their eyes feasted on, nor did they forsake the idols of Egypt.

"Then I thought I would pour out my wrath upon them and spend my anger against them in the midst of the land of Egypt. ⁹ But I acted for the sake of my name, that it should not be profaned in the sight of the nations among whom they dwelt, in whose sight I made myself known to them in bringing them out of the land of Egypt. ¹⁰ So I led them out of the land of Egypt and brought them into the wilderness. ¹¹ I gave them my statutes and showed them my ordinances, by whose observance man shall live. ¹² Moreover I gave them my sabbaths, as a sign between me and them, that they might know that I the LORD sanctify them. ¹³ But the house of Israel rebelled against me in the wilderness; they did not walk in my statutes but rejected my ordinances, by whose observance man shall live; and my sabbaths they greatly profaned.

"Then I thought I would pour out my wrath upon them in the wilderness, to make a full end of them. ¹⁴ But I acted for the sake of my name, that it should not be profaned in the sight of the nations, in whose sight I had brought them out. ¹⁵ Moreover I swore to them in the wilderness that I would not bring them into the land which I had given them, a land flowing with milk and honey, the most glorious of all lands, ¹⁶ because they rejected my ordinances and did not walk in my statutes, and profaned my sabbaths; for their heart went after their idols. ¹⁷ Nevertheless my eye spared them, and I did not destroy them or make a full end of them in the wilderness.

18 "And I said to their children in the wilderness, Do not walk in the statutes of your fathers, nor observe their ordinances, nor defile yourselves with their idols. ¹⁹ I the LORD am your God; walk in my statutes, and be careful to observe my ordinances, ²⁰ and hallow my sabbaths that they may be a sign between me and you,

---

20.1–44: The fall and rise of Israel (compare Ps. 106). **1–4:** Setting: August 14, 591 B.C. *Elders* of the Exile, 14.1–11. **5–8:** Apostasy in Egypt, where Israel served idols (Jos.24.14). There is some chronological confusion: God's promise to Israel was traditionally in a Palestinian setting (Gen.28.13–15); his revelation, *I am the LORD your God*, in the wilderness (Ex.20.2). **9–26:** Apostasy in the wilderness. *For the sake of my name* (36.22; Jer.14.7; Ps. 106.8) expresses the important concept that Israel's delivery from Egypt, the wilderness, and eventually from the Exile, was not accomplished because of Israel's intrinsic worth, but to demonstrate to all who would see that God is faithful and he alone is God (v. 44; Num.14.13–19). **12–13:** Of interest is the picture here of the institution of the *sabbath* in the wilderness period (Ex.31.13); compare the emphasis on the divine institution of the sabbath at creation in the "P" source in Genesis (Gen.2.1–3). The proper observance of the sabbath (see Jer.17.19–27 n.) became

that you may know that I the LORD am your God. [21] But the children rebelled against me; they did not walk in my statutes, and were not careful to observe my ordinances, by whose observance man shall live; they profaned my sabbaths.

"Then I thought I would pour out my wrath upon them and spend my anger against them in the wilderness. [22] But I withheld my hand, and acted for the sake of my name, that it should not be profaned in the sight of the nations, in whose sight I had brought them out. [23] Moreover I swore to them in the wilderness that I would scatter them among the nations and disperse them through the countries, [24] because they had not executed my ordinances, but had rejected my statutes and profaned my sabbaths, and their eyes were set on their fathers' idols. [25] Moreover I gave them statutes that were not good and ordinances by which they could not have life; [26] and I defiled them through their very gifts in making them offer by fire all their first-born, that I might horrify them; I did it that they might know that I am the LORD.

27 "Therefore, son of man, speak to the house of Israel and say to them, Thus says the Lord GOD: In this again your fathers blasphemed me, by dealing treacherously with me. [28] For when I had brought them into the land which I swore to give them, then wherever they saw any high hill or any leafy tree, there they offered their sacrifices and presented the provocation of their offering; there they sent up their soothing odors, and there they poured out their drink offerings. [29] (I said to them, What is the high place to which you go? So its name is called Bamah[t] to this day.) [30] Wherefore

say to the house of Israel, Thus says the Lord GOD: Will you defile yourselves after the manner of your fathers and go astray after their detestable things? [31] When you offer your gifts and sacrifice your sons by fire, you defile yourselves with all your idols to this day. And shall I be inquired of by you, O house of Israel? As I live, says the Lord GOD, I will not be inquired of by you.

32 "What is in your mind shall never happen–the thought, 'Let us be like the nations, like the tribes of the countries, and worship wood and stone.'

33 "As I live, says the Lord GOD, surely with a mighty hand and an outstretched arm, and with wrath poured out, I will be king over you. [34] I will bring you out from the peoples and gather you out of the countries where you are scattered, with a mighty hand and an outstretched arm, and with wrath poured out; [35] and I will bring you into the wilderness of the peoples, and there I will enter into judgment with you face to face. [36] As I entered into judgment with your fathers in the wilderness of the land of Egypt, so I will enter into judgment with you, says the Lord GOD. [37] I will make you pass under the rod, and I will let you go in by number.[u] [38] I will purge out the rebels from among you, and those who transgress against me; I will bring them out of the land where they sojourn, but they shall not enter the land of Israel. Then you will know that I am the LORD.

39 "As for you, O house of Israel, thus says the Lord GOD: Go serve every one of you his idols, now and

t That is *High Place*
u Gk: Heb *bring you into the bond of the covenant*

---

increasingly important in post-exilic Judaism (Mt.12.1–8; Jn.9.13–16). **25–26:** This seems to contradict Jer.7.31, Lev.18.21, and the nature of God himself. One may interpret it as God's allowing his people to degenerate to this level so that they might conclusively learn his superiority to any man-made deity (Jer.19.4–6); these events, however, post-date the wilderness period. **27–29:** Apostasy in Canaan. The emphasis is on the fertility cult associated with the high places (6.1–7; 16.15–22). **30–31:** In view of their constant faithlessness, they should not presume to approach God now. **32–39:** As in the Sinai wilderness (Num.14.13–25), the unfaithful will be purged in the Syrian *wilderness*. But Israel will be preserved as God's people.

hereafter, if you will not listen to me; but my holy name you shall no more profane with your gifts and your idols.

40 "For on my holy mountain, the mountain height of Israel, says the Lord GOD, there all the house of Israel, all of them, shall serve me in the land; there I will accept them, and there I will require your contributions and the choicest of your gifts, with all your sacred offerings. [41] As a pleasing odor I will accept you, when I bring you out from the peoples, and gather you out of the countries where you have been scattered; and I will manifest my holiness among you in the sight of the nations. [42] And you shall know that I am the LORD, when I bring you into the land of Israel, the country which I swore to give to your fathers. [43] And there you shall remember your ways and all the doings with which you have polluted yourselves; and you shall loathe yourselves for all the evils that you have committed. [44] And you shall know that I am the LORD, when I deal with you for my name's sake, not according to your evil ways, nor according to your corrupt doings, O house of Israel, says the Lord GOD."

45[v] And the word of the LORD came to me: [46] "Son of man, set your face toward the south, preach against the south, and prophesy against the forest land in the Negeb; [47] say to the forest of the Negeb, Hear the word of the LORD: Thus says the Lord GOD, Behold, I will kindle a fire in you, and it shall devour every green tree in you and every dry tree; the blazing flame shall not be quenched, and all faces from south to north shall be scorched by it. [48] All flesh shall see that I the LORD have kindled it; it shall not be quenched." [49] Then I said, "Ah Lord GOD! they are saying of me, 'Is he not a maker of allegories?'"

21[w] The word of the LORD came to me: [2] "Son of man, set your face toward Jerusalem and preach against the sanctuaries; prophesy against the land of Israel [3] and say to the land of Israel, Thus says the LORD: Behold, I am against you, and will draw forth my sword out of its sheath, and will cut off from you both righteous and wicked. [4] Because I will cut off from you both righteous and wicked, therefore my sword shall go out of its sheath against all flesh from south to north; [5] and all flesh shall know that I the LORD have drawn my sword out of its sheath; it shall not be sheathed again. [6] Sigh therefore, son of man; sigh with breaking heart and bitter grief before their eyes. [7] And when they say to you, 'Why do you sigh?' you shall say, 'Because of the tidings. When it comes, every heart will melt and all hands will be feeble, every spirit will faint and all knees will be weak as water. Behold, it comes and it will be fulfilled,'" says the Lord GOD.

8 And the word of the LORD came to me: [9] "Son of man, prophesy and say, Thus says the Lord, Say:

A sword, a sword is sharpened
    and also polished,
[10] sharpened for slaughter,
    polished to flash like lightning!
Or do we make mirth? You have despised the rod, my son, with everything of wood. [11] So the sword is given to be polished, that it may be handled; it is sharpened and polished to be given into the hand of the slayer. [12] Cry and wail, son of man, for it is against

v Ch 21.1 in Heb   *w* Ch 21.6 in Heb

40–44: After the new Exodus (Jer.23.7–8) God will restore his people to Zion (17.22–24) and their sacrifices will again be acceptable. (Ps.51.15–19).

    20.45–49: Oracle against the south (i.e. Judah), which will be consumed by the invader from the north (Jer.5.14–17). One should read "south," not *Negeb*, in vv. 46–47.

    21.1–32: Oracles on the sword, one of four conventional instruments of God's judgment (14.21; Is.34.5; Rev.6.8; compare 6.11 and Jeremiah's three, Jer.14.12; compare Jer.5.6). **1–7:** God draws his sword. Because of its heterodoxy (*sanctuaries;* ch. 20), Judah (*all flesh,* v. 4) will be cut down; all men (*all flesh,* v. 5) will see the terrifying judgment (Jer.4.9). **8–17:** Song of the sword (Jer.50.35–37). God's judgment is irrevocable. His flashing sword reaps its

my people; it is against all the princes of Israel; they are delivered over to the sword with my people. Smite therefore upon your thigh. ¹³ For it will not be a testing–what could it do if you despise the rod?" says the Lord GOD.

14 "Prophesy therefore, son of man; clap your hands and let the sword come down twice, yea thrice, the sword for those to be slain; it is the sword for the great slaughter, which encompasses them, ¹⁵ that their hearts may melt, and many fall at all their gates. I have given the glittering sword; ah! it is made like lightning, it is polished*ˣ* for slaughter. ¹⁶ Cut sharply to right*ʸ* and left where your edge is directed. ¹⁷ I also will clap my hands, and I will satisfy my fury; I the LORD have spoken."

18 The word of the LORD came to me again: ¹⁹ "Son of man, mark two ways for the sword of the king of Babylon to come; both of them shall come forth from the same land. And make a signpost, make it at the head of the way to a city; ²⁰ mark a way for the sword to come to Rabbah of the Ammonites and to Judah and to*ᶻ* Jerusalem the fortified. ²¹ For the king of Babylon stands at the parting of the way, at the head of the two ways, to use divination; he shakes the arrows, he consults the teraphim, he looks at the liver. ²² Into his right hand comes the lot for Jerusalem,*ᵃ* to open the mouth with a cry,*ᵇ* to lift up the voice with shouting, to set battering rams against the gates, to cast up mounds, to build siege towers. ²³ But to them it will seem like a false divination; they have sworn solemn oaths; but he brings their guilt to remembrance, that they may be captured.

24 "Therefore thus says the Lord GOD: Because you have made your guilt to be remembered, in that your transgressions are uncovered, so that in all your doings your sins appear–because you have come to remembrance, you shall be taken in them.*ᶜ* ²⁵ And you, O unhallowed wicked one, prince of Israel, whose day has come, the time of your final punishment, ²⁶ thus says the Lord GOD: Remove the turban, and take off the crown; things shall not remain as they are; exalt that which is low, and abase that which is high. ²⁷ A ruin, ruin, ruin I will make it; there shall not be even a trace*ᵈ* of it until he comes whose right it is; and to him I will give it.

28 "And you, son of man, prophesy, and say, Thus says the Lord GOD concerning the Ammonites, and concerning their reproach; say, A sword, a sword is drawn for the slaughter, it is polished to glitter*ᵉ* and to flash like lightning– ²⁹ while they see for you false visions, while they divine lies for you–to be laid on the necks of the unhallowed wicked, whose day has come, the time of their final punishment. ³⁰ Return it to its sheath. In the place where you were created, in the land of your origin, I will judge you. ³¹ And I will pour out my indignation upon you; I will blow upon you with the fire of my wrath; and I will deliver you into the hands of brutal men, skilful to destroy. ³² You shall be fuel for the fire; your blood shall be in the midst of the land; you shall be no more remembered; for I the LORD have spoken."

x Tg: Heb *wrapped up*
y Gk Syr Vg: Heb *right, set*   z Gk Syr: Heb *in*
a Heb *Jerusalem, to set battering rams*
b Gk: Heb *with slaughter*   c Gk: Heb *with the hand*
d Cn: Heb *not even this*   e Cn: Heb *to contain*

---

grim toll across the land (6.3). **12:** *Smite upon thy thigh,* a sign of mourning (Jer.31.19). **18–24:** The sword of Nebuchadrezzar. Perhaps from Riblah (compare 2 Kg.25.6), Nebuchadrezzar determines which rebel to attack first by using divination: belomancy (i.e. casting of arrows with names of projected victims on the heads); consultation of teraphim, an oracular device the use of which is unclear (Hos.3.4); and hepatoscopy (analytical observation of the configurations and markings of sheep livers). The sword is about to fall–on Jerusalem! *Rabbah,* Ammonite capital (Jer.49.3). **25–27:** The sword will cut down Zedekiah, Judah's king (Jer.21.7). **28–32:** The sword against Ammon (v. 20). With familiar phraseology (compare v. 28 with v. 8), Judah's co-conspirators, the Ammonites, will also succumb to the sword of God's wrath (25.1–7). This

22 Moreover the word of the LORD came to me, saying, [2] "And you, son of man, will you judge, will you judge the bloody city? Then declare to her all her abominable deeds. [3] You shall say, Thus says the Lord GOD: A city that sheds blood in the midst of her, that her time may come, and that makes idols to defile herself! [4] You have become guilty by the blood which you have shed, and defiled by the idols which you have made; and you have brought your day near, the appointed time[f] of your years has come. Therefore I have made you a reproach to the nations, and a mocking to all the countries. [5] Those who are near and those who are far from you will mock you, you infamous one, full of tumult.

[6] "Behold, the princes of Israel in you, every one according to his power, have been bent on shedding blood. [7] Father and mother are treated with contempt in you; the sojourner suffers extortion in your midst; the fatherless and the widow are wronged in you. [8] You have despised my holy things, and profaned my sabbaths. [9] There are men in you who slander to shed blood, and men in you who eat upon the mountains; men commit lewdness in your midst. [10] In you men uncover their fathers' nakedness; in you they humble women who are unclean in their impurity. [11] One commits abomination with his neighbor's wife; another lewdly defiles his daughter-in-law; another in you defiles his sister, his father's daughter. [12] In you men take bribes to shed blood; you take interest and increase and make gain of your neighbors by extortion; and you

have forgotten me, says the Lord GOD.

[13] "Behold, therefore, I strike my hands together at the dishonest gain which you have made, and at the blood which has been in the midst of you. [14] Can your courage endure, or can your hands be strong, in the days that I shall deal with you? I the LORD have spoken, and I will do it. [15] I will scatter you among the nations and disperse you through the countries, and I will consume your filthiness out of you. [16] And I[g] shall be profaned through you in the sight of the nations; and you shall know that I am the LORD."

[17] And the word of the LORD came to me: [18] "Son of man, the house of Israel has become dross to me; all of them, silver[h] and bronze and tin and iron and lead in the furnace, have become dross. [19] Therefore thus says the Lord GOD: Because you have all become dross, therefore, behold, I will gather you into the midst of Jerusalem. [20] As men gather silver and bronze and iron and lead and tin into a furnace, to blow the fire upon it in order to melt it; so I will gather you in my anger and in my wrath, and I will put you in and melt you. [21] I will gather you and blow upon you with the fire of my wrath, and you shall be melted in the midst of it. [22] As silver is melted in a furnace, so you shall be melted in the midst of it; and you shall know that I the LORD have poured out my wrath upon you."

[23] And the word of the LORD came to me: [24] "Son of man, say to her, You are a land that is not cleansed,

f Two Mss Gk Syr Vg Tg: Heb *until*
g Gk Syr Vg: Heb *you*
h Transposed from the end of the verse. Compare verse 20

---

oracle, as also vv. 18–24, may come from the time of the assassination of Gedaliah (Jer.40.13–41.18).

22.1–31: Oracles of indictment. 1–16: This writ of indictment contains a catalogue of sins (18.5–18) including idolatry (6.2–14; 14.3–5), injustice (18.12), violence (7.23), slander (Jer.6.28), adultery and fornication (18.6; Jer.3.1–4), and extortion–a list reminiscent of the regulations in the Holiness Code, Lev. chs. 17–26. In scorn and anger (*strike my hands together*, 6.11; 21.14,17) God will wreak punishment upon this *bloody city* (Nah.3.1, referring to Nineveh). **17–22:** The judgment will be like a smelter in which base metals are removed; so Judah must endure the rigorous refining process and be purified of her baseness (Is.1.22–25; Jer.6.27–30). **23–31:** This oracle seems to come after Jerusalem's fall (587 B.C.; v. 31) and describes Judah's sinfulness in

or rained upon in the day of indignation. ²⁵ Her princes^i in the midst of her are like a roaring lion tearing the prey; they have devoured human lives; they have taken treasure and precious things; they have made many widows in the midst of her. ²⁶ Her priests have done violence to my law and have profaned my holy things; they have made no distinction between the holy and the common, neither have they taught the difference between the unclean and the clean, and they have disregarded my sabbaths, so that I am profaned among them. ²⁷ Her princes in the midst of her are like wolves tearing the prey, shedding blood, destroying lives to get dishonest gain. ²⁸ And her prophets have daubed for them with whitewash, seeing false visions and divining lies for them, saying, 'Thus says the Lord GOD,' when the LORD has not spoken. ²⁹ The people of the land have practiced extortion and committed robbery; they have oppressed the poor and needy, and have extorted from the sojourner without redress. ³⁰ And I sought for a man among them who should build up the wall and stand in the breach before me for the land, that I should not destroy it; but I found none. ³¹ Therefore I have poured out my indignation upon them; I have consumed them with the fire of my wrath; their way have I requited upon their heads, says the Lord GOD."

23 The word of the LORD came to me: ² "Son of man, there were two women, the daughters of one mother; ³ they played the harlot in Egypt; they played the harlot in their youth; there their breasts were pressed and their virgin bosoms handled. ⁴ Oho'lah was the name of the elder and Ohol'ibah the name of her sister. They became mine, and they bore sons and daughters. As for their names, Oho'lah is Sama'ria, and Ohol'ibah is Jerusalem.

5 "Oho'lah played the harlot while she was mine; and she doted on her lovers the Assyrians, ⁶ warriors clothed in purple, governors and commanders, all of them desirable young men, horsemen riding on horses. ⁷ She bestowed her harlotries upon them, the choicest men of Assyria all of them; and she defiled herself with all the idols of every one on whom she doted. ⁸ She did not give up her harlotry which she had practiced since her days in Egypt; for in her youth men had lain with her and handled her virgin bosom and poured out their lust upon her. ⁹ Therefore I delivered her into the hands of her lovers, into the hands of the Assyrians, upon whom she doted. ¹⁰ These uncovered her nakedness; they seized her sons and her daughters; and her they slew with the sword; and she became a byword among women, when judgment had been executed upon her.

11 "Her sister Ohol'ibah saw this, yet she was more corrupt than she in her doting and in her harlotry, which

i Gk: Heb *a conspiracy of her prophets*

---

retrospect. All classes of Judean society were corrupt (Jer.8.8–10): princes, priests (Jer.2.8; Zeph.3.4), nobles (Mic.7.3), prophets (13.10–16), and people (12.19); and all must be punished (Jer.6.27).

23.1–49: The allegory of the sisters, Oholah and Oholibah (compare ch. 16). **1–4:** Introduction. Israel's apostasy began in Egypt (20.5–9). The word-play *Oholah*, "she who has a tent" (i.e. Samaria), and *Oholibah*, "my tent [is] in her" (i.e. Jerusalem), suggests that though Samaria had a sanctuary (*tent*), THE sanctuary was in Jerusalem, thus emphasizing the enormity of Judah's apostasy. Or it may refer to the pagan sanctuaries (16.16) found in both lands. On the marrying of sisters, see Gen.31.41; Lev.18.18. **5–10:** Oholah. Like Hosea (8.9–10), Isaiah (7.1–9), and Jeremiah (4.30; same word for "lovers" in Ezek.23.9), Ezekiel viewed foreign alliances as disloyalty to God, though alternatives were not always politically available. Jehu (842–815 B.C.) surrendered to Shalmaneser III of Assyria; Jehoahaz (815–801) paid tribute to Adad-Nirari III, as did Menahem (745–738) to Tiglath-Pileser III (2 Kg.15.19–29) and Hoshea (732–724) to Shalmaneser V (2 Kg.17.1–14). **11–21:** Oholibah. Judah, like Samaria, was tributary to Assyria, Ahaz (735–715 B.C.) to Tiglath-Pileser III (2 Kg.16.7–9), Hezekiah (715–687)

was worse than that of her sister. [12] She doted upon the Assyrians, governors and commanders, warriors clothed in full armor, horsemen riding on horses, all of them desirable young men. [13] And I saw that she was defiled; they both took the same way. [14] But she carried her harlotry further; she saw men portrayed upon the wall, the images of the Chalde'ans portrayed in vermilion, [15] girded with belts on their loins, with flowing turbans on their heads, all of them looking like officers, a picture of Babylonians whose native land was Chalde'a. [16] When she saw them she doted upon them, and sent messengers to them in Chalde'a. [17] And the Babylonians came to her into the bed of love, and they defiled her with their lust; and after she was polluted by them, she turned from them in disgust. [18] When she carried on her harlotry so openly and flaunted her nakedness, I turned in disgust from her, as I had turned from her sister. [19] Yet she increased her harlotry, remembering the days of her youth, when she played the harlot in the land of Egypt [20] and doted upon her paramours there, whose members were like those of asses, and whose issue was like that of horses. [21] Thus you longed for the lewdness of your youth, when the Egyptians[j] handled your bosom and pressed[k] your young breasts."

22 Therefore, O Ohol'ibah, thus says the Lord GOD: "Behold, I will rouse against you your lovers from whom you turned in disgust, and I will bring them against you from every side: [23] the Babylonians and all the Chalde'ans, Pekod and Sho'a and Ko'a, and all the Assyrians with them, desirable young men, governors and commanders all of them, officers and warriors,[l] all of them riding on horses. [24] And they shall come against you from the north[m] with chariots and wagons and a host of peoples; they shall set themselves against you on every side with buckler, shield, and helmet, and I will commit the judgment to them, and they shall judge you according to their judgments. [25] And I will direct my indignation against you, that they may deal with you in fury. They shall cut off your nose and your ears, and your survivors shall fall by the sword. They shall seize your sons and your daughters, and your survivors shall be devoured by fire. [26] They shall also strip you of your clothes and take away your fine jewels. [27] Thus I will put an end to your lewdness and your harlotry brought from the land of Egypt; so that you shall not lift up your eyes to the Egyptians or remember them any more. [28] For thus says the Lord GOD: Behold, I will deliver you into the hands of those whom you hate, into the hands of those from whom you turned in disgust; [29] and they shall deal with you in hatred, and take away all the fruit of your labor, and leave you naked and bare, and the nakedness of your harlotry shall be uncovered. Your lewdness and your harlotry [30] have brought this upon you, because you played the harlot with the nations, and polluted yourself with their idols. [31] You have gone the way of your sister; therefore I will give her cup into your hand. [32] Thus says the Lord GOD:

j Two Mss: Heb *from Egypt*
k Cn: Heb *for the sake of*
l Compare verses 6 and 12: Heb *called*
m Gk: The meaning of the Hebrew word is unknown

to Sennacherib (2 Kg.18.1–36), and Manasseh (687–642) to Esarhaddon. Judah made alliances with Babylon; Hezekiah with Merodach-Baladan (2 Kg.20.12–21), Jehoiakim and Zedekiah with Nebuchadrezzar (2 Kg.24.1; compare Jer.22.18–23; 2 Kg.24.17; compare Jer.27.1–22) as well as with Egypt (Jer.2.18,36), and in both instances probably others not known to us (Hos. 7.11). The prophets' objections were based on the inherent, and demonstrated, dangers of syncretism and apostasy (2 Kg.16.7–19). **22–35:** Such faithlessness, religious and political, will be punished. *The Babylonians*, their Aramean mercenaries (*Pekod*, Jer.50.21; *Shoa* and *Koa*), and *Assyrian* auxiliaries will devastate the land (*strip you; leave you naked*). *From the north*, the usual invasion route from Mesopotamia into Palestine (Jer.4.6; 6.1; 25.9). The oracle of the cup

[1028]

"You shall drink your sister's cup
   which is deep and large;
you shall be laughed at and held in
   derision,
   for it contains much;
[33] you will be filled with drunkenness
   and sorrow.
A cup of horror and desolation,
   is the cup of your sister Sama'ria;
[34] you shall drink it and drain it out,
   and pluck out your hair,*n*
   and tear your breasts;
for I have spoken, says the Lord God.
[35] Therefore thus says the Lord God:
Because you have forgotten me and
cast me behind your back, therefore
bear the consequences of your lewdness and harlotry."

36 The Lord said to me: "Son of
man, will you judge Oho'lah and
Ohol'ibah? Then declare to them their
abominable deeds. [37] For they have
committed adultery, and blood is upon
their hands; with their idols they have
committed adultery; and they have
even offered up to them for food the
sons whom they had borne to me.
[38] Moreover this they have done to
me: they have defiled my sanctuary
on the same day and profaned my
sabbaths. [39] For when they had
slaughtered their children in sacrifice
to their idols, on the same day they
came into my sanctuary to profane it.
And lo, this is what they did in my
house. [40] They even sent for men to
come from far, to whom a messenger
was sent, and lo, they came. For them
you bathed yourself, painted your
eyes, and decked yourself with ornaments; [41] you sat upon a stately

couch, with a table spread before it
on which you had placed my incense
and my oil. [42] The sound of a carefree multitude was with her; and with
men of the common sort drunkards*o*
were brought from the wilderness; and
they put bracelets upon the hands of
the women, and beautiful crowns upon
their heads.

43 "Then I said, Do not men now
commit adultery*p* when they practice
harlotry with her? [44] For they have
gone in to her, as men go in to a harlot.
Thus they went in to Oho'lah and to
Ohol'ibah to commit lewdness.*q*
[45] But righteous men shall pass judgment on them with the sentence of
adulteresses, and with the sentence
of women that shed blood; because
they are adulteresses, and blood is upon
their hands."

46 For thus says the Lord God:
"Bring up a host against them, and
make them an object of terror and a
spoil. [47] And the host shall stone them
and dispatch them with their swords;
they shall slay their sons and their
daughters, and burn up their houses.
[48] Thus will I put an end to lewdness
in the land, that all women may take
warning and not commit lewdness as
you have done. [49] And your lewdness
shall be requited upon you, and you
shall bear the penalty for your sinful
idolatry; and you shall know that I am
the Lord God."

24 In the ninth year, in the tenth
month, on the tenth day of the
month, the word of the Lord came to

n Compare Syr: Heb *gnaw its sherds*
o Heb uncertain   *p* Compare Gk: Heb obscure
q Gk: Heb *a woman of lewdness*

---

of wrath (vv. 32–34; Jer.25.15–29; Hab.2.16) assigns Samaria's fate to Jerusalem. **36–49:** As
the adulteress is stoned (Lev.20.10), so the adultery (i.e. human sacrifice, pagan worship, profanation of the sabbath) of Samaria and Judah (Jer.4.30) has been and will be punished–with
death.

24.1–27: The beginning of the end. 1–14: The allegory of the caldron (Jer.1.13–19) combines
two themes (perhaps from two oracles). In the *caldron* (i.e. Jerusalem, 11.3–12) everyone, the
good and bad (21.4; Mic.2.2–3), will be boiled as the besiegers heap wood (siege equipment)
around it. The contents will be thoroughly boiled, the pot emptied (i.e. after the siege), and the
bones burned (a reference to the sacking of the city). Verses 6 and 11 introduce the theme of
corrosion, referring to Jerusalem's bloody past (22.2–12; Gen.4.10–11). Recalling the theme of
refining (22.17–22), this corrosion must be burned out. **1:** The date of the oracle is January 15,
588 B.C.

me: ² "Son of man, write down the name of this day, this very day. The king of Babylon has laid siege to Jerusalem this very day. ³ And utter an allegory to the rebellious house and say to them, Thus says the Lord GOD:

Set on the pot, set it on,
    pour in water also;
⁴ put in it the pieces of flesh,
    all the good pieces, the thigh and
      the shoulder;
    fill it with choice bones.
⁵ Take the choicest one of the flock,
    pile the logs*ʳ* under it;
    boil its pieces,*ˢ*
      seethe*ᵗ* also its bones in it.

6 "Therefore thus says the Lord GOD: Woe to the bloody city, to the pot whose rust is in it, and whose rust has not gone out of it! Take out of it piece after piece, without making any choice.*ᵘ* ⁷ For the blood she has shed is still in the midst of her; she put it on the bare rock, she did not pour it upon the ground to cover it with dust. ⁸ To rouse my wrath, to take vengeance, I have set on the bare rock the blood she has shed, that it may not be covered. ⁹ Therefore thus says the Lord GOD: Woe to the bloody city! I also will make the pile great. ¹⁰ Heap on the logs, kindle the fire, boil well the flesh, and empty out the broth,*ᵛ* and let the bones be burned up. ¹¹ Then set it empty upon the coals, that it may become hot, and its copper may burn, that its filthiness may be melted in it, its rust consumed. ¹² In vain I have wearied myself;*ʷ* its thick rust does not go out of it by fire. ¹³ Its rust is your filthy lewdness. Because I would have cleansed you and you were not cleansed from your filthiness, you shall not be cleansed any more till I have satisfied my fury upon you. ¹⁴ I the LORD have spoken; it shall come to pass, I will do it; I will not go back, I will not spare, I will not repent; according to your ways and your doings I will judge you, says the Lord GOD."

15 Also the word of the LORD came to me: ¹⁶ "Son of man, behold, I am about to take the delight of your eyes away from you at a stroke; yet you shall not mourn or weep nor shall your tears run down. ¹⁷ Sigh, but not aloud; make no mourning for the dead. Bind on your turban, and put your shoes on your feet; do not cover your lips, nor eat the bread of mourners*ˣ*." ¹⁸ So I spoke to the people in the morning, and at evening my wife died. And on the next morning I did as I was commanded.

19 And the people said to me, "Will you not tell us what these things mean for us, that you are acting thus?" ²⁰ Then I said to them, "The word of the LORD came to me: ²¹ 'Say to the house of Israel, Thus says the Lord GOD: Behold, I will profane my sanctuary, the pride of your power, the delight of your eyes, and the desire of your soul; and your sons and your daughters whom you left behind shall fall by the sword. ²² And you shall do as I have done; you shall not cover your lips, nor eat the bread of mourners.*ˣ* ²³ Your turbans shall be on your heads and your shoes on your feet; you shall not mourn or weep, but you shall pine away in your iniquities and groan to one another. ²⁴ Thus shall Ezekiel be to you a sign; according to all that he has done you shall do. When this comes, then you will know that I am the Lord GOD.'

25 "And you, son of man, on the day when I take from them their stronghold, their joy and glory, the delight of their eyes and their heart's desire, and also their sons and daughters,

r Compare verse 10: Heb *the bones*
s Two Mss: Heb *its boilings*
t Cn: Heb *its bones seethe*
u Heb *no lot has fallen upon it*
v Compare Gk: Heb *mix the spices*
w Cn: Heb uncertain   *x* Vg Tg: Heb *men*

24.15–27: Oracle at the death of Ezekiel's wife. Ezekiel was instructed to forego the customary rites of mourning (Jer.16.5–9; Mic.1.8) as a sign to the people that the loss of cherished persons and things would bring a numbing, inexpressible grief (compare Jer.16.1–4). **25–27:** When word of the fall of Jerusalem reached Ezekiel (33.21–22), his tongue would be loosed (3.24–27), and he would proclaim a new message.

²⁶ on that day a fugitive will come to you to report to you the news. ²⁷ On that day your mouth will be opened to the fugitive, and you shall speak and be no longer dumb. So you will be a sign to them; and they will know that I am the LORD."

25 The word of the LORD came to me: ² "Son of man, set your face toward the Ammonites, and prophesy against them. ³ Say to the Ammonites, Hear the word of the Lord GOD: Thus says the Lord GOD, Because you said, 'Aha!' over my sanctuary when it was profaned, and over the land of Israel when it was made desolate, and over the house of Judah when it went into exile; ⁴ therefore I am handing you over to the people of the East for a possession, and they shall set their encampments among you and make their dwellings in your midst; they shall eat your fruit, and they shall drink your milk. ⁵ I will make Rabbah a pasture for camels and the cities of the Ammonites*ʸ* a fold for flocks. Then you will know that I am the LORD. ⁶ For thus says the Lord GOD: Because you have clapped your hands and stamped your feet and rejoiced with all the malice within you against the land of Israel, ⁷ therefore, behold, I have stretched out my hand against you, and will hand you over as spoil to the nations; and I will cut you off from the peoples and will make you perish out of the countries; I will destroy you. Then you will know that I am the LORD.

8 "Thus says the Lord GOD: Be-cause Moab*ᶻ* said, Behold, the house of Judah is like all the other nations, ⁹ therefore I will lay open the flank of Moab from the cities*ᵃ* on its frontier, the glory of the country, Beth-jesh′-imoth, Ba′al-me′on, and Kiriatha′im. ¹⁰ I will give it along with the Ammon-ites to the people of the East as a possession, that it*ᵇ* may be remem-bered no more among the nations, ¹¹ and I will execute judgments upon Moab. Then they will know that I am the LORD.

12 "Thus says the Lord GOD: Be-cause Edom acted revengefully against the house of Judah and has grievously offended in taking vengeance upon them, ¹³ therefore thus says the Lord GOD, I will stretch out my hand against Edom, and cut off from it man and beast; and I will make it desolate; from Teman even to Dedan they shall fall by the sword. ¹⁴ And I will lay my vengeance upon Edom by the hand of my people Israel; and they shall do in Edom according to my anger and ac-cording to my wrath; and they shall know my vengeance, says the Lord GOD.

15 "Thus says the Lord GOD: Be-cause the Philistines acted revengefully and took vengeance with malice of heart to destroy in never-ending en-mity; ¹⁶ therefore thus says the Lord GOD, Behold, I will stretch out my hand against the Philistines, and I will cut off the Cher′ethites, and de-stroy the rest of the seacoast. ¹⁷ I will

y Cn: Heb lacks *the cities of*
z Gk Old Latin: Heb *Moab and Seir*
a Heb *cities from its cities*
b Cn: Heb *the Ammonites*

25.1–32.32: Oracles against the nations. Compare Is. chs. 13–23; Jer. chs. 46–51. Seven nations (Ammon, Moab, Edom, Philistia, Tyre, Sidon, and Egypt; compare Dt.7.1) will be punished before Israel is restored (36.5–7).

25.1–17: Oracles against Ammon, Moab, Edom, and Philistia. 1–7: Against Ammon (21.28–32; Am.1.13–15; Jer.49.1–6). Ammon, which had seized one-time Israelite territory (Jer.49.1), is to be occupied by *the people of the East* (Is.11.14), i.e. Arab tribes, whose expansion during this period pushed the Edomites into southern Judah (vv. 12–14). This Arab expansion eventually produced the Nabatean empire (compare 2 Cor.11:32). **8–11:** Against Moab. Compare Jer.48.1–47. The Arab expansion would also envelop Moab. **12–14:** Against Edom. Compare Is. ch. 34; Jer.49.7–22. **15–17:** Against Philistia. Compare Jer. ch. 47. *The Cherethites*, who lived between Gerar and Sharuhen (1 Sam.30.14), were perhaps originally Cretans (Jer. 47.4).

execute great vengeance upon them with wrathful chastisements. Then they will know that I am the LORD, when I lay my vengeance upon them."

26 In the eleventh year, on the first day of the month, the word of the LORD came to me: [2] "Son of man, because Tyre said concerning Jerusalem, 'Aha, the gate of the peoples is broken, it has swung open to me; I shall be replenished, now that she is laid waste,' [3] therefore thus says the Lord GOD: Behold, I am against you, O Tyre, and will bring up many nations against you, as the sea brings up its waves. [4] They shall destroy the walls of Tyre, and break down her towers; and I will scrape her soil from her, and make her a bare rock. [5] She shall be in the midst of the sea a place for the spreading of nets; for I have spoken, says the Lord GOD; and she shall become a spoil to the nations; [6] and her daughters on the mainland shall be slain by the sword. Then they will know that I am the LORD.

7 "For thus says the Lord GOD: Behold, I will bring upon Tyre from the north Nebuchadrez'zar king of Babylon, king of kings, with horses and chariots, and with horsemen and a host of many soldiers. [8] He will slay with the sword your daughters on the mainland; he will set up a siege wall against you, and throw up a mound against you, and raise a roof of shields against you. [9] He will direct the shock of his battering rams against your walls, and with his axes he will break down your towers. [10] His horses will be so many that their dust will cover you;

your walls will shake at the noise of the horsemen and wagons and chariots, when he enters your gates as one enters a city which has been breached. [11] With the hoofs of his horses he will trample all your streets; he will slay your people with the sword; and your mighty pillars will fall to the ground. [12] They will make a spoil of your riches and a prey of your merchandise; they will break down your walls and destroy your pleasant houses; your stones and timber and soil they will cast into the midst of the waters. [13] And I will stop the music of your songs, and the sound of your lyres shall be heard no more. [14] I will make you a bare rock; you shall be a place for the spreading of nets; you shall never be rebuilt; for I the LORD have spoken, says the Lord GOD.

15 "Thus says the Lord GOD to Tyre: Will not the coastlands shake at the sound of your fall, when the wounded groan, when slaughter is made in the midst of you? [16] Then all the princes of the sea will step down from their thrones, and remove their robes, and strip off their embroidered garments; they will clothe themselves with trembling; they will sit upon the ground and tremble every moment, and be appalled at you. [17] And they will raise a lamentation over you, and say to you,

'How you have vanished[c] from the seas,
  O city renowned,
that was mighty on the sea,
  you and your inhabitants,

c Gk Old Latin Aquila: Heb *vanished, O inhabited one,*

26.1–28.19: Oracles against Tyre. 26.1–21: Tyre is to be destroyed by Nebuchadrezzar. Note the four divisions of the oracle, each with the introductory "Thus says the Lord GOD" (vv. 3,7,15,19). 26.1–6: Announcement of the judgment. For its failure to aid its ally Jerusalem (Jer.27.3), and because of its inordinate pride (28.2–10), Tyre is to fall. 4: *Rock*, in Hebrew a play on the word "Tyre," which could also be read as "rock." 7–14: With mighty siege works, Nebuchadrezzar will besiege the city, which lay a half mile off-shore on an island, and he will occupy its suburbs (*daughters*) on the mainland. Nebuchadrezzar's thirteen-year siege of Tyre apparently began shortly after Jerusalem's fall (*the eleventh year* of v. 1 should perhaps be read "the twelfth year" with the Septuagint; namely 586 B.C.), and ended in a negotiated settlement (29.18). Tyre finally fell to Alexander the Great in 332 B.C. 14: Compare vv. 4–5. 15–18: Lamentation of *the princes of the sea*, perhaps cities in trade alliance with Tyre. 19–21:

who imposed your terror
　on all the mainland!*d*
[18] Now the isles tremble
　on the day of your fall;
yea, the isles that are in the sea
　are dismayed at your passing.'

19 "For thus says the Lord GOD: When I make you a city laid waste, like the cities that are not inhabited, when I bring up the deep over you, and the great waters cover you, [20] then I will thrust you down with those who descend into the Pit, to the people of old, and I will make you to dwell in the nether world, among primeval ruins, with those who go down to the Pit, so that you will not be inhabited or have a place*e* in the land of the living. [21] I will bring you to a dreadful end, and you shall be no more; though you be sought for, you will never be found again, says the Lord GOD."

27 The word of the LORD came to me: [2] "Now you, son of man, raise a lamentation over Tyre, [3] and say to Tyre, who dwells at the entrance to the sea, merchant of the peoples on many coastlands, thus says the Lord GOD:

"O Tyre, you have said,
　'I am perfect in beauty.'
[4] Your borders are in the heart of
　　the seas;
　your builders made perfect your
　　beauty.
[5] They made all your planks
　of fir trees from Senir;
they took a cedar from Lebanon

to make a mast for you.
[6] Of oaks of Bashan
　they made your oars;
they made your deck of pines
　from the coasts of Cyprus,
　inlaid with ivory.
[7] Of fine embroidered linen from
　　Egypt
　was your sail,
　serving as your ensign;
blue and purple from the coasts of
　　Eli'shah
　was your awning.
[8] The inhabitants of Sidon and Arvad
　were your rowers;
skilled men of Zemer*f* were in you,
　they were your pilots.
[9] The elders of Gebal and her skilled
　　men were in you,
　caulking your seams;
all the ships of the sea with their
　　mariners were in you,
　to barter for your wares.

10 "Persia and Lud and Put were in your army as your men of war; they hung the shield and helmet in you; they gave you splendor. [11] The men of Arvad and Helech*g* were upon your walls round about, and men of Gamad were in your towers; they hung their shields upon your walls round about; they made perfect your beauty.

12 "Tarshish trafficked with you because of your great wealth of every kind; silver, iron, tin, and lead they exchanged for your wares. [13] Javan,

d Cn: Heb *her inhabitants*
e Gk: Heb *I will give beauty*
f Compare Gen 10.18: Heb *your skilled men, O Tyre*
g Or *and your army*

The waters of the primordial deep (Gen.1.2) will cover the wasted city, which will *descend into the Pit* (Sheol, see 31.15–18; Is.14.15), the abode of the dead.

　27.1–36: Lamentation over Tyre. The good ship Tyre was constructed of the best materials (*I am perfect;* compare 28.2–10). Royal *purple* dye was the chief export product of Phoenicia; the word "Phoenicia" comes from the Greek word for "purple" (the word "Canaan" also means "purple"). *Senir* is Mount Hermon (Dt.3.9). *Bashan* is east of the Sea of Galilee. *Elishah* is probably Cyprus. *Arvad*, like Tyre, was an island city, two miles off-shore. *Gebal* was later known as Byblos. **10–25a:** A prose intrusion into the lament over Tyre. **10–11:** Tyre's mercenaries included men from *Lud*, usually identified with Lydia in Asia Minor (Gen.10.13), but see 30.1–5 n. *Put*, perhaps Cyrene, east of Libya (30.5). *Helech*, possibly Cilicia. The identity of *Gamad* is uncertain; perhaps the word should be read Gomerim, i.e. the Cimmerians in Cappadocia. **12–25a:** Tyre's commercial empire is described generally from west to east (*Tarshish*, see Jer.10.9 n.; *Jawan*, Ionians, i.e. Greeks, Gen.10.2; *Tubal* and *Meshech*, see

Tubal, and Meshech traded with you; they exchanged the persons of men and vessels of bronze for your merchandise. 14 Beth-togar'mah exchanged for your wares horses, war horses, and mules. 15 The men of Rhodes[h] traded with you; many coastlands were your own special markets, they brought you in payment ivory tusks and ebony. 16 Edom[i] trafficked with you because of your abundant goods; they exchanged for your wares emeralds, purple, embroidered work, fine linen, coral, and agate. 17 Judah and the land of Israel traded with you; they exchanged for your merchandise wheat, olives and early figs,[j] honey, oil, and balm. 18 Damascus trafficked with you for your abundant goods, because of your great wealth of every kind; wine of Helbon, and white wool, 19 and wine[k] from Uzal they exchanged for your wares; wrought iron, cassia, and calamus were bartered for your merchandise. 20 Dedan traded with you in saddlecloths for riding. 21 Arabia and all the princes of Kedar were your favored dealers in lambs, rams, and goats; in these they trafficked with you. 22 The traders of Sheba and Ra'amah traded with you; they exchanged for your wares the best of all kinds of spices, and all precious stones, and gold. 23 Haran, Canneh, Eden,[l] Asshur, and Chilmad traded with you. 24 These traded with you in choice garments, in clothes of blue and embroidered work, and in carpets of colored stuff, bound with cords and made secure; in these they traded with you.[m] 25 The ships of Tarshish traveled for you with your merchandise.[n]

"So you were filled and heavily laden
    in the heart of the seas.

26 Your rowers have brought you out
    into the high seas.
The east wind has wrecked you
    in the heart of the seas.
27 Your riches, your wares, your merchandise,
    your mariners and your pilots,
your caulkers, your dealers in
    merchandise,
and all your men of war who are
    in you,
with all your company
    that is in your midst,
sink into the heart of the seas
    on the day of your ruin.
28 At the sound of the cry of your pilots
    the countryside shakes,
29 and down from their ships
    come all that handle the oar.
The mariners and all the pilots of
    the sea
    stand on the shore
30 and wail aloud over you,
    and cry bitterly.
They cast dust on their heads
    and wallow in ashes;
31 they make themselves bald for you,
    and gird themselves with
      sackcloth,
and they weep over you in bitterness
    of soul,
    with bitter mourning.
32 In their wailing they raise a
    lamentation for you,
    and lament over you:
'Who was ever destroyed[o] like Tyre
    in the midst of the sea?
33 When your wares came from the seas,
    you satisfied many peoples;

h Gk: Heb *Dedan*   i Another reading is *Aram*
j Cn: Heb *wheat of minnith and pannag*
k Gk: Heb *Vedan and Javan*
l Cn: Heb *Eden the traders of Sheba*
m Cn: Heb *in your market*
n Cn: Heb *your travelers your merchandise*
o Tg Vg: Heb *like silence*

38.1–9 n.; *Beth-togarmah*, see 38.1–9 n.), from south to north (*Helbon*, famed wine center thirteen miles north of Damascus), from southwest to northeast (*Uzal*, modern Sana in Yemen; *Dedan*, in west central Arabia; *Sheba*, in southwest Arabia; *Haran*, on the Balikh River in Mesopotamia, Gen.11.31–32; *Eden*, in Assyrian records Bit-Adini, the Beth-eden of Am.1.5, and *Canneh* southeast of Haran; *Asshur*, south of Nineveh; *Chilmad*, an unidentified Mesopotamian city). *Calamus*, sweet cane (Jer.6.20), was used for oil and sacrifice. **25b–36:** This section continues vv. 1–9. The sinking of the ship by the *east wind* (19.12; Jer.18.17). The sudden

with your abundant wealth and
merchandise
you enriched the kings of the
earth.
34 Now you are wrecked by the seas,
in the depths of the waters;
your merchandise and all your crew
have sunk with you.
35 All the inhabitants of the coastlands
are appalled at you;
and their kings are horribly afraid,
their faces are convulsed.
36 The merchants among the peoples
hiss at you;
you have come to a dreadful end
and shall be no more for ever.' "

28 The word of the LORD came
to me: 2 "Son of man, say to
the prince of Tyre, Thus says the
Lord GOD:
"Because your heart is proud,
and you have said, 'I am a god,
I sit in the seat of the gods,
in the heart of the seas,'
yet you are but a man, and no god,
though you consider yourself as
wise as a god—
3 you are indeed wiser than Daniel;
no secret is hidden from you;
4 by your wisdom and your
understanding
you have gotten wealth for
yourself,
and have gathered gold and silver
into your treasuries;
5 by your great wisdom in trade
you have increased your wealth,
and your heart has become proud
in your wealth—
6 therefore thus says the Lord GOD:
"Because you consider yourself
as wise as a god,

7 therefore, behold, I will bring
strangers upon you,
the most terrible of the nations;
and they shall draw their swords
against the beauty of your
wisdom
and defile your splendor.
8 They shall thrust you down into the
Pit,
and you shall die the death of the
slain
in the heart of the seas.
9 Will you still say, 'I am a god,'
in the presence of those who slay
you,
though you are but a man, and no
god,
in the hands of those who wound
you?
10 You shall die the death of the
uncircumcised
by the hand of foreigners;
for I have spoken, says the Lord
GOD."

11 Moreover the word of the LORD
came to me: 12 "Son of man, raise a
lamentation over the king of Tyre, and
say to him, Thus says the Lord GOD:
"You were the signet of perfection,*p*
full of wisdom
and perfect in beauty.
13 You were in Eden, the garden of
God;
every precious stone was your
covering,
carnelian, topaz, and jasper,
chrysolite, beryl, and onyx,
sapphire,*q* carbuncle, and emerald;
and wrought in gold were your
settings

p Heb obscure
q Or *lapis lazuli*

---

end of the great commercial city brings fear and lamentation to seamen, merchants, and
inhabitants of the coastlands.
28.1–10: Oracle against Tyre, apparently using mythological themes, including the Canaanite
story of Dan'el (see 14.12–23 n.) in which Dan'el is the wise judge of widows and orphans. Pride
leads one to regard himself as God. Thus the prince of Tyre sat *in the seat of the gods* (compare
Is.14.13–14); but he will be slain by *the most terrible of the nations*, Babylonia (30.10–11), and
come to an ignominious end (*the death of the uncircumcized*) in Sheol (31.14–18).
28.11–19: Lamentation over the king of Tyre, based on a variant version of the Eden story.
Man, created as a perfect being, dwelt in Eden, with a covering of precious stones (compare
the twelve precious stones of the ephod in Ex.28.17–20 and the description of the heavenly
Jerusalem in Rev.4.1–6; 21.15–21). But pride and idolatry caused his banishment by the guardian

and your engravings.[r]
On the day that you were created
  they were prepared.
[14] With an anointed guardian cherub
  I placed you;[s]
  you were on the holy mountain of
    God;
  in the midst of the stones of fire
  you walked.
[15] You were blameless in your ways
  from the day you were created,
  till iniquity was found in you.
[16] In the abundance of your trade
  you were filled with violence, and
  you sinned;
  so I cast you as a profane thing from
    the mountain of God,
  and the guardian cherub drove you
    out
  from the midst of the stones of fire.
[17] Your heart was proud because of
  your beauty;
  you corrupted your wisdom for
    the sake of your splendor.
I cast you to the ground;
  I exposed you before kings,
  to feast their eyes on you.
[18] By the multitude of your iniquities,
  in the unrighteousness of your
    trade
  you profaned your sanctuaries;
so I brought forth fire from the midst
  of you;
  it consumed you,
and I turned you to ashes upon the
  earth
  in the sight of all who saw you.
[19] All who know you among the
  peoples
  are appalled at you;
you have come to a dreadful end
  and shall be no more for ever."
20 The word of the LORD came to
me: [21] "Son of man, set your face toward Sidon, and prophesy against her
[22] and say, Thus says the Lord GOD:
"Behold, I am against you, O Sidon,
  and I will manifest my glory in
    the midst of you.
And they shall know that I am the
  LORD
  when I execute judgments in her,
  and manifest my holiness in her;
[23] for I will send pestilence into her,
  and blood into her streets;
  and the slain shall fall in the midst
    of her,
  by the sword that is against her on
    every side.
Then they will know that I am the
  LORD.

24 "And for the house of Israel there shall be no more a brier to prick or a thorn to hurt them among all their neighbors who have treated them with contempt. Then they will know that I am the Lord GOD.

25 "Thus says the Lord GOD: When I gather the house of Israel from the peoples among whom they are scattered, and manifest my holiness in them in the sight of the nations, then they shall dwell in their own land which I gave to my servant Jacob. [26] And they shall dwell securely in it, and they shall build houses and plant vineyards. They shall dwell securely, when I execute judgments upon all their neighbors who have treated them with contempt. Then they will know that I am the LORD their God."

29 In the tenth year, in the tenth month, on the twelfth day of the month, the word of the LORD came to me: [2] "Son of man, set your face against Pharaoh king of Egypt, and prophesy against him and against all Egypt;

r Heb uncertain   s Heb uncertain

cherub (Gen.3.24). **16:** *The mountain of God* in Canaanite myth was Mount Sapon, modern Jebel Aqra', north of Ugarit.
    28.20–23: Oracle against Sidon, north of Tyre, an ally of Jerusalem against Nebuchadrezzar (Jer.27.3). **22–23:** Compare 20.41; 36.23.
    28.24–26: Restoration of Israel. An editorial addition, concluding the first section of the oracles concerning foreign nations. **24:** Compare Num.33.55. **25–26:** Compare 34.28; Jer. 23.6; Lev.25.19.
    29.1–32.32: Against Egypt. 29.1–16: Against Pharaoh (January 7, 587 B.C.). Hophra's attack against Nebuchadrezzar in the spring of 588 had failed to relieve Jerusalem (vv. 6–9;

[3] speak, and say, Thus says the Lord GOD:

> "Behold, I am against you,
> Pharaoh king of Egypt,
> the great dragon that lies
> in the midst of his streams,
> that says, 'My Nile is my own;
> I made it.'[t]
> [4] I will put hooks in your jaws,
> and make the fish of your streams
> stick to your scales;
> and I will draw you up out of the
> midst of your streams,
> with all the fish of your streams
> which stick to your scales.
> [5] And I will cast you forth into the
> wilderness,
> you and all the fish of your
> streams;
> you shall fall upon the open field,
> and not be gathered and buried.
> To the beasts of the earth and to the
> birds of the air
> I have given you as food.

6 "Then all the inhabitants of Egypt shall know that I am the LORD. Because you[u] have been a staff of reed to the house of Israel; [7] when they grasped you with the hand, you broke, and tore all their shoulders; and when they leaned upon you, you broke, and made all their loins to shake;[v] [8] therefore thus says the Lord GOD: Behold, I will bring a sword upon you, and will cut off from you man and beast; [9] and the land of Egypt shall be a desolation and a waste. Then they will know that I am the LORD.

"Because you[w] said, 'The Nile is mine, and I made it,' [10] therefore, behold, I am against you, and against your streams, and I will make the land of Egypt an utter waste and desolation, from Migdol to Syene, as far as the border of Ethiopia. [11] No foot of man shall pass through it, and no foot of beast shall pass through it; it shall be uninhabited forty years. [12] And I will make the land of Egypt a desolation in the midst of desolated countries; and her cities shall be a desolation forty years among cities that are laid waste. I will scatter the Egyptians among the nations, and disperse them among the countries.

13 "For thus says the Lord GOD: At the end of forty years I will gather the Egyptians from the peoples among whom they were scattered; [14] and I will restore the fortunes of Egypt, and bring them back to the land of Pathros, the land of their origin; and there they shall be a lowly kingdom. [15] It shall be the most lowly of the kingdoms, and never again exalt itself above the nations; and I will make them so small that they will never again rule over the nations. [16] And it shall never again be the reliance of the house of Israel, recalling their iniquity, when they turn to them for aid. Then they will know that I am the Lord GOD."

17 In the twenty-seventh year, in the first month, on the first day of the month, the word of the LORD came to me: [18] "Son of man, Nebuchadrez'-zar king of Babylon made his army labor hard against Tyre; every head was made bald and every shoulder was rubbed bare; yet neither he nor his army got anything from Tyre to pay for the labor that he had performed against it. [19] Therefore thus says the Lord GOD: Behold, I will give the land of

t Syr Compare Gk: Heb *I have made myself*
u Gk Syr Vg: Heb *they*
v Syr: Heb *stand*   w Gk Syr Vg: Heb *he*

Jer.37.1–10). Hophra is depicted as the great sea dragon (Hebrew "tannin"; Is.27.1; Job ch. 41) whom God will catch and let his body become carrion (32.1–8). *His streams*, the Nile delta and canals. *Fish of your streams*, the Egyptians and their mercenaries. **10:** *Migdol* (southwest of Pelusium, 30.15; Jer.44.1) and *Syene* (Aswan, at the First Cataract of the Nile) are the northern and southern limits of Egypt. **11:** *Forty years*, 4.6; Num.14.33. **14:** *Pathros*, see Jer.44.1 n.

29.17–21: Egypt as "wages" for Nebuchadrezzar. This is Ezekiel's latest dated oracle, April 26, 571 B.C., shortly after Ahmosis II forced Hophra to make him co-regent. Nebuchadrezzar will get sufficient booty from Egypt to compensate for his lack of booty from the siege of Tyre (26.7; Jer.46.2–26). *Horn* may refer to the re-establishment of the Davidic line in Israel (Ps.132.17).

Egypt to Nebuchadrez'zar king of Babylon; and he shall carry off its wealth[x] and despoil it and plunder it; and it shall be the wages for his army. 20 I have given him the land of Egypt as his recompense for which he labored, because they worked for me, says the Lord GOD.

21 "On that day I will cause a horn to spring forth to the house of Israel, and I will open your lips among them. Then they will know that I am the LORD."

30 The word of the LORD came to me: 2 "Son of man, prophesy, and say, Thus says the Lord GOD:
"Wail, 'Alas for the day!'
3   For the day is near,
   the day of the LORD is near;
it will be a day of clouds,
   a time of doom for the nations.
4 A sword shall come upon Egypt,
   and anguish shall be in Ethiopia,
when the slain fall in Egypt,
   and her wealth is carried away,
   and her foundations are torn
     down.
5 Ethiopia, and Put, and Lud, and all Arabia, and Libya,[y] and the people of the land that is in league, shall fall with them by the sword.

6 "Thus says the LORD:
Those who support Egypt shall fall,
   and her proud might shall come
     down;
from Migdol to Syene
   they shall fall within her by the
     sword,
says the Lord GOD.
7 And she[z] shall be desolated in the midst of desolated countries
and her cities shall be in the midst of cities that are laid waste.

8 Then they will know that I am the
   LORD,
when I have set fire to Egypt,
   and all her helpers are broken.

9 "On that day swift[a] messengers shall go forth from me to terrify the unsuspecting Ethiopians; and anguish shall come upon them on the day of Egypt's doom; for, lo, it comes!

10 "Thus says the Lord GOD:
I will put an end to the wealth[b] of
   Egypt,
by the hand of Nebuchadrez'zar
   king of Babylon.
11 He and his people with him, the
   most terrible of the nations,
shall be brought in to destroy the
   land;
and they shall draw their swords
   against Egypt,
   and fill the land with the slain.
12 And I will dry up the Nile,
   and will sell the land into the hand
   of evil men;
I will bring desolation upon the land
   and everything in it,
by the hand of foreigners;
   I, the LORD, have spoken.

13 "Thus says the Lord GOD:
I will destroy the idols,
   and put an end to the images, in
     Memphis;
there shall no longer be a prince in
   the land of Egypt;
so I will put fear in the land of
   Egypt.
14 I will make Pathros a desolation,
   and will set fire to Zo'an,
   and will execute acts of judgment
     upon Thebes.

x Or *multitude*   y Gk Compare Syr Vg: Heb *Cub*
z Gk: Heb *they*   a Gk Syr: Heb *in ships*
b Or *multitude*

30.1–26: The doom of Egypt. 1–5: The day of the LORD since the time of Amos (Am.5.18–20) was God's judgment day (15.5; Is.2.12; Jer.30.7; Zeph.1.14–18); later it became the day of Israel's restoration and remained doomsday for the Gentiles. *Sword*, 21.3–17. *Put*, see 27.10–11 n. Because of its regular juxtaposition with Put (27.10; 38.5; [with Cush (Ethiopia)]; Is.66.19), *Lud* is probably not Lydia in Asia Minor, but should be sought in northeast Africa. **6–9:** Egypt's mercenaries (27.10–11) will collapse before the onslaught; Egypt will be reduced to ashes (28.18). *Migdol* to *Syene*, see 29.10 n. **10–12:** Nebuchadrezzar (26.7), king of *the most terrible of the nations* (28.7), is God's instrument (Jer.27.6). **13–19:** All Egypt will be destroyed. *Memphis*, the ancient capital of lower Egypt. *Pathros*, see Jer.44.1 n. *Zoan*, in the Greek period

¹⁵ And I will pour my wrath upon
Pelusium,
the stronghold of Egypt,
and cut off the multitude of
Thebes.
¹⁶ And I will set fire to Egypt;
Pelusium shall be in great agony;
Thebes shall be breached,
and its walls broken down.ᶜ
¹⁷ The young men of On and of
Pibe'seth shall fall by the
sword;
and the women shall go into
captivity.
¹⁸ At Tehaph'nehes the day shall be
dark,
when I break there the dominion
of Egypt,
and her proud might shall come to
an end;
she shall be covered by a cloud,
and her daughters shall go into
captivity.
¹⁹ Thus I will execute acts of judgment
upon Egypt.
Then they will know that I am
the LORD."

20 In the eleventh year, in the first
month, on the seventh day of the
month, the word of the LORD came to
me: ²¹ "Son of man, I have broken the
arm of Pharaoh king of Egypt; and lo,
it has not been bound up, to heal it by
binding it with a bandage, so that it
may become strong to wield the sword.
²² Therefore thus says the Lord GOD:
Behold, I am against Pharaoh king of
Egypt, and will break his arms, both
the strong arm and the one that was
broken; and I will make the sword fall
from his hand. ²³ I will scatter the
Egyptians among the nations, and disperse them throughout the lands.
²⁴ And I will strengthen the arms of the
king of Babylon, and put my sword in

his hand; but I will break the arms of
Pharaoh, and he will groan before him
like a man mortally wounded. ²⁵ I will
strengthen the arms of the king of Babylon, but the arms of Pharaoh shall fall;
and they shall know that I am the
LORD. When I put my sword into the
hand of the king of Babylon, he shall
stretch it out against the land of Egypt;
²⁶ and I will scatter the Egyptians
among the nations and disperse them
throughout the countries. Then they
will know that I am the LORD."

31 In the eleventh year, in the third
month, on the first day of the
month, the word of the LORD came to
me: ² "Son of man, say to Pharaoh
king of Egypt and to his multitude:
"Whom are you like in your
greatness?
³ Behold, I will liken you toᵈ a
cedar in Lebanon,
with fair branches and forest shade,
and of great height,
its top among the clouds.ᵉ
⁴ The waters nourished it,
the deep made it grow tall,
making its rivers flowᶠ
round the place of its planting,
sending forth its streams
to all the trees of the forest.
⁵ So it towered high
above all the trees of the forest;
its boughs grew large
and its branches long,
from abundant water in its shoots.
⁶ All the birds of the air
made their nests in its boughs;
under its branches all the beasts of
the field
brought forth their young;
and under its shadow
dwelt all great nations.

c Cn: Heb *and Memphis, distresses by day*
d Cn: Heb *Behold, Assyria*
e Gk: Heb *thick boughs*   f Gk: Heb *going*

Tanis, in the northeast delta region. *Thebes* is present-day Karnak (Jer.46.25). *Pelusium*, east
of Zoan. *On* is Heliopolis (see Jer.43.13 n.). *Pibeseth*, Bubastis. *Tehaphnehes*, Tahpanhes (Jer.
43.7). **20–26:** April 29, 587 B.C. Nebuchadrezzar had broken one arm of Hophra the year before
(see 29.1–16 n.); the next time, he will break both arms.

    31.1–18: Allegory of the cedar (compare ch. 17). Date, June 21, 587 B.C. Ezekiel uses an an-
cient Babylonian myth to emphasize that, as with Tyre (28.1–5), the cause for Egypt's fall was
pride (and political unreliability, 29.6–9). **4:** *The deep* (Hebrew *tehom;* compare Tiamat, the
Babylonian dragon of the watery chaos; see Is.51.9–11 n.), ancient mythological opponent of

7 It was beautiful in its greatness,
  in the length of its branches;
for its roots went down
  to abundant waters.
8 The cedars in the garden of God
    could not rival it,
  nor the fir trees equal its boughs;
the plane trees were as nothing
  compared with its branches;
no tree in the garden of God
  was like it in beauty.
9 I made it beautiful
  in the mass of its branches,
and all the trees of Eden envied it,
  that were in the garden of God.

10 "Therefore thus says the Lord GOD: Because it[g] towered high and set its top among the clouds,[h] and its heart was proud of its height, 11 I will give it into the hand of a mighty one of the nations; he shall surely deal with it as its wickedness deserves. I have cast it out. 12 Foreigners, the most terrible of the nations, will cut it down and leave it. On the mountains and in all the valleys its branches will fall, and its boughs will lie broken in all the watercourses of the land; and all the peoples of the earth will go from its shadow and leave it. 13 Upon its ruin will dwell all the birds of the air, and upon its branches will be all the beasts of the field. 14 All this is in order that no trees by the waters may grow to lofty height or set their tops among the clouds,[h] and that no trees that drink water may reach up to them in height; for they are all given over to death, to the nether world among mortal men, with those who go down to the Pit.

15 "Thus says the Lord GOD: When it goes down to Sheol I will make the deep mourn for[i] it, and restrain its

rivers, and many waters shall be stopped; I will clothe Lebanon in gloom for it, and all the trees of the field shall faint because of it. 16 I will make the nations quake at the sound of its fall, when I cast it down to Sheol with those who go down to the Pit; and all the trees of Eden, the choice and best of Lebanon, all that drink water, will be comforted in the nether world. 17 They also shall go down to Sheol with it, to those who are slain by the sword; yea, those who dwelt under its shadow among the nations shall perish.[j] 18 Whom are you thus like in glory and in greatness among the trees of Eden? You shall be brought down with the trees of Eden to the nether world; you shall lie among the uncircumcised, with those who are slain by the sword.

"This is Pharaoh and all his multitude, says the Lord GOD."

32 In the twelfth year, in the twelfth month, on the first day of the month, the word of the LORD came to me: 2 "Son of man, raise a lamentation over Pharaoh king of Egypt, and say to him:
"You consider yourself a lion among
  the nations,
but you are like a dragon in the
  seas;
you burst forth in your rivers,
  trouble the waters with your feet,
  and foul their rivers.
3 Thus says the Lord GOD:
  I will throw my net over you
  with a host of many peoples;
  and I[k] will haul you up in my
    dragnet.
4 And I will cast you on the ground,

---

g Syr Vg: Heb *you*   *h* Gk: Heb *thick boughs*
i Gk: Heb *mourn for, I have covered*
j Compare Gk: Heb obscure   *k* Gk Vg: Heb *they*

---

the gods, nourished the tree so that it reached into the heavens and sheltered all life. **7–9:** The splendor of the great cedar, Egypt, was incomparable (28.11–19), surpassing those *in the garden of God* (thus rivaling God, Gen.11.1–9). **10–18:** But God will cut it down; the life it sheltered will be dispersed, and it will go down to Sheol (28.8–10) where it will lie not with the honored dead, *the trees of Eden*, but with those who died untimely, violent, or dishonorable deaths. Later the great world tree, or tree of life, became a motif in Near Eastern (e.g. Persian) apocalypticism.

    32.1–16: Lament over Pharaoh. The date is March 3, 585 B.C. Though Pharaoh thought himself *a lion* (symbol of royal power, see 19.1–9 n.; compare the lion-bodied sphinx), he is only a sea monster whom God will capture with a net (12.13), as Marduk captured Tiamat

on the open field I will fling you,
and will cause all the birds of the
　air to settle on you,
and I will gorge the beasts of the
　whole earth with you.
⁵ I will strew your flesh upon the
　mountains,
and fill the valleys with your
　carcass.*l*
⁶ I will drench the land even to the
　mountains
with your flowing blood;
and the watercourses will be full
　of you.
⁷ When I blot you out, I will cover
　the heavens,
and make their stars dark;
I will cover the sun with a cloud,
and the moon shall not give its
　light.
⁸ All the bright lights of heaven
will I make dark over you,
and put darkness upon your land,
　　　　　　says the Lord GOD.
9 "I will trouble the hearts of many
peoples, when I carry you captive*m*
among the nations, into the countries
which you have not known. ¹⁰ I will
make many peoples appalled at you,
and their kings shall shudder because
of you, when I brandish my sword before them; they shall tremble every moment, every one for his own life, on the
day of your downfall. ¹¹ For thus says
the Lord GOD: The sword of the king
of Babylon shall come upon you. ¹² I
will cause your multitude to fall by the
swords of mighty ones, all of them most
terrible among the nations.
　"They shall bring to nought the pride
　　of Egypt,
and all its multitude shall perish.
¹³ I will destroy all its beasts
　from beside many waters;

and no foot of man shall trouble them
　any more,
nor shall the hoofs of beasts
　trouble them.
¹⁴ Then I will make their waters clear,
and cause their rivers to run like
　oil, says the Lord GOD.
¹⁵ When I make the land of Egypt
　desolate
and when the land is stripped of
　all that fills it,
when I smite all who dwell in it,
then they will know that I am the
　LORD.
¹⁶ This is a lamentation which shall be
chanted; the daughters of the nations
shall chant it; over Egypt, and over all
her multitude, shall they chant it, says
the Lord GOD."
17 In the twelfth year, in the first
month,*n* on the fifteenth day of the
month, the word of the LORD came to
me: ¹⁸ "Son of man, wail over the multitude of Egypt, and send them down,
her and the daughters of majestic nations, to the nether world, to those who
have gone down to the Pit:
¹⁹ 'Whom do you surpass in beauty?
　Go down, and be laid with the
　　uncircumcised.'
²⁰ They shall fall amid those who are
slain by the sword,*o* and with her shall
lie all her multitudes.*p* ²¹ The mighty
chiefs shall speak of them, with their
helpers, out of the midst of Sheol:
'They have come down, they lie still,
the uncircumcised, slain by the sword.'
22 "Assyria is there, and all her
company, their graves round about her,
all of them slain, fallen by the sword;

l Symmachus Syr Vg: Heb *your height*
m Gk: Heb *bring your destruction*
n Gk: Heb lacks *in the first month*
o Gk Syr: Heb *sword, the sword is delivered*
p Gk: Heb *they have drawn her away and all her multi-*
　tudes

(see 31.4 n.), and will expose on land for carrion (29.1–16). Verses 7–8 recall the day of the
LORD (see 30.1–5 n.; Is.13.10; Jl.2.2) in which God overcomes all that oppose him. The recurring *sword* of God (vv. 10–12; 21.1–32; 30.25; compare Lev.26.33; Is.34.5–6; Jer.12.12) recalls
the sword-wielding Baal depicted in statues found by archaeologists. Egypt will become a
lifeless wasteland (Jer.4.23–28), mourned by professional mourning women (Jer.9.17–18).
　32.17–32: Egypt in the underworld (April 27, 586 B.C.). Like Tyre (28.10), Egypt will join
those in that section of the underworld reserved for the uncircumcized and those who are
executed or who die violent or untimely deaths. They do not enjoy the status of the honored
war-dead, who were properly buried (v. 27). In its dishonorable demise Egypt will join others

23 whose graves are set in the uttermost parts of the Pit, and her company is round about her grave; all of them slain, fallen by the sword, who spread terror in the land of the living.

24 "Elam is there, and all her multitude about her grave; all of them slain, fallen by the sword, who went down uncircumcised into the nether world, who spread terror in the land of the living, and they bear their shame with those who go down to the Pit. 25 They have made her a bed among the slain with all her multitude, their graves round about her, all of them uncircumcised, slain by the sword; for terror of them was spread in the land of the living, and they bear their shame with those who go down to the Pit; they are placed among the slain.

26 "Meshech and Tubal are there, and all their multitude, their graves round about them, all of them uncircumcised, slain by the sword; for they spread terror in the land of the living. 27 And they do not lie with the fallen mighty men of old*q* who went down to Sheol with their weapons of war, whose swords were laid under their heads, and whose shields*r* are upon their bones; for the terror of the mighty men was in the land of the living. 28 So you shall be broken and lie among the uncircumcised, with those who are slain by the sword.

29 "Edom is there, her kings and all her princes, who for all their might are laid with those who are slain by the sword; they lie with the uncircumcised, with those who go down to the Pit.

30 "The princes of the north are there, all of them, and all the Sido'-nians, who have gone down in shame with the slain, for all the terror which they caused by their might; they lie uncircumcised with those who are slain by the sword, and bear their shame with those who go down to the Pit.

31 "When Pharaoh sees them, he will comfort himself for all his multitude, Pharaoh and all his army, slain by the sword, says the Lord GOD. 32 For he*s* spread terror in the land of the living; therefore he shall be laid among the uncircumcised, with those who are slain by the sword, Pharaoh and all his multitude, says the Lord GOD."

33 The word of the LORD came to me: 2 "Son of man, speak to your people and say to them, If I bring the sword upon a land, and the people of the land take a man from among them, and make him their watchman; 3 and if he sees the sword coming upon the land and blows the trumpet and warns the people; 4 then if any one who hears the sound of the trumpet does not take warning, and the sword comes and takes him away, his blood shall be upon his own head. 5 He heard the sound of the trumpet, and did not take warning; his blood shall be upon himself. But if he had taken warning, he would have saved his life. 6 But if the watchman sees the sword coming and does not blow the trumpet, so that the people are not warned, and the sword comes, and takes any one of them; that man is taken away in his iniquity, but his blood I will require at the watchman's hand.

7 "So you, son of man, I have made a watchman for the house of Israel; whenever you hear a word from my mouth, you shall give them warning from me. 8 If I say to the wicked, O wicked man, you shall surely die, and you do not speak to warn the wicked to turn from his way, that wicked man shall die in his iniquity, but his blood I will require at your hand. 9 But if you warn the wicked to turn from his way, and he does not turn from his way;

q Gk Old Latin: Heb *of the uncircumcised*
r Cn: Heb *iniquities*
s Cn: Heb *I*

who were objects of God's wrath (Is.14.9–11), such as *Assyria* (Nah. chs. 1–3); *Elam* (Jer.49.34–39); *Meshech* and *Tubal* (see 38.2 n.; Gen.10.2 n.); *Edom* (25.12–14); *Sidon* (28.20–23); *princes of the north* (v. 30), unnamed rulers in Phoenicia and Syria.

33.1–39.29: Oracles of restoration. 33.1–20: Responsibility. 1–9: The prophet as watchman (Is.21.6; Jer.6.17) applies Ezekiel's doctrine of individual responsibility. Compare 3.16–21.

he shall die in his iniquity, but you will have saved your life.

10 "And you, son of man, say to the house of Israel, Thus have you said: 'Our transgressions and our sins are upon us, and we waste away because of them; how then can we live?' ¹¹ Say to them, As I live, says the Lord GOD, I have no pleasure in the death of the wicked, but that the wicked turn from his way and live; turn back, turn back from your evil ways; for why will you die, O house of Israel? ¹² And you, son of man, say to your people, The righteousness of the righteous shall not deliver him when he transgresses; and as for the wickedness of the wicked, he shall not fall by it when he turns from his wickedness; and the righteous shall not be able to live by his righteousness*ᵗ* when he sins. ¹³ Though I say to the righteous that he shall surely live, yet if he trusts in his righteousness and commits iniquity, none of his righteous deeds shall be remembered; but in the iniquity that he has committed he shall die. ¹⁴ Again, though I say to the wicked, 'You shall surely die,' yet if he turns from his sin and does what is lawful and right, ¹⁵ if the wicked restores the pledge, gives back what he has taken by robbery, and walks in the statutes of life, committing no iniquity; he shall surely live, he shall not die. ¹⁶ None of the sins that he has committed shall be remembered against him; he has done what is lawful and right, he shall surely live.

17 "Yet your people say, 'The way of the Lord is not just'; when it is their own way that is not just. ¹⁸ When the righteous turns from his righteousness, and commits iniquity, he shall die for it. ¹⁹ And when the wicked turns from his wickedness, and does what is lawful and right, he shall live by it. ²⁰ Yet you say, 'The way of the Lord is not

just.' O house of Israel, I will judge each of you according to his ways."

21 In the twelfth year of our exile, in the tenth month, on the fifth day of the month, a man who had escaped from Jerusalem came to me and said, "The city has fallen." ²² Now the hand of the LORD had been upon me the evening before the fugitive came; and he had opened my mouth by the time the man came to me in the morning; so my mouth was opened, and I was no longer dumb.

23 The word of the LORD came to me: ²⁴ "Son of man, the inhabitants of these waste places in the land of Israel keep saying, 'Abraham was only one man, yet he got possession of the land; but we are many; the land is surely given us to possess.' ²⁵ Therefore say to them, Thus says the Lord GOD: You eat flesh with the blood, and lift up your eyes to your idols, and shed blood; shall you then possess the land? ²⁶ You resort to the sword, you commit abominations and each of you defiles his neighbor's wife; shall you then possess the land? ²⁷ Say this to them, Thus says the Lord GOD: As I live, surely those who are in the waste places shall fall by the sword; and him that is in the open field I will give to the beasts to be devoured; and those who are in strongholds and in caves shall die by pestilence. ²⁸ And I will make the land a desolation and a waste; and her proud might shall come to an end; and the mountains of Israel shall be so desolate that none will pass through. ²⁹ Then they will know that I am the LORD, when I have made the land a desolation and a waste because of all their abominations which they have committed.

30 "As for you, son of man, your people who talk together about you

ᵗ Heb *by it*

Death (vv. 8–9) may refer to premature death as contrasted with blessed longevity. **10–20:** On individual responsibility. This oracle re-emphasizes 14.12–23 and 18.5–32.

33.21–33: Miscellanea. 21–22: January 19, 586 B.C. (read "eleventh" for *twelfth*). A few months after the fall of Jerusalem, word reached Ezekiel and his tongue was loosed (3.24–27). Perhaps these two verses, which are unrelated to this context, should follow 24.27. **23–29:** Expansion on the problem of possession of Palestinian property formerly belonging to de-

by the walls and at the doors of the houses, say to one another, each to his brother, 'Come, and hear what the word is that comes forth from the LORD.' ³¹ And they come to you as people come, and they sit before you as my people, and they hear what you say but they will not do it; for with their lips they show much love, but their heart is set on their gain. ³² And, lo, you are to them like one who sings love songs*u* with a beautiful voice and plays well on an instrument, for they hear what you say, but they will not do it. ³³ When this comes–and come it will!– then they will know that a prophet has been among them."

34 The word of the LORD came to me: ² "Son of man, prophesy against the shepherds of Israel, prophesy, and say to them, even to the shepherds, Thus says the Lord GOD: Ho, shepherds of Israel who have been feeding yourselves! Should not shepherds feed the sheep? ³ You eat the fat, you clothe yourselves with the wool, you slaughter the fatlings; but you do not feed the sheep. ⁴ The weak you have not strengthened, the sick you have not healed, the crippled you have not bound up, the strayed you have not brought back, the lost you have not sought, and with force and harshness you have ruled them. ⁵ So they were scattered, because there was no shepherd; and they became food for all the wild beasts. ⁶ My sheep were scattered, they wandered over all the mountains and on every high hill; my sheep were scattered over all the face of the earth, with none to search or seek for them.

7 "Therefore, you shepherds, hear the word of the LORD: ⁸ As I live, says the Lord GOD, because my sheep have become a prey, and my sheep have become food for all the wild beasts, since there was no shepherd; and because my shepherds have not searched for my sheep, but the shepherds have fed themselves, and have not fed my sheep; ⁹ therefore, you shepherds, hear the word of the LORD: ¹⁰ Thus says the Lord GOD, Behold, I am against the shepherds; and I will require my sheep at their hand, and put a stop to their feeding the sheep; no longer shall the shepherds feed themselves. I will rescue my sheep from their mouths, that they may not be food for them.

11 "For thus says the Lord GOD: Behold, I, I myself will search for my sheep, and will seek them out. ¹² As a shepherd seeks out his flock when some of his sheep*v* have been scattered abroad, so will I seek out my sheep; and I will rescue them from all places where they have been scattered on a day of clouds and thick darkness. ¹³ And I will bring them out from the peoples, and gather them from the countries, and will bring them into their own land; and I will feed them on the mountains of Israel, by the fountains, and in all the inhabited places of the country. ¹⁴ I will feed them with good pasture, and upon the mountain heights of Israel shall be their pasture; there they shall lie down in good grazing land, and on fat pasture they shall feed on the mountains of Israel. ¹⁵ I myself will be the shepherd of my sheep, and I will make them lie down, says the Lord GOD. ¹⁶ I will seek the lost, and I will bring back the strayed, and I will bind up the crippled, and I will strengthen the weak, and the fat and

u Cn: Heb *like a love song*
v Cn: Heb *when he is among his sheep*

---

portees. Note the three scourges in v. 27 (14.21; 21.3–5). **30–33:** Consistent with human nature, the people heard what they wanted to hear. But the day approaches when they will be reminded that with the words of God's love were also the words of God's justice (Jer.5.12–13). *Song*, oracles may have been chanted (2 Kg.3.15).
    34.1–31: The shepherds of Israel. 1–10: The shepherds (i.e. kings) had misused their people (Jer.23.13–17) and scattered them (Jer.10.21; 23.1–4). This oracle applies the doctrine of individual responsibility (18.5–32) to the rulers, who are also subject to God's law (2 Sam.12.1–15). *Wild beasts*, Judah's attackers, especially Babylonia. **11–16:** God is the Good Shepherd (Is.40.11; Jer.31.10) who will gather the dispersed and injured flock. This passage suggests a

the strong I will watch over;*w* I will feed them in justice.

17 "As for you, my flock, thus says the Lord GOD: Behold, I judge between sheep and sheep, rams and he-goats. 18 Is it not enough for you to feed on the good pasture, that you must tread down with your feet the rest of your pasture; and to drink of clear water, that you must foul the rest with your feet? 19 And must my sheep eat what you have trodden with your feet, and drink what you have fouled with your feet?

20 "Therefore, thus says the Lord GOD to them: Behold, I, I myself will judge between the fat sheep and the lean sheep. 21 Because you push with side and shoulder, and thrust at all the weak with your horns, till you have scattered them abroad, 22 I will save my flock, they shall no longer be a prey; and I will judge between sheep and sheep. 23 And I will set up over them one shepherd, my servant David, and he shall feed them: he shall feed them and be their shepherd. 24 And I, the LORD, will be their God, and my servant David shall be prince among them; I, the LORD, have spoken.

25 "I will make with them a covenant of peace and banish wild beasts from the land, so that they may dwell securely in the wilderness and sleep in the woods. 26 And I will make them and the places round about my hill a blessing; and I will send down the showers in their season; they shall be showers of blessing. 27 And the trees of the field shall yield their fruit, and the earth shall yield its increase, and they shall be secure in their land; and they shall know that I am the LORD, when I break the bars of their yoke, and deliver them from the hand of those who enslaved them. 28 They shall no more be a prey to the nations, nor shall the beasts of the land devour them; they shall dwell securely, and none shall make them afraid. 29 And I will provide for them prosperous*x* plantations so that they shall no more be consumed with hunger in the land, and no longer suffer the reproach of the nations. 30 And they shall know that I, the LORD their God, am with them, and that they, the house of Israel, are my people, says the Lord GOD. 31 And you are my sheep, the sheep of my pasture,*y* and I am your God, says the Lord GOD."

35 The word of the LORD came to me: 2 "Son of man, set your face against Mount Se'ir, and prophesy against it, 3 and say to it, Thus says the Lord GOD: Behold, I am against you, mount Se'ir, and I will stretch out my hand against you, and I will make you a desolation and a waste. 4 I will lay your cities waste, and you shall become a desolation; and you shall know that I am the LORD. 5 Because you cherished perpetual enmity, and gave over the people of Israel to the power of the sword at the time of their calamity, at the time of their final punishment; 6 therefore, as I live, says the Lord GOD, I will prepare you

w Gk Syr Vg: Heb *destroy*
x Gk Syr Old Latin: Heb *for renown*
y Gk Old Latin: Heb *pasture you are men*

return to theocracy (Hos.8.4; 1 Sam.8.7). **17–22:** Sheep, good and bad, are found in the flock; the bad must be separated out and punished (Mt.25.31–32). The figure may have a double meaning and refer also to the nations which oppress Israel. **23–24:** God will place his *servant David* (2 Sam.3.18), i.e. a restored monarchy, over his people (37.22–25; Jer.23.5–6). *One shepherd*, see Hos.1.11; Jn.10.16. **25–31:** Using the oldest term for covenant making (see Jer.31.31–34), the prophet affirms that God will make a *covenant of peace* (37.26; Heb.13.20). God, again resident on Mount Zion (*my hill*), will preserve the proper sequence of seasons (Gen.8.21–22), assuring his people of continuous prosperity (Am.9.13–14), free from fear of destruction within (*wild beasts*, Lev.26.6) and without (*prey of nations*).

35.1–15: The oracle against Edom is an editorial expansion of an oracle of Ezekiel, using Ezekiel's phraseology (compare vv. 1–3 with 6.1–3). Properly belonging with 25.12–14, it was placed here to be contrasted with ch. 36 (especially 36.5), forming the prelude to Israel's restoration. It reflects the growing intensity of Jewish hatred for Edom subsequent to Edom's occupation of southern Judah (Jer.49.7–22). In contrast with Egypt (29.13–16), Edom will remain

for blood, and blood shall pursue you; because you are guilty of blood,[z] therefore blood shall pursue you. [7] I will make Mount Se'ir a waste and a desolation; and I will cut off from it all who come and go. [8] And I will fill your mountains with the slain; on your hills and in your valleys and in all your ravines those slain with the sword shall fall. [9] I will make you a perpetual desolation, and your cities shall not be inhabited. Then you will know that I am the LORD.

10 "Because you said, 'These two nations and these two countries shall be mine, and we will take possession of them,'–although the LORD was there– [11] therefore, as I live, says the Lord GOD, I will deal with you according to the anger and envy which you showed because of your hatred against them; and I will make myself known among you,[a] when I judge you. [12] And you shall know that I, the LORD, have heard all the revilings which you uttered against the mountains of Israel, saying, 'They are laid desolate, they are given us to devour.' [13] And you magnified yourselves against me with your mouth, and multiplied your words against me; I heard it. [14] Thus says the Lord GOD: For the rejoicing of the whole earth I will make you desolate. [15] As you rejoiced over the inheritance of the house of Israel, because it was desolate, so I will deal with you; you shall be desolate, Mount Se'ir, and all Edom, all of it. Then they will know that I am the LORD.

36 "And you, son of man, prophesy to the mountains of Israel, and say, O mountains of Israel, hear the word of the LORD. [2] Thus says the Lord GOD: Because the enemy said of you, 'Aha!' and, 'The ancient heights have become our possession,' [3] therefore prophesy, and say, Thus says the

Lord GOD: Because, yea, because they made you desolate, and crushed you from all sides, so that you became the possession of the rest of the nations, and you became the talk and evil gossip of the people; [4] therefore, O mountains of Israel, hear the word of the Lord GOD: Thus says the Lord GOD to the mountains and the hills, the ravines and the valleys, the desolate wastes and the deserted cities, which have become a prey and derision to the rest of the nations round about; [5] therefore thus says the Lord GOD: I speak in my hot jealousy against the rest of the nations, and against all Edom, who gave my land to themselves as a possession with wholehearted joy and utter contempt, that they might possess[b] it and plunder it. [6] Therefore prophesy concerning the land of Israel, and say to the mountains and hills, to the ravines and valleys, Thus says the Lord GOD: Behold, I speak in my jealous wrath, because you have suffered the reproach of the nations; [7] therefore thus says the Lord GOD: I swear that the nations that are round about you shall themselves suffer reproach.

8 "But you, O mountains of Israel, shall shoot forth your branches, and yield your fruit to my people Israel; for they will soon come home. [9] For, behold, I am for you, and I will turn to you, and you shall be tilled and sown; [10] and I will multiply men upon you, the whole house of Israel, all of it; the cities shall be inhabited and the waste places rebuilt; [11] and I will multiply upon you man and beast; and they shall increase and be fruitful; and I will cause you to be inhabited as in your former times, and will do more good to you than ever before. Then you

z Gk: Heb *you have hated blood*
a Gk: Heb *them*
b One Ms: Heb *drive out*

forever desolate. *Mount Seir* is the plateau rising east of the Arabah in which Sela, the Edomite capital, was located.

36.1–39.29: The new Israel. 36.1–38: Prophecy to the mountains of Israel; the restoration of Israel. 36.1–7: Mountains of Israel, the highlands, represent all Israel (Dt.3.25). Though dispossessed by *Edom* (35.1–15) and surrounding nations (Neh.2.19), Israel will be restored to her heritage (Mal.1.2–5). **8–15:** The land will surpass its pristine productivity (*at your beginnings*,

will know that I am the LORD. ¹² Yea, I will let men walk upon you, even my people Israel; and they shall possess you, and you shall be their inheritance, and you shall no longer bereave them of children. ¹³ Thus says the Lord GOD: Because men say to you, 'You devour men, and you bereave your nation of children,' ¹⁴ therefore you shall no longer devour men and no longer bereave your nation of children, says the Lord GOD; ¹⁵ and I will not let you hear any more the reproach of the nations, and you shall no longer bear the disgrace of the peoples and no longer cause your nation to stumble, says the Lord GOD."

16 The word of the LORD came to me: ¹⁷ "Son of man, when the house of Israel dwelt in their own land, they defiled it by their ways and their doings; their conduct before me was like the uncleanness of a woman in her impurity. ¹⁸ So I poured out my wrath upon them for the blood which they had shed in the land, for the idols with which they had defiled it. ¹⁹ I scattered them among the nations, and they were dispersed through the countries; in accordance with their conduct and their deeds I judged them. ²⁰ But when they came to the nations, wherever they came, they profaned my holy name, in that men said of them, 'These are the people of the LORD, and yet they had to go out of his land.' ²¹ But I had concern for my holy name, which the house of Israel caused to be profaned among the nations to which they came.

22 "Therefore say to the house of Israel, Thus says the Lord GOD: It is not for your sake, O house of Israel, that I am about to act, but for the sake of my holy name, which you have profaned among the nations to which you came. ²³ And I will vindicate the holiness of my great name, which has been profaned among the nations, and which you have profaned among them; and the nations will know that I am the LORD, says the Lord GOD, when through you I vindicate my holiness before their eyes. ²⁴ For I will take you from the nations, and gather you from all the countries, and bring you into your own land. ²⁵ I will sprinkle clean water upon you, and you shall be clean from all your uncleannesses, and from all your idols I will cleanse you. ²⁶ A new heart I will give you, and a new spirit I will put within you; and I will take out of your flesh the heart of stone and give you a heart of flesh. ²⁷ And I will put my spirit within you, and cause you to walk in my statutes and be careful to observe my ordinances. ²⁸ You shall dwell in the land which I gave to your fathers; and you shall be my people, and I will be your God. ²⁹ And I will deliver you from all your uncleannesses; and I will summon the grain and make it abundant and lay no famine upon you. ³⁰ I will make the fruit of the tree and the increase of the field abundant, that you may never again suffer the disgrace of famine among the nations. ³¹ Then you will remember your evil ways, and your deeds that were not good; and you will loathe yourselves for your iniquities and your abominable deeds. ³² It is not for your sake that I will act, says the Lord GOD; let that be known to you. Be ashamed and confounded for your ways, O house of Israel.

33 "Thus says the Lord GOD: On the day that I cleanse you from all

---

the Exodus; Hos.11.1–4; Jer.2.1–3). **14:** *No longer devour men,* the hilltops will not serve again as fertility cult sanctuaries (6.1–14; Dt.12.1–3,29–31), perhaps involving human sacrifices. **16–21:** The land was defiled by Israel's offering of pagan sacrifices, thereby profaning God's name (Lev.18.21; 20.3). **17:** *Uncleanness,* due to menstruation (18.6; Lev.15.19–30). **22–32:** As in ch. 20, God reminds Israel that he will restore them, his people (Ex.6.7; Lev.20.24), for the sake of his name; like Ezekiel (12.6; 24.27) they will be a sign, for all nations. **26:** The *new heart* (18.31) will be created by God's spirit (ch. 37; Is.44.3; Rom.8.3–6); he will *cleanse* them (Ex.30.17–21), for man cannot make himself clean. **33–36:** The skeptical nations (v. 20) will recognize Israel's restoration (Jer.31.23–28) as God's act. **37–38:** *Like a flock,* see ch. 34.

your iniquities, I will cause the cities to be inhabited, and the waste places shall be rebuilt: [34] And the land that was desolate shall be tilled, instead of being the desolation that it was in the sight of all who passed by. [35] And they will say, 'This land that was desolate has become like the garden of Eden; and the waste and desolate and ruined cities are now inhabited and fortified.' [36] Then the nations that are left round about you shall know that I, the LORD, have rebuilt the ruined places, and replanted that which was desolate; I, the LORD, have spoken, and I will do it.

37 "Thus says the Lord GOD: This also I will let the house of Israel ask me to do for them: to increase their men like a flock. [38] Like the flock for sacrifices,[c] like the flock at Jerusalem during her appointed feasts, so shall the waste cities be filled with flocks of men. Then they will know that I am the LORD."

37 The hand of the LORD was upon me, and he brought me out by the Spirit of the LORD, and set me down in the midst of the valley;[d] it was full of bones. [2] And he led me round among them; and behold, there were very many upon the valley;[d] and lo, they were very dry. [3] And he said to me, "Son of man, can these bones live?" And I answered, "O Lord GOD, thou knowest." [4] Again he said to me, "Prophesy to these bones, and say to them, O dry bones, hear the word of the LORD. [5] Thus says the Lord GOD to these bones: Behold, I will cause breath[e] to enter you, and you shall live. [6] And I will lay sinews upon you, and will cause flesh to come upon you, and cover you with skin, and put breath[e] in you, and you shall live; and you shall know that I am the LORD."

7 So I prophesied as I was com-

manded; and as I prophesied, there was a noise, and behold, a rattling; and the bones came together, bone to its bone. [8] And as I looked, there were sinews on them, and flesh had come upon them, and skin had covered them; but there was no breath in them. [9] Then he said to me, "Prophesy to the breath, prophesy, son of man, and say to the breath,[f] Thus says the Lord GOD: Come from the four winds, O breath,[f] and breathe upon these slain, that they may live." [10] So I prophesied as he commanded me, and the breath came into them, and they lived, and stood upon their feet, an exceedingly great host.

11 Then he said to me, "Son of man, these bones are the whole house of Israel. Behold, they say, 'Our bones are dried up, and our hope is lost; we are clean cut off.' [12] Therefore prophesy, and say to them, Thus says the Lord GOD: Behold, I will open your graves, and raise you from your graves, O my people; and I will bring you home into the land of Israel. [13] And you shall know that I am the LORD, when I open your graves, and raise you from your graves, O my people. [14] And I will put my Spirit within you, and you shall live, and I will place you in your own land; then you shall know that I, the LORD, have spoken, and I have done it, says the LORD."

15 The word of the LORD came to me: [16] "Son of man, take a stick and write on it, 'For Judah, and the children of Israel associated with him'; then take another stick and write upon it, 'For Joseph (the stick of E'phraim) and all the house of Israel associated with him'; [17] and join them together

c Heb *flock of holy things*   d Or *plain*
e Or *spirit*   f Or *wind* or *spirit*

37.1–14: Vision of the valley of dry bones. 1: *Valley*, "plain" in 3.22; 8.4. The *bones* are the exiles, who have no more hope of resuscitating the kingdom of Israel than of putting flesh on a skeleton and calling it to life. **9:** Hebrew "rûah" means "spirit, breath, wind"; thus there is a constant word-play here. *Four winds* may refer to God's omnipresence (1.17). **14:** This vision has no direct connection with the Christian doctrine of resurrection.

37.15–28: Oracle of the two sticks (Zech.11.7–14) envisions the re-unification of the long-divided land and the establishment of a united Israel, ruled by one king; then the situation

into one stick, that they may become one in your hand. ¹⁸ And when your people say to you, 'Will you not show us what you mean by these?' ¹⁹ say to them, Thus says the Lord GOD: Behold, I am about to take the stick of Joseph (which is in the hand of E'phraim) and the tribes of Israel associated with him; and I will join*g* with it the stick of Judah, and make them one stick, that they may be one in my hand. ²⁰ When the sticks on which you write are in your hand before their eyes, ²¹ then say to them, Thus says the Lord GOD: Behold, I will take the people of Israel from the nations among which they have gone, and will gather them from all sides, and bring them to their own land; ²² and I will make them one nation in the land, upon the mountains of Israel; and one king shall be king over them all; and they shall be no longer two nations, and no longer divided into two kingdoms. ²³ They shall not defile themselves any more with their idols and their detestable things, or with any of their transgressions; but I will save them from all the backslidings in which they have sinned, and will cleanse them; and they shall be my people, and I will be their God.

24 "My servant David shall be king over them; and they shall all have one shepherd. They shall follow my ordinances and be careful to observe my statutes. ²⁵ They shall dwell in the land where your fathers dwelt that I

gave to my servant Jacob; they and their children and their children's children shall dwell there for ever; and David my servant shall be their prince for ever. ²⁶ I will make a covenant of peace with them; it shall be an everlasting covenant with them; and I will bless*h* them and multiply them, and will set my sanctuary in the midst of them for evermore. ²⁷ My dwelling place shall be with them; and I will be their God, and they shall be my people. ²⁸ Then the nations will know that I the LORD sanctify Israel, when my sanctuary is in the midst of them for evermore."

38 The word of the LORD came to me: ² "Son of man, set your face toward Gog, of the land of Magog, the chief prince of Meshech and Tubal, and prophesy against him ³ and say, Thus says the Lord GOD: Behold, I am against you, O Gog, chief prince of Meshech and Tubal; ⁴ and I will turn you about, and put hooks into your jaws, and I will bring you forth, and all your army, horses and horsemen, all of them clothed in full armor, a great company, all of them with buckler and shield, wielding swords; ⁵ Persia, Cush, and Put are with them, all of them with shield and helmet; ⁶ Gomer and all his hordes; Beth-togar'mah from the uttermost parts of the north with all his hordes–many peoples are with you.

7 "Be ready and keep ready, you

g Heb *join them*   *h* Tg: Heb *give*

---

earlier predicted will prevail (34.28): law-abiding living (11.20) in the promised land (28.25) under the Davidic king (34.23–24); the covenant of peace (34.25); and the re-established central sanctuary (45.1–8). **25:** *Prince,* the king (compare 12.10; 34.24).

38.1–39.29: The Gog and Magog oracles describe in apocalyptic language the coming of the foe from the north (38.15; Jer.6.22) against God's people living peacefully in the promised land (38.8,11–12). After a cataclysmic battle the aggressor forces will be completely defeated, and God will be acknowledged by all nations as the undisputed victor (38.23; 39.21–29; 36.22–23). Since the foe from the north in Jeremiah (Jer.25.9) and Ezekiel (Ezek.26.7) was Babylon, it is probable that the foe here described is a grandiose surrogate for Babylon. The conflict is that preceding the fall of Babylon, and the victory includes Israel's restoration to its land (34.11–16; 36.8–38; Jer.31.23–28). The limited scope and goal of these oracles has been expanded to cosmic proportions by the writer of Rev.20.7–10. **38.1–9:** *Gog,* king of *Magog,* both unidentified, though general location is in the north. *Meshech,* Assyrian "Mushku," south of Gomer, west of the Anti-Taurus mountains (27.13). *Tubal,* Assyrian "Tabal," south of Beth-togarmah, east of the Anti-Taurus mountains. *Cush,* Ethiopia. *Put,* see 30.5 n. *Gomer,* Assyrian "Gimirrai," Cimmerians in central Asia Minor (Gen.10.2–3). *Beth-togarmah,* Assyrian "Til-garimmu," east of the

and all the hosts that are assembled about you, and be a guard for them. [8] After many days you will be mustered; in the latter years you will go against the land that is restored from war, the land where people were gathered from many nations upon the mountains of Israel, which had been a continual waste; its people were brought out from the nations and now dwell securely, all of them. [9] You will advance, coming on like a storm, you will be like a cloud covering the land, you and all your hordes, and many peoples with you.

10 "Thus says the Lord GOD: On that day thoughts will come into your mind, and you will devise an evil scheme [11] and say, 'I will go up against the land of unwalled villages; I will fall upon the quiet people who dwell securely, all of them dwelling without walls, and having no bars or gates'; [12] to seize spoil and carry off plunder; to assail the waste places which are now inhabited, and the people who were gathered from the nations, who have gotten cattle and goods, who dwell at the center of the earth. [13] Sheba and Dedan and the merchants of Tarshish and all its villages will say to you, 'Have you come to seize spoil? Have you assembled your hosts to carry off plunder, to carry away silver and gold, to take away cattle and goods, to seize great spoil?'

14 "Therefore, son of man, prophesy, and say to Gog, Thus says the Lord GOD: On that day when my people Israel are dwelling securely, you will bestir yourself[i] [15] and come from your place out of the uttermost parts of the north, you and many peoples with you, all of them riding on horses, a great host, a mighty army; [16] you will come up against my people Israel, like a cloud covering the land. In the latter days I will bring you against my land, that the nations may know me, when through you, O Gog, I vindicate my holiness before their eyes.

17 "Thus says the Lord GOD: Are you he of whom I spoke in former days by my servants the prophets of Israel, who in those days prophesied for years that I would bring you against them? [18] But on that day, when Gog shall come against the land of Israel, says the Lord GOD, my wrath will be roused. [19] For in my jealousy and in my blazing wrath I declare, On that day there shall be a great shaking in the land of Israel; [20] the fish of the sea, and the birds of the air, and beasts of the field, and all creeping things that creep on the ground, and all the men that are upon the face of the earth, shall quake at my presence, and the mountains shall be thrown down, and the cliffs shall fall, and every wall shall tumble to the ground. [21] I will summon every kind of terror[j] against Gog,[k] says the Lord GOD; every man's sword will be against his brother. [22] With pestilence and bloodshed I will enter into judgment with him; and I will rain upon him and his hordes and the many peoples that are with him, torrential rains and hailstones, fire and brimstone. [23] So I will show my greatness and my holiness and make myself known in the eyes of many nations. Then they will know that I am the LORD.

39 "And you, son of man, prophesy against Gog, and say, Thus says the Lord GOD· Behold, I am against you, O Gog, chief prince

i Gk: Heb *will you not know?*
j Gk: Heb *a sword to all my mountains*
k Heb *him*

southernmost Halys River, southeast of Gomer (27.14). Though people and places in apocalyptic literature can often be identified, they are part of the literary equipment and should rarely be taken literally. *In the latter years* corresponds to "in the latter days" (Hos.3.5; Jer. 30.24) before the re-establishment of David's line (34.23–24; Jer.23.5–6). **10–23:** The plot against God's defenseless people is doomed to defeat. God will marshal all the forces of nature against Gog (Ps.18.7–15; Is.24.18–20; 30.27–33; Jl.2.28–32). **12:** *Center*, see 5.5 n. **13:** *Sheba*, 27.22. *Dedan*, 25.13. *Tarshish*, see Jer.10.9 n.

39.1–20: Gog's defeat. The magnitude of the opposing forces, and thus of God's victory, is

of Meshech and Tubal; 2 and I will turn you about and drive you forward, and bring you up from the uttermost parts of the north, and lead you against the mountains of Israel; 3 then I will strike your bow from your left hand, and will make your arrows drop out of your right hand. 4 You shall fall upon the mountains of Israel, you and all your hordes and the peoples that are with you; I will give you to birds of prey of every sort and to the wild beasts to be devoured. 5 You shall fall in the open field; for I have spoken, says the Lord GOD. 6 I will send fire on Magog and on those who dwell securely in the coastlands; and they shall know that I am the LORD.

7 "And my holy name I will make known in the midst of my people Israel; and I will not let my holy name be profaned any more; and the nations shall know that I am the LORD, the Holy One in Israel. 8 Behold, it is coming and it will be brought about, says the Lord GOD. That is the day of which I have spoken.

9 "Then those who dwell in the cities of Israel will go forth and make fires of the weapons and burn them, shields and bucklers, bows and arrows, handpikes and spears, and they will make fires of them for seven years; 10 so that they will not need to take wood out of the field or cut down any out of the forests, for they will make their fires of the weapons; they will despoil those who despoiled them, and plunder those who plundered them, says the Lord GOD.

11 "On that day I will give to Gog a place for burial in Israel, the Valley of the Travelers*l* east of the sea; it will block the travelers, for there Gog and all his multitude will be buried; it will be called the Valley of Hamon-gog.*m* 12 For seven months the house of Israel will be burying them, in order to cleanse the land. 13 All the people of the land will bury them; and it will redound to their honor on the day that I show my glory, says the Lord GOD. 14 They will set apart men to pass through the land continually and bury*n* those remaining upon the face of the land, so as to cleanse it; at the end of seven months they will make their search. 15 And when these pass through the land and any one sees a man's bone, then he shall set up a sign by it, till the buriers have buried it in the Valley of Hamon-gog. 16 (A city Hamo'nah*o* is there also.) Thus shall they cleanse the land.

17 "As for you, son of man, thus says the Lord GOD: Speak to the birds of every sort and to all beasts of the field, 'Assemble and come, gather from all sides to the sacrificial feast which I am preparing for you, a great sacrificial feast upon the mountains of Israel, and you shall eat flesh and drink blood. 18 You shall eat the flesh of the mighty, and drink the blood of the princes of the earth–of rams, of lambs, and of goats, of bulls, all of them fatlings of Bashan. 19 And you shall eat fat till you are filled, and drink blood till you are drunk, at the sacrificial feast which I am preparing for you. 20 And you shall be filled at my table with horses and riders, with mighty men and all kinds of warriors,' says the Lord GOD.

21 "And I will set my glory among the nations; and all the nations shall see my judgment which I have executed, and my hand which I have laid on them. 22 The house of Israel shall know that I am the LORD their God, from that day forward. 23 And the nations shall know that the house of Israel went into captivity for their iniquity, because they dealt so

l Or *Abarim*   *m* That is *the multitude of Gog*
n Gk Syr: Heb *bury the travelers*
o That is *Multitude*

---

emphasized by the huge quantities of war material (enough *wood* for fuel for *seven years*) and by the *seven months* required to remove the enemy dead to the region east of the Dead Sea. The slaughter of those who dared oppose God and oppress his people is regarded as a sacrifice to God's glory. **21–29:** Conclusion of the oracles–the victory and restoration told in familiar terms (5.8; 28.26; 34.30).

treacherously with me that I hid my face from them and gave them into the hand of their adversaries, and they all fell by the sword. ²⁴ I dealt with them according to their uncleanness and their transgressions, and hid my face from them.

25 "Therefore thus says the Lord GOD: Now I will restore the fortunes of Jacob, and have mercy upon the whole house of Israel; and I will be jealous for my holy name. ²⁶ They shall forget their shame, and all the treachery they have practiced against me, when they dwell securely in their land with none to make them afraid, ²⁷ when I have brought them back from the peoples and gathered them from their enemies' lands, and through them have vindicated my holiness in the sight of many nations. ²⁸ Then they shall know that I am the LORD their God because I sent them into exile among the nations, and then gathered them into their own land. I will leave none of them remaining among the nations any more; ²⁹ and I will not hide my face any more from them, when I pour out my Spirit upon the house of Israel, says the Lord GOD."

40 In the twenty-fifth year of our exile, at the beginning of the year, on the tenth day of the month, in the fourteenth year after the city was conquered, on that very day, the hand of the LORD was upon me, ² and brought me in the visions of God into the land of Israel, and set me down upon a very high mountain, on which was a structure like a city opposite me.*p* ³ When he brought me there, behold, there was a man, whose appearance was like bronze, with a line of flax and a measuring reed in his hand; and he was standing in the gateway. ⁴ And the man said to me, "Son of man, look with your eyes, and hear with your ears, and set your mind upon all that I shall show you, for you were brought here in order that I might show it to you; declare all that you see to the house of Israel."

5 And behold, there was a wall all around the outside of the temple area, and the length of the measuring reed in the man's hand was six long cubits, each being a cubit and a handbreadth in length; so he measured the thickness of the wall, one reed; and the height, one reed. ⁶ Then he went into the gateway facing east, going up its steps, and measured the threshold of the gate, one reed deep;*q* ⁷ and the side rooms, one reed long, and one reed broad; and the space between the side rooms, five cubits; and the threshold of the gate by the vestibule of the gate at the inner end, one reed. ⁸ Then he measured the vestibule of the gateway, eight cubits; ⁹ and its jambs, two cubits; and the vestibule of the gate was at the inner end. ¹⁰ And there were three side rooms on either side of the east gate; the three were of the same size; and the jambs on either side were of the same size. ¹¹ Then he measured the breadth of

p Gk: Heb *on the south*
q Heb *deep, and one threshold, one reed deep*

40.1–48.35: The vision of the restored temple and land. This section is really a continuation of the theme of chs. 33–39, but because of its unified description of Israel's religious and political restoration it may be separated from the less homogeneous preceding section. The temple, though somewhat idealized, is the Solomonic temple, in which Ezekiel probably served as priest before his exile (1.3) and which was destroyed in 587 B.C. **40.1–47: The temple area, gates, outer and inner courts. 1–5:** April 28, 573 B.C. On the twenty-fifth anniversary of his exile, Ezekiel is transported in a vision (compare 8.2–3) to the temple mountain (*very high mountain*, 17.22; Mic.4.1). **3:** The *reed* was about ten feet, four inches long. **5:** The *long cubit* was about 20.68 inches; the ordinary cubit was about 17.5 inches. The equal height and width of the outer retaining wall corresponds to the symmetry of the enclosure itself (42.16–20). **6–16:** The detailed description of the east or processional gate (10.19) makes it possible to compare it with Solomonic gateways found at Megiddo, Gezer, and Hazor, all having the same design and essentially the same dimensions. After ascending seven steps (vv. 22,26) one came to the temple gate which had a double entrance vestibule, the second narrower than the first,

the opening of the gateway, ten cubits; and the breadth of the gateway, thirteen cubits. [12] There was a barrier before the side rooms, one cubit on either side; and the side rooms were six cubits on either side. [13] Then he measured the gate from the back[r] of the one side room to the back[r] of the other, a breadth of five and twenty cubits, from door to door. [14] He measured also the vestibule, twenty cubits; and round about the vestibule of the gateway was the court.[s] [15] From the front of the gate at the entrance to the end of the inner vestibule of the gate was fifty cubits. [16] And the gateway had windows round about, narrowing inwards into their jambs in the side rooms, and likewise the vestibule had windows round about inside, and on the jambs were palm trees.

17 Then he brought me into the outer court; and behold, there were chambers and a pavement, round about the court; thirty chambers fronted on the pavement. [18] And the pavement ran along the side of the gates, corresponding to the length of the gates; this was the lower pavement. [19] Then he measured the distance from the inner front of[t] the lower gate to the outer front of the inner court, a hundred cubits.

Then he went before me to the north, [20] and behold, there was a gate[u] which faced toward the north, belonging to the outer court. He measured its length and its breadth. [21] Its side rooms, three on either side, and its jambs and its vestibule were of the same size as those of the first gate; its length was fifty cubits, and its breadth twenty-five cubits. [22] And its windows, its vestibule, and its palm trees were of the same size as those of the gate which faced toward the east; and seven steps led up to it; and its vestibule was on the inside. [23] And opposite the gate on the north, as on the east, was a gate to the inner court; and he measured from gate to gate, a hundred cubits.

24 And he led me toward the south, and behold, there was a gate on the south; and he measured its jambs and its vestibule; they had the same size as the others. [25] And there were windows round about in it and in its vestibule, like the windows of the others; its length was fifty cubits, and its breadth twenty-five cubits. [26] And there were seven steps leading up to it, and its vestibule was on the inside; and it had palm trees on its jambs, one on either side. [27] And there was a gate on the south of the inner court; and he measured from gate to gate toward the south, a hundred cubits.

28 Then he brought me to the inner court by the south gate, and he measured the south gate; it was of the same size as the others. [29] Its side rooms, its jambs, and its vestibule were of the same size as the others; and there were windows round about in it and in its vestibule; its length was fifty cubits, and its breadth twenty-five cubits. [30] And there were vestibules round about, twenty-five cubits long and five cubits broad. [31] Its vestibule faced the outer court, and palm trees were on its jambs, and its stairway had eight steps.

32 Then he brought me to the inner

r Compare Gk: Heb *roof*
s Compare Gk: Heb *and he made the jambs sixty cubits, and to the jamb of the court was the gateway round about*
t Compare Gk: Heb *from before*
u Gk: Heb *a hundred cubits on the east and on the north.* [20]*And the gate*

---

and closed off from the interior by doors. The wall joined the gate at the entrance vestibules; the remainder of the gate extended into the outer court. The interior had three chambers, or guardrooms, on either side separated by heavy piers. Passing the last pier, one entered the outer court, or possibly first into an inner vestibule and then the outer court. The side chambers had back doors opening into the outer court. The windows, as the temple itself, were of Phoenician, or Tyrian, design, narrowing inwards. Palm trees were a common Near Eastern decorative motif. **17–19:** The thirty chambers were probably for the use of people and Levites worshiping in the outer court. **20–27:** Northern and southern gates were similar to the east gate. **28–37:** Eight steps above the outer court were the gates leading to the inner court corresponding to

court on the east side, and he measured the gate; it was of the same size as the others. 33 Its side rooms, its jambs, and its vestibule were of the same size as the others; and there were windows round about in it and in its vestibule; its length was fifty cubits, and its breadth twenty-five cubits. 34 Its vestibule faced the outer court, and it had palm trees on its jambs, one on either side; and its stairway had eight steps.

35 Then he brought me to the north gate, and he measured it; it had the same size as the others. 36 Its side rooms, its jambs, and its vestibule were of the same size as the others;*v* and it had windows round about; its length was fifty cubits, and its breadth twenty-five cubits. 37 Its vestibule*w* faced the outer court, and it had palm trees on its jambs, one on either side; and its stairway had eight steps.

38 There was a chamber with its door in the vestibule of the gate,*x* where the burnt offering was to be washed. 39 And in the vestibule of the gate were two tables on either side, on which the burnt offering and the sin offering and the guilt offering were to be slaughtered. 40 And on the outside of the vestibule*y* at the entrance of the north gate were two tables; and on the other side of the vestibule of the gate were two tables. 41 Four tables were on the inside, and four tables on the outside of the side of the gate, eight tables, on which the sacrifices were to be slaughtered. 42 And there were also four tables of hewn stone for the burnt offering, a cubit and a half long, and a cubit and a half broad, and one cubit high, on which the instruments were to be laid with which the burnt offerings and the sacrifices were slaughtered.

43 And hooks, a handbreadth long, were fastened round about within. And on the tables the flesh of the offering was to be laid.

44 Then he brought me from without into the inner court, and behold, there were two chambers*z* in the inner court, one*a* at the side of the north gate facing south, the other at the side of the south*b* gate facing north. 45 And he said to me, This chamber which faces south is for the priests who have charge of the temple, 46 and the chamber which faces north is for the priests who have charge of the altar; these are the sons of Zadok, who alone among the sons of Levi may come near to the LORD to minister to him. 47 And he measured the court, a hundred cubits long, and a hundred cubits broad, foursquare; and the altar was in front of the temple.

48 Then he brought me to the vestibule of the temple and measured the jambs of the vestibule, five cubits on either side; and the breadth of the gate was fourteen cubits; and the side-walls of the gate were three cubits*c* on either side. 49 The length of the vestibule was twenty cubits, and the breadth twelve*d* cubits; and ten steps led up*e* to it; and there were pillars beside the jambs on either side.

41 Then he brought me to the nave, and measured the jambs; on each side six cubits was the breadth of the jambs.*f* 2 And the breadth of the en-

v One Ms Compare verses 29 and 33: Heb lacks *were of the same size as the others*
w Gk Vg Compare verses 26, 31, 34: Heb *jambs*
x Cn: Heb *at the jambs of the gates*
y Cn: Heb *to him who goes up*
z Gk: Heb *and from without to the inner gate were chambers for singers*
a Gk: Heb *which*
b Gk: Heb *east*
c Gk: Heb *and the breadth of the gate was three cubits*
d Gk: Heb *eleven*
e Gk: Heb *and by steps which went up*
f Compare Gk: Heb *tent*

those leading to the outer court. The temple was built on a succession of terraces. **38–43:** At the east gate leading to the inner court were the facilities for the preparation of the sacrifices (Lev.1.1–7.38). **44–47:** On the north and south sides of the square inner court were buildings for the use of the Zadokite priests (43.19; 44.15–16).

    40.48–41.26: The temple arrangements. 48–49: The temple was ten steps (about ten feet; see 41.8) above the level of the inner court. In front of the vestibule were Solomon's free-standing pillars (1 Kg.7.15–22). **41.1–4:** The tripartite temple division is known also from the thirteenth century Canaanite temple at Hazor and the eighth century temple at Tell Tainat (Hattina) in

trance was ten cubits; and the sidewalls of the entrance were five cubits on either side; and he measured the length of the nave forty cubits, and its breadth, twenty cubits. ³ Then he went into the inner room and measured the jambs of the entrance, two cubits; and the breadth of the entrance, six cubits; and the sidewalls*g* of the entrance, seven cubits. ⁴ And he measured the length of the room, twenty cubits, and its breadth, twenty cubits, beyond the nave. And he said to me, This is the most holy place.

5 Then he measured the wall of the temple, six cubits thick; and the breadth of the side chambers, four cubits, round about the temple. ⁶ And the side chambers were in three stories, one over another, thirty in each story. There were offsets*h* all around the wall of the temple to serve as supports for the side chambers, so that they should not be supported by the wall of the temple. ⁷ And the side chambers became broader as they rose*i* from story to story, corresponding to the enlargement of the offset*j* from story to story round about the temple; on the side of the temple a stairway led upward, and thus one went up from the lowest story to the top story through the middle story. ⁸ I saw also that the temple had a raised platform round about; the foundations of the side chambers measured a full reed of six long cubits. ⁹ The thickness of the outer wall of the side chambers was five cubits; and the part of the platform which was left free was five cubits.*k* Between the platform*l* of the temple and the ¹⁰ chambers of the court was a breadth of twenty cubits round about the temple on every side. ¹¹ And the doors of the side chambers opened on the part of the platform that

was left free, one door toward the north, and another door toward the south; and the breadth of the part that was left free was five cubits round about.

12 The building that was facing the temple yard on the west side was seventy cubits broad; and the wall of the building was five cubits thick round about, and its length ninety cubits.

13 Then he measured the temple, a hundred cubits long; and the yard and the building with its walls, a hundred cubits long; ¹⁴ also the breadth of the east front of the temple and the yard, a hundred cubits.

15 Then he measured the length of the building facing the yard which was at the west and its walls*m* on either side, a hundred cubits.

The nave of the temple and the inner room and the outer*n* vestibule ¹⁶ were paneled*o* and round about all three had windows with recessed*p* frames. Over against the threshold the temple was paneled with wood round about, from the floor up to the windows (now the windows were covered), ¹⁷ to the space above the door, even to the inner room, and on the outside. And on all the walls round about in the inner room and the nave were carved likenesses*q* ¹⁸ of cherubim and palm trees, a palm tree between cherub and cherub. Every cherub had two faces: ¹⁹ the face of a man toward the palm tree on the one side, and the face of a young lion toward the palm tree on the other side. They were carved on the

g Gk: Heb *breadth*
h Gk Compare 1 Kg 6.6: Heb *they entered*
i Cn: Heb *it was surrounded*
j Gk: Heb *for the encompassing of the temple*
k Syr: Heb lacks *five cubits*
l Cn: Heb *house of the side chambers*
m Cn: The meaning of the Hebrew term is unknown
n Gk: Heb *of the court* *o* Gk: Heb *the thresholds*
p Cn Compare Gk 1 Kg 6.4: The meaning of the Hebrew term is unknown
q Cn: Heb *measures and carved*

northern Syria. *The vestibule* (40.48–49) was 35½ by 20½ feet; *the nave* (41.1–2), 35½ by 71 feet; and *the inner room* (41.3–4), or *most holy place,* which Ezekiel did not enter (Lev.16.1–34), 35½ by 35½ feet (1 Kg.6.1–8.66; Ex.26.31–37). **5–11:** The three tiers of thirty chambers per tier on the sides of the temple (1 Kg.6.5–10) were probably for equipment for the temple services, storage, and the temple treasures (1 Kg.14.26; 2 Kg.14.14). **12–15a:** The purpose of the auxiliary building is unknown; earlier it may have served as a stable for sacred horses, now removed (2 Kg.23.11). **15b–26:** The windows were like those in the gates (40.16); for the

whole temple round about; [20] from the floor to above the door cherubim and palm trees were carved on the wall.[r]

21 The doorposts of the nave were squared; and in front of the holy place was something resembling [22] an altar of wood, three cubits high, two cubits long, and two cubits broad;[s] its corners, its base,[t] and its walls were of wood. He said to me, "This is the table which is before the LORD." [23] The nave and the holy place had each a double door. [24] The doors had two leaves apiece, two swinging leaves for each door. [25] And on the doors of the nave were carved cherubim and palm trees, such as were carved on the walls; and there was a canopy of wood in front of the vestibule outside. [26] And there were recessed windows and palm trees on either side, on the sidewalls of the vestibule.[u]

42 Then he led me out into the inner[v] court, toward the north, and he brought me to the chambers which were opposite the temple yard and opposite the building on the north. [2] The length of the building which was on the north side[w] was[x] a hundred cubits, and the breadth fifty cubits. [3] Adjoining the twenty cubits which belonged to the inner court, and facing the pavement which belonged to the outer court, was gallery[y] against gallery[y] in three stories. [4] And before the chambers was a passage inward, ten cubits wide and a hundred cubits long,[z] and their doors were on the north. [5] Now the upper chambers were narrower, for the galleries[y] took more away from them than from the lower and middle chambers in the building. [6] For they were in three stories, and they had no pillars like the pillars of

the outer[a] court; hence the upper chambers were set back from the ground more than the lower and the middle ones. [7] And there was a wall outside parallel to the chambers, toward the outer court, opposite the chambers, fifty cubits long. [8] For the chambers on the outer court were fifty cubits long, while those opposite the temple were a hundred cubits long. [9] Below these chambers was an entrance on the east side, as one enters them from the outer court, [10] where the outside wall begins.[b]

On the south[c] also, opposite the yard and opposite the building, there were chambers [11] with a passage in front of them; they were similar to the chambers on the north, of the same length and breadth, with the same exits[d] and arrangements and doors. [12] And below the south chambers was an entrance on the east side, where one enters the passage, and opposite them was a dividing wall.[e]

13 Then he said to me, "The north chambers and the south chambers opposite the yard are the holy chambers, where the priests who approach the LORD shall eat the most holy offerings; there they shall put the most holy offerings–the cereal offering, the sin offering, and the guilt offering, for the place is holy. [14] When the priests enter the holy place, they shall not go out of it into the outer court without

r Cn Compare verse 25: Heb *and the wall*
s Gk: Heb lacks *two cubits broad*   t Gk: Heb *length*
u Cn: Heb *vestibule. And the side chambers of the temple and the canopies*   v Gk: Heb *outer*
w Gk: Heb *door*   x Gk: Heb *before the length*
y The meaning of the Hebrew word is unknown
z Gk Syr: Heb *a way of one cubit*
a Gk: Heb lacks *outer*
b Cn: Heb *And in the breadth of the wall of the court*   c Gk: Heb *east*
d Heb *and all their exits*
e Cn: Heb *And according to the entrances of the chambers that were toward the south was an entrance at the head of the way, the way before the dividing wall toward the east as one enters them*

decorative motifs, see 1 Kg.6.29–30; on the *cherubim*, see 1.5 n. **22:** The *table* (perhaps for the bread of the Presence), see 1 Kg.6.20–22; Lev.24.5–9.

42.1–14: The priests' chambers. The description is unclear. Perhaps the three stories of chambers were arranged terrace-fashion against the north and south terrace-walls retaining the inner court, with staircases leading to the upper stories and halls on each level into which the chamber doors opened. A second, smaller, apartment-building was opposite, on the outer court side. In them the priests were to store their share of the sacrifices (44.28–31; Lev.2.1–10; 7.7–10), eat their meals, and leave the garments they wore for the services before entering the outer

laying there the garments in which they minister, for these are holy; they shall put on other garments before they go near to that which is for the people."

15 Now when he had finished measuring the interior of the temple area, he led me out by the gate which faced east, and measured the temple area round about. [16] He measured the east side with the measuring reed, five hundred cubits by the measuring reed. [17] Then he turned and measured[f] the north side, five hundred cubits by the measuring reed. [18] Then he turned and measured[f] the south side, five hundred cubits by the measuring reed. [19] Then he turned to the west side and measured, five hundred cubits by the measuring reed. [20] He measured it on the four sides. It had a wall around it, five hundred cubits long and five hundred cubits broad, to make a separation between the holy and the common.

43 Afterward he brought me to the gate, the gate facing east. [2] And behold, the glory of the God of Israel came from the east; and the sound of his coming was like the sound of many waters; and the earth shone with his glory. [3] And[g] the vision I saw was like the vision which I had seen when he came to destroy the city, and[h] like the vision which I had seen by the river Chebar; and I fell upon my face. [4] As the glory of the LORD entered the temple by the gate facing east, [5] the Spirit lifted me up, and brought me into the inner court; and behold, the glory of the LORD filled the temple.

6 While the man was standing beside me, I heard one speaking to me out of the temple; [7] and he said to me, "Son of man, this is the place of my throne and the place of the soles of my feet, where I will dwell in the midst of the people of Israel for ever. And the house of Israel shall no more defile my holy name, neither they, nor their kings, by their harlotry, and by the dead bodies[i] of their kings, [8] by setting their threshold by my threshold and their doorposts beside my doorposts, with only a wall between me and them. They have defiled my holy name by their abominations which they have committed, so I have consumed them in my anger. [9] Now let them put away their idolatry and the dead bodies[i] of their kings far from me, and I will dwell in their midst for ever.

10 "And you, son of man, describe to the house of Israel the temple and its appearance and plan,[j] that they may be ashamed of their iniquities. [11] And if they are ashamed of all that they have done, portray[k] the temple, its arrangement, its exits and its entrances, and its whole form; and make known to them all its ordinances and all its laws; and write it down in their sight, so that they may observe and perform all its laws[l] and all its ordinances. [12] This is the law of the temple: the whole territory round about upon the top of the mountain shall be most holy. Behold, this is the law of the temple.

13 "These are the dimensions of the altar by cubits (the cubit being a cubit and a handbreadth): its base

f Gk: Heb *measuring reed round about. He measured*
g Gk: Heb *And like the vision*
h Syr: Heb *and the visions*
i Or *the monuments*
j Gk: Heb *the temple that they may measure the pattern*
k Gk: Heb *the form of*
l Compare Gk: Heb *its whole form*

---

court. **15–20:** The total temple area was five hundred cubits square (861.63 feet square; see 40.5 n.).

43.1–12: Return of the glory of God. As God on his throne-chariot had forsaken the temple by the east gate (10.18–19; 11.22–23), so he returns from the same direction and re-consecrates the purified temple by his Presence (Ex.40.34–38; 1 Kg.8.10–11). *Thundering of many waters*, 1.24; Rev.14.2; 19.6. Like the brightness of the sun, *the earth shone with his glory* (Is.60.1–3). **6–12:** The restored temple is to be restricted to purely religious uses, as commanded by God; especially discouraged is any influence from the crown (ch. 8; 1 Kg.7.1–12; 11.33; Am.7.13). **43.13–26: The altar of burnt offering. 13–17:** The altar was built in three superimposed squares of sixteen, fourteen, and twelve cubits respectively, resting on a foundation platform,

shall be one cubit high,*m* and one cubit broad, with a rim of one span around its edge. And this shall be the height*x* of the altar: [14] from the base on the ground to the lower ledge, two cubits, with a breadth of one cubit; and from the smaller ledge to the larger ledge, four cubits, with a breadth of one cubit; [15] and the altar hearth, four cubits; and from the altar hearth projecting upward, four horns, one cubit high.*n* [16] The altar hearth shall be square, twelve cubits long by twelve broad. [17] The ledge also shall be square, fourteen cubits long by fourteen broad, with a rim around it half a cubit broad, and its base one cubit round about. The steps of the altar shall face east."

18 And he said to me, "Son of man, thus says the Lord GOD: These are the ordinances for the altar: On the day when it is erected for offering burnt offerings upon it and for throwing blood against it, [19] you shall give to the Levitical priests of the family of Zadok, who draw near to me to minister to me, says the Lord GOD, a bull for a sin offering. [20] And you shall take some of its blood, and put it on the four horns of the altar, and on the four corners of the ledge, and upon the rim round about; thus you shall cleanse the altar and make atonement for it. [21] You shall also take the bull of the sin offering, and it shall be burnt in the appointed place belonging to the temple, outside the sacred area. [22] And on the second day you shall offer a he-goat without blemish for a sin offering; and the altar shall be cleansed, as it was cleansed with the bull. [23] When you have finished cleansing it, you shall offer a bull without blemish and a ram from the flock

without blemish. [24] You shall present them before the LORD, and the priests shall sprinkle salt upon them and offer them up as a burnt offering to the LORD. [25] For seven days you shall provide daily a goat for a sin offering; also a bull and a ram from the flock, without blemish, shall be provided. [26] Seven days shall they make atonement for the altar and purify it, and so consecrate it. [27] And when they have completed these days, then from the eighth day onward the priests shall offer upon the altar your burnt offerings and your peace offerings; and I will accept you, says the Lord GOD."

44 Then he brought me back to the outer gate of the sanctuary, which faces east; and it was shut. [2] And he*o* said to me, "This gate shall remain shut; it shall not be opened, and no one shall enter by it; for the LORD, the God of Israel, has entered by it; therefore it shall remain shut. [3] Only the prince may sit in it to eat bread before the LORD; he shall enter by way of the vestibule of the gate, and shall go out by the same way."

4 Then he brought me by way of the north gate to the front of the temple; and I looked, and behold, the glory of the LORD filled the temple of the LORD; and I fell upon my face. [5] And the LORD said to me, "Son of man, mark well, see with your eyes, and hear with your ears all that I shall tell you concerning all the ordinances of the temple of the LORD and all its laws; and mark well those who may be admitted to*p* the temple and all those who are to be excluded from the sanctuary. [6] And say to the rebellious house,*q* to the house of Israel, Thus says the Lord GOD:

m Gk: Heb lacks *high*   *x* Gk: Heb *back*
n Gk: Heb lacks *one cubit high*   *o* Cn: Heb *the* LORD
p Cn: Heb *the entrance of*   *q* Gk: Heb lacks *house*

"the bosom of the earth," with steps on the east leading to the *altar hearth*, "the mountain of God," like the Mesopotamian ziggurats (see Gen.11.4 n.). The total height of the altar is twelve cubits (20.68 feet). **18–26:** On the analogy of earlier consecratory rites (Ex.29.36–37; 40.1–38; Lev.8.14–15), the priests of Zadok (44.5–31) are to dedicate the altar.

44.1–31: Temple ordinances. 44.1–5: The outer east gate should remain closed, perhaps symbolizing its consecration by God's entrance and God's continued presence (43.7). The prince (see 37.15–28 n.) apparently entered from the temple side for the ceremonial meal (Lev.7.15; Dt.12.7), and thus the gate remained closed (compare 46.1). **6–9:** No more foreigners may

O house of Israel, let there be an end to all your abominations, [7] in admitting foreigners, uncircumcised in heart and flesh, to be in my sanctuary, profaning it,[r] when you offer to me my food, the fat and the blood. You[s] have broken my covenant, in addition to all your abominations. [8] And you have not kept charge of my holy things; but you have set foreigners to keep my charge in my sanctuary.

9 "Therefore[t] thus says the Lord GOD: No foreigner, uncircumcised in heart and flesh, of all the foreigners who are among the people of Israel, shall enter my sanctuary. [10] But the Levites who went far from me, going astray from me after their idols when Israel went astray, shall bear their punishment. [11] They shall be ministers in my sanctuary, having oversight at the gates of the temple, and serving in the temple; they shall slay the burnt offering and the sacrifice for the people, and they shall attend on the people, to serve them. [12] Because they ministered to them before their idols and became a stumbling block of iniquity to the house of Israel, therefore I have sworn concerning them, says the Lord GOD, that they shall bear their punishment. [13] They shall not come near to me, to serve me as priest, nor come near any of my sacred things and the things that are most sacred; but they shall bear their shame, because of the abominations which they have committed. [14] Yet I will appoint them to keep charge of the temple, to do all its service and all that is to be done in it.

15 "But the Levitical priests, the sons of Zadok, who kept the charge of my sanctuary when the people of Israel went astray from me, shall come near to me to minister to me; and they shall attend on me to offer me the fat and the blood, says the Lord GOD; [16] they shall enter my sanctuary, and they shall approach my table, to minister to me, and they shall keep my charge. [17] When they enter the gates of the inner court, they shall wear linen garments; they shall have nothing of wool on them, while they minister at the gates of the inner court, and within. [18] They shall have linen turbans upon their heads, and linen breeches upon their loins; they shall not gird themselves with anything that causes sweat. [19] And when they go out into the outer court to the people, they shall put off the garments in which they have been ministering, and lay them in the holy chambers; and they shall put on other garments, lest they communicate holiness to the people with their garments. [20] They shall not shave their heads or let their locks grow long; they shall only trim the hair of their heads. [21] No priest shall drink wine, when he enters the inner court. [22] They shall not marry a widow, or a divorced woman, but only a virgin of the stock of the house of Israel, or a widow who is the widow of a priest. [23] They shall teach my people the difference between the holy and the common, and show them how to distinguish between the unclean and the clean. [24] In a controversy they shall act as judges, and they shall judge it according to my judgments. They shall keep my laws and my statutes in all my appointed feasts,

r Gk: Heb *it my temple*
s Gk Syr Vg: Heb *they*
t Gk: Heb *for you*

---

serve in the temple (Jos.9.23; Num.31.30,47), nor *uncircumcised* in heart (Dt.30.6; Lev.26.41; Jer.4.4). **10–14:** Because they had been party to Israel's apostasy, the Levites are demoted from being priests to temple servants (compare Dt.17.18–18.8). **15–31:** The priesthood. Solomon elevated *Zadok* to be chief priest after Abiathar's defection and banishment (2 Sam.15.24–29; 1 Kg.1.7–8; 2.26–27). 1 Chr.6.50–53 and 24.31 trace the lineage back to Eleazar, Aaron's son. Their present status is perhaps derived from Hilkiah's role in Josiah's reform (2 Kg.22.11–14; 23.4,24). **16:** *My table,* the table in the nave (41.22) or the altar. **17:** *Linen garments,* see 9.2 n. **19:** The care of the garments, compare 42.14; Hag.2.10–12. **20:** The care of the *hair,* Lev.21.5; Dt.14.1–2. **21:** *No wine* before service, Lev.10.9. **22:** Proper *marriage,* Lev.21.7,13–15. **23:** Teaching of the people, Lev.10.11. **24:** *Judges,* Dt.21.1–5. **25:** Defilement by a dead person,

and they shall keep my sabbaths holy. [25] They shall not defile themselves by going near to a dead person; however, for father or mother, for son or daughter, for brother or unmarried sister they may defile themselves. [26] After he is defiled,[u] he shall count for himself seven days, and then he shall be clean.[v] [27] And on the day that he goes into the holy place, into the inner court, to minister in the holy place, he shall offer his sin offering, says the Lord GOD.

[28] "They shall have no[w] inheritance; I am their inheritance: and you shall give them no possession in Israel; I am their possession. [29] They shall eat the cereal offering, the sin offering, and the guilt offering; and every devoted thing in Israel shall be theirs. [30] And the first of all the first fruits of all kinds, and every offering of all kinds from all your offerings, shall belong to the priests; you shall also give to the priests the first of your coarse meal, that a blessing may rest on your house. [31] The priests shall not eat of anything, whether bird or beast, that has died of itself or is torn.

45 "When you allot the land as a possession, you shall set apart for the LORD a portion of the land as a holy district, twenty-five thousand cubits long and twenty[x] thousand cubits broad; it shall be holy throughout its whole extent. [2] Of this a square plot of five hundred by five hundred cubits shall be for the sanctuary, with fifty cubits for an open space around it. [3] And in the holy district you shall measure off a section twenty-five thousand cubits long and ten thousand broad, in which shall be the sanctuary, the most holy place. [4] It shall be the holy portion of the land; it shall be for the priests, who minister in the sanctuary and approach the LORD to minister to him; and it shall be a place for their houses and a holy place for the sanctuary. [5] Another section, twenty-five thousand cubits long and ten thousand cubits broad, shall be for the Levites who minister at the temple, as their possession for cities to live in.[y]

6 "Alongside the portion set apart as the holy district you shall assign for the possession of the city an area five thousand cubits broad, and twenty-five thousand cubits long; it shall belong to the whole house of Israel.

7 "And to the prince shall belong the land on both sides of the holy district and the property of the city, alongside the holy district and the property of the city, on the west and on the east, corresponding in length to one of the tribal portions, and extending from the western to the eastern boundary of the land. [8] It is to be his property in Israel. And my princes shall no more oppress my people; but they shall let the house of Israel have the land according to their tribes.

9 "Thus says the Lord GOD: Enough, O princes of Israel! Put away violence and oppression, and execute justice and righteousness; cease your evictions of my people, says the Lord GOD.

10 "You shall have just balances, a just ephah, and a just bath. [11] The ephah and the bath shall be of the same measure, the bath containing one tenth of a homer, and the ephah one tenth of a homer; the homer shall be the

u Syr: Heb *cleansed*
v Syr: Heb lacks *and then he shall be clean*
w Vg: Heb *as an*   *x* Gk: Heb *ten*
y Gk: Heb *twenty chambers*

Lev.21.1–3. **28:** *No inheritance*, Jos.13.14; Num.18.20–32. **29:** Eating sacrifices and *first fruits*, Lev.2.3–10; 6.14–18; Dt.18.3–5. **31:** Eating of unslaughtered *meat*, Lev.7.24.

45.1–9: The distribution of land (continued in 47.13–48.35) is completely idealistic. The *holy district* is divided into two sections, each 25,000 by 10,000 cubits; the northern section is for the Levites, the southern for the Zadokite priests. The latter included the five hundred cubit square section for the temple area plus an enclosure-space fifty cubits deep not mentioned earlier (42.20). The 25,000 by 5,000 cubit property of Jerusalem south of the holy district (v. 6) made with the holy district (v. 1) an area 25,000 cubits (8.3 miles) square.

45.10–12: Weights and measures. For present-day equivalents of *bath, ephah, homer, shekel,*

standard measure. [12] The shekel shall be twenty gerahs; five shekels shall be five shekels, and ten shekels shall be ten shekels, and your mina shall be fifty shekels.[z]

13 "This is the offering which you shall make: one sixth of an ephah from each homer of wheat, and one sixth of an ephah from each homer of barley, [14] and as the fixed portion of oil,[a] one tenth of a bath from each cor (the cor,[b] like the homer, contains ten baths); [15] and one sheep from every flock of two hundred, from the families[c] of Israel. This is the offering for cereal offerings, burnt offerings, and peace offerings, to make atonement for them, says the Lord GOD. [16] All the people of the land shall give[d] this offering to the prince in Israel. [17] It shall be the prince's duty to furnish the burnt offerings, cereal offerings, and drink offerings, at the feasts, the new moons, and the sabbaths, all the appointed feasts of the house of Israel: he shall provide the sin offerings, cereal offerings, burnt offerings, and peace offerings, to make atonement for the house of Israel.

18 "Thus says the Lord GOD: In the first month, on the first day of the month, you shall take a young bull without blemish, and cleanse the sanctuary. [19] The priest shall take some of the blood of the sin offering and put it on the doorposts of the temple, the four corners of the ledge of the altar, and the posts of the gate of the inner court. [20] You shall do the same on the seventh day of the month for any one who has sinned through error or ignorance; so you shall make atonement for the temple.

21 "In the first month, on the fourteenth day of the month, you shall celebrate the feast of the passover, and for seven days unleavened bread shall be eaten. [22] On that day the prince shall provide for himself and all the people of the land a young bull for a sin offering. [23] And on the seven days of the festival he shall provide as a burnt offering to the LORD seven young bulls and seven rams without blemish, on each of the seven days; and a he-goat daily for a sin offering. [24] And he shall provide as a cereal offering an ephah for each bull, an ephah for each ram, and a hin of oil to each ephah. [25] In the seventh month, on the fifteenth day of the month and for the seven days of the feast, he shall make the same provision for sin offerings, burnt offerings, and cereal offerings, and for the oil.

46 "Thus says the Lord GOD: The gate of the inner court that faces east shall be shut on the six working days; but on the sabbath day it shall be opened and on the day of the new moon it shall be opened. [2] The prince shall enter by the vestibule of the gate from without, and shall take his stand by the post of the gate. The priests shall offer his burnt offering and his peace offerings, and he shall worship at the threshold of the gate. Then he shall go out, but the gate shall not be shut until evening. [3] The people of the land shall worship at the entrance of that gate before the LORD on the sabbaths and on the new moons. [4] The burnt offering that the prince offers to the LORD on the sabbath day shall be six lambs without blemish and a ram without blemish; [5] and the cereal offering with

z Gk: Heb *twenty shekels, twenty-five shekels, fifteen shekels shall be your mina*
a Cn: Heb *oil, the bath the oil*
b Vg: Heb *homer*
c Gk: Heb *watering places*
d Gk Compare Syr: Heb *shall be to*

---

gerah, and *mina*, see pp. 1530–1531. **13–17:** The people will bring token gifts to the prince, who, as their representative, will offer them to God.

45.18–25: Festival regulations: *passover* (Ex.23.15; Dt.16.1–8; Lev.23.4–8) and *tabernacles* (Ex.23.16; Dt.16.13–15; Lev.23.33–36); omitted are the festival of first fruits (Ex.23.16; Dt. 16.9–12; Lev.23.15–21) and the day of atonement (Lev.23.26–32). **24:** *A hin*, see p. 1530.

46.1–18: Regulations regarding the prince. 46.1–8: The prince (see 37.15–28 n.) shall bring his offerings (45.13–16) through the *east gate* of the *inner court* to its inner vestibule where he will stand (2 Kg.11.14) by the ritually cleansed doorway (45.18–19), while the priests offer

the ram shall be an ephah, and the cereal offering with the lambs shall be as much as he is able, together with a hin of oil to each ephah. 6 On the day of the new moon he shall offer a young bull without blemish, and six lambs and a ram, which shall be without blemish; 7 as a cereal offering he shall provide an ephah with the bull and an ephah with the ram, and with the lambs as much as he is able, together with a hin of oil to each ephah. 8 When the prince enters, he shall go in by the vestibule of the gate, and he shall go out by the same way.

9 "When the people of the land come before the LORD at the appointed feasts, he who enters by the north gate to worship shall go out by the south gate; and he who enters by the south gate shall go out by the north gate: no one shall return by way of the gate by which he entered, but each shall go out straight ahead. 10 When they go in, the prince shall go in with them; and when they go out, he shall go out.

11 "At the feasts and the appointed seasons the cereal offering with a young bull shall be an ephah, and with a ram an ephah, and with the lambs as much as one is able to give, together with a hin of oil to an ephah. 12 When the prince provides a freewill offering, either a burnt offering or peace offerings as a freewill offering to the LORD, the gate facing east shall be opened for him; and he shall offer his burnt offering or his peace offerings as he does on the sabbath day. Then he shall go out, and after he has gone out the gate shall be shut.

13 "He shall provide a lamb a year old without blemish for a burnt offering to the LORD daily; morning by morning he shall provide it. 14 And he shall provide a cereal offering with it morning by morning, one sixth of an ephah, and one third of a hin of oil to moisten the flour, as a cereal offering to the LORD; this is the ordinance for the continual burnt offering.*e* 15 Thus the lamb and the meal offering and the oil shall be provided, morning by morning, for a continual burnt offering.

16 "Thus says the Lord GOD: If the prince makes a gift to any of his sons out of*f* his inheritance, it shall belong to his sons, it is their property by inheritance. 17 But if he makes a gift out of his inheritance to one of his servants, it shall be his to the year of liberty; then it shall revert to the prince; only his sons may keep a gift from his inheritance. 18 The prince shall not take any of the inheritance of the people, thrusting them out of their property; he shall give his sons their inheritance out of his own property, so that none of my people shall be dispossessed of his property."

19 Then he brought me through the entrance, which was at the side of the gate, to the north row of the holy chambers for the priests; and there I saw a place at the extreme western end of them. 20 And he said to me, "This is the place where the priests shall boil the guilt offering and the sin offering, and where they shall bake the cereal offering, in order not to bring them out into the outer court and so communicate holiness to the people."

21 Then he brought me forth to the outer court, and led me to the four corners of the court; and in each corner of the court there was a court—

e Cn: Heb *perpetual ordinances continually*
f Gk: Heb *it is his inheritance*

the sacrifices on the altar directly ahead. The people stand in the outer court. For the sacrifices, see Ex.29.38–42; Num.28.3–15. *New moon*, first day of the month; note the increasingly strong emphasis on the sabbath. **9–10:** The great festival crowds require regulations for controlled egress. **11–15:** When the prince makes a *free-will offering* (Lev.22.18–23), the east gate (v. 1) will also be opened. The prince must also provide for daily sacrifices (Ex.29.38–42; 1 Kg.18.29; 2 Kg.16.15). **16–18:** Crown property could not be disposed of permanently. When given to a non-relative, it had to be returned on the *year of liberty* (jubilee year, Lev.25.8–17).

46.19–20: The priests' quarters, see 42.1–14. *Communicate holiness,* see 42.14; 44.19. **21–24:** The temple kitchens, for the common-meal sacrifices.

²² in the four corners of the court were small*ᵍ* courts, forty cubits long and thirty broad; the four were of the same size. ²³ On the inside, around each of the four courts was a row of masonry, with hearths made at the bottom of the rows round about. ²⁴ Then he said to me, "These are the kitchens where those who minister at the temple shall boil the sacrifices of the people."

47 Then he brought me back to the door of the temple; and behold, water was issuing from below the threshold of the temple toward the east (for the temple faced east); and the water was flowing down from below the south end of the threshold of the temple, south of the altar. ² Then he brought me out by way of the north gate, and led me round on the outside to the outer gate, that faces toward the east;*ʰ* and the water was coming out on the south side.

3 Going on eastward with a line in his hand, the man measured a thousand cubits, and then led me through the water; and it was ankle-deep. ⁴ Again he measured a thousand, and led me through the water; and it was knee-deep. Again he measured a thousand, and led me through the water; and it was up to the loins. ⁵ Again he measured a thousand, and it was a river that I could not pass through, for the water had risen; it was deep enough to swim in, a river that could not be passed through. ⁶ And he said to me, "Son of man, have you seen this?"

Then he led me back along the bank of the river. ⁷ As I went back, I saw upon the bank of the river very many trees on the one side and on the other. ⁸ And he said to me, "This water flows toward the eastern region and goes down into the Arabah; and when it enters the stagnant waters of the sea,*ⁱ* the water will become fresh. ⁹ And wherever the river*ʲ* goes every living creature which swarms will live, and there will be very many fish; for this water goes there, that the waters of the sea*ᵏ* may become fresh; so everything will live where the river goes. ¹⁰ Fishermen will stand beside the sea; from En-ge′di to En-eg′laim it will be a place for the spreading of nets; its fish will be of very many kinds, like the fish of the Great Sea. ¹¹ But its swamps and marshes will not become fresh; they are to be left for salt. ¹² And on the banks, on both sides of the river, there will grow all kinds of trees for food. Their leaves will not wither nor their fruit fail, but they will bear fresh fruit every month, because the water for them flows from the sanctuary. Their fruit will be for food, and their leaves for healing."

13 Thus says the Lord GOD: "These are the boundaries by which you shall divide the land for inheritance among the twelve tribes of Israel. Joseph shall have two portions. ¹⁴ And you shall divide it equally; I swore to give it to your fathers, and this land shall fall to you as your inheritance.

15 "This shall be the boundary of the land: On the north side, from the Great Sea by way of Hethlon to the entrance of Hamath, and on to Zedad,*ˡ* ¹⁶ Bero′thah, Sib′raim (which lies on the border between Damascus and Hamath), as far as Hazer-hatticon,

g Gk Syr Vg: The meaning of the Hebrew word is uncertain
h Heb obscure
i Compare Syr: Heb *into the sea to the sea those that were made to issue forth*
j Gk Syr Vg Tg: Heb *two rivers*
k Compare Syr: Heb.lacks *the waters of the sea*
l Gk: Heb *the entrance of Zedad, Hamath*

47.1–12: The sacred river. This figure, known from Ugaritic (Canaanite) and Mesopotamian sources, is also found in Jl.3.18; Zech.14.8; and Rev. ch. 22. From the throne of God (the temple; 43.7) issued the waters of life by which the saline waters of the Dead Sea become fresh, and in the desolate wilderness of Judah fruit trees flourish, making a new Paradise, as it were, and man (the Jews) will benefit. **8:** *Arabah,* the valley south of the Dead Sea. **10:** *En-gedi to En-eglaim* ('Ain Feshkha, about one and one-half miles south of Khirbet Qumran), northwest coast of the Dead Sea.

47.13–20: Israel's boundaries (Num.34.1–12): north, apparently that of David's empire in north Syria (2 Sam.8.5–12; Num.34.7–9); east, *Hazar-enon,* between Damascus and Palmyra,

which is on the border of Hauran. 17 So the boundary shall run from the sea to Hazar-e'non, which is on the northern border of Damascus, with the border of Hamath to the north.*m* This shall be the north side.

18 "On the east side, the boundary shall run from Hazar-e'non*n* between Hauran and Damascus;*m* along the Jordan between Gilead and the land of Israel; to the eastern sea and as far as Tamar.*o* This shall be the east side.

19 "On the south side, it shall run from Tamar as far as the waters of Meribath-ka'desh, thence along the Brook of Egypt to the Great Sea. This shall be the south side.

20 "On the west side, the Great Sea shall be the boundary to a point opposite the entrance of Hamath. This shall be the west side.

21 "So you shall divide this land among you according to the tribes of Israel. 22 You shall allot it as an inheritance for yourselves and for the aliens who reside among you and have begotten children among you. They shall be to you as native-born sons of Israel; with you they shall be allotted an inheritance among the tribes of Israel. 23 In whatever tribe the alien resides, there you shall assign him his inheritance, says the Lord GOD.

48 "These are the names of the tribes: Beginning at the northern border, from the sea by way*p* of Hethlon to the entrance of Hamath, as far as Hazar-e'non (which is on the northern border of Damascus over against Hamath), and*q* extending from the east side to the west,*r* Dan, one portion. 2 Adjoining the territory

of Dan, from the east side to the west, Asher, one portion. 3 Adjoining the territory of Asher, from the east side to the west, Naph'tali, one portion. 4 Adjoining the territory of Naph'tali, from the east side to the west, Manas'seh, one portion. 5 Adjoining the territory of Manas'seh, from the east side to the west, E'phraim, one portion. 6 Adjoining the territory of E'phraim, from the east side to the west, Reuben, one portion. 7 Adjoining the territory of Reuben, from the east side to the west, Judah, one portion.

8 "Adjoining the territory of Judah, from the east side to the west, shall be the portion which you shall set apart, twenty-five thousand cubits in breadth, and in length equal to one of the tribal portions, from the east side to the west, with the sanctuary in the midst of it. 9 The portion which you shall set apart for the LORD shall be twenty-five thousand cubits in length, and twenty*s* thousand in breadth. 10 These shall be the allotments of the holy portion: the priests shall have an allotment measuring twenty-five thousand cubits on the northern side, ten thousand cubits in breadth on the western side, ten thousand in breadth on the eastern side, and twenty-five thousand in length on the southern side, with the sanctuary of the LORD in the midst of it. 11 This shall be for the consecrated priests, the sons*t* of Zadok, who kept my charge, who did not go astray

m Heb obscure
n Cn: Heb lacks *Hazar-enon*
o Compare Syr: Heb *you shall measure*
p Compare 47.15: Heb *by the side of the way*
q Cn: Heb *and they shall be his*
r Gk Compare verses 2–8: Heb *the east side the west*
s Compare 45.1: Heb *ten*
t One Ms Gk: Heb *of the sons*

---

to the Dead Sea (Num.34.10–12); south, along the southern Negeb to *the Brook of Egypt* (Num.34.3–5); west, the Mediterranean Sea (Num.34.6). *Sibraim*, the same as Sepharvaim (see Is.36.19 n.). 21–23: Proselytes (*aliens*) and Jews should be treated alike (Num.15.29; Lev. 19.33–34).

48.1–29: The allotment of the land. All tribes receive equal allotments west of the Jordan, with Ephraim and Manasseh each given a portion and Levi, as the priestly tribe (see Jos.14.3–4), omitted. This division of the country ignores geographical reality. 1–7: Seven tribes north of the holy district, with Judah immediately contiguous to it. 1: *Hethlon*, Heitala, east of Tripoli (47.15). *Entrance to Hamath*, territory between Riblah and Kadesh on the Orontes River. 8–22: The properties of the Zadokite priests and the Levites, like that of the prince on either side, were to be held in perpetuity (45.1–9). The size of Jerusalem, with the surrounding open

when the people of Israel went astray, as the Levites did. ¹² And it shall belong to them as a special portion from the holy portion of the land, a most holy place, adjoining the territory of the Levites. ¹³ And alongside the territory of the priests, the Levites shall have an allotment twenty-five thousand cubits in length and ten thousand in breadth. The whole length shall be twenty-five thousand cubits and the breadth twenty^u thousand. ¹⁴ They shall not sell or exchange any of it; they shall not alienate this choice portion of the land, for it is holy to the LORD.

15 "The remainder, five thousand cubits in breadth and twenty-five thousand in length, shall be for ordinary use for the city, for dwellings and for open country. In the midst of it shall be the city; ¹⁶ and these shall be its dimensions: the north side four thousand five hundred cubits, the south side four thousand five hundred, the east side four thousand five hundred, and the west side four thousand and five hundred. ¹⁷ And the city shall have open land: on the north two hundred and fifty cubits, on the south two hundred and fifty, on the east two hundred and fifty, and on the west two hundred and fifty. ¹⁸ The remainder of the length alongside the holy portion shall be ten thousand cubits to the east, and ten thousand to the west, and it shall be alongside the holy portion. Its produce shall be food for the workers of the city. ¹⁹ And the workers of the city, from all the tribes of Israel, shall till it. ²⁰ The whole portion which you shall set apart shall be twenty-five thousand cubits square, that is, the holy portion together with the property of the city. 21 "What remains on both sides of the holy portion and of the property of the city shall belong to the prince.

Extending from the twenty-five thousand cubits of the holy portion to the east border, and westward from the twenty-five thousand cubits to the west border, parallel to the tribal portions, it shall belong to the prince. The holy portion with the sanctuary of the temple in its midst, ²² and the property of the Levites and the property of the city,^v shall be in the midst of that which belongs to the prince. The portion of the prince shall lie between the territory of Judah and the territory of Benjamin.

23 "As for the rest of the tribes: from the east side to the west, Benjamin, one portion. ²⁴ Adjoining the territory of Benjamin, from the east side to the west, Simeon, one portion. ²⁵ Adjoining the territory of Simeon, from the east side to the west, Is'sachar, one portion. ²⁶ Adjoining the territory of Is'sachar, from the east side to the west, Zeb'ulun, one portion. ²⁷ Adjoining the territory of Zeb'ulun, from the east side to the west, Gad, one portion. ²⁸ And adjoining the territory of Gad to the south, the boundary shall run from Tamar to the waters of Meribath-ka'desh, thence along the Brook of Egypt to the Great Sea. ²⁹ This is the land which you shall allot as an inheritance among the tribes of Israel, and these are their several portions, says the Lord GOD.

30 "These shall be the exits of the city: On the north side, which is to be four thousand five hundred cubits by measure, ³¹ three gates, the gate of Reuben, the gate of Judah, and the gate of Levi, the gates of the city being named after the tribes of Israel. ³² On the east side, which is to be four thousand five hundred cubits, three gates, the gate of Joseph, the gate of Benja-

u Gk: Heb *ten*
v Cn: Heb *and from the property of the Levites and from the property of the city*

---

area, was exactly ten times that of the temple (42.20), i.e. 5,000 cubits square (1.6 miles). **15:** *Ordinary use*, see 22.26; 42.20; 44.23. **23–29:** Five tribes south of Jerusalem and the holy district beginning with Benjamin.

48.30–35: The new Jerusalem. Three gates on each of the city's four sides, with each gate named after a tribe, including Levi, and with Ephraim and Manasseh combined in Joseph

min, and the gate of Dan. [33] On the south side, which is to be four thousand five hundred cubits by measure, three gates, the gate of Simeon, the gate of Is'sachar, and the gate of Zeb'ulun. [34] On the west side, which is to be four thousand five hundred cubits, three gates,[w] the gate of Gad, the gate of Asher, and the gate of Naph'tali. [35] The circumference of the city shall be eighteen thousand cubits. And the name of the city henceforth shall be, The LORD is there."

w One Ms Gk Syr: Heb *their gates three*

(compare Rev.21.12–14). **35:** The new city receives a new name (Is.62.2), "The LORD is there" (Yahweh-shammah); for other names see Jer.3.17; Zech.8.3; Is.1.26 n.; 60.14 (compare Jer. 23.6).

THE BOOK OF DANIEL

The six stories and four dream-visions of the book of Daniel make up the first great work of apocalyptic, later examples of which are 1 Enoch, Syriac Baruch, and the New Testament book of Revelation. These apocalypses come from times of national or community tribulation, and are not actual history, but, through symbols and signs, are interpretations of current history with its background and predictions of a future where tribulations and sorrows will give place to triumph and peace. The Apocalyptists usually set forth their messages under the name of some ancient worthy, e.g. Adam, Enoch, Noah, Abraham, or some other figure of note.

This book appears under the name of Daniel, or Dan'el, a worthy twice referred to in Ezekiel (Ezek.14.14; 28.3), and whose name appears also in the North Canaanite clay-tablet texts found at Ras Shamra. The author was a pious Jew living under the persecution of Antiochus Epiphanes, 167–164 B.C. (see "Survey of . . . Bible Lands," §15). To encourage his suffering fellow-believers he tells six stories, set in earlier days in Babylon just before and just after the Persian conquest, which illustrate how faithful Jews, loyally practicing their religion, were enabled by divine aid to triumph over their enemies. Then in four visions he ventures to interpret current history and predict the coming consummation when the "saints" will have ultimate victory. His book was originally written in Aramaic, and the section from 2.4b to 7.28 is still in Aramaic, though the remainder is now in Hebrew.

IN THE THIRD YEAR OF THE REIGN OF Jehoi'akim king of Judah, Nebuchadnez'zar king of Babylon came to Jerusalem and besieged it. ² And the Lord gave Jehoi'akim king of Judah into his hand, with some of the vessels of the house of God; and he brought them to the land of Shinar, to the house of his god, and placed the vessels in the treasury of his god. ³ Then the king commanded Ash'penaz, his chief eunuch, to bring some of the people of Israel, both of the royal family and of the nobility, ⁴ youths without blemish, handsome and skilful in all wisdom, endowed with knowledge, understanding learning, and competent to serve in the king's palace, and to teach them the letters and language of the Chalde'ans. ⁵ The king assigned them a daily portion of the rich food which the king ate, and of the wine which he drank. They were to be educated for three years, and at the end of that time they were to stand before the king. ⁶ Among these were Daniel, Hanani'ah, Mish'a-el, and Azari'ah of the tribe of Judah. ⁷ And the chief of the eunuchs gave them names: Daniel he called Belteshaz'zar, Hanani'ah he called Shadrach, Mish'a-el he called Meshach, and Azari'ah he called Abed'nego.

8 But Daniel resolved that he would not defile himself with the king's rich food, or with the wine which he drank; therefore he asked the chief of the eunuchs to allow him not to defile himself. ⁹ And God gave Daniel favor and compassion in the sight of the chief of the eunuchs; ¹⁰ and the chief of the eunuchs said to Daniel, "I fear lest my lord the king, who appointed your food and your drink, should see that you were in poorer condition than the youths who are of your own

---

1.1–21: Daniel and his friends. A story to teach how faithful observance of the law is rewarded. **1:** The *third year* of Jehoiakim was 606 B.C. *Nebuchadnezzar* is a Jewish form of the name Nabuchadrezzar, who in 597 B.C. carried away temple treasure and captives to Babylon (2 Kg.24.10–15), in v. 2 called by the ancient name *Shinar* (Gen.10.10; Is.11.11). **2:** *His god* at Babylon was Marduk. **3–5:** Promising *youths* among the captives were trained for *three years* to be royal pages. **6:** As such they were given Babylonian names and provided with food and drink from the royal table. **8:** *Defile himself*, i.e. by eating food not permitted by Jewish dietary laws. **10:** *Poorer condition*, lit. "your faces looking sorrowful." **20:** *Magicians and enchanters*

age. So you would endanger my head with the king." ¹¹ Then Daniel said to the steward whom the chief of the eunuchs had appointed over Daniel, Hanani′ah, Mish′a-el, and Azari′ah; ¹² "Test your servants for ten days; let us be given vegetables to eat and water to drink. ¹³ Then let our appearance and the appearance of the youths who eat the king's rich food be observed by you, and according to what you see deal with your servants." ¹⁴ So he hearkened to them in this matter, and tested them for ten days. ¹⁵ At the end of ten days it was seen that they were better in appearance and fatter in flesh than all the youths who ate the king's rich food. ¹⁶ So the steward took away their rich food and the wine they were to drink, and gave them vegetables.

17 As for these four youths, God gave them learning and skill in all letters and wisdom; and Daniel had understanding in all visions and dreams. ¹⁸ At the end of the time, when the king had commanded that they should be brought in, the chief of the eunuchs brought them in before Nebuchadnez′zar. ¹⁹ And the king spoke with them, and among them all none was found like Daniel, Hanani′ah, Mish′a-el, and Azari′ah; therefore they stood before the king. ²⁰ And in every matter of wisdom and understanding concerning which the king inquired of them, he found them ten times better than all the magicians and enchanters that were in all his kingdom. ²¹ And Daniel continued until the first year of King Cyrus.

2 In the second year of the reign of Nebuchadnez′zar, Nebuchad-

nez′zar had dreams; and his spirit was troubled, and his sleep left him. ² Then the king commanded that the magicians, the enchanters, the sorcerers, and the Chalde′ans be summoned, to tell the king his dreams. So they came in and stood before the king. ³ And the king said to them, "I had a dream, and my spirit is troubled to know the dream." ⁴ Then the Chalde′ans said to the king,ᵃ "O king, live for ever! Tell your servants the dream, and we will show the interpretation." ⁵ The king answered the Chalde′ans, "The word from me is sure: if you do not make known to me the dream and its interpretation, you shall be torn limb from limb, and your houses shall be laid in ruins. ⁶ But if you show the dream and its interpretation, you shall receive from me gifts and rewards and great honor. Therefore show me the dream and its interpretation." ⁷ They answered a second time, "Let the king tell his servants the dream, and we will show its interpretation." ⁸ The king answered, "I know with certainty that you are trying to gain time, because you see that the word from me is sure ⁹ that if you do not make the dream known to me, there is but one sentence for you. You have agreed to speak lying and corrupt words before me till the times change. Therefore tell me the dream, and I shall know that you can show me its interpretation." ¹⁰ The Chalde′ans answered the king, "There is not a man on earth who can meet the king's demand; for no great and powerful king has asked such a thing of any magician or enchanter or Chal-

a Heb adds *in Aramaic,* indicating that the text from this point to the end of chapter 7 is in Aramaic

here probably stand merely as names for court sages whose learning and wisdom were surpassed by that divinely given to Daniel and his friends (v. 17). **21:** The *first year* of *Cyrus* at Babylon was 538 B.C. (Ezra 1.1), almost seventy years after Daniel's coming to Babylon.
2.1–49: Nebuchadnezzar's dream. A story to teach the feebleness of human wisdom compared with that conferred by God. **1:** *Second year* is a slip (compare "third year" in 1.5–6,17,20). **2:** *Chaldeans* here means not an ethnic group but a caste of wise men. In ancient as in modern times it was believed that important matters were revealed in *dreams* (Gen.20.3; 41.1–32; Mt.27.19). **4–11:** Cuneiform tablets on divination through dreams are still extant. If the king would *tell* the dream they could consult dream-books and find the interpretation, but asking them to *show* the dream itself was unheard of and *difficult* beyond human skill. **11:** The word

de'an. [11] The thing that the king asks is difficult, and none can show it to the king except the gods, whose dwelling is not with flesh."

12 Because of this the king was angry and very furious, and commanded that all the wise men of Babylon be destroyed. [13] So the decree went forth that the wise men were to be slain, and they sought Daniel and his companions, to slay them. [14] Then Daniel replied with prudence and discretion to Ar'ioch, the captain of the king's guard, who had gone out to slay the wise men of Babylon; [15] he said to Ar'ioch, the king's captain, "Why is the decree of the king so severe?" Then Ar'ioch made the matter known to Daniel. [16] And Daniel went in and besought the king to appoint him a time, that he might show to the king the interpretation.

17 Then Daniel went to his house and made the matter known to Hanani'ah, Mish'a-el, and Azari'ah, his companions, [18] and told them to seek mercy of the God of heaven concerning this mystery, so that Daniel and his companions might not perish with the rest of the wise men of Babylon. [19] Then the mystery was revealed to Daniel in a vision of the night. Then Daniel blessed the God of heaven. [20] Daniel said:

"Blessed be the name of God for
　　ever and ever.
to whom belong wisdom and
　　might.
[21] He changes times and seasons;
　he removes kings and sets up
　　kings;
　he gives wisdom to the wise
　　and knowledge to those who have
　　understanding;
[22] he reveals deep and mysterious
　　things;
　he knows what is in the darkness,
　　and the light dwells with him.

23 To thee, O God of my fathers,
　I give thanks and praise,
for thou hast given me wisdom and
　　strength,
　and hast now made known to me
　　what we asked of thee,
　for thou hast made known to us
　　the king's matter."

24 Therefore Daniel went in to Ar'ioch, whom the king had appointed to destroy the wise men of Babylon; he went and said thus to him, "Do not destroy the wise men of Babylon; bring me in before the king, and I will show the king the interpretation."

25 Then Ar'ioch brought in Daniel before the king in haste, and said thus to him: "I have found among the exiles from Judah a man who can make known to the king the interpretation." [26] The king said to Daniel, whose name was Belteshaz'zar, "Are you able to make known to me the dream that I have seen and its interpretation?" [27] Daniel answered the king, "No wise men, enchanters, magicians, or astrologers can show to the king the mystery which the king has asked, [28] but there is a God in heaven who reveals mysteries, and he has made known to King Nebuchadnez'zar what will be in the latter days. Your dream and the visions of your head as you lay in bed are these: [29] To you, O king, as you lay in bed came thoughts of what would be hereafter, and he who reveals mysteries made known to you what is to be. [30] But as for me, not because of any wisdom that I have more than all the living has this mystery been revealed to me, but in order that the interpretation may be made known to the king, and that you may know the thoughts of your mind.

31 "You saw, O king, and behold, a great image. This image, mighty and of exceeding brightness, stood before you, and its appearance was frighten-

gods is used, since these Chaldeans were polytheists. **14:** On the ground of 1.20, Daniel and his friends were counted among the court's *wise men.* In what follows, Daniel represents the ideal sage. **18:** This is a *mystery*, but through prayer even mysteries may be *revealed* by God's wisdom (v. 30). **26:** *Belteshazzar*, as 1.7; 4.8,9. **28:** *In the latter day* is eschatological, referring to the end of this present world, a matter known only to God. **33:** *Legs*, i.e. the lower legs, the

ing. ³² The head of this image was of fine gold, its breast and arms of silver, its belly and thighs of bronze, ³³ its legs of iron, its feet partly of iron and partly of clay. ³⁴ As you looked, a stone was cut out by no human hand, and it smote the image on its feet of iron and clay, and broke them in pieces; ³⁵ then the iron, the clay, the bronze, the silver, and the gold, all together were broken in pieces, and became like the chaff of the summer threshing floors; and the wind carried them away, so that not a trace of them could be found. But the stone that struck the image became a great mountain and filled the whole earth.

36 "This was the dream; now we will tell the king its interpretation. ³⁷ You, O king, the king of kings, to whom the God of heaven has given the kingdom, the power, and the might, and the glory, ³⁸ and into whose hand he has given, wherever they dwell, the sons of men, the beasts of the field, and the birds of the air, making you rule over them all—you are the head of gold. ³⁹ After you shall arise another kingdom inferior to you, and yet a third kingdom of bronze, which shall rule over all the earth. ⁴⁰ And there shall be a fourth kingdom, strong as iron, because iron breaks to pieces and shatters all things; and like iron which crushes, it shall break and crush all these. ⁴¹ And as you saw the feet and toes partly of potter's clay and partly of iron, it shall be a divided kingdom; but some of the firmness of iron shall be in it, just as you saw iron mixed with the miry clay. ⁴² And as the toes of the feet were partly iron and partly

clay, so the kingdom shall be partly strong and partly brittle. ⁴³ As you saw the iron mixed with miry clay, so they will mix with one another in marriage,*b* but they will not hold together, just as iron does not mix with clay. ⁴⁴ And in the days of those kings the God of heaven will set up a kingdom which shall never be destroyed, nor shall its sovereignty be left to another people. It shall break in pieces all these kingdoms and bring them to an end, and it shall stand for ever; ⁴⁵ just as you saw that a stone was cut from a mountain by no human hand, and that it broke in pieces the iron, the bronze, the clay, the silver, and the gold. A great God has made known to the king what shall be hereafter. The dream is certain, and its interpretation sure."

46 Then King Nebuchadnez'zar fell upon his face, and did homage to Daniel, and commanded that an offering and incense be offered up to him. ⁴⁷ The king said to Daniel, "Truly, your God is God of gods and Lord of kings, and a revealer of mysteries, for you have been able to reveal this mystery." ⁴⁸ Then the king gave Daniel high honors and many great gifts, and made him ruler over the whole province of Babylon, and chief prefect over all the wise men of Babylon. ⁴⁹ Daniel made request of the king, and he appointed Shadrach, Meshach, and Abed'nego over the affairs of the province of Babylon; but Daniel remained at the king's court.

3 King Nebuchadnez'zar made an image of gold, whose height was

b Aram *by the seed of men*

---

upper legs being the *thighs*. **34:** The image was of human construction, but the *stone* was quarried supernaturally. This could become a *mountain* filling the *whole earth* because the earth was pictured as a disk beneath the heavenly vault. **36–45:** For this writer the five kingdoms are the Babylonian, Median, Persian, Greek, and the coming universal kingdom of God. **41:** The declining strength of the fourth kingdom means the divided kingdoms of the Seleucids and Ptolemies (see "Survey of . . . Bible Lands," §14) whose rulers, though they intermarried, did not hold together. **46–49:** That the king *did homage* to Daniel, recognized his God, and gave him and his friends *honors*, was to symbolize how oppressing nations would presently treat Israel.

3.1–30: The three youths in the fiery furnace. A story to show how martyrdom is preferable to apostasy. **1:** Huge *images* of deities were common in ancient times. This one was gold-

sixty cubits and its breadth six cubits. He set it up on the plain of Dura, in the province of Babylon. ² Then King Nebuchadnez'zar sent to assemble the satraps, the prefects, and the governors, the counselors, the treasurers, the justices, the magistrates, and all the officials of the provinces to come to the dedication of the image which King Nebuchadnez'zar had set up. ³ Then the satraps, the prefects, and the governors, the counselors, the treasurers, the justices, the magistrates, and all the officials of the provinces, were assembled for the dedication of the image that King Nebuchadnez'zar had set up; and they stood before the image that Nebuchadnez'zar had set up. ⁴ And the herald proclaimed aloud, "You are commanded, O peoples, nations, and languages, ⁵ that when you hear the sound of the horn, pipe, lyre, trigon, harp, bagpipe, and every kind of music, you are to fall down and worship the golden image that King Nebuchadnez'zar has set up; ⁶ and whoever does not fall down and worship shall immediately be cast into a burning fiery furnace." ⁷ Therefore, as soon as all the peoples heard the sound of the horn, pipe, lyre, trigon, harp, bagpipe, and every kind of music, all the peoples, nations, and languages fell down and worshiped the golden image which King Nebuchadnez'zar had set up.

8 Therefore at that time certain Chalde'ans came forward and maliciously accused the Jews. ⁹ They said to King Nebuchadnez'zar, "O king, live for ever! ¹⁰ You, O king, have made a decree, that every man who hears the sound of the horn, pipe, lyre, trigon, harp, bagpipe, and every kind of music, shall fall down and worship the golden image; ¹¹ and whoever does not fall down and worship shall be cast into a burning fiery furnace. ¹² There

are certain Jews whom you have appointed over the affairs of the province of Babylon: Shadrach, Meshach, and Abed'nego. These men, O king, pay no heed to you; they do not serve your gods or worship the golden image which you have set up."

13 Then Nebuchadnez'zar in furious rage commanded that Shadrach, Meshach, and Abed'nego be brought. Then they brought these men before the king. ¹⁴ Nebuchadnez'zar said to them, "Is it true, O Shadrach, Meshach, and Abed'nego, that you do not serve my gods or worship the golden image which I have set up? ¹⁵ Now if you are ready when you hear the sound of the horn, pipe, lyre, trigon, harp, bagpipe, and every kind of music, to fall down and worship the image which I have made, well and good; but if you do not worship, you shall immediately be cast into a burning fiery furnace; and who is the god that will deliver you out of my hands?"

16 Shadrach, Meshach, and Abed'nego answered the king, "O Nebuchadnez'zar, we have no need to answer you in this matter. ¹⁷ If it be so, our God whom we serve is able to deliver us from the burning fiery furnace; and he will deliver us out of your hand, O king.^{c} ¹⁸ But if not, be it known to you, O king, that we will not serve your gods or worship the golden image which you have set up."

19 Then Nebuchadnez'zar was full of fury, and the expression of his face was changed against Shadrach, Meshach, and Abed'nego. He ordered the furnace heated seven times more than it was wont to be heated. ²⁰ And he ordered certain mighty men of his army to bind Shadrach, Meshach, and Abed'nego, and to cast them into the

c Or *Behold, our God . . . king.* Or *If our God is able to deliver us, he will deliver us from the burning fiery furnace and out of your hand, O king.*

plated. *Dura* is unidentifiable. **2:** Ceremonies of *dedication* are well attested (1 Kg.8.63; 2 Chr. 7.9; Neh.12.27; and title of Ps. 30), at which *officials* were expected to appear, for they represented the various *peoples, nations, languages* of the kingdom. **5:** The *trigon* was a stringed instrument. The meaning of the Aramaic word translated *bagpipe* is uncertain; some think it means a drum. **6:** Punishment by burning alive was not uncommon (Gen.38.24; Jos.7.15). The *furnace* was the local kiln-type oven, with openings at top and at ground level. **19:** The

burning fiery furnace. ²¹ Then these men were bound in their mantles,*d* their tunics,*d* their hats, and their other garments, and they were cast into the burning fiery furnace. ²² Because the king's order was strict and the furnace very hot, the flame of the fire slew those men who took up Shadrach, Meshach, and Abed'nego. ²³ And these three men, Shadrach, Meshach, and Abed'nego, fell bound into the burning fiery furnace.

24 Then King Nebuchadnez'zar was astonished and rose up in haste. He said to his counselors, "Did we not cast three men bound into the fire?" They answered the king, "True, O king." ²⁵ He answered, "But I see four men loose, walking in the midst of the fire, and they are not hurt; and the appearance of the fourth is like a son of the gods."

26 Then Nebuchadnez'zar came near to the door of the burning fiery furnace and said, "Shadrach, Meshach, and Abed'nego, servants of the Most High God, come forth, and come here!" Then Shadrach, Meshach, and Abed'nego came out from the fire. ²⁷ And the satraps, the prefects, the governors, and the king's counselors gathered together and saw that the fire had not had any power over the bodies of those men; the hair of their heads was not singed, their mantles*d* were not harmed, and no smell of fire had come upon them. ²⁸ Nebuchadnez'zar said, "Blessed be the God of Shadrach, Meshach, and Abed'nego, who has sent his angel and delivered his servants, who trusted in him, and set at nought the king's command, and yielded up their bodies rather than serve and worship any god except their own God. ²⁹ Therefore I make a decree: Any people, nation, or language that speaks anything against the God of Shadrach, Meshach, and Abed'nego shall be torn limb from limb, and their houses laid in ruins; for there is no other god who is able to deliver in this way." ³⁰ Then the king promoted Shadrach, Meshach, and Abed'nego in the province of Babylon.

4*e* King Nebuchadnez'zar to all peoples, nations, and languages, that dwell in all the earth: Peace be multiplied to you! ² It has seemed good to me to show the signs and wonders that the Most High God has wrought toward me.

³ How great are his signs,
   how mighty his wonders!
His kingdom is an everlasting
      kingdom,
   and his dominion is from
      generation to generation.

4*f* I, Nebuchadnez'zar, was at ease in my house and prospering in my palace. ⁵ I had a dream which made me afraid; as I lay in bed the fancies and the visions of my head alarmed me. ⁶ Therefore I made a decree that all the wise men of Babylon should be brought before me, that they might make known to me the interpretation of the dream. ⁷ Then the magicians, the enchanters, the Chalde'ans, and the astrologers came in; and I told them the dream, but they could not make known to me its interpretation. ⁸ At last Daniel came in before me–he who was named Belteshaz'zar after the name of my god, and in whom is the spirit of the holy gods*g*–and I told him the dream, saying, ⁹ "O Belteshaz'zar,

d The meaning of the Aramaic word is uncertain
e Ch 3.31 in Aram   f Ch 4.1 in Aram
g Or Spirit of the holy God

---

seven times is merely rhetorical. **21:** Usually victims were stripped; the binding and clothing here heightens the miracle of their deliverance. **22:** They were cast in at the top opening, flames from which *slew* the soldiers. The king was looking into the ground level opening and saw where they fell. **25:** *A son of the gods;* a celestial being (v. 28). **26:** They emerged from the ground level opening. **29:** This dismemberment of person and property was not uncommon punishment (2.5).

4.1–37: Nebuchadnezzar's madness. A story to show how helpless is the greatest heathen power against Israel's God. **1:** Many ancient monarchs imagined they ruled *all the earth.* **6:** As in 2.2 court sages are expected to be skilled interpreters of dreams. **9:** For Daniel's office

chief of the magicians, because I know that the spirit of the holy gods[g] is in you and that no mystery is difficult for you, here is[h] the dream which I saw; tell me its interpretation. 10 The visions of my head as I lay in bed were these: I saw, and behold, a tree in the midst of the earth; and its height was great. 11 The tree grew and became strong, and its top reached to heaven, and it was visible to the end of the whole earth. 12 Its leaves were fair and its fruit abundant, and in it was food for all. The beasts of the field found shade under it, and the birds of the air dwelt in its branches, and all flesh was fed from it.

13 "I saw in the visions of my head as I lay in bed, and behold, a watcher, a holy one, came down from heaven. 14 He cried aloud and said thus, 'Hew down the tree and cut off its branches, strip off its leaves and scatter its fruit; let the beasts flee from under it and the birds from its branches. 15 But leave the stump of its roots in the earth, bound with a band of iron and bronze, amid the tender grass of the field. Let him be wet with the dew of heaven; let his lot be with the beasts in the grass of the earth; 16 let his mind be changed from a man's, and let a beast's mind be given to him; and let seven times pass over him. 17 The sentence is by the decree of the watchers, the decision by the word of the holy ones, to the end that the living may know that the Most High rules the kingdom of men, and gives it to whom he will, and sets over it the lowliest of men.' 18 This dream I, King Nebuchadnezzar, saw. And you, O Belteshaz'zar, declare the interpretation, because all

the wise men of my kingdom are not able to make known to me the interpretation, but you are able, for the spirit of the holy gods[i] is in you."

19 Then Daniel, whose name was Belteshaz'zar, was dismayed for a moment, and his thoughts alarmed him. The king said, "Belteshaz'zar, let not the dream or the interpretation alarm you." Belteshaz'zar answered, "My lord, may the dream be for those who hate you and its interpretation for your enemies! 20 The tree you saw, which grew and became strong, so that its top reached to heaven, and it was visible to the end of the whole earth; 21 whose leaves were fair and its fruit abundant, and in which was food for all; under which beasts of the field found shade, and in whose branches the birds of the air dwelt— 22 it is you, O king, who have grown and become strong. Your greatness has grown and reaches to heaven, and your dominion to the ends of the earth. 23 And whereas the king saw a watcher, a holy one, coming down from heaven and saying, 'Hew down the tree and destroy it, but leave the stump of its roots in the earth, bound with a band of iron and bronze, in the tender grass of the field; and let him be wet with the dew of heaven; and let his lot be with the beasts of the field, till seven times pass over him'; 24 this is the interpretation, O king: It is a decree of the Most High, which has come upon my lord the king, 25 that you shall be driven from among men, and your dwelling shall be with the beasts of the field; you shall be made to eat grass

g Or *Spirit of the holy God*
h Cn: Aram *visions of*
i Or *Spirit of the holy God*

---

compare 2.48; 5.11. What the *spirit of the holy gods* (v. 18; 5.11) means is quite obscure. **10:** *Tree*, see Ezek.31.3–14. It is the world-tree at the center of the earth disk, whose branches touch the heavenly vault and stretch in all directions to where this vault touches the rim of the disk (see 2.34 n.). **13,17,23:** The *watcher* was a celestial being (see, in the pseudepigraphic literature, 1 Enoch 12.2,3; Jubilees 4.15), who *cried aloud* to his attendants (v. 14); such celestial beings, as a kind of heavenly council, execute the *sentence* given by God. **16:** The *seven times* means a conventional number of years. **19:** *Dismayed*, i.e. embarrassed and perplexed, so he uses a stereotyped formula of aversion. **22:** The tree is *you*, for a tree not uncommonly symbolized a man (Pss.1.3; 37.35; Jer.17.8). **25:** The king will suffer temporarily from "insania zoanthropia," a form of insanity in which a man acts like a beast (v. 33). History knows of no

like an ox, and you shall be wet with the dew of heaven, and seven times shall pass over you, till you know that the Most High rules the kingdom of men, and gives it to whom he will. 26 And as it was commanded to leave the stump of the roots of the tree, your kingdom shall be sure for you from the time that you know that Heaven rules. 27 Therefore, O king, let my counsel be acceptable to you; break off your sins by practicing righteousness, and your iniquities by showing mercy to the oppressed, that there may perhaps be a lengthening of your tranquillity."

28 All this came upon King Nebuchadnez'zar. 29 At the end of twelve months he was walking on the roof of the royal palace of Babylon, 30 and the king said, "Is not this great Babylon, which I have built by my mighty power as a royal residence and for the glory of my majesty?" 31 While the words were still in the king's mouth, there fell a voice from heaven, "O King Nebuchadnez'zar, to you it is spoken: The kingdom has departed from you, 32 and you shall be driven from among men, and your dwelling shall be with the beasts of the field; and you shall be made to eat grass like an ox; and seven times shall pass over you, until you have learned that the Most High rules the kingdom of men and gives it to whom he will." 33 Immediately the word was fulfilled upon Nebuchadnez'zar. He was driven from among men, and ate grass like an ox, and his body was wet with the dew of heaven till his hair grew as long as eagles' feathers, and his nails were like birds' claws.

34 At the end of the days I, Nebuchadnez'zar, lifted my eyes to heaven, and my reason returned to me, and I blessed the Most High, and praised and honored him who lives for ever;
for his dominion is an everlasting dominion,
and his kingdom endures from generation to generation;
35 all the inhabitants of the earth are accounted as nothing;
and he does according to his will in the host of heaven
and among the inhabitants of the earth;
and none can stay his hand or say to him, "What doest thou?"
36 At the same time my reason returned to me; and for the glory of my kingdom, my majesty and splendor returned to me. My counselors and my lords sought me, and I was established in my kingdom, and still more greatness was added to me. 37 Now I, Nebuchadnez'zar, praise and extol and honor the King of heaven; for all his works are right and his ways are just; and those who walk in pride he is able to abase.

5 King Belshaz'zar made a great feast for a thousand of his lords, and drank wine in front of the thousand.

2 Belshaz'zar, when he tasted the wine, commanded that the vessels of gold and of silver which Nebuchadnez'zar his father had taken out of the temple in Jerusalem be brought, that the king and his lords, his wives, and his concubines might drink from them. 3 Then they brought in the golden and silver vessels*j* which had been taken out of the temple, the house of God in Jerusalem; and the king and his lords, his wives, and his

j Theodotion Vg: Aram *golden vessels*

---

such affliction affecting Nebuchadnezzar, but some later tale may have associated it with him. The tale may have originally been told of Nabonidus, to judge from a Dead Sea Scroll text. **30:** Nebuchadnezzar had a reputation as a builder. **36:** His *counselors* were his ministers of state, his *lords* his courtiers.

5.1–31: Belshazzar's feast. A story to show that divine punishment is visited on sacrilege. **1:** *Belshazzar*, son of Nabonidus the last Neo-Babylonian ruler, was only viceroy during his father's absences. *Great feast* probably means a state banquet. **2:** For the *vessels* see 1.2; Ezra 1.7–11. *His father*, i.e. his predecessor, for three kings ruled between Nebuchadnezzar and Nabonidus. From vv. 11,13,18,22, however, we see that this writer thought Nebuchadnezzar

concubines drank from them. ⁴ They drank wine, and praised the gods of gold and silver, bronze, iron, wood, and stone.

5 Immediately the fingers of a man's hand appeared and wrote on the plaster of the wall of the king's palace, opposite the lampstand; and the king saw the hand as it wrote. ⁶ Then the king's color changed, and his thoughts alarmed him; his limbs gave way, and his knees knocked together. ⁷ The king cried aloud to bring in the enchanters, the Chalde'ans, and the astrologers. The king said to the wise men of Babylon, "Whoever reads this writing, and shows me its interpretation, shall be clothed with purple, and have a chain of gold about his neck, and shall be the third ruler in the kingdom." ⁸ Then all the king's wise men came in, but they could not read the writing or make known to the king the interpretation. ⁹ Then King Belshaz'zar was greatly alarmed, and his color changed; and his lords were perplexed.

10 The queen, because of the words of the king and his lords, came into the banqueting hall; and the queen said, "O king, live for ever! Let not your thoughts alarm you or your color change. ¹¹ There is in your kingdom a man in whom is the spirit of the holy gods.ᵏ In the days of your father light and understanding and wisdom, like the wisdom of the gods, were found in him, and King Nebuchadnez'zar, your father, made him chief of the magicians, enchanters, Chalde'ans, and astrologers,ˡ ¹² because an excellent spirit, knowledge, and understanding to interpret dreams, explain riddles, and solve problems were found in this Daniel, whom the king named Belteshaz'zar. Now let Daniel be called, and he will show the interpretation."

13 Then Daniel was brought in before the king. The king said to Daniel, "You are that Daniel, one of the exiles of Judah, whom the king my father brought from Judah. ¹⁴ I have heard of you that the spirit of the holy godsᵏ is in you, and that light and understanding and excellent wisdom are found in you. ¹⁵ Now the wise men, the enchanters, have been brought in before me to read this writing and make known to me its interpretation; but they could not show the interpretation of the matter. ¹⁶ But I have heard that you can give interpretations and solve problems. Now if you can read the writing and make known to me its interpretation, you shall be clothed with purple, and have a chain of gold about your neck, and shall be the third ruler in the kingdom."

17 Then Daniel answered before the king, "Let your gifts be for yourself, and give your rewards to another; nevertheless I will read the writing to the king and make known to him the interpretation. ¹⁸ O king, the Most High God gave Nebuchadnez'zar your father kingship and greatness and glory and majesty; ¹⁹ and because of the greatness that he gave him, all peoples, nations, and languages trembled and feared before him; whom he would he slew, and whom he would he kept alive; whom he would he raised up, and whom he would he put down. ²⁰ But when his heart was lifted up and his spirit was hardened so that he dealt proudly, he was deposed from his kingly throne, and his glory was taken from him; ²¹ he was driven from among men, and his mind was made like that of a beast, and his dwelling was with the wild asses; he was fed grass like an ox, and his body was wet with the dew of heaven, until he knew that the Most High God rules the kingdom of men, and sets over it whom he will. ²² And you his son, Belshaz'zar, have not humbled your heart,

k Or *Spirit of the holy God*
l Aram repeats *the king your father*

was his real father. **4:** During the drinking, libations were poured out to heathen deities. **5:** This sacrilege brought forth *the fingers of a man's hand* writing a message of doom. **7:** The *writing*, we learn from v. 25, was Aramaic, but the message was cryptic and needed *interpretation. Third ruler* means he would rank third in the kingdom. **10–11:** The *queen* was the queen-

though you knew all this, 23 but you have lifted up yourself against the Lord of heaven; and the vessels of his house have been brought in before you, and you and your lords, your wives, and your concubines have drunk wine from them; and you have praised the gods of silver and gold, of bronze, iron, wood, and stone, which do not see or hear or know, but the God in whose hand is your breath, and whose are all your ways, you have not honored.

24 "Then from his presence the hand was sent, and this writing was inscribed. 25 And this is the writing that was inscribed: MENE, MENE, TEKEL, and PARSIN. 26 This is the interpretation of the matter: MENE, God has numbered the days of your kingdom and brought it to an end; 27 TEKEL, you have been weighed in the balances and found wanting; 28 PERES, your kingdom is divided and given to the Medes and Persians."

29 Then Belshaz'zar commanded, and Daniel was clothed with purple, a chain of gold was put about his neck, and proclamation was made concerning him, that he should be the third ruler in the kingdom.

30 That very night Belshaz'zar the Chalde'an king was slain. 31 And Darius the Mede received the kingdom, being about sixty-two years old.

6 It pleased Darius to set over the kingdom a hundred and twenty satraps, to be throughout the whole kingdom; 2 and over them three presi-dents, of whom Daniel was one, to whom these satraps should give ac-count, so that the king might suffer no loss. 3 Then this Daniel became dis-tinguished above all the other presi-dents and satraps, because an excel-lent spirit was in him; and the king planned to set him over the whole king-dom. 4 Then the presidents and the satraps sought to find a ground for complaint against Daniel with regard to the kingdom; but they could find no ground for complaint or any fault, because he was faithful, and no error or fault was found in him. 5 Then these men said, "We shall not find any ground for complaint against this Daniel unless we find it in connection with the law of his God."

6 Then these presidents and satraps came by agreement*m* to the king and said to him, "O King Darius, live for ever! 7 All the presidents of the king-dom, the prefects and the satraps, the counselors and the governors are agreed that the king should establish an ordinance and enforce an interdict, that whoever makes petition to any god or man for thirty days, except to you, O king, shall be cast into the den of lions. 8 Now, O king, establish the interdict and sign the document, so that it cannot be changed, according to the law of the Medes and the Persians, which cannot be revoked." 9 Therefore King Darius signed the document and interdict.

m Or *thronging*

---

mother. **25–28:** All three words represent weights, *mene* a mina, *tekel* a shekel, *parsin* two half-minas, but they may also be read as the verbs "to number," "to weigh," and "to divide." So the meaning may be that Evil-merodach, who succeeded Nebuchadnezzar, weighs a mina, his successor Neriglissar also a mina, his successor Labashi-Marduk only a shekel, Nabonidus and Belshazzar half a mina each, but that now by the judgment of numbering, weighing, and dividing the Neo-Babylonian kingdom is to be conquered by the Medo-Persians. **31:** No such person as *Darius the Mede* is known to history. It was Cyrus who overthrew the Neo-Baby-lonian power. Perhaps it means Cyrus's general Gobyras, who was about *sixty-two*.

    6.1–28: Daniel in the lions' den. A story to show how God will deliver his faithful servants. **1:** Darius I set up the satrapies (i.e. provinces, each governed by a satrap), but *Darius* here means the Mede of 5.31. Jewish tradition increased the twenty-odd satrapies into over one hundred and twenty (Est.1.1; 8.9). **2–5:** Each satrap had a military chief and a civil secretary, these being the *three presidents*. The king, however, planned to appoint Daniel as grand vizier. From this pinnacle jealous fellow officials seek to topple him, using his religion as their lever. **7:** Their request is that for a month the king should be treated as divine. From vv. 17,23,24 it appears that the *den* was thought of as a pit. **8:** For the unchangeableness of Medo-Persian

10 When Daniel knew that the document had been signed, he went to his house where he had windows in his upper chamber open toward Jerusalem; and he got down upon his knees three times a day and prayed and gave thanks before his God, as he had done previously. ¹¹ Then these men came by agreement^m and found Daniel making petition and supplication before his God. ¹² Then they came near and said before the king, concerning the interdict, "O king! Did you not sign an interdict, that any man who makes petition to any god or man within thirty days except to you, O king, shall be cast into the den of lions?" The king answered, "The thing stands fast, according to the law of the Medes and Persians, which cannot be revoked." ¹³ Then they answered before the king, "That Daniel, who is one of the exiles from Judah, pays no heed to you, O king, or the interdict you have signed, but makes his petition three times a day."

14 Then the king, when he heard these words, was much distressed, and set his mind to deliver Daniel; and he labored till the sun went down to rescue him. ¹⁵ Then these men came by agreement^m to the king, and said to the king, "Know, O king, that it is a law of the Medes and Persians that no interdict or ordinance which the king establishes can be changed."

16 Then the king commanded, and Daniel was brought and cast into the den of lions. The king said to Daniel, "May your God, whom you serve continually, deliver you!" ¹⁷ And a stone was brought and laid upon the mouth of the den, and the king sealed it with his own signet and with the signet of his lords, that nothing might be changed concerning Daniel. ¹⁸ Then the king went to his palace, and spent the night fasting; no diversions were brought to him, and sleep fled from him.

19 Then, at break of day, the king arose and went in haste to the den of lions. ²⁰ When he came near to the den where Daniel was, he cried out in a tone of anguish and said to Daniel, "O Daniel, servant of the living God, has your God, whom you serve continually, been able to deliver you from the lions?" ²¹ Then Daniel said to the king, "O king, live for ever! ²² My God sent his angel and shut the lions' mouths, and they have not hurt me, because I was found blameless before him; and also before you, O king, I have done no wrong." ²³ Then the king was exceedingly glad, and commanded that Daniel be taken up out of the den. So Daniel was taken up out of the den, and no kind of hurt was found upon him, because he had trusted in his God. ²⁴ And the king commanded, and those men who had accused Daniel were brought and cast into the den of lions–they, their children, and their wives; and before they reached the bottom of the den the lions overpowered them and broke all their bones in pieces.

25 Then King Darius wrote to all the peoples, nations, and languages that dwell in all the earth: "Peace be multiplied to you. ²⁶ I make a decree, that in all my royal dominion men tremble and fear before the God of Daniel,

for he is the living God,
    enduring for ever;
his kingdom shall never be
    destroyed,
    and his dominion shall be to the
    end.
²⁷ He delivers and rescues,
    he works signs and wonders

m Or *thronging*

---

law see Est.1.19; 8.8. **10:** Daniel had a roof-chamber with windows allowing him to face Jerusalem in prayer (1 Kg.8.44,48). For the three daily prayers see Ps.55.17, and for kneeling 2 Chr.6.13; Ezra 9.5; Acts 20.36. **14:** The monarch sees through the conspiracy but is helpless. **17:** The pit was *sealed* by affixing the royal seal to cords across the stone. **22:** For shutting the lions' mouths see 1 Macc.2.60; Heb.11.33. **24:** Well recognized family solidarity is involved here, as punishment falls also on the families of the accusers (compare Num.16.25–33; Jos.7.24;

in heaven and on earth,
he who has saved Daniel
    from the power of the lions."
28 So this Daniel prospered during
the reign of Darius and the reign of
Cyrus the Persian.

7 In the first year of Belshaz'zar
    king of Babylon, Daniel had a
dream and visions of his head as he
lay in his bed. Then he wrote down
the dream, and told the sum of the
matter. ² Daniel said, "I saw in my
vision by night, and behold, the four
winds of heaven were stirring up the
great sea. ³ And four great beasts
came up out of the sea, different from
one another. ⁴ The first was like a lion
and had eagles' wings. Then as I looked
its wings were plucked off, and it was
lifted up from the ground and made
to stand upon two feet like a man; and
the mind of a man was given to it.
⁵ And behold, another beast, a second
one, like a bear. It was raised up on
one side; it had three ribs in its mouth
between its teeth; and it was told,
'Arise, devour much flesh.' ⁶ After
this I looked, and lo, another, like a
leopard, with four wings of a bird on
its back; and the beast had four heads;
and dominion was given to it. ⁷ After
this I saw in the night visions, and behold, a fourth beast, terrible and dreadful and exceedingly strong; and it had
great iron teeth; it devoured and broke
in pieces, and stamped the residue with
its feet. It was different from all the
beasts that were before it; and it had
ten horns. ⁸ I considered the horns,

and behold, there came up among
them another horn, a little one, before
which three of the first horns were
plucked up by the roots; and behold,
in this horn were eyes like the eyes
of a man, and a mouth speaking great
things. ⁹ As I looked,
thrones were placed
    and one that was ancient of days
        took his seat;
his raiment was white as snow,
    and the hair of his head like pure
        wool;
his throne was fiery flames,
    its wheels were burning fire.
¹⁰ A stream of fire issued
    and came forth from before him;
a thousand thousands served him,
    and ten thousand times ten
        thousand stood before him;
the court sat in judgment,
    and the books were opened.
¹¹ I looked then because of the sound
of the great words which the horn was
speaking. And as I looked, the beast
was slain, and its body destroyed and
given over to be burned with fire. ¹² As
for the rest of the beasts, their dominion
was taken away, but their lives were
prolonged for a season and a time.
¹³ I saw in the night visions,
    and behold, with the clouds of
        heaven
    there came one like a son of man,
    and he came to the Ancient of Days
        and was presented before him.
¹⁴ And to him was given dominion
    and glory and kingdom,
    that all peoples, nations, and
        languages

---

2 Sam.21.6,9; Est.9.13). **28:** Cyrus, whose reign over Babylon began in 538 B.C., was the first
Iranian to rule there, but this writer obviously thinks of his *Darius the Mede* as preceding him.
7.1–28: The vision of the four beasts. A vision of the passing of kingdoms to make way for
the kingdom of God. **1:** *The first year,* i.e. 554 B.C., when he began to act as viceroy for his
father. *The sum,* i.e. the main substance. **2:** In accord with the view that there were four kingdoms (see ch. 2), *four* winds appropriately introduce the beasts symbolizing these kingdoms.
4–8: The winged lion represents the Babylonian empire, the bear the Medes, the four-headed
winged leopard the Persians, the dragon-like beast the Greeks, whose ten horns represent the
ten rulers who succeeded Alexander. The *little horn* (compare 8.9) is Antiochus Epiphanes,
who gained his throne by uprooting others. **9–14: The divine judgment.** God, the Ancient
One, appears on his fiery throne surrounded by his court (1 Kg.22.19); the record books are
examined and judgment is given. **11–12:** The Greek empire will be destroyed, but the remnant
of the others will continue until absorbed into the final kingdom. **13–14:** God will then give

should serve him;
his dominion is an everlasting
    dominion,
  which shall not pass away,
and his kingdom one
    that shall not be destroyed.
15 "As for me, Daniel, my spirit within me was anxious and the visions of my head alarmed me. 16 I approached one of those who stood there and asked him the truth concerning all this. So he told me, and made known to me the interpretation of the things. 17 'These four great beasts are four kings who shall arise out of the earth. 18 But the saints of the Most High shall receive the kingdom, and possess the kingdom for ever, for ever and ever.'

19 "Then I desired to know the truth concerning the fourth beast, which was different from all the rest, exceedingly terrible, with its teeth of iron and claws of bronze; and which devoured and broke in pieces, and stamped the residue with its feet; 20 and concerning the ten horns that were on its head, and the other horn which came up and before which three of them fell, the horn which had eyes and a mouth that spoke great things, and which seemed greater than its fellows. 21 As I looked, this horn made war with the saints, and prevailed over them, 22 until the Ancient of Days came, and judgment was given for the saints of the Most High, and the time came when the saints received the kingdom.

23 "Thus he said: 'As for the fourth
    beast,
  there shall be a fourth kingdom on
    earth,
  which shall be different from all
    the kingdoms,
and it shall devour the whole
    earth,

  and trample it down, and break
    it to pieces.
24 As for the ten horns,
  out of this kingdom
    ten kings shall arise,
  and another shall arise after them;
he shall be different from the former
    ones,
  and shall put down three kings.
25 He shall speak words against the
    Most High,
  and shall wear out the saints of the
    Most High,
  and shall think to change the
    times and the law;
and they shall be given into his hand
  for a time, two times, and half a
    time.
26 But the court shall sit in judgment,
  and his dominion shall be taken
    away,
  to be consumed and destroyed to
    the end.
27 And the kingdom and the
    dominion
  and the greatness of the kingdoms
    under the whole heaven
  shall be given to the people of
    the saints of the Most High;
their kingdom shall be an
    everlasting kingdom,
  and all dominions shall serve and
    obey them.'

28 "Here is the end of the matter. As for me, Daniel, my thoughts greatly alarmed me, and my color changed; but I kept the matter in my mind."

8 In the third year of the reign of King Belshaz'zar a vision appeared to me, Daniel, after that which appeared to me at the first. 2 And I saw in the vision; and when I saw, I was in Susa the capital, which is in the province of Elam; and I saw in the vision, and I was at the river U'lai. 3 I raised my eyes and saw, and be-

---

the messianic king a universal and *everlasting* dominion. **16:** At the seer's request an angel gives him the *interpretation*. **21:** Antiochus Epiphanes persecuted the righteous (see "Survey of . . . Bible Lands," §15). **25–28:** Catalogue of Antiochus' enormities with prediction of their end after three and a half years (i.e. *a time, two times, and a half a time;* compare 8.14; 9.27; 12.7,11,12). After his end the expected messianic kingdom will be established.

8.1–27: The vision of the ram and the he-goat. 1–2: The vision is dated two years later than the previous one (7.1), placing the seer in *Susa*, the winter capital of the Persian kings. The *Ulai*

hold, a ram standing on the bank of the river. It had two horns; and both horns were high, but one was higher than the other, and the higher one came up last. [4] I saw the ram charging westward and northward and southward; no beast could stand before him, and there was no one who could rescue from his power; he did as he pleased and magnified himself.

5 As I was considering, behold, a he-goat came from the west across the face of the whole earth, without touching the ground; and the goat had a conspicuous horn between his eyes. [6] He came to the ram with the two horns, which I had seen standing on the bank of the river, and he ran at him in his mighty wrath. [7] I saw him come close to the ram, and he was enraged against him and struck the ram and broke his two horns; and the ram had no power to stand before him, but he cast him down to the ground and trampled upon him; and there was no one who could rescue the ram from his power. [8] Then the he-goat magnified himself exceedingly; but when he was strong, the great horn was broken, and instead of it there came up four conspicuous horns toward the four winds of heaven.

9 Out of one of them came forth a little horn, which grew exceedingly great toward the south, toward the east, and toward the glorious land. [10] It grew great, even to the host of heaven; and some of the host of the stars it cast down to the ground, and trampled upon them. [11] It magnified itself, even up to the Prince of the host; and the continual burnt offering was taken away from him, and the place of his

sanctuary was overthrown. [12] And the host was given over to it together with the continual burnt offering through transgression;[n] and truth was cast down to the ground, and the horn acted and prospered. [13] Then I heard a holy one speaking; and another holy one said to the one that spoke, "For how long is the vision concerning the continual burnt offering, the transgression that makes desolate, and the giving over of the sanctuary and host to be trampled under foot?"[o] [14] And he said to him,[p] "For two thousand and three hundred evenings and mornings; then the sanctuary shall be restored to its rightful state."

15 When I, Daniel, had seen the vision, I sought to understand it; and behold, there stood before me one having the appearance of a man. [16] And I heard a man's voice between the banks of the U'lai, and it called, "Gabriel, make this man understand the vision." [17] So he came near where I stood; and when he came, I was frightened and fell upon my face. But he said to me, "Understand, O son of man, that the vision is for the time of the end."

18 As he was speaking to me, I fell into a deep sleep with my face to the ground; but he touched me and set me on my feet. [19] He said, "Behold, I will make known to you what shall be at the latter end of the indignation; for it pertains to the appointed time of the end. [20] As for the ram which you saw with the two horns, these are the kings of Media and Persia. [21] And the he-goat[q] is the king of Greece; and the

n Heb obscure   o Heb obscure
p Theodotion Gk Syr Vg: Heb *me*
q Or *shaggy he-goat*

---

is the Eulaeus. **3–4:** The two-horned ram is the Medo-Persian empire (v. 20), the advance of the Persians being irresistible. **5–7:** The he-goat from the west is Alexander the Great (v. 21), who overthrew the Persian empire. **8:** Alexander's empire was divided, the four *conspicuous* leaders being Cassander, Lysimachus, Seleucus, and Ptolemy. **9–14:** From the Seleucids sprang Antiochus Epiphanes who in 167 B.C. conquered Palestine, violated the *sanctuary*, and prohibited worship there (vv. 23–25; see "Survey of . . . Bible Lands," §15). The angels comment and calculate that this will continue about three and a half years (*two thousand and three hundred evenings and mornings* are one thousand, one hundred and fifty days; see 7.25–28 n.). The *sanctuary* was *restored* on 25th Chislev (December 14th) 164 B.C. **16:** *A man's voice* i.e. a celestial being speaking human language. **17:** *The end*, compare v. 19; 11.35; 12.4,9,13. **23–24:**

great horn between his eyes is the first king. ²² As for the horn that was broken, in place of which four others arose, four kingdoms shall arise from his^r nation, but not with his power. ²³ And at the latter end of their rule, when the transgressors have reached their full measure, a king of bold countenance, one who understands riddles, shall arise. ²⁴ His power shall be great,^s and he shall cause fearful destruction, and shall succeed in what he does, and destroy mighty men and the people of the saints. ²⁵ By his cunning he shall make deceit prosper under his hand, and in his own mind he shall magnify himself. Without warning he shall destroy many; and he shall even rise up against the Prince of princes; but, by no human hand, he shall be broken. ²⁶ The vision of the evenings and the mornings which has been told is true; but seal up the vision, for it pertains to many days hence."

27 And I, Daniel, was overcome and lay sick for some days; then I rose and went about the king's business; but I was appalled by the vision and did not understand it.

9 In the first year of Darius the son of Ahasu-e′rus, by birth a Mede, who became king over the realm of the Chalde′ans— ² in the first year of his reign, I, Daniel, perceived in the books the number of years which, according to the word of the LORD to Jeremiah the prophet, must pass before the end of the desolations of Jerusalem, namely, seventy years.

3 Then I turned my face to the Lord God, seeking him by prayer and supplications with fasting and sackcloth and ashes. ⁴ I prayed to the LORD my God and made confession, saying,

"O Lord, the great and terrible God, who keepest covenant and steadfast love with those who love him and keep his commandments, ⁵ we have sinned and done wrong and acted wickedly and rebelled, turning aside from thy commandments and ordinances; ⁶ we have not listened to thy servants the prophets, who spoke in thy name to our kings, our princes, and our fathers, and to all the people of the land. ⁷ To thee, O Lord, belongs righteousness, but to us confusion of face, as at this day, to the men of Judah, to the inhabitants of Jerusalem, and to all Israel, those that are near and those that are far away, in all the lands to which thou hast driven them, because of the treachery which they have committed against thee. ⁸ To us, O Lord, belongs confusion of face, to our kings, to our princes, and to our fathers, because we have sinned against thee. ⁹ To the Lord our God belong mercy and forgiveness; because we have rebelled against him, ¹⁰ and have not obeyed the voice of the LORD our God by following his laws, which he set before us by his servants the prophets. ¹¹ All Israel has transgressed thy law and turned aside, refusing to obey thy voice. And the curse and oath which are written in the law of Moses the servant of God have been poured out upon us, because we have sinned against him. ¹² He has confirmed his words, which he spoke against us and against our rulers who ruled us, by bringing upon us a great calamity; for under the whole heaven there has not been done the like of what has been done against Jerusalem. ¹³ As it is written in the law

r Theodotion Gk Vg: Heb *the*
s Theodotion and Beatty papyrus of Gk: Heb repeats *but not with his power* from verse 22

The shameless insolence, "double talk," and ruthlessness of Antiochus were notorious. *The saints* are the godly Jews (7.25,27). **25**: *The Prince of princes* is God, to whom Antiochus' self-deification (11.36) was an affront, and by whom he was *broken* (2 Macc.9.5). **26–27**: Since Daniel is pictured as being in Susa in 552 B.C., and the vision concerns events of 164, the account is to be preserved for that time, for naturally Daniel did *not understand it.*

9.1–27: The prophecy of the seventy weeks, expounding a prophecy of Jeremiah. **1**: According to this writer's chronology the *first year* of *Darius* the Mede was 538 B.C. *Ahasuerus* means Xerxes, a fictitious parent for a fictitious Darius. **2**: The *seventy years* are referred to in Jer. 25.11,12; 29.10. **4–19**: With Daniel's prayer of confession compare Neh. chs. 1 and 9. **11**: For

of Moses, all this calamity has come upon us, yet we have not entreated the favor of the LORD our God, turning from our iniquities and giving heed to thy truth. ¹⁴ Therefore the LORD has kept ready the calamity and has brought it upon us; for the LORD our God is righteous in all the works which he has done, and we have not obeyed his voice. ¹⁵ And now, O Lord our God, who didst bring thy people out of the land of Egypt with a mighty hand, and hast made thee a name, as at this day, we have sinned, we have done wickedly. ¹⁶ O Lord, according to all thy righteous acts, let thy anger and thy wrath turn away from thy city Jerusalem, thy holy hill; because for our sins, and for the iniquities of our fathers, Jerusalem and thy people have become a byword among all who are round about us. ¹⁷ Now therefore, O our God, hearken to the prayer of thy servant and to his supplications, and for thy own sake, O Lord,*ᵗ* cause thy face to shine upon thy sanctuary, which is desolate. ¹⁸ O my God, incline thy ear and hear; open thy eyes and behold our desolations, and the city which is called by thy name; for we do not present our supplications before thee on the ground of our righteousness, but on the ground of thy great mercy. ¹⁹ O LORD, hear; O LORD, forgive; O LORD, give heed and act; delay not, for thy own sake, O my God, because thy city and thy people are called by thy name."

20 While I was speaking and praying, confessing my sin and the sin of my people Israel, and presenting my supplication before the LORD my God for the holy hill of my God; ²¹ while I was speaking in prayer, the man Gabriel, whom I had seen in the vision at the first, came to me in swift flight at the time of the evening sacrifice. ²² He came*ᵘ* and he said to me, "O Daniel, I have now come out to give you wisdom and understanding. ²³ At the beginning of your supplications a word went forth, and I have come to tell it to you, for you are greatly beloved; therefore consider the word and understand the vision.

24 "Seventy weeks of years are decreed concerning your people and your holy city, to finish the transgression, to put an end to sin, and to atone for iniquity, to bring in everlasting righteousness, to seal both vision and prophet, and to anoint a most holy place.*ᵛ* ²⁵ Know therefore and understand that from the going forth of the word to restore and build Jerusalem to the coming of an anointed one, a prince, there shall be seven weeks. Then for sixty-two weeks it shall be built again with squares and moat, but in a troubled time. ²⁶ And after the sixty-two weeks, an anointed one shall be cut off, and shall have nothing; and the people of the prince who is to come shall destroy the city and the sanctuary. Its*ʷ* end shall come with a flood, and to the end there shall be war; desolations are decreed. ²⁷ And he shall make a strong covenant with many for one week; and for half of the week he shall cause sacrifice and offering to cease; and upon the wing of abominations shall come one who makes deso-

t Theodotion Vg Compare Syr: Heb *for the Lord's sake*
u Gk Syr: Heb *made to understand*
v Or *thing* or *one*   *w* Or *his*

---

this *curse* see Dt.28.15–45. **13:** For what was *written* see Lev.26.14–22. **17:** The *desolate* sanctuary is a hint of Antiochus' "abomination of desolation" (v. 27; 8.13; see 11.29–31 n.). **21:** Gabriel is called *the man* because he appeared in human form (8.15). **24:** Jeremiah's seventy years (see v. 2. n.) mean *seventy weeks of years*, or 490 years (i.e. 70 × 7 years), after which the messianic kingdom will come, fulfilling both *vision and prophet*. **25–27:** As we do not know his date for the *going forth of the word*, we can only guess that his princely *anointed one* may have been Cyrus, or Zerubbabel, or Jeshua, and the one *cut off* Philopator, or Jason, or Onias III. The *prince who is to come* is doubtless Antiochus, who wrought such *desolation*, made *a covenant* with the Hellenizing Jews, and offered the *abominations* of heathen sacrifice in the temple. *Seven weeks*, i.e. forty-nine years. *Sixty-two weeks*, i.e. 434 years. *One week*, i.e. seven years. *Half a week*, i.e. three and one-half years; see 7.25–28 n.

late, until the decreed end is poured out on the desolator."

10 In the third year of Cyrus king of Persia a word was revealed to Daniel, who was named Belteshaz'zar. And the word was true, and it was a great conflict. And he understood the word and had understanding of the vision.

2 In those days I, Daniel, was mourning for three weeks. ³ I ate no delicacies, no meat or wine entered my mouth, nor did I anoint myself at all, for the full three weeks. ⁴ On the twenty-fourth day of the first month, as I was standing on the bank of the great river, that is, the Tigris, ⁵ I lifted up my eyes and looked, and behold, a man clothed in linen, whose loins were girded with gold of Uphaz. ⁶ His body was like beryl, his face like the appearance of lightning, his eyes like flaming torches, his arms and legs like the gleam of burnished bronze, and the sound of his words like the noise of a multitude. ⁷ And I, Daniel, alone saw the vision, for the men who were with me did not see the vision, but a great trembling fell upon them, and they fled to hide themselves. ⁸ So I was left alone and saw this great vision, and no strength was left in me; my radiant appearance was fearfully changed, and I retained no strength. ⁹ Then I heard the sound of his words; and when I heard the sound of his words, I fell on my face in a deep sleep with my face to the ground.

10 And behold, a hand touched me and set me trembling on my hands and knees. ¹¹ And he said to me, "O

Daniel, man greatly beloved, give heed to the words that I speak to you, and stand upright, for now I have been sent to you." While he was speaking this word to me, I stood up trembling. ¹² Then he said to me, "Fear not, Daniel, for from the first day that you set your mind to understand and humbled yourself before your God, your words have been heard, and I have come because of your words. ¹³ The prince of the kingdom of Persia withstood me twenty-one days; but Michael, one of the chief princes, came to help me, so I left him there with the prince of the kingdom of Persiaˣ ¹⁴ and came to make you understand what is to befall your people in the latter days. For the vision is for days yet to come."

15 When he had spoken to me according to these words, I turned my face toward the ground and was dumb. ¹⁶ And behold, one in the likeness of the sons of men touched my lips; then I opened my mouth and spoke. I said to him who stood before me, "O my lord, by reason of the vision pains have come upon me, and I retain no strength. ¹⁷ How can my lord's servant talk with my lord? For now no strength remains in me, and no breath is left in me."

18 Again one having the appearance of a man touched me and strengthened me. ¹⁹ And he said, "O man greatly beloved, fear not, peace be with you; be strong and of good courage." And when he spoke to me,

x Theodotion Compare Gk: Heb *I was left there with the kings of Persia*

10.1–21: A vision of the last days (which continues through 12.13, ch. 10 being prologue, ch. 11 the vision, ch. 12 the epilogue). **1:** *The third year of Cyrus*, 535 B.C. For the first *conflict* see v. 13. **4:** *Tigris* is a gloss on *great river*, for Babylon is on the Euphrates. **5:** The *man* was a celestial being, probably Gabriel, in human form, but having angelic splendor. *Uphaz*, see Jer.10.9. **7:** His companions did not see the vision but were affected by the supernatural presence, as in Acts 9.7. **12–13:** *Michael . . . came to help*, as in 9.21–23 Gabriel is God's response to supplication. Conflict in heaven among the angelic patrons of the nations had delayed his coming three weeks, and he got away because *Michael*, the Jews' patron angel (v. 21), had helped him against the patron angel of Persia. In vv. 20–21 he says he must return, when he expects to be involved with the patron angel of Greece also. That they *withstood* him suggests they did not want Daniel to be told the things which were *to befall* the Jews in *days yet to come*.

I was strengthened and said, "Let my lord speak, for you have strengthened me." [20] Then he said, "Do you know why I have come to you? But now I will return to fight against the prince of Persia; and when I am through with him, lo, the prince of Greece will come. [21] But I will tell you what is inscribed in the book of truth: there is none who contends by my side against these except Michael, your prince. [1] And as for me, in the first year of Darius the Mede, I stood up to confirm and strengthen him.

2 "And now I will show you the truth. Behold, three more kings shall arise in Persia; and a fourth shall be far richer than all of them; and when he has become strong through his riches, he shall stir up all against the kingdom of Greece. [3] Then a mighty king shall arise, who shall rule with great dominion and do according to his will. [4] And when he has arisen, his kingdom shall be broken and divided toward the four winds of heaven, but not to his posterity, nor according to the dominion with which he ruled; for his kingdom shall be plucked up and go to others besides these.

5 "Then the king of the south shall be strong, but one of his princes shall be stronger than he and his dominion shall be a great dominion. [6] After some years they shall make an alliance, and the daughter of the king of the south shall come to the king of the north to make peace; but she shall not retain the strength of her arm, and he and

his offspring shall not endure; but she shall be given up, and her attendants, her child, and he who got possession of[y] her.

7 "In those times a branch[z] from her roots shall arise in his place; he shall come against the army and enter the fortress of the king of the north, and he shall deal with them and shall prevail. [8] He shall also carry off to Egypt their gods with their molten images and with their precious vessels of silver and of gold; and for some years he shall refrain from attacking the king of the north. [9] Then the latter shall come into the realm of the king of the south but shall return into his own land.

10 "His sons shall wage war and assemble a multitude of great forces, which shall come on and overflow and pass through, and again shall carry the war as far as his fortress. [11] Then the king of the south, moved with anger, shall come out and fight with the king of the north; and he shall raise a great multitude, but it shall be given into his hand. [12] And when the multitude is taken, his heart shall be exalted, and he shall cast down tens of thousands, but he shall not prevail. [13] For the king of the north shall again raise a multitude, greater than the former; and after some years[a] he shall come on with a great army and abundant supplies.

14 "In those times many shall rise against the king of the south; and the

y Or *supported*
z Gk: Heb *from a branch*
a Heb *at the end of the times years*

11.1–12.13: Interpretation of the vision of history unfolding. 1: The angel had been the guardian angel of *Darius the Mede* and *now*, treating Daniel as an official of Cyrus, proceeds to unfold history. **2:** If the *three more* are those after Cyrus they are probably Cambyses, Darius I, and Xerxes I, who warred with the Greeks. Some suggest that Darius III, the last king of Persia, is the *fourth;* others believe Artaxerxes is meant. **3:** The *mighty king* is Alexander the Great. **4:** For his kingdom broken into four, see 8.8 n. None of his successors were of *his posterity.* **5:** The kings of *the south* are the Ptolemies, those of *the north* the Seleucids. Here the *king* is Ptolemy I, and the prince who was *stronger* is Seleucus I. **6:** The *alliance* was that of about 250 B.C., when Ptolemy II gave his daughter Bernice to Antiochus II; but Bernice, her *attendants*, her *child*, and her husband fell, owing to the plotting of Laodice, mother of Seleucus II. **7–8:** The *branch* is Ptolemy III, who captured the *fortress* of Seleucia and brought back immense booty. **9:** A reference to the campaign of Seleucus II against Egypt in 242 B.C., which came to disaster. **10:** *His sons* were Seleucus III and Antiochus III, the latter of whom attacked Egypt. **11–13:** Ptolemy IV sent armies through Palestine and defeated Antiochus at

men of violence among your own people shall lift themselves up in order to fulfil the vision; but they shall fail. ¹⁵ Then the king of the north shall come and throw up siegeworks, and take a well-fortified city. And the forces of the south shall not stand, or even his picked troops, for there shall be no strength to stand. ¹⁶ But he who comes against him shall do according to his own will, and none shall stand before him; and he shall stand in the glorious land, and all of it shall be in his power. ¹⁷ He shall set his face to come with the strength of his whole kingdom, and he shall bring terms of peace*ᵇ* and perform them. He shall give him the daughter of women to destroy the kingdom;*ᶜ* but it shall not stand or be to his advantage. ¹⁸ Afterward he shall turn his face to the coastlands, and shall take many of them; but a commander shall put an end to his insolence; indeed*ᵈ* he shall turn his insolence back upon him. ¹⁹ Then he shall turn his face back toward the fortresses of his own land; but he shall stumble and fall, and shall not be found.

20 "Then shall arise in his place one who shall send an exactor of tribute through the glory of the kingdom; but within a few days he shall be broken, neither in anger nor in battle. ²¹ In his place shall arise a contemptible person to whom royal majesty has not been given; he shall come in without warning and obtain the kingdom by flatteries. ²² Armies shall be utterly swept away before him and broken, and the prince of the covenant also. ²³ And from the time that an alliance is made with him he shall act deceitfully; and he shall become strong with a small people. ²⁴ Without warning he shall come into the richest parts*ᵉ* of the province; and he shall do what neither his fathers nor his fathers' fathers have done, scattering among them plunder, spoil, and goods. He shall devise plans against strongholds, but only for a time. ²⁵ And he shall stir up his power and his courage against the king of the south with a great army; and the king of the south shall wage war with an exceedingly great and mighty army; but he shall not stand, for plots shall be devised against him. ²⁶ Even those who eat his rich food shall be his undoing; his army shall be swept away, and many shall fall down slain. ²⁷ And as for the two kings, their minds shall be bent on mischief; they shall speak lies at the same table, but to no avail; for the end is yet to be at the time appointed. ²⁸ And he shall return to his land with great substance, but his heart shall be set against the holy covenant. And he shall work his will, and return to his own land.

29 "At the time appointed he shall return and come into the south; but it shall not be this time as it was before. ³⁰ For ships of Kittim shall come against him, and he shall be afraid and withdraw, and shall turn back and be enraged and take action against the holy covenant. He shall turn back and

b Gk: Heb *upright ones*　　*c* Heb *her* or *it*
d Heb obscure　　*e* Or *among the richest men*

Raphia, but Antiochus in turn crushed the Egyptians at Banias. **14:** A reference to the Egyptian insurrections under the child king, Ptolemy V. **15–17:** Antiochus III campaigned against Egypt, taking possession of Palestine, then made peace with Egypt, sealing it by marrying his daughter to the youthful Ptolemy. **18–19:** Antiochus undertook a campaign to capture the *coast lands* of Asia Minor, but, checked by the Roman *commander*, he started plundering on his return journey and died at Elymais. **20:** Seleucus IV succeeded him and to help pay the Roman indemnity sent to Jerusalem an *exactor*, Heliodorus, to seize the temple treasure. He failed and died ingloriously. **21–45:** These verses concern Antiochus IV Epiphanes, the *contemptible person* who attained power by guile. **22–24:** His southern campaign, during which he deposed *the prince*, i.e. the high-priest Onias III, by *alliance* appointed Jason as high-priest, and let his troops plunder Palestine. **25–28:** His Egyptian campaign. In 169 he invaded Egypt and captured Ptolemy VI. Troubles at home forced him to leave Egypt, and on his way back with great booty, he sacked Jerusalem and plundered the treasury. **29–31:** The second campaign against Egypt, when Romans, coming in *ships* from *Kittim* (Cyprus), forced him to withdraw. Being

give heed to those who forsake the holy covenant. [31] Forces from him shall appear and profane the temple and fortress, and shall take away the continual burnt offering. And they shall set up the abomination that makes desolate. [32] He shall seduce with flattery those who violate the covenant; but the people who know their God shall stand firm and take action. [33] And those among the people who are wise shall make many understand, though they shall fall by sword and flame, by captivity and plunder, for some days. [34] When they fall, they shall receive a little help. And many shall join themselves to them with flattery; [35] and some of those who are wise shall fall, to refine and to cleanse them[f] and to make them white, until the time of the end, for it is yet for the time appointed.

36 "And the king shall do according to his will; he shall exalt himself and magnify himself above every god, and shall speak astonishing things against the God of gods. He shall prosper till the indignation is accomplished; for what is determined shall be done. [37] He shall give no heed to the gods of his fathers, or to the one beloved by women; he shall not give heed to any other god, for he shall magnify himself above all. [38] He shall honor the god of fortresses instead of these; a god whom his fathers did not know he shall honor with gold and silver, with precious stones and costly gifts. [39] He shall deal with the strongest fortresses by the help of a foreign god; those who acknowledge him he shall magnify with honor. He shall make them rulers

over many and shall divide the land for a price.

40 "At the time of the end the king of the south shall attack[g] him; but the king of the north shall rush upon him like a whirlwind, with chariots and horsemen, and with many ships; and he shall come into countries and shall overflow and pass through. [41] He shall come into the glorious land. And tens of thousands shall fall, but these shall be delivered out of his hand: Edom and Moab and the main part of the Ammonites. [42] He shall stretch out his hand against the countries, and the land of Egypt shall not escape. [43] He shall become ruler of the treasures of gold and of silver, and all the precious things of Egypt; and the Libyans and the Ethiopians shall follow in his train. [44] But tidings from the east and the north shall alarm him, and he shall go forth with great fury to exterminate and utterly destroy many. [45] And he shall pitch his palatial tents between the sea and the glorious holy mountain; yet he shall come to his end, with none to help him.

12 "At that time shall arise Michael, the great prince who has charge of your people. And there shall be a time of trouble, such as never has been since there was a nation till that time; but at that time your people shall be delivered, every one whose name shall be found written in the book. [2] And many of those who sleep in the dust of the earth shall awake, some to everlasting life, and some to shame and

f Gk: Heb *among them*
g Heb *thrust at*

---

enraged he attacked Jerusalem again in 167 B.C., setting up the *abomination that makes desolate*, i.e. a heathen altar in the temple (see "Survey of . . . Bible Lands," §15). 33–35: The resistance movement. Some Hellenizing Jews sided with Antiochus, forsaking the *covenant*, but the *wise*, though persecuted, maintained resistance. The *little help* is the Maccabean success, the revolt of Mattathias and his son, Judas Maccabeus (1 Macc. ch. 2). 36–39: Antiochus' march towards his doom. He abandoned *the gods of his fathers* and the Tammuz-Adonis cult, being interested in Zeus Olympius and claiming divine honors for himself. 40–45: Predictions that Ptolemy will provoke another war with disastrous results, so that Antiochus will conquer Libya to the west of Egypt and Ethiopia to the south, but on his way back will perish somewhere along the coastal route. None of these predictions was fulfilled. 12.1–13: The final consummation. 1: These campaigns of Antiochus only introduce the great tribulation which precedes the end of the age. *Michael*, see 10.12–13 n. 2: The general resurrection, with judgment to *shame* or to

everlasting contempt. [3] And those who are wise shall shine like the brightness of the firmament; and those who turn many to righteousness, like the stars for ever and ever. [4] But you, Daniel, shut up the words, and seal the book, until the time of the end. Many shall run to and fro, and knowledge shall increase."

5 Then I Daniel looked, and behold, two others stood, one on this bank of the stream and one on that bank of the stream. [6] And I[h] said to the man clothed in linen, who was above the waters of the stream, "How long shall it be till the end of these wonders?" [7] The man clothed in linen, who was above the waters of the stream, raised his right hand and his left hand toward heaven; and I heard him swear by him who lives for ever that it would be for a time, two times, and half a time; and that when the shattering of the power of the holy people comes to

an end all these things would be accomplished. [8] I heard, but I did not understand. Then I said, "O my lord, what shall be the issue of these things?" [9] He said, "Go your way, Daniel, for the words are shut up and sealed until the time of the end. [10] Many shall purify themselves, and make themselves white, and be refined; but the wicked shall do wickedly; and none of the wicked shall understand; but those who are wise shall understand. [11] And from the time that the continual burnt offering is taken away, and the abomination that makes desolate is set up, there shall be a thousand two hundred and ninety days. [12] Blessed is he who waits and comes to the thousand three hundred and thirty-five days. [13] But go your way till the end; and you shall rest, and shall stand in your allotted place at the end of the days."

h Gk Vg: Heb *he*

---

life. **4**: Knowledge of these matters is to be *shut up* till the end. **6–7**: When will the end be? One angelic response to Daniel's question: it will be in three and a half years (see 7.25–28 n.). **8–12**: Two new and variant calculations setting the end somewhat later, i.e. 1,290 days and 1,335 days, perhaps added after the three and one-half years (1,150 days) had passed. **13**: The promise that Daniel will have a place in that final consummation.

THE BOOK OF HOSEA

The book of Hosea stands first in that part of the Latter Prophets called the Book of the Twelve, also known as the Minor Prophets because of the brevity of the books in comparison with Isaiah, Jeremiah, and Ezekiel (see Introduction to the Old Testament, p. xxv). By the second century B.C. these twelve constituted a unit (see Sir.49.10). See p. xxvii.

Hosea's ministry to the northern kingdom followed closely upon that of Amos (see Introduction to Amos). While Amos had spoken as a southerner to a prosperous Israel enjoying an era of peace, Hosea spoke as a native to his own people who were suffering from war with Assyria and in virtual anarchy. Four Israelite kings were assassinated within fourteen years after the death of Jeroboam II. After the Assyrian conquest of 733–732, which resulted in the fall of Damascus, Samaria itself soon fell to the Assyrians (721).

Not all aspects of Hosea's life are clear. It can best be reconstructed, however, from the first three chapters by observing that Hosea deals with Gomer as the LORD deals with Israel; the prophet's personal life is an incarnation of God's redeeming love. Accordingly the sensitive prophet, obedient to his call to take "a wife of harlotry," married the prostitute Gomer. She bore three children, of whom Hosea was presumably not the father (2.4–5), and then left him. But Hosea brought her back publicly (3.1–5) and took her again to himself.

Hosea's ministry dramatizes his message. Though the book is divided into two uneven parts (chs. 1–3; 4–14) and presents serious textual difficulties, it is thoroughly unified by the dominant theme of divine compassion and the love that will not let Israel go. At the heart of Hosea's preaching is a gospel of redeeming love.

THE WORD OF THE LORD THAT came to Hose′a the son of Be-e′ri, in the days of Uzzi′ah, Jotham, Ahaz, and Hezeki′ah, kings of Judah, and in the days of Jerobo′am the son of Jo′ash, king of Israel.

2 When the LORD first spoke through Hose′a, the LORD said to Hose′a, " Go, take to yourself a wife of harlotry and have children of harlotry, for the land commits great harlotry by forsaking the LORD." ³ So he went and took Gomer the daughter of Dib-la′im, and she conceived and bore him a son.

4 And the LORD said to him, "Call his name Jezreel; for yet a little while, and I will punish the house of Jehu for the blood of Jezreel, and I will put an end to the kingdom of the house of Israel. ⁵ And on that day, I will break the bow of Israel in the valley of Jezreel."

6 She conceived again and bore a daughter. And the LORD said to him, "Call her name Not pitied, for I will

1.1: Superscription. The conviction that *the word of the LORD* comes to a prophet (Jl.1.1; Mic.1.1; Zeph.1.1; Hag.1.1; Zech.1.1) is fundamental to Hebrew prophecy; it asserts that the prophet's inspiration and authority are not from himself but God, who has revealed his will to him (Ezek.2.3–5; 3.10–11; Am.3.7; Zech.1.6), whose personal agent he is (Ex.4.15–16; Is.6.8), and whom alone he must obey (1 Kg. ch. 13; Am.7.14–17; Acts 4.18–20). *Hosea* means "salvation" or "deliverance." *The kings of Judah*, see Is.1.1 n., and Mic.1.1 n. Hosea prophesied not only during the reign of Jeroboam II (786–746 B.C.; see Introduction to Amos), but also after his death.

1.2–3.5: Hosea's disciplinary actions against his unfaithful wife and her children and his redemptive love for them exemplify God's dealings with harlotrous Israel and form a living basis for his preaching. Time–the reign of Jeroboam II.

1.2–9: Hosea marries the prostitute Gomer and gives her children prophetically significant names (Is.7.3; 8.3) at the LORD's command. **2:** *For the land* . . . expresses the essence of Israel's sin and her need of redemption. **4–5:** *Jezreel*, meaning "God sows," points backward to the sin of the house of *Jehu* (1 Kg.19.15–17; 2 Kg. chs. 9–10) and forward to Israel's restoration (Hos.2.21–23). Jeroboam II belonged to the dynasty of Jehu. **6:** Because of her sin Israel will *not* be *pitied*, and the name of the second child (Hebrew *Lo-ruhamah*) will be a living reminder

no more have pity on the house of
Israel, to forgive them at all. ⁷ But I
will have pity on the house of Judah,
and I will deliver them by the LORD
their God; I will not deliver them by
bow, nor by sword, nor by war, nor by
horses, nor by horsemen."

8 When she had weaned Not pitied,
she conceived and bore a son. ⁹ And
the LORD said, "Call his name Not my
people, for you are not my people and
I am not your God."ᵃ

10ᵇ Yet the number of the people
of Israel shall be like the sand of the
sea, which can be neither measured
nor numbered; and in the place where
it was said to them, "You are not my
people," it shall be said to them, "Sons
of the living God." ¹¹ And the people
of Judah and the people of Israel shall
be gathered together, and they shall
appoint for themselves one head; and
they shall go up from the land, for great
shall be the day of Jezreel.

2 ᶜ Say to your brother,ᵈ "My people," and to your sister,ᵉ "She
has obtained pity."

² "Plead with your mother, plead—
    for she is not my wife,
  and I am not her husband—
that she put away her harlotry from
    her face,
  and her adultery from between
    her breasts;
³ lest I strip her naked
  and make her as in the day she
    was born,
and make her like a wilderness,
  and set her like a parched
    land,
  and slay her with thirst.

⁴ Upon her children also I will have
    no pity,
  because they are children of
    harlotry.
⁵ For their mother has played the
    harlot;
  she that conceived them has
    acted shamefully.
For she said, 'I will go after my
    lovers,
  who give me my bread and my
    water,
  my wool and my flax, my oil and
    my drink.'
⁶ Therefore I will hedge up herᶠ way
    with thorns;
  and I will build a wall against her,
  so that she cannot find her paths.
⁷ She shall pursue her lovers,
  but not overtake them;
  and she shall seek them,
  but shall not find them.
Then she shall say, 'I will go
  and return to my first husband,
  for it was better with me then
    than now.'
⁸ And she did not know
  that it was I who gave her
  the grain, the wine, and the oil,
  and who lavished upon her silver
  and gold which they used for
    Ba'al.
⁹ Therefore I will take back
  my grain in its time,
  and my wine in its season;
  and I will take away my wool and
    my flax,
  which were to cover her
    nakedness.

a Heb *I am not yours*   b Ch 2.1 in Heb
c Ch 2.3 in Heb   d Gk: Heb *brothers*
e Gk Vg: Heb *sisters*   f Gk Syr: Heb *your*

---

of this. **7**: This verse, which exempts *Judah*, is a later addition. **8–9**: The name of the third
child (Hebrew *Lo-ammi*) signifies the breaking of the covenant relationship between the LORD
and Israel (Ex.6.7; 19.5; compare Is.40.1; Jer.31.31–34).

    1.10–2.1: Israel's punishment is not final; afterwards she *shall be like the sand of the sea*
(compare Gen.22.17) and again as God's *sons* (compare Rom.9.25–26). Though these words
may have been uttered at a different time, the thought is genuinely Hosean (see 14.4–7).

    2.2–13: Israel will suffer public shame and personal privation like a harlot, because she has
adulterated the worship of the LORD with Canaanite Baalism. **3**: Is.47.2–3; Ezek.16.37–39;
Rev.17.16. **5**: Jer.2.23–25; 3.1–2. Israel's *lovers* and their gifts refer to the immoral fertility
rites of Canaanite religion. **7**: Hosea takes the metaphor of marriage from the cult of Baal,
and boldly calls the LORD *husband*. **8**: The LORD, the universal Creator, is the giver of all good
gifts, though Israel may fail to acknowledge this (Gen.1.29–30; Dt.7.13; Jas.1.17). **9**: Am.4.6–8.

10 Now I will uncover her lewdness
     in the sight of her lovers,
     and no one shall rescue her out of
       my hand.
11 And I will put an end to all her
       mirth,
     her feasts, her new moons, her
       sabbaths,
     and all her appointed feasts.
12 And I will lay waste her vines and
       her fig trees,
     of which she said,
   'These are my hire,
     which my lovers have given me.'
   I will make them a forest,
     and the beasts of the field shall
       devour them.
13 And I will punish her for the feast
       days of the Ba′als
     when she burned incense to them
   and decked herself with her ring and
       jewelry,
     and went after her lovers,
     and forgot me, says the LORD.

14 "Therefore, behold, I will allure
       her,
     and bring her into the wilderness,
     and speak tenderly to her.
15 And there I will give her her
       vineyards,
     and make the Valley of Achor
       a door of hope.
   And there she shall answer as in the
       days of her youth,
     as at the time when she came out
       of the land of Egypt.
16 "And in that day, says the LORD,
   you will call me, 'My husband,' and no

longer will you call me, 'My Ba′al.'
17 For I will remove the names of the
   Ba′als from her mouth, and they shall
   be mentioned by name no more.
18 And I will make for you[g] a covenant on that day with the beasts of
   the field, the birds of the air, and the
   creeping things of the ground; and I
   will abolish[h] the bow, the sword, and
   war from the land; and I will make
   you lie down in safety. 19 And I will
   betroth you to me for ever; I will betroth you to me in righteousness and
   in justice, in steadfast love, and in
   mercy. 20 I will betroth you to me in
   faithfulness; and you shall know the
   LORD.
21 "And in that day, says the LORD,
     I will answer the heavens
     and they shall answer the earth;
22 and the earth shall answer the
       grain, the wine, and the oil,
     and they shall answer Jezreel;[i]
23   and I will sow him[j] for myself in
       the land.
   And I will have pity on Not pitied,
     and I will say to Not my people,
     'You are my people';
     and he shall say, 'Thou art my
       God.' "

3 And the LORD said to me, "Go
   again, love a woman who is beloved of a paramour and is an adulteress; even as the LORD loves the people
   of Israel, though they turn to other
   gods and love cakes of raisins." 2 So I
   bought her for fifteen shekels of silver

g Heb *them*   h Heb *break*
i That is *God sows*   j Cn: Heb *her*

11: Is.1.12–17; Am.5.21–24. 13: *Baals*, see v. 16 n. *Incense* was peculiarly associated with pagan worship (Jer.44.8,17). *Decked herself*, compare Is.3.16–22.

2.14–23: The LORD will woo Israel back, renew his covenant with her, and betroth her to himself forever. 14: The *wilderness* signifies Israel's early years after the Exodus when she was faithful to the covenant (Ex. chs. 19–24; Jer.2.2–3; compare Ezek.20.33–38). 15: When entering the Promised Land Israel sinned at *the Valley of Achor* (Jos.7.20–26; Is.65.10). 16: *Baal*, often used as a proper name of the leading Canaanite deity, means "master," "lord." 17–23: The climax of the chapter promises the removal of the *Baals*, the establishment of a universal *covenant* (Lev.26.6; Job 5.23; Is.11.6–9; Ezek.34.25–31), the abolition of *war* (Ps.46.9; Is.2.4), and betrothal to the LORD in *steadfast love* and *faithfulness*.

3.1–5: The restoration of Gomer. Hosea buys back his adulterous wife, disciplines her, and affirms his devotion. In a like manner the LORD will restore Israel. 1: *Even as the LORD loves the people of Israel, though they turn to other gods;* these words disclose the central message of this book: divine love necessitates both Israel's temporary chastisement and her ultimate redemption. *Cakes of raisins* were used in pagan festivals (Is.16.7; Jer.7.18). 2: *Shekel*, about

and a homer and a lethech of barley.
³ And I said to her, "You must dwell as mine for many days; you shall not play the harlot, or belong to another man; so will I also be to you." ⁴ For the children of Israel shall dwell many days without king or prince, without sacrifice or pillar, without ephod or teraphim. ⁵ Afterward the children of Israel shall return and seek the LORD their God, and David their king; and they shall come in fear to the LORD and to his goodness in the latter days.

4 Hear the word of the LORD, O
    people of Israel;
  for the LORD has a controversy
    with the inhabitants of the land.
  There is no faithfulness or kindness,
    and no knowledge of God in the
    land;
² there is swearing, lying, killing,
    stealing, and committing
    adultery;
  they break all bounds and murder
    follows murder.
³ Therefore the land mourns,
    and all who dwell in it languish,
  and also the beasts of the field,
    and the birds of the air;
  and even the fish of the sea are
    taken away.

⁴ Yet let no one contend,
    and let none accuse,
  for with you is my contention, O
    priest.ᵏ
⁵ You shall stumble by day,

  the prophet also shall stumble
    with you by night;
  and I will destroy your mother.
⁶ My people are destroyed for lack
    of knowledge;
  because you have rejected
    knowledge,
  I reject you from being a priest to
    me.
  And since you have forgotten the
    law of your God,
  I also will forget your children.

⁷ The more they increased,
    the more they sinned against me;
  I will change their glory into
    shame.
⁸ They feed on the sin of my people;
    they are greedy for their iniquity.
⁹ And it shall be like people, like
    priest;
  I will punish them for their ways,
    and requite them for their deeds.
¹⁰ They shall eat, but not be satisfied;
    they shall play the harlot, but not
    multiply;
  because they have forsaken the
    LORD
  to cherish harlotry.

¹¹ Wine and new wine
    take away the understanding.
¹² My people inquire of a thing of
    wood,
  and their staff gives them oracles.
  For a spirit of harlotry has led them
    astray,

k Cn: Heb uncertain

---

eleven grams; *homer*, about six and one-half bushels; *lethech*, about three bushels. From whom Hosea *bought her* is not indicated. True redemption is costly (Ps.49.7–8; 1 Cor.6.19–20; 7.23; Gal.4.4–5); Hosea redeemed his wife by love and for a price. **4:** During the period of corrective punishment Israel will be deprived of her civil and ceremonial institutions. *Pillar*, Gen.31.45. *Ephod*, see Jg.8.24–28 n.; 1 Sam.2.18 n. *Teraphim*, household gods (Gen.31.19). **5:** The phrase *and David their king* is probably a later Judean addition.

4.1–14.9: Because of her constant rebellion, the judgment of the LORD is upon Israel; yet she will eventually be restored. These themes are elaborated in a series of discourses written after the death of Jeroboam II. The lack of clear order may in part reflect the style of the prophet and may in part be due to editorial rearrangement.

4.1–8.14: All Israel has forgotten the LORD and has sought help from other gods and other nations. 4.1–3: *The LORD has a controversy* with his people because they love neither him nor their fellow Israelites (Mic.6.2). *Faithfulness, kindness (steadfast love)*, and *knowledge of God* are major theological terms in Hosea (2.19–20; 4.6; 5.4,7; 6.3,6; 10.12; 11.3–4,12b; 12.6). **4–6:** The controversy is first of all with the priest and prophet; for, having rejected the knowledge and teaching of God, they have destroyed his people. **7–14:** Sin has infected them all, *like people, like priest.* **13:** A reference to high-place sanctuaries and their sacred trees (Jer.2.20).

and they have left their God to
  play the harlot.
13 They sacrifice on the tops of the
  mountains,
  and make offerings upon the hills,
under oak, poplar, and terebinth,
  because their shade is good.

Therefore your daughters play the
  harlot,
  and your brides commit adultery.
14 I will not punish your daughters
  when they play the harlot,
  nor your brides when they commit
  adultery;
for the men themselves go aside with
  harlots,
  and sacrifice with cult prostitutes,
and a people without understanding
  shall come to ruin.

15 Though you play the harlot, O
  Israel,
  let not Judah become guilty.
Enter not into Gilgal,
  nor go up to Beth-a'ven,
  and swear not, "As the LORD
  lives."
16 Like a stubborn heifer,
  Israel is stubborn;
can the LORD now feed them
  like a lamb in a broad pasture?

17 E'phraim is joined to idols,
  let him alone.
18 A band*l* of drunkards, they give
  themselves to harlotry;
  they love shame more than their
  glory.*m*
19 A wind has wrapped them*n* in its
  wings,
  and they shall be ashamed
  because of their altars.*o*

5 Hear this, O priests!
  Give heed, O house of Israel!

Hearken, O house of the king!
  For the judgment pertains to you;
for you have been a snare at Mizpah,
  and a net spread upon Tabor.
2 And they have made deep the pit of
  Shittim;*p*
  but I will chastise all of them.

3 I know E'phraim,
  and Israel is not hid from me;
for now, O E'phraim, you have
  played the harlot,
  Israel is defiled.
4 Their deeds do not permit them
  to return to their God.
For the spirit of harlotry is within
  them,
  and they know not the LORD.

5 The pride of Israel testifies to his
  face;
  E'phraim*q* shall stumble in his
  guilt;
  Judah also shall stumble with
  them.
6 With their flocks and herds they
  shall go
  to seek the LORD,
but they will not find him;
  he has withdrawn from them.
7 They have dealt faithlessly with the
  LORD;
  for they have borne alien children.
Now the new moon shall devour
  them with their fields.

8 Blow the horn in Gib'e-ah,
  the trumpet in Ramah.
Sound the alarm at Beth-a'ven;
  tremble,*r* O Benjamin!
9 E'phraim shall become a desolation
  in the day of punishment;
  among the tribes of Israel

l Cn: Heb uncertain
m Cn Compare Gk: Heb of this line uncertain
n Heb *her*   *o* Gk Syr: Heb *sacrifices*
p Cn: Heb uncertain   *q* Heb *Israel and Ephraim*
r Cn Compare Gk: Heb *after you*

14: *Cult prostitutes*, see Gen.38.15 n.; Dt.23.17 n. 15: *Beth-aven* is Bethel (Am.5.5). 5.1–2:
Israel's leaders have been a snare, so God will chastise all of them. *Tabor*, Mount Tabor, where
there seems to have been a sanctuary (compare Dt.33.19; Jg.4.6). *Mizpah*, either the city in
Transjordan (Jg.10.17) or north of Jerusalem (1 Sam.7.5). 3–4: The spirit of harlotry is so
confirmed within them that they cannot return to their God. 5b: 1.7. 6: Contrast Jer.29.13.
7: *Alien children*, sons faithless to the LORD. *New moon*, perhaps referring to the new moon
festivals. 8–14: In the day of punishment the LORD will become the enemy of Israel (Am.9.2–4).

I declare what is sure.

¹⁰ The princes of Judah have become
    like those who remove the
      landmark;
    upon them I will pour out
      my wrath like water.

¹¹ E′phraim is oppressed, crushed in
    judgment,
    because he was determined to go
      after vanity.ˢ

¹² Therefore I am like a moth to
    E′phraim,
    and like dry rot to the house of
      Judah.

¹³ When E′phraim saw his sickness,
    and Judah his wound,
    then E′phraim went to Assyria,
    and sent to the great king.ᵗ
    But he is not able to cure you
      or heal your wound.

¹⁴ For I will be like a lion to E′phraim,
    and like a young lion to the house
      of Judah.
    I, even I, will rend and go away,
    I will carry off, and none shall
      rescue.

¹⁵ I will return again to my place,
    until they acknowledge their guilt
      and seek my face,
    and in their distress they seek me,
      saying,

6 "Come, let us return to the LORD;
    for he has torn, that he may heal
      us;
    he has stricken, and he will bind
      us up.

² After two days he will revive us;
    on the third day he will raise us
      up,
    that we may live before him.

³ Let us know, let us press on to know
    the LORD;
    his going forth is sure as the
      dawn;
    he will come to us as the showers,

    as the spring rains that water the
      earth."

⁴ What shall I do with you, O
    E′phraim?
    What shall I do with you, O
      Judah?
    Your love is like a morning cloud,
      like the dew that goes early away.

⁵ Therefore I have hewn them by the
    prophets,
    I have slain them by the words
      of my mouth,
    and my judgment goes forth as the
      light.ᵘ

⁶ For I desire steadfast love and not
    sacrifice,
    the knowledge of God, rather
      than burnt offerings.

⁷ But atᵛ Adam they transgressed
    the covenant;
    there they dealt faithlessly with
      me.

⁸ Gilead is a city of evildoers,
    tracked with blood.

⁹ As robbers lie in waitʷ for a man,
    so the priests are banded
      together;ˣ
    they murder on the way to Shechem,
      yea, they commit villainy.

¹⁰ In the house of Israel I have seen
    a horrible thing;
    E′phraim's harlotry is there, Israel
      is defiled.

¹¹ For you also, O Judah, a harvest is
    appointed.

    When I would restore the fortunes
      of my people,

7 ¹ when I would heal Israel,
    the corruption of E′phraim is
      revealed,
    and the wicked deeds of Sama′ria;

s Gk: Heb *a command*
t Cn: Heb *a king that will contend*
u Gk Syr: Heb *thy judgment goes forth*
v Cn: Heb *like*   *w* Cn: Heb uncertain
x Syr: Heb *a company*

This section refers to the Syro-Ephraimitic War (2 Kg.15.27–30). **10:** *Remove the landmark,*
Dt.19.14; Pr.22.28. **5.15–6.3:** If Israel will but return to the LORD, he will heal her sickness and
revive her. **6.3:** *Spring rains,* the latter rains, Dt.11.14. **4–6:** What the LORD really desires is
steadfast love and *knowledge* of him (4.1–3). **6:** This verse epitomizes much of Hosea's message
(2.19–20; compare Mt.9.13; 12.7). *Love and not sacrifice,* compare Am.5.23,24; Mic.6.6–8.
7–11: By her harlotry Ephraim has transgressed the Sinaitic covenant (Ex.24.3–8; Dt.5.1–3).
7: *Adam,* geographical allusion uncertain; compare Jos.3.16. **7.1–7:** Because of her wicked

for they deal falsely,
  the thief breaks in,
  and the bandits raid without.
2 But they do not consider
  that I remember all their evil
    works.
Now their deeds encompass them,
  they are before my face.
3 By their wickedness they make the
    king glad,
  and the princes by their treachery.
4 They are all adulterers;
  they are like a heated oven,
whose baker ceases to stir the fire,
  from the kneading of the dough
    until it is leavened.
5 On the day of our king the princes
  became sick with the heat of wine;
  he stretched out his hand with
    mockers.
6 For like an oven their hearts burn*y*
  with intrigue;
all night their anger smolders;
  in the morning it blazes like a
    flaming fire.
7 All of them are hot as an oven,
  and they devour their rulers.
All their kings have fallen;
  and none of them calls upon me.

8 E'phraim mixes himself with the
    peoples;
  E'phraim is a cake not turned.
9 Aliens devour his strength,
  and he knows it not;
gray hairs are sprinkled upon him,
  and he knows it not.
10 The pride of Israel witnesses
  against him;
  yet they do not return to the
    LORD their God,
  nor seek him, for all this.

11 E'phraim is like a dove,
  silly and without sense,
  calling to Egypt, going to Assyria.

12 As they go, I will spread over them
  my net;
I will bring them down like birds
  of the air;
I will chastise them for their
  wicked deeds.*z*
13 Woe to them, for they have strayed
  from me!
Destruction to them, for they
  have rebelled against me!
I would redeem them,
  but they speak lies against me.

14 They do not cry to me from the
  heart,
  but they wail upon their beds;
for grain and wine they gash
  themselves,
  they rebel against me.
15 Although I trained and
  strengthened their arms,
  yet they devise evil against me.
16 They turn to Ba'al;*a*
  they are like a treacherous bow,
their princes shall fall by the sword
  because of the insolence of their
  tongue.
This shall be their derision in the
  land of Egypt.

8 Set the trumpet to your lips,
  for*b* a vulture is over the house
  of the LORD,
because they have broken my
  covenant,
  and transgressed my law.
2 To me they cry,
  My God, we Israel know thee.
3 Israel has spurned the good;
  the enemy shall pursue him.

4 They made kings, but not through
  me.

y Gk Syr: Heb *brought near*
z Cn: Heb *according to the report to their congregation*
a Cn: Heb uncertain
b Cn: Heb *as*

---

deeds, Samaria will also be punished. **4:** The time between the kneading of the dough and its fermentation is apparently when the oven was the hottest. **5:** *The day of our king*, perhaps at the celebration of enthronement. **8–10:** Ephraim is a half-baked cake. **11–13:** Ephraim is like a silly dove. *Calling to Egypt . . .*, seeking alliances. **14–16:** Because they turn to Baal the Israelites shall bear the consequences. *Gash themselves*, Dt.14.1; 1 Kg.18.28. **8.1:** *The trumpet* warns of the approach of the enemy (compare Jer.6.1; Neh.4.18–20; Jl.2.1). *Vulture*, an eagle, the Assyrian army (Jer.49.22). **4:** Probably an allusion to the rapid succession of kings

They set up princes, but without
  my knowledge.
With their silver and gold they made
  idols
for their own destruction.
5 I have*c* spurned your calf, O
  Sama'ria.
My anger burns against them.
How long will it be
  till they are pure 6 in Israel?*d*

A workman made it;
  it is not God.
The calf of Sama'ria
  shall be broken to pieces.*e*

7 For they sow the wind,
  and they shall reap the whirlwind.
The standing grain has no heads,
  it shall yield no meal;
if it were to yield,
  aliens would devour it.
8 Israel is swallowed up;
  already they are among the
    nations
  as a useless vessel.
9 For they have gone up to Assyria,
  a wild ass wandering alone;
  E'phraim has hired lovers.
10 Though they hire allies among the
    nations,
  I will soon gather them up.
And they shall cease*f* for a little
    while
  from anointing*g* king and princes.

11 Because E'phraim has multiplied
    altars for sinning,
  they have become to him altars
    for sinning.
12 Were I to write for him my laws
    by ten thousands,
  they would be regarded as a
    strange thing.
13 They love sacrifice;*h*

they sacrifice flesh and eat it;
  but the LORD has no delight in
    them.
Now he will remember their iniquity,
  and punish their sins;
  they shall return to Egypt.
14 For Israel has forgotten his Maker,
  and built palaces;
and Judah has multiplied fortified
  cities;
but I will send a fire upon his
  cities,
and it shall devour his strongholds.

9 Rejoice not, O Israel!
  Exult not*i* like the peoples;
for you have played the harlot,
  forsaking your God.
You have loved a harlot's hire
  upon all threshing floors.
2 Threshing floor and winevat shall
    not feed them,
  and the new wine shall fail them.
3 They shall not remain in the land
    of the LORD;
  but E'phraim shall return to
    Egypt,
  and they shall eat unclean food in
    Assyria.

4 They shall not pour libations of wine
    to the LORD;
  and they shall not please him with
    their sacrifices.
Their bread*j* shall be like mourners'
    bread;
  all who eat of it shall be defiled;
for their bread shall be for their
    hunger only;
  it shall not come to the house of
    the LORD.

c Heb *He has*
d Gk: Heb *for from Israel*
e Or *shall go up in flames*
f Gk: Heb *begin*   *g* Gk: Heb *burden*
h Cn: Heb uncertain   *i* Gk: Heb *to exultation*
j Cn: Heb *to them*

after Jeroboam II (see Introduction). **5:** *Your calf,* see 1 Kg.12.28,29. *A workman made it,*
compare Is.40.19,20. **7–10:** As punishment for political defection, Israel shall be without king
and princes. **11–14:** As punishment for religious defection, Israel *shall return to Egypt* (compare
9.3,6). **14:** Reliance on palaces and walled cities alone is sin. *Fire,* Am.1.4,7.
  9,1–11.12: Israel has rejected the LORD and must undergo punishment that will bring loss of
king, children, places of worship, and country. **9.1–17:** Israel is destined for prey and slaughter
and to be deprived of land and cultus (2.11; 8.11–14; 11.5). **1:** *Harlot's hire,* the pay of the sacred
prostitute (see Gen.38.17; Mic.1.7). **4:** *Mourners' bread,* unclean because of association with

5 What will you do on the day of
appointed festival,
and on the day of the feast of the
LORD?
6 For behold, they are going to
Assyria;[k]
Egypt shall gather them,
Memphis shall bury them.
Nettles shall possess their precious
things of silver;
thorns shall be in their tents.

7 The days of punishment have come,
the days of recompense have
come;
Israel shall know it.
The prophet is a fool,
the man of the spirit is mad,
because of your great iniquity
and great hatred.
8 The prophet is the watchman of
E'phraim,
the people of my God,
yet a fowler's snare is on all his ways,
and hatred in the house of his
God.
9 They have deeply corrupted
themselves
as in the days of Gib'e-ah:
he will remember their iniquity,
he will punish their sins.

10 Like grapes in the wilderness,
I found Israel.
Like the first fruit on the fig tree,
in its first season,
I saw your fathers.
But they came to Ba'al-pe'or,
and consecrated themselves to
Ba'al,[l]
and became detestable like the
thing they loved.
11 E'phraim's glory shall fly away like
a bird–
no birth, no pregnancy, no
conception!
12 Even if they bring up children,

I will bereave them till none is
left.
Woe to them
when I depart from them!
13 E'phraim's sons, as I have seen, are
destined for a prey;[m]
E'phraim must lead forth his sons
to slaughter.
14 Give them, O LORD–
what wilt thou give?
Give them a miscarrying womb
and dry breasts.

15 Every evil of theirs is in Gilgal;
there I began to hate them.
Because of the wickedness of their
deeds
I will drive them out of my house.
I will love them no more;
all their princes are rebels.

16 E'phraim is stricken,
their root is dried up,
they shall bear no fruit.
Even though they bring forth,
I will slay their beloved children.
17 My God will cast them off,
because they have not hearkened
to him;
they shall be wanderers among
the nations.

10 Israel is a luxuriant vine
that yields its fruit.
The more his fruit increased
the more altars he built;
as his country improved
he improved his pillars.
2 Their heart is false;
now they must bear their guilt.
The LORD[n] will break down their
altars,
and destroy their pillars.

3 For now they will say:
"We have no king,

k Cn: Heb *from destruction*   l Heb *shame*
m Cn Compare Gk: Heb uncertain   n Heb *he*

---

the dead. **6:** *Memphis,* the capital of Lower Egypt. **7:** *Man of the spirit,* that is, the prophet (see
Mic.3.8 n.). **8:** *Watchman,* compare Ezek.33.6–8. **9:** 1 Sam. ch. 10. **10–17:** *In the wilderness*
Israel covenanted herself to the LORD, but in Canaan she *consecrated* herself to the fertility god
Baal; therefore the LORD will make her barren. **10:** *Baal-peor,* Num.25.1–18. **15:** *Gilgal,* 4.15.
Drive them out of my house, as a husband his faithless wife. **10.1–2:** In Canaan Israel *increased*

for we fear not the LORD,
　and a king, what could he do for
　　us?"
⁴ They utter mere words;
　with empty oaths they make
　　covenants;
　so judgment springs up like
　　poisonous weeds
　in the furrows of the field.
⁵ The inhabitants of Sama'ria tremble
　for the calf*o* of Beth-a'ven.
　Its people shall mourn for it,
　and its idolatrous priests shall
　　wail*p* over it,
　over its glory which has departed
　　from it.
⁶ Yea, the thing itself shall be carried
　　to Assyria,
　as tribute to the great king.*q*
　E'phraim shall be put to shame,
　and Israel shall be ashamed of his
　　idol.*r*

⁷ Sama'ria's king shall perish,
　like a chip on the face of the
　　waters.
⁸ The high places of Aven, the sin of
　　Israel,
　shall be destroyed.
　Thorn and thistle shall grow up
　on their altars;
　and they shall say to the mountains,
　　Cover us,
　and to the hills, Fall upon us.

⁹ From the days of Gib'e-ah, you
　　have sinned, O Israel;
　there they have continued.
　Shall not war overtake them in
　　Gib'e-ah?
¹⁰ I will come*s* against the wayward
　　people to chastise them;
　and nations shall be gathered
　　against them
　when they are chastised*t* for their
　　double iniquity.

¹¹ E'phraim was a trained heifer
　　that loved to thresh,
　and I spared her fair neck;
　but I will put E'phraim to the yoke,
　　Judah must plow,
　Jacob must harrow for himself.
¹² Sow for yourselves righteousness,
　reap the fruit*u* of steadfast love;
　break up your fallow ground,
　for it is the time to seek the LORD,
　that he may come and rain
　　salvation upon you.

¹³ You have plowed iniquity,
　you have reaped injustice,
　you have eaten the fruit of lies.
　Because you have trusted in your
　　chariots*v*
　and in the multitude of your
　　warriors,
¹⁴ therefore the tumult of war shall arise
　　among your people,
　and all your fortresses shall be
　　destroyed,
　as Shalman destroyed Beth-ar'bel on
　　the day of battle;
　mothers were dashed in pieces with
　　their children.
¹⁵ Thus it shall be done to you, O house
　　of Israel,*w*
　because of your great wickedness.
　In the storm*x* the king of Israel
　shall be utterly cut off.

When Israel was a child, I loved
　him,
　and out of Egypt I called my son.
² The more I*y* called them,
　the more they went from me;*z*
　they kept sacrificing to the Ba'als,
　and burning incense to idols.

o Gk Syr: Heb *calves*　　*p* Cn: Heb *exult*
q Cn: Heb *a king that will contend*
r Cn: Heb *counsel*
s Cn Compare Gk: Heb *in my desire*
t Gk: Heb *bound*　*u* Gk: Heb *according to*
v Gk: Heb *way*　*w* Gk: Heb *O Bethel*
x Cn: Heb *dawn*　*y* Gk: Heb *they*
z Gk: Heb *them*

in sin as she increased in prosperity. *Pillars*, Ex.23.24. **3–10:** Israel's *king shall perish*, for she *sinned* by establishing the monarchy *in the days of Saul*. **5:** *Calf*, 8.5. **8:** Am.9.1; Lk.23.30; Rev.6.16. *Aven* means "wickedness," a reference to Bethel. **9:** *Gibeah*, see Jg. ch. 19. **11–12:** Repentance, shown by acts of *righteousness*, will bring *salvation*. **12:** Compare 6.3; Is.44.3; 45.8; 55.10; Jer.4.3; 2 Cor.9.10). **13–15:** Rebellious Israel shall hear *the tumult of war*. **14:** *Shalman . . . Beth-arbel*, the allusion is unknown and the text uncertain. **11.1–7:** The LORD, as a loving and patient father, must now chastise his disobedient and wilful son. **1:** Ex.4.22;

³ Yet it was I who taught E′phraim to
    walk,
  I took them up in my*ᵃ* arms;
  but they did not know that I healed
    them.
⁴ I led them with cords of
    compassion,*ᵇ*
  with the bands of love,
  and I became to them as one
    who eases the yoke on their jaws,
  and I bent down to them and fed
    them.

⁵ They shall return to the land of
    Egypt,
  and Assyria shall be their king,
  because they have refused to
    return to me.
⁶ The sword shall rage against their
    cities,
  consume the bars of their gates,
  and devour them in their
    fortresses.*ᶜ*
⁷ My people are bent on turning away
    from me;*ᵈ*
  so they are appointed to the yoke,
  and none shall remove it.

⁸ How can I give you up, O E′phraim!
  How can I hand you over, O
    Israel!
  How can I make you like Admah!
  How can I treat you like Zeboi′im!
  My heart recoils within me,
    my compassion grows warm and
    tender.
⁹ I will not execute my fierce anger,
  I will not again destroy E′phraim;
  for I am God and not man,
    the Holy One in your midst,
  and I will not come to destroy.*ᵉ*

¹⁰ They shall go after the Lᴏʀᴅ,
  he will roar like a lion;

yea, he will roar,
  and his sons shall come trembling
    from the west;
¹¹ they shall come trembling like birds
    from Egypt,
  and like doves from the land of
    Assyria;
  and I will return them to their
    homes, says the Lᴏʀᴅ.
¹²*ᶠ* E′phraim has encompassed me
    with lies,
  and the house of Israel with
    deceit;
  but Judah is still known by*ᵍ* God,
  and is faithful to the Holy One.

12 E′phraim herds the wind,
  and pursues the east wind all
    day long;
  they multiply falsehood and
    violence;
  they make a bargain with Assyria,
  and oil is carried to Egypt.

² The Lᴏʀᴅ has an indictment against
    Judah,
  and will punish Jacob according to
    his ways,
  and requite him according to his
    deeds.
³ In the womb he took his brother by
    the heel,
  and in his manhood he strove with
    God.
⁴ He strove with the angel and
    prevailed,
  he wept and sought his favor.
  He met God at Bethel,
    and there God spoke with him*ʰ*–
⁵ the Lᴏʀᴅ the God of hosts,

a Gk Syr Vg: Heb *his*   *b* Heb *man*
c Cn: Heb *counsels*
d The meaning of the Hebrew is uncertain
e Cn: Heb *into the city*   *f* Ch 12.1 in Heb
g Cn Compare Gk: Heb *roams with*
h Gk Syr: Heb *us*

Mt.2.15. **3:** Jer.31.1–3. **8–9:** The Lᴏʀᴅ's compassion restrains his anger, for he *will not come to destroy* (Mk.2.17). *Admah, Zeboiim*, cities destroyed along with Sodom and Gomorrah (Gen. ch. 19; Dt.29.23). **10:** Contrast 5.14. **11:** *Doves*, contrast 7.11. *Egypt* and *Assyria*, contrast 9.3. **12:** *But Judah is still . . .* , some regard the last part of this verse as a Judean gloss (compare 1.7).
    12.1–14.9: Rebellion and restoration. Although the Lᴏʀᴅ led Israel by the prophets, she turned to Baal and died. Yet the Lᴏʀᴅ is the savior, and if Israel will acknowledge him, he will restore her to abundant life, because he loves her. **12.2–6:** Israel should hold fast to God's love and justice, as Jacob strove with the angel at the Jabbok River. **3:** *Took his brother by the heel*, Gen.25.26. **4:** *Strove with the angel*, Gen.32.22–30. *Met God at Bethel*, Gen.28.11–17;

the LORD is his name:
⁶ "So you, by the help of your God,
　　return,
　hold fast to love and justice,
　and wait continually for your
　　God."

⁷ A trader, in whose hands are false
　　balances,
　he loves to oppress.
⁸ E'phraim has said, "Ah, but I am
　　rich,
　I have gained wealth for myself";
but all his riches can never offset*ⁱ*
　the guilt he has incurred.
⁹ I am the LORD your God
　from the land of Egypt;
I will again make you dwell in
　　tents,
　as in the days of the appointed
　　feast.

¹⁰ I spoke to the prophets;
　it was I who multiplied visions,
　and through the prophets gave
　　parables.
¹¹ If there is iniquity in Gilead
　they shall surely come to nought;
　if in Gilgal they sacrifice bulls,
　their altars also shall be like stone
　　heaps
　on the furrows of the field.
¹² (Jacob fled to the land of Aram,
　there Israel did service for a wife,
　and for a wife he herded sheep.)
¹³ By a prophet the LORD brought
　Israel up from Egypt,
　and by a prophet he was
　　preserved.
¹⁴ E'phraim has given bitter
　　provocation;
　so his LORD will leave his
　　bloodguilt upon him,
　and will turn back upon him his
　　reproaches.

13 When E'phraim spoke, men
　　trembled;
　he was exalted in Israel;
　but he incurred guilt through Ba'al
　　and died.
² And now they sin more and more,
　and make for themselves molten
　　images,
　idols skilfully made of their silver,
　all of them the work of craftsmen.
Sacrifice to these, they say.*ʲ*
Men kiss calves!
³ Therefore they shall be like the
　　morning mist
　or like the dew that goes early
　　away,
　like the chaff that swirls from the
　　threshing floor
　or like smoke from a window.

⁴ I am the LORD your God
　from the land of Egypt;
　you know no God but me,
　and besides me there is no savior.
⁵ It was I who knew you in the
　　wilderness,
　in the land of drought;
⁶ but when they had fed*ᵏ* to the full,
　they were filled, and their heart
　　was lifted up;
　therefore they forgot me.
⁷ So I will be to them like a lion,
　like a leopard I will lurk beside
　　the way.
⁸ I will fall upon them like a bear
　　robbed of her cubs,
　I will tear open their breast,
　and there I will devour them like a
　　lion,
　as a wild beast would rend them.

⁹ I will destroy you, O Israel;
　who*ˡ* can help you?

i　Cn Compare Gk: Heb obscure
j　Gk: Heb *to these they say sacrifices of*
k　Cn: Heb *according to their pasture*
l　Gk Syr: Heb *for in me*

35.5–8. **9**: As a punishment, the LORD will again make Israel *dwell in tents*, as in the wilderness during the Exodus. **10–14**: Because Israel spurned the prophets, she will be held responsible for her bitter *provocation* (Am.3.2; compare Gal.6.7). **12**: Perhaps by a Judean editor. **13.1–3**: Through the sin of Canaanite idolatry, Israel died (2.13; compare Rom.6.23; 8.13). **2**: *Men kiss calves*, at Dan and Bethel. *Morning mist*, compare 6.4. **4–13**: Because they forgot their savior, the LORD will rend and destroy the Israelites, and neither king nor princes will save them. **4**: Ex.20.2; Is.45.21. **14–16**: The LORD will not redeem his rebellious people from Death;

10 Where*m* now is your king, to save
      you;
   where are all*n* your princes,*o* to
      defend you*p*–
   those of whom you said,
      "Give me a king and princes"?
11 I have given you kings in my anger,
      and I have taken them away in
      my wrath.

12 The iniquity of E'phraim is bound
      up,
   his sin is kept in store.
13 The pangs of childbirth come for
      him,
   but he is an unwise son;
   for now he does not present himself
      at the mouth of the womb.

14 Shall I ransom them from the power
      of Sheol?
   Shall I redeem them from Death?
   O Death, where*q* are your plagues?
   O Sheol, where*q* is your
      destruction?
   Compassion is hid from my eyes.

15 Though he may flourish as the reed
      plant,*r*
   the east wind, the wind of the
      Lord, shall come,
   rising from the wilderness;
   and his fountain shall dry up,
      his spring shall be parched;
   it shall strip his treasury
      of every precious thing.
16*s* Sama'ria shall bear her guilt,
   because she has rebelled against
      her God;
   they shall fall by the sword,
      their little ones shall be dashed in
      pieces,
   and their pregnant women ripped
      open.

14 Return, O Israel, to the Lord
      your God,
   for you have stumbled because
      of your iniquity.

2 Take with you words
      and return to the Lord;
   say to him,
      "Take away all iniquity;
   accept that which is good
      and we will render
      the fruit*t* of our lips.
3 Assyria shall not save us,
      we will not ride upon horses;
   and we will say no more, 'Our God,'
      to the work of our hands.
   In thee the orphan finds mercy."

4 I will heal their faithlessness;
      I will love them freely,
   for my anger has turned from
      them.
5 I will be as the dew to Israel;
      he shall blossom as the lily,
      he shall strike root as the poplar;*u*
6 his shoots shall spread out;
      his beauty shall be like the olive,
      and his fragrance like Lebanon.
7 They shall return and dwell beneath
      my*v* shadow,
   they shall flourish as a garden;*w*
   they shall blossom as the vine,
      their fragrance shall be like the
      wine of Lebanon.

8 O E'phraim, what have I to do with
      idols?
   It is I who answer and look after
      you.*x*
   I am like an evergreen cypress,
      from me comes your fruit.

9 Whoever is wise, let him understand
      these things;
   whoever is discerning, let him
      know them;
   for the ways of the Lord are right,
      and the upright walk in them,
      but transgressors stumble in them.

m Gk Syr Vg: Heb *I will be*
n Cn: Heb *in all*   *o* Cn: Heb *cities*
p Cn Compare Gk: Heb *and your judges*
q Gk Syr: Heb *I will be*   *r* Cn: Heb *among brothers*
s Ch 14.1 in Heb   *t* Gk Syr: Heb *bulls*
u Cn: Heb *Lebanon*   *v* Heb *his*
w Cn: Heb *they shall grow grain*   *x* Heb *him*

Samaria shall bear her guilt. **14:** Quoted in 1 Cor.15.55. **14.1–3:** *Israel* may still return to the
Lord her God, for with him there is mercy (Ps.130.7–8; Is.55.6–9). **3:** The futility of foreign
alliances and idols. **4–7:** And because he loves freely, he will heal and bring Israel back to
fruitful life (Is.54.5–8). **8:** The Lord alone guides and sustains Israel (2.8). **9:** A later postscript, in the style of wisdom literature (compare Pr.4.11–12; see also Ec.12.9–14 n.).

THE BOOK OF JOEL

Of Joel himself nothing is known except that he was the son of Pethuel (1.1). Like Obadiah, even his name ("the LORD is God") is not unique, for he shares it with a dozen other Old Testament figures. From his book it appears that he lived in Judah during the Persian period of Jewish history (539–331 B.C.). He was not only well acquainted with the temple at Jerusalem, but was so much interested in its priesthood and services that, like Haggai and Zechariah, he is to be considered a "cultic prophet," that is, a prophet who could exercise his ministry within the life of the temple, even using liturgical forms, and whose message may have been transmitted through priestly circles. As such, Joel helps to mark a notable change in Old Testament prophecy. Taking the characteristic forms of classical prophecy, he expands their apocalyptic and liturgical dimensions.

The dates of Joel's ministry cannot be determined with precision. The majority of historical references in his book, the absence of any mention of the Assyrians or Babylonians, and the heavy borrowing from earlier prophets point to the period from about 400 to 350 B.C.

Joel viewed a locust plague which ravished the country as God's judgment on his people and called them to repentance (1.2–2.27). Using this catastrophe as a dire warning, he went on to depict the advent of the Day of the LORD and its final judgments and blessings (2.28–3.21).

HE WORD OF THE LORD THAT came to Joel, the son of Pethu'el:

2 Hear this, you aged men,
give ear, all inhabitants of the
land!
Has such a thing happened in your
days,
or in the days of your fathers?
3 Tell your children of it,
and let your children tell their
children,
and their children another
generation.

4 What the cutting locust left,
the swarming locust has eaten.
What the swarming locust left,
the hopping locust has eaten,
and what the hopping locust left,
the destroying locust has eaten.

5 Awake, you drunkards, and weep;
and wail, all you drinkers of wine,
because of the sweet wine,
for it is cut off from your mouth.
6 For a nation has come up against
my land,

powerful and without number;
its teeth are lions' teeth,
and it has the fangs of a lioness.
7 It has laid waste my vines,
and splintered my fig trees;
it has stripped off their bark and
thrown it down;
their branches are made white.

8 Lament like a virgin girded with
sackcloth
for the bridegroom of her youth.
9 The cereal offering and the drink
offering are cut off
from the house of the LORD.
The priests mourn,
the ministers of the LORD.
10 The fields are laid waste,
the ground mourns;
because the grain is destroyed,
the wine fails,
the oil languishes.

11 Be confounded, O tillers of the soil,
wail, O vinedressers,
for the wheat and the barley;
because the harvest of the field
has perished.

1.1–2.27: The locust plague. 1.1: Superscription. *The word of the LORD . . .* , see Hos.1.1 n. *Pethuel* does not occur elsewhere. **2–7:** The land is devastated by a swarm of locusts, described as a nation with lions' teeth (v. 6; compare 2.4–9; Rev.9.7–8). **8–14:** The whole community is

¹² The vine withers,
    the fig tree languishes.
Pomegranate, palm, and apple,
    all the trees of the field are
        withered;
and gladness fails
    from the sons of men.

¹³ Gird on sackcloth and lament, O
        priests,
    wail, O ministers of the altar.
Go in, pass the night in sackcloth,
    O ministers of my God!
Because cereal offering and drink
        offering
are withheld from the house of
    your God.

¹⁴ Sanctify a fast,
    call a solemn assembly.
Gather the elders
    and all the inhabitants of the land
to the house of the LORD your God;
    and cry to the LORD.

¹⁵ Alas for the day!
For the day of the LORD is near,
    and as destruction from the
        Almighty it comes.
¹⁶ Is not the food cut off
    before our eyes,
joy and gladness
    from the house of our God?

¹⁷ The seed shrivels under the clods,^a
    the storehouses are desolate;
the granaries are ruined
    because the grain has failed.
¹⁸ How the beasts groan!
    The herds of cattle are perplexed
because there is no pasture for them;
    even the flocks of sheep are
        dismayed.

¹⁹ Unto thee, O LORD, I cry.
For fire has devoured

the pastures of the wilderness,
and flame has burned
    all the trees of the field.
²⁰ Even the wild beasts cry to thee
    because the water brooks are
        dried up,
and fire has devoured
    the pastures of the wilderness

2 Blow the trumpet in Zion;
    sound the alarm on my holy
        mountain!
Let all the inhabitants of the land
    tremble,
    for the day of the LORD is coming,
    it is near,
² a day of darkness and gloom,
    a day of clouds and thick
        darkness!
Like blackness there is spread upon
    the mountains
a great and powerful people;
    their like has never been from of old,
    nor will be again after them
    through the years of all
        generations.

³ Fire devours before them,
    and behind them a flame burns.
The land is like the garden of Eden
    before them,
    but after them a desolate
        wilderness,
    and nothing escapes them.

⁴ Their appearance is like the
        appearance of horses,
    and like war horses they run.
⁵ As with the rumbling of chariots,
    they leap on the tops of the
        mountains,
like the crackling of a flame of fire
    devouring the stubble,
like a powerful army
    drawn up for battle.

a Heb uncertain

called upon to lament and return to the LORD. **13–14:** *Ministers of the altar* of burnt offering, who serve in the inner court (see Ezek.43.18–27). *A fast*, 2 Kg.18.6; Jer.36.6; Jon.3.5. **15–20:** The lament. **15:** This calamitous day portends the final day of the LORD which comes as destruction from the Almighty (Zeph.1.14–18). **19–20:** *Fire* and *flame* epitomize the most severe destruction. **2.1–11:** The cry of alarm at the approaching catastrophe. **1:** The priests blow the ram's horn (shofar) to warn of the imminent danger (Hos.5.8; Am.3.6; Zeph.1.16; Rev.8.6–13). **4–9:** The locusts, which symbolize that dreadful day, approach with the relentless and devas-

⁶ Before them peoples are in anguish,
    all faces grow pale.
⁷ Like warriors they charge,
    like soldiers they scale the wall.
They march each on his way,
    they do not swerve*b* from their
      paths.
⁸ They do not jostle one another,
    each marches in his path;
they burst through the weapons
    and are not halted.
⁹ They leap upon the city,
    they run upon the walls;
they climb up into the houses,
    they enter through the windows
      like a thief.

¹⁰ The earth quakes before them,
    the heavens tremble.
The sun and the moon are darkened,
    and the stars withdraw their
      shining.
¹¹ The LORD utters his voice
    before his army,
for his host is exceedingly great;
    he that executes his word is
      powerful.
For the day of the LORD is great and
    very terrible;
    who can endure it?

¹² "Yet even now," says the LORD,
    "return to me with all your heart,
with fasting, with weeping, and with
      mourning;
¹³   and rend your hearts and not
    your garments."
Return to the LORD, your God,
    for he is gracious and merciful,
slow to anger, and abounding in
    steadfast love,
    and repents of evil.
¹⁴ Who knows whether he will not turn
    and repent,

and leave a blessing behind him,
a cereal offering and a drink offering
    for the LORD, your God?

¹⁵ Blow the trumpet in Zion;
    sanctify a fast;
call a solemn assembly;
¹⁶   gather the people.
Sanctify the congregation;
    assemble the elders;
gather the children,
    even nursing infants.
Let the bridegroom leave his room,
    and the bride her chamber.

¹⁷ Between the vestibule and the altar
    let the priests, the ministers of
      the LORD, weep
and say, "Spare thy people, O LORD,
    and make not thy heritage a
      reproach,
a byword among the nations.
Why should they say among the
    peoples,
    'Where is their God?' "

¹⁸ Then the LORD became jealous for
    his land,
    and had pity on his people.
¹⁹ The LORD answered and said to his
    people,
"Behold, I am sending to you
    grain, wine, and oil,
    and you will be satisfied;
and I will no more make you
    a reproach among the nations.

²⁰ "I will remove the northerner far
    from you,
    and drive him into a parched and
      desolate land,
his front into the eastern sea,

b Gk Syr Vg: Heb *take a pledge*

tating force of a powerful *army* (2.25; Rev.9.7–10). **6**: Nah.2.10. **10**: At the time of the
divine visitation the sun, moon, and stars refuse to shine (Am.8.9). **11**: Rev.6.17. **12–17**: A
call to repentance, by which total calamity may yet be averted. **13**: The pleas to *rend your
hearts* and *return to the LORD* express the preaching of the classical prophets, placed here in a
cultic context. *Gracious and merciful . . .* is a frequent designation of the LORD (Ex.34.6;
Neh.9.17,31; Ps.86.15). **14**: Characteristically Joel regards temple offerings as *a blessing.* **15**:
1.14. **17**: *Between the vestibule* (1 Kg.6.3) *and the altar* of burnt offering (2 Chr.4.1); this was
in the inner court of the priests. **18–27**: God's gracious answer promises the remission of the
plague (vv. 20,25), the return of fertility (vv. 19,21–24), and the restoration of the covenant
(vv. 26–27). **18**: *Jealous* includes the meaning zealous (Dt.4.24). **20**: *The northerner* refers to

and his rear into the western sea;
the stench and foul smell of him will
rise,
for he has done great things.

21 "Fear not, O land;
be glad and rejoice,
for the LORD has done great things!
22 Fear not, you beasts of the field,
for the pastures of the wilderness
are green;
the tree bears its fruit,
the fig tree and vine give their full
yield.

23 "Be glad, O sons of Zion,
and rejoice in the LORD, your
God;
for he has given the early rain for
your vindication,
he has poured down for you
abundant rain,
the early and the latter rain, as
before.

24 "The threshing floors shall be full
of grain,
the vats shall overflow with wine
and oil.
25 I will restore to you the years
which the swarming locust has
eaten,
the hopper, the destroyer, and the
cutter,
my great army, which I sent
among you.

26 "You shall eat in plenty and be
satisfied,
and praise the name of the LORD
your God,
who has dealt wondrously with
you.

And my people shall never again be
put to shame.
27 You shall know that I am in the
midst of Israel,
and that I, the LORD, am your
God and there is none else.
And my people shall never again
be put to shame.

28c "And it shall come to pass
afterward,
that I will pour out my spirit on all
flesh;
your sons and your daughters shall
prophesy,
your old men shall dream dreams,
and your young men shall see
visions.
29 Even upon the menservants and
maidservants
in those days, I will pour out my
spirit.

30 "And I will give portents in the
heavens and on the earth, blood and
fire and columns of smoke. 31 The sun
shall be turned to darkness, and the
moon to blood, before the great and
terrible day of the LORD comes. 32 And
it shall come to pass that all who call
upon the name of the LORD shall be
delivered; for in Mount Zion and in
Jerusalem there shall be those who
escape, as the LORD has said, and
among the survivors shall be those
whom the LORD calls.

3 *d* "For behold, in those days and
at that time, when I restore the
fortunes of Judah and Jerusalem, 2 I
will gather all the nations and bring
them down to the valley of Jehosh'-
aphat, and I will enter into judgment

c Ch 3.1 in Heb   *d* Ch 4.1 in Heb

---

the destructive agent, probably the locusts. **27:** By his gifts of abundance the LORD's people
will know that he alone is their God (Is.45.5,6,18; Ezek.36.11; 39.28) and dwells in their
midst (3.17,21).
    2.28–3.21: The day of the LORD. 2.28–32: The outpouring of the spirit and the signs fore-
telling the great day. **28–29:** For Joel *all flesh* meant primarily the Jews (3.2,17,19–21; Ezek.
39.29); for Peter at Pentecost it included all nations (Acts 2.17). **30–31:** *The heavens* and *the
earth* will warn of *the great and terrible day* (Mk.13.24; Rev.6.12). **31:** Here *blood* indicates
color. **32:** Those who worship the LORD (Gen.4.26; 12.8; Ps.116.13) will be delivered (Acts
2.21; Rom.10.13). **32b:** Ob.17. **3.1–3:** The day of judgment on all the nations. The trial will be
held in *the valley of Jehoshaphat* ("the LORD judges"), called *the valley of decision* in v. 14

with them there, on account of my
people and my heritage Israel, because they have scattered them among
the nations, and have divided up my
land, ³ and have cast lots for my people, and have given a boy for a harlot,
and have sold a girl for wine, and have
drunk it.

4 "What are you to me, O Tyre and
Sidon, and all the regions of Philistia?
Are you paying me back for something? If you are paying me back, I
will requite your deed upon your own
head swiftly and speedily. ⁵ For you
have taken my silver and my gold, and
have carried my rich treasures into
your temples.ᵉ ⁶ You have sold the
people of Judah and Jerusalem to the
Greeks, removing them far from their
own border. ⁷ But now I will stir them
up from the place to which you have
sold them, and I will requite your deed
upon your own head. ⁸ I will sell your
sons and your daughters into the hand
of the sons of Judah, and they will sell
them to the Sabe'ans, to a nation far
off; for the LORD has spoken."

⁹ Proclaim this among the nations:
Prepare war,
    stir up the mighty men.
Let all the men of war draw near,
    let them come up.
¹⁰ Beat your plowshares into swords,
    and your pruning hooks into
        spears;
let the weak say, "I am a warrior."

¹¹ Hasten and come,
    all you nations round about,
    gather yourselves there.

Bring down thy warriors, O LORD.
¹² Let the nations bestir themselves,
    and come up to the valley of
        Jehosh'aphat;
for there I will sit to judge
    all the nations round about.

¹³ Put in the sickle,
    for the harvest is ripe.
Go in, tread,
    for the wine press is full.
The vats overflow,
    for their wickedness is great.

¹⁴ Multitudes, multitudes,
    in the valley of decision!
For the day of the LORD is near
    in the valley of decision.
¹⁵ The sun and the moon are darkened,
    and the stars withdraw their
        shining.

¹⁶ And the LORD roars from Zion,
    and utters his voice from
        Jerusalem,
    and the heavens and the earth
        shake.
But the LORD is a refuge to his
        people,
    a stronghold to the people of
        Israel.

¹⁷ "So you shall know that I am the
        LORD your God,
    who dwell in Zion, my holy
        mountain.
And Jerusalem shall be holy
    and strangers shall never again
        pass through it.

e Or *palaces*

(Jer.25.31). Joel probably had no exact spot in mind, although the context (2.32; 3.1,16,17,21) points to the general area of Jerusalem, and tradition locates it in the Kidron valley. **3a:** Ob.11. **4–8:** *Tyre* (Is. ch. 23; Ezek.26.1–28.19; Am.1.9–10; Zech.9.3–4), *Sidon* (Ezek.28.20–26; Zech.9.2), *and Philistia* (Is.14.29–31; Jer. ch. 47; Ezek.25.15–17; Am.1.6–8; Zeph.2.4–7; Zech. 9.5–7) will receive their recompense first (this prose paragraph may be a later addition). **6–8:** Because the Philistines and Phoenicians sold Israelites as slaves to Gentiles (Ezek.27.13; Am. 1.6,9), their children will be sold to the *Sabeans*, famous traders from southwest Arabia. **9–12:** The holy war between the LORD's warriors and all the nations round about (compare Ezek. chs. 38–39). **10:** The picture in Is.2.4 and Mic.4.3 is reversed. **13–17:** *The day of the LORD is near.* **13:** The inordinate wickedness of the Gentiles is compared to the harvest which is ripe and vats which overflow (Is.63.1–6; Mt.3.10–12; Mk.4.29; Rev.14.15–20). **16:** Am.1.2. **17:** Jerusalem shall now be holy, as the LORD's earthly tabernacle (Is.1.24–28; 52.1; Zech.8.3;

¹⁸ "And in that day
the mountains shall drip sweet wine,
and the hills shall flow with milk,
and all the stream beds of Judah
shall flow with water;
and a fountain shall come forth from
the house of the LORD
and water the valley of Shittim.

¹⁹ "Egypt shall become a desolation
and Edom a desolate wilderness,

for the violence done to the people
of Judah,
because they have shed innocent
blood in their land.
²⁰ But Judah shall be inhabited for
ever,
and Jerusalem to all generations.
²¹ I will avenge their blood, and I will
not clear the guilty,^g
for the LORD dwells in Zion."

g Gk Syr: Heb *I will hold innocent their blood which I
have not held innocent*

14.21; Rev.21.2–3,27). **18–21:** *The divine blessings* bestowed *in that day* include the paradisiacal fertility of the land, the destruction of Israel's ancient enemies, and the restoration of Judah. **18:** *mountains*, Am.9.13; *fountain*, Ezek.47.1–12 n. **19:** *Edom*, Ob.11 n. **20–21:** Is.12.6; Zech. 2.10–12.

THE BOOK OF AMOS

During the long and peaceful reign of Jeroboam II (786–746 B.C.) Israel attained a height of territorial expansion and national prosperity never again reached. The military security and economic affluence which characterized this age were taken by many Israelites as signs of the LORD's special favor toward them which they felt they deserved because of their extravagant support of the official shrines.

Into this scene stepped the prophet Amos, probably sometime during the decade 760–750 B.C. A native of the small Judean village of Tekoa, he was called by God from a shepherd's task (7.14–15) to the difficult mission of preaching harsh words in a smooth season. He denounced Israel, as well as her neighbors, for reliance upon military might, and for grave injustice in social dealings, abhorrent immorality, and shallow, meaningless piety. Amos' forceful, uncompromising preaching brought him into conflict with the religious authorities of his day. His personal confrontation with the priest Amaziah (7.10–17) remains one of the unforgettable scenes in Hebrew prophecy.

Expelled from the royal sanctuary at Bethel and commanded not to prophesy there again, Amos probably returned to Judah and wrote down the essence of his public preaching in substantially its present form. The book falls into three parts, chs. 1–2, oracles against Israel's neighbors; chs. 3–6, indictment of Israel herself for sin and injustice; and chs. 7–9, visions of Israel's coming doom. Amos became the first in a brilliant succession of writing prophets whose words have left their indelible stamp on later thought about God and man.

THE WORDS OF AMOS, WHO WAS among the shepherds of Teko'a, which he saw concerning Israel in the days of Uzzi'ah king of Judah and in the days of Jerobo'am the son of Jo'ash, king of Israel, two years*a* before the earthquake. ² And he said:

"The LORD roars from Zion,
  and utters his voice from
    Jerusalem;
the pastures of the shepherds mourn,
  and the top of Carmel withers."

³ Thus says the LORD:
"For three transgressions of
    Damascus,
  and for four, I will not revoke the
    punishment;*b*

because they have threshed Gilead
  with threshing sledges of iron.
⁴ So I will send a fire upon the house
    of Haz'ael,
  and it shall devour the strongholds
    of Ben-ha'dad.
⁵ I will break the bar of Damascus,
  and cut off the inhabitants from
    the Valley of Aven,*c*
  and him that holds the scepter from
    Beth-eden;
  and the people of Syria shall go
    into exile to Kir,"
      says the LORD.

⁶ Thus says the LORD:

a Or *during two years*
b Heb *cause it to return*   c Or *On*

1.1: Superscription. *He saw,* see Nah.1.1 n. *Uzziah* reigned over the southern kingdom from 783 to 742 B.C. The *earthquake,* mentioned again in Zech.14.5, cannot be precisely dated. **1.2–2.16: Indictment of neighboring peoples, Israel, and Judah.** Amos applies the same standards to Israel's neighbors and to Israel. **2:** This verse occurs in similar form in Jl.3.16 (compare Jer.25.30). Some scholars consider it an editorial addition. It sounds the solemn theme of the whole section. **3,6,9, etc.:** *Thus says the LORD* and the conclusion *says the LORD* (Hebrew, "the oracle of Yahweh") are standard formulas identifying prophetic oracles. The expression *for three transgressions . . . and for four* indicates "more than enough" (Job 33.14; Pr.30.18). Here *transgression* means rebellion. **3–5:** Against Damascus (compare Is.17.1–3; Jer.49.23–27; Zech. 9.1–4). *Damascus* was the capital of *Syria; Hazael* and *Ben-hadad* III were rulers (2 Kg.13.3); and *Kir* is called the place of Syrian origins (Am.9.7) and exile (2 Kg.16.9). *The Valley of Aven,* perhaps to be read "the Valley of On," may be between the Lebanon and Anti-Lebanon ranges. *Beth-eden* is the Bit-idini of the Assyrian records, by the Euphrates. The Syrian conquest of

"For three transgressions of Gaza,
  and for four, I will not revoke the
    punishment;[b]
because they carried into exile a
    whole people
  to deliver them up to Edom.
[7] So I will send a fire upon the wall
      of Gaza,
  and it shall devour her
    strongholds.
[8] I will cut off the inhabitants from
      Ashdod,
  and him that holds the scepter
    from Ash'kelon;
I will turn my hand against Ekron;
  and the remnant of the Philistines
    shall perish,"
                    says the Lord GOD.

[9] Thus says the LORD:
"For three transgressions of Tyre,
  and for four, I will not revoke the
    punishment;[b]
because they delivered up a whole
    people to Edom,
  and did not remember the
    covenant of brotherhood.
[10] So I will send a fire upon the wall of
      Tyre,
  and it shall devour her
    strongholds."

[11] Thus says the LORD:
"For three transgressions of Edom,
  and for four, I will not revoke the
    punishment;[b]
because he pursued his brother with
    the sword,
  and cast off all pity,
and his anger tore perpetually,
  and he kept his wrath[d] for ever.
[12] So I will send a fire upon Teman,
  and it shall devour the strongholds
    of Bozrah."

[13] Thus says the LORD:
"For three transgressions of the
    Ammonites,
  and for four, I will not revoke the
    punishment;[b]
because they have ripped up women
    with child in Gilead,
  that they might enlarge their
    border.
[14] So I will kindle a fire in the wall of
    Rabbah,
  and it shall devour her
    strongholds,
with shouting in the day of battle,
  with a tempest in the day of the
    whirlwind;
[15] and their king shall go into exile,
  he and his princes together,"
                    says the LORD.

2 Thus says the LORD:
  "For three transgressions of Moab,
    and for four, I will not revoke the
      punishment;[e]
because he burned to lime
    the bones of the king of Edom.
[2] So I will send a fire upon Moab,
  and it shall devour the
    strongholds of Ker'ioth,
and Moab shall die amid uproar,
  amid shouting and the sound of
    the trumpet;
[3] I will cut off the ruler from its midst,
  and will slay all its princes with
    him,"
                    says the LORD.

[4] Thus says the LORD:
"For three transgressions of Judah,
  and for four, I will not revoke the
    punishment;[e]

b Heb *cause it to return*
d Gk Syr Vg: Heb *his wrath kept*
e Heb *cause it to return*

Gilead, 2 Kg.10.32–33. **6–8:** Against Philistia. Four Philistine cities are condemned because of their slave traffic with Edom (2 Chr.21.16–17; Jl.3.4–8; Zeph.2.4–7). **9–10:** Against Tyre (see Jl.3.4–8). *Covenant of brotherhood,* compare 1 Kg.9.13. **11–12:** Against Edom. This oracle, recalling later oracles against Edom (see Introduction to Obadiah), is regarded by many as secondary. *Brother,* that is, Judah, Mal.1.2. **13–15:** Against the Ammonites (Zeph. 2.8–11), who are to be punished because of inhuman atrocities against Israelites in Trans-jordan in *Gilead.* **2.1–3:** Against Moab, Israel's ancient enemy to the south-east of the Jordan (Is.15.1–16.14). *Burned to lime,* perhaps involving a desecration (compare 2 Kg.23.16–20; Is.33.12). **4–5:** Against Judah. In part because of its language, many consider this oracle a later addition, but it is consistent with Amos' view that all nations stand accountable before God. **6–16:**

because they have rejected the law
   of the LORD,
  and have not kept his statutes,
but their lies have led them astray,
  after which their fathers walked.
5 So I will send a fire upon Judah,
  and it shall devour the strongholds
   of Jerusalem."

6 Thus says the LORD:
"For three transgressions of Israel,
  and for four, I will not revoke the
   punishment;*e*
because they sell the righteous for
  silver,
  and the needy for a pair of shoes–
7 they that trample the head of the
  poor into the dust of the earth,
  and turn aside the way of the
   afflicted;
a man and his father go in to the
  same maiden,
  so that my holy name is profaned;
8 they lay themselves down beside
  every altar
  upon garments taken in pledge;
and in the house of their God they
  drink
  the wine of those who have been
   fined.

9 "Yet I destroyed the Amorite before
  them,
  whose height was like the height
   of the cedars,
  and who was as strong as the oaks;
I destroyed his fruit above,
  and his roots beneath.
10 Also I brought you up out of the
  land of Egypt,
  and led you forty years in the
   wilderness,
  to possess the land of the Amorite.
11 And I raised up some of your sons
  for prophets,

and some of your young men for
  Nazirites.
Is it not indeed so, O people of
  Israel?"
           says the LORD.

12 "But you made the Nazirites drink
  wine,
  and commanded the prophets,
  saying, 'You shall not prophesy.'

13 "Behold, I will press you down in
  your place,
  as a cart full of sheaves presses
   down.
14 Flight shall perish from the swift,
  and the strong shall not retain his
   strength,
  nor shall the mighty save his life;
15 he who handles the bow shall not
  stand,
  and he who is swift of foot shall
   not save himself,
  nor shall he who rides the horse
   save his life;
16 and he who is stout of heart among
  the mighty
  shall flee away naked in that day,"
           says the LORD.

3 Hear this word that the LORD has
spoken against you, O people of
Israel, against the whole family which
I brought up out of the land of Egypt:
2 "You only have I known
  of all the families of the earth;
therefore I will punish you
  for all your iniquities.

3 "Do two walk together,
  unless they have made an
   appointment?
4 Does a lion roar in the forest,
  when he has no prey?
Does a young lion cry out from his
  den,

e Heb *cause it to return*

Against Israel. Using the same literary form, Amos shows that Israel and her neighbors are
judged by the same standards. **7–8:** *Same maiden*, cult prostitutes. **9:** *Amorites*, the pre-Israelite
inhabitants of Canaan (see Ezek.16.3). **11:** *Nazirites*, Num.6.2 n.; Jg.13.5 n.
    3.1–6.14: Israel's sinfulness and God's punishment. Three sections, each with the same opening
exhortation (3.1; 4.1; 5.1).
    3.1–15: The privileges of election create a greater responsibility (Lk.12.48b). Because Israel
had been favored above *all the families of the earth* (Ex.19.4–6; Dt.7.6), the neighboring nations

if he has taken nothing?
5 Does a bird fall in a snare on the
    earth,
  when there is no trap for it?
Does a snare spring up from the
    ground,
  when it has taken nothing?
6 Is a trumpet blown in a city,
  and the people are not afraid?
Does evil befall a city,
  unless the LORD has done it?
7 Surely the Lord GOD does nothing,
  without revealing his secret
  to his servants the prophets.
8 The lion has roared;
  who will not fear?
The Lord GOD has spoken;
  who can but prophesy?"

9 Proclaim to the strongholds in
    Assyria,*f*
  and to the strongholds in the land
    of Egypt,
and say, "Assemble yourselves upon
    the mountains of Sama′ria,
  and see the great tumults within
    her,
  and the oppressions in her midst."
10 "They do not know how to do
    right," says the LORD,
  "those who store up violence and
    robbery in their strongholds."
11 Therefore thus says the Lord GOD:
  "An adversary shall surround the
    land,
  and bring down your defenses
    from you,
  and your strongholds shall be
    plundered."

12 Thus says the LORD: "As the
shepherd rescues from the mouth of
the lion two legs, or a piece of an ear,

so shall the people of Israel who dwell
in Sama′ria be rescued, with the corner of a couch and part*g* of a bed."

13 "Hear, and testify against the house
    of Jacob,"
  says the Lord GOD, the God of
    hosts,
14 "that on the day I punish Israel for
    his transgressions,
  I will punish the altars of Bethel,
and the horns of the altar shall be
    cut off
  and fall to the ground.
15 I will smite the winter house with
    the summer house;
  and the houses of ivory shall
    perish,
and the great houses*h* shall come to
    an end,"
                    says the LORD.

4 "Hear this word, you cows of
    Bashan,
  who are in the mountain of
    Sama′ria,
who oppress the poor, who crush the
    needy,
  who say to their husbands, 'Bring,
    that we may drink!'
2 The Lord GOD has sworn by his
    holiness
  that, behold, the days are coming
    upon you,
when they shall take you away with
    hooks,
  even the last of you with fishhooks.
3 And you shall go out through the
    breaches,
  every one straight before her;

f Gk: Heb *Ashdod*
g The meaning of the Hebrew word is uncertain
h Or *many houses*

---

are assembled to witness her chastisement. **3–8:** The call to prophesy cannot be resisted. **6:**
Israel's God is operative in history, sending calamity (*evil*) as corrective discipline (Job 2.10;
Is.45.7). **7:** The Old Testament concept of revelation is grounded in the conviction that the
God who is Lord over nature and history discloses his will to *his* chosen *servants* (2.11; Gen.
18.17–19; Ex.4.15–16; Jer.7.25; Dan.9.10; Lk.1.70). **12:** Although a few may be rescued from
the catastrophe (5.3), the burden of Amos' message is the thoroughness of the divine punishment (9.1). **15:** Houses of ivory, see 1 Kg.22.39 n.
    4.1–13: Israel's luxurious excesses and vain piety. Israel has not heeded the LORD's repeated
warnings. **1–3:** The wealthy and greedy women of *Samaria*, being as guilty as their husbands,
will also be punished (compare Is.3.16–26). *Cows of Bashan*, Ps.22.12. **4–5:** Israel's love of

and you shall be cast forth into
  Harmon,"
           says the LORD.

4 "Come to Bethel, and transgress;
  to Gilgal, and multiply
    transgression;
bring your sacrifices every morning,
  your tithes every three days;
5 offer a sacrifice of thanksgiving of
  that which is leavened,
  and proclaim freewill offerings,
    publish them;
  for so you love to do, O people of
    Israel!"
           says the Lord GOD.

6 "I gave you cleanness of teeth in all
  your cities,
  and lack of bread in all your
    places,
yet you did not return to me,"
           says the LORD.

7 "And I also withheld the rain from
  you
  when there were yet three months
    to the harvest;
I would send rain upon one city,
  and send no rain upon another
    city;
one field would be rained upon,
  and the field on which it did not
    rain withered;
8 so two or three cities wandered to
  one city
  to drink water, and were not
    satisfied;
yet you did not return to me,"
           says the LORD.

9 "I smote you with blight and
  mildew;
I laid waste*i* your gardens and
  your vineyards;
  your fig trees and your olive trees
    the locust devoured;

yet you did not return to me,"
           says the LORD.

10 "I sent among you a pestilence after
  the manner of Egypt;
  I slew your young men with the
    sword;
I carried away your horses;*j*
  and I made the stench of your
    camp go up into your nostrils;
yet you did not return to me,"
           says the LORD.

11 "I overthrew some of you,
  as when God overthrew Sodom
    and Gomor'rah,
  and you were as a brand plucked
    out of the burning;
yet you did not return to me,"
           says the LORD.

12 "Therefore thus I will do to you, O
  Israel;
  because I will do this to you,
  prepare to meet your God, O
    Israel!"

13 For lo, he who forms the mountains,
  and creates the wind,
  and declares to man what is his
    thought;
who makes the morning darkness,
  and treads on the heights of the
    earth–
  the LORD, the God of hosts, is his
    name!

5 Hear this word which I take up
  over you in lamentation, O house
of Israel:
2 "Fallen, no more to rise,
  is the virgin Israel;
  forsaken on her land,
  with none to raise her up."

i Cn: Heb *the multitude of*
j Heb *with the captivity of your horses*

---

manifold public rites at the chief sanctuaries is satirized. **6–12:** Having ignored the LORD's
repeated warnings through nature and history, Israel must now prepare to meet her God, who
is characterized by patient love and inexorable justice. **13:** This doxology, like those in 5.8–9
and 9.5–6, with which it shares the refrain *the LORD is his name*, is probably a later addition.
5.1–6.14: The horror and finality of Israel's deserved punishment. 5.1–3: A lament for the

³ For thus says the Lord GOD:
"The city that went forth a thousand
shall have a hundred left,
and that which went forth a hundred
shall have ten left
to the house of Israel."

⁴ For thus says the LORD to the house
of Israel:
"Seek me and live;
⁵   but do not seek Bethel,
and do not enter into Gilgal
or cross over to Beer-sheba;
for Gilgal shall surely go into exile,
and Bethel shall come to nought."

⁶ Seek the LORD and live,
lest he break out like fire in the
house of Joseph,
and it devour, with none to quench
it for Bethel,
⁷ O you who turn justice to
wormwood,
and cast down righteousness to
the earth!

⁸ He who made the Plei′ades and
Orion,
and turns deep darkness into the
morning,
and darkens the day into night,
who calls for the waters of the sea,
and pours them out upon the
surface of the earth,
the LORD is his name,
⁹ who makes destruction flash forth
against the strong,
so that destruction comes upon
the fortress.

¹⁰ They hate him who reproves in the
gate,
and they abhor him who speaks
the truth.
¹¹ Therefore because you trample
upon the poor
and take from him exactions of
wheat,

you have built houses of hewn stone,
but you shall not dwell in them;
you have planted pleasant
vineyards,
but you shall not drink their wine.
¹² For I know how many are your
transgressions,
and how great are your sins—
you who afflict the righteous, who
take a bribe,
and turn aside the needy in the
gate.
¹³ Therefore he who is prudent will
keep silent in such a time;
for it is an evil time.

¹⁴ Seek good, and not evil,
that you may live;
and so the LORD, the God of hosts,
will be with you,
as you have said.
¹⁵ Hate evil, and love good,
and establish justice in the gate;
it may be that the LORD, the God of
hosts,
will be gracious to the remnant of
Joseph.

¹⁶ Therefore thus says the LORD, the
God of hosts, the Lord:
"In all the squares there shall be
wailing;
and in all the streets they shall say,
'Alas! alas!'
They shall call the farmers to
mourning
and to wailing those who are
skilled in lamentation,
¹⁷ and in all vineyards there shall be
wailing,
for I will pass through the midst
of you,"

says the LORD.

¹⁸ Woe to you who desire the day of
the LORD!
Why would you have the day of
the LORD?
It is darkness, and not light;

---

fallen and forsaken nation. *Went forth a thousand*, a reference to military forces. **4–7,14–15:**
There is yet time to seek the LORD and live. **8–9:** The second doxology (see 4.13 n.). **10–13,**
16–17: Amos warns Israel again about the nature and effect of her transgressions. **18–20:**
The day of the LORD, in which Israelites piously expected to be vindicated against their enemies,

19 as if a man fled from a lion,
   and a bear met him;
 or went into the house and leaned
   with his hand against the wall,
   and a serpent bit him.
20 Is not the day of the LORD darkness,
   and not light,
 and gloom with no brightness in
   it?

21 "I hate, I despise your feasts,
   and I take no delight in your
   solemn assemblies.
22 Even though you offer me your
   burnt offerings and cereal
   offerings,
   I will not accept them,
 and the peace offerings of your fatted
   beasts
   I will not look upon.
23 Take away from me the noise of
   your songs;
   to the melody of your harps I will
   not listen.
24 But let justice roll down like waters,
   and righteousness like an
   ever-flowing stream.

25 "Did you bring to me sacrifices
and offerings the forty years in the
wilderness, O house of Israel? 26 You
shall take up Sakkuth your king, and
Kaiwan your star-god, your images,*k*
which you made for yourselves;
27 therefore I will take you into exile
beyond Damascus," says the LORD,
whose name is the God of hosts.

6 "Woe to those who are at ease in
   Zion,
   and to those who feel secure on
   the mountain of Sama'ria,

the notable men of the first of the
   nations,
   to whom the house of Israel come!
2 Pass over to Calneh, and see;
   and thence go to Hamath the
   great;
 then go down to Gath of the
   Philistines.
 Are they better than these kingdoms?
   Or is their territory greater than
   your territory,
3 O you who put far away the evil day,
   and bring near the seat of
   violence?

4 "Woe to those who lie upon beds of
   ivory,
   and stretch themselves upon their
   couches,
 and eat lambs from the flock,
   and calves from the midst of the
   stall;
5 who sing idle songs to the sound of
   the harp,
   and like David invent for
   themselves instruments of
   music;
6 who drink wine in bowls,
   and anoint themselves with the
   finest oils,
   but are not grieved over the ruin
   of Joseph!
7 Therefore they shall now be the
   first of those to go into exile,
   and the revelry of those who
   stretch themselves shall pass
   away."

8 The Lord GOD has sworn by
   himself
 (says the LORD, the God of hosts):
   "I abhor the pride of Jacob,

k Heb *your images, your star-god*

---

will be darkness and gloom (Am.8.9–14; see Zeph.1.14–18 n.). Amos' profound reinterpretation
of this popular concept is among his most significant contributions. **21–27:** The LORD delights
not in an abundance of festivals and sacrifices but in *justice* and *righteousness*. Verse 24 expresses
the heart of Amos' preaching. **25:** In the desert Israel had a pure, direct relation with God which
rendered sacrifices unnecessary (Jer.2.2–3; Hos.2.14–20; 9.10). **26:** *Sakkuth* and *Kaiwan*
designate known Assyrian deities (Acts 7.42–43). **6.1–7:** The Israelites, who feel themselves
secure in their false confidence and lie upon beds of ivory in luxurious self-indulgence, will be
the first of those whom God will send into exile. **2:** Compare Is.10.9–11; 2 Chr.26.6. *Calneh*
and *Hamath*, important commercial centers in Syria, represent wealth and security. **5:** *David*,
1 Chr.23.5; Neh.12.36. **8–14:** Because Israel has turned faith into pride (Is.28.1; Hos.5.5; Am.

and hate his strongholds;
and I will deliver up the city and
all that is in it."

9 And if ten men remain in one
house, they shall die. [10] And when a
man's kinsman, he who burns him,[l]
shall take him up to bring the bones
out of the house, and shall say to him
who is in the innermost parts of the
house, "Is there still any one with
you?" he shall say, "No"; and he shall
say, "Hush! We must not mention the
name of the LORD."

[11] For behold, the LORD commands,
and the great house shall be
smitten into fragments,
and the little house into bits.
[12] Do horses run upon rocks?
Does one plow the sea with oxen?
But you have turned justice into
poison
and the fruit of righteousness into
wormwood–
[13] you who rejoice in Lo-debar,[n]
who say, "Have we not by our
own strength
taken Karnaim[o] for ourselves?"
[14] "For behold, I will raise up against
you a nation,
O house of Israel," says the LORD,
the God of hosts;
"and they shall oppress you from
the entrance of Hamath
to the Brook of the Arabah."

7 Thus the Lord GOD showed me:
behold, he was forming locusts in
the beginning of the shooting up of the
latter growth; and lo, it was the latter
growth after the king's mowings.
[2] When they had finished eating the
grass of the land, I said,

"O Lord GOD, forgive, I beseech
thee!
How can Jacob stand?
He is so small!"
[3] The LORD repented concerning this;
"It shall not be," said the LORD.

4 Thus the Lord GOD showed me:
behold, the Lord GOD was calling for a
judgment by fire, and it devoured the
great deep and was eating up the land.
[5] Then I said,
"O Lord GOD, cease, I beseech thee!
How can Jacob stand?
He is so small!"
[6] The LORD repented concerning this;
"This also shall not be," said the
Lord GOD.

7 He showed me: behold, the Lord
was standing beside a wall built with
a plumb line, with a plumb line in his
hand. [8] And the LORD said to me,
"Amos, what do you see?" And I said,
"A plumb line." Then the Lord said,
"Behold, I am setting a plumb line
in the midst of my people Israel;
I will never again pass by them;
[9] the high places of Isaac shall be
made desolate,
and the sanctuaries of Israel shall
be laid waste,
and I will rise against the house
of Jerobo'am with the sword."

10 Then Amazi'ah the priest of
Bethel sent to Jerobo'am king of Israel, saying, "Amos has conspired
against you in the midst of the house
of Israel; the land is not able to bear
all his words. [11] For thus Amos has
said,

l Or *who makes a burning for him*
n Or *a thing of nought*
o Or *horns*

8.7) and justice into poison, she will be thoroughly punished. **9–10:** The sequel to siege or pestilence. *Not mention the name of the LORD*, perhaps out of fear of further judgment. **14:** From
Hamath to the *Arabah*, the farthest extent of Israelite territory (see 2 Kg.14.25).
   7.1–9.15: Five visions of God's judgment, and a prophecy of restoration. 7.1–9: The first three
visions. **1–3:** Judgment by locusts (Jl.1.2–7 n.). **4–6:** Judgment by fire (see 1.4). The judgments
are halted when Amos pleads. **7–9:** *Plumb line* (2 Kg.21.13–15). The people are found warped
beyond correction; God decrees an irrevocable sentence of destruction.
   7.10–17: Amos and Amaziah. A prose biographical incident, introduced here perhaps because
of the threat against the house of Jeroboam in v. 9. Amaziah was the official priest of the royal

'Jerobo'am shall die by the sword,
and Israel must go into exile
away from his land.' "
12 And Amazi'ah said to Amos, "O
seer, go, flee away to the land of
Judah, and eat bread there, and prophesy there; 13 but never again prophesy
at Bethel, for it is the king's sanctuary,
and it is a temple of the kingdom."

14 Then Amos answered Amazi'ah,
"I am no prophet, nor a prophet's son;*p*
but I am a herdsman, and a dresser
of sycamore trees, 15 and the LORD
took me from following the flock, and
the LORD said to me, 'Go, prophesy
to my people Israel.'
16 "Now therefore hear the word of
the LORD.
You say, 'Do not prophesy against
Israel,
and do not preach against the
house of Isaac.'
17 Therefore thus says the LORD:
'Your wife shall be a harlot in the
city,
and your sons and your daughters
shall fall by the sword,
and your land shall be parceled
out by line;
you yourself shall die in an unclean
land,
and Israel shall surely go into
exile away from its land.' "

8 Thus the Lord GOD showed me:
behold, a basket of summer fruit.*q*
2 And he said, "Amos, what do you
see?" And I said, "A basket of summer fruit."*q* Then the LORD said to
me,
"The end*r* has come upon my
people Israel;
I will never again pass by them.
3 The songs of the temple*s* shall
become wailings in that day,"
says the Lord GOD;

"the dead bodies shall be many;
in every place they shall be cast
out in silence."*t*

4 Hear this, you who trample upon the
needy,
and bring the poor of the land to
an end,
5 saying, "When will the new moon
be over,
that we may sell grain?
And the sabbath,
that we may offer wheat for sale,
that we may make the ephah small
and the shekel great,
and deal deceitfully with false
balances,
6 that we may buy the poor for silver
and the needy for a pair of
sandals,
and sell the refuse of the wheat?"

7 The LORD has sworn by the pride
of Jacob:
"Surely I will never forget any of
their deeds.
8 Shall not the land tremble on this
account,
and every one mourn who dwells
in it,
and all of it rise like the Nile,
and be tossed about and sink
again, like the Nile of Egypt?"

9 "And on that day," says the Lord
GOD,
"I will make the sun go down at
noon,
and darken the earth in broad
daylight.
10 I will turn your feasts into
mourning,
and all your songs into
lamentation;

p Or one of the sons of the prophets
q Heb qayits   r Heb qets
s Or palace   t Or be silent!

---

sanctuary at Bethel. **14**: Amos asserts that he is not a professional prophet (1 Sam.9.6–10;
Mic.3.5–8,11) or a member of a prophetic guild (2 Kg.2.3 n.; 1 Sam.10.5; 1 Kg.22.6), but a layman whom the LORD took and sent to prophesy to his people (3.3–8; 2 Sam.7.8).
8.1–3: Fourth vision. *A basket of* ripe *summer fruit* symbolizes the immediacy of Israel's *end.*
8.4–14: The indictment of Israel and the coming of the day of mourning (see 5.18–20 n.).
5–6: The merchants are impatient for the holy days to pass so they can resume their fraudulent

I will bring sackcloth upon all loins,
  and baldness on every head;
I will make it like the mourning for
  an only son,
  and the end of it like a bitter day.

11 "Behold, the days are coming," says
  the Lord GOD,
  "when I will send a famine on the
  land;
not a famine of bread, nor a thirst
  for water,
but of hearing the words of the
  LORD.
12 They shall wander from sea to sea,
  and from north to east;
they shall run to and fro, to seek the
  word of the LORD,
  but they shall not find it.

13 "In that day the fair virgins and the
  young men
  shall faint for thirst.
14 Those who swear by Ash'imah of
  Sama'ria,
  and say, 'As thy god lives, O Dan,'
and, 'As the way of Beer-sheba lives,'
  they shall fall, and never rise
  again."

9 I saw the LORD standing beside[u]
  the altar, and he said:
"Smite the capitals until the
  thresholds shake,
  and shatter them on the heads of
  all the people;[v]
and what are left of them I will slay
  with the sword;
  not one of them shall flee away,
  not one of them shall escape.

2 "Though they dig into Sheol,
  from there shall my hand take
  them;

though they climb up to heaven,
  from there I will bring them down.
3 Though they hide themselves on the
  top of Carmel,
from there I will search out and
  take them;
and though they hide from my sight
  at the bottom of the sea,
there I will command the serpent,
  and it shall bite them.
4 And though they go into captivity
  before their enemies,
there I will command the sword,
  and it shall slay them;
and I will set my eyes upon them
  for evil and not for good."

5 The Lord, GOD of hosts,
he who touches the earth and it
  melts,
  and all who dwell in it mourn,
and all of it rises like the Nile,
  and sinks again, like the Nile of
  Egypt;
6 who builds his upper chambers in
  the heavens,
  and founds his vault upon the
  earth;
who calls for the waters of the sea,
  and pours them out upon the
  surface of the earth—
the LORD is his name.

7 "Are you not like the Ethiopians to
  me,
  O people of Israel?" says the
  LORD.
"Did I not bring up Israel from the
  land of Egypt,
  and the Philistines from Caphtor
  and the Syrians from Kir?
8 Behold, the eyes of the Lord GOD
  are upon the sinful kingdom,

u Or upon   v Heb all of them

---

business (Is.1.13–17; Lev.19.35–36; Dt.25.13–16). **13–14:** The patron deities of pagan shrines, from farthest north (*Dan*) to farthest south (*Beer-sheba*), will be of no help in that day.

9.1–4: Fifth vision. The last pronouncement is the most dreadful. **1:** *Thresholds shake,* see Is.6.4. **2:** *Sheol,* the place of the dead (Job 10.19–22; Is.14.11,15), which offers man no hiding place from God (Ps.139.7–12). **3:** *Serpent,* mythological dragon inhabiting the deep sea (Job 41.1–34 n.).

9.5–6: The third doxology, see 4.13 n. The Lord of nature and history (9.1–4) is also the Creator.

9.7–10: Israel has no claim to special privilege in the moral realm, for the LORD will destroy

and I will destroy it from the
surface of the ground;
except that I will not utterly
destroy the house of Jacob,"
says the LORD.

9 "For lo, I will command,
and shake the house of Israel
among all the nations
as one shakes with a sieve,
but no pebble shall fall upon the
earth.
10 All the sinners of my people shall
die by the sword,
who say, 'Evil shall not overtake
or meet us.'

11 "In that day I will raise up
the booth of David that is fallen
and repair its breaches,
and raise up its ruins,
and rebuild it as in the days of
old;
12 that they may possess the remnant
of Edom

and all the nations who are called
by my name,"
says the LORD who does this.

13 "Behold, the days are coming," says
the LORD,
"when the plowman shall overtake
the reaper
and the treader of grapes him
who sows the seed;
the mountains shall drip sweet wine,
and all the hills shall flow with it.
14 I will restore the fortunes of my
people Israel,
and they shall rebuild the ruined
cities and inhabit them;
they shall plant vineyards and drink
their wine,
and they shall make gardens and
eat their fruit.
15 I will plant them upon their land,
and they shall never again be
plucked up
out of the land which I have given
them,"
says the LORD your God.

every sinful kingdom. Here Amos' universalism (see 1.2–2.16 n.) complements the doctrine of election (3.2). **7:** *Caphtor,* see Jg.13.1 n. *Kir,* see 1.5 n.
9.11–15: Prophecies of the restoration of the Davidic dynasty (vs. 11–12) **and the glorious age to come** (vs. 13–15). This section, so affirmative in its emphasis, is generally considered a later addition. It expands, however, genuine elements in Amos' own thought (compare 3.12; 5.3,4,6, 11–15) and also illustrates a basic concept that the full prophetic word contains both judgment and salvation (see Introduction to Micah). **11–12:** Note the use of this passage by James at the meeting of the apostles and the elders of the church at Jerusalem in Acts 15.16–17. **13:** See Jl.3.18–21 n.

THE BOOK OF OBADIAH

Nothing is known of the person of the prophet Obadiah; even his name is not distinctive (see v. 1 n.). The problems of date and composition of his brief work, the shortest book in the Old Testament, are not easily solved. Some of the oracles in the book were spoken, or written, soon after Jerusalem fell to the Babylonians in 587 (586) B.C. Obadiah may not himself have written all of the present book, but may have drawn upon collections of sayings transmitted orally among prophetic circles. This could account for the similarity between vv. 1–9 and Jer.49.7–22. But the work is dominated by the theme of justice and judgment, and may well be the product of one man.

Verses 1–14 indict the Edomites for outrageous and hostile actions when their Israelite brothers were in peril. Starting from these recent events in the experience of his people, Obadiah, like Joel (see Introduction to Joel), moves on to portray their future consummation. Verses 15–18 announce the day of the LORD's recompense upon the nations for their shameful behavior. A final section (vv. 19–21) proclaims the return of Israel's exiles to the Promised Land, their dominion over Edom, and the LORD's universal sovereignty.

1 THE VISION OF OBADI'AH.

Thus says the Lord GOD concerning
    Edom:
We have heard tidings from the
    LORD,
  and a messenger has been sent
    among the nations:
  "Rise up! let us rise against her for
    battle!"
2 Behold, I will make you small
    among the nations,
  you shall be utterly despised.
3 The pride of your heart has
    deceived you,
  you who live in the clefts of the
    rock,[a]
  whose dwelling is high,
who say in your heart,
  "Who will bring me down to the
    ground?"
4 Though you soar aloft like the eagle,
  though your nest is set among the
    stars,
  thence I will bring you down,
       says the LORD.

5 If thieves came to you,

if plunderers by night–
how you have been destroyed!–
  would they not steal only enough
    for themselves?
If grape gatherers came to you,
  would they not leave gleanings?
6 How Esau has been pillaged,
  his treasures sought out!
7 All your allies have deceived you,
  they have driven you to the
    border;
your confederates have prevailed
  against you;
your trusted friends have set a
  trap under you–
  there is no understanding of it.
8 Will I not on that day, says the
    LORD,
  destroy the wise men out of Edom,
  and understanding out of Mount
    Esau?
9 And your mighty men shall be
    dismayed, O Teman,
  so that every man from Mount
    Esau will be cut off by slaughter.
10 For the violence done to your
    brother Jacob,

a Or *Sela*

1: Introduction. *Vision*, see Nah.1.1 n. *Obadiah*, meaning "Servant of the LORD," is the name of twelve different persons in the Old Testament. *Edom*, southeast of Palestine. **2–4:** The humbling of Edom. The non-Israelite *nations*, the Gentiles, will share in the spectacle. **3:** The same Hebrew word means *rock* and Sela, an Edomite fortress also called Teman (v. 9) and Petra. **4:** *Says the LORD*, see Am.1.3 n. **5–7:** The pillaging and betrayal of Edom. **6:** *Esau*, Jacob's twin, was the father of the Edomites (Gen.25.30; 36.1). **8–11:** The destruction of Edom.

shame shall cover you,
and you shall be cut off for ever.

11 On the day that you stood aloof,
on the day that strangers carried
off his wealth,
and foreigners entered his gates
and cast lots for Jerusalem,
you were like one of them.

12 But you should not have gloated
over the day of your brother
in the day of his misfortune;
you should not have rejoiced over
the people of Judah
in the day of their ruin;
you should not have boasted
in the day of distress.

13 You should not have entered the
gate of my people
in the day of his calamity;
you should not have gloated over his
disaster
in the day of his calamity;
you should not have looted his goods
in the day of his calamity.

14 You should not have stood at the
parting of the ways
to cut off his fugitives;
you should not have delivered up
his survivors
in the day of distress.

15 For the day of the LORD is near upon
all the nations.
As you have done, it shall be done
to you,
your deeds shall return on your
own head.

16 For as you have drunk upon my
holy mountain,

all the nations round about shall
drink;
they shall drink, and stagger,[b]
and shall be as though they had
not been.

17 But in Mount Zion there shall be
those that escape,
and it shall be holy;
and the house of Jacob shall possess
their own possessions.

18 The house of Jacob shall be a fire,
and the house of Joseph a flame,
and the house of Esau stubble;
they shall burn them and consume
them,
and there shall be no survivor to
the house of Esau;
for the LORD has spoken.

19 Those of the Negeb shall possess
Mount Esau,
and those of the Shephe'lah the
land of the Philistines;
they shall possess the land of
E'phraim and the land of
Sama'ria
and Benjamin shall possess Gilead.

20 The exiles in Halah[c] who are of
the people of Israel
shall possess[d] Phoenicia as far
as Zar'ephath;
and the exiles of Jerusalem who
are in Sephar'ad
shall possess the cities of the
Negeb.

21 Saviors shall go up to Mount Zion
to rule Mount Esau;
and the kingdom shall be the
LORD's.

b Cn: Heb *swallow*
c Cn: Heb *this army*   *d* Cn: Heb *which*

8: Compare Zeph.1.9,10; 3.16; Hag.2.23. Edom was renowned for her *wise men* (Jer.49.7).
10–11: *Jacob* was the father of the Israelites (Gen.49.2; Is.43.1). By failing to help his brother in
his adversity, Edom became as guilty as the *foreigners* who *entered his gates.* Obadiah shares this
bitterness against Edom with other writers of the sixth and fifth centuries B.C. (Ps.137.7; Is.
34.5–7; 63.1–6; Lam.4.21; Ezek.25.12–14; Mal.1.2–5; see also, from an earlier period, Am.
1.11–12). 12–14: Eight-fold indictment of Edom, cast in a very forceful, repetitive style. 15–18:
The day of the LORD's judgment *upon all the nations,* especially Edom. But Israel shall be saved.
15: *The day of the LORD,* see Am.5.18 n. 16: Compare Jer.25.15–29. 17: Jl.2.32. 19–21: The
division of the land, and the LORD's kingship. 19: *Negeb* is the arid south; *Shephelah,* the
western foothills. *Gilead* is in Transjordan. 20: *Halah* (the Hebrew text is uncertain) is in
northern Mesopotamia (2 Kg.17.6); *Sepharad,* perhaps in Asia Minor. 21: The immediate
reference of this verse is political: Israel will dominate Edom. But it carries also a broader
theological reference: power belongs to the LORD, and he shall reign over all (Pss.22.28; 47;
99.1–2).

THE BOOK OF JONAH

The book of Jonah is unique among the prophetic books. It contains no collection of oracles in verse against Israel and foreign nations, but presents a prose narrative about the prophet himself. Instead of portraying a prophet who is an obedient servant of the LORD, calling his people to repentance, it features a recalcitrant prophet who flees from his mission and sulks when his hearers repent.

The book is a didactic narrative which has taken older material from the realm of popular legend and put it to new, more consequential use. Its two parts, chs. 1–2 and 3–4, are now united by having in common a central character (Jonah), a similar plot (his ironical conversion of the heathen), and an identical theme (the breadth of God's saving love).

The principal figure of this artful story is an obscure Galilean prophet from Gath-hepher who counseled Jeroboam II (786–746 B.C.) in a successful conflict with the Syrians (2 Kg.14.25) and with whom some of the earlier traditional material was probably associated. Its author, however, probably lived in the post-exilic period because he shows the influence of Jeremiah and Second Isaiah, and opposes the type of narrow Jewish nationalism exhibited in Ezra and Nehemiah. Although the linguistic evidence is indecisive, a date sometime in the fifth or fourth century B.C. seems indicated.

With skill and finesse this little book calls Israel to repentance and reminds her of her mission to preach to all the nations the wideness of God's mercy and his forgiveness (Gen.12.1–3; Is.42.6–7; 49.6). In spirit, therefore, it remains truly prophetic and justifies its place in the Book of the Twelve Prophets.

NOW THE WORD OF THE LORD came to Jonah the son of Amit'tai, saying, 2 "Arise, go to Nin'eveh, that great city, and cry against it; for their wickedness has come up before me." 3 But Jonah rose to flee to Tarshish from the presence of the LORD. He went down to Joppa and found a ship going to Tarshish; so he paid the fare, and went on board, to go with them to Tarshish, away from the presence of the LORD.

4 But the LORD hurled a great wind upon the sea, and there was a mighty tempest on the sea, so that the ship threatened to break up. 5 Then the mariners were afraid, and each cried to his god; and they threw the wares that were in the ship into the sea, to lighten it for them. But Jonah had gone down into the inner part of the ship and had lain down, and was fast asleep. 6 So the captain came and said to him, "What do you mean, you sleeper? Arise, call upon your god! Perhaps the god will give a thought to us, that we do not perish."

7 And they said to one another, "Come, let us cast lots, that we may know on whose account this evil has come upon us." So they cast lots, and the lot fell upon Jonah. 8 Then they said to him, "Tell us, on whose account this evil has come upon us? What is your occupation? And whence do you come? What is your country? And of what people are you?" 9 And he said to them, "I am a Hebrew; and I fear the LORD, the God of heaven, who made the sea and the dry land." 10 Then the men were exceedingly afraid, and said to him, "What is this that you have done!" For the men knew that he was fleeing from the presence of the LORD, because he had told them.

1.1–16: Jonah's first call to preach to Nineveh, although unheeded, results in the conversion of the heathen sailors. **1–3:** Jonah rebels against the divine commission and attempts to flee from God. **1:** *The word of the LORD*, Hos.1.1 n. The word Jonah means "dove." **2:** For the *wickedness* of the Assyrian capital, *Nineveh*, see Nah. ch. 3. **3:** *Tarshish*, probably in southern Spain (Is.23.1–12; Ezek.27.12,25), represents the farthest point to which Jonah could sail. **4–16:** The LORD procures Jonah's recall. He causes a great tempest; for *the LORD, the God of heaven*, rules

11 Then they said to him, "What shall we do to you, that the sea may quiet down for us?" For the sea grew more and more tempestuous. 12 He said to them, "Take me up and throw me into the sea; then the sea will quiet down for you; for I know it is because of me that this great tempest has come upon you." 13 Nevertheless the men rowed hard to bring the ship back to land, but they could not, for the sea grew more and more tempestuous against them. 14 Therefore they cried to the LORD, "We beseech thee, O LORD, let us not perish for this man's life, and lay not on us innocent blood; for thou, O LORD, hast done as it pleased thee." 15 So they took up Jonah and threw him into the sea; and the sea ceased from its raging. 16 Then the men feared the LORD exceedingly, and they offered a sacrifice to the LORD and made vows.

17*a* And the LORD appointed a great fish to swallow up Jonah; and Jonah was in the belly of the fish three days and three nights.

2 Then Jonah prayed to the LORD his God from the belly of the fish, 2 saying,

"I called to the LORD, out of my distress,
  and he answered me;
out of the belly of Sheol I cried,
  and thou didst hear my voice.
3 For thou didst cast me into the deep,
  into the heart of the seas,
and the flood was round about me;

all thy waves and thy billows
  passed over me.
4 Then I said, 'I am cast out
  from thy presence;
how shall I again look
  upon thy holy temple?'
5 The waters closed in over me,
  the deep was round about me;
weeds were wrapped about my head
6   at the roots of the mountains.
I went down to the land
  whose bars closed upon me for ever;
yet thou didst bring up my life from the Pit,
  O LORD my God.
7 When my soul fainted within me,
  I remembered the LORD;
and my prayer came to thee,
  into thy holy temple.
8 Those who pay regard to vain idols
  forsake their true loyalty.
9 But I with the voice of thanksgiving
  will sacrifice to thee;
what I have vowed I will pay.
  Deliverance belongs to the LORD!"

10 And the LORD spoke to the fish, and it vomited out Jonah upon the dry land.

3 Then the word of the LORD came to Jonah the second time, saying, 2 "Arise, go to Nin'eveh, that great city, and proclaim to it the message that I tell you." 3 So Jonah arose and went to Nin'eveh, according to the word of the LORD. Now Nin'eveh was an exceedingly great city, three days' journey in breadth. 4 Jonah began to go into

a Ch 2.1 in Heb

---

the sea and the dry land (Pss.65.5–7; 107.23–32; 139.7–12; Mk.4.35–41; Acts ch. 27). **16:** Jonah becomes a missionary of his God in spite of himself.

1.17–2.10: Jonah is miraculously saved and returned to *dry land*. The *great fish* is not the principal item in the story; like the tempest, the east wind, the plant, and the worm, it is an obedient agent of God's purpose. **17:** Mt.12.38–41.

2.1–9: Jonah's prayer. This psalm of thanksgiving (instead of an expected petition for help) may originally have been independent of the prose narrative. But it now serves to express Jonah's thanks for his deliverance (v. 9). **2:** Pss.18.6; 120.1. *Sheol*, or *Pit* (v. 6), is the region of darkness and death (Ps.88.3–12). **3a:** Ps.88.6. **3b:** Ps.42.7. **6:** *Land*, of the departed, Sheol.

3.1–4.11: Jonah's second call to preach to Nineveh, although reluctantly and grudgingly obeyed, results in the wholesale conversion of the heathen city. **3:** *Exceedingly great city;* excavations have revealed a city about three miles in length and somewhat less than one and one-half miles wide. The message of the story, not the size of the city, is of primary import.

the city, going a day's journey. And he cried, "Yet forty days, and Nin'eveh shall be overthrown!" [5] And the people of Nin'eveh believed God; they proclaimed a fast, and put on sackcloth, from the greatest of them to the least of them.

6 Then tidings reached the king of Nin'eveh, and he arose from his throne, removed his robe, and covered himself with sackcloth, and sat in ashes. [7] And he made proclamation and published through Nin'eveh, "By the decree of the king and his nobles: Let neither man nor beast, herd nor flock, taste anything; let them not feed, or drink water, [8] but let man and beast be covered with sackcloth, and let them cry mightily to God; yea, let every one turn from his evil way and from the violence which is in his hands. [9] Who knows, God may yet repent and turn from his fierce anger, so that we perish not?"

10 When God saw what they did, how they turned from their evil way, God repented of the evil which he had said he would do to them; and he did not do it.

4 But it displeased Jonah exceedingly, and he was angry. [2] And he prayed to the LORD and said, "I pray thee, LORD, is not this what I said when I was yet in my country? That is why I made haste to flee to Tarshish; for I knew that thou art a gracious God and merciful, slow to anger, and abounding in steadfast love, and repentest of evil. [3] Therefore now, O LORD, take my life from me, I beseech thee, for it is better for me to die than to live." [4] And the LORD said, "Do you do well to be angry?" [5] Then Jonah went out of the city and sat to the east of the city, and made a booth for himself there. He sat under it in the shade, till he should see what would become of the city.

6 And the LORD God appointed a plant,[b] and made it come up over Jonah, that it might be a shade over his head, to save him from his discomfort. So Jonah was exceedingly glad because of the plant.[b] [7] But when dawn came up the next day, God appointed a worm which attacked the plant,[b] so that it withered. [8] When the sun rose, God appointed a sultry east wind, and the sun beat upon the head of Jonah so that he was faint; and he asked that he might die, and said, "It is better for me to die than to live." [9] But God said to Jonah, "Do you do well to be angry for the plant?"[b] And he said, "I do well to be angry, angry enough to die." [10] And the LORD said, "You pity the plant,[b] for which you did not labor, nor did you make it grow, which came into being in a night, and perished in a night. [11] And should not I pity Nin'eveh, that great city, in which there are more than a hundred and twenty thousand persons who do not know their right hand from their left, and also much cattle?"

b Heb *qiqayon*, probably *the castor oil plant*

5–10: Again Jonah is a successful missionary in spite of himself. **6:** *Sackcloth* and *ashes*, traditional signs of mourning and repentance (2 Sam.3.31; Job 42.6; Dan.9.3; Mt.11.21). **7–9:** The pagan *king* sets a better example than Jonah (4.1). **10:** Repentance and deliverance are themes dominating the story of Jonah and its use in the New Testament (Mt.12.38–41; Lk.11.29–32). **4.1–11:** Note the similarity between the reactions of Jonah in this episode and the prophet Elijah in 1 Kg.19.1–18. **4.2b:** Ex.34.6–7 n. **11:** God has concern for every creature in his universe, even the *cattle*.

THE BOOK OF MICAH

The superscription to this book indicates that Micah was a younger contemporary of Isaiah. The characteristics of the era in which Micah spoke were similar, therefore, to those seen in the ministries of Hosea and Isaiah. The prosperous half-century of peace enjoyed by the northern kingdom of Israel was ended by the death of Jeroboam II and the westward advance of the Assyrians. In 731 B.C. the fall of Damascus marked the end of Syria's freedom; a brief decade later brought the same fate to Israel and its capital at Samaria. Although the kingdom of Judah was spared at that time from the Assyrian yoke, the anti-Assyrian policies of Hezekiah brought Sennacherib of Assyria to Judah in 701 B.C., and Judah was left a weak vassal state.

But unlike Isaiah, Micah was neither of noble descent nor a native of the capital. He came, rather, from the common people, being a citizen of the small village of Moresheth in the Judean foothills southwest of Jerusalem. Therefore Micah looked upon the corruptions and pretensions of the capital through different eyes. Perhaps it was this difference which accounts for Micah's prophecy of the fall of Jerusalem (3.9–12), a major note distinguishing him from his contemporaries and for which he was long remembered (Jer.26.18).

Micah stands solidly with Amos, Hosea, and Isaiah as a fierce champion of pure worship of the LORD and shares with them both the word of judgment against his people (1.2–3.12; 6.1–7.7) and the promise of divine forgiveness and hope in a future restoration. The latter theme of the prophet comes to us in a post-exilic expanded and edited form in 4.1–5.15. The picture of the restored Jerusalem in 7.8–20 comes from the post-exilic period.

T HE WORD OF THE LORD THAT came to Micah of Mo'resheth in the days of Jotham, Ahaz, and Hezeki'ah, kings of Judah, which he saw concerning Sama'ria and Jerusalem.

2 Hear, you peoples, all of you;
hearken, O earth, and all that is in
it;
and let the Lord GOD be a witness
against you,
the Lord from his holy temple.
3 For behold, the LORD is coming
forth out of his place,
and will come down and tread
upon the high places of the
earth.
4 And the mountains will melt under
him
and the valleys will be cleft,
like wax before the fire,
like waters poured down a steep
place.
5 All this is for the transgression of
Jacob
and for the sins of the house of
Israel.
What is the transgression of Jacob?
Is it not Sama'ria?
And what is the sin of the house*a*
of Judah?
Is it not Jerusalem?
6 Therefore I will make Sama'ria a
heap in the open country,
a place for planting vineyards;
and I will pour down her stones into
the valley,
and uncover her foundations.
7 All her images shall be beaten to
pieces,

a Gk Tg Compare Syr: Heb *what are the high places*

1.1: Superscription. *The word of the* LORD . . . *which he saw*, see Hos.1.1 n. and Nah.1.1 n. *Jotham* reigned over Judah from 750 to 735 B.C.; *Ahaz* from 735 to 715; and *Hezekiah* from 715 to 687.
    1.2–3.12: Threats directed against Samaria and Jerusalem because of the corruption of their religious and political leaders form the first major section of Micah's book. 1.2–7: Samaria will be destroyed when the LORD comes in judgment to punish *the house of Israel* for its *transgression*. This oracle is to be dated before 721 B.C. 2: Compare Is.1.2; Hab.2.20. 8–16: In a

all her hires shall be burned with
fire,
and all her idols I will lay waste;
for from the hire of a harlot she
gathered them,
and to the hire of a harlot they
shall return.

8 For this I will lament and wail;
I will go stripped and naked;
I will make lamentation like the
jackals,
and mourning like the ostriches.
9 For her wound[b] is incurable;
and it has come to Judah,
it has reached to the gate of my
people,
to Jerusalem.

10 Tell it not in Gath,
weep not at all;
in Beth-le-aph′rah
roll yourselves in the dust.
11 Pass on your way,
inhabitants of Shaphir,
in nakedness and shame;
the inhabitants of Za′anan
do not come forth;
the wailing of Beth-e′zel
shall take away from you its
standing place.
12 For the inhabitants of Maroth
wait anxiously for good,
because evil has come down from
the LORD
to the gate of Jerusalem.
13 Harness the steeds to the chariots,
inhabitants of Lachish;
you were[c] the beginning of sin
to the daughter of Zion,
for in you were found
the transgressions of Israel.
14 Therefore you shall give parting
gifts
to Mo′resheth-gath;

the houses of Achzib shall be a
deceitful thing
to the kings of Israel.
15 I will again bring a conqueror upon
you,
inhabitants of Mare′shah;
the glory of Israel
shall come to Adullam.
16 Make yourselves bald and cut off
your hair,
for the children of your delight;
make yourselves as bald as the eagle,
for they shall go from you into
exile.

2 Woe to those who devise
wickedness
and work evil upon their beds!
When the morning dawns, they
perform it,
because it is in the power of their
hand.
2 They covet fields, and seize them;
and houses, and take them away;
they oppress a man and his house,
a man and his inheritance.
3 Therefore thus says the LORD:
Behold, against this family I am
devising evil,
from which you cannot remove
your necks;
and you shall not walk haughtily,
for it will be an evil time.
4 In that day they shall take up a taunt
song against you,
and wail with bitter lamentation,
and say, "We are utterly ruined;
he changes the portion of my
people;
how he removes it from me!
Among our captors[d] he divides
our fields."

b Gk Syr Vg: Heb *wounds*
c Cn: Heb *it was*
d Cn: Heb *the rebellious*

series of forceful literary puns on the names of the areas to be devastated, the prophet laments
that *the wound* of his people *is incurable* and that God *will bring a conqueror* even *to the gate
of Jerusalem.* This *lament*, perhaps acted out by the prophet himself, *stripped* and *naked* (v. 8),
may refer to the campaign of 701 B.C. 2.1-11: Because of their uncleanness, which Micah
depicts with clarity (v. 2) and bitter realism (v. 11), the Israelites must experience a grievous
destruction, for the LORD will hold the nation responsible for its social and moral abuses.
1-2: Ps.36.4; Is.5.8-12; 32.7; Am.8.4. 3: *An evil time,* Jer.18.11; compare Am.5.13. 4: A
taunt song, compare Hab.2.6. 6: Micah quotes the popular preaching of the false prophets

⁵ Therefore you will have none to
    cast the line by lot
    in the assembly of the L*ORD*.

⁶ "Do not preach"–thus they preach–
    "one should not preach of such
       things;
    disgrace will not overtake us."
⁷ Should this be said, O house of
     Jacob?
    Is the Spirit of the L*ORD*
     impatient?
    Are these his doings?
Do not my words do good
    to him who walks uprightly?
⁸ But you rise against my people*ᵉ* as
    an enemy;
    you strip the robe from the
     peaceful,*ᶠ*
from those who pass by trustingly
    with no thought of war.
⁹ The women of my people you drive
    out
    from their pleasant houses;
from their young children you take
    away
    my glory for ever.
¹⁰ Arise and go,
    for this is no place to rest;
because of uncleanness that destroys
    with a grievous destruction.
¹¹ If a man should go about and utter
    wind and lies,
    saying, "I will preach to you of
    wine and strong drink,"
    he would be the preacher for this
     people!

¹² I will surely gather all of you, O
     Jacob,
    I will gather the remnant of Israel;
I will set them together
    like sheep in a fold,
like a flock in its pasture,
    a noisy multitude of men.
¹³ He who opens the breach will go up
    before them;

they will break through and pass
    the gate,
    going out by it.
Their king will pass on before them,
    the L*ORD* at their head.

3 And I said:
    Hear, you heads of Jacob
    and rulers of the house of Israel!
Is it not for you to know justice?–
²   you who hate the good and love
    the evil,
who tear the skin from off my
    people,
and their flesh from off their
    bones;
³ who eat the flesh of my people,
    and flay their skin from off them,
and break their bones in pieces,
    and chop them up like meat*ᵍ* in
    a kettle,
    like flesh in a caldron.

⁴ Then they will cry to the L*ORD*,
    but he will not answer them;
he will hide his face from them at
    that time,
because they have made their
    deeds evil.

⁵ Thus says the L*ORD* concerning the
    prophets
who lead my people astray,
who cry "Peace"
    when they have something to eat,
but declare war against him
    who puts nothing into their
    mouths.
⁶ Therefore it shall be night to you,
    without vision,
    and darkness to you, without
    divination.
The sun shall go down upon the
    prophets,
    and the day shall be black over
    them;

e Cn: Heb *yesterday my people rose*
f Cn: Heb *from before a garment*
g Gk: Heb *as*

(Is.30.10; Jer.5.31; Am.2.12. **12–13**: This picture of the restored remnant of all Israel, which
presupposes the capture of the country and its destruction, was probably contributed by an
exilic or post-exilic editor. **3.1–4**: The avaricious and irresponsible deeds of Israel's *rulers*.
2: Compare Is.5.20. Micah here uses the figures of a butcher and wild beast. **4**: Futile *cry to
the* L*ORD*, compare Is.1.15. **5–8**: The mercenary prophets and seers, who prostitute their
solemn office, shall be cut off from God, the source of true revelation. **7**: *Seers*, see 1 Sam.9.9.

⁷ the seers shall be disgraced,
  and the diviners put to shame;
they shall all cover their lips,
  for there is no answer from God.
⁸ But as for me, I am filled with
    power,
  with the Spirit of the LORD,
  and with justice and might,
to declare to Jacob his transgression
  and to Israel his sin.

⁹ Hear this, you heads of the house
    of Jacob
  and rulers of the house of Israel,
who abhor justice
  and pervert all equity,
¹⁰ who build Zion with blood
  and Jerusalem with wrong.
¹¹ Its heads give judgment for a bribe,
  its priests teach for hire,
  its prophets divine for money;
yet they lean upon the LORD and say,
  "Is not the LORD in the midst of
    us?
  No evil shall come upon us."
¹² Therefore because of you
  Zion shall be plowed as a field;
Jerusalem shall become a heap of
    ruins,
  and the mountain of the house a
    wooded height.

4 It shall come to pass in the latter
    days
  that the mountain of the house of
    the LORD
shall be established as the highest of
    the mountains,
  and shall be raised up above the
    hills;

and peoples shall flow to it,
² and many nations shall come,
  and say:
"Come, let us go up to the mountain
  of the LORD,
to the house of the God of Jacob;
that he may teach us his ways
  and we may walk in his paths."
For out of Zion shall go forth the
    law,
  and the word of the LORD from
    Jerusalem.
³ He shall judge between many
    peoples,
  and shall decide for strong
    nations afar off;
and they shall beat their swords into
    plowshares,
  and their spears into pruning
    hooks;
nation shall not lift up sword against
    nation,
  neither shall they learn war any
    more;
⁴ but they shall sit every man under
  his vine and under his fig tree,
  and none shall make them afraid;
for the mouth of the LORD of
  hosts has spoken.

⁵ For all the peoples walk
  each in the name of its god,
but we will walk in the name of the
  LORD our God
  for ever and ever.

⁶ In that day, says the LORD,
  I will assemble the lame
and gather those who have been
    driven away,

8: In contrast with the false officials, Micah's call has imbued him with power, justice, and might, because it filled him with *the Spirit of the LORD* (Is.11.2; 61.1; Ezek.2.2). **9–12:** The first section reaches its climax with Micah's bold assertion that, because of corruption which permeates all of its rulers, Jerusalem and the temple itself shall be destroyed. **9:** This recalls Am.5.6–7. **10:** Compare Hab.2.12. **12:** This was quoted at the trial of Jeremiah (Jer.26.18).
   4.1–5.15: Prophecies of Israel's glorious future and the restoration of the Davidic kingdom constitute the second major section of the book. Though many scholars date the origin of these prophecies in the post-exilic period, they are quite possibly based on genuine oracles of Micah, edited in their present form after the Exile. **1–5:** The exaltation of Jerusalem as a center of worship by the nations; the new age of peace. Verses 1–3 are duplicated in Is.2.2–4. Here, as sometimes elsewhere in the prophetic books, the author of a passage may be unknown, as with Is. chs. 40–66. **1:** *The mountain of the house,* Mount Zion. *Highest of the mountains,* compare Ezek.40.2. **4:** Compare Zech.3.10. **5:** Compare Is.2.5. **6–8:** The LORD's gracious

and those whom I have afflicted;
7 and the lame I will make the
remnant;
and those who were cast off, a
strong nation;
and the LORD will reign over them
in Mount Zion
from this time forth and for
evermore.

8 And you, O tower of the flock,
hill of the daughter of Zion,
to you shall it come,
the former dominion shall come,
the kingdom of the daughter of
Jerusalem.

9 Now why do you cry aloud?
Is there no king in you?
Has your counselor perished,
that pangs have seized you like
a woman in travail?
10 Writhe and groan,*h* O daughter of
Zion,
like a woman in travail;
for now you shall go forth from the
city
and dwell in the open country;
you shall go to Babylon.
There you shall be rescued,
there the LORD will redeem you
from the hand of your enemies.

11 Now many nations
are assembled against you,
saying, "Let her be profaned,
and let our eyes gaze upon Zion."
12 But they do not know
the thoughts of the LORD,
they do not understand his plan,
that he has gathered them as
sheaves to the threshing floor.
13 Arise and thresh,

O daughter of Zion,
for I will make your horn iron
and your hoofs bronze;
you shall beat in pieces many
peoples,
and shall*i* devote their gain to the
LORD,
their wealth to the Lord of the
whole earth.

5*j* Now you are walled about with
a wall;*k*
siege is laid against us;
with a rod they strike upon the
cheek
the ruler of Israel.

2*l* But you, O Bethlehem Eph'rathah,
who are little to be among the
clans of Judah,
from you shall come forth for me
one who is to be ruler in Israel,
whose origin is from of old,
from ancient days.
3 Therefore he shall give them up
until the time
when she who is in travail has
brought forth;
then the rest of his brethren shall
return
to the people of Israel.
4 And he shall stand and feed his flock
in the strength of the LORD,
in the majesty of the name of the
LORD his God.
And they shall dwell secure, for now
he shall be great
to the ends of the earth.

5 And this shall be peace,

h Heb uncertain *i* Gk Syr Tg: Heb *I will*
j Ch 4.14 in Heb
k Cn Compare Gk: Heb obscure
l Ch 5.1 in Heb

exaltation of the lame and rejected, for whom he will restore his kingdom (Is.40.9–11; Ezek.
34.11–16; 37.24–28; Zeph.3.19; Jn.10.7–16). **4.9–5.1:** In three paragraphs the humiliation and
travail which Israel must experience in the near future (see "now" in 4.9,11, and 5.1) are contrasted with her final triumph. **4.9:** Compare 5.3 and Jer.8.19. **10:** The reference to exile in
Babylon is a later addition (Is.48.20; 52.9–12). **5.2–6:** The shepherd king who is to be ruler of
Israel will be born not in Jerusalem, but, like David, in Bethlehem, among the insignificant
clans of Judah. **2:** *Bethlehem*, Gen.35.19; Ru.4.11; 1 Sam.17.12. *Me*, refers to God. *From of old*
could mean from the days of David, rather than pre-existence from the beginning of time.
The New Testament interprets this statement as a prophecy of the birth of Christ (Mt.2.6;
compare also Jn.7.40–43). **6:** *The land of Nimrod*, synonymous with Assyria (Gen.10.9–11).

when the Assyrian comes into our
  land
and treads upon our soil,*m*
that we will raise against him seven
  shepherds
and eight princes of men;
⁶ they shall rule the land of Assyria
  with the sword,
and the land of Nimrod with the
  drawn sword;*n*
and they*o* shall deliver us from the
  Assyrian
when he comes into our land
and treads within our border.

⁷ Then the remnant of Jacob shall be
  in the midst of many peoples
like dew from the Lord,
  like showers upon the grass,
which tarry not for men
  nor wait for the sons of men.
⁸ And the remnant of Jacob shall be
  among the nations,
  in the midst of many peoples,
like a lion among the beasts of the
  forest,
like a young lion among the flocks
  of sheep,
which, when it goes through, treads
  down
and tears in pieces, and there is
  none to deliver.
⁹ Your hand shall be lifted up over
  your adversaries,
and all your enemies shall be cut
  off.

¹⁰ And in that day, says the Lord,
  I will cut off your horses from
    among you
and will destroy your chariots;
¹¹ and I will cut off the cities of your
  land
and throw down all your
  strongholds;

¹² and I will cut off sorceries from your
  hand,
and you shall have no more
  soothsayers;
¹³ and I will cut off your images
  and your pillars from among you,
and you shall bow down no more
  to the work of your hands;
¹⁴ and I will root out your Ashe′rim
  from among you
and destroy your cities.
¹⁵ And in anger and wrath I will
  execute vengeance
upon the nations that did not obey.

6 Hear what the Lord says:
  Arise, plead your case before the
    mountains,
  and let the hills hear your voice.
² Hear, you mountains, the
    controversy of the Lord,
  and you enduring foundations
    of the earth;
for the Lord has a controversy with
    his people,
  and he will contend with Israel.

³ "O my people, what have I done
    to you?
  In what have I wearied you?
    Answer me!
⁴ For I brought you up from the land
    of Egypt,
  and redeemed you from the house
    of bondage;
  and I sent before you Moses,
    Aaron, and Miriam.
⁵ O my people, remember what
    Balak king of Moab devised,
  and what Balaam the son of Be′or
    answered him,
  and what happened from Shittim to
    Gilgal,

m Gk: Heb *in our palaces*
n Cn: Heb *in its entrances*
o Heb *he*

7–9: Then *the remnant* shall be a blessing upon those who receive them and a curse upon those who reject them (Gen.12.2–3; Gal.3.8). **10–15:** *And in that day* the Lord will abolish war in Israel (4.3), purify her worship, and punish disobedient nations. **10:** Zech.9.10. **13–14:** *pillars* and *Asherim*, pagan cult-objects (see Ex.34.13 n.).

  6.1–7.7: A series of laments, threats, and denunciations, directed against all classes of Israelites, forms the third major section. As extensions of themes sounded in the first section (1.2–3.12), these oracles, if not Micah's, are consonant with his thought. **6.1–8:** The Lord has a *controversy* with his people because they have forgotten his saving acts of old and what it means *to walk*

that you may know the saving acts
of the LORD."

6 "With what shall I come before the
LORD,
and bow myself before God on
high?
Shall I come before him with burnt
offerings,
with calves a year old?
7 Will the LORD be pleased with
thousands of rams,
with ten thousands of rivers of oil?
Shall I give my first-born for my
transgression,
the fruit of my body for the sin of
my soul?"
8 He has showed you, O man, what is
good;
and what does the LORD require
of you
but to do justice, and to love
kindness,*p*
and to walk humbly with your
God?

9 The voice of the LORD cries to the
city—
and it is sound wisdom to fear
thy name:
"Hear, O tribe and assembly of the
city!*q*
10 Can I forget*r* the treasures of
wickedness in the house of the
wicked,
and the scant measure that is
accursed?
11 Shall I acquit the man with wicked
scales
and with a bag of deceitful
weights?
12 Your*s* rich men are full of violence;
your*s* inhabitants speak lies,
and their tongue is deceitful in
their mouth.

13 Therefore I have begun*t* to smite
you,
making you desolate because of
your sins.
14 You shall eat, but not be satisfied,
and there shall be hunger in your
inward parts;
you shall put away, but not save,
and what you save I will give to
the sword.
15 You shall sow, but not reap;
you shall tread olives, but not
anoint yourselves with oil;
you shall tread grapes, but not
drink wine.
16 For you have kept the statutes of
Omri,*u*
and all the works of the house of
Ahab;
and you have walked in their
counsels;
that I may make you a desolation,
and your*v* inhabitants a
hissing;
so you shall bear the scorn of the
peoples."*w*

7 Woe is me! For I have become
as when the summer fruit has
been gathered,
as when the vintage has been
gleaned:
there is no cluster to eat,
no first-ripe fig which my soul
desires.
2 The godly man has perished from
the earth,
and there is none upright among
men;
they all lie in wait for blood,
and each hunts his brother with
a net.

p Or *steadfast love*
q Cn Compare Gk: Heb *and who has appointed it yet*
r Cn: Heb uncertain   *s* Heb *whose*
t Gk Syr Vg: Heb *have made sick*
u Gk Syr Vg Tg: Heb *the statutes of Omri are kept*
v Heb *its*   *w* Gk: Heb *my people*

humbly with God (Is.3.13; Hos.4.1–3; 12.2). **5:** Num.22.1–6; 25.1–5; Jos.4.19–24. **8:** In this
single sentence the prophet sums up the legal, ethical, and spiritual requirements of religion,
and sounds major notes of Amos (Am.5.24), Hosea (Hos.2.19–20; 6.6), and Isaiah (Is.7.9;
30.15). **9–16:** Jerusalem, which is as wicked as was Samaria (see v. 16), must be destroyed.
7.1–7: Not only the prince and the judge, but the best and most upright of Jerusalem's inhabitants, were corrupt, and the godly man's enemies were his neighbors and the men of his own
house. There was no basis for mutual confidence.

3 Their hands are upon what is evil,
  to do it diligently;
  the prince and the judge ask for
    a bribe,
and the great man utters the evil
    desire of his soul;
  thus they weave it together.
4 The best of them is like a brier,
  the most upright of them a thorn
    hedge.
The day of their[x] watchmen, of
  their[x] punishment, has come;
  now their confusion is at hand.
5 Put no trust in a neighbor,
  have no confidence in a friend;
guard the doors of your mouth
  from her who lies in your bosom;
6 for the son treats the father with
    contempt,
  the daughter rises up against her
    mother,
  the daughter-in-law against her
    mother-in-law;
  a man's enemies are the men of
    his own house.
7 But as for me, I will look to the
    LORD,
  I will wait for the God of my
    salvation;
  my God will hear me.

8 Rejoice not over me, O my enemy;
  when I fall, I shall rise;
when I sit in darkness,
  the LORD will be a light to me.
9 I will bear the indignation of the
    LORD
  because I have sinned against
    him,
until he pleads my cause
  and executes judgment for me.
He will bring me forth to the light;
  I shall behold his deliverance.
10 Then my enemy will see,
  and shame will cover her who said
    to me,
  "Where is the LORD your God?"
My eyes will gloat over her;

now she will be trodden down
  like the mire of the streets.

11 A day for the building of your walls!
  In that day the boundary shall be
    far extended.
12 In that day they will come to you,
  from Assyria to[y] Egypt,
  and from Egypt to the River,
  from sea to sea and from
    mountain to mountain.
13 But the earth will be desolate
  because of its inhabitants,
  for the fruit of their doings.

14 Shepherd thy people with thy staff,
  the flock of thy inheritance,
who dwell alone in a forest
  in the midst of a garden land;
let them feed in Bashan and Gilead
  as in the days of old.

15 As in the days when you came out
    of the land of Egypt
  I will show them[z] marvelous
    things.

16 The nations shall see and be
    ashamed
  of all their might;
  they shall lay their hands on their
    mouths;
  their ears shall be deaf;
17 they shall lick the dust like a
    serpent,
  like the crawling things of the
    earth;
  they shall come trembling out of
    their strongholds,
  they shall turn in dread to the
    LORD our God,
  and they shall fear because of thee.

18 Who is a God like thee, pardoning
    iniquity
  and passing over transgression

x Heb *your*
y Cn: Heb *and cities o*
z Heb *him*

7.8–20: God will show his steadfast love to Israel, and shame will cover her enemies. This final section was probably written in the early post-exilic period; compare Ps. 137; Is. chs. 33; 40–66. **8–10:** The prophet speaks as Israel. **9:** Jer.10.19. **10:** Ps.79.10; Jl.2.17. **11–13:** Addressed to Jerusalem. **14:** A prayer to God. Compare Jer.50.19. **15:** The LORD speaks. **16–17:** The nations

for the remnant of his inheritance?
He does not retain his anger for ever
because he delights in steadfast
love.
[19] He will again have compassion upon
us,
he will tread our iniquities under
foot.

Thou wilt cast all our[a] sins
into the depths of the sea.
[20] Thou wilt show faithfulness to Jacob
and steadfast love to Abraham,
as thou hast sworn to our fathers
from the days of old.

a Gk Syr Vg Tg: Heb *their*

will be dumb, deaf, and humbled. Israel speaks. **18–20:** Israel praises God for his forgiveness and faithfulness. **20:** Gen.12.1–3; 17.6–8; Lk.1.55.

THE BOOK OF NAHUM

As is typical of Hebrew prophecy, Nahum's words were prompted by the dramatic events of international history. The proud Assyrian empire, whose power had for centuries been felt and feared from Mesopotamia to the Mediterranean, crumbled quickly after the death of Asshurbanipal (about 630 B.C.). Under the combined assaults of the vigorous Medes from north of Persia and the Chaldeans from southern Babylonia, the ancient capital city of Asshur fell in 614 B.C. When the renowned Nineveh was destroyed in 612, Assyrian domination of the Near East was ended.

The fervent reaction to the overthrow of Assyria, expressed by the peoples long subjected to its yoke, is nowhere more clearly seen than in the book of Nahum. The core of the book is a superb, vivid poem extolling Nineveh's destruction, which Nahum felt to be inevitable. The prophet spells out the reason for the Assyrian downfall in unequivocal terms: it is the LORD's judgment upon an unscrupulous, defiant nation.

This basic theme forms both the strength and weakness of Nahum's thought. It asserts boldly that the LORD is the avenger of cruelty and immorality. But it fails, perhaps only because of a resolute singleness of purpose, to indicate the consequences of this divine justice for Israel itself.

The date of Nahum's triumphal ode lies close to the event it foretells, probably between 626 and 612 B.C. Its author is identified only by his name; even the location of Elkosh (1.1) is uncertain.

AN ORACLE CONCERNING NIN'EVEH. The book of the vision of Nahum of Elkosh.

2 The LORD is a jealous God and avenging,
the LORD is avenging and wrathful;
the LORD takes vengeance on his adversaries
and keeps wrath for his enemies.
3 The LORD is slow to anger and of great might,
and the LORD will by no means clear the guilty.

His way is in whirlwind and storm,
and the clouds are the dust of his feet.
4 He rebukes the sea and makes it dry,
he dries up all the rivers;
Bashan and Carmel wither,
the bloom of Lebanon fades.

5 The mountains quake before him,
the hills melt;
the earth is laid waste before him,
the world and all that dwell therein.

6 Who can stand before his indignation?
Who can endure the heat of his anger?
His wrath is poured out like fire,
and the rocks are broken asunder by him.
7 The LORD is good,
a stronghold in the day of trouble;
he knows those who take refuge in him.
8 But with an overflowing flood
he will make a full end of his adversaries,[a]

a Gk: Heb her place

1.1: Title. *Oracle*, literally "burden," is a technical term describing the prophetic word (Is.13.1; Jer.23.33–40 n.; Hab.1.1; Zech.9.1; Mal.1.1). The prophet "saw" this word (Am.1.1; Mic.1.1; Hab.1.1) as a *vision* (Ob.1). *Elkosh* may be a village in Galilee, known to Jerome as Elkesi, but more probably was located in SW Judah.

1.2–14: The coming of the avenging LORD. An incomplete acrostic psalm, probably inserted either by Nahum or an editor to introduce the prophet's own poem on Nineveh's fall (mainly 1.15–3.19). Now in some disorder, it runs at least through v. 9, but its precise junction with the main poem is unclear. 2: *Jealous*, see Ex.34.14 n. 3b: Is.29.6. 4: *Bashan, Carmel*, and *Lebanon* were regions famous for their fertility. 11: *Counseled villainy;* alternate translation, "a wicked

and will pursue his enemies into
    darkness.
9 What do you plot against the LORD?
    He will make a full end;
    he will not take vengeance[b]
    twice on his foes.[c]
10 Like entangled thorns they are
    consumed,[d]
    like dry stubble.
11 Did one not[e] come out from you,
    who plotted evil against the
    LORD,
    and counseled villainy?

12 Thus says the LORD,
    "Though they be strong and many,[f]
    they will be cut off and pass away.
    Though I have afflicted you,
    I will afflict you no more.
13 And now I will break his yoke from
    off you
    and will burst your bonds
    asunder."

14 The LORD has given commandment
    about you:
    "No more shall your name be
    perpetuated;
    from the house of your gods I will
    cut off
    the graven image and the molten
    image.
    I will make your grave, for you are
    vile."

15[g] Behold, on the mountains the feet
    of him
    who brings good tidings,
    who proclaims peace!
Keep your feasts, O Judah,
    fulfil your vows,
for never again shall the wicked
    come against you,
he is utterly cut off.

2 The shatterer has come up against
    you.
Man the ramparts;
    watch the road;
gird your loins;
    collect all your strength.

2 (For the LORD is restoring the
    majesty of Jacob
    as the majesty of Israel,
for plunderers have stripped them
    and ruined their branches.)

3 The shield of his mighty men is red,
    his soldiers are clothed in scarlet.
The chariots flash like flame[h]
    when mustered in array;
    the chargers[i] prance.
4 The chariots rage in the streets,
    they rush to and fro through the
    squares;
they gleam like torches,
    they dart like lightning.
5 The officers are summoned,
    they stumble as they go,
they hasten to the wall,
    the mantelet is set up.
6 The river gates are opened,
    the palace is in dismay;
7 its mistress[j] is stripped, she is
    carried off,
    her maidens lamenting,
moaning like doves,
    and beating their breasts.
8 Nin′eveh is like a pool
    whose waters[k] run away.
"Halt! Halt!" they cry;
    but none turns back.
9 Plunder the silver,

b Gk: Heb *rise up*   c Cn: Heb *distress*
d Heb *are consumed, drunken as with their drink*
e Cn: Heb *fully*   f Heb uncertain
g Ch 2.1 in Heb
h Cn: The meaning of the Hebrew word is uncertain
i Cn Compare Gk Syr: Heb *cypresses*
j The meaning of the Hebrew is uncertain
k Cn Compare Gk: Heb *from the days that she has become, and they*

---

counselor," which may refer to a specific person (the same word, "wicked," later transliterated
"Belial," is used in v. 15).
   1.15–3.19: The sack of Nineveh. The LORD's punishment of the defiant Assyrians and Israel's
proclamation of the good news. **15:** Is.40.9; 52.7; Rom.10.15. Read here 2.2. **2.1–13:** The
assault upon Nineveh. The plundering of its treasures and the terror of its inhabitants will
come because the LORD of hosts is against that rapacious city (Is.5.26–30; Jer.5.15–17). **1:**
Nahum is so thoroughly convinced of the LORD's destruction of Nineveh that he can say the
enemy already *has come up.* **7:** *Its mistress* is either Nineveh's queen or its patron goddess

plunder the gold!
There is no end of treasure,
  or wealth of every precious thing.

[10] Desolate! Desolation and ruin!
Hearts faint and knees tremble,
anguish is on all loins,
  all faces grow pale!
[11] Where is the lions' den,
  the cave[l] of the young lions,
where the lion brought his prey,
  where his cubs were, with none to
    disturb?
[12] The lion tore enough for his whelps
  and strangled prey for his
    lionesses;
he filled his caves with prey
  and his dens with torn flesh.

[13] Behold, I am against you, says
the LORD of hosts, and I will burn
your[m] chariots in smoke, and the
sword shall devour your young lions; I
will cut off your prey from the earth,
and the voice of your messengers shall
no more be heard.

3 Woe to the bloody city,
  all full of lies and booty—
no end to the plunder!
[2] The crack of whip, and rumble of
    wheel,
galloping horse and bounding
    chariot!
[3] Horsemen charging,
  flashing sword and glittering spear,
hosts of slain,
  heaps of corpses,
dead bodies without end—
  they stumble over the bodies!
[4] And all for the countless harlotries
    of the harlot,
  graceful and of deadly charms,
who betrays nations with her
    harlotries,
  and peoples with her charms.

[5] Behold, I am against you,
  says the LORD of hosts,
  and will lift up your skirts over
    your face;
and I will let nations look on your
    nakedness
  and kingdoms on your shame.
[6] I will throw filth at you
  and treat you with contempt,
  and make you a gazingstock.
[7] And all who look on you will shrink
    from you and say,
Wasted is Nin'eveh; who will
    bemoan her?
  whence shall I seek comforters for
    her?[n]

[8] Are you better than Thebes[o]
  that sat by the Nile,
with water around her,
  her rampart a sea,
  and water her wall?
[9] Ethiopia was her strength,
  Egypt too, and that without limit;
  Put and the Libyans were her[p]
    helpers.

[10] Yet she was carried away,
  she went into captivity;
her little ones were dashed in pieces
  at the head of every street;
for her honored men lots were cast,
  and all her great men were bound
    in chains.
[11] You also will be drunken,
  you will be dazed;
you will seek
  a refuge from the enemy.
[12] All your fortresses are like fig trees
  with first-ripe figs—
if shaken they fall
  into the mouth of the eater.
[13] Behold, your troops
  are women in your midst.

l Cn: Heb *pasture*   *m* Heb *her*
n Gk: Heb *you*   *o* Heb *No-amon*
p Gk: Heb *your*

Ishtar. **11:** *Lion* often symbolizes the destroyer (Is.5.29; Jer.4.7; Hos.5.14; Mic.5.8). **3.1–19:**
The arrogant Assyrian empire will pass away and its capital, a city of rapine and blood, will
fall because the LORD is against it. **4:** The LORD condemns Nineveh for treacherous and
deceitful dealings with other nations. Compare Jeremiah's indictment of Jerusalem (5.1–3,26–31)
and the judgment against Babylon (Rome) in Rev.17.1–6; 18.1–24. **5–7:** Such immorality is
an offense to God and man and will not go unpunished. **8:** The Egyptian capital *Thebes*
(Hebrew, No-amon) had been captured by the Assyrians themselves in 663 B.C. **10:** Ps.137.8–9.

The gates of your land
  are wide open to your foes;
  fire has devoured your bars.
14 Draw water for the siege,
  strengthen your forts;
  go into the clay,
    tread the mortar,
    take hold of the brick mold!
15 There will the fire devour you,
  the sword will cut you off.
  It will devour you like the locust.

Multiply yourselves like the locust,
  multiply like the grasshopper!
16 You increased your merchants
  more than the stars of the
  heavens.
  The locust spreads its wings and
  flies away.
17 Your princes are like grasshoppers,

your scribes*q* like clouds of
  locusts
settling on the fences
  in a day of cold—
when the sun rises, they fly away;
  no one knows where they are.

18 Your shepherds are asleep,
  O king of Assyria;
  your nobles slumber.
Your people are scattered on the
  mountains
  with none to gather them.
19 There is no assuaging your hurt,
  your wound is grievous.
All who hear the news of you
  clap their hands over you.
For upon whom has not come
  your unceasing evil?

q Or *marshals*

14–15: Nahum's warnings are satirical, for Nineveh is already doomed. **15:** *Locust* indicates both vast multitudes and destructive swarms. **18:** *Shepherds*, ruling officials (compare Zech. 11.4–17 n.). **19:** *Clap their hands*, compare Ps.47.1–4. *Upon whom*, compare Is.37.10–13.

THE BOOK OF HABAKKUK

In the present book of Habakkuk at least three distinct literary forms can be recognized. The section 1.2–2.5 is constructed as a dialogue between the prophet and God; the next section (2.6–20), consisting of five woes against a wicked nation, is cast in classical prophetic style; and ch. 3 is a lengthy poem, similar in structure to the Psalms and in its final form obviously meant for liturgical use. Moreover, various historical allusions discernible in the three sections point to different periods. These materials, therefore, may not originally have been a unit. But they are connected by the common theme of theodicy (justification of the ways of God) and now appear as the work of a Hebrew prophet who lived during the height of Babylonian power, most likely in the decade 608–598 B.C.

Although a certain Habakkuk appears in the apocryphal story of Bel and the Dragon, nothing is known about the life of the Old Testament prophet, not even his father's name. His thought, however, is laid bare by the searching questions he asks.

The author is confronting honestly the profoundly disturbing problem of why a just God is "silent when the wicked swallows up the man more righteous than he" (1.13). To this perennial question the prophet receives an answer which is eternally valid: God is still sovereign, and in his own way and at the proper time will deal with the wicked; "but the righteous shall live by his faith" (2.4).

THE ORACLE OF God WHICH Habak′kuk the prophet saw.
² O LORD, how long shall I cry for help,
and thou wilt not hear?
Or cry to thee "Violence!"
and thou wilt not save?
³ Why dost thou make me see wrongs and look upon trouble?
Destruction and violence are before me;
strife and contention arise.
⁴ So the law is slacked and justice never goes forth.
For the wicked surround the righteous,
so justice goes forth perverted.

⁵ Look among the nations, and see;
wonder and be astounded.
For I am doing a work in your days that you would not believe if told.
⁶ For lo, I am rousing the Chalde′ans,
that bitter and hasty nation,
who march through the breadth of the earth,
to seize habitations not their own.
⁷ Dread and terrible are they;
their justice and dignity proceed from themselves.
⁸ Their horses are swifter than leopards,
more fierce than the evening wolves;
their horsemen press proudly on.
Yea, their horsemen come from afar;
they fly like an eagle swift to devour.
⁹ They all come for violence;
terror*a* of them goes before them.
They gather captives like sand.

a Cn: Heb uncertain

1.1: Title. *Oracle*, see Nah.1.1 n.
1.2–2.5: A dialogue in two cycles (1.2–11; 1.12–2.5), between the prophet and God, raising the question of the LORD's just government of the world. **1.2–11: The first cycle. 1.2–4:** Habakkuk protests that God neither hears nor acts (compare Ps.22.1–2) and thereby negates *law* and *justice*. This section may originally have been concerned with unrighteous members of the Israelite community; in its present context it is directed against the Chaldeans (vv. 6–11, 15–17). **2:** Ps.13.1–2; Jer.14.9; Rev.6.9–10. **3:** Jer.20.8,10. **4:** Ps.119.126; Is.59.12–14; Jer. 12.1–4. **5–11:** The LORD replies that the Chaldeans, wicked as they are, are the instrument of his own choosing (Is.10.5–27; 41.2–3; 42.24; 44.28; 45.1–6; Jer.5.14–19; 27.6–7; ch. 51). **5:** Quoted in Acts 13.41. **6:** The *Chaldeans*, or neo-Babylonians, ruled the ancient Near East from 612 to 539 B.C. (see Introduction to Nahum). **7–11:** This tyrannical nation administers a *justice* all its own and worships its own *might*.

¹⁰ At kings they scoff,
    and of rulers they make sport.
They laugh at every fortress,
    for they heap up earth and take it.
¹¹ Then they sweep by like the wind
    and go on,
guilty men, whose own might is
    their god!

¹² Art thou not from everlasting,
    O LORD my God, my Holy One?
We shall not die.
O LORD, thou hast ordained them
    as a judgment;
and thou, O Rock, hast
    established them for
    chastisement.
¹³ Thou who art of purer eyes than to
    behold evil
and canst not look on wrong,
why dost thou look on faithless men,
    and art silent when the wicked
    swallows up
the man more righteous than he?
¹⁴ For thou makest men like the fish of
    the sea,
like crawling things that have no
    ruler.
¹⁵ He brings all of them up with a
    hook,
he drags them out with his net,
he gathers them in his seine;
    so he rejoices and exults.
¹⁶ Therefore he sacrifices to his net
    and burns incense to his seine;
for by them he lives in luxury,ᵇ
    and his food is rich.
¹⁷ Is he then to keep on emptying his
    net,

and mercilessly slaying nations
    for ever?

2 I will take my stand to watch,
    and station myself on the tower,
and look forth to see what he will
    say to me,
and what I will answer concerning
    my complaint.
² And the LORD answered me:
    "Write the vision;
make it plain upon tablets,
    so he may run who reads it.
³ For still the vision awaits its time;
    it hastens to the end–it will not
    lie.
If it seem slow, wait for it;
    it will surely come, it will not
    delay.
⁴ Behold, he whose soul is not
    upright in him shall fail,ᶜ
but the righteous shall live by
    his faith.ᵈ
⁵ Moreover, wine is treacherous;
    the arrogant man shall not abide.ᵉ
His greed is as wide as Sheol;
    like death he has never enough.
He gathers for himself all nations,
    and collects as his own all
    peoples."

⁶ Shall not all these take up their taunt
against him, in scoffing derision of him,
and say,
    "Woe to him who heaps up what
    is not his own–
    for how long?–
    and loads himself with pledges!"

b Heb *his portion is fat*   *c* Cn: Heb *is puffed up*
d Or *faithfulness*
e The Hebrew of these two lines is obscure

1.12–2.5: The second cycle. Habakkuk asks how long the Holy One will look on while faithless men persecute those more righteous than they; he then takes his *stand* to receive the LORD's answer. **12:** *Rock*, a metaphor frequently applied to God (Dt.32.4,18,30,31; 2 Sam.23.3; Pss.18.2,31; 92.15; 95.1; Is.30.29; and elsewhere). **13:** The heart of Habakkuk's problem (see Ps.5.4–6). **2.1:** The "watchtower" indicates both the prophet's eager desire for, and confidence in, the LORD's reply (Pss.5.3; 130.5–6; Is.21.8; Hos.9.8). **2.2–5:** The LORD responds with the assurance that although the prophet may not see its final issue, the divine justice is inexorable and will come in due time; in the meanwhile the *righteous* man must *live* faithfully. **2:** The LORD's answer is to be as *plain* as a highway sign (Is.8.1; Rev.1.19). **3:** Num.23.19; Dan.8.19; 2 Pet.3.8–10; Heb.10.37. **4:** The heart of the matter is that the *righteous* man who is faithful to God and his word *shall live* and the unrighteous *shall fail.* Here the contrast is primarily between Israelites and Chaldeans; but the verse has, properly, received wider application (Rom.1.17; Gal.3.11; Heb.10.38–39). **2.6–20: The five woes.** These are directed against a nation that plunders *peoples,* obtains

7 Will not your debtors suddenly
     arise,
  and those awake who will make
     you tremble?
  Then you will be booty for them.
8 Because you have plundered many
     nations,
  all the remnant of the peoples
     shall plunder you,
  for the blood of men and violence
     to the earth,
  to cities and all who dwell therein.

9 Woe to him who gets evil gain for
     his house,
  to set his nest on high,
  to be safe from the reach of
     harm!
10 You have devised shame to your
     house
  by cutting off many peoples;
  you have forfeited your life.
11 For the stone will cry out from the
     wall,
  and the beam from the woodwork
     respond.

12 Woe to him who builds a town with
     blood,
  and founds a city on iniquity!
13 Behold, is it not from the LORD of
     hosts
  that peoples labor only for fire,
  and nations weary themselves for
     nought?
14 For the earth will be filled
  with the knowledge of the glory of
     the LORD,
  as the waters cover the sea.

15 Woe to him who makes his
     neighbors drink
  of the cup of his wrath,ƒ and
  makes them drunk,
  to gaze on their shame!

16 You will be sated with contempt
     instead of glory.
  Drink, yourself, and stagger!g
  The cup in the LORD's right hand
  will come around to you,
  and shame will come upon your
     glory!
17 The violence done to Lebanon will
     overwhelm you;
  the destruction of the beasts will
     terrify you,h
  for the blood of men and violence
     to the earth,
  to cities and all who dwell therein.

18 What profit is an idol
  when its maker has shaped it,
  a metal image, a teacher of lies?
  For the workman trusts in his own
     creation
  when he makes dumb idols!
19 Woe to him who says to a wooden
     thing, Awake;
  to a dumb stone, Arise!
  Can this give revelation?
  Behold, it is overlaid with gold and
     silver,
  and there is no breath at all in it.

20 But the LORD is in his holy temple;
  let all the earth keep silence
     before him.

3 A prayer of Habak′kuk the
   prophet, according to Shigion′oth.
2 O LORD, I have heard the report of
     thee,
  and thy work, O LORD, do I fear.
  In the midst of the years renew it;
  in the midst of the years make it
     known;
  in wrath remember mercy.
3 God came from Teman,

ƒ Cn: Heb *joining to your wrath*
g Cn Compare Gk Syr: Heb *be uncircumcised*
h Gk Syr: Heb *them*

gain by violence, *builds* towns *with blood*, shamelessly degrades its *neighbors*, and *trusts* in *idols*.
Applied originally to the Assyrians, Babylonians, or Macedonians, they have universal reference,
indicting all human tyranny. **14:** Is.11.9. **20:** Ps.11.4; Zeph.1.7; Zech.2.13.
  3.1–19: Habakkuk's prayer. This is really a hymn, extolling the marching forth of the LORD
in victory *for the salvation of his people.* This magnificent poem exhibits the characteristics of a
psalm, including liturgical directions, and was probably added later, possibly from the circles
of cultic prophecy (see Introduction to Joel). *Shigionoth, Selah,* and *choirmaster* are technical

and the Holy One from Mount
Paran.
His glory covered the heavens,
and the earth was full of his praise.
Selah
4 His brightness was like the light,
rays flashed from his hand;
and there he veiled his power.
5 Before him went pestilence,
and plague followed close behind.
6 He stood and measured the earth;
he looked and shook the nations;
then the eternal mountains were
scattered,
the everlasting hills sank low.
His ways were as of old.
7 I saw the tents of Cushan in
affliction;
the curtains of the land of Mid'ian
did tremble.
8 Was thy wrath against the rivers, O
LORD?
Was thy anger against the rivers,
or thy indignation against the sea,
when thou didst ride upon thy
horses,
upon thy chariot of victory?
9 Thou didst strip the sheath from thy
bow,
and put the arrows to the string.*i*
Selah
Thou didst cleave the earth with
rivers.
10 The mountains saw thee, and
writhed;
the raging waters swept on;
the deep gave forth its voice,
it lifted its hands on high.
11 The sun and moon stood still in their
habitation*j*
at the light of thine arrows as they
sped,
at the flash of thy glittering spear.
12 Thou didst bestride the earth in
fury,
thou didst trample the nations in
anger.

13 Thou wentest forth for the
salvation of thy people,
for the salvation of thy anointed.
Thou didst crush the head of the
wicked,*k*
laying him bare from thigh to
neck.*l*
Selah
14 Thou didst pierce with thy*m* shafts
the head of his warriors,*n*
who came like a whirlwind to
scatter me,
rejoicing as if to devour the poor
in secret.
15 Thou didst trample the sea with
thy horses,
the surging of mighty waters.

16 I hear, and my body trembles,
my lips quiver at the sound;
rottenness enters into my bones,
my steps totter*o* beneath me.
I will quietly wait for the day of
trouble
to come upon people who invade
us.

17 Though the fig tree do not blossom,
nor fruit be on the vines,
the produce of the olive fail
and the fields yield no food,
the flock be cut off from the fold
and there be no herd in the stalls,
18 yet I will rejoice in the LORD,
I will joy in the God of my
salvation.
19 GOD, the Lord, is my strength;
he makes my feet like hinds' feet,
he makes me tread upon my high
places.

To the choirmaster: with stringed*p*
instruments.

i Cn: Heb obscure
j Heb uncertain
k Cn: Heb *head from the house of the wicked*
l Heb obscure
m Heb *his*
n Vg Compare Gk Syr: Heb uncertain
o Cn Compare Gk: Heb *I tremble because*
p Heb *my stringed*

---

terms in the Psalter (Pss. 7, title; 4, title). **3,7:** God appears from the region of Sinai and
marches toward Edom, as at the Exodus (Dt.33.2; Jg.5.4). **8b:** Dt.33.26. **13:** *Anointed* indicates
either the king or the nation. **18:** The psalm reaches its height by rejoicing in the LORD as the
saving God (Pss.25.5; 27.1; 68.19–20) and thus exhibits a clear thematic connection with chs.
1–2 (see also 3.12–14,16).

THE BOOK OF ZEPHANIAH

The superscription to Zephaniah's book traces his ancestry back to Hezekiah and dates his ministry in the reign of Josiah (640–609 B.C.). Since the name Hezekiah is uncommon in the Old Testament, here it presumably refers to the famous Judean king (715–687 B.C.), who was favorably influenced by the preaching of Isaiah and Micah. Zephaniah's intimate knowledge of Jerusalem and its court circles, his failure to denounce the king personally, and the absence of any concern with the poor of the land support the inference that he was of royal descent.

His condemnation of the corrupt practices and religious perversions (1.4–6,8,9,12; 3.1–3,7), officially legislated against by Deuteronomy, indicates that Zephaniah prophesied before Josiah's reforms of 621 B.C. (2 Kg. ch. 23). The allusion to imminent threat from the north (see 1.10 n.), perhaps the barbaric Scythian hordes, further suggests the decade about 630 for Zephaniah's public ministry.

The book can be divided into three sections, coinciding with its three chapters. Chapter 1 proclaims doom on Judah for its religious syncretism, in the form of the destructive day of the LORD, which is "near and hastening fast." Chapter 2 extends the divine judgment to other nations (especially Israel's ancient enemies), which are also guilty; however, a humble seeking after righteousness may mitigate the wrath of that day. Chapter 3 promises comfort and consolation to those who wait patiently for the LORD and "serve him with one accord." The inhabitants of Jerusalem shall rejoice that the LORD their King is in their midst to save them and gather them home (3.20).

THE WORD OF THE LORD WHICH came to Zephani'ah the son of Cushi, son of Gedali'ah, son of Amari'ah, son of Hezeki'ah, in the days of Josi'ah the son of Amon, king of Judah.

2 "I will utterly sweep away everything
from the face of the earth," says the LORD.
3 "I will sweep away man and beast;
I will sweep away the birds of the air
and the fish of the sea.
I will overthrow[a] the wicked;
I will cut off mankind
from the face of the earth," says the LORD.
4 "I will stretch out my hand against Judah,

and against all the inhabitants of Jerusalem;
and I will cut off from this place the remnant of Ba'al
and the name of the idolatrous priests;[b]
5 those who bow down on the roofs
to the host of the heavens;
those who bow down and swear to the LORD
and yet swear by Milcom;
6 those who have turned back from following the LORD,
who do not seek the LORD or inquire of him."

7 Be silent before the Lord GOD!

a Cn: Heb *the stumbling blocks*
b Compare Gk: Heb *idolatrous priests with the priests*

1.1: **Superscription:** *The word of the LORD*, see Hos.1.1 n. Three others in the Old Testament are named *Zephaniah* (2 Kg.25.18; 1 Chr.6.36; Zech.6.10,14). Elsewhere *Cushi* means "Ethiopian" or "Cushite."

1.2–6: **The threat of universal destruction** caused by Judah's religious syncretism. Zephaniah vigorously condemns the adulteration of the pure worship of the LORD with elements of Canaanite (*Baal*), Ammonite (*Milcom*), and Assyrian (*host of the heavens*) religions. **2–3:** *Man, mankind,* and *earth* are alliterative in Hebrew, as in Gen. ch. 2 (see Gen.2.7 n.), suggesting the negation of creation. *Says the LORD*, see Am.1.3 n.

1.7–9: **Court officials and royal family will be punished** *on the day of the LORD's sacrifice.* **7:** Hab.2.20; Zech.2.13. **9:** *Leaps over the threshold*, a pagan religious practice (1 Sam.5.5 n.).

For the day of the LORD is at
hand;
the LORD has prepared a sacrifice
and consecrated his guests.
8 And on the day of the LORD's
sacrifice–
"I will punish the officials and the
king's sons
and all who array themselves in
foreign attire.
9 On that day I will punish
every one who leaps over the
threshold,
and those who fill their master's
house
with violence and fraud."

10 "On that day," says the LORD,
"a cry will be heard from the Fish
Gate,
a wail from the Second Quarter,
a loud crash from the hills.
11 Wail, O inhabitants of the Mortar!
For all the traders are no more;
all who weigh out silver are cut
off.
12 At that time I will search
Jerusalem with lamps,
and I will punish the men
who are thickening upon their lees,
those who say in their hearts,
'The LORD will not do good,
nor will he do ill.'
13 Their goods shall be plundered,
and their houses laid waste.
Though they build houses,
they shall not inhabit them;
though they plant vineyards,
they shall not drink wine from
them."

14 The great day of the LORD is near,

near and hastening fast;
the sound of the day of the LORD is
bitter,
the mighty man cries aloud there.
15 A day of wrath is that day,
a day of distress and anguish,
a day of ruin and devastation,
a day of darkness and gloom,
a day of clouds and thick darkness,
16 a day of trumpet blast and battle
cry
against the fortified cities
and against the lofty battlements.

17 I will bring distress on men,
so that they shall walk like the
blind,
because they have sinned against
the LORD;
their blood shall be poured out like
dust,
and their flesh like dung.
18 Neither their silver nor their gold
shall be able to deliver them
on the day of the wrath of the
LORD.
In the fire of his jealous wrath,
all the earth shall be consumed;
for a full, yea, sudden end
he will make of all the inhabitants
of the earth.

2 Come together and hold
assembly,
O shameless nation,
2 before you are driven away
like the drifting chaff,^{c}
before there comes upon you
the fierce anger of the LORD,
before there comes upon you

c Cn Compare Gk Syr: Heb *before a decree is born; like
chaff a day has passed away*

1.10–13: **Merchants and traders will be cut off** and the religiously indifferent will be desolate
on that day. **10:** The enemy will approach Jerusalem from the north, first through *the Fish
Gate* (Neh.3.1–6; 12.39; compare Jer.1.13–16). **11:** *Traders,* literally, "people of Canaan."
12: *Thickening,* a figure drawn from wine-making to portray indolence.
  1.14–18: **The day of the LORD is at hand,** a day of *wrath* and *ruin,* of *distress* and *devastation.*
On this day neither *silver* nor *gold* shall *deliver* sinful man from the *fire* of the LORD's zeal.
Zephaniah elaborates the preaching of Amos (Am.5.18–20; 8.9–14) that the day of the LORD
will be darkness and not light, woe and not weal, upon Israel as well as the Gentiles (see also
Is.13.9–16; Ezek.7.19; Jl.1.15; 2.1–2). **18:** *End,* compare Ezek.7.2–7.
  2.1–3: **The humble of the land who seek the LORD in righteousness** *may be hidden* from his
fierce anger. **3:** *Seek,* Is.55.6–9; Am.5.6–7. *Humble,* compare 3.12–13.

the day of the wrath of the LORD.
³ Seek the LORD, all you humble of
   the land,
   who do his commands;
seek righteousness, seek humility;
   perhaps you may be hidden
   on the day of the wrath of the
   LORD.
⁴ For Gaza shall be deserted,
   and Ash'kelon shall become a
      desolation;
Ashdod's people shall be driven out
   at noon,
   and Ekron shall be uprooted.

⁵ Woe to you inhabitants of the
      seacoast,
   you nation of the Cher'ethites!
The word of the LORD is against you,
   O Canaan, land of the Philistines;
   and I will destroy you till no
      inhabitant is left.
⁶ And you, O seacoast, shall be
      pastures,
   meadows for shepherds
   and folds for flocks.
⁷ The seacoast shall become the
      possession
   of the remnant of the house of
      Judah,
   on which they shall pasture,
and in the houses of Ash'kelon
   they shall lie down at evening.
For the LORD their God will be
   mindful of them
   and restore their fortunes.

⁸ "I have heard the taunts of Moab
   and the revilings of the
      Ammonites,
how they have taunted my people
   and made boasts against their
      territory.
⁹ Therefore, as I live," says the LORD
      of hosts,
   the God of Israel,
   "Moab shall become like Sodom,

and the Ammonites like
   Gomor'rah,
a land possessed by nettles and salt
   pits,
   and a waste for ever.
The remnant of my people shall
   plunder them,
   and the survivors of my nation
   shall possess them."
¹⁰ This shall be their lot in return for
   their pride,
   because they scoffed and boasted
   against the people of the LORD of
      hosts.
¹¹ The LORD will be terrible against
      them;
   yea, he will famish all the gods of
      the earth,
   and to him shall bow down,
   each in its place,
   all the lands of the nations.

¹² You also, O Ethiopians,
   shall be slain by my sword.

¹³ And he will stretch out his hand
   against the north,
   and destroy Assyria;
and he will make Nin'eveh a
      desolation,
   a dry waste like the desert.
¹⁴ Herds shall lie down in the midst of
      her,
   all the beasts of the field;*d*
   the vulture*e* and the hedgehog
   shall lodge in her capitals;
   the owl*f* shall hoot in the window,
   the raven*g* croak on the threshold;
   for her cedar work will be laid
      bare.
¹⁵ This is the exultant city
   that dwelt secure,
   that said to herself,
   "I am and there is none else."
What a desolation she has become,

d Tg Compare Gk: Heb *nation*
e The meaning of the Hebrew word is uncertain
f Cn: Heb *a voice*   *g* Gk Vg: Heb *desolation*

2.4–15: Against the nations. 4–7: The Philistines shall be desolated because *the word of the LORD* is against them (see Jl.3.4–8). **8–11:** The Moabites and Ammonites, traditional enemies of Israel who lived in Transjordan, shall be annihilated, becoming *like Sodom* and *Gomorrah* (Is. chs. 15–16; 25.10–12; Jer.48.1–49.6; Ezek 25.8–11; Am.1.13–2.3). **9:** Gen.19.24–28,30–38. **12–15:** The Ethiopians shall be slain, and the Assyrians humiliated because of their arrogance (Is.10.5–34). **12:** Is. ch. 18. **14:** The Hebrew text is uncertain. **15:** See Nah.3.4 n.

a lair for wild beasts!
Every one who passes by her
hisses and shakes his fist.

3 Woe to her that is rebellious and
    defiled,
    the oppressing city!
2 She listens to no voice,
    she accepts no correction.
She does not trust in the LORD,
    she does not draw near to her
        God.

3 Her officials within her
    are roaring lions;
her judges are evening wolves
    that leave nothing till the morning.
4 Her prophets are wanton,
    faithless men;
her priests profane what is sacred,
    they do violence to the law.
5 The LORD within her is righteous,
    he does no wrong;
every morning he shows forth his
        justice,
    each dawn he does not fail;
but the unjust knows no shame.

6 "I have cut off nations;
    their battlements are in ruins;
I have laid waste their streets
    so that none walks in them;
their cities have been made desolate,
    without a man, without an
        inhabitant.
7 I said, 'Surely she will fear me,
    she will accept correction;
she will not lose sight*h*
    of all that I have enjoined upon
        her.'
But all the more they were eager
    to make all their deeds corrupt."

8 "Therefore wait for me," says the
        LORD,
    "for the day when I arise as a
        witness.

For my decision is to gather nations,
    to assemble kingdoms,
to pour out upon them my
        indignation,
    all the heat of my anger;
for in the fire of my jealous wrath
    all the earth shall be consumed.

9 "Yea, at that time I will change the
        speech of the peoples
    to a pure speech,
that all of them may call on the name
        of the LORD
    and serve him with one accord.
10 From beyond the rivers of Ethiopia
    my suppliants, the daughter of
        my dispersed ones,
    shall bring my offering.

11 "On that day you shall not be put to
        shame
    because of the deeds by which
        you have rebelled against me;
for then I will remove from your
        midst
    your proudly exultant ones,
and you shall no longer be haughty
    in my holy mountain.
12 For I will leave in the midst of you
    a people humble and lowly.
They shall seek refuge in the name
        of the LORD,
13   those who are left in Israel;
they shall do no wrong
    and utter no lies,
nor shall there be found in their
        mouth
    a deceitful tongue.
For they shall pasture and lie down,
    and none shall make them
        afraid."

14 Sing aloud, O daughter of Zion;
    shout, O Israel!
Rejoice and exult with all your heart,
    O daughter of Jerusalem!

h Gk Syr: Heb and her dwelling will not be cut off

3.1–7: Woe to Jerusalem, because her *officials*, *judges*, *prophets*, and *priests* are *corrupt* and
do not fear the *righteous* LORD, though he has continually warned them (compare Am.4.6–12).
    3.8–13: On that day the nations will be converted and a righteous remnant will be left in Israel.
9: The gift of *a pure speech* symbolizes forgiveness (Is.6.5–7), removes the curse of Babel
(Gen.11.1–9), and anticipates Pentecost (Acts 2.1–11). **13:** Ezek.34.13–16; Zech.8.3,16.
    3.14–20: The glorious gospel of salvation, promising the joy of restoration to Jerusalem. This

15 The LORD has taken away the
judgments against you,
he has cast out your enemies.
The King of Israel, the LORD, is
in your midst;
you shall fear evil no more.
16 On that day it shall be said to
Jerusalem:
"Do not fear, O Zion;
let not your hands grow weak.
17 The LORD, your God, is in your
midst,
a warrior who gives victory;
he will rejoice over you with
gladness,
he will renew you[i] in his love;
he will exult over you with loud
singing
18 as on a day of festival.[j]
"I will remove disaster[k] from you,

so that you will not bear reproach
for it.
19 Behold, at that time I will deal
with all your oppressors.
And I will save the lame
and gather the outcast,
and I will change their shame into
praise
and renown in all the earth.
20 At that time I will bring you home,
at the time when I gather you
together;
yea, I will make you renowned and
praised
among all the peoples of the earth,
when I restore your fortunes
before your eyes," says the LORD.

i Gk Syr: Heb *he will be silent*
j Gk Syr: Heb obscure
k Cn: Heb *they were*

passage is generally held to be a later addition. **14–15:** These verses have the form of a psalm
of the enthronement of the LORD (compare Pss. 47; 97). **14:** Zech.9.9. **15:** Is.12.6; 40.2; 41.10.
17: Ex.15.3; Is.12.2; 62.5. **19–20:** The major elements of post-exilic eschatology are found here:
destruction of the enemy (Ob.15,16; Mic.5.9; Zech.12.9), ingathering of the exiles (Mic.4.6–7;
Zech.10.8–12), and return to the Holy Land (Is.61.1–5; Zech.8.7–8). By making Israel *renowned*
(literally "a name") *and praised among all the peoples of the earth* the LORD fulfils his promise
to the patriarchs (Gen.12.2–3).

THE BOOK OF HAGGAI

When Cyrus conquered Babylon, he not only published a decree (538 B.C.) allowing the captive Jews to return to Palestine but also encouraged them to rebuild the temple at Jerusalem (Ezra 1.1–4). It is possible that under Sheshbazzar's leadership rebuilding was immediately attempted. By 520 B.C., however, no significant progress was evident. A successful effort was then begun, and the new temple was completed in the spring of 515 B.C.

Assisted by Zechariah (see Introduction to Zechariah), the man principally responsible for this major accomplishment was the prophet Haggai. In five addresses, dating from the sixth through the ninth months of 520 B.C., he exhorted Zerubbabel the governor and Joshua the high priest, the joint leaders of the Judean community, to assume official leadership in the reconstruction of the temple, and urged the priests to purify the cultic worship. These twin projects were, first of all, urgent practical steps toward unifying the disrupted religious life of the community. But Haggai saw them also as necessary preparations for the messianic age. Upon the completion of these enterprises the wonderful era foreseen by earlier prophets would come; for God would bless his people with fruitfulness and prosperity, overthrow the Gentiles, and establish Zerubbabel as the messianic king on the throne of David.

IN THE SECOND YEAR OF DARIUS THE king, in the sixth month, on the first day of the month, the word of the LORD came by Haggai the prophet to Zerub'babel the son of She-al'ti-el, governor of Judah, and to Joshua the son of Jehoz'adak, the high priest, 2 "Thus says the LORD of hosts: This people say the time has not yet come to rebuild the house of the LORD." 3 Then the word of the LORD came by Haggai the prophet, 4 "Is it a time for you yourselves to dwell in your paneled houses, while this house lies in ruins? 5 Now therefore thus says the LORD of hosts: Consider how you have fared. 6 You have sown much, and harvested little; you eat, but you never have enough; you drink, but you never have your fill; you clothe yourselves, but no one is warm; and he who earns wages earns wages to put them into a bag with holes.

7 "Thus says the LORD of hosts: Consider how you have fared. 8 Go up to the hills and bring wood and build the house, that I may take pleasure in it and that I may appear in my glory, says the LORD. 9 You have looked for much, and, lo, it came to little; and when you brought it home, I blew it away. Why? says the LORD of hosts. Because of my house that lies in ruins, while you busy yourselves each with his own house. 10 Therefore the heavens above you have withheld the dew, and the earth has withheld its produce. 11 And I have called for a drought upon the land and the hills, upon the grain, the new wine, the oil, upon what the ground brings forth, upon men and cattle, and upon all their labors."

12 Then Zerub'babel the son of She-al'ti-el, and Joshua the son of Jehoz'adak, the high priest, with all the remnant of the people, obeyed the voice of the LORD their God, and the words of Haggai the prophet, as the LORD their God had sent him; and the people feared before the LORD. 13 Then Haggai, the messenger of the LORD, spoke to the people with the LORD's message, "I am with you, says the LORD." 14 And the LORD stirred

---

1.1–15a: Because the people have neglected the temple, God has punished them. 1: *Darius* was king of the Persian empire from 521 to 485 B.C. *The sixth month of his second year*, mid-August to mid-September 520 B.C. *Haggai* means "festal." *Zerubbabel*, the grandson of Jehoiachin (2 Kg.24.8–17), was a royal descent from David; as the Persian-appointed governor of Judah, he shared authority with Joshua, the high priest, who also had come from Babylon. **4:** The temple had been plundered and burned in 587 B.C. (2 Kg.25.8–17). **5–11:** The poor conditions in Judah were God's punishment for the neglect of his house. **13:** *The messenger*

up the spirit of Zerub'babel the son of She-al'ti-el, governor of Judah, and the spirit of Joshua the son of Jehoz'-adak, the high priest, and the spirit of all the remnant of the people; and they came and worked on the house of the LORD of hosts, their God, ¹⁵ on the twenty-fourth day of the month, in the sixth month.

2 In the second year of Darius the king, ¹ in the seventh month, on the twenty-first day of the month, the word of the LORD came by Haggai the prophet, ² "Speak now to Zerub'babel the son of She-al'ti-el, governor of Judah, and to Joshua the son of Jehoz'-adak, the high priest, and to all the remnant of the people, and say, ³ 'Who is left among you that saw this house in its former glory? How do you see it now? Is it not in your sight as nothing? ⁴ Yet now take courage, O Zerub'-babel, says the LORD; take courage, O Joshua, son of Jehoz'adak, the high priest; take courage, all you people of the land, says the LORD; work, for I am with you, says the LORD of hosts, ⁵ according to the promise that I made you when you came out of Egypt. My Spirit abides among you; fear not. ⁶ For thus says the LORD of hosts: Once again, in a little while, I will shake the heavens and the earth and the sea and the dry land; ⁷ and I will shake all nations, so that the treasures of all nations shall come in, and I will fill this house with splendor, says the LORD of hosts. ⁸ The silver is mine, and the gold is mine, says the LORD of hosts. ⁹ The latter splendor of this house shall be

greater than the former, says the LORD of hosts; and in this place I will give prosperity, says the LORD of hosts.' "

10 On the twenty-fourth day of the ninth month, in the second year of Darius, the word of the LORD came by Haggai the prophet, ¹¹ "Thus says the LORD of hosts: Ask the priests to decide this question, ¹² 'If one carries holy flesh in the skirt of his garment, and touches with his skirt bread, or pottage, or wine, or oil, or any kind of food, does it become holy?' " The priests answered, "No." ¹³ Then said Haggai, "If one who is unclean by contact with a dead body touches any of these, does it become unclean?" The priests answered, "It does become unclean." ¹⁴ Then Haggai said, "So is it with this people, and with this nation before me, says the LORD; and so with every work of their hands; and what they offer there is unclean. ¹⁵ Pray now, consider what will come to pass from this day onward. Before a stone was placed upon a stone in the temple of the LORD, ¹⁶ how did you fare?^a When one came to a heap of twenty measures, there were but ten; when one came to the winevat to draw fifty measures, there were but twenty. ¹⁷ I smote you and all the products of your toil with blight and mildew and hail; yet you did not return to me, says the LORD. ¹⁸ Consider from this day onward, from the twenty-fourth day of the ninth month. Since the day that the foundation of the LORD'S temple was laid, consider: ¹⁹ Is the seed yet in

a Gk: Heb *since they were*

of the LORD, see Mal.3.1. **15a:** It is best to regard this as the date for the oracle in 2.15–19, which originally may have stood at this point.

1.15b–2.9: The new temple to be more splendid than the old. 2.1: *The seventh month,* mid-September to mid-October. **3:** A few of the people then present may have seen Solomon's temple before its destruction. **5:** Haggai sees God's *Spirit* standing in Israel's midst and is reminded of the Exodus (Ex.13.21–22; 14.19–20). **6:** Referred to and partially quoted in Heb.12.26. **7:** *Treasures of all nations;* compare Is.40.14; 60.6; 61.6.

2.10–14: The offering made by a defiled people is unclean. 10: *The ninth month,* mid-November to mid-December. **14:** The people condemned here may be the Samaritans, who opposed the work of the post-exilic community (Ezra 4.1–5; Neh.4.7–8).

2.15–19: When the foundation of the temple is laid, God will bless his people. This section may have stood after 1.1–14. *The twenty-fourth day* (v. 18; see 1.15a n.) probably marks the laying of the foundation stone. **17:** See Am.4.9. **18:** *Ninth,* probably error for "sixth" or a gloss. **19:** Good harvests were signs of God's favor; see Ps.128.

the barn? Do the vine, the fig tree, the pomegranate, and the olive tree still yield nothing? From this day on I will bless you."

20 The word of the LORD came a second time to Haggai on the twenty-fourth day of the month, 21 "Speak to Zerub'babel, governor of Judah, saying, I am about to shake the heavens and the earth, 22 and to overthrow the throne of kingdoms; I am about to destroy the strength of the kingdoms of the nations, and overthrow the chariots and their riders; and the horses and their riders shall go down, every one by the sword of his fellow. 23 On that day, says the LORD of hosts, I will take you, O Zerub'babel my servant, the son of She-al'ti-el, says the LORD, and make you like a signet ring; for I have chosen you, says the LORD of hosts."

2.20–23: When the LORD establishes the kingdom, Zerubbabel will be his messiah. **21**: Compare 2.6; Jl.3.16. **22**: *Overthrow the chariots*, God will again redeem his people, as at the Exodus (Ex.15.1). Haggai links Israel's earlier traditions with the coming messianic age. **23**: *My servant*, Num.12.7–8; 2 Sam.3.18; Is.42.1; Jer.27.6; see Zech.3.8 n. *Signet ring*, compare Jer.22.24.

THE BOOK OF ZECHARIAH

Zechariah, whose prophecies date from 520 to 518 B.C. and are found in chapters 1–8, was contemporary with Haggai (Ezra 5.1; 6.14) and shared his zeal for a rebuilt temple, a purified community, and the coming of the messianic age (see Introduction to Haggai). Like Haggai also, Zechariah forms a link between earlier prophecy (especially Ezekiel) and mature apocalyptic (Dan. chs. 7–12). But Zechariah differs from his contemporary in the form and presentation of his message, employing the literary style of night visions and dialogues between God, seer, and interpreting angel. With him, therefore, both the form and imagery of Jewish apocalyptic thought are developed into major proportions.

Chapters 9–14, which nowhere claim to be from Zechariah, portray nothing of the early Persian period but speak rather of the Greeks (9.13). Instead of Joshua and Zerubbabel, unnamed shepherds lead the community. Instead of peace and rebuilding, there are expectations of universal warfare and the siege of Jerusalem. Style, vocabulary, and theological ideas differentiate these chapters from Zechariah's work. Though they may contain some pre-exilic bits, they were written during the Greek period, principally in the fourth and third centuries B.C., by unknown authors. Since the eschatological and messianic themes found in the first section are here further elaborated, the authors are spiritual disciples of Zechariah. The pictures of the messianic Prince of Peace and the Good Shepherd smitten for the flock remarkably foreshadow the New Testament delineation of Christ.

IN THE EIGHTH MONTH, IN THE SECOND year of Darius, the word of the LORD came to Zechari'ah the son of Berechi'ah, son of Iddo, the prophet, saying, ² "The LORD was very angry with your fathers. ³ Therefore say to them, Thus says the LORD of hosts: Return to me, says the LORD of hosts, and I will return to you, says the LORD of hosts. ⁴ Be not like your fathers, to whom the former prophets cried out, 'Thus says the LORD of hosts, Return from your evil ways and from your evil deeds.' But they did not hear or heed me, says the LORD. ⁵ Your fathers, where are they? And the prophets, do they live for ever? ⁶ But my words and my statutes, which I commanded my servants the prophets, did they not overtake your fathers? So they repented and said, As the LORD of hosts purposed to deal with us for our ways and deeds, so has he dealt with us."

7 On the twenty-fourth day of the eleventh month which is the month of Shebat, in the second year of Darius, the word of the LORD came to Zechari'ah the son of Berechi'ah, son of Iddo, the prophet; and Zechari'ah said, ⁸ "I saw in the night, and behold, a man riding upon a red horse! He was standing among the myrtle trees in the glen; and behind him were red, sorrel, and white horses. ⁹ Then I said, 'What are these, my lord?' The angel who talked with me said to me, 'I will show you what they are.' ¹⁰ So the man who was standing among the myrtle trees answered, 'These are they whom the LORD has sent to patrol the

---

1.1–6: Introduction: a call to repentance. 1: Mid-October to mid-November 520 B.C. *Zechariah*, meaning "The LORD is renowned," was the *son of* the priest *Iddo* (Ezra 5.1; 6.14; Neh.12.16). The presence of the phrase *the son of Berechiah* is due probably to a scribal confusion with the son of Jeberechiah in Is.8.2, with whom Zechariah the son of Jehoiada (2 Chr.24.20–22) is also confused in Mt.23.35. Zechariah had prophetic and priestly interests (see Introduction to Joel). **4:** The *prophets* had continually invited repentance (Is.1.16–20; 30.15; 55.6–9; Jer. 3.12,22; 4.3–4; Hos.10.12; 14.1–7; Am.5.4,6,14). **6:** Both law (*statutes*) and prophecy (*words*) continue valid. So *they repented . . .* , perhaps an editorial addition (contrast 7.11).

1.7–6.15: The word of the LORD to Zechariah in a series of eight visions. There is a standard pattern: (a) vision, (b) question, (c) answer. **1.7:** Mid-January to mid-February, 519 B.C.

1.8–17: The first vision: divine horsemen patrolling the earth. 9: *My lord*, i.e., *the angel*. **10:** Job 1.6–7; 2.1–2. **11:** *Remains at rest*, the catastrophic Day of Judgment has not yet ap-

earth.' ¹¹ And they answered the angel of the LORD who was standing among the myrtle trees, 'We have patrolled the earth, and behold, all the earth remains at rest.' ¹² Then the angel of the LORD said, 'O LORD of hosts, how long wilt thou have no mercy on Jerusalem and the cities of Judah, against which thou hast had indignation these seventy years?' ¹³ And the LORD answered gracious and comforting words to the angel who talked with me. ¹⁴ So the angel who talked with me said to me, 'Cry out, Thus says the LORD of hosts: I am exceedingly jealous for Jerusalem and for Zion. ¹⁵ And I am very angry with the nations that are at ease; for while I was angry but a little they furthered the disaster. ¹⁶ Therefore, thus says the LORD, I have returned to Jerusalem with compassion; my house shall be built in it, says the LORD of hosts, and the measuring line shall be stretched out over Jerusalem. ¹⁷ Cry again, Thus says the LORD of hosts: My cities shall again overflow with prosperity, and the LORD will again comfort Zion and again choose Jerusalem.' "

18ᵃ And I lifted my eyes and saw, and behold, four horns! ¹⁹ And I said to the angel who talked with me, "What are these?" And he answered me, "These are the horns which have scattered Judah, Israel, and Jerusalem." ²⁰ Then the LORD showed me four smiths. ²¹ And I said, "What are these coming to do?" He answered, "These are the horns which scattered Judah, so that no man raised his head; and these have come to terrify them, to cast down the horns of the nations who lifted up their horns against the land of Judah to scatter it."

2ᵇ And I lifted my eyes and saw, and behold, a man with a measuring line in his hand! ² Then I said, "Where are you going?" And he said to me, "To measure Jerusalem, to see what is its breadth and what is its length." ³ And behold, the angel who talked with me came forward, and another angel came forward to meet him, ⁴ and said to him, "Run, say to that young man, 'Jerusalem shall be inhabited as villages without walls, because of the multitude of men and cattle in it. ⁵ For I will be to her a wall of fire round about, says the LORD, and I will be the glory within her.' "

6 Ho! ho! Flee from the land of the north, says the LORD; for I have spread you abroad as the four winds of the heavens, says the LORD. ⁷ Ho! Escape to Zion, you who dwell with the daughter of Babylon. ⁸ For thus said the LORD of hosts, after his glory sent me to the nations who plundered you, for he who touches you touches the apple of his eye: ⁹ "Behold, I will shake my hand over them, and they shall become plunder for those who served them. Then you will know that the LORD of hosts has sent me. ¹⁰ Sing and rejoice, O daughter of Zion; for lo, I come and I will dwell in the midst of you, says the LORD. ¹¹ And many nations shall join themselves to the LORD in that day, and shall be my people; and I will dwell in the midst of you, and you shall know that the LORD

a Ch 2.1 in Heb   *b* Ch 2.5 in Heb

---

peared (Hag.2.6). **12:** The *seventy years* refer to the period from 587 to 519 B.C. (Jer.25.11; 29.10). **15:** Ps.123.4; Am.6.1. **17:** 8.3; Is.44.26; 51.3; 54.8–10; Jer.31.38–39.

1.18–21: The second vision: four horns and four smiths. The *four horns* symbolize the powerful nations of the world (compare Ps.75.4,5; Dan.7.19–27) which the *smiths* (the LORD's agents of destruction) will scatter (Is.54.16–17; Hag.2.21–22).

2.1–5: The third vision: a man going to measure Jerusalem. 1: *Measuring line*, see Ezek. 40.3–4; Rev.11.1; 21.15–17. **5:** God is Jerusalem's guard and glory. (Is.4.5 n.; Ezek. 43.2–5).

2.6–13: An appeal to the exiles. 6: Babylonia is the *land of the north* (6.6,8; Jer.3.18; 46.20; compare Jer.51.45–49). **8:** *Apple of his eye* indicates special favor and affection (Dt.32.10; see Ps.17.8 n.). **10:** Is.54.1–3; 65.18–19; Zeph.3.14; Ezek.43.6–9. **11:** 8.20–23. **12:** This is the only Old Testament reference to Palestine as *the holy land*. The concept reappears in the Apocrypha (Wisdom of Solomon 12.3; 2 Macc.1.7). **13:** Hab.2.20; Zeph.1.7.

of hosts has sent me to you. [12] And the LORD will inherit Judah as his portion in the holy land, and will again choose Jerusalem."

13 Be silent, all flesh, before the LORD; for he has roused himself from his holy dwelling.

3 Then he showed me Joshua the high priest standing before the angel of the LORD, and Satan standing at his right hand to accuse him. [2] And the LORD said to Satan, "The LORD rebuke you, O Satan! The LORD who has chosen Jerusalem rebuke you! Is not this a brand plucked from the fire?" [3] Now Joshua was standing before the angel, clothed with filthy garments. [4] And the angel said to those who were standing before him, "Remove the filthy garments from him." And to him he said, "Behold, I have taken your iniquity away from you, and I will clothe you with rich apparel." [5] And I said, "Let them put a clean turban on his head." So they put a clean turban on his head and clothed him with garments; and the angel of the LORD was standing by.

6 And the angel of the LORD enjoined Joshua, [7] "Thus says the LORD of hosts: If you will walk in my ways and keep my charge, then you shall rule my house and have charge of my courts, and I will give you the right of access among those who are standing here. [8] Hear now, O Joshua the high priest, you and your friends who sit before you, for they are men of good omen: behold, I will bring my servant the Branch. [9] For behold, upon the stone which I have set before Joshua, upon a single stone with seven facets, I will engrave its inscription, says the LORD of hosts, and I will remove the guilt of this land in a single day. [10] In that day, says the LORD of hosts, every one of you will invite his neighbor under his vine and under his fig tree."

4 And the angel who talked with me came again, and waked me, like a man that is wakened out of his sleep. [2] And he said to me, "What do you see?" I said, "I see, and behold, a lampstand all of gold, with a bowl on the top of it, and seven lamps on it, with seven lips on each of the lamps which are on the top of it. [3] And there are two olive trees by it, one on the right of the bowl and the other on its left." [4] And I said to the angel who talked with me, "What are these, my lord?" [5] Then the angel who talked with me answered me, "Do you not know what these are?" I said, "No, my lord." [6] Then he said to me, "This is the word of the LORD to Zerub'babel: Not by might, nor by power, but by my Spirit, says the LORD of hosts. [7] What are you, O great mountain? Before Zerub'babel you shall become a plain; and he shall bring forward the top stone amid shouts of 'Grace, grace to it!' " [8] Moreover the word of the LORD came to me, saying, [9] "The hands of Zerub'babel have laid the foundation of this house; his hands shall also complete it. Then you will know that the LORD of hosts has sent me to you. [10] For whoever has despised the day of small things

3.1–10: The fourth vision: Joshua and Satan. 1: *Joshua*, see Hag.1.1 n. In the Old Testament *Satan* (literally, "the Adversary") is not the incarnation of evil but a functionary of the heavenly court who accuses man of wrong (1 Chr.21.1; see Job 1.6–8 n.). God then acquits ("justifies") or condemns the defendant. **3–4:** *Filthy garments* represent the sin of both priest and people. **5:** The *clean turban* (Ex.28.4) and *garments* (Lev.8.1–9) symbolize purity, in preparation for the advent of the Messiah. **7:** *Access*, to the heavenly courts; Joshua will present Jerusalem's prayers to heaven. **8:** *The Branch*, a Davidic figure who is to usher in the messianic age (compare Ps.132.17; Is.4.2; 11.1; Jer.23.5; 33.15), here refers to Zerubbabel (see 6.9–15 n.). **9:** *Stone* may symbolize Joshua's high-priesthood (Ex.28.9–12; see Zech.6.9–15 n.). **10:** Mic.4.4.

    4.1–14: The fifth vision: a golden lampstand and two olive trees. This vision emphasizes the important position held by Joshua and Zerubbabel (v. 14) in the restored Jewish community. **2:** Contrast Ex.25.31–40. The stand with seven lamps may signify the unified community, or God's presence in *the whole earth* (v. 10b; compare Rev.5.6). **3,11–14:** Rev.11.4. The *two olive trees* may provide oil for the lamps (v. 12), or merely flank them. **6–10a:** Through God's

shall rejoice, and shall see the plummet in the hand of Zerub'babel.

"These seven are the eyes of the LORD, which range through the whole earth." [11] Then I said to him, "What are these two olive trees on the right and the left of the lampstand?" [12] And a second time I said to him, "What are these two branches of the olive trees, which are beside the two golden pipes from which the oil[c] is poured out?" [13] He said to me, "Do you not know what these are?" I said, "No, my lord." [14] Then he said, "These are the two anointed who stand by the Lord of the whole earth."

5 Again I lifted my eyes and saw, and behold, a flying scroll! [2] And he said to me, "What do you see?" I answered, "I see a flying scroll; its length is twenty cubits, and its breadth ten cubits." [3] Then he said to me, "This is the curse that goes out over the face of the whole land; for every one who steals shall be cut off henceforth according to it, and every one who swears falsely shall be cut off henceforth according to it. [4] I will send it forth, says the LORD of hosts, and it shall enter the house of the thief, and the house of him who swears falsely by my name; and it shall abide in his house and consume it, both timber and stones."

5 Then the angel who talked with me came forward and said to me, "Lift your eyes, and see what this is that goes forth." [6] And I said, "What is it?" He said, "This is the ephah that goes forth." And he said, "This is their iniquity[d] in all the land." [7] And behold,

the leaden cover was lifted, and there was a woman sitting in the ephah! [8] And he said, "This is Wickedness." And he thrust her back into the ephah, and thrust down the leaden weight upon its mouth. [9] Then I lifted my eyes and saw, and behold, two women coming forward! The wind was in their wings; they had wings like the wings of a stork, and they lifted up the ephah between earth and heaven. [10] Then I said to the angel who talked with me, "Where are they taking the ephah?" [11] He said to me, "To the land of Shinar, to build a house for it; and when this is prepared, they will set the ephah down there on its base."

6 And again I lifted my eyes and saw, and behold, four chariots came out from between two mountains; and the mountains were mountains of bronze. [2] The first chariot had red horses, the second black horses, [3] the third white horses, and the fourth chariot dappled gray[e] horses. [4] Then I said to the angel who talked with me, "What are these, my lord?" [5] And the angel answered me, "These are going forth to the four winds of heaven, after presenting themselves before the LORD of all the earth. [6] The chariot with the black horses goes toward the north country, the white ones go toward the west country,[f] and the dappled ones go toward the south country." [7] When the steeds came out, they were impatient to get off and patrol the earth. And he said, "Go, patrol the earth." So they patrolled the earth. [8] Then

c Cn: Heb *gold*　　d Gk Compare Syr: Heb *eye*
e Compare Gk: The meaning of the Hebrew word is uncertain　　f Cn: Heb *after them*

Spirit Zerubbabel will complete the temple. **12:** Perhaps a gloss; no pipes have been previously mentioned. **14:** *Anointed,* literally, "sons of oil," is not the usual designation for "messiah."

5.1–4: The sixth vision: a flying scroll. 1: The *scroll* represents the word of God materialized (Ezek.2.9–3.3; Rev.10.8–11; see Jer.36.1–3). **2:** A cubit, about eighteen inches. **3:** The *curse* is to purify both civil and cultic life (compare Dt.27.14–26).

5.5–11: The seventh vision: a woman in an ephah. Judah will be purified by sending its sin, personified as a woman in an ephah, to Babylon, where the ephah will be worshiped. **6:** *Ephah,* here a container with the capacity of an ephah, about six gallons. **11:** *Shinar,* Babylonia (Gen. 10.10; Dan.1.2). *House* here means temple. *On its base,* as though the ephah were an image.

6.1–8: The eighth vision: four chariots. Although details are not clear, this vision probably refers to the inauguration of the messianic age with its judgment upon all the earth. **1–3:** See Rev.6.2–8. **8:** *North country,* Babylonia, see 2.6 n.

he cried to me, "Behold, those who go toward the north country have set my Spirit at rest in the north country."

9 And the word of the LORD came to me: ¹⁰ "Take from the exiles Heldai, Tobi'jah, and Jedai'ah, who have arrived from Babylon; and go the same day to the house of Josi'ah, the son of Zephani'ah. ¹¹ Take from them silver and gold, and make a crown,^g and set it upon the head of Joshua, the son of Jehoz'adak, the high priest; ¹² and say to him, 'Thus says the LORD of hosts, "Behold, the man whose name is the Branch: for he shall grow up in his place, and he shall build the temple of the LORD. ¹³ It is he who shall build the temple of the LORD, and shall bear royal honor, and shall sit and rule upon his throne. And there shall be a priest by his throne, and peaceful understanding shall be between them both." ' ¹⁴ And the crown^h shall be in the temple of the LORD as a reminder to Heldai,ⁱ Tobi'-jah, Jedai'ah, and Josi'ah^j the son of Zephani'ah.

15 "And those who are far off shall come and help to build the temple of the LORD; and you shall know that the LORD of hosts has sent me to you. And this shall come to pass, if you will diligently obey the voice of the LORD your God."

7 In the fourth year of King Darius, the word of the LORD came to Zechari'ah in the fourth day of the ninth month, which is Chislev. ² Now the people of Bethel had sent Share'-zer and Reg'em-mel'ech and their men, to entreat the favor of the LORD, ³ and to ask the priests of the house of the LORD of hosts and the prophets, "Should I mourn and fast in the fifth month, as I have done for so many years?" ⁴ Then the word of the LORD of hosts came to me; ⁵ "Say to all the people of the land and the priests, When you fasted and mourned in the fifth month and in the seventh, for these seventy years, was it for me that you fasted? ⁶ And when you eat and when you drink, do you not eat for yourselves and drink for yourselves? ⁷ When Jerusalem was inhabited and in prosperity, with her cities round about her, and the South and the lowland were inhabited, were not these the words which the LORD proclaimed by the former prophets?"

8 And the word of the LORD came to Zechari'ah, saying, ⁹ "Thus says the LORD of hosts, Render true judgments, show kindness and mercy each to his brother, ¹⁰ do not oppress the widow, the fatherless, the sojourner, or the poor; and let none of you devise evil against his brother in your heart." ¹¹ But they refused to hearken, and turned a stubborn shoulder, and stopped their ears that they might not hear. ¹² They made their hearts like adamant lest they should hear the law and the words which the LORD of hosts had sent by his Spirit through the former prophets. Therefore great wrath came from the LORD of hosts. ¹³ "As I called, and they would not hear, so they called, and I would not hear," says the LORD of hosts, ¹⁴ "and I scattered them with a whirlwind among all the nations which they had not known. Thus the

g Gk Mss: Heb *crowns*   h Gk: Heb *crowns*
i With verse 10: Heb *Helem*
j With verse 10: Heb *Hen*

6.9–15: The crowning of the messianic leader. This section abounds with difficulties. Originally it probably directed the crowning of Zerubbabel as messianic king, but was revised to refer to Joshua. **11:** Zerubbabel should be read for, or perhaps along with, *Joshua.* **12:** *Branch* is a messianic designation (see 3.8 n.; Hag.2.20–23). **15:** The new age will see the return of the exiles, conversion of the Gentiles, and completion of the temple (8.20–23; Ob.19–21; Mic.2.12; 4.1–5,6–8; Zeph.3.9–10,20; Mal.1.11). This verse is probably an addition.

7.1–14: An answer to an inquiry about fasting. 1: Mid-November to mid-December 518 B.C. **5:** The temple at Jerusalem was burned *in the fifth month* and Gedaliah the governor was murdered *in the seventh* (2 Kg.25.8–9,25). *These seventy years,* see 1.12 n. **9–10:** This is the essence of prophetic moral teaching (Is.1.16–17; 55.6–9; 58.6–12; Jer.7.5–7; Am.5.14–15,21–24; Mic.6.8). **12:** Neh.9.3; Jer.5.3; 7.25–26; 11.10; Dan.9.11–14. **13:** Is.1.15; Jer.7.13–15.

land they left was desolate, so that no one went to and fro, and the pleasant land was made desolate."

8 And the word of the LORD of hosts came to me, saying, 2 "Thus says the LORD of hosts: I am jealous for Zion with great jealousy, and I am jealous for her with great wrath. 3 Thus says the LORD: I will return to Zion, and will dwell in the midst of Jerusalem, and Jerusalem shall be called the faithful city, and the mountain of the LORD of hosts, the holy mountain. 4 Thus says the LORD of hosts: Old men and old women shall again sit in the streets of Jerusalem, each with staff in hand for very age. 5 And the streets of the city shall be full of boys and girls playing in its streets. 6 Thus says the LORD of hosts: If it is marvelous in the sight of the remnant of this people in these days, should it also be marvelous in my sight, says the LORD of hosts? 7 Thus says the LORD of hosts: Behold, I will save my people from the east country and from the west country; 8 and I will bring them to dwell in the midst of Jerusalem; and they shall be my people and I will be their God, in faithfulness and in righteousness."

9 Thus says the LORD of hosts: "Let your hands be strong, you who in these days have been hearing these words from the mouth of the prophets, since the day that the foundation of the house of the LORD of hosts was laid, that the temple might be built. 10 For before those days there was no wage for man or any wage for beast, neither was there any safety from the foe for him who went out or came in; for I set every man against his fellow. 11 But now I will not deal with the remnant of this people as in the former days, says the LORD of hosts. 12 For there shall be a sowing of peace; the vine shall yield its fruit, and the ground shall give its increase, and the heavens shall give their dew; and I will cause the remnant of this people to possess all these things. 13 And as you have been a byword of cursing among the nations, O house of Judah and house of Israel, so will I save you and you shall be a blessing. Fear not, but let your hands be strong."

14 For thus says the LORD of hosts: "As I purposed to do evil to you, when your fathers provoked me to wrath, and I did not relent, says the LORD of hosts, 15 so again have I purposed in these days to do good to Jerusalem and to the house of Judah; fear not. 16 These are the things that you shall do: Speak the truth to one another, render in your gates judgments that are true and make for peace, 17 do not devise evil in your hearts against one another, and love no false oath, for all these things I hate, says the LORD."

18 And the word of the LORD of hosts came to me, saying, 19 "Thus says the LORD of hosts: The fast of the fourth month, and the fast of the fifth, and the fast of the seventh, and the fast of the tenth, shall be to the house of Judah seasons of joy and gladness, and cheerful feasts; therefore love truth and peace.

20 "Thus says the LORD of hosts: Peoples shall yet come, even the inhabitants of many cities; 21 the inhabitants of one city shall go to another, saying, 'Let us go at once to entreat the favor of the LORD, and to seek the LORD of hosts; I am going.'

8.1–23: The LORD will return to Zion and do good to Jerusalem and Judah. Ten sections introduced by the words, "Thus says the LORD of hosts" (except in v. 3 where the words "of hosts" are not present). 2: Jl.2.18 n. 3: Is.1.26; 11.9; 62.11–12; Jer.31.23. 4–5: Is.65.19–20. 7: *East country* and *west country*, i.e. from all the lands of the dispersion. 8: The covenant shall be reaffirmed (Ex.6.7; Jer.31.33). 9: Hag.1.6–11; 2.4–9,15–19. 13: Jer.29.18; Gen.12.2–3. 14–17: God still demands right living (see 7.9–10 n.; Eph.4.25–32; 1 Th.5.12–22). 18–19: These fasts commemorated the fall and humiliation of Jerusalem. In *the fourth month* the Babylonians breached the walls of Jerusalem, and in *the tenth month* they had begun the siege (2 Kg.25.1–4; Jer.39.2; 52.4–7); for the other months, see 7.5 n. 20–23: The prophecy of Zechariah ends on a note of universalism (compare Is.2.3; 45.14,24).

²² Many peoples and strong nations shall come to seek the LORD of hosts in Jerusalem, and to entreat the favor of the LORD. ²³ Thus says the LORD of hosts: In those days ten men from the nations of every tongue shall take hold of the robe of a Jew, saying, 'Let us go with you, for we have heard that God is with you.'"

9   An Oracle

The word of the LORD is against the
    land of Hadrach
  and will rest upon Damascus.
For to the LORD belong the cities of
    Aram,ᵏ
  even as all the tribes of Israel;
² Hamath also, which borders thereon,
  Tyre and Sidon, though they are
    very wise.
³ Tyre has built herself a rampart,
  and heaped up silver like dust,
  and gold like the dirt of the
    streets.
⁴ But lo, the Lord will strip her of her
    possessions
  and hurl her wealth into the sea,
  and she shall be devoured by fire.

⁵ Ash'kelon shall see it, and be afraid;
  Gaza too, and shall writhe in
    anguish;
  Ekron also, because its hopes are
    confounded.
The king shall perish from Gaza;
  Ash'kelon shall be uninhabited;
⁶ a mongrel people shall dwell in
    Ashdod;
  and I will make an end of the
    pride of Philistia.
⁷ I will take away its blood from its
    mouth,

and its abominations from
    between its teeth;
it too shall be a remnant for our God;
  it shall be like a clan in Judah,
  and Ekron shall be like the
    Jeb'usites.
⁸ Then I will encamp at my house as
    a guard,
  so that none shall march to and
    fro;
no oppressor shall again overrun
    them,
  for now I see with my own eyes.

⁹ Rejoice greatly, O daughter of Zion!
  Shout aloud, O daughter of
    Jerusalem!
Lo, your king comes to you;
  triumphant and victorious is he,
  humble and riding on an ass,
  on a colt the foal of an ass.
¹⁰ I will cut off the chariot from
    E'phraim
  and the war horse from
    Jerusalem;
  and the battle bow shall be cut off,
  and he shall command peace to
    the nations;
his dominion shall be from sea to
    sea,
  and from the River to the ends of
    the earth.

¹¹ As for you also, because of the blood
    of my covenant with you,
  I will set your captives free from
    the waterless pit.
¹² Return to your stronghold, O
    prisoners of hope;
  today I declare that I will restore
    to you double.
¹³ For I have bent Judah as my bow;

ᵏ Cn: Heb *the eye of Adam* (or *man*)

9.1–11.17: The restoration of Israel; the day of the LORD.

9.1–8: The shattering of Israel's enemies foreshadows the messianic era (see Zeph.3.14–20 n.) here may be a reflection of Alexander the Great's conquests after 333 B.C. **1–6:** These cities of Syria (*Aram*) and *Philistia* fall within the ideal limits of the promised land (Gen.15.18–21; Ex.23.31). **7:** When converted, the Philistines will observe Jewish dietary laws (compare Gen.9.4; Lev.11.2–47; Dt.14.3–21). *Jebusites*, 2 Sam.5.6–9 n.

9.9–10: The Prince of Peace. 9: Not two animals (Mt.21.5) but one (Jn.12.14–15) young animal is meant. The *triumphant* king comes as a *humble* and peaceful monarch. **10:** Pss.46.8–10; 72.8; Is.11.6–9; 57.19; Hos.2.18; Mic.4.1–4; compare Eph.2.14–18.

9.11–17: The ingathering of dispersed Israelites. 11: *Blood of my covenant*, Ex.24.8; Mk.14.24;

I have made E'phraim its arrow.
I will brandish your sons, O Zion,
  over your sons, O Greece,
  and wield you like a warrior's
    sword.

14 Then the LORD will appear over
    them,
  and his arrow go forth like
    lightning;
  the Lord GOD will sound the
    trumpet,
  and march forth in the whirlwinds
    of the south.
15 The LORD of hosts will protect them,
  and they shall devour and tread
    down the slingers;*l*
and they shall drink their blood*m*
    like wine,
  and be full like a bowl,
  drenched like the corners of the
    altar.

16 On that day the LORD their God will
    save them
  for they are the flock of his
    people;
for like the jewels of a crown
  they shall shine on his land.
17 Yea, how good and how fair it shall
    be!
  Grain shall make the young men
    flourish,
  and new wine the maidens.

10 Ask rain from the LORD
    in the season of the spring rain,
  from the LORD who makes the storm
    clouds,
  who gives men showers of rain,
  to every one the vegetation in the
    field.
2 For the teraphim utter nonsense,
  and the diviners see lies;
the dreamers tell false dreams,
  and give empty consolation.

Therefore the people wander like
    sheep;
  they are afflicted for want of a
    shepherd.

3 "My anger is hot against the
    shepherds,
  and I will punish the leaders;*n*
for the LORD of hosts cares for his
  flock, the house of Judah,
  and will make them like his proud
    steed in battle.
4 Out of them shall come the
    cornerstone,
  out of them the tent peg,
  out of them the battle bow,
  out of them every ruler.
5 Together they shall be like mighty
    men in battle,
  trampling the foe in the mud of
    the streets;
they shall fight because the LORD is
    with them,
  and they shall confound the riders
    on horses.

6 "I will strengthen the house of
    Judah,
  and I will save the house of
    Joseph.
I will bring them back because I
  have compassion on them,
  and they shall be as though I had
    not rejected them;
for I am the LORD their God and
  I will answer them.
7 Then E'phraim shall become like a
    mighty warrior,
  and their hearts shall be glad as
    with wine.
Their children shall see it and
  rejoice,
  their hearts shall exult in the
    LORD.

l Cn: Heb *the slingstones*
m Gk: Heb *be turbulent*
n Or *he-goats*

Heb.9.20–22. **12:** Is.40.1–2,9–10; 61.7. **13:** *Judah* and *Ephraim*, the southern and northern kingdoms. **16–17:** Ezek.34.25–31 n.; Jer.31.12–14.
    10.1–2: The LORD alone controls nature, and gives rain. **1:** 14.17; Jl.2.18–27; Am.4.7–8.
2: *Teraphim,* see Ezek.21.18–24 n.
    10.3–12: The LORD alone controls history, and will gather in his redeemed. **6–7:** Both Israel and Judah will be saved. **6:** 8.7–8; Is.41.17–20; 54.8. **8–12:** The restoration. **8:** Is.43.1–7, 14–21; Jer.23.3. **10:** Dt.30.1–5; Hos.11.11. **12:** 14.9; Mic.4.5.

8 "I will signal for them and gather
    them in,
    for I have redeemed them,
    and they shall be as many as of
      old.
9 Though I scattered them among the
    nations,
    yet in far countries they shall
      remember me,
    and with their children they shall
      live and return.
10 I will bring them home from the
      land of Egypt,
    and gather them from Assyria;
    and I will bring them to the land of
      Gilead and to Lebanon,
    till there is no room for them.
11 They shall pass through the sea of
      Egypt,*o*
    and the waves of the sea shall be
      smitten,
    and all the depths of the Nile
      dried up.
    The pride of Assyria shall be laid
      low,
    and the scepter of Egypt shall
      depart.
12 I will make them strong in the
      LORD
    and they shall glory*p* in his
      name,"
      says the LORD.

‖ ‖ Open your doors, O Lebanon,
    that the fire may devour your
      cedars!
2 Wail, O cypress, for the cedar has
      fallen,
    for the glorious trees are ruined!
    Wail, oaks of Bashan,
    for the thick forest has been
      felled!
3 Hark, the wail of the shepherds,
    for their glory is despoiled!
    Hark, the roar of the lions,

for the jungle of the Jordan is laid
waste!

4 Thus said the LORD my God: "Become shepherd of the flock doomed to slaughter. 5 Those who buy them slay them and go unpunished; and those who sell them say, 'Blessed be the LORD, I have become rich'; and their own shepherds have no pity on them. 6 For I will no longer have pity on the inhabitants of this land, says the LORD. Lo, I will cause men to fall each into the hand of his shepherd, and each into the hand of his king; and they shall crush the earth, and I will deliver none from their hand."

7 So I became the shepherd of the flock doomed to be slain for those who trafficked in the sheep. And I took two staffs; one I named Grace, the other I named Union. And I tended the sheep. 8 In one month I destroyed the three shepherds. But I became impatient with them, and they also detested me. 9 So I said, "I will not be your shepherd. What is to die, let it die; what is to be destroyed, let it be destroyed; and let those that are left devour the flesh of one another." 10 And I took my staff Grace, and I broke it, annulling the covenant which I had made with all the peoples. 11 So it was annulled on that day, and the traffickers in the sheep, who were watching me, knew that it was the word of the LORD. 12 Then I said to them, "If it seems right to you, give me my wages; but if not, keep them." And they weighed out as my wages thirty shekels of silver. 13 Then the LORD said to me, "Cast it into the treasury"*q* –the lordly price at which I was paid

o Cn: Heb distress
p Gk: Heb walk
q Syr: Heb to the potter

11.1–3: The fall of the tyrants. *Cedars, shepherds,* and *lions* refer to the rulers. **1:** Lebanon's cedars were proverbial symbols of strength (Ezek.31.2–9). **2:** *Oaks of Bashan,* Is.2.13; Ezek.27.6; compare Ps.22.12; Am.4.1. **3:** *Jungle of the Jordan,* Jer.12.5 n.
    11.4–17: The two shepherds. Because they have despised him, God allows the Israelites to be abused by their rulers and breaks his covenant with them. **4–14:** The prophet portrays a good shepherd rejected by his sheep. **5:** *Those who buy* and *sell* are the Ptolemaic overlords; *their own shepherds* are native appointees. **8:** *The three shepherds,* probably contemporary officials, cannot now be identified. **12–13:** *Thirty shekels,* the price of a slave (Ex.21.32; com-

off by them. So I took the thirty shekels of silver and cast them into the treasury*q* in the house of the LORD. ¹⁴ Then I broke my second staff Union, annulling the brotherhood between Judah and Israel.

15 Then the LORD said to me, "Take once more the implements of a worthless shepherd. ¹⁶ For lo, I am raising up in the land a shepherd who does not care for the perishing, or seek the wandering,*r* or heal the maimed, or nourish the sound, but devours the flesh of the fat ones, tearing off even their hoofs.
¹⁷ Woe to my worthless shepherd,
  who deserts the flock!
May the sword smite his arm
  and his right eye!
Let his arm be wholly withered,
  his right eye utterly blinded!"

12 An Oracle

The word of the LORD concerning Israel: Thus says the LORD, who stretched out the heavens and founded the earth and formed the spirit of man within him: ² "Lo, I am about to make Jerusalem a cup of reeling to all the peoples round about; it will be against Judah also in the siege against Jerusalem. ³ On that day I will make Jerusalem a heavy stone for all the peoples; all who lift it shall grievously hurt themselves. And all the nations of the earth will come together against it. ⁴ On that day, says the LORD, I will strike every horse with panic, and its rider with madness. But upon the house of Judah I will open my eyes, when I strike every horse of the peoples with blindness. ⁵ Then the clans of Judah shall say to themselves, 'The inhabitants of Jerusalem have strength through the LORD of hosts, their God.'

6 "On that day I will make the clans of Judah like a blazing pot in the midst of wood, like a flaming torch among sheaves; and they shall devour to the right and to the left all the peoples round about, while Jerusalem shall still be inhabited in its place, in Jerusalem.

7 "And the LORD will give victory to the tents of Judah first, that the glory of the house of David and the glory of the inhabitants of Jerusalem may not be exalted over that of Judah. ⁸ On that day the LORD will put a shield about the inhabitants of Jerusalem so that the feeblest among them on that day shall be like David, and the house of David shall be like God, like the angel of the LORD, at their head. ⁹ And on that day I will seek to destroy all the nations that come against Jerusalem.

10 "And I will pour out on the house of David and the inhabitants of Jerusalem a spirit of compassion and supplication, so that, when they look on him whom they have pierced, they shall mourn for him, as one mourns for an only child, and weep bitterly over him, as one weeps over a first-born. ¹¹ On that day the mourning in Jerusalem will be as great as the mourning for Hadadrim'mon in the plain of Megid'do. ¹² The land shall mourn, each family by itself; the family of the house of David by itself, and their wives by themselves; the family of the house of Nathan by itself, and their wives by themselves; ¹³ the family of

q Sry: Heb *to the potter*
r Syr Compare Gk Vg: Heb *the youth*

pare Mt.26.15; 27.9). **15–17:** The prophet portrays a worthless shepherd who exploits the sheep (Ezek.34.2–10; Mic.3.1–7; Jn.10.1,8–13).
    12.1–14.21: The coming great day of the LORD, when he shall cleanse Jerusalem from sin, re-establish the covenant, and reign over all the earth.
    12.1–13.6: Jerusalem shall lament her sin and be purged of idolatry. 12.1: Is.42.5. **2:** Ps.75.8; Is.51.17–23. **7–8:** The ideal king will be from *the house of David*. **10–14:** With the picture of Jerusalem mourning over a prophet or king whom it has martyred compare Is.52.13–53.12; Mt.23.37; Jn.19.34–37; Rev.1.7. **10:** *Only child* and *first-born*, see Lk.2.7; Jn.1.14,18. **11:** *Hadad-rimmon*, a popular fertility god whose seasonal death was widely mourned (compare Ezek.8.14; Hos.7.14). **13:** Compare Num.3.21. **13.1:** Ps.46.4; Ezek.47.1–12; Jl.3.18; Jn.4.10–

the house of Levi by itself, and their wives by themselves; the family of the Shim'e-ites by itself, and their wives by themselves; 14 and all the families that are left, each by itself, and their wives by themselves.

13 "On that day there shall be a fountain opened for the house of David and the inhabitants of Jerusalem to cleanse them from sin and uncleanness.

2 "And on that day, says the LORD of hosts, I will cut off the names of the idols from the land, so that they shall be remembered no more; and also I will remove from the land the prophets and the unclean spirit. 3 And if any one again appears as a prophet, his father and mother who bore him will say to him, 'You shall not live, for you speak lies in the name of the LORD'; and his father and mother who bore him shall pierce him through when he prophesies. 4 On that day every prophet will be ashamed of his vision when he prophesies; he will not put on a hairy mantle in order to deceive, 5 but he will say, 'I am no prophet, I am a tiller of the soil; for the land has been my possession*t* since my youth.' 6 And if one asks him, 'What are these wounds on your back?' he will say, 'The wounds I received in the house of my friends.' "

7 "Awake, O sword, against my
    shepherd,
  against the man who stands next
    to me,"
            says the LORD of hosts.
"Strike the shepherd, that the sheep
    may be scattered;
  I will turn my hand against the
    little ones.
8 In the whole land, says the LORD,
  two thirds shall be cut off and
    perish,

and one third shall be left alive.
9 And I will put this third into the fire,
  and refine them as one refines
    silver,
  and test them as gold is tested.
They will call on my name,
  and I will answer them.
I will say, 'They are my people';
  and they will say, 'The LORD is
    my God.' "

14 Behold, a day of the LORD is coming, when the spoil taken from you will be divided in the midst of you. 2 For I will gather all the nations against Jerusalem to battle, and the city shall be taken and the houses plundered and the women ravished; half of the city shall go into exile, but the rest of the people shall not be cut off from the city. 3 Then the LORD will go forth and fight against those nations as when he fights on a day of battle. 4 On that day his feet shall stand on the Mount of Olives which lies before Jerusalem on the east; and the Mount of Olives shall be split in two from east to west by a very wide valley; so that one half of the Mount shall withdraw northward, and the other half southward. 5 And the valley of my mountains shall be stopped up, for the valley of the mountains shall touch the side of it; and you shall flee as you fled from the earthquake in the days of Uzzi'ah king of Judah. Then the LORD your*u* God will come, and all the holy ones with him.*v*

6 On that day there shall be neither cold nor frost.*w* 7 And there shall be continuous day (it is known to the LORD), not day and not night, for at evening time there shall be light.

t Cn: Heb *for man has caused me to possess*
u Heb *my*
v Gk Syr Vg Tg: Heb *you*
w Compare Gk Syr Vg Tg: Heb uncertain

14; 7.38; Rev.21.6; 22.1–2. **2–6**: Professional prophecy, fallen into disrepute, will cease. **2**: Hos.2.17; Zeph.1.4; 3.4. **3**: Jer.23.9–22. **4**: 2 Kg.1.8. **5**: Am.7.14. **6**: Compare 1 Kg.18.28.
    13.7–9: God's shepherd, smitten for the sheep. A separate messianic oracle (Mt.26.31; Mk. 14.27), closely linked with chs. 9–11. After the death of the shepherd, a remnant of his flock will be purified and saved. **7**: *Man*, here the shepherd-king. **8**: Is.6.13. **9**: *Refine*, Is.1.25–26; 48.10. *My people . . . my God*, signifies the re-establishing of the covenant (Hos.2.21–23).
    14.1–21: The final warfare and the final victory (Is.66.15–23; Ezek. chs. 38–39; Jl.3.9–21;

8 On that day living waters shall flow out from Jerusalem, half of them to the eastern sea and half of them to the western sea; it shall continue in summer as in winter.

9 And the LORD will become king over all the earth; on that day the LORD will be one and his name one.

10 The whole land shall be turned into a plain from Geba to Rimmon south of Jerusalem. But Jerusalem shall remain aloft upon its site from the Gate of Benjamin to the place of the former gate, to the Corner Gate, and from the Tower of Han'anel to the king's wine presses. [11] And it shall be inhabited, for there shall be no more curse;[x] Jerusalem shall dwell in security.

12 And this shall be the plague with which the LORD will smite all the peoples that wage war against Jerusalem: their flesh shall rot while they are still on their feet, their eyes shall rot in their sockets, and their tongues shall rot in their mouths. [13] And on that day a great panic from the LORD shall fall on them, so that each will lay hold on the hand of his fellow, and the hand of the one will be raised against the hand of the other; [14] even Judah will fight against Jerusalem. And the wealth of all the nations round about shall be collected, gold, silver, and garments in great abundance. [15] And a plague like this plague shall fall on the horses, the mules, the camels, the asses, and whatever beasts may be in those camps.

16 Then every one that survives of all the nations that have come against Jerusalem shall go up year after year to worship the King, the LORD of hosts, and to keep the feast of booths. [17] And if any of the families of the earth do not go up to Jerusalem to worship the King, the LORD of hosts, there will be no rain upon them. [18] And if the family of Egypt do not go up and present themselves, then upon them shall[y] come the plague with which the LORD afflicts the nations that do not go up to keep the feast of booths. [19] This shall be the punishment to Egypt and the punishment to all the nations that do not go up to keep the feast of booths.

20 And on that day there shall be inscribed on the bells of the horses, "Holy to the LORD." And the pots in the house of the LORD shall be as the bowls before the altar; [21] and every pot in Jerusalem and Judah shall be sacred to the LORD of hosts, so that all who sacrifice may come and take of them and boil the flesh of the sacrifice in them. And there shall no longer be a trader in the house of the LORD of hosts on that day.

x Or *ban of utter destruction*
y Gk Syr: Heb *shall not*

Mk.13.7–27; Rev. chs. 20–22). **5:** See Am.1.1 n. **6–7:** Is.24.23; Rev.22.5. **8:** 13.1. **9:** Dt.6.4; Ps.99.1–5; Mal.1.11; Rev.11.15–18; 15.3–4. **10–11:** Compare 2 Kg.23.8; Jer.31.38–40. **12–15:** 14.3; Ex.7.4–5. **16–19:** *Booths*, Lev.23.33–36 n. Originally a nature festival (note *rain*), in the post-exilic period this feast was probably associated with renewing the covenant and celebrating the kingship of God. **17:** Ex.34.21–24; Jn.7.2. **18–19:** Compare Is. ch. 19; Jer. ch. 46; Ezek. chs. 29–32. **20–21:** Lev.27.30–33; Jl.3.17; Rev.21.27. **21b:** The meaning of this sentence is not clear. Either no *trader* will be needed because everything will be holy, or nothing will be permitted that defiles pure worship (Jn.2.16).

THE BOOK OF MALACHI

Nothing is known about the person of Malachi. Even his name, which means "My messenger," may be only an appellation, based on 3.1 (compare 2.7). The book, however, presents a substantial amount of information about its author's viewpoints. Living probably in the period 500–450 B.C., this Jew was devoted to the temple and held a high view of the priesthood and its responsibilities. He speaks frequently of the covenant (2.4,5,8,10,14; 3.1) and shows great respect for the priestly "instruction" (torah, 2.6–9). Instead of adopting the oracular style normally used by prophets, Malachi employs a distinctive question-and-answer method of stating his argument. Nevertheless, his emphases upon sin, judgment, and repentance and upon the advent of the day of the LORD (3.1–5,7; 4.1–3,6) mark him as a prophet, and he may best be understood as a "cultic prophet" (see Introduction to Joel).

One central theme dominates Malachi's thought: fidelity to the LORD's covenant and its teachings. From this standpoint he both condemns the priests for corrupting worship and misleading the people (1.6–2.9; 3.3–4) and charges his brethren to remain faithful to their Jewish wives and thus have "godly offspring" (2.13–16). In exhorting Israel to faithfulness Malachi gives also striking descriptions of the worship of the LORD by the Gentiles (1.11,14b), the ideal priest (2.5–7), and the blessing of obedience (3.10–12,16–17; 4.2–3). He asserts, further, the fatherhood of God (2.10) and adds to the concept of the day of the LORD (Zeph.1.14–18) the figure of the appointed forerunner (3.1–4; compare 4.5–6). It is fitting that these pages, which point so clearly to the New Covenant, conclude the books of the prophets and precede, in our English Bibles, the New Testament.

THE ORACLE OF THE WORD OF THE LORD to Israel by Mal'achi.[a]

2 "I have loved you," says the LORD. But you say, "How hast thou loved us?" "Is not Esau Jacob's brother?" says the LORD. "Yet I have loved Jacob [3] but I have hated Esau; I have laid waste his hill country and left his heritage to jackals of the desert." [4] If Edom says, "We are shattered but we will rebuild the ruins," the LORD of hosts says, "They may build, but I will tear down, till they are called the wicked country, the people with whom the LORD is angry for ever." [5] Your own eyes shall see this, and you shall say, "Great is the LORD, beyond the border of Israel!"

6 "A son honors his father, and a servant his master. If then I am a father, where is my honor? And if I am a master, where is my fear? says the LORD of hosts to you, O priests, who despise my name. You say, 'How have we despised thy name?' [7] By offering polluted food upon my altar. And you say, 'How have we polluted it?'[b] By thinking that the LORD's table may be despised. [8] When you offer blind animals in sacrifice, is that no evil? And when you offer those that are lame or sick, is that no evil? Present that to your governor; will he be pleased with you or show you favor? says the LORD of hosts. [9] And now entreat the favor of God, that he may be gracious to us. With such a gift from your hand, will he show favor to any of you? says the LORD of hosts. [10] Oh, that there were one among you who would shut the doors, that you might

a Or my messenger   b Gk: Heb thee

1.1: Superscription: Compare Zech.9.1; 12.1. Oracle, see Nah.1.1 n. The word of the LORD, see Hos.1.1 n.

1.2–5: God loves Israel. 2: Esau, Jacob's twin brother, was the ancestor of the Edomites (Gen.25.24–26,30; 36.1). **2–3:** Rom.9.13. **2–5:** Is. ch. 34; 63.1–6; Jer.49.7–22; Ezek.25.12–14; Am.1.11–12; see Introduction to Obadiah.

1.6–2.9: The priests have despised their God and their solemn vocation. 6: Ex.20.12; Pr.30.11. **8:** Blind or lame animals were unacceptable for sacrifice (Lev.22.17–25; Dt.15.21). **10:** Shut the doors of the temple to halt vain worship (Is.1.13; Am.5.21–24). **11:** In contrast with Judah's

not kindle fire upon my altar in vain! I have no pleasure in you, says the LORD of hosts, and I will not accept an offering from your hand. ¹¹ For from the rising of the sun to its setting my name is great among the nations, and in every place incense is offered to my name, and a pure offering; for my name is great among the nations, says the LORD of hosts. ¹² But you profane it when you say that the LORD's table is polluted, and the food for it*c* may be despised. ¹³ 'What a weariness this is,' you say, and you sniff at me,*d* says the LORD of hosts. You bring what has been taken by violence or is lame or sick, and this you bring as your offering! Shall I accept that from your hand? says the LORD. ¹⁴ Cursed be the cheat who has a male in his flock, and vows it, and yet sacrifices to the Lord what is blemished; for I am a great King, says the LORD of hosts, and my name is feared among the nations.

2 "And now, O priests, this command is for you. ² If you will not listen, if you will not lay it to heart to give glory to my name, says the LORD of hosts, then I will send the curse upon you and I will curse your blessings; indeed I have already cursed them, because you do not lay it to heart. ³ Behold, I will rebuke your offspring, and spread dung upon your faces, the dung of your offerings, and I will put you out of my presence.*e* ⁴ So shall you know that I have sent this command to you, that my covenant with Levi may hold, says the LORD of hosts. ⁵ My covenant with him was a covenant of life and peace, and I gave them to him, that he might fear; and he feared me, he stood in awe of my name. ⁶ True instruction*f* was in his mouth,

and no wrong was found on his lips. He walked with me in peace and uprightness, and he turned many from iniquity. ⁷ For the lips of a priest should guard knowledge, and men should seek instruction*f* from his mouth, for he is the messenger of the LORD of hosts. ⁸ But you have turned aside from the way; you have caused many to stumble by your instruction;*f* you have corrupted the covenant of Levi, says the LORD of hosts, ⁹ and so I make you despised and abased before all the people, inasmuch as you have not kept my ways but have shown partiality in your instruction."*f*

10 Have we not all one father? Has not one God created us? Why then are we faithless to one another, profaning the covenant of our fathers? ¹¹ Judah has been faithless, and abomination has been committed in Israel and in Jerusalem; for Judah has profaned the sanctuary of the LORD, which he loves, and has married the daughter of a foreign god. ¹² May the LORD cut off from the tents of Jacob, for the man who does this, any to witness*g* or answer, or to bring an offering to the LORD of hosts!

13 And this again you do. You cover the LORD's altar with tears, with weeping and groaning because he no longer regards the offering or accepts it with favor at your hand. ¹⁴ You ask, "Why does he not?" Because the LORD was witness to the covenant between you and the wife of your youth, to whom you have been faithless, though she is your companion and your wife by covenant. ¹⁵ Has not the one God

c Heb *its fruit, its food*
d Another reading is *it*
e Cn Compare Gk Syr: Heb *and he shall bear you to it*
f Or *law*   *g* Cn Compare Gk: Heb *arouse*

---

present corrupt practices, the Gentiles render a *pure offering* to the LORD (compare v. 14b; Ps.102.15; Jl.2.28; Zeph.3.9–10). **2.3:** Ex.29.14; Nah.3.6. **4:** *Levi* was the priestly tribe (Num. 3.45; 18.21–24; Dt.33.8–11). **5:** Num.25.12–13. **7:** Lev.10.11; Dt.21.5. **8–9:** Mic.3.11; Mt. 23.1–36.
  2.10–16: God hates divorce and demands marital fidelity. 10: The fatherhood and unity of God imply the brotherhood and unity of man (v. 15; compare Dt.32.6,18; Is.63.16; 64.8; Jer.31.1–3; Hos.11.1; Eph.4.6). **11:** *The daughter of a foreign god* refers to heathen women. **14–16:** Marriage is a sacred *covenant*, honorable among godly men (Gen.2.24; Ezek.16.8; Hos.2.19; Mk.10.2–9; Eph.5.21–33.

made[h] and sustained for us the spirit of life?[i] And what does he desire? Godly offspring. So take heed to yourselves, and let none be faithless to the wife of his youth. [16] "For I hate[j] divorce, says the LORD the God of Israel, and covering one's garment with violence, says the LORD of hosts. So take heed to yourselves and do not be faithless."

17 You have wearied the LORD with your words. Yet you say, "How have we wearied him?" By saying, "Every one who does evil is good in the sight of the LORD, and he delights in them." Or by asking, "Where is the God of justice?"

3 "Behold, I send my messenger to prepare the way before me, and the Lord whom you seek will suddenly come to his temple; the messenger of the covenant in whom you delight, behold, he is coming, says the LORD of hosts. [2] But who can endure the day of his coming, and who can stand when he appears?

"For he is like a refiner's fire and like fullers' soap; [3] he will sit as a refiner and purifier of silver, and he will purify the sons of Levi and refine them like gold and silver, till they present right offerings to the LORD. [4] Then the offering of Judah and Jerusalem will be pleasing to the LORD as in the days of old and as in former years.

5 "Then I will draw near to you for judgment; I will be a swift witness against the sorcerers, against the adulterers, against those who swear falsely, against those who oppress the hireling in his wages, the widow and the orphan, against those who thrust aside the sojourner, and do not fear me, says the LORD of hosts.

6 "For I the LORD do not change; therefore you, O sons of Jacob, are not consumed. [7] From the days of your fathers you have turned aside from my statutes and have not kept them. Return to me, and I will return to you, says the LORD of hosts. But you say, 'How shall we return?' [8] Will man rob God? Yet you are robbing me. But you say, 'How are we robbing thee?' In your tithes and offerings. [9] You are cursed with a curse, for you are robbing me; the whole nation of you. [10] Bring the full tithes into the storehouse, that there may be food in my house; and thereby put me to the test, says the LORD of hosts, if I will not open the windows of heaven for you and pour down for you an overflowing blessing. [11] I will rebuke the devourer[k] for you, so that it will not destroy the fruits of your soil; and your vine in the field shall not fail to bear, says the LORD of hosts. [12] Then all nations will call you blessed, for you will be a land of delight, says the LORD of hosts.

13 "Your words have been stout against me, says the LORD. Yet you say, 'How have we spoken against thee?' [14] You have said, 'It is vain to serve God. What is the good of our keeping his charge or of walking as in mourning before the LORD of hosts? [15] Henceforth we deem the arrogant blessed; evildoers not only prosper but when they put God to the test they escape.' "

h Or has he not made one?
i Cn: Heb and a remnant of spirit was his
j Cn: Heb he hates   k Or devouring locust

2.17–3.5: The LORD will send his messenger to prepare for the coming of the day of judgment. 17: Job 21.7–16; Hab.1.2–4,13. **3.1–4:** The *messenger* or angel (Gen.16.7; 22.11; Ex.3.2; Is.63.9) will prepare for *the day of* God's *coming* (Is.40.3; Mt.11.10; Mk.1.2; Lk.1.17,76; 7.27) first by purifying the priesthood. **2:** Mt.3.10–12. **5:** God himself will appear for *judgment* against the wicked and godless (Zeph.1.14–18; 3.1–8; Mk.13.14–37; 2 Th.2.1–12).

3.6–12: If the people will return to God with a full measure of devotion, he will bless them. 6: Num.23.19; Heb.13.8; Jas.1.17. **8–9:** The *tithes* required by the law (Lev.27.30; Num.18.21–24) were being withheld; therefore the *curse* of crop failure resulted (v. 11). **10:** Dt.28.2–12; Ezek.34.25–31. **12:** Is.61.6–9; 62.4.

3.13–4.3: When the day of judgment comes, the true worshipers will be spared. 14: Job 21.15; Is.58.3. **16:** *A book of remembrance*, compare Ex.32.32–34; Ps.69.28; Is.4.3; 65.6; Dan.7.10;

16 Then those who feared the LORD spoke with one another; the LORD heeded and heard them, and a book of remembrance was written before him of those who feared the LORD and thought on his name. [17] "They shall be mine, says the LORD of hosts, my special possession on the day when I act, and I will spare them as a man spares his son who serves him. [18] Then once more you shall distinguish between the righteous and the wicked, between one who serves God and one who does not serve him.

4[1] "For behold, the day comes, burning like an oven, when all the arrogant and all evildoers will be stubble; the day that comes shall burn them up, says the LORD of hosts, so that it will leave them neither root nor branch. [2] But for you who fear my name the sun of righteousness shall rise, with healing in its wings. You shall go forth leaping like calves from the stall. [3] And you shall tread down the wicked, for they will be ashes under the soles of your feet, on the day when I act, says the LORD of hosts.

4 "Remember the law of my servant Moses, the statutes and ordinances that I commanded him at Horeb for all Israel.

5 "Behold, I will send you Eli'jah the prophet before the great and terrible day of the LORD comes. [6] And he will turn the hearts of fathers to their children and the hearts of children to their fathers, lest I come and smite the land with a curse."[m]

l Ch 4.1–6 are Ch 3.19–24 in the Hebrew
m Or *ban of utter destruction*

12.1; Rev.20.12; 21.27. **4.1:** Compare 3.2–5. **2:** *The sun of* God's *righteousness* symbolizes health and vindication (2 Sam.23.4; Ps.84.11; Is.60.1).

4.4–6: Two appendices: the first (v. 4) exhorts obedience to the law of Moses; the second (v. 5–6) identifies the forerunner with *Elijah*. Standing at the very end of the prophetic corpus, these two appendices serve to link *the law* and *the prophet*. **4:** *Horeb*, Mount Sinai (Dt.5.1–3), is also the place where God revealed himself to Elijah (1 Kg.19.1–18). **5:** A commentary on 3.1. For an expansion of this tradition, see Mt.11.7–15; 17.10–13; Mk.6.14–16; compare Ecclesiasticus 48.10. **6:** *Turn the hearts* . . . applied specifically to John the Baptist in Lk.1.17.

THE
NEW TESTAMENT

INTRODUCTION TO THE NEW TESTAMENT

THE NEW TESTAMENT comprises the twenty-seven books which constitute the second of the two portions into which the Bible is naturally divided. A more appropriate word than "testament" to designate the character of these books is "covenant." This is the word which the Bible uses in referring to the relationship that God established with his people. In a sublime passage written more than five hundred years before Christ, the prophet Jeremiah predicted that the covenant relation of God with his people, instituted through Moses on Mount Sinai, would give place in the future to a more inward and personal one (Jer.31. 31–34). In accord with this prophecy the Apostle Paul regarded the Christian dispensation as based on a new covenant, which he contrasted with the old covenant enshrined in the books of Moses (2 Cor.3.6–15). Another early Christian writer, doubtless thinking of the words of Jesus when he instituted the Last Supper (Mt.26.28; Mk.14.24; 1 Cor.11.25), declared that by his sacrificial death Christ became the mediator of a new covenant (Heb.9.15–20; compare 10.16). It is quite understandable, therefore, that the two collections of documents which belong respectively to the two dispensations of God's dealings with his people have been brought together in one volume as "The Holy Bible, containing the Old and New Testaments."

Unlike the books of the Old Testament, which originated during a period extending over many centuries, the books of the New Testament were written within a period of somewhat less than one hundred years. These books fall into four different literary forms. Four of them are "Gospels" because they tell the "gospel" (a word derived from the Anglo-Saxon gōd-spell, meaning "good tidings") of Jesus Christ, that is, his birth, baptism, ministry of teaching and healing, death, and resurrection. Church history is represented in the Acts of the Apostles, which is an account of the spread of the Christian faith during the first thirty or so years after the death and resurrection of Jesus Christ. Twenty-one of the books of the New Testament are in the form of letters. The last book of the New Testament is an apocalypse, that is, a revelation (Greek apokalypsis) or disclosure of God's will for the future.

Jesus himself left no literary remains; information regarding his words and works comes from his immediate followers (the apostles) and their disciples. At first this information was circulated orally. As far as we know today, the first attempt to produce a written Gospel was made by John Mark, who according to tradition was a disciple of the Apostle Peter. This Gospel, along with a collection of sayings of Jesus and several other special sources, formed the basis of the Gospels attributed to Matthew and Luke. The reasons for regarding the Gospel of Mark as one of the sources of Matthew and Luke include the following facts. (1) Apart from details Mark contains very little that is not in Matthew or in Luke. (2) When Mark and Matthew differ as to sequence of matter, Luke agrees with Mark, and when Mark and Luke differ as to sequence, Matthew agrees with Mark. (3) Matthew and Luke never agree as to sequence against Mark. Because these three Gospels have so much in common, they are generally called the Synoptic Gospels (from the Greek word *synopsis*, a seeing together).

In contrast to the Synoptics, which relate mainly Jesus' public teaching and ministry to the crowds in Galilee, the Gospel according to John contains information regarding Jesus' early Judean ministry as well as extensive discourses to the disciples concerning the union of the Christian with Christ (chs. 14–17). John contains no parables in the Synoptic sense, and he frequently weaves the words of Jesus so closely with his own interpretation of them that it is sometimes difficult to find the break between the two.

The letters in the New Testament were written by various teachers in the primitive church to congregations and to individuals in order to provide further instruction in the Christian faith and to correct certain abuses and disorders which had arisen. The letter-form happily combines the advantages inherent in both conversation and treatise. By their nature letters permit the writer to communicate with the recipients in a personal and indeed affectionate manner; at the same time, they also allow the writer to treat abstract subjects with accuracy and fulness.

The New Testament letters fall into two main groups, those attributed to Paul and those attributed to other writers. Within each group the present sequence seems to have been determined in accord with the length of the letters, the longest standing first. The present titles of the letters were not part of the original documents, and would not have been needed until the individual letters had been gathered into a collection.

The language in which the books of the New Testament were written was the koine or common Greek of the time. This form of Greek, which lacks many of the subtle refinements of classical Greek of an earlier period, was known and used by most of the peoples of the Roman Empire to whom the first Christian missionaries carried the gospel. Noticeably different grades of koine Greek are found in the several New Testament documents. The most highly literary as regards sentence structure and vocabulary are the Letter to the Hebrews and the two books written by Luke (the Gospel and the Acts). Those which are the furthest removed from classical Greek standards and closest to colloquial Greek are the Gospel of Mark and the book of Revelation. Furthermore, since all the authors represented in the New Testament appear to have been either Jews or Jewish proselytes before becoming Christians, it is natural that their use of koine Greek was colored by their familiarity with the special characteristics of the Greek translation of the Hebrew Old Testament (the Septuagint). Here and there the Gospels and the first half of Acts preserve in Greek certain turns of expression which reflect an underlying Aramaic idiom, which was the mother tongue of Jesus and his disciples.

The original manuscripts of the several books of the New Testament have long since disappeared. Three sources of information exist today for our knowledge of the text of the New Testament. They are Greek manuscripts, early translations into other languages (primarily Syriac, Latin, and Coptic), and quotations from the New Testament made by early ecclesiastical writers. The total number of Greek manuscripts of all or parts of the New Testament is close to five thousand. Of this number the most important are, in general, the oldest; more than three hundred, written on papyrus or parchment, date from the second to the eighth century. In evaluating the significance of this rich store of manuscripts, it should be recalled that the writings of many ancient classical authors have survived in only a few copies (or even in only one), and that not infrequently these copies date from the late Middle Ages, separated from the time of the composition of the originals by more than a thousand years.

Before the invention of printing with movable type (about A.D. 1450–1455) all literary works had to be copied by hand. Owing to the rapid expansion of the early church and the growing demand for additional copies of the Christian Scriptures, sometimes speed in the preparation of manuscripts seemed to be of greater importance than strict accuracy of detail. Consequently unintentional errors, inevitable in all transcription, were multiplied in what was copied. At other times alterations were deliberately made; for example, scribes would occasionally improve the grammar and style, correct real or imagined errors in history and geography, adjust quotations from the Old Testament in accord with current copies of the Greek Septuagint, and harmonize differing accounts in the Synoptic Gospels. Thus, not only inadvertence but also well-intentioned efforts resulted in the creation of thousands of divergencies in the manuscripts of the New Testament. It should be added, however, that the great majority of these variant readings involve inconsequential details, such as alternative spellings, differing order of words, and interchange of synonyms. Among the relatively few variants which involve the essential meaning of the text, modern scholars are usually able to determine with more or less probability what the original text was. (For examples of various kinds of additions to the text, see Mt.6.13 note *n*; 23.13 note *v*; Mk.9.43 note *n*; Lk.12.39 note *q*; 17.35 note *b*; 22.42 note *l*; 24.11 note *v*; Jn.5.3 note *k*; Acts 8.36 note *h*.)

As long as copies of the books of the New Testament were written on scrolls, practical difficulties of length prevented the collection of many of the books of the New Testament into one scroll. In the second century, however, the adoption by many Christians of the codex or leaf-form of manuscript permitted the gathering, for example, of all of the Gospels or all of Paul's letters into one volume. This process of assembling various books in a single codex was accompanied by the development of the idea of the canon of the New Testament.

The word "canon" is a Greek word borrowed from a Semitic root, meaning a stalk or a reed, which could be used for measuring. By extension the word came to denote a rule, norm, or list (of books). Why, how, and when the present books of the New Testament were finally gathered into one collection are questions difficult to answer because of the lack of explicit information. It is possible, however, to reconstruct some of the influences which must have contributed to the emergence of the canon of the New Testament.

The Bible of the earliest Christians was the Old Testament (2 Tim.3.15–17). Of equal authority to these writings were the remembered words of Jesus (Acts 20.35; 1 Cor.7.10,12; 9.14; 1 Tim.5.18). Parallel with the oral circulation of Jesus' teaching were apostolic interpretations of his person and significance for the life of the church. It is natural that when the gospels and the apostolic letters were written, incorporating these two kinds of authoritative materials, they would be treasured, circulated, and read in services of worship (Col.4.16; 1 Th.5.27; Rev.1.3).

At first a local church would have only a few apostolic letters and perhaps one or two gospels. During the course of the second century most churches came to acknowledge a canon which included the present four Gospels, the Acts, thirteen letters of Paul, 1 Peter, and 1 John. Seven books still lacked general recognition: Hebrews, James, 2 Peter, 2 and 3 John, Jude, and Revelation. On the other hand, certain writings, such as the Letter of Barnabas or the Shepherd of Hermas, were accepted as Scripture by several ecclesiastical writers, though rejected by the majority. During the third century there was a sifting of the disputed books; certain of them came to be acknowledged as canonical and others were rejected as apocryphal. The fourth century was marked by authoritative pronouncements, first by bishops of provincial churches and later by synods or councils. St. Athanasius in his Festal Letter for A.D. 367 was the first to name the twenty-seven books of the New Testament as exclusively canonical.

Various external circumstances assisted in the process of canonization of the New Testament books. The emergence of heretical sects with their own sacred books made it imperative for the church to determine the limits of the canon. Likewise, when Christians were persecuted for their faith it became a matter of the utmost importance to know which books could be renounced and which could not be handed over to the imperial police without incurring the guilt of sacrilege.

The tests of canonicity which were most frequently applied seem to have been apostolic authorship, or at least apostolic content, and general harmony with the Old Testament and the rest of the New Testament. Prior, however, to the issuing of pronouncements by church councils was the intuitive insight of individual Christians who had discerned the inherent significance of the canonical books. In the most basic sense neither individuals nor councils created the canon, but only came to recognize and acknowledge the self-authenticating quality of these writings, which imposed themselves as canonical upon the church.

THE GOSPEL ACCORDING TO

MATTHEW

The Gospel according to Matthew is a manual of Christian teaching in which Jesus Christ, Lord of the new-yet-old community, the church, is described particularly as the fulfiller and fulfilment of God's will disclosed in the Old Testament. Jesus is set forth as Israel's Messiah in whom God's purpose culminates and by whose words and life his followers, the true Israel, may gain divine forgiveness and fellowship.

The accounts of Jesus' deeds and words, drawn from Christian sources both oral and written, are arranged in a generally biographical order: chs. 1–2, Birth of Jesus; 3.1–12, Activity of John the Baptist; 3.13–4.11, Baptism and temptation of Jesus; 4.12–18.35, Jesus' preaching and teaching in Galilee; chs. 19–20, Journey to Jerusalem; chs. 21–27, The last week, concluding with Jesus' crucifixion and burial; ch. 28, The resurrection; Jesus' commission to his disciples.

Within this natural framework the accounts of what Jesus said or did are grouped by common subject matter. The five discourses of Jesus, a noteworthy feature of this Gospel (see 7.28 n.), are collections of teachings on specific themes: chs. 5–7, The Sermon on the Mount; ch. 10, Instructions for missionary disciples; ch. 13, The parables of the kingdom of God; ch. 18, On sincere discipleship; chs. 24–25, On the end of this age.

This Gospel is anonymous. The unknown Christian teacher who prepared it during the last third of the first century may have used as one of his sources a collection of Jesus' sayings that the apostle Matthew is said to have made. In time a title containing Matthew's name, and signifying apostolic authority, came to identify the whole.

THE BOOK OF THE GENEALOGY OF Jesus Christ, the son of David, the son of Abraham.

2 Abraham was the father of Isaac, and Isaac the father of Jacob, and Jacob the father of Judah and his brothers, ³ and Judah the father of Perez and Zerah by Tamar, and Perez the father of Hezron, and Hezron the father of Ram,ᵃ ⁴ and Ramᵃ the father of Ammin′adab, and Ammin′-adab the father of Nahshon, and Nahshon the father of Salmon, ⁵ and Salmon the father of Bo′az by Rahab, and Bo′az the father of Obed by Ruth, and Obed the father of Jesse, ⁶ and Jesse the father of David the king.

And David was the father of Solomon by the wife of Uri′ah, ⁷ and Solomon the father of Rehobo′am, and Rehobo′am the father of Abi′jah, and Abi′jah the father of Asa,ᵇ ⁸ and Asaᵇ

the father of Jehosh′aphat, and Jehosh′aphat the father of Joram, and Joram the father of Uzzi′ah, ⁹ and Uzzi′ah the father of Jotham, and Jotham the father of Ahaz, and Ahaz the father of Hezeki′ah, ¹⁰ and Hezeki′ah the father of Manas′seh, and Manas′-seh the father of Amos,ᶜ and Amosᶜ the father of Josi′ah, ¹¹ and Josi′ah the father of Jechoni′ah and his brothers, at the time of the deportation to Babylon.

12 And after the deportation to Babylon: Jechoni′ah was the father of She-al′ti-el,ᵈ and She-al′ti-elᵈ the father of Zerub′babel, ¹³ and Zerub′-babel the father of Abi′ud, and Abi′ud the father of Eli′akim, and Eli′akim the father of Azor, ¹⁴ and Azor the father of Zadok, and Zadok the father

a Greek Aram
b Greek Asaph
c Other authorities read Amon
d Greek Salathiel

1.1–17: Jesus' royal descent (Lk.3.23–38) is traced through David the king (22.41–45; Rom. 1.3) back to Abraham the patriarch (Gal.3.16). 3–6: Ru.4.18–22; 1 Chr.2.1–15. 11: The deportation, 2 Kg.24.8–16; Jer.27.20. 12: Jeconiah, or Jehoiachin (2 Kg.24.6; 1 Chr.3.16). Shealtiel apparently transmitted the line of legal descent from Jeconiah to Zerubbabel (Ezra 3.2; Hag.2.2; Lk.3.27), although the Chronicler traces it through Pedaiah (1 Chr.3.16–19). 13–16: The persons from Abiud to Jacob are otherwise unknown. 16: Christ, the Greek translation of

of Achim, and Achim the father of Eli'ud, [15] and Eli'ud the father of Elea'zar, and Elea'zar the father of Matthan, and Matthan the father of Jacob, [16] and Jacob the father of Joseph the husband of Mary, of whom Jesus was born, who is called Christ.

17 So all the generations from Abraham to David were fourteen generations, and from David to the deportation to Babylon fourteen generations, and from the deportation to Babylon to the Christ fourteen generations.

18 Now the birth of Jesus Christ[f] took place in this way. When his mother Mary had been betrothed to Joseph, before they came together she was found to be with child of the Holy Spirit; [19] and her husband Joseph, being a just man and unwilling to put her to shame, resolved to divorce her quietly. [20] But as he considered this, behold, an angel of the Lord appeared to him in a dream, saying, "Joseph, son of David, do not fear to take Mary your wife, for that which is conceived in her is of the Holy Spirit; [21] she will bear a son, and you shall call his name Jesus, for he will save his people from their sins." [22] All this took place to fulfil what the Lord had spoken by the prophet:
[23] "Behold, a virgin shall conceive and
    bear a son,
  and his name shall be called
    Emman'u-el"
(which means, God with us). [24] When Joseph woke from sleep, he did as the angel of the Lord commanded him; he took his wife, [25] but knew her not until she had borne a son; and he called his name Jesus.

2 Now when Jesus was born in Bethlehem of Judea in the days of Herod the king, behold, wise men from the East came to Jerusalem, saying, [2] "Where is he who has been born king of the Jews? For we have seen his star in the East, and have come to worship him." [3] When Herod the king heard this, he was troubled, and all Jerusalem with him; [4] and assembling all the chief priests and scribes of the people, he inquired of them where the Christ was to be born. [5] They told him, "In Bethlehem of Judea; for so it is written by the prophet:
[6] 'And you, O Bethlehem, in the land
    of Judah,
  are by no means least among the
    rulers of Judah;
  for from you shall come a ruler
  who will govern my people
    Israel.' "
7 Then Herod summoned the wise men secretly and ascertained from them what time the star appeared; [8] and he sent them to Bethlehem, saying, "Go and search diligently for the child, and when you have found him bring me word, that I too may come and worship him." [9] When they had heard the king they went their way; and lo, the star which they had seen in the East went before them, till it came to rest over the place where the child was. [10] When they saw the star, they rejoiced exceedingly with great joy; [11] and going into the house they saw the child with Mary his mother, and they fell down and worshiped him. Then, opening their treasures, they offered him gifts, gold and frankincense and myrrh. [12] And being warned in a dream not to return to Herod, they

f Other ancient authorities read *of the Christ*

the Hebrew word "Messiah," which means "anointed one" (compare Lev.4.3,5,16; 2 Sam.1.14,16).
   1.18–2.23: Jesus' birth and infancy (Lk.1.26–2.40). **20:** *Angel*, see Heb.1.14 n. **21:** The Hebrew and Aramaic forms of *Jesus* and *he will save* are similar. The point could be suggested by translating, "You shall call his name 'Savior' because he will save." **22–23:** See Is.7.14 n. **25:** *Until:* According to Catholic teaching, the Semitic idiom in the use of *until* here does not imply that they had conjugal relations after the birth of Jesus.
   2.1–12: The wise men (Magi). **1:** *Herod* the Great died early in 4 B.C. The *wise men*, a learned class in ancient Persia. **2:** Jer.23.5; Num.24.17. **5:** Jn.7.42. **6:** Mic.5.2. **11:** See Lk.2.7 n.

departed to their own country by another way.

13 Now when they had departed, behold, an angel of the Lord appeared to Joseph in a dream and said, "Rise, take the child and his mother, and flee to Egypt, and remain there till I tell you; for Herod is about to search for the child, to destroy him." 14 And he rose and took the child and his mother by night, and departed to Egypt, 15 and remained there until the death of Herod. This was to fulfil what the Lord had spoken by the prophet, "Out of Egypt have I called my son."

16 Then Herod, when he saw that he had been tricked by the wise men, was in a furious rage, and he sent and killed all the male children in Bethlehem and in all that region who were two years old or under, according to the time which he had ascertained from the wise men. 17 Then was fulfilled what was spoken by the prophet Jeremiah:

18 "A voice was heard in Ramah,
wailing and loud lamentation,
Rachel weeping for her children;
she refused to be consoled,
because they were no more."

19 But when Herod died, behold, an angel of the Lord appeared in a dream to Joseph in Egypt, saying, 20 "Rise, take the child and his mother, and go to the land of Israel, for those who sought the child's life are dead."

21 And he rose and took the child and his mother, and went to the land of Israel. 22 But when he heard that Archela'us reigned over Judea in place of his father Herod, he was afraid to go there, and being warned in a dream he withdrew to the district of Galilee. 23 And he went and dwelt in a city called Nazareth, that what was spoken by the prophets might be fulfilled, "He shall be called a Nazarene."

3 In those days came John the Baptist, preaching in the wilderness of Judea, 2 "Repent, for the kingdom of heaven is at hand." 3 For this is he who was spoken of by the prophet Isaiah when he said,

"The voice of one crying in the
wilderness:
Prepare the way of the Lord,
make his paths straight."

4 Now John wore a garment of camel's hair, and a leather girdle around his waist; and his food was locusts and wild honey. 5 Then went out to him Jerusalem and all Judea and all the region about the Jordan, 6 and they were baptized by him in the river Jordan, confessing their sins.

7 But when he saw many of the Pharisees and Sad'ducees coming for baptism, he said to them, "You brood of vipers! Who warned you to flee from the wrath to come? 8 Bear fruit that

---

2.13–23: Escape to Egypt and return. 15: *Out of Egypt . . .*, a quotation from Hos.11.1, where the reference is to Israel (compare Ex.4.22). **18:** Quoted from Jer.31.15. *Rachel*, wife of Jacob, died in childbirth and according to Gen.35.16–20 was buried near Bethlehem. *Ramah*, north of Jerusalem, was the scene of national grief (Jer.40.1) inflicted by an enemy. **22:** *Archelaus* reigned from 4 B.C. to A.D. 6 and was replaced by a Roman procurator. **23:** There is a similarity in sound and possibly in meaning between the Aramaic word for *Nazareth* and the Hebrew word translated *branch* (Is.11.1).

3.1–12: Activity of John the Baptist (Mk.1.1–8; Lk.3.1–18; Jn.1.6–8,19–28). **1:** *John* resembled the Old Testament prophets (compare v. 4 with 2 Kg.1.8; Zech.13.4). Christian faith understood him to fulfil Is.40.3; Mal.3.1; 4.5 (see 3.3; 17.10–12). His influence outside Christianity is attested by Acts 18.25; 19.1–7. *Those days*, namely, when Jesus began his public life. *The wilderness of Judea* lay east and southeast of Jerusalem. **2:** *Repent*, literally "return," meant to come back to the way of life charted by the covenant between God and Israel (Ex.19.3–6; 24.3–8; Jer.31.31–34). *The kingdom*, see 4.17 n. **3:** Is.40.3. **6:** See Mk.1.4 n. **7:** *Pharisees* and *Sadducees* formed two major divisions among the Jews (for differences between them, see 22.23 n. and Acts 23.6–10). A third Jewish sect in Palestine was the Essenes (see Josephus, *B. J.*, II, viii, 2–13); their beliefs and practices are reflected in the Dead Sea Scrolls found at Qumran (see "Survey of . . . Bible Lands," §15, end). *The wrath to come*, God's judgment (1 Th.

befits repentance, ⁹ and do not presume to say to yourselves, 'We have Abraham as our father'; for I tell you, God is able from these stones to raise up children to Abraham. ¹⁰ Even now the axe is laid to the root of the trees; every tree therefore that does not bear good fruit is cut down and thrown into the fire.

11 "I baptize you with water for repentance, but he who is coming after me is mightier than I, whose sandals I am not worthy to carry; he will baptize you with the Holy Spirit and with fire. ¹² His winnowing fork is in his hand, and he will clear his threshing floor and gather his wheat into the granary, but the chaff he will burn with unquenchable fire."

13 Then Jesus came from Galilee to the Jordan to John, to be baptized by him. ¹⁴ John would have prevented him, saying, "I need to be baptized by you, and do you come to me?" ¹⁵ But Jesus answered him, "Let it be so now; for thus it is fitting for us to fulfil all righteousness." Then he consented. ¹⁶ And when Jesus was baptized, he went up immediately from the water, and behold, the heavens were opened*g* and he saw the Spirit of God descending like a dove, and alighting on him; ¹⁷ and lo, a voice from heaven, saying, "This is my beloved Son,*h* with whom I am well pleased."

4 Then Jesus was led up by the Spirit into the wilderness to be tempted by the devil. ² And he fasted forty days and forty nights, and afterward he was hungry. ³ And the tempter came and said to him, "If you are the Son of God, command these stones to become loaves of bread." ⁴ But he answered, "It is written,

'Man shall not live by bread alone, but by every word that proceeds from the mouth of God.'"

⁵ Then the devil took him to the holy city, and set him on the pinnacle of the temple, ⁶ and said to him, "If you are the Son of God, throw yourself down; for it is written,

'He will give his angels charge of you,'

and

'On their hands they will bear you up, lest you strike your foot against a stone.'"

⁷ Jesus said to him, "Again it is written, 'You shall not tempt the Lord your God.'" ⁸ Again, the devil took him to a very high mountain, and showed him all the kingdoms of the world and the glory of them; ⁹ and he said to him, "All these I will give you, if you will fall down and worship me." ¹⁰ Then Jesus said to him, "Begone, Satan! for it is written,

'You shall worship the Lord your God and him only shall you serve.'"

¹¹ Then the devil left him, and behold, angels came and ministered to him.

12 Now when he heard that John had been arrested, he withdrew into Galilee; ¹³ and leaving Nazareth he went and dwelt in Caper′na-um by the sea, in the territory of Zeb′ulun and

g Other ancient authorities add *to him*
h Or *my Son, my* (or *the*) *Beloved*

1.10). **8–10:** See Lk.3.7–9 n.; Jn.8.33. **11–12:** See Lk.12.49 n.; Acts 2.17–21; 19.1–7; 18.24–26. **3.13–17:** Jesus' baptism (Mk.1.9–11; Lk.3.21–22; Jn.1.31–34). **13–15:** Jesus recognized John's authority and identified himself with those who responded in faith to John's call. **16–17:** A description of the surge of certainty and self-understanding that came to Jesus at his baptism. The language, akin to Old Testament speech, portrays a spiritual experience which words cannot adequately describe. *Beloved Son,* see Mk.1.11 n.

4.1–11: Jesus' temptation (Mk.1.12–13; Lk.4.1–13; Heb.2.18; 4.15). The accounts illustrate Jesus' habitual refusal to allow his sense of mission to be influenced by concern for his safety or for merely practical interests. **1:** *The devil, tempter* (v. 3), and *Satan* (v. 10) are names for evil conceived as a personal will actively hostile to God (see Lk.13.11,16 n.). **2:** *Forty,* compare Ex.34.28; 1 Kg.19.8. **3:** *If you are the Son of God;* but see the declaration in 3.17. **4:** Dt.8.3. **5:** *The holy city,* Jerusalem. **6:** Ps.91.11–12. **7:** Dt.6.16. **10:** Dt.6.13.

Naph'tali, [14] that what was spoken by the prophet Isaiah might be fulfilled:

[15] "The land of Zeb'ulun and the land of Naph'tali,
toward the sea, across the Jordan,
Galilee of the Gentiles–
[16] the people who sat in darkness have seen a great light,
and for those who sat in the region and shadow of death
light has dawned."

[17] From that time Jesus began to preach, saying, "Repent, for the kingdom of heaven is at hand."

18 As he walked by the Sea of Galilee, he saw two brothers, Simon who is called Peter and Andrew his brother, casting a net into the sea; for they were fishermen. [19] And he said to them, "Follow me, and I will make you fishers of men." [20] Immediately they left their nets and followed him. [21] And going on from there he saw two other brothers, James the son of Zeb'edee and John his brother, in the boat with Zeb'edee their father, mending their nets, and he called them. [22] Immediately they left the boat and their father, and followed him.

23 And he went about all Galilee, teaching in their synagogues and preaching the gospel of the kingdom and healing every disease and every infirmity among the people. [24] So his fame spread throughout all Syria, and they brought him all the sick, those afflicted with various diseases and pains, demoniacs, epileptics, and paralytics, and he healed them. [25] And great crowds followed him from Galilee and the Decap'olis and Jerusalem and Judea and from beyond the Jordan.

5 Seeing the crowds, he went up on the mountain, and when he sat down his disciples came to him. [2] And he opened his mouth and taught them, saying:

3 "Blessed are the poor in spirit, for theirs is the kingdom of heaven.

4 "Blessed are those who mourn, for they shall be comforted.

5 "Blessed are the meek, for they shall inherit the earth.

6 "Blessed are those who hunger and thirst for righteousness, for they shall be satisfied.

7 "Blessed are the merciful, for they shall obtain mercy.

8 "Blessed are the pure in heart, for they shall see God.

9 "Blessed are the peacemakers, for they shall be called sons of God.

10 "Blessed are those who are per-

4.12–25: Beginnings of Jesus' activity in Galilee. 12–17: Mk.1.14–15; Lk.4.14–15. **15–16:** Is.9.1–2. **17:** *From that time*, the arrest of John (v. 12). *The kingdom of heaven* is Matthew's usual way of expressing the equivalent phrase, "the kingdom of God," found in parallel accounts in the other gospels. In asserting that God's *kingdom is at hand* Jesus meant that all God's past dealings with his creation were coming to climax and fruition. Jesus taught both the present reality of God's rule (Lk.10.18; 11.20; 17.21) and its future realization (Mt.6.10). See Mk.1.15 n. **18–22:** Mk.1.16–20; Lk.5.1–11; Jn.1.35–42. **24:** *Demoniacs*, persons controlled in body or will, or in both, by evil forces (Mt.8.16,28; 9.32; 15.22; Mk.5.15; see Lk.13.11,16 n.). *Demons*, see Lk.4.33 n. **25:** *Decapolis*, see Mk.5.20 n.

5.1–7.27: The Sermon on the Mount sounds the keynote of the new age which Jesus came to introduce. Internal analysis and comparison with Luke's Gospel suggest that the Evangelist (in accord with his habit of synthesis) has inserted into this account of the Sermon portions of Jesus' teaching given on other occasions. **1:** *He sat down*, the usual position of Jewish rabbis while teaching (compare Lk.4.20–21).

5.3–12: The Beatitudes (Lk.6.17,20–23) proclaim God's favor toward those who aspire to live under his rule. **3:** *Poor in spirit*, those who feel a deep sense of spiritual poverty (Is.66.2). **4:** *Comforted*, the word implies strengthening as well as consolation. **5:** Ps.37.11. **6:** Is.55.1–2; Jn.4.14; 6.48–51. **8:** Purity of *heart* is single-mindedness or sincerity, freedom from mixed motives; it is not synonymous with chastity, but includes it (Ps.24.4; Heb.12.14). *See God*, 1 Cor.13.12; 1 Jn.3.2; Rev. 22.4. **9:** *Peacemakers* are not merely "peaceable," but those who work earnestly to "make" peace. **10:** 1 Pet.3.14; 4.14. **12:** 2 Chr.36.15–16; Mt.23.37; Acts 7.52.

secuted for righteousness' sake, for theirs is the kingdom of heaven.

11 "Blessed are you when men revile you and persecute you and utter all kinds of evil against you falsely on my account. [12] Rejoice and be glad, for your reward is great in heaven, for so men persecuted the prophets who were before you.

13 "You are the salt of the earth; but if salt has lost its taste, how shall its saltness be restored? It is no longer good for anything except to be thrown out and trodden under foot by men.

14 "You are the light of the world. A city set on a hill cannot be hid. [15] Nor do men light a lamp and put it under a bushel, but on a stand, and it gives light to all in the house. [16] Let your light so shine before men, that they may see your good works and give glory to your Father who is in heaven.

17 "Think not that I have come to abolish the law and the prophets; I have come not to abolish them but to fulfil them. [18] For truly, I say to you, till heaven and earth pass away, not an iota, not a dot, will pass from the law until all is accomplished. [19] Whoever then relaxes one of the least of these commandments and teaches men so, shall be called least in the kingdom of heaven; but he who does them and teaches them shall be called great in the kingdom of heaven. [20] For I tell you, unless your righteousness exceeds that of the scribes and Pharisees, you will never enter the kingdom of heaven.

21 "You have heard that it was said to the men of old, 'You shall not kill; and whoever kills shall be liable to judgment.' [22] But I say to you that every one who is angry with his brother[i] shall be liable to judgment; whoever insults[j] his brother shall be liable to the council, and whoever says, 'You fool!' shall be liable to the hell[k] of fire. [23] So if you are offering your gift at the altar, and there remember that your brother has something against you, [24] leave your gift there before the altar and go; first be reconciled to your brother, and then come and offer your gift. [25] Make friends quickly with your accuser, while you are going with him to court, lest your accuser hand you over to the judge, and the judge to the guard, and you be put in prison; [26] truly, I say to you, you will never get out till you have paid the last penny.

27 "You have heard that it was said, 'You shall not commit adultery.' [28] But I say to you that every one who looks at a woman lustfully has already committed adultery with her in his heart. [29] If your right eye causes you to sin, pluck it out and throw it away; it is better that you lose one of your members than that your whole body be thrown into hell.[k] [30] And if your right hand causes you to sin, cut it off and throw it away; it is better that you lose one of your members than that your whole body go into hell.[k]

31 "It was also said, 'Whoever divorces his wife, let him give her a certificate of divorce.' [32] But I say to you that every one who divorces his wife, except on the ground of unchastity, makes her an adulteress; and

i Other ancient authorities insert *without cause*
j Greek *says Raca to* (an obscure term of abuse)
k Greek *Gehenna*

5.13–16: The witness of the disciples. 13: Mk.9.49–50; Lk.14.34–35. **14:** Phil.2.15; Jn.8.12. **15:** See Mk.4.21 n. **16:** 1 Pet.2.12.

5.17–20: The relation of Jesus' message to the Jewish law was a great concern to followers with a Jewish background. **17:** *The prophets* in the Hebrew Scriptures comprise the books of Joshua, Judges, Samuel, Kings, Isaiah, Jeremiah, Ezekiel, and the twelve minor prophets (see Lk.24.27 n., 44 n.). **18:** Mk.13.31; Lk.16.17. **19:** *Relaxes*, or "sets aside." *Teaches*, Jas.3.1. **20:** *Righteousness*, one's acceptance of God's requirements and one's being accepted by God (Lk.18.10–14).

5.21–48: Illustrations of the true understanding of the Law. 21: Ex.20.13; Dt.5.17; 16.18. **25–26:** Lk.12.57–59. **26:** *Penny*, see Lk.12.59 n. **27:** Ex.20.14; Dt.5.18. **29–30:** Mk.9.43–48; Mt.18.8–9. **31:** *It was also said*, Dt.24.1–4. **32:** The expression *except . . . unchastity* occurs also

whoever marries a divorced woman commits adultery.

33 "Again you have heard that it was said to the men of old, 'You shall not swear falsely, but shall perform to the Lord what you have sworn.' 34 But I say to you, Do not swear at all, either by heaven, for it is the throne of God, 35 or by the earth, for it is his footstool, or by Jerusalem, for it is the city of the great King. 36 And do not swear by your head, for you cannot make one hair white or black. 37 Let what you say be simply 'Yes' or 'No'; anything more than this comes from evil.[1]

38 "You have heard that it was said, 'An eye for an eye and a tooth for a tooth.' 39 But I say to you, Do not resist one who is evil. But if any one strikes you on the right cheek, turn to him the other also; 40 and if any one would sue you and take your coat, let him have your cloak as well; 41 and if any one forces you to go one mile, go with him two miles. 42 Give to him who begs from you, and do not refuse him who would borrow from you.

43 "You have heard that it was said, 'You shall love your neighbor and hate your enemy.' 44 But I say to you, Love your enemies and pray for those who persecute you, 45 so that you may be sons of your Father who is in heaven; for he makes his sun rise on the evil and on the good, and sends rain on the just and on the unjust. 46 For if you love those who love you, what reward have you? Do not even the tax collectors do the same? 47 And if you salute only your brethren, what more

are you doing than others? Do not even the Gentiles do the same? 48 You, therefore, must be perfect, as your heavenly Father is perfect.

6 "Beware of practicing your piety before men in order to be seen by them; for then you will have no reward from your Father who is in heaven.

2 "Thus, when you give alms, sound no trumpet before you, as the hypocrites do in the synagogues and in the streets, that they may be praised by men. Truly, I say to you, they have received their reward. 3 But when you give alms, do not let your left hand know what your right hand is doing, 4 so that your alms may be in secret; and your Father who sees in secret will reward you.

5 "And when you pray, you must not be like the hypocrites; for they love to stand and pray in the synagogues and at the street corners, that they may be seen by men. Truly, I say to you, they have received their reward. 6 But when you pray, go into your room and shut the door and pray to your Father who is in secret; and your Father who sees in secret will reward you.

7 "And in praying do not heap up empty phrases as the Gentiles do; for they think that they will be heard for their many words. 8 Do not be like them, for your Father knows what you need before you ask him. 9 Pray then like this:

Our Father who art in heaven,
Hallowed be thy name.

1 Or the evil one

in 19.9; it is absent from the accounts in Mk.10.11–12 and Lk.16.18 (compare also Rom.7.2–3; 1 Cor.7.10–11). **33–37:** Lev.19.12; Num.30.2; Dt.23.21; Mt.23.16–22; Jas.5.12. **35:** Is.66.1. **38:** Ex.21.23–24; Lev.24.19–20; Dt.19.21. Though this principle *controlled* retaliation in primitive society, it did not justify it. **39–42:** Lk.6.29–30; Rom.12.17; 1 Cor.6.7; 1 Pet.2.19; 3.9. **43–48:** Lk.6.27–28,32–36. **45:** To be *sons of* God is to pattern attitudes after God's. The words *son of* commonly mean that one shows the quality named or trait of character implied (see 23.31 n.; Lk.6.35; 10.6; Jn.8.39–47).

6.1–34: Teachings in practical piety; Jesus emphasizes a sincere response to God that identifies oneself with his purposes. **1:** 23.5. **5:** Lk.18.10–14. **9–13:** The Lord's Prayer (compare Lk.11.2–4) falls into two parts relating to God and to man; after the opening invocation, there are three petitions concerning God's glory, followed by those concerning our needs. The phrase, *on earth as it is in heaven* (v. 10), belongs to each of the first three petitions. On the basis of David's prayer (1 Chr.29.11–13) the early church added an appropriate concluding doxology (see note *n*). **9:** Is.63.16; 64.8. **13:** 2 Th.3.3; Jas.1.13. **14–15:** 18.35; Mk.11.25–26; Eph.4.32;

10 Thy kingdom come.
  Thy will be done,
    On earth as it is in heaven.
11 Give us this day our daily bread;*m*
12 And forgive us our debts,
    As we also have forgiven our
      debtors;
13 And lead us not into temptation,
    But deliver us from evil.*n*
14 For if you forgive men their trespasses, your heavenly Father also will forgive you; 15 but if you do not forgive men their trespasses, neither will your Father forgive your trespasses.

16 "And when you fast, do not look dismal, like the hypocrites, for they disfigure their faces that their fasting may be seen by men. Truly, I say to you, they have received their reward. 17 But when you fast, anoint your head and wash your face, 18 that your fasting may not be seen by men but by your Father who is in secret; and your Father who sees in secret will reward you.

19 "Do not lay up for yourselves treasures on earth, where moth and rust*o* consume and where thieves break in and steal, 20 but lay up for yourselves treasures in heaven, where neither moth nor rust*o* consumes and where thieves do not break in and steal. 21 For where your treasure is, there will your heart be also.

22 "The eye is the lamp of the body. So, if your eye is sound, your whole body will be full of light; 23 but if your eye is not sound, your whole body will be full of darkness. If then the light in you is darkness, how great is the darkness!

24 "No one can serve two masters; for either he will hate the one and love the other, or he will be devoted to the one and despise the other. You cannot serve God and mammon.*x*

25 "Therefore I tell you, do not be anxious about your life, what you shall eat or what you shall drink, nor about your body, what you shall put on. Is not life more than food, and the body more than clothing? 26 Look at the birds of the air: they neither sow nor reap nor gather into barns, and yet your heavenly Father feeds them. Are you not of more value than they? 27 And which of you by being anxious can add one cubit to his span of life?*p* 28 And why are you anxious about clothing? Consider the lilies of the field, how they grow; they neither toil nor spin; 29 yet I tell you, even Solomon in all his glory was not arrayed like one of these. 30 But if God so clothes the grass of the field, which today is alive and tomorrow is thrown into the oven, will he not much more clothe you, O men of little faith? 31 Therefore do not be anxious, saying, 'What shall we eat?' or 'What shall we drink?' or 'What shall we wear?' 32 For the Gentiles seek all these things; and your heavenly Father knows that you need them all. 33 But seek first his kingdom and his righteousness, and all these things shall be yours as well.

34 "Therefore do not be anxious about tomorrow, for tomorrow will be anxious for itself. Let the day's own trouble be sufficient for the day.

7 "Judge not, that you be not judged. 2 For with the judgment you pronounce you will be judged, and the measure you give will be the measure you get. 3 Why do you see the speck that is in your brother's eye, but do not notice the log that is in your own eye? 4 Or how can you say to your brother,

m Or our bread for the morrow
n Or the evil one. Other authorities, some ancient, add, in some form, *For thine is the kingdom and the power and the glory, for ever. Amen.*
o Or worm
x Mammon is a Semitic word for money or riches
p Or to his stature

Col.3.13. **16–18**: Acceptable fasting (Is.58.5). **19–21**: The uselessness of trusting in worldly goods (Jas.5.2–3). **22–23**: Lk.11.34–36. **24**: Lk.16.13. **25–33**: Lk.12.22–31. **25**: Lk.10.41; 12.11; Phil.4.6. **27**: A *cubit*, about 18 inches. "Cubit" may be used figuratively of length of life (see Ps.39.5 for a similar usage); or in the literal sense Jesus could note that growing in stature (see note *p*) is natural to life and beyond control by anxiety. **29**: 1 Kg.10.4–7. **30**: *Men of little faith* are unwilling to rest in the assurance that God cares about their lives (8.26; 14.31; 16.8). **33**: Mk.10.29–30; Lk.18.29–30.

'Let me take the speck out of your eye,' when there is the log in your own eye? [5] You hypocrite, first take the log out of your own eye, and then you will see clearly to take the speck out of your brother's eye.

6 "Do not give dogs what is holy; and do not throw your pearls before swine, lest they trample them under foot and turn to attack you.

7 "Ask, and it will be given you; seek, and you will find; knock, and it will be opened to you. [8] For every one who asks receives, and he who seeks finds, and to him who knocks it will be opened. [9] Or what man of you, if his son asks him for bread, will give him a stone? [10] Or if he asks for a fish, will give him a serpent? [11] If you then, who are evil, know how to give good gifts to your children, how much more will your Father who is in heaven give good things to those who ask him! [12] So whatever you wish that men would do to you, do so to them; for this is the law and the prophets.

13 "Enter by the narrow gate; for the gate is wide and the way is easy,[q] that leads to destruction, and those who enter by it are many. [14] For the gate is narrow and the way is hard, that leads to life, and those who find it are few.

15 "Beware of false prophets, who come to you in sheep's clothing but inwardly are ravenous wolves. [16] You will know them by their fruits. Are grapes gathered from thorns, or figs from thistles? [17] So, every sound tree bears good fruit, but the bad tree bears evil fruit. [18] A sound tree cannot bear evil fruit, nor can a bad tree bear good fruit. [19] Every tree that does not bear good fruit is cut down and thrown into the fire. [20] Thus you will know them by their fruits.

21 "Not every one who says to me, 'Lord, Lord,' shall enter the kingdom of heaven, but he who does the will of my Father who is in heaven. [22] On that day many will say to me, 'Lord, Lord, did we not prophesy in your name, and cast out demons in your name, and do many mighty works in your name?' [23] And then will I declare to them, 'I never knew you; depart from me, you evildoers.'

24 "Every one then who hears these words of mine and does them will be like a wise man who built his house upon the rock; [25] and the rain fell, and the floods came, and the winds blew and beat upon that house, but it did not fall, because it had been founded on the rock. [26] And every one who hears these words of mine and does not do them will be like a foolish man who built his house upon the sand; [27] and the rain fell, and the floods came, and the winds blew and beat against that house, and it fell; and great was the fall of it."

28 And when Jesus finished these sayings, the crowds were astonished at his teaching, [29] for he taught them as one who had authority, and not as their scribes.

8 When he came down from the mountain, great crowds followed him; [2] and behold, a leper came to him

q Other ancient authorities read *for the way is wide and easy*

7.1–27: Illustrations of the practical meaning of Jesus message. 1–5: Judgment of others (Lk.6.37–38,41–42; Mk.4.24; Rom.2.1; 14.10). **7–11:** Encouragement to prayer (6.8; Mk.11.23–24; Jn.15.7; 1 Jn.3.22; 5.14). **12:** Lk.6.31; Mt.22.39–40; Rom.13.8–10. **13–14:** Lk.13.23–24; Jer.21.8; Ps. 1; Dt.30.19; Jn.10.7; 14.6. **15–20:** Lk.6.43–45. **15:** 24.11,24; Ezek.22.27; 1 Jn.4.1; Jn.10.12. *Sheep* often symbolize a group of followers in a religious sense (Ezek.34.1–24; Lk. 12.32). **16:** 3.8; 12.33–35; Lk.6.43–45. **19:** 3.10; Lk.13.6–9; Jas.3.10–12. **22:** *That day,* the day of judgment. Jesus speaks as the divine judge. **24–27:** Lk.6.47–49; Jas.1.22–25. **28:** *When Jesus finished these sayings,* this (or a similar) formula marks the conclusion of each of the five main discourses in the gospel (see Introduction and 11.1; 13.53; 19.1; 26.1). **29:** *Unlike their scribes,* Jesus speaks on his own responsibility without appeal to traditional authority (Mk.1.22; 11.18; Lk.4.32).

8.1–9.38: Events in Galilee. 8.2–4: Mk.1.40–44; Lk.5.12–14. *Leprosy,* a skin disorder of an uncertain nature. Several diseases were possibly referred to by this name (see Lev.13.1–59 n.;

and knelt before him, saying, "Lord, if you will, you can make me clean." [3] And he stretched out his hand and touched him, saying, "I will; be clean." And immediately his leprosy was cleansed. [4] And Jesus said to him, "See that you say nothing to any one; but go, show yourself to the priest, and offer the gift that Moses commanded, for a proof to the people."[r]

5 As he entered Caper'na-um, a centurion came forward to him, beseeching him [6] and saying, "Lord, my servant is lying paralyzed at home, in terrible distress." [7] And he said to him, "I will come and heal him." [8] But the centurion answered him, "Lord, I am not worthy to have you come under my roof; but only say the word, and my servant will be healed. [9] For I am a man under authority, with soldiers under me; and I say to one, 'Go,' and he goes, and to another, 'Come,' and he comes, and to my slave, 'Do this,' and he does it." [10] When Jesus heard him, he marveled, and said to those who followed him, "Truly, I say to you, not even[s] in Israel have I found such faith. [11] I tell you, many will come from east and west and sit at table with Abraham, Isaac, and Jacob in the kingdom of heaven, [12] while the sons of the kingdom will be thrown into the outer darkness; there men will weep and gnash their teeth." [13] And to the centurion Jesus said, "Go; be it done for you as you have believed." And the servant was healed at that very moment.

14 And when Jesus entered Peter's house, he saw his mother-in-law lying sick with a fever; [15] he touched her hand, and the fever left her, and she rose and served him. [16] That evening they brought to him many who were possessed with demons; and he cast out the spirits with a word, and healed all who were sick. [17] This was to fulfil what was spoken by the prophet Isaiah, "He took our infirmities and bore our diseases."

18 Now when Jesus saw great crowds around him, he gave orders to go over to the other side. [19] And a scribe came up and said to him, "Teacher, I will follow you wherever you go." [20] And Jesus said to him, "Foxes have holes, and birds of the air have nests; but the Son of man has nowhere to lay his head." [21] Another of the disciples said to him, "Lord, let me first go and bury my father." [22] But Jesus said to him, "Follow me, and leave the dead to bury their own dead."

23 And when he got into the boat, his disciples followed him. [24] And behold, there arose a great storm on the sea, so that the boat was being swamped by the waves; but he was asleep. [25] And they went and woke him, saying, "Save, Lord; we are perishing." [26] And he said to them, "Why are you afraid, O men of little faith?" Then he rose and rebuked the winds and the sea; and there was a great calm. [27] And the men marveled, saying, "What sort of man is this, that even winds and sea obey him?"

28 And when he came to the other side, to the country of the Gadarenes,[t]

r Greek *to them*
s Other ancient authorities read *with no one*
t Other ancient authorities read *Gergesenes;* some, *Gerasenes*

Num.5.1–4). Its presence excluded the sufferer from associating with others. *Make me clean,* the leper seeks not merely healing but the freedom to rejoin the Jewish community. **4:** Lev. 14.2–32. **5–13:** Lk.7.1–10; Jn.4.46–53. The *centurion,* a non-Jewish military officer, is convinced that diseases are as obedient to Jesus as soldiers are to him. **10:** *Faith* refers to the centurion's trust and recognition of Jesus' power (v. 13; Mk.11.23 n., 24 n.). **11–12:** See Lk. 14.15 n.; Is.49.12; 59.19; Mt.13.42,50; 22.13; 24.51; 25.30. **14–17:** Mk.1.29–34; Lk.4.38–41. **16:** *Demons,* see 4.24 n.; 12.22 n.; Lk.4.33 n.; 7.33 n.; 13.16 n. **17:** Is.53.4. **18–22:** Mk.4.35; Lk.8.22; 9.57–60. **18:** *The other side,* the eastern shore of the Sea of Galilee. **20:** *Son of man,* see Mk.2.10 n. **22:** *Follow me,* Jesus implies that obedience to his call must take precedence over every other duty or love (compare 10.37). *Leave the dead,* i.e. the spiritually dead, who are not alive to the greater demands of the kingdom of God. **23–27:** Mk.4.36–41; Lk.8.22–24. **25:** See Lk.8.24 n. **28–34:** Mk.5.1–20; Lk.8.26–39. **31:** See v. 16 n.

two demoniacs met him, coming out of the tombs, so fierce that no one could pass that way. [29] And behold, they cried out, "What have you to do with us, O Son of God? Have you come here to torment us before the time?" [30] Now a herd of many swine was feeding at some distance from them. [31] And the demons begged him, "If you cast us out, send us away into the herd of swine." [32] And he said to them, "Go." So they came out and went into the swine; and behold, the whole herd rushed down the steep bank into the sea, and perished in the waters. [33] The herdsmen fled, and going into the city they told everything, and what had happened to the demoniacs. [34] And behold, all the city came out to meet Jesus; and when they saw him, they begged him to leave their neighborhood.

9 And getting into a boat he crossed over and came to his own city. [2] And behold, they brought to him a paralytic, lying on his bed; and when Jesus saw their faith he said to the paralytic, "Take heart, my son; your sins are forgiven." [3] And behold, some of the scribes said to themselves, "This man is blaspheming." [4] But Jesus, knowing[u] their thoughts, said, "Why do you think evil in your hearts? [5] For which is easier, to say, 'Your sins are forgiven,' or to say, 'Rise and walk'? [6] But that you may know that the Son of man has authority on earth to forgive sins"–he then said to the paralytic– "Rise, take up your bed and go home." [7] And he rose and went home. [8] When the crowds saw it, they were afraid, and they glorified God, who had given such authority to men.

9 As Jesus passed on from there, he saw a man called Matthew sitting at the tax office; and he said to him, "Follow me." And he rose and followed him.

10 And as he sat at table[v] in the house, behold, many tax collectors and sinners came and sat down with Jesus and his disciples. [11] And when the Pharisees saw this, they said to his disciples, "Why does your teacher eat with tax collectors and sinners?" [12] But when he heard it, he said, "Those who are well have no need of a physician, but those who are sick. [13] Go and learn what this means, 'I desire mercy, and not sacrifice.' For I came not to call the righteous, but sinners."

14 Then the disciples of John came to him, saying, "Why do we and the Pharisees fast,[w] but your disciples do not fast?" [15] And Jesus said to them, "Can the wedding guests mourn as long as the bridegroom is with them? The days will come, when the bridegroom is taken away from them, and then they will fast. [16] And no one puts a piece of unshrunk cloth on an old garment, for the patch tears away from the garment, and a worse tear is made. [17] Neither is new wine put into old wineskins; if it is, the skins burst, and the wine is spilled, and the skins are destroyed; but new wine is put into fresh wineskins, and so both are preserved."

18 While he was thus speaking to them, behold, a ruler came in and knelt before him, saying, "My daughter has just died; but come and lay your hand on her, and she will live." [19] And Jesus rose and followed him, with his disciples. [20] And behold, a woman who had suffered from a hemorrhage for twelve years came up behind him and touched the fringe of his garment; [21] for she

u Other ancient authorities read *seeing*
v Greek *reclined*
w Other ancient authorities add *much* or *often*

9.1–8: Healing a paralytic (Mk.2.1–12; Lk.5.17–26). **1:** *His own city,* Capernaum. **8:** 7.28–29. **9–13:** Mk.2.13–17; Lk.5.27–32. **10:** Lk.7.34; 15.1–2. **13:** Hos.6.6; Mt.12.7; 15.2–6. Jesus uses a Biblical quotation to challenge a conventional religious idea (see Lk.5.32 n.). **14–17:** Mk.2.18–22; Lk.5.33–39. **15:** Jesus recognizes the principle of fasting, but denies that it fits the circumstances of his life. **16–17:** The two pictorial sayings defend the practices of John's disciples and the practices of his own disciples; Jesus insists that the two ways should not be joined. **18–26:** Mk.5.21–43; Lk.8.40–56. **18:** *A ruler,* a leader in a synagogue. **21:** The Greek word here translated *be made well* (also v. 22; Mk.5.23,28,34; 10.52; Lk.8.36,48,50;

said to herself, "If I only touch his garment, I shall be made well." ²² Jesus turned, and seeing her he said, "Take heart, daughter; your faith has made you well." And instantly the woman was made well. ²³ And when Jesus came to the ruler's house, and saw the flute players, and the crowd making a tumult, ²⁴ he said, "Depart; for the girl is not dead but sleeping." And they laughed at him. ²⁵ But when the crowd had been put outside, he went in and took her by the hand, and the girl arose. ²⁶ And the report of this went through all that district.

27 And as Jesus passed on from there, two blind men followed him, crying aloud, "Have mercy on us, Son of David." ²⁸ When he entered the house, the blind men came to him; and Jesus said to them, "Do you believe that I am able to do this?" They said to him, "Yes, Lord." ²⁹ Then he touched their eyes, saying, "According to your faith be it done to you." ³⁰ And their eyes were opened. And Jesus sternly charged them, "See that no one knows it." ³¹ But they went away and spread his fame through all that district.

32 As they were going away, behold, a dumb demoniac was brought to him. ³³ And when the demon had been cast out, the dumb man spoke; and the crowds marveled, saying, "Never was anything like this seen in Israel." ³⁴ But the Pharisees said, "He casts out demons by the prince of demons."[a]

35 And Jesus went about all the cities and villages, teaching in their synagogues and preaching the gospel of the kingdom, and healing every disease and every infirmity. ³⁶ When he saw the crowds, he had compassion for them, because they were harassed and helpless, like sheep without a shepherd. ³⁷ Then he said to his disciples, "The harvest is plentiful, but the laborers are few; ³⁸ pray therefore the Lord of the harvest to send out laborers into his harvest."

10 And he called to him his twelve disciples and gave them authority over unclean spirits, to cast them out, and to heal every disease and every infirmity. ² The names of the twelve apostles are these: first, Simon, who is called Peter, and Andrew his brother; James the son of Zeb'edee, and John his brother; ³ Philip and Bartholomew; Thomas and Matthew the tax collector; James the son of Alphaeus, and Thaddaeus;[x] ⁴ Simon the Cananaean, and Judas Iscariot, who betrayed him.

5 These twelve Jesus sent out, charging them, "Go nowhere among the Gentiles, and enter no town of the Samaritans, ⁶ but go rather to the lost sheep of the house of Israel. ⁷ And preach as you go, saying, 'The kingdom of heaven is at hand.' ⁸ Heal the sick, raise the dead, cleanse lepers, cast out demons. You received without paying, give without pay. ⁹ Take no gold, nor silver, nor copper in your belts, ¹⁰ no bag for your journey, nor two tunics, nor sandals, nor a staff; for the laborer deserves his food. ¹¹ And whatever town or village you enter, find out who is worthy in it, and stay with him until

a Other ancient authorities omit this verse
x Other ancient authorities read *Lebbaeus* or *Lebbaeus called Thaddaeus*

17.19; 18.42) carries with it the idea of rescue from impending destruction or from a superior power. **22:** Mk.11.23 n., 24 n. **23:** Jer.9.17–18. **24:** Jesus speaks in the perspective of the kingdom of God in which physical death is not finally destructive of a person's existence but is a temporary cessation of personal activity (and analogous to sleeping). Verse 18 and the crowd's attitude clearly assert the fact of physical death. **27–31:** 20.29–34. **29:** 9.22 n. **30:** 8.4. **32–34:** 12.22–24; Lk.11.14–15. **34:** See 12.24 n.; Mk.3.22 n.; Jn.7.20. **35–38:** 4.23–25. **36:** Mk.6.34; Mt.14.14; 15.32; Num.27.17; Ezek.34.1–6; Zech.10.2.

    10.1–11.1: Commissioning and instruction of the Twelve. 10.1–4: Mk.6.7; 3.13–19; Lk.9.1; 6.12–16. **1:** *Unclean spirits*, see Mk.1.23 n. **5–15:** Mk.6.8–11; Lk.9.2–5; 10.3–12. **5:** 15.21–28; Lk.9.52; Jn.4.9. **6:** 15.24. **7:** The primary message. Through acceptance, or at least openness to this message and its bearer, healing would follow (see 4.17 n.; 4.23; 9.21,35). **9:** Lk.22.35–36. **10:** *Tunic*, a short-sleeved garment of knee-length, held in at the waist by a girdle (Mk.1.6).

you depart. [12] As you enter the house, salute it. [13] And if the house is worthy, let your peace come upon it; but if it is not worthy, let your peace return to you. [14] And if any one will not receive you or listen to your words, shake off the dust from your feet as you leave that house or town. [15] Truly, I say to you, it shall be more tolerable on the day of judgment for the land of Sodom and Gomor'rah than for that town.

16 "Behold, I send you out as sheep in the midst of wolves; so be wise as serpents and innocent as doves. [17] Beware of men; for they will deliver you up to councils, and flog you in their synagogues, [18] and you will be dragged before governors and kings for my sake, to bear testimony before them and the Gentiles. [19] When they deliver you up, do not be anxious how you are to speak or what you are to say; for what you are to say will be given to you in that hour; [20] for it is not you who speak, but the Spirit of your Father speaking through you. [21] Brother will deliver up brother to death, and the father his child, and children will rise against parents and have them put to death; [22] and you will be hated by all for my name's sake. But he who endures to the end will be saved. [23] When they persecute you in one town, flee to the next; for truly, I say to you, you will not have gone through all the towns of Israel, before the Son of man comes.

24 "A disciple is not above his teacher, nor a servant[y] above his master; [25] it is enough for the disciple to be like his teacher, and the servant[y] like his master. If they have called the master of the house Be-el'zebul, how much more will they malign those of his household.

26 "So have no fear of them; for nothing is covered that will not be revealed, or hidden that will not be known. [27] What I tell you in the dark, utter in the light; and what you hear whispered, proclaim upon the housetops. [28] And do not fear those who kill the body but cannot kill the soul; rather fear him who can destroy both soul and body in hell.[z] [29] Are not two sparrows sold for a penny? And not one of them will fall to the ground without your Father's will. [30] But even the hairs of your head are all numbered. [31] Fear not, therefore; you are of more value than many sparrows. [32] So every one who acknowledges me before men, I also will acknowledge before my Father who is in heaven; [33] but whoever denies me before men, I also will deny before my Father who is in heaven.

34 "Do not think that I have come to bring peace on earth; I have not come to bring peace, but a sword. [35] For I have come to set a man against his father, and a daughter against her mother, and a daughter-in-law against her mother-in-law; [36] and a man's foes will be those of his own household. [37] He who loves father or mother more than me is not worthy of me; and he who loves son or daughter more than me is not worthy of me; [38] and he who does not take his cross and follow me is not worthy of me. [39] He who finds his life will lose it, and he who loses his life for my sake will find it.

40 "He who receives you receives me, and he who receives me receives

[y] Or *slave*   [z] Greek *Gehenna*

Deserves, 1 Cor.9.14. **15:** Life and death depend on man's response to God's kingdom. *Sodom and Gomorrah* illustrate God's judgment on wickedness (Gen.18.16–33; ch. 19). **16–25:** 24.9,13; Mk.13.9–13; Lk.21.12–17,19. **20:** Jn.16.7–11. **21:** 10.35–36; Lk.12.52–53. **22:** *My name's sake,* "because of me and my cause." **23:** The words stress the urgency of the disciples' task. **25:** Lk.6.40; Jn.13.16; 15.20; Mt.9.34; 12.24; Mk.3.22. **26–33:** Lk.12.2–9. **28:** Heb.10.31. **29–33:** 6.26–33. **29:** See Lk.12.6 n. **31:** 12.12. **32–33:** Jesus claims to mediate God's will; a favorable response to him is a response to God (compare vv. 40–42). **34–36:** Lk.12.51–53. **35:** Mic.7.6. **37–39:** 16.24–25; Mk.8.34–35; Lk.9.23–24; 14.26–27; 17.33. **37:** Compare the stronger form of expression in Lk.14.26. **38:** A *cross,* a Roman means of execution, was carried by the condemned man to the scene of death. Jesus sees that the acceptance of his message with its promise also brings seeming destruction (v. 34). Only those who in faith accept the threat of destruction

him who sent me. ⁴¹ He who receives a prophet because he is a prophet shall receive a prophet's reward, and he who receives a righteous man because he is a righteous man shall receive a righteous man's reward. ⁴² And whoever gives to one of these little ones even a cup of cold water because he is a disciple, truly, I say to you, he shall not lose his reward."

‖‖ And when Jesus had finished instructing his twelve disciples, he went on from there to teach and preach in their cities.

2 Now when John heard in prison about the deeds of the Christ, he sent word by his disciples ³ and said to him, "Are you he who is to come, or shall we look for another?" ⁴ And Jesus answered them, "Go and tell John what you hear and see: ⁵ the blind receive their sight and the lame walk, lepers are cleansed and the deaf hear, and the dead are raised up, and the poor have good news preached to them. ⁶ And blessed is he who takes no offense at me."

7 As they went away, Jesus began to speak to the crowds concerning John: "What did you go out into the wilderness to behold? A reed shaken by the wind? ⁸ Why then did you go out? To see a man*a* clothed in soft raiment? Behold, those who wear soft raiment are in kings' houses. ⁹ Why then did you go out? To see a prophet?*b* Yes, I tell you, and more than a prophet. ¹⁰ This is he of whom it is written,

'Behold, I send my messenger before thy face,

who shall prepare thy way before thee.'

¹¹ Truly, I say to you, among those born of women there has risen no one greater than John the Baptist; yet he who is least in the kingdom of heaven is greater than he. ¹² From the days of John the Baptist until now the kingdom of heaven has suffered violence,*c* and men of violence take it by force. ¹³ For all the prophets and the law prophesied until John; ¹⁴ and if you are willing to accept it, he is Eli'jah who is to come. ¹⁵ He who has ears to hear,*d* let him hear.

16 "But to what shall I compare this generation? It is like children sitting in the market places and calling to their playmates,

¹⁷ 'We piped to you, and you did not dance;

we wailed, and you did not mourn.'

¹⁸ For John came neither eating nor drinking, and they say, 'He has a demon'; ¹⁹ the Son of man came eating and drinking, and they say, 'Behold, a glutton and a drunkard, a friend of tax collectors and sinners!' Yet wisdom is justified by her deeds."*e*

20 Then he began to upbraid the cities where most of his mighty works had been done, because they did not repent. ²¹ "Woe to you, Chora'zin! woe to you, Beth-sa'ida! for if the mighty works done in you had been done in Tyre and Sidon, they would have repented long ago in sackcloth

a Or *What then did you go out to see? A man . . .*
b Other ancient authorities read *What then did you go out to see? A prophet?*
c Or *has been coming violently*
d Other ancient authorities omit *to hear*
e Other ancient authorities read *children* (Lk 7.35)

---

will find life (v. 39; 5.11–12; 16.24; Mk.8.34–35; 10.29–31; Lk.9.24–25; 14.27; 17.33; Jn.12.25). **42**: *Little ones*, see 18.6 n. **11.1**: *Finished*, see 7.28 n.
   11.2–12.50: Narratives illustrating the authority claimed by Jesus. 11.2–19: Jesus and John (Lk.7.18–35; 16.16). **2–3**: *The Christ*, i.e. the Messiah who *is to come*. **4–5**: Jesus performs the works of the predicted Messiah (Is.29.18–19; 35.5–6; 61.1; compare Lk.4.18–19). **6**: Jesus invites John to answer his own question, basing his decision on what he hears of Jesus' activities interpreted in comparison with Isaiah's words (compare Lk.4.17–21). **7–15**: John was important because he introduced the new manifestation (or "coming") of God's kingdom. **10**: From Mal.3.1; compare Mk.1.2. **14**: Mal.4.5; Lk.1.17; Mk.9.11–13. Biblical prophecy depends on human acceptance of God's terms for fulfilment. If John's message were accepted, his activity would become that foretold in Elijah's name. Jesus seems not to have expected the literal return of *Elijah* (17.10–13; Mk.9.9–13). **18**: See Lk.7.33 n. **23**: Is.14.13,15. **25–30**: Lk.10.21–

and ashes. ²² But I tell you, it shall be more tolerable on the day of judgment for Tyre and Sidon than for you. ²³ And you, Caper'na-um, will you be exalted to heaven? You shall be brought down to Hades. For if the mighty works done in you had been done in Sodom, it would have remained until this day. ²⁴ But I tell you that it shall be more tolerable on the day of judgment for the land of Sodom than for you."

25 At that time Jesus declared, "I thank thee, Father, Lord of heaven and earth, that thou hast hidden these things from the wise and understanding and revealed them to babes; ²⁶ yea, Father, for such was thy gracious will.ᶠ ²⁷ All things have been delivered to me by my Father; and no one knows the Son except the Father, and no one knows the Father except the Son and any one to whom the Son chooses to reveal him. ²⁸ Come to me, all who labor and are heavy laden, and I will give you rest. ²⁹ Take my yoke upon you, and learn from me; for I am gentle and lowly in heart, and you will find rest for your souls. ³⁰ For my yoke is easy, and my burden is light."

12 At that time Jesus went through the grainfields on the sabbath; his disciples were hungry, and they began to pluck heads of grain and to eat. ² But when the Pharisees saw it, they said to him, "Look, your disciples are doing what is not lawful to do on the sabbath." ³ He said to them, "Have you not read what David did, when he was hungry, and those who were with him:

4 how he entered the house of God and ate the bread of the Presence, which it was not lawful for him to eat nor for those who were with him, but only for the priests? ⁵ Or have you not read in the law how on the sabbath the priests in the temple profane the sabbath, and are guiltless? ⁶ I tell you, something greater than the temple is here. ⁷ And if you had known what this means, 'I desire mercy, and not sacrifice,' you would not have condemned the guiltless. ⁸ For the Son of man is lord of the sabbath."

9 And he went on from there, and entered their synagogue. ¹⁰ And behold, there was a man with a withered hand. And they asked him, "Is it lawful to heal on the sabbath?" so that they might accuse him. ¹¹ He said to them, "What man of you, if he has one sheep and it falls into a pit on the sabbath, will not lay hold of it and lift it out? ¹² Of how much more value is a man than a sheep! So it is lawful to do good on the sabbath." ¹³ Then he said to the man, "Stretch out your hand." And the man stretched it out, and it was restored, whole like the other. ¹⁴ But the Pharisees went out and took counsel against him, how to destroy him.

15 Jesus, aware of this, withdrew from there. And many followed him, and he healed them all, ¹⁶ and ordered them not to make him known. ¹⁷ This was to fulfil what was spoken by the prophet Isaiah:

18 "Behold, my servant whom I have chosen,

f Or *so it was well-pleasing before thee*

---

22. **25:** 9.13; 10.42; see 16.17 n.; Lk.10.21–22; 24.16. **27:** Jesus claimed a special relation to God which he could share with others (Jn.3.35; 13.3). **29:** The rabbis spoke of the *yoke* of the Law. Jesus regarded his claim as more demanding and more rewarding (5.17–20).

12.1–14: Jesus and sabbath laws (Mk.2.23–3.6; Lk.6.1–11). **1:** Dt.23.25. **2:** The objection rested on the traditional interpretation that plucking grain by hand was an activity forbidden by Ex.20.8–11. **3–4:** 1 Sam.21.1–6; Lev.24.5–9. **5:** Num.28.9–10. **6:** Since no penalty was exacted from those who set aside provisions of the Law for the sake of some human need or some more significant service to God, Jesus' disciples eat because of their need and serve him who is greater than the institutions of the Law (see vv. 41–42). **7:** Hos.6.6; Mt.9.13. **8:** Jesus claims, by virtue of his mission as the Messiah, authority over man's obedience to God (11.27; Jn.5.1–18). **11–12:** The rabbis agreed with the principle of attending to accidental injury and danger on the sabbath, but they thought that chronic conditions should wait (Lk.13.14). For Jesus it was important to restore a person to useful life. **12:** 10.31.

   12.15–21: Work of healing (Mk.3.7–12; Lk.6.17–19; 4.40). **17–21:** Is.42.1–4.

my beloved with whom my soul
   is well pleased.
I will put my Spirit upon him,
   and he shall proclaim justice to the
      Gentiles.
¹⁹ He will not wrangle or cry aloud,
   nor will any one hear his voice
      in the streets;
²⁰ he will not break a bruised reed
   or quench a smoldering wick,
      till he brings justice to victory;
²¹   and in his name will the
         Gentiles hope."

22 Then a blind and dumb demoniac was brought to him, and he healed
him, so that the dumb man spoke and
saw. ²³ And all the people were
amazed, and said, "Can this be the
Son of David?" ²⁴ But when the
Pharisees heard it they said, "It is only
by Be-el′zebul, the prince of demons,
that this man casts out demons."
²⁵ Knowing their thoughts, he said to
them, "Every kingdom divided against
itself is laid waste, and no city or house
divided against itself will stand; ²⁶ and
if Satan casts out Satan, he is divided
against himself; how then will his kingdom stand? ²⁷ And if I cast out demons
by Be-el′zebul, by whom do your sons
cast them out? Therefore they shall be
your judges. ²⁸ But if it is by the Spirit
of God that I cast out demons, then
the kingdom of God has come upon
you. ²⁹ Or how can one enter a strong
man's house and plunder his goods, unless he first binds the strong man? Then
indeed he may plunder his house.
³⁰ He who is not with me is against me,

and he who does not gather with me
scatters. ³¹ Therefore I tell you, every
sin and blasphemy will be forgiven
men, but the blasphemy against the
Spirit will not be forgiven. ³² And whoever says a word against the Son of
man will be forgiven; but whoever
speaks against the Holy Spirit will not
be forgiven, either in this age or in
the age to come.

33 "Either make the tree good, and
its fruit good; or make the tree bad,
and its fruit bad; for the tree is known
by its fruit. ³⁴ You brood of vipers!
how can you speak good, when you are
evil? For out of the abundance of the
heart the mouth speaks. ³⁵ The good
man out of his good treasure brings
forth good, and the evil man out of his
evil treasure brings forth evil. ³⁶ I
tell you, on the day of judgment men
will render account for every careless
word they utter; ³⁷ for by your words
you will be justified, and by your words
you will be condemned."

38 Then some of the scribes and
Pharisees said to him, "Teacher, we
wish to see a sign from you." ³⁹ But
he answered them, "An evil and adulterous generation seeks for a sign; but
no sign shall be given to it except the
sign of the prophet Jonah. ⁴⁰ For as
Jonah was three days and three nights
in the belly of the whale, so will the
Son of man be three days and three
nights in the heart of the earth. ⁴¹ The
men of Nin′eveh will arise at the judgment with this generation and condemn
it; for they repented at the preaching of

12.22–37: Sources of Jesus' power (Mk.3.20–30; Lk.11.14–23; 12.10). **22–24**: The dumbness
here said to be caused by demonic possession is said in Lk.11.14 to describe the demon itself.
The Biblical writers speak either of *healing* the victim or casting out the demon (v. 24; 9.32–33;
Lk.11.14–15). **23**: *Son of David*, a title of the Messiah (21.9). **24**: The issue is how to account
for Jesus' manifest power. The Pharisees attribute it to evil forces hostile to mankind (see
Lk.7.33 n.). *Beelzebul*, see 2 Kg.1.2 n.; Mk.3.22 n. **27**: *Your sons*, your disciples (compare
1 Pet.5.13). Exorcising demons was not limited to Jesus and his followers (7.22–23; Mk.9.38;
Acts 19.13–19). **28**: Lk.4.18–20. **31–32**: The unforgivable sin is the utter rebellion against God
that denies him as the doer of his own acts (Lk.12.10). **32**: Mk.3.28–30. **33–36**: 7.16–20; Mk.
7.14–23; Lk.6.43–45. **33**: *Make*, recognize that fruit and tree will be alike (Jas.3.11–12). **36**:
Careless, useless; "barren" in Jas.2.20. **37**: Compare Rom.2.6.
   12.38–42: Request for a sign (Lk.11.16,29–32). **39**: *Adulterous* was used by Old Testament
prophets to describe Israel's turning away from God (Jer.3.8; Ezek.23.37; Hos.2.2–10). *Sign*,
compare v. 40. **40**: *Whale*, "sea monster" (compare Jon.1.17). **41**: Jon.3.5; Mt.11.20–24; 12.6.
42: 1 Kg.10.1–10; 2 Chr.9.1–9.

Jonah, and behold, something greater than Jonah is here. [42] The queen of the South will arise at the judgment with this generation and condemn it; for she came from the ends of the earth to hear the wisdom of Solomon, and behold, something greater than Solomon is here.

43 "When the unclean spirit has gone out of a man, he passes through waterless places seeking rest, but he finds none. [44] Then he says, 'I will return to my house from which I came.' And when he comes he finds it empty, swept, and put in order. [45] Then he goes and brings with him seven other spirits more evil than himself, and they enter and dwell there; and the last state of that man becomes worse than the first. So shall it be also with this evil generation."

46 While he was still speaking to the people, behold, his mother and his brothers stood outside, asking to speak to him.[g] [48] But he replied to the man who told him, "Who is my mother, and who are my brothers?" [49] And stretching out his hand toward his disciples, he said, "Here are my mother and my brothers! [50] For whoever does the will of my Father in heaven is my brother, and sister, and mother."

13 That same day Jesus went out of the house and sat beside the sea. [2] And great crowds gathered about him, so that he got into a boat and sat there; and the whole crowd stood on the beach. [3] And he told them many things in parables, saying: "A sower went out to sow. [4] And as he sowed, some seeds fell along the path, and the birds came and devoured them. [5] Other seeds fell on rocky ground, where they had not much soil, and immediately they sprang up, since they had no depth of soil, [6] but when the sun rose they were scorched; and since they had no root they withered away. [7] Other seeds fell upon thorns, and the thorns grew up and choked them. [8] Other seeds fell on good soil and brought forth grain, some a hundredfold, some sixty, some thirty. [9] He who has ears,[h] let him hear."

10 Then the disciples came and said to him, "Why do you speak to them in parables?" [11] And he answered them, "To you it has been given to know the secrets of the kingdom of heaven, but to them it has not been given. [12] For to him who has will more be given, and he will have abundance; but from him who has not, even what he has will be taken away. [13] This is why I speak to them in parables, because seeing they do not see, and hearing they do not hear, nor do they understand. [14] With them indeed is fulfilled the prophecy of Isaiah which says:

'You shall indeed hear but never understand,

g Other ancient authorities insert verse 47, *Some one told him, "Your mother and your brothers are standing outside, asking to speak to you"*
h Other ancient authorities add here and in verse 43 *to hear*

12.43–45: The return of the unclean spirit (Lk.11.24–26; see Mk.1.23 n.). **43:** Waterless places, or deserts, supposed to be the favorite abode of demons (compare Is.13.21–22; 34.14). **44:** *My house*, the man himself. *Empty*, though evil has been temporarily expelled, nothing good has been put in its place.

12.46–50: Jesus' true family (Mk.3.31–35; Lk.8.19–21). See 13.55 n.

13.1–52: Teaching in parables (Mk.4.1–34; Lk.8.4–18; 13.18–21). **1:** *The sea*, of Galilee. **3:** *Parables* are stories describing situations in everyday life which, as Jesus used them, convey a spiritual meaning. In general the teaching of each parable relates to a single point, and apart from this the details may, or may not, have a particular meaning. Jesus used this method of teaching because: (a) it gave vivid, memorable expression to his teachings; (b) it led those who heard to reflect on his words and bear responsibility for their decision to accept or oppose his claim; (c) it probably reduced specific grounds for contention by hostile listeners. **3b–8: The sower,** explained in vv. 18–23 (see Mk.4.1–9). **11:** The disciples heard and accepted the message about God's kingdom and by their faith had access to deeper understanding (see Mk.4.11 n.). **12:** 25.29; Mk.4.24–25; Lk.8.18; 19.26. **13:** The parables do not obscure truth but present it; men receive the message through their physical senses but do not comprehend (see 11.25 n.).

and you shall indeed see but never
perceive.
[15] For this people's heart has grown
dull,
and their ears are heavy of
hearing,
and their eyes they have closed,
lest they should perceive with their
eyes,
and hear with their ears,
and understand with their heart,
and turn for me to heal them.'
[16] But blessed are your eyes, for they
see, and your ears, for they hear.
[17] Truly, I say to you, many prophets
and righteous men longed to see what
you see, and did not see it, and to
hear what you hear, and did not hear
it.
18 "Hear then the parable of the
sower. [19] When any one hears the
word of the kingdom and does not
understand it, the evil one comes and
snatches away what is sown in his
heart; this is what was sown along the
path. [20] As for what was sown on rocky
ground, this is he who hears the word
and immediately receives it with joy;
[21] yet he has no root in himself, but
endures for a while, and when tribulation or persecution arises on account
of the word, immediately he falls away.[i]
[22] As for what was sown among thorns,
this is he who hears the word, but the
cares of the world and the delight in
riches choke the word, and it proves
unfruitful. [23] As for what was sown
on good soil, this is he who hears the
word and understands it; he indeed
bears fruit, and yields, in one case a
hundredfold, in another sixty, and in
another thirty."
24 Another parable he put before
them, saying, "The kingdom of heaven
may be compared to a man who sowed

good seed in his field; [25] but while men
were sleeping, his enemy came and
sowed weeds among the wheat, and
went away. [26] So when the plants came
up and bore grain, then the weeds appeared also. [27] And the servants[j] of
the householder came and said to him,
'Sir, did you not sow good seed in your
field? How then has it weeds?' [28] He
said to them, 'An enemy has done
this.' The servants[j] said to him, 'Then
do you want us to go and gather them?'
[29] But he said, 'No; lest in gathering
the weeds you root up the wheat along
with them. [30] Let both grow together
until the harvest; and at harvest time
I will tell the reapers, Gather the
weeds first and bind them in bundles to
be burned, but gather the wheat into
my barn.' "

31 Another parable he put before
them, saying, "The kingdom of heaven
is like a grain of mustard seed which a
man took and sowed in his field; [32] it
is the smallest of all seeds, but when
it has grown it is the greatest of shrubs
and becomes a tree, so that the birds
of the air come and make nests in its
branches."

33 He told them another parable.
"The kingdom of heaven is like leaven
which a woman took and hid in three
measures of flour, till it was all leavened."

34 All this Jesus said to the crowds
in parables; indeed he said nothing to
them without a parable. [35] This was
to fulfil what was spoken by the
prophet:[k]
"I will open my mouth in parables,
I will utter what has been hidden
since the foundation of the
world."

i Or *stumbles*
j Or *slaves*
k Other ancient authorities read *the prophet Isaiah*

14–15: Is.6.9–10; Mk.8.18; see Acts 28.26 n. 16–17: See Lk.10.23–24 n. 17: *See . . . hear*,
Jesus' message about God's kingdom. 18–23: Response to Jesus' message affected by the circumstances of human life. 22: 19.23. 24–30: **Weeds in the wheat.** God allows good and evil
to exist together until the close of human history (vv. 36–43). 31–32: **The mustard seed.** (Lk.
13.18–19). The beginnings of God's kingdom are small, but it has an inherent nature that will
grow to its intended end, startlingly different in size from its beginning. 32: Dan.4.12. 33:
Leaven (Lk.13.20–21). God's rule, like *leaven* working in a hidden way, will pervade man's life,
giving it a new quality. 35: *The prophet*, i.e. Asaph the seer (2 Chr.29.30), the author of Ps. 78,

36 Then he left the crowds and went into the house. And his disciples came to him, saying, "Explain to us the parable of the weeds of the field." 37 He answered, "He who sows the good seed is the Son of man; 38 the field is the world, and the good seed means the sons of the kingdom; the weeds are the sons of the evil one, 39 and the enemy who sowed them is the devil; the harvest is the close of the age, and the reapers are angels. 40 Just as the weeds are gathered and burned with fire, so will it be at the close of the age. 41 The Son of man will send his angels, and they will gather out of his kingdom all causes of sin and all evildoers, 42 and throw them into the furnace of fire; there men will weep and gnash their teeth. 43 Then the righteous will shine like the sun in the kingdom of their Father. He who has ears, let him hear.

44 "The kingdom of heaven is like treasure hidden in a field, which a man found and covered up; then in his joy he goes and sells all that he has and buys that field.

45 "Again, the kingdom of heaven is like a merchant in search of fine pearls, 46 who, on finding one pearl of great value, went and sold all that he had and bought it.

47 "Again, the kingdom of heaven is like a net which was thrown into the sea and gathered fish of every kind; 48 when it was full, men drew it ashore and sat down and sorted the good into vessels but threw away the bad. 49 So it will be at the close of the age. The angels will come out and separate the evil from the righteous, 50 and throw them into the furnace of fire; there men will weep and gnash their teeth.

51 "Have you understood all this?" They said to him, "Yes." 52 And he said to them, "Therefore every scribe who has been trained for the kingdom of heaven is like a householder who brings out of his treasure what is new and what is old."

53 And when Jesus had finished these parables, he went away from there, 54 and coming to his own country he taught them in their synagogue, so that they were astonished, and said, "Where did this man get this wisdom and these mighty works? 55 Is not this the carpenter's son? Is not his mother called Mary? And are not his brothers James and Joseph and Simon and Judas? 56 And are not all his sisters with us? Where then did this man get all this?" 57 And they took offense at him. But Jesus said to them, "A prophet is not without honor except in his own country and in his own house." 58 And he did not do many mighty works there, because of their unbelief.

14 At that time Herod the tetrarch heard about the fame of Jesus; 2 and he said to his servants, "This is John the Baptist, he has been raised from the dead; that is why these powers are at work in him." 3 For Herod had seized John and bound him and put him in prison, for the sake of Hero'-di-as, his brother Philip's wife;*l* 4 because John said to him, "It is not law-

l Other ancient authorities read *his brother's wife*

from which (v. 2) the quotation is taken. **42**: See Lk.12.49 n. **43**: Dan.12.3. **44–46: Hidden treasure and the pearl of great value. 44**: Some men respond in whole-hearted dedication to Jesus' message without any other thought than to have what it yields. **45–46**: Some men dedicate themselves to God's kingdom because, being able to judge the value of other claims being made on them, they value it more. **47–50: The dragnet. 52**: *Scribe*, an expert in the Mosaic law, having become a disciple of Jesus is able to preserve past insights and enlarge them.

13.53–17.27: Events of decisive acceptance or rejection of Jesus. 13.53–58: Rejection at home. 53: *Finished*, see 7.28 n. **54**: *His own country*, Nazareth (Lk.4.16,23). **55**: *Brothers*, regarded by Protestants as children of Mary, younger than Jesus. In Semitic usage, besides its ordinary meaning, the word *brothers* may also refer to persons of varying degrees of blood relationship; here (and in Mt. 12.46; Mk.3.31–32; 6.3; Lk.8.19–20; Jn.2.12; 7.3,5; Acts 1.14; 1 Cor.9.5; Gal.1.19) Catholic tradition regards them as relatives of Jesus, not blood brothers (see also Mt.1.25 n.; Lk.2.7 n.). **58**: See Mk.6.5–6 n.

14.1–12: Death of John (Mk.6.14–29; Lk.9.7–9). **1**: *Herod* Antipas, son of Herod the Great

ful for you to have her." 5 And though he wanted to put him to death, he feared the people, because they held him to be a prophet. 6 But when Herod's birthday came, the daughter of Hero'di-as danced before the company, and pleased Herod, 7 so that he promised with an oath to give her whatever she might ask. 8 Prompted by her mother, she said, "Give me the head of John the Baptist here on a platter." 9 And the king was sorry; but because of his oaths and his guests he commanded it to be given; 10 he sent and had John beheaded in the prison, 11 and his head was brought on a platter and given to the girl, and she brought it to her mother. 12 And his disciples came and took the body and buried it; and they went and told Jesus.

13 Now when Jesus heard this, he withdrew from there in a boat to a lonely place apart. But when the crowds heard it, they followed him on foot from the towns. 14 As he went ashore he saw a great throng; and he had compassion on them, and healed their sick. 15 When it was evening, the disciples came to him and said, "This is a lonely place, and the day is now over; send the crowds away to go into the villages and buy food for themselves." 16 Jesus said, "They need not go away; you give them something to eat." 17 They said to him, "We have only five loaves here and two fish." 18 And he said, "Bring them here to me." 19 Then he ordered the crowds to sit down on the grass; and taking the five loaves and the two fish he looked up to heaven, and blessed, and broke and gave the loaves to the disciples, and the disciples gave them to the crowds. 20 And they all ate and were satisfied. And they took up twelve baskets full of the broken pieces left over. 21 And

those who ate were about five thousand men, besides women and children.

22 Then he made the disciples get into the boat and go before him to the other side, while he dismissed the crowds. 23 And after he had dismissed the crowds, he went up on the mountain by himself to pray. When evening came, he was there alone, 24 but the boat by this time was many furlongs distant from the land,*m* beaten by the waves; for the wind was against them. 25 And in the fourth watch of the night he came to them, walking on the sea. 26 But when the disciples saw him walking on the sea, they were terrified, saying, "It is a ghost!" And they cried out for fear. 27 But immediately he spoke to them, saying, "Take heart, it is I; have no fear."

28 And Peter answered him, "Lord, if it is you, bid me come to you on the water." 29 He said, "Come." So Peter got out of the boat and walked on the water and came to Jesus; 30 but when he saw the wind,*n* he was afraid, and beginning to sink he cried out, "Lord, save me." 31 Jesus immediately reached out his hand and caught him, saying to him, "O man of little faith, why did you doubt?" 32 And when they got into the boat, the wind ceased. 33 And those in the boat worshiped him, saying, "Truly you are the Son of God."

34 And when they had crossed over, they came to land at Gennes'aret. 35 And when the men of that place recognized him, they sent round to all that region and brought to him all that were sick, 36 and besought him that they might only touch the fringe of his garment; and as many as touched it were made well.

m Other ancient authorities read *was out on the sea*
n Other ancient authorities read *strong wind*

Tetrarch, ruler of a minor political unit. **3:** *Philip*, not the tetrarch of Lk.3.1, but a half-brother of *Herod* Antipas. **4:** Lev.18.16; 20.21. **6:** *The daughter* was Salome (Josephus, *Ant*.xviii.5.4).
    14.13–21: Five thousand fed (Mk.6.30–44; Lk.9.10–17; Jn.6.1–13). **13:** After John's death Jesus faced a new stage in his life (compare his reaction to John's imprisonment, Mk.1.14–15). **14:** 20.25–28.
    14.22–36: Jesus walks on water (Mk.6.45–52; Jn.6.15–21). **24:** A *furlong*, about one-eighth of a mile. **25:** *The fourth watch*, see Mk.6.48 n. **26:** Lk.24.37. **33:** Mk.6.51–52.

15 Then Pharisees and scribes came
to Jesus from Jerusalem and
said, 2 "Why do your disciples transgress the tradition of the elders? For
they do not wash their hands when
they eat." 3 He answered them, "And
why do you transgress the commandment of God for the sake of your tradition? 4 For God commanded, 'Honor
your father and your mother,' and, 'He
who speaks evil of father or mother,
let him surely die.' 5 But you say, 'If
any one tells his father or his mother,
What you would have gained from me
is given to God,[o] he need not honor
his father.' 6 So, for the sake of your
tradition, you have made void the
word[p] of God. 7 You hypocrites!
Well did Isaiah prophesy of you, when
he said:
8 'This people honors me with their
lips,
but their heart is far from me;
9 in vain do they worship me,
teaching as doctrines the precepts of
men.' "
10 And he called the people to him
and said to them, "Hear and understand: 11 not what goes into the mouth
defiles a man, but what comes out of
the mouth, this defiles a man." 12 Then
the disciples came and said to him,
"Do you know that the Pharisees were
offended when they heard this saying?"
13 He answered, "Every plant which
my heavenly Father has not planted
will be rooted up. 14 Let them alone;
they are blind guides. And if a blind
man leads a blind man, both will fall
into a pit." 15 But Peter said to him,
"Explain the parable to us." 16 And
he said, "Are you also still without understanding? 17 Do you not see that
whatever goes into the mouth passes
into the stomach, and so passes on?[q]
18 But what comes out of the mouth
proceeds from the heart, and this defiles a man. 19 For out of the heart come
evil thoughts, murder, adultery, fornication, theft, false witness, slander.
20 These are what defile a man; but to
eat with unwashed hands does not defile a man."
21 And Jesus went away from there
and withdrew to the district of Tyre
and Sidon. 22 And behold, a Canaanite
woman from that region came out and
cried, "Have mercy on me, O Lord,
Son of David; my daughter is severely
possessed by a demon." 23 But he did
not answer her a word. And his disciples came and begged him, saying,
"Send her away, for she is crying
after us." 24 He answered, "I was sent
only to the lost sheep of the house of
Israel." 25 But she came and knelt
before him, saying, "Lord, help me."
26 And he answered, "It is not fair to
take the children's bread and throw it
to the dogs." 27 She said, "Yes, Lord,
yet even the dogs eat the crumbs that
fall from their masters' table." 28 Then
Jesus answered her, "O woman, great
is your faith! Be it done for you as you
desire." And her daughter was healed
instantly.
29 And Jesus went on from there
and passed along the Sea of Galilee.

o Or *an offering*
p Other ancient authorities read *law*
q Or *is evacuated*

15.1–20: Tradition of the elders (Mk.7.1–23). **2:** *The tradition of the elders*, the rabbinical exposition of the Law of Moses. **4:** Ex.20.12; Dt.5.16; Ex.21.17; Lev.20.9. **7–9:** Is.29.13 (see Mk.7.6–7 n.). **10–20:** The teaching here depends on the principle in the Law that certain physical conditions can and do render an individual unfit to share in the worship of the community. **11:** *Defiles*, renders unfit to share in public ritual (Acts 10.14–15; 1 Tim.4.3). **13:** Is.60.21. **14:** Lk.6.39; Mt.23.16,24. **19–20:** Violations of the rights and interests of another hinder worship (5.23–24).

15.21–28: The Canaanite woman (Mk.7.24–30). **22:** The woman, though a Gentile, speaks to Jesus as the Jewish Messiah. **24:** 10.6,23. Jesus consistently said that his primary mission was to call Jews back to God. The Gentile woman's claim must be based on her own personal acceptance of his message. The distinction is between his mission and his willingness to respond to faith wherever found. **27:** The woman accepts Jesus' mission and as a Gentile asks his help.

15.29–31: Healings (Mk.7.31–37).

And he went up on the mountain, and sat down there. [30] And great crowds came to him, bringing with them the lame, the maimed, the blind, the dumb, and many others, and they put them at his feet, and he healed them, [31] so that the throng wondered, when they saw the dumb speaking, the maimed whole, the lame walking, and the blind seeing; and they glorified the God of Israel.

32 Then Jesus called his disciples to him and said, "I have compassion on the crowd, because they have been with me now three days, and have nothing to eat; and I am unwilling to send them away hungry, lest they faint on the way." [33] And the disciples said to him, "Where are we to get bread enough in the desert to feed so great a crowd?" [34] And Jesus said to them, "How many loaves have you?" They said, "Seven, and a few small fish." [35] And commanding the crowd to sit down on the ground, [36] he took the seven loaves and the fish, and having given thanks he broke them and gave them to the disciples, and the disciples gave them to the crowds. [37] And they all ate and were satisfied; and they took up seven baskets full of the broken pieces left over. [38] Those who ate were four thousand men, besides women and children. [39] And sending away the crowds, he got into the boat and went to the region of Mag'adan.

16 And the Pharisees and Sad'ducees came, and to test him they asked him to show them a sign from heaven. [2] He answered them,[r] "When it is evening, you say, 'It will be fair weather; for the sky is red.' [3] And in the morning, 'It will be stormy today, for the sky is red and threaten-

ing.' You know how to interpret the appearance of the sky, but you cannot interpret the signs of the times. [4] An evil and adulterous generation seeks for a sign, but no sign shall be given to it except the sign of Jonah." So he left them and departed.

5 When the disciples reached the other side, they had forgotten to bring any bread. [6] Jesus said to them, "Take heed and beware of the leaven of the Pharisees and Sad'ducees." [7] And they discussed it among themselves, saying, "We brought no bread." [8] But Jesus, aware of this, said, "O men of little faith, why do you discuss among yourselves the fact that you have no bread? [9] Do you not yet perceive? Do you not remember the five loaves of the five thousand, and how many baskets you gathered? [10] Or the seven loaves of the four thousand, and how many baskets you gathered? [11] How is it that you fail to perceive that I did not speak about bread? Beware of the leaven of the Pharisees and Sad'ducees." [12] Then they understood that he did not tell them to beware of the leaven of bread, but of the teaching of the Pharisees and Sad'ducees.

13 Now when Jesus came into the district of Caesare'a Philip'pi, he asked his disciples, "Who do men say that the Son of man is?" [14] And they said, "Some say John the Baptist, others say Eli'jah, and others Jeremiah or one of the prophets." [15] He said to them, "But who do you say that I am?" [16] Simon Peter replied, "You are the Christ, the Son of the living God." [17] And Jesus answered him, "Blessed are you, Simon

r Other ancient authorities omit the following words to the end of verse 3

15.32–39: **Four thousand fed** (see Mk.8.1–10 n.). **39:** *Magadan* was apparently on the west side of the Sea of Galilee.

16.1–4: **Demand for signs** (Mk.8.11–13; Lk.11.16,29; 12.54–56). **3:** *The signs of the times* may refer to 15.29–31; compare 11.2–6. **4:** See 12.39 n., 40 n.; Jon.3.4–5.

16.5–12: **Leaven of the Pharisees** (Mk.8.14–21; Lk.12.1). **5:** *The other side*, the eastern shore of the Sea of Galilee. **6:** *Leaven*, see Mk.8.15 n. **9:** 14.17–21. **10:** 15.34–38.

16.13–23: **Peter's confession** (Mk.8.27–33; Lk.9.18–22). **13:** See Mk.8.27 n. *Son of man* here is equivalent to "I." **16:** Peter asserts that Jesus is the Messiah, not merely one of the prophets (v. 14). He identifies Jesus with the figure of Mal.3.1–4 (compare Mk.1.2; Mt.1.16; Jn.1.49; 11.27). **17:** *Simon* was Peter's personal name. *Bar-Jona* identifies Simon as "son of

Bar-Jona! For flesh and blood has not revealed this to you, but my Father who is in heaven. [18] And I tell you, you are Peter,[s] and on this rock[t] I will build my church, and the powers of death[u] shall not prevail against it. [19] I will give you the keys of the kingdom of heaven, and whatever you bind on earth shall be bound in heaven, and whatever you loose on earth shall be loosed in heaven." [20] Then he strictly charged the disciples to tell no one that he was the Christ.

21 From that time Jesus began to show his disciples that he must go to Jerusalem and suffer many things from the elders and chief priests and scribes, and be killed, and on the third day be raised. [22] And Peter took him and began to rebuke him, saying, "God forbid, Lord! This shall never happen to you." [23] But he turned and said to Peter, "Get behind me, Satan! You are a hindrance[v] to me; for you are not on the side of God, but of men."

24 Then Jesus told his disciples, "If any man would come after me, let him deny himself and take up his cross and follow me. [25] For whoever would save his life will lose it, and whoever loses his life for my sake will find it. [26] For what will it profit a man, if he gains the whole world and forfeits his life? Or what shall a man give in return for his life? [27] For the Son of man is to come with his angels in the glory of his Father, and then he will repay every man for what he has done. [28] Truly, I say to you, there are some standing here who will not taste death before they see the Son of man coming in his kingdom."

17 And after six days Jesus took with him Peter and James and John his brother, and led them up a high mountain apart. [2] And he was transfigured before them, and his face shone like the sun, and his garments became white as light. [3] And behold, there appeared to them Moses and Eli'jah, talking with him. [4] And Peter said to Jesus, "Lord, it is well that we are here; if you wish, I will make three booths here, one for you and one for Moses and one for Eli'jah." [5] He was still speaking, when lo, a bright cloud overshadowed them, and a voice from the cloud said, "This is my beloved Son,[w] with whom I am well pleased; listen to him." [6] When the disciples heard this, they fell on their faces, and were filled with awe. [7] But Jesus came and touched them, saying, "Rise, and have no fear." [8] And when they lifted up their eyes, they saw no one but Jesus only.

9 And as they were coming down the mountain, Jesus commanded them, "Tell no one the vision, until the Son

s Greek *Petros*   t Greek *petra*
u Greek *the gates of Hades*
v Greek *stumbling block*
w Or *my Son, my* (or *the*) *Beloved*

John." *Flesh and blood*, human beings (1 Cor.15.50; Gal.1.16; Eph.6.12). *Revealed*, understanding spiritual realities involves God's disclosure (see 11.25 n.; Lk.24.16; 1 Cor.1.18–25; 2.6–16). **18:** The Greek text involves a play on two words, *Petros* ("Peter") and *petra* ("rock"). Palestinian Aramaic, which Jesus usually spoke, used the same word for both proper name and common noun: "You are *Kepha* [Cephas; compare 1 Cor.15.5; Gal.2.9], and on this *kepha* [rock] I will build . . ." For the view that all the apostles also form the foundation of the church, see Eph.2.20; Rev.21.14. *Church*, see Gal.1.13 n. **19:** *The keys of the kingdom* are a symbol of Peter's power as the leader of the church. *Bind* and *loose* are technical rabbinic terms meaning "forbid" and "permit" some action about which a question has arisen. Later the authority of binding and loosing was also conferred upon all the apostles (18.18). **20:** See Mk.8.30 n. **21:** See Lk.9.22 n. **22–23:** See Mk.8.32 n., 33 n.

16.24–28: On discipleship (Mk.8.34–9.1; Lk.9.23–27). **24:** See 10.38 n. **25:** See Mk.8.35 n. **26:** Here *life* is not merely physical existence, but the higher or spiritual life of man, his real self (compare Lk.9.25; 12.15). **27:** Ps.62.12; Mt.10.33; Lk.12.8–9; Rom.2.6; 1 Jn.2.28; Rev.22.12. **28:** See Mk.9.1 n.; 1 Cor.16.22; 1 Th.4.15–18; Jas.5.7; Rev.1.7.

17.1–8: The transfiguration. See notes on the parallel passages, Mk.9.2–8; Lk.9.28–36.

17.9–13: Prophecies about Elijah (Mk.9.9–13). **9:** See Mk.8.30 n. **10:** See 11.14 n. **12:** *Elijah has already come*, in the person of John the Baptist.

of man is raised from the dead."
¹⁰ And the disciples asked him, "Then
why do the scribes say that first Eli′jah
must come?" ¹¹ He replied, "Eli′jah
does come, and he is to restore all
things; ¹² but I tell you that Eli′jah has
already come, and they did not know
him, but did to him whatever they
pleased. So also the Son of man will
suffer at their hands." ¹³ Then the
disciples understood that he was speaking to them of John the Baptist.

14 And when they came to the
crowd, a man came up to him and
kneeling before him said, ¹⁵ "Lord,
have mercy on my son, for he is an
epileptic and he suffers terribly; for
often he falls into the fire, and often
into the water. ¹⁶ And I brought him
to your disciples, and they could not
heal him." ¹⁷ And Jesus answered,
"O faithless and perverse generation,
how long am I to be with you? How
long am I to bear with you? Bring him
here to me." ¹⁸ And Jesus rebuked
him, and the demon came out of him,
and the boy was cured instantly.
¹⁹ Then the disciples came to Jesus
privately and said, "Why could we not
cast it out?" ²⁰ He said to them, "Because of your little faith. For truly, I say
to you, if you have faith as a grain of
mustard seed, you will say to this
mountain, 'Move from here to there,'
and it will move; and nothing will be
impossible to you."ˣ

22 As they were gatheringʸ in
Galilee, Jesus said to them, "The Son
of man is to be delivered into the
hands of men, ²³ and they will kill him,

and he will be raised on the third day."
And they were greatly distressed.

24 When they came to Caper′-
na-um, the collectors of the half-shekel
tax went up to Peter and said, "Does
not your teacher pay the tax?" ²⁵ He
said, "Yes." And when he came home,
Jesus spoke to him first, saying, "What
do you think, Simon? From whom do
kings of the earth take toll or tribute?
From their sons or from others?"
²⁶ And when he said, "From others,"
Jesus said to him, "Then the sons are
free. ²⁷ However, not to give offense
to them, go to the sea and cast a hook,
and take the first fish that comes up,
and when you open its mouth you will
find a shekel; take that and give it to
them for me and for yourself."

18 At that time the disciples came to
Jesus, saying, "Who is the greatest in the kingdom of heaven?" ² And
calling to him a child, he put him in
the midst of them, ³ and said, "Truly,
I say to you, unless you turn and become like children, you will never enter
the kingdom of heaven. ⁴ Whoever
humbles himself like this child, he is
the greatest in the kingdom of heaven.

5 "Whoever receives one such child
in my name receives me; ⁶ but whoever causes one of these little ones
who believe in me to sin,ᶻ it would be
better for him to have a great millstone
fastened round his neck and to be
drowned in the depth of the sea.

x Other ancient authorities insert verse 21, "*But this
kind never comes out except by prayer and fasting*"
y Other ancient authorities read *abode*
z Greek *causes . . . to stumble*

17.14–21: An epileptic child healed (Mk.9.14–29; Lk.9.37–42). 15: To be *epileptic* was
attributed to the baleful influences of the moon, a demonic force (compare Ps.121.6). 20:
Little faith as distinguished from unbelief (13.58). Jesus' saying is in figurative language; faith is
concerned with God's will, not with moving mountains (compare 21.21–22; Mk.11.22–23;
Lk.17.6; 1 Cor.13.2; Jas.1.6).

17.22–23: The Passion foretold a second time (Mk.9.30–32; Lk.9.43–45). Compare 16.21;
20.17–19.

17.24–27: Money for the temple tax. 24: The half-shekel tax was paid by Jewish males annually to support the temple. On the value see 26.15 n. (Ex.30.13; 38.26).

18.1–35: Sayings on humility and forgiveness. 1–5: True greatness (Mk.9.33–37; Lk.9.46–48).
3: *Turn and become like children*, turn away from self-chosen goals and relate oneself to God as
to a father. Childlike relations to a parent, not childish behavior, are in view (Mk.10.15;
Lk.18.17; 1 Pet.2.2). 6: *Little ones*, disciples of Jesus, whom he calls "children" (Mk.10.24;
compare Mt.11.25).

7 "Woe to the world for temptations to sin![a] For it is necessary that temptations come, but woe to the man by whom the temptation comes! [8] And if your hand or your foot causes you to sin,[z] cut it off and throw it away; it is better for you to enter life maimed or lame than with two hands or two feet to be thrown into the eternal fire. [9] And if your eye causes you to sin,[z] pluck it out and throw it away; it is better for you to enter life with one eye than with two eyes to be thrown into the hell[b] of fire.

10 "See that you do not despise one of these little ones; for I tell you that in heaven their angels always behold the face of my Father who is in heaven.[c] [12] What do you think? If a man has a hundred sheep, and one of them has gone astray, does he not leave the ninety-nine on the mountains and go in search of the one that went astray? [13] And if he finds it, truly, I say to you, he rejoices over it more than over the ninety-nine that never went astray. [14] So it is not the will of my[d] Father who is in heaven that one of these little ones should perish.

15 "If your brother sins against you, go and tell him his fault, between you and him alone. If he listens to you, you have gained your brother. [16] But if he does not listen, take one or two others along with you, that every word may be confirmed by the evidence of two or three witnesses. [17] If he refuses to listen to them, tell it to the church; and if he refuses to listen even to the church, let him be to you as a Gentile and a tax collector. [18] Truly, I say to you, whatever you bind on earth shall be bound in heaven, and whatever you loose on earth shall be loosed in heaven. [19] Again I say to you, if two of you agree on earth about anything they ask, it will be done for them by my Father in heaven. [20] For where two or three are gathered in my name, there am I in the midst of them."

21 Then Peter came up and said to him, "Lord, how often shall my brother sin against me, and I forgive him? As many as seven times?" [22] Jesus said to him, "I do not say to you seven times, but seventy times seven.[e]

23 "Therefore the kingdom of heaven may be compared to a king who wished to settle accounts with his servants. [24] When he began the reckoning, one was brought to him who owed him ten thousand talents;[f] [25] and as he could not pay, his lord ordered him to be sold, with his wife and children and all that he had, and payment to be made. [26] So the servant fell on his knees, imploring him, 'Lord, have patience with me, and I will pay you everything.' [27] And out of pity for him the lord of that servant released him and forgave him the debt. [28] But that same servant, as he went out, came upon one of his fellow servants who owed him a hundred denarii;[g] and seizing him by the throat he said, 'Pay what you owe.' [29] So his fellow servant fell down and besought him, 'Have patience with me, and I will pay you.' [30] He refused and went and put him in prison till he should pay the debt. [31] When his fellow servants saw what had taken place, they were greatly distressed, and they went and reported to their lord all that had taken

a Greek *stumbling blocks*
z Greek *causes . . . to stumble*   *b* Greek *Gehenna*
c Other ancient authorities add verse 11, *For the Son of man came to save the lost*
d Other ancient authorities read *your*
e Or *seventy-seven times*
f This talent was more than fifteen years' wages of a laborer
g The denarius was a day's wage for a laborer

18.7–9: Warnings of hell (Mk.9.42–48; Lk.17.1–2). **8–9:** In vivid language Jesus speaks of the terrible danger in yielding to temptation (5.29–30).
18.10–14: The lost sheep (Lk.15.3–7). **10:** *Little ones,* see v. 6 n. *Angels,* see Acts 12.15 n.
18.15–20: Discipline among followers (Lk.17.3). 1 Cor.6.1–6; Gal.6.1; Jas.5.19–20; Lev.19.17. **16:** Dt.19.15. **17:** The guilty person excludes himself from the group of followers. **18:** See 16.19 n.; Jn.20.21–23 n.
18.21–35: Forgiveness. 21–22: Lk.17.4. Forgiveness is beyond calculating. **23:** 25.19. **25:** Lk.7.42. **26:** 8.2; 17.14. **32–33:** Lk.7.41–43.

place. ³² Then his lord summoned him and said to him, 'You wicked servant! I forgave you all that debt because you besought me; ³³ and should not you have had mercy on your fellow servant, as I had mercy on you?' ³⁴ And in anger his lord delivered him to the jailers,*h* till he should pay all his debt. ³⁵ So also my heavenly Father will do to every one of you, if you do not forgive your brother from your heart."

19 Now when Jesus had finished these sayings, he went away from Galilee and entered the region of Judea beyond the Jordan; ² and large crowds followed him, and he healed them there.

3 And Pharisees came up to him and tested him by asking, "Is it lawful to divorce one's wife for any cause?" ⁴ He answered, "Have you not read that he who made them from the beginning made them male and female, ⁵ and said, 'For this reason a man shall leave his father and mother and be joined to his wife, and the two shall become one flesh'? ⁶ So they are no longer two but one flesh. What therefore God has joined together, let not man put asunder." ⁷ They said to him, "Why then did Moses command one to give a certificate of divorce, and to put her away?" ⁸ He said to them, "For your hardness of heart Moses allowed you to divorce your wives, but from the beginning it was not so. ⁹ And I say to you: whoever divorces his wife, except for unchastity,*j* and marries another, commits adultery."*k*

10 The disciples said to him, "If such is the case of a man with his wife, it is not expedient to marry." ¹¹ But he said to them, "Not all men can receive this saying, but only those to whom it is given. ¹² For there are eunuchs who have been so from birth, and there are eunuchs who have been made eunuchs by men, and there are eunuchs who have made themselves eunuchs for the sake of the kingdom of heaven. He who is able to receive this, let him receive it."

13 Then children were brought to him that he might lay his hands on them and pray. The disciples rebuked the people; ¹⁴ but Jesus said, "Let the children come to me, and do not hinder them; for to such belongs the kingdom of heaven." ¹⁵ And he laid his hands on them and went away.

16 And behold, one came up to him, saying, "Teacher, what good deed must I do, to have eternal life?" ¹⁷ And he said to him, "Why do you ask me about what is good? One there is who is good. If you would enter life, keep the commandments." ¹⁸ He said to him, "Which?" And Jesus said, "You shall not kill, You shall not commit adultery, You shall not steal, You shall not bear false witness, ¹⁹ Honor your father and mother, and, You shall love your neighbor as yourself." ²⁰ The young man said to him, "All these I have observed; what do I still lack?" ²¹ Jesus said to him, "If you

h Greek *torturers*
j Other ancient authorities, after *unchastity*, read *makes her commit adultery*
k Other ancient authorities insert *and he who marries a divorced woman commits adultery*

19.1–20.34: From Galilee to Jerusalem (Mk.10.1–52; Lk.18.15–19.27).
19.1–12: Marriage and divorce (Mk.10.1–12). **1:** *Finished*, see 7.28 n. **3:** The Mosaic law gives no answer to this question and the rabbis differed in their opinions. **4–6:** Gen.1.27; 2.24. Jesus appeals to God's purpose of unity in marriage as shown in the account of creation. **7:** Dt.24.1–4. **8:** See Mk.10.5 n. **9:** See 5.32 n.; Lk.16.18; 1 Cor.7.10–13. **11–12:** Jesus recognizes a place for voluntary celibacy in the service of God's kingdom (compare 1 Cor.7.1–9).
19.13–15: Blessing the children (Mk.10.13–16; Lk.18.15–17). **14:** See Mk.10.15 n.; compare Mt.18.2–4; 1 Cor.14.20.
19.16–30: The rich young man (Mk.10.17–31; Lk.18.18–30). **16:** Lk.10.25; Lev.18.5. The question concerns the way of life which Jesus will guarantee as satisfying God (see Lk.18.26 n.). **17:** Jesus replies that the good way of life is obedience to God's will (15.2–3,6). **18:** Ex.20.12–16; Dt.5.16–20; Rom.13.9; Jas.2.11. **19:** Lev.19.18; Mt.22.39; Rom.13.8; Jas.2.8–9. **21:** Jesus consistently turned men's attention from concern over their own religious standing, calling them to involve themselves in the basic, vital interests of others. Neither wealth, poverty, nor formal

would be perfect, go, sell what you possess and give to the poor, and you will have treasure in heaven; and come, follow me." 22 When the young man heard this he went away sorrowful; for he had great possessions.

23 And Jesus said to his disciples, "Truly, I say to you, it will be hard for a rich man to enter the kingdom of heaven. 24 Again I tell you, it is easier for a camel to go through the eye of a needle than for a rich man to enter the kingdom of God." 25 When the disciples heard this they were greatly astonished, saying, "Who then can be saved?" 26 But Jesus looked at them and said to them, "With men this is impossible, but with God all things are possible." 27 Then Peter said in reply, "Lo, we have left everything and followed you. What then shall we have?" 28 Jesus said to them, "Truly, I say to you, in the new world, when the Son of man shall sit on his glorious throne, you who have followed me will also sit on twelve thrones, judging the twelve tribes of Israel. 29 And every one who has left houses or brothers or sisters or father or mother or children or lands, for my name's sake, will receive a hundredfold,*l* and inherit eternal life. 30 But many that are first will be last, and the last first.

20 "For the kingdom of heaven is like a householder who went out early in the morning to hire laborers for his vineyard. 2 After agreeing with the laborers for a denarius*m* a day, he sent them into his vineyard.

3 And going out about the third hour he saw others standing idle in the market place; 4 and to them he said, 'You go into the vineyard too, and whatever is right I will give you.' So they went. 5 Going out again about the sixth hour and the ninth hour, he did the same. 6 And about the eleventh hour he went out and found others standing; and he said to them, 'Why do you stand here idle all day?' 7 They said to him, 'Because no one has hired us.' He said to them, 'You go into the vineyard too.' 8 And when evening came, the owner of the vineyard said to his steward, 'Call the laborers and pay them their wages, beginning with the last, up to the first.' 9 And when those hired about the eleventh hour came, each of them received a denarius. 10 Now when the first came, they thought they would receive more; but each of them also received a denarius. 11 And on receiving it they grumbled at the householder, 12 saying, 'These last worked only one hour, and you have made them equal to us who have borne the burden of the day and the scorching heat.' 13 But he replied to one of them, 'Friend, I am doing you no wrong; did you not agree with me for a denarius? 14 Take what belongs to you, and go; I choose to give to this last as I give to you. 15 Am I not allowed to do what I choose with what belongs to me? Or do you begrudge my generosity?'*n* 16 So the last will be first, and the first last."

l Other ancient authorities read *manifold*
m The denarius was a day's wage for a laborer
n Or *is your eye evil because I am good?*

piety was so important as sharing in the working out of God's life-giving design for all men (5.23–24,43–48; 6.33). Eternal life will be found through utter dependence on God, not through a ritual that wealth makes possible (see Lk.12.33 n.; Acts 2.44–45; 4.34,35). 24: See Mk.10.25 n. 28: *The new world* refers to the consummation of God's purpose (compare Rom.8.18–25). 29: *Inherit eternal life* means *enter the kingdom of God* (vv. 23,24), and *inherit the kingdom* (25.34). 30: 20.16; Mk.10.31; Lk.13.30.

20.1–16: Laborers in the vineyard. 1: *Early*, approximately six a.m. 3: About nine a.m. 5: About noon and three p.m. 6: About five p.m. 8: Lev.19.13; Dt.24.14–15. 9: *Denarius*, smaller coins existed (see Lk.12.59 n.); therefore payment could have been made on an hourly basis. 14: The point of the parable is the willingness of the owner to exceed conventional practices, and his freedom to do so within the limits of agreement. 15: The first sentence is not a statement of economic theory except as it claims the right to enter into differing contracts. The second sentence expresses the sense of the Greek text, which is literally translated in note *n*. 16: Compare 19.30.

17 And as Jesus was going up to Jerusalem, he took the twelve disciples aside, and on the way he said to them, 18 "Behold, we are going up to Jerusalem; and the Son of man will be delivered to the chief priests and scribes, and they will condemn him to death, 19 and deliver him to the Gentiles to be mocked and scourged and crucified, and he will be raised on the third day."

20 Then the mother of the sons of Zeb′edee came up to him, with her sons, and kneeling before him she asked him for something. 21 And he said to her, "What do you want?" She said to him, "Command that these two sons of mine may sit, one at your right hand and one at your left, in your kingdom." 22 But Jesus answered, "You do not know what you are asking. Are you able to drink the cup that I am to drink?" They said to him, "We are able." 23 He said to them, "You will drink my cup, but to sit at my right hand and at my left is not mine to grant, but it is for those for whom it has been prepared by my Father." 24 And when the ten heard it, they were indignant at the two brothers. 25 But Jesus called them to him and said, "You know that the rulers of the Gentiles lord it over them, and their great men exercise authority over them. 26 It shall not be so among you; but whoever would be great among you must be your servant, 27 and whoever would be first among you must be your slave; 28 even as the Son of man came not to be served but to serve, and to give his life as a ransom for many."

29 And as they went out of Jericho, a great crowd followed him. 30 And behold, two blind men sitting by the roadside, when they heard that Jesus was passing by, cried out,*o* "Have mercy on us, Son of David!" 31 The crowd rebuked them, telling them to be silent; but they cried out the more, "Lord, have mercy on us, Son of David!" 32 And Jesus stopped and called them, saying, "What do you want me to do for you?" 33 They said to him, "Lord, let our eyes be opened." 34 And Jesus in pity touched their eyes, and immediately they received their sight and followed him.

21 And when they drew near to Jerusalem and came to Beth′phage, to the Mount of Olives, then Jesus sent two disciples, 2 saying to them, "Go into the village opposite you, and immediately you will find an ass tied, and a colt with her; untie them and bring them to me. 3 If any one says anything to you, you shall say, 'The Lord has need of them,' and he will send them immediately." 4 This took place to fulfil what was spoken by the prophet, saying,

5 "Tell the daughter of Zion,
Behold, your king is coming to you,
    humble, and mounted on an ass,
    and on a colt, the foal of an ass."

6 The disciples went and did as Jesus had directed them; 7 they brought the ass and the colt, and put their garments on them, and he sat thereon. 8 Most of the crowd spread their garments on the road, and others cut branches from the trees and spread

o Other ancient authorities insert *Lord*

20.17–19: **The Passion foretold a third time** (Mk.10.32–34; Lk.18.31–34); compare 16.21; 17.22.

20.20–28: **James and John seek honor** (Mk.10.35–45; Lk.22.24–27). **22:** *Cup*, see Lk.22.42 n. **23:** Acts 12.2; Rev.1.9; Mt.13.11. **26:** See Mk.9.35. **28:** 26.39; 1 Tim.2.5–6; Jn.13.15–16; Tit.2.14; 1 Pet.1.18. The thought seems to be based on Is. ch. 53.

20.29–34: **Two blind men of Jericho** (Mk.10.46–52; Lk.18.35–43). Jesus responds not to the Messianic title *Son of David* (v. 30) but to the cry of need (v. 34; compare 15.22–28).

21.1–27.66: **The last week** (Mk.11.1–15.47; Lk.19.28–23.56).

21.1–9: **Palm Sunday** (Mk.11.1–10; Lk.19.28–38; Jn.12.12–18). **1:** See Mk.11.1 n. **5:** Is. 62.11; Zech.9.9. The Hebrew text refers not to two animals but to one. The reference to the two in v. 7 may have arisen through misunderstanding the form of Hebrew poetic expression in Zech.9.9. **8:** Tokens of honor (2 Kg.9.13). **9:** Ps.118.26. *Hosanna*, originally a Hebrew invoca-

them on the road. [9] And the crowds that went before him and that followed him shouted, "Hosanna to the Son of David! Blessed is he who comes in the name of the Lord! Hosanna in the highest!" [10] And when he entered Jerusalem, all the city was stirred, saying, "Who is this?" [11] And the crowds said, "This is the prophet Jesus from Nazareth of Galilee."

12 And Jesus entered the temple of God[p] and drove out all who sold and bought in the temple, and he overturned the tables of the moneychangers and the seats of those who sold pigeons. [13] He said to them, "It is written, 'My house shall be called a house of prayer'; but you make it a den of robbers."

14 And the blind and the lame came to him in the temple, and he healed them. [15] But when the chief priests and the scribes saw the wonderful things that he did, and the children crying out in the temple, "Hosanna to the Son of David!" they were indignant; [16] and they said to him, "Do you hear what these are saying?" And Jesus said to them, "Yes; have you never read,

'Out of the mouth of babes and
   sucklings
thou hast brought perfect praise'?"

[17] And leaving them, he went out of the city to Bethany and lodged there.

18 In the morning, as he was returning to the city, he was hungry. [19] And seeing a fig tree by the wayside he went to it, and found nothing on it but leaves only. And he said to it, "May no fruit ever come from you again!"

And the fig tree withered at once. [20] When the disciples saw it they marveled, saying, "How did the fig tree wither at once?" [21] And Jesus answered them, "Truly, I say to you, if you have faith and never doubt, you will not only do what has been done to the fig tree, but even if you say to this mountain, 'Be taken up and cast into the sea,' it will be done. [22] And whatever you ask in prayer, you will receive, if you have faith."

23 And when he entered the temple, the chief priests and the elders of the people came up to him as he was teaching, and said, "By what authority are you doing these things, and who gave you this authority?" [24] Jesus answered them, "I also will ask you a question; and if you tell me the answer, then I also will tell you by what authority I do these things. [25] The baptism of John, whence was it? From heaven or from men?" And they argued with one another, "If we say, 'From heaven,' he will say to us, 'Why then did you not believe him?' [26] But if we say, 'From men,' we are afraid of the multitude; for all hold that John was a prophet." [27] So they answered Jesus, "We do not know." And he said to them, "Neither will I tell you by what authority I do these things.

28 "What do you think? A man had two sons; and he went to the first and said, 'Son, go and work in the vineyard today.' [29] And he answered, 'I will not'; but afterward he repented and went. [30] And he went to the second and said the same; and he an-

p Other ancient authorities omit *of God*

---

tion addressed to God, meaning, "O save!"; later it was used as a cry of joyous acclamation. **11:** The identification reflects an unchanged attitude toward Jesus. His parable (see Mk.11.1 n.) is seen and not understood (Jn.6.14; 7.40; Acts 3.22; Mk.6.15; Lk.13.33).

   21.12–17: Cleansing the temple (Mk.11.11,15–19; Lk.19.45–48; Jn.2.13–17). **12:** The animals for sale were acceptable for sacrifice; the money changers converted Gentile coins into Jewish money that could properly be presented in the temple (Ex.30.13; Lev.1.14). **13:** Is.56.7; Jer.7.11. **15:** Lk.19.39; Mt.21.9. *Hosanna*, see v. 9 n. **16:** Ps.8.2.

   21.18–22: Fig tree cursed (Mk.11.12–14,20–25). See Mk.11.13 n. **19:** The leaves of the fig tree normally appear after the fruit. **21:** See 17.20 n.

   21.23–32: Jesus' authority (Mk.11.27–33; Lk.20.1–8). Jn.2.18–22. **26:** 11.9; 14.5; Lk.1.76. **27:** Jesus declined to answer because his listeners declined to heed. **28–32:** 20.1; 21.33; Lk. 15.11–32. **32:** Lk.7.29–30. *The way of righteousness* led to reconciliation with God by faith.

swered, 'I go, sir,' but did not go. 31 Which of the two did the will of his father?" They said, "The first." Jesus said to them, "Truly, I say to you, the tax collectors and the harlots go into the kingdom of God before you. 32 For John came to you in the way of righteousness, and you did not believe him, but the tax collectors and the harlots believed him; and even when you saw it, you did not afterward repent and believe him.

33 "Hear another parable. There was a householder who planted a vineyard, and set a hedge around it, and dug a wine press in it, and built a tower, and let it out to tenants, and went into another country. 34 When the season of fruit drew near, he sent his servants to the tenants, to get his fruit; 35 and the tenants took his servants and beat one, killed another, and stoned another. 36 Again he sent other servants, more than the first; and they did the same to them. 37 Afterward he sent his son to them, saying, 'They will respect my son.' 38 But when the tenants saw the son, they said to themselves, 'This is the heir; come, let us kill him and have his inheritance.' 39 And they took him and cast him out of the vineyard, and killed him. 40 When therefore the owner of the vineyard comes, what will he do to those tenants?" 41 They said to him, "He will put those wretches to a miserable death, and let out the vineyard to other tenants who will give him the fruits in their seasons."

42 Jesus said to them, "Have you never read in the scriptures:

'The very stone which the builders rejected
has become the head of the corner;
this was the Lord's doing,
and it is marvelous in our eyes'?

43 Therefore I tell you, the kingdom of God will be taken away from you and given to a nation producing the fruits of it."q

45 When the chief priests and the Pharisees heard his parables, they perceived that he was speaking about them. 46 But when they tried to arrest him, they feared the multitudes, because they held him to be a prophet.

22 And again Jesus spoke to them in parables, saying, 2 "The kingdom of heaven may be compared to a king who gave a marriage feast for his son, 3 and sent his servants to call those who were invited to the marriage feast; but they would not come. 4 Again he sent other servants, saying, 'Tell those who are invited, Behold, I have made ready my dinner, my oxen and my fat calves are killed, and everything is ready; come to the marriage feast.' 5 But they made light of it and went off, one to his farm, another to his business, 6 while the rest seized his servants, treated them shamefully, and killed them. 7 The king was angry, and he sent his troops and destroyed those murderers and burned their city. 8 Then he said to his servants, 'The wedding is ready, but those invited were not worthy. 9 Go therefore to the thoroughfares, and invite to the marriage feast as many as you find.' 10 And those servants went out into the streets and gathered all whom they found, both bad and good; so the wedding hall was filled with guests.

11 "But when the king came in to look at the guests, he saw there a man who had no wedding garment; 12 and he said to him, 'Friend, how did you get in here without a wedding garment?' And he was speechless. 13 Then the king said to the attendants, 'Bind him hand and foot, and cast him into the outer darkness; there men will weep

q Other ancient authorities add verse 44, "*And he who falls on this stone will be broken to pieces; but when it falls on any one, it will crush him*"

21.33–46: Parable of the vineyard (Mk.12.1–12; Lk.20.9–19). **33:** Compare Is.5.1–7, which forms the background of Jesus' parable. **34:** 22.3. **41:** 8.11; Acts 13.46; 18.6; 28.28. **42:** Jesus agrees with his listeners' answer (v. 41) and quotes Ps.118.22–23 to support his teaching (Acts 4.11; 1 Pet.2.7).

22.1–14: The marriage feast (Lk.14.16–24). **3:** 21.34. **10:** 13.47. **13:** 8.12.

and gnash their teeth.' ¹⁴ For many are called, but few are chosen."

15 Then the Pharisees went and took counsel how to entangle him in his talk. ¹⁶ And they sent their disciples to him, along with the Hero'dians, saying, "Teacher, we know that you are true, and teach the way of God truthfully, and care for no man; for you do not regard the position of men. ¹⁷ Tell us, then, what you think. Is it lawful to pay taxes to Caesar, or not?" ¹⁸ But Jesus, aware of their malice, said, "Why put me to the test, you hypocrites? ¹⁹ Show me the money for the tax." And they brought him a coin.ʳ ²⁰ And Jesus said to them, "Whose likeness and inscription is this?" ²¹ They said, "Caesar's." Then he said to them, "Render therefore to Caesar the things that are Caesar's, and to God the things that are God's." ²² When they heard it, they marveled; and they left him and went away.

23 The same day Sad'ducees came to him, who say that there is no resurrection; and they asked him a question, ²⁴ saying, "Teacher, Moses said, 'If a man dies, having no children, his brother must marry the widow, and raise up children for his brother.' ²⁵ Now there were seven brothers among us; the first married, and died, and having no children left his wife to his brother. ²⁶ So too the second and third, down to the seventh. ²⁷ After them all, the woman died. ²⁸ In the resurrection, therefore, to which of the

seven will she be wife? For they all had her."

29 But Jesus answered them, "You are wrong, because you know neither the scriptures nor the power of God. ³⁰ For in the resurrection they neither marry nor are given in marriage, but are like angelsˢ in heaven. ³¹ And as for the resurrection of the dead, have you not read what was said to you by God, ³² 'I am the God of Abraham, and the God of Isaac, and the God of Jacob'? He is not God of the dead, but of the living." ³³ And when the crowd heard it, they were astonished at his teaching.

34 But when the Pharisees heard that he had silenced the Sad'ducees, they came together. ³⁵ And one of them, a lawyer, asked him a question, to test him. ³⁶ "Teacher, which is the great commandment in the law?" ³⁷ And he said to him, "You shall love the Lord your God with all your heart, and with all your soul, and with all your mind. ³⁸ This is the great and first commandment. ³⁹ And a second is like it, You shall love your neighbor as yourself. ⁴⁰ On these two commandments depend all the law and the prophets."

41 Now while the Pharisees were gathered together, Jesus asked them a question, ⁴² saying, "What do you think of the Christ? Whose son is he?" They said to him, "The son of David."

r Greek *a denarius*
s Other ancient authorities add *of God*

22.15–22: **Paying taxes to Caesar** (Mk.12.13–17; Lk.20.20–26). 15: Mk.3.6; 8.15. 16: *Herodians*, Mk.3.6 n. In asking Jesus for a pronouncement affecting all Jews, his enemies thought to bring him into conflict with sectarian views. 17: If Jesus approved paying taxes he would offend the nationalistic parties; if he disapproved payment he could be reported as disloyal to the empire. 21: Rom.13.7; 1 Pet.2.17.

22.23–33: **Question about the resurrection** (Mk.12.18–27; Lk.20.27–40). 23: Belief in the *resurrection* was held by the Pharisees in Jesus' day, but rejected by the Sadducees (Acts 4.1–2; 23.6–10). 24: Dt.25.5. 29: The Sadducees fail to see God's purpose and do not trust his *power*. 31–32: Ex.3.6. The idea here is that men who are related to God in faith have life even though physically dead. Resurrection is the divine act by which men will achieve the fulness of life intended in creation and lost through sin and death (see Lk.20.34–36 n.).

22.34–40: **The great commandment** (Mk.12.28–34; Lk.10.25–28). 37: Dt.6.5. 39: Lev.19.18; Compare Mt.19.19; Rom.13.9; Gal.5.14; Jas.2.8. 40: The Law contains many ways of applying to life the principle of love.

22.41–46: **David's son** (Mk.12.35–37; Lk.20.41–44). 44: The first *Lord* refers to God, the

43 He said to them, "How is it then that David, inspired by the Spirit,*t* calls him Lord, saying,

44 'The Lord said to my Lord,

Sit at my right hand,

till I put thy enemies under thy feet'?

45 If David thus calls him Lord, how is he his son?" 46 And no one was able to answer him a word, nor from that day did any one dare to ask him any more questions.

23 Then said Jesus to the crowds and to his disciples, 2 "The scribes and the Pharisees sit on Moses' seat; 3 so practice and observe whatever they tell you, but not what they do; for they preach, but do not practice. 4 They bind heavy burdens, hard to bear,*u* and lay them on men's shoulders; but they themselves will not move them with their finger. 5 They do all their deeds to be seen by men; for they make their phylacteries broad and their fringes long, 6 and they love the place of honor at feasts and the best seats in the synagogues, 7 and salutations in the market places, and being called rabbi by men. 8 But you are not to be called rabbi, for you have one teacher, and you are all brethren. 9 And call no man your father on earth, for you have one Father, who is in heaven. 10 Neither be called masters, for you have one master, the Christ. 11 He who is greatest among you shall be your servant; 12 whoever exalts himself will be humbled, and whoever humbles himself will be exalted.

13 "But woe to you, scribes and Pharisees, hypocrites! because you shut the kingdom of heaven against men; for you neither enter yourselves, nor allow those who would enter to go in.*v* 15 Woe to you, scribes and Pharisees, hypocrites! for you traverse sea and land to make a single proselyte, and when he becomes a proselyte, you make him twice as much a child of hell*w* as yourselves.

16 "Woe to you, blind guides, who say, 'If any one swears by the temple, it is nothing; but if any one swears by the gold of the temple, he is bound by his oath.' 17 You blind fools! For which is greater, the gold or the temple that has made the gold sacred? 18 And you say, 'If any one swears by the altar, it is nothing; but if any one swears by the gift that is on the altar, he is bound by his oath.' 19 You blind men! For which is greater, the gift or the altar that makes the gift sacred? 20 So he who swears by the altar, swears by it and by everything on it; 21 and he who swears by the temple, swears by it and by him who dwells in it; 22 and he who swears by heaven, swears by the throne of God and by him who sits upon it.

23 "Woe to you, scribes and Pharisees, hypocrites! for you tithe mint and dill and cummin, and have neglected the weightier matters of the law, justice and mercy and faith; these you ought to have done, without neglecting the others. 24 You blind guides, straining out a gnat and swallowing a camel!

25 "Woe to you, scribes and Pharisees, hypocrites! for you cleanse the outside of the cup and of the plate, but inside they are full of extortion and rapacity. 26 You blind Pharisee! first cleanse the inside of the cup and of the plate, that the outside also may be clean.

t Or *David in the Spirit*
u Other ancient authorities omit *hard to bear*
v Other authorities add here (or after verse 12) verse 14, *Woe to you, scribes and Pharisees, hypocrites! for you devour widows' houses and for a pretense you make long prayers; therefore you will receive the greater condemnation*
w Greek *Gehenna*

second *Lord* is taken here to refer to the Messiah (see Ps.110.1; Acts 2.34–35; Heb.1.13; 10.12–13).
23.1–36: Woe to scribes and Pharisees. 4: Lk.11.46; Mt.11.28–30; Acts 15.10. **5:** 6.1; 5.16; Ex.13.9; Dt.6.8. **6–7:** Mk.12.38–39; Lk.11.43; 14.7–11; 20.46. **8:** Jas.3.1. **12:** Lk.14.11; 18.14; Mt.18.4; 1 Pet.5.6. **13:** Lk.11.52. **15:** Acts 2.10; 6.5; 13.43. **16:** 5.33–37; 15.14. **17:** Ex.30.29. **21:** 1 Kg.8.13; Ps.26.8. **23–24:** Lk.11.42; Lev.27.30; Mic.6.8. **25–26:** Lk.11.39–41; Mk.7.4. **27–28:** Lk.11.44; Acts 23.3; Ps.5.9. **28:** See Lk.20.20 n. **29–32:** Lk.11.47–48; Acts 7.51–53.

27 "Woe to you, scribes and Pharisees, hypocrites! for you are like whitewashed tombs, which outwardly appear beautiful, but within they are full of dead men's bones and all uncleanness. [28] So you also outwardly appear righteous to men, but within you are full of hypocrisy and iniquity.

29 "Woe to you, scribes and Pharisees, hypocrites! for you build the tombs of the prophets and adorn the monuments of the righteous, [30] saying, 'If we had lived in the days of our fathers, we would not have taken part with them in shedding the blood of the prophets.' [31] Thus you witness against yourselves, that you are sons of those who murdered the prophets. [32] Fill up, then, the measure of your fathers. [33] You serpents, you brood of vipers, how are you to escape being sentenced to hell?[w] [34] Therefore I send you prophets and wise men and scribes, some of whom you will kill and crucify, and some you will scourge in your synagogues and persecute from town to town, [35] that upon you may come all the righteous blood shed on earth, from the blood of innocent Abel to the blood of Zechari'ah the son of Barachi'ah, whom you murdered between the sanctuary and the altar. [36] Truly, I say to you, all this will come upon this generation.

37 "O Jerusalem, Jerusalem, killing the prophets and stoning those who are sent to you! How often would I have gathered your children together as a hen gathers her brood under her wings, and you would not! [38] Behold, your house is forsaken and desolate.[x] [39] For I tell you, you will not see me again, until you say, 'Blessed is he who comes in the name of the Lord.' "

24 Jesus left the temple and was going away, when his disciples came to point out to him the buildings of the temple. [2] But he answered them, "You see all these, do you not? Truly, I say to you, there will not be left here one stone upon another, that will not be thrown down."

3 As he sat on the Mount of Olives, the disciples came to him privately, saying, "Tell us, when will this be, and what will be the sign of your coming and of the close of the age?" [4] And Jesus answered them, "Take heed that no one leads you astray. [5] For many will come in my name, saying, 'I am the Christ,' and they will lead many astray. [6] And you will hear of wars and rumors of wars; see that you are not alarmed; for this must take place, but the end is not yet. [7] For nation will rise against nation, and kingdom against kingdom, and there will be

w Greek *Gehenna*
x Other ancient authorities omit *and desolate*

31: *Sons of* has two meanings: descendants, or, those of similar character. The scribes and Pharisees would admit to being descendants *of those who murdered the prophets.* Jesus insists that their attitudes are also similar (v. 28). 33: 3.7; Lk.3.7. 34–36: Lk.11.49–51. 34: See Lk.11.49 n.; Mt.10.17,23; 2 Chr.36.15–16. *Prophets and wise men and scribes* are terms of Jewish origin applied here to Christian missionaries. 35: Gen.4.8; Heb.11.4; 2 Chr.24.20–22; Zech.1.1. The identifying words *son of Barachiah* (not in Lk.11.51) probably were mistakenly added to the text of Matthew at an early date because of confusion over which *Zechariah* was meant. The meaning of the sentence is to indicate the sweep of time from the first to the last victim of murder mentioned in the Old Testament (2 Chronicles stands last in the order of books in the Hebrew Bible).

23.37–39: Lament over Jerusalem (Lk.13.34–35). 37: The words *how often* suggest repeated efforts, made perhaps during an earlier Judean ministry (see Lk.4.44 n.). 38: 1 Kg.9.7; Jer.12.7; 22.5. 39: 21.9; Ps.118.26.

24.1–3: Destruction of the temple foretold (Mk.13.1–2; Lk.21.5–7). 1: These verses, together with the discourse that follows, seem to merge teachings about an immediate destruction of Jerusalem with details associated in Scripture with the end of human history. These teachings were set down by the Evangelist in the light of events between A.D. 30 and 70. It is difficult to be certain what the original form of Jesus' words was. 3: Lk.17.20–21; Mt.13.39,40,49; 16.27.

24.4–36: On the end of the age (Mk.13.3–37; Lk.21.8–36). 5: 1 Jn.2.18. 6–7: Rev.6.3–8,

famines and earthquakes in various places: [8] all this is but the beginning of the birth-pangs.

9 "Then they will deliver you up to tribulation, and put you to death; and you will be hated by all nations for my name's sake. [10] And then many will fall away,[y] and betray one another, and hate one another. [11] And many false prophets will arise and lead many astray. [12] And because wickedness is multiplied, most men's love will grow cold. [13] But he who endures to the end will be saved. [14] And this gospel of the kingdom will be preached throughout the whole world, as a testimony to all nations; and then the end will come.

15 "So when you see the desolating sacrilege spoken of by the prophet Daniel, standing in the holy place (let the reader understand), [16] then let those who are in Judea flee to the mountains; [17] let him who is on the housetop not go down to take what is in his house; [18] and let him who is in the field not turn back to take his mantle. [19] And alas for those who are with child and for those who give suck in those days! [20] Pray that your flight may not be in winter or on a sabbath. [21] For then there will be great tribulation, such as has not been from the beginning of the world until now, no, and never will be. [22] And if those days had not been shortened, no human being would be saved; but for the sake of the elect those days will be shortened. [23] Then if any one says to you, 'Lo, here is the Christ!' or 'There he is!' do not believe it. [24] For false Christs and false prophets will arise

and show great signs and wonders, so as to lead astray, if possible, even the elect. [25] Lo, I have told you beforehand. [26] So, if they say to you, 'Lo, he is in the wilderness,' do not go out; if they say, 'Lo, he is in the inner rooms,' do not believe it. [27] For as the lightning comes from the east and shines as far as the west, so will be the coming of the Son of man. [28] Wherever the body is, there the eagles[z] will be gathered together.

29 "Immediately after the tribulation of those days the sun will be darkened, and the moon will not give its light, and the stars will fall from heaven, and the powers of the heavens will be shaken; [30] then will appear the sign of the Son of man in heaven, and then all the tribes of the earth will mourn, and they will see the Son of man coming on the clouds of heaven with power and great glory; [31] and he will send out his angels with a loud trumpet call, and they will gather his elect from the four winds, from one end of heaven to the other.

32 "From the fig tree learn its lesson: as soon as its branch becomes tender and puts forth its leaves, you know that summer is near. [33] So also, when you see all these things, you know that he is near, at the very gates. [34] Truly, I say to you, this generation will not pass away till all these things take place. [35] Heaven and earth will pass away, but my words will not pass away.

36 "But of that day and hour no one knows, not even the angels of heaven,

[y] Or *stumble*
[z] Or *vultures*

12–17. 8: *The birth-pangs* signal the imminence of the new age, which was announced at the beginning of Jesus' public ministry as "at hand" (4.17), but is to be realized only after a period of witness to Jesus' message (v. 14). Verses 5–14 seem to include a larger community of followers than the original disciples. 9: 10.17–18,22; Jn.15.18; 16.2. 13: 10.22; Rev.2.7. 14: 28.19; Rom. 10.18. 15: Dan.9.27; 11.31; 12.11; see Mk.13.14 n. 17–18: Lk.17.31. 21: Dan.12.1; Jl.2.2. 28: See Lk.17.37 n.; Job 39.30. 29–31: The language here is drawn from the Old Testament; God's victory over sin is to be established by the Son of man whom he sends (Rev.8.12; Is.13.10; 34.4; Ezek.32.7; Jl.2.10–11; Zeph.1.15). 30: 16.27; Dan.7.13; Rev.1.7. 31: 1 Cor.15.52; 1 Th.4.16; Is.27.13; Zech.2.10; 9.14. 34: 10.23; 16.28. The normal meaning of *this generation* would be "men of our time," and the words would refer to a period of 20–30 years. What Jesus meant, however, is uncertain. 35: 5.18; Lk.16.17. 36: Acts 1.6–7. 37–39: Lk.17.26–27; Gen.6.5–8;

nor the Son,[a] but the Father only.
[37] As were the days of Noah, so will
be the coming of the Son of man.
[38] For as in those days before the
flood they were eating and drinking,
marrying and giving in marriage, until
the day when Noah entered the ark,
[39] and they did not know until the
flood came and swept them all away,
so will be the coming of the Son of
man. [40] Then two men will be in the
field; one is taken and one is left.
[41] Two women will be grinding at
the mill; one is taken and one is left.
[42] Watch therefore, for you do not
know on what day your Lord is coming. [43] But know this, that if the
householder had known in what part
of the night the thief was coming, he
would have watched and would not
have let his house be broken into.
[44] Therefore you also must be ready;
for the Son of man is coming at an hour
you do not expect.

45 "Who then is the faithful and
wise servant, whom his master has
set over his household, to give them
their food at the proper time?
[46] Blessed is that servant whom his
master when he comes will find so doing. [47] Truly, I say to you, he will set
him over all his possessions. [48] But
if that wicked servant says to himself,
'My master is delayed,' [49] and begins
to beat his fellow servants, and eats
and drinks with the drunken, [50] the
master of that servant will come on a
day when he does not expect him and
at an hour he does not know, [51] and
will punish[b] him, and put him with the
hypocrites; there men will weep and
gnash their teeth.

25 "Then the kingdom of heaven
shall be compared to ten maidens who took their lamps and went to
meet the bridegroom.[c] [2] Five of them

were foolish, and five were wise. [3] For
when the foolish took their lamps,
they took no oil with them; [4] but the
wise took flasks of oil with their
lamps. [5] As the bridegroom was delayed, they all slumbered and slept.
[6] But at midnight there was a cry,
'Behold, the bridegroom! Come out to
meet him.' [7] Then all those maidens
rose and trimmed their lamps. [8] And
the foolish said to the wise, 'Give us
some of your oil, for our lamps are going out.' [9] But the wise replied, 'Perhaps there will not be enough for us
and for you; go rather to the dealers
and buy for yourselves.' [10] And while
they went to buy, the bridegroom
came, and those who were ready went
in with him to the marriage feast; and
the door was shut. [11] Afterward the
other maidens came also, saying,
'Lord, lord, open to us.' [12] But he
replied, 'Truly, I say to you, I do
not know you.' [13] Watch therefore, for
you know neither the day nor the
hour.

14 "For it will be as when a man
going on a journey called his servants
and entrusted to them his property;
[15] to one he gave five talents,[d] to
another two, to another one, to each
according to his ability. Then he went
away. [16] He who had received the five
talents went at once and traded with
them; and he made five talents more.
[17] So also, he who had the two talents
made two talents more. [18] But he who
had received the one talent went and
dug in the ground and hid his master's
money. [19] Now after a long time the
master of those servants came and
settled accounts with them. [20] And he
who had received the five talents came

a Other ancient authorities omit *nor the Son*
b Or *cut him in pieces*
c Other ancient authorities add *and the bride*
d This talent was more than fifteen years' wages of a
laborer

7.6–24. **40–41:** Lk.17.34–35. **42:** Mk.13.35; Lk.12.40; 21.34–46; Mt.25.13. **43–51:** Lk.12.39–46.
43: 1 Th.5.2; Rev.3.3.

25.1–46: Teachings on the coming of the kingdom. 1–13: The parable of the wise and foolish
maidens is based on the Palestinian custom that *the bridegroom* fetched his bride from her
parents' home to his own. **1:** Lk.12.35–38; Mk.13.34. **2:** 7.24–27. **10:** Rev.19.9. **11–12:** Lk.
13.25; Mt.7.21–23. **13:** 24.42; Mk.13.35; Lk.12.40.
25.14–30: Parable of the talents. Lk.19.12–27. **15:** On the value of this *talent* see note *d*.

forward, bringing five talents more, saying, 'Master, you delivered to me five talents; here I have made five talents more.' [21] His master said to him, 'Well done, good and faithful servant; you have been faithful over a little, I will set you over much; enter into the joy of your master.' [22] And he also who had the two talents came forward, saying, 'Master, you delivered to me two talents; here I have made two talents more.' [23] His master said to him, 'Well done, good and faithful servant; you have been faithful over a little, I will set you over much; enter into the joy of your master.' [24] He also who had received the one talent came forward, saying, 'Master, I knew you to be a hard man, reaping where you did not sow, and gathering where you did not winnow; [25] so I was afraid, and I went and hid your talent in the ground. Here you have what is yours.' [26] But his master answered him, 'You wicked and slothful servant! You knew that I reap where I have not sowed, and gather where I have not winnowed? [27] Then you ought to have invested my money with the bankers, and at my coming I should have received what was my own with interest. [28] So take the talent from him, and give it to him who has the ten talents. [29] For to every one who has will more be given, and he will have abundance; but from him who has not, even what he has will be taken away. [30] And cast the worthless servant into the outer darkness; there men will weep and gnash their teeth.'

31 "When the Son of man comes in his glory, and all the angels with him, then he will sit on his glorious throne. [32] Before him will be gathered all the nations, and he will separate them one from another as a shepherd separates the sheep from the goats, [33] and he will place the sheep at his right hand, but the goats at the left. [34] Then the King will say to those at his right hand, 'Come, O blessed of my Father, inherit the kingdom prepared for you from the foundation of the world; [35] for I was hungry and you gave me food, I was thirsty and you gave me drink, I was a stranger and you welcomed me, [36] I was naked and you clothed me, I was sick and you visited me, I was in prison and you came to me.' [37] Then the righteous will answer him, 'Lord, when did we see thee hungry and feed thee, or thirsty and give thee drink? [38] And when did we see thee a stranger and welcome thee, or naked and clothe thee? [39] And when did we see thee sick or in prison and visit thee?' [40] And the King will answer them, 'Truly, I say to you, as you did it to one of the least of these my brethren, you did it to me.' [41] Then he will say to those at his left hand, 'Depart from me, you cursed, into the eternal fire prepared for the devil and his angels; [42] for I was hungry and you gave me no food, I was thirsty and you gave me no drink, [43] I was a stranger and you did not welcome me, naked and you did not clothe me, sick and in prison and you did not visit me.' [44] Then they also will answer, 'Lord, when did we see thee hungry or thirsty or a stranger or naked or sick or in prison, and did not minister to thee?' [45] Then he will answer them, 'Truly, I say to you, as you did it not to one of the least of these, you did it not to me.' [46] And they will go away into eternal punishment, but the righteous into eternal life."

21: Lk.16.10. **29:** The statement, *From him who has not . . . taken away*, illustrates Jesus' way of speaking in two settings at once: as the master's servant had his original talent, yet had earned nothing by it, so men can have their earthly existence and all that derives from it, yet lack merit in the final judgment (v. 30). **30:** *Worthless*, without value to his master.

25.31–46: The Great Judgment. 31: 16.27; 19.28. **32:** Ezek.34.17. *The nations*, probably those who do not know the God of Israel (compare Rom.2.13–16). **34:** Lk.12.32; Mt.5.3; Rev.13.8; 17.8. **35–36:** Is.58.7; Jas.1.27; 2.15–16; Heb.13.2; 2 Tim.1.16. **40:** 10.42; Mk.9.41; Heb.6.10; Pr.19.17. **41:** Mk.9.48; Rev.20.10. **46:** Dan.12.2; Jn.5.29. *Go away into eternal life* expresses the same idea as *inherit the kingdom* (v. 34).

26 When Jesus had finished all these sayings, he said to his disciples, 2 "You know that after two days the Passover is coming, and the Son of man will be delivered up to be crucified."

3 Then the chief priests and the elders of the people gathered in the palace of the high priest, who was called Ca′iaphas, 4 and took counsel together in order to arrest Jesus by stealth and kill him. 5 But they said, "Not during the feast, lest there be a tumult among the people."

6 Now when Jesus was at Bethany in the house of Simon the leper, 7 a woman came up to him with an alabastar flask of very expensive ointment, and she poured it on his head, as he sat at table. 8 But when the disciples saw it, they were indignant, saying, "Why this waste? 9 For this ointment might have been sold for a large sum, and given to the poor." 10 But Jesus, aware of this, said to them, "Why do you trouble the woman? For she has done a beautiful thing to me. 11 For you always have the poor with you, but you will not always have me. 12 In pouring this ointment on my body she has done it to prepare me for burial. 13 Truly, I say to you, wherever this gospel is preached in the whole world, what she has done will be told in memory of her."

14 Then one of the twelve, who was called Judas Iscariot, went to the chief priests 15 and said, "What will you give me if I deliver him to you?" And they paid him thirty pieces of silver.

16 And from that moment he sought an opportunity to betray him.

17 Now on the first day of Unleavened Bread the disciples came to Jesus, saying, "Where will you have us prepare for you to eat the passover?" 18 He said, "Go into the city to a certain one, and say to him, 'The Teacher says, My time is at hand; I will keep the passover at your house with my disciples.' " 19 And the disciples did as Jesus had directed them, and they prepared the passover.

20 When it was evening, he sat at table with the twelve disciples;*e* 21 and as they were eating, he said, "Truly, I say to you, one of you will betray me." 22 And they were very sorrowful, and began to say to him one after another, "Is it I, Lord?" 23 He answered, "He who has dipped his hand in the dish with me, will betray me. 24 The Son of man goes as it is written of him, but woe to that man by whom the Son of man is betrayed! It would have been better for that man if he had not been born." 25 Judas, who betrayed him, said, "Is it I, Master?"*f* He said to him, "You have said so."

26 Now as they were eating, Jesus took bread, and blessed, and broke it, and gave it to the disciples and said, "Take, eat; this is my body." 27 And he took a cup, and when he had given thanks he gave it to them, saying, "Drink of it, all of you; 28 for this is my blood of the*g* covenant, which is poured out for many for the forgiveness

e Other authorities omit *disciples*
f Or *Rabbi*
g Other ancient authorities insert *new*

26.1–27.66: Jesus' death (Mk.14.1–15.47; Lk.22.1–23.56; Jn.13.1–19.42). **26.1**: *Finished*, see 7.28 n. **2–5**: Mk.14.1–2; Lk.22.1–2; Jn.11.47–53. **2**: *The Passover* commemorated the escape from Egypt under Moses (Ex.12.1–20). **6–13**: Mk.14.3–9; Jn.12.1–8. A similar event is reported in Lk.7.36–50. **6**: The identity of this Simon is unknown. **7**: Jn.12.3; see Lk.7.37 n., 46. **10**: The *beautiful thing* is what is good and fitting under the circumstances of impending death. The same Greek words are translated "good works" in 5.16. **12**: Jn.19.40. **14–16**: Mk.14.10–11; Lk.22.3–6. **14**: See Mk.14.10 n. **15**: Ex.21.32; Zech.11.12. The value of the *thirty pieces of silver* is uncertain. Matthew's quotation refers to silver shekels; at four denarii to the shekel this was one hundred and twenty days' wages (20.2).
26.17–29: The Last Supper. 17–19: Mk.14.12–16; Lk.22.7–13. **17**: See Lk.22.7 n. **18**: Lk.22.10 n., 11 n. Jn.7.6; 12.23; 13.1; 17.1. **19**: 21.6; Dt.16.5–8. **20–25**: Mk.14.17–21; Lk.22.14,21–23; Jn.13.21–30. **24**: Ps.41.9; Lk.24.25; 1 Cor.15.3; Acts 17.2–3; Mt.18.7. **25**: Judas' question is phrased to imply that the answer will be in the negative. **26–29**: Mk.14.22–25; Lk.22.15–20; 1 Cor.10.16; 11.23–26; Mt.14.19; 15.36; see Lk.22.17 n. **28**: Heb.9.20; Mt.20.28;

of sins. [29] I tell you I shall not drink again of this fruit of the vine until that day when I drink it new with you in my Father's kingdom."

30 And when they had sung a hymn, they went out to the Mount of Olives. [31] Then Jesus said to them, "You will all fall away because of me this night; for it is written, 'I will strike the shepherd, and the sheep of the flock will be scattered.' [32] But after I am raised up, I will go before you to Galilee." [33] Peter declared to him, "Though they all fall away because of you, I will never fall away." [34] Jesus said to him, "Truly, I say to you, this very night, before the cock crows, you will deny me three times." [35] Peter said to him, "Even if I must die with you, I will not deny you." And so said all the disciples.

36 Then Jesus went with them to a place called Gethsem'ane, and he said to his disciples, "Sit here, while I go yonder and pray." [37] And taking with him Peter and the two sons of Zeb'edee, he began to be sorrowful and troubled. [38] Then he said to them, "My soul is very sorrowful, even to death; remain here, and watch[h] with me." [39] And going a little farther he fell on his face and prayed, "My Father, if it be possible, let this cup pass from me; nevertheless, not as I will, but as thou wilt." [40] And he came to the disciples and found them sleeping; and he said to Peter, "So, could you not watch[h] with me one hour? [41] Watch[h] and pray that you may not enter into temptation; the spirit indeed is willing, but the flesh is

weak." [42] Again, for the second time, he went away and prayed, "My Father, if this cannot pass unless I drink it, thy will be done." [43] And again he came and found them sleeping, for their eyes were heavy. [44] So, leaving them again, he went away and prayed for the third time, saying the same words. [45] Then he came to the disciples and said to them, "Are you still sleeping and taking your rest? Behold, the hour is at hand, and the Son of man is betrayed into the hands of sinners. [46] Rise, let us be going; see, my betrayer is at hand."

47 While he was still speaking, Judas came, one of the twelve, and with him a great crowd with swords and clubs, from the chief priests and the elders of the people. [48] Now the betrayer had given them a sign, saying, "The one I shall kiss is the man; seize him." [49] And he came up to Jesus at once and said, "Hail, Master!"[i] And he kissed him. [50] Jesus said to him, "Friend, why are you here?"[j] Then they came up and laid hands on Jesus and seized him. [51] And behold, one of those who were with Jesus stretched out his hand and drew his sword, and struck the slave of the high priest, and cut off his ear. [52] Then Jesus said to him, "Put your sword back into its place; for all who take the sword will perish by the sword. [53] Do you think that I cannot appeal to my Father, and he will at once send me more than twelve legions of angels? [54] But how

h Or keep awake
i Or Rabbi
j Or do that for which you have come

Mk.1.4; Ex.24.6–8; see Mk.14.24 n. In the background of Jesus' words are several important ideas of Jewish religion: man's sins lead to death; God has rescued his people, as from Egypt, and may be trusted to deliver from death itself; God forgives men in mercy if they obey him; God will make a new covenant (Jer.31.31–34). **29:** See Lk.14.15; 22.18,30; Rev.19.9.

26.30–56: Gethsemane. 30–35: Mk.14.26–31; Lk.22.31–34,39; Jn.14.31; 18.1; 13.36–38. **30:** Probably the *hymn* was Psalms 115–118. **31:** Zech.13.7; Jn.16.32. **32:** 28.7,10,16. **36–46:** Mk.14.32–42; Lk.22.40–46. **38:** Jn.12.27; Heb.5.7–8; Ps.42.6. *My soul*, i.e. "I." **39:** Ezek. 23.31–34; Jn.18.11; Mt.20.22. Jesus does not desire death but accepts God's will even including death. *Cup*, see Lk.22.42 n. **41:** 6.13; Lk.11.4. *Temptation*, "testing," in which man's best intentions may give way. **42:** Jn.4.34; 5.30; 6.38. **45:** 26.18 n.; Jn.12.23; 13.1; 17.1. **47–56:** Mk.14.43–52; Lk.22.47–53; Jn.18.2–11. **50:** *Friend*, "comrade." The synoptic gospels do not report Judas' movements on this night (compare Jn.13.30; 18.3). **51:** Jn.18.10. **52:** Gen.9.6; Rev.13.10. **53:** *Twelve legions*, 72,000. **54:** Faith in God can not claim his promise (4.6) so as to counteract his purpose. **55:** Lk.19.47; Jn.18.19–21.

then should the scriptures be fulfilled, that it must be so?" [55] At that hour Jesus said to the crowds, "Have you come out as against a robber, with swords and clubs to capture me? Day after day I sat in the temple teaching, and you did not seize me. [56] But all this has taken place, that the scriptures of the prophets might be fulfilled." Then all the disciples forsook him and fled.

57 Then those who had seized Jesus led him to Ca'iaphas the high priest, where the scribes and the elders had gathered. [58] But Peter followed him at a distance, as far as the courtyard of the high priest, and going inside he sat with the guards to see the end. [59] Now the chief priests and the whole council sought false testimony against Jesus that they might put him to death, [60] but they found none, though many false witnesses came forward. At last two came forward [61] and said, "This fellow said, 'I am able to destroy the temple of God, and to build it in three days.'" [62] And the high priest stood up and said, "Have you no answer to make? What is it that these men testify against you?" [63] But Jesus was silent. And the high priest said to him, "I adjure you by the living God, tell us if you are the Christ, the Son of God." [64] Jesus said to him, "You have said so. But I tell you, hereafter you will see the Son of man seated at the right hand of Power, and coming on the clouds of heaven." [65] Then the high priest tore his robes, and said, "He has uttered blasphemy. Why do we still need witnesses? You have now heard his blasphemy. [66] What is your judgment?" They answered, "He deserves death." [67] Then they spat in his face, and struck him; and some slapped him,

[68] saying, "Prophesy to us, you Christ! Who is it that struck you?"

69 Now Peter was sitting outside in the courtyard. And a maid came up to him, and said, "You also were with Jesus the Galilean." [70] But he denied it before them all, saying, "I do not know what you mean." [71] And when he went out to the porch, another maid saw him, and she said to the bystanders, "This man was with Jesus of Nazareth." [72] And again he denied it with an oath, "I do not know the man." [73] After a little while the bystanders came up and said to Peter, "Certainly you are also one of them, for your accent betrays you." [74] Then he began to invoke a curse on himself and to swear, "I do not know the man." And immediately the cock crowed. [75] And Peter remembered the saying of Jesus, "Before the cock crows, you will deny me three times." And he went out and wept bitterly.

27 When morning came, all the chief priests and the elders of the people took counsel against Jesus to put him to death; [2] and they bound him and led him away and delivered him to Pilate the governor.

3 When Judas, his betrayer, saw that he was condemned, he repented and brought back the thirty pieces of silver to the chief priests and the elders, [4] saying, "I have sinned in betraying innocent blood." They said, "What is that to us? See to it yourself." [5] And throwing down the pieces of silver in the temple, he departed; and he went and hanged himself. [6] But the chief priests, taking the pieces of silver, said, "It is not lawful to put them into the treasury, since they are blood money." [7] So they took counsel, and bought with them the potter's field, to bury

26.57–75: Jesus before Caiaphas. 57: The reference is to the Jewish supreme court (the Sanhedrin; see Jn.11.47 n.). **59:** See Mk.14.55 n. **61:** 24.2; 27.40; Acts 6.14; Jn.2.19. **63:** 27.11; Jn.18.33. **64:** 16.28; Dan.7.13; Ps.110.1. **65:** Num.14.6; Acts 14.14; Lev.24.16. **66:** Lev.24.16. **73:** Peter spoke with a Galilean accent differing from the Judean. **75:** Compare v. 34.

27.1–26: Jesus before Pilate. 1–2: Mk.15.1; Lk.23.1; Jn.18.28–32. Jewish law required that the Sanhedrin take formal action by daylight. Apparently 26.57–68 describes a pre-dawn hearing. **3–10:** Acts 1.16–20. The details of Judas' end are obscure. Each account connects him in

strangers in. [8] Therefore that field has been called the Field of Blood to this day. [9] Then was fulfilled what had been spoken by the prophet Jeremiah, saying, "And they took the thirty pieces of silver, the price of him on whom a price had been set by some of the sons of Israel, [10] and they gave them for the potter's field, as the Lord directed me."

11 Now Jesus stood before the governor; and the governor asked him, "Are you the King of the Jews?" Jesus said, "You have said so." [12] But when he was accused by the chief priests and elders, he made no answer. [13] Then Pilate said to him, "Do you not hear how many things they testify against you?" [14] But he gave him no answer, not even to a single charge; so that the governor wondered greatly.

15 Now at the feast the governor was accustomed to release for the crowd any one prisoner whom they wanted. [16] And they had then a notorious prisoner, called Barab'bas.[k] [17] So when they had gathered, Pilate said to them, "Whom do you want me to release for you, Barab'bas[k] or Jesus who is called Christ?" [18] For he knew that it was out of envy that they had delivered him up. [19] Besides, while he was sitting on the judgment seat, his wife sent word to him, "Have nothing to do with that righteous man, for I have suffered much over him today in a dream." [20] Now the chief priests and the elders persuaded the people to ask for Barab'bas and destroy Jesus. [21] The governor again said to them, "Which of the two do you want me to release for you?" And they said, "Barab'bas." [22] Pilate said to them, "Then what shall I do with Jesus who

is called Christ?" They all said, "Let him be crucified." [23] And he said, "Why, what evil has he done?" But they shouted all the more, "Let him be crucified."

24 So when Pilate saw that he was gaining nothing, but rather that a riot was beginning, he took water and washed his hands before the crowd, saying, "I am innocent of this man's blood;[l] see to it yourselves." [25] And all the people answered, "His blood be on us and on our children!" [26] Then he released for them Barab'bas, and having scourged Jesus, delivered him to be crucified.

27 Then the soldiers of the governor took Jesus into the praetorium, and they gathered the whole battalion before him. [28] And they stripped him and put a scarlet robe upon him, [29] and plaiting a crown of thorns they put it on his head, and put a reed in his right hand. And kneeling before him they mocked him, saying, "Hail, King of the Jews!" [30] And they spat upon him, and took the reed and struck him on the head. [31] And when they had mocked him, they stripped him of the robe, and put his own clothes on him, and led him away to crucify him.

32 As they went out, they came upon a man of Cyre'ne, Simon by name; this man they compelled to carry his cross. [33] And when they came to a place called Gol'gotha (which means the place of a skull), [34] they offered him wine to drink, mingled with gall; but when he tasted it, he would not drink it. [35] And when they had

---

k Other ancient authorities read *Jesus Barabbas*
l Other authorities read *this righteous blood* or *this righteous man's blood*

---

death with a cemetery for foreigners in Jerusalem. **9–10:** Zech.11.12–13; Jer.18.1–3; 32.6–15. **11–14:** Mk.15.2–5; Lk.23.2–5; Jn.18.29–19.16. **14:** Lk.23.9; Mt.26.62; Mk.14.60; 1 Tim.6.13. **15–26:** Mk.15.6–15; Lk.23.18–25; Jn.18.38–40; 19.4–16. **19:** Lk.23.4. **21:** Acts 3.13–14. **24:** Dt.21.6–9; Ps.26.6. **25:** Acts 5.28; Jos.2.19. **26:** Scourging with a multi-thonged whip ordinarily preceded execution. **27.27–44: The crucifixion. 27–31:** Mk.15.16–20; Jn.19.1–3. **27:** The *praetorium* was the governor's residence. *The battalion* at full strength numbered about five hundred men. **32–44:** Mk.15.21–32; Lk.23.26,33–43; Jn.19.17–24. **32:** The procession included Jesus, two other prisoners, a centurion, and a few soldiers. *Simon*, see Mk.15.21 n. **34:** *Gall*, any bitter liquid,

crucified him, they divided his garments among them by casting lots; [36] then they sat down and kept watch over him there. [37] And over his head they put the charge against him, which read, "This is Jesus the King of the Jews." [38] Then two robbers were crucified with him, one on the right and one on the left. [39] And those who passed by derided him, wagging their heads [40] and saying, "You who would destroy the temple and build it in three days, save yourself! If you are the Son of God, come down from the cross." [41] So also the chief priests, with the scribes and elders, mocked him, saying, [42] "He saved others; he cannot save himself. He is the King of Israel; let him come down now from the cross, and we will believe in him. [43] He trusts in God; let God deliver him now, if he desires him; for he said, 'I am the Son of God.' " [44] And the robbers who were crucified with him also reviled him in the same way.

45 Now from the sixth hour there was darkness over all the land[m] until the ninth hour. [46] And about the ninth hour Jesus cried with a loud voice, "Eli, Eli, la'ma sabach-tha'ni?" that is, "My God, my God, why hast thou forsaken me?" [47] And some of the bystanders hearing it said, "This man is calling Eli'jah." [48] And one of them at once ran and took a sponge, filled it with vinegar, and put it on a reed, and gave it to him to drink. [49] But the others said, "Wait, let us see whether Eli'jah will come to save him."[n] [50] And Jesus cried again with a loud voice and yielded up his spirit.

51 And behold, the curtain of the temple was torn in two, from top to bottom; and the earth shook, and the rocks were split; [52] the tombs also were opened, and many bodies of the saints who had fallen asleep were raised, [53] and coming out of the tombs after his resurrection they went into the holy city and appeared to many. [54] When the centurion and those who were with him, keeping watch over Jesus, saw the earthquake and what took place, they were filled with awe, and said, "Truly this was the Son[x] of God!"

55 There were also many women there, looking on from afar, who had followed Jesus from Galilee, ministering to him; [56] among whom were Mary Mag'dalene, and Mary the mother of James and Joseph, and the mother of the sons of Zeb'edee.

57 When it was evening, there came a rich man from Arimathe'a, named Joseph, who also was a disciple of Jesus. [58] He went to Pilate and asked for the body of Jesus. Then Pilate ordered it to be given to him. [59] And Joseph took the body, and wrapped it in a clean linen shroud, [60] and laid it in his own new tomb, which he had hewn in the rock; and he rolled a great stone to the door of the tomb, and departed. [61] Mary Mag'dalene and the other Mary were there, sitting opposite the sepulchre.

62 Next day, that is, after the day of Preparation, the chief priests and

m Or *earth*
n Other ancient authorities insert *And another took a spear and pierced his side, and out came water and blood*
x Or *a son*

possibly the myrrh of Mk.15.23. **35:** Ps.22.18. **37:** Indication of the offense was customary. Since the Romans recognized the ruling Herods, it seems implied that Jesus was alleged to be a pretender and revolutionary. **39:** Ps.22.7–8; 109.25. **40:** 26.61; Acts 6.14; Jn.2.19. **42–43:** The taunts stress religious aspects of Jesus' works and words. *Israel* (rather than *the Jews*, v. 37) refers to the religious community rather than the political state. **43:** Ps.22.8.
27.45–66: The death of Jesus. 45–56: Mk.15.33–41; Lk.23.44–49; Jn.19.28–37. **45:** From about noon to about three p.m. **46:** *Eli . . . sabachthani*, quoted from Ps.22.1. **47:** *Elijah* (similar in sound to *Eli*) was expected to usher in the final period (Mal.4.5–6; Mt.27.49). **48:** Ps.69.21. The *vinegar* was a cheap, sour wine of the poor. The motive in offering it may have been to revive him and hence prolong the ordeal. **51:** Heb.9.8; 10.19; Ex.26.31–35; Mt.28.2; see Mk.15.38 n. **56:** *James*, possibly the James of 10.3; Lk.24.10; Acts 1.13. **57–61:** Mk.15.42–47; Lk.23.50–56; Jn.19.38–42; Acts 13.29. **58:** Bodies of the executed were normally denied burial. **60:** See Mk.16.3–5 n.; Acts 13.29. **61:** 27.56. **62:** *Next day*, the sabbath (Mk.15.42).

the Pharisees gathered before Pilate
[63] and said, "Sir, we remember how
that impostor said, while he was still
alive, 'After three days I will rise
again.' [64] Therefore order the sepulchre to be made secure until the third
day, lest his disciples go and steal him
away, and tell the people, 'He has
risen from the dead,' and the last fraud
will be worse than the first." [65] Pilate
said to them, "You have a guard[o] of
soldiers; go, make it as secure as you
can."[p] [66] So they went and made
the sepulchre secure by sealing the
stone and setting a guard.

28 Now after the sabbath, toward
the dawn of the first day of the
week, Mary Mag'dalene and the other
Mary went to see the sepulchre. [2] And
behold, there was a great earthquake;
for an angel of the Lord descended
from heaven and came and rolled
back the stone, and sat upon it. [3] His
appearance was like lightning, and his
raiment white as snow. [4] And for fear
of him the guards trembled and
became like dead men. [5] But the angel
said to the women, "Do not be afraid;
for I know that you seek Jesus who
was crucified. [6] He is not here; for he
has risen, as he said. Come, see the
place where he[q] lay. [7] Then go
quickly and tell his disciples that he
has risen from the dead, and behold,
he is going before you to Galilee; there
you will see him. Lo, I have told you."
[8] So they departed quickly from the
tomb with fear and great joy, and ran

to tell his disciples. [9] And behold,
Jesus met them and said, "Hail!" And
they came up and took hold of his feet
and worshiped him. [10] Then Jesus said
to them, "Do not be afraid; go and tell
my brethren to go to Galilee, and there
they will see me."

11 While they were going, behold,
some of the guard went into the city
and told the chief priests all that had
taken place. [12] And when they had
assembled with the elders and taken
counsel, they gave a sum of money to
the soldiers [13] and said, "Tell people,
'His disciples came by night and stole
him away while we were asleep.'
[14] And if this comes to the governor's
ears, we will satisfy him and keep you
out of trouble." [15] So they took the
money and did as they were directed;
and this story has been spread among
the Jews to this day.

16 Now the eleven disciples went
to Galilee, to the mountain to which
Jesus had directed them. [17] And when
they saw him they worshiped him; but
some doubted. [18] And Jesus came and
said to them, "All authority in heaven
and on earth has been given to me.
[19] Go therefore and make disciples of
all nations, baptizing them in the name
of the Father and of the Son and of
the Holy Spirit, [20] teaching them to
observe all that I have commanded
you; and lo, I am with you always, to
the close of the age."

o Or *Take a guard*
p Greek *know*
q Other ancient authorities read *the Lord*

28.1–15: The first Easter (Mk.16.1–8; Lk.24.1–11; Jn.20.1–10). **4:** *The guards*, 27.62–66.
7: 26.32; 28.16; Jn.21.1–23; 1 Cor.15.3–4,12,20. **8:** Compare Lk.24.9,22–23; the sequence of
events cannot be worked out. Each account is a separate summary of early Christian testimony
to the fact of Jesus' resurrection. **9:** Jn.20.14–18.

28.11–15: Bribing the guard. 11: 27.62–66. **15:** *This day*, i.e. the time when the Gospel
according to Matthew was written.

28:16–20: Jesus' commission to his disciples. 17: 1 Cor.15.5–6; Jn.21.1–23; Lk.24.11. **18:**
11.27; Lk.10.22; Phil.2.9; Eph.1.20–22. *All authority*, compare Dan.7.14. **19:** *All nations*, contrast 10.5, and compare Mk.16.15; Lk.24.47; Acts 1.8. According to Hebrew usage *in the name
of* means in the possession and protection of (Ps.124.8). **20:** *I am with you*, 18.20; Acts 18.10.

THE GOSPEL ACCORDING TO

MARK

The Gospel according to Mark is commonly thought to have been the first written of the Gospels in the New Testament (see pp. 1167–1168). The Evangelist presents Jesus of Nazareth as the Son of God (1.1,11; 5.7; 9.7; 14.61–62; 15.39) whose ministry was characterized by a succession of mighty works which, to those who had eyes to see, were signs of the presence of God's power and kingdom.

This Gospel is largely a collection of narratives that depict Jesus as being almost constantly active (a favorite word in Mark is "immediately," which occurs about forty times in sixteen chapters). On the other hand, Mark records fewer words of Jesus than does any of the other Gospels; it contains one collection of sayings in the form of a discourse (ch. 13) and a few parables.

The main divisions are: 1.1–13, Opening events of Jesus' public life (John the Baptist; baptism and temptation of Jesus); 1.14–9.50, Jesus' preaching, teaching, and healing in Galilee; ch. 10, Journey to Jerusalem; chs. 11–15, The last week, concluding with Jesus' crucifixion and burial; 16.1–8, The resurrection. This arrangement of the story of Jesus, beginning with the preaching of John, preserves the form and to some degree the content of the first Christian missionary message. The early disciples illustrated their claim that Jesus was the divinely appointed Christ (1.1; 8.29) by retelling significant moments from his days in Galilee and the last week of his life (compare Acts 10.34–43).

Though the Gospel is anonymous, an ancient Christian tradition may well be correct in ascribing it to John Mark (Acts 12.12; 15.37), who is said to have composed it at Rome as a summary of Peter's preaching (compare 1 Pet.5.13). The date of writing, though uncertain, was probably prior to the fall of Jerusalem in A.D. 70.

THE BEGINNING OF THE GOSPEL of Jesus Christ, the Son of God.*a* 2 As it is written in Isaiah the prophet,*b*

"Behold, I send my messenger
  before thy face,
who shall prepare thy way;
3 the voice of one crying in the
    wilderness:
Prepare the way of the Lord,
  make his paths straight–"

4 John the baptizer appeared*c* in the wilderness, preaching a baptism of repentance for the forgiveness of sins. 5 And there went out to him all the country of Judea, and all the people of Jerusalem; and they were baptized by him in the river Jordan, confessing their sins. 6 Now John was clothed with camel's hair, and had a leather girdle around his waist, and ate locusts and wild honey. 7 And he preached, saying, "After me comes he who is mightier than I, the thong of whose sandals I am not worthy to stoop down and untie. 8 I have baptized you with water; but he will baptize you with the Holy Spirit."

9 In those days Jesus came from Nazareth of Galilee and was baptized by John in the Jordan. 10 And when he came up out of the water, immediately he saw the heavens opened and the Spirit descending upon him like a

a Other ancient authorities omit *the Son of God*
b Other ancient authorities read *in the prophets*
c Other ancient authorities read *John was baptizing*

1.1–8: Activity of John the Baptist (Mt.3.1–12; Lk.3.1–20; Jn.1.6,15,19–28). **1:** *The gospel* (i.e. the good news) begins with John's call to repentance. **2:** Mal.3.1 (God is the speaker); Mt.11.10; Lk.7.27. **3:** Is.40.3. **4:** Acts 13.24. John called men to baptism *with water*, thereby symbolizing recognition and confession of sin together with acceptance of God's judgment and forgiveness. **8:** Baptism *with the Holy Spirit* would draw men into spiritual communion with God (Acts 2.17–21; Jl.2.28–29).
1.9–11: Jesus' baptism (Mt.3.13–17; Lk.3.21–22; Jn.1.29–34). **11:** *Beloved*, similar in meaning to *chosen* (Is.42.1), refers to an act of will rather than of feeling (Ps.2.7; Lk.9.35; 2 Pet.1.17).

dove; [11] and a voice came from heaven, "Thou art my beloved Son;[d] with thee I am well pleased."

12 The Spirit immediately drove him out into the wilderness. [13] And he was in the wilderness forty days, tempted by Satan; and he was with the wild beasts; and the angels ministered to him.

14 Now after John was arrested, Jesus came into Galilee, preaching the gospel of God, [15] and saying, "The time is fulfilled, and the kingdom of God is at hand; repent, and believe in the gospel."

16 And passing along by the Sea of Galilee, he saw Simon and Andrew the brother of Simon casting a net in the sea; for they were fishermen. [17] And Jesus said to them, "Follow me and I will make you become fishers of men." [18] And immediately they left their nets and followed him. [19] And going on a little farther, he saw James the son of Zeb'edee and John his brother, who were in their boat mending the nets. [20] And immediately he called them; and they left their father Zeb'edee in the boat with the hired servants, and followed him.

21 And they went into Caper'na-um; and immediately on the sabbath he entered the synagogue and taught. [22] And they were astonished at his teaching, for he taught them as one who had authority, and not as the scribes. [23] And immediately there was in their synagogue a man with an unclean spirit; [24] and he cried out, "What have you to do with us, Jesus of Nazareth? Have you come to destroy us? I know who you are, the Holy One of God." [25] But Jesus rebuked him, saying, "Be silent, and come out of him!" [26] And the unclean spirit, convulsing him and crying with a loud voice, came out of him. [27] And they were all amazed, so that they questioned among themselves, saying, "What is this? A new teaching! With authority he commands even the unclean spirits, and they obey him." [28] And at once his fame spread everywhere throughout all the surrounding region of Galilee.

29 And immediately he[e] left the synagogue, and entered the house of Simon and Andrew, with James and John. [30] Now Simon's mother-in-law lay sick with a fever, and immediately they told him of her. [31] And he came and took her by the hand and lifted her up, and the fever left her; and she served them.

32 That evening, at sundown, they brought to him all who were sick or possessed with demons. [33] And the whole city was gathered together about the door. [34] And he healed many who were sick with various diseases, and cast out many demons; and he would not permit the demons to speak, because they knew him.

35 And in the morning, a great while before day, he rose and went out to a lonely place, and there he prayed. [36] And Simon and those who were with him pursued him, [37] and they found him and said to him, "Every one is searching for you." [38] And he said to them, "Let us go on to the next towns, that I may preach there also; for that is why I came out." [39] And he went throughout all Galilee, preaching in their synagogues and casting out demons.

d Or *my Son, my* (or *the*) *Beloved*
e Other ancient authorities read *they*

1.12–13: Jesus' temptation (Mt.4.1–11; Lk.4.1–13).
    1.14–39: Beginnings of Jesus' activity in Galilee. 14–15: Mt.4.12–17; Lk.4.14–15. **15:** Jesus' message summarized. The whole of Mark is an expansion of this verse. *Repent*, return to God's way; *believe the gospel*, accept the message (see Mt.4.17 n.). **16–20:** Mt.4.18–22; Lk.5.1–11; Jn.1.35–42. **21–22:** Mt.7.28–29; Lk.4.31–32. **23–28:** Lk.4.33–37. **23:** The *spirit*, or demon, was called *unclean* because the effect of the condition was to separate men from the worship of God. **27:** See Mt.7.29 n. **29–34:** Mt.8.14–17; Lk.4.38–41. **32:** The sabbath ended at sunset. **34:** See vv. 43–44 n. **35–39:** Mt.4.23–25; Lk.4.42–44. **35:** See Lk.3.21 n. **38:** He *came out* from Capernaum (2.1).

40 And a leper came to him beseeching him, and kneeling said to him, "If you will, you can make me clean." ⁴¹ Moved with pity, he stretched out his hand and touched him, and said to him, "I will; be clean." ⁴² And immediately the leprosy left him, and he was made clean. ⁴³ And he sternly charged him, and sent him away at once, ⁴⁴ and said to him, "See that you say nothing to any one; but go, show yourself to the priest, and offer for your cleansing what Moses commanded, for a proof to the people."ᶠ ⁴⁵ But he went out and began to talk freely about it, and to spread the news, so that Jesusᵍ could no longer openly enter a town, but was out in the country; and people came to him from every quarter.

2 And when he returned to Caper'na-um after some days, it was reported that he was at home. ² And many were gathered together, so that there was no longer room for them, not even about the door; and he was preaching the word to them. ³ And they came, bringing to him a paralytic carried by four men. ⁴ And when they could not get near him because of the crowd, they removed the roof above him; and when they had made an opening, they let down the pallet on which the paralytic lay. ⁵ And when Jesus saw their faith, he said to the paralytic, "My son, your sins are forgiven." ⁶ Now some of the scribes were sitting there, questioning in their hearts, ⁷ "Why does this man speak thus? It is blasphemy! Who can forgive sins but God alone?" ⁸ And immediately Jesus, perceiving in his spirit that they thus questioned within themselves, said to them, "Why do you question thus in your hearts? ⁹ Which is easier, to say to the paralytic, 'Your sins are forgiven,' or to say, 'Rise, take up your pallet and walk'? ¹⁰ But that you may know that the Son of man has authority on earth to forgive sins"– he said to the paralytic– ¹¹ "I say to you, rise, take up your pallet and go home." ¹² And he rose, and immediately took up the pallet and went out before them all; so that they were all amazed and glorified God, saying, "We never saw anything like this!"

13 He went out again beside the sea; and all the crowd gathered about him, and he taught them. ¹⁴ And as he passed on, he saw Levi the son of Alphaeus sitting at the tax office, and he said to him, "Follow me." And he rose and followed him.

15 And as he sat at table in his house, many tax collectors and sinners were sitting with Jesus and his disciples; for there were many who followed him. ¹⁶ And the scribes ofʰ the Pharisees, when they saw that he was eating with sinners and tax col-

f Greek *to them*
g Greek *he*
h Other ancient authorities read *and*

1.40–9.50: Ministry and controversy, chiefly in Galilee. 1.40–45: Mt.8.2–4; Lk.5.12–16. **43–44:** Jesus wished the healing to carry with it a spiritual obligation. He apparently feared that rumors of miracles would gather the curious and foster cries for help only in physical terms, thus hindering his message (v. 45).

2.1–12: Healing a paralytic (Mt.9.1–8; Lk.5.17–26). **2:** *The word* was everything he had to say to men about God's purposes. **4:** *The roof* was flat, probably of sticks and packed earth. **7:** The Jewish leaders sense in Jesus' words (v. 5) either some claim of his own or the assertion of a way of forgiveness different from that taught by the scribes. **10:** *Son of man*, a title which Jesus used of himself, probably seemed to his listeners to carry either of two meanings: (a) that Jesus called himself a typical human being in accordance with the common meaning of *son of* (see Mt.5.45 n.); or (b) that Jesus (contrary to the humble conditions of his daily life) linked himself to the prophesied figure of Dan.7.13–14 who was popularly regarded as the coming Messiah (see Acts 7.56 n.). Jesus nowhere fully discloses his own understanding of the term (but see 8.32 n.). However, each meaning by itself, as well as both together (see Mt.25.29 n.), could have appealed to him. It was also characteristic of him to speak in such a way as to oblige his hearers to determine their own personal attitudes toward him as part of the process of understanding his words (see Mt.13.3 n.).

2.13–17: The call of Levi (Mt.9.9–13; Lk.5.27–32). **13:** *The sea*, of Galilee. **14:** *Levi*, Mat-

lectors, said to his disciples, "Why does he eat[i] with tax collectors and sinners?" 17 And when Jesus heard it, he said to them, "Those who are well have no need of a physician, but those who are sick; I came not to call the righteous, but sinners."

18 Now John's disciples and the Pharisees were fasting; and people came and said to him, "Why do John's disciples and the disciples of the Pharisees fast, but your disciples do not fast?" 19 And Jesus said to them, "Can the wedding guests fast while the bridegroom is with them? As long as they have the bridegroom with them, they cannot fast. 20 The days will come, when the bridegroom is taken away from them, and then they will fast in that day. 21 No one sews a piece of unshrunk cloth on an old garment; if he does, the patch tears away from it, the new from the old, and a worse tear is made. 22 And no one puts new wine into old wineskins; if he does, the wine will burst the skins, and the wine is lost, and so are the skins; but new wine is for fresh skins."[j]

23 One sabbath he was going through the grainfields; and as they made their way his disciples began to pluck heads of grain. 24 And the Pharisees said to him, "Look, why are they doing what is not lawful on the sabbath?" 25 And he said to them, "Have you never read what David did, when he was in need and was hungry, he and those who were with him: 26 how he entered the house of God, when Abi'athar was high priest, and

ate the bread of the Presence, which it is not lawful for any but the priests to eat, and also gave it to those who were with him?" 27 And he said to them, "The sabbath was made for man, not man for the sabbath; 28 so the Son of man is lord even of the sabbath."

3 Again he entered the synagogue, and a man was there who had a withered hand. 2 And they watched him, to see whether he would heal him on the sabbath, so that they might accuse him. 3 And he said to the man who had the withered hand, "Come here." 4 And he said to them, "Is it lawful on the sabbath to do good or to do harm, to save life or to kill?" But they were silent. 5 And he looked around at them with anger, grieved at their hardness of heart, and said to the man, "Stretch out your hand." He stretched it out, and his hand was restored. 6 The Pharisees went out, and immediately held counsel with the Hero'di-ans against him, how to destroy him.

7 Jesus withdrew with his disciples to the sea, and a great multitude from Galilee followed; also from Judea 8 and Jerusalem and Idume'a and from beyond the Jordan and from about Tyre and Sidon a great multitude, hearing all that he did, came to him. 9 And he told his disciples to have a boat ready for him because of the crowd, lest they should crush him; 10 for he had healed many, so that all

i Other ancient authorities add *and drink*
j Other ancient authorities omit *but new wine is for fresh skins*

---

thew. This experience was not necessarily Matthew's first contact with Jesus (v. 15). **17:** See Lk.5.32 n.

2.18–22: Fasting (Mt.9.14–17; Lk.5.33–39). **19–20:** Is.62.5; Lk.17.22. The implication is that Jesus comes as a *bridegroom* for his followers (the bride). Fasting was inappropriate to a wedding, and to joyous association with himself (see Jn.3.27–29 n.).

2.23–3.6: Jesus and sabbath laws (Mt.12.1–14; Lk.6.1–11). **2.24:** The Pharisees attack Jesus by attacking his disciples (vv. 16,18). **26:** *Abiathar* was *high priest* during David's reign (2 Sam. 15.35); his father Ahimelech was priest at the time David ate the consecrated bread (1 Sam. 21.1–6). **27:** Ex.23.12; Dt.5.14. **3.3–4:** Jesus, acting by the principle stated in 2.27, equated acts to meet human need with acts *lawful on the sabbath*. **6:** *Herodians*, apparently a group supporting the royal family. Nothing definite is known about them, but probably their interests were secular. The Pharisees sought allies wherever they might be found (12.13).

3.7–12: Work of healing (Mt.4.24–25; 12.15–21; Lk.6.17–19; 4.41). **7–8:** 1.28,38,45. Jesus' fame has spread. **10:** 5.29,34; 6.54–56. **12:** 1.43–44.

who had diseases pressed upon him to touch him. ¹¹ And whenever the unclean spirits beheld him, they fell down before him and cried out, "You are the Son of God." ¹² And he strictly ordered them not to make him known.

13 And he went up on the mountain, and called to him those whom he desired; and they came to him. ¹⁴ And he appointed twelve,ᵏ to be with him, and to be sent out to preach ¹⁵ and have authority to cast out demons: ¹⁶ Simonˣ whom he surnamed Peter; ¹⁷ James the son of Zeb'edee and John the brother of James, whom he surnamed Bo-aner'ges, that is, sons of thunder; ¹⁸ Andrew, and Philip, and Bartholomew, and Matthew, and Thomas, and James the son of Alphaeus, and Thaddaeus, and Simon the Cananaean, ¹⁹ and Judas Iscariot, who betrayed him.

Then he went home; ²⁰ and the crowd came together again, so that they could not even eat. ²¹ And when his family heard it, they went out to seize him, for people were saying, "He is beside himself." ²² And the scribes who came down from Jerusalem said, "He is possessed by Be-el'zebul, and by the prince of demons he casts out the demons." ²³ And he called them to him, and said to them in parables, "How can Satan cast out Satan? ²⁴ If a kingdom is divided against itself, that kingdom cannot stand. ²⁵ And if a house is divided against itself, that house will not be able to stand. ²⁶ And if Satan has risen up against himself and is divided, he cannot

stand, but is coming to an end. ²⁷ But no one can enter a strong man's house and plunder his goods, unless he first binds the strong man; then indeed he may plunder his house.

28 "Truly, I say to you, all sins will be forgiven the sons of men, and whatever blasphemies they utter; ²⁹ but whoever blasphemes against the Holy Spirit never has forgiveness, but is guilty of an eternal sin"– ³⁰ for they had said, "He has an unclean spirit."

31 And his mother and his brothers came; and standing outside they sent to him and called him. ³² And a crowd was sitting about him; and they said to him, "Your mother and your brothersˡ are outside, asking for you." ³³ And he replied, "Who are my mother and my brothers?" ³⁴ And looking around on those who sat about him, he said, "Here are my mother and my brothers! ³⁵ Whoever does the will of God is my brother, and sister, and mother."

4 Again he began to teach beside the sea. And a very large crowd gathered about him, so that he got into a boat and sat in it on the sea; and the whole crowd was beside the sea on the land. ² And he taught them many things in parables, and in his teaching he said to them: ³ "Listen! A sower went out to sow. ⁴ And as he sowed, some seed fell along the path, and the birds came and devoured it. ⁵ Other seed fell on rocky ground, where it

k Other ancient authorities add *whom also he named apostles*
x Other authorities read *demons*. ¹⁶ *So he appointed the twelve: Simon*
l Other early authorities add *and your sisters*

3.13–19a: The Twelve chosen (Mt.10.1–4; Lk.6.12–16). Jesus invited the Twelve to live intimately with him, adopting his way of life as well as his message. Spiritual strength came through the community he established (see 6.7–13 n.). **13:** Lk.6.12. **18:** This *Alphaeus* was apparently not identical with Levi's father (2.14). *Simon the Cananaean* belonged to a Jewish patriotic group also called Zealots (Lk.6.15; Acts 1.13).

3.19b–30: Questions about Jesus' power (Mt.12.22–37; Lk.11.14–23; 12.10; 6.43–45). **21:** *His family* (perhaps his mother and his brothers, v. 31) were concerned both for his safety, amidst the intense emotions rising round him, and his sanity. **22:** The Pharisees attribute his acts to demonic power (see Lk.7.33 n.; Jn.10.20). *Beelzebul*, a pagan god (see 2 Kg.1.2 n.) identified with Satan. **24–27:** Inner division is destructive. **29:** Mt.12.31–32 n. **31–35:** *Brothers*, see Mt.13.55 n.

4.1–34: Teaching in parables (Mt. ch. 13; Lk.8.4–18; 13.18–21). On Jesus' use of parables, see Mt.13.3 n. **3:** The *sower* scattered seed broadcast. **5:** The rock lay just below the surface of the

had not much soil, and immediately it sprang up, since it had no depth of soil; [6] and when the sun rose it was scorched, and since it had no root it withered away. [7] Other seed fell among thorns and the thorns grew up and choked it, and it yielded no grain. [8] And other seeds fell into good soil and brought forth grain, growing up and increasing and yielding thirtyfold and sixtyfold and a hundredfold." [9] And he said, "He who has ears to hear, let him hear."

10 And when he was alone, those who were about him with the twelve asked him concerning the parables. [11] And he said to them, "To you has been given the secret of the kingdom of God, but for those outside everything is in parables; [12] so that they may indeed see but not perceive, and may indeed hear but not understand; lest they should turn again, and be forgiven." [13] And he said to them, "Do you not understand this parable? How then will you understand all the parables? [14] The sower sows the word. [15] And these are the ones along the path, where the word is sown; when they hear, Satan immediately comes and takes away the word which is sown in them. [16] And these in like manner are the ones sown upon rocky ground, who, when they hear the word, immediately receive it with joy; [17] and they have no root in themselves, but endure for a while; then, when tribulation or persecution arises on account of the word, immediately they fall away.*m* [18] And others are the ones sown among thorns; they are those who hear the word, [19] but the cares of the world, and the delight in riches, and the desire for other things, enter in and choke the word, and it proves unfruitful. [20] But those that were sown upon the good soil are the ones who hear the word and accept it and bear fruit, thirtyfold and sixtyfold and a hundredfold."

21 And he said to them, "Is a lamp brought in to be put under a bushel, or under a bed, and not on a stand? [22] For there is nothing hid, except to be made manifest; nor is anything secret, except to come to light. [23] If any man has ears to hear, let him hear." [24] And he said to them, "Take heed what you hear; the measure you give will be the measure you get, and still more will be given you. [25] For to him who has will more be given; and from him who has not, even what he has will be taken away."

26 And he said, "The kingdom of God is as if a man should scatter seed upon the ground, [27] and should sleep and rise night and day, and the seed should sprout and grow, he knows not how. [28] The earth produces of itself, first the blade, then the ear, then the full grain in the ear. [29] But when the grain is ripe, at once he puts in the sickle, because the harvest has come."

30 And he said, "With what can we compare the kingdom of God, or what parable shall we use for it? [31] It is like a grain of mustard seed, which, when sown upon the ground, is the smallest of all the seeds on earth; [32] yet when it is sown it grows up and becomes the greatest of all shrubs, and puts forth large branches, so that the birds of the air can make nests in its shade."

33 With many such parables he spoke the word to them, as they were able to hear it; [34] he did not speak to them without a parable, but privately

m Or *stumble*

---

ground. **11:** *Has been given,* i.e. by God. Jesus distinguished between his followers' spiritual opportunities and those of other men (Lk.10.23–24). **12:** An adaptation of Is.6.9–10. **13–20:** See Mt.13.18–23 n. **21:** *A bushel,* (Greek "modios"), a pan or container holding about eight quarts (Mt.5.15; Lk.8.16; 11.33). **22:** Mt.10.26; Lk.8.17; 12.2. **24–25:** Mt.7.2; 13.12; Lk.6.38. **26–29: The seed growing secretly** (Mt.13.24–30). The growth of God's kingdom in the world is beyond man's understanding or control. Yet he may recognize its progress and play a part in it. **29:** Jl.3.13. **30–32: The mustard seed** (see Mt.13.31–32 n.; Lk.13.18–19). **32:** Dan.4.12,21; Ezek.17.23; 31.6. **33–34:** Mt.13.34–35.

to his own disciples he explained everything.

35 On that day, when evening had come, he said to them, "Let us go across to the other side." 36 And leaving the crowd, they took him with them in the boat, just as he was. And other boats were with him. 37 And a great storm of wind arose, and the waves beat into the boat, so that the boat was already filling. 38 But he was in the stern, asleep on the cushion; and they woke him and said to him, "Teacher, do you not care if we perish?" 39 And he awoke and rebuked the wind, and said to the sea, "Peace! Be still!" And the wind ceased, and there was a great calm. 40 He said to them, "Why are you afraid? Have you no faith?" 41 And they were filled with awe, and said to one another, "Who then is this, that even wind and sea obey him?"

5 They came to the other side of the sea, to the country of the Ger'-asenes.[n] 2 And when he had come out of the boat, there met him out of the tombs a man with an unclean spirit, 3 who lived among the tombs; and no one could bind him any more, even with a chain; 4 for he had often been bound with fetters and chains, but the chains he wrenched apart, and the fetters he broke in pieces; and no one had the strength to subdue him. 5 Night and day among the tombs and on the mountains he was always crying out, and bruising himself with stones. 6 And when he saw Jesus from afar, he ran and worshiped him; 7 and crying out with a loud voice, he said, "What have you to do with me, Jesus, Son of the Most High God? I adjure you by God, do not torment me." 8 For he had said to him, "Come out of the man, you unclean spirit!" 9 And Jesus[o] asked

him, "What is your name?" He replied, "My name is Legion; for we are many." 10 And he begged him eagerly not to send them out of the country. 11 Now a great herd of swine was feeding there on the hillside; 12 and they begged him, "Send us to the swine, let us enter them." 13 So he gave them leave. And the unclean spirits came out, and entered the swine; and the herd, numbering about two thousand, rushed down the steep bank into the sea, and were drowned in the sea.

14 The herdsmen fled, and told it in the city and in the country. And people came to see what it was that had happened. 15 And they came to Jesus, and saw the demoniac sitting there, clothed and in his right mind, the man who had had the legion; and they were afraid. 16 And those who had seen it told what had happened to the demoniac and to the swine. 17 And they began to beg Jesus[p] to depart from their neighborhood. 18 And as he was getting into the boat, the man who had been possessed with demons begged him that he might be with him. 19 But he refused, and said to him, "Go home to your friends, and tell them how much the Lord has done for you, and how he has had mercy on you." 20 And he went away and began to proclaim in the Decap'olis how much Jesus had done for him; and all men marveled.

21 And when Jesus had crossed again in the boat to the other side, a great crowd gathered about him; and he was beside the sea. 22 Then came one of the rulers of the synagogue, Ja'irus by name; and seeing him, he fell at his feet, 23 and besought him, say-

n Other ancient authorities read Gergesenes, some
Gadarenes
o Greek he   p Greek him

4.35–41: Wind and sea calmed (Mt.8.18,23–27; Lk.8.22–25). Jesus' authority is shown to extend to the world of natural forces. 38: Teacher, see Lk.8.24 n. 40: Faith trusts God to achieve his purpose, even through apparent destruction (Mt.6.25–33; 10.38 n.; Mk.14.35–36).
   5.1–43: Preaching tour. 1–20: The Gerasene demoniac (Mt.8.28–34; Lk.8.26–39). 7: 1.24.
9: A legion, a major unit in the Roman army, consisted of four thousand to six thousand men. Jesus would have the man witness in an area where he was known. 20: Decapolis, a federation of about ten cities in eastern Palestine.
   5.21–43: Jairus' daughter raised (Mt.9.18–26; Lk.8.40–56). 23: See Mt.9.21 n. 25: Lev.

ing, "My little daughter is at the point of death. Come and lay your hands on her, so that she may be made well, and live." ²⁴ And he went with him.

And a great crowd followed him and thronged about him. ²⁵ And there was a woman who had had a flow of blood for twelve years, ²⁶ and who had suffered much under many physicians, and had spent all that she had, and was no better but rather grew worse. ²⁷ She had heard the reports about Jesus, and came up behind him in the crowd and touched his garment. ²⁸ For she said, "If I touch even his garments, I shall be made well." ²⁹ And immediately the hemorrhage ceased; and she felt in her body that she was healed of her disease. ³⁰ And Jesus, perceiving in himself that power had gone forth from him, immediately turned about in the crowd, and said, "Who touched my garments?" ³¹ And his disciples said to him, "You see the crowd pressing around you, and yet you say, 'Who touched me?'" ³² And he looked around to see who had done it. ³³ But the woman, knowing what had been done to her, came in fear and trembling and fell down before him, and told him the whole truth. ³⁴ And he said to her, "Daughter, your faith has made you well; go in peace, and be healed of your disease."

35 While he was still speaking, there came from the ruler's house some who said, "Your daughter is dead. Why trouble the Teacher any further?" ³⁶ But ignoring*q* what they said, Jesus said to the ruler of the synagogue, "Do not fear, only believe." ³⁷ And he allowed no one to follow him except Peter and James and John the brother of James. ³⁸ When they came to the house of the ruler of the synagogue, he saw a tumult, and people weeping and wailing loudly. ³⁹ And when he had entered, he said to them, "Why do you make a tumult and weep? The child is not dead but sleeping." ⁴⁰ And they laughed at him. But he put them all outside, and took the child's father and mother and those who were with him, and went in where the child was. ⁴¹ Taking her by the hand he said to her, "Tal′itha cu′mi"; which means, "Little girl, I say to you, arise." ⁴² And immediately the girl got up and walked (she was twelve years of age), and they were immediately overcome with amazement. ⁴³ And he strictly charged them that no one should know this, and told them to give her something to eat.

6 He went away from there and came to his own country; and his disciples followed him. ² And on the sabbath he began to teach in the synagogue; and many who heard him were astonished, saying, "Where did this man get all this? What is the wisdom given to him? What mighty works are wrought by his hands! ³ Is not this the carpenter, the son of Mary and brother of James and Joses and Judas and Simon, and are not his sisters here with us?" And they took offense*r* at him. ⁴ And Jesus said to them, "A prophet is not without honor, except in his own country, and among his own kin, and in his own house." ⁵ And he could do no mighty work there, except that he laid his hands upon a few sick people and healed them. ⁶ And he marveled because of their unbelief.

And he went about among the villages teaching.

7 And he called to him the twelve,

q Or *overhearing.* Other ancient authorities read *hearing*
r Or *stumbled*

15.25–30. **28:** 5.23. **30:** Lk.5.17. **34:** *Has made you well,* see Mt.9.21 n. **36:** 4.40. **39:** See Mt. 9.24 n. **41:** The phrase *talitha cumi* preserves the actual (as distinct from translated) Aramaic words of Jesus (see 2 Kg.18.26 n.).

6.1–6: Rejection at home (Mt.13.53–58; Lk.4.16–30). **3:** See Mt. 13.55 n. **5–6:** Jesus required faith on the part of those who sought healing for themselves or for others (occasional apparent exceptions occur; e.g. Jn.5.13).

6.7–13: Commissioning and instruction of the Twelve (Mt.10.1,9–11,14; Lk.9.1–6). See 3.13–19 n. **7:** The disciples share Jesus' *authority* over malign, destructive forces (vv. 7–9); his

and began to send them out two by two, and gave them authority over the unclean spirits. [8] He charged them to take nothing for their journey except a staff; no bread, no bag, no money in their belts; [9] but to wear sandals and not put on two tunics. [10] And he said to them, "Where you enter a house, stay there until you leave the place. [11] And if any place will not receive you and they refuse to hear you, when you leave, shake off the dust that is on your feet for a testimony against them." [12] So they went out and preached that men should repent. [13] And they cast out many demons, and anointed with oil many that were sick and healed them.

14 King Herod heard of it; for Jesus'[s] name had become known. Some[t] said, "John the baptizer has been raised from the dead; that is why these powers are at work in him." [15] But others said, "It is Eli'jah." And others said, "It is a prophet, like one of the prophets of old." [16] But when Herod heard of it he said, "John, whom I beheaded, has been raised." [17] For Herod had sent and seized John, and bound him in prison for the sake of Hero'di-as, his brother Philip's wife; because he had married her. [18] For John said to Herod, "It is not lawful for you to have your brother's wife." [19] And Hero'di-as had a grudge against him, and wanted to kill him. But she could not, [20] for Herod feared John, knowing that he was a righteous and holy man, and kept him safe. When he heard him, he was much perplexed; and yet he heard him gladly. [21] But an opportunity came when Herod on his birthday gave a banquet for his courtiers and officers and the leading men of Galilee. [22] For when Hero'di-as' daughter came in and

danced, she pleased Herod and his guests; and the king said to the girl, "Ask me for whatever you wish, and I will grant it." [23] And he vowed to her, "Whatever you ask me, I will give you, even half of my kingdom." [24] And she went out, and said to her mother, "What shall I ask?" And she said, "The head of John the baptizer." [25] And she came in immediately with haste to the king, and asked, saying, "I want you to give me at once the head of John the Baptist on a platter." [26] And the king was exceedingly sorry; but because of his oaths and his guests he did not want to break his word to her. [27] And immediately the king sent a soldier of the guard and gave orders to bring his head. He went and beheaded him in the prison, [28] and brought his head on a platter, and gave it to the girl; and the girl gave it to her mother. [29] When his disciples heard of it, they came and took his body, and laid it in a tomb.

30 The apostles returned to Jesus, and told him all that they had done and taught. [31] And he said to them, "Come away by yourselves to a lonely place, and rest a while." For many were coming and going, and they had no leisure even to eat. [32] And they went away in the boat to a lonely place by themselves. [33] Now many saw them going, and knew them, and they ran there on foot from all the towns, and got there ahead of them. [34] As he went ashore he saw a great throng, and he had compassion on them, because they were like sheep without a shepherd; and he began to teach them many things. [35] And when it grew late, his disciples came to him and said, "This is a lonely place, and the hour is now late; [36] send them away, to go into the country and

s Greek *his*   *t* Other ancient authorities read *he*

refusal to engage in self-seeking (v. 10), or violence (v. 11); his message (v. 12; 1.14–15); and his sympathy for human suffering (v. 13). **9:** *Tunics,* see Mt.10.10 n. **12:** 1.14–15. **13:** Jas.5.14; Is.1.6; Lk.10.34.

    6.14–29: Death of John (Mt.14.1–12; Lk.9.7–9). **14:** *Herod* Antipas, son of Herod the Great. **20:** Mt.21.26.

    6.30–44: Five thousand fed (Mt.14.13–21; Lk.9.10–17; Jn.6.1–13; compare Mk.8.1–10). **34:** *Sheep without a shepherd,* a familiar picture of aimlessness (Num.27.17; 1 Kg.22.17; Ezek.34.5).

villages round about and buy themselves something to eat." [37] But he answered them, "You give them something to eat." And they said to him, "Shall we go and buy two hundred denarii[u] worth of bread, and give it to them to eat?" [38] And he said to them, "How many loaves have you? Go and see." And when they had found out, they said, "Five, and two fish." [39] Then he commanded them all to sit down by companies upon the green grass. [40] So they sat down in groups, by hundreds and by fifties. [41] And taking the five loaves and the two fish he looked up to heaven, and blessed, and broke the loaves, and gave them to the disciples to set before the people; and he divided the two fish among them all. [42] And they all ate and were satisfied. [43] And they took up twelve baskets full of broken pieces and of the fish. [44] And those who ate the loaves were five thousand men.

45 Immediately he made his disciples get into the boat and go before him to the other side, to Beth-sa'ida, while he dismissed the crowd. [46] And after he had taken leave of them, he went up on the mountain to pray. [47] And when evening came, the boat was out on the sea, and he was alone on the land. [48] And he saw that they were making headway painfully, for the wind was against them. And about the fourth watch of the night he came to them, walking on the sea. He meant to pass by them, [49] but when they saw him walking on the sea they thought it was a ghost, and cried out; [50] for they all saw him, and were terrified. But immediately he spoke to them and said, "Take heart, it is I; have no fear."

[51] And he got into the boat with them and the wind ceased. And they were utterly astounded, [52] for they did not understand about the loaves, but their hearts were hardened.

53 And when they had crossed over, they came to land at Gennes'aret, and moored to the shore. [54] And when they got out of the boat, immediately the people recognized him, [55] and ran about the whole neighborhood and began to bring sick people on their pallets to any place where they heard he was. [56] And wherever he came, in villages, cities, or country, they laid the sick in the market places, and besought him that they might touch even the fringe of his garment; and as many as touched it were made well.

7 Now when the Pharisees gathered together to him, with some of the scribes, who had come from Jerusalem, [2] they saw that some of his disciples ate with hands defiled, that is, unwashed. [3] (For the Pharisees, and all the Jews, do not eat unless they wash their hands,[v] observing the tradition of the elders; [4] and when they come from the market place, they do not eat unless they purify[w] themselves;[a] and there are many other traditions which they observe, the washing of cups and pots and vessels of bronze.[x]) [5] And the Pharisees and the scribes asked him, "Why do your disciples not live[y] according to the tradition of the elders, but eat with hands defiled?" [6] And he said to

u The denarius was a day's wage for a laborer
v One Greek word is of uncertain meaning and is not translated
w Other ancient authorities read *baptize*
a Other ancient authorities read *and they do not eat anything from the market unless they purify it*
x Other ancient authorities add *and beds*
y Greek *walk*

6.45–52: Jesus walks on water (Mt.14.22–33; Jn.6.15–21). **48:** *The fourth watch*, just prior to dawn. *He meant to pass by them* describes the way Jesus appeared to his disciples. **52:** The disciples miss the true import of Jesus' acts through lack of faith (Mk.3.5; 8.17; Jn.12.40; Rom.11.7,25; 2 Cor.3.14; Eph.4.18; but compare Mt.14.33).

6.53–56: Belief in Jesus' power to heal (Mt.14.34–36). Compare Mt.4.24; Mk.1.32–34; 3.10; Lk.4.40–41; 6.18,19.

7.1–23: Tradition of the elders (Mt.15.1–20). Whereas the common people were moved by elemental needs, and Jesus was aroused to compassion for human suffering (6.53–56), the religious leaders were concerned with details of ritual. **3:** See Lk.11.38 n. **4:** Mt.23.25; Lk.11.39. **5:** Gal.1.14. **6–7:** Is.29.13, according to the Septuagint. **11:** *Given to God* verbally, but in fact

them, "Well did Isaiah prophesy of you hypocrites, as it is written,

'This people honors me with their lips,
but their heart is far from me;
[7] in vain do they worship me,
teaching as doctrines the precepts of men.'

[8] You leave the commandment of God, and hold fast the tradition of men."

9 And he said to them, "You have a fine way of rejecting the commandment of God, in order to keep your tradition! [10] For Moses said, 'Honor your father and your mother'; and, 'He who speaks evil of father or mother, let him surely die'; [11] but you say, 'If a man tells his father or his mother, What you would have gained from me is Corban' (that is, given to God)[z]– [12] then you no longer permit him to do anything for his father or mother, [13] thus making void the word of God through your tradition which you hand on. And many such things you do."

14 And he called the people to him again, and said to them, "Hear me, all of you, and understand: [15] there is nothing outside a man which by going into him can defile him; but the things which come out of a man are what defile him."[a] [17] And when he had entered the house, and left the people, his disciples asked him about the parable. [18] And he said to them, "Then are you also without understanding? Do you not see that whatever goes into a man from outside cannot defile him, [19] since it enters, not his heart but his stomach, and so passes on?"[b] (Thus he declared all foods clean.) [20] And he said, "What comes out of a man is what defiles a man. [21] For from within, out of the heart of man, come evil thoughts, fornication, theft, murder, adultery, [22] coveting, wickedness, deceit, licentiousness, envy, slander, pride, foolishness. [23] All these evil things come from within, and they defile a man."

24 And from there he arose and went away to the region of Tyre and Sidon.[c] And he entered a house, and would not have any one know it; yet he could not be hid. [25] But immediately a woman, whose little daughter was possessed by an unclean spirit, heard of him, and came and fell down at his feet. [26] Now the woman was a Greek, a Syrophoeni'cian by birth. And she begged him to cast the demon out of her daughter. [27] And he said to her, "Let the children first be fed, for it is not right to take the children's bread and throw it to the dogs." [28] But she answered him, "Yes, Lord; yet even the dogs under the table eat the children's crumbs." [29] And he said to her, "For this saying you may go your way; the demon has left your daughter." [30] And she went home, and found the child lying in bed, and the demon gone.

31 Then he returned from the region of Tyre, and went through Sidon to the Sea of Galilee, through the region of the Decap'olis. [32] And they brought to him a man who was deaf and had an impediment in his speech; and they besought him to lay his hand upon him. [33] And taking him aside from the multitude privately, he put his fingers into his ears, and he spat and touched his tongue; [34] and looking up to heaven, he sighed, and said to him, "Eph'phatha," that is, "Be opened." [35] And his ears were opened, his tongue was released, and he spoke plainly. [36] And he charged them to tell no one; but the more he charged them, the more zealously they proclaimed it. [37] And they were astonished beyond measure, saying, "He has done all things well; he even makes the deaf hear and the dumb speak."

z Or *an offering*
a Other ancient authorities add verse 16, "*If any man has ears to hear, let him hear*"
b Or *is evacuated*
c Other ancient authorities omit *and Sidon*

retained for private use. **15:** See Mt.15.10–20 n. **19:** *Clean,* i.e., ritually. **21–23:** Gal.5.19–21.
   7.24–30: The Syrophoenician woman (Mt.15.21–28). **27:** See Mt.15.24 n. **28:** See Mt.15.27 n.
   7.31–37: Healings (Mt.15.29–31). **31:** *Decapolis,* see 5.20 n. **34:** *Ephphatha,* an Aramaic word (see 5.41 n.).

8 In those days, when again a great crowd had gathered, and they had nothing to eat, he called his disciples to him, and said to them, [2] "I have compassion on the crowd, because they have been with me now three days, and have nothing to eat; [3] and if I send them away hungry to their homes, they will faint on the way; and some of them have come a long way." [4] And his disciples answered him, "How can one feed these men with bread here in the desert?" [5] And he asked them, "How many loaves have you?" They said, "Seven." [6] And he commanded the crowd to sit down on the ground; and he took the seven loaves, and having given thanks he broke them and gave them to his disciples to set before the people; and they set them before the crowd. [7] And they had a few small fish; and having blessed them, he commanded that these also should be set before them. [8] And they ate, and were satisfied; and they took up the broken pieces left over, seven baskets full. [9] And there were about four thousand people. [10] And he sent them away; and immediately he got into the boat with his disciples, and went to the district of Dalmanu'tha.*d*

11 The Pharisees came and began to argue with him, seeking from him a sign from heaven, to test him. [12] And he sighed deeply in his spirit, and said, "Why does this generation seek a sign? Truly, I say to you, no sign shall be given to this generation." [13] And he left them, and getting into the boat again he departed to the other side.

14 Now they had forgotten to bring bread; and they had only one loaf with them in the boat. [15] And he cautioned them, saying, "Take heed, beware of the leaven of the Pharisees and the leaven of Herod."*e* [16] And they discussed it with one another, saying, "We have no bread." [17] And being aware of it, Jesus said to them, "Why do you discuss the fact that you have no bread? Do you not yet perceive or understand? Are your hearts hardened? [18] Having eyes do you not see, and having ears do you not hear? And do you not remember? [19] When I broke the five loaves for the five thousand, how many baskets full of broken pieces did you take up?" They said to him, "Twelve." [20] "And the seven for the four thousand, how many baskets full of broken pieces did you take up?" And they said to him, "Seven." [21] And he said to them, "Do you not yet understand?"

22 And they came to Beth-sa'ida. And some people brought to him a blind man, and begged him to touch him. [23] And he took the blind man by the hand, and led him out of the village; and when he had spit on his eyes and laid his hands upon him, he asked him, "Do you see anything?" [24] And he looked up and said, "I see men; but they look like trees, walking." [25] Then again he laid his hands upon his eyes; and he looked intently and was restored, and saw everything clearly. [26] And he sent him away to his home, saying, "Do not even enter the village."

27 And Jesus went on with his disciples, to the villages of Caesare'a

d Other ancient authorities read *Magadan* or *Magdala*
e Other ancient authorities read *the Herodians*

8.1–10: Four thousand fed (Mt.15.32–39). This narrative repeats the thought of 6.30–44. Some regard these passages as alternate ways of describing one original event, the details of which we can no longer determine. **10:** *Dalmanutha*, the location is unknown (see note *d* and Mt.15.39).

8.11–13: Sayings on signs (Mt.16.1–4; 12.38–39; Lk.11.29; 11.16; 12.54–56).

8.14–21: Leaven of the Pharisees (Mt.16.5–12; Lk.12.1). **14–15:** Jesus joins two ideas. **15:** *Leaven* here seems to refer to settled conviction which affects all of life as leaven raises dough. **17–18:** Is.6.9–10; Jer.5.21; Ezek.12.2; Mt.13.10–15; Mk.6.52; Jn.12.36–41. **19:** 6.41–44. **20:** 8.1–10.

8.22–26: A blind man healed. 10.46–52; Jn.9.1–7. **22:** *Bethsaida*, 6.45; Lk.9.10.

8.27–33: Peter's confession (Mt.16.13–23; Lk.9.18–22). **27:** *Caesarea Philippi* was a site of

Philip'pi; and on the way he asked his disciples, "Who do men say that I am?" ²⁸ And they told him, "John the Baptist; and others say, Eli'jah; and others one of the prophets." ²⁹ And he asked them, "But who do you say that I am?" Peter answered him, "You are the Christ." ³⁰ And he charged them to tell no one about him.

31 And he began to teach them that the Son of man must suffer many things, and be rejected by the elders and the chief priests and the scribes, and be killed, and after three days rise again. ³² And he said this plainly. And Peter took him, and began to rebuke him. ³³ But turning and seeing his disciples, he rebuked Peter, and said, "Get behind me, Satan! For you are not on the side of God, but of men."

34 And he called to him the multitude with his disciples, and said to them, "If any man would come after me, let him deny himself and take up his cross and follow me. ³⁵ For whoever would save his life will lose it; and whoever loses his life for my sake and the gospel's will save it. ³⁶ For what does it profit a man, to gain the whole world and forfeit his life? ³⁷ For what can a man give in return for his life? ³⁸ For whoever is ashamed of me and of my words in this adulterous and sinful generation, of him will the Son of man also be ashamed, when he comes in the glory of his Father with the holy

9 angels." ¹ And he said to them, "Truly, I say to you, there are some standing here who will not taste death before they see that the kingdom of God has come with power."

2 And after six days Jesus took with him Peter and James and John, and led them up a high mountain apart by themselves; and he was transfigured before them, ³ and his garments became glistening, intensely white, as no fuller on earth could bleach them. ⁴ And there appeared to them Eli'jah with Moses; and they were talking to Jesus. ⁵ And Peter said to Jesus, "Master,*f* it is well that we are here; let us make three booths, one for you and one for Moses and one for Eli'jah." ⁶ For he did not know what to say, for they were exceedingly afraid. ⁷ And a cloud overshadowed them, and a voice came out of the cloud, "This is my beloved Son;*g* listen to him." ⁸ And suddenly looking around they no longer saw any one with them but Jesus only.

9 And as they were coming down the mountain, he charged them to tell no one what they had seen, until the Son of man should have risen from the dead. ¹⁰ So they kept the matter to themselves, questioning what the rising from the dead meant. ¹¹ And they asked him, "Why do the scribes say that first Eli'jah must come?" ¹² And he said to them, "Eli'jah does come first

f Or *Rabbi*　　*g* Or *my Son, my* (or *the*) *Beloved*

pagan worship. **28:** 6.14–16. **29:** Jn.6.66–69. **30:** Jesus consistently sought to repress sensational reports (see 1.43–44 n.). **31:** First prediction of the Passion (compare 9.30–32; 10.33–34). **32:** The idea that the *Son of man* (the Messiah) was to suffer was in complete contrast to Jewish expectation (see 2.10 n.; 9.10 n.; Mt.16.22). **33:** Jesus saw in Peter's words a continuation of Satan's temptation (Mt.4.10; Lk.4.8).

8.34–9.1: On discipleship (Mt.16.24–28; Lk.9.23–27). **8.34:** See Mt.10.38 n. **35:** Mt.10.39; Lk.17.33; Jn.12.25. The apparent contradiction here is overcome because man's existence depends on God. **38:** See Mt.12.39 n. **9.1:** *Taste*, become personally acquainted with.

9.2–8: The transfiguration (Mt.17.1–8; Lk.9.28–36). By this narrative the author means to describe a vision of Jesus in heavenly glory as the Messiah (see Lk.9.28–36 n.). **2:** *Transfigured*, having a non-earthly appearance. **4:** The prophet *Elijah* was expected to appear on earth before the Messiah appeared (Mal.4.5–6). *Moses*, the lawgiver, the traditional author of the first five books of the Bible, which formed the basic authority in Jewish religion. **5:** *Three booths*, temporary shelters. **7:** Mt.3.17; Jn.12.28–29; 2 Pet.1.17–18.

9.9–13: Prophecies about Elijah (Mt.17.9–13). **10:** The disciples could not associate belief in resurrection with the Son of man (v. 9; see 2.10 n.). **11:** See Mt.11.14 n. **13:** *Elijah has come* in the person of *John* (Mt.11.14; Lk.1.17,76), and John was treated as Elijah had been treated (1 Kg.19.2,10).

to restore all things; and how is it written of the Son of man, that he should suffer many things and be treated with contempt? [13] But I tell you that Eli'jah has come, and they did to him whatever they pleased, as it is written of him."

14 And when they came to the disciples, they saw a great crowd about them, and scribes arguing with them. [15] And immediately all the crowd, when they saw him, were greatly amazed, and ran up to him and greeted him. [16] And he asked them, "What are you discussing with them?" [17] And one of the crowd answered him, "Teacher, I brought my son to you, for he has a dumb spirit; [18] and wherever it seizes him, it dashes him down; and he foams and grinds his teeth and becomes rigid; and I asked your disciples to cast it out, and they were not able." [19] And he answered them, "O faithless generation, how long am I to be with you? How long am I to bear with you? Bring him to me." [20] And they brought the boy to him; and when the spirit saw him, immediately it convulsed the boy, and he fell on the ground and rolled about, foaming at the mouth. [21] And Jesus[h] asked his father, "How long has he had this?" And he said, "From childhood. [22] And it has often cast him into the fire and into the water, to destroy him; but if you can do anything, have pity on us and help us." [23] And Jesus said to him, "If you can! All things are possible to him who believes." [24] Immediately the father of the child cried out[i] and said, "I believe; help my unbelief!" [25] And when Jesus saw that a crowd came running together, he rebuked the unclean spirit, saying to it, "You dumb and deaf spirit, I command you, come out of him, and never enter him again." [26] And after crying out and convulsing him terribly, it came out, and the boy was like a corpse; so that most of them said, "He is dead." [27] But Jesus took him by the hand and lifted him up, and he arose. [28] And when he had entered the house, his disciples asked him privately, "Why could we not cast it out?" [29] And he said to them, "This kind cannot be driven out by anything but prayer."[j]

30 They went on from there and passed through Galilee. And he would not have any one know it; [31] for he was teaching his disciples, saying to them, "The Son of man will be delivered into the hands of men, and they will kill him; and when he is killed, after three days he will rise." [32] But they did not understand the saying, and they were afraid to ask him.

33 And they came to Caper'na-um; and when he was in the house he asked them, "What were you discussing on the way?" [34] But they were silent; for on the way they had discussed with one another who was the greatest. [35] And he sat down and called the twelve; and he said to them, "If any one would be first, he must be last of all and servant of all." [36] And he took a child, and put him in the midst of them; and taking him in his

h Greek he
i Other ancient authorities add with tears
j Other ancient authorities add and fasting

9.14–29: Epileptic child healed (Mt.17.14–21; Lk.9.37–42). **15:** Perhaps the crowd was *amazed* by the coincidence of the disciples' failure (v. 18) and Jesus' unexpected return. **18:** In modern diagnosis the symptoms point to an epileptic seizure. **19:** Failure is attributed to wrong attitude (v. 29); the disciple must speak from faith not argument (see Lk.10.20 n.; Mk. 11.23 n., 24 n.). **28:** A reasonable question in the light of 6.7,13 where spiritual power accompanied the message. **29:** Prayer to God is faith in God, and contrasts with the argumentative attitude in v. 14. The potency in faith rests with God and is not under the believer's control.

9.30–32: The Passion foretold again (Mt.17.22–23; Lk.9.43–45); compare 8.31; 10.33. **31:** The burden of Jesus' teaching was on his coming violent death and resurrection (8.31; 10.33–34; see Lk.9.22 n.). **32:** See 9.10 n.; Jn.12.16.

9.33–37: True greatness (Mt.18.1–5; Lk.9.46–48). **34:** Lk.22.24. **35:** 10.43–44; Mt.20.26–27; 23.11; Lk.9.48; 22.26. **36:** 10.16. **37:** *In my name* means "because of regard for who and what I am."

arms, he said to them, [37] "Whoever receives one such child in my name receives me; and whoever receives me, receives not me but him who sent me."

38 John said to him, "Teacher, we saw a man casting out demons in your name,[k] and we forbade him, because he was not following us." [39] But Jesus said, "Do not forbid him; for no one who does a mighty work in my name will be able soon after to speak evil of me. [40] For he that is not against us is for us. [41] For truly, I say to you, whoever gives you a cup of water to drink because you bear the name of Christ, will by no means lose his reward.

42 "Whoever causes one of these little ones who believe in me to sin,[l] it would be better for him if a great millstone were hung round his neck and he were thrown into the sea. [43] And if your hand causes you to sin,[l] cut it off; it is better for you to enter life maimed than with two hands to go to hell,[m] to the unquenchable fire.[n] [45] And if your foot causes you to sin,[l] cut it off; it is better for you to enter life lame than with two feet to be thrown into hell.[m, n] [47] And if your eye causes you to sin,[l] pluck it out; it is better for you to enter the kingdom of God with one eye than with two eyes to be thrown into hell,[m] [48] where their worm does not die, and the fire is not quenched. [49] For every one will be salted with fire.[o] [50] Salt is good; but if the salt has lost its saltness, how will you season it? Have salt in yourselves, and be at peace with one another."

10 And he left there and went to the region of Judea and beyond the Jordan, and crowds gathered to him again; and again, as his custom was, he taught them.

2 And Pharisees came up and in order to test him asked, "Is it lawful for a man to divorce his wife?" [3] He answered them, "What did Moses command you?" [4] They said, "Moses allowed a man to write a certificate of divorce, and to put her away." [5] But Jesus said to them, "For your hardness of heart he wrote you this commandment. [6] But from the beginning of creation, 'God made them male and female.' [7] 'For this reason a man shall leave his father and mother and be joined to his wife,[p] [8] and the two shall become one flesh.' So they are no longer two but one flesh. [9] What therefore God has joined together, let not man put asunder."

10 And in the house the disciples asked him again about this matter. [11] And he said to them, "Whoever divorces his wife and marries another, commits adultery against her; [12] and if she divorces her husband and marries another, she commits adultery."

13 And they were bringing children to him, that he might touch them; and the disciples rebuked them. [14] But when Jesus saw it he was indignant, and said to them, "Let the children come to me, do not hinder them; for to

k Other ancient authorities add *who does not follow us*
l Greek *stumble*   m Greek *Gehenna*
n Verses 44 and 46 (which are identical with verse 48) are omitted by the best ancient authorities
o Other ancient authorities add *and every sacrifice will be salted with salt*
p Other ancient authorities omit *and be joined to his wife*

9.38–41: The unknown exorcist (Lk.9.49–50). **39–40:** Mt.12.30; Lk.11.23. Each saying arose in a situation which gave it specific meaning. Num.11.27–29. **41:** Mt.10.42; Mk.9.37.
9.42–48: Warnings of hell (Mt.18.6–9; 5.29–30; Lk.17.1–2). **42:** *Little ones*, followers (see Mt.18.6 n.). The *great mill stone* was turned by a donkey. **48:** Is.66.24. **49–50:** Salty disciples. Mt.5.13; Lk.14.34–35. **50a:** Mt.5.13. **50b:** Perhaps the meaning is: "Maintain peacefully your own distinct character and service."
10.1–52: From Galilee to Jerusalem (Mt.19.1–20.34; Lk.18.15–19.27). **1–12:** On marriage and divorce (Mt.19.1–12). **1:** Lk.9.51; Jn.10.40; 11.7. **2:** See Mt.19.3 n. **3–4:** See Dt.24.1–4 n. **5:** Jesus is saying that the Law was shaped to the character of those for whom it was written. **6:** Gen.1.27; 5.2. **7–8:** Gen.2.24. **11:** See Mt.5.31–32 n. **12:** This provision was not applicable to Palestine, where women could not sue for divorce.
10.13–16: Blessing the children (Mt.19.13–15; Lk.18.15–17). **14:** Mt.5.3–12. **15:** To receive the kingdom as a child is to depend in trustful simplicity on what God offers.

such belongs the kingdom of God. ¹⁵ Truly, I say to you, whoever does not receive the kingdom of God like a child shall not enter it." ¹⁶ And he took them in his arms and blessed them, laying his hands upon them.

17 And as he was setting out on his journey, a man ran up and knelt before him, and asked him, "Good Teacher, what must I do to inherit eternal life?" ¹⁸ And Jesus said to him, "Why do you call me good? No one is good but God alone. ¹⁹ You know the commandments: 'Do not kill, Do not commit adultery, Do not steal, Do not bear false witness, Do not defraud, Honor your father and mother.' " ²⁰ And he said to him, "Teacher, all these I have observed from my youth." ²¹ And Jesus looking upon him loved him, and said to him, "You lack one thing; go, sell what you have, and give to the poor, and you will have treasure in heaven; and come, follow me." ²² At that saying his countenance fell, and he went away sorrowful; for he had great possessions.

23 And Jesus looked around and said to his disciples, "How hard it will be for those who have riches to enter the kingdom of God!" ²⁴ And the disciples were amazed at his words. But Jesus said to them again, "Children, how hard it is* to enter the kingdom of God! ²⁵ It is easier for a camel to go through the eye of a needle than for a rich man to enter the kingdom of God." ²⁶ And they were exceedingly astonished, and said to him,* "Then who can be saved?" ²⁷ Jesus looked at them and said, "With men it is im-

possible, but not with God; for all things are possible with God." ²⁸ Peter began to say to him, "Lo, we have left everything and followed you." ²⁹ Jesus said, "Truly, I say to you, there is no one who has left house or brothers or sisters or mother or father or children or lands, for my sake and for the gospel, ³⁰ who will not receive a hundredfold now in this time, houses and brothers and sisters and mothers and children and lands, with persecutions, and in the age to come eternal life. ³¹ But many that are first will be last, and the last first."

32 And they were on the road, going up to Jerusalem, and Jesus was walking ahead of them; and they were amazed, and those who followed were afraid. And taking the twelve again, he began to tell them what was to happen to him, ³³ saying, "Behold, we are going up to Jerusalem; and the Son of man will be delivered to the chief priests and the scribes, and they will condemn him to death, and deliver him to the Gentiles; ³⁴ and they will mock him, and spit upon him, and scourge him, and kill him; and after three days he will rise."

35 And James and John, the sons of Zeb′edee, came forward to him, and said to him, "Teacher, we want you to do for us whatever we ask of you." ³⁶ And he said to them, "What do you want me to do for you?" ³⁷ And they said to him, "Grant us to sit, one at your right hand and one at your left, in your glory." ³⁸ But Jesus said to

r Other ancient authorities add *for those who trust in riches*
s Other ancient authorities read *to one another*

10.17–31: The rich man (Mt.19.16–30; Lk.18.18–30). **17**: Lk.10.25; Mk.1.40. **19**: Ex.20.12–16; Dt.5.16–20. **21**: Jesus' invitation to *sell . . . give . . . come* is a drastic test of the questioner's concern for spiritual satisfaction (see Lk.12.33–34 n.). **24**: It was supposed that wealth made possible the performance of religious duties. Jesus' point is that men by nature do not submit to God's rule (compare v. 15), but sincere submission is essential to salvation. **25**: A proverbial expression denoting a human impossibility (compare v. 27). **26**: To *be saved* is to enter the kingdom (v. 25). **28**: 1.16–20.
10.32–34: The Passion foretold a third time (Mt.20.17–19; Lk.18.31–34); compare 8.31; 9.31. **32**: *Walking ahead of them*, a vivid picture of Jesus' resolute demeanor (compare Lk.9.51) despite the sufferings which awaited him at Jerusalem (see 8.31 n.). **34**: See Mt.10.38 n.; Mk. 14.65; 15.19,26–32.
10.35–45: James and John seek honor (Mt.20.20–28; Lk.22.24–27). **37**: See Mt.19.28 n.

them, "You do not know what you are asking. Are you able to drink the cup that I drink, or to be baptized with the baptism with which I am baptized?" ³⁹ And they said to him, "We are able." And Jesus said to them, "The cup that I drink you will drink; and with the baptism with which I am baptized, you will be baptized; ⁴⁰ but to sit at my right hand or at my left is not mine to grant, but it is for those for whom it has been prepared." ⁴¹ And when the ten heard it, they began to be indignant at James and John. ⁴² And Jesus called them to him and said to them, "You know that those who are supposed to rule over the Gentiles lord it over them, and their great men exercise authority over them. ⁴³ But it shall not be so among you; but whoever would be great among you must be your servant, ⁴⁴ and whoever would be first among you must be slave of all. ⁴⁵ For the Son of man also came not to be served but to serve, and to give his life as a ransom for many."

46 And they came to Jericho; and as he was leaving Jericho with his disciples and a great multitude, Bartimae'us, a blind beggar, the son of Timae'us, was sitting by the roadside. ⁴⁷ And when he heard that it was Jesus of Nazareth, he began to cry out and say, "Jesus, Son of David, have mercy on me!" ⁴⁸ And many rebuked him, telling him to be silent; but he cried out all the more, "Son of David, have mercy on me!" ⁴⁹ And Jesus stopped and said, "Call him." And they called the blind man, saying to him, "Take heart; rise, he is calling you." ⁵⁰ And throwing off

his mantle he sprang up and came to Jesus. ⁵¹ And Jesus said to him, "What do you want me to do for you?" And the blind man said to him, "Master,ᵗ let me receive my sight." ⁵² And Jesus said to him, "Go your way; your faith has made you well." And immediately he received his sight and followed him on the way.

‖ And when they drew near to Jerusalem, to Beth'phage and Bethany, at the Mount of Olives, he sent two of his disciples, ² and said to them, "Go into the village opposite you, and immediately as you enter it you will find a colt tied, on which no one has ever sat; untie it and bring it. ³ If any one says to you, 'Why are you doing this?' say, 'The Lord has need of it and will send it back here immediately.'" ⁴ And they went away, and found a colt tied at the door out in the open street; and they untied it. ⁵ And those who stood there said to them, "What are you doing, untying the colt?" ⁶ And they told them what Jesus had said; and they let them go. ⁷ And they brought the colt to Jesus, and threw their garments on it; and he sat upon it. ⁸ And many spread their garments on the road, and others spread leafy branches which they had cut from the fields. ⁹ And those who went before and those who followed cried out, "Hosanna! Blessed is he who comes in the name of the Lord! ¹⁰ Blessed is the kingdom of our father David that is coming! Hosanna in the highest!"

11 And he entered Jerusalem, and went into the temple; and when he had

t Or *Rabbi*

The seats symbolize positions of special dignity. **38:** Lk.12.50; Jn.18.11; Mk.14.36. *Cup*, see Lk.22.42 n. Acceptance of *baptism* symbolizes acceptance of God's way (see 1.4 n.). **42:** *Are supposed to rule*, or "are recognized as rulers." **45:** *A ransom*, that which is given to gain release. Jesus speaks of his life and death as achieving freedom for men, but does not spell out details (14.24; Lk.4.18; 1 Tim.2.5–6).

10.46–52: Blind Bartimaeus (Mt.20.29–34; Lk.18.35–43). **46:** *Bartimaeus* means "son of Timaeus" in Aramaic. **50:** *Mantle*, the outer garment. **52:** See Mt.9.21 n.; Mk.11.23 n., 24 n.

11.1–15.47: The last week (Mt.21.1–27.66; Lk.19.28–23.56).

11.1–11: Palm Sunday (Mt.21.1–9; Lk.19.28–38). **1:** Jesus dramatized his offer of himself as the Messiah, putting his emphasis on humility. Like a parable, his action had to be understood and accepted. **7–10:** Jn.12.12–15. **9:** Ps.118.26; Mt.21.15; 23.39; Zech.9.9. *Hosanna*, see Mt. 21.9 n. **11:** Mt.21.10–11,17.

looked round at everything, as it was already late, he went out to Bethany with the twelve.

12 On the following day, when they came from Bethany, he was hungry. [13] And seeing in the distance a fig tree in leaf, he went to see if he could find anything on it. When he came to it, he found nothing but leaves, for it was not the season for figs. [14] And he said to it, "May no one ever eat fruit from you again." And his disciples heard it.

15 And they came to Jerusalem. And he entered the temple and began to drive out those who sold and those who bought in the temple, and he overturned the tables of the money-changers and the seats of those who sold pigeons; [16] and he would not allow any one to carry anything through the temple. [17] And he taught, and said to them, "Is it not written, 'My house shall be called a house of prayer for all the nations'? But you have made it a den of robbers." [18] And the chief priests and the scribes heard it and sought a way to destroy him; for they feared him, because all the multitude was astonished at his teaching. [19] And when evening came they[u] went out of the city.

20 As they passed by in the morning, they saw the fig tree withered away to its roots. [21] And Peter remembered and said to him, "Master,[v] look! The fig tree which you cursed has withered." [22] And Jesus answered them, "Have faith in God. [23] Truly, I say to you, whoever says to this mountain, 'Be taken up and cast into the sea,' and does not doubt in his heart, but believes that what he says will come to pass, it will be done for him. [24] There-fore I tell you, whatever you ask in prayer, believe that you have received[a] it, and it will be yours. [25] And whenever you stand praying, forgive, if you have anything against any one; so that your Father also who is in heaven may forgive you your trespasses."[w]

27 And they came again to Jerusalem. And as he was walking in the temple, the chief priests and the scribes and the elders came to him, [28] and they said to him, "By what authority are you doing these things, or who gave you this authority to do them?" [29] Jesus said to them, "I will ask you a question; answer me, and I will tell you by what authority I do these things. [30] Was the baptism of John from heaven or from men? Answer me." [31] And they argued with one another, "If we say, 'From heaven,' he will say, 'Why then did you not believe him?' [32] But shall we say, 'From men'?'–they were afraid of the people, for all held that John was a real prophet. [33] So they answered Jesus, "We do not know." And Jesus said to them, "Neither will I tell you by what authority I do these things."

12 And he began to speak to them in parables. "A man planted a vineyard, and set a hedge around it, and dug a pit for the wine press, and built a tower, and let it out to tenants, and went into another country. [2] When the time came, he sent a servant to the tenants, to get from them some of the fruit of the vineyard. [3] And they took him and beat him, and sent him away empty-handed. [4] Again he sent

u Other ancient authorities read *he*   v Or *Rabbi*
a Other ancient authorities read *are receiving*
w Other ancient authorities add verse 26, "*But if you do not forgive, neither will your Father who is in heaven forgive your trespasses*"

11.12–14: Fig tree cursed (Mt.21.18–19; compare Lk.13.6–9). **12:** Monday. **13:** The leaves showed the possibility of green fruit. Jesus' meaning, probably symbolic, is not clear.
    11.15–19: Cleansing the temple (Mt.21.12–13; Lk.19.45–48; Jn.2.13–17). **15:** See Mt.21.12 n. **17:** Is.56.7; Jer.7.11. **19:** Lk.21.37–38.
    11.20–25: The meaning of the withered fig tree (Mt.21.18–22). **23:** See Mt.17.20 n. Jesus emphasizes not power in faith but the power of God, his illustration being figurative. Faith will command only according to God's will (Mt.4.3–4; Mk.14.35–36). **24:** See Lk.11.9 n. What God wills is possible both to himself and to the man who shares his will. **25:** Mt.6.14–15; 18.35.
    11.27–33: On Jesus' authority (Mt.21.23–27; Lk.20.1–8; Jn.2.18–22). See Mt.21.27 n.
    12.1–12: Parable of the vineyard (Mt.21.33–46; Lk.20.9–19). Is.5.1–7. **10:** Ps.118.22–23.

to them another servant, and they wounded him in the head, and treated him shamefully. ⁵ And he sent another, and him they killed; and so with many others, some they beat and some they killed. ⁶ He had still one other, a beloved son; finally he sent him to them, saying, 'They will respect my son.' ⁷ But those tenants said to one another, 'This is the heir; come, let us kill him, and the inheritance will be ours.' ⁸ And they took him and killed him, and cast him out of the vineyard. ⁹ What will the owner of the vineyard do? He will come and destroy the tenants, and give the vineyard to others. ¹⁰ Have you not read this scripture:

'The very stone which the builders rejected
has become the head of the corner;
¹¹ this was the Lord's doing,
and it is marvelous in our eyes'?"

12 And they tried to arrest him, but feared the multitude, for they perceived that he had told the parable against them; so they left him and went away.

13 And they sent to him some of the Pharisees and some of the Hero'di-ans, to entrap him in his talk. ¹⁴ And they came and said to him, "Teacher, we know that you are true, and care for no man; for you do not regard the position of men, but truly teach the way of God. Is it lawful to pay taxes to Caesar, or not? ¹⁵ Should we pay them, or should we not?" But knowing their hypocrisy, he said to them, "Why put me to the test? Bring me a coin,ˣ and let me look at it." ¹⁶ And they brought one. And he said to them, "Whose likeness and inscription is this?" They said to him, "Caesar's." ¹⁷ Jesus said to them, "Render to Caesar the things that are Caesar's, and to God the things that are God's." And they were amazed at him.

18 And Sad'ducees came to him, who say that there is no resurrection; and they asked him a question, saying, ¹⁹ "Teacher, Moses wrote for us that if a man's brother dies and leaves a wife, but leaves no child, the manʸ must take the wife, and raise up children for his brother. ²⁰ There were seven brothers; the first took a wife, and when he died left no children; ²¹ and the second took her, and died, leaving no children; and the third likewise; ²² and the seven left no children. Last of all the woman also died. ²³ In the resurrection whose wife will she be? For the seven had her as wife."

24 Jesus said to them, "Is not this why you are wrong, that you know neither the scriptures nor the power of God? ²⁵ For when they rise from the dead, they neither marry nor are given in marriage, but are like angels in heaven. ²⁶ And as for the dead being raised, have you not read in the book of Moses, in the passage about the bush, how God said to him, 'I am the God of Abraham, and the God of Isaac, and the God of Jacob'? ²⁷ He is not God of the dead, but of the living; you are quite wrong."

28 And one of the scribes came up and heard them disputing with one another, and seeing that he answered them well, asked him, "Which commandment is the first of all?" ²⁹ Jesus answered, "The first is, 'Hear, O Israel: The Lord our God, the Lord is one; ³⁰ and you shall love the Lord your God with all your heart, and with all your soul, and with all your mind, and with all your strength.' ³¹ The second is this, 'You shall love your neighbor as yourself.' There is no other commandment greater than these." ³² And the scribe said to him, "You are right, Teacher; you have truly said

x Greek *a denarius*   y Greek *his brother*

12.13–17: **Paying taxes to Caesar** (Mt.22.15–22; Lk.20.20–26). **13:** 3.6 n.; Lk.11.53–54. **14:** See Mt.22.16 n. **17:** Rom.13.7.

12.18–27: **Question about the resurrection** (Mt.22.23–33; Lk.20.27–40). **18:** See Mt.22.23 n. **19:** Dt.25.5. **24:** See Mt.22.29 n. **26:** Ex.3.6; see Mt.22.31–32 n.; Lk.20.34–36 n.

12.28–34: **The great commandment** (Mt.22.34–40; Lk.10.25–28). **29:** The words of Dt.6.4, which are both preface to, and part of, the first commandment, define qualitatively the whole-

that he is one, and there is no other but he; ³³ and to love him with all the heart, and with all the understanding, and with all the strength, and to love one's neighbor as oneself, is much more than all whole burnt offerings and sacrifices." ³⁴ And when Jesus saw that he answered wisely, he said to him, "You are not far from the kingdom of God." And after that no one dared to ask him any question.

35 And as Jesus taught in the temple, he said, "How can the scribes say that the Christ is the son of David? ³⁶ David himself, inspired by^z the Holy Spirit, declared,

'The Lord said to my Lord,
  Sit at my right hand,
till I put thy enemies under thy feet.'
³⁷ David himself calls him Lord; so how is he his son?" And the great throng heard him gladly.

38 And in his teaching he said, "Beware of the scribes, who like to go about in long robes, and to have salutations in the market places ³⁹ and the best seats in the synagogues and the places of honor at feasts, ⁴⁰ who devour widows' houses and for a pretense make long prayers. They will receive the greater condemnation."

41 And he sat down opposite the treasury, and watched the multitude putting money into the treasury. Many rich people put in large sums. ⁴² And a poor widow came, and put in two copper coins, which make a penny. ⁴³ And he called his disciples to him, and said to them, "Truly, I say to you, this poor widow has put in more than

all those who are contributing to the treasury. ⁴⁴ For they all contributed out of their abundance; but she out of her poverty has put in everything she had, her whole living."

13 And as he came out of the temple, one of his disciples said to him, "Look, Teacher, what wonderful stones and what wonderful buildings!" ² And Jesus said to him, "Do you see these great buildings? There will not be left here one stone upon another, that will not be thrown down."

3 And as he sat on the Mount of Olives opposite the temple, Peter and James and John and Andrew asked him privately, ⁴ "Tell us, when will this be, and what will be the sign when these things are all to be accomplished?" ⁵ And Jesus began to say to them, "Take heed that no one leads you astray. ⁶ Many will come in my name, saying, 'I am he!' and they will lead many astray. ⁷ And when you hear of wars and rumors of wars, do not be alarmed; this must take place, but the end is not yet. ⁸ For nation will rise against nation, and kingdom against kingdom; there will be earthquakes in various places, there will be famines; this is but the beginning of the birth-pangs.

9 "But take heed to yourselves; for they will deliver you up to councils; and you will be beaten in synagogues; and you will stand before governors and kings for my sake, to bear testimony before them. ¹⁰ And the gospel

z Or *himself, in*

ness of the love that God requires. **33:** 1 Sam.15.22; Hos.6.6; Mic.6.6–8; Mt.9.13. Sacrifices were offered only at the temple in Jerusalem.
  12.35–37: David's son (Mt.22.41–46; Lk.20.41–44). **36:** See Mt.22.44 n.
  12.38–40: Sayings on pride and humility. 38: Mt.23.1; Lk.20.45. **39:** Mt.23.6; Lk.20.46. The *best seats* were at the front, facing the congregation (Jas.2.2,3). The *places of honor* were the couches at the host's table (Lk.11.43; 14.7–11). **40:** Lk.20.47.
  12.41–44: The widow's offering (Lk.21.1–4). **41:** See Lk.21.1 n. **42:** See Lk.12.59 n. **43:** See Lk.21.2 n.
  13.1–2: Destruction of Jerusalem foretold (Mt.24.1–3; Lk.21.5–7). See Mt.24.1 n. **1:** *The temple*, begun by Herod the Great, was as yet unfinished. **2:** Lk.19.43–44; Mk.14.58; 15.29; Jn.2.19; Acts 6.14. This temple was destroyed A.D. 70.
  13.3–37: On the end of the age (Mt.24.4–36; Lk.21.8–36). **4:** Lk.17.20. **6:** Jn.8.24; 1 Jn.2.18. **8:** *Birth-pangs*, see Mt.24.8 n. **9–13:** Mt.10.17–22. **11:** Jn.14.26; 16.7–11; Lk.12.11–12. **13:** Jn.

[1232]

must first be preached to all nations. [11] And when they bring you to trial and deliver you up, do not be anxious beforehand what you are to say; but say whatever is given you in that hour, for it is not you who speak, but the Holy Spirit. [12] And brother will deliver up brother to death, and the father his child, and children will rise against parents and have them put to death; [13] and you will be hated by all for my name's sake. But he who endures to the end will be saved.

14 "But when you see the desolating sacrilege set up where it ought not to be (let the reader understand), then let those who are in Judea flee to the mountains; [15] let him who is on the housetop not go down, nor enter his house, to take anything away; [16] and let him who is in the field not turn back to take his mantle. [17] And alas for those who are with child and for those who give suck in those days! [18] Pray that it may not happen in winter. [19] For in those days there will be such tribulation as has not been from the beginning of the creation which God created until now, and never will be. [20] And if the Lord had not shortened the days, no human being would be saved; but for the sake of the elect, whom he chose, he shortened the days. [21] And then if any one says to you, 'Look, here is the Christ!' or 'Look, there he is!' do not believe it. [22] False Christs and false prophets will arise and show signs and wonders, to lead astray, if possible, the elect. [23] But take heed; I have told you all things beforehand.

24 "But in those days, after that tribulation, the sun will be darkened, and the moon will not give its light, [25] and the stars will be falling from heaven, and the powers in the heavens will be shaken. [26] And then they will see the Son of man coming in clouds with great power and glory. [27] And then he will send out the angels, and gather his elect from the four winds, from the ends of the earth to the ends of heaven.

28 "From the fig tree learn its lesson: as soon as its branch becomes tender and puts forth its leaves, you know that summer is near. [29] So also, when you see these things taking place, you know that he is near, at the very gates. [30] Truly, I say to you, this generation will not pass away before all these things take place. [31] Heaven and earth will pass away, but my words will not pass away.

32 "But of that day or that hour no one knows, not even the angels in heaven, nor the Son, but only the Father. [33] Take heed, watch;[a] for you do not know when the time will come. [34] It is like a man going on a journey, when he leaves home and puts his servants in charge, each with his work, and commands the doorkeeper to be on the watch. [35] Watch therefore –for you do not know when the master of the house will come, in the evening, or at midnight, or at cockcrow, or in the morning– [36] lest he come suddenly and find you asleep. [37] And what I say to you I say to all: Watch."

14 It was now two days before the Passover and the feast of Unleavened Bread. And the chief priests and the scribes were seeking how to arrest him by stealth, and kill him; [2] for they said, "Not during the feast, lest there be a tumult of the people."

3 And while he was at Bethany in the house of Simon the leper, as he sat at table, a woman came with an alabaster flask of ointment of pure nard, very costly, and she broke the flask

a Other ancient authorities add *and pray*

15.18–21. **14:** Dan.9.27; 11.31; 12.11. *The desolating sacrilege*, the intrusion of Gentile practices into the temple. **17:** Lk.23.29. **22:** Mt.7.15; Jn.4.48. **26:** 8.38; Mt.10.23; Dan.7.13; 1 Th.4.13–18. **30:** See Mt.24.34 n.; Mk.9.1. **31:** Mt.5.18; Lk.16.17. **32:** Acts 1.7. **33:** Eph.6.18; Col.4.2. **34:** Mt.25.14. **35:** Lk.12.35–40. Domestic division of the night into four parts.

    14.1–15.47: Jesus' death (Mt.26.1–27.66; Lk.22.1–23.56; Jn.13.1–19.42). **14.1:** *The feast of Unleavened Bread* was part of the commemoration of the escape from Egypt under Moses

and poured it over his head. [4] But there were some who said to themselves indignantly, "Why was the ointment thus wasted? [5] For this ointment might have been sold for more than three hundred denarii,[b] and given to the poor." And they reproached her. [6] But Jesus said, "Let her alone; why do you trouble her? She has done a beautiful thing to me. [7] For you always have the poor with you, and whenever you will, you can do good to them; but you will not always have me. [8] She has done what she could; she has anointed my body beforehand for burying. [9] And truly, I say to you, wherever the gospel is preached in the whole world, what she has done will be told in memory of her."

10 Then Judas Iscariot, who was one of the twelve, went to the chief priests in order to betray him to them. [11] And when they heard it they were glad, and promised to give him money. And he sought an opportunity to betray him.

12 And on the first day of Unleavened Bread, when they sacrificed the passover lamb, his disciples said to him, "Where will you have us go and prepare for you to eat the passover?" [13] And he sent two of his disciples, and said to them, "Go into the city, and a man carrying a jar of water will meet you; follow him, [14] and wherever he enters, say to the householder, 'The Teacher says, Where is my guest room, where I am to eat the passover with my disciples?' [15] And he will show you a large upper room furnished and ready; there prepare for us." [16] And

the disciples set out and went to the city, and found it as he had told them; and they prepared the passover.

17 And when it was evening he came with the twelve. [18] And as they were at table eating, Jesus said, "Truly, I say to you, one of you will betray me, one who is eating with me." [19] They began to be sorrowful, and to say to him one after another, "Is it I?" [20] He said to them, "It is one of the twelve, one who is dipping bread into the dish with me. [21] For the Son of man goes as it is written of him, but woe to that man by whom the Son of man is betrayed! It would have been better for that man if he had not been born."

22 And as they were eating, he took bread, and blessed, and broke it, and gave it to them, and said, "Take; this is my body." [23] And he took a cup, and when he had given thanks he gave it to them, and they all drank of it. [24] And he said to them, "This is my blood of the[c] covenant, which is poured out for many. [25] Truly, I say to you, I shall not drink again of the fruit of the vine until that day when I drink it new in the kingdom of God."

26 And when they had sung a hymn, they went out to the Mount of Olives. [27] And Jesus said to them, "You will all fall away; for it is written, 'I will strike the shepherd, and the sheep will be scattered.' [28] But after I am raised up, I will go before you to Galilee." [29] Peter said to him, "Even though they all fall away, I will not."

b The denarius was a day's wage for a laborer
c Other ancient authorities insert *new*

(Ex.12.1–20). **3–9:** See Mt.26.6 n. *Nard* was imported from India. **5:** On the value of a denarius, see note *b*. **6:** See Mt.26.10 n. **7:** Dt.15.11. **8:** The woman has shown personal regard for Jesus within her ability and opportunity. Jn.19.40. **10–11:** Mt.26.14–16; Lk.22.3–6. **10:** *One of the twelve;* the words do not so much identify *Judas* as intensify the horror of the betrayal. Judas makes possible a change in the priests' plans (vv. 1–2).

    14.12–25: The Last Supper. **12–16:** Mt.26.17–19; Lk.22.7–13; see 22.10 n. **14:** See Lk.22.12 n. **17–21:** Mt.26.20–25; Lk.22.14,21–23; Jn.13.21–30. **18:** Ps.41.9. **19:** The question was so worded as to imply that the answer would be negative. **22–25:** Mt.26.26–29; Lk.22.15–20; 1 Cor.11.23–26. **23:** 1 Cor.10.16. **24:** See Mt.26.28 n. Jesus speaks of his blood as being the mediating reality in a new relationship between God and men (see 10.45 n.). **25:** Lk.13.29; see 22.16 n.

    14.26–52: Gethsemane. **26–31:** Mt.26.30–35; Lk.22.39,31–34. **26:** Jn.18.1–2. **27:** Zech.13.7;

³⁰ And Jesus said to him, "Truly, I say to you, this very night, before the cock crows twice, you will deny me three times." ³¹ But he said vehemently, "If I must die with you, I will not deny you." And they all said the same.

32 And they went to a place which was called Gethsem'ane; and he said to his disciples, "Sit here, while I pray." ³³ And he took with him Peter and James and John, and began to be greatly distressed and troubled. ³⁴ And he said to them, "My soul is very sorrowful, even to death; remain here, and watch."ᵈ ³⁵ And going a little farther, he fell on the ground and prayed that, if it were possible, the hour might pass from him. ³⁶ And he said, "Abba, Father, all things are possible to thee; remove this cup from me; yet not what I will, but what thou wilt." ³⁷ And he came and found them sleeping, and he said to Peter, "Simon, are you asleep? Could you not watchᵈ one hour? ³⁸ Watchᵈ and pray that you may not enter into temptation; the spirit indeed is willing, but the flesh is weak." ³⁹ And again he went away and prayed, saying the same words. ⁴⁰ And again he came and found them sleeping, for their eyes were very heavy; and they did not know what to answer him. ⁴¹ And he came the third time, and said to them, "Are you still sleeping and taking your rest? It is enough; the hour has come; the Son of man is betrayed into the hands of sinners. ⁴² Rise, let us be going; see, my betrayer is at hand."

43 And immediately, while he was still speaking, Judas came, one of the twelve, and with him a crowd with swords and clubs, from the chief priests and the scribes and the elders. ⁴⁴ Now the betrayer had given them a sign, saying, "The one I shall kiss is the man; seize him and lead him away under guard." ⁴⁵ And when he came, he went up to him at once, and said, "Master!"ᵉ And he kissed him. ⁴⁶ And they laid hands on him and seized him. ⁴⁷ But one of those who stood by drew his sword, and struck the slave of the high priest and cut off his ear. ⁴⁸ And Jesus said to them, "Have you come out as against a robber, with swords and clubs to capture me? ⁴⁹ Day after day I was with you in the temple teaching, and you did not seize me. But let the scriptures be fulfilled." ⁵⁰ And they all forsook him, and fled.

51 And a young man followed him, with nothing but a linen cloth about his body; and they seized him, ⁵² but he left the linen cloth and ran away naked.

53 And they led Jesus to the high priest; and all the chief priests and the elders and the scribes were assembled. ⁵⁴ And Peter had followed him at a distance, right into the courtyard of the high priest; and he was sitting with the guards, and warming himself at the fire. ⁵⁵ Now the chief priests and the whole council sought testimony against Jesus to put him to death; but they found none. ⁵⁶ For many bore false witness against him, and their witness did not agree. ⁵⁷ And some stood up and bore false witness against him, saying, ⁵⁸ "We heard him say, 'I will de-

ᵈ Or *keep awake*   ᵉ Or *Rabbi*

Jn.16.32. **28:** 16.7. **30:** 14.66–72; Jn.13.36–38; 18.17–18,25–27. **32–42:** Mt.26.36–46; Lk.22.40–46. **32:** Jn.18.1; Heb.5.7–8. **34:** Jn.12.27. **35–36:** Jesus would not accept for himself the possibility of anything contrary to God's will (see 11.23–24 n.). *Abba*, "father" in Aramaic (see Rom.8.15 n.; Gal.4.6). **36:** *Cup*, see Lk.22.42 n. **38:** Mt.6.13; Lk.11.4. **43–52:** Mt.26.47–56; Lk.22.47–53; Jn.18.2–11. **43:** See Mt.26.50 n. **49:** Lk.19.47; Jn.18.19–21. **51:** The young man's identity is not disclosed. Perhaps he was sleeping in the house where Jesus ate the Last Supper and rose hastily from bed to follow Jesus to Gethsemane. If the house was that of Mary, the mother of John Mark (where the disciples met at a later date; Acts 12.12), it is possible that the *young man* was the Evangelist himself.

14.53–72: Jesus before Caiaphas. 55: At least two witnesses who agreed were required by Num.35.30 and Dt.19.15 (compare Mt.18.16). **58:** 13.2; 15.29; Acts 6.14; Jn.2.19. **61–62:** *The*

stroy this temple that is made with hands, and in three days I will build another, not made with hands.' " [59] Yet not even so did their testimony agree. [60] And the high priest stood up in the midst, and asked Jesus, "Have you no answer to make? What is it that these men testify against you?" [61] But he was silent and made no answer. Again the high priest asked him, "Are you the Christ, the Son of the Blessed?" [62] And Jesus said, "I am; and you will see the Son of man seated at the right hand of Power, and coming with the clouds of heaven." [63] And the high priest tore his garments, and said, "Why do we still need witnesses? [64] You have heard his blasphemy. What is your decision?" And they all condemned him as deserving death. [65] And some began to spit on him, and to cover his face, and to strike him, saying to him, "Prophesy!" And the guards received him with blows.

66 And as Peter was below in the courtyard, one of the maids of the high priest came; [67] and seeing Peter warming himself, she looked at him, and said, "You also were with the Nazarene, Jesus." [68] But he denied it, saying, "I neither know nor understand what you mean." And he went out into the gateway.[f] [69] And the maid saw him, and began again to say to the bystanders, "This man is one of them." [70] But again he denied it. And after a little while again the bystanders said to Peter, "Certainly you are one of them; for you are a Galilean." [71] But he began to invoke a curse on himself and to swear, "I do not know this man of whom you speak." [72] And immediately the cock crowed a second time. And Peter remembered how Jesus had said to him, "Before the cock crows

twice, you will deny me three times." And he broke down and wept.

15 And as soon as it was morning the chief priests, with the elders and scribes, and the whole council held a consultation; and they bound Jesus and led him away and delivered him to Pilate. [2] And Pilate asked him, "Are you the King of the Jews?" And he answered him, "You have said so." [3] And the chief priests accused him of many things. [4] And Pilate again asked him, "Have you no answer to make? See how many charges they bring against you." [5] But Jesus made no further answer, so that Pilate wondered.

6 Now at the feast he used to release for them one prisoner for whom they asked. [7] And among the rebels in prison, who had committed murder in the insurrection, there was a man called Barab′bas. [8] And the crowd came up and began to ask Pilate to do as he was wont to do for them. [9] And he answered them, "Do you want me to release for you the King of the Jews?" [10] For he perceived that it was out of envy that the chief priests had delivered him up. [11] But the chief priests stirred up the crowd to have him release for them Barab′bas instead. [12] And Pilate again said to them, "Then what shall I do with the man whom you call the King of the Jews?" [13] And they cried out again, "Crucify him." [14] And Pilate said to them, "Why, what evil has he done?" But they shouted all the more, "Crucify him." [15] So Pilate, wishing to satisfy the crowd, released for them Barab′bas; and having scourged Jesus, he delivered him to be crucified.

_f_ Or *fore-court*. Other ancient authorities add *and the cock crowed*

Blessed . . . Power, Jewish ways of referring to God. **62:** Dan.7.13 combined with the thought of Ps.110.1. **63:** Acts 14.14; Jl.2.12–13. **64:** Lev.24.16. **66:** 14.30. **70:** See Mt.26.73 n. **72:** Before dawn, compare 13.35. *He broke down*, the meaning of the Greek is uncertain.
     15.1–15: Jesus before Pilate. 1: See Mt.27.1–2 n.; Lk.23.1; Jn.18.28–32. **2–5:** Mt.27.11–14; Lk.23.2–5; Jn.18.29–38. **6–15:** Mt.27.15–26; Lk.23.18–25; Jn.18.38–40; 19.4–16. **7:** The *insurrection* is unrecorded; the crime was more serious than that of brigandage (15.27; Jn.18.40). **11:** Acts 3.14. **13:** According to Jewish law a religious curse was implicit in crucifixion (Dt. 21.23). **15:** See Mt.27.26 n.

16 And the soldiers led him away inside the palace (that is, the praetorium); and they called together the whole battalion. [17] And they clothed him in a purple cloak, and plaiting a crown of thorns they put it on him. [18] And they began to salute him, "Hail, King of the Jews!" [19] And they struck his head with a reed, and spat upon him, and they knelt down in homage to him. [20] And when they had mocked him, they stripped him of the purple cloak, and put his own clothes on him. And they led him out to crucify him.

21 And they compelled a passer-by, Simon of Cyre'ne, who was coming in from the country, the father of Alexander and Rufus, to carry his cross. [22] And they brought him to the place called Gol'gotha (which means the place of a skull). [23] And they offered him wine mingled with myrrh; but he did not take it. [24] And they crucified him, and divided his garments among them, casting lots for them, to decide what each should take. [25] And it was the third hour, when they crucified him. [26] And the inscription of the charge against him read, "The King of the Jews." [27] And with him they crucified two robbers, one on his right and one on his left.[g] [29] And those who passed by derided him, wagging their heads, and saying, "Aha! You who would destroy the temple and build it in three days, [30] save yourself, and come down from the cross!" [31] So also the chief priests mocked him to one another with the scribes, saying, "He saved others; he cannot save himself. [32] Let the Christ, the King of Israel, come down now from the cross, that we may see and believe." Those who were crucified with him also reviled him.

33 And when the sixth hour had come, there was darkness over the whole land[h] until the ninth hour. [34] And at the ninth hour Jesus cried with a loud voice, "E'lo-i, E'lo-i, la'ma sabach-tha'ni?" which means, "My God, my God, why hast thou forsaken me?" [35] And some of the bystanders hearing it said, "Behold, he is calling Eli'jah." [36] And one ran and, filling a sponge full of vinegar, put it on a reed and gave it to him to drink, saying, "Wait, let us see whether Eli'jah will come to take him down." [37] And Jesus uttered a loud cry, and breathed his last. [38] And the curtain of the temple was torn in two, from top to bottom. [39] And when the centurion, who stood facing him, saw that he thus[i] breathed his last, he said, "Truly this man was the Son[x] of God!"

40 There were also women looking on from afar, among whom were Mary Mag'dalene, and Mary the mother of James the younger and of Joses, and Salo'me, [41] who, when he was in Galilee, followed him, and ministered to him; and also many other women who came up with him to Jerusalem.

42 And when evening had come, since it was the day of Preparation, that is, the day before the sabbath, [43] Joseph of Arimathe'a, a respected member of the council, who was also himself looking for the kingdom of

g Other ancient authorities insert verse 28, *And the scripture was fulfilled which says, "He was reckoned with the transgressors"*
h Or *earth*
i Other ancient authorities insert *cried out and*
x Or *a son*

15.16–47: The crucifixion. 16–20: Mt.27.27–31; Lk.23.11; Jn.19.1–3. **16:** See Mt.27.27 n. **21–32:** Mt.27.32–44; Lk.23.33–43; Jn.19.17–24. **21:** The men named were probably known to the Christians who first read Mark. A connection with the *Rufus* mentioned in Rom.16.13 is possible but not established. **23:** *Wine . . . with myrrh* was a sedative. **24:** Ps.22.18. **25:** About 9 a.m. **29:** 13.2; 14.58; Jn.2.19. **31:** Ps.22.7–8. **33:** See Mt.27.45 n. **34:** See Mt.27.46 n. **36:** Ps.69.21; see Mt.27.48 n. **38:** The veil closed off the Holy of Holies (Heb.9.3), the inner sanctuary which represented God's presence with his people (compare 2 Kg.19.14–15; 2 Chr. 6.1–2,18–21). The damage to the veil, whatever the underlying event may have been, symbolized for Christian faith the unhindered access to God achieved for all by Jesus' death (Heb.10.19–20). **41:** Lk.8.1–3. **42–47:** Mt.27.57–61; Lk.23.50–56; Jn.19.38–42. **42:** Late on Friday afternoon. **46:** Acts 13.29.

God, took courage and went to Pilate, and asked for the body of Jesus. ⁴⁴ And Pilate wondered if he were already dead; and summoning the centurion, he asked him whether he was already dead.*ʲ* ⁴⁵ And when he learned from the centurion that he was dead, he granted the body to Joseph. ⁴⁶ And he bought a linen shroud, and taking him down, wrapped him in the linen shroud, and laid him in a tomb which had been hewn out of the rock; and he rolled a stone against the door of the tomb. ⁴⁷ Mary Mag'dalene and Mary the mother of Joses saw where he was laid.

16 And when the sabbath was past, Mary Mag'dalene, and Mary the mother of James, and Salo'me, bought spices, so that they might go and anoint him. ² And very early on the first day of the week they went to the tomb when the sun had risen. ³ And they were saying to one another, "Who will roll away the stone for us from the door of the tomb?" ⁴ And looking up, they saw that the stone was rolled back –it was very large. ⁵ And entering the tomb, they saw a young man sitting on the right side, dressed in a white robe; and they were amazed. ⁶ And he said to them, "Do not be amazed; you seek Jesus of Nazareth, who was cruci-

fied. He has risen, he is not here; see the place where they laid him. ⁷ But go, tell his disciples and Peter that he is going before you to Galilee; there you will see him, as he told you." ⁸ And they went out and fled from the tomb; for trembling and astonishment had come upon them; and they said nothing to any one, for they were afraid.

9 Now when he rose early on the first day of the week, he appeared first to Mary Magdalene, from whom he had cast out seven demons. ¹⁰ She went and told those who had been with him, as they mourned and wept. ¹¹ But when they heard that he was alive and had been seen by her, they would not believe it.

12 After this he appeared in another form to two of them, as they were walking into the country. ¹³ And they went back and told the rest, but they did not believe them.

14 Afterward he appeared to the eleven themselves as they sat at table; and he upbraided them for their unbelief and hardness of heart, because they had not believed those who saw him after he had risen. ¹⁵ And he said to them, "Go into all the world and

ʲ Other ancient authorities read *whether he had been some time dead*

16.1–8: The first Easter (Mt.28.1–10; Lk.24.1–11; Jn.20.1–10). **1:** Lk.23.56; Jn.19.39. *Sabbath* ended at sundown on Saturday. The women came to complete the rites of burial. **3–4:** The disk-shaped *stone* rolled edgeways in a gutter to close the opening of the tomb. **5:** The main chamber of a tomb was normally furnished with niches to receive the bodies. The young man's clothes indicate him to be a heavenly messenger. **7:** 14.28; Jn.21.1–23; Mt.28.7. **8:** *For they were afraid.* The Greek expression is unusual in style and abrupt in effect, especially if, as is possible, it originally ended the Gospel. In contrast with Mt.28.8–10, where fear is part of an emotional state that includes joy (v. 8) and is controlled by worship (v. 9) and acceptance of mission (v. 10), fear here (probably in the sense of overwhelming awe) is the pervasive consequence of amazement (v. 5) and of trembling and astonishment (v. 8) that resulted in flight and silence (v. 8). On the silence of the women compare Mt.28.8 n.; Lk.24.9–11, 22–24, and vv. 9–10 below.

16.9–20: The traditional close of the Gospel of Mark. Nothing is certainly known either about how this Gospel originally ended or about the origin of vv. 9–20, which cannot have been part of the original text of Mark. Certain important witnesses to the text, including some ancient ones, end the Gospel with v. 8. Though it is possible that the compiler of the Gospel intended this abrupt ending, one can find hints that he intended to describe events after the resurrection: for example, Mk.14.28 looks forward to an account of at least one experience of the disciples with Jesus in Galilee after the resurrection, while the friendly reference to Peter (16.7) may anticipate the recounting of the otherwise unrecorded moment of reconciliation between Peter

preach the gospel to the whole creation. [16] He who believes and is baptized will be saved; but he who does not
believe will be condemned. [17] And these
signs will accompany those who believe: in my name they will cast out demons; they will speak in new tongues;
[18] they will pick up serpents, and if they
drink any deadly thing, it will not hurt
them; they will lay their hands on the
sick, and they will recover."
19 So then the Lord Jesus, after he
had spoken to them, was taken up into

heaven, and sat down at the right hand
of God. [20] And they went forth and
preached everywhere, while the Lord
worked with them and confirmed the
message by the signs that attended it.
Amen.[k]

k Some of the most ancient authorities bring the book
to a close at the end of verse 8. One authority concludes the book by adding after verse 8 the following:
*But they reported briefly to Peter and those with him
all that they had been told. And after this, Jesus himself
sent out by means of them, from east to west, the sacred
and imperishable proclamation of eternal salvation.*
Other authorities include the preceding passage and
continue with verses 9–20. In most authorities verses
9–20 follow immediately after verse 8; a few authorities insert additional material after verse 14.

and his Lord (compare Lk.24.34; 1 Cor.15.5). If such accounts as these were originally part
of Mark's Gospel, the loss of them took place very shortly after the Gospel was written, under
circumstances beyond present knowledge. Many witnesses, some ancient, end the Gospel with
vv. 9–20, thus showing that from early Christian times these verses have been accepted traditionally and generally as part of the canonical Gospel of Mark. Additionally, a variety of
witnesses give the short paragraph in note k along with vv. 9–20, thus showing that differences
existed in ancient practice. The most likely accounting for the origin of these verses as a unit
is that, having been compiled early in the second century as a didactic summary of grounds
for belief in Jesus' resurrection, they were appended to the Gospel by the middle of the second
century. On the Christian belief in continuing unrecorded memories about Jesus in the first
century see Lk.1.1–2; Jn.20.30; 21.25; Acts 20.35 n.; 1 Cor.15.3; also compare Mt.28.20; Jn.
16.12–33; Rev.1.12–16 n.; 2.18.

16.9–18: Post-resurrection appearances of Jesus. 9–10: Mary is associated with other women
in vv. 1,7–8 and parallels; she is apparently alone in Jn.20.1–2,11–19. *Seven demons*, Lk.8.2;
11: Lk.24.11,22–25; Jn.20.19–29; 1 Cor.15.5.Here, as in Jn.20.19–29, the disciples are convinced
of the truth of Jesus' resurrection by their own immediate experience with him, though they
should have heeded the witness of others as later generations must do (Jn.20.29). 12–13: Lk.
24.12–35. 13: Compare Lk.24.34. 14–18: Mt.28.19; Lk.24.47. 14: At the close of this verse a
few ancient authorities as old as the fourth century add the following: "And they excused
themselves, saying, 'This age of lawlessness and unbelief is under Satan, who does not allow
the truth and power of God to prevail over the unclean things of the spirits. Therefore reveal
your righteousness now' — thus they spoke to Christ. And Christ replied to them, 'The term
of years for Satan's power has been fulfilled, but other terrible things draw near. And for those
who have sinned I was delivered over to death, that they may return to the truth and sin no
more, that they may inherit the spiritual and incorruptible glory of righteousness which is in
heaven.'" 16: Acts 2.37–42; 10.47–48; Rom.10.9. 17–18: The reality of faith in men's lives as
they respond to the apostolic witness is signified by events that both correspond with biblically
recorded happenings in the lives of the apostles and conform to apostolic statements about the
gifts of the Spirit (for example, 1 Cor.12.8–11, 28; 14.2–5; Heb.2.3–4): exorcism (Acts 8.6–7;
16.18; 19.11–20); new tongues (see Acts 2.4–11 n.; 10.46; 19.6; 1 Cor.12.10,28; 14.2–33);healing
(Acts 28.8; 1 Cor.12.9; Jas.5.13–16). Instances of picking up snakes and drinking poison, without injury to the believer in either case, lack New Testament parallels. However, the former
resembles the harmless accidental attack upon Paul in Acts 28.3–6, and the latter appears
occasionally in Christian literature from the second century onward.

16.19–20: Jesus' exaltation. 19: For the concept of Jesus' exaltation, Phil.2.9–11; Heb.1.3;
for the language *was taken up*, Acts 1.2,11,22; 1 Tim.3.16 (seemingly a Christian hymn); for
the image of the *right hand of God*, Ps.110.1 n.; Acts 7.55; Heb.1.3. 20: Vv. 17–18; Heb.2.3–4.

LUKE

The Gospel according to Luke sets forth the words and works of Jesus as the divine-human Savior, whose compassion and tenderness extended to all who were needy. The universal mission of Jesus is emphasized (a) by tracing his genealogy back to Adam, the father of the race (3.38; contrast Mt.1.1–2); (b) by including references which commend members of a despised people, the Samaritans (10.30–37; 17.11–19; see Acts 8.5 n.); (c) by indicating that women have a new place of importance among the followers of Jesus (7.36–50; 8.3; 10.38–42); and (d) by promising that the Gentiles would have an opportunity to accept the gospel (2.32; 3.6; 24.47; compare 15.4 n.).

In addition to presenting the story of Jesus' work in Galilee and his last week in Jerusalem, Luke includes more episodes of Jesus' final journey to Jerusalem than do the other Evangelists. This special section (9.51–18.14) also preserves many of the most beloved of Jesus' parables (such as the Good Samaritan, the Prodigal Son, the Unjust Judge, and others).

The major divisions are: chs. 1–2, Births of John and Jesus; the boy Jesus in the temple; 3.1–22, Activity of John; baptism of Jesus; 3.23–38, Genealogy of Jesus; 4.1–13, Temptation of Jesus; 4.14–9.50, Jesus' activity, chiefly in Galilee; 9.51–19.27, Journey to Jerusalem; 19.28–23.56, The last week, concluding with Jesus' crucifixion and burial; ch. 24, The resurrection; commissioning the disciples.

Although the Gospel is anonymous and the evidence pertaining to the identity of its author is inconclusive, there are many considerations supporting the early Christian tradition that the author was the physician Luke, a Gentile convert and a friend of Paul's (Col.4.14; 2 Tim.4.11; Philem.24). The Gospel appears to have been written during the last third of the first century, although the precise date is unknown.

INASMUCH AS MANY HAVE UNDERtaken to compile a narrative of the things which have been accomplished among us, ² just as they were delivered to us by those who from the beginning were eyewitnesses and ministers of the word, ³ it seemed good to me also, having followed all things closely*a* for some time past, to write an orderly account for you, most excellent Theoph'ilus, ⁴ that you may know the truth concerning the things of which you have been informed.

5 In the days of Herod, king of Judea, there was a priest named Zechari'ah,*b* of the division of Abi'jah; and he had a wife of the daughters of Aaron, and her name was Elizabeth.

⁶ And they were both righteous before God, walking in all the commandments and ordinances of the Lord blameless. ⁷ But they had no child, because Elizabeth was barren, and both were advanced in years.

8 Now while he was serving as priest before God when his division was on duty, ⁹ according to the custom of the priesthood, it fell to him by lot to enter the temple of the Lord and burn incense. ¹⁰ And the whole multitude of the people were praying outside at the hour of incense. ¹¹ And there appeared to him an angel of the Lord standing on the right side of the altar of incense. ¹² And Zechari'ah was troubled when he saw him, and fear fell upon him.

a Or *accurately*   *b* Greek *Zacharias*

1.1–4: Introduction. 1: Jn.20.30–31; 21.25. The writers of the gospels used sources of information now lost (see 6.17–49 n.). **2:** Acts 1.21; 10.39; Heb.2.3; 1 Jn.1.1. **3:** See Acts 1.1 n. *Theophilus*, an unknown Christian, perhaps of social prominence (*most excellent*, see Acts 23.26 n.). **4:** Jn.20.31.

1.5–2.40: The births of John and Jesus (Mt.1.18–2.23). **1.5:** *Herod* the Great reigned 37–4 B.C. The date intended here is approximately 7–6 B.C. *The division of Abijah*, 1 Chr.24.10. **8–9:**

13 But the angel said to him, "Do not be afraid, Zechari′ah, for your prayer is heard, and your wife Elizabeth will bear you a son, and you shall call his name John. 14 And you will have joy and gladness, and many will rejoice at his birth; 15 for he will be great before the Lord, and he shall drink no wine nor strong drink, and he will be filled with the Holy Spirit, even from his mother's womb. 16 And he will turn many of the sons of Israel to the Lord their God, 17 and he will go before him in the spirit and power of Eli′jah, to turn the hearts of the fathers to the children, and the disobedient to the wisdom of the just, to make ready for the Lord a people prepared." 18 And Zechari′ah said to the angel, "How shall I know this? For I am an old man, and my wife is advanced in years." 19 And the angel answered him, "I am Gabriel, who stand in the presence of God; and I was sent to speak to you, and to bring you this good news. 20 And behold, you will be silent and unable to speak until the day that these things come to pass, because you did not believe my words, which will be fulfilled in their time." 21 And the people were waiting for Zechari′ah, and they wondered at his delay in the temple. 22 And when he came out, he could not speak to them, and they perceived that he had seen a vision in the temple; and he made signs to them and remained dumb. 23 And when his time of service was ended, he went to his home.

24 After these days his wife Elizabeth conceived, and for five months she hid herself, saying, 25 "Thus the Lord has done to me in the days when he looked on me, to take away my reproach among men."

26 In the sixth month the angel Gabriel was sent from God to a city of Galilee named Nazareth, 27 to a virgin betrothed to a man whose name was Joseph, of the house of David; and the virgin's name was Mary. 28 And he came to her and said, "Hail, O favored one, the Lord is with you!"*c* 29 But she was greatly troubled at the saying, and considered in her mind what sort of greeting this might be. 30 And the angel said to her, "Do not be afraid, Mary, for you have found favor with God. 31 And behold, you will conceive in your womb and bear a son, and you shall call his name Jesus. 32 He will be great, and will be called the Son of the Most High; and the Lord God will give to him the throne of his father David, 33 and he will reign over the house of Jacob for ever; and of his kingdom there will be no end." 34 And Mary said to the angel, "How shall this be, since I have no husband?" 35 And the angel said to her,
"The Holy Spirit will come upon you, and the power of the Most High will overshadow you; therefore the child to be born*d* will be called holy, the Son of God. 36 And behold, your kinswoman Elizabeth in her old age has also conceived a son; and this is the sixth month with her who was called barren. 37 For with God nothing will be impossible." 38 And Mary said, "Behold, I am the handmaid of the Lord; let it be to me according to your word." And the angel departed from her.

39 In those days Mary arose and

c Other ancient authorities add *"Blessed are you among women!"*
d Other ancient authorities add *of you*

---

2 Chr.31.2; Ex.30.1,6–8. **14–17**: Canticle in honor of John. **15**: Num.6.1–4; Lk.7.33. **17**: Mal.4.5–6; Mt.11.14. **19**: Dan.8.16; 9.21. **25**: Among Jews barrenness was regarded as a sign of divine disfavor and therefore a *reproach* (see Gen.16.2 n.; 30.23; 1 Sam.1.1–18; Ps.128.3). **26–38**: The birth of Jesus is foretold (the Annunciation). **31**: Mt.1.21. **33**: Mt.28.18; Dan.2.44.

went with haste into the hill country, to a city of Judah, [40] and she entered the house of Zechari′ah and greeted Elizabeth. [41] And when Elizabeth heard the greeting of Mary, the babe leaped in her womb; and Elizabeth was filled with the Holy Spirit [42] and she exclaimed with a loud cry, "Blessed are you among women, and blessed is the fruit of your womb! [43] And why is this granted me, that the mother of my Lord should come to me? [44] For behold, when the voice of your greeting came to my ears, the babe in my womb leaped for joy. [45] And blessed is she who believed that there would be[e] a fulfilment of what was spoken to her from the Lord." [46] And Mary said,

"My soul magnifies the Lord,
[47] and my spirit rejoices in God my
    Savior,
[48] for he has regarded the low estate
    of his handmaiden.
For behold, henceforth all
    generations will call me blessed;
[49] for he who is mighty has done great
    things for me,
    and holy is his name.
[50] And his mercy is on those who fear
    him
    from generation to generation.
[51] He has shown strength with his arm,
    he has scattered the proud in the
    imagination of their hearts,
[52] he has put down the mighty from
    their thrones,
    and exalted those of low degree;
[53] he has filled the hungry with good
    things,
    and the rich he has sent empty away.
[54] He has helped his servant Israel,
    in remembrance of his mercy,
[55] as he spoke to our fathers,
    to Abraham and to his posterity for
    ever."

[56] And Mary remained with her about three months, and returned to her home.

57 Now the time came for Elizabeth to be delivered, and she gave birth to a son. [58] And her neighbors and kinsfolk heard that the Lord had shown great mercy to her, and they rejoiced with her. [59] And on the eighth day they came to circumcise the child; and they would have named him Zechari′ah after his father, [60] but his mother said, "Not so; he shall be called John." [61] And they said to her, "None of your kindred is called by this name." [62] And they made signs to his father, inquiring what he would have him called. [63] And he asked for a writing tablet, and wrote, "His name is John." And they all marveled. [64] And immediately his mouth was opened and his tongue loosed, and he spoke, blessing God. [65] And fear came on all their neighbors. And all these things were talked about through all the hill country of Judea; [66] and all who heard them laid them up in their hearts, saying, "What then will this child be?" For the hand of the Lord was with him.

67 And his father Zechari′ah was filled with the Holy Spirit, and prophesied, saying,
[68] "Blessed be the Lord God of Israel,
    for he has visited and redeemed his
        people,
[69] and has raised up a horn of salvation
        for us
    in the house of his servant David,
[70] as he spoke by the mouth of his
        holy prophets from of old,
[71] that we should be saved from our
        enemies,
    and from the hand of all who hate us;
[72] to perform the mercy promised to
        our fathers,

e Or believed, for there will be

42: 11.27–28. **46–55**: The "Magnificat" (so called from the first word of the Latin translation) is based largely on Hannah's prayer in 1 Sam.2.1–10. _Magnifies_, i.e. declares the greatness of. **47**: 1 Tim.2.3; Tit.3.4; Jude 25. **55**: Gen.17.7; 18.18; 22.17; Mic.7.20. **57–66**: Birth of John the Baptist. **59**: Lev.12.3; Gen.17.12; Lk.2.21. **63**: See v. 13. **65**: _Fear_ (rendered "awe" in 5.26) indicates recognition of the limits of human understanding and power before God (2.9; 7.16; Acts 2.43,46–47; 5.5,11; 19.17). **67–79**: The "Benedictus," so called from the first word in the Latin translation. **69**: _A horn of salvation_ is here a king who will bring salvation (a horn is a

and to remember his holy covenant,
73 the oath which he swore to our
    father Abraham, 74 to grant us
that we, being delivered from the
    hand of our enemies,
might serve him without fear,
75 in holiness and righteousness before
    him all the days of our life.
76 And you, child, will be called the
    prophet of the Most High;
for you will go before the Lord to
    prepare his ways,
77 to give knowledge of salvation to
    his people
in the forgiveness of their sins,
78 through the tender mercy of our
    God,
when the day shall dawn upon* us
    from on high
79 to give light to those who sit in
    darkness and in the shadow of
    death,
to guide our feet into the way of
    peace."
80 And the child grew and became
strong in spirit, and he was in the
wilderness till the day of his manifestation to Israel.

2 In those days a decree went out
from Caesar Augustus that all the
world should be enrolled. 2 This was
the first enrollment, when Quirin'i-us
was governor of Syria. 3 And all went
to be enrolled, each to his own city.
4 And Joseph also went up from Galilee, from the city of Nazareth, to Judea,
to the city of David, which is called
Bethlehem, because he was of the
house and lineage of David, 5 to be enrolled with Mary, his betrothed, who

was with child. 6 And while they were
there, the time came for her to be delivered. 7 And she gave birth to her
first-born son and wrapped him in
swaddling cloths, and laid him in a
manger, because there was no place for
them in the inn.

8 And in that region there were
shepherds out in the field, keeping
watch over their flock by night. 9 And
an angel of the Lord appeared to them,
and the glory of the Lord shone around
them, and they were filled with fear.
10 And the angel said to them, "Be
not afraid; for behold, I bring you good
news of a great joy which will come
to all the people; 11 for to you is born
this day in the city of David a Savior,
who is Christ the Lord. 12 And this will
be a sign for you: you will find a babe
wrapped in swaddling cloths and lying
in a manger." 13 And suddenly there
was with the angel a multitude of the
heavenly host praising God and saying,
14 "Glory to God in the highest,
    and on earth peace among men with
        whom he is pleased!"*

15 When the angels went away
from them into heaven, the shepherds
said to one another, "Let us go over
to Bethlehem and see this thing that
has happened, which the Lord has
made known to us." 16 And they
went with haste, and found Mary and
Joseph, and the babe lying in a manger. 17 And when they saw it they
made known the saying which had

f Or *whereby the dayspring will visit*. Other ancient
authorities read *since the dayspring has visited*
g Other ancient authorities read *peace, good will among
men*

---

symbol of effective strength; see Ps.18.1–3; 92.10–11; 132.17–18). **76:** Mal.4.5; Lk.7.26. **77:**
Mk.1.4. **78:** Mal.4.2; Eph.5.14. *The day* will be when God fulfils his purpose to bless mankind.
79: Is.9.2; Mt.4.16; Lk.4.18. **80:** These words cover a period of approximately thirty years.
The day of his manifestation, 3.2,3.
   2.1–40: The birth of Jesus (Mt.1.18–2.23). **1:** About 6–5 B.C. (see 1.5 n.). The emperor
Augustus reigned from 27 B.C. to A.D. 14. *World* here refers to the Roman Empire. **7:** According
to Catholic teaching, the expression *first-born son* is used here simply as a Semitic legal term
and does not necessarily imply subsequent births. *Swaddling cloths*, strips of cloth customarily
wrapped around a newly born infant. **9:** *Fear*, see 1.65 n. **11:** *The city of David*, Bethlehem. Three
great Christian claims about Jesus are that he is *Savior*, *Christ* (the Messiah), and *Lord* (see
Mt.1.21 n.; 16.16 n.; Jn.4.42; Acts 2.36; 5.31; Phil.2.11). **14:** 3.22; 19.38. *Peace . . .* , the lack
of one letter in the later Greek manuscripts accounts for the rendering in note g. *Men with
whom he is pleased* means "those whom God has chosen in accord with his good pleasure."

been told them concerning this child; ¹⁸ and all who heard it wondered at what the shepherds told them. ¹⁹ But Mary kept all these things, pondering them in her heart. ²⁰ And the shepherds returned, glorifying and praising God for all they had heard and seen, as it had been told them.

21 And at the end of eight days, when he was circumcised, he was called Jesus, the name given by the angel before he was conceived in the womb.

22 And when the time came for their purification according to the law of Moses, they brought him up to Jerusalem to present him to the Lord ²³ (as it is written in the law of the Lord, "Every male that opens the womb shall be called holy to the Lord") ²⁴ and to offer a sacrifice according to what is said in the law of the Lord, "a pair of turtledoves, or two young pigeons." ²⁵ Now there was a man in Jerusalem, whose name was Simeon, and this man was righteous and devout, looking for the consolation of Israel, and the Holy Spirit was upon him. ²⁶ And it had been revealed to him by the Holy Spirit that he should not see death before he had seen the Lord's Christ. ²⁷ And inspired by the Spirit^h he came into the temple; and when the parents brought in the child Jesus, to do for him according to the custom of the law, ²⁸ he took him up in his arms and blessed God and said,

²⁹ "Lord, now lettest thou thy servant
    depart in peace,
according to thy word;
³⁰ for mine eyes have seen thy
    salvation
³¹ which thou hast prepared in the
    presence of all peoples,

³² a light for revelation to the Gentiles,
    and for glory to thy people Israel."

33 And his father and his mother marveled at what was said about him; ³⁴ and Simeon blessed them and said to Mary his mother,

"Behold, this child is set for the fall
    and rising of many in Israel,
and for a sign that is spoken against
³⁵ (and a sword will pierce through
    your own soul also),
that thoughts out of many hearts may
    be revealed."

36 And there was a prophetess, Anna, the daughter of Phan′u-el, of the tribe of Asher; she was of a great age, having lived with her husband seven years from her virginity, ³⁷ and as a widow till she was eighty-four. She did not depart from the temple, worshiping with fasting and prayer night and day. ³⁸ And coming up at that very hour she gave thanks to God, and spoke of him to all who were looking for the redemption of Jerusalem.

39 And when they had performed everything according to the law of the Lord, they returned into Galilee, to their own city, Nazareth. ⁴⁰ And the child grew and became strong, filled with wisdom; and the favor of God was upon him.

41 Now his parents went to Jerusalem every year at the feast of the Passover. ⁴² And when he was twelve years old, they went up according to custom; ⁴³ and when the feast was ended, as they were returning, the boy Jesus stayed behind in Jerusalem. His parents did not know it, ⁴⁴ but supposing him to be in the company they went a day's journey, and they sought him among their kinsfolk and acquaint-

h Or in the Spirit

21: See Mt.1.21 n. **22–24:** Lev.12.2–8. **23:** Ex.13.2,12. **25–38:** *Simeon* and *Anna*, not otherwise known, express faith in Jesus as Savior, Christ, and universal Lord (see v. 11 n.). **25:** *The consolation of Israel* was the salvation which the Messiah was to bring (vv. 26,38; 23.51). **26:** *The Lord's Christ*, the Christ of God (9.20). **29–32:** The "Nunc Dimittis," so called from the first words of the Latin translation. **29:** *Lettest . . . depart*, the figure is taken from the manumission of a slave. *In peace*, i.e. in a state of peace with God. **30:** 3.6; Is.52.10. **32:** Is.42.6; 49.6; Acts 13.47; 26.23. **33:** Luke could call Joseph the *father* of Jesus notwithstanding 1.34–35 since he was Mary's husband and Jesus' legal father (compare Mt.13.55; Lk.3.23). **36:** Jos.19.24.
    2.41–52: The boy Jesus at Jerusalem. This is the only information in the Bible on Jesus

ances; [45] and when they did not find him, they returned to Jerusalem, seeking him. [46] After three days they found him in the temple, sitting among the teachers, listening to them and asking them questions; [47] and all who heard him were amazed at his understanding and his answers. [48] And when they saw him they were astonished; and his mother said to him, "Son, why have you treated us so? Behold, your father and I have been looking for you anxiously." [49] And he said to them, "How is it that you sought me? Did you not know that I must be in my Father's house?" [50] And they did not understand the saying which he spoke to them. [51] And he went down with them and came to Nazareth, and was obedient to them; and his mother kept all these things in her heart.

52 And Jesus increased in wisdom and in stature,[i] and in favor with God and man.

3 In the fifteenth year of the reign of Tibe′ri-us Caesar, Pontius Pilate being governor of Judea, and Herod being tetrarch of Galilee, and his brother Philip tetrarch of the region of Iturae′a and Trachoni′tis, and Lysa′ni-as tetrarch of Abile′ne, [2] in the high-priesthood of Annas and Ca′iaphas, the word of God came to John the son of Zechari′ah in the wilderness; [3] and he went into all the region about the Jordan, preaching a baptism of repentance for the forgiveness of sins. [4] As it is written in the book of the words of Isaiah the prophet,
"The voice of one crying in the
  wilderness:
Prepare the way of the Lord,
  make his paths straight.
[5] Every valley shall be filled,
  and every mountain and hill shall
    be brought low,
and the crooked shall be made
    straight,
  and the rough ways shall be made
    smooth;
[6] and all flesh shall see the salvation
  of God.''

7 He said therefore to the multitudes that came out to be baptized by him, "You brood of vipers! Who warned you to flee from the wrath to come? [8] Bear fruits that befit repentance, and do not begin to say to yourselves, 'We have Abraham as our father'; for I tell you, God is able from these stones to raise up children to Abraham. [9] Even now the axe is laid to the root of the trees; every tree therefore that does not bear good fruit is cut down and thrown into the fire."

10 And the multitudes asked him, "What then shall we do?" [11] And he answered them, "He who has two coats, let him share with him who has none; and he who has food, let him do likewise." [12] Tax collectors also came to be baptized, and said to him,

i Or *years*

---

maturing. **41:** Ex.23.15; Dt.16.1–8. **46:** *The teachers* were the experts in the Jewish religion. **48:** Mk.3.31–35. **50–51:** 2.19. **52:** 1 Sam.2.26; Lk.1.80; 2.40.

3.1–20: Activity of John the Baptist (Mt.3.1–12; Mk.1.1–8). **1:** The year A.D. 26 or 27 is meant. *Pilate*, a Roman procurator, had final authority in *Judea* (23.1). The remainder of the kingdom of Herod the Great was divided between his sons *Herod* Antipas (9.7; 23.6,7) and *Philip*. For *tetrarch*, see Mt.14.1 n. *Abilene*, north of Philip's rule, was closely associated with it during the first century. **2:** Annas and his son-in-law Caiaphas (Jn.18.13) controlled the Jewish temple and priests. Caiaphas was the high priest (Mt.26.3; Jn.11.49); Annas, though retired, retained his prestige (Acts 4.6). Luke contrasts the powers men recognize with the authority of the word of God (1 Cor.1.26–31). *John*, see Mt.3.1 n. **3:** See Mk.1.4 n. **4–6:** Is.40.3–5. **5:** The language expresses the idea of moral and spiritual renewal, but the coming of God's salvation also meant judgment (v. 7; Am.5.18–20). **7:** *Viper*, a poisonous reptile that frequented the area (Is.30.6; 59.5; Mt.12.34; 23.33). *Wrath*, see Mt.3.7 n. **8:** John demands right living based on a sincere search for God's will (Mt.7.15–20; Gal.5.22–23) and suited to the protestations of repentance (see Mt.3.2 n.). The claim to have *Abraham as father* was a claim to privileged standing with God through natural birth (Jn.8.33,39; Rom.2.28,29). **9:** *Fire*, a symbol of judgment (Mt.7.19; 13.40–42; Heb.6.7–8). **10–11:** 6.29; Acts 2.44–45; 4.32–35. **12–13:** 19.2,8. **15:** Acts

"Teacher, what shall we do?" [13] And he said to them, "Collect no more than is appointed you." [14] Soldiers also asked him, "And we, what shall we do?" And he said to them, "Rob no one by violence or by false accusation, and be content with your wages."

15 As the people were in expectation, and all men questioned in their hearts concerning John, whether perhaps he were the Christ, [16] John answered them all, "I baptize you with water; but he who is mightier than I is coming, the thong of whose sandals I am not worthy to untie; he will baptize you with the Holy Spirit and with fire. [17] His winnowing fork is in his hand, to clear his threshing floor, and to gather the wheat into his granary, but the chaff he will burn with unquenchable fire."

18 So, with many other exhortations, he preached good news to the people. [19] But Herod the tetrarch, who had been reproved by him for Hero'di-as, his brother's wife, and for all the evil things that Herod had done, [20] added this to them all, that he shut up John in prison.

21 Now when all the people were baptized, and when Jesus also had been baptized and was praying, the heaven was opened, [22] and the Holy Spirit descended upon him in bodily form, as a dove, and a voice came from heaven, "Thou art my beloved Son;[j] with thee I am well pleased."[k]

23 Jesus, when he began his ministry, was about thirty years of age, being the son (as was supposed) of Joseph,

the son of Heli, [24] the son of Matthat, the son of Levi, the son of Melchi, the son of Jan'na-i, the son of Joseph, [25] the son of Mattathi'as, the son of Amos, the son of Nahum, the son of Esli, the son of Nag'ga-i, [26] the son of Ma'ath, the son of Mattathi'as, the son of Sem'e-in, the son of Josech, the son of Joda, [27] the son of Jo-an'an, the son of Rhesa, the son of Zerub'babel, the son of She-al'ti-el,[l] the son of Neri, [28] the son of Melchi, the son of Addi, the son of Cosam, the son of Elma'dam, the son of Er, [29] the son of Joshua, the son of Elie'zer, the son of Jorim, the son of Matthat, the son of Levi, [30] the son of Simeon, the son of Judah, the son of Joseph, the son of Jonam, the son of Eli'akim, [31] the son of Me'le-a, the son of Menna, the son of Mat'tatha, the son of Nathan, the son of David, [32] the son of Jesse, the son of Obed, the son of Bo'az, the son of Sala, the son of Nahshon, [33] the son of Ammin'adab, the son of Admin, the son of Arni, the son of Hezron, the son of Perez, the son of Judah, [34] the son of Jacob, the son of Isaac, the son of A-braham, the son of Terah, the son of Nahor, [35] the son of Serug, the son of Re'u, the son of Peleg, the son of Eber, the son of Shelah, [36] the son of Ca-i'nan, the son of Arphax'ad, the son of Shem, the son of Noah, the son of Lamech, [37] the son of Methuselah, the son of Enoch, the son of Jared, the son of Maha'lale-el, the son of Ca-i'nan, [38] the son of Enos, the son of

j Or *my Son, my* (or *the*) *Beloved*
k Other ancient authorities read *today I have begotten thee*
l Greek *Salathiel*

13.25; Jn.1.19–22; Lk.7.19. **16**: Acts 1.5; 11.16; 19.4. **18**: *He preached good news,* or "preached the gospel," refers to the message of forgiveness (v. 3) and the advent of a new relationship between men and God (vv. 15–17). **19–20**: Mt.14.3–4; Mk.6.17–18.
3.21–22: Jesus' baptism (Mt.3.13–17; Mk.1.9–11; Jn.1.29–34). See Mt.3.16–17 n. **21**: Prayer was part of many recorded momentous events in Jesus' life (e.g. Mk.1.35; Lk.5.16; 6.12; 9.18, 28; 11.1; 22.41–46). **22**: *Beloved,* see Mk.1.11 n.; Ps.2.7; Is.42.1; Lk.9.35.
3.23–38: The genealogy of Jesus is traced through Old Testament lines back to Adam, the first man (compare Mt.1.1–17). By linking Jesus' line with God's original creation Luke shows Jesus' common humanity, as contrasted with Matthew's emphasis on Jesus' Jewish lineage (see Mt.1.1 n.). **23**: Jesus' age is approximate (Jn.8.57). The persons named from *Heli* to *Zerubbabel* (v. 27) are otherwise unknown. For the rest of the genealogy, compare Gen.5.3–32; 11.10–26; Ru.4.18–22; 1 Chr.1.1–4,24–28; 2.1–15.

Seth, the son of Adam, the son of God.

4 And Jesus, full of the Holy Spirit, returned from the Jordan, and was led by the Spirit [2] for forty days in the wilderness, tempted by the devil. And he ate nothing in those days; and when they were ended, he was hungry. [3] The devil said to him, "If you are the Son of God, command this stone to become bread." [4] And Jesus answered him, "It is written, 'Man shall not live by bread alone.'" [5] And the devil took him up, and showed him all the kingdoms of the world in a moment of time, [6] and said to him, "To you I will give all this authority and their glory; for it has been delivered to me, and I give it to whom I will. [7] If you, then, will worship me, it shall all be yours." [8] And Jesus answered him, "It is written,

'You shall worship the Lord your God,

and him only shall you serve.'"

[9] And he took him to Jerusalem, and set him on the pinnacle of the temple, and said to him, "If you are the Son of God, throw yourself down from here; [10] for it is written,

'He will give his angels charge of you, to guard you,'

[11] and

'On their hands they will bear you up,

lest you strike your foot against a stone.'"

[12] And Jesus answered him, "It is said, 'You shall not tempt the Lord your God.'" [13] And when the devil had ended every temptation, he departed from him until an opportune time.

14 And Jesus returned in the power of the Spirit into Galilee, and a report concerning him went out through all the surrounding country. [15] And he taught in their synagogues, being glorified by all.

16 And he came to Nazareth, where he had been brought up; and he went to the synagogue, as his custom was, on the sabbath day. And he stood up to read; [17] and there was given to him the book of the prophet Isaiah. He opened the book and found the place where it was written,

[18] "The Spirit of the Lord is upon me, because he has anointed me to preach good news to the poor.

He has sent me to proclaim release to the captives

and recovering of sight to the blind, to set at liberty those who are oppressed,

[19] to proclaim the acceptable year of the Lord."

[20] And he closed the book, and gave it back to the attendant, and sat down; and the eyes of all in the synagogue were fixed on him. [21] And he began to say to them, "Today this scripture has been fulfilled in your hearing." [22] And all spoke well of him, and wondered at the gracious words which proceeded out of his mouth; and they said, "Is not this Joseph's son?" [23] And he said to them, "Doubtless you will quote to me this proverb, 'Physician, heal yourself; what we have heard you did at Caper'na-um, do here also in your own

4.1–13: Jesus' temptation (Mt.4.1–11; Mk.1.12–13). The order of temptations differs from Matthew's but the testing remains the same. **1:** *Full of the Holy Spirit* is a Christian phrase (Acts 2.4; 6.3,5; 7.55; 11.24); the work of Jesus and the church begins as God acts through individuals. **2:** Dt.9.9; 1 Kg.19.8; see Mt.4.2 n. **3–4:** See Mt.4.3–4 n.; Dt.8.3. **5–8:** Dt.6.13; 1 Jn.5.19. **9–12:** See Mt.4.5–7; Ps.91.11–12; Dt.6.16. **13:** *Until an opportune time,* to renew temptation (compare Mk.8.33; Lk.22.28).

4.14–9.50: Events and teachings in Galilee. **4.14–15:** Jesus' return to Galilee (Mt.4.12–17; Mk.1.14–15). **14:** 5.17.

4.16–30: In the synagogue at Nazareth (Mt.13.53–58; Mk.6.1–6). **16:** Jesus' *custom* was not merely to worship in the synagogue but to present his message there (v. 15; Mt.4.23; 9.35). Details of synagogue worship are mentioned here and in vv. 17,20 (compare Acts 13.15). **17:** The *book* was a scroll, which Jesus unrolled. **18–19:** Is.61.1,2; 58.6; see Mt.3.1 n.; Lk.13.11, 16 n. **21:** *Fulfilled,* see Mt.11.4–6 n. **23:** The popular reaction became increasingly hostile as

country.' " 24 And he said, "Truly, I say to you, no prophet is acceptable in his own country. 25 But in truth, I tell you, there were many widows in Israel in the days of Eli'jah, when the heaven was shut up three years and six months, when there came a great famine over all the land; 26 and Eli'jah was sent to none of them but only to Zar'ephath, in the land of Sidon, to a woman who was a widow. 27 And there were many lepers in Israel in the time of the prophet Eli'sha; and none of them was cleansed, but only Na'aman the Syrian." 28 When they heard this, all in the synagogue were filled with wrath. 29 And they rose up and put him out of the city, and led him to the brow of the hill on which their city was built, that they might throw him down headlong. 30 But passing through the midst of them he went away.

31 And he went down to Caper'-na-um, a city of Galilee. And he was teaching them on the sabbath; 32 and they were astonished at his teaching, for his word was with authority. 33 And in the synagogue there was a man who had the spirit of an unclean demon; and he cried out with a loud voice, 34 "Ah!*m* What have you to do with us, Jesus of Nazareth? Have you come to destroy us? I know who you are, the Holy One of God." 35 But Jesus rebuked him, saying, "Be silent, and come out of him!" And when the demon had thrown him down in the midst, he came out of him, having done him no harm. 36 And they were

all amazed and said to one another, "What is this word? For with authority and power he commands the unclean spirits, and they come out." 37 And reports of him went out into every place in the surrounding region.

38 And he arose and left the synagogue, and entered Simon's house. Now Simon's mother-in-law was ill with a high fever, and they besought him for her. 39 And he stood over her and rebuked the fever, and it left her; and immediately she rose and served them.

40 Now when the sun was setting, all those who had any that were sick with various diseases brought them to him; and he laid his hands on every one of them and healed them. 41 And demons also came out of many, crying, "You are the Son of God!" But he rebuked them, and would not allow them to speak, because they knew that he was the Christ.

42 And when it was day he departed and went into a lonely place. And the people sought him and came to him, and would have kept him from leaving them; 43 but he said to them, "I must preach the good news of the kingdom of God to the other cities also; for I was sent for this purpose." 44 And he was preaching in the synagogues of Judea.*n*

5 While the people pressed upon him to hear the word of God, he was standing by the lake of Gennes'-

m Or *Let us alone*
n Other ancient authorities read *Galilee*

---

the magnitude of Jesus' message sank home. **24–27:** According to the Old Testament, foreigners sometimes knew God's help when Israel did not (1 Kg.17.1,8–16; 18.1; 2 Kg.5.1–14).

4.31–37: The synagogue at Capernaum (Mt.7.28–29; Mk.1.21–28). **32:** *Teaching* here means the substance of what Jesus taught. **33:** See Mk.1.23 n. Demons were thought of in Jesus' day as non-material existences of a personal sort, hostile to human welfare and rebellious against God. The gospels reflect widespread dread of demons and a general sense of helplessness before demonic activity. Jesus is portrayed here and elsewhere (compare 11.20–22) as one who can deliver from demonic oppression and from Satan himself, evil's supreme embodiment (see Mt.4.24 n.; 12.22 n.; Lk.7.33 n.; 13.16 n.).

4.38–44: Healing and preaching (Mt.8.14–17; Mk.1.29–39). **40:** *Every one,* Jesus gives attention to individuals, illustrating vv. 18–19. **41:** *Demons,* see v. 33 n. **44:** This is the only express mention outside the Fourth Gospel of Jesus' early Judean ministry (but compare the implications of Mt.23.37 and Lk.13.34). The original text, however, is uncertain, for *Galilee* appears in some ancient witnesses here as well as in the parallel accounts (Mt.4.23; Mk.1.39).

5.1–11: The unexpected catch (Mt.4.18–22; Mk.1.16–20). **1:** *Lake of Gennesaret,* Sea of Gali-

aret. [2] And he saw two boats by the lake; but the fishermen had gone out of them and were washing their nets. [3] Getting into one of the boats, which was Simon's, he asked him to put out a little from the land. And he sat down and taught the people from the boat. [4] And when he had ceased speaking, he said to Simon, "Put out into the deep and let down your nets for a catch." [5] And Simon answered, "Master, we toiled all night and took nothing! But at your word I will let down the nets." [6] And when they had done this, they enclosed a great shoal of fish; and as their nets were breaking, [7] they beckoned to their partners in the other boat to come and help them. And they came and filled both the boats, so that they began to sink. [8] But when Simon Peter saw it, he fell down at Jesus' knees, saying, "Depart from me, for I am a sinful man, O Lord." [9] For he was astonished, and all that were with him, at the catch of fish which they had taken; [10] and so also were James and John, sons of Zeb'edee, who were partners with Simon. And Jesus said to Simon, "Do not be afraid; henceforth you will be catching men." [11] And when they had brought their boats to land, they left everything and followed him.

12 While he was in one of the cities, there came a man full of leprosy; and when he saw Jesus, he fell on his face and besought him, "Lord, if you will, you can make me clean." [13] And he stretched out his hand, and touched him, saying, "I will; be clean." And immediately the leprosy left him. [14] And he charged him to tell no one; but "go and show yourself to the priest, and make an offering for your cleansing, as Moses commanded, for a proof to the people."*o* [15] But so much the more the report went abroad con-cerning him; and great multitudes gathered to hear and to be healed of their infirmities. [16] But he withdrew to the wilderness and prayed.

17 On one of those days, as he was teaching, there were Pharisees and teachers of the law sitting by, who had come from every village of Galilee and Judea and from Jerusalem; and the power of the Lord was with him to heal.*p* [18] And behold, men were bringing on a bed a man who was para-lyzed, and they sought to bring him in and lay him before Jesus;*q* [19] but finding no way to bring him in, be-cause of the crowd, they went up on the roof and let him down with his bed through the tiles into the midst before Jesus. [20] And when he saw their faith he said, "Man, your sins are forgiven you." [21] And the scribes and the Pharisees began to question, saying, "Who is this that speaks blasphemies? Who can forgive sins but God only?" [22] When Jesus perceived their ques-tionings, he answered them, "Why do you question in your hearts? [23] Which is easier, to say, 'Your sins are for-given you,' or to say, 'Rise and walk'? [24] But that you may know that the Son of man has authority on earth to forgive sins"–he said to the man who was paralyzed–"I say to you, rise, take up your bed and go home." [25] And immediately he rose before them, and took up that on which he lay, and went home, glorifying God. [26] And amaze-ment seized them all, and they glorified God and were filled with awe, saying, "We have seen strange things today."

27 After this he went out, and saw a tax collector, named Levi, sitting at the tax office; and he said to him, "Follow me." [28] And he left every-thing, and rose and followed him.

o Greek *to them*
p Other ancient authorities read *was present to heal them*
q Greek *him*

lee. **8:** Although the great catch is not described as a miracle, Peter sees in Jesus' guidance a more-than-human power, and he responds by personal self-judgment.

5.12–16: A leper healed (Mt.8.1–4; Mk.1.40–45). **12:** *Leprosy*, see Mt.8.2–4 n. **14:** Lev.13.2–3; 14.2–32. **16:** See 3.21 n.

5:17–26: Forgiveness of sins (Mt.9.1–8; Mk.2.1–12). **17:** *Power*, 4.14. **24:** *Son of man*, see Mk.2.10 n.

29 And Levi made him a great feast in his house; and there was a large company of tax collectors and others sitting at table*r* with them. 30 And the Pharisees and their scribes murmured against his disciples, saying, "Why do you eat and drink with tax collectors and sinners?" 31 And Jesus answered them, "Those who are well have no need of a physician, but those who are sick; 32 I have not come to call the righteous, but sinners to repentance."

33 And they said to him, "The disciples of John fast often and offer prayers, and so do the disciples of the Pharisees, but yours eat and drink." 34 And Jesus said to them, "Can you make wedding guests fast while the bridegroom is with them? 35 The days will come, when the bridegroom is taken away from them, and then they will fast in those days." 36 He told them a parable also: "No one tears a piece from a new garment and puts it upon an old garment; if he does, he will tear the new, and the piece from the new will not match the old. 37 And no one puts new wine into old wineskins; if he does, the new wine will burst the skins and it will be spilled, and the skins will be destroyed. 38 But new wine must be put into fresh wineskins. 39 And no one after drinking old wine desires new; for he says, 'The old is good.' "*s*

6 On a sabbath,*t* while he was going through the grainfields, his disciples plucked and ate some heads of grain, rubbing them in their hands. 2 But some of the Pharisees said, "Why are you doing what is not lawful to do on the sabbath?" 3 And Jesus answered, "Have you not read what David did when he was hungry, he and those who were with him: 4 how he entered the house of God, and took and ate the bread of the Presence, which it is not lawful for any but the priests to eat, and also gave it to those with him?" 5 And he said to them, "The Son of man is lord of the sabbath."

6 On another sabbath, when he entered the synagogue and taught, a man was there whose right hand was withered. 7 And the scribes and the Pharisees watched him, to see whether he would heal on the sabbath, so that they might find an accusation against him. 8 But he knew their thoughts, and he said to the man who had the withered hand, "Come and stand here." And he rose and stood there. 9 And Jesus said to them, "I ask you, is it lawful on the sabbath to do good or to do harm, to save life or to destroy it?" 10 And he looked around on them all, and said to him, "Stretch out your hand." And he did so, and his hand was restored. 11 But they were filled with fury and discussed with one another what they might do to Jesus.

12 In these days he went out to the mountain to pray; and all night he continued in prayer to God. 13 And when it was day, he called his disciples, and

r Greek *reclining*
s Other ancient authorities read *better*
t Other ancient authorities read *On the second first sabbath* (on the second sabbath after the first)

5.27–32: Call of Levi (Matthew) (Mt.9.9–13; Mk.2.13–17). **32:** Jesus sought to draw in (i.e. *call*) outcasts whom the Pharisees excluded from society. *Call*, however, also meant "invite" (as to a banquet); Jesus' invitation to the Messianic banquet (see 12.37 n.; Rev.3.20 n.) was extended not to the self-judged righteous but to *sinners* (Mt.8.11–12; compare Lk.14.15–24).

5.33–39: On fasting (Mt.9.14–17; Mk.2.18–22). **34–35:** See Mk.2.19–20 n. **36–37:** See Mt. 9.16–17 n. **39:** This sentence explains why the disciples of John and of the Pharisees (v. 33) continued their religious forms notwithstanding Jesus' message; pious conservatism prevented their accepting the new revelation.

6.1–11: Jesus and sabbath laws (see Mt.12.1–14 n.; Mk.2.23–3.6). **1:** Dt.23.25. **2:** Ex.20.10; 23.12; Dt.5.14. **3:** 1 Sam.21.1–6. **4:** Lev.24.5–9.

6.12–16: Choosing the Twelve (Mt.10.1–4; Mk.3.13–19). **12:** See 3.21 n. **13:** The *disciples* were a larger group of followers from whom Jesus chose twelve for close companionship (Acts 1.21–22). *Apostle* means "appointed representative" and was not always limited to the Twelve (Rom.16.7; Acts 14.14).

chose from them twelve, whom he named apostles; ¹⁴ Simon, whom he named Peter, and Andrew his brother, and James and John, and Philip, and Bartholomew, ¹⁵ and Matthew, and Thomas, and James the son of Alphaeus, and Simon who was called the Zealot, ¹⁶ and Judas the son of James, and Judas Iscariot, who became a traitor.

17 And he came down with them and stood on a level place, with a great crowd of his disciples and a great multitude of people from all Judea and Jerusalem and the seacoast of Tyre and Sidon, who came to hear him and to be healed of their diseases; ¹⁸ and those who were troubled with unclean spirits were cured. ¹⁹ And all the crowd sought to touch him, for power came forth from him and healed them all.

20 And he lifted up his eyes on his disciples, and said:

"Blessed are you poor, for yours is the kingdom of God.

21 "Blessed are you that hunger now, for you shall be satisfied.

"Blessed are you that weep now, for you shall laugh.

22 "Blessed are you when men hate you, and when they exclude you and revile you, and cast out your name as evil, on account of the Son of man! ²³ Rejoice in that day, and leap for joy, for behold, your reward is great in heaven; for so their fathers did to the prophets.

24 "But woe to you that are rich, for you have received your consolation.

25 "Woe to you that are full now, for you shall hunger.

"Woe to you that laugh now, for you shall mourn and weep.

26 "Woe to you, when all men speak well of you, for so their fathers did to the false prophets.

27 "But I say to you that hear, Love your enemies, do good to those who hate you, ²⁸ bless those who curse you, pray for those who abuse you. ²⁹ To him who strikes you on the cheek, offer the other also; and from him who takes away your coat do not withhold even your shirt. ³⁰ Give to every one who begs from you; and of him who takes away your goods do not ask them again. ³¹ And as you wish that men would do to you, do so to them.

32 "If you love those who love you, what credit is that to you? For even sinners love those who love them. ³³ And if you do good to those who do good to you, what credit is that to you? For even sinners do the same. ³⁴ And if you lend to those from whom you hope to receive, what credit is that to you? Even sinners lend to sinners, to receive as much again. ³⁵ But love your enemies, and do good, and lend, expecting nothing in return;ᵛ and your reward will be great, and you will be sons of the Most High; for he is kind to the ungrateful and the selfish. ³⁶ Be merciful, even as your Father is merciful.

37 "Judge not, and you will not be judged; condemn not, and you will not be condemned; forgive, and you will

---

v Other ancient authorities read *despairing of no man*

6.17–49: The Sermon on the Plain. Luke gives here a number of Jesus' sayings found in the Sermon on the Mount (Mt. chs. 5–7). He has fewer teachings than appear there; he gives others found elsewhere in Matthew. Verses 24–26 are without parallel. The "sermons" in the gospels were formed from collections of memorized words of Jesus to instruct Christian converts (compare Jn.20.30–31; 21.25). **17–19:** Mt.4.24–25; 12.15–21; Mk.3.7–12. **17:** The setting for the discourse in vv. 20–49 (compare Mt.5.1–2). Each gospel distinguishes between the crowds in general and Jesus' followers. The teachings are primarily for the latter, though not exclusively so (7.1). **18:** *Unclean spirits,* see Mk.1.23 n. **20–23:** Mt.5.3–12; Lk.4.18–19. **24–26:** Material satisfactions will not last (11.38–52; 17.1; 21.23; 22.22). **25:** 12.19–20; 16.25; Jas.5.1–5. **27–30:** Mt.5.39–42; Rom.12.17; 13.8–10. **29:** The reference is to a robber who grabs the outer garment (*coat*). He is not to be restrained from taking the *shirt* also. **31:** Mt.7.12. **32–36:** Mt.5.44–48. **35:** *The Most High,* a common expression referring to God. **37–42:** Mt.7.1–5. **39:** Mt.15.14.

be forgiven; [38] give, and it will be given to you; good measure, pressed down, shaken together, running over, will be put into your lap. For the measure you give will be the measure you get back."

39 He also told them a parable: "Can a blind man lead a blind man? Will they not both fall into a pit? [40] A disciple is not above his teacher, but every one when he is fully taught will be like his teacher. [41] Why do you see the speck that is in your brother's eye, but do not notice the log that is in your own eye? [42] Or how can you say to your brother, 'Brother, let me take out the speck that is in your eye,' when you yourself do not see the log that is in your own eye? You hypocrite, first take the log out of your own eye, and then you will see clearly to take out the speck that is in your brother's eye.

43 "For no good tree bears bad fruit, nor again does a bad tree bear good fruit; [44] for each tree is known by its own fruit. For figs are not gathered from thorns, nor are grapes picked from a bramble bush. [45] The good man out of the good treasure of his heart produces good, and the evil man out of his evil treasure produces evil; for out of the abundance of the heart his mouth speaks.

46 "Why do you call me 'Lord, Lord,' and not do what I tell you? [47] Every one who comes to me and hears my words and does them, I will show you what he is like: [48] he is like a man building a house, who dug deep, and laid the foundation upon rock; and when a flood arose, the stream broke against that house, and could not shake it, because it had been well built.[w] [49] But he who hears and does not do them is like a man who built a house

on the ground without a foundation; against which the stream broke, and immediately it fell, and the ruin of that house was great."

7 After he had ended all his sayings in the hearing of the people he entered Caper'na-um. [2] Now a centurion had a slave who was dear[x] to him, who was sick and at the point of death. [3] When he heard of Jesus, he sent to him elders of the Jews, asking him to come and heal his slave. [4] And when they came to Jesus, they besought him earnestly, saying, "He is worthy to have you do this for him, [5] for he loves our nation, and he built us our synagogue." [6] And Jesus went with them. When he was not far from the house, the centurion sent friends to him, saying to him, "Lord, do not trouble yourself, for I am not worthy to have you come under my roof; [7] therefore I did not presume to come to you. But say the word, and let my servant be healed. [8] For I am a man set under authority, with soldiers under me: and I say to one, 'Go,' and he goes; and to another, 'Come,' and he comes; and to my slave, 'Do this,' and he does it." [9] When Jesus heard this he marveled at him, and turned and said to the multitude that followed him, "I tell you, not even in Israel have I found such faith." [10] And when those who had been sent returned to the house, they found the slave well.

11 Soon afterward[y] he went to a city called Na'in, and his disciples and a great crowd went with him. [12] As he drew near to the gate of the city, behold, a man who had died was being carried out, the only son of his

w Other ancient authorities read *founded upon the rock*
x Or *valuable*
y Other ancient authorities read *Next day*

40: Mt.10.24–25; Jn.13.16. **41–42:** Mt.7.3–5. **43–45:** Mt.7.16–21; 12.33–35; Jas.3.11–12. **45:** Mk.7.14–23. **46–49:** Mt.7.24–27; Jas.1.22–25. The differences between Matthew and Luke probably derive from different collections of words of Jesus.

7.1–10: The centurion's slave. This narrative appears to be another version of the story recounted in Mt.8.5–13 (compare Jn.4.46–53). **3:** *Elders*, leaders in the Jewish community. **5:** Acts 10.2. **9:** Though Luke lacks the climactic utterance of Mt.8.13, his intent is the same: the faith of a Gentile is acceptable to Jesus (4.27; 5.32).

7.11–17: The widow's son at Nain. Mk.5.21–24,35–43; Jn.11.1–44; 1 Kg.17.17–24; 2 Kg.4.32–

mother, and she was a widow; and a large crowd from the city was with her. ¹³ And when the Lord saw her, he had compassion on her and said to her, "Do not weep." ¹⁴ And he came and touched the bier, and the bearers stood still. And he said, "Young man, I say to you, arise." ¹⁵ And the dead man sat up, and began to speak. And he gave him to his mother. ¹⁶ Fear seized them all; and they glorified God, saying, "A great prophet has arisen among us!" and "God has visited his people!" ¹⁷ And this report concerning him spread through the whole of Judea and all the surrounding country.

18 The disciples of John told him of all these things. ¹⁹ And John, calling to him two of his disciples, sent them to the Lord, saying, "Are you he who is to come, or shall we look for another?" ²⁰ And when the men had come to him, they said, "John the Baptist has sent us to you, saying, 'Are you he who is to come, or shall we look for another?'" ²¹ In that hour he cured many of diseases and plagues and evil spirits, and on many that were blind he bestowed sight. ²² And he answered them, "Go and tell John what you have seen and heard: the blind receive their sight, the lame walk, lepers are cleansed, and the deaf hear, the dead are raised up, the poor have good news preached to them. ²³ And blessed is he who takes no offense at me."

24 When the messengers of John had gone, he began to speak to the crowds concerning John: "What did you go out into the wilderness to behold? A reed shaken by the wind? ²⁵ What then did you go out to see? A man clothed in soft clothing? Behold, those who are gorgeously appareled and live in luxury are in kings' courts. ²⁶ What then did you go out to see? A prophet? Yes, I tell you, and more than a prophet. ²⁷ This is he of whom it is written,

'Behold, I send my messenger
    before thy face,
who shall prepare thy way before
    thee.'

²⁸ I tell you, among those born of women none is greater than John; yet he who is least in the kingdom of God is greater than he." ²⁹ (When they heard this all the people and the tax collectors justified God, having been baptized with the baptism of John; ³⁰ but the Pharisees and the lawyers rejected the purpose of God for themselves, not having been baptized by him.)

31 "To what then shall I compare the men of this generation, and what are they like? ³² They are like children sitting in the market place and calling to one another,

'We piped to you, and you did not
    dance;
we wailed, and you did not weep.'

³³ For John the Baptist has come eating no bread and drinking no wine; and you say, 'He has a demon.' ³⁴ The Son of man has come eating and drinking; and you say, 'Behold, a glutton and a drunkard, a friend of tax collectors and sinners!' ³⁵ Yet wisdom is justified by all her children."

36 One of the Pharisees asked him to eat with him, and he went into the Pharisee's house, and took his place at

---

37; Lk.4.25–26. **13:** *Lord* is used frequently in Luke as a title for Jesus. **16:** *Fear,* see 1.65 n. **7.18–35:** Jesus and John (Mt.11.2–19). **19:** *Lord,* see v. 13 n. *He who is to come,* the Messiah (see Mt.11.2–3 n.). **21–22:** Is.29.18–19; 35.5–6; 61.1; Lk.4.18–19. An appeal to John to believe because of the evidence that God's purposes were being realized. **27:** Mal.3.1; Mk.1.2. **29:** *Justified,* in the sense that they accepted Jesus' word about John and God's purpose through him, in contrast with the thought of v. 30. **30:** Not all Pharisees are referred to here (see Mt. 3.7 n.). The *lawyers,* also called scribes, were experts in Jewish law. **33:** *Demon* possession is appealed to to explain unconventional behavior (Mt.11.18; Mk.3.22; Lk.8.27) or attitudes considered basically false (Jn.7.20; 10.20; 1 Tim.4.1). See 4.33 n.
7.36–50: The woman who was a sinner (compare Mt.26.6–13; Mk.14.3–9; Jn.12.1–8). **36:** 11.37; 14.1. **37:** Mt.9.10; Lk.5.29–30; 7.34. Houses seem to have been somewhat open to in-

table. 37 And behold, a woman of the city, who was a sinner, when she learned that he was at table in the Pharisee's house, brought an alabaster flask of ointment, 38 and standing behind him at his feet, weeping, she began to wet his feet with her tears, and wiped them with the hair of her head, and kissed his feet, and anointed them with the ointment. 39 Now when the Pharisee who had invited him saw it, he said to himself, "If this man were a prophet, he would have known who and what sort of woman this is who is touching him, for she is a sinner." 40 And Jesus answering said to him, "Simon, I have something to say to you." And he answered, "What is it, Teacher?" 41 "A certain creditor had two debtors; one owed five hundred denarii, and the other fifty. 42 When they could not pay, he forgave them both. Now which of them will love him more?" 43 Simon answered, "The one, I suppose, to whom he forgave more." And he said to him, "You have judged rightly." 44 Then turning toward the woman he said to Simon, "Do you see this woman? I entered your house, you gave me no water for my feet, but she has wet my feet with her tears and wiped them with her hair. 45 You gave me no kiss, but from the time I came in she has not ceased to kiss my feet. 46 You did not anoint my head with oil, but she has anointed my feet with ointment. 47 Therefore I tell you, her sins, which are many, are forgiven, for she loved much; but he who is forgiven little, loves little." 48 And he said to

her, "Your sins are forgiven." 49 Then those who were at table with him began to say among themselves, "Who is this, who even forgives sins?" 50 And he said to the woman, "Your faith has saved you; go in peace."

8 Soon afterward he went on through cities and villages, preaching and bringing the good news of the kingdom of God. And the twelve were with him, 2 and also some women who had been healed of evil spirits and infirmities: Mary, called Mag'-dalene, from whom seven demons had gone out, 3 and Jo-an'na, the wife of Chu'za, Herod's steward, and Susanna, and many others, who provided for them[z] out of their means.

4 And when a great crowd came together and people from town after town came to him, he said in a parable: 5 "A sower went out to sow his seed; and as he sowed, some fell along the path, and was trodden under foot, and the birds of the air devoured it. 6 And some fell on the rock; and as it grew up, it withered away, because it had no moisture. 7 And some fell among thorns; and the thorns grew with it and choked it. 8 And some fell into good soil and grew, and yielded a hundredfold." As he said this, he called out, "He who has ears to hear, let him hear."

9 And when his disciples asked him what this parable meant, 10 he said, "To you it has been given to know the secrets of the kingdom of God; but for others they are in parables, so that

z Other ancient authorities read *him*

trusion of this sort (Mk.1.33; 2.2). The woman may have intended to anoint Jesus' head, a sign of regard (v. 46) as well as of personal grooming (Mt.6.17), but was overcome by a sense of humility and gratitude for his message (5.32). **39:** Jesus does not share the Pharisee's concern (compare Mk.1.41 with Mk.7.3–4). **41:** *Denarius*, see 10.35 note *i*. **42:** Mt.18.25. **44–46:** Jesus notes contrasts in responses to himself. **47:** The conclusion: the woman knows the meaning of forgiveness, the host does not. *For she loved much*, her great love proves that her many sins have been forgiven. **48:** Mt.9.2; Mk.2.5; 11.23 n., 24 n.; Lk.5.20.

    8.1–3: On tour. 1: Mt.4.23; 9.35; Mk.3.14; Lk.23.49. **2:** Mt.27.55–56; Mk.15.40–41. *Mary, called Magdalene*, apparently came from Magdala on the Sea of Galilee. There is no evidence to identify her with the woman in 7.36–50. **3:** Herod's *steward* was probably a domestic administrator, as in Mt.20.8. *Others*, i.e. other women.

    8.4–15: Parable of the sower (Mt.13.1–23; Mk.4.1–20). **4:** *Parable*, see Mt.13.3 n. **5:** See Mk.4.3 n. **6:** See Mk.4.5 n. **10:** See Mk.4.11 n.; Mt.13.11 n.; Is.6.9–10; Jer.5.21; Ezek.12.2.

seeing they may not see, and hearing they may not understand. ¹¹ Now the parable is this: The seed is the word of God. ¹² The ones along the path are those who have heard; then the devil comes and takes away the word from their hearts, that they may not believe and be saved. ¹³ And the ones on the rock are those who, when they hear the word, receive it with joy; but these have no root, they believe for a while and in time of temptation fall away. ¹⁴ And as for what fell among the thorns, they are those who hear, but as they go on their way they are choked by the cares and riches and pleasures of life, and their fruit does not mature. ¹⁵ And as for that in the good soil, they are those who, hearing the word, hold it fast in an honest and good heart, and bring forth fruit with patience.

16 "No one after lighting a lamp covers it with a vessel, or puts it under a bed, but puts it on a stand, that those who enter may see the light. ¹⁷ For nothing is hid that shall not be made manifest, nor anything secret that shall not be known and come to light. ¹⁸ Take heed then how you hear; for to him who has will more be given, and from him who has not, even what he thinks that he has will be taken away."

19 Then his mother and his brothers came to him, but they could not reach him for the crowd. ²⁰ And he was told, "Your mother and your brothers are standing outside, desiring to see you." ²¹ But he said to them, "My mother and my brothers are those who hear the word of God and do it."

22 One day he got into a boat with his disciples, and he said to them, "Let us go across to the other side of the lake." So they set out, ²³ and as they sailed he fell asleep. And a storm of wind came down on the lake, and they were filling with water, and were in danger. ²⁴ And they went and woke him, saying, "Master, Master, we are perishing!" And he awoke and rebuked the wind and the raging waves; and they ceased, and there was a calm. ²⁵ He said to them, "Where is your faith?" And they were afraid, and they marveled, saying to one another, "Who then is this, that he commands even wind and water, and they obey him?"

26 Then they arrived at the country of the Ger′asenes,ᵃ which is opposite Galilee. ²⁷ And as he stepped out on land, there met him a man from the city who had demons; for a long time he had worn no clothes, and he lived not in a house but among the tombs. ²⁸ When he saw Jesus, he cried out and fell down before him, and said with a loud voice, "What have you to do with me, Jesus, Son of the Most High God? I beseech you, do not torment me." ²⁹ For he had commanded the unclean spirit to come out of the man. (For many a time it had seized him; he was kept under guard, and bound with chains and fetters, but he broke the bonds and was driven by the demon into the desert.) ³⁰ Jesus then asked him, "What is your name?" And he said, "Legion"; for many demons had entered him. ³¹ And they begged him not to command them to depart into the abyss. ³² Now a large herd of swine was

ᵃ Other ancient authorities read *Gadarenes*, others *Gergesenes*

11: 1 Th.2.13; 1 Pet.1.23. **15:** The words *honest and good*, here spoken of the heart (compare Mk.7.21–23), echo the classical Greek description of the true gentleman.

8.16–18: On obedient listening (Mk.4.21–25). **16:** See Mk.4.21 n. **17:** See Mk.4.22 n. **18:** See Mt.13.12 n.

8.19–21: Jesus' true family (Mt.12.46–50; Mk.3.31–35). **19:** *Brothers*, see Mt.13.55 n. **21:** 11.28.

8.22–25: Wind and sea calmed (Mt.8.18,23–27; Mk.4.35–41). See notes on the passage in Mark. **24:** *Master* and the titles for Jesus in the parallels express aspects of the disciples' attitude toward Jesus (Mt.17.4; Mk.9.5; 11.21; 14.45; Lk.17.13; Jn.1.38).

8.26–39: The Gerasene demoniac (Mt.8.28–34; Mk.5.1–20). **27:** *Demons*, see 4.33 n. **31:** *Abyss*, a place of confinement for demonic forces which, though hostile to God, are ultimately

feeding there on the hillside; and they begged him to let them enter these. So he gave them leave. [33] Then the demons came out of the man and entered the swine, and the herd rushed down the steep bank into the lake and were drowned.

34 When the herdsmen saw what had happened, they fled, and told it in the city and in the country. [35] Then people went out to see what had happened, and they came to Jesus, and found the man from whom the demons had gone, sitting at the feet of Jesus, clothed and in his right mind; and they were afraid. [36] And those who had seen it told them how he who had been possessed with demons was healed. [37] Then all the people of the surrounding country of the Ger'-asenes[a] asked him to depart from them; for they were seized with great fear; so he got into the boat and returned. [38] The man from whom the demons had gone begged that he might be with him; but he sent him away, saying, [39] "Return to your home, and declare how much God has done for you." And he went away, proclaiming throughout the whole city how much Jesus had done for him.

40 Now when Jesus returned, the crowd welcomed him, for they were all waiting for him. [41] And there came a man named Ja'irus, who was a ruler of the synagogue; and falling at Jesus' feet he besought him to come to his house, [42] for he had an only daughter, about twelve years of age, and she was dying.

As he went, the people pressed round him. [43] And a woman who had had a flow of blood for twelve years[b] and could not be healed by any one, [44] came up behind him, and touched the fringe of his garment; and im-

mediately her flow of blood ceased. [45] And Jesus said, "Who was it that touched me?" When all denied it, Peter[c] said, "Master, the multitudes surround you and press upon you!" [46] But Jesus said, "Some one touched me; for I perceive that power has gone forth from me." [47] And when the woman saw that she was not hidden, she came trembling, and falling down before him declared in the presence of all the people why she had touched him, and how she had been immediately healed. [48] And he said to her, "Daughter, your faith has made you well; go in peace."

49 While he was still speaking, a man from the ruler's house came and said, "Your daughter is dead; do not trouble the Teacher any more." [50] But Jesus on hearing this answered him, "Do not fear; only believe, and she shall be well." [51] And when he came to the house, he permitted no one to enter with him, except Peter and John and James, and the father and mother of the child. [52] And all were weeping and bewailing her; but he said, "Do not weep; for she is not dead but sleeping." [53] And they laughed at him, knowing that she was dead. [54] But taking her by the hand he called, saying, "Child, arise." [55] And her spirit returned, and she got up at once; and he directed that something should be given her to eat. [56] And her parents were amazed; but he charged them to tell no one what had happened.

9 And he called the twelve together and gave them power and authority over all demons and to cure dis-

a Other ancient authorities read *Gadarenes*, others *Gergesenes*
b Other ancient authorities add *and had spent all her living upon physicians*
c Other ancient authorities add *and those who were with him*

---

under his control (Rev.9.1–11; 11.7; 17.8; 20.1–3). The words attribute to Jesus a judicial authority (as Mt.7.21–23; 11.20–24). **36:** *Was healed,* see Mt.9.21 n. **37:** *Depart,* 5.8.

    8.40–56: Jairus' daughter raised (Mt.9.18–26; Mk.5.21–43). See notes on the parallel passages. **43:** Lev.15.25–30. **46:** 5.17. **48:** See Mt.9.21 n., 22; Lk.7.50; 17.19; 18.42. **50:** See Mt.9.21 n.

    9.1–6: Commissioning and instruction of the Twelve (Mt.9.35; 10.1,9–11,14; Mk.6.7–13; Lk.10.4–11). See notes on the passages in Matthew and Mark. **3:** *Tunic,* see Mt.10.10 n.

eases, [2] and he sent them out to preach the kingdom of God and to heal. [3] And he said to them, "Take nothing for your journey, no staff, nor bag, nor bread, nor money; and do not have two tunics. [4] And whatever house you enter, stay there, and from there depart. [5] And wherever they do not receive you, when you leave that town shake off the dust from your feet as a testimony against them." [6] And they departed and went through the villages, preaching the gospel and healing everywhere.

7 Now Herod the tetrarch heard of all that was done, and he was perplexed, because it was said by some that John had been raised from the dead, [8] by some that Eli'jah had appeared, and by others that one of the old prophets had risen. [9] Herod said, "John I beheaded; but who is this about whom I hear such things?" And he sought to see him.

10 On their return the apostles told him what they had done. And he took them and withdrew apart to a city called Beth-sa'ida. [11] When the crowds learned it, they followed him; and he welcomed them and spoke to them of the kingdom of God, and cured those who had need of healing. [12] Now the day began to wear away; and the twelve came and said to him, "Send the crowd away, to go into the villages and country round about, to lodge and get provisions; for we are here in a lonely place." [13] But he said to them, "You give them something to eat." They said, "We have no more than five loaves and two fish—unless we are to go and buy food for all these people." [14] For there were about five thousand men. And he said to his disciples, "Make them sit down in companies, about fifty each." [15] And they did so, and made them all sit down. [16] And taking the five loaves and the two fish he looked up to heaven, and blessed and broke them, and gave them to the disciples to set before the crowd. [17] And all ate and were satisfied. And they took up what was left over, twelve baskets of broken pieces.

18 Now it happened that as he was praying alone the disciples were with him; and he asked them, "Who do the people say that I am?" [19] And they answered, "John the Baptist; but others say, Eli'jah; and others, that one of the old prophets has risen." [20] And he said to them, "But who do you say that I am?" And Peter answered, "The Christ of God." [21] But he charged and commanded them to tell this to no one, [22] saying, "The Son of man must suffer many things, and be rejected by the elders and chief priests and scribes, and be killed, and on the third day be raised."

23 And he said to all, "If any man would come after me, let him deny himself and take up his cross daily and follow me. [24] For whoever would save his life will lose it; and whoever loses his life for my sake, he will save it. [25] For what does it profit a man if he gains the whole world and loses or forfeits himself? [26] For whoever is ashamed of me and of my words, of him will the Son of man be ashamed when he comes in his glory and the glory of the Father and of the holy angels. [27] But I tell you truly,

---

9.7–9: Herod asks about Jesus (Mt.14.1–2; Mk.6.14–16). See notes on the parallel passages; compare Mt.16.14; Lk.9.18–19.
9.10–17: Five thousand fed (Mt.14.13–21; Mk.6.30–44; Jn.6.1–14). See notes on the parallel passages. **13:** 2 Kg.4.42–44. **16:** 22.19; 24.30–31; Acts 2.42; 20.11; 27.35.
9.18–22: Peter's confession (Mt.16.13–23; Mk.8.27–33). See notes on the parallel passages. **18:** See 3.21 n. **19:** 9.7; Mk.9.11–13; see Mt.14.2. **22:** 9.43–45; 18.31–34; 17.25; see Mk. 9.31 n. Jesus accepted rejection because he insisted that he himself be freely followed.
9.23–27: On discipleship (Mt.16.24–28; Mk.8.34–9.1). See notes on the parallel passages. **23:** The language suggests that Jesus frequently spoke in this way (see Mt.10.38 n.). **26:** Mt. 10.33; Lk.12.9; 1 Jn.2.28. **27:** *Taste death,* die (compare Jn.8.52; Heb.2.9).

there are some standing here who will not taste death before they see the kingdom of God."

28 Now about eight days after these sayings he took with him Peter and John and James, and went up on the mountain to pray. ²⁹ And as he was praying, the appearance of his countenance was altered, and his raiment became dazzling white. ³⁰ And behold, two men talked with him, Moses and Eli'jah, ³¹ who appeared in glory and spoke of his departure, which he was to accomplish at Jerusalem. ³² Now Peter and those who were with him were heavy with sleep, and when they wakened they saw his glory and the two men who stood with him. ³³ And as the men were parting from him, Peter said to Jesus, "Master, it is well that we are here; let us make three booths, one for you and one for Moses and one for Eli'jah"—not knowing what he said. ³⁴ As he said this, a cloud came and overshadowed them; and they were afraid as they entered the cloud. ³⁵ And a voice came out of the cloud, saying, "This is my Son, my Chosen;ᵈ listen to him!" ³⁶ And when the voice had spoken, Jesus was found alone. And they kept silence and told no one in those days anything of what they had seen.

37 On the next day, when they had come down from the mountain, a great crowd met him. ³⁸ And behold, a man from the crowd cried, "Teacher, I beg you to look upon my son, for he is my only child; ³⁹ and behold, a spirit

seizes him, and he suddenly cries out; it convulses him till he foams, and shatters him, and will hardly leave him. ⁴⁰ And I begged your disciples to cast it out, but they could not." ⁴¹ Jesus answered, "O faithless and perverse generation, how long am I to be with you and bear with you? Bring your son here." ⁴² While he was coming, the demon tore him and convulsed him. But Jesus rebuked the unclean spirit, and healed the boy, and gave him back to his father. ⁴³ And all were astonished at the majesty of God.

But while they were all marveling at everything he did, he said to his disciples, ⁴⁴ "Let these words sink into your ears; for the Son of man is to be delivered into the hands of men." ⁴⁵ But they did not understand this saying, and it was concealed from them, that they should not perceive it; and they were afraid to ask him about this saying.

46 And an argument arose among them as to which of them was the greatest. ⁴⁷ But when Jesus perceived the thought of their hearts, he took a child and put him by his side, ⁴⁸ and said to them, "Whoever receives this child in my name receives me, and whoever receives me receives him who sent me; for he who is least among you all is the one who is great."

49 John answered, "Master, we saw a man casting out demons in your name, and we forbade him, because he

ᵈ Other ancient authorities read *my Beloved*

9.28–36: The transfiguration (Mt.17.1–8; Mk.9.2–8). This event began as prayer (v. 29; see 3.21 n.) and grew into an intense religious experience, the exact nature of which is uncertain (Mt.17.9 uses the word "vision"). The aura of unnatural brilliance is associated with mystical experiences elsewhere (Ex.34.29–35; Acts 9.3). **31:** *Departure,* death. **32:** Apparently the experience took place at night. **35:** *Chosen* has about the same meaning as *beloved* in the parallel passages (see Mk.1.11 n.; Lk.3.22; Jn.12.28–30).

9.37–43a: Epileptic child healed (Mt.17.14–21; Mk.9.14–29). See notes on the parallel passages. **43:** Acts 2.22.

9.43b–45: The Passion foretold again (Mt.17.22–23; Mk.9.30–32); compare 9.22; 18.31–33. **44:** 9.22; 18.31–34; 17.25. **45:** The comment is based on the point of view that (a) the Messiah's death was not part of the disciples' Jewish faith, and (b) spiritual truth must be revealed (see 24.16 n.; Mt.16.17 n.; 1 Cor.2.14).

9.46–48: True greatness (Mt.18.1–5; Mk.9.33–37). **47:** 18.17. **48:** See 10.16 n.; Mk.9.35 n.

9.49–50: The unknown exorcist (Mk.9.38–41). **49:** 11.19. **50:** 11.23; see Mk.9.39–40 n.

does not follow with us." ⁵⁰ But Jesus said to him, "Do not forbid him; for he that is not against you is for you."

51 When the days drew near for him to be received up, he set his face to go to Jerusalem. ⁵² And he sent messengers ahead of him, who went and entered a village of the Samaritans, to make ready for him; ⁵³ but the people would not receive him, because his face was set toward Jerusalem. ⁵⁴ And when his disciples James and John saw it, they said, "Lord, do you want us to bid fire come down from heaven and consume them?"*e* ⁵⁵ But he turned and rebuked them.*f* ⁵⁶ And they went on to another village.

57 As they were going along the road, a man said to him, "I will follow you wherever you go." ⁵⁸ And Jesus said to him, "Foxes have holes, and birds of the air have nests; but the Son of man has nowhere to lay his head." ⁵⁹ To another he said, "Follow me." But he said, "Lord, let me first go and bury my father." ⁶⁰ But he said to him, "Leave the dead to bury their own dead; but as for you, go and proclaim the kingdom of God." ⁶¹ Another said, "I will follow you, Lord; but let me first say farewell to those at my home." ⁶² Jesus said to him, "No one who puts his hand to the plow and looks back is fit for the kingdom of God."

10 After this the Lord appointed seventy*g* others, and sent them on ahead of him, two by two, into every town and place where he himself was about to come. ² And he said to them, "The harvest is plentiful, but the laborers are few; pray therefore the Lord of the harvest to send out laborers into his harvest. ³ Go your way; behold, I send you out as lambs in the midst of wolves. ⁴ Carry no purse, no bag, no sandals; and salute no one on the road. ⁵ Whatever house you enter, first say, 'Peace be to this house!' ⁶ And if a son of peace is there, your peace shall rest upon him; but if not, it shall return to you. ⁷ And remain in the same house, eating and drinking what they provide, for the laborer deserves his wages; do not go from house to house. ⁸ Whenever you enter a town and they receive you, eat what is set before you; ⁹ heal the sick in it and say to them, 'The kingdom of God has come near to you.' ¹⁰ But whenever you enter a town and they do not receive you, go into its streets and say, ¹¹ 'Even the dust of your town that clings to our feet, we wipe off against you; nevertheless know this, that the kingdom of God has come near.' ¹² I tell you, it shall be more tolerable on that day for Sodom than for that town.

13 "Woe to you, Chora'zin! woe to you, Beth-sa'ida! for if the mighty works done in you had been done in Tyre and Sidon, they would have repented long ago, sitting in sackcloth and ashes. ¹⁴ But it shall be more tolerable in the judgment for Tyre and Sidon than for you. ¹⁵ And you, Caper'na-um, will you be exalted to heaven? You shall be brought down to Hades.

16 "He who hears you hears me, and

e Other ancient authorities add *as Elijah did*
f Other ancient authorities add *and he said, "You do not know what manner of spirit you are of; for the Son of man came not to destroy men's lives but to save them"*
g Other ancient authorities read *seventy-two*

9.51–18.14: Events and teachings on the way to Jerusalem. 9.51–56: The hostile Samaritans (compare Jn.4.9). **51:** *Messengers,* whose errand was to arrange for lodging and food (Mt.10.5 was at an earlier stage of time and purpose). **53:** The Samaritans *would not* help pilgrims going to keep a feast at what they regarded as the wrong sanctuary (compare Jn.4.20). **54:** Mk.3.17; 2 Kg.1.9–16.

9.57–62: Claims of discipleship (Mt.8.19–22). **60:** See Mt.8.22 n. **61:** Phil.3.13; Heb.6.4–6.

10.1–16: Mission of the Seventy (Mt.9.37–38; 10.7–16). **1:** 9.1–5,51–52; Mk.6.7–11. **2:** Mt.9.37–38; Jn.4.35. **4:** *Salute no one,* which might cause delay. **5:** 1 Sam.25.6. **6:** *Son of peace,* a peaceful person (compare Mt.5.45 n.). **7:** 1 Cor.9.4–14; 1 Tim.5.18; Dt.24.15. **9:** 11.20. **11:** Acts 13.51. **12:** Mt.11.24; Gen.19.24–28; Jude 7. **13–15:** Mt.11.21–23; Lk.6.24–26. **15:** The words echo Is.14.13–15 (see also v. 18). **16:** Mt.10.40; 18.5; Mk.9.37; Lk.9.48; Jn.13.20; 12.48; Gal.4.14.

he who rejects you rejects me, and he who rejects me rejects him who sent me."

17 The seventy[g] returned with joy, saying, "Lord, even the demons are subject to us in your name!" 18 And he said to them, "I saw Satan fall like lightning from heaven. 19 Behold, I have given you authority to tread upon serpents and scorpions, and over all the power of the enemy; and nothing shall hurt you. 20 Nevertheless do not rejoice in this, that the spirits are subject to you; but rejoice that your names are written in heaven."

21 In that same hour he rejoiced in the Holy Spirit and said, "I thank thee, Father, Lord of heaven and earth, that thou hast hidden these things from the wise and understanding and revealed them to babes; yea, Father, for such was thy gracious will.[h] 22 All things have been delivered to me by my Father; and no one knows who the Son is except the Father, or who the Father is except the Son and any one to whom the Son chooses to reveal him."

23 Then turning to the disciples he said privately, "Blessed are the eyes which see what you see! 24 For I tell you that many prophets and kings desired to see what you see, and did not see it, and to hear what you hear, and did not hear it."

25 And behold, a lawyer stood up to put him to the test, saying, "Teacher, what shall I do to inherit eternal life?" 26 He said to him, "What is written in the law? How do you read?" 27 And he answered, "You shall love the Lord your God with all your heart, and with all your soul, and with all your strength, and with all your mind; and your neighbor as yourself." 28 And he said to him, "You have answered right; do this, and you will live."

29 But he, desiring to justify himself, said to Jesus, "And who is my neighbor?" 30 Jesus replied, "A man was going down from Jerusalem to Jericho, and he fell among robbers, who stripped him and beat him, and departed, leaving him half dead. 31 Now by chance a priest was going down that road; and when he saw him he passed by on the other side. 32 So likewise a Levite, when he came to the place and saw him, passed by on the other side. 33 But a Samaritan, as he journeyed, came to where he was; and when he saw him, he had compassion, 34 and went to him and bound up his wounds, pouring on oil and wine; then he set him on his own beast and brought him to an inn, and took care of him. 35 And the next day he took out two denarii[i] and gave them to the

g Other ancient authorities read *seventy-two*
h Or *so it was well-pleasing before thee*
i The denarius was a day's wage for a laborer

10.17–20: Return of the Seventy. 17: *Even the demons are subject to us,* unlike the Twelve (9.1), the Seventy had not been promised this power (see 13.16 n.). **18:** *I saw Satan fall . . . from heaven,* compare Jn.12.31; Rev.12.7–12. **19:** *Authority,* Mk.6.7; Lk.22.29. *The enemy,* Satan (Mt.13.39). **20:** Jesus regarded exorcism as not in itself a sign of God's kingdom (11.19). *Written in heaven,* Dan.12.1; Ps.69.28; Ex.32.32; Phil.4.3; Heb.12.23; Rev.3.5; 13.8; 21.27.

10.21–22: Prayer of Jesus (see 3.21 n. and Mt.11.25–27 n.). **21:** 1 Cor.1.26–29. *In the Holy Spirit,* in spiritual ecstasy. **22:** Mt.28.18; Jn.3.35; 13.3; 10.15; 17.25. **23–24:** Mt.13.16–17; Jn.8.56; Heb.11.13; 1 Pet.1.10–12. Jesus speaks both of spiritual perception guided by faith (Mk.4.9; Lk.8.10), and of the fulfilment of God's purpose (2.26–32).

10.25–28: A lawyer's question (Mt.22.23–40; Mk.12.28–31). **25:** Mt.19.16 n.; Mk.10.17; Lk.18.18. *Inherit,* see Mt.19.29 n. **27:** See Mk.12.29 n., 31 n. Rom.13.8–10; Gal.5.14; and Jas. 2.8 implicitly link Dt.6.4–5 and Lev.19.18, stressing as here (vv. 29–37) the principle that acts of love are the final requirement of the law (compare Dt.6.4ff. and notes; Lev.19.17–18 n.). **28:** Mk.12.34; Lev.18.1–5.

10.29–37: The Good Samaritan. 29: The questioner intended to prove his right to eternal life by defining the limits of his duty, and showing how he had fulfilled it. *Justify himself* means to show himself to be righteous, acceptable to God (18.9–14). **30:** *Robbers,* the Greek word is used of Barabbas (Jn.18.40) and those crucified with Jesus (Mk.15.27; Mt.27.38). **31–33:** The *priest* represented the highest religious leadership among the Jews; the *Levite* (v. 32) was the

innkeeper, saying, 'Take care of him; and whatever more you spend, I will repay you when I come back.' ³⁶ Which of these three, do you think, proved neighbor to the man who fell among the robbers?" ³⁷ He said, "The one who showed mercy on him." And Jesus said to him, "Go and do likewise."

38 Now as they went on their way, he entered a village; and a woman named Martha received him into her house. ³⁹ And she had a sister called Mary, who sat at the Lord's feet and listened to his teaching. ⁴⁰ But Martha was distracted with much serving; and she went to him and said, "Lord, do you not care that my sister has left me to serve alone? Tell her then to help me." ⁴¹ But the Lord answered her, "Martha, Martha, you are anxious and troubled about many things; ⁴² one thing is needful.^j Mary has chosen the good portion, which shall not be taken away from her."

He was praying in a certain place, and when he ceased, one of his disciples said to him, "Lord, teach us to pray, as John taught his disciples." ² And he said to them, "When you pray, say:

"Father, hallowed be thy name. Thy kingdom come. ³ Give us each day our daily bread;^k ⁴ and forgive us our sins, for we ourselves forgive every one who is indebted to us; and lead us not into temptation."

5 And he said to them, "Which of you who has a friend will go to him at midnight and say to him, 'Friend, lend me three loaves; ⁶ for a friend of mine has arrived on a journey, and I have nothing to set before him'; ⁷ and he will answer from within, 'Do not bother me; the door is now shut, and my children are with me in bed; I cannot get up and give you anything'? ⁸ I tell you, though he will not get up and give him anything because he is his friend, yet because of his importunity he will rise and give him whatever he needs. ⁹ And I tell you, Ask, and it will be given you; seek, and you will find; knock, and it will be opened to you. ¹⁰ For every one who asks receives, and he who seeks finds, and to him who knocks it will be opened. ¹¹ What father among you, if his son asks for^l a fish, will instead of a fish give him a serpent; ¹² or if he asks for an egg, will give him a scorpion? ¹³ If you then, who are evil, know how to give good gifts to your children, how much more will the heavenly Father give the Holy Spirit to those who ask him!"

14 Now he was casting out a demon that was dumb; when the demon had gone out, the dumb man spoke, and the people marveled. ¹⁵ But some of them said, "He casts out demons by Be-el'-zebul, the prince of demons"; ¹⁶ while others, to test him, sought from him a sign from heaven. ¹⁷ But he, knowing their thoughts, said to them, "Every kingdom divided against itself is laid waste, and a divided household falls. ¹⁸ And if Satan also is divided against himself, how will his kingdom stand?

j Other ancient authorities read *few things are needful, or only one*
k Or *our bread for the morrow*
l Other ancient authorities insert *bread, will give him a stone; or if he asks for*

---

designated lay-associate of the priest. In contrast it was a *Samaritan*, a foreigner not expected to show sympathy to Jews (see Jn.4.9 n.; Acts 8.5 n.), who *had compassion.* **34**: *Oil and wine,* ancient medication. **35**: *Denarii,* see Mt.20.2 n.

10.38–42: Martha and Mary, compare Jn.11.1 where they are introduced as well-known persons living at Bethany. **42**: With delicate ambiguity Jesus rebuked Martha's choice of values; a simple meal (one dish) is sufficient for hospitality. Jesus approved Mary's preference for listening to his teaching as contrasted with Martha's unneeded acts of hospitality.

11.1–13: Sayings on prayer. 1–4: See Mt.6.9–13 n.; Lk.3.21 n. 4: Mk.11.25; Mt.18.35. **5–8**: Lk.18.1–5. **9–13**: Mt.7.7–11. **9**: Mt.18.19; 21.22; Mk.11.24; Jas.1.5–8; 1 Jn.5.14–15; Jn.14.13; 15.7; 17.23–24.

11.14–26: Sources of Jesus' power (Mt.12.22–30; Mk.3.22–27). **14**: Mt.9.32–34; see 12.22–24 n. **15**: See Mk.3.22 n. **16**: Mt.12.38; 16.1–4; Mk.8.11–12; Jn.2.18; 6.30; 1 Cor.1.22. **19**:

For you say that I cast out demons by Be-el'zebul. ¹⁹ And if I cast out demons by Be-el'zebul, by whom do your sons cast them out? Therefore they shall be your judges. ²⁰ But if it is by the finger of God that I cast out demons, then the kingdom of God has come upon you. ²¹ When a strong man, fully armed, guards his own palace, his goods are in peace; ²² but when one stronger than he assails him and overcomes him, he takes away his armor in which he trusted, and divides his spoil. ²³ He who is not with me is against me, and he who does not gather with me scatters.

24 "When the unclean spirit has gone out of a man, he passes through waterless places seeking rest; and finding none he says, 'I will return to my house from which I came.' ²⁵ And when he comes he finds it swept and put in order. ²⁶ Then he goes and brings seven other spirits more evil than himself, and they enter and dwell there; and the last state of that man becomes worse than the first."

27 As he said this, a woman in the crowd raised her voice and said to him, "Blessed is the womb that bore you, and the breasts that you sucked!" ²⁸ But he said, "Blessed rather are those who hear the word of God and keep it!"

29 When the crowds were increasing, he began to say, "This generation is an evil generation; it seeks a sign, but no sign shall be given to it except the sign of Jonah. ³⁰ For as Jonah became a sign to the men of Nin'eveh, so will the Son of man be to this generation. ³¹ The queen of the South will arise at the judgment with the men of this generation and condemn them; for she came from the ends of the earth to hear the wisdom of Solomon, and behold, something greater than Solomon is here. ³² The men of Nin'eveh will arise at the judgment with this generation and condemn it; for they repented at the preaching of Jonah, and behold, something greater than Jonah is here.

33 "No one after lighting a lamp puts it in a cellar or under a bushel, but on a stand, that those who enter may see the light. ³⁴ Your eye is the lamp of your body; when your eye is sound, your whole body is full of light; but when it is not sound, your body is full of darkness. ³⁵ Therefore be careful lest the light in you be darkness. ³⁶ If then your whole body is full of light, having no part dark, it will be wholly bright, as when a lamp with its rays gives you light."

37 While he was speaking, a Pharisee asked him to dine with him; so he went in and sat at table. ³⁸ The Pharisee was astonished to see that he did not first wash before dinner. ³⁹ And the Lord said to him, "Now you Pharisees cleanse the outside of the cup and of the dish, but inside you are full of extortion and wickedness. ⁴⁰ You fools! Did not he who made the outside make the inside also? ⁴¹ But give for alms those things which are within; and behold, everything is clean for you.

42 "But woe to you Pharisees! for you tithe mint and rue and every herb, and neglect justice and the love of God; these you ought to have done, without neglecting the others. ⁴³ Woe to you

---

See Mt.12.27 n. **20:** Ex.8.19. *Finger* stands for God's power. **23:** Mt.12.30. Jesus used similar language for a different point in Mk.9.38–40; Lk.9.49–50. **24–26:** See Mt.12.43–45 n. **28:** 8.21.
 11.29–32: Request for a sign. 29: Mt.12.39. **30:** Jon.3.4. **31:** 1 Kg.10.1–10; 2 Chr.9.1–9. **32:** Mt.12.6.
 11.33–36: Concerning light (Mt.5.15; 6.22–23). **33:** See Mk.4.21 n.
 11.37–54: Against Pharisees and lawyers (Mt.23.1–36, in different order). **37:** 7.36; 14.1. **38:** *Wash before dinner*, ceremonial washing (literally "baptize before dinner"; compare Mk. 7.1–5). **39–41:** Mt.23.25–26. Jesus turns back the Pharisees' criticism that the outside is unwashed by insisting that the inner life is equal in importance to the outer (v. 40); indeed, that it exercises a cleansing or corrupting power over the outward (v. 41; Mk.7.23). **41:** Tit.1.15. **42:** Mt.23.23; Lev.27.30; Mic.6.8. **43:** See Mk.12.38–39 n. **44:** Mt.23.27. **45:** *Lawyer*, a teacher

Pharisees! for you love the best seat in the synagogues and salutations in the market places. ⁴⁴ Woe to you! for you are like graves which are not seen, and men walk over them without knowing it."

45 One of the lawyers answered him, "Teacher, in saying this you reproach us also." ⁴⁶ And he said, "Woe to you lawyers also! for you load men with burdens hard to bear, and you yourselves do not touch the burdens with one of your fingers. ⁴⁷ Woe to you! for you build the tombs of the prophets whom your fathers killed. ⁴⁸ So you are witnesses and consent to the deeds of your fathers; for they killed them, and you build their tombs. ⁴⁹ Therefore also the Wisdom of God said, 'I will send them prophets and apostles, some of whom they will kill and persecute,' ⁵⁰ that the blood of all the prophets, shed from the foundation of the world, may be required of this generation, ⁵¹ from the blood of Abel to the blood of Zechari′ah, who perished between the altar and the sanctuary. Yes, I tell you, it shall be required of this generation. ⁵² Woe to you lawyers! for you have taken away the key of knowledge; you did not enter yourselves, and you hindered those who were entering."

53 As he went away from there, the scribes and the Pharisees began to press him hard, and to provoke him to speak of many things, ⁵⁴ lying in wait for him, to catch at something he might say.

12 In the meantime, when so many thousands of the multitude had gathered together that they trod upon one another, he began to say to his disciples first, "Beware of the leaven of the Pharisees, which is hypocrisy. ² Nothing is covered up that will not be revealed, or hidden that will not be known. ³ Therefore whatever you have said in the dark shall be heard in the light, and what you have whispered in private rooms shall be proclaimed upon the housetops.

4 "I tell you, my friends, do not fear those who kill the body, and after that have no more that they can do. ⁵ But I will warn you whom to fear: fear him who, after he has killed, has power to cast into hell;ᵐ yes, I tell you, fear him! ⁶ Are not five sparrows sold for two pennies? And not one of them is forgotten before God. ⁷ Why, even the hairs of your head are all numbered. Fear not; you are of more value than many sparrows.

8 "And I tell you, every one who acknowledges me before men, the Son of man also will acknowledge before the angels of God; ⁹ but he who denies me before men will be denied before the angels of God. ¹⁰ And every one who speaks a word against the Son of man will be forgiven; but he who blasphemes against the Holy Spirit will not be forgiven. ¹¹ And when they bring you before the synagogues and the rulers and the authorities, do not be anxious how or what you are to answer or what you are to say; ¹² for the Holy Spirit will teach you in that very hour what you ought to say."

13 One of the multitude said to him, "Teacher, bid my brother

m Greek *Gehenna*

---

of the Jewish law. **46:** Mt.23.4. **47–48:** Mt.23.29–32; Acts 7.51–53. **49–51:** Mt.23.34–36. **49:** 1 Cor.1.24; Col.2.3. *The Wisdom of God* is either the title of an otherwise unknown book, or (more probably) a reference to the divine decrees as interpreted by Jesus (compare Jesus' personification of wisdom in 7.35); in Mt.23.34 the words are attributed to Jesus himself. **51:** See Mt.23.35 n. **52:** Mt.23.13. *The key of knowledge*, the clue to proper understanding of God's purpose. The lawyers have not *entered*, i.e. have rejected God's rule, and keep others from it.

12.1–12: Encouragement of disciples (Mt.10.26–33). **1:** Mt.16.6,12; see Mk.8.15 n. **2:** See Mk.4.22 n. **3:** Similar to but different from Mt.10.27. **5:** Heb.10.31. **6:** Mt.10.29. The *penny* (assarion) was one-sixteenth of a denarius (see 12.59 n.). **7:** 21.18; Acts 27.34; Mt.12.12. **9:** Mk.8.38; Lk.9.26; 2 Tim.2.12. **10:** See Mt.12.31 n.; Mk.3.28–29. **11:** Mt.10.19; Mk.13.11; Lk.21.14–15. **12:** 2 Tim.4.17.

12.13–21: Parable of the rich fool. 13: According to Dt.21.17 the elder received double the

divide the inheritance with me." [14] But he said to him, "Man, who made me a judge or divider over you?" [15] And he said to them, "Take heed, and beware of all covetousness; for a man's life does not consist in the abundance of his possessions." [16] And he told them a parable, saying, "The land of a rich man brought forth plentifully; [17] and he thought to himself, 'What shall I do, for I have nowhere to store my crops?' [18] And he said, 'I will do this: I will pull down my barns, and build larger ones; and there I will store all my grain and my goods. [19] And I will say to my soul, Soul, you have ample goods laid up for many years; take your ease, eat, drink, be merry.' [20] But God said to him, 'Fool! This night your soul is required of you; and the things you have prepared, whose will they be?' [21] So is he who lays up treasure for himself, and is not rich toward God."

22 And he said to his disciples, "Therefore I tell you, do not be anxious about your life, what you shall eat, nor about your body, what you shall put on. [23] For life is more than food, and the body more than clothing. [24] Consider the ravens: they neither sow nor reap, they have neither storehouse nor barn, and yet God feeds them. Of how much more value are you than the birds! [25] And which of you by being anxious can add a cubit to his span of life?[n] [26] If then you are not able to do as small a thing as that, why are you anxious about the rest? [27] Consider the lilies, how they grow; they neither toil nor spin;[o] yet I tell you, even Solomon in all his glory was not arrayed like one of these. [28] But if God so clothes the grass which is alive in the field today and tomorrow is thrown into the oven, how much more will he clothe you, O men of little faith! [29] And do not seek what you are to eat and what you are to drink, nor be of anxious mind. [30] For all the nations of the world seek these things; and your Father knows that you need them. [31] Instead, seek his[p] kingdom, and these things shall be yours as well.

32 "Fear not, little flock, for it is your Father's good pleasure to give you the kingdom. [33] Sell your possessions, and give alms; provide yourselves with purses that do not grow old, with a treasure in the heavens that does not fail, where no thief approaches and no moth destroys. [34] For where your treasure is, there will your heart be also.

35 "Let your loins be girded and your lamps burning, [36] and be like men who are waiting for their master to come home from the marriage feast, so that they may open to him at once when he comes and knocks. [37] Blessed are those servants whom the master finds awake when he comes; truly, I say to you, he will gird himself and have them sit at table, and he will come and serve them. [38] If he comes in the second watch, or in the third, and finds them so, blessed are those servants! [39] But know this, that if the householder had known at what hour the thief was coming, he[q] would not have left his house to be broken into. [40] You also must be ready; for the Son of man is coming at an unexpected hour."

n Or *to his stature*
o Other ancient authorities read *Consider the lilies; they neither spin nor weave*
p Other ancient authorities read *God's*
q Other ancient authorities add *would have watched and*

younger's share. **15:** *A man's life*, i.e. full human experience (1 Tim.6.6–10). **20:** Jer.17.11; Job 27.8; Ps.39.6; Lk.12.33–34.
    12.22–34: On anxiety (Mt.6.25–33,19–21). **24:** 12.6–7. **25:** See Mt.6.27 n. **27:** 1 Kg.10.1–10. **30:** Mt.6.8. **32:** *Flock* refers to the Messiah's people (Ezek. ch. 34). **33–34:** Compare Mt.6.19–21; Mk.10.21; Lk.18.22; Acts 2.45; 4.32–35. Jesus spoke against abuse, not possession, of property (v. 15).
    12.35–48: On watchfulness (Mt.24.43–51). **35:** Eph.6.14; Mt.25.1–13; Mk.13.33–37. **37:** The language suggests that Jesus' mind moved to the Messianic banquet (13.29; 22.16), to which a marriage feast served as an analogy. **38:** The time, between 9 p.m. and 3 a.m. **39–40:** Mt.

41 Peter said, "Lord, are you telling this parable for us or for all?" [42] And the Lord said, "Who then is the faithful and wise steward, whom his master will set over his household, to give them their portion of food at the proper time? [43] Blessed is that servant whom his master when he comes will find so doing. [44] Truly, I say to you, he will set him over all his possessions. [45] But if that servant says to himself, 'My master is delayed in coming,' and begins to beat the menservants and the maidservants, and to eat and drink and get drunk, [46] the master of that servant will come on a day when he does not expect him and at an hour he does not know, and will punish[r] him, and put him with the unfaithful. [47] And that servant who knew his master's will, but did not make ready or act according to his will, shall receive a severe beating. [48] But he who did not know, and did what deserved a beating, shall receive a light beating. Every one to whom much is given, of him will much be required; and of him to whom men commit much they will demand the more.

49 "I came to cast fire upon the earth; and would that it were already kindled! [50] I have a baptism to be baptized with; and how I am constrained until it is accomplished! [51] Do you think that I have come to give peace on earth? No, I tell you, but rather division; [52] for henceforth in one house there will be five divided, three against two and two against three; [53] they will be divided, father against son and son against father, mother against daughter and daughter against her mother, mother-in-law against her daughter-in-law and daughter-in-law against her mother-in-law."

54 He also said to the multitudes, "When you see a cloud rising in the west, you say at once, 'A shower is coming'; and so it happens. [55] And when you see the south wind blowing, you say, 'There will be scorching heat'; and it happens. [56] You hypocrites! You know how to interpret the appearance of earth and sky; but why do you not know how to interpret the present time?

57 "And why do you not judge for yourselves what is right? [58] As you go with your accuser before the magistrate, make an effort to settle with him on the way, lest he drag you to the judge, and the judge hand you over to the officer, and the officer put you in prison. [59] I tell you, you will never get out till you have paid the very last copper."

13 There were some present at that very time who told him of the Galileans whose blood Pilate had mingled with their sacrifices. [2] And he answered them, "Do you think that these Galileans were worse sinners than all the other Galileans, because they suffered thus? [3] I tell you, No; but unless you repent you will all likewise perish. [4] Or those eighteen upon whom

r Or *cut him in pieces*

24.43–44; 1 Th.5.2; Rev.3.3; 16.15; 2 Pet.3.10. **42:** Mt.24.45–51. **47–48:** Dt.25.2–3; Num. 15.29–30; Lk.8.18; 19.26.

12.49–56: On the end of the age. 49: *Fire*, a symbol of judgment (Mt.3.11; 7.19; Mk.9.48; Lk.3.16). **50:** Mk.10.38–39; Jn.12.27. **51–53:** Mt.10.34–36; Lk.21.16; Mic.7.6. **54–56:** Mt. 16.2–3. Winds from the west blew off the Mediterranean; those from the south off the desert. Jesus says there are many signs of spiritual crisis that men neglect.

12.57–59: Mt.5.25–26. **59:** The *copper* (lepton) was the smallest Greek coin in circulation. There were two lepta to a quadrans ("penny" in Mt.5.26; Mk.12.42), eight to an assarion ("penny" in Lk.12.6) and one hundred and twenty-eight to a denarius, the daily wage in Mt.20.2.

13.1–9: On repentance. 2: The reports carried with them questions of a deeper meaning. Jewish faith thought painful experiences were signs of God's judgment (Jn.9.2–3). Jesus does not argue here (as in Mt.5.45) for a disconnection between natural and moral good and evil. Here suffering represents God's judgment and is a call to repentance lest spiritual catastrophe overtake his hearers. **4:** *Siloam*, a section of Jerusalem. **6–9:** Mt.21.18–20; Mk.11.12–14,20–21. **7:** Mt.3.10; 7.19; Lk.3.9.

the tower in Silo′am fell and killed them, do you think that they were worse offenders than all the others who dwelt in Jerusalem? ⁵ I tell you, No; but unless you repent you will all likewise perish.″

6 And he told this parable: "A man had a fig tree planted in his vineyard; and he came seeking fruit on it and found none. ⁷ And he said to the vinedresser, 'Lo, these three years I have come seeking fruit on this fig tree, and I find none. Cut it down; why should it use up the ground?' ⁸ And he answered him, 'Let it alone, sir, this year also, till I dig about it and put on manure. ⁹ And if it bears fruit next year, well and good; but if not, you can cut it down.' "

10 Now he was teaching in one of the synagogues on the sabbath. ¹¹ And there was a woman who had had a spirit of infirmity for eighteen years; she was bent over and could not fully straighten herself. ¹² And when Jesus saw her, he called her and said to her, "Woman, you are freed from your infirmity." ¹³ And he laid his hands upon her, and immediately she was made straight, and she praised God. ¹⁴ But the ruler of the synagogue, indignant because Jesus had healed on the sabbath, said to the people, "There are six days on which work ought to be done; come on those days and be healed, and not on the sabbath day." ¹⁵ Then the Lord answered him, "You hypocrites! Does not each of you on the sabbath untie his ox or his ass from the manger, and lead it away to water it? ¹⁶ And ought not this woman, a daughter of Abraham whom Satan bound for eighteen years, be loosed from this bond on the sabbath day?" ¹⁷ As he said this, all his adversaries were put to shame; and all

the people rejoiced at all the glorious things that were done by him.

18 He said therefore, "What is the kingdom of God like? And to what shall I compare it? ¹⁹ It is like a grain of mustard seed which a man took and sowed in his garden; and it grew and became a tree, and the birds of the air made nests in its branches."

20 And again he said, "To what shall I compare the kingdom of God? ²¹ It is like leaven which a woman took and hid in three measures of flour, till it was all leavened."

22 He went on his way through towns and villages, teaching, and journeying toward Jerusalem. ²³ And some one said to him, "Lord, will those who are saved be few?" And he said to them, ²⁴ "Strive to enter by the narrow door; for many, I tell you, will seek to enter and will not be able. ²⁵ When once the householder has risen up and shut the door, you will begin to stand outside and to knock at the door, saying, 'Lord, open to us.' He will answer you, 'I do not know where you come from.' ²⁶ Then you will begin to say, 'We ate and drank in your presence, and you taught in our streets.' ²⁷ But he will say, 'I tell you, I do not know where you come from; depart from me, all you workers of iniquity!' ²⁸ There you will weep and gnash your teeth, when you see Abraham and Isaac and Jacob and all the prophets in the kingdom of God and you yourselves thrust out. ²⁹ And men will come from east and west, and from north and south, and sit at table in the kingdom of God. ³⁰ And behold, some are last who will be first, and some are first who will be last."

31 At that very hour some Pharisees came, and said to him, "Get away from here, for Herod wants to

---

13.10–17: An infirm woman healed. 14: Ex.20.9–10; Mt.12.11–12; Lk.6.6–11; 14.1–6; Jn.5.1–18. **16:** Jesus attributes physical (and psychical) disorders to the work of *Satan* (see Mt.4.1 n.; 12.24 n.). They are in conflict with God's purpose of salvation in his covenant with Abraham, and are the concern of his saving activity (4.18; Mt.8.14–17).

13.18–21: Parables of mustard seed and leaven (see Mt.13.31–33 n.; Mk.4.30–32).

13.22–30: On the end of the age. 22–24: Mt.7.13–14; Jn.10.7; Lk.9.51 n. **25:** Mt.25.10–12. **26–29:** The host clearly is meant to be the Messiah (compare 14.15–24).

kill you." ³² And he said to them, "Go and tell that fox, 'Behold, I cast out demons and perform cures today and tomorrow, and the third day I finish my course. ³³ Nevertheless I must go on my way today and tomorrow and the day following; for it cannot be that a prophet should perish away from Jerusalem.' ³⁴ O Jerusalem, Jerusalem, killing the prophets and stoning those who are sent to you! How often would I have gathered your children together as a hen gathers her brood under her wings, and you would not! ³⁵ Behold, your house is forsaken. And I tell you, you will not see me until you say, 'Blessed is he who comes in the name of the Lord!' "

14 One sabbath when he went to dine at the house of a ruler who belonged to the Pharisees, they were watching him. ² And behold, there was a man before him who had dropsy. ³ And Jesus spoke to the lawyers and Pharisees, saying, "Is it lawful to heal on the sabbath, or not?" ⁴ But they were silent. Then he took him and healed him, and let him go. ⁵ And he said to them, "Which of you, having a son⁸ or an ox that has fallen into a well, will not immediately pull him out on a sabbath day?" ⁶ And they could not reply to this.

7 Now he told a parable to those who were invited, when he marked how they chose the places of honor, saying to them, ⁸ "When you are invited by any one to a marriage feast, do not sit down in a place of honor, lest a more eminent man than you be invited by him; ⁹ and he who invited you both will come and say to you, 'Give place to this man,' and then you will begin with shame to take the lowest place. ¹⁰ But when you are invited, go and sit in the lowest place, so that when your host comes he may say to you, 'Friend, go up higher'; then you will be honored in the presence of all who sit at table with you. ¹¹ For every one who exalts himself will be humbled, and he who humbles himself will be exalted."

12 He said also to the man who had invited him, "When you give a dinner or a banquet, do not invite your friends or your brothers or your kinsmen or rich neighbors, lest they also invite you in return, and you be repaid. ¹³ But when you give a feast, invite the poor, the maimed, the lame, the blind, ¹⁴ and you will be blessed, because they cannot repay you. You will be repaid at the resurrection of the just."

15 When one of those who sat at table with him heard this, he said to him, "Blessed is he who shall eat bread in the kingdom of God!" ¹⁶ But he said to him, "A man once gave a great banquet, and invited many; ¹⁷ and at the time for the banquet he sent his servant to say to those who had been invited, 'Come; for all is now ready.' ¹⁸ But they all alike began to make excuses. The first said to him, 'I have bought a field, and I must go out and see it; I pray you, have me excused.' ¹⁹ And another said, 'I have bought five yoke of oxen, and I go to examine them; I pray you, have

s Other ancient authorities read *an ass*

13.31–33: **Words to Herod Antipas. 31:** *Here,* Herod's domain (Galilee and Perea). **32:** *Behold . . .* , no cunning threats of *that fox* can shorten *my course. Third day,* not literally; a short and limited time is meant. **33:** *It cannot be . . .* , bitter irony.

13.34–35: **Lament over Jerusalem** (Mt.23.37–39). **34:** *How often,* see Mt.23.37 n. **35:** Jer. 22.5; Ps.118.26.

14.1–6: **Healing the man with dropsy.** Mt.12.9–14; Mk.3.1–6; Lk.6.6–11; 13.10–17.

14.7–14: **On humility. 8:** Prov.25.6–7; Lk.11.43; 20.46. **12:** Jas.2.2–4; Mt.5.43–48. **14:** Jesus appeals not to a spirit of material gain, i.e. a hope of reward in the judgment, but rather to man's faith that the principle of love will be vindicated (Col.3.23–24).

14.15–24: **The great banquet** (Mt.22.1–10; compare also Mt.8.11; 26.29; see Lk.5.32 n.; 13.29). The point is that though men suppose they highly prize the thought of sharing God's kingdom, they may in fact be rejecting appeals to act so that they may enter it. **15:** Lk.22.16,

me excused.' 20 And another said, 'I have married a wife, and therefore I cannot come.' 21 So the servant came and reported this to his master. Then the householder in anger said to his servant, 'Go out quickly to the streets and lanes of the city, and bring in the poor and maimed and blind and lame.' 22 And the servant said, 'Sir, what you commanded has been done, and still there is room.' 23 And the master said to the servant, 'Go out to the highways and hedges, and compel people to come in, that my house may be filled. 24 For I tell you,*a* none of those men who were invited shall taste my banquet.' "

25 Now great multitudes accompanied him; and he turned and said to them, 26 "If any one comes to me and does not hate his own father and mother and wife and children and brothers and sisters, yes, and even his own life, he cannot be my disciple. 27 Whoever does not bear his own cross and come after me, cannot be my disciple. 28 For which of you, desiring to build a tower, does not first sit down and count the cost, whether he has enough to complete it? 29 Otherwise, when he has laid a foundation, and is not able to finish, all who see it begin to mock him, 30 saying, 'This man began to build, and was not able to finish.' 31 Or what king, going to encounter another king in war, will not sit down first and take counsel whether he is able with ten thousand to meet him who comes against him with twenty thousand? 32 And if not, while the other is yet a great way off, he sends an embassy and asks terms of peace. 33 So therefore, whoever of you does

not renounce all that he has cannot be my disciple.

34 "Salt is good; but if salt has lost its taste, how shall its saltness be restored? 35 It is fit neither for the land nor for the dunghill; men throw it away. He who has ears to hear, let him hear."

15 Now the tax collectors and sinners were all drawing near to hear him. 2 And the Pharisees and the scribes murmured, saying, "This man receives sinners and eats with them."

3 So he told them this parable: 4 "What man of you, having a hundred sheep, if he has lost one of them, does not leave the ninety-nine in the wilderness, and go after the one which is lost, until he finds it? 5 And when he has found it, he lays it on his shoulders, rejoicing. 6 And when he comes home, he calls together his friends and his neighbors, saying to them, 'Rejoice with me, for I have found my sheep which was lost.' 7 Just so, I tell you, there will be more joy in heaven over one sinner who repents than over ninety-nine righteous persons who need no repentance.

8 "Or what woman, having ten silver coins,*t* if she loses one coin, does not light a lamp and sweep the house and seek diligently until she finds it? 9 And when she has found it, she calls together her friends and neighbors, saying, 'Rejoice with me, for I have found the coin which I had lost.' 10 Just so, I tell you, there is joy before the angels of God over one sinner who repents."

11 And he said, "There was a man

a The Greek word for *you* here is plural
t The drachma, rendered here by *silver coin*, was about a day's wage for a laborer

---

18,28–30; Rev.19.9. **20:** Dt.24.5; 1 Cor.7.33. **24:** *You* is plural here; Jesus drops the parabolic form and speaks to the guests (v. 15) in his own person.

14.25–35: Conditions of discipleship. 26–27: Mt.10.37–38. **26:** Jn.12.25. *Hate* is used in vigorous, vivid hyperbole; the parallel passage in Mt.10.37 reflects Jesus' meaning. **27:** See Mt.10.38 n. **31–32:** Possibly Jesus alludes to some contemporary event. **33:** 9.57–62; 12.33; 18.29–30; Phil.3.7. **34–35:** Mt.5.13; Mk.9.49–50.

15.1–32: Parables about the lost. 3–7: The lost sheep. Mt.18.12–14. The parable illustrates God's concern for men who lack ability to find him; he seeks them. **4:** The phrase *until he finds it* is in harmony with Luke's universalism (see Introduction and contrast "if" in Mt.18.13). **8–10: The lost coin.** This parable intensifies the picture of human helplessness and divine con-

who had two sons; ¹² and the younger of them said to his father, 'Father, give me the share of property that falls to me.' And he divided his living between them. ¹³ Not many days later, the younger son gathered all he had and took his journey into a far country, and there he squandered his property in loose living. ¹⁴ And when he had spent everything, a great famine arose in that country, and he began to be in want. ¹⁵ So he went and joined himself to one of the citizens of that country, who sent him into his fields to feed swine. ¹⁶ And he would gladly have fed on[u] the pods that the swine ate; and no one gave him anything. ¹⁷ But when he came to himself he said, 'How many of my father's hired servants have bread enough and to spare, but I perish here with hunger! ¹⁸ I will arise and go to my father, and I will say to him, "Father, I have sinned against heaven and before you; ¹⁹ I am no longer worthy to be called your son; treat me as one of your hired servants." ' ²⁰ And he arose and came to his father. But while he was yet at a distance, his father saw him and had compassion, and ran and embraced him and kissed him. ²¹ And the son said to him, 'Father, I have sinned against heaven and before you; I am no longer worthy to be called your son.'[v] ²² But the father said to his servants, 'Bring quickly the best robe, and put it on him; and put a ring on his hand, and shoes on his feet; ²³ and bring the fatted calf and kill it, and let us eat and make merry; ²⁴ for this my son was dead, and is alive again; he was lost, and is found.' And they began to make merry.

25 "Now his elder son was in the field; and as he came and drew near to the house, he heard music and dancing. ²⁶ And he called one of the servants and asked what this meant. ²⁷ And he said to him, 'Your brother has come, and your father has killed the fatted calf, because he has received him safe and sound.' ²⁸ But he was angry and refused to go in. His father came out and entreated him, ²⁹ but he answered his father, 'Lo, these many years I have served you, and I never disobeyed your command; yet you never gave me a kid, that I might make merry with my friends. ³⁰ But when this son of yours came, who has devoured your living with harlots, you killed for him the fatted calf!' ³¹ And he said to him, 'Son, you are always with me, and all that is mine is yours. ³² It was fitting to make merry and be glad, for this your brother was dead, and is alive; he was lost, and is found.' "

16 He also said to the disciples, "There was a rich man who had a steward, and charges were brought to him that this man was wasting his goods. ² And he called him and said to him, 'What is this that I hear about you? Turn in the account of your stewardship, for you can no longer be steward.' ³ And the steward said to himself, 'What shall I do, since my master is taking the stewardship away from me? I am not strong enough to dig, and I am ashamed to beg. ⁴ I have decided what to do, so that people may receive me into their houses when I am put out of the stewardship.' ⁵ So, summoning his master's debtors one by one, he said to the first, 'How much do you owe my master?' ⁶ He said, 'A hundred measures of oil.' And he said to him, 'Take your bill, and sit

u Other ancient authorities read filled his belly with
v Other ancient authorities add treat me as one of your hired servants

cern. The *coin* was approximately equivalent to the denarius (see note *t*). **11–32: The lost son. 12:** See 12.13 n. **15:** *Swine*, the culminating indignity for a Jew. **22–24:** His place as son is freely restored. The parable illustrates God's acceptance of those who rebel and return. **22:** Gen.41.42; Zech.3.4. **24:** 1 Tim.5.6; Eph.2.1; Lk.9.60. **25–32:** Jesus' aim was to portray the difference between God's loving forgiveness and the self-centered complacency that not only denies love, but cannot understand it.

16.1–13: The dishonest steward. The point is in v. 8, the application in v. 9: the dishonest steward was prudent in using the things of this life to ensure the future; believers should do the

down quickly and write fifty.' [7] Then he said to another, 'And how much do you owe?' He said, 'A hundred measures of wheat.' He said to him, 'Take your bill, and write eighty.' [8] The master commended the dishonest steward for his shrewdness; for the sons of this world[w] are more shrewd in dealing with their own generation than the sons of light. [9] And I tell you, make friends for yourselves by means of unrighteous mammon,[a] so that when it fails they may receive you into the eternal habitations.

10 "He who is faithful in a very little is faithful also in much; and he who is dishonest in a very little is dishonest also in much. [11] If then you have not been faithful in the unrighteous mammon,[a] who will entrust to you the true riches? [12] And if you have not been faithful in that which is another's, who will give you that which is your own? [13] No servant can serve two masters; for either he will hate the one and love the other, or he will be devoted to the one and despise the other. You cannot serve God and mammon."[a]

14 The Pharisees, who were lovers of money, heard all this, and they scoffed at him. [15] But he said to them, "You are those who justify yourselves before men, but God knows your hearts; for what is exalted among men is an abomination in the sight of God.

16 "The law and the prophets were until John; since then the good news of the kingdom of God is preached,

and every one enters it violently. [17] But it is easier for heaven and earth to pass away, than for one dot of the law to become void.

18 "Every one who divorces his wife and marries another commits adultery, and he who marries a woman divorced from her husband commits adultery.

19 "There was a rich man, who was clothed in purple and fine linen and who feasted sumptuously every day. [20] And at his gate lay a poor man named Laz'arus, full of sores, [21] who desired to be fed with what fell from the rich man's table; moreover the dogs came and licked his sores. [22] The poor man died and was carried by the angels to Abraham's bosom. The rich man also died and was buried; [23] and in Hades, being in torment, he lifted up his eyes, and saw Abraham far off and Laz'arus in his bosom. [24] And he called out, 'Father Abraham, have mercy upon me, and send Laz'arus to dip the end of his finger in water and cool my tongue; for I am in anguish in this flame.' [25] But Abraham said, 'Son, remember that you in your lifetime received your good things, and Laz'arus in like manner evil things; but now he is comforted here, and you are in anguish. [26] And besides all this, between us and you a great chasm has been fixed, in order that those who would pass from here to you may not be able, and none may cross from there to us.' [27] And he said, 'Then I beg you,

w Greek *age*
a Mammon is a Semitic word for money or riches

---

same. **8:** *The master* is the rich man of v. 1. *Sons of light*, those who are spiritually enlightened. The phrase appears in Jn.12.36; Eph.5.8; 1 Th.5.5, as well as in the Dead Sea Scrolls, where it is contrasted with the sons of darkness. **10:** Mt.25.21; Lk.19.17. **13:** See Mt.6.24 n. **14–15:** Mt. 19.16–30; Lk.18.9–14. *What is exalted*, that is, what is given a regard due only to God. **17:** Mt.5.17–18; Lk.21.33. **18:** Mt.5.31–32; 19.9; Mk.10.11–12; 1 Cor.7.10–11.

16.19–31: The rich man and Lazarus. It is not known whether Jesus alluded here to a contemporary incident. The main point (vv. 27–31) is that the Old Testament speaks an urgent and sufficient call to repentance (v. 17). As a whole the story seems to illustrate vv. 10–15. Jesus draws details from contemporary ways of expressing Jewish faith, including items not found in the Old Testament. **19:** The *rich man*, though unnamed, is commonly called "Dives" (Latin for "rich man"). **20:** The person named here is not to be identified with the Lazarus of Jn.11.1–44; 12.1,9. **21–22:** The moral quality of Lazarus is passed over to illustrate the fatal deficiency in the life of the other and the impossibility of changing his condemnation. **22:** See 23.42 n. **29:** Jn.5.45–47; Acts 15.21. **30:** 3.8; 19.9.

father, to send him to my father's house, 28 for I have five brothers, so that he may warn them, lest they also come into this place of torment.' 29 But Abraham said, 'They have Moses and the prophets; let them hear them.' 30 And he said, 'No, father Abraham; but if some one goes to them from the dead, they will repent.' 31 He said to him, 'If they do not hear Moses and the prophets, neither will they be convinced if some one should rise from the dead.' "

17 And he said to his disciples, "Temptations to sinˣ are sure to come; but woe to him by whom they come! 2 It would be better for him if a millstone were hung round his neck and he were cast into the sea, than that he should cause one of these little ones to sin.ʸ 3 Take heed to yourselves; if your brother sins, rebuke him, and if he repents, forgive him; 4 and if he sins against you seven times in the day, and turns to you seven times, and says, 'I repent,' you must forgive him."

5 The apostles said to the Lord, "Increase our faith!" 6 And the Lord said, "If you had faith as a grain of mustard seed, you could say to this sycamine tree, 'Be rooted up, and be planted in the sea,' and it would obey you.

7 "Will any one of you, who has a servant plowing or keeping sheep, say to him when he has come in from the field, 'Come at once and sit down at table'? 8 Will he not rather say to him, 'Prepare supper for me, and gird yourself and serve me, till I eat and drink; and afterward you shall eat and drink'? 9 Does he thank the servant because he did what was commanded? 10 So you also, when you have done all that is commanded you, say, 'We are unworthy servants; we have only done what was our duty.' "

11 On the way to Jerusalem he was passing along between Sama'ria and Galilee. 12 And as he entered a village, he was met by ten lepers, who stood at a distance 13 and lifted up their voices and said, "Jesus, Master, have mercy on us." 14 When he saw them he said to them, "Go and show yourselves to the priests." And as they went they were cleansed. 15 Then one of them, when he saw that he was healed, turned back, praising God with a loud voice; 16 and he fell on his face at Jesus' feet, giving him thanks. Now he was a Samaritan. 17 Then said Jesus, "Were not ten cleansed? Where are the nine? 18 Was no one found to return and give praise to God except this foreigner?" 19 And he said to him, "Rise and go your way; your faith has made you well."

20 Being asked by the Pharisees when the kingdom of God was coming, he answered them, "The kingdom of God is not coming with signs to be observed; 21 nor will they say, 'Lo, here it is!' or 'There!' for behold, the kingdom of God is in the midst of you."ᶻ

22 And he said to the disciples, "The days are coming when you will desire to see one of the days of the Son of man, and you will not see it. 23 And they will say to you, 'Lo, there!' or 'Lo, here!' Do not go, do not follow them.

x Greek *stumbling blocks*
y Greek *stumble*
z Or *within you*

17.1–2: Mt.18.6,7; Mk.9.42; 1 Cor.8.12. **2:** *Little ones,* disciples (see Mt.18.6 n.). **5:** Mk. 11.23 n., 24 n. **6:** *Sycamine,* mulberry. **7–10:** Man's relation to God makes obedience to God a duty to be fulfilled and not an occasion for reward.

17.11–19: Ten lepers cleansed. **12:** Lev.13.45–46; see Mt.8.2 n. **14:** *Priest,* Lev.13.2–3; 14.2–32. **18:** 7.9. **19:** Mt.9.22; Mk.5.34; Lk.8.48; 18.42. *Made you well,* see Mt.9.21 n.; Mk. 11.23 n., 24 n.

17.20–21: The kingdom is in the midst of you. **20:** 19.11; 21.7; Acts 1.6. **21:** The reality of God's *kingdom* is present to be accepted. The questioners had in mind a kingdom bringing material benefits.

17.22–37: The end of the age. Mt. ch. 24 has similar teachings, in a different order and setting. **22:** Mt.9.15; Mk.2.20; Lk.5.35. **23–24:** Mt.24.23,26,27; Mk.13.21; Rev.1.7. **23:** *Lo, there* is the Son of man! etc. **24:** The coming will be sudden and visible to all. **25:** 9.22. **26–27:**

²⁴ For as the lightning flashes and lights up the sky from one side to the other, so will the Son of man be in his day.ᵃ ²⁵ But first he must suffer many things and be rejected by this generation. ²⁶ As it was in the days of Noah, so will it be in the days of the Son of man. ²⁷ They ate, they drank, they married, they were given in marriage, until the day when Noah entered the ark, and the flood came and destroyed them all. ²⁸ Likewise as it was in the days of Lot–they ate, they drank, they bought, they sold, they planted, they built, ²⁹ but on the day when Lot went out from Sodom fire and sulphur rained from heaven and destroyed them all– ³⁰ so will it be on the day when the Son of man is revealed. ³¹ On that day, let him who is on the housetop, with his goods in the house, not come down to take them away; and likewise let him who is in the field not turn back. ³² Remember Lot's wife. ³³ Whoever seeks to gain his life will lose it, but whoever loses his life will preserve it. ³⁴ I tell you, in that night there will be two in one bed; one will be taken and the other left. ³⁵ There will be two women grinding together; one will be taken and the other left."ᵇ ³⁷ And they said to him, "Where, Lord?" He said to them, "Where the body is, there the eaglesᶜ will be gathered together."

18 And he told them a parable, to the effect that they ought always to pray and not lose heart. ² He said, "In a certain city there was a judge who neither feared God nor regarded man; ³ and there was a widow in that city who kept coming to him and saying, 'Vindicate me against my adversary.' ⁴ For a while he refused; but afterward he said to himself, 'Though I neither fear God nor regard man, ⁵ yet because this widow bothers me, I will vindicate her, or she will wear me out by her continual coming.'" ⁶ And the Lord said, "Hear what the unrighteous judge says. ⁷ And will not God vindicate his elect, who cry to him day and night? Will he delay long over them? ⁸ I tell you, he will vindicate them speedily. Nevertheless, when the Son of man comes, will he find faith on earth?"

9 He also told this parable to some who trusted in themselves that they were righteous and despised others: ¹⁰ "Two men went up into the temple to pray, one a Pharisee and the other a tax collector. ¹¹ The Pharisee stood and prayed thus with himself, 'God, I thank thee that I am not like other men, extortioners, unjust, adulterers, or even like this tax collector. ¹² I fast twice a week, I give tithes of all that I get.' ¹³ But the tax collector, standing far off, would not even lift up his eyes to heaven, but beat his breast, saying, 'God, be merciful to me a sinner!' ¹⁴ I tell you, this man went down to his house justified rather than the other; for every one who exalts himself will be humbled, but he who humbles himself will be exalted."

15 Now they were bringing even infants to him that he might touch

---

a Other ancient authorities omit *in his day*
b Other ancient authorities add verse 36, "Two men will be in the field; one will be taken and the other left"
c Or *vultures*

Mt.24.37–39; Gen.6.5–8; 7.6–24. **28–30:** Gen.18.16–19.28. **31:** Mt.24.17–18; Mk.13.15–16; Lk.21.21. **32:** Gen.19.26. **33:** See Mt.10.38 n., 39. **34–35:** Mt.24.40–41. **37:** Mt.24.28. Jesus' answer is a significant appeal to faith. The questioners wish to know *where* the Messiah and his people will be located. Instead of answering them directly, Jesus warns: As surely as vultures find the carcass, so surely will divine judgment come; therefore always be ready!

18.1–8: The unjust judge. 1: The point is carefully stated (compare 11.5–8), perhaps because the details are incongruous (as in 16.1–9). **7:** Rev.6.10; Mt.24.22; Rom.8.33; Col.3.12; 2 Tim. 2.10. **8:** *Comes*, from heaven, in judgment. *Faith*, a requisite for this persistent prayer (v. 1).

18.9–14: Pharisee and tax collector. 9: *Righteous*, that is, acceptable to God because of their ritual observance (vv. 11–12; see Mt.5.20 n.). **11:** Mt.6.5; Mk.11.25. **12:** *Twice a week*, Mondays and Thursdays. **14:** *Justified* means "accepted by God," "right with God." God receives those who in contrition implore his mercy rather than those who parade their supposed virtues (15.7).

18.15–19.27: From Galilee to Jerusalem (Mt.19.1–20.34; Mk.10.1–52).

them; and when the disciples saw it, they rebuked them. [16] But Jesus called them to him, saying, "Let the children come to me, and do not hinder them; for to such belongs the kingdom of God. [17] Truly, I say to you, whoever does not receive the kingdom of God like a child shall not enter it."

18 And a ruler asked him, "Good Teacher, what shall I do to inherit eternal life?" [19] And Jesus said to him, "Why do you call me good? No one is good but God alone. [20] You know the commandments: 'Do not commit adultery, Do not kill, Do not steal, Do not bear false witness, Honor your father and mother.'" [21] And he said, "All these I have observed from my youth." [22] And when Jesus heard it, he said to him, "One thing you still lack. Sell all that you have and distribute to the poor, and you will have treasure in heaven; and come, follow me." [23] But when he heard this he became sad, for he was very rich. [24] Jesus looking at him said, "How hard it is for those who have riches to enter the kingdom of God! [25] For it is easier for a camel to go through the eye of a needle than for a rich man to enter the kingdom of God." [26] Those who heard it said, "Then who can be saved?" [27] But he said, "What is impossible with men is possible with God." [28] And Peter said, "Lo, we have left our homes and followed you." [29] And he said to them, "Truly, I say to you, there is no man who has left house or wife or brothers or parents or children, for the sake of the kingdom of God, [30] who will not receive manifold more in this time, and in the age to come eternal life."

31 And taking the twelve, he said to them, "Behold, we are going up to Jerusalem, and everything that is written of the Son of man by the prophets will be accomplished. [32] For he will be delivered to the Gentiles, and will be mocked and shamefully treated and spit upon; [33] they will scourge him and kill him, and on the third day he will rise." [34] But they understood none of these things; this saying was hid from them, and they did not grasp what was said.

35 As he drew near to Jericho, a blind man was sitting by the roadside begging; [36] and hearing a multitude going by, he inquired what this meant. [37] They told him, "Jesus of Nazareth is passing by." [38] And he cried, "Jesus, Son of David, have mercy on me!" [39] And those who were in front rebuked him, telling him to be silent; but he cried out all the more, "Son of David, have mercy on me!" [40] And Jesus stopped, and commanded him to be brought to him; and when he came near, he asked him, [41] "What do you want me to do for you?" He said, "Lord, let me receive my sight." [42] And Jesus said to him, "Receive your sight; your faith has made you well." [43] And immediately he received his sight and followed him, glorifying God; and all the people, when they saw it, gave praise to God.

19 He entered Jericho and was passing through. [2] And there was a man named Zacchae′us; he was a chief

---

18.15–17: Blessing the children (Mt.19.13–15; 18.3; Mk.10.13–16). **16–17:** God's kingdom is shared by those who depend in trustful simplicity on God as on a father.

18.18–30: The rich ruler (Mt.19.16–30; Mk.10.17–31). **18:** 10.25. **20:** See Mt.19.18 n. The order of the commandments, varying from the Hebrew Scripture, follows the ancient Greek translation of the Old Testament. **22:** See 12.33 n. **25:** See Mk.10.25 n. **26:** To *be saved* refers to the same spiritual experience as to *inherit eternal life* (v. 18), and to *enter the kingdom of God* (v. 25). The heart of this story lies in the questioner's sense of personal lack notwithstanding his opportunity (because of his wealth) to fulfil all ritual requirements. **27:** Gen.18.14; Job 42.2; Jer.32.17; Lk.1.37. **28:** 5.1–11.

18.31–34: The Passion foretold again (Mt.20.17–19; Mk.10.32–34); compare 9.22,44–45; 17.25.

18.35–43: A blind man healed (Mt.20.29–34; Mk.10.46–52). Mt.9.27–31; Mk.8.22; Jn.9.1–3. **42:** See Mt.9.21 n.; Mk.11.23 n., 24 n.

tax collector, and rich. ³ And he sought to see who Jesus was, but could not, on account of the crowd, because he was small of stature. ⁴ So he ran on ahead and climbed up into a sycamore tree to see him, for he was to pass that way. ⁵ And when Jesus came to the place, he looked up and said to him, "Zacchae′us, make haste and come down; for I must stay at your house today." ⁶ So he made haste and came down, and received him joyfully. ⁷ And when they saw it they all murmured, "He has gone in to be the guest of a man who is a sinner." ⁸ And Zacchae′us stood and said to the Lord, "Behold, Lord, the half of my goods I give to the poor; and if I have defrauded any one of anything, I restore it fourfold." ⁹ And Jesus said to him, "Today salvation has come to this house, since he also is a son of Abraham. ¹⁰ For the Son of man came to seek and to save the lost."

11 As they heard these things, he proceeded to tell a parable, because he was near to Jerusalem, and because they supposed that the kingdom of God was to appear immediately. ¹² He said therefore, "A nobleman went into a far country to receive a kingdom and then return. ¹³ Calling ten of his servants, he gave them ten pounds,ᵉ and said to them, 'Trade with these till I come.' ¹⁴ But his citizens hated him and sent an embassy after him, saying, 'We do not want this man to reign over us.' ¹⁵ When he returned, having received the kingdom, he commanded these servants, to whom he had given the money, to be called to him, that

he might know what they had gained by trading. ¹⁶ The first came before him, saying, 'Lord, your pound has made ten pounds more.' ¹⁷ And he said to him, 'Well done, good servant! Because you have been faithful in a very little, you shall have authority over ten cities.' ¹⁸ And the second came, saying, 'Lord, your pound has made five pounds.' ¹⁹ And he said to him, 'And you are to be over five cities.' ²⁰ Then another came, saying, 'Lord, here is your pound, which I kept laid away in a napkin; ²¹ for I was afraid of you, because you are a severe man; you take up what you did not lay down, and reap what you did not sow.' ²² He said to him, 'I will condemn you out of your own mouth, you wicked servant! You knew that I was a severe man, taking up what I did not lay down and reaping what I did not sow? ²³ Why then did you not put my money into the bank, and at my coming I should have collected it with interest?' ²⁴ And he said to those who stood by, 'Take the pound from him, and give it to him who has the ten pounds.' ²⁵ (And they said to him, 'Lord, he has ten pounds!') ²⁶ 'I tell you, that to every one who has will more be given; but from him who has not, even what he has will be taken away. ²⁷ But as for these enemies of mine, who did not want me to reign over them, bring them here and slay them before me.' "

28 And when he had said this, he went on ahead, going up to Jerusalem. ²⁹ When he drew near to

ᵉ The mina, rendered here by *pound*, was about three months' wages for a laborer

---

19.1–10: Zacchaeus. 1: *Jericho* was on a main trade route, and was an important customs center. **2:** As *chief tax collector* Zacchaeus had contracted for the right to collect revenues in the district. His neighbors despised him for thus sharing in the Roman domination (v. 7). **7:** 5.29–30; 15.1–2. **8:** *I give*, henceforward, a vow. *Fourfold*, Ex.22.1; Lev.6.5; Num.5.6–7. **9:** *Salvation*, or the kingdom of God, *has come* in Jesus' message and Zacchaeus' response (17.20–21; see 18.26 n.).

19.11–27: Parable of the pounds. Compare the somewhat similar parable of the talents (Mt.25.14–30). **11:** 9.51 n.; 13.22; 17.11; 18.31. **12:** The details here may reflect contemporary events. **13:** *Ten*, only three are mentioned later. **17:** 16.10. **21:** *You take up . . . lay down*, probably a current proverbial expression for a grasping person. **26:** See Mt.13.12 n. **27:** Though all are judged, only the hostile are punished.

19.28–23.56: The last week (Mt.21.1–27.66; Mk.11.1–15.47).

Beth'phage and Bethany, at the mount that is called Olivet, he sent two of the disciples, [30] saying, "Go into the village opposite, where on entering you will find a colt tied, on which no one has ever yet sat; untie it and bring it here. [31] If any one asks you, 'Why are you untying it?' you shall say this, 'The Lord has need of it.' " [32] So those who were sent went away and found it as he had told them. [33] And as they were untying the colt, its owners said to them, "Why are you untying the colt?" [34] And they said, "The Lord has need of it." [35] And they brought it to Jesus, and throwing their garments on the colt they set Jesus upon it. [36] And as he rode along, they spread their garments on the road. [37] As he was now drawing near, at the descent of the Mount of Olives, the whole multitude of the disciples began to rejoice and praise God with a loud voice for all the mighty works that they had seen, [38] saying, "Blessed is the King who comes in the name of the Lord! Peace in heaven and glory in the highest!" [39] And some of the Pharisees in the multitude said to him, "Teacher, rebuke your disciples." [40] He answered, "I tell you, if these were silent, the very stones would cry out."

41 And when he drew near and saw the city he wept over it, [42] saying, "Would that even today you knew the things that make for peace! But now they are hid from your eyes. [43] For the days shall come upon you, when your enemies will cast up a bank about you and surround you, and hem you in on every side, [44] and dash you to the ground, you and your children within you, and they will not leave one stone upon another in you; because you did not know the time of your visitation."

45 And he entered the temple and began to drive out those who sold, [46] saying to them, "It is written, 'My house shall be a house of prayer'; but you have made it a den of robbers."

47 And he was teaching daily in the temple. The chief priests and the scribes and the principal men of the people sought to destroy him; [48] but they did not find anything they could do, for all the people hung upon his words.

20 One day, as he was teaching the people in the temple and preaching the gospel, the chief priests and the scribes with the elders came up [2] and said to him, "Tell us by what authority you do these things, or who it is that gave you this authority." [3] He answered them, "I also will ask you a question; now tell me, [4] Was the baptism of John from heaven or from men?" [5] And they discussed it with one another, saying, "If we say, 'From heaven,' he will say, 'Why did you not believe him?' [6] But if we say, 'From men,' all the people will stone us; for they are convinced that John was a prophet." [7] So they answered that they did not know whence it was. [8] And Jesus said to them, "Neither will I tell you by what authority I do these things."

9 And he began to tell the people this parable: "A man planted a vineyard, and let it out to tenants, and went into another country for a long while. [10] When the time came, he sent a servant to the tenants, that they should give him some of the fruit of the vine-

---

19.28–44: Palm Sunday (Mt.21.1–9; Mk.11.1–10). Jn.12.12–18. **29:** *Olivet* means "olive grove." **32:** 22.13. **35:** See Mk.11.1 n. **36:** 2 Kg.9.13. **37:** The road traversed a ridge into the valley of the Kidron. **38:** Ps.118.26; Zech.9.9; Lk.13.35. **39–40:** Mt.21.15–16; Hab.2.11. **41:** 13.33–34. **43:** 21.20–24; 21.6; Is.29.3; Jer.6.6; Ezek.4.2. *Your enemies*, the Roman armies. *A bank*, a palisade. **44:** Ps.137.8–9; Hos.10.14–15; 13.16; see 1 Pet.2.12 n. *Your children*, the city's inhabitants. *The time of your visitation*, the time of Christ's ministry.

19.45–46: Cleansing the temple (Mt.21.12–13; Mk.11.15–19; Jn.2.13–17). **45:** See Mt.21.12 n.; Ex.30.13; Lev.1.14. **46:** Is.56.7; Jer.7.11.

20.1–8: On Jesus' authority (Mt.21.23–27; Mk.11.27–33; Jn.2.18–22).

20.9–19: Parable of the vineyard (Mt.21.33–46; Mk.12.1–12). **9:** Is.5.1–7; Mt.25.14. **13:** The

yard; but the tenants beat him, and sent him away empty-handed. [11] And he sent another servant; him also they beat and treated shamefully, and sent him away empty-handed. [12] And he sent yet a third; this one they wounded and cast out. [13] Then the owner of the vineyard said, 'What shall I do? I will send my beloved son; it may be they will respect him.' [14] But when the tenants saw him, they said to themselves, 'This is the heir; let us kill him, that the inheritance may be ours.' [15] And they cast him out of the vineyard and killed him. What then will the owner of the vineyard do to them? [16] He will come and destroy those tenants, and give the vineyard to others." When they heard this, they said, "God forbid!" [17] But he looked at them and said, "What then is this that is written:

'The very stone which the builders rejected
has become the head of the corner'?
[18] Every one who falls on that stone will be broken to pieces; but when it falls on any one it will crush him."

[19] The scribes and the chief priests tried to lay hands on him at that very hour, but they feared the people; for they perceived that he had told this parable against them. [20] So they watched him, and sent spies, who pretended to be sincere, that they might take hold of what he said, so as to deliver him up to the authority and jurisdiction of the governor. [21] They asked him, "Teacher, we know that you speak and teach rightly, and show no partiality, but truly teach the way of God. [22] Is it lawful for us to give tribute to Caesar, or not?" [23] But he perceived their craftiness, and said to them, [24] "Show me a coin.*f* Whose likeness and inscription has it?" They said, "Caesar's." [25] He said to them, "Then render to Caesar the things that are Caesar's, and to God the things that are God's." [26] And they were not able in the presence of the people to catch him by what he said; but marveling at his answer they were silent.

[27] There came to him some Sad'-ducees, those who say that there is no resurrection, [28] and they asked him a question, saying, "Teacher, Moses wrote for us that if a man's brother dies, having a wife but no children, the man*g* must take the wife and raise up children for his brother. [29] Now there were seven brothers; the first took a wife, and died without children; [30] and the second [31] and the third took her, and likewise all seven left no children and died. [32] Afterward the woman also died. [33] In the resurrection, therefore, whose wife will the woman be? For the seven had her as wife."

[34] And Jesus said to them, "The sons of this age marry and are given in marriage; [35] but those who are accounted worthy to attain to that age and to the resurrection from the dead neither marry nor are given in marriage, [36] for they cannot die any more, because they are equal to angels and are sons of God, being sons of the resurrection. [37] But that the dead are raised, even Moses showed, in the passage about the bush, where he calls the Lord the God of Abraham and the

f Greek *denarius*   *g* Greek *his brother*

---

use of *beloved* (not present in Matthew and Mark) identifies the *son* with Jesus. **16:** Acts 13.46; 18.6; 28.28. **17:** Ps.118.22–23; Acts 4.11; 1 Pet.2.7. **18:** Is.8.14–15. **19:** Lk.19.47.

20.20–26: Paying taxes to Caesar (Mt.22.15–22; Mk.12.13–17). **20:** *Sincere* translates a Greek word which normally means "correct according to the law," i.e. "righteous." It is used here in the same sense of false pretense that it has in Mt.23.28. **25:** Rom.13.7; Lk.23.2.

20.27–40: Question about the resurrection. (Mt.22.23–33; Mk.12.18–27). **27:** Acts 4.1–2; 23.6–10. **28:** Dt.25.5; Gen.38.8. **34–36:** Luke makes the same point as Matthew and Mark, but in somewhat different language: human relations in the home do not exist in the same way beyond death. Jesus distinguishes two ages and kinds of existence. Men are part of this age by the fact of physical birth, and of the age to come by resurrection (v. 36; Rom.1.4). **38:** God is not frustrated by physical death. **39:** Mk.12.28. **40:** Mk.12.34; Mt.22.46.

God of Isaac and the God of Jacob. [38] Now he is not God of the dead, but of the living; for all live to him." [39] And some of the scribes answered, "Teacher, you have spoken well." [40] For they no longer dared to ask him any question.

41 But he said to them, "How can they say that the Christ is David's son? [42] For David himself says in the Book of Psalms,

'The Lord said to my Lord,
Sit at my right hand,
[43] till I make thy enemies a stool for
    thy feet.'
[44] David thus calls him Lord; so how is he his son?"

45 And in the hearing of all the people he said to his disciples, [46] "Beware of the scribes, who like to go about in long robes, and love salutations in the market places and the best seats in the synagogues and the places of honor at feasts, [47] who devour widows' houses and for a pretense make long prayers. They will receive the greater condemnation."

21 He looked up and saw the rich putting their gifts into the treasury; [2] and he saw a poor widow put in two copper coins. [3] And he said, "Truly I tell you, this poor widow has put in more than all of them; [4] for they all contributed out of their abundance, but she out of her poverty put in all the living that she had."

5 And as some spoke of the temple, how it was adorned with noble stones and offerings, he said, [6] "As for these things which you see, the days will come when there shall not be left here one stone upon another that will not be thrown down." [7] And they asked him, "Teacher, when will this be, and what will be the sign when this is about to take place?" [8] And he said, "Take heed that you are not led astray; for many will come in my name, saying, 'I am he!' and, 'The time is at hand!' Do not go after them. [9] And when you hear of wars and tumults, do not be terrified; for this must first take place, but the end will not be at once."

10 Then he said to them, "Nation will rise against nation, and kingdom against kingdom; [11] there will be great earthquakes, and in various places famines and pestilences; and there will be terrors and great signs from heaven. [12] But before all this they will lay their hands on you and persecute you, delivering you up to the synagogues and prisons, and you will be brought before kings and governors for my name's sake. [13] This will be a time for you to bear testimony. [14] Settle it therefore in your minds, not to meditate beforehand how to answer; [15] for I will give you a mouth and wisdom, which none of your adversaries will be able to withstand or contradict. [16] You will be delivered up even by parents and brothers and kinsmen and friends, and some of you they will put to death; [17] you will be hated by all for my name's sake. [18] But not a hair of your head will perish. [19] By your endurance you will gain your lives.

20 "But when you see Jerusalem

20.41–44: David's son (Mt.22.41–46; Mk.12.35–37). **42**: Ps.110.1; see Mt.22.44 n. **44**: The question is: How can the Messiah be David's descendant if David calls him *Lord?*
    20.45–47: On pride and humility. 45: Mt.23.1; Mk.12.37. **46**: Mt.23.6; see Mk.12.39 n.; Lk.11.43; 14.7–11.
    21.1–4: The widow's offering (Mk.12.41–44). **1**: *The treasury* refers here to a container to receive offerings; in Jn.8.20 to a room in the temple. **2**: The *copper* coin (lepton) was of little monetary value (see 12.59 n.) but of great spiritual significance because of its cost to this giver.
    21.5–7: Destruction of the temple foretold (Mt.24.1–3; Mk.13.1–2). **5**: See Mt.24.1 n. **6**: See Mk.13.2 n. **7**: 17.20; Acts 1.6.
    21.8–36: On the end of the age (Mt.24.4–36; Mk.13.3–37). **8**: 17.23; Mk.13.21; 1 Jn.2.18. **10**: 2 Chr.15.6; Is.19.2. **12–17**: Mt.10.17–22. **12**: Acts 25.24; Jn.16.2. **13**: Phil.1.12. **14–15**: 12.11–12. **16**: 12.52–53. **17**: Mt.10.22; Jn.15.18–25. **18**: 12.7; Mt.10.30; Acts 27.34; 1 Sam. 14.45. **19**: *Gain your lives*, or "win your souls." Mk.13.13; Mt.10.22; Rev.2.7. **20–22**: 19.41–44;

surrounded by armies, then know that its desolation has come near. ²¹ Then let those who are in Judea flee to the mountains, and let those who are inside the city depart, and let not those who are out in the country enter it; ²² for these are days of vengeance, to fulfil all that is written. ²³ Alas for those who are with child and for those who give suck in those days! For great distress shall be upon the earth and wrath upon this people; ²⁴ they will fall by the edge of the sword, and be led captive among all nations; and Jerusalem will be trodden down by the Gentiles, until the times of the Gentiles are fulfilled.

25 "And there will be signs in sun and moon and stars, and upon the earth distress of nations in perplexity at the roaring of the sea and the waves, ²⁶ men fainting with fear and with foreboding of what is coming on the world; for the powers of the heavens will be shaken. ²⁷ And then they will see the Son of man coming in a cloud with power and great glory. ²⁸ Now when these things begin to take place, look up and raise your heads, because your redemption is drawing near."

29 And he told them a parable: "Look at the fig tree, and all the trees; ³⁰ as soon as they come out in leaf, you see for yourselves and know that the summer is already near. ³¹ So also, when you see these things taking place, you know that the kingdom of God is near. ³² Truly, I say to you, this generation will not pass away till all has taken place. ³³ Heaven and earth will pass away, but my words will not pass away.

34 "But take heed to yourselves lest your hearts be weighed down with dissipation and drunkenness and cares of this life, and that day come upon you suddenly like a snare; ³⁵ for it will come upon all who dwell upon the face of the whole earth. ³⁶ But watch at all times, praying that you may have strength to escape all these things that will take place, and to stand before the Son of man."

37 And every day he was teaching in the temple, but at night he went out and lodged on the mount called Olivet. ³⁸ And early in the morning all the people came to him in the temple to hear him.

22 Now the feast of Unleavened Bread drew near, which is called the Passover. ² And the chief priests and the scribes were seeking how to put him to death; for they feared the people.

3 Then Satan entered into Judas called Iscariot, who was of the number of the twelve; ⁴ he went away and conferred with the chief priests and officers how he might betray him to them. ⁵ And they were glad, and engaged to give him money. ⁶ So he agreed, and sought an opportunity to betray him to them in the absence of the multitude.

7 Then came the day of Unleavened Bread, on which the passover lamb had to be sacrificed. ⁸ So Jesus*ʰ* sent Peter and John, saying, "Go and prepare the passover for us, that we may eat it." ⁹ They said to him, "Where will you have us prepare it?" ¹⁰ He said to them, "Behold, when you have entered the city, a man carrying a jar

h Greek *he*

23.28–31; 17.31. **24:** Rom.11.25; Is.63.18; Dan.8.13; Rev.11.2. *The times of the Gentiles* represent spiritual opportunity that God previously had given Jews and now extends to non-Jews (20.16; Mk.13.10; Rom.11.25). **25:** Rev.6.12–13; Is.13.10; Jl.2.10; Zeph.1.15. **27:** Dan.7.13–14. **28:** *Redemption*, 2.38; Eph.4.30. **33:** 16.17. **34:** 8.14; 12.22,45; Mk.4.19; 1 Th.5.6–7. **36:** Mt.7.21–23; Mk.13.33; 2 Cor.5.10. **37:** Mt.21.17; Mk.11.19; Lk.19.47. **38:** See Jn.7.52 note *r*.
 22.1–23.56: Jesus' death (Mt.26.1–27.66; Mk.14.1–15.47; Jn.13.1–19.42). **22.1–2:** Mt.26.2–5; Mk.14.1–2; Jn.11.47–53. **3–6:** Mt.26.14–16; Mk.14.10–11; Jn.13.2. **5:** See Mt.26.15 n.
 22.7–38: The Last Supper. 7–13: Mt.26.17–19; Mk.14.12–16. **7:** Ex.12.18–20; Dt.16.5–8.
 10: The plans rest on some prearrangement, apparently; a man carrying a jar of water would be doing woman's work and would be readily noticeable. The procedure hid the intended place of

of water will meet you; follow him into the house which he enters, [11] and tell the householder, 'The Teacher says to you, Where is the guest room, where I am to eat the passover with my disciples?' [12] And he will show you a large upper room furnished; there make ready." [13] And they went, and found it as he had told them; and they prepared the passover.

14 And when the hour came, he sat at table, and the apostles with him. [15] And he said to them, "I have earnestly desired to eat this passover with you before I suffer; [16] for I tell you I shall not eat it[i] until it is fulfilled in the kingdom of God." [17] And he took a cup, and when he had given thanks he said, "Take this, and divide it among yourselves; [18] for I tell you that from now on I shall not drink of the fruit of the vine until the kingdom of God comes." [19] And he took bread, and when he had given thanks he broke it and gave it to them, saying, "This is my body which is given for you. Do this in remembrance of me." [20] And likewise the cup after supper, saying, "This cup which is poured out for you is the new covenant in my blood.[j] [21] But behold the hand of him who betrays me is with me on the table. [22] For the Son of man goes as it has been determined; but woe to that man by whom he is betrayed!" [23] And they began to question one another, which of them it was that would do this.

24 A dispute also arose among them, which of them was to be regarded as the greatest. [25] And he said to them, "The kings of the Gentiles exercise lordship over them; and those in authority over them are called benefactors. [26] But not so with you; rather let the greatest among you become as the youngest, and the leader as one who serves. [27] For which is the greater, one who sits at table, or one who serves? Is it not the one who sits at table? But I am among you as one who serves.

28 "You are those who have continued with me in my trials; [29] and I assign to you, as my Father assigned to me, a kingdom, [30] that you may eat and drink at my table in my kingdom, and sit on thrones judging the twelve tribes of Israel.

31 "Simon, Simon, behold, Satan demanded to have you,[k] that he might sift you[k] like wheat, [32] but I have prayed for you that your faith may not fail; and when you have turned again, strengthen your brethren." [33] And he said to him, "Lord, I am ready to go with you to prison and to death." [34] He said, "I tell you, Peter, the cock will not crow this day, until you three times deny that you know me."

35 And he said to them, "When I sent you out with no purse or bag or

i Other ancient authorities read *never eat it again*
j Other authorities omit, in whole or in part, verses 19b–20 (*which is given . . . in my blood*)
k The Greek word for *you* here is plural; in verse 32 it is singular

the meal from Jesus' enemies. **11:** The identity of the householder is unknown (see Mk.14.51 n.). **12:** The *upper room* was on the second floor, probably served by an outside staircase. **14–23:** Mt.26.20–29; Mk.14.17–25; Jn.13.21–30. **14:** *The hour*, of the meal, after sundown. **15:** 12.49–50. **16:** Jesus thinks of the meal as pointing forward to the meal celebrating the fulfilling of God's kingdom (13.28–29; 14.15; 22.28–30). **17:** Some Jewish meals included prayers over the cup of wine and several such prayers might be offered during the meal (see v. 20). Luke's order of events may be related to this fact, or to variations among early Christians in the way they observed the Lord's Supper. Jesus transformed a Jewish devotional meal into a continuing expression of association with himself in death and victory. **19:** 1 Cor.11.23–26. **21:** Ps.41.9; Jn.13.21–30. **24–30:** Mt.20.25–28; Mk.10.42–45. **24:** 9.46; Mk.9.34; Jn.13.3–16. **25:** *Benefactors*, a title bestowed on Hellenistic kings. **26:** See Mk.9.35 n. **28:** *My trials*, 4.13; Heb.2.18; 4.15. **29:** Mk.14.25; Heb.9.20. **30:** Mk. 10.37; Rev.3.21; 20.4. **31–34:** Mt.26.33–35; Mk.14.29–31; Jn.13.37–38. **31:** Job.1.6–12; Am.9.9. See note *k*. **34:** Vv. 54–62. **35:** 10.4. **36:** The *sword* apparently meant to Jesus a preparation to live by one's own resources against hostility. The natural meaning of v. 38 is that the disciples supposed he spoke of an actual sword, only to learn that two swords were sufficient for the whole enterprise, i.e. were not to be used at all. **37:** Is.53.12.

sandals, did you lack anything?" They said, "Nothing." [36] He said to them, "But now, let him who has a purse take it, and likewise a bag. And let him who has no sword sell his mantle and buy one. [37] For I tell you that this scripture must be fulfilled in me, 'And he was reckoned with transgressors'; for what is written about me has its fulfilment." [38] And they said, "Look, Lord, here are two swords." And he said to them, "It is enough."

[39] And he came out, and went, as was his custom, to the Mount of Olives; and the disciples followed him. [40] And when he came to the place he said to them, "Pray that you may not enter into temptation." [41] And he withdrew from them about a stone's throw, and knelt down and prayed, [42] "Father, if thou art willing, remove this cup from me; nevertheless not my will, but thine, be done."[l] [45] And when he rose from prayer, he came to the disciples and found them sleeping for sorrow, [46] and he said to them, "Why do you sleep? Rise and pray that you may not enter into temptation."

[47] While he was still speaking, there came a crowd, and the man called Judas, one of the twelve, was leading them. He drew near to Jesus to kiss him; [48] but Jesus said to him, "Judas, would you betray the Son of man with a kiss?" [49] And when those who were about him saw what would follow, they said, "Lord, shall we strike with the sword?" [50] And one of them struck the slave of the high priest and cut off his right ear. [51] But Jesus said, "No more of this!" And he touched his ear and healed him. [52] Then Jesus said to the chief priests and officers of

the temple and elders, who had come out against him, "Have you come out as against a robber, with swords and clubs? [53] When I was with you day after day in the temple, you did not lay hands on me. But this is your hour, and the power of darkness."

[54] Then they seized him and led him away, bringing him into the high priest's house. Peter followed at a distance; [55] and when they had kindled a fire in the middle of the courtyard and sat down together, Peter sat among them. [56] Then a maid, seeing him as he sat in the light and gazing at him, said, "This man also was with him." [57] But he denied it, saying, "Woman, I do not know him." [58] And a little later some one else saw him and said, "You also are one of them." But Peter said, "Man, I am not." [59] And after an interval of about an hour still another insisted, saying, "Certainly this man also was with him; for he is a Galilean." [60] But Peter said, "Man, I do not know what you are saying." And immediately, while he was still speaking, the cock crowed. [61] And the Lord turned and looked at Peter. And Peter remembered the word of the Lord, how he had said to him, "Before the cock crows today, you will deny me three times." [62] And he went out and wept bitterly.

[63] Now the men who were holding Jesus mocked him and beat him; [64] they also blindfolded him and asked him, "Prophesy! Who is it that

---

Other ancient authorities add verses 43 and 44:
[43]And there appeared to him an angel from heaven, strengthening him. [44]And being in an agony he prayed more earnestly; and his sweat became like great drops of blood falling down upon the ground.

22.39–53: Gethsemane. 39–46: Mt.26.30,36–46; Mk.14.26,32–42. **39:** Jn.18.1–2. **41:** Heb.5.7–8; Lk.11.4. **42:** *Cup,* metaphor for that which is allotted by God, whether blessing (Ps. 16.5; 116.13) or judgement (Is.51.17; Lam.4.21). It here refers to Jesus' suffering and death; cf. Mt.20.22; Mk.10.38. **43–44:** Although it is probable that these verses were not part of the original Gospel of Luke (since important early manuscripts lack them), they were known to Christian writers of the second century and reflect tradition from the first century concerning the sufferings of Jesus. **43:** Mt.4.11; see Acts 12.15 n. **44:** 2 Cor.8.9; Phil.2.6–8; Heb.2.9,17–18; 4.15; 5.8; 1 Pet. 2.21–24;4.1. **47–53:** Mt.26.47–56; Mk.14.43–52; Jn.18.3–11. **47:** See Mt.26.50 n. **52:** Only Luke says that the prospect of arresting Jesus had attracted the leaders of the Jewish religion (compare Mt.26.47,57; Mk.14.43; Jn.18.3). **22.54–71: Jesus before Caiaphas. 54–55:** Jn.18.12–16. **56–62:** Jn.18.16–18,25–27. **59:** See Mt.26.73 n. **61:** 7.13; 22.34. **63–65:** Jn.18.22–24. **66:** See Mt.27.1 n.

struck you?" 65 And they spoke many other words against him, reviling him.

66 When day came, the assembly of the elders of the people gathered together, both chief priests and scribes; and they led him away to their council, and they said, 67 "If you are the Christ, tell us." But he said to them, "If I tell you, you will not believe; 68 and if I ask you, you will not answer. 69 But from now on the Son of man shall be seated at the right hand of the power of God." 70 And they all said, "Are you the Son of God, then?" And he said to them, "You say that I am." 71 And they said, "What further testimony do we need? We have heard it ourselves from his own lips."

23 Then the whole company of them arose, and brought him before Pilate. 2 And they began to accuse him, saying, "We found this man perverting our nation, and forbidding us to give tribute to Caesar, and saying that he himself is Christ a king." 3 And Pilate asked him, "Are you the King of the Jews?" And he answered him, "You have said so." 4 And Pilate said to the chief priests and the multitudes, "I find no crime in this man." 5 But they were urgent, saying, "He stirs up the people, teaching throughout all Judea, from Galilee even to this place."

6 When Pilate heard this, he asked whether the man was a Galilean. 7 And when he learned that he belonged to Herod's jurisdiction, he sent him over to Herod, who was himself in Jerusalem at that time. 8 When Herod saw Jesus, he was very glad, for he had long desired to see him, because he had heard about him, and he was hoping to see some sign done by him. 9 So he questioned him at some length; but he made

no answer. 10 The chief priests and the scribes stood by, vehemently accusing him. 11 And Herod with his soldiers treated him with contempt and mocked him; then, arraying him in gorgeous apparel, he sent him back to Pilate. 12 And Herod and Pilate became friends with each other that very day, for before this they had been at enmity with each other.

13 Pilate then called together the chief priests and the rulers and the people, 14 and said to them, "You brought me this man as one who was perverting the people; and after examining him before you, behold, I did not find this man guilty of any of your charges against him; 15 neither did Herod, for he sent him back to us. Behold, nothing deserving death has been done by him; 16 I will therefore chastise him and release him."*m*

18 But they all cried out together, "Away with this man, and release to us Barab′bas"– 19 a man who had been thrown into prison for an insurrection started in the city, and for murder. 20 Pilate addressed them once more, desiring to release Jesus; 21 but they shouted out, "Crucify, crucify him!" 22 A third time he said to them, "Why, what evil has he done? I have found in him no crime deserving death; I will therefore chastise him and release him." 23 But they were urgent, demanding with loud cries that he should be crucified. And their voices prevailed. 24 So Pilate gave sentence that their demand should be granted. 25 He released the man who had been thrown into prison for insurrection and mur-

m Here, or after verse 19, other ancient authorities add verse 17, *Now he was obliged to release one man to them at the festival*

23.1–5,13–25: Jesus before Pilate. 1: Mt.27.1–2; Mk.15.1; Jn.18.28. **2:** 20.25. The charge is phrased to sound like treason. **3:** Mt.27.11–12; Mk.15.2–3; Jn.18.29–38; Lk.22.70. **4:** 23.14, 22,41; Mt.27.24; Jn.19.4,6; Acts 13.28. Pilate refused to take religious ideas in a political sense. Here and in the following verses Luke seems anxious to show that Pilate sought to free Jesus, but yielded at length to pressures. **6–12: Jesus before Herod Antipas.** This episode is reported only by Luke. *Herod* was a son of Herod the Great (see 3.1 n.). **8:** 9.9; Acts 4.27–28. **9:** Mk. 15.5. **11:** Mk.15.17–19; Jn.19.2–3. **14:** Vv. 4,22,41. **16:** Jn.19.12–14. **18–25:** Mt.27.20–26; Mk.15.11–15; Jn.18.38–40; 19.14–16; Acts 3.13–14.

der, whom they asked for; but Jesus he delivered up to their will.

26 And as they led him away, they seized one Simon of Cyre'ne, who was coming in from the country, and laid on him the cross, to carry it behind Jesus. ²⁷ And there followed him a great multitude of the people, and of women who bewailed and lamented him. ²⁸ But Jesus turning to them said, "Daughters of Jerusalem, do not weep for me, but weep for yourselves and for your children. ²⁹ For behold, the days are coming when they will say, 'Blessed are the barren, and the wombs that never bore, and the breasts that never gave suck!' ³⁰ Then they will begin to say to the mountains, 'Fall on us'; and to the hills, 'Cover us.' ³¹ For if they do this when the wood is green, what will happen when it is dry?"

32 Two others also, who were criminals, were led away to be put to death with him. ³³ And when they came to the place which is called The Skull, there they crucified him, and the criminals, one on the right and one on the left. ³⁴ And Jesus said, "Father, forgive them; for they know not what they do."*n* And they cast lots to divide his garments. ³⁵ And the people stood by, watching; but the rulers scoffed at him, saying, "He saved others; let him save himself, if he is the Christ of God, his Chosen One!" ³⁶ The soldiers also mocked him, coming up and offering him vinegar, ³⁷ and saying, "If you are the King of the Jews, save yourself!" ³⁸ There was also an inscription over him,*o*

"This is the King of the Jews."

39 One of the criminals who were hanged railed at him, saying, "Are you not the Christ? Save yourself and us!" ⁴⁰ But the other rebuked him, saying, "Do you not fear God, since you are under the same sentence of condemnation? ⁴¹ And we indeed justly; for we are receiving the due reward of our deeds; but this man has done nothing wrong." ⁴² And he said, "Jesus, remember me when you come into*p* your kingdom." ⁴³ And he said to him, "Truly, I say to you, today you will be with me in Paradise."

44 It was now about the sixth hour, and there was darkness over the whole land*q* until the ninth hour, ⁴⁵ while the sun's light failed;*r* and the curtain of the temple was torn in two. ⁴⁶ Then Jesus, crying with a loud voice, said, "Father, into thy hands I commit my spirit!" And having said this he breathed his last. ⁴⁷ Now when the centurion saw what had taken place, he praised God, and said, "Certainly this man was innocent!" ⁴⁸ And all the multitudes who assembled to see the sight, when they saw what had taken place, returned home beating their breasts. ⁴⁹ And all his acquaintances and the women who had followed him from Galilee stood at a distance and saw these things.

n Other ancient authorities omit the sentence *And Jesus . . . what they do*
o Other ancient authorities add *in letters of Greek and Latin and Hebrew*
p Other ancient authorities read *in*
q Or *earth*
r Or *the sun was eclipsed.* Other ancient authorities read *the sun was darkened*

23.26–56: The crucifixion. 26: See Mt.27.32 n.; Mk.15.21 n.; Jn.19.17. **28–32:** 21.23–24; 19.41–44. **30:** Hos.10.8. **31:** A proverbial saying which, in this context, probably means: If the innocent Jesus meets such a fate, what will be the fate of the guilty Jerusalem (v. 28)? Compare 1 Pet.4.17–18. **33–43:** Mt.27.33–44; Mk.15.22–32; Jn.19.17–24. **34:** Num.15.27–31; Acts 7.60; Ps.22.18. **35:** 4.23. **36:** Ps.69.21; see Mt.27.48 n.; Mk.15.23. **41:** Vv. 4,14,22. **42:** The robber's appeal may be based on the charge against Jesus (vv. 2,3,38); he thinks in terms of 21.27–28. Jesus promises him much more than he had asked, intimating also that God's kingly power is a present reality, not merely future (Mt.6.10). *Paradise* (like "Abraham's bosom" in 16.22) was a contemporary Jewish term for the lodging place of the righteous dead prior to resurrection. **43:** 2 Cor.12.3; Rev.2.7. **44–49:** Mt.27.45–56; Mk.15.33–41; Jn.19.25–30. **44:** See Mt.27.45 n. **45:** Ex.26.31–35; Heb.9.8; 10.19–20. *The sun's light failed*, the translation is uncertain; see note *r*. **46:** Ps.31.5. **48:** The cause of this popular agitation is not clear (Zech.12.10). **49:** 8.1–3;

50 Now there was a man named Joseph from the Jewish town of Ari-mathe′a. He was a member of the council, a good and righteous man, ⁵¹ who had not consented to their purpose and deed, and he was looking for the kingdom of God. ⁵² This man went to Pilate and asked for the body of Jesus. ⁵³ Then he took it down and wrapped it in a linen shroud, and laid him in a rock-hewn tomb, where no one had ever yet been laid. ⁵⁴ It was the day of Preparation, and the sabbath was beginning.ˢ ⁵⁵ The women who had come with him from Galilee followed, and saw the tomb, and how his body was laid; ⁵⁶ then they returned, and prepared spices and ointments.

On the sabbath they rested according to the commandment.

24 But on the first day of the week, at early dawn, they went to the tomb, taking the spices which they had prepared. ² And they found the stone rolled away from the tomb, ³ but when they went in they did not find the body.ᵗ ⁴ While they were perplexed about this, behold, two men stood by them in dazzling apparel; ⁵ and as they were frightened and bowed their faces to the ground, the men said to them, "Why do you seek the living among the dead?ᵘ ⁶ Remember how he told you, while he was still in Galilee, ⁷ that the Son of man must be delivered into the hands of sinful men, and be crucified, and on the third day rise." ⁸ And they remembered his words, ⁹ and returning from the tomb they told all this to the eleven and to all the rest. ¹⁰ Now it was Mary Mag′-dalene and Jo-an′na and Mary the mother of James and the other women with them who told this to the apostles; ¹¹ but these words seemed to them an idle tale, and they did not believe them.ᵛ

13 That very day two of them were going to a village named Emma′us, about seven milesʷ from Jerusalem, ¹⁴ and talking with each other about all these things that had happened. ¹⁵ While they were talking and discussing together, Jesus himself drew near and went with them. ¹⁶ But their eyes were kept from recognizing him. ¹⁷ And he said to them, "What is this conversation which you are holding with each other as you walk?" And they stood still, looking sad. ¹⁸ Then one of them, named Cle′opas, answered him, "Are you the only visitor to Jerusalem who does not know the things that have happened there in these days?" ¹⁹ And he said to them, "What things?" And they said to him, "Concerning Jesus of Nazareth, who was a prophet mighty in deed and word before God and all the people, ²⁰ and how our chief priests and rulers delivered him up to be condemned to death, and crucified him. ²¹ But we had hoped that he was the one to redeem Israel. Yes, and besides all this, it is now the third day since this happened. ²² Moreover, some women of our company amazed us. They were at the tomb early in the morning ²³ and did not find his body;

s Greek *was dawning*
t Other ancient authorities add *of the Lord Jesus*
u Other ancient authorities add *He is not here, but has risen*
v Other ancient authorities add verse 12, *But Peter rose and ran to the tomb; stooping and looking in, he saw the linen cloths by themselves; and he went home wondering at what had happened*
w Greek *sixty stadia;* some ancient authorities read *a hundred and sixty stadia*

23.55–56; 24.10; Ps.38.11. **50–56:** Mt.27.57–61; Mk.15.42–47; Jn.19.38–42; Acts 13.29. **51:** The council was the Sanhedrin (see Jn.11.47 n.). **52:** Mt.27.58. **53:** Acts 13.29. **54:** *The sabbath* began at sundown. Luke, having non-Jewish readers in mind, wishes to indicate the urgency of the burial in Jewish custom. **56:** Mk.16.1; Ex.12.16; 20.10.

    24.1–11: The first Easter (Mt.28.1–10; Mk.16.1–8; Jn.20.1,11–18). **1:** See Mk.16.1 n. **2:** See Mk.16.3 n. **4:** See Mk.16.5 n. **6:** 9.22; 13.32–33. *You* here suggests that Jesus' disciples as a group often included others than those of the inner circle. **9:** See Mt.28.8 n.; Mk.16.8. **10:** Mk.16.1; Lk.8.1–3; Jn.19.25; 20.2. **12:** This verse (see note *v*), though appearing in valuable ancient manuscripts, seems to be an addition to the original text of Luke based on Jn.20.3–10.

    24.13–35: On the road to Emmaus. 16: See Mt.16.17 n.; Jn.20.14; 21.4. The distinction is

and they came back saying that they had even seen a vision of angels, who said that he was alive. ²⁴ Some of those who were with us went to the tomb, and found it just as the women had said; but him they did not see." ²⁵ And he said to them, "O foolish men, and slow of heart to believe all that the prophets have spoken! ²⁶ Was it not necessary that the Christ should suffer these things and enter into his glory?" ²⁷ And beginning with Moses and all the prophets, he interpreted to them in all the scriptures the things concerning himself.

28 So they drew near to the village to which they were going. He appeared to be going further, ²⁹ but they constrained him, saying, "Stay with us, for it is toward evening and the day is now far spent." So he went in to stay with them. ³⁰ When he was at table with them, he took the bread and blessed, and broke it, and gave it to them. ³¹ And their eyes were opened and they recognized him; and he vanished out of their sight. ³² They said to each other, "Did not our hearts burn within us*c* while he talked to us on the road, while he opened to us the scriptures?" ³³ And they rose that same hour and returned to Jerusalem; and they found the eleven gathered together and those who were with them, ³⁴ who said, "The Lord has risen indeed, and has appeared to Simon!"

³⁵ Then they told what had happened on the road, and how he was known to them in the breaking of the bread.

36 As they were saying this, Jesus himself stood among them.*x* ³⁷ But they were startled and frightened, and supposed that they saw a spirit. ³⁸ And he said to them, "Why are you troubled, and why do questionings rise in your hearts? ³⁹ See my hands and my feet, that it is I myself; handle me, and see; for a spirit has not flesh and bones as you see that I have."*y* ⁴¹ And while they still disbelieved for joy, and wondered, he said to them, "Have you anything here to eat?" ⁴² They gave him a piece of broiled fish, ⁴³ and he took it and ate before them.

44 Then he said to them, "These are my words which I spoke to you, while I was still with you, that everything written about me in the law of Moses and the prophets and the psalms must be fulfilled." ⁴⁵ Then he opened their minds to understand the scriptures, ⁴⁶ and said to them, "Thus it is written, that the Christ should suffer and on the third day rise from the dead, ⁴⁷ and that repentance and forgiveness of sins should be preached in his name to all nations,*z* beginning from Jerusalem. ⁴⁸ You are witnesses of

c Other ancient authorities omit *within us*
x Other ancient authorities add *and said to them,* "Peace *to you!*"
y Other ancient authorities add verse 40, *And when he had said this, he showed them his hands and his feet*
z Or nations. *Beginning from Jerusalem you are witnesses*

---

between perception and recognition. **19:** Mt.21.11; Lk.7.16; 13.33; Acts 3.22; 10.38. **25:** Mk.12.24. **26:** *Necessary* because of the divine plan. **27:** *Moses,* the traditional author of the first five books of the Old Testament. *The prophets,* a major section of the Jewish Scriptures (see v. 44 n.; Mt.5.17 n.; Acts 28.23). **28:** Mk.6.48. **30:** Mk.6.41; 14.22; Lk.9.16; 22.19. **34:** Mk.16.7; 1 Cor.15.5. Peter's experience, doubtless of tremendous effect for the beginnings of Christianity, is not described.

24.36–53: Commissioning of the disciples. 36–43: Jn.20.19–23; 1 Cor.15.5. The experience with Jesus, affirmed in v. 36, is tentatively interpreted in v. 37 as encounter with the dead, but this explanation is rejected in v. 39. **39:** *Handle me,* 1 Jn.1.1. **44:** Vv. 26–27; Acts 28.23. The Psalms formed the opening, and the longest, part of the third division of the Jewish Scriptures (see p. xxi). **45:** 24.32. **46:** Hos.6.2; 1 Cor.15.3–4. **47:** Acts 1.4–8; Mt.28.19. **48:** 1.2; Acts 1.8. **49:** Acts 2.1–4; Jn.14.26; 20.21–23. The words allude to the energy of the Holy Spirit referred to in Jl.2.28–32 (compare Acts 2.1–21). The new age has begun but its power is not yet freely felt. **51:** Acts 1.9–11. **52–53:** Acts 1.12–14.

Supplementary Note: The words and passages printed as textual notes at 24.3 *t*, 5 *u*, 11 *v*, 36 *x*, 40 *y*, and 52 *b* have traditionally been accepted as part of the canonical Gospel of Luke and therefore as inspired Scripture.

these things. ⁴⁹ And behold, I send the promise of my Father upon you; but stay in the city, until you are clothed with power from on high."

50 Then he led them out as far as Bethany, and lifting up his hands he blessed them. ⁵¹ While he blessed them, he parted from them, and was carried up into heaven.^a ⁵² And they^b returned to Jerusalem with great joy, ⁵³ and were continually in the temple blessing God.

a Other ancient authorities omit *and was carried up into heaven*
b Other ancient authorities add *worshiped him, and*

JOHN

The Fourth Gospel explains the mystery of the person of Jesus. Like other men, he is yet unlike them, standing above them in unique, solitary grandeur. Whence this uniqueness? The Synoptic Gospels present it, but do not account for it. John takes us behind the scenes of Jesus' earthly ministry, letting us see the eternal origin and divine nature of this Man who was more than man. He was eternally present with God, active in creating the world, the source of the moral and spiritual nature ("life," "light") of man. Hence, when he became Man, he "made . . . known" the eternal God, whom "no one has ever seen" (1.14,18).

As do the other Evangelists, John records real events, but goes beyond them in interpreting these events. He uses symbols from common experience – such as bread, water, light, life, shepherd, door – and contrasting images from the thought-world of the time – such as light/darkness, truth/lies, love/hatred – to make the meaning of Christ clear and gripping. After a magnificent prologue (1.1–18) he sets forth Jesus Christ as the object of faith (1.19–4.54), depicts his conflict with unbelievers (chs. 5–12), his fellowship with believers (chs. 13–17), his death and resurrection (chs. 18–20), and concludes with an epilogue (ch. 21).

Who is the author? Tradition says it was the apostle John. Many scholars, however, suggest a disciple of John who recorded his preaching as Mark did that of Peter. In any case, the historic basis of the Gospel has become increasingly recognized. When it appeared, whether around A.D. 90–100 or much earlier as some now hold, it was accepted as an authentic and apostolic testimony to Jesus (21.24), written that men might "believe that Jesus is the Christ, the Son of God," and thus "have life in his name" (20.31).

I N THE BEGINNING WAS THE WORD, and the Word was with God, and the Word was God. ² He was in the beginning with God; ³ all things were made through him, and without him was not anything made that was made. ⁴ In him was life,ᵃ and the life was the light of men. ⁵ The light shines in the darkness, and the darkness has not overcome it.

6 There was a man sent from God, whose name was John. ⁷ He came for testimony, to bear witness to the light, that all might believe through him. ⁸ He was not the light, but came to bear witness to the light.

9 The true light that enlightens every man was coming into the world.

¹⁰ He was in the world, and the world was made through him, yet the world knew him not. ¹¹ He came to his own home, and his own people received him not. ¹² But to all who received him, who believed in his name, he gave power to become children of God; ¹³ who were born, not of blood nor of the will of the flesh nor of the will of man, but of God.

14 And the Word became flesh and dwelt among us, full of grace and truth; we have beheld his glory, glory as of the only Son from the Father. ¹⁵ (John bore witness to him, and cried, "This was he of whom I said,

a Or *was not anything made. That which has been made was life in him*

1.1–18: The Prologue. 1–2: The *Word* (Greek "logos") of God is more than speech; it is God in action, creating (Gen.1.3; Ps.33.6), revealing (Amos 3.7–8), redeeming (Ps.107.19–20). Jesus is this *Word* (v. 14). He was eternal (*in the beginning;* compare Gen.1.1); personal (*with God*); divine (*was God*). *Was*, not "became" (contrast v. 14). 3: He was sole agent of creation (Gen. 1.1; Pr.8.27–30; Col.1.16–17; Heb.1.2). 4: Apart from him both physical (Col.1.17) and spiritual life would recede into nothingness (5.39–40; 8.12). 5: *Darkness* is total evil in conflict with God; it cannot *overcome*. 6–8: John, climaxing the Old Testament prophets, was *sent* (commissioned by God, Mal.3.1) to point to Jesus (vv. 19–34). 9: *True light* is real, underived light, contrasted not with false light, but with such as John, who was but a lamp (5.35). 11: *His own people*, the Jews. 14–17: God's *glory* dwelt ("tabernacled") in the *flesh* (human nature) of Jesus,

'He who comes after me ranks before me, for he was before me.' ") ¹⁶ And from his fulness have we all received, grace upon grace. ¹⁷ For the law was given through Moses; grace and truth came through Jesus Christ. ¹⁸ No one has ever seen God; the only Son,ᵇ who is in the bosom of the Father, he has made him known.

19 And this is the testimony of John, when the Jews sent priests and Levites from Jerusalem to ask him, "Who are you?" ²⁰ He confessed, he did not deny, but confessed, "I am not the Christ." ²¹ And they asked him, "What then? Are you Eli′jah?" He said, "I am not." "Are you the prophet?" And he answered, "No." ²² They said to him then, "Who are you? Let us have an answer for those who sent us. What do you say about yourself?" ²³ He said, "I am the voice of one crying in the wilderness, 'Make straight the way of the Lord,' as the prophet Isaiah said."

24 Now they had been sent from the Pharisees. ²⁵ They asked him, "Then why are you baptizing, if you are neither the Christ, nor Eli′jah, nor the prophet?" ²⁶ John answered them, "I baptize with water; but among you stands one whom you do not know, ²⁷ even he who comes after me, the thong of whose sandal I am not worthy to untie." ²⁸ This took place in Bethany beyond the Jordan, where John was baptizing.

29 The next day he saw Jesus coming toward him, and said, "Behold, the Lamb of God, who takes away the sin of the world! ³⁰ This is he of whom I said, 'After me comes a man who ranks before me, for he was before me.' ³¹ I myself did not know him; but for this I came baptizing with water, that he might be revealed to Israel." ³² And John bore witness, "I saw the Spirit descend as a dove from heaven, and it remained on him. ³³ I myself did not know him; but he who sent me to baptize with water said to me, 'He on whom you see the Spirit descend and remain, this is he who baptizes with the Holy Spirit.' ³⁴ And I have seen and have borne witness that this is the Son of God."

35 The next day again John was standing with two of his disciples; ³⁶ and he looked at Jesus as he walked, and said, "Behold, the Lamb of God!" ³⁷ The two disciples heard him say this, and they followed Jesus. ³⁸ Jesus turned, and saw them following, and said to them, "What do you seek?" And they said to him, "Rabbi" (which means Teacher), "where are you staying?" ³⁹ He said to them, "Come and see." They came and saw where he was staying; and they stayed with him that day, for it was about the tenth hour. ⁴⁰ One of the two who heard John speak, and followed him, was Andrew, Simon Peter's brother. ⁴¹ He first found his brother Simon, and said to him, "We have found the Messiah" (which means Christ). ⁴² He brought him to Jesus. Jesus looked at him, and said, "So you are Simon the

ᵇ Other ancient authorities read *God*

---

as did his *grace* (redeeming love) and *truth* (faithfulness to his promises). These are available to *all*, exhaustless (*grace upon grace*), a fulfilment of the *law* of *Moses*. **18:** *The bosom of the Father*, complete communion (vv. 1–2). Men *see* God in Jesus (14.9).

1.19–34: The testimony of John. 19: *Jews*, the religious authorities. **20:** *The Christ*, the Messiah. **21:** *Elijah* (2 Kg.2.11) was expected to return to prepare the Messiah's way (Mal.4.5). John is unconscious of this role, but Jesus later ascribed it to him (see Mt.11.14 n.; Mk.9.13 n.). *The prophet* was likewise an expected Messianic forerunner (6.14; 7.40; see Dt.18.15). **23:** As a *voice* John fulfils a prophetic role announcing the Messiah's coming (Is.40.3). **25:** *Why are you baptizing*, performing an official rite, without official status? **27:** *To untie a sandal thong* was a slave's task. **29:** *Lamb*, Ex. ch. 12; Is.53.7. *Of God*, provided by God. **30:** He outranks me, *for he was* (existed) *before me*. **31–33:** John's knowledge of Jesus' significance was given him by God at the baptism. **34:** *Son of God*, the Messiah (v. 49; 11.27).

1.35–51: The testimony of Jesus' first disciples. 39: *Come and see*, a call to personal following

son of John? You shall be called Cephas" (which means Peter[c]).

43 The next day Jesus decided to go to Galilee. And he found Philip and said to him, "Follow me." [44] Now Philip was from Beth-sa'ida, the city of Andrew and Peter. [45] Philip found Nathan'a-el, and said to him, "We have found him of whom Moses in the law and also the prophets wrote, Jesus of Nazareth, the son of Joseph." [46] Nathan'a-el said to him, "Can anything good come out of Nazareth?" Philip said to him, "Come and see." [47] Jesus saw Nathan'a-el coming to him, and said of him, "Behold, an Israelite indeed, in whom is no guile!" [48] Nathan'a-el said to him, "How do you know me?" Jesus answered him, "Before Philip called you, when you were under the fig tree, I saw you." [49] Nathan'a-el answered him, "Rabbi, you are the Son of God! You are the King of Israel!" [50] Jesus answered him, "Because I said to you, I saw you under the fig tree, do you believe? You shall see greater things than these." [51] And he said to him, "Truly, truly, I say to you, you will see heaven opened, and the angels of God ascending and descending upon the Son of man."

2 On the third day there was a marriage at Cana in Galilee, and the mother of Jesus was there; [2] Jesus also was invited to the marriage, with his disciples. [3] When the wine gave out, the mother of Jesus said to him, "They have no wine." [4] And Jesus said to her, "O woman, what have you to do with me? My hour has not yet come." [5] His mother said to the servants, "Do whatever he tells you." [6] Now six stone jars were standing there, for the Jewish rites of purification, each holding twenty or thirty gallons. [7] Jesus said to them, "Fill the jars with water." And they filled them up to the brim. [8] He said to them, "Now draw some out, and take it to the steward of the feast." So they took it. [9] When the steward of the feast tasted the water now become wine, and did not know where it came from (though the servants who had drawn the water knew), the steward of the feast called the bridegroom [10] and said to him, "Every man serves the good wine first; and when men have drunk freely, then the poor wine; but you have kept the good wine until now." [11] This, the first of his signs, Jesus did at Cana in Galilee, and manifested his glory; and his disciples believed in him.

12 After this he went down to Caper'na-um, with his mother and his brothers and his disciples; and there they stayed for a few days.

13 The Passover of the Jews was at hand, and Jesus went up to Jerusalem. [14] In the temple he found those who were selling oxen and sheep and pigeons, and the money-changers at their business. [15] And making a whip of cords, he drove them all, with the sheep and oxen, out of the temple; and he poured out the coins of the money-changers and overturned their tables.

c From the word for *rock* in Aramaic and Greek respectively

(8.12). *The tenth hour*, about 4 p.m. **42:** In Aramaic *Cephas* (Greek *Peter*) means *Rock*. **45:** *Moses . . . prophets*, the Old Testament points to Christ. **46:** *Nathanael*, probably the same person as Bartholomew (Mt.10.3; Mk.3.18; Lk.6.14), lived in Cana, near Nazareth (21.2). **47:** *No guile*, no qualities of Jacob before he became Israel (Gen.27.35; 32.28). **51:** What Jacob saw in vision (Gen.28.12) is now a reality in Jesus. *Son of man*, a messenger from heaven to make God known (3.13), and to be the final judge (5.27; see Mk.2.10 n.).

2.1–12: The wedding at Cana. 4: *Woman*, a term of solemn and respectful address (compare 19.26). The *hour* of Jesus' self-disclosure was determined by God, not by Mary's desires. His final manifestation was at the cross (7.30; 8.20; 12.23,27; 13.1; 17.1). **6:** *Rites of purification* were ceremonial, not hygienic. **8:** *Steward*, head-waiter or toastmaster. **11:** Jesus' miracles were not wonders to astound, but *signs* pointing to *his glory* (God's presence in him). *First*, for the second see 4.46–54. **12:** *Brothers*, see Mt.13.55 n.

2.13–25: The cleansing of the temple (compare Mt.21.12–17; Mk.11.15–19; Lk.19.45–48). **14:** Animals were sold for sacrifice; Roman money was changed into Jewish money to pay the temple tax. **15–16:** Not an outburst of temper, but the energy of righteousness against religious

16 And he told those who sold the pigeons, "Take these things away; you shall not make my Father's house a house of trade." 17 His disciples remembered that it was written, "Zeal for thy house will consume me." 18 The Jews then said to him, "What sign have you to show us for doing this?" 19 Jesus answered them, "Destroy this temple, and in three days I will raise it up." 20 The Jews then said, "It has taken forty-six years to build this temple, and will you raise it up in three days?" 21 But he spoke of the temple of his body. 22 When therefore he was raised from the dead, his disciples remembered that he had said this; and they believed the scripture and the word which Jesus had spoken.

23 Now when he was in Jerusalem at the Passover feast, many believed in his name when they saw the signs which he did; 24 but Jesus did not trust himself to them, 25 because he knew all men and needed no one to bear witness of man; for he himself knew what was in man.

3 Now there was a man of the Pharisees, named Nicode'mus, a ruler of the Jews. 2 This man came to Jesus*d* by night and said to him, "Rabbi, we know that you are a teacher come from God; for no one can do these signs that you do, unless God is with him." 3 Jesus answered him, "Truly, truly, I say to you, unless one is born anew,*e* he cannot see the kingdom of God." 4 Nicode'mus said to him, "How can a man be born when he is old? Can he enter a second time into his mother's womb and be born?" 5 Jesus answered,

"Truly, truly, I say to you, unless one is born of water and the Spirit, he cannot enter the kingdom of God. 6 That which is born of the flesh is flesh, and that which is born of the Spirit is spirit.*f* 7 Do not marvel that I said to you, 'You must be born anew.'*e* 8 The wind*f* blows where it wills, and you hear the sound of it, but you do not know whence it comes or whither it goes; so it is with every one who is born of the Spirit." 9 Nicode'mus said to him, "How can this be?" 10 Jesus answered him, "Are you a teacher of Israel, and yet you do not understand this? 11 Truly, truly, I say to you, we speak of what we know, and bear witness to what we have seen; but you do not receive our testimony. 12 If I have told you earthly things and you do not believe, how can you believe if I tell you heavenly things? 13 No one has ascended into heaven but he who descended from heaven, the Son of man.*g* 14 And as Moses lifted up the serpent in the wilderness, so must the Son of man be lifted up, 15 that whoever believes in him may have eternal life."*h*

16 For God so loved the world that he gave his only Son, that whoever believes in him should not perish but have eternal life. 17 For God sent the Son into the world, not to condemn the world, but that the world might be saved through him. 18 He who believes in him is not condemned; he who does not believe is condemned already, because he has not believed in the name

d Greek *him*   *e* Or *from above*
f The same Greek word means both *wind* and *spirit*
g Other ancient authorities add *who is in heaven*
h Some interpreters hold that the quotation continues through verse 21

---

leaders to whom religion had become a business. *My Father's house* is a claim to lordship. **17:** Ps.69.9. **23–25:** Faith which rests merely on *signs* and not on him to whom they point is shallow and unstable.

3.1–21: Jesus and official Judaism. 1: *The Pharisees* were the most devout of Jews. *A ruler*, a member of the Sanhedrin (see 11.47 n.). **3:** *The kingdom of God* is entered, not by moral achievement, but by a transformation wrought by God. **5:** Birth into the new order is through *water* (referring to baptism; 1.33; Eph.5.26) and *the Spirit* (Ezek.36.25–27; Tit.3.5). **6:** Like begets like. **8–9:** See note *f* and Ezek.37.5–10. **12:** *Earthly things*, such as the parable of the wind; *heavenly things*, supreme spiritual realities. **13–15:** Jesus *descended from heaven* to bring *eternal life* (participation in God's life), through being *lifted up* on the cross (Num.21.9). **16:** Luther called this verse "the Gospel in miniature." **17–20:** God's purpose is to save; men judge themselves by hiding their *evil deeds* from the *light* of Christ's holiness.

of the only Son of God. [19] And this is the judgment, that the light has come into the world, and men loved darkness rather than light, because their deeds were evil. [20] For every one who does evil hates the light, and does not come to the light, lest his deeds should be exposed. [21] But he who does what is true comes to the light, that it may be clearly seen that his deeds have been wrought in God.

22 After this Jesus and his disciples went into the land of Judea; there he remained with them and baptized. [23] John also was baptizing at Ae'non near Salim, because there was much water there; and people came and were baptized. [24] For John had not yet been put in prison.

25 Now a discussion arose between John's disciples and a Jew over purifying. [26] And they came to John, and said to him, "Rabbi, he who was with you beyond the Jordan, to whom you bore witness, here he is, baptizing, and all are going to him." [27] John answered, "No one can receive anything except what is given him from heaven. [28] You yourselves bear me witness, that I said, I am not the Christ, but I have been sent before him. [29] He who has the bride is the bridegroom; the friend of the bridegroom, who stands and hears him, rejoices greatly at the bridegroom's voice; therefore this joy of mine is now full. [30] He must increase, but I must decrease."[i]

31 He who comes from above is above all; he who is of the earth belongs to the earth, and of the earth he speaks; he who comes from heaven is above all. [32] He bears witness to what he has seen and heard, yet no one receives his testimony; [33] he who receives his testimony sets his seal to this, that God is true. [34] For he whom God has sent utters the words of God, for it is not by measure that he gives the Spirit; [35] the Father loves the Son, and has given all things into his hand. [36] He who believes in the Son has eternal life; he who does not obey the Son shall not see life, but the wrath of God rests upon him.

4 Now when the Lord knew that the Pharisees had heard that Jesus was making and baptizing more disciples than John [2] (although Jesus himself did not baptize, but only his disciples), [3] he left Judea and departed again to Galilee. [4] He had to pass through Sama'ria. [5] So he came to a city of Sama'ria, called Sy'char, near the field that Jacob gave to his son Joseph. [6] Jacob's well was there, and so Jesus, wearied as he was with his journey, sat down beside the well. It was about the sixth hour.

7 There came a woman of Sama'ria to draw water. Jesus said to her, "Give me a drink." [8] For his disciples had gone away into the city to buy food. [9] The Samaritan woman said to him, "How is it that you, a Jew, ask a drink of me, a woman of Sama'ria?" For Jews have no dealings with Samaritans. [10] Jesus answered her, "If you knew the gift of God, and who it is that is saying to you, 'Give me a drink,' you would have asked him, and he would have given you living water." [11] The woman said to him, "Sir, you have nothing to draw with, and the well

i Some interpreters hold that the quotation continues through verse 36

3.22–36: Further testimony of John (compare 1.19–34). **25:** *Purifying*, Jewish religious ceremonies. **27–29:** John was only the *friend of the bridegroom*, leading Israel, the bride, to Jesus, the bridegroom. He *rejoices* in their union (see Mk.2.19–20 n.). **32–35:** *No one*, a generalization about the Jews. The author and others do believe, and attest that Jesus authentically speaks *the words of God*. **36:** Unbelief is disobedience. *Wrath* is the consuming fire of God's holiness.
4.1–42: Jesus and the Samaritans. 1–3: *The Pharisees*, hostile to John, now turn on Jesus. **4:** *Samaria*, between Judea and Galilee, with a mixed people (see Acts 8.5 n.). **5:** Gen.33.19; 48.22; Jos.24.32. **6:** *Wearied*, shows Jesus' humanity. *The sixth hour*, about noon. **5:** Gen. 33.19; 48.22; Jos.24.32. **9:** Rabbis avoided speaking to a *woman* in public (v. 27). *Jews* held *Samaritans* in contempt, as religious apostates (2 Kg.17.24–34). **10:** *Living water*, Jer.2.13;

is deep; where do you get that living water? ¹² Are you greater than our father Jacob, who gave us the well, and drank from it himself, and his sons, and his cattle?" ¹³ Jesus said to her, "Every one who drinks of this water will thirst again, ¹⁴ but whoever drinks of the water that I shall give him will never thirst; the water that I shall give him will become in him a spring of water welling up to eternal life." ¹⁵ The woman said to him, "Sir, give me this water, that I may not thirst, nor come here to draw."

16 Jesus said to her, "Go, call your husband, and come here." ¹⁷ The woman answered him, "I have no husband." Jesus said to her, "You are right in saying, 'I have no husband'; ¹⁸ for you have had five husbands, and he whom you now have is not your husband; this you said truly." ¹⁹ The woman said to him, "Sir, I perceive that you are a prophet. ²⁰ Our fathers worshiped on this mountain; and you say that in Jerusalem is the place where men ought to worship." ²¹ Jesus said to her, "Woman, believe me, the hour is coming when neither on this mountain nor in Jerusalem will you worship the Father. ²² You worship what you do not know; we worship what we know, for salvation is from the Jews. ²³ But the hour is coming, and now is, when the true worshipers will worship the Father in spirit and truth, for such the Father seeks to worship him. ²⁴ God is spirit, and those who worship him must worship in spirit and truth." ²⁵ The woman said to him, "I know that Messiah is coming (he who is called Christ); when he comes, he will show us all things." ²⁶ Jesus said to her, "I who speak to you am he."

27 Just then his disciples came.

They marveled that he was talking with a woman, but none said, "What do you wish?" or, "Why are you talking with her?" ²⁸ So the woman left her water jar, and went away into the city, and said to the people, ²⁹ "Come, see a man who told me all that I ever did. Can this be the Christ?" ³⁰ They went out of the city and were coming to him.

31 Meanwhile the disciples besought him, saying, "Rabbi, eat." ³² But he said to them, "I have food to eat of which you do not know." ³³ So the disciples said to one another, "Has any one brought him food?" ³⁴ Jesus said to them, "My food is to do the will of him who sent me, and to accomplish his work. ³⁵ Do you not say, 'There are yet four months, then comes the harvest'? I tell you, lift up your eyes, and see how the fields are already white for harvest. ³⁶ He who reaps receives wages, and gathers fruit for eternal life, so that sower and reaper may rejoice together. ³⁷ For here the saying holds true, 'One sows and another reaps.' ³⁸ I sent you to reap that for which you did not labor; others have labored, and you have entered into their labor."

39 Many Samaritans from that city believed in him because of the woman's testimony, "He told me all that I ever did." ⁴⁰ So when the Samaritans came to him, they asked him to stay with them; and he stayed there two days. ⁴¹ And many more believed because of his word. ⁴² They said to the woman, "It is no longer because of your words that we believe, for we have heard for ourselves, and we know that this is indeed the Savior of the world."

43 After the two days he de-

17.13. **14:** Jesus' gift is God's life in man. **19–20:** *A prophet* should be able to settle rival religious claims. **21:** *This mountain,* i.e. Mount Gerizim, where the Samaritans had had a temple. Jesus means that the place of worship is not of primary importance. **24:** Worship *in spirit* is man's response to God's gift of himself (*the Father seeks,* v. 23). *In truth,* in accord with God's nature seen in Christ. **27:** See v. 9 n. **35:** *Already,* see v. 30. **36:** *Wages,* the reward of gathering believers. **37–38:** Jesus *sows* (vv. 7–26), the disciples *reap;* the harvest comes from the *labor* of Jesus' life, death, and resurrection (12.23–24). **39–42:** Faith based on the testimony of another (*the woman*) is vindicated in personal experience.

parted to Galilee. ⁴⁴ For Jesus himself testified that a prophet has no honor in his own country. ⁴⁵ So when he came to Galilee, the Galileans welcomed him, having seen all that he had done in Jerusalem at the feast, for they too had gone to the feast.

46 So he came again to Cana in Galilee, where he had made the water wine. And at Caper′na-um there was an official whose son was ill. ⁴⁷ When he heard that Jesus had come from Judea to Galilee, he went and begged him to come down and heal his son, for he was at the point of death. ⁴⁸ Jesus therefore said to him, "Unless you see signs and wonders you will not believe." ⁴⁹ The official said to him, "Sir, come down before my child dies." ⁵⁰ Jesus said to him, "Go; your son will live." The man believed the word that Jesus spoke to him and went his way. ⁵¹ As he was going down, his servants met him and told him that his son was living. ⁵² So he asked them the hour when he began to mend, and they said to him, "Yesterday at the seventh hour the fever left him." ⁵³ The father knew that was the hour when Jesus had said to him, "Your son will live"; and he himself believed, and all his household. ⁵⁴ This was now the second sign that Jesus did when he had come from Judea to Galilee.

5 After this there was a feast of the Jews, and Jesus went up to Jerusalem.

2 Now there is in Jerusalem by the Sheep Gate a pool, in Hebrew called Beth-za′tha,ʲ which has five porticoes. ³ In these lay a multitude of invalids, blind, lame, paralyzed.ᵏ ⁵ One man was there, who had been ill for thirty-eight years. ⁶ When Jesus saw him and knew that he had been lying there a long time, he said to him, "Do you want to be healed?" ⁷ The sick man answered him, "Sir, I have no man to put me into the pool when the water is troubled, and while I am going another steps down before me." ⁸ Jesus said to him, "Rise, take up your pallet, and walk." ⁹ And at once the man was healed, and he took up his pallet and walked.

Now that day was the sabbath. ¹⁰ So the Jews said to the man who was cured, "It is the sabbath, it is not lawful for you to carry your pallet." ¹¹ But he answered them, "The man who healed me said to me, 'Take up your pallet, and walk.'" ¹² They asked him, "Who is the man who said to you, 'Take up your pallet, and walk'?" ¹³ Now the man who had been healed did not know who it was, for Jesus had withdrawn, as there was a crowd in the place. ¹⁴ Afterward, Jesus found him in the temple, and said to him, "See, you are well! Sin no more, that nothing worse befall you." ¹⁵ The man went away and told the Jews that it was Jesus who had healed him. ¹⁶ And this was why the Jews perse-

ʲ Other ancient authorities read *Bethesda*, others *Bethsaida*
ᵏ Other ancient authorities insert, wholly or in part, *waiting for the moving of the water; ⁴ for an angel of the Lord went down at certain seasons into the pool, and troubled the water: whoever stepped in first after the troubling of the water was healed of whatever disease he had*

4.43–54: Jesus and the Gentiles. Illustrates v. 42, Jesus as *Savior of the world* (Jew, Samaritan, Gentile–everyone; compare Is.43.3,11; 45.22). **46:** *An official*, a Gentile military officer. **48:** *You* is plural here, addressed to all who base faith on mere signs (compare v. 45). **49:** He desires life for his child, not a display. **50:** The official *believed* that Jesus' *word* had effected the cure, and he did not return to his home (which was only about eighteen miles away) until the next day (v. 52). **52:** *Seventh hour*, about 1 p.m. **53:** *Believed*, in the deepest sense. **54:** *Second*, for the first see 2.1–11.

5.1–18: Healing the lame man on the sabbath. 3: After the word *paralyzed* later manuscripts add an explanatory statement; see note *k*. **7:** *When the water is troubled* is explained by the addition to v. 3. Movement caused by an intermittent spring was attributed to divine action. **13:** *Jesus had withdrawn* to avoid publicity. **14:** There are *worse* things than illness. **16:** *The Jews*, the religious authorities, opposed Jesus for his break with their legalism. **17:** God continually gives life and judges evil, as does Jesus. **18:** *Equal*, see 10.30–33.

cuted Jesus, because he did this on the sabbath. ¹⁷ But Jesus answered them, "My Father is working still, and I am working." ¹⁸ This was why the Jews sought all the more to kill him, because he not only broke the sabbath but also called God his own Father, making himself equal with God.

19 Jesus said to them, "Truly, truly, I say to you, the Son can do nothing of his own accord, but only what he sees the Father doing; for whatever he does, that the Son does likewise. ²⁰ For the Father loves the Son, and shows him all that he himself is doing; and greater works than these will he show him, that you may marvel. ²¹ For as the Father raises the dead and gives them life, so also the Son gives life to whom he will. ²² The Father judges no one, but has given all judgment to the Son, ²³ that all may honor the Son, even as they honor the Father. He who does not honor the Son does not honor the Father who sent him. ²⁴ Truly, truly, I say to you, he who hears my word and believes him who sent me, has eternal life; he does not come into judgment, but has passed from death to life.

25 "Truly, truly, I say to you, the hour is coming, and now is, when the dead will hear the voice of the Son of God, and those who hear will live. ²⁶ For as the Father has life in himself, so he has granted the Son also to have life in himself, ²⁷ and has given him authority to execute judgment, because he is the Son of man. ²⁸ Do not marvel at this; for the hour is coming when all who are in the tombs will hear his voice ²⁹ and come forth, those who have done good, to the resurrection of life, and those who have done evil, to the resurrection of judgment.

30 "I can do nothing on my own authority; as I hear, I judge; and my judgment is just, because I seek not my own will but the will of him who sent me. ³¹ If I bear witness to myself, my testimony is not true; ³² there is another who bears witness to me, and I know that the testimony which he bears to me is true. ³³ You sent to John, and he has borne witness to the truth. ³⁴ Not that the testimony which I receive is from man; but I say this that you may be saved. ³⁵ He was a burning and shining lamp, and you were willing to rejoice for a while in his light. ³⁶ But the testimony which I have is greater than that of John; for the works which the Father has granted me to accomplish, these very works which I am doing, bear me witness that the Father has sent me. ³⁷ And the Father who sent me has himself borne witness to me. His voice you have never heard, his form you have never seen; ³⁸ and you do not have his word abiding in you, for you do not believe him whom he has sent. ³⁹ You search the scriptures, because you think that in them you have eternal life; and it is they that bear witness to me; ⁴⁰ yet you refuse to come to me that you may have life. ⁴¹ I do not receive glory from men. ⁴² But I know that you have not the love of God within you. ⁴³ I have come in my Father's name, and you do not receive me; if another comes in his own name, him you will

---

5.19–29: Jesus' relation to God. 19–20: Jesus' sonship involves the identity of his will and actions with the Father's. The *greater works* are giving life (v. 21) and judgment (v. 22). **24:** He who *believes* on the basis of Jesus' word *has passed* into the realm where death does not reign. **25:** The *coming* age is already present in Jesus. To *hear* with the comprehension of faith makes the spiritually *dead* live. **26–29:** They will share in the final *resurrection of life*.

5.30–40: Evidence of Jesus' relation to God. 30: Jesus' judgment is that of God, and therefore *just*, without favoritism or error. **32:** *Another*, the Father. **33–40:** God witnesses to Jesus through the ministry of *John* the Baptist (vv. 33–35), through Jesus' *works* (v. 36), and through *the scriptures* (vv. 37–40).

5.41–47: Jesus condemns the Jews. 41: No human standards apply to him. **42:** No *love of God*, no love of Jesus. **43–44:** Judgment based on human pride. **45:** 9.28; Rom.2.17. **47:** Lk.16.29,31.

receive. ⁴⁴ How can you believe, who receive glory from one another and do not seek the glory that comes from the only God? ⁴⁵ Do not think that I shall accuse you to the Father; it is Moses who accuses you, on whom you set your hope. ⁴⁶ If you believed Moses, you would believe me, for he wrote of me. ⁴⁷ But if you do not believe his writings, how will you believe my words?"

6 After this Jesus went to the other side of the Sea of Galilee, which is the Sea of Tibe'ri-as. ² And a multitude followed him, because they saw the signs which he did on those who were diseased. ³ Jesus went up on the mountain, and there sat down with his disciples. ⁴ Now the Passover, the feast of the Jews, was at hand. ⁵ Lifting up his eyes, then, and seeing that a multitude was coming to him, Jesus said to Philip, "How are we to buy bread, so that these people may eat?" ⁶ This he said to test him, for he himself knew what he would do. ⁷ Philip answered him, "Two hundred denarii*l* would not buy enough bread for each of them to get a little." ⁸ One of his disciples, Andrew, Simon Peter's brother, said to him, ⁹ "There is a lad here who has five barley loaves and two fish; but what are they among so many?" ¹⁰ Jesus said, "Make the people sit down." Now there was much grass in the place; so the men sat down, in number about five thousand. ¹¹ Jesus then took the loaves, and when he had given thanks, he distributed them to those who were seated; so also the fish, as much as they wanted. ¹² And when they had eaten their fill, he told his dis-

ciples, "Gather up the fragments left over, that nothing may be lost." ¹³ So they gathered them up and filled twelve baskets with fragments from the five barley loaves, left by those who had eaten. ¹⁴ When the people saw the sign which he had done, they said, "This is indeed the prophet who is to come into the world!"

15 Perceiving then that they were about to come and take him by force to make him king, Jesus withdrew again to the mountain by himself.

16 When evening came, his disciples went down to the sea, ¹⁷ got into a boat, and started across the sea to Caper'na-um. It was now dark, and Jesus had not yet come to them. ¹⁸ The sea rose because a strong wind was blowing. ¹⁹ When they had rowed about three or four miles,*m* they saw Jesus walking on the sea and drawing near to the boat. They were frightened, ²⁰ but he said to them, "It is I; do not be afraid." ²¹ Then they were glad to take him into the boat, and immediately the boat was at the land to which they were going.

22 On the next day the people who remained on the other side of the sea saw that there had been only one boat there, and that Jesus had not entered the boat with his disciples, but that his disciples had gone away alone. ²³ However, boats from Tibe'ri-as came near the place where they ate the bread after the Lord had given thanks. ²⁴ So when the people saw that Jesus was not there, nor his disciples, they themselves got into the boats and went to Caper'na-um, seeking Jesus.

l The denarius was a day's wage for a laborer
m Greek *twenty-five or thirty stadia*

6.1–15: Feeding the five thousand; the only miracle recorded by all four gospels (Mt.14.13–21; Mk.6.32–44; Lk.9.10–17). **1:** *Tiberias,* named for the Emperor Tiberius. **6:** *To test* Philip's faith. **7:** *Two hundred denarii,* for the value of the denarius, see note *l.* **9:** *Barley loaves,* food of the poor. **12:** *Gather,* an act of reverential economy toward the gift of God. **13:** *Twelve baskets,* one for each disciple. **15:** *To make him king,* as a political Messiah opposing Rome; but Jesus would not accept this (18.36).

6.16–21: Jesus walks on the sea (Mt.14.22–27; Mk.6.45–51). Jesus is greater than a political ruler (v. 15); he is Lord of the elements (Ps.107.29–30). **17:** *Not yet come,* probably they expected to meet Jesus along the shore. **20–21:** Jesus' presence dispels fear.

6.22–71: Jesus, the bread of life. 22–25: Note the clamor for more bread. **26:** *Signs,* point-

25 When they found him on the other side of the sea, they said to him, "Rabbi, when did you come here?" 26 Jesus answered them, "Truly, truly, I say to you, you seek me, not because you saw signs, but because you ate your fill of the loaves. 27 Do not labor for the food which perishes, but for the food which endures to eternal life, which the Son of man will give to you; for on him has God the Father set his seal." 28 Then they said to him, "What must we do, to be doing the works of God?" 29 Jesus answered them, "This is the work of God, that you believe in him whom he has sent." 30 So they said to him, "Then what sign do you do, that we may see, and believe you? What work do you perform? 31 Our fathers ate the manna in the wilderness; as it is written, 'He gave them bread from heaven to eat.'" 32 Jesus then said to them, "Truly, truly, I say to you, it was not Moses who gave you the bread from heaven; my Father gives you the true bread from heaven. 33 For the bread of God is that which comes down from heaven, and gives life to the world." 34 They said to him, "Lord, give us this bread always."

35 Jesus said to them, "I am the bread of life; he who comes to me shall not hunger, and he who believes in me shall never thirst. 36 But I said to you that you have seen me and yet do not believe. 37 All that the Father gives me will come to me; and him who comes to me I will not cast out. 38 For I have come down from heaven, not to do my own will, but the will of him who sent me; 39 and this is the will of him who sent me, that I should lose nothing of all that he has given me, but raise it up at the last day. 40 For this is the will of my Father, that every one who sees the Son and believes in him should have eternal life; and I will raise him up at the last day."

41 The Jews then murmured at him, because he said, "I am the bread which came down from heaven." 42 They said, "Is not this Jesus, the son of Joseph, whose father and mother we know? How does he now say, 'I have come down from heaven'?" 43 Jesus answered them, "Do not murmur among yourselves. 44 No one can come to me unless the Father who sent me draws him; and I will raise him up at the last day. 45 It is written in the prophets, 'And they shall all be taught by God.' Every one who has heard and learned from the Father comes to me. 46 Not that any one has seen the Father except him who is from God; he has seen the Father. 47 Truly, truly, I say to you, he who believes has eternal life. 48 I am the bread of life. 49 Your fathers ate the manna in the wilderness, and they died. 50 This is the bread which comes down from heaven, that a man may eat of it and not die. 51 I am the living bread which came down from heaven; if any one eats of this bread, he will live for ever; and the bread which I shall give for the life of the world is my flesh."

52 The Jews then disputed among themselves, saying, "How can this

---

ing to Jesus as food for the soul. **27**: *Son of man*, see 1.51 n. *Seal*, God's authentication, perhaps at the baptism (1.32). **28**: *Works*, 3.21; Rev.2.26. **29**: *Work*, singular number; not many works (v. 28), but obedient trust (*believe*) is the one thing pleasing to God (1 Jn.3.23). *Him . . . sent*, Jesus who reveals God. **30**: *See*, as a proof; but faith cannot be proved. **31**: The Messiah was expected to reproduce the miracle of the giving of manna (Ex.16.4,15; Num.11.8; Ps.78.24; 105.40). **36–40**: Jesus himself is God's gift of sustenance for time and eternity. Belief or unbelief involves a mystery known only to God, but no one who *comes* is rejected (v. 37). Faith is God's gift, not a human achievement; it gives *eternal life* now and issues in resurrection *at the last day*. **44–45**: The *drawing* is not coercive or mechanical. *Prophets*, Is.54.13; compare Jl. 2.28–29. Had they *heard* and *learned* God's voice in their scriptures, they would have recognized its accents in him who alone has direct communion with God. **51**: *The living bread . . . is my flesh*, the One who became flesh (assumed complete human nature, 1.14) offered himself to God in death, thus releasing his life *for the life of the world*. **53**: The separation of the *blood*

man give us his flesh to eat?" [53] So Jesus said to them, "Truly, truly, I say to you, unless you eat the flesh of the Son of man and drink his blood, you have no life in you; [54] he who eats my flesh and drinks my blood has eternal life, and I will raise him up at the last day. [55] For my flesh is food indeed, and my blood is drink indeed. [56] He who eats my flesh and drinks my blood abides in me, and I in him. [57] As the living Father sent me, and I live because of the Father, so he who eats me will live because of me. [58] This is the bread which came down from heaven, not such as the fathers ate and died; he who eats this bread will live for ever." [59] This he said in the synagogue, as he taught at Caper'na-um.

60 Many of his disciples, when they heard it, said, "This is a hard saying; who can listen to it?" [61] But Jesus, knowing in himself that his disciples murmured at it, said to them, "Do you take offense at this? [62] Then what if you were to see the Son of man ascending where he was before? [63] It is the spirit that gives life, the flesh is of no avail; the words that I have spoken to you are spirit and life. [64] But there are some of you that do not believe." For Jesus knew from the first who those were that did not believe, and who it was that would betray him. [65] And he said, "This is why I told you that no one can come to me unless it is granted him by the Father."

66 After this many of his disciples drew back and no longer went about with him. [67] Jesus said to the twelve, "Do you also wish to go away?" [68] Simon Peter answered him, "Lord, to whom shall we go? You have the words of eternal life; [69] and we have believed, and have come to know, that you are the Holy One of God." [70] Jesus answered them, "Did I not choose you, the twelve, and one of you is a devil?" [71] He spoke of Judas the son of Simon Iscariot, for he, one of the twelve, was to betray him.

7 After this Jesus went about in Galilee; he would not go about in Judea, because the Jews[n] sought to kill him. [2] Now the Jews' feast of Tabernacles was at hand. [3] So his brothers said to him, "Leave here and go to Judea, that your disciples may see the works you are doing. [4] For no man works in secret if he seeks to be known openly. If you do these things, show yourself to the world." [5] For even his brothers did not believe in him. [6] Jesus said to them, "My time has not yet come, but your time is always here. [7] The world cannot hate you, but it hates me because I testify of it that its works are evil. [8] Go to the feast yourselves; I am not[o] going up to this feast, for my time has not yet fully come." [9] So saying, he remained in Galilee.

10 But after his brothers had gone up to the feast, then he also went up, not publicly but in private.[11] The Jews were looking for him at the feast,

---

n Or *Judeans*
o Other ancient authorities add *yet*

from the *flesh* emphasizes the reality of Jesus' death. **54:** To *eat* and *drink* is to believe (v. 47), to appropriate, assimilate, and *abide* in Christ (v. 56). **58:** Since Christ is *bread . . . from heaven* (compare vv. 32–35), to eat him is to *live for ever*. **60:** *Hard saying* means offensive or difficult, but not obscure. **62–63:** The ascension, by which Jesus will be taken away as regards the flesh, will indicate that he has been speaking of spiritual realities and not the actual eating of his flesh. **64–65:** These truths can be discerned only by faith, which is God's gift, not man's achievement (Eph.2.8). **66–71:** To receive God's gift of faith is to *know* God in Christ; to refuse it is to become an ally of the *devil*. Faith and unbelief mark the great divisions among men.

7.1–52: Jesus, the water of life. 2: *Tabernacles* (or Booths), a feast which began on the fifteenth of the seventh month (Sept.-Oct.), commemorating the wilderness wanderings (Lev. 23.39–43; Dt.16.13–15). **3–5:** Jesus' *brothers* (see Mt.13.55 n.) challenge him to declare himself *to the world* of pilgrims at the feast; his claims (chs. 5 and 6) must be verified at Jerusalem. **6–8:** Jesus' *time*, or *hour* (v. 30; see 2.4 n.; 8.20; 12.23; 17.1), was the time for his self-manifestation on the cross. **10:** Compare Jesus' *private* journey with the public one in 12.12–15, and the reasons for both in v. 8 and 12.23. **11–13:** Subdued debate (*muttering*) over

and saying, "Where is he?" ¹² And there was much muttering about him among the people. While some said, "He is a good man," others said, "No, he is leading the people astray." ¹³ Yet for fear of the Jews no one spoke openly of him.

14 About the middle of the feast Jesus went up into the temple and taught. ¹⁵ The Jews marveled at it, saying, "How is it that this man has learning,ᵖ when he has never studied?" ¹⁶ So Jesus answered them, "My teaching is not mine, but his who sent me; ¹⁷ if any man's will is to do his will, he shall know whether the teaching is from God or whether I am speaking on my own authority. ¹⁸ He who speaks on his own authority seeks his own glory; but he who seeks the glory of him who sent him is true, and in him there is no falsehood. ¹⁹ Did not Moses give you the law? Yet none of you keeps the law. Why do you seek to kill me?" ²⁰ The people answered, "You have a demon! Who is seeking to kill you?" ²¹ Jesus answered them, "I did one deed, and you all marvel at it. ²² Moses gave you circumcision (not that it is from Moses, but from the fathers), and you circumcise a man upon the sabbath. ²³ If on the sabbath a man receives circumcision, so that the law of Moses may not be broken, are you angry with me because on the sabbath I made a man's whole body well? ²⁴ Do not judge by appearances, but judge with right judgment."

25 Some of the people of Jerusalem therefore said, "Is not this the man whom they seek to kill? ²⁶ And here he is, speaking openly, and they say nothing to him! Can it be that the authorities really know that this is the Christ? ²⁷ Yet we know where this man comes from; and when the Christ appears, no one will know where he comes from." ²⁸ So Jesus proclaimed, as he taught in the temple, "You know me, and you know where I come from? But I have not come of my own accord; he who sent me is true, and him you do not know. ²⁹ I know him, for I come from him, and he sent me." ³⁰ So they sought to arrest him; but no one laid hands on him, because his hour had not yet come. ³¹ Yet many of the people believed in him; they said, "When the Christ appears, will he do more signs than this man has done?"

32 The Pharisees heard the crowd thus muttering about him, and the chief priests and Pharisees sent officers to arrest him. ³³ Jesus then said, "I shall be with you a little longer, and then I go to him who sent me; ³⁴ you will seek me and you will not find me; where I am you cannot come." ³⁵ The Jews said to one another, "Where does this man intend to go that we shall not find him? Does he intend to go to the Dispersion among the Greeks and teach the Greeks? ³⁶ What does he mean by saying, 'You will seek me and you will not find me,' and, 'Where I am you cannot come'?"

37 On the last day of the feast, the great day, Jesus stood up and pro-

ᵖ Or *this man knows his letters*

Jesus' character is prompted by *fear of the Jews* (see 5.16 n.). **15:** Wherein lay the authority of Jesus' teaching (Mk.1.22) without the accreditation of official rabbinic study? **16–18:** Jesus' *teaching* came *from God*, not from himself, a fact that can be recognized by him who wills to obey God's *will*. **19–24:** The law of Moses condemns their desire to *kill* Jesus for healing on the sabbath (5.18), for it enjoins circumcision even when the eighth day falls on a sabbath (Lev.12.3). If circumcision, why not healings? **25–31:** Possibility of Jesus' messiahship is denied because his origin is known, whereas it was believed that the Messiah's origin would be mysterious. Jesus' human origin is apparent, but not his true origin in God, whose authority he bears (*sent*). **32–36:** The *chief priests* (Sadducees) and *Pharisees*, inveterate enemies, unite in sending *officers* (temple police) to arrest Jesus. This leads Jesus to speak of his death (*I go to him who sent me*). Later the Jews will seek deliverance in the Messiah, but *will not find* him, for he will have ascended to where they *cannot come* because they are unbelievers (contrast 8.21 with 12.26; 17.24). They miss the point, thinking that he is going to the Jews dispersed among the *Greeks* (Gentiles). **37–39:** For seven days water was carried in a golden pitcher from the Pool of Siloam to the

claimed, "If any one thirst, let him come to me and drink. [38] He who believes in me, as[q] the scripture has said, 'Out of his heart shall flow rivers of living water.' " [39] Now this he said about the Spirit, which those who believed in him were to receive; for as yet the Spirit had not been given, because Jesus was not yet glorified.

40 When they heard these words, some of the people said, "This is really the prophet." [41] Others said, "This is the Christ." But some said, "Is the Christ to come from Galilee? [42] Has not the scripture said that the Christ is descended from David, and comes from Bethlehem, the village where David was?" [43] So there was a division among the people over him. [44] Some of them wanted to arrest him, but no one laid hands on him.

45 The officers then went back to the chief priests and Pharisees, who said to them, "Why did you not bring him?" [46] The officers answered, "No man ever spoke like this man!" [47] The Pharisees answered them, "Are you led astray, you also? [48] Have any of the authorities or of the Pharisees believed in him? [49] But this crowd, who do not know the law, are accursed." [50] Nicode′mus, who had gone to him before, and who was one of them, said to them, [51] "Does our law judge a man without first giving him a hearing and learning what he does?" [52] They replied, "Are you from Galilee too? Search and you will see that no prophet is to rise from Galilee."

8 [53] They went each to his own house, [1] but Jesus went to the Mount of Olives. [2] Early in the morning he came again to the temple; all the people came to him, and he sat down and taught them. [3] The scribes and the Pharisees brought a woman who had been caught in adultery, and placing her in the midst [4] they said to him, "Teacher, this woman has been caught in the act of adultery. [5] Now in the law Moses commanded us to stone such. What do you say about her?" [6] This they said to test him, that they might have some charge to bring against him. Jesus bent down and wrote with his finger on the ground. [7] And as they continued to ask him, he stood up and said to them, "Let him who is without sin among you be the first to throw a stone at her." [8] And once more he bent down and wrote with his finger on the ground. [9] But when they heard it, they went away, one by one, beginning with the eldest, and Jesus was left alone with the woman standing before him. [10] Jesus looked up and said to her, "Woman, where are they? Has no one condemned you?" [11] She said, "No one, Lord." And Jesus said, "Neither do I

q Or *let him come to me, and let him who believes in me drink.* As

r The most ancient authorities omit 7.53–8.11; other authorities add the passage here or after 7.36 or after 21.25 or after Luke 21.38, with variations of text.

temple as a reminder of the water from the rock in the desert (Num.20.2–13), and as a symbol of hope for the coming Messianic deliverance (Is.12.3). Jesus is the true water of life, who turns the symbol into reality (Is.44.3; 55.1). Believers become channels of life to others, through Christ's *Spirit* given at Pentecost after he was *glorified* (crucified, risen, ascended). The gift of the *Spirit* is a mark of the Messianic age (Jl.2.28–29; Acts 2.14–21). **40–44:** There is a division among the people over superficial matters. That he is from God is important. *The prophet . . . the Christ*, see 1.20–21 n. **42:** *Descended from David*, 2 Sam.7.12–13; Ps.89.3–4; 132.11–12. *Bethlehem*, Mic.5.2. **49:** *Crowd*, the masses who are indifferent to scrupulous Pharisaic observances. **52:** Sarcasm, expressing the contempt of Jerusalem aristocrats for Galilean peasants.

7.53–8.11: The woman caught in adultery. This account, omitted in many ancient manuscripts, appears to be an authentic incident in Jesus' ministry, though not belonging originally to John's Gospel. **8.2:** *Early*, Lk.21.38; Acts 5.21. *Sat down*, Mt.5.1; 23.2; Mk.9.35. **5:** *The law of Moses*, Lev.20.10; Dt.22.23–24. **7:** *Without sin*, Mt.23.28; Rom.2.1. **8:** *Wrote*. According to several later manuscripts, Jesus *wrote . . . on the ground* "the sins of each of them" (compare Jer.17.13). **11:** *Do not sin again*, 5.14.

8.12–59: Jesus, the light of life. Great golden lamps in the temple court were lit during the feast of Tabernacles (7.2): therefore the appropriateness of Jesus' claim in v. 12 (Is.49.6; 60.1–3).

condemn you; go, and do not sin again."

12 Again Jesus spoke to them, saying, "I am the light of the world; he who follows me will not walk in darkness, but will have the light of life." 13 The Pharisees then said to him, "You are bearing witness to yourself; your testimony is not true." 14 Jesus answered, "Even if I do bear witness to myself, my testimony is true, for I know whence I have come and whither I am going, but you do not know whence I come or whither I am going. 15 You judge according to the flesh, I judge no one. 16 Yet even if I do judge, my judgment is true, for it is not I alone that judge, but I and he*s* who sent me. 17 In your law it is written that the testimony of two men is true; 18 I bear witness to myself, and the Father who sent me bears witness to me." 19 They said to him therefore, "Where is your Father?" Jesus answered, "You know neither me nor my Father; if you knew me, you would know my Father also." 20 These words he spoke in the treasury, as he taught in the temple; but no one arrested him, because his hour had not yet come.

21 Again he said to them, "I go away, and you will seek me and die in your sin; where I am going, you cannot come." 22 Then said the Jews, "Will he kill himself, since he says, 'Where I am going, you cannot come'?" 23 He said to them, "You are from below, I am from above; you are of this world, I am not of this world. 24 I told you that you would die in your sins, for you will die in your sins unless

you believe that I am he." 25 They said to him, "Who are you?" Jesus said to them, "Even what I have told you from the beginning.*t* 26 I have much to say about you and much to judge; but he who sent me is true, and I declare to the world what I have heard from him." 27 They did not understand that he spoke to them of the Father. 28 So Jesus said, "When you have lifted up the Son of man, then you will know that I am he, and that I do nothing on my own authority but speak thus as the Father taught me. 29 And he who sent me is with me; he has not left me alone, for I always do what is pleasing to him." 30 As he spoke thus, many believed in him.

31 Jesus then said to the Jews who had believed in him, "If you continue in my word, you are truly my disciples, 32 and you will know the truth, and the truth will make you free." 33 They answered him, "We are descendants of Abraham, and have never been in bondage to any one. How is it that you say, 'You will be made free'?"

34 Jesus answered them, "Truly, truly, I say to you, every one who commits sin is a slave to sin. 35 The slave does not continue in the house for ever; the son continues for ever. 36 So if the Son makes you free, you will be free indeed. 37 I know that you are descendants of Abraham; yet you seek to kill me, because my word finds no place in you. 38 I speak of what I have seen with my Father, and you do what you have heard from your father."

s Other ancient authorities read *the Father*
t Or *Why do I talk to you at all?*

13–18: Jesus answers the objection to his bearing self-witness: (a) he comes from the world above; hence, he alone among men understands who he is (Mt.11.27); (b) the joint witness of the Father and the Son fulfils the Jewish requirement of *two* witnesses (Dt.19.15). **19:** The question reveals judgment *according to the flesh* (v. 15); they have no ears to hear God speaking in Jesus. **22:** Suicide leads to hell, they suggest. **23–24:** Jesus reiterates his source *from above* (in God); to believe in him is the only escape from sin and death. **25–27:** An indirect claim to oneness with God, which they miss. **28–29:** The oneness is based on obedience, of which the cross is the final proof (12.32). **32:** *Truth*, not knowledge in general, but saving truth (14.6). *Free*, from sin and its slavery (v. 34). **33–38:** As *descendants of Abraham* the Jews had the truth of the Mosaic law; yet the law left them *slaves to sin*. The freedom of sonship to God comes only through *the Son.* **39–47:** Their desire *to kill* Jesus forfeits their claim to be heirs of Abra-

39 They answered him, "Abraham is our father." Jesus said to them, "If you were Abraham's children, you would do what Abraham did, ⁴⁰ but now you seek to kill me, a man who has told you the truth which I heard from God; this is not what Abraham did. ⁴¹ You do what your father did." They said to him, "We were not born of fornication; we have one Father, even God." ⁴² Jesus said to them, "If God were your Father, you would love me, for I proceeded and came forth from God; I came not of my own accord, but he sent me. ⁴³ Why do you not understand what I say? It is because you cannot bear to hear my word. ⁴⁴ You are of your father the devil, and your will is to do your father's desires. He was a murderer from the beginning, and has nothing to do with the truth, because there is no truth in him. When he lies, he speaks according to his own nature, for he is a liar and the father of lies. ⁴⁵ But, because I tell the truth, you do not believe me. ⁴⁶ Which of you convicts me of sin? If I tell the truth, why do you not believe me? ⁴⁷ He who is of God hears the words of God; the reason why you do not hear them is that you are not of God."

48 The Jews answered him, "Are we not right in saying that you are a Samaritan and have a demon?" ⁴⁹ Jesus answered, "I have not a demon; but I honor my Father, and you dishonor me. ⁵⁰ Yet I do not seek my own glory; there is One who seeks it and he will be the judge. ⁵¹ Truly, truly, I say to you, if any one keeps my word, he will never see death." ⁵² The Jews said to him, "Now we know that you have a demon. Abraham died, as did the prophets; and you say, 'If any one keeps my word, he will never taste death.' ⁵³ Are you greater than our father Abraham, who died? And the prophets died! Who do you claim to be?" ⁵⁴ Jesus answered, "If I glorify myself, my glory is nothing; it is my Father who glorifies me, of whom you say that he is your God. ⁵⁵ But you have not known him; I know him. If I said, I do not know him, I should be a liar like you; but I do know him and I keep his word. ⁵⁶ Your father Abraham rejoiced that he was to see my day; he saw it and was glad." ⁵⁷ The Jews then said to him, "You are not yet fifty years old, and have you seen Abraham?"ᵘ ⁵⁸ Jesus said to them, "Truly, truly, I say to you, before Abraham was, I am." ⁵⁹ So they took up stones to throw at him; but Jesus hid himself, and went out of the temple.

9 As he passed by, he saw a man blind from his birth. ² And his disciples asked him, "Rabbi, who sinned, this man or his parents, that he was born blind?" ³ Jesus answered, "It was not that this man sinned, or his parents, but that the works of God might be made manifest in him. ⁴ We must work the works of him who sent me, while it is day; night comes, when no one can work. ⁵ As long as I am in the world, I am the light of the world." ⁶ As he said this, he spat on the ground and made clay of the spittle and anointed the man's eyes with the clay, ⁷ saying to him, "Go, wash in the pool of Silo'am" (which means Sent). So he went and washed and came back seeing. ⁸ The neighbors and those who had

ᵘ Other ancient authorities read *has Abraham seen you?*

---

ham's faith and true children of God. They insist (v. 41) that *God* is their father. Their murderous intention and resistance to the truth belie this and brand them as children of *the devil* (v. 44). The fault is in them and not in Jesus (v. 46). **48:** *The Jews* turn to insult and calumny. **50–54:** God is judge, and will vindicate believers in Jesus with eternal life. **56:** Refusal to believe severs them from *Abraham*, who *rejoiced* in the hope of the coming of the Messiah (Heb.11.17). **58:** The *I am* is the divine name (Ex.3.14), a claim to pre-existence and oneness with God (10.30–33).

    9.1–41: Jesus manifests himself as the light of life. 2–3: Suffering was attributed to sin, either of the parents or of the man prenatally. Jesus denies this and shifts attention from cause to purpose; this is an opportunity for God to act. **6:** *Spittle* was considered to have medicinal

seen him before as a beggar, said, "Is not this the man who used to sit and beg?" [9] Some said, "It is he"; others said, "No, but he is like him." He said, "I am the man." [10] They said to him, "Then how were your eyes opened?" [11] He answered, "The man called Jesus made clay and anointed my eyes and said to me, 'Go to Silo′am and wash'; so I went and washed and received my sight." [12] They said to him, "Where is he?" He said, "I do not know."

13 They brought to the Pharisees the man who had formerly been blind. [14] Now it was a sabbath day when Jesus made the clay and opened his eyes. [15] The Pharisees again asked him how he had received his sight. And he said to them, "He put clay on my eyes, and I washed, and I see." [16] Some of the Pharisees said, "This man is not from God, for he does not keep the sabbath." But others said, "How can a man who is a sinner do such signs?" There was a division among them. [17] So they again said to the blind man, "What do you say about him, since he has opened your eyes?" He said, "He is a prophet."

18 The Jews did not believe that he had been blind and had received his sight, until they called the parents of the man who had received his sight, [19] and asked them, "Is this your son, who you say was born blind? How then does he now see?" [20] His parents answered, "We know that this is our son, and that he was born blind; [21] but how he now sees we do not know, nor do we know who opened his eyes. Ask him; he is of age, he will speak for himself." [22] His parents said this because they feared the Jews, for the Jews had already agreed that if any one should confess him to be Christ, he was to be put out of the synagogue. [23] Therefore his parents said, "He is of age, ask him."

24 So for the second time they called the man who had been blind, and said to him, "Give God the praise; we know that this man is a sinner." [25] He answered, "Whether he is a sinner, I do not know; one thing I know, that though I was blind, now I see." [26] They said to him, "What did he do to you? How did he open your eyes?" [27] He answered them, "I have told you already, and you would not listen. Why do you want to hear it again? Do you too want to become his disciples?" [28] And they reviled him, saying, "You are his disciple, but we are disciples of Moses. [29] We know that God has spoken to Moses, but as for this man, we do not know where he comes from." [30] The man answered, "Why, this is a marvel! You do not know where he comes from, and yet he opened my eyes. [31] We know that God does not listen to sinners, but if any one is a worshiper of God and does his will, God listens to him. [32] Never since the world began has it been heard that any one opened the eyes of a man born blind. [33] If this man were not from God, he could do nothing." [34] They answered him, "You were born in utter sin, and would you teach us?" And they cast him out.

35 Jesus heard that they had cast him out, and having found him he said, "Do you believe in the Son of man?"*v* [36] He answered, "And who is he, sir, that I may believe in him?" [37] Jesus said to him, "You have seen him, and it is he who speaks to you." [38] He said, "Lord, I believe"; and he

v Other ancient authorities read *the Son of God*

value. **7**: *Sent*, a symbol of Jesus as "sent" from God to give light. **13–14**: The *Pharisees* would consider making *clay* as work, a breach of sabbath laws. **17**: The miracle authenticates Jesus as a messenger from God. **18–23**: The *parents* are interrogated to avoid the possibility of mistaken identity. **22**: *Put out*, excommunicated (v. 34). **24**: Not "*Give God the praise* rather than Jesus," but a technical phrase adjuring the man to tell the truth (Jos.7.19). One who broke the sabbath must be *a sinner*. **25**: Recovered sight was more important than Pharisaic tradition. **31**: *We know*, from Old Testament teachings (Ps.66.18; Pr.15.29). **34**: Anger usurps reason. **35–41**: Judgment was not the purpose, but the result, of Jesus' coming (3.17). Belief opens the

worshiped him. ³⁹ Jesus said, "For judgment I came into this world, that those who do not see may see, and that those who see may become blind." ⁴⁰ Some of the Pharisees near him heard this, and they said to him, "Are we also blind?" ⁴¹Jesus said to them, "If you were blind, you would have no guilt; but now that you say, 'We see,' your guilt remains.

10 "Truly, truly, I say to you, he who does not enter the sheepfold by the door but climbs in by another way, that man is a thief and a robber; ² but he who enters by the door is the shepherd of the sheep. ³ To him the gatekeeper opens; the sheep hear his voice, and he calls his own sheep by name and leads them out. ⁴ When he has brought out all his own, he goes before them, and the sheep follow him, for they know his voice. ⁵ A stranger they will not follow, but they will flee from him, for they do not know the voice of strangers." ⁶ This figure Jesus used with them, but they did not understand what he was saying to them.

7 So Jesus again said to them, "Truly, truly, I say to you, I am the door of the sheep. ⁸ All who came before me are thieves and robbers; but the sheep did not heed them. ⁹ I am the door; if any one enters by me, he will be saved, and will go in and out and find pasture. ¹⁰ The thief comes only to steal and kill and destroy; I came that they may have life, and have it abundantly. ¹¹ I am the good shepherd. The good shepherd lays down his life for the sheep. ¹² He who is a hireling and not a shepherd, whose own the sheep are not, sees the wolf coming and leaves the sheep and flees; and the wolf snatches them and scatters them. ¹³ He flees because he is a hireling and cares nothing for the sheep. ¹⁴ I am the good shepherd; I know my own and my own know me, ¹⁵ as the Father knows me and I know the Father; and I lay down my life for the sheep. ¹⁶ And I have other sheep, that are not of this fold; I must bring them also, and they will heed my voice. So there shall be one flock, one shepherd. ¹⁷ For this reason the Father loves me, because I lay down my life, that I may take it again. ¹⁸ No one takes it from me, but I lay it down of my own accord. I have power to lay it down, and I have power to take it again; this charge I have received from my Father."

19 There was again a division among the Jews because of these words. ²⁰ Many of them said, "He has a demon, and he is mad; why listen to him?" ²¹ Others said, "These are not the sayings of one who has a demon. Can a demon open the eyes of the blind?"

22 It was the feast of the Dedication at Jerusalem; ²³ it was winter, and Jesus was walking in the temple, in the portico of Solomon. ²⁴ So the Jews gathered round him and said to him, "How long will you keep us in suspense? If you are the Christ, tell us plainly." ²⁵ Jesus answered them, "I told you, and you do not believe. The works that I do in my Father's name, they bear witness to me; ²⁶ but you do not believe, because you do not belong to my sheep. ²⁷ My sheep hear my voice, and I know them, and they follow me; ²⁸ and I give them eternal

---

eyes of the spirit (*he worshiped him*), unbelief blinds *the Pharisees*. Proud refusal to admit spiritual blindness demonstrates their *guilt* (v. 41).
10.1–42: Jesus, the shepherd who gives his life. 1–6: The details are strikingly true to life. **7:** Christ is the *door* into God's fold. **8:** Refers to Messianic pretenders, whose political ambitions men of faith did not *heed*. **9:** Christ provides (a) escape from the perils of sin, (b) freedom, and (c) spiritual sustenance (the bread, water, and light of life, chs. 6–9). **10:** *Life*, see 3.13–15 n. *Abundantly*, beyond measure (Ps.23.5). **11:** Jesus fulfils Old Testament promises that God himself will come to shepherd his people (Is.40.11; Jer.23.1–6; Ezek.34, esp. v. 11). **16:** *Other sheep*, the Gentiles. *One flock*, Eph.2.11–22. **19–21:** 7.43; 8.48; 9.16. **22:** *Dedication*, commemorating the rededication of the temple in 164 B.C. after its desecration by Antiochus Epiphanes (see "Survey of . . . Bible Lands," §15). **24–30:** Evidence of Jesus' oneness with God

life, and they shall never perish, and no one shall snatch them out of my hand. [29] My Father, who has given them to me,[w] is greater than all, and no one is able to snatch them out of the Father's hand. [30] I and the Father are one."

31 The Jews took up stones again to stone him. [32] Jesus answered them, "I have shown you many good works from the Father; for which of these do you stone me?" [33] The Jews answered him, "It is not for a good work that we stone you but for blasphemy; because you, being a man, make yourself God." [34] Jesus answered them, "Is it not written in your law, 'I said, you are gods'? [35] If he called them gods to whom the word of God came (and scripture cannot be broken), [36] do you say of him whom the Father consecrated and sent into the world, 'You are blaspheming,' because I said, 'I am the Son of God'? [37] If I am not doing the works of my Father, then do not believe me; [38] but if I do them, even though you do not believe me, believe the works, that you may know and understand that the Father is in me and I am in the Father." [39] Again they tried to arrest him, but he escaped from their hands.

40 He went away again across the Jordan to the place where John at first baptized, and there he remained. [41] And many came to him; and they said, "John did no sign, but everything that John said about this man was true." [42] And many believed in him there.

Now a certain man was ill, Laz′-arus of Bethany, the village of Mary and her sister Martha. [2] It was Mary who anointed the Lord with ointment and wiped his feet with her hair, whose brother Laz′arus was ill. [3] So the sisters sent to him, saying, "Lord, he whom you love is ill." [4] But when Jesus heard it he said, "This illness is not unto death; it is for the glory of God, so that the Son of God may be glorified by means of it."

5 Now Jesus loved Martha and her sister and Laz′arus. [6] So when he heard that he was ill, he stayed two days longer in the place where he was. [7] Then after this he said to the disciples, "Let us go into Judea again." [8] The disciples said to him, "Rabbi, the Jews were but now seeking to stone you, and are you going there again?" [9] Jesus answered, "Are there not twelve hours in the day? If any one walks in the day, he does not stumble, because he sees the light of this world. [10] But if any one walks in the night, he stumbles, because the light is not in him." [11] Thus he spoke, and then he said to them, "Our friend Laz′arus has fallen asleep, but I go to awake him out of sleep." [12] The disciples said to him, "Lord, if he has fallen asleep, he will recover." [13] Now Jesus had spoken of his death, but they thought that he meant taking rest in sleep. [14] Then Jesus told them plainly, "Laz′arus is dead; [15] and for your sake I am glad that I was not there, so that you may believe. But let us go to him." [16] Thomas, called the Twin, said to his fellow disciples, "Let us also go, that we may die with him."

17 Now when Jesus came, he found that Laz′arus[x] had already been in the tomb four days. [18] Bethany was

w Other ancient authorities read *What my Father has given to me*

x Greek *he*

demands faith for its interpretation (see 8.58 n.). **31–39:** Two arguments: (a) In the light of Ps.82.6, titles are less important than realities; (b) Jesus' works authenticate him, for they are the kind which God does. **40:** Jesus withdraws to Perea for safety. **41:** 1.26–36.

11.1–57: The raising of Lazarus, the crowning miracle or *sign* (12.17–18), revealing Jesus as the giver of life (5.25–29), and precipitating his death (11.53). **1:** *Bethany*, v. 18. **2:** 12.1–3. **4:** *Death*, i.e. final death. **6:** The action of Jesus is never hurried. **9:** His life would end when God willed; his enemies could not shorten it. **11:** *Sleep* is a common New Testament description of death (see Mt.9.24 n.; Mk.5.39; Acts 7.60; 1 Cor.15.6). **15:** The miracle will confirm their faith. **16:** Courageous loyalty, not cynicism. **20:** As in Lk.10.38–42, Martha is active,

near Jerusalem, about two miles[y] off, [19] and many of the Jews had come to Martha and Mary to console them concerning their brother. [20] When Martha heard that Jesus was coming, she went and met him, while Mary sat in the house. [21] Martha said to Jesus, "Lord, if you had been here, my brother would not have died. [22] And even now I know that whatever you ask from God, God will give you." [23] Jesus said to her, "Your brother will rise again." [24] Martha said to him, "I know that he will rise again in the resurrection at the last day." [25] Jesus said to her, "I am the resurrection and the life;[z] he who believes in me, though he die, yet shall he live, [26] and whoever lives and believes in me shall never die. Do you believe this?" [27] She said to him, "Yes, Lord; I believe that you are the Christ, the Son of God, he who is coming into the world."

[28] When she had said this, she went and called her sister Mary, saying quietly, "The Teacher is here and is calling for you." [29] And when she heard it, she rose quickly and went to him. [30] Now Jesus had not yet come to the village, but was still in the place where Martha had met him. [31] When the Jews who were with her in the house, consoling her, saw Mary rise quickly and go out, they followed her, supposing that she was going to the tomb to weep there. [32] Then Mary, when she came where Jesus was and saw him, fell at his feet, saying to him, "Lord, if you had been here, my brother would not have died." [33] When Jesus saw her weeping, and the Jews who came with her also weeping, he was deeply moved in spirit and

troubled; [34] and he said, "Where have you laid him?" They said to him, "Lord, come and see." [35] Jesus wept. [36] So the Jews said, "See how he loved him!" [37] But some of them said, "Could not he who opened the eyes of the blind man have kept this man from dying?"

[38] Then Jesus, deeply moved again, came to the tomb; it was a cave, and a stone lay upon it. [39] Jesus said, "Take away the stone." Martha, the sister of the dead man, said to him, "Lord, by this time there will be an odor, for he has been dead four days." [40] Jesus said to her, "Did I not tell you that if you would believe you would see the glory of God?" [41] So they took away the stone. And Jesus lifted up his eyes and said, "Father, I thank thee that thou hast heard me. [42] I knew that thou hearest me always, but I have said this on account of the people standing by, that they may believe that thou didst send me." [43] When he had said this, he cried with a loud voice, "Laz'arus, come out." [44] The dead man came out, his hands and feet bound with bandages, and his face wrapped with a cloth. Jesus said to them, "Unbind him, and let him go."

[45] Many of the Jews therefore, who had come with Mary and had seen what he did, believed in him; [46] but some of them went to the Pharisees and told them what Jesus had done. [47] So the chief priests and the Pharisees gathered the council, and said, "What are we to do? For this man performs many signs. [48] If we let him go on thus, every one will believe in him, and the Romans

y Greek *fifteen stadia*
z Other ancient authorities omit *and the life*
a Greek *our place*

Mary contemplative. **21–22:** Disappointment blends with faint hope, *even now.* **24:** Belief in *the resurrection at the last day* was widespread among pious Jews in Jesus' day. **25–26:** Jesus is not only the agent of final resurrection, but gives eternal life now (Rom.6.4–5; Col.2.12; 3.1). The body dies, but the person *shall never die.* **27:** Martha rests her perplexity on the mystery of Jesus' person as the Messiah. **32:** See v. 21. **33:** *Moved*, stirred with indignation, probably at the power of death (12.27). **34:** *Laid*, buried. **35:** Jesus' humanity was real. **39:** *Dead four days;* popular belief imagined that the soul lingered near the body for three days, then left. **40:** *Glory of God*, i.e. God acting to reveal his nature as lifegiver. **41–42:** God hears even Jesus' unspoken thoughts, but Jesus wishes the people to know that he is no magician, but one sent from God. **47:** *Council*, the Sanhedrin, the official Jewish court, made up of seventy priests,

will come and destroy both our holy place[a] and our nation." [49] But one of them, Ca'iaphas, who was high priest that year, said to them, "You know nothing at all; [50] you do not understand that it is expedient for you that one man should die for the people, and that the whole nation should not perish." [51] He did not say this of his own accord, but being high priest that year he prophesied that Jesus should die for the nation, [52] and not for the nation only, but to gather into one the children of God who are scattered abroad. [53] So from that day on they took counsel how to put him to death.

54 Jesus therefore no longer went about openly among the Jews, but went from there to the country near the wilderness, to a town called E'phraim; and there he stayed with the disciples.

55 Now the Passover of the Jews was at hand, and many went up from the country to Jerusalem before the Passover, to purify themselves. [56] They were looking for Jesus and saying to one another as they stood in the temple, "What do you think? That he will not come to the feast?" [57] Now the chief priests and the Pharisees had given orders that if any one knew where he was, he should let them know, so that they might arrest him.

12 Six days before the Passover, Jesus came to Bethany, where Laz'arus was, whom Jesus had raised from the dead. [2] There they made him a supper; Martha served, and Laz'arus was one of those at table with him. [3] Mary took a pound of costly ointment of pure nard and anointed the feet of Jesus and wiped his feet with her hair; and the house was filled with the fragrance of the ointment. [4] But Judas Iscariot, one of his disciples (he who was to betray him), said, [5] "Why was this ointment not sold for three hundred denarii[b] and given to the poor?" [6] This he said, not that he cared for the poor but because he was a thief, and as he had the money box he used to take what was put into it. [7] Jesus said, "Let her alone, let her keep it for the day of my burial. [8] The poor you always have with you, but you do not always have me."

9 When the great crowd of the Jews learned that he was there, they came, not only on account of Jesus but also to see Laz'arus, whom he had raised from the dead. [10] So the chief priests planned to put Laz'arus also to death, [11] because on account of him many of the Jews were going away and believing in Jesus.

12 The next day a great crowd who had come to the feast heard that Jesus was coming to Jerusalem. [13] So they took branches of palm trees and went out to meet him, crying, "Hosanna! Blessed is he who comes in the name of the Lord, even the King of Israel!" [14] And Jesus found a young ass and sat upon it; as it is written,
[15] "Fear not, daughter of Zion;
 behold, your king is coming,
 sitting on an ass's colt!"

b The denarius was a day's wage for a laborer

---

scribes, and elders, presided over by the high priest. **49–53:** An unconscious prophecy with deep theological meaning–Jesus' death would redeem not only the Jews but believers in all nations. **54:** *Ephraim*, about fifteen miles north of Jerusalem.

12.1–11: The anointing at Bethany. In the full knowledge of a plot against his life (11.53,57), Jesus returns to the vicinity of Jerusalem. **1:** *Bethany*, 11.18. **4–5:** Judas's reaction is a sign of his defection. **5:** *Three hundred denarii*, see note *b*. **6:** *Take*, pilfer. **7:** Jesus foresees his death; the anointing is the last rite in preparation for burial. **8:** Such spontaneous love will not neglect the poor.

12.12–19: Palm Sunday. Jesus dramatically manifests himself as the Messiah. **13:** *Hosanna*, see Mt.21.9 n. *In the name of*, with the authority of God. *King of Israel*, the Messiah. **14–15:** Zech.9.9. Warlike kings rode on horses and in chariots; the king of peace, *on an ass's colt*. **16:** The cross, resurrection, ascension, and Pentecost clarified many Old Testament passages.

[16] His disciples did not understand this at first; but when Jesus was glorified, then they remembered that this had been written of him and had been done to him. [17] The crowd that had been with him when he called Laz'arus out of the tomb and raised him from the dead bore witness. [18] The reason why the crowd went to meet him was that they heard he had done this sign. [19] The Pharisees then said to one another, "You see that you can do nothing; look, the world has gone after him."

20 Now among those who went up to worship at the feast were some Greeks. [21] So these came to Philip, who was from Beth-sa'ida in Galilee, and said to him, "Sir, we wish to see Jesus." [22] Philip went and told Andrew; Andrew went with Philip and they told Jesus. [23] And Jesus answered them, "The hour has come for the Son of man to be glorified. [24] Truly, truly, I say to you, unless a grain of wheat falls into the earth and dies, it remains alone; but if it dies, it bears much fruit. [25] He who loves his life loses it, and he who hates his life in this world will keep it for eternal life. [26] If any one serves me, he must follow me; and where I am, there shall my servant be also; if any one serves me, the Father will honor him.

27 "Now is my soul troubled. And what shall I say? 'Father, save me from this hour'? No, for this purpose I have come to this hour. [28] Father, glorify thy name." Then a voice came from heaven, "I have glorified it, and I will glorify it again." [29] The crowd standing by heard it and said that it had thundered. Others said, "An angel has spoken to him." [30] Jesus answered, "This voice has come for your sake, not for mine. [31] Now is the judgment of this world, now shall the ruler of this world be cast out; [32] and I, when I am lifted up from the earth, will draw all men to myself." [33] He said this to show by what death he was to die. [34] The crowd answered him, "We have heard from the law that the Christ remains for ever. How can you say that the Son of man must be lifted up? Who is this Son of man?" [35] Jesus said to them, "The light is with you for a little longer. Walk while you have the light, lest the darkness overtake you; he who walks in the darkness does not know where he goes. [36] While you have the light, believe in the light, that you may become sons of light."

When Jesus had said this, he departed and hid himself from them. [37] Though he had done so many signs before them, yet they did not believe in him; [38] it was that the word spoken by the prophet Isaiah might be fulfilled:

"Lord, who has believed our report,
and to whom has the arm of the
Lord been revealed?"

[39] Therefore they could not believe. For Isaiah again said,

[40] "He has blinded their eyes and
hardened their heart,
lest they should see with their eyes
and perceive with their heart,
and turn for me to heal them."

[41] Isaiah said this because he saw his glory and spoke of him. [42] Nevertheless many even of the authorities believed in him, but for fear of the Pharisees they did not confess it, lest they should be put out of the synagogue: [43] for they loved the praise of men more than the praise of God.

44 And Jesus cried out and said, "He who believes in me, believes not in me but in him who sent me. [45] And he who sees me sees him who sent me.

12.20–50: Jesus' public ministry concludes. 20: *Greeks*, Gentiles. **23–24:** *The hour*, see 2.4 n. **25–26:** Mt.10.39; Mk.8.35; Lk.9.24; 14.26. **27–30:** Mk.14.32–42. A *voice . . . from heaven* was a common sign of divine reassurance (Mk.1.11; 9.7; Acts 9.7). **31–33:** Reality reverses appearances: Jesus' death judges the *world*, not him; defeats Satan, not Jesus; draws, not repels, *all* men. **34–36a:** All evidence is in; it is time to act! *Sons of light*, see Lk.16.8 n. **36b–43:** Refusal to *believe* evidence (*so many signs*) induces spiritual blindness (Is.6.9–10; Mt.13.14–15; see Acts 28.26 n.). **44–50:** Summary of Jesus' teaching.

[46] I have come as light into the world, that whoever believes in me may not remain in darkness. [47] If any one hears my sayings and does not keep them, I do not judge him; for I did not come to judge the world but to save the world. [48] He who rejects me and does not receive my sayings has a judge; the word that I have spoken will be his judge on the last day. [49] For I have not spoken on my own authority; the Father who sent me has himself given me commandment what to say and what to speak. [50] And I know that his commandment is eternal life. What I say, therefore, I say as the Father has bidden me."

13 Now before the feast of the Passover, when Jesus knew that his hour had come to depart out of this world to the Father, having loved his own who were in the world, he loved them to the end. [2] And during supper, when the devil had already put it into the heart of Judas Iscariot, Simon's son, to betray him, [3] Jesus, knowing that the Father had given all things into his hands, and that he had come from God and was going to God, [4] rose from supper, laid aside his garments, and girded himself with a towel. [5] Then he poured water into a basin, and began to wash the disciples' feet, and to wipe them with the towel with which he was girded. [6] He came to Simon Peter; and Peter said to him, "Lord, do you wash my feet?" [7] Jesus answered him, "What I am doing you do not know now, but afterward you will understand." [8] Peter said to him, "You shall never wash my feet." Jesus answered him, "If I do not wash you, you have no part in me." [9] Simon Peter said to him, "Lord, not my feet only but also my hands and my head!" [10] Jesus said to him, "He who has

bathed does not need to wash, except for his feet,[c] but he is clean all over; and you[x] are clean, but not every one of you." [11] For he knew who was to betray him; that was why he said, "You are not all clean."

12 When he had washed their feet, and taken his garments, and resumed his place, he said to them, "Do you know what I have done to you? [13] You call me Teacher and Lord; and you are right, for so I am. [14] If I then, your Lord and Teacher, have washed your feet, you also ought to wash one another's feet. [15] For I have given you an example, that you also should do as I have done to you. [16] Truly, truly, I say to you, a servant[d] is not greater than his master; nor is he who is sent greater than he who sent him. [17] If you know these things, blessed are you if you do them. [18] I am not speaking of you all; I know whom I have chosen; it is that the scripture may be fulfilled, 'He who ate my bread has lifted his heel against me.' [19] I tell you this now, before it takes place, that when it does take place you may believe that I am he. [20] Truly, truly, I say to you, he who receives any one whom I send receives me; and he who receives me receives him who sent me."

21 When Jesus had thus spoken, he was troubled in spirit, and testified, "Truly, truly, I say to you, one of you will betray me." [22] The disciples looked at one another, uncertain of whom he spoke. [23] One of his disciples, whom Jesus loved, was lying close to the breast of Jesus; [24] so Simon Peter beckoned to him and said, "Tell us who it is of whom he speaks." [25] So lying thus, close to the breast of Jesus, he said to him, "Lord, who is it?"

c Other ancient authorities omit *except for his feet*
x The Greek word for *you* here is plural
d Or *slave*

13.1–38: The Last Supper. Preparation for the teaching (chs. 14–17) and events (chs. 18–21) to follow. **1:** *To the end.* the utmost. **5:** Lk.22.27. **6–9:** Though incongruous, Peter must let Jesus *wash* him, the reason made plain *afterward* in the cross. **11:** Outward washing alone does not cleanse (Lk.11.39–41; Heb.10.22). **15:** 1 Pet.2.21. **16:** Mt.10.24; Lk.6.40. **17:** Lk.11.28; Jas.1.25. **18:** Ps.41.9. **21–30:** The betrayer must be dissuaded, or dismissed. Jesus honors him by seating him next to himself, handing him a *morsel* (Ru.2.14), concealing his treachery from

26 Jesus answered, "It is he to whom I shall give this morsel when I have dipped it." So when he had dipped the morsel, he gave it to Judas, the son of Simon Iscariot. 27 Then after the morsel, Satan entered into him. Jesus said to him, "What you are going to do, do quickly." 28 Now no one at the table knew why he said this to him. 29 Some thought that, because Judas had the money box, Jesus was telling him, "Buy what we need for the feast"; or, that he should give something to the poor. 30 So, after receiving the morsel, he immediately went out; and it was night.

31 When he had gone out, Jesus said, "Now is the Son of man glorified, and in him God is glorified; 32 if God is glorified in him, God will also glorify him in himself, and glorify him at once. 33 Little children, yet a little while I am with you. You will seek me; and as I said to the Jews so now I say to you, 'Where I am going you cannot come.' 34 A new commandment I give to you, that you love one another; even as I have loved you, that you also love one another. 35 By this all men will know that you are my disciples, if you have love for one another."

36 Simon Peter said to him, "Lord, where are you going?" Jesus answered, "Where I am going you cannot follow me now; but you shall follow afterward." 37 Peter said to him, "Lord, why cannot I follow you now? I will lay down my life for you." 38 Jesus answered, "Will you lay down your life for me? Truly, truly, I say to you, the cock will not crow, till you have denied me three times.

14 "Let not your hearts be troubled; believe[e] in God, believe also in me. 2 In my Father's house are many rooms; if it were not so, would I have told you that I go to prepare a place for you? 3 And when I go and prepare a place for you, I will come again and will take you to myself, that where I am you may be also. 4 And you know the way where I am going."[f] 5 Thomas said to him, "Lord, we do not know where you are going; how can we know the way?" 6 Jesus said to him, "I am the way, and the truth, and the life; no one comes to the Father, but by me. 7 If you had known me, you would have known my Father also; henceforth you know him and have seen him."

8 Philip said to him, "Lord, show us the Father, and we shall be satisfied." 9 Jesus said to him, "Have I been with you so long, and yet you do not know me, Philip? He who has seen me has seen the Father; how can you say, 'Show us the Father'? 10 Do you not believe that I am in the Father and the Father in me? The words that I say to you I do not speak on my own authority; but the Father who dwells in me does his works. 11 Believe me that I am in the Father and the Father in me; or else believe me for the sake of the works themselves.

12 "Truly, truly, I say to you, he who believes in me will also do the works that I do; and greater works than

e Or *you believe*
f Other ancient authorities read *where I am going you know, and the way you know*

---

all but the beloved disciple. Refusal of light brings *night* (12.35). **31–35:** The death that Judas has gone to arrange will *glorify* (reveal the essence of) both Father and Son as holy love. The disciples are now the organ of this love. **36–38:** Peter is not yet ready to *follow* Jesus to death; *afterward*, according to tradition, he was martyred.

14.1–17.26: Jesus' farewell discourse and prayer; an interpretation of Jesus' completed work on earth and relation to both believers and the world after his resurrection and ascension. It is a meditation, which–like a love-letter–is difficult to outline.

14.1–31: The believers' relation to the glorified Christ; no separation, but deepened fellowship. **1:** Belief in God has new meaning in Jesus. **2–3:** For him to *go*, through death and resurrection, to his *Father's house* (with *rooms* for all) was to *prepare a place* of permanent fellowship with him (13.33,36). **4–7:** Access to God is solely through Jesus (Mt.11.27; Jn.1.18; 6.46; Acts 4.12). **8–11:** Knowledge of God is solely through the person, *words*, and *works* of Jesus. **12–17:** *Greater works* (of a more exalted nature because redemption is achieved) will be done by the

these will he do, because I go to the Father. [13] Whatever you ask in my name, I will do it, that the Father may be glorified in the Son; [14] if you ask[g] anything in my name, I will do it.

15 "If you love me, you will keep my commandments. [16] And I will pray the Father, and he will give you another Counselor, to be with you for ever, [17] even the Spirit of truth, whom the world cannot receive, because it neither sees him nor knows him; you know him, for he dwells with you, and will be in you.

18 "I will not leave you desolate; I will come to you. [19] Yet a little while, and the world will see me no more, but you will see me; because I live, you will live also. [20] In that day you will know that I am in my Father, and you in me, and I in you. [21] He who has my commandments and keeps them, he it is who loves me; and he who loves me will be loved by my Father, and I will love him and manifest myself to him." [22] Judas (not Iscariot) said to him, "Lord, how is it that you will manifest yourself to us, and not to the world?" [23] Jesus answered him, "If a man loves me, he will keep my word, and my Father will love him, and we will come to him and make our home with him. [24] He who does not love me does not keep my words; and the word which you hear is not mine but the Father's who sent me.

25 "These things I have spoken to you, while I am still with you. [26] But the Counselor, the Holy Spirit, whom the Father will send in my name, he will teach you all things, and bring to your remembrance all that I have said to you. [27] Peace I leave with you; my peace I give to you; not as the world gives do I give to you. Let not your hearts be troubled, neither let them be afraid. [28] You heard me say to you, 'I go away, and I will come to you.' If you loved me, you would have rejoiced, because I go to the Father; for the Father is greater than I. [29] And now I have told you before it takes place, so that when it does take place, you may believe. [30] I will no longer talk much with you, for the ruler of this world is coming. He has no power over me; [31] but I do as the Father has commanded me, so that the world may know that I love the Father. Rise, let us go hence.

15 "I am the true vine, and my Father is the vinedresser. [2] Every branch of mine that bears no fruit, he takes away, and every branch that does bear fruit he prunes, that it may bear more fruit. [3] You are already made clean by the word which I have spoken to you. [4] Abide in me, and I in you. As the branch cannot bear fruit by itself, unless it abides in the vine, neither can you, unless you abide in me. [5] I am the vine, you are the branches. He who abides in me, and I in him, he it is that bears much fruit, for apart from me you can do nothing. [6] If a man does not abide in me, he is cast forth as a branch and withers; and the branches are gathered, thrown into the fire and burned. [7] If you abide in me, and my words abide in you, ask whatever you will, and it shall be done for you. [8] By this my Father is glorified, that you bear much fruit, and so prove

g Other ancient authorities add *me*

believers through prayer (vv. 13,15), obedience (v. 15), and the Holy Spirit (*Counselor*, vv. 16, 17). **16:** *Counselor*, the same word is translated "advocate" in 1 Jn.2.1. **18-20:** The Spirit imparts Christ's life (Acts 2.33) and unites the believer to God. **21-24:** Fellowship with Christ is dependent on *love* which issues in obedience. **25-27:** The *Holy Spirit* interprets Christ's teachings (v. 26), and imparts his peace (v. 27). **28-31:** To *go* to the Father meant Jesus' self-chosen conflict with *the ruler of this world*, whose *power* would be broken by death and resurrection.

15.1-27: The pattern of the Christian believer's life. Three dimensions are set forth: (a) **1-11:** The believer's relation to Christ–*abide*. As *the true vine* Jesus was the true Israel, fulfilling the vocation in which the old Israel had failed (Is.5.1-7; Jer.2.21; Ezek.19.10-14). The *fruit* bearing (Gal.5.22-23) of the new Israel (the church) springs from union (actual incorporation) with

to be my disciples. ⁹ As the Father has loved me, so have I loved you; abide in my love. ¹⁰ If you keep my commandments, you will abide in my love, just as I have kept my Father's commandments and abide in his love. ¹¹ These things I have spoken to you, that my joy may be in you, and that your joy may be full.

12 "This is my commandment, that you love one another as I have loved you. ¹³ Greater love has no man than this, that a man lay down his life for his friends. ¹⁴ You are my friends if you do what I command you. ¹⁵ No longer do I call you servants,*ʰ* for the servant*ⁱ* does not know what his master is doing; but I have called you friends, for all that I have heard from my Father I have made known to you. ¹⁶ You did not choose me, but I chose you and appointed you that you should go and bear fruit and that your fruit should abide; so that whatever you ask the Father in my name, he may give it to you. ¹⁷ This I command you, to love one another.

18 "If the world hates you, know that it has hated me before it hated you. ¹⁹ If you were of the world, the world would love its own; but because you are not of the world, but I chose you out of the world, therefore the world hates you. ²⁰ Remember the word that I said to you, 'A servant*ⁱ* is not greater than his master.' If they persecuted me, they will persecute you; if they kept my word, they will keep yours also. ²¹ But all this they will do to you on

my account, because they do not know him who sent me. ²² If I had not come and spoken to them, they would not have sin; but now they have no excuse for their sin. ²³ He who hates me hates my Father also. ²⁴ If I had not done among them the works which no one else did, they would not have sin; but now they have seen and hated both me and my Father. ²⁵ It is to fulfil the word that is written in their law, 'They hated me without a cause.' ²⁶ But when the Counselor comes, whom I shall send to you from the Father, even the Spirit of truth, who proceeds from the Father, he will bear witness to me; ²⁷ and you also are witnesses, because you have been with me from the beginning.

16 "I have said all this to you to keep you from falling away. ² They will put you out of the synagogues; indeed, the hour is coming when whoever kills you will think he is offering service to God. ³ And they will do this because they have not known the Father, nor me. ⁴ But I have said these things to you, that when their hour comes you may remember that I told you of them.

"I did not say these things to you from the beginning, because I was with you. ⁵ But now I am going to him who sent me; yet none of you asks me, 'Where are you going?' ⁶ But because I have said these things to you, sorrow has filled your hearts. ⁷ Nevertheless I tell you the truth: it is to your advan-

h Or *slaves*   *i* Or *slave*

---

him (v. 5), through prayer (v. 7), and loving obedience (vv. 9,10), issuing in *joy* (v. 11). (b) **12–17:** The relation of believers to one another–*love*. The measure is determined by Jesus' death (v. 13). Fellowship with Jesus (vv. 14,15), *fruit* bearing, and prayer (v. 16), are all dependent on obeying his *command* to *love* (v. 17). (c) **18–27:** The believer's relation to the world—separation (the world hates the church because it hates Christ who has judged it, vv. 18–25; Ps.35.19; 69.4), and bearing *witness* to Christ in the power of the Holy *Spirit* (vv. 26–27; Acts 1.21–22; 5.32).

16.1–33: The Christian's relation to the world. 1–4a: Forewarning of conflict. It is to be expected that the world, even the religious world, will persecute the followers of Christ (vv. 2–3; Acts 22.3–5; 26.9–11). **4b–11:** The work of the *Counselor* (Holy Spirit) through the church. *Sorrow* at Jesus' departure is transformed by *the truth* that his death and resurrection make possible the Spirit's work (vv. 6–7). He can then *convince the world* that sin is unbelief in Jesus (v. 9), that the cross reveals God's *righteousness* (v. 10), and brings *judgment* by triumphing over evil (v. 11; 12.31; 14.30; 1 Cor.2.8; Col.2.15). **12–15:** The guidance of the *Spirit* into the full

tage that I go away, for if I do not go away, the Counselor will not come to you; but if I go, I will send him to you. [8] And when he comes, he will convince[x] the world concerning sin and righteousness and judgment: [9] concerning sin, because they do not believe in me; [10] concerning righteousness, because I go to the Father, and you will see me no more; [11] concerning judgment, because the ruler of this world is judged.

12 "I have yet many things to say to you, but you cannot bear them now. [13] When the Spirit of truth comes, he will guide you into all the truth; for he will not speak on his own authority, but whatever he hears he will speak, and he will declare to you the things that are to come. [14] He will glorify me, for he will take what is mine and declare it to you. [15] All that the Father has is mine; therefore I said that he will take what is mine and declare it to you.

16 "A little while, and you will see me no more; again a little while, and you will see me." [17] Some of his disciples said to one another, "What is this that he says to us, 'A little while, and you will not see me, and again a little while, and you will see me'; and, 'because I go to the Father'?" [18] They said, "What does he mean by 'a little while'? We do not know what he means." [19] Jesus knew that they wanted to ask him; so he said to them, "Is this what you are asking yourselves, what I meant by saying, 'A little while, and you will not see me, and again a little while, and you will see me'? [20] Truly, truly, I say to you, you will weep and lament, but the world will rejoice; you will be sorrowful, but your sorrow will turn into joy. [21] When a

woman is in travail she has sorrow, because her hour has come; but when she is delivered of the child, she no longer remembers the anguish, for joy that a child[j] is born into the world. [22] So you have sorrow now, but I will see you again and your hearts will rejoice, and no one will take your joy from you. [23] In that day you will ask nothing of me. Truly, truly, I say to you, if you ask anything of the Father, he will give it to you in my name. [24] Hitherto you have asked nothing in my name; ask, and you will receive, that your joy may be full.

25 "I have said this to you in figures; the hour is coming when I shall no longer speak to you in figures but tell you plainly of the Father. [26] In that day you will ask in my name; and I do not say to you that I shall pray the Father for you; [27] for the Father himself loves you, because you have loved me and have believed that I came from the Father. [28] I came from the Father and have come into the world; again, I am leaving the world and going to the Father."

29 His disciples said, "Ah, now you are speaking plainly, not in any figure! [30] Now we know that you know all things, and need none to question you; by this we believe that you came from God." [31] Jesus answered them, "Do you now believe? [32] The hour is coming, indeed it has come, when you will be scattered, every man to his home, and will leave me alone; yet I am not alone, for the Father is with me. [33] I have said this to you, that in me you may have peace. In the world you have tribulation; but be of good cheer, I have overcome the world."

x Or *convict*   *j* Greek *a human being*

truth about the historic Jesus (*will glorify*, will reveal the essential nature of). **16–24:** Temporary *sorrow* over Jesus' death yields to *joy* over his resurrection and abiding presence (vv. 20–22). This is sustained by prayer in Jesus' *name* (nature, all that the cross and resurrection reveal him to be, vv. 23–24). **25–33:** The pledge of triumph. Jesus' *going to the Father* (v. 28) makes plain all his teachings, reveals God's *love* (v. 27), empowers prayer (v. 26), and offers *peace* even in *tribulation* (v. 33). **32:** Mk.14.27; Zech.13.7. **33:** 14.27; 15.18; Rom.8.37; 2 Cor. 2.14; Rev.3.21.

17.1–26: Jesus' high priestly prayer. This falls naturally into three parts: (a) **1–5:** Jesus' prayer for himself. The *hour* (see 2.4 n.) of Jesus' perfect obedience unto death *has come*, secur-

17 When Jesus had spoken these words, he lifted up his eyes to heaven and said, "Father, the hour has come; glorify thy Son that the Son may glorify thee, ² since thou hast given him power over all flesh, to give eternal life to all whom thou hast given him. ³ And this is eternal life, that they know thee the only true God, and Jesus Christ whom thou hast sent. ⁴ I glorified thee on earth, having accomplished the work which thou gavest me to do; ⁵ and now, Father, glorify thou me in thy own presence with the glory which I had with thee before the world was made.

6 "I have manifested thy name to the men whom thou gavest me out of the world; thine they were, and thou gavest them to me, and they have kept thy word. ⁷ Now they know that everything that thou hast given me is from thee; ⁸ for I have given them the words which thou gavest me, and they have received them and know in truth that I came from thee; and they have believed that thou didst send me. ⁹ I am praying for them; I am not praying for the world but for those whom thou hast given me, for they are thine; ¹⁰ all mine are thine, and thine are mine, and I am glorified in them. ¹¹ And now I am no more in the world, but they are in the world, and I am coming to thee. Holy Father, keep them in thy name, which thou hast given me, that they may be one, even as we are one. ¹² While I was with them, I kept them in thy name, which thou hast given me; I have guarded them, and none of them is lost but the son of perdition, that the scripture might be fulfilled. ¹³ But now I am coming to thee; and these things I speak in the world, that they may have my joy fulfilled in themselves. ¹⁴ I

have given them thy word; and the world has hated them because they are not of the world, even as I am not of the world. ¹⁵ I do not pray that thou shouldst take them out of the world, but that thou shouldst keep them from the evil one.*k* ¹⁶ They are not of the world, even as I am not of the world. ¹⁷ Sanctify them in the truth; thy word is truth. ¹⁸ As thou didst send me into the world, so I have sent them into the world. ¹⁹ And for their sake I consecrate myself, that they also may be consecrated in truth.

20 "I do not pray for these only, but also for those who believe in me through their word, ²¹ that they may all be one; even as thou, Father, art in me, and I in thee, that they also may be in us, so that the world may believe that thou hast sent me. ²² The glory which thou hast given me I have given to them, that they may be one even as we are one, ²³ I in them and thou in me, that they may become perfectly one, so that the world may know that thou hast sent me and hast loved them even as thou hast loved me. ²⁴ Father, I desire that they also, whom thou hast given me, may be with me where I am, to behold my glory which thou hast given me in thy love for me before the foundation of the world. ²⁵ O righteous Father, the world has not known thee, but I have known thee; and these know that thou hast sent me. ²⁶ I made known to them thy name, and I will make it known, that the love with which thou hast loved me may be in them, and I in them."

18 When Jesus had spoken these words, he went forth with his disciples across the Kidron valley, where

k Or *from evil*

ing *eternal life* for men through knowledge (personal acquaintance) of God and his Son. *Having accomplished* his *work* (19.30), Jesus awaits the restoration of his pre-incarnate *glory*. (b) **6–19**: Jesus' prayer for his disciples, left *in the world* after his ascension (v. 11), is that they may *be one* as are the Father and the Son (v. 11), have *joy* (v. 13), be victorious over the *evil one* (v. 15), and fulfil their mission of representing Christ to *the world* (vv. 16–19). (c) **20–26**: Jesus' prayer for the Church universal is that it may be indwelt by the Father and the Son and express their unity in *love*, thus fulfilling its mission of leading *the world* to *believe*.

    18.1–19.42: Arrest, trial, crucifixion, and burial of Jesus. 18.1: *Kidron valley*, between Jerusalem

there was a garden, which he and his disciples entered. ² Now Judas, who betrayed him, also knew the place; for Jesus often met there with his disciples. ³ So Judas, procuring a band of soldiers and some officers from the chief priests and the Pharisees, went there with lanterns and torches and weapons. ⁴ Then Jesus, knowing all that was to befall him, came forward and said to them, "Whom do you seek?" ⁵ They answered him, "Jesus of Nazareth." Jesus said to them, "I am he." Judas, who betrayed him, was standing with them. ⁶ When he said to them, "I am he," they drew back and fell to the ground. ⁷ Again he asked them, "Whom do you seek?" And they said, "Jesus of Nazareth." ⁸ Jesus answered, "I told you that I am he; so, if you seek me, let these men go." ⁹ This was to fulfil the word which he had spoken, "Of those whom thou gavest me I lost not one." ¹⁰ Then Simon Peter, having a sword, drew it and struck the high priest's slave and cut off his right ear. The slave's name was Malchus. ¹¹ Jesus said to Peter, "Put your sword into its sheath; shall I not drink the cup which the Father has given me?"

12 So the band of soldiers and their captain and the officers of the Jews seized Jesus and bound him. ¹³ First they led him to Annas; for he was the father-in-law of Ca'iaphas, who was high priest that year. ¹⁴ It was Ca'iaphas who had given counsel to the Jews that it was expedient that one man should die for the people.

15 Simon Peter followed Jesus, and so did another disciple. As this disciple was known to the high priest, he entered the court of the high priest along with Jesus, ¹⁶ while Peter stood outside at the door. So the other disciple, who was known to the high priest, went out and spoke to the maid who kept the door, and brought Peter in. ¹⁷ The maid who kept the door said to Peter, "Are not you also one of this man's disciples?" He said, "I am not." ¹⁸ Now the servants[l] and officers had made a charcoal fire, because it was cold, and they were standing and warming themselves; Peter also was with them, standing and warming himself.

19 The high priest then questioned Jesus about his disciples and his teaching. ²⁰ Jesus answered him, "I have spoken openly to the world; I have always taught in synagogues and in the temple, where all Jews come together; I have said nothing secretly. ²¹ Why do you ask me? Ask those who have heard me, what I said to them; they know what I said." ²² When he had said this, one of the officers standing by struck Jesus with his hand, saying, "Is that how you answer the high priest?" ²³ Jesus answered him, "If I have spoken wrongly, bear witness to the wrong; but if I have spoken rightly, why do you strike me?" ²⁴ Annas then sent him bound to Ca'iaphas the high priest.

25 Now Simon Peter was standing and warming himself. They said to him, "Are not you also one of his disciples?" He denied it and said, "I am not." ²⁶ One of the servants[l] of the high priest, a kinsman of the man whose ear Peter had cut off, asked, "Did I not see you in the garden with him?" ²⁷ Peter again denied it; and at once the cock crowed.

28 Then they led Jesus from the house of Ca'iaphas to the praetorium. It was early. They themselves did not enter the praetorium, so that they might not be defiled, but might eat the pass-

l Or slaves

and the Mount of Olives. *A garden,* Gethsemane. **3:** Both Roman *soldiers* and *officers* of the Jewish temple police made the arrest. **4:** Jesus' fate is self-chosen; he, not Judas or the soldiers, determines his death. **9:** 6.39; 10.28; 17.12. **11:** *Cup,* see Lk.22.42 n. **13:** *Annas,* though deposed by the Romans in A.D. 15, was still the leading influence among the Jews through his son-in-law and four sons who succeeded him. **19–21:** An informal trial, designed to indict Jesus for training disciples secretly as revolutionaries. **24:** He is sent to *Caiaphas* for formal trial before the Sanhedrin (Mt.26.57–75; Mk.14.53–72; Lk.22.54–71). **27:** 13.38. **28:** *Prae-*

over. ²⁹ So Pilate went out to them and said, "What accusation do you bring against this man?" ³⁰ They answered him, "If this man were not an evildoer, we would not have handed him over." ³¹ Pilate said to them, "Take him yourselves and judge him by your own law." The Jews said to him, "It is not lawful for us to put any man to death." ³² This was to fulfil the word which Jesus had spoken to show by what death he was to die.

33 Pilate entered the praetorium again and called Jesus, and said to him, "Are you the King of the Jews?" ³⁴ Jesus answered, "Do you say this of your own accord, or did others say it to you about me?" ³⁵ Pilate answered, "Am I a Jew? Your own nation and the chief priests have handed you over to me; what have you done?" ³⁶ Jesus answered, "My kingship is not of this world; if my kingship were of this world, my servants would fight, that I might not be handed over to the Jews; but my kingship is not from the world." ³⁷ Pilate said to him, "So you are a king?" Jesus answered, "You say that I am a king. For this I was born, and for this I have come into the world, to bear witness to the truth. Every one who is of the truth hears my voice." ³⁸ Pilate said to him, "What is truth?"

After he had said this, he went out to the Jews again, and told them, "I find no crime in him. ³⁹ But you have a custom that I should release one man for you at the Passover; will you have me release for you the King of the Jews?" ⁴⁰ They cried out again, "Not this man, but Barab'bas!" Now Barab'bas was a robber.

19 Then Pilate took Jesus and scourged him. ² And the soldiers plaited a crown of thorns, and put it on his head, and arrayed him in a purple robe; ³ they came up to him, saying, "Hail, King of the Jews!" and struck him with their hands. ⁴ Pilate went out again, and said to them, "See, I am bringing him out to you, that you may know that I find no crime in him." ⁵ So Jesus came out, wearing the crown of thorns and the purple robe. Pilate said to them, "Behold the man!" ⁶ When the chief priests and the officers saw him, they cried out, "Crucify him, crucify him!" Pilate said to them, "Take him yourselves and crucify him, for I find no crime in him." ⁷ The Jews answered him, "We have a law, and by that law he ought to die, because he has made himself the Son of God." ⁸ When Pilate heard these words, he was the more afraid; ⁹ he entered the praetorium again and said to Jesus, "Where are you from?" But Jesus gave no answer. ¹⁰ Pilate therefore said to him, "You will not speak to me? Do you not know that I have power to release you, and power to crucify you?" ¹¹ Jesus answered him, "You would have no power over me unless it had been given you from above; therefore he who delivered me to you has the greater sin."

12 Upon this Pilate sought to release him, but the Jews cried out, "If you release this man, you are not Caesar's friend; every one who makes himself a king sets himself against Caesar." ¹³ When Pilate heard these words, he brought Jesus out and sat down on the judgment seat at a place

---

torium, governor's residence. *Defiled*, entering a Gentile's house would make them ceremonially unclean. **29–31:** The Jews tried religious cases, but could not administer the death penalty. **32:** Crucifixion (3.14; 12.32), rather than the Jewish method of stoning. **33–37:** The Jews charged Jesus with political treason. Jesus is king of *truth*, from God's world. **40:** *Robber*, a political revolutionary, a "bandit-patriot." **19.1–5:** Though Pilate found (18.38) Jesus innocent of political insurrection, he has him *scourged* (brutally whipped). **7:** Lev.24.16; Mk.14.61–64; Jn.5.18; 10.33. **9:** Unable to understand the charge, Pilate is superstitiously afraid (Mt.27.19). **11:** God controls evil, without setting aside human responsibility. The high priest, who *delivered* Jesus to Pilate, bore the greater responsibility. **12:** A threat of blackmail. **14:** *Sixth hour*, about noon. **17:** *Skull*, a place of skull-like appearance just outside the city walls (v. 20). **19–22:** The trilingual caption expressed Pilate's contempt (v. 14). **23:** A Roman custom. **24:**

called The Pavement, and in Hebrew, Gab'batha. 14 Now it was the day of Preparation of the Passover; it was about the sixth hour. He said to the Jews, "Behold your King!" 15 They cried out, "Away with him, away with him, crucify him!" Pilate said to them, "Shall I crucify your King?" The chief priests answered, "We have no king but Caesar." 16 Then he handed him over to them to be crucified.

17 So they took Jesus, and he went out, bearing his own cross, to the place called the place of a skull, which is called in Hebrew Gol'gotha. 18 There they crucified him, and with him two others, one on either side, and Jesus between them. 19 Pilate also wrote a title and put it on the cross; it read, "Jesus of Nazareth, the King of the Jews." 20 Many of the Jews read this title, for the place where Jesus was crucified was near the city; and it was written in Hebrew, in Latin, and in Greek. 21 The chief priests of the Jews then said to Pilate, "Do not write, 'The King of the Jews,' but, 'This man said, I am King of the Jews.'" 22 Pilate answered, "What I have written I have written."

23 When the soldiers had crucified Jesus they took his garments and made four parts, one for each soldier; also his tunic. But the tunic was without seam, woven from top to bottom; 24 so they said to one another, "Let us not tear it, but cast lots for it to see whose it shall be." This was to fulfil the scripture,

"They parted my garments among them,
and for my clothing they cast lots."

25 So the soldiers did this. But standing by the cross of Jesus were his mother, and his mother's sister, Mary the wife of Clopas, and Mary Mag'-dalene. 26 When Jesus saw his mother, and the disciple whom he loved standing near, he said to his mother, "Woman, behold, your son!" 27 Then he said to the disciple, "Behold, your mother!" And from that hour the disciple took her to his own home.

28 After this Jesus, knowing that all was now finished, said (to fulfil the scripture), "I thirst." 29 A bowl full of vinegar stood there; so they put a sponge full of the vinegar on hyssop and held it to his mouth. 30 When Jesus had received the vinegar, he said, "It is finished"; and he bowed his head and gave up his spirit.

31 Since it was the day of Preparation, in order to prevent the bodies from remaining on the cross on the sabbath (for that sabbath was a high day), the Jews asked Pilate that their legs might be broken, and that they might be taken away. 32 So the soldiers came and broke the legs of the first, and of the other who had been crucified with him; 33 but when they came to Jesus and saw that he was already dead, they did not break his legs. 34 But one of the soldiers pierced his side with a spear, and at once there came out blood and water. 35 He who saw it has borne witness–his testimony is true, and he knows that he tells the truth–that you also may believe. 36 For these things took place that the scripture might be fulfilled, "Not a bone of him shall be broken." 37 And again another scripture says, "They shall look on him whom they have pierced."

38 After this Joseph of Arimathe'a, who was a disciple of Jesus, but secretly, for fear of the Jews, asked Pilate that he might take away the body of Jesus, and Pilate gave him leave. So he came and took away his body. 39 Nicode'mus also, who had at first come to him by night, came bringing a mixture of myrrh and aloes, about a hundred pounds' weight. 40 They took the body of Jesus, and bound it in

Providence controlled even the soldiers' behavior (Ps.22.18). **26–27:** Indicates Jesus' real humanity and concern for human values. **28:** *I thirst*, Ps.69.21. **29:** *Vinegar*, sour wine. **30:** *Finished*, all that God has sent him to do for the redemption of the world (17.4). **31:** *High day*, especially holy since it fell on the Passover. **34:** *Blood and water* indicate the reality of Jesus' humanity, and perhaps also the new covenant and baptism (Mk.14.24; 1 Cor.10.16; Jn.3.5;

linen cloths with the spices, as is the burial custom of the Jews. ⁴¹ Now in the place where he was crucified there was a garden, and in the garden a new tomb where no one had ever been laid. ⁴² So because of the Jewish day of Preparation, as the tomb was close at hand, they laid Jesus there.

20 Now on the first day of the week Mary Mag′dalene came to the tomb early, while it was still dark, and saw that the stone had been taken away from the tomb. ² So she ran, and went to Simon Peter and the other disciple, the one whom Jesus loved, and said to them, "They have taken the Lord out of the tomb, and we do not know where they have laid him." ³ Peter then came out with the other disciple, and they went toward the tomb. ⁴ They both ran, but the other disciple outran Peter and reached the tomb first; ⁵ and stooping to look in, he saw the linen cloths lying there, but he did not go in. ⁶ Then Simon Peter came, following him, and went into the tomb; he saw the linen cloths lying, ⁷ and the napkin, which had been on his head, not lying with the linen cloths but rolled up in a place by itself. ⁸ Then the other disciple, who reached the tomb first, also went in, and he saw and believed; ⁹ for as yet they did not know the scripture, that he must rise from the dead. ¹⁰ Then the disciples went back to their homes.

11 But Mary stood weeping outside the tomb, and as she wept she stooped to look into the tomb; ¹² and she saw two angels in white, sitting where the body of Jesus had lain, one at the head and one at the feet. ¹³ They said to her, "Woman, why are you weeping?" She said to them, "Because they have taken away my Lord, and I do not know where they have laid him." ¹⁴ Saying this, she turned round and saw Jesus standing, but she did not know that it was Jesus. ¹⁵ Jesus said to her, "Woman, why are you weeping? Whom do you seek?" Supposing him to be the gardener, she said to him, "Sir, if you have carried him away, tell me where you have laid him, and I will take him away." ¹⁶ Jesus said to her, "Mary." She turned and said to him in Hebrew, "Rab-bo′ni!" (which means Teacher). ¹⁷ Jesus said to her, "Do not hold me, for I have not yet ascended to the Father; but go to my brethren and say to them, I am ascending to my Father and your Father, to my God and your God." ¹⁸ Mary Mag′dalene went and said to the disciples, "I have seen the Lord"; and she told them that he had said these things to her.

19 On the evening of that day, the first day of the week, the doors being shut where the disciples were, for fear of the Jews, Jesus came and stood among them and said to them, "Peace be with you." ²⁰ When he had said this, he showed them his hands and his side. Then the disciples were glad when they saw the Lord. ²¹ Jesus said to them again, "Peace be with you. As the Father has sent me, even so I send you." ²² And when he had said this, he breathed on them, and said to them, "Receive the Holy Spirit. ²³ If you for-

---

1 Jn.5.6–8). **36:** Jesus fulfils the passover (Ex.12.46; 1 Cor.5.7). **37:** Zech.12.10. **38:** *Joseph of Arimathea*, Mt.27.57–60; Mk.15.43; Lk.23.50–53. **39:** *Nicodemus*, 3.1–15; 7.50–52.
   20.1–31: The resurrection. 1: *First day*, Sunday. **2–3:** The empty tomb indicates actual resurrection, not mere immortality. **4:** *The other disciple* was younger. **6:** Peter shows characteristic boldness. **7:** Jesus' body had escaped without *the linen cloths* being unwound. *The napkin*, which had been wrapped about *his head* (compare 11.44), lay apart, still *rolled up*. **8:** *Believed*, faith grasped the evidence that Jesus had not been resuscitated from a swoon, or stolen; he had been transformed without corruption into his resurrection body (Acts 2.24–31). **9:** *The scripture*, the Old Testament (compare Lk.24.27,32,44–46; Acts 2.24–28). **16–17:** The old title, *Teacher*, and Mary's effort to *hold* (cling to) him, were to be abandoned for the new relation with him as the *ascended* Lord (compare chs. 14–17). **20:** *Hands, side*, identifying marks; also signs of glory through suffering (Lk.24.25–26). **21–23:** The church embodies Christ's mission of forgiveness, but only as his life is *breathed* into her (see Mt.16.19 n.). **24–27:** Thomas

give the sins of any, they are forgiven; if you retain the sins of any, they are retained."

24 Now Thomas, one of the twelve, called the Twin, was not with them when Jesus came. [25] So the other disciples told him, "We have seen the Lord." But he said to them, "Unless I see in his hands the print of the nails, and place my finger in the mark of the nails, and place my hand in his side, I will not believe."

26 Eight days later, his disciples were again in the house, and Thomas was with them. The doors were shut, but Jesus came and stood among them, and said, "Peace be with you." [27] Then he said to Thomas, "Put your finger here, and see my hands; and put out your hand, and place it in my side; do not be faithless, but believing." [28] Thomas answered him, "My Lord and my God!" [29] Jesus said to him, "Have you believed because you have seen me? Blessed are those who have not seen and yet believe."

30 Now Jesus did many other signs in the presence of the disciples, which are not written in this book; [31] but these are written that you may believe that Jesus is the Christ, the Son of God, and that believing you may have life in his name.

21 After this Jesus revealed himself again to the disciples by the Sea of Tibe'ri-as; and he revealed himself in this way. [2] Simon Peter, Thomas called the Twin, Nathan'a-el of Cana in Galilee, the sons of Zeb'edee, and two others of his disciples were together. [3] Simon Peter said to them, "I am going fishing." They said to him, "We will go with you." They went out

and got into the boat; but that night they caught nothing.

4 Just as day was breaking, Jesus stood on the beach; yet the disciples did not know that it was Jesus. [5] Jesus said to them, "Children, have you any fish?" They answered him, "No." [6] He said to them, "Cast the net on the right side of the boat, and you will find some." So they cast it, and now they were not able to haul it in, for the quantity of fish. [7] That disciple whom Jesus loved said to Peter, "It is the Lord!" When Simon Peter heard that it was the Lord, he put on his clothes, for he was stripped for work, and sprang into the sea. [8] But the other disciples came in the boat, dragging the net full of fish, for they were not far from the land, but about a hundred yards[m] off.

9 When they got out on land, they saw a charcoal fire there, with fish lying on it, and bread. [10] Jesus said to them, "Bring some of the fish that you have just caught." [11] So Simon Peter went aboard and hauled the net ashore, full of large fish, a hundred and fifty-three of them; and although there were so many, the net was not torn. [12] Jesus said to them, "Come and have breakfast." Now none of the disciples dared ask him, "Who are you?" They knew it was the Lord. [13] Jesus came and took the bread and gave it to them, and so with the fish. [14] This was now the third time that Jesus was revealed to the disciples after he was raised from the dead.

15 When they had finished breakfast, Jesus said to Simon Peter, "Simon, son of John, do you love me more than these?" He said to him, "Yes, Lord; you know that I love you." He said to

m Greek *two hundred cubits*

---

wanted visible proof. **28:** Climax of the book. **29:** Faith now rests on the apostolic testimony. **30–31:** Purpose of the Gospel according to John.

21.1–25: Epilogue. A post-resurrection appearance in Galilee (*Tiberias*, see 6.1 n.). **2–3:** Indicates Peter's natural leadership. **4–6:** Obedience to Jesus' command is rewarded. **9–14:** Jesus' feeding of the disciples is a prelude to his command to Peter to *feed* others. **15–17:** *These*, other disciples (Mk.14.29). The triple question is reminiscent of Peter's triple denial (18.17, 25–27). **18–19:** According to tradition Peter was martyred under Nero at Rome about A.D. 64–68. **20–22:** Each is to *follow* his Lord, regardless of others. *Until I come*, the second coming.

him, "Feed my lambs." [16] A second time he said to him, "Simon, son of John, do you love me?" He said to him, "Yes, Lord; you know that I love you." He said to him, "Tend my sheep." [17] He said to him the third time, "Simon, son of John, do you love me?" Peter was grieved because he said to him the third time, "Do you love me?" And he said to him, "Lord, you know everything; you know that I love you." Jesus said to him, "Feed my sheep. [18] Truly, truly, I say to you, when you were young, you girded yourself and walked where you would; but when you are old, you will stretch out your hands, and another will gird you and carry you where you do not wish to go." [19] (This he said to show by what death he was to glorify God.) And after this he said to him, "Follow me."

20 Peter turned and saw following them the disciple whom Jesus loved, who had lain close to his breast at the supper and had said, "Lord, who is it that is going to betray you?" [21] When Peter saw him, he said to Jesus, "Lord, what about this man?" [22] Jesus said to him, "If it is my will that he remain until I come, what is that to you? Follow me!" [23] The saying spread abroad among the brethren that this disciple was not to die; yet Jesus did not say to him that he was not to die, but, "If it is my will that he remain until I come, what is that to you?"

24 This is the disciple who is bearing witness to these things, and who has written these things; and we know that his testimony is true.

25 But there are also many other things which Jesus did; were every one of them to be written, I suppose that the world itself could not contain the books that would be written.

23: A rumor that the End would come before the beloved disciple's death was falsely based.
24: *We know*, confirmation by the church where the Gospel of John was written.

THE ACTS OF THE APOSTLES

The book of Acts continues the narrative of Luke's Gospel by tracing the story of the Christian movement from the resurrection of Jesus to the time when the apostle Paul was in Rome preaching the gospel unhindered. Most of the first half of Acts is occupied with the Jerusalem church and its relationships, while the latter half is dominated by Paul. The progress of the book is mainly geographical; from Jerusalem the word spreads to Samaria (8.5), the seacoast (8.40), Damascus (9.10), Antioch and Cyprus (11.19), Asia Minor (13.13), Europe (16.11), and finally Rome itself (28.16).

As in the Gospel of Luke (see Lk.1.1 n.), the author makes use of sources. The first half of Acts contains various traditions of the Jerusalem church and also a document which seems to reflect the interests of the church at Antioch (parts of chs. 6–8; 11.19–30; 12.24–13.12; and perhaps other passages).

Much of the latter part of the book is narrated in the first person plural, beginning at 16.10. Many believe that Luke "the beloved physician" (Col.4.14; 2 Tim.4.11; compare Philem.24) wrote these sections. Either his travel diary was incorporated in the work by someone else, or, more probably, he wrote both Luke and Acts, using the "we" style to indicate events of which he was an eyewitness.

Luke's purpose was to awaken faith by showing the triumphant progress of the Good News and to defend Christians against the charge that they were destructive of Jewish institutions and a troublesome element in the empire. But he had also an interest in history for its own sake and in the men and women of the story, in the details of lodging, entertainment, and travel, and all that constitutes local color. From every point of view, the New Testament would be infinitely poorer without this first book of church history.

I N THE FIRST BOOK, O THE-OPH′ILUS, I have dealt with all that Jesus began to do and teach, ² until the day when he was taken up, after he had given commandment through the Holy Spirit to the apostles whom he had chosen. ³ To them he presented himself alive after his passion by many proofs, appearing to them during forty days, and speaking of the kingdom of God. ⁴ And while staying*a* with them he charged them not to depart from Jerusalem, but to wait for the promise of the Father, which, he said, "you heard from me, ⁵ for John baptized with water, but before many days you shall be baptized with the Holy Spirit."

6 So when they had come together, they asked him, "Lord, will you at this time restore the kingdom to Israel?" ⁷ He said to them, "It is not for you to know times or seasons which the Father has fixed by his own authority. ⁸ But you shall receive power when the Holy Spirit has come upon you; and you shall be my witnesses in Jerusalem and in all Judea and Sama′ria and to the end of the earth." ⁹ And when he had said this, as they were looking on, he was lifted up, and a cloud took him out of their sight. ¹⁰ And while they were gazing into heaven as he went, behold, two men stood by them in white robes, ¹¹ and said, "Men of Galilee, why do you stand looking into

a Or *eating*

1.1–5: Introduction; the risen Christ. The author links his volume with *the first book*, the Gospel of Luke. **1**: *Theophilus*, "lover of God"; perhaps a Roman official to whom the two books were addressed, or any reader who loves God (see Lk.1.3 n.). **3**: Some of the *many proofs* are given in Lk.24.13–53. **4**: The Greek words for *staying* and *eating* (see note *a*) are identical. **5**: John the Baptist had predicted that the Messiah would baptize his people *with the Holy Spirit* (Mk.1.8; Mt.3.11; Lk.3.16; Jn.1.33). The idea is found also in the Dead Sea scrolls (see "Survey of . . . Bible Lands," §15, end).

1.6–11: The ascension. This takes place after forty days (v. 3); but compare Lk.24.50–51. **6**: Since he was promised "the throne of his father David" (Lk.1.32), the disciples would expect Jesus to *restore the kingdom to Israel*. **8**: For apostles as *witnesses* see Lk.24.48; Acts 1.22; 2.32.

heaven? This Jesus, who was taken up from you into heaven, will come in the same way as you saw him go into heaven."

12 Then they returned to Jerusalem from the mount called Olivet, which is near Jerusalem, a sabbath day's journey away; [13] and when they had entered, they went up to the upper room, where they were staying, Peter and John and James and Andrew, Philip and Thomas, Bartholomew and Matthew, James the son of Alphaeus and Simon the Zealot and Judas the son of James. [14] All these with one accord devoted themselves to prayer, together with the women and Mary the mother of Jesus, and with his brothers.

15 In those days Peter stood up among the brethren (the company of persons was in all about a hundred and twenty), and said, [16] "Brethren, the scripture had to be fulfilled, which the Holy Spirit spoke beforehand by the mouth of David, concerning Judas who was guide to those who arrested Jesus. [17] For he was numbered among us, and was allotted his share in this ministry. [18] (Now this man bought a field with the reward of his wickedness; and falling headlong[b] he burst open in the middle and all his bowels gushed out. [19] And it became known to all the inhabitants of Jerusalem, so that the field was called in their language Akel'dama, that is, Field of Blood.) [20] For it is written in the book of Psalms,

'Let his habitation become desolate,
and let there be no one to live in it';
and

'His office let another take.'

[21] So one of the men who have accompanied us during all the time that the Lord Jesus went in and out among us, [22] beginning from the baptism of John until the day when he was taken up from us—one of these men must become with us a witness to his resurrection." [23] And they put forward two, Joseph called Barsab'bas, who was surnamed Justus, and Matthi'as. [24] And they prayed and said, "Lord, who knowest the hearts of all men, show which one of these two thou hast chosen [25] to take the place in this ministry and apostleship from which Judas turned aside, to go to his own place." [26] And they cast lots for them, and the lot fell on Matthi'as; and he was enrolled with the eleven apostles.

2 When the day of Pentecost had come, they were all together in one place. [2] And suddenly a sound came from heaven like the rush of a mighty wind, and it filled all the house where they were sitting. [3] And there appeared to them tongues as of fire, distributed and resting on each one of them. [4] And they were all filled with the Holy Spirit and began to speak in other tongues, as the Spirit gave them utterance.

5 Now there were dwelling in Jerusalem Jews, devout men from every nation under heaven. [6] And at this sound the multitude came together, and they were bewildered, because each one heard them speaking in his own language. [7] And they were amazed and wondered, saying, "Are

b Or *swelling up*

1.12–26: The gathering of the Twelve. The gospels agree that the Eleven remained together; now the sacred number, corresponding to the tribes of Israel, is restored, in anticipation of the coming age (Lk.22.29–30). **12:** *Olivet* means "olive grove." *A sabbath day's journey*, a little more than half a mile. **13:** The same list as in Lk.6.14–16, but in a different order. **14:** *Brothers*, see Mt.13.55 n. **18:** *Falling headlong*, literally "flat" or "prone," but here the meaning is uncertain; according to Mt.27.5, Judas hanged himself. **22:** *The baptism of John* is regarded as the beginning of the gospel (10.37; Mk.1.1–4). Every apostle is *a witness* to Jesus' *resurrection;* this includes Paul (1 Cor.15.8–9).

2.1–47: The day of Pentecost (Lev.23.15–21). Jewish tradition held that the Law was given on this day, seven weeks after Passover. **1–13:** The gift of the Holy Spirit. **3:** John had promised a baptism of the Holy Spirit and *fire* (Lk.3.16). **4–11:** The *other tongues* in the Corinthian church were an incoherent form of speech (1 Cor.14.1–33); here Luke thinks of a gift of foreign lan-

not all these who are speaking Galileans? [8] And how is it that we hear, each of us in his own native language? [9] Par'thians and Medes and E'lamites and residents of Mesopota'mia, Judea and Cappado'cia, Pontus and Asia, [10] Phryg'ia and Pamphyl'ia, Egypt and the parts of Libya belonging to Cyre'ne, and visitors from Rome, both Jews and proselytes, [11] Cretans and Arabians, we hear them telling in our own tongues the mighty works of God." [12] And all were amazed and perplexed, saying to one another, "What does this mean?" [13] But others mocking said, "They are filled with new wine."

14 But Peter, standing with the eleven, lifted up his voice and addressed them, "Men of Judea and all who dwell in Jerusalem, let this be known to you, and give ear to my words. [15] For these men are not drunk, as you suppose, since it is only the third hour of the day; [16] but this is what was spoken by the prophet Joel:

[17] 'And in the last days it shall be, God declares,
　that I will pour out my Spirit upon all flesh,
　and your sons and your daughters shall prophesy,
　and your young men shall see visions,
　and your old men shall dream dreams;
[18] yea, and on my menservants and my maidservants in those days
　I will pour out my Spirit; and they shall prophesy.
[19] And I will show wonders in the heaven above
　and signs on the earth beneath,
　blood, and fire, and vapor of smoke;
[20] the sun shall be turned into darkness
　and the moon into blood,

before the day of the Lord comes, the great and manifest day.
[21] And it shall be that whoever calls on the name of the Lord shall be saved.'

22 "Men of Israel, hear these words: Jesus of Nazareth, a man attested to you by God with mighty works and wonders and signs which God did through him in your midst, as you yourselves know— [23] this Jesus, delivered up according to the definite plan and foreknowledge of God, you crucified and killed by the hands of lawless men. [24] But God raised him up, having loosed the pangs of death, because it was not possible for him to be held by it. [25] For David says concerning him,

'I saw the Lord always before me,
　for he is at my right hand that I may not be shaken;
[26] therefore my heart was glad, and my tongue rejoiced;
　moreover my flesh will dwell in hope.
[27] For thou wilt not abandon my soul to Hades,
　nor let thy Holy One see corruption.
[28] Thou hast made known to me the ways of life;
　thou wilt make me full of gladness with thy presence.'

29 "Brethren, I may say to you confidently of the patriarch David that he both died and was buried, and his tomb is with us to this day. [30] Being therefore a prophet, and knowing that God had sworn with an oath to him that he would set one of his descendants upon his throne, [31] he foresaw and spoke of the resurrection of the Christ, that he was not abandoned to Hades, nor did his flesh see corruption. [32] This Jesus God raised up, and of that we all are witnesses. [33] Being therefore exalted at the right hand of God, and

---

guages, as though the story of the tower of Babel (Gen.11.1–9) had been reversed. **13:** *Filled with new wine* suggests the ecstatic utterance of 1 Cor. ch. 14. **14–36:** Peter's sermon. **15:** *Third hour*, about 9 a.m. **17:** The gift of the Spirit to *all flesh*, and not just to chosen individuals, is a mark of the Messianic age (Jl.2.28–32). Like Paul (1 Cor.12.13), Acts usually assumes that all Christians receive the Spirit (10.44–48). **23:** *Definite plan*, see Lk.24.26 n. **24:** *God raised him up*, see 1 Cor.15.4–8. **25:** Ps.16.8–11. **30:** Ps.132.11. **31:** Ps.16.10. **36:** Early Christians

having received from the Father the promise of the Holy Spirit, he has poured out this which you see and hear. [34] For David did not ascend into the heavens; but he himself says,

'The Lord said to my Lord, Sit at my right hand,
[35] till I make thy enemies a stool for thy feet.'

[36] Let all the house of Israel therefore know assuredly that God has made him both Lord and Christ, this Jesus whom you crucified."

37 Now when they heard this they were cut to the heart, and said to Peter and the rest of the apostles, "Brethren, what shall we do?" [38] And Peter said to them, "Repent, and be baptized every one of you in the name of Jesus Christ for the forgiveness of your sins; and you shall receive the gift of the Holy Spirit. [39] For the promise is to you and to your children and to all that are far off, every one whom the Lord our God calls to him." [40] And he testified with many other words and exhorted them, saying, "Save yourselves from this crooked generation." [41] So those who received his word were baptized, and there were added that day about three thousand souls. [42] And they devoted themselves to the apostles' teaching and fellowship, to the breaking of bread and the prayers.

43 And fear came upon every soul; and many wonders and signs were done through the apostles. [44] And all who believed were together and had all things in common; [45] and they sold their possessions and goods and dis-

tributed them to all, as any had need. [46] And day by day, attending the temple together and breaking bread in their homes, they partook of food with glad and generous hearts, [47] praising God and having favor with all the people. And the Lord added to their number day by day those who were being saved.

3 Now Peter and John were going up to the temple at the hour of prayer, the ninth hour. [2] And a man lame from birth was being carried, whom they laid daily at that gate of the temple which is called Beautiful to ask alms of those who entered the temple. [3] Seeing Peter and John about to go into the temple, he asked for alms. [4] And Peter directed his gaze at him, with John, and said, "Look at us." [5] And he fixed his attention upon them, expecting to receive something from them. [6] But Peter said, "I have no silver and gold, but I give you what I have; in the name of Jesus Christ of Nazareth, walk." [7] And he took him by the right hand and raised him up; and immediately his feet and ankles were made strong. [8] And leaping up he stood and walked and entered the temple with them, walking and leaping and praising God. [9] And all the people saw him walking and praising God, [10] and recognized him as the one who sat for alms at the Beautiful Gate of the temple; and they were filled with wonder and amazement at what had happened to him.

11 While he clung to Peter and John, all the people ran together to them in the portico called Solomon's,

---

believed that Jesus was not only *Christ*, the Messiah on earth, but also the heavenly *Lord*; vv. 34–35 use Ps.110.1 to prove this. **37–42:** The call to repentance. **39:** Is.57.19; Jl.2.32. **42:** *The breaking of bread*, apparently a common meal which included the Lord's Supper (see 1 Cor.11.17–34). **43–47:** Description of the early church. **44:** Jerusalem Christians for a time, like the Essenes (see Mt.3.7 n.), *had everything in common* (4.32–35), but 5.4 suggests that this was not a universal rule.

    3.1–10: Healing at the Beautiful Gate. Two of the chief disciples manifest "the signs of a true apostle" (2 Cor.12.12; Mt.10.8). **1:** *Ninth hour*, about 3 p.m., when sacrifice was offered with prayer (Ex.29.39; Lev.6.20; Josephus, *Ant.* xiv.4.3). **2:** The *gate . . . called Beautiful* was probably on the east side of the temple. **6:** Christians and others healed and cast out demons *in the name of Jesus* (19.13; Mk.9.38; Mt.7.22).

    3.11–26: Peter's preaching. In a second sermon Peter gives a fuller account of the Christian message. **11:** *The portico called Solomon's* was probably on the east side of the temple. **13:**

astounded. [12] And when Peter saw it he addressed the people, "Men of Israel, why do you wonder at this, or why do you stare at us, as though by our own power or piety we had made him walk? [13] The God of Abraham and of Isaac and of Jacob, the God of our fathers, glorified his servant[c] Jesus, whom you delivered up and denied in the presence of Pilate, when he had decided to release him. [14] But you denied the Holy and Righteous One, and asked for a murderer to be granted to you, [15] and killed the Author of life, whom God raised from the dead. To this we are witnesses. [16] And his name, by faith in his name, has made this man strong whom you see and know; and the faith which is through Jesus[d] has given the man this perfect health in the presence of you all.

[17] "And now, brethren, I know that you acted in ignorance, as did also your rulers. [18] But what God foretold by the mouth of all the prophets, that his Christ should suffer, he thus fulfilled. [19] Repent therefore, and turn again, that your sins may be blotted out, that times of refreshing may come from the presence of the Lord, [20] and that he may send the Christ appointed for you, Jesus, [21] whom heaven must receive until the time for establishing all that God spoke by the mouth of his holy prophets from of old. [22] Moses said, 'The Lord God will raise up for you a prophet from your brethren as he raised me up. You shall listen to him in whatever he tells you. [23] And it shall be that every soul that does not listen to that prophet shall be destroyed from the people.' [24] And all the prophets who have spoken, from Samuel and those who came afterwards, also proclaimed these days. [25] You are the sons of the prophets and of the covenant which God gave to your fathers, saying to Abraham, 'And in your posterity shall all the families of the earth be blessed.' [26] God, having raised up his servant,[c] sent him to you first, to bless you in turning every one of you from your wickedness."

4 And as they were speaking to the people, the priests and the captain of the temple and the Sad'ducees came upon them, [2] annoyed because they were teaching the people and proclaiming in Jesus the resurrection from the dead. [3] And they arrested them and put them in custody until the morrow, for it was already evening. [4] But many of those who heard the word believed; and the number of the men came to about five thousand.

5 On the morrow their rulers and elders and scribes were gathered together in Jerusalem, [6] with Annas the high priest and Ca'iaphas and John and Alexander, and all who were of the high-priestly family. [7] And when they had set them in the midst, they inquired, "By what power or by what name did you do this?" [8] Then Peter, filled with the Holy Spirit, said to them, "Rulers of the people and elders, [9] if we are being examined today concerning a good deed done to a cripple, by what means this man has been healed, [10] be it known to you all, and to all the people of Israel, that by the name of Jesus Christ of Nazareth, whom you crucified, whom God raised from the dead, by him this man is standing before you well. [11] This is the stone which was rejected by you builders, but

c Or *child*   d Greek *him*

Servant, the word can be translated "child" (see note c), but in the Greek version of Is.52.13 it is used for the suffering Servant of the Lord; compare the prayers in Acts 4.25,27,30. **15:** *Author*, the word can mean "pioneer" or "founder" (of a new city). **22:** Jesus is successor of Moses as well as David (Dt.18.15–16). **23:** Dt.18.19; Lev.23.29. **25:** Gen.22.18.

4.1–31: Arrest and release of Peter and John. The first of many incidents in which the apostles defend the faith before the authorities. **1–2:** The *priests* in control of *the temple* were usually Sadducees, who denied the *resurrection from the dead* (23.6–8). **5–6:** Perhaps the *rulers* are priests; with the *elders and scribes* they made up the Sanhedrin, or council, of which *the high priest* was head (see Jn.11.47 n.). *Annas* held this office A.D. 6–14, and *Caiaphas* was his son-in-

which has become the head of the corner. ¹² And there is salvation in no one else, for there is no other name under heaven given among men by which we must be saved."

13 Now when they saw the boldness of Peter and John, and perceived that they were uneducated, common men, they wondered; and they recognized that they had been with Jesus. ¹⁴ But seeing the man that had been healed standing beside them, they had nothing to say in opposition. ¹⁵ But when they had commanded them to go aside out of the council, they conferred with one another, ¹⁶ saying, "What shall we do with these men? For that a notable sign has been performed through them is manifest to all the inhabitants of Jerusalem, and we cannot deny it. ¹⁷ But in order that it may spread no further among the people, let us warn them to speak no more to any one in this name." ¹⁸ So they called them and charged them not to speak or teach at all in the name of Jesus. ¹⁹ But Peter and John answered them, "Whether it is right in the sight of God to listen to you rather than to God, you must judge; ²⁰ for we cannot but speak of what we have seen and heard." ²¹ And when they had further threatened them, they let them go, finding no way to punish them, because of the people; for all men praised God for what had happened. ²² For the man on whom this sign of healing was performed was more than forty years old.

23 When they were released they went to their friends and reported what the chief priests and the elders had said to them. ²⁴ And when they heard it, they lifted their voices together to God and said, "Sovereign Lord, who didst make the heaven and the earth and the sea and everything in them, ²⁵ who by the mouth of our father David, thy servant,^{c} didst say by the Holy Spirit,

'Why did the Gentiles rage,
  and the peoples imagine vain things?
²⁶ The kings of the earth set themselves
    in array,
  and the rulers were gathered
    together,
  against the Lord and against his
    Anointed'–^{e}

²⁷ for truly in this city there were gathered together against thy holy servant^c Jesus, whom thou didst anoint, both Herod and Pontius Pilate, with the Gentiles and the peoples of Israel, ²⁸ to do whatever thy hand and thy plan had predestined to take place. ²⁹ And now, Lord, look upon their threats, and grant to thy servants^f to speak thy word with all boldness, ³⁰ while thou stretchest out thy hand to heal, and signs and wonders are performed through the name of thy holy servant^c Jesus." ³¹ And when they had prayed, the place in which they were gathered together was shaken; and they were all filled with the Holy Spirit and spoke the word of God with boldness.

32 Now the company of those who believed were of one heart and soul, and no one said that any of the things which he possessed was his own, but they had everything in common. ³³ And with great power the apostles gave their testimony to the resurrection of the Lord Jesus, and great grace was upon them all. ³⁴ There was not a needy person among them, for as many as were possessors of lands or houses sold them, and brought the pro-

c Or *child* e Or *Christ* f Or *slaves*

---

law (Jn.18.13); *John* may be Jonathan, who succeeded Caiaphas. **11:** The stone which was rejected (Ps.118.22) is also identified with Jesus in Mk.12.10; 1 Pet.2.7. Essenes (see Mt.3.7 n.) and Christians used this and other Old Testament "stone" passages in teaching. **13:** Like Jesus (Jn.7.15), the apostles were considered *uneducated* because they lacked rabbinical training. **25–26:** Ps.2.1–2. **27:** *Servant,* see 3.13 n. **29:** Here *servants* is the Greek word for "slaves," as throughout Paul's letters; it was customary for Semites to call themselves slaves of their gods.
    4.32–5.11: The sharing of goods. Christians took care of their needy (Rom.12.8; 1 Cor.13.3; Heb.13.16), but it was only in Jerusalem that this type of communal living (similar to that of the

ceeds of what was sold [35] and laid it at the apostles' feet; and distribution was made to each as any had need. [36] Thus Joseph who was surnamed by the apostles Barnabas (which means, Son of encouragement), a Levite, a native of Cyprus, [37] sold a field which belonged to him, and brought the money and laid it at the apostles' feet.

5 But a man named Anani'as with his wife Sapphi'ra sold a piece of property, [2] and with his wife's knowledge, [2] he kept back some of the proceeds, and brought only a part and laid it at the apostles' feet. [3] But Peter said, "Anani'as, why has Satan filled your heart to lie to the Holy Spirit and to keep back part of the proceeds of the land? [4] While it remained unsold, did it not remain your own? And after it was sold, was it not at your disposal? How is it that you have contrived this deed in your heart? You have not lied to men but to God." [5] When Anani'as heard these words, he fell down and died. And great fear came upon all who heard of it. [6] The young men rose and wrapped him up and carried him out and buried him.

7 After an interval of about three hours his wife came in, not knowing what had happened. [8] And Peter said to her, "Tell me whether you sold the land for so much." And she said, "Yes, for so much." [9] But Peter said to her, "How is it that you have agreed together to tempt the Spirit of the Lord? Hark, the feet of those that have buried your husband are at the door, and they will carry you out." [10] Immediately she fell down at his feet and died. When the young men came in they found her dead, and they carried her out and buried her beside her husband. [11] And great fear came upon the whole church, and upon all who heard of these things.

12 Now many signs and wonders were done among the people by the hands of the apostles. And they were all together in Solomon's Portico. [13] None of the rest dared join them, but the people held them in high honor. [14] And more than ever believers were added to the Lord, multitudes both of men and women, [15] so that they even carried out the sick into the streets, and laid them on beds and pallets, that as Peter came by at least his shadow might fall on some of them. [16] The people also gathered from the towns around Jerusalem, bringing the sick and those afflicted with unclean spirits, and they were all healed.

17 But the high priest rose up and all who were with him, that is, the party of the Sad'ducees, and filled with jealousy [18] they arrested the apostles and put them in the common prison. [19] But at night an angel of the Lord opened the prison doors and brought them out and said, [20] "Go and stand in the temple and speak to the people all the words of this Life." [21] And when they heard this, they entered the temple at daybreak and taught.

Now the high priest came and those who were with him and called together the council and all the senate of Israel, and sent to the prison to have them brought. [22] But when the officers came, they did not find them in the prison, and they returned and reported, [23] "We found the prison securely locked and the sentries standing at the doors, but when we opened it we found no one inside." [24] Now when the captain of the temple and the chief priests heard these words, they were much perplexed about them, wondering what this would come to. [25] And some one came and

---

Essenes) was practiced for a time. **5.3:** The apostles, or perhaps the church, represent *the Holy Spirit*. **4:** The property was at Ananias's *disposal* until he pretended to dedicate all his goods.
    5.12–42: Second arrest of the apostles. The motif of obeying God rather than men, and the divided opinion of the council, are repeated (compare ch. 4). **12:** *Solomon's Portico,* see 3.11 n. **16:** Compare Mk.1.32–34. **19:** *An angel . . . opened the prison doors,* as in 12.6–11; compare 16.25–26. **21:** *Senate,* which means "body of elders," is another word for *council* or Sanhedrin

told them, "The men whom you put in prison are standing in the temple and teaching the people." 26 Then the captain with the officers went and brought them, but without violence, for they were afraid of being stoned by the people. 27 And when they had brought them, they set them before the council. And the high priest questioned them, 28 saying, "We strictly charged you not to teach in this name, yet here you have filled Jerusalem with your teaching and you intend to bring this man's blood upon us." 29 But Peter and the apostles answered, "We must obey God rather than men. 30 The God of our fathers raised Jesus whom you killed by hanging him on a tree. 31 God exalted him at his right hand as Leader and Savior, to give repentance to Israel and forgiveness of sins. 32 And we are witnesses to these things, and so is the Holy Spirit whom God has given to those who obey him."

33 When they heard this they were enraged and wanted to kill them. 34 But a Pharisee in the council named Gama′li-el, a teacher of the law, held in honor by all the people, stood up and ordered the men to be put outside for a while. 35 And he said to them, "Men of Israel, take care what you do with these men. 36 For before these days Theu′das arose, giving himself out to be somebody, and a number of men, about four hundred, joined him; but he was slain and all who followed him were dispersed and came to nothing. 37 After him Judas the Galilean arose in the days of the census and drew away some of the people after him; he also perished, and all who followed him were scattered. 38 So in the present case I tell you, keep away from these men and let them alone; for if this plan or this undertaking is of men, it will fail; 39 but if it is of God, you will not be able to overthrow them. You might even be found opposing God!"

40 So they took his advice, and when they had called in the apostles, they beat them and charged them not to speak in the name of Jesus, and let them go. 41 Then they left the presence of the council, rejoicing that they were counted worthy to suffer dishonor for the name. 42 And every day in the temple and at home they did not cease teaching and preaching Jesus as the Christ.

6 Now in these days when the disciples were increasing in number, the Hellenists murmured against the Hebrews because their widows were neglected in the daily distribution. 2 And the twelve summoned the body of the disciples and said, "It is not right that we should give up preaching the word of God to serve tables. 3 Therefore, brethren, pick out from among you seven men of good repute, full of the Spirit and of wisdom, whom we may appoint to this duty. 4 But we will devote ourselves to prayer and to the ministry of the word." 5 And what they said pleased the whole multitude, and they chose Stephen, a man

---

(see Jn.11.47 n.). **30:** The cross was a pole or *tree* to which a crossbeam was fixed. **31:** *Leader*, the word is translated *Author* in 3.15. *Savior*, a name given by the ancients to one who saves a city, rescues, or heals; the New Testament uses it of Jesus as healer and deliverer from sin and death. **34–37:** *Gamaliel*, a famous liberal rabbi; the speech here fits his tolerant attitude. *Theudas*, according to Josephus (*Ant.* xx.5.1), raised his revolt later than this. *Judas the Galilean* revolted in A.D. 6.

6.1–7: Choice of the Seven. These are traditionally regarded as the first deacons (Phil.1.1; 1 Tim.3.8–13), but their functions are more like those of presbyters or bishops (20.17,28), for Stephen teaches (vv. 9–10) and does not merely *serve tables* (v. 2). **1:** *The Hellenists*, Greek-speaking Jews or Jews who have adopted Greek customs; the *Hebrews* probably spoke Aramaic and were more conservative (compare 21.20). **2:** *To serve tables*, perhaps to wait at meals (Jesus thought this compatible with *the word of God*, Lk.22.27); the phrase can also include financial administration. **5:** *Stephen, Philip*, and the other names are Greek. *Proselyte*, a Gentile convert to Judaism, prior to becoming a Christian. **6:** *Laid . . . hands*, see 1 Tim.4.14 n.

full of faith and of the Holy Spirit, and Philip, and Proch'orus, and Nica'nor, and Ti'mon, and Par'menas, and Nicola'us, a proselyte of Antioch. 6 These they set before the apostles, and they prayed and laid their hands upon them.

7 And the word of God increased; and the number of the disciples multiplied greatly in Jerusalem, and a great many of the priests were obedient to the faith.

8 And Stephen, full of grace and power, did great wonders and signs among the people. 9 Then some of those who belonged to the synagogue of the Freedmen (as it was called), and of the Cyre'nians, and of the Alexandrians, and of those from Cili'cia and Asia, arose and disputed with Stephen. 10 But they could not withstand the wisdom and the Spirit with which he spoke. 11 Then they secretly instigated men, who said, "We have heard him speak blasphemous words against Moses and God." 12 And they stirred up the people and the elders and the scribes, and they came upon him and seized him and brought him before the council, 13 and set up false witnesses who said, "This man never ceases to speak words against this holy place and the law; 14 for we have heard him say that this Jesus of Nazareth will destroy this place, and will change the customs which Moses delivered to us." 15 And gazing at him, all who sat in the council saw that his face was like the face of an angel.

7 And the high priest said, "Is this so?" 2 And Stephen said:

"Brethren and fathers, hear me. The God of glory appeared to our father Abraham, when he was in Mesopota'mia, before he lived in Haran, 3 and said to him, 'Depart from your land and from your kindred and go into the land which I will show you.' 4 Then he departed from the land of the Chalde'ans, and lived in Haran. And after his father died, God removed him from there into this land in which you are now living; 5 yet he gave him no inheritance in it, not even a foot's length, but promised to give it to him in possession and to his posterity after him, though he had no child. 6 And God spoke to this effect, that his posterity would be aliens in a land belonging to others, who would enslave them and ill-treat them four hundred years. 7 'But I will judge the nation which they serve,' said God, 'and after that they shall come out and worship me in this place.' 8 And he gave him the covenant of circumcision. And so Abraham became the father of Isaac, and circumcised him on the eighth day; and Isaac became the father of Jacob, and Jacob of the twelve patriarchs.

9 "And the patriarchs, jealous of Joseph, sold him into Egypt; but God was with him, 10 and rescued him out of all his afflictions, and gave him favor and wisdom before Pharaoh, king of Egypt, who made him governor over Egypt and over all his household. 11 Now there came a famine throughout all Egypt and Canaan, and great affliction, and our fathers could find no food. 12 But when Jacob heard that there was grain in Egypt, he sent forth our fathers the first time. 13 And at the second visit Joseph made himself known to his brothers, and Joseph's family became known to Pharaoh. 14 And Joseph sent and

---

6.8–8.1a: **Preaching and martyrdom of Stephen.** Like Jesus, Stephen was charged with prophesying against the temple, and forgave his persecutors. **6.9:** *Freedmen*, former slaves, either Jews or proselytes; an inscription found in Jerusalem is thought to refer to this *synagogue*. **14:** *Jesus . . . will destroy this place*, Mk.14.58; Jn.2.19. Stephen saw more clearly than others that Jesus' teaching would *change the customs* (Mk.7.18–19; Mt.23.25–26; Lk.11.39–41). Christianity now begins to emerge as a world religion. **7.2–50:** Early Christian preaching often included the stories of *Abraham* (v. 2), *Joseph* (v. 9), *Moses* (v. 20), and others (compare 13.16–24; Heb.11.4–40). **6:** *Four hundred years*, so Gen.15.13; more precisely, 430 years (Ex. 12.40; see Gal.3.17 n.). **14:** *Seventy-five*, according to the Septuagint of Gen.46.27; Ex.1.5.

called to him Jacob his father and all his kindred, seventy-five souls; ¹⁵ and Jacob went down into Egypt. And he died, himself and our fathers, ¹⁶ and they were carried back to Shechem and laid in the tomb that Abraham had bought for a sum of silver from the sons of Hamor in Shechem.

17 "But as the time of the promise drew near, which God had granted to Abraham, the people grew and multiplied in Egypt ¹⁸ till there arose over Egypt another king who had not known Joseph. ¹⁹ He dealt craftily with our race and forced our fathers to expose their infants, that they might not be kept alive. ²⁰ At this time Moses was born, and was beautiful before God. And he was brought up for three months in his father's house; ²¹ and when he was exposed, Pharaoh's daughter adopted him and brought him up as her own son. ²² And Moses was instructed in all the wisdom of the Egyptians, and he was mighty in his words and deeds.

23 "When he was forty years old, it came into his heart to visit his brethren, the sons of Israel. ²⁴ And seeing one of them being wronged, he defended the oppressed man and avenged him by striking the Egyptian. ²⁵ He supposed that his brethren understood that God was giving them deliverance by his hand, but they did not understand. ²⁶ And on the following day he appeared to them as they were quarreling and would have reconciled them, saying, 'Men, you are brethren, why do you wrong each other?' ²⁷ But the man who was wronging his neighbor thrust him aside, saying, 'Who made you a ruler and a judge over us? ²⁸ Do you want to kill me as you killed the Egyptian yesterday?' ²⁹ At this retort Moses fled, and became an exile in the land of Mid'ian, where he became the father of two sons.

30 "Now when forty years had passed, an angel appeared to him in the wilderness of Mount Sinai, in a flame of fire in a bush. ³¹ When Moses saw it he wondered at the sight; and as he drew near to look, the voice of the Lord came, ³² 'I am the God of your fathers, the God of Abraham and of Isaac and of Jacob.' And Moses trembled and did not dare to look. ³³ And the Lord said to him, 'Take off the shoes from your feet, for the place where you are standing is holy ground. ³⁴ I have surely seen the ill-treatment of my people that are in Egypt and heard their groaning, and I have come down to deliver them. And now come, I will send you to Egypt.'

35 "This Moses whom they refused, saying, 'Who made you a ruler and a judge?' God sent as both ruler and deliverer by the hand of the angel that appeared to him in the bush. ³⁶ He led them out, having performed wonders and signs in Egypt and at the Red Sea, and in the wilderness for forty years. ³⁷ This is the Moses who said to the Israelites, 'God will raise up for you a prophet from your brethren as he raised me up.' ³⁸ This is he who was in the congregation in the wilderness with the angel who spoke to him at Mount Sinai, and with our fathers; and he received living oracles to give to us. ³⁹ Our fathers refused to obey him, but thrust him aside, and in their hearts they turned to Egypt, ⁴⁰ saying to Aaron, 'Make for us gods to go before us; as for this Moses who led us out from the land of Egypt, we do not know what has become of him.' ⁴¹ And they made a calf in those days, and offered a sacrifice to the idol and rejoiced in the works of their hands. ⁴² But God turned and gave them over to worship the host of heaven, as it is written in the book of the prophets:

'Did you offer to me slain beasts and
          sacrifices,

16: *Shechem;* but according to Gen.50.13 Jacob was buried at Hebron. *Abraham;* but according to Gen.33.19 and Jos.24.32 it was Jacob who bought the tomb at Shechem. 37: *A prophet,* 3.22. 42–43: Amos 5.25–27 is quoted to suggest that the Hebrews had always been idolaters. The *book*

forty years in the wilderness, O house of Israel?

[43] And you took up the tent of Moloch,
and the star of the god Rephan,
the figures which you made to worship;
and I will remove you beyond Babylon.'

44 "Our fathers had the tent of witness in the wilderness, even as he who spoke to Moses directed him to make it, according to the pattern that he had seen. [45] Our fathers in turn brought it in with Joshua when they dispossessed the nations which God thrust out before our fathers. So it was until the days of David, [46] who found favor in the sight of God and asked leave to find a habitation for the God of Jacob. [47] But it was Solomon who built a house for him. [48] Yet the Most High does not dwell in houses made with hands; as the prophet says,

[49] 'Heaven is my throne,
and earth my footstool.
What house will you build for me,
says the Lord,
or what is the place of my rest?
[50] Did not my hand make all these things?'

51 "You stiff-necked people, uncircumcised in heart and ears, you always resist the Holy Spirit. As your fathers did, so do you. [52] Which of the prophets did not your fathers persecute? And they killed those who announced beforehand the coming of the Righteous One, whom you have now betrayed and murdered, [53] you who

received the law as delivered by angels and did not keep it."

54 Now when they heard these things they were enraged, and they ground their teeth against him. [55] But he, full of the Holy Spirit, gazed into heaven and saw the glory of God, and Jesus standing at the right hand of God; [56] and he said, "Behold, I see the heavens opened, and the Son of man standing at the right hand of God." [57] But they cried out with a loud voice and stopped their ears and rushed together upon him. [58] Then they cast him out of the city and stoned him; and the witnesses laid down their garments at the feet of a young man named Saul. [59] And as they were stoning Stephen, he prayed, "Lord Jesus, receive my spirit." [60] And he knelt down and cried with a loud voice, "Lord, do not hold this sin against them." And when he had said this, he fell asleep. 8 [1] And Saul was consenting to his death.

And on that day a great persecution arose against the church in Jerusalem; and they were all scattered throughout the region of Judea and Sama'ria, except the apostles. [2] Devout men buried Stephen, and made great lamentation over him. [3] But Saul was ravaging the church, and entering house after house, he dragged off men and women and committed them to prison.

4 Now those who were scattered went about preaching the word. [5] Philip went down to a city of Sama'ria, and proclaimed to them the Christ. [6] And the multitudes with one accord

---

of the (twelve minor) *prophets* was thought of as a unit. **44–50:** Up to v. 42 Stephen has been on common ground with his hearers; now he argues that God *does not dwell in houses made with hands* (Is.66.1–2) and that it was wrong for *Solomon* to build *a house for him.* The Letter to the Hebrews (chs. 8 and 9) likewise regards the tent (tabernacle) as the true type of worship, and ignores the temple. **51:** *Uncircumcised in heart and ears,* Ex.33.3,5; Jer.9.26; Rom.2.29. **53:** *The law,* being *delivered by angels,* is considered valid; but Paul used this Jewish tradition to argue that the law is secondary (Gal.3.19). **56:** *Son of man* in the gospels usually denotes Jesus as the glorified heavenly judge (see Mk.2.10 n.); elsewhere in the New Testament the phrase is found only here and in Rev.1.13.

8.1b–40: Spread of the gospel to Samaria and the seacoast. Christianity now first reaches non-Jewish regions. **3:** *Saul was ravaging the church,* Gal.1.13. **5:** *Samaria* was inhabited by mixed remnants of the northern tribes who worshiped the Lord God and used the Pentateuch. Jews despised them as mongrels. In one tradition the disciples are forbidden to visit their towns (Mt.10.5), but according to others Jesus was friendly to Samaritans (Lk.10.30–37; 17.11–19;

gave heed to what was said by Philip, when they heard him and saw the signs which he did. ⁷ For unclean spirits came out of many who were possessed, crying with a loud voice; and many who were paralyzed or lame were healed. ⁸ So there was much joy in that city.

9 But there was a man named Simon who had previously practiced magic in the city and amazed the nation of Sama′ria, saying that he himself was somebody great. ¹⁰ They all gave heed to him, from the least to the greatest, saying, "This man is that power of God which is called Great." ¹¹ And they gave heed to him, because for a long time he had amazed them with his magic. ¹² But when they believed Philip as he preached good news about the kingdom of God and the name of Jesus Christ, they were baptized, both men and women. ¹³ Even Simon himself believed, and after being baptized he continued with Philip. And seeing signs and great miracles performed, he was amazed.

14 Now when the apostles at Jerusalem heard that Sama′ria had received the word of God, they sent to them Peter and John, ¹⁵ who came down and prayed for them that they might receive the Holy Spirit; ¹⁶ for it had not yet fallen on any of them, but they had only been baptized in the name of the Lord Jesus. ¹⁷ Then they laid their hands on them and they received the Holy Spirit. ¹⁸ Now when Simon saw that the Spirit was given through the laying on of the apostles' hands, he offered them money, ¹⁹ saying, "Give me also this power, that any one on whom I lay my hands may receive the Holy Spirit." ²⁰ But Peter said to him, "Your silver perish with you, because you thought you could obtain the gift of God with money! ²¹ You have neither part nor lot in this matter, for your heart is not right before God. ²² Repent therefore of this wickedness of yours, and pray to the Lord that, if possible, the intent of your heart may be forgiven you. ²³ For I see that you are in the gall of bitterness and in the bond of iniquity." ²⁴ And Simon answered, "Pray for me to the Lord, that nothing of what you have said may come upon me."

25 Now when they had testified and spoken the word of the Lord, they returned to Jerusalem, preaching the gospel to many villages of the Samaritans.

26 But an angel of the Lord said to Philip, "Rise and go toward the south⁽ᵍ⁾ to the road that goes down from Jerusalem to Gaza." This is a desert road. ²⁷ And he rose and went. And behold, an Ethiopian, a eunuch, a minister of the Can′dace, queen of the Ethiopians, in charge of all her treasure, had come to Jerusalem to worship ²⁸ and was returning; seated in his chariot, he was reading the prophet Isaiah. ²⁹ And the Spirit said to Philip, "Go up and join this chariot." ³⁰ So Philip ran to him, and heard him reading Isaiah the prophet, and asked, "Do you understand what you are reading?" ³¹ And he said, "How can I, unless some one guides me?" And he invited Philip to come up and sit with him. ³² Now the passage of the scripture which he was reading was this:

"As a sheep led to the slaughter
  or a lamb before its shearer is dumb,
  so he opens not his mouth.
³³ In his humiliation justice was
    denied him.
Who can describe his generation?

g Or at noon

Jn.4.4–42). **14–17:** In Acts believers usually receive the Holy Spirit at baptism (2.38; 19.5–6), or before baptism (10.44). Here the Samaritans *received the Holy Spirit* (v. 17) some time subsequent to baptism, and only after the apostles' visit. **17:** *Laid . . . hands,* see 1 Tim.4.14 n. **18:** The term "simony" (buying church offices) is derived from this account. **27:** *Ethiopian* at this time meant "Nubian." *The Candace* was the title of the *queen of the Ethiopians.* **28:** *He was reading* aloud to himself (as was customary in antiquity); hence Philip *heard him* (v. 30). **30–35:** In the book of Isaiah the early Christians found many prophecies

For his life is taken up from the earth."

34 And the eunuch said to Philip, "About whom, pray, does the prophet say this, about himself or about some one else?" 35 Then Philip opened his mouth, and beginning with this scripture he told him the good news of Jesus. 36 And as they went along the road they came to some water, and the eunuch said, "See, here is water! What is to prevent my being baptized?"*h* 38 And he commanded the chariot to stop, and they both went down into the water, Philip and the eunuch, and he baptized him. 39 And when they came up out of the water, the Spirit of the Lord caught up Philip; and the eunuch saw him no more, and went on his way rejoicing. 40 But Philip was found at Azo'tus, and passing on he preached the gospel to all the towns till he came to Caesare'a.

9 But Saul, still breathing threats and murder against the disciples of the Lord, went to the high priest 2 and asked him for letters to the synagogues at Damascus, so that if he found any belonging to the Way, men or women, he might bring them bound to Jerusalem. 3 Now as he journeyed he approached Damascus, and suddenly a light from heaven flashed about him. 4 And he fell to the ground and heard a voice saying to him, "Saul, Saul, why do you persecute me?" 5 And he said, "Who are you, Lord?" And he said, "I am Jesus, whom you are persecuting; 6 but rise and enter the city, and you will be told what you are to do." 7 The men who were traveling with him stood speechless, hearing the voice

but seeing no one. 8 Saul arose from the ground; and when his eyes were opened, he could see nothing; so they led him by the hand and brought him into Damascus. 9 And for three days he was without sight, and neither ate nor drank.

10 Now there was a disciple at Damascus named Anani'as. The Lord said to him in a vision, "Anani'as." And he said, "Here I am, Lord." 11 And the Lord said to him, "Rise and go to the street called Straight, and inquire in the house of Judas for a man of Tarsus named Saul; for behold, he is praying, 12 and he has seen a man named Anani'as come in and lay his hands on him so that he might regain his sight." 13 But Anani'as answered, "Lord, I have heard from many about this man, how much evil he has done to thy saints at Jerusalem; 14 and here he has authority from the chief priests to bind all who call upon thy name." 15 But the Lord said to him, "Go, for he is a chosen instrument of mine to carry my name before the Gentiles and kings and the sons of Israel; 16 for I will show him how much he must suffer for the sake of my name." 17 So Anani'as departed and entered the house. And laying his hands on him he said, "Brother Saul, the Lord Jesus who appeared to you on the road by which you came, has sent me that you may regain your sight and be filled with the Holy Spirit." 18 And immediately something like scales fell from his eyes and he re-

h Other ancient authorities add all or most of verse 37, *And Philip said, "If you believe with all your heart, you may." And he replied, "I believe that Jesus Christ is the Son of God."*

---

of Christ; Is.53.7–8 deals with the servant of the Lord (see Acts 3.13 n., and compare Mt.8.17). **40:** *Caesarea*, important Palestinian seaport where the Roman procurator had his headquarters.
9.1–22: Conversion of Saul of Tarsus. Slightly different versions are found in 22.4–16; 26.9–18; compare Paul's account, Gal.1.13–17. **2:** *The Way*, i.e. the true way of the Lord, was one of the earliest names for Christianity. Those *belonging to* it *at Damascus* were probably from Jerusalem; the empire granted the Jews the right to extradite offenders. **3:** The glory of God (or Christ) is often described as light (2 Cor.3.18; 4.6). **4–5:** In persecuting the disciples, he persecuted *Jesus* (Mt.10.40; 25.40). **11:** *The street called Straight*, perhaps Darb el-Mostakim, which runs through Damascus from east to west. **15:** Saul, like the prophets, was chosen for a special purpose (Jer.1.5; Gal.1.15); *instrument*, literally "vessel" (as in Rom.9.22–23; 2 Cor.4.7), emphasizes his domination by Christ.

gained his sight. Then he rose and was baptized, [19] and took food and was strengthened.

For several days he was with the disciples at Damascus. [20] And in the synagogues immediately he proclaimed Jesus, saying, "He is the Son of God." [21] And all who heard him were amazed, and said, "Is not this the man who made havoc in Jerusalem of those who called on this name? And he has come here for this purpose, to bring them bound before the chief priests." [22] But Saul increased all the more in strength, and confounded the Jews who lived in Damascus by proving that Jesus was the Christ.

23 When many days had passed, the Jews plotted to kill him, [24] but their plot became known to Saul. They were watching the gates day and night, to kill him; [25] but his disciples took him by night and let him down over the wall, lowering him in a basket.

26 And when he had come to Jerusalem he attempted to join the disciples; and they were all afraid of him, for they did not believe that he was a disciple. [27] But Barnabas took him, and brought him to the apostles, and declared to them how on the road he had seen the Lord, who spoke to him, and how at Damascus he had preached boldly in the name of Jesus. [28] So he went in and out among them at Jerusalem, [29] preaching boldly in the name of the Lord. And he spoke and disputed against the Hellenists; but they were seeking to kill him. [30] And when the brethren knew it, they brought him down to Caesare'a, and sent him off to Tarsus.

31 So the church throughout all Judea and Galilee and Sama'ria had peace and was built up; and walking in the fear of the Lord and in the comfort of the Holy Spirit it was multiplied.

32 Now as Peter went here and there among them all, he came down also to the saints that lived at Lydda. [33] There he found a man named Aene'as, who had been bedridden for eight years and was paralyzed. [34] And Peter said to him, "Aene'as, Jesus Christ heals you; rise and make your bed." And immediately he rose. [35] And all the residents of Lydda and Sharon saw him, and they turned to the Lord.

36 Now there was at Joppa a disciple named Tabitha, which means Dorcas.[x] She was full of good works and acts of charity. [37] In those days she fell sick and died; and when they had washed her, they laid her in an upper room. [38] Since Lydda was near Joppa, the disciples, hearing that Peter was there, sent two men to him entreating him, "Please come to us without delay." [39] So Peter rose and went with them. And when he had come, they took him to the upper room. All the widows stood beside him weeping, and showing tunics and other garments which Dorcas made while she was with them. [40] But Peter put them all outside and knelt down and prayed; then turning to the body he said, "Tabitha, rise." And she opened her eyes, and when she saw Peter she sat up. [41] And he gave her his hand and lifted her up. Then calling the saints and widows he presented her alive. [42] And it became known throughout all Joppa, and many believed in the Lord. [43] And he stayed in Joppa for many days with one Simon, a tanner.

10 At Caesare'a there was a man named Cornelius, a centurion of what was known as the Italian Cohort, [2] a devout man who feared God with

x The name Tabitha in Aramaic and the name Dorcas in Greek mean *gazelle*

9.23–31: Saul's first visit to Jerusalem. In Gal.1.15–20 Paul implies that his first visit was three years after his conversion. **25:** 2 Cor.11.32–33. **30:** *Tarsus*, Paul's home city (22.3).

9.32–43: Peter's journey to Lydda and Joppa. 32: *Lydda*, in the plain of Sharon (v. 35), about ten miles SE of Joppa (v. 36). **39:** *Widows*, see 1 Tim.5.3–16 n. **43:** *A tanner* was practically an outcast; Jewish law regarded his work as defiling.

10.1–48: The conversion of Cornelius. Luke ascribes to Peter the honor of converting the first

all his household, gave alms liberally to the people, and prayed constantly to God. ³ About the ninth
hour of the day he saw clearly in a
vision an angel of God coming in and
saying to him, "Cornelius." ⁴ And he
stared at him in terror, and said, "What
is it, Lord?" And he said to him, "Your
prayers and your alms have ascended
as a memorial before God. ⁵ And now
send men to Joppa, and bring one
Simon who is called Peter; ⁶ he is lodging with Simon, a tanner, whose
house is by the seaside." ⁷ When the
angel who spoke to him had departed,
he called two of his servants and a devout soldier from among those that
waited on him, ⁸ and having related
everything to them, he sent them to
Joppa.

9 The next day, as they were on
their journey and coming near the city,
Peter went up on the housetop to
pray, about the sixth hour. ¹⁰ And he
became hungry and desired something
to eat; but while they were preparing
it, he fell into a trance ¹¹ and saw the
heaven opened, and something descending, like a great sheet, let down by
four corners upon the earth. ¹² In it
were all kinds of animals and reptiles
and birds of the air. ¹³ And there came
a voice to him, "Rise, Peter; kill and
eat." ¹⁴ But Peter said, "No, Lord; for
I have never eaten anything that is
common or unclean." ¹⁵ And the voice
came to him again a second time,
"What God has cleansed, you must
not call common." ¹⁶ This happened
three times, and the thing was taken
up at once to heaven.

17 Now while Peter was inwardly
perplexed as to what the vision which
he had seen might mean, behold, the
men that were sent by Cornelius, having

made inquiry for Simon's house, stood
before the gate ¹⁸ and called out to ask
whether Simon who was called Peter
was lodging there. ¹⁹ And while Peter
was pondering the vision, the Spirit
said to him, "Behold, three men are
looking for you. ²⁰ Rise and go down,
and accompany them without hesita-
tion; for I have sent them." ²¹ And
Peter went down to the men and said,
"I am the one you are looking for;
what is the reason for your coming?"
²² And they said, "Cornelius, a centurion, an upright and God-fearing
man, who is well spoken of by the
whole Jewish nation, was directed by a
holy angel to send for you to come to
his house, and to hear what you have
to say." ²³ So he called them in to be
his guests.

The next day he rose and went off
with them, and some of the brethren from Joppa accompanied him.
²⁴ And on the following day they entered Caesare′a. Cornelius was expecting them and had called together his
kinsmen and close friends. ²⁵ When
Peter entered, Cornelius met him and
fell down at his feet and worshiped
him. ²⁶ But Peter lifted him up, saying, "Stand up; I too am a man."
²⁷ And as he talked with him, he
went in and found many persons
gathered; ²⁸ and he said to them,
"You yourselves know how unlawful
it is for a Jew to associate with or to visit
any one of another nation; but God
has shown me that I should not call
any man common or unclean. ²⁹ So
when I was sent for, I came without
objection. I ask then why you sent for
me."

30 And Cornelius said, "Four days
ago, about this hour, I was keeping the
ninth hour of prayer in my house; and

Gentile; but see 11.19–21. **1**: *Italian Cohort*, probably the Cohors II. Italica Civium Romano-
rum. **2**: Cornelius *feared God*, i.e. worshiped him, but had not adopted the Jewish religion.
3: *Ninth hour*, about 3 p.m. **9**: *The sixth hour*, about noon, the usual Roman time for luncheon.
14: *Common*, ritually impure; only certain mammals, fish, and insects might be eaten (Lev.11).
15: *God . . . cleansed* all foods through Jesus' word (Mk.7.14–19), but Peter did not realize
this until now; some Jewish Christians continued even later to insist on food laws (15.29;
Col.2.21). **26**: *I too am a man*, 14.15; Rev.19.10. **28**: Food laws made association with Gentiles

behold, a man stood before me in bright apparel, ³¹ saying, 'Cornelius, your prayer has been heard and your alms have been remembered before God. ³² Send therefore to Joppa and ask for Simon who is called Peter; he is lodging in the house of Simon, a tanner, by the seaside.' ³³ So I sent to you at once, and you have been kind enough to come. Now therefore we are all here present in the sight of God, to hear all that you have been commanded by the Lord."

34 And Peter opened his mouth and said: "Truly I perceive that God shows no partiality, ³⁵ but in every nation any one who fears him and does what is right is acceptable to him. ³⁶ You know the word which he sent to Israel, preaching good news of peace by Jesus Christ (he is Lord of all), ³⁷ the word which was proclaimed throughout all Judea, beginning from Galilee after the baptism which John preached: ³⁸ how God anointed Jesus of Nazareth with the Holy Spirit and with power; how he went about doing good and healing all that were oppressed by the devil, for God was with him. ³⁹ And we are witnesses to all that he did both in the country of the Jews and in Jerusalem. They put him to death by hanging him on a tree; ⁴⁰ but God raised him on the third day and made him manifest; ⁴¹ not to all the people but to us who were chosen by God as witnesses, who ate and drank with him after he rose from the dead. ⁴² And he commanded us to preach to the people, and to testify that he is the one ordained by God to be judge of the living and the dead. ⁴³ To him all the prophets bear witness that every one who believes in him re-

ceives forgiveness of sins through his name."

44 While Peter was still saying this, the Holy Spirit fell on all who heard the word. ⁴⁵ And the believers from among the circumcised who came with Peter were amazed, because the gift of the Holy Spirit had been poured out even on the Gentiles. ⁴⁶ For they heard them speaking in tongues and extolling God. Then Peter declared, ⁴⁷ "Can any one forbid water for baptizing these people who have received the Holy Spirit just as we have?" ⁴⁸ And he commanded them to be baptized in the name of Jesus Christ. Then they asked him to remain for some days.

11 Now the apostles and the brethren who were in Judea heard that the Gentiles also had received the word of God. ² So when Peter went up to Jerusalem, the circumcision party criticized him, ³ saying, "Why did you go to uncircumcised men and eat with them?" ⁴ But Peter began and explained to them in order: ⁵ "I was in the city of Joppa praying; and in a trance I saw a vision, something descending, like a great sheet, let down from heaven by four corners; and it came down to me. ⁶ Looking at it closely I observed animals and beasts of prey and reptiles and birds of the air. ⁷ And I heard a voice saying to me, 'Rise, Peter; kill and eat.' ⁸ But I said, 'No, Lord; for nothing common or unclean has ever entered my mouth.' ⁹ But the voice answered a second time from heaven, 'What God has cleansed you must not call common.' ¹⁰ This happened three times, and all was drawn up again into heaven. ¹¹ At that very moment three men arrived

difficult. **30**: See v. 3 n. **34**: *No partiality*, literally "God accepts no one's face"; compare Rom.2.11 where Paul teaches that Jews have no special privilege. **36–43**: This sums up the gospel, beginning with the baptism of John and ending with the statement that Christ is judge (3.20–21). **38**: *God anointed Jesus*, Lk.3.22; 4.14. **41**: Jesus was seen only by those *chosen* (Lk.24.48; Acts 1.8,22). **42**: *Judge of the living and the dead*, 1 Pet.4.5; 2 Tim.4.1. **44–48**: They knew by the *speaking in tongues* (2.4–11) that *the Holy Spirit* fell before baptism (see 8.14–17 n.). **45**: All *believers* were still *from among the circumcised*, unless the incident of 11.20 took place previously.

11.1–18: Peter's defense. The baptism of Gentiles requires explanation. **2**: *The circumcision*

at the house in which we were, sent to me from Caesare'a. [12] And the Spirit told me to go with them, making no distinction. These six brethren also accompanied me, and we entered the man's house. [13] And he told us how he had seen the angel standing in his house and saying, 'Send to Joppa and bring Simon called Peter; [14] he will declare to you a message by which you will be saved, you and all your household.' [15] As I began to speak, the Holy Spirit fell on them just as on us at the beginning. [16] And I remembered the word of the Lord, how he said, 'John baptized with water, but you shall be baptized with the Holy Spirit.' [17] If then God gave the same gift to them as he gave to us when we believed in the Lord Jesus Christ, who was I that I could withstand God?" [18] When they heard this they were silenced. And they glorified God, saying, "Then to the Gentiles also God has granted repentance unto life."

19 Now those who were scattered because of the persecution that arose over Stephen traveled as far as Phoeni'cia and Cyprus and Antioch, speaking the word to none except Jews. [20] But there were some of them, men of Cyprus and Cyre'ne, who on coming to Antioch spoke to the Greeks[i] also, preaching the Lord Jesus. [21] And the hand of the Lord was with them, and a great number that believed turned to the Lord. [22] News of this came to the ears of the church in Jerusalem, and they sent Barnabas to Antioch. [23] When he came and saw the grace

of God, he was glad; and he exhorted them all to remain faithful to the Lord with steadfast purpose; [24] for he was a good man, full of the Holy Spirit and of faith. And a large company was added to the Lord. [25] So Barnabas went to Tarsus to look for Saul; [26] and when he had found him, he brought him to Antioch. For a whole year they met with[j] the church, and taught a large company of people; and in Antioch the disciples were for the first time called Christians.

27 Now in these days prophets came down from Jerusalem to Antioch. [28] And one of them named Ag'abus stood up and foretold by the Spirit that there would be a great famine over all the world; and this took place in the days of Claudius. [29] And the disciples determined, every one according to his ability, to send relief to the brethren who lived in Judea; [30] and they did so, sending it to the elders by the hand of Barnabas and Saul.

12 About that time Herod the king laid violent hands upon some who belonged to the church. [2] He killed James the brother of John with the sword; [3] and when he saw that it pleased the Jews, he proceeded to arrest Peter also. This was during the days of Unleavened Bread. [4] And when he had seized him, he put him in prison, and delivered him to four squads of soldiers to guard him, intending after the Passover to bring him

i Other ancient authorities read *Hellenists*
j Or *were guests of*

---

party, of conservative Jewish Christians, arises as soon as Gentiles are admitted (15.1–5; 21.20; Gal.2.12). **16:** See 1.5 n.

11.19–26: Mission to the Greeks in Antioch. Stephen's death and the ensuing *persecution* led to the Gentile mission (8.1b–4). **19:** *Antioch* on the Orontes, in Syria. **20:** This mission *to the Greeks* may have occurred before Peter's conversion of Cornelius (see 10.45 n.). **22:** *Barnabas* came from Cyprus (4.36) and there were Cypriots in Antioch. **25–26:** *Saul* was in *Tarsus;* compare Gal.1.21. *Christians*, a Latin word meaning "partisans of Christ," perhaps at first a term of reproach.

11.27–30: Famine relief sent to Jerusalem through Barnabas and Paul. **27:** *Prophets* were numerous in the early church (see 13.1 n.; 1 Cor.12.28–29). **28:** *Agabus*, 21.10–11. The *famine . . . in the days of Claudius* (A.D. 41–54) probably occurred in A.D. 46.

12.1–19: Herod Agrippa's persecution. James the son of Zebedee is martyred; Peter is arrested but escapes. **1:** *Herod* Agrippa I, grandson of Herod the Great and the Maccabean Mariamne, was made king by Claudius A.D. 41. He was popular because he favored Pharisaism.

out to the people. ⁵ So Peter was kept in prison; but earnest prayer for him was made to God by the church.

6 The very night when Herod was about to bring him out, Peter was sleeping between two soldiers, bound with two chains, and sentries before the door were guarding the prison; ⁷ and behold, an angel of the Lord appeared, and a light shone in the cell; and he struck Peter on the side and woke him, saying, "Get up quickly." And the chains fell off his hands. ⁸ And the angel said to him, "Dress yourself and put on your sandals." And he did so. And he said to him, "Wrap your mantle around you and follow me." ⁹ And he went out and followed him; he did not know that what was done by the angel was real, but thought he was seeing a vision. ¹⁰ When they had passed the first and the second guard, they came to the iron gate leading into the city. It opened to them of its own accord, and they went out and passed on through one street; and immediately the angel left him. ¹¹ And Peter came to himself, and said, "Now I am sure that the Lord has sent his angel and rescued me from the hand of Herod and from all that the Jewish people were expecting."

12 When he realized this, he went to the house of Mary, the mother of John whose other name was Mark, where many were gathered together and were praying. ¹³ And when he knocked at the door of the gateway, a maid named Rhoda came to answer. ¹⁴ Recognizing Peter's voice, in her joy she did not open the gate but ran in and told that Peter was standing at the gate. ¹⁵ They said to her, "You are mad." But she insisted that it was so. They said, "It is his angel!" ¹⁶ But Peter continued knocking; and when

they opened, they saw him and were amazed. ¹⁷ But motioning to them with his hand to be silent, he described to them how the Lord had brought him out of the prison. And he said, "Tell this to James and to the brethren." Then he departed and went to another place.

18 Now when day came, there was no small stir among the soldiers over what had become of Peter. ¹⁹ And when Herod had sought for him and could not find him, he examined the sentries and ordered that they should be put to death. Then he went down from Judea to Caesare'a, and remained there.

20 Now Herod was angry with the people of Tyre and Sidon; and they came to him in a body, and having persuaded Blastus, the king's chamberlain, they asked for peace, because their country depended on the king's country for food. ²¹ On an appointed day Herod put on his royal robes, took his seat upon the throne, and made an oration to them. ²² And the people shouted, "The voice of a god, and not of man!" ²³ Immediately an angel of the Lord smote him, because he did not give God the glory; and he was eaten by worms and died.

24 But the word of God grew and multiplied.

25 And Barnabas and Saul returned from*ᵏ* Jerusalem when they had fulfilled their mission, bringing with them John whose other name was Mark.

13 Now in the church at Antioch there were prophets and teachers, Barnabas, Simeon who was called Niger, Lucius of Cyre'ne, Man'a-en a member of the court of Herod the tetrarch, and Saul. ² While they were

ᵏ Other ancient authorities read *to*

4: *Passover* season, i.e. the days of unleavened bread (v. 3). 12: *John . . . Mark* accompanied Paul and Barnabas as far as Perga (12.25–13.13; compare also Mk.14.51 n.). 15: It was believed that a person's guardian *angel* represented him in heaven (Gen.48.16; Mt.18.10).
12.20–24: Death of Herod Agrippa. This was in the spring of A.D. 44. Josephus (*Ant.* xix.8.2) tells how he was stricken by a mortal illness immediately after the people hailed him as a god.
12.25–13.12: Barnabas and Saul in Cyprus. The beginning of Paul's first missionary journey.
13.1: *Prophets and teachers* were important in the early church (see 11.27 n.; 1 Cor.12.28;

worshiping the Lord and fasting, the Holy Spirit said, "Set apart for me Barnabas and Saul for the work to which I have called them." ³ Then after fasting and praying they laid their hands on them and sent them off.

4 So, being sent out by the Holy Spirit, they went down to Seleu'cia; and from there they sailed to Cyprus. ⁵ When they arrived at Sal'amis, they proclaimed the word of God in the synagogues of the Jews. And they had John to assist them. ⁶ When they had gone through the whole island as far as Paphos, they came upon a certain magician, a Jewish false prophet, named Bar-Jesus. ⁷ He was with the proconsul, Sergius Paulus, a man of intelligence, who summoned Barnabas and Saul and sought to hear the word of God. ⁸ But El'ymas the magician (for that is the meaning of his name) withstood them, seeking to turn away the proconsul from the faith. ⁹ But Saul, who is also called Paul, filled with the Holy Spirit, looked intently at him ¹⁰ and said, "You son of the devil, you enemy of all righteousness, full of all deceit and villainy, will you not stop making crooked the straight paths of the Lord? ¹¹ And now, behold, the hand of the Lord is upon you, and you shall be blind and unable to see the sun for a time." Immediately mist and darkness fell upon him and he went about seeking people to lead him by the hand. ¹² Then the proconsul believed, when he saw what had oc-

curred, for he was astonished at the teaching of the Lord.

13 Now Paul and his company set sail from Paphos, and came to Perga in Pamphyl'ia. And John left them and returned to Jerusalem; ¹⁴ but they passed on from Perga and came to Antioch of Pisid'ia. And on the sabbath day they went into the synagogue and sat down. ¹⁵ After the reading of the law and the prophets, the rulers of the synagogue sent to them, saying, "Brethren, if you have any word of exhortation for the people, say it." ¹⁶ So Paul stood up, and motioning with his hand said:

"Men of Israel, and you that fear God, listen. ¹⁷ The God of this people Israel chose our fathers and made the people great during their stay in the land of Egypt, and with uplifted arm he led them out of it. ¹⁸ And for about forty years he bore with*ᵐ* them in the wilderness. ¹⁹ And when he had destroyed seven nations in the land of Canaan, he gave them their land as an inheritance, for about four hundred and fifty years. ²⁰ And after that he gave them judges until Samuel the prophet. ²¹ Then they asked for a king; and God gave them Saul the son of Kish, a man of the tribe of Benjamin, for forty years. ²² And when he had removed him, he raised up David to be their king; of whom he testified and said, 'I have found in David the son of Jesse a man after my heart, who will do all my will.' ²³ Of

m Other ancient authorities read *cared for* (Dt 1.31)

Eph.4.11). *Niger* means "black." *Cyrene* had a large Jewish colony. **2–3:** Paul declared that he received his apostleship "not from men nor through man" (Gal.1.1). *The Holy Spirit* called them; when the others *laid their hands on them* it was not to make them apostles but to bless them for the new work (see 1 Tim.4.14 n.). **4:** *Seleucia* Pieria, Antioch's seaport, about 16 miles west. **5:** *Salamis*, largest city of Cyprus, north of modern Famagusta. **6:** *Paphos*, capital of the island, located in the extreme west. *Bar-Jesus*, "son of Jesus (or Joshua)." **7:** The island was a senatorial province ruled by a *proconsul*. **8:** *Elymas* does not mean "Bar-Jesus." Perhaps his name was Elymas, son of Jesus (or Joshua). **9:** *Saul* was his Jewish name, *Paul* his Roman name. A new source, using the latter, may begin here.

13.13–52: Journey to Antioch of Pisidian and Iconium. Paul's first work in inner Asia Minor. **13:** *Perga* is inland from Attalia, main seaport of Pamphylia ("region of all tribes"), which lies south of the Taurus range, between Cilicia and Lycia. **14:** Strictly, *Antioch* near *Pisidia*, near the modern Yalovach. **15:** One lesson each from *the law and the prophets* was customary. **19:** *Seven nations*, Dt.7.1; Jos.14.1. The rabbis reckoned almost *four hundred and fifty years* from the entrance into Canaan to the building of the temple. **22:** Ps.89.20; 1 Sam.13.14. **23:** *Savior*,

this man's posterity God has brought to Israel a Savior, Jesus, as he promised. ²⁴ Before his coming John had preached a baptism of repentance to all the people of Israel. ²⁵ And as John was finishing his course, he said, 'What do you suppose that I am? I am not he. No, but after me one is coming, the sandals of whose feet I am not worthy to untie.'

26 "Brethren, sons of the family of Abraham, and those among you that fear God, to us has been sent the message of this salvation. ²⁷ For those who live in Jerusalem and their rulers, because they did not recognize him nor understand the utterances of the prophets which are read every sabbath, fulfilled these by condemning him. ²⁸ Though they could charge him with nothing deserving death, yet they asked Pilate to have him killed. ²⁹ And when they had fulfilled all that was written of him, they took him down from the tree, and laid him in a tomb. ³⁰ But God raised him from the dead; ³¹ and for many days he appeared to those who came up with him from Galilee to Jerusalem, who are now his witnesses to the people. ³² And we bring you the good news that what God promised to the fathers, ³³ this he has fulfilled to us their children by raising Jesus; as also it is written in the second psalm,

'Thou art my Son,
     today I have begotten thee.'
³⁴ And as for the fact that he raised him from the dead, no more to return to corruption, he spoke in this way,
'I will give you the holy and sure
     blessings of David.'
³⁵ Therefore he says also in another psalm,
'Thou wilt not let thy Holy One see
     corruption.'
³⁶ For David, after he had served the counsel of God in his own generation, fell asleep, and was laid with his fathers, and saw corruption; ³⁷ but he whom God raised up saw no corruption. ³⁸ Let it be known to you therefore, brethren, that through this man forgiveness of sins is proclaimed to you, ³⁹ and by him every one that believes is freed from everything from which you could not be freed by the law of Moses. ⁴⁰ Beware, therefore, lest there come upon you what is said in the prophets:
⁴¹ 'Behold, you scoffers, and wonder,
     and perish;
for I do a deed in your days,
a deed you will never believe, if one
     declares it to you.' "

42 As they went out, the people begged that these things might be told them the next sabbath. ⁴³ And when the meeting of the synagogue broke up, many Jews and devout converts to Judaism followed Paul and Barnabas, who spoke to them and urged them to continue in the grace of God.

44 The next sabbath almost the whole city gathered together to hear the word of God. ⁴⁵ But when the Jews saw the multitudes, they were filled with jealousy, and contradicted what was spoken by Paul, and reviled him. ⁴⁶ And Paul and Barnabas spoke out boldly, saying, "It was necessary that the word of God should be spoken first to you. Since you thrust it from you, and judge yourselves unworthy of eternal life, behold, we turn to the Gentiles. ⁴⁷ For so the Lord has commanded us, saying,
'I have set you to be a light for the
     Gentiles,
that you may bring salvation to the
     uttermost parts of the earth.' "
48 And when the Gentiles heard this, they were glad and glorified the word of God; and as many as were

see 5.31 n. **25:** Mk.1.7; Lk.3.16; Mt.3.11; Jn.1.20. **26–41:** For argument and style compare 2.14–36. **33:** Ps.2.7. **34:** Is.55.3. **35:** Ps.16.10. **38–39:** Paul's letters usually speak of justification, not *forgiveness of sins. Freed*, Greek "justified" or "acquitted." **41:** Hab.1.5. **46:** In Corinth also (18.6) Paul went first to the Jews and then *to the Gentiles.* His churches usually included Jews. **47:** Is.49.6. **51:** *They shook off the dust* (Lk.10.11) to show that their responsi-

ordained to eternal life believed. [49] And the word of the Lord spread throughout all the region. [50] But the Jews incited the devout women of high standing and the leading men of the city, and stirred up persecution against Paul and Barnabas, and drove them out of their district. [51] But they shook off the dust from their feet against them, and went to Ico'nium. [52] And the disciples were filled with joy and with the Holy Spirit.

14 Now at Ico'nium they entered together into the Jewish synagogue, and so spoke that a great company believed, both of Jews and of Greeks. [2] But the unbelieving Jews stirred up the Gentiles and poisoned their minds against the brethren. [3] So they remained for a long time, speaking boldly for the Lord, who bore witness to the word of his grace, granting signs and wonders to be done by their hands. [4] But the people of the city were divided; some sided with the Jews, and some with the apostles. [5] When an attempt was made by both Gentiles and Jews, with their rulers, to molest them and to stone them, [6] they learned of it and fled to Lystra and Derbe, cities of Lycao'nia, and to the surrounding country; [7] and there they preached the gospel.

[8] Now at Lystra there was a man sitting, who could not use his feet; he was a cripple from birth, who had never walked. [9] He listened to Paul speaking; and Paul, looking intently at him and seeing that he had faith to be made well, [10] said in a loud voice, "Stand upright on your feet." And he sprang up and walked. [11] And when the crowds saw what Paul had done, they lifted up their voices, saying in Lycao'nian, "The gods have come down to us in the likeness of men!" [12] Barnabas they called Zeus, and Paul, because he was the chief speaker, they called Hermes. [13] And the priest of Zeus, whose temple was in front of the city, brought oxen and garlands to the gates and wanted to offer sacrifice with the people. [14] But when the apostles Barnabas and Paul heard of it, they tore their garments and rushed out among the multitude, crying, [15] "Men, why are you doing this? We also are men, of like nature with you, and bring you good news, that you should turn from these vain things to a living God who made the heaven and the earth and the sea and all that is in them. [16] In past generations he allowed all the nations to walk in their own ways; [17] yet he did not leave himself without witness, for he did good and gave you from heaven rains and fruitful seasons, satisfying your hearts with food and gladness." [18] With these words they scarcely restrained the people from offering sacrifice to them.

[19] But Jews came there from Antioch and Ico'nium; and having persuaded the people, they stoned Paul and dragged him out of the city, supposing that he was dead. [20] But when the disciples gathered about him, he rose up and entered the city; and on the next day he went on with Barnabas to Derbe. [21] When they had preached the gospel to that city and had made many disciples, they returned to Lystra and to Ico'nium and to Antioch, [22] strengthening the souls of the disciples, exhorting them to continue in

---

bility ended (18.6). *Iconium*, modern Konya, an important road-junction in the central plain.
14.1–28: Ministry in the Iconium region and return. Conclusion of the first missionary journey. **2**: 17.5,13. **6**: *Lystra*, a Roman colony, modern Hatun-Serai, 25 miles southwest of Konya. *Derbe*, probably Kerti, a mound near Beydilli. **11–12**: According to a myth of this region, *Zeus* and *Hermes* visited Baucis and Philemon *in the likeness of men*, and rewarded their hospitality. Paul, *the chief speaker*, was hailed as the messenger of the gods (compare Gal.4.14), not the chief god. **15–17**: Compare 17.22–31. Paul, like Peter (10.26), rejects worship of himself. **19**: Paul tells of being *stoned* once (2 Cor.11.25). **23**: In Acts, Paul's churches are ruled by *elders* (compare 20.17). The word is not used in letters attributed to Paul except in 1 Timothy and Titus.

the faith, and saying that through many tribulations we must enter the kingdom of God. ²³ And when they had appointed elders for them in every church, with prayer and fasting they committed them to the Lord in whom they believed.

24 Then they passed through Pisid'ia, and came to Pamphyl'ia. ²⁵ And when they had spoken the word in Perga, they went down to Attali'a; ²⁶ and from there they sailed to Antioch, where they had been commended to the grace of God for the work which they had fulfilled. ²⁷ And when they arrived, they gathered the church together and declared all that God had done with them, and how he had opened a door of faith to the Gentiles. ²⁸ And they remained no little time with the disciples.

15 But some men came down from Judea and were teaching the brethren, "Unless you are circumcised according to the custom of Moses, you cannot be saved." ² And when Paul and Barnabas had no small dissension and debate with them, Paul and Barnabas and some of the others were appointed to go up to Jerusalem to the apostles and the elders about this question. ³ So, being sent on their way by the church, they passed through both Phoeni'cia and Sama'ria, reporting the conversion of the Gentiles, and they gave great joy to all the brethren. ⁴ When they came to Jerusalem, they were welcomed by the church and the apostles and the elders, and they declared all that God had done with them. ⁵ But some believers who belonged to the party of the Pharisees rose up, and said, "It is necessary to circumcise them, and to charge them to keep the law of Moses."

6 The apostles and the elders were gathered together to consider this matter. ⁷ And after there had been much debate, Peter rose and said to them, "Brethren, you know that in the early days God made choice among you, that by my mouth the Gentiles should hear the word of the gospel and believe. ⁸ And God who knows the heart bore witness to them, giving them the Holy Spirit just as he did to us; ⁹ and he made no distinction between us and them, but cleansed their hearts by faith. ¹⁰ Now therefore why do you make trial of God by putting a yoke upon the neck of the disciples which neither our fathers nor we have been able to bear? ¹¹ But we believe that we shall be saved through the grace of the Lord Jesus, just as they will."

12 And all the assembly kept silence; and they listened to Barnabas and Paul as they related what signs and wonders God had done through them among the Gentiles. ¹³ After they finished speaking, James replied, "Brethren, listen to me. ¹⁴ Simeon has related how God first visited the Gentiles, to take out of them a people for his name. ¹⁵ And with this the words of the prophets agree, as it is written,

¹⁶ 'After this I will return,
and I will rebuild the dwelling of
David, which has fallen;
I will rebuild its ruins,
and I will set it up,
¹⁷ that the rest of men may seek the
Lord,
and all the Gentiles who are called
by my name,
¹⁸ says the Lord, who has made these
things known from of old.'
¹⁹ Therefore my judgment is that we should not trouble those of the Gentiles

---

15.1–35: Controversy over admission of Gentiles. The Jerusalem church guides developments on the mission field (8.14; 11.1–3). **1:** *Some men,* not identified here or in Gal.2.4; 5.12. **2:** *Were appointed;* Paul says he went "by revelation" (Gal.2.2; see Acts 11.27–30 n.). *Apostles and . . . elders,* or presbyters, rule the Jerusalem church; see 6.1–7 n. **5:** The strict believers of v. 1 were probably *Pharisees* (see 11.2 n.). **7:** *In the early days,* compare 10.9–48. **10:** The *yoke* is that of the Law (Mt.11.29–30; 23.4). **11:** *We shall be saved through . . . grace,* Rom.3.24. **13:** *James,* the brother of the Lord (see Gal.1.19 n.). **14:** *Simeon,* the Semitic form of Peter's given name. **16–18:** Am.9.11–12; Jer.12.15; Is.45.21. **20:** *What is strangled* may mean the same as

who turn to God, [20] but should write to them to abstain from the pollutions of idols and from unchastity and from what is strangled[n] and from blood. [21] For from early generations Moses has had in every city those who preach him, for he is read every sabbath in the synagogues."

22 Then it seemed good to the apostles and the elders, with the whole church, to choose men from among them and send them to Antioch with Paul and Barnabas. They sent Judas called Barsab′bas, and Silas, leading men among the brethren, [23] with the following letter: "The brethren, both the apostles and the elders, to the brethren who are of the Gentiles in Antioch and Syria and Cili′cia, greeting. [24] Since we have heard that some persons from us have troubled you with words, unsettling your minds, although we gave them no instructions, [25] it has seemed good to us, having come to one accord, to choose men and send them to you with our beloved Barnabas and Paul, [26] men who have risked their lives for the sake of our Lord Jesus Christ. [27] We have therefore sent Judas and Silas, who themselves will tell you the same things by word of mouth. [28] For it has seemed good to the Holy Spirit and to us to lay upon you no greater burden than these necessary things: [29] that you abstain from what has been sacrificed to idols and from blood and from what is strangled[n] and from unchastity. If you keep yourselves from these, you will do well. Farewell."

30 So when they were sent off, they went down to Antioch; and having gathered the congregation together, they delivered the letter. [31] And when they read it, they rejoiced at the exhortation. [32] And Judas and Silas, who were themselves prophets, exhorted the brethren with many words and strengthened them. [33] And after they had spent some time, they were sent off in peace by the brethren to those who had sent them.[o] [35] But Paul and Barnabas remained in Antioch, teaching and preaching the word of the Lord, with many others also.

36 And after some days Paul said to Barnabas, "Come, let us return and visit the brethren in every city where we proclaimed the word of the Lord, and see how they are." [37] And Barnabas wanted to take with them John called Mark. [38] But Paul thought best not to take with them one who had withdrawn from them in Pamphyl′ia, and had not gone with them to the work. [39] And there arose a sharp contention, so that they separated from each other; Barnabas took Mark with him and sailed away to Cyprus, [40] but Paul chose Silas and departed, being commended by the brethren to the grace of the Lord. [41] And he went through Syria and Cili′cia, strengthening the churches.

16 And he came also to Derbe and to Lystra. A disciple was there, named Timothy, the son of a Jewish woman who was a believer; but his father was a Greek. [2] He was well spoken of by the brethren at Lystra and Ico′nium. [3] Paul wanted Timothy

n Other early authorities omit *and from what is strangled*
o Other ancient authorities insert verse 34, *But it seemed good to Silas to remain there*

---

blood (omitted by some manuscripts), i.e. meat not ritually butchered. *Pollutions of idols*, i.e. food sacrificed to them. The rabbis taught that these, and *unchastity*, had been forbidden to Noah's sons, therefore to all mankind. **22:** *Paul* is told of the decree in 21.25 as though for the first time. He did not absolutely forbid food offered to idols (1 Cor.10.27–29) and he rejected other restrictions on food (Gal.2.11–12; Col.2.21). *Silas* may be the Silvanus of 2 Cor.1.19; 1 Th.1.1; 2 Th.1.1.

15.36–41: Departure on second missionary journey. 37–38: *John called Mark . . . had withdrawn*, see 12.12 n.; 13.13. **39:** The *contention* may also have involved the eating together of Jews and Gentiles (see 10.28 n.; Gal.2.13).

16.1–5: Timothy joins Paul. If *Timothy*, being *the son of a Jewish woman*, was considered a Jew, Paul *circumcised him* without inconsistency despite his rejection of the rite for Gentiles.

to accompany him; and he took him and circumcised him because of the Jews that were in those places, for they all knew that his father was a Greek. [4] As they went on their way through the cities, they delivered to them for observance the decisions which had been reached by the apostles and elders who were at Jerusalem. [5] So the churches were strengthened in the faith, and they increased in numbers daily.

6 And they went through the region of Phry'gia and Galatia, having been forbidden by the Holy Spirit to speak the word in Asia. [7] And when they had come opposite My'sia, they attempted to go into Bithyn'ia, but the Spirit of Jesus did not allow them; [8] so, passing by My'sia, they went down to Tro'as. [9] And a vision appeared to Paul in the night: a man of Macedo'nia was standing beseeching him and saying, "Come over to Macedo'nia and help us." [10] And when he had seen the vision, immediately we sought to go on into Macedo'nia, concluding that God had called us to preach the gospel to them.

11 Setting sail therefore from Tro'as, we made a direct voyage to Sam'o-thrace, and the following day to Ne-ap'-olis, [12] and from there to Philip'pi, which is the leading city of the district[x] of Macedo'nia, and a Roman colony. We remained in this city some days; [13] and on the sabbath day we went outside the gate to the riverside, where we supposed there was a place of prayer; and we sat down and spoke to the women who had come together. [14] One who heard us was a woman named Lydia, from the city of Thyati'ra, a seller of purple goods, who was a worshiper of God. The Lord opened her heart to give heed to what was said by Paul. [15] And when she was baptized, with her household, she besought us, saying, "If you have judged me to be faithful to the Lord, come to my house and stay." And she prevailed upon us.

16 As we were going to the place of prayer, we were met by a slave girl who had a spirit of divination and brought her owners much gain by soothsaying. [17] She followed Paul and us, crying, "These men are servants of the Most High God, who proclaim to you the way of salvation." [18] And this she did for many days. But Paul was annoyed, and turned and said to the spirit, "I charge you in the name of Jesus Christ to come out of her." And it came out that very hour.

19 But when her owners saw that their hope of gain was gone, they seized Paul and Silas and dragged them into the market place before the rulers; [20] and when they had brought them to the magistrates they said, "These men are Jews and they are disturbing our city. [21] They advocate customs which it is not lawful for us Romans to accept or practice." [22] The crowd joined in attacking them; and the magistrates tore the garments off them and gave orders to beat them with rods. [23] And when they had inflicted many blows upon them, they threw them into prison, charging the jailer to keep them safely. [24] Having received this charge, he put them into the inner

x The Greek text is uncertain

16.6–10: Through Asia Minor to Troas. Journey through the interior to the Aegean. **6:** *The region* is probably the country northwest of Iconium where both Phrygians and Galatians lived. *Asia,* the Roman province of Asia (in Asia Minor) included western Phrygia. **7:** *Opposite Mysia* (the region east of Troas) would be near Nacoleia, modern Seyitgazi. *Bithynia* was north of here. **9:** *Macedonia,* a Roman province in Europe including Philippi, Thessalonica, and Beroea.

16.11–40: Paul and Silas in Philippi. Paul enters Europe for the first time. **12:** *Philippi* was *the leading city,* but not the capital, *of Macedonia. A Roman colony* was often founded to provide land for veteran soldiers; as such it had special civic rights. **13:** *A place of prayer,* probably a synagogue. **17:** Pagans sometimes spoke of the God of Israel or the highest god of their pantheon as *the Most High God* (Num.24.16; Is.14.14; Dan.3.26). **20:** *Magistrates,* Greek "generals"; here probably praetors. **21:** *Not lawful,* because Jews were forbidden to make converts

prison and fastened their feet in the stocks.

25 But about midnight Paul and Silas were praying and singing hymns to God, and the prisoners were listening to them, [26] and suddenly there was a great earthquake, so that the foundations of the prison were shaken; and immediately all the doors were opened and every one's fetters were unfastened. [27] When the jailer woke and saw that the prison doors were open, he drew his sword and was about to kill himself, supposing that the prisoners had escaped. [28] But Paul cried with a loud voice, "Do not harm yourself, for we are all here." [29] And he called for lights and rushed in, and trembling with fear he fell down before Paul and Silas, [30] and brought them out and said, "Men, what must I do to be saved?" [31] And they said, "Believe in the Lord Jesus, and you will be saved, you and your household." [32] And they spoke the word of the Lord to him and to all that were in his house. [33] And he took them the same hour of the night, and washed their wounds, and he was baptized at once, with all his family. [34] Then he brought them up into his house, and set food before them; and he rejoiced with all his household that he had believed in God.

35 But when it was day, the magistrates sent the police, saying, "Let those men go." [36] And the jailer reported the words to Paul, saying, "The magistrates have sent to let you go; now therefore come out and go in peace." [37] But Paul said to them, "They have beaten us publicly, uncondemned, men who are Roman citizens, and have thrown us into prison; and do they now cast us out secretly? No! let them come themselves and take us out." [38] The police reported these words to the magistrates, and they were afraid when they heard that they were Roman citizens; [39] so they came and apologized to them. And they took them out and asked them to leave the city. [40] So they went out of the prison, and visited Lydia; and when they had seen the brethren, they exhorted them and departed.

17 Now when they had passed through Amphip'olis and Apollo'nia, they came to Thessaloni'ca, where there was a synagogue of the Jews. [2] And Paul went in, as was his custom, and for three weeks[p] he argued with them from the scriptures, [3] explaining and proving that it was necessary for the Christ to suffer and to rise from the dead, and saying, "This Jesus, whom I proclaim to you, is the Christ." [4] And some of them were persuaded, and joined Paul and Silas; as did a great many of the devout Greeks and not a few of the leading women. [5] But the Jews were jealous, and taking some wicked fellows of the rabble, they gathered a crowd, set the city in an uproar, and attacked the house of Jason, seeking to bring them out to the people. [6] And when they could not find them, they dragged Jason and some of the brethren before the city authorities, crying, "These men who have turned the world upside down have come here also, [7] and Jason has received them; and they are all acting against the decrees of Caesar, saying that there is another king, Jesus." [8] And the people and the city authorities were disturbed when they heard this. [9] And when they had taken security from Jason and the rest, they let them go.

10 The brethren immediately sent

p Or sabbaths

---

of *Romans*. **24:** *The stocks* tortured prisoners by forcing their legs apart. **35:** *Police*, lictors, whose symbol of office was a bundle of rods, sometimes bound around an axe (the fasces). **37–38:** By law *Roman citizens* were protected against scourging (yet see 2 Cor.11.25).
    17.1–15: From Thessalonica to Athens. Paul founds churches in Thessalonica and Beroea. **1:** *Amphipolis and Apollonia* were on the Via Egnatia between Philippi and *Thessalonica*, capital of the province. **6–7:** *City authorities*, i.e. "politarchs," a Macedonian title. **14–15:** *Timothy* must soon have joined Paul at Athens (1 Th.3.2).

Paul and Silas away by night to Beroe'a; and when they arrived they went into the Jewish synagogue. [11] Now these Jews were more noble than those in Thessaloni'ca, for they received the word with all eagerness, examining the scriptures daily to see if these things were so. [12] Many of them therefore believed, with not a few Greek women of high standing as well as men. [13] But when the Jews of Thessaloni'ca learned that the word of God was proclaimed by Paul at Beroe'a also, they came there too, stirring up and inciting the crowds. [14] Then the brethren immediately sent Paul off on his way to the sea, but Silas and Timothy remained there. [15] Those who conducted Paul brought him as far as Athens; and receiving a command for Silas and Timothy to come to him as soon as possible, they departed.

16 Now while Paul was waiting for them at Athens, his spirit was provoked within him as he saw that the city was full of idols. [17] So he argued in the synagogue with the Jews and the devout persons, and in the market place every day with those who chanced to be there. [18] Some also of the Epicurean and Stoic philosophers met him. And some said, "What would this babbler say?" Others said, "He seems to be a preacher of foreign divinities"–because he preached Jesus and the resurrection. [19] And they took hold of him and brought him to the Are-op'agus, saying, "May we know what this new teaching is which you present? [20] For you bring some strange things to our ears; we wish to know therefore what these things mean." [21] Now all the Athenians and the foreigners who lived there spent their time in nothing except telling or hearing something new.

22 So Paul, standing in the middle of the Are-op'agus, said: "Men of Athens, I perceive that in every way you are very religious. [23] For as I passed along, and observed the objects of your worship, I found also an altar with this inscription, 'To an unknown god.' What therefore you worship as unknown, this I proclaim to you. [24] The God who made the world and everything in it, being Lord of heaven and earth, does not live in shrines made by man, [25] nor is he served by human hands, as though he needed anything, since he himself gives to all men life and breath and everything. [26] And he made from one every nation of men to live on all the face of the earth, having determined allotted periods and the boundaries of their habitation, [27] that they should seek God, in the hope that they might feel after him and find him. Yet he is not far from each one of us, [28] for

'In him we live and move and have
     our being';

as even some of your poets have said,
'For we are indeed his offspring.'
[29] Being then God's offspring, we ought not to think that the Deity is like gold, or silver, or stone, a representation by the art and imagination of man. [30] The times of ignorance God overlooked, but now he commands all men everywhere to repent, [31] because he has fixed a day on which he will judge the world in righteousness by a man whom he has appointed, and of this he has given assurance to all men by raising him from the dead."

17.16–34: Paul at Athens. The apostle is portrayed as the first Christian philosopher, using Stoic and Jewish arguments. **17:** *The market place* or Agora has now been excavated. **18:** *Babbler*, literally "cock-sparrow," one who picks up scraps of learning. *Jesus and* Anastasis (= *resurrection*) were mistaken for two *foreign divinities.* **19:** Either the council of *the Areopagus*, or the hill itself. **21:** *The Athenians* at this time were famous for their curiosity. **22:** *Religious*, i.e. addicted to worship of gods. **23:** One who did not know which god to thank or propitiate might set up an altar *to an unknown god.* **26:** *From one*, i.e. one man (Adam). **28:** The first quotation is sometimes attributed to Epimenides; the second is from Aratus' *Phaenomena.* **32:** *Some mocked*, as in 1 Cor.15.12,35.

32 Now when they heard of the resurrection of the dead, some mocked; but others said, "We will hear you again about this." 33 So Paul went out from among them. 34 But some men joined him and believed, among them Dionys'ius the Are-op'agite and a woman named Dam'aris and others with them.

18 After this he left Athens and went to Corinth. 2 And he found a Jew named Aq'uila, a native of Pontus, lately come from Italy with his wife Priscilla, because Claudius had commanded all the Jews to leave Rome. And he went to see them; 3 and because he was of the same trade he stayed with them, and they worked, for by trade they were tentmakers. 4 And he argued in the synagogue every sabbath, and persuaded Jews and Greeks. 5 When Silas and Timothy arrived from Macedo'nia, Paul was occupied with preaching, testifying to the Jews that the Christ was Jesus. 6 And when they opposed and reviled him, he shook out his garments and said to them, "Your blood be upon your heads! I am innocent. From now on I will go to the Gentiles." 7 And he left there and went to the house of a man named Titius*q* Justus, a worshiper of God; his house was next door to the synagogue. 8 Crispus, the ruler of the synagogue, believed in the Lord, together with all his household; and many of the Corinthians hearing Paul believed and were baptized. 9 And the Lord said to Paul one night in a vision, "Do not be afraid, but speak and do not be silent; 10 for I am with you, and no man shall attack you to harm you; for I have many people in this city."

11 And he stayed a year and six months, teaching the word of God among them.

12 But when Gallio was proconsul of Acha'ia, the Jews made a united attack upon Paul and brought him before the tribunal, 13 saying, "This man is persuading men to worship God contrary to the law." 14 But when Paul was about to open his mouth, Gallio said to the Jews, "If it were a matter of wrongdoing or vicious crime, I should have reason to bear with you, O Jews; 15 but since it is a matter of questions about words and names and your own law, see to it yourselves; I refuse to be a judge of these things." 16 And he drove them from the tribunal. 17 And they all seized Sos'thenes, the ruler of the synagogue, and beat him in front of the tribunal. But Gallio paid no attention to this.

18 After this Paul stayed many days longer, and then took leave of the brethren and sailed for Syria, and with him Priscilla and Aq'uila. At Cen'chre-ae he cut his hair, for he had a vow. 19 And they came to Ephesus, and he left them there; but he himself went into the synagogue and argued with the Jews. 20 When they asked him to stay for a longer period, he declined; 21 but on taking leave of them he said, "I will return to you if God wills," and he set sail from Ephesus. 22 When he had landed at Caesare'a, he went up and greeted the church, and then went down to Antioch. 23 After spending some time there he departed and went from place to place through the region of Galatia

q Other early authorities read *Titus*

18.1–17: Founding of the church in Corinth. See 1 Cor. chs. 1–4 for Paul's own account. **2:** Claudius' edict expelling the Jews from Rome was issued probably in A.D. 49. *Priscilla*, the Prisca of 1 Cor.16.19. **3:** *Tentmakers;* the Greek word usually means "leather-workers." **8:** *Crispus*, one of the few Corinthians baptized personally by Paul (1 Cor.1.14). **12:** *Gallio*, brother of the philosopher Seneca, *proconsul of Asia* about A.D. 51. The *tribunal* has been excavated. **17:** *Sosthenes* may be the one mentioned in 1 Cor.1.1.

18.18–23: End of the second missionary journey and beginning of the third. Paul returns to Antioch and goes back to Asia Minor. **18:** Paul *cut his hair* as a temporary Nazirite *vow* (21.24; Num.6.1–21). *Cenchreae*, the eastern port of Corinth. **23:** *The region of Galatia and Phrygia*, see 16.6 n. Paul perhaps came near Pessinus and Gordium and then turned west.

and Phryg'ia, strengthening all the disciples.

24 Now a Jew named Apol'los, a native of Alexandria, came to Ephesus. He was an eloquent man, well versed in the scriptures. [25] He had been instructed in the way of the Lord; and being fervent in spirit, he spoke and taught accurately the things concerning Jesus, though he knew only the baptism of John. [26] He began to speak boldly in the synagogue; but when Priscilla and Aq'uila heard him, they took him and expounded to him the way of God more accurately. [27] And when he wished to cross to Acha'ia, the brethren encouraged him, and wrote to the disciples to receive him. When he arrived, he greatly helped those who through grace had believed, [28] for he powerfully confuted the Jews in public, showing by the scriptures that the Christ was Jesus.

19 While Apol'los was at Corinth, Paul passed through the upper country and came to Ephesus. There he found some disciples. [2] And he said to them, "Did you receive the Holy Spirit when you believed?" And they said, "No, we have never even heard that there is a Holy Spirit." [3] And he said, "Into what then were you baptized?" They said, "Into John's baptism." [4] And Paul said, "John baptized with the baptism of repentance, telling the people to believe in the one who was to come after him, that is, Jesus." [5] On hearing this, they were baptized in the name of the Lord Jesus. [6] And when Paul had laid his hands upon them, the Holy Spirit came on them;

and they spoke with tongues and prophesied. [7] There were about twelve of them in all.

8 And he entered the synagogue and for three months spoke boldly, arguing and pleading about the kingdom of God; [9] but when some were stubborn and disbelieved, speaking evil of the Way before the congregation, he withdrew from them, taking the disciples with him, and argued daily in the hall of Tyran'nus.[r] [10] This continued for two years, so that all the residents of Asia heard the word of the Lord, both Jews and Greeks.

11 And God did extraordinary miracles by the hands of Paul, [12] so that handkerchiefs or aprons were carried away from his body to the sick, and diseases left them and the evil spirits came out of them. [13] Then some of the itinerant Jewish exorcists undertook to pronounce the name of the Lord Jesus over those who had evil spirits, saying, "I adjure you by the Jesus whom Paul preaches." [14] Seven sons of a Jewish high priest named Sceva were doing this. [15] But the evil spirit answered them, "Jesus I know, and Paul I know; but who are you?" [16] And the man in whom the evil spirit was leaped on them, mastered all of them, and overpowered them, so that they fled out of that house naked and wounded. [17] And this became known to all residents of Ephesus, both Jews and Greeks; and fear fell upon them all; and the name of the Lord Jesus was extolled. [18] Many also

r Other ancient authorities add *from the fifth hour to the tenth*

18.24–28: Apollos in Ephesus. For his activity in Corinth see 1 Cor.1.12; 3.1–9,21–23. **24:** An Alexandrian *well versed in the scriptures* would probably interpret them allegorically. **25:** He knew something *concerning Jesus* but was ignorant of such Christian rites as baptism in Jesus' name (19.5).

19.1–40: Paul's long ministry in Ephesus. This period of more than two years (v. 10; compare 20.31) forms the background of 1 and 2 Corinthians. **1:** *The upper country*, inner Asia Minor (18.23). *Disciples* elsewhere in Acts means Christians; these perhaps belonged to John the Baptist. **2:** All who read the Old Testament would know of *a Holy Spirit*. The reference may be to outward signs of the Spirit's presence. **5–6:** See 8.14–17 n. **9:** *The Way*, see 9.2 n. Some manuscripts add that Paul lectured "from the fifth hour to the tenth," i.e. from 11 a.m. to 4 p.m., when, because of the heat of the day, the hall would not be used by Tyrannus. **12:** 5.15. **13:** Jewish and pagan sources show that non-Christians used *the name of the Lord Jesus* in

of those who were now believers came, confessing and divulging their practices. ¹⁹ And a number of those who practiced magic arts brought their books together and burned them in the sight of all; and they counted the value of them and found it came to fifty thousand pieces of silver. ²⁰ So the word of the Lord grew and prevailed mightily.

21 Now after these events Paul resolved in the Spirit to pass through Macedo′nia and Acha′ia and go to Jerusalem, saying, "After I have been there, I must also see Rome." ²² And having sent into Macedo′nia two of his helpers, Timothy and Eras′tus, he himself stayed in Asia for a while.

23 About that time there arose no little stir concerning the Way. ²⁴ For a man named Deme′trius, a silversmith, who made silver shrines of Ar′temis, brought no little business to the craftsmen. ²⁵ These he gathered together, with the workmen of like occupation, and said, "Men, you know that from this business we have our wealth. ²⁶ And you see and hear that not only at Ephesus but almost throughout all Asia this Paul has persuaded and turned away a considerable company of people, saying that gods made with hands are not gods. ²⁷ And there is danger not only that this trade of ours may come into disrepute but also that the temple of the great goddess Ar′temis may count for nothing, and that she may even be deposed from her magnificence, she whom all Asia and the world worship."

28 When they heard this they were enraged, and cried out, "Great is Ar′temis of the Ephesians!" ²⁹ So the city was filled with the confusion; and they rushed together into the theater,

dragging with them Ga′ius and Aristar′chus, Macedo′nians who were Paul's companions in travel. ³⁰ Paul wished to go in among the crowd, but the disciples would not let him; ³¹ some of the A′si-archs also, who were friends of his, sent to him and begged him not to venture into the theater. ³² Now some cried one thing, some another; for the assembly was in confusion, and most of them did not know why they had come together. ³³ Some of the crowd prompted Alexander, whom the Jews had put forward. And Alexander motioned with his hand, wishing to make a defense to the people. ³⁴ But when they recognized that he was a Jew, for about two hours they all with one voice cried out, "Great is Ar′temis of the Ephesians!" ³⁵ And when the town clerk had quieted the crowd, he said, "Men of Ephesus, what man is there who does not know that the city of the Ephesians is temple keeper of the great Ar′temis, and of the sacred stone that fell from the sky?ˢ ³⁶ Seeing then that these things cannot be contradicted, you ought to be quiet and do nothing rash. ³⁷ For you have brought these men here who are neither sacrilegious nor blasphemers of our goddess. ³⁸ If therefore Deme′trius and the craftsmen with him have a complaint against any one, the courts are open, and there are proconsuls; let them bring charges against one another. ³⁹ But if you seek anything further,ᵗ it shall be settled in the regular assembly. ⁴⁰ For we are in danger of being charged with rioting today, there being no cause that we can give to justify this commotion." ⁴¹ And when he had said this, he dismissed the assembly.

s The meaning of the Greek is uncertain
t Other ancient authorities read *about other matters*

exorcism (Mk.9.38–41). **19:** Ephesus was such a noted center of *magic* that magical books were often called "Ephesian writings." **21:** Rom.1.13–15; 15.22–25. **22:** *Erastus*, Rom.16.23; 2 Tim. 4.20; an inscription from Corinth mentions a Roman official (an aedile) by this name. **24:** *Shrines*, perhaps miniature temples or statues. **27:** *Artemis*, Ephesus' chief divinity; her *temple* was one of the seven wonders of the ancient world. **31:** *Asiarchs*, an honorific title given civic benefactors in the Roman province of Asia. **35:** Cities and peoples were sometimes honored with the title of *temple keeper* to a god.

20 After the uproar ceased, Paul sent for the disciples and having exhorted them took leave of them and departed for Macedo'nia. ² When he had gone through these parts and had given them much encouragement, he came to Greece. ³ There he spent three months, and when a plot was made against him by the Jews as he was about to set sail for Syria, he determined to return through Macedo'nia. ⁴ Sop'ater of Beroe'a, the son of Pyrrhus, accompanied him; and of the Thessalo'nians, Aristar'chus and Secun'dus; and Ga'ius of Derbe, and Timothy; and the Asians, Tych'icus and Troph'imus. ⁵ These went on and were waiting for us at Tro'as, ⁶ but we sailed away from Philip'pi after the days of Unleavened Bread, and in five days we came to them at Tro'as, where we stayed for seven days.

7 On the first day of the week, when we were gathered together to break bread, Paul talked with them, intending to depart on the morrow; and he prolonged his speech until midnight. ⁸ There were many lights in the upper chamber where we were gathered. ⁹ And a young man named Eu'tychus was sitting in the window. He sank into a deep sleep as Paul talked still longer; and being overcome by sleep, he fell down from the third story and was taken up dead. ¹⁰ But Paul went down and bent over him, and embracing him said, "Do not be alarmed, for his life is in him." ¹¹ And when Paul had gone up and had broken bread and eaten, he conversed with them a long while, until daybreak, and so departed. ¹² And they took the lad away alive, and were not a little comforted.

13 But going ahead to the ship, we set sail for Assos, intending to take Paul aboard there; for so he had arranged, intending himself to go by land. ¹⁴ And when he met us at Assos, we took him on board and came to Mityle'ne. ¹⁵ And sailing from there we came the following day opposite Chi'os; the next day we touched at Samos; and*ᵘ* the day after that we came to Mile'tus. ¹⁶ For Paul had decided to sail past Ephesus, so that he might not have to spend time in Asia; for he was hastening to be at Jerusalem, if possible, on the day of Pentecost.

17 And from Mile'tus he sent to Ephesus and called to him the elders of the church. ¹⁸ And when they came to him, he said to them:

"You yourselves know how I lived among you all the time from the first day that I set foot in Asia, ¹⁹ serving the Lord with all humility and with tears and with trials which befell me through the plots of the Jews; ²⁰ how I did not shrink from declaring to you anything that was profitable, and teaching you in public and from house to house, ²¹ testifying both to Jews and to Greeks of repentance to God and of faith in our Lord Jesus Christ. ²² And now, behold, I am going to Jerusalem, bound in the Spirit, not knowing what shall befall me there; ²³ except that the Holy Spirit testifies to me in every city that imprisonment and afflictions await me. ²⁴ But I do not account my life of any value nor as precious to myself, if only I may accomplish my course and the ministry which I received from the Lord Jesus, to testify to the gospel of the grace of God. ²⁵ And now, behold, I know that all you among whom I have gone preaching the kingdom will see my face no more. ²⁶ Therefore I testify to you this

u Other ancient authorities add *after remaining at Trogyllium*

20.1–6: The last visit to Greece. The companions may be carrying relief money to Jerusalem (24.17; 1 Cor.16.1–4; 2 Cor.8.23). **4:** *Sopater*, perhaps the Sosipater of Rom.16.21. **6:** *Days of Unleavened Bread,* 12.3; see Mk.14.1 n.
20.7–21.14: Paul's return to Palestine. This concludes the third missionary journey. **20.7:** *The first day of the week,* Sunday. *To break bread,* see 2.42 n. **17:** *Miletus,* modern Balat, then an important port at the mouth of the Maeander. **24–25:** *Accomplish my course . . . testify,* a

day that I am innocent of the blood of all of you, ²⁷ for I did not shrink from declaring to you the whole counsel of God. ²⁸ Take heed to yourselves and to all the flock, in which the Holy Spirit has made you overseers, to care for the church of God^v which he obtained with the blood of his own Son.^w ²⁹ I know that after my departure fierce wolves will come in among you, not sparing the flock; ³⁰ and from among your own selves will arise men speaking perverse things, to draw away the disciples after them. ³¹ Therefore be alert, remembering that for three years I did not cease night or day to admonish every one with tears. ³² And now I commend you to God and to the word of his grace, which is able to build you up and to give you the inheritance among all those who are sanctified. ³³ I coveted no one's silver or gold or apparel. ³⁴ You yourselves know that these hands ministered to my necessities, and to those who were with me. ³⁵ In all things I have shown you that by so toiling one must help the weak, remembering the words of the Lord Jesus, how he said, 'It is more blessed to give than to receive.' "

36 And when he had spoken thus, he knelt down and prayed with them all. ³⁷ And they all wept and embraced Paul and kissed him, ³⁸ sorrowing most of all because of the word he had spoken, that they should see his face no more. And they brought him to the ship.

21 And when we had parted from them and set sail, we came by a straight course to Cos, and the next day to Rhodes, and from there to Pat′ara.^x ² And having found a ship crossing to Phoeni′cia, we went aboard, and set sail. ³ When we had come in sight of Cyprus, leaving it on the left we sailed to Syria, and landed at Tyre; for there the ship was to unload its cargo. ⁴ And having sought out the disciples, we stayed there for seven days. Through the Spirit they told Paul not to go on to Jerusalem. ⁵ And when our days there were ended, we departed and went on our journey; and they all, with wives and children, brought us on our way till we were outside the city; and kneeling down on the beach we prayed and bade one another farewell. ⁶ Then we went on board the ship, and they returned home.

7 When we had finished the voyage from Tyre, we arrived at Ptolema′is; and we greeted the brethren and stayed with them for one day. ⁸ On the morrow we departed and came to Caesare′a; and we entered the house of Philip the evangelist, who was one of the seven, and stayed with him. ⁹ And he had four unmarried daughters, who prophesied. ¹⁰ While we were staying for some days, a prophet named Ag′abus came down from Judea. ¹¹ And coming to us he took Paul's girdle and bound his own feet and hands, and said, "Thus says the Holy Spirit, 'So shall the Jews at Jerusalem bind the man who owns this girdle and deliver him into the hands of the Gentiles.' " ¹² When we heard this, we and the people there begged him not to go up to Jerusalem. ¹³ Then Paul answered, "What are you doing, weeping and breaking my heart? For I am ready not only to be imprisoned but even to die at Jerusalem for the name of the Lord Jesus." ¹⁴ And when he would not be persuaded, we ceased and said, "The will of the Lord be done."

15 After these days we made ready and went up to Jerusalem. ¹⁶ And some

v Other ancient authorities read *of the Lord*
w Greek *with the blood of his Own* or *with his own blood*
x Other ancient authorities add *and Myra*

---

premonition of martyrdom (2 Tim.4.6). **28:** *Overseers,* Greek "bishops" (compare Tit.1.5–7), the elders of v. 17. As in 1 Pet.2.25, the bishop is a shepherd. **29–30:** Mt.7.15; Mk.13.22. **34:** 1 Cor.9.1–18; 2 Cor.11.7–11. **35:** A saying of Jesus not found in the gospels. **21.7:** *Ptolemais,* modern Acre, near Haifa. **8:** *Philip the evangelist,* though not an apostle, did similar work. *One of the Seven,* see 6.1–7 n. **10–11:** *Agabus* (11.28), like Old Testament prophets (Is.20.2–6), performed a symbolic act.

of the disciples from Caesare'a went with us, bringing us to the house of Mnason of Cyprus, an early disciple, with whom we should lodge.

17 When we had come to Jerusalem, the brethren received us gladly. 18 On the following day Paul went in with us to James; and all the elders were present. 19 After greeting them, he related one by one the things that God had done among the Gentiles through his ministry. 20 And when they heard it, they glorified God. And they said to him, "You see, brother, how many thousands there are among the Jews of those who have believed; they are all zealous for the law, 21 and they have been told about you that you teach all the Jews who are among the Gentiles to forsake Moses, telling them not to circumcise their children or observe the customs. 22 What then is to be done? They will certainly hear that you have come. 23 Do therefore what we tell you. We have four men who are under a vow; 24 take these men and purify yourself along with them and pay their expenses, so that they may shave their heads. Thus all will know that there is nothing in what they have been told about you but that you yourself live in observance of the law. 25 But as for the Gentiles who have believed, we have sent a letter with our judgment that they should abstain from what has been sacrificed to idols and from blood and from what is strangled*y* and from unchastity." 26 Then Paul took the men, and the next day he purified himself with them and went into the temple, to give notice when the days of purification would be fulfilled and the offering presented for every one of them.

27 When the seven days were almost completed, the Jews from Asia, who had seen him in the temple, stirred up all the crowd, and laid hands on him, 28 crying out, "Men of Israel, help! This is the man who is teaching men everywhere against the people and the law and this place; moreover he also brought Greeks into the temple, and he has defiled this holy place." 29 For they had previously seen Troph'imus the Ephesian with him in the city, and they supposed that Paul had brought him into the temple. 30 Then all the city was aroused, and the people ran together; they seized Paul and dragged him out of the temple, and at once the gates were shut. 31 And as they were trying to kill him, word came to the tribune of the cohort that all Jerusalem was in confusion. 32 He at once took soldiers and centurions, and ran down to them; and when they saw the tribune and the soldiers, they stopped beating Paul. 33 Then the tribune came up and arrested him, and ordered him to be bound with two chains. He inquired who he was and what he had done. 34 Some in the crowd shouted one thing, some another; and as he could not learn the facts because of the uproar, he ordered him to be brought into the barracks. 35 And when he came to the steps, he was actually carried by the soldiers because of the violence of the crowd; 36 for the mob of the people followed, crying, "Away with him!"

37 As Paul was about to be brought

y Other early authorities omit *and from what is strangled*

21.15–26: Paul's conformity to Judaism. He takes a vow in order to allay suspicions. **20:** On Jewish Christians who were *zealous for the law*, see 11.2; 15.5; and the Introduction to Galatians. **21:** The charge was untrue (16.3; 1 Cor.9.20; 10.32). **23–24:** The temporary Nazirite *vow* was a later development out of Num.6.1–21. **25:** He is told of the decree as though he had not heard of it (see 15.22 n.).

21.27–22.29: Paul's arrest and defense. Seized after a disturbance in the temple, Paul tells of his conversion. **21.28:** It was a capital offense to bring *Greeks into the temple;* an inscription stating this has been discovered. **29:** *Trophimus,* 20.4; 2 Tim.4.20. **31:** A military *tribune* commanded a *cohort;* this would have been stationed at the Antonia, near the temple. **33:** Paul's case came into the hands of Roman, not Jewish, authorities. **38:** For *the Egyptian,* see Josephus,

into the barracks, he said to the tribune, "May I say something to you?" And he said, "Do you know Greek? ³⁸ Are you not the Egyptian, then, who recently stirred up a revolt and led the four thousand men of the Assassins out into the wilderness?" ³⁹ Paul replied, "I am a Jew, from Tarsus in Cili′cia, a citizen of no mean city; I beg you, let me speak to the people." ⁴⁰ And when he had given him leave, Paul, standing on the steps, motioned with his hand to the people; and when there was a great hush, he spoke to them in the Hebrew language, saying:

22 "Brethren and fathers, hear the defense which I now make before you."

2 And when they heard that he addressed them in the Hebrew language, they were the more quiet. And he said:

3 "I am a Jew, born at Tarsus in Cili′cia, but brought up in this city at the feet of Gama′li-el, educated according to the strict manner of the law of our fathers, being zealous for God as you all are this day. ⁴ I persecuted this Way to the death, binding and delivering to prison both men and women, ⁵ as the high priest and the whole council of elders bear me witness. From them I received letters to the brethren, and I journeyed to Damascus to take those also who were there and bring them in bonds to Jerusalem to be punished.

6 "As I made my journey and drew near to Damascus, about noon a great light from heaven suddenly shone about me. ⁷ And I fell to the ground and heard a voice saying to me, 'Saul, Saul, why do you persecute me?' ⁸ And I answered, 'Who are you, Lord?' And he said to me, 'I am Jesus of Nazareth whom you are persecuting.' ⁹ Now those who were with me saw the light but did not hear the voice of the one who was speaking to me. ¹⁰ And I said, 'What shall I do, Lord?' And the Lord said to me, 'Rise, and go into Damascus, and there you will be told all that is appointed for you to do.' ¹¹ And when I could not see because of the brightness of that light, I was led by the hand by those who were with me, and came into Damascus.

12 "And one Anani′as, a devout man according to the law, well spoken of by all the Jews who lived there, ¹³ came to me, and standing by me said to me, 'Brother Saul, receive your sight.' And in that very hour I received my sight and saw him. ¹⁴ And he said, 'The God of our fathers appointed you to know his will, to see the Just One and to hear a voice from his mouth; ¹⁵ for you will be a witness for him to all men of what you have seen and heard. ¹⁶ And now why do you wait? Rise and be baptized, and wash away your sins, calling on his name.'

17 "When I had returned to Jerusalem and was praying in the temple, I fell into a trance ¹⁸ and saw him saying to me, 'Make haste and get quickly out of Jerusalem, because they will not accept your testimony about me.' ¹⁹ And I said, 'Lord, they themselves know that in every synagogue I imprisoned and beat those who believed in thee. ²⁰ And when the blood of Stephen thy witness was shed, I also was standing by and approving, and keeping the garments of those who killed him.' ²¹ And he said to me, 'Depart; for I will send you far away to the Gentiles.' "

22 Up to this word they listened to him; then they lifted up their voices and said, "Away with such a fellow from the earth! For he ought not to live." ²³ And as they cried out and waved their garments and threw dust into the air, ²⁴ the tribune commanded him to be brought into the barracks, and ordered him to be examined by scourging, to find out why they shouted thus against him. ²⁵ But

---

War ii.13.5. **40**: *Hebrew*, probably Aramic. **22.3**: *Brought up*, educated. *Gamaliel*, see 5.34 n. **4–21**: In 9.7 the companions heard the voice but saw no one; otherwise the account is similar

when they had tied him up with the thongs, Paul said to the centurion who was standing by, "Is it lawful for you to scourge a man who is a Roman citizen, and uncondemned?" ²⁶ When the centurion heard that, he went to the tribune and said to him, "What are you about to do? For this man is a Roman citizen." ²⁷ So the tribune came and said to him, "Tell me, are you a Roman citizen?" And he said, "Yes." ²⁸ The tribune answered, "I bought this citizenship for a large sum." Paul said, "But I was born a citizen." ²⁹ So those who were about to examine him withdrew from him instantly; and the tribune also was afraid, for he realized that Paul was a Roman citizen and that he had bound him.

30 But on the morrow, desiring to know the real reason why the Jews accused him, he unbound him, and commanded the chief priests and all the council to meet, and he brought Paul down and set him before them.

23 And Paul, looking intently at the council, said, "Brethren, I have lived before God in all good conscience up to this day." ² And the high priest Anani'as commanded those who stood by him to strike him on the mouth. ³ Then Paul said to him, "God shall strike you, you whitewashed wall! Are you sitting to judge me according to the law, and yet contrary to the law you order me to be struck?" ⁴ Those who stood by said, "Would you revile God's high priest?" ⁵ And Paul said, "I did not know, brethren, that he was the high priest; for it is written, 'You shall not speak evil of a ruler of your people.'"

6 But when Paul perceived that one part were Sad'ducees and the other Pharisees, he cried out in the council, "Brethren, I am a Pharisee, a son of Pharisees; with respect to the hope and the resurrection of the dead I am on trial." ⁷ And when he had said this, a dissension arose between the Pharisees and the Sad'ducees; and the assembly was divided. ⁸ For the Sad'ducees say that there is no resurrection, nor angel, nor spirit; but the Pharisees acknowledge them all. ⁹ Then a great clamor arose; and some of the scribes of the Pharisees' party stood up and contended, "We find nothing wrong in this man. What if a spirit or an angel spoke to him?" ¹⁰ And when the dissension became violent, the tribune, afraid that Paul would be torn in pieces by them, commanded the soldiers to go down and take him by force from among them and bring him into the barracks.

11 The following night the Lord stood by him and said, "Take courage, for as you have testified about me at Jerusalem, so you must bear witness also at Rome."

12 When it was day, the Jews made a plot and bound themselves by an oath neither to eat nor drink till they had killed Paul. ¹³ There were more than forty who made this conspiracy. ¹⁴ And they went to the chief priests and elders, and said, "We have strictly bound ourselves by an oath to taste no food till we have killed Paul. ¹⁵ You therefore, along with the council, give notice now to the tribune to bring him down to you, as though you were going to determine his case more exactly. And we are ready to kill him before he comes near."

to 9.1–18. **24:** The *scourging* was to extract evidence, not for punishment. **25:** *A Roman citizen*, still uncondemned, was protected from scourging; see 16.37–38 n. **28:** In Claudius' reign *citizenship* was often purchased *for a large sum*.

22.30–23.10: Paul before the Sanhedrin; the tribune brings him before it to get evidence, not to try him. **23.2:** *Ananias, high priest* in the reigns of Claudius and Nero, was assassinated about A.D. 66. **3:** *Whitewashed wall* is obscure; perhaps a tomb (compare Mt.23.27), which is unclean. **5:** Quoted from Ex.22.28. **6:** *Paul* claims to be a *Pharisee* (26.5; Phil.3.5). For his *hope* of the *resurrection* see 1 Cor. ch. 15; Phil.3.11. **8:** *Sadducees* denied the *resurrection*, see Mt.22.23 n.

16 Now the son of Paul's sister heard of their ambush; so he went and entered the barracks and told Paul. 17 And Paul called one of the centurions and said, "Take this young man to the tribune; for he has something to tell him." 18 So he took him and brought him to the tribune and said, "Paul the prisoner called me and asked me to bring this young man to you, as he has something to say to you." 19 The tribune took him by the hand, and going aside asked him privately, "What is it that you have to tell me?" 20 And he said, "The Jews have agreed to ask you to bring Paul down to the council tomorrow, as though they were going to inquire somewhat more closely about him. 21 But do not yield to them; for more than forty of their men lie in ambush for him, having bound themselves by an oath neither to eat nor drink till they have killed him; and now they are ready, waiting for the promise from you." 22 So the tribune dismissed the young man, charging him, "Tell no one that you have informed me of this."

23 Then he called two of the centurions and said, "At the third hour of the night get ready two hundred soldiers with seventy horsemen and two hundred spearmen to go as far as Caesare'a. 24 Also provide mounts for Paul to ride, and bring him safely to Felix the governor." 25 And he wrote a letter to this effect:

26 "Claudius Lys'ias to his Excellency the governor Felix, greeting. 27 This man was seized by the Jews, and was about to be killed by them, when I came upon them with the soldiers and rescued him, having learned that he was a Roman citizen. 28 And desiring to know the charge on which they accused him, I brought him down to their council. 29 I found that he was accused about questions of their law, but charged with nothing deserving death or imprisonment. 30 And when it was disclosed to me that there would be a plot against the man, I sent him to you at once, ordering his accusers also to state before you what they have against him."

31 So the soldiers, according to their instructions, took Paul and brought him by night to Antip'atris. 32 And on the morrow they returned to the barracks, leaving the horsemen to go on with him. 33 When they came to Caesare'a and delivered the letter to the governor, they presented Paul also before him. 34 On reading the letter, he asked to what province he belonged. When he learned that he was from Cili'cia 35 he said, "I will hear you when your accusers arrive." And he commanded him to be guarded in Herod's praetorium.

24 And after five days the high priest Anani'as came down with some elders and a spokesman, one Tertul'lus. They laid before the governor their case against Paul; 2 and when he was called, Tertul'lus began to accuse him, saying:

"Since through you we enjoy much peace, and since by your provision, most excellent Felix, reforms are introduced on behalf of this nation, 3 in every way and everywhere we accept this with all gratitude. 4 But, to detain you no further, I beg you in your kindness to hear us briefly. 5 For we have found this man a pestilent fellow, an agitator among all the Jews throughout the world, and a ringleader of the sect of the Nazarenes. 6 He even tried

---

23.11–35: Paul is sent to Caesarea. 23: *Third hour*, between 9 and 10 p.m. The number of soldiers is surprising. The Greek word translated *spearmen* is obscure; it may mean "bowmen" or "bodyguards." 24: Antonius *Felix*, procurator of Judea, brother of a favorite freedman of Claudius. 26: *His Excellency*, the word used in addressing Theophilus (Lk.1.3). 35: The *praetorium*, formerly Herod's palace, now headquarters of the procurators.

24.1–27: Paul before Felix. The apostle denies the charges, and the governor postpones the case. 5: *Sect*, the word is usually used in a bad sense (24.14; 28.22). *Nazarenes*, Christians as followers of Jesus of Nazareth (2.22); a meaning not found elsewhere in early Christian literature.

to profane the temple, but we seized him.[z] [8] By examining him yourself you will be able to learn from him about everything of which we accuse him."

9 The Jews also joined in the charge, affirming that all this was so. 10 And when the governor had motioned to him to speak, Paul replied:

"Realizing that for many years you have been judge over this nation, I cheerfully make my defense. [11] As you may ascertain, it is not more than twelve days since I went up to worship at Jerusalem; [12] and they did not find me disputing with any one or stirring up a crowd, either in the temple or in the synagogues, or in the city. [13] Neither can they prove to you what they now bring up against me. [14] But this I admit to you, that according to the Way, which they call a sect, I worship the God of our fathers, believing everything laid down by the law or written in the prophets, [15] having a hope in God which these themselves accept, that there will be a resurrection of both the just and the unjust. [16] So I always take pains to have a clear conscience toward God and toward men. [17] Now after some years I came to bring to my nation alms and offerings. [18] As I was doing this, they found me purified in the temple, without any crowd or tumult. But some Jews from Asia— [19] they ought to be here before you and to make an accusation, if they have anything against me. [20] Or else let these men themselves say what wrongdoing they found when I stood before the council, [21] except this one thing which I cried out while standing among them, 'With respect to the resurrection of the dead I am on trial before you this day.' "

22 But Felix, having a rather accurate knowledge of the Way, put them off, saying, "When Lys'ias the tribune comes down, I will decide your case." [23] Then he gave orders to the centurion that he should be kept in custody but should have some liberty, and that none of his friends should be prevented from attending to his needs.

24 After some days Felix came with his wife Drusil'la, who was a Jewess; and he sent for Paul and heard him speak upon faith in Christ Jesus. [25] And as he argued about justice and self-control and future judgment, Felix was alarmed and said, "Go away for the present; when I have an opportunity I will summon you." [26] At the same time he hoped that money would be given him by Paul. So he sent for him often and conversed with him. [27] But when two years had elapsed, Felix was succeeded by Porcius Festus; and desiring to do the Jews a favor, Felix left Paul in prison.

25 Now when Festus had come into his province, after three days he went up to Jerusalem from Caesare'a. [2] And the chief priests and the principal men of the Jews informed him against Paul; and they urged him, [3] asking as a favor to have the man sent to Jerusalem, planning an ambush to kill him on the way. [4] Festus replied that Paul was being kept at Caesare'a, and that he himself intended to go there shortly. [5] "So," said he, "let the men of authority among you go down with me, and if there is anything wrong about the man, let them accuse him."

6 When he had stayed among them not more than eight or ten days, he went down to Caesare'a; and the next day he took his seat on the tribunal and ordered Paul to be brought. [7] And when he had come, the Jews who had

z Other ancient authorities add *and we would have judged him according to our law.* [7]*But the chief captain Lysias came and came with great violence took him out of our hands,* [8]*commanding his accusers to come before you.*

14: *The Way,* see 9.2 n. 17: *To bring . . . alms,* see 20.1–6 n. 24: *Drusilla* was sister of Herod Agrippa II and Bernice (25.13). 25–26: The behavior of *Felix* is like that of Herod Antipas (Mk.6.20). Compare 18.14–17. 27: *When two years had elapsed,* either from Felix's appointment or Paul's arrest.

25.1–12: **Appeal to the emperor.** Paul insists on a Roman trial and Festus sends him to Rome.

gone down from Jerusalem stood about him, bringing against him many serious charges which they could not prove. [8] Paul said in his defense, "Neither against the law of the Jews, nor against the temple, nor against Caesar have I offended at all." [9] But Festus, wishing to do the Jews a favor, said to Paul, "Do you wish to go up to Jerusalem, and there be tried on these charges before me?" [10] But Paul said, "I am standing before Caesar's tribunal, where I ought to be tried; to the Jews I have done no wrong, as you know very well. [11] If then I am a wrongdoer, and have committed anything for which I deserve to die, I do not seek to escape death; but if there is nothing in their charges against me, no one can give me up to them. I appeal to Caesar." [12] Then Festus, when he had conferred with his council, answered, "You have appealed to Caesar; to Caesar you shall go."

13 Now when some days had passed, Agrippa the king and Berni'ce arrived at Caesare'a to welcome Festus. [14] And as they stayed there many days, Festus laid Paul's case before the king, saying, "There is a man left prisoner by Felix; [15] and when I was at Jerusalem, the chief priests and the elders of the Jews gave information about him, asking for sentence against him. [16] I answered them that it was not the custom of the Romans to give up any one before the accused met the accusers face to face, and had opportunity to make his defense concerning the charge laid against him. [17] When therefore they came together here, I made no delay, but on the next day took my seat on the tribunal and ordered the man to be brought in. [18] When the accusers stood up, they brought no charge in his case of such evils as I supposed; [19] but they had

certain points of dispute with him about their own superstition and about one Jesus, who was dead, but whom Paul asserted to be alive. [20] Being at a loss how to investigate these questions, I asked whether he wished to go to Jerusalem and be tried there regarding them. [21] But when Paul had appealed to be kept in custody for the decision of the emperor, I commanded him to be held until I could send him to Caesar." [22] And Agrippa said to Festus, "I should like to hear the man myself." "Tomorrow," said he, "you shall hear him."

23 So on the morrow Agrippa and Berni'ce came with great pomp, and they entered the audience hall with the military tribunes and the prominent men of the city. Then by command of Festus Paul was brought in. [24] And Festus said, "King Agrippa and all who are present with us, you see this man about whom the whole Jewish people petitioned me, both at Jerusalem and here, shouting that he ought not to live any longer. [25] But I found that he had done nothing deserving death; and as he himself appealed to the emperor, I decided to send him. [26] But I have nothing definite to write to my lord about him. Therefore I have brought him before you, and, especially before you, King Agrippa, that, after we have examined him, I may have something to write. [27] For it seems to me unreasonable, in sending a prisoner, not to indicate the charges against him."

26 Agrippa said to Paul, "You have permission to speak for yourself." Then Paul stretched out his hand and made his defense:

2 "I think myself fortunate that it is before you, King Agrippa, I am to make my defense today against all the accusations of the Jews, [3] because you

---

9–10: Paul fears being turned over to a Jewish court; therefore he insists on *Caesar's tribunal*, i.e. trial according to Roman law. **11–12:** He appeals *to Caesar* in the person of his governor, and Festus decides that the emperor himself should hear the case.

25.13–26.32: Paul's defense before Agrippa. A model defense of Christianity. **25.13:** *Agrippa the king*, Herod Agrippa II, who ruled parts of Palestine. He and *Bernice* were children of Herod Agrippa I (12.1–23). **25:** *Emperor*, literally Augustus, one of the imperial titles.

are especially familiar with all customs and controversies of the Jews; therefore I beg you to listen to me patiently.

4 "My manner of life from my youth, spent from the beginning among my own nation and at Jerusalem, is known by all the Jews. [5] They have known for a long time, if they are willing to testify, that according to the strictest party of our religion I have lived as a Pharisee. [6] And now I stand here on trial for hope in the promise made by God to our fathers, [7] to which our twelve tribes hope to attain, as they earnestly worship night and day. And for this hope I am accused by Jews, O king! [8] Why is it thought incredible by any of you that God raises the dead?

9 "I myself was convinced that I ought to do many things in opposing the name of Jesus of Nazareth. [10] And I did so in Jerusalem; I not only shut up many of the saints in prison, by authority from the chief priests, but when they were put to death I cast my vote against them. [11] And I punished them often in all the synagogues and tried to make them blaspheme; and in raging fury against them, I persecuted them even to foreign cities.

12 "Thus I journeyed to Damascus with the authority and commission of the chief priests. [13] At midday, O king, I saw on the way a light from heaven, brighter than the sun, shining round me and those who journeyed with me. [14] And when we had all fallen to the ground, I heard a voice saying to me in the Hebrew language, 'Saul, Saul, why do you persecute me? It hurts you to kick against the goads.' [15] And I said, 'Who are you, Lord?' And the Lord said, 'I am Jesus whom you are persecuting. [16] But rise and stand upon your feet; for I have appeared to you for this purpose, to appoint you to serve and bear witness to the things in which you have seen me and to those in which I will appear to you, [17] delivering you from the people and from the Gentiles—to whom I send you [18] to open their eyes, that they may turn from darkness to light and from the power of Satan to God, that they may receive forgiveness of sins and a place among those who are sanctified by faith in me.'

19 "Wherefore, O King Agrippa, I was not disobedient to the heavenly vision, [20] but declared first to those at Damascus, then at Jerusalem and throughout all the country of Judea, and also to the Gentiles, that they should repent and turn to God and perform deeds worthy of their repentance. [21] For this reason the Jews seized me in the temple and tried to kill me. [22] To this day I have had the help that comes from God, and so I stand here testifying both to small and great, saying nothing but what the prophets and Moses said would come to pass: [23] that the Christ must suffer, and that, by being the first to rise from the dead, he would proclaim light both to the people and to the Gentiles."

24 And as he thus made his defense, Festus said with a loud voice, "Paul, you are mad; your great learning is turning you mad." [25] But Paul said, "I am not mad, most excellent Festus, but I am speaking the sober truth. [26] For the king knows about these things, and to him I speak freely; for I am persuaded that none of these things has escaped his notice, for this was not done in a corner. [27] King Agrippa, do you believe the prophets? I know that you believe." [28] And Agrippa said to Paul, "In a short time you think to make me a Christian!" [29] And Paul said, "Whether short or long, I would to God that not only you but also all who hear me this day might become such as I am—except for these chains."

26.3: Agrippa was perhaps well acquainted with Judaism, but was not a practicing Jew. **4:** *My nation,* Cilicia. **8:** *You,* i.e. the Jewish people. **12–20:** A third account of Paul's conversion (9.1–8; 22.4–16). Here he adds that *all had fallen to the ground.* **17:** *The people,* i.e. the Jewish people. **23:** *That the Christ must suffer,* 8.32–35; Lk.24.26. **32:** See 25.11–12 n.

30 Then the king rose, and the governor and Berni'ce and those who were sitting with them; ³¹ and when they had withdrawn, they said to one another, "This man is doing nothing to deserve death or imprisonment." ³² And Agrippa said to Festus, "This man could have been set free if he had not appealed to Caesar."

27 And when it was decided that we should sail for Italy, they delivered Paul and some other prisoners to a centurion of the Augustan Cohort, named Julius. ² And embarking in a ship of Adramyt'tium, which was about to sail to the ports along the coast of Asia, we put to sea, accompanied by Aristar'chus, a Macedo'nian from Thessaloni'ca. ³ The next day we put in at Sidon; and Julius treated Paul kindly, and gave him leave to go to his friends and be cared for. ⁴ And putting to sea from there we sailed under the lee of Cyprus, because the winds were against us. ⁵ And when we had sailed across the sea which is off Cili'cia and Pamphyl'ia, we came to Myra in Ly'cia. ⁶ There the centurion found a ship of Alexandria sailing for Italy, and put us on board. ⁷ We sailed slowly for a number of days, and arrived with difficulty off Cni'dus, and as the wind did not allow us to go on, we sailed under the lee of Crete off Salmo'ne. ⁸ Coasting along it with difficulty, we came to a place called Fair Havens, near which was the city of Lase'a.

9 As much time had been lost, and the voyage was already dangerous because the fast had already gone by, Paul advised them, ¹⁰ saying, "Sirs, I perceive that the voyage will be with injury and much loss, not only of the cargo and the ship, but also of our lives." ¹¹ But the centurion paid more attention to the captain and to the owner of the ship than to what Paul said. ¹² And because the harbor was not suitable to winter in, the majority advised to put to sea from there, on the chance that somehow they could reach Phoenix, a harbor of Crete, looking northeast and southeast,ᵃ and winter there.

13 And when the south wind blew gently, supposing that they had obtained their purpose, they weighed anchor and sailed along Crete, close inshore. ¹⁴ But soon a tempestuous wind, called the northeaster, struck down from the land; ¹⁵ and when the ship was caught and could not face the wind, we gave way to it and were driven. ¹⁶ And running under the lee of a small island called Cauda,ᵇ we managed with difficulty to secure the boat; ¹⁷ after hoisting it up, they took measuresᶜ to undergird the ship; then, fearing that they should run on the Syr'tis, they lowered the gear, and so were driven. ¹⁸ As we were violently storm-tossed, they began next day to throw the cargo overboard; ¹⁹ and the third day they cast out with their own hands the tackle of the ship. ²⁰ And when neither sun nor stars appeared for many a day, and no small tempest lay on us, all hope of our being saved was at last abandoned.

21 As they had been long without food, Paul then came forward among them and said, "Men, you should have listened to me, and should not have set sail from Crete and incurred this injury and loss. ²² I now bid you take heart; for there will be no loss of life among you, but only of the ship. ²³ For this very night there stood by me an angel of the God to whom I belong and whom I worship, ²⁴ and he said, 'Do not be afraid, Paul; you must stand before Caesar; and lo, God has granted you all those who sail with

a Or *southwest and northwest*
b Other ancient authorities read *Clauda*
c Greek *helps*

27.1–44: The voyage to Malta. A dangerous winter voyage ends in shipwreck. **1:** *The Augustan Cohort.* A unit of this name was stationed in Syria in the first century. **4:** *Under the lee of Cyprus*, apparently east of the island. **7:** *The lee of Crete*, to its south; *Salmone* is at the eastern end. **9:** *The fast*, the Day of Atonement, in September or October. **17:** *The Syrtis*, a dangerous

you.' 25 So take heart, men, for I have faith in God that it will be exactly as I have been told. 26 But we shall have to run on some island."

27 When the fourteenth night had come, as we were drifting across the sea of A'dria, about midnight the sailors suspected that they were nearing land. 28 So they sounded and found twenty fathoms; a little farther on they sounded again and found fifteen fathoms. 29 And fearing that we might run on the rocks, they let out four anchors from the stern, and prayed for day to come. 30 And as the sailors were seeking to escape from the ship, and had lowered the boat into the sea, under pretense of laying out anchors from the bow, 31 Paul said to the centurion and the soldiers, "Unless these men stay in the ship, you cannot be saved." 32 Then the soldiers cut away the ropes of the boat, and let it go.

33 As day was about to dawn, Paul urged them all to take some food, saying, "Today is the fourteenth day that you have continued in suspense and without food, having taken nothing. 34 Therefore I urge you to take some food; it will give you strength, since not a hair is to perish from the head of any of you." 35 And when he had said this, he took bread, and giving thanks to God in the presence of all he broke it and began to eat. 36 Then they all were encouraged and ate some food themselves. 37 (We were in all two hundred and seventy-six[d] persons in the ship.) 38 And when they had eaten enough, they lightened the ship, throwing out the wheat into the sea.

39 Now when it was day, they did not recognize the land, but they noticed a bay with a beach, on which they planned if possible to bring the ship ashore. 40 So they cast off the anchors and left them in the sea, at the same time loosening the ropes that tied the rudders; then hoisting the foresail to the wind they made for the beach. 41 But striking a shoal[e] they ran the vessel aground; the bow stuck and remained immovable, and the stern was broken up by the surf. 42 The soldiers' plan was to kill the prisoners, lest any should swim away and escape; 43 but the centurion, wishing to save Paul, kept them from carrying out their purpose. He ordered those who could swim to throw themselves overboard first and make for the land, 44 and the rest on planks or on pieces of the ship. And so it was that all escaped to land.

28 After we had escaped, we then learned that the island was called Malta. 2 And the natives showed us unusual kindness, for they kindled a fire and welcomed us all, because it had begun to rain and was cold. 3 Paul had gathered a bundle of sticks and put them on the fire, when a viper came out because of the heat and fastened on his hand. 4 When the natives saw the creature hanging from his hand, they said to one another, "No doubt this man is a murderer. Though he has escaped from the sea, justice has not allowed him to live." 5 He, however, shook off the creature into the fire and suffered no harm. 6 They waited, expecting him to swell up or suddenly fall down dead; but when they had waited a long time and saw no misfortune come to him, they changed their minds and said that he was a god.

7 Now in the neighborhood of that place were lands belonging to the chief man of the island, named Publius, who received us and entertained us hospitably for three days. 8 It happened that the father of Publius lay

d Other ancient authorities read *seventy-six* or *about seventy-six*
e Greek *place of two seas*

---

shoal west of Cyrene. **27:** *Adria* apparently included the sea as far as north Africa. **41:** *A shoal*, Greek "a place of two seas," probably the bay now named for St. Paul.

28.1–10: Paul in Malta. Unharmed though bitten by a viper, Paul heals the father of Publius. **2:** The *natives* were non-Greeks who spoke a Semitic language. **7:** *Chief man*, a Greek term for a high official in Malta.

sick with fever and dysentery; and Paul visited him and prayed, and putting his hands on him healed him. ⁹ And when this had taken place, the rest of the people on the island who had diseases also came and were cured. ¹⁰ They presented many gifts to us;ᶠ and when we sailed, they put on board whatever we needed.

11 After three months we set sail in a ship which had wintered in the island, a ship of Alexandria, with the Twin Brothers as figurehead. ¹² Putting in at Syracuse, we stayed there for three days. ¹³ And from there we made a circuit and arrived at Rhe′gium; and after one day a south wind sprang up, and on the second day we came to Pute′oli. ¹⁴ There we found brethren, and were invited to stay with them for seven days. And so we came to Rome. ¹⁵ And the brethren there, when they heard of us, came as far as the Forum of Ap′pius and Three Taverns to meet us. On seeing them Paul thanked God and took courage. ¹⁶ And when we came into Rome, Paul was allowed to stay by himself, with the soldier that guarded him.

17 After three days he called together the local leaders of the Jews; and when they had gathered, he said to them, "Brethren, though I had done nothing against the people or the customs of our fathers, yet I was delivered prisoner from Jerusalem into the hands of the Romans. ¹⁸ When they had examined me, they wished to set me at liberty, because there was no reason for the death penalty in my case. ¹⁹ But when the Jews objected, I was compelled to appeal to Caesar–though I had no charge to bring against my nation. ²⁰ For this reason therefore I have asked to see you and speak with you, since it is because of the hope of Israel that I am bound with this chain." ²¹ And they said to him, "We have received no letters from Judea about you, and none of the brethren coming here has reported or spoken any evil about you. ²² But we desire to hear from you what your views are; for with regard to this sect we know that everywhere it is spoken against."

23 When they had appointed a day for him, they came to him at his lodging in great numbers. And he expounded the matter to them from morning till evening, testifying to the kingdom of God and trying to convince them about Jesus both from the law of Moses and from the prophets. ²⁴ And some were convinced by what he said, while others disbelieved. ²⁵ So, as they disagreed among themselves, they departed, after Paul had made one statement: "The Holy Spirit was right in saying to your fathers through Isaiah the prophet:

²⁶ 'Go to this people, and say,
    You shall indeed hear but never
       understand,
    and you shall indeed see but never
       perceive.
²⁷ For this people's heart has grown
       dull,
    and their ears are heavy of hearing,
    and their eyes they have closed;
    lest they should perceive with their
       eyes,
    and hear with their ears,
    and understand with their heart,
    and turn for me to heal them.'
²⁸ Let it be known to you then that

ᶠ Or *honored us with many honors*

28.11–16: The journey to Rome. Paul goes by sea to Syracuse, Rhegium, and Puteoli, then by land to the capital. **11:** *The Twin Brothers*, Castor and Pollux, were worshiped by sailors. **13:** *Rhegium*, modern Reggio Calabria. **13:** *Puteoli*, Pozzuoli, on the north side of the Bay of Naples. **15:** The *Forum of Appius* was forty-three miles from Rome, and the *Three Taverns* thirty-three miles, both on the Via Appia. **16:** *By himself*, apparently in his own quarters, under house arrest or with a light chain (v. 20).

28.17–28: Paul and the Jews of Rome. Rejected by the Jews, he again turns to the Gentiles (see 13.46 n.). **20:** The *chain* may be actual or a metaphor of his restriction. **23:** *The prophets*, see Mt.5.17 n. **26:** Christians often used Is.6.9–10 to explain the Jews' rejection of the gospel (see Mt.13.14–15 n.; Jn.12.40; compare the ideas of Rom. chs. 9–11).

this salvation of God has been sent to the Gentiles; they will listen."*g*

30 And he lived there two whole years at his own expense,*h* and welcomed all who came to him, 31 preaching the kingdom of God and teaching about the Lord Jesus Christ quite openly and unhindered.

g Other ancient authorities add verse 29, *And when he had said these words, the Jews departed, holding much dispute among themselves*
h Or *in his own hired dwelling*

28.30–31: Conclusion. Though under house arrest (v. 16) Paul preached *unhindered* for *two whole years.* Thus the author concludes his narrative of the spread of the gospel from Jerusalem (1.8) to Rome, the capital of the empire.

THE LETTER OF PAUL TO THE

ROMANS

This first of Paul's letters in the canonical order is also the longest, the weightiest, and the most influential of them. Written at the height of his career (between A.D. 54 and 58), it conveys the full richness of his experience of Christ as well as the full maturity of his thought.

For several years—years of intense missionary activity and of more than ordinary stress—Paul had been engaged in collecting contributions from the Gentile churches of Greece and Asia Minor for the needy Jerusalem church. It was his hope that these gifts would allay certain suspicions of him and his work which some members of that church felt and which had been a source of anxiety to him. The collection was now complete, and Paul, apparently in Corinth (15.25–27; compare 1 Cor.16.3–5), was awaiting an opportunity to go to Jerusalem with it. He intended afterwards to carry the gospel to Spain (15.28) and, on his way, to stop at Rome where the church had already been established by others. He writes to the Roman church to announce this intention and to explain his understanding of the gospel, partly perhaps with a view to securing the support of that church for his work farther to the west.

After the salutation and thanksgiving, Paul describes first the world's need of redemption (1.18–3.20). He then discusses God's saving act in Christ: its nature (3.21–4.25) and the new life which it has made available (5.1–8.39). After a section dealing with the role of the Jewish nation in God's plan (chs. 9–11), the letter closes with ethical teaching and some personal remarks (chs. 12–16).

PAUL, A SERVANT*a* OF JESUS CHRIST, called to be an apostle, set apart for the gospel of God ² which he promised beforehand through his prophets in the holy scriptures, ³ the gospel concerning his Son, who was descended from David according to the flesh ⁴ and designated Son of God in power according to the Spirit of holiness by his resurrection from the dead, Jesus Christ our Lord, ⁵ through whom we have received grace and apostleship to bring about the obedience of faith for the sake of his name among all the nations, ⁶ including yourselves who are called to belong to Jesus Christ;

7 To all God's beloved in Rome, who are called to be saints:

Grace to you and peace from God our Father and the Lord Jesus Christ.

8 First, I thank my God through Jesus Christ for all of you, because your faith is proclaimed in all the world. ⁹ For God is my witness, whom I serve with my spirit in the gospel of his Son, that without ceasing I mention you always in my prayers, ¹⁰ asking that somehow by God's will I may now at last succeed in coming to you. ¹¹ For I long to see you, that I may impart to you some spiritual gift to strengthen you, ¹² that is, that we may be mutually encouraged by each other's faith, both yours and mine. ¹³ I want you to know, brethren, that I have often intended to come to you (but thus far

a Or *slave*

1.1–7: Salutation. Ancient Greek letters customarily began with the names of the sender and of the recipient and a short greeting. Paul expands the usual form to express his Christian faith as well. **3–4:** God's *Son*, who came into the world physically *descended from David*, was manifested and installed in his true status at the resurrection. The *Spirit of holiness*, the Holy Spirit. **7:** *Saints*, those who belong to God, consecrated to his service. *Grace . . . and peace*, see 2 Th.1.2 n.

1.8–15: Thanksgiving. After the salutation in ancient letters there usually came a short prayer of thanksgiving or of petition on behalf of the person addressed. This element also Paul expands in a characteristically Christian way.

have been prevented), in order that I may reap some harvest among you as well as among the rest of the Gentiles. [14] I am under obligation both to Greeks and to barbarians, both to the wise and to the foolish: [15] so I am eager to preach the gospel to you also who are in Rome.

16 For I am not ashamed of the gospel: it is the power of God for salvation to every one who has faith, to the Jew first and also to the Greek. [17] For in it the righteousness of God is revealed through faith for faith; as it is written, "He who through faith is righteous shall live."[b]

18 For the wrath of God is revealed from heaven against all ungodliness and wickedness of men who by their wickedness suppress the truth. [19] For what can be known about God is plain to them, because God has shown it to them. [20] Ever since the creation of the world his invisible nature, namely, his eternal power and deity, has been clearly perceived in the things that have been made. So they are without excuse; [21] for although they knew God they did not honor him as God or give thanks to him, but they became futile in their thinking and their senseless minds were darkened. [22] Claiming to be wise, they became fools, [23] and exchanged the glory of the immortal God for images resembling mortal man or birds or animals or reptiles.

24 Therefore God gave them up in the lusts of their hearts to impurity, to the dishonoring of their bodies among themselves, [25] because they exchanged the truth about God for a lie and wor-

shiped and served the creature rather than the Creator, who is blessed for ever! Amen.

26 For this reason God gave them up to dishonorable passions. Their women exchanged natural relations for unnatural, [27] and the men likewise gave up natural relations with women and were consumed with passion for one another, men committing shameless acts with men and receiving in their own persons the due penalty for their error.

28 And since they did not see fit to acknowledge God, God gave them up to a base mind and to improper conduct. [29] They were filled with all manner of wickedness, evil, covetousness, malice. Full of envy, murder, strife, deceit, malignity, they are gossips, [30] slanderers, haters of God, insolent, haughty, boastful, inventors of evil, disobedient to parents, [31] foolish, faithless, heartless, ruthless. [32] Though they know God's decree that those who do such things deserve to die, they not only do them but approve those who practice them.

2 Therefore you have no excuse, O man, whoever you are, when you judge another; for in passing judgment upon him you condemn yourself, because you, the judge, are doing the very same things. [2] We know that the judgment of God rightly falls upon those who do such things. [3] Do you suppose, O man, that when you judge those who do such things and yet do them yourself, you will escape the judgment of God? [4] Or do you presume upon the riches of his kindness

b Or *The righteous shall live by faith*

1.16–17: The theme of the letter. In Christ God has acted powerfully to save men, offering righteousness and new life, to be received in faith. **17:** *The righteousness of God* is a state of pardon, or acceptance with God, which is not man's achievement but God's gift, originating in God's own righteous nature. *Through faith for faith*, faith is the sole condition of salvation. *He who . . . shall live*, from Hab.2.4; compare Gal.3.11; Phil.3.9; Heb.10.38.

1.18–32: God's judgment upon sin. 18: *Wrath*, see Col.3.6 n. **19:** *What can be known*, i.e. apart from God's revelation to Israel and in Christ. **20–21:** Men have denied the knowledge of God that was given with their creation. **24,26,28:** *God gave them up*, because in turning from God they violated their true nature, becoming involved in terrible and destructive perversions; God has let the process of death work itself out. **29–31:** Gal.5.19–21.

2.1–11: Jews are under judgment, as well as pagans (1.18–32). **5:** *The day of wrath*, God's

and forbearance and patience? Do you not know that God's kindness is meant to lead you to repentance? [5] But by your hard and impenitent heart you are storing up wrath for yourself on the day of wrath when God's righteous judgment will be revealed. [6] For he will render to every man according to his works: [7] to those who by patience in well-doing seek for glory and honor and immortality, he will give eternal life; [8] but for those who are factious and do not obey the truth, but obey wickedness, there will be wrath and fury. [9] There will be tribulation and distress for every human being who does evil, the Jew first and also the Greek, [10] but glory and honor and peace for every one who does good, the Jew first and also the Greek. [11] For God shows no partiality.

[12] All who have sinned without the law will also perish without the law, and all who have sinned under the law will be judged by the law. [13] For it is not the hearers of the law who are righteous before God, but the doers of the law who will be justified. [14] When Gentiles who have not the law do by nature what the law requires, they are a law to themselves, even though they do not have the law. [15] They show that what the law requires is written on their hearts, while their conscience also bears witness and their conflicting thoughts accuse or perhaps excuse them [16] on that day when, according to my gospel, God judges the secrets of men by Christ Jesus.

[17] But if you call yourself a Jew and rely upon the law and boast of your relation to God [18] and know his will and approve what is excellent, because you are instructed in the law, [19] and if you are sure that you are a guide to the blind, a light to those who are in darkness, [20] a corrector of the foolish, a teacher of children, having in the law the embodiment of knowledge and truth— [21] you then who teach others, will you not teach yourself? While you preach against stealing, do you steal? [22] You who say that one must not commit adultery, do you commit adultery? You who abhor idols, do you rob temples? [23] You who boast in the law, do you dishonor God by breaking the law? [24] For, as it is written, "The name of God is blasphemed among the Gentiles because of you."

[25] Circumcision indeed is of value if you obey the law; but if you break the law, your circumcision becomes uncircumcision. [26] So, if a man who is uncircumcised keeps the precepts of the law, will not his uncircumcision be regarded as circumcision? [27] Then those who are physically uncircumcised but keep the law will condemn you who have the written code and circumcision but break the law. [28] For he is not a real Jew who is one outwardly, nor is true circumcision something external and physical. [29] He is a Jew who is one inwardly, and real circumcision is a matter of the heart, spiritual and not literal. His praise is not from men but from God.

3 Then what advantage has the Jew? Or what is the value of circum-

---

condemnation of sin, already manifest (1.18), will be consummated in the final judgment. **9–10:** The Jew *first*, because privileges granted to the covenant people (3.1–8) increase responsibility (1.16; Amos 3.2; Lk.12.48).

2.12–16: Rule of judgment: law of Moses for the Jew; law of conscience for the Gentile. **14–15:** Paul recognizes (despite 1.18–32) that there are morally sensitive and responsible Gentiles, however far short they may fall of God's righteous demands. **17–24:** Many Jews, though possessing God's written law, fall short of even ordinary morality. **23:** *Do you . . . the law?*, may also be translated, "You dishonor God by breaking the law." **24:** Is.52.5. **25:** *Circumcision becomes uncircumcision*, in the sense that the Jewish violator of the law stands before God precisely where the pagan violator stands (Jer.9.25–26). **28:** Mt.3.9; Jn.8.39; Gal.6.15. **29:** *Circumcision . . . of the heart*, Dt.10.16; Jer.4.4; 9.26; Ezek.44.9.

3.1–8: The advantage of the Jews as the covenant people cannot be denied. To them were given the *oracles*, i.e. the Scriptures, and particularly the promises they contain. God's *faithful-*

cision? ² Much in every way. To begin with, the Jews are entrusted with the oracles of God. ³ What if some were unfaithful? Does their faithlessness nullify the faithfulness of God? ⁴ By no means! Let God be true though every man be false, as it is written,

"That thou mayest be justified in thy words,
and prevail when thou art judged."

⁵ But if our wickedness serves to show the justice of God, what shall we say? That God is unjust to inflict wrath on us? (I speak in a human way.) ⁶ By no means! For then how could God judge the world? ⁷ But if through my falsehood God's truthfulness abounds to his glory, why am I still being condemned as a sinner? ⁸ And why not do evil that good may come?–as some people slanderously charge us with saying. Their condemnation is just.

9 What then? Are we Jews any better off?ᶜ No, not at all; for Iᵈ have already charged that all men, both Jews and Greeks, are under the power of sin, ¹⁰ as it is written:

"None is righteous, no, not one;
¹¹ no one understands, no one seeks for God.
¹² All have turned aside, together they have gone wrong;
no one does good, not even one."
¹³ "Their throat is an open grave,
they use their tongues to deceive."
"The venom of asps is under their lips."
¹⁴ "Their mouth is full of curses and bitterness."

¹⁵ "Their feet are swift to shed blood,
¹⁶ in their paths are ruin and misery,
¹⁷ and the way of peace they do not know."
¹⁸ "There is no fear of God before their eyes."

19 Now we know that whatever the law says it speaks to those who are under the law, so that every mouth may be stopped, and the whole world may be held accountable to God. ²⁰ For no human being will be justified in his sight by works of the law, since through the law comes knowledge of sin.

21 But now the righteousness of God has been manifested apart from law, although the law and the prophets bear witness to it, ²² the righteousness of God through faith in Jesus Christ for all who believe. For there is no distinction; ²³ since all have sinned and fall short of the glory of God, ²⁴ they are justified by his grace as a gift, through the redemption which is in Christ Jesus, ²⁵ whom God put forward as an expiation by his blood, to be received by faith. This was to show God's righteousness, because in his divine forbearance he had passed over former sins; ²⁶ it was to prove at the present time that he himself is righteous and that he justifies him who has faith in Jesus.

27 Then what becomes of our boasting? It is excluded. On what principle? On the principle of works? No, but on the principle of faith. ²⁸ For we

c Or *at any disadvantage?*   d Greek *we*

---

ness in making the promises is not invalidated by the failure of the Jews to keep their part of the covenant; nor can that failure be excused on the plea that, because of it, God's truth will shine more brightly when he fulfils his part (Paul will discuss this problem more fully in chs. 9–11). **4**: Ps.51.4.

3.9–20: All are guilty. Jew and Greek, despite the former's advantages, stand on the same ground, *under the power of sin.* **10–18**: Ps.14.1–2; 53.1–2; 5.9; 140.3; 10.7; Is.59.7–8; Ps.36.1. The law succeeds only in making men aware of their condition. That indeed was God's purpose in giving it (7.7; see Gal.3.19–29 n.).

3.21–26: The true righteousness, now revealed in Christ, rests not upon obedience to law, but on faith in God's act of *redemption . . . in Christ Jesus.* **21**: *The law and the prophets*, the Hebrew scriptures. **24**: *Redemption* means a ransoming or "buying back" (as of a slave or captive), and therefore emancipation or deliverance. Slaves of sin are set free through God's act in Christ (Eph.1.7; Col.1.14; Heb.9.15). **25**: *Expiation by his blood*, a reference to the death of Christ as a sacrifice for sin (1 Jn.2.2), demonstrating the seriousness with which God regards sin (despite his *forbearance*); it also reveals the measure of his love (Jn.3.16).

hold that a man is justified by faith apart from works of law. ²⁹ Or is God the God of Jews only? Is he not the God of Gentiles also? Yes, of Gentiles also, ³⁰ since God is one; and he will justify the circumcised on the ground of their faith and the uncircumcised through their faith. ³¹ Do we then overthrow the law by this faith? By no means! On the contrary, we uphold the law.

4 What then shall we say aboutᵉ Abraham, our forefather according to the flesh? ² For if Abraham was justified by works, he has something to boast about, but not before God. ³ For what does the scripture say? "Abraham believed God, and it was reckoned to him as righteousness." ⁴ Now to one who works, his wages are not reckoned as a gift but as his due. ⁵ And to one who does not work but trusts him who justifies the ungodly, his faith is reckoned as righteousness. ⁶ So also David pronounces a blessing upon the man to whom God reckons righteousness apart from works:

⁷ "Blessed are those whose iniquities are forgiven, and whose sins are covered;
⁸ blessed is the man against whom the Lord will not reckon his sin."

⁹ Is this blessing pronounced only upon the circumcised, or also upon the uncircumcised? We say that faith was reckoned to Abraham as righteousness. ¹⁰ How then was it reckoned to him? Was it before or after he had been circumcised? It was not after, but before he was circumcised. ¹¹ He received cir-

cumcision as a sign or seal of the righteousness which he had by faith while he was still uncircumcised. The purpose was to make him the father of all who believe without being circumcised and who thus have righteousness reckoned to them, ¹² and likewise the father of the circumcised who are not merely circumcised but also follow the example of the faith which our father Abraham had before he was circumcised.

13 The promise to Abraham and his descendants, that they should inherit the world, did not come through the law but through the righteousness of faith. ¹⁴ If it is the adherents of the law who are to be the heirs, faith is null and the promise is void. ¹⁵ For the law brings wrath, but where there is no law there is no transgression.

16 That is why it depends on faith, in order that the promise may rest on grace and be guaranteed to all his descendants—not only to the adherents of the law but also to those who share the faith of Abraham, for he is the father of us all, ¹⁷ as it is written, "I have made you the father of many nations" —in the presence of the God in whom he believed, who gives life to the dead and calls into existence the things that do not exist. ¹⁸ In hope he believed against hope, that he should become the father of many nations; as he had been told, "So shall your descendants be." ¹⁹ He did not weaken in faith when he considered his own body, which was as good as dead because he

ᵉ Other ancient authorities read *was gained by*

3.27–31: Boasting is excluded. *On the principle of works* there might be ground for boasting, but if salvation is by faith, pride *is excluded*. **30:** Since *God is one*, he will deal with Jews and Gentiles on the same basis.

4.1–8: Abraham justified by faith, not by works. **2:** *But not before God;* the full statement would be: "But actually if he had anything to boast about, it was not before God." **3:** According to Paul's understanding of Gen.15.6, Abraham's faith in God was credited to him as righteousness. **6–8:** God's blessing belongs not to those who perfectly obey the law (as though that were possible), but to those who in faith accept God's free gift of forgiveness (Ps.32.1–2). **9–12:** This justification of Abraham occurred *before he was circumcised,* and therefore cannot have been dependent upon circumcision; it depended only upon faith. **11:** Gen.17.10. **12:** *Follow the example,* i.e. rely only on faith, as Abraham did.

4.13–25: The true descendants of Abraham are those who have faith in Christ, whether Jews or Gentiles. To them the benefits promised to Abraham belong (Gen.17.4–6; 22.17–18; Gal. 3.29). **17:** Gen.17.5. **18:** Gen.15.5. **19:** Gen.17.17; 18.11; Heb.11.12. **22–23:** See v. 3.

was about a hundred years old, or when he considered the barrenness of Sarah's womb. ²⁰ No distrust made him waver concerning the promise of God, but he grew strong in his faith as he gave glory to God, ²¹ fully convinced that God was able to do what he had promised. ²² That is why his faith was "reckoned to him as righteousness." ²³ But the words, "it was reckoned to him," were written not for his sake alone, ²⁴ but for ours also. It will be reckoned to us who believe in him that raised from the dead Jesus our Lord, ²⁵ who was put to death for our trespasses and raised for our justification.

5 Therefore, since we are justified by faith, we*ʲ* have peace with God through our Lord Jesus Christ. ² Through him we have obtained access*ᵍ* to this grace in which we stand, and we*ʰ* rejoice in our hope of sharing the glory of God. ³ More than that, we*ʰ* rejoice in our sufferings, knowing that suffering produces endurance, ⁴ and endurance produces character, and character produces hope, ⁵ and hope does not disappoint us, because God's love has been poured into our hearts through the Holy Spirit which has been given to us.

6 While we were still weak, at the right time Christ died for the ungodly. ⁷ Why, one will hardly die for a righteous man–though perhaps for a good man one will dare even to die. ⁸ But God shows his love for us in that while we were yet sinners Christ died for us. ⁹ Since, therefore, we are now justified by his blood, much more shall we be saved by him from the wrath of God. ¹⁰ For if while we were enemies we were reconciled to God by the death of his Son, much more, now that we are reconciled, shall we be saved by his life. ¹¹ Not only so, but we also rejoice in God through our Lord Jesus Christ, through whom we have now received our reconciliation.

12 Therefore as sin came into the world through one man and death through sin, and so death spread to all men because all men sinned– ¹³ sin indeed was in the world before the law was given, but sin is not counted where there is no law. ¹⁴ Yet death reigned from Adam to Moses, even over those whose sins were not like the transgression of Adam, who was a type of the one who was to come.

15 But the free gift is not like the trespass. For if many died through one man's trespass, much more have the grace of God and the free gift in the grace of that one man Jesus Christ abounded for many. ¹⁶ And the free gift is not like the effect of that one man's sin. For the judgment following one trespass brought condemnation, but the free gift following many trespasses brings justification. ¹⁷ If, because of one man's trespass, death reigned through that one man, much more will those who receive the abundance of grace and the free gift of righteousness reign in life through the one man Jesus Christ.

18 Then as one man's trespass led to condemnation for all men, so one man's act of righteousness leads to acquittal and life for all men. ¹⁹ For as by one man's disobedience many

f Other ancient authorities read *let us*
g Other ancient authorities add *by faith*
h Or *let us*

5.1–11: Consequences of justification. 1–5: When we rely utterly upon God's grace and not at all upon ourselves, *we have peace*, i.e. reconciliation, or a state of harmony *with God. Hope of . . . the glory of God*, though we had fallen short of the glorious destiny God intended for us (3.23), we now find ourselves confidently expecting it. **6–11:** Christ in his death has borne the consequences of our sin and thus has reconciled us to God. Note that Paul never speaks of a reconciliation of God to us; it is we who were estranged. **9–10:** Being *now justified* (and reconciled) *by Christ's death*, we *shall . . . be saved* in the final Judgment *by his life*, i.e. through our participation in his present *life* as the risen Lord. **11:** *Now*, under the gospel.
    5.12–21: Adam and Christ; analogy and contrast. Sin and death for all men followed upon Adam's disobedience (Gen.2.17; 3.17–19). **13–16:** 1 Cor.15.21–23,45–49. **18:** *Acquittal and*

were made sinners, so by one man's obedience many will be made righteous. [20] Law came in, to increase the trespass; but where sin increased, grace abounded all the more, [21] so that, as sin reigned in death, grace also might reign through righteousness to eternal life through Jesus Christ our Lord.

What shall we say then? Are we to continue in sin that grace may abound? [2] By no means! How can we who died to sin still live in it? [3] Do you not know that all of us who have been baptized into Christ Jesus were baptized into his death? [4] We were buried therefore with him by baptism into death, so that as Christ was raised from the dead by the glory of the Father, we too might walk in newness of life.

5 For if we have been united with him in a death like his, we shall certainly be united with him in a resurrection like his. [6] We know that our old self was crucified with him so that the sinful body might be destroyed, and we might no longer be enslaved to sin. [7] For he who has died is freed from sin. [8] But if we have died with Christ, we believe that we shall also live with him. [9] For we know that Christ being raised from the dead will never die again; death no longer has dominion over him. [10] The death he died he died to sin, once for all, but the life he lives he lives to God. [11] So you also must consider yourselves dead to sin and alive to God in Christ Jesus.

12 Let not sin therefore reign in your mortal bodies, to make you obey their passions. [13] Do not yield your members to sin as instruments of wickedness, but yield yourselves to God as men who have been brought from death to life, and your members to God as instruments of righteousness. [14] For sin will have no dominion over you, since you are not under law but under grace.

15 What then? Are we to sin because we are not under law but under grace? By no means! [16] Do you not know that if you yield yourselves to any one as obedient slaves, you are slaves of the one whom you obey, either of sin, which leads to death, or of obedience, which leads to righteousness? [17] But thanks be to God, that you who were once slaves of sin have become obedient from the heart to the standard of teaching to which you were committed, [18] and, having been set free from sin, have become slaves of righteousness. [19] I am speaking in human terms, because of your natural limitations. For just as you once yielded your members to impurity and to greater and greater iniquity, so now yield your members to righteousness for sanctification.

20 When you were slaves of sin, you were free in regard to righteousness. [21] But then what return did you get from the things of which you are now ashamed? The end of those things is death. [22] But now that you have been set free from sin and have become slaves of God, the return you get is sanctification and its end, eternal

---

life for all followed upon Christ's perfect obedience. **20:** *Law . . . to increase the trespass*, this is explained in 7.7–13.

6.1–14: Dying and rising with Christ. Paul's insistence that salvation is entirely a gracious and undeserved gift of God may seem to have laid him open to the charge of encouraging sin. This charge Paul vigorously rejects. When the Christian is *baptized*, he is united with Christ. We share in his death and in the *newness of life* (v. 4), which his resurrection has made possible for us. But this death is a *death . . . to sin*, and the new life is *life . . . to God* (v. 10). *How then can we who died to sin still live in it?* (v. 2). **6:** *The sinful body*, not the physical body as such, but the sinful self. **13:** *Your members*, all the organs and functions of the person.

6.15–23: The two slaveries. In rejecting again the same charge (see v. 1 n.), Paul draws an analogy from slavery. The sinner is sin's slave; but if he becomes God's slave, how can he longer obey his old master? **19:** *Sanctification*, the process and result of being entirely devoted, consecrated, to God (v. 22).

life. ²³ For the wages of sin is death, but the free gift of God is eternal life in Christ Jesus our Lord.

7 Do you not know, brethren–for I am speaking to those who know the law–that the law is binding on a person only during his life? ² Thus a married woman is bound by law to her husband as long as he lives; but if her husband dies she is discharged from the law concerning the husband. ³ Accordingly, she will be called an adulteress if she lives with another man while her husband is alive. But if her husband dies she is free from that law, and if she marries another man she is not an adulteress.

4 Likewise, my brethren, you have died to the law through the body of Christ, so that you may belong to another, to him who has been raised from the dead in order that we may bear fruit for God. ⁵ While we were living in the flesh, our sinful passions, aroused by the law, were at work in our members to bear fruit for death. ⁶ But now we are discharged from the law, dead to that which held us captive, so that we serve not under the old written code but in the new life of the Spirit.

7 What then shall we say? That the law is sin? By no means! Yet, if it had not been for the law, I should not have known sin. I should not have known what it is to covet if the law had not said, "You shall not covet." ⁸ But sin,

finding opportunity in the commandment, wrought in me all kinds of covetousness. Apart from the law sin lies dead. ⁹ I was once alive apart from the law, but when the commandment came, sin revived and I died; ¹⁰ the very commandment which promised life proved to be death to me. ¹¹ For sin, finding opportunity in the commandment, deceived me and by it killed me. ¹² So the law is holy, and the commandment is holy and just and good.

13 Did that which is good, then, bring death to me? By no means! It was sin, working death in me through what is good, in order that sin might be shown to be sin, and through the commandment might become sinful beyond measure. ¹⁴ We know that the law is spiritual; but I am carnal, sold under sin. ¹⁵ I do not understand my own actions. For I do not do what I want, but I do the very thing I hate. ¹⁶ Now if I do what I do not want, I agree that the law is good. ¹⁷ So then it is no longer I that do it, but sin which dwells within me. ¹⁸ For I know that nothing good dwells within me, that is, in my flesh. I can will what is right, but I cannot do it. ¹⁹ For I do not do the good I want, but the evil I do not want is what I do. ²⁰ Now if I do what I do not want, it is no longer I that do it, but sin which dwells within me.

21 So I find it to be a law that when I want to do right, evil lies close at

---

7.1–6: **An analogy from marriage.** One who has died to sin is no more bound to it than is a woman to her deceased husband. **1–2:** *The law* here probably means Roman law. **4–6:** *The law* here refers to God's commandments, as in chs. 2–4.

7.7–13: **The law and sin.** **7:** Though the law is *holy . . . and good* (v. 12), it not only makes man conscious of sin (see Gal.3.19 n.), but also incites to sin (e.g. covetousness; compare Ex.20.17; Dt.5.21). **9:** Probably a reminiscence of a thoughtless, carefree boyhood brought to an end (*death*) by the dawning sense of moral obligation and guilt. **10:** Lev.18.5. **13:** The real enemy is sin, which uses even *what is good* (the law) to make a man more sinful than he would otherwise be.

7.14–23: **The inner conflict.** Sin is personified as an evil power that enters a man's life and brings his true self into slavery to its rule or *law* (still another use of this term). **14:** *The law is spiritual*, divine in origin and nature, and holy (v. 12). *I am carnal*, Greek "fleshly," referring not merely to man's physical nature, but to his whole nature in so far as he is ruled by selfish interests (compare v. 18 and v. 25). **17:** In emphasizing the reality of sin's power over a man's *inmost self* (v. 22), Paul seems almost to deny one's responsibility for sin (compare v. 20). Other passages in his letters, however, prevent our inferring that he means this (e.g. Rom.1.31– 2.5).

hand. ²² For I delight in the law of God, in my inmost self, ²³ but I see in my members another law at war with the law of my mind and making me captive to the law of sin which dwells in my members. ²⁴ Wretched man that I am! Who will deliver me from this body of death? ²⁵ Thanks be to God through Jesus Christ our Lord! So then, I of myself serve the law of God with my mind, but with my flesh I serve the law of sin.

8 There is therefore now no condemnation for those who are in Christ Jesus. ² For the law of the Spirit of life in Christ Jesus has set me free from the law of sin and death. ³ For God has done what the law, weakened by the flesh, could not do: sending his own Son in the likeness of sinful flesh and for sin,*ⁱ* he condemned sin in the flesh, ⁴ in order that the just requirement of the law might be fulfilled in us, who walk not according to the flesh but according to the Spirit. ⁵ For those who live according to the flesh set their minds on the things of the flesh, but those who live according to the Spirit set their minds on the things of the Spirit. ⁶ To set the mind on the flesh is death, but to set the mind on the Spirit is life and peace. ⁷ For the mind that is set on the flesh is hostile to God;

it does not submit to God's law, indeed it cannot; ⁸ and those who are in the flesh cannot please God.

9 But you are not in the flesh, you are in the Spirit, if in fact the Spirit of God dwells in you. Any one who does not have the Spirit of Christ does not belong to him. ¹⁰ But if Christ is in you, although your bodies are dead because of sin, your spirits are alive because of righteousness. ¹¹ If the Spirit of him who raised Jesus from the dead dwells in you, he who raised Christ Jesus from the dead will give life to your mortal bodies also through his Spirit which dwells in you.

12 So then, brethren, we are debtors, not to the flesh, to live according to the flesh– ¹³ for if you live according to the flesh you will die, but if by the Spirit you put to death the deeds of the body you will live. ¹⁴ For all who are led by the Spirit of God are sons of God. ¹⁵ For you did not receive the spirit of slavery to fall back into fear, but you have received the spirit of sonship. When we cry, "Abba! Father!" ¹⁶ it is the Spirit himself bearing witness with our spirit that we are children of God, ¹⁷ and if children, then heirs, heirs of God and fellow heirs with Christ, provided we suffer with

i Or *and as a sin offering*

7.24–25: Despair and release. Threatened by utter defeat in the struggle with our enemy entrenched in our own souls, we cast ourselves upon God's mercy in Christ; only then do we find freedom from both the guilt and the power of sin. **24:** *This body of death*, i.e. the body, which is the instrument of sin, is under the dominion of death. **25:** *Flesh*, compare "carnal," v. 14 n.

8.1–4: God's saving act. 1: *Condemnation* means more than judgment; it means doom. There is to be no doom or death *for us*, because God has sentenced sin to death (*condemned sin*, v. 3). **2:** *The Spirit* is the divine principle (*law*) of life in the new order which God has created through Christ. To be *in Christ* is to belong to this new order and thus to know the Spirit, who is the actual presence of God in our midst and in our hearts. **4:** Only through the power of *the Spirit* can we hope for the righteousness which *the law* requires but cannot enable us in our weakness to attain.

8.5–11: Life in the flesh and in the Spirit. 5: To live *according to the flesh* (see 7.14 n.) is to be dominated by selfish passions; to *live according to* (or *in*, v. 9) *the Spirit* is to belong to the new community of faith where God dwells as the Spirit. **9–10:** Note the similar, almost interchangeable, use of "the Spirit of God," "the Spirit of Christ," and "Christ." **10:** Gal.2.20; Eph.3.17. **11:** Jn.5.21.

8.12–17: The Spirit and sonship. The Spirit does not make slaves of us, but sons. **15:** *Abba*, the Aramaic word meaning "Father," which Jesus used in his own prayers (Mk.14.36) and which passed into the liturgy of the early church. **16:** The fact that *the Spirit* prompts this ecstatic prayer proves our sonship (Gal.4.6).

him in order that we may also be glorified with him.

18 I consider that the sufferings of this present time are not worth comparing with the glory that is to be revealed to us. [19] For the creation waits with eager longing for the revealing of the sons of God; [20] for the creation was subjected to futility, not of its own will but by the will of him who subjected it in hope; [21] because the creation itself will be set free from its bondage to decay and obtain the glorious liberty of the children of God. [22] We know that the whole creation has been groaning in travail together until now; [23] and not only the creation, but we ourselves, who have the first fruits of the Spirit, groan inwardly as we wait for adoption as sons, the redemption of our bodies. [24] For in this hope we were saved. Now hope that is seen is not hope. For who hopes for what he sees? [25] But if we hope for what we do not see, we wait for it with patience.

26 Likewise the Spirit helps us in our weakness; for we do not know how to pray as we ought, but the Spirit himself intercedes for us with sighs too deep for words. [27] And he who searches the hearts of men knows what is the mind of the Spirit, because[j] the Spirit intercedes for the saints according to the will of God.

28 We know that in everything God works for good[k] with those who love him,[l] who are called according to his purpose. [29] For those whom he foreknew he also predestined to be conformed to the image of his Son, in order that he might be the first-born among many brethren. [30] And those whom he predestined he also called; and those whom he called he also justified; and those whom he justified he also glorified.

31 What then shall we say to this? If God is for us, who is against us? [32] He who did not spare his own Son but gave him up for us all, will he not also give us all things with him? [33] Who shall bring any charge against God's elect? It is God who justifies; [34] who is to condemn? Is it Christ Jesus, who died, yes, who was raised from the dead, who is at the right hand of God, who indeed intercedes for us?[m] [35] Who shall separate us from the love of Christ? Shall tribulation, or distress, or persecution, or famine, or nakedness, or peril, or sword? [36] As it is written,

"For thy sake we are being killed all
    the day long;
we are regarded as sheep to be
    slaughtered."

[37] No, in all these things we are more than conquerors through him who loved us. [38] For I am sure that neither death, nor life, nor angels, nor principalities, nor things present, nor things to come, nor powers, [39] nor height,

j Or *that*
k Other ancient authorities read *in everything he works for good,* or *everything works for good*
l Greek *God*   *m* Or *It is Christ Jesus . . . for us*

8.18–25: The hope of fulfilment. 18: The Christian life involves *sufferings* (this was more obviously true then than now), but Paul rejoices in the sure hope of *glory* (5.2). **20:** *Of him,* God (Gen.3.17). **21:** When man (in Christ) is finally restored to his true nature and destiny, nature will also share in the freedom from *bondage to decay* and in the *glorious liberty.* **22–23:** Nature is thought of as sharing in the stress, anxiety, and pain which we ourselves feel as we wait for the promised *redemption. The first fruits of the Spirit,* the Spirit, already received, is an advanced installment of the full sonship we are yet to receive. *Our bodies,* as usually in Paul, our "selves," our "personalities." **24–25:** 1 Cor.2.9; 2 Cor.5.7; Heb.11.1.

8.26–30: Human weakness is sustained by the Spirit's intercession and by the knowledge of God's loving purpose. **28:** *His purpose,* or plan, is set forth in vv. 29–30. **29:** *To be conformed to . . . his Son* is to share the resurrection life of Christ, to be a "fellow heir" (compare v. 17), to be *glorified.*

8.31–39: Our confidence in God. 31: Ps.118.6. **32:** 4.25; 5.8; Jn.3.16. **35:** To be a Christian in the first century was both difficult and dangerous. **36:** Ps.44.22. **38:** *Neither death, nor life,* i.e. whether we live or die we shall not be separated. *Angels . . . principalities . . . powers* are supernatural beings, whether evil or good, and of various ranks (see Eph.6.12 n.). **39:** *Height* and

nor depth, nor anything else in all creation, will be able to separate us from the love of God in Christ Jesus our Lord.

9 I am speaking the truth in Christ, I am not lying; my conscience bears me witness in the Holy Spirit, [2] that I have great sorrow and unceasing anguish in my heart. [3] For I could wish that I myself were accursed and cut off from Christ for the sake of my brethren, my kinsmen by race. [4] They are Israelites, and to them belong the sonship, the glory, the covenants, the giving of the law, the worship, and the promises; [5] to them belong the patriarchs, and of their race, according to the flesh, is the Christ. God who is over all be blessed for ever.[n] Amen.

6 But it is not as though the word of God had failed. For not all who are descended from Israel belong to Israel, [7] and not all are children of Abraham because they are his descendants; but "Through Isaac shall your descendants be named." [8] This means that it is not the children of the flesh who are the children of God, but the children of the promise are reckoned as descendants. [9] For this is what the promise said, "About this time I will return and Sarah shall have a son." [10] And not only so, but also when Rebecca had conceived children by one man, our forefather Isaac, [11] though they were not yet born and had done nothing either good or bad, in order that God's purpose of election might continue, not because of works but because of his

call, [12] she was told, "The elder will serve the younger." [13] As it is written, "Jacob I loved, but Esau I hated."

14 What shall we say then? Is there injustice on God's part? By no means! [15] For he says to Moses, "I will have mercy on whom I have mercy, and I will have compassion on whom I have compassion." [16] So it depends not upon man's will or exertion, but upon God's mercy. [17] For the scripture says to Pharaoh, "I have raised you up for the very purpose of showing my power in you, so that my name may be proclaimed in all the earth." [18] So then he has mercy upon whomever he wills, and he hardens the heart of whomever he wills.

19 You will say to me then, "Why does he still find fault? For who can resist his will?" [20] But who are you, a man, to answer back to God? Will what is molded say to its molder, "Why have you made me thus?" [21] Has the potter no right over the clay, to make out of the same lump one vessel for beauty and another for menial use? [22] What if God, desiring to show his wrath and to make known his power, has endured with much patience the vessels of wrath made for destruction, [23] in order to make known the riches of his glory for the vessels of mercy, which he has prepared beforehand for glory, [24] even us whom he has called, not from the Jews only but also from the Gentiles? [25] As indeed he says in Hose'a,

"Those who were not my people

n Or *Christ, who is God over all, blessed for ever*

---

depth, the highest point to which the stars rise and the abyss out of which they were thought to ascend; i.e. no supposed astrological power can separate us from Christ or defeat God's purpose for us.

9.1–5: The problem of Israel's unbelief. 3: Ex.32.32. **4:** *Sonship*, Ex.4.22; Jer.31.9. *Glory*, God's presence (Ex.16.10; 24.16). *Covenants*, plural because the covenant with Israel was often renewed (Gen.6.18; 9.9; 15.8; 17.2,7,9; Ex.2.24). *Giving the law*, Ex.20.1–17; Dt.5.1–21. *Worship*, in tabernacle and temple.

9.6–13: God's promise to Israel has not failed, because the promise was not made to Abraham's physical descendants merely as such, but to those whom God chose. **7:** Gen.21.12. **9:** Gen.18.10. **10–12:** Gen.25.21,23. **13:** Mal.1.2–3.

9.14–29: God's right to choose. 15: Ex.33.19. **17:** Ex.9.16. **19–21:** Is.29.16; 45.9; 64.8; Jer.18.6. **24:** God's choice or election is not limited to *the Jews* (compare 3.29). **25–26:** The passage *in Hosea* (Hos.2.23; 1.10) refers to God's reclaiming of Israel after she had forsaken God and lost her covenant status; Paul (as also 1 Pet.2.10) applies the promise to the Gentiles.

I will call 'my people,'
and her who was not beloved
I will call 'my beloved.' "
26 "And in the very place where it was
said to them, 'You are not my
people,'
they will be called 'sons of the living
God.' "
27 And Isaiah cries out concerning
Israel: "Though the number of the
sons of Israel be as the sand of the sea,
only a remnant of them will be saved;
28 for the Lord will execute his sentence upon the earth with rigor and
dispatch." 29 And as Isaiah predicted,
"If the Lord of hosts had not left us
children,
we would have fared like Sodom and
been made like Gomor′rah."
30 What shall we say, then? That
Gentiles who did not pursue righteousness have attained it, that is, righteousness through faith; 31 but that Israel
who pursued the righteousness which
is based on law did not succeed in fulfilling that law. 32 Why? Because they
did not pursue it through faith, but as
if it were based on works. They have
stumbled over the stumbling stone,
33 as it is written,
"Behold, I am laying in Zion a stone
that will make men stumble,
a rock that will make them fall;
and he who believes in him will not
be put to shame."

10 Brethren, my heart's desire and
prayer to God for them is that
they may be saved. 2 I bear them witness that they have a zeal for God,
but it is not enlightened. 3 For, being
ignorant of the righteousness that

comes from God, and seeking to establish their own, they did not submit to
God's righteousness. 4 For Christ is the
end of the law, that every one who has
faith may be justified.

5 Moses writes that the man who
practices the righteousness which is
based on the law shall live by it. 6 But
the righteousness based on faith says,
Do not say in your heart, "Who will
ascend into heaven?" (that is, to bring
Christ down) 7 or "Who will descend
into the abyss?" (that is, to bring Christ
up from the dead). 8 But what does
it say? The word is near you, on your
lips and in your heart (that is, the word
of faith which we preach); 9 because,
if you confess with your lips that Jesus
is Lord and believe in your heart that
God raised him from the dead, you will
be saved. 10 For man believes with his
heart and so is justified, and he confesses with his lips and so is saved.
11 The scripture says, "No one who believes in him will be put to shame."
12 For there is no distinction between
Jew and Greek; the same Lord is
Lord of all and bestows his riches upon
all who call upon him. 13 For, "every
one who calls upon the name of the
Lord will be saved."

14 But how are men to call upon
him in whom they have not believed?
And how are they to believe in him of
whom they have never heard? And
how are they to hear without a
preacher? 15 And how can men
preach unless they are sent? As it is
written, "How beautiful are the feet of
those who preach good news!" 16 But
they have not all obeyed the gospel; for

27–29: God's promises never included all Israelites (Is.10.22; 1.9). *Sodom* and *Gomorrah*, Gen.19.24–25.   **9.30–10.13: True righteousness is by faith. 9.30:** 3.22; 10.6,20; Gal.2.16; 3.24; Phil.3.9; Heb. 11.7. **33:** Is.28.16 and 8.14–15. The "stone" is a symbol of God's help, but if neglected it becomes an instrument of judgment. Christ is this *stone*. **10.4:** Gal.3.23–26. **5:** Lev.18.5; Gal.3.12. One must actually *practice* the law if one is to find life through it; this Paul has already shown to be impossible (3.9–20). But one has only to *accept* the free gift of the salvation in Christ (vv. 6–9; compare Dt.30.11–14). **10:** Both faith and confession are essential for justification and salva-tion. **11:** Is.28.16. **13:** Jl.2.32. The early Christians often applied to Jesus Old Testament references to the *Lord*, which in their original context refer to God.

  10.14–21: Israel responsible for its failure. 14–18: The nation cannot claim that it has not had the opportunity of hearing the gospel **15:** Is.52.7. **16:** Is.53.1. **18:** Ps.19.4. **19–21:** Nor

Isaiah says, "Lord, who has believed what he has heard from us?" ¹⁷ So faith comes from what is heard, and what is heard comes by the preaching of Christ.

18 But I ask, have they not heard? Indeed they have; for

"Their voice has gone out to all the
        earth,
and their words to the ends of the
        world."

¹⁹ Again I ask, did Israel not understand? First Moses says,

"I will make you jealous of those
        who are not a nation;
with a foolish nation I will make you
        angry."

²⁰ Then Isaiah is so bold as to say,

"I have been found by those who did
        not seek me;
I have shown myself to those who did
        not ask for me."

²¹ But of Israel he says, "All day long I have held out my hands to a disobedient and contrary people."

I ask, then, has God rejected his people? By no means! I myself am an Israelite, a descendant of Abraham, a member of the tribe of Benjamin. ² God has not rejected his people whom he foreknew. Do you not know what the scripture says of Eli'jah, how he pleads with God against Israel? ³ "Lord, they have killed thy prophets, they have demolished thy altars, and I alone am left, and they seek my life." ⁴ But what is God's reply to him? "I have kept for myself seven thousand men who have not bowed the knee to Ba'al." ⁵ So too at the present time there is a remnant, chosen by grace. ⁶ But if it is by grace, it is no longer

on the basis of works; otherwise grace would no longer be grace.

7 What then? Israel failed to obtain what it sought. The elect obtained it, but the rest were hardened, ⁸ as it is written,

"God gave them a spirit of stupor,
eyes that should not see and ears
        that should not hear,
down to this very day."

⁹ And David says,

"Let their table become a snare and
        a trap,
a pitfall and a retribution for them;
¹⁰ let their eyes be darkened so that
        they cannot see,
and bend their backs for ever."

11 So I ask, have they stumbled so as to fall? By no means! But through their trespass salvation has come to the Gentiles, so as to make Israel jealous. ¹² Now if their trespass means riches for the world, and if their failure means riches for the Gentiles, how much more will their full inclusion mean!

13 Now I am speaking to you Gentiles. Inasmuch then as I am an apostle to the Gentiles, I magnify my ministry ¹⁴ in order to make my fellow Jews jealous, and thus save some of them. ¹⁵ For if their rejection means the reconciliation of the world, what will their acceptance mean but life from the dead? ¹⁶ If the dough offered as first fruits is holy, so is the whole lump; and if the root is holy, so are the branches.

17 But if some of the branches were broken off, and you, a wild olive shoot, were grafted in their place to share the richness^o of the olive tree, ¹⁸ do not boast over the branches. If you do

o Other ancient authorities read *rich root*

---

can Israel claim that it has not understood the gospel; even Gentiles have been able to understand it. **19**: Dt.32.21. **20–21**: Is.65.1–2.

11.1–16: Israel's rejection not final. 1–6: As in Elijah's time (1 Kg.19.10,18), there is a *remnant* of the faithful. Paul as a Jew is no more alone than Elijah was. **7–12:** The resistance to the gospel on the part of the masses of Jews is providential; God has *hardened* their *hearts* for a loving purpose, namely, that the Gentiles might have an opportunity to hear and receive the gospel. **8**: Is.29.10. **9**: Ps.69.22–23. **13–16**: The *reconciliation* of Gentiles will have the effect of making Israelites *jealous* and thus of drawing *some of them* to Christ. **16**: *The dough* and *the root* (Num.15.19–20 Septuagint; Jer.11.16–17) stand for the patriarchs, through whom all Israel has been consecrated.

11.17–24: The metaphor of the olive tree. The tree, including root and branches, is Israel.

boast, remember it is not you that support the root, but the root that supports you. [19] You will say, "Branches were broken off so that I might be grafted in." [20] That is true. They were broken off because of their unbelief, but you stand fast only through faith. So do not become proud, but stand in awe. [21] For if God did not spare the natural branches, neither will he spare you. [22] Note then the kindness and the severity of God: severity toward those who have fallen, but God's kindness to you, provided you continue in his kindness; otherwise you too will be cut off. [23] And even the others, if they do not persist in their unbelief, will be grafted in, for God has the power to graft them in again. [24] For if you have been cut from what is by nature a wild olive tree, and grafted, contrary to nature, into a cultivated olive tree, how much more will these natural branches be grafted back into their own olive tree.

25 Lest you be wise in your own conceits, I want you to understand this mystery, brethren: a hardening has come upon part of Israel, until the full number of the Gentiles come in, [26] and so all Israel will be saved; as it is written,

"The Deliverer will come from Zion,
he will banish ungodliness from
Jacob";
[27] "and this will be my covenant with
them
when I take away their sins."

[28] As regards the gospel they are enemies of God, for your sake; but as regards election they are beloved for the sake of their forefathers. [29] For the gifts and the call of God are irrevocable. [30] Just as you were once disobedient to God but now have received mercy because of their disobedience, [31] so they have now been disobedient in order that by the mercy shown to you they also may[p] receive mercy. [32] For God has consigned all men to disobedience, that he may have mercy upon all.

33 O the depth of the riches and wisdom and knowledge of God! How unsearchable are his judgments and how inscrutable his ways! [34] "For who has known the mind of the Lord,
or who has been his counselor?"
[35] "Or who has given a gift to him
that he might be repaid?"
[36] For from him and through him and to him are all things. To him be glory for ever. Amen.

12 I appeal to you therefore, brethren, by the mercies of God, to present your bodies as a living sacrifice, holy and acceptable to God, which is your spiritual worship. [2] Do not be conformed to this world[q] but be transformed by the renewal of your mind, that you may prove what is the will of God, what is good and acceptable and perfect.[r]

3 For by the grace given to me I bid every one among you not to think of

p Other ancient authorities add *now*
q Greek *age*
r Or *what is the good and acceptable and perfect will of God*

The branches broken off are the unbelieving Jews; the branches grafted in are Gentiles who believe in Christ. **20–22:** Having been made a part of the tree only because of faith (not merit or works), Gentile believers have no reason for pride, else God who has grafted them into the tree may later cut them off. **24:** The restoration of Israel will be easier than the call of the Gentiles.

11.25–36: All Israel will be saved. 25–26: A *mystery*, a truth once hidden, but now revealed by God. The *full number of the Gentiles* may mean the elect from among the Gentiles; and *all Israel* may mean Israel as a whole, not every particular Israelite. **26–27:** Is.59.20–21; 27.9. **28–32:** Although temporarily *enemies* of the *gospel*, the *election* of the Jews is *irrevocable*. **33:** The wonder of God's providence. **34:** Is.40.13. **35:** Job 35.7; 41.11. **36:** 1 Cor.8.6; 11.12; Col.1.16; Heb.2.10.

12.1–8: The consecrated life. 1: *Bodies*, as usually in Paul, means "selves." *Living sacrifice*, as contrasted to the sacrifice of a slain beast. **2:** Christians are to live as belonging to the coming age, not this present age (Eph.4.23; 1 Jn.2.15). *Prove* means "have sure knowledge of."

himself more highly than he ought to think, but to think with sober judgment, each according to the measure of faith which God has assigned him. [4] For as in one body we have many members, and all the members do not have the same function, [5] so we, though many, are one body in Christ, and individually members one of another. [6] Having gifts that differ according to the grace given to us, let us use them: if prophecy, in proportion to our faith; [7] if service, in our serving; he who teaches, in his teaching; [8] he who exhorts, in his exhortation; he who contributes, in liberality; he who gives aid, with zeal; he who does acts of mercy, with cheerfulness.

9 Let love be genuine; hate what is evil, hold fast to what is good; [10] love one another with brotherly affection; outdo one another in showing honor. [11] Never flag in zeal, be aglow with the Spirit, serve the Lord. [12] Rejoice in your hope, be patient in tribulation, be constant in prayer. [13] Contribute to the needs of the saints, practice hospitality.

14 Bless those who persecute you; bless and do not curse them. [15] Rejoice with those who rejoice, weep with those who weep. [16] Live in harmony with one another; do not be haughty, but associate with the lowly;[s] never be conceited. [17] Repay no one evil for evil, but take thought for what is noble in the sight of all. [18] If possible, so far as it depends upon you, live peaceably with all. [19] Beloved, never avenge yourselves, but leave it[t] to the wrath of God; for it is written, "Vengeance is mine, I will repay, says the Lord."

[20] No, "if your enemy is hungry, feed him; if he is thirsty, give him drink; for by so doing you will heap burning coals upon his head." [21] Do not be overcome by evil, but overcome evil with good.

13 Let every person be subject to the governing authorities. For there is no authority except from God, and those that exist have been instituted by God. [2] Therefore he who resists the authorities resists what God has appointed, and those who resist will incur judgment. [3] For rulers are not a terror to good conduct, but to bad. Would you have no fear of him who is in authority? Then do what is good, and you will receive his approval, [4] for he is God's servant for your good. But if you do wrong, be afraid, for he does not bear the sword in vain; he is the servant of God to execute his wrath on the wrongdoer. [5] Therefore one must be subject, not only to avoid God's wrath but also for the sake of conscience. [6] For the same reason you also pay taxes, for the authorities are ministers of God, attending to this very thing. [7] Pay all of them their dues, taxes to whom taxes are due, revenue to whom revenue is due, respect to whom respect is due, honor to whom honor is due.

8 Owe no one anything, except to love one another; for he who loves his neighbor has fulfilled the law. [9] The commandments, "You shall not commit adultery, You shall not kill, You shall not steal, You shall not covet," and any other commandment, are

s Or *give yourselves to humble tasks*
t Greek *give place*

3: *Measure of faith*, measure of the Spirit which one has received by faith (1 Cor.4.7). **4–8:** 1 Cor. 12.4–31. **8:** *He who gives aid*, or "he who rules."

   12.9–21: The Christian's duty. 9–18: The law of love (compare 1 Cor.13). **13:** *Hospitality*, see 16.1–2 n.; Heb.13.2 n.; 3 Jn.5–8 n. **14:** Mt.5.44. **19:** The vindication of justice is God's prerogative, not ours (Dt.32.35). We are neither wise enough nor good enough to punish our enemies justly. **20:** To *heap burning coals . . .* , is to make the enemy feel ashamed by meeting his *evil* with *good* (Pr.25.21–22).

   13.1–7: The Christian and the state. Though the Christian has no right to punish (12.19–21), the state does have that right and the Christian must respect it. Paul's confidence that the Roman state is, on the whole, just and beneficent is matched in 1 Pet.2.13–17; 3.13.

   13.8–10: Love fulfils the law. 8a: Pay every debt; do not stand under any obligation except the obligation to love. **8b–10:** Mk.12.31; Jas.2.8.

summed up in this sentence, "You shall love your neighbor as yourself." [10] Love does no wrong to a neighbor; therefore love is the fulfilling of the law.

11 Besides this you know what hour it is, how it is full time now for you to wake from sleep. For salvation is nearer to us now than when we first believed; [12] the night is far gone, the day is at hand. Let us then cast off the works of darkness and put on the armor of light; [13] let us conduct ourselves becomingly as in the day, not in reveling and drunkenness, not in debauchery and licentiousness, not in quarreling and jealousy. [14] But put on the Lord Jesus Christ, and make no provision for the flesh, to gratify its desires.

14 As for the man who is weak in faith, welcome him, but not for disputes over opinions. [2] One believes he may eat anything, while the weak man eats only vegetables. [3] Let not him who eats despise him who abstains, and let not him who abstains pass judgment on him who eats; for God has welcomed him. [4] Who are you to pass judgment on the servant of another? It is before his own master that he stands or falls. And he will be upheld, for the Master is able to make him stand.

5 One man esteems one day as better than another, while another man esteems all days alike. Let every one be fully convinced in his own mind. [6] He who observes the day, observes it in honor of the Lord. He also who eats, eats in honor of the Lord, since he gives thanks to God; while he who abstains, abstains in honor of the Lord and gives thanks to God. [7] None of us lives to himself, and none of us dies to himself. [8] If we live, we live to the Lord,

and if we die, we die to the Lord; so then, whether we live or whether we die, we are the Lord's. [9] For to this end Christ died and lived again, that he might be Lord both of the dead and of the living.

10 Why do you pass judgment on your brother? Or you, why do you despise your brother? For we shall all stand before the judgment seat of God; [11] for it is written,

"As I live, says the Lord, every knee
    shall bow to me,
and every tongue shall give
    praise*u* to God."

[12] So each of us shall give account of himself to God.

13 Then let us no more pass judgment on one another, but rather decide never to put a stumbling block or hindrance in the way of a brother. [14] I know and am persuaded in the Lord Jesus that nothing is unclean in itself; but it is unclean for any one who thinks it unclean. [15] If your brother is being injured by what you eat, you are no longer walking in love. Do not let what you eat cause the ruin of one for whom Christ died. [16] So do not let your good be spoken of as evil. [17] For the kingdom of God is not food and drink but righteousness and peace and joy in the Holy Spirit; [18] he who thus serves Christ is acceptable to God and approved by men. [19] Let us then pursue what makes for peace and for mutual upbuilding. [20] Do not, for the sake of food, destroy the work of God. Everything is indeed clean, but it is wrong for any one to make others fall by what he eats; [21] it is right not to eat meat or drink wine or do anything that

u Or *confess*

13.11–14: The imminence of Christ's second coming makes it the more urgent that Christians *conduct* themselves *becomingly*. **14:** To *put on the Lord Jesus Christ* is to enter fully into the new order of existence which God has created through Christ (see 6.1–14 n.).
14.1–23: Love respects the scruples of others. Some Christians have scruples about eating meat (v. 2), about observing the sabbath (vv. 5–6), about drinking wine (v. 21). Paul regards these scruples as unnecessary (v. 14) and designates the man who is troubled by them *weak* or *weak in faith* (v. 1). But the "strong" must not pass judgment on the *weak* (v. 10). **11:** Is.45.23.
13–15: The "strong" must also restrict his own liberty if he finds that his example is injuring a brother who has scruples (1 Cor.8.9–13; 10.23–29a). **17–21:** More important than our rights to eat and drink as we please is our obligation not to *destroy the work of God* by making our

makes your brother stumble.*[v]* [22] The faith that you have, keep between yourself and God; happy is he who has no reason to judge himself for what he approves. [23] But he who has doubts is condemned, if he eats, because he does not act from faith; for whatever does not proceed from faith is sin.*[w]*

15 We who are strong ought to bear with the failings of the weak, and not to please ourselves; [2] let each of us please his neighbor for his good, to edify him. [3] For Christ did not please himself; but, as it is written, "The reproaches of those who reproached thee fell on me." [4] For whatever was written in former days was written for our instruction, that by steadfastness and by the encouragement of the scriptures we might have hope. [5] May the God of steadfastness and encouragement grant you to live in such harmony with one another, in accord with Christ Jesus, [6] that together you may with one voice glorify the God and Father of our Lord Jesus Christ.

[7] Welcome one another, therefore, as Christ has welcomed you, for the glory of God. [8] For I tell you that Christ became a servant to the circumcised to show God's truthfulness, in order to confirm the promises given to the patriarchs, [9] and in order that the Gentiles might glorify God for his mercy. As it is written,

"Therefore I will praise thee among
   the Gentiles,
and sing to thy name";
[10] and again it is said,
"Rejoice, O Gentiles, with his
   people";

[11] and again,
"Praise the Lord, all Gentiles,
   and let all the peoples praise him";
[12] and further Isaiah says,
"The root of Jesse shall come,
he who rises to rule the Gentiles;
in him shall the Gentiles hope."

[13] May the God of hope fill you with all joy and peace in believing, so that by the power of the Holy Spirit you may abound in hope.

[14] I myself am satisfied about you, my brethren, that you yourselves are full of goodness, filled with all knowledge, and able to instruct one another. [15] But on some points I have written to you very boldly by way of reminder, because of the grace given me by God [16] to be a minister of Christ Jesus to the Gentiles in the priestly service of the gospel of God, so that the offering of the Gentiles may be acceptable, sanctified by the Holy Spirit. [17] In Christ Jesus, then, I have reason to be proud of my work for God. [18] For I will not venture to speak of anything except what Christ has wrought through me to win obedience from the Gentiles, by word and deed, [19] by the power of signs and wonders, by the power of the Holy Spirit, so that from Jerusalem and as far round as Illyr'icum I have fully preached the gospel of Christ, [20] thus making it my ambition to preach the gospel, not where Christ has already been named, lest I build on another man's foundation, [21] but as it is written,

v Other ancient authorities add *or be upset or be weakened*
w Other authorities, some ancient, insert here Ch 16.25–27

---

brother stumble (1 Cor.10.23–24). **22:** *Happy is he* who is free from misgivings as to the rightness of his practices, whether of eating or of not eating. **23:** Whatever is done against one's conscience *is sin.*

15.1–13: The strong should bear patiently burdens laid on them by *the failings of the weak.* **3:** A reference to the self-abasement of the pre-existent Christ (2 Cor.8.9; Phil.2.5–8), quoting Ps.69.9. **8–12:** Christ must needs have been a Jew to prove God's *truthfulness,* who had given *promises to the patriarchs;* but the promised salvation was also for the Gentiles, as Paul emphasizes with quotations from Ps.18.49; Dt.32.43; Ps.117.1; and Is.11.10.

15.14–23: Personal notes. 14–16: An apology for Paul's apparent boldness in writing so long a letter to a church with which he had had no earlier connections. **14:** *Able to instruct one another,* a suggestion that the Roman church was not under the oversight of another apostle (compare v. 20). **19:** *Sign and wonders,* a reference to apostolic miracles (1 Cor.12.10; 2 Cor.

"They shall see who have never
been told of him,
and they shall understand who
have never heard of him."
22 This is the reason why I have so
often been hindered from coming to
you. [23] But now, since I no longer
have any room for work in these regions, and since I have longed for many
years to come to you, [24] I hope to see
you in passing as I go to Spain, and to
be sped on my journey there by you,
once I have enjoyed your company for
a little. [25] At present, however, I am
going to Jerusalem with aid for the
saints. [26] For Macedo'nia and Acha'ia
have been pleased to make some contribution for the poor among the saints
at Jerusalem; [27] they were pleased to do
it, and indeed they are in debt to them,
for if the Gentiles have come to share in
their spiritual blessings, they ought also
to be of service to them in material
blessings. [28] When therefore I have
completed this, and have delivered to
them what has been raised,[x] I shall go
on by way of you to Spain; [29] and I
know that when I come to you I shall
come in the fulness of the blessing[y]
of Christ.

30 I appeal to you, brethren, by our
Lord Jesus Christ and by the love of the
Spirit, to strive together with me in your
prayers to God on my behalf, [31] that I
may be delivered from the unbelievers
in Judea, and that my service for Jerusalem may be acceptable to the saints,
[32] so that by God's will I may come to
you with joy and be refreshed in your

company. [33] The God of peace be with
you all. Amen.

16 I commend to you our sister
Phoebe, a deaconess of the
church at Cen'chre-ae, [2] that you may
receive her in the Lord as befits the
saints, and help her in whatever she
may require from you, for she has been
a helper of many and of myself as well.

3 Greet Prisca and Aq'uila, my fellow workers in Christ Jesus, [4] who
risked their necks for my life, to whom
not only I but also all the churches of
the Gentiles give thanks; [5] greet also the
church in their house. Greet my beloved Epae'netus, who was the first
convert in Asia for Christ. [6] Greet
Mary, who has worked hard among
you. [7] Greet Androni'cus and Ju'nias,
my kinsmen and my fellow prisoners;
they are men of note among the apostles, and they were in Christ before
me. [8] Greet Amplia'tus, my beloved in
the Lord. [9] Greet Urba'nus, our fellow
worker in Christ, and my beloved Sta-
chys. [10] Greet Apel'les, who is approved in Christ. Greet those who belong to the family of Aristobu'lus.
[11] Greet my kinsman Hero'dion. Greet
those in the Lord who belong to the
family of Narcis'sus. [12] Greet those
workers in the Lord, Tryphae'na and
Trypho'sa. Greet the beloved Persis,
who has worked hard in the Lord.
[13] Greet Rufus, eminent in the Lord,
also his mother and mine. [14] Greet

x Greek *sealed to them this fruit*
y Other ancient authorities insert *of the gospel*

12.12; Gal.3.5). *Illyricum,* modern Albania. **21:** Is.52.15. **23:** *No longer . . . any room,* Paul
conceives of his work as primarily that of an evangelist taking the gospel to new territories.
25: *Aid for the saints,* 1 Cor.16.1–4; 2 Cor.8–9; and probably Gal.2.10. **30–31:** Paul anticipates
that he may have trouble in Jerusalem (Acts 21.7–28.31). *My service for Jerusalem,* the offering
he is bringing.
  16.1–23: Greetings. 1–2: Because ancient inns and hotels were often infested with prostitutes
and bandits, Christians who traveled usually depended upon the hospitality of their brethren
(see 12.13 n.). *Deaconess* may mean simply "helper." *Cenchreae* was close to Corinth, its
nearest seaport on the eastern side. **3–16:** Except for *Prisca and Aquila* (Acts ch. 18; 1 Cor.16.19;
2 Tim.4.19), nothing is known about these persons beyond what is contained here. **5:** *The
church in their house,* most congregations in the earliest period met in the homes of members
(see Philem.2 n.). **6:** See v. 12. **7:** *Kinsmen,* fellow Jews (9.3). *Of note among the apostles,* i.e.
distinguished apostles. **11:** *Kinsman,* see v. 7 n. **12:** *Persis,* the name of a woman. **13:** *Rufus,*
see Mk.15.21 n. *His mother and mine,* Paul felt for her the affection of a son. **16:** The *holy kiss,*

Asyn'critus, Phlegon, Hermes, Pat'robas, Hermas, and the brethren who are with them. ¹⁵ Greet Philol'ogus, Julia, Nereus and his sister, and Olym'pas, and all the saints who are with them. ¹⁶ Greet one another with a holy kiss. All the churches of Christ greet you.

17 I appeal to you, brethren, to take note of those who create dissensions and difficulties, in opposition to the doctrine which you have been taught; avoid them. ¹⁸ For such persons do not serve our Lord Christ, but their own appetites,ᶻ and by fair and flattering words they deceive the hearts of the simple-minded. ¹⁹ For while your obedience is known to all, so that I rejoice over you, I would have you wise as to what is good and guileless as to what is evil; ²⁰ then the God of peace will soon crush Satan under your feet. The grace of our Lord Jesus Christ be with you.ᵃ

21 Timothy, my fellow worker, greets you; so do Lucius and Jason and Sosip'ater, my kinsmen.

22 I Tertius, the writer of this letter, greet you in the Lord.

23 Ga'ius, who is host to me and to the whole church, greets you. Eras'tus, the city treasurer, and our brother Quartus, greet you.ᵇ

25 Now to him who is able to strengthen you according to my gospel and the preaching of Jesus Christ, according to the revelation of the mystery which was kept secret for long ages ²⁶ but is now disclosed and through the prophetic writings is made known to all nations, according to the command of the eternal God, to bring about the obedience of faith– ²⁷ to the only wise God be glory for evermore through Jesus Christ! Amen.

z Greek *their own belly* (Phil 3.19)
a Other ancient authorities omit this sentence
b Other ancient authorities insert verse 24, *The grace of our Lord Jesus Christ be with you all. Amen.*

a symbol of brotherly love among Christians, became a regular part of the liturgical rites in the church (1 Cor.16.20; 2 Cor.13.12; 1 Th.5.26; 1 Pet.5.14). **17:** Gal.1.8–9; 2 Th.3.6,14; 2 Jn.10. **22:** *Tertius* is the amanuensis, or secretary, who wrote down what Paul dictated (see Col.4.18 n. and compare 1 Pet.5.12).

16.25–27: The benediction. 25: *Preaching,* another word for "gospel" (1 Cor.1.21–24). **26:** *The prophetic writings* (the Old Testament) held a secret (v. 25) which became known only when Christ appeared.

THE FIRST LETTER OF PAUL TO THE

CORINTHIANS

This is one of the most valuable of Paul's letters, not only for the light it throws upon the character and mind of the apostle and for its vigorous presentation of the gospel, but also for the vivid pictures it brings us of the actual life of a particular local church at the middle of the first century.

The church at Corinth was situated near the center of the Roman province of Achaia in one of the most important cities of Greece. Paul had himself brought the Christian message to Corinth and it was through his work that the church had been established there (Acts 18.1–11). One gathers from the two letters to the Corinthians that Paul's subsequent relations with this church were disturbed from time to time by doubts and suspicions on both sides, but that for no church did Paul feel a deeper affection. It is clear that he is writing from Ephesus (16.8; compare Acts 19.1–40), just across the Aegean Sea from Corinth. The allusion to the "contribution for the saints" (16.1; compare 2 Cor.9.1–2) shows that the letter must be dated earlier than Romans, but hardly more than two or three years earlier (see Introduction to Romans).

The whole letter is concerned directly or indirectly with doctrinal and ethical problems that were disturbing the Corinthian church. In settling these local problems Paul has bequeathed to the Church universal some of the most exalted chapters in his correspondence, such as the hymn on Christian love (ch. 13) and the teaching on the resurrection (ch. 15).

P AUL, CALLED BY THE WILL OF God to be an apostle of Christ Jesus, and our brother Sos'thenes,

2 To the church of God which is at Corinth, to those sanctified in Christ Jesus, called to be saints together with all those who in every place call on the name of our Lord Jesus Christ, both their Lord and ours:

3 Grace to you and peace from God our Father and the Lord Jesus Christ.

4 I give thanks to God[a] always for you because of the grace of God which was given you in Christ Jesus, [5] that in every way you were enriched in him with all speech and all knowledge– [6] even as the testimony to Christ was confirmed among you– [7] so that you are not lacking in any spiritual gift, as you wait for the revealing of our Lord Jesus Christ; [8] who will sustain you to the end, guiltless in the day of our Lord Jesus Christ. [9] God is faithful, by whom you were called into the fellowship of his Son, Jesus Christ our Lord.

10 I appeal to you, brethren, by the name of our Lord Jesus Christ, that all of you agree and that there be no dissensions among you, but that you be united in the same mind and the same judgment. [11] For it has been reported to me by Chlo'e's people that there is quarreling among you, my brethren. [12] What I mean is that each one of you says, "I belong to Paul," or "I belong to Apol'los," or "I belong to Cephas," or "I belong to Christ." [13] Is Christ divided? Was Paul crucified for you? Or were you baptized in the name of Paul? [14] I am thankful[b] that I baptized none of you except Crispus and

a Other ancient authorities read *my God*
b Other ancient authorities read *I thank God*

1.1–3: Salutation, see Rom.1.1–7 n. *Sosthenes*, perhaps the person referred to in Acts 18.17. **3:** *Grace . . . peace,* see 2 Th.1.2 n.

1.4–9: Thanksgiving, see Rom.1.8–15 n. Paul touches felicitously upon themes which he will discuss more critically later in the letter, namely, his readers' advanced understanding (*knowledge*) of the gospel, their eloquence (*speech*), and the variety of their *spiritual gifts*. **7–8:** *The revealing . . .* and *the day . . .* are allusions to the final time of judgment and salvation.

1.10–17: Dissensions at Corinth. 11: *Chloe's people*, members of her household who have either written or visited Paul. **12:** *Apollos*, Acts 18.24–28. *Cephas*, Peter (see Mt.16.18 n.).

Ga'ius; ¹⁵ lest any one should say that you were baptized in my name. ¹⁶ (I did baptize also the household of Steph'anas. Beyond that, I do not know whether I baptized any one else.) ¹⁷ For Christ did not send me to baptize but to preach the gospel, and not with eloquent wisdom, lest the cross of Christ be emptied of its power.

18 For the word of the cross is folly to those who are perishing, but to us who are being saved it is the power of God. ¹⁹ For it is written,
"I will destroy the wisdom of the
    wise,
and the cleverness of the clever I will
    thwart."
²⁰ Where is the wise man? Where is the scribe? Where is the debater of this age? Has not God made foolish the wisdom of the world? ²¹ For since, in the wisdom of God, the world did not know God through wisdom, it pleased God through the folly of what we preach to save those who believe. ²² For Jews demand signs and Greeks seek wisdom, ²³ but we preach Christ crucified, a stumbling block to Jews and folly to Gentiles, ²⁴ but to those who are called, both Jews and Greeks, Christ the power of God and the wisdom of God. ²⁵ For the foolishness of God is wiser than men, and the weakness of God is stronger than men.

26 For consider your call, brethren; not many of you were wise according to worldly standards, not many were powerful, not many were of noble birth; ²⁷ but God chose what is foolish in the world to shame the wise, God chose

what is weak in the world to shame the strong, ²⁸ God chose what is low and despised in the world, even things that are not, to bring to nothing things that are, ²⁹ so that no human being might boast in the presence of God. ³⁰ He is the source of your life in Christ Jesus, whom God made our wisdom, our righteousness and sanctification and redemption; ³¹ therefore, as it is written, "Let him who boasts, boast of the Lord."

2 When I came to you, brethren, I did not come proclaiming to you the testimony^c of God in lofty words or wisdom. ² For I decided to know nothing among you except Jesus Christ and him crucified. ³ And I was with you in weakness and in much fear and trembling; ⁴ and my speech and my message were not in plausible words of wisdom, but in demonstration of the Spirit and of power, ⁵ that your faith might not rest in the wisdom of men but in the power of God.

6 Yet among the mature we do impart wisdom, although it is not a wisdom of this age or of the rulers of this age, who are doomed to pass away. ⁷ But we impart a secret and hidden wisdom of God, which God decreed before the ages for our glorification. ⁸ None of the rulers of this age understood this; for if they had, they would not have crucified the Lord of glory. ⁹ But, as it is written,
"What no eye has seen, nor ear
    heard,
nor the heart of man conceived,

c Other ancient authorities read *mystery* (or *secret*)

14–17: Not to be taken to mean that Paul regarded baptism as unimportant, but only that he himself had not baptized many persons at Corinth. *Crispus*, Acts 18.8. *Gaius*, Rom.16.23. **16:** *Stephanus*, 1 Cor.16.15. **17:** *Eloquent wisdom*, some at Corinth took pride in their ability to talk in a sophisticated, philosophical way; over against this stands the cross.
1.18–2.5: The gospel is not a new philosophy, but a message to be accepted and lived. **19:** Is.29.14. **20–21:** The saved are not *the wise* of this world (or the *powerful* or *noble*, v. 26), but *those who believe*. **23:** *Christ crucified*, the living, risen Christ who was crucified. **28:** *Things that are not*, perhaps a technical philosophical term used sarcastically by critics of the gospel. **31:** Jer.9.23–24.
2.6–16: Spiritual wisdom. The Spirit imparts a deeper wisdom than any human effort can achieve, a wisdom which only the *mature* (those who have been *taught by the Spirit*) can understand. **7:** *Secret and hidden wisdom*, redemption in Christ, soon to be fully manifested, and now present through the Spirit. **8:** *The rulers of this age*, the demonic powers (Eph.6.12) which actuated Pilate and others. Not recognizing Christ for what he was, they crucified him; but his

what God has prepared for those who love him,"
¹⁰ God has revealed to us through the Spirit. For the Spirit searches everything, even the depths of God. ¹¹ For what person knows a man's thoughts except the spirit of the man which is in him? So also no one comprehends the thoughts of God except the Spirit of God. ¹² Now we have received not the spirit of the world, but the Spirit which is from God, that we might understand the gifts bestowed on us by God. ¹³ And we impart this in words not taught by human wisdom but taught by the Spirit, interpreting spiritual truths to those who possess the Spirit.*d*

14 The unspiritual*e* man does not receive the gifts of the Spirit of God, for they are folly to him, and he is not able to understand them because they are spiritually discerned. ¹⁵ The spiritual man judges all things, but is himself to be judged by no one. ¹⁶ "For who has known the mind of the Lord so as to instruct him?" But we have the mind of Christ.

3 But I, brethren, could not address you as spiritual men, but as men of the flesh, as babes in Christ. ² I fed you with milk, not solid food; for you were not ready for it; and even yet you are not ready, ³ for you are still of the flesh. For while there is jealousy and strife among you, are you not of the flesh, and behaving like ordinary men? ⁴ For when one says, "I belong to Paul," and another, "I belong to Apol′los," are you not merely men?

5 What then is Apol′los? What is Paul? Servants through whom you be-lieved, as the Lord assigned to each. ⁶ I planted, Apol′los watered, but God gave the growth. ⁷ So neither he who plants nor he who waters is anything, but only God who gives the growth. ⁸ He who plants and he who waters are equal, and each shall receive his wages according to his labor. ⁹ For we are God's fellow workers; you are God's field, God's building.

10 According to the grace of God given to me, like a skilled master builder I laid a foundation, and another man is building upon it. Let each man take care how he builds upon it. ¹¹ For no other foundation can any one lay than that which is laid, which is Jesus Christ. ¹² Now if any one builds on the foundation with gold, silver, precious stones, wood, hay, straw— ¹³ each man's work will become manifest; for the Day will disclose it, because it will be revealed with fire, and the fire will test what sort of work each one has done. ¹⁴ If the work which any man has built on the foundation survives, he will receive a reward. ¹⁵ If any man's work is burned up, he will suffer loss, though he himself will be saved, but only as through fire.

16 Do you not know that you are God's temple and that God's Spirit dwells in you? ¹⁷ If any one destroys God's temple, God will destroy him. For God's temple is holy, and that temple you are.

18 Let no one deceive himself. If any one among you thinks that he is

---

d Or interpreting spiritual truths in spiritual language; or comparing spiritual things with spiritual
e Or natural

---

cross was the means of his victory over them (Col.2.14–15). **9:** Compare Is.64.4. **10–12:** *The Spirit* we have received is God's own Spirit, who knows what is in God as our own spirits know what is in us. **15:** Perhaps Paul means that the spiritual man is not to be judged by the unspiritual (4.3–4). **16:** The man with the Spirit has the *mind of Christ*, and no one is in position to instruct *Christ. The Lord* (Is.40.13, referring to God) is here applied to Christ.

3.1–9: Paul has apparently been criticized at Corinth for preaching too simple a gospel. He explains that, though he has wisdom to impart (2.6), he could impart it only to the spiritually mature; and the Corinthians did not qualify. They still do not, as the party spirit shows.

3.10–23: The responsibility of teachers. 10–15: Paul turns from criticism of the church's members to a warning to one of its teachers. Paul suspects that he is not building well and warns of the Judgment Day (v. 13). **16–17:** Since the church is *God's temple*, those who divide and destroy it are guilty of a terrible desecration. **18–20:** The most divisive and harmful party seems

wise in this age, let him become a fool that he may become wise. ¹⁹ For the wisdom of this world is folly with God. For it is written, "He catches the wise in their craftiness," ²⁰ and again, "The Lord knows that the thoughts of the wise are futile." ²¹ So let no one boast of men. For all things are yours, ²² whether Paul or Apol'los or Cephas or the world or life or death or the present or the future, all are yours; ²³ and you are Christ's; and Christ is God's.

4 This is how one should regard us, as servants of Christ and stewards of the mysteries of God. ² Moreover it is required of stewards that they be found trustworthy. ³ But with me it is a very small thing that I should be judged by you or by any human court. I do not even judge myself. ⁴ I am not aware of anything against myself, but I am not thereby acquitted. It is the Lord who judges me. ⁵ Therefore do not pronounce judgment before the time, before the Lord comes, who will bring to light the things now hidden in darkness and will disclose the purposes of the heart. Then every man will receive his commendation from God.

6 I have applied all this to myself and Apol'los for your benefit, brethren, that you may learn by us not to go beyond what is written, that none of you may be puffed up in favor of one against another. ⁷ For who sees anything different in you? What have you that you did not receive? If then you received it, why do you boast as if it were not a gift?

8 Already you are filled! Already you have become rich! Without us you have become kings! And would that you did reign, so that we might share the rule with you! ⁹ For I think that God has exhibited us apostles as last of all, like men sentenced to death; because we have become a spectacle to the world, to angels and to men. ¹⁰ We are fools for Christ's sake, but you are wise in Christ. We are weak, but you are strong. You are held in honor, but we in disrepute. ¹¹ To the present hour we hunger and thirst, we are ill-clad and buffeted and homeless, ¹² and we labor, working with our own hands. When reviled, we bless; when persecuted, we endure; ¹³ when slandered, we try to conciliate; we have become, and are now, as the refuse of the world, the offscouring of all things.

14 I do not write this to make you ashamed, but to admonish you as my beloved children. ¹⁵ For though you have countless guides in Christ, you do not have many fathers. For I became your father in Christ Jesus through the gospel. ¹⁶ I urge you, then, be imitators of me. ¹⁷ Therefore I sent*g* to you Timothy, my beloved and faithful child in the Lord, to remind you of my ways in Christ, as I teach them everywhere in every church. ¹⁸ Some are arrogant, as though I were not coming to you. ¹⁹ But I will come to you soon, if the Lord wills, and I will find out not the talk of these arrogant people but their power. ²⁰ For the kingdom of God does not consist in talk but in power. ²¹ What

g Or *am sending*

---

to be the "wisdom" party–those who pretend to possess superior intellectualism. Paul refutes their pretensions by quoting Job 5.13 and Ps.94.11. **21–23:** You do not belong to any human leader; all of these leaders belong to you, as indeed does everything else. But this is true only because you belong to Christ and thus to God (4.7).

4.1–7: The teachers themselves, as *servants of Christ*, are answerable only to him. **4–5:** Since only the Lord knows the heart, both boasting and blaming are ruled out. **6:** If this is true for such teachers as Paul and Apollos, it is true also for the parties. **7:** See 3.21–23 n.

4.8–13: A highly ironical statement, by which Paul hopes to shame his critics. **9:** A reference to triumphal processions in which returning military conquerors displayed their trophies and their captives. **10:** 1.18–25. **12:** Paul's *labor*, Acts. 18.2–3.

4.14–21: Fatherly admonition and warning. 15: The *guide* (translated "custodian," Gal.3.24) was the slave who looked after a child's needs when not in school. A wide gulf separated this slave and the father; Paul implies such a gulf between himself and any other teacher at Corinth. **17:** *Timothy*, one of Paul's most faithful helpers (Acts 16.1–3). **19,20:** *Power*, of the Spirit.

do you wish? Shall I come to you with a rod, or with love in a spirit of gentleness?

5 It is actually reported that there is immorality among you, and of a kind that is not found even among pagans; for a man is living with his father's wife. ² And you are arrogant! Ought you not rather to mourn? Let him who has done this be removed from among you.

3 For though absent in body I am present in spirit, and as if present, I have already pronounced judgment ⁴ in the name of the Lord Jesus on the man who has done such a thing. When you are assembled, and my spirit is present, with the power of our Lord Jesus, ⁵ you are to deliver this man to Satan for the destruction of the flesh, that his spirit may be saved in the day of the Lord Jesus.*h*

6 Your boasting is not good. Do you not know that a little leaven leavens the whole lump? ⁷ Cleanse out the old leaven that you may be a new lump, as you really are unleavened. For Christ, our paschal lamb, has been sacrificed. ⁸ Let us, therefore, celebrate the festival, not with the old leaven, the leaven of malice and evil, but with the unleavened bread of sincerity and truth.

9 I wrote to you in my letter not to associate with immoral men; ¹⁰ not at all meaning the immoral of this world, or the greedy and robbers, or idolaters, since then you would need to go out of the world. ¹¹ But rather I wrote*i* to you

not to associate with any one who bears the name of brother if he is guilty of immorality or greed, or is an idolater, reviler, drunkard, or robber–not even to eat with such a one. ¹² For what have I to do with judging outsiders? Is it not those inside the church whom you are to judge? ¹³ God judges those outside. "Drive out the wicked person from among you."

6 When one of you has a grievance against a brother, does he dare go to law before the unrighteous instead of the saints? ² Do you not know that the saints will judge the world? And if the world is to be judged by you, are you incompetent to try trivial cases? ³ Do you not know that we are to judge angels? How much more, matters pertaining to this life! ⁴ If then you have such cases, why do you lay them before those who are least esteemed by the church? ⁵ I say this to your shame. Can it be that there is no man among you wise enough to decide between members of the brotherhood, ⁶ but brother goes to law against brother, and that before unbelievers?

7 To have lawsuits at all with one another is defeat for you. Why not rather suffer wrong? Why not rather be defrauded? ⁸ But you yourselves wrong and defraud, and that even your own brethren.

9 Do you not know that the unrighteous will not inherit the kingdom of God? Do not be deceived; neither the

h Other ancient authorities omit *Jesus*
i Or *now I write*

5.1–13: A case for church discipline. 1: *Reported*, possibly by Chloe's people (1.11). Both Roman and Jewish law (Lev.18.7–8) forbade marriage between a man and his stepmother. **2:** Paul is as much shocked by the complacency of the congregation in tolerating this sin as by the sin itself. **5:** Membership in the church protects one from Satan's destructive power; this man does not deserve such protection. Once excluded, he will be subject to disease and death (*the destruction of the flesh*), but there is hope that his soul may be saved in the final judgment (see 1 Tim.1.20 n.). **7:** *Paschal lamb*, Ex.12.21; Mk.14.12; Lk.22.7. **8:** Our new life is a continuing festival of thanksgiving and communion, with bread unleavened by *malice and evil*. **9:** An earlier *letter*, which has been lost (unless a fragment of it is now found in 2 Cor.6.14–7.1). **11:** Immoral people are bound to be met with in public social life, but they must not be tolerated as brothers (compare Dt.17.2–7).

6.1–8: Lawsuits in pagan courts. Christians ought to settle their differences outside of court, for they will participate with Christ in the final judgment of pagan magistrates; how absurd then that they should now abide by the judgments of outsiders! **7–8:** A rebuke to both sides of every lawsuit.

immoral, nor idolaters, nor adulterers, nor sexual perverts, [10] nor thieves, nor the greedy, nor drunkards, nor revilers, nor robbers will inherit the kingdom of God. [11] And such were some of you. But you were washed, you were sanctified, you were justified in the name of the Lord Jesus Christ and in the Spirit of our God.

12 "All things are lawful for me," but not all things are helpful. "All things are lawful for me," but I will not be enslaved by anything. [13] "Food is meant for the stomach and the stomach for food"—and God will destroy both one and the other. The body is not meant for immorality, but for the Lord, and the Lord for the body. [14] And God raised the Lord and will also raise us up by his power. [15] Do you not know that your bodies are members of Christ? Shall I therefore take the members of Christ and make them members of a prostitute? Never! [16] Do you not know that he who joins himself to a prostitute becomes one body with her? For, as it is written, "The two shall become one flesh." [17] But he who is united to the Lord becomes one spirit with him. [18] Shun immorality. Every other sin which a man commits is outside the body; but the immoral man sins against his own body. [19] Do you not know that your body is a temple of the Holy Spirit within you, which you have from God? You are not your own; [20] you were bought with a price. So glorify God in your body.

7 Now concerning the matters about which you wrote. It is well for a man not to touch a woman. [2] But because of the temptation to immorality,

each man should have his own wife and each woman her own husband. [3] The husband should give to his wife her conjugal rights, and likewise the wife to her husband. [4] For the wife does not rule over her own body, but the husband does; likewise the husband does not rule over his own body, but the wife does. [5] Do not refuse one another except perhaps by agreement for a season, that you may devote yourselves to prayer; but then come together again, lest Satan tempt you through lack of self-control. [6] I say this by way of concession, not of command. [7] I wish that all were as I myself am. But each has his own special gift from God, one of one kind and one of another.

8 To the unmarried and the widows I say that it is well for them to remain single as I do. [9] But if they cannot exercise self-control, they should marry. For it is better to marry than to be aflame with passion.

10 To the married I give charge, not I but the Lord, that the wife should not separate from her husband [11] (but if she does, let her remain single or else be reconciled to her husband)—and that the husband should not divorce his wife.

12 To the rest I say, not the Lord, that if any brother has a wife who is an unbeliever, and she consents to live with him, he should not divorce her. [13] If any woman has a husband who is an unbeliever, and he consents to live with her, she should not divorce him. [14] For the unbelieving husband is consecrated through his wife, and the unbelieving wife is consecrated through her husband. Otherwise, your children would be unclean, but as it is they are

---

6.9–20: A warning against laxity. Corinth was known in antiquity as a particularly licentious city. **13:** The libertines argued that satisfying sexual desire was like taking food to satisfy one's hunger. Paul rejects this analogy. **16:** Immorality involves the whole *body*, which for Paul means the whole personal life (compare Gen.2.24; Mt.19.5; Eph.5.31). **20:** We belong to Christ, who has *bought* us with his own blood.

7.1–16: Directions about marriage. 1: Paul's reasons for favoring celibacy (v. 8) are given in vv. 26,32–34. **3–4:** Equality of *conjugal rights* between husband and wife and the need for mutual consideration. **10–11:** *Not I, but the Lord*, a possible reference to the teaching of Jesus found in Mk.10.2–9. **12:** *I say, not the Lord*, Paul can cite no remembered saying of Jesus as authority for what he now writes. **14:** *Is consecrated*, is brought in some sense within the sphere

holy. ¹⁵ But if the unbelieving partner desires to separate, let it be so; in such a case the brother or sister is not bound. For God has called us*l* to peace. ¹⁶ Wife, how do you know whether you will save your husband? Husband, how do you know whether you will save your wife?

17 Only, let every one lead the life which the Lord has assigned to him, and in which God has called him. This is my rule in all the churches. ¹⁸ Was any one at the time of his call already circumcised? Let him not seek to remove the marks of circumcision. Was any one at the time of his call uncircumcised? Let him not seek circumcision. ¹⁹ For neither circumcision counts for anything nor uncircumcision, but keeping the commandments of God. ²⁰ Every one should remain in the state in which he was called. ²¹ Were you a slave when called? Never mind. But if you can gain your freedom, avail yourself of the opportunity.*x* ²² For he who was called in the Lord as a slave is a freedman of the Lord. Likewise he who was free when called is a slave of Christ. ²³ You were bought with a price; do not become slaves of men. ²⁴ So, brethren, in whatever state each was called, there let him remain with God.

25 Now concerning the unmarried,*y* I have no command of the Lord, but I give my opinion as one who by the Lord's mercy is trustworthy. ²⁶ I think that in view of the present*m* distress it is well for a person to remain as he is. ²⁷ Are you bound to a wife? Do not seek to be free. Are you free from a wife? Do not seek marriage. ²⁸ But if you marry, you do not sin, and if a girl*z* marries she does not sin. Yet those who marry will have worldly troubles, and I would spare you that. ²⁹ I mean, brethren, the appointed time has grown very short; from now on, let those who have wives live as though they had none, ³⁰ and those who mourn as though they were not mourning, and those who rejoice as though they were not rejoicing, and those who buy as though they had no goods, ³¹ and those who deal with the world as though they had no dealings with it. For the form of this world is passing away.

32 I want you to be free from anxieties. The unmarried man is anxious about the affairs of the Lord, how to please the Lord; ³³ but the married man is anxious about worldly affairs, how to please his wife, ³⁴ and his interests are divided. And the unmarried woman or girl*z* is anxious about the affairs of the Lord, how to be holy in body and spirit; but the married woman is anxious about worldly affairs, how to please her husband. ³⁵ I say this for your own benefit, not to lay any restraint upon you, but to promote good order and to secure your undivided devotion to the Lord.

36 If any one thinks that he is not behaving properly toward his betrothed,*z* if his passions are strong, and it has to

l Other ancient authorities read *you*
x Or *make use of your present condition instead*
y Greek *virgins*
m Or *impending*
z Greek *virgin*

---

of salvation. *They are holy*, i.e. regarded as Christian children. **15:** *The brother or sister*, the Christian partner.

7.17–24: Because the end of the world is fast approaching, it is better for everyone to remain as he is and not try to change his outward situation. **25–35:** Paul repeats his counsel about marriage, justifying his caution with a reference to the shortness of the time and the desirability of not being involved in the distracting obligations of family life. **36–38:** These difficult verses may also be freely rendered as follows: "If a father thinks that he is acting unfairly toward his unmarried daughter, when she is past the bloom of her youth, and if it has to be, let him do as he thinks right. He commits no sin; she and her suitor should be allowed to marry. ³⁷ But if a father is firmly established in his heart, being free from all external constraint and having a legal right to carry out his own wishes, and in his own heart has determined to keep his unmarried daughter at home, he will do well. ³⁸ In short, he who gives his daughter in marriage does well; and he who refrains from giving her in marriage will do better."

be, let him do as he wishes: let them marry–it is no sin. [37] But whoever is firmly established in his heart, being under no necessity but having his desire under control, and has determined this in his heart, to keep her as his betrothed,[z] he will do well. [38] So that he who marries his betrothed[z] does well; and he who refrains from marriage will do better.

39 A wife is bound to her husband as long as he lives. If the husband dies, she is free to be married to whom she wishes, only in the Lord. [40] But in my judgment she is happier if she remains as she is. And I think that I have the Spirit of God.

8 Now concerning food offered to idols: we know that "all of us possess knowledge." "Knowledge" puffs up, but love builds up. [2] If any one imagines that he knows something, he does not yet know as he ought to know. [3] But if one loves God, one is known by him.

4 Hence, as to the eating of food offered to idols, we know that "an idol has no real existence," and that "there is no God but one." [5] For although there may be so-called gods in heaven or on earth–as indeed there are many "gods" and many "lords"– [6] yet for us there is one God, the Father, from whom are all things and for whom we exist, and one Lord, Jesus Christ, through whom are all things and through whom we exist.

7 However, not all possess this knowledge. But some, through being hitherto accustomed to idols, eat food as really offered to an idol; and their conscience, being weak, is defiled. [8] Food will not commend us to God. We are no worse off if we do not eat, and no better off if we do. [9] Only take care lest this liberty of yours somehow become a stumbling block to the weak. [10] For if any one sees you, a man of knowledge, at table in an idol's temple, might he not be encouraged, if his conscience is weak, to eat food offered to idols? [11] And so by your knowledge this weak man is destroyed, the brother for whom Christ died. [12] Thus, sinning against your brethren and wounding their conscience when it is weak, you sin against Christ. [13] Therefore, if food is a cause of my brother's falling, I will never eat meat, lest I cause my brother to fall.

9 Am I not free? Am I not an apostle? Have I not seen Jesus our Lord? Are not you my workmanship in the Lord? [2] If to others I am not an apostle, at least I am to you; for you are the seal of my apostleship in the Lord.

3 This is my defense to those who would examine me. [4] Do we not have the right to our food and drink? [5] Do we not have the right to be accompanied by a wife,[n] as the other apostles and the brothers of the Lord and Cephas? [6] Or is it only Barnabas and I

z Greek *virgin* n Greek *a sister as wife*

8.1–13: May a Christian eat food consecrated to a pagan god? Much of the meat sold in the market places had come from animals sacrificed in pagan temples. Many Christians had scruples about eating such meat (Rom. ch. 14). Others, however, felt superior to such scruples and contemptuous toward those troubled by them. These superior people with their "*knowledge*" Paul rebukes for their lack of *love* (v. 1). **2–3:** The true blessedness consists, not in knowing, but in being known by God, and it is in love that one is thus known. **6:** Mal.2.10; Jn.1.3; Rom.11.36; Eph.4.6; Col.1.16. **10:** Social clubs and guilds held banquets in pagan temples; since no real acknowledgment or worship of the idol was involved for him, many a Christian felt that there was no proper objection to his attending. But Paul warns of the influence by example upon a brother for whom such indulgence would be a violation of conscience and therefore destructive.

9.1–14: Paul's rights as an apostle. Paul himself practiced the principle of self-restraint that he has just been preaching. For the good of the church, he has refrained from asserting his rights as an apostle (1 Th.2.6). **1:** Acts 9.3–6,17; Gal.1.11–16; 1 Cor.15.8–9. **2:** The Corinthian church is itself proof of the effectiveness and authenticity of Paul's *apostleship*. **4:** That is, at the expense of the church. **5:** *Brothers of the Lord*, see Mt.13.55 n. For Peter's wife, compare

who have no right to refrain from working for a living? [7] Who serves as a soldier at his own expense? Who plants a vineyard without eating any of its fruit? Who tends a flock without getting some of the milk?

8 Do I say this on human authority? Does not the law say the same? [9] For it is written in the law of Moses, "You shall not muzzle an ox when it is treading out the grain." Is it for oxen that God is concerned? [10] Does he not speak entirely for our sake? It was written for our sake, because the plowman should plow in hope and the thresher thresh in hope of a share in the crop. [11] If we have sown spiritual good among you, is it too much if we reap your material benefits? [12] If others share this rightful claim upon you, do not we still more?

Nevertheless, we have not made use of this right, but we endure anything rather than put an obstacle in the way of the gospel of Christ. [13] Do you not know that those who are employed in the temple service get their food from the temple, and those who serve at the altar share in the sacrificial offerings? [14] In the same way, the Lord commanded that those who proclaim the gospel should get their living by the gospel.

15 But I have made no use of any of these rights, nor am I writing this to secure any such provision. For I would rather die than have any one deprive me of my ground for boasting. [16] For if I preach the gospel, that gives me no ground for boasting. For necessity is laid upon me. Woe to me if I do not preach the gospel! [17] For if I do this of my own will, I have a reward; but if not of my own will, I am entrusted with a commission. [18] What then is my reward? Just this: that in my preaching I may make the gospel free of charge, not making full use of my right in the gospel.

19 For though I am free from all men, I have made myself a slave to all, that I might win the more. [20] To the Jews I became as a Jew, in order to win Jews; to those under the law I became as one under the law–though not being myself under the law–that I might win those under the law. [21] To those outside the law I became as one outside the law–not being without law toward God but under the law of Christ–that I might win those outside the law. [22] To the weak I became weak, that I might win the weak. I have become all things to all men, that I might by all means save some. [23] I do it all for the sake of the gospel, that I may share in its blessings.

24 Do you not know that in a race all the runners compete, but only one receives the prize? So run that you may obtain it. [25] Every athlete exercises self-control in all things. They do it to receive a perishable wreath, but we an imperishable. [26] Well, I do not run aimlessly, I do not box as one beating the air; [27] but I pommel my body and subdue it, lest after preaching to others I myself should be disqualified.

10 I want you to know, brethren, that our fathers were all under the cloud, and all passed through the sea, [2] and all were baptized into Moses in the cloud and in the sea, [3] and

---

Mk.1.30. **6:** Paul was a tent-maker by trade (Acts 18.3). **9:** The ox has a right to eat the grain (Dt.25.4). **14:** Lk.10.7; compare 1 Tim.5.18.

9.15–27: Paul waives his apostolic rights. 15–18: He deserves no credit for preaching the gospel–this he cannot help–but he does take pride in doing it without compensation; and the ground of this pride he will not give up. **19–23:** Paul returns to the general topic of ch. 8; the Christian is free except from the obligation to love. If taken in context this passage will not be misunderstood: here are consideration and tact, not cowardice and compromise. **24–27:** The importance of self-discipline out of consideration for the "weaker" consciences of others.

10.1–13: A warning against overconfidence. Baptism and partaking the Lord's supper are not enough to guarantee salvation, any more than corresponding acts sufficed for the ancient Hebrews. **2:** *Cloud, sea,* Ex.13.21; 14.22. **3–4:** Ex.16.4–35; 17.6; Num.20.7–11. A later legend

all ate the same supernatural[o] food [4] and all drank the same supernatural[o] drink. For they drank from the supernatural[o] Rock which followed them, and the Rock was Christ. [5] Nevertheless with most of them God was not pleased; for they were overthrown in the wilderness.

6 Now these things are warnings for us, not to desire evil as they did. [7] Do not be idolaters as some of them were; as it is written, "The people sat down to eat and drink and rose up to dance." [8] We must not indulge in immorality as some of them did, and twenty-three thousand fell in a single day. [9] We must not put the Lord[p] to the test, as some of them did and were destroyed by serpents; [10] nor grumble, as some of them did and were destroyed by the Destroyer. [11] Now these things happened to them as a warning, but they were written down for our instruction, upon whom the end of the ages has come. [12] Therefore let any one who thinks that he stands take heed lest he fall. [13] No temptation has overtaken you that is not common to man. God is faithful, and he will not let you be tempted beyond your strength, but with the temptation will also provide the way of escape, that you may be able to endure it.

14 Therefore, my beloved, shun the worship of idols. [15] I speak as to sensible men; judge for yourselves what I say. [16] The cup of blessing which we bless, is it not a participation[q] in the blood of Christ? The bread which we break, is it not a participation[q] in the body of Christ? [17] Because there is one bread, we who are many are one body, for we all partake of the one bread. [18] Consider the people of Israel;[a] are not those who eat the sacrifices partners in the altar? [19] What do I imply then? That food offered to idols is anything, or that an idol is anything? [20] No, I imply that what pagans sacrifice they offer to demons and not to God. I do not want you to be partners with demons. [21] You cannot drink the cup of the Lord and the cup of demons. You cannot partake of the table of the Lord and the table of demons. [22] Shall we provoke the Lord to jealousy? Are we stronger than he?

23 "All things are lawful," but not all things are helpful. "All things are lawful," but not all things build up. [24] Let no one seek his own good, but the good of his neighbor. [25] Eat whatever is sold in the meat market without raising any question on the ground of conscience. [26] For "the earth is the Lord's, and everything in it." [27] If one of the unbelievers invites you to dinner and you are disposed to go, eat whatever is set before you without raising any question on the ground of conscience. [28] (But if some one says to you, "This has been offered in sacrifice," then out of consideration for the man who informed you, and for conscience' sake– [29] I mean his conscience, not yours–do not eat it.) For why should my liberty be determined by another man's scruples? [30] If I partake with thankfulness, why am I denounced because of that for which I give thanks?

o Greek *spiritual*
p Other ancient authorities read *Christ*
q Or *communion*   a Greek *Israel according to the flesh*

---

told of the Rock following the people in the desert. Paul sees the *Rock* as a symbol of Christ, perhaps as the very work of the pre-existent Christ. **5:** Num.14.29–30. **7:** Ex.32.4,6. **8:** Num. 25.1–18. **9:** Num.21.5–6. **10:** Num.16.14,49.

10.14–22: Remembering the rather liberal attitude expressed earlier (8.4–10), Paul warns against actual participation in pagan worship. To eat at a friend's table, or even at a banquet in a temple, food consecrated to an idol is one thing; taking part in a pagan religious rite (comparable to the Lord's supper in the church) is quite another. **19–20:** Idols do not exist; but demons stand behind them (Dt.32.17) and use them to destroy those who worship them. **21:** 2 Cor.6.15–16.

10.23–11.1: A full return to the topic of ch. 8 (compare 6.12–13). **26:** Ps.24.1; 50.12. **28:** 8.7,10–12. **32:** 8.13.

31 So, whether you eat or drink, or whatever you do, do all to the glory of God. [32] Give no offense to Jews or to Greeks or to the church of God, [33] just as I try to please all men in everything I do, not seeking my own advantage, but that of many, that they may be saved. [1] Be imitators of me, as I am of Christ.

2 I commend you because you remember me in everything and maintain the traditions even as I have delivered them to you. [3] But I want you to understand that the head of every man is Christ, the head of a woman is her husband, and the head of Christ is God. [4] Any man who prays or prophesies with his head covered dishonors his head, [5] but any woman who prays or prophesies with her head unveiled dishonors her head—it is the same as if her head were shaven. [6] For if a woman will not veil herself, then she should cut off her hair; but if it is disgraceful for a woman to be shorn or shaven, let her wear a veil. [7] For a man ought not to cover his head, since he is the image and glory of God; but woman is the glory of man. [8] (For man was not made from woman, but woman from man. [9] Neither was man created for woman, but woman for man.) [10] That is why a woman ought to have a veil[r] on her head, because of the angels. [11] (Nevertheless, in the Lord woman is not independent of man nor man of woman; [12] for as woman was made from man, so man is now born of woman. And all things are from God.) [13] Judge for yourselves; is it proper for a woman to pray to God with her head

uncovered? [14] Does not nature itself teach you that for a man to wear long hair is degrading to him, [15] but if a woman has long hair, it is her pride? For her hair is given to her for a covering. [16] If any one is disposed to be contentious, we recognize no other practice, nor do the churches of God.

17 But in the following instructions I do not commend you, because when you come together it is not for the better but for the worse. [18] For, in the first place, when you assemble as a church, I hear that there are divisions among you; and I partly believe it, [19] for there must be factions among you in order that those who are genuine among you may be recognized. [20] When you meet together, it is not the Lord's supper that you eat. [21] For in eating, each one goes ahead with his own meal, and one is hungry and another is drunk. [22] What! Do you not have houses to eat and drink in? Or do you despise the church of God and humiliate those who have nothing? What shall I say to you? Shall I commend you in this? No, I will not.

23 For I received from the Lord what I also delivered to you, that the Lord Jesus on the night when he was betrayed took bread, [24] and when he had given thanks, he broke it, and said, "This is my body which is for[s] you. Do this in remembrance of me." [25] In the same way also the cup, after supper, saying, "This cup is the new covenant in my blood. Do this, as often as you drink it, in remembrance of me." [26] For as often as you eat this

r Greek *authority* (the veil being a symbol of this)
s Other ancient authorities read *broken for*

11.2–16: A discussion of **ways of worship** (extending through ch. 14). 2: *The traditions*, see 2 Th.2.15 n. 3–5: A play on the word *head*. A man dishonors Christ by worshiping with his head covered; a woman dishonors both her husband and Christ by worshiping otherwise. 10: *Angels* were thought of as administering the divine order (see 1 Tim.5.21 n.). A woman worshiping in the presence of men with bare head shows disrespect for this order. 11: Paul guards against a wrong inference from what he has said about the subordination of women. 16: Paul shuts off further discussion, appealing to the example of other churches (14.36).

11.17–34: **Directions concerning the Lord's supper.** 18–19: *Factions*, cliques, perhaps corresponding to social classes, at the supper (compare also 1.11–12). 20–21: The Lord's supper took place in connection with a common meal, which came to be known as the agape, or love feast (Jude 12). 23–25: Mt.26.26–29; Mk.14.22–25; Lk.22.14–20. 25: *New covenant in my blood*,

bread and drink the cup, you proclaim the Lord's death until he comes.

27 Whoever, therefore, eats the bread or drinks the cup of the Lord in an unworthy manner will be guilty of profaning the body and blood of the Lord. [28] Let a man examine himself, and so eat of the bread and drink of the cup. [29] For any one who eats and drinks without discerning the body eats and drinks judgment upon himself. [30] That is why many of you are weak and ill, and some have died.*t* [31] But if we judged ourselves truly, we should not be judged. [32] But when we are judged by the Lord, we are chastened*u* so that we may not be condemned along with the world.

33 So then, my brethren, when you come together to eat, wait for one another– [34] if any one is hungry, let him eat at home–lest you come together to be condemned. About the other things I will give directions when I come.

12 Now concerning spiritual gifts,*x* brethren, I do not want you to be uninformed. [2] You know that when you were heathen, you were led astray to dumb idols, however you may have been moved. [3] Therefore I want you to understand that no one speaking by the Spirit of God ever says "Jesus be cursed!" and no one can say "Jesus is Lord" except by the Holy Spirit.

4 Now there are varieties of gifts, but the same Spirit; [5] and there are varieties of service, but the same Lord; [6] and there are varieties of working, but it is the same God who inspires them all in every one. [7] To each is given the manifestation of the Spirit for the common good. [8] To one is given through the Spirit the utterance of wisdom, and to another the utterance of knowledge according to the same Spirit, [9] to another faith by the same Spirit, to another gifts of healing by the one Spirit, [10] to another the working of miracles, to another prophecy, to another the ability to distinguish between spirits, to another various kinds of tongues, to another the interpretation of tongues. [11] All these are inspired by one and the same Spirit, who apportions to each one individually as he wills.

12 For just as the body is one and has many members, and all the members of the body, though many, are one body, so it is with Christ. [13] For by one Spirit we were all baptized into one body–Jews or Greeks, slaves or free–and all were made to drink of one Spirit.

14 For the body does not consist of one member but of many. [15] If the foot should say, "Because I am not a hand, I do not belong to the body," that would not make it any less a part of the body. [16] And if the ear should say, "Because I am not an eye, I do not belong to the body," that would not make it any less a part of the body. [17] If the whole body were an eye, where would be the hearing? If the whole body were an ear, where would be the sense of smell? [18] But as it is, God arranged the organs in the body, each one of them, as he chose. [19] If all

t Greek *have fallen asleep* (as in 15.6, 20)
u Or *when we are judged we are being chastened by the Lord*   *x* Or *spiritual persons*

---

the old covenant was also confirmed with blood (Ex.24.8). **26:** *You proclaim*, the celebration is "a living sermon." **29:** *Without discerning the body*, without realizing the sacred meaning of his action. **33–34:** *Wait for one another*, apparently those who came early left too little food for others. *Eat at home*, Paul says, if you cannot control your hunger.

12.1–11: Spiritual gifts. 2: A reference to the highly emotional, orgiastic practices in certain pagan cults. Ecstasy is not enough to prove that one is *moved* by the Holy Spirit. **4–11:** The real test is whether the gift comes from the one God and contributes to *the common good* (v. 7). Note the suggestion of the Trinity, *Spirit . . . Lord . . . God* (vv. 4–5). **10:** *Miracles*, see Gal.3.5 n. *Prophecy*, inspired preaching. *Ability to distinguish between spirits*, power to recognize whether a man is a true or a false prophet (1 Jn.4.1). *Interpretation of tongues*, ability to put into intelligible words what the ecstatics were saying (14.9–19).

12.12–31: The body and its members, a figure of the church, which is the body of Christ

were a single organ, where would the body be? 20 As it is, there are many parts, yet one body. 21 The eye cannot say to the hand, "I have no need of you," nor again the head to the feet, "I have no need of you." 22 On the contrary, the parts of the body which seem to be weaker are indispensable, 23 and those parts of the body which we think less honorable we invest with the greater honor, and our unpresentable parts are treated with greater modesty, 24 which our more presentable parts do not require. But God has so composed the body, giving the greater honor to the inferior part, 25 that there may be no discord in the body, but that the members may have the same care for one another. 26 If one member suffers, all suffer together; if one member is honored, all rejoice together.

27 Now you are the body of Christ and individually members of it. 28 And God has appointed in the church first apostles, second prophets, third teachers, then workers of miracles, then healers, helpers, administrators, speakers in various kinds of tongues. 29 Are all apostles? Are all prophets? Are all teachers? Do all work miracles? 30 Do all possess gifts of healing? Do all speak with tongues? Do all interpret? 31 But earnestly desire the higher gifts.

And I will show you a still more excellent way.

13 If I speak in the tongues of men and of angels, but have not love, I am a noisy gong or a clanging cymbal. 2 And if I have prophetic powers, and understand all mysteries and all knowledge, and if I have all faith, so as to remove mountains, but have not love, I am nothing. 3 If I give away all I have, and if I deliver my body to be burned,[v] but have not love, I gain nothing.

4 Love is patient and kind; love is not jealous or boastful; 5 it is not arrogant or rude. Love does not insist on its own way; it is not irritable or resentful; 6 it does not rejoice at wrong, but rejoices in the right. 7 Love bears all things, believes all things, hopes all things, endures all things.

8 Love never ends; as for prophecies, they will pass away; as for tongues, they will cease; as for knowledge, it will pass away. 9 For our knowledge is imperfect and our prophecy is imperfect; 10 but when the perfect comes, the imperfect will pass away. 11 When I was a child, I spoke like a child, I thought like a child, I reasoned like a child; when I became a man, I gave up childish ways. 12 For now we see in a mirror dimly, but then face to face. Now I know in part; then I shall understand fully, even as I have been fully understood. 13 So faith, hope, love abide, these three; but the greatest of these is love.

v Other ancient authorities read *body that I may glory*

(Rom.12.4–5; Eph.4.14–16; Col.3.14). **28:** *Helpers, administrators,* probably also known as deacons and bishops (see Phil.1.1 n.).

13.1–13: This chapter, wonderfully significant when considered alone, is even more meaningful in its context. Paul is still discussing spiritual gifts (12.1–11); the great gift of the Spirit is not tongues or even prophecy, but *love.* This *love* is not love in an ordinary or general sense, but the love which is known within the church, the very love of God poured out in Christ (Rom.5.5). **1:** *Gong . . . cymbal,* probably a reference to the noisy accompaniments of pagan worship. **2:** 14.2; Mt.17.20; 21.21. **3:** The reading in note *v* probably represents an ancient attempt to avoid what might be regarded as an absurdity: How could one accept a martyr's death unless one is moved by love? But Paul knows that pride or perverted self-interest can conceivably move one to make such a sacrifice. **4–7:** The reverse of the proud, contemptuous, divisive spirit manifested in the behavior of some at Corinth. **8–13:** *Knowledge* and ability to express it (whether in *prophecies* or *tongues*) are too faulty for one to take pride in them. **12:** *A mirror,* a polished metal surface, not yielding a clear image. **13:** *Love* is *greatest* because it is God's love poured into our hearts; *faith* and *hope* are our response to what God has first done (1 Jn.4.19). The triad appears elsewhere in Paul's letters (Rom.5.1–5; Phil.1.9–10; Col.1.4–5; 1 Th.1.3; 5.8; 2 Th.1.3–4).

14 Make love your aim, and earnestly desire the spiritual gifts, especially that you may prophesy. [2] For one who speaks in a tongue speaks not to men but to God; for no one understands him, but he utters mysteries in the Spirit. [3] On the other hand, he who prophesies speaks to men for their upbuilding and encouragement and consolation. [4] He who speaks in a tongue edifies himself, but he who prophesies edifies the church. [5] Now I want you all to speak in tongues, but even more to prophesy. He who prophesies is greater than he who speaks in tongues, unless some one interprets, so that the church may be edified.

6 Now, brethren, if I come to you speaking in tongues, how shall I benefit you unless I bring you some revelation or knowledge or prophecy or teaching? [7] If even lifeless instruments, such as the flute or the harp, do not give distinct notes, how will any one know what is played? [8] And if the bugle gives an indistinct sound, who will get ready for battle? [9] So with yourselves; if you in a tongue utter speech that is not intelligible, how will any one know what is said? For you will be speaking into the air. [10] There are doubtless many different languages in the world, and none is without meaning; [11] but if I do not know the meaning of the language, I shall be a foreigner to the speaker and the speaker a foreigner to me. [12] So with yourselves; since you are eager for manifestations of the Spirit, strive to excel in building up the church.

13 Therefore, he who speaks in a tongue should pray for the power to interpret. [14] For if I pray in a tongue, my spirit prays but my mind is unfruitful. [15] What am I to do? I will pray with the spirit and I will pray with the mind also; I will sing with the spirit and I will sing with the mind also. [16] Otherwise, if you bless[w] with the spirit, how can any one in the position of an outsider[x] say the "Amen" to your thanksgiving when he does not know what you are saying? [17] For you may give thanks well enough, but the other man is not edified. [18] I thank God that I speak in tongues more than you all; [19] nevertheless, in church I would rather speak five words with my mind, in order to instruct others, than ten thousand words in a tongue.

20 Brethren, do not be children in your thinking; be babes in evil, but in thinking be mature. [21] In the law it is written, "By men of strange tongues and by the lips of foreigners will I speak to this people, and even then they will not listen to me, says the Lord." [22] Thus, tongues are a sign not for believers but for unbelievers, while prophecy is not for unbelievers but for believers. [23] If, therefore, the whole church assembles and all speak in tongues, and outsiders or unbelievers enter, will they not say that you are mad? [24] But if all prophesy, and an unbeliever or outsider enters, he is convicted by all, he is called to account by all, [25] the secrets of his heart are disclosed; and so, falling on his face, he will worship God and declare that God is really among you.

26 What then, brethren? When you come together, each one has a hymn, a lesson, a revelation, a tongue, or an interpretation. Let all things be done for edification. [27] If any speak in a tongue, let there be only two or at most three, and each in turn; and let one interpret. [28] But if there is no one to interpret, let each of them keep silence in church and speak to himself and to God. [29] Let two or three prophets speak, and let the others

w That is, *give thanks to God*
x Or *him that is without gifts*

14.1–40: Speaking in tongues is subordinate to prophecy (see 12.10 n.). **16:** *Say the "Amen,"* Neh.8.6; 1 Chr.16.36; Ps.106.48. **18:** For other evidence that Paul himself had ecstatic experiences, see 2 Cor.12.1–4. **21:** *Law*, the Old Testament (Is.28.11–12). **25:** *The secrets . . . are disclosed*, compare Jn.4.16–19. **26:** *A hymn*, Eph.5.19. *A lesson*, a teaching. **34:** 1 Tim.2.11–12;

weigh what is said. [30] If a revelation is made to another sitting by, let the first be silent. [31] For you can all prophesy one by one, so that all may learn and all be encouraged; [32] and the spirits of prophets are subject to prophets. [33] For God is not a God of confusion but of peace.

As in all the churches of the saints, [34] the women should keep silence in the churches. For they are not permitted to speak, but should be subordinate, as even the law says. [35] If there is anything they desire to know, let them ask their husbands at home. For it is shameful for a woman to speak in church. [36] What! Did the word of God originate with you, or are you the only ones it has reached?

[37] If any one thinks that he is a prophet, or spiritual, he should acknowledge that what I am writing to you is a command of the Lord. [38] If any one does not recognize this, he is not recognized. [39] So, my brethren, earnestly desire to prophesy, and do not forbid speaking in tongues; [40] but all things should be done decently and in order.

[15] Now I would remind you, brethren, in what terms I preached to you the gospel, which you received, in which you stand, [2] by which you are saved, if you hold it fast—unless you believed in vain.

[3] For I delivered to you as of first importance what I also received, that Christ died for our sins in accordance with the scriptures, [4] that he was buried, that he was raised on the third day in accordance with the scriptures, [5] and that he appeared to Cephas, then to the twelve. [6] Then he appeared to more than five hundred brethren at one time, most of whom are still alive, though some have fallen asleep. [7] Then he appeared to James, then to all the apostles. [8] Last of all, as to one untimely born, he appeared also to me. [9] For I am the least of the apostles, unfit to be called an apostle, because I persecuted the church of God. [10] But by the grace of God I am what I am, and his grace toward me was not in vain. On the contrary, I worked harder than any of them, though it was not I, but the grace of God which is with me. [11] Whether then it was I or they, so we preach and so you believed.

[12] Now if Christ is preached as raised from the dead, how can some of you say that there is no resurrection of the dead? [13] But if there is no resurrection of the dead, then Christ has not been raised; [14] if Christ has not been raised, then our preaching is in vain and your faith is in vain. [15] We are even found to be misrepresenting God, because we testified of God that he raised Christ, whom he did not raise if it is true that the dead are not raised. [16] For if the dead are not raised, then Christ has not been raised. [17] If Christ has not been raised, your faith is futile and you are still in your sins. [18] Then those also who have fallen asleep in Christ have perished. [19] If for this life only we have hoped in Christ, we are of all men most to be pitied.

[20] But in fact Christ has been raised from the dead, the first fruits of those who have fallen asleep. [21] For as by a man came death, by a man has come also the resurrection of the dead. [22] For as in Adam all die, so also in Christ shall all be made alive. [23] But each in his own order: Christ

---

1 Pet.3.1. **36:** Paul ends discussion of a troublesome issue in a similar way in 11.16 and Phil.3.15.
    15.1–11: Paul's gospel. A restatement against the background of reports that some at Corinth deny the resurrection. **3:** *Scriptures*, Is.53.5–12. **4:** *Scriptures*, Ps.16.10 (compare Acts 2.31). **7:** *James*, "the Lord's brother" of Gal.1.19. **8:** *One untimely born*, the meaning is obscure; Paul perhaps is referring to the separation in time between his own experience and those of the others. For other accounts of Paul's encounter with the risen Christ, see 9.1; Gal.1.16; Acts 9.3–6
    15.12–34: The significance of the resurrection. 18: 1 Th.4.16. **21–22:** Rom.5.12–18. **23:**

the first fruits, then at his coming those who belong to Christ. 24 Then comes the end, when he delivers the kingdom to God the Father after destroying every rule and every authority and power. 25 For he must reign until he has put all his enemies under his feet. 26 The last enemy to be destroyed is death. 27 "For God*z* has put all things in subjection under his feet." But when it says, "All things are put in subjection under him," it is plain that he is excepted who put all things under him. 28 When all things are subjected to him, then the Son himself will also be subjected to him who put all things under him, that God may be everything to every one.

29 Otherwise, what do people mean by being baptized on behalf of the dead? If the dead are not raised at all, why are people baptized on their behalf? 30 Why am I in peril every hour? 31 I protest, brethren, by my pride in you which I have in Christ Jesus our Lord, I die every day! 32 What do I gain if, humanly speaking, I fought with beasts at Ephesus? If the dead are not raised, "Let us eat and drink, for tomorrow we die." 33 Do not be deceived: "Bad company ruins good morals." 34 Come to your right mind, and sin no more. For some have no knowledge of God. I say this to your shame.

35 But some one will ask, "How are the dead raised? With what kind of body do they come?" 36 You foolish man! What you sow does not come to life unless it dies. 37 And what you sow is not the body which is to be,

but a bare kernel, perhaps of wheat or of some other grain. 38 But God gives it a body as he has chosen, and to each kind of seed its own body. 39 For not all flesh is alike, but there is one kind for men, another for animals, another for birds, and another for fish. 40 There are celestial bodies and there are terrestrial bodies; but the glory of the celestial is one, and the glory of the terrestrial is another. 41 There is one glory of the sun, and another glory of the moon, and another glory of the stars; for star differs from star in glory.

42 So is it with the resurrection of the dead. What is sown is perishable, what is raised is imperishable. 43 It is sown in dishonor, it is raised in glory. It is sown in weakness, it is raised in power. 44 It is sown a physical body, it is raised a spiritual body. If there is a physical body, there is also a spiritual body. 45 Thus it is written, "The first man Adam became a living being"; the last Adam became a life-giving spirit. 46 But it is not the spiritual which is first but the physical, and then the spiritual. 47 The first man was from the earth, a man of dust; the second man is from heaven. 48 As was the man of dust, so are those who are of the dust; and as is the man of heaven, so are those who are of heaven. 49 Just as we have borne the image of the man of dust, we shall*a* also bear the image of the man of heaven. 50 I tell you this, brethren: flesh and blood cannot inherit the

z Greek *he*
a Other ancient authorities read *let us*

Coming, the glorious return of Christ at the end of the age (1 Th.2.19; 4.13–17). **24–27**: *His enemies* are the demonic powers dominating the present age; one of these is *death*. **27**: Ps.8.6. *His feet*, Christ's. **29**: A practice otherwise unknown. Presumably Christians accepted baptism in the names of their loved ones who had died without being baptized in order that the latter might share in the final resurrection. Without advocating this practice, Paul makes it a point in his argument. **31**: *I die*, i.e. I risk death, *every day*. **32**: One cannot say with assurance whether the fighting *with beasts* is to be taken literally or is merely a strong metaphor (compare 4.9). In any case, Paul had bitter and dangerous enemies. The quotation is from Is.22.13. **33**: Paul quotes a Greek proverb (attributed to the Attic poet Menander), warning the Corinthians not to associate with those who deny the resurrection.

15.35–58: The nature of the resurrection. 35–44: Greeks had no trouble in conceiving of the immortality of the soul, but the idea of the raised body was difficult. Paul's point is that there are many kinds of "bodies"; the resurrection body will be a new body (not *perishable*, v. 42, or *physical*, v. 44), which God will provide. **45–47**: Gen.2.7. **50**: Jn.3.6. **51–52**: *Mystery*, a

kingdom of God, nor does the perishable inherit the imperishable. 51 Lo! I tell you a mystery. We shall not all sleep, but we shall all be changed, [52] in a moment, in the twinkling of an eye, at the last trumpet. For the trumpet will sound, and the dead will be raised imperishable, and we shall be changed. [53] For this perishable nature must put on the imperishable, and this mortal nature must put on immortality. [54] When the perishable puts on the imperishable, and the mortal puts on immortality, then shall come to pass the saying that is written:

"Death is swallowed up in victory."
[55] "O death, where is thy victory?
     O death, where is thy sting?"
[56] The sting of death is sin, and the power of sin is the law. [57] But thanks be to God, who gives us the victory through our Lord Jesus Christ.

58 Therefore, my beloved brethren, be steadfast, immovable, always abounding in the work of the Lord, knowing that in the Lord your labor is not in vain.

16 Now concerning the contribution for the saints: as I directed the churches of Galatia, so you also are to do. [2] On the first day of every week, each of you is to put something aside and store it up, as he may prosper, so that contributions need not be made when I come. [3] And when I arrive, I will send those whom you accredit by letter to carry your gift to Jerusalem. [4] If it seems advisable that I should go also, they will accompany me.

5 I will visit you after passing through Macedo'nia, for I intend to pass through Macedo'nia, [6] and perhaps I will stay with you or even spend the winter, so that you may speed me on my journey, wherever I go. [7] For I do not want to see you now just in passing; I hope to spend some time with you, if the Lord permits. [8] But I will stay in Ephesus until Pentecost, [9] for a wide door for effective work has opened to me, and there are many adversaries.

10 When Timothy comes, see that you put him at ease among you, for he is doing the work of the Lord, as I am. [11] So let no one despise him. Speed him on his way in peace, that he may return to me; for I am expecting him with the brethren.

12 As for our brother Apol'los, I strongly urged him to visit you with the other brethren, but it was not at all his will[b] to come now. He will come when he has opportunity.

13 Be watchful, stand firm in your faith, be courageous, be strong. [14] Let all that you do be done in love.

15 Now, brethren, you know that the household of Steph'anas were the first converts in Acha'ia, and they have devoted themselves to the service of the saints; [16] I urge you to be subject to such men and to every fellow worker and laborer. [17] I rejoice at the coming of Steph'anas and Fortuna'tus and Acha'icus, because they have made up for your absence; [18] for they refreshed my spirit as well as yours. Give recognition to such men.

19 The churches of Asia send greetings. Aq'uila and Prisca, together with the church in their house, send you hearty greetings in the Lord. [20] All the brethren send greetings. Greet one another with a holy kiss.

b Or God's will for him

---

secret made known in Christ. *We shall not all sleep*, we shall not all die before the Lord's coming (1 Th.4.13–17). **54–55:** Is.25.8; Hos.13.14. **57:** *God gives us the victory* over sin now (Rom. 8.1–2) and hereafter over death (Rom.8.11). **58:** *Immovable*, not shaken by false teaching.
    16.1–24: Final messages. 1: *Contribution*, Rom.15.25–29; 2 Cor. chs. 8–9; Gal.2.10. **5:** Acts 19.21. **8–9:** Acts 18.19; 19.9. **10:** *Timothy*, see Introduction to 2 Timothy. *Apollos*, Acts 18.24–26. **15:** *Stephanus*, 1.16. **17:** Perhaps these men brought the letter mentioned in 7.1 and are to carry back Paul's reply. **19:** *Asia*, a Roman province in western Asia Minor. *Aquila and Prisca* are mentioned in Acts 18.2; Rom.16.3; 2 Tim.4.19. *The Church . . . in their house,*

21 I, Paul, write this greeting with my own hand. 22 If any one has no love for the Lord, let him be accursed. Our Lord, come!c 23 The grace of the Lord Jesus be with you. 24 My love be with you all in Christ Jesus. Amen.

c Greek *Maranatha*

---

see Philem.1 n. **20:** *Holy kiss*, see Rom.16.16 n. **21:** Paul adds his personal signature (2 Th.3.17), after dictating the rest; perhaps Sosthenes (1.1) had served as his secretary (compare Rom. 16.22). **22:** *Our Lord, come!* is the preferable rendering of the word *Maranatha* (transliterated from two Aramaic words); an equally legitimate rendering, but less probable in this context, is "Our Lord has come."

CORINTHIANS

Relations between Paul and the Corinthian church had deteriorated during the period after 1 Corinthians was written. Having made a "painful visit" to the church (2.1), the apostle refrained from making a second visit because he had reason to believe that it too would be painful. Instead, he had written a severe letter (not known to us) "out of much affliction and anguish of heart and with many tears" (2.4) and sent it to Corinth, presumably by Titus, one of his fellow-workers. So anxious was he about the effects of this letter that he found it impossible to wait for Titus' return. He left Ephesus, hoping to meet Titus in Troas. Disappointed there, he went on to Macedonia (2.12–13), where Titus rejoined him, bringing a most reassuring report on the attitude of the Corinthian church toward him (7.13–16). In relief and gratitude, Paul wrote this letter. In it he takes occasion to speak at length about the offering for the church at Jerusalem (8.1–9.15), which was now almost complete.

Chapters 10 to 13 constitute a vigorous defense of Paul and his work and are written in a tone so different from that of chapters 1 to 9 that many scholars believe they are a fragment of another letter written to Corinth at some other time.

Because so much of 2 Corinthians is a response to the words and feelings of others, which are not recorded in the letter, it is difficult sometimes to follow the apostle's argument. Its pages preserve much, however, that illuminates Paul's own life, ministry, and the concern which he felt for the churches he had established (4.5; 5.20; 6.1–10; 11.22–33; 12.2–10).

PAUL, AN APOSTLE OF CHRIST JESUS by the will of God, and Timothy our brother.

To the church of God which is at Corinth, with all the saints who are in the whole of Acha'ia:

2 Grace to you and peace from God our Father and the Lord Jesus Christ.

3 Blessed be the God and Father of our Lord Jesus Christ, the Father of mercies and God of all comfort, 4 who comforts us in all our affliction, so that we may be able to comfort those who are in any affliction, with the comfort with which we ourselves are comforted by God. 5 For as we share abundantly in Christ's sufferings, so through Christ we share abundantly in comfort too.[a] 6 If we are afflicted, it is for your comfort and salvation; and if we are comforted, it is for your comfort, which you experience when you patiently endure the same sufferings that we suffer. 7 Our hope for you is unshaken; for we know that as you share in our sufferings, you will also share in our comfort.

8 For we do not want you to be ignorant, brethren, of the affliction we experienced in Asia; for we were so utterly, unbearably crushed that we despaired of life itself. 9 Why, we felt that we had received the sentence of death; but that was to make us rely not on ourselves but on God who raises the dead; 10 he delivered us from so deadly a peril, and he will deliver us; on him we have set our hope that he will deliver us again. 11 You also must help us by prayer, so that many will give thanks on our behalf for the bless-

a Or, *For as the sufferings of Christ abound for us, so also our comfort abounds through Christ*

1.1–14: Salutation and thanksgiving, see Rom.1.1–7 n. and 1.8–15 n. The thanksgiving reflects the relief which Paul felt as a result of the news that Titus brought him (see Introduction). **1:** *Timothy*, see Introduction to 2 Timothy. *Achaia*, the Roman province in which Corinth was located. **2:** *Grace . . . peace*, see 2 Th.1.2 n. **8–10:** It is not known what this terrible trial was; some identify it with the experience mentioned in 1 Cor.15.32. **8:** *Asia*, a Roman province in western Asia Minor.

ing granted us in answer to many prayers.

12 For our boast is this, the testimony of our conscience that we have behaved in the world, and still more toward you, with holiness and godly sincerity, not by earthly wisdom but by the grace of God. 13 For we write you nothing but what you can read and understand; I hope you will understand fully, 14 as you have understood in part, that you can be proud of us as we can be of you, on the day of the Lord Jesus.

15 Because I was sure of this, I wanted to come to you first, so that you might have a double pleasure;*b* 16 I wanted to visit you on my way to Macedo'nia, and to come back to you from Macedo'nia and have you send me on my way to Judea. 17 Was I vacillating when I wanted to do this? Do I make my plans like a worldly man, ready to say Yes and No at once? 18 As surely as God is faithful, our word to you has not been Yes and No. 19 For the Son of God, Jesus Christ, whom we preached among you, Silva'nus and Timothy and I, was not Yes and No; but in him it is always Yes. 20 For all the promises of God find their Yes in him. That is why we utter the Amen through him, to the glory of God. 21 But it is God who establishes us with you in Christ, and has commissioned us; 22 he has put his seal upon us and given us his Spirit in our hearts as a guarantee.

23 But I call God to witness against me–it was to spare you that I refrained from coming to Corinth. 24 Not that we lord it over your faith; we work with you for your joy, for you stand firm in your faith. 1 For I made up my mind not to make you another painful visit. 2 For if I cause you pain, who is there to make me glad but the one whom I have pained? 3 And I wrote as I did, so that when I came I might not suffer pain from those who should have made me rejoice, for I felt sure of all of you, that my joy would be the joy of you all. 4 For I wrote you out of much affliction and anguish of heart and with many tears, not to cause you pain but to let you know the abundant love that I have for you.

5 But if any one has caused pain, he has caused it not to me, but in some measure–not to put it too severely– to you all. 6 For such a one this punishment by the majority is enough; 7 so you should rather turn to forgive and comfort him, or he may be overwhelmed by excessive sorrow. 8 So I beg you to reaffirm your love for him. 9 For this is why I wrote, that I might test you and know whether you are obedient in everything. 10 Any one whom you forgive, I also forgive. What I have forgiven, if I have forgiven anything, has been for your sake in the presence of Christ, 11 to keep Satan from gaining the advantage over us; for we are not ignorant of his designs.

12 When I came to Tro'as to preach the gospel of Christ, a door was opened for me in the Lord; 13 but my mind could not rest because I did not find my brother Titus there. So I took leave of them and went on to Macedo'nia.

14 But thanks be to God, who in Christ always leads us in triumph, and through us spreads the fragrance of the knowledge of him everywhere. 15 For we are the aroma of Christ to God

b Other ancient authorities read favor

1.15–3.3: Paul's recent relations with the church, see Introduction. **1.16:** Paul *wanted* to go to both Macedonia and Corinth in order (among other reasons) to receive their contributions to the offering, which he would then take *to Judea*. **17–20:** His critics accused him of being *vacillating*. **22:** The *Spirit*, already given, is an advance installment of what is in store for Christians (5.5; Eph.1.13); God will finish what he has begun (Rom.8.16–17,23; Eph.1.14; Phil.1.6). **2.3–4:** Many identify the letter referred to with chs. 10–13 (see Introduction), but there is no ground for certainty. **12–13:** *A door was opened*, there was a good opportunity for preaching Christ. *Titus*, like Timothy, was one of Paul's helpers (see Introduction to Titus). **14:** A reference to the triumphal processions of conquerors returning to their capitals. The

among those who are being saved and among those who are perishing, ¹⁶ to one a fragrance from death to death, to the other a fragrance from life to life. Who is sufficient for these things? ¹⁷ For we are not, like so many, peddlers of God's word; but as men of sincerity, as commissioned by God, in the sight of God we speak in Christ.

3 Are we beginning to commend ourselves again? Or do we need, as some do, letters of recommendation to you, or from you? ² You yourselves are our letter of recommendation, written on your*c* hearts, to be known and read by all men; ³ and you show that you are a letter from Christ delivered by us, written not with ink but with the Spirit of the living God, not on tablets of stone but on tablets of human hearts.

4 Such is the confidence that we have through Christ toward God. ⁵ Not that we are competent of ourselves to claim anything as coming from us; our competence is from God, ⁶ who has made us competent to be ministers of a new covenant, not in a written code but in the Spirit; for the written code kills, but the Spirit gives life.

7 Now if the dispensation of death, carved in letters on stone, came with such splendor that the Israelites could not look at Moses' face because of its brightness, fading as this was, ⁸ will not the dispensation of the Spirit be attended with greater splendor? ⁹ For if there was splendor in the dispensation of condemnation, the dispensa-tion of righteousness must far exceed it in splendor. ¹⁰ Indeed, in this case, what once had splendor has come to have no splendor at all, because of the splendor that surpasses it. ¹¹ For if what faded away came with splendor, what is permanent must have much more splendor.

12 Since we have such a hope, we are very bold, ¹³ not like Moses, who put a veil over his face so that the Israelites might not see the end of the fading splendor. ¹⁴ But their minds were hardened; for to this day, when they read the old covenant, that same veil remains unlifted, because only through Christ is it taken away. ¹⁵ Yes, to this day whenever Moses is read a veil lies over their minds; ¹⁶ but when a man turns to the Lord the veil is removed. ¹⁷ Now the Lord is the Spirit, and where the Spirit of the Lord is, there is freedom. ¹⁸ And we all, with unveiled face, beholding*d* the glory of the Lord, are being changed into his likeness from one degree of glory to another; for this comes from the Lord who is the Spirit.

4 Therefore, having this ministry by the mercy of God,*e* we do not lose heart. ² We have renounced disgrace-ful, underhanded ways; we refuse to practice cunning or to tamper with God's word, but by the open state-ment of the truth we would commend ourselves to every man's conscience in the sight of God. ³ And even if our

c Other ancient authorities read *our*
d Or *reflecting*
e Greek *as we have received mercy*

fragrance is the odor of incense in connection either with such processions or with sacrifice (Col.2.15). **16**: The decisiveness of one's acceptance or rejection of the gospel. **17**: *Peddlers*, a reference presumably to the "false apostles" of 11.4,13. **3.1**: Apparently Paul had been accused of commending himself. **3**: The church at Corinth (Paul's *letter of recommendation*) was the work of God; Paul was only the instrument (v. 5). *Tablets of stone*, like the *written code* (v. 6), suggest the covenant with Moses (Ex.24.12); Christ has instituted a new covenant.

3.4–18: **The new covenant** (see Jer.31.31 n.). **6**: *Kills*, produces not life but despair and death. For Paul's view of the purpose and effect of the law, see Gal.3.19–29 n. and Rom.7.7–13 n. **7**: *Dispensation of death*, existence under the law (Ex.34.29–35). **13**: Paul interprets Moses' *veil* as his effort to hide from the people how temporary the old covenant was to be. **14**: *The old covenant*, the books of the law. **15–17**: In Christ one sees the transiency of the old and knows the *freedom* and *glory* of the new. Paul here comes very close to identifying the Spirit, known within the church, with the risen Lord Jesus. **18**: 4.6; 1 Jn.3.2.

4.1–18: **The apostle's ministry. 2**: Probably an oblique reference to the methods of the "false apostles" (11.13). **3–4**: Paul has apparently been accused of not making the gospel clear.

gospel is veiled, it is veiled only to those who are perishing. ⁴ In their case the god of this world has blinded the minds of the unbelievers, to keep them from seeing the light of the gospel of the glory of Christ, who is the likeness of God. ⁵ For what we preach is not ourselves, but Jesus Christ as Lord, with ourselves as your servants*f* for Jesus' sake. ⁶ For it is the God who said, "Let light shine out of darkness," who has shone in our hearts to give the light of the knowledge of the glory of God in the face of Christ.

7 But we have this treasure in earthen vessels, to show that the transcendent power belongs to God and not to us. ⁸ We are afflicted in every way, but not crushed; perplexed, but not driven to despair; ⁹ persecuted, but not forsaken; struck down, but not destroyed; ¹⁰ always carrying in the body the death of Jesus, so that the life of Jesus may also be manifested in our bodies. ¹¹ For while we live we are always being given up to death for Jesus' sake, so that the life of Jesus may be manifested in our mortal flesh. ¹² So death is at work in us, but life in you.

13 Since we have the same spirit of faith as he had who wrote, "I believed, and so I spoke," we too believe, and so we speak, ¹⁴ knowing that he who raised the Lord Jesus will raise us also with Jesus and bring us with you into his presence. ¹⁵ For it is all for your sake, so that as grace extends to more and more people it may increase thanksgiving, to the glory of God.

16 So we do not lose heart. Though

our outer nature is wasting away, our inner nature is being renewed every day. ¹⁷ For this slight momentary affliction is preparing for us an eternal weight of glory beyond all comparison, ¹⁸ because we look not to the things that are seen but to the things that are unseen; for the things that are seen are transient, but the things that are unseen are eternal.

5 For we know that if the earthly tent we live in is destroyed, we have a building from God, a house not made with hands, eternal in the heavens. ² Here indeed we groan, and long to put on our heavenly dwelling, ³ so that by putting it on we may not be found naked. ⁴ For while we are still in this tent, we sigh with anxiety; not that we would be unclothed, but that we would be further clothed, so that what is mortal may be swallowed up by life. ⁵ He who has prepared us for this very thing is God, who has given us the Spirit as a guarantee.

6 So we are always of good courage; we know that while we are at home in the body we are away from the Lord, ⁷ for we walk by faith, not by sight. ⁸ We are of good courage, and we would rather be away from the body and at home with the Lord. ⁹ So whether we are at home or away, we make it our aim to please him. ¹⁰ For we must all appear before the judgment seat of Christ, so that each one may receive good or evil, according to what he has done in the body.

11 Therefore, knowing the fear of the Lord, we persuade men; but what

f Or *slaves*

God of this world, Satan. **6**: Gen.1.3. **7**: *Earthen vessels*, a reference to the weakness of the body (Gen.2.7) and indeed to all human limitations. **10–11**: In his sufferings and perils Paul shares in Jesus' death; but it is given to him also to share in the life of the risen, victorious Christ. **12**: The apostle "dies" (i.e. suffers) that the Corinthians and others may know the life in Christ (v. 15). **13**: A reference to the courage and faithfulness of the psalmist in the midst of troubles (Ps.116.10). **17**: Paul considers all of his sufferings as a *slight momentary affliction*.

5.1–10: Continuing to think of his sufferings and constant peril, Paul uses the figures of a *tent* and a *building from God* in speaking of death and resurrection. This *building* is the "spiritual body" of 1 Cor.15.44–50. **3**: *Naked*, Paul hopes that the Lord will come and that he will receive his new body before he has had to put off the old one. **4**: 1 Cor.15.51–54. **5**: See 1.22 n. **6–8**: Believers are never *away from the Lord* in the absolute sense; but as long as they are in the body, they are to a degree separated from him (1 Cor.13.12).

we are is known to God, and I hope it is known also to your conscience. [12] We are not commending ourselves to you again but giving you cause to be proud of us, so that you may be able to answer those who pride themselves on a man's position and not on his heart. [13] For if we are beside ourselves, it is for God; if we are in our right mind, it is for you. [14] For the love of Christ controls us, because we are convinced that one has died for all; therefore all have died. [15] And he died for all, that those who live might live no longer for themselves but for him who for their sake died and was raised.

16 From now on, therefore, we regard no one from a human point of view; even though we once regarded Christ from a human point of view, we regard him thus no longer. [17] Therefore, if any one is in Christ, he is a new creation;*g* the old has passed away, behold, the new has come. [18] All this is from God, who through Christ reconciled us to himself and gave us the ministry of reconciliation; [19] that is, in Christ God was reconciling*h* the world to himself, not counting their trespasses against them, and entrusting to us the message of reconciliation. [20] So we are ambassadors for Christ, God making his appeal through us. We beseech you on behalf of Christ, be reconciled to God. [21] For our sake he made him to be sin who knew no sin, so that in him we might become the righteousness of God.

6 Working together with him, then, we entreat you not to accept the grace of God in vain. [2] For he says,

"At the acceptable time I have
    listened to you,
and helped you on the day of
    salvation."

Behold, now is the acceptable time; behold, now is the day of salvation. [3] We put no obstacle in any one's way, so that no fault may be found with our ministry, [4] but as servants of God we commend ourselves in every way: through great endurance, in afflictions, hardships, calamities, [5] beatings, imprisonments, tumults, labors, watching, hunger; [6] by purity, knowledge, forbearance, kindness, the Holy Spirit, genuine love, [7] truthful speech, and the power of God; with the weapons of righteousness for the right hand and for the left; [8] in honor and dishonor, in ill repute and good repute. We are treated as impostors, and yet are true; [9] as unknown, and yet well known; as dying, and behold we live; as punished, and yet not killed; [10] as sorrowful, yet always rejoicing; as poor, yet making many rich; as having nothing, and yet possessing everything.

11 Our mouth is open to you, Corinthians; our heart is wide. [12] You are not restricted by us, but you are restricted in your own affections. [13] In return—I speak as to children—widen your hearts also.

14 Do not be mismated with unbelievers. For what partnership have righteousness and iniquity? Or what

g Or *creature*   *h* Or *God was in Christ reconciling*

5.11–6.13: Further defense of his ministry. 5.13: *Beside ourselves* no doubt refers to a criticism levelled against Paul. **14:** *The love of Christ*, Christ's love for us. *All have died*, to "die" in this sense is to live no longer for oneself but for Christ (v. 15). **16–17:** Once Paul thought of Christ simply as a man shamefully crucified; he now knows him as the risen Lord, head of a *new creation* into which the believer is incorporated. **18:** *Reconciled*, Rom.5.10; Col.1.20; Heb.1.3. **20:** *Be reconciled*, accept God's forgiveness in Christ. **21:** Paul does not say "made him a sinner"; the sinless Christ bore the burden of our sin that we might be acquitted (Gal. 3.13). **6.1–2:** Quoting Is.49.8 Paul urges his readers to respond faithfully to God's grace in Christ. *Now*, before the Lord returns. **4–5:** 11.23–29. **10:** *Rich*, with spiritual gifts. **11:** I have been frank with you, *Corinthians*, for you are in my *heart*. **12:** Any restraint upon our relations has been owing to you, not to me.

6.14–7.1: A parenthesis on relations with pagans. This passage represents not only an abrupt change of subject, but also an interruption, because 7.2 seems to follow directly upon 6.13. It has been suggested that a fragment of some other letter to Corinth (possibly that mentioned in

fellowship has light with darkness? [15] What accord has Christ with Be'lial?[i] Or what has a believer in common with an unbeliever? [16] What agreement has the temple of God with idols? For we are the temple of the living God; as God said,

"I will live in them and move
among them,
and I will be their God,
and they shall be my people.
[17] Therefore come out from them,
and be separate from them, says
the Lord,
and touch nothing unclean;
then I will welcome you,
[18] and I will be a father to you,
and you shall be my sons and
daughters,
says the Lord Almighty."

7 Since we have these promises, beloved, let us cleanse ourselves from every defilement of body and spirit, and make holiness perfect in the fear of God.

2 Open your hearts to us; we have wronged no one, we have corrupted no one, we have taken advantage of no one. [3] I do not say this to condemn you, for I said before that you are in our hearts, to die together and to live together. [4] I have great confidence in you; I have great pride in you; I am filled with comfort. With all our affliction, I am overjoyed.

5 For even when we came into Macedo'nia, our bodies had no rest but we were afflicted at every turn–fighting without and fear within. [6] But God, who comforts the downcast, comforted us by the coming of Titus, [7] and not only by his coming but also by the

comfort with which he was comforted in you, as he told us of your longing, your mourning, your zeal for me, so that I rejoiced still more. [8] For even if I made you sorry with my letter, I do not regret it (though I did regret it), for I see that that letter grieved you, though only for a while. [9] As it is, I rejoice, not because you were grieved, but because you were grieved into repenting; for you felt a godly grief, so that you suffered no loss through us. [10] For godly grief produces a repentance that leads to salvation and brings no regret, but worldly grief produces death. [11] For see what earnestness this godly grief has produced in you, what eagerness to clear yourselves, what indignation, what alarm, what longing, what zeal, what punishment! At every point you have proved yourselves guiltless in the matter. [12] So although I wrote to you, it was not on account of the one who did the wrong, nor on account of the one who suffered the wrong, but in order that your zeal for us might be revealed to you in the sight of God. [13] Therefore we are comforted.

And besides our own comfort we rejoiced still more at the joy of Titus, because his mind has been set at rest by you all. [14] For if I have expressed to him some pride in you, I was not put to shame; but just as everything we said to you was true, so our boasting before Titus has proved true. [15] And his heart goes out all the more to you, as he remembers the obedience of you all, and the fear and trembling with which you received him. [16] I rejoice, because I have perfect confidence in you.

i Greek Beliar

---

1 Cor.5.9–11) was accidentally inserted here when the letters of Paul were first collected and published. **6.15:** *Belial*, another name for Satan; it appears in the intertestamental literature. **16:** 1 Cor.3.16. **16–18:** Paul makes a continuous statement out of a number of Old Testament passages, rather loosely quoted: Lev.26.12; Ezek.37.27; Is.52.11; 2 Sam.7.14. **7.1:** *Make holiness perfect*, be completely dedicated to God.

    7.2–16: Paul's joy at the restoration of good relations. **2–4:** After the "parenthesis" of 6.14–7.1 this statement follows naturally upon 6.13. **5–16:** See Introduction. **5:** *Bodies*, a way of referring to his suffering and anxiety. **8:** 2.3–4. **11:** *Punishment*, a penalty of some kind imposed on an unnamed opponent of the apostle (2.5–9). **12:** *The one who suffered the wrong*, probably Paul himself.

8 We want you to know, brethren, about the grace of God which has been shown in the churches of Macedo'nia, 2 for in a severe test of affliction, their abundance of joy and their extreme poverty have overflowed in a wealth of liberality on their part. 3 For they gave according to their means, as I can testify, and beyond their means, of their own free will, 4 begging us earnestly for the favor of taking part in the relief of the saints— 5 and this, not as we expected, but first they gave themselves to the Lord and to us by the will of God. 6 Accordingly we have urged Titus that as he had already made a beginning, he should also complete among you this gracious work. 7 Now as you excel in everything—in faith, in utterance, in knowledge, in all earnestness, and in your love for us—see that you excel in this gracious work also.

8 I say this not as a command, but to prove by the earnestness of others that your love also is genuine. 9 For you know the grace of our Lord Jesus Christ, that though he was rich, yet for your sake he became poor, so that by his poverty you might become rich. 10 And in this matter I give my advice: it is best for you now to complete what a year ago you began not only to do but to desire, 11 so that your readiness in desiring it may be matched by your completing it out of what you have. 12 For if the readiness is there, it is acceptable according to what a man has, not according to what he has not. 13 I do not mean that others should be eased and you burdened, 14 but that as a matter of equality your abundance at the present time should supply their want, so that their abundance may supply your want,

that there may be equality. 15 As it is written, "He who gathered much had nothing over, and he who gathered little had no lack."

16 But thanks be to God who puts the same earnest care for you into the heart of Titus. 17 For he not only accepted our appeal, but being himself very earnest he is going to you of his own accord. 18 With him we are sending the brother who is famous among all the churches for his preaching of the gospel; 19 and not only that, but he has been appointed by the churches to travel with us in this gracious work which we are carrying on, for the glory of the Lord and to show our good will. 20 We intend that no one should blame us about this liberal gift which we are administering, 21 for we aim at what is honorable not only in the Lord's sight but also in the sight of men. 22 And with them we are sending our brother whom we have often tested and found earnest in many matters, but who is now more earnest than ever because of his great confidence in you. 23 As for Titus, he is my partner and fellow worker in your service; and as for our brethren, they are messengers*j* of the churches, the glory of Christ. 24 So give proof, before the churches, of your love and of our boasting about you to these men.

9 Now it is superfluous for me to write to you about the offering for the saints, 2 for I know your readiness, of which I boast about you to the people of Macedo'nia, saying that Acha'ia has been ready since last year; and your zeal has stirred up most of them. 3 But I am sending the brethren so that our boasting about you may not prove vain in this case, so that you

j Greek *apostles*

8.1–9.15: The offering for the relief of the Jerusalem church (Gal.2.1–10; 1 Cor.16.1–4; Rom.15.25–27). **8.9:** *Though he was rich,* a reference to Christ's pre-existence. **10:** The raising of funds at Corinth had perhaps been interrupted by the rift between Paul and the church, a rift now healed. **14:** *Your abundance* suggests that the Corinthian church was in better economic condition than some of Paul's other churches (compare the Macedonians' extreme poverty, 8.1–2). **15:** Ex.16.18. **18:** *The brother,* like *our brother* in v. 22, is unidentified. One gathers from v. 23 that two men had been appointed by the churches to assist Paul in the collection and, no doubt at Paul's insistence, to "audit" the accounts (vv. 20–21). **9.2:** *Achaia,* see 1.1 n. **3:** *The*

may be ready, as I said you would be; [4] lest if some Macedo'nians come with me and find that you are not ready, we be humiliated–to say nothing of you–for being so confident. [5] So I thought it necessary to urge the brethren to go on to you before me, and arrange in advance for this gift you have promised, so that it may be ready not as an exaction but as a willing gift.

[6] The point is this: he who sows sparingly will also reap sparingly, and he who sows bountifully will also reap bountifully. [7] Each one must do as he has made up his mind, not reluctantly or under compulsion, for God loves a cheerful giver. [8] And God is able to provide you with every blessing in abundance, so that you may always have enough of everything and may provide in abundance for every good work. [9] As it is written,

"He scatters abroad, he gives to the
        poor;
    his righteousness[k] endures for ever."
[10] He who supplies seed to the sower and bread for food will supply and multiply your resources[l] and increase the harvest of your righteousness.[k] [11] You will be enriched in every way for great generosity, which through us will produce thanksgiving to God; [12] for the rendering of this service not only supplies the wants of the saints but also overflows in many thanksgivings to God. [13] Under the test of this service, you[m] will glorify God by your obedience in acknowledging the gospel of Christ, and by the generosity of your contribution for them and for all others; [14] while they long for you and pray for you, because of the surpassing grace of God in you. [15] Thanks be to God for his inexpressible gift!

10 I, Paul, myself entreat you, by the meekness and gentleness of Christ–I who am humble when face to face with you, but bold to you when I am away!– [2] I beg of you that when I am present I may not have to show boldness with such confidence as I count on showing against some who suspect us of acting in worldly fashion. [3] For though we live in the world we are not carrying on a worldly war, [4] for the weapons of our warfare are not worldly but have divine power to destroy strongholds. [5] We destroy arguments and every proud obstacle to the knowledge of God, and take every thought captive to obey Christ, [6] being ready to punish every disobedience, when your obedience is complete.

[7] Look at what is before your eyes. If any one is confident that he is Christ's, let him remind himself that as he is Christ's, so are we. [8] For even if I boast a little too much of our authority, which the Lord gave for building you up and not for destroying you, I shall not be put to shame. [9] I would not seem to be frightening you with letters. [10] For they say, "His letters are weighty and strong, but his bodily presence is weak, and his speech of no account." [11] Let such people understand

k Or *benevolence*
l Greek *sowing*
m Or *they*

---

brethren, presumably the same ones spoken of in 8.18,22–23. **9**: Ps.112.9. **10**: A reminiscence of Is.55.10. **11–12**: The gift *which through us* is to be delivered at Jerusalem will be the occasion of *many thanksgivings to God* on the part of those who receive it. **15**: *Thanks . . . to God*, not only for the generosity he inspires, but also, and much more, for the *gift* of Christ himself.

10.1–18: On the problem which the abrupt change of tone presents, see Introduction. Some identify 10.1–13.10 with the "painful" letter referred to in 2.3–9; 7.8–12. This identification is questionable, but one can see grounds for holding that these chapters were not originally a part of the same letter as chs. 1–9. **1**: *I who am humble*, Paul is ironically quoting his opponents, as he often does in these last four chapters. **6**: The "disobedient" ones will be punished when the church as a whole returns to its loyalty and *obedience* to Paul, as he is sure it will eventually do. **7–12**: The critics are probably members of the Corinthian church as well as "false apostles" from outside. They have apparently accused him of weakness and empty *boasting*. **10**: 2.3.

that what we say by letter when absent, we do when present. ¹² Not that we venture to class or compare ourselves with some of those who commend themselves. But when they measure themselves by one another, and compare themselves with one another, they are without understanding.

13 But we will not boast beyond limit, but will keep to the limits God has apportioned us, to reach even to you. ¹⁴ For we are not overextending ourselves, as though we did not reach you; we were the first to come all the way to you with the gospel of Christ. ¹⁵ We do not boast beyond limit, in other men's labors; but our hope is that as your faith increases, our field among you may be greatly enlarged, ¹⁶ so that we may preach the gospel in lands beyond you, without boasting of work already done in another's field. ¹⁷ "Let him who boasts, boast of the Lord." ¹⁸ For it is not the man who commends himself that is accepted, but the man whom the Lord commends.

I wish you would bear with me in a little foolishness. Do bear with me! ² I feel a divine jealousy for you, for I betrothed you to Christ to present you as a pure bride to her one husband. ³ But I am afraid that as the serpent deceived Eve by his cunning, your thoughts will be led astray from a sincere and pure devotion to Christ. ⁴ For if some one comes and preaches another Jesus than the one we preached, or if you receive a different spirit from the one you received,

or if you accept a different gospel from the one you accepted, you submit to it readily enough. ⁵ I think that I am not in the least inferior to these superlative apostles. ⁶ Even if I am unskilled in speaking, I am not in knowledge; in every way we have made this plain to you in all things.

7 Did I commit a sin in abasing myself so that you might be exalted, because I preached God's gospel without out cost to you? ⁸ I robbed other churches by accepting support from them in order to serve you. ⁹ And when I was with you and was in want, I did not burden any one, for my needs were supplied by the brethren who came from Macedo'nia. So I refrained and will refrain from burdening you in any way. ¹⁰ As the truth of Christ is in me, this boast of mine shall not be silenced in the regions of Acha'ia. ¹¹ And why? Because I do not love you? God knows I do!

12 And what I do I will continue to do, in order to undermine the claim of those who would like to claim that in their boasted mission they work on the same terms as we do. ¹³ For such men are false apostles, deceitful workmen, disguising themselves as apostles of Christ. ¹⁴ And no wonder, for even Satan disguises himself as an angel of light. ¹⁵ So it is not strange if his servants also disguise themselves as servants of righteousness. Their end will correspond to their deeds.

16 I repeat, let no one think me foolish; but even if you do, accept me as a fool, so that I too may boast a little.

13–14: Paul is not doing more than God commissioned him to do when he exercises his authority as an apostle in the church at Corinth. **15–16:** A hint perhaps that his opponents were exploiting *other men's labors;* for Paul's missionary policy, compare Rom.15.20. On Paul's hopes of working west of Achaia, see Acts 19.21; Rom.1.11–15; 15.23–28. **17:** Jer.9.24.

11.1–15: Paul's reply to various charges. 2: Hos.2.19–20; Eph.5.26–27. **3:** Gen.3.4. **5–6:** That Paul as a speaker was being compared to others to his disadvantage appears also in 10.10 and, less clearly, in 1 Cor.2.1–5. **7–11:** Even Paul's honorable and generous determination not to be a financial burden had been perversely twisted into a charge against him. On the matter of Paul's support, see Acts 18.1–4; 2 Th.3.7–9; 1 Cor.9.3–7; and especially Phil.4.10–20. Why he accepted aid of this kind only from the Philippian church we are not told. **8:** *I robbed,* a natural exaggeration (compare v. 9). Those who *disguise themselves as apostles of Christ* are in reality *servants* of Satan; they have not manifested the same disinterestedness as Paul and are seeking to force him through their criticisms to surrender a practice which embarrasses them. **10:** *Achaia,* see 1.1 n.

[17] (What I am saying I say not with the Lord's authority but as a fool, in this boastful confidence; [18] since many boast of worldly things, I too will boast.) [19] For you gladly bear with fools, being wise yourselves! [20] For you bear it if a man makes slaves of you, or preys upon you, or takes advantage of you, or puts on airs, or strikes you in the face. [21] To my shame, I must say, we were too weak for that!

But whatever any one dares to boast of–I am speaking as a fool–I also dare to boast of that. [22] Are they Hebrews? So am I. Are they Israelites? So am I. Are they descendants of Abraham? So am I. [23] Are they servants of Christ? I am a better one–I am talking like a madman–with far greater labors, far more imprisonments, with countless beatings, and often near death. [24] Five times I have received at the hands of the Jews the forty lashes less one. [25] Three times I have been beaten with rods; once I was stoned. Three times I have been shipwrecked; a night and a day I have been adrift at sea; [26] on frequent journeys, in danger from rivers, danger from robbers, danger from my own people, danger from Gentiles, danger in the city, danger in the wilderness, danger at sea, danger from false brethren; [27] in toil and hardship, through many a sleepless night, in hunger and thirst, often without food, in cold and ex-posure. [28] And, apart from other things, there is the daily pressure upon me of my anxiety for all the churches. [29] Who is weak, and I am not weak? Who is made to fall, and I am not indignant?

30 If I must boast, I will boast of the things that show my weakness. [31] The God and Father of the Lord Jesus, he who is blessed for ever, knows that I do not lie. [32] At Damascus, the governor under King Ar'etas guarded the city of Damascus in order to seize me, [33] but I was let down in a basket through a window in the wall, and escaped his hands.

12 I must boast; there is nothing to be gained by it, but I will go on to visions and revelations of the Lord. [2] I know a man in Christ who fourteen years ago was caught up to the third heaven–whether in the body or out of the body I do not know, God knows. [3] And I know that this man was caught up into Paradise–whether in the body or out of the body I do not know, God knows– [4] and he heard things that cannot be told, which man may not utter. [5] On behalf of this man I will boast, but on my own behalf I will not boast, except of my weaknesses. [6] Though if I wish to boast, I shall not be a fool, for I shall be speaking the truth. But I refrain from it, so that no one may think more of me than he sees in me or hears from me. [7] And to keep me from being too elated by the

---

11.16–33: Paul's claims to consideration. Paul indulges in the "little foolishness" spoken of in v. 1. He knows it is foolish to boast, and perhaps even wrong, but feels that the attitudes of some at Corinth have forced him to assert his claims (12.11). **22:** Apparently the authenticity of Paul's Judaism was called into question (Rom.9.1–3; 11.1; Gal.1.13–14; Phil.3.4–6; compare Acts 22.3; 26.4–6). **23–27:** Very little is known about these hardships; the book of Acts refers to only a few of them. **24:** *Forty lashes*, a Jewish punishment; only thirty-nine were administered lest by a miscount the number exceed the maximum prescribed in Dt.25.3. **25:** *Beaten with rods*, a Roman punishment (Acts 16.22–23). *Stoned*, Acts 14.19. **32–33:** This item would seem logically to belong after v. 27; perhaps it is an afterthought (see also Acts 9.23–25). *Aretas* IV was king of Nabataea, southeast of Palestine. Apparently Damascus was under his jurisdiction at the time of Paul's escape.

12.1–13: Strength in weakness. Though Paul speaks of the *abundance of revelations* (v. 7), he refers specifically to only one of them. **2:** *I know a man*, an oblique reference to himself (see v. 7). *The third heaven*, the highest bliss. Nothing is otherwise known of this experience unless it is that referred to in Gal.1.16 and 1 Cor.15.8; but this is not probable. **4:** *Things that cannot be told*, because they are too sacred. **5:** Paul deserves no credit for these *revelations*; therefore he will not speak of them as though they were his own. **7–9:** Some have thought that

abundance of revelations, a thorn was given me in the flesh, a messenger of Satan, to harass me, to keep me from being too elated. [8] Three times I besought the Lord about this, that it should leave me; [9] but he said to me, "My grace is sufficient for you, for my power is made perfect in weakness." I will all the more gladly boast of my weaknesses, that the power of Christ may rest upon me. [10] For the sake of Christ, then, I am content with weaknesses, insults, hardships, persecutions, and calamities; for when I am weak, then I am strong.

11 I have been a fool! You forced me to it, for I ought to have been commended by you. For I was not at all inferior to these superlative apostles, even though I am nothing. [12] The signs of a true apostle were performed among you in all patience, with signs and wonders and mighty works. [13] For in what were you less favored than the rest of the churches, except that I myself did not burden you? Forgive me this wrong!

14 Here for the third time I am ready to come to you. And I will not be a burden, for I seek not what is yours but you; for children ought not to lay up for their parents, but parents for their children. [15] I will most gladly spend and be spent for your souls. If I love you the more, am I to be loved the less? [16] But granting that I myself did not burden you, I was crafty, you say, and got the better of you by guile. [17] Did I take advantage of you through any of those whom I sent to you? [18] I urged Titus to go, and sent the brother with him. Did Titus take advantage of you? Did we not act in the same spirit? Did we not take the same steps?

19 Have you been thinking all along that we have been defending ourselves before you? It is in the sight of God that we have been speaking in Christ, and all for your upbuilding, beloved. [20] For I fear that perhaps I may come and find you not what I wish, and that you may find me not what you wish; that perhaps there may be quarreling, jealousy, anger, selfishness, slander, gossip, conceit, and disorder. [21] I fear that when I come again my God may humble me before you, and I may have to mourn over many of those who sinned before and have not repented of the impurity, immorality, and licentiousness which they have practiced.

13 This is the third time I am coming to you. Any charge must be sustained by the evidence of two or three witnesses. [2] I warned those who sinned before and all the others, and I warn them now while absent, as I did when present on my second visit, that if I come again I will not spare them— [3] since you desire proof that Christ is speaking in me. He is not weak in dealing with you, but is powerful in you. [4] For he was crucified in weakness, but lives by the power of God. For we are weak in him, but in dealing with you we shall live with him by the power of God.

5 Examine yourselves, to see whether you are holding to your faith. Test yourselves. Do you not realize that Jesus Christ is in you?—unless in-

---

the thorn . . . in the flesh was illness or a physical disability; others have suggested that it was the opposition of his fellow Jews. No firm decision is possible. **12:** A reference to apostolic miracles (Rom.15.19; Gal.3.5). **13:** See 11.7–11 n. *Forgive me this wrong,* for the irony compare 11.21a.

12.14–13.10: Paul plans to visit Corinth again. This *third* visit cannot be identified with assurance. Some suppose it to be the visit referred to in retrospect in 2.1; others, that it is the visit in prospect when chs. 1–9 were written. **12.17–18:** Is this the sending of *Titus* and *the brother* mentioned in 8.16–19? If so, chs. 10–13 cannot have been written earlier than chs. 1–9, unless ch. 8 be regarded as a separate note about the collection written earlier still. See Introduction and 10.1–18 n. **19–21:** For his readers' sake, as well as for his own, Paul wants the coming visit to be happy and mutually rewarding. If chs. 10–13 are the "painful" letter referred to in 2.3–4, we know from chs. 1–9 that Paul's hopes were fulfilled. **13.1:** *Witnesses,* Dt.19.15. **2–4:** Paul will vigorously assert his apostolic authority in dealing with wrongdoing at Corinth, but

deed you fail to meet the test! ⁶ I hope you will find out that we have not failed. ⁷ But we pray God that you may not do wrong–not that we may appear to have met the test, but that you may do what is right, though we may seem to have failed. ⁸ For we cannot do anything against the truth, but only for the truth. ⁹ For we are glad when we are weak and you are strong. What we pray for is your improvement. ¹⁰ I write this while I am away from you, in order that when I come I may not have to be severe in my use of the authority which the Lord has given me for building up and not for tearing down.

11 Finally, brethren, farewell. Mend your ways, heed my appeal, agree with one another, live in peace, and the God of love and peace will be with you. ¹² Greet one another with a holy kiss. ¹³ All the saints greet you.

14 The grace of the Lord Jesus Christ and the love of God and the fellowship of[n] the Holy Spirit be with you all.

n Or *and participation in*

it will be Christ's authority. **5–9:** Paul hopes that he will not need to exert his authority, but that the church will discipline itself.
    13.11–14: Conclusion. 12: The liturgical *kiss*, see Rom.16.16 n. **14:** The fullest of Paul's benedictions at the end of his letters (for the Trinitarian form, compare 1 Cor.12.4–6). The order is significant; the *grace of Christ* leads one toward the *love of God*, and the love of God when actualized through the *Spirit* produces *fellowship* with God and man.

THE LETTER OF PAUL TO THE

GALATIANS

Often called the Magna Charta of Christian liberty, the Letter to the Galatians deals with the question whether a Gentile must become a Jew before he can become a Christian. Certain Judaizing teachers had infiltrated the churches of Galatia in central Asia Minor, which Paul had previously founded (Acts 16.6), declaring that in addition to having faith in Jesus Christ a Christian was obligated to keep the Mosaic law. Paul insists, on the contrary, that a man becomes right with God only by faith in Christ and not by the performance of good works, ritual observances, and the like (2.16; 3.24–25; 5.1; 6.12–15).

So serious was the crisis in Galatia that Paul dispenses with his customary expression of thanksgiving and commendation, and plunges directly into a vigorous defense of his apostolic authority and the validity of his teaching (1.1–2.21). The central part of the letter is an exposition of the doctrine of justification by faith alone (3.1–4.31). Lest some should imagine that this doctrine leads to a life of indifference to the moral code, Paul concludes with certain practical applications of his teaching (5.1–6.18).

The importance of this brief letter is hard to overestimate. Written perhaps about A.D. 55 during Paul's third missionary journey, it gives many autobiographical details of the apostle's earlier life and evangelistic activity. Here are set forth, with impassioned eloquence, the true function of the Mosaic law and its relation to God's grace manifested in Christ. The declaration of the principles reiterated in these six chapters made Christianity a world religion instead of a Jewish sect.

PAUL AN APOSTLE–NOT FROM MEN nor through man, but through Jesus Christ and God the Father, who raised him from the dead– ² and all the brethren who are with me,

To the churches of Galatia:

3 Grace to you and peace from God the Father and our Lord Jesus Christ, ⁴ who gave himself for our sins to deliver us from the present evil age, according to the will of our God and Father; ⁵ to whom be the glory for ever and ever. Amen.

6 I am astonished that you are so quickly deserting him who called you in the grace of Christ and turning to a different gospel– ⁷ not that there is another gospel, but there are some who trouble you and want to pervert the gospel of Christ. ⁸ But even if we, or an angel from heaven, should preach to you a gospel contrary to that which we preached to you, let him be accursed. ⁹ As we have said before, so now I say again, If any one is preaching to you a gospel contrary to that which you received, let him be accursed.

10 Am I now seeking the favor of men, or of God? Or am I trying to please men? If I were still pleasing men, I should not be a servant*a* of Christ.

11 For I would have you know, brethren, that the gospel which was preached by me is not man's*b* gospel. ¹² For I did not receive it from man, nor was I taught it, but it came through a revelation of Jesus Christ. ¹³ For you have heard of my former life in Judaism, how I persecuted the church of

a Or *slave* *b* Greek *according to man*

1.1–5: The Salutation (see Rom.1.1–7 n.) emphasizes both Paul's divinely given authority as an apostle and the atoning death of *Jesus Christ, who gave himself for our sins* (Mk.10.45; 1 Tim.2.6). **3:** *Grace* and *peace,* see 2 Th.1.2 n. **4:** *The present evil age* is in contrast to the coming age to be inaugurated at the return of Christ. Man's deliverance through Christ's self-giving rests upon *the will of God.*

1.6–10: The Galatian apostasy from the true gospel. **8–9:** A solemn anathema. **10:** 1 Th.2.4.

1.11–24: Paul's vindication of his apostleship. 11: Despite his severity, Paul addresses the Galatians as *brethren. Man's gospel,* a merely human message. **12:** *Through a revelation,* at

God violently and tried to destroy it; [14] and I advanced in Judaism beyond many of my own age among my people, so extremely zealous was I for the traditions of my fathers. [15] But when he who had set me apart before I was born, and had called me through his grace, [16] was pleased to reveal his Son to[c] me, in order that I might preach him among the Gentiles, I did not confer with flesh and blood, [17] nor did I go up to Jerusalem to those who were apostles before me, but I went away into Arabia; and again I returned to Damascus.

18 Then after three years I went up to Jerusalem to visit Cephas, and remained with him fifteen days. [19] But I saw none of the other apostles except James the Lord's brother. [20] (In what I am writing to you, before God, I do not lie!) [21] Then I went into the regions of Syria and Cili′cia. [22] And I was still not known by sight to the churches of Christ in Judea; [23] they only heard it said, "He who once persecuted us is now preaching the faith he once tried to destroy." [24] And they glorified God because of me.

2 Then after fourteen years I went up again to Jerusalem with Barnabas, taking Titus along with me. [2] I went up by revelation; and I laid before them (but privately before those who were of repute) the gospel which I preach among the Gentiles, lest somehow I should be running or had run in vain. [3] But even Titus, who was with

me, was not compelled to be circumcised, though he was a Greek. [4] But because of false brethren secretly brought in, who slipped in to spy out our freedom which we have in Christ Jesus, that they might bring us into bondage– [5] to them we did not yield submission even for a moment, that the truth of the gospel might be preserved for you. [6] And from those who were reputed to be something (what they were makes no difference to me; God shows no partiality)–those, I say, who were of repute added nothing to me; [7] but on the contrary, when they saw that I had been entrusted with the gospel to the uncircumcised, just as Peter had been entrusted with the gospel to the circumcised [8] (for he who worked through Peter for the mission to the circumcised worked through me also for the Gentiles), [9] and when they perceived the grace that was given to me, James and Cephas and John, who were reputed to be pillars, gave to me and Barnabas the right hand of fellowship, that we should go to the Gentiles and they to the circumcised; [10] only they would have us remember the poor, which very thing I was eager to do.

11 But when Cephas came to Antioch I opposed him to his face, because he stood condemned. [12] For before certain men came from James, he ate with the Gentiles; but when they came he drew back and separated

c Greek *in*

---

the time of Paul's conversion (Acts 9.3–6). **13:** *I persecuted*, compare Acts 8.3; 9.21; 22.4. The *church* is the people of God, whom he has called into fellowship with himself through the redemptive work of Jesus Christ. The word may refer either to the total number of believers throughout the world, or to those in one locality, whether gathered for worship or scattered by persecution. **14:** Acts 22.3. **15–17:** Paul's conversion and commission as an apostle were due to the sovereign plan of God, not to human teachers (1.1). **17:** *Arabia*, that is, the Nabataean kingdom, of which the capital was Petra. *Damascus*, Acts 9.19–25; 2 Cor.11.32–33. **18:** *Cephas*, the Aramaic equivalent of "Peter" (see Mt.16.18 n.). *Fifteen days*, a relatively short time. **19:** *The Lord's brother*, see Mt.13.55 n. **21:** *Cilicia*, of which Tarsus (see Acts 9.30 n.) was the capital.

2.1–10: Paul's apostleship recognized in Jerusalem. This visit is probably the one mentioned in Acts 15.2. *Titus*, one of Paul's most trusted helpers (2 Cor.7.6; 8.6,16–17). **2–3:** Although the Judaizers had apparently demanded that *Titus, a Greek*, should be circumcised, the apostles at Jerusalem, by not enforcing that demand, approved of Paul's work among the Gentiles (v. 9; see Acts 16.1–5 n.). On *Titus*, see Introduction to Titus. **4:** *False brethren*, Acts 15.1. **10:** *The poor*, Acts 11.29–30; 24.17; 1 Cor.16.1–3; 2 Cor.8.1–15. **11–14:** Peter's inconsistency

himself, fearing the circumcision party. [13] And with him the rest of the Jews acted insincerely, so that even Barnabas was carried away by their insincerity. [14] But when I saw that they were not straightforward about the truth of the gospel, I said to Cephas before them all, "If you, though a Jew, live like a Gentile and not like a Jew, how can you compel the Gentiles to live like Jews?" [15] We ourselves, who are Jews by birth and not Gentile sinners, [16] yet who know that a man is not justified[d] by works of the law but through faith in Jesus Christ, even we have believed in Christ Jesus, in order to be justified by faith in Christ, and not by works of the law, because by works of the law shall no one be justified. [17] But if, in our endeavor to be justified in Christ, we ourselves were found to be sinners, is Christ then an agent of sin? Certainly not! [18] But if I build up again those things which I tore down, then I prove myself a transgressor. [19] For I through the law died to the law, that I might live to God. [20] I have been crucified with Christ; it is no longer I who live, but Christ who lives in me; and the life I now live in the flesh I live by faith in the Son of God, who loved me and gave himself for me. [21] I do not nullify the grace of God; for if justification[e] were through the law, then Christ died to no purpose.

3 O foolish Galatians! Who has bewitched you, before whose eyes Jesus Christ was publicly portrayed as crucified? [2] Let me ask you only this: Did you receive the Spirit by works of the law, or by hearing with faith? [3] Are you so foolish? Having begun with the Spirit, are you now ending with the flesh? [4] Did you experience so many things in vain?–if it really is in vain. [5] Does he who supplies the Spirit to you and works miracles among you do so by works of the law, or by hearing with faith?

6 Thus Abraham "believed God, and it was reckoned to him as righteousness." [7] So you see that it is men of faith who are the sons of Abraham. [8] And the scripture, foreseeing that God would justify the Gentiles by faith, preached the gospel beforehand to Abraham, saying, "In you shall all the nations be blessed." [9] So then, those who are men of faith are blessed with Abraham who had faith.

10 For all who rely on works of the law are under a curse; for it is written, "Cursed be every one who does not abide by all things written in the book of the law, and do them." [11] Now it is evident that no man is justified before God by the law; for "He who through faith is righteous shall live";[f] [12] but the law does not rest on faith, for "He who does them shall live by them." [13] Christ redeemed us from the curse of the law, having become a curse for us–for it is written, "Cursed be every one who hangs on a tree"– [14] that in Christ Jesus the blessing of Abraham might come upon the Gentiles, that

d Or *reckoned righteous;* and so elsewhere
e Or *righteousness*
f Or *the righteous shall live by faith*

---

and Paul's steadfastness. *Cephas,* see 1.18 n. After his vision (Acts 10.10–35) Peter had recognized that God makes no distinction between Jew and Gentile. But at Antioch, when criticized for table fellowship with converted Gentiles, Peter yielded to the narrow prejudices of the Judaizers (v. 12); his inconsistency was contagious (v. 13). **15–21:** A statement of the fundamental difference between the law and the gospel, concluding with a declaration of Paul's own living faith. **20:** Paul's mystical union with Christ does not destroy his own personality, but sustains and molds his Christian life (compare Jesus' reference to the vine and the branches, Jn.15.1–5).

3.1–18: An appeal to experience and to scripture, proving that justification is by faith, not works. **5:** *Miracles,* wrought *among* (lit. "in") the Galatians, attest the truth of the gospel (on apostolic miracles, compare Rom.15.19; 1 Cor.12.10; 2 Cor.12.12). **6–7:** *Abraham* is typical of all *men of faith* (Gen.15.6; Rom.4.16). **8:** Gen.12.3; compare 18.18; Acts 3.25. **10:** Dt.27.26. **11:** Hab.2.4. **12:** Lev.18.5; Rom.10.5. **13:** Dt.21.23. **16:** *Offspring,* the word used in Gen.12.7

we might receive the promise of the Spirit through faith.

15 To give a human example, brethren: no one annuls even a man's will,[g] or adds to it, once it has been ratified. [16] Now the promises were made to Abraham and to his offspring. It does not say, "And to offsprings," referring to many; but, referring to one, "And to your offspring," which is Christ. [17] This is what I mean: the law, which came four hundred and thirty years afterward, does not annul a covenant previously ratified by God, so as to make the promise void. [18] For if the inheritance is by the law, it is no longer by promise; but God gave it to Abraham by a promise.

19 Why then the law? It was added because of transgressions, till the offspring should come to whom the promise had been made; and it was ordained by angels through an intermediary. [20] Now an intermediary implies more than one; but God is one.

21 Is the law then against the promises of God? Certainly not; for if a law had been given which could make alive, then righteousness would indeed be by the law. [22] But the scripture consigned all things to sin, that what was promised to faith in Jesus Christ might be given to those who believe.

23 Now before faith came, we were confined under the law, kept under restraint until faith should be revealed. [24] So that the law was our custodian until Christ came, that we might be justified by faith. [25] But now that faith has come, we are no longer under a custodian; [26] for in Christ Jesus you are all sons of God, through faith. [27] For as many of you as were baptized into Christ have put on Christ. [28] There is neither Jew nor Greek, there is neither slave nor free, there is neither male nor female; for you are all one in Christ Jesus. [29] And if you are Christ's, then you are Abraham's offspring, heirs according to promise.

4 I mean that the heir, as long as he is a child, is no better than a slave, though he is the owner of all the estate; [2] but he is under guardians and trustees until the date set by the father. [3] So with us; when we were children, we were slaves to the elemental spirits of the universe. [4] But when the time had fully come, God sent forth his Son, born of woman, born under the law, [5] to redeem those who were under the law, so that we might receive adoption as sons. [6] And because you are sons, God has sent the Spirit of his Son into our hearts, crying, "Abba! Father!" [7] So through God you are no longer a slave but a son, and if a son then an heir.

8 Formerly, when you did not know God, you were in bondage to beings that by nature are no gods; [9] but now that you have come to know God, or rather to be known by God, how can

g Or *covenant* (as in verse 17)

---

and 22.17–18 is literally "seed." **17**: The faith-principle is older and more fundamental than the Mosaic law. Paul follows the chronology found in some manuscripts of the Septuagint of Ex.12.40, according to which the 430 years included the sojourn of the patriarchs in Palestine and in Egypt; on the other hand the Hebrew text of Ex.12.40 refers the 430 years solely to the sojourn in Egypt (see also Acts 7.6 n.).

3.19–29: The true purpose of the Mosaic law. Though the law could not make men righteous (v. 21), it revealed God's will so that men might recognize their *transgressions* (vv. 19 and 22; Rom.3.20; 7.7). It is like a *custodian* (see 1 Cor.4.15 n.) who has temporary charge of a child (vv. 24–25). It was not even given by God directly, but (according to later Jewish belief) through *angels* (v. 19; Dt.33.2, Septuagint; see Acts 7.38,53 n.; Heb.2.2). **29**: *Abraham's offspring*, by spiritual kinship (see vv. 6–7 n.).

4.1–31: Bondage under the law; freedom in Christ. 3: *Elemental spirits of the universe*, a better translation is "rudimentary notions of the world," referring to elementary religious observances (vv. 9–10; Col.2.8,20). **4**: The pre-existent Christ became incarnate at a time determined by God in order to ransom those who were in bondage *under the law*. **6**: *Abba*, the Aramaic word meaning "Father" (see Rom.8.15 n.). **4.8–20: Paul reproves the Galatians** for their spiritual immaturity. **9**: *Elemental spirits*, see

you turn back again to the weak and beggarly elemental spirits, whose slaves you want to be once more? [10] You observe days, and months, and seasons, and years! [11] I am afraid I have labored over you in vain.

12 Brethren, I beseech you, become as I am, for I also have become as you are. You did me no wrong; [13] you know it was because of a bodily ailment that I preached the gospel to you at first; [14] and though my condition was a trial to you, you did not scorn or despise me, but received me as an angel of God, as Christ Jesus. [15] What has become of the satisfaction you felt? For I bear you witness that, if possible, you would have plucked out your eyes and given them to me. [16] Have I then become your enemy by telling you the truth?[h] [17] They make much of you, but for no good purpose; they want to shut you out, that you may make much of them. [18] For a good purpose it is always good to be made much of, and not only when I am present with you. [19] My little children, with whom I am again in travail until Christ be formed in you! [20] I could wish to be present with you now and to change my tone, for I am perplexed about you.

21 Tell me, you who desire to be under law, do you not hear the law? [22] For it is written that Abraham had two sons, one by a slave and one by a free woman. [23] But the son of the slave was born according to the flesh, the son of the free woman through promise. [24] Now this is an allegory: these women are two covenants. One is from Mount Sinai, bearing children for slavery; she is Hagar. [25] Now Hagar is Mount Sinai in Arabia;[i] she corresponds to the present Jerusalem, for she is in slavery with her children. [26] But the Jerusalem above is free, and she is our mother. [27] For it is written,

"Rejoice, O barren one who does not bear;
break forth and shout, you who are not in travail;
for the children of the desolate one are many more than the children of her that is married."

[28] Now we,[j] brethren, like Isaac, are children of promise. [29] But as at that time he who was born according to the flesh persecuted him who was born according to the Spirit, so it is now. [30] But what does the scripture say? "Cast out the slave and her son; for the son of the slave shall not inherit with the son of the free woman." [31] So, brethren, we are not children of the slave but of the free woman.

5 For freedom Christ has set us free; stand fast therefore, and do not submit again to a yoke of slavery.

2 Now I, Paul, say to you that if you receive circumcision, Christ will be of no advantage to you. [3] I testify again to every man who receives circumcision that he is bound to keep the whole law. [4] You are severed from Christ, you who would be justified by the law; you have fallen away from grace. [5] For through the Spirit, by faith, we wait for the hope of righteousness. [6] For in Christ Jesus neither circumcision nor uncircumcision is of

h Or *by dealing truly with you*
i Other ancient authorities read *For Sinai is a mountain in Arabia*
j Other ancient authorities read *you*

---

v. 3 n. **10:** They still observe Jewish fast-*days*, new moons (*months;* Col.2.16), Passover *seasons*, and sabbatical *years*. **13–14:** On his first visit through the region of Galatia (Acts 16.6) an illness (was it eye trouble? see v. 15) detained Paul; though he was a care to the Galatians, they treated him with special consideration. **17:** *They,* the Judaizing teachers. **19:** *My little children,* Paul addresses the Galatians as their father in Jesus Christ (1 Cor.4.15).
   4.21–31: Allegory of Hagar and Sarah, showing that those who rely upon the law instead of having faith in God's promise are to be excluded from the inheritance. **22:** Gen.16.15; 21.2,9. **26:** The church is *our mother.* **27:** Is.54.1. **29–30:** Gen.21.9–12.
   5.1–26: The nature of Christian liberty. 2–12: To seek justification by legal works is futile; Christ and the Mosaic law of circumcision are mutually exclusive. Faith alone justifies, but the

any avail, but faith working^x through love. ⁷ You were running well; who hindered you from obeying the truth? ⁸ This persuasion is not from him who calls you. ⁹ A little leaven leavens the whole lump. ¹⁰ I have confidence in the Lord that you will take no other view than mine; and he who is troubling you will bear his judgment, whoever he is. ¹¹ But if I, brethren, still preach circumcision, why am I still persecuted? In that case the stumbling block of the cross has been removed. ¹² I wish those who unsettle you would mutilate themselves!

13 For you were called to freedom, brethren; only do not use your freedom as an opportunity for the flesh, but through love be servants of one another. ¹⁴ For the whole law is fulfilled in one word, "You shall love your neighbor as yourself." ¹⁵ But if you bite and devour one another take heed that you are not consumed by one another.

16 But I say, walk by the Spirit, and do not gratify the desires of the flesh. ¹⁷ For the desires of the flesh are against the Spirit, and the desires of the Spirit are against the flesh; for these are opposed to each other, to prevent you from doing what you would. ¹⁸ But if you are led by the Spirit you are not under the law. ¹⁹ Now the works of the flesh are plain: fornication, impurity, licentiousness, ²⁰ idolatry, sorcery, enmity, strife, jealousy, anger, selfishness, dissension, party spirit, ²¹ envy,^{k} drunkenness, carousing, and the like. I warn you, as I warned you before, that those who do such things shall not inherit the kingdom of God. ²² But the fruit of the Spirit is love, joy, peace, patience, kindness, goodness, faithfulness, ²³ gentleness, self-control; against such there is no law. ²⁴ And those who belong to Christ Jesus have crucified

the flesh with its passions and desires.
25 If we live by the Spirit, let us also walk by the Spirit. ²⁶ Let us have no self-conceit, no provoking of one another, no envy of one another.

6 Brethren, if a man is overtaken in any trespass, you who are spiritual should restore him in a spirit of gentleness. Look to yourself, lest you too be tempted. ² Bear one another's burdens, and so fulfil the law of Christ. ³ For if any one thinks he is something, when he is nothing, he deceives himself. ⁴ But let each one test his own work, and then his reason to boast will be in himself alone and not in his neighbor. ⁵ For each man will have to bear his own load.

6 Let him who is taught the word share all good things with him who teaches.

7 Do not be deceived; God is not mocked, for whatever a man sows, that he will also reap. ⁸ For he who sows to his own flesh will from the flesh reap corruption; but he who sows to the Spirit will from the Spirit reap eternal life. ⁹ And let us not grow weary in well-doing, for in due season we shall reap, if we do not lose heart. ¹⁰ So then, as we have opportunity, let us do good to all men, and especially to those who are of the household of faith.

11 See with what large letters I am writing to you with my own hand. ¹² It is those who want to make a good showing in the flesh that would compel you to be circumcised, and only in order that they may not be persecuted for the cross of Christ. ¹³ For even those who receive circumcision do not themselves keep the law, but they desire to have you circumcised that they may glory in your flesh. ¹⁴ But far be it from me to glory except in the cross

x Or *made effective*
k Other ancient authorities add *murder*

---

faith that justifies is not alone–it produces good works *through love* (v. 6). **12:** A bitterly satirical wish. **13–25:** Though free from the law, Christians must not abuse their liberty. **13:** Mt.20.26. **14:** Lev.19.18; compare Rom.13.8–10. **17:** Rom.7.15–23.
6.1–10: Exhortations to charity and zeal. 2: *The law of Christ* is the law of love. **6:** The church is obligated to support its teachers. **10:** *To all men*, for Christian love is not limited. **11–18:**

of our Lord Jesus Christ, by which[l] the world has been crucified to me, and I to the world. 15 For neither circumcision counts for anything, nor uncircumcision, but a new creation. 16 Peace and mercy be upon all who walk by this rule, upon the Israel of God.

17 Henceforth let no man trouble me; for I bear on my body the marks of Jesus.

18 The grace of our Lord Jesus Christ be with your spirit, brethren. Amen.

l Or *through whom*

Autographic postscript. **15:** Final declaration of what really matters in Christianity (see 5.2–12 n.; 1 Cor.7.19). **16:** The church is God's *Israel* (3.7,9,14,29). **18:** The addition of the word *brethren* to the benediction softens the severity of the whole letter.

EPHESIANS

Regarded by many as the most sublime of all of the apostle Paul's writings, the theme of this brief letter is God's eternal purpose in establishing and completing the universal Church of Jesus Christ. Though drawn from various backgrounds and nationalities, the members of this community have been called by God the Father, redeemed and forgiven through his Son, and incorporated into a fellowship that is sealed and directed by the divine, indwelling Spirit (this Trinitarian emphasis, in a lyrical mood, appears in 1.5,12,13; 2.18–20; 3.14,16,17; 4.4–6). In developing such luminous figures of the church as the body of Christ (1.23; 4.16), the building or temple of God (2.20–22), and the bride of Christ (5.23–32), the author suggests the glorious privilege and destiny of believers as well as their duties.

Written while Paul was a prisoner (3.1; 4.1; 6.20), probably at about the same time as his Letter to the Colossians, Ephesians shares with that letter many of the same phrases and expressions (see the cross references). Its contents may be divided into two main sections, the first chiefly doctrinal (chs. 1–3), the second hortatory and practical (chs. 4–6). Because important early manuscripts and church fathers make no reference to Ephesus in 1.1 (see note *a*), and because the letter contains no local allusions or personal greetings, most scholars regard it as an encyclical or "circular letter," of which copies were distributed by Tychicus (6.21–22) to several churches in Asia Minor. When Paul's correspondence was collected into a corpus, a copy of this letter was probably secured from Ephesus, the capital of the Roman province of Asia, and the present title was then affixed.

Paul, an apostle of Christ Jesus by the will of God,

To the saints who are also faithful*a* in Christ Jesus:

2 Grace to you and peace from God our Father and the Lord Jesus Christ.

3 Blessed be the God and Father of our Lord Jesus Christ, who has blessed us in Christ with every spiritual blessing in the heavenly places, 4 even as he chose us in him before the foundation of the world, that we should be holy and blameless before him. 5 He destined us in love*b* to be his sons through Jesus Christ, according to the purpose of his will, 6 to the praise of his glorious grace which he freely bestowed on us in the Beloved. 7 In him we have redemption through his blood, the forgiveness of our trespasses, according to the riches of his grace 8 which he lavished upon us. 9 For he has made known to us in all wisdom and insight the mystery of his will, according to his purpose which he set forth in Christ 10 as a plan for the fulness of time, to unite all things in him, things in heaven and things on earth.

11 In him, according to the purpose of him who accomplishes all things according to the counsel of his will, 12 we who first hoped in Christ have been destined and appointed to live for the praise of his glory. 13 In him you also, who have heard the word of truth, the gospel of your salvation, and have believed in him, were sealed with the

a Other ancient authorities read *who are at Ephesus and faithful*
b Or *before him in love, having destined us*

1.1–2: Salutation, see Introduction and Rom.1.1–7 n. **2:** *Grace . . . peace,* see 2 Th.1.2 n.
1.3–23: Thanksgiving for blessings and prayer for spiritual wisdom (see Rom.1.8–15 n.).
3: *In the heavenly places,* an expression, found only in this letter (1.20; 2.6; 3.10; 6.12), referring to the unseen spiritual world behind and above the material universe. **4–10:** God *chose us . . .* and *destined us* to be *his sons* in accord with his eternal *purpose in Christ . . . to unite* heaven and earth in him. **6:** *To his praise,* a refrain thrice repeated, referring to the Father (v. 6), the Son (v. 12), and Holy Spirit (vv. 13–14). **7:** *Redemption through his blood,* Mk.10.45; 14.24; see Heb.9.11 n. **9:** The word *mystery* everywhere in Ephesians (except 5.32) and Colossians refers to God's age-long purpose, now disclosed to his chosen, to call Gentiles as well as Jews to share in Christ's redemptive work (3.4–6). **10:** *Fulness of time,* Gal.4.4. **13:** *You also,* "you

promised Holy Spirit, [14] which is the guarantee of our inheritance until we acquire possession of it, to the praise of his glory.

15 For this reason, because I have heard of your faith in the Lord Jesus and your love[c] toward all the saints, [16] I do not cease to give thanks for you, remembering you in my prayers, [17] that the God of our Lord Jesus Christ, the Father of glory, may give you a spirit of wisdom and of revelation in the knowledge of him, [18] having the eyes of your hearts enlightened, that you may know what is the hope to which he has called you, what are the riches of his glorious inheritance in the saints, [19] and what is the immeasurable greatness of his power in us who believe, according to the working of his great might [20] which he accomplished in Christ when he raised him from the dead and made him sit at his right hand in the heavenly places, [21] far above all rule and authority and power and dominion, and above every name that is named, not only in this age but also in that which is to come; [22] and he has put all things under his feet and has made him the head over all things for the church, [23] which is his body, the fulness of him who fills all in all.

2 And you he made alive, when you were dead through the trespasses and sins [2] in which you once walked, following the course of this world, following the prince of the power of the air, the spirit that is now at work in the sons of disobedience. [3] Among these we all once lived in the passions of our flesh, following the desires of body and mind, and so we were by nature children of wrath, like the rest of mankind. [4] But God, who is rich in mercy, out of the great love with which he loved us, [5] even when we were dead through our trespasses, made us alive together with Christ (by grace you have been saved), [6] and raised us up with him, and made us sit with him in the heavenly places in Christ Jesus, [7] that in the coming ages he might show the immeasurable riches of his grace in kindness toward us in Christ Jesus. [8] For by grace you have been saved through faith; and this is not your own doing, it is the gift of God– [9] not because of works, lest any man should boast. [10] For we are his workmanship, created in Christ Jesus for good works, which God prepared beforehand, that we should walk in them.

11 Therefore remember that at one time you Gentiles in the flesh, called the uncircumcision by what is called the circumcision, which is made in the flesh by hands– [12] remember that you were at that time separated from Christ, alienated from the commonwealth of Israel, and strangers to the covenants of promise, having no hope and without God in the world. [13] But now in Christ Jesus you who once were far off have been brought near in the blood of Christ. [14] For he is our peace, who has made us both one, and has broken down the dividing wall of hostility, [15] by abolishing in his flesh the law of commandments and ordinances, that he might create in himself one

c Other ancient authorities omit *your love*

Gentiles as well as we Jews." *Promised*, Lk.24.49; Jn.14.26; Acts 1.4; 2.33. **14:** *Guarantee*, see 2 Cor.1.22 n. **22–23:** The church, as the *fulness* of Christ, is the complement of his mystic person; he is the *head*, the church *is his body*.

2.1–22: Christ's benefits, for both Gentiles and Jews. **1:** *Dead*, v. 5; Col.2.13. **2:** *The prince of the power of the air*, Satan (6.11–12; Col.1.13). **3:** *By nature*, man's state apart from God's grace in Christ. *Wrath*, see Col.3.6 n. **5:** *Grace*, God's unmerited favor shown to mankind in Christ. **8:** *Through faith*, as the channel; Paul never says, "saved because of faith." *This*, namely, your salvation. **10:** *Good works* are the result, not the cause, of salvation. *Beforehand* ascribes the whole matter to God. **11:** *Called . . . called*, since the distinction between Jew and Gentile is removed in Christ (Col.3.11) the terms "circumcision" and "uncircumcision" are obsolete. **12:** The plight of the Gentiles apart from Christ. **13–22:** *But now* the reconciling work of Christ avails also for Gentiles, *who once were far off* from God and his people. *In the blood of Christ*, by the new covenant (see 1.7 n.). **14–16:** Christ has not only *broken down the . . . hostility* be-

new man in place of the two, so making peace, [16] and might reconcile us both to God in one body through the cross, thereby bringing the hostility to an end. [17] And he came and preached peace to you who were far off and peace to those who were near; [18] for through him we both have access in one Spirit to the Father. [19] So then you are no longer strangers and sojourners, but you are fellow citizens with the saints and members of the household of God, [20] built upon the foundation of the apostles and prophets, Christ Jesus himself being the cornerstone, [21] in whom the whole structure is joined together and grows into a holy temple in the Lord; [22] in whom you also are built into it for a dwelling place of God in the Spirit.

3 For this reason I, Paul, a prisoner for Christ Jesus on behalf of you Gentiles— [2] assuming that you have heard of the stewardship of God's grace that was given to me for you, [3] how the mystery was made known to me by revelation, as I have written briefly. [4] When you read this you can perceive my insight into the mystery of Christ, [5] which was not made known to the sons of men in other generations as it has now been revealed to his holy apostles and prophets by the Spirit; [6] that is, how the Gentiles are fellow heirs, members of the same body, and partakers of the promise in Christ Jesus through the gospel.

7 Of this gospel I was made a min-

ister according to the gift of God's grace which was given me by the working of his power. [8] To me, though I am the very least of all the saints, this grace was given, to preach to the Gentiles the unsearchable riches of Christ, [9] and to make all men see what is the plan of the mystery hidden for ages in[d] God who created all things; [10] that through the church the manifold wisdom of God might now be made known to the principalities and powers in the heavenly places. [11] This was according to the eternal purpose which he has realized in Christ Jesus our Lord, [12] in whom we have boldness and confidence of access through our faith in him. [13] So I ask you not to[e] lose heart over what I am suffering for you, which is your glory.

14 For this reason I bow my knees before the Father, [15] from whom every family in heaven and on earth is named, [16] that according to the riches of his glory he may grant you to be strengthened with might through his Spirit in the inner man, [17] and that Christ may dwell in your hearts through faith; that you, being rooted and grounded in love, [18] may have power to comprehend with all the saints what is the breadth and length and height and depth, [19] and to know the love of Christ which surpasses knowledge, that you may be filled with all the fulness of God.

20 Now to him who by the power

d Or *by*   *e* Or *I ask that I may not*

---

tween Jew and Gentile (*made us both one*), but has reconciled *both to God in one body,* the church. **16:** *Both,* Jew and Gentile. **17:** Is.52.7; 57.19. **18:** The unity of Christians *in one body,* the church (v. 16), is based on their participation *in one Spirit.* **19:** *Strangers,* v. 12. **20–22:** *The foundation,* laid by *the apostles and* Christian *prophets* (3.5; 4.11; Acts 13.1). The *whole structure* depends upon Christ as the *cornerstone* (a Messianic designation, compare Is.28.16; Mt.21.42). Christians are built into a growing *temple* or *dwelling place of God* (1 Cor.3.16–17; 1 Pet.2.4–5).

3.1–20: A prayer for wisdom, interrupted by a parenthesis on Paul's mission to the Gentiles (vv. 2–13). **1:** Paul was *a prisoner* because he had aroused the hostility of the Jews by advocating the equality of the *Gentiles* in the church (Acts 21.21,28; 22.21–22). **2:** Col.1.25. **3:** *Mystery,* see 1.9 n. *By revelation,* 1.17; Acts 9.3–4; Gal.1.12. *Briefly,* in 1.9–10. **5:** Christian *prophets,* see 2.20. **6:** The content of the *mystery,* v. 3. **7:** *Minister,* Col.1.23,25. **8:** *Least,* 1 Cor.15.9. *Unsearchable,* in their nature, extent, and application (v. 19; Rom.11.33). **10:** By means of *the church* God's *manifold* ("richly variegated," as a tapestry) *wisdom* in the plan of redemption is displayed to angelic beings (1 Cor.4.9). **12:** 2.18. **14–19:** Paul's prayer. **14:** *For this reason,* resumes v. 1. **14–15:** *Father, family,* a play on words in Greek ("pater," "patria"); God is the Author of all fatherhood. **18:** *The breadth . . . and depth,* of Christ's love. **20–21:** The

at work within us is able to do far more abundantly than all that we ask or think, ²¹ to him be glory in the church and in Christ Jesus to all generations, for ever and ever. Amen.

4 I therefore, a prisoner for the Lord, beg you to lead a life worthy of the calling to which you have been called, ² with all lowliness and meekness, with patience, forbearing one another in love, ³ eager to maintain the unity of the Spirit in the bond of peace. ⁴ There is one body and one Spirit, just as you were called to the one hope that belongs to your call, ⁵ one Lord, one faith, one baptism, ⁶ one God and Father of us all, who is above all and through all and in all. ⁷ But grace was given to each of us according to the measure of Christ's gift. ⁸ Therefore it is said,

"When he ascended on high he led
     a host of captives,
and he gave gifts to men."

⁹ (In saying, "He ascended," what does it mean but that he had also descended into the lower parts of the earth? ¹⁰ He who descended is he who also ascended far above all the heavens, that he might fill all things.) ¹¹ And his gifts were that some should be apostles, some prophets, some evangelists, some pastors and teachers, ¹² to equip the saints for the work of ministry, for building up the body of Christ, ¹³ until we all attain to the unity of the faith and of the knowledge of the Son of God, to mature manhood, to the measure of the stature of the fulness of Christ; ¹⁴ so that we may no longer be children, tossed to and fro and carried about with every wind of doctrine, by the cunning of men, by their craftiness in deceitful wiles. ¹⁵ Rather, speaking the truth in love, we are to grow up in every way into him who is the head, into Christ, ¹⁶ from whom the whole body, joined and knit together by every joint with which it is supplied, when each part is working properly, makes bodily growth and upbuilds itself in love.

17 Now this I affirm and testify in the Lord, that you must no longer live as the Gentiles do, in the futility of their minds; ¹⁸ they are darkened in their understanding, alienated from the life of God because of the ignorance that is in them, due to their hardness of heart; ¹⁹ they have become callous and have given themselves up to licentiousness, greedy to practice every kind of uncleanness. ²⁰ You did not so learn Christ!– ²¹ assuming that you have heard about him and were taught in him, as the truth is in Jesus. ²² Put off your old nature which belongs to your former manner of life and is corrupt through deceitful lusts, ²³ and be renewed in the spirit of your minds, ²⁴and put on the new nature, created after the likeness of God in true righteousness and holiness.

25 Therefore, putting away falsehood, let every one speak the truth with his neighbor, for we are members one of another. ²⁶ Be angry but do not sin; do not let the sun go down on your anger, ²⁷ and give no opportunity to the devil. ²⁸ Let the thief no longer steal, but rather let him labor, doing honest work with his hands, so that he may be able to give to those in need. ²⁹ Let no evil talk come out of your mouths, but only such as is good

---

doxology celebrates God's boundless generosity and his *glory* both *in the church and in Jesus Christ.*
     4.1–6.20: Ethical implications of the doctrinal teaching in chs.1–3. **4.1–16: An appeal to maintain the unity of the faith. 2:** Col.3.12–13. **4–6:** Seven elements of unity. **7–16:** Christian unity amid diversity of spiritual gifts. **8:** Ps.68.18. *Captives*, the enemies of Christ's kingdom (Col.2.15). **9:** *Lower parts*, the region of the grave. **10:** The same Christ, after his burial, was exalted that he might fill all things with himself. **11:** *Pastors and teachers*, two aspects of one ministry. **12:** All Christians are to be equipped *for the work of* active spiritual service. **15:** The verb means both *speaking* and doing.
     4.17–5.20: An appeal to renounce pagan ways. 4.17–19: Rom.1.21–25. **22:** *Put off*, like filthy, worn-out clothes (Col.3.9; see Rom.6.6 n.). **25:** Zech.8.16; Rom.12.5. **26:** If angry, let it neither

for edifying, as fits the occasion, that it may impart grace to those who hear. ³⁰ And do not grieve the Holy Spirit of God, in whom you were sealed for the day of redemption. ³¹ Let all bitterness and wrath and anger and clamor and slander be put away from you, with all malice, ³² and be kind to one another, tenderhearted, forgiving one another, as God in Christ forgave you.

5 Therefore be imitators of God, as beloved children. ² And walk in love, as Christ loved us and gave himself up for us, a fragrant offering and sacrifice to God.

3 But fornication and all impurity or covetousness must not even be named among you, as is fitting among saints. ⁴ Let there be no filthiness, nor silly talk, nor levity, which are not fitting; but instead let there be thanksgiving. ⁵ Be sure of this, that no fornicator or impure man, or one who is covetous (that is, an idolater), has any inheritance in the kingdom of Christ and of God. ⁶ Let no one deceive you with empty words, for it is because of these things that the wrath of God comes upon the sons of disobedience. ⁷ Therefore do not associate with them, ⁸ for once you were darkness, but now you are light in the Lord; walk as children of light ⁹ (for the fruit of light is found in all that is good and right and true), ¹⁰ and try to learn what is pleasing to the Lord. ¹¹ Take no part in the unfruitful works of darkness, but instead expose them. ¹² For it is a shame even to speak of the things that they do in secret; ¹³ but when anything is exposed by the light it becomes visible,

for anything that becomes visible is light. ¹⁴ Therefore it is said,

"Awake, O sleeper, and arise from the dead,
and Christ shall give you light."

15 Look carefully then how you walk, not as unwise men but as wise, ¹⁶ making the most of the time, because the days are evil. ¹⁷ Therefore do not be foolish, but understand what the will of the Lord is. ¹⁸ And do not get drunk with wine, for that is debauchery; but be filled with the Spirit, ¹⁹ addressing one another in psalms and hymns and spiritual songs, singing and making melody to the Lord with all your heart, ²⁰ always and for everything giving thanks in the name of our Lord Jesus Christ to God the Father.

21 Be subject to one another out of reverence for Christ. ²² Wives, be subject to your husbands, as to the Lord. ²³ For the husband is the head of the wife as Christ is the head of the church, his body, and is himself its Savior. ²⁴ As the church is subject to Christ, so let wives also be subject in everything to their husbands. ²⁵ Husbands, love your wives, as Christ loved the church and gave himself up for her, ²⁶ that he might sanctify her, having cleansed her by the washing of water with the word, ²⁷ that he might present the church to himself in splendor, without spot or wrinkle or any such thing, that she might be holy and without blemish. ²⁸ Even so husbands should love their wives as their own bodies. He who loves his wife loves himself. ²⁹ For no man ever hates his own flesh, but nourishes and cherishes it, as Christ does the church, ³⁰ because we are members of his body. ³¹ "For this reason a man

be in a sinful spirit nor prolonged (Ps.4.4; Jas.1.19–20). **28**: *Give*, not merely in restitution, but in liberality. **29**: Col.3.8. *As God . . . forgave*, Christian conduct is the corollary of Christian doctrine (Phil.2.5–8; Col.3.1–3). **5.1**: *Imitators of God*, in forgiving (4.32) and in loving. **2**: *Gave himself up* to death as a sacrifice *for us*. **4**: *Levity*, of a licentious nature. **5**: *Covetous*, see Col.3.5 n. **6**: *Wrath*, see Col.3.6 n. **9**: Gal.5.22–23. **11**: Gal.5.19–21. **14**: Quoted perhaps from an early Christian hymn based on Is.60.1. **16**: Col.4.5. **19**: Col.3.16.

5.21–6.9: The Christian household (Col.3.18–4.1): husband and wife (5.21–33), children and parents (6.1–4), masters and slaves (6.5–9). **5.21**: The general principle is that of mutual subjection (Phil.2.3), on which the following applications rest. **23**: Being *the head of the wife* involves responsibility for cherishing and protecting her (vv. 25,29). **25**: *Gave*, see 5.2 n. **26**:

shall leave his father and mother and be joined to his wife, and the two shall become one flesh." [32] This mystery is a profound one, and I am saying that it refers to Christ and the church; [33] however, let each one of you love his wife as himself, and let the wife see that she respects her husband.

6 Children, obey your parents in the Lord, for this is right. [2] "Honor your father and mother" (this is the first commandment with a promise), [3] "that it may be well with you and that you may live long on the earth." [4] Fathers, do not provoke your children to anger, but bring them up in the discipline and instruction of the Lord.

5 Slaves, be obedient to those who are your earthly masters, with fear and trembling, in singleness of heart, as to Christ; [6] not in the way of eye-service, as men-pleasers, but as servants[f] of Christ, doing the will of God from the heart, [7] rendering service with a good will as to the Lord and not to men, [8] knowing that whatever good any one does, he will receive the same again from the Lord, whether he is a slave or free. [9] Masters, do the same to them, and forbear threatening, knowing that he who is both their Master and yours is in heaven, and that there is no partiality with him.

10 Finally, be strong in the Lord and in the strength of his might. [11] Put on the whole armor of God, that you may be able to stand against the wiles of the devil. [12] For we are not contending against flesh and blood, but against the principalities, against the powers, against the world rulers of this present darkness, against the spiritual hosts of wickedness in the heavenly places. [13] Therefore take the whole armor of God, that you may be able to withstand in the evil day, and having done all, to stand. [14] Stand therefore, having girded your loins with truth, and having put on the breastplate of righteousness, [15] and having shod your feet with the equipment of the gospel of peace; [16] besides all these, taking the shield of faith, with which you can quench all the flaming darts of the evil one. [17] And take the helmet of salvation, and the sword of the Spirit, which is the word of God. [18] Pray at all times in the Spirit, with all prayer and supplication. To that end keep alert with all perseverance, making supplication for all the saints, [19] and also for me, that utterance may be given me in opening my mouth boldly to proclaim the mystery of the gospel, [20] for which I am an ambassador in chains; that I may declare it boldly, as I ought to speak.

21 Now that you also may know how I am and what I am doing, Tych'icus the beloved brother and faithful minister in the Lord will tell you everything. [22] I have sent him to you for this very purpose, that you may know how we are, and that he may encourage your hearts.

23 Peace be to the brethren, and love with faith, from God the Father and the Lord Jesus Christ. [24] Grace be with all who love our Lord Jesus Christ with love undying.

f Or slaves

Christian baptism. **27:** 2 Cor.11.2; Rev.21.2. **31:** Gen.2.24. **32:** *This mystery*, namely Christ's spiritual union with our humanity, is of great significance in understanding the nature of human marriage. **33:** Here, implicitly, polygamy is made impossible. **6.2:** Ex.20.12. **3:** Dt.5.16. **4:** Col.3.21. **8:** Col.3.22; on slavery, see Introduction to Philemon. **9:** God shows *no partiality* to social status (Col.3.25–4.1).

    6.10–20: God's armor and the Christian's warfare. 12: *Flesh and blood*, that is, mere mortal beings. *Principalities . . . hosts of wickedness*, organized forces of malevolent spirit beings (see Rom.8.38 n.; Rev.12.7–9). **13–17:** The armor which God wears (Is.11.5; 59.17) and supplies. **15:** Is.52.7. **17:** *The sword* (the one offensive weapon mentioned here) is the word which God speaks through his servants (Hos.6.5; Mt.10.19–20; compare Heb.4.12). **18–20:** Persevering prayer (Col.4.2–4) is an aid in standing (v. 14). **19:** *Mystery*, see 1.9 n.

    6.21–24: Personal matters and benediction. 24: *Grace . . . with love undying*, a worthy conclusion, returning to the fundamental thought of 1.3–14.

THE LETTER OF PAUL TO THE

PHILIPPIANS

This letter, one of the most cordial and affectionate we have from Paul's hand, was addressed to the Christians at Philippi in Macedonia. They formed the first congregation established through the apostle on European soil (Acts 16.11–15), and Paul's relations with them in all the years afterward seem to have been extraordinarily close and happy.

Except that Paul was then in prison and awaiting trial (1.12–26), it is impossible to speak confidently of the time and place of the writing of this letter. Because of references to the praetorian guard and to Caesar's household and also because the situation reflected in the letter bears some resemblance to that described at the very end of the book of Acts, most scholars put its composition during the period of Paul's imprisonment at Rome (about A.D. 61–63); but the indications are by no means conclusive and other scholars have proposed Caesarea or Ephesus at earlier stages in Paul's career.

The immediate occasion of Paul's writing was the return to Philippi of Epaphroditus (2.25–29), who had been sent by the church there with a gift for Paul (4.18). The apostle took this opportunity to describe his own situation and state of mind to his Philippian brethren, to thank them for their gift, and to give them certain needed instructions. The entire letter breathes Paul's radiant joy and serene happiness in Christ, even while in prison and in danger of death (2.2; 3.8–14; 4.11–13).

PAUL AND TIMOTHY, SERVANTS[a] OF Christ Jesus,

To all the saints in Christ Jesus who are at Philip'pi, with the bishops[b] and deacons: 2 Grace to you and peace from God our Father and the Lord Jesus Christ.

3 I thank my God in all my remembrance of you, 4 always in every prayer of mine for you all making my prayer with joy, 5 thankful for your partnership in the gospel from the first day until now. 6 And I am sure that he who began a good work in you will bring it to completion at the day of Jesus Christ. 7 It is right for me to feel thus about you all, because I hold you in my heart, for you are all partakers with me of grace, both in my imprisonment and in the defense and confirmation of the gospel. 8 For God is my witness, how I yearn for you all with the affection of Christ Jesus. 9 And it is my prayer that your love may abound more and more, with knowledge and all discernment, 10 so that you may approve what is excellent, and may be pure and blameless for the day of Christ, 11 filled with the fruits of righteousness which come through Jesus Christ, to the glory and praise of God.

12 I want you to know, brethren, that what has happened to me has really served to advance the gospel, 13 so that it has become known throughout the whole praetorian guard[c] and to all the rest that my imprisonment is for Christ; 14 and most of the brethren have been made confident in the Lord because of my imprisonment, and are much more bold to speak the word of God without fear.

15 Some indeed preach Christ from

a Or slaves   b Or overseers
c Greek in the whole praetorium

1.1–2: **Salutation**, see Rom.1.1–7 n. **1**: *Bishops and deacons*, i.e. "overseers" and "assistants" (compare 1 Cor.12.28). **2**: *Grace . . . peace*, see 2 Th.1.2 n.

1.3–11: **Thanksgiving**, see Rom.1.8–15 n. **5**: *Partnership*, see Introduction. **6**: *The day of Jesus Christ*, the day when he will return and the present age will end (1 Cor.1.8; compare 2 Th.2.3 and 2 Pet.3.10).

1.12–26: **Paul's present circumstances.** **12**: See v. 7. **13**: Paul is under military guard; and now all the members of the local headquarters (compare note *c*) know why he is there, and so have heard at least the name of Christ. **15–18**: That some of Paul's fellow-Christians regarded

envy and rivalry, but others from good will. [16] The latter do it out of love, knowing that I am put here for the defense of the gospel; [17] the former proclaim Christ out of partisanship, not sincerely but thinking to afflict me in my imprisonment. [18] What then? Only that in every way, whether in pretense or in truth, Christ is proclaimed; and in that I rejoice.

19 Yes, and I shall rejoice. For I know that through your prayers and the help of the Spirit of Jesus Christ this will turn out for my deliverance, [20] as it is my eager expectation and hope that I shall not be at all ashamed, but that with full courage now as always Christ will be honored in my body, whether by life or by death. [21] For to me to live is Christ, and to die is gain. [22] If it is to be life in the flesh, that means fruitful labor for me. Yet which I shall choose I cannot tell. [23] I am hard pressed between the two. My desire is to depart and be with Christ, for that is far better. [24] But to remain in the flesh is more necessary on your account. [25] Convinced of this, I know that I shall remain and continue with you all, for your progress and joy in the faith, [26] so that in me you may have ample cause to glory in Christ Jesus, because of my coming to you again.

27 Only let your manner of life be worthy of the gospel of Christ, so that whether I come and see you or am absent, I may hear of you that you stand firm in one spirit, with one mind striving side by side for the faith of the gospel, [28] and not frightened in anything by your opponents. This is a clear omen to them of their destruction, but of your salvation, and that from God. [29] For it has been granted to you that for the sake of Christ you should not only believe in him but also suffer for his sake, [30] engaged in the same conflict which you saw and now hear to be mine.

2 So if there is any encouragement in Christ, any incentive of love, any participation in the Spirit, any affection and sympathy, [2] complete my joy by being of the same mind, having the same love, being in full accord and of one mind. [3] Do nothing from selfishness or conceit, but in humility count others better than yourselves. [4] Let each of you look not only to his own interests, but also to the interests of others. [5] Have this mind among yourselves, which is yours in Christ Jesus, [6] who, though he was in the form of God, did not count equality with God a thing to be grasped, [7] but emptied himself, taking the form of a servant,[d] being born in the likeness of men. [8] And being found in human form he humbled himself and became obedient unto death, even death on a cross. [9] Therefore God has highly exalted him and bestowed on him the name which is above every name, [10] that at the name of Jesus every knee should bow, in heaven and on earth and under the earth, [11] and every tongue confess that Jesus Christ is Lord, to the glory of God the Father.

12 Therefore, my beloved, as you have always obeyed, so now, not only as in my presence but much more in my absence, work out your own salvation with fear and trembling; [13] for God

d Or *slave*

him with suspicion and ill-will appears in Galatians and in 1 and 2 Corinthians (especially 2 Cor. chs. 10–13). **21–24:** His life is not his own but belongs utterly to Christ; therefore *to depart and be with Christ* is *gain;* but this would mean loss to his churches. **25–26:** It is not known whether Paul's expectation was fulfilled or not. **28–30:** The *omen* consists in the church's brave, united witness to Christ even at the cost of *conflict* and suffering.

2.1–18: Humility and the example of Christ. 1–2: The "if" is rhetorical; with Christ's *encouragement* and moved by God's *love* for them, they are to *complete* Paul's *joy.* **3:** He has reason to fear that they are somewhat divided by petty jealousies (4.2). **6:** *In the form of God,* that is, pre-existent and divine (Jn.1.1–3; Col.1.15). *A thing to be grasped,* and never relinquished. **7:** *But emptied himself,* the extreme limit of self-denial. *Servant,* perhaps an allusion to Is.52.13–53.12. *Born,* Jn.1.14. **8:** Mt.26.39; Jn.10.18; Rom.5.19; Heb.5.8; 12.2. **9:** *Exalted,* at the resurrection. *The name* is "Lord" (see 1 Th.1.1 n.). **10–11:** Compare Is.45.23. **12:** *With fear and*

is at work in you, both to will and to work for his good pleasure.

14 Do all things without grumbling or questioning, 15 that you may be blameless and innocent, children of God without blemish in the midst of a crooked and perverse generation, among whom you shine as lights in the world, 16 holding fast the word of life, so that in the day of Christ I may be proud that I did not run in vain or labor in vain. 17 Even if I am to be poured as a libation upon the sacrificial offering of your faith, I am glad and rejoice with you all. 18 Likewise you also should be glad and rejoice with me.

19 I hope in the Lord Jesus to send Timothy to you soon, so that I may be cheered by news of you. 20 I have no one like him, who will be genuinely anxious for your welfare. 21 They all look after their own interests, not those of Jesus Christ. 22 But Timothy's worth you know, how as a son with a father he has served with me in the gospel. 23 I hope therefore to send him just as soon as I see how it will go with me; 24 and I trust in the Lord that shortly I myself shall come also.

25 I have thought it necessary to send to you Epaphrodi'tus my brother and fellow worker and fellow soldier, and your messenger and minister to my need, 26 for he has been longing for you all, and has been distressed because you heard that he was ill. 27 Indeed he was ill, near to death. But God had mercy on him, and not only on him but on me also, lest I should have sorrow upon sorrow. 28 I am the more eager to send him, therefore, that you may rejoice at seeing him again, and that I may be less anxious. 29 So receive him in the Lord with all joy; and honor such men, 30 for he nearly died for the work of Christ, risking his life to complete your service to me.

3 Finally, my brethren, rejoice in the Lord. To write the same things to you is not irksome to me, and is safe for you.

2 Look out for the dogs, look out for the evil-workers, look out for those who mutilate the flesh. 3 For we are the true circumcision, who worship God in spirit,*e* and glory in Christ Jesus, and put no confidence in the flesh. 4 Though I myself have reason for confidence in the flesh also. If any other man thinks he has reason for confidence in the flesh, I have more: 5 circumcised on the eighth day, of the people of Israel, of the tribe of Benjamin, a Hebrew born of Hebrews; as to the law a Pharisee, 6 as to zeal a persecutor of the church, as to righteousness under the law blameless. 7 But whatever gain I had, I counted as loss for the sake of Christ. 8 Indeed I count everything as loss because of the surpassing worth of knowing Christ Jesus my Lord. For his sake I have suffered the loss of all things, and count them as refuse, in order that I may gain Christ 9 and be found in him, not having a righteousness of my own, based on law, but that which is through faith in Christ, the

e Other ancient authorities read *worship by the Spirit of God*

---

trembling, humbly and with constant dependence on God's help. **14:** *Without grumbling,* compare 1 Cor.10.9–10. **16:** *Day of Christ,* see 1.6 n. **17:** A reminder that Paul stands in danger of condemnation and death.

   2.19–30: Timothy and Epaphroditus. 19: *Timothy,* Acts 16.1–3; 1 Cor.16.10–11; see Introduction to 2 Timothy. **23–24:** A reference to the uncertainty of how his impending trial will end (1.19,26). **25:** *Epaphroditus,* see Introduction and 4.18.

   3.1–11: A warning. 1: *The same things,* he has given this warning before. **2:** A bitter and ironical reference to those who preach the necessity of circumcision (compare Gal.5.12). **3:** *True circumcision,* Jer.4.4; Rom.2.28–29; Gal.6.14–15; Col.2.11–13. *The flesh,* outward states or rites. **5:** *A Hebrew* . . . , though living in a Greek city (Tarsus) Paul's family spoke the language of Palestine (Acts 21.40; 22.2). *Pharisee,* one who carefully observed the Jewish law. **6:** *A persecutor,* Acts 9.1–2; 1 Cor.15.9; Gal.1.13. *Under the law blameless,* so far as its external requirements are concerned. No contradiction need be found between this statement and what Paul says in Rom.3.20 and 7.7–25. **9:** *The righteousness from God,* a free gift, dependent only

righteousness from God that depends on faith; [10] that I may know him and the power of his resurrection, and may share his sufferings, becoming like him in his death, [11] that if possible I may attain the resurrection from the dead.

12 Not that I have already obtained this or am already perfect; but I press on to make it my own, because Christ Jesus has made me his own. [13] Brethren, I do not consider that I have made it my own; but one thing I do, forgetting what lies behind and straining forward to what lies ahead, [14] I press on toward the goal for the prize of the upward call of God in Christ Jesus. [15] Let those of us who are mature be thus minded; and if in anything you are otherwise minded, God will reveal that also to you. [16] Only let us hold true to what we have attained.

17 Brethren, join in imitating me, and mark those who so live as you have an example in us. [18] For many, of whom I have often told you and now tell you even with tears, live as enemies of the cross of Christ. [19] Their end is destruction, their god is the belly, and they glory in their shame, with minds set on earthly things. [20] But our commonwealth is in heaven, and from it we await a Savior, the Lord Jesus Christ, [21] who will change our lowly body to be like his glorious body, by the power which enables him even to subject all things to himself.

4 Therefore, my brethren, whom I love and long for, my joy and crown, stand firm thus in the Lord, my beloved.

2 I entreat Eu-o'dia and I entreat Syn'tyche to agree in the Lord. [3] And I ask you also, true yokefellow, help these women, for they have labored side by side with me in the gospel together with Clement and the rest of my fellow workers, whose names are in the book of life.

4 Rejoice in the Lord always; again I will say, Rejoice. [5] Let all men know your forbearance. The Lord is at hand. [6] Have no anxiety about anything, but in everything by prayer and supplication with thanksgiving let your requests be made known to God. [7] And the peace of God, which passes all understanding, will keep your hearts and your minds in Christ Jesus.

8 Finally, brethren, whatever is true, whatever is honorable, whatever is just, whatever is pure, whatever is lovely, whatever is gracious, if there is any excellence, if there is anything worthy of praise, think about these things. [9] What you have learned and received and heard and seen in me, do; and the God of peace will be with you.

10 I rejoice in the Lord greatly that now at length you have revived your concern for me; you were indeed concerned for me, but you had no opportunity. [11] Not that I complain of want; for I have learned, in whatever state I am, to be content. [12] I know how to be abased, and I know how to abound; in any and all circumstances I have learned the secret of facing plenty and hunger, abundance and want. [13] I can do all things in him who strengthens me.

14 Yet it was kind of you to share

upon man's willingness humbly to receive it (Rom.1.16–4.25). **10–11:** Actually to know Christ as risen and living is to have *power* to suffer like him and for him, and to possess the sure hope of rising and living with him.

3.12–21: Confession and exhortation. 12–14: Though righteousness is God's gift, Christians are not relieved of the obligation of serious effort. *The prize* is God's *upward call* to share his glory (Rom.5.2). **18–19:** *Many*, presumably professing Christians, but probably not the Judaizers of 3.2, whom the description scarcely fits. **20:** *Our commonwealth*, our real homeland. **21:** Rom.8.23; 1 Cor.15.47–57; 2 Cor.5.1–5; Col.3.1–4.

4.1–23: Final appeals. 1: *Joy and crown*, 1 Th.2.19–20. **2:** *Euodia . . . Syntyche*, two women in the Philippian church who had been disagreeing. **3:** *True yokefellow*, probably a leader in the church at Philippi. The Greek word for *yokefellow* may be understood as a proper name, Syzygus. **5:** Ps.119.151. **10:** A reference to the gift which Epaphroditus brought; see Introduc-

my trouble. ¹⁵ And you Philippians yourselves know that in the beginning of the gospel, when I left Macedo´nia, no church entered into partnership with me in giving and receiving except you only; ¹⁶ for even in Thessaloni´ca you sent me help*f* once and again. ¹⁷ Not that I seek the gift; but I seek the fruit which increases to your credit. ¹⁸ I have received full payment, and more; I am filled, having received from Epaphrodi´tus the gifts you sent, a fragrant offering, a sacrifice acceptable and pleasing to God. ¹⁹ And my God will supply every need of yours according to his riches in glory in Christ Jesus. ²⁰ To our God and Father be glory for ever and ever. Amen.

21 Greet every saint in Christ Jesus. The brethren who are with me greet you. ²² All the saints greet you, especially those of Caesar's household. 23 The grace of the Lord Jesus Christ be with your spirit.

f Other ancient authorities read *money for my needs*

tion and 2.25–30. **14:** *My trouble*, the deprivations and disappointments attendant upon imprisonment. **16:** According to Acts 17.1, Paul had gone to Thessalonica immediately after his stay in Philippi. **22:** *Caesar's household*, those in the service of the emperor, who at that time was Nero.

COLOSSIANS

Colossae was a rather insignificant town of Phrygia in Asia Minor, not far from Ephesus. Paul had sent Epaphras, a Colossian, to preach there (1.7; 4.12). Subsequently the apostle heard the disquieting news of the activity of false teachers in the newly founded church, and he wrote this letter to correct their erroneous speculations. These teachers, who claimed to possess superior knowledge of divine matters (2.18), advocated a theosophical mixture of ascetic (2.16,20–23) and ritualistic (2.16–18) practices, some of which had certain parallels in the Jewish sect of the Essenes (see "Survey of . . . Bible Lands," § 15, end).

The letter falls into two main parts, the doctrinal section (1.1–3.4), and the practical exhortations (3.5–4.18). In the first part Paul emphasizes the supremacy and all-sufficiency of Christ in the cosmos (1.15–17), in the church (1.18–20), and in the individual (2.9–12). In the second part he counteracts the ascetic and legalistic tendencies by urging a spiritual morality and a social ethic bound together by Christian love (3.5–4.1).

Written in the early 60's while Paul was in prison (4.3,10,18) and at about the same time as the letter to the Ephesians (with which it has many similarities; see the cross references), this letter to Colossae was dispatched by Tychicus (4.7,8), who also carried Paul's letter to Philemon (see Introduction to Philemon).

Though the precise form of the Colossian heresy has long since passed away, Paul's letter retains its freshness and relevance in combatting other types of inadequate Christologies and sub-Christian practices which have troubled the church from age to age.

PAUL, AN APOSTLE OF CHRIST JESUS by the will of God, and Timothy our brother,

2 To the saints and faithful brethren in Christ at Colos'sae:

Grace to you and peace from God our Father.

3 We always thank God, the Father of our Lord Jesus Christ, when we pray for you, 4 because we have heard of your faith in Christ Jesus and of the love which you have for all the saints, 5 because of the hope laid up for you in heaven. Of this you have heard before in the word of the truth, the gospel 6 which has come to you, as indeed in the whole world it is bearing fruit and growing—so among yourselves, from the day you heard and understood the grace of God in truth, 7 as you learned it from Ep'aphras our beloved fellow servant. He is a faithful minister of Christ on our[a] behalf 8 and has made known to us your love in the Spirit.

9 And so, from the day we heard of it, we have not ceased to pray for you, asking that you may be filled with the knowledge of his will in all spiritual wisdom and understanding, 10 to lead a life worthy of the Lord, fully pleasing to him, bearing fruit in every good work and increasing in the knowledge of God. 11 May you be strengthened with all power, according to his glorious might, for all endurance and patience with joy, 12 giving thanks to the Father, who has qualified us[b] to share in the inheritance of the saints in light. 13 He has delivered us from the dominion of darkness and transferred us to the kingdom of his beloved Son, 14 in

a Other ancient authorities read your
b Other ancient authorities read you

1.1–2: Salutation, see Rom.1.1–7 n. **2:** *Grace . . . peace,* see 2 Th.1.2 n.
1.3–14: Thanksgiving and intercession, see Rom.1.8–15 n. **3:** Eph.1.16. **4:** Philem.5. **4–5:** *Faith . . . love . . . hope,* 1 Cor.13.13. **6:** *The whole world,* in every quarter of the Roman Empire (v. 23). **7:** *Epaphras,* the founder of the church at Colossae, is now with Paul (4.12; Philem.23). **8–9:** Eph.1.15–17. **9–11:** A petition for sensitivity to God's will, issuing in Christian conduct and sustained by divine strength. **13:** *Delivered,* rescued from Satan's power (Mt.6.13 note *n;* Acts 26.18).

whom we have redemption, the forgiveness of sins.

15 He is the image of the invisible God, the first-born of all creation; [16] for in him all things were created, in heaven and on earth, visible and invisible, whether thrones or dominions or principalities or authorities–all things were created through him and for him. [17] He is before all things, and in him all things hold together. [18] He is the head of the body, the church; he is the beginning, the first-born from the dead, that in everything he might be pre-eminent. [19] For in him all the fulness of God was pleased to dwell, [20] and through him to reconcile to himself all things, whether on earth or in heaven, making peace by the blood of his cross.

21 And you, who once were estranged and hostile in mind, doing evil deeds, [22] he has now reconciled in his body of flesh by his death, in order to present you holy and blameless and irreproachable before him, [23] provided that you continue in the faith, stable and steadfast, not shifting from the hope of the gospel which you heard, which has been preached to every creature under heaven, and of which I, Paul, became a minister.

24 Now I rejoice in my sufferings for your sake, and in my flesh I complete what is lacking in Christ's afflictions for the sake of his body, that is, the church, [25] of which I became a minister according to the divine office which was given to me for you, to make the word of God fully known,

[26] the mystery hidden for ages and generations*c* but now made manifest to his saints. [27] To them God chose to make known how great among the Gentiles are the riches of the glory of this mystery, which is Christ in you, the hope of glory. [28] Him we proclaim, warning every man and teaching every man in all wisdom, that we may present every man mature in Christ. [29] For this I toil, striving with all the energy which he mightily inspires within me.

2 For I want you to know how greatly I strive for you, and for those at La-odice'a, and for all who have not seen my face, [2] that their hearts may be encouraged as they are knit together in love, to have all the riches of assured understanding and the knowledge of God's mystery, of Christ, [3] in whom are hid all the treasures of wisdom and knowledge. [4] I say this in order that no one may delude you with beguiling speech. [5] For though I am absent in body, yet I am with you in spirit, rejoicing to see your good order and the firmness of your faith in Christ.

6 As therefore you received Christ Jesus the Lord, so live in him, [7] rooted and built up in him and established in the faith, just as you were taught, abounding in thanksgiving.

8 See to it that no one makes a prey of you by philosophy and empty deceit, according to human tradition, according to the elemental spirits of the uni-

c Or *from angels and men*

1.15–23: The supremacy of Christ in the universe and in the church. **15:** The *image* perfectly reveals *the invisible God* (Jn.1.18; 2 Cor.4.4; Heb.1.3). *First-born* expresses priority to and supremacy over *all creation* (v. 17). **16:** Every *created* thing had its origin *in him* and exists *for him*. *Thrones . . . authorities* refer to various ranks of angels (Eph.6.12). **17:** Christ holds together the universe (Heb.1.3). **18:** *Head of . . . the church,* Eph.1.22–23; 4.15. *The beginning,* the origin or source (Rev.3.14). *First-born from the dead,* Acts 26.23; Rom.14.9; Rev.1.5. **19:** *The fulness of God,* a technical term for the plenitude of deity (see 2.9 n.). The verse may also be translated, "For it pleased God that in him [i.e. the Son] all the fulness of deity should dwell." **20:** *Blood of his cross,* the sacrificial death of Christ. **22:** *To present you,* the purpose and effect of the reconciliation (Eph.5.27).

1.24–2.7: Paul's interest in the Colossians, justifying his intervention in the affairs of a church where he was personally unknown (2.1). **1.24:** Because of the mystical union of the believers with Christ, what Paul suffers *for the sake of . . . the church* can be called *Christ's afflictions* (2 Cor. 1.5; 4.10). **26:** *Mystery,* 2.2; 4.3; see Eph.1.9 n. **2.1:** *Laodicea,* chief city of Phrygia in Asia Minor, near Colosse (Rev.3.14–22).

verse, and not according to Christ.
⁹ For in him the whole fulness of deity
dwells bodily, ¹⁰ and you have come
to fulness of life in him, who is the head
of all rule and authority. ¹¹ In him also
you were circumcised with a circumcision made without hands, by putting
off the body of flesh in the circumcision
of Christ; ¹² and you were buried with
him in baptism, in which you were also
raised with him through faith in the
working of God, who raised him from
the dead. ¹³ And you, who were dead
in trespasses and the uncircumcision
of your flesh, God made alive together
with him, having forgiven us all our
trespasses, ¹⁴ having canceled the bond
which stood against us with its legal
demands; this he set aside, nailing it
to the cross. ¹⁵ He disarmed the principalities and powers and made a public example of them, triumphing over
them in him.ᵈ

16 Therefore let no one pass judgment on you in questions of food and
drink or with regard to a festival or a
new moon or a sabbath. ¹⁷ These are
only a shadow of what is to come; but
the substance belongs to Christ. ¹⁸ Let
no one disqualify you, insisting on self-
abasement and worship of angels, taking his stand on visions, puffed up without reason by his sensuous mind, ¹⁹ and
not holding fast to the Head, from
whom the whole body, nourished and
knit together through its joints and
ligaments, grows with a growth that is
from God.

20 If with Christ you died to the elemental spirits of the universe, why do

you live as if you still belonged to the
world? Why do you submit to regulations, ²¹ "Do not handle, Do not taste,
Do not touch" ²² (referring to things
which all perish as they are used),
according to human precepts and doctrines? ²³ These have indeed an appearance of wisdom in promoting rigor
of devotion and self-abasement and
severity to the body, but they are of no
value in checking the indulgence of
the flesh.ᵉ

3 If then you have been raised with
Christ, seek the things that are
above, where Christ is, seated at the
right hand of God. ² Set your minds on
things that are above, not on things that
are on earth. ³ For you have died, and
your life is hid with Christ in God.
⁴ When Christ who is our life appears,
then you also will appear with him in
glory.

5 Put to death therefore what is
earthly in you: fornication, impurity,
passion, evil desire, and covetousness,
which is idolatry. ⁶ On account of these
the wrath of God is coming.ᶠ ⁷ In these
you once walked, when you lived in
them. ⁸ But now put them all away:
anger, wrath, malice, slander, and foul
talk from your mouth. ⁹ Do not lie to
one another, seeing that you have put
off the old nature with its practices
¹⁰ and have put on the new nature,
which is being renewed in knowledge
after the image of its creator. ¹¹ Here
there cannot be Greek and Jew, circum-

d Or *in it* (that is, the cross)
e Or *are of no value, serving only to indulge the flesh*
f Other ancient authorities add *upon the sons of disobedience*

2.8–23: **Warning against false teaching. 8:** Here *philosophy* refers to "vain speculation."
Elemental spirits, see Gal.4.3 n. **9:** *In him*, the exalted Christ. *The whole fulness of deity*, not
merely the divine attributes but the divine nature. *Dwells*, eternally. **10:** Eph.1.21–22. **13:**
Eph.2.1,5. **14:** *The bond*, the record of our transgressions (Eph.2.15; 1 Pet.2.24). **15:** *Principalities and powers*, see 1.16 n. *Made a public example*, as captives, stripped of armor, displayed in proof of victory. **16–23:** The Colossian error involved excessive ritualism, asceticism,
and the worship of angels. **16.** *Festival . . . new moon . . . sabbath*, annual, monthly, and weekly
observances. **19:** *The Head*, Christ (Eph.1.22; 4.15). **20:** *You died*, compare Rom.6.6–11;
Gal.2.19. *Elemental spirits*, see Gal.4.3 n. *Regulations*, such as those quoted in v. 21.
   3.1–17: The true Christian life. 1: *Raised*, 2.12. *Seated*, see Heb.1.3. **3:** *You have died* to the
world (2.20); *your* new *life is* secure *in God*, hidden *with Christ* from the world. **4:** Jn.14.6;
1 Jn.2.28; 3.2. **5:** The covetous man sets up another object of worship besides God (Eph.5.5).
6: *The wrath of God*, God's steadfast and holy hatred of sin (Rom.1.18–32). *Is coming*, the
Day of Judgment. **10:** *Image*, Gen.1.26–27; Eph.2.10; 4.24. **11:** Gal.3.28. **12:** *Put on then*,

cised and uncircumcised, barbarian, Scyth'ian, slave, free man, but Christ is all, and in all.

12 Put on then, as God's chosen ones, holy and beloved, compassion, kindness, lowliness, meekness, and patience, [13] forbearing one another and, if one has a complaint against another, forgiving each other; as the Lord has forgiven you, so you also must forgive. [14] And above all these put on love, which binds everything together in perfect harmony. [15] And let the peace of Christ rule in your hearts, to which indeed you were called in the one body. And be thankful. [16] Let the word of Christ dwell in you richly, teach and admonish one another in all wisdom, and sing psalms and hymns and spiritual songs with thankfulness in your hearts to God. [17] And whatever you do, in word or deed, do everything in the name of the Lord Jesus, giving thanks to God the Father through him.

18 Wives, be subject to your husbands, as is fitting in the Lord. [19] Husbands, love your wives, and do not be harsh with them. [20] Children, obey your parents in everything, for this pleases the Lord. [21] Fathers, do not provoke your children, lest they become discouraged. [22] Slaves, obey in everything those who are your earthly masters, not with eyeservice, as men-pleasers, but in singleness of heart, fearing the Lord. [23] Whatever your task, work heartily, as serving the Lord and not men, [24] knowing that from the Lord you will receive the inheritance as your reward; you are serving the Lord Christ. [25] For the wrongdoer will be paid back for the wrong he has done, and there is no partiality.

4 Masters, treat your slaves justly and fairly, knowing that you also have a Master in heaven.

2 Continue steadfastly in prayer, being watchful in it with thanksgiving; [3] and pray for us also, that God may open to us a door for the word, to declare the mystery of Christ, on account of which I am in prison, [4] that I may make it clear, as I ought to speak.

5 Conduct yourselves wisely toward outsiders, making the most of the time. [6] Let your speech always be gracious, seasoned with salt, so that you may know how you ought to answer every one.

7 Tych'icus will tell you all about my affairs; he is a beloved brother and faithful minister and fellow servant in the Lord. [8] I have sent him to you for this very purpose, that you may know how we are and that he may encourage your hearts, [9] and with him Ones'imus, the faithful and beloved brother, who is one of yourselves. They will tell you of everything that has taken place here.

10 Aristar'chus my fellow prisoner greets you, and Mark the cousin of Barnabas (concerning whom you have received instructions–if he comes to you, receive him), [11] and Jesus who is called Justus. These are the only men of the circumcision among my fellow workers for the kingdom of God, and they have been a comfort to me. [12] Ep'-aphras, who is one of yourselves, a servant[g] of Christ Jesus, greets you, always remembering you earnestly in

g Or *slave*

---

as a consequence of having put on (v. 10) the new nature, to which these virtues belong. **15:** *Rule*, literally "be umpire." **17:** *Do everything* for Jesus' sake, that it may be as though he were doing it (v. 11).

   3.18–4.6: The Christian's duties as regards family (vv. 18–20), masters and slaves (3.22–4.1), prayer, and social intercourse (4.2–6). **3.18–4.1:** Eph.5.22–6.9. **3.22:** *Slaves, obey;* the case of Onesimus was then engaging Paul's attention (see Introduction to Philemon). *Eyeservice*, zealous service performed only when one's master is watching. **4.3:** *Open . . . a door*, see Rev. 3.8 n. **5:** Eph.5.16. **6:** *Gracious*, courteous. *With salt*, with spiritual understanding (Mk.9.50).

   4.7–18: Epilogue, personal messages (vv. 7–9), greetings (vv. 10–15), and final instructions (vv. 16–18). **7:** *Tychicus*, Eph.6.21–22. **9:** *Onesimus*, Philem.10. **10:** Acts 19.29; 27.2; Philem.24. **11:** *Jesus*, the Greek form of a fairly common Jewish name. **12:** 1.7; Philem.23. **14:** 2 Tim.4.10–

his prayers, that you may stand mature and fully assured in all the will of God. [13] For I bear him witness that he has worked hard for you and for those in La-odice'a and in Hi-erap'olis. [14] Luke the beloved physician and Demas greet you. [15] Give my greetings to the brethren at La-odice'a, and to Nympha and the church in her house. [16] And when this letter has been read among you, have it read also in the church of the La-odice'ans; and see that you read also the letter from La-odice'a. [17] And say to Archip'pus, "See that you fulfil the ministry which you have received in the Lord."

18 I, Paul, write this greeting with my own hand. Remember my fetters. Grace be with you.

11; Philem.24. **15:** *Church in . . . house,* see Philem.2 n. **16:** *The letter* left at *Laodicea,* either the letter to the Ephesians or some other Pauline letter no longer extant. **18:** *I . . . with my own hand,* up to this point Paul had been dictating (see 2 Th.3.17 n.).

THESSALONIANS

During his second missionary journey (Acts 15.40–18.22) and after being driven out of Philippi, Paul, together with Silas and Timothy, came to Thessalonica, the capital of Macedonia (Acts 17.1). Here he preached in the synagogue for three sabbaths, proclaiming Jesus as the Messiah, and proving from the Scriptures the necessity of his death and resurrection (Acts 17.3). Some Jews were convinced; many of the Greeks who had been previously attracted to the religion of Israel were also persuaded. A successful ministry, mainly among Gentiles, continued for some time. The Jews, annoyed at seeing the fruit of their missionary labors joining Paul, accused him of sedition (Acts 17.7) and aroused such a disturbance that Paul and Silas were sent away by their friends by night to Beroea. When word of the apostle's success there reached Thessalonica, his opponents followed him to Beroea and hunted him out of town again. Paul moved on to Athens and shortly afterwards to Corinth.

Paul was anxious about the immature congregation in Thessalonica, deprived of its leadership and persecuted by the synagogue. The attack upon the gospel was apparently reinforced by questioning the apostle's character and motives, accusing him of error, guile, greed, impurity, and dishonesty (2.3–6). Paul sent Timothy to strengthen and encourage the young congregation. When he returned with good news of their faith and loyalty, Paul wrote the first letter to express his gratitude and joy at their perseverance, to exhort them to Christian conduct, and to answer two questions that perplexed them: namely, Is a Christian deprived of the blessings of the kingdom if he dies before Christ's second advent? and, When will Christ come in glory? He deals with the first question in 4.13–18, and with the second question in 5.1–11.

The letter was written from Corinth, perhaps early in the 50's. It is the earliest of Paul's extant correspondence.

PAUL, SILVA′NUS, AND TIMOTHY, To the church of the Thessalo′nians in God the Father and the Lord Jesus Christ:

Grace to you and peace.

2 We give thanks to God always for you all, constantly mentioning you in our prayers, [3] remembering before our God and Father your work of faith and labor of love and steadfastness of hope in our Lord Jesus Christ. [4] For we know, brethren beloved by God, that he has chosen you; [5] for our gospel came to you not only in word, but also in power and in the Holy Spirit and with full conviction. You know what kind of men we proved to be among you for your sake. [6] And you became imitators of us and of the Lord, for you received the word in much affliction, with joy inspired by the Holy Spirit; [7] so that you became an example to all the believers in Macedo′nia and in Acha′ia. [8] For not only has the word of the Lord sounded forth from you in Macedo′nia and Acha′ia, but your faith in God has gone forth everywhere, so that we need not say anything. [9] For they themselves report concerning us what a welcome we had among you, and how you turned to God from idols, to serve a living and true God, [10] and to wait for his Son from heaven, whom he

---

1.1: Salutation, see Rom.1.1–7 n. *Silvanus,* identical with Silas (Acts 15.22,40; 16.19–25; 17.4). *Timothy,* see Introduction to 2 Timothy. *Church,* see Gal.1.13 n. *Lord,* the title of Israel's covenant God, is applied by Christians to the risen and glorified Jesus (Phil.2.9–11). *Grace . . . and peace,* see 2 Th.1.2 n.

1.2–10: Thanksgiving, see Rom.1.8–15 n. Paul is grateful that the Thessalonians have persevered, though aware that much yet needs to be accomplished in them. **4:** Israel's privileges as God's *chosen* are transferred to the church. **5:** *Our gospel* is not just words; the saving power of God is at work in it. **7–8:** *Macedonia,* of which Thessalonica was the capital. *Achaia,* Greece

raised from the dead, Jesus who delivers us from the wrath to come.

2 For you yourselves know, brethren, that our visit to you was not in vain; [2] but though we had already suffered and been shamefully treated at Philip'pi, as you know, we had courage in our God to declare to you the gospel of God in the face of great opposition. [3] For our appeal does not spring from error or uncleanness, nor is it made with guile; [4] but just as we have been approved by God to be entrusted with the gospel, so we speak, not to please men, but to please God who tests our hearts. [5] For we never used either words of flattery, as you know, or a cloak for greed, as God is witness; [6] nor did we seek glory from men, whether from you or from others, though we might have made demands as apostles of Christ. [7] But we were gentle[a] among you, like a nurse taking care of her children. [8] So, being affectionately desirous of you, we were ready to share with you not only the gospel of God but also our own selves, because you had become very dear to us.

9 For you remember our labor and toil, brethren; we worked night and day, that we might not burden any of you, while we preached to you the gospel of God. [10] You are witnesses, and God also, how holy and righteous and blameless was our behavior to you believers; [11] for you know how, like a father with his children, we exhorted each one of you and encouraged you and charged you [12] to lead a life worthy of God, who calls you into his own kingdom and glory.

13 And we also thank God constantly for this, that when you received the word of God which you heard from us, you accepted it not as the word of men but as what it really is, the word of God, which is at work in you believers. [14] For you, brethren, became imitators of the churches of God in Christ Jesus which are in Judea; for you suffered the same things from your own countrymen as they did from the Jews, [15] who killed both the Lord Jesus and the prophets, and drove us out, and displease God and oppose all men [16] by hindering us from speaking to the Gentiles that they may be saved–so as always to fill up the measure of their sins. But God's wrath has come upon them at last![b]

17 But since we were bereft of you, brethren, for a short time, in person not in heart, we endeavored the more eagerly and with great desire to see you face to face; [18] because we wanted to come to you–I, Paul, again and again–but Satan hindered us. [19] For what is our hope or joy or crown of boasting before our Lord Jesus at his coming? Is it not you? [20] For you are our glory and joy.

3 Therefore when we could bear it no longer, we were willing to be left behind at Athens alone, [2] and we sent Timothy, our brother and God's servant in the gospel of Christ, to establish you in your faith and to exhort you, [3] that no one be moved by these afflictions. You yourselves know that this is to be our lot. [4] For when we were with you, we told you beforehand that we were to suffer affliction; just as it has come to pass, and as you know. [5] For this reason, when I could bear it no

a Other ancient authorities read *babes*
b Or *completely,* or *for ever*

(where Paul was then). **10:** The return of the risen Christ is the hope of God's people. *The wrath,* i.e. of God, which is not anger or irritation, but justice.

2.1–16: Paul's life and work at Thessalonica. 2: *Philippi,* Acts 16.19–40. **3–8:** The opponents of the gospel accused Paul of heresy, immorality, trickery, and greed. He replies by reminding his readers of his conduct among them. **9:** Paul supported himself by working at his trade (Acts 18.3) so as not to burden the church. **14–16:** The severe language reflects the strenuous struggle between Paul and the Jews (Acts 14.2,5,19; 17.5,13; 21.21; 25.2,7).

2.17–3.13: Paul's affection for the Thessalonians. 2.18: Behind obstacles Paul recognizes the activity of Satan, the adversary of God's kingly rule (see Mt.4.1 n.; Rom.16.20; 2 Cor.11.14; 1 Tim.1.20). **3.3:** *Afflictions* are normal, not exceptional. **5:** *Tempter,* see 2.18 n. **6:** *Timothy*

longer, I sent that I might know your faith, for fear that somehow the tempter had tempted you and that our labor would be in vain.

6 But now that Timothy has come to us from you, and has brought us the good news of your faith and love and reported that you always remember us kindly and long to see us, as we long to see you– 7 for this reason, brethren, in all our distress and affliction we have been comforted about you through your faith; 8 for now we live, if you stand fast in the Lord. 9 For what thanksgiving can we render to God for you, for all the joy which we feel for your sake before our God, 10 praying earnestly night and day that we may see you face to face and supply what is lacking in your faith?

11 Now may our God and Father himself, and our Lord Jesus, direct our way to you; 12 and may the Lord make you increase and abound in love to one another and to all men, as we do to you, 13 so that he may establish your hearts unblamable in holiness before our God and Father, at the coming of our Lord Jesus with all his saints.

4 Finally, brethren, we beseech and exhort you in the Lord Jesus, that as you learned from us how you ought to live and to please God, just as you are doing, you do so more and more. 2 For you know what instructions we gave you through the Lord Jesus. 3 For this is the will of God, your sanctification: that you abstain from unchastity; 4 that each one of you know how to take a wife for himself*x* in holiness and honor, 5 not in the passion of lust like heathen who do not know God; 6 that no man transgress, and wrong his brother in this matter,*c* because the Lord is an avenger in all these things, as we solemnly forewarned you. 7 For God has not called us for uncleanness, but in holiness. 8 Therefore whoever disregards this, disregards not man but God, who gives his Holy Spirit to you.

9 But concerning love of the brethren you have no need to have any one write to you, for you yourselves have been taught by God to love one another; 10 and indeed you do love all the brethren throughout Macedo'nia. But we exhort you, brethren, to do so more and more, 11 to aspire to live quietly, to mind your own affairs, and to work with your hands, as we charged you; 12 so that you may command the respect of outsiders, and be dependent on nobody.

13 But we would not have you ignorant, brethren, concerning those who are asleep, that you may not grieve as others do who have no hope. 14 For since we believe that Jesus died and rose again, even so, through Jesus, God will bring with him those who have fallen asleep. 15 For this we declare to you by the word of the Lord, that we who are alive, who are left until the coming of the Lord, shall not precede those who have fallen asleep. 16 For the Lord himself will descend from heaven with a cry of command, with the archangel's call, and with the sound of the trumpet of God. And the dead in Christ will rise first; 17 then we who are alive, who are left, shall be caught up together

x Or *how to control his own body*
c Or *defraud his brother in business*

---

has come, see Introduction. **7:** *Distress and affliction*, Acts 18.6,12. **10:** The prayer was answered some years later (Acts 20.1–2). **13:** The heart is not the organ of feeling as in modern speech, but the controlling center of personality. *Saints*, all who belong to God.

4.1–12: Exhortation to purity. 3: The Gentile world was notorious for sexual license (1 Cor. 6.18). **8:** Paul's supreme argument for purity of life–the indwelling Holy Spirit (1 Cor.3.16–17). **9:** *Taught by God*, Is.54.13. **11:** *Work with your hands*, see 2.9 n. **12:** *Outsiders*, not belonging to God's people.

4.13–5.11: Questions concerning the coming of the Lord. 4.13: *Those who are asleep*, a common metaphor for the dead (see Mt.9.24 n.; Jn.11.11 n.). **14:** The Christian is united with Christ in his death and resurrection (Rom.6.3). **15:** *The word of the Lord*, authoritative revelation, not private opinion. **16:** Mt.24.30–31; Mk.13.26–27; 1 Cor.15.52. **5.1:** Some *brethren* desired an

with them in the clouds to meet the Lord in the air; and so we shall always be with the Lord. [18] Therefore comfort one another with these words.

5 But as to the times and the seasons, brethren, you have no need to have anything written to you. [2] For you yourselves know well that the day of the Lord will come like a thief in the night. [3] When people say, "There is peace and security," then sudden destruction will come upon them as travail comes upon a woman with child, and there will be no escape. [4] But you are not in darkness, brethren, for that day to surprise you like a thief. [5] For you are all sons of light and sons of the day; we are not of the night or of darkness. [6] So then let us not sleep, as others do, but let us keep awake and be sober. [7] For those who sleep sleep at night, and those who get drunk are drunk at night. [8] But, since we belong to the day, let us be sober, and put on the breastplate of faith and love, and for a helmet the hope of salvation. [9] For God has not destined us for wrath, but to obtain salvation through our Lord Jesus Christ, [10] who died for us so that whether we wake or sleep we might live with him. [11] Therefore encourage one another and build one another up, just as you are doing.

[12] But we beseech you, brethren, to respect those who labor among you and are over you in the Lord and admonish you, [13] and to esteem them very highly in love because of their work. Be at peace among yourselves. [14] And we exhort you, brethren, admonish the idlers, encourage the fainthearted, help the weak, be patient with them all. [15] See that none of you repays evil for evil, but always seek to do good to one another and to all. [16] Rejoice always, [17] pray constantly, [18] give thanks in all circumstances; for this is the will of God in Christ Jesus for you. [19] Do not quench the Spirit, [20] do not despise prophesying, [21] but test everything; hold fast what is good, [22] abstain from every form of evil.

[23] May the God of peace himself sanctify you wholly; and may your spirit and soul and body be kept sound and blameless at the coming of our Lord Jesus Christ. [24] He who calls you is faithful, and he will do it.

[25] Brethren, pray for us.

[26] Greet all the brethren with a holy kiss.

[27] I adjure you by the Lord that this letter be read to all the brethren.

[28] The grace of our Lord Jesus Christ be with you.

---

eschatological time-table (Acts 1.6–7). **2:** Paul reiterates Jesus' warning (Mt.24.43–44; Lk. 12.39–40). *Woman with child*, a common prophetic expression for the suddenness of the day of the Lord (Is.13.8; Jer.6.24; Hos.13.13). **5:** Lk.16.8. **6:** *Let us not sleep*, in carelessness and sin. **8:** The Christian's armor (compare Rom.13.12; 2 Cor.6.7; 10.4; Eph.6.13–17). **10:** *Whether we wake or sleep*, whether we are alive or dead when Christ returns. **11:** Paul frequently pictures the church as a temple under construction. The builder is God, but Christians can take part in the work of building (1 Cor.3.9; Eph.2.20).

5.12–28: Concluding exhortation. 19: *Do not quench* the fire of *the Spirit* (compare Mt.3.11; Acts 2.3; 2 Tim.1.6). **20:** *Prophesying*, not only prediction, but the inspired word of preaching (see Acts 11.27 n.). **21:** *Test everything*, see 1 Jn.4.1–3. **23:** *Spirit and soul and body*, Paul does not think of a person as having three parts, but as a unity which may be viewed from three different points of view: his relation to God, his personal vitality, and his physical body. **24:** *Will do it*, v. 23. **26:** *Holy kiss*, see Rom.16.16 n. **27:** Col.4.16.

THESSALONIANS

The congregation in Thessalonica continued to experience sharp opposition from the synagogue, which regarded the new fellowship as an heretical sect. Pressed from without by hostility and stirred within by expectation of the second coming of Christ and by a vivid sense of the presence and power of the Holy Spirit, the erroneous opinion arose that the day of the Lord had already come (2.2).

Paul's second letter followed soon after the first (see Introduction to 1 Thessalonians). It was written to encourage the congregation in its difficult situation and to counter the theological and practical consequences of the false teaching. He reminds his readers of the apostolic tradition concerning the day of the Lord, and declares that the rebellion against God must first take place and the man of lawlessness be revealed (2.3–8). He also rebukes those who use the teaching as justification for a life of idleness, pointing to his own example in their midst and reiterating his precept, "If any one will not work, let him not eat" (3.10).

The letters to the Thessalonians are of special value for their revelation of the personal characteristics of Paul as a missionary and for the light they shed on life in the early Christian community. Paul's intensity and affection are impressively conveyed, and we sense across the centuries the power of his personality.

PAUL, SILVA'NUS, AND TIMOTHY, To the church of the Thessalo'nians in God our Father and the Lord Jesus Christ:

2 Grace to you and peace from God the Father and the Lord Jesus Christ.

3 We are bound to give thanks to God always for you, brethren, as is fitting, because your faith is growing abundantly, and the love of every one of you for one another is increasing. [4] Therefore we ourselves boast of you in the churches of God for your steadfastness and faith in all your persecutions and in the afflictions which you are enduring.

5 This is evidence of the righteous judgment of God, that you may be made worthy of the kingdom of God, for which you are suffering– [6] since indeed God deems it just to repay with affliction those who afflict you, [7] and to grant rest with us to you who are afflicted, when the Lord Jesus is revealed from heaven with his mighty angels in flaming fire, [8] inflicting vengeance upon those who do not know God and upon those who do not obey the gospel of our Lord Jesus. [9] They shall suffer the punishment of eternal destruction and exclusion from the presence of the Lord and from the glory of his might, [10] when he comes on that day to be glorified in his saints, and to be marveled at in all who have believed, because our testimony to you was believed. [11] To this end we always pray for you, that our God may make you worthy of his call, and may fulfil every good resolve and work of faith by his power, [12] so that the name of our Lord Jesus may be glorified in you, and you in him, according to the grace of our God and the Lord Jesus Christ.

1.1–2: Salutation, see Rom.1.1–7 n. *Silvanus, Timothy,* see 1 Th.1.1 n. **2:** *Grace and peace* combine the conventional Greek and Hebrew salutations; the apostle's greeting, however, is not merely his own good wishes but the grace and peace of God given in Jesus Christ.

1.3–4: Thanksgiving, see Rom.1.8–15 n.

1.5–12: The judgment of God. Reference to *afflictions* (v. 4) leads to a digression of remarkable intensity (see 1 Th.2.14 n.). **9:** *Eternal destruction,* not annihilation, but endless ruin in separation from Christ. **10:** *That day,* see 2 Tim.1.12 n. *Glorified in his saints,* what Christ has done for his people will be seen to redound to his glory. **12:** *The name,* the character and fame (Phil.2.9).

2 Now concerning the coming of our Lord Jesus Christ and our assembling to meet him, we beg you, brethren, ² not to be quickly shaken in mind or excited, either by spirit or by word, or by letter purporting to be from us, to the effect that the day of the Lord has come. ³ Let no one deceive you in any way; for that day will not come, unless the rebellion comes first, and the man of lawlessness*a* is revealed, the son of perdition, ⁴ who opposes and exalts himself against every so-called god or object of worship, so that he takes his seat in the temple of God, proclaiming himself to be God. ⁵ Do you not remember that when I was still with you I told you this? ⁶ And you know what is restraining him now so that he may be revealed in his time. ⁷ For the mystery of lawlessness is already at work; only he who now restrains it will do so until he is out of the way. ⁸ And then the lawless one will be revealed, and the Lord Jesus will slay him with the breath of his mouth and destroy him by his appearing and his coming. ⁹ The coming of the lawless one by the activity of Satan will be with all power and with pretended signs and wonders, ¹⁰ and with all wicked deception for those who are to perish, because they refused to love the truth and so be saved. ¹¹ Therefore God sends upon them a strong delusion, to make them believe what is false, ¹² so that all may be condemned who did not believe the truth but had pleasure in unrighteousness.

13 But we are bound to give thanks to God always for you, brethren beloved by the Lord, because God chose you from the beginning*b* to be saved, through sanctification by the Spirit*c* and belief in the truth. ¹⁴ To this he called you through our gospel, so that you may obtain the glory of our Lord Jesus Christ. ¹⁵ So then, brethren, stand firm and hold to the traditions which you were taught by us, either by word of mouth or by letter.

16 Now may our Lord Jesus Christ himself, and God our Father, who loved us and gave us eternal comfort and good hope through grace, ¹⁷ comfort your hearts and establish them in every good work and word.

3 Finally, brethren, pray for us, that the word of the Lord may speed on and triumph, as it did among you, ² and that we may be delivered from wicked and evil men; for not all have faith. ³ But the Lord is faithful; he will strengthen you and guard you from evil.*d* ⁴ And we have confidence in the Lord about you, that you are doing and will do the things which we command. ⁵ May the Lord direct your hearts to the love of God and to the steadfastness of Christ.

6 Now we command you, brethren, in the name of our Lord Jesus Christ, that you keep away from any brother who is living in idleness and not in accord with the tradition that you received from us. ⁷ For you yourselves

a Other ancient authorities read *sin*
b Other ancient authorities read *as the first converts*
c Or *of spirit*
d Or *the evil one*

2.1–12: The day of the Lord. *The rebellion and the man of lawlessness* will precede the second coming of Christ. **2:** The new teaching originated in or was supported by the utterances of an ecstatic individual, or perhaps in a letter purporting to come from Paul. **3–4:** The day of the Lord (2 Pet.3.10) will be preceded by persecutions, false prophets, and a "desolating sacrilege" (Dan.9.27; 11.31; 12.11; Mt. ch. 24; Mk. ch. 13; Lk.21.5–36). **6:** The man of lawlessness has not yet come because something (v. 7, someone) is *restraining* him. Paul assumes that his readers understand this reference, but we do not. There are three main conjectures, none of which is entirely satisfactory: (a) The Roman empire and emperor; (b) A supernatural power; (c) Satan himself. **7:** *The mystery of lawlessness,* the counterfeit and opponent of the mystery of godliness (Col.1.26; 1 Tim.3.16). **11:** Rom.1.28.

2.13–17: Thanksgiving and exhortation. 13: 1.3; Eph.1.4; 1 Pet.1.2. **15:** *The traditions* would involve doctrinal, moral, and liturgical teaching, as 1 Corinthians shows. **16:** 1 Th.3.11; 1 Pet.1.3.

3.1–18: Closing appeals, rebukes, and prayer. 2: Rom.15.31. **3:** *Evil,* Mt.6.13. **6–15:** Paul

know how you ought to imitate us; we were not idle when we were with you, [8] we did not eat any one's bread without paying, but with toil and labor we worked night and day, that we might not burden any of you. [9] It was not because we have not that right, but to give you in our conduct an example to imitate. [10] For even when we were with you, we gave you this command: If any one will not work, let him not eat. [11] For we hear that some of you are living in idleness, mere busybodies, not doing any work. [12] Now such persons we command and exhort in the Lord Jesus Christ to do their work in quietness and to earn their own living.

[13] Brethren, do not be weary in well-doing.

[14] If any one refuses to obey what we say in this letter, note that man, and have nothing to do with him, that he may be ashamed. [15] Do not look on him as an enemy, but warn him as a brother.

[16] Now may the Lord of peace himself give you peace at all times in all ways. The Lord be with you all.

[17] I, Paul, write this greeting with my own hand. This is the mark in every letter of mine; it is the way I write. [18] The grace of our Lord Jesus Christ be with you all.

---

rebukes those who, because of the supposed imminence of Christ's coming, had ceased to work and were living on the generosity of others. **8:** 1 Th.2.9; Acts 18.3. **11:** *Busybodies*, 1 Th.4.11. **13:** Gal.6.9. **15:** A caution against falling into extremes. **17:** Paul adds a concluding note in his own handwriting as a guarantee of genuineness (see 2.2 n.).

THE FIRST LETTER OF PAUL TO

TIMOTHY

The two letters to Timothy and the one to Titus, commonly called the Pastorals, are similar in character and in the problems they raise concerning authorship. It is difficult to ascribe them in their present form to the apostle Paul. The vocabulary and style of the letters differ widely from the acknowledged letters of Paul; some of his leading theological ideas are entirely absent (e.g. the union of the believer with Christ, the power and witness of the Spirit, freedom from the law), and some expressions bear a different meaning from that in his customary usage (e.g. "the faith" as a synonym for the Christian religion rather than the believer's relationship to Christ).

A few scholars, attempting to maintain Pauline authorship, account for the differences by assuming changes in his environment as well as modifications in his vocabulary, style, and thought. But in view of the widespread custom of pseudonymous authorship in antiquity it is easier to assume that a loyal disciple of Paul used several previously unpublished messages of the apostle and expanded them to deal with conditions confronting the church a generation after Paul's death. (On pseudonymous authorship see the Introduction to 2 Peter).

The First Letter to Timothy has a double purpose: to provide guidance in the problems of church administration, and to oppose false teaching of a speculative and moralistic type. Thus, it offers suggestions for the regulation of worship (2.1–15), lays down the qualifications of bishops (3.1–7) and deacons (3.8–13), and gives instructions as to the attitude of church leaders toward false asceticism (4.1–16) and toward individual members (5.1–12), particularly widows (5.13–16), presbyters (5.17), and slaves (6.1–2). It also warns strongly against antinomian teachers who lack understanding, wander into vain discussions, and end by making shipwreck of their faith (6.3–20). The author is especially sharp in reproving those who seek to make profit out of religion (6.3–10). The letter attacks gnostic asceticism, namely the attitude of one who claims to possess the true knowledge (gnosis) and is therefore superior to the claims of the body, renouncing marriage and abstaining from certain foods (4.3). The speculative mythology of gnosticism is also denounced as "godless and silly myths" (4.7) and "what is falsely called knowledge" (6.20).

For information concerning the person of Timothy, see the Introduction to 2 Timothy.

PAUL, AN APOSTLE OF CHRIST JESUS by command of God our Savior and of Christ Jesus our hope,

2 To Timothy, my true child in the faith:

Grace, mercy, and peace from God the Father and Christ Jesus our Lord.

3 As I urged you when I was going to Macedo'nia, remain at Ephesus that you may charge certain persons not to teach any different doctrine, [4] nor to occupy themselves with myths and endless genealogies which promote speculations rather than the divine training[a] that is in faith; [5] whereas the aim of our charge is love that issues from a pure heart and a good conscience and sincere faith. [6] Certain persons by swerving from these have wandered away into vain discussion, [7] desiring to be teachers of the law, without understanding either what they are saying or the things about which they make assertions.

a Or stewardship, or order

1.1–2: Salutation, see Rom.1.1–7 n. **2:** *Timothy,* see Introduction to 2 Timothy. *Mercy* is added to *grace and peace* (compare 2 Tim.1.2 and see 2 Th.1.2 n.).

1.3–20: The defense of the truth. 4: *Myths and endless genealogies,* probably Jewish speculations (compare Tit.1.14; 3.9). *The divine training* pictures the Christian life as the discipline of servants in a large household (see note *a*). **5:** The goal of preaching is love: not romantic sentiment, but sharing God's generosity with one's neighbor. **6:** The neglect of love leads to empty

8 Now we know that the law is good, if any one uses it lawfully, [9] understanding this, that the law is not laid down for the just but for the lawless and disobedient, for the ungodly and sinners, for the unholy and profane, for murderers of fathers and murderers of mothers, for manslayers, [10] immoral persons, sodomites, kidnapers, liars, perjurers, and whatever else is contrary to sound doctrine, [11] in accordance with the glorious gospel of the blessed God with which I have been entrusted.

12 I thank him who has given me strength for this, Christ Jesus our Lord, because he judged me faithful by appointing me to his service, [13] though I formerly blasphemed and persecuted and insulted him; but I received mercy because I had acted ignorantly in unbelief, [14] and the grace of our Lord overflowed for me with the faith and love that are in Christ Jesus. [15] The saying is sure and worthy of full acceptance, that Christ Jesus came into the world to save sinners. And I am the foremost of sinners; [16] but I received mercy for this reason, that in me, as the foremost, Jesus Christ might display his perfect patience for an example to those who were to believe in him for eternal life. [17] To the King of ages, immortal, invisible, the only God, be honor and glory for ever and ever.[b] Amen.

18 This charge I commit to you, Timothy, my son, in accordance with the prophetic utterances which pointed to you, that inspired by them you may wage the good warfare, [19] holding faith and a good conscience. By rejecting conscience, certain persons have made shipwreck of their faith, [20] among them Hymenae'us and Alexander, whom I have delivered to Satan that they may learn not to blaspheme.

2 First of all, then, I urge that supplications, prayers, intercessions, and thanksgivings be made for all men, [2] for kings and all who are in high positions, that we may lead a quiet and peaceable life, godly and respectful in every way. [3] This is good, and it is acceptable in the sight of God our Savior, [4] who desires all men to be saved and to come to the knowledge of the truth. [5] For there is one God, and there is one mediator between God and men, the man Christ Jesus, [6] who gave himself as a ransom for all, the testimony to which was borne at the proper time. [7] For this I was appointed a preacher and apostle (I am telling the truth, I am not lying), a teacher of the Gentiles in faith and truth.

8 I desire then that in every place the men should pray, lifting holy hands without anger or quarreling; [9] also that women should adorn themselves modestly and sensibly in seemly apparel, not with braided hair or gold or pearls or costly attire [10] but by good deeds, as befits women who profess religion. [11] Let a woman learn in silence with all submissiveness. [12] I permit no woman to teach or to have authority over men; she is to keep silent. [13] For Adam was formed first, then Eve;

b Greek *to the ages of ages*

---

talk. **12–14:** The Lord displayed his grace in making an apostle out of Saul the persecutor (Acts 9.4; 1 Cor.15.9; Gal.1.13; Phil.3.6). **15:** *The saying is sure*, a formula characteristic of the letters to Timothy and Titus (3.1; 4.9; 2 Tim.2.11; Tit.3.8). **20:** *Hymenaeus*, 2 Tim.2.17. *Alexander*, 2 Tim.4.14. *Satan* was regarded as the source of suffering and disease as well as moral evil (Lk.13.16; 2 Cor.12.7). Under the power of Satan, the sufferer may be moved to repentance (see 1 Cor.5.5 n.).

2.1–15: The regulation of worship. 2: The Christian prays even for bad rulers (Rom.13.1). *A quiet and peaceable life*, a poignant petition in view of the persecutions of the early church. **4:** One of the strongest affirmations of the universality of God's grace. **5:** *Mediator*, Heb.9.15; 12.24. **6:** *Ransom*, Mt.20.28; Mk.10.45. **8:** *Lifting holy hands*, a common posture for prayer (Ps.141.2). **9:** *Seemly apparel*, 1 Pet.3.3–6. **11:** *In silence*, 1 Cor.14.34–35. **12:** 1 Cor.11.2–16; compare Eph.5.22–33. **13:** Gen.2.7,21–22. **14:** Gen.3.1–6. **15:** This much debated verse has

14 and Adam was not deceived, but the woman was deceived and became a transgressor. 15 Yet woman will be saved through bearing children,*c* if she continues*d* in faith and love and holiness, with modesty.

3 The saying is sure: If any one aspires to the office of bishop, he desires a noble task. 2 Now a bishop must be above reproach, the husband of one wife, temperate, sensible, dignified, hospitable, an apt teacher, 3 no drunkard, not violent but gentle, not quarrelsome, and no lover of money. 4 He must manage his own household well, keeping his children submissive and respectful in every way; 5 for if a man does not know how to manage his own household, how can he care for God's church? 6 He must not be a recent convert, or he may be puffed up with conceit and fall into the condemnation of the devil;*f* 7 moreover he must be well thought of by outsiders, or he may fall into reproach and the snare of the devil.*f*

8 Deacons likewise must be serious, not double-tongued, not addicted to much wine, not greedy for gain; 9 they must hold the mystery of the faith with a clear conscience. 10 And let them also be tested first; then if they prove themselves blameless let them serve as deacons. 11 The women likewise must be serious, no slanderers, but temperate, faithful in all things. 12 Let deacons be the husband of one wife, and let them manage their children and their households well; 13 for those who serve well as deacons gain a good

standing for themselves and also great confidence in the faith which is in Christ Jesus.

14 I hope to come to you soon, but I am writing these instructions to you so that, 15 if I am delayed, you may know how one ought to behave in the household of God, which is the church of the living God, the pillar and bulwark of the truth. 16 Great indeed, we confess, is the mystery of our religion:
He*h* was manifested in the flesh,
    vindicated*i* in the Spirit,
        seen by angels,
preached among the nations,
believed on in the world,
        taken up in glory.

4 Now the Spirit expressly says that in later times some will depart from the faith by giving heed to deceitful spirits and doctrines of demons, 2 through the pretensions of liars whose consciences are seared, 3 who forbid marriage and enjoin abstinence from foods which God created to be received with thanksgiving by those who believe and know the truth. 4 For everything created by God is good, and nothing is to be rejected if it is received with thanksgiving; 5 for then it is consecrated by the word of God and prayer.

6 If you put these instructions before the brethren, you will be a good minister of Christ Jesus, nourished on the words of the faith and of the good doctrine which you have followed.

c Or *by the birth of the child*
d Greek *they continue*   f Or *slanderer*
h Greek *Who;* other ancient authorities read *God;*
others, *Which*   i Or *justified*

---

also been translated (a) "she will be saved through the birth of the Child" [referring to Jesus Christ], or (b) "she will be brought safely through childbirth."
    3.1–16: Problems of administration. 1–7: The qualifications of a bishop (literally "overseer").
2: *Hospitable,* see 3 Jn.5 n. **6:** The devil accuses believers before God's judgment seat (Job 1.6–11; Rev.12.10). **8–13:** The qualifications of deacons (compare Acts 6.1–6). **11:** Women also shared in the work of the deacons (Rom.16.1). **14–16:** Practical problems in perspective; administration is not a necessary evil but a spiritual task in the household of God (1 Cor.12.28). **16:** Christ is the content of *the mystery.*
    4.1–16: False teachers. 1: *The* Holy *Spirit,* speaking through New Testament prophets (compare Acts 20.23; 21.11). *Later times,* the period before the day of the Lord (Mt.24.24; 1 Jn.2.18). *Deceitful spirits,* see 1 Jn.4.1 n.; 2 Jn.7. *Doctrines of demons,* Eph.6.12; Jas.3.15; Rev.16.13–14. **3–5:** Gnostic teachers forbade legitimate *marriage* and certain *foods* (Col.2.16). The author's reply stresses the goodness of God's creation (Tit.1.15); since, however, the creation can be misused, *everything* should be *consecrated by the word of God and prayer.*

[7] Have nothing to do with godless and silly myths. Train yourself in godliness; [8] for while bodily training is of some value, godliness is of value in every way, as it holds promise for the present life and also for the life to come. [9] The saying is sure and worthy of full acceptance. [10] For to this end we toil and strive,[j] because we have our hope set on the living God, who is the Savior of all men, especially of those who believe.

11 Command and teach these things. [12] Let no one despise your youth, but set the believers an example in speech and conduct, in love, in faith, in purity. [13] Till I come, attend to the public reading of scripture, to preaching, to teaching. [14] Do not neglect the gift you have, which was given you by prophetic utterance when the council of elders laid their hands upon you. [15] Practice these duties, devote yourself to them, so that all may see your progress. [16] Take heed to yourself and to your teaching; hold to that, for by so doing you will save both yourself and your hearers.

5 Do not rebuke an older man but exhort him as you would a father; treat younger men like brothers, [2] older women like mothers, younger women like sisters, in all purity.

3 Honor widows who are real widows. [4] If a widow has children or grandchildren, let them first learn their religious duty to their own family and make some return to their parents; for this is acceptable in the sight of God. [5] She who is a real widow, and is left all alone, has set her hope on God and continues in supplications and prayers night and day; [6] whereas she who is self-indulgent is dead even while she lives. [7] Command this, so that they may be without reproach. [8] If any one does not provide for his relatives, and especially for his own family, he has disowned the faith and is worse than an unbeliever.

9 Let a widow be enrolled if she is not less than sixty years of age, having been the wife of one husband; [10] and she must be well attested for her good deeds, as one who has brought up children, shown hospitality, washed the feet of the saints, relieved the afflicted, and devoted herself to doing good in every way. [11] But refuse to enrol younger widows; for when they grow wanton against Christ they desire to marry, [12] and so they incur condemnation for having violated their first pledge. [13] Besides that, they learn to be idlers, gadding about from house to house, and not only idlers but gossips and busybodies, saying what they should not. [14] So I would have younger widows marry, bear children, rule their households, and give the enemy no occasion to revile us. [15] For some have already strayed after Satan. [16] If any believing woman[l] has relatives who are widows, let her assist them; let the church not be burdened, so that it may assist those who are real widows.

17 Let the elders who rule well be considered worthy of double honor, especially those who labor in preaching and teaching; [18] for the scripture says, "You shall not muzzle an ox when it is treading out the grain," and, "The

j Other ancient authorities read *suffer reproach*
l Other ancient authorities read *man or woman;* others, simply *man*

7: *Myths,* theological speculations (1.4; Tit.1.14). **13:** The church adopted many liturgical practices of the synagogue, including *public reading of scripture, preaching, teaching.* **14:** The laying on of hands (see 5.22 n.) is not an empty gesture but expresses the donation and reception of a gift; e.g. Jesus blesses children (Mk.10.16); he heals with a touch (Mk.6.5); the Spirit is given to the baptized (Acts 8.17; 19.6); men are set aside for special tasks in the church (Acts 6.6; 13.3).

5.1–6.2: The pastor and the flock. 5.3–16: Three classes of *widows* are mentioned: (a) *real* widows are older women who depend upon the church for support (Acts 6.1); (b) *enrolled* widows are Christian workers whose qualifications are detailed; they pledge themselves to the service of Christ; (c) *younger* widows are encouraged to remarry. **3:** *Real widows* are not to be treated as burdens but with honor. **17–22:** *Elders,* see Tit.1.5–7 n. **18:** Dt.25.4; Mt.10.10;

laborer deserves his wages." ¹⁹ Never admit any charge against an elder except on the evidence of two or three witnesses. ²⁰ As for those who persist in sin, rebuke them in the presence of all, so that the rest may stand in fear. ²¹ In the presence of God and of Christ Jesus and of the elect angels I charge you to keep these rules without favor, doing nothing from partiality. ²² Do not be hasty in the laying on of hands, nor participate in another man's sins; keep yourself pure.

23 No longer drink only water, but use a little wine for the sake of your stomach and your frequent ailments.

24 The sins of some men are conspicuous, pointing to judgment, but the sins of others appear later. ²⁵ So also good deeds are conspicuous; and even when they are not, they cannot remain hidden.

6 Let all who are under the yoke of slavery regard their masters as worthy of all honor, so that the name of God and the teaching may not be defamed. ² Those who have believing masters must not be disrespectful on the ground that they are brethren; rather they must serve all the better since those who benefit by their service are believers and beloved.

Teach and urge these duties. ³ If any one teaches otherwise and does not agree with the sound words of our Lord Jesus Christ and the teaching which accords with godliness, ⁴ he is puffed up with conceit, he knows nothing; he has a morbid craving for controversy and for disputes about words, which produce envy, dissension, slander, base suspicions, ⁵ and wrangling among men who are depraved in mind and bereft of the truth, imagining that godliness is a means of gain. ⁶ There is great gain in godliness with contentment; ⁷ for we brought nothing into the world, and*ᵐ* we cannot take anything out of the world; ⁸ but if we have food and clothing, with these we shall be content. ⁹ But those who desire to be rich fall into temptation, into a snare, into many senseless and hurtful desires that plunge men into ruin and destruction. ¹⁰ For the love of money is the root of all evils; it is through this craving that some have wandered away from the faith and pierced their hearts with many pangs.

11 But as for you, man of God, shun all this; aim at righteousness, godliness, faith, love, steadfastness, gentleness. ¹² Fight the good fight of the faith; take hold of the eternal life to which you were called when you made the good confession in the presence of many witnesses. ¹³ In the presence of God who gives life to all things, and of Christ Jesus who in his testimony before Pontius Pilate made the good confession, ¹⁴ I charge you to keep the commandment unstained and free from reproach until the appearing of our Lord Jesus Christ; ¹⁵ and this will be made manifest at the proper time by the blessed and only Sovereign, the King of kings and Lord of lords, ¹⁶ who alone has immortality and dwells in unapproachable light, whom no man has ever seen or can see. To him be honor and eternal dominion. Amen.

17 As for the rich in this world,

m Other ancient authorities insert it is certain that

Lk.10.7; 1 Cor.9.9–14. **19:** *Two or three witnesses*, Dt.19.15; Mt.18.16. **21:** *Elect angels*, chosen by God as his ministers (see 1 Cor.11.10 n.; Heb.1.14 n.). **22:** *Laying on of hands* may refer to ordination (see 4.14 n.) or to the restoration of penitents after discipline. **6.1–2:** Slaves and masters (1 Cor.7.21–23; Eph.6.5–9), see Introduction to Philemon.
   6.3–20: Final directions. 3–5: *Sound words*, the apostolic testimony. The false teachers are conceited, contentious, and greedy. **6:** 2 Cor.9.8. **10:** Frequently misquoted: it is the *love of money* which *is the root of all evils*. **12:** *Confession*, a word from the language of worship, signifying adoration and praise of God; in baptism, or before the Roman tribunal, the believer praises God by affirming that Jesus is Lord. **14:** *The commandment*, here probably synonymous with the Christian way of life. **16:** God *alone has immortality*, 1.17; Jn.5.26. *Unapproachable light*, Ps.104.2. *No mere man . . . can see* God (Jn.1.18; 1 Jn.4.12), but the Son can and will

charge them not to be haughty, nor to set their hopes on uncertain riches but on God who richly furnishes us with everything to enjoy. [18] They are to do good, to be rich in good deeds, liberal and generous, [19] thus laying up for themselves a good foundation for the future, so that they may take hold of the life which is life indeed.

20 O Timothy, guard what has been entrusted to you. Avoid the godless chatter and contradictions of what is falsely called knowledge, [21] for by professing it some have missed the mark as regards the faith.
Grace be with you.

---

reveal him (Mt.11.27; 1 Jn.3.2; Rev.22.4). **17–19:** Warnings to the wealthy. **20:** Gnostic pretensions are dealt a final blow in the reference to *what is falsely called knowledge.*

THE SECOND LETTER OF PAUL TO

TIMOTHY

From the book of Acts we learn that Timothy was the son of a Greek and a Jewish woman who had become a Christian (Acts 16.1). Owing to the training he had received from his mother and his grandmother (2 Tim.1.5; 3.15), he already was a Christian when Paul came to his home town in Lystra, Asia Minor, and took him away to be his helper in missionary work. Thereafter he is often mentioned in Acts and in the opening sentences of several of Paul's letters (e.g. 1 and 2 Thessalonians and 2 Corinthians).

The Second Letter to Timothy is an earnest pastoral from a veteran missionary to a younger colleague, urging endurance as the main quality of a preacher of the gospel. Timothy is urged to rekindle the gift of God within him (1.3–7); he is not to be ashamed of witnessing to the Lord (1.8–18); and is to take his share of suffering as a good soldier of Jesus Christ (2.1–13). As he encounters false teachers with "godless chatter," he must endeavor to be a sound workman, handling the word rightly (2.14–19), to purify himself from what is ignoble, so as to be a vessel fit for the Master's use (2.20–26). In this he can be helped by the example of Paul (3.10–17), who is now at the end of his career and awaits the crown of righteousness. The farewell words (4.6–8) are a moving testimony of Christian fortitude and hope in the face of certain martyrdom.

For questions of date and authorship, see the Introduction to 1 Timothy.

PAUL, AN APOSTLE OF CHRIST JESUS by the will of God according to the promise of the life which is in Christ Jesus,

2 To Timothy, my beloved child:
Grace, mercy, and peace from God the Father and Christ Jesus our Lord.

3 I thank God whom I serve with a clear conscience, as did my fathers, when I remember you constantly in my prayers. ⁴ As I remember your tears, I long night and day to see you, that I may be filled with joy. ⁵ I am reminded of your sincere faith, a faith that dwelt first in your grandmother Lo'is and your mother Eunice and now, I am sure, dwells in you. ⁶ Hence I remind you to rekindle the gift of God that is within you through the laying on of my hands; ⁷ for God did not give us a spirit of timidity but a spirit of power and love and self-control.

8 Do not be ashamed then of testifying to our Lord, nor of me his prisoner, but share in suffering for the gospel in the power of God, ⁹ who saved us and called us with a holy calling, not in virtue of our works but in virtue of his own purpose and the grace which he gave us in Christ Jesus ages ago, ¹⁰ and now has manifested through the appearing of our Savior Christ Jesus, who abolished death and brought life and immortality to light through the gospel. ¹¹ For this gospel I was appointed a preacher and apostle and teacher, ¹² and therefore I suffer as I do. But I am not

---

1.1–2: Salutation, see Rom.1.1–7 n. *Grace* . . . see 2 Th.1.2 n. and 1 Tim.1.2 n.

1.3–7: Thanksgiving and exhortation, see Rom.1.8–15 n. **5:** Timothy's family, see Introduction. **6:** God does not regret or withdraw his gifts, but they can become ineffective through one's neglect of them; hence Timothy is encouraged to *rekindle the gift of God. Laying on . . . hands,* see 1 Tim.4.14 n. **7:** Throughout the letter Timothy is exhorted to courage and endurance, which are possibilities, not because of native human qualities, but through the gift of the Holy Spirit (Rom.8.15; Eph.1.17).

1.8–2.13: An appeal to show courage. Timothy was apparently overawed by his surroundings and did not make his witness boldly. **1.9:** In the gospel God invites men to become his own, not as a reward of their accomplishments, but because he is gracious (Eph.1.3–4). **10:** *The appearing,* the Incarnation of Christ. *Abolished death,* Rom.6.9; 8.2; Heb.2.14–15. *Life and immortality,* immortal life (Rom.8.11). **12:** *That Day,* the second coming of Christ (v. 18; 2 Th.1.10). **13:** *The pattern of sound words,* the apostolic testimony to the gospel. **15:** *Asia,* the Roman province

ashamed, for I know whom I have believed, and I am sure that he is able to guard until that Day what has been entrusted to me.[a] [13] Follow the pattern of the sound words which you have heard from me, in the faith and love which are in Christ Jesus; [14] guard the truth that has been entrusted to you by the Holy Spirit who dwells within us.

15 You are aware that all who are in Asia turned away from me, and among them Phy'gelus and Hermog'enes. [16] May the Lord grant mercy to the household of Onesiph'orus, for he often refreshed me; he was not ashamed of my chains, [17] but when he arrived in Rome he searched for me eagerly and found me– [18] may the Lord grant him to find mercy from the Lord on that Day–and you well know all the service he rendered at Ephesus.

2 You then, my son, be strong in the grace that is in Christ Jesus, [2] and what you have heard from me before many witnesses entrust to faithful men who will be able to teach others also. [3] Share in suffering as a good soldier of Christ Jesus. [4] No soldier on service gets entangled in civilian pursuits, since his aim is to satisfy the one who enlisted him. [5] An athlete is not crowned unless he competes according to the rules. [6] It is the hard-working farmer who ought to have the first share of the crops. [7] Think over what I say, for the Lord will grant you understanding in everything.

8 Remember Jesus Christ, risen from the dead, descended from David, as preached in my gospel, [9] the gospel for which I am suffering and wearing fetters like a criminal. But the word of God is not fettered. [10] Therefore I endure everything for the sake of the elect, that they also may obtain sal-

vation in Christ Jesus with its eternal glory. [11] The saying is sure:

If we have died with him, we shall also live with him;
[12] if we endure, we shall also reign with him;
if we deny him, he also will deny us;
[13] if we are faithless, he remains faithful–
for he cannot deny himself.

14 Remind them of this, and charge them before the Lord[b] to avoid disputing about words, which does no good, but only ruins the hearers. [15] Do your best to present yourself to God as one approved, a workman who has no need to be ashamed, rightly handling the word of truth. [16] Avoid such godless chatter, for it will lead people into more and more ungodliness, [17] and their talk will eat its way like gangrene. Among them are Hymenae'us and Phile'tus, [18] who have swerved from the truth by holding that the resurrection is past already. They are upsetting the faith of some. [19] But God's firm foundation stands, bearing this seal: "The Lord knows those who are his," and, "Let every one who names the name of the Lord depart from iniquity."

20 In a great house there are not only vessels of gold and silver but also of wood and earthenware, and some for noble use, some for ignoble. [21] If any one purifies himself from what is ignoble, then he will be a vessel for noble use, consecrated and useful to the master of the house, ready for any good work. [22] So shun youthful passions and aim at righteousness, faith, love, and peace, along with those who call upon the Lord from a pure heart.

a Or *what I have entrusted to him*
b Other ancient authorities read *God*

---

of that name in Asia Minor. **18:** *That Day*, see v. 12 n. **2.3–7:** Three illustrations (*soldier*, *athlete*, *farmer*) having the same point: hold nothing back from commitment to your work. **9:** *The word . . . is not fettered*, Phil.1.12–14. **11:** *The saying* is rhythmical in structure; it may be from an early Christian hymn. *We shall also live with him*, Rom.6.5–11; Gal.6.14; Col.2.12. **12:** *If we deny him*, Mt.10.32–33; Mk.8.38; Lk.12.9. **13:** Rom.3.3–4.

2.14–4.5: The pastor and the flock. 2.15: The task of preaching demands work and discipline. **17:** *Hymenaeus*, 1 Tim.1.20. **19:** *Seal*, an inscription involving quotations from Num.16.5 and Is.26.13, one bearing on predestination, the other on free will. **20:** *In a great house*, such

23 Have nothing to do with stupid, senseless controversies; you know that they breed quarrels. 24 And the Lord's servant must not be quarrelsome but kindly to every one, an apt teacher, forbearing, 25 correcting his opponents with gentleness. God may perhaps grant that they will repent and come to know the truth, 26 and they may escape from the snare of the devil, after being captured by him to do his will.*c*

3 But understand this, that in the last days there will come times of stress. 2 For men will be lovers of self, lovers of money, proud, arrogant, abusive, disobedient to their parents, ungrateful, unholy, 3 inhuman, implacable, slanderers, profligates, fierce, haters of good, 4 treacherous, reckless, swollen with conceit, lovers of pleasure rather than lovers of God, 5 holding the form of religion but denying the power of it. Avoid such people. 6 For among them are those who make their way into households and capture weak women, burdened with sins and swayed by various impulses, 7 who will listen to anybody and can never arrive at a knowledge of the truth. 8 As Jannes and Jambres opposed Moses, so these men also oppose the truth, men of corrupt mind and counterfeit faith; 9 but they will not get very far, for their folly will be plain to all, as was that of those two men.

10 Now you have observed my teaching, my conduct, my aim in life, my faith, my patience, my love, my steadfastness, 11 my persecutions, my sufferings, what befell me at Antioch, at Ico'nium, and at Lystra, what per-

secutions I endured; yet from them all the Lord rescued me. 12 Indeed all who desire to live a godly life in Christ Jesus will be persecuted, 13 while evil men and impostors will go on from bad to worse, deceivers and deceived. 14 But as for you, continue in what you have learned and have firmly believed, knowing from whom you learned it 15 and how from childhood you have been acquainted with the sacred writings which are able to instruct you for salvation through faith in Christ Jesus. 16 All scripture is inspired by God and*d* profitable for teaching, for reproof, for correction, and for training in righteousness, 17 that the man of God may be complete, equipped for every good work.

4 I charge you in the presence of God and of Christ Jesus who is to judge the living and the dead, and by his appearing and his kingdom: 2 preach the word, be urgent in season and out of season, convince, rebuke, and exhort, be unfailing in patience and in teaching. 3 For the time is coming when people will not endure sound teaching, but having itching ears they will accumulate for themselves teachers to suit their own likings, 4 and will turn away from listening to the truth and wander into myths. 5 As for you, always be steady, endure suffering, do the work of an evangelist, fulfil your ministry.

6 For I am already on the point of being sacrificed; the time of my departure has come. 7 I have fought the good fight, I have finished the race, I

c Or by him, to do his (that is, God's) will
d Or Every scripture inspired by God is also

---

as the church is (compare Rom.9.19–24). **25:** *Correcting with gentleness,* nothing is gained by becoming angry; patience and avoidance of controversy may lead some to repentance. **3.1:** *The last days,* which have already begun (compare v. 5; Acts 2.16–17). *Times of stress,* Mt.24.4–5; Mk.13.22; 2 Th.2.3–12. **2:** Rom.1.29–31. **5:** Having the outward *form,* but lacking the vital *power* (1 Cor.2.5; 4.19–20; 1 Th.1.5; Tit.1.16). **6–7:** Love of novelty was a feature of life in ancient times also. **8:** The names *Jannes* and *Jambres* are not given in Ex.7.11, but are supplied by Jewish tradition. **11:** Acts 13.14–52; 14.1–20; 16.1–5; 2 Cor.6.4–10. **15:** *The sacred writings,* the books of the Old Testament, which the church interpreted as pointing to Jesus Christ. **16:** *All scripture,* the Old Testament. *Inspired by God,* compare Gen.2.7 where God breathes life into man. **4.1:** *His appearing,* Christ's second coming. *His kingdom,* the rule of Christ as king. **3:** 3.1. **5:** *Evangelist,* Acts 21.8; Eph.4.11.

have kept the faith. [8] Henceforth there is laid up for me the crown of righteousness, which the Lord, the righteous judge, will award to me on that Day, and not only to me but also to all who have loved his appearing.

[9] Do your best to come to me soon. [10] For Demas, in love with this present world, has deserted me and gone to Thessaloni′ca; Crescens has gone to Galatia,[e] Titus to Dalmatia. [11] Luke alone is with me. Get Mark and bring him with you; for he is very useful in serving me. [12] Tych′icus I have sent to Ephesus. [13] When you come, bring the cloak that I left with Carpus at Tro′as, also the books, and above all the parchments. [14] Alexander the coppersmith did me great harm; the Lord will requite him for his deeds. [15] Beware of him yourself, for he strongly opposed our message. [16] At my first defense no one took my part; all deserted me. May it not be charged against them! [17] But the Lord stood by me and gave me strength to proclaim the message fully, that all the Gentiles might hear it. So I was rescued from the lion's mouth. [18] The Lord will rescue me from every evil and save me for his heavenly kingdom. To him be the glory for ever and ever. Amen.

[19] Greet Prisca and Aq′uila, and the household of Onesiph′orus. [20] Eras′tus remained at Corinth; Troph′imus I left ill at Mile′tus. [21] Do your best to come before winter. Eubu′lus sends greetings to you, as do Pudens and Linus and Claudia and all the brethren.

[22] The Lord be with your spirit. Grace be with you.

e Other ancient authorities read *Gaul*

4.6–22: Concluding exhortations. 8: Among Jews crowns or wreaths of leaves or of flowers were worn as symbols of joy and honor at feasts and weddings. The Greeks gave wreaths to the winners of athletic contests (1 Cor.9.25). **14:** *Alexander*, Acts 19.33; 1 Tim.1.20. **17:** *The lion's mouth*, a common Old Testament metaphor for a violent death (Ps.7.2; 17.12; 22.21). **19:** *Prisca and Aquila*, Acts 18.2,18; Rom.16.3; 1 Cor.16.19. *Onesiphorus*, 1.16–17. **20:** *Trophimus*, Acts 20.4; 21.29. **21:** *Winter*, when navigation was suspended.

THE LETTER OF PAUL TO

TITUS

Though not mentioned in the Acts of the Apostles, Titus is frequently referred to in Paul's letters (particularly in 2 Corinthians and Galatians). Born of Gentile parents (Gal.2.3), he was one of the delegation from Antioch who accompanied Paul and Barnabas to Jerusalem at the time of the apostolic council (Acts 15.2; Gal.2.1,3). During Paul's third missionary journey Titus was twice sent on urgent missions to Corinth and succeeded in restoring harmony between that church and its apostolic founder (see Introduction to 2 Corinthians). Later he was entrusted with the organization of the church on the island of Crete (Tit. 1.5). Subsequently he is said to have gone to Dalmatia, a region on the eastern shore of the Adriatic sea (2 Tim.4.10).

The Letter to Titus has three main topics, corresponding to its chapter divisions. The first sets forth what is required of elders or bishops in the face of various false teachers and local shortcomings. The second suggests the proper approach to different groups in the church: older men (vv. 1–2), older women (vv. 3–5), younger men (vv. 6–8), and slaves (vv. 9–10), and concludes with a summary of what is expected of believers in view of God's grace (vv. 11–15). The third unfolds this ethical program, advising Christians to avoid hatred and wrangling and to manifest the meekness, gentleness, obedience, and courtesy made possible by God's mercy in Christ.

For questions of date and authorship, see the Introduction to 1 Timothy.

PAUL, A SERVANT*a* OF God AND AN apostle of Jesus Christ, to further the faith of God's elect and their knowledge of the truth which accords with godliness, ² in hope of eternal life which God, who never lies, promised ages ago ³ and at the proper time manifested in his word through the preaching with which I have been entrusted by command of God our Savior;

4 To Titus, my true child in a common faith:

Grace and peace from God the Father and Christ Jesus our Savior.

5 This is why I left you in Crete, that you might amend what was defective, and appoint elders in every town as I directed you, ⁶ if any man is blameless, the husband of one wife, and his children are believers and not open to the charge of being profligate or insubordinate. ⁷ For a bishop, as God's steward, must be blameless; he must not be arrogant or quick-tempered or a drunkard or violent or greedy for gain, ⁸ but hospitable, a lover of goodness, master of himself, upright, holy, and self-controlled; ⁹ he must hold firm to the sure word as taught, so that he may be able to give instruction in sound doctrine and also to confute those who contradict it. ¹⁰ For there are many insubordinate men, empty talkers and deceivers, especially the circumcision party; ¹¹ they must be silenced, since they are upsetting whole families by teaching

a Or *slave*

1.1–4: Salutation, see Rom.1.1–7 n. **1:** The church is *God's elect*, the chosen people. **2–3:** The good news of Christ was *promised ages ago* (Lk.24.44; Acts 3.18; Rom.1.2) and revealed at the *proper time* (Mk.1.15; Gal.4.4); the stress is on God's initiative and sovereignty. *Who never lies*, contrast v. 12. **4:** *Grace and peace*, see 2 Th.1.2 n.

1.5–16: Administration of the church in Crete. **5:** *Elder* and *bishop* (v. 7) are two terms for the same officer in the church. **7:** The *bishop* is pictured as *God's steward*, the servant who manages the affairs of a large household. **10:** *The circumcision party* maintained that Christians are subject to the law of Moses and to Jewish traditions (Acts 15.1–29; see Introduction to Galatians). **12:** Quoted from the Cretan poet Epimenides. In ancient parlance "to Cretanize" was to be a liar. **14:** *Jewish myths*, see 1 Tim.1.4 n.

for base gain what they have no right to teach. [12] One of themselves, a prophet of their own, said, "Cretans are always liars, evil beasts, lazy gluttons." [13] This testimony is true. Therefore rebuke them sharply, that they may be sound in the faith, [14] instead of giving heed to Jewish myths or to commands of men who reject the truth. [15] To the pure all things are pure, but to the corrupt and unbelieving nothing is pure; their very minds and consciences are corrupted. [16] They profess to know God, but they deny him by their deeds; they are detestable, disobedient, unfit for any good deed.

2 But as for you, teach what befits sound doctrine. [2] Bid the older men be temperate, serious, sensible, sound in faith, in love, and in steadfastness. [3] Bid the older women likewise to be reverent in behavior, not to be slanderers or slaves to drink; they are to teach what is good, [4] and so train the young women to love their husbands and children, [5] to be sensible, chaste, domestic, kind, and submissive to their husbands, that the word of God may not be discredited. [6] Likewise urge the younger men to control themselves. [7] Show yourself in all respects a model of good deeds, and in your teaching show integrity, gravity, [8] and sound speech that cannot be censured, so that an opponent may be put to shame, having nothing evil to say of us. [9] Bid slaves to be submissive to their masters and to give satisfaction in every respect; they are not to be refractory, [10] nor to pilfer, but to show entire and true fidelity, so that in everything they may adorn the doctrine of God our Savior.

[11] For the grace of God has appeared for the salvation of all men, [12] training us to renounce irreligion and worldly passions, and to live sober, upright, and godly lives in this world, [13] awaiting our blessed hope, the appearing of the glory of our great God and Savior[c] Jesus Christ, [14] who gave himself for us to redeem us from all iniquity and to purify for himself a people of his own who are zealous for good deeds.

[15] Declare these things; exhort and reprove with all authority. Let no one disregard you.

3 Remind them to be submissive to rulers and authorities, to be obedient, to be ready for any honest work, [2] to speak evil of no one, to avoid quarreling, to be gentle, and to show perfect courtesy toward all men. [3] For we ourselves were once foolish, disobedient, led astray, slaves to various passions and pleasures, passing our days in malice and envy, hated by men and hating one another; [4] but when the goodness and loving kindness of God our Savior appeared, [5] he saved us, not because of deeds done by us in righteousness, but in virtue of his own mercy, by the washing of regeneration and renewal in the Holy Spirit, [6] which he poured out upon us richly through Jesus Christ our Savior, [7] so that we might be justified by his grace and become heirs in hope of eternal life. [8] The saying is sure.

I desire you to insist on these things, so that those who have believed in God may be careful to apply them-

c Or *of the great God and our Savior*

2.1–3.11: **The pastor and the flock.** Advice is given on relationships to *older men* (v. 2), *older women* (vv. 3–5), *younger men* (vv. 6–8), *slaves* (vv. 9–10). **5:** *Submissive to their husbands*, see Eph.5.21 n. **7:** Titus himself is to set the example. **9:** *Slaves*, 1 Cor.7.21–23; Eph.6.5–8; Col. 3.22; 1 Tim.6.1–2; see Introduction to Philemon. **14:** *Who gave himself*, Mt.20.28; Mk.10.45; Gal.1.4. *To redeem . . . iniquity*, to ransom us from slavery to sin (Ps.130.8). *To purify . . . a people*, Ezek.37.23; 1 Pet.2.9. **3.1:** *Be submissive*, see 1 Tim.2.2 n. *Honest work*, see 1 Th.2.9 n. **5:** *The washing of regeneration* combines two pictures descriptive of baptism: the washing away of sins (Acts 22.16; Eph.5.26), and rebirth, the beginning of a new life (Jn.3.5). *Renewal in the Holy Spirit*, the restoration of the relationship to God which was lost through sin (2 Cor.5.17). **9:** *Genealogies*, see 1 Tim.1.4 n. **10:** See 2 Jn.10 n.

selves to good deeds;[d] these are excellent and profitable to men. [9] But avoid stupid controversies, genealogies, dissensions, and quarrels over the law, for they are unprofitable and futile. [10] As for a man who is factious, after admonishing him once or twice, have nothing more to do with him, [11] knowing that such a person is perverted and sinful; he is self-condemned.

12 When I send Artemas or Tych'-icus to you, do your best to come to me at Nicop'olis, for I have decided to spend the winter there. [13] Do your best to speed Zenas the lawyer and Apol'los on their way; see that they lack nothing. [14] And let our people learn to apply themselves to good deeds,[d] so as to help cases of urgent need, and not to be unfruitful.

15 All who are with me send greetings to you. Greet those who love us in the faith.

Grace be with you all.

d Or *enter honorable occupations*

3.12–15: Final instructions. 12: *Tychicus,* Acts 20.4; Eph.6.21; Col.4.7; 2 Tim.4.12. **13:** *Apollos,* Acts 18.24; 1 Cor.1.12; 16.12.

THE LETTER OF PAUL TO

PHILEMON

What should be done when a runaway slave who has robbed his master repents of his misdeeds and becomes a Christian? The Letter to Philemon, a resident of Colossae in Phrygia, is a model of Christian tactfulness in seeking to effect reconciliation between Onesimus, the runaway slave, and his master, who according to Roman law had absolute authority over the person and life of his slave.

While Paul was under house arrest at Rome (about A.D. 61–63, see Acts 28.30 n.), Onesimus came under his influence and was converted (v. 10; compare Col.4.9). Paul persuaded him to return to his master, Philemon, who had previously become a Christian as a result of Paul's earlier preaching in Asia Minor (v. 19) and whose home was now a meeting place of a Christian congregation.

When it is realized that in the ancient world slavery was regarded as a legitimate and necessary segment of the social order, and that severe laws punished those who interfered with the rights of slave-owners, it is not surprising that neither Jesus nor any of the apostles attacked the institution of slavery as such. At the same time Jesus' teaching of the essential worth of every human soul (Mt.6.26; 10.24–31; Lk. ch. 15) and the church's recognition of the brotherhood of all Christian believers (Gal.3.28; Eph.6.5–9; Col.3.11) were destined to reorganize society. This Letter to Philemon reveals yet another side of the apostle Paul. In a situation which involved no doctrinal or ecclesiastical dispute, he writes with a delicate appreciation of the legal rights of Philemon, while inculcating at the same time a principle (v. 16) which would soften the harshness of slavery and eventually operate to banish it altogether.

PAUL, A PRISONER FOR CHRIST Jesus, and Timothy our brother,

To Phile′mon our beloved fellow worker [2] and Ap′phia our sister and Archip′pus our fellow soldier, and the church in your house:

3 Grace to you and peace from God our Father and the Lord Jesus Christ.

4 I thank my God always when I remember you in my prayers, [5] because I hear of your love and of the faith which you have toward the Lord Jesus and all the saints, [6] and I pray that the sharing of your faith may promote the knowledge of all the good that is ours in Christ. [7] For I have derived much joy and comfort from your love, my brother, because the hearts of the saints have been refreshed through you.

8 Accordingly, though I am bold enough in Christ to command you to do what is required, [9] yet for love's sake I prefer to appeal to you—I, Paul, an ambassador[a] and now a prisoner also for Christ Jesus— [10] I appeal to you for my child, Ones′imus, whose father I have become in my imprisonment. [11] (Formerly he was useless to you, but now he is indeed useful[b] to you and to me.) [12] I am sending him back to you, sending my very heart. [13] I would have been glad to keep him with me, in order that he might serve me on your behalf during my imprisonment for the gospel; [14] but I preferred to do

a Or *an old man*
b The name Onesimus means *useful* or (compare verse 20) *beneficial*

1–3: **Salutation**, see Rom.1.1–7 n. **1**: *Prisoner*, see Introduction. **2**: *Sister*, in the faith. *The church in your house*, in the first century Christians met for worship in private homes (Rom.16.5; 1 Cor.16.19; Col.4.15). **3**: *Grace . . . peace*, see 2 Th.1.2 n.
4–7: **Thanksgiving**, see Rom.1.8–15 n. **7**: *Refreshed through* Philemon's charitable acts.
8–20: **Paul's plea for Onesimus. 9**: *Ambassador*, 2 Cor.5.20. **10**: *My child* in the Christian faith (see Gal.4.19 n.). *Onesimus*, see note *b*. **14**: Though as an apostle Paul had the right to

nothing without your consent in order that your goodness might not be by compulsion but of your own free will.

15 Perhaps this is why he was parted from you for a while, that you might have him back for ever, [16] no longer as a slave but more than a slave, as a beloved brother, especially to me but how much more to you, both in the flesh and in the Lord. [17] So if you consider me your partner, receive him as you would receive me. [18] If he has wronged you at all, or owes you anything, charge that to my account. [19] I, Paul, write this with my own hand, I will repay it–to say nothing of your owing me even your own self. [20] Yes, brother, I want some benefit from you in the Lord. Refresh my heart in Christ.

21 Confident of your obedience, I write to you, knowing that you will do even more than I say. [22] At the same time, prepare a guest room for me, for I am hoping through your prayers to be granted to you.

23 Ep'aphras, my fellow prisoner in Christ Jesus, sends greetings to you, [24] and so do Mark, Aristar'chus, Demas, and Luke, my fellow workers.

25 The grace of the Lord Jesus Christ be with your spirit.

---

command (v. 8), he leaves the matter to Philemon's free choice. **15:** *Was parted*, a tactful expression for "ran away." *Back forever*, suggesting God's providential oversight. **18:** Paul avoids speaking bluntly of the theft. **21:** *More than I say*, perhaps a gentle hint that Philemon should grant Onesimus his freedom.

21–25: Concluding hopes and greetings. 22: While Philemon's *guest*, Paul will be able to observe how Onesimus has been treated. **23:** Col.1.7; 4.12. **24:** Col.4.10,14.

THE LETTER TO THE HEBREWS

This anonymous treatise contains the longest sustained argument of any book in the Bible. With a careful and closely knit discussion, the unknown author moves with confidence step by step through an elaborate proof of the pre-eminence of Christianity over Judaism.

The recipients of the letter were on the point of giving up their Christian faith and returning to the Jewish beliefs and practices of their ancestors. To win them back to a firm adherence to Christianity the author emphasizes three main points: (a) The superiority of Jesus Christ to the prophets (1.1–3), to the angels (1.5–2.18), and to Moses himself (3.1–6); (b) The superiority of Christ's priesthood to the Levitical priesthood (4.14–7.28); and (c) The superiority of Christ's sacrifice offered in the heavenly sanctuary to the many animal sacrifices offered on earth by the Levitical priests (8.1–10.39). At frequent and appropriate junctures within the theological discussion the author inserts earnest admonitions based on the argument in the immediately preceding section.

From internal considerations it appears that the letter was written prior to the fall of Jerusalem and the destruction of the temple in A.D. 70. At an early date the church recognized the intrinsic worth of this "word of exhortation" (13.22), and Christians of all ages have been inspired by the great chapter on faith (ch. 11) as well as by the author's profound interpretation of the significance of the person and work of Jesus Christ, "the same yesterday and today and forever" (13.8).

IN MANY AND VARIOUS WAYS God spoke of old to our fathers by the prophets; ² but in these last days he has spoken to us by a Son, whom he appointed the heir of all things, through whom also he created the world. ³ He reflects the glory of God and bears the very stamp of his nature, upholding the universe by his word of power. When he had made purification for sins, he sat down at the right hand of the Majesty on high, ⁴ having become as much superior to angels as the name he has obtained is more excellent than theirs.

5 For to what angel did God ever say,
"Thou art my Son,
today I have begotten thee"?
Or again,
"I will be to him a father,
and he shall be to me a son"?
⁶ And again, when he brings the firstborn into the world, he says,
"Let all God's angels worship him."
⁷ Of the angels he says,
"Who makes his angels winds,
and his servants flames of fire."
⁸ But of the Son he says,
"Thy throne, O God,ᵃ is for ever
and ever,
the righteous scepter is the scepter
of thyᵇ kingdom.
⁹ Thou hast loved righteousness and
hated lawlessness;
therefore God, thy God, has
anointed thee
with the oil of gladness beyond thy
comrades."
¹⁰ And,

---

a Or *God is thy throne*
b Other ancient authorities read *his*

1.1–4: The prologue, a stately declaration of the author's theme, namely the superiority of Christianity to Judaism. Note the contrasts between *of old* and *in these last days, to our fathers* and *to us, by the prophets* and *by a Son;* yet it is the same God who spoke then and speaks now. God's *Son,* who is the exact counterpart of the Father (v. 3), not only had part in the creation (Jn.1.1–3), but continues to sustain *the universe* (Col.1.15–17). Having accomplished his priestly work of *purification for sins* (v. 3), he was enthroned in royal splendor. Thus Christ is prophet (in him God spoke forth), priest, and king.

1.5–2.18: The superiority of Christ to angels. 1.5–13: Seven quotations from the Old Testament. **5:** Ps.2.7 and 2 Sam.7.14. **6:** Dt.32.43 Septuagint, compare Ps.97.7. **7:** Ps.104.4. **8–9:** Ps.45.6–7. **10–12:** Ps.102.25–27. **13:** Ps.110.1. **14:** As to their nature, angels are *spirits;* as to

"Thou, Lord, didst found the earth
    in the beginning,
and the heavens are the work of thy
    hands;
11 they will perish, but thou remainest;
    they will all grow old like a garment,
12 like a mantle thou wilt roll them up,
    and they will be changed.[c]
  But thou art the same,
    and thy years will never end."
13 But to what angel has he ever said,
  "Sit at my right hand,
  till I make thy enemies
  a stool for thy feet"?
14 Are they not all ministering spirits
sent forth to serve, for the sake of those
who are to obtain salvation?

2 Therefore we must pay the closer
attention to what we have heard,
lest we drift away from it. 2 For if the
message declared by angels was valid
and every transgression or disobedience received a just retribution, 3 how
shall we escape if we neglect such a
great salvation? It was declared at first
by the Lord, and it was attested to us
by those who heard him, 4 while God
also bore witness by signs and wonders
and various miracles and by gifts of the
Holy Spirit distributed according to
his own will.

5 For it was not to angels that God
subjected the world to come, of which
we are speaking. 6 It has been testified
somewhere,
  "What is man that thou art mindful
    of him,
  or the son of man, that thou carest
    for him?

7 Thou didst make him for a little
    while lower than the angels,
  thou hast crowned him with glory
    and honor,[d]
8 putting everything in subjection
    under his feet."
Now in putting everything in subjection
to him, he left nothing outside his control. As it is, we do not yet see everything in subjection to him. 9 But we
see Jesus, who for a little while was
made lower than the angels, crowned
with glory and honor because of the
suffering of death, so that by the grace
of God he might taste death for
every one.

10 For it was fitting that he, for
whom and by whom all things exist,
in bringing many sons to glory, should
make the pioneer of their salvation
perfect through suffering. 11 For he
who sanctifies and those who are
sanctified have all one origin. That is
why he is not ashamed to call them
brethren, 12 saying,
  "I will proclaim thy name to my
    brethren,
  in the midst of the congregation I
    will praise thee."
13 And again,
  "I will put my trust in him."
And again,
  "Here am I, and the children God
    has given me."
14 Since therefore the children
share in flesh and blood, he himself
likewise partook of the same nature,

c Other ancient authorities add *like a garment*
d Other ancient authorities insert *and didst set him over
the works of thy hands*

---

their function, they are *sent . . . to serve*. **2.1–4: Warning and exhortation.** The superior status
of the Son to angels authenticates his message and lays a greater obligation on those who *heard*.
2: *The message declared by angels*, see Acts 7.53 n.; Gal.3.19 n.
  2.5–18: The suffering of Jesus. Though Jesus, in his humiliation, was *for a little while . . . lower
than the angels* (v. 9), his suffering was temporary and enabled him to *become a merciful and
faithful high priest* (v. 7). **6–8:** Quoted from Ps.8.4–6; *for a little while* (v. 7) agrees with the
Septuagint, not the Hebrew. **9:** Jesus' exaltation is the consequence of his humiliation (12.2;
Phil.2.6–11). *By the grace of God;* some ancient witnesses read "apart from God." *Taste death*,
experience its full bitterness (Mt.26.39). **10–18:** The high destiny of man, described in Ps. 8, is
to be attained through the work of Christ. **10:** *It was fitting*, it was in accord with God's gracious
nature. The idea, "to make perfect," is characteristic of this letter (5.9; 7.19,28; 9.9; 10.1,14;
11.40; 12.23) and means "to make complete, to bring to maturity." Christ as *pioneer* goes before
and points out the way to his followers (12.2); the same Greek word is translated "Author"
(Acts 3.15) and "Leader" (Acts 5.31). **11:** *He who sanctifies*, Jesus Christ; *those who are sanctified*, see 10.10 n. *One origin*, God. **12:** Ps.22.22. **13:** Is.8.17–18. **14–15:** The eternal Son became

that through death he might destroy him who has the power of death, that is, the devil, [15] and deliver all those who through fear of death were subject to lifelong bondage. [16] For surely it is not with angels that he is concerned but with the descendants of Abraham. [17] Therefore he had to be made like his brethren in every respect, so that he might become a merciful and faithful high priest in the service of God, to make expiation for the sins of the people. [18] For because he himself has suffered and been tempted, he is able to help those who are tempted.

3 Therefore, holy brethren, who share in a heavenly call, consider Jesus, the apostle and high priest of our confession. [2] He was faithful to him who appointed him, just as Moses also was faithful in[e] God's house. [3] Yet Jesus has been counted worthy of as much more glory than Moses as the builder of a house has more honor than the house. [4] (For every house is built by some one, but the builder of all things is God.) [5] Now Moses was faithful in all God's house as a servant, to testify to the things that were to be spoken later, [6] but Christ was faithful over God's[f] house as a son. And we are his house if we hold fast our confidence and pride in our hope.[g]

7 Therefore, as the Holy Spirit says,
"Today, when you hear his voice,

[8] do not harden your hearts as in the rebellion,
on the day of testing in the wilderness,
[9] where your fathers put me to the test
and saw my works for forty years.
[10] Therefore I was provoked with that generation,
and said, 'They always go astray in their hearts;
they have not known my ways.'
[11] As I swore in my wrath,
'They shall never enter my rest.' "

[12] Take care, brethren, lest there be in any of you an evil, unbelieving heart, leading you to fall away from the living God. [13] But exhort one another every day, as long as it is called "today," that none of you may be hardened by the deceitfulness of sin. [14] For we share in Christ, if only we hold our first confidence firm to the end, [15] while it is said,

"Today, when you hear his voice,
do not harden your hearts as in the rebellion."

[16] Who were they that heard and yet were rebellious? Was it not all those who left Egypt under the leadership of Moses? [17] And with whom was he provoked forty years? Was it not with those who sinned, whose bodies fell in the wilderness? [18] And to whom did he

e Other ancient authorities insert *all*
f Greek *his*
g Other ancient authorities insert *firm to the end*

man in order to overcome the devil and to free men from the fear of death (Rom.6.23). **17:** As high priest the Son is both sympathetic (*merciful;* compare 5.2–3) and trustworthy (*faithful;* compare 3.2,6), *to make expiation* continually for *sins* that bring death and the fear of it to his *people* (vv. 14–15). **18:** At Gethsemane, and elsewhere, Jesus was *tempted* to escape the death of the cross (5.7–8); therefore he can help those who *are tempted* to apostatize.

3.1–6: Christ is superior to Moses. 1: *Holy brethren*, the readers are addressed in terms that remind them of their position and responsibility in sharing *in a heavenly* calling, as distinguished from the calling of Israel to an earthly Canaan. As *apostle, Jesus* is God's envoy to men; as *high priest*, he is man's representative before God. **2:** Tactfully the author first refers to what Jesus and Moses have in common, namely faithfulness to their respective tasks. **3–5:** As to position, Jesus (a son) is superior to Moses (a servant in God's house; Num.12.7). **6:** *We are his house*, the community of faithful believers.

3.7–4.13: Warning and exhortation, based on the terrible fate of Israel in the desert (Ps. 95.7–11). **3.8:** *Rebellion* and *testing* are translations of the Hebrew names, Meribah and Massah, in Ps.95.8 (Ex.17.1–7; Num.20.1–13; Dt.33.8). **11:** *My rest*, the peaceful settlement of the promised land of Canaan (4.1–4). **12:** Jer.17.5–6. **13:** *The deceitfulness of sin*, the specious attractiveness of unbelief, leading to apostasy (v. 12). **16–18:** A series of questions (based on Num.14.1–35) suggests the lessons to be drawn from Israel's tragic failure.

swear that they should never enter his rest, but to those who were disobedient? ¹⁹ So we see that they were unable to enter because of unbelief.

4 Therefore, while the promise of entering his rest remains, let us fear lest any of you be judged to have failed to reach it. ² For good news came to us just as to them; but the message which they heard did not benefit them, because it did not meet with faith in the hearers.ʰ ³ For we who have believed enter that rest, as he has said,

"As I swore in my wrath,
'They shall never enter my rest,' "
although his works were finished from the foundation of the world. ⁴ For he has somewhere spoken of the seventh day in this way, "And God rested on the seventh day from all his works." ⁵ And again in this place he said,

"They shall never enter my rest."
⁶ Since therefore it remains for some to enter it, and those who formerly received the good news failed to enter because of disobedience, ⁷ again he sets a certain day, "Today," saying through David so long afterward, in the words already quoted,

"Today, when you hear his voice,
do not harden your hearts."
⁸ For if Joshua had given them rest, Godⁱ would not speak later of another day. ⁹ So then, there remains a sabbath rest for the people of God; ¹⁰ for whoever enters God's rest also ceases from his labors as God did from his.

11 Let us therefore strive to enter that rest, that no one fall by the same sort of disobedience. ¹² For the word of God is living and active, sharper than any two-edged sword, piercing to the division of soul and spirit, of joints and marrow, and discerning the thoughts and intentions of the heart. ¹³ And before him no creature is hidden, but all are open and laid bare to the eyes of him with whom we have to do.

14 Since then we have a great high priest who has passed through the heavens, Jesus, the Son of God, let us hold fast our confession. ¹⁵ For we have not a high priest who is unable to sympathize with our weaknesses, but one who in every respect has been tempted as we are, yet without sin. ¹⁶ Let us then with confidence draw near to the throne of grace, that we may receive mercy and find grace to help in time of need.

5 For every high priest chosen from among men is appointed to act on behalf of men in relation to God, to offer gifts and sacrifices for sins. ² He can deal gently with the ignorant and wayward, since he himself is beset with weakness. ³ Because of this he is bound to offer sacrifice for his own sins as well as for those of the people. ⁴ And one does not take the honor upon himself, but he is called by God, just as Aaron was.

h Other manuscripts read *they were not united in faith with the hearers*
i Greek *he*

4.1–13: The rest which God promised. 1: God's *promise*, which must be fulfilled, *remains* for Christians to appropriate (v. 6). **2:** *The hearers*, Num.13.30–14.10. **3:** Ps.95.11. **4:** Gen.2.2. **5:** Ps.95.11. **6:** See v. 1 n. **7:** Ps.95.7–8. **7–8:** The possession of Canaan under *Joshua* was not the promised *rest*, otherwise *David* would not have spoken centuries later of a *rest* still remaining. **9–10:** *Sabbath rest*, points back to God's rest after the work of creation (Gen.2.2), and forward to the eternal satisfaction of rest after the toils of this life. **11–13: An exhortation** to diligence, reinforced by a reminder that *the word of God* can discern all secret *intentions of the heart.*

4.14–5.14: The theme of **Jesus our high priest** is resumed (compare 2.17–18); he has the two qualifications of a priest, divine appointment (5.4) and the ability to *sympathize with our weaknesses* (4.15). **4.15–16:** The force of his temptations was all the fiercer because he never yielded; therefore he is tender *to sympathize* and strong to aid. **16:** At God's *throne of grace* men *receive mercy* for past sins and *find grace* for present and future *need*. **5.1:** *Gifts and sacrifices*, cereal and animal sacrifices. **2:** The Old Testament provides no atoning sacrifice for deliberate and defiant sins (see Num.15.30 n.; Dt.17.12), but only for "unwitting" offenses committed by

5 So also Christ did not exalt himself to be made a high priest, but was appointed by him who said to him,
"Thou art my Son,
today I have begotten thee";
6 as he says also in another place,
"Thou art a priest for ever,
after the order of Melchiz′edek."
7 In the days of his flesh, Jesus[j] offered up prayers and supplications, with loud cries and tears, to him who was able to save him from death, and he was heard for his godly fear. 8 Although he was a Son, he learned obedience through what he suffered; 9 and being made perfect he became the source of eternal salvation to all who obey him, 10 being designated by God a high priest after the order of Melchiz′edek.

11 About this we have much to say which is hard to explain, since you have become dull of hearing. 12 For though by this time you ought to be teachers, you need some one to teach you again the first principles of God's word. You need milk, not solid food; 13 for every one who lives on milk is unskilled in the word of righteousness, for he is a child. 14 But solid food is for the mature, for those who have their faculties trained by practice to distinguish good from evil.

6 Therefore let us leave the elementary doctrine of Christ and go on to maturity, not laying again a foundation of repentance from dead works and of faith toward God, 2 with in-

struction[k] about ablutions, the laying on of hands, the resurrection of the dead, and eternal judgment. 3 And this we will do if God permits.[l] 4 For it is impossible to restore again to repentance those who have once been enlightened, who have tasted the heavenly gift, and have become partakers of the Holy Spirit, 5 and have tasted the goodness of the word of God and the powers of the age to come, 6 if they then commit apostasy, since they crucify the Son of God on their own account and hold him up to contempt. 7 For land which has drunk the rain that often falls upon it, and brings forth vegetation useful to those for whose sake it is cultivated, receives a blessing from God. 8 But if it bears thorns and thistles, it is worthless and near to being cursed; its end is to be burned.

9 Though we speak thus, yet in your case, beloved, we feel sure of better things that belong to salvation. 10 For God is not so unjust as to overlook your work and the love which you showed for his sake in serving the saints, as you still do. 11 And we desire each one of you to show the same earnestness in realizing the full assurance of hope until the end, 12 so that you may not be sluggish, but imitators of those who through faith and patience inherit the promises.

13 For when God made a promise

j Greek he
k Other ancient manuscripts read of instruction
l Other ancient manuscripts read let us do this if God permits

the ignorant and wayward (Lev. ch. 4). **4:** Aaron, Ex.28.1. **5:** Ps.2.7. **6:** The order of Melchizedek, according to the rank which Melchizedek held (Ps.110.4; see 7.1–10 n.). **7–8:** Jesus' agonizing prayer in Gethsemane (Mk.14.32–42) was heard in the sense that he learned obedience by submitting to the divine will, which involved death and resurrection. **9:** Made perfect, Jesus completed his divinely appointed discipline for priesthood (see 2.10 n.). Eternal salvation, not merely temporary deliverance, such as the Levitical law provided (9.12). **10:** Melchizedek, see 7.1–10 n. **11–14:** The author deplores the spiritual immaturity of his readers. **12–14:** Milk stands for rudimentary teachings; solid food, more advanced doctrinal teaching (1 Cor.3.1–2).

6.1–20: Exhortation and declaration of purpose. Despite misgivings as to the capacity of his readers (5.11–14), and taking the elements of Christian knowledge for granted (6.1–3), the author is resolved to proceed to more advanced subjects. Though it would be useless to address himself to those who have apostatized from the faith (vv. 4–6), who are like worthless land (vv. 7–8), he is persuaded that this gloomy picture does not represent the condition of his readers (vv. 9–12), whom he addresses for the first and only time as beloved (v. 9). **13–20:** The certainty of God's promises. To encourage patient waiting (v. 12) the author mentions the example of Abraham

to Abraham, since he had no one greater by whom to swear, he swore by himself, [14] saying, "Surely I will bless you and multiply you." [15] And thus Abraham,[m] having patiently endured, obtained the promise. [16] Men indeed swear by a greater than themselves, and in all their disputes an oath is final for confirmation. [17] So when God desired to show more convincingly to the heirs of the promise the unchangeable character of his purpose, he interposed with an oath, [18] so that through two unchangeable things, in which it is impossible that God should prove false, we who have fled for refuge might have strong encouragement to seize the hope set before us. [19] We have this as a sure and steadfast anchor of the soul, a hope that enters into the inner shrine behind the curtain, [20] where Jesus has gone as a forerunner on our behalf, having become a high priest for ever after the order of Melchiz'edek.

7 For this Melchiz'edek, king of Salem, priest of the Most High God, met Abraham returning from the slaughter of the kings and blessed him; [2] and to him Abraham apportioned a tenth part of everything. He is first, by translation of his name, king of righteousness, and then he is also king of Salem, that is, king of peace. [3] He is without father or mother or genealogy, and has neither beginning of days nor end of life, but resembling the Son of God he continues a priest for ever.

[4] See how great he is! Abraham the patriarch gave him a tithe of the spoils. [5] And those descendants of Levi who receive the priestly office have a commandment in the law to take tithes from the people, that is, from their brethren, though these also are descended from Abraham. [6] But this man who has not their genealogy received tithes from Abraham and blessed him who had the promises. [7] It is beyond dispute that the inferior is blessed by the superior. [8] Here tithes are received by mortal men; there, by one of whom it is testified that he lives. [9] One might even say that Levi himself, who receives tithes, paid tithes through Abraham, [10] for he was still in the loins of his ancestor when Melchiz'edek met him.

11 Now if perfection had been attainable through the Levit'ical priesthood (for under it the people received the law), what further need would there have been for another priest to arise after the order of Melchiz'edek, rather than one named after the order of Aaron? [12] For when there is a change in the priesthood, there is necessarily a change in the law as well. [13] For the one of whom these things are spoken belonged to another tribe, from which no one has ever served at the altar. [14] For it is evident that our Lord was descended from Judah, and in connection with that tribe Moses said nothing about priests.

15 This becomes even more evident when another priest arises in the likeness of Melchiz'edek, [16] who has become a priest, not according to a legal requirement concerning bodily descent but by the power of an indestructible life. [17] For it is witnessed of him,

m Greek *he*

(v. 15). **13–14:** Gen.22.16–17. **18:** *Two unchangeable things*, God's promise and God's oath. **19:** *The inner shrine*, the Holy of Holies (9.3) of the tabernacle, *behind the curtain* or veil (Ex. 26.31–35), restricted to the high priest alone (Lev.16.2); as *forerunner*, however, Jesus secures our unhindered access to God. **20:** *Melchizedek*, here the author picks up the argument of 5.10.

    7.1–28: The priesthood of Melchizedek and the Levitical priesthood compared. 1–10: From details in Gen.14.17–20 the author deduces that the mysterious priest-king, Melchizedek, was greater than either Abraham or his descendent, Levi. **3:** Nothing more is implied than that Melchizedek's ancestors, birth, and death are not recorded in Scripture. **8:** *Mortal men*, the Levitical priests. *One* who *lives*, Melchizedek, whose death is not recorded. **11–25:** The Levitical priesthood is inadequate, because it is provisional and temporary (vv. 11–14). On the other hand, a *priest . . . in the likeness of Melchizedek* is eternal (Ps.110.4), and his office is neither

"Thou art a priest for ever,
after the order of Melchiz'edek."
[18] On the one hand, a former commandment is set aside because of its weakness and uselessness [19] (for the law made nothing perfect); on the other hand, a better hope is introduced, through which we draw near to God.

20 And it was not without an oath. [21] Those who formerly became priests took their office without an oath, but this one was addressed with an oath,

"The Lord has sworn
and will not change his mind,
'Thou art a priest for ever.' "
[22] This makes Jesus the surety of a better covenant.

23 The former priests were many in number, because they were prevented by death from continuing in office; [24] but he holds his priesthood permanently, because he continues for ever. [25] Consequently he is able for all time to save those who draw near to God through him, since he always lives to make intercession for them.

26 For it was fitting that we should have such a high priest, holy, blameless, unstained, separated from sinners, exalted above the heavens. [27] He has no need, like those high priests, to offer sacrifices daily, first for his own sins and then for those of the people; he did this once for all when he offered up himself. [28] Indeed, the law appoints men in their weakness as high priests, but the word of the oath, which came later than the law, appoints a Son who has been made perfect for ever.

8 Now the point in what we are saying is this: we have such a high priest, one who is seated at the right hand of the throne of the Majesty in heaven, [2] a minister in the sanctuary and the true tent[n] which is set up not by man but by the Lord. [3] For every high priest is appointed to offer gifts and sacrifices; hence it is necessary for this priest also to have something to offer. [4] Now if he were on earth, he would not be a priest at all, since there are priests who offer gifts according to the law. [5] They serve a copy and shadow of the heavenly sanctuary; for when Moses was about to erect the tent,[n] he was instructed by God, saying, "See that you make everything according to the pattern which was shown you on the mountain." [6] But as it is, Christ[o] has obtained a ministry which is as much more excellent than the old as the covenant he mediates is better, since it is enacted on better promises. [7] For if that first covenant had been faultless, there would have been no occasion for a second.

8 For he finds fault with them when he says:

"The days will come, says the Lord,
when I will establish a new covenant
with the house of Israel
and with the house of Judah;
[9] not like the covenant that I made
with their fathers
on the day when I took them by
the hand
to lead them out of the land of
Egypt;
for they did not continue in my
covenant,
and so I paid no heed to them, says
the Lord.
[10] This is the covenant that I will make
with the house of Israel
after those days, says the Lord:
I will put my laws into their minds,
and write them on their hearts,

n Or *tabernacle*   *o* Greek *he*

---

inherited nor transmitted (vv. 15–19). Unlike the Levitical priests, Jesus was appointed with a divine oath (Ps.110.4); furthermore, being immortal Jesus *holds his priesthood permanently* (vv. 20–25). **26–28:** Summary of the merits of our high priest, Jesus the Son of God.
8.1–13: The heavenly sanctuary and the new covenant. 1–6: The chief *point . . . is this, we have . . . a high priest* who is also the enthroned king, ministering on our behalf in the heavenly sanctuary, of which the earthly tabernacle erected by Moses was *a copy* (v. 5; Ex.25.40). **7–12:** The *new covenant*, of which Jeremiah prophesied (Jer.31.31–34), surpasses the *first covenant* in

and I will be their God,
and they shall be my people.
11 And they shall not teach every one
his fellow
or every one his brother, saying,
'Know the Lord,'
for all shall know me,
from the least of them to the
greatest.
12 For I will be merciful toward their
iniquities,
and I will remember their sins no
more."
13 In speaking of a new covenant he treats the first as obsolete. And what is becoming obsolete and growing old is ready to vanish away.

9 Now even the first covenant had regulations for worship and an earthly sanctuary. 2 For a tent*p* was prepared, the outer one, in which were the lampstand and the table and the bread of the Presence;*q* it is called the Holy Place. 3 Behind the second curtain stood a tent*p* called the Holy of Holies, 4 having the golden altar of incense and the ark of the covenant covered on all sides with gold, which contained a golden urn holding the manna, and Aaron's rod that budded, and the tables of the covenant; 5 above it were the cherubim of glory overshadowing the mercy seat. Of these things we cannot now speak in detail.

6 These preparations having thus been made, the priests go continually into the outer tent,*p* performing their ritual duties; 7 but into the second only the high priest goes, and he but once a year, and not without taking blood which he offers for himself and for the errors of the people. 8 By this the Holy Spirit indicates that the way into the sanctuary is not yet opened as long as the outer tent*p* is still standing 9 (which is symbolic for the present age). According to this arrangement, gifts and sacrifices are offered which cannot perfect the conscience of the worshiper, 10 but deal only with food and drink and various ablutions, regulations for the body imposed until the time of reformation.

11 But when Christ appeared as a high priest of the good things that have come,*r* then through the greater and more perfect tent*p* (not made with hands, that is, not of this creation) 12 he entered once for all into the Holy Place, taking*s* not the blood of goats and calves but his own blood, thus securing an eternal redemption. 13 For if the sprinkling of defiled persons with the blood of goats and bulls and with the ashes of a heifer sanctifies for the purification of the flesh, 14 how much more shall the blood of Christ, who through the eternal Spirit offered himself without blemish to God, purify your*t* conscience from dead works to serve the living God.

p Or *tabernacle*
q Greek *the presentation of the loaves*
r Other manuscripts read *good things to come*
s Greek *through*
t Other manuscripts read *our*

promising a universal and personal knowledge of God. **13:** Even in Jeremiah's day the old covenant was treated as *obsolete* (Jer.31.31–32).
9.1–10: The ministry of the Levitical priests (Ex.25.10–40). **2:** *The bread of the Presence*, Lev.24.5–9. **3:** Ex.26.31–33. **4:** *The golden altar of incense* stood in the Holy Place (Ex.30.6). *Ark of the covenant*, the chest containing the tables of the Law (Ex.25.10–22). *Urn . . . manna*, Ex.16.32–34. *Aaron's rod*, Num.17.1–10. **7:** Lev. ch. 16. *Errors of the people*, see 5.2 n. **9–10:** *Perfect*, see 2.10 n. *The conscience*, Levitical sacrifices cannot produce an inward purity. **10:** *The time of reformation*, the period of the new covenant, inaugurated by the death of Christ.
9.11–10.18: Characteristics of the sacrifice of Christ. The offering of the blood of Christ is incomparably superior to sacrifices of *the blood of goats and calves* (9.13–14), because (a) it is the life (Lev.17.11) of a person, the Christ, not of irrational beasts (10.4); (b) Christ was both priest and sacrificial victim (9.12); (c) the offering was *made once for all* (9.12,25–26; 10.11–12); (d) it was made in the heavenly tabernacle (9.24); (e) it was a voluntary act (10.9; compare Jn.10.17–18), accomplished through his *eternal Spirit* (9.14); and therefore (f) the efficacy of his sacrifice remains *for all time* (10.14). **9.13:** Lev.16.6,16; Num.19.9,17–18. **14:** *The eternal Spirit*, or "his eternal spirit." **15:** Christ's death redeemed also the Old Testament saints (11.39–40),

15 Therefore he is the mediator of a new covenant, so that those who are called may receive the promised eternal inheritance, since a death has occurred which redeems them from the transgressions under the first covenant.[u] 16 For where a will[u] is involved, the death of the one who made it must be established. 17 For a will[u] takes effect only at death, since it is not in force as long as the one who made it is alive. 18 Hence even the first covenant was not ratified without blood. 19 For when every commandment of the law had been declared by Moses to all the people, he took the blood of calves and goats, with water and scarlet wool and hyssop, and sprinkled both the book itself and all the people, 20 saying, "This is the blood of the covenant which God commanded you." 21 And in the same way he sprinkled with the blood both the tent[p] and all the vessels used in worship. 22 Indeed, under the law almost everything is purified with blood, and without the shedding of blood there is no forgiveness of sins.

23 Thus it was necessary for the copies of the heavenly things to be purified with these rites, but the heavenly things themselves with better sacrifices than these. 24 For Christ has entered, not into a sanctuary made with hands, a copy of the true one, but into heaven itself, now to appear in the presence of God on our behalf. 25 Nor was it to offer himself repeatedly, as the high priest enters the Holy Place yearly with blood not his own; 26 for then he would have had to suffer repeatedly since the foundation of the world. But as it is, he has appeared once for all at the end of the age to put away sin by the sacrifice of himself. 27 And just as it is appointed for men to die once, and after that comes judgment, 28 so Christ,

having been offered once to bear the sins of many, will appear a second time, not to deal with sin but to save those who are eagerly waiting for him.

10 For since the law has but a shadow of the good things to come instead of the true form of these realities, it can never, by the same sacrifices which are continually offered year after year, make perfect those who draw near. 2 Otherwise, would they not have ceased to be offered? If the worshipers had once been cleansed, they would no longer have any consciousness of sin. 3 But in these sacrifices there is a reminder of sin year after year. 4 For it is impossible that the blood of bulls and goats should take away sins.

5 Consequently, when Christ[v] came into the world, he said,

"Sacrifices and offerings thou hast
    not desired,
but a body hast thou prepared for
    me;
6 in burnt offerings and sin offerings
    thou hast taken no pleasure.
7 Then I said, 'Lo, I have come to do
    thy will, O God,'
as it is written of me in the roll of
    the book."

8 When he said above, "Thou hast neither desired nor taken pleasure in sacrifices and offerings and burnt offerings and sin offerings" (these are offered according to the law), 9 then he added, "Lo, I have come to do thy will." He abolishes the first in order to establish the second. 10 And by that will we have been sanctified through the offering of the body of Jesus Christ once for all.

11 And every priest stands daily at his service, offering repeatedly the same sacrifices, which can never take

p Or *tabernacle*
u The Greek word here used means both *covenant* and *will*   v Greek *he*

and inaugurated the new covenant (Rom.3.24–25; 1 Cor.11.25). **15–17:** See note *u*. **18–20:** Ex.24.6–8. **28:** *The sins of many*, Is.53.12; Mk.10.45; Rom.5.19; Rev.7.9–10. *A second time*, Acts 1.10–11; Phil.3.20. **10.1:** Insubstantial *shadow* is contrasted with *the true form*. *Draw near*, i.e. to God (7.25). **2:** *Consciousness of sin*, see 9.9 n. **5–9:** Ps.40.6–8 Septuagint. **8:** 1 Sam.15.22; Ps.50.8–15; Is.1.10–17; Jer.7.21–26; Hos.6.6. **10:** *Sanctified*, ceremonially cleansed and dedi-

away sins. ¹² But when Christ^w had offered for all time a single sacrifice for sins, he sat down at the right hand of God, ¹³ then to wait until his enemies should be made a stool for his feet. ¹⁴ For by a single offering he has perfected for all time those who are sanctified. ¹⁵ And the Holy Spirit also bears witness to us; for after saying, ¹⁶ "This is the covenant that I will
make with them
after those days, says the Lord:
I will put my laws on their hearts,
and write them on their minds,"
¹⁷ then he adds,
"I will remember their sins and their
misdeeds no more."
¹⁸ Where there is forgiveness of these, there is no longer any offering for sin.

19 Therefore, brethren, since we have confidence to enter the sanctuary by the blood of Jesus, ²⁰ by the new and living way which he opened for us through the curtain, that is, through his flesh, ²¹ and since we have a great priest over the house of God, ²² let us draw near with a true heart in full assurance of faith, with our hearts sprinkled clean from an evil conscience and our bodies washed with pure water. ²³ Let us hold fast the confession of our hope without wavering, for he who promised is faithful; ²⁴ and let us consider how to stir up one another to love and good works, ²⁵ not neglecting to meet together, as is the habit of some, but encouraging one another, and all the more as you see the Day drawing near.

26 For if we sin deliberately after receiving the knowledge of the truth, there no longer remains a sacrifice for sins, ²⁷ but a fearful prospect of judgment, and a fury of fire which will consume the adversaries. ²⁸ A man who has violated the law of Moses dies without mercy at the testimony of two or three witnesses. ²⁹ How much worse punishment do you think will be deserved by the man who has spurned the Son of God, and profaned the blood of the covenant by which he was sanctified, and outraged the Spirit of grace? ³⁰ For we know him who said, "Vengeance is mine, I will repay." And again, "The Lord will judge his people." ³¹ It is a fearful thing to fall into the hands of the living God.

32 But recall the former days when, after you were enlightened, you endured a hard struggle with sufferings, ³³ sometimes being publicly exposed to abuse and affliction, and sometimes being partners with those so treated. ³⁴ For you had compassion on the prisoners, and you joyfully accepted the plundering of your property, since you knew that you yourselves had a better possession and an abiding one. ³⁵ Therefore do not throw away your confidence, which has a great reward. ³⁶ For you have need of endurance, so that you may do the will of God and receive what is promised.
³⁷ "For yet a little while,
and the coming one shall come and
shall not tarry;
³⁸ but my righteous one shall live by
faith,
and if he shrinks back,
my soul has no pleasure in him."
³⁹ But we are not of those who shrink back and are destroyed, but of those who have faith and keep their souls.

w Greek *this one*

cated. **11–12:** A priest stands, a king sits; Christ is both (1.3). **14:** *Sanctified*, see v. 10 n. **16–17:** The new covenant assures full and final remission of sins (Jer.31.33–34).
10.19–39: Exhortations and warnings. 19–25: Three privileges and duties of Christians: *let us draw near* to God in faith and worship (v. 22); *let us hold fast* the public *confession of our hope* (v. 23); *let us consider* how we can help others in love (v. 24). **25:** *The Day* of Christ's second coming (see 9.28 n.). **26–31:** The fate of the wilful sinner (see 5.2 n. and 6.4–6). **28:** Dt.17.2–6. **30:** Dt.32.35–36. **32–39:** Memory of past victories should inspire present *endurance*. **37:** Is. 26.20 Septuagint. **37–38:** Hab.2.3–4.
11.1–40: Roll call of heroes and heroines of faith, designed to reinforce the exhortation in 10.35–39. **1:** Instead of defining faith comprehensively, the author describes those aspects of

Now faith is the assurance of things hoped for, the conviction of things not seen. ² For by it the men of old received divine approval. ³ By faith we understand that the world was created by the word of God, so that what is seen was made out of things which do not appear.

4 By faith Abel offered to God a more acceptable sacrifice than Cain, through which he received approval as righteous, God bearing witness by accepting his gifts; he died, but through his faith he is still speaking. ⁵ By faith Enoch was taken up so that he should not see death; and he was not found, because God had taken him. Now before he was taken he was attested as having pleased God. ⁶ And without faith it is impossible to please him. For whoever would draw near to God must believe that he exists and that he rewards those who seek him. ⁷ By faith Noah, being warned by God concerning events as yet unseen, took heed and constructed an ark for the saving of his household; by this he condemned the world and became an heir of the righteousness which comes by faith.

8 By faith Abraham obeyed when he was called to go out to a place which he was to receive as an inheritance; and he went out, not knowing where he was to go. ⁹ By faith he sojourned in the land of promise, as in a foreign land, living in tents with Isaac and Jacob, heirs with him of the same promise. ¹⁰ For he looked forward to the city which has foundations, whose builder and maker is God. ¹¹ By faith Sarah herself received power to conceive, even when she was past the age, since she considered him faithful who had promised. ¹² Therefore from one man, and him as good as dead, were born descendants as many as the stars of heaven and as the innumerable grains of sand by the seashore.

13 These all died in faith, not having received what was promised, but having seen it and greeted it from afar, and having acknowledged that they were strangers and exiles on the earth. ¹⁴ For people who speak thus make it clear that they are seeking a homeland. ¹⁵ If they had been thinking of that land from which they had gone out, they would have had opportunity to return. ¹⁶ But as it is, they desire a better country, that is, a heavenly one. Therefore God is not ashamed to be called their God, for he has prepared for them a city.

17 By faith Abraham, when he was tested, offered up Isaac, and he who had received the promises was ready to offer up his only son, ¹⁸ of whom it was said, "Through Isaac shall your descendants be named." ¹⁹ He considered that God was able to raise men even from the dead; hence, figuratively speaking, he did receive him back. ²⁰ By faith Isaac invoked future blessings on Jacob and Esau. ²¹ By faith Jacob, when dying, blessed each of the sons of Joseph, bowing in worship over the head of his staff. ²² By faith Joseph, at the end of his life, made mention of the exodus of the Israelites and gave directions concerning his burial.ˣ

23 By faith Moses, when he was born, was hid for three months by his parents, because they saw that the child was beautiful; and they were not afraid of the king's edict. ²⁴ By faith Moses, when he was grown up, refused to be called the son of Pharaoh's daughter, ²⁵ choosing rather to share ill-treatment with the

x Greek *bones*

it which bear upon his argument. **4:** Gen.4.3–10. **5:** Gen.5.21–24. **6:** A general axiom referring to the existence and the moral government of God. **7:** Gen.6.13–22. **8–9:** Gen.12.1–8. **10:** *The city* is the heavenly Jerusalem (v. 16; Gal.4.26; Rev.21.2). *Foundations*, contrasted with tents (v. 9). **11:** Gen.17.19; 18.11–14; 21.2. **12:** Gen.15.5–6; 22.17; 32.12; Rom.4.19. **16:** *A city*, see v. 10 n. **17:** Gen.22.1–10. **18:** Gen.21.12. **19:** Abraham received Isaac *back* when he was told to offer a ram instead of his son (Gen.22.13). **20:** Gen.27.27–29,39–40. **21:** Gen. ch. 48; 47.31 Septuagint. **22:** Gen.50.24–25; Ex.13.19. **23:** Ex.2.2; 1.22. **24–25:** Ex.2.10–15.

people of God than to enjoy the fleeting pleasures of sin. ²⁶ He considered abuse suffered for the Christ greater wealth than the treasures of Egypt, for he looked to the reward. ²⁷ By faith he left Egypt, not being afraid of the anger of the king; for he endured as seeing him who is invisible. ²⁸ By faith he kept the Passover and sprinkled the blood, so that the Destroyer of the first-born might not touch them.

29 By faith the people crossed the Red Sea as if on dry land; but the Egyptians, when they attempted to do the same, were drowned. ³⁰ By faith the walls of Jericho fell down after they had been encircled for seven days. ³¹ By faith Rahab the harlot did not perish with those who were disobedient, because she had given friendly welcome to the spies.

32 And what more shall I say? For time would fail me to tell of Gideon, Barak, Samson, Jephthah, of David and Samuel and the prophets– ³³ who through faith conquered kingdoms, enforced justice, received promises, stopped the mouths of lions, ³⁴ quenched raging fire, escaped the edge of the sword, won strength out of weakness, became mighty in war, put foreign armies to flight. ³⁵ Women received their dead by resurrection. Some were tortured, refusing to accept release, that they might rise again to a better life. ³⁶ Others suffered mocking and scourging, and even chains and imprisonment. ³⁷ They were stoned, they were sawn in two,ʸ they were killed with the sword; they went about in skins of sheep and goats,

destitute, afflicted, ill-treated– ³⁸ of whom the world was not worthy– wandering over deserts and mountains, and in dens and caves of the earth.

39 And all these, though well attested by their faith, did not receive what was promised, ⁴⁰ since God had foreseen something better for us, that apart from us they should not be made perfect.

12 Therefore, since we are surrounded by so great a cloud of witnesses, let us also lay aside every weight, and sin which clings so closely, and let us run with perseverance the race that is set before us, ² looking to Jesus the pioneer and perfecter of our faith, who for the joy that was set before him endured the cross, despising the shame, and is seated at the right hand of the throne of God.

3 Consider him who endured from sinners such hostility against himself, so that you may not grow weary or fainthearted. ⁴ In your struggle against sin you have not yet resisted to the point of shedding your blood. ⁵ And have you forgotten the exhortation which addresses you as sons?–

"My son, do not regard lightly the
   discipline of the Lord,
nor lose courage when you are
   punished by him.
⁶ For the Lord disciplines him
   whom he loves,
and chastises every son whom he
   receives."

⁷ It is for discipline that you have to endure. God is treating you as sons; for what son is there whom his father does not discipline? ⁸ If you are left without

ʸ Other manuscripts add *they were tempted*

26: *Abuse suffered for the Christ*, 13.13 (see 1 Cor.10.3–4 n.). **27:** *Him who is invisible*, Jn.1.18; Col.1.15; 1 Tim.1.17; 6.16. **28:** Ex.12.21–30. **29:** Ex.14.21–31. **30:** Jos.6.12–21. **31.** Jos.2.1–21; 6.22–25. **32:** Jg. chs. 6–8; 4–5; 13–16; 11–12; 1 Sam. chs. 16–30; 2 Sam. chs. 1–24; 1 Kg.1.1–2.11; 1 Sam.1–12; 15.1–16.13. **33:** *Lions*, Dan. ch. 6. **34:** *Fire*, Dan. ch. 3. **35:** 1 Kg.17.17–24; 2 Kg.4.25–37; 2 Macc.7.9,14. **37:** 2 Chr.24.20–22; Jer.26.23; 2 Macc.5.27; 6.12–7.42. **38:** *Caves*, 2 Macc.6.11; 10.6. **40:** See 9.15 n.

12.1–29: Exhortations and warnings. 1–11: Suffering, its joy and discipline. **1:** *Witnesses*, those mentioned in ch. 11. *Weight*, encumbrance. *The race*, 1 Cor.9.24–27. *Sin*, not a particular "besetting sin," but sin in general. **2:** *Pioneer and perfecter*, see 2.10 n. *Our faith*, literally "the faith." *For the joy*, may also be translated "instead of the joy" (of unbroken life in heaven, Phil.2.6). **5–6:** Pr.3.11–12. **8:** *All have participated*, namely, all sons of God (v. 6). **9:** *Father*

discipline, in which all have participated, then you are illegitimate children and not sons. ⁹ Besides this, we
have had earthly fathers to discipline
us and we respected them. Shall we not
much more be subject to the Father of
spirits and live? ¹⁰ For they disciplined us for a short time at their pleasure, but he disciplines us for our good,
that we may share his holiness. ¹¹ For
the moment all discipline seems painful rather than pleasant; later it yields
the peaceful fruit of righteousness to
those who have been trained by it.

12 Therefore lift your drooping
hands and strengthen your weak
knees, ¹³ and make straight paths for
your feet, so that what is lame may not
be put out of joint but rather be healed.
¹⁴ Strive for peace with all men, and
for the holiness without which no one
will see the Lord. ¹⁵ See to it that no
one fail to obtain the grace of God; that
no "root of bitterness" spring up and
cause trouble, and by it the many become defiled; ¹⁶ that no one be immoral or irreligious like Esau, who
sold his birthright for a single meal.
¹⁷ For you know that afterward, when
he desired to inherit the blessing, he
was rejected, for he found no chance
to repent, though he sought it with
tears.

18 For you have not come to what
may be touched, a blazing fire, and
darkness, and gloom, and a tempest,
¹⁹ and the sound of a trumpet, and a
voice whose words made the hearers
entreat that no further messages be
spoken to them. ²⁰ For they could not
endure the order that was given, "If
even a beast touches the mountain,
it shall be stoned." ²¹ Indeed, so terrifying was the sight that Moses said,
"I tremble with fear." ²² But you have
come to Mount Zion and to the city
of the living God, the heavenly
Jerusalem, and to innumerable angels
in festal gathering, ²³ and to the as-
semblyᶻ of the first-born who are enrolled in heaven, and to a judge who is
God of all, and to the spirits of just
men made perfect, ²⁴ and to Jesus, the
mediator of a new covenant, and to the
sprinkled blood that speaks more
graciously than the blood of Abel.

25 See that you do not refuse him
who is speaking. For if they did not
escape when they refused him who
warned them on earth, much less
shall we escape if we reject him who
warns from heaven. ²⁶ His voice then
shook the earth; but now he has promised, "Yet once more I will shake not
only the earth but also the heaven."
²⁷ This phrase, "Yet once more," indicates the removal of what is shaken,
as of what has been made, in order that
what cannot be shaken may remain.
²⁸ Therefore let us be grateful for receiving a kingdom that cannot be
shaken, and thus let us offer to God acceptable worship, with reverence and
awe; ²⁹ for our God is a consuming fire.

13 Let brotherly love continue.
² Do not neglect to show hospitality to strangers, for thereby some
have entertained angels unawares.
³ Remember those who are in prison,
as though in prison with them; and
those who are ill-treated, since you also
are in the body. ⁴ Let marriage be held
in honor among all, and let the marriage bed be undefiled; for God will

z Or *angels, and to the festal gathering and assembly*

of spirits, God is the author of man's spiritual being (Num.16.22; Ec.12.7; Zech.12.1). **12:**
Is.35.3. **14–17:** The necessity of peace and purity. **15:** Dt.29.18 Septuagint. **16:** Gen.25.29–34.
17: *Chance to repent*, or "place for a change of mind in his father" (Gen.27.30–40). **18–29:** The
two covenants contrasted. **18–19:** *What may be touched*, Mount Sinai (Ex.19.12–22; 20.18–21;
Dt.4.11–12; 5.22–27). **20:** Ex.19.12–13. **21:** Dt.9.19. **22:** *Mount Zion . . . the heavenly
Jerusalem*, contrast v. 18 and see 11.10 n. **24:** Abel's blood cried for vengeance (11.4; Gen.4.10);
the sprinkled blood of Jesus, which established the new covenant (9.14; 13.20), calls *more
graciously* for man's forgiveness. **25:** *Who warns*, the Greek may also be translated "who is."
26: Hag.2.6. **29:** Dt.4.24; 9.3; 2 Th.1.7–8; compare Mt.3.12.
    13.1–17: Concluding admonitions. **2:** *Strangers*, Christian brethren from other places (see

judge the immoral and adulterous. ⁵ Keep your life free from love of money, and be content with what you have; for he has said, "I will never fail you nor forsake you." ⁶ Hence we can confidently say,

"The Lord is my helper,
I will not be afraid;
what can man do to me?"

7 Remember your leaders, those who spoke to you the word of God; consider the outcome of their life, and imitate their faith. ⁸ Jesus Christ is the same yesterday and today and for ever. ⁹ Do not be led away by diverse and strange teachings; for it is well that the heart be strengthened by grace, not by foods, which have not benefited their adherents. ¹⁰ We have an altar from which those who serve the tent*a* have no right to eat. ¹¹ For the bodies of those animals whose blood is brought into the sanctuary by the high priest as a sacrifice for sin are burned outside the camp. ¹² So Jesus also suffered outside the gate in order to sanctify the people through his own blood. ¹³ Therefore let us go forth to him outside the camp and bear the abuse he endured. ¹⁴ For here we have no lasting city, but we seek the city which is to come. ¹⁵ Through him then let us continually offer up a sacrifice of praise to God, that is, the fruit of lips that acknowledge his name. ¹⁶ Do not neglect to do good and to share what

you have, for such sacrifices are pleasing to God.

17 Obey your leaders and submit to them; for they are keeping watch over your souls, as men who will have to give account. Let them do this joyfully, and not sadly, for that would be of no advantage to you.

18 Pray for us, for we are sure that we have a clear conscience, desiring to act honorably in all things. ¹⁹ I urge you the more earnestly to do this in order that I may be restored to you the sooner.

20 Now may the God of peace who brought again from the dead our Lord Jesus, the great shepherd of the sheep, by the blood of the eternal covenant, ²¹ equip you with everything good that you may do his will, working in you*b* that which is pleasing in his sight, through Jesus Christ; to whom be glory for ever and ever. Amen.

22 I appeal to you, brethren, bear with my word of exhortation, for I have written to you briefly. ²³ You should understand that our brother Timothy has been released, with whom I shall see you if he comes soon. ²⁴ Greet all your leaders and all the saints. Those who come from Italy send you greetings. ²⁵ Grace be with all of you. Amen.

a Or *tabernacle*
b Other ancient authorities read *us*

Rom.16.1–2 n.; 1 Pet.4.9 n.). *Angels*, Gen.18.1–8; 19.1–3. **3:** Mt.25.35–46. **5:** Jos.1.5. **6:** Ps. 118.6. **9:** *Foods*, 9.10. **11:** Lev.16.27. **12:** *Sanctify*, see 10.10 n. **14:** *City*, see 11.10 n.; 12.22 n. **15:** *A sacrifice* of thanksgiving (Lev.7.12; Ps.50.14,23; Hos.14.2). **17:** *Leaders*, v. 7. **18–25:** Personal messages (vv. 18–19), benediction (vv. 20–21), and postscript (vv. 22–25). **22:** *Briefly*, considering the extent of the subject.

THE LETTER OF

JAMES

The Letter of James is a sermon in the form of a letter. It is epigrammatic in style, hortatory in content; there are about sixty imperatives in the letter's one hundred and eight verses. The author presupposes knowledge of the gospel on the part of his readers, and is concerned to remind them how Christians ought to live. The letter is a remarkably pure specimen of the ethical teaching found in the Sermon on the Mount (Mt. chs. 5–7).

It is sometimes asserted that James is in conflict with Paul on the question of faith and works. The difference between the two, however, is largely one of emphasis and vocabulary. For Paul faith is the believer's loyal relationship to Christ; for James it is mere assent to theological statements (see 2.14–16 n.). Whereas James speaks of works, Paul speaks of fruits of the Spirit (Gal.5.22–23); for him "works" are "works of the law" (Gal.3.3,5) and are opposed to faith. On the other hand, Paul would have shared James' horror at an empty belief in God (Jas.2.18–19); his motto for the Christian life is "faith working through love" (Gal.5.6).

Of authorship and date not much is known. The tradition that it was written by James the brother of the Lord has little support from ancient times. The indications of the letter itself—its excellent Greek with vivid metaphor and facile use of idiom, its apparent knowledge of 1 Peter (compare Jas.1.1 with 1 Pet.1.1; and 4.10 with 1 Pet.5.6) and of certain letters of Paul—suggest a Hellenistic Christian as its author and a date toward the end of the first century.

JAMES, A SERVANT OF God AND OF the Lord Jesus Christ,

To the twelve tribes in the Dispersion:

Greeting.

2 Count it all joy, my brethren, when you meet various trials, 3 for you know that the testing of your faith produces steadfastness. 4 And let steadfastness have its full effect, that you may be perfect and complete, lacking in nothing.

5 If any of you lacks wisdom, let him ask God, who gives to all men generously and without reproaching, and it will be given him. 6 But let him ask in faith, with no doubting, for he who doubts is like a wave of the sea that is driven and tossed by the wind. 7, 8 For that person must not suppose that a double-minded man, unstable in all his ways, will receive anything from the Lord.

9 Let the lowly brother boast in his exaltation, 10 and the rich in his humiliation, because like the flower of the grass he will pass away. 11 For the sun rises with its scorching heat and withers the grass; its flower falls, and its beauty perishes. So will the rich man fade away in the midst of his pursuits.

12 Blessed is the man who endures trial, for when he has stood the test he will receive the crown of life which God has promised to those who love him. 13 Let no one say when he is tempted, "I am tempted by God"; for God cannot be tempted with evil and he himself tempts no one; 14 but each person is tempted when he is lured and enticed by his own desire. 15 Then desire when it has conceived gives birth to sin; and sin when it is full-grown brings forth death.

16 Do not be deceived, my beloved brethren. 17 Every good endowment and every perfect gift is

1.1: **Salutation.** 1: The phrase *twelve tribes in the Dispersion* describes Jews scattered throughout the world. Its use here testifies to the church's sense of being a pilgrim people as well as the heir of Israel (Phil.3.20; 1 Pet.1.1).

1.2–18: **The blessings of trials.** Trials are a ground for rejoicing. 5: *Wisdom*, see 3.13 n. 6: *The sea*, Is.57.20; Jer.49.23. 7–8: His entire conduct reflects his inconstancy of purpose (Mt. 6.24). 10–11: Is.40.6–7. 12: *The crown of life*, see 2 Tim.4.8 n. 13: Temptation is not from God,

from above, coming down from the Father of lights with whom there is no variation or shadow due to change.[a] 18 Of his own will he brought us forth by the word of truth that we should be a kind of first fruits of his creatures.

19 Know this, my beloved brethren. Let every man be quick to hear, slow to speak, slow to anger, 20 for the anger of man does not work the righteousness of God. 21 Therefore put away all filthiness and rank growth of wickedness and receive with meekness the implanted word, which is able to save your souls.

22 But be doers of the word, and not hearers only, deceiving yourselves. 23 For if any one is a hearer of the word and not a doer, he is like a man who observes his natural face in a mirror; 24 for he observes himself and goes away and at once forgets what he was like. 25 But he who looks into the perfect law, the law of liberty, and perseveres, being no hearer that forgets but a doer that acts, he shall be blessed in his doing.

26 If any one thinks he is religious, and does not bridle his tongue but deceives his heart, this man's religion is vain. 27 Religion that is pure and undefiled before God and the Father is this: to visit orphans and widows in their affliction, and to keep oneself unstained from the world.

2 My brethren, show no partiality as you hold the faith of our Lord Jesus Christ, the Lord of glory. 2 For if a man with gold rings and in fine clothing comes into your assembly, and a poor man in shabby clothing also comes in, 3 and you pay attention to the one who wears the fine clothing and say, "Have a seat here, please," while you say to the poor man, "Stand there," or, "Sit at my feet," 4 have you not made distinctions among yourselves, and become judges with evil thoughts? 5 Listen, my beloved brethren. Has not God chosen those who are poor in the world to be rich in faith and heirs of the kingdom which he has promised to those who love him? 6 But you have dishonored the poor man. Is it not the rich who oppress you, is it not they who drag you into court? 7 Is it not they who blaspheme the honorable name which was invoked over you?

8 If you really fulfil the royal law, according to the scripture, "You shall love your neighbor as yourself," you do well. 9 But if you show partiality, you commit sin, and are convicted by the law as transgressors. 10 For whoever keeps the whole law but fails in one point has become guilty of all of it. 11 For he who said, "Do not commit adultery," said also, "Do not kill." If you do not commit adultery but do kill, you have become a transgressor of the law. 12 So speak and so act as those who are to be judged under the law of liberty. 13 For judgment is without mercy to one who has shown no mercy; yet mercy triumphs over judgment.

14 What does it profit, my brethren,

a Other ancient authorities read *variation due to a shadow of turning*

---

but from within man. **17:** *Father of lights*, creator of the heavenly bodies (Gen.1.14–18; Ps. 136.7). **18:** God makes us his children through knowledge of his truth (1 Jn.3.9). The *first fruits* of harvest were holy and were frequently offered to God (Num.15.21; Dt.18.4).

1.19–27: True worship. 19–20: *Anger*, see Eph.4.26 n. **21:** *Put away*, strip off as dirty clothing. *The implanted word*, the gospel which has been received and is now growing. James uses a variety of expressions for the gospel: perfect law (v. 25), law of liberty (v. 25; 2.12), royal law (2.8). **22:** *Be doers . . . , not hearers only*, Mt.7.24–27; Rom.2.13. **25:** *The perfect law*, the Jewish description of the Old Testament law, is here applied to the gospel, the "law" through which a man obtains freedom. *Blessed*, Ps.1.1; Mt.5.3–11. The word points to the happiness of the man who has God's favor. **26–27:** Religion consists of more than devotional exercises (Mt.25.35–36).

2.1–13: The respect due to the poor. 1: God shows no partiality; the disciple must not. **2:** *Assembly*, literally "synagogue." **5:** Lk.6.20; 1 Cor.1.26–29. **7:** *The honorable name* is that of Christ (see 2 Th.1.12 n.). **8:** Lev.19.18. **10:** *The law* forms a unity; therefore violating any one part breaks the entire law. **11:** Ex.20.13–14; Dt.5.17–18. **13:** *No mercy*, Mt.6.14–15; 18.21–35.

if a man says he has faith but has not works? Can his faith save him? [15] If a brother or sister is ill-clad and in lack of daily food, [16] and one of you says to them, "Go in peace, be warmed and filled," without giving them the things needed for the body, what does it profit? [17] So faith by itself, if it has no works, is dead.

18 But some one will say, "You have faith and I have works." Show me your faith apart from your works, and I by my works will show you my faith. [19] You believe that God is one; you do well. Even the demons believe– and shudder. [20] Do you want to be shown, you shallow man, that faith apart from works is barren? [21] Was not Abraham our father justified by works, when he offered his son Isaac upon the altar? [22] You see that faith was active along with his works, and faith was completed by works, [23] and the scripture was fulfilled which says, "Abraham believed God, and it was reckoned to him as righteousness"; and he was called the friend of God. [24] You see that a man is justified by works and not by faith alone. [25] And in the same way was not also Rahab the harlot justified by works when she received the messengers and sent them out another way? [26] For as the body apart from the spirit is dead, so faith apart from works is dead.

3 Let not many of you become teachers, my brethren, for you know that we who teach shall be judged with greater strictness. [2] For we all make many mistakes, and if any one makes no mistakes in what he says he is a perfect man, able to bridle the whole body also. [3] If we put bits into the mouths of horses that they may obey us, we guide their whole bodies. [4] Look at the ships also; though they are so great and are driven by strong winds, they are guided by a very small rudder wherever the will of the pilot directs. [5] So the tongue is a little member and boasts of great things. How great a forest is set ablaze by a small fire!

6 And the tongue is a fire. The tongue is an unrighteous world among our members, staining the whole body, setting on fire the cycle of nature,[b] and set on fire by hell.[c] [7] For every kind of beast and bird, of reptile and sea creature, can be tamed and has been tamed by humankind, [8] but no human being can tame the tongue–a restless evil, full of deadly poison. [9] With it we bless the Lord and Father, and with it we curse men, who are made in the likeness of God. [10] From the same mouth come blessing and cursing. My brethren, this ought not to be so. [11] Does a spring pour forth from the same opening fresh water and brackish? [12] Can a fig tree, my brethren, yield olives, or a grapevine figs? No more can salt water yield fresh.

13 Who is wise and understanding among you? By his good life let him show his works in the meekness of wisdom. [14] But if you have bitter jealousy and selfish ambition in your hearts, do not boast and be false to the truth. [15] This wisdom is not such as comes down from above, but is earthly, unspiritual, devilish. [16] For where jealousy and selfish ambition exist, there will be disorder and every vile

b Or *wheel of birth* ― *c* Greek *Gehenna*

2.14–26: Faith and works. See Introduction. **14:** Faith without works is counterfeit; such faith cannot save (Mt.25.31–46; Gal.5.6). **19:** Faith here is subscription to sound theology, whereas for Paul it is trust in Jesus Christ and communion with him. **21:** Gen.22.1–14. **23:** Gen.15.6 (compare Rom.4.3–25; Gal.3.6–14). *The friend of God,* 2 Chr.20.7; Is.41.8. **25:** *Rahab,* Jos.2.1–21. Abraham and Rahab represent two extremes: the friend of God and the harlot; but both were justified by God. **26:** Where there are no works, faith is no more alive than a body without spirit.

3.1–18: True wisdom. Two besetting sins of the teacher are rebuked: intemperate speech (vv. 1–12) and arrogance (vv. 13–18). **13:** True *wisdom* is not a human achievement, but is from God, and it reveals itself in a good life (v. 17). **14:** *Hearts,* see 1 Th.3.13 n. **17:** Wisdom

practice. [17] But the wisdom from above is first pure, then peaceable, gentle, open to reason, full of mercy and good fruits, without uncertainty or insincerity. [18] And the harvest of righteousness is sown in peace by those who make peace.

4 What causes wars, and what causes fightings among you? Is it not your passions that are at war in your members? [2] You desire and do not have; so you kill. And you covet[d] and cannot obtain; so you fight and wage war. You do not have, because you do not ask. [3] You ask and do not receive, because you ask wrongly, to spend it on your passions. [4] Unfaithful creatures! Do you not know that friendship with the world is enmity with God? Therefore whoever wishes to be a friend of the world makes himself an enemy of God. [5] Or do you suppose it is in vain that the scripture says, "He yearns jealously over the spirit which he has made to dwell in us"? [6] But he gives more grace; therefore it says, "God opposes the proud, but gives grace to the humble." [7] Submit yourselves therefore to God. Resist the devil and he will flee from you. [8] Draw near to God and he will draw near to you. Cleanse your hands, you sinners, and purify your hearts, you men of double mind. [9] Be wretched and mourn and weep. Let your laughter be turned to mourning and your joy to dejection. [10] Humble yourselves before the Lord and he will exalt you.

11 Do not speak evil against one another, brethren. He that speaks evil against a brother or judges his brother, speaks evil against the law and judges

the law. But if you judge the law, you are not a doer of the law but a judge. [12] There is one lawgiver and judge, he who is able to save and to destroy. But who are you that you judge your neighbor?

13 Come now, you who say, "Today or tomorrow we will go into such and such a town and spend a year there and trade and get gain"; [14] whereas you do not know about tomorrow. What is your life? For you are a mist that appears for a little time and then vanishes. [15] Instead you ought to say, "If the Lord wills, we shall live and we shall do this or that." [16] As it is, you boast in your arrogance. All such boasting is evil. [17] Whoever knows what is right to do and fails to do it, for him it is sin.

5 Come now, you rich, weep and howl for the miseries that are coming upon you. [2] Your riches have rotted and your garments are motheaten. [3] Your gold and silver have rusted, and their rust will be evidence against you and will eat your flesh like fire. You have laid up treasure[e] for the last days. [4] Behold, the wages of the laborers who mowed your fields, which you kept back by fraud, cry out; and the cries of the harvesters have reached the ears of the Lord of hosts. [5] You have lived on the earth in luxury and in pleasure; you have fattened your hearts in a day of slaughter. [6] You have condemned, you have killed the righteous man; he does not resist you.

7 Be patient, therefore, brethren,

d Or *you kill and you covet*
e Or *will eat your flesh, since you have stored up fire*

---

and godliness are intimately connected. The supreme example is Jesus Christ (Jn.14.6; 1 Cor. 1.30).

4.1–5.6: The contrast between godliness and worldliness. 4.1: *Passions*, Rom.7.5–25; 1 Pet. 2.11–12. **4:** The prophets pictured the covenant as a marriage between God and Israel. Those who break covenant are *unfaithful creatures*, adulterers (Is.1.21; Jer.3.6–10; Hos.2.2). *Enmity with God*, Mt.6.24; Lk.16.13. **5:** God longs for men's friendship. For the quotation compare Ex.20.5; Dt.4.24; Zech.8.2. **6:** Pr.3.34; 1 Pet.5.5. **9:** Is.32.11; Jer.4.13; Mic.2.4. **10:** Mt.23.12; 1 Pet.5.6. **12:** *One*, God. **13–17:** The author rebukes the presumption of those who plan their future with complacency, forgetting that they live by the mercy of God. Human life is as evanescent as morning mist. **5.1–6:** The rich are addressed as examples of the folly of accumulating riches.

until the coming of the Lord. Behold, the farmer waits for the precious fruit of the earth, being patient over it until it receives the early and the late rain. ⁸ You also be patient. Establish your hearts, for the coming of the Lord is at hand. ⁹ Do not grumble, brethren, against one another, that you may not be judged; behold, the Judge is standing at the doors. ¹⁰ As an example of suffering and patience, brethren, take the prophets who spoke in the name of the Lord. ¹¹ Behold, we call those happy who were steadfast. You have heard of the steadfastness of Job, and you have seen the purpose of the Lord, how the Lord is compassionate and merciful.

12 But above all, my brethren, do not swear, either by heaven or by earth or with any other oath, but let your yes be yes and your no be no, that you may not fall under condemnation.

13 Is any one among you suffering? Let him pray. Is any cheerful? Let him sing praise. ¹⁴ Is any among you sick? Let him call for the elders of the church, and let them pray over him, anointing him with oil in the name of the Lord; ¹⁵ and the prayer of faith will save the sick man, and the Lord will raise him up; and if he has committed sins, he will be forgiven. ¹⁶ Therefore confess your sins to one another, and pray for one another, that you may be healed. The prayer of a righteous man has great power in its effects. ¹⁷ Eli′jah was a man of like nature with ourselves and he prayed fervently that it might not rain, and for three years and six months it did not rain on the earth. ¹⁸ Then he prayed again and the heaven gave rain, and the earth brought forth its fruit.

19 My brethren, if any one among you wanders from the truth and some one brings him back, ²⁰ let him know that whoever brings back a sinner from the error of his way will save his soul from death and will cover a multitude of sins.

5.7–20: Concluding encouragement. 7–9: Three references to the coming of the Lord stand in contrast to the preceding passage; seeking riches is vain, but he who waits patiently for the Lord will be rewarded. **11:** Job 1.21–22; 2.10; Ps.111.4. **12:** Mt.5.34–37. **13–15:** This passage is cited by those churches that make a practice of anointing the sick (formerly called the sacrament of extreme unction by the Roman Catholic Church). **14:** *Oil* was a common medicinal remedy (Is.1.6; Mk.6.13; see Lk.10.34 n.). Here it is invested with special significance through connection with the divine name (see 2 Th.1.12 n.). **17:** 1 Kg.17.1; 18.1; Lk.4.25. **19:** God's *truth* is that which leads to righteousness. It is a closing indication of the practical character of the letter. **20:** *Cover . . . sins*, see 1 Pet.4.8 n.

THE FIRST LETTER OF

PETER

The First Letter of Peter was written to give encouragement and hope to Christians in the northern part of Asia Minor who were undergoing persecution. The congregations, composed mainly of Gentile converts (1.14; 2.10; 4.3), are urged not to be surprised at the "fiery ordeal" which has come upon them. They are to rejoice even in their trials, which they share with their brotherhood throughout the world (5.9). By participating in the sufferings of Christ (4.13) they will demonstrate the genuineness of their faith (1.6,7).

After the salutation (1.1–2) the author recalls the significance of God's deed in Christ (1.3–12), on the basis of which he exhorts his readers to holiness (1.13–2.10). He then discusses the obligations of Christians in time of suffering, with repeated reference to the example of Christ (2.11–4.6). In view of the nearness of Christ's coming, he admonishes them to live as "good stewards" (4.7–11). After restating his message in summary form (4.12–19), he concludes with various exhortations and greetings (5.1–14).

A number of scholars have found it impossible to accept the tradition of Peter's authorship because of the letter's excellent Greek style (contrast Mt.26.73; Acts 4.13) and its apparent reflections of several letters of Paul (compare 2.6,8 with Rom.9.32–33; and 3.1–7 with Eph. 5.22–28). It may well be, however, that Peter stands in the background as author, but that the actual composition of the letter was entrusted to Silvanus (5.12), the missionary companion of Paul (2 Cor.1.19; 1 Th.1.1; 2 Th.1.1). It apparently was written from Rome (see 5.13 n.), perhaps after the outbreak of the Neronian persecution in A.D. 64.

PETER, AN APOSTLE OF JESUS Christ,

To the exiles of the Dispersion in Pontus, Galatia, Cappado'cia, Asia, and Bithyn'ia, ² chosen and destined by God the Father and sanctified by the Spirit for obedience to Jesus Christ and for sprinkling with his blood:

May grace and peace be multiplied to you.

3 Blessed be the God and Father of our Lord Jesus Christ! By his great mercy we have been born anew to a living hope through the resurrection of Jesus Christ from the dead, ⁴ and to an inheritance which is imperishable, undefiled, and unfading, kept in heaven for you, ⁵ who by God's power are guarded through faith for a salvation ready to be revealed in the last time. ⁶ In this you rejoice,ᵃ though now for a little while you may have to suffer various trials, ⁷ so that the genuineness of your faith, more precious than gold which though perishable is tested by fire, may redound to praise and glory and honor at the revelation of Jesus Christ. ⁸ Without having seenᵇ him youᶜ love him; though you do not now see him youᶜ believe in him and rejoice with unutterable and exalted joy. ⁹ As the out-

a Or Rejoice in this
b Other ancient authorities read known
c Or omit you

1.1–2: Salutation, see Rom.1.1–7 n. **1:** *Exiles of the Dispersion,* see Jas.1.1 n. **2:** The transcendent origin of man's redemption, involving *God the Father,* the *Spirit,* and *Jesus Christ. Chosen and destined,* see Eph.1.4–10 n.; 1 Th.1.4 n. *Obedience to Jesus Christ* is the goal to which God's election and sanctification point. *Sprinkling with his blood,* forgiveness is based on Christ's sacrificial death (see Mt.26.28 n.; Heb.9.11–10.18 n.). *Grace and peace,* see 2 Th.1.2 n.

1.3–12: Rejoice in what God has done. *Living hope,* not forlorn or dead. *The resurrection of Jesus Christ* is the foundation of Christian hope, for in him God has shown what he intends to do for his people (1 Cor.15.20–28). **4:** *Inheritance* expresses the forward-looking character of the Christian life; the greater part of the riches is yet to come. **5:** *Faith* puts man in God's keeping. *Salvation* is *ready to be revealed;* it is accomplished, but not fully manifest; the decisive battle of the war has been won, though the struggle continues. **10–12:** The prophets, and even angels, sought to understand what God was doing for the redemption of his people.

come of your faith you obtain the salvation of your souls.

10 The prophets who prophesied of the grace that was to be yours searched and inquired about this salvation; [11] they inquired what person or time was indicated by the Spirit of Christ within them when predicting the sufferings of Christ and the subsequent glory. [12] It was revealed to them that they were serving not themselves but you, in the things which have now been announced to you by those who preached the good news to you through the Holy Spirit sent from heaven, things into which angels long to look.

13 Therefore gird up your minds, be sober, set your hope fully upon the grace that is coming to you at the revelation of Jesus Christ. [14] As obedient children, do not be conformed to the passions of your former ignorance, [15] but as he who called you is holy, be holy yourselves in all your conduct; [16] since it is written, "You shall be holy, for I am holy." [17] And if you invoke as Father him who judges each one impartially according to his deeds, conduct yourselves with fear throughout the time of your exile. [18] You know that you were ransomed from the futile ways inherited from your fathers, not with perishable things such as silver or gold, [19] but with the precious blood of Christ, like that of a lamb without blemish or spot. [20] He was destined before the foundation of the world but was made manifest at the end of the times for your sake. [21] Through him you have confidence in God, who raised him from the dead and gave him glory, so that your faith and hope are in God.[d]

22 Having purified your souls by your obedience to the truth for a sincere love of the brethren, love one another earnestly from the heart. [23] You have been born anew, not of perishable seed but of imperishable, through the living and abiding word of God; [24] for
"All flesh is like grass
and all its glory like the flower of
  grass.
The grass withers, and the flower
  falls,
[25] but the word of the Lord abides for
  ever."
That word is the good news which was preached to you.

2 So put away all malice and all guile and insincerity and envy and all slander. [2] Like newborn babes, long for the pure spiritual milk, that by it you may grow up to salvation; [3] for you have tasted the kindness of the Lord.

4 Come to him, to that living stone, rejected by men but in God's sight chosen and precious; [5] and like living stones be yourselves built into a spiritual house, to be a holy priesthood, to offer spiritual sacrifices acceptable to God through Jesus Christ. [6] For it stands in scripture:
"Behold, I am laying in Zion a stone,
  a cornerstone chosen and
  precious,
and he who believes in him will not
  be put to shame."
[7] To you therefore who believe, he is precious, but for those who do not believe,
"The very stone which the builders
  rejected

d Or so that your faith is hope in God

1.13–2.10: **An appeal for holiness.** 1.13: *At the revelation*, at the second coming. 14: *Former ignorance*, Acts 17.30; Eph.4.17–18. 16: Lev.11.44–45. 20: Redemption through Christ was not a sudden whim of God, but was planned *before the foundation of the world*. 23–25: The Christian has been *born anew* by the creative *word of God*. Man is frail, but the word that works in him *abides* for ever (Is.40.6–9). 2.2: *Pure spiritual milk*, unadulterated nourishment supplied by the gospel. 3: Ps.34.8. 4: Ps.118.22; Is.28.16; Mt.21.42. 5–8: The images are mixed: a spiritual house being built of living stones, then a holy priesthood offering spiritual sacrifices. Christ is the rock of destiny: to those who believe, he is chosen and precious; to those who reject him, he is *a rock that makes them fall*. 6: Is.28.16. 7: Ps.118.22. 8: Is.8.14–15. 9–10: As Gentiles they were *no people* (Hos.2.23); now they are *God's own people*, chosen, holy, *a*

has become the head of the corner,"
8 and
"A stone that will make men
stumble,
a rock that will make them fall";
for they stumble because they disobey
the word, as they were destined to do.

9 But you are a chosen race, a
royal priesthood, a holy nation, God's
own people,*e* that you may declare
the wonderful deeds of him who called
you out of darkness into his marvelous light. 10 Once you were no
people but now you are God's people;
once you had not received mercy but
now you have received mercy.

11 Beloved, I beseech you as aliens
and exiles to abstain from the passions
of the flesh that wage war against
your soul. 12 Maintain good conduct
among the Gentiles, so that in case
they speak against you as wrongdoers,
they may see your good deeds and
glorify God on the day of visitation.

13 Be subject for the Lord's sake to
every human institution,*f* whether it be
to the emperor as supreme, 14 or to
governors as sent by him to punish
those who do wrong and to praise those
who do right. 15 For it is God's will
that by doing right you should put to
silence the ignorance of foolish men.
16 Live as free men, yet without using
your freedom as a pretext for evil; but
live as servants of God. 17 Honor all
men. Love the brotherhood. Fear
God. Honor the emperor.

18 Servants, be submissive to your
masters with all respect, not only to the
kind and gentle but also to the overbearing. 19 For one is approved if,
mindful of God, he endures pain while
suffering unjustly. 20 For what credit
is it, if when you do wrong and are
beaten for it you take it patiently? But
if when you do right and suffer for it
you take it patiently, you have God's
approval. 21 For to this you have been
called, because Christ also suffered
for you, leaving you an example, that
you should follow in his steps. 22 He
committed no sin; no guile was found
on his lips. 23 When he was reviled,
he did not revile in return; when he
suffered, he did not threaten; but he
trusted to him who judges justly. 24 He
himself bore our sins in his body on
the tree,*g* that we might die to sin and
live to righteousness. By his wounds
you have been healed. 25 For you were
straying like sheep, but have now returned to the Shepherd and Guardian
of your souls.

3 Likewise you wives, be submissive
to your husbands, so that some,
though they do not obey the word,
may be won without a word by the
behavior of their wives, 2 when they
see your reverent and chaste behavior.
3 Let not yours be the outward adorning with braiding of hair, decoration of
gold, and wearing of fine clothing, 4 but
let it be the hidden person of the heart
with the imperishable jewel of a gentle
and quiet spirit, which in God's sight
is very precious. 5 So once the holy
women who hoped in God used to
adorn themselves and were submissive
to their husbands, 6 as Sarah obeyed
Abraham, calling him lord. And you
are now her children if you do right
and let nothing terrify you.

7 Likewise you husbands, live con-

e Greek *a people for his possession*
f Or *every institution ordained for men*
g Or *carried up . . . to the tree*

---

royal priesthood (Ex.19.6). *Into his marvelous light*, in which God dwells (Is.57.15; 1 Tim.6.16).
2.11–4.11: The obligation of Christians. 2.11: *That wage war*, Rom.7.23. **12:** *Day of visita-*
tion, when God makes the truth known to them. **13–17:** Respect for civil authority. **14:**
Governors, of Roman provinces. **16:** *Live as servants of God*, only so can you *live as free men*.
17: *Fear God. Honor the emperor*, Pr.24.21; Mt.22.21; Rom.13.7. **18–25:** Obedience to masters.
The Christian servant must have respect even for harsh and unjust masters. **21–25:** The example
of Christ is set forth in language that echoes Is.53.5–12. **24:** *The tree*, the cross (see Acts 5.30 n.).
25: *Shepherd and Guardian*, synonymous terms, referring to Christ (5.4; Jn.10.11,14; Heb.13.20).
3.1–7: Wives and husbands. **1:** An unbelieving husband *may be won* (converted) by example
without argument. **4:** *Hidden*, Eph.3.16. **6:** Gen.18.12. **7:** 1 Th.4.4. **8–12:** Love of the brethren.

siderately with your wives, bestowing honor on the woman as the weaker sex, since you are joint heirs of the grace of life, in order that your prayers may not be hindered.

8 Finally, all of you, have unity of spirit, sympathy, love of the brethren, a tender heart and a humble mind. ⁹ Do not return evil for evil or reviling for reviling; but on the contrary bless, for to this you have been called, that you may obtain a blessing. ¹⁰ For

"He that would love life
and see good days,
let him keep his tongue from evil
and his lips from speaking guile;
¹¹ let him turn away from evil and
do right;
let him seek peace and pursue it.
¹² For the eyes of the Lord are upon
the righteous,
and his ears are open to their prayer.
But the face of the Lord is against
those that do evil."

13 Now who is there to harm you if you are zealous for what is right? ¹⁴ But even if you do suffer for righteousness' sake, you will be blessed. Have no fear of them, nor be troubled, ¹⁵ but in your hearts reverence Christ as Lord. Always be prepared to make a defense to any one who calls you to account for the hope that is in you, yet do it with gentleness and reverence; ¹⁶ and keep your conscience clear, so that, when you are abused, those who revile your good behavior in Christ may be put to shame. ¹⁷ For it is better to suffer for doing right, if that should be God's will, than for doing wrong. ¹⁸ For Christ also died[h] for sins once for all, the righteous for the

unrighteous, that he might bring us to God, being put to death in the flesh but made alive in the spirit; ¹⁹ in which he went and preached to the spirits in prison, ²⁰ who formerly did not obey, when God's patience waited in the days of Noah, during the building of the ark, in which a few, that is, eight persons, were saved through water. ²¹ Baptism, which corresponds to this, now saves you, not as a removal of dirt from the body but as an appeal to God for a clear conscience, through the resurrection of Jesus Christ, ²² who has gone into heaven and is at the right hand of God, with angels, authorities, and powers subject to him.

4 Since therefore Christ suffered in the flesh,[i] arm yourselves with the same thought, for whoever has suffered in the flesh has ceased from sin, ² so as to live for the rest of the time in the flesh no longer by human passions but by the will of God. ³ Let the time that is past suffice for doing what the Gentiles like to do, living in licentiousness, passions, drunkenness, revels, carousing, and lawless idolatry. ⁴ They are surprised that you do not now join them in the same wild profligacy, and they abuse you; ⁵ but they will give account to him who is ready to judge the living and the dead. ⁶ For this is why the gospel was preached even to the dead, that though judged in the flesh like men, they might live in the spirit like God.

7 The end of all things is at hand; therefore keep sane and sober for your prayers. ⁸ Above all hold unfail-

h Other ancient authorities read *suffered*
i Other ancient authorities add *for us*; some *for you*

9: Rom.12.17; 1 Th.5.15. **10:** Ps.34.12–16. **13–17:** Patience in persecution. Be ready to defend your hope as a Christian, but do so with gentleness and reverence. **18–22:** The example of Christ (compare 2.21–25). **18:** *Put to death in the flesh* asserts that he really died. *Made alive in the spirit*, death did not hold him; he rose to new life (1 Cor.15.35–50). **19–20:** This difficult passage may mean that Christ announced his completed work in the realm of the dead to those who in Noah's day had been disobedient (compare 4.6). **21:** Mention of the flood (Gen. chs. 6–8) leads to a comparison with baptism: then water destroyed; now in baptism it saves. **22:** *At the right hand of God*, the place of honor (Ps.110.1). *Authorities and powers*, angelic beings (see Col.1.16 n.). **4.1–6:** Spiritual liberation through suffering. **1:** *Since therefore*, refers back to 3.18. **4:** *Now join*, as you once did. **6:** *Preached . . . to the dead*, see 3.19–20 n. **7–11:** Since the end is near, be sober stewards of God's diverse gifts (1 Cor.12.14–26). **8:** *Love covers . . .*

ing your love for one another, since love covers a multitude of sins. [9] Practice hospitality ungrudgingly to one another. [10] As each has received a gift, employ it for one another, as good stewards of God's varied grace: [11] whoever speaks, as one who utters oracles of God; whoever renders service, as one who renders it by the strength which God supplies; in order that in everything God may be glorified through Jesus Christ. To him belong glory and dominion for ever and ever. Amen.

12 Beloved, do not be surprised at the fiery ordeal which comes upon you to prove you, as though something strange were happening to you. [13] But rejoice in so far as you share Christ's sufferings, that you may also rejoice and be glad when his glory is revealed. [14] If you are reproached for the name of Christ, you are blessed, because the spirit of glory[j] and of God rests upon you. [15] But let none of you suffer as a murderer, or a thief, or a wrongdoer, or a mischief-maker; [16] yet if one suffers as a Christian, let him not be ashamed, but under that name let him glorify God. [17] For the time has come for judgment to begin with the household of God; and if it begins with us, what will be the end of those who do not obey the gospel of God? [18] And

"If the righteous man is scarcely saved,
where will the impious and sinner appear?"

[19] Therefore let those who suffer according to God's will do right and entrust their souls to a faithful Creator.

5 So I exhort the elders among you, as a fellow elder and a witness of the sufferings of Christ as well as a partaker in the glory that is to be revealed. [2] Tend the flock of God that is your charge,[k] not by constraint but willingly,[l] not for shameful gain but eagerly, [3] not as domineering over those in your charge but being examples to the flock. [4] And when the chief Shepherd is manifested you will obtain the unfading crown of glory. [5] Likewise you that are younger be subject to the elders. Clothe yourselves, all of you, with humility toward one another, for "God opposes the proud, but gives grace to the humble."

6 Humble yourselves therefore under the mighty hand of God, that in due time he may exalt you. [7] Cast all your anxieties on him, for he cares about you. [8] Be sober, be watchful. Your adversary the devil prowls around like a roaring lion, seeking some one to devour. [9] Resist him, firm in your faith, knowing that the same experience of suffering is required of your brotherhood throughout the world. [10] And after you have suffered a little while, the God of all grace, who has called you to his eternal glory in Christ, will himself restore, establish, and strengthen[m] you. [11] To him be the dominion for ever and ever. Amen.

12 By Silva'nus, a faithful brother as I regard him, I have written briefly to you, exhorting and declaring that

---

j Other ancient authorities insert *and of power*
k Other ancient authorities add *exercising the oversight*
l Other ancient authorities add *as God would have you*
m Other ancient authorities read *restore, establish, strengthen and settle*

---

sins, Pr.10.12; Lk.7.47; 1 Cor.13.7. **9:** *Practice hospitality*, provide lodging for Christian travelers (see Heb.13.2 n.; 3 Jn.5–8 n.).

4.12–19: Recapitulation of previous exhortations. **12:** *Fiery ordeal*, persecutions (1.6–7). **13:** Rom.8.17; 2 Tim.2.12. **14:** 2.20; Is.11.2. **16:** Phil.1.20. *Christian*, see Acts 11.26 n. **18:** Pr.11.31 Septuagint. *Scarcely*, with difficulty. **19:** 2.20.

5.1–14: Concluding exhortations and greetings. 1: *Elders*, church officials. **3:** *Not domineering*, Mk.10.42. **4:** *The chief Shepherd*, Christ (see 2.25 n.). **5:** *Clothe yourselves*, humility is not natural to anyone; it must be put on like clothing. The quotation is from Pr.3.34. **7:** Ps.55.22. **8:** *Roaring*, the rage of hunger. **9:** *Resist*, the devil (compare Eph.6.11–18). **10:** God has *called*; he will also *strengthen*. **12:** *Silvanus*, probably identical with Silas (Acts 15.22,40; 16.19; 17.4).

this is the true grace of God; stand fast in it. [13] She who is at Babylon, who is likewise chosen, sends you greetings; and so does my son Mark. [14] Greet one another with the kiss of love. Peace to all of you that are in Christ.

13: *Babylon*, a cryptic name for Rome (see Rev.17.1 n.). *My son*, in a spiritual sense (see Philem. 10 n.). *Mark*, see Acts 12.12 n.; Col.4.10; Philem.24. **14:** *Kiss*, see Rom.16.16 n.

THE SECOND LETTER OF
PETER

This brief letter has a double purpose: to undergird faith in the second coming of Christ, and to warn against false teachers. The author recalls the apostolic witness as the basis of the church's proclamation (1.16), points to the Messianic prophecies of the Old Testament which have been confirmed by the coming of Christ (1.19–21), and explains the delay of the second coming as due to the patience and forbearance of God, who desires "that all should reach repentance" (3.9).

The false teachers are vigorously denounced as licentious (2.2,10,13,14), greedy (2.3,14,15) and despisers of authority (2.10). They will be visited by God's judgment, as were the fallen angels, the sinful world in the time of Noah, and the cities of Sodom and Gomorrah; the godly, however, will be rescued, as Lot was (2.4–9).

The tradition that this letter is the work of the apostle Peter was questioned in early times, and internal indications are almost decisive against it. It is dependent upon the Letter of Jude (compare 2.1–8 with Jude 4–16), and the author refers to all the letters of Paul (3.15) in a way that presupposes not only that they had been collected into a corpus, but that they were regarded as equal to "the other scriptures"—conditions which did not exist in the lifetime of Peter. Most scholars therefore regard the letter as the work of one who was deeply indebted to Peter and who published it under his master's name early in the second century. In this connection the following considerations should be borne in mind. (1) In antiquity pseudonymous authorship was a widely accepted literary convention. Therefore the use of an apostle's name in reasserting his teaching was not regarded as dishonest but merely a way of reminding the church of what it had received from God through that apostle. (2) The authority of New Testament books is dependent, not upon their human authorship, but upon their intrinsic significance, which the church, under the guidance of the Spirit, has recognized as the authentic voice of apostolic teaching. For this reason, therefore, what is traditionally known as the Second Letter of Peter was included in the canon of Scripture (on the canon, see p. 1170).

SIMEON[x] PETER, A SERVANT AND apostle of Jesus Christ,

To those who have obtained a faith of equal standing with ours in the righteousness of our God and Savior Jesus Christ:[a]

2 May grace and peace be multiplied to you in the knowledge of God and of Jesus our Lord.

3 His divine power has granted to us all things that pertain to life and godliness, through the knowledge of him who called us to[b] his own glory and excellence, 4 by which he has granted to us his precious and very great promises, that through these you may escape from the corruption that is in the world because of passion, and become partakers of the divine nature. 5 For this very reason make every effort to supplement your faith with virtue, and virtue with knowledge, 6 and knowledge with self-control, and self-control with steadfastness, and steadfastness with godliness, 7 and godliness with brotherly affection, and brotherly affection with love. 8 For if these things are yours and abound, they keep you from being ineffective or unfruitful in the knowledge of our Lord Jesus Christ. 9 For whoever lacks

x Other authorities read *Simon*
a Or *of our God and the Savior Jesus Christ*
b Or *by*

1.1–2: Salutation, see Rom.1.1–7 n. **1:** *God and Savior,* see Tit.2.13. **2:** *Knowledge* is one of the author's favorite words (1.3,5,6,8; 2.20; 3.18). *Grace and peace,* see 2 Th.1.2 n.

1.3–21: Exhortation to holiness. Man's salvation is the result of God's goodness. One must hold firmly *his precious and very great promises,* and thus escape the corruption of the world. **5:** *Faith* should lead to Christian virtues, of which seven are listed, concluding with *love* (1

these things is blind and shortsighted and has forgotten that he was cleansed from his old sins. ¹⁰ Therefore, brethren, be the more zealous to confirm your call and election, for if you do this you will never fall; ¹¹ so there will be richly provided for you an entrance into the eternal kingdom of our Lord and Savior Jesus Christ.

12 Therefore I intend always to remind you of these things, though you know them and are established in the truth that you have. ¹³ I think it right, as long as I am in this body,ᶜ to arouse you by way of reminder, ¹⁴ since I know that the putting off of my bodyᶜ will be soon, as our Lord Jesus Christ showed me. ¹⁵ And I will see to it that after my departure you may be able at any time to recall these things.

16 For we did not follow cleverly devised myths when we made known to you the power and coming of our Lord Jesus Christ, but we were eyewitnesses of his majesty. ¹⁷ For when he received honor and glory from God the Father and the voice was borne to him by the Majestic Glory, "This is my beloved Son,ᵈ with whom I am well pleased," ¹⁸ we heard this voice borne from heaven, for we were with him on the holy mountain. ¹⁹ And we have the prophetic word made more sure. You will do well to pay attention to this as to a lamp shining in a dark place, until the day dawns and the morning star rises in your hearts. ²⁰ First of all you must understand this, that no prophecy of scripture is a matter of one's own interpretation, ²¹ because no prophecy ever came by the impulse of man, but men moved by the Holy Spirit spoke from God.ᵉ

2 But false prophets also arose among the people, just as there will be false teachers among you, who will secretly bring in destructive heresies, even denying the Master who bought them, bringing upon themselves swift destruction. ² And many will follow their licentiousness, and because of them the way of truth will be reviled. ³ And in their greed they will exploit you with false words; from of old their condemnation has not been idle, and their destruction has not been asleep.

4 For if God did not spare the angels when they sinned, but cast them into hellᶠ and committed them to pits of nether gloom to be kept until the judgment; ⁵ if he did not spare the ancient world, but preserved Noah, a herald of righteousness, with seven other persons, when he brought a flood upon the world of the ungodly; ⁶ if by turning the cities of Sodom and Gomor'rah to ashes he condemned them to extinction and made them an example to those who were to be ungodly; ⁷ and if he rescued righteous Lot, greatly distressed by the licentiousness of the wicked ⁸ (for by what that righteous man saw and heard as he lived among them, he was vexed in his righteous soul day after day with their lawless deeds), ⁹ then the Lord knows how to rescue the godly from trial, and to keep the unrighteous under punishment until the day of judgment, ¹⁰ and especially those who indulge in the lust of defiling passion and despise authority.

c Greek *tent*   *d* Or *my Son, my* (or *the*) *Beloved*
e Other authorities read *moved by the Holy Spirit holy men of God spoke*
f Greek *Tartarus*

Cor.13.13). **11**: *Kingdom*, Col.1.13. **16**: Apostolic tradition is not a collection of *myths*, but is based upon the experience of *eyewitnesses*. **17–18**: A reference to the transfiguration (Mt. 17.1–8; Mk.9.2–8; Lk.9.28–36). **19**: This testimony confirms the prophecies of the Old Testament, which must be studied diligently until the coming of the Lord. **20–21**: Since *prophecy* is God's gift, its *interpretation* must be in accord with his intention.

2.1–22: Attack upon false teachers. The language follows closely the Letter of Jude (vv. 4–16) in the denunciation of heretics. **1**: The future tense gives an atmosphere of prophecy; but in vv. 14–19 and 3.5 the present tense is used. False teachers are already present. **4–10a**: God's past judgments indicate what is in store for these men. **5**: Gen.6.6–8; 8.18. **6**: Gen.19.24. **7**: Gen.19.16,29. **11**: See Jude 9–10 n. **15**: Num.22.5,7. **16**: Num.22.21,23,28,30–31. **19**: *Slaves*,

Bold and wilful, they are not afraid to revile the glorious ones, [11] whereas angels, though greater in might and power, do not pronounce a reviling judgment upon them before the Lord. [12] But these, like irrational animals, creatures of instinct, born to be caught and killed, reviling in matters of which they are ignorant, will be destroyed in the same destruction with them, [13] suffering wrong for their wrongdoing. They count it pleasure to revel in the daytime. They are blots and blemishes, reveling in their dissipation,[g] carousing with you. [14] They have eyes full of adultery, insatiable for sin. They entice unsteady souls. They have hearts trained in greed. Accursed children! [15] Forsaking the right way they have gone astray; they have followed the way of Balaam, the son of Be'or, who loved gain from wrongdoing, [16] but was rebuked for his own transgression; a dumb ass spoke with human voice and restrained the prophet's madness.

17 These are waterless springs and mists driven by a storm; for them the nether gloom of darkness has been reserved. [18] For, uttering loud boasts of folly, they entice with licentious passions of the flesh men who have barely escaped from those who live in error. [19] They promise them freedom, but they themselves are slaves of corruption; for whatever overcomes a man, to that he is enslaved. [20] For if, after they have escaped the defilements of the world through the knowledge of our Lord and Savior Jesus Christ, they are again entangled in them and overpowered, the last state has become worse for them than the first. [21] For it would have been better for them never to have known the way of righteousness than after knowing it to turn back from the holy commandment delivered to them. [22] It has happened to them according to the true proverb, The dog turns back to his own vomit, and the sow is washed only to wallow in the mire.

3 This is now the second letter that I have written to you, beloved, and in both of them I have aroused your sincere mind by way of reminder; [2] that you should remember the predictions of the holy prophets and the commandment of the Lord and Savior through your apostles. [3] First of all you must understand this, that scoffers will come in the last days with scoffing, following their own passions [4] and saying, "Where is the promise of his coming? For ever since the fathers fell asleep, all things have continued as they were from the beginning of creation." [5] They deliberately ignore this fact, that by the word of God heavens existed long ago, and an earth formed out of water and by means of water, [6] through which the world that then existed was deluged with water and perished. [7] But by the same word the heavens and earth that now exist have been stored up for fire, being kept until the day of judgment and destruction of ungodly men.

8 But do not ignore this one fact, beloved, that with the Lord one day is as a thousand years, and a thousand

g Other ancient authorities read *love feasts*

Jn.8.34; Rom.6.6,16. **20**: *The last state*, Mt.12.45; Lk.11.26. **21**: *The holy commandments delivered to them*, 1 Tim.6.14; Jude 3. **22**: Pr.26.11.

3.1–18: The day of the Lord. Scoffers ridicule the hope of Christ's second coming. Delay is no proof that he will not come, for God does not measure time as men do. The delay shows God's patience and his desire that men should repent. Because the day of the Lord will come according to his promise, Christians should await it in holiness and godliness. **3**: The coming of scoffers is a sign of *the last days* (see 2 Tim.3.1 n.). **4**: *Ever since the fathers fell asleep* expresses the viewpoint of a later generation. The scoffers apparently argued that the universe is immutable, and therefore there would be no end. **5**: God's *word* is not just chatter; it is creative, and by it the world was brought into being (Gen.1.6–10). **6–7**: So far from being immutable the world has already been destroyed once, by the deluge (Gen.7.11), and, so the author affirms, it will be destroyed again, by fire. **8**: God's measure of time is cited from Ps.90.4.

years as one day. ⁹ The Lord is not slow about his promise as some count slowness, but is forbearing toward you,ʰ not wishing that any should perish, but that all should reach repentance. ¹⁰ But the day of the Lord will come like a thief, and then the heavens will pass away with a loud noise, and the elements will be dissolved with fire, and the earth and the works that are upon it will be burned up.

11 Since all these things are thus to be dissolved, what sort of persons ought you to be in lives of holiness and godliness, ¹² waiting for and hastening*i* the coming of the day of God, because of which the heavens will be kindled and dissolved, and the elements will melt with fire! ¹³ But according to his promise we wait for new heavens and a new earth in which righteousness dwells.

14 Therefore, beloved, since you wait for these, be zealous to be found by him without spot or blemish, and at peace. ¹⁵ And count the forbearance of our Lord as salvation. So also our beloved brother Paul wrote to you according to the wisdom given him, ¹⁶ speaking of this as he does in all his letters. There are some things in them hard to understand, which the ignorant and unstable twist to their own destruction, as they do the other scriptures. ¹⁷ You therefore, beloved, knowing this beforehand, beware lest you be carried away with the error of lawless men and lose your own stability. ¹⁸ But grow in the grace and knowledge of our Lord and Savior Jesus Christ. To him be the glory both now and to the day of eternity. Amen.

h Other ancient authorities read *on your account*
i Or *earnestly desiring*

10: *Day of the Lord*, see Am.5.18–20 n.; Jl.2.28–32 n. *Like a thief*, Mt.24.43; Lk.12.39. **12:** In apocalyptic writings *fire* plays a prominent role in the destruction of the world. **13–14:** Freely quoted from Is.65.17; 66.22. In Isaiah and Rev. ch. 21 the thought is not the destruction but the renewal and transformation of the universe. **15–16:** The author knows several letters of Paul and equates them with *the other scriptures*.

THE FIRST LETTER OF

JOHN

Though 1 John has been traditionally called a letter, it lacks the salutation and epistolary ending characteristic of letters. In form and content it resembles a theological treatise or sermon, written with obvious affection and concern for the spiritual welfare of those to whom it is addressed.

The author of 1 John does not mention his name; in 2 and 3 John he calls himself "the elder." The close kinship between these letters and the Fourth Gospel in vocabulary, literary style, and theological ideas indicates that they came from the same pen.

Though it is impossible to date 1 John with precision, most scholars believe that it was written toward the end of the first Christian century. Whether its circulation preceded, accompanied, or followed that of the Gospel of John cannot be determined, but it is evident that the two are in some sense companions.

This letter has a twofold purpose: to deepen the spiritual life of its readers (1.3–4), and to correct the heretical views of certain gnostic teachers who denied that God had really become man in Jesus (4.2; compare 2 Jn.7). Doctrine and ethics, theology and behavior, are inextricably woven together throughout the letter. The truth is not so much argued as affirmed. Though, in a broad sense, there is order and progression in the letter, yet the various themes are frequently reintroduced, and often blend into one another, like the leading refrains of a great musical composition.

THAT WHICH WAS FROM THE beginning, which we have heard, which we have seen with our eyes, which we have looked upon and touched with our hands, concerning the word of life– 2 the life was made manifest, and we saw it, and testify to it, and proclaim to you the eternal life which was with the Father and was made manifest to us– 3 that which we have seen and heard we proclaim also to you, so that you may have fellowship with us; and our fellowship is with the Father and with his Son Jesus Christ. 4 And we are writing this that our*a* joy may be complete.

5 This is the message we have heard from him and proclaim to you, that God is light and in him is no darkness at all. 6 If we say we have fellowship with him while we walk in darkness, we lie and do not live according to the truth; 7 but if we walk in the light, as he is in the light, we have fellowship with one another, and the blood of Jesus his Son cleanses us from all sin. 8 If we say we have no sin, we deceive ourselves, and the truth is not in us. 9 If we confess our sins, he is faithful and just, and will forgive our sins and cleanse us from all unrighteousness. 10 If we say we have not sinned, we make him a liar, and his word is not in us.

2 My little children, I am writing this to you so that you may not sin; but if any one does sin, we have an advocate with the Father, Jesus

a Other ancient authorities read *your*

1.1–4: Introduction. 1–2: *From the beginning,* compare Gen.1.1; Jn.1.1. *We,* the apostolic group. *The word of life,* namely Christ, eternally *with the Father,* and *made manifest* in his Incarnation (see Jn.1.1–2 n.). *Heard, seen, looked upon, touched* refer to the evidence of the senses, refuting the gnostic heresy that Christ was not really human. **3–4:** The purpose of writing is the attainment of *fellowship* (oneness with Christ) and Christian joy (Jn.15.11; 17.13).

1.5–10: Right attitude toward sin. 5: *God is light,* absolute holiness without taint of evil. **6:** *Walk in darkness,* habitual and intentional evil conduct (Jn.3.19; 1 Jn.2.11). **8–9:** Denial of *sin* (guilt, sinful nature) is self-deception; confession brings forgiveness. **10:** Denial of acts of sin contradicts God's declaration (Ps.14.1–2; 53.1–3).

2.1–6: Obedience. 1: *That you may not sin* is the ultimate goal of Christian living (Rom.6.11).

Christ the righteous; [2] and he is the expiation for our sins, and not for ours only but also for the sins of the whole world. [3] And by this we may be sure that we know him, if we keep his commandments. [4] He who says "I know him" but disobeys his commandments is a liar, and the truth is not in him; [5] but whoever keeps his word, in him truly love for God is perfected. By this we may be sure that we are in him: [6] he who says he abides in him ought to walk in the same way in which he walked.

7 Beloved, I am writing you no new commandment, but an old commandment which you had from the beginning; the old commandment is the word which you have heard. [8] Yet I am writing you a new commandment, which is true in him and in you, because[b] the darkness is passing away and the true light is already shining. [9] He who says he is in the light and hates his brother is in the darkness still. [10] He who loves his brother abides in the light, and in it[c] there is no cause for stumbling. [11] But he who hates his brother is in the darkness and walks in the darkness, and does not know where he is going, because the darkness has blinded his eyes.

12 I am writing to you, little children, because your sins are forgiven for his sake. [13] I am writing to you, fathers, because you know him who is from the beginning. I am writing to you, young men, because you have overcome the evil one. I write to you, chil-

dren, because you know the Father. [14] I write to you, fathers, because you know him who is from the beginning. I write to you, young men, because you are strong, and the word of God abides in you, and you have overcome the evil one.

15 Do not love the world or the things in the world. If any one loves the world, love for the Father is not in him. [16] For all that is in the world, the lust of the flesh and the lust of the eyes and the pride of life, is not of the Father but is of the world. [17] And the world passes away, and the lust of it; but he who does the will of God abides for ever.

18 Children, it is the last hour; and as you have heard that antichrist is coming, so now many antichrists have come; therefore we know that it is the last hour. [19] They went out from us, but they were not of us; for if they had been of us, they would have continued with us; but they went out, that it might be plain that they all are not of us. [20] But you have been anointed by the Holy One, and you all know.[d] [21] I write to you, not because you do not know the truth, but because you know it, and know that no lie is of the truth. [22] Who is the liar but he who denies that Jesus is the Christ? This is the antichrist, he who denies the Father and the Son. [23] No one who denies the Son has the Father. He who confesses the

b Or *that*
c Or *him*
d Other ancient authorities read *you know everything*

Advocate, one who pleads the cause of another (see Jn.14.16 n.). **2:** *Expiation*, 4.10. **3–5:** Obedience to God's *commandments* tests whether we know him, and measures the perfection (completeness) of our *love for God* (Jn.14.15,21,23; 15.10). **6:** Jesus is the pattern of obedience.
    2.7–11: Love of the brethren. 8: The *commandment* to love, though old, is never obsolete or antiquated, but ever *new*, being the law of the new age and overcoming the *darkness* of evil (1.5; Rom.13.12–14). **9–11:** Hatred of a *brother* (fellow Christian) is incompatible with membership in Christ's kingdom of *light*.
    2.12–14: True relationship to God in Christ. 12: *Little children*, the whole Christian group (2.1,18,28). **14:** *Fathers*, the aged. *Young men*, youth.
    2.15–17: True appraisal of the world. 15: *The world*, all that is alienated from and at enmity with God (Jas.1.27). **16:** *Lust of the flesh*, unlawful physical gratification; *lust of the eyes*, sinful delights of mind or emotions; *pride of life*, empty trust in possessions.
    2.18–29: Loyalty to the true faith. 18: *Antichrist*, any concentration of enmity against God; in this case, false teachers (4.3). **19:** They left the Christian fellowship because they were not really Christians. **20–21:** Christians have received the enlightening grace of the Holy Spirit,

Son has the Father also. ²⁴ Let what you heard from the beginning abide in you. If what you heard from the beginning abides in you, then you will abide in the Son and in the Father. ²⁵ And this is what he has promised us,*ᵉ* eternal life.

26 I write this to you about those who would deceive you; ²⁷ but the anointing which you received from him abides in you, and you have no need that any one should teach you; as his anointing teaches you about everything, and is true, and is no lie, just as it has taught you, abide in him.

28 And now, little children, abide in him, so that when he appears we may have confidence and not shrink from him in shame at his coming. ²⁹ If you know that he is righteous, you may be sure that every one who does right is born of him.

3 See what love the Father has given us, that we should be called children of God; and so we are. The reason why the world does not know us is that it did not know him. ² Beloved, we are God's children now; it does not yet appear what we shall be, but we know that when he appears we shall be like him, for we shall see him as he is. ³ And every one who thus hopes in him purifies himself as he is pure.

4 Every one who commits sin is guilty of lawlessness; sin is lawlessness. ⁵ You know that he appeared to take away sins, and in him there is no sin. ⁶ No one who abides in him sins; no one who sins has either seen him or known him. ⁷ Little children, let no one de-

ceive you. He who does right is righteous, as he is righteous. ⁸ He who commits sin is of the devil; for the devil has sinned from the beginning. The reason the Son of God appeared was to destroy the works of the devil. ⁹ No one born of God commits sin; for God's*ᶠ* nature abides in him, and he cannot sin because he is*ᵍ* born of God. ¹⁰ By this it may be seen who are the children of God, and who are the children of the devil: whoever does not do right is not of God, nor he who does not love his brother.

11 For this is the message which you have heard from the beginning, that we should love one another, ¹² and not be like Cain who was of the evil one and murdered his brother. And why did he murder him? Because his own deeds were evil and his brother's righteous. ¹³ Do not wonder, brethren, that the world hates you. ¹⁴ We know that we have passed out of death into life, because we love the brethren. He who does not love abides in death. ¹⁵ Any one who hates his brother is a murderer, and you know that no murderer has eternal life abiding in him. ¹⁶ By this we know love, that he laid down his life for us; and we ought to lay down our lives for the brethren. ¹⁷ But if any one has the world's goods and sees his brother in need, yet closes his heart against him, how does God's love abide in him? ¹⁸ Little children, let us not love in word or speech but in deed and in truth.

e Other ancient authorities read *you*
f Greek *his*
g Or *for the offspring of God abide in him, and they cannot sin because they are*

and therefore can discern *the truth* (v. 27; 1 Cor.2.15–16). **22–23:** Gnostics denied that the historic man Jesus was the Christ (2 Jn.7). **27:** Jn.14.26. **28:** 4.17. **29:** 3.7–10; 4.7.
 3.1–10: Filial relation expressed in right conduct. 1–2: God's *love* in making us his *children* (Jn.1.12) progressively produces resemblance to him, here and hereafter. **3:** Hope of complete moral likeness to Christ motivates purity of life (Mt.5.8). **5:** Jn.1.29. **6:** *Sins,* habitually and constantly (3 Jn.11). **8:** Jn.8.44; Acts 13.10; Heb.2.14. **9:** 5.18.
 3.11–18: Love of the brethren. 11–12: Abel's *righteous deeds* stirred Cain's hatred (Gen.4.8; Heb.11.4; Jude 11). **13:** *The world* likewise *hates* the church (Jn.15.18–19). **14–15:** Murder, which takes life, robs the *murderer* of *eternal life.* **16:** Jesus, in contrast to taking life, *laid down his life* (Jn.15.13). He is our pattern. **17:** *To lay down our lives* may take the form of daily sacrifice for others *in need.* **18:** *Word,* intention without *deed; speech,* hypocrisy, not *truth* (Jas.1.22).

19 By this we shall know that we are of the truth, and reassure our hearts before him 20 whenever our hearts condemn us; for God is greater than our hearts, and he knows everything. 21 Beloved, if our hearts do not condemn us, we have confidence before God; 22 and we receive from him whatever we ask, because we keep his commandments and do what pleases him. 23 And this is his commandment, that we should believe in the name of his Son Jesus Christ and love one another, just as he has commanded us. 24 All who keep his commandments abide in him, and he in them. And by this we know that he abides in us, by the Spirit which he has given us.

4 Beloved, do not believe every spirit, but test the spirits to see whether they are of God; for many false prophets have gone out into the world. 2 By this you know the Spirit of God: every spirit which confesses that Jesus Christ has come in the flesh is of God, 3 and every spirit which does not confess Jesus is not of God. This is the spirit of antichrist, of which you heard that it was coming, and now it is in the world already. 4 Little children, you are of God, and have overcome them; for he who is in you is greater than he who is in the world. 5 They are of the world, therefore what they say is of the world, and the world listens to them. 6 We are of God. Whoever knows God listens to us, and he who is not of God

does not listen to us. By this we know the spirit of truth and the spirit of error.

7 Beloved, let us love one another; for love is of God, and he who loves is born of God and knows God. 8 He who does not love does not know God; for God is love. 9 In this the love of God was made manifest among us, that God sent his only Son into the world, so that we might live through him. 10 In this is love, not that we loved God but that he loved us and sent his Son to be the expiation for our sins. 11 Beloved, if God so loved us, we also ought to love one another. 12 No man has ever seen God; if we love one another, God abides in us and his love is perfected in us.

13 By this we know that we abide in him and he in us, because he has given us of his own Spirit. 14 And we have seen and testify that the Father has sent his Son as the Savior of the world. 15 Whoever confesses that Jesus is the Son of God, God abides in him, and he in God. 16 So we know and believe the love God has for us. God is love, and he who abides in love abides in God, and God abides in him. 17 In this is love perfected with us, that we may have confidence for the day of judgment, because as he is so are we in this world. 18 There is no fear in love, but perfect love casts out fear. For fear has to do with punishment, and he who fears is not perfected in love. 19 We love, because he first loved us. 20 If any one says, "I love God," and hates his brother, he is a liar;

3.19–24: The Christian's assurance. 19: *This*, the *love* described in v. 18. **20:** *God*, who *knows* everything, judges us by the abiding relation of love to others, rather than by our passing moods (Jn.21.17). **21–22:** *Confidence* in prayer results from obedience to God, and strengthens assurance (5.14). **23–24:** Belief *in the name* (the total person) *of Jesus Christ* and *love* are the basic ingredients of obedience (Jn.6.28–29; 13.34; 15.17; Acts 16.31), wrought in us by the Holy *Spirit*.

4.1–6: Discernment of truth and error. 1–2: Note the contrast between *spirits* (supernatural powers claimed by *false prophets*) and the Holy *Spirit* (Jn.16.13–15). **3:** 2 Jn.7. **4:** *He who is in the world*, the devil (3.10; Jn.8.44; 12.31). **5:** *They*, the false prophets. **6:** *We*, the Christian teachers. *Whoever knows God* discriminates between *truth* and *error* (Jn.5.37–38; 8.47; 10.4–5).

4.7–21: The blessedness of love. 7–10: That *God is love* is seen in sending *his Son* as *the expiation* (atonement) *for our sins* (2.2). **11–12:** *To love one another* is the only authentication that we know God, *whom no man has ever seen*. **13–18:** The Holy *Spirit* testifies that *Jesus*, God's *Son*, has revealed his *Father* as *love*. When his love is *perfected* (matured) in us, *fear* of *judgment* is allayed. **19–21:** *Love* originates in *God*. Failure to *love* is visible evidence of a breach with the unseen God, and a violation of his *commandment*.

for he who does not love his brother whom he has seen, cannot[h] love God whom he has not seen. [21] And this commandment we have from him, that he who loves God should love his brother also.

5 Every one who believes that Jesus is the Christ is a child of God, and every one who loves the parent loves the child. [2] By this we know that we love the children of God, when we love God and obey his commandments. [3] For this is the love of God, that we keep his commandments. And his commandments are not burdensome. [4] For whatever is born of God overcomes the world; and this is the victory that overcomes the world, our faith. [5] Who is it that overcomes the world but he who believes that Jesus is the Son of God?

6 This is he who came by water and blood, Jesus Christ, not with the water only but with the water and the blood. [7] And the Spirit is the witness, because the Spirit is the truth. [8] There are three witnesses, the Spirit, the water, and the blood; and these three agree. [9] If we receive the testimony of men, the testimony of God is greater; for this is the testimony of God that he has borne witness to his Son. [10] He who believes in the Son of God has the testimony in himself. He who does not believe God has made him a liar, because he has not believed in the testimony that God has borne to his Son. [11] And this is

the testimony, that God gave us eternal life, and this life is in his Son. [12] He who has the Son has life; he who has not the Son of God has not life.

13 I write this to you who believe in the name of the Son of God, that you may know that you have eternal life. [14] And this is the confidence which we have in him, that if we ask anything according to his will he hears us. [15] And if we know that he hears us in whatever we ask, we know that we have obtained the requests made of him. [16] If any one sees his brother committing what is not a mortal sin, he will ask, and God[i] will give him life for those whose sin is not mortal. There is sin which is mortal; I do not say that one is to pray for that. [17] All wrongdoing is sin, but there is sin which is not mortal.

18 We know that any one born of God does not sin, but He who was born of God keeps him, and the evil one does not touch him.

19 We know that we are of God, and the whole world is in the power of the evil one.

20 And we know that the Son of God has come and has given us understanding, to know him who is true; and we are in him who is true, in his Son Jesus Christ. This is the true God and eternal life. [21] Little children, keep yourselves from idols.

h Other ancient authorities read *how can he*
i Greek *he*

5.1–12: Victorious faith issuing in eternal life. **1:** Jn.8.42. **3:** *Love of God* involves obedience to his will. *Not burdensome*, Mt.11.30. **4:** Jn.16.33. *That overcomes*, or "that have overcome." **6–8:** The Spirit's witness is to *the water* (Jesus' baptism) and to *the blood* (the cross). **9:** Jn.5.32, 36; 8.18. **11–12:** *Eternal life* is *in* (living union with) Jesus, God's *Son*, and nowhere else.
5.13–21: Conclusion. 13: Jn.17.3; 20.31. **14:** Mt.7.7. **15:** 3.22. **16:** *Sin which is mortal* is not an act, but a state. It is not forbidden to pray even concerning this. **18–20:** *We know*, thrice repeated (compare v. 13). **18:** *Does not sin*, see 3.6 n. **19:** *World*, see 2.15 n. **20:** *The true God*, in contrast to the gnostic view of God. **21:** *Idols*, any rival to God (1 Cor.10.14).

JOHN

Language, literary style, and ideas, along with early church tradition, make it highly probable that this letter came from the same pen which produced 1 John and the Fourth Gospel. The tone of the author's admonitions indicates that he was well known to his readers and was one whose spiritual authority they acknowledged. Unlike 1 John, which appears to have been addressed to several churches, this letter was written to one specific church ("the elect lady," v. 1), probably one of the churches of Asia Minor.

The letter yields no definite evidence regarding date. The kinship of situation and ideas with those reflected in 1 John suggests a date near the end of the first century (see Introduction to 1 John).

The author repeats in briefer form the main teaching of 1 John, and adds a warning against showing hospitality to false teachers, lest this might further the spread of error (vv. 7–11).

THE ELDER TO THE ELECT LADY and her children, whom I love in the truth, and not only I but also all who know the truth, ² because of the truth which abides in us and will be with us for ever:

3 Grace, mercy, and peace will be with us, from God the Father and from Jesus Christ the Father's Son, in truth and love.

4 I rejoiced greatly to find some of your children following the truth, just as we have been commanded by the Father. ⁵ And now I beg you, lady, not as though I were writing you a new commandment, but the one we have had from the beginning, that we love one another. ⁶ And this is love, that we follow his commandments; this is the commandment, as you have heard from the beginning, that you follow love. ⁷ For many deceivers have gone out into the world, men who will not acknowledge the coming of Jesus Christ in the flesh; such a one is the deceiver and the antichrist. ⁸ Look to yourselves, that you may not lose what you*a* have worked for, but may win a full reward. ⁹ Any one who goes ahead and does not abide in the doctrine of Christ does not have God; he who abides in the doctrine has both the Father and the Son. ¹⁰ If any one comes to you and does not bring this doctrine, do not receive him into the house or give him any greeting; ¹¹ for he who greets him shares his wicked work.

12 Though I have much to write to you, I would rather not use paper and ink, but I hope to come to see you and talk with you face to face, so that our joy may be complete.

13 The children of your elect sister greet you.

a Other ancient authorities read *we*

1: *Elect lady*, probably refers to a local church, the members of which are called *her children*. 2: *The truth* about Jesus, in contrast to false teaching (v. 7). 4: *Some*, not all; heresy has crept in. 5–6: 1 Jn.2.7; 5.3; Jn.13.34. 7: *Deceivers*, who taught that the Christ was not indissolubly united with the man Jesus (1 Jn.2.22), or that Jesus' body was not a real body of *flesh* and blood (1 Jn.4.2–3). 8: *Full reward*, eternal life (Jn.20.31; 1 Jn.2.25; 5.11–12). 9: *Goes ahead*, i.e. treats the Christian revelation as a mere stepping-stone to more "advanced" doctrine (compare 1 Jn.2.22–23 n.). 10–11: Hospitality to false teachers incurs responsibility for their *wicked work* (contrast 3 Jn.5–8). 13: *Elect sister*, sister church (see v. 1 n.).

JOHN

Of the three Johannine letters, this one alone is written to an individual. It reflects a period in the church's life when organization was loose and churches were bound together by letters from those in authority and by personal visits of their representatives and traveling missionaries. In the unknown church to which this letter was directed, a certain Diotrephes, who liked "to put himself first" (v. 9), had challenged the spiritual authority of "the elder," refusing to receive messengers from him and putting "out of the church" those who showed them hospitality (v. 10). The elder, therefore, writes to a respected and influential member of the church named Gaius (v. 1), who has cordially welcomed the messengers and provided for their further needs (vv. 5–6). He encourages Gaius to continue this practice, indicating that he will deal with Diotrephes on a subsequent visit (v. 10). He also reinforces certain truths set forth in 1 and 2 John (v. 11).

The authorship and date parallel those of 1 and 2 John (see Introductions to 1 and 2 John).

THE ELDER TO THE BELOVED Ga'ius, whom I love in the truth. 2 Beloved, I pray that all may go well with you and that you may be in health; I know that it is well with your soul. ³ For I greatly rejoiced when some of the brethren arrived and testified to the truth of your life, as indeed you do follow the truth. ⁴ No greater joy can I have than this, to hear that my children follow the truth.

5 Beloved, it is a loyal thing you do when you render any service to the brethren, especially to strangers, ⁶ who have testified to your love before the church. You will do well to send them on their journey as befits God's service. ⁷ For they have set out for his sake and have accepted nothing from the heathen. ⁸ So we ought to support such men, that we may be fellow workers in the truth.

9 I have written something to the church; but Diot'rephes, who likes to put himself first, does not acknowledge my authority. ¹⁰ So if I come, I will bring up what he is doing, prating against me with evil words. And not content with that, he refuses himself to welcome the brethren, and also stops those who want to welcome them and puts them out of the church.

11 Beloved, do not imitate evil but imitate good. He who does good is of God; he who does evil has not seen God. ¹² Deme'trius has testimony from every one, and from the truth itself; I testify to him too, and you know my testimony is true.

13 I had much to write to you, but I would rather not write with pen and ink; ¹⁴ I hope to see you soon, and we will talk together face to face. 15 Peace be to you. The friends greet you. Greet the friends, every one of them.

1: *Gaius*, see Introduction. **3:** *Truth of your life*, behavior contrasting with that of Diotrephes (vv. 9–10) in receiving emissaries from the elder. **5–8:** Commendation for, and encouragement to continue, rendering *service* to traveling missionaries, who were dependent on the church rather than on *the heathen* (non-Christians). Such support is true participation (contrast 2 Jn. 10–11). **9–10:** *Written something*, probably a letter of apostolic counsel no longer extant. *Diotrephes*, see Introduction. Personal ambition rejects *authority*. *Brethren*, emissaries of the elder (contrast 1 Jn.2.19). **11:** 1 Jn.3.6–10. **12:** *Demetrius*, perhaps the bearer of this letter. **13:** 2 Jn.12. **15:** *Friends*, fellow-Christians.

JUDE

The Letter of Jude was written to warn against false teachers who had made their way into the church. Little is said of the content of their teaching, but the letter gives a vivid sketch of their character and methods. They are immoral (vv. 4,7,16) and covetous men (vv. 11,16), who reject authority (vv. 8,11). Grumblers, malcontents, loud-mouthed boasters (v. 16), they are crisply characterized as "worldly people, devoid of the Spirit" (v. 19). Because they lack brotherly love (v. 12), it is not surprising that they create divisions in congregations (v. 19). Their doom is sure. Like their spiritual prototypes—the disobedient Israelites in the wilderness, the cities of Sodom and Gomorrah, and the fallen angels (vv. 5–7)—they will experience God's judgment.

The author urges his readers to "contend for the faith which was once for all delivered to the saints" (v. 3), standing firm against the persuasive innovation of those who pervert the grace of God into immorality and deny the Lord Jesus Christ. He concludes his brief but trenchant letter with a beautiful and moving doxology (vv. 24–25).

The destination of the letter cannot be determined. Its author may well be, as tradition affirms, the brother of James and of the Lord. Otherwise it is difficult to see why a pseudonymous author should have chosen the name of one so obscure. It was probably written about the year 80.

JUDE, A SERVANT OF JESUS CHRIST and brother of James,

To those who are called, beloved in God the Father and kept for Jesus Christ:

2 May mercy, peace, and love be multiplied to you.

3 Beloved, being very eager to write to you of our common salvation, I found it necessary to write appealing to you to contend for the faith which was once for all delivered to the saints. [4] For admission has been secretly gained by some who long ago were designated for this condemnation, ungodly persons who pervert the grace of our God into licentiousness and deny our only Master and Lord, Jesus Christ.[a]

5 Now I desire to remind you, though you were once for all fully informed, that he[b] who saved a people out of the land of Egypt, afterward destroyed those who did not believe. [6] And the angels that did not keep their own position but left their proper dwelling have been kept by him in eternal chains in the nether gloom until the judgment of the great day; [7] just as Sodom and Gomor'rah and the surrounding cities, which likewise acted immorally and indulged in unnatural lust, serve as an example by undergoing a punishment of eternal fire.

8 Yet in like manner these men in their dreamings defile the flesh, reject authority, and revile the glorious ones.[c] [9] But when the archangel Michael, contending with the devil, disputed about the body of Moses, he did not presume

a Or the only Master and our Lord Jesus Christ
b Ancient authorities read Jesus or the Lord or God
c Greek glories

1–2: Salutation, see Rom.1.1–7 n. **1:** God has *called* the Christians, shown them his love, and keeps them for the coming of *Jesus Christ.*

3–4: Occasion of the letter. The emergence of false teachers has stimulated the author to warn his readers against those who pervert the gospel and deny Christ. **3:** *The faith,* a synonym for the gospel. *The saints,* see Rom.1.7 n.

5–16: False teachers. 5–7: The Israelites in the wilderness, the rebellious angels, and Sodom and Gomorrah (Gen. ch. 19) are illustrations of how God judges the disobedient. **8:** In spite of warnings, the heretics defy authority, revile angels, and live licentiously. **9–10:** The author refers to a Jewish tradition according to which Michael, though provoked to anger by Satan (who had charged that Moses, being a murderer, was not worthy of burial), refrained from pronouncing *a reviling judgment.* The heretics, however, are very free with intemperate lan-

to pronounce a reviling judgment upon him, but said, "The Lord rebuke you." [10] But these men revile whatever they do not understand, and by those things that they know by instinct as irrational animals do, they are destroyed. [11] Woe to them! For they walk in the way of Cain, and abandon themselves for the sake of gain to Balaam's error, and perish in Korah's rebellion. [12] These are blemishes[d] on your love feasts, as they boldly carouse together, looking after themselves; waterless clouds, carried along by winds; fruitless trees in late autumn, twice dead, uprooted; [13] wild waves of the sea, casting up the foam of their own shame; wandering stars for whom the nether gloom of darkness has been reserved for ever.

14 It was of these also that Enoch in the seventh generation from Adam prophesied, saying, "Behold, the Lord came with his holy myriads, [15] to execute judgment on all, and to convict all the ungodly of all their deeds of ungodliness which they have committed in such an ungodly way, and of all the harsh things which ungodly sinners have spoken against him." [16] These are grumblers, malcontents, following their own passions, loud-mouthed boasters, flattering people to gain advantage.

17 But you must remember, beloved, the predictions of the apostles of our Lord Jesus Christ; [18] they said to you, "In the last time there will be scoffers, following their own ungodly passions." [19] It is these who set up divisions, worldly people, devoid of the Spirit. [20] But you, beloved, build yourselves up on your most holy faith; pray in the Holy Spirit; [21] keep yourselves in the love of God; wait for the mercy of our Lord Jesus Christ unto eternal life. [22] And convince some, who doubt; [23] save some, by snatching them out of the fire; on some have mercy with fear, hating even the garment spotted by the flesh.[e]

24 Now to him who is able to keep you from falling and to present you without blemish before the presence of his glory with rejoicing, [25] to the only God, our Savior through Jesus Christ our Lord, be glory, majesty, dominion, and authority, before all time and now and for ever. Amen.

d Or *reefs*
e The Greek text in this sentence is uncertain at several points

guage. **11:** *The way of Cain*, Gen.4.9; Heb.11.4; 1 Jn.3.12. *Balaam*, Num. chs. 22–24; Rev.2.14. *Korah*, Num. ch. 16. **12:** Apparently the heretics are within the fellowship, even attending the love feasts (see 1 Cor.11.20–21 n., and 2 Pet.2.13 note *g*), and hence were the more dangerous. **14:** *Behold* . . . , quoted from the book of Enoch, 1.9.

17–23: Exhortations. Recall the apostolic tradition, avoid the heretics, grow in faith, wait for the mercy of Jesus Christ, care for the erring. **18:** *In the last time*, 1 Jn.2.18; 1 Pet.1.5. **19:** *Divisions* in the church (1 Cor.1.12–13). **20–21:** Note the Trinitarian reference.

24–25: Doxology.

THE REVELATION TO JOHN

(The Apocalypse)

The book of Revelation, or Apocalypse, is a fitting close of the Holy Scriptures, for its final chapters depict the consummation toward which the whole Biblical message of redemption is focused. It may be described as an inspired picture-book which, by an accumulation of magnificent poetic imagery, makes a powerful appeal to the reader's imagination. Many of the details of its pictures are intended to contribute to the total impression and are not to be isolated and interpreted with wooden literalism.

Throughout the centuries the Apocalypse has been the object of widely divergent systems of interpretation. It offers its deepest truths to those who keep in mind the following considerations. (1) This book comprises the substance of many visions which repeat with kaleidoscopic variety certain great principles of God's just and merciful government of all his creation. By centering attention on these principles, the church in all ages has been comforted and sustained despite the fiercest antagonisms of both human and demonic foes. (2) This book contains many symbols involving numbers, strange beasts, and other apocalyptic figures. Though the key for understanding some of these symbols has been lost, in other cases a comparison with the prophetic symbolism in the Old Testament, especially Daniel and Ezekiel, sheds light upon the author's meaning.

Though parts of the book may have been reduced to writing before the fall of Jerusalem in A.D. 70, it is probable that the author, whose name was John (1.1,4,9; 22.8), put the book in its present form toward the end of the reign of the Emperor Domitian (A.D. 81–96), by whom he had been exiled to the rocky island of Patmos (1.9). Since that time the book's sublime visions of God and the glorious cadences of heavenly anthems have inspired countless poets, hymn writers, artists, and ordinary readers down through the ages.

THE REVELATION OF JESUS CHRIST, which God gave him to show to his servants what must soon take place; and he made it known by sending his angel to his servant John, [2] who bore witness to the word of God and to the testimony of Jesus Christ, even to all that he saw. [3] Blessed is he who reads aloud the words of the prophecy, and blessed are those who hear, and who keep what is written therein; for the time is near.

4 John to the seven churches that are in Asia:

Grace to you and peace from him who is and who was and who is to come, and from the seven spirits who are before his throne, [5] and from Jesus Christ the faithful witness, the firstborn of the dead, and the ruler of kings on earth.

To him who loves us and has freed us from our sins by his blood [6] and made us a kingdom, priests to his God and Father, to him be glory and dominion for ever and ever. Amen. [7] Behold, he is coming with the clouds, and every eye will see him, every one who pierced him; and all tribes of the earth will wail on account of him. Even so. Amen.

1.1–3: **The prologue.** This revelation came from God through Jesus Christ and was communicated to John by an angel (referred to again in 22.16). **3:** *Blessed is* . . . , the first of seven beatitudes in Revelation (compare 14.13; 16.15; 19.9; 20.6; 22.7,14) is pronounced upon the reader of this prophetic book in services of worship and upon the listening worshipers who heed its message. The solemn words, *the time is near*, provide a motive for obedience.

1.4–8: **Introductory salutation** to seven representative churches in the Roman province of Asia (in western Asia Minor). *Seven* suggests the idea of completeness and totality. **4:** *Grace . . . and peace*, see 2 Th.1.2 n. The *seven spirits* are either angelic beings or, more likely, a symbolic reference to the manifold energies of the Spirit of God (Is.11.2). **5:** He *loves* continually; he *has freed us* once for all. **8:** *Alpha* and *Omega*, the first and last letters of the

[1493]

8 "I am the Alpha and the Omega," says the Lord God, who is and who was and who is to come, the Almighty.

9 I John, your brother, who share with you in Jesus the tribulation and the kingdom and the patient endurance, was on the island called Patmos on account of the word of God and the testimony of Jesus. [10] I was in the Spirit on the Lord's day, and I heard behind me a loud voice like a trumpet [11] saying, "Write what you see in a book and send it to the seven churches, to Ephesus and to Smyrna and to Per'gamum and to Thyati'ra and to Sardis and to Philadelphia and to La-odice'a."

12 Then I turned to see the voice that was speaking to me, and on turning I saw seven golden lampstands, [13] and in the midst of the lampstands one like a son of man, clothed with a long robe and with a golden girdle round his breast; [14] his head and his hair were white as white wool, white as snow; his eyes were like a flame of fire, [15] his feet were like burnished bronze, refined as in a furnace, and his voice was like the sound of many waters; [16] in his right hand he held seven stars, from his mouth issued a sharp two-edged sword, and his face was like the sun shining in full strength.

17 When I saw him, I fell at his feet as though dead. But he laid his right hand upon me, saying, "Fear not, I am the first and the last, [18] and the living one; I died, and behold I am alive for evermore, and I have the keys of Death and Hades. [19] Now write what you see, what is and what is to take place hereafter. [20] As for the mystery of the seven stars which you saw in my right hand, and the seven golden lampstands, the seven stars are the angels of the seven churches and the seven lampstands are the seven churches.

2 "To the angel of the church in Ephesus write: 'The words of him who holds the seven stars in his right hand, who walks among the seven golden lampstands.

2 "'I know your works, your toil and your patient endurance, and how you cannot bear evil men but have tested those who call themselves apostles but are not, and found them to be false; [3] I know you are enduring patiently and bearing up for my name's sake, and you have not grown weary. [4] But I have this against you, that you have abandoned the love you had at first. [5] Remember then from what you have fallen, repent and do the works you did at first. If not, I will come to you and remove your lampstand from its place, unless you repent. [6] Yet this you have, you hate the works of the Nicola'itans, which I also hate. [7] He who has an ear, let him hear what the Spirit says to the churches. To him who conquers I will grant to eat of the tree of life, which is in the paradise of God.'

Greek alphabet (like our "A to Z"); hence, the beginning and end of all things (Is.44.6).
1.9–20: Preparatory vision on *Patmos*, a rocky island, about ten by five miles, in the Aegean, where John had been exiled (see Introduction). **10:** *Lord's day*, Sunday. **12–16:** In the midst of the churches (see v. 20) stands the exalted Christ, whose royalty, eternity, wisdom, and immutability are suggested by means of symbols; the effect is that of terrifying majesty (compare v. 17 with Is.6.5). *Son of man*, see Mk.2.10 n. *Two-edged sword*, the word of God (Heb.4.12). **18:** *Hades*, used here with its synonym *death*, is the abode of the dead; Christ has *the keys* to release those confined within its gates (Mt.16.18 note *u*; Jn.5.25–29). **20:** Angels are assigned to *the seven churches*, as also to nations (Dan.10.13; 12.1) and individuals (Mt.18.10).
2.1–3.22: The letters to the seven churches, each containing an address, a descriptive phrase referring to the risen Lord, a commendation or condemnation of the church addressed, an admonition, and a concluding promise and exhortation to the faithful. **2.1–7: The first letter** is appropriately sent to *Ephesus*, the most important city of proconsular Asia. **1:** Christ *walks among* his churches (1.20). **2:** *Evil men*, compare the warning to the Ephesian elders in Acts 20.29–30. **6:** To *hate* evil is the counterpart of the love of the good (Is.61.8; Zech.8.17). The *Nicolaitans* (probably not connected with the Nicolaus of Acts 6.5) taught that Christians were free to eat food offered to idols and to practice immorality in the name of religion (v. 14). **7:** *Conquers*, a military term, suggesting continuous vigilance. *Tree of life*, Gen.2.9.

8 "And to the angel of the church in Smyrna write: 'The words of the first and the last, who died and came to life.

9 "'I know your tribulation and your poverty (but you are rich) and the slander of those who say that they are Jews and are not, but are a synagogue of Satan. [10] Do not fear what you are about to suffer. Behold, the devil is about to throw some of you into prison, that you may be tested, and for ten days you will have tribulation. Be faithful unto death, and I will give you the crown of life. [11] He who has an ear, let him hear what the Spirit says to the churches. He who conquers shall not be hurt by the second death.'

12 "And to the angel of the church in Per'gamum write: 'The words of him who has the sharp two-edged sword.

13 "'I know where you dwell, where Satan's throne is; you hold fast my name and you did not deny my faith even in the days of An'tipas my witness, my faithful one, who was killed among you, where Satan dwells. [14] But I have a few things against you: you have some there who hold the teaching of Balaam, who taught Balak to put a stumbling block before the sons of Israel, that they might eat food sacrificed to idols and practice immorality. [15] So you also have some who hold the teaching of the Nicola'itans. [16] Repent then. If not, I will come to you soon and war against them with the sword of my mouth. [17] He who has an ear, let him hear what the Spirit says to the churches. To him who conquers I will give some of the hidden manna, and I will give him a white stone, with a new name written on the stone which no one knows except him who receives it.'

18 "And to the angel of the church in Thyati'ra write: 'The words of the Son of God, who has eyes like a flame of fire, and whose feet are like burnished bronze.

19 "'I know your works, your love and faith and service and patient endurance, and that your latter works exceed the first. [20] But I have this against you, that you tolerate the woman Jez'ebel, who calls herself a prophetess and is teaching and beguiling my servants to practice immorality and to eat food sacrificed to idols. [21] I gave her time to repent, but she refuses to repent of her immorality. [22] Behold, I will throw her on a sickbed, and those who commit adultery with her I will throw into great tribulation, unless they repent of her doings; [23] and I will strike her children dead. And all the churches shall know that I am he who searches mind and heart, and I will give to each of you as your works deserve. [24] But to the rest of you in Thyati'ra, who do not hold this teaching, who have not learned what some call the deep things of Satan, to you I say, I do not lay upon you any other burden; [25] only hold fast what you have, until I come. [26] He who conquers and who keeps my works until the end, I will give him power over the nations, [27] and he shall rule them with a rod of iron, as when earthen pots are broken in pieces, even as I myself have received power from my Father; [28] and

---

2.8–11: **The second letter,** sent to *Smyrna*, commends the church for its perseverance amid *tribulation* and *poverty*. **8:** Is.44.6. **10:** *Ten days*, not a lengthy period (Dan.1.12). *Crown of life*, supreme blessedness. **11:** *The second death*, the final condemnation of sinners (20.14; Mt. 10.28).

2.12–17: **The third letter** is sent to *Pergamum*, a noted center of idolatrous worship. **14–15:** See v. 6; Num.25.1–2; 31.16. **17:** *Manna . . . name*, Ps.78.24; Is.62.2. *White*, the color symbolizing victory and joy.

2.18–29: **The fourth letter** is sent to *Thyatira*, a commercial center renowned for its many trade guilds, which periodically sponsored idolatrous feasts. **18:** Dan.10.6. **20:** *Jezebel*, a *false prophetess*, resembling Ahab's wicked and idolatrous queen (1 Kg.16.31; 2 Kg.9.22,30). **23:** *Her children*, those who follow her teachings. **24:** *Deep things of Satan*, a withering reference to heretical teachings (contrast 1 Cor.2.10). **26–27:** The conquerors will share in Christ's Messianic rule (Ps.2.8–9). **28:** *The morning star* is Christ himself (22.16).

I will give him the morning star. ²⁹ He who has an ear, let him hear what the Spirit says to the churches.'

3 "And to the angel of the church in Sardis write: 'The words of him who has the seven spirits of God and the seven stars.

" 'I know your works; you have the name of being alive, and you are dead. ² Awake, and strengthen what remains and is on the point of death, for I have not found your works perfect in the sight of my God. ³ Remember then what you received and heard; keep that, and repent. If you will not awake, I will come like a thief, and you will not know at what hour I will come upon you. ⁴ Yet you have still a few names in Sardis, people who have not soiled their garments; and they shall walk with me in white, for they are worthy. ⁵ He who conquers shall be clad thus in white garments, and I will not blot his name out of the book of life; I will confess his name before my Father and before his angels. ⁶ He who has an ear, let him hear what the Spirit says to the churches.'

7 "And to the angel of the church in Philadelphia write: 'The words of the holy one, the true one, who has the key of David, who opens and no one shall shut, who shuts and no one opens.

8 " 'I know your works. Behold, I have set before you an open door, which no one is able to shut; I know that you have but little power, and yet you have kept my word and have not denied my name. ⁹ Behold, I will make those of the synagogue of Satan who say that they are Jews and are not, but lie–behold, I will make them come and bow down before your feet, and learn that I have loved you. ¹⁰ Because you have kept my word of patient endurance, I will keep you from the hour of trial which is coming on the whole world, to try those who dwell upon the earth. ¹¹ I am coming soon; hold fast what you have, so that no one may seize your crown. ¹² He who conquers, I will make him a pillar in the temple of my God; never shall he go out of it, and I will write on him the name of my God, and the name of the city of my God, the new Jerusalem which comes down from my God out of heaven, and my own new name. ¹³ He who has an ear, let him hear what the Spirit says to the churches.'

14 "And to the angel of the church in La-odice′a write: 'The words of the Amen, the faithful and true witness, the beginning of God's creation. 15 " 'I know your works: you are neither cold nor hot. Would that you were cold or hot! ¹⁶ So, because you are lukewarm, and neither cold nor hot, I will spew you out of my mouth. ¹⁷ For you say, I am rich, I have prospered, and I need nothing; not knowing that you are wretched, pitiable, poor, blind, and naked. ¹⁸ Therefore I counsel you to buy from me gold refined by fire, that you may be rich, and white garments to clothe you and to keep the shame of your nakedness from being seen, and salve to anoint your eyes, that you may see. ¹⁹ Those

---

3.1–6: **The fifth letter** is sent to *Sardis*, notorious for its luxury and licentiousness. **1**: *You have the name*, its Christianity was only nominal. **3**: *Received*, the gospel. *Like a thief*, just when unexpected (16.15; Mt.24.42–44; 1 Th.5.2). **4–5**: Those who have maintained spiritual purity will enjoy Christ's companionship here and will be acknowledged before God in heaven. **5**: *Book of life*, the register of God containing the names of the redeemed (13.8; 17.8; 20.12,15; Ex.32.32; Ps.69.28; Dan.12.1; Mal.3.16; Lk.10.20).

3.7–13: **The sixth letter** is sent to *Philadelphia*, a small town in Lydia. **7**: *Key of David*, a symbol of authority (Is.22.22). **8**: *An open door*, of opportunity (1 Cor.16.9; 2 Cor.2.12). **9**: Is.43.4; 60.14. **10**: The Philadelphian church, though feeble (v. 8), will be sustained during the coming persecution. **12**: *A pillar*, steadfast and permanent (Gal.2.9). *New Jerusalem*, 21.2.

3.14–22: **The seventh letter** is sent to *Laodicea*, a proud and wealthy city near Colossae (Col. 4.13–16). **14**: *The Amen* is Jesus Christ (2 Cor.1.20). *The beginning of God's creation*, Christ is the principle and source of all creation (Jn.1.3; Col.1.15,18). **15–16**: Their lukewarm Christianity is nauseating. **17**: Complacent and self-satisfied, they are spiritually poverty-stricken

whom I love, I reprove and chasten;
so be zealous and repent. ²⁰ Behold,
I stand at the door and knock; if any
one hears my voice and opens the door,
I will come in to him and eat with him,
and he with me. ²¹ He who conquers,
I will grant him to sit with me on my
throne, as I myself conquered and sat
down with my Father on his throne.
²² He who has an ear, let him hear
what the Spirit says to the churches.' "

4 After this I looked, and lo, in
heaven an open door! And the
first voice, which I had heard speaking to me like a trumpet, said, "Come
up hither, and I will show you what
must take place after this." ² At once
I was in the Spirit, and lo, a throne
stood in heaven, with one seated on
the throne! ³ And he who sat there appeared like jasper and carnelian, and
round the throne was a rainbow that
looked like an emerald. ⁴ Round the
throne were twenty-four thrones, and
seated on the thrones were twenty-four
elders, clad in white garments, with
golden crowns upon their heads.
⁵ From the throne issue flashes of
lightning, and voices and peals of thunder, and before the throne burn seven
torches of fire, which are the seven
spirits of God; ⁶ and before the throne
there is as it were a sea of glass, like
crystal.

And round the throne, on each side
of the throne, are four living creatures,
full of eyes in front and behind: ⁷ the
first living creature like a lion, the second living creature like an ox, the third

living creature with the face of a man,
and the fourth living creature like a flying eagle. ⁸ And the four living creatures, each of them with six wings, are
full of eyes all round and within, and
day and night they never cease to sing,

"Holy, holy, holy, is the Lord God
    Almighty,
who was and is and is to come!"
⁹ And whenever the living creatures
give glory and honor and thanks to him
who is seated on the throne, who
lives for ever and ever, ¹⁰ the twenty-
four elders fall down before him who
is seated on the throne and worship
him who lives for ever and ever; they
cast their crowns before the throne,
singing,
¹¹ "Worthy art thou, our Lord and
    God,
to receive glory and honor and
    power,
for thou didst create all things,
and by thy will they existed and were
    created."

5 And I saw in the right hand of
him who was seated on the throne
a scroll written within and on the
back, sealed with seven seals; ² and I
saw a strong angel proclaiming with a
loud voice, "Who is worthy to open the
scroll and break its seals?" ³ And
no one in heaven or on earth or under
the earth was able to open the scroll
or to look into it, ⁴ and I wept much
that no one was found worthy to open
the scroll or to look into it. ⁵ Then one
of the elders said to me, "Weep not;
lo, the Lion of the tribe of Judah, the
Root of David, has conquered, so that

(Hos.12.8). **19:** God's chastening has beneficent motives (Pr.3.12; Heb.12.5–11). **20:** An
invitation to share the joys of the Messianic banquet in the coming age (compare Mt.26.29).
21: *To sit with me*, a promise of reigning with Christ in glory (22.5; Lk.22.30).
   4.1–5.14: Vision of the glory of God and of the Lamb. 4.1: *The first voice*, mentioned in 1.10.
2: *A throne*, Ezek.1.26–28. **3:** The glory of the divine presence is described in terms of precious
gems. **4:** *Twenty-four elders*, probably angelic beings of the heavenly court, symbolizing the
twelve patriarchs of the Old Testament and the twelve apostles of the New Testament. **5:** *Seven
spirits*, 1.4. **6:** *A sea of glass* suggests the distance between God and his creatures, even in heaven.
Four living creatures, angelic beings representing man and all beasts (Ezek.1.5,10). *Full of
eyes*, symbolizing unceasing watchfulness. **8:** *Six wings . . . Holy, holy, holy*, Is.6.2–3. **10:**
Cast their crowns, acknowledging that all power comes from God. **11:** *They existed* in God's
mind from all eternity. **5.1:** *A scroll*, containing the fixed purposes of God for the future
(Ezek.2.9–10). *Sealed*, therefore both unalterable and unknown to others. **3–4:** No created
being is worthy to carry out God's plan, only the Messianic king can do so; for his titles (*Lion . . .*

he can open the scroll and its seven seals."

6 And between the throne and the four living creatures and among the elders, I saw a Lamb standing, as though it had been slain, with seven horns and with seven eyes, which are the seven spirits of God sent out into all the earth; ⁷ and he went and took the scroll from the right hand of him who was seated on the throne. ⁸ And when he had taken the scroll, the four living creatures and the twenty-four elders fell down before the Lamb, each holding a harp, and with golden bowls full of incense, which are the prayers of the saints; ⁹ and they sang a new song, saying,

"Worthy art thou to take the scroll
and to open its seals,
for thou wast slain and by thy blood
didst ransom men for God
from every tribe and tongue and
people and nation,
¹⁰ and hast made them a kingdom and
priests to our God,
and they shall reign on earth."

¹¹ Then I looked, and I heard around the throne and the living creatures and the elders the voice of many angels, numbering myriads of myriads and thousands of thousands, ¹² saying with a loud voice, "Worthy is the Lamb who was slain, to receive power and wealth and wisdom and might and honor and glory and blessing!" ¹³ And I heard every creature in heaven and on earth and under the earth and in the sea, and all therein, saying, "To him who sits

upon the throne and to the Lamb be blessing and honor and glory and might for ever and ever!" ¹⁴ And the four living creatures said, "Amen!" and the elders fell down and worshiped.

6 Now I saw when the Lamb opened one of the seven seals, and I heard one of the four living creatures say, as with a voice of thunder, "Come!" ² And I saw, and behold, a white horse, and its rider had a bow; and a crown was given to him, and he went out conquering and to conquer.

3 When he opened the second seal, I heard the second living creature say, "Come!" ⁴ And out came another horse, bright red; its rider was permitted to take peace from the earth, so that men should slay one another; and he was given a great sword.

5 When he opened the third seal, I heard the third living creature say, "Come!" And I saw, and behold, a black horse, and its rider had a balance in his hand; ⁶ and I heard what seemed to be a voice in the midst of the four living creatures saying, "A quart of wheat for a denarius,ᵃ and three quarts of barley for a denarius;ᵃ but do not harm oil and wine!"

7 When he opened the fourth seal, I heard the voice of the fourth living creature say, "Come!" ⁸ And I saw, and behold, a pale horse, and its rider's name was Death, and Hades followed him; and they were given power over a

a The denarius was a day's wage for a laborer

Root), compare Gen.49.9–10; Is.11.1,10. **6–9:** *The Lamb . . . slain*, refers to Christ's sacrificial death, by which God's purposes contained in the scroll are accomplished (Is.53.7; Jn.1.29,36; 1 Pet.1.19). *Seven horns . . . seven eyes*, plentitude of power and insight. *Seven spirits*, 1.4. **8:** *The prayers of the saints* on earth are joined with the worship rendered to the *Lamb* by heavenly creatures. **9–10:** *A new song*, because Christ has inaugurated a new era (14.3). The *Lamb* is adored in terms similar to the adoration rendered to God (4.11). *A kingdom and priests*, the vocation promised to Israel (Ex.19.6; Is.61.6) is extended to the church (1 Pet.2.9). **11–12:** The sevenfold praise of *myriads* in heaven honoring the sacrificial *Lamb*. **13:** Universal praise to the Creator and to the Redeemer as equal in majesty.

6.1–17: The opening of the first six seals of the scroll, and the pictorial enactment of what is written therein. **1–8:** *Come!* [the word can also be translated "Go!"], addressed successively to each of the four horsemen (Zech.6.1–3) who accomplish God's purposes (Lev.26.21–39). **2:** The *white horse* symbolizes a conquering power that none can resist (in 19.11–13 the reference is to Christ). **4:** The *red horse* symbolizes war and bloodshed. **5:** The *black horse* symbolizes famine, which follows upon war. **8:** The *pale horse* symbolizes pestilence and death. *A fourth*

fourth of the earth, to kill with sword and with famine and with pestilence and by wild beasts of the earth.

9 When he opened the fifth seal, I saw under the altar the souls of those who had been slain for the word of God and for the witness they had borne; [10] they cried out with a loud voice, "O Sovereign Lord, holy and true, how long before thou wilt judge and avenge our blood on those who dwell upon the earth?" [11] Then they were each given a white robe and told to rest a little longer, until the number of their fellow servants and their brethren should be complete, who were to be killed as they themselves had been.

12 When he opened the sixth seal, I looked, and behold, there was a great earthquake; and the sun became black as sackcloth, the full moon became like blood, [13] and the stars of the sky fell to the earth as the fig tree sheds its winter fruit when shaken by a gale; [14] the sky vanished like a scroll that is rolled up, and every mountain and island was removed from its place. [15] Then the kings of the earth and the great men and the generals and the rich and the strong, and every one, slave and free, hid in the caves and among the rocks of the mountains, [16] calling to the mountains and rocks, "Fall on us and hide us from the face of him who is seated on the throne, and from the wrath of the Lamb; [17] for the great day of their wrath has come, and who can stand before it?"

7 After this I saw four angels standing at the four corners of the earth, holding back the four winds of the earth, that no wind might blow on earth or sea or against any tree. [2] Then I saw another angel ascend from the rising of the sun, with the seal of the living God, and he called with a loud voice to the four angels who had been given power to harm earth and sea, [3] saying, "Do not harm the earth or the sea or the trees, till we have sealed the servants of our God upon their foreheads." [4] And I heard the number of the sealed, a hundred and forty-four thousand sealed, out of every tribe of the sons of Israel, [5] twelve thousand sealed out of the tribe of Judah, twelve thousand of the tribe of Reuben, twelve thousand of the tribe of Gad, [6] twelve thousand of the tribe of Asher, twelve thousand of the tribe of Naph'tali, twelve thousand of the tribe of Manas'seh, [7] twelve thousand of the tribe of Simeon, twelve thousand of the tribe of Levi, twelve thousand of the tribe of Is'sachar, [8] twelve thousand of the tribe of Zeb'ulun, twelve thousand of the tribe of Joseph, twelve thousand sealed out of the tribe of Benjamin.

9 After this I looked, and behold, a great multitude which no man could number, from every nation, from all tribes and peoples and tongues, standing before the throne and before the Lamb, clothed in white robes, with palm branches in their hands, [10] and crying out with a loud voice, "Salvation belongs to our God who sits upon

part indicates wide but not total devastation. *Pestilence*, Ex.9.3; 2 Sam.24.13; Ezek.5.12. *Wild beasts*, Ezek.5.17; 29.5; 33.27.

6.9–17: The fifth and sixth seals describe the prayers of the martyrs in heaven (vv. 9–11) and their effects on earth (vv. 12–17). **9:** The souls of the martyrs are said to be *under the altar* because they had been sacrificed (Phil.2.17; 2 Tim.4.6). **10:** *How long?* is a cry for divine vindication. **11:** *White robe*, see 2.17 n. and 7.9 n. **12–14:** The *great earthquake* and cosmic catastrophes are not to be understood literally, but represent social upheavals and divine judgment in the Day of the Lord (Is.34.4; Jl.2.30–31; Am.8.9). **15–17:** All classes of society seek to escape from God.

7.1–17: An interlude between the sixth and seventh seals: two visions (vv. 1–8 and vv. 9–17) which provide assurance that God's people are secure from the plagues and judgments. **3:** The seal (Ezek.9.4–6) marks those under God's protection. **4:** The explicit number (144,000) symbolizes completeness; not one of the redeemed is missing. **9:** *A great multitude* of the redeemed, so many they cannot be counted. *White robes* and *palm branches* symbolize righteousness and victory. **12:** A sevenfold ascription of praise to God. **14:** *The blood of the Lamb of God* cleanses

the throne, and to the Lamb!" [11] And all the angels stood round the throne and round the elders and the four living creatures, and they fell on their faces before the throne and worshiped God, [12] saying, "Amen! Blessing and glory and wisdom and thanksgiving and honor and power and might be to our God for ever and ever! Amen."

13 Then one of the elders addressed me, saying, "Who are these, clothed in white robes, and whence have they come?" [14] I said to him, "Sir, you know." And he said to me, "These are they who have come out of the great tribulation; they have washed their robes and made them white in the blood of the Lamb.

[15] Therefore are they before the throne
of God,
and serve him day and night
within his temple;
and he who sits upon the throne
will shelter them with his
presence.
[16] They shall hunger no more, neither
thirst any more;
the sun shall not strike them, nor
any scorching heat.
[17] For the Lamb in the midst of the
throne will be their shepherd,
and he will guide them to springs
of living water;
and God will wipe away every tear
from their eyes."

8 When the Lamb opened the seventh seal, there was silence in heaven for about half an hour. [2] Then I saw the seven angels who stand before God, and seven trumpets were given to them. [3] And another angel came and stood at the altar with a golden censer; and he was given much incense to mingle with the prayers of all the saints upon the golden altar before the throne; [4] and the smoke of the incense rose with the prayers of the saints from the hand of the angel before God. [5] Then the angel took the censer and filled it with fire from the altar and threw it on the earth; and there were peals of thunder, voices, flashes of lightning, and an earthquake.

6 Now the seven angels who had the seven trumpets made ready to blow them.

7 The first angel blew his trumpet, and there followed hail and fire, mixed with blood, which fell on the earth; and a third of the earth was burnt up, and a third of the trees were burnt up, and all green grass was burnt up.

8 The second angel blew his trumpet, and something like a great mountain, burning with fire, was thrown into the sea; [9] and a third of the sea became blood, a third of the living creatures in the sea died, and a third of the ships were destroyed.

10 The third angel blew his trumpet, and a great star fell from heaven, blazing like a torch, and it fell on a third of the rivers and on the fountains of water. [11] The name of the star is Wormwood. A third of the waters became wormwood, and many men died of the water, because it was made bitter.

12 The fourth angel blew his trumpet, and a third of the sun was struck, and a third of the moon, and a third of the stars, so that a third of their light was darkened; a third of the day was kept from shining, and likewise a third of the night.

13 Then I looked, and I heard an eagle crying with a loud voice, as it flew in midheaven, "Woe, woe, woe to

---

from sin (Jn.1.29; 1 Jn.1.7). **15:** To *serve* God implies activity in heaven. *Shelter them with his presence*, literally "spread his tabernacle over them." **16:** Is.49.10; Ps.121.6. **17:** A paradox, the *Lamb* is a *shepherd* (Ps.23.1–2; Ezek.34.23–24; Jn.10.11). *Springs of living water*, 21.6; 22.1,17; Jn.4.10; 7.37. *Wipe away every tear*, 21.4; Is.25.8.

    8.1–5: The seventh seal is opened. *Incense . . . prayers*, Ps.141.2. **5:** Ezek.10.2.

    8.6–9.21: The first six trumpets introduce new convulsions of nature, in judgment upon the wicked (compare the plagues of Egypt, Ex.9.23,25; 7.17–21; 10.21–23). These calamities are not consecutive nor are they to be taken literally. **8.11:** *Wormwood*, a bitter drug symbolizing

those who dwell on the earth, at the blasts of the other trumpets which the three angels are about to blow!"

9 And the fifth angel blew his trumpet, and I saw a star fallen from heaven to earth, and he was given the key of the shaft of the bottomless pit; ² he opened the shaft of the bottomless pit, and from the shaft rose smoke like the smoke of a great furnace, and the sun and the air were darkened with the smoke from the shaft. ³ Then from the smoke came locusts on the earth, and they were given power like the power of scorpions of the earth; ⁴ they were told not to harm the grass of the earth or any green growth or any tree, but only those of mankind who have not the seal of God upon their foreheads; ⁵ they were allowed to torture them for five months, but not to kill them, and their torture was like the torture of a scorpion, when it stings a man. ⁶ And in those days men will seek death and will not find it; they will long to die, and death will fly from them.

7 In appearance the locusts were like horses arrayed for battle; on their heads were what looked like crowns of gold; their faces were like human faces, ⁸ their hair like women's hair, and their teeth like lions' teeth; ⁹ they had scales like iron breastplates, and the noise of their wings was like the noise of many chariots with horses rushing into battle. ¹⁰ They have tails like scorpions, and stings, and their power of hurting men for five months lies in their tails. ¹¹ They have as king over them the angel of the bottomless pit; his name in Hebrew is Abad'don, and in Greek he is called Apol'lyon.*b*

12 The first woe has passed; behold, two woes are still to come.

13 Then the sixth angel blew his trumpet, and I heard a voice from the four horns of the golden altar before God, ¹⁴ saying to the sixth angel who had the trumpet, "Release the four angels who are bound at the great river Euphra'tes." ¹⁵ So the four angels were released, who had been held ready for the hour, the day, the month, and the year, to kill a third of mankind. ¹⁶ The number of the troops of cavalry was twice ten thousand times ten thousand; I heard their number. ¹⁷ And this was how I saw the horses in my vision: the riders wore breastplates the color of fire and of sapphire*c* and of sulphur, and the heads of the horses were like lions' heads, and fire and smoke and sulphur issued from their mouths. ¹⁸ By these three plagues a third of mankind was killed, by the fire and smoke and sulphur issuing from their mouths. ¹⁹ For the power of the horses is in their mouths and in their tails; their tails are like serpents, with heads, and by means of them they wound.

20 The rest of mankind, who were not killed by these plagues, did not repent of the works of their hands nor give up worshiping demons and idols of gold and silver and bronze and stone and wood, which cannot either see or hear or walk; ²¹ nor did they repent of their murders or their sorceries or their immorality or their thefts.

10 Then I saw another mighty angel coming down from heaven, wrapped in a cloud, with a rainbow over his head, and his face was like the

b Or *Destroyer*　　*c* Greek *hyacinth*

---

divine chastisements (Jer.9.15; 23.15). **13**: *An eagle* announces impending judgment. *Woe . . .*, thrice repeated because the last three plagues are especially grievous.
　9.1–12: The plague of demonic locusts, which combine the terrors of evil spirits and of invading horsemen (probably Parthians). **1**: *A star fallen from heaven,* one of the fallen angels, perhaps Satan himself (v. 11; Lk.10.18). **3**: *Locusts,* Ex.10.12–15. **4**: God's servants are not to be harmed (7.3). **11**: The name *Abaddon,* which means "Destruction," denotes the depths of Sheol (Job.26.6; see Pr.15.11 n.). **14**: The *Euphrates* was at the eastern border of the Roman empire, where invasion by the Parthians was feared. **16–19**: As with the locusts, the details regarding the two hundred million cavalry are not to be understood literally. **20–21**: Compare the hardness of Pharaoh's heart despite the plagues (Ex.8.15,19).

sun, and his legs like pillars of fire. ² He had a little scroll open in his hand. And he set his right foot on the sea, and his left foot on the land, ³ and called out with a loud voice, like a lion roaring; when he called out, the seven thunders sounded. ⁴ And when the seven thunders had sounded, I was about to write, but I heard a voice from heaven saying, "Seal up what the seven thunders have said, and do not write it down." ⁵ And the angel whom I saw standing on sea and land lifted up his right hand to heaven ⁶ and swore by him who lives for ever and ever, who created heaven and what is in it, the earth and what is in it, and the sea and what is in it, that there should be no more delay, ⁷ but that in the days of the trumpet call to be sounded by the seventh angel, the mystery of God, as he announced to his servants the prophets, should be fulfilled.

8 Then the voice which I had heard from heaven spoke to me again, saying, "Go, take the scroll which is open in the hand of the angel who is standing on the sea and on the land." ⁹ So I went to the angel and told him to give me the little scroll; and he said to me, "Take it and eat; it will be bitter to your stomach, but sweet as honey in your mouth." ¹⁰ And I took the little scroll from the hand of the angel and ate it; it was sweet as honey in my mouth, but when I had eaten it my stomach was made bitter. ¹¹ And I was told, "You must again prophesy

about many peoples and nations and tongues and kings."

11 Then I was given a measuring rod like a staff, and I was told: "Rise and measure the temple of God and the altar and those who worship there, ² but do not measure the court outside the temple; leave that out, for it is given over to the nations, and they will trample over the holy city for forty-two months. ³ And I will grant my two witnesses power to prophesy for one thousand two hundred and sixty days, clothed in sackcloth."

4 These are the two olive trees and the two lampstands which stand before the Lord of the earth. ⁵ And if any one would harm them, fire pours from their mouth and consumes their foes; if any one would harm them, thus he is doomed to be killed. ⁶ They have power to shut the sky, that no rain may fall during the days of their prophesying, and they have power over the waters to turn them into blood, and to smite the earth with every plague, as often as they desire. ⁷ And when they have finished their testimony, the beast that ascends from the bottomless pit will make war upon them and conquer them and kill them, ⁸ and their dead bodies will lie in the street of the great city which is allegorically*d* called Sodom and Egypt, where their Lord was crucified. ⁹ For three days and a half men from the peoples and tribes and tongues and nations gaze at their

d Greek *spiritually*

10.1–11.13: An interlude between the sixth and seventh trumpets; two visions (10.1–11 and 11.1–13) provide consolation and assurance for the seer and for his fellow-believers. **10.1–2:** The smallness of the *little scroll* is emphasized in contrast to the *mighty angel* holding it. **6:** *No more delay* in the accomplishment of God's will. **7:** *The mystery of God*, Rom.16.25–26. **8:** *The scroll*, which is not the sealed scroll of 5.1, is a special message from God to John. **9:** Ezek.2.8; 3.1–3. **10:** *Sweet*, because it contains God's words; *bitter*, because it involves his terrible judgments. **11:** *You must*, in accord with the divine will, *again prophesy;* the second part of the book (chs. 12–22) contains these prophecies.

11.1–13: The measuring of the temple and the two witnesses. 1: The sanctuary *and those who worship there* are measured with a view to their preservation (as in Zech.2.1–5; compare Ezek. 40.3–42.20). **2:** *The court outside*, the court of the Gentiles. *Forty-two months* = 1260 days = 3½ years (Dan.7.25; 12.7). **3:** *My two witnesses*, unnamed but resembling Zerubbabel and Joshua (Zech.3.1–4.14) as well as Elijah (vv. 5–6; 2 Kg.1.10) and Moses (v. 6; Ex.7.17,19). Clothed in *sackcloth*, a sign that their prophecy was of repentance. **7:** *The beast* (or "the monster") is the Antichrist (17.8; Dan.7.3,7,21). **8:** The name *Sodom* is applied to Jerusalem

dead bodies and refuse to let them be placed in a tomb, ¹⁰ and those who dwell on the earth will rejoice over them and make merry and exchange presents, because these two prophets had been a torment to those who dwell on the earth. ¹¹ But after the three and a half days a breath of life from God entered them, and they stood up on their feet, and great fear fell on those who saw them. ¹² Then they heard a loud voice from heaven saying to them, "Come up hither!" And in the sight of their foes they went up to heaven in a cloud. ¹³ And at that hour there was a great earthquake, and a tenth of the city fell; seven thousand people were killed in the earthquake, and the rest were terrified and gave glory to the God of heaven.

14 The second woe has passed; behold, the third woe is soon to come.

15 Then the seventh angel blew his trumpet, and there were loud voices in heaven, saying, "The kingdom of the world has become the kingdom of our Lord and of his Christ, and he shall reign for ever and ever." ¹⁶ And the twenty-four elders who sit on their thrones before God fell on their faces and worshiped God, ¹⁷ saying,

"We give thanks to thee, Lord God
  Almighty, who art and who
  wast,
  that thou hast taken thy great
  power and begun to reign.
¹⁸ The nations raged, but thy wrath
  came,
  and the time for the dead to be
  judged,
  for rewarding thy servants, the
  prophets and saints,
  and those who fear thy name,
  both small and great,

and for destroying the destroyers of the earth."

19 Then God's temple in heaven was opened, and the ark of his covenant was seen within his temple; and there were flashes of lightning, voices, peals of thunder, an earthquake, and heavy hail.

12 And a great portent appeared in heaven, a woman clothed with the sun, with the moon under her feet, and on her head a crown of twelve stars; ² she was with child and she cried out in her pangs of birth, in anguish for delivery. ³ And another portent appeared in heaven; behold, a great red dragon, with seven heads and ten horns, and seven diadems upon his heads. ⁴ His tail swept down a third of the stars of heaven, and cast them to the earth. And the dragon stood before the woman who was about to bear a child, that he might devour her child when she brought it forth; ⁵ she brought forth a male child, one who is to rule all the nations with a rod of iron, but her child was caught up to God and to his throne, ⁶ and the woman fled into the wilderness, where she has a place prepared by God, in which to be nourished for one thousand two hundred and sixty days.

7 Now war arose in heaven, Michael and his angels fighting against the dragon; and the dragon and his angels fought, ⁸ but they were defeated and there was no longer any place for them in heaven. ⁹ And the great dragon was thrown down, that ancient serpent, who is called the Devil and Satan, the deceiver of the whole world—he was thrown down to the earth, and his angels were thrown

---

in Is.1.10. **11–12:** The witnesses are resuscitated (compare Ezek.37.5,10) and taken to heaven (2 Kg.2.11). **14–19:** The seventh trumpet announces (v. 15) the consummation of God's kingdom (10.7).
12.1–17: The vision of the woman, the child, and the dragon portrays the conflict between Christ and Satan. **1:** The *woman* appears to be the heavenly representative of God's people, first as Israel (from whom Jesus the Messiah was born, v. 5), then as the Christian Church (which is persecuted by the dragon, v. 13). **3:** *Dragon*, identified in v. 9 as *the Devil* or *Satan*. His enormous size and power are suggested in v. 4. **5:** Ps.2.9. **6:** The church is sustained by God. **7:** *Michael*, an archangel and the champion of Israel (Dan.10.13,21; 12.1; Jude 9). *The dragon*

down with him. [10] And I heard a loud voice in heaven, saying, "Now the salvation and the power and the kingdom of our God and the authority of his Christ have come, for the accuser of our brethren has been thrown down, who accuses them day and night before our God. [11] And they have conquered him by the blood of the Lamb and by the word of their testimony, for they loved not their lives even unto death. [12] Rejoice then, O heaven and you that dwell therein! But woe to you, O earth and sea, for the devil has come down to you in great wrath, because he knows that his time is short!"

13 And when the dragon saw that he had been thrown down to the earth, he pursued the woman who had borne the male child. [14] But the woman was given the two wings of the great eagle that she might fly from the serpent into the wilderness, to the place where she is to be nourished for a time, and times, and half a time. [15] The serpent poured water like a river out of his mouth after the woman, to sweep her away with the flood. [16] But the earth came to the help of the woman, and the earth opened its mouth and swallowed the river which the dragon had poured from his mouth. [17] Then the dragon was angry with the woman, and went off to make war on the rest of her offspring, on those who keep the commandments of God and bear testimony to Jesus. And he stood[e] on the sand of the sea.

13 And I saw a beast rising out of the sea, with ten horns and seven heads, with ten diadems upon its horns and a blasphemous name upon its heads. [2] And the beast that I saw was like a leopard, its feet were like a bear's, and its mouth was like a lion's mouth. And to it the dragon gave his power and his throne and great authority. [3] One of its heads seemed to have a mortal wound, but its mortal wound was healed, and the whole earth followed the beast with wonder. [4] Men worshiped the dragon, for he had given his authority to the beast, and they worshiped the beast, saying, "Who is like the beast, and who can fight against it?"

5 And the beast was given a mouth uttering haughty and blasphemous words, and it was allowed to exercise authority for forty-two months; [6] it opened its mouth to utter blasphemies against God, blaspheming his name and his dwelling, that is, those who dwell in heaven. [7] Also it was allowed to make war on the saints and to conquer them.[f] And authority was given it over every tribe and people and tongue and nation, [8] and all who dwell on earth will worship it, every one whose name has not been written before the foundation of the world in the book of life of the Lamb that was slain. [9] If any one has an ear, let him hear:
[10] If any one is to be taken captive,
    to captivity he goes;
if any one slays with the sword,
   with the sword must he be slain.
Here is a call for the endurance and faith of the saints.

11 Then I saw another beast which rose out of the earth; it had two horns like a lamb and it spoke like a dragon. [12] It exercises all the authority of the first beast in its presence, and makes the earth and its inhabitants worship the first beast, whose mortal wound was healed. [13] It works great signs,

e Other ancient authorities read *And I stood*, connecting the sentence with 13.1
f Other ancient authorities omit this sentence

---

and his angels, see Eph.6.12 n. **9:** Lk.10.18. **10:** *The accuser*, Job 1.9–11. **11:** *They have conquered*, through both divine and human effort. **16:** Aid comes from an unexpected quarter.
    13.1–18: The two beasts. 1–10: The *beast* from *the sea* combines the powers of the four beasts of Dan. ch. 7 and represents the Roman empire, incited by the *dragon* (v. 2) to persecute *the saints* (v. 7). **5:** The sovereignty of God, even amid persecution, is implied by the use of passive verbs here and in vv. 7,10,14,15 (compare 6.4; see 17.17 n.). **8:** *Book of life*, see 3.5 n. **10:** Jer.15.2; Mt.26.52. **11–18:** The *beast* from *the earth*, called the false prophet (19.20), enforces Emperor worship (v. 12), and produces *great signs* (v. 13) to deceive the people (v. 14;

even making fire come down from heaven to earth in the sight of men; ¹⁴ and by the signs which it is allowed to work in the presence of the beast, it deceives those who dwell on earth, bidding them make an image for the beast which was wounded by the sword and yet lived; ¹⁵ and it was allowed to give breath to the image of the beast so that the image of the beast should even speak, and to cause those who would not worship the image of the beast to be slain. ¹⁶ Also it causes all, both small and great, both rich and poor, both free and slave, to be marked on the right hand or the forehead, ¹⁷ so that no one can buy or sell unless he has the mark, that is, the name of the beast or the number of its name. ¹⁸ This calls for wisdom: let him who has understanding reckon the number of the beast, for it is a human number, its number is six hundred and sixty-six.ᵍ

14 Then I looked, and lo, on Mount Zion stood the Lamb, and with him a hundred and forty-four thousand who had his name and his Father's name written on their foreheads. ² And I heard a voice from heaven like the sound of many waters and like the sound of loud thunder; the voice I heard was like the sound of harpers playing on their harps, ³ and they sing a new song before the throne and before the four living creatures and before the elders. No one could learn that song except the hundred and forty-four thousand who had been redeemed from the earth. ⁴ It is these

who have not defiled themselves with women, for they are chaste;ʰ it is these who follow the Lamb wherever he goes; these have been redeemed from mankind as first fruits for God and the Lamb, ⁵ and in their mouth no lie was found, for they are spotless.

6 Then I saw another angel flying in midheaven, with an eternal gospel to proclaim to those who dwell on earth, to every nation and tribe and tongue and people; ⁷ and he said with a loud voice, "Fear God and give him glory, for the hour of his judgment has come; and worship him who made heaven and earth, the sea and the fountains of water."

8 Another angel, a second, followed, saying, "Fallen, fallen is Babylon the great, she who made all nations drink the wine of her impure passion."

9 And another angel, a third, followed them, saying with a loud voice, "If any one worships the beast and its image, and receives a mark on his forehead or on his hand, ¹⁰ he also shall drink the wine of God's wrath, poured unmixed into the cup of his anger, and he shall be tormented with fire and sulphur in the presence of the holy angels and in the presence of the Lamb. ¹¹ And the smoke of their torment goes up for ever and ever; and they have no rest, day or night, these worshipers of the beast and its image, and whoever receives the mark of its name."

12 Here is a call for the endurance

g Other ancient authorities read *six hundred and sixteen*
h Greek *virgins*

---

compare Dt.13.1–5; Mt.24.24; 2 Th.2.9). **16–17:** *Marked* in imitation of the sealing of God's servants (7.2–4), resulting in economic boycott against the Christians. **18:** Since Hebrew and Greek letters have numerical equivalents, *the number of the beast* (666) is the sum of the separate letters of his name. Of countless explanations, the most probable is *Neron Caesar* (in Hebrew letters), which, if spelled without the final *n*, also accounts for the variant reading, 616 (see note *g*).

14.1–20: An interlude of three visions intended to reassure the church amid trials and persecutions. **1–5:** The Lamb and those redeemed from the earth; as in 7.4, the one hundred and forty-four thousand is a symbolic expression for the whole number of the faithful. **3:** *They,* the one hundred and forty-four thousand. *New Song,* compare 5.8–10. **4:** *They are chaste,* in contrast to the devotees of the pagan cults (2.20–22). *First fruits,* Ex.23.19; Jas.1.18. **6–13:** Three angels announce the coming judgment. **6:** God's *eternal* purpose is soon to be fulfilled (10.7). **8:** An anticipation of ch. 18. **10:** *Wine of God's wrath,* Jer.25.15–16; 51.7. *Unmixed,* not diluted. *Tormented with fire,* in Gehenna (see 19.20 n.; 20.10). **11:** *Smoke,* 18.9, 18–19.3.

of the saints, those who keep the commandments of God and the faith of Jesus.

13 And I heard a voice from heaven saying, "Write this: Blessed are the dead who die in the Lord henceforth." "Blessed indeed," says the Spirit, "that they may rest from their labors, for their deeds follow them!"

14 Then I looked, and lo, a white cloud, and seated on the cloud one like a son of man, with a golden crown on his head, and a sharp sickle in his hand. 15 And another angel came out of the temple, calling with a loud voice to him who sat upon the cloud, "Put in your sickle, and reap, for the hour to reap has come, for the harvest of the earth is fully ripe." 16 So he who sat upon the cloud swung his sickle on the earth, and the earth was reaped.

17 And another angel came out of the temple in heaven, and he too had a sharp sickle. 18 Then another angel came out from the altar, the angel who has power over fire, and he called with a loud voice to him who had the sharp sickle, "Put in your sickle, and gather the clusters of the vine of the earth, for its grapes are ripe." 19 So the angel swung his sickle on the earth and gathered the vintage of the earth, and threw it into the great wine press of the wrath of God; 20 and the wine press was trodden outside the city, and blood flowed from the wine press, as high as a horse's bridle, for one thousand six hundred stadia.[i]

15 Then I saw another portent in heaven, great and wonderful, seven angels with seven plagues, which are the last, for with them the wrath of God is ended.

2 And I saw what appeared to be a sea of glass mingled with fire, and those who had conquered the beast and its image and the number of its name, standing beside the sea of glass with harps of God in their hands. 3 And they sing the song of Moses, the servant of God, and the song of the Lamb, saying,

"Great and wonderful are thy deeds,
O Lord God the Almighty!
Just and true are thy ways,
O King of the ages![j]
4 Who shall not fear and glorify thy
   name, O Lord?
For thou alone art holy.
All nations shall come and worship
   thee,
for thy judgments have been
   revealed."

5 After this I looked, and the temple of the tent of witness in heaven was opened, 6 and out of the temple came the seven angels with the seven plagues, robed in pure bright linen, and their breasts girded with golden girdles. 7 And one of the four living creatures gave the seven angels seven golden bowls full of the wrath of God who lives for ever and ever; 8 and the temple was filled with smoke from the glory of God and from his power, and no one could enter the temple until the seven plagues of the seven angels were ended.

16 Then I heard a loud voice from the temple telling the seven angels, "Go and pour out on the earth the seven bowls of the wrath of God."

2 So the first angel went and poured his bowl on the earth, and foul and evil sores came upon the men who bore the mark of the beast and worshiped its image.

i About two hundred miles
j Other ancient authorities read *the nations*

13: *Blessed*, see 1.3 n. *Their deeds*, the fruits of Christian character (Gal.5.22–23). **14–20:** The final judgment of God (Jl.3.13), involving the ingathering of the saints by *one like a son of man* (vv. 14–16) and the assembling of the wicked for destruction (vv. 17–20; Is.63.1–6).

15.1–16.21: The seven bowls of the wrath of God. 15.2–4: Preparatory vision of the victorious martyrs in heaven (8.3–5). **2:** *Sea*, see 4.6 n. **3:** Ex.15.1–18. **7:** *Golden bowls*, resembling the bronze basins used by the priests in the sacrificial ritual (Ex.27.3). **8:** *Smoke*, Is.6.1–4.

16.1–21: The pouring of the bowls (compare the plagues inflicted on Egypt, Ex. chs. 7–12). The descriptive details are not to be understood literally, but as contributing to the general

3 The second angel poured his bowl into the sea, and it became like the blood of a dead man, and every living thing died that was in the sea.

4 The third angel poured his bowl into the rivers and the fountains of water, and they became blood. [5] And I heard the angel of water say,

"Just art thou in these thy
        judgments,
thou who art and wast, O Holy One.
[6] For men have shed the blood of
        saints and prophets,
and thou hast given them blood to
        drink.
It is their due!"
[7] And I heard the altar cry,
"Yea, Lord God the Almighty,
true and just are thy judgments!"

8 The fourth angel poured his bowl on the sun, and it was allowed to scorch men with fire; [9] men were scorched by the fierce heat, and they cursed the name of God who had power over these plagues, and they did not repent and give him glory.

10 The fifth angel poured his bowl on the throne of the beast, and its kingdom was in darkness; men gnawed their tongues in anguish [11] and cursed the God of heaven for their pain and sores, and did not repent of their deeds.

12 The sixth angel poured his bowl on the great river Euphra'tes, and its water was dried up, to prepare the way for the kings from the east. [13] And I saw, issuing from the mouth of the dragon and from the mouth of the beast and from the mouth of the false prophet, three foul spirits like frogs; [14] for they are demonic spirits, performing signs, who go abroad to the kings of the whole world, to assemble them for battle on the great day of God the Almighty. [15] ("Lo, I am coming like a thief! Blessed is he who is awake, keeping his garments that he may not go naked and be seen exposed!") [16] And they assembled them at the place which is called in Hebrew Armaged'don.

17 The seventh angel poured his bowl into the air, and a loud voice came out of the temple, from the throne, saying, "It is done!" [18] And there were flashes of lightning, voices, peals of thunder, and a great earthquake such as had never been since men were on the earth, so great was that earthquake. [19] The great city was split into three parts, and the cities of the nations fell, and God remembered great Babylon, to make her drain the cup of the fury of his wrath. [20] And every island fled away, and no mountains were to be found; [21] and great hailstones, heavy as a hundredweight, dropped on men from heaven, till men cursed God for the plague of the hail, so fearful was that plague.

17 Then one of the seven angels who had the seven bowls came and said to me, "Come, I will show you the judgment of the great harlot who is seated upon many waters, [2] with whom the kings of the earth have committed fornication, and with the wine of whose fornication the dwellers on earth have become drunk." [3] And he carried me away in the Spirit into a wilderness, and I saw a woman sitting on a scarlet beast which was full of blasphemous names, and it had seven heads and ten horns. [4] The woman was arrayed in purple and scarlet, and bedecked with gold and jewels and pearls, holding in her hand a golden cup full of abominations and the impurities of her fornication; [5] and on her fore-

---

effect of intense calamity and terror. **2:** Ex.9.10–11; Dt.28.35. **3–4:** Ex.7.17–21. **5:** *The angel that has control* of *water*. **6:** Divine retribution. **10:** Ex.10.21. **13:** *Foul spirits*, 1 Tim.4.1; 1 Jn.4.3. **15:** *Like a thief*, see 3.3 n. *Blessed*, see 1.3 n. **16:** *They*, the frog-like spirits. *Armageddon*, "Hill of Megiddo," the site of several decisive battles in Israel's history (compare Jg.5.19; 2 Kg.9.27; 2 Chr.35.22). **19:** *The great city*, Rome. **21:** *Hail*, Ex.9.23.

17.1–18.24: The fall of Babylon, which is Rome, the city on *seven hills* (17.9,18) and the archpersecutor of the saints (17.6). **17.2:** Jer.51.7. **3:** *Scarlet beast*, the Roman empire (see 13.1 n.). *Blasphemous names*, divine titles given to Roman emperors. **5:** *On her forehead*, as was custom-

head was written a name of mystery: "Babylon the great, mother of harlots and of earth's abominations." [6] And I saw the woman, drunk with the blood of the saints and the blood of the martyrs of Jesus.

When I saw her I marveled greatly. [7] But the angel said to me, "Why marvel? I will tell you the mystery of the woman, and of the beast with seven heads and ten horns that carries her. [8] The beast that you saw was, and is not, and is to ascend from the bottomless pit and go to perdition; and the dwellers on earth whose names have not been written in the book of life from the foundation of the world, will marvel to behold the beast, because it was and is not and is to come. [9] This calls for a mind with wisdom: the seven heads are seven mountains on which the woman is seated; [10] they are also seven kings, five of whom have fallen, one is, the other has not yet come, and when he comes he must remain only a little while. [11] As for the beast that was and is not, it is an eighth but it belongs to the seven, and it goes to perdition. [12] And the ten horns that you saw are ten kings who have not yet received royal power, but they are to receive authority as kings for one hour, together with the beast. [13] These are of one mind and give over their power and authority to the beast; [14] they will make war on the Lamb, and the Lamb will conquer them, for he is Lord of lords and King of kings, and those with him are called and chosen and faithful."

15 And he said to me, "The waters that you saw, where the harlot is seated, are peoples and multitudes and nations and tongues. [16] And the ten horns that you saw, they and the beast will hate the harlot; they will make her desolate and naked, and devour her flesh and burn her up with fire, [17] for God has put it into their hearts to carry out his purpose by being of one mind and giving over their royal power to the beast, until the words of God shall be fulfilled. [18] And the woman that you saw is the great city which has dominion over the kings of the earth."

18 After this I saw another angel coming down from heaven, having great authority; and the earth was made bright with his splendor. [2] And he called out with a mighty voice,

"Fallen, fallen is Babylon the great!
It has become a dwelling place of
   demons,
a haunt of every foul spirit,
a haunt of every foul and hateful
   bird;
[3] for all nations have drunk[k] the wine
   of her impure passion,
and the kings of the earth have
   committed fornication with her,
and the merchants of the earth have
   grown rich with the wealth of
   her wantonness."

[4] Then I heard another voice from heaven saying,

"Come out of her, my people,
lest you take part in her sins,
lest you share in her plagues;
[5] for her sins are heaped high as
   heaven,
and God has remembered her
   iniquities.
[6] Render to her as she herself has
   rendered,
and repay her double for her deeds;
mix a double draught for her in the
   cup she mixed.
[7] As she glorified herself and played
   the wanton,

k Other ancient authorities read *fallen by*

---

ary with Roman harlots. **8:** *The beast* now represents the Emperor Nero, commonly expected to return to life and power (v. 11). **12:** These are probably local governors and satraps. **14:** The victory of Christ over the empire of the Antichrist. **17:** By divine overruling, the forces of iniquity fulfil the purposes of God (compare the passive verbs in 6.4; see 13.5 n.).

    18.1–24: Dirge over the fallen city (Rome), with echoes from the taunt songs in Is. chs. 23–24; ch. 47; Jer. chs. 50–51; Ezek. chs. 26–27. **1–3:** Angelic announcement of doom (Is.21.9; Jer. 50.39). **4–8:** Summons to God's people to leave the doomed city. **6:** Ps.137.8. **9–20:** Lamenta-

so give her a like measure of torment
and mourning.
Since in her heart she says, 'A queen
I sit,
I am no widow, mourning I shall
never see,'
8 so shall her plagues come in a single
day,
pestilence and mourning and
famine,
and she shall be burned with fire;
for mighty is the Lord God who
judges her."

9 And the kings of the earth, who committed fornication and were wanton with her, will weep and wail over her when they see the smoke of her burning; 10 they will stand far off, in fear of her torment, and say,

"Alas! alas! thou great city,
thou mighty city, Babylon!
In one hour has thy judgment
come."

11 And the merchants of the earth weep and mourn for her, since no one buys their cargo any more, 12 cargo of gold, silver, jewels and pearls, fine linen, purple, silk and scarlet, all kinds of scented wood, all articles of ivory, all articles of costly wood, bronze, iron and marble, 13 cinnamon, spice, incense, myrrh, frankincense, wine, oil, fine flour and wheat, cattle and sheep, horses and chariots, and slaves, that is, human souls.

14 "The fruit for which thy soul longed
has gone from thee,
and all thy dainties and thy splendor
are lost to thee, never to be
found again!"

15 The merchants of these wares, who gained wealth from her, will stand far off, in fear of her torment, weeping and mourning aloud,

16 "Alas, alas, for the great city
that was clothed in fine linen, in
purple and scarlet,
bedecked with gold, with jewels, and
with pearls!

17 In one hour all this wealth has been
laid waste."

And all shipmasters and seafaring men, sailors and all whose trade is on the sea, stood far off 18 and cried out as they saw the smoke of her burning, "What city was like the great city?" 19 And they threw dust on their heads, as they wept and mourned, crying out,

"Alas, alas, for the great city
where all who had ships at sea
grew rich by her wealth!
In one hour she has been laid waste.
20 Rejoice over her, O heaven,
O saints and apostles and prophets,
for God has given judgment for you
against her!"

21 Then a mighty angel took up a stone like a great millstone and threw it into the sea, saying,

"So shall Babylon the great city be
thrown down with violence,
and shall be found no more;
22 and the sound of harpers and
minstrels, of flute players and
trumpeters,
shall be heard in thee no more;
and a craftsman of any craft
shall be found in thee no more;
and the sound of the millstone
shall be heard in thee no more;
23 and the light of a lamp
shall shine in thee no more;
and the voice of bridegroom and
bride
shall be heard in thee no more;
for thy merchants were the great
men of the earth,
and all nations were deceived by
thy sorcery.
24 And in her was found the blood of
prophets and of saints,
and of all who have been slain on
earth."

19 After this I heard what seemed to be the loud voice of a great multitude in heaven, crying,

"Hallelujah! Salvation and glory and
power belong to our God,

---

tion of those who have been enriched by the wicked city: kings (vv. 9–10), merchants (vv. 11–16), and mariners (vv. 17–20). **21–24:** Symbolic action representing the total destruction of the city (Jer.51.63–64).

19.1–10: Praises in heaven for the destruction of Rome (vv. 1–5) and for the marriage of the

² for his judgments are true and just;
  he has judged the great harlot who
    corrupted the earth with her
    fornication,
  and he has avenged on her the blood
    of his servants."
³ Once more they cried,
  "Hallelujah! The smoke from her
    goes up for ever and ever."
⁴ And the twenty-four elders and the four living creatures fell down and worshiped God who is seated on the throne, saying, "Amen. Hallelujah!"
⁵ And from the throne came a voice crying,
  "Praise our God, all you his servants,
  you who fear him, small and great."
⁶ Then I heard what seemed to be the voice of a great multitude, like the sound of many waters and like the sound of mighty thunderpeals, crying,
  "Hallelujah! For the Lord our God
    the Almighty reigns.
⁷ Let us rejoice and exult and give
    him the glory,
  for the marriage of the Lamb has
    come,
  and his Bride has made herself
    ready;
⁸ it was granted her to be clothed with
    fine linen, bright and pure"—
for the fine linen is the righteous deeds of the saints.

9 And the angel said[l] to me, "Write this: Blessed are those who are invited to the marriage supper of the Lamb." And he said to me, "These are true words of God." ¹⁰ Then I fell down at his feet to worship him, but he said to me, "You must not do that! I am a fellow servant with you and your brethren who hold the testimony of Jesus. Worship God." For the testimony of Jesus is the spirit of prophecy.

11 Then I saw heaven opened, and behold, a white horse! He who sat upon it is called Faithful and True, and in righteousness he judges and makes war. ¹² His eyes are like a flame of fire, and on his head are many diadems; and he has a name inscribed which no one knows but himself. ¹³ He is clad in a robe dipped in[m] blood, and the name by which he is called is The Word of God. ¹⁴ And the armies of heaven, arrayed in fine linen, white and pure, followed him on white horses. ¹⁵ From his mouth issues a sharp sword with which to smite the nations, and he will rule them with a rod of iron; he will tread the wine press of the fury of the wrath of God the Almighty. ¹⁶ On his robe and on his thigh he has a name inscribed, King of kings and Lord of lords.

17 Then I saw an angel standing in the sun, and with a loud voice he called to all the birds that fly in midheaven, "Come, gather for the great supper of God, ¹⁸ to eat the flesh of kings, the flesh of captains, the flesh of mighty men, the flesh of horses and their riders, and the flesh of all men, both free and slave, both small and great." ¹⁹ And I saw the beast and the kings of the earth with their armies gathered to make war against him who sits upon the horse and against his army. ²⁰ And the beast was captured, and with it the false prophet who in its presence had worked the signs by which he deceived those who had received the mark of the beast and those who worshiped its image. These two were thrown alive into the lake of fire that burns with sulphur. ²¹ And the rest were slain by the sword of him who sits upon the horse, the sword that

l Greek *he said*
m Other ancient authorities read *sprinkled with*

Lamb (vv. 6–9). **5:** Ps.115.13. **7:** *His bride*, the church (Eph.5.23–32). **8:** The church is holy as her members are holy (7.14; compare Mt.22.11). **9:** *Blessed*, see 1.3 n. **10:** An aside (compare 22.8–9). **11–21:** **The victory of Christ and his heavenly armies** over the beast and his cohorts. **12:** *A name . . . which no one knows*, the greatness of Christ surpasses human knowledge (Mt.11.27). **13:** As revealer of God he is called *The Word of God* (Jn.1.1,14). **15:** 1.16; Ps.2.9. **16:** 17.14; Dt.10.17. **17–18:** *An angel* summons the birds of prey (Ezek.39.4,17–20). **19–21:** The final battle between Christ and Antichrist (anticipated in 16.13–16). **20:** *The false prophet*, the second beast of 13.11–15. *The lake of fire* is Gehenna (see 14.10 n.; Mt.18.9 note *b*).

issues from his mouth; and all the birds were gorged with their flesh.

20 Then I saw an angel coming down from heaven, holding in his hand the key of the bottomless pit and a great chain. [2] And he seized the dragon, that ancient serpent, who is the Devil and Satan, and bound him for a thousand years, [3] and threw him into the pit, and shut it and sealed it over him, that he should deceive the nations no more, till the thousand years were ended. After that he must be loosed for a little while.

4 Then I saw thrones, and seated on them were those to whom judgment was committed. Also I saw the souls of those who had been beheaded for their testimony to Jesus and for the word of God, and who had not worshiped the beast or its image and had not received its mark on their foreheads or their hands. They came to life, and reigned with Christ a thousand years. [5] The rest of the dead did not come to life until the thousand years were ended. This is the first resurrection. [6] Blessed and holy is he who shares in the first resurrection! Over such the second death has no power, but they shall be priests of God and of Christ, and they shall reign with him a thousand years.

7 And when the thousand years are ended, Satan will be loosed from his prison [8] and will come out to deceive the nations which are at the four corners of the earth, that is, Gog and Magog, to gather them for battle; their number is like the sand of the sea. [9] And they marched up over the broad earth and surrounded the camp of the saints and the beloved city; but fire came down from heaven[n] and consumed them, [10] and the devil who had deceived them was thrown into the lake of fire and sulphur where the beast and the false prophet were, and they will be tormented day and night for ever and ever.

11 Then I saw a great white throne and him who sat upon it; from his presence earth and sky fled away, and no place was found for them. [12] And I saw the dead, great and small, standing before the throne, and books were opened. Also another book was opened, which is the book of life. And the dead were judged by what was written in the books, by what they had done. [13] And the sea gave up the dead in it, Death and Hades gave up the dead in them, and all were judged by what they had done. [14] Then Death and Hades were thrown into the lake of fire. This is the second death, the lake of fire; [15] and if any one's name was not found written in the book of life, he was thrown into the lake of fire.

21 Then I saw a new heaven and a new earth; for the first heaven and the first earth had passed away,

n Other ancient authorities read *from God, out of heaven,* or *out of heaven from God*

20.1–6: The binding of Satan and the reign of the martyrs. 2: As other numerals in this book are to be understood symbolically and not literally, so this period of *a thousand years* represents the perfection and completion of the martyrs' reign with Christ, untroubled by Satan's wiles. One must beware of reading more into this passage than is warranted; e.g. nothing is said here about a reign on earth. **4:** *Thrones* of judgment (Dan.7.9,22,27; Mt.19.28; Lk.22.30). *Those . . . beheaded for their testimony*, martyrs (in 6.9–10 the souls of the martyrs, under the altar, cry for vengeance). *Its mark*, 13.16–17; 14.9. **6:** *Blessed*, see 1.3 n. *Priests*, 1.6; 5.10. *Second death*, see 2.11 n. **7–10: The loosing of Satan and the final conflict.** *Gog and Magog*, Ezek. chs. 38–39. **9:** *The beloved city*, Jerusalem, symbol of the Church universal. *Fire*, 2 Kg.1.10–12. **11–15: The final judgment. 12:** *Books*, containing the record of men's deeds (Dan.7.10). *Book of life*, see 3.5 n. *Judged . . . by what they had done*, Mt.16.27; Rom.2.6. **13–14:** *Death and Hades* (the temporary abode of the dead) are personified. **14:** *The second death*, see 2.11 n.; Mt.25.41.

21.1–22.5: Vision of the new Jerusalem. 21.1: The *new heaven and new earth*, predicted by Isaiah (Is.65.17; 66.22); all creation will be renewed, freed from imperfections, and transformed by the glory of God (Rom.8.19–21). *The sea*, a symbol of turbulence and unrest. **2:** *New Jerusalem*, the church (Gal.4.26). *Prepared as a bride*, suggesting all that is beautiful and

and the sea was no more. 2 And I saw
the holy city, new Jerusalem, coming
down out of heaven from God, prepared as a bride adorned for her husband; 3 and I heard a loud voice from
the throne saying, "Behold, the dwelling of God is with men. He will dwell
with them, and they shall be his people,[o] and God himself will be with
them;[p] 4 he will wipe away every tear
from their eyes, and death shall be no
more, neither shall there be mourning
nor crying nor pain any more, for the
former things have passed away."

5 And he who sat upon the throne
said, "Behold, I make all things new."
Also he said, "Write this, for these
words are trustworthy and true." 6 And
he said to me, "It is done! I am the
Alpha and the Omega, the beginning
and the end. To the thirsty I will give
from the fountain of the water of life
without payment. 7 He who conquers
shall have this heritage, and I will be
his God and he shall be my son. 8 But
as for the cowardly, the faithless, the
polluted, as for murderers, fornicators,
sorcerers, idolaters, and all liars, their
lot shall be in the lake that burns with
fire and sulphur, which is the second
death."

9 Then came one of the seven angels
who had the seven bowls full of the
seven last plagues, and spoke to me,
saying, "Come, I will show you the
Bride, the wife of the Lamb." 10 And
in the Spirit he carried me away to a
great, high mountain, and showed me
the holy city Jerusalem coming down
out of heaven from God, 11 having the
glory of God, its radiance like a most
rare jewel, like a jasper, clear as
crystal. 12 It had a great, high wall,
with twelve gates, and at the gates
twelve angels, and on the gates the
names of the twelve tribes of the
sons of Israel were inscribed; 13 on
the east three gates, on the north three
gates, on the south three gates, and on
the west three gates. 14 And the wall
of the city had twelve foundations, and
on them the twelve names of the twelve
apostles of the Lamb.

15 And he who talked to me had a
measuring rod of gold to measure the
city and its gates and walls. 16 The city
lies foursquare, its length the same as
its breadth; and he measured the city
with his rod, twelve thousand
stadia;[q] its length and breadth and
height are equal. 17 He also measured
its wall, a hundred and forty-four cubits
by a man's measure, that is, an angel's.
18 The wall was built of jasper, while
the city was pure gold, clear as glass.
19 The foundations of the wall of the
city were adorned with every jewel;
the first was jasper, the second sapphire, the third agate, the fourth emerald, 20 the fifth onyx, the sixth carnelian, the seventh chrysolite, the eighth
beryl, the ninth topaz, the tenth chryso-
prase, the eleventh jacinth, the twelfth
amethyst. 21 And the twelve gates were
twelve pearls, each of the gates made
of a single pearl, and the street of the
city was pure gold, transparent as
glass.

22 And I saw no temple in the city,
for its temple is the Lord God the
Almighty and the Lamb. 23 And the
city has no need of sun or moon to

o Other ancient authorities read *peoples*
p Other ancient authorities add *and be their God*
q About fifteen hundred miles

---

lovely (19.7–9). **3:** Ezek.37.27. **4:** 7.16; Is.25.8; 35.10. **5:** The speaker is God himself. **6:** *Alpha* and *Omega*, see 1.8 n. *Water of life*, Is.55.1; Jn.4.13; 7.37. **7:** *He who conquers*, compare the concluding words of each of the seven letters in chs. 2 and 3. **8:** *The cowardly* fall away in time of persecution. *Sorcerers*, literally "poisoners," those dealing in philters and poisons (Acts 19.19). *The lake*, see 19.20 n. *The second death*, contrasted to the water of life in v. 6 (see 2.11 n.).

21.9–27: The measuring of the city. Since the city is symbolical, so are its measurements (all of which are multiples of 12). **9:** *The seven bowls*, see ch. 16. **10:** *High mountain*, Ezek.40.2. **11:** *Jasper*, 4.3. **14:** *Apostles*, Eph.2.20. **15–18:** *The city* is represented as being a cube, symbol of perfection; its beauty and magnificence are suggested by the precious stones (Ex.28.17–21). **19:** Is.54.11–12. **21:** *The street*, the paving of the streets. **22–23:** *No temple . . . no sun* are

shine upon it, for the glory of God is its light, and its lamp is the Lamb. ²⁴ By its light shall the nations walk; and the kings of the earth shall bring their glory into it, ²⁵ and its gates shall never be shut by day–and there shall be no night there; ²⁶ they shall bring into it the glory and the honor of the nations. ²⁷ But nothing unclean shall enter it, nor any one who practices abomination or falsehood, but only those who are written in the Lamb's book of life.

22 Then he showed me the river of the water of life, bright as crystal, flowing from the throne of God and of the Lamb ² through the middle of the street of the city; also, on either side of the river, the tree of life′ with its twelve kinds of fruit, yielding its fruit each month; and the leaves of the tree were for the healing of the nations. ³ There shall no more be anything accursed, but the throne of God and of the Lamb shall be in it, and his servants shall worship him; ⁴ they shall see his face, and his name shall be on their foreheads. ⁵ And night shall be no more; they need no light of lamp or sun, for the Lord God will be their light, and they shall reign for ever and ever.

6 And he said to me, "These words are trustworthy and true. And the Lord, the God of the spirits of the prophets, has sent his angel to show his servants what must soon take place. ⁷ And behold, I am coming soon."

Blessed is he who keeps the words of the prophecy of this book.

8 I John am he who heard and saw these things. And when I heard and saw them, I fell down to worship at the feet of the angel who showed them to me; ⁹ but he said to me, "You must not do that! I am a fellow servant with you and your brethren the prophets, and with those who keep the words of this book. Worship God."

10 And he said to me, "Do not seal up the words of the prophecy of this book, for the time is near. ¹¹ Let the evildoer still do evil, and the filthy still be filthy, and the righteous still do right, and the holy still be holy."

12 "Behold, I am coming soon, bringing my recompense, to repay every one for what he has done. ¹³ I am the Alpha and the Omega, the first and the last, the beginning and the end."

14 Blessed are those who wash their robes,ˢ that they may have the right to the tree of life and that they may enter the city by the gates. ¹⁵ Outside are the dogs and sorcerers and fornicators and murderers and idolaters, and every one who loves and practices falsehood.

16 "I Jesus have sent my angel to you with this testimony for the churches. I am the root and the offspring of David, the bright morning star."

17 The Spirit and the Bride say, "Come." And let him who hears say, "Come." And let him who is thirsty

r Or *the Lamb. In the midst of the street of the city, and on either side of the river, was the tree of life*, etc.
s Other ancient authorities read *do his commandments*

needed because the Presence and Glory of God pervades the entire community (Is.24.23; 60.1, 19). *Its lamp is the Lamb*, Jn.8.12. **25**: Is.60.11. **27**: *Book of life*, see 3.5 n.

22.1–5: The river and the tree of life. 1: *The river* of blessings from God (compare Gen.2.10; Ps.46.4). **2**: *The tree*, used here generically of many trees *on either side of the river* (Ezek.47.12). **3**: *The throne of God and of the Lamb* is one throne (Jn.10.30). **4**: To *see his face* will be the crowning joy of heaven (Mt.5.8; 1 Jn.3.2; compare 1 Cor.13.12). *On their foreheads*, see 7.3 n.; contrast 13.16. **5**: Those who *worship* God (v. 3) *shall reign* with him in eternal triumph.

22.6–21: Epilogue, consisting of warnings and exhortations. **6**: *He said*, an angel (v. 8), perhaps the one referred to in 1.1. *These words*, i.e. the contents of this book. **7**: A parenthesis, reporting the words of Christ (compare 16.15); the quotation marks after the word *soon* should be moved to stand after the word *place* (v. 6). *Blessed*, see 1.3 n. **8–9**: 19.10. **10**: *Do not seal*, this book is intended for all to read. **11**: The end of the age is too near to allow time for change. **12**: *Bringing my recompense*, Is.40.10; Jer.17.10. **13**: Christ applies God's title to himself (see 1.8 n.). **14**: *Blessed*, see 1.3 n. *Wash*, 7.14. *The city*, heavenly Jerusalem. **15**: *Dogs*, impure,

come, let him who desires take the water of life without price.

18 I warn every one who hears the words of the prophecy of this book: if any one adds to them, God will add to him the plagues described in this book, ¹⁹ and if any one takes away from the words of the book of this prophecy, God will take away his share in the tree of life and in the holy city, which are described in this book.

20 He who testifies to these things says, "Surely I am coming soon." Amen. Come, Lord Jesus!

21 The grace of the Lord Jesus be with all the saints.*t* Amen.

t Other ancient authorities omit *all*; others omit *the saints*

lascivious persons (Phil.3.2). *Sorcerers*, see 21.8 n. **16**: *Root . . . of David*, Is.11.1,10; Mt.1.1. **17**: *The Bride*, the church. "*Come*," addressed to Jesus, as v. 20. **18–19**: A solemn warning against perversion of the teachings of *this book* (compare Dt.4.2; 12.32). **21**: A fitting conclusion to this book and to the Bible.

HOW TO READ THE BIBLE WITH UNDERSTANDING

THE DIVERSITY AND THE UNITY OF THE SCRIPTURES

THE BIBLE belongs to the whole world as no other book does. Parts or the whole of it are available in more than a thousand languages. Christians everywhere pay lip service to it as the supreme authority for their faith. Phrases from its pages have become current speech, and allusions to its stories are widely understood. Yet relatively few people are familiar with it as a whole, and acquaintance for the most part is limited to a small selection of passages. Much is not easy to understand, and not all is equally rewarding for all purposes. What every reader should first understand is the range and variety of the Bible, and what parts can best serve the purpose for which he turns to it.

The opening chapters of the Old Testament deal with human origins. They are not to be read as history, but neither are they to be dismissed as childish myths. They are marked by profound spiritual insight. They teach that God created man to be obedient to him, and that in that obedience man's well-being lay. By disobedience man turned from the true source of his life, so that before Adam and Eve were ejected from the Garden, he hid himself from God. These chapters think of sin not as a theological abstraction, but as something real which recoils upon man to his own hurt. It broke up the first family, brought murder and strife and corruption, and ate like a canker into the heart of man.

These chapters are followed by the stories of the patriarchs, which preserve ancient traditions now known to reflect the conditions of the times of which they tell, though they cannot be treated as strictly historical. That they contain genuine historical memories is increasingly recognized today. Yet here again, it is not for history but for religion that they are preserved, and they have much of abiding value to say to us today. Every reader should be alert to understand not merely God's dealings with the patriarchs, but what he is saying to us through these stories. To take a single illustration, the story of Abraham's narrowly averted sacrifice of Isaac is more than a memory of times when human sacrifice was common, or of the first awakening in Israel's ancestors of the recognition that God did not desire it. It is the story of a man who loved God more than all else and who was willing to surrender to God even the son in whose life his own was bound. There are sacrifices which God does not ask; there are none a man should be unwilling to make.

With the story of the Exodus and the settlement in Canaan we come nearer to historical light, though we are still dealing with idealized history. The main purpose of this narrative is to bring the reader to realize that God chose Israel to be his people and delivered her by his power, thus revealing his own character and laying on her the constraint of obedience. God's election of Israel was to privilege indeed, but it was also to service, and the privilege was bound up with the service.

Into this story the legal sections of the Old Testament have been fitted, and especially all the provisions for the sacrificial ritual of the shrine. Much bears the marks of the social and religious background of the times from which it comes, and not a little is without authority for the Christian. He does not observe the Jewish dietary laws, and in many countries the care for the helpless and needy is no longer left to his charity but is organized by the state; and for the Christian, animal sacrifices are superseded by the sacrifice of Christ. It is to be observed, however, that while the Letter to the Hebrews links the death of Christ with the ritual of the Day of Atonement, other references in the New Testament allude rather to the Suffering Servant of Isaiah 53. That chapter contains the most remarkable thought on sacrifice found in the Old Testament. The Servant was one who willingly gave himself to be sacrificed, a morally blameless man instead of a physically unblemished animal, and his sacrifice was wider in its efficacy than any sacrifice mentioned in the Pentateuch. It availed even for Gentiles, who in penitence confessed that the sufferings he endured should rightly have been theirs. It was because the death of Jesus picked up the meaning of sacrifice in the Old Testament at this, its highest point both in the nature and in the efficacy of the sacrifice, that, for the Christian, ritual sacrifice was superseded in the Cross. For the Jew sacrifice ended when the Temple was destroyed, because perforce it must end. For the Christian it ended when the great concept of Isaiah 53 found its fulfilment at Calvary.

When we come to the books of Samuel and Kings we have much very good history. The unsurpassed account of the reign of David probably comes from the time of Solomon, and it is without equal as historical writing in the literature of any country of the world at so early an age. Not all in these books is of the same historical value, and especially in the stories of Elijah and Elisha there are legendary elements. There is variety of literary forms within a single book. All in these books, as also in the later books of Chronicles, Ezra, and Nehemiah, is concerned with the lessons of history as much as with the history itself. For here, as everywhere, the Bible is a religious book, concerned to remember the past for what it has to say to the present.

The prophetic books offer special difficulty to the modern reader. They contain utterances of the prophets to their contemporaries, often with no indication but their contents to tell us the circumstances of their delivery, and not arranged chronologically. They expose the political and social ills of Israel, the hollow religiosity and the denial of human brotherhood, the rapacity of the rich and the sexual laxity, in a way that may seem to have little relevance to our day. Yet all their oracles spring from enduring religious principles, which are valid in every generation, so that the reader here once more should seek to penetrate beneath all that belongs to the age of the prophets to that which is of abiding significance, that he may then convert it into the terms of his own life and his own day.

The prophetic oracles are mostly in poetry, but the poetic book of the Old Testament *par excellence* is the book of Psalms. Here we have poems which were created for religious use, many of them probably to accompany the ritual of sacrifice and feast, and they have continued to serve a religious use in public and in private throughout the years. There are verses which grate on our ears, and not all the psalms reach the same heights. But as a whole, they can still nourish the spirit of devotion, and can express the aspirations of our hearts as we set aside the ephemeral and allow them to serve as the vehicle of our approach to God.

Of the wisdom books of the Old Testament, two may be mentioned here. The book of Proverbs is mainly a collection of poetic observations used in the instruction of youth, and governed throughout by the conviction that the fear of the Lord is the beginning of wisdom, and that the way of wisdom is the way of integrity and of obedience to his will. The book of Job carries one of the profoundest messages to be found in the Old Testament. Through its story of a godly man who suffered grievous pain and loss, and who was tormented by the friends who came to comfort him till he was goaded into an appeal both *to* God and *against* him until God answered him out of the whirlwind to remind him of the folly of passing judgment on God out of his ignorance, the author teaches that more important than the discovery of the reasons for suffering is the finding of God *in* suffering. So far from being cut off from God by his suffering, as Job's friends supposed and as Job himself feared, he comes to a new understanding of God through his suffering. His past knowledge of God was but as hearsay compared with the experience he now has, so that instead of continuing to be tormented by questions, he rests in God.

When we pass from the Old Testament to the New, we move in a different world. Yet the two Testaments are bound together in a very real way. Here in the first three Gospels we have stories of Jesus which are linked together by the use of common sources, while in the fourth Gospel we have an independent account which is more concerned to interpret the significance of our Lord. None of the Gospels offers a biography of Jesus, yet by their study we may come to know him better than others may be known from full and careful biographies. By the intimate study of the Gospels we may know much about Jesus; but better than that, we may come to know him and to be infused with something of his spirit.

History is represented in the New Testament by the book of Acts. Yet here again history is not recorded merely for its own sake. The reader is told of the spread of Christianity until in the person of Paul it is carried to Rome, though a great deal that he would like to know is left unrecorded. Yet he can see the spirit of the early church, and can understand its message. More important, he can realize that from the beginning it was perceived that the Christian faith is not something to be enjoyed alone, but to be shared. It is something that is given to the church so that it may be communicated to all men, and only in sharing it with all men is it truly possessed.

In the letters of the New Testament we have reflected some of the churches which were founded by the apostles, and — more important — we have unfolded the significance of the Christian message. The death and resurrection of Jesus are seen not simply as facts of history, but as charged with meaning for us. When the Cross of Christ becomes the organ of our surrender by faith to him, in a profound sense we die with him and are born anew in him. His resurrection becomes the organ of our renewed life, whose essential character lies in the union of our life with him, so that he lives in us, and we are linked with his character and purpose and live no longer unto ourselves but become extensions of his personality in the world. The Son of God lifts us to become the sons of God, in whom our Father is to be seen, and heirs of God, whose heritage is to share his spirit and purpose.

The final book of the New Testament came out of a time of suffering and persecution, like the book of Daniel in the Old Testament, whose character it so much shares. Neither should be read as a cryptic plan of the ages, but as the expression of an undying hope in God and a grand faith that humble loyalty to him transmutes suffering for him into a privilege. The wise reader is less concerned with the intricate symbolism than with the spirit which penetrates it all.

That there is a place for the study of every detail of the Bible in the light of the situation out of which it arose, with all the illumination that philology and archaeology and ancient history can provide, is not for a moment here forgotten. But more important than that is the recognition that in this book are the living oracles of God, which may speak to us and nourish our spirit when we approach them in true devotion and humility. We should always remember the variety of literary forms found in the Bible, and should read a passage in the light of its own particular literary character. Legend should be read as legend, and poetry as poetry, and not with a dull prosaic and literalistic mind.

Of the great themes which run through the Bible and impart to it a unity despite its diversity the wise reader is ever aware. Throughout, God is One who reveals himself to men and who desires their fellowship. He reveals himself in history and through persons, until he finally reveals himself in One who is both God and man. In both Testaments it is the same God who is revealed, and this above all else gives unity to the Bible. At the same time it must be recognized that much in the Old Testament is superseded in the New, and there are ideas of God in the Old Testament which are not to be approved. For though both Testaments bring us revelation of God, the revelation came through men who could

not always apprehend it in its fulness. Just as light is modified by the glass through which it passes, while none derives from the glass itself, so revelation whose sole origin is in God is modified and often marred by the personalities through which it comes. That is why the perfect revelation could come only through the perfect Man, and why the incarnation was already implicit in the self-revealing purpose of God.

In both Testaments God is revealed as compassionate and saving. He had compassion on Israel in her Egyptian bondage, and on men who were in the deeper bondage of sin. It has already been said that from the earliest pages of the Bible it was perceived that fundamentally sin is disobedience to God and that by its very nature it curses man. Throughout the Bible God is concerned to save men from sin, but in the New Testament we have the supreme expression of that concern when God in Christ stooped to take upon himself the curse of sin, that by the sacrifice on the Cross deliverance might be wrought. The saving character of God was revealed in bringing Israel out of Egypt; but it was revealed on a new level at Golgotha.

Again, in both Testaments religion is seen in terms of covenant, and the covenant is the response in gratitude for the deliverance that has been accomplished. When Israel was saved from Egypt she went to the sacred mount and there pledged herself in the covenant to the God who had saved her. The deliverance was the unconstrained act of God, whose initiative in grace is the same throughout the Bible. So in the New Testament the Cross is freely accepted by him in whom the character of God is perfectly revealed, and it becomes the organ of our salvation, laying upon us its constraint to bind ourselves in the new covenant to him. In Old Testament and in New the covenant calls for obedience. It is not a bargain but a pledge. That Israel was often faithless to the covenant does not alter its essential character. Her obedience consisted in the cherishing of the revelation that had been given to her in the context of her deliverance and in reflecting the will of God in all her life. In due time she was instructed by the prophets that her faith was not for her alone. She had been chosen by God that through her he might reach all nations, and her election involved her mission. The new covenant in Christ calls for the cherishing of the larger revelation of God given to us in the life and death and resurrection of Christ, and in obedience to his divine will.

Yet another theme which runs through the

Bible and belongs to its unity is faith. Faith is something more than a belief about God. When the Israelites stepped on to the sand left by the receding Red Sea, they showed more than a belief about God. And Christian faith is more than an intellectual persuasion. It is the abandonment of ourselves to Christ, something that carries us into him, so that henceforth we live in him and he in us, as the vine and the branch live in each other indissolubly.

In both Testaments the theme of judgment figures. When Adam sinned and isolated himself from God, his self-judgment led to the judgment of exclusion from the Garden. And continually in the Old Testament we find the same thing. The prophets announced the coming judgment when Israel by her disobedience cut herself off from God. All judgment begins in self-judgment. So, too, in the New Testament: "He who does not believe is condemned already" (Jn.3.18). This is the reverse side of the teaching that man's well-being consists in walking in obedience to God. When he does not obey God he walks to disaster, because without God his wisdom is but folly. Yet the judgment of God is ever tempered with mercy. His mercy is shown in his patience and in sending his servants the prophets to warn and to reclaim. It is shown, too, in the sparing of the remnant. Sometimes it is a righteous remnant, spared for its own loyalty, and sometimes it is a remnant spared to preserve for a generation, whose response shall be wiser than its own, the reve-

lation it so lightly regards. From the earliest pages of the Bible the thought of the remnant appears. Noah and his family are a remnant spared at the flood, and throughout the prophetic words of judgment there appear promises of the remnant that shall remain—the remnant to whom alone the heritage of the covenant belongs, and through whom it is to be shared with those who do not belong to Israel according to the flesh. And in the New Testament the Church consists first of a remnant of Israel. The first disciples were all Jews, who inherited the revelation of the Old Covenant and also the new revelation from the same God given in Christ, and who brought the response of faith and obedience, and then shared their heritage with Gentiles who brought the same response.

A rich diversity of types of literature marks the Bible. There is progress in revelation; part of the Old Testament was outgrown before the Old Testament was itself complete, and more was superseded in the New Testament. Yet amid the diversity runs a unity, and in all the progress there is the thread of a true continuity which derives from the God who speaks through it all. The end of true study of the Bible is to hear his voice, and all who have ears to hear may hear it. The wise student of the Bible will welcome every aid to understand its background and meaning, but his supreme need is one no other can supply. It is the humble desire to find God in his word, and to hear his word that it may find response in gratitude and obedience.

MODERN APPROACHES TO BIBLICAL STUDY

Opening the Old Testament can be at first quite disconcerting to the average reader. If Moses wrote the Pentateuch (the Torah, see p. xxviii), he would appear to have done it in a very sporadic fashion, with laws and narrative put together in a puzzling mixture. And how was the book of Jeremiah assembled, with its personal sayings, the biography (Jer. chaps. 37–45), and prose discourses? So many of the prophetical books have the character of pieces in an anthology, to which no indication of the date or life-setting have been provided. More basically, are we to think of the Old Testament as a *literary* work? In its final form it is literature, but how was it put together, especially since oral tradition (the prophets were *preachers*) must have played a role? These questions can also be addressed to the New Testament. How did the synoptic Gospels come to be written? What was the role of the early Christian community in the formation of the oral and written traditions about Jesus? It is problems such as these that gave rise to the scientific approach to the Bible in modern times — an approach that is manifested in the introductions and notes of the present edition of the Bible.

1. Literary Criticism

During the nineteenth and twentieth centuries scholars attempted to answer these questions by the method of literary criticism. This approach aimed primarily at questions of authorship (did John write the Gospel attributed to him?), and the formation of the *written* documents (how were the J, E, P, and D documents (see p. xxviii) put together to form the Pentateuch?). This method achieved many good results. For example, we can now better grasp the message of Is.40–55 when we read these chapters in the light of the exilic period rather than as coming from the Isaiah of 700 B.C. It must be acknowledged, however, that new insights from archaeology and history have revealed definite limitations of this method. Among other things, it failed to take seriously the *oral* traditions that lay behind the final written form of a biblical book, nor did it adequately examine questions of the origin or life-setting of the individual units within a book. This task was taken over by the method called "form criticism."

2. Form Criticism

The method of form criticism was first used by German scholars (Hermann Gunkel for the Old Testament; Martin Dibelius for the New Testament), who employed the term *Formgeschichte* (lit. "form history"). It was recognized that within the Bible certain definite literary genres or forms could be identified. Gunkel analyzed the Psalter into Hymns, Laments, Thanksgiving Songs, Liturgies, etc. The analysis rested upon a study of literary style, which was correlated with the life-setting (*Sitz im Leben*) of the individual Psalm. Often similar genres in the literature of Israel's neighbors, especially Egypt and Mesopotamia, served to suggest or confirm such analysis, which eventually was applied to all parts of the Bible.

The existence of various literary genres in the Bible had always been admitted, but they had not been studied in and for themselves or used as tools in the analysis of biblical literature. In a sense, they were taken for granted, just as we take for granted the several genres in our own literatures. Any newspaper presents its readers with many and various literary genres: advertisements, obituary notices, editorials, letters to the editor, human interest stories, the comics, etc. In all these cases fixed written forms can be recognized. Each has its own specific characteristics: certain expressions or formulae and perhaps even a given structure. The modern reader is oblivious to all these details. He is so attuned to the literary expressions of his own culture that he automatically "shifts gears" as he moves from one genre to another. But it is a different experience when he exposes himself to a literature as ancient and varied as the Bible.

The difference between the peoples of the ancient Semitic world, its way of thinking, and our own style, quickly dawns upon us. It would not do to exaggerate these differences, but the fact remains that the mode of expression of the people of biblical times is a challenge to our understanding. Thus, their way of writing history does not conform to ours, as we quickly learn from the story of David's rise in 1 Sam.16 — 2 Sam.5, or from the "throne succession" narrative in 2 Sam.9ff. The reader's task is to ascertain and respect the various literary types, whether historical, epic, saga, or legend, that occur in the Bible; otherwise he will fail to comprehend the literary riches preserved in the various parts of Scripture.

In contrast to an earlier generation of Bible readers, we are very much aware of the role played by oral tradition in the gradual formation of the Scriptures. Many of the biblical books have a long pre-history of oral transmission. Ancient man retained in his memory far more than he wrote. Thus we read of Jeremiah being commissioned by the LORD to write "all the words that I have spoken to you . . . from the day of Josiah until today" (36.2). It would appear that it was only after a twenty-year period of preaching that Jeremiah resorted to writing. In his case, and in that of other prophets as well, it is easy to imagine that many of their listeners remembered certain sayings and even put them in writing. We know that Isaiah had a group of disciples (Is.8.16). The wisdom-sayings were cultivated at the Jerusalem court (Pr. 25.1), as was the case in Egypt. But many of these sayings doubtless were first coined among the common people. Similarly, the laws circulated by oral tradition before they became fixed in writing. They were proclaimed at the great feasts, such as that of the covenant renewal, and only later reduced to the codes we find in the Bible (Covenant [see Ex.20.22–23.33n.], Priestly, and Deuteronomic Codes). The stories of the Judges (Jephthah, Samson, Deborah, and others) circulated by word of mouth among the people concerned (in Transjordan and in Judah) before they were incorporated into a *book* such as Judges. The Gospels too have been analyzed in the light of the several units that went into their composition: the sayings of Jesus, the miracle stories, the Passion narratives, etc. Scholars came to recognize that some of these had their life-setting in the primitive Church. Such literary units reflect concerns which became particularly acute in the history of the community — such as the attitude to the synagogue, the delay of the parousia (= second coming), etc. — and the gospel material was shaped to meet the needs of the growing Church. Thus, several parables reflect their new life-setting (see p. 1532); they shift the emphasis which Jesus would have placed on the coming of the kingdom to the second coming of Christ (e.g., the parable of the ten maidens, Mt.25.1–13).

The life-setting of any piece of literature is a particularly important element. To a given life-setting there corresponds a certain range of literary genres. Thus, Israelite liturgy is the general life-setting within which the Psalms were composed and utilized. It was in the temple and in association with various feasts that the Songs of Praise, Thanksgivings, Laments, etc., were used. And we are better able to understand the structures and motifs of a given genre if we can locate it within its proper life-setting. In everyday life we understand the life-setting implicit in a wedding invitation, in an obituary notice, etc. In a similar vein, we must be sensitive to the life-setting of a given prophetic oracle, or a given wisdom saying. It is also important to recognize that the life-setting changes as a biblical tradition is handed down within a community. This fact is especially important for understanding the Gospels. Thus, one may distinguish between the historical life-setting in Jesus' own experience, into which one of his sayings may fit (Mk.2.27, "the sabbath was made for man, not man for the sabbath"), from the life-setting in the Christian community which applied one of the Lord's sayings to a particular situation in the life of the Church (Mt.28.19–20, "Go therefore and make disciples of all nations, baptizing them in the name of the Father and of the Son and of the Holy Spirit, teaching them . . ."). Furthermore, as will be indicated in the following section dealing with redaction criticism, there is a third life-setting — the place of, and emphasis given to, a particular section within a Gospel. Thus, one can see the different ways in which the tradition concerning John the Baptist is used in the Gospels of Matthew and Mark. Each evangelist has his own way of emphasizing the traditions about Jesus, and gives these a specific life-setting within his own Gospel.

3. Redaction Criticism

The intensely analytical method of form criticism called forth another approach, synthetic in character. This is the method of "redaction criticism" (*Redaktionsgeschichte*, lit. "redaction history"), which studies the document in its final form from the theological point of view of the author who arranged, modified, and edited — and may even have created new forms — the traditional material that was available to him. This method is most clearly illustrated by the differences among the Synoptic Gospels, which show that Matthew's viewpoint goes beyond Mark's, and that Luke's is different from either — despite the similarities among them all that warrant for them the term "synoptic." Now there is another life-setting to take into consideration: the life-setting of the Gospel itself — how a given form is used in a Gospel. A similar synthetic approach is applicable to the Old Testament. It is not enough to recognize a unit or given literary genre. One must also consider its function within the larger work of which it forms a part. Thus, the various episodes in the book of Judges have been brought together to contribute to a higher unity, the theme of which is clearly enunciated in ch. 2 of that book: the cycle of apostasy, enslavement, repentance, and deliverance (Jg.2.16–20). As the annotation on this passage states, the author "wishes his readers to understand that the history he is about to relate teaches the lesson that Israel was prosperous and free only when she was loyal to her God." Indeed, the book of Judges itself is a part of a larger composition: Joshua, Judges, 1–2 Samuel, 1–2 Kings. This corpus has been given the name "Deuteronomistic History," because it interprets the history of Israel from Joshua to the Exile in the light of the teaching of the book of Deuteronomy (see the Introductions to Judges and Kings). It is interesting, furthermore, to compare the treatment given to a particular unit by the Deuteronomistic historians with that accorded by the Chronicler in his history. In 2 Sam.24.1, the bare fact is recorded that "the anger of the LORD was kindled against Israel, and he incited David against them. . . ." And David is condemned for taking a census on this occasion. But in 1 Chr.21.1 we read, "Satan stood up against Israel, and incited David to number Israel." The point of view of the redactor has shaped the text — hence the name, redaction criticism.

4. Transmission (or Tradition) History

Another term that is frequently used in this kind of study of the biblical text is "transmission history" (*Überlieferungsgeschichte;* also called "tradition history," *Traditionsgeschichte*). This means the recognition of the growth and gradual formation of the stories that have been handed down — from simple forms in the beginning, to large complexes

that can be recognized in the books as we now have them. Thus, the manner in which the Yahwist writer in the J document has put together the material belonging to pre-history (Gen.2–11), and has also worked out the sequence of the patriarchal narratives (e.g., that of Abraham), can come alive by the study of the history of the transmission of a unit. And very often this kind of analysis lends itself to conclusions about the history of Israel and its beliefs, enabling us to date certain ideas and movements as very old or as relatively late.

5. Summary

Current biblical scholarship employs all the methods which we have briefly described. It is concerned to determine the given literary genre of a biblical book or most often a given section of it (form criticism). Further, it may be possible to discover how this genre was handed down (transmission history), and came to be incorporated by a collector or editor (redaction criticism) into a continuous narrative, and ultimately became part of a written document (literary criticism). The methods do not exclude one another; in fact, they are mutually complementary. But they are not merely methods; they are not intellectual exercises for an elite. Every perceptive reader of the Bible can profit from the several approaches. We shall try to illustrate the advantages in the case of the Decalogue.

The literary genre of the Decalogue can be described as apodictic law. As opposed to casuistic law, which stipulates a course of action in given circumstances, the apodictic law is a forceful command or prohibition. There are several such laws in the Old Testament (for example, Ex.23.1–9; Lev.18.6–23). A motive clause may be appended to a law, as in the case of the sabbath law and honoring one's parents. Unfortunately, there is as yet no way of tracing the history of the development of the Decalogue, even though we can make many worthwhile observations about it. As is well known, there is more than one version of it: Ex.20.1–17, and Dt.5.6–22. A comparison of the two passages reveals something of the transmission history.

In general, the Decalogue in Deuteronomy is couched in language that is characteristic of this book: "as the LORD your God commanded you" (5.12–16; compare 4.5; 5.32); "that it may go well with you in the land which the LORD your God gives you" (5.16,

29; 6.18). The familiar sabbath law is strengthened in Deuteronomy ("observe") as against Exodus ("remember"). A more striking difference is the motive clause: creation in six days and rest on the seventh (Ex.20.11), in contrast to the Exodus from Egypt (Dt.5.15). Originally, one may presume, there was no motive given; in the course of time, two different motives were offered.

The treatment of the second commandment is particularly interesting. The prohibition of a graven image (Ex.20.4; Dt.5.8) referred originally to an image of the LORD (see Ex. 34.17). But both versions of the Decalogue, by adding the phrase "the likeness of anything . . . ," refer the prohibition to images of other gods — presumably at a time when *this* was the great temptation. The continuation, "you shall not bow down to them or serve them" refers now to the "other gods," and thus the second commandment stands in the shadow of the first; the prohibition of images (of the LORD) and of foreign gods is viewed as one and the same. The "false witness" in Ex.20.16 and Dt.5.20 calls for comment. In the Deuteronomy passage "false witness" is, more literally, "vain witness" (empty, and eventually, deceitful). One may reasonably surmise that the form in Exodus is the original. It is found frequently outside the Decalogue (for example, Ps.27.12; Pr.6.19), whereas "vain witness" is found only in the Deuteronomic version of the Decalogue.

We may conclude, then, that the form of the Decalogue has had a complicated transmission history. What is suggested by the fact that it is found in two different books? The form in Exodus has the flavor of the editing given to the Deuteronomistic history (Joshua to Kings): Egypt is "the house of bondage" (Ex.20.2); reverence for "the name of the LORD your God" (Ex.20.70). The import of

such touches is to include the Decalogue within the sweep of Israel's salvation history as it is presented here. In Deuteronomy the role of the Decalogue is slightly different — it has become the sovereign will of God, mediated through Moses in a farewell speech. It is followed by the Deuteronomic code (Dt. chaps. 12–26), which serves as a commentary on, or interpretation of, this Decalogue. But this life-setting of the Decalogue within the framework of the book of Deuteronomy is not necessarily the life-setting which the Decalogue had in the life of Israel. Here we are on somewhat uncertain ground. But it seems safe to say that *one* life-setting for the Decalogue has been the cult, perhaps at the covenant renewal ceremony, or the Feast of Tabernacles.

We have discussed the Decalogue merely as an example of how literary analysis of a biblical text can proceed. Basically the same approach can be used throughout the Old and New Testaments. And the reader will find Bible reading more challenging, as well as more informative, if he studies the text along these lines. He will understand how truly the Old Testament is a precipitate, as it were, from the life of Israel, the People of God. Similarly, the role of the Church in the formation of the New Testament, especially the Gospels, will stand out. We have not mentioned the Pauline Epistles, but the reader will not fail to be impressed with the manner in which the "good news" is mediated by Paul, in contrast to the way in which it is presented in the four Gospels. In short, there is no book, or part of a book, in the Bible that does not have a literary form and a history behind its incorporation and transmission within the Scriptures. If we pay attention to this aspect of biblical literature, we shall be well on our way to understanding it.

CHARACTERISTICS OF HEBREW POETRY

I. POETRY IN THE BIBLE

Hebrew poetry has had a long and varied history, extending from the beginnings of Israel's life up to modern times. The earliest phases are represented by the poetical parts of the Old Testament. These are, in relation to the total extent of the Old Testament, quite substantial: Psalms, Proverbs, Song of Solomon, Lamentations, almost the whole of Job, much of the prophetic literature, and many passages in the narrative literature (e.g., Ex.15.1–18; Jg.5.2–31). In all, this amounts to about one third of the Old Testament; but it is presumably only a fraction of the entire body of Hebrew poetry produced during the Old Testament period. The Hebrew poetic tradition is continued in the Apocrypha (Wisdom of Solomon, Sirach, and several passages in other books (e.g., Judith), and in parts of the Pseudepigrapha and of the literature of the Qumran sect (the Dead Sea Scrolls). In the New Testament much of the teaching of Jesus is expressed in poetic form; and there are passages of poetry in Lk.1–2 and in several other books, notably Revelation.

It is significant that the Hebrew poetic form is clear even when the poems have been transmitted in Greek. In translating from one language to another there is the double problem of reproducing both the spirit and the form of the original. For technical reasons, and because of the dissimilarity between poetic structure in different languages, it may be difficult to reproduce the form satisfactorily. In order to preserve and communicate the spirit, it is often necessary in translation to adopt a different poetic form, or even to translate into rhythmical prose. The many attempts which have been made to render the *Iliad* and the *Odyssey* into English verse and prose show how formidable the undertaking can be. In some ways the translation of ancient Hebrew poetry presents a less intractable problem, because its formal characteristics are in the main simple and flexible.

II. THE FORMS OF HEBREW POETRY

Although there are gaps in our knowledge of the forms of ancient Hebrew poetry, and important points are still open to dispute, its general structure is sufficiently clear. Three main formal characteristics have been attributed to it: A. Parallelism; B. Meter; C. Strophic Arrangement.

A. Parallelism

This feature (sometimes referred to also as "thought rhyme") is a balance not only of form but also of the thought between successive members in a poem. The terminology applied to these members varies considerably, but in this article the poetic unit printed as a line in the Revised Standard Version will be called a "stich" (Gr. *stichos*, "line"), and combinations of two and three of these units will be termed "distichs" and "tristichs" respectively. A distich is a couplet of two lines, and a tristich is a three-line poetic unit. The following from Ps.19.1 is a distich, or couplet, in which this balance of thought and form is evident:

> The heavens are telling the glory of God;
> and the firmament proclaims his handiwork.

As an example of a tristich we may take Ps.100.1:

> Make a joyful noise to the LORD, all the lands!
> Serve the LORD with gladness!
> Come into his presence with singing!

Parallelism appears in four main forms: (1) Synonymous, (2) Antithetic, (3) Formal, (4) Climactic; and it may be (5) Internal or External, and (6) Complete or Incomplete.

(1) In Synonymous Parallelism the same thought is expressed in successive stichs; for example,

> The ox knows its owner,
>> and the ass its master's crib. (Is.1.3a)

and

> But let justice roll down like waters,
>> and righteousness like an ever-flowing stream. (Am.5.24)

In these distichs, the second stich simply repeats the sense of the first in slightly different terms.

(2) In Antithetic Parallelism the thought expressed in the second stich is in contrast to that in the first; for example,

> for the LORD knows the way of the righteous,
>> but the way of the wicked will perish. (Ps.1.6)

and

> A wise son makes a glad father,
>> but a foolish son is a sorrow to his mother. (Pr.10.1)

This type of parallelism is particularly characteristic of the Wisdom Literature. It also occurs frequently in the sayings of Jesus; for example,

> A sound tree cannot bear evil fruit,
>> nor can a bad tree bear good fruit. (Mt.7.18)

and

> He who finds his life will lose it,
>> and he who loses his life for my sake will find it. (Mt.10.39)

(3) Formal Parallelism, also called Synthetic Parallelism, contains neither repetition in different terms nor contrasted assertions. In it the thought of the first stich is carried further and completed in the second; for example,

> The LORD looks down from heaven
>> upon the children of men. (Ps.14.2a)

Here there is a formal balance of clause with clause, but no such correspondence in content as we find in Synonymous and Antithetic Parallelism. The balance is emphasized by two factors: the clearly marked caesura or break between the stichs, and the correspondence in rhythm or meter (see below, section B).

(4) In Climactic Parallelism the characteristics of Synonymous and Formal Parallelism are combined. The second stich echoes or repeats part of the first and also adds to it an element which carries forward or completes the sense; for example,

> Ascribe to the LORD, O heavenly beings,
>> ascribe to the LORD glory and strength. (Ps. 29.1)

and

> Pray to your Father who is in secret;
>> and your Father who sees in secret will reward you. (Mt.6.6b)

(5) All the examples quoted above are instances of Internal Parallelism, in which the balance of form and thought is between the individual stichs within a distich or tristich. In External Parallelism there is balance not only *within* but *between* distichs. So in Is.1.27–28:

[1524]

> Zion shall be redeemed by justice,
>   and those in her who repent, by righteousness.
> But rebels and sinners shall be destroyed together,
>   and those who forsake the LORD shall be consumed.

There is here Internal Synonymous Parallelism *within* each of the two distichs and External Antithetic Parallelism *between* the distichs. Compare Is.1.10:

> Hear the word of the LORD,
>   you rulers of Sodom!
> Give ear to the teachings of our God,
>   you people of Gomorrah!

By contrast, here each distich has Internal Formal Parallelism, and there is External Parallelism between the distichs. External Parallelism gives scope for still more elaborate patterns, as in Ps.30.8–10:

> To thee, O LORD, I cried;
>   and to the LORD I made supplication;
> "What profit is there in my death,
>   if I go down to the Pit?
> Will the dust praise thee?
>   Will it tell of thy faithfulness?
> Hear, O LORD, and be gracious to me!
>   O LORD, be thou my helper!"

The first, third, and fourth distichs have Internal Synonymous Parallelism, but the second has Internal Formal Parallelism. There is External Synonymous Parallelism between the first and fourth distichs and between the second and third, giving the pattern a, b, b, a.

(6) Complete Parallelism occurs when each term in the first stich is matched by a corresponding term in the second, as in the following example from Psalm 146.2:

> I-will-praise the-LORD as-long-as-I-live;
>   I-will-sing-praises to-my-God while-I-have-being.

(The hyphens link words which together represent a single term in the Hebrew.) In Incomplete Parallelism one or more terms in the first stich have no counterpart in the second, as in the following:

> Our-inheritance has-been-turned-over to-strangers,
>   our-homes to-aliens. (Lam.5.2)

Here there is nothing in the second stich to correspond to "has-been-turned-over" in the first. Incomplete Parallelism may occur without compensation, as in the example just given, or with compensation, as in Lam.5.11:

> Women are-ravished in-Zion,
>   virgins in-the-towns-of Judah.

In this verse the second stich contains no counterpart to "are-ravished" in the first, but the *two* terms "in-the-towns-of" and "Judah" in the second stich correspond to the *one* term "in-Zion" in the first.

These varied forms of parallelism provide almost innumerable possibilities of changing poetic patterns. One feature, however, remains constant. In a distich or tristich each stich is separated from what follows or precedes by an emphatic rhythmic break (a caesura); there may be a completion of the sense in what follows, but there is always a marked pause. The feature

[1525]

known as enjambement (running over without rhetorical pause from one line to another so that closely related words fall in different lines) is foreign to Hebrew poetry.

Even a superficial study of the poetic parts of the Bible make it abundantly clear that parallelism is a formal characteristic of Hebrew poetry; and this is further borne out by the fact that the same feature also appears in other ancient Near Eastern literatures. There is, unfortunately, less clarity about the second formal characteristic, namely meter.

B. Meter

It is reasonable to suppose that parallelism is complemented by metrical or rhythmical patterns and that each stich is composed of a number of metrical units. But the evidence about the nature of the patterns of meter from ancient Near Eastern parallels and from writers such as Josephus, Origen, and Jerome is inadequate. Of the varied theories which have been advanced in modern times the one which commands the widest agreement is that the meter is determined in terms of accented syllables and that the number of unaccented syllables is of no significance. This means that as a rule each word counts as one unit; but where a word has a secondary accent in addition to the main one, it counts as two units, and where a word loses its accent because of its close connection with the following word, it does not count as a unit. The metrical value of a stich is indicated by the number of stressed syllables which it contains. By far the most frequent metrical pattern is 3 + 3, that is, a distich with three stressed syllables in each stich. This is the characteristic meter of Hebrew proverbs; and it abounds in the Wisdom Literature, but it is also very frequent in some parts of the prophetic books and in the Psalms. The following example is from Wisdom Literature:

> Mán that-is-bórn of-a-wóman
> is-of-féw dáys, and-full-of-tróuble.
> He-comes-fórth like-a-flówer, and-wíthers;
> he-flées like-a-shádow and-contínues-not. (Job 14.1–2)

The shorter 2 + 2 meter is well adapted to the expression of intense emotion and urgency; for example,

> Céase to-do-évil,
> léarn to-do-góod;
> séek jústice,
> córrect oppréssion;
> defénd the-fátherless,
> pléad for-the-wídow. (Is.1.16d–17)

The unequal metrical pattern 3 + 2 is known as the Qinah ("lament") meter, because it is the prevailing meter used in the book of Lamentations and occurs frequently in laments, although it is not confined to this type of composition. The unfulfilled expectation of a third beat in the second stich creates a peculiarly haunting effect. So in the two following passages:

> Fállen, no-móre to-ríse,
> is-the-vírgin Ísrael. (Amos 5.2a)

> Give-éar-to my-wórds, O-Lórd;
> give-héed-to my-gróaning.
> Héarken to-the-sound-of my-crý,
> my-kíng and-my-Gód. (Ps.5.1–2b)

Other metrical patterns which occur less frequently are 4 + 4, 2 + 2 + 2, 3 + 3 + 3. The last of these is memorably illustrated in a familiar psalm:

Líft-up your-héads, O-gátes!
and-be-lífted-up, O-áncient dóors!
that-the-Kíng-of glóry may-come-ín.
Whó-is the-Kíng-of glóry?
The-LÓRD, stróng and-míghty,
the-LÓRD, míghty in-báttle! (Ps.24.7–8)

A Hebrew poem is not necessarily composed in a single meter throughout. Indeed, the variation of meter can be most effective. A good instance of this is Ps.46, in which 4 + 4 meter predominates (verses 1–2, 4–6, 8–10), with 3 + 3 distichs rounding off each section (verses 3, 7, 11), so that the metrical pattern suggests that the poem is constructed in three stanzas.

C. Strophic Arrangement

Ps.46 is by no means the only poem in the Old Testament in which a recurring refrain appears to indicate a grouping of distichs or tristichs into larger patterns resembling stanzas. For instance, in Pss.42 and 43 (which form one psalm), the following refrain occurs at 42.5, 11, and 43.5:

Why are you cast down, O my soul,
and why are you disquieted within me?
Hope in God; for I shall again praise him,
my help and my God.

Again in Is.9.8–10.4 and 5.25–30, which are probably parts of a single poem, the following refrain appears to mark off recognizable stanzas:

For all this his anger is not turned away
and his hand is stretched out still.
(9.12b, 17c, 21b; 10.4b; 5.25c)

Ps.107.1–32 contains the double refrain,

Then they cried to the LORD in their trouble,
and he delivered them from their distress; . . .
Let them thank the LORD for his steadfast love,
for his wonderful works to the sons of men!

at verses 6, 8, 13, 15, 19, 21, 28, 31; but it does not mark off regular strophes.

Strophic arrangement is the least convincing of the formal characteristics attributed to Hebrew poetry. Some Hebrew poems do indeed fall into recognizable sections; but, with the exception of poems of a special type (see below, section III, A), these sections are not strictly regular. Moreover, the term "strophe" is inappropriate, since it implies the recurrence of regular metrical patterns in a fixed number of poetic lines. All the indications are that such rigid structures were alien to ancient Hebrew poetry, which in meter and in the grouping of distichs and tristichs was as flexible as it manifestly was in the use of parallelism.

III. THE TECHNIQUES OF HEBREW POETRY

In addition to the structural forms of Hebrew poetry, certain technical devices were used to secure particular effects. These are: A. Acrostic Patterns; B. Alliteration; C. Assonance; D. Paranomasia.

A. Acrostic Patterns

The sole instances of deliberately contrived sequences of lines (see above, II, C) are acrostic poems. Acrostic patterns occur in varying degrees of complexity. In Ps.34.1–21 the successive verses begin with the letters of the Hebrew alphabet in the appropriate order (verse 22 is outside the pattern). Pss.9 and 10 form a single poem with an imperfectly preserved acrostic pattern in which pairs of verses begin with successive letters of the Hebrew alphabet. Varied acrostic patterns appear in Lam.1; 2; 3; 4: in 1; 2; and 3 the distichs are grouped in threes (in 3 *all* the distichs in a given group begin with the same letter; in 1 and 2 only the first distich in each group) and in 4 the grouping is in pairs. The most elaborate acrostic poem in the Bible is Ps.119, in which there are twenty-two sections (corresponding to the successive letters of the alphabet) each consisting of eight distichs, and every distich in a given section begins with the same letter.

Various reasons have been suggested for the adoption of this somewhat exacting technical pattern: to serve as a mnemonic device; to exploit the supposed magical power of an alphabetic acrostic; or to express completeness of grief, aspiration, penitence, hope, or devotion. The last of these would be particularly appropriate to Ps.119 and the acrostics in the book of Lamentations.

B. Alliteration

Effect is sometimes gained by the juxtaposition of words or syllables which begin with the same consonant; for example, in Ps.122.6–7, where *sh* and *l* recur:

> *sha'ălu shĕlom Yĕrushalayim*
> *yishlayu 'ohăbhayikh*
> *yĕhi shalom bĕḥelekh*
> *shalwah bĕ'armĕnothayikh.*

Similarly, in Ps.93.4 the occurrence of doubled consonants and particularly of *m*, brings out effectively the menacing reverberation of the flood waters:

> *miqqoloth mayim rabbim*
> *'addir mimmishbĕre yam*
> *'addir bammarom Yahweh.*

C. Assonance

There is no systematic use of rhyme in ancient Hebrew poetry; but the recurrence of the same vowel sound is often deliberately contrived. Where this occurs in suffixes such as *-enu* ("our," "us") and *-ehu* ("it"), something approximating to rhyme appears. Thus in Ps.90.17 we find

> *wihi no'am 'ădhonay 'ĕlohenu 'alenu*
> *uma'aseh yadhenu konenah 'alenu*
> *uma'aseh yadhenu konĕnehu.*

In Is.53.4–5 the echoing suffixes *-enu* ("our") and *-hu* ("him") produce a wailing effect and also, together with the emphatic repetition of the pronoun *hu'* ("he") and the final *lanu* ("for us"), bring out the contrast between the Servant and those for whom he suffered.

D. Onomatopoeia

The use of words which sound like what they describe has already been illustrated from Ps.93.4 (see above, section III, B). Another outstanding example of this is the description in the Song of Deborah of the thudding hoofs of galloping horses:

> *'az ḥalĕmu 'iqqebhe sus*
> *middahăroth dahăroth 'abbiraw* (Jg.5.22)

E. Paranomasia

A pointed play on words occurs more frequently in the Bible than is evident from an English rendering. In predicting national disaster Amos makes an effective play on the name "Gilgal" and the verb *galah* ("go into exile"):

> *ki haggilgal galoh yighleh.*

Again, when Amos sees a basket of "summer fruit" (*qayiṣ*) it is a token that the 'end' (*qeṣ*) is coming on Israel (Am.8.12). Isaiah says that God looked for 'justice' (*mishpaṭ*) and 'righteousness' (*ṣĕdhaqah*) but found only 'bloodshed' (*mispaḥ*) and the 'cry' (*ṣĕ'aqah*) of the oppressed (Is.5.7b). In Jer.31.16–19 the words "come back," "bring back," "be restored," "turned away" all come from the same verb (*shubh*). It is probably impossible to reproduce in translation this sustained play on similar and contrasted meanings.

IV. CONCLUSION

The supreme quality of ancient Hebrew poetry is seen in the concentrated expression, within a limited compass, of experience, emotion, and aspiration. This is seen in the ancient war songs and dirges, the love poems in the Song of Songs, many of the hymns, laments, and thanksgivings in the Psalter, and in the terse oracles of Amos and of Isaiah of Jerusalem. Apart from Job and (probably) Isa.40–55, there is no sustained poetic composition of any great length in the Old Testament, and nothing which is epic in character. Though the tradition of the Psalmists is continued in the later period, e.g., in the poems in Lk.1–2 and (with significant differences) the Qumran *Hymns of Thanksgiving*, it is on the whole the didactic and reflective notes which tend to predominate, as in Sirach and the Wisdom of Solomon. In the sayings of Jesus the form and spirit of classical prophecy and of Wisdom are fused in a new and creative manifestation of the Hebrew poetic genius.

LITERARY FORMS IN THE GOSPELS

An analysis of the teaching of Jesus reported in the four Gospels reveals a variety of literary forms. Sometimes he conveyed his teaching by means of parables; at other times he used proverbs and plays on words (puns). Many passages in the Gospels are arranged in strophic, or poetic, form, and frequently one is struck by the vigorous, picturesque language by which the teaching is conveyed. Examples within each of these catagories, considered in reverse order, include the following.

§ 1 **Picturesque speech.** Like other persons of the Near East, Jesus made use of striking contrasts and vivid metaphors. Using exaggerated and colorful expressions, he frequently drew attention to the ridiculous and the illogical behavior of the self-righteous. For example, instead of saying in prosaic and commonplace terms that some people are inconsistent when judging others and themselves, Jesus put it thus:

Why do you see the speck that is in your brother's eye, but do not notice the log that is in your own eye?... You hypocrite, first take the log out of your own eye, and then you will see clearly to take the speck out of your brother's eye (Mt.7.3,5).

By taking into account the presence of picturesque expression in the Gospels the reader can sometimes avoid misinterpreting the meaning. For example, the hard saying preserved in the third Gospel, "If any one comes to me and does not hate his own father and mother and wife and children and brothers and sisters, yes, and even his own life, he cannot be my disciple" (Lk.14.26), must be understood in the light of the frequent use of overstatement as characteristic of the speech of Near Easterners. It is obvious that Jesus, so far from intending to increase the sum total of hatred in the world, states a principle in a startling, hyperbolic manner, and leaves it to his hearers to discover whatever qualifications are necessary in the light of his other pronouncements. The saying means that if one is to be a follower of Jesus, he must be prepared to choose between natural affection and loyalty to his Master. The same idea is expressed in Matthew's less rigorous version of Jesus' saying: "He who loves father or mother more than me is not worthy of me, and he who loves son or daughter more than me is not worthy of me" (Mt.10.37).

One should, of course, be alert to the danger of diluting Jesus' teaching by finding overstatement in passages where it is not present. For example, Jesus' command to the rich man who inquired what he should do to inherit eternal life, "Sell all that you have and distribute to the poor, and you will have treasure in heaven; and come, follow me" (Lk.18.22), should not be discounted as exaggerated hyperbole, meaning merely, "Sell ten percent of what you have...." The context makes it absolutely clear that the questioner as well as the disciples understood Jesus' words in their literal sense.

§ 2 **Poetic, rhythmical parallelism.** Hebrew poetry, illustrated in the Old Testament Psalter, is characterized by parallelism of members. Sometimes the parallelism is synonymous and sometimes antithetic (see pp. 1523–24).

In view of the frequency of Jesus' quotations from and allusions to the Psalms, it is not surprising that we find much of his teaching cast into the mold of Semitic poetry. Synonymous parallelism appears in the saying recorded in Lk.6.26–27:

Love your enemies,
  do good to those who hate you,
  bless those who curse you,
  pray for those who abuse you.

Antithetic parallelism is illustrated by Mt. 7.17–18:

Every sound tree bears good fruit,
  but the bad tree bears evil fruit.
A sound tree cannot bear evil fruit,
  nor can a bad tree bear good fruit.

Besides these two basic types of parallelism, several other kinds have been identified. What is called step parallelism, for example, occurs when the second line takes up a thought contained in the first line and, repeating it, makes it, as it were, a step toward the development of a further thought, which is the climax of the whole. An example of step parallelism is found in Lk.9.48 (the italics indicate the repeated member which serves as a step, and the vertical line stands before the climax):

Whoever receives this child in my name
  receives me,

and whoever receives me | receives him
who sent me.

For other passages that exhibit an elaborate
rhythmical pattern, see Mt.6.19–21; 23.16–22;
Mk.2.21–22; 9.43–48; Lk.11.31–32; 17.26–30.

§ **3 Plays on words.** The Old Testament
contains not a few instances of plays on
words (for examples see pp. 1528f. and the
notes on Gen.11.9; Jer.1.11–12; Am.8.1–2).
The text of the Gospels, which has been transmitted to us in Greek, contains more than one
instance where the original Aramaic of Jesus'
mother tongue probably involved a word-play.
It is understandable that very few such puns
in Aramaic could be reproduced in Greek.
In one case, however, it happens that the
Greek word *pneuma*, just as the Aramaic
rūhâ, means both "wind" and "spirit." In
Jn.3.8 Jesus is quoted as saying to Nicodemus,
"The *pneuma* blows where it wills, and you
hear the sound of it, but you do not know
whence it comes or whither it goes; so it is
with everyone who is born of the *pneuma*."

One of the most noteworthy of Jesus'
sayings about the church involves a play on
words. According to Mt.16.13ff. at Caesarea
Philippi, in response to Jesus' question to his
disciples who they thought he was, Simon
Peter confessed, "You are the Christ, the Son
of the living God." After declaring that
Peter had spoken this by divine revelation,
Jesus retorted, "And I tell you, you are Peter
[Greek *Petros*], and on this rock [Greek *petra*]
I will build my church." In Jesus' mother
tongue the play is even closer, for in Aramaic
the word *kēphâ* serves as a proper name
(Cephas) and also means "a rock, a stone."
Jesus' statement therefore would have been,
"And I tell you, you are *Kēphâ*, and on this
kēphâ I will build my church" (there remains
a difference in gender, for the common noun
is feminine and the proper name is, of course,
masculine; compare French *pierre* (f.), "a
stone," and *Pierre* (m.), "Peter").

Another passage which probably involved a
pun is Mt.23.24, where the Greek text is unable to reproduce the jingle that is present in
what is presumed to be the original Aramaic.
In his condemnation of the inconsistency of
certain scribes and Pharisees, Jesus reproached them for "straining out a gnat and
swallowing a camel." Since in Aramaic the
word for "gnat" or "louse" is *qalmâ* and the
word for "camel" is *gamlâ*, the pun provides
added piquancy to the picturesque speech used
by Jesus: he is describing a punctilious
Pharisee who, in view of Lev.11.41ff., which
forbids the eating of what swarms or crawls

on the earth, is careful to strain out a *qalmâ*
that may have fallen into his food or wine,
but is quite unconcerned over gulping down
a whole *gamlâ*!

§ **4 Proverbs.** Every language has pithy
sayings or maxims that express a truth crisply
and forcefully. Because proverbs frequently
express only one side of a truth, it happens
that mutually contradictory proverbs may
circulate, each of which is true when applied
to the appropriate life-setting. The common
saying, "Penny wise, pound foolish," correctly describes one who is scrupulous about
small transactions, but extravagant in great
ones. On the other hand, the proverb, "Take
care of the pennies, and the dollars will take
care of themselves," is also true. More than
once the Bible presents two proverbs which,
though contradictory, are both true when
applied to appropriate circumstances. In Pr.
26.4 the writer cautions his reader, "Answer
not a fool according to his folly, lest you be
like him yourself"; in the very next verse,
however, he advises, "Answer a fool according
to his folly, lest he be wise in his own eyes."
It is left to the reader to know when it is
appropriate to heed one or the other of these
two antithetical proverbs.

It is not surprising that Jesus sometimes
cast his teaching in the form of proverbs.
Since, however, these brief, salty sayings
stress one side of a truth, they should not be
exalted as maxims of inflexible conduct. On
the contrary, one categorical statement must
be interpreted in the light of another that may
counsel the opposite of the first. For example,
Jesus' command, "Judge not, that you be not
judged" (Mt.7.1), has sometimes been taken
as a blanket prohibition against making judgments concerning right and wrong, good and
evil. In the same context, however, the
evangelist includes another of Jesus' pithy
sayings, one which presupposes the necessity
of forming judgments: "Do not give dogs
what is holy; and do not throw your pearls
before swine" (Mt.7.6). To obey this command against desecrating what is holy, one
obviously must judge who is doggish and who
is swinish. Spiritual prudence will know when
it is appropriate to follow one precept and
when it is appropriate to follow the other.

Similarly Jesus' proverb-like prohibition,
"Do not resist one who is evil" (Mt.5.39), is
not to be taken to mean that his disciples are
never to resist evil in any kind of way. In the
light of Jesus' other teachings as well as his
use of force to drive out the money-changers
from the temple precincts (Mk.12.15), it is

clear that the principle which he inculcates in this crisp maxim is non-retaliation for a malicious wrong inflicted by a personal enemy.

§ **5 Parables.** In all the teaching of Jesus there is no feature more striking than the parables. Although other religious teachers had made use of parabolic stories (see Jg. 9.7–15; 2 Sam.12.1–6), in quantity and in excellence his parables are acknowledged to be outstanding. About sixty examples, from what was probably a larger number, have been preserved in the synoptic Gospels. The fourth Gospel nowhere uses the word "parable," but it contains several parabolic sayings in the form of allegories (for example, Jn.10.1–18; 15.1–11).

The old definition of a parable as "an earthly story with a heavenly meaning" contains a certain amount of truth, but one must beware against seeking an elaborate allegorical meaning for every detail in a parable. That is, many details in Jesus' parables are present in order to make the story "live," and were not included primarily to instruct or edify the hearer. Defined more precisely, in Jesus' teaching a parable is a comparison drawn from nature or common experience in life and designed to illustrate some moral or religious truth, on the assumption that what is valid in one sphere is valid also in the other. The distinctions between parable and simile and metaphor are not easily defined. Often there is scarcely any difference, for all of them involve an aspect of comparison, but generally the metaphor and simile are short while the parable is more extended. "You are the salt of the earth" (Mt.5.13) is a metaphor; "Be wise as serpents" (Mt.10.16) is a simile; but "The kingdom of heaven is like leaven which a woman took and hid in three measures of meal, till it was all leavened" (Mt.13.33) is a parable.

The proper method of interpreting Jesus' parables is to make a thorough inquiry into the "life-setting" in his ministry when the parable was first uttered, and to seek out the chief point which, in that setting, it was intended to teach. In other words, To whom did Jesus speak the parable? and, Why did he speak it? Usually the details in a parable provide nothing more than the necessary background in order to make the story realistic, and are not to be assigned, point by point, special meanings in the manner of an allegory. An analysis of Jesus' parables reveals that most of them are intended either (*a*) to portray a type of human character or disposition for

warning or example, or (*b*) to reveal a principle of God's government of the world and men. In other words, Jesus' parables usually teach a certain kind of conduct which his hearers are to emulate or avoid (matters of ethics), or they disclose something of the character of God and his dealings with men (matters of theology). Examples of the former class of parables include The Two Builders (Mt.7.24–27), The Two Sons (Mt.21.28–32), The Pharisee and the Tax Collector (Lk. 18.9–14), and The Good Samaritan (Lk. 10.30–37); examples of the latter include the several parables concerning the Kingdom of Heaven (Mt. chap. 13; 20.1–15), The Seed Growing Secretly (Mk.4.26–29), The Great Supper (Lk.14.16–24), and The Lost Coin (Lk.15.8–10).

Finally, it should be observed that when Christian teachers and evangelists retold Jesus' parables in the early church, they occasionally introduced small changes so as to apply the stories to new situations or to bring out the application more vividly. An example of the latter is the slight modification in the order of the wording in Matthew and Luke's retelling of the parable of The Wicked Tenants. According to Mark 12.8, when the owner of the vineyard sent his son to the tenants to get some of the fruit, they "killed him, and cast him out of the vineyard." Matthew and Luke, however, finding in the parable a parallel to what happened to Jesus when he was crucified *outside* the city walls, altered the sequence of the clauses so as to read, "they cast him out of the vineyard, and killed him" (Mt.21.39; Lk.20.15).

There was also a tendency to turn parables that Jesus addressed to the crowd or to opponents, into parables for the disciples. For example, according to Luke (15.4–10) Jesus told the parable of the Lost Sheep as an answer to criticisms leveled against him by Pharisees and scribes (15.2). When Matthew recounts the same parable (18.12–14), however, it is no longer addressed to Jesus' opponents; it has now become part of Jesus' instruction to his disciples (18.1), that is, to the church, on the subject of how Christians are to relate to other Christians (cf. 18.15–17).

In other cases the parables of Jesus were remembered long after the circumstances that gave rise to them had been forgotten. More than once, therefore, we find that the Evangelists, impressed by the sublimity of Jesus' teaching, recount his parables without mentioning the specific situation in which they were first narrated.

SURVEY OF THE GEOGRAPHY, HISTORY, AND
ARCHAEOLOGY OF THE BIBLE LANDS

1. THE LANDS

§ 1 **Lands of the Near East.** Seen from the tower of the Russian monastery on the Mount of Olives, Palestine looks like a gable roof pitching eastward and westward. The north-south road, which from the days of old has linked together the highland towns and villages, runs straight along the roof top. To the east barren hills slope down gently at first, and soon precipitously, toward the deep rift of the Jordan valley and of the Dead Sea, the northeastern shore of which is in full sight. The eastern sky line is formed by the Transjordan ridge, which marks the limit of the Syrian desert. On the western horizon the Mediterranean Sea and the coastal plain are visible in the distant haze, while the western slopes of the highlands, past Jerusalem and its suburbs, remain partly hidden, owing to the steep descent.

Toward the south the barren expanses and parched hills of the Negeb isolate Palestine from the countries adjoining the Red Sea: Arabia, the Sinai peninsula wedged between the Gulf of 'Aqaba and the Gulf of Suez, and the lands of the Nile, accessible by way of the isthmus which bridges Asia and Africa. The Negeb thus had economic and strategic importance, for it was the gateway to the Middle East by sea or overland route, as well as Egypt's Asiatic frontier, where the soldiers of Pharaoh guarded the approach to the kingdom.

The topography north of the Syrian border somewhat resembles the Palestinian relief with its successive zones running parallel to the shore line. The Syrian system, however, has a different geological origin. The plain along the shore is reduced to a narrow strip interrupted by rocky spurs projecting from the mountainside. The Lebanon range rises abruptly from the seaboard, culminating at 10,131 feet. Passes are few and high. North of Lebanon the coastal range is noticeably lower. The Orontes and the Litani, flowing respectively northward and southward, drain the depression of the Beqa'a, which is the plain or valley between the Lebanon and the Anti-Lebanon mountains and which leads into the Jordan rift. In their lower course, the Orontes and the Litani turn westward at a sharp angle, dramatically breaking through the barrier of the mountains. East of the Beqa'a, Mount Hermon and the Anti-Lebanon range reach altitudes of respectively 9,232 and 8,625 feet, contrasting with the smaller hills fanning out farther to the northeast. Mountain streams flowing eastward (for example the Pharpar and Abana) irrigate the gardens of Damascus and of the villages which line the northwestern reaches of the Syrian desert.

The arc-shaped ranges of the Taurus and Anti-Taurus, broken only by the watergaps through which the Euphrates and the Tigris reach their lower course, isolate the Anatolian plateau from the Syrian tableland and the plains of Mesopotamia. At all times immigrants, invaders, and merchants from the East, heading for the Mediterranean seaboard, have journeyed along the crescent of fertile land which bends around the northern portion of the Syrian desert. The most important migration ever to follow this route was the migration of the Arameans, who settled in the Syrian districts of the interior, while the coastline continued to be held by the seafaring Phoenicians and while wandering Arabs grazed their flocks on the desert pastures. It is in the wake of the Aramean migration that Abraham and his kin made their first appearance in Palestine, which their descendants were to regard as their homeland.

The above geographical survey sets the stage for the struggle of the Empires, amidst which most of the events of Biblical history took place. The first act, in the second millennium, was the drive of the Hittites from Anatolia against Egypt. It resulted ultimately in a stalemate, and Palestine, at first neutralized between the two rivals, achieved political independence under the Hebrew kings. The second phase was marked by the expeditions of the Assyrian and Neo-Babylonian rulers. They failed to establish their domination permanently over Egypt, but the autonomy of the Hebrew states was brought to an end.

§ 2 **The land of Canaan.** Having considered Palestine in its geographical setting, we shall now describe its main natural divisions. The Jordan rift parts the country lengthwise from north to south. Western Palestine, between the sea and the river, is a well-defined unit, while Transjordan has no eastern boundary other than the precarious limit between the desert and the sown. The river Jordan is formed by the union of mountain streams from the eastern and southern slopes of Mount Hermon. For some ten miles it flows through the Huleh basin, the lower part of it forming a shallow lake partly covered by thickets of papyrus. For the next ten miles it descends from an altitude of 223 feet above sea level to 695 feet below sea level, as it enters the Lake of Tiberias, or Sea of Galilee. The lower course of the Jordan is less precipitous. From the Lake of Tiberias to the Dead Sea, 95 miles south as the crow flies and 1,285 feet below sea level, the river meanders in an impenetrable jungle (Jer.12.5) of tamarisks, oleanders, and other shrubs, often less than one mile across, to the right and left of which the terrace of the valley (called today the Ghor or Rift), with its sterile layers of marl, extends to the foot of the Transjordan ridge and of the Palestinian highlands. South of the Dead Sea the desert valley of the Arabah prolongs the Jordan rift toward the south, rising gradually to an altitude of 656 feet above sea level, about halfway between the southern shore of the Dead Sea and the Gulf of 'Aqaba.

The boundaries of ancient regions of the Transjordan ridge are clearly defined by the eastern tributaries of the Jordan and of the Dead Sea: north of the Yarmuk, Bashan; between the Yarmuk and the Jabbok, Gilead; between the Jabbok and the Arnon, the kingdom of Sihon and Ammon; between the Arnon and the Zered, Moab; south of the Zered, Edom.

We turn now to the natural divisions of western Palestine, from north to south. Galilee is bounded on the north by the lower course of the Litani, and on the south by the great plain which cuts diagonally from the sea to the Jordan rift. Upper Galilee reaches an altitude of 3,962 feet at Jebel Jermaq, contrasting with the smaller hills of lower Galilee; Mount Tabor, five miles east of Nazareth, is only 1,929 feet high. The Galilean relief is confused. There is no clear-cut parting of the waters flowing westward to the sea and eastward into the depths of the Jordan valley. The geological dislocation of the Galilean range has resulted in a number of basins and plains locked between rocky ridges, but relatively fertile if properly drained, while numerous olive groves thrive on artificial terraces.

At the foot of the Galilean hills lies the Plain of Esdraelon (or Jezreel), bounded on the south by the Carmel range, the northern edge of the highlands of Samaria, and Mount Gilboa. The central part of the Plain of Esdraelon communicates with the Plain of

Acco through the gap of the River Kishon, between Mount Carmel and a spur of the Galilean hills, and with the Jordan rift. It is a zone of great agricultural wealth and of strategic importance, as evidenced by a row of fortified cities guarding the access to central Palestine and to the Jordan, including Jokneam, Megiddo, Taanach, Ibleam, and Beth-shean.

The highlands of Samaria and Ephraim rise up from the fertile Plain of Sharon to a maximum height of 3,332 feet. Ascending from the Plain of Esdraelon, the road of the highlands linked together Samaria and Shechem, which controlled the pass between Mount Gerizim and Mount Ebal. Farther south the road followed the watershed almost continually, passing at or near Shiloh, Bethel, Mizpah, Ramah, Gibeah, and Jerusalem. From Shechem a path along the Wadi Far'a gave easy access to the Jordan valley, while mountain roads linked Jericho with Bethel

and Jerusalem. The western slopes of Samaria and Ephraim were rich in olive groves and vineyards, the eastern slopes being used as grazing grounds.

The natural divisions of southern Palestine are as follows. (1) The Philistine plain, along the sea. (2) The Shephelah, or Judean lowlands, guarded by the fortress of Lachish. (3) The "Hill Country of Judah," with a maximum altitude of 3,345 feet; the road from Jerusalem to Bethlehem and Hebron follows the watershed most of the time. (4) East of the watershed, the Wilderness of Judah overlooks the precipice of the Dead Sea. (5) The slopes to the south and southwest of the range extend toward the Negeb, without clear-cut limits. The Negeb of Judah and the desert provide extensive grazing grounds. The vineyards of the highlands were famous, and grains were cultivated on a large scale in the Shephelah and in the plain.

2. THE PEOPLE

§ 3 **Anthropological data.** The Israelites referred to the inhabitants of Palestine, whom they conquered in the time of Joshua, as Canaanites. The majority was of Semitic origin. The Bible names several of their clans, together with the remnants of aboriginal populations. Early in the second millennium important elements of non-Semitic peoples, including Hittites of Anatolia and Hurrians (Horites) from the upper course of the Euphrates, settled in Canaan and mingled with the Semites, or retained their separate identity, like the Hittites of Hebron, from whom Abraham purchased the cave of Machpelah (Gen. ch. 23). The Hurrian contribution to Palestinian culture can be shown by a study of names of persons and places as well as by the products of their arts and crafts. There is evidence of Mediterranean influences in Canaanite art as early as 1500 B.C. A century later written documents attest the presence of elements of population from the Aegean area in the coastal regions of Palestine and in the Egyptian fortress-cities of the Plain of Esdraelon. Another wave brought in the Philistines from Crete, who settled on the southern coastal plain and made deep inroads in the districts of the interior, prior to the conquest of Canaan by the Israelites.

§ 4 **Canaanite city-states.** Canaanite settlement followed a pattern of decentraliza-

tion. Small city-states existed side by side in the neutralized no man's land which lay between the overlords of Anatolia and Egypt. The sovereignty of the Pharaohs over Palestine was more nominal than real. They regarded the fortresses of the Plain of Esdraelon and a few posts along the seaboard as adequate for the security of their northern advanced border. For the rest they relied on rivalries among the Canaanite chieftains to make a general rebellion unlikely. The economy of Canaanite Palestine was a rural economy, drawing its resources from agriculture and animal husbandry. Towns were market places and administrative or defense centers, rather than commercial or industrial centers. They contrasted sharply with the Phoenician cities, which subsisted primarily on trade from overseas.

§ 5 **The archaeology of Canaan.** Archaeological excavations have unearthed the remains of Canaanite towns built on hilltops or on some rocky ledge in the fork of two ravines. The area of such towns seldom exceeded twenty acres. Methods of fortification varied with local conditions. Sloping embankments, eventually faced with huge stones, were common. The walls, usually of sun-dried bricks, were built on foundations of field stones on the shoulder of the embankment. They were often reinforced with rectangular towers. Some larger towns and cities had a double line of fortifications, or an acropolis having its own rampart within the perimeter of the city. City gates were as a rule flanked with towers; two or three pairs of massive piers protruded from either side of the gateway, leaving a passage wide enough to admit one or two chariots; wooden doors equipped with bronze hinge pivots revolving in stone sockets closed the passage. The esplanade outside the gate was used as a market place, open air court room, and meeting place for the city elders.

Supplying the city with water was a vital problem. Springs outside the walls could be intercepted by enemies. In order to obviate this danger several cities had underground passages leading from within the city-walls to a spring which could be walled in and concealed from without. It is presumably through the water shaft of the Jebusites that David's warriors conquered Jerusalem (2 Sam.5.8). Cisterns and reservoirs formed by damming up a ravine collected rain water, while regular wells, wherever possible, tapped the underground water table.

Each Canaanite city-state had its place or places of worship, within or without the walls. So-called high places were open air enclosures marking the area sacred to the gods of the city. The divine power was thought to inhabit a pillar of stone, the *masṣebah*, while a row of raised stones symbolized the families or clans of the worshipers. A sacred tree or a wooden post called the *asherah* played a role similar to that of the *masṣebah*. A well or basin and a stone altar completed the main furnishings of the high place. In several instances, small rectangular temples, easily identified by utensils used in sacrificial worship, replaced or supplemented the original high place.

Natural caves in the vicinity of the town and sometimes within its perimeter were used for the burial of the dead. When such caves were not available, tombs were dug out of the rock. They consisted of a vertical shaft, eight to ten feet deep, giving access to one or several burial chambers. The dead were laid out on a layer of pebbles or a bench of hewn stones, and were provided with familiar objects, weapons, utensils, and provisions.

3. THE PEOPLE OF THE COVENANT

§ 6 The Patriarchs. The name "Patriarchs" is given to Abraham, Isaac, and Jacob (Israel) and his sons, for whom the twelve tribes were named. The book of Genesis is our primary source for the history of the Patriarchal era. The narratives appear sometimes in duplicate or even triplicate form, suggesting the use of previous written sources or oral traditions. They refer to the Patriarchs as persons, although it is clear that the history of the Hebrew clans is reflected in the history of their founders.

Within each generation individuals belonging to the same ancestral stock were dropped from the privileged line of descent. They were regarded as the ancestors of related tribes or nations upon which the Israelites looked with suspicion or hostility, while keeping the memory of their common origin. Such were Lot, "father" of the Moabites and Ammonites; Ishmael, "father" of the Arabs; the sons of Abraham by his concubines, who were sent away "eastward to the east country" (Gen.25.6); and Esau, "father" of the Edomites.

One may gather from Genesis that Abraham stemmed from Aramean shepherds and herdsmen from the Fertile Crescent, who frequented the markets of such important centers as Haran and Ur of the Chaldeans. The Aramean origin of the Patriarchs is further evidenced by the linguistic shift from Aramean to Hebrew, as recorded in Genesis: Abram and Sarai changed their names to Abraham and Sarah when they settled in Canaan (Gen.17.5,15). This linguistic evolution was complete in the days of Jacob, who was nicknamed "the Aramean" (Dt.26.5) but who gave the Hebrew name "Galeed" to a stone marker which he erected jointly with his kinsmen, who called it in Aramaic "Jegarsahadutha" (Gen.31.47).

Certain cultural features extant in the Patriarchal narratives have their counterpart in the laws of Hammurabi and in the documents of Nuzi, a Hurian colony in northern Mesopotamia; and tablets dating from the eighteenth century B.C. found at the Amorite city of Mari on the Euphrates illuminate many aspects of the cultural backgrounds of the Patriarchal period.

The Patriarchs and their people can be described as semi-nomads who grazed their flocks of sheep and goats in the unsettled areas of Palestine and came into contact with the sedentary populations when trading their cattle, cheese, butter, and wool for articles manufactured by Canaanite craftsmen. Their activity revolved around a number of centers or encampments generally located in the vicinity of urban markets. Each of these encampments had its place of worship, sacred to the god of the clan, and marked with a sacred tree or grove, in the shadow of which an altar was built or a *maṣṣebah* erected, much in the manner of Canaanite high places.

The main encampments of the Patriarchs are recorded in Genesis: Shechem, their first station in Canaan (Gen.12.6–7); the encampment between Bethel and Ai, where Abram and Lot parted (Gen.12.8; 13.3–11); Mamre, where God appeared to Abraham, a short distance north of Hebron, where the cave of Machpelah became the main burial place of the Patriarchs (Gen.13.18; 18.1; 23.7–20); Beer-sheba in the Negeb, where they concluded an agreement with local rulers concerning grazing rights (Gen.21.25–34).

The Jacob narratives suggest a strong tendency toward a sedentary way of life. On his return from the Aramean countries, Jacob built a house at Succoth in the Jordan valley (Gen.33.17). At Shechem he owned a field and a well (Gen.33.19; compare Jn.4.6). Later he is said to have occupied permanently the encampment at Mamre, while he sent his sons to graze their flocks as far as Dothan in northern Samaria (Gen.35.27; 37.17).

The main historical substance of the story of Joseph and his brothers amounts to the following. A famine drove the Israelites out of Canaan. They descended into Egypt and were resettled in pasture lands on the eastern border of the Delta. The attraction which Egypt exercised upon them is well illustrated by tomb-paintings discovered at Beni-hasan in Middle Egypt, representing a caravan of Semitic immigrants in many-colored robes being introduced to the governor. The welcome received by the sons of Jacob and the elevation of Joseph to a position of authority may suggest that the descent of the Israelites occurred when foreign kings of Asiatic origin, the Hyksos, ruled Egypt.

§ 7 **The days of Moses.** "Now there arose a new king over Egypt, who did not know Joseph." These words in Ex.1.8 refer to the restoration of a national Egyptian dynasty after the expulsion of the Hyksos rulers. Foreigners were regarded with suspicion and hostility. The Israelites were drafted into forced labor under the whip of harsh overseers. A man of the tribe of Levi, Moses, who had to flee for his life after killing one of these Egyptian taskmasters and who sought asylum among Midianite tribesmen, came back to Egypt for the God-inspired purpose of liberating his people. The Israelites fled by night, were miraculously saved from being recaptured by Egyptian forces sent after them, and journeyed to Mount Horeb, or Sinai.

If one assumes Canaan to have been the goal of the Israelites, their march to Horeb through the wild gorges of the peninsula appears preposterous. But we should remember that the Biblical record in no way implies that they chose one of the normal routes from Egypt to Canaan. Nor was their choice guided primarily by strategic considerations. There is ample evidence that Moses' immediate objective was to lead the people to the place where God had ordered them to convene.

The historical contents of the Biblical traditions relative to the covenant at Horeb may be summarized as follows. First, the tribes named after the sons of Jacob (Israel) were for the first time constituted as one nation under the God who had been the protector of the Patriarchs, and whose name Yahweh (see Ex.3.15 note *f*) covered his mysterious identity. Second, the entire legislation of the Israelites had its leading principle in the covenant, established when the Decalogue was given to Moses. There is little doubt that the statutes, eventually revised to meet new situations, originated in the Mosaic institution. They embody provisions already found in legal codes of the ancient Near East, but the integrating factor, namely ethical monotheism, was unique. Third, the religious organization of Israel was derived, as a whole, from the Sinaitic institution. The worship of the nation revolved around the ark of the covenant, which was the monument of God's presence among his people.

The Biblical descriptions of the ark seem to combine two different conceptions. According to one tradition, the ark was a wooden chest in which the stone tables of the Law were kept. Another tradition regarded the ark as the portable throne of God, who was said to reside invisibly between the cherubim. These were two figures facing each other whose wings overshadowed the "mercy seat," which the author of Exodus regarded as identical with, or structurally related to, the lid of the chest.

The most important station of the Israelites

on their journey to Canaan was Kadesh-barnea in the wastelands of the Negeb, on a caravan road from the Isthmus of Suez to Beer-sheba (Num.13.26; 20.1). From Kadesh an exploring party was sent to reconnoiter the border of Canaan, but a direct invasion from the south proved impossible, and the Israelites detoured via Edom and the territory of Moab, from whence they were to strike from the east (Num. chs. 13–14 and ch. 20ff.).

The chronology of the Exodus is far from certain. We do not know who Joseph's Pharaoh was, nor under whose reign the Israelites fled from Egypt. Numerical data in the Bible, such as the forty years' wandering in the wilderness, cannot be related to Egyptian chronology. They belong in a pattern of symbolism, the meaning of which escapes us. The fact that several Canaanite cities were destroyed in the second half of the thirteenth century B.C., in the opinion of leading archaeologists, suggests a general invasion of Canaan, which can possibly be ascribed to the forces of Joshua. This might substantiate the dating of the Exodus during the reign of Rameses II (see Ex. 1.8 n.).

§ 8 **The conquest of Canaan.** The pattern of the conquest as recorded in the book of Joshua is one of grand strategy. After the death of Moses the host of Israel under the command of Joshua marched from their encampment down the ridge of Moab, crossed the Jordan, and captured Jericho and Ai, thus gaining a foothold in the central highlands (Jos. chs. 2–8). From thence a successful campaign against the local chieftains, who had formed a league under Adonizedek, "king" of Jerusalem, gave Joshua control of the south (Jos. ch. 10). A sweeping move northward resulted in the defeat of the "king" of Hazor and his associates in Galilee (Jos.11.1–15).

One suspects some artificiality in this literary scheme. The Old Testament itself suggests that unrelated actions were fought by individual clans or by foreign groups allied to the Israelites, like the Calebites who occupied a district southwest of Hebron (Jos.14. 6–15). Furthermore the book of Judges makes it plain that in several instances the Israelites had been unable to dislodge the Canaanites from their strongholds. An outstanding example was Jerusalem, which remained in the hands of the Jebusites until it was captured by David (Jg.1.19,21).

The settlement of the tribes is described by the author of the book of Joshua, who gives an outline of their borders and a list of their principal cities (Jos. chs. 13–21). Reuben, Gad, and the half of Manasseh settled in Transjordan on lands formerly held by defeated local chieftains, Sihon the Amorite and Og, "king" of Bashan. Asher, Naphtali, Zebulun, and Issachar occupied the districts of Galilee and part of the Plain of Esdraelon. A third group composed of the western half of Manasseh and of Ephraim, jointly known as the "house of Joseph," settled in central Palestine. On the southern border of Ephraim dwelt Benjamin and Dan, but part of the Danites emigrated to the springs of the Jordan. Southern Palestine fell to Judah, in the inheritance of which Simeon was assigned ill-defined possessions, while the estates granted to the Levites were distributed throughout the territory of other tribes.

The social significance of the settlement cannot be exaggerated. The tribes, originally nomadic groups of tent-dwellers, now became identified with assigned territories, and the bonds of clansmen descended from a common ancestor were gradually replaced by the solidarity of villagers born in the land they were tilling.

The population of the districts thus apportioned was far from homogeneous. Israelites lived side by side with the Canaanites whom they had overrun but only partially conquered. Canaanite cities were still holding their own in various parts of the country. Some districts were solidly occupied by foreign elements, like the enclave of Caleb in the south of Judah (Jos.15.13–19), or the four cities of the Gibeonites (Jos.9.17) which were to play an important part in subsequent political and religious developments.

The national existence of the Israelites was at first most precarious. The incurable individualism of the tribes, their rivalries and feuds, prevented them from presenting a solid front against the recurrent hostility of their neighbors. The adoption by the Israelites of the way of life of the Canaanites, intermarriages, and participation in local religious cults, were equally pernicious. The book of Judges is full of these problems of coexistence. The ephemeral authority of inspired leaders such as Deborah (Jg.4.4–5.31) and Gideon (Jg.6.11–8.28) could help solve major crises, but offered no permanent remedy against the ingrained anarchy of the Israelites, who had lost the rugged virtues of tribesmen and had not yet matured as citizens.

4. THE HEBREW KINGDOMS

§ 9 Rise of the monarchy. The end of the second millennium B.C., around 1300–1000, was characterized by a general movement of monarchic centralization which did away with the old feudal pattern. Self-supporting states emerged, each under the authority of its king, who had nothing but the title in common with the Canaanite "kings" who lorded it over their kinsmen and the tenants of their estates. Ammon and Moab in Transjordan, as well as the Arameans in Syria, constituted themselves typical monarchies. In the highlands of Samaria, Abimelech, son of Gideon (Jerubbaal), had himself proclaimed king at Shechem (Jg.9.1–57), but he was unable to cope with problems of Hebrew-Canaanite relationships and the attempt proved abortive.

The pressure of external events prompted the Israelites to unite permanently under the scepter of Saul. The Ammonites raided the Israelites of Transjordan and threatened the eastern border of Palestine. In the west the danger came from the Philistines. This people seems to have been ubiquitous, but their principal habitat was the southern half of the coastal plain. Numerous samples of painted pottery, decorated with a combination of geometric patterns and over-stylized figures of birds, have been found in this region and are commonly attributed to Philistine craftsmen. The nation was organized as a federation of five cities, Ashdod, Ashkelon, Gaza, Gath, and Ekron, under their "tyrants." But textual as well as archaeological evidence shows that they were well on the way to infiltrate and eventually to subjugate the whole of Palestine. They held a strict monopoly on iron, a metal which was not used in Palestine prior to 1200 B.C. They controlled the major part of the Shephelah and the Plain of Sharon. Philistine raiding parties plundered the countryside of Judah and Ephraim. Shiloh was ransacked and the ark of the covenant was carried away as a war trophy (1 Sam.4.11). It even seems that the Philistines occupied for some time a strategic outpost in the highlands of Benjamin, intercepting the road between Geba and Michmash.

In the face of such perils the Israelites called Saul, a tribesman of warlike Benjamin, to reign over them. This was in a sense a departure from the religious ideal of Moses, who envisioned Israel as a theocratic nation under God-appointed leaders, but not under a monarch chosen by popular acclaim. Samuel, the last of such leaders who judged Israel, tried in vain to dissuade the people, but their desire prevailed (1 Sam. ch. 8).

The monarchy of Saul had all the characteristics of an emergency dictatorship. He established his capital at Gibeah in the heart of Benjamin. The foundations of his palace-fortress have been unearthed from the hillock of Tell el-Ful, five short miles north of Jerusalem.

A vigorous action neutralized the Ammonite threat. The Philistines were dislodged from their strategic positions and thrown back into the lowlands, but Saul's attack of the Philistine forces holding the Plain of Esdraelon resulted in the defeat of the Israelites. Saul and his son Jonathan were slain and their armor exhibited in the temple of Ashtaroth at Beth-shan (1 Sam.31.10), perhaps to be identified with a little shrine which is dated, on archaeological evidence, from the eleventh to the tenth century B.C.

Even if the monarchy of Saul had not met its tragic fate, it is doubtful whether it could have ever achieved a reasonable measure of stability. The urgent problem of non-Israelite minorities had been treated high-handedly, and Saul had manifested his intolerance as well as his total lack of moral or political restraint in ordering the massacre of the Gibeonites (2 Sam.21.1), in violation of the solemn pledge given them by Joshua. Nor were his policies toward the other tribes of Israel much better advised. The banishment of young David, whom he feared as a potential rival, did much to stir up feelings of suspicion and resentment between the men of Judah and the Israelites of central Palestine.

§ 10 David and Solomon. After precarious days as an outlaw in the wilderness of Judah and a refugee among the Philistines, David was anointed by the men of Judah to reign in Hebron, shortly after 1000 B.C. (2 Sam.2.1–4). After seven difficult years, during which he managed to gain some influence over the northern tribes, he was proclaimed king over the entire nation and made Jerusalem, which he had just captured from the Jebusites, his capital (2 Sam.5.6–10). This was excellent politics, for Jerusalem could be considered neutral ground between Judah and Benjamin. One would no longer think of the king as a man of a tribe eager to lord it over the others, but as the permanent leader and arbiter of the nation, including foreign minorities to which some consideration was to be given.

At first unanimous popular support enabled David to fight the foreign wars to a finish. Ammon was thoroughly defeated, the Philistines were driven back into the plain, and the frontiers of Israel were firmly secured. Yet the particularism of the tribes flared up once again when a party of malcontents led by Absalom, David's own son, forced the king into temporary exile. The revolt was put down with great difficulty (2 Sam. chs. 15–18), and much unfinished business was left for his successor.

David is said to have reigned thirty-three years in Jerusalem (1 Kg.2.11). Toward the end he prevented a crisis of succession by having Solomon anointed and enthroned (1 Kg. ch. 1).

The outstanding achievement of the new reign, to which the Old Testament ascribes a conventional duration of forty years, was the building of the temple. Like all important constructions of this period it required foreign cooperation. Hiram of Tyre provided specialized craftsmen and timber from Lebanon (1 Kg.5.1–12). The temple was part of a compound which integrated the king's palace with the dwelling of the Lord. This arrangement, inspired by the Oriental conception of the king being the incarnation of the divinity, was regarded with misgivings by the prophets, who feared an encroachment upon the transcendence of God (compare Ezek.43.8). The temple of Jerusalem, as a national sanctuary, never completely superseded the shrines of the country, and their persistent survival is denounced in the historical and prophetical writings.

The house of the Lord consisted essentially of a long nave in which were ten lampstands, a table for the bread of the Presence, and the altar of incense. From thence one gained access to the inner sanctuary, a chamber (30′ x 30′ x 30′) containing the ark, which David had brought back from Kiriath-jearim, and two cherubim, fifteen feet high, made of olive wood and overlaid with gold. The "house" was entered from the east by means of a vestibule flanked with pillars of bronze. The altar of burnt offering stood in the courtyard in front of the temple, where the sacrificial service took place. The carved ivories found at Arslan Tash and Megiddo, engraved with winged figures and floral or geometrical patterns, constitute a valid analogy to the decoration of the temple and its furnishings.

In the administrative order the division of the country into fiscal districts, not without some gerrymandering, provided a better integration of minority groups with the Israelites. A new system of government replaced the arbitrary rule of petty tyrants and their satellites. There arose a class of responsible officials similar to the Egyptian scribes, and the names of departmental heads have been preserved in the Bible (1 Kg.4.1–19). Foreign trade and industry were a royal monopoly. The king's commercial agents are mentioned among other crown officials. Special reference is made to the purchase of chariots and teams of horses for the army or for re-exportation abroad (1 Kg.10.26–29). The occupation of the Negeb made possible the exploitation of iron and copper mines east of the Arabah and the establishment of a naval base at Elath (Ezion-geber), the ruins of which have been excavated near 'Aqaba at a site known today as Tell el-Kheleifeh. A fleet manned by Phoenician sailors sailed periodically to south Arabia, India, and east Africa, bringing back gold, gems, and exotic products (1 Kg.9.26–28; 10.22).

§ 11 The divided monarchy: Judah and Israel. The chronology of David and Solomon may be regarded as conventionalized. Beginning with the schism of Jeroboam and the divided monarchy, however, dates and correlations of the chronologies of Israel and Judah multiply and the historical perspective becomes clearer, though some problems are still much debated. The dates which are given here are in accord with the system proposed by Edwin R. Thiele; for a full conspectus of these, as well as the dates of an alternative system developed by William F. Albright, see the Chronological Table, pp. 1548f.

The personal prestige of Solomon and his efficient administration had driven underground those who favored a divided monarchy. Rehoboam, who succeeded his father in 931 B.C., made himself unpopular from the start (1 Kg. ch. 12). His arrogance and an increased taxation recklessly enforced undid the superficial unity which had been painstakingly achieved. The Israelites of central and northern Palestine seceded under Jeroboam, leaving Judah alone in the south. The common frontier, at first hotly contested, cut transversally through the territory of Benjamin. The dynastic stability of the kingdom of Judah, faithful to the house of David, compensated for the limited extent of its territory; on the other hand, the kingdom of Israel went through eight crises of royal succession during the two centuries of its existence.

Jeroboam fortified Shechem and made it the first capital of the northern kingdom

(1 Kg.12.25). Later he seems to have taken up royal residence at Tirzah, famed for its beauty (1 Kg.14.17; S. of S.6.4). This city remained the capital of the ten tribes until about 880 B.C., when Omri established himself on the hill of Samaria (1 Kg.16.23–24). Archaeological excavations have laid bare the foundations of the palace at Samaria. The entire area was surrounded by a double casemated wall. In a room of the king's house were found carved plaques of ivory, partly gilded and inlaid, which had been used to decorate wooden pieces of furniture. They show an eclectic inspiration, combining Egyptian, Oriental, and Mediterranean motifs: the child Horus on a lotus flower, the so-called djed pillar flanked by deities, lilies, and palmated ornaments, various types of sphinxes and winged figures, a woman's head in a rectangular frame, and animals. They are similar to ivories discovered in the ruins of Hadatu (Arslan Tash), where the Assyrians had carried them as war booty from the palace of Hazael in Damascus. Storehouses contained a large number of broken jars which, judging from inscriptions penned in ancient Hebrew script, contained the oil and wine delivered to the royal treasury in payment of taxes. These inscriptions have made it possible to establish a list of fiscal districts of the northern kingdom, which must have reached a high level of prosperity.

Foreign trade was flourishing. A wealthy class of traders and craftsmen began to develop in urban centers. Close political and economic relations were established between the kingdom of Israel and the Phoenician city-state of Sidon. This, however, did much to bring about a recrudescence of pagan cults which were bitterly opposed by Elijah and other prophets.

A similar evolution took place in the kingdom of Judah. The economy was still predominantly rural. Uzziah (Azariah) did much to intensify the cultivation of the royal domain and ordered the digging of cisterns and the building of watchtowers in the countryside (2 Chr.26.10). Meanwhile craftsmen and merchants set up their shops in the streets of the capital and regional centers such as Hebron and Lachish. The exploitation of the mines in the Arabah and the maritime enterprises of Solomon went on with some intermittence, depending on whether or not the kings of Judah were able to guarantee the security of the caravans through the Negeb and on the Edomite border.

§ **12** Political relations between Judah and

Israel ranged from open hostility to an uneasy coexistence abundant in plots and intrigues, and even to occasional confederation, as, for example, the ill-fated expedition of Jehoshaphat and Ahab against the Syrians (1 Kg.22.29–40), or the campaign of Jehoshaphat and Jehoram of Israel against Mesha, recorded in 2 Kg.3.4–27 and on the so-called Moabite Stone, discovered in 1868 and preserved in the Louvre at Paris.

While Judah felt relatively secure once its northern frontier had been stabilized, the Israelites were much more vulnerable. They had a standing quarrel with the kingdom of Damascus for the possession of Gilead, and their own territory was repeatedly invaded by the Syrian forces. Worse yet, the westward expansion of the Assyrian empire had begun and could not be stopped despite ineffectual attempts by Samaria and Damascus to lay aside their differences and offer a united front against the invaders. The progress of the Assyrians may be followed by means of the Biblical record and of cuneiform texts, from the battle of Qarqar on the Orontes, when Ahab and the Syrians were defeated in 853 B.C., to the imposition of tributes successively upon Jehu (841–814), Menahem (752–742), and Hoshea, the last king of Israel (732–722). The final act was the long siege of Samaria by the armies of Shalmaneser V. Sargon II, who succeeded his brother Shalmaneser in 722 B.C., claimed the ultimate victory. A large number of Israelites from central Palestine was deported, and displaced tribes from the Babylonian borderlands were relocated on the territory of Israel (2 Kg. ch. 17).

The next blow fell on Judah. The campaign of Sennacherib, Sargon's successor, is recorded at length on a hexagonal prism of clay inscribed in Assyrian cuneiform. In 701 B.C. the Assyrians invaded the Philistine plain and the Shephelah and besieged Lachish, the fall of which is represented with great topographic accuracy on reliefs from the palace of Nineveh, preserved in the British Museum (see also 2 Kg. ch. 18). Meanwhile Hezekiah (716–687) worked feverishly to strengthen the fortifications of Jerusalem. A tunnel-aqueduct was hewn from the solid rock to divert the waters of the Gihon to the pool of Siloam, located within the walls (2 Kg.20.20). An inscription in ancient Hebrew script relates the details of the enterprise. Jerusalem, already surrounded, was unexpectedly delivered, owing to an epidemic which all but annihilated the Assyrian forces (2 Kg.19.35).

A troubled period followed, during which

the Assyrians meddled continually with the affairs of the kingdom of Judah. Josiah (640–609 B.C.) seems to have gained some brief authority over the territory of Israel, presumably with the agreement of the Assyrian overlords. He initiated a general religious reform, following the discovery of an unknown scroll of the Law in 622 (2 Kg. chs. 22–23). The character of his reformation suggests a definite relation between the scroll discovered in the temple and the book of Deuteronomy. Despite Josiah's efforts, however, a strong current of syncretism still pervaded the religion of the temple. In politics an influential party advocated an Egyptian alliance, which was consistently opposed by the prophets.

The rise of the Neo-Babylonian empire after the collapse of the Assyrian monarchy in 612 B.C. ushered in a new era of hostilities.

Under Nebuchadnezzar "the Chaldeans," following the same itinerary as Sennacherib, captured Lachish, which apparently had been reoccupied by the Judeans. Letters written in ancient Hebrew script, discovered in the ruins in 1935, refer to miscellaneous events which preceded the beginning of the siege of the city in 588 B.C. One of these letters had been sent to the commander of Lachish by a subordinate in charge of an outpost. He notified him that the fire signals from Azekah, ten miles north of Lachish, had ceased; obviously Azekah had just succumbed. Thereafter the siege of Jerusalem followed in short order. The walls were stormed and the temple destroyed in the summer of 586 B.C. The elite of the people of Judah were deported, while proletarians were left in the country under the rule of Babylonian governors.

5. POST-EXILIC PALESTINE

§ **13 The remnant that returned.** The Babylonian captivity resulted in a drastic reappraisal by the Jews of their cultural and religious heritage. The exiles had to abandon their way of life as landowners and to adapt themselves to their new environment. They took up various professions, international trade, and banking, as one may gather from numerous tablets of contracts in Neo-Babylonian cuneiform. Soon, however, Babylonian was replaced by Aramaic as the common language in commercial transactions, and this change may account for the fact that part of the book of Daniel is written in Aramaic, and that the so-called square letters of the Aramaic alphabet replaced the ancient Hebrew script.

It became clear that no matter how many exiles might eventually return to the homeland, a substantial number, and these not the least wealthy or the least influential, would stay in Babylonia and even prosper there. The same could be said of the voluntary expatriates who settled in Egypt in increasing numbers. From now on there would be an "Israel abroad."

This all demanded a reinterpretation of Israel's religious heritage, the ritual and sacrificial elements of which had been stressed by the priestly caste at the expense of spiritual values, much to the dismay of the prophets. But now that the temple lay in ruins, the religious life of the exiles had to feed on past memories; henceforward the emphasis would be on the teaching of the Law and the collecting of the utterances of Israel's sages and prophets.

Meanwhile, some of the exiles had not given up dreams of a restoration. Ezekiel outlined for them the ideal image of Israel as a theocracy in conformity with pre-monarchic conceptions, and the ideal temple, which would stand in absolute isolation from everything profane. The Lord God would have nothing in common with earthly rulers.

The dream came true. The armies of Cyrus, king of Persia since 555 B.C., king of the Medes and Persians since 549, entered Babylon and put an end to the domination of the Chaldeans. The new empire was conceived as a commonwealth of provinces enjoying a large degree of autonomy under the control of their viceroys or satraps. Seals and coins, in fact the earliest coins known to have been minted in Palestine, were inscribed with the word *Yehud*, which was the name of the Persian province of Judea. These coins were used along with the royal gold currency.

The edict of 538 B.C. authorized the exiles to return to their country (Ezra 1.2–4; 6.2–5). This was in execution of a general policy of relocation of "displaced persons" on a voluntary basis. A considerable number of Jews availed themselves of the edict; they organized convoys to journey back to Palestine, where they often found their old homes occupied by the proletarians left by the Chaldeans.

The facts and circumstances of the restoration are recorded in the books of Ezra and

Nehemiah, two scribes who had been endowed with official authority as royal commissioners. The historical substance of these books can be given credit, although the sequence and chronology of the events which they relate pose serious problems. Documentary and archaeological evidence shows that the relocation of the exiles was particularly concentrated in the vicinity of Jerusalem and in the southern part of the Shephelah. Southern Palestine came to be known as Idumea, for the Edomites had settled there after the Babylonian conquest.

The first achievement of the returning exiles was the building of the second temple. The construction had begun under the administration of Zerubbabel, a royal commissioner, who seems to have been subsequently recalled. After several interruptions the work was completed in the spring of 515 B.C. during the reign of Darius. The new sanctuary reproduced the structure of the temple of Solomon, with the essential difference that the invisible presence of God was no longer attached to a man-made object as it had been to the ark.

Next the walls and gates of Jerusalem were repaired under Nehemiah, who organized the men of Judah in gangs, each responsible for a particular section of the rampart. The dedication took place in 443 B.C., during the reign of Artaxerxes I (Longimanus). The work of restoration had been fiercely opposed by Sanballat, governor of Samaria, and Tobiah, the Ammonite. The Samaritans are mentioned in this context for the first time as an organized group hostile to the Jews (Neh.4.2). They were the descendants of the colonists established by the Assyrians in the territory of Israel. They had adopted the religion of the Jews, on the theory that it was fitting to worship the tutelary god of their new country. The center of their cult was the summit of Mount Gerizim; here the few hundred Samaritans who live today in Nablus still gather annually for their Passover rites.

§ 14 **The invasion of Hellenism.** The conquests of Alexander the Great, from the time of his landing in Troas (334 B.C.) to his death in Babylon (323), revolutionized the political, economic, and cultural life of the entire Near East, including Egypt. In the ensuing struggle for Alexander's succession, Judea was claimed by the Ptolemies of Egypt, until it passed under the allegiance of the Seleucids of Antioch in 198 B.C., when Antiochus the Great defeated the Egyptian forces at Panias. Hellenistic culture spread through the

countries of the Near East at an amazing rate. Greek came to be spoken and written almost everywhere. International trade flourished. The Nabatean caravan leaders, who specialized in the south Arabian transit in competition with the maritime enterprises of the Ptolemies, were soon to organize themselves as an independent state, being followed later by the Palmyrenians, who monopolized the communications with central Asia. Archaeological and documentary evidence points to the importance of Marisa in Idumea, where hellenized Sidonian merchants acted as commercial agents for the Ptolemies. An artistic syncretism developed which combined the traditions of Greek and Oriental architecture, and a similar movement of integration took place between Oriental and Greek cults and mystery religions.

This cultural revolution affected the Jews in various ways. They seem to have been treated with fairness by the Ptolemies, who had adopted a policy of broad tolerance. The so-called "Letter of Aristeas" attributes to Ptolemy Philadelphus (285–246 B.C.) the initiative in having the sacred writings of the Jews translated into Greek. Whether or not the details of the story are authentic, it appears that the Greek version of the Bible known as the Septuagint had its beginnings at Alexandria in the course of the third century B.C. There were precedents for such a translation of the Bible, parts of which had been rendered into Aramaic and into the Samaritan dialect. The Septuagint, as it was transmitted to the Christian church, was not completed until the beginning of the first century B.C. It was made to include, in addition to the books of the Hebrew Bible, the books of the Maccabees, the historical novels of Tobit and Judith, the Greek additions to Daniel and Esther, the book of Baruch, the Wisdom of Solomon, and Ecclesiasticus. These writings, known as the Apocrypha, are not included in the canon of Protestant Bibles (see p. xxviii). Some of them may be translations of Hebrew or Aramaic originals. Important fragments of a Hebrew and Aramaic text of several of these books were discovered at Qumran by the Dead Sea.

§ 15 The Seleucid policy of imposing Greek culture and customs upon subjugated peoples contrasted with the tolerance of the Ptolemies. To be sure, Hellenism had made inroads among the Jews themselves. There was a strong party favoring the adoption of the new culture, even to the point of apostasy from the Mosaic observances, and it is hinted by some ancient writers that the profanation of the second temple, which Antiochus Epiphanes dedicated to Zeus Olympius in 167 B.C., was not opposed by the Hellenist Jews, who rather welcomed the assimilation of the Lord God to the highest god of paganism.

This was more, however, than the orthodox could bear. They revolted. Their leader, Judas "the Maccabee," of the priestly family of the Hasmoneans, campaigned successfully against the Syrians. The temple was purified in 164 B.C.; this is the origin of the Hanukkah festival of the Jews (Jn.10.22). The autonomy of the Jews was recognized grudgingly by the Seleucid overlords. After the death of Judas in 160 B.C., the Jewish state of the Hasmoneans continued until 40 B.C., thus outlasting the Seleucids, whose discords were brought to an end when Pompey made Syria a Roman province in 63 B.C.

Our sources for the history of the entire period are the books of the Maccabees, Josephus, and archaeological evidence, especially Jewish coinage. The latter reflects the growing ambition of the Hasmoneans, who at first were recognized only as high priests and ethnarchs of the Jewish community but who, beginning with Aristobulus (104–103 B.C.), assumed the title of kings, despite the opposition of the Pharisees.

Growing political and religious divisions weakened the dynasty. The Sadducees, a politically-minded aristocracy, were not adverse to what they regarded as necessary concessions to the spirit of the times. The Pharisees, on the contrary, strove to maintain the separateness of the nation by refining upon the legal observances of the Mosaic code. Another religious sect, related to or identical with the Essenes described by Josephus, sought refuge in complete isolation from national life. Theirs was an ideal of ethical asceticism with strong eschatological overtones, as evidenced by the Zadokite documents discovered in Cairo in 1896, and the scrolls discovered more recently in caves near the ruins of the ancient community center of a Jewish sect at Qumran by the Dead Sea. These documents throw some light on the way of life and the preaching of John the Baptist, and indirectly on the environment of early Christianity.

§ **16 Rome's order.** When Augustus became Emperor in 27 B.C., Syria, which had been under Roman protectorate since its conquest by Pompey, was given the status of an imperial province, governed by a legate.

For reasons of political expediency Palestine and adjacent territories were left under the authority of local princes. After the collapse of the Hasmonean dynasty, Herod the Great had been made king by senatorial decree. He reigned from 37 to 4 B.C., courting the Romans and ridding himself of his enemies astutely and ruthlessly.

Herod's building programs show his versatility: dungeon-like fortress-palaces in secluded parts of the country, where he could retire and plot without being observed, and seek refuge if need be; luxurious country estates in the valley of the Jordan, and a winter palace south of Jericho; public buildings, often inspired by political considerations, as in pagan Ashkelon, Herod's birthplace, and Samaria, where a temple was built to the Emperor Augustus; monumental enclosures around the burial grounds of Machpelah in Hebron and at Mamre, north of the town. The perennial problem of supplying Jerusalem with water was solved by the construction of an aqueduct leading from two groups of springs south of Bethlehem. The fortress covering the northwestern angle of Jerusalem, known as the Tower of the Ovens, was rebuilt as a fortified residence with sumptuous courtyards and apartments.

The construction of the temple of Jerusalem was Herod's chief undertaking. The "house" was surrounded by extensive courtyards lined with porticoes. Josephus describes the successive precincts, access to which was restricted to certain categories of persons according to their degree of consecration to God. Gentiles were admitted only in the outer zone, the limits of which were marked by a railing, trespassers being threatened with death.

After the death of Herod in 4 B.C., Palestine passed under the rule of tetrarchs: Archelaus (4 B.C.–A.D. 6), over Judea and Samaria; Herod Antipas (4 B.C.–A.D. 39), over Samaria; Philip (4 B.C.–A.D. 34), over the districts of Iturea and Trachonitis, southeast of Mount Hermon. Palestine was unified again under Herod Agrippa I, who ruled the tetrarchy of Philip from A.D. 37, Galilee from 39, Samaria and Judea from 41, until his death in 44. Later Herod Agrippa II acquired the tetrarchy of Philip and several Galilean towns from respectively A.D. 53 and 56 to about 100. During the intervals between these reigns, the northern districts were administered directly by the imperial legate of Syria, while Samaria and Judea were placed under the jurisdiction of a Roman procurator residing at Caesarea on the sea (see p. 1550).

§ **17** The sequence of political events in the preceding section supplies the chronological framework for the life of Christ and the activity of his first disciples. Jesus was born about four or five years before the Christian era. (His birth occurred sometime prior to the death of Herod the Great, who, according to Josephus, died shortly before April 12, 4 B.C. The traditional Christian calendar was devised about A.D. 525 by Dionysius Exiguus, a Roman abbot, who unfortunately erred by four or five years in his calculations.) According to Luke (3.1) Jesus was baptized by John in the fifteenth year of Tiberius Caesar. If one counts from the death of Augustus, this comes to A.D. 28/29; but if, as some think more probable, one reckons from the year of the association of Tiberius with Augustus as joint ruler, the date is A.D. 26/27. Luke goes on to say that Pontius Pilate was governor of Judea, Herod [Antipas] tetrarch of Galilee, his brother Philip tetrarch of Ituraea and Trachonitis, and Lysanias tetrarch of Abilene. Pilate is known from extra-Biblical sources, and his name occurs in an inscription recently discovered at Caesarea. The year of the crucifixion is uncertain, though the year 30 has a high degree of probability. At the time of Paul, Damascus was in the hands of Aretas (Hareitat), king of the Nabateans, about A.D. 37 to 40 (2 Cor.11.32). Acts 18.12 records the presence of Paul in Corinth under the proconsulate of Gallio, A.D. 51/52. According to Acts 24.27 Paul had been in prison for two years when Felix, procurator of Judea, was recalled by Nero, and the apostle was sent to Rome by Festus (Acts 25.11–12), who took office about A.D. 60.

The history of the Herodians and of the procurators abounds in riots and attempted rebellions against the ruling power. The glens of upper Galilee were haunted by frustrated Jewish patriots, malcontents, and outlaws of every description. The revolt against the Romans broke out under Vespasian in the summer of A.D. 66. The events of the war are recorded with the utmost detail by Josephus, from the initial successes of the Jews to the siege and destruction of Jerusalem by Titus in 70. The local currency of these years illustrates vividly the general march of events. The Jews had minted silver shekels (erroneously attributed to the Maccabees) as a symbol of national independence. The rapidly deteriorating situation of the Jewish nationalists, when the Roman armies, at first surprised, began to react, is shown by the poorer standards and the scarcity of the Jewish silver shekels from the third year of independence onward, when bronze tokens were used as substitutes. The triumphal arch of Titus, erected at Rome in 71, and imperial coins bearing the words *Iudaea capta*, marked the victory of the Roman arms. A garrison of desperadoes held out until 73 in the fortress of Masada, a formidable Maccabean stronghold, whose spectacular ruins uncovered by archaeologists make vivid Josephus's account of its fall (*Jewish War* VII.viii.3ff.).

Another revolt broke out under Hadrian in A.D. 132. References to and letters from the leader, Simon ben Koziba, nicknamed Bar Kochba, have been found in the caves of Murabba'at and Nahal Hever in the desert of Judah. The Romans were at first unable to stem the rebellion, but reinforcements arrived, and Jerusalem, which had fallen to Bar Kochba's men, was recaptured in 134. The insurrection was brought to an end one year later when Bar Kochba was buried under the ruins of the fortified village of Bittir, where he had made his last stand. Jerusalem was renamed Colonia Aelia Capitolina, and a shrine was dedicated to Zeus and Hadrian in the temple area.

The collapse of Israel as a nation ushered in a new era. Judaism had to forgo its earthly ties, and the Messianic hope had to be reinterpreted. The seed of David was extinct, the temple would not be rebuilt, and the people were scattered among the Gentiles. There remained only the Book, and in the reading of the sacred page Israel would slowly discover its mission in the world.

The church had received from its Founder the mission to preach the gospel to all creatures. Thus the word was proclaimed "in Jerusalem, and in all Judea and Samaria, and to the end of the earth" (Acts 1.8), and the power of God confirmed the word. Was this not the true fulfilment of the prophecy of Joel, "I will pour out my spirit on all flesh" (Jl.2.28)? The eternal had broken through into time. Almost from the start the church made a clean departure from historical contingencies, straining forward to what lies ahead: not Israel among the nations, but the nations as the new Israel, brought to the obedience of Christ.

MEASURES AND WEIGHTS IN THE BIBLE

1. HEBREW MEASURES OF LENGTH

Hebrew	RSV	Equivalence	U.S. Measures
'ammāh	cubit	2 spans	17.49 inches
zéreth	span	3 handbreadths	8.745 inches
ṭṓphaḥ, ṭéphaḥ	handbreadth	4 fingers	2.915 inches
'esḅa'	finger		0.728 inch

The cubit described in Ezekiel (40.5; 43.13) is equal to seven (not six) handbreadths, namely 20.405 inches.

2. MEASURES OF LENGTH IN THE NEW TESTAMENT

Greek	RSV	U.S. Measures
pēchus	cubit	about 1½ feet
orguia	fathom	about 72.44 inches
stadion	furlong, stadia, or the equivalent in miles	about 606 feet
milion	mile	about 4,879 feet

3. HEBREW MEASURES OF CAPACITY

a. Dry Measures

Hebrew	RSV	Equivalence	U.S. Measures
hṓmer	homer	} 2 lethechs	6.524 bushels
kōr	measure, cor		
léthekh	lethech	5 ephahs	3.262 bushels
'éphāh	ephah, measure	3 seahs	20.878 quarts
se'āh	measure	$3\frac{1}{3}$ omers	6.959 quarts
'ōmer	omer	$1\frac{4}{5}$ kabs	2.087 quarts
'issārôn	tenth part (of ephah)		
qabh			1.159 quarts

b. Liquid Measures

Hebrew	RSV	Equivalence	U.S. Measures
kōr	measure, cor	10 baths	60.738 gallons
bath	bath	6 hins	6.073 gallons
hîn	hin	3 kabs	1.012 gallons
qabh	kab	4 logs	1.349 quarts
lōgh	log		0.674 pint

4. MEASURES OF CAPACITY IN THE NEW TESTAMENT

Greek	RSV	Equivalence	U.S. Measures
batos	measure	(Hebrew) bath	
koros	measure	(Hebrew) kōr	see Table 3
saton	measure	(Hebrew) se'āh	
metrētēs	measure		10.3 gallons
choinix	quart		0.98 dry quart
modios	bushel	(Latin) modius	7.68 dry quarts
xestēs	pot	(Latin) sextarius	0.96 dry pint, or 1.12 fluid pints

5. HEBREW WEIGHTS

Hebrew	RSV	Equivalence	U.S. Avoirdupois
kikkār	talent	60 minas	75.558 pounds
māneh	mina	50 shekels	20.148 ounces
shéqel	shekel	2 bekas	176.29 grains
béqa'	beka, half a shekel	10 gerahs	88.14 grains
gērāh	gerah		8.81 grains

The practice of weighing unmarked ingots of metal used in commercial transactions prior to the invention of money explains that the names of the units of weight were used later as indications of value, and as names for monetary standards. There is, however, no direct relation between the shekel-weight and the weight of a shekel piece.

6. WEIGHTS IN THE NEW TESTAMENT

Greek	RSV	Equivalence	U.S. Avoirdupois
talenton	talent	(Hebrew) talent	see Table 5
mna	pound	(Hebrew) mina	see Table 5
litra	pound	(Latin) libra	0.719 pound

CHRONOLOGICAL TABLES OF RULERS

A. THE UNITED MONARCHY. The length of Saul's reign is not known; David and Solomon are each said to have ruled for forty years, which is often used as a general and somewhat indefinite number. Their reigns must have fallen between about 1020 and 922 (931) B.C., perhaps as follows:

Saul	1020–1000 B.C.
David	1000–961 (or 1000–965) B.C.
Solomon	961–922 (or 965–931) B.C.

B. THE DIVIDED MONARCHY, JUDAH AND ISRAEL. Problems of chronology of the kings of Israel and Judah permit no easy solution. The following tables are based upon two widely accepted systems of chronology, one developed by W. F. Albright, and the other by E. R. Thiele. The dates of Thiele's system, which are enclosed within parentheses, are presented in simplified form apart from coregencies and simultaneous claims to the throne. The two columns show the chronological relationships of the kings of the two kingdoms.

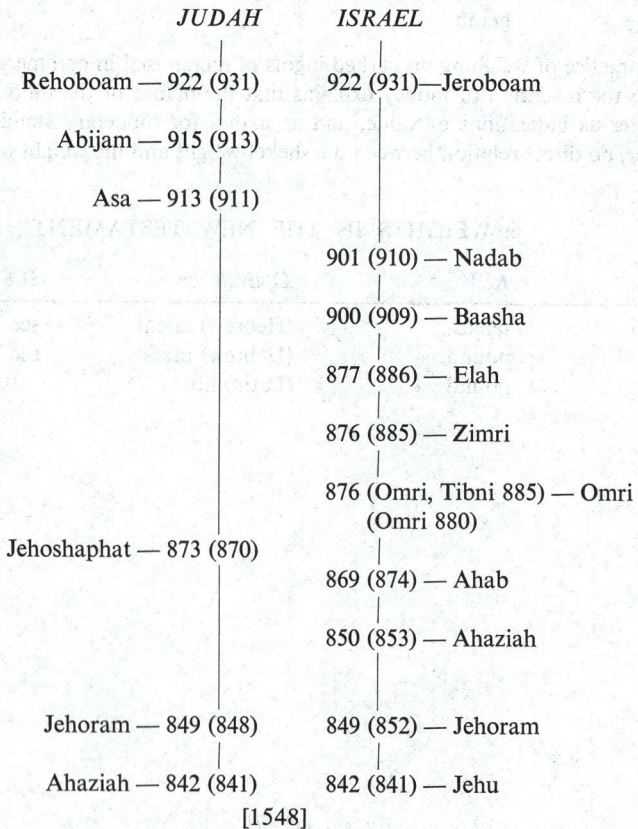

JUDAH	ISRAEL
Rehoboam — 922 (931)	922 (931)—Jeroboam
Abijam — 915 (913)	
Asa — 913 (911)	
	901 (910) — Nadab
	900 (909) — Baasha
	877 (886) — Elah
	876 (885) — Zimri
	876 (Omri, Tibni 885) — Omri (Omri 880)
Jehoshaphat — 873 (870)	
	869 (874) — Ahab
	850 (853) — Ahaziah
Jehoram — 849 (848)	849 (852) — Jehoram
Ahaziah — 842 (841)	842 (841) — Jehu

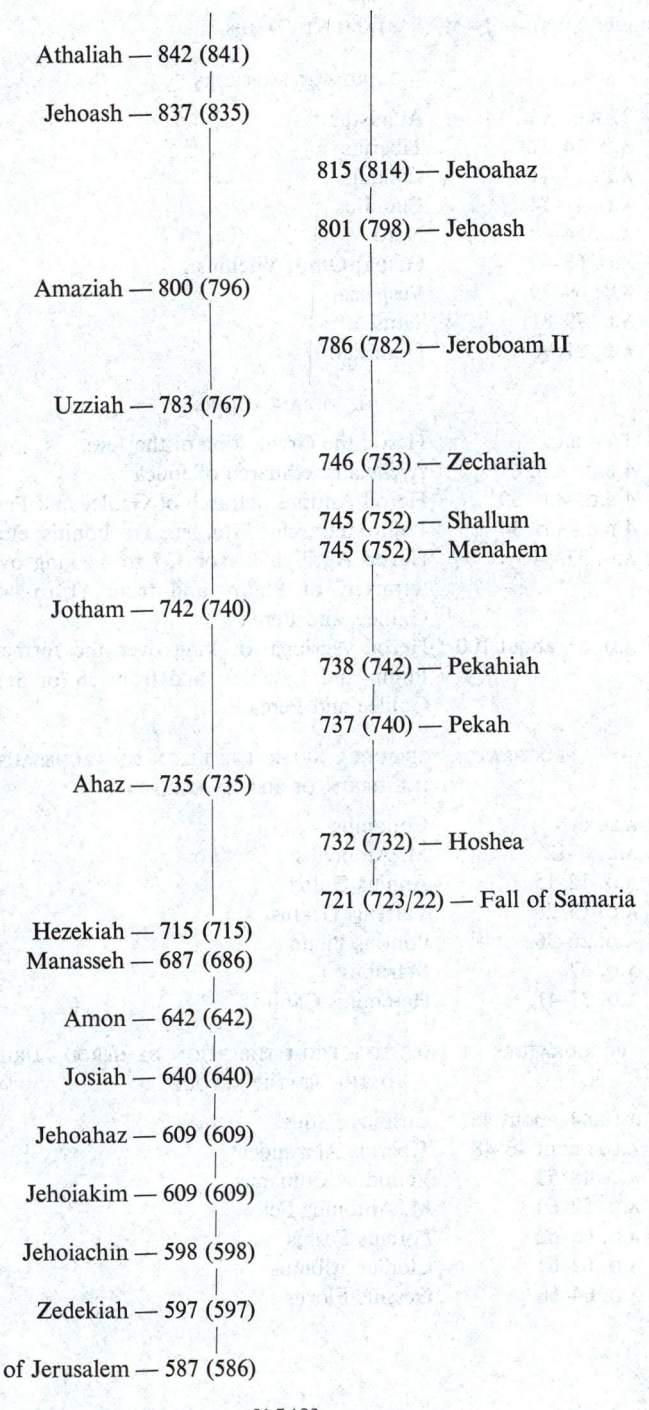

Athaliah — 842 (841)

Jehoash — 837 (835)

815 (814) — Jehoahaz

801 (798) — Jehoash

Amaziah — 800 (796)

786 (782) — Jeroboam II

Uzziah — 783 (767)

746 (753) — Zechariah

745 (752) — Shallum
745 (752) — Menahem

Jotham — 742 (740)

738 (742) — Pekahiah

737 (740) — Pekah

Ahaz — 735 (735)

732 (732) — Hoshea

721 (723/22) — Fall of Samaria

Hezekiah — 715 (715)
Manasseh — 687 (686)

Amon — 642 (642)

Josiah — 640 (640)

Jehoahaz — 609 (609)

Jehoiakim — 609 (609)

Jehoiachin — 598 (598)

Zedekiah — 597 (597)

Fall of Jerusalem — 587 (586)

[1549]

C. Rulers During New Testament Times.

ROMAN EMPERORS

27 B.C.–A.D. 14	Augustus
A.D. 14–37	Tiberius
A.D. 37–41	Caligula
A.D. 41–54	Claudius
A.D. 54–68	Nero
A.D. 68–69	Galba; Otho; Vitellius
A.D. 69–79	Vespasian
A.D. 79–81	Titus
A.D. 81–96	Domitian

HERODIAN RULERS

37–4 B.C.	Herod the Great, king of the Jews
4 B.C.–A.D. 6	Archelaus, ethnarch of Judea
4 B.C.–A.D. 39	Herod Antipas, tetrarch of Galilee and Perea
4 B.C.–A.D. 34	Philip, tetrarch of Ituraea, Trachonitis, etc.
A.D. 37–44	Herod Agrippa I, from 37 to 44 king over the former tetrarchy of Philip, and from 41 to 44 over Judea, Galilee, and Perea
A.D. 53–about 100	Herod Agrippa II, king over the former tetrarchy of Philip and Lysanias, and from 56 (or 61) over parts of Galilee and Perea

PROCURATORS OF JUDEA AFTER THE REIGN OF ARCHELAUS TO THE REIGN OF HEROD AGRIPPA I

A.D. 6–8	Coponius
A.D. 9–12	M. Ambivius
A.D. 12–15	Annius Rufus
A.D. 15–26	Valerius Gratus
A.D. 26–36	Pontius Pilate
A.D. 37	Marullus
A.D. 37–41	Herennius Capito

PROCURATORS OF PALESTINE FROM THE REIGN OF HEROD AGRIPPA I TO THE JEWISH REVOLT

A.D. 44–about 46	Cuspius Fadus
A.D. about 46–48	Tiberius Alexander
A.D. 48–52	Ventidius Cumanus
A.D. 52–60	M. Antonius Felix
A.D. 60–62	Porcius Festus
A.D. 62–64	Clodius Albinus
A.D. 64–66	Gessius Florus

ENGLISH VERSIONS OF THE BIBLE

THE TYNDALE–KING JAMES TRADITION

Prior to the sixteenth century, translations of the Bible into English were made from the Latin Vulgate instead of from the Hebrew or Greek, and were recorded only in manuscript copies.

To the Anglo-Saxon period belong the paraphrases of the Biblical narrative put into verse by Caedmon, herdsman for the abbey at Whitby (about A.D. 670); a version of the Psalms attributed to Aldhelm, bishop of Sherborne (640–709); a translation of the Gospel of John by the Venerable Bede (d. 735); portions of Exodus and the Acts of the Apostles, and some of the Psalms, by King Alfred (849–901); and a translation of the Heptateuch (Genesis through Judges) by Aelfric, abbot of Eynsham (955–1020). Four complete manuscripts and five fragmentary manuscripts remain of the Anglo-Saxon Gospels; these date from the eleventh to the thirteenth centuries. The famous Lindisfarne Gospels and the Rushworth Gospels are Latin manuscripts written toward the close of the seventh century, with interlinear Anglo-Saxon glosses (translations) inserted three centuries later. There were many Anglo-Saxon Psalters, with the Latin text and an interlinear Anglo-Saxon gloss.

To the Middle English period (1150–1500) belong the Ormulum, a metrical paraphrase of the Gospels, with interspersed moralizations; the Psalter of Richard Rolle (d. 1349), a prose version with commentary; and a prose version of the Psalms which has been attributed to William of Shoreham (about 1270–1350).

The first English versions of the entire Bible were the two associated with the work of John Wyclif, made by translation from the Latin Vulgate between 1380 and 1397. They were copied by hand, and there remain some one hundred and eighty manuscripts, mostly of the second version.

We do not know what part of the work upon the first version was done by Wyclif himself. But that is of no consequence; he inspired it all, including the making of the second version after his death in 1384. Both versions were made by scholars who were his immediate associates. Nicholas Hereford was largely responsible for the first version, which was completed before Wyclif's death. John Purvey, Wyclif's secretary, was responsible for the second version, which was completed by 1397.

Five hundred years earlier, King Alfred had written that he translated the Latin "hwilum word be worde, hwilum andgit of andgite"–that is, "sometimes word for word, sometimes meaning for meaning."

The first version of the Wyclif Bible was a careful literal translation of the Latin Vulgate, with the English words following the order of the Latin words as closely as possible. Purvey gives a striking example of the mischief that may thus be wrought. In 1 Sam.2.10 the Latin has *Dominum formidabunt adversarii eius*, which the first version renders, "The Lord shulen drede the adversaries of hym." This follows the Latin word order, but ignores the Latin inflections which show that "adversaries" is the subject of the verb, that the verb for "shall dread" is plural, and that "the Lord" is its object. Purvey changes the translation to read, "Adversaries of the Lord shulen drede hym."

In the "General Prologue" to the second version Purvey states that it is best "to translate late after the sentence and not only after the words, so that the sentence be as open, or opener, in English as in Latin" – that is, so that the meaning be as clear, or clearer.

The sixteenth century brought the Bible in English to the common people as a printed book. Beginning with the first of Tyndale's translations in 1526, there appeared in rapid succession eight English versions of the Bible, culminating in the King James Version published in 1611.

The first English version of the Scriptures to be made by direct translation from the Hebrew and Greek was the work of William Tyndale. His New Testament, 1526, was followed by his translation of the Pentateuch in 1530 and of Jonah in 1531. In 1534 he issued a revision of his translation of the New Testament, and in 1535 *The New Testament yet once again corrected by William Tyndale*. These became the basis of all later revisions and the main source of the authorized versions of the New Testament in English.

Tyndale was bitterly opposed. He was accused of perverting the meaning of the Scriptures, and his New Testaments were ordered to be burned as "untrue translations," intended "for the advancement and setting forth of Luther's abominable heresies." He was finally betrayed into the hands of his enemies, and in October 1536, was executed and burned at the stake.

In 1535 appeared an English translation of the Bible by Miles Coverdale. This was the first complete Bible to be printed in English. It was not a direct translation from the original languages, but was based upon two Latin versions and upon the translations by Tyndale into English, and by Luther and Zwingli into German.

In 1537 a folio volume was published entitled *The Bible, which is all the Holy Scriptures, in which are contayned the Olde and Newe Testaments, truely and purely translated into Englysh, by Thomas Matthew*. "Thomas Matthew" was a pseudonym adopted by John Rogers, a friend of Tyndale, who took Tyndale's manuscript translations of the books of the Old Testament from Joshua to Second Chronicles, together with Tyndale's printed translations of the Pentateuch and the New Testament, and published them in this one volume, which he completed by adding Coverdale's version of the rest of the Old Testament and the Apocrypha.

In 1539 Richard Taverner, a layman and a lawyer, clerk of the signet to the king, published a revision of Matthew's Bible, one edition of which was issued in parts in order that people who could not afford to purchase the whole Bible might buy one or more parts. He was a good Greek scholar, and made some changes in the translation of the New Testament which have been kept in later versions.

Meanwhile at Paris, in early 1538, Miles Coverdale had begun a new revision of Matthew's Bible, for which he had been commissioned by Sir Thomas Cromwell, Secretary to King Henry VIII, and Vicar General. The Great Bible, as this was called, was published at London in April 1539. It was the first authorized English version, and a copy was ordered to be placed in every church.

Under Queen Mary the printing of the English Bible ceased and its use in the churches was forbidden. Many English citizens sought refuge on the Continent, and a group of these at Geneva undertook the revision of the English Bible. The Geneva version appeared in 1560. It was set in Roman type instead of the old blackface, and it was a book easy to handle, instead of an unwieldy folio. It was the first English version to use numbered verses, each set off as a separate paragraph.

The Geneva Bible was never authorized, but it became at once the people's book, the household Bible of the English-speaking nations, and it held this place for three-quarters of a century. It was the Bible used by Shakespeare and John Bunyan; and it was the Bible of the Puritans who settled New England. Between 1560 and 1644 at least one hundred and forty editions of the Geneva Bible or New Testament were printed, and it lasted longer in competition with the King James Version than any other English version.

Queen Elizabeth renewed the injunction that a copy of "the whole Bible of the largest volume in English" be placed in every church, and encouraged its reading. Because not enough copies of the Great Bible were available, Archbishop Parker proposed that the bishops themselves make a new revision of the English Bible. The resulting version, known as the Bishops' Bible, was published in 1568. It was authorized by Convocation, and its possession enjoined upon the churches. In 1572 another edition was published, with considerable revision of the New Testament. This revised edition, reprinted in 1602, became the basis of the revision under King James.

In 1582 an English translation of the New Testament was published at Rheims, made from the Latin by Roman Catholic scholars led by Gregory Martin, who had been trained at Oxford University. A similar translation was made of the Old Testament, but not published until 1609. The distinctive characteristic of the Rhemish version of the New Testament is the closeness with which it adheres to the Latin.

On February 10, 1604, after a conference "for hearing and for the determining things pretended to be amiss in the church," King James I ordained: "That a translation be made of the whole Bible, as consonant as can be to the original Hebrew and Greek; and this to be set out and printed without any marginal notes, and only to be used in all churches of England in time of divine service." He appointed fifty-four men as translators, forty-eight of whom are named in the records that have come down to us. They worked in six companies, to each of which was assigned a section of the Bible. Two companies met at Oxford, two at Cambridge, and two at Westminster.

It was provided that each company would

consider the work of each other company, and that differences would be resolved by correspondence if possible, and if not, be referred to the general meeting at the end. This was a meeting at London of a committee of six, made up of two representatives from the companies at each of the three centers, which devoted nine months to bringing together and finally editing the work. It was then seen through the press by Dr. Thomas Bilson, bishop of Winchester, and Dr. Myles Smith, of Oxford University; and Smith wrote an extended and informative preface, entitled "The Translators to the Reader." This version of the Bible, with a dedication to King James, was published in 1611.

It is a strange fact that no evidence has yet been found that the King James Version was ever authorized in the sense of being publicly sanctioned by Convocation or by Parliament. But it did not need that. Bishop Westcott, writing one hundred years ago, said: "From the middle of the seventeenth century, the King's Bible has been the acknowledged Bible of the English-speaking nations throughout the world simply because it is the best. A revision which embodied the ripe fruits of nearly a century of labour, and appealed to the religious instinct of a great Christian people, gained by its own internal character a vital authority which could never have been secured by any edict of sovereign rulers."

To this may be added the verdict of Sir Frederic Kenyon: "It is the simple truth that, as literature, the English Authorized Version is superior to the original Greek. It was the good fortune of the English nation that its Bible was produced at a time when the genius of the language for noble prose was at its height, and when a natural sense of style was not infected by self-conscious scholarship. The beauty of the language commended the teaching of the sacred books and made them dear to the heart of the people, while it made an indelible and enduring impression alike on literature and on popular speech" (*The Story of the Bible*, London, 1936).

An outstanding merit of the King James Version is the music of its cadences. The translators were men experienced in the public reading of the Scriptures and in the conduct of public worship. Their choice of the final wording of a passage was often determined by a marvelously sure instinct for what would sound well when read aloud. Take as an example the successive translations of Pr.3.17, part of a discourse in praise of wisdom, where Coverdale, the Great Bible, and the Bishops' Bible agree in reading: "Her wayes are pleas-

ant wayes and all her paths are peaceable."

The Geneva Bible has: "Her wayes are wayes of pleasure and all her paths prosperitie."

The King James Version gives to the verse a perfect melody: "Her wayes are wayes of pleasantnesse, and all her pathes are peace."

The English Bible owes more to William Tyndale than to any other man, not only because he was the first to translate the Bible from the original Hebrew and Greek, but because the basic structure of his translation has endured through all subsequent changes. It has been estimated that about sixty per cent of the text of the English Bible achieved its final literary form before the King James Version appeared, and that in the King James Version at least one-third of the New Testament is worded exactly as in Tyndale's New Testament, while the sentences of the remaining two-thirds follow the general pattern of the underlying structure of Tyndale's New Testament.

Among the hundreds of phrases and sentences which the King James translators owed to Tyndale, and which have been kept by revisers of our own time, are: "You cannot serve God and mammon" (Mt.6.24); "Consider the lilies of the field, how they grow" (Mt.6.28); "where two or three are gathered in my name, there am I in the midst of them" (Mt.18.20); "It is more blessed to give than to receive" (Acts 20.35); "the unsearchable riches of Christ" (Eph.3.8); "out of darkness into his marvelous light" (1 Pet.2.9).

To Coverdale and the Great Bible we owe such phrases as "till heaven and earth pass away" (Mt.5.18); "none of us lives to himself, and none of us dies to himself" (Rom.14.7); "death is swallowed up in victory" (1 Cor. 15.54); "the world has been crucified to me, and I to the world" (Gal.6.14).

From Taverner come these readings: "If any man will come after me, let him deny himself and take up his cross and follow me" (Mt.16.24); "according to thy word" (Lk. 2.29); "a certain creditor" (7.41); "Master, it is good for us to be here" (9.33); "he would have given thee living water" (Jn.4.10).

From the Geneva Bible come such phrases as: "his word was with authority" (Lk.4.32); "in all these things we are more than conquerors through him that loved us" (Rom. 8.37); "we have the mind of Christ" (1 Cor. 2.16); "all the fulness of God" (Eph.3.19); "the eyes of him with whom we have to do" (Heb.4.13); "so great a cloud of witnesses" (Heb.12.1).

Among the phrases which appeared first in

the Bishops' Bible are "persecuted for righteousness' sake" (Mt.5.10); "faithless and perverse generation" (Mt.17.17); "overcome evil with good" (Rom.12.21); "was made in the likeness of men" (Phil.2.7); "the power of his resurrection" (Phil.3.10).

We owe to the Rheims Version such expressions as "Why, what evil has he done?" (Mt.27.23); "owe no one anything" (Rom. 13.8); "the ministry of reconciliation" (2 Cor. 5.18); "to me to live is Christ, and to die is gain" (Phil.1.21).

For two and a half centuries the King James Version maintained its place as the Authorized Version of the English-speaking peoples, without any serious consideration of its revision. But in the 1850's a movement toward revision began to gather strength, and in 1870 the Convocation of the Province of Canterbury appointed a Committee to undertake it. The Revised Version of the New Testament was published in 1881, of the Old Testament in 1885, and of the Apocrypha in 1895. The American Standard Version, a variant edition containing the renderings preferred by the American scholars who had cooperated in the work of revision, was published in 1901.

In 1928 the copyright of the American Standard Version was acquired by the International Council of Religious Education, and thus passed into the ownership of the churches of the United States and Canada which were associated in this Council through their boards of education and publication. The Council appointed a committee of scholars to have charge of the text of the American Standard Version and to undertake inquiry as to whether further revision was necessary. After more than two years of study and experimental work, this committee decided that there was need for a thorough revision of the version of 1901, which would stay as close to the Tyndale-King James tradition as it could in the light of present knowledge of the Hebrew and Greek texts and their meaning on the one hand, and present usage of English on the other.

In 1937 the revision was authorized by vote of the Council, which directed that the resulting version should "embody the best results of modern scholarship as to the meaning of the Scriptures, and express this meaning in English diction which is designed for use in public and private worship and preserves those qualities which have given to the King James Version a supreme place in English literature."

The Revised Standard Version of the New Testament was published in 1946, of the Old Testament in 1952, and of the Apocrypha in 1957. The publication of the Revised Standard Version of the Bible was authorized in 1951 by vote of the National Council of the Churches of Christ in the U.S.A.

The revised versions of 1881–1901 made permanent advances in their recognition of the principle that Hebrew poetry is to be translated as poetry, in characteristic parallelism, and in their giving due weight to the text of the ancient Greek manuscripts of the New Testament which had been discovered since 1611.

But the Revised New Testament of 1881, said Charles H. Spurgeon, the great London preacher, was "strong in Greek, weak in English." The revisers were literalists, especially in the New Testament. Their ideal of translation was a meticulous word-for-word reproduction of the Greek text in English words, using the same English word for a given Greek word whenever possible, leaving no Greek word without translation into a correspondent English word, following the order of the Greek words rather than the order natural to English, and attempting to translate the tenses and the definite article with a precision alien to English idioms. The result is that the Revised Version and the American Standard Version are distinctly "translation English."

The problem of the archaic language of the King James Version was ineffectively handled by the revisers, who changed some of the misleading words but actually increased the use of other archaic terms, such as aforetime, haply, holden, howbeit, would fain, must needs, peradventure. Where the King James Version reads, "this is the will of God in Christ Jesus concerning you" (1 Th.5.18), the 1881–1901 revisers changed it to "this is the will of God in Christ Jesus to you-ward" (so also in Rom. 8.18, Gal.5.10, Col.1.25). A full account of archaic words and obsolete meanings in the King James Version and the revised versions of 1881–1901 is given in *The Bible Word Book*, by Ronald Bridges and Luther A. Weigle.

It is one of the ironies of history that the King James Version remained unrevised for two hundred and sixty years, then was revised with the utmost care, but that almost immediately there began the period which Sir Frederic Kenyon has called the Age of Discoveries, since it "has seen discovery after discovery widening our knowledge of the Bible text and its early history, and testing the results at which the scholars of 1881 had arrived by evidence with which they were totally unacquainted." (For a description of some of these discoveries, see pp. xii, xiii, 1544 above.)

The Revised Standard Version has taken full account of the new knowledge of the history, geography, religions, and cultures of Bible lands, and of the rich new resources for understanding the vocabulary, grammar, and idioms of the Biblical and related languages. It also breaks away from the literalism and mechanical exactitude of the revisions of 1881–1901, and returns to the basic structure and more natural cadence of the Tyndale-King James tradition. The review of the Revised Standard Version in *The Scotsman* of Edinburgh concluded with the statement: "In general it may be claimed, whatever criticism may be directed to this or that minor detail of text or diction, that here we have the most significant and adequate of existing revisions, the one most tenacious in its style and form of the tradition of the English Bible."

Paraphrases and new translations, usually of the New Testament, have appeared from time to time, such as those by Henry Hammond, 1653; Richard Baxter, 1685; Daniel Mace, 1729; Edward Harwood, 1768; Andrews Norton, 1855; Leicester Sawyer, 1858. A group of scholars produced The Twentieth Century New Testament, 1898–1901; thereafter have come new translations by R. F. Weymouth, 1903; James Moffatt, 1913; Edgar J. Goodspeed, 1923; and J. B. Phillips, 1947–1958. Moffatt's translation of the Old Testament appeared in 1924; and a translation of the Old Testament by J. M. Powis Smith and other scholars (1927) was published with the Goodspeed New Testament as The Bible: An American Translation. The third quarter of this century has witnessed the publication of a variety of new Bible translations which makes it one of the more important eras in the history of the English Bible. In 1955 the Jewish Publication Society, whose first translation of the Scriptures (the Old Testament) had appeared in 1917, initiated a new translation of the Scriptures in English for the Jewish people. The first part was published in 1962, entitled The Torah, The Five Books of Moses: A New Translation of the Holy Scriptures According to the Masoretic Text. It is the work of a committee of outstanding scholars, with Professor Harry M. Orlinsky as Editor-in-Chief. It is notable for its perceptive rendition of the Hebrew vocabulary and syntax into contemporary English.

In this period a number of important Protestant and Catholic English translations were completed. One of these was The New English Bible, published March 16, 1970, and of which a first edition of the New Testament had appeared in 1961. At that time, Professor C. H. Dodd, Director of the enterprise and Chairman of the New Testament translation panel, stated that this is "not another revision of an old version, but a genuinely new translation of the original, which should be frankly contemporary in vocabulary, idiom, style and rhythm — not to supersede the Authorized Version, but as a second version alongside it." It is to be classed with other modern translations made by James Moffatt, by Edgar Goodspeed, and by J. B. Phillips, as alive as Phillips, though less paraphrastic. For example, it does not join in Phillips' "Give one another a hearty handshake all around for my sake," but has "Greet one another with the kiss of peace" (Rom.16.16). British usage is followed in such terms as "corn," "fortnight," "pounds," "pence," and "farthing." In the Gospels and Acts the expression "the Christ" is replaced in forty-five cases by "the Messiah."

The New English Bible was made under the direction of a Joint Committee of Protestant Churches of Great Britain, with representatives from the Roman Catholic Church participating as advisers at a later stage of the project. The Joint Committee appointed three panels of scholars to deal respectively with the Old Testament, the Apocrypha, and the New Testament, and a panel to act as literary advisers. From the beginning Dr. C. H. Dodd served as Director of the project. Sir Godfrey Driver was Joint Director beginning in 1965. The New English Bible is attractively presented in several formats. It has been widely acclaimed, and the popularity of the edition containing the Old Testament, the New Testament, and the Apocrypha reflects the increasing interest of Protestant Churches in the last of these.

The first English Bible made from the original Hebrew and Greek languages which received Roman Catholic approval was The Revised Standard Version Catholic Edition, of which the New Testament was published in 1965 and the complete Bible in 1966. In it the deuterocanonical books, which comprise what others call the Apocrypha (but without 1 Esdras, 2 Esdras, and the Prayer of Manasseh), are placed among the Old Testament books in accord with Catholic usage. It was prepared by the Catholic Biblical Association of Great Britain with the consent of the Revised Standard Version Bible Committee and the Division of Christian Education of the National Council of the Churches of Christ in the U.S.A. The Reverend Professor Reginald C. Fuller and Dom Bernard Orchard provided major leadership in this step toward a Common Bible. There are no changes in the Old Testament text; the sixty-seven changes in the New Testament, made for liturgical and theological reasons, are carefully noted in an appendix. A significant further advance toward a Common Bible was achieved with the publication of the RSV without any changes whatever in the Oxford Annotated Bible with the Apocrypha (1966), to which Richard Cardinal Cushing of Boston granted the imprimatur. This edition was heralded by *The Reader's Digest* in a special article entitled, "At Last: One Bible for All Christians."

The first English translation of the Bible made from the original languages by Catholic scholars was The Jerusalem Bible, published in 1966. With close comparison with the Hebrew and Greek, it is based on the French translation made under the direction of l'École Biblique of Jerusalem by a committee of scholars headed by Père Roland de Vaux, O.P., and popularly known as La Bible de Jérusalem. The English translation was made by a British Committee headed by Alexander Jones, L.S.S., of Christ's College, Liverpool. The translation is well done and has been warmly received. At the same time it must be acknowledged that occasionally the French idiom intrudes. "Yahweh" is used instead of the surrogate, the LORD. The volume is provided with useful introductions and notes, and "thee," "thou," and "thine" disappear from the text.

The New American Bible, published September 30, 1970 (St. Jerome's Day in the ecclesiastical calendar), carries on its title page the statement that it is "translated from the original languages with critical use of all the ancient sources," that the translation is by members of the Catholic Biblical Association of America, and that it is sponsored by the Bishops' Committee of the Confraternity of Christian Doctrine. The version is the final outcome of a movement which began in response to the encyclical letter of Pope Pius XII, issued September 30, 1943, and urging translation of the Scriptures from the original languages. The work of translation was begun in 1944, and the first volume, Genesis to Ruth, was published on September 30, 1952. Later volumes appeared in due time, copyrighted by the Confraternity of Christian Doctrine. The Chairman of the Editorial Board for the Old Testament was the late Professor Louis F. Hartman, and the Chairman of the Editorial Board for the New Testament was Msgr. Myles M. Bourke. A few years before the end of the work, four Protestant scholars were added to the Committee. The completed work represents capable and dedicated scholarship and renders the Scriptures in modern American idiom. The deuterocanonical books appear among the books of the Old Testament. The book of Psalms provides a rendering marked by a certain liturgical and literary timbre. The introductions and notes reflect the notable accomplishments of Catholic scholarship in biblical interpretation.

In contrast to all these, the Revised Standard Version stands in the Tyndale-King James Version tradition, and presents a different approach to Bible translation, conscious of its historic connections with the history of the Christian Church in Great Britain and America. The Revised Standard Version has its distinctive approach to translation, presenting, as it does, a somewhat more literal, less paraphrastic rendering which lets the reader know what the original Hebrew and Greek texts say.

The ecumenicity of our times is in various degrees represented in these newer translations, but perhaps most of all in the Revised Standard Version. The committee which produced the Revised Standard Version is a continuing committee, holding meetings at regular intervals and having charge of the RSV text. In 1959 a few changes were authorized for subsequent printings of the Revised Standard Version, growing out of a study of suggestions made to the Committee by various readers. Meanwhile the Committee has become both international and ecumenical, with the appointment of Catholic and Protestant members from Great Britain, Canada, and the United States. A prominent American Jewish scholar is a member of the Old Testament section.

The Second Edition of the New Testament (1971) profits from the results of textual and linguistic studies undertaken since the version was first issued in 1946. It incorporates suggestions from many sources, including two special denominational committees. In certain important readings (such as the ending of Mark's Gospel and John 7.53—8.11) the text of the second edition has been adjusted to agree with the forthcoming third edition of the United Bible Societies' Greek New Testament, for which there is now available a companion volume written by Bruce M. Metzger (*A Textual Commentary on the Greek New Testament*, London and New York, 1971). The Committee looks forward also to the preparation of a second edition of the Old Testament.

There are many aids to the study of the Revised Standard Version. In 1957 the Complete Concordance of the Revised Standard

Version was published, and in 1962 the Oxford University Press issued a useful selective concordance, The Oxford Concise Concordance to the Revised Standard Version. Provision has been made for the study of the history of the Tyndale-King James tradition by the publication of The New Testament Octapla (1962) and The Genesis Octapla (1965). The first of these volumes contains the full text, in parallel columns on facing pages, of the New Testament as translated by Tyndale, the Great Bible, the Geneva Bible, the Bishops' Bible, the Rheims Version, the King James Version, the American Standard Version, and the Revised Standard Version. The second volume contains the full text of the Book of Genesis as translated by the same authorities, except that Catholic scholarship is represented by the Douay Version (1609). These two volumes, edited by Luther A. Weigle, contain comprehensive introductions indicating significant steps in the development of the Tyndale-King James tradition.

INDEX TO THE ANNOTATIONS

The following index lists important names, institutions, and ideas which are mentioned in the annotations. In order to gain the fullest information, the Scriptural reference as well as the annotation itself should be read, and all cross references should be consulted.

Gnosticism, 1 Tim.4.3–5; 6.20; 1 Jn.2.22–23; Introd. to 1 Jn., p. 1484
God Almighty, Gen.17.1
Gods, pagan
　Ashtaroth, Jg.2.13; 2 Sam.7.3–4
　Bel, Is.46.1–4
　Chemosh, Num.21.29; Jg.11.24
　Day Star and Dawn, Is.14.12–15
　Hadad-rimmon, Zech.12.11
　Ishtar, Jer.44.15–28
　Marduk, Jer.50.2–3
　Milcom, 2 Sam.12.30
　Nabu, Is.46.1–4
　Sakkuth and Kaiwan, Am.5.26
　Tammuz, Is.17.9–11; Ezek.8.14–18; Dan. 11.36–39
　see also Asherah, Baal, Dagon
Golden Rule, the, Mt.7.12
Good and evil, Gen.2.9; Is.7.15
Grace, Job 33.23–28; Is.55.6–9; Eph.2.5; 2 Th.1.2
Great Commandment, Lev.19.17–18; Dt.6. 4–5; 10.19; Mt.22.34–40
Greek language, the, pp. xiv–xv, 1168
Guilt offering, Lev.5.14–6.7; Sam.6.3

Hallel, Egyptian, Ps.113
Hallelujah, Pss.105; 113; 146
Harem, 2 Sam.5.13–16; 1 Kg.2.13–25; Est. 2.3,9
Healing, Pss.30; 32; 38; 39; 41; 42; 43; 51; 88; 102; 103; 116
Heaven, joy of, Rev.22.4
Heaven, the third, 2 Cor. 12.2
Heavenly places, Eph.1.3
Hebrews, origins of the, Gen.10.21–31; Ex. 1.15; 1 Sam.4.6; 14.21; p. 1535
Hell, Mt.18.7–9
Herod Agrippa I, Acts 12.1
Herod Agrippa II, Acts 25.13
Herod Antipas, Lk.3.1
Herod the Great, Lk.1.5
Herodians, Mk.3.6
High places, 1 Kg.3.1–2; 2 Kg.23.4–14; Ezek.6.1–14; p. 1536
Hittites, Gen. 10.15–20; 23.3; 1 Sam.26.5–6; Ezek.16.1–7
Holiness, Ex.19.12; Lev.6.27–28; 19.1–37
Holiness Code, Lev.17.1–26.46
Holy City, Pss.46.4–7; 87.1–6
Holy One, Is.1.4
Holy Spirit, as Counselor, Jn.14.16; 16.4b–11
Holy War, Ex.17.14; Num.31.9–12; Dt.3.22; 20.1–20; 1 Sam.15.3
Horites (Hurrians), Gen.36.20; p. 1535
Horn of salvation, Lk.1.69
Hosanna, Ps.118.25; Mt.21.9
Hospitality, Christian, Heb.13.2
Hosts, Lord of, 1 Sam.1.3
House-churches, Philem.2
Hyksos, p. 1537

Idolatry, Dt.12.32–13.18; Jg.17.1–6; 1 Sam. 7.3–4; Job 12.6; Is.44.9–20; 57.1–13; Jer.

10.1–16; 19.3–15; Ezek.8.16–18; 14.1–11; Hos.13.1–3; Zeph.1.2–6
Image of God, Gen.1.26; 5.3; 9.3–6
Immanuel, Is.7.10–17
Immorality, 1 Cor.6.16
"In Christ," Rom.8.2; Gal.2.20
Inheritance, Gen.25.31–34; Lev.25.10,23; Num.27.1–11; Dt.21.15–17; 1 Kg.21.1–4; see also Birthright
Interest, Ex.22.25; Dt.23.19–20; Neh.5.7–10; Ps.15.5
Iron Age, 1 Sam.13.19–22

Jachin and Boaz, 1 Kg.7.15–22
Jerusalem, fall of, 2 Kg.24.1–17; 24.20b–25.7; Mt.24.1; p. 1542
Jerusalem, new, Is.60.1–22; 65.24–25; Ezek. 48.30–35
Jesus, baptism of, Mt.3.13–17
Jesus, birth of, Mt.1.18; Lk.2.1–40
Jesus, brothers and sisters of, Mk.6.3
Jesus, high priestly prayer of, Jn.17.1–26
Jesus, mission of, Mt.15.24
Jesus, name of, Mt.1.21
Jesus, temptation of, Mt.4.1–11
John the Baptist, Mt.3.1–12
Jubilee, Lev.25.8–24
Judas, death of, Mt.27.3–10; Acts 1.16–20
Judges, Jg.2.16; 10.1–5
Judgment, divine, 2 Th.1.5–12
Judgment, Last, Dan.7.9–14; Jl.3.1–3; Mt. 25.31–46; Rev.20.11–15

Kingdom of God, Pss.93; 145.10–13a; Dan. 2.36–45; 7.11–14; Mt.4.17
Kingdom of heaven, Mt.4.17
Kingship of God, 1 Sam.4.3–4; Pss.93; 95–100; Is.43.14–15
Kiss, the holy, Rom.16.16
Knowledge, Pr.1.7; Is.1.2–3; Jer.9.23–24; Hos.4.1–3
Knowledge, tree of, Gen.2.9

Laments of Jeremiah, Jer.11.18–12.6; 15. 10–21; 17.14–18; 18.18–23; 20.7–13, 14–18
Language of the New Testament, the, pp. xiv–xv, 1168
Languages of the Old Testament, the, pp. xii–xiii, xxvi
Languages, origins of, Gen.11.1–9
Last supper, the, Mt.26.17–29
Law, Ex.20.22–23.33; Introd. to Lev., p. 122; Lev.1.1; 17.1–16; Introd. to Dt., p. 214; Dt.6.8–9; Introd. to Ezra, p. 573; Neh.8.1–12; Pss.19.7–14; 119; Is.1.10; Jer.8.8–9; see also Covenant Code, Deuteronomic Code, Holiness Code, Priestly Code, Clean and unclean, Dietary Practices.
Law, purpose of the Mosaic, Gal.3.19–29
Lawyer, Lk.11.45
Laying on of hands, the, 1 Tim.4.14
Lazarus, the raising of, Jn.11.1–57
Legion, a Roman, Mk.5.9

20

NOTES

NOTES

THE APOCRYPHA

EXPANDED EDITION

REVISED STANDARD VERSION

THE OXFORD ANNOTATED APOCRYPHA

THE APOCRYPHA

OF THE OLD TESTAMENT

REVISED STANDARD VERSION

EXPANDED EDITION CONTAINING
THE THIRD AND FOURTH BOOKS
OF THE MACCABEES AND PSALM 151

Translated from the Greek and Latin Languages
Being the Version Set Forth A.D. 1611, Revised A.D. 1894
Compared with the Most Ancient Authorities
And Revised A.D. 1957
Introductions, Comments, Cross References, Chronological Tables of Rulers, and Index

EDITED BY

BRUCE M. METZGER

NEW YORK   OXFORD UNIVERSITY PRESS

TABLE OF CONTENTS

The Editor's Preface, vii

Preface to the Apocrypha, ix

Introduction to the Apocrypha, xi

Abbreviations, xxiii

THE BOOKS OF THE APOCRYPHA

For further information concerning the history and significance of the Old Testament Apocrypha, reference may be made to Bruce M. Metzger, *An Introduction to the Apocrypha* (New York: Oxford University Press, 1957). For extensive introductions to and commentaries on apocryphal and pseudepigraphical books, the most comprehensive work in English is the two volumes edited by R. H. Charles, *The Apocrypha and Pseudepigrapha of the Old Testament* (Oxford: at the Clarendon Press, 1913).

THE EDITOR'S PREFACE

THIS ANNOTATED EDITION of the books of the Apocrypha (like THE NEW OXFORD ANNOTATED BIBLE) is intended to serve both the general reader and the student of biblical literature. Besides containing the several books or parts of books that have been customarily reckoned as the Apocrypha, or the Deuterocanonical writings (see pp. xii and xiii below), the present edition includes three other texts that are highly regarded by Eastern Orthodox Churches, namely, 3 and 4 Maccabees and Psalm 151. It supplies the following helps:

1. A general introduction presents information concerning the meanings and usage of the word "apocrypha," the types of literature represented in apocryphal books, divergent attitudes in the Christian Church toward the Apocrypha, and the pervasive influence of the Apocrypha.

2. Each of the books of the Apocrypha has an introduction dealing with aspects of its composition, date, and contents.

3. Each chapter is provided with annotations which explain literary, historical, geographical, and religious matters in the text. In addition to the comments there are selected cross references to other passages of the Apocrypha and the Bible which shed light upon the verse under consideration. The words in bold-face type at the beginning of each section of the annotations serve as an outline of the subject matter.

4. The tables of rulers during the inter-testamental period provide a chronological framework for the history of the period between the Old and the New Testaments.

5. An index to the chief annotations directs attention to comments on important persons, places, and ideas in the Apocrypha.

The following persons contributed to the OXFORD ANNOTATED APOCRYPHA:

The introductions and annotations for individual books of the Apocrypha were written by Walter J. Harrelson, The Divinity School, Vanderbilt University, Nashville, Tennessee (1 Esdras); Robert C. Dentan, Emeritus, General Theological Seminary, New York City (Tobit, Judith); Floyd V. Filson, Emeritus, McCormick Theological Seminary, Chicago, Illinois (Additions to Esther, Wisdom of Solomon); Herbert G. May, Emeritus, Graduate School of Theology, Oberlin College, Oberlin, Ohio (Baruch, Letter of Jeremiah); Sherman E. Johnson, Emeritus, Church Divinity School of the Pacific, Berkeley, California (1, 2, and 4 Maccabees); and Demetrios J. Constantelos, Stockton State College, Pomona, New Jersey (3 Maccabees). The editor is responsible for the introductions and annotations for the remaining books of the Apocrypha, as well as for

[vii]

the general introduction, the chronological tables, and the chart of titles given to books associated with Ezra and Nehemiah.

It remains to be mentioned that the translation of the three additional texts included in this expanded edition of the Apocrypha (3 and 4 Maccabees and Psalm 151) was prepared by a subcommittee of the Revised Standard Version Bible Committee, comprised of Demetrios J. Constantelos, Robert A. Kraft, Sherman E. Johnson, Allen P. Wikgren, and Bruce M. Metzger, who also served as chairman of the subcommittee.

The editor expresses his gratitude to those named above, as well as to Father Eugene H. Maly, Mt. St. Mary's Seminary of the West, Norwood, Ohio, and to the late Luther A. Weigle, Sterling Professor of Religious Education and Dean of the Divinity School, Emeritus, Yale University, New Haven, Connecticut, for their willingness to read the introductions and annotations and for their judicious counsel concerning several features of this annotated edition of the Apocrypha. May its varied helps prove useful in bringing about a wider appreciation of the literature that forms a bridge between the Old and New Testaments.

Princeton Theological Seminary   BRUCE M. METZGER
Princeton, New Jersey

PREFACE TO THE APOCRYPHA

IN RESPONSE to the request of the General Convention of the Protestant Episcopal Church, October, 1952, the Division of Christian Education of the National Council of the Churches of Christ in the U.S.A. organized a committee of scholars to undertake revision of the English translation of the Apocrypha; and its publication was authorized by the General Board, NCCCUSA, December 12, 1952. The scholars accepting this assignment were Millar Burrows, Winkley Professor of Biblical Theology, Yale University; Henry J. Cadbury, Hollis Professor of Divinity, Harvard University; Clarence T. Craig, Dean and Professor of New Testament, Drew Theological Seminary; Floyd V. Filson, Dean and Professor of New Testament Literature and History, McCormick Theological Seminary; Frederick C. Grant, Professor of Biblical Theology, Union Theological Seminary; Bruce M. Metzger, Professor of New Testament, Princeton Theological Seminary; Robert H. Pfeiffer, Hancock Professor of Hebrew and other Oriental Languages, Harvard University; Allen P. Wikgren, Professor of New Testament, University of Chicago; and Luther A. Weigle, Sterling Professor of Religious Education and Dean of the Divinity School, Emeritus, Yale University, who was appointed chairman of the Committee. A great loss was sustained in the death, August 20, 1953, of Dean Craig. In 1954, J. Carter Swaim, Professor of New Testament at Western Theological Seminary, Pittsburgh, became Executive Director, Department of the English Bible, in the Division of Christian Education, NCCCUSA, and was added to the membership of the Committee. Roy G. Ross, General Secretary of the National Council of the Churches of Christ in the U.S.A., and Paul C. Payne, Chairman, and Gerald E. Knoff, Executive Secretary, of its Division of Christian Education, have been members of the Committee ex officio.

The work has involved the preparation and circulation of mimeographed drafts of translation, the discussion and resolution of all disputed points in face-to-face conference, the circulation of new drafts embodying the decisions reached in conference, and a final review of each book in the light of written agenda proposed by the members of the Committee and of the Advisory Board made up of representatives appointed by denominations which accepted the invitation to review the drafts. This procedure is similar to that followed by the Committee which prepared the Revised Standard Version of the Bible, containing the Old and New Testaments; and, in general, similar principles of translation have been followed.

The Apocrypha here translated are those books and portions of books which appear in the Latin Vulgate, either as part of the Old Testament or as an appendix, but are not in the Hebrew Bible. With the exception of 2 Esdras these books appear in the Greek version of the Old Testament which is known as the Septuagint, but they are not included in the Hebrew Canon of Holy Scripture.

Because of their inclusion in the Latin Vulgate, the Church throughout the medieval period looked upon these books as belonging to the Scriptures, though not unaware of their lack of canonical status among the Jews. In 1546, the Council of Trent decreed that the Canon of the Old Testament includes them (except the Prayer of Manasseh and

1 and 2 Esdras), and condemned any one who "does not accept these entire books, with all their parts, as they have customarily been read in the Catholic Church and are found in the ancient editions of the Latin Vulgate, as sacred and canonical."

In Luther's German translation of the Bible (1534) the Apocrypha stand between the Old Testament and the New Testament, with the title: "Apocrypha, that is, books which are not held equal to the sacred Scriptures, and nevertheless are useful and good to read." Coverdale's English translation of the Bible (1535) gave them the same position, with the title: "Apocrypha. The books and treatises which among the fathers of old are not reckoned to be of like authority with the other books of the Bible, neither are they found in the Canon of the Hebrew."

The Apocrypha had a place in all the sixteenth century English translations of the Bible, and in the King James Version (1611). The Thirty-nine Articles of the Church of England say concerning the Apocrypha: "And the other books (as Jerome saith) the Church doth read for example of life, and instruction of manners; but yet doth it not apply them to establish any doctrine." The Puritans opposed every use of them that would suggest that they possessed any authority; and the Westminster Confession (1648) declares: "The books commonly called Apocrypha, not being of divine inspiration, are no part of the Canon of Scripture; and therefore are of no authority in the Church of God, nor to be otherwise approved, or made use of, than other human writings."

The basic Greek text of the books of the Apocrypha from which the present translation was made is the edition of the Septuagint prepared by Alfred Rahlfs, published by the Württemberg Bible Society, Stuttgart, 1935. This text is based mainly upon the Codex Vaticanus (4th century A.D.), the Codex Sinaiticus (4th century), and the Codex Alexandrinus (5th century). For the book of Tobit the Greek text found in the codices Vaticanus and Alexandrinus was followed; and for the Additions to Daniel (namely, Susanna, the Prayer of Azariah and the Song of the Three Young Men, and Bel and the Dragon) the translators used the Greek version of Theodotion. In both these cases the Committee's procedure was in accord with general usage.

The basic text followed in the case of 2 Esdras is the Old Latin version edited by Robert L. Bensly. This was supplemented by consulting the Latin text edited by Bruno Violet, as well as the several Oriental versions of 2 Esdras, namely, the Syriac, Ethiopic, Arabic (two forms, referred to as Arabic 1 and Arabic 2), Armenian, and Georgian versions. In addition, account was taken of a few verses of the fifteenth chapter of 2 Esdras which have been preserved in Greek (Oxyrhynchus Papyrus number 1010).

In the translation of Sirach, constant reference was made to the medieval Hebrew fragments of a large part of this book, which were discovered at the end of the nineteenth century. Throughout the work of translating the books of the Apocrypha consideration was given to variant readings, including those in the *apparatus criticus* of Rahlfs as well as those in other editions of the Septuagint or of single books of the Apocrypha. Likewise, a search was made for all portions of the Apocrypha preserved in the Greek papyri from Egypt, and the text of these fragments was collated with that of Rahlfs.

The quarrels over the authority of the Apocrypha are now largely matters of the past. A generation that has witnessed the discovery of the Dead Sea Scrolls will probably agree with the statement by Professor Frank C. Porter, in Hastings' Dictionary of the Bible (1901), that "modern historical interest, on the other hand, is putting the Apocrypha in their true place as significant documents of a most important era in religious history."

—1957

INTRODUCTION TO THE APOCRYPHA

1. Meanings and usage of the word "apocrypha."
2. Kinds of literature in the Apocrypha.
3. Divergent attitudes in the Christian Church toward the Apocrypha.
4. The pervasive influence of the Apocrypha.
5. Other apocryphal and pseudepigraphical literature.

1. Meanings and usage of the word "apocrypha."

The word "apocrypha" is used in a variety of ways that can be confusing to the general reader. Confusion arises partly from the ambiguity of the ancient usage of the word, and partly from the modern application of the term to different groups of books. Etymologically the word means "things that are hidden," but why it was chosen to describe certain books is not clear. Some have suggested that the books were "hidden" or withdrawn from common use because they were deemed to contain mysterious or esoteric lore, too profound to be communicated to any except the initiated (compare 2 Esd.14.45–46). Others have suggested that the term was employed by those who held that such books deserved to be "hidden" because they were spurious or heretical. Thus it appears that in antiquity the term had an honorable significance as well as a derogatory one, depending upon the point of view of those who made use of the word.

According to traditional usage "Apocrypha" has been the designation applied to the fifteen books, or portions of books, listed below. (In many earlier editions of the Apocrypha, the Letter of Jeremiah is incorporated as the final chapter of the Book of Baruch; hence in these editions there are fourteen books.)

The First Book of Esdras
The Second Book of Esdras
Tobit
Judith
The Additions to the Book of Esther
The Wisdom of Solomon
Ecclesiasticus, or the Wisdom of Jesus the Son of Sirach
Baruch
The Letter of Jeremiah
The Prayer of Azariah and the Song of the Three Young Men
Susanna

Bel and the Dragon
The Prayer of Manasseh
The First Book of the Maccabees
The Second Book of the Maccabees

In addition, the present expanded edition includes these three texts which are of special interest to Eastern Orthodox readers (see p. xiii):

The Third Book of the Maccabees
The Fourth Book of the Maccabees
Psalm 151

None of these books is included in the Hebrew canon of holy Scripture. All of them, however, with the exception of 2 Esdras, are present in copies of the Greek version of the Old Testament known as the Septuagint. The Old Latin translations of the Old Testament, made from the Septuagint, also include them, along with 2 Esdras. As a consequence, many of the early Church Fathers quoted most of these books as authoritative Scripture (see sect. 3 below).

At the end of the fourth century Pope Damasus commissioned Jerome, the most learned biblical scholar of his day, to prepare a standard Latin version of the Scriptures (the Latin Vulgate). In the Old Testament Jerome followed the Hebrew canon and by means of prefaces called the reader's attention to the separate category of the apocryphal books. Subsequent copyists of the Latin Bible, however, were not always careful to transmit Jerome's prefaces, and during the medieval period the Western Church generally regarded these books as part of the holy Scriptures. In 1546 the Council of Trent decreed that the canon of the Old Testament includes them (except the Prayer of Manasseh and 1 and 2 Esdras). Subsequent editions of the Latin Vulgate text, officially approved by the Roman Catholic Church, contain these books incorporated within the sequence of the Old Testament books. Thus Tobit and Judith stand after Nehemiah; the Wisdom of Solomon and Ecclesiasticus stand after the Song of Solomon; Baruch (with the Letter of Jeremiah as chapter 6) stands after Lamentations; and 1 and 2 Maccabees conclude the books of the Old Testament. An appendix after the New Testament contains the Prayer of Manasseh and 1 and 2 Esdras, without implying canonical status.

Editions of the Bible prepared by Protestants have followed the Hebrew canon. The disputed books have generally been placed in a separate section, usually bound between the Old and New Testaments, but occasionally placed after the close of the New Testament.

Modern Roman Catholic scholars commonly employ a distinction introduced by Sixtus of Sienna in 1566 to designate the two groups of books. The terms "protocanonical" and "deuterocanonical" are used to signify respectively those books of Scripture that were received by the entire Church from the beginning as inspired, and those whose inspiration came to be recognized later, after the matter had been disputed by certain Fathers and local churches. Thus Roman Catholics accept as fully canonical those books and parts of books which Protestants call the Apocrypha (except the Prayer of Manasseh and 1 and 2 Esdras, which both groups regard as apocryphal). In short, as a popular Roman Catholic Catechism puts it, "*Deuterocanonical* does not mean *Apocryphal*, but simply 'later added to the canon.' "

The Eastern Orthodox Churches recognize several other books as authoritative. Editions of the Old Testament approved by the Holy Synod of the Greek Orthodox Church contain, besides the Deuterocanonical books, 1 Esdras, Psalm 151, the Prayer of Manasseh, and 3 Maccabees, while 4 Maccabees stands in an appendix. Slavonic Bibles approved by the Russian Orthodox Church contain, besides the Deuterocanonical books, 1 and 2 Esdras (called 2 and 3 Esdras), Psalm 151, and 3 Maccabees.

Besides the books that are included in the present edition, many other Jewish and Jewish-Christian works have survived from the period between about 200 B.C. to about A.D. 200. Since most of these profess to have been written by ancient worthies of Israel, who lived long before the books were actually composed, they are generally called "pseudepigrapha" (for a description of several of the more noteworthy pseudepigrapha, see sect. 5 below).

2. Kinds of literature in the Apocrypha.

The books of the Apocrypha represent several different literary genres, including the historical, novelistic, didactic, devotional, epistolary, and apocalyptic types. Though several of the books combine material belonging to more than one of these genres, most of the books can be classified as predominantly of one type or another. Thus 1 Esdras, 1 Maccabees, and, in a certain sense, 2 Maccabees belong to the genre of historical writing. Second Maccabees, which is characterized by bombastic rhetoric, fiery arguments, exaggerated numbers, and superabundant use of invectives against the enemies of Jewish orthodoxy, falls more precisely into the category, then so popular in the Hellenistic world, known as "pathetic history"—a type of literature that uses all possible means to strike the imagination and move the emotions of the reader.

Ostensibly historical but actually quite imaginative are the books of Tobit, Judith, Susanna, and Bel and the Dragon, which may be called moralistic novels. In fact, the last two are noteworthy as ancient examples of the detective story.

Of a serious and didactic nature are the two treatises on wisdom, the Wisdom of Solomon and Ecclesiasticus, or the Wisdom of Jesus the Son of Sirach. The latter shows particularly close connections with the style and content of the Old Testament book of Proverbs, from which it is a natural development.

The Prayer of Manasseh takes its place with devotional literature of a relatively high order. The psalmody of the Prayer of Azariah and the Song of the Three Young Men is of a decidedly liturgical cast.

The Old Testament contains no books that are in the form of a letter, but twenty-one of the twenty-seven books of the New Testament are in epistolary form. The Letter of Jeremiah, which dates from inter-testamental times, may have provided later writers with an example of how this literary form could be used for religious purposes, a form which offers the possibility of combining profound theological content with a direct personal approach to the reader.

Finally, 2 Esdras, a book which purports to reveal the future, is a specimen of that type of literature called apocalyptic. An apocalypse is literally "an unveiling." Like the last six chapters of Daniel in the Old Testament and the book of Revelation in the New Testament, which also are apocalypses, 2 Esdras includes many symbols involving mysterious numbers, strange beasts, and the disclosure of hitherto hidden truths through angelic visitants.

Despite the diversities of literary form, most of which are parallel to, or developments from, similar genres in the Old Testament, the attentive reader of the Apocrypha will be struck by the absence of the prophetic element. From first to last the apocryphal books bear testimony to the assertion of the Jewish historian Josephus (*Against Apion*, i.8), that "the exact succession of the prophets" had been broken after the close of the Hebrew canon of the Old Testament. Sometimes there is a direct confession that the gift of prophecy had departed (1 Macc.9.27); at other times a hope is expressed that it might one day return (1 Macc.4.46; 14.41). When a writer imitates the prophetic character, as in the book of Baruch, he repeats with slight modifications the language of the older prophets. But the introductory phrase, "Thus says the LORD," which occurs so frequently in the Old Testament, is conspicuous by its absence from the books of the Apocrypha.

3. Divergent attitudes in the Christian Church toward the Apocrypha.

Ecclesiastical opinions concerning the nature and worth of the books of the Apocrypha have varied with age and place.

None of the authors of the books of the New Testament makes a direct quotation from any of the fifteen books of the Apocrypha, although frequent quotations occur from most of the thirty-nine books of the Hebrew canon of the Old Testament. On the other hand, several New Testament writers make occasional allusions to one or more apocryphal books. For example, what seem to be literary echoes from the Wisdom of Solomon are present in Paul's Letter to the Romans (compare Rom.1.20–29 with Wis.13.5,8; 14.24,27; and Rom.9.20–23 with Wis.12.12,20; 15.7) and in his correspondence with the Corinthians (compare 2 Cor.5.1,4 with Wis.9.15). The short Letter of James, a typical bit of "wisdom literature" in the New Testament, contains allusions not only to the Old Testament book of Proverbs but to gnomic sayings in Sirach as well (compare Jas.1.19 with Sir.5.11; and Jas.1.13 with Sir.15.11–12).

During the early Christian centuries most Greek and Latin Church Fathers, such as Irenaeus, Tertullian, Clement of Alexandria, and Cyprian (none of whom knew any Hebrew), quoted passages from the Apocrypha as "Scripture," "divine Scripture," "inspired," and the like. In this period only an occasional Father made an effort to learn the limits of the Palestinian Jewish canon (as

Melito of Sardis) or to distinguish between the Hebrew text of Daniel and the addition of the story of Susanna in the Greek version (as Africanus).

In the fourth century many Greek Fathers (including Eusebius, Athanasius, Cyril of Jerusalem, Gregory of Nazianzus, Amphilochius, and Epiphanius) came to recognize a distinction between the books in the Hebrew canon and the rest, though the latter were still customarily cited as Scripture. During the following centuries usage fluctuated in the East, but at the important Synod of Jerusalem in 1672 the books of Wisdom, Judith, Tobit, Bel and the Dragon, Susanna, Maccabees, and Ecclesiasticus were expressly designated as canonical.

In the Latin Church, on the other hand, though opinion has not been unanimous, a generally high regard for the books of the Apocrypha has prevailed. More than one local synodical council (e.g. Hippo, A.D. 393, and Carthage, 397 and 419) justified and authorized their use as Scripture. The so-called *Decretum Gelasianum*, a Latin document handed down most frequently under the name of Pope Gelasius (A.D. 492–496), but in some manuscripts as the work of Damasus (366–384) or Hormisdas (514–523), contains, among other material, lists of the books to be read as divine Scripture and of books to be avoided as apocryphal. The former list, which is not present in all the manuscripts, includes among the biblical books Tobit, Judith, Wisdom, Ecclesiasticus, and 1 and 2 Maccabees. Irrespective of the problem of its authorship (many scholars today believe it to be the work of a cleric who lived in south Gaul), the list without doubt reflects the views of the Roman Church at the beginning of the sixth century.

There were, however, occasional voices raised to question the legitimacy of regarding the disputed books as Scripture. At the close of the fourth century, Jerome spoke out decidedly for the Hebrew canon, declaring unreservedly that books which were outside that canon should be classed as apocryphal. When he prepared his celebrated revision of the Latin Bible, the Vulgate, he scrupulously separated the apocryphal Additions to Daniel and Esther, marking them with prefatory notes as absent from the original Hebrew. But, as was remarked above, subsequent scribes were not always careful to transmit Jerome's explanatory material, and during the Middle Ages most readers of the Latin Bible made no distinction between the two classes of books. It is noteworthy, however, that throughout these centuries more than one highly respected ecclesiastical writer (such as Gregory the Great, Walafrid Strabo, Hugh of St. Victor, Hugh of St. Cher, and Nicholas of Lyra), being influenced by the great authority of Jerome, raised theoretical doubts about the disputed books.

Toward the close of the fourteenth century John Wyclif ("the father of English prose") and his disciples, Nicholas of Hereford and John Purvey, produced the first English version of the Bible. This translation, having been rendered from the Latin Vulgate, included all of the disputed books, with the exception of 2 Esdras. In the Prologue to the Old Testament, however, a distinction is made between the books of the Hebrew canon, which are thereupon enumerated, and the others which, the writer says, "shal be set among apocrifa, that is, with outen autorite of bileue." In the case of the books of Esther and Daniel, the translators included a rendering of Jerome's notes calling the reader's attention to the additions.

In the controversies that arose at the time of the Reformation, Protestant leaders soon recognized the need to distinguish between books that were authoritative for the establishment of doctrine and those that were not. Thus, disputes over the doctrines of Purgatory and of the efficacy of prayers and Masses for the dead inevitably involved discussion concerning the authority of 2 Maccabees, which contains what was held to be scriptural warrant for them (12.43–45).

The first extensive discussion of the canon from the Protestant point of view was a treatise in Latin, *De Canonicis Scripturis Libellus*, published at Wittenberg in 1520 by Andreas Bodenstein, who is commonly known as Carlstadt, the name of his birthplace. Besides distinguishing the canonical books of the Hebrew Old Testament from the books of the Apocrypha, Carlstadt classified the latter into two divisions. Of one group, containing Wisdom, Ecclesiasticus, Judith, Tobit, and 1 and 2 Maccabees, he says, "These are Apocrypha, that is, are outside the Hebrew canon; yet they are holy writings" (sect. 114). In explaining his view of the status and worth of such books as Tobit, Wisdom, and Ecclesiasticus, he writes:

> What they contain is not to be despised at once; still it is not right that a Christian should relieve, much less slake, his thirst with them. . . . Before all things the best books must be read, that is, those which are canonical beyond all controversy; afterwards, if one has the time, it is allowed to peruse the controverted books, provided that you have the set purpose of comparing and collating the non-canonical books with those which are truly canonical (sect. 118).

The second group of apocryphal books, namely 1 and 2 Esdras, Baruch, Prayer of Manasseh, and the Additions to Daniel, Carlstadt declared to be filled with ridiculous puerilities worthy of the censor's ban, and therefore to be contemptuously discarded.

The first Bible in a modern vernacular to segregate the apocryphal books from the others was the Dutch Bible published by Jacob van Liesveldt in 1526 at Antwerp. After Malachi there follows a section embodying the Apocrypha, which is entitled, "The books which are not in the canon, that is to say, which one does not find among the Jews in the Hebrew."

The first edition of the Swiss-German Bible, prepared by ministers of the Church in Zurich, was published in six volumes (Zurich, 1527–29), the fifth of which contains the Apocrypha. The title page of this volume states, "These are the books which are not reckoned as biblical by the ancients, nor are found among the Hebrews." A one-volume edition of the Zurich Bible, which appeared in 1530, contains the apocryphal books grouped together after the New Testament. In commenting on the attitude of Protestants respecting the disputed books, Œcolampadius, perhaps on the whole the best representative of the Swiss Reformers, declared in a formal statement issued in 1530: "We do not despise Judith, Tobit, Ecclesiasticus, Baruch, the last two books of Esdras, the three books of Maccabees, the Additions to Daniel; but we do not allow them divine authority with the others."

In reaction to Protestant criticism of the disputed books, on April 8, 1546, the Council of Trent gave what is regarded by Roman Catholics as the first infallible and effectually promulgated declaration on the canon of the holy Scriptures. After enumerating the books, which in the Old Testament include Tobit, Judith, Wisdom, Ecclesiasticus, Baruch, and the two books of Maccabees, the decree pronounces an anathema upon any one who "does not accept as sacred and canonical the aforesaid books in their entirety and with all their parts, as they have been accustomed to be read in the Catholic Church and as they are contained in the old Latin Vulgate Edition" (trans. by Father H. J. Schroeder). The reference to "books in their entirety and with all their parts" is intended to cover the Letter of Jeremiah as chapter 6 of Baruch, the Additions to Esther, and the chapters in Daniel concerning the Song of the Three Young Men, Susanna, and Bel and the Dragon. It is noteworthy, however, that the Prayer of Manasseh and 1 and 2 Esdras, though included in some manuscripts of the Latin Vulgate, were denied canonical status by the Council. In the official edition of the Vulgate, published in 1592, these three are printed as an appendix after the New Testament, "lest they should perish altogether."

In England, though Protestants were unanimous in declaring that the apocryphal books were not to be used to establish any doctrine, differences arose as to the proper use and place of non-canonical books. The milder view prevailed in the Church of England, and the lectionary attached to the Book of Common Prayer, from 1549 onward, has always contained prescribed lessons from the Apocrypha. In reply to those who urged the discontinuance of reading lessons from apocryphal books, as being inconsistent with the sufficiency of Scripture, the bishops at the Savoy Conference, held in 1661, replied that the same objection could be raised against the preaching of sermons, and that it was much to be desired that all sermons should give as useful instruction as did the chapters selected from the Apocrypha.

A more strict point of view was taken by the Puritans, who felt uneasy that there should be any books included within the covers of the Bible besides those which they regarded as authoritative. In time this aversion to associating merely human books with those acknowledged as the only sacred and canonical ones found a natural expression in the publication of editions of the Bible from which the section devoted to the Apocrypha was omitted. The earliest copies of the English Bible which excluded the Apocrypha are certain Geneva Bibles printed in 1599 mainly in the Low Countries. The omission of the sheets containing the Apocrypha was presumably due to those responsible for binding the copies, for the titles of the apocryphal books occur in the table of contents at the beginning of the edition.

It would seem that the practice of issuing copies of the Bible without the Apocrypha continued, for in 1615 George Abbot, Archbishop of Canterbury, who had been one of the translators of the King James Version of 1611, directed public notices to be given that no Bibles were to be bound up and sold without the Apocrypha on pain of a whole year's imprisonment. Despite the severe penalty, however, not a few printings of the King James Version appeared in London and Cambridge without the Apocrypha; copies lacking the disputed books are dated 1616, 1618, 1620, 1622, 1626, 1627, 1629, 1630, and 1633. Like the copies of the Geneva Bible of 1599, these seem to have been the work of publishers who wished to satisfy a growing demand for less bulky and less expensive editions of the Bible.

During subsequent centuries the editions of Bibles that lacked the books of the Apocrypha came to outnumber by far those that included them, and soon it became difficult to obtain ordinary editions of the King James Version containing the Apocrypha.

4. The pervasive influence of the Apocrypha.

Most readers will probably be surprised to learn how pervasive the influence of the Apocrypha has been over the centuries. Not only have these books inspired homilies, meditations, and liturgical forms, but poets, dramatists, composers, and artists have drawn freely upon them for subject matter. Common proverbs and familiar names are derived from their pages. Even the discovery of the New World was due in part to the influence of a passage in 2 Esdras upon Christopher Columbus. In what follows the reader will find a representative selection of such examples, most of them chosen from the editor's book, *An Introduction to the Apocrypha*, and arranged under the headings of (*a*) English Literature, (*b*) Music, (*c*) Art, and (*d*) Miscellaneous.

(*a*) English Literature. Sometime during the ninth or the tenth century an unknown poet, using the West-Saxon dialect, turned the story of Judith into an Old English epic of twelve cantos, transforming at the same time the heroine into a Christian. It is thought that the poem was written to celebrate the prowess of Æthelflæd, "The Lady of the Mercians," who, like the indomitable Judith, delivered her people from the fury of invaders, the heathen Northmen.

During the fourteenth and fifteenth centuries a poem called "The Pistill [i.e. Epistle] of Swete Susan" circulated in Scotland. Written in stanzas of thirteen lines and characterized by an unusual combination of alliteration and rhyme, the ancient apocryphal story was adorned with many imaginative details by the author, thought to have been a certain Huchown (Hugh) of Ayrshire in western Scotland.

How conversant Shakespeare was with the contents of the Bible is a question which, like many another concerning the bard of Avon, has been keenly debated. In any case, it is a fact that two of the poet's daughters bore the names of two of the chief heroines of the Apocrypha—Susanna and Judith—and, what is of greater significance, allusions to about eighty passages from eleven books of the Apocrypha have been identified in his plays.

Noteworthy among American writers who have drawn upon the Apocrypha for themes as well as subject matter is Henry Wadsworth Longfellow. His *New England Tragedies* contains references to 1 and 2 Maccabees, and the chief episodes of the courageous Maccabean uprising are included in his poetic dramatization, *Judas Maccabaeus*.

(*b*) Music. More than one hymn writer has drawn inspiration, as well as, in some cases, the words themselves, from the Apocrypha. For example, the exalted hymn of thanksgiving, "Nun danket alle Gott," written by Pastor Martin Rinkart about 1636 when the devastating Thirty Years War was nearing its end, is dependent upon Luther's translation of Sir.50.22–24. Two stanzas of the hymn, as translated by Catherine Winkworth, will show the amount of borrowing (here printed in italics):

Now thank we all our God	O may this bounteous God
With heart and hands and voices,	*Through all our life be near us,*
Who wondrous things hath done,	*With ever joyful hearts*
In whom His world rejoices;	*And blessed peace to cheer us;*
Who, from our mother's arms,	*And keep us in His grace,*
Hath blessed us on our way	And guide us when perplexed,
With countless gifts of love,	*And free us from all ills*
And still is ours today.	In this world and the next.

Strange though it may seem, ideas included in the Christmas hymn, "It Came upon the Midnight Clear," are traceable to the Old Testament Apocrypha. In the New Testament accounts of the Nativity, nothing is said of the exact time of Jesus' birth. The subsequent identification of the hour of his birth as midnight is doubtless due to the influence of a remarkable passage in the Wisdom of Solomon. At an early century in the Christian era the imagination of more than one Church Father was caught by pseudo-Solomon's vivid reference to the time when God's "all-powerful word [the Logos] leaped from heaven, from the royal throne," namely when "night in its swift course was now half gone" (Wis.18.14–15). Despite the context of the passage, which speaks of the destruction of the first-born Egyptians at the time of the Exodus, the words were interpreted as referring to the Incarnation of the eternal Word of God, Jesus Christ. Thus by a curious, not to say ironical, twist of fortune, a passage which tells of a stern warrior with a sharp sword filling a doomed land with death has had a share in fixing popular traditions concerning the time and circumstances of the birth of the Prince of Peace.

The influence of the Apocrypha can also be traced in many an anthem, cantata, oratorio, and opera. Handel's oratorios *Susanna* and *Judas Maccabaeus*, as well as his *Alexander Balus*, an historical sequel to the latter, will occur at once to music lovers. At an early date in operatic history the stirring story of

Judith was found to lend itself admirably to dramatic presentation. Italian and German operas on this theme were written by Andrea Salvadori, Marco da Gangliano, Martin Opitz, and Joachim Beccau. In the nineteenth century the noted Russian pianist and composer, Anton Rubenstein, published *The Maccabees*, an opera of monumental proportions, the libretto of which was written by one of his collaborators, Dr. H. S. von Mosenthal.

(*c*) Art. During the Renaissance and later, many painters chose subjects from the books of the Apocrypha. Almost every large gallery in Europe and America has one or more works of the old masters depicting Judith, Tobit, or Susanna, who were the three most popular subjects from the Apocrypha.

Besides paintings, down through the ages artists in almost every other medium have chosen themes from the Apocrypha. Were space available here for an inventory, examples could be cited from such divergent types of *objets d'art* as mosaics, frescoes, gems, ivories, sarcophagi, enameled plaques, terra cottas, stained glass, manuscript illumination, sculpture, and tapestries.

(*d*) Miscellaneous. The influence of the Apocrypha in everyday life can be observed in the currency of such names as Edna, Susanna (or one of its many derivatives, such as Susan, Suzanne, and Sue), Judith (or Judy), Raphael, and Tobias (or Toby).

The word "macabre," according to the opinion of several lexicographers, may be derived ultimately from "Maccabee," alluding to the grisly and gruesome tortures inflicted upon the Jewish martyrs.

Some of the most common expressions and proverbs have come from the Apocrypha. The sententious sayings, "A good name endures for ever" and "You can't touch pitch without being defiled," are derived from Sir.41.13 and 13.1. The noble affirmation in 1 Esd.4.41, "Great is Truth, and mighty above all things" (King James Version), or its Latin form, *Magna est veritas, et praevalet*, has been used frequently as a motto or maxim in a wide variety of contexts.

A passage from the Apocrypha encouraged Christopher Columbus in the enterprise that resulted in his discovery of the New World. To be sure, the verse in 2 Esdras is an erroneous comment upon the Genesis narrative of creation, and Columbus was mistaken in attributing its authority to the "prophet Ezra" of the Old Testament, but—for all that—it played a significant part in pushing back the earth's horizons, both figuratively and literally. The words of 2 Esd.6.42 concerning God's work of creation ("On the third day thou didst command the waters to be gathered together in the seventh part of the earth; six parts thou didst dry up and keep so that some of them might be planted and cultivated and be of service before thee") led Columbus to reason that, if only one-seventh of the earth's surface is covered with water, the ocean between the west coast of Europe and the east coast of Asia could be no great width and might be navigated in a few days with a fair wind. It was partly by quoting this verse from what was regarded as an authoritative book that Columbus managed to persuade Ferdinand and Isabella of Spain to provide the necessary financial support for his voyage.

5. Other apocryphal and pseudepigraphical literature.

Besides the fifteen books or parts of books which are traditionally called the Apocrypha, there are many other Jewish or Jewish-Christian works, dating from the centuries immediately before and after the beginning of the Christian era, which for a time were popular among certain groups of Jews and in early Eastern Churches. It is customary to classify these writings as Palestinian pseudepigrapha (those composed in Hebrew or Aramaic) and Alexandrian pseudepigrapha (those composed in Greek). Of the scores of such documents which are known to have circulated more or less widely, the following have been chosen as representative examples. (For a definition of pseudepigrapha, see p. xiii.)

(*a*) Palestinian pseudepigrapha. The Book of Jubilees is a legendary expansion of Gen.1.1–Ex.12.47, written in Hebrew not long before 100 B.C. by an unknown author of nationalist and rigoristic outlook, who deplored contemporary laxity. It attempts to show that the Mosaic law, with its prescriptions about feasts, the Sabbath offerings, abstinence from blood and from fornication (which for the writer includes intermarriage with Gentiles), was promulgated in patriarchal times, and indeed existed eternally with God in heaven. Events recorded in Genesis are dated exactly (but fictitiously) according to the jubilee (every forty-nine years) and its subdivisions. The book has been transmitted in its entirety in an Ethiopic translation, and portions of the text survive in Greek, Latin, and Syriac versions. At about the middle of the present century five fragmentary manuscripts of Jubilees, written in a good style of Hebrew, were discovered at Qumran by the Dead Sea. These manuscripts, which preserve portions of fifteen of the fifty chapters of the book, show that the Latin and Ethiopic versions are faithful translations of the original.

In addition to the 150 psalms comprising the Book of Psalms in the Hebrew Bible, during the intertestamental period other psalms were composed in Hebrew and in other languages. One of these, which celebrates the prowess of young David in slaying Goliath, is appended (as Ps. 151) to the Psalter in Greek manuscripts. Part of this psalm came to be incorporated in the Ethiopian coronation ritual.

The Psalms of Solomon is a collection of eighteen songs of generally exalted sentiments, composed in Hebrew during the last century B.C. They are extant today in Greek and Syriac. The author, who is usually thought to reflect Pharisaic polemic against Sadducean dominance in the religious ceremonial of his day, looked forward to the time when the Messiah would reign as king at Jerusalem. According to an extended description of the coming Messiah (chs. 17–18), he is to be sinless, strong through the spirit of holiness, gaining his wisdom from God, shepherding the flock of the Lord with fidelity and righteousness, and conquering the entire heathen world without warfare, "by the word of his mouth."

The book of Enoch, also called 1 Enoch or Ethiopic Enoch, is a heterogeneous collection of apocalypses and other material written by several authors in Aramaic (or Hebrew) during the last two centuries B.C. It embodies a series of revelations, of which Enoch is the professed recipient, on such matters as the origin of evil, the angels and their destinies, the nature of Gehenna and Paradise, and the pre-existent Messiah. Interspersed throughout the lengthy and rambling work are sections which have been called "the book of celestial physics." These sections, which are one of the curiosities of ancient pseudo-scientific literature, set forth contemporary speculations concerning such meteorological and astronomical phenomena as lightning, hail, snow, the twelve winds, the heavenly luminaries, and the like. The entire work is preserved in an Ethiopic translation, which includes what have been thought to be Christian interpolations in chs. 37–71, where the Messiah is called the Son of Man. Portions of the book are extant in Greek and Latin; recently eight manuscripts of part of the work (but not chs. 37–71) have turned up in Aramaic at Qumran. It is of interest that a quotation from the book of Enoch (1.9) occurs in the New Testament letter of Jude (vv. 14–15).

(*b*) Alexandrian pseudepigrapha. Third Maccabees is a religious novel written in Greek by an Alexandrian Jew sometime between 100 B.C. and A.D. 70. The title is a misnomer, for the book has nothing to do with the Maccabees. With many legendary embellishments the author recounts three stories of conflict between Ptolemy IV (221–203 B.C.) and the Jews of Egypt. The most dramatic section describes how the Jews were herded into the hippodrome near Alexandria, to be trampled under the feet of intoxicated elephants. After the king's purpose had been several times providentially delayed, it was finally foiled by a vision of angels which turned the elephants upon the persecutors.

Fourth Maccabees is a Greek philosophical treatise addressed to Jews on the supremacy of devout reason over the passions of body and soul. In the form of a Stoic diatribe, or popular address, the author begins with a philosophical exposition of his theme, which he then illustrates with examples drawn from 2 Maccabees. He describes at length the gruesome tortures that tested the fortitude of Eleazar, the seven brothers, and their mother, all of whom preferred death to committing apostasy. The book was probably written by a Hellenistic Jew of Alexandria at some time later than 2 Maccabees and before A.D. 70.

From what has been said above the reader will be able to form some opinion of the importance of apocryphal and pseudepigraphical literature, both for its own sake as well as for the information it supplies concerning the development of Jewish life and thought just prior to the beginning of the Christian era. The stirring political fortunes of the Jews in the time of the Maccabees; the rise of what has been called normative Judaism, and the emergence of the sects of the Pharisees and the Sadducees; the lush growth of popular belief in the activities of angels and demons, and the use of apotropaic magic to avert the malevolent influence of the latter; the growing preoccupation concerning original sin and its relation to the "evil inclination" present in every person; the blossoming of apocalyptic hopes relating to the coming Messiah, the resurrection of the body, and the vindication of the righteous—all these and many other topics receive welcome light from the books of the Apocrypha.

ALPHABETICAL LIST OF ABBREVIATIONS OF

THE BOOKS OF THE APOCRYPHA

*The abbreviations for the books of the Bible are
those used in* THE NEW OXFORD ANNOTATED BIBLE.

MISCELLANEOUS ABBREVIATIONS

Ant.	Josephus, *Antiquities of the Jews*
Arab	Arabic
Arm	Armenian
Arrian	Flavius Arrianus (Greek historian, 2nd cent. A.D.)
Ch., chs.	Chapter, chapters
Cn	Correction; made where the text has suffered in transmission and the versions provide no satisfactory restoration, but where the Standard Bible Committee agrees with the judgment of competent scholars as to the most probable restoration of the original text.
e.g.	for example

Ethiop	Ethiopic
Georg	Georgian
Enoch	The Book of Enoch (see pp. xxi–xxii)
Gk	Greek
Heb	Hebrew
Her	Herodotus (Greek historian, 5th cent. B.C.)
i.e.	that is
Josephus	Flavius Josephus (Jewish historian, about A.D. 37 to about 100)
Lat	Latin
lit.	literally
LXX	Septuagint
Ms(s)	Manuscript(s)
n.	note
Polyb	Polybius (Greek historian, 2nd cent. B.C.)
Syr	Syriac
Vg	Vulgate
v., vv.	Verse, verses

OTHER EXPLANATIONS

In the annotations italics are used to designate the words which are quoted verbatim from the text of the Apocrypha. In the notes belonging to the Revised Standard Version (designated by italic letters and standing at the foot of the second column of the text of the Apocrypha) alternative renderings or readings are printed in italics.

THE FIRST BOOK OF

ESDRAS

The book which is known in the Apocrypha as 1 Esdras is called 3 Esdras in the Latin Vulgate Bible, where it is now placed (since the Council of Trent) in an appendix after the New Testament. None of the other apocryphal books is so intimately connected with the Old Testament. Beginning somewhat abruptly with a description of the great passover held by King Josiah in Jerusalem (about 621 B.C.), the book reproduces the substance of 2 Chr.35.1–36.23, the whole of Ezra, and Neh.7.38–8.12, breaking off in the middle of a sentence after an account of Ezra's reforms (about 398 B.C.). There are numerous minor discrepancies between the apocryphal and canonical accounts, including a rearrangement of the materials; and the story of the three young men in the court of Darius (3.1–5.6) has no parallel in the Old Testament.

The origin of the book is a matter of dispute. It is not a translation of the Masoretic Hebrew text of the Old Testament, though it may represent some other Hebrew or Aramaic original. The book is quite independent of the Septuagint Greek version of the canonical Ezra-Nehemiah. The Jewish historian Josephus followed 1 Esdras rather than the Septuagint as his authority for the history of the period.

The purpose of the unknown author was to emphasize the contribution of Josiah, Zerubbabel, and Ezra to the reform of Israelite worship. The book was written after Daniel (about 165 B.C.) and before Josephus wrote his *Antiquities of the Jewish People* (A.D. 93–94). A date late in the second century B.C. is probable.

JOSIAH KEPT THE PASSOVER TO HIS Lord in Jerusalem; he killed the passover lamb on the fourteenth day of the first month, ²having placed the priests according to their divisions, arrayed in their garments, in the temple of the Lord. ³And he told the Levites, the temple servants of Israel, that they should sanctify themselves to the Lord and put the holy ark of the Lord in the house which Solomon the king, the son of David, had built; ⁴and he said, "You need no longer carry it upon your shoulders. Now worship the Lord your God and serve his people Israel; and prepare yourselves by your families and kindred, ⁵in accordance with the directions of David king of Israel and the magnificence of Solomon his son. Stand in order in the temple according to the grouping of the fathers' houses of you Levites, who minister before your brethren the people of Israel, ⁶and kill the passover lamb and prepare the sacrifices for your brethren, and keep the passover according to the commandment of the Lord which was given to Moses."

7 And Josiah gave to the people who were present thirty thousand lambs and kids, and three thousand calves; these were given from the king's possessions, as he promised, to the people and the priests and Levites. ⁸And Hilkiah, Zechariah, and Jehiel,ᵃ the chief officers of the temple, gave to the priests for the passover two thousand six hundred sheep and three hundred calves. ⁹And Jeconiah and Shemaiah and Nethanel his brother, and Hashabiah and Ochiel and Joram, captains over thousands, gave the Levites for the passover five thousand sheep and seven hundred calves.

10 And this is what took place. The priests and the Levites, properly arrayed and having the unleavened

a Gk *Esyelus*

1.1–33: Josiah's passover; his effort to intercept the Egyptians at Megiddo, and his death (2 Chr.35.1–27). According to 2 Kg.23.21–23 the passover celebration concluded Josiah's religious reform, the account of which is omitted in 1 Esdras. **7–9:** The list of offerings

[1]

bread, stood according to kindred [11]and the grouping of the fathers' houses, before the people, to make the offering to the Lord as it is written in the book of Moses; this they did in the morning. [12]They roasted the passover lamb with fire, as required; and they boiled the sacrifices in brass pots and caldrons, with a pleasing odor, [13]and carried them to all the people. Afterward they prepared the passover for themselves and for their brethren the priests, the sons of Aaron, [14]because the priests were offering the fat until night; so the Levites prepared it for themselves and for their brethren the priests, the sons of Aaron. [15]And the temple singers, the sons of Asaph, were in their place according to the arrangement made by David, and also Asaph, Zechariah, and Eddinus, who represented the king. [16]The gatekeepers were at each gate; no one needed to depart from his duties, for their brethren the Levites prepared the passover for them.

17 So the things that had to do with the sacrifices to the Lord were accomplished that day: the passover was kept [18]and the sacrifices were offered on the altar of the Lord, according to the command of King Josiah. [19]And the people of Israel who were present at that time kept the passover and the feast of unleavened bread seven days. [20]No passover like it had been kept in Israel since the times of Samuel the prophet; [21]none of the kings of Israel had kept such a passover as was kept by Josiah and the priests and the Levites and the men of Judah and all of Israel who were dwelling in Jerusalem. [22]In the eighteenth year of the reign of Josiah this passover was kept. [23]And the deeds of Josiah were upright in the sight of

his Lord, for his heart was full of godliness. [24]The events of his reign have been recorded in the past, concerning those who sinned and acted wickedly toward the Lord beyond any other people or kingdom, and how they grieved the Lord[b] deeply, so that the words of the Lord rose up against Israel.

25 After all these acts of Josiah, it happened that Pharaoh, king of Egypt, went to make war at Carchemish on the Euphrates, and Josiah went out against him. [26]And the king of Egypt sent word to him saying, "What have we to do with each other, king of Judea? [27]I was not sent against you by the Lord God, for my war is at the Euphrates. And now the Lord is with me! The Lord is with me, urging me on! Stand aside, and do not oppose the Lord."

28 But Josiah did not turn back to his chariot, but tried to fight with him, and did not heed the words of Jeremiah the prophet from the mouth of the Lord. [29]He joined battle with him in the plain of Megiddo, and the commanders came down against King Josiah. [30]And the king said to his servants, "Take me away from the battle, for I am very weak." And immediately his servants took him out of the line of battle. [31]And he got into his second chariot; and after he was brought back to Jerusalem he died, and was buried in the tomb of his fathers. [32]And in all Judea they mourned for Josiah. Jeremiah the prophet lamented for Josiah, and the principal men, with the women,[c] have made lamentation for him to this day; it was ordained that this should always be done throughout the whole nation of Israel. [33]These things are written in the book of the histories

b Gk *him*   *c* Or *their wives*

---

differs slightly from that in 2 Chr.35.7–9. **15:** *Zechariah* and *Eddinus* appear in 2 Chr.35.15 as Heman and Jeduthun. **17–33:** 1 Esdras follows the account in 2 Chr.35.16–27 faithfully, apart from the omission of the Pharaoh's name, Josiah's disguising himself, and his being struck by an arrow.

of the kings of Judea; and every one of the acts of Josiah, and his splendor, and his understanding of the law of the Lord, and the things that he had done before and these that are now told, are recorded in the book of the kings of Israel and Judah.

34 And the men of the nation took Jeconiah the son of Josiah, who was twenty-three years old, and made him king in succession to Josiah his father. ³⁵And he reigned three months in Judah and Jerusalem. Then the king of Egypt deposed him from reigning in Jerusalem, ³⁶and fined the nation a hundred talents of silver and a talent of gold. ³⁷And the king of Egypt made Jehoiakim his brother king of Judea and Jerusalem. ³⁸Jehoiakim put the nobles in prison, and seized his brother Zarius and brought him up out of Egypt.

39 Jehoiakim was twenty-five years old when he began to reign in Judea and Jerusalem, and he did what was evil in the sight of the Lord. ⁴⁰And Nebuchadnezzar king of Babylon came up against him, and bound him with a chain of brass and took him away to Babylon. ⁴¹Nebuchadnezzar also took some of the holy vessels of the Lord, and carried them away, and stored them in his temple in Babylon. ⁴²But the things that are reported about Jehoiakim*d* and his uncleanness and impiety are written in the chronicles of the kings.

43 Jehoiachin*e* his son became king in his stead; when he was made king he was eighteen years old, ⁴⁴and he reigned three months and ten days

in Jerusalem. He did what was evil in the sight of the Lord. ⁴⁵So after a year Nebuchadnezzar sent and removed him to Babylon, with the holy vessels of the Lord, ⁴⁶and made Zedekiah king of Judea and Jerusalem.

Zedekiah was twenty-one years old, and he reigned eleven years. ⁴⁷He also did what was evil in the sight of the Lord, and did not heed the words that were spoken by Jeremiah the prophet from the mouth of the Lord. ⁴⁸And though King Nebuchadnezzar had made him swear by the name of the Lord, he broke his oath and rebelled; and he stiffened his neck and hardened his heart and transgressed the laws of the Lord, the God of Israel. ⁴⁹Even the leaders of the people and of the priests committed many acts of sacrilege and lawlessness beyond all the unclean deeds of all the nations, and polluted the temple of the Lord which had been hallowed in Jerusalem. ⁵⁰So the God of their fathers sent by his messenger to call them back, because he would have spared them and his dwelling place. ⁵¹But they mocked his messengers, and whenever the Lord spoke, they scoffed at his prophets, ⁵²until in his anger against his people because of their ungodly acts he gave command to bring against them the kings of the Chaldeans. ⁵³These slew their young men with the sword around their holy temple, and did not spare young man or virgin, old

d Gk *him*
e Gk *Jehoiakim*

1.34–58: The last kings of Judah; Jerusalem's fall to the Babylonians (2 Chr.36.1–21). **34:** The expression *men of the nation* corresponds to the "people of the land" of 2 Chr.36.1; in pre-exilic times these were conservative landowners who often came to the support of reforming kings or who themselves instituted reforms (2 Kg.12.18,20; 21.24; 23.30). *Jeconiah*, also called Jehoahaz (2 Kg.23.30–31; 2 Chr.36.1–2) and Shallum (Jer.22.11). **38:** The author has misunderstood 2 Chr.36.4. Neco of Egypt removed Jehoahaz from the throne and installed Josiah's elder son Eliakim as king, changing his name to Jehoiakim. Jehoahaz was taken to Egypt where presumably he died (Jer.22.10–12). 1 Esdras has *Jehoiakim* bring up his brother *Zarius* from Egypt; the name *Zarius* is apparently an orthographic corruption (through confusion of the Hebrew letters *d* and *r*) of Zedekiah, who was a brother of Jehoiakim (2 Kg.24.17). **39:** 1 Esdras omits the length of Jehoiakim's reign, which was eleven years (2 Chr.36.5). **43:** 1 Esdras mistakenly

man or child, for he gave them all into their hands. ⁵⁴And all the holy vessels of the Lord, great and small, and the treasure chests of the Lord, and the royal stores, they took and carried away to Babylon. ⁵⁵And they burned the house of the Lord and broke down the walls of Jerusalem and burned their towers with fire, ⁵⁶and utterly destroyed all its glorious things. The survivors he led away to Babylon with the sword, ⁵⁷and they were servants to him and to his sons until the Persians began to reign, in fulfilment of the word of the Lord by the mouth of Jeremiah: ⁵⁸"Until the land has enjoyed its sabbaths, it shall keep sabbath all the time of its desolation until the completion of seventy years."

2 In the first year of Cyrus as king of the Persians, that the word of the Lord by the mouth of Jeremiah might be accomplished, ²the Lord stirred up the spirit of Cyrus king of the Persians, and he made a proclamation throughout all his kingdom and also put it in writing:

3 "Thus says Cyrus king of the Persians: The Lord of Israel, the Lord Most High, has made me king of the world, ⁴and he has commanded me to build him a house at Jerusalem, which is in Judea. ⁵If any one of you, therefore, is of his people, may his Lord be with him, and let him go up to Jerusalem, which is in Judea, and build the house of the Lord of Israel—he is the Lord who dwells in Jerusalem, ⁶and let each man, wherever he may live, be helped by the men of his place with gold and silver, ⁷with gifts, and with horses and cattle, besides the other things added as votive offerings for the temple of the Lord which is in Jerusalem."

8 Then arose the heads of families of the tribes of Judah and Benjamin, and the priests and the Levites, and all whose spirit the Lord had stirred to go up to build the house in Jerusalem for the Lord; ⁹and their neighbors helped them with everything, with silver and gold, with horses and cattle, and with a very great number of votive offerings from many whose hearts were stirred.

10 Cyrus the king also brought out the holy vessels of the Lord which Nebuchadnezzar had carried away from Jerusalem and stored in his temple of idols. ¹¹When Cyrus king of the Persians brought these out, he gave them to Mithridates his treasurer, ¹²and by him they were given to Sheshbazzar*f* the governor of Judea. ¹³The number of these was: a thousand gold cups, a thousand silver cups, twenty-nine silver censers, thirty gold bowls, two thousand four hundred and ten silver bowls, and a thousand other vessels. ¹⁴All the vessels were handed over, gold and silver, five thousand four hundred and sixty-nine, ¹⁵and they were carried back by Sheshbazzar*f* with the returning exiles from Babylon to Jerusalem.

f Gk *Sanabassarus*

---

gives Jehoiakim (see note *e*) as the name of that king's son and successor, rather than Jehoiachin; but the king's age at the beginning of his reign is correctly given (*eighteen years;* not eight, as in 2 Chr.36.9). **58:** To *keep sabbath* means that the land is to continue in a state of "sabbath" rest (i.e., to lie untended as in the seventh or sabbatical years) until the exiles return (Jer.25.11–12; 29.10; compare Lev.25.1–7; 26.27–39).

    2.1–15: Cyrus of Persia permits the exiles to return (Ezra 1.1–11). The text is virtually identical with that in Ezra, although the inventory of the sacred vessels appears to be better preserved in 1 Esdras than in Ezra. **1:** *First year of Cyrus,* i.e. 538 B.C.

    2.16–30: Opposition to the rebuilding of the temple and the city walls (Ezra 4.7–24). A misplaced account of opposition to rebuilding the walls of Jerusalem in the time of Artaxerxes I (464–423 B.C.). Cyrus was succeeded by Cambyses (529–521), who was followed by Darius I (521–485). Josephus (*Antiq.* xi. ii.1–3) substitutes Cambyses for Artaxerxes, thus providing the correct sequence of Persian kings. The original location of the passage was probably between

16 But in the time of Artaxerxes king of the Persians, Bishlam, Mithridates, Tabeel, Rehum, Beltethmus, Shimshai the scribe, and the rest of their associates, living in Samaria and other places, wrote him the following letter, against those who were living in Judea and Jerusalem:

17 "To King Artaxerxes our lord, Your servants Rehum the recorder and Shimshai the scribe and the other judges of their council in Coelesyria and Phoenicia: [18]Now be it known to our lord the king that the Jews who came up from you to us have gone to Jerusalem and are building that rebellious and wicked city, repairing its market places and walls and laying the foundations for a temple. [19]Now if this city is built and the walls finished, they will not only refuse to pay tribute but will even resist kings. [20]And since the building of the temple is now going on, we think it best not to neglect such a matter, [21]but to speak to our lord the king, in order that, if it seems good to you, search may be made in the records of your fathers. [22]You will find in the chronicles what has been written about them, and will learn that this city was rebellious, troubling both kings and other cities, [23]and that the Jews were rebels and kept setting up blockades in it from of old. That is why this city was laid waste. [24]Therefore we now make known to you, O lord and king, that if this city is built and its

walls finished, you will no longer have access to Coelesyria and Phoenicia."

25 Then the king, in reply to Rehum the recorder and Beltethmus and Shimshai the scribe and the others associated with them and living in Samaria and Syria and Phoenicia, wrote as follows:

26 "I have read the letter which you sent me. So I ordered search to be made, and it has been found that this city from of old has fought against kings, [27]and that the men in it were given to rebellion and war, and that mighty and cruel kings ruled in Jerusalem and exacted tribute from Coelesyria and Phoenicia. [28]Therefore I have now issued orders to prevent these men from building the city and to take care that nothing more be done [29]and that such wicked proceedings go no further to the annoyance of kings."

30 Then, when the letter from King Artaxerxes was read, Rehum and Shimshai the scribe and their associates went in haste to Jerusalem, with horsemen and a multitude in battle array, and began to hinder the builders. And the building of the temple in Jerusalem ceased until the second year of the reign of Darius king of the Persians.

3 Now King Darius gave a great banquet for all that were under him and all that were born in his house and all the nobles of Media and Persia [2]and all the satraps and

---

Ezra ch. 10 and Neh. ch. 1. **16**: The name *Beltethmus* is a Greek transliteration of the Aramaic title of the office held by *Rehum;* the same mistake occurs in v. 25. **17**: The persons named are officials of the Persian province called "Beyond the River" (Ezra 4.10), which included the lands of Syria, Phoenicia, and Palestine. *Rehum* is designated "the commander" in Ezra 4.8f.; the translation *recorder* is supported by Josephus. **20**: The account differs considerably from that in Ezra 4.14, which contains no reference to the rebuilding of the *temple* at this point (compare Ezra 4.24, however, where work on the *temple* is said to have stopped). **25**: *Rehum* the governor is again identified as the *recorder* rather than as the commander of Persian forces in Samaria (Ezra 4.17). As in v. 16 the name *Beltethmus* is a transliteration of the Aramaic title of *Rehum* and is not the name of a third addressee. **30**: An erroneous reference (as also in Ezra 4.24) to the halting of work on the *temple*.

3.1–5.6: The three young bodyguards in the court of Darius. This famous story, found only in 1 Esdras among the several works attributed to Ezra, provides sufficient reason for the preservation of the book throughout the centuries. The story probably originated outside the Jewish

generals and governors that were under him in the hundred and twenty-seven satrapies from India to Ethiopia. ³They ate and drank, and when they were satisfied they departed; and Darius the king went to his bedroom, and went to sleep, and then awoke.

4 Then the three young men of the bodyguard, who kept guard over the person of the king, said to one another, ⁵"Let each of us state what one thing is strongest; and to him whose statement seems wisest, Darius the king will give rich gifts and great honors of victory. ⁶He shall be clothed in purple, and drink from gold cups, and sleep on a gold bed, and have a chariot with gold bridles, and a turban of fine linen, and a necklace about his neck; ⁷and because of his wisdom he shall sit next to Darius and shall be called kinsman of Darius."

8 Then each wrote his own statement, and they sealed them and put them under the pillow of Darius the king, ⁹and said, "When the king wakes, they will give him the writing; and to the one whose statement the king and the three nobles of Persia judge to be wisest the victory shall be given according to what is written." ¹⁰The first wrote, "Wine is strongest." ¹¹The second wrote, "The king is strongest." ¹²The third wrote, "Women are strongest, but truth is victor over all things."

13 When the king awoke, they took the writing and gave it to him, and he read it. ¹⁴Then he sent and summoned all the nobles of Persia and Media and the satraps and generals and governors and prefects, ¹⁵and he took his seat in the council chamber, and the writing was read in their presence. ¹⁶And he said, "Call the young men, and they shall explain their statements." So they were summoned, and came in. ¹⁷And they said to them, "Explain to us what you have written."

Then the first, who had spoken of the strength of wine, began and said: ¹⁸"Gentlemen, how is wine the strongest? It leads astray the minds of all who drink it. ¹⁹It makes equal the mind of the king and the orphan, of the slave and the free, of the poor and the rich. ²⁰It turns every thought to feasting and mirth, and forgets all sorrow and debt. ²¹It makes all hearts feel rich, forgets kings and satraps, and makes every one talk in millions.ᵍ ²²When men drink they forget to be friendly with friends and brothers, and before long they draw their swords. ²³And when they recover from the wine, they do not remember what they have done. ²⁴Gentlemen, is not wine the strongest, since it forces men to do these things?" When he had said this, he stopped speaking.

g Gk talents

---

community as a popular tale praising the relative strength of wine, kings, and women (the original order was perhaps kings, wine, and women). The praise of the strength of truth (4.33–41; compare 3.12) was added later in the transmission of the story, perhaps by a Greek-speaking editor (this part of the story has close parallels to Greek thought and literature). The author of 1 Esdras, adopting the story, needed only to identify the third youth with Zerubbabel (4.13) and to add a sequel to the tale, relating how Darius rewarded Zerubbabel by supporting the rebuilding of Jerusalem and its temple (4.42–5.6). The version of the story found in Josephus (*Antiq.* XI. iii.2–9) differs from the one given here in several particulars.

3.1–17a: The contest planned. 1–3: Apparently Darius' banquet was held at Susa, though the location is not explicitly mentioned. **2:** During Darius' reign (521–485 B.C.) there were actually only about twenty provinces (*satrapies*); this number was increased during Seleucid times (after 312 B.C.), and the total *one hundred twenty-seven* became conventional in later literature (Est.1.1; Josephus, *Antiq.* XI. iii.2). **4–12:** The three bodyguards decide upon a form of entertainment for the king that would bring riches and honor to one of them. According to Josephus (*Antiq.* XI. iii.2) it was the king who proposed the contest. **13–17a:** The entire court is assembled to hear the guardsmen defend their respective answers; such a scene is entirely consonant with court practices in the ancient world.

3.17b–24: In praise of the strength of wine. *Wine* is the great leveler in society; it takes away man's capacity for discernment and remembrance, overpowering king and commoner alike.

4 Then the second, who had spoken of the strength of the king, began to speak: ²"Gentlemen, are not men strongest, who rule over land and sea and all that is in them? ³But the king is stronger; he is their lord and master, and whatever he says to them they obey. ⁴If he tells them to make war on one another, they do it; and if he sends them out against the enemy, they go, and conquer mountains, walls, and towers. ⁵They kill and are killed, and do not disobey the king's command; if they win the victory, they bring everything to the king—whatever spoil they take and everything else. ⁶Likewise those who do not serve in the army or make war but till the soil, whenever they sow, reap the harvest and bring some to the king; and they compel one another to pay taxes to the king. ⁷And yet he is only one man! If he tells them to kill, they kill; if he tells them to release, they release; ⁸if he tells them to attack, they attack; if he tells them to lay waste, they lay waste; if he tells them to build, they build; ⁹if he tells them to cut down, they cut down; if he tells them to plant, they plant. ¹⁰All his people and his armies obey him. Moreover, he reclines, he eats and drinks and sleeps, ¹¹but they keep watch around him and no one may go away to attend to his own affairs, nor do they disobey him. ¹²Gentlemen, why is not the king the strongest, since he is to be obeyed in this fashion?" And he stopped speaking.

13 Then the third, that is Zerubbabel, who had spoken of women and truth, began to speak: ¹⁴"Gentlemen, is not the king great, and are not men many, and is not wine strong? Who then is their master, or who is their lord? Is it not women? ¹⁵Women gave birth to the king and to every people that rules over sea and land. ¹⁶From women they came; and women brought up the very men who plant the vineyards from which comes wine. ¹⁷Women make men's clothes; they bring men glory; men cannot exist without women. ¹⁸If men gather gold and silver or any other beautiful thing, and then see a woman lovely in appearance and beauty, ¹⁹they let all those things go, and gape at her, and with open mouths stare at her, and all prefer her to gold or silver or any other beautiful thing. ²⁰A man leaves his own father, who brought him up, and his own country, and cleaves to his wife. ²¹With his wife he ends his days, with no thought of his father or his mother or his country. ²²Hence you must realize that women rule over you!

"Do you not labor and toil, and bring everything and give it to women? ²³A man takes his sword, and goes out to travel and rob and steal and to sail the sea and rivers; ²⁴he faces lions, and he walks in darkness, and when he steals and robs and plunders, he brings it back to the woman he loves. ²⁵A man loves his wife more than his father or his mother. ²⁶Many men have lost their minds because of women, and have become slaves because of them. ²⁷Many have perished, or stumbled, or sinned, because of women. ²⁸And now do you not believe me?

"Is not the king great in his power? Do not all lands fear to touch him? ²⁹Yet I have seen him with Apame, the king's concubine, the daughter of the illustrious Bartacus; she would sit at the king's right hand ³⁰and take the crown from the king's head and put it on her own, and slap the king with her left hand. ³¹At this the king

---

4.1–12: In praise of the strength of kings. The arbitrary power of oriental kings here portrayed is quite true to the actual situation in the ancient world. No polemic against kingship need be seen in the passage.

4.13–32: In praise of the strength of women. The third youth, identified for the first time as *Zerubbabel* (v. 13), depicts the strength of *women*, who give birth to kings, who receive from men the treasures won in warfare and heroic deeds, who can humiliate their masters, including kings, and yet are sought after and fawned upon by those whom they humiliate. **29:** The king's concubine *Apame*, daughter of Bartacus, cannot be identified.

would gaze at her with mouth agape. If she smiles at him, he laughs; if she loses her temper with him, he flatters her, that she may be reconciled to him. ³²Gentlemen, why are not women strong, since they do such things?"

33 Then the king and the nobles looked at one another; and he began to speak about truth: ³⁴"Gentlemen, are not women strong? The earth is vast, and heaven is high, and the sun is swift in its course, for it makes the circuit of the heavens and returns to its place in one day. ³⁵Is he not great who does these things? But truth is great, and stronger than all things. ³⁶The whole earth calls upon truth, and heaven blesses her. All God's*ʰ* works quake and tremble, and with him there is nothing unrighteous. ³⁷Wine is unrighteous, the king is unrighteous, women are unrighteous, all the sons of men are unrighteous, all their works are unrighteous, and all such things. There is no truth in them and in their unrighteousness they will perish. ³⁸But truth endures and is strong for ever, and lives and prevails for ever and ever. ³⁹With her there is no partiality or preference, but she does what is righteous instead of anything that is unrighteous or wicked. All men approve her deeds, ⁴⁰and there is nothing unrighteous in her judgment. To her belongs the strength and the kingship and the power and the majesty of all the ages. Blessed be the God of

truth!" ⁴¹He ceased speaking; then all the people shouted, and said, "Great is truth, and strongest of all!"

42 Then the king said to him, "Ask what you wish, even beyond what is written, and we will give it to you, for you have been found to be the wisest. And you shall sit next to me, and be called my kinsman." ⁴³Then he said to the king, "Remember the vow which you made to build Jerusalem, in the day when you became king, ⁴⁴and to send back all the vessels that were taken from Jerusalem, which Cyrus set apart when he began*ⁱ* to destroy Babylon, and vowed to send them back there. ⁴⁵You also vowed to build the temple, which the Edomites burned when Judea was laid waste by the Chaldeans. ⁴⁶And now, O lord the king, this is what I ask and request of you, and this befits your greatness. I pray therefore that you fulfil the vow whose fulfilment you vowed to the King of heaven with your own lips."

47 Then Darius the king rose, and kissed him, and wrote letters for him to all the treasurers and governors and generals and satraps, that they should give escort to him and all who were going up with him to build Jerusalem. ⁴⁸And he wrote letters to all the governors in Coelesyria and Phoenicia and to those in Lebanon, to bring cedar

h Gk *All the works*
i Cn: Gk *vowed*

4.33–41: In praise of the strength of truth. The strength of *truth*, an addition to the original story probably made prior to the story's adaptation to the Jewish author's purpose, is portrayed in imagery akin to the depiction of truth in Greek literature. The Jewish adapter of the story may have modified the original somewhat to make truth more nearly akin to Hebraic ideas of truth (firmness, reliability). The closing references to truth suggest that it is virtually equivalent to the will of God: "Blessed be the God of truth!" (v. 40). The audience responds (v. 41) with the declaration, "Great is truth, and strongest of all!" The Latin proverb *magna est veritas et praevalet* ("Great is truth, and it prevails") is the most famous line from the Vulgate text of 1 Esdras.

4.42–57: Zerubbabel's reward. Darius authorizes Zerubbabel to return to Jerusalem and rebuild the temple, with generous support from the Persian treasury. **43:** The historically improbable vow of Darius to rebuild Jerusalem and its temple upon his accession to the kingship is not otherwise attested; indeed, the author has already recounted Cyrus' proclamation authorizing the return of the exiles and the restoration of the temple vessels (2.1–15). **45:** *The Edomites* are credited with having burned the temple, contrary to 1.55 (see Ob.11–14). **48–57:** Darius magnificently supports the program outlined by Zerubbabel. The historical background

timber from Lebanon to Jerusalem, and to help him build the city. [49]And he wrote for all the Jews who were going up from his kingdom to Judea, in the interest of their freedom, that no officer or satrap or governor or treasurer should forcibly enter their doors; [50]that all the country which they would occupy should be theirs without tribute; that the Idumeans should give up the villages of the Jews which they held; [51]that twenty talents a year should be given for the building of the temple until it was completed, [52]and an additional ten talents a year for burnt offerings to be offered on the altar every day, in accordance with the commandment to make seventeen offerings; [53]and that all who came from Babylonia to build the city should have their freedom, they and their children and all the priests who came. [54]He wrote also concerning their support and the priests' garments in which[j] they were to minister. [55]He wrote that the support for the Levites should be provided until the day when the temple should be finished and Jerusalem built. [56]He wrote that land and wages should be provided for all who guarded the city. [57]And he sent back from Babylon all the vessels which Cyrus had set apart; everything that Cyrus had ordered to be done, he also commanded to be done and to be sent to Jerusalem.

58 When the young man went out, he lifted up his face to heaven toward Jerusalem, and praised the King of heaven, saying, [59]"From thee is the victory; from thee is wisdom; and thine is the glory. I am thy servant. [60]Blessed art thou, who hast given me wisdom; I give thee thanks, O Lord of our fathers."

61 So he took the letters, and went to Babylon and told this to all his brethren. [62]And they praised the God of their fathers, because he had given them release and permission [63]to go up and build Jerusalem and the temple which is called by his name; and they feasted, with music and rejoicing, for seven days.

5 After this the heads of fathers' houses were chosen to go up, according to their tribes, with their wives and sons and daughters, and their menservants and maidservants, and their cattle. [2]And Darius sent with them a thousand horsemen to take them back to Jerusalem in safety, with the music of drums and flutes; [3]and all their brethren were making merry. And he made them go up with them.

4 These are the names of the men who went up, according to their fathers' houses in the tribes, over their groups: [5]the priests, the sons of Phinehas, son of Aaron; Jeshua the son of Jozadak, son of Seraiah, and Joakim the son of Zerubbabel, son of Shealtiel, of the house of David, of the lineage of Phares, of the tribe of Judah, [6]who spoke wise words before Darius the king of the Persians, in the second year of his reign, in the month of Nisan, the first month.

7 These are the men of Judea who

j Gk in what priestly garments

---

is reflected more accurately in the decree issued by Darius after the governor of Samaria had complained about the rebuilding of the temple (Ezra 6.1–13; 1 Esd.6.23–34). The decree of Cyrus allowing the exiles to return and restore the temple and its cult (2.1–15) is no doubt historical, and Darius confirmed this decree (6.23–34); but Zerubbabel's return was hardly supported by Darius in the manner here portrayed.

4.58–60: Zerubbabel's prayer. The language of this prayer is similar to a prayer of Daniel (Dan.2.20–23) and may be dependent upon it.

4.61–5.6: Preparations for the return. Zerubbabel journeys (perhaps from Susa) to Babylon and there recruits leaders for the returning exiles (5.4–6). The list of the leaders is hopelessly confused. *Jeshua* (5.5) is clearly the leading priest, and *Zerubbabel* is the hero of the story, not his son *Joakim*. In Neh.12.10,26, Joakim appears as the son of Jeshua; 1 Chr.3.17–24 gives a different genealogy for Zerubbabel (where he is said to be a grandson of Jehoiachin).

5.7–46: A list of the returning exiles (Ezra 2.1–70 and Neh.7.6–73a). The list in 1 Esdras

came up out of their sojourn in captivity, whom Nebuchadnezzar king of Babylon had carried away to Babylon [8]and who returned to Jerusalem and the rest of Judea, each to his own town. They came with Zerubbabel and Jeshua, Nehemiah, Seraiah, Resaiah, Bigvai,[k] Mordecai, Bilshan,[l] Mispar,[m] Reeliah, Rehum, and Baanah, their leaders.

9 The number of the men of the nation and their leaders: the sons of Parosh, two thousand one hundred and seventy-two. The sons of Shephatiah, four hundred and seventy-two. [10]The sons of Arah, seven hundred and fifty-six. [11]The sons of Pahathmoab, of the sons of Jeshua and Joab, two thousand eight hundred and twelve. [12]The sons of Elam, one thousand two hundred and fifty-four. The sons of Zattu, nine hundred and forty-five. The sons of Chorbe, seven hundred and five. The sons of Bani, six hundred and forty-eight. [13]The sons of Bebai, six hundred and twenty-three. The sons of Azgad, one thousand three hundred and twenty-two. [14]The sons of Adonikam, six hundred and sixty-seven. The sons of Bigvai, two thousand and sixty-six. The sons of Adin, four hundred and fifty-four. [15]The sons of Ater, namely of Hezekiah, ninety-two. The sons of Kilan and Azetas, sixty-seven. The sons of Azaru, four hundred and thirty-two. [16]The sons of Annias, one hundred and one. The sons of Arom. The sons of Bezai, three hundred and twenty-three. The sons of Jorah,[n] one hundred and twelve. [17]The sons of Baiterus, three thousand and five. The sons of Bethlehem,[o] one hundred and twenty-three. [18]The men of Netophah, fifty-five. The men of Anathoth, one hundred and fifty-eight. The men of Bethasmoth, forty-two. [19]The men of Kiriatharim, twenty-five. The men of Chephirah and Beeroth, seven hundred

and forty-three. [20]The Chadiasans and Ammidians, four hundred and twenty-two. The men of Ramah[p] and Geba, six hundred and twenty-one. [21]The men of Michmas,[q] one hundred and twenty-two. The men of Bethel,[r] fifty-two. The sons of Magbish,[s] one hundred and fifty-six. [22]The sons of the other Elam[t] and Ono, seven hundred and twenty-five. The sons of Jericho, three hundred and forty-five. [23]The sons of Senaah, three thousand three hundred and thirty.

24 The priests: the sons of Jedaiah the son of Jeshua, of the sons of Anasib, nine hundred and seventy-two. The sons of Immer, one thousand and fifty-two. [25]The sons of Pashhur, one thousand two hundred and forty-seven. The sons of Harim, one thousand and seventeen.

26 The Levites: the sons of Jeshua and Kadmiel and Bannas and Sudias, seventy-four. [27]The temple singers: the sons of Asaph, one hundred and twenty-eight. [28]The gatekeepers: the sons of Shallum, the sons of Ater, the sons of Talmon, the sons of Akkub, the sons of Hatita, the sons of Shobai, in all one hundred and thirty-nine.

29 The temple servants: the sons of Ziha,[u] the sons of Hasupha, the sons of Tabbaoth, the sons of Keros, the sons of Siaha,[v] the sons of Padon, the sons of Lebanah, the sons of Hagabah, [30]the sons of Akkub, the sons of Uthai, the sons of Ketab, the sons of Hagab, the sons of Shamlai,[w] the sons of Hana, the sons of Cathua, the sons of Gahar,[x] [31]the sons of Reaiah,[y] the sons of Rezin,[z] the sons of Nekoda,[a] the sons of Chezib, the sons of Gazzam,[b] the sons of Uzza, the sons of

k Gk *Eneneus*   l Gk *Beelsarus*
m Gk *Aspharasus*   n Gk *Arsiphurith*
o Gk *Bethlomon*   p Gk *Kirama*
q Gk *Macalon*   r Gk *Betolio*
s Gk *Niphis*   t Gk *Calamolalus*
u Gk *Esau*   v Gk *Sua*
w Gk *Subai*   x Gk *Geddur*   y Gk *Jairus*
z Gk *Daisan*   a Gk *Noeba*   b Gk *Gazera*

---

differs from that in Ezra at many points, both as to names and numbers. The totals, however, are almost identical. The numbers of the priests and Levites are almost identical in the three lists, an indication that priestly and Levitical genealogies were more carefully preserved than the other lists. **24–25:** Only four divisions of priests are given, while in 1 Chr. ch. 24 twenty-four

Paseah,[c] the sons of Hasrah, the sons of Besai,[d] the sons of Asnah, the sons of the Meunites,[e] the sons of Nephisim, the sons of Bakbuk,[f] the sons of Hakupha, the sons of Asur, the sons of Pharakim, the sons of Bazluth, [32]the sons of Mehida, the sons of Cutha, the sons of Charea, the sons of Barkos, the sons of Sisera,[g] the sons of Temah, the sons of Neziah, the sons of Hatipha.

33 The sons of Solomon's servants: the sons of Hassophereth,[h] the sons of Peruda, the sons of Jaalah, the sons of Lozon, the sons of Giddel,[i] the sons of Shephatiah, [34]the sons of Hattil,[j] the sons of Pochereth-hazzebaim, the sons of Sarothie, the sons of Masiah, the sons of Gas, the sons of Addus, the sons of Subas, the sons of Apherra, the sons of Barodis, the sons of Shaphat, the sons of Ami.[k]

35 All the temple servants and the sons of Solomon's servants were three hundred and seventy-two.

36 The following are those who came up from Telmelah[l] and Telharsha, under the leadership of Cherub, Addan, and Immer, [37]though they could not prove by their fathers' houses or lineage that they belonged to Israel: the sons of Delaiah the son of Tobiah, the sons of Nekoda, six hundred and fifty-two.

38 Of the priests the following had assumed the priesthood but were not found registered: the sons of Habaiah, the sons of Hakkoz, the sons of Jaddus who had married Agia, one of the daughters of Barzillai, and was called by his name. [39]And when the genealogy of these men was sought in the register and was not found, they were excluded

from serving as priests. [40]And Nehemiah and Attharias[m] told them not to share in the holy things until a high priest should appear wearing Urim and Thummim.[n]

41 All those of Israel, twelve or more years of age, besides menservants and maidservants, were forty-two thousand three hundred and sixty; [42]their menservants and maidservants were seven thousand three hundred and thirty-seven; there were two hundred and forty-five musicians and singers. [43]There were four hundred and thirty-five camels, and seven thousand and thirty-six horses, two hundred and forty-five mules, and five thousand five hundred and twenty-five asses.

44 Some of the heads of families, when they came to the temple of God which is in Jerusalem, vowed that they would erect the house on its site, to the best of their ability, [45]and that they would give to the sacred treasury for the work a thousand minas of gold, five thousand minas of silver, and one hundred priests' garments.

46 The priests, the Levites, and some of the people[o] settled in Jerusalem and its vicinity; and the temple singers, the gatekeepers, and all Israel in their towns.

47 When the seventh month came, and the sons of Israel were each in his own home, they gathered as one man in the square before the first gate toward the east. [48]Then Jeshua the son of Jozadak, with his fellow priests, and Zerubbabel the son of Shealtiel,

c Gk *Phinoe*   d Gk *Basthai*   e Gk *Maani*
f Gk *Acub* or *Acuph* or *Acum*   g Gk *Serar*
h Gk *Assaphioth*   i Gk *Isdael*
j Gk *Agia*   k Gk *Allon*   l Gk *Thermeleth*
m Or *the governor*   n Gk *Manifestation and Truth*
o Or *those who were of the people*

divisions appear. **40:** The name *Nehemiah* is not found in the lists in Ezra and Nehemiah; "the governor" (see note *m*) orders the community to await the appearance of a high priest before participating in the holy things. The name is an addition to the text, arising from the circumstance that Nehemiah served as governor of Judah under appointment by Artaxerxes I (Neh.5.14). *Urim and Thummim* are the sacred lots used by the priests to receive oracular decisions (Ex.28.30; Lev.8.8; Dt.33.8; 1 Sam.14.41). **41:** The total exceeds the sum of the several groups listed, it being assumed that others were present who are not specifically mentioned in the list.

5.47–73: Work on the temple commences and is interrupted (Ezra 3.1–4.5; compare Josephus, *Antiq.* xi. iv.1–3). This section is confused because the building of the temple is placed both in

with his kinsmen, took their places and prepared the altar of the God of Israel, [49]to offer burnt offerings upon it, in accordance with the directions in the book of Moses the man of God. [50]And some joined them from the other peoples of the land. And they erected the altar in its place, for all the peoples of the land were hostile to them and were stronger than they; and they offered sacrifices at the proper times and burnt offerings to the Lord morning and evening. [51]They kept the feast of booths, as it is commanded in the law, and offered the proper sacrifices every day, [52]and thereafter the continual offerings and sacrifices on sabbaths and at new moons and at all the consecrated feasts. [53]And all who had made any vow to God began to offer sacrifices to God, from the new moon of the seventh month, though the temple of God was not yet built. [54]And they gave money to the masons and the carpenters, and food and drink [55]and carts*p* to the Sidonians and the Tyrians, to bring cedar logs from Lebanon and convey them in rafts to the harbor of Joppa, according to the decree which they had in writing from Cyrus king of the Persians.

56 In the second year after their coming to the temple of God in Jerusalem, in the second month, Zerubbabel the son of Shealtiel and Jeshua the son of Jozadak made a beginning, together with their brethren and the Levitical priests and all who had come to Jerusalem from the captivity; [57]and

they laid the foundation of the temple of God on the new moon of the second month in the second year after they came to Judea and Jerusalem. [58]And they appointed the Levites who were twenty or more years of age to have charge of the work of the Lord. And Jeshua arose, and his sons and brethren and Kadmiel his brother and the sons of Jeshua Emadabun and the sons of Joda son of Iliadun, with their sons and brethren, all the Levites, as one man pressing forward the work on the house of God.

So the builders built the temple of the Lord. [59]And the priests stood arrayed in their garments, with musical instruments and trumpets, and the Levites, the sons of Asaph, with cymbals, [60]praising the Lord and blessing him, according to the directions of David king of Israel; [61]and they sang hymns, giving thanks to the Lord, because his goodness and his glory are for ever upon all Israel. [62]And all the people sounded trumpets and shouted with a great shout, praising the Lord for the erection of the house of the Lord. [63]Some of the Levitical priests and heads of fathers' houses, old men who had seen the former house, came to the building of this one with outcries and loud weeping, [64]while many came with trumpets and a joyful noise, [65]so that the people could not hear the trumpets because of the weeping of the people.

For the multitude sounded the trum-

p The Greek text is uncertain at this point

---

the reign of Cyrus (538–529 B.C.) and that of Darius (521–485 B.C.). A first return of exiles under Sheshbazzar and a second return under Zerubbabel and Jeshua have been merged. The true sequence of events is that Sheshbazzar returned to Judah shortly after 538 B.C., restored the sacrificial altar, resumed the cultic services, and laid the foundation of the temple. The work was halted until the return of additional exiles under Zerubbabel and Jeshua; when the work was resumed, opposition from Samaria, the capital of the province to which Judah belonged, quickly developed. Haggai and Zechariah encouraged the community to complete the temple, and work was begun once more; the temple was finally dedicated in 516 B.C. **47–55:** It is highly doubtful that Zerubbabel and Jeshua were involved in the initial work under Sheshbazzar; the events recorded here belong to the period of rebuilding begun in the second year of Darius, not Cyrus. **51:** The *feast of booths* is observed for one week beginning on the fifteenth day of the seventh month (Lev.23.39). **54:** Minted *money* was in use in the Persian period. **56:** Apparently the *second year* of Cyrus is intended, but the second year of Darius is the correct date. **59–65:** The author erroneously speaks of the temple's being built at this time; the ceremony described

pets loudly, so that the sound was heard afar; 66and when the enemies of the tribe of Judah and Benjamin heard it, they came to find out what the sound of the trumpets meant. 67And they learned that those who had returned from captivity were building the temple for the Lord God of Israel. 68So they approached Zerubbabel and Jeshua and the heads of the fathers' houses and said to them, "We will build with you. 69For we obey your Lord just as you do, and we have been sacrificing to him ever since the days of Esarhaddon*q* king of the Assyrians, who brought us here." 70But Zerubbabel and Jeshua and the heads of the fathers' houses in Israel said to them, "You have nothing to do with us in building the house for the Lord our God, 71for we alone will build it for the Lord of Israel, as Cyrus the king of the Persians has commanded us." 72But the peoples of the land pressed hard*r* upon those in Judea, cut off their supplies, and hindered their building; 73and by plots and demagoguery and uprisings they prevented the completion of the building as long as King Cyrus lived. And they were kept from building for two years, until the reign of Darius.

6 Now in the second year of the reign of Darius, the prophets Haggai and Zechariah the son of Iddo prophesied to the Jews who were in Judea and Jerusalem; they prophesied to them in the name of the Lord God of Israel. 2Then Zerubbabel the son of Shealtiel and Jeshua the son of Jozadak arose and began to build the house of the Lord which is in Jerusalem, with the help of the prophets of the Lord who were with them.

3 At the same time Sisinnes the governor of Syria and Phoenicia and Sathrabuzanes and their associates came to them and said, 4"By whose order are you building this house and this roof and finishing all the other things? And who are the builders that are finishing these things?" 5Yet the elders of the Jews were dealt with kindly, for the providence of the Lord was over the captives; 6and they were not prevented from building until word could be sent to Darius concerning them and a report made.

7 A copy of the letter which Sisinnes the governor of Syria and Phoenicia, and Sathrabuzanes, and their associates the local rulers in Syria and Phoenicia, wrote and sent to Darius:

8 "To King Darius, greeting. Let it be fully known to our lord the king that, when we went to the country of Judea and entered the city of Jerusalem, we found the elders of the Jews, who had been in captivity, 9building in the city of Jerusalem a great new house for the Lord, of hewn stone, with costly timber laid in the walls. 10These operations are going on rapidly, and the work is prospering in their hands and being completed with all splendor and care. 11Then we asked these elders, 'At whose command are you building this house and laying the foundations of this structure?' 12And in order that we might inform you in writing who the leaders are, we questioned them and asked them for a list of the names of those who are at their head. 13They answered us, 'We are the servants of the Lord who created the heaven and

q Gk *Asbasareth*
r The Greek text is uncertain at this point

---

in Ezra 3.10–13 occurred when the foundation of the temple was laid. **66–73:** Enemies interrupt the work; they hear the sound of celebration, a detail not found in Ezra. **69:** Instead of *Esarhaddon,* Josephus (*Antiq.* xi. iv.3) reads Shalmaneser (as in 2 Kg. ch. 17). **73:** The *two years* from the reign of Cyrus to that of Darius (compare 2.30) is a mistake; Ezra lacks this detail, although in Ezra 4.24 the cessation of work until the time of Darius introduces a similar confusion.

6.1–7.15: The temple completed (Ezra 4.24–6.22). Haggai and Zechariah encourage the resumption of work on the temple and succeed in gaining support for Zerubbabel and Jeshua (= Joshua; compare Hag.1.1–4; 2.1–4; Zech.4.9; 6.15). **6.3:** *Sisinnes* is Tattenai, governor of the province "Beyond the River"; *Sathrabuzanes* is Shetherbozenai (Ezra 5.3). **14:** *A king of*

the earth. [14]And the house was built many years ago by a king of Israel who was great and strong, and it was finished. [15]But when our fathers sinned against the Lord of Israel who is in heaven, and provoked him, he gave them over into the hands of Nebuchadnezzar king of Babylon, king of the Chaldeans; [16]and they pulled down the house, and burned it, and carried the people away captive to Babylon. [17]But in the first year that Cyrus reigned over the country of Babylonia, King Cyrus wrote that this house should be rebuilt. [18]And the holy vessels of gold and of silver, which Nebuchadnezzar had taken out of the house in Jerusalem and stored in his own temple, these Cyrus the king took out again from the temple in Babylon, and they were delivered to Zerubbabel and Sheshbazzar[s] the governor [19]with the command that he should take all these vessels back and put them in the temple at Jerusalem, and that this temple of the Lord should be rebuilt on its site. [20]Then this Sheshbazzar,[s] after coming here, laid the foundations of the house of the Lord which is in Jerusalem, and although it has been in process of construction from that time until now, it has not yet reached completion.' [21]Now therefore, if it seems wise, O king, let search be made in the royal archives of our lord[t] the king that are in Babylon; [22]and if it is found that the building of the house of the Lord in Jerusalem was done with the consent of King Cyrus, and if it is approved by our lord the king, let him send us directions concerning these things."

23 Then King Darius commanded that search be made in the royal archives that were deposited in Babylon. And in Ecbatana, the fortress which is in the country of Media, a scroll[u] was found in which this was recorded: [24]"In the first year of the reign of Cyrus, King Cyrus ordered the building of the house of the Lord in Jerusalem, where they sacrifice with perpetual fire; [25]its height to be sixty cubits and its breadth sixty cubits, with three courses of hewn stone and one course of new native timber; the cost to be paid from the treasury of Cyrus the king; [26]and that the holy vessels of the house of the Lord, both of gold and of silver, which Nebuchadnezzar took out of the house in Jerusalem and carried away to Babylon, should be restored to the house in Jerusalem, to be placed where they had been."

27 So Darius[v] commanded Sisinnes the governor of Syria and Phoenicia, and Sathrabuzanes, and their associates, and those who were appointed as local rulers in Syria and Phoenicia, to keep away from the place, and to permit Zerubbabel, the servant of the Lord and governor of Judea, and the elders of the Jews to build this house of the Lord on its site. [28]"And I command that it be built completely, and that full effort be made to help the men who have returned from the captivity of Judea, until the house of the Lord is finished; [29]and that out of the tribute of Coelesyria and Phoenicia a portion be scrupulously given to these men, that is, to Zerubbabel the governor, for sacrifices to the Lord, for bulls and rams and lambs, [30]and likewise wheat and salt and wine and oil, regularly every year, without quibbling, for daily use as the priests in Jerusalem may indicate, [31]in order that libations may be made to the Most High God for the king and his children, and prayers be offered for their life."

32 And he commanded that if any should transgress or nullify any of the things herein written,[w] a beam should

s Gk *Sanabassarus*
t Other authorities read *of Cyrus*
u Other authorities read *passage*   *v* Gk *he*
w Other authorities read *stated above* or *added in writing*

Israel, namely Solomon. **18:** *Zerubbabel* is an addition; only Sheshbazzar is mentioned in Ezra 5.14 and in Josephus (*Antiq.* XI. iv.4). **23:** *Ecbatana* was the summer residence of Darius. **32:** Ezra 6.11 prescribes that violators of the decree be impaled and their house be made a

be taken out of his house and he should be hanged upon it, and his property should be forfeited to the king.

33 "Therefore may the Lord, whose name is there called upon, destroy every king and nation that shall stretch out their hands to hinder or damage that house of the Lord in Jerusalem.

34 "I, King Darius, have decreed that it be done with all diligence as here prescribed."

7 Then Sisinnes the governor of Coelesyria and Phoenicia, and Sathrabuzanes, and their associates, following the orders of King Darius, ²supervised the holy work with very great care, assisting the elders of the Jews and the chief officers of the temple. ³And the holy work prospered, while the prophets Haggai and Zechariah prophesied; ⁴and they completed it by the command of the Lord God of Israel. So with the consent of Cyrus and Darius and Artaxerxes, kings of the Persians, ⁵the holy house was finished by the twenty-third day of the month of Adar, in the sixth year of King Darius. ⁶And the people of Israel, the priests, the Levites, and the rest of those from the captivity who joined them, did according to what was written in the book of Moses. ⁷They offered at the dedication of the temple of the Lord one hundred bulls, two hundred rams, four hundred lambs, ⁸and twelve he-goats for the sin of all Israel, according to the number of the twelve leaders of the tribes of Israel; ⁹and the priests and the Levites stood arrayed in their garments, according to kindred, for the services of the Lord God of Israel in accordance with the

book of Moses; and the gatekeepers were at each gate.

10 The people of Israel who came from the captivity kept the passover on the fourteenth day of the first month, after the priests and the Levites were purified together. ¹¹Not all of the returned captives were purified, but the Levites were all purified together,ˣ ¹²and they sacrificed the passover lamb for all the returned captives and for their brethren the priests and for themselves. ¹³And the people of Israel who came from the captivity ate it, all those who had separated themselves from the abominations of the peoples of the land and sought the Lord. ¹⁴And they kept the feast of unleavened bread seven days, rejoicing before the Lord, ¹⁵because he had changed the will of the king of the Assyrians concerning them, to strengthen their hands for the service of the Lord God of Israel.

8 After these things, when Artaxerxes the king of the Persians was reigning, Ezra came, the son of Seraiah, son of Azariah, son of Hilkiah, son of Shallum, ²son of Zadok, son of Ahitub, son of Amariah, son of Uzzi, son of Bukki, son of Abishua, son of Phineas, son of Eleazar, son of Aaron the chief priest. ³This Ezra came up from Babylon as a scribe skilled in the law of Moses, which was given by the God of Israel; ⁴and the king showed him honor, for he found favor before the kingʸ in all his requests. ⁵There came up with him to Jerusalem some of the people of Israel and some of the priests

x The Greek text of this verse is uncertain   *y* Gk *him*

---

dunghill (2 Kg.10.27; Dan.2.5). **7.4:** *Artaxerxes* (see 8.1–9.36 n.) is erroneously named here (as also in Ezra 6.14); the name is omitted by Josephus because of the anachronism. **5:** The date intended is February-March, 516 B.C. **7–8:** Compare the account of the dedication of the first temple (1 Kg.8.5,63). **9:** Compare Ezra 6.18. **13:** Contrary to Ezra 6.21 the account here seems to suggest that only the returned exiles participated in the passover. **15:** The expression *king of the Assyrians* may be used because the Persian empire comprised the former empire of Assyria. Josephus refers to the Persian king (*Antiq.* xi. iv.8).

    8.1–9.55: The history of Ezra (Ezra 7.1–10.44 and Neh.7.73–8.12). Ezra, whose name appears as author or central personality in 1 Esdras, is first introduced at this point in the document.

    8.1–9.36: Ezra leads a group of exiles from Babylonia. The author ignores the work of Nehemiah (Neh. chs. 1–7), as Sirach ignores the work of Ezra (Sir.49.13). It is probable that

and Levites and temple singers and gatekeepers and temple servants, ⁶in the seventh year of the reign of Artaxerxes, in the fifth month (this was the king's seventh year); for they left Babylon on the new moon of the first month and arrived in Jerusalem on the new moon of the fifth month, by the prosperous journey which the Lord gave them.ᶻ ⁷For Ezra possessed great knowledge, so that he omitted nothing from the law of the Lord or the commandments, but taught all Israel all the ordinances and judgments.

8 The following is a copy of the written commission from Artaxerxes the king which was delivered to Ezra the priest and reader of the law of the Lord:

9 "King Artaxerxes to Ezra the priest and reader of the law of the Lord, greeting. ¹⁰In accordance with my gracious decision, I have given orders that those of the Jewish nation and of the priests and Levites and others in our realm, who freely choose to do so, may go with you to Jerusalem. ¹¹Let as many as are so disposed, therefore, depart with you as I and the seven friends who are my counselors have decided, ¹²in order to look into matters in Judea and Jerusalem, in accordance with what is in the law of the Lord, ¹³and to carry to Jerusalem the gifts for the Lord of Israel which I and my friends have vowed, and to collect for the Lord in Jerusalem all the gold and silver that may be found in the country of Babylonia, ¹⁴together with what is given by the nation for the temple of their Lord which is in Jerusalem, both gold and silver for bulls and rams and lambs and

what goes with them, ¹⁵so as to offer sacrifices upon the altar of their Lord which is in Jerusalem. ¹⁶And whatever you and your brethren are minded to do with the gold and silver, perform it in accordance with the will of your God; ¹⁷and deliver the holy vessels of the Lord which are given you for the use of the temple of your God which is in Jerusalem. ¹⁸And whatever else occurs to you as necessary for the temple of your God, you may provide out of the royal treasury.

19 "And I, Artaxerxes the king, have commanded the treasurers of Syria and Phoenicia that whatever Ezra the priest and reader of the law of the Most High God sends for, they shall take care to give him, ²⁰up to a hundred talents of silver, and likewise up to a hundred cors of wheat, a hundred baths of wine, and salt in abundance. ²¹Let all things prescribed in the law of God be scrupulously fulfilled for the Most High God, so that wrath may not come upon the kingdom of the king and his sons. ²²You are also informed that no tribute or any other tax is to be laid on any of the priests or Levites or temple singers or gatekeepers or temple servants or persons employed in this temple, and that no one has authority to impose any tax upon them.

23 "And you, Ezra, according to the wisdom of God, appoint judges and justices to judge all those who know the law of your God, throughout all Syria and Phoenicia; and those who do not know it you shall teach. ²⁴And all who transgress the law of your God or the law of the kingdom shall be strictly punished, whether by death or

z Other authorities add *for him* or *upon him*

Ezra came to Judea under Artaxerxes II (404–358 B.C.) rather than under Artaxerxes I (464–423 B.C.).
8.1–7: Ezra identified. 1–2: The genealogy is briefer than that in Ezra 7.1–5. **6:** *The seventh year* of Artaxerxes II was 398 or 397 B.C. (If Ezra came in the seventh year of Artaxerxes I, the date would be 458 or 457 B.C.). **7:** Ezra comes specifically as a teacher of *the law of the Lord.*
8.8–24: The letter of Artaxerxes to Ezra (Ezra 7.12–26). **11:** *The seven friends* or counselors of the king are referred to in Est.1.14 and Herodotus, *Hist.* III. 84. **20:** The *talent* was 75.5 U.S. pounds; the *cor* 6.5 bushels; and the *bath* about 6 gallons. **22:** Temple personnel are exempt from all taxes. **23–24:** Ezra is given authority to appoint judges throughout the entire province in order to maintain the Jewish law.

some other punishment, either fine or imprisonment."

25 Blessed be the Lord alone, who put this into the heart of the king, to glorify his house which is in Jerusalem, [26]and who honored me in the sight of the king and his counselors and all his friends and nobles. [27]I was encouraged by the help of the Lord my God, and I gathered men from Israel to go up with me.

28 These are the principal men, according to their fathers' houses and their groups, who went up with me from Babylon, in the reign of Artaxerxes the king: [29]Of the sons of Phineas, Gershom. Of the sons of Ithamar, Gamael. Of the sons of David, Hattush the son of Shecaniah. [30]Of the sons of Parosh, Zechariah, and with him a hundred and fifty men enrolled. [31]Of the sons of Pahathmoab, Eliehoenai the son of Zerahiah, and with him two hundred men. [32]Of the sons of Zattu, Shecaniah the son of Jahaziel, and with him three hundred men. Of the sons of Adin, Obed the son of Jonathan, and with him two hundred and fifty men. [33]Of the sons of Elam, Jeshaiah the son of Gotholiah, and with him seventy men. [34]Of the sons of Shephatiah, Zeraiah the son of Michael, and with him seventy men. [35]Of the sons of Joab, Obadiah the son of Jehiel, and with him two hundred and twelve men. [36]Of the sons of Bani, Shelomith the son of Josiphiah, and with him a hundred and sixty men. [37]Of the sons of Bebai, Zechariah the son of Bebai, and with him twenty-eight men. [38]Of the sons of Azgad, Johanan the son of Hakkatan, and with him a hundred and ten men. [39]Of the sons of Adonikam, the last ones, their names being Eliphelet, Jeuel, and Shemaiah, and with them seventy men.

[40]Of the sons of Bigvai, Uthai the son of Istalcurus, and with him seventy men.

41 I assembled them at the river called Theras, and we encamped there three days, and I inspected them. [42]When I found there none of the sons of the priests or of the Levites, [43]I sent word to Eliezar, Iduel, Maasmas, [44]Elnathan, Shemaiah, Jarib, Nathan, Elnathan, Zechariah, and Meshullam, who were leaders and men of understanding; [45]and I told them to go to Iddo, who was the leading man at the place of the treasury, [46]and ordered them to tell Iddo and his brethren and the treasurers at that place to send us men to serve as priests in the house of our Lord. [47]And by the mighty hand of our Lord they brought us competent men of the sons of Mahli the son of Levi, son of Israel, namely Sherebiah[a] with his sons and kinsmen, eighteen; [48]also Hashabiah and Annunus and Jeshaiah his brother, of the sons of Hananiah, and their sons, twenty men; [49]and of the temple servants, whom David and the leaders had given for the service of the Levites, two hundred and twenty temple servants; the list of all their names was reported.

50 There I proclaimed a fast for the young men before our Lord, to seek from him a prosperous journey for ourselves and for our children and the cattle that were with us. [51]For I was ashamed to ask the king for foot soldiers and horsemen and an escort to keep us safe from our adversaries; [52]for we had said to the king, "The power of our Lord will be with those who seek him, and will support them in every way." [53]And again we prayed to our Lord about these things, and we found him very merciful.

54 Then I set apart twelve of the

a Gk *Asebebias*

8.25–60: Ezra leads the exiles to Jerusalem (Ezra 7.27–8.30). **28–40:** The list of those who returned differs in a few particulars from that found in Ezra 8.1–14. **41:** *The river . . . Theras* (Ahava in Ezra 8.21) is probably a tributary of the Euphrates. **42–49:** Because neither priests nor Levites were among the group first assembled by Ezra, special measures had to be taken to secure the required number of both. **50:** Fasting prior to an important undertaking was common

leaders of the priests, Sherebiah and Hashabiah, and ten of their kinsmen with them; ⁵⁵and I weighed out to them the silver and the gold and the holy vessels of the house of our Lord, which the king himself and his counselors and the nobles and all Israel had given. ⁵⁶I weighed and gave to them six hundred and fifty talents of silver, and silver vessels worth a hundred talents, and a hundred talents of gold, ⁵⁷and twenty golden bowls, and twelve bronze vessels of fine bronze that glittered like gold. ⁵⁸And I said to them, "You are holy to the Lord, and the vessels are holy, and the silver and the gold are vowed to the Lord, the Lord of our fathers. ⁵⁹Be watchful and on guard until you deliver them to the leaders of the priests and the Levites, and to the heads of the fathers' houses of Israel, in Jerusalem, in the chambers of the house of our Lord." ⁶⁰So the priests and the Levites who took the silver and the gold and the vessels which had been in Jerusalem carried them to the temple of the Lord.

61 We departed from the river Theras on the twelfth day of the first month; and we arrived in Jerusalem by the mighty hand of our Lord which was upon us; he delivered us from every enemy on the way, and so we came to Jerusalem. ⁶²When we had been there three days, the silver and the gold were weighed and delivered in the house of our Lord to Meremoth the priest, son of Uriah; ⁶³and with him was Eleazar the son of Phinehas,

and with them were Jozabad the son of Jeshua and Moeth the son of Binnui,^b the Levites. ⁶⁴The whole was counted and weighed, and the weight of everything was recorded at that very time. ⁶⁵And those who had come back from captivity offered sacrifices to the Lord, the God of Israel, twelve bulls for all Israel, ninety-six rams, ⁶⁶seventy-two lambs, and as a thank offering twelve he-goats—all as a sacrifice to the Lord. ⁶⁷And they delivered the king's orders to the royal stewards and to the governors of Coelesyria and Phoenicia; and these officials^c honored the people and the temple of the Lord.

68 After these things had been done, the principal men came to me and said, ⁶⁹"The people of Israel and the leaders and the priests and the Levites have not put away from themselves the alien peoples of the land and their pollutions, the Canaanites, the Hittites, the Perizzites, the Jebusites, the Moabites, the Egyptians, and the Edomites. ⁷⁰For they and their sons have married the daughters of these people,^d and the holy race has been mixed with the alien peoples of the land; and from the beginning of this matter the leaders and the nobles have been sharing in this iniquity."

71 As soon as I heard these things, I rent my garments and my holy mantle, and pulled out hair from my head and beard, and sat down in anxiety and grief. ⁷²And all who were ever moved

b Gk *Sabannus*
c Gk *they*
d Gk *their daughters*

(2 Chr.20.3; Est.4.16; Jer.36.9). **58:** *Holy* objects could be entrusted only to those who were *holy* themselves.

8.61–67: Arrival in Jerusalem (Ezra 8.31–36). The treasures are placed in the temple storehouses (*chambers*, v. 59), sacrifices are offered to God, and the king's orders delivered to the provincial officers; the latter have no choice but to obey.

8.68–9.36: Mixed marriages in Judah (Ezra 9.1–10.44). No sooner does Ezra arrive than he is presented with evidence that the community has been corrupted by mixed marriages. The older legislation had warned against marriage with the population of Canaan upon entrance into the land (Dt.7.3) but had not expressly forbidden mixed marriages. Strong warnings had been issued, however, against Israel's adopting the abominable practices of the surrounding nations (Lev.18.24–30). During the exile Israel had been able to survive only on the basis of maintaining a relatively high level of racial integrity. The strict separation carried out by Ezra is therefore understandable; in the exile standards were probably higher on this issue than they were in Judah. (Nehemiah also faced the same problem; Neh.10.28–30; 13.3, 23–30).

at^e the word of the Lord of Israel gathered round me, as I mourned over this iniquity, and I sat grief-stricken until the evening sacrifice. ⁷³Then I rose from my fast, with my garments and my holy mantle rent, and kneeling down and stretching forth my hands to the Lord ⁷⁴I said,

"O Lord, I am ashamed and confounded before thy face. ⁷⁵For our sins have risen higher than our heads, and our mistakes have mounted up to heaven ⁷⁶from the times of our fathers, and we are in great sin to this day. ⁷⁷And because of our sins and the sins of our fathers we with our brethren and our kings and our priests were given over to the kings of the earth, to the sword and captivity and plundering, in shame until this day. ⁷⁸And now in some measure mercy has come to us from thee, O Lord, to leave to us a root and a name in thy holy place, ⁷⁹and to uncover a light for us in the house of the Lord our God, and to give us food in the time of our servitude. ⁸⁰Even in our bondage we were not forsaken by our Lord, but he brought us into favor with the kings of the Persians, so that they have given us food ⁸¹and glorified the temple of our Lord, and raised Zion from desolation, to give us a stronghold in Judea and Jerusalem.

82 "And now, O Lord, what shall we say, when we have these things? For we have transgressed thy commandments, which thou didst give by thy servants the prophets, saying, ⁸³'The land which you are entering to take possession of it is a land polluted with the pollution of the aliens of the land, and they have filled it with their uncleanness. ⁸⁴Therefore do not give your daughters in marriage to their sons, and do not take their daughters for your sons; ⁸⁵and do not seek ever to have peace with them, in order that

you may be strong and eat the good things of the land and leave it for an inheritance to your children for ever.' ⁸⁶And all that has happened to us has come about because of our evil deeds and our great sins. For thou, O Lord, didst lift the burden of our sins ⁸⁷and give us such a root as this; but we turned back again to transgress thy law by mixing with the uncleanness of the peoples of the land. ⁸⁸Wast thou not angry enough with us to destroy us without leaving a root or seed or name? ⁸⁹O Lord of Israel, thou art true; for we are left as a root this day. ⁹⁰Behold, we are now before thee in our iniquities; for we can no longer stand in thy presence because of these things."

91 While Ezra was praying and making his confession, weeping and lying upon the ground before the temple, there gathered about him a very great throng from Jerusalem, men and women and youths; for there was great weeping among the multitude. ⁹²Then Shecaniah the son of Jehiel, one of the men of Israel, called out, and said to Ezra, "We have sinned against the Lord, and have married foreign women from the peoples of the land; but even now there is hope for Israel. ⁹³Let us take an oath to the Lord about this, that we will put away all our foreign wives, with their children, ⁹⁴as seems good to you and to all who obey the law of the Lord. ⁹⁵Arise^f and take action, for it is your task, and we are with you to take strong measures." ⁹⁶Then Ezra arose and had the leaders of the priests and Levites of all Israel take oath that they would do this. And they took the oath.

9   Then Ezra rose and went from the court of the temple to the chamber

e Or *zealous for*
f Other authorities read *as seems good to you." And all who obeyed the law of the Lord rose and said to Ezra, "Arise*

8.74–90: **Ezra's prayer** (Ezra 9.6–15). Ezra speaks for the entire community, acknowledging the sin of all and the justice of their punishment by God. 82–85: The prophetic books contain no such statement; the author may have in mind Lev.18.19–30.
    8.91–9.36: **The people repent and dismiss their foreign wives** (Ezra 10.1–44). 9.4: *The ruling*

of Jehohanan the son of Eliashib, [2]and spent the night there; and he did not eat bread or drink water, for he was mourning over the great iniquities of the multitude. [3]And a proclamation was made throughout Judea and Jerusalem to all who had returned from the captivity that they should assemble at Jerusalem, [4]and that if any did not meet there within two or three days, in accordance with the decision of the ruling elders, their cattle should be seized for sacrifice and the men themselves[g] expelled from the multitude of those who had returned from the captivity.

5 Then the men of the tribe of Judah and Benjamin assembled at Jerusalem within three days; this was the ninth month, on the twentieth day of the month. [6]And all the multitude sat in the open square before the temple, shivering because of the bad weather that prevailed. [7]Then Ezra rose and said to them, "You have broken the law and married foreign women, and so have increased the sin of Israel. [8]Now then make confession and give glory to the Lord the God of our fathers, [9]and do his will; separate yourselves from the peoples of the land and from your foreign wives." [10]Then all the multitude shouted and said with a loud voice, "We will do as you have said. [11]But the multitude is great and it is winter, and we are not able to stand in the open air. This is not a work we can do in one day or two, for we have sinned too much in these things. [12]So let the leaders of the multitude stay, and let all those in our settlements who have foreign wives come at the time appointed, [13]with the elders and judges of each place, until we are freed from the wrath of the Lord over this matter." [14]Jonathan the son of Asahel and Jahzeiah the son of Tikvah[h] undertook the matter on these terms, and Meshullam and Levi and Shabbethai served with them as judges. [15]And those who had returned from the captivity acted in accordance with all this.

16 Ezra the priest chose for himself the leading men of their fathers' houses, all of them by name; and on the new moon of the tenth month they began their sessions to investigate the matter. [17]And the cases of the men who had foreign wives were brought to an end by the new moon of the first month.

18 Of the priests those who were brought in and found to have foreign wives were: [19]of the sons of Jeshua the son of Jozadak and his brethren, Maaseiah, Eliezar, Jarib, and Jodan. [20]They pledged themselves to put away their wives, and to give rams in expiation of their error. [21]Of the sons of Immer: Hanani and Zebadiah and Maaseiah and Shemaiah and Jehiel and Azariah. [22]Of the sons of Pashhur: Elioenai, Maaseiah, Ishmael, and Nathanael, and Gedaliah, and Elasah.[i]

23 And of the Levites: Jozabad and Shimei and Kelaiah, who was Kelita, and Pethahiah and Judah and Jonah. [24]Of the temple singers: Eliashib and Zaccur.[j] [25]Of the gatekeepers: Shallum and Telem.[k]

26 Of Israel: of the sons of Parosh: Ramiah, Izziah, Malchijah, Mijamin, and Eleazar, and Asibias, and Benaiah. [27]Of the sons of Elam: Mattaniah and

g Gk *he himself*   h Gk *Thocanus*
i Gk *Salthas* or *Saloas*
j Gk *Bacchurus*
k Gk *Tolbanes*

---

elders issue orders for the entire community to assemble within two or three days; Ezra is the religious, not the political, authority in the land. **7**: *The law*, i.e. Dt.7.3. **8**: To *give glory to the Lord* is to acknowledge themselves to be in the wrong (compare Jos.7.19). **11–13**: Because of the severe winter weather, it is agreed that the separation should take place in the local districts, and the multitude is dismissed. **16–17**: Three months are required to settle the cases, from the first of the *tenth month* (Tebet = December-January) to the first of the *first month* (Nisan = March-April). **18–36**: The list of those who put away foreign wives, including priests, Levites, and the laity. The list was probably preserved in the temple archives. **20**: An offering of a ram as a guilt offering (Ezra 10.19) was made *in expiation* of the sin. **22**: *Gedaliah*, Greek "Ocidelos" (the parallel in Ezra 10.22 reads "Jozabad"; compare Ezra 10.18).

Zechariah, Jehiel[l] and Abdi, and Jeremoth and Elijah. [28]Of the sons of Zattu:[m] Elioenai,[n] Eliashib, Othoniah, Jeremoth, and Zabad and Zerdaiah. [29]Of the sons of Bebai: Jehohanan and Hananiah and Zabbai and Emathis. [30]Of the sons of Bani:[o] Meshullam,[p] Malluch,[q] Adaiah, Jashub, and Sheal and Jeremoth. [31]Of the sons of Addi: Naathus and Moossias, Laccunus and Naidus, and Bescaspasmys and Sesthel, and Belnuus and Manasseas. [32]Of the sons of Annan: Elionas and Asaias and Melchias and Sabbaias and Simon Chosamaeus. [33]Of the sons of Hashum: Mattenai and Mattattah and Zabad and Eliphelet and Manasseh and Shimei. [34]Of the sons of Bani: Jeremai, Maadai,[r] Amram,[s] Joel, Mamdai and Bedeiah and Vaniah, Carabasion and Eliashib and Machnadebai,[t] Eliasis, Binnui, Elialis, Shimei, Shelemiah, Nethaniah. Of the sons of Ezora: Shashai, Azarel, Azael, Shemaiah,[u] Amariah,[v] Joseph. [35]Of the sons of Nebo:[w] Mattithiah,[x] Zabad, Iddo, Joel, Benaiah. [36]All these had married foreign women, and they put them away with their children.

37 The priests and the Levites and the men of Israel settled in Jerusalem and in the country. On the new moon of the seventh month, when the sons of Israel were in their settlements, [38]the whole multitude gathered with one accord into the open square before the east gate of the temple; [39]and they told Ezra the chief priest and reader to bring the law of Moses which had been given by the Lord God of Israel. [40]So Ezra the chief priest brought the law, for all the multitude, men and women, and all

the priests to hear the law, on the new moon of the seventh month. [41]And he read aloud in the open square before the gate of the temple from early morning until midday, in the presence of both men and women; and all the multitude gave attention to the law. [42]Ezra the priest and reader of the law stood on the wooden platform which had been prepared; [43]and beside him stood Mattathiah, Shema, Anaiah,[y] Azariah, Uriah, Hezekiah, and Baalsamus on his right hand, [44]and on his left Pedaiah, Mishael, Malchijah, Lothasubus, Nabariah, and Zechariah. [45]Then Ezra took up the book of the law in the sight of the multitude, for he had the place of honor in the presence of all. [46]And when he opened the law, they all stood erect. And Ezra blessed the Lord God Most High, the God of hosts, the Almighty; [47]and all the multitude answered, "Amen." And they lifted up their hands, and fell to the ground and worshiped the Lord. [48]Jeshua and Anniuth and Sherebiah, Jamin,[z] Akkub, Shabbethai, Hodiah, Maaseiah[a] and Kelita, Azariah and Jozabad, Hanan, Pelaiah, the Levites, taught the law of the Lord,[b] at the same time explaining what was read.

49 Then Attharates[c] said to Ezra the chief priest and reader, and to the

l Gk *Jezrielus* m Gk *Zamoth*
n Gk *Eliadas* o Gk *Mani*
p Gk *Olamus* q Gk *Mamuchus*
r Gk *Momdius* s Gk *Maerus*
t Gk *Mamnitanemus*
u Gk *Samatus* v Gk *Zambris*
w Gk *Nooma* x Gk *Mazitias*
y Gk *Ananias* z Gk *Jadinus*
a Gk *Maiannas*
b Other authorities add *and read the law of the Lord to the multitude*
c Or *the governor*

9.37–55: Ezra's public reading of the law (Neh.7.73–8.12). **37:** *The new moon* or first day *of the seventh month* was a day of holy convocation (Lev.23.23–24; Num.29.1), the day of the New Year. **39:** Ezra is not identified elsewhere as the *chief priest* (in Neh.8.2 he is called the priest). *The law of Moses* is either the present Pentateuch or (more probably) the major legal portions of it. **42:** The *platform* erected for Ezra probably continued the tradition whereby kings would appear before the people to reaffirm the covenant law on the festal occasion at the turn of the year (compare 2 Chr.20.5; 23.13; 29.4). **48:** The Levites explained the law to the people, perhaps translating it (or its difficult portions) into Aramaic for those who may not have been familiar with Hebrew. **49:** *Attharates* is a corruption of *tirshatha*, "governor," in Neh.8.9. 1 Esdras does not intend to indicate that Nehemiah, whom some have identified with Attharates the governor, was a participant in the festivity (in Neh.8.9 the name of Nehemiah is

Levites who were teaching the multitude, and to all, [50]"This day is holy to the Lord"—now they were all weeping as they heard the law—[51]"so go your way, eat the fat and drink the sweet, and send portions to those who have none; [52]for the day is holy to the Lord; and do not be sorrowful, for the Lord will exalt you." [53]And the Levites commanded all the people, saying,

"This day is holy; do not be sorrowful." [54]Then they all went their way, to eat and drink and enjoy themselves, and to give portions to those who had none, and to make great rejoicing; [55]because they were inspired by the words which they had been taught. And they came together.*[d]*

d The Greek text ends abruptly: compare Nehemiah 8.13

an intrusion). **50–55:** The people are to rejoice even though the words of the law cause them to recognize their sin. **55:** The book ends abruptly; originally it may have continued with the story of the great celebration of the feast of booths (Neh.8.13–18). This would have been a fitting conclusion to the work, since it begins with the account of Josiah's great passover celebration.

THE SECOND BOOK OF

ESDRAS

The book commonly known as 2 Esdras differs from the other fourteen books of the Apocrypha in being an apocalypse (for the characteristics of apocalyptic literature, see p. xii above). The main part of 2 Esdras is a series of seven revelations (3.1–5.20; 5.21–6.34; 6.35–9.25; 9.38–10.59; 11.1–12.51; 13.1–58; 14.1–48), in which the seer is instructed by the angel Uriel concerning some of the great mysteries of the moral world.

The problems concerning the composition and transmission of 2 Esdras are extremely complicated. The author of the central portion (chs. 3–14) was an unknown Palestinian Jew who probably wrote in Hebrew or Aramaic near the close of the first century A.D. Subsequently his book was translated into Greek. About the middle of the next century an unknown Christian editor added in Greek an introductory section, which now comprises chs. 1–2. Nearly a century later another unknown Christian appended chs. 15–16, also in Greek.

The Semitic original and almost all of the Greek text have been lost (only 15.57–59 survives on a scrap of Greek papyrus). Before the text of the central section (chs. 3–14) perished, however, translations were made into several other languages, namely Syriac, Coptic, Ethiopic, Arabic (two independent versions), Armenian, and Georgian. In the West the entire book (chs. 1–16) circulated in several Old Latin versions. A later form of the Latin text is printed, since the Council of Trent, as an appendix to the New Testament in the Roman Catholic Vulgate Bible, where it is called the Fourth Book of Esdras.

The purpose of the original author of 2 Esdras was not only to denounce the wickedness of Rome (under the image of "Babylon") and to lament the sorrows that had befallen Jerusalem, but to wrestle with one of the most perplexing of all religious questions, the problem of theodicy, that is the reconciliation of God's justice, wisdom, power, and goodness with the many evils that beset mankind. In spite of the essentially pessimistic outlook of the book, the seer's strong religious faith enabled him to rise above the fires of adversity to high spiritual levels. His agonizing is both honorable and pathetic as he seeks "to justify the ways of God to man."

THE SECOND BOOK OF THE PROPHET Ezra the son of Seraiah, son of Azariah, son of Hilkiah, son of Shallum, son of Zadok, son of Ahitub, ²son of Ahijah, son of Phinehas, son of Eli, son of Amariah, son of Azariah, son of Meraioth, son of Arna, son of Uzzi, son of Borith, son of Abishua, son of Phinehas, son of Eleazar, ³son of Aaron, of the tribe of Levi, who was a captive in the country of the Medes in the reign of Artaxerxes, king of the Persians.

4 The word of the Lord came to me, saying, ⁵"Go and declare to my people their evil deeds, and to their children the iniquities which they have committed against me, so that they may tell their children's children ⁶that the sins of their parents have increased in them, for they have forgotten me and have offered sacrifices to strange gods. ⁷Was it not I who brought them out of the land of Egypt, out of the house of bondage? But they have angered me and despised my counsels. ⁸Pull out the hair of your head and hurl all evils upon them, for they have not obeyed my law—they are a rebellious people. ⁹How long shall I endure them, on

---

1.1–2.48: Ezra is commanded to reprove the Jewish people. 1.1–3: The genealogy of Ezra, who is of priestly descent (compare the somewhat different genealogies in Ezra 7.1–5 and 1 Esd.8.1–2). 3: *Artaxerxes* II, reigned 404–358 B.C.

1.4–11: Ezra receives a prophetic call. 4: The expression, *the word of the Lord came . . .*, so typical of prophetic authorization, is absent from the canonical book of Ezra. 5: Is.58.1. 8: The command to *pull out his hair* is to be connected with Ezra's denunciation (*hurl all evils*) of his

whom I have bestowed such great benefits? [10]For their sake I have overthrown many kings; I struck down Pharaoh with his servants, and all his army. [11]I have destroyed all nations before them, and scattered in the east the people of two provinces, Tyre and Sidon; I have slain all their enemies.

12 "But speak to them and say, Thus says the Lord: [13]Surely it was I who brought you through the sea, and made safe highways for you where there was no road; I gave you Moses as leader and Aaron as priest; [14]I provided light for you from a pillar of fire, and did great wonders among you. Yet you have forgotten me, says the Lord.

15 "Thus says the Lord Almighty: The quails were a sign to you; I gave you camps for your protection, and in them you complained. [16]You have not exulted in my name at the destruction of your enemies, but to this day you still complain. [17]Where are the benefits which I bestowed on you? When you were hungry and thirsty in the wilderness, did you not cry out to me, [18]saying, 'Why hast thou led us into this wilderness to kill us? It would have been better for us to serve the Egyptians than to die in this wilderness.' [19]I pitied your groanings and gave you manna for food; you ate the bread of angels. [20]When you were thirsty, did I not cleave the rock so that waters flowed in abundance? Because of the heat I covered you with the leaves of trees. [21]I divided fertile lands among you; I drove out the Canaanites, the Perizzites, and the Philistines before you. What more can I do for you? says the Lord. [22]Thus says the Lord Al-

mighty: When you were in the wilderness, at the bitter stream, thirsty and blaspheming my name, [23]I did not send fire upon you for your blasphemies, but threw a tree into the water and made the stream sweet.

24 "What shall I do to you, O Jacob? You would not obey me, O Judah. I will turn to other nations and will give them my name, that they may keep my statutes. [25]Because you have forsaken me, I also will forsake you. When you beg mercy of me, I will show you no mercy. [26]When you call upon me, I will not listen to you; for you have defiled your hands with blood, and your feet are swift to commit murder. [27]It is not as though you had forsaken me; you have forsaken yourselves, says the Lord.

28 "Thus says the Lord Almighty: Have I not entreated you as a father entreats his sons or a mother her daughters or a nurse her children, [29]that you should be my people and I should be your God, and that you should be my sons and I should be your father? [30]I gathered you as a hen gathers her brood under her wings. But now, what shall I do to you? I will cast you out from my presence. [31]When you offer oblations to me, I will turn my face from you; for I have rejected your feast days, and new moons, and circumcisions of the flesh. [32]I sent to you my servants the prophets, but you have taken and slain them and torn their bodies in pieces; their blood I will require of you, says the Lord.

33 "Thus says the Lord Almighty: Your house is desolate; I will drive you out as the wind drives straw; [34]and your sons will have no children, be-

---

people. **10**: Ex.14.28. **11**: The author is confused; *Tyre and Sidon*, which were cities, not *provinces*, lay to the west of the land of the Medes (v. 3).

1.12–23: Summary of God's mercies to Israel. **13**: Ex.14.29. **14**: Ex.13.21. **15**: Ex.16.13; Ps.105.40. **17–18**: Num.14.3. **19**: *The bread of angels*, Ps. 78.25; Wis.16.20. **20**: Num.20.11; Wis.11.4. **22–23**: Ex.15.22–25.

1.24–32: The casting-off of Israel. **26**: Is.1.15; 59.7. **29**: Jer.24.7; Heb.8.10. **30**: The similarity with Mt.23.37 and Lk.13.34 suggests that the author of this part of 2 Esdras was a Jewish Christian. **32**: Compare Mt. 23.34–35.

1.33–40: God will give Israel's houses to another people. **35–36**: Gentile Christians are meant

cause with you they have neglected my commandment and have done what is evil in my sight. ³⁵I will give your houses to a people that will come, who without having heard me will believe. Those to whom I have shown no signs will do what I have commanded. ³⁶They have seen no prophets, yet will recall their former state.ᵃ ³⁷I call to witness the gratitude of the people that is to come, whose children rejoice with gladness; though they do not see me with bodily eyes, yet with the spirit they will believe the things I have said.

38 "And now, father, look with pride and see the people coming from the east; ³⁹to them I will give as leaders Abraham, Isaac, and Jacob and Hosea and Amos and Micah and Joel and Obadiah and Jonah ⁴⁰and Nahum and Habakkuk, Zephaniah, Haggai, Zechariah and Malachi, who is also called the messenger of the Lord.

2 "Thus says the Lord: I brought this people out of bondage, and I gave them commandments through my servants the prophets; but they would not listen to them, and made my counsels void. ²The mother who bore them says to them, 'Go, my children, because I am a widow and forsaken. ³I brought you up with gladness; but with mourning and sorrow I have lost you, because you have sinned before the Lord God and have done what is evil in my sight. ⁴But now what can I do for you? For I am a widow and forsaken. Go, my children, and ask for mercy from the Lord.' ⁵I call upon you, father, as a witness in addition to the mother of the children, because they would not

keep my covenant, ⁶that you may bring confusion upon them and bring their mother to ruin, so that they may have no offspring. ⁷Let them be scattered among the nations, let their names be blotted out from the earth, because they have despised my covenant.

8 "Woe to you, Assyria, who conceal the unrighteous in your midst! O wicked nation, remember what I did to Sodom and Gomorrah, ⁹whose land lies in lumps of pitch and heaps of ashes. So will I do to those who have not listened to me, says the Lord Almighty."

10 Thus says the Lord to Ezra: "Tell my people that I will give them the kingdom of Jerusalem, which I was going to give to Israel. ¹¹Moreover, I will take back to myself their glory, and will give to these others the everlasting habitations, which I had prepared for Israel.ᵇ ¹²The tree of life shall give them fragrant perfume, and they shall neither toil nor become weary. ¹³Ask and you will receive; pray that your days may be few, that they may be shortened. The kingdom is already prepared for you; watch! ¹⁴Call, O call heaven and earth to witness, for I left out evil and created good, because I live, says the Lord.

15 "Mother, embrace your sons; bring them up with gladness, as does the dove; establish their feet, because I have chosen you, says the Lord. ¹⁶And I will raise up the dead from their places, and will bring them out from their tombs, because I recognize

ᵃ Other authorities read *their iniquities*
ᵇ Lat *those*

(compare Rom.10.14–20). **37:** *With bodily eyes,* Jn.20.29. **38:** God is represented as addressing Ezra as *father* of the nation. **39–40:** The three patriarchs and the twelve minor prophets, arranged in the order of the Septuagint.

2.1–9: The Lord's anger against Israel. 2: *The mother who bore them,* Jerusalem (Is.54.1; Gal.4.26–27). *Go . . . ,* Bar.4.19. **3:** Bar.4.11. **5:** The writer addresses Ezra as *father.* **6:** *To ruin,* in the fall of Jerusalem, A.D. 70. **8:** By the name *Assyria,* Israel's ancient foe, the author refers cryptically to Rome. *Sodom and Gomorrah,* Gen.19.24.

2.10–14: Israel's habitation to be given to others. 10: *My people,* i.e. the Christians (compare Hos.2.23). **11:** *Everlasting habitations,* Lk.16.9. **12:** Rev.2.7; 22.2,14. **13:** Mt.7.7–8; Lk.11.9–10; Mt.25.34.

2.15–32: Exhortation to good works. 15: *Mother,* probably a reference to the church.

my name in them. [17]Do not fear, mother of the sons, for I have chosen you, says the Lord. [18]I will send you help, my servants Isaiah and Jeremiah. According to their counsel I have consecrated and prepared for you twelve trees loaded with various fruits, [19]and the same number of springs flowing with milk and honey, and seven mighty mountains on which roses and lilies grow; by these I will fill your children with joy. [20]Guard the rights of the widow, secure justice for the fatherless, give to the needy, defend the orphan, clothe the naked, [21]care for the injured and the weak, do not ridicule a lame man, protect the maimed, and let the blind man have a vision of my splendor. [22]Protect the old and the young within your walls; [23]when you find any who are dead, commit them to the grave and mark it,[c] and I will give you the first place in my resurrection. [24]Pause and be quiet, my people, because your rest will come. [25]Good nurse, nourish your sons, and strengthen their feet. [26]Not one of the servants whom I have given you will perish, for I will require them from among your number. [27]Do not be anxious, for when the day of tribulation and anguish comes, others shall weep and be sorrowful, but you shall rejoice and have abundance. [28]The nations shall envy you but they shall not be able to do anything against you, says the Lord. [29]My hands will cover you, that your sons may not see Gehenna. [30]Rejoice, O mother, with your sons, because I will deliver you, says the Lord. [31]Remember your sons that sleep, because I will bring them out of the hiding places of the earth, and will show mercy to them; for I am merciful, says the Lord Almighty. [32]Embrace your children until I come,

and proclaim mercy to them; because my springs run over, and my grace will not fail."

33 I, Ezra, received a command from the Lord on Mount Horeb to go to Israel. When I came to them they rejected me and refused the Lord's commandment. [34]Therefore I say to you, O nations that hear and understand, "Await your shepherd; he will give you everlasting rest, because he who will come at the end of the age is close at hand. [35]Be ready for the rewards of the kingdom, because the eternal light will shine upon you for evermore. [36]Flee from the shadow of this age, receive the joy of your glory; I publicly call on my Savior to witness.[d] [37]Receive what the Lord has entrusted to you and be joyful, giving thanks to him who has called you to heavenly kingdoms. [38]Rise and stand, and see at the feast of the Lord the number of those who have been sealed. [39]Those who have departed from the shadow of this age have received glorious garments from the Lord. [40]Take again your full number, O Zion, and conclude the list of your people who are clothed in white, who have fulfilled the law of the Lord. [41]The number of your children, whom you desired, is full; beseech the Lord's power that your people, who have been called from the beginning, may be made holy."

42 I, Ezra, saw on Mount Zion a great multitude, which I could not number, and they all were praising the Lord with songs. [43]In their midst was a young man of great stature, taller than any of the others, and on the head of each of them he placed a crown, but he was more exalted than they. And I

---

c Or *seal it;* or *mark them and commit them to the grave*
d Other authorities read *I testify that my Savior has been commissioned by the Lord*

18: *Twelve trees,* Rev.22.2.   **19:** *Milk and honey,* Dt.31.20.   **23:** *Find any . . . dead,* compare Tob.1.17–19.   **26:** Jn.17.12.   **29:** *Gehenna,* place of torment.

    2.33–41: Rejected by Israel, Ezra turns to the Gentiles. 33: *On Mount Horeb,* like a second Moses (Ex.3.1; 2 Chr.5.10). **35:** *The eternal light,* Is.60.20; Rev.21.23; 22.5. **40:** *Zion,* Heb. 12.22–23. *Clothed in white,* Rev.3.4; 6.11; 7.14. **41:** *The number . . . is full,* see 4.36–37 n.; Rev. 6.11. *Called,* Rom.8.29–30.

    2.42–48: Ezra's vision of a great multitude. 42: Rev.7.9. **43:** *A young man,* compare v. 47 and Enoch 46.1.

was held spellbound. [44]Then I asked an angel, "Who are these, my lord?" [45]He answered and said to me, "These are they who have put off mortal clothing and have put on the immortal, and they have confessed the name of God; now they are being crowned, and receive palms." [46]Then I said to the angel, "Who is that young man who places crowns on them and puts palms in their hands?" [47]He answered and said to me, "He is the Son of God, whom they confessed in the world." So I began to praise those who had stood valiantly for the name of the Lord. [48]Then the angel said to me, "Go, tell my people how great and many are the wonders of the Lord God which you have seen."

3 In the thirtieth year after the destruction of our city, I Salathiel, who am also called Ezra, was in Babylon. I was troubled as I lay on my bed, and my thoughts welled up in my heart, [2]because I saw the desolation of Zion and the wealth of those who lived in Babylon. [3]My spirit was greatly agitated, and I began to speak anxious words to the Most High, and said, [4]"O sovereign Lord, didst thou not speak at the beginning when thou didst form the earth—and that without help—and didst command the dust[e] [5]and it gave[f] thee Adam, a lifeless body? Yet he was the workmanship of thy hands, and thou didst breathe into him the breath of life, and he was made alive in thy presence. [6]And thou didst lead him into the garden which thy right hand had planted before the earth appeared. [7]And thou didst lay upon

him one commandment of thine; but he transgressed it, and immediately thou didst appoint death for him and for his descendants. From him there sprang nations and tribes, peoples and clans, without number. [8]And every nation walked after its own will and did ungodly things before thee and scorned thee, and thou didst not hinder them. [9]But again, in its time thou didst bring the flood upon the inhabitants of the world and destroy them. [10]And the same fate befell them: as death came upon Adam, so the flood upon them. [11]But thou didst leave one of them, Noah with his household, and all the righteous who have descended from him.

12 "When those who dwelt on earth began to multiply, they produced children and peoples and many nations, and again they began to be more ungodly than were their ancestors. [13]And when they were committing iniquity before thee, thou didst choose for thyself one of them, whose name was Abraham; [14]and thou didst love him, and to him only didst thou reveal the end of the times, secretly by night. [15]Thou didst make with him an everlasting covenant, and promise him that thou wouldst never forsake his descendants; and thou gavest to him Isaac, and to Isaac thou gavest Jacob and Esau. [16]And thou didst set apart Jacob for thyself, but Esau thou didst reject; and Jacob became a great multitude. [17]And when thou didst lead his descendants out of Egypt, thou didst bring them to Mount Sinai. [18]Thou

e Syr Ethiop
f Syr

3.1–5.20: The first vision. 3.1–3: Introduction. 1: *The thirtieth year after the destruction* of Jerusalem by Nebuchadnezzar in 587/6 B.C. (2 Kg.25.1ff.) would be 557/6 B.C. The date specified may imply that the author was writing about A.D.100 (i.e. thirty years after the fall of Jerusalem in A.D.70). *Salathiel* is the Greek form of Shealtiel (Ezra 3.2; 5.2; Neh.12.1). The words *who am also called Ezra* are an anachronistic gloss; Ezra lived a century later.
3.4–36: The author raises perplexing questions. Whence comes sin with its consequent misery? How can Israel's continuing affliction be reconciled with God's justice? 4–5: The creation of Adam. 6–8: Adam's sin brings death on all mankind. 7: The words *immediately thou didst appoint death* imply that Adam was not originally intended to be mortal (compare Wis.1.13–14; 2.23–24). 8: Gen.6.12. 9–11: The flood (Gen.6.11ff.). 12–16: The choice of Abraham (Gen. 12.1; 17.5). 14: *By night*, Gen.15.5,12,17. 17–19: The Exodus and the giving of the law. 18:

didst bend down the heavens and shake[g] the earth, and move the world, and make the depths to tremble, and trouble the times. [19]And thy glory passed through the four gates of fire and earthquake and wind and ice, to give the law to the descendants of Jacob, and thy commandment to the posterity of Israel.

20 "Yet thou didst not take away from them their evil heart, so that thy law might bring forth fruit in them. [21]For the first Adam, burdened with an evil heart, transgressed and was overcome, as were also all who were descended from him. [22]Thus the disease became permanent; the law was in the people's heart along with the evil root, but what was good departed, and the evil remained. [23]So the times passed and the years were completed, and thou didst raise up for thyself a servant, named David. [24]And thou didst command him to build a city for thy name, and in it to offer thee oblations from what is thine. [25]This was done for many years; but the inhabitants of the city transgressed, [26]in everything doing as Adam and all his descendants had done, for they also had the evil heart. [27]So thou didst deliver the city into the hands of thy enemies.

28 "Then I said in my heart, Are the deeds of those who inhabit Babylon any better? Is that why she has gained dominion over Zion? [29]For when I came here I saw ungodly deeds without number, and my soul has seen many sinners during these thirty years.[h] And my heart failed me, [30]for I have seen how thou dost endure those who sin, and hast spared those who act wickedly, and hast destroyed thy people, and hast preserved thy enemies, [31]and hast not shown to any one how thy way may be comprehended.[i] Are the deeds of Babylon better than those of Zion? [32]Or has another nation known thee besides Israel? Or what tribes have so believed thy covenants as these tribes of Jacob? [33]Yet their reward has not appeared and their labor has borne no fruit. For I have traveled widely among the nations and have seen that they abound in wealth, though they are unmindful of thy commandments. [34]Now therefore weigh in a balance our iniquities and those of the inhabitants of the world; and so it will be found which way the turn of the scale will incline. [35]When have the inhabitants of the earth not sinned in thy sight? Or what nation has kept thy commandments so well? [36]Thou mayest indeed find individual men who have kept thy commandments, but nations thou wilt not find."

4 Then the angel that had been sent to me, whose name was Uriel, answered [2]and said to me, "Your understanding has utterly failed regarding this world, and do you think you can comprehend the way of the Most High?" [3]Then I said, "Yes, my lord." And he replied to me, "I have been sent to show you three ways, and to put before you three problems. [4]If you can solve one of them for me, I also will show you the way you desire to see, and will teach you why the heart is evil."

5 I said, "Speak on, my lord." And he said to me, "Go, weigh for me the weight of fire, or measure for

g Syr Ethiop Arab 1 Georg: Lat *didst set fast*
h Ethiop Arab 1 Arm: Lat Syr *in this thirtieth year*
i Syr: Lat *how this way should be forsaken*

Compare Ex.19.16–18; Ps. 68.7–8. **20–27:** The tendency to sin is universal and permanent. **20:** *Evil heart*, the evil *yeser* (see Sir.15.14 n.). **28–36:** The deeds of Babylon compared with those of Israel. **28:** *Babylon*, i.e. Rome (Rev.14.8). **29:** *Came here*, to Rome. The first *thirty years* of the Babylonian exile are meant. **30:** Here the author expresses the essence of the problem. **34:** For God's balance, compare Job 31.6; Ps. 62.9; Pr.16.2; Dan.5.27; Enoch 41.1; 61.8. **36:** *Individual men* among the Gentiles.

    4.1–5.19: The reply: God's ways are beyond human comprehension.

    4.1–12: The limitations of the human mind (Wis.9.16). **1:** The name *Uriel* in Hebrew means "the fire of God." According to Enoch 20.2 Uriel is a watcher over the world and over Tartarus, the lowest part of hell (compare 2 Pet.2.4 marg.).

me a measure[j] of wind, or call back for me the day that is past."

6 I answered and said, "Who of those that have been born can do this, that you ask me concerning these things?"

7 And he said to me, "If I had asked you, 'How many dwellings are in the heart of the sea, or how many streams are at the source of the deep, or how many streams are above the firmament, or which are the exits of hell, or which are the entrances[k] of paradise?' [8]perhaps you would have said to me, 'I never went down into the deep, nor as yet into hell, neither did I ever ascend into heaven.' [9]But now I have asked you only about fire and wind and the day, things through which you have passed and without which you cannot exist,[l] and you have given me no answer about them!" [10]And he said to me, "You cannot understand the things with which you have grown up; [11]how then can your mind comprehend the way of the Most High? And how can one who is already worn out[m] by the corrupt world understand incorruption?"[n] When I heard this, I fell on my face[o] [12]and said to him, "It would be better for us not to be here than to come here and live in ungodliness, and to suffer and not understand why."

13 He answered me and said, "I went into a forest of trees of the plain, and they made a plan [14]and said, 'Come, let us go and make war against the sea, that it may recede before us, and that we may make for ourselves more forests.' [15]And in like manner the waves of the sea also made a plan and said, 'Come, let us go up and subdue the forest of the plain so that there also we may gain more territory for ourselves.' [16]But the plan of the forest was in vain, for the fire came and consumed it; [17]likewise also the plan of the waves of the sea, for the sand stood firm and stopped them. [18]If now you

were a judge between them, which would you undertake to justify, and which to condemn?"

19 I answered and said, "Each has made a foolish plan, for the land is assigned to the forest, and to the sea is assigned a place to carry its waves."

20 He answered me and said, "You have judged rightly, but why have you not judged so in your own case? [21]For as the land is assigned to the forest and the sea to its waves, so also those who dwell upon earth can understand only what is on the earth, and he who is above the heavens can understand what is above the height of the heavens."

22 Then I answered and said, "I beseech you, my lord, why[p] have I been endowed with the power of understanding? [23]For I did not wish to inquire about the ways above, but about those things which we daily experience: why Israel has been given over to the Gentiles as a reproach; why the people whom you loved has been given over to godless tribes, and the law of our fathers has been made of no effect and the written covenants no longer exist; [24]and why we pass from the world like locusts, and our life is like a mist,[q] and we are not worthy to obtain mercy. [25]But what will he do for his name, by which we are called? It is about these things that I have asked."

26 He answered me and said, "If you are alive, you will see, and if you live long,[r] you will often marvel, because the age is hastening swiftly to its end. [27]For it will not be able to bring the things that have been promised to the righteous in their appointed times, because this age is full of sadness

j Syr Ethiop Arab Georg: Lat *a blast*
k Syr Compare Ethiop Arab 2 Arm: Latin omits *of hell, or which are the entrances*
l Other Latin manuscripts read *from which you cannot be separated*
m The text here is uncertain
n Syr Ethiop *the way of the incorruptible?*
o Syr Ethiop Arab 1: Latin is corrupt
p Syr Ethiop Arm: Latin is corrupt
q Syr Ethiop Arab Georg: Lat *a trembling*
r Syr: Lat *live*

4.13–21: Parable of the conflict between the forest and the sea. 21: Is.55.8–9; Jn.3.31; 1 Cor. 2.14.

4.22–32: Additional questions. 26–32: The angel answers that the new age, soon to dawn,

and infirmities. [28]For the evil about which[s] you ask me has been sown, but the harvest of it has not yet come. [29]If therefore that which has been sown is not reaped, and if the place where the evil has been sown does not pass away, the field where the good has been sown will not come. [30]For a grain of evil seed was sown in Adam's heart from the beginning, and how much ungodliness it has produced until now, and will produce until the time of threshing comes! [31]Consider now for yourself how much fruit of ungodliness a grain of evil seed has produced. [32]When heads of grain without number are sown, how great a threshing floor they will fill!"

33 Then I answered and said, "How long[t] and when will these things be? Why are our years few and evil?" [34]He answered me and said, "You do not hasten faster than the Most High, for your haste is for yourself,[u] but the Highest hastens on behalf of many. [35]Did not the souls of the righteous in their chambers ask about these matters, saying, 'How long are we to remain here?'[v] And when will come the harvest of our reward?' [36]And Jeremiel the archangel answered them and said, 'When the number of those like yourselves is completed;[w] for he has weighed the age in the balance, [37]and measured the times by measure, and numbered the times by number; and he will not move or arouse them until that measure is fulfilled.'"

38 Then I answered and said, "O sovereign Lord, but all of us also are full of ungodliness. [39]And it is perhaps on account of us that the time of threshing is delayed for the righteous— on account of the sins of those who dwell on earth."

40 He answered me and said, "Go and ask a woman who is with child if, when her nine months have been completed, her womb can keep the child within her any longer."

41 And I said, "No, lord, it cannot."

And he said to me, "In Hades the chambers of the souls are like the womb. [42]For just as a woman who is in travail makes haste to escape the pangs of birth, so also do these places hasten to give back those things that were committed to them from the beginning. [43]Then the things that you desire to see will be disclosed to you."

44 I answered and said, "If I have found favor in your sight, and if it is possible, and if I am worthy, [45]show me this also: whether more time is to come than has passed, or whether for us the greater part has gone by. [46]For I know what has gone by, but I do not know what is to come."

47 And he said to me, "Stand at my right side, and I will show you the interpretation of a parable."

48 So I stood and looked, and behold, a flaming furnace passed by before me, and when the flame had gone by I looked, and behold, the smoke remained. [49]And after this a cloud full of water passed before me and poured down a heavy and violent rain, and when the rainstorm had

s Syr Ethiop: Latin is uncertain
t Syr Ethiop: Latin is uncertain
u Syr Ethiop Arab Arm: the Latin is corrupt
v Syr Ethiop Arab 2 Georg: Lat *How long do I hope thus?*
w Syr Ethiop Arab 2: Lat *number of seeds is completed for you*

---

will solve all problems; but first the evil which is sown must be reaped. **30:** *A grain of evil seed,* the evil *yeser* (see Sir.15.14 n.).

4.33–43: The seer asks when the new age will come; he is told that first the predetermined number of the righteous must be completed. **35:** *The righteous,* i.e. the righteous dead. *Chambers,* literally "storehouses" or "garners"; according to rabbinical teaching the souls of the righteous dead are beneath the throne of God (compare Rev.6.9f.). **36:** *Jeremiel,* probably the same as Remiel, the seventh of seven archangels mentioned in Enoch 20.1–8. *Completed,* 2.41; Rev.6.11. **36–37:** *Weighed ... measured ... numbered,* God has determined the times and periods of history (see Sir.36.8 n.). **41:** *Chambers,* see v. 35 n.

4.44–50: The seer asks what proportion of time remains; he is told by a parable that the end is near.

passed, drops remained in the cloud.

50 And he said to me, "Consider it for yourself; for as the rain is more than the drops, and the fire is greater than the smoke, so the quantity that passed was far greater; but drops and smoke remained."

51 Then I prayed and said, "Do you think that I shall live until those days? Or who will be alive in those days?"

52 He answered me and said, "Concerning the signs about which you ask me, I can tell you in part; but I was not sent to tell you concerning your life, for I do not know.

5 "Now concerning the signs: behold, the days are coming when those who dwell on earth shall be seized with great terror,ˣ and the way of truth shall be hidden, and the land shall be barren of faith. ²And unrighteousness shall be increased beyond what you yourself see, and beyond what you heard of formerly. ³And the land which you now see ruling shall be waste and untrodden,ʸ and men shall see it desolate. ⁴But if the Most High grants that you live, you shall see it thrown into confusion after the third period;ᶻ

and the sun shall suddenly shine forth at night,
and the moon during the day.
⁵Blood shall drip from wood,
and the stone shall utter its voice;
the peoples shall be troubled,
and the stars shall fall.ᵃ
⁶And one shall reign whom those who dwell on earth do not expect, and the birds shall fly away together; ⁷and the sea of Sodom shall cast up fish; and

one whom the many do not know shall make his voice heard by night, and all shall hear his voice.ᵇ ⁸There shall be chaos also in many places, and fire shall often break out, and the wild beasts shall roam beyond their haunts, and menstruous women shall bring forth monsters. ⁹And salt waters shall be found in the sweet, and all friends shall conquer one another; then shall reason hide itself, and wisdom shall withdraw into its chamber,¹⁰and it shall be sought by many but shall not be found, and unrighteousness and unrestraint shall increase on earth. ¹¹And one country shall ask its neighbor, 'Has righteousness, or any one who does right, passed through you?' And it will answer, 'No.' ¹²And at that time men shall hope but not obtain; they shall labor but their ways shall not prosper. ¹³These are the signs which I am permitted to tell you, and if you pray again, and weep as you do now, and fast for seven days, you shall hear yet greater things than these."

14 Then I awoke, and my body shuddered violently, and my soul was so troubled that it fainted. ¹⁵But the angel who had come and talked with me held me and strengthened me and set me on my feet.

16 Now on the second night Phaltiel, a chief of the people, came to me and said, "Where have you been? And

x Syr: Ethiop *confusion*: Latin is uncertain
y Syr: Latin is corrupt
z Literally *after the third*; Ethiop *after three months*; Arm *after the third vision*; Georg *after the third day*
a Ethiop Compare Syr and Arab: Latin is uncertain
b Cn: Lat *fish; and it shall make its voice heard by night, which the many have not known, but all shall hear its voice.*

4.51–5.13: **The seer asks whether the end will come during his own lifetime;** he is given a description of the signs which will precede the end (compare Mt.24.4–31; Mk.13.5–27; Lk.21.8–28). **5.2:** Mt.24.12. **3:** *The land which you now see ruling*, i.e. the Roman Empire. **4:** The reference to *the third period* is cryptic (compare 14.11–13). **5:** *The stone shall utter its voice*, Hab.2.11; Lk.19.40. **6:** *The birds*, foreseeing impending disasters, *shall fly away.* **7:** *The sea of Sodom*, i.e. the Dead Sea. **8a:** Syriac, "a fissure shall arise over wide regions" (compare Zech.14.4). *Shall often break out*, or "shall burst forth for a long period." **10–11:** Is.59.14–15. **13:** For the author, fasting prepared one to receive a divine revelation; he refers to three fasts each of seven days (5.20; 6.35; 12.51).

5.14–19: Conclusion of the vision. 14: *Then I awoke*, from the dream-vision. *My soul . . . fainted*, Pss. 84.2; 107.5; Jon.2.7; compare Is.6.5; Dan.10.17b. **16:** *Phaltiel*, the historical reference is uncertain; compare Paltiel in Num.34.26; 2 Sam.3.15.

why is your face sad? [17]Or do you not know that Israel has been entrusted to you in the land of their exile? [18]Rise therefore and eat some bread, so that you may not forsake us, like a shepherd who leaves his flock in the power of cruel wolves."

19 Then I said to him, "Depart from me and do not come near me for seven days, and then you may come to me."

He heard what I said and left me. [20]So I fasted seven days, mourning and weeping, as Uriel the angel had commanded me.

21 And after seven days the thoughts of my heart were very grievous to me again. [22]Then my soul recovered the spirit of understanding, and I began once more to speak words in the presence of the Most High. [23]And I said, "O sovereign Lord, from every forest of the earth and from all its trees thou hast chosen one vine, [24]and from all the lands of the world thou hast chosen for thyself one region,[c] and from all the flowers of the world thou hast chosen for thyself one lily, [25]and from all the depths of the sea thou hast filled for thyself one river, and from all the cities that have been built thou hast consecrated Zion for thyself, [26]and from all the birds that have been created thou hast named for thyself one dove, and from all the flocks that have been made thou hast provided for thyself one sheep, [27]and from all the multitude of peoples thou hast gotten for thyself one people; and to this people, whom thou hast loved, thou hast given the law which is approved by all. [28]And now, O Lord, why hast thou given over the one to the many, and dishonored[d] the one root beyond the others, and scattered thine only one among the

many? [29]And those who opposed thy promises have trodden down those who believed thy covenants. [30]If thou dost really hate thy people, they should be punished at thy own hands."

31 When I had spoken these words, the angel who had come to me on a previous night was sent to me, [32]and he said to me, "Listen to me, and I will instruct you; pay attention to me, and I will tell you more."

33 And I said, "Speak, my lord." And he said to me, "Are you greatly disturbed in mind over Israel?[e] Or do you love him more than his Maker does?"

34 And I said, "No, my lord, but because of my grief I have spoken; for every hour I suffer agonies of heart, while I strive to understand the way of the Most High and to search out part of his judgment."

35 And he said to me, "You cannot." And I said, "Why not, my lord? Why then was I born? Or why did not my mother's womb become my grave, that I might not see the travail of Jacob and the exhaustion of the people of Israel?"

36 He said to me, "Count up for me those who have not yet come, and gather for me the scattered raindrops, and make the withered flowers bloom again for me; [37]open for me the closed chambers, and bring forth for me the winds shut up in them, or show me the picture of a voice; and then I will explain to you the travail that you ask to understand."[f]

38 And I said, "O sovereign Lord, who is able to know these things except he whose dwelling is not with men? [39]As for me, I am without wis-

c Ethiop: Lat *pit*
d Syr Ethiop Arab: Lat *prepared*
e Or *You are greatly distracted in mind over Israel.*
f Lat *see*

5.21–6.34: The second vision. 5.21–30: The seer reiterates his complaints of divine inequity in dealing with Israel. 23–28: Most of the figures representing Israel have been drawn from the Old Testament: the *vine* (v. 23), Ps. 80.8–15; the *lily* (v. 24), S. of S.2.2 (interpreted allegorically); Hos.14.5; the *river* (v. 25), Is.8.6; the city of *Zion* (v. 25), Ps. 132.13; the *dove* (v. 26), Ps.74.19; the *sheep* (v. 26), Ps. 79.13; Is.53.7; the *root* (v. 28), Enoch 93.8, compare Rom.11.17–18. **33:** It is unthinkable that man should love Israel more than God their *Maker does* (8.47). **35:** Job 3.11; 10.18–19. **36–40:** If the seer cannot understand the things of earth, how can he

dom, and how can I speak concerning the things which thou hast asked me?"

40 He said to me, "Just as you cannot do one of the things that were mentioned, so you cannot discover my judgment, or the goal of the love that I have promised my people."

41 And I said, "Yet behold, O Lord, thou dost have charge of those who are alive at the end, but what will those do who were before us, or we, or those who come after us?"

42 He said to me, "I shall liken my judgment to a circle;*g* just as for those who are last there is no slowness, so for those who are first there is no haste."

43 Then I answered and said, "Couldst thou not have created at one time those who have been and those who are and those who will be, that thou mightest show thy judgment the sooner?"

44 He replied to me and said, "The creation cannot make more haste than the Creator, neither can the world hold at one time those who have been created in it."

45 And I said, "How hast thou said to thy servant that thou*h* wilt certainly give life at one time to thy creation? If therefore all creatures will live at one time*i* and the creation will sustain them, it might even now be able to support all of them present at one time."

46 He said to me, "Ask a woman's womb, and say to it, 'If you bear ten*j* children, why one after another?' Request it therefore to produce ten at one time."

47 I said, "Of course it cannot, but only each in its own time."

48 He said to me, "Even so have I given the womb of the earth to those who from time to time are sown in it. 49For as an infant does not bring forth, and a woman who has become old does not bring forth any longer, so have I organized the world which I created."

50 Then I inquired and said, "Since thou hast now given me the opportunity, let me speak before thee. Is our mother, of whom thou hast told me, still young? Or is she now approaching old age?"

51 He replied to me, "Ask a woman who bears children, and she will tell you. 52Say to her, 'Why are those whom you have borne recently not like those whom you bore before, but smaller in stature?' 53And she herself will answer you, 'Those born in the strength of youth are different from those born during the time of old age, when the womb is failing.' 54Therefore you also should consider that you and your contemporaries are smaller in stature than those who were before you, 55and those who come after you will be smaller than you, as born of a creation which already is aging and passing the strength of youth."

56 And I said, "O Lord, I beseech thee, if I have found favor in thy sight, show thy servant through whom thou dost visit thy creation."

6 And he said to me, "At the beginning of the circle of the earth,*k*

g Or *crown*
h Syr Ethiop Arab 1: Latin text is uncertain
i Latin omits *If . . . one time*
j Syr Ethiop Arab 2 Arm: Latin text is corrupt
k The text is uncertain: compare Syr *The beginning by the hand of man, but the end by my own hands. For as before the land of the world existed there, and before:* Ethiop *At first by the Son of Man, and afterwards myself. For before the earth and the lands were created, and before*

---

expect to fathom the judgments and purpose of God? **40:** *My . . . I*, the angel speaks in God's name.

5.41–55: The place of successive generations in the divine plan for the world. The seer inquires about the status of those who have died before the messianic age shall begin (v. 41); he is told, in effect, that the last shall be as the first, and the first as the last (v. 42). He inquires why all generations of men could not have lived at the same time, namely at the beginning of the messianic age (v. 43); the reply is that generations must follow one another (vv. 44–49). *Mother* earth has become old and the last generations are inferior to the early ones (vv. 50–55). **52:** *Smaller in stature*, compare Gen.6.4 (the Nephilim, "giants"); Num.13.33.

5.56–6.6: The end of the age. As God alone created the world (without an intermediate agency), so he will bring about its end by himself alone (7.39–44).

before the portals of the world were in place, and before the assembled winds blew, [2]and before the rumblings of thunder sounded, and before the flashes of lightning shone, and before the foundations of paradise were laid, [3]and before the beautiful flowers were seen, and before the powers of movement[l] were established, and before the innumerable hosts of angels were gathered together, [4]and before the heights of the air were lifted up, and before the measures of the firmaments were named, and before the footstool of Zion was established, [5]and before the present years were reckoned; and before the imaginations of those who now sin were estranged, and before those who stored up treasures of faith were sealed—[6]then I planned these things, and they were made through me and not through another, just as the end shall come through me and not through another."

7 And I answered and said, "What will be the dividing of the times? Or when will be the end of the first age and the beginning of the age that follows?"

8 He said to me, "From Abraham to Isaac,[m] because from him were born Jacob and Esau, for Jacob's hand held Esau's heel from the beginning. [9]For Esau is the end of this age, and Jacob is the beginning of the age that follows. [10]For the beginning of a man is his hand, and the end of a man is his heel;[n] between the heel and the hand seek for nothing else, Ezra!"

11 I answered and said, "O sovereign Lord, if I have found favor in thy sight, [12]show thy servant the end of thy signs which thou didst show me in part on a previous night."

13 He answered and said to me,

"Rise to your feet and you will hear a full, resounding voice. [14]And if the place where you are standing is greatly shaken [15]while the voice is speaking, do not be terrified; because the word concerns the end, and the foundations of the earth will understand [16]that the speech concerns them. They will tremble and be shaken, for they know that their end must be changed."

17 When I heard this, I rose to my feet and listened, and behold, a voice was speaking, and its sound was like the sound of many waters. [18]And it said, "Behold, the days are coming, and it shall be that when I draw near to visit the inhabitants of the earth, [19]and when I require from the doers of iniquity the penalty of their iniquity, and when the humiliation of Zion is complete, [20]and when the seal is placed upon the age which is about to pass away, then I will show these signs: the books shall be opened before the firmament, and all shall see it together. [21]Infants a year old shall speak with their voices, and women with child shall give birth to premature children at three or four months, and these shall live and dance. [22]Sown places shall suddenly appear unsown, and full storehouses shall suddenly be found to be empty; [23]and the trumpet shall sound aloud, and when all hear it, they shall suddenly be terrified. [24]At that time friends shall make war on friends like enemies, and the earth and those who inhabit it shall be terrified, and the springs of the fountains shall stand still, so that for three hours they shall not flow.

25 "And it shall be that whoever

l Or *earthquake*
m Other authorities read *Abraham*
n Syr: Latin is defective here

6.7–10: The dividing of the times. In allegorical language the seer is told that the present corrupt age (symbolized by *Esau*) will be followed immediately, without a break, by the glorious age to come (symbolized by *Jacob*).

6.11–28: The signs of the end of the age. 12: *Thou didst show me in part*, 4.51–5.13. **17:** *I rose to my feet*, presumably the author had previously been lying down, experiencing a dream-vision. *Many waters*, Rev.1.15; 14.2; 19.6. **20:** *The books shall be opened*, i.e. the celestial books in which are written the deeds of men (Dan.7.10; 12.1; Mal.3.16; Rev.20.12; compare Ex.32.32; Ps. 69.28; Lk.10.20; Heb.12.23). **23:** *The trumpet*, 1 Cor.15.52; 1 Thess.4.16. **26:** *The men who*

remains after all that I have foretold
to you shall himself be saved and shall
see my salvation and the end of my
world. 26And they shall see the men
who were taken up, who from their
birth have not tasted death; and the
heart of the earth's[o] inhabitants shall be
changed and converted to a different
spirit. 27For evil shall be blotted out,
and deceit shall be quenched; 28faith-
fulness shall flourish, and corruption
shall be overcome, and the truth, which
has been so long without fruit, shall be
revealed."

29 While he spoke to me, behold,
little by little the place where I was
standing began to rock to and fro.[p]
30And he said to me, "I have come to
show you these things this night.[q] 31If
therefore you will pray again and fast
again for seven days, I will again declare to you greater things than these,[r]
32because your voice has surely been
heard before the Most High; for the
Mighty One has seen your uprightness
and has also observed the purity which
you have maintained from your youth.
33Therefore he sent me to show you all
these things, and to say to you: 'Believe
and do not be afraid! 34Do not be
quick to think vain thoughts concerning the former times, lest you be hasty
concerning the last times.' "

35 Now after this I wept again and
fasted seven days as before, in order to
complete the three weeks as I had been
told. 36And on the eighth night my
heart was troubled within me again,
and I began to speak in the presence of
the Most High. 37For my spirit was
greatly aroused, and my soul was in
distress.

38 I said, "O Lord, thou didst speak
at the beginning of creation, and didst
say on the first day, 'Let heaven and
earth be made,' and thy word accomplished the work. 39And then the Spirit
was hovering, and darkness and silence
embraced everything; the sound of
man's voice was not yet there.[s] 40Then
thou didst command that a ray of light
be brought forth from thy treasuries,
so that thy works might then appear.

41 "Again, on the second day, thou
didst create the spirit of the firmament,
and didst command him to divide and
separate the waters, that one part
might move upward and the other part
remain beneath.

42 "On the third day thou didst
command the waters to be gathered
together in the seventh part of the
earth; six parts thou didst dry up and
keep so that some of them might be
planted and cultivated and be of service before thee. 43For thy word went
forth, and at once the work was done.
44For immediately fruit came forth in
endless abundance and of varied appeal to the taste; and flowers of inimi-
table color; and odors of inexpressible
fragrance. These were made on the
third day.

45 "On the fourth day thou didst
command the brightness of the sun,
the light of the moon, and the arrangement of the stars to come into
being; 46and thou didst command them
to serve man, who was about to be
formed.

47 "On the fifth day thou didst
command the seventh part, where the

o Syr Compare Ethiop Arab 1 Arm: Latin omits *earth's*
p Syr Ethiop Compare Arab Arm: Latin is corrupt
q Syr Compare Ethiop: Latin is corrupt
r Syr Ethiop Arab 1 Arm: Latin adds *by day*
s Syr Ethiop: Lat *was not yet from thee*

---

were taken up, such as Enoch (Gen.5.24; Sir.44.16) and Elijah (2 Kg.2.11–12); compare also 14.9. *Shall be . . . converted*, by the preaching of Elijah (Mal.4.6).

6.29–34: Conclusion of the vision. 34: The seer is cautioned against being oversolicitous.

6.35–9.25: The third vision. 6.35–37: Introduction. 35: *I . . . fasted seven days*, see 5.13 n. *The three weeks* (compare Dan.10.2–3), so far only two fasts of seven days have been mentioned (here and at 5.20); presumably the author is thinking also of another fast prior to the first vision (3.1–5.20), not mentioned in the present form of the book.

6.38–59: The seer recounts God's work in creation. If the world was created for Israel (v. 55), why has the nation not possessed its inheritance? **38–54:** Gen. ch. 1. **38:** *Thy word accomplished the work*, Ps. 33.6; Heb.11.3; 2 Pet.3.5. **40:** God's *treasuries* are in heaven. **41:** *The spirit of the*

water had been gathered together, to bring forth living creatures, birds, and fishes; and so it was done. [48]The dumb and lifeless water produced living creatures, as it was commanded,[t] that therefore the nations might declare thy wondrous works.

49 "Then thou didst keep in existence two living creatures;[u] the name of one thou didst call Behemoth and the name of the other Leviathan. [50]And thou didst separate one from the other, for the seventh part where the water had been gathered together could not hold them both. [51]And thou didst give Behemoth one of the parts which had been dried up on the third day, to live in it, where there are a thousand mountains; [52]but to Leviathan thou didst give the seventh part, the watery part; and thou hast kept them to be eaten by whom thou wilt, and when thou wilt.

53 "On the sixth day thou didst command the earth to bring forth before thee cattle, beasts, and creeping things; [54]and over these thou didst place Adam, as ruler over all the works which thou hadst made; and from him we have all come, the people whom thou hast chosen.

55 "All this I have spoken before thee, O Lord, because thou hast said that it was for us that thou didst create this world.[v] [56]As for the other nations which have descended from Adam, thou hast said that they are nothing, and that they are like spittle, and thou hast compared their abundance to a drop from a bucket. [57]And now, O Lord, behold, these nations, which are reputed as nothing, domineer over us and devour us. [58]But we thy people, whom thou hast called thy first-born,

only begotten, zealous for thee,[w] and most dear, have been given into their hands. [59]If the world has indeed been created for us, why do we not possess our world as an inheritance? How long will this be so?"

7 When I had finished speaking these words, the angel who had been sent to me on the former nights was sent to me again, [2]and he said to me, "Rise, Ezra, and listen to the words that I have come to speak to you."

3 I said, "Speak, my lord." And he said to me, "There is a sea set in a wide expanse so that it is broad[x] and vast, [4]but it has an entrance set in a narrow place, so that it is like a river. [5]If any one, then, wishes to reach the sea, to look at it or to navigate it, how can he come to the broad part unless he passes through the narrow part? [6]Another example: There is a city built and set on a plain, and it is full of all good things; [7]but the entrance to it is narrow and set in a precipitous place, so that there is fire on the right hand and deep water on the left; [8]and there is only one path lying between them, that is, between the fire and the water, so that only one man can walk upon that path. [9]If now that city is given to a man for an inheritance, how will the heir receive his inheritance unless he passes through the danger set before him?"

10 I said, "He cannot, lord." And he said to me, "So also is Israel's portion. [11]For I made the world for their sake, and when Adam transgressed my statutes, what had been made was

t The text of this verse is uncertain
u Syr Ethiop: Lat *two souls*
v Syr Ethiop Arab 2: Lat *the first-born world* Compare Arab 1 *first world*
w The meaning of the Latin text is obscure
x Syr Compare Ethiop Arab 1: Lat *deep*

---

firmament is an angel (compare the angel with power over fire, Rev.14.18, and the angel of water, Rev.16.5). **46**: Ps. 8.6–8. **49–52**: *Behemoth* and *Leviathan* are two primeval monsters (compare Job 7.12; 26.12–13; Ps.74.12–15; 89.10–11; Is.30.7; 51.9–10). **55**: The idea that the world was created for the sake of Israel (7.11) is not found in the Old Testament, but was deduced by Jewish rabbis from such passages as Ex.4.22; Dt.10.15; 14.2. **56**: *A drop from a bucket*, Is.40.15.

7.1–25: The angel instructs the seer. The wickedness of this world makes the path to the next world narrow and dangerous. **1**: *The former nights*, at the beginning of each vision. **11**: Though *the world* was created for Israel's *sake*, that inheritance was spoiled *when Adam transgressed* (compare Rom.5.18–20). **12** and **13**: *The entrances*, Ethiopic, "the ways," i.e. the paths of life

judged. ¹²And so the entrances of this world were made narrow and sorrowful and toilsome; they are few and evil, full of dangers and involved in great hardships. ¹³But the entrances of the greater world are broad and safe, and really yield the fruit of immortality. ¹⁴Therefore unless the living pass through the difficult and vain experiences, they can never receive those things that have been reserved for them. ¹⁵But now why are you disturbed, seeing that you are to perish? And why are you moved, seeing that you are mortal? ¹⁶And why have you not considered in your mind what is to come, rather than what is now present?"

17 Then I answered and said, "O sovereign Lord, behold, thou hast ordained in thy law that the righteous shall inherit these things, but that the ungodly shall perish. ¹⁸The righteous therefore can endure difficult circumstances while hoping for easier ones; but those who have done wickedly have suffered the difficult circumstances and will not see the easier ones."

19 And he said to me, "You are not a better judge than God, or wiser than the Most High! ²⁰Let many perish who are now living, rather than that the law of God which is set before them be disregarded! ²¹For God strictly commanded those who came into the world, when they came, what they should do to live, and what they should observe to avoid punishment. ²²Nevertheless they were not obedient, and spoke against him;

they devised for themselves vain thoughts,

²³and proposed to themselves wicked frauds;
they even declared that the Most High does not exist,
and they ignored his ways!
²⁴They scorned his law,
and denied his covenants;
they have been unfaithful to his statutes,
and have not performed his works.

25 "Therefore, Ezra, empty things are for the empty, and full things are for the full. ²⁶For behold, the time will come, when the signs which I have foretold to you will come to pass, that the city which now is not seen shall appear,^{y} and the land which now is hidden shall be disclosed. ²⁷And every one who has been delivered from the evils that I have foretold shall see my wonders. ²⁸For my son the Messiah^z shall be revealed with those who are with him, and those who remain shall rejoice four hundred years. ²⁹And after these years my son the Messiah shall die, and all who draw human breath. ³⁰And the world shall be turned back to primeval silence for seven days, as it was at the first beginnings; so that no one shall be left. ³¹And after seven days the world, which is not yet awake, shall be roused, and that which is corruptible shall perish. ³²And the earth shall give up those who are asleep in it, and the dust those who dwell silently in it; and the chambers shall give up the souls which have been committed to them. ³³And the Most High shall be

y Arm: Lat Syr *that the bride shall appear, even the city appearing*
z Syr Arab 1: Ethiop *my Messiah;* Arab 2 *the Messiah;* Arm *the Messiah of God;* Lat *my son Jesus*

here on earth, and in the world of immortality. **13:** *The greater world,* Syriac, "the future world." **14:** *Things . . . reserved for them,* 1 Cor.2.9. **15–16:** The seer should not brood over difficulties and death; though inevitable, they are but preliminary to something better (2 Cor. 4.18). **17–18:** The seer inquires whether the future bliss is only for the righteous Jews, or for all the Jews. **19–25:** The angel replies that those who disregard the Mosaic law will be punished. **25:** Mt.13.12.

7.26–44: The messianic kingdom and the end of the world. 26: *The signs . . . foretold,* 6.20–24. *The city,* the heavenly Jerusalem. *The land,* the heavenly paradise. **28:** *Those who remain,* after the tribulations that will precede the inauguration of the messianic kingdom. *Four hundred years,* so the Latin and Arabic 1; Syriac, "thirty years"; Arabic 2, "one thousand years"; Ethiopic and Armenian omit. **31:** *The world . . . not yet awake,* i.e. the world to come. **32:** Dan.12.2. *Chambers,* see 4.35 n. **33:** *Judgment,* Syriac adds, "and then comes the end." *Away,*

revealed upon the seat of judgment, and compassion shall pass away, and patience shall be withdrawn;[a] [34]but only judgment shall remain, truth shall stand, and faithfulness shall grow strong. [35]And recompense shall follow, and the reward shall be manifested; righteous deeds shall awake, and unrighteous deeds shall not sleep.[b] [36]Then the pit[c] of torment shall appear, and opposite it shall be the place of rest; and the furnace of hell[d] shall be disclosed, and opposite it the paradise of delight. [37]Then the Most High will say to the nations that have been raised from the dead, 'Look now, and understand whom you have denied, whom you have not served, whose commandments you have despised! [38]Look on this side and on that; here are delight and rest, and there are fire and torments!' Thus he will[e] speak to them on the day of judgment—[39]a day that has no sun or moon or stars,[40]or cloud or thunder or lightning or wind or water or air, or darkness or evening or morning, [41]or summer or spring or heat or winter[f] or frost or cold or hail or rain or dew, [42]or noon or night, or dawn or shining or brightness or light, but only the splendor of the glory of the Most High, by which all shall see what has been determined for them. [43]For it will last for about a week of years. [44]This is my judgment and its prescribed order; and to you alone have I shown these things."

[45] I answered and said, "O sovereign Lord, I said then and I say now:[g] Blessed are those who are alive and keep thy commandments! [46]But what of those for whom I prayed? For who among the living is there that has not sinned, or who among men that has not transgressed thy covenant? [47]And now I see that the world to come will bring delight to few, but torments to many. [48]For an evil heart has grown up in us, which has alienated us from God,[h] and has brought us into corruption and the ways of death, and has shown us the paths of perdition and removed us far from life—and that not just a few of us but almost all who have been created!"

[49] He answered me and said, "Listen to me, Ezra,[i] and I will instruct you, and will admonish you yet again. [50]For this reason the Most High has made not one world but two. [51]For whereas you have said that the righteous are not many but few, while the ungodly abound, hear the explanation for this.

[52] "If you have just a few precious stones, will you add to them lead and clay?"[j]

[53] I said, "Lord, how could that be?"

[54] And he said to me, "Not only

a Lat *gather together*
b The passage from verse [36] to verse [105], formerly missing, has been restored to the text
c Syr Ethiop: Lat *place*
d Lat *gehenna*
e Syr Ethiop Arab 1: Lat *thou shalt*
f Or *storm*
g Syr: Lat *And I answered, "I said then, O Lord, and I say now:*
h Cn: Lat Syr Ethiop *from these*
i Syr Arab 1: Lat Syr Ethiop omit *Ezra*
j Arab 1: Lat Syr Ethiop are corrupt

Syriac adds, "and pity shall be far off." The final judgment will be conducted in strict accord with justice and truth. **34:** *Grow strong,* i.e. triumph. **35:** *Righteous deeds shall awake,* acts of charity hitherto concealed shall be disclosed (compare Mt.25.35–46). **[36–105]:** These verses are lacking from the standard editions of the Latin Vulgate and from the King James version. They are present in the Syriac, Ethiopic, Arabic, and Armenian versions, and in two Latin manuscripts. The section was probably deliberately cut out of an ancestor of most extant Latin manuscripts because of dogmatic reasons, for the passage contains an emphatic denial of the value of prayers for the dead (v. [105]). **[36]:** *Pit,* Rev.9.2. *Opposite,* Lk.16.23–24. **[37]:** Mt. 25.31ff. **[39–43]:** Description of the day of judgment. **[42]:** *Only* the uncreated light *of the Most High* will serve to illuminate the judgment scene (compare Is.60.19–20; Rev.21.23). **[43]:** *A week of years,* seven years.

7.[45–61]: The small number of the saved (contrast Lk.13.23–30). **[48]:** *An evil heart,* see 3.20 n. **[49]:** 5.32. **[52]:** The question implies that the number of the elect cannot be increased by adding base elements.

that, but ask the earth and she will tell you; defer to her, and she will declare it to you. [55]Say to her, 'You produce gold and silver and brass, and also iron and lead and clay; [56]but silver is more abundant than gold, and brass than silver, and iron than brass, and lead than iron, and clay than lead.' [57]Judge therefore which things are precious and desirable, those that are abundant or those that are rare?"

[58] I said, "O sovereign Lord, what is plentiful is of less worth, for what is more rare is more precious."

[59] He answered me and said, "Weigh within yourself[k] what you have thought, for he who has what is hard to get rejoices more than he who has what is plentiful. [60]So also will be the judgment[l] which I have promised; for I will rejoice over the few who shall be saved, because it is they who have made my glory to prevail now, and through them my name has now been honored. [61]And I will not grieve over the multitude of those who perish; for it is they who are now like a mist, and are similar to a flame and smoke—they are set on fire and burn hotly, and are extinguished."

[62] I replied and said, "O earth, what have you brought forth, if the mind is made out of the dust like the other created things! [63]For it would have been better if the dust itself had not been born, so that the mind might not have been made from it. [64]But now the mind grows with us, and therefore we are tormented, because we perish and know it. [65]Let the human race lament, but let the beasts of the field be glad; let all who have been born lament, but let the four-footed beasts and the flocks rejoice! [66]For it is much better with them than with us; for they do not look for a judgment, nor do they know of any torment or

salvation promised to them after death. [67]For what does it profit us that we shall be preserved alive but cruelly tormented? [68]For all who have been born are involved in iniquities, and are full of sins and burdened with transgressions. [69]And if we were not to come into judgment after death, perhaps it would have been better for us."

[70] He answered me and said, "When the Most High made the world and Adam and all who have come from him, he first prepared the judgment and the things that pertain to the judgment. [71]And now understand from your own words, for you have said that the mind grows with us. [72]For this reason, therefore, those who dwell on earth shall be tormented, because though they had understanding they committed iniquity, and though they received the commandments they did not keep them, and though they obtained the law they dealt unfaithfully with what they received. [73]What, then, will they have to say in the judgment, or how will they answer in the last times? [74]For how long the time is that the Most High has been patient with those who inhabit the world, and not for their sake, but because of the times which he has foreordained!"

[75] I answered and said, "If I have found favor in thy sight, O Lord, show this also to thy servant: whether after death, as soon as every one of us yields up his soul, we shall be kept in rest until those times come when thou wilt renew the creation, or whether we shall be tormented at once?"

[76] He answered me and said, "I will show you that also, but do not be associated with those who have shown scorn, nor number yourself among those who are tormented. [77]For you

k Syr Ethiop Arab 1: Latin is corrupt here
l Syr Arab 1: Lat *creation*

7.[62–74]: The seer's lament over the human race. [63]: 4.12. **[64]:** The possession of reasoning powers intensifies sufferings. **[67]:** The author identifies himself with sinners (contrast 6.32–34). **[70]:** *Things that pertain to the judgment*, according to rabbinical teaching, before the beginning of the world God created Paradise and Gehenna.
7.[75–101]: The state of the departed after death and before the judgment. [77]: *A treasure of*

have a treasure of works laid up with the Most High; but it will not be shown to you until the last times. [78]Now, concerning death, the teaching is: When the decisive decree has gone forth from the Most High that a man shall die, as the spirit leaves the body to return again to him who gave it, first of all it adores the glory of the Most High. [79]And if it is one of those who have shown scorn and have not kept the way of the Most High, and who have despised his law, and who have hated those who fear God—[80]such spirits shall not enter into habitations, but shall immediately wander about in torments, ever grieving and sad, in seven ways. [81]The first way, because they have scorned the law of the Most High. [82]The second way, because they cannot now make a good repentance that they may live. [83]The third way, they shall see the reward laid up for those who have trusted the covenants of the Most High. [84]The fourth way, they shall consider the torment laid up for themselves in the last days. [85]The fifth way, they shall see how the habitations of the others are guarded by angels in profound quiet. [86]The sixth way, they shall see how some of them will pass over*m* into torments. [87]The seventh way, which is worse*n* than all the ways that have been mentioned, because they shall utterly waste away in confusion and be consumed with shame,*o* and shall wither with fear at seeing the glory of the Most High before whom they sinned while they were alive, and before whom they are to be judged in the last times.

[88] "Now this is the order of those who have kept the ways of the Most High, when they shall be separated from their mortal body.*p* [89]During the time that they lived in it,*q* they laboriously served the Most High, and withstood danger every hour, that they might keep the law of the Lawgiver perfectly. [90]Therefore this is the teaching concerning them: [91]First of all, they shall see with great joy the glory of him who receives them, for they shall have rest in seven orders. [92]The first order, because they have striven with great effort to overcome the evil thought which was formed with them, that it might not lead them astray from life into death. [93]The second order, because they see the perplexity in which the souls of the ungodly wander, and the punishment that awaits them. [94]The third order, they see the witness which he who formed them bears concerning them, that while they were alive they kept the law which was given them in trust. [95]The fourth order, they understand the rest which they now enjoy, being gathered into their chambers and guarded by angels in profound quiet, and the glory which awaits them in the last days. [96]The fifth order, they rejoice that they have now escaped what is corruptible, and shall inherit what is to come; and besides they see the straits and toil*r* from which they have been delivered, and the spacious liberty which they are to receive and enjoy in immortality. [97]The sixth order, when it is shown to them how their face is to shine like the sun, and how they are to be made like the light of the stars, being incorruptible from then on. [98]The seventh order, which is greater than all that have been mentioned, because they shall rejoice with

m Cn: the text of this verse is corrupt
n Lat *greater*
o Syr Ethiop: Latin is corrupt
p Literally *the corruptible vessel*
q Syr Ethiop: Latin is corrupt
r Syr Ethiop: Lat *fulness*

---

works, 8.33,36. *Will not be shown,* see v. 35 n. **[78]**: Ec.12.7. The first act of the departed spirit (whether righteous or wicked) is to adore God. **[80–87]**: Seven kinds of torment for the wicked. **[80]**: *Habitations,* Lk.16.9; elsewhere called "chambers," see 4.35 n. **[83]**: Compare Lk.16.23. **[85]**: *The others,* i.e. the righteous. **[88–99]**: Seven kinds of joyous rest for the righteous. The author implies that the *mortal body* has been merely a prison-house for the spirit (contrast 1 Cor.15.53; 2 Cor.5.2–4). **[92]**: *The evil thought,* the evil *yeser* (see Sir.15.14 n.). **[95]**: *Chambers,* see 4.35 n. *In the last days,* better, "at their latter end." **[97]**: *Shine,* v. [125]; Dan.12.3;

boldness, and shall be confident without confusion, and shall be glad without fear, for they hasten to behold the face of him whom they served in life and from whom they are to receive their reward when glorified. [99]This is the order of the souls of the righteous, as henceforth is announced;*s* and the aforesaid are the ways of torment which those who would not give heed shall suffer hereafter."

[100] I answered and said, "Will time therefore be given to the souls, after they have been separated from the bodies, to see what you have described to me?"

[101] He said to me, "They shall have freedom for seven days, so that during these seven days they may see the things of which you have been told, and afterwards they shall be gathered in their habitations."

[102] I answered and said, "If I have found favor in thy sight, show further to me, thy servant, whether on the day of judgment the righteous will be able to intercede for the ungodly or to entreat the Most High for them, [103]fathers for sons or sons for parents, brothers for brothers, relatives for their kinsmen, or friends*t* for those who are most dear."

[104] He answered me and said, "Since you have found favor in my sight, I will show you this also. The day of judgment is decisive*u* and displays to all the seal of truth. Just as now a father does not send his son, or a son his father, or a master his servant, or a friend his dearest friend, to be ill*v* or sleep or eat or be healed in his stead, [105]so no one shall ever pray for another on that day, neither shall any one lay a burden on another;*w* for then every one shall bear his own righteousness or unrighteousness."

36 [106] I answered and said, "How then do we find that first Abraham prayed for the people of Sodom, and Moses for our fathers who sinned in the desert, 37[107]and Joshua after him for Israel in the days of Achan, 38[108]and Samuel in the days of Saul,*x* and David for the plague, and Solomon for those in the sanctuary, 39[109]and Elijah for those who received the rain, and for the one who was dead, that he might live, 40[110]and Hezekiah for the people in the days of Sennacherib, and many others prayed for many? 41[111]If therefore the righteous have prayed for the ungodly now, when corruption has increased and unrighteousness has multiplied, why will it not be so then as well?"

42 [112] He answered me and said, "This present world is not the end; the full glory does not*y* abide in it;*z* therefore those who were strong prayed for the weak. 43[113]But the day of judgment will be the end of this age and the beginning*a* of the immortal age to come, in which corruption has passed away, 44[114]sinful indulgence has come to an end, unbelief has been cut off, and righteousness has increased and truth has appeared. 45[115]Therefore no one will then be able to have mercy on him who has been condemned in the judgment, or to harm*b* him who is victorious."

46 [116] I answered and said, "This is my first and last word, that it would

s Syr: Latin is corrupt here
t Syr Ethiop Arab 1: Lat *kinsmen for their nearest, friends* (literally *the confident*) *for their dearest*
u Lat *bold*
v Syr Ethiop Arm: Lat *understand*
w Syr: Latin omits *on that . . . another*
x Syr Ethiop Arab 1: Latin omits *in the days of Saul*
y Latin omits *not*
z Or *the glory does not continuously abide in it*
a Latin omits *the beginning*
b Syr Ethiop: Lat *overwhelm*

Mt.13.43. **[98]:** *To behold the face* of God (Mt.5.8; Heb.12.14; 1 Jn.3.2; Rev.22.4). *Reward,* 1 Cor.3.14; Rev.22.12. **[101]:** *Habitations,* see v. [80] n.
    7.[102–115]: No intercession for the wicked on the day of judgment (compare Dt.24.16; Jer. 31.30). **[106]:** Gen.18.23; Ex.32.11. **[107]:** Jos.7.6–7. **[108]:** *Samuel,* 1 Sam.7.9; 12.23. *David,* 2 Sam.24.17. *Solomon,* 1 Kg.8.22–23,30. **[109]:** 1 Kg.18.42,45; 17.20–21. **[110]:** 2 Kg.19.15–19. **[112–115]:** During the present order intercession *for the weak* is possible, but the day of judgment means the closing of all accounts on the basis of strict justice (see v. 33 n.).
    7.[116–131]: The seer laments the fate of the mass of humanity. **[116]:** *My first . . . word,* 3.5ff.

have been better if the earth had not produced Adam, or else, when it had produced him, had restrained him from sinning. 47[117]For what good is it to all that they live in sorrow now and expect punishment after death? 48[118]O Adam, what have you done? For though it was you who sinned, the fall was not yours alone, but ours also who are your descendants. 49[119]For what good is it to us, if an eternal age has been promised to us, but we have done deeds that bring death? 50[120]And what good is it that an everlasting hope has been promised us, but we have miserably failed? 51[121]Or that safe and healthful habitations have been reserved for us, but we have lived wickedly? 52[122]Or that the glory of the Most High will defend those who have led a pure life, but we have walked in the most wicked ways? 53[123]Or that a paradise shall be revealed, whose fruit remains unspoiled and in which are abundance and healing, but we shall not enter it, 54[124]because we have lived in unseemly places? 55[125]Or that the faces of those who practiced self-control shall shine more than the stars, but our faces shall be blacker than darkness? 56[126]For while we lived and committed iniquity we did not consider what we should suffer after death."

57 [127] He answered and said, "This is the meaning of the contest which every man who is born on earth shall wage, 58[128]that if he is defeated he shall suffer what you have said, but if he is victorious he shall receive what I have said.^{c} 59[129]For this is the way of which Moses, while he was alive, spoke to the people, saying, 'Choose for yourself life, that you may live!' 60[130]But they did not believe him, or the proph-

ets after him, or even myself who have spoken to them. 61[131]Therefore there shall not be^d grief at their destruction, so much as joy over those to whom salvation is assured."

62 [132] I answered and said, "I know, O Lord, that the Most High is now called merciful, because he has mercy on those who have not yet come into the world; 63[133]and gracious, because he is gracious to those who turn in repentance to his law; 64[134]and patient, because he shows patience toward those who have sinned, since they are his own works; 65[135]and bountiful, because he would rather give than take away;^{e} 66[136]and abundant in compassion, because he makes his compassions abound more and more to those now living and to those who are gone and to those yet to come, 67[137]for if he did not make them abound, the world with those who inhabit it would not have life; 68[138]and he is called giver, because if he did not give out of his goodness so that those who have committed iniquities might be relieved of them, not one ten-thousandth of mankind could have life; 69[139]and judge, because if he did not pardon those who were created by his word and blot out the multitude of their sins,^{f} 70[140]there would probably be left only very few of the innumerable multitude."

8 He answered me and said, "The Most High made this world for the sake of many, but the world to come for the sake of few. 2But I will tell you a parable, Ezra. Just as, when you ask the earth, it will tell you that it provides very much clay from which earthen-

c Syr Ethiop Arab 1: Lat *I say*
d Syr: Lat *was not*
e Or *is ready to give according to requests*
f Lat *contempts*

---

[118]: 4.30–31. [123]: *Fruit*, compare Ezek.47.12; Rev.22.2. [125]: *Shine more than the stars*, Dan.12.3; compare Mt.13.43. *Darkness*, Mt.8.12; 22.13; Jude 13. [127–129]: Man is responsible for his choices (Dt.30.19).

7.[132]–8.3: The seer acknowledges (and implicitly appeals to) God's mercy. Will a merciful God permit so many to perish? He is told that nothing can alter their doom, for *many have been created, but few shall be saved* (8.3). [132–139]: For the sevenfold attributes of God, compare Ex.34.6–7. [132]: *O Lord*, better, "sir." [135]: Acts 20.35. [138]: *Life*, i.e. eternal life. 8.2: *A parable*, an analogous illustration (as in 7.[54–57]). 3: Mt.22.14.

ware is made, but only a little dust from which gold comes; so is the course of the present world. [3]Many have been created, but few shall be saved."

4 I answered and said, "Then drink your fill of understanding, O my soul, and drink wisdom, O my heart![g] [5]For not of your own will did you come into the world,[h] and against your will you depart, for you have been given only a short time to live. [6]O Lord who art over us, grant to thy servant that we may pray before thee, and give us seed for our heart and cultivation of our understanding so that fruit may be produced, by which every mortal who bears the likeness[i] of a human being may be able to live. [7]For thou alone dost exist, and we are a work of thy hands, as thou hast declared. [8]And because thou dost give life to the body which is now fashioned in the womb, and dost furnish it with members, what thou hast created is preserved in fire and water, and for nine months the womb[j] which thou hast formed endures thy creation which has been created in it. [9]But that which keeps and that which is kept shall both be kept by thy keeping.[k] And when the womb gives up again what has been created in it, [10]thou hast commanded that from the members themselves (that is, from the breasts) milk should be supplied which is the fruit of the breasts, [11]so that what has been fashioned may be nourished for a time; and afterwards thou wilt guide him in thy mercy. [12]Thou hast brought him up in thy righteousness, and instructed him in thy law,

and reproved him in thy wisdom. [13]Thou wilt take away his life, for he is thy creation; and thou wilt make him live, for he is thy work. [14]If then thou wilt suddenly and quickly[l] destroy him who with so great labor was fashioned by thy command, to what purpose was he made? [15]And now I will speak out: About all mankind thou knowest best; but I will speak about thy people, for whom I am grieved, [16]and about thy inheritance, for whom I lament, and about Israel, for whom I am sad, and about the seed of Jacob, for whom I am troubled. [17]Therefore I will pray before thee for myself and for them, for I see the failings of us who dwell in the land, [18]and[m] I have heard of the swiftness of the judgment that is to come. [19]Therefore hear my voice, and understand my words, and I will speak before thee."

The beginning of the words of Ezra's prayer, before he was taken up. He said: [20]"O Lord who inhabitest eternity,[n] whose eyes are exalted[o] and whose upper chambers are in the air, [21]whose throne is beyond measure and whose glory is beyond comprehension, before whom the hosts of angels stand trembling [22]and at whose command they are changed to wind and fire,[p] whose word is sure and whose utterances are certain, whose ordinance is strong and whose com-

g Syr: Lat *let it feed on what it understands*
h Syr: Latin is corrupt here   i Syr: Lat *place*
j Literally *what thou hast formed*
k Syr: Latin is corrupt here
l Syr: Lat *shalt with a light command*
m Literally *but*   n Or *abidest for ever*
o Another Latin text reads *whose are the highest heavens*
p Syr: Lat *they whose service takes the form of wind and fire*

8.4–36: The seer implores God to show mercy upon his creation. 4–19a: Why should God wonderfully fashion and sustain all mankind, only to destroy the great majority? **4–5:** The pre-existence of the soul is implied here (Wis.8.19). **7:** Is.44.6; 45.11; 60.21. **14:** *Was fashioned by thy command*, Ps. 139.14–15. **15–16:** The seer leaves the fate of *mankind* in God's hands, and speaks particularly about Israel, God's *inheritance* (Ps.28.9). **19b–36:** A beautiful and liturgically structured prayer (invocation to God, whose attributes are recalled, vv. 20–23; petitions, interspersed with confession and intercessions, vv. 24–35; concluding ascription of praise, v. 36). This prayer also occurs separately, with the title "Confessio Esdrae," in the section of canticles and hymns contained in many manuscripts of the Latin Vulgate Bible. This circumstance accounts for the presence (in v. 19b) of a superscription in the third person. **19b:** The words, *before he was taken up*, indicate that the belief was current that Ezra, like Enoch and Elijah, was translated to heaven without dying. **22:** *Wind and fire*, Ps.104.4; Heb.1.7.

mand is terrible, ²³whose look dries up the depths and whose indignation makes the mountains melt away, and whose truth is established for ever^q— ²⁴hear, O Lord, the prayer of thy servant, and give ear to the petition of thy creature; attend to my words. ²⁵For as long as I live I will speak, and as long as I have understanding I will answer. ²⁶O look not upon the sins of thy people, but at those who have served thee in truth. ²⁷Regard not the endeavors of those who act wickedly, but the endeavors of those who have kept thy covenants amid afflictions. ²⁸Think not on those who have lived wickedly in thy sight; but remember those who have willingly acknowledged that thou art to be feared. ²⁹Let it not be thy will to destroy those who have had the ways of cattle; but regard those who have gloriously taught thy law.^r ³⁰Be not angry with those who are deemed worse than beasts; but love those who have always put their trust in thy glory. ³¹For we and our fathers have passed our lives in ways that bring death;^s but thou, because of us sinners, art called merciful. ³²For if thou hast desired to have pity on us, who have no works of righteousness, then thou wilt be called merciful. ³³For the righteous, who have many works laid up with thee, shall receive their reward in consequence of their own deeds. ³⁴But what is man, that thou art angry with him; or what is a corruptible race, that thou art so bitter against it? ³⁵For in truth there is no one among those who have been born who has not acted wickedly, and among those who have

existed^t there is no one who has not transgressed. ³⁶For in this, O Lord, thy righteousness and goodness will be declared, when thou art merciful to those who have no store of good works."

37 He answered me and said, "Some things you have spoken rightly, and it will come to pass according to your words. ³⁸For indeed I will not concern myself about the fashioning of those who have sinned, or about their death, their judgment, or their destruction; ³⁹but I will rejoice over the creation of the righteous, over their pilgrimage also, and their salvation, and their receiving their reward. ⁴⁰As I have spoken, therefore, so it shall be.

41 "For just as the farmer sows many seeds upon the ground and plants a multitude of seedlings, and yet not all that have been sown will come up^u in due season, and not all that were planted will take root; so also those who have been sown in the world will not all be saved."

42 I answered and said, "If I have found favor before thee, let me speak.^v ⁴³For if the farmer's seed does not come up, because it has not received thy rain in due season, or if it has been ruined by too much rain, it perishes.^w ⁴⁴But man, who has been formed by thy hands and is called thy own image because he is made like thee, and for whose sake thou hast formed all things —hast thou also made him like the

q Arab 2: other authorities read *bears witness*
r Syr *have received the brightness of thy law*
s Syr Ethiop: the Latin text is uncertain
t Syr: the Latin text is corrupt
u Syr Ethiop *will live;* Lat *will be saved*
v Or *If I have found favor, let me speak before thee*
w Cn: Compare Syr Arab 1 Arm Georg: the Latin is corrupt

23: *Dries up,* Is.50.2; 51.10. *Mountains melt,* Mic.1.4; Sir.16.18–19. **32:** Rom.3.19–26. **33:** 7.[77].

8.37–40: The divine reply to the seer's prayer: God will rejoice in the righteous and forget the sinners (the central petition of the prayer—mercy on the wicked—is ignored). **39:** *Their pilgrimage,* i.e. their return home to God (compare 2 Cor.5.6–8). **40:** Instead of *I have spoken,* the reading of the Ethiopic, "you have spoken," is to be preferred in view of v. 37 and the irony of the divine reply: "it is to be as you have *spoken,* but not as you had intended" (in vv. 26–36 the seer prayed God to ignore the wicked and their doings and pay attention to the righteous only; this, the Almighty replies, he will do, but in the sense of being unconcerned about the *destruction* of the wicked, v. 38).

8.41–45: Mankind is like the farmer's seed; only a few individuals will escape destruction. **45:** An anguished entreaty: *spare thy people,* Jl.2.17.

farmer's seed? [45]No, O Lord[x] who art over us! But spare thy people and have mercy on thy inheritance, for thou hast mercy on thy own creation."

46 He answered me and said, "Things that are present are for those who live now, and things that are future are for those who will live hereafter. [47]For you come far short of being able to love my creation more than I love it. But you have often compared yourself[y] to the unrighteous. Never do so! [48]But even in this respect you will be praiseworthy before the Most High, [49]because you have humbled yourself, as is becoming for you, and have not deemed yourself to be among the righteous in order to receive[z] the greatest glory. [50]For many miseries will affect those who inhabit the world in the last times, because they have walked in great pride. [51]But think of your own case, and inquire concerning the glory of those who are like yourself, [52]because it is for you that paradise is opened, the tree of life is planted, the age to come is prepared, plenty is provided, a city is built, rest is appointed,[a] goodness is established and wisdom perfected beforehand. [53]The root of evil is sealed up from you, illness is banished from you, and death[b] is hidden; hell has fled and corruption has been forgotten;[c] [54]sorrows have passed away, and in the end the treasure of immortality is made manifest. [55]Therefore do not ask any more questions about the multitude of those who perish. [56]For they also received freedom, but they despised the Most High, and were contemptuous of his law, and forsook his ways. [57]Moreover

they have even trampled upon his righteous ones, [58]and said in their hearts that there is no God—though knowing full well that they must die. [59]For just as the things which I have predicted await[d] you, so the thirst and torment which are prepared await them. For the Most High did not intend that men should be destroyed; [60]but they themselves who were created have defiled the name of him who made them, and have been ungrateful to him who prepared life for them. [61]Therefore my judgment is now drawing near; [62]I have not shown this to all men, but only to you and a few like you."

Then I answered and said, [63]"Behold, O Lord, thou hast now shown me a multitude of the signs which thou wilt do in the last times, but thou hast not shown me when thou wilt do them."

9 He answered me and said, "Measure carefully in your mind, and when you see that a certain part of the predicted signs are past, [2]then you will know that it is the very time when the Most High is about to visit the world which he has made. [3]So when there shall appear in the world earthquakes, tumult of peoples, intrigues of nations, wavering of leaders, confusion of princes, [4]then you will know that it was of these that the Most High spoke from the days that were of old, from the beginning. [5]For just as with everything that has occurred in the world,

x Ethiop Arab Compare Syr: Latin omits *O Lord*
y Syr Ethiop: Lat *brought yourself near*
z Or *righteous; so that you will receive*
a Syr: Lat *allowed*
b Syr Ethiop Arm: Latin omits *death*
c Syr: Lat *Hades and corruption have fled into oblivion,* or *corruption has fled into Hades to be forgotten*
d Syr: Lat *will receive*

8.46–62: The final divine reply: The seer is assured that his lot is with the blessed, and is advised to think no more about sinners, who deserve their doom because they have *despised the Most High* (v. 56). **46–47:** The seer's objection (v. 44) is invalid, for the simile of the seeds suits the *present* corruptible order; *the future* has standards of its own. Moreover, God's love for his *creation* far exceeds man's love (see 5.33 n.). **48:** *In this respect,* i.e. the seer's humility (compare Lk.18.13–14). **52:** The future joys of heaven are already in existence and may be contemplated now (1 Pet.1.4). *Tree of life,* 7.[123]; Rev.2.7; 22.2. **53:** *Hell* is personified (as in Rev.6.8). **56:** *Freedom,* i.e. free will. **58:** Ps.14.1; 53.1. **59:** *The things . . . predicted,* in vv. 52–54. *Thirst,* in the fire of hell (Lk.16.24). *The Most High did not intend* man's destruction (Mt.18.14; 1 Tim.2.4). **62:** *A few like you,* i.e. prophets (apocalyptists) like the seer.

8.63–9.13: **The end, and the signs which will precede it** (4.51–5.13; 6.11–24). **8.63:** *When,* 4.33;

the beginning is evident,[e] and the end manifest; [6]so also are the times of the Most High: the beginnings are manifest in wonders and mighty works, and the end in requital[f] and in signs. [7]And it shall be that every one who will be saved and will be able to escape on account of his works, or on account of the faith by which he has believed, [8]will survive the dangers that have been predicted, and will see my salvation in my land and within my borders, which I have sanctified for myself from the beginning. [9]Then those who have now abused my ways shall be amazed, and those who have rejected them with contempt shall dwell in torments. [10]For as many as did not acknowledge me in their lifetime, although they received my benefits, [11]and as many as scorned my law while they still had freedom, and did not understand but despised it[g] while an opportunity of repentance was still open to them, [12]these must in torment acknowledge it[h] after death. [13]Therefore, do not continue to be curious as to how the ungodly will be punished; but inquire how the righteous will be saved, those to whom the age belongs and for whose sake the age was made."[i]

14 I answered and said, [15]"I said before, and I say now, and will say it again: there are more who perish than those who will be saved, [16]as a wave is greater than a drop of water."

17 He answered me and said, "As is the field, so is the seed; and as are the flowers, so are the colors; and as is the work, so is the product; and as is the farmer, so is the threshing floor. [18]For there was a time in this age when I was preparing for those who now

exist, before the world was made for them to dwell in, and no one opposed me then, for no one existed; [19]but now those who have been created in this world which is supplied both with an unfailing table and an inexhaustible pasture,[j] have become corrupt in their ways. [20]So I considered my world, and behold, it was lost, and my earth, and behold, it was in peril because of the devices of those who[k] had come into it. [21]And I saw and spared some[l] with great difficulty, and saved for myself one grape out of a cluster, and one plant out of a great forest.[m] [22]So let the multitude perish which has been born in vain, but let my grape and my plant be saved, because with much labor I have perfected them. [23]But if you will let seven days more pass—do not fast during them, however; [24]but go into a field of flowers where no house has been built, and eat only of the flowers of the field, and taste no meat and drink no wine, but eat only flowers, [25]and pray to the Most High continually—then I will come and talk with you."

26 So I went, as he directed me, into the field which is called Ardat;[n] and there I sat among the flowers and ate of the plants of the field, and the nourishment they afforded satisfied me. [27]And after seven days, as I lay on the grass, my heart was troubled again as it was before. [28]And my mouth was opened, and I began to

e Syr: Ethiop *in the word:* Latin is corrupt
f Syr: Lat Ethiop *in effects*
g Or *me*   h Or *me*
i Syr: Lat *saved, and whose is the age and for whose sake the age was made and when*   j Cn: Lat *law*
k Cn: Lat *devices which*   l Lat *them*
m Syr Ethiop Arab 1: Lat *tribe*
n Syr Ethiop *Arpad:* Arm *Ardab*

contrast Acts 1.7. **9.3:** The messianic woes on earth. **9–12:** The state of the wicked immediately after death. **11:** Opportunity of repentance (Wis.12.10,20; Heb.12.17). **12:** *Acknowledge*, their earlier opportunity of repentance; or the word may be translated "be brought to know."

9.14–25: Recapitulation: The seer again deplores the fate of the wicked, and the small number of the saved is explained a last time. **19:** Restore "law" (see note *j*) to the text: the meaning is that despite God's gracious provision of earthly sustenance and divine law, men *have become corrupt.* **21–22:** The preservation of a small remnant is the result of God's grace. **24:** Likewise Daniel and his companions ate only vegetables (Dan.1.8–16; compare 2 Macc.5.27).

9.26–10.59: The fourth vision. 9.26–28: Introduction. 26: *Ardat*, an unknown location, probably of symbolical or mystic significance.

speak before the Most High, and said,
[29]"O Lord, thou didst show thyself
among us, to our fathers in the wilderness when they came out from Egypt
and when they came into the untrodden and unfruitful wilderness; [30]and
thou didst say, 'Hear me, O Israel,
and give heed to my words, O descendants of Jacob. [31]For behold, I sow my
law in you, and it shall bring forth fruit
in you, and you shall be glorified
through it for ever.' [32]But though our
fathers received the law, they did not
keep it, and did not observe the statutes; yet the fruit of the law did not
perish—for it could not, because it was
thine. [33]Yet those who received it
perished, because they did not keep
what had been sown in them. [34]And
behold, it is the rule that, when the
ground has received seed, or the sea a
ship, or any dish food or drink, and
when it happens that what was sown
or what was launched or what was put
in is destroyed, [35]they are destroyed,
but the things that held them remain;
yet with us it has not been so. [36]For
we who have received the law and
sinned will perish, as well as our heart
which received it; [37]the law, however,
does not perish but remains in its
glory."

[38] When I said these things in my
heart, I lifted up my eyes[o] and saw a
woman on my right, and behold, she
was mourning and weeping with a loud
voice, and was deeply grieved at heart,
and her clothes were rent, and there
were ashes on her head. [39]Then I dismissed the thoughts with which I had
been engaged, and turned to her [40]and
said to her, "Why are you weeping,
and why are you grieved at heart?"
[41] And she said to me, "Let me
alone, my lord, that I may weep for
myself and continue to mourn, for I
am greatly embittered in spirit and
deeply afflicted."

[42] And I said to her, "What has
happened to you? Tell me."

[43] And she said to me, "Your
servant was barren and had no child,
though I lived with my husband
thirty years. [44]And every hour and
every day during those thirty years I
besought the Most High, night and
day. [45]And after thirty years God
heard your handmaid, and looked
upon my low estate, and considered
my distress, and gave me a son. And I
rejoiced greatly over him, I and my
husband and all my neighbors;[p] and
we gave great glory to the Mighty One.
[46]And I brought him up with much
care. [47]So when he grew up and I came
to take a wife for him, I set a day for
the marriage feast.

[10] "But it happened that when my
son entered his wedding chamber,
he fell down and died. [2]Then we all
put out the lamps, and all my neighbors[q] attempted to console me; and I
remained quiet until evening of the
second day. [3]But when they all had
stopped consoling me, that I might be
quiet, I got up in the night and fled,
and came to this field, as you see. [4]And
now I intend not to return to the city,
but to stay here, and I will neither eat
nor drink, but without ceasing mourn
and fast until I die."

[5] Then I broke off the reflections
with which I was still engaged, and
answered her in anger and said,
[6]"You most foolish of women, do you
not see our mourning, and what has
happened to us? [7]For Zion, the
mother of us all, is in deep grief and
great affliction. [8]It is most appropriate to mourn now, because we are all

o Syr Arab Arm: Lat *I looked about me with my eyes*
p Literally *all my fellow citizens*
q Literally *all my fellow citizens*

9.29–37: **The abiding glory of the Mosaic law,** contrasted with Israel. **29:** Ex.19.9; 24.10;
Dt.4.12.

9.38–10.24: **The seer speaks with a disconsolate woman. 38:** *Ashes on her head,* a sign of
mourning. **47:** It was customary for the father to arrange for the wedding (see Sir.7.25 n.).
10.2: *Lamps,* because weddings took place at night. **2:** *I remained quiet,* shows the depth of her
grief, for ordinarily there was loud lamentation. **7:** *Zion, the mother of us all,* Gal.4.26.

mourning, and to be sorrowful, because we are all sorrowing; you are sorrowing for one son, but we, the whole world, for our mother.*ʳ* ⁹Now ask the earth, and she will tell you that it is she who ought to mourn over so many who have come into being upon her. ¹⁰And from the beginning all have been born of her, and others will come; and behold, almost all go to perdition, and a multitude of them are destined for destruction. ¹¹Who then ought to mourn the more, she*ˢ* who lost so great a multitude, or you who are grieving for one? ¹²But if you say to me, 'My lamentation is not like the earth's, for I have lost the fruit of my womb, which I brought forth in pain and bore in sorrow; ¹³but it is with the earth according to the way of the earth—the multitude that is now in it goes as it came'; ¹⁴then I say to you, 'As you brought forth in sorrow, so the earth also has from the beginning given her fruit, that is, man, to him who made her.' ¹⁵Now, therefore, keep your sorrow to yourself, and bear bravely the troubles that have come upon you. ¹⁶For if you acknowledge the decree of God to be just, you will receive your son back in due time, and will be praised among women. ¹⁷Therefore go into the city to your husband."

18 She said to me, "I will not do so; I will not go into the city, but I will die here."

19 So I spoke again to her, and said, ²⁰"Do not say that, but let yourself be persuaded because of the troubles of Zion, and be consoled because of the sorrow of Jerusalem. ²¹For you see that our sanctuary has been laid waste, our altar thrown down, our temple destroyed; ²²our harp has been laid low, our song has been silenced, and our rejoicing has been ended; the light of our lampstand has been put out, the ark of our covenant has been plundered, our holy things have been polluted, and the name by which we are called has been profaned; our free men*ᵗ* have suffered abuse, our priests have been burned to death, our Levites have gone into captivity, our virgins have been defiled, and our wives have been ravished; our righteous men have been carried off, our little ones have been cast out, our young men have been enslaved and our strong men made powerless. ²³And, what is more than all, the seal of Zion—for she has now lost the seal of her glory, and has been given over into the hands of those that hate us. ²⁴Therefore shake off your great sadness and lay aside your many sorrows, so that the Mighty One may be merciful to you again, and the Most High may give you rest, a relief from your troubles."

25 While I was talking to her, behold, her face suddenly shone exceedingly, and her countenance flashed like lightning, so that I was too frightened to approach her, and my heart was terrified. While*ᵘ* I was wondering what this meant, ²⁶behold, she suddenly uttered a loud and fearful cry, so that the earth shook at the sound. ²⁷And I looked, and behold, the woman was no longer visible to me, but there was an established city,*ᵛ* and a place of huge foundations showed itself. Then I was afraid, and cried with a loud voice and said, ²⁸"Where is the angel Uriel,

r Compare Syr: Latin is corrupt
s Syr
t Or *children*
u Syr Ethiop Arab 1: Latin omits *I was too . . . terrified. While*
v Syr Ethiop Arab: Lat *a city was being built*

16: To *acknowledge* the justice of God's *decree* is equivalent to pious submission to his will. *You will receive your son back in due time*, i.e. in the birth of another son, after returning to her husband (v. 17). **21–23:** A pathetic account of the utter ruin of Israel. **22:** *Harp* symbolizes the service of praise. The extinction of the perpetually burning *lamp* marked the cessation of temple services. *Our holy things* are enumerated in 1 Macc.4.49–51. The name Israel was bestowed by God (Gen.32.28). **23:** *The seal* of a nation is symbolic of its independence.

10.25–28: A vision of the heavenly Jerusalem. 27: *An established city*, Heb.11.10; Rev.21.9–21. **28:** *At first*, 4.1.

who came to me at first? For it was he who brought me into this overpowering bewilderment; my end has become corruption, and my prayer a reproach."

29 As I was speaking these words, behold, the angel who had come to me at first came to me, and he looked upon me; [30]and behold, I lay there like a corpse and I was deprived of my understanding. Then he grasped my right hand and strengthened me and set me on my feet, and said to me, [31]"What is the matter with you? And why are you troubled? And why are your understanding and the thoughts of your mind troubled?"

32 I said, "Because you have forsaken me! I did as you directed, and went out into the field, and behold, I saw, and still see, what I am unable to explain."

33 He said to me, "Stand up like a man, and I will instruct you."

34 I said, "Speak, my lord; only do not forsake me, lest I die before my time.[w] [35]For I have seen what I did not know, and I have heard what I do not understand. [36]Or is my mind deceived, and my soul dreaming? [37]Now therefore I entreat you to give your servant an explanation of this bewildering vision."

38 He answered me and said, "Listen to me and I will inform you, and tell you about the things which you fear, for the Most High has revealed many secrets to you. [39]For he has seen your righteous conduct, that you have sorrowed continually for your people, and mourned greatly over Zion. [40]This therefore is the meaning of the vision. [41]The woman who appeared to you a little while ago, whom you saw mourning and began to console—[42]but you do not now see the form of a woman,

but an established city[x] has appeared to you—[43]and as for her telling you about the misfortune of her son, this is the interpretation: [44]This woman whom you saw, whom you now behold as an established city, is Zion.[y] [45]And as for her telling you that she was barren for thirty years, it is because there were three thousand[y] years in the world before any offering was offered in it.[z] [46]And after three thousand[y] years Solomon built the city, and offered offerings; then it was that the barren woman bore a son. [47]And as for her telling you that she brought him up with much care, that was the period of residence in Jerusalem. [48]And as for her saying to you, 'When my son entered his wedding chamber he died,' and that misfortune had overtaken her,[a] that was the destruction which befell Jerusalem. [49]And behold, you saw her likeness, how she mourned for her son, and you began to console her for what had happened.[b] [50]For now the Most High, seeing that you are sincerely grieved and profoundly distressed for her, has shown you the brilliance of her glory, and the loveliness of her beauty. [51]Therefore I told you to remain in the field where no house had been built, [52]for I knew that the Most High would reveal these things to you. [53]Therefore I told you to go into the field where there was no foundation of any building, [54]for no work of man's building could endure in a place where the city of the Most High was to be revealed.

55 "Therefore do not be afraid, and do not let your heart be terrified; but go in and see the splendor and vastness

w Syr Ethiop Arab: Lat *die to no purpose*
x Syr Ethiop Arab: Lat *a city to be built*
y Syr Ethiop Arab Arm: Latin is corrupt
z Cn: Lat Syr Arab Arm *her*   a Or *him*
b Most Latin manuscripts and Arab 2 add *these were the things to be opened to you*

10.29–59: Interpretation of the vision. **30:** *Like a corpse*, Rev.1.17; compare Dan.8.18; 10.9. **32:** *And still see*, the vision is still before the seer's eyes. *Unable to explain*, compare 2 Cor.12.3–4 (also of an ecstatic experience). **33:** *Stand up*, 5.15; 6.13,17. **44:** *Zion*, i.e. the heavenly Jerusalem. **45:** *In it*, in the world. **46:** *A son*, i.e. the earthly Jerusalem. **49:** The *likeness*, or model, of the earthly city is the heavenly Zion, who *mourned for her son* (the ruined earthly Jerusalem). For the idea of a heavenly counterpart or model, compare Ex.25.9,40; Heb.8.5. **55–56:** 1 Cor.

of the building, as far as it is possible for your eyes to see it, [56]and afterward you will hear as much as your ears can hear. [57]For you are more blessed than many, and you have been called before the Most High, as but few have been. [58]But tomorrow night you shall remain here, [59]and the Most High will show you in those dream visions what the Most High will do to those who dwell on earth in the last days."

So I slept that night and the following one, as he had commanded me.

11 On the second night I had a dream, and behold, there came up from the sea an eagle that had twelve feathered wings and three heads. [2]And I looked, and behold, he spread his wings over[c] all the earth, and all the winds of heaven blew upon him, and the clouds were gathered about him.[d] [3]And I looked, and out of his wings there grew opposing wings; but they became little, puny wings. [4]But his heads were at rest; the middle head was larger than the other heads, but it also was at rest with them. [5]And I looked, and behold, the eagle flew with his wings, to reign over the earth and over those who dwell in it. [6]And I saw how all things under heaven were subjected to him, and no one spoke against him, not even one creature that was on the earth. [7]And I looked, and behold, the eagle rose upon his talons, and uttered a cry to his wings, saying, [8]"Do not all watch at the same time; let each sleep in his own place, and watch in his turn; [9]but let the heads be reserved for the last."

10 And I looked, and behold, the voice did not come from his heads, but from the midst of his body. [11]And I counted his opposing wings, and behold, there were eight of them. [12]And I looked, and behold, on the right side one wing arose, and it reigned over all the earth. [13]And while it was reigning it came to its end and disappeared, so that its place was not seen. Then the next wing arose and reigned, and it continued to reign a long time. [14]And while it was reigning its end came also, so that it disappeared like the first. [15]And behold, a voice sounded, saying to it, [16]"Hear me, you who have ruled the earth all this time; I announce this to you before you disappear. [17]After you no one shall rule as long as you, or even half as long."

18 Then the third wing raised itself up, and held the rule like the former ones, and it also disappeared. [19]And so it went with all the wings; they wielded power one after another and then were never seen again. [20]And I looked, and behold, in due course the wings that followed[e] also rose up on the right[f] side, in order to rule. There were some of them that ruled, yet disappeared suddenly; [21]and others of them rose up, but did not hold the rule.

22 And after this I looked, and behold, the twelve wings and the two little wings disappeared; [23]and nothing remained on the eagle's body except the three heads that were at rest and six little wings. [24]And I looked, and behold, two little wings separated from the six and remained under the head that was on the right side; but four remained in their place. [25]And I looked, and behold, these little wings[g] planned to set themselves up and hold

c Arab 2 Arm: Lat Syr *in*
d Syr Compare Ethiop Arab: Latin omits *the clouds* and *about him*
e Syr Arab 2 *the little wings*
f Some Ethiopic manuscripts read *left*
g Syr: Lat *underwings*

2.9; 2 Cor.12.4. *Go in and see*, the city is conceived as still standing before Ezra. **57**: *You have been called before the Most High*, Arabic 1, "your name is known [or recognized] before the Most High," i.e. God has singled you out for honor (Is.45.3–4).
    11.1–12.51: The fifth vision (the eagle vision). 11.1: *From the sea*, Dan.7.3; Rev.13.1. *An eagle*, symbol of the Roman Empire. **2**: *Spread his wings*, asserted his dominion. *The winds*, 13.2; Dan.7.2. **3**: *Opposing wings*, symbolizing usurpers who revolted against the Roman emperors. *But they became little*, i.e. they were subdued. **4**: *Were at rest*, i.e. were not troubled by the opposing wings. **13**: *It came to its end*, i.e. the ruler perished.

the rule. [26]And I looked, and behold, one was set up, but suddenly disappeared; [27]a second also, and this disappeared more quickly than the first. [28]And I looked, and behold, the two that remained were planning between themselves to reign together; [29]and while they were planning, behold, one of the heads that were at rest (the one which was in the middle) awoke; for it was greater than the other two heads. [30]And I saw how it allied the two heads with itself, [31]and behold, the head turned with those that were with it, and it devoured the two little wings[h] which were planning to reign. [32]Moreover this head gained control of the whole earth, and with much oppression dominated its inhabitants; and it had greater power over the world than all the wings that had gone before.

33 And after this I looked, and behold, the middle head also suddenly disappeared, just as the wings had done. [34]But the two heads remained, which also ruled over the earth and its inhabitants. [35]And I looked, and behold, the head on the right side devoured the one on the left.

36 Then I heard a voice saying to me, "Look before you and consider what you see." [37]And I looked, and behold, a creature like a lion was aroused out of the forest, roaring; and I heard how he uttered a man's voice to the eagle, and spoke, saying, [38]"Listen and I will speak to you. The Most High says to you, [39]'Are you not the one that remains of the four beasts which I had made to reign in my world, so that the end of my times might come through them? [40]You, the fourth that has come, have conquered all the beasts that have gone before; and you have held sway over the world with much terror, and over all the earth with grievous oppression; and for so long you have dwelt on the

earth with deceit.[i] [41]And you have judged the earth, but not with truth; [42]for you have afflicted the meek and injured the peaceable; you have hated those who tell the truth, and have loved liars; you have destroyed the dwellings of those who brought forth fruit, and have laid low the walls of those who did you no harm. [43]And so your insolence has come up before the Most High, and your pride to the Mighty One. [44]And the Most High has looked upon his times, and behold, they are ended, and his ages are completed! [45]Therefore you will surely disappear, you eagle, and your terrifying wings, and your most evil little wings, and your malicious heads, and your most evil talons, and your whole worthless body, [46]so that the whole earth, freed from your violence, may be refreshed and relieved, and may hope for the judgment and mercy of him who made it.' "

12 While the lion was saying these words to the eagle, I looked, [2]and behold, the remaining head disappeared. And the two wings that had gone over to it arose[j] and set themselves up to reign, and their reign was brief and full of tumult. [3]And I looked, and behold, they also disappeared, and the whole body of the eagle was burned, and the earth was exceedingly terrified.

Then I awoke in great perplexity of mind and great fear, and I said to my spirit, [4]"Behold, you have brought this upon me, because you search out the ways of the Most High. [5]Behold, I am still weary in mind and very weak in my spirit, and not even a little strength is left in me, because of the great fear with which I have been terrified this night. [6]Therefore I will now beseech the Most High that he may strengthen me to the end."

h Syr: Lat *underwings*
i Syr Arab Arm: Lat Ethiop *The fourth came, however, and conquered . . . and held sway . . . and for so long dwelt*
j Ethiop: Latin omits *arose*

36: *Look before you,* the seer is alerted to the special importance of what follows. **43:** Dan.5.20.
12.3b–39: The interpretation of the vision. 3b–9: The seer awakes and asks for an interpretation of the vision. **11:** *The fourth kingdom* in Daniel's vision (Dan.7.7) symbolized the Greek or

7 And I said, "O sovereign Lord, if I have found favor in thy sight, and if I have been accounted righteous before thee beyond many others, and if my prayer has indeed come up before thy face, [8]strengthen me and show me, thy servant, the interpretation and meaning of this terrifying vision, that thou mayest fully comfort my soul. [9]For thou hast judged me worthy to be shown the end of the times and the last events of the times."

10 He said to me, "This is the interpretation of this vision which you have seen: [11]The eagle which you saw coming up from the sea is the fourth kingdom which appeared in a vision to your brother Daniel. [12]But it was not explained to him as I now explain or have explained it to you. [13]Behold, the days are coming when a kingdom shall arise on earth, and it shall be more terrifying than all the kingdoms that have been before it. [14]And twelve kings shall reign in it, one after another. [15]But the second that is to reign shall hold sway for a longer time than any other of the twelve. [16]This is the interpretation of the twelve wings which you saw. [17]As for your hearing a voice that spoke, coming not from the eagle's[k] heads but from the midst of his body, this is the interpretation: [18]In the midst of[l] the time of that kingdom great struggles shall arise, and it shall be in danger of falling; nevertheless it shall not fall then, but shall regain its former power.[m] [19]As for your seeing eight little wings[n] clinging to his wings, this is the interpretation: [20]Eight kings shall arise in it, whose times shall be short and their years swift; [21]and two of them shall perish when the middle of its time draws near; and four shall

be kept for the time when its end approaches; but two shall be kept until the end. [22]As for your seeing three heads at rest, this is the interpretation: [23]In its last days the Most High will raise up three kings,[o] and they[p] shall renew many things in it, and shall rule the earth [24]and its inhabitants more oppressively than all who were before them; therefore they are called the heads of the eagle. [25]For it is they who shall sum up his wickedness and perform his last actions. [26]As for your seeing that the large head disappeared, one of the kings[q] shall die in his bed, but in agonies. [27]But as for the two who remained, the sword shall devour them. [28]For the sword of one shall devour him who was with him; but he also shall fall by the sword in the last days. [29]As for your seeing two little wings[r] passing over to[s] the head which was on the right side, [30]this is the interpretation: It is these whom the Most High has kept for the eagle's[t] end; this was the reign which was brief and full of tumult, as you have seen.

31 "And as for the lion whom you saw rousing up out of the forest and roaring and speaking to the eagle and reproving him for his unrighteousness, and as for all his words that you have heard, [32]this is the Messiah[u] whom the Most High has kept until the end of days, who will arise from the posterity of David, and will come and speak to

k Syr Arm: Lat *After*
l Syr Arm: Lat *After*
m Ethiop Arab 1 Arm: Lat Syr *beginning*
n Syr: Lat *underwings*
o Syr Ethiop Arab Arm: Lat *kingdoms*
p Syr Ethiop Arm: Lat *he*
q Lat *them*
r Arab 1: Lat *underwings*
s Syr Ethiop: Latin omits *to*
t Lat *his*
u Literally *anointed one*

Macedonian Empire; here, however, it is reinterpreted (compare v. 12) to refer to the Roman Empire (see 11.1 n.). **13:** *The days are coming*, the seer is represented as prophesying during the exile. **17:** 11.10; compare 11.15. **18:** There is nothing in the vision which corresponds to what is said in this verse. The author probably refers to *the time* of *great struggles* for power which followed the death of Nero A.D. 68. **19:** *Little wings*, 11.3,11. *Clinging to his wings*, Armenian, "sprouting out around his great wings." **20:** *In it*, within the Roman Empire. **21:** *Its time*, the time of the kingdom. *Its end*, the end of the kingdom. **23:** *Its last days*, the last days of the kingdom. **23–24:** 11.30–32. **28:** *But ... days*, there is nothing corresponding to this in the vision. **30:** *As you have seen*, v. 3. **31:** *The lion*, 11.37ff. **32:** *Whom the Most High has kept until the end*

them;[v] he will denounce them for their ungodliness and for their wickedness, and will cast up before them their contemptuous dealings. [33]For first he will set them living before his judgment seat, and when he has reproved them, then he will destroy them. [34]But he will deliver in mercy the remnant of my people, those who have been saved throughout my borders, and he will make them joyful until the end comes, the day of judgment, of which I spoke to you at the beginning. [35]This is the dream that you saw, and this is its interpretation. [36]And you alone were worthy to learn this secret of the Most High. [37]Therefore write all these things that you have seen in a book, and put it in a hidden place; [38]and you shall teach them to the wise among your people, whose hearts you know are able to comprehend and keep these secrets. [39]But wait here seven days more, so that you may be shown whatever it pleases the Most High to show you." Then he left me.

40 When all the people heard that the seven days were past and I had not returned to the city, they all gathered together, from the least to the greatest, and came to me and spoke to me, saying, [41]"How have we offended you, and what harm have we done you, that you have forsaken us and sit in this place? [42]For of all the prophets you alone are left to us, like a cluster of grapes from the vintage, and like a lamp in a dark place, and like a haven for a ship saved from a storm. [43]Are not the evils which have befallen us sufficient? [44]Therefore if you forsake us, how much better it would have been for us if we also had been consumed in the burning of Zion! [45]For we are no

better than those who died there." And they wept with a loud voice.

Then I answered them and said, [46]"Take courage, O Israel; and do not be sorrowful, O house of Jacob; [47]for the Most High has you in remembrance, and the Mighty One has not forgotten you in your struggle. [48]As for me, I have neither forsaken you nor withdrawn from you; but I have come to this place to pray on account of the desolation of Zion, and to seek mercy on account of the humiliation of our[w] sanctuary. [49]Now go, every one of you to his house, and after these days I will come to you." [50]So the people went into the city, as I told them to do. [51]But I sat in the field seven days, as the angel[x] had commanded me; and I ate only of the flowers of the field, and my food was of plants during those days.

13 After seven days I dreamed a dream in the night; [2]and behold, a wind arose from the sea and stirred up all its waves. [3]And I looked, and behold, this wind made something like the figure of a man come up out of the heart of the sea. And I looked, and behold,[y] that man flew[z] with the clouds of heaven; and wherever he turned his face to look, everything under his gaze trembled, [4]and whenever his voice issued from his mouth, all who heard his voice melted as wax melts[a] when it feels the fire.

5 After this I looked, and behold, an innumerable multitude of men were gathered together from the four winds

v Syr: Latin omits *of days . . . and speak*
w Syr Ethiop: Lat *your*
x Literally *he*
y Syr: Latin omits *this wind . . . and behold*
z Syr Ethiop Arab Arm: Lat *grew strong*
a Syr: Lat *burned as the earth rests*

---

of days, the pre-existent Messiah in heaven (Dan.7.13–14; Enoch 48.6; 62.7). *He will denounce them*, 13.37. **34:** *He will make them joyful*, 7.28. **35:** *The dream*, 11.1. **37:** The seer is bidden to compose an esoteric book. **37–38:** To *put the book in a hidden place* suggests that it is an apocryphal book, which only the elect (*the wise*) can *comprehend*. **39:** *He*, the angel Uriel (see 4.1 n.).

12.40–51: The seer comforts those who were grieved because of his absence. **40:** *The seven days*, 9.23,27. **42:** *A lamp*, 2 Pet.1.19. **49:** *These days*, v. 39. **51:** 9.24–26.

13.1–58: The sixth vision (the man from the sea). **3:** *Something like the figure of a man*, the Messiah (Dan.7.13); compare v. 32 "my Son," i.e. the Son of God. *Flew with the clouds*, Is.19.1;

of heaven to make war against the man who came up out of the sea. [6]And I looked, and behold, he carved out for himself a great mountain, and flew up upon it. [7]And I tried to see the region or place from which the mountain was carved, but I could not.

8 After this I looked, and behold, all who had gathered together against him, to wage war with him, were much afraid, yet dared to fight. [9]And behold, when he saw the onrush of the approaching multitude, he neither lifted his hand nor held a spear or any weapon of war; [10]but I saw only how he sent forth from his mouth as it were a stream of fire, and from his lips a flaming breath, and from his tongue he shot forth a storm of sparks.[b] [11]All these were mingled together, the stream of fire and the flaming breath and the great storm, and fell on the onrushing multitude which was prepared to fight, and burned them all up, so that suddenly nothing was seen of the innumerable multitude but only the dust of ashes and the smell of smoke. When I saw it, I was amazed.

12 After this I saw the same man come down from the mountain and call to him another multitude which was peaceable. [13]Then many people[c] came to him, some of whom were joyful and some sorrowful; some of them were bound, and some were bringing others as offerings.

Then in great fear I awoke; and I besought the Most High, and said, [14]"From the beginning thou hast shown thy servant these wonders, and hast deemed me worthy to have my prayer heard by thee; [15]now show me also the interpretation of this dream. [16]For as I consider it in my mind, alas for those who will be left in those days! And still more, alas for those who are not left! [17]For those who are not left will be sad, [18]because they understand what is reserved for the last days, but cannot attain it. [19]But alas for those also who are left, and for that very reason! For they shall see great dangers and much distress, as these dreams show. [20]Yet it is better[d] to come into these things,[e] though incurring peril, than to pass from the world like a cloud, and not to see what shall happen in the last days."

He answered me and said, [21]"I will tell you the interpretation of the vision, and I will also explain to you the things which you have mentioned. [22]As for what you said about those who are left, this is the interpretation: [23]He who brings the peril at that time will himself protect those who fall into peril, who have works and have faith in the Almighty. [24]Understand therefore that those who are left are more blessed than those who have died. [25]This is the interpretation of the vision: As for your seeing a man come up from the heart of the sea, [26]this is he whom the Most High has been keeping for many ages, who will himself deliver his creation; and he will direct those who are left. [27]And as for your seeing wind and fire and a storm coming out of his mouth, [28]and as for his not holding a spear or weapon of war, yet destroying the onrushing multitude which came to conquer him, this is the interpretation: [29]Behold, the days are coming when the Most High will deliver those who are on the earth. [30]And bewilderment of

b Compare Syr: Latin is corrupt
c Lat Syr Arab 2 literally *the faces of many people*
d Ethiop Compare Arab 2: Lat *easier*
e Syr: Lat *this*

Dan.7.13; Rev.1.7. **4:** *As wax melts*, Mic.1.4; Jdt.16.15. **6:** *Carved out*, Dan.2.45. **10:** Is.11.4. **13a:** *Some . . . were bound*, Jews who came from captivity. *Others as offerings*, Is.66.20.

13.13b–20: The seer prays that God will interpret the vision to him. **14:** *From the beginning*, when the seer first began to have the visions. *My prayer*, 9.25ff. **19:** *For that very reason*, better, "for this reason—" (the reason follows).

13.21–56: The interpretation of the vision. **21:** *Things . . . mentioned*, in vv. 16–20. **22:** *Left*, Syriac and Arabic 1 add, "and of those who do not survive." **23:** *He who brings the peril*, the Messiah, whose advent is preceded by the messianic woes. **26:** *He whom the Most High has been keeping for many ages*, the pre-existent heavenly Messiah (v. 52; 12.32). **27–28:** Vv. 9–11.

mind shall come over those who dwell on the earth. ³¹And they shall plan to make war against one another, city against city, place against place, people against people, and kingdom against kingdom. ³²And when these things come to pass and the signs occur which I showed you before, then my Son will be revealed, whom you saw as a man coming up from the sea.*ᶠ* ³³And when all the nations hear his voice, every man shall leave his own land and the warfare that they have against one another; ³⁴and an innumerable multitude shall be gathered together, as you saw, desiring to come and conquer him. ³⁵But he will stand on the top of Mount Zion. ³⁶And Zion will come and be made manifest to all people, prepared and built, as you saw the mountain carved out without hands. ³⁷And he, my Son, will reprove the assembled nations for their ungodliness (this was symbolized by the storm), ³⁸and will reproach them to their face with their evil thoughts and the torments with which they are to be tortured (which were symbolized by the flames), and will destroy them without effort by the law*ᵍ* (which was symbolized by the fire). ³⁹And as for your seeing him gather to himself another multitude that was peaceable, ⁴⁰these are the ten tribes which were led away from their own land into captivity in the days of King Hoshea, whom Shalmaneser the king of the Assyrians led captive; he took them across the river, and they were taken into another land. ⁴¹But they formed this plan for themselves, that they would leave the multitude of the nations and go to a more distant region, where mankind had never lived, ⁴²that there at least they might keep their statutes which they had

not kept in their own land. ⁴³And they went in by the narrow passages of the Euphrates river. ⁴⁴For at that time the Most High performed signs for them, and stopped the channels of the river until they had passed over. ⁴⁵Through that region there was a long way to go, a journey of a year and a half; and that country is called Arzareth.*ʰ*

46 "Then they dwelt there until the last times; and now, when they are about to come again, ⁴⁷the Most High will stop*ⁱ* the channels of the river again, so that they may be able to pass over. Therefore you saw the multitude gathered together in peace. ⁴⁸But those who are left of your people, who are found within my holy borders, shall be saved.*ʲ* ⁴⁹Therefore when he destroys the multitude of the nations that are gathered together, he will defend the people who remain. ⁵⁰And then he will show them very many wonders."

51 I said, "O sovereign Lord, explain this to me: Why did I see the man coming up from the heart of the sea?"

52 He said to me, "Just as no one can explore or know what is in the depths of the sea, so no one on earth can see my Son or those who are with him, except in the time of his day.*ᵏ* ⁵³This is the interpretation of the dream which you saw. And you alone have been enlightened about this, ⁵⁴because you have forsaken your own ways and have applied yourself to mine, and have searched out my law; ⁵⁵for you have devoted your life to wisdom, and called

f Syr and most Latin manuscripts omit *from the sea*
g Syr: Lat *and the law*
h That is *Another Land*
i Syr: Lat *stops*
j Syr: Latin omits *shall be saved*
k Syr: Ethiop *except when his time and his day have come.* Latin omits *his*

31: Is.19.2; Mt.24.7. **32:** *Then my son will be revealed*, 7.28; Mt.24.30; Mk.13.26. **34:** Rev.16.16; 19.19. **36:** *Zion*, the heavenly Jerusalem (7.26; Rev.21.2, 9f.). *Without hands*, Dan.2.34,45. **37:** 12.32. **40:** 2 Kg.17.1–6. *The ten tribes*, the Northern Kingdom. *The river*, the Euphrates. **44:** *Stopped . . . the river*, Jos.3.14–16. **45:** *Arzareth*, Hebrew for "Another Land" (see note *h*; compare Dt.29.28). **47:** *Will stop . . . the river*, Is.11.15–16. **49:** *The people that remain*, presumably Israel, including the ten tribes who have returned to Palestine (v. 48). **50:** *Then*, in the messianic age. **52:** *Those . . . with him*, perhaps angels (Mt.24.31; 25.31). *Except . . . day*, until the day on which the Messiah appears.

understanding your mother. [56]Therefore I have shown you this, for there is a reward laid up with the Most High. And after three more days I will tell you other things, and explain weighty and wondrous matters to you."

57 Then I arose and walked in the field, giving great glory and praise to the Most High because of his wonders, which he did from time to time, [58]and because he governs the times and whatever things come to pass in their seasons. And I stayed there three days.

14 On the third day, while I was sitting under an oak, behold, a voice came out of a bush opposite me and said, "Ezra, Ezra." [2]And I said, "Here I am, Lord," and I rose to my feet. [3]Then he said to me, "I revealed myself in a bush and spoke to Moses, when my people were in bondage in Egypt; [4]and I sent him and led[l] my people out of Egypt; and I led him up on Mount Sinai, where I kept him with me many days; [5]and I told him many wondrous things, and showed him the secrets of the times and declared to him[m] the end of the times. Then I commanded him, saying, [6]'These words you shall publish openly, and these you shall keep secret.' [7]And now I say to you: [8]Lay up in your heart the signs that I have shown you, the dreams that you have seen, and the interpretations that you have heard; [9]for you shall be taken up from among men, and henceforth you shall live with my Son and with those who are like you, until the times are ended. [10]For the age has lost its youth, and the times begin to grow old. [11]For the age is divided into twelve parts, and nine[n] of its parts have already passed, [12]as well as half of the tenth part; so two of its parts remain, besides half of the tenth part.[o]

[13]Now therefore, set your house in order, and reprove your people; comfort the lowly among them, and instruct those that are wise.[p] And now renounce the life that is corruptible, [14]and put away from you mortal thoughts; cast away from you the burdens of man, and divest yourself now of your weak nature, [15]and lay to one side the thoughts that are most grievous to you, and hasten to escape from these times. [16]For evils worse than those which you have now seen happen shall be done hereafter. [17]For the weaker the world becomes through old age, the more shall evils be multiplied among[q] its inhabitants. [18]For truth shall go farther away, and falsehood shall come near. For the eagle[r] which you saw in the vision is already hastening to come."

19 Then I answered and said, "Let me speak in thy presence, Lord.[s] [20]For behold, I will go, as thou hast commanded me, and I will reprove the people who are now living; but who will warn those who will be born hereafter? For the world lies in darkness, and its inhabitants are without light. [21]For thy law has been burned, and so no one knows the things which have been done or will be done by thee. [22]If then I have found favor before thee, send the Holy Spirit into me, and I will write everything that has happened in the world from the beginning, the things which were written in thy law, that men may be able to find the path, and that those who wish to live in the last days may live."

l Other authorities read *he led*
m Syr Ethiop Arab Arm: Latin omits *declared to him*
n Cn: Lat Ethiop *ten*
o Syr omits verses 11, 12: Ethiop *For the world is divided into ten parts, and has come to the tenth, and half of the tenth remains. Now . . .*
p Latin omits *and . . . wise*
q Literally *upon*
r Syr Ethiop Arab Arm: Latin is corrupt
s Most Latin manuscripts omit *Let me speak*

14.1–48: The seventh vision (the legend of Ezra and the holy Scriptures). **1–18**: God speaks to Ezra. **1**: *A bush*, compare Ex.3.4. **4**: *Many days*, forty days (Ex.34.28). **9**: *My son*, the preexistent heavenly Messiah (7.28; 13.32,52). **10**: 5.50–55. **13**: *House*, of Israel. **14**: 2 Cor.5.4. **16**: Mt.24.8. **18**: *The eagle*, ch. 11.

14.19–26: Ezra's prayer for inspiration to restore the holy Scriptures. **20**: *Without light*, without the light of God's law (Ps.19.8b). **21**: 4.23. **22**: *The Holy Spirit* will guide Ezra in

23 He answered me and said, "Go and gather the people, and tell them not to seek you for forty days. [24]But prepare for yourself many writing tablets, and take with you Sarea, Dabria, Selemia, Ethanus, and Asiel— these five, because they are trained to write rapidly; [25]and you shall come here, and I will light in your heart the lamp of understanding, which shall not be put out until what you are about to write is finished. [26]And when you have finished, some things you shall make public, and some you shall deliver in secret to the wise; tomorrow at this hour you shall begin to write."

27 Then I went as he commanded me, and I gathered all the people together, and said, [28]"Hear these words, O Israel. [29]At first our fathers dwelt as aliens in Egypt, and they were delivered from there, [30]and received the law of life, which they did not keep, which you also have transgressed after them. [31]Then land was given to you for a possession in the land of Zion; but you and your fathers committed iniquity and did not keep the ways which the Most High commanded you. [32]And because he is a righteous judge, in due time he took from you what he had given. [33]And now you are here, and your brethren are farther in the interior.[t] [34]If you, then, will rule over your minds and discipline your hearts, you shall be kept alive, and after death you shall obtain mercy. [35]For after death the judgment will come, when we shall live again; and then the names of the righteous will become manifest, and the deeds of the ungodly will be disclosed. [36]But let no one come to me now, and let no one seek me for forty days."

37 So I took the five men, as he commanded me, and we proceeded to the field, and remained there. [38]And on the next day, behold, a voice called me, saying, "Ezra, open your mouth and drink what I give you to drink." [39]Then I opened my mouth, and behold, a full cup was offered to me; it was full of something like water, but its color was like fire. [40]And I took it and drank; and when I had drunk it, my heart poured forth understanding, and wisdom increased in my breast, for my spirit retained its memory; [41]and my mouth was opened, and was no longer closed. [42]And the Most High gave understanding to the five men, and by turns they wrote what was dictated, in characters which they did not know.[u] They sat forty days, and wrote during the daytime, and ate their bread at night. [43]As for me, I spoke in the daytime and was not silent at night. [44]So during the forty days ninety-four[v] books were written. [45]And when the forty days were ended, the Most High spoke to me, saying, "Make public the twenty-four[w] books that you wrote first and let the worthy and the unworthy read them; [46]but keep

t Syr Ethiop Arm: Lat *are among you*
u Syr Compare Ethiop Arab 2 Arm: Latin is corrupt
v Syr Ethiop Arab 1 Arm: Latin is corrupt
w Syr Arab 1: Latin omits *twenty-four*

rewriting the law, which has been burned (v. 21). **23:** *Forty days*, Ex.24.18; 34.28; Dt.9.9,18. **24:** *Many*, compare v. 44. **26:** *Some things . . . make public*, namely, the rewritten books of the Old Testament. *Some . . . deliver in secret*, namely, the apocalypses (see 12.37–38 n.).
   14.27–36: The last words of Ezra. 29: *Aliens*, Gen.47.4. **30:** *The law*, which, if observed, would confer *life*. **33:** *Farther*, 13.45. **34:** *Kept alive*, i.e. spiritually alive. **36:** *Forty days*, v. 23.
   14.37–48: The restoration of the holy Scriptures. 37: *The five men*, v. 24. **39:** *A full cup* of inspiration, containing the fire of the Spirit (v. 22). **41:** *Was opened*, in fluent speech. **42:** *In characters which they did not know*, in a new Hebrew script, the (modern) square characters. **45:** *The twenty-four books* of the Hebrew canon comprise the five books of the Law (Gen., Ex., Lev., Num., Dt.), eight books of the Prophets (the former prophets, Jos., Jg., 1 and 2 Sam. [as one book], 1 and 2 Kg. [as one book]; the latter prophets, Is., Jer., Ezek., and the Twelve [counted as one book]), and eleven books of the Writings (Ps., Pr., Job, S. of S., Ru., Lam., Ec., Est., Dan., Ezra-Neh. [as one book], 1 and 2 Chr. [as one book]). **46:** *The seventy* are esoteric, apocalyptic books (see 12.37–38 n.).

the seventy that were written last, in order to give them to the wise among your people. [47]For in them is the spring of understanding, the fountain of wisdom, and the river of knowledge." [48]And I did so.[x]

15[y] The Lord says, "Behold, speak in the ears of my people the words of the prophecy which I will put in your mouth, [2]and cause them to be written on paper; for they are trustworthy and true. [3]Do not fear the plots against you, and do not be troubled by the unbelief of those who oppose you. [4]For every unbeliever shall die in his unbelief."

5 "Behold," says the Lord, "I bring evils upon the world, the sword and famine and death and destruction. [6]For iniquity has spread throughout every land, and their harmful deeds have reached their limit. [7]Therefore," says the Lord, [8]"I will be silent no longer concerning their ungodly deeds which they impiously commit, neither will I tolerate their wicked practices. Behold, innocent and righteous blood cries out to me, and the souls of the righteous cry out continually. [9]I will surely avenge them," says the Lord, "and will receive to myself all the innocent blood from among them. [10]Behold, my people is led like a flock to the slaughter; I will not allow them to live any longer in the land of Egypt, [11]but I will bring them out with a mighty hand and with an uplifted arm, and will smite Egypt with plagues, as before, and will destroy all its land."

12 Let Egypt mourn, and its foundations, for the plague of chastisement and punishment that the Lord will bring upon it. [13]Let the farmers that till the ground mourn, because their seed shall fail and their trees shall be ruined by blight and hail and by a terrible tempest. [14]Alas for the world and for those who live in it! [15]For the sword and misery draw near them, and nation shall rise up to fight against nation, with swords in their hands. [16]For there shall be unrest among men; growing strong against one another, they shall in their might have no respect for their king or the chief of their leaders. [17]For a man will desire to go into a city, and shall not be able. [18]For because of their pride the cities shall be in confusion, the houses shall be destroyed, and people shall be afraid. [19]A man shall have no pity upon his neighbors, but shall make an assault upon their houses with the sword, and plunder their goods, because of hunger for bread and because of great tribulation.

20 "Behold," says God, "I call together all the kings of the earth to fear me, from the rising sun and from the south, from the east and from Lebanon; to turn and repay what they have given them. [21]Just as they have done to my elect until this day, so I will do, and will repay into their bosom." Thus says the Lord God: [22]"My right hand will not spare the sinners, and my sword will not cease from those who shed innocent blood on the earth." [23]And a fire will go forth from his wrath, and will consume the foundations of the earth, and the sinners, like straw that is kindled. [24]"Woe to those

x Syr adds *in the seventh year of the sixth week, five thousand years and three months and twelve days after creation.*
At that time Ezra was caught up, and taken to the place of those who are like him, after he had written all these things. And he was called the Scribe of the knowledge of the Most High for ever and ever. Ethiop Arab 1 Arm have a similar ending
y Chapters 15 and 16 (except 15.57–59 which has been found in Greek) are extant only in Latin

---

15.1–16.78: An appendix. 15.1–4: The certainty of this prophecy. **1:** *Which I will put in your mouth,* Is.51.16; Jer.1.9.

15.5–11: God will take vengeance upon the wicked. 9: *All the innocent blood,* i.e. all the souls of the righteous (compare Rev.6.10; 19.2). **10:** Ps.44.22; Is.53.7. **11:** *Will smite Egypt . . . as before,* perhaps an allusion to the occurrence during the reign of Gallienus (A.D. 260–268) of a terrible famine, followed by a plague, which killed two-thirds of the population of Alexandria.

15.12–27: The signs of the end. 15: *Nation . . . against nation,* Mt.24.7; Mk.13.8; Lk.21.10. **18:** Lk.21.26.

who sin and do not observe my commandments," says the Lord; 25"I will not spare them. Depart, you faithless children! Do not pollute my sanctuary." 26For the Lord knows all who transgress against him; therefore he will hand them over to death and slaughter. 27For now calamities have come upon the whole earth, and you shall remain in them; for God will not deliver you, because you have sinned against him.

28 Behold, a terrifying sight, appearing from the east! 29The nations of the dragons of Arabia shall come out with many chariots, and from the day that they set out, their hissing shall spread over the earth, so that all who hear them fear and tremble. 30Also the Carmonians, raging in wrath, shall go forth like wild boars of the forest, and with great power they shall come, and engage them in battle, and shall devastate a portion of the land of the Assyrians with their teeth. 31And then the dragons, remembering their origin, shall become still stronger; and if they combine in great power and turn to pursue them, 32then these shall be disorganized and silenced by their power, and shall turn and flee. 33And from the land of the Assyrians an enemy in ambush shall beset them and destroy one of them, and fear and trembling shall come upon their army, and indecision upon their kings.

34 Behold, clouds from the east, and from the north to the south; and their appearance is very threatening, full of wrath and storm. 35They shall dash against one another and shall pour out a heavy tempest upon the earth, and their own tempest; and there shall be blood from the sword as high as a horse's belly 36and a man's thigh and a camel's hock. 37And there

shall be fear and great trembling upon the earth; and those who see that wrath shall be horror-stricken, and they shall be seized with trembling. 38And, after that, heavy storm clouds shall be stirred up from the south, and from the north, and another part from the west. 39And the winds from the east shall prevail over the cloud that was^z raised in wrath, and shall dispel it; and the tempest that was to cause destruction by the east wind shall be driven violently toward the south and west. 40And great and mighty clouds, full of wrath and tempest, shall rise, to destroy all the earth and its inhabitants, and shall pour out upon every high and lofty place*a* a terrible tempest, 41fire and hail and flying swords and floods of water, that all the fields and all the streams may be filled with the abundance of those waters. 42And they shall destroy cities and walls, mountains and hills, trees of the forests, and grass of the meadows, and their grain. 43And they shall go on steadily to Babylon, and shall destroy her. 44They shall come to her and surround her; they shall pour out the tempest and all its wrath upon her; then the dust and smoke shall go up to heaven, and all who are about her shall wail over her. 45And those who survive shall serve those who have destroyed her.

46 And you, Asia, who share in the glamour of Babylon and the glory of her person—47woe to you, miserable wretch! For you have made yourself like her; you have decked out your daughters in harlotry to please and glory in your lovers, who have always lusted after you. 48You have imitated that hateful harlot in all her deeds and devices; therefore God says, 49"I

z Literally *that he*
a Or *eminent person*

15.28–63: A vision of warfare. This section is thought to reflect events of the third century A.D., including the attack of King Sapor I of Persia (A.D. 240–273) upon the Roman province of Syria. **30:** *The Carmonians,* from Carmania (Kirman), the southern province of the Parthian empire. *Like wild boars,* Ps.80.13. **35:** *As high as . . . ,* Rev.14.20. **43:** *Babylon,* i.e. Rome. **47–48:** Rev.14.8; 17.4–5. **49:** Rev.18.7–8.

will send evils upon you, widowhood, poverty, famine, sword, and pestilence, to lay waste your houses and bring you to destruction and death. [50]And the glory of your power shall wither like a flower, when the heat rises that is sent upon you. [51]You shall be weakened like a wretched woman who is beaten and wounded, so that you cannot receive your mighty lovers. [52]Would I have dealt with you so violently," says the Lord, [53]"if you had not always killed my chosen people, exulting and clapping your hands and talking about their death when you were drunk? [54]Trick out the beauty of your face! [55]The reward of a harlot is in your bosom, therefore you shall receive your recompense. [56]As you will do to my chosen people," says the Lord, "so God will do to you, and will hand you over to adversities. [57]Your children shall die of hunger, and you shall fall by the sword, and your cities shall be wiped out, and all your people who are in the open country shall fall by the sword. [58]And those who are in the mountains and highlands[b] shall perish of hunger, and they shall eat their own flesh in hunger for bread and drink their own blood in thirst for water. [59]Unhappy above all others, you shall come and suffer fresh afflictions. [60]And as they pass they shall wreck the hateful[c] city, and shall destroy a part of your land and abolish a portion of your glory, as they return from devastated Babylon. [61]And you shall be broken down by them like stubble, and they shall be like fire to you. [62]And they shall devour you and your cities, your land and your mountains; they shall burn with fire all your forests and your fruitful trees. [63]They shall carry your children away captive, and shall plunder your wealth, and abolish the glory of your countenance."

16 Woe to you, Babylon and Asia! Woe to you, Egypt and Syria!

[2]Gird yourselves with sackcloth and haircloth, and wail for your children, and lament for them; for your destruction is at hand. [3]The sword has been sent upon you, and who is there to turn it back? [4]A fire has been sent upon you, and who is there to quench it? [5]Calamities have been sent upon you, and who is there to drive them away? [6]Can one drive off a hungry lion in the forest, or quench a fire in the stubble, when once it has begun to burn? [7]Can one turn back an arrow shot by a strong archer? [8]The Lord God sends calamities, and who will drive them away? [9]Fire will go forth from his wrath, and who is there to quench it? [10]He will flash lightning, and who will not be afraid? He will thunder, and who will not be terrified? [11]The Lord will threaten, and who will not be utterly shattered at his presence? [12]The earth and its foundations quake, the sea is churned up from the depths, and its waves and the fish also shall be troubled at the presence of the Lord and before the glory of his power. [13]For his right hand that bends the bow is strong, and his arrows that he shoots are sharp and will not miss when they begin to be shot to the ends of the world. [14]Behold, calamities are sent forth and shall not return until they come over the earth. [15]The fire is kindled, and shall not be put out until it consumes the foundations of the earth. [16]Just as an arrow shot by a mighty archer does not return, so the calamities that are sent upon the earth shall not return. [17]Alas for me! Alas for me! Who will deliver me in those days?

18 The beginning of sorrows, when there shall be much lamentation; the beginning of famine, when many shall perish; the beginning of wars, when the powers shall be terrified; the beginning of calamities, when all shall

b Gk: Latin omits *and highlands*
c Another reading is *idle* or *unprofitable*

16.1–34: Denunciation of Babylon, Asia, Egypt, and Syria. 1: *Babylon,* i.e. Rome. **2:** *Sackcloth and haircloth,* signs of mourning. **12:** Ps.18.15. **15:** *Until it consumes . . . the earth,* an

tremble. What shall they do in these circumstances, when the calamities come? ¹⁹Behold, famine and plague, tribulation and anguish are sent as scourges for the correction of men. ²⁰Yet for all this they will not turn from their iniquities, nor be always mindful of the scourges. ²¹Behold, provisions will be so cheap upon earth that men will imagine that peace is assured for them, and then the calamities shall spring up on the earth—the sword, famine, and great confusion. ²²For many of those who live on the earth shall perish by famine; and those who survive the famine shall die by the sword. ²³And the dead shall be cast out like dung, and there shall be no one to console them; for the earth shall be left desolate, and its cities shall be demolished. ²⁴No one shall be left to cultivate the earth or to sow it. ²⁵The trees shall bear fruit, and who will gather it? ²⁶The grapes shall ripen, and who will tread them? For in all places there shall be great solitude; ²⁷one man will long to see another, or even to hear his voice. ²⁸For out of a city, ten shall be left; and out of the field, two who have hidden themselves in thick groves and clefts in the rocks. ²⁹As in an olive orchard three or four olives may be left on every tree, ³⁰or as when a vineyard is gathered some clusters may be left by those who search carefully through the vineyard, ³¹so in those days three or four shall be left by those who search their houses with the sword. ³²And the earth shall be left desolate, and its fields shall be for briers, and its roads and all its paths shall bring forth thorns, because no sheep will go along them. ³³Virgins shall mourn because they have no bridegrooms; women shall mourn because they have no husbands; their daughters shall mourn, because they have no helpers. ³⁴Their bridegrooms shall be killed in war, and their husbands shall perish of famine.

35 Listen now to these things, and understand them, O servants of the Lord. ³⁶Behold the word of the Lord, receive it; do not disbelieve what the Lord says.*ᵈ* ³⁷Behold, the calamities draw near, and are not delayed. ³⁸Just as a woman with child, in the ninth month, when the time of her delivery draws near, has great pains about her womb for two or three hours beforehand, and when the child comes forth from the womb, there will not be a moment's delay, ³⁹so the calamities will not delay in coming forth upon the earth, and the world will groan, and pains will seize it on every side.

40 "Hear my words, O my people; prepare for battle, and in the midst of the calamities be like strangers on the earth. ⁴¹Let him that sells be like one who will flee; let him that buys be like one who will lose; ⁴²let him that does business be like one who will not make a profit; and let him that builds a house be like one who will not live in it; ⁴³let him that sows be like one who will not reap; so also him that prunes the vines, like one who will not gather the grapes; ⁴⁴them that marry, like those who will have no children; and them that do not marry, like those who are widowed. ⁴⁵Because those who labor, labor in vain; ⁴⁶for strangers shall gather their fruits, and plunder their goods, and overthrow their houses, and take their children captive; for in captivity and famine they will beget their children. ⁴⁷Those who conduct business, do it only to be plundered; the more they adorn their cities, their houses and possessions, and their persons, ⁴⁸the more angry I will be with them for their sins," says the Lord. ⁴⁹Just as a respectable and virtuous woman abhors a harlot, ⁵⁰so righteousness shall abhor iniquity, when she decks herself out, and shall accuse her to her face, when he comes who will defend him who searches out every sin on earth.

d Cn: Lat *do not believe the gods of whom the Lord speaks*

---

apocalyptic idea from Persian eschatology (compare 2 Pet.3.10). **29:** Is.17.6. **16.35–50: God's people are warned of impending disasters. 38:** 4.40. **41:** 1 Cor.7.29–31.

51 Therefore do not be like her or her works. [52]For behold, just a little while, and iniquity will be removed from the earth, and righteousness will reign over us. [53]Let no sinner say that he has not sinned; for God[e] will burn coals of fire on the head of him who says, "I have not sinned before God and his glory." [54]Behold, the Lord knows all the works of men, their imaginations and their thoughts and their hearts. [55]He said, "Let the earth be made," and it was made; "Let the heaven be made," and it was made. [56]At his word the stars were fixed, and he knows the number of the stars. [57]It is he who searches the deep and its treasures, who has measured the sea and its contents; [58]who has enclosed the sea in the midst of the waters, and by his word has suspended the earth over the water; [59]who has spread out the heaven like an arch, and founded it upon the waters; [60]who has put springs of water in the desert, and pools on the tops of the mountains, to send rivers from the heights to water the earth; [61]who formed man, and put a heart in the midst of his body, and gave him breath and life and understanding [62]and the spirit of Almighty God; who made all things and searches out hidden things in hidden places. [63]Surely he knows your imaginations and what you think in your hearts! Woe to those who sin and want to hide their sins! [64]Because the Lord will strictly examine all their works, and will make a public spectacle of all of you. [65]And when your sins come out before men, you shall be put to shame; and your own iniquities shall stand as your accusers in that day. [66]What will you do? Or how will you hide your sins before God and his angels? [67]Behold, God is the judge, fear him! Cease from your sins, and forget your iniquities, never to commit them again; so God will lead you forth and deliver you from all tribulation.

68 For behold, the burning wrath of a great multitude is kindled over you, and they shall carry off some of you and shall feed you what was sacrificed to idols. [69]And those who consent to eat shall be held in[f] derision and contempt, and be trodden under foot. [70]For in many places[g] and in neighboring cities there shall be a great insurrection against those who fear the Lord. [71]They shall be like mad men, sparing no one, but plundering and destroying those who continue to fear the Lord. [72]For they shall destroy and plunder their goods, and drive them out of their houses. [73]Then the tested quality of my elect shall be manifest, as gold that is tested by fire.

74 "Hear, my elect," says the Lord. "Behold, the days of tribulation are at hand, and I will deliver you from them. [75]Do not fear or doubt, for God is your guide. [76]You who keep my commandments and precepts," says the Lord God, "do not let your sins pull you down, or your iniquities prevail over you." [77]Woe to those who are choked by their sins and overwhelmed by their iniquities, as a field is choked with underbrush and its path[h] overwhelmed with thorns, so that no one can pass through! [78]It is shut off and given up to be consumed by fire.

e Literally *he*
f Literally *consent to them shall be for these in*
g. The Latin is uncertain
h Another reading is *seed*

16.51–67: The impossibility of hiding sin from God.
16.68–78: Though persecuted, God's elect will be delivered. **73**: Zech.13.9; 1 Pet.1.7.

TOBIT

A fascinating amalgam of *Arabian Nights* romance, kindly Jewish piety, and sound moral teaching, Tobit is one of the most popular of the books of the Apocrypha. Originally composed in Hebrew or Aramaic, probably sometime during the second century B.C., its author is unknown, as is also the place where he wrote it, although Jerusalem, Antioch, and Alexandria have all been suggested as possibilities.

Besides the intrinsic interest of the tale, which is compounded in large part of themes derived from ancient folklore, the book's principal value lies in the picture it gives of Jewish culture and religious life in an age not too remote, either in time or temper, from that of the New Testament.

The ostensible setting of the story is the Assyrian capital, Nineveh, where the people of Northern Israel had been taken captive in the latter part of the eighth century B.C. (2 Kg.17.1–6). There, it is said, dwelt the pious Tobit, who, despite his many charitable deeds, became blind and poor (chs. 1–2). But God heard his prayer, as well as the prayer of demon-haunted Sarah in faraway Media, and sent the angel Raphael to save them both (ch. 3). When Tobit commissioned his son Tobias to collect a deposit of money he had made long before in Media, the angel accompanied him and revealed magic formulas which would heal his father's blindness and exorcise Sarah's demon-lover, Asmodeus (chs. 4–6). Tobias successfully completed his mission and married Sarah (chs. 7–14).

The book exists in numerous recensions and versions which differ considerably from one another in matters of detail.

THE BOOK OF THE ACTS[a] OF TOBIT the son of Tobiel, son of Ananiel, son of Aduel, son of Gabael, of the descendants of Asiel and the tribe of Naphtali, ²who in the days of Shalmaneser,[b] king of the Assyrians, was taken into captivity from Thisbe, which is to the south of Kedesh Naphtali in Galilee above Asher.

3 I, Tobit, walked in the ways of truth and righteousness all the days of my life, and I performed many acts of charity to my brethren and countrymen who went with me into the land of the Assyrians, to Nineveh. ⁴Now when I was in my own country, in the land of Israel, while I was still a young man, the whole tribe of Naphtali my forefather deserted the house of Jerusalem. This was the place which had been chosen from among all the tribes of Israel, where all the tribes should sacrifice and where the temple of the dwelling of the Most High was consecrated and established for all generations for ever.

5 All the tribes that joined in apostasy used to sacrifice to the calf[c] Baal, and so did the house of Naphtali my forefather. ⁶But I alone went often to Jerusalem for the feasts, as it is ordained for all Israel by an everlasting decree. Taking the first fruits and the tithes of my produce and the first shearings, I would give these to the priests, the sons of Aaron, at the altar. ⁷Of all my produce I would give a tenth to the sons of Levi who ministered at Jerusalem; a second tenth I would sell,

a Gk *words*
b Gk *Enemessarus*
c Other authorities read *heifer*

1.1–2: Title. 2: *Shalmaneser* (or rather Sargon; see v. 15 n.) took Samaria, the capital of Israel, in 722 B.C. and transported a large part of the population to Assyria (2 Kg.17.1–6). *Thisbe* is unidentified. *Kedesh Naphtali*, 2 Kg.15.29. *Asher* is probably Hazor.
1.3–3.6: Tobit's own account of his virtuous life and unhappy fate.
1.3–22: Tobit's piety brings him into conflict with the king. 3: *Nineveh* was the capital of Assyria. **4:** Since the rebellion of the northern tribes against Jerusalem (1 Kg.12.19–20) occurred about 922 B.C., Tobit could not have been *still a young man*, or even born, when it happened. Such chronological, and other historical, difficulties make it clear that the story is fiction (compare v. 15 n., 6.1 n., 9.2 n., 14.15 n.). **5:** *Calf*, 1 Kg.12.28–29. **6–8:** During the apostasy, Tobit alone remains loyal to the divinely-appointed temple in Jerusalem. **6:** *An everlasting decree*, Dt.12.11,

and I would go and spend the proceeds each year at Jerusalem; ⁸the third tenth I would give to those to whom it was my duty, as Deborah my father's mother had commanded me, for I was left an orphan by my father. ⁹When I became a man I married Anna, a member of our family, and by her I became the father of Tobias.

10 Now when I was carried away captive to Nineveh, all my brethren and my relatives ate the food of the Gentiles; ¹¹but I kept myself from eating it, ¹²because I remembered God with all my heart. ¹³Then the Most High gave me favor and good appearance in the sight of Shalmaneser,*b* and I was his buyer of provisions. ¹⁴So I used to go into Media, and once at Rages in Media I left ten talents of silver in trust with Gabael, the brother of Gabrias. ¹⁵But when Shalmaneser*b* died, Sennacherib his son reigned in his place; and under him the highways were unsafe, so that I could no longer go into Media.

16 In the days of Shalmaneser*b* I performed many acts of charity to my brethren. ¹⁷I would give my bread to the hungry and my clothing to the naked; and if I saw any one of my people dead and thrown out behind the wall of Nineveh, I would bury him. ¹⁸And if Sennacherib the king put to death any who came fleeing from Judea, I buried them secretly. For in his anger he put many to death. When the bodies were sought by the king, they were not found. ¹⁹Then one of

the men of Nineveh went and informed the king about me, that I was burying them; so I hid myself. When I learned that I was being searched for, to be put to death, I left home in fear. ²⁰Then all my property was confiscated and nothing was left to me except my wife Anna and my son Tobias.

21 But not fifty*d* days passed before two of Sennacherib's*e* sons killed him, and they fled to the mountains of Ararat. Then Esarhaddon,*f* his son, reigned in his place; and he appointed Ahikar, the son of my brother Anael, over all the accounts of his kingdom and over the entire administration. ²²Ahikar interceded for me, and I returned to Nineveh. Now Ahikar was cupbearer, keeper of the signet, and in charge of administration of the accounts, for Esarhaddon*f* had appointed him second to himself.*g* He was my nephew.

3 When I arrived home and my wife Anna and my son Tobias were restored to me, at the feast of Pentecost, which is the sacred festival of the seven weeks, a good dinner was prepared for me and I sat down to eat. ²Upon seeing the abundance of food I said to my son, "Go and bring whatever poor man of our brethren you may find who is mindful of the Lord, and I will wait for you." ³But he came back and said, "Father, one of our people has been strangled and thrown into the market

b Gk *Enemessarus*
d Other authorities read *fifty-five*
e Gk *his*   *f* Gk *Sacherdonus*
g Or *a second time*

13–14. 10–12: Even in captivity among Gentiles Tobit refuses to violate the dietary laws. 14: *Media* is the northern part of modern Iran, east of Assyria. *Rages* was an important city whose ruins are located about five miles southeast of modern Teheran. *Ten talents*, at least $10,000. 15–20: Tobit arouses Sennacherib's wrath and flees the country. 15: *Shalmaneser* actually died before the fall of Samaria, which was taken by Sargon. *Sennacherib* succeeded his father Sargon in 705 B.C. 17: It was for the Jews a great calamity that a dead body should lie unburied. 21–22: Under a new king, *Esarhaddon* (681–669 B.C.), Tobit is able to return. 21: *Ahikar* was a legendary ancient wise man whose story survives in several oriental languages. An Aramaic version of his adventures, dating from the fifth century B.C., was found among the Jewish papyri at Elephantine in upper Egypt (see also 14.10 n.).

    2.1–14: Another act of charity results in Tobit's blindness and impoverishment. 1: *Pentecost* ... *seven weeks*, approximately, after Passover (Lev.23.15–21; Dt.16.9–11). 2: Generosity toward the poor is one of the virtues taught by this book (4.7–11,16). 3: *Strangled*, presumably executed (compare 1.18). Leaving the body unburied was intended as additional punishment, so

place." 4So before I tasted anything I sprang up and removed the body[h] to a place of shelter until sunset. 5And when I returned I washed myself and ate my food in sorrow. 6Then I remembered the prophecy of Amos, how he said,

"Your feasts shall be turned into
  mourning,
and all your festivities into
  lamentation."
And I wept.

7 When the sun had set I went and dug a grave and buried the body.[h] 8And my neighbors laughed at me and said, "He is no longer afraid that he will be put to death for doing this; he once ran away, and here he is burying the dead again!" 9On the same night I returned from burying him, and because I was defiled I slept by the wall of the courtyard, and my face was uncovered. 10I did not know that there were sparrows on the wall and their fresh droppings fell into my open eyes and white films formed on my eyes. I went to physicians, but they did not help me. Ahikar, however, took care of me until he[i] went to Elymais.

11 Then my wife Anna earned money at women's work. 12She used to send the product to the owners. Once when they paid her wages, they also gave her a kid; 13and when she returned to me it began to bleat. So I said to her, "Where did you get the kid? It is not stolen, is it? Return it to the owners; for it is not right to eat what is stolen." 14And she said, "It was given to me as a gift in addition to my wages." But I did not believe her, and told her to return it to the owners; and I blushed for her. Then she replied to me, "Where are your charities and your righteous deeds? You seem to know everything!"

3 Then in my grief I wept, and I prayed in anguish, saying, 2"Righteous art thou, O Lord; all thy deeds and all thy ways are mercy and truth, and thou dost render true and righteous judgment for ever. 3Remember me and look favorably upon me; do not punish me for my sins and for my unwitting offenses and those which my fathers committed before thee. 4For they disobeyed thy commandments, and thou gavest us over to plunder, captivity, and death; thou madest us a byword of reproach in all the nations among which we have been dispersed. 5And now thy many judgments are true in exacting penalty from me for my sins and those of my fathers, because we did not keep thy commandments. For we did not walk in truth before thee. 6And now deal with me according to thy pleasure; command my spirit to be taken up, that I may depart and become dust. For it is better for me to die than to live, because I have heard false reproaches, and great is the sorrow within me. Command that I now be released from my distress to go to the eternal abode; do not turn thy face away from me."

7 On the same day, at Ecbatana in Media, it also happened that Sarah, the daughter of Raguel, was reproached by her father's maids, 8because she had been given to seven husbands, and the evil demon Asmodeus had slain each of them before he had been with her as his wife. So the maids[j] said to her, "Do you not know that you strangle your husbands? You already have had seven and have had no benefit from[k] any of them. 9Why do you beat us? If they are dead, go with them! May we never see a son or daughter of yours!"

h Gk *him*   *i* Other authorities read *I*   *j* Gk *they*
k Other authorities read *have not borne the name of*

Tobit's act of charity was an act of defiance toward the king. **5:** *Washed myself*, ceremonially, after touching a corpse (Num.19.11–13). **9:** *Defiled*, from handling the corpse. **10:** *Elymais*, a city, or possibly a region, in Persia (1 Macc.6.1).

  3.1–6: Tobit's prayer.

  3.7–17: God hears the prayer of Tobit, and also of Sarah, plagued by a demon-lover. From this point on the story is told in the third person. **7–10:** Sarah contemplates suicide. **7:** *Ecbatana*,

10 When she heard these things she was deeply grieved, even to the thought of hanging herself. But she said, "I am the only child of my father; if I do this, it will be a disgrace to him, and I shall bring his old age down in sorrow to the grave."[l] [11]So she prayed by her window and said, "Blessed art thou, O Lord my God, and blessed is thy holy and honored name for ever. May all thy works praise thee for ever. [12]And now, O Lord, I have turned my eyes and my face toward thee. [13]Command that I be released from the earth and that I hear reproach no more. [14]Thou knowest, O Lord, that I am innocent of any sin with man, [15]and that I did not stain my name or the name of my father in the land of my captivity. I am my father's only child, and he has no child to be his heir, no near kinsman or kinsman's[m] son for whom I should keep myself as wife. Already seven husbands of mine are dead. Why should I live? But if it be not pleasing to thee to take my life, command that respect be shown to me and pity be taken upon me, and that I hear reproach no more."

16 The prayer of both was heard in the presence of the glory of the great God. [17]And Raphael[n] was sent to heal the two of them: to scale away the white films from Tobit's eyes; to give Sarah the daughter of Raguel in marriage to Tobias the son of Tobit, and to bind Asmodeus the evil demon, because Tobias was entitled to possess her. At that very moment Tobit returned and entered his house and Sarah the daughter of Raguel came down from her upper room.

4 On that day Tobit remembered the money which he had left in trust with Gabael at Rages in Media, and he said to himself: [2]"I have asked for death. Why do I not call my son Tobias so that I may explain to him about the money[o] before I die?" [3]So he called him and said, "My son, when I die, bury me, and do not neglect your mother. Honor her all the days of your life; do what is pleasing to her, and do not grieve her. [4]Remember, my son, that she faced many dangers for you while you were yet unborn. When she dies, bury her beside me in the same grave.

5 "Remember the Lord our God all your days, my son, and refuse to sin or to transgress his commandments. Live uprightly all the days of your life, and do not walk in the ways of wrongdoing. [6]For if you do what is true, your ways will prosper through your deeds. [7]Give alms from your possessions to all who live uprightly, and do not let your eye begrudge the gift when you make it. Do not turn your face away from any poor man, and the face of God will not be turned away from you. [8]If you have many possessions, make your gift from them in proportion; if few, do not be afraid to give according to the little you have. [9]So you will be laying up a good treasure for yourself against the day of necessity. [10]For charity delivers from death and keeps you from entering the darkness; [11]and for all who practice it charity is an excellent offering in the presence of the Most High.

12 "Beware, my son, of all immo-

l Gk *to Hades*   *m* Gk *his*
n Other authorities read *the great Raphael. And he*
o Other authorities omit *about the money*

capital of Media, in Persia. **8:** The name *Asmodeus* means "destroyer." **11–15:** Sarah's prayer. **11:** *Blessed art thou* is the traditional beginning of a Jewish prayer (compare 8.5, 15 and see Jdt.13.17 n.). **16–17:** The angel Raphael is sent in answer to both the prayers. **17:** The name *Raphael* means "God heals." *Entitled to possess her*, 6.11. The phrase *at that very moment* is a dramatic device which heightens the interest of the story.

4.1–21: Preparing to send his son for the trust-money, Tobit imparts his philosophy of life. 1: *The money . . . at Rages*, 1.14. **5–19:** This section of general ethical counsel epitomizes the moral teaching of the book. There are many close parallels with other books of wisdom, such as Proverbs and Sirach. **6:** Morality guarantees prosperity; a dogma of orthodox Hebrew wisdom (Ps.1.1–3, Pr.10.27–30). **7–11:** The value of almsgiving; the emphasis is typical of the period (12.8–9; 14.10–11; Sir.3.30; 35.2; Mt.6.2–4). **12–13:** One should marry within his own

rality. First of all take a wife from among the descendants of your fathers and do not marry a foreign woman, who is not of your father's tribe; for we are the sons of the prophets. Remember, my son, that Noah, Abraham, Isaac, and Jacob, our fathers of old, all took wives from among their brethren. They were blessed in their children, and their posterity will inherit the land. [13]So now, my son, love your brethren, and in your heart do not disdain your brethren and the sons and daughters of your people by refusing to take a wife for yourself from among them. For in pride there is ruin and great confusion; and in shiftlessness there is loss and great want, because shiftlessness is the mother of famine. [14]Do not hold over till the next day the wages of any man who works for you, but pay him at once; and if you serve God you will receive payment.

"Watch yourself, my son, in everything you do, and be disciplined in all your conduct. [15]And what you hate, do not do to any one. Do not drink wine to excess or let drunkenness go with you on your way. [16]Give of your bread to the hungry, and of your clothing to the naked. Give all your surplus to charity, and do not let your eye begrudge the gift when you make it. [17]Place your bread on the grave of the righteous, but give none to sinners. [18]Seek advice from every wise man, and do not despise any useful counsel. [19]Bless the Lord God on every occasion; ask him that your ways may be made straight and that all your paths and plans may prosper. For none of the nations has understanding; but the Lord himself gives all good things, and according to his will he humbles whomever he wishes.

"So, my son, remember my commands, and do not let them be blotted out of your mind. [20]And now let me explain to you about the ten talents of silver which I left in trust with Gabael the son of Gabrias at Rages in Media. [21]Do not be afraid, my son, because we have become poor. You have great wealth if you fear God and refrain from every sin and do what is pleasing in his sight."

5 Then Tobias answered him, "Father, I will do everything that you have commanded me; [2]but how can I obtain the money when I do not know the man?" [3]Then Tobit gave him the receipt, and said to him, "Find a man to go with you and I will pay him wages as long as I live; and go and get the money." [4]So he went to look for a man; and he found Raphael, who was an angel, [5]but Tobias[p] did not know it. Tobias[p] said to him, "Can you go with me to Rages in Media? Are you acquainted with that region?" [6]The angel replied, "I will go with you; I am familiar with the way, and I have stayed with our brother Gabael." [7]Then Tobias said to him, "Wait for me, and I shall tell my father." [8]And he said to him, "Go, and do not delay." So he went in and said to his father, "I have found some one to go with me." He said, "Call him to me, so that I may learn to what tribe he belongs, and whether he is a reliable man to go with you."

9 So Tobias[p] invited him in; he entered and they greeted each other. [10]Then Tobit said to him, "My

p Gk *he*

---

family group; this is a keynote of the book (1.9; 3.15; 6.11–12). **13:** *Pride,* Pr.16.18. *Shiftlessness,* Pr.19.15; Sir.22.1–2. **14:** Lev.19.13. **15:** *What you hate, do not do,* the Golden Rule (Mt.7.12) in negative form, which was enunciated also by the great Jewish teacher, Hillel (flourished in the time of Herod the Great, 37–4 B.C.). *Wine,* Pr.23.29–35; Sir.31.29–31. **16:** Compare vv. 7–11. **17:** Placing food on graves was a pagan practice, forbidden in the Old Testament (Dt.26.14) and deprecated by many Jews (compare Sir.30.18). Some interpret the verse as a reference to the meals provided the mourners at funerals (compare Jer.16.7; Ezek.24.17). **19:** A sound moral life needs to be sustained by prayer.

5.1–21: Raphael, in the disguise of Azarias, is employed as Tobias' guide. 5: *Tobias did not know it,* as frequently in folklore, where angels (or gods) traveling in disguise are a favorite

brother, to what tribe and family do you belong? Tell me." [11]But he answered, "Are you looking for a tribe and a family or for a man whom you will pay to go with your son?" And Tobit said to him, "I should like to know, my brother, your people and your name." [12]He replied, "I am Azarias the son of the great Ananias, one of your relatives." [13]Then Tobit said to him, "You are welcome, my brother. Do not be angry with me because I tried to learn your tribe and family. You are a relative of mine, of a good and noble lineage. For I used to know Ananias and Jathan, the sons of the great Shemaiah, when we went together to Jerusalem to worship and offered the first-born of our flocks and the tithes of our produce. They did not go astray in the error of our brethren. My brother, you come of good stock. [14]But tell me, what wages am I to pay you—a drachma a day, and expenses for yourself as for my son? [15]And besides, I will add to your wages if you both return safe and sound." So they agreed to these terms.

16 Then he said to Tobias, "Get ready for the journey, and good success to you both." So his son made the preparations for the journey. And his father said to him, "Go with this man; God who dwells in heaven will prosper your way, and may his angel attend you." So they both went out and departed, and the young man's dog was with them.

17 But Anna,[q] his mother, began to weep, and said to Tobit, "Why have you sent our child away? Is he not the staff of our hands as he goes in and out before us? [18]Do not add money to money, but consider it rubbish as com-

pared to our child. [19]For the life that is given to us by the Lord is enough for us." [20]And Tobit said to her, "Do not worry, my sister; he will return safe and sound, and your eyes will see him. [21]For a good angel will go with him; his journey will be successful, and he will come back safe and sound." So she stopped weeping.

6 Now as they proceeded on their way they came at evening to the Tigris river and camped there. [2]Then the young man went down to wash himself. A fish leaped up from the river and would have swallowed the young man; [3]and the angel said to him, "Catch the fish." So the young man seized the fish and threw it up on the land. [4]Then the angel said to him, "Cut open the fish and take the heart and liver and gall and put them away safely." [5]So the young man did as the angel told him; and they roasted and ate the fish.

And they both continued on their way until they came near to Ecbatana. [6]Then the young man said to the angel, "Brother Azarias, of what use is the liver and heart and gall of the fish?" [7]He replied, "As for the heart and the liver, if a demon or evil spirit gives trouble to any one, you make a smoke from these before the man or woman, and that person will never be troubled again. [8]And as for the gall, anoint with it a man who has white films in his eyes, and he will be cured."

9 When they approached Ecbatana,[r] [10]the angel said to the young man, "Brother, today we shall stay with Raguel. He is your relative, and he has

---

q Other authorities omit *Anna*
r Other authorities read *Rages*

---

theme (compare Gen. ch. 18; Heb.13.2). **12**: In Hebrew *Azarias* means "God helps." **14**: A *drachma* was the normal day's wage for an artisan, about sixteen cents. **16**: The *dog* is a surprising feature of the story, but plays no special role (see 11.4 n.). **21**: Pleasing irony; Tobit does not know that Raphael is the *good angel.*

    6.1–8: On the journey, Raphael instructs Tobias in obtaining magical medicines from a man-eating fish. 1: *The Tigris* is actually west of Nineveh, so they would not have crossed it going to Persia (see 1.4 n.). **6–8**: Belief in the healing properties of the fish's organs is typical of folklore.

    6.9–17: Raphael prepares Tobias to seek the hand of Sarah. 12: *According to the law of Moses,*

an only daughter named Sarah. I will suggest that she be given to you in marriage, [11]because you are entitled to her and to her inheritance, for you are her only eligible kinsman. [12]The girl is also beautiful and sensible. Now listen to my plan. I will speak to her father, and as soon as we return from Rages we will celebrate the marriage. For I know that Raguel, according to the law of Moses, cannot give her to another man without incurring the penalty of death, because you rather than any other man are entitled to the inheritance."

13 Then the young man said to the angel, "Brother Azarias, I have heard that the girl has been given to seven husbands and that each died in the bridal chamber. [14]Now I am the only son my father has, and I am afraid that if I go in I will die as those before me did, for a demon is in love with her, and he harms no one except those who approach her. So now I fear that I may die and bring the lives of my father and mother to the grave in sorrow on my account. And they have no other son to bury them."

15 But the angel said to him, "Do you not remember the words with which your father commanded you to take a wife from among your own people? Now listen to me, brother, for she will become your wife; and do not worry about the demon, for this very night she will be given to you in marriage. [16]When you enter the bridal chamber, you shall take live ashes of incense and lay upon them some of the heart and liver of the fish so as to make a smoke. [17]Then the demon will smell it and flee away, and will never again return. And when you approach her, rise up, both of you, and cry out to the merciful God, and he will save you and have mercy on you. Do not be afraid, for she was destined for you from eternity. You will save her, and she will go with you, and I suppose that you will have children by her." When Tobias heard these things, he fell in love with her and yearned deeply for her.

7 When they reached Ecbatana and arrived at the house of Raguel, Sarah met them and greeted them. They returned her greeting, and she brought them into the house. [2]Then Raguel said to his wife Edna, "How much the young man resembles my cousin Tobit!" [3]And Raguel asked them, "Where are you from, brethren?" They answered him, "We belong to the sons of Naphtali, who are captives in Nineveh." [4]So he said to them, "Do you know our brother Tobit?" And they said, "Yes, we do." And he asked them, "Is he in good health?" [5]They replied, "He is alive and in good health." And Tobias said, "He is my father." [6]Then Raguel sprang up and kissed him and wept. [7]And he blessed him and exclaimed, "Son of that good and noble man!" When he heard that Tobit had lost his sight, he was stricken with grief and wept. [8]And his wife Edna and his daughter Sarah wept. They received them very warmly; and they killed a ram from the flock and set large servings of food before them.

Then Tobias said to Raphael, "Brother Azarias, speak of those things which you talked about on the journey, and let the matter be settled." [9]So he communicated the proposal to Raguel. And Raguel said to Tobias, "Eat, drink, and be merry; [10]for it is your right to take my child. But let me

---

presumably Num.36.6–8, although there is no mention of a death penalty. **14:** *To bury them*, one of the chief concerns of this book (see 1.17 n.; 4.3–4; 14.10). **17:** *Cry out . . . to God*, magic is not enough, prayer is necessary too. *From eternity*, "marriages are made in heaven" (compare Gen.24.14).

7.1–8a: Tobias and Raphael arrive at the home of Sarah's father. 1: *Ecbatana*, 3.7. The following conversation implies that Sarah and her family had not previously been aware of Tobias' existence. **4–5:** The Syriac and Latin Vulgate omit the conversation about Tobit's health, probably on account of his blindness.

explain the true situation to you. ¹¹I have given my daughter to seven husbands, and when each came to her he died in the night. But for the present be merry." And Tobias said, "I will eat nothing here until you make a binding agreement with me." ¹²So Raguel said, "Take her right now, in accordance with the law. You are her relative, and she is yours. The merciful God will guide you both for the best." ¹³Then he called his daughter Sarah, and taking her by the hand he gave her to Tobias to be his wife, saying, "Here she is; take her according to the law of Moses, and take her with you to your father." And he blessed them. ¹⁴Next he called his wife Edna, and took a scroll and wrote out the contract; and they set their seals to it. ¹⁵Then they began to eat.

16 And Raguel called his wife Edna and said to her, "Sister, make up the other room, and take her into it." ¹⁷So she did as he said, and took her there; and the girlˢ began to weep. But the motherˢ comforted her daughter in her tears, and said to her, ¹⁸"Be brave, my child; the Lord of heaven and earth grant you joyᵗ in place of this sorrow of yours. Be brave, my daughter."

8 When they had finished eating, they escorted Tobias in to her. ²As he went he remembered the words of Raphael, and he took the live ashes of incense and put the heart and liver of the fish upon them and made a smoke. ³And when the demon smelled the odor he fled to the remotest parts of Egypt, and the angel bound him. ⁴When the door was shut and the two were alone, Tobias got up from the bed and said, "Sister, get up, and let us pray that the Lord may have mercy upon us." ⁵And Tobias began to pray,

"Blessed art thou, O God of our fathers,
and blessed be thy holy and glorious name for ever.
Let the heavens and all thy creatures bless thee.
⁶Thou madest Adam and gavest him Eve his wife
as a helper and support.
From them the race of mankind has sprung.
Thou didst say, 'It is not good that the man should be alone;
let us make a helper for him like himself.'
⁷And now, O Lord, I am not taking this sister of mine because of lust, but with sincerity. Grant that I may find mercy and may grow old together with her." ⁸And she said with him, "Amen." ⁹Then they both went to sleep for the night.

But Raguel arose and went and dug a grave, ¹⁰with the thought, "Perhaps he too will die." ¹¹Then Raguel went into his house ¹²and said to his wife Edna, "Send one of the maids to see whether he is alive; and if he is not, let us bury him without any one knowing about it." ¹³So the maid opened the door and went in, and found them both asleep. ¹⁴And she came out and told them that he was alive. ¹⁵Then Raguel blessed God and said,

"Blessed art thou, O God, with every pure and holy blessing.
Let thy saints and all thy creatures bless thee;
let all thy angels and thy chosen people bless thee for ever.

s Gk *she*
t Other authorities read *favor*

7.8b–18: Tobias proposes and the wedding takes place. 13: *Taking her by the hand*, like a modern father "giving away the bride," he marries her to Tobias. 14: Signing *the contract* was the only other ceremony required.

8.1–9a: On the wedding night, Tobias routs the demon. 3: *Egypt* was the traditional home of magic and witchcraft (compare Ex.7.11). 4: See 6.17 n. 5–8: Tobias and Sarah join in prayer before consummating the marriage. 5: *Blessed art thou*, see 3.11 n.

8.9b–21: Raguel's fears are happily disappointed and he provides an extended wedding feast. 9b: *Dug a grave*, because he did not, of course, know that Tobias was provided with an effective means to drive away the demon. 19: For joy Raguel doubles the usual length of a wedding

¹⁶Blessed art thou, because thou hast
made me glad.
It has not happened to me as I
expected;
but thou hast treated us according to thy great mercy.
¹⁷Blessed art thou, because thou hast
had compassion on two only
children.
Show them mercy, O Lord;
and bring their lives to fulfilment
in health and happiness and
mercy."
¹⁸Then he ordered his servants to fill in
the grave.

19 After this he gave a wedding feast
for them which lasted fourteen days.
²⁰And before the days of the feast were
over, Raguel declared by oath to
Tobias^u that he should not leave until
the fourteen days of the wedding feast
were ended, ²¹that then he should take
half of Raguel's^v property and return
in safety to his father, and that the
rest would be his "when my wife and I
die."

9 Then Tobias called Raphael and
said to him, ²"Brother Azarias,
take a servant and two camels with you
and go to Gabael at Rages in Media
and get the money for me; and bring
him to the wedding feast. ³For Raguel
has sworn that I should not leave; ⁴but
my father is counting the days, and if
I delay long he will be greatly distressed." ⁵So Raphael made the journey and stayed over night with Gabael.
He gave him the receipt, and Gabael^w
brought out the money bags with their
seals intact and gave them to him. ⁶In
the morning they both got up early

and came to the wedding feast.
And Gabael blessed Tobias and his
wife.^x

10 Now his father Tobit was counting each day, and when the days
for the journey had expired and they
did not arrive, ²he said, "Is it possible
that he has been detained?^y Or is it
possible that Gabael has died and there
is no one to give him the money?"
³And he was greatly distressed. ⁴And
his wife said to him, "The lad has
perished; his long delay proves it."
Then she began to mourn for him, and
said, ⁵"Am I not distressed, my child,
that I let you go, you who are the light
of my eyes?" ⁶But Tobit said to her,
"Be still and stop worrying; he is well."
⁷And she answered him, "Be still and
stop deceiving me; my child has
perished." And she went out every day
to the road by which they had left;
she ate nothing in the daytime, and
throughout the nights she never stopped
mourning for her son Tobias, until
the fourteen days of the wedding feast
had expired which Raguel had sworn
that he should spend there.

At that time Tobias said to Raguel,
"Send me back, for my father and
mother have given up hope of ever
seeing me again." ⁸But his father-in-
law said to him, "Stay with me, and I
will send messengers to your father,
and they will inform him how things
are with you." ⁹Tobias replied, "No,
send me back to my father." ¹⁰So
Raguel arose and gave him his wife

u Gk *him*   v Gk *his*   w Gk *he*
x Cn: Gk *And Tobias blessed his wife*
y One Gk Ms Lat: Gk *they are put to shame* or *they are
disappointed*

feast (11.19; Jg.14.12). The oath complicates Tobias' affairs and makes necessary Raphael's
solitary mission in the next chapter.

9.1–6: Raphael goes to Rages and obtains the money from Gabael. 2: From Ecbatana to *Rages*
was a journey which, according to the ancient historian Arrian (*Anabasis*, III. 19–20), took
Alexander's army eleven days of forced marches; the author evidently supposed it to be much
shorter (see 1.4 n.). **3:** *Has sworn*, 8.20. **4:** Tobias' tender concern for his father is typical of the
spirit of the book. The son's unwillingness to prolong his visit is thoroughly justified by the
touching description of his parent's uneasiness in 10.1–7.

10.1–7a: Tobias' father and mother grow anxious at their son's absence. 1: In *counting each
day*, Tobit had naturally made no allowance for a two-week wedding celebration. **4:** *The lad has
perished*, the mother's feminine tendency to suspect the worst and her husband's courageous
attempts to console her illustrate the author's fine sensitivity to human feeling.

Sarah and half of his property in slaves, cattle, and money. ¹¹And when he had blessed them he sent them away, saying, "The God of heaven will prosper you, my children, before I die." ¹²He said also to his daughter, "Honor your father-in-law and your mother-in-law; they are now your parents. Let me hear a good report of you." And he kissed her. And Edna said to Tobias, "The Lord of heaven bring you back safely, dear brother, and grant me to see your children by my daughter Sarah, that I may rejoice before the Lord. See, I am entrusting my daughter to you; do nothing to grieve her."

11 After this Tobias went on his way, praising God because he had made his journey a success. And he blessed Raguel and his wife Edna.

So he continued on his way until they came near to Nineveh. ²Then Raphael said to Tobias, "Are you not aware, brother, of how you left your father? ³Let us run ahead of your wife and prepare the house. ⁴And take the gall of the fish with you." So they went their way, and the dog went along behind them.

5 Now Anna sat looking intently down the road for her son. ⁶And she caught sight of him coming, and said to his father, "Behold, your son is coming, and so is the man who went with him!"

7 Raphael said, "I know, Tobias, that your father will open his eyes. ⁸You therefore must anoint his eyes with the gall; and when they smart he will rub them, and will cause the white films to fall away, and he will see you."

9 Then Anna ran to meet them, and embraced her son, and said to him, "I have seen you, my child; now I am ready to die." And they both wept. ¹⁰Tobit started toward the door, and stumbled. But his son ran to him ¹¹and took hold of his father, and he sprinkled the gall upon his father's eyes, saying, "Be of good cheer, father." ¹²And when his eyes began to smart he rubbed them, ¹³and the white films scaled off from the corners of his eyes. ¹⁴Then he saw his son and embraced him, and he wept and said, "Blessed art thou, O God, and blessed is thy name for ever, and blessed are all thy holy angels. ¹⁵For thou hast afflicted me, but thou hast had mercy upon me; here I see my son Tobias!" And his son went in rejoicing, and he reported to his father the great things that had happened to him in Media.

16 Then Tobit went out to meet his daughter-in-law at the gate of Nineveh, rejoicing and praising God. Those who saw him as he went were amazed because he could see. ¹⁷And Tobit gave thanks before them that God had been merciful to him. When Tobit came near to Sarah his daughter-in-law, he blessed her, saying, "Welcome, daughter! Blessed is God who has brought you to us, and blessed are your father and your mother." So there was rejoicing among all his brethren in Nineveh. ¹⁸Ahikar and his nephew Nadab*z* came, ¹⁹and Tobias' marriage was celebrated for seven days with great festivity.

12 Tobit then called his son Tobias and said to him, "My son, see to the wages of the man who went with you; and he must also be given more." ²He replied, "Father, it would do me

z Other authorities read *Nasbas*

10.7b–12: Tobias and Sarah start for home. 11: *The God of heaven* was a favorite name for Israel's God in the Persian period and later (Jdt.5.8; Ezra 1.2).

11.1–15: Tobias and Raphael precede Sarah into the city and heal Tobit's blindness. 4: *The dog* appears again for the first time since 5.16; perhaps his presence in the story is a survival from an older folk tale, in which he had a real function. **14:** *Blessed art thou*, see 3.11 n.

11.16–19: Tobit meets his daughter-in-law and celebrates the marriage. 18: *Ahikar . . . Nadab*, see 14.10 n. **19:** *Seven days*, apparently the normal period of a wedding celebration (see 8.19 n.).

12.1–22: Raphael, being offered his wages, gives good advice and discloses his true identity. 1–5: Tobias generously wishes to reward Raphael far beyond the amount agreed upon (5.14).

no harm to give him half of what I have brought back. ³For he has led me back to you safely, he cured my wife, he obtained the money for me, and he also healed you." ⁴The old man said, "He deserves it." ⁵So he called the angel and said to him, "Take half of all that you two have brought back."

6 Then the angel*ᵃ* called the two of them privately and said to them: "Praise God and give thanks to him; exalt him and give thanks to him in the presence of all the living for what he has done for you. It is good to praise God and to exalt his name, worthily declaring the works of God. Do not be slow to give him thanks. ⁷It is good to guard the secret of a king, but gloriously to reveal the works of God. Do good, and evil will not overtake you. ⁸Prayer is good when accompanied by fasting, almsgiving, and righteousness. A little with righteousness is better than much with wrongdoing. It is better to give alms than to treasure up gold. ⁹For almsgiving delivers from death, and it will purge away every sin. Those who perform deeds of charity and of righteousness will have fulness of life; ¹⁰but those who commit sin are the enemies of their own lives.

11 "I will not conceal anything from you. I have said, 'It is good to guard the secret of a king, but gloriously to reveal the works of God.' ¹²And so, when you and your daughter-in-law Sarah prayed, I brought a reminder of your prayer before the Holy One; and when you buried the dead, I was like-wise present with you. ¹³When you did not hesitate to rise and leave your dinner in order to go and lay out the dead, your good deed was not hidden from me, but I was with you. ¹⁴So now God sent me to heal you and your daughter-in-law Sarah. ¹⁵I am Raphael, one of the seven holy angels who present the prayers of the saints and enter into the presence of the glory of the Holy One."

16 They were both alarmed; and they fell upon their faces, for they were afraid. ¹⁷But he said to them, "Do not be afraid; you will be safe. But praise God for ever. ¹⁸For I did not come as a favor on my part, but by the will of our God. Therefore praise him for ever. ¹⁹All these days I merely appeared to you and did not eat or drink, but you were seeing a vision. ²⁰And now give thanks to God, for I am ascending to him who sent me. Write in a book everything that has happened." ²¹Then they stood up; but they saw him no more. ²²So they confessed the great and wonderful works of God, and acknowledged that the angel of the Lord had appeared to them.

13 Then Tobit wrote a prayer of rejoicing, and said:
"Blessed is God who lives for ever,
    and blessed is his kingdom.
²For he afflicts, and he shows mercy;
    he leads down to Hades, and
      brings up again,
    and there is no one who can
      escape his hand.

a Gk *he*

6–10: In the style of a Jewish teacher of wisdom, Raphael delivers a brief exhortation on the good life, similar to that of Tobit in ch. 4. **8:** *Prayer . . . fasting, almsgiving, and righteousness* ("piety") are mentioned together also in Mt.6.1–18 (on almsgiving, compare 4.7–11 and see Sir.3.30 n.). **11:** V. 7. **12–15:** Raphael reveals himself as an angelic intercessor who brings the prayers of men into the presence of God. From v. 15 we learn that there are six others. "Uriel" is named in 2 Esd.4.1; "Gabriel" and "Michael," respectively, in Dan.9.21 and 10.13. The growth of angelology was characteristic of the Judaism of the period; this was partly due to an increasing sense of God's transcendence and partly, perhaps, to Persian influences. **17:** *Do not be afraid*, compare Mt.28.5,10.
    13.1–18: Tobit's hymn of praise. Some scholars believe that chs. 13 and 14 were added to the book much later in order to give substance to the words of 12.22a and to round out the account of Tobit's life. The hymn contains numerous echoes of Old Testament passages and has no particular appropriateness to Tobit's personal situation. **1–6:** Exhortation to the exiles. **2:**

[3]Acknowledge him before the nations,
O sons of Israel;
for he has scattered us among
them.
[4]Make his greatness known there,
and exalt him in the presence of
all the living;
because he is our Lord and God,
he is our Father for ever.
[5]He will afflict us for our iniquities;
and again he will show mercy,
and will gather us from all the
nations
among whom you[b] have been
scattered.
[6]If you turn to him with all your heart
and with all your soul,
to do what is true before him,
then he will turn to you
and will not hide his face from
you.
But see what he will do with you;
give thanks to him with your
full voice.
Praise the Lord of righteousness,
and exalt the King of the ages.
I give him thanks in the land of my
captivity,
and I show his power and majesty
to a nation of sinners.
Turn back, you sinners, and do
right before him;
who knows if he will accept you
and have mercy on you?
[7]I exalt my God;
my soul exalts the King of heaven,
and will rejoice in his majesty.
[8]Let all men speak,
and give him thanks in
Jerusalem.
[9]O Jerusalem, the holy city,
he will afflict you for the deeds
of your sons,
but again he will show mercy to
the sons of the righteous.
[10]Give thanks worthily to the Lord,
and praise the King of the ages,
that his tent may be raised for
you again with joy.

May he cheer those within you who
are captives,
and love those within you who
are distressed,
to all generations for ever.
[11]Many nations will come from afar
to the name of the Lord God,
bearing gifts in their hands, gifts
for the King of heaven.
Generations of generations will give
you joyful praise.
[12]Cursed are all who hate you;
blessed for ever will be all who
love you.
[13]Rejoice and be glad for the sons of
the righteous;
for they will be gathered together,
and will praise the Lord of the
righteous.
[14]How blessed are those who love
you!
They will rejoice in your peace.
Blessed are those who grieved over
all your afflictions;
for they will rejoice for you upon
seeing all your glory,
and they will be made glad for
ever.
[15]Let my soul praise God the great
King.
[16]For Jerusalem will be built with
sapphires and emeralds,
her[c] walls with precious stones,
and her towers and battlements
with pure gold.
[17]The streets of Jerusalem will be
paved[d] with beryl and ruby and
stones of Ophir;
[18] all her lanes will cry 'Hallelujah!'
and will give praise,
saying, 'Blessed is God, who has
exalted you for ever.' "

14 Here Tobit ended his words of
praise. [2]He was fifty-eight years
old when he lost his sight, and after
eight years he regained it. He gave

b Other authorities read *we*
c Gk *your*
d Or *inlaid*

---

1 Sam.2.6–8; Lk.1.52–53. 4: *Our Father*, Is.63.16; 64.8; Sir.23.1,4; Mt.6.9. 7: The psalmist offers his own praise. 8–18: God's favor to Jerusalem. 10: *Tent*, temple. 16–18: That *Jerusalem will be built* with precious stones is an echo of Is.54.11–12 (compare Rev.21.18–21).

alms, and he continued to fear the Lord God and to praise him. [3]When he had grown very old he called his son and grandsons, and said to him, "My son, take your sons; behold, I have grown old and am about to depart this life. [4]Go to Media, my son, for I fully believe what Jonah the prophet said about Nineveh, that it will be overthrown. But in Media there will be peace for a time. Our brethren will be scattered over the earth from the good land, and Jerusalem will be desolate. The house of God in it will be burned down and will be in ruins for a time. [5]But God will again have mercy on them, and bring them back into their land; and they will rebuild the house of God,[e] though it will not be like the former one until the times of the age are completed. After this they will return from the places of their captivity, and will rebuild Jerusalem in splendor. And the house of God will be rebuilt there with a glorious building for all generations for ever, just as the prophets said of it. [6]Then all the Gentiles will turn to fear the Lord God in truth, and will bury their idols. [7]All the Gentiles will praise the Lord, and his people will give thanks to God, and the Lord will exalt his people. And all who love the Lord God in truth and righteousness will rejoice, showing mercy to our brethren.

8 "So now, my son, leave Nineveh, because what the prophet Jonah said will surely happen. [9]But keep the law and the commandments, and be merciful and just, so that it may be well with you. [10]Bury me properly, and your mother with me. And do not live in Nineveh any longer. See, my son, what Nadab[f] did to Ahikar who had reared him, how he brought him from light into darkness, and with what he repaid him. But Ahikar was saved, and the other received repayment as he himself went down into the darkness. Ahikar[g] gave alms and escaped the deathtrap which Nadab[h] had set for him; but Nadab[f] fell into the trap and perished. [11]So now, my children, consider what almsgiving accomplishes and how righteousness delivers." As he said this he died in his bed. He was a hundred and fifty-eight years old; and Tobias[h] gave him a magnificent funeral. [12]And when Anna died he buried her with his father.

Then Tobias returned with his wife and his sons to Ecbatana, to Raguel his father-in-law. [13]He grew old with honor, and he gave his father-in-law and mother-in-law magnificent funerals. He inherited their property and that of his father Tobit. [14]He died in Ecbatana of Media at the age of a hundred and twenty-seven years. [15]But before he died he heard of the destruction of Nineveh, which Nebuchadnezzar and Ahasuerus had captured. Before his death he rejoiced over Nineveh.

e Gk *house*
f Other authorities read *Aman*
g Other authorities read *Manasses*
h Gk *he*

14.1–12: Tobit's final counsel, and death. 3–8: He advises his son to leave Nineveh, which is to be destroyed, and predicts the future course of Israel's history. **4:** *What Jonah the prophet said,* Jon.3.4 (Jonah's prophecy, however, was not fulfilled, Jon.3.10). **6:** That *the Gentiles will turn* to Judaism was a characteristic belief of the post-exilic age (e.g. Zech.8.20–23). **10:** *Bury me properly,* see 6.14 n. Nadab (also Nasbas or Nadin) is the villain of the *Ahikar* story (see 1.21 n.). *Gave alms,* 4.7–11. **15:** *Nebuchadnezzar . . . Ahasuerus,* i.e. Xerxes (Est.1.1). Both names are anachronistic; Nineveh's conquerors were Nabopolassar and Cyaxares (see 1.4 n.).

JUDITH

Rising slowly to a climax of unforgettable horror, the plot of Judith is a masterpiece of ancient Jewish narrative art. Although obviously a work of fiction, the atmosphere of the tale is entirely realistic, untouched by the aura of the marvelous which envelops such books as Jonah and Tobit. This is not to say that it is irreligious, but that its religion is of a national, legal, and practical type which tends to equate piety with patriotism and to encourage the belief that God helps those who help themselves. In mood and theme the book is closely akin to the book of Esther in the canonical Old Testament, but the character of its heroine is far more positive than Esther's. Judith observes the Mosaic law with scrupulous devotion; she does not, like Esther, demur when duty calls; the impulse to save her people is her own, and the grim stratagem which brings deliverance is of her own devising.

The first part of the book (chs. 1–7) describes at somewhat wearisome length how Nebuchadnezzar's general, Holofernes, invaded the west and at length laid siege to the Jewish town of Bethulia, hoping to starve it into submission. Judith, a beautiful and pious widow, is introduced in ch. 8, and the rest of the story relates how she beguiled Holofernes into entertaining her in his tent, where, when he had become thoroughly drunk, she decapitated him.

The story was probably written in Hebrew during the latter part of the second century B.C. It has been transmitted to us today in three slightly different Greek versions, two Latin versions, a Syriac version, as well as several later Hebrew recensions. The stirring narrative has inspired numerous works of painting, sculpture, and literature, notably an Anglo-Saxon epic of which extensive fragments survive.

IN THE TWELFTH YEAR OF THE REIGN of Nebuchadnezzar, who ruled over the Assyrians in the great city of Nineveh, in the days of Arphaxad, who ruled over the Medes in Ecbatana—²he is the king who built walls about Ecbatana with hewn stones three cubits thick and six cubits long; he made the walls seventy cubits high and fifty cubits wide; ³at the gates he built towers a hundred cubits high and sixty cubits wide at the foundations; ⁴and he made its gates, which were seventy cubits high and forty cubits wide, so that his armies could march out in force and his infantry form their ranks—⁵it was in those days that King Nebuchadnezzar made war against King Arphaxad in the great plain which is on the borders of Ragae. ⁶He was joined by all the people of the hill country and all those who lived along the Euphrates and the Tigris and the Hydaspes and in the plain where Arioch ruled the Elymaeans. Many nations joined the forces of the Chaldeans.

7 Then Nebuchadnezzar king of the Assyrians sent to all who lived in Persia and to all who lived in the west, those who lived in Cilicia and Damascus and Lebanon and Antilebanon and

---

1.1–6: Nebuchadnezzar declares war on Arphaxad, king of Media. 1: *Nebuchadnezzar* (605 [or 604]–562 B.C.) was second ruler over the Neo-Babylonian Empire (not *over the Assyrians*). It was he who destroyed Jerusalem in 587–86 B.C. and carried the Jews off into their Babylonian Exile (2 Kg.24.1–25.26). The author of the book of Judith, in complete disregard of history, represents him as flourishing after the Exile (4.3; 5.19). Some scholars believe that the historical confusion of the book, of which this is but one example, is deliberate, intended to stamp the work unmistakably as fiction. *Arphaxad* is unknown. *The Medes* inhabited the northern part of modern Iran and had their capital at *Ecbatana* (Tob.3.7). **5:** *Ragae*, called Rages in Tob.1.14 (see note there). **6:** *Euphrates . . . Tigris*, the principal rivers of Mesopotamia (modern Iraq). *Hydaspes*, a river in India, but here evidently placed in Mesopotamia. *Arioch*, unknown. *Elymaeans*, Elamites. *Chaldeans*, the Neo-Babylonians (see v. 1 n.).

1.7–11: The Persians and the western nations refuse Nebuchadnezzar's plea for help. 7–10: The nations enumerated correspond to modern Syria, Lebanon, Palestine, and Egypt. **7:** *Persia*, the south of modern Iran.

all who lived along the seacoast, ⁸and those among the nations of Carmel and Gilead, and Upper Galilee and the great Plain of Esdraelon, ⁹and all who were in Samaria and its surrounding towns, and beyond the Jordan as far as Jerusalem and Bethany and Chelous and Kadesh and the river of Egypt, and Tahpanhes and Raamses and the whole land of Goshen, ¹⁰even beyond Tanis and Memphis, and all who lived in Egypt as far as the borders of Ethiopia. ¹¹But all who lived in the whole region disregarded the orders of Nebuchadnezzar king of the Assyrians, and refused to join him in the war; for they were not afraid of him, but looked upon him as only one man,ᵃ and they sent back his messengers empty-handed and shamefaced.

12 Then Nebuchadnezzar was very angry with this whole region, and swore by his throne and kingdom that he would surely take revenge on the whole territory of Cilicia and Damascus and Syria, that he would kill them by the sword, and also all the inhabitants of the land of Moab, and the people of Ammon, and all Judea, and every one in Egypt, as far as the coasts of the two seas. ¹³In the seventeenth year he led his forces against King Arphaxad, and defeated him in battle, and overthrew the whole army of Arphaxad, and all his cavalry and all his chariots. ¹⁴Thus he took possession of his cities, and came to Ecbatana, captured its towers, plundered its markets, and turned its beauty into shame. ¹⁵He captured Arphaxad in the mountains of Ragae and struck him down with hunting spears; and he utterly destroyed him, to this day. ¹⁶Then he returned with them to Nineveh, he and all his com-

bined forces, a vast body of troops; and there he and his forces rested and feasted for one hundred and twenty days.

2 In the eighteenth year, on the twenty-second day of the first month, there was talk in the palace of Nebuchadnezzar king of the Assyrians about carrying out his revenge on the whole region, just as he had said. ²He called together all his officers and all his nobles and set forth to them his secret plan and recounted fully, with his own lips, all the wickedness of the region;ᵇ ³and it was decided that every one who had not obeyed his command should be destroyed. ⁴When he had finished setting forth his plan, Nebuchadnezzar king of the Assyrians called Holofernes, the chief general of his army, second only to himself, and said to him,

5 "Thus says the Great King, the lord of the whole earth: When you leave my presence, take with you men confident in their strength, to the number of one hundred and twenty thousand foot soldiers and twelve thousand cavalry. ⁶Go and attack the whole west country, because they disobeyed my orders. ⁷Tell them to prepare earth and water, for I am coming against them in my anger, and will cover the whole face of the earth with the feet of my armies, and will hand them over to be plundered by my troops,ᶜ ⁸till their wounded shall fill their valleys, and every brook and river shall be filled with their dead, and over-flow; ⁹and I will lead them away captive to the ends of the whole earth. ¹⁰You shall go and seize all their terri-

<hr>

ᵃ Or *a man*
ᵇ The meaning of the Greek of the last clause of this verse is uncertain　　ᶜ Gk *them*

<hr>

1.12–16: Angry at the western nations, Nebuchadnezzar defeats Arphaxad without their assistance. **12:** *The two seas*, presumably the Red and the Mediterranean.

2.1–13: Nebuchadnezzar orders Holofernes to lead a punitive expedition against the West. **4:** Next to Judith, *Holofernes* is the principal character of the book. So far as is known, Nebuchadnezzar had no such general, but the name is found in classical authors of a much later period. His career may have been suggested by memories of a Persian general of similar name who was a leader in the expedition which invaded the West under Artaxerxes III about 350 B.C. (Diodorus Siculus, *Hist.* XXXI. 19; see 12.11 n.). **7:** *Earth and water* were characteristic signs of submission demanded by Persian (not Assyrian or Babylonian) kings (Herodotus, *Hist.* VI. 48).

tory for me in advance. They will yield themselves to you, and you shall hold them for me till the day of their punishment. [11]But if they refuse, your eye shall not spare and you shall hand them over to slaughter and plunder throughout your whole region. [12]For as I live, and by the power of my kingdom, what I have spoken my hand will execute. [13]And you—take care not to transgress any of your sovereign's commands, but be sure to carry them out just as I have ordered you; and do not delay about it."

14 So Holofernes left the presence of his master, and called together all the commanders, generals, and officers of the Assyrian army, [15]and mustered the picked troops by divisions as his lord had ordered him to do, one hundred and twenty thousand of them, together with twelve thousand archers on horseback, [16]and he organized them as a great army is marshaled for a campaign. [17]He collected a vast number of camels and asses and mules for transport, and innumerable sheep and oxen and goats for provision; [18]also plenty of food for every man, and a huge amount of gold and silver from the royal palace. [19]So he set out with his whole army, to go ahead of King Nebuchadnezzar and to cover the whole face of the earth to the west with their chariots and horsemen and picked troops of infantry. [20]Along with them went a mixed crowd like a swarm of locusts, like the dust of the earth—a multitude that could not be counted.

21 They marched for three days from Nineveh to the plain of Bectileth, and camped opposite Bectileth near the mountain which is to the north of Upper Cilicia. [22]From there Holofernes[d] took his whole army, his infantry, cavalry, and chariots, and went up into the hill country [23]and ravaged Put and Lud, and plundered all the people of Rassis and the Ishmaelites who lived along the desert, south of the country of the Chelleans. [24]Then he followed[e] the Euphrates and passed through Mesopotamia and destroyed all the hilltop cities along the brook Abron, as far as the sea. [25]He also seized the territory of Cilicia, and killed every one who resisted him, and came to the southern borders of Japheth, fronting toward Arabia. [26]He surrounded all the Midianites, and burned their tents and plundered their sheepfolds. [27]Then he went down into the plain of Damascus during the wheat harvest, and burned all their fields and destroyed their flocks and herds and sacked their cities and ravaged their lands and put to death all their young men with the edge of the sword.

28 So fear and terror of him fell upon all the people who lived along the seacoast, at Sidon and Tyre, and those who lived in Sur and Ocina and all who lived in Jamnia. Those who lived in Azotus and Ascalon feared him exceedingly.

3 So they sent messengers to sue for peace, and said, [2]"Behold, we the servants of Nebuchadnezzar, the Great King, lie prostrate before you. Do with us whatever you will. [3]Behold, our buildings, and all our land, and all

---

d Gk *he*   *e* Or *crossed*

2.14–27: Holofernes brings an enormous army to Damascus. 21: The *three days* march is impossible, since *Nineveh*, the capital of Assyria, is at least three hundred miles from *Bectileth* (an unidentified site), which is described as *north of Upper Cilicia.* Cilicia is in southeastern Asia Minor. **23:** *Put and Lud*, probably in Asia Minor. *Rassis*, unknown. *Ishmaelites*, Arabs (Gen. 16.11–12). *Chelleans*, unknown. **24:** The geography here is confused. *Abron*, unknown. The natural line of march would be directly south from Cilicia to Damascus. **26:** *Midianites*, archaic for Arabs (Jg.6.1–6). **27:** *Damascus*, the ancient and beautiful capital of Syria, was noted for its fertile surroundings.

2.28–3.8: Through fear the people of the seacoast submit voluntarily. 2.28: *Sidon and Tyre*, on the Phoenician coast, west of Damascus. *Sur and Ocina*, unknown. *Jamnia*, just north of *Azotus* (Ashdod) *and Ascalon* (Ashkelon), important Philistine cities in southwest Palestine.

our wheat fields, and our flocks and herds, and all our sheepfolds with their tents, lie before you; do with them whatever you please. ⁴Our cities also and their inhabitants are your slaves; come and deal with them in any way that seems good to you."

5 The men came to Holofernes and told him all this. ⁶Then he went down to the seacoast with his army and stationed garrisons in the hilltop cities and took picked men from them as his allies. ⁷And these people and all in the country round about welcomed him with garlands and dances and tambourines. ⁸And he demolished all their shrines* and cut down their sacred groves; for it had been given to him to destroy all the gods of the land, so that all nations should worship Nebuchadnezzar only, and all their tongues and tribes should call upon him as god.

9 Then he came to the edge of Esdraelon, near Dothan, fronting the great ridge of Judea; ¹⁰here he camped between Geba and Scythopolis, and remained for a whole month in order to assemble all the supplies for his army.

4 By this time the people of Israel living in Judea heard of everything that Holofernes, the general of Nebuchadnezzar the king of the Assyrians, had done to the nations, and how he had plundered and destroyed all

their temples; ²they were therefore very greatly terrified at his approach, and were alarmed both for Jerusalem and for the temple of the Lord their God. ³For they had only recently returned from the captivity, and all the people of Judea were newly gathered together, and the sacred vessels and the altar and the temple had been consecrated after their profanation. ⁴So they sent to every district of Samaria, and to Kona and Beth-horon and Belmain and Jericho and to Choba and Aesora and the valley of Salem, ⁵and immediately seized all the high hilltops and fortified the villages on them and stored up food in preparation for war—since their fields had recently been harvested. ⁶And Joakim, the high priest, who was in Jerusalem at that time, wrote to the people of Bethulia and Betomesthaim, which faces Esdraelon opposite the plain near Dothan, ⁷ordering them to seize the passes up into the hills, since by them Judea could be invaded, and it was easy to stop any who tried to enter, for the approach was narrow, only wide enough for two men at the most.

8 So the Israelites did as Joakim the high priest and the senate of the whole people of Israel, in session at Jerusalem, had given order. ⁹And every man of Israel cried out to God with great

f Syr: Gk *borders*

3.8: Holofernes seems here to go beyond his original commission, which was merely punitive; now he seeks to impose religious unity by forcing all men to worship Nebuchadnezzar alone. The language is suggested directly by such passages as Dan. chs. 3 and 6, and indirectly by the persecutions of Antiochus Epiphanes as related in 1 Macc.1.10–2.26 and 2 Macc. chs. 6–7. Holofernes' invasion thus becomes a threat to Israel's religious integrity as well as her national security.

3.9–4.15: When Holofernes reaches the soil of Palestine, the Jews prepare to resist. 3.9: *Esdraelon* is the great plain which cuts across Palestine just north of Mt. Carmel. *Dothan* is a short distance south of the plain. *Scythopolis* is identical with Beth-shan, located at the junction of Esdraelon and the Jordan Valley. **4.3:** The statement that *they had only recently returned from the captivity* is flagrantly anachronistic, since it was Nebuchadnezzar who had begun the captivity (compare 1.1 n.), and the return took place nearly fifty years later under the Persian Empire, which had succeeded the Babylonian (Ezra 1.1–3). **4:** The inclusion of *Samaria* is quite unrealistic, since the people of Judea (v. 1) and the Samaritans were separate and increasingly hostile communities in the post-exilic era. **6:** The name of the high priest, *Joakim*, is no doubt derived from Neh.12.26. The identification of *Bethulia*, the center of the story's action, is one of the major puzzles of the book; the most probable suggestion is that it is a pseudonym for Shechem (see 6.11 n.; 7.18 n.; and 10.10 n.). **8:** *Senate*, an anachronism of the author (see 1.1 n. and 1 Macc.12.6 n.).

fervor, and they humbled themselves with much fasting. [10]They and their wives and their children and their cattle and every resident alien and hired laborer and purchased slave—they all girded themselves with sackcloth. [11]And all the men and women of Israel, and their children, living at Jerusalem, prostrated themselves before the temple and put ashes on their heads and spread out their sackcloth before the Lord. [12]They even surrounded the altar with sackcloth and cried out in unison, praying earnestly to the God of Israel not to give up their infants as prey and their wives as booty, and the cities they had inherited to be destroyed, and the sanctuary to be profaned and desecrated to the malicious joy of the Gentiles. [13]So the Lord heard their prayers and looked upon their affliction; for the people fasted many days throughout Judea and in Jerusalem before the sanctuary of the Lord Almighty. [14]And Joakim the high priest and all the priests who stood before the Lord and ministered to the Lord, with their loins girded with sackcloth, offered the continual burnt offerings and the vows and freewill offerings of the people. [15]With ashes upon their turbans, they cried out to the Lord with all their might to look with favor upon the whole house of Israel.

5 When Holofernes, the general of the Assyrian army, heard that the people of Israel had prepared for war and had closed the passes in the hills and had fortified all the high hilltops and set up barricades in the plains, [2]he was very angry. So he called together all the princes of Moab and the commanders of Ammon and all the governors of the coastland, [3]and said to them, "Tell me, you Canaanites, what people is this that lives in the hill country? What cities do they inhabit? How large is their army, and in what does their power or strength consist? Who rules over them as king, leading their army? [4]And why have they alone, of all who live in the west, refused to come out and meet me?"

5 Then Achior, the leader of all the Ammonites, said to him, "Let my lord now hear a word from the mouth of your servant, and I will tell you the truth about this people that dwells in the nearby mountain district. No falsehood shall come from your servant's mouth. [6]This people is descended from the Chaldeans. [7]At one time they lived in Mesopotamia, because they would not follow the gods of their fathers who were in Chaldea. [8]For they had left the ways of their ancestors, and they worshiped the God of heaven, the God they had come to know; hence they drove them out from the presence of their gods; and they fled to Mesopotamia, and lived there for a long time. [9]Then their God commanded them to leave the place where they were living and go to the land of Canaan. There they settled, and prospered, with much gold and silver and very many cattle. [10]When a famine spread over Canaan they went down to Egypt and lived there as long as they had food; and

---

14: *The continual burnt offerings* were the prescribed daily sacrifices (Ex.29.38–42); the *freewill offerings* were presented voluntarily as occasion required (Lev.22.18–30).
    5.1–24: Holofernes is advised by Achior that the Jews are invincible as long as they keep God's law. 2: *Moab* was the region directly east of the Dead Sea, while *Ammon* lay north and east of it. Both nations were traditional enemies of the Jews (Jg.3.12–30; 2 Sam.10–12; 2 Kg.3.4–27; 24.2). **3:** The circumstance that Israel inhabited the rugged *hill country* had often helped her to preserve her independence in the past. **5–21:** To explain the character of the Jews, Achior summarizes their entire history from Abraham to the return from exile. **6–9:** The migration of Abraham and the prosperity of his descendants (Gen.11.27–37.1). **6:** *Chaldeans,* Abraham came from Ur of the Chaldees (Gen.11.27–31). **7:** *Mesopotamia* here is the region in the north around Haran (Gen.11.31). Late Jewish tradition ascribed the migration of Abraham's family to a desire to escape the influence of polytheism. **8:** *The God of heaven* was a favorite name for Israel's God during the Persian period and later (Tob.10.11; Ezra 1.2). **10–13:** The descent into

there they became a great multitude—so great that they could not be counted. [11]So the king of Egypt became hostile to them; he took advantage of them and set them to making bricks, and humbled them and made slaves of them. [12]Then they cried out to their God, and he afflicted the whole land of Egypt with incurable plagues; and so the Egyptians drove them out of their sight. [13]Then God dried up the Red Sea before them, [14]and he led them by the way of Sinai and Kadesh-barnea, and drove out all the people of the wilderness. [15]So they lived in the land of the Amorites, and by their might destroyed all the inhabitants of Heshbon; and crossing over the Jordan they took possession of all the hill country. [16]And they drove out before them the Canaanites and the Perizzites and the Jebusites and the Shechemites and all the Gergesites, and lived there a long time. [17]As long as they did not sin against their God they prospered, for the God who hates iniquity is with them. [18]But when they departed from the way which he had appointed for them, they were utterly defeated in many battles and were led away captive to a foreign country; the temple of their God was razed to the ground, and their cities were captured by their enemies. [19]But now they have returned to their God, and have come back from the places to which they were scattered, and have occupied Jerusalem, where their sanctuary is, and have settled in the hill country, because it was uninhabited. [20]Now therefore, my master and lord, if there is any unwitting error in this people and they sin against their God and we find out their offense, then we will go up and defeat them. [21]But if there is no transgression in their nation, then let my lord pass them by; for their Lord will defend them, and their God will protect them, and we shall be put to shame before the whole world."

22 When Achior had finished saying this, all the men standing around the tent began to complain; Holofernes' officers and all the men from the seacoast and from Moab insisted that he must be put to death. [23]"For," they said, "we will not be afraid of the Israelites; they are a people with no strength or power for making war. [24]Therefore let us go up, Lord Holofernes, and they will be devoured by your vast army."

6 When the disturbance made by the men outside the council died down, Holofernes, the commander of the Assyrian army, said to Achior and all the Moabites in the presence of all the foreign contingents:

2 "And who are you, Achior, and you hirelings of Ephraim, to prophesy among us as you have done today and tell us not to make war against the people of Israel because their God will defend them? Who is God except Nebuchadnezzar? [3]He will send his forces and will destroy them from the face of the earth, and their God will not deliver them—we the king's[f] servants will destroy them as one man. They cannot resist the might of our cavalry. [4]We will burn them up,[g] and their mountains will be drunk with their blood, and their fields will be full of their dead. They[h] cannot withstand us, but will utterly perish. So says King Nebuchadnezzar, the lord of the whole earth. For he has spoken; none of his words shall be in vain.

f Gk *his*
g Other authorities add *with it*
h Gk *The track of their feet*

Egypt and the Exodus (Gen.37.2–Ex.18.27). **14**: *Sinai,* Ex.19.1–Num.10.10. *Kadesh-barnea,* Num.20.1. **15–16**: The conquests in Transjordan and Canaan (Num.20.14–Jos.11.23). **15**: *Amorites . . . Heshbon,* Num.21.21–32. **17**: *They prospered,* the philosophy of Deuteronomy (28.1–14). **18**: The exile (see 1.1 n.). **19**: The return from exile (Ezra chs. 1–3); see 4.3 n. **22–24**: Holofernes' other advisers oppose the view of Achior.

   6.1–21: **For his presumption, Achior is handed over to the Jews to perish with them in the fall of Bethulia. 1–9**: Holofernes' denunciation of Achior. **2**: By calling Achior and his Ammonite

5 "But you, Achior, you Ammonite hireling, who have said these words on the day of your iniquity, you shall not see my face again from this day until I take revenge on this race that came out of Egypt. [6]Then the sword of my army and the spear[i] of my servants shall pierce your sides, and you shall fall among their wounded, when I return. [7]Now my slaves are going to take you back into the hill country and put you in one of the cities beside the passes, [8]and you will not die until you perish along with them. [9]If you really hope in your heart that they will not be taken, do not look downcast! I have spoken and none of my words shall fail."

10 Then Holofernes ordered his slaves, who waited on him in his tent, to seize Achior and take him to Bethulia and hand him over to the men of Israel. [11]So the slaves took him and led him out of the camp into the plain, and from the plain they went up into the hill country and came to the springs below Bethulia. [12]When the men of the city saw them,[j] they caught up their weapons and ran out of the city to the top of the hill, and all the slingers kept them from coming up by casting stones at them. [13]However, they got under the shelter of the hill and they bound Achior and left him lying at the foot of the hill, and returned to their master.

14 Then the men of Israel came down from their city and found him; and they untied him and brought him into Bethulia and placed him before the magistrates of their city, [15]who in those days were Uzziah the son of Micah, of the tribe of Simeon, and Chabris the son of Gothoniel, and Charmis the son of Melchiel. [16]They called together all the elders of the city, and all their young men and their women ran to the assembly; and they set Achior in the midst of all their people, and Uzziah asked him what had happened. [17]He answered and told them what had taken place at the council of Holofernes, and all that he had said in the presence of the Assyrian leaders, and all that Holofernes had said so boastfully against the house of Israel. [18]Then the people fell down and worshiped God, and cried out to him, and said,

19 "O Lord God of heaven, behold their arrogance, and have pity on the humiliation of our people, and look this day upon the faces of those who are consecrated to thee."

20 Then they consoled Achior, and praised him greatly. [21]And Uzziah took him from the assembly to his own house and gave a banquet for the elders; and all that night they called on the God of Israel for help.

7 The next day Holofernes ordered his whole army, and all the allies who had joined him, to break camp and move against Bethulia, and to seize the passes up into the hill country and make war on the Israelites. [2]So all their warriors moved their camp that day; their force of men of war was one hundred and seventy thousand infantry and twelve thousand cavalry, together with the baggage and the foot soldiers handling it, a very great multitude. [3]They encamped in the valley near Bethulia, beside the spring, and they spread out in breadth over Dothan as far as Balbaim and in length from Bethulia to Cyamon, which faces Esdraelon.

i Lat Syr: Gk *people*
j Other authorities add *on the top of the hill*

4 When the Israelites saw their vast numbers they were greatly terrified, and every one said to his neighbor, "These men will now lick up the face of the whole land; neither the high mountains nor the valleys nor the hills will bear their weight." ⁵Then each man took up his weapons, and when they had kindled fires on their towers they remained on guard all that night.

6 On the second day Holofernes led out all his cavalry in full view of the Israelites in Bethulia, ⁷and examined the approaches to the city, and visited the springs that supplied their water, and seized them and set guards of soldiers over them, and then returned to his army.

8 Then all the chieftains of the people of Esau and all the leaders of the Moabites and the commanders of the coastland came to him and said, ⁹"Let our lord hear a word, lest his army be defeated. ¹⁰For these people, the Israelites, do not rely on their spears but on the height of the mountains where they live, for it is not easy to reach the tops of their mountains. ¹¹Therefore, my lord, do not fight against them in battle array, and not a man of your army will fall. ¹²Remain in your camp, and keep all the men in your forces with you; only let your servants take possession of the spring of water that flows from the foot of the mountain—¹³for this is where all the people of Bethulia get their water. So thirst will destroy them, and they will give up their city. We and our people will go up to the tops of the nearby mountains and camp there to keep watch that not a man gets out of the city. ¹⁴They and their wives and children will waste away with famine, and before the sword reaches them they

will be strewn about in the streets where they live. ¹⁵So you will pay them back with evil, because they rebelled and did not receive you peaceably."

16 These words pleased Holofernes and all his servants, and he gave orders to do as they had said. ¹⁷So the army of the Ammonites moved forward, together with five thousand Assyrians, and they encamped in the valley and seized the water supply and the springs of the Israelites. ¹⁸And the sons of Esau and the sons of Ammon went up and encamped in the hill country opposite Dothan; and they sent some of their men toward the south and the east, toward Acraba, which is near Chusi beside the brook Mochmur. The rest of the Assyrian army encamped in the plain, and covered the whole face of the land, and their tents and supply trains spread out in great number, and they formed a vast multitude.

19 The people of Israel cried out to the Lord their God, for their courage failed, because all their enemies had surrounded them and there was no way of escape from them. ²⁰The whole Assyrian army, their infantry, chariots, and cavalry, surrounded them for thirty-four days, until all the vessels of water belonging to every inhabitant of Bethulia were empty; ²¹their cisterns were going dry, and they did not have enough water to drink their fill for a single day, because it was measured out to them to drink. ²²Their children lost heart, and the women and young men fainted from thirst and fell down in the streets of the city and in the passages through the gates; there was no strength left in them any longer.

23 Then all the people, the young men, the women, and the children,

---

7.8–18: They cut off the city's water supply by seizing the springs. 8: *Esau* means Edom, southeast of the Dead Sea. These people have not previously been mentioned, but were also traditional enemies of the Jews (see e.g. Ob.18). 18: The localities of *Acraba* and *Chusi* and the valley of *Mochmur* have all been identified with sites in the neighborhood of Shechem (see 4.6 n.).

7.19–28: Driven to desperation, the citizens of Bethulia urge their leaders to capitulate. 23: *Uzziah*, 6.15.

gathered about Uzziah and the rulers of the city and cried out with a loud voice, and said before all the elders, 24"God be judge between you and us! For you have done us a great injury in not making peace with the Assyrians. 25For now we have no one to help us; God has sold us into their hands, to strew us on the ground before them with thirst and utter destruction. 26Now call them in and surrender the whole city to the army of Holofernes and to all his forces, to be plundered. 27For it would be better for us to be captured by them;*k* for we will be slaves, but our lives will be spared, and we shall not witness the death of our babes before our eyes, or see our wives and children draw their last breath. 28We call to witness against you heaven and earth and our God, the Lord of our fathers, who punishes us according to our sins and the sins of our fathers. Let him not do this day the things which we have described!"

29 Then great and general lamentation arose throughout the assembly, and they cried out to the Lord God with a loud voice. 30And Uzziah said to them, "Have courage, my brothers! Let us hold out for five more days; by that time the Lord our God will restore to us his mercy, for he will not forsake us utterly. 31But if these days pass by, and no help comes for us, I will do what you say."

32 Then he dismissed the people to their various posts, and they went up on the walls and towers of their city. The women and children he sent home. And they were greatly depressed in the city.

8 At that time Judith heard about these things: she was the daughter of Merari the son of Ox, son of Joseph, son of Oziel, son of Elkiah, son of Ananias, son of Gideon, son of Raphaim, son of Ahitub, son of Elijah, son of Hilkiah, son of Eliab, son of Nathanael, son of Salamiel, son of Sarasadai, son of Israel. 2Her husband Manasseh, who belonged to her tribe and family, had died during the barley harvest. 3For as he stood overseeing the men who were binding sheaves in the field, he was overcome by the burning heat, and took to his bed and died in Bethulia his city. So they buried him with his fathers in the field between Dothan and Balamon. 4Judith had lived at home as a widow for three years and four months. 5She set up a tent for herself on the roof of her house, and girded sackcloth about her loins and wore the garments of her widowhood. 6She fasted all the days of her widowhood, except the day before the sabbath and the sabbath itself, the day before the new moon and the day of the new moon, and the feasts and days of rejoicing of the house of Israel. 7She was beautiful in appearance, and had a very lovely face; and her husband Manasseh had left her gold and silver, and men and women slaves, and cattle, and fields; and she maintained this estate. 8No one spoke ill of her, for she feared God with great devotion.

9 When Judith heard the wicked words spoken by the people against the ruler, because they were faint for lack of water, and when she heard all that Uzziah said to them, and how he promised them under oath to surrender the city to the Assyrians after five days, 10she sent her maid, who was in charge of all she possessed, to summon*l* Chabris and Charmis, the elders

k Other authorities add *than to die of thirst*
l Some authorities add *Uzziah and* (See verses 28 and 35)

7.29–32: Uzziah advises a delay of five days.

8.1–8: The character of Judith. 1: The name *Judith* means "Jewess." Her ancestors cannot be identified: some of the names are unparalleled in the Old Testament. 2–3: Her husband had died of sunstroke (compare 2 Kg.4.18–20). 6: The rigorous piety which is her outstanding quality is of the rabbinical or Pharisaical type. She omits fasting only on days when it is forbidden. 7: Beauty and wealth are normal elements in the character of a romantic heroine.

8.9–27: Judith presents sound theological arguments against Uzziah's proposal. 12: Note the

of her city. [11]They came to her, and she said to them,

"Listen to me, rulers of the people of Bethulia! What you have said to the people today is not right; you have even sworn and pronounced this oath between God and you, promising to surrender the city to our enemies unless the Lord turns and helps us within so many days. [12]Who are you, that have put God to the test this day, and are setting yourselves up in the place of[m] God among the sons of men? [13]You are putting the Lord Almighty to the test—but you will never know anything! [14]You cannot plumb the depths of the human heart, nor find out what a man is thinking; how do you expect to search out God, who made all these things, and find out his mind or comprehend his thought? No, my brethren, do not provoke the Lord our God to anger. [15]For if he does not choose to help us within these five days, he has power to protect us within any time he pleases, or even to destroy us in the presence of our enemies. [16]Do not try to bind the purposes of the Lord our God; for God is not like man, to be threatened, nor like a human being, to be won over by pleading. [17]Therefore, while we wait for his deliverance, let us call upon him to help us, and he will hear our voice, if it pleases him.

18 "For never in our generation, nor in these present days, has there been any tribe or family or people or city of ours which worshiped gods made with hands, as was done in days gone by— [19]and that was why our fathers were handed over to the sword, and to be plundered, and so they suffered a great catastrophe before our enemies. [20]But we know no other god but him, and therefore we hope that he will not disdain us or any of our nation. [21]For if we are captured all Judea will be captured and our sanctuary will be plundered; and he will exact of us[n] the penalty for its desecration. [22]And the slaughter of our brethren and the captivity of the land and the desolation of our inheritance—all this he will bring upon our heads among the Gentiles, wherever we serve as slaves; and we shall be an offense and a reproach in the eyes of those who acquire us. [23]For our slavery will not bring us into favor, but the Lord our God will turn it to dishonor.

24 "Now therefore, brethren, let us set an example to our brethren, for their lives depend upon us, and the sanctuary and the temple and the altar rest upon us. [25]In spite of everything let us give thanks to the Lord our God, who is putting us to the test as he did our forefathers. [26]Remember what he did with Abraham, and how he tested Isaac, and what happened to Jacob in Mesopotamia in Syria, while he was keeping the sheep of Laban, his mother's brother. [27]For he has not tried us with fire, as he did them, to search their hearts, nor has he taken revenge upon us; but the Lord scourges those who draw near to him, in order to admonish them."

28 Then Uzziah said to her, "All that you have said has been spoken out of a true heart, and there is no one who can deny your words. [29]Today is not the first time your wisdom has been shown, but from the beginning of your life all the people have recognized your understanding, for your heart's disposition is right. [30]But the people were very thirsty, and they compelled us to do for them what we have promised, and made us take an oath which we cannot break. [31]So pray for us, since

m Or *above*
n Gk *our blood*

---

neat balance of her antitheses: it is not for us to *put God to the test* (Dt.6.16); he is (v. 25) putting us to the test. **16:** *God is not like man*, Num.23.19; 1 Sam.15.29. **18:** The people are safe because they have been entirely loyal to God (compare 5.21). Judith's optimistic judgment of her contemporaries stands in sharp contrast to the attitude of the great prophets, but is similar to that of Ps.44.17–18. **27:** Their present sufferings are not punitive, but educative.

8.28–35: Answering Uzziah's plea, she personally pledges to deliver the city. 30–31: The vow,

you are a devout woman, and the Lord will send us rain to fill our cisterns and we will no longer be faint."

32 Judith said to them, "Listen to me. I am about to do a thing which will go down through all generations of our descendants. [33]Stand at the city gate tonight, and I will go out with my maid; and within the days after which you have promised to surrender the city to our enemies, the Lord will deliver Israel by my hand. [34]Only, do not try to find out what I plan; for I will not tell you until I have finished what I am about to do."

35 Uzziah and the rulers said to her, "Go in peace, and may the Lord God go before you, to take revenge upon our enemies." [36]So they returned from the tent and went to their posts.

9 Then Judith fell upon her face, and put ashes on her head, and uncovered the sackcloth she was wearing; and at the very time when that evening's incense was being offered in the house of God in Jerusalem, Judith cried out to the Lord with a loud voice, and said,

2 "O Lord God of my father Simeon, to whom thou gavest a sword to take revenge on the strangers who had loosed the girdle*o* of a virgin to defile her, and uncovered her thigh to put her to shame, and polluted her womb to disgrace her; for thou hast said, 'It shall not be done'—yet they did it. [3]So thou gavest up their rulers to be slain, and their bed, which was ashamed of the deceit they had practiced, to be stained with blood, and thou didst strike down slaves along with princes, and princes on their thrones; [4]and thou gavest their wives for a prey and their daughters to captivity, and all their

booty to be divided among thy beloved sons, who were zealous for thee, and abhorred the pollution of their blood, and called on thee for help—O God, my God, hear me also, a widow.

5 "For thou hast done these things and those that went before and those that followed; thou hast designed the things that are now, and those that are to come. Yea, the things thou didst intend came to pass, [6]and the things thou didst will presented themselves and said, 'Lo, we are here'; for all thy ways are prepared in advance, and thy judgment is with foreknowledge.

7 "Behold now, the Assyrians are increased in their might; they are exalted, with their horses and riders; they glory in the strength of their foot soldiers; they trust in shield and spear, in bow and sling, and know not that thou art the Lord who crushest wars; the Lord is thy name. [8]Break their strength by thy might, and bring down their power in thy anger; for they intend to defile thy sanctuary, and to pollute the tabernacle where thy glorious name rests, and to cast down the horn of thy altar with the sword. [9]Behold their pride, and send thy wrath upon their heads; give to me, a widow, the strength to do what I plan. [10]By the deceit of my lips strike down the slave with the prince and the prince with his servant; crush their arrogance by the hand of a woman.

11 "For thy power depends not upon numbers, nor thy might upon men of strength; for thou art God of the lowly, helper of the oppressed, upholder of the weak, protector of the forlorn, savior of those without hope. [12]Hear,

o Cn: Gk *womb*

---

though wrong, as Judith said, had been made and its consequences could be avoided only by an act of God. **33:** Judith promises that God will act through her.

    9.1–14: Judith's prayer. 1: *Evening's incense,* Ex.30.8; Ps.141.2. It may have become customary to offer prayer regularly at this time of day. **2:** *My father Simeon,* the patriarch, son of Jacob, who, with Levi, avenged their sister Dinah (Gen.34.25–26). **4:** God's special care for the *widow* was an article of Israel's faith (Dt.10.18; Ps.146.9). **5–6:** God's absolute foreknowledge and control of history, both past and future (Is.44.6–8). **10:** The author of the book apparently feels no moral inconsistency in having Judith pray for divine help in practicing *deceit* (see v. 13 n.). That an enemy should be destroyed *by the hand of a woman* would be not only remarkable, but particularly ignominious (Jg.9.54). **11:** *Thy power depends not upon*

O hear me, God of my father, God of the inheritance of Israel, Lord of heaven and earth, Creator of the waters, King of all thy creation, hear my prayer! [13]Make my deceitful words to be their wound and stripe, for they have planned cruel things against thy covenant, and against thy consecrated house, and against the top of Zion, and against the house possessed by thy children. [14]And cause thy whole nation and every tribe to know and understand that thou art God, the God of all power and might, and that there is no other who protects the people of Israel but thou alone!"

10 When Judith[p] had ceased crying out to the God of Israel, and had ended all these words, [2]she rose from where she lay prostrate and called her maid and went down into the house where she lived on sabbaths and on her feast days; [3]and she removed the sackcloth which she had been wearing, and took off her widow's garments, and bathed her body with water, and anointed herself with precious ointment, and combed her hair and put on a tiara, and arrayed herself in her gayest apparel, which she used to wear while her husband Manasseh was living. [4]And she put sandals on her feet, and put on her anklets and bracelets and rings, and her earrings and all her ornaments, and made herself very beautiful, to entice the eyes of all men who might see her. [5]And she gave her maid a bottle of wine and a flask of oil, and

filled a bag with parched grain and a cake of dried fruit and fine bread; and she wrapped up all her vessels and gave them to her to carry.

6 Then they went out to the city gate of Bethulia, and found Uzziah standing there with the elders of the city, Chabris and Charmis. [7]When they saw her, and noted how her face was altered and her clothing changed, they greatly admired her beauty, and said to her, [8]"May the God of our fathers grant you favor and fulfil your plans, that the people of Israel may glory and Jerusalem may be exalted." And she worshiped God.

9 Then she said to them, "Order the gate of the city to be opened for me, and I will go out and accomplish the things about which you spoke with me." So they ordered the young men to open the gate for her, as she had said. [10]When they had done this, Judith went out, she and her maid with her; and the men of the city watched her until she had gone down the mountain and passed through the valley and they could no longer see her.

11 The women[q] went straight on through the valley; and an Assyrian patrol met her [12]and took her into custody, and asked her, "To what people do you belong, and where are you coming from, and where are you going?" She replied, "I am a daughter of the Hebrews, but I am fleeing from them, for they are about to be handed over to you to be devoured. [13]I am on

p Gk *she*   *q* Gk *They*

---

numbers, Jg.7.2; 1 Sam.14.6. **12:** *King of all thy creation*, a favorite late Jewish title for God. **13:** This prayer for God's blessing on a lie has been frequently criticized as a serious, and basic, moral blemish in the book. While Judith's conduct may, in the abstract, seem indefensible, it has often been imitated by both Jews and Christians in similar circumstances of crisis; the moral question is complex and the practical solution sometimes agonizing.

10.1–5: Judith beautifies herself. 2: *Went down into the house*, from the roof where she apparently lived (presumably in a tent) except on the sabbath and festivals. **4:** The Latin version states that God gave her a supernatural beauty because her motive in adorning herself was virtuous, not lustful. **5:** *Vessels*, for cooking her food in accordance with the Jewish dietary laws.

10.6–10: She leaves the city with the elders' blessing. 8: *She worshiped God*, prayer and acts of piety accompany every one of her decisive acts. **10:** *Down the mountain . . . through the valley*, the geographical location of Bethulia, on the mountain with the "Assyrian" camp at the entrance of the valley leading up to it, could hardly be described more clearly.

10.11–23: Arriving at the enemy lines, she is brought into Holofernes' presence. 13: *I will*

my way to the presence of Holofernes the commander of your army, to give him a true report; and I will show him a way by which he can go and capture all the hill country without losing one of his men, captured or slain."

14 When the men heard her words, and observed her face—she was in their eyes marvelously beautiful—they said to her, 15"You have saved your life by hurrying down to the presence of our lord. Go at once to his tent; some of us will escort you and hand you over to him. 16And when you stand before him, do not be afraid in your heart, but tell him just what you have said, and he will treat you well."

17 They chose from their number a hundred men to accompany her and her maid, and they brought them to the tent of Holofernes. 18There was great excitement in the whole camp, for her arrival was reported from tent to tent, and they came and stood around her as she waited outside the tent of Holofernes while they told him about her. 19And they marveled at her beauty, and admired the Israelites, judging them by her, and every one said to his neighbor, "Who can despise these people, who have women like this among them? Surely not a man of them had better be left alive, for if we let them go they will be able to ensnare the whole world!"

20 Then Holofernes' companions and all his servants came out and led her into the tent. 21Holofernes was resting on his bed, under a canopy which was woven with purple and gold and emeralds and precious stones. 22When they told him of her he came forward to the front of the tent, with

silver lamps carried before him. 23And when Judith came into the presence of Holofernes*r* and his servants, they all marveled at the beauty of her face; and she prostrated herself and made obeisance to him, and his slaves raised her up.

Then Holofernes said to her, "Take courage, woman, and do not be afraid in your heart, for I have never hurt any one who chose to serve Nebuchadnezzar, the king of all the earth. 2And even now, if your people who live in the hill country had not slighted me, I would never have lifted my spear against them; but they have brought all this on themselves. 3And now tell me why you have fled from them and have come over to us—since you have come to safety. 4Have courage; you will live, tonight and from now on. No one will hurt you, but all will treat you well, as they do the servants of my lord King Nebuchadnezzar."

5 Judith replied to him, "Accept the words of your servant, and let your maidservant speak in your presence, and I will tell nothing false to my lord this night. 6And if you follow out the words of your maidservant, God will accomplish something through you, and my lord will not fail to achieve his purposes. 7Nebuchadnezzar the king of the whole earth lives, and as his power endures, who has sent you to direct every living soul, not only do men serve him because of you, but also the beasts of the field and the cattle and the birds of the air will live by your power under Nebuchadnezzar and all his house. 8For we have heard of your wisdom and skill, and it is reported

r Gk *him*

---

show him a way. The first of her "deceitful words" (see 9.13 n.). **21:** The *canopy* was some kind of decorated mosquito net. The Anglo-Saxon poem of Judith describes it thus: "There was hung|All golden a fair fly-net round the bed|Of the folk-leader, that the baleful one,|The chief of warriors, might look through on each|Child of the brave who came therein, and none|Might look on him . . . ."

11.1–4: Holofernes graciously receives her.

11.5–23: Judith's explanation of her flight commends her to the general and his advisers. 6: The idea that God can work through heathen kings and their armies is fairly common in the Old Testament (Is.10.5; 44.28; Jer.25.9). **7:** This verse is as obscure in the Greek as in the English.

throughout the whole world that you are the one good man in the whole kingdom, thoroughly informed and marvelous in military strategy.

9 "Now as for the things Achior said in your council, we have heard his words, for the men of Bethulia spared him and he told them all he had said to you. ¹⁰Therefore, my lord and master, do not disregard what he said, but keep it in your mind, for it is true: our nation cannot be punished, nor can the sword prevail against them, unless they sin against their God.

11 "And now, in order that my lord may not be defeated and his purpose frustrated, death will fall upon them, for a sin has overtaken them by which they are about to provoke their God to anger when they do what is wrong. ¹²Since their food supply is exhausted and their water has almost given out, they have planned to kill their cattle and have determined to use all that God by his laws has forbidden them to eat. ¹³They have decided to consume the first fruits of the grain and the tithes of the wine and oil, which they had consecrated and set aside for the priests who minister in the presence of our God at Jerusalem—although it is not lawful for any of the people so much as to touch these things with their hands. ¹⁴They have sent men to Jerusalem, because even the people living there have been doing this, to bring back to them permission from the senate. ¹⁵When the word reaches them and they proceed to do this, on that very day they will be handed over to you to be destroyed.

16 "Therefore, when I, your servant, learned all this, I fled from them; and God has sent me to accomplish with you things that will astonish the whole world, as many as shall hear about them. ¹⁷For your servant is religious, and serves the God of heaven day and night; therefore, my lord, I will remain with you, and every night your servant will go out into the valley, and I will pray to God and he will tell me when they have committed their sins. ¹⁸And I will come and tell you, and then you shall go out with your whole army, and not one of them will withstand you. ¹⁹Then I will lead you through the middle of Judea, till you come to Jerusalem; and I will set your throne*s* in the midst of it; and you will lead them like sheep that have no shepherd, and not a dog will so much as open its mouth to growl at you. For this has been told me, by my foreknowledge; it was announced to me, and I was sent to tell you."

20 Her words pleased Holofernes and all his servants, and they marveled at her wisdom and said, ²¹"There is not such a woman from one end of the earth to the other, either for beauty of face or wisdom of speech!" ²²And Holofernes said to her, "God has done well to send you before the people, to lend strength to our hands and to bring destruction upon those who have slighted my lord. ²³You are not only beautiful in appearance, but wise in speech; and if you do as you have said, your God shall be my God, and you shall live in the house of King Nebuchadnezzar and be renowned throughout the whole world."

12 Then he commanded them to bring her in where his silver dishes were kept, and ordered them to set a table for her with some of his own food and to serve her with his own wine. ²But Judith said, "I cannot eat

s Or chariot

9: *The things Achior said,* compare 5.5–21. **11–15:** She declares that the imminent fall of Bethulia is due to the circumstance that its citizens are about to appropriate to common use food which the Mosaic law assigned to God and the temple. **13:** *First fruits,* Ex.23.19. *Tithes,* Lev.27.30. **14:** *Senate,* the Sanhedrin, the supreme religious authority of later Judaism. **17:** *God of heaven,* see 5.8 n. By telling him that *every night* she *will go out into the valley* Judith is preparing a ruse for her eventual escape (13.10). The Anglo-Saxon poem, no doubt for moral reasons, omits this element in the story.
12.1–9: For three days Judith remains and establishes a pattern of conduct. 2: Once again

it, lest it be an offense; but I will be provided from the things I have brought with me." [3]Holofernes said to her, "If your supply runs out, where can we get more like it for you? For none of your people is here with us." [4]Judith replied, "As your soul lives, my lord, your servant will not use up the things I have with me before the Lord carries out by my hand what he has determined to do."

5 Then the servants of Holofernes brought her into the tent, and she slept until midnight. Along toward the morning watch she arose [6]and sent to Holofernes and said, "Let my lord now command that your servant be permitted to go out and pray." [7]So Holofernes commanded his guards not to hinder her. And she remained in the camp for three days, and went out each night to the valley of Bethulia, and bathed at the spring in the camp.[t] [8]When she came up from the spring she prayed the Lord God of Israel to direct her way for the raising up of her people. [9]So she returned clean and stayed in the tent until she ate her food toward evening.

10 On the fourth day Holofernes held a banquet for his slaves only, and did not invite any of his officers. [11]And he said to Bagoas, the eunuch who had charge of all his personal affairs, "Go now and persuade the Hebrew woman who is in your care to join us and eat and drink with us. [12]For it will be a disgrace if we let such a woman go without enjoying her company, for if

we do not embrace her she will laugh at us." [13]So Bagoas went out from the presence of Holofernes, and approached her and said, "This beautiful maidservant will please come to my lord and be honored in his presence, and drink wine and be merry with us, and become today like one of the daughters of the Assyrians who serve in the house of Nebuchadnezzar." [14]And Judith said, "Who am I, to refuse my lord? Surely whatever pleases him I will do at once, and it will be a joy to me until the day of my death!" [15]So she got up and arrayed herself in all her woman's finery, and her maid went and spread on the ground for her before Holofernes the soft fleeces which she had received from Bagoas for her daily use, so that she might recline on them when she ate.

16 Then Judith came in and lay down, and Holofernes' heart was ravished with her and he was moved with great desire to possess her; for he had been waiting for an opportunity to deceive her, ever since the day he first saw her. [17]So Holofernes said to her, "Drink now, and be merry with us!" [18]Judith said, "I will drink now, my lord, because my life means more to me today than in all the days since I was born." [19]Then she took and ate and drank before him what her maid had prepared. [20]And Holofernes was greatly pleased with her, and drank a great quantity of wine, much more than he had ever drunk in any one day since he was born.

t Other authorities omit *in the camp*

the narrative stresses Judith's meticulous observance of the Jewish dietary laws, even in the presence of the Gentiles. Her behavior contrasts markedly with that of Esther (Est.2.20; compare Dan.1.8). **6–7:** Since she had gone out every night, her departure after Holofernes' assassination would occasion no surprise. **8:** Her prayer was genuine enough, but not for the purpose previously announced (11.17).

12.10–20: Judith invited to Holofernes' banquet. 11: *Bagoas* is a well-known Persian name, spelled "Bigvai" in Ezra 2.2 and the Elephantine papyri. Diodorus Siculus (*Hist.* XVI. 47) mentions an officer Bagoas in the army of Artaxerxes III (see 2.4 n.). In oriental kingdoms the officer in charge of the women was normally a *eunuch;* eunuchs often attained also to positions of considerable responsibility in the state (Dan.1.3; Acts 8.27). **14:** Judith pretends to be pleased by his obviously dishonorable intentions toward her. Her real thoughts are paraphrased in the Anglo-Saxon poem as follows: ". . . the Saviour's handmaid then|Gloried, intently mindful how she might|Take from the hateful one most easily|His life. . . ."

13 When evening came, his slaves quickly withdrew, and Bagoas closed the tent from outside and shut out the attendants from his master's presence; and they went to bed, for they all were weary because the banquet had lasted long. ²So Judith was left alone in the tent, with Holofernes stretched out on his bed, for he was overcome with wine.

3 Now Judith had told her maid to stand outside the bedchamber and to wait for her to come out, as she did every day; for she said she would be going out for her prayers. And she had said the same thing to Bagoas. ⁴So every one went out, and no one, either small or great, was left in the bedchamber. Then Judith, standing beside his bed, said in her heart, "O Lord God of all might, look in this hour upon the work of my hands for the exaltation of Jerusalem. ⁵For now is the time to help thy inheritance, and to carry out my undertaking for the destruction of the enemies who have risen up against us."

6 She went up to the post at the end of the bed, above Holofernes' head, and took down his sword that hung there. ⁷She came close to his bed and took hold of the hair of his head, and said, "Give me strength this day, O Lord God of Israel!" ⁸And she struck his neck twice with all her might, and severed his head from his body. ⁹Then she tumbled his body off the bed and pulled down the canopy from the posts; after a moment she went out, and gave Holofernes' head to her maid, ¹⁰who placed it in her food bag.

Then the two of them went out together, as they were accustomed to go for prayer; and they passed through the camp and circled around the valley and went up the mountain to Bethulia and came to its gates. ¹¹Judith called out from afar to the watchmen at the gates, "Open, open the gate! God, our God, is still with us, to show his power in Israel, and his strength against our enemies, even as he has done this day!"

12 When the men of her city heard her voice, they hurried down to the city gate and called together the elders of the city. ¹³They all ran together, both small and great, for it was unbelievable that she had returned; they opened the gate and admitted them, and they kindled a fire for light, and gathered around them. ¹⁴Then she said to them with a loud voice, "Praise God, O praise him! Praise God, who has not withdrawn his mercy from the house of Israel, but has destroyed our enemies by my hand this very night!"

15 Then she took the head out of the bag and showed it to them, and said, "See, here is the head of Holofernes, the commander of the Assyrian army, and here is the canopy beneath which he lay in his drunken stupor. The Lord has struck him down by the hand of a woman. ¹⁶As the Lord lives, who has protected me in the way I went, it was my face that tricked him to his destruction, and yet he committed no act of sin with me, to defile and shame me."

17 All the people were greatly astonished, and bowed down and worshiped God, and said with one accord, "Blessed art thou, our God, who hast brought into contempt this day the enemies of thy people."

18 And Uzziah said to her, "O

13.1–10a: Judith beheads Holofernes. 4–7: Judith's prayer before she decapitates the enemy of her people is both the most dramatic and most horrifying moment of the story. In the Anglo-Saxon version, the prayer becomes an invocation of the Holy Trinity. **9:** *Pulled down the canopy* (10.21) and carried it off as a trophy (v. 15). **10a:** Even the bag in which she brought her food (10.5) is now seen to have been part of a well-laid plan.

13.10b–20: She escapes and returns to her own people. 10b: Her established habit of leaving the camp each night for prayer (11.17; 12.7) permits her an easy escape. **17:** *Blessed art thou, our God,* is the most common formula of late Jewish prayers (see Tob.3.11 n.). **18:** Uzziah's words are reminiscent of those spoken concerning Jael under similar circumstances (Jg.5.24); also of Melchizedek's greeting to Abraham (Gen.14.19–20).

daughter, you are blessed by the Most High God above all women on earth; and blessed be the Lord God, who created the heavens and the earth, who has guided you to strike the head of the leader of our enemies. ¹⁹Your hope will never depart from the hearts of men, as they remember the power of God. ²⁰May God grant this to be a perpetual honor to you, and may he visit you with blessings, because you did not spare your own life when our nation was brought low, but have avenged our ruin, walking in the straight path before our God." And all the people said, "So be it, so be it!"

14 Then Judith said to them, "Listen to me, my brethren, and take this head and hang it upon the parapet of your wall. ²And as soon as morning comes and the sun rises, let every valiant man take his weapons and go out of the city, and set a captain over them, as if you were going down to the plain against the Assyrian outpost; only do not go down. ³Then they will seize their arms and go into the camp and rouse the officers of the Assyrian army; and they will rush into the tent of Holofernes, and will not find him. Then fear will come over them, and they will flee before you, ⁴and you and all who live within the borders of Israel shall pursue them and cut them down as they flee. ⁵But before you do all this, bring Achior the Ammonite to me, and let him see and recognize the man who despised the house of Israel and sent him to us as if to his death."

6 So they summoned Achior from the house of Uzziah. And when he came and saw the head of Holofernes in the hand of one of the men at the gathering of the people, he fell down on his face and his spirit failed him. ⁷And when they raised him up he fell at Judith's feet, and knelt before her, and said, "Blessed are you in every tent of Judah! In every nation those who hear your name will be alarmed. ⁸Now tell me what you have done during these days."

Then Judith described to him in the presence of the people all that she had done, from the day she left until the moment of her speaking to them. ⁹And when she had finished, the people raised a great shout and made a joyful noise in their city. ¹⁰And when Achior saw all that the God of Israel had done, he believed firmly in God, and was circumcised, and joined the house of Israel, remaining so to this day.

11 As soon as it was dawn they hung the head of Holofernes on the wall, and every man took his weapons, and they went out in companies to the passes in the mountains. ¹²And when the Assyrians saw them they sent word to their commanders, and they went to the generals and the captains and to all their officers. ¹³So they came to Holofernes' tent and said to the steward in charge of all his personal affairs, "Wake up our lord, for the slaves have been so bold as to come down against us to give battle, in order to be destroyed completely."

14 So Bagoas went in and knocked at the door of the tent, for he supposed that he was sleeping with Judith. ¹⁵But when no one answered, he opened it and went into the bedchamber and found him thrown down on the platform dead, with his head cut off and missing. ¹⁶And he cried out with a

---

14.1–10: Achior identifies the head of Holofernes and is converted to Judaism. 1–4: Judith suggests tactics which will put the enemy to flight with minimum effort by the Jewish forces. In the Latin version, v. 5 is omitted and vv. 6–7, more logically, precede vv. 1–4. 5: *Achior*, the Ammonite leader whom Holofernes had left to be destroyed with the Jews (5.5–6.21). The full irony of the situation is evident when one remembers that Achior had been told he would see that face again only on the day of Holofernes' vengeance (6.5). 10: The author seems to have forgotten that the conversion of an Ammonite to Judaism is strictly forbidden by the law (Dt.23.3).

14.11–19: The enemy discovers Holofernes' death. 11–13: As Judith had planned, the threatening movements of the Jews lead to the discovery of Holofernes' body.

loud voice and wept and groaned and shouted, and rent his garments. [17]Then he went to the tent where Judith had stayed, and when he did not find her he rushed out to the people and shouted, [18]"The slaves have tricked us! One Hebrew woman has brought disgrace upon the house of King Nebuchadnezzar! For look, here is Holofernes lying on the ground, and his head is not on him!"

19 When the leaders of the Assyrian army heard this, they rent their tunics and were greatly dismayed, and their loud cries and shouts arose in the midst of the camp.

15 When the men in the tents heard it, they were amazed at what had happened. [2]Fear and trembling came over them, so that they did not wait for one another, but with one impulse all rushed out and fled by every path across the plain and through the hill country. [3]Those who had camped in the hills around Bethulia also took to flight. Then the men of Israel, every one that was a soldier, rushed out upon them. [4]And Uzziah sent men to Betomasthaim and Bebai and Choba and Kola, and to all the frontiers of Israel, to tell what had taken place and to urge all to rush out upon their enemies to destroy them. [5]And when the Israelites heard it, with one accord they fell upon the enemy,[u] and cut them down as far as Choba. Those in Jerusalem and all the hill country also came, for they were told what had happened in the camp of the enemy; and those in Gilead and in Galilee outflanked them with great slaughter, even

beyond Damascus and its borders. [6]The rest of the people of Bethulia fell upon the Assyrian camp and plundered it, and were greatly enriched. [7]And the Israelites, when they returned from the slaughter, took possession of what remained, and the villages and towns in the hill country and in the plain got a great amount of booty, for there was a vast quantity of it.

8 Then Joakim the high priest, and the senate of the people of Israel who lived at Jerusalem, came to witness the good things which the Lord had done for Israel, and to see Judith and to greet her. [9]And when they met her they all blessed her with one accord and said to her, "You are the exaltation of Jerusalem, you are the great glory of Israel, you are the great pride of our nation! [10]You have done all this singlehanded; you have done great good to Israel, and God is well pleased with it. May the Almighty Lord bless you for ever!" And all the people said, "So be it!"

11 So all the people plundered the camp for thirty days. They gave Judith the tent of Holofernes and all his silver dishes and his beds and his bowls and all his furniture; and she took them and loaded her mule and hitched up her carts and piled the things on them.

12 Then all the women of Israel gathered to see her, and blessed her, and some of them performed a dance for her; and she took branches in her hands and gave them to the women who were with her; [13]and they crowned

u Gk *them*

15.1–7: The Assyrians, fleeing in panic, are slaughtered and despoiled by the Jews. 3: *Those who had camped in the hills* were the Edomites and Ammonites (7.18). **4:** As with so many place names in this book, *Betomasthaim and Bebai and Choba and Kola* have never been satisfactorily identified. **5:** *Gilead*, which was situated in the northern part of Transjordan, and *Galilee*, in the north of Palestine proper, lay on either flank of the enemy's northeastward flight through *Damascus* and back toward Assyria.

15.8–13: Judith is led in triumph to Jerusalem. 11: The *thirty days* of plundering is obviously unrealistic. While the people apparently intend that Judith herself shall have Holofernes' treasure, she accepts the gifts only with the intention of dedicating them to God (16.19). **12:** *A dance*, compare 1 Sam.18.6; Ps.149.3–9. *Branches*, Ps.118.27; 1 Macc.13.51; 2 Macc.10.7. **13:** The reference to *olive wreaths* seems to indicate a late date for the book, for the custom is Greek, not Jewish. The destination of the procession is the temple in Jerusalem (16.18).

themselves with olive wreaths, she and those who were with her; and she went before all the people in the dance, leading all the women, while all the men of Israel followed, bearing their arms and wearing garlands and with songs on their lips.

16 Then Judith began this thanksgiving before all Israel, and all the people loudly sang this song of praise. ²And Judith said,

Begin a song to my God with tambourines,
sing to my Lord with cymbals.
Raise to him a new psalm;ᵛ
exalt him, and call upon his name.
³For God is the Lord who crushes wars;
for he has delivered me out of the hands of my pursuers,
and brought me into his camp, in the midst of the people.

⁴The Assyrian came down from the mountains of the north;
he came with myriads of his warriors;
their multitude blocked up the valleys,
their cavalry covered the hills.
⁵He boasted that he would burn up my territory,
and kill my young men with the sword,
and dash my infants to the ground
and seize my children as prey,
and take my virgins as booty.

⁶But the Lord Almighty has foiled them
by the hand of a woman.
⁷For their mighty one did not fall by the hands of the young men,

nor did the sons of the Titans smite him,
nor did tall giants set upon him;
but Judith the daughter of Merari undid him
with the beauty of her countenance.

⁸For she took off her widow's mourning
to exalt the oppressed in Israel.
She anointed her face with ointment
and fastened her hair with a tiara
and put on a linen gown to deceive him.
⁹Her sandal ravished his eyes, her beauty captivated his mind, and the sword severed his neck.
¹⁰The Persians trembled at her boldness,
the Medes were daunted at her daring.

¹¹Then my oppressed people shouted for joy;
my weak people shoutedʷ and the enemyˣ trembled;
they lifted up their voices, and the enemyˣ were turned back.
¹²The sons of maidservants have pierced them through;
they were wounded like the children of fugitives,
they perished before the army of my Lord.

¹³I will sing to my God a new song:
O Lord, thou art great and glorious,
wonderful in strength, invincible.

v Other authorities read *a psalm and praise*
w Other authorities read *feared*
x Gk *they*

16.1–17: Judith's thanksgiving psalm. In the book of Tobit (ch. 13) a prayer composed by Tobit occupies a similar position at the end of the story. It is Israel, personified as a woman, who sings the hymn; Judith herself is referred to only in the third person (v. 7). 2–3: A call to praise (compare Ex.15.21; Jg.5.2). 2: The phrase "a new" psalm (compare v. 13) is a cliché drawn from the Psalter (e.g. Pss.96.1; 98.1). 4–12: Description of the victory. 7: *Sons of the Titans* is Greek; perhaps the original had "sons of Rephaim" (compare Dt.3.11). 13–16: A general hymn of praise. 13: *I will sing . . . a new song*, Ps.144.9. The hymn begins in the next

¹⁴Let all thy creatures serve thee,
    for thou didst speak, and they
    were made.
Thou didst send forth thy Spirit,ʸ
    and it formed them;
    there is none that can resist thy
    voice.
¹⁵For the mountains shall be shaken
    to their foundations with the
    waters;
    at thy presence the rocks shall
    melt like wax,
but to those who fear thee
    thou wilt continue to show
    mercy.
¹⁶For every sacrifice as a fragrant
    offering is a small thing,
    and all fat for burnt offerings to
    thee is a very little thing,
but he who fears the Lord shall be
    great for ever.

¹⁷Woe to the nations that rise up
    against my people!
The Lord Almighty will take
    vengeance on them in the day
    of judgment;
fire and worms he will give to their
    flesh;
    they shall weep in pain for ever.

18 When they arrived at Jerusalem they worshiped God. As soon as the people were purified, they offered their burnt offerings, their freewill offerings, and their gifts. ¹⁹Judith also dedicated to God all the vessels of Holofernes, which the people had given her; and the canopy which she took for herself from his bedchamber she gave as a votive offering to the Lord. ²⁰So the people continued feasting in Jerusalem before the sanctuary for three months, and Judith remained with them.

21 After this every one returned home to his own inheritance, and Judith went to Bethulia, and remained on her estate, and was honored in her time throughout the whole country. ²²Many desired to marry her, but she remained a widow all the days of her life after Manasseh her husband died and was gathered to his people. ²³She became more and more famous, and grew old in her husband's house, until she was one hundred and five years old. She set her maid free. She died in Bethulia, and they buried her in the cave of her husband Manasseh, ²⁴and the house of Israel mourned for her seven days. Before she died she distributed her property to all those who were next of kin to her husband Manasseh, and to her own nearest kindred. ²⁵And no one ever again spread terror among the people of Israel in the days of Judith, or for a long time after her death.

ʸ Or *breath*

---

line. 14: Pss.33.6; 104.30. 16: *Every sacrifice . . . is a small thing;* to compare sacrifice unfavorably with moral obedience ("to fear the Lord") is a commonplace of Old Testament religion, especially in later times (1 Sam.15.22; Pss.40.6–8; 50.8–15; 51.16–17; Hos.6.6; compare Sir.34.18–19). 17: Concluding anathema on Israel's enemies (compare Jg.5.31). *Fire and worms,* Is.66.24; Sir.7.17. As in Dan.12.2, the punishment of the wicked is eternal.

16.18–20: A victory celebration in Jerusalem. 20: *Three months,* Syriac, "a month of days." 16.21–25: Judith remains a widow and dies at a ripe old age. 24: She *distributed her property,* according to the Mosaic law (Num.27.11).

THE ADDITIONS TO THE BOOK OF

ESTHER

Translated in the order of the Greek version of Esther but with the chapter and verse numbers of the King James Version

After the book of Esther had been translated from Hebrew into Greek, six Additions totaling 107 verses were incorporated at various points in the narrative. These supplementary sections were also included in the Old Latin translation, which was based on the Greek. In the fourth century A.D. Jerome, when making the Latin Vulgate Bible, removed all of the Additions and placed them at the end of the book of Esther. Rearranged in their proper chronological order, and with chapter and verse numbering which reflects Jerome's order, the six Additions are: 11.2–12.6, Mordecai saves the king's life; 13.1–7, The king's letter ordering the massacre of the Jews; 13.8–14, The prayers of Mordecai and Esther; 15.1–16, Esther risks her life to appeal to the king; 16.1–24, The king's second letter, denouncing Haman and directing his subjects to help the Jews; 10.4–11.1, Mordecai's dream interpreted and the book of Esther attested as genuine.

Some of the Additions were probably introduced by Lysimachus, an Alexandrian Jew who lived at Jerusalem and who translated the canonical book of Esther about 114 B.C. (11.1). Other Additions appear to have been inserted several years later, either by Lysimachus or by another person.

The purpose of the Additions is partly to make the story more vivid but chiefly to supply a religious element that is lacking in the canonical book of Esther, which never mentions God or religious practices. The Additions make frequent reference to God, emphasize his choice of Abraham and Israel, and give prominence to prayer. They occasionally contradict the canonical book of Esther, and have little or no historical value.

‖‖ ²IN THE SECOND YEAR OF THE reign of Artaxerxes the Great, on the first day of Nisan, Mordecai the son of Jair, son of Shimei, son of Kish, of the tribe of Benjamin, had a dream. ³He was a Jew, dwelling in the city of Susa, a great man, serving in the court of the king. ⁴He was one of the captives whom Nebuchadnezzar king of Babylon had brought from Jerusalem with Jeconiah king of Judea. And this was his dream:

5 Behold, noise*a* and confusion, thunders and earthquake, tumult upon the earth! ⁶And behold, two great dragons came forward, both ready to fight, and they roared terribly. ⁷And at their roaring every nation prepared for war, to fight against the nation of the righteous. ⁸And behold, a day of darkness and gloom, tribulation and distress, affliction and great tumult upon the earth! ⁹And the whole righteous nation was troubled; they feared the evils that threatened them, and were ready to perish. ¹⁰Then they cried to God; and from their cry, as though from a tiny spring, there came a great river, with abundant water; ¹¹light came, and the sun rose, and the lowly were exalted and consumed those held in honor.

12 Mordecai saw in this dream what

a Or *voices*

11.2–12: Mordecai's dream of impending conflict between two *dragons* (Mordecai and Haman; compare 10.7) pictures how the *righteous nation* Israel, threatened with annihilation, is delivered by God. **2:** *Artaxerxes* is Xerxes I (486 [or 485]–465 B.C.). His *second year* was 485 [or 484] B.C. **4:** This verse dates Mordecai's captivity in 597 B.C. (2 Kg.24.15); v. 2 dates his dream 112 years later. **7:** *Nation of the righteous*, that is, the Jews. **10:** The expressions *tiny spring* and *great river* refer to Esther (10.6). **12:** Mordecai knows that the *dream* forecasts God's action, but does not yet grasp the interpretation given in 10.6–12.

[96]

God had determined to do, and after he awoke he had it on his mind and sought all day to understand it in every detail.

12 Now Mordecai took his rest in the courtyard with Gabatha and Tharra, the two eunuchs of the king who kept watch in the courtyard. ²He overheard their conversation and inquired into their purposes, and learned that they were preparing to lay hands upon Artaxerxes the king; and he informed the king concerning them. ³Then the king examined the two eunuchs, and when they confessed they were led to execution. ⁴The king made a permanent record of these things, and Mordecai wrote an account of them. ⁵And the king ordered Mordecai to serve in the court and rewarded him for these things. ⁶But Haman, the son of Hammedatha, a Bougaean, was in great honor with the king, and he sought to injure Mordecai and his people because of the two eunuchs of the king.

*Esther 1.1–3.13 follows
here in the Greek*

13 This is a copy of the letter: "The Great King, Artaxerxes, to the rulers of the hundred and twenty-seven provinces from India to Ethiopia and to the governors under them, writes thus:

2 "Having become ruler of many nations and master of the whole world, not elated with presumption of authority but always acting reasonably and with kindness, I have determined to settle the lives of my subjects in lasting tranquillity and, in order to make my kingdom peaceable and open to travel throughout all its extent, to re-establish the peace which all men desire.

3 "When I asked my counselors how this might be accomplished, Haman, who excels among us in sound judgment, and is distinguished for his unchanging good will and steadfast fidelity, and has attained the second place in the kingdom, ⁴pointed out to us that among all the nations in the world there is scattered a certain hostile people, who have laws contrary to those of every nation and continually disregard the ordinances of the kings, so that the unifying of the kingdom which we honorably intend cannot be brought about. ⁵We understand that this people, and it alone, stands constantly in opposition to all men, perversely following a strange manner of life and laws, and is ill-disposed to our government, doing all the harm they can so that our kingdom may not attain stability.

6 "Therefore we have decreed that those indicated to you in the letters of Haman, who is in charge of affairs and is our second father, shall all, with their wives and children, be utterly destroyed by the sword of their enemies, without pity or mercy, on the fourteenth day of the twelfth month, Adar, of this present year, ⁷so that those who have long been and are now hostile may in one day go down in violence to Hades, and leave our government completely secure and untroubled hereafter."

12.1–6: Mordecai saves the king's life when two eunuchs posted to protect the king plot instead to kill him. **5:** The king rewards Mordecai (in Est.6.3, however, it is said later that "nothing has been done for him"). **6:** It is implied that Haman shared in the plot and so resented Mordecai's action. *Bougaean* represents a Greek word which in Est.3.1 translates the Hebrew word Agagite (compare 1 Sam.15.8).

13.1–7: The king's letter ordering the massacre of the Jews. This addition follows Est.3.1–13, in which Haman has induced Artaxerxes to send a letter to all provinces of his kingdom, ordering complete annihilation of *a certain hostile people*, the Jews, because they observe *a strange manner of life and laws;* they observe the Mosaic law. **6:** *Our second father* implies that Haman ranked second only to the king. *Fourteenth day*, according to 16.20 (and Est.3.13; 8.12; 9.1) it was the thirteenth day. *Adar*, February–March.

*Esther 3.14–4.17 follows
here in the Greek*

8 Then Mordecai[b] prayed to the Lord, calling to remembrance all the works of the Lord. He said:

9 "O Lord, Lord, King who rulest over all things, for the universe is in thy power and there is no one who can oppose thee if it is thy will to save Israel. [10]For thou hast made heaven and earth and every wonderful thing under heaven, [11]and thou art Lord of all, and there is no one who can resist thee, who art the Lord. [12]Thou knowest all things; thou knowest, O Lord, that it was not in insolence or pride or for any love of glory that I did this, and refused to bow down to this proud Haman. [13]For I would have been willing to kiss the soles of his feet, to save Israel! [14]But I did this, that I might not set the glory of man above the glory of God, and I will not bow down to any one but to thee, who art my Lord; and I will not do these things in pride. [15]And now, O Lord God and King, God of Abraham, spare thy people; for the eyes of our foes are upon us[c] to annihilate us, and they desire to destroy the inheritance that has been thine from the beginning. [16]Do not neglect thy portion, which thou didst redeem for thyself out of the land of Egypt. [17]Hear my prayer, and have mercy upon thy inheritance; turn our mourning into feasting, that we may live and sing praise to thy name, O Lord; do not destroy the mouth of those who praise thee."

18 And all Israel cried out mightily, for their death was before their eyes.

14 And Esther the queen, seized with deathly anxiety, fled to the Lord; [2]she took off her splendid apparel and put on the garments of distress and mourning, and instead of costly perfumes she covered her head with ashes and dung, and she utterly humbled her body, and every part that she loved to adorn she covered with her tangled hair. [3]And she prayed to the Lord God of Israel, and said:

"O my Lord, thou only art our King; help me, who am alone and have no helper but thee, [4]for my danger is in my hand. [5]Ever since I was born I have heard in the tribe of my family that thou, O Lord, didst take Israel out of all the nations, and our fathers from among all their ancestors, for an everlasting inheritance, and that thou didst do for them all that thou didst promise. [6]And now we have sinned before thee, and thou hast given us into the hands of our enemies, [7]because we glorified their gods. Thou art righteous, O Lord! [8]And now they are not satisfied that we are in bitter slavery, but they have covenanted with their idols [9]to abolish what thy mouth has ordained and to destroy thy inheritance, to stop the mouths of those who praise thee and to quench thy altar and the glory of thy house, [10]to open the mouths of the nations for the praise of vain idols, and to magnify for ever a mortal king. [11]O Lord, do not surrender thy scepter to what has no being; and do not let them mock at our downfall; but turn their plan against themselves, and make an example of the man who began this against us. [12]Remember, O Lord;

b Gk he   c Gk *for they are looking upon us*

13.8–14.19: The prayers of Mordecai and Esther. The canonical book of Esther never mentions God or prayer or calls Israel God's chosen people. These prayers are added to give the book a deeply religious tone. They call God *Lord* and *King* and *Lord God of Abraham*. He is righteous, has created and rules all things, has redeemed his people Israel from Egypt, answers prayer, and can save them now. **13.12–14:** Mordecai did not *bow down* to Haman, as the king's other servants did (Est.3.2), because such homage is due only to God. **18:** All Israel echoed Mordecai's prayer.

14.1–19: Esther joins in her people's prayer for deliverance. 1–2: She discards every trace of queenly attire and elegance and prays as an unworthy member of Israel. **6–7:** Her people's captivity is due to their sinfulness and idolatry while living in Palestine (Dan.9.16); Israel does not deserve to be saved. **11:** Esther begs God not to let pagan idols, that have no real existence,

make thyself known in this time of our affliction, and give me courage, O King of the gods and Master of all dominion! [13]Put eloquent speech in my mouth before the lion, and turn his heart to hate the man who is fighting against us, so that there may be an end of him and those who agree with him. [14]But save us by thy hand, and help me, who am alone and have no helper but thee, O Lord. [15]Thou hast knowledge of all things; and thou knowest that I hate the splendor of the wicked and abhor the bed of the uncircumcised and of any alien. [16]Thou knowest my necessity—that I abhor the sign of my proud position, which is upon my head on the days when I appear in public. I abhor it like a menstruous rag, and I do not wear it on the days when I am at leisure. [17]And thy servant has not eaten at Haman's table, and I have not honored the king's feast or drunk the wine of the libations. [18]Thy servant has had no joy since the day that I was brought here until now, except in thee, O Lord God of Abraham. [19]O God, whose might is over all, hear the voice of the despairing, and save us from the hands of evildoers. And save me from my fear!"

15 On the third day, when she ended her prayer, she took off the garments in which she had worshiped, and arrayed herself in splendid attire. [2]Then, majestically adorned, after invoking the aid of the all-seeing God and Savior, she took her two maids with her, [3]leaning daintily on one, [4]while the other followed carrying her train. [5]She was radiant with perfect beauty, and she looked happy, as if beloved, but her heart was frozen

with fear. [6]When she had gone through all the doors, she stood before the king. He was seated on his royal throne, clothed in the full array of his majesty, all covered with gold and precious stones. And he was most terrifying.

7 Lifting his face, flushed with splendor, he looked at her in fierce anger. And the queen faltered, and turned pale and faint, and collapsed upon the head of the maid who went before her. [8]Then God changed the spirit of the king to gentleness, and in alarm he sprang from his throne and took her in his arms until she came to herself. And he comforted her with soothing words, and said to her, [9]"What is it, Esther? I am your brother. Take courage; [10]you shall not die, for our law applies only to the people.[d] Come near."

11 Then he raised the golden scepter and touched it to her neck; [12]and he embraced her, and said, "Speak to me." [13]And she said to him, "I saw you, my lord, like an angel of God, and my heart was shaken with fear at your glory. [14]For you are wonderful, my lord, and your countenance is full of grace." [15]But as she was speaking, she fell fainting. [16]And the king was agitated, and all his servants sought to comfort her.

Esther 5.3–8.12 follows
here in the Greek

16 The following is a copy of this letter:
"The Great King, Artaxerxes, to the rulers of the provinces from India

d The meaning of the Greek text of this clause is obscure

---

rule the world. **16–18:** Esther says she hates her position as queen and wife of the king, and has never *eaten at Haman's table* or *honored the king's feast* (but compare Est.2.18, as well as Est.5.5 and 7.1).

    15.1–16: Esther risks her life to appeal to the king. This passage expands and exaggerates Est.5.1–2. Any one who entered the king's presence without his summons or permission was put to death, unless the king forgave the intrusion (Est.4.11). To avoid personal danger and to induce the king to reverse his decree, Esther enhanced her charm by splendid attire; then with fearful heart she entered the king's presence. The king's initial anger was changed to tender concern by her fright and fainting; she then could plead for her people.

    16.1–24: The king's second letter, denouncing Haman and directing his subjects to help the

to Ethiopia, one hundred and twenty-seven satrapies, and to those who are loyal to our government, greeting.

2 "The more often they are honored by the too great kindness of their benefactors, the more proud do many men become. ³They not only seek to injure our subjects, but in their inability to stand prosperity they even undertake to scheme against their own benefactors. ⁴They not only take away thankfulness from among men, but, carried away by the boasts of those who know nothing of goodness, they suppose that they will escape the evil-hating justice of God, who always sees everything. ⁵And often many of those who are set in places of authority have been made in part responsible for the shedding of innocent blood, and have been involved in irremediable calamities, by the persuasion of friends who have been entrusted with the administration of public affairs, ⁶when these men by the false trickery of their evil natures beguile the sincere good will of their sovereigns.

7 "What has been wickedly accomplished through the pestilent behavior of those who exercise authority unworthily, can be seen not so much from the more ancient records which we hand on as from investigation of matters close at hand. ⁸For the future we will take care to render our kingdom quiet and peaceable for all men, ⁹by changing our methods and always judging what comes before our eyes with more equitable consideration. ¹⁰For Haman, the son of Hammedatha, a Macedonian (really an alien to the Persian blood, and quite devoid of our kindliness), having become our guest, ¹¹so far enjoyed the good will that we have for every nation that he was called our father and was continually bowed down to by all as the person second to the royal throne. ¹²But, unable to

restrain his arrogance, he undertook to deprive us of our kingdom and our life, ¹³and with intricate craft and deceit asked for the destruction of Mordecai, our savior and perpetual benefactor, and of Esther, the blameless partner of our kingdom, together with their whole nation. ¹⁴He thought that in this way he would find us undefended and would transfer the kingdom of the Persians to the Macedonians.

15 "But we find that the Jews, who were consigned to annihilation by this thrice accursed man, are not evildoers but are governed by most righteous laws ¹⁶and are sons of the Most High, the most mighty living God, who has directed the kingdom both for us and for our fathers in the most excellent order.

17 "You will therefore do well not to put in execution the letters sent by Haman the son of Hammedatha, ¹⁸because the man himself who did these things has been hanged at the gate of Susa, with all his household. For God, who rules over all things, has speedily inflicted on him the punishment he deserved.

19 "Therefore post a copy of this letter publicly in every place, and permit the Jews to live under their own laws. ²⁰And give them reinforcements, so that on the thirteenth day of the twelfth month, Adar, on that very day they may defend themselves against those who attack them at the time of their affliction. ²¹For God, who rules over all things, has made this day to be a joy to his chosen people instead of a day of destruction for them.

22 "Therefore you shall observe this with all good cheer as a notable day among your commemorative festivals, ²³so that both now and hereafter it may mean salvation for us and the loyal Persians, but that for those who

---

Jews. 10–14: Haman, already executed (Est.7.6–10), is (falsely) called a *Macedonian* trying to overthrow Persian rule. 15–16: The king commends the Mosaic *laws*, praises the Jews, and recognizes God's rule. All Persian subjects are commanded to ignore Haman's letter (according to 13.1–6 it was really the king's letter) and help the Jews defend themselves on the thirteenth

plot against us it may be a reminder of destruction.

24 "Every city and country, without exception, which does not act accordingly, shall be destroyed in wrath with spear and fire. It shall be made not only impassable for men, but also most hateful for all time to beasts and birds."

This is followed in the Greek by 8.13–10.3, where the Hebrew Esther ends. The Greek version adds the following:

10 ⁴And Mordecai said, "These things have come from God. ⁵For I remember the dream that I had concerning these matters, and none of them has failed to be fulfilled. ⁶The tiny spring which became a river, and there was light and the sun and abundant water—the river is Esther, whom the king married and made queen. ⁷The two dragons are Haman and myself. ⁸The nations are those that gathered to destroy the name of the Jews. ⁹And my nation, this is Israel, who cried out to God and were saved.

The Lord has saved his people; the Lord has delivered us from all these evils; God has done great signs and wonders, which have not occurred among the nations. ¹⁰For this purpose he made two lots, one for the people of God and one for all the nations. ¹¹And these two lots came to the hour and moment and day of decision before God and among all the nations. ¹²And God remembered his people and vindicated his inheritance. ¹³So they will observe these days in the month of Adar, on the fourteenth and fifteenth of that month, with an assembly and joy and gladness before God, from generation to generation for ever among his people Israel."

11 ¹In the fourth year of the reign of Ptolemy and Cleopatra, Dositheus, who said that he was a priest and a Levite,ᵉ and Ptolemy his son brought to Egyptᶠ the preceding Letter of Purim, which they said was genuine and had been translated by Lysimachus the son of Ptolemy, one of the residents of Jerusalem.

ᵉ Or *priest, and Levitas*
ᶠ Cn: Gk *brought in*

---

day of Adar, the prescribed day of annihilation. **24:** Destruction faces every place which does not defend and respect the Jews.

10.4–11.1: Mordecai's dream interpreted and the book of Esther attested as genuine. This passage interprets the dream of 11.5–11. The threat to Israel is here ascribed not to one man, Haman, as in the canonical Esther, but to a general anti-Semitic hostility against the Jews. **13:** As in Est.9.20–22, Israel is to celebrate this deliverance annually. **11.1:** *Fourth year*, that is 114–113 B.C. *Letter of Purim*, a reference not merely to Mordecai's letter (Est.9.20–22) but to the entire book of Esther. *Lysimachus* is a Greek name; on his work of translating the Hebrew book of Esther into Greek, see the Introduction.

THE WISDOM OF SOLOMON

The Wisdom of Solomon, which the Latin Vulgate Bible entitles simply the book of Wisdom, professes to have been written by Solomon (7.1–14 and 8.17–9.18 recall Solomon's prayer for wisdom in 1 Kg.3.6–9 and 2 Chr.1.8–10). Internal evidence, however, indicates that the book was composed in Greek by an unknown Hellenistic Jew, probably at Alexandria during the latter part of the first century B.C. He no doubt used traditional wisdom material, which perhaps included for the earlier chapters material originally written in Hebrew and then translated into Greek. Such a supposition helps to account for the fact that the word "wisdom" occurs twenty-nine times in the first ten chapters, where the concept of wisdom is personified, while in the last nine chapters the word appears only twice and with a much vaguer meaning. Whatever oral or written sources were used, however, it is probable that one man wrote the entire book.

The literary style of the book varies from poetic patches of high lyrical quality to plodding and pedestrian prose. Impersonating King Solomon, the author promises reward and immortality to the righteous and warns the wicked of judgment (chs. 1–5); praises wisdom and describes her nature and works (chs. 6–9); illustrates wisdom's guidance of God's people from Adam to Moses and recalls God's judgment on the Egyptians and Canaanites (chs. 10–12); explains the origin and folly of idolatry (chs. 13–15); and contrasts God's plagues on the Egyptians and his kindness to his people (chs. 16–19).

L OVE RIGHTEOUSNESS, YOU RULERS OF the earth,
think of the Lord with uprightness,
and seek him with sincerity of
heart;
²because he is found by those who do
not put him to the test,
and manifests himself to those who
do not distrust him.
³For perverse thoughts separate men
from God,
and when his power is tested, it
convicts the foolish;
⁴because wisdom will not enter a
deceitful soul,
nor dwell in a body enslaved to sin.
⁵For a holy and disciplined spirit will
flee from deceit,
and will rise and depart from foolish
thoughts,
and will be ashamed at the approach
of unrighteousness.

⁶For wisdom is a kindly spirit and
will not free a blasphemer from the
guilt of his words;
because God is witness of his inmost
feelings,
and a true observer of his heart, and
a hearer of his tongue.
⁷Because the Spirit of the Lord has
filled the world,
and that which holds all things
together knows what is said;
⁸therefore no one who utters
unrighteous things will escape
notice,
and justice, when it punishes, will
not pass him by.
⁹For inquiry will be made into the
counsels of an ungodly man,
and a report of his words will come
to the Lord,
to convict him of his lawless deeds;
¹⁰because a jealous ear hears all things,
and the sound of murmurings does
not go unheard.
¹¹Beware then of useless murmuring,
and keep your tongue from slander;
because no secret word is without
result,ᵃ

a Or *will go unpunished*

1.1–5.23: Commendation of wisdom as guide to happiness and immortality. 1.1–5: *Rulers* (compare 6.1) are urged to *love righteousness* and seek God. *Wisdom* dwells only in a sincere, holy, and disciplined soul.

1.6–11: The ungodly will not escape punishment; God knows their unrighteous thoughts, words, and deeds and will judge them. **6:** *A kindly spirit,* literally "a spirit that loves man"; wisdom's concern for man's welfare will not tolerate blasphemous or unrighteous words.

and a lying mouth destroys the soul.

¹²Do not invite death by the error of
    your life,
nor bring on destruction by the
    works of your hands;
¹³because God did not make death,
and he does not delight in the death
    of the living.
¹⁴For he created all things that they
    might exist,
and the generative forces[b] of the
    world are wholesome,
and there is no destructive poison in
    them;
and the dominion[c] of Hades is not
    on earth.
¹⁵For righteousness is immortal.

¹⁶But ungodly men by their words and
    deeds summoned death;[d]
considering him a friend, they pined
    away,
and they made a covenant with
    him,
because they are fit to belong to his
    party.

2 For they reasoned unsoundly,
    saying to themselves,
"Short and sorrowful is our life,
and there is no remedy when a
    man comes to his end,
and no one has been known to
    return from Hades.
²Because we were born by mere
    chance,
and hereafter we shall be as though
    we had never been;
because the breath in our nostrils is
    smoke,
and reason is a spark kindled by the
    beating of our hearts.
³When it is extinguished, the body
    will turn to ashes,
and the spirit will dissolve like
    empty air.

⁴Our name will be forgotten in time,
and no one will remember our
    works;
our life will pass away like the traces
    of a cloud,
and be scattered like mist
that is chased by the rays of the sun
and overcome by its heat.
⁵For our allotted time is the passing
    of a shadow,
and there is no return from our
    death,
because it is sealed up and no one
    turns back.

⁶"Come, therefore, let us enjoy the
    good things that exist,
and make use of the creation to the
    full as in youth.
⁷Let us take our fill of costly wine
    and perfumes,
and let no flower of spring pass by
    us.
⁸Let us crown ourselves with
    rosebuds before they wither.
⁹Let none of us fail to share in our
    revelry,
everywhere let us leave signs of
    enjoyment,
because this is our portion, and this
    our lot.
¹⁰Let us oppress the righteous poor
    man;
let us not spare the widow
nor regard the gray hairs of the
    aged.
¹¹But let our might be our law of
    right,
for what is weak proves itself to be
    useless.

¹²"Let us lie in wait for the righteous
    man,
because he is inconvenient to us
    and opposes our actions;

b Or *the creatures*   *c* Or *palace*   *d* Gk *him*

1.12–15: God has made man for immortality. 15: Righteous living leads to immortality.
    1.16–2.24: The reasoning of the materialist or sensualist. 2.1–5: The ungodly say that life is
short, birth the result of *mere chance*, life without real meaning, and physical death the end of
existence. 6–9: They encourage one another to live lives of sensual satisfaction before death
snuffs out existence. 10–20: They urge one another to oppress *righteous*, helpless folk, whose
godly words and lives reproach them, and to persecute, torture, and kill those who call *God*

he reproaches us for sins against
the law,
and accuses us of sins against our
training.
¹³He professes to have knowledge of
God,
and calls himself a child*e* of the
Lord.
¹⁴He became to us a reproof of our
thoughts;
¹⁵the very sight of him is a burden
to us,
because his manner of life is unlike
that of others,
and his ways are strange.
¹⁶We are considered by him as
something base,
and he avoids our ways as
unclean;
he calls the last end of the
righteous happy,
and boasts that God is his father.
¹⁷Let us see if his words are true,
and let us test what will happen at
the end of his life;
¹⁸for if the righteous man is God's
son, he will help him,
and will deliver him from the hand
of his adversaries.
¹⁹Let us test him with insult and
torture,
that we may find out how gentle
he is,
and make trial of his forbearance.
²⁰Let us condemn him to a shameful
death,
for, according to what he says, he
will be protected."

²¹Thus they reasoned, but they were
led astray,
for their wickedness blinded them,
²²and they did not know the secret
purposes of God,
nor hope for the wages of holiness,
nor discern the prize for blameless
souls;
²³for God created man for
incorruption,
and made him in the image of his
own eternity,*f*
²⁴but through the devil's envy death
entered the world,
and those who belong to his party
experience it.

3 But the souls of the righteous
are in the hand of God,
and no torment will ever touch
them.
²In the eyes of the foolish they
seemed to have died,
and their departure was thought to
be an affliction,
³and their going from us to be their
destruction;
but they are at peace.
⁴For though in the sight of men they
were punished,
their hope is full of immortality.
⁵Having been disciplined a little,
they will receive great good,
because God tested them and found
them worthy of himself;
⁶like gold in the furnace he tried
them,
and like a sacrificial burnt offering
he accepted them.
⁷In the time of their visitation they
will shine forth,
and will run like sparks through
the stubble.
⁸They will govern nations and rule
over peoples,
and the Lord will reign over them
for ever.
⁹Those who trust in him will
understand truth,

e Or *servant*
f Other ancient authorities read *nature*

their *father*. **21–24:** Such false reasoning arises from *wickedness* and consequent failure to
know God. God made man in his image to be immortal, but *the devil's envy* (compare 1.16)
brought *death* into *the world*.
  3.1–9: The blessed estate of the righteous. Though affliction, suffering, and the early death of
the righteous may seem to be divine punishment, after death their *souls* are forever safe and at
peace with God; they enjoy sure *immortality*. **7–9:** Their discipline and testing will be followed
by a divine *visitation;* God will vindicate them, let them share in his rule over all peoples, and
give them understanding of his ways.

and the faithful will abide with him
in love,
because grace and mercy are upon
his elect,
and he watches over his holy ones.[g]

10But the ungodly will be punished
as their reasoning deserves,
who disregarded the righteous
man[h]
and rebelled against the Lord;
11for whoever despises wisdom and
instruction is miserable.
Their hope is vain, their labors are
unprofitable,
and their works are useless.
12Their wives are foolish, and their
children evil;
13their offspring are accursed.
For blessed is the barren woman
who is undefiled,
who has not entered into a sinful
union;
she will have fruit when God
examines souls.
14Blessed also is the eunuch whose
hands have done no lawless
deed,
and who has not devised wicked
things against the Lord;
for special favor will be shown him
for his faithfulness,
and a place of great delight in the
temple of the Lord.
15For the fruit of good labors is
renowned,
and the root of understanding does
not fail.
16But children of adulterers will not
come to maturity,
and the offspring of an unlawful
union will perish.
17Even if they live long they will be
held of no account,
and finally their old age will be
without honor.

18If they die young, they will have
no hope
and no consolation in the day of
decision.
19For the end of an unrighteous
generation is grievous.

4 Better than this is childlessness
with virtue,
for in the memory of virtue[i] is
immortality,
because it is known both by God
and by men.
2When it is present, men imitate[j]
it,
and they long for it when it has
gone;
and throughout all time it marches
crowned in triumph,
victor in the contest for prizes that
are undefiled.
3But the prolific brood of the
ungodly will be of no use,
and none of their illegitimate
seedlings will strike a deep root
or take a firm hold.
4For even if they put forth boughs
for a while,
standing insecurely they will be
shaken by the wind,
and by the violence of the winds
they will be uprooted.
5The branches will be broken off
before they come to maturity,
and their fruit will be useless,
not ripe enough to eat, and good
for nothing.
6For children born of unlawful
unions
are witnesses of evil against their
parents when God examines
them.[k]

g The text of this line is uncertain, and it is omitted here
by some ancient authorities. Compare 4.15
h Or *what is right*   i Gk *it*
j Other ancient authorities read *honor*
k Gk *at their examination*

3.10–4.6: The punishment of the ungodly. The ungodly will meet a sad end, because disregarding what *the righteous* could teach them *they rebelled against the Lord* (v. 10). In Israel the possession of many children and a long life were often considered proof of God's favor. But the
barren woman and the *eunuch* are also blessed by God (vv. 13–14); a virtuous life is what counts,
for it alone assures *immortality*. The wicked, even if they *live long* (v. 17) and have many children
(4.3), have *no* justified *hope* for the future; their children usually die early, are *of no account*,
and attest their parents' wickedness (3.16–18).

⁷But the righteous man, though he
die early, will be at rest.
⁸For old age is not honored for
length of time,
nor measured by number of years;
⁹but understanding is gray hair for
men,
and a blameless life is ripe old age.

¹⁰There was one who pleased God
and was loved by him,
and while living among sinners he
was taken up.
¹¹He was caught up lest evil change
his understanding
or guile deceive his soul.
¹²For the fascination of wickedness
obscures what is good,
and roving desire perverts the
innocent mind.
¹³Being perfected in a short time, he
fulfilled long years;
¹⁴for his soul was pleasing to the
Lord,
therefore he took him quickly from
the midst of wickedness.
¹⁵Yet the peoples saw and did not
understand,
nor take such a thing to heart,
that God's grace and mercy are
with his elect,
and he watches over his holy ones.

¹⁶The righteous man who has died
will condemn the ungodly who
are living,
and youth that is quickly perfected*
will condemn the prolonged old
age of the unrighteous man.
¹⁷For they will see the end of the wise
man,
and will not understand what the
Lord purposed for him,
and for what he kept him safe.

¹⁸They will see, and will have
contempt for him,
but the Lord will laugh them to
scorn.
After this they will become
dishonored corpses,
and an outrage among the dead
for ever;
¹⁹because he will dash them
speechless to the ground,
and shake them from the
foundations;
they will be left utterly dry and
barren,
and they will suffer anguish,
and the memory of them will
perish.

²⁰They will come with dread when
their sins are reckoned up,
and their lawless deeds will convict
them to their face.

5 Then the righteous man will
stand with great confidence
in the presence of those who have
afflicted him,
and those who make light of his
labors.
²When they see him, they will be
shaken with dreadful fear,
and they will be amazed at his
unexpected salvation.
³They will speak to one another in
repentance,
and in anguish of spirit they will
groan, and say,
⁴"This is the man whom we once
held in derision
and made a byword of reproach—
we fools!
We thought that his life was
madness
and that his end was without honor.

l Or *ended*

4.7–19: The blessedness of the righteous despite premature death. The righteous man who dies
young has three advantages: he *will be at rest* with God (v. 7); *a blameless life* means more than
long years; and early death ends the danger of falling into evil. **10–15:** Enoch is an example of a
good man *perfected in a short time;* he lived 365 years, several hundred years less than any
other listed in Gen. ch. 5. **14–15:** *The peoples . . . did not understand* that God was good to
Enoch in removing him *from the midst of wickedness.* The wicked, who have contempt for such
good men, will be judged by God for their sins.
  4.20–5.14: The confusion and remorse of the ungodly at the judgment. 5.3–14: The wicked who
have persecuted the righteous will repent; they will see that their lawless, godless way has done

⁵Why has he been numbered among
　　the sons of God?
And why is his lot among the
　　saints?
⁶So it was we who strayed from the
　　way of truth,
and the light of righteousness did
　　not shine on us,
and the sun did not rise upon
　　us.
⁷We took our fill of the paths of
　　lawlessness and destruction,
and we journeyed through
　　trackless deserts,
but the way of the Lord we have
　　not known.
⁸What has our arrogance profited
　　us?
And what good has our boasted
　　wealth brought us?

⁹"All those things have vanished
　　like a shadow,
and like a rumor that passes
　　by;
¹⁰like a ship that sails through the
　　billowy water,
and when it has passed no trace
　　can be found,
nor track of its keel in the waves;
¹¹or as, when a bird flies through the
　　air,
no evidence of its passage is found;
the light air, lashed by the beat of
　　its pinions
and pierced by the force of its
　　rushing flight,
is traversed by the movement of its
　　wings,
and afterward no sign of its coming
　　is found there;
¹²or as, when an arrow is shot at a
　　target,
the air, thus divided, comes
　　together at once,
so that no one knows its pathway.

¹³So we also, as soon as we were born,
　　ceased to be,
and we had no sign of virtue to
　　show,
but were consumed in our
　　wickedness."
¹⁴Because the hope of the ungodly
　　man is like chaffᵐ carried by
　　the wind,
and like a light hoarfrostⁿ driven
　　away by a storm;
it is dispersed like smoke before
　　the wind,
and it passes like the remembrance
　　of a guest who stays but a day.

¹⁵But the righteous live for ever,
and their reward is with the Lord;
the Most High takes care of them.
¹⁶Therefore they will receive a
　　glorious crown
and a beautiful diadem from the
　　hand of the Lord,
because with his right hand he will
　　cover them,
and with his arm he will shield
　　them.
¹⁷The Lordᵒ will take his zeal as his
　　whole armor,
and will arm all creation to repelᵖ
　　his enemies;
¹⁸he will put on righteousness as a
　　breastplate,
and wear impartial justice as a
　　helmet;
¹⁹he will take holiness as an
　　invincible shield,
²⁰and sharpen stern wrath for a
　　sword,
and creation will join with him to
　　fight against the madmen.
²¹Shafts of lightning will fly with
　　true aim,

m Or *dust*
n Other authorities read *spider's web*
o Gk He
p Or *punish*

---

them no good. **5:** *Sons of God*, either angels, or God's holy people. **6–7:** *Way of truth . . . way of the Lord*, the way which the righteous chose and followed. **9:** *All those things*, namely their wealth and pleasure in tormenting the righteous, give no permanent pleasure or benefit; they vanish without a trace.

5.15–23: The future bliss of the righteous and the misery of the ungodly at the judgment. 17–23: The Lord will put on his full armor (*breastplate, helmet, shield, sword;* compare Eph.6.11–17), and with *lightning*, hail, raging waters, rushing rivers, and mighty winds will fight and overwhelm

and will leap to the target as from a
well-drawn bow of clouds,
²²and hailstones full of wrath will be
hurled as from a catapult;
the water of the sea will rage
against them,
and rivers will relentlessly
overwhelm them;
²³a mighty wind will rise against them,
and like a tempest it will winnow
them away.
Lawlessness will lay waste the
whole earth,
and evil-doing will overturn the
thrones of rulers.

6 Listen therefore, O kings, and
understand;
learn, O judges of the ends of the
earth.
²Give ear, you that rule over
multitudes,
and boast of many nations.
³For your dominion was given you
from the Lord,
and your sovereignty from the Most
High,
who will search out your works and
inquire into your plans.
⁴Because as servants of his kingdom
you did not rule rightly,
nor keep the law,
nor walk according to the purpose
of God,
⁵he will come upon you terribly and
swiftly,
because severe judgment falls on
those in high places.
⁶For the lowliest man may be
pardoned in mercy,
but mighty men will be mightily
tested.
⁷For the Lord of all will not stand
in awe of any one,

nor show deference to greatness;
because he himself made both small
and great,
and he takes thought for all alike.
⁸But a strict inquiry is in store for
the mighty.
⁹To you then, O monarchs, my
words are directed,
that you may learn wisdom and not
transgress.
¹⁰For they will be made holy who
observe holy things in holiness,
and those who have been taught
them will find a defense.
¹¹Therefore set your desire on my
words;
long for them, and you will be
instructed.

¹²Wisdom is radiant and unfading,
and she is easily discerned by those
who love her,
and is found by those who seek her.
¹³She hastens to make herself known
to those who desire her.
¹⁴He who rises early to seek her will
have no difficulty,
for he will find her sitting at his
gates.
¹⁵To fix one's thought on her is
perfect understanding,
and he who is vigilant on her
account will soon be free from
care,
¹⁶because she goes about seeking
those worthy of her,
and she graciously appears to them
in their paths,
and meets them in every thought.

¹⁷The beginning of wisdom*q* is the
most sincere desire for
instruction,

q Gk Her beginning

---

the wicked. **23:** The statement that *evil-doing* overthrows *thrones* recalls 1.1 and prepares for
6.1–11.

6.1–9.18: Commendation of wisdom as the guide of life. 6.1–11: Further admonition to rulers,
who receive their authority from God and must answer to him for lawless, godless acts; for he
treats alike lowly and *mighty, small and great* (vv. 6–7). *Monarchs* need *wisdom*, and will receive
it if they desire it (vv. 9–11).

6.12–16: Wisdom is easily found; for she seeks out those who desire to know her, and gives
them understanding (compare Pr. ch. 8, which also refers to rulers).

6.17–20: The steps from the love of wisdom to immortality. A sorites (a form of logic much

and concern for instruction is love
of her,
[18]and love of her is the keeping of her
laws,
and giving heed to her laws is
assurance of immortality,
[19]and immortality brings one near to
God;
[20]so the desire for wisdom leads to a
kingdom.

[21]Therefore if you delight in thrones
and scepters, O monarchs over
the peoples,
honor wisdom, that you may reign
for ever.
[22]I will tell you what wisdom is and
how she came to be,
and I will hide no secrets from
you,
but I will trace her course from the
beginning of creation,
and make the knowledge of her
clear,
and I will not pass by the truth;
[23]neither will I travel in the company
of sickly envy,
for envy[r] does not associate with
wisdom.
[24]A multitude of wise men is the
salvation of the world,
and a sensible king is the stability
of his people.
[25]Therefore be instructed by my
words, and you will profit.

7 I also am mortal, like all men,
a descendant of the first-formed
child of earth;
and in the womb of a mother I was
molded into flesh,
[2]within the period of ten months,
compacted with blood,

from the seed of a man and the
pleasure of marriage.
[3]And when I was born, I began to
breathe the common air,
and fell upon the kindred earth,
and my first sound was a cry, like
that of all.
[4]I was nursed with care in swaddling
cloths.
[5]For no king has had a different
beginning of existence;
[6]there is for all mankind one
entrance into life, and a common
departure.

[7]Therefore I prayed, and
understanding was given me;
I called upon God, and the spirit
of wisdom came to me.
[8]I preferred her to scepters and
thrones,
and I accounted wealth as nothing
in comparison with her.
[9]Neither did I liken to her any
priceless gem,
because all gold is but a little sand
in her sight,
and silver will be accounted as clay
before her.
[10]I loved her more than health and
beauty,
and I chose to have her rather than
light,
because her radiance never ceases.
[11]All good things came to me along
with her,
and in her hands uncounted wealth.
[12]I rejoiced in them all, because
wisdom leads them;
but I did not know that she was
their mother.
[13]I learned without guile and I impart

r Gk *this*

used by the Stoics), tracing the path from desire for *wisdom* to its results in *immortality* and
fellowship with God. **20:** *A kingdom,* God's eternal kingdom, in which rulers and others who
truly desire wisdom participate.
    6.21–25: A promise of instruction in the nature of wisdom. The writer speaks in the name of
Solomon. **24:** The beneficial results of wisdom: *wise men* save *the world;* rulers guided by wisdom give *stability* to their *people.*
    7.1–22a: Solomon received wisdom from God. 1–10: Recognizing his need for wisdom, Solo-
mon *prayed* for and received it, and valued it above every other gift (1 Kg.3.5–15). **11–22a:**
With the gift of wisdom Solomon received *all good things, friendship with God,* and *unerring
knowledge* of the world, the heavenly bodies, and plant and animal life.

without grudging;
I do not hide her wealth,
[14]for it is an unfailing treasure for
men;
those who get it obtain friendship
with God,
commended for the gifts that come
from instruction.

[15]May God grant that I speak with
judgment
and have thoughts worthy of what
I have received,
for he is the guide even of wisdom
and the corrector of the wise.
[16]For both we and our words are in
his hand,
as are all understanding and skill
in crafts.
[17]For it is he who gave me unerring
knowledge of what exists,
to know the structure of the world
and the activity of the elements;
[18]the beginning and end and middle
of times,
the alternations of the solstices and
the changes of the seasons,
[19]the cycles of the year and the
constellations of the stars,
[20]the natures of animals and the
tempers of wild beasts,
the powers of spirits[s] and the
reasonings of men,
the varieties of plants and the
virtues of roots;
[21]I learned both what is secret and
what is manifest,
[22]for wisdom, the fashioner of all
things, taught me.

For in her there is a spirit that is
intelligent, holy,
unique, manifold, subtle,
mobile, clear, unpolluted,
distinct, invulnerable, loving the
good, keen,

irresistible, [23]beneficent, humane,
steadfast, sure, free from anxiety,
all-powerful, overseeing all,
and penetrating through all
spirits
that are intelligent and pure and
most subtle.
[24]For wisdom is more mobile than
any motion;
because of her pureness she pervades
and penetrates all things.
[25]For she is a breath of the power of
God,
and a pure emanation of the glory
of the Almighty;
therefore nothing defiled gains
entrance into her.
[26]For she is a reflection of eternal
light,
a spotless mirror of the working of
God,
and an image of his goodness.
[27]Though she is but one, she can do
all things,
and while remaining in herself, she
renews all things;
in every generation she passes into
holy souls
and makes them friends of God,
and prophets;
[28]for God loves nothing so much
as the man who lives with
wisdom.
[29]For she is more beautiful than the
sun,
and excels every constellation of
the stars.
Compared with the light she is
found to be superior,
[30]for it is succeeded by the night,
but against wisdom evil does not
prevail.

8 She reaches mightily from one
end of the earth to the other,
and she orders all things well.

s Or *winds*

7.22b–8.1: The nature and beneficial works of wisdom. 22b–23: Wisdom's twenty-one (3 × 7)
attributes. **24:** She is a pure, freely moving, and all-penetrating *spirit*. **25–26:** She emanates
from God; his *power, glory*, purity, *light*, and *goodness* are expressed through her (compare
Jn.1.1–14; Heb.1.1–3). **7.27–8.1:** She is everywhere, *orders all things well*, and *can do all things*.
Her greatest work is to enter *holy souls* and make them *friends of God, and prophets*. *Evil* cannot
defeat her.

²I loved her and sought her from
  my youth,
and I desired to take her for my
  bride,
and I became enamored of her
  beauty.
³She glorifies her noble birth by
  living with God,
and the Lord of all loves her.
⁴For she is an initiate in the
  knowledge of God,
and an associate in his works.
⁵If riches are a desirable possession
  in life,
what is richer than wisdom who
  effects all things?
⁶And if understanding is effective,
who more than she is fashioner of
  what exists?
⁷And if any one loves righteousness,
her labors are virtues;
for she teaches self-control and
  prudence,
justice and courage;
nothing in life is more profitable
  for men than these.
⁸And if any one longs for wide
  experience,
she knows the things of old, and
  infers the things to come;
she understands turns of speech
  and the solutions of riddles;
she has foreknowledge of signs and
  wonders
and of the outcome of seasons and
  times.
⁹Therefore I determined to take
  her to live with me,
knowing that she would give me
  good counsel
and encouragement in cares and
  grief.
¹⁰Because of her I shall have glory
  among the multitudes
and honor in the presence of the

elders, though I am young.
¹¹I shall be found keen in judgment,
and in the sight of rulers I shall be
  admired.
¹²When I am silent they will wait
  for me,
and when I speak they will give
  heed;
and when I speak at greater length
they will put their hands on their
  mouths.
¹³Because of her I shall have
  immortality,
and leave an everlasting
  remembrance to those who
  come after me.
¹⁴I shall govern peoples,
and nations will be subject to me;
¹⁵dread monarchs will be afraid of
  me when they hear of me;
among the people I shall show
  myself capable, and courageous
  in war.
¹⁶When I enter my house, I shall
  find rest with her,
for companionship with her has
  no bitterness,
and life with her has no pain, but
  gladness and joy.
¹⁷When I considered these things
  inwardly,
and thought upon them in my mind,
that in kinship with wisdom there
  is immortality,
¹⁸and in friendship with her, pure
  delight,
and in the labors of her hands,
  unfailing wealth,
and in the experience of her
  company, understanding,
and renown in sharing her words,
I went about seeking how to get
  her for myself.
¹⁹As a child I was by nature
  well endowed,

8.2–16: Solomon desires to take wisdom as his bride. 4–6: She is *God's associate in his works*, and his agent in making all things (Pr.8.22–30; compare Jn.1.3; Col.1.16; Heb.1.2). **7:** She *teaches self-control, prudence, justice,* and *courage,* which (according to Plato and the Stoics) are the four cardinal virtues. **8:** She knows the past and the future, and so can give good counsel. **10–16:** *Because of her* Solomon receives *honor* and respect, *immortality,* a great empire, *rest* and *joy.*

8.17–21: Considering all the benefits conferred by wisdom, Solomon prays to God to grant her to him. 19–20: The Platonic view of the soul as pre-existent.

and a good soul fell to my lot;
[20]or rather, being good, I entered an
undefiled body.
[21]But I perceived that I would not
possess wisdom unless God gave
her to me—
and it was a mark of insight to
know whose gift she was—
so I appealed to the Lord and
besought him,
and with my whole heart I said:

9 "O God of my fathers and Lord
of mercy,
who hast made all things by thy
word,
[2]and by thy wisdom hast formed
man,
to have dominion over the creatures
thou hast made,
[3]and rule the world in holiness and
righteousness,
and pronounce judgment in
uprightness of soul,
[4]give me the wisdom that sits by
thy throne,
and do not reject me from among
thy servants.
[5]For I am thy slave and the son of
thy maidservant,
a man who is weak and short-lived,
with little understanding of
judgment and laws;
[6]for even if one is perfect among
the sons of men,
yet without the wisdom that comes
from thee he will be regarded as
nothing.
[7]Thou hast chosen me to be king of
thy people
and to be judge over thy sons and
daughters.
[8]Thou hast given command to build
a temple on thy holy mountain,
and an altar in the city of thy
habitation,
a copy of the holy tent which thou

didst prepare from the
beginning.
[9]With thee is wisdom, who knows
thy works
and was present when thou didst
make the world,
and who understands what is
pleasing in thy sight
and what is right according to thy
commandments.
[10]Send her forth from the holy
heavens,
and from the throne of thy glory
send her,
that she may be with me and toil,
and that I may learn what is
pleasing to thee.
[11]For she knows and understands all
things,
and she will guide me wisely in my
actions
and guard me with her glory.
[12]Then my works will be acceptable,
and I shall judge thy people justly,
and shall be worthy of the throne[t]
of my father.
[13]For what man can learn the
counsel of God?
Or who can discern what the Lord
wills?
[14]For the reasoning of mortals is
worthless,
and our designs are likely to fail,
[15]for a perishable body weighs down
the soul,
and this earthy tent burdens the
thoughtful[u] mind.
[16]We can hardly guess at what is on
earth,
and what is at hand we find with
labor;
but who has traced out what is in
the heavens?
[17]Who has learned thy counsel,
unless thou hast given wisdom

t Gk *thrones*   *u* Or *anxious*

9.1–18: Solomon's prayer for wisdom (1 Kg.3.6–9). **1–2:** God *made all things* by his *word* and *wisdom* (compare Jn.1.1–3); here "word" and "wisdom" are synonyms. **6–9:** The *king* needs *wisdom* to learn God's will and to know what is right. **10–12:** Only by wisdom's presence and guidance can the king govern well. **13–15:** Man's *perishable body*, though not called evil (compare 8.20), *burdens* and *hampers* the mind. **16–17:** Man knows even earthly things imperfectly; only through *wisdom*, also called *the holy Spirit*, can he learn heavenly things (1 Cor.2.7–12).

and sent thy holy Spirit from on
  high?
[18]And thus the paths of those on
  earth were set right,
and men were taught what pleases
  thee,
and were saved by wisdom."

10 Wisdom[v] protected the
  first-formed father of the
world, when he alone had been
  created;
she delivered him from his
  transgression,
[2]and gave him strength to rule all
  things.
[3]But when an unrighteous man
  departed from her in his anger,
he perished because in rage he slew
  his brother.
[4]When the earth was flooded
  because of him, wisdom again
  saved it,
steering the righteous man by a
  paltry piece of wood.

[5]Wisdom[w] also, when the nations
  in wicked agreement had been
  confounded,
recognized the righteous man and
  preserved him blameless before
  God,
and kept him strong in the face
  of his compassion for his child.

[6]Wisdom[w] rescued a righteous man
  when the ungodly were
  perishing;
he escaped the fire that descended
  on the Five Cities.[x]
[7]Evidence of their wickedness still
  remains:
a continually smoking wasteland,
plants bearing fruit that does not
  ripen,
and a pillar of salt standing as a

monument to an unbelieving
  soul.
[8]For because they passed wisdom
  by,
they not only were hindered from
  recognizing the good,
but also left for mankind a
  reminder of their folly,
so that their failures could never
  go unnoticed.

[9]Wisdom rescued from troubles
  those who served her.
[10]When a righteous man fled from
  his brother's wrath,
she guided him on straight paths;
she showed him the kingdom of
  God,
and gave him knowledge of
  angels;[y]
she prospered him in his labors,
and increased the fruit of his toil.
[11]When his oppressors were covetous,
she stood by him and made him
  rich.
[12]She protected him from his
  enemies,
and kept him safe from those who
  lay in wait for him;
in his arduous contest she gave him
  the victory,
so that he might learn that godliness
  is more powerful than anything.

[13]When a righteous man was sold,
  wisdom[z] did not desert him,
but delivered him from sin.
She descended with him into the
  dungeon,
[14]and when he was in prison she did
  not leave him,
until she brought him the scepter
  of a kingdom

v Gk *She*   w Gk *She*
x Or *Pentapolis*
y Or *of holy things*
z Gk *she*

18: *Wisdom* guides, teaches, and saves men. The remaining chapters of the book tell how wisdom saved Israel and her ancestors, though references to wisdom by name almost disappear after ch. 10.

   10.1–12.27: Historical illustrations of the power of wisdom. 10.1–11.4: From Adam to Moses. 10.1–2: Adam (Gen.1.26–5.5). **3:** Cain (Gen.4.1–16). *Perished*, spiritual death. **4:** Noah (Gen. 5.28–9.29). **5:** Abraham (Gen.11.26–25.10). *Nations*, Gen.11.1–9. **6–8:** *A righteous man*, Lot (Gen. ch. 19). **9–12:** Jacob (Gen.25.19–49.33, especially ch. 28). **13–14:** Joseph (Gen. chs.

and authority over his masters.
Those who accused him she showed
  to be false,
and she gave him everlasting honor.

¹⁵A holy people and blameless race
wisdom*a* delivered from a nation
  of oppressors.
¹⁶She entered the soul of a servant
  of the Lord,
and withstood dread kings with
  wonders and signs.
¹⁷She gave to holy men the reward
  of their labors;
she guided them along a marvelous
  way,
and became a shelter to them by
  day,
and a starry flame through the
  night.
¹⁸She brought them over the Red Sea,
and led them through deep waters;
¹⁹but she drowned their enemies,
and cast them up from the depth
  of the sea.
²⁰Therefore the righteous plundered
  the ungodly;
they sang hymns, O Lord, to thy
  holy name,
and praised with one accord thy
  defending hand,
²¹because wisdom opened the mouth
  of the dumb,
and made the tongues of babes
  speak clearly.

11 Wisdom*a* prospered their works
    by the hand of a holy prophet.
²They journeyed through an
  uninhabited wilderness,
and pitched their tents in untrodden
  places.
³They withstood their enemies and
  fought off their foes.

⁴When they thirsted they called
  upon thee,
and water was given them out of
  flinty rock,
and slaking of thirst from hard
  stone.
⁵For through the very things by
  which their enemies were
  punished,
they themselves received benefit
  in their need.
⁶Instead of the fountain of an
  ever-flowing river,
stirred up and defiled with blood
⁷in rebuke for the decree to slay the
  infants,
thou gavest them abundant water
  unexpectedly,
⁸showing by their thirst at that time
how thou didst punish their
  enemies.
⁹For when they were tried, though
  they were being disciplined in
  mercy,
they learned how the ungodly were
  tormented when judged in wrath.
¹⁰For thou didst test them as a father
  does in warning,
but thou didst examine the
  ungodly*b* as a stern king does in
  condemnation.
¹¹Whether absent or present, they
  were equally distressed,
¹²for a twofold grief possessed them,
and a groaning at the memory of
  what had occurred.
¹³For when they heard that through
  their own punishments
the righteous*c* had received benefit,
they perceived it was the
  Lord's doing.
¹⁴For though they had mockingly
  rejected him who long before

a Gk *she*   *b* Gk *those*   *c* Gk *they*

37–50). **15–21:** Through Moses wisdom delivered Israel from Egypt (Ex.1.1–15.21, especially chs. 12–15).

   11.1–12.2: The contrast between the fortunes of Israel and Egypt. 11.1–4: Wisdom guided Israel through the wilderness (Ex.15.22–17.16). **1:** *A holy prophet,* that is, Moses (Dt.18.15,18).

   11.5–14: How water was used to bless the Israelites and to punish the Egyptians. Israel's thirst was God's discipline in *mercy* (v. 9); *water* from the *rock* (vv. 4, 7) showed that God could help in every need. But the Egyptians were *judged in wrath;* the Nile was turned to *blood* (vv. 6–9). They suffered *twofold grief:* the *memory* of their own punishment and the knowledge that through it Israel had been blessed and Moses vindicated (vv. 11–14).

had been cast out and exposed,
at the end of the events they
marveled at him,
for their thirst was not like that of
the righteous.

15In return for their foolish and
wicked thoughts,
which led them astray to worship
irrational serpents and worthless
animals,
thou didst send upon them a
multitude of irrational creatures
to punish them,
16that they might learn that one is
punished by the very things by
which he sins.
17For thy all-powerful hand,
which created the world out of
formless matter,
did not lack the means to send
upon them a multitude of bears,
or bold lions,
18or newly created unknown beasts
full of rage,
or such as breathe out fiery
breath,
or belch forth a thick pall of
smoke,
or flash terrible sparks from their
eyes;
19not only could their damage
exterminate men,*d*
but the mere sight of them could
kill by fright.
20Even apart from these, men*e* could
fall at a single breath
when pursued by justice
and scattered by the breath of thy
power.
But thou hast arranged all things
by measure and number and
weight.

21For it is always in thy power to

show great strength,
and who can withstand the might
of thy arm?
22Because the whole world before
thee is like a speck that tips the
scales,
and like a drop of morning dew
that falls upon the ground.
23But thou art merciful to all, for
thou canst do all things,
and thou dost overlook men's sins,
that they may repent.
24For thou lovest all things that
exist,
and hast loathing for none of the
things which thou hast made,
for thou wouldst not have made
anything if thou hadst hated
it.
25How would anything have endured
if thou hadst not willed it?
Or how would anything not called
forth by thee have been
preserved?
26Thou sparest all things, for they
are thine, O Lord who lovest the
living.

12 For thy immortal spirit is in
all things.
2Therefore thou dost correct little
by little those who trespass,
and dost remind and warn them
of the things wherein they sin,
that they may be freed from
wickedness and put their trust
in thee, O Lord.

3Those who dwelt of old in thy holy
land
4thou didst hate for their detestable
practices,
their works of sorcery and unholy
rites,

d Gk *them*
e Gk *they*

11.15–20: The plague of frogs and lice. The wicked man is *punished by the very things by which he sins;* the Egyptians worshiped *irrational creatures,* and were punished by frogs, flies, lice, locusts (Ex. chs. 8 and 10). But God was merciful; he could have sent *bears, lions,* or newly created fierce *beasts,* or killed the Egyptians by *a single breath.*

11.21–12.2: God's universal love. God is almighty, but he is *merciful to all,* withholding punishment to give time to *repent.* He loves and preserves *all,* and corrects *little by little those who trespass* in order to lead them to repentance.

12.3–11: An example of God's patience and mercy. He hated the pagan peoples of Canaan

[5]their merciless slaughter[f] of
children,
and their sacrificial feasting on
human flesh and blood.
These initiates from the midst of
a heathen cult,[g]
[6]these parents who murder helpless
lives,
thou didst will to destroy by the
hands of our fathers,
[7]that the land most precious of all
to thee
might receive a worthy colony of
the servants[h] of God.
[8]But even these thou didst spare,
since they were but men,
and didst send wasps[i] as
forerunners of thy army,
to destroy them little by little,
[9]though thou wast not unable to
give the ungodly into the hands
of the righteous in battle,
or to destroy them at one blow by
dread wild beasts or thy stern
word.
[10]But judging them little by little
thou gavest them a chance to
repent,
though thou wast not unaware
that their origin[j] was evil
and their wickedness inborn,
and that their way of thinking
would never change.
[11]For they were an accursed race
from the beginning,
and it was not through fear of any
one that thou didst leave them
unpunished for their sins.

[12]For who will say, "What hast thou
done?"
Or who will resist thy judgment?
Who will accuse thee for the
destruction of nations which
thou didst make?
Or who will come before thee to
plead as an advocate for
unrighteous men?
[13]For neither is there any god
besides thee, whose care is for
all men,[k]
to whom thou shouldst prove that
thou hast not judged unjustly;
[14]nor can any king or monarch
confront thee about those whom
thou hast punished.
[15]Thou art righteous and rulest all
things righteously,
deeming it alien to thy power
to condemn him who does not
deserve to be punished.
[16]For thy strength is the source of
righteousness,
and thy sovereignty over all causes
thee to spare all.
[17]For thou dost show thy strength
when men doubt the
completeness of thy power,
and dost rebuke any insolence
among those who know it.[l]
[18]Thou who art sovereign in strength
dost judge with mildness,
and with great forbearance thou
dost govern us;
for thou hast power to act whenever
thou dost choose.

[19]Through such works thou hast
taught thy people
that the righteous man must be
kind,
and thou hast filled thy sons with
good hope,
because thou givest repentance for
sins.
[20]For if thou didst punish with such
great care and indulgence[m]

f Cn: Gk *slaughterers*
g The Greek text of this line is uncertain
h Or *children*   i Or *hornets*
j Or *nature*   k Or *all things*
l The Greek text of this line is uncertain
m Some ancient authorities omit *and indulgence;* others
read *and entreaty*

(Ex.23.23; Dt.7.1) for their evil *practices;* but he judged them *little by little* (v. 8; compare
Ex.23.29–30), giving them *a chance to repent* (v. 10; compare 2 Esd.9.11; Heb.12.17).
    12.12–18: God's supreme power delights in benevolence. God, *sovereign,* all-powerful, is
answerable to no one; he is *righteous,* condemns no man unjustly, and judges with *mildness*
and *forbearance.* He cares *for all men* (v. 13) and rules *all things* (v. 15).
    12.19–22: God's mercy is an example to Israel. Israel may think that God has *judged* them

the enemies of thy servants[n] and
those deserving of death,
granting them time and opportunity
to give up their wickedness,
[21]with what strictness thou hast
judged thy sons,
to whose fathers thou gavest oaths
and covenants full of good
promises!
[22]So while chastening us thou
scourgest our enemies ten
thousand times more,
so that we may meditate upon thy
goodness when we judge,
and when we are judged we may
expect mercy.

[23]Therefore those who in folly of
life lived unrighteously
thou didst torment through their
own abominations.
[24]For they went far astray on the
paths of error,
accepting as gods those animals
which even their enemies[o]
despised;
they were deceived like foolish
babes.
[25]Therefore, as to thoughtless
children,
thou didst send thy judgment to
mock them.
[26]But those who have not heeded
the warning of light rebukes
will experience the deserved
judgment of God.
[27]For when in their suffering they
became incensed
at those creatures which they had
thought to be gods, being
punished by means of them,
they saw and recognized as the true
God him whom they had before
refused to know.

Therefore the utmost condemnation
came upon them.

13 For all men who were ignorant
of God were foolish by nature;
and they were unable from the
good things that are seen to
know him who exists,
nor did they recognize the craftsman
while paying heed to his
works;
[2]but they supposed that either fire
or wind or swift air,
or the circle of the stars, or
turbulent water,
or the luminaries of heaven were
the gods that rule the world.
[3]If through delight in the beauty
of these things men[p] assumed
them to be gods,
let them know how much better
than these is their Lord,
for the author of beauty created
them.
[4]And if men[p] were amazed at their
power and working,
let them perceive from them
how much more powerful is he
who formed them.
[5]For from the greatness and beauty
of created things
comes a corresponding perception
of their Creator.
[6]Yet these men are little to be
blamed,
for perhaps they go astray
while seeking God and desiring to
find him.
[7]For as they live among his works
they keep searching,
and they trust in what they see,
because the things that are seen
are beautiful.

n Or *children*   *o* Gk *they*   *p* Gk *they*

---

strictly (v. 21), but he *scourges* Israel's *enemies* far *more;* he chastens Israel in *mercy* and for
their own good.
    12.23–27: Further comments on the punishment of the Egyptians (in accord with the principle
set forth in 11.16). The Egyptians were tormented by the *animals* that they worshiped. **27:**
Though the Egyptians *recognized* Israel's God as *the true God*, they refused to let Israel go.
The utmost condemnation, i.e. the death of their first-born sons.
    **13.1–15.17: The origin and folly of idolatry. 13.1–9: Nature-worship is the least culpable form
of false worship.** *Ignorant, foolish* men, misled by the *beauty* and *power* of *created things,* thought
them *gods.* **6–7:** The author partly excuses such idolatry as arising from honest search for God.

8Yet again, not even they are to be
    excused;
9for if they had the power to know
    so much
that they could investigate the
    world,
how did they fail to find sooner
    the Lord of these things?

10But miserable, with their hopes set
    on dead things, are the men
who give the name "gods" to the
    works of men's hands,
gold and silver fashioned with
    skill,
and likenesses of animals,
or a useless stone, the work of an
    ancient hand.
11A skilled woodcutter may saw down
    a tree easy to handle
and skilfully strip off all its bark,
and then with pleasing workmanship
make a useful vessel that serves
    life's needs,
12and burn the castoff pieces of his
    work
to prepare his food, and eat his fill.
13But a castoff piece from among
    them, useful for nothing,
a stick crooked and full of knots,
he takes and carves with care in his
    leisure,
and shapes it with skill gained in
    idleness;*q*
he forms it like the image of a man,
14or makes it like some worthless
    animal,
giving it a coat of red paint and
    coloring its surface red
and covering every blemish in it
    with paint;
15then he makes for it a niche that
    befits it,
and sets it in the wall, and fastens
    it there with iron.
16So he takes thought for it, that it
    may not fall,

because he knows that it cannot
    help itself,
for it is only an image and has
    need of help.
17When he prays about possessions
    and his marriage and children,
he is not ashamed to address a
    lifeless thing.
18For health he appeals to a thing
    that is weak;
for life he prays to a thing that is
    dead;
for aid he entreats a thing that is
    utterly inexperienced;
for a prosperous journey, a thing
    that cannot take a step;
19for money-making and work and
    success with his hands
he asks strength of a thing whose
    hands have no strength.

14 Again, one preparing to sail
    and about to voyage over
    raging waves
calls upon a piece of wood more
    fragile than the ship which
    carries him.
2For it was desire for gain that
    planned that vessel,
and wisdom was the craftsman who
    built it;
3but it is thy providence, O Father,
    that steers its course,
because thou hast given it a path
    in the sea,
and a safe way through the waves,
4showing that thou canst save from
    every danger,
so that even if a man lacks skill, he
    may put to sea.
5It is thy will that the works of thy
    wisdom should not be without
    effect;
therefore men trust their lives even
    to the smallest piece of wood,
and passing through the billows on

q Other authorities read with intelligent skill

8–9: Yet it cannot be *excused;* such idolaters should have discerned *the Lord* of created things.
    13.10–19: The folly of image-worship (compare the Letter of Jeremiah). A *woodcutter* fells a
tree, makes of some knotty *castoff* piece an *image* of *man* or *animal,* and calls it his god, although
it cannot stand or act and has no life.
    14.1–7: The folly of the seafarer who trusts in a wooden image on a ship's prow. Though men

a raft they come safely to land.
⁶For even in the beginning, when
　arrogant giants were perishing,
the hope of the world took refuge
　on a raft,
and guided by thy hand left to the
　world the seed of a new
　generation.
⁷For blessed is the wood by which
　righteousness comes.

⁸But the idol made with hands is
　accursed, and so is he who made
　it;
because he did the work, and the
　perishable thing was named a
　god.
⁹For equally hateful to God are the
　ungodly man and his
　ungodliness,
¹⁰for what was done will be punished
　together with him who did it.
¹¹Therefore there will be a visitation
　also upon the heathen idols,
because, though part of what God
　created, they became an
　abomination,
and became traps for the souls of
　men
and a snare to the feet of the
　foolish.

¹²For the idea of making idols was
　the beginning of fornication,
and the invention of them was the
　corruption of life,
¹³for neither have they existed from
　the beginning
nor will they exist for ever.
¹⁴For through the vanity of men
　they entered the world,
and therefore their speedy end has
　been planned.
¹⁵For a father, consumed with grief
　at an untimely bereavement,

made an image of his child, who
　had been suddenly taken from
　him;
and he now honored as a god
　what was once a dead human
　being,
and handed on to his dependents
　secret rites and initiations.
¹⁶Then the ungodly custom, grown
　strong with time, was kept as a
　law,
and at the command of monarchs
　graven images were worshiped.
¹⁷When men could not honor
　monarchs*ʳ* in their presence,
　since they lived at a distance,
they imagined their appearance
　far away,
and made a visible image of the
　king whom they honored,
so that by their zeal they might
　flatter the absent one as though
　present.
¹⁸Then the ambition of the craftsman
　impelled
even those who did not know the
　king to intensify their worship.
¹⁹For he, perhaps wishing to please
　his ruler,
skilfully forced the likeness to take
　more beautiful form,
²⁰and the multitude, attracted by the
　charm of his work,
now regarded as an object of
　worship the one whom shortly
　before they had honored as a
　man.
²¹And this became a hidden trap for
　mankind,
because men, in bondage to
　misfortune or to royal authority,
bestowed on objects of stone or
　wood the name that ought not
　to be shared.

r Gk *them*

---

planned the vessel, a safe voyage is God's doing. **6:** God saved Noah and his family in the ark
(Gen. chs. 6–8). **7:** *The wood* refers not (as some have thought) to the cross of Christ but to
Noah's ark, which carried forward God's righteous will.
　14.8–11: Idolaters will be punished. 9: Contrast 11.24–26.
　14.14–21: The origins of idolatry. A grief-stricken *father* made and *worshiped* an *image* of his
dead child (vv. 15–16). Subjects living at a distance made and worshiped images of their king
(v. 17); moreover skilled craftsmen made the image *more beautiful* than the king (vv. 18–20).
(Euhemerus, about 300 B.C., taught that all gods were deified mortals.)

²²Afterward it was not enough for
them to err about the knowledge
of God,
but they live in great strife due to
ignorance,
and they call such great evils
peace.
²³For whether they kill children in
their initiations, or celebrate
secret mysteries,
or hold frenzied revels with strange
customs,
²⁴they no longer keep either their
lives or their marriages pure,
but they either treacherously kill
one another, or grieve one
another by adultery,
²⁵and all is a raging riot of blood and
murder, theft and deceit,
corruption, faithlessness, tumult,
perjury,
²⁶confusion over what is good,
forgetfulness of favors,
pollution of souls, sex perversion,
disorder in marriage, adultery, and
debauchery.
²⁷For the worship of idols not to be
named
is the beginning and cause and end
of every evil.
²⁸For their worshipers*s* either rave
in exultation, or prophesy lies,
or live unrighteously, or readily
commit perjury;
²⁹for because they trust in lifeless
idols
they swear wicked oaths and
expect to suffer no harm.
³⁰But just penalties will overtake
them on two counts:
because they thought wickedly of
God in devoting themselves to
idols,
and because in deceit they swore
unrighteously through contempt
for holiness.

³¹For it is not the power of the things
by which men swear,*t*
but the just penalty for those who
sin,
that always pursues the
transgression of the unrighteous.

15 But thou, our God, art kind
and true,
patient, and ruling all things*u* in
mercy.
²For even if we sin we are thine,
knowing thy power;
but we will not sin, because we
know that we are accounted
thine.
³For to know thee is complete
righteousness,
and to know thy power is the root
of immortality.
⁴For neither has the evil intent of
human art misled us,
nor the fruitless toil of painters,
a figure stained with varied colors,
⁵whose appearance arouses yearning
in fools,
so that they desire*v* the lifeless
form of a dead image.
⁶Lovers of evil things and fit for
such objects of hope*w*
are those who either make or
desire or worship them.

⁷For when a potter kneads the soft
earth
and laboriously molds each vessel
for our service,
he fashions out of the same clay
both the vessels that serve clean uses
and those for contrary uses, making
all in like manner;
but which shall be the use of each
of these
the worker in clay decides.

s Gk *they*   *t* Or *of the oaths men swear*
u Or *ruling the universe*
v Gk *and he desires*   *w* Gk *such hopes*

14.22–31: **The evil results of idolatry** (Rom.1.24–32). Ignorance of God, *strife*, moral wrong,
and perversion (v. 26), will bring sure punishment.
    15.1–17: **The contrast between the worshipers of the true God and idolaters. 1–5:** The purifying
influence of the worship of the true God on the life of Israel. **3:** *To know* God is *righteousness*
and true life (compare Jn.17.3). **6–17:** The folly and wickedness of making and worshiping
clay idols. For financial profit *a potter* molds from one mass of *clay* both useful *vessels* and

8With misspent toil, he forms a
    futile god from the same clay—
this man who was made of earth
    a short time before
and after a little while goes to the
    earth from which he was taken,
when he is required to return the
    soul that was lent him.
9But he is not concerned that he is
    destined to die
or that his life is brief,
but he competes with workers in
    gold and silver,
and imitates workers in copper;
and he counts it his glory that he
    molds counterfeit gods.
10His heart is ashes, his hope is
    cheaper than dirt,
and his life is of less worth than
    clay,
11because he failed to know the one
    who formed him
and inspired him with an active
    soul
and breathed into him a living
    spirit.
12But hex considered our existence
    an idle game,
and life a festival held for profit,
for he says one must get money
    however one can, even by base
    means.
13For this man, more than all others,
    knows that he sins
when he makes from earthy matter
    fragile vessels and graven images.

14But most foolish, and more
    miserable than an infant,
are all the enemies who oppressed
    thy people.
15For they thought that all their
    heathen idols were gods,
though these have neither the use
    of their eyes to see with,
nor nostrils with which to draw
    breath,

nor ears with which to hear,
nor fingers to feel with,
and their feet are of no use for
    walking.
16For a man made them,
and one whose spirit is borrowed
    formed them;
for no man can form a god which
    is like himself.
17He is mortal, and what he makes
    with lawless hands is dead,
for he is better than the objects he
    worships,
sincey he has life, but they never
    have.

18The enemies of thy peoplez worship
    even the most hateful animals,
which are worse than all others,
    when judged by their lack of
    intelligence;
19and even as animals they are not
    so beautiful in appearance that
    one would desire them,
but they have escaped both the
    praise of God and his blessing.

16 Therefore those men were
    deservedly punished through
    such creatures,
and were tormented by a multitude
    of animals.
2Instead of this punishment thou
    didst show kindness to thy
    people,
and thou didst prepare quails to
    eat,
a delicacy to satisfy the desire of
    appetite;
3in order that those men, when
    they desired food,
might lose the least remnant of
    appetitea
because of the odious creatures
    sent to them,

x Other authorities read *they*
y Other authorities read *of which*
z Gk *They*
a Gk *loathe the necessary appetite*

---

counterfeit gods; cheap imitations of gold, silver, and copper *images.* **14–17:** The stupidity of
Israel's *enemies,* who worship useless, lifeless images.
  15.18–19.22: The contrast between **God's treatment of the Egyptians and of the Israelites**
(compare 11.1–14). **16.1–4:** The Egyptians, *tormented* by the *animals* they worshiped (Ex. chs. 8
and 10), lost all appetite (v. 3); the Israelites, after brief hunger, enjoyed *quails* (Num. ch. 11).

while thy people,[b] after suffering
want a short time,
might partake of delicacies.
⁴For it was necessary that upon
those oppressors inexorable want
should come,
while to these it was merely shown
how their enemies were being
tormented.

⁵For when the terrible rage of wild
beasts came upon thy people[c]
and they were being destroyed by
the bites of writhing serpents,
thy wrath did not continue to the
end;
⁶they were troubled for a little
while as a warning,
and received a token of deliverance
to remind them of thy law's
command.
⁷For he who turned toward it was
saved, not by what he saw,
but by thee, the Savior of all.
⁸And by this also thou didst
convince our enemies
that it is thou who deliverest from
every evil.
⁹For they were killed by the bites
of locusts and flies,
and no healing was found for them,
because they deserved to be
punished by such things;
¹⁰but thy sons were not conquered
even by the teeth of venomous
serpents,
for thy mercy came to their help
and healed them.
¹¹To remind them of thy oracles
they were bitten,
and then were quickly delivered,
lest they should fall into deep
forgetfulness
and become unresponsive[d] to thy
kindness.
¹²For neither herb nor poultice cured
them,
but it was thy word, O Lord,

which heals all men.
¹³For thou hast power over life and
death;
thou dost lead men down to the
gates of Hades and back again.
¹⁴A man in his wickedness kills
another,
but he cannot bring back the
departed spirit,
nor set free the imprisoned soul.

¹⁵To escape from thy hand is
impossible;
¹⁶for the ungodly, refusing to know
thee,
were scourged by the strength of
thy arm,
pursued by unusual rains and hail
and relentless storms,
and utterly consumed by fire.
¹⁷For—most incredible of all—in
the water, which quenches all
things,
the fire had still greater effect,
for the universe defends the
righteous.
¹⁸At one time the flame was
restrained,
so that it might not consume the
creatures sent against the
ungodly,
but that seeing this they might
know
that they were being pursued by
the judgment of God;
¹⁹and at another time even in the
midst of water it burned more
intensely than fire,
to destroy the crops of the
unrighteous land.
²⁰Instead of these things thou didst
give thy people the food of
angels,
and without their toil thou didst
supply them from heaven with
bread ready to eat,

b Gk *they*   c Gk *them*
d The meaning of the Greek is obscure

5–14: The Egyptians were killed by *bites of locusts and flies* (not mentioned in Exodus); Israel, bitten by serpents (Num.21.6–9), suffered briefly as a *warning* (vv. 6,11), and were *quickly* healed by God's *word* (vv. 11–12). God has *power over life and death* (vv. 13–14).
    16.15–29: How fire from God punished the Egyptians. 20: The food of angels is manna,

providing every pleasure and suited
to every taste.

²¹For thy sustenance manifested thy
sweetness toward thy children;
and the bread, ministering*e* to the
desire of the one who took it,
was changed to suit every one's
liking.

²²Snow and ice withstood fire without
melting,
so that they might know that the
crops of their enemies
were being destroyed by the fire
that blazed in the hail
and flashed in the showers of
rain;

²³whereas the fire,*f* in order that the
righteous might be fed,
even forgot its native power.

²⁴For the creation, serving thee who
hast made it,
exerts itself to punish the
unrighteous,
and in kindness relaxes on behalf
of those who trust in thee.

²⁵Therefore at that time also, changed
into all forms,
it served thy all-nourishing bounty,
according to the desire of those
who had need,*g*

²⁶so that thy sons, whom thou didst
love, O·Lord, might learn
that it is not the production of
crops that feeds man,
but that thy word preserves those
who trust in thee.

²⁷For what was not destroyed by fire
was melted when simply warmed
by a fleeting ray of the sun,

²⁸to make it known that one must rise
before the sun to give thee
thanks,
and must pray to thee at the
dawning of the light;

²⁹for the hope of an ungrateful man

will melt like wintry frost,
and flow away like waste water.

17 Great are thy judgments and
hard to describe;
therefore uninstructed souls have
gone astray.

²For when lawless men supposed
that they held the holy nation
in their power,
they themselves lay as captives of
darkness and prisoners of long
night,
shut in under their roofs, exiles
from eternal providence.

³For thinking that in their secret
sins they were unobserved
behind a dark curtain of
forgetfulness,
they were scattered, terribly*h*
alarmed,
and appalled by specters.

⁴For not even the inner chamber
that held them protected them
from fear,
but terrifying sounds rang out
around them,
and dismal phantoms with gloomy
faces appeared.

⁵And no power of fire was able to
give light,
nor did the brilliant flames of the
stars
avail to illumine that hateful
night.

⁶Nothing was shining through to
them
except a dreadful, self-kindled
fire,
and in terror they deemed the
things which they saw
to be worse than that unseen
appearance.

e Gk *and it, ministering*
f Gk *this*
g Or *who made supplication*
h Or, with other authorities, *unobserved, they were
darkened behind a dark curtain of forgetfulness, terribly*

suited to the taste of each Israelite (vv. 20–21,25). **22–27:** The *fire* God sent executed his judgment; now he kept fire from melting *snow and ice* (a poetical expression for the manna; compare
19.21); now *a fleeting ray of the sun* melted it (Ex.16.21). **28–29:** Man should *rise* at dawn to
thank God, for God's blessing escapes the *ungrateful man* as fast as the rising sun melts *wintry
frost.*

    17.1–18.4: The contrast between the Egyptians and the Israelites during the plague of darkness.
God's judgment made *lawless men* (the Egyptians) terrified *captives of darkness*, unaided by

⁷The delusions of their magic art
lay humbled,
and their boasted wisdom was
scornfully rebuked.
⁸For those who promised to drive
off the fears and disorders of a
sick soul
were sick themselves with ridiculous
fear.
⁹For even if nothing disturbing
frightened them,
yet, scared by the passing of beasts
and the hissing of serpents,
¹⁰they perished in trembling fear,
refusing to look even at the air,
though it nowhere could be
avoided.
¹¹For wickedness is a cowardly thing,
condemned by its own
testimony;*i*
distressed by conscience, it has
always exaggerated*j* the
difficulties.
¹²For fear is nothing but surrender
of the helps that come from
reason;
¹³and the inner expectation of help,
being weak,
prefers ignorance of what causes
the torment.
¹⁴But throughout the night, which
was really powerless,
and which beset them from the
recesses of powerless Hades,
they all slept the same sleep,
¹⁵and now were driven by monstrous
specters,
and now were paralyzed by their
souls' surrender,
for sudden and unexpected fear
overwhelmed them.
¹⁶And whoever was there fell down,
and thus was kept shut up in a
prison not made of iron;
¹⁷for whether he was a farmer or a
shepherd
or a workman who toiled in the
wilderness,
he was seized, and endured the

inescapable fate;
for with one chain of darkness they
all were bound.
¹⁸Whether there came a whistling
wind,
or a melodious sound of birds in
wide-spreading branches,
or the rhythm of violently rushing
water,
¹⁹or the harsh crash of rocks hurled
down,
or the unseen running of leaping
animals,
or the sound of the most savage
roaring beasts,
or an echo thrown back from a
hollow of the mountains,
it paralyzed them with terror.
²⁰For the whole world was illumined
with brilliant light,
and was engaged in unhindered
work,
²¹while over those men alone heavy
night was spread,
an image of the darkness that was
destined to receive them;
but still heavier than darkness
were they to themselves.

18 But for thy holy ones there
was very great light.
Their enemies*k* heard their voices
but did not see their forms,
and counted them happy for not
having suffered,
²and were thankful that thy holy
ones,*k* though previously wronged,
were doing them no injury;
and they begged their pardon for
having been at variance with
them.*l*
³Therefore thou didst provide a
flaming pillar of fire
as a guide for thy people's*m*
unknown journey,
and a harmless sun for their
glorious wandering.

i The Greek text of this line is uncertain and probably
corrupt
j Other ancient authorities read *anticipated*   *k* Gk *they*
l The meaning of the Greek of this line is uncertain
m Gk *their*

---

their *magic art* or *boasted wisdom* (Ex.10.21–23). **18.1**: *Thy holy ones*, the Israelites. **3**: *Pillar
of fire . . . a harmless sun* (Ex.13.21–22). Most details here come from the author's imagination
or from Jewish tradition.

⁴For their enemies*n* deserved to be
  deprived of light and imprisoned
  in darkness,
those who had kept thy sons
  imprisoned,
through whom the imperishable
  light of the law was to be given
  to the world.

⁵When they had resolved to kill the
  babes of thy holy ones,
and one child had been exposed
  and rescued,
thou didst in punishment take
  away a multitude of their
  children;
and thou didst destroy them all
  together by a mighty flood.
⁶That night was made known
  beforehand to our fathers,
so that they might rejoice in sure
  knowledge of the oaths in which
  they trusted.
⁷The deliverance of the righteous
  and the destruction of their
  enemies
were expected by thy people.
⁸For by the same means by which
  thou didst punish our enemies
thou didst call us to thyself and
  glorify us.
⁹For in secret the holy children of
  good men offered sacrifices,
and with one accord agreed to the
  divine law,
that the saints would share alike
  the same things,
both blessings and dangers;
and already they were singing the
  praises of the fathers.*o*
¹⁰But the discordant cry of their
  enemies echoed back,
and their piteous lament for their
  children was spread abroad.
¹¹The slave was punished with the
  same penalty as the master,
and the common man suffered the

same loss as the king;
¹²and they all together, by the one
  form of death,
had corpses too many to count.
For the living were not sufficient
  even to bury them,
since in one instant their most
  valued children had been
  destroyed.
¹³For though they had disbelieved
  everything because of their
  magic arts,
yet, when their first-born were
  destroyed, they acknowledged
  thy people to be God's son.
¹⁴For while gentle silence enveloped
  all things,
and night in its swift course was
  now half gone,
¹⁵thy all-powerful word leaped from
  heaven, from the royal throne,
into the midst of the land that was
  doomed,
a stern warrior ¹⁶carrying the sharp
  sword of thy authentic command,
and stood and filled all things
  with death,
and touched heaven while standing
  on the earth.
¹⁷Then at once apparitions in dreadful
  dreams greatly troubled them,
and unexpected fears assailed them;
¹⁸and one here and another there,
  hurled down half dead,
made known why they were dying;
¹⁹for the dreams which disturbed
  them forewarned them of this,
so that they might not perish
  without knowing why they
  suffered.

²⁰The experience of death touched
  also the righteous,
and a plague came upon the
  multitude in the desert,

n Gk *those men*
o Other authorities read *dangers, the fathers already leading the songs of praise*

**18.5–25: The contrast between the visitation of death on the Egyptians and on the Israelites.
5:** *Resolved,* Ex.1.16. *Exposed and rescued,* Ex.2.1–10. *A multitude of their children,* the Egyptian
first-born (Ex.12.29). *Didst destroy them,* Ex.14.27–28. **6:** *That night,* the first Passover. **15:**
God's *all-powerful word,* as a *stern warrior, leaped from heaven* and carried out God's judgment
(this recalls Rev.19.13 rather than Jn.1.1–18). **20–25:** When *a plague* struck Israel *in the desert,*

but the wrath did not long
   continue.
21For a blameless man was quick to
   act as their champion;
he brought forward the shield of
   his ministry,
prayer and propitiation by incense;
he withstood the anger and put an
   end to the disaster,
showing that he was thy servant.
22He conquered the wrath*p* not by
   strength of body,
and not by force of arms,
but by his word he subdued the
   punisher,
appealing to the oaths and
   covenants given to our fathers.
23For when the dead had already
   fallen on one another in heaps,
he intervened and held back the
   wrath,
and cut off its way to the living.
24For upon his long robe the whole
   world was depicted,
and the glories of the fathers were
   engraved on the four rows of
   stones,
and thy majesty on the diadem
   upon his head.
25To these the destroyer yielded,
   these he*q* feared;
for merely to test the wrath was
   enough.

19 But the ungodly were assailed
   to the end by pitiless anger,
for God*r* knew in advance even
   their future actions,
2that, though they themselves had
   permitted*s* thy people to depart
and hastily sent them forth,
they would change their minds
   and pursue them.
3For while they were still busy at
   mourning,
and were lamenting at the graves
   of their dead,

they reached another foolish
   decision,
and pursued as fugitives those
   whom they had begged and
   compelled to depart.
4For the fate they deserved drew
   them on to this end,
and made them forget what had
   happened,
in order that they might fill up the
   punishment which their torments
   still lacked,
5and that thy people might
   experience*t* an incredible journey,
but they themselves might meet a
   strange death.

6For the whole creation in its nature
   was fashioned anew,
complying with thy commands,
that thy children*u* might be kept
   unharmed.
7The cloud was seen overshadowing
   the camp,
and dry land emerging where water
   had stood before,
an unhindered way out of the Red
   Sea,
and a grassy plain out of the raging
   waves,
8where those protected by thy hand
   passed through as one nation,
after gazing on marvelous wonders.
9For they ranged like horses,
and leaped like lambs,
praising thee, O Lord, who didst
   deliver them.
10For they still recalled the events
   of their sojourn,
how instead of producing animals
   the earth brought forth gnats,
and instead of fish the river spewed
   out vast numbers of frogs.
11Afterward they saw also a new

p Cn: Gk *multitude*   q Other authorities read *they*
r Gk *he*
s Other authorities read *had changed their minds to permit*
t Other authorities read *accomplish*   u Or *servants*

Aaron stopped the destroying angel of God from inflicting further death (Num.16.41–50).
24: From Ex. ch. 28 and Jewish tradition.
  19.1–21: God judged the Egyptians and delivered Israel at the Red Sea. 1–5: The Egyptians'
foolish decision to pursue Israel and enslave them again. **6–12:** God worked changes in nature
to deliver Israel. **7:** *Cloud,* Ex.13.21–22. *Dry land,* Ex.14.21–22. **10:** Ex. ch. 8. **11–12:** Num.

kind[v] of birds,
when desire led them to ask for
luxurious food;
[12]for, to give them relief, quails came
up from the sea.

[13]The punishments did not come
upon the sinners
without prior signs in the violence
of thunder,
for they justly suffered because of
their wicked acts;
for they practiced a more bitter
hatred of strangers.
[14]Others had refused to receive
strangers when they came to
them,
but these made slaves of guests
who were their benefactors.
[15]And not only so, but punishment
of some sort will come upon the
former
for their hostile reception of the
aliens;
[16]but the latter, after receiving them
with festal celebrations,
afflicted with terrible sufferings
those who had already shared the
same rights.
[17]They were stricken also with loss
of sight—
just as were those at the door of
the righteous man—
when, surrounded by yawning
darkness,

each tried to find the way through
his own door.

[18]For the elements changed[w] places
with one another,
as on a harp the notes vary the
nature of the rhythm,
while each note remains the same.[x]
This may be clearly inferred from
the sight of what took place.
[19]For land animals were transformed
into water creatures,
and creatures that swim moved
over to the land.
[20]Fire even in water retained its
normal power,
and water forgot its fire-quenching
nature.
[21]Flames, on the contrary, failed to
consume
the flesh of perishable creatures
that walked among them,
nor did they melt[y] the crystalline,
easily melted kind of heavenly
food.

[22]For in everything, O Lord, thou
hast exalted and glorified thy
people;
and thou hast not neglected to
help them at all times and in all
places.

v Or *production*
w Gk *changing*
x The meaning of this verse is uncertain
y Cn: Gk *nor could be melted*

---

ch. 11; compare Ex.16.13. **13–17:** The Egyptians treated *strangers* worse than did the men of Sodom, and so deserved greater *punishment*. **14:** *Others,* men of Sodom (Gen.19.1–11). *These,* the Egyptians. *Guests,* Israel was invited to Egypt (Gen.45.16–20). **17:** Gen.19.11; Ex.10.21–23. **18–21:** In the plagues and at the Red Sea nature and *animals* changed their customary action to effect God's redemptive purpose. **19:** *Land animals,* apparently a reference to Israel and their cattle crossing the Red Sea. *Creatures that swim,* frogs (Ex.8.1–7). **20–21:** 16.17. *Heavenly food,* the manna. **22:** The lesson of the preceding historical survey.

ECCLESIASTICUS, OR THE WISDOM
OF JESUS THE SON OF

SIRACH

Ecclesiasticus, or the Wisdom of Jesus the Son of Sirach, is the only book in the Apocrypha of which the name of the author is known (50.27). From internal hints we may infer that Joshua ben Sira (which is Hebrew for "Jesus the son of Sirach") was a Jewish scribe, that is, a professional teacher of the Old Testament law. The invitation in 51.23 suggests that the author conducted an academy, probably in Jerusalem, where he lectured to young men on ethical and religious subjects. About 180 B.C. this seasoned scribe and sage committed to writing the distilled wisdom that he had been accustomed to impart orally. Though the material is loosely arranged and the author almost desultory in passing from one subject to another, it appears that he intended to compose a work in two volumes (chs. 1–23 and 24–51), each of which commences with an encomium on wisdom.

Soon after 132 B.C. Ben Sira's grandson (see the Prologue) translated the original Hebrew text into Greek. About three or four centuries later a Syriac translation was made from a Hebrew text that differed considerably from that which underlies the Greek translation. Five fragmentary Hebrew manuscripts, which date from the medieval period, preserve a little more than two-thirds of the book. In the relatively few places where they overlap, these Hebrew manuscripts sometimes present quite different readings, and not infrequently a word in one manuscript is represented by a synonym in another. There is no unanimity of opinion concerning the importance of these Hebrew manuscripts; some scholars maintain that they are secondary, having been translated from an inferior form of the Greek, while others believe that they derive from Ben Sira's original Hebrew text, though embodying certain modifications adopted from the Greek and Syriac versions. In 1952 several tiny fragments of the Hebrew text, dating from about the time of Christ, were discovered in a cave near Qumran by the Dead Sea. This new evidence confirms the antiquity of the corresponding readings in the medieval Hebrew manuscripts.

In the Latin Church during the third century A.D. the book of Sirach came to be known as Ecclesiasticus, which means "The Church Book." This rather nondescript title was apparently meant to suggest that the book is the most important of the several deuterocanonical books which, though not in the Palestinian Jewish canon of the Scriptures, are accepted as inspired by the Roman Catholic Church.

Sirach is a significant link in the history of the development of ancient Jewish thought. It is the last great example of the type of wisdom literature represented in the Old Testament book of Proverbs, and the first specimen of that form of Judaism which subsequently developed into the rabbinical schools of the Pharisees and the Sadducees.

The Prologue

WHEREAS MANY GREAT TEACHINGS have been given to us through the law and the prophets and the others that followed them, on account of which we should praise Israel for instruction and wisdom; and since it is necessary not only that the readers themselves should acquire understanding but also that those who love learning should be able to help the outsiders by both speaking and writing, my grandfather Jesus, after devoting himself especially to the reading of the law and the prophets and the other books of our fathers, and after acquiring considerable proficiency in them, was himself also led to write something pertaining to instruction and wisdom, in order that, by becoming conversant with this also, those who love learning should make even greater progress in living according to the law.

You are urged therefore to read

with good will and attention, and to be indulgent*ᵃ* in cases where, despite our diligent labor in translating, we may seem to have rendered some phrases imperfectly. For what was originally expressed in Hebrew does not have exactly the same sense when translated into another language. Not only this work, but even the law itself, the prophecies, and the rest of the books differ not a little as originally expressed.

When I came to Egypt in the thirty-eighth year of the reign of Euergetes and stayed for some time, I found opportunity for no little instruction.*ᵇ* It seemed highly necessary that I should myself devote some pains and labor to the translation of the following book, using in that period of time great watchfulness and skill in order to complete and publish the book for those living abroad who wished to gain learning, being prepared in character to live according to the law.

All wisdom comes from the
Lord
  and is with him for ever.
²The sand of the sea, the drops of
  rain,
  and the days of eternity—who
  can count them?
³The height of heaven, the breadth
  of the earth,
  the abyss, and wisdom—who
  can search them out?
⁴Wisdom was created before all
  things,
  and prudent understanding from
  eternity.*ᶜ*
⁶The root of wisdom—to whom has
  it been revealed?

Her clever devices—who knows
  them?*ᵈ*
⁸There is One who is wise, greatly
  to be feared,
  sitting upon his throne.
⁹The Lord himself created wisdom;*ᵉ*
  he saw her and apportioned
  her,
  he poured her out upon all his
  works.
¹⁰She dwells with all flesh according
  to his gift,
  and he supplied her to those
  who love him.

¹¹The fear of the Lord is glory and
  exultation,
  and gladness and a crown of
  rejoicing.
¹²The fear of the Lord delights the
  heart,
  and gives gladness and joy and
  long life.
¹³With him who fears the Lord it
  will go well at the end;
  on the day of his death he will
  be blessed.

¹⁴To fear the Lord is the beginning
  of wisdom;
  she is created with the faithful
  in the womb.
¹⁵She made*ᶠ* among men an eternal
  foundation,
  and among their descendants
  she will be trusted.

a Or *Please read therefore with good will and attention, and be indulgent*
b Other authorities read *a copy affording no little instruction*
c Other authorities add as verse 5, *The source of wisdom is God's word in the highest heaven, and her ways are the eternal commandments.*
d Other authorities add as verse 7, *The knowledge of wisdom—to whom was it manifested? And her abundant experience—who has understood it?*
e Gk *her*
f Gk *made as nest*

1.1–10: **The origin of wisdom.** 1: The opening statement, *all wisdom comes from the Lord*, serves as a text on which the author's discourse is based (compare Pr.3.13–20). 2–3: Illustrations of the impossibility of fathoming the depths of divine wisdom (18.5; Rom.11.33). 3: *Height of heaven*, Ps.103.11. 8: *Sitting upon his throne*, Ps.47.8; Is.6.1. 9: *The Lord . . . created wisdom*, Pr.8.22–31. 10: *All flesh*, mankind in general. *According to his gift*, i.e. in measured quantity, but *to those who love him*, i.e. to Israel, he gave wisdom unstintedly.

1.11–20: **The fear of the Lord leads to obedience of the divine law.** In the wisdom literature the fear of the Lord is roughly equivalent to religion and piety (Job 28.28; Ps.111.10; Pr.1.7; 9.10). 12: *Long life*, v. 20; Pr.3.16. 15a: Syriac, "With faithful men is she, and she has been established

¹⁶To fear the Lord is wisdom's full
  measure;
  she satisfiesᵍ men with her
    fruits;
¹⁷she fills their whole house with
    desirable goods,
  and their storehouses with her
    produce.
¹⁸The fear of the Lord is the crown
    of wisdom,
  making peace and perfect health
    to flourish.
¹⁹He saw her and apportioned her;
  he rained down knowledge and
    discerning comprehension,
  and he exalted the glory of those
    who held her fast.
²⁰To fear the Lord is the root of
    wisdom,
  and her branches are long life.ʰ

²²Unrighteous anger cannot be
    justified,
  for a man's anger tips the scale
    to his ruin.
²³A patient man will endure until
    the right moment,
  and then joy will burst forth for
    him.
²⁴He will hide his words until the
    right moment,
  and the lips of many will tell of
    his good sense.
²⁵In the treasuries of wisdom are
    wise sayings,
  but godliness is an abomination
    to a sinner.
²⁶If you desire wisdom, keep the
    commandments,
  and the Lord will supply it for
    you.

²⁷For the fear of the Lord is wisdom
    and instruction,
  and he delights in fidelity and
    meekness.
²⁸Do not disobey the fear of the
    Lord;
  do not approach him with a
    divided mind.
²⁹Be not a hypocrite in men's sight,ⁱ
  and keep watch over your lips.
³⁰Do not exalt yourself lest you fall,
  and thus bring dishonor upon
    yourself.
The Lord will reveal your secrets
  and cast you down in the midst
    of the congregation,
because you did not come in the
    fear of the Lord,
  and your heart was full of deceit.

2 My son, if you come forward
    to serve the Lord,
  prepare yourself for temptation.ʲ
²Set your heart right and be
    steadfast,
  and do not be hasty in time of
    calamity.
³Cleave to him and do not depart,
  that you may be honored at the
    end of your life.
⁴Accept whatever is brought upon
    you,
  and in changes that humble you
    be patient.
⁵For gold is tested in the fire,
  and acceptable men in the
    furnace of humiliation.
⁶Trust in him, and he will help you;

g Gk *intoxicates*
h Other authorities add as verse 21, *The fear of the Lord
drives away sins; and where it abides, it will turn away
all anger.*
i Syr: Gk *in the mouths of men*   *j* Or *trials*

from eternity." **16:** *Her fruits*, Pr.8.19; 11.30. **17:** Wis.7.11. **20:** *Long life*, v. 12; Pr.4.10.
  1.22–30: Wisdom is shown in the exercise of patience, self-control, and humility. 22: Pr.29.22.
24: *Will hide his words*, a patient man is not hasty to speak. **26:** 19.20; Ec.12.13. **27:** Pr.15.33.
28: Obedience is the result of trust. *A divided mind*, 2.12; Jas.1.6–8; 4.8. **29:** *Hypocrite*, 32.15;
33.2. **30:** *Do not exalt yourself*, Mt.23.12. *In the . . . congregation*, 4.7; 7.7; Pr.5.14. *Full of
deceit*, 19.26.
  2.1–6: Serving God faithfully. 1: *My son*, the usual mode of a Jewish teacher's address to his
pupil (7.3; Pr.2.1; 3.1). *Prepare . . . for temptation*, Jas.1.2–4 and 12–15. **2:** *Do not be hasty*, i.e.
do not be impatient and fearful, but calm and self-possessed (Is.52.12; 1 Pet.4.12). **3:** *Cleave
to him*, to God (Dt.10.20). *At the end of your life*, 1.13. **4:** *Accept* divinely appointed adversities
(Job 2.10; Jas.1.2). *Be patient*, Jas.5.7–8. **5:** Pr.17.3; 27.21; Wis.3.6; Jas.1.12; 1 Pet.1.7.
6: Ps.37.3,5.

make your ways straight, and
  hope in him.

⁷You who fear the Lord, wait for
    his mercy;
  and turn not aside, lest you fall.
⁸You who fear the Lord, trust in
    him,
  and your reward will not fail;
⁹you who fear the Lord, hope for
    good things,
  for everlasting joy and mercy.
¹⁰Consider the ancient generations
    and see:
  who ever trusted in the Lord
    and was put to shame?
  Or who ever persevered in the fear
    of the Lord*ᵏ* and was
    forsaken?
  Or who ever called upon him
    and was overlooked?
¹¹For the Lord is compassionate and
    merciful;
  he forgives sins and saves in
    time of affliction.

¹²Woe to timid hearts and to slack
    hands,
  and to the sinner who walks
    along two ways!
¹³Woe to the faint heart, for it has
    no trust!
  Therefore it will not be sheltered.
¹⁴Woe to you who have lost your
    endurance!
  What will you do when the
    Lord punishes you?
¹⁵Those who fear the Lord will not
    disobey his words,
  and those who love him will
    keep his ways.

¹⁶Those who fear the Lord will seek
    his approval,
  and those who love him will be
    filled with the law.
¹⁷Those who fear the Lord will
    prepare their hearts,
  and will humble themselves
    before him.
¹⁸Let us fall*ˡ* into the hands of the
    Lord,
  but not into the hands of men;
  for as his majesty is,
    so also is his mercy.

3 Listen to me your father, O
  children;
  and act accordingly, that you
    may be kept in safety.
²For the Lord honored the father
    above the children,
  and he confirmed the right of
    the mother over her sons.
³Whoever honors his father atones
    for sins,
⁴ and whoever glorifies his mother
    is like one who lays up
    treasure.
⁵Whoever honors his father will be
    gladdened by his own children,
  and when he prays he will be
    heard.
⁶Whoever glorifies his father will
    have long life,
  and whoever obeys the Lord
    will refresh his mother;
⁷ he will serve his parents as his
    masters.*ᵐ*
⁸Honor your father by word and
    deed,

k Gk *of him*   *l* Gk *We shall fall*
m In other authorities this line is preceded by *Whoever
fears the Lord will honor his father,*

2.7–11: The reward of those who fear the Lord. 7: *Wait for his mercy,* Jdt.8.17. 9: *Everlasting joy,* Is.35.10; 51.11; 61.7. 10: Ps.37.25. 11: *Compassionate and merciful,* Ex.34.6–7; Ps.103.8–9; 145.8; Jon.4.2.
   2.12–14: A threefold woe against the unfaithful. 12: *Timid hearts,* 22.18; Dt.20.8. *Slack hands,* 25.23; Heb.12.12. 14: *Endurance,* compare v. 1.
   2.15–18: Characteristics of those who fear the Lord. 15: Jn.14.15; 15.10. 16: *Will be filled with the law,* will be in heart and mind saturated with the Mosaic statutes (32.15). 17: *Will humble themselves,* 3.18; 7.17; 18.21. 18: 2 Sam.24.14.
   3.1–16: Filial duty and its reward (Ex.20.12; Dt.5.16; Eph.6.1–3). In accord with the Jewish doctrine that the observance of the Mosaic law is meritorious, Sirach teaches that the keeping of the commandment to honor one's parents (Ex.20.12) *atones for sins* (vv. 14–15); contrast the teaching in Lk.17.10. 4: *Lays up treasure,* Mt.6.20. 6: *Will refresh,* will give rest from

that a blessing from him may
come upon you.
⁹For a father's blessing strengthens
the houses of the children,
but a mother's curse uproots
their foundations.

¹⁰Do not glorify yourself by
dishonoring your father,
for your father's dishonor is no
glory to you.
¹¹For a man's glory comes from
honoring his father,
and it is a disgrace for children
not to respect their mother.
¹²O son, help your father in his old
age,
and do not grieve him as long
as he lives;
¹³even if he is lacking in
understanding, show
forbearance;
in all your strength do not
despise him.
¹⁴For kindness to a father will not
be forgotten,
and against your sins it will be
credited to you;
¹⁵in the day of your affliction it will
be remembered in your favor;
as frost in fair weather, your sins
will melt away.
¹⁶Whoever forsakes his father is like
a blasphemer,
and whoever angers his mother
is cursed by the Lord.

¹⁷My son, perform your tasks in
meekness;
then you will be loved by those
whom God accepts.
¹⁸The greater you are, the more you
must humble yourself;
so you will find favor in the sight
of the Lord."
²⁰For great is the might of the Lord;
he is glorified by the humble.
²¹Seek not what is too difficult for
you,
nor investigate what is beyond
your power.
²²Reflect upon what has been
assigned to you,
for you do not need what is
hidden.
²³Do not meddle in what is beyond
your tasks,
for matters too great for human
understanding have been shown
you.
²⁴For their hasty judgment has led
many astray,
and wrong opinion has caused
their thoughts to slip."

²⁶A stubborn mind will be afflicted
at the end,
and whoever loves danger will
perish by it.
²⁷A stubborn mind will be burdened
by troubles,
and the sinner will heap sin
upon sin.
²⁸The affliction of the proud has no
healing,
for a plant of wickedness has
taken root in him.
²⁹The mind of the intelligent man
will ponder a parable,
and an attentive ear is the wise
man's desire.

n Other authorities add as verse 19, *Many are lofty and
renowned, but to the meek he reveals his secrets.*
o Other authorities add as verse 25, *If you have no eyes
you will be without light; if you lack knowledge do not
profess to have it.*

anxieties (Pr.29.17). **9**: Hebrew, "The blessing of a father establishes the root, but the curse of
a mother uproots the young plant." **10**: *Your father's dishonor,* i.e. the dishonor brought
upon a father by his son. **13**: Or, "Even if his mind fail, be considerate with him." **14–15**: Compare v. 3. *Will not be forgotten . . . will be credited . . . will be remembered* by God. **16**: Lev.20.9;
Dt.27.16; Pr.19.26; 30.11,17. *Forsakes,* Hebrew and Syriac, "despises."

3.17–24: On humility. **17**: Hebrew, "My son, when in prosperity walk with humility, and
you will be loved more than a giver of gifts." **18**: Mt.20.26–28; Phil.2.3–8; 1 Pet.5.5–6. **21**:
Ps.131.1; Jer.45.5; Rom.12.16. **22**: Dt.29.29. **23**: 1 Cor.2.9. **24**: Or, "their conceit has misled
many," referring perhaps to speculations of Greek philosophers.

3.26–31: Retribution and reward. **26**: Pr.28.14; Rom.2.5. **28**: *Has no healing,* i.e. adversity
works no reformation in *the proud.* **29**: Hebrew, "the ear that listens to wisdom rejoices."

30 Water extinguishes a blazing fire:
so almsgiving atones for sin.
31 Whoever requites favors gives
thought to the future;
at the moment of his falling he
will find support.

4 My son, deprive not the poor
of his living,
and do not keep needy eyes
waiting.
2 Do not grieve the one who is
hungry,
nor anger a man in want.
3 Do not add to the troubles of an
angry mind,
nor delay your gift to a beggar.
4 Do not reject an afflicted suppliant,
nor turn your face away from
the poor.
5 Do not avert your eye from the
needy,
nor give a man occasion to
curse you;
6 for if in bitterness of soul he calls
down a curse upon you,
his Creator will hear his
prayer.

7 Make yourself beloved in the
congregation;
bow your head low to a great
man.
8 Incline your ear to the poor,
and answer him peaceably and
gently.
9 Deliver him who is wronged from
the hand of the wrongdoer;
and do not be fainthearted in
judging a case.
10 Be like a father to orphans,
and instead of a husband to
their mother;
you will then be like a son of the
Most High,
and he will love you more than
does your mother.

11 Wisdom exalts her sons
and gives help to those who
seek her.
12 Whoever loves her loves life,
and those who seek her early
will be filled with joy.
13 Whoever holds her fast will obtain
glory,
and the Lord will bless the place
she[p] enters.
14 Those who serve her will minister
to the Holy One;[q]
the Lord loves those who love
her.
15 He who obeys her will judge the
nations,
and whoever gives heed to her
will dwell secure.
16 If he has faith in her he will obtain
her;
and his descendants will remain
in possession of her.
17 For at first she will walk with him
on tortuous paths,
she will bring fear and cowardice
upon him,
and will torment him by her
discipline
until she trusts him,
and she will test him with her
ordinances.
18 Then she will come straight
back to him and gladden
him,
and will reveal her secrets to
him.
19 If he goes astray she will forsake
him,
and hand him over to his
ruin.

p Or *he*
q Or *at the holy place*

30: That *almsgiving atones for sin* accords with the Jewish doctrine of the efficacy of good works (Tob.4.7–11; contrast Gal.2.16; Eph.2.9); see also 7.10 n.; 29.11 n.

4.1–10: Duties toward the poor (7.32–36; 29.8–13; Dt.15.7–11). **1:** *Do not keep needy eyes waiting*, when they look for help. **4:** Mt.5.42. **6:** Ex.22.23; Dt.15.9; Pr.17.5. **7:** *Make yourself beloved*, by giving alms to the poor. **7:** *A great man*, Hebrew, "the ruler of the city." **10:** Job 29.16; 31.18; Ps.82.3; Is.1.17; Jas.1.27.

4.11–19: The rewards of wisdom. 11: 6.27. **12:** Pr.3.16–17; 8.17; Wis.8.17–18. **14–15:** The disciples of wisdom are like priests and judges. **18:** *Secrets*, 39.7; Job 11.6; Dan.2.21–22.

²⁰Observe the right time, and beware
of evil;ʳ
and do not bring shame on
yourself.
²¹For there is a shame which brings
sin,
and there is a shame which is
glory and favor.
²²Do not show partiality, to your
own harm,
or deference, to your downfall.
²³Do not refrain from speaking at
the crucial time,ˢ
and do not hide your wisdom.ᵗ
²⁴For wisdom is known through
speech,
and education through the words
of the tongue.
²⁵Never speak against the truth,
but be mindful of your
ignorance.
²⁶Do not be ashamed to confess your
sins,
and do not try to stop the current
of a river.
²⁷Do not subject yourself to a foolish
fellow,
nor show partiality to a ruler.
²⁸Strive even to death for the truth
and the Lord God will fight for
you.

²⁹Do not be reckless in your speech,
or sluggish and remiss in your
deeds.
³⁰Do not be like a lion in your home,
nor be a faultfinder with your
servants.
³¹Let not your hand be extended to
receive,
but withdrawn when it is time
to repay.

5 Do not set your heart on your
wealth,

nor say, "I have enough."
²Do not follow your inclination and
strength,
walking according to the desires
of your heart.
³Do not say, "Who will have power
over me?"
for the Lord will surely punish
you.

⁴Do not say, "I sinned, and what
happened to me?"
for the Lord is slow to anger.
⁵Do not be so confident of
atonement
that you add sin to sin.
⁶Do not say, "His mercy is great,
he will forgiveᵘ the multitude of
my sins,"
for both mercy and wrath are with
him,
and his anger rests on sinners.
⁷Do not delay to turn to the Lord,
nor postpone it from day to
day;
for suddenly the wrath of the Lord
will go forth,
and at the time of punishment
you will perish.

⁸Do not depend on dishonest
wealth,
for it will not benefit you in the
day of calamity.
⁹Do not winnow with every wind,
nor follow every path:
the double-tongued sinner does
that.
¹⁰Be steadfast in your understanding,
and let your speech be consistent.

r Or *an evil man*
s Cn: Gk *at a time of salvation*
t So some Gk Mss and Heb Syr Vg: other Gk Mss omit
and do not hide your wisdom
u Heb: Gk *he* (or *it*) *will atone for*

4.20–5.3: Precepts for everyday life. 22: That is, a man should not be afraid of offending another so long as he does what is right; even if it results in his *own harm*, he will have no cause for shame. **26:** That is, it is as futile to hide one's sins from God as to try to stop a river from flowing. **30:** *Like a lion*, wild, hasty, relentless, destructive. **31:** Compare Acts 20.35. **5.1:** *Enough*, Hebrew, "the power." **3:** Ps.12.4.

5.4–7: Warnings against presuming on God's mercy. 4: Ec.8.11. **5:** That is, do not continue sinning, *confident of* God's forgiveness. **6:** God's *mercy and wrath*, 16.11–12. **7:** *Postpone it*, i.e. postpone repentance.

5.8–6.1: Honesty and sincerity. 5.8: Pr.10.2; 11.4; Ezek.7.19. **9:** A condemnation of time-

¹¹Be quick to hear,
  and be deliberate in answering.
¹²If you have understanding, answer
    your neighbor;
  but if not, put your hand on
    your mouth.
¹³Glory and dishonor come from
    speaking,
  and a man's tongue is his
    downfall.

¹⁴Do not be called a slanderer,
  and do not lie in ambush with
    your tongue;
for shame comes to the thief,
  and severe condemnation to the
    double-tongued.
¹⁵In great or small matters do not
    act amiss,

𝟨 and do not become an enemy
    instead of a friend;
  for a bad name incurs shame
  and reproach:
  so fares the double-tongued
    sinner.

²Do not exalt yourself through your
    soul's counsel,
  lest your soul be torn in pieces
    like a bull.ᵛ
³You will devour your leaves and
    destroy your fruit,
  and will be left like a withered
    tree.
⁴An evil soul will destroy him who
    has it,
  and make him the laughingstock
    of his enemies.

⁵A pleasant voice multiplies friends,
  and a gracious tongue multiplies
    courtesies.
⁶Let those that are at peace with
    you be many,

but let your advisers be one in a
    thousand.
⁷When you gain a friend, gain him
    through testing,
  and do not trust him hastily.
⁸For there is a friend who is such
    at his own convenience,
  but will not stand by you in
    your day of trouble.
⁹And there is a friend who changes
    into an enemy,
  and will disclose a quarrel to
    your disgrace.
¹⁰And there is a friend who is a table
    companion,
  but will not stand by you in
    your day of trouble.
¹¹In your prosperity he will make
    himself your equal,
  and be bold with your
    servants;
¹²but if you are brought low he will
    turn against you,
  and will hide himself from your
    presence.
¹³Keep yourself far from your
    enemies,
  and be on guard toward your
    friends.

¹⁴A faithful friend is a sturdy shelter:
  he that has found one has found
    a treasure.
¹⁵There is nothing so precious as a
    faithful friend,
  and no scales can measure his
    excellence.
¹⁶A faithful friend is an elixir of
    life;
  and those who fear the Lord will
    find him.
¹⁷Whoever fears the Lord directs his
    friendship aright,

ᵛ The meaning of the Greek of this verse is obscure

servers, who speak according to expediency rather than truth. **11**: Jas.1.19. **12**: *Hand on . . . mouth*, Job 21.5; 29.9; 40.4. **13**: Pr.18.21; Mt.12.37.

6.2–4: Self-control; a warning against lustful passions. Hebrew (freely), "Be not a slave to your passions, lest they consume your strength; they will eat up your leaves [figurative for youth], and destroy your fruit [offspring], and leave you as a dried-up tree. For unbridled passion destroys its possessor, and makes him the sport of his enemies."

6.5–17: True and false friendship. 5: 20.13; Pr.15.1. **6–7:** Care in choosing friends. **8–13:** False friendship. **9:** Pr.25.9–10. **10:** 37.5. **11b:** Hebrew (one manuscript) and Syriac, "and when you are in adversity, he will desert you." **13:** *Friends*, i.e. false friends. **14–17:** True

for as he is, so is his neighbor also.

[18]My son, from your youth up choose
instruction,
and until you are old you will
keep finding wisdom.
[19]Come to her like one who plows
and sows,
and wait for her good harvest.
For in her service you will toil a
little while,
and soon you will eat of her
produce.
[20]She seems very harsh to the
uninstructed;
a weakling will not remain with
her.
[21]She will weigh him down like a
heavy testing stone,
and he will not be slow to cast
her off.
[22]For wisdom is like her name,
and is not manifest to many.

[23]Listen, my son, and accept my
judgment;
do not reject my counsel.
[24]Put your feet into her fetters,
and your neck into her collar.
[25]Put your shoulder under her and
carry her,
and do not fret under her bonds.
[26]Come to her with all your soul,
and keep her ways with all your
might.
[27]Search out and seek, and she will
become known to you;
and when you get hold of her,
do not let her go.
[28]For at last you will find the rest
she gives,
and she will be changed into joy
for you.

[29]Then her fetters will become for
you a strong protection,
and her collar a glorious robe.
[30]Her yoke[w] is a golden ornament,
and her bonds are a cord of blue.
[31]You will wear her like a glorious robe,
and put her on like a crown of
gladness.

[32]If you are willing, my son, you will
be taught,
and if you apply yourself you
will become clever.
[33]If you love to listen you will gain
knowledge,
and if you incline your ear you
will become wise.
[34]Stand in the assembly of the elders.
Who is wise? Cleave to him.
[35]Be ready to listen to every[x]
narrative,
and do not let wise proverbs
escape you.
[36]If you see an intelligent man, visit
him early;
let your foot wear out his
doorstep.
[37]Reflect on the statutes of the Lord,
and meditate at all times on his
commandments.
It is he who will give insight to[y]
your mind,
and your desire for wisdom will
be granted.

7 Do no evil, and evil will never
befall you.
2 Stay away from wrong, and it
will turn away from you.
[3]My son, do not sow the furrows of
injustice,

w Heb: Gk *Upon her*
x Heb: Gk adds *divine*
y Heb: Gk *will confirm*

---

friends are beyond value, and are the gift of God. **17b:** That is, *his neighbor* is as dear to him
as he is to himself.
    6.18–37: The blessings of wisdom. 18: 22.6. **19:** *Wait for the harvest,* Jas.5.7–8. **22:** *Wisdom
is like her name,* Hebrew, "Discipline [*musar*] is like her name," perhaps a play on the Hebrew
participle *musar,* meaning "removed, withdrawn"; hence the path of discipline *is not manifest
to many.* **25:** *Put your shoulder under her,* wisdom is like a yoke. *Under her bonds,* Hebrew,
"at her counsels." **27:** *Do not let her go,* Pr.4.13. **28:** *Rest,* compare Mt.11.29. **30:** *A cord of
blue,* Num.15.38. **31:** *A crown of gladness,* 1.11; 15.6; Pr.4.9; 16.31. **34:** 8.9. **37:** The law
(*statutes, commandments*) is the source of wisdom. *Meditate,* Jos.1.8; Ps.1.2.
    7.1–3: The avoidance of sin. 3: Job 4.8; Pr.22.8; Gal.6.8. *Sevenfold,* 35.11.

and you will not reap a sevenfold
crop.

⁴Do not seek from the Lord the
highest office,
nor the seat of honor from the
king.
⁵Do not assert your righteousness
before the Lord,
nor display your wisdom before
the king.
⁶Do not seek to become a judge,
lest you be unable to remove
iniquity,
lest you be partial to a powerful man,
and thus put a blot on your
integrity.
⁷Do not offend against the public,
and do not disgrace yourself
among the people.

⁸Do not commit a sin twice;
even for one you will not go
unpunished.
⁹Do not say, "He will consider the
multitude of my gifts,
and when I make an offering to
the Most High God he will
accept it."
¹⁰Do not be fainthearted in your
prayer,
nor neglect to give alms.

¹¹Do not ridicule a man who is bitter
in soul,
for there is One who abases and
exalts.
¹²Do not devise* a lie against your
brother,
nor do the like to a friend.
¹³Refuse to utter any lie,

for the habit of lying serves no
good.
¹⁴Do not prattle in the assembly of
the elders,
nor repeat yourself in your prayer.

¹⁵Do not hate toilsome labor,
or farm work, which were
created by the Most High.
¹⁶Do not count yourself among the
crowd of sinners;
remember that wrath does not
delay.
¹⁷Humble yourself greatly,
for the punishment of the
ungodly is fire and worms.*

¹⁸Do not exchange a friend for money,
or a real brother for the gold of
Ophir.
¹⁹Do not deprive yourself of a wise
and good wife,
for her charm is worth more
than gold.
²⁰Do not abuse a servant who
performs his work faithfully,
or a hired laborer who devotes
himself to you.
²¹Let your soul love* an intelligent
servant;
do not withhold from him his
freedom.

²²Do you have cattle? Look after them;
if they are profitable to you, keep
them.
²³Do you have children? Discipline
them,

z Heb: Gk *plow*
a The Hebrew text reads *for the expectation of man is worms*
b The Hebrew text reads *Love like yourself*

7.4–7: Conduct in public life. 4: Pr.25.6–7. **6:** *A judge,* Hebrew, "a ruler."
7.8–10: A warning against presuming upon God's forgiveness without amendment of life. **10:** According to Jewish teaching, *to give alms* is the highest form of righteousness (see 3.30 n. and 29.11 n.; compare Mt.6.1).
7.11–17: Precepts for right conduct of life. 11: *Bitter in soul,* because of poverty (4.2; Pr.17.5). *Abases and exalts,* 1 Sam.2.7; Lk.1.52–53. **14:** Mt.6.7. **15:** Pr.24.27. **16:** *Wrath,* 5.7. **17:** *Humble,* 2.17. A motive for humility is the thought that the body is destined to corruption. *Fire and worms,* Is.66.24; Jdt.16.17; Mk.9.48.
7.18–21: Duties to a friend, a wife, and a servant. 18: *Ophir,* 1 Kg.9.28; Job 22.24; 28.16. **19:** *Do not deprive,* Hebrew, "reject not," referring to divorce (v. 26). **21:** After six years of service a Hebrew slave was entitled to *freedom* (Ex.21.2; Lev.25.39–43; Dt.15.12–15).
7.22–25: Duties to cattle, and to children. 23: Hebrew (one manuscript) and Syriac, "Do

and make them obedient[c] from
their youth.
²⁴Do you have daughters? Be
concerned for their chastity,[d]
and do not show yourself too
indulgent with them.
²⁵Give a daughter in marriage; you
will have finished a great task.
But give her to a man of
understanding.

²⁶If you have a wife who pleases
you,[e] do not cast her out;
but do not trust yourself to one
whom you detest.
²⁷With all your heart honor your
father,
and do not forget the birth pangs
of your mother.
²⁸Remember that through your
parents[f] you were born;
and what can you give back to
them that equals their gift to
you?

²⁹With all your soul fear the Lord,
and honor his priests.
³⁰With all your might love your Maker,
and do not forsake his ministers.
³¹Fear the Lord and honor the priest,
and give him his portion, as is
commanded you:
the first fruits, the guilt offering,
the gift of the shoulders,
the sacrifice of sanctification,
and the first fruits of the holy
things.

³²Stretch forth your hand to the poor,

so that your blessing may be
complete.
³³Give graciously to all the living,
and withhold not kindness from
the dead.
³⁴Do not fail those who weep,
but mourn with those who
mourn.
³⁵Do not shrink from visiting a sick
man,
because for such deeds you will
be loved.
³⁶In all you do, remember the end
of your life,
and then you will never sin.

8 Do not contend with a powerful
man,
lest you fall into his hands.
²Do not quarrel with a rich man,
lest his resources outweigh yours;
for gold has ruined many,
and has perverted the minds of
kings.
³Do not argue with a chatterer,
nor heap wood on his fire.

⁴Do not jest with an ill-bred person,
lest your ancestors be disgraced.
⁵Do not reproach a man who is
turning away from sin;
remember that we all deserve
punishment.
⁶Do not disdain a man when he is old,
for some of us are growing old.
⁷Do not rejoice over any one's death;
remember that we all must die.

c Gk *bend their necks*   *d* Gk *body*
e Heb Syr omit *who pleases you*   *f* Gk *them*

---

you have sons? Correct them, and choose wives for them while they are young." **24:** 26.10–11;
42.9–11. **25:** Marriages were arranged by the father (see v. 23 n. and 36.21 n.).
   7.26–28: Duties to one's wife and parents. 26: *Do not cast her out,* see v. 19 n. **27–28:** An
expansion of Ex.20.12.
   7.29–31: Duties to God and to the priesthood. In supporting and showing honor to God's
ministers one indirectly honors God himself. **31:** *As is commanded,* Ex.29.27; Lev.7.31–34;
Num.18.8–20; Dt.18.3.
   7.32–36: Various duties: to give alms, respect the dead, comfort mourners, visit the sick.
32: Dt.14.28–29. **33b:** Hebrew, "deny not respect to the dead," by providing honorable burial
(38.16–18; Tob.1.17) and showing solicitude for their dependents. **34:** Rom.12.15. **35:** Mt.
25.36. **36:** Ec.11.9–12.7.
   8.1–19: Warnings concerning various kinds of men. 1–3: A prudent man will avoid quarreling
with the *powerful,* the *rich,* and the *chatterer.* **2:** *Lest his resources outweigh yours,* as a bribe in
perverting *the minds of kings.* **4:** *Be disgraced,* by his railing. **5–7:** Have respect for the penitent,

⁸Do not slight the discourse of the
　　sages,
　　but busy yourself with their
　　　maxims;
　　because from them you will gain
　　　instruction
　　and learn how to serve great men.
⁹Do not disregard the discourse of
　　the aged,
　　for they themselves learned from
　　　their fathers;
　　because from them you will gain
　　　understanding
　　and learn how to give an answer
　　　in time of need.

¹⁰Do not kindle the coals of a sinner,
　　lest you be burned in his flaming
　　　fire.
¹¹Do not get up and leave an
　　insolent fellow,
　　lest he lie in ambush against
　　　your words.
¹²Do not lend to a man who is
　　stronger than you;
　　but if you do lend anything, be
　　　as one who has lost it.
¹³Do not give surety beyond your
　　means,
　　but if you give surety, be con-
　　　cerned as one who must pay.

¹⁴Do not go to law against a judge,
　　for the decision will favor him
　　　because of his standing.
¹⁵Do not travel on the road with a
　　foolhardy fellow,
　　lest he be burdensome to you;
　　for he will act as he pleases,
　　and through his folly you will
　　　perish with him.
¹⁶Do not fight with a wrathful man,
　　and do not cross the wilderness
　　　with him;
　　because blood is as nothing in his
　　　sight,

and where no help is at hand,
　　he will strike you down.
¹⁷Do not consult with a fool,
　　for he will not be able to keep
　　　a secret.
¹⁸In the presence of a stranger do
　　nothing that is to be kept secret,
　　for you do not know what he
　　　will divulge.*g*
¹⁹Do not reveal your thoughts to
　　every one,
　　lest you drive away your good
　　　luck.*h*

9 Do not be jealous of the wife
　　of your bosom,
　　and do not teach her an evil
　　　lesson to your own hurt.
²Do not give yourself to a woman
　　so that she gains mastery over
　　　your strength.
³Do not go to meet a loose woman,
　　lest you fall into her snares.
⁴Do not associate with a woman
　　singer,
　　lest you be caught in her intrigues.
⁵Do not look intently at a virgin,
　　lest you stumble and incur
　　　penalties for her.
⁶Do not give yourself to harlots
　　lest you lose your inheritance.
⁷Do not look around in the streets
　　of a city,
　　nor wander about in its deserted
　　　sections.
⁸Turn away your eyes from a shapely
　　woman,
　　and do not look intently at
　　　beauty belonging to another;
　　many have been misled by a
　　　woman's beauty,
　　and by it passion is kindled like
　　　a fire.
⁹Never dine with another man's wife,

g Or *it will bring forth*
h Heb: Gk *let him not return a favor to you*

---

the aged, and the departed. **8–9:** Learn from men of experience. **10–11:** Warnings against associating with sinners. **12–13:** Warnings concerning lending, and giving *surety*. **14–19:** Warnings concerning various social relationships.

　　9.1–9: Warnings concerning women. 1: *Jealous,* Num.5.14–15. **2:** Pr.31.3. **3:** Pr.23.27. **5:** Job 31.1; Mt.5.28. **6:** Pr.29.3; Lk.15.13. **8:** *Belonging to another* man's wife. **9:** *Into destruction* refers to the adulterer's punishment (Lev.20.10; Dt.22.22).

nor revel with her at wine;
lest your heart turn aside to her,
and in blood[i] you be plunged
into destruction.

[10]Forsake not an old friend,
for a new one does not compare
with him.
A new friend is like new wine;
when it has aged you will drink
it with pleasure.

[11]Do not envy the honors of a
sinner,
for you do not know what his
end will be.
[12]Do not delight in what pleases the
ungodly;
remember that they will not be
held guiltless as long as they
live.

[13]Keep far from a man who has the
power to kill,
and you will not be worried by
the fear of death.
But if you approach him, make no
misstep,
lest he rob you of your life.
Know that you are walking in the
midst of snares,
and that you are going about
on the city battlements.

[14]As much as you can, aim to know
your neighbors,
and consult with the wise.
[15]Let your conversation be with men
of understanding,
and let all your discussion be
about the law of the Most
High.
[16]Let righteous men be your dinner
companions,
and let your glorying be in the
fear of the Lord.
[17]A work will be praised for the skill
of the craftsmen;

so a people's leader is proved
wise by his words.
[18]A babbler is feared in his city,
and the man who is reckless in
speech will be hated.

[10] A wise magistrate will educate
his people,
and the rule of an understanding
man will be well ordered.
[2]Like the magistrate of the people,
so are his officials;
and like the ruler of the city, so
are all its inhabitants.
[3]An undisciplined king will ruin his
people,
but a city will grow through the
understanding of its rulers.
[4]The government of the earth is in
the hands of the Lord,
and over it he will raise up the
right man for the time.
[5]The success of a man is in the
hands of the Lord,
and he confers his honor upon
the person of the scribe.[j]

[6]Do not be angry with your neighbor
for any injury,
and do not attempt anything by
acts of insolence.
[7]Arrogance is hateful before the
Lord and before men,
and injustice is outrageous to
both.
[8]Sovereignty passes from nation to
nation
on account of injustice and
insolence and wealth.
[9]How can he who is dust and ashes
be proud?
for even in life his bowels
decay.[k]
[10]A long illness baffles the physician;[l]
the king of today will die
tomorrow.

i Heb: Gk *by your spirit*
j Or *the official*
k Heb: Gk is obscure
l Heb Vg: Gk is uncertain

9.10–18: Precepts concerning various kinds of persons. 11: Ps.37.1; 73.3 and 17. **15b**: Ps.1.2.
16b: 10.22.
 10.1–5: Concerning rulers. 4: Pr.8.15–16; Wis.6.1–3. *For the* right *time.*
 10.6–18: Concerning arrogance and pride, especially in rulers (Pr.16.18). **6**: Lev.19.17;

¹¹For when a man is dead,
　　he will inherit creeping things,
　　and wild beasts, and worms.
¹²The beginning of man's pride is to
　　depart from the Lord;
　　his heart has forsaken his
　　Maker.
¹³For the beginning of pride is sin,
　　and the man who clings to it
　　pours out abominations.
　Therefore the Lord brought upon
　　them extraordinary afflictions,
　and destroyed them utterly.
¹⁴The Lord has cast down the thrones
　　of rulers,
　　and has seated the lowly in their
　　place.
¹⁵The Lord has plucked up the roots
　　of the nations,ᵐ
　　and has planted the humble in
　　their place.
¹⁶The Lord has overthrown the lands
　　of the nations,
　　and has destroyed them to the
　　foundations of the earth.
¹⁷He has removed some of them and
　　destroyed them,
　　and has extinguished the memory
　　of them from the earth.
¹⁸Pride was not created for men,
　　nor fierce anger for those born of
　　women.

¹⁹What race is worthy of honor?
　　The human race.
　What race is worthy of honor?
　　Those who fear the Lord.
　What race is unworthy of honor?
　　The human race.
　What race is unworthy of honor?
　　Those who transgress the
　　commandments.
²⁰Among brothers their leader is
　　worthy of honor,
　　and those who fear the Lord are
　　worthy of honor in his eyes.ⁿ

²²The rich, and the eminent, and the
　　poor—
　　their glory is the fear of the
　　Lord.
²³It is not right to despise an
　　intelligent poor man,
　　nor is it proper to honor a sinful
　　man.
²⁴The nobleman, and the judge, and
　　the ruler will be honored,
　　but none of them is greater than
　　the man who fears the Lord.
²⁵Free men will be at the service of
　　a wise servant,
　　and a man of understanding will
　　not grumble.

²⁶Do not make a display of your wis-
　　dom when you do your work,
　　nor glorify yourself at a time
　　when you are in want.
²⁷Better is a man who works and has
　　an abundance of everything,
　　than one who goes about
　　boasting, but lacks bread.
²⁸My son, glorify yourself with
　　humility,
　　and ascribe to yourself honor
　　according to your worth.
²⁹Who will justify the man that sins
　　against himself?
　And who will honor the man
　　that dishonors his own life?
³⁰A poor man is honored for his
　　knowledge,
　　while a rich man is honored for
　　his wealth.
³¹A man honored in poverty, how
　　much more in wealth!
　　And a man dishonored in wealth,
　　how much more in poverty!

‖ The wisdom of a humble man
‖ will lift up his head,

m Some authorities read *proud nations*
n Other authorities add as verse 21, *The fear of the Lord
is the beginning of acceptance; obduracy and pride are
the beginning of rejection.*

Mt.18.21. **11:** Job 17.14; Is.14.11. **12:** Dt.8.14. **14:** 1 Sam.2.8; Lk.1.52. **16:** Is.40.15–17;
Wis.11.21–22.
　　10.19–25: True honor. 19: Jer.9.23–24; 1 Cor.1.26–31; 2 Cor.10.17; Jas.1.9. **23:** Jas.2.1–4.
25: Pr.17.2.
　　10.26–11.1: Wrong and right estimation of self. 27: Pr.12.9. **11.1:** 39.4; compare Gen.41.40;
Dan.6.3.

and will seat him among the
great.

[2]Do not praise a man for his good
looks,
nor loathe a man because of his
appearance.
[3]The bee is small among flying
creatures,
but her product is the best of
sweet things.
[4]Do not boast about wearing fine
clothes,
nor exalt yourself in the day that
you are honored;
for the works of the Lord are
wonderful,
and his works are concealed
from men.
[5]Many kings have had to sit on the
ground,
but one who was never thought
of has worn a crown.
[6]Many rulers have been greatly
disgraced,
and illustrious men have been
handed over to others.

[7]Do not find fault before you
investigate;
first consider, and then
reprove.
[8]Do not answer before you have
heard,
nor interrupt a speaker in the
midst of his words.
[9]Do not argue about a matter which
does not concern you,
nor sit with sinners when they
judge a case.

[10]My son, do not busy yourself with
many matters;
if you multiply activities you will
not go unpunished,
and if you pursue you will not
overtake,
and by fleeing you will not
escape.
[11]There is a man who works, and
toils, and presses on,
but is so much the more in want.
[12]There is another who is slow and
needs help,
who lacks strength and abounds
in poverty;
but the eyes of the Lord look upon
him for his good;
he lifts him out of his low estate
[13]and raises up his head,
so that many are amazed at him.

[14]Good things and bad, life and
death,
poverty and wealth, come from
the Lord.[o]
[17]The gift of the Lord endures for
those who are godly,
and what he approves will have
lasting success.
[18]There is a man who is rich through
his diligence and self-denial,
and this is the reward allotted to
him:
[19]when he says, "I have found rest,
and now I shall enjoy[p] my
goods!"
he does not know how much time
will pass
until he leaves them to others
and dies.
[20]Stand by your covenant[q] and
attend to it,
and grow old in your work.

[21]Do not wonder at the works of a
sinner,
but trust in the Lord and keep at
your toil;

o Other authorities add as verses 15 and 16, [15]*Wisdom, understanding, and knowledge of the law come from the Lord; affection and the ways of good works come from him.* [16]*Error and darkness were created with sinners; evil will grow old with those who take pride in malice.*
p Gk *eat of*
q Heb *task*

11.2–9: Warnings against hasty judgments, based on *looks* (v. 2), size (v. 3), or *clothes* (v. 4); compare 1 Sam.16.7. **6:** 1 Sam.15.28; Est.7.10. **8:** Pr.18.13. **9b:** Ps.1.1.

11.10–13: Discretion in conduct. 11: Pr.10.3; Ec.9.11. **12b:** Ps.34.15.

11.14–28: All things come from God. 14: A summary of the following section (1 Sam.2.7; Job 1.21; Is.45.7). **19:** Lk.12.19. **21:** 9.11; Pr.3.31; 23.17. *Keep at your toil,* Hebrew and Syriac, "abide in his light."

for it is easy in the sight of the Lord
to enrich a poor man quickly
and suddenly.
22 The blessing of the Lord is*r* the
reward of the godly,
and quickly God causes his
blessing to flourish.
23 Do not say, "What do I need,
and what prosperity could be
mine in the future?"
24 Do not say, "I have enough,
and what calamity could
happen to me in the future?"
25 In the day of prosperity, adversity
is forgotten,
and in the day of adversity,
prosperity is not remembered.
26 For it is easy in the sight of the
Lord
to reward a man on the day of
death according to his
conduct.
27 The misery of an hour makes one
forget luxury,
and at the close of a man's life
his deeds will be revealed.
28 Call no one happy before his
death;
a man will be known through
his children.
29 Do not bring every man into your
home,
for many are the wiles of the
crafty.
30 Like a decoy partridge in a cage,
so is the mind of a proud man,
and like a spy he observes your
weakness;*s*
31 for he lies in wait, turning good
into evil,
and to worthy actions he will
attach blame.
32 From a spark of fire come many
burning coals,

and a sinner lies in wait to shed
blood.
33 Beware of a scoundrel, for he
devises evil,
lest he give you a lasting
blemish.
34 Receive a stranger into your home
and he will upset you with
commotion,
and will estrange you from your
family.

12 If you do a kindness, know to
whom you do it,
and you will be thanked for your
good deeds.
2 Do good to a godly man, and you
will be repaid—
if not by him, certainly by the
Most High.
3 No good will come to the man who
persists in evil
or to him who does not give
alms.
4 Give to the godly man, but do not
help the sinner.
5 Do good to the humble, but do
not give to the ungodly;
hold back his bread, and do not
give it to him,
lest by means of it he subdue
you;
for you will receive twice as much
evil
for all the good which you do to
him.
6 For the Most High also hates
sinners
and will inflict punishment on
the ungodly.*t*
7 Give to the good man, but do not
help the sinner.

r Gk *is in*
s Heb: Gk *downfall*
t Other authorities add *and he is keeping them for the
mighty day of their punishment*

26–27: Sirach's theology does not include a future life. **28:** *Through his children*, Hebrew,
"by his latter end," i.e. a man's circumstances at the time of his death indicate the kind of life
he has lived.
  11.29–34: Care in choosing companions. 31: Hebrew, "The backbiter turns good to evil."
32: Pr.1.11.
  12.1–7: The need of discretion in almsgiving (Mt.7.6). **3:** Hebrew, "No good comes to him
who helps the wicked, nor is it an act of benevolence which he has done." **4–5:** Contrast
Lk.6.27–31; Gal.6.10.

[8]A friend will not be known[u] in
   prosperity,
   nor will an enemy be hidden in
     adversity.
[9]A man's enemies are grieved when
   he prospers,
   and in his adversity even his
     friend will separate from him.
[10]Never trust your enemy,
   for like the rusting of copper, so
     is his wickedness.
[11]Even if he humbles himself and
   goes about cringing,
   watch yourself, and be on your
     guard against him;
and you will be to him like one
   who has polished a mirror,
   and you will know that it was
     not hopelessly tarnished.
[12]Do not put him next to you,
   lest he overthrow you and take
     your place;
do not have him sit at your right,
   lest he try to take your seat of
     honor,
and at last you will realize the
   truth of my words,
   and be stung by what I have
     said.

[13]Who will pity a snake charmer
   bitten by a serpent,
   or any who go near wild beasts?
[14]So no one will pity a man who
   associates with a sinner
   and becomes involved in his sins.
[15]He will stay with you for a time,
   but if you falter, he will not
     stand by you.

[16]An enemy will speak sweetly with
   his lips,
   but in his mind he will plan to
     throw you into a pit;
an enemy will weep with his eyes,
   but if he finds an opportunity

his thirst for blood will be
   insatiable.
[17]If calamity befalls you, you will .
   find him there ahead of you;
   and while pretending to help
     you, he will trip you by the
     heel;
[18]he will shake his head, and clap
   his hands,
   and whisper much, and change
     his expression.

13 Whoever touches pitch will
   be defiled,
   and whoever associates with a
     proud man will become like
     him.
[2]Do not lift a weight beyond your
   strength,
   nor associate with a man
     mightier and richer than
     you.
How can the clay pot associate
   with the iron kettle?
The pot will strike against it,
   and will itself be broken.
[3]A rich man does wrong, and he
   even adds reproaches;
   a poor man suffers wrong, and
     he must add apologies.
[4]A rich man[v] will exploit you if you
   can be of use to him,
   but if you are in need he will
     forsake you.
[5]If you own something, he will live
   with you;
   he will drain your resources and
     he will not care.
[6]When he needs you he will deceive
   you,
   he will smile at you and give you
     hope.
He will speak to you kindly and
   say, "What do you need?"

u Other authorities read *punished*
v Gk *He*

12.8-18: False friends (compare 6.5–17). **9a:** Hebrew, "When a man is prosperous, even his
enemy is friendly" (Pr.19.4,6). **11c,d:** As one can prevent tarnish on a metal mirror by constantly polishing it, so the dangers of false friendship can be avoided by constant watchfulness.
18: *Shake his head,* a gesture of derisive triumph (13.7; Job 16.4; Ps.22.7; Mt.27.39). *Whisper,*
secretly conspiring (Ps.41.7). *Change his expression,* openly showing his enmity.
   13.1–20: Warnings concerning associates. 1: A summary of what follows. **3:** *He must add*

⁷He will shame you with his foods,
until he has drained you two or
three times;
and finally he will deride you.
Should he see you afterwards, he
will forsake you,
and shake his head at you.

⁸Take care not to be led astray,
and not to be humiliated in your
feasting.ʷ
⁹When a powerful man invites you,
be reserved;
and he will invite you the more
often.
¹⁰Do not push forward, lest you be
repulsed;
and do not remain at a distance,
lest you be forgotten.
¹¹Do not try to treat him as an equal,
nor trust his abundance of words;
for he will test you through much
talk,
and while he smiles he will be
examining you.
¹²Cruel is he who does not keep
words to himself;
he will not hesitate to injure or
to imprison.
¹³Keep words to yourself and be very
watchful,
for you are walking about with
your own downfall.ˣ

¹⁵Every creature loves its like,
and every person his neighbor;
¹⁶all living beings associate by species,
and a man clings to one like
himself.
¹⁷What fellowship has a wolf with a
lamb?
No more has a sinner with a
godly man.
¹⁸What peace is there between a
hyena and a dog?
And what peace between a rich
man and a poor man?
¹⁹Wild asses in the wilderness are

the prey of lions;
likewise the poor are pastures
for the rich.
²⁰Humility is an abomination to a
proud man;
likewise a poor man is an
abomination to a rich one.

²¹When a rich man totters, he is
steadied by friends,
but when a humble man falls, he
is even pushed away by friends.
²²If a rich man slips, his helpers are
many;
he speaks unseemly words, and
they justify him.
If a humble man slips, they even
reproach him;
he speaks sensibly, and receives
no attention.
²³When the rich man speaks all are
silent,
and they extol to the clouds what
he says.
When the poor man speaks they
say, "Who is this fellow?"
And should he stumble, they
even push him down.

²⁴Riches are good if they are free
from sin,
and poverty is evil in the
opinion of the ungodly.
²⁵A man's heart changes his
countenance,
either for good or for evil.ʸ
²⁶The mark of a happy heart is a
cheerful face,
but to devise proverbs requires
painful thinking.

14 Blessed is the man who does
not blunder with his lips
and need not suffer grief for sin.
²Blessed is he whose heart does

w Other authorities read *folly*
x Other authorities add *When you hear these things in
your sleep, wake up!* ¹⁴*During all your life love the
Lord, and call on him for your salvation.*
y Other authorities add *and a glad heart makes a cheerful
countenance*

---

apologies, as though it were he who committed the wrong. **7:** Compare Pr.23.1–3. *Shake his
head*, see 12.18 n. **15:** 27.9. **17:** 2 Cor.6.14. **19:** Job 24.5. **20:** Pr.29.27.
13.21–14.2: The rich and the poor. **21–23:** Pr.14.20; 19.4,7. **26a:** Pr.15.13. **26b:** Ec.12.12.
14.2: Rom.14.22; 1 Jn.3.21.

not condemn him,
and who has not given up his hope.

³Riches are not seemly for a stingy
man;
and of what use is property to
an envious man?
⁴Whoever accumulates by depriving
himself, accumulates for others;
and others will live in luxury on
his goods.
⁵If a man is mean to himself, to
whom will he be generous?
He will not enjoy his own riches.
⁶No one is meaner than the man
who is grudging to himself,
and this is the retribution for
his baseness;
⁷even if he does good, he does it
unintentionally,
and betrays his baseness in the end.
⁸Evil is the man with a grudging eye;
he averts his face and disregards
people.
⁹A greedy man's eye is not satisfied
with a portion,
and mean injustice withers the
soul.
¹⁰A stingy man's eye begrudges bread,
and it is lacking at his table.

¹¹My son, treat yourself well,
according to your means,
and present worthy offerings to
the Lord.
¹²Remember that death will not delay,
and the decree² of Hades has
not been shown to you.
¹³Do good to a friend before you die,
and reach out and give to him
as much as you can.
¹⁴Do not deprive yourself of a happy
day;
let not your share of desired
good pass by you.

¹⁵Will you not leave the fruit of your
labors to another,
and what you acquired by toil
to be divided by lot?
¹⁶Give, and take, and beguile yourself,
because in Hades one cannot
look for luxury.
¹⁷All living beings become old like a
garment,
for the decree*a* from of old is,
"You must surely die!"
¹⁸Like flourishing leaves on a
spreading tree
which sheds some and puts
forth others,
so are the generations of flesh and
blood:
one dies and another is born.
¹⁹Every product decays and ceases to
exist,
and the man who made it will
pass away with it.

²⁰Blessed is the man who meditates
on*b* wisdom
and who reasons intelligently.
²¹He who reflects in his mind on her
ways
will also ponder her secrets.
²²Pursue wisdom*c* like a hunter,
and lie in wait on her paths.
²³He who peers through her
windows
will also listen at her doors;
²⁴he who encamps near her house
will also fasten his tent peg to
her walls;
²⁵he will pitch his tent near her,
and will lodge in an excellent
lodging place;
²⁶he will place his children under
her shelter,
and will camp under her boughs;

z Gk *covenant*   a Gk *covenant*
b Other authorities read *dies in*   c Gk *her*

14.3–19: Envy and avarice. 4: 11.19–20; Job 27.16–17; Pr.13.22; Ec.6.2; Lk.12.16–21.
8: *Averts his face,* 4.4; Tob.4.7. 10: Pr.23.6–7. The Hebrew and Syriac add, "A good eye
[i.e. a liberal man] causes bread to increase, and 'A dry spring sends forth water' [this appears
to be a proverb] upon his table." 11–16: Wealth should be used wisely during life, for it must
be left behind at death. 13: Tob.4.7; Lk.14.13. 14: Ec.5.18. 15: V. 4. 16: Ec.9.10. *Hades,*
Hebrew "sheol." 17: *Like a garment,* Ps.102.26; compare Is.40.6; Jas.1.10; 1 Pet.1.24. 18:
Ec.1.4. 19: Contrast Rev.14.13.
    14.20–15.10: The search for wisdom and its blessings (Pr.8.32–35). 26a: Hebrew, "He builds

²⁷he will be sheltered by her from
   the heat,
  and will dwell in the midst of her
   glory.

15 The man who fears the Lord
   will do this,
  and he who holds to the law will
   obtain wisdom.ᵈ
²She will come to meet him like a
   mother,
  and like the wife of his youth
   she will welcome him.
³She will feed him with the bread
   of understanding,
  and give him the water of
   wisdom to drink.
⁴He will lean on her and will not
   fall,
  and he will rely on her and will
   not be put to shame.
⁵She will exalt him above his
   neighbors,
  and will open his mouth in the
   midst of the assembly.
⁶He will find gladness and a crown
   of rejoicing,
  and will acquire an everlasting
   name.
⁷Foolish men will not obtain her,
  and sinful men will not see
   her.
⁸She is far from men of pride,
  and liars will never think of
   her.

⁹A hymn of praise is not fitting on
   the lips of a sinner,
  for it has not been sent from the
   Lord.
¹⁰For a hymn of praise should be

uttered in wisdom,
  and the Lord will prosper it.

¹¹Do not say, "Because of the Lord
   I left the right way";
  for heᵉ will not do what he hates.
¹²Do not say, "It was he who led me
   astray";
  for he has no need of a sinful
   man.
¹³The Lord hates all abominations,
  and they are not loved by those
   who fear him.
¹⁴It was he who created man in the
   beginning,
  and he left him in the power of
   his own inclination.
¹⁵If you will, you can keep the
   commandments,
  and to act faithfully is a matter
   of your own choice.
¹⁶He has placed before you fire and
   water:
  stretch out your hand for
   whichever you wish.
¹⁷Before a manᶠ are life and death,
  and whichever he chooses will be
   given to him.
¹⁸For great is the wisdom of the
   Lord;
  he is mighty in power and sees
   everything;
¹⁹his eyes are on those who fear him,
  and he knows every deed of
   man.
²⁰He has not commanded any one
   to be ungodly,
  and he has not given any one
   permission to sin.

d Gk *her*
e Heb: Gk *you*   *f* Gk *men*

---

his nest in her foliage." **15.1:** Hebrew prefixes "For," connecting 14.20–27 (telling how wisdom must be sought) with 15.1–8 (telling how wisdom will welcome those who seek her). *The law* is identified with wisdom (1.26; 19.20; 21.11; 24.23). **2b:** Hebrew, "Like a young bride she will embrace him." **3:** Pr.9.2,5. **9–10:** Compare Pr.27.21b.

    15.11–20: Free will and responsibility for sin (17.1–12). **11–12:** Jas.1.13. **13b:** Hebrew, "and he does not let them come near those who fear him." **14:** Gen.1.27. *Inclination*, the Hebrew word *yeṣer* is a technical term, used here in a neutral sense meaning "free will." Elsewhere *yeṣer* is sometimes used in a good sense (Is.26.3; 1 Chr.29.18); but usually it refers to an evil tendency or inclination toward sin (Gen.6.5; 8.21; compare 2 Esd.4.30–31). In postbiblical times the doctrine arose of a good and an evil *yeṣer* which every person possesses. **16:** *Fire and water*, representing opposite extremes. *Fire* here has no eschatological significance. **17:** Dt.30.19; Jer.21.8. **18–19:** Ps.33.13,18; 34.15; Heb.4.13.

16 Do not desire a multitude
of useless children,
nor rejoice in ungodly sons.
2If they multiply, do not rejoice in
them,
unless the fear of the Lord is in
them.
3Do not trust in their survival,
and do not rely on their
multitude;
for one is better than a thousand,*g*
and to die childless is better
than to have ungodly children.
4For through one man of
understanding a city will be
filled with people,
but through a tribe of lawless
men it will be made desolate.
5Many such things my eye has seen,
and my ear has heard things
more striking than these.

6In an assembly of sinners a fire will
be kindled,
and in a disobedient nation
wrath was kindled.
7He was not propitiated for the
ancient giants
who revolted in their might.
8He did not spare the neighbors of
Lot,
whom he loathed on account of
their insolence.
9He showed no pity for a nation
devoted to destruction,
for those destroyed in their sins;
10nor for the six hundred thousand
men on foot,
who rebelliously assembled in
their stubbornness.
11Even if there is only one stiff-necked
person,
it will be a wonder if he remains
unpunished.

For mercy and wrath are with the
Lord;*h*
he is mighty to forgive, and he
pours out wrath.
12As great as his mercy, so great is
also his reproof;
he judges a man according to
his deeds.
13The sinner will not escape with his
plunder,
and the patience of the godly
will not be frustrated.
14He will make room for every act
of mercy;
every one will receive in
accordance with his deeds.*i*

17Do not say, "I shall be hidden from
the Lord,
and who from on high will
remember me?
Among so many people I shall not
be known,
for what is my soul in the
boundless creation?
18Behold, heaven and the highest
heaven,
the abyss and the earth, will
tremble at his visitation.
19The mountains also and the
foundations of the earth
shake with trembling when he
looks upon them.
20And no mind will reflect on this.
Who will ponder his ways?
21Like a tempest which no man can
see,
so most of his works are
concealed.

g The text of this line is uncertain
h Gk *him*
i Other authorities add 15*The Lord hardened Pharaoh so
that he did not know him; in order that his works might
be known under heaven.* 16*His mercy is manifest to the
whole of creation, and he divided his light and darkness
with a plumb line.*

16.1–5: The misfortune of having ungodly children. 3c: Hebrew and Syriac, "For better is
one who does the will [of the Lord] than a thousand [godless children]."
16.6–23: The certainty of punishment for sin. 6: *A fire will be kindled,* 21.9; compare Num.
16.35. **7:** *Ancient giants,* Gen.6.4; Wis.14.6; Bar.3.26–28. **8:** Gen.19.14–25. **10:** 46.8; Num.
11.21. **11:** *Mercy and wrath,* 5.6. **12b:** Ps.62.12. **16b** (in note *i*): Hebrew, "and his light and his
darkness he has apportioned to the children of men." **17d:** Hebrew, "and what is my soul
among the multitudes of spirits of all the children of men?" **18–19:** A parenthetical meditation
on the supreme power of God. **20–22:** Hebrew, continuing the thought of v. 17, "In truth, he
[God] does not set his heart on me [pays no attention to me]; and as for my ways, who will

²²Who will announce his acts of
    justice?
  Or who will await them? For
    the covenant is far off."
²³This is what one devoid of
    understanding thinks;
  a senseless and misguided man
    thinks foolishly.

²⁴Listen to me, my son, and acquire
    knowledge,
  and pay close attention to my
    words.
²⁵I will impart instruction by weight,
  and declare knowledge accurately.

²⁶The works of the Lord have existed
    from the beginning by his
    creation,ʲ
  and when he made them, he
    determined their divisions.
²⁷He arranged his works in an eternal
    order,
  and their dominionᵏ for allˡ
    generations;
  they neither hunger nor grow weary,
  and they do not cease from their
    labors.
²⁸They do not crowd one another
    aside,
  and they will never disobey his
    word.
²⁹After this the Lord looked upon
    the earth,
  and filled it with his good things;
³⁰with all kinds of living beings he
    covered its surface,
  and to it they return.

17 The Lord created man out of
    earth,
  and turned him back to it again.

²He gave to menᵐ few days, a
    limited time,
  but granted them authority over
    the things upon the earth.ⁿ
³He endowed them with strength
    like his own,ᵒ
  and made them in his own image.
⁴He placed the fear of themᵖ in all
    living beings,
  and granted them dominion
    over beasts and birds.�q
⁶He made for themʳ tongue and eyes;
  he gave them ears and a mind
    for thinking.
⁷He filled them with knowledge
    and understanding,
  and showed them good and evil.
⁸He set his eye upon their hearts
  to show them the majesty of his
    works.ˢ
¹⁰And they will praise his holy name,
  to proclaim the grandeur of his
    works.
¹¹He bestowed knowledge upon them,
  and allotted to them the law of life.
¹²He established with them an eternal
    covenant,
  and showed them his judgments.
¹³Their eyes saw his glorious majesty,
  and their ears heard the glory of
    his voice.
¹⁴And he said to them, "Beware of
    all unrighteousness."ᵗ
  And he gave commandment to
    each of them concerning his
    neighbor.

j Heb: Gk *judgment*   *k* Or *elements*
l Gk *their*   *m* Gk *them*   *n* Gk *it*
o Cn: Gk *proper to them*   *p* Syr: Gk *him*
q Other authorities add ⁵*They obtained the use of the five operations of the Lord; as sixth he distributed to them the gift of mind, and as seventh reason, the interpreter of his operations.*   *r* Syr: Gk *Inclination and*
s Other authorities add ⁹*and he gave them to boast of his marvels for ever*   *t* Or *every unrighteous man*

---

mark them? ²¹ If I sin, no eye will see me, or if I deal untruly in all secrecy, who will know it? ²² My righteous dealing, who shall declare it? And what hope is there? For the decree is distant" (i.e. the decreed reward for righteousness is remote and uncertain). **23:** Sirach's own view of the ideas expressed in vv. 17–22.

16.24–17.14: Divine wisdom seen in creation. 16.27–28: 43.10; Is.40.26. **29:** *After this,* compare Gen.1.20–31. **30:** *To it,* the earth (Gen.3.19; Ps.104.29). **17.1:** Gen.2.7; 3.19; Ps.146.4. **2a:** Literally, "He granted them days by number, and a set time" (Gen.6.3; Ps.90.10). **3:** Gen. 1.26–27. **4:** Gen.1.28; Ps.8.6–8. **5** (in note *q*): *The five operations,* or "powers" (i.e. the five senses). **7:** Gen.2.17. **11:** Syriac, "He set before them the covenant" (Dt.4.44). *The law of life,* the law which gives life (45.5; Bar.4.1). **12:** *Eternal covenant,* Ex.19.16–24.18. **14:** A summary of all the prohibitory commandments.

¹⁵Their ways are always before him,
they will not be hid from his
eyes.ᵘ
¹⁷He appointed a ruler for every
nation,
but Israel is the Lord's own
portion.ᵛ
¹⁹All their works are as the sun
before him,
and his eyes are continually
upon their ways.
²⁰Their iniquities are not hidden
from him,
and all their sins are before the
Lord.ʷ
²²A man's almsgiving is like a signet
with the Lord,ˣ
and he will keep a person's
kindness like the apple of his eye.
²³Afterward he will arise and requite
them,
and he will bring their
recompense on their heads.
²⁴Yet to those who repent he grants
a return,
and he encourages those whose
endurance is failing.

²⁵Turn to the Lord and forsake your
sins;
pray in his presence and lessen
your offenses.
²⁶Return to the Most High and turn
away from iniquity,ʸ
and hate abominations intensely.
²⁷Who will sing praises to the Most
High in Hades,
as do those who are alive and
give thanks?
²⁸From the dead, as from one who
does not exist, thanksgiving
has ceased;
he who is alive and well sings
the Lord's praises.
²⁹How great is the mercy of the Lord,
and his forgiveness for those

who turn to him!
³⁰For all things cannot be in men,ᶻ
since a son of man is not immortal.
³¹What is brighter than the sun? Yet
its light fails.ᵃ
So flesh and blood devise evil.
³²He marshals the host of the height
of heaven;
but all men are dust and ashes.

18 He who lives for ever created
the whole universe;
2 the Lord alone will be declared
righteous.ᵇ
⁴To none has he given power to
proclaim his works;
and who can search out his
mighty deeds?
⁵Who can measure his majestic
power?
And who can fully recount his
mercies?
⁶It is not possible to diminish or
increase them,
nor is it possible to trace the
wonders of the Lord.
⁷When a man has finished, he is
just beginning,
and when he stops, he will be
at a loss.
⁸What is man, and of what use is
he?
What is his good and what is
his evil?

u Other authorities add ¹⁶*Their ways from youth tend
toward evil, and they are unable to make for themselves
hearts of flesh in place of their stony hearts.* ¹⁷*For in
the division of the nations of the whole earth*
v Other authorities add ¹⁸*whom, being his first-born, he
brings up with discipline, and allotting to him the light of
his love, he does not neglect him.*
w Other authorities add ²¹*But the Lord, who is gracious
and knows his creatures, has neither left nor abandoned
them, but spared them.*   x Gk *him*
y Other authorities add *for he will lead you out of darkness to the light of health*
z The Greek text of this line is uncertain
a Or *suffers eclipse*
b Other authorities add *and there is no other beside him;*
³*he steers the world with the span of his hand, and all
things obey his will; for he is king of all things, by his
power separating among them the holy things from the
profane.*

17.15–24: The divine judge. 17: Dt.32.8–9. **22:** *Almsgiving,* 29.12–13. *Apple of his eye,*
Dt.32.10; Ps.17.8; Pr.7.2. **23:** *Arise,* in judgment. **24:** *A return,* to God's favor.
    17.25–32: Exhortation to turn to God. 25–26: Jer.3.12. **27–28:** Ps.6.5; 115.17; Is.38.18;
Bar.2.17. **30:** Syriac, "For it is not like this in man [i.e. only God has such mercy and forgive-
ness (18.13)], nor is his [i.e. God's] thought like the thoughts of the children of men." **31:**
Syriac, "So is man who has the inclination [see 15.14 n.] of flesh and blood."
    18.1–14: The majesty of God. 4b: Ps.106.2. **8:** Ps.8.4. **9:** Compare Ps.90.10.

⁹The number of a man's days is
   great if he reaches a hundred
   years.
¹⁰Like a drop of water from the sea
   and a grain*c* of sand
   so are a few years in the day of
   eternity.
¹¹Therefore the Lord is patient with
   them
   and pours out his mercy upon
   them.
¹²He sees and recognizes that their
   end will be evil;
   therefore he grants them
   forgiveness in abundance.
¹³The compassion of man is for his
   neighbor,
   but the compassion of the Lord
   is for all living beings.
   He rebukes and trains and teaches
   them,
   and turns them back, as a
   shepherd his flock.
¹⁴He has compassion on those who
   accept his discipline
   and who are eager for his
   judgments.

¹⁵My son, do not mix reproach with
   your good deeds,
   nor cause grief by your words
   when you present a gift.
¹⁶Does not the dew assuage the
   scorching heat?
   So a word is better than a gift.
¹⁷Indeed, does not a word surpass a
   good gift?
   Both are to be found in a
   gracious man.
¹⁸A fool is ungracious and abusive,
   and the gift of a grudging man
   makes the eyes dim.

¹⁹Before you speak, learn,
   and before you fall ill, take care
   of your health.
²⁰Before judgment, examine yourself,

and in the hour of visitation
   you will find forgiveness.
²¹Before falling ill, humble yourself,
   and when you are on the point
   of sinning, turn back.
²²Let nothing hinder you from
   paying a vow promptly,
   and do not wait until death to
   be released from it.
²³Before making a vow,*d* prepare
   yourself;
   and do not be like a man who
   tempts the Lord.
²⁴Think of his wrath on the day of
   death,
   and of the moment of vengeance
   when he turns away his face.
²⁵In the time of plenty think of the
   time of hunger;
   in the days of wealth think of
   poverty and need.
²⁶From morning to evening
   conditions change,
   and all things move swiftly
   before the Lord.

²⁷A wise man is cautious in
   everything,
   and in days of sin he guards
   against wrongdoing.
²⁸Every intelligent man knows
   wisdom,
   and he praises the one who finds
   her.
²⁹Those who understand sayings
   become skilled themselves,
   and pour forth apt proverbs.

³⁰Do not follow your base desires,
   but restrain your appetites.
³¹If you allow your soul to take
   pleasure in base desire,
   it will make you the
   laughingstock of your enemies.
³²Do not revel in great luxury,

c Gk *pebble*
d Or *offering a prayer*

18.15–18: The right spirit in giving alms. 15: Do not humiliate the receiver of charity (41.22).
16b: Syriac, "So a [kindly] word changes [the character of] a gift." **17a:** Syriac, "For there is a
good word which is better than a gift."
   18.19–29: The need of foresight. 22: Dt.23.21; Ec.5.4. **24:** 7.36.
   18.30–19.3: An exhortation to self-control. 33: Hebrew, "Do not be a squanderer and a

lest you become impoverished
by its expense.
33Do not become a beggar by feasting
with borrowed money,
when you have nothing in your
purse.

19 A workman who is a drunkard
will not become rich;
he who despises small things
will fail little by little.
2Wine and women lead intelligent
men astray,
and the man who consorts with
harlots is very reckless.
3Decay and worms will inherit him,
and the reckless soul will be
snatched away.

4One who trusts others too quickly
is lightminded,
and one who sins does wrong to
himself.
5One who rejoices in wickedness*e*
will be condemned,*f*
6   and for one who hates gossip
evil is lessened.
7Never repeat a conversation,
and you will lose nothing at
all.
8With friend or foe do not report
it,
and unless it would be a sin for
you, do not disclose it;
9for some one has heard you and
watched you,
and when the time comes he
will hate you.
10Have you heard a word? Let it die
with you.
Be brave! It will not make you
burst!
11With such a word a fool will suffer
pangs
like a woman in labor with a
child.

12Like an arrow stuck in the flesh of
the thigh,
so is a word inside a fool.
13Question a friend, perhaps he did
not do it;
but if he did anything, so that
he may do it no more.
14Question a neighbor, perhaps he
did not say it;
but if he said it, so that he may
not say it again.
15Question a friend, for often it is
slander;
so do not believe everything you
hear.
16A person may make a slip without
intending it.
Who has never sinned with his
tongue?
17Question your neighbor before you
threaten him;
and let the law of the Most
High take its course.*g*

20All wisdom is the fear of the
Lord,
and in all wisdom there is the
fulfilment of the law.*h*
22But the knowledge of wickedness
is not wisdom,
nor is there prudence where
sinners take counsel.
23There is a cleverness which is
abominable,
but there is a fool who merely
lacks wisdom.

e Other authorities read *heart*
f Other authorities add *but he who withstands pleasures
crowns his life.* 6He who controls his tongue will live
without strife,
g Other authorities add *and do not be angry.* 18The fear
of the Lord is the beginning of acceptance, and wisdom
obtains his love. 19The knowledge of the Lord's commandments is life-giving discipline; and those who do
what is pleasing to him enjoy the fruit of the tree of
immortality.
h Other authorities add, *and the knowledge of his omnipotence.* 21When a servant says to his master, "I will not
act as you wish," even if later he does it, he angers the
one who supports him.

---

drunkard, else there will be nothing in your purse." **19.1:** *Will fail . . . little,* Hebrew, "will
become altogether naked," i.e. destitute.
      19.4–12: A warning against too much talking. 7b: Syriac, "then no one will reproach you"
(Pr.25.9–10). **8:** *Unless* by keeping silent *it would be a sin.* **9:** Pr.25.10.
      19.13–17: On administering reproof. 16: Jas.3.2. **17:** Lev.19.17; Mt.18.15; Lk.17.3.
      19.20–30: Wisdom and craftiness contrasted. 20: Jas.1.25. **21** (in note *h*): Mt.21.28–32. **23:**
Who merely lacks wisdom, and is guileless.

²⁴Better is the God-fearing man who
   lacks intelligence,
   than the highly prudent man
   who transgresses the law.
²⁵There is a cleverness which is
   scrupulous but unjust,
   and there are people who distort
   kindness to gain a verdict.
²⁶There is a rascal bowed down in
   mourning,ⁱ
   but inwardly he is full of deceit.
²⁷He hides his face and pretends not
   to hear;
   but where no one notices, he
   will forestall you.
²⁸And if by lack of strength he is
   prevented from sinning,
   he will do evil when he finds an
   opportunity.
²⁹A man is known by his appearance,
   and a sensible man is known
   by his face, when you meet
   him.
³⁰A man's attire and open-mouthed
   laughter,
   and a man's manner of walking,
   show what he is.

20 There is a reproof which is
   not timely;
   and there is a man who keeps
   silent but is wise.
²How much better it is to reprove
   than to stay angry!
   And the one who confesses his
   fault will be kept from loss.ʲ
⁴Like a eunuch's desire to violate a
   maiden
   is a man who executes
   judgments by violence.
⁵There is one who by keeping silent
   is found wise,
   while another is detested for
   being too talkative.
⁶There is one who keeps silent
   because he has no answer,
   while another keeps silent

because he knows when to
   speak.
⁷A wise man will be silent until the
   right moment,
   but a braggart and fool goes
   beyond the right moment.
⁸Whoever uses too many words will
   be loathed,
   and whoever usurps the right to
   speak will be hated.

⁹There may be good fortune for a
   man in adversity,
   and a windfall may result in a
   loss.
¹⁰There is a gift that profits you
   nothing,
   and there is a gift that brings a
   double return.
¹¹There are losses because of glory,
   and there are men who have
   raised their heads from humble
   circumstances.
¹²There is a man who buys much for
   a little,
   but pays for it seven times over.
¹³The wise man makes himself
   beloved through his words,
   but the courtesies of fools are
   wasted.
¹⁴A fool's gift will profit you nothing,
   for he has many eyes instead of
   one.
¹⁵He gives little and upbraids much,
   he opens his mouth like a
   herald;
   today he lends and tomorrow he
   asks it back;
   such a one is a hateful man.
¹⁶A fool will say, "I have no friend,
   and there is no gratitude for my
   good deeds;
   those who eat my bread speak
   unkindly."

i Gk *blackness*
j Other authorities add ³*How good it is to show repentance when you are reproved, for so you will escape
   deliberate sin!*

30: Instead of *and . . . laughter*, the Syriac reads, "proclaims his deeds," i.e. his occupation.
   20.1–26: Use and abuse of the tongue. 1–8: Proper times for speech and for silence. 2: Syriac,
"He that reproves a sinner gets no thanks, but let him that makes confession be kept back from
hurt" (i.e. be spared humiliation). **5:** Pr.17.28. **7:** V. 20b; Ec.3.7.
   20.9–17: Paradoxes. 13: 6.5. *Are wasted*, are thrown away. **14:** Syriac, "for he looks for
sevenfold repayment."

¹⁷How many will ridicule him, and
  how often!

¹⁸A slip on the pavement is better
  than a slip of the tongue;
so the downfall of the wicked
  will occur speedily.
¹⁹An ungracious man is like a story
  told at the wrong time,
which is continually on the lips
  of the ignorant.
²⁰A proverb from a fool's lips will
  be rejected,
for he does not tell it at its
  proper time.

²¹A man may be prevented from
  sinning by his poverty,
so when he rests he feels no
  remorse.
²²A man may lose his life through
  shame,
or lose it because of his foolish
  look.
²³A man may for shame make
  promises to a friend,
and needlessly make him an
  enemy.

²⁴A lie is an ugly blot on a man;
  it is continually on the lips of
  the ignorant.
²⁵A thief is preferable to a habitual
  liar,
but the lot of both is ruin.
²⁶The disposition of a liar brings
  disgrace,
and his shame is ever with him.

²⁷He who speaks wisely will advance
  himself,
and a sensible man will please
  great men.

²⁸Whoever cultivates the soil will
  heap up his harvest,
and whoever pleases great men
  will atone for injustice.
²⁹Presents and gifts blind the eyes of
  the wise;
like a muzzle on the mouth they
  avert reproofs.
³⁰Hidden wisdom and unseen treasure,
  what advantage is there in either
  of them?
³¹Better is the man who hides his folly
  than the man who hides his
  wisdom.^k

21   Have you sinned, my son?
  Do so no more,
but pray about your former sins.
²Flee from sin as from a snake;
  for if you approach sin, it will
  bite you.
Its teeth are lion's teeth,
  and destroy the souls of men.
³All lawlessness is like a two-edged
  sword;
there is no healing for its wound.

⁴Terror and violence will lay waste
  riches;
thus the house of the proud will
  be laid waste.
⁵The prayer of a poor man goes from
  his lips to the ears of God,^l
and his judgment comes speedily.
⁶Whoever hates reproof walks in
  the steps of the sinner,
but he that fears the Lord will
  repent in his heart.
⁷He who is mighty in speech is
  known from afar;

k Other authorities add ³²*Unwearied patience in seeking
the Lord is better than a masterless charioteer of one's
own life.*   l Gk *his ears*

20.18–20: **Concerning inappropriate speech. 19:** Syriac, "As the fat tail of a sheep [Ex.29.22],
eaten without salt, so is a word spoken out of season."
   20.21–23: **Sin unintentionally avoided, and intentionally committed. 22:** 4.20–21. **23:** *Make
him an enemy,* because of inability to fulfil the promises.
   20.24–26: **Lying.** Ps.5.6; Pr.12.22; 13.5.
   20.27–31: **The reward of the wise. 27:** *Will please,* Syriac, "will rule." **28:** Pr.12.11. **29:**
Presents and gifts, i.e. bribes (Dt.16.19; Pr.17.8). **30:** 41.14–15.
   21.1–10: **Warnings against sin. 2–3:** The characteristics of sin are subtlety, strength, and
deadliness. **5:** 35.17–19. **5b:** Syriac, "and it ascends unto the presence of the eternal Judge."
7: Syriac, "The wise man recognizes him that is before him, and discerns the sinner in a mo-

but the sensible man, when he
　　slips, is aware of it.

8A man who builds his house with
　　other people's money
　　is like one who gathers stones
　　for his burial mound.*m*
9An assembly of the wicked is like
　　tow gathered together,
　　and their end is a flame of fire.
10The way of sinners is smoothly
　　paved with stones,
　　but at its end is the pit of Hades.

11Whoever keeps the law controls
　　his thoughts,
　　and wisdom is the fulfilment of
　　the fear of the Lord.
12He who is not clever cannot be
　　taught,
　　but there is a cleverness which
　　increases bitterness.
13The knowledge of a wise man will
　　increase like a flood,
　　and his counsel like a flowing
　　spring.
14The mind of a fool is like a broken
　　jar;
　　it will hold no knowledge.

15When a man of understanding
　　hears a wise saying,
　　he will praise it and add to it;
　　when a reveler hears it, he dislikes
　　it
　　and casts it behind his back.
16A fool's narration is like a burden
　　on a journey,
　　but delight will be found in the
　　speech of the intelligent.
17The utterance of a sensible man
　　will be sought in the assembly,
　　and they will ponder his words
　　in their minds.

18Like a house that has vanished, so
　　is wisdom to a fool;

and the knowledge of the
　　ignorant is unexamined talk.
19To a senseless man education is
　　fetters on his feet,
　　and like manacles on his right
　　hand.
20A fool raises his voice when he
　　laughs,
　　but a clever man smiles quietly.
21To a sensible man education is like
　　a golden ornament,
　　and like a bracelet on the right
　　arm.
22The foot of a fool rushes into a
　　house,
　　but a man of experience stands
　　respectfully before it.
23A boor peers into the house from
　　the door,
　　but a cultivated man remains
　　outside.
24It is ill-mannered for a man to
　　listen at a door,
　　and a discreet man is grieved by
　　the disgrace.
25The lips of strangers will speak of
　　these things,*n*
　　but the words of the prudent
　　will be weighed in the balance.
26The mind of fools is in their mouth,
　　but the mouth of wise men is
　　in*o* their mind.
27When an ungodly man curses his
　　adversary,*p*
　　he curses his own soul.
28A whisperer defiles his own soul
　　and is hated in his neighborhood.

22 The indolent may be compared
　　to a filthy stone,
　　and every one hisses at his disgrace.
2The indolent may be compared to
　　the filth of dunghills;

m Other authorities read *for the winter*
n The Greek text of this line is uncertain
o Other authorities omit *in*
p Or *curses Satan*

ment." **8:** That is, he prepares for his own destruction. **9:** 16.6. **10:** *Smoothly paved,* Pr.14.12;
16.25; Mt.7.13.
　　21.11–28: The contrast between the wise man and the fool. 15: *Dislikes,* Syriac, "mocks at."
18a: Syriac, "As a prison-house is wisdom to a fool." **21:** This verse should follow v. 19.
20: 19.30; Ec.7.6. **22:** Pr.25.17. **28:** 5.14; 28.13.
　　22.1–18: Concerning laziness and foolishness. 1b: Syriac, "Everyone flees from the stench

any one that picks it up will
shake it off his hand.

³It is a disgrace to be the father of
an undisciplined son,
and the birth of a daughter is a
loss.
⁴A sensible daughter obtains her
husband,
but one who acts shamefully
brings grief to her father.
⁵An impudent daughter disgraces
father and husband,
and will be despised by both.
⁶Like music in mourning is a tale
told at the wrong time,
but chastising and discipline are
wisdom at all times.

⁷He who teaches a fool is like
one who glues potsherds
together,
or who rouses a sleeper from
deep slumber.
⁸He who tells a story to a fool tells
it to a drowsy man;
and at the end he will say,
"What is it?"*q*
¹¹Weep for the dead, for he lacks
the light;
and weep for the fool, for he
lacks intelligence;
weep less bitterly for the dead, for
he has attained rest;
but the life of the fool is worse
than death.
¹²Mourning for the dead lasts seven
days,
but for a fool or an ungodly man
it lasts all his life.

¹³Do not talk much with a foolish
man,
and do not visit an unintelligent
man;
guard yourself from him to escape
trouble,
and you will not be soiled when
he shakes himself off;

avoid him and you will find rest,
and you will never be wearied by
his madness.
¹⁴What is heavier than lead?
And what is its name except
"Fool"?
¹⁵Sand, salt, and a piece of iron
are easier to bear than a stupid
man.

¹⁶A wooden beam firmly bonded
into a building
will not be torn loose by an
earthquake;
so the mind firmly fixed on a
reasonable counsel
will not be afraid in a crisis.
¹⁷A mind settled on an intelligent
thought
is like the stucco decoration on
the wall of a colonnade.*r*
¹⁸Fences set on a high place
will not stand firm against the
wind;
so a timid heart with a fool's
purpose
will not stand firm against any
fear.

¹⁹A man who pricks an eye will
make tears fall,
and one who pricks the heart
makes it show feeling.
²⁰One who throws a stone at birds
scares them away,
and one who reviles a friend will
break off the friendship.
²¹Even if you have drawn your sword
against a friend,
do not despair, for a renewal of
friendship is possible.
²²If you have opened your mouth
against your friend,
do not worry, for reconciliation
is possible;
but as for reviling, arrogance,

q Other authorities add ⁹*Children who are brought up in
a good life, conceal the lowly birth of their parents.*
¹⁰*Children who are disdainfully and boorishly haughty
stain the nobility of their kindred.*
r Or *on a smooth wall*

---

thereof." **3–6**: 16.1–5. **4**: *Obtains*, Hebrew, "becomes a treasure to." **5**: 42.11. **6**: Pr.25.20.
7: A thankless task. **12**: *Seven days*, Gen.50.10; Jdt.16.24. **13b**: *An unintelligent man*, Syriac,
"a pig in the way" (compare v. 13d). **15**: *Sand*, Job 6.3; Pr.27.3.

disclosure of secrets, or a
treacherous blow—
in these cases any friend will
flee.

23Gain the trust of your neighbor in
his poverty,
that you may rejoice with him
in his prosperity;
stand by him in time of affliction,
that you may share with him in
his inheritance.*s*
24The vapor and smoke of the
furnace precede the fire;
so insults precede bloodshed.
25I will not be ashamed to protect
a friend,
and I will not hide from him;
26but if some harm should happen
to me because of him,
whoever hears of it will beware
of him.

27O that a guard were set over my
mouth,
and a seal of prudence upon my
lips,
that it may keep me from falling,
so that my tongue may not
destroy me!*t*

23 O Lord, Father and Ruler
of my life,
do not abandon me to their
counsel,
and let me not fall because of
them!
2O that whips were set over my
thoughts,
and the discipline of wisdom
over my mind!*u*
That they may not spare me in my
errors,
and that it may not pass by my*v*
sins;
3in order that my mistakes may not
be multiplied,
and my sins may not abound;
then I will not fall before my
adversaries,

and my enemy will not rejoice
over me.
4O Lord, Father and God of my life,
do not give me haughty eyes,
5 and remove from me evil desire.
6Let neither gluttony nor lust
overcome me,
and do not surrender me to a
shameless soul.

7Listen, my children, to instruction
concerning speech;
the one who observes it will
never be caught.
8The sinner is overtaken through
his lips,
the reviler and the arrogant are
tripped by them.
9Do not accustom your mouth to
oaths,
and do not habitually utter the
name of the Holy One;
10for as a servant who is continually
examined under torture
will not lack bruises,
so also the man who always swears
and utters the Name
will not be cleansed from sin.
11A man who swears many oaths will
be filled with iniquity,
and the scourge will not leave
his house;
if he offends, his sin remains on
him,
and if he disregards it, he sins
doubly;
if he has sworn needlessly, he will
not be justified,
for his house will be filled with
calamities.

12There is an utterance which is
comparable to death;*w*
may it never be found in the
inheritance of Jacob!

s Other authorities add *For one should not always despise
restricted circumstances, nor admire a rich man who
is stupid.*
t Or *Who will set a guard . . . destroy me?*
u Or *Who will set whips . . . my mind?*   v Gk *their*
w Other authorities read *clothed about with death*

22.19–26: The preservation of friendship. 25: *A friend*, Syriac adds, "who becomes poor."
22.27–23.6: A prayer for self-control. 27: Ps.141.3.
23.7–15: The proper use of the tongue (compare Jas.3.5–12). **11:** Lev.5.4. **12a:** Lev.24.15–16.

For all these errors will be far from
the godly,
and they will not wallow in
sins.
13Do not accustom your mouth to
lewd vulgarity,
for it involves sinful speech.
14Remember your father and
mother
when*x* you sit among great
men;
lest you be forgetful in their
presence,
and be deemed a fool on
account of your habits;
then you will wish that you had
never been born,
and you will curse the day of
your birth.
15A man accustomed to use insulting
words
will never become disciplined
all his days.

16Two sorts of men multiply sins,
and a third incurs wrath.
The soul heated like a burning fire
will not be quenched until it is
consumed;
a man who commits fornication
with his near of kin*y*
will never cease until the fire
burns him up.
17To a fornicator all bread tastes
sweet;
he will never cease until he dies.
18A man who breaks his marriage
vows
says to himself, "Who sees me?
Darkness surrounds me, and the
walls hide me,
and no one sees me. Why should
I fear?
The Most High will not take notice
of my sins."
19His fear is confined to the eyes of
men,
and he does not realize that the
eyes of the Lord

are ten thousand times brighter
than the sun;
they look upon all the ways of
men,
and perceive even the hidden
places.
20Before the universe was created, it
was known to him;
so it was also after it was
finished.
21This man will be punished in the
streets of the city,
and where he least suspects it,
he will be seized.
22So it is with a woman who leaves
her husband
and provides an heir by a
stranger.
23For first of all, she has disobeyed
the law of the Most High;
second, she has committed
an offense against her
husband;
and third, she has committed
adultery through harlotry
and brought forth children by
another man.
24She herself will be brought before
the assembly,
and punishment will fall on her
children.
25Her children will not take root,
and her branches will not bear
fruit.
26She will leave her memory for a
curse,
and her disgrace will not be
blotted out.
27Those who survive her will
recognize
that nothing is better than the
fear of the Lord,
and nothing sweeter than to heed
the commandments of the
Lord.*z*

x Gk for
y Gk in the body of his flesh
z Other authorities add 28*It is a great honor to follow*
God, and to be received by him is long life.

23.16–27: Sins of the flesh. 16: *The fire,* of passion. **17:** *All bread,* a euphemism (Syriac,
"all flesh"). **18:** Job 24.15. **19:** 15.19; Pr.15.3. **21–22:** Lev.20.10; Dt.22.21–23. **24–25:** Dt.23.2;
Wis.3.16–19; 4.3–6.

24

Wisdom will praise herself,
and will glory in the midst
of her people.*a*
²In the assembly of the Most High
she will open her mouth,
and in the presence of his host
she will glory:
³"I came forth from the mouth of
the Most High,
and covered the earth like a mist.
⁴I dwelt in high places,
and my throne was in a pillar of
cloud.
⁵Alone I have made the circuit of
the vault of heaven
and have walked in the depths
of the abyss.
⁶In the waves of the sea, in the
whole earth,
and in every people and nation
I have gotten a possession.
⁷Among all these I sought a resting
place;
I sought in whose territory I
might lodge.

⁸"Then the Creator of all things
gave me a commandment,
and the one who created me
assigned a place for my tent.
And he said, 'Make your dwelling
in Jacob,
and in Israel receive your
inheritance.'
⁹From eternity, in the beginning,
he created me,
and for eternity I shall not cease
to exist.
¹⁰In the holy tabernacle I ministered
before him,
and so I was established in Zion.
¹¹In the beloved city likewise he
gave me a resting place,
and in Jerusalem was my
dominion.
¹²So I took root in an honored people,
in the portion of the Lord, who
is their inheritance.

¹³"I grew tall like a cedar in Lebanon,

and like a cypress on the heights
of Hermon.
¹⁴I grew tall like a palm tree in
En-ge'di,*b*
and like rose plants in Jericho;
like a beautiful olive tree in the
field,
and like a plane tree I grew
tall.
¹⁵Like cassia and camel's thorn I
gave forth the aroma of spices,
and like choice myrrh I spread
a pleasant odor,
like galbanum, onycha, and stacte,
and like the fragrance of
frankincense in the tabernacle.
¹⁶Like a terebinth I spread out my
branches,
and my branches are glorious
and graceful.
¹⁷Like a vine I caused loveliness to
bud,
and my blossoms became
glorious and abundant
fruit.*c*

¹⁹"Come to me, you who desire
me,
and eat your fill of my produce.
²⁰For the remembrance of me is
sweeter than honey,
and my inheritance sweeter than
the honeycomb.
²¹Those who eat me will hunger for
more,
and those who drink me will
thirst for more.
²²Whoever obeys me will not be put
to shame,
and those who work with my
help will not sin."

²³All this is the book of the covenant
of the Most High God,
the law which Moses
commanded us

a Or *will glorify herself in the midst of the people.*
b Other authorities read *on the beaches*
c Other authorities add ¹⁸*I am the mother of beautiful love, of fear, of knowledge, and of holy hope; being eternal, I therefore am given to all my children, to those who are named by him.*

24.1–34: Praise of wisdom. 3–22: Pr.8.22–9.12. **4:** *Pillar of cloud,* Ex.33.9–10. **6:** *Have gotten a possession,* Syriac and Latin, "have ruled." **19:** Is.55.1 **20:** Ps.19.10.

as an inheritance for the
congregations of Jacob.[d]
²⁵It fills men with wisdom, like the
Pishon,
and like the Tigris at the time
of the first fruits.
²⁶It makes them full of understanding,
like the Euphrates,
and like the Jordan at harvest
time.
²⁷It makes instruction shine forth
like light,
like the Gihon at the time of
vintage.
²⁸Just as the first man did not know
her perfectly,
the last one has not fathomed
her;
²⁹for her thought is more abundant
than the sea,
and her counsel deeper than the
great abyss.

³⁰I went forth like a canal from a
river
and like a water channel into a
garden.
³¹I said, "I will water my orchard
and drench my garden
plot";
and lo, my canal became a
river,
and my river became a sea.
³²I will again make instruction shine
forth like the dawn,
and I will make it shine afar;
³³I will again pour out teaching like
prophecy,
and leave it to all future
generations.
³⁴Observe that I have not labored
for myself alone,
but for all who seek instruction.[e]

25 My soul takes pleasure in
three things,

and they are beautiful in the
sight of the Lord and of men:[f]
agreement between brothers,
friendship between neighbors,
and a wife and husband who
live in harmony.
²My soul hates three kinds of
men,
and I am greatly offended at
their life:
a beggar who is proud, a rich man
who is a liar,
and an adulterous old man who
lacks good sense.

³You have gathered nothing in your
youth;
how then can you find anything
in your old age?
⁴What an attractive thing is judgment
in gray-haired men,
and for the aged to possess good
counsel!
⁵How attractive is wisdom in the
aged,
and understanding and counsel
in honorable men!
⁶Rich experience is the crown of the
aged,
and their boast is the fear of the
Lord.

⁷With nine thoughts I have gladdened
my heart,
and a tenth I shall tell with my
tongue:
a man rejoicing in his children;
a man who lives to see the
downfall of his foes;
⁸happy is he who lives with an
intelligent wife,

d Other authorities add ²⁴"*Do not cease to be strong in
the Lord, cleave to him so that he may strengthen you;
the Lord Almighty alone is God, and besides him there
is no savior.*"
e Gk *it*
f Syr Vg: Gk *In three things I was beautified and I stood
in beauty before the Lord and men*

25: Gen.2.11,14.   **26:** Jos.3.15.   **30–34:** The author compares himself to an irrigation canal
leading off from the great river of wisdom.   **34:** 33.17.
    25.1–2: Three beautiful and three hateful things.
    25.3–6: The attractiveness of wisdom in the aged.
    25.7–11: Ten happy thoughts. 8a: Hebrew and Syriac add, "and does not plow with ox and
ass" (compare Dt.22.10).

and he who has not made a slip
   with his tongue,
and he who has not served a
   man inferior to himself;
⁹happy is he who has gained good
   sense,
and he who speaks to attentive
   listeners.
¹⁰How great is he who has gained
   wisdom!
But there is no one superior to
   him who fears the Lord.
¹¹The fear of the Lord surpasses
   everything;
to whom shall be likened the
   one who holds it fast?ᵍ

¹³Any wound, but not a wound of
   the heart!
Any wickedness, but not the
   wickedness of a wife!
¹⁴Any attack, but not an attack from
   those who hate!
And any vengeance, but not the
   vengeance of enemies!
¹⁵There is no venomʰ worse than a
   snake's venom,ʰ
and no wrath worse than an
   enemy's wrath.

¹⁶I would rather dwell with a lion
   and a dragon
than dwell with an evil wife.
¹⁷The wickedness of a wife changes
   her appearance,
and darkens her face like that of
   a bear.
¹⁸Her husband takes his meals among
   the neighbors,
and he cannot help sighingⁱ
   bitterly.
¹⁹Any iniquity is insignificant
   compared to a wife's iniquity;
may a sinner's lot befall her!
²⁰A sandy ascent for the feet of the
   aged—

such is a garrulous wife for a
   quiet husband.
²¹Do not be ensnared by a woman's
   beauty,
and do not desire a woman for
   her possessions.ʲ
²²There is wrath and impudence and
   great disgrace
when a wife supports her
   husband.
²³A dejected mind, a gloomy face,
and a wounded heart are caused
   by an evil wife.
Drooping hands and weak knees
are caused by the wife who
   does not make her husband
   happy.
²⁴From a woman sin had its
   beginning,
and because of her we all die.
²⁵Allow no outlet to water,
and no boldness of speech in an
   evil wife.
²⁶If she does not go as you
   direct,
separate her from yourself.

26 Happy is the husband of a
   good wife;
the number of his days will be
   doubled.
²A loyal wife rejoices her husband,
and he will complete his years
   in peace.
³A good wife is a great blessing;
she will be granted among the
   blessings of the man who fears
   the Lord.
⁴Whether rich or poor, his heart is
   glad,
and at all times his face is
   cheerful.

g Other authorities add ¹²*The fear of the Lord is the
beginning of love for him, and faith is the beginning of
clinging to him.*
h Cn: Gk *head*
i Other authorities read *and listening he sighs*
j Heb Syr: Some Gk authorities read *for her beauty*

25.13–26: Wicked and virtuous women. 15: *An enemy's*, Syriac, "a woman's." **16:** Pr.21.19;
25.24. **20a:** It is tedious and wearisome. **21:** 42.12. **24:** Gen.3.6; 2 Cor.11.3; 1 Tim.2.14.
26b: Literally, "cut her off from your flesh," that is, divorce her (Dt.24.1); hitherto they had
been "one flesh" (Gen.2.24).
   26.1–4: The happiness of the husband of a good wife (Pr.31.10–31). **2:** *Rejoices*, Hebrew,
"makes fat" (v.13). **3:** 36.24; Pr.12.4.

⁵Of three things my heart is afraid,
  and of a fourth I am frightened:ᵏ
The slander of a city, the gathering
  of a mob,
  and false accusation—all these
  are worse than death.
⁶There is grief of heart and sorrow
  when a wife is envious of a
  rival,
  and a tongue-lashing makes it
  known to all.
⁷An evil wife is an ox yoke which
  chafes;
  taking hold of her is like grasping
  a scorpion.
⁸There is great anger when a wife
  is drunken;
  she will not hide her shame.
⁹A wife's harlotry shows in her
  lustful eyes,
  and she is known by her eyelids.
¹⁰Keep strict watch over a headstrong
  daughter,
  lest, when she finds liberty, she
  use it to her hurt.
¹¹Be on guard against her impudent
  eye,
  and do not wonder if she sins
  against you.
¹²As a thirsty wayfarer opens his
  mouth
  and drinks from any water near
  him,
  so will she sit in front of every post
  and open her quiver to the arrow.

¹³A wife's charm delights her husband,
  and her skill puts fat on his bones.
¹⁴A silent wife is a gift of the Lord,
  and there is nothing so precious
  as a disciplined soul.
¹⁵A modest wife adds charm to charm,
  and no balance can weigh the
  value of a chaste soul.
¹⁶Like the sun rising in the heights
  of the Lord,
  so is the beauty of a good wife in
  her well-ordered home.

¹⁷Like the shining lamp on the holy
  lampstand,
  so is a beautiful face on a stately
  figure.
¹⁸Like pillars of gold on a base of
  silver,
  so are beautiful feet with a
  steadfast heart.ˡ

²⁸At two things my heart is grieved,
  and because of a third anger
  comes over me:
  a warrior in want through poverty,
  and intelligent men who are
  treated contemptuously;
  a man who turns back from
  righteousness to sin—
  the Lord will prepare him for the
  sword!

²⁹A merchant can hardly keep from
  wrongdoing,
  and a tradesman will not be
  declared innocent of sin.

27 Many have committed sin
  for a trifle,ᵐ
  and whoever seeks to get rich
  will avert his eyes.
²As a stake is driven firmly into a
  fissure between stones,

k The Greek of this line is uncertain
l Other authorities add verses 19–27:
¹⁹*My son, keep sound the bloom of your youth,
  and do not give your strength to strangers.*
²⁰*Seek a fertile field within the whole plain,
  and sow it with your own seed, trusting in your fine
  stock.*
²¹*So your offspring will survive
  and, having confidence in their good descent, will grow
  great.*
²²*A harlot is regarded as spittle,
  and a married woman as a tower of death to her
  lovers.*
²³*A godless wife is given as a portion to a lawless man,
  but a pious wife is given to the man who fears the Lord.*
²⁴*A shameless woman constantly acts disgracefully,
  but a modest daughter will even be embarrassed before
  her husband.*
²⁵*A headstrong wife is regarded as a dog,
  but one who has a sense of shame will fear the Lord.*
²⁶*A wife honoring her husband will seem wise to all,
  but if she dishonors him in her pride she will be known
  to all as ungodly.*
*Happy is the husband of a good wife;
  for the number of his years will be doubled.*
²⁷*A loud-voiced and garrulous wife is regarded as a war
  trumpet for putting the enemy to flight,
  and every person like this lives in the anarchy of war.*
m One ancient authority reads *gain*

26.5–12: A wicked wife. 10: 42.11.
  26.13–18: A good wife. 18: *With . . . heart,* other witnesses read, "upon firm heels."
  26.28–27.3: Miscellaneous observations. 26.28: *A warrior,* Syriac, "a wealthy man." **27.1:**
Pr.28.21.

so sin is wedged in between
selling and buying.
³If a man is not steadfast and zealous
in the fear of the Lord,
his house will be quickly
overthrown.

⁴When a sieve is shaken, the refuse
remains;
so a man's filth remains in his
thoughts.
⁵The kiln tests the potter's vessels;
so the test of a man is in his
reasoning.
⁶The fruit discloses the cultivation
of a tree;
so the expression of a thought
discloses the cultivation of a
man's mind.
⁷Do not praise a man before you
hear him reason,
for this is the test of men.

⁸If you pursue justice, you will
attain it
and wear it as a glorious robe.
⁹Birds flock with their kind;
so truth returns to those who
practice it.
¹⁰A lion lies in wait for prey;
so does sin for the workers of
iniquity.

¹¹The talk of the godly man is
always wise,
but the fool changes like the
moon.
¹²Among stupid people watch for a
chance to leave,
but among thoughtful people
stay on.
¹³The talk of fools is offensive,
and their laughter is wantonly
sinful.
¹⁴The talk of men given to swearing
makes one's hair stand on end,

and their quarrels make a man
stop his ears.
¹⁵The strife of the proud leads to
bloodshed,
and their abuse is grievous to
hear.

¹⁶Whoever betrays secrets destroys
confidence,
and he will never find a
congenial friend.
¹⁷Love your friend and keep faith
with him;
but if you betray his secrets, do
not run after him.
¹⁸For as a man destroys his enemy,
so you have destroyed the
friendship of your neighbor.
¹⁹And as you allow a bird to escape
from your hand,
so you have let your neighbor
go, and will not catch him
again.
²⁰Do not go after him, for he is too
far off,
and has escaped like a gazelle
from a snare.
²¹For a wound may be bandaged,
and there is reconciliation after
abuse,
but whoever has betrayed secrets is
without hope.

²²Whoever winks his eye plans evil
deeds,
and no one can keep him from
them.
²³In your presence his mouth is all
sweetness,
and he admires your words;
but later he will twist his speech
and with your own words he
will give offense.
²⁴I have hated many things, but none
to be compared to him;
even the Lord will hate him.

27.4–7: Tests in life. 6: Mt.7.17.
27.8–10: Reward and retribution.
27.11–15: Kinds of talk.
27.16–21: Against disclosing secrets (Pr.20.19; 25.9). 18: *Enemy*, Syriac, "inheritance."
21: *Without hope*, of reconciliation (22.22).
27.22–24: Hypocrisy. 22: *Winks*, with insincerity (Ps.35.19; Pr.6.13; 10.10).

25Whoever throws a stone straight
    up throws it on his own head;
    and a treacherous blow opens up
      wounds.
26He who digs a pit will fall into it,
    and he who sets a snare will be
      caught in it.
27If a man does evil, it will roll back
    upon him,
    and he will not know where it
      came from.
28Mockery and abuse issue from the
    proud man,*n*
    but vengeance lies in wait for
      him like a lion.
29Those who rejoice in the fall of the
    godly will be caught in a
      snare,
    and pain will consume them
      before their death.

30Anger and wrath, these also are
    abominations,
    and the sinful man will possess
      them.

28 He that takes vengeance will
    suffer vengeance from the
      Lord,
    and he will firmly establish*o* his
      sins.
2Forgive your neighbor the wrong
    he has done,
    and then your sins will be
      pardoned when you pray.
3Does a man harbor anger against
    another,
    and yet seek for healing from
      the Lord?
4Does he have no mercy toward a
    man like himself,
    and yet pray for his own sins?
5If he himself, being flesh, maintains
    wrath,
    who will make expiation for his
      sins?
6Remember the end of your life, and
    cease from enmity,

remember destruction and death,
    and be true to the
      commandments.
7Remember the commandments,
    and do not be angry with your
      neighbor;
    remember the covenant of the
      Most High, and overlook
      ignorance.

8Refrain from strife, and you will
    lessen sins;
    for a man given to anger will
      kindle strife,
9and a sinful man will disturb
    friends
    and inject enmity among those
      who are at peace.
10In proportion to the fuel for the
    fire, so will be the burning,
    and in proportion to the
      obstinacy of strife will be
      the burning;*p*
in proportion to the strength of the
    man will be his anger,
    and in proportion to his wealth
      he will heighten his wrath.
11A hasty quarrel kindles fire,
    and urgent strife sheds blood.
12If you blow on a spark, it will glow;
    if you spit on it, it will be put out;
    and both come out of your mouth.

13Curse the whisperer and deceiver,
    for he has destroyed many who
      were at peace.
14Slander*q* has shaken many,
    and scattered them from nation
      to nation,
    and destroyed strong cities,
    and overturned the houses of
      great men.
15Slander*q* has driven away
    courageous women,

n Other authorities read *proud men*
o Other authorities read *closely observe*
p Other authorities place this line at the end of the verse,
   or omit it
q Gk *a third tongue*

27.25–29: Retribution (Ps.7.14–16; 9.15–16; Pr.26.27; Ec.10.8).
    27.30–28.7: Vengeance. 1: Dt.32.35; Rom.12.19. **2:** Mt.6.14; Mk.11.25. **3:** Mt.18.23–35.
4: Mt.5.7. **6:** 7.36.
    28.8–12: Strife and quarrels. 8: Pr.15.18. **10:** Pr.26.20–21; Jas.3.5. **12:** Pr.15.1.
    28.13–26: Slander and an evil tongue (51.2–6; Jas.3.5–12). **15:** *Has driven away,* from their

and deprived them of the fruit
of their toil.

¹⁶Whoever pays heed to slander^r
will not find rest,
nor will he settle down in peace.

¹⁷The blow of a whip raises a welt,
but a blow of the tongue crushes
the bones.

¹⁸Many have fallen by the edge of
the sword,
but not so many as have fallen
because of the tongue.

¹⁹Happy is the man who is protected
from it,
who has not been exposed to its
anger,
who has not borne its yoke,
and has not been bound with its
fetters;

²⁰for its yoke is a yoke of iron,
and its fetters are fetters of
bronze;

²¹its death is an evil death,
and Hades is preferable to it.

²²It will not be master over the
godly,
and they will not be burned in its
flame.

²³Those who forsake the Lord will
fall into its power;
it will burn among them and
will not be put out.
It will be sent out against them like
a lion;
like a leopard it will mangle
them.

²⁴See that you fence in your property
with thorns,
lock up your silver and gold,

²⁵make balances and scales for your
words,
and make a door and a bolt for
your mouth.

²⁶Beware lest you err with your
tongue,^s
lest you fall before him who lies
in wait.

29 He that shows mercy will
lend to his neighbor,

and he that strengthens him with
his hand keeps the
commandments.

²Lend to your neighbor in the time
of his need;
and in turn, repay your neighbor
promptly.

³Confirm your word and keep faith
with him,
and on every occasion you will
find what you need.

⁴Many persons regard a loan as a
windfall,
and cause trouble to those who
help them.

⁵A man will kiss another's hands
until he gets a loan,
and will lower his voice in
speaking of his neighbor's
money;
but at the time for repayment he
will delay,
and will pay in words of
unconcern,
and will find fault with the
time.

⁶If the lender^t exerts pressure, he
will hardly get back half,
and will regard that as a
windfall.
If he does not, the borrower^u has
robbed him of his money,
and he has needlessly made him
his enemy;
he will repay him with curses and
reproaches,
and instead of glory will repay
him with dishonor.

⁷Because of such wickedness,
therefore,^v many have refused
to lend;
they have been afraid of being
defrauded needlessly.

⁸Nevertheless, be patient with a
man in humble circumstances,

r Gk *it*
s Gk *with it*
t Gk *he*
u Gk *he*
v Other authorities read *It is not because of wickedness
that*

---

homes. **16:** The statement refers primarily to the husband. **17:** Pr.25.15. **25b:** 22.27; Ps.141.3.
29.1–13: Concerning loans (Ex.22.25; Lev.25.36; Mt.5.42; Lk.6.35). **2:** Pr.19.17. **4:** 8.12.

and do not make him wait for
your alms.
⁹Help a poor man for the
commandment's sake,
and because of his need do not
send him away empty.
¹⁰Lose your silver for the sake of a
brother or a friend,
and do not let it rust under a
stone and be lost.
¹¹Lay up your treasure according to
the commandments of the
Most High,
and it will profit you more than
gold.
¹²Store up almsgiving in your
treasury,
and it will rescue you from all
affliction;
¹³more than a mighty shield and
more than a heavy spear,
it will fight on your behalf
against your enemy.

¹⁴A good man will be surety for his
neighbor,
but a man who has lost his
sense of shame will fail him.
¹⁵Do not forget all the kindness of
your surety,
for he has given his life for you.
¹⁶A sinner will overthrow the
prosperity of his surety,
¹⁷ and one who does not feel grateful will abandon his rescuer.
¹⁸Being surety has ruined many men
who were prosperous,
and has shaken them like a wave
of the sea;
it has driven men of power into exile,
and they have wandered among
foreign nations.
¹⁹The sinner who has fallen into
suretyship
and pursues gain will fall into
lawsuits.

²⁰Assist your neighbor according to
your ability,
but take heed to yourself lest
you fall.
²¹The essentials for life are water
and bread
and clothing and a house to
cover one's nakedness.
²²Better is the life of a poor man
under the shelter of his roof
than sumptuous food in another
man's house.
²³Be content with little or much.ʷ
²⁴It is a miserable life to go from
house to house,
and where you are a stranger you
may not open your mouth;
²⁵you will play the host and provide
drink without being thanked,
and besides this you will hear
bitter words:
²⁶"Come here, stranger, prepare the
table,
and if you have anything at
hand, let me have it to eat."
²⁷"Give place, stranger, to an
honored person;
my brother has come to stay
with me; I need my house."
²⁸These things are hard to bear for
a man who has feeling:
scolding about lodgingˣ and
the reproach of the
moneylender.

30 He who loves his son will
whip him often,
in order that he may rejoice at
the way he turns out.
²He who disciplines his son will
profit by him,
and will boast of him among
acquaintances.

w Other authorities add *and you will not hear reproach
for your sojourning.*
x Or *from the household,* or (Syr) *from the host*

10: *Rust,* Mt.6.19; Jas.5.3. **11:** Syriac, "Lay up for yourself a treasure of righteousness [i.e.
through almsgiving] and love, and it shall profit you more than all that you have" (see 3.30 n.
and compare Mt.19.21; Lk.12.33).
 29.14–20: Concerning suretyship. 14: Contrast Pr.6.1–5; 17.18. **20:** 8.13.
 29.21–28: On contentment and hospitality. 21: 39.26. **23:** Phil.4.11; 1 Tim.6.8; Heb.13.5.
28: Syriac adds, "Give very freely to the poor, and feed him from that which is at hand; if he is

³He who teaches his son will make
his enemies envious,
and will glory in him in the
presence of friends.
⁴The*ʸ* father may die, and yet he
is not dead,
for he has left behind him one
like himself;
⁵while alive he saw and rejoiced,
and when he died he was not
grieved;
⁶he has left behind him an avenger
against his enemies,
and one to repay the kindness
of his friends.

⁷He who spoils his son will bind up
his wounds,
and his feelings will be troubled
at every cry.
⁸A horse that is untamed turns out
to be stubborn,
and a son unrestrained turns out
to be wilful.
⁹Pamper a child, and he will frighten
you;
play with him, and he will give
you grief.
¹⁰Do not laugh with him, lest you
have sorrow with him,
and in the end you will gnash
your teeth.
¹¹Give him no authority in his
youth,
and do not ignore his errors.
¹²Bow down his neck in his
youth,*ᶻ*
and beat his sides while he is
young,
lest he become stubborn and
disobey you,
and you have sorrow of soul
from him.*ᵃ*
¹³Discipline your son and take pains
with him,

that you may not be offended by
his shamelessness.

¹⁴Better off is a poor man who is well
and strong in constitution
than a rich man who is severely
afflicted in body.
¹⁵Health and soundness are better
than all gold,
and a robust body than countless
riches.
¹⁶There is no wealth better than
health of body,
and there is no gladness above
joy of heart.
¹⁷Death is better than a miserable
life,
and eternal rest*ᵇ* than chronic
sickness.

¹⁸Good things poured out upon a
mouth that is closed
are like offerings of food placed
upon a grave.
¹⁹Of what use to an idol is an
offering of fruit?
For it can neither eat nor smell.
So is he who is afflicted by the
Lord;
²⁰he sees with his eyes and groans,
like a eunuch who embraces a
maiden and groans.

²¹Do not give yourself over to sorrow,
and do not afflict yourself
deliberately.
²²Gladness of heart is the life of man,
and the rejoicing of a man is
length of days.
²³Delight your soul and comfort your
heart,
and remove sorrow far from you,

y Gk *His*
z Other authorities omit this line and the preceding line
a Other authorities omit this line
b Some authorities omit *eternal rest*

---

naked, clothe him; thus you will be lending unto God, and he will repay you sevenfold" (compare Is.58.7; Mt.25.35–36).

30.1–13: On bringing up children. 1: Pr.13.24; 23.13–14; 29.15. **2:** Pr.29.17. **11:** 7.23. **13:** *Take pains with him,* Hebrew, "make his yoke heavy."

30:14–20: Concerning health. 18: Tob.4.17. **19:** Let.Jer.27–28; Bel 3 (compare Ps.115.5–7). **20:** *Groans,* with regret.

30.21–25: Gladness of heart (Ec.11.9–10). **21:** 38.20; Pr.12.25. **22:** 15.13; 17.22. **23:** 38.18–19.

for sorrow has destroyed many,
   and there is no profit in it.
24 Jealousy and anger shorten life,
   and anxiety brings on old age
     too soon.
25 A man of cheerful and good heart
   will give heed to the food he
     eats.

31 Wakefulness over wealth
   wastes away one's flesh,
   and anxiety about it removes
     sleep.
2 Wakeful anxiety prevents slumber,
   and a severe illness carries off
     sleep.*c*
3 The rich man toils as his wealth
   accumulates,
   and when he rests he fills himself
     with his dainties.
4 The poor man toils as his livelihood
   diminishes,
   and when he rests he becomes
     needy.

5 He who loves gold will not be
   justified,
   and he who pursues money will
     be led astray*d* by it.
6 Many have come to ruin because
   of gold,
   and their destruction has met
     them face to face.
7 It is a stumbling block to those
   who are devoted to it,
   and every fool will be taken
     captive by it.
8 Blessed is the rich man who is
   found blameless,
   and who does not go after gold.
9 Who is he? And we will call him
   blessed,
   for he has done wonderful things
     among his people.
10 Who has been tested by it and
   been found perfect?
   Let it be for him a ground for
     boasting.

Who has had the power to
   transgress and did not
   transgress,
   and to do evil and did not do it?
11 His prosperity will be established,
   and the assembly will relate his
     acts of charity.

12 Are you seated at the table of a
   great man?*e*
   Do not be greedy*f* at it,
   and do not say, "There is
     certainly much upon it!"
13 Remember that a greedy*g* eye is
   a bad thing.
   What has been created more
     greedy*g* than the eye?
   Therefore it sheds tears from
     every face.
14 Do not reach out your hand for
   everything you see,
   and do not crowd your neighbor*h*
     at the dish.
15 Judge your neighbor's feelings by
   your own,
   and in every matter be
     thoughtful.
16 Eat like a human being what is set
   before you,
   and do not chew greedily, lest
     you be hated.
17 Be the first to stop eating, for the
   sake of good manners,
   and do not be insatiable, lest
     you give offense.
18 If you are seated among many
   persons,
   do not reach out your hand
     before they do.

19 How ample a little is for a well-
   disciplined man!
   He does not breathe heavily
     upon his bed.

c Other authorities read *sleep carries off a severe illness*
d Heb Syr: Gk *will be filled*
e Heb Syr: Gk *at a great table*
f Gk *open your throat*
g Gk *evil*   *h* Gk *him*

31.1–11: **The right attitude toward wealth. 1:** 1 Tim.6.9–10. **4:** The opposite of v. 3 (compare 11.11).
   31.12–30: **Temperance in food and drink. 12:** Pr.23.1–3. **15b:** Hebrew, "and keep in mind your own dislikes." **16:** *Like a human being*, and not like an animal. **17:** 37.29.

²⁰Healthy sleep depends on moderate
  eating;
he rises early, and feels fit.*ⁱ*
The distress of sleeplessness and
  of nausea
and colic are with the glutton.
²¹If you are overstuffed with food,
  get up in the middle of the
  meal, and you will have relief.
²²Listen to me, my son, and do not
  disregard me,
and in the end you will appreciate
  my words.
In all your work be industrious,
  and no sickness will overtake you.

²³Men will praise the one who is
  liberal with food,
and their testimony to his
  excellence is trustworthy.
²⁴The city will complain of the one
  who is niggardly with food,
and their testimony to his
  niggardliness is accurate.

²⁵Do not aim to be valiant over wine,
  for wine has destroyed many.
²⁶Fire and water prove*ʲ* the temper
  of steel,
so wine tests hearts in the strife
  of the proud.
²⁷Wine is like life to men,
  if you drink it in moderation.
What is life to a man who is
  without wine?
It has been created to make men
  glad.
²⁸Wine drunk in season and
  temperately
is rejoicing of heart and gladness
  of soul.
²⁹Wine drunk to excess is bitterness
  of soul,
with provocation and stumbling.
³⁰Drunkenness increases the anger
  of a fool to his injury,
reducing his strength and adding
  wounds.

³¹Do not reprove your neighbor at
  a banquet of wine,
and do not despise him in his
  merrymaking;
speak no word of reproach to him,
and do not afflict him by making
  demands of him.

32 If they make you master of
  the feast, do not exalt
  yourself;
be among them as one of
  them;
take good care of them and then
  be seated;
² when you have fulfilled your
  duties, take your place,
that you may be merry on their
  account
and receive a wreath for your
  excellent leadership.

³Speak, you who are older, for it is
  fitting that you should,
but with accurate knowledge,
and do not interrupt the
  music.
⁴Where there is entertainment, do
  not pour out talk;
do not display your cleverness
  out of season.
⁵A ruby seal in a setting of gold
  is a concert of music at a
  banquet of wine.
⁶A seal of emerald in a rich setting
  of gold
is the melody of music with
  good wine.

⁷Speak, young man, if there is need
  of you,
but no more than twice, and
  only if asked.
⁸Speak concisely, say much in few
  words;
be as one who knows and yet
  holds his tongue.

i Gk his soul is with him
j Gk The furnace by dipping proves

22: *Be industrious*, Hebrew, "be moderate," which suits the context better. **23:** Pr.22.9. **25:** Is.5.22. **27:** Ps.104.15; Pr.31.6–7.
  31.31–32.13: Etiquette at a banquet. 2: *A wreath*, Syriac, "honor." **7–9:** Advice for younger guests.

9Among the great do not act as
their equal;
and when another is speaking,
do not babble.

10Lightning speeds before the
thunder,
and approval precedes a modest
man.
11Leave in good time and do not be
the last;
go home quickly and do not
linger.
12Amuse yourself there, and do what
you have in mind,
but do not sin through proud
speech.
13And for these things bless him who
made you
and satisfies you with his good
gifts.

14He who fears the Lord will accept
his discipline,
and those who rise early to seek
him[k] will find favor.
15He who seeks the law will be filled
with it,
but the hypocrite will stumble
at it.
16Those who fear the Lord will form
true judgments,
and like a light they will kindle
righteous deeds.
17A sinful man will shun reproof,
and will find a decision according
to his liking.

18A man of judgment will not
overlook an idea,
and an insolent[l] and proud
man will not cower in
fear.[m]
19Do nothing without deliberation;
and when you have acted, do not
regret it.

20Do not go on a path full of
hazards,
and do not stumble over stony
ground.
21Do not be overconfident on a
smooth[n] way,
22 and give good heed to your
paths.[o]
23Guard[p] yourself in every act,
for this is the keeping of the
commandments.

24He who believes the law gives heed
to the commandments,
and he who trusts the Lord will
not suffer loss.

33 No evil will befall the man
who fears the Lord,
but in trial he will deliver him
again and again.
2A wise man will not hate the law,
but he who is hypocritical about
it is like a boat in a storm.
3A man of understanding will trust
in the law;
for him the law is as dependable
as an inquiry by means of
Urim.

4Prepare what to say, and thus you
will be heard;
bind together your instruction,
and make your answer.
5The heart of a fool is like a cart
wheel,
and his thoughts like a turning
axle.
6A stallion is like a mocking
friend;
he neighs under every one who
sits on him.

k Other authorities omit *to seek him*
l Heb: Gk *alien*
m The meaning of this line is uncertain. Other authorities
add the phrases *and after acting, with him, without
deliberation*
n Or *an unexplored*
o Syr Vg: Gk *and beware of your children*
p Heb Syr: Gk *Trust*

32.14–33.6: The God-fearing man contrasted with the sinner. 32.14: 18.14; Job 5.17; Heb.
12.5–7. **17:** *A decision*, i.e. an interpretation (of the law). **20b:** Hebrew and Syriac, "Do not
trip over the same obstacle twice." **24a:** Hebrew and Syriac, "He who observes the law preserves himself" (Pr.19.16). **33.1:** Pr.12.21; 1 Pet.3.13. **2:** Hebrew, "He that hates the law is not
wise, and is tossed about like a boat in a storm." **3:** *Urim*, 45.10; Ex.28.30; Num.27.21; 1 Sam.
14.41–42.

⁷Why is any day better than
  another,
  when all the daylight in the
    year is from the sun?
⁸By the Lord's decision they were
    distinguished,
  and he appointed the different
    seasons and feasts;
⁹some of them he exalted and
    hallowed,
  and some of them he made
    ordinary days.
¹⁰All men are from the ground,
  and Adam was created of the
    dust.
¹¹In the fulness of his knowledge
    the Lord distinguished them
  and appointed their different
    ways;
¹²some of them he blessed and
    exalted,
  and some of them he made
    holy and brought near to
      himself;
  but some of them he cursed and
    brought low,
  and he turned them out of their
    place.
¹³As clay in the hand of the potter—
  for all his ways are as he
    pleases—
  so men are in the hand of him
    who made them,
  to give them as he decides.

¹⁴Good is the opposite of evil,
  and life the opposite of death;
  so the sinner is the opposite of
    the godly.
¹⁵Look upon all the works of the
    Most High;
  they likewise are in pairs, one
    the opposite of the other.

¹⁶I was the last on watch;

I was like one who gleans after
  the grape-gatherers;
by the blessing of the Lord I
  excelled,
and like a grape-gatherer I filled
  my wine press.
¹⁷Consider that I have not labored
    for myself alone,
  but for all who seek instruction.
¹⁸Hear me, you who are great among
    the people,
  and you leaders of the
    congregation, hearken.

¹⁹To son or wife, to brother or
    friend,
  do not give power over yourself,
    as long as you live;
  and do not give your property to
    another,
  lest you change your mind and
    must ask for it.
²⁰While you are still alive and have
    breath in you,
  do not let any one take your
    place.
²¹For it is better that your children
    should ask from you
  than that you should look to the
    hand of your sons.
²²Excel in all that you do;
  bring no stain upon your honor.
²³At the time when you end the days
    of your life,
  in the hour of death, distribute
    your inheritance.

²⁴Fodder and a stick and burdens
    for an ass;
  bread and discipline and work
    for a servant.
²⁵Set your slave to work, and you
    will find rest;
  leave his hands idle, and he will
    seek liberty.

33.7–15: **Divinely ordained diversities in nature. 10:** Gen.2.7; Job 10.9. **11:** *Ways*, destinies.
12: *Blessed*, Gen.9.1; 12.2. *Made holy*, ordained to the priesthood (Num.16.5,10; Ezek.40.46;
42.13; 45.4). *Cursed*, Gen.9.25. **13:** Is.29.16; 45.9; 64.8; Jer.18.4,6; Wis.15.7–8; Rom.9.21.
15: 42.24 (compare Ec.3.2–8).
33.16–18: **The author's qualifications as a teacher** (24.30–34). **17:** 24.34; Wis.6.1–2.
33.19–23: **On preserving one's financial independence.**
33.24–31: **On the treatment of slaves** (7.20–21). The rights of slaves were defined in the

26Yoke and thong will bow the neck,
and for a wicked servant there
are racks and tortures.
27Put him to work, that he may not
be idle,
for idleness teaches much evil.
28Set him to work, as is fitting for
him,
and if he does not obey, make
his fetters heavy.
29Do not act immoderately toward
anybody,
and do nothing without
discretion.

30If you have a servant, let him be
as yourself,
because you have bought him
with blood.
31If you have a servant, treat him as
a brother,
for as your own soul you will
need him.
If you ill-treat him, and he leaves
and runs away,
which way will you go to seek
him?

34 A man of no understanding
has vain and false hopes,
and dreams give wings to fools.
2As one who catches at a shadow
and pursues the wind,
so is he who gives heed to
dreams.
3The vision of dreams is this against
that,
the likeness of a face confronting
a face.
4From an unclean thing what will
be made clean?
And from something false what
will be true?
5Divinations and omens and dreams
are folly,

and like a woman in travail the
mind has fancies.
6Unless they are sent from the Most
High as a visitation,
do not give your mind to them.
7For dreams have deceived many,
and those who put their hope in
them have failed.
8Without such deceptions the law
will be fulfilled,
and wisdom is made perfect in
truthful lips.

9An educated*q* man knows many
things,
and one with much experience
will speak with understanding.
10He that is inexperienced knows
few things,
but he that has traveled acquires
much cleverness.
11I have seen many things in my
travels,
and I understand more than I
can express.
12I have often been in danger of
death,
but have escaped because of
these experiences.

13The spirit of those who fear the
Lord will live,
for their hope is in him who
saves them.
14He who fears the Lord will not be
timid,
nor play the coward, for he is
his hope.
15Blessed is the soul of the man who
fears the Lord!
To whom does he look? And
who is his support?
16The eyes of the Lord are upon
those who love him,

q Other authorities read A traveled

Mosaic law (Ex.21.2–6,20–21,26–27; Lev.25.46; Dt.15.12–18). **30** and **31**: Syriac, "If you have
(only) one servant. . . ."
   34.1–8: The vanity of dreams and omens (Dt.13.2–5; 18.9–14; Ec.5.7; Jer.29.8). **3a**: Syriac,
"A dream of the night is like a mirror," i.e. the image in each is insubstantial. **4**: Job 14.4. **6**:
Allowance is made for God-given dreams (Gen.37.5ff.; Jg.7.13ff.; Job 33.15–18).
   34.9–12: Experience as a teacher.
   34.13–17: The blessedness of those who fear God. 14: Ps.112.6–7; Pr.3.23–26; 28.1. **16:** *Eyes,*
Ps.33.18; 34.15. *Shelter,* Ps.61.2–4; 91.1–4; Is.25.4.

a mighty protection and strong
support,
a shelter from the hot wind and a
shade from noonday sun,
a guard against stumbling and
a defense against falling.
[17]He lifts up the soul and gives light
to the eyes;
he grants healing, life, and
blessing.

[18]If one sacrifices from what has
been wrongfully obtained, the
offering is blemished;[r]
the gifts[s] of the lawless are not
acceptable.
[19]The Most High is not pleased
with the offerings of the
ungodly;
and he is not propitiated for sins
by a multitude of sacrifices.
[20]Like one who kills a son before his
father's eyes
is the man who offers a sacrifice
from the property of the poor.
[21]The bread of the needy is the life
of the poor;
whoever deprives them of it is
a man of blood.
[22]To take away a neighbor's living
is to murder him;
to deprive an employee of his
wages is to shed blood.

[23]When one builds and another
tears down,
what do they gain but toil?
[24]When one prays and another
curses,
to whose voice will the Lord
listen?
[25]If a man washes after touching a
dead body, and touches it
again,
what has he gained by his
washing?
[26]So if a man fasts for his sins,

and goes again and does the
same things,
who will listen to his prayer?
And what has he gained by
humbling himself?

35 He who keeps the law makes
many offerings;
he who heeds the commandments
sacrifices a peace offering.
[2]He who returns a kindness offers
fine flour,
and he who gives alms sacrifices
a thank offering.
[3]To keep from wickedness is pleasing
to the Lord,
and to forsake unrighteousness
is atonement.
[4]Do not appear before the Lord
empty-handed,
[5] for all these things are to be
done because of the
commandment.
[6]The offering of a righteous man
anoints the altar,
and its pleasing odor rises before
the Most High.
[7]The sacrifice of a righteous man is
acceptable,
and the memory of it will not
be forgotten.
[8]Glorify the Lord generously,
and do not stint the first fruits
of your hands.
[9]With every gift show a cheerful
face,
and dedicate your tithe with
gladness.
[10]Give to the Most High as he has
given,
and as generously as your hand
has found.
[11]For the Lord is the one who
repays,
and he will repay you sevenfold.

r Other authorities read *is made in mockery*
s Other authorities read *mockeries*

34.18–26: Unacceptable sacrifices (1 Sam.15.22; Ps.51.16–19; Pr.15.8; 21.3; Hos.6.6; Am.
5.21–24; Mt.23.23). **21:** Lev.19.13; Dt.24.14–15; Tob.4.14. **25:** Num.19.11–13; 2 Pet.2.22.
    35.1–11: Acceptable sacrifices (Is.1.11–18; Mic.6.6–8; Mk.12.33). **1:** *Peace offering*, Lev.3.1–
17. **2:** *Fine flour*, Lev.2.1–16. *Thank offering*, Lev.7.12. **3:** Dan.4.27. **4:** Ex.23.15; Dt.16.16. **8:**
7.31; Pr.3.9; 22.9. **9:** 2 Cor.9.7. **10:** Tob.4.8. **11:** Pr.19.17; 2 Cor.9.8.

¹²Do not offer him a bribe, for he
  will not accept it;
and do not trust to an
  unrighteous sacrifice;
for the Lord is the judge,
  and with him is no partiality.
¹³He will not show partiality in the
  case of a poor man;
and he will listen to the prayer
  of one who is wronged.
¹⁴He will not ignore the supplication
  of the fatherless,
nor the widow when she pours
  out her story.
¹⁵Do not the tears of the widow run
  down her cheek
as she cries out against him
  who has caused them to
  fall?
¹⁶He whose service is pleasing to the
  Lord will be accepted,
and his prayer will reach to the
  clouds.
¹⁷The prayer of the humble pierces
  the clouds,
and he will not be consoled until
  it reaches the Lord;ᵗ
he will not desist until the Most
  High visits him,
and does justice for the righteous,
  and executes judgment.
¹⁸And the Lord will not delay,
  neither will he be patient with
  them,
till he crushes the loins of the
  unmerciful
and repays vengeance on the
  nations;
till he takes away the multitude of
  the insolent,
and breaks the scepters of the
  unrighteous;
¹⁹till he repays man according to his
  deeds,

and the works of men according
  to their devices;
till he judges the case of his people
  and makes them rejoice in his
  mercy.
²⁰Mercy is as welcome when he
  afflicts them
as clouds of rain in the time of
  drought.

36 Have mercy upon us, O
  Lord, the God of all, and
  look upon us,
² and cause the fear of thee to fall
  upon all the nations.
³Lift up thy hand against foreign
  nations
and let them see thy might.
⁴As in us thou hast been sanctified
  before them,
so in them be thou magnified
  before us;
⁵and let them know thee, as we
  have known
that there is no God but thee,
  O Lord.
⁶Show signs anew, and work further
  wonders;
make thy hand and thy right
  arm glorious.
⁷Rouse thy anger and pour out thy
  wrath;
destroy the adversary and wipe
  out the enemy.
⁸Hasten the day, and remember the
  appointed time,ᵘ
and let people recount thy
  mighty deeds.
⁹Let him who survives be consumed
  in the fiery wrath,
and may those who harm thy
  people meet destruction.

ᵗ Or *until the Lord draws near*
ᵘ Other authorities read *remember thy oath*

35.12–20: God's mercy and justice. 12: *Unrighteous sacrifice*, Hebrew and Syriac, "sacrifice
of violence (or extortion)," i.e. derived from unjust dealing (34.20). *No partiality*, Dt.10.17;
Job 34.19; Wis.6.7; Acts 10.34; Gal.2.6. **14–15:** Ex.22.22. **18:** *Will not delay*, in executing
judgment (2 Pet.3.9). Here and in vv. 19–20 the author has in mind the pagan oppressors of
God's chosen people.
  36.1–17: A prayer for the deliverance and restoration of Israel. 2–3: Ps.79.6; Is.19.16; Jer.
10.25. **4:** Ezek.20.41; 28.25. **5:** 1 Kg.8.43,60. **7:** Ps.79.6. **8a:** Hebrew and Syriac, "Hasten the
end" (of the present age). **8b:** Hebrew and Syriac, "For who may say to thee, 'What doest
thou?'" i.e. God has *appointed* the *time* of the coming of the Messianic era (see 2 Esd.4.36–37 n.;

¹⁰Crush the heads of the rulers of
the enemy,
who say, "There is no one but
ourselves."
¹¹Gather all the tribes of Jacob,
and give*ᵛ* them their inheritance,
as at the beginning.
¹²Have mercy, O Lord, upon the
people called by thy name,
upon Israel, whom thou hast
likened to a*ʷ* first-born son.
¹³Have pity on the city of thy
sanctuary,*ˣ*
Jerusalem, the place of thy
rest.
¹⁴Fill Zion with the celebration of
thy wondrous deeds,
and thy temple*ʸ* with thy
glory.
¹⁵Bear witness to those whom thou
didst create in the beginning,
and fulfil the prophecies spoken
in thy name.
¹⁶Reward those who wait for thee,
and let thy prophets be found
trustworthy.
¹⁷Hearken, O Lord, to the prayer of
thy servants,
according to the blessing of
Aaron for thy people,
and all who are on the earth will
know
that thou art the Lord, the God
of the ages.

¹⁸The stomach will take any food,
yet one food is better than
another.
¹⁹As the palate tastes the kinds of
game,
so an intelligent mind detects
false words.
²⁰A perverse mind will cause grief,
but a man of experience will pay
him back.
²¹A woman will accept any man,
but one daughter is better than
another.
²²A woman's beauty gladdens the
countenance,
and surpasses every human
desire.
²³If kindness and humility mark her
speech,
her husband is not like other
men.
²⁴He who acquires a wife gets his
best possession,*ᶻ*
a helper fit for him and a pillar
of support.*ᵃ*
²⁵Where there is no fence, the
property will be plundered;
and where there is no wife, a
man will wander about and
sigh.
²⁶For who will trust a nimble
robber
that skips from city to city?
So who will trust a man that has
no home,
and lodges wherever night finds
him?

37 Every friend will say, "I too
am a friend";
but some friends are friends
only in name.
²Is it not a grief to the death
when a companion and friend
turns to enmity?
³O evil imagination, why were you
formed
to cover the land with deceit?
⁴Some companions rejoice in the
happiness of a friend,
but in time of trouble are
against him.

v Other authorities read I gave
w Other authorities read hast named thy
x Or on thy holy city
y Heb Syr: Gk Vg people
z Heb: Gk enters upon a possession
a Heb: Gk rest

Acts 1.7–8). **11**: Jer.31.10. **12**: Dan.9.18–19. **13**: Ps.132.14. **17**: *The blessing of Aaron for thy
people*, Num.6.23–26; Hebrew and Syriac, "thy good favor toward thy people." *The God of
the ages*, the eternal God (Gen.21.33; Is.40.28).
   36.18–26: Concerning discrimination (vv. 18–20, in general; vv. 21–26, in choosing a wife).
19: Job 12.11; 34.3. **21a**: *Will accept*, because the marriage was arranged by her father (see
7.25 n.). **24**: *A helper fit for him*, Gen.2.18. **26**: *Home*, literally "nest."
   37.1–6: False friends (6.7–13). **3**: *Evil imagination*, the evil *yeser* (see 15.14 n.). **4**: *Happi-*

⁵Some companions help a friend
  for their stomachs' sake,
  and in the face of battle take up
    the shield.
⁶Do not forget a friend in your heart,
  and be not unmindful of him in
    your wealth.

⁷Every counselor praises counsel,
  but some give counsel in their
    own interest.
⁸Be wary of a counselor,
  and learn first what is his
    interest—
  for he will take thought for
    himself—
  lest he cast the lot against you
⁹   and tell you, "Your way is
    good,"
  and then stand aloof to see what
    will happen to you.
¹⁰Do not consult with one who looks
  at you suspiciously;
  hide your counsel from those
    who are jealous of you.
¹¹Do not consult with a woman
  about her rival
  or with a coward about war,
  with a merchant about barter
  or with a buyer about selling,
  with a grudging man about
    gratitude
  or with a merciless man about
    kindness,
  with an idler about any work
  or with a man hired for a year
    about completing his work,
  with a lazy servant about a big
    task—
  pay no attention to these in any
    matter of counsel.
¹²But stay constantly with a godly
  man
  whom you know to be a keeper
    of the commandments,
  whose soul is in accord with your
    soul,

and who will sorrow with you if
  you fail.
¹³And establish the counsel of your
  own heart,
  for no one is more faithful to
    you than it is.
¹⁴For a man's soul sometimes keeps
  him better informed
  than seven watchmen sitting
    high on a watchtower.
¹⁵And besides all this pray to the
  Most High
  that he may direct your way in
    truth.

¹⁶Reason is the beginning of every
  work,
  and counsel precedes every
    undertaking.
¹⁷As a clue to changes of heart
¹⁸   four turns of fortune appear,
  good and evil, life and death;
  and it is the tongue that
    continually rules them.
¹⁹A man may be shrewd and the
  teacher of many,
  and yet be unprofitable to
    himself.
²⁰A man skilled in words may be
  hated;
  he will be destitute of all
    food,
²¹for grace was not given him by the
  Lord,
  since he is lacking in all wisdom.
²²A man may be wise to his own
  advantage,
  and the fruits of his
    understanding may be
    trustworthy on his lips.
²³A wise man will instruct his own
  people,
  and the fruits of his
    understanding will be
    trustworthy.
²⁴A wise man will have praise heaped
  upon him,

---

ness, arising from feasting (see v. 5). **6:** *In your heart*, Hebrew, "in war." *In your wealth*, Hebrew,
"when you take the spoil."
    37.7–15: Concerning counselors. 14: *Watchmen*, probably astrologers are meant.
    37.16–26: True and false wisdom. 17–18: Hebrew, "The roots of the heart's counsels send
out four branches." **18:** Pr.18.21. **21:** *Grace*, graciousness.

and all who see him will call him happy.

²⁵The life of a man is numbered by days,
but the days of Israel are without number.

²⁶He who is wise among his people will inherit confidence,ᵇ
and his name will live for ever.

²⁷My son, test your soul while you live;
see what is bad for it and do not give it that.

²⁸For not everything is good for every one,
and not every person enjoys everything.

²⁹Do not have an insatiable appetite for any luxury,
and do not give yourself up to food;

³⁰for overeating brings sickness,
and gluttony leads to nausea.

³¹Many have died of gluttony,
but he who is careful to avoid it prolongs his life.

38 Honor the physician with the honor due him,ᶜ according to your need of him,
for the Lord created him;

²for healing comes from the Most High,
and he will receive a gift from the king.

³The skill of the physician lifts up his head,
and in the presence of great men he is admired.

⁴The Lord created medicines from the earth,
and a sensible man will not despise them.

⁵Was not water made sweet with a tree
in order that hisᵈ power might be known?

⁶And he gave skill to men
that heᵉ might be glorified in his marvelous works.

⁷By them he heals and takes away pain;

⁸ the pharmacist makes of them a compound.
His works will never be finished;
and from him healthᶠ is upon the face of the earth.

⁹My son, when you are sick do not be negligent,
but pray to the Lord, and he will heal you.

¹⁰Give up your faults and direct your hands aright,
and cleanse your heart from all sin.

¹¹Offer a sweet-smelling sacrifice,
and a memorial portion of fine flour,
and pour oil on your offering,
as much as you can afford.ᵍ

¹²And give the physician his place,
for the Lord created him;
let him not leave you, for there is need of him.

¹³There is a time when success lies in the hands of physicians,ʰ

¹⁴ for they too will pray to the Lord
that he should grant them success in diagnosisⁱ
and in healing, for the sake of preserving life.

¹⁵He who sins before his Maker,

b Other authorities read *honor*
c Other authorities omit *with the honor due him*
d Or *its*   e Or *they*   f Or *peace*
g Heb: Vulgate omits *as much as you can afford;* Greek is obscure
h Gk *in their hands*   i Heb: Gk *rest*

25: *Is numbered by days*, i.e. is of limited duration, contrasted with the nation of *Israel* (39.9; 44.13–14; 2 Macc. 14.15).

37.27–31: Temperance (31.16–22).

38.1–15: Concerning physicians. 1: *Created him*, i.e. established his profession. 5: Ex.15.23–25. 8: *His works*, God's works. 9–14: In sickness turn first to God, by prayer, repentance, and sacrifice (contrast 2 Chr.16.12); then call the physician. 12: *Created*, see v. 1 n. 15: Severe illness, according to Jewish ideas, is divine judgment for sin (Job 5.17–18; 1 Cor.11.30). The Hebrew text, however, reads, "He who sins before his Maker will behave himself proudly before the physician."

may he fall into the care^j of a
physician.

^{16}My son, let your tears fall for the
dead,
and as one who is suffering
grievously begin the lament.
Lay out his body with the honor
due him,
and do not neglect his burial.
^{17}Let your weeping be bitter and
your wailing fervent;
observe the mourning according
to his merit,
for one day, or two, to avoid
criticism;
then be comforted for your
sorrow.
^{18}For sorrow results in death,
and sorrow of heart saps one's
strength.
^{19}In calamity sorrow continues,
and the life of the poor man
weighs down his heart.
^{20}Do not give your heart to
sorrow;
drive it away, remembering the
end of life.
^{21}Do not forget, there is no coming
back;
you do the dead^k no good, and
you injure yourself.
^{22}"Remember my doom, for yours is
like it:
yesterday it was mine, and
today it is yours."
^{23}When the dead is at rest, let his
remembrance cease,
and be comforted for him when
his spirit has departed.

^{24}The wisdom of the scribe depends
on the opportunity of
leisure;
and he who has little business
may become wise.
^{25}How can he become wise who
handles the plow,

and who glories in the shaft of
a goad,
who drives oxen and is occupied
with their work,
and whose talk is about^l bulls?
^{26}He sets his heart on plowing
furrows,
and he is careful about fodder
for the heifers.
^{27}So too is every craftsman and
master workman
who labors by night as well as
by day;
those who cut the signets of
seals,
each is diligent in making a
great variety;
he sets his heart on painting a
lifelike image,
and he is careful to finish his
work.
^{28}So too is the smith sitting by the
anvil,
intent upon his handiwork in
iron;
the breath of the fire melts his
flesh,
and he wastes away in^m the heat
of the furnace;
he inclines his ear to the sound of
the hammer,^{n}
and his eyes are on the pattern
of the object.
He sets his heart on finishing his
handiwork,
and he is careful to complete its
decoration.
^{29}So too is the potter sitting at his
work
and turning the wheel with his
feet;
he is always deeply concerned over
his work,
and all his output is by
number.
^{30}He moulds the clay with his arm

j Gk *hands*   *k* Gk *him*   *l* Or *among*
m Cn Compare Syr: Gk *contends with*
n Cn: Gk *the sound of the hammer renews his ear*

38.16–23: On mourning for the dead (22.11–12). **16d**: Hebrew, "and do not hide yourself
when he has become a corpse." **18**: *Death*, Hebrew "harm." **22**: Lugubrious counsel from the
dead man. **23**: 2 Sam.12.20.
   38.24–39.11: Various craftsmen contrasted with the scribe, a student of divine wisdom.

and makes it pliable with his
feet;
he sets his heart to finish the
glazing,
and he is careful to clean the
furnace.

31All these rely upon their hands,
and each is skilful in his own
work.
32Without them a city cannot be
established,
and men can neither sojourn nor
live there.
33Yet they are not sought out for
the council of the people,
nor do they attain eminence in
the public assembly.
They do not sit in the judge's
seat,
nor do they understand the
sentence of judgment;
they cannot expound discipline or
judgment,
and they are not found using
proverbs.
34But they keep stable the fabric of
the world,
and their prayer is in the practice
of their trade.

39 On the other hand he who
devotes himself
to the study of the law of the
Most High
will seek out the wisdom of all the
ancients,
and will be concerned with
prophecies;
2he will preserve the discourse of
notable men
and penetrate the subtleties of
parables;
3he will seek out the hidden meanings
of proverbs
and be at home with the
obscurities of parables.

4He will serve among great men
and appear before rulers;
he will travel through the lands of
foreign nations,
for he tests the good and the evil
among men.
5He will set his heart to rise early
to seek the Lord who made
him,
and will make supplication
before the Most High;
he will open his mouth in
prayer
and make supplication for his
sins.

6If the great Lord is willing,
he will be filled with the spirit
of understanding;
he will pour forth words*o* of
wisdom
and give thanks to the Lord in
prayer.
7He will direct his counsel and
knowledge aright,
and meditate on his secrets.
8He will reveal instruction in his
teaching,
and will glory in the law of the
Lord's covenant.
9Many will praise his understanding,
and it will never be blotted
out;
his memory will not disappear,
and his name will live through
all generations.
10Nations will declare his wisdom,
and the congregation will
proclaim his praise;
11if he lives long, he will leave a
name greater than a
thousand,
and if he goes to rest, it is
enough*p* for him.

o Other authorities read *his words*
p Cn: the meaning of the Greek is uncertain

38.32: Craftsmen are necessary for the well-being of the social structure. **39.1:** The threefold division of the Hebrew canon: the law, wisdom (= the writings), and the prophets (given third place here in deference to wisdom; compare the Prologue to Sirach and see 2 Esd.14.45 n.). **2–3:** These verses refer to the oral traditions of the sages. *He will preserve*, in his memory (Pr.4.21; 22.17–18). **4:** *Will travel*, 51.13. **6:** Jas.4.15. **9:** *It*, Syriac, "his name." **11:** *It*, i.e. his name, which survives him and keeps him in remembrance.

¹²I have yet more to say, which I
have thought upon,
and I am filled, like the moon
at the full.
¹³Listen to me, O you holy sons,
and bud like a rose growing by
a stream of water;
¹⁴send forth fragrance like
frankincense,
and put forth blossoms like a lily.
Scatter the fragrance, and sing a
hymn of praise;
bless the Lord for all his works;
¹⁵ascribe majesty to his name
and give thanks to him with
praise,
with songs on your lips, and with
lyres;
and this you shall say in
thanksgiving:
¹⁶"All things are the works of the
Lord, for they are very good,
and whatever he commands will
be done in his time."

¹⁷No one can say, "What is this?"
"Why is that?"
for in God's^q time all things
will be sought after.
At his word the waters stood in a
heap,
and the reservoirs of water at
the word of his mouth.
¹⁸At his command whatever pleases
him is done,
and none can limit his saving
power.
¹⁹The works of all flesh are before him,
and nothing can be hid from his
eyes.
²⁰From everlasting to everlasting he
beholds them,
and nothing is marvelous to him.
²¹No one can say, "What is this?"
"Why is that?"
for everything has been created
for its use.

²²His blessing covers the dry land
like a river,
and drenches it like a flood.
²³The nations will incur his wrath,
just as he turns fresh water into
salt.
²⁴To the holy his ways are straight,
just as they are obstacles to the
wicked.
²⁵From the beginning good things
were created for good people,
just as evil things for sinners.
²⁶Basic to all the needs of man's
life
are water and fire and iron and
salt
and wheat flour and milk and
honey,
the blood of the grape, and oil
and clothing.
²⁷All these are for good to the
godly,
just as they turn into evils for
sinners.

²⁸There are winds that have been
created for vengeance,
and in their anger they scourge
heavily;
in the time of consummation they
will pour out their strength
and calm the anger of their
Maker.
²⁹Fire and hail and famine and
pestilence,
all these have been created for
vengeance;
³⁰the teeth of wild beasts, and
scorpions and vipers,
and the sword that punishes the
ungodly with destruction;
³¹they will rejoice in his commands,
and be made ready on earth for
their service,
and when their times come they
will not transgress his word.

q Gk *his*

39.12–35: In praise of God the creator. 12–15: Introduction to Sirach's eulogy. 15: *In thanks-giving,* Hebrew, "with a shout." 16: Gen.1.31; 1 Tim.4.4. 17a: Rom.9.20. 17c: Ps.33.6–7; 147.15,18. 18: Ps.135.6. 19: 16.17–19; Heb.4.13. 22: *A river,* the Nile is meant. *A flood,* the Euphrates is meant. 23b: Ps.107.33. 24: Hos.14.9. 25b: 40.10. 26: 29.21. 29: 40.9; Ex.9.23. 30: Dt.32.24; Wis.16.5. 31: *They,* the previously mentioned instruments appointed

³²Therefore from the beginning I
have been convinced,
and have thought this out and
left it in writing:
³³The works of the Lord are all
good,
and he will supply every need in
its hour.
³⁴And no one can say, "This is worse
than that,"
for all things will prove good in
their season.
³⁵So now sing praise with all your
heart and voice,
and bless the name of the Lord.

40 Much labor was created for
every man,
and a heavy yoke is upon the
sons of Adam,
from the day they come forth from
their mother's womb
till the day they return to′ the
mother of all.
²Their perplexities and fear of
heart—
their anxious thought is the day
of death,
³from the man who sits on a
splendid throne
to the one who is humbled in
dust and ashes,
⁴from the man who wears purple
and a crown
to the one who is clothed in
burlap;
⁵there is anger and envy and trouble
and unrest,
and fear of death, and fury and
strife.
And when one rests upon his bed,
his sleep at night confuses his
mind.
⁶He gets little or no rest,
and afterward in his sleep, as
though he were on watch,

he is troubled by the visions of his
mind
like one who has escaped from
the battle-front;
⁷at the moment of his rescue he
wakes up,
and wonders that his fear came
to nothing.
⁸With all flesh, both man and beast,
and upon sinners seven times
more,
⁹are death and bloodshed and strife
and sword,
calamities, famine and affliction
and plague.
¹⁰All these were created for the
wicked,
and on their account the flood
came.
¹¹All things that are from the earth
turn back to the earth,
and what is from the waters
returns to the sea.
¹²All bribery and injustice will be
blotted out,
but good faith will stand for
ever.
¹³The wealth of the unjust will dry
up like a torrent,
and crash like a loud clap of
thunder in a rain.
¹⁴A generous man will be made glad;
likewise transgressors will
utterly fail.
¹⁵The children of the ungodly will
not put forth many branches;
they are unhealthy roots upon
sheer rock.
¹⁶The reeds by any water or river bank
will be plucked up before any
grass.
¹⁷Kindness is like a garden of
blessings,
and almsgiving endures for ever.

r Other authorities read *are buried in*

---

to execute God's wrath. **33a:** V. 16. **34:** *In their season*, compare Ec.3.1–8. **35:** Ps.145.21.
40.1–11: The miseries of mankind. 1: Gen.3.19; Job 7.1–2; 14.1; Ec.1.3; 2.23. **4:** *Purple*,
Hebrew, "a turban," which was worn by the high priest (Ex.28.37). **8:** *Seven times*, 35.11.
11b: Hebrew and Syriac, "and what is from above (returns) on high" (Ec.12.7).
40.12–17: Injustice will be blotted out. 17: *Almsgiving*, see 7.10 n. The verse in Hebrew reads,
"But kindness shall never be moved, and righteousness abides forever."

18Life is sweet for the self-reliant and
the worker,*s*
but he who finds treasure is
better off than both.
19Children and the building of a
city establish a man's name,
but a blameless wife is accounted
better than both.
20Wine and music gladden the
heart,
but the love of wisdom is better
than both.
21The flute and the harp make
pleasant melody,
but a pleasant voice is better
than both.
22The eye desires grace and
beauty,
but the green shoots of grain
more than both.
23A friend or a companion never
meets one amiss,
but a wife with her husband is
better than both.
24Brothers and help are for a time
of trouble,
but almsgiving rescues better
than both.
25Gold and silver make the foot
stand sure,
but good counsel is esteemed
more than both.
26Riches and strength lift up the
heart,
but the fear of the Lord is
better than both.
There is no loss in the fear of the
Lord,
and with it there is no need to
seek for help.
27The fear of the Lord is like a
garden of blessing,
and covers a man*t* better than
any glory.

28My son, do not lead the life of a
beggar;

it is better to die than to
beg.
29When a man looks to the table of
another,
his existence cannot be
considered as life.
He pollutes himself with another
man's food,
but a man who is intelligent and
well instructed guards against
that.
30In the mouth of the shameless
begging is sweet,
but in his stomach a fire is
kindled.

41 O death, how bitter is the
reminder of you
to one who lives at peace among
his possessions,
to a man without distractions, who
is prosperous in everything,
and who still has the vigor to
enjoy his food!
2O death, how welcome is your
sentence
to one who is in need and is
failing in strength,
very old and distracted over
everything;
to one who is contrary, and has
lost his patience!
3Do not fear the sentence of
death;
remember your former days and
the end of life;
this is the decree from the Lord
for all flesh,
4 and how can you reject the
good pleasure of the Most
High?
Whether life is for ten or a hundred
or a thousand years,
there is no inquiry about it in
Hades.

s Cn: Gk *self-reliant worker*
t Gk *him*

40.18–27: The joys of life. 23b: *A wife with her husband*, Hebrew, "a prudent wife." **27a:**
V. 17a.
40.28–30: A beggar's life is no life at all (29.24).
41.1–42.14: A series of contrasts. 41.1–7: *Death*—bitter to some, welcome to others. **3–4:**
38.20–23. **3b:** Hebrew, "Remember that the former and the latter (share it) with you."

5The children of sinners are
abominable children,
and they frequent the haunts of
the ungodly.
6The inheritance of the children of
sinners will perish,
and on their posterity will be a
perpetual reproach.
7Children will blame an ungodly
father,
for they suffer reproach because
of him.
8Woe to you, ungodly men,
who have forsaken the law of the
Most High God!
9When you are born, you are born
to a curse;
and when you die, a curse is your
lot.
10Whatever is from the dust returns
to dust;
so the ungodly go from curse to
destruction.

11The mourning of men is about their
bodies,
but the evil name of sinners will
be blotted out.
12Have regard for your name, since
it will remain for you
longer than a thousand great
stores of gold.
13The days of a good life are
numbered,
but a good name endures for ever.

14My children, observe instruction
and be at peace;
hidden wisdom and unseen treasure,
what advantage is there in either
of them?
15Better is the man who hides his
folly
than the man who hides his
wisdom.
16Therefore show respect for my
words:
For it is not good to retain every
kind of shame,

and not everything is confidently
esteemed by every one.

17Be ashamed of immorality, before
your father or mother;
and of a lie, before a prince or a
ruler;
18of a transgression, before a judge
or magistrate;
and of iniquity, before a
congregation or the people;
of unjust dealing, before your
partner or friend;
19 and of theft, in the place where
you live.
Be ashamed before the truth of
God and his covenant.
Be ashamed of selfish behavior
at meals,*u*
of surliness in receiving and giving,
20 and of silence, before those who
greet you;
of looking at a woman who is a
harlot,
21 and of rejecting the appeal of a
kinsman;
of taking away some one's portion
or gift,
and of gazing at another man's
wife;
22of meddling with his maidservant—
and do not approach her bed;
of abusive words, before friends—
and do not upbraid after making
a gift;
23of repeating and telling what you
hear,
and of revealing secrets.
Then you will show proper shame,
and will find favor with every
man.

42 Of the following things do
not be ashamed,
and do not let partiality lead
you to sin:
2of the law of the Most High and
his covenant,

u Gk of fixing the elbow on the bread

5–13: A contrast between the memorials left by the ungodly and the just. **10:** 40.11. **12:** Pr.22.1.
41.14–42.14: True and false shame. 41.14–16: Introductory section. **17–23:** Things to be
ashamed of. **21:** Pr.6.29; Mt.5.28. **22:** 18.15. **23:** 27.16. **42.1–8:** Things of which one must

and of rendering judgment to
acquit the ungodly;

3of keeping accounts with a partner
or with traveling companions,
and of dividing the inheritance
of friends;

4of accuracy with scales and
weights,
and of acquiring much or little;

5of profit from dealing with
merchants,
and of much discipline of
children,
and of whipping a wicked
servant severely.*ᵛ*

6Where there is an evil wife, a seal
is a good thing;
and where there are many hands,
lock things up.

7Whatever you deal out, let it be
by number and weight,
and make a record of all that you
give out or take in.

8Do not be ashamed to instruct the
stupid or foolish
or the aged man who quarrels
with the young.
Then you will be truly instructed,
and will be approved before all
men.

9A daughter keeps her father secretly
wakeful,
and worry over her robs him of
sleep;
when she is young, lest she do not
marry,
or if married, lest she be hated;

10while a virgin, lest she be defiled
or become pregnant in her
father's house;
or having a husband, lest she prove
unfaithful,
or, though married, lest she be
barren.

11Keep strict watch over a headstrong
daughter,
lest she make you a laughingstock
to your enemies,
a byword in the city and notorious*ʷ*
among the people,
and put you to shame before the
great multitude.

12Do not look upon any one for
beauty,
and do not sit in the midst of
women;

13for from garments comes the moth,
and from a woman comes
woman's wickedness.

14Better is the wickedness of a man
than a woman who does
good;
and it is a woman who brings
shame and disgrace.

15I will now call to mind the works
of the Lord,
and will declare what I have
seen.
By the words of the Lord his works
are done.

16The sun looks down on everything
with its light,
and the work of the Lord is full
of his glory.

17The Lord has not enabled his holy
ones
to recount all his marvelous
works,
which the Lord the Almighty has
established
that the universe may stand firm
in his glory.

18He searches out the abyss, and the
hearts of men,*ˣ*
and considers their crafty devices.

v Gk *making the side of a wicked servant bleed*
w Gk *called out*
x Gk *and the heart*

---

not be ashamed. **1**: Lev.19.15; Dt.1.17; Pr.24.23. **5c**: 33.26–29. **6**: *Many hands*, in the house-hold.

42.9–11: **A father's concern for his daughter** (7.24–25; 26.10–12).

42.12–14: **Concerning women** (9.1–9). **12**: 25.21. Hebrew, "Let her not parade her charms before men, or spend her time conversing with married women."

42.15–43.33: **In praise of God, the Creator.**

42.15–25: **The omnipotence and omniscience of God. 17**: *Holy ones*, the angels; Sirach means that even the angels lack sufficient power to declare all the wonders of his mighty works.

For the Most High knows all that
  may be known,
and he looks into the signs[y] of
  the age.
[19]He declares what has been and
  what is to be,
and he reveals the tracks of
  hidden things.
[20]No thought escapes him,
  and not one word is hidden from
  him.
[21]He has ordained the splendors of
  his wisdom,
  and he is from everlasting and to
  everlasting.
Nothing can be added or taken
  away,
  and he needs no one to be his
  counselor.
[22]How greatly to be desired are all
  his works,
  and how sparkling they are to
  see![z]
[23]All these things live and remain
  for ever
  for every need, and are all
  obedient.
[24]All things are twofold, one opposite
  the other,
  and he has made nothing
  incomplete.
[25]One confirms the good things of
  the other,
  and who can have enough of
  beholding his glory?

43 The pride of the heavenly
  heights is the clear
  firmament,
  the appearance of heaven in a
  spectacle of glory.
[2]The sun, when it appears, making
  proclamation as it goes
  forth,
  is a marvelous instrument, the
  work of the Most High.
[3]At noon it parches the land;

and who can withstand its
  burning heat?
[4]A man tending[a] a furnace works
  in burning heat,
but the sun burns the mountains
  three times as much;
it breathes out fiery vapors,
  and with bright beams it blinds
  the eyes.
[5]Great is the Lord who made it;
  and at his command it hastens
  on its course.

[6]He made the moon also, to serve
  in its season[b]
  to mark the times and to be an
  everlasting sign.
[7]From the moon comes the sign for
  feast days,
  a light that wanes when it has
  reached the full.
[8]The month is named for the moon,
  increasing marvelously in its
  phases,
an instrument of the hosts on
  high
  shining forth in the firmament
  of heaven.

[9]The glory of the stars is the beauty
  of heaven,
  a gleaming array in the heights
  of the Lord.
[10]At the command of the Holy One
  they stand as ordered,
  they never relax in their
  watches.
[11]Look upon the rainbow, and
  praise him who made it,
  exceedingly beautiful in its
  brightness.
[12]It encircles the heaven with its
  glorious arc;
  the hands of the Most High
  have stretched it out.

y Gk *sign*   z The Greek of this line is uncertain
a Other authorities read *blowing*
b The Greek text of this line is uncertain

20: Ps.139.4; Is.29.15. **21**: *His counselor*, Hebrew, "his instructor" (see Is.40.13–14). **24**: 33.15.
  43.1–5: The splendor of the firmament and the sun. **1**: Ex.24.10. **2**: Ps.19.1–5.
  43.6–8: The splendor of the moon. **6**: Gen.1.16. The Hebrews followed a lunar calendar.
  43.9–12: The glory of the stars and the rainbow. **10**: *They stand* like sentinels on high. **11–12**:
50.7; Gen.9.13; Ezek.1.28.

¹³By his command he sends the
driving snow
and speeds the lightnings of his
judgment.
¹⁴Therefore the storehouses are
opened,
and the clouds fly forth like
birds.
¹⁵In his majesty he amasses the
clouds,
and the hailstones are broken in
pieces.
¹⁶At his appearing the mountains
are shaken;
at his will the south wind blows.
¹⁷The voice of his thunder rebukes
the earth;
so do the tempest from the
north and the whirlwind.
He scatters the snow like birds
flying down,
and its descent is like locusts
alighting.
¹⁸The eye marvels at the beauty of
its whiteness,
and the mind is amazed at its
falling.
¹⁹He pours the hoarfrost upon the
earth like salt,
and when it freezes, it becomes
pointed thorns.
²⁰The cold north wind blows,
and ice freezes over the water;
it rests upon every pool of water,
and the water puts it on like a
breastplate.
²¹He consumes the mountains and
burns up the wilderness,
and withers the tender grass like
fire.
²²A mist quickly heals all things;
when the dew appears, it
refreshes from the heat.

²³By his counsel he stilled the great
deep
and planted islands in it.
²⁴Those who sail the sea tell of its
dangers,
and we marvel at what we hear.
²⁵For in it are strange and marvelous
works,
all kinds of living things, and
huge creatures of the sea.
²⁶Because of him his messenger finds
the way,
and by his word all things hold
together.

²⁷Though we speak much we cannot
reach the end,
and the sum of our words is:
"He is the all."
²⁸Where shall we find strength to
praise him?
For he is greater than all his
works.
²⁹Terrible is the Lord and very
great,
and marvelous is his power.
³⁰When you praise the Lord, exalt
him as much as you can;
for he will surpass even that.
When you exalt him, put forth all
your strength,
and do not grow weary, for you
cannot praise him enough.
³¹Who has seen him and can describe
him?
Or who can extol him as he is?
³²Many things greater than these lie
hidden,
for we have seen but few of his
works.
³³For the Lord has made all things,
and to the godly he has granted
wisdom.

44 Let us now praise famous
men,
and our fathers in their
generations.

43.13–26: Marvels of nature. 13: *Snow,* Hebrew, "lightning." **14:** Job 38.22; Jer.51.16.
20: *Blows,* Hebrew, "he causes to blow." **23:** Ps.104.25–26. **26b:** Col.1.17.
   43.27–33: God is greater than all his works. 27: *He is the all,* not to be taken in a pantheistic
sense. **28a:** Hebrew, "Let us praise him the more, since we cannot fathom (him)" (Job 11.7;
Ps.145.3).
   44.1–50.24: In praise of famous men. 44.1–15: Introduction. **1:** *Famous men,* Hebrew and
Syriac, "men of piety." *Generations,* i.e. historical sequence.

²The Lord apportioned to them*ᶜ*
   great glory,
   his majesty from the beginning.
³There were those who ruled in
   their kingdoms,
   and were men renowned for
   their power,
giving counsel by their
   understanding,
   and proclaiming prophecies;
⁴leaders of the people in their
   deliberations
   and in understanding of
   learning for the people,
   wise in their words of instruction;
⁵those who composed musical tunes,
   and set forth verses in writing;
⁶rich men furnished with resources,
   living peaceably in their
   habitations—
⁷all these were honored in their
   generations,
   and were the glory of their times.
⁸There are some of them who have
   left a name,
   so that men declare their praise.
⁹And there are some who have no
   memorial,
   who have perished as though
   they had not lived;
they have become as though they
   had not been born,
   and so have their children after
   them.
¹⁰But these were men of mercy,
   whose righteous deeds have not
   been forgotten;
¹¹their prosperity will remain with
   their descendants,
   and their inheritance to their
   children's children.*ᵈ*
¹²Their descendants stand by the
   covenants;
   their children also, for their sake.
¹³Their posterity will continue for ever,
   and their glory will not be
   blotted out.
¹⁴Their bodies were buried in peace,

and their name lives to all
   generations.
¹⁵Peoples will declare their wisdom,
   and the congregation proclaims
   their praise.

¹⁶Enoch pleased the Lord, and was
   taken up;
   he was an example of repentance
   to all generations.

¹⁷Noah was found perfect and
   righteous;
   in the time of wrath he was
   taken in exchange;
therefore a remnant was left to the
   earth
   when the flood came.
¹⁸Everlasting covenants were made
   with him
   that all flesh should not be
   blotted out by a flood.

¹⁹Abraham was the great father of
   a multitude of nations,
   and no one has been found like
   him in glory;
²⁰he kept the law of the Most High,
   and was taken into covenant
   with him;
he established the covenant in his
   flesh,
   and when he was tested he was
   found faithful.
²¹Therefore the Lord*ᵉ* assured him
   by an oath
   that the nations would be blessed
   through his posterity;
   that he would multiply him like
   the dust of the earth,
   and exalt his posterity like the
   stars,
and cause them to inherit from
   sea to sea
   and from the River to the ends
   of the earth.

c Heb: Gk *created*
d Heb Compare Vg Syr: The Greek of this verse is
   uncertain   *e* Gk *he*

44.16–18: Enoch and Noah. 16: 49.14; Gen.5.24; Heb.11.5. **17a:** Gen.6.9; Heb.11.7. **18:**
Gen.8.20–22; 9.12–17.
   44.19–23: Abraham, Isaac, and Jacob. 19: *Father*, Gen.17.4; Mt.3.9. **20:** *Kept the law*,
Gen.26.5. *In his flesh*, Gen.17.10–14. *Tested*, Gen.22.1–14; 1 Macc.2.52; Heb.11.17. **21:** Gen.

²²To Isaac also he gave the same
assurance
for the sake of Abraham his
father.

²³The blessing of all men and the
covenant
he made to rest upon the head
of Jacob;
he acknowledged him with his
blessings,
and gave him his inheritance;*f*
he determined his portions,
and distributed them among
twelve tribes.

45 From his descendants the
Lord*g* brought forth a man
of mercy,
who found favor in the sight of
all flesh
and was beloved by God and man,
Moses, whose memory is blessed.
²He made him equal in glory to the
holy ones,
and made him great in the fears
of his enemies.
³By his words he caused signs to
cease;
the Lord*g* glorified him in the
presence of kings.
He gave him commands for his
people,
and showed him part of his glory.
⁴He sanctified him through
faithfulness and meekness;
he chose him out of all mankind.
⁵He made him hear his voice,
and led him into the thick
darkness,
and gave him the commandments
face to face,
the law of life and knowledge,
to teach Jacob the covenant,
and Israel his judgments.

⁶He exalted Aaron, the brother of
Moses,*h*

a holy man like him, of the tribe
of Levi.
⁷He made an everlasting covenant
with him,
and gave him the priesthood of
the people.
He blessed him with splendid
vestments,
and put a glorious robe upon
him.
⁸He clothed him with superb
perfection,
and strengthened him with the
symbols of authority,
the linen breeches, the long robe,
and the ephod.
⁹And he encircled him with
pomegranates,
with very many golden bells
round about,
to send forth a sound as he walked,
to make their ringing heard in
the temple
as a reminder to the sons of his
people;
¹⁰with a holy garment, of gold and blue
and purple, the work of an
embroiderer;
with the oracle of judgment, Urim
and Thummim;
¹¹ with twisted scarlet, the work
of a craftsman;
with precious stones engraved like
signets,
in a setting of gold, the work of
a jeweler,
for a reminder, in engraved letters,
according to the number of the
tribes of Israel;
¹²with a gold crown upon his turban,
inscribed like a signet with
"Holiness,"
a distinction to be prized, the work
of an expert,
the delight of the eyes, richly
adorned.

f Heb: Gk *by inheritance*
g Gk *he*   *h* Gk *him*

22.16–18; Gal.3.8. *River*, the Euphrates. **22:** Gen.17.19; 26.3–5. **23:** Gen.27.28; 28.14.
45.1–5: Moses. 1: Ex.11.3. **2:** *Holy ones*, the angels. **3:** Ex.7–10. *Part*, Ex.33.18–23. **4:** *Meekness.* Num.12.3. **5:** Ex.20.21; 24.18; Dt.6.1–2.
45.6–22: Aaron. 6: Ex.4.14. **7:** Ex.28.1–4. **8–13:** Ex. ch. 28. **10:** *Urim*, see 33.3 n.

¹³Before his time there never were
such beautiful things.
No outsider ever put them on,
but only his sons
and his descendants perpetually.
¹⁴His sacrifices shall be wholly burned
twice every day continually.
¹⁵Moses ordained him,
and anointed him with holy
oil;
it was an everlasting covenant for
him
and for his descendants all the
days of heaven,
to minister to the Lord*ⁱ* and serve
as priest
and bless his people in his
name.
¹⁶He chose him out of all the living
to offer sacrifice to the Lord,
incense and a pleasing odor as a
memorial portion,
to make atonement for the
people.*ʲ*
¹⁷In his commandments he gave him
authority in statutes and*ᵏ*
judgments,
to teach Jacob the testimonies,
and to enlighten Israel with his
law.
¹⁸Outsiders conspired against him,
and envied him in the wilderness,
Dathan and Abiram and their men
and the company of Korah, in
wrath and anger.
¹⁹The Lord saw it and was not
pleased,
and in the wrath of his anger
they were destroyed;
he wrought wonders against them
to consume them in flaming
fire.
²⁰He added glory to Aaron
and gave him a heritage;
he allotted to him the first of the
first fruits,
he prepared bread of first fruits
in abundance;

²¹for they eat the sacrifices to the
Lord,
which he gave to him and his
descendants.
²²But in the land of the people he
has no inheritance,
and he has no portion among
the people;
for the Lord*ˡ* himself is his*ᵐ*
portion and inheritance.

²³Phinehas the son of Eleazar is the
third in glory,
for he was zealous in the fear of
the Lord,
and stood fast, when the people
turned away,
in the ready goodness of his soul,
and made atonement for Israel.
²⁴Therefore a covenant of peace was
established with him,
that he should be leader of the
sanctuary and of his people,
that he and his descendants should
have
the dignity of the priesthood for
ever.
²⁵A covenant was also established
with David,
the son of Jesse, of the tribe of
Judah:
the heritage of the king is from
son to son only;
so the heritage of Aaron is for
his descendants.
²⁶May the Lord*ⁿ* grant you wisdom
in your heart
to judge his people in
righteousness,
so that their prosperity may not
vanish,
and that their glory may endure
throughout their generations.*ᵒ*

i Gk *him*
j Other authorities read *thy people*
k Heb: Gk *in covenants of*
l Gk *he*
m Other authorities read *your*
n Gk *he*
o The Greek of this line is obscure

14: Num.28.3–4. **15:** Lev. ch. 8. *Bless*, Num. 6.23–27. **18:** Num. ch. 16. *Outsiders*, as in
v. 13, those who were not of the family of Aaron. **22:** Num.18.20; Dt.12.12.
45.23–26: Phinehas (Num.25.10–13; Ps.106.30; 1 Macc.2.54). **25:** 2 Sam.7.12. **26:** You . . .
your, the reference is to Simon, son of Onias (see 50.1 n.), and his successors.

46 Joshua the son of Nun was mighty in war,
and was the successor of Moses in prophesying.
He became, in accordance with his name,
a great savior of God's[p] elect,
to take vengeance on the enemies that rose against them,
so that he might give Israel its inheritance.
2How glorious he was when he lifted his hands
and stretched out his sword against the cities!
3Who before him ever stood so firm?
For he waged the wars of the Lord.
4Was not the sun held back by his hand?
And did not one day become as long as two?
5He called upon the Most High, the Mighty One,
when enemies pressed him on every side,
6and the great Lord answered him with hailstones of mighty power.
He hurled down war upon that nation,
and at the descent of Beth-horon[q] he destroyed those who resisted,
so that the nations might know his armament,
that he was fighting in the sight of the Lord;
for he wholly followed the Mighty One.
7And in the days of Moses he did a loyal deed,
he and Caleb the son of Jephunneh:
they withstood the congregation,[r] restrained the people from sin,
and stilled their wicked murmuring.

8And these two alone were preserved out of six hundred thousand people on foot,
to bring them into their inheritance, into a land flowing with milk and honey.
9And the Lord gave Caleb strength, which remained with him to old age,
so that he went up to the hill country,
and his children obtained it for an inheritance;
10so that all the sons of Israel might see that it is good to follow the Lord.

11The judges also, with their respective names,
those whose hearts did not fall into idolatry
and who did not turn away from the Lord—
may their memory be blessed!
12May their bones revive from where they lie,
and may the name of those who have been honored
live again in their sons!

13Samuel, beloved by his Lord, a prophet of the Lord, established the kingdom
and anointed rulers over his people.
14By the law of the Lord he judged the congregation,
and the Lord watched over Jacob.
15By his faithfulness he was proved to be a prophet,
and by his words he became known as a trustworthy seer.
16He called upon the Lord, the Mighty One,

p Gk *his*
q Compare Joshua 10.11: Greek lacks *of Beth-horon*
r Other authorities read *the enemy*

46.1–10: Joshua and Caleb. 1: *His name* means "Jehovah is salvation." **2–8:** Jos. chs. 6–11. **4:** Jos.10.12–14. **6:** Jos.10.11. **7:** Num.14.6–10; 1 Macc.2.55–56. **8:** Num.11.21; 14.38; 26.65. **9:** Jos.14.6–11.

46.11–12: The judges. 12: *Bones revive* (49.10), the meaning is to be interpreted in the light of the last line of the verse.

46.13–20: Samuel. 13: *Anointed rulers,* 1 Sam.10.1; 16.13. **15:** 1 Sam.3.19–20. **16–18:** 1 Sam. 7.9–11. **19:** 1 Sam.12.3. **20:** 1 Sam.28.18–19.

when his enemies pressed him on
every side,
and he offered in sacrifice a
sucking lamb.
[17]Then the Lord thundered from
heaven,
and made his voice heard with
a mighty sound;
[18]and he wiped out the leaders of the
people of Tyre
and all the rulers of the Philistines.
[19]Before the time of his eternal sleep,
Samuel[s] called men to witness
before the Lord and his
anointed:
"I have not taken any one's
property,
not so much as a pair of shoes."
And no man accused him.
[20]Even after he had fallen asleep he
prophesied
and revealed to the king his
death,
and lifted up his voice out of the
earth in prophecy,
to blot out the wickedness of
the people.

47 And after him Nathan rose
up
to prophesy in the days of David.
[2]As the fat is selected from the
peace offering,
so David was selected from the
sons of Israel.
[3]He played with lions as with young
goats,
and with bears as with lambs of
the flock.
[4]In his youth did he not kill a giant,
and take away reproach from
the people,
when he lifted his hand with a
stone in the sling
and struck down the boasting of
Goliath?
[5]For he appealed to the Lord, the
Most High,

and he gave him strength in his
right hand
to slay a man mighty in war,
to exalt the power[t] of his people.
[6]So they glorified him for his ten
thousands,
and praised him for the blessings
of the Lord,
when the glorious diadem was
bestowed upon him.
[7]For he wiped out his enemies on
every side,
and annihilated his adversaries
the Philistines;
he crushed their power[t] even
to this day.
[8]In all that he did he gave thanks
to the Holy One, the Most High,
with ascriptions of glory;
he sang praise with all his heart,
and he loved his Maker.
[9]He placed singers before the altar,
to make sweet melody with their
voices.
[10]He gave beauty to the feasts,
and arranged their times
throughout the year,[u]
while they praised God's[v] holy
name,
and the sanctuary resounded
from early morning.
[11]The Lord took away his sins,
and exalted his power[w] for ever;
he gave him the covenant of kings
and a throne of glory in Israel.

[12]After him rose up a wise son
who fared amply[x] because of him;
[13]Solomon reigned in days of peace,
and God gave him rest on every
side,
that he might build a house for
his name
and prepare a sanctuary to stand
for ever.
[14]How wise you became in your youth!

s Gk *he*   *t* Gk *horn*
u Gk *to completion*   *v* Gk *his*
w Gk *horn*   *x* Gk *lived in a broad place*

47.1–11: David. 1: 2 Sam.7.2–3; 12.1; 1 Chr.17.1. **2:** *The fat*, the portion reserved for sacrifice (Lev.3.3–5). **3:** 1 Sam.17.34. **4:** 1 Sam.17.49–51. **6:** 1 Sam.18.7. **7:** 2 Sam.5.7; 8.1. **9:** 1 Chr.16.4. **11:** 2 Sam.12.13.
47.12–22: Solomon. 13–17: 1 Kg.4.21–32. **14:** Compare the address to Elijah in 48.4–11.

You overflowed like a river with
understanding.

¹⁵Your soul covered the earth,
and you filled it with parables
and riddles.

¹⁶Your name reached to far-off
islands,
and you were loved for your
peace.

¹⁷For your songs and proverbs and
parables,
and for your interpretations, the
countries marveled at you.

¹⁸In the name of the Lord God,
who is called the God of Israel,
you gathered gold like tin
and amassed silver like lead.

¹⁹But you laid your loins beside
women,
and through your body you were
brought into subjection.

²⁰You put a stain upon your honor,
and defiled your posterity,
so that you brought wrath upon
your children
and they were grieved*ʸ* at your
folly,

²¹so that the sovereignty was divided
and a disobedient kingdom arose
out of Ephraim.

²²But the Lord will never give up
his mercy,
nor cause any of his works to
perish;
he will never blot out the
descendants of his chosen one,
nor destroy the posterity of him
who loved him;
so he gave a remnant to Jacob,
and to David a root of his stock.

²³Solomon rested with his fathers,
and left behind him one of his
sons,
ample in*ᶻ* folly and lacking in
understanding,

Rehoboam, whose policy caused
the people to revolt.
Also Jeroboam the son of Nebat,
who caused Israel to sin
and gave to Ephraim a sinful
way.

²⁴Their sins became exceedingly many,
so as to remove them from their
land.

²⁵For they sought out every sort of
wickedness,
till vengeance came upon them.

48

Then the prophet Elijah
arose like a fire,
and his word burned like a torch.

²He brought a famine upon them,
and by his zeal he made them
few in number.

³By the word of the Lord he shut
up the heavens,
and also three times brought
down fire.

⁴How glorious you were, O Elijah,
in your wondrous deeds!
And who has the right to boast
which you have?

⁵You who raised a corpse from
death
and from Hades, by the word
of the Most High;

⁶who brought kings down to
destruction,
and famous men from their beds;

⁷who heard rebuke at Sinai
and judgments of vengeance at
Horeb;

⁸who anointed kings to inflict
retribution,
and prophets to succeed you.*ᵃ*

⁹You who were taken up by a
whirlwind of fire,
in a chariot with horses of fire;

ʸ Other authorities read *I was grieved*
ᶻ Heb (with a play on the name Rehoboam) Syr: Gk
the people's
ᵃ Heb: Gk *him*

18: 1 Kg.10.21,27. 19: 1 Kg.11.1. 21: 1 Kg.12.15–20. 22: 2 Sam.7.15; Ps.89.33. *Nor . . . perish,*
Hebrew, "He will let none of his words fall to the ground."

47.23–25: Solomon's successors. 23: *Rehoboam,* 1 Kg.11.43; 12.10–14. *Jeroboam,* 1 Kg.12.28–
30. 24: 2 Kg.17.6,18.

48.1–11: Elijah. 1: 1 Kg.17.1. *Torch,* Hebrew, "furnace." 2: Jas.5.17. 3: 1 Kg.18.38; 2 Kg.
1.10–12. 5: 1 Kg.17.21–22. 6: 2 Kg.1.16. 7: 1 Kg.19.8. 8: 1 Kg.19.15–16. 9: 2 Kg.2.11. 10:
Mal. 4.5–6.

¹⁰you who are ready*b* at the
  appointed time, it is written,
to calm the wrath of God before
  it breaks out in fury,
to turn the heart of the father to
  the son,
and to restore the tribes of
  Jacob.
¹¹Blessed are those who saw you,
  and those who have been
  adorned*c* in love;
for we also shall surely live.*d*

¹²It was Elijah who was covered by
  the whirlwind,
and Elisha was filled with his
  spirit;
in all his days he did not tremble
  before any ruler,
and no one brought him into
  subjection.
¹³Nothing was too hard for him,
  and when he was dead his body
  prophesied.
¹⁴As in his life he did wonders,
  so in death his deeds were
  marvelous.

¹⁵For all this the people did not
  repent,
and they did not forsake their
  sins,
till they were carried away captive
  from their land
and were scattered over all the
  earth;
the people were left very few in
  number,
but with rulers from the house
  of David.
¹⁶Some of them did what was
  pleasing to God,*e*
but others multiplied sins.

¹⁷Hezekiah fortified his city,
  and brought water into the
  midst of it;

he tunneled the sheer rock with iron
  and built pools for water.
¹⁸In his days Sennacherib came up,
  and sent the Rabshakeh;*f*
he lifted up his hand against
  Zion
and made great boasts in his
  arrogance.
¹⁹Then their hearts were shaken and
  their hands trembled,
and they were in anguish, like
  women in travail.
²⁰But they called upon the Lord who
  is merciful,
spreading forth their hands
  toward him;
and the Holy One quickly heard
  them from heaven,
and delivered them by the hand
  of Isaiah.
²¹The Lord*g* smote the camp of the
  Assyrians,
and his angel wiped them
  out.
²²For Hezekiah did what was
  pleasing to the Lord,
and he held strongly to the ways
  of David his father,
which Isaiah the prophet
  commanded,
who was great and faithful in
  his vision.
²³In his days the sun went backward,
  and he lengthened the life of
  the king.
²⁴By the spirit of might he saw the
  last things,
and comforted those who
  mourned in Zion.
²⁵He revealed what was to occur to
  the end of time,
and the hidden things before
  they came to pass.

b Heb: Gk *are for reproofs*
c Other authorities read *who have died*
d The text and meaning of this verse are uncertain
e Gk lacks *to God*
f Other authorities add *and departed*
g Gk *he*

48.12–16: Elisha and subsequent generations. 12: 2 Kg.2.9,13. **13:** 2 Kg.13.20–21. **15:** 2 Kg.
18.11–12.
  48.17–25: Hezekiah and Isaiah. 17: 2 Kg.20.20. **18:** 2 Kg.18.13,17; Is.36.1. *Made . . .
boasts,* Hebrew and Syriac, "blasphemed God." **20:** 2 Kg.19.15–20. **21:** 2 Kg.19.35; Is.37.36;
1 Macc.7.41. **22:** 2 Kg.18.3. **23:** 2 Kg.20.10–11; Is.38.8. **24–25:** Is.40.1; 42.9.

49

The memory of Josiah is like a blending of incense prepared by the art of the perfumer; it is sweet as honey to every mouth, and like music at a banquet of wine.

2 He was led aright in converting the people, and took away the abominations of iniquity.

3 He set his heart upon the Lord; in the days of wicked men he strengthened godliness.

4 Except David and Hezekiah and Josiah they all sinned greatly, for they forsook the law of the Most High; the kings of Judah came to an end;

5 for they gave their power to others, and their glory to a foreign nation,

6 who set fire to the chosen city of the sanctuary, and made her streets desolate, according to the word[h] of Jeremiah.

7 For they had afflicted him; yet he had been consecrated in the womb as prophet, to pluck up and afflict and destroy, and likewise to build and to plant.

8 It was Ezekiel who saw the vision of glory which God[i] showed him above the chariot of the cherubim.

9 For God[i] remembered his enemies with storm, and did good to those who directed their ways aright.[j]

10 May the bones of the twelve prophets revive from where they lie, for they comforted the people of Jacob and delivered them with confident hope.

11 How shall we magnify Zerubbabel? He was like a signet on the right hand,

12 and so was Jeshua the son of Jozadak; in their days they built the house and raised a temple[k] holy to the Lord, prepared for everlasting glory.

13 The memory of Nehemiah also is lasting; he raised for us the walls that had fallen, and set up the gates and bars and rebuilt our ruined houses.

14 No one like Enoch has been created on earth, for he was taken up from the earth.

15 And no man like Joseph[l] has been born, and his bones are cared for.

16 Shem and Seth were honored among men, and Adam above every living being in the creation.

50

The leader of his brethren and the pride of his people[m] was Simon the high priest, son of Onias, who in his life repaired the house,

h Gk *by the hand*   i Gk *he*
j The text and meaning of this verse are uncertain
k Other authorities read *people*
l Heb Syr: Greek adds *the leader of his brothers, the support of the people*
m Heb Syr: Greek lacks this line. Compare 49.15

49.1–3: Josiah (2 Kg.22.1). **2a**: Hebrew, "For he was grieved over our backslidings" (2 Kg. 22.11–13). **3**: 2 Kg.23.3,25.

49.4–10: **The last kings and the last prophets. 5–7**: 2 Chr.36.17–19. *Jeremiah*, Jer.1.5–10; 39.8. **8–9**: Ezek.1.3–15; 13.11; 38.9,16,22. **10**: *Bones*, see 46.12 n.

49.11–16: **Zerubbabel, Jeshua, Nehemiah, and others. 11**: Ezra 3.2; Hag.2.23. **12**: Ezra 3.2; Hag.1.12; 2.2; Zech.3.1. **13**: Neh.7.1. **14**: 44.16. **15**: Gen.39.1ff.; 50.25–26. **16**: Gen.5.3,32.

50.1–24: **Simon, son of Onias** (see 45.26 n.). **1**: Simon II was high priest about 219–196 B.C.

and in his time fortified the
temple.
2He laid the foundations for the
high double walls,[n]
the high retaining walls for the
temple enclosure.
3In his days a cistern for water was
quarried out,[o]
a reservoir like the sea in
circumference.
4He considered how to save his
people from ruin,
and fortified the city to
withstand a siege.
5How glorious he was when the
people gathered round him
as he came out of the inner
sanctuary![p]
6Like the morning star among the
clouds,
like the moon when it is full;
7like the sun shining upon the
temple of the Most High,
and like the rainbow gleaming
in glorious clouds;
8like roses in the days of the first
fruits,
like lilies by a spring of water,
like a green shoot on Lebanon[q]
on a summer day;
9like fire and incense in the censer,
like a vessel of hammered gold
adorned with all kinds of
precious stones;
10like an olive tree putting forth its
fruit,
and like a cypress towering in
the clouds.
11When he put on his glorious robe
and clothed himself with superb
perfection
and went up to the holy altar,
he made the court of the
sanctuary glorious.
12And when he received the portions
from the hands of the priests,
as he stood by the hearth of the
altar
with a garland of brethren around
him,

he was like a young cedar on
Lebanon;
and they surrounded him like the
trunks of palm trees,
13 all the sons of Aaron in their
splendor
with the Lord's offering in their
hands,
before the whole congregation
of Israel.
14Finishing the service at the altars,
and arranging the offering to the
Most High, the Almighty,
15he reached out his hand to the cup
and poured a libation of the
blood of the grape;
he poured it out at the foot of the
altar,
a pleasing odor to the Most
High, the King of all.
16Then the sons of Aaron shouted,
they sounded the trumpets of
hammered work,
they made a great noise to be heard
for remembrance before the
Most High.
17Then all the people together made
haste
and fell to the ground upon their
faces
to worship their Lord,
the Almighty, God Most High.
18And the singers praised him with
their voices
in sweet and full-toned melody.[r]
19And the people besought the Lord
Most High
in prayer before him who is
merciful,
till the order of worship of the
Lord was ended;
so they completed his service.
20Then Simon[s] came down, and
lifted up his hands
over the whole congregation of
the sons of Israel,

n The meaning of this phrase is obscure
o Cn Compare Heb: Gk *was diminished*
p Gk *the house of the veil*
q Or *a sprig of frankincense*
r Other authorities read *in sweet melody throughout the house*   s Gk *he*

(Josephus, *Antiquities*, XII.iv.10). *Onias* is the Greek form of Johanan. *The house*, of God. **16:** *Trumpets*, Num.10.2; 31.6. **20:** *The blessing*, namely Num.6.24–27. *His name*, only the high

to pronounce the blessing of the
Lord with his lips,
and to glory in his name;
²¹and they bowed down in worship
a second time,
to receive the blessing from the
Most High.

²²And now bless the God of all,
who in every way does great things;
who exalts our days from birth,
and deals with us according to
his mercy.
²³May he give us*ᵗ* gladness of heart,
and grant that peace may be in
our days in Israel,
as in the days of old.
²⁴May he entrust to us his mercy!
And let him deliver us in our*ᵘ* days!

²⁵With two nations my soul is vexed,
and the third is no nation:
²⁶Those who live on Mount Seir,*ᵛ*
and the Philistines,
and the foolish people that dwell
in Shechem.

²⁷Instruction in understanding and
knowledge
I have written in this book,
Jesus the son of Sirach, son of
Eleazar, of Jerusalem,*ʷ*
who out of his heart poured
forth wisdom.
²⁸Blessed is he who concerns himself
with these things,
and he who lays them to heart
will become wise.
²⁹For if he does them, he will be
strong for all things,
for the light of the Lord is his path.

51 I will give thanks to thee, O
Lord and King,

and will praise thee as God my
Savior.
I give thanks to thy name,
2 for thou hast been my protector
and helper
and hast delivered my body from
destruction
and from the snare of a
slanderous tongue,
from lips that utter lies.
Before those who stood by
thou wast my helper, ³and didst
deliver me,
in the greatness of thy mercy
and of thy name,
from the gnashings of teeth about
to devour me,*ˣ*
from the hand of those who
sought my life,
from the many afflictions that I
endured,
⁴from choking fire on every side
and from the midst of fire which
I did not kindle,
⁵from the depths of the belly of Hades,
from an unclean tongue and
lying words—
6 the slander of an unrighteous
tongue to the king.
My soul drew near to death,
and my life was very near to
Hades beneath.
⁷They surrounded me on every side,
and there was no one to help me;
I looked for the assistance of men,
and there was none.
⁸Then I remembered thy mercy, O
Lord,
and thy work from of old,
that thou dost deliver those who
wait for thee

t Other authorities read *you*
u Other authorities read *his*
v Heb Vg: Gk *on the mountain of Samaria*
w The text of this line is uncertain
x Cn Compare Vg: Gk *when I was about to be devoured*

priest (and only once a year, on the Day of Atonement), could utter the ineffable name "Yahweh." **22–24:** Doxology. **24:** Hebrew, "May his love abide upon Simon, and may he keep in him the covenant of Phinehas; may one never be cut off from him; and as for his offspring, (may it be) as the days of heaven."

    50.25–26: A fragment. 26: *Those . . . on Mount Seir*, Edomites. *People . . . in Shechem*, Samaritans.

    50.27–29: The author's epilogue.

    51.1–30: Appendix. 1–12: A hymn of thanksgiving for deliverance. **10a:** Hebrew, "Yea, I exalted Jehovah (saying), 'Thou art my Father [Ps.89.26], for thou art the Mighty One of my

and dost save them from the
hand of their enemies.
⁹And I sent up my supplication
from the earth,
and prayed for deliverance from
death.
¹⁰I appealed to the Lord, the Father
of my lord,
not to forsake me in the days
of affliction,
at the time when there is no
help against the proud.
¹¹I will praise thy name continually,
and will sing praise with
thanksgiving.
My prayer was heard,
12 for thou didst save me from
destruction
and rescue me from an evil plight.
Therefore I will give thanks to
thee and praise thee,
and I will bless the name of the
Lord.

¹³While I was still young, before I
went on my travels,
I sought wisdom openly in my
prayer.
¹⁴Before the temple I asked for her,
and I will search for her to the last.
¹⁵From blossom toʸ ripening grape
my heart delighted in her;
my foot entered upon the straight
path;
from my youth I followed her steps.
¹⁶I inclined my ear a little and
received her,
and I found for myself much
instruction.
¹⁷I made progress therein;
to him who gives me wisdom I
will give glory.
¹⁸For I resolved to live according to
wisdom,ᶻ
and I was zealous for the good;
and I shall never be put to shame.
¹⁹My soul grappled with wisdom,ᶻ

and in my conduct I was strict;ᵃ
I spread out my hands to the
heavens,
and lamented my ignorance of her.
²⁰I directed my soul to her,
and through purification I
found her.
I gained understandingᵇ with her
from the first,
therefore I will not be forsaken.
²¹My heart was stirred to seek her,
therefore I have gained a good
possession.
²²The Lord gave me a tongue as my
reward,
and I will praise him with it.

²³Draw near to me, you who are
untaught,
and lodge in my school.
²⁴Why do you say you are lacking
in these things,ᶜ
and why are your souls very
thirsty?
²⁵I opened my mouth and said,
Get these thingsᵈ for yourselves
without money.
²⁶Put your neck under the yoke,
and let your souls receive
instruction;
it is to be found close by.
²⁷See with your eyes that I have
labored little
and found for myself much rest.
²⁸Get instruction with a large sum
of silver,
and you will gain by it much gold.
²⁹May your soul rejoice in his mercy,
and may you not be put to
shame when you praise him.
³⁰Do your work before the appointed
time,
and in God'sᵉ time he will give
you your reward.

y Other authorities read As from   z Gk her
a The Greek text of this line is uncertain   b Gk heart
c Cn Compare Heb Syr: The Greek text of this line is
uncertain
d Greek lacks these things   e Gk his

salvation.' " 13–30: A concluding poem (serving the purpose of a modern preface) in which the
author tell͏ how he acquired wisdom and sought to impart it to others. The poem (like Ps.25 and
Pr.31.10–31) is an acrostic; the verses begin with the successive letters of the Hebrew alphabet. 13: *Travels*, 34.11; 39.4. 22: *Tongue*, eloquence. 26: *The yoke*, of wisdom (compare
Mt.11.29–30). 30: *Your work*, of learning wisdom.

BARUCH

The book which goes under the name of Baruch purports to have been written during the Babylonian captivity by Baruch, the companion and secretary of the prophet Jeremiah (Jer. 32.12; 36.4), and sent to Jerusalem to be read on feast days as a confession of sins (1.14). The first part, which is in prose, comprises an introduction (1.1–14) and a confession of Israel's guilt (1.15–3.8). The second part is made up of two poems, one lauding wisdom as God's special gift to Israel (3.9–4.4) and the other dealing with the themes of comfort and restoration (4.5–5.9). Diverse authorship of the two parts is indicated by differing viewpoints, literary forms, and diction. For example, God is spoken of in quite different ways in the two parts; the word "Lord" appears forty-nine times in the first part but not once in the second part, where it is replaced by the word "God." Furthermore, only in the second part does one find the expressions "the Everlasting," "everlasting Savior," and "the Holy One."

That the book was written originally in Hebrew is suggested by the decidedly Hebraic cast of many sentences. In fact, the Greek text, particularly in the first part, is often incomprehensible without re-translating it back into Hebrew. Today the book is extant in Greek, from which a number of other ancient versions were made, including two in Latin, two in Syriac, and others in Coptic, Armenian, Ethiopic, and Arabic.

The date at which the several component parts of the book were brought together is disputed. According to a widely held opinion its final redaction took place sometime between about 150 and 60 B.C.

THESE ARE THE WORDS OF THE BOOK which Baruch the son of Neraiah, son of Mahseiah, son of Zedekiah, son of Hasadiah, son of Hilkiah, wrote in Babylon, ²in the fifth year, on the seventh day of the month, at the time when the Chaldeans took Jerusalem and burned it with fire. ³And Baruch read the words of this book in the hearing of Jeconiah the son of Jehoiakim, king of Judah, and in the hearing of all the people who came to hear the book, ⁴and in the hearing of the mighty men and the princes, and in the hearing of the elders, and in the hearing of all the people, small and great, all who dwelt in Babylon by the river Sud.

5 Then they wept, and fasted, and prayed before the Lord; ⁶and they collected money, each giving what he could; ⁷and they sent it to Jerusalem to Jehoiakim the high priest,ᵃ the son of Hilkiah, son of Shallum, and to the priests, and to all the people who were present with him in Jerusalem. ⁸At the same time, on the tenth day of Sivan, Baruchᵇ took the vessels of the house of the Lord, which had been carried away from the temple, to return them to the land of Judah—the silver vessels which Zedekiah the son of Josiah, king of Judah, had made, ⁹after Nebuchadnezzar king of Babylon had carried away from Jerusalem Jeconiah and the princes and the prisoners and the mighty men and the people of the land, and brought them to Babylon.

10 And they said: "Herewith we send you money; so buy with the money burnt offerings and sin offerings and incense, and prepare a cereal offering, and offer them upon the altar of the Lord our God; ¹¹and pray for the life

a Gk the priest   b Gk he

1.1–14: Historical introduction. 1–2: Authorship and date. **1:** *Baruch*, Jeremiah's secretary (Jer.36.4). **2:** *Fifth year*, after the fall of Jerusalem in 587/6 B.C. **3–4:** The book is read before the exiles. **3:** *Jeconiah*, also called Jehoiachin (2 Kg.24.15; Jer.24.1). **4:** *Sud*, unknown. **5–14:** A gift of money, the temple vessels, and the book are sent to Jerusalem. **5:** The word *Lord* occurs only in the first part of the book (1.1–3.8). **7:** *Jehoiakim the high priest*, otherwise unknown. **8:** *Sivan*, the third month (May-June). For the return of gold and *silver vessels*, see Ezra 1.7–11. **9:** Jer.24.1. **11:** Jer.29.7. *Belshazzar* was actually the son of Nabonidus. *Like the days of heaven*, without end (Dt.11.21).

o.^b Nebuchadnezzar king of Babylon, and for the life of Belshazzar his son, that their days on earth may be like the days of heaven. ¹²And the Lord will give us strength, and he will give light to our eyes, and we shall live under the protection^c of Nebuchadnezzar king of Babylon, and under the protection^c of Belshazzar his son, and we shall serve them many days and find favor in their sight. ¹³And pray for us to the Lord our God, for we have sinned against the Lord our God, and to this day the anger of the Lord and his wrath have not turned away from us. ¹⁴And you shall read this book which we are sending you, to make your confession in the house of the Lord on the days of the feasts and at appointed seasons.

15 "And you shall say: 'Righteousness belongs to the Lord our God, but confusion of face, as at this day, to us, to the men of Judah, to the inhabitants of Jerusalem, ¹⁶and to our kings and our princes and our priests and our prophets and our fathers, ¹⁷because we have sinned before the Lord, ¹⁸and have disobeyed him, and have not heeded the voice of the Lord our God, to walk in the statutes of the Lord which he set before us. ¹⁹From the day when the Lord brought our fathers out of the land of Egypt until today, we have been disobedient to the Lord our God, and we have been negligent, in not heeding his voice. ²⁰So to this day there have clung to us the calamities and the curse which the Lord declared through Moses his servant at the time when he brought our fathers out of the land of Egypt to give to us a land flowing with milk and honey. ²¹We did not heed the voice of the Lord our God in all the words of the prophets whom he sent to us, but we each followed the intent of his own wicked heart by

serving other gods and doing what is evil in the sight of the Lord our God.

2 "'So the Lord confirmed his word, which he spoke against us, and against our judges who judged Israel, and against our kings and against our princes and against the men of Israel and Judah. ²Under the whole heaven there has not been done the like of what he has done in Jerusalem, in accordance with what is written in the law of Moses, ³that we should eat, one the flesh of his son and another the flesh of his daughter. ⁴And he gave them into subjection to all the kingdoms around us, to be a reproach and a desolation among all the surrounding peoples, where the Lord has scattered them. ⁵They were brought low and not raised up, because we sinned against the Lord our God, in not heeding his voice.

6 "'Righteousness belongs to the Lord our God, but confusion of face to us and our fathers, as at this day. ⁷All those calamities with which the Lord threatened us have come upon us. ⁸Yet we have not entreated the favor of the Lord by turning away, each of us, from the thoughts of his wicked heart. ⁹And the Lord has kept the calamities ready, and the Lord has brought them upon us, for the Lord is righteous in all his works which he has commanded us to do. ¹⁰Yet we have not obeyed his voice, to walk in the statutes of the Lord which he set before us.

11 "'And now, O Lord God of Israel, who didst bring thy people out of the land of Egypt with a mighty hand and with signs and wonders and with great power and outstretched arm, and hast made thee a name, as at this day, ¹²we have sinned, we have been ungodly, we have done wrong, O Lord our

^c Gk *in the shadow*

1.15–3.8: Confession of sin, for the Jerusalem community (1.15–2.5), and for the exiles (2.6–3.8); compare 1.15 and 2.6. **1.15–2.5:** Disobedience brought the judgment of exile. **1.15–18:** Based on Dan.9.7–10. **15:** Ezra 9.7. **20:** Dt. ch. 28; Jer.11.3–5. **21:** Jer.7.25–26; Dan.9.5. **2.1–2:** Dan.9.12–13. **3:** Lev.26.29; Dt.28.53; Jer.19.9; Lam.4.10. **5:** Dt.28.13. **2.6–10:** Confession of guilt. **8:** Dan.9.13. **9:** Dan.9.14. **11–26:** Supplication and confession. **11–14:** Dan.

God, against all thy ordinances. ¹³Let thy anger turn away from us, for we are left, few in number, among the nations where thou hast scattered us. ¹⁴Hear, O Lord, our prayer and our supplication, and for thy own sake deliver us, and grant us favor in the sight of those who have carried us into exile; ¹⁵that all the earth may know that thou art the Lord our God, for Israel and his descendants are called by thy name. ¹⁶O Lord, look down from thy holy habitation, and consider us. Incline thy ear, O Lord, and hear; ¹⁷open thy eyes, O Lord, and see; for the dead who are in Hades, whose spirit has been taken from their bodies, will not ascribe glory or justice to the Lord, ¹⁸but the person that is greatly distressed,*d* that goes about bent over and feeble, and the eyes that are failing, and the person that hungers, will ascribe to thee glory and righteousness, O Lord. ¹⁹For it is not because of any righteous deeds of our fathers or our kings that we bring before thee our prayer for mercy, O Lord our God. ²⁰For thou hast sent thy anger and thy wrath upon us, as thou didst declare by thy servants the prophets, saying: ²¹"Thus says the Lord: Bend your shoulders and serve the king of Babylon, and you will remain in the land which I gave to your fathers. ²²But if you will not obey the voice of the Lord and will not serve the king of Babylon, ²³I will make to cease from the cities of Judah and from the region about Jerusalem the voice of mirth and the voice of gladness, the voice of the bridegroom and the voice of the bride, and the whole land will be a desolation without inhabitants."

24 "'But we did not obey thy voice, to serve the king of Babylon; and thou hast confirmed thy words, which thou didst speak by thy servants the prophets, that the bones of our kings and the bones of our fathers would be brought out of their graves;*e* ²⁵and behold, they have been cast out to the heat of day and the frost of night. They perished in great misery, by famine and sword and pestilence. ²⁶And the house which is called by thy name thou hast made as it is to-day, because of the wickedness of the house of Israel and the house of Judah.

27 "'Yet thou hast dealt with us, O Lord our God, in all thy kindness and in all thy great compassion, ²⁸as thou didst speak by thy servant Moses on the day when thou didst command him to write thy law in the presence of the people of Israel, saying, ²⁹"If you will not obey my voice, this very great multitude will surely turn into a small number among the nations, where I will scatter them. ³⁰For I know that they will not obey me, for they are a stiff-necked people. But in the land of their exile they will come to themselves, ³¹and they will know that I am the Lord their God. I will give them a heart that obeys and ears that hear; ³²and they will praise me in the land of their exile, and will remember my name, ³³and will turn from their stubbornness and their wicked deeds; for they will remember the ways of their fathers, who sinned before the Lord. ³⁴I will bring them again into the land which I swore to give to their fathers, to Abraham and to Isaac and to Jacob, and they will rule over it; and I will increase them, and they will not be diminished. ³⁵I will make an everlasting covenant with them to be their God and they shall be my people; and I will never again remove my people Israel from the land which I have given them."

3 "'O Lord Almighty, God of Israel, the soul in anguish and the

d The meaning of the Greek is uncertain
e Gk *their place*

9.15–17. **13**: Dt.4.27; Jer.42.2. **16**: Dt.26.15. **17**: Pss.6.5; 30.9; Is.38.18; Sir.17.27–28. *Hades*, Sheol. **21**: Jer.27.11–12. **23**: Jer.7.34. **25**: Jer.36.30. **26**: Jer.7.14. **27–35**: Repentance and restoration under an everlasting covenant. **28–29**: Dt.28.58,62. **30**: 1 Kg.8.47. **31**: Jer.24.7. **33**: Dt.9.6. **34**: Lev.26.42; Dt.6.10; Jer.32.37. **35**: Jer.32.38–40; Ezek.36.26–29; Am.9.15. **3.1–8**: Impassioned plea of repentant exiles ("though penitent we are still in exile!").

wearied spirit cry out to thee. ²Hear, O Lord, and have mercy, for we have sinned before thee. ³For thou art enthroned for ever, and we are perishing for ever. ⁴O Lord Almighty, God of Israel, hear now the prayer of the dead of Israel and of the sons of those who sinned before thee, who did not heed the voice of the Lord their God, so that calamities have clung to us. ⁵Remember not the iniquities of our fathers, but in this crisis remember thy power and thy name. ⁶For thou art the Lord our God, and thee, O Lord, will we praise. ⁷For thou hast put the fear of thee in our hearts in order that we should call upon thy name; and we will praise thee in our exile, for we have put away from our hearts all the iniquity of our fathers who sinned before thee. ⁸Behold, we are today in our exile where thou hast scattered us, to be reproached and cursed and punished for all the iniquities of our fathers who forsook the Lord our God.' ''

⁹Hear the commandments of life,
O Israel;
give ear, and learn wisdom!
¹⁰Why is it, O Israel, why is it that
you are in the land of your
enemies,
that you are growing old in a
foreign country,
that you are defiled with the
dead,
¹¹   that you are counted among
those in Hades?
¹²You have forsaken the fountain of
wisdom.
¹³If you had walked in the way of
God,
you would be dwelling in peace
for ever.
¹⁴Learn where there is wisdom,

where there is strength,
where there is understanding,
that you may at the same time
discern
where there is length of days,
and life,
where there is light for the eyes,
and peace.

¹⁵Who has found her place?
And who has entered her
storehouses?
¹⁶Where are the princes of the
nations,
and those who rule over the
beasts on the earth;
¹⁷those who have sport with the
birds of the air,
and who hoard up silver and
gold,
in which men trust,
and there is no end to their
getting;
¹⁸those who scheme to get silver,
and are anxious,
whose labors are beyond
measure?
¹⁹They have vanished and gone down
to Hades,
and others have arisen in their
place.

²⁰Young men have seen the light of
day,
and have dwelt upon the
earth;
but they have not learned the way
to knowledge,
nor understood her paths,
nor laid hold of her.
²¹Their sons have strayed far from
her*f* way.
²²She has not been heard of in
Canaan,
nor seen in Teman;

f Other authorities read *their*

4: *The dead of Israel,* the Israelites in exile (v. 11; Is.59.10b; Lam.3.6). 7: Jer.32.40b. 8: The fathers' sins (2.33; 3.4–5) are visited on the sons (Lam.5.7).
   3.9–4.4: Wisdom, found by God, was given to Israel and is the law. 3.9–14: Introduction to the poem. 10: *Growing old,* the exile has been long (contrast 1.2). 11: Pss.28.1; 88.4. 12: Pr.18.4; Jer.2.13. 14: Pr.3.16; 8.14. 15–28: The rulers of the world and the mighty have not found wisdom. 15: Job 28.12. 16b–17a: Jer.27.6; Dan.2.38; Jdt.11.7. 22: *Canaan,* Ezek.28.3–5 associates Tyre (in Canaan) with wisdom. *Teman,* in Edom, was reputed for its wisdom (Jer.49.7;

²³the sons of Hagar, who seek for
   understanding on the earth,
  the merchants of Merran and
   Teman,
  the story-tellers and the seekers
   for understanding,
have not learned the way to
  wisdom,
  nor given thought to her paths.

²⁴O Israel, how great is the house
  of God!
  And how vast the territory that
  he possesses!
²⁵It is great and has no bounds;
  it is high and immeasurable.
²⁶The giants were born there, who
  were famous of old,
  great in stature, expert in war.
²⁷God did not choose them,
  nor give them the way to
  knowledge;
²⁸so they perished because they had
  no wisdom,
  they perished through their
  folly.

²⁹Who has gone up into heaven,
  and taken her,
  and brought her down from the
  clouds?
³⁰Who has gone over the sea, and
  found her,
  and will buy her for pure gold?
³¹No one knows the way to her,
  or is concerned about the path
  to her.
³²But he who knows all things knows
  her,
  he found her by his
  understanding.
He who prepared the earth for all
  time
  filled it with four-footed
  creatures;

³³he who sends forth the light, and
  it goes,
  called it, and it obeyed him in
  fear;
³⁴the stars shone in their watches,
  and were glad;
  he called them, and they said,
  "Here we are!"
  They shone with gladness for
  him who made them.
³⁵This is our God;
  no other can be compared to
  him!
³⁶He found the whole way to
  knowledge,
  and gave her to Jacob his
  servant
  and to Israel whom he loved.
³⁷Afterward she appeared upon earth
  and lived among men.

4 She is the book of the
  commandments of God,
  and the law that endures for
  ever.
All who hold her fast will live,
  and those who forsake her will
  die.
²Turn, O Jacob, and take her;
  walk toward the shining of her
  light.
³Do not give your glory to another,
  or your advantages to an alien
  people.
⁴Happy are we, O Israel,
  for we know what is pleasing to
  God.

⁵Take courage, my people,
  O memorial of Israel!
⁶It was not for destruction
  that you were sold to the nations,
but you were handed over to your
  enemies
  because you angered God.

Ob.8–9). **23:** *Merran*, probably a corruption which arose in the Hebrew text for "Midian," a son of Keturah (Gen.25.2). **24:** *House of God*, the created world. **26:** Gen.6.4; Wis.14.6; compare the book of Enoch 7.1–6. **29–37:** God found wisdom and gave her to Israel (Sir.24.1–12). **29–30:** Dt.30.12–13; Job 28.13–14. **32–34:** Job 28.23–26; Pr.8.22–31. **33:** *Light*, Gen.1.3. **34:** *Stars . . . were glad*, Job 38.7. **37:** Many church fathers took this as an allusion to the Incarnation. **4.1–3:** Wisdom is *the law* (the Torah). **1:** Sir.24.23. **2:** Is.60.3.

    4.5–5.9: Poem of comfort and restoration. 4.5–20: Israel provoked God, and Zion now mourns for her captive children. **5:** *Take courage, my people* (compare vv. 21,27,30), inspired

[7] For you provoked him who made
you,
by sacrificing to demons and
not to God.
[8] You forgot the everlasting God,
who brought you up,
and you grieved Jerusalem, who
reared you.
[9] For she saw the wrath that came
upon you from God,
and she said:
"Hearken, you neighbors of Zion,
God has brought great sorrow
upon me;
[10] for I have seen the captivity of my
sons and daughters,
which the Everlasting brought
upon them.
[11] With joy I nurtured them,
but I sent them away with
weeping and sorrow.
[12] Let no one rejoice over me, a widow
and bereaved of many;
I was left desolate because of the
sins of my children,
because they turned away from
the law of God.
[13] They had no regard for his statutes;
they did not walk in the ways
of God's commandments,
nor tread the paths of discipline
in his righteousness.
[14] Let the neighbors of Zion come;
remember the capture of my
sons and daughters,
which the Everlasting brought
upon them.
[15] For he brought against them a
nation from afar,
a shameless nation, of a strange
language,
who had no respect for an old man,
and had no pity for a child.
[16] They led away the widow's
beloved sons,
and bereaved the lonely woman
of her daughters.

[17] "But I, how can I help you?
[18] For he who brought these calamities
upon you
will deliver you from the hand
of your enemies.
[19] Go, my children, go;
for I have been left desolate.
[20] I have taken off the robe of peace
and put on the sackcloth of my
supplication;
I will cry to the Everlasting all
my days.

[21] "Take courage, my children, cry
to God,
and he will deliver you from the
power and hand of the enemy.
[22] For I have put my hope in the
Everlasting to save you,
and joy has come to me from
the Holy One,
because of the mercy which soon
will come to you
from your everlasting Savior.[g]
[23] For I sent you out with sorrow and
weeping,
but God will give you back to
me with joy and gladness for
ever.
[24] For as the neighbors of Zion have
now seen your capture,
so they soon will see your
salvation by God,
which will come to you with great
glory
and with the splendor of the
Everlasting.
[25] My children, endure with patience
the wrath that has come upon
you from God.
Your enemy has overtaken you,
but you will soon see their
destruction
and will tread upon their necks.
[26] My tender sons have traveled
rough roads;

g Or *from the Everlasting, your Savior*

---

by Is.40.1. **7:** *Demons,* Dt.32.16–17; Ps.106.37; 1 Cor.10.20. **9b–16:** Jerusalem speaks to her *neighbors* (i.e. neighboring cities). **12:** *Widow,* Lam.1.1. **15:** Dt.28.49–50; Jer.6.15. **17–29:** Jerusalem encourages her exiled children. **17–18:** Only God can help. **20:** *Robe of peace,* garment worn in time of prosperity. *Sackcloth of my supplication,* garment worn by a suppliant. **23:** Ps.126.6; Jer.31.12–13. **24:** Is.60.1–3. **25:** *The wrath* is only temporary (Is.54.7–8).

they were taken away like a
   flock carried off by the enemy.

27"Take courage, my children, and
   cry to God,
for you will be remembered by
   him who brought this upon you.
28For just as you purposed to go
   astray from God,
return with tenfold zeal to seek
   him.
29For he who brought these calamities
   upon you
will bring you everlasting joy
   with your salvation."

30Take courage, O Jerusalem,
   for he who named you will
   comfort you.
31Wretched will be those who
   afflicted you
and rejoiced at your fall.
32Wretched will be the cities which
   your children served as slaves;
wretched will be the city which
   received your sons.
33For just as she rejoiced at your fall
   and was glad for your ruin,
so she will be grieved at her own
   desolation.
34And I will take away her pride in
   her great population,
and her insolence will be turned
   to grief.
35For fire will come upon her from
   the Everlasting for many days,
and for a long time she will be
   inhabited by demons.

36Look toward the east, O Jerusalem,
   and see the joy that is coming
   to you from God!
37Behold, your sons are coming,
   whom you sent away;
they are coming, gathered from
   east and west,

at the word of the Holy One,
   rejoicing in the glory of God.

5 Take off the garment of your sorrow and affliction, O Jerusalem,
and put on for ever the beauty
   of the glory from God.
2Put on the robe of the righteousness
   from God;
put on your head the diadem of
   the glory of the Everlasting.
3For God will show your splendor
   everywhere under heaven.
4For your name will for ever be
   called by God,
"Peace of righteousness and
   glory of godliness."

5Arise, O Jerusalem, stand upon the
   height
and look toward the east,
and see your children gathered
   from west and east,
at the word of the Holy One,
rejoicing that God has
   remembered them.
6For they went forth from you on
   foot,
led away by their enemies;
but God will bring them back to you,
   carried in glory, as on a royal
   throne.
7For God has ordered that every
   high mountain and the
   everlasting hills be made low
and the valleys filled up, to
   make level ground,
so that Israel may walk safely in
   the glory of God.
8The woods and every fragrant tree
   have shaded Israel at God's
   command.
9For God will lead Israel with joy,
   in the light of his glory,
with the mercy and righteousness
   that come from him.

4.30–5.9: Jerusalem encouraged with promises concerning the destruction of her enemy and
the return of her children. **30:** *He who named you*, see 5.4 n. **31–35:** Contrast the attitude
toward Babylon in 1.11–12. **35:** *Fire*, Jer.51.58. *Demons*, Is.13.21. **36:** Is.40.9–11. **37:** Is.43.5.
5.1–9: Glorification of Jerusalem and return of the exiles. **1–2:** Is.61.3,10. **4:** Is.60.14;
62.4; Jer.33.16; Ezek.48.35. *Peace of righteousness*, Is.32.17. **5:** Is.49.18; 60.4. **6:** Is.49.22;
66.20. **7:** Is.42.16–17.

THE LETTER OF JEREMIAH

The so-called Letter of Jeremiah, which professes to be a copy of a letter sent by Jeremiah in 597 B.C. to those Jews who were about to be taken as captives to Babylon (v. 1), is an earnest though rambling discourse against the folly of idolatry. It can be characterized as an impassioned sermon on Jer.10.11, a verse (in Aramaic) which provides the exiled Jews with a response when invited to participate in the worship of idols: "Thus shall you say to them: 'The gods who did not make the heavens and the earth shall perish from the earth and from under the heavens.'" Elaborating upon this text, the author draws upon Jer.10.3–9,14 and Ps.115.4–8 (compare also Is.40.18–20; 41.6–7) for a variety of arguments to prove the utter impotence, whether for good or ill, of gods of wood and silver and gold. The style of the tractate is florid and declamatory, with no logical connection in the sequence of its statements. In a mechanical way the author divides his homily into sections by a refrain repeated with slight variations, insisting that "this shows that they are no gods" (vv. 16, 23, 29b, 40a, 44b, 52, 56b, 65, 69).

On the basis of linguistic and historical considerations most scholars date the Letter of Jeremiah in the Hellenistic period. The seven generations of exile mentioned in v. 3, at forty years for a generation, would imply a date 280 years after the exile in 597, that is 317 B.C. Others think that the Letter is still later, dating it in the Maccabean period. The original language was most probably Hebrew (see, for example, v. 72 n.), though some think that it was written in either Aramaic or Greek. The oldest manuscript remains of the book is a tiny fragment of Greek papyrus containing several words from vv. 43–44; it was discovered in Cave VII at Qumran by the Dead Sea, and is thought to date from about 100 B.C.

The Letter stands at different places in various manuscripts and versions. It appears as a separate book between Lamentations and Ezekiel in two ancient Greek manuscripts of the Old Testament (the fourth century codex Vaticanus and the fifth century codex Alexandrinus), in the Syriac Hexaplar manuscript at Milan, and in the Arabic version. In other Greek and Syriac manuscripts, as well as the Latin version, it is attached to the apocryphal book of Baruch, and consequently many English translations include it as the final (sixth) chapter of that book. Since, however, the Letter is an independent composition and has nothing to do with Baruch, the Revised Standard Version prints it as a separate book.

---

6 [h] A COPY OF A LETTER WHICH JEREMIAH sent to those who were to be taken to Babylon as captives by the king of the Babylonians, to give them the message which God had commanded him.

2 Because of the sins which you have committed before God, you will be taken to Babylon as captives by Nebuchadnezzar, king of the Babylonians. ³Therefore when you have come to Babylon you will remain there for many years, for a long time, up to seven generations; after that I will bring you away from there in peace. ⁴Now in Babylon you will see gods made of silver and gold and wood, which are carried on men's shoulders and inspire fear in the heathen. ⁵So take care not to become at all like the foreigners or to let fear for these gods[i] possess you, when you see the multitude before and behind them worshiping them. ⁶But say in your heart, "It is thou, O Lord, whom we must worship." ⁷For my angel is with you, and he is watching your lives.

6.1–7: Historical introduction. 1: The exile of 597 B.C. (2 Kg.24.10–17). *Letter*, according to Jer.29.1 a letter is sent to Babylon. *King of the Babylonians*, but "king of Babylon" in the book of Jeremiah (Jer.20.4; 21.2; etc.). **2:** Jer.16.10. **3:** *Seven generations*, contrast seventy years in Jer.29.10, forty years in Ezek.4.6, seventy weeks of years in Dan.9.24. **4:** *Silver and gold*, overlaid on wood (v. 55; Is.40.19; Jer.10.3–4). *Carried on men's shoulders*, perhaps an allusion to the Babylonian New Year procession, or a reflection of Is.46.7; Jer.10.5. **5:** *Like the foreigners*, Jer.10.2. **7:** *My angel*, Ex.23.23; 32.34.

8 Their tongues are smoothed by the craftsman, and they themselves are overlaid with gold and silver; but they are false and cannot speak. [9]People[j] take gold and make crowns for the heads of their gods, as they would for a girl who loves ornaments; [10]and sometimes the priests secretly take gold and silver from their gods and spend it upon themselves, [11]and even give some of it to the harlots in the brothel. They deck their gods[k] out with garments like men—these gods of silver and gold and wood, [12]which cannot save themselves from rust and corrosion. When they have been dressed in purple robes, [13]their faces are wiped because of the dust from the temple, which is thick upon them. [14]Like a local ruler the god[l] holds a scepter, though unable to destroy any one who offends it. [15]It has a dagger in its right hand, and has an axe; but it cannot save itself from war and robbers. [16]Therefore they evidently are not gods; so do not fear them.

17 For just as one's dish is useless when it is broken, so are the gods of the heathen,[m] when they have been set up in the temples. Their eyes are full of the dust raised by the feet of those who enter. [18]And just as the gates are shut on every side upon a man who has offended a king, as though he were sentenced to death, so the priests make their temples secure with doors and locks and bars, in order that they may not be plundered by robbers. [19]They light lamps, even more than they light for themselves, though their gods[n] can see none of them. [20]They are[o] just like a beam of the temple, but men say their hearts have melted, when worms from the earth devour them and their robes. They do not notice [21]when their faces have been blackened by the smoke of the temple. [22]Bats, swallows, and birds light on their bodies and heads; and so do cats. [23]From this you will know that they are not gods; so do not fear them.

24 As for the gold which they wear for beauty—they will not shine unless some one wipes off the rust; for even when they were being cast, they had no feeling. [25]They are bought at any cost, but there is no breath in them. [26]Having no feet, they are carried on men's shoulders, revealing to mankind their worthlessness. [27]And those who serve them are ashamed because through them these gods[n] are made to stand, lest they fall to the ground. If any one sets one of them upright, it cannot move of itself; and if it is tipped over, it cannot straighten itself; but gifts are placed before them just as before the dead. [28]The priests sell the sacrifices that are offered to these gods[p] and use the money; and likewise their wives preserve some with salt, but give none to the poor or helpless. [29]Sacrifices to them may be touched by women in menstruation or at childbirth. Since you know by these things that they are not gods, do not fear them.

j Gk *They*
k Gk *them*
l Gk *he*
m Gk *of them*
n Gk *they*
o Gk *It is*
p Gk *to them*

8–73: Condemnation of idolatry. 8–16: Idols are decked out like people. 8: *Craftsman,* Is. 40.20. **11:** *Harlots,* probably cult prostitutes. *In the brothel,* alternate translation, "on the roof." **12:** *Purple robes,* Jer.10.9. **14:** *Scepter,* Est.5.2. *Destroy,* put to death. **15:** *Dagger,* the Hebrew word behind the Greek could also mean "sword." Archaeologists have found representations of deities bearing scepters, swords, daggers, and battle-axes.

17–23: Uselessness and helplessness of idols. 17: *Dish . . . broken,* Jer.19.11; 22.28. **18:** *Gates* of the palace or doors of courtyard prison (Jer.32.2). **19:** Ps.115.5. *Lamps* have been found in excavated temples. **22:** This is the earliest Jewish reference to *cats,* which were first domesticated in Egypt.

24–29: Idols are unable to feel or move. 25: *Any cost,* great cost. *No breath,* Ps.135.17; Jer.10.14; Hab.2.19. **26:** Is.46.7. **27:** *Cannot move,* Is.46.7; Jer.10.4. *Gifts* for *the dead,* Ps. 106.28; Sir.30.18–19. **29:** Lev.12.1–8.

30 For why should they be called gods? Women serve meals for gods of silver and gold and wood; [31]and in their temples the priests sit with their clothes rent, their heads and beards shaved, and their heads uncovered. [32]They howl and shout before their gods as some do at a funeral feast for a man who has died. [33]The priests take some of the clothing of their gods[q] to clothe their wives and children. [34]Whether one does evil to them or good, they will not be able to repay it. They cannot set up a king or depose one. [35]Likewise they are not able to give either wealth or money; if one makes a vow to them and does not keep it, they will not require it. [36]They cannot save a man from death or rescue the weak from the strong. [37]They cannot restore sight to a blind man; they cannot rescue a man who is in distress. [38]They cannot take pity on a widow or do good to an orphan. [39]These things that are made of wood and overlaid with gold and silver are like stones from the mountain, and those who serve them will be put to shame. [40]Why then must any one think that they are gods, or call them gods?

Besides, even the Chaldeans themselves dishonor them; [41]for when they see a dumb man, who cannot speak, they bring him and pray Bel[r] that the man may speak, as though Bel[s] were able to understand. [42]Yet they themselves cannot perceive this and abandon them, for they have no sense. [43]And the women, with cords about them, sit along the passageways, burning bran for incense; and when one of them is led off by one of the passers-by and is lain with, she derides the woman next to her, because she was not as attractive as herself and her cord was not broken. [44]Whatever is done for them is false. Why then must any one think that they are gods, or call them gods?

45 They are made by carpenters and goldsmiths; they can be nothing but what the craftsmen wish them to be. [46]The men that make them will certainly not live very long themselves; how then can the things that are made by them be gods? [47]They have left only lies and reproach for those who come after. [48]For when war or calamity comes upon them, the priests consult together as to where they can hide themselves and their gods.[t] [49]How then can one fail to see that these are not gods, for they cannot save themselves from war or calamity? [50]Since they are made of wood and overlaid with gold and silver, it will afterward be known that they are false. [51]It will be manifest to all the nations and kings that they are not gods but the work of men's hands, and that there is no work of God in them. [52]Who then can fail to know that they are not gods?[u]

53 For they cannot set up a king over a country or give rain to men. [54]They cannot judge their own cause or deliver one who is wronged, for they have no power; they are like crows between heaven and earth. [55]When fire breaks out in a temple of wooden

q Gk them
r Or they bring Bel and pray
s Gk he
t Gk them
u The Greek text of this verse is uncertain

30–40a: Idols cannot repay good or evil, or help mankind. 30: *Women*, there were only male ministrants in the Jewish temple. **31–32:** Ritual lamentations for dying gods (such as Tammuz, Ezek.8.14; compare Lev.21.5,10; Ezek.24.17). **34b:** Job 12.18; Dan.2.21. **35b:** Dt.23.21. **36:** On the contrary, the Lord can do this (Dt.32.39; Ps.49.15). **37:** Ps.146.8. **38:** Dt.10.18; Ps. 146.9; Jer.7.6. **39:** Hab.2.19.

40b–44: The Chaldeans dishonor their own idols. 41: *Bel*, Marduk (Is.46.1). **43:** A similar Babylonian practice is described by Herodotus (*Hist.* i. 199), according to which cult prostitutes sat among roped-off passageways.

45–52: Idols are but the work of man's hands. 45: Ps.115.4; Is.40.19; Jer.10.9. **47:** Idolaters bequeath lies and reproach, not real gods, to posterity. **50:** *Afterward*, when the veneer has been exposed for what it is. *False*, a fraud.

53–56: The impotence of idols. 53: V. 34b. *Give rain*, Dt.11.14; 28.12; Ps.147.8.

gods overlaid with gold or silver, their priests will flee and escape, but the gods[v] will be burnt in two like beams. [56]Besides, they can offer no resistance to a king or any enemies. Why then must any one admit or think that they are gods?

57 Gods made of wood and overlaid with silver and gold are not able to save themselves from thieves and robbers. [58]Strong men will strip them of their gold and silver and of the robes they wear, and go off with this booty, and they will not be able to help themselves. [59]So it is better to be a king who shows his courage, or a household utensil that serves its owner's need, than to be these false gods; better even the door of a house that protects its contents, than these false gods; better also a wooden pillar in a palace, than these false gods.

60 For sun and moon and stars, shining and sent forth for service, are obedient. [61]So also the lightning, when it flashes, is widely seen; and the wind likewise blows in every land. [62]When God commands the clouds to go over the whole world, they carry out his command. [63]And the fire sent from above to consume mountains and woods does what it is ordered. But these idols[w] are not to be compared

with them in appearance or power. [64]Therefore one must not think that they are gods nor call them gods, for they are not able either to decide a case or to do good to men. [65]Since you know then that they are not gods, do not fear them.

66 For they can neither curse nor bless kings; [67]they cannot show signs in the heavens and[x] among the nations, or shine like the sun or give light like the moon. [68]The wild beasts are better than they are, for they can flee to cover and help themselves. [69]So we have no evidence whatever that they are gods; therefore do not fear them.

70 Like a scarecrow in a cucumber bed, that guards nothing, so are their gods of wood, overlaid with gold and silver. [71]In the same way, their gods of wood, overlaid with gold and silver, are like a thorn bush in a garden, on which every bird sits; or like a dead body cast out in the darkness. [72]By the purple and linen[y] that rot upon them you will know that they are not gods; and they will finally themselves be consumed, and be a reproach in the land. [73]Better therefore is a just man who has no idols, for he will be far from reproach.

v Gk *they*   w Gk *these things*
x Other ancient authorities omit *and*
y Cn: Gk *marble*, Syr *silk*

57–65: Idols are helpless, useless, and not to be compared with celestial phenomena. **60:** Gen.1.14–18. **61–62:** Job 38.24–27; Ps.97.4. **63:** *Fire,* lightning. **64:** *Decide a case,* the true God does this (Ex.18.19; Ps.43.1).

66–69: The helplessness of idols. **67:** *Signs,* portents (Jer.10.2; Jl.2.30; Mt.16.1).

70–73: Idols are compared with a scarecrow, thorn bush, and corpse. **70:** *Scarecrow,* Jer.10.5. **71:** *Thorn bush,* an ordinary, useless shrub (compare Jg.9.14–15). **72:** The Greek text (*marble,* see note *y*) is a misinterpretation of the Hebrew word *shesh,* which means both "linen" and "marble" ("alabaster"). **73:** The conclusion of the matter.

THE PRAYER OF AZARIAH AND THE

SONG OF THE THREE YOUNG MEN

Additions to Daniel, inserted between 3.23 and 3.24

The ancient Greek and Latin versions of the book of Daniel contain a number of additions which are not present in the original Hebrew and Aramaic text. Besides many minor accretions throughout the book there are three lengthy Additions, now included among the Apocrypha as separate books under the respective titles: The Prayer of Azariah and the Song of the Three Young Men; Susanna; Bel and the Dragon.

The date when these Additions were composed is probably sometime in the second or first century B.C. Whether they were written originally in Hebrew, Aramaic, or Greek has been debated by scholars. Of the three Additions the Prayer of Azariah and the Song of the Three Young Men has the best claim to have been composed in Hebrew.

According to the book of Daniel, three Jewish captives in Babylon, named Shadrach, Meshach, and Abednego, refused to worship the golden image which Nebuchadnezzar had set up. By way of punishment for their refusal they were bound and thrown into the burning fiery furnace (Dan.3.23). Then follows the interpolation, which has three sections: vv. 1–22, the prayer of Azariah (Azariah is his Hebrew name; Abednego, his pagan name; see Dan.1.7); vv. 23–27, details about the furnace; vv. 28–68, the song of the three. This song is in two parts: the first is a liturgy addressed to God (vv. 29–34), and the second is a series of exhortations addressed to all creatures, animate and inanimate, to praise the Lord (vv. 35–68). Both parts of the song possess a certain solemnity and majestic rhythm owing to the presence of a regularly recurring refrain, which may have been used as the response of the congregation. The unknown hymnwriter derived much of his inspiration from the antiphonal liturgies in Pss. 136 and 148.

AND THEY WALKED ABOUT IN THE midst of the flames, singing hymns to God and blessing the Lord. ²Then Azariah stood and offered this prayer; in the midst of the fire he opened his mouth and said: ³"Blessed art thou, O Lord, God of
 our fathers, and worthy of
 praise;
 and thy name is glorified for
 ever.
⁴For thou art just in all that thou
 hast done to us,
 and all thy works are true and
 thy ways right,
 and all thy judgments are truth.
⁵Thou hast executed true judgments
 in all that thou hast brought
 upon us
 and upon Jerusalem, the holy
 city of our fathers,
 for in truth and justice thou hast

brought all this upon us
 because of our sins.
⁶For we have sinfully and lawlessly
 departed from thee,
 and have sinned in all things
 and have not obeyed thy
 commandments;
⁷we have not observed them or done
 them,
 as thou hast commanded us that
 it might go well with us.
⁸So all that thou hast brought upon
 us,
 and all that thou hast done to
 us,
 thou hast done in true judgment.
⁹Thou hast given us into the hands
 of lawless enemies, most
 hateful rebels,
 and to an unjust king, the most
 wicked in all the world.
¹⁰And now we cannot open our mouths;

1–22: The prayer of Azariah. 1: *They,* the three men mentioned in Dan.3.23. **3:** 1 Chr. 29.10,20. **4:** Neh.9.33; Rev.16.7; 19.2. **6–7:** Is.59.12–13; Dan.9.5–8; Bar.1.17–18. **8–10:**

shame and disgrace have befallen
    thy servants and worshipers.
[11]For thy name's sake do not give us
    up utterly,
    and do not break thy covenant,
[12] and do not withdraw thy mercy
    from us,
  for the sake of Abraham thy beloved
    and for the sake of Isaac thy
    servant
    and Israel thy holy one,
[13]to whom thou didst promise
    to make their descendants as
    many as the stars of heaven
    and as the sand on the shore of
    the sea.
[14]For we, O Lord, have become
    fewer than any nation,
    and are brought low this day in all
    the world because of our sins.
[15]And at this time there is no prince,
    or prophet, or leader,
    no burnt offering, or sacrifice, or
    oblation, or incense,
    no place to make an offering
    before thee or to find mercy.
[16]Yet with a contrite heart and a
    humble spirit may we be
    accepted,
    as though it were with burnt
    offerings of rams and bulls,
    and with tens of thousands of
    fat lambs;
[17] such may our sacrifice be in thy
    sight this day,
    and may we wholly follow thee,
  for there will be no shame for
    those who trust in thee.
[18]And now with all our heart we
    follow thee,
    we fear thee and seek thy face.
[19]Do not put us to shame,
    but deal with us in thy forbearance
    and in thy abundant mercy.
[20]Deliver us in accordance with thy
    marvelous works,

and give glory to thy name, O
    Lord!
Let all who do harm to thy servants
    be put to shame;
[21] let them be disgraced and
    deprived of all power and
    dominion,
    and let their strength be broken.
[22]Let them know that thou art the
    Lord, the only God,
    glorious over the whole world."

23 Now the king's servants who
threw them in did not cease feeding
the furnace fires with naphtha, pitch,
tow, and brush. [24]And the flame
streamed out above the furnace forty-
nine cubits, [25]and it broke through and
burned those of the Chaldeans whom
it caught about the furnace. [26]But the
angel of the Lord came down into the
furnace to be with Azariah and his
companions, and drove the fiery flame
out of the furnace, [27]and made the
midst of the furnace like a moist
whistling wind, so that the fire did not
touch them at all or hurt or trouble
them.

28 Then the three, as with one
mouth, praised and glorified and
blessed God in the furnace, saying:
[29]"Blessed art thou, O Lord, God of
    our fathers,
    and to be praised and highly
    exalted for ever;
[30]And blessed is thy glorious, holy
    name
    and to be highly praised and
    highly exalted for ever;
[31]Blessed art thou in the temple of
    thy holy glory
    and to be extolled and highly
    glorified for ever.
[32]Blessed art thou, who sittest upon
    cherubim and lookest upon
    the deeps,

Lev.26.14,38; Dt.28.15,63–64. **12:** *Abraham thy beloved,* 2 Chr.20.7; Is.41.8; Jas.2.23. **13:** Gen.15.5; 22.17. **14:** Dt.28.63; Jer.42.2; Bar.2.13. **15:** Lam.2.9; Hos.3.4; 2 Esd.10.21–22. **16:** Ps.51.16–17; Hos.6.6. **19:** Ps.25.3. **21:** Ps.35.26. **22:** Ps.83.18.
    23–27: The continued stoking of the furnace, and the descent of the angel of the Lord. 23: *Naphtha,* a natural petroleum.
    28–69: Song of the three young men. 32–37: Ps.148. **35:** Pss.103.22; 145.10.

and to be praised and highly
exalted for ever.
³³Blessed art thou upon the throne
of thy kingdom
and to be extolled and highly
exalted for ever.
³⁴Blessed art thou in the firmament
of heaven
and to be sung and glorified for
ever.

³⁵"Bless the Lord, all works of the
Lord,
sing praise to him and highly
exalt him for ever.
³⁶Bless the Lord, you heavens,
sing praise to him and highly
exalt him for ever.
³⁷Bless the Lord, you angels of the
Lord,
sing praise to him and highly
exalt him for ever.
³⁸Bless the Lord, all waters above
the heaven,
sing praise to him and highly
exalt him for ever.
³⁹Bless the Lord, all powers,
sing praise to him and highly
exalt him for ever.
⁴⁰Bless the Lord, sun and moon,
sing praise to him and highly
exalt him for ever.
⁴¹Bless the Lord, stars of heaven,
sing praise to him and highly
exalt him for ever.
⁴²Bless the Lord, all rain and
dew,
sing praise to him and highly
exalt him for ever.
⁴³Bless the Lord, all winds,
sing praise to him and highly
exalt him for ever.
⁴⁴Bless the Lord, fire and heat,
sing praise to him and highly
exalt him for ever.
⁴⁵Bless the Lord, winter cold and
summer heat,
sing praise to him and highly
exalt him for ever.
⁴⁶Bless the Lord, dews and snows,

sing praise to him and highly
exalt him for ever.
⁴⁷Bless the Lord, nights and days,
sing praise to him and highly
exalt him for ever.
⁴⁸Bless the Lord, light and darkness,
sing praise to him and highly
exalt him for ever.
⁴⁹Bless the Lord, ice and cold,
sing praise to him and highly
exalt him for ever.
⁵⁰Bless the Lord, frosts and snows,
sing praise to him and highly
exalt him for ever.
⁵¹Bless the Lord, lightnings and
clouds,
sing praise to him and highly
exalt him for ever.
⁵²Let the earth bless the Lord;
let it sing praise to him and
highly exalt him for ever.
⁵³Bless the Lord, mountains and
hills,
sing praise to him and highly
exalt him for ever.
⁵⁴Bless the Lord, all things that
grow on the earth,
sing praise to him and highly
exalt him for ever.
⁵⁵Bless the Lord, you springs,
sing praise to him and highly
exalt him for ever.
⁵⁶Bless the Lord, seas and rivers,
sing praise to him and highly
exalt him for ever.
⁵⁷Bless the Lord, you whales and all
creatures that move in the
waters,
sing praise to him and highly
exalt him for ever.
⁵⁸Bless the Lord, all birds of the air,
sing praise to him and highly
exalt him for ever.
⁵⁹Bless the Lord, all beasts and
cattle,
sing praise to him and highly
exalt him for ever.
⁶⁰Bless the Lord, you sons of men,
sing praise to him and highly
exalt him for ever.

37: Pss.103.20; 148.2. **38**: Ps.148.4. **39**: *All powers*, i.e. with heavenly bodies or angels.
40: Ps.148.3. **44**: Ps.148.8. **53**: Ps.148.9. **58–59**: Ps.148.10.

SONG OF THE THREE YOUNG MEN *"Give thanks to the Lord"*

[61]Bless the Lord, O Israel,
    sing praise to him and highly
      exalt him for ever.
[62]Bless the Lord, you priests of the
    Lord,
    sing praise to him and highly
      exalt him for ever.
[63]Bless the Lord, you servants of the
    Lord,
    sing praise to him and highly
      exalt him for ever.
[64]Bless the Lord, spirits and souls of
    the righteous,
    sing praise to him and highly
      exalt him for ever.
[65]Bless the Lord, you who are holy
    and humble in heart,
    sing praise to him and highly
      exalt him for ever.

[66]Bless the Lord, Hananiah, Azariah,
    and Mishael,
    sing praise to him and highly
      exalt him for ever;
for he has rescued us from Hades
    and saved us from the hand
    of death,
and delivered us from the midst
    of the burning fiery furnace;
from the midst of the fire he has
    delivered us.
[67]Give thanks to the Lord, for he is
    good,
for his mercy endures for ever.
[68]Bless him, all who worship the
    Lord, the God of gods,
    sing praise to him and give
    thanks to him,
for his mercy endures for ever."

61–62: Ps.135.19. **63:** Ps.134.1. **65:** *Holy and humble in heart*, Pss.18.25,27; 86.1–2; Zeph.2.3. **67–68:** Pss.106.1; 136.1–2.

SUSANNA

Of the cycle of traditions concerning Daniel which were added to the book of Daniel when it was translated into Greek the story of Susanna is undoubtedly the gem. One of the finest short stories in world literature, it is based on the familiar motif of the triumph of virtue over villainy, the narrow escape from death of an innocent victim. While inculcating lessons of morality and trust in God, the story is a model of artistic fiction. Plot, surprise, struggle, and unfolding character are present in just the right proportion, and the whole is told succinctly and pungently.

In Hebrew the name Susanna means "a lily" and the name Daniel means "God has judged." Both are obviously appropriate names for the heroine and hero in a story that tells how Susanna was cleared of a false charge of adultery through the timely intervention of a sagacious and brave youth.

The position of this addition in the book of Daniel varies in the manuscripts. In the Septuagint and the Latin Vulgate the account of Susanna follows the last chapter of Daniel (which in Hebrew is ch. 12), and is numbered ch. 13. In the Greek text of Theodotion, however, as well as the Old Latin, Coptic, and Arabic versions the story of Susanna forms the introduction to the book of Daniel, being prefixed to ch. 1. It may be that this latter position was thought more appropriate because the addition describes Daniel as "a young lad" (v. 45).

Concerning date and original language, see the first part of the Introduction to the Prayer of Azariah and the Song of the Three Young Men.

THERE WAS A MAN LIVING IN BABYlon whose name was Joakim. ²And he took a wife named Susanna, the daughter of Hilkiah, a very beautiful woman and one who feared the Lord. ³Her parents were righteous, and had taught their daughter according to the law of Moses. ⁴Joakim was very rich, and had a spacious garden adjoining his house; and the Jews used to come to him because he was the most honored of them all.

5 In that year two elders from the people were appointed as judges. Concerning them the Lord had said: "Iniquity came forth from Babylon, from elders who were judges, who were supposed to govern the people." ⁶These men were frequently at Joakim's house, and all who had suits at law came to them.

7 When the people departed at noon, Susanna would go into her husband's garden to walk. ⁸The two elders used to see her every day, going in and walking about, and they began to desire her. ⁹And they perverted their minds and turned away their eyes from looking to Heaven or remembering righteous judgments. ¹⁰Both were overwhelmed with passion for her, but they did not tell each other of their distress, ¹¹for they were ashamed to disclose their lustful desire to possess her. ¹²And they watched eagerly, day after day, to see her.

13 They said to each other, "Let us go home, for it is mealtime." ¹⁴And when they went out, they parted from each other. But turning back, they met again; and when each pressed the other for the reason, they confessed their lust. And then together they arranged for a time when they could find her alone.

1–4: **Introduction.** The setting of the story is Babylon during the exile. **1:** The name *Joakim* means "the Lord will establish." **2:** The names *Susanna* and *Hilkiah* mean respectively "lily" and "the Lord is my portion." **4:** Some Jews prospered during the exile (Jer.29.5).

5–14: **The two lustful elders. 5:** *In that year*, apparently the year of Joakim's marriage (v. 2). The *two elders* are identified by Jewish tradition to be the two false prophets mentioned in Jer. 29.21–23. The quotation ("*Iniquity . . . people*") is either an unwritten prophetic saying or an allusion to Jer.23.14–15. **9:** *Heaven*, a metonym for God (see 1 Macc.3.18 n. and compare Lk.15.18).

15 Once, while they were watching for an opportune day, she went in as before with only two maids, and wished to bathe in the garden, for it was very hot. [16]And no one was there except the two elders, who had hid themselves and were watching her. [17]She said to her maids, "Bring me oil and ointments, and shut the garden doors so that I may bathe." [18]They did as she said, shut the garden doors, and went out by the side doors to bring what they had been commanded; and they did not see the elders, because they were hidden.

19 When the maids had gone out, the two elders rose and ran to her, and said: [20]"Look, the garden doors are shut, no one sees us, and we are in love with you; so give your consent, and lie with us. [21]If you refuse, we will testify against you that a young man was with you, and this was why you sent your maids away."

22 Susanna sighed deeply, and said, "I am hemmed in on every side. For if I do this thing, it is death for me; and if I do not, I shall not escape your hands. [23]I choose not to do it and to fall into your hands, rather than to sin in the sight of the Lord."

24 Then Susanna cried out with a loud voice, and the two elders shouted against her. [25]And one of them ran and opened the garden doors. [26]When the household servants heard the shouting in the garden, they rushed in at the side door to see what had happened to her. [27]And when the elders told their tale, the servants were greatly ashamed, for nothing like this had ever been said about Susanna.

28 The next day, when the people gathered at the house of her husband Joakim, the two elders came, full of their wicked plot to have Susanna put to death. [29]They said before the people, "Send for Susanna, the daughter of Hilkiah, who is the wife of Joakim." [30]So they sent for her. And she came, with her parents, her children, and all her kindred.

31 Now Susanna was a woman of great refinement, and beautiful in appearance. [32]As she was veiled, the wicked men ordered her to be unveiled, that they might feast upon her beauty. [33]But her family and friends and all who saw her wept.

34 Then the two elders stood up in the midst of the people, and laid their hands upon her head. [35]And she, weeping, looked up toward heaven, for her heart trusted in the Lord. [36]The elders said, "As we were walking in the garden alone, this woman came in with two maids, shut the garden doors, and dismissed the maids. [37]Then a young man, who had been hidden, came to her and lay with her. [38]We were in a corner of the garden, and when we saw this wickedness we ran to them. [39]We saw them embracing, but we could not hold the man, for he was too strong for us, and he opened the doors and dashed out. [40]So we seized this woman and asked her who the young man was, but she would not tell us. These things we testify."

41 The assembly believed them, because they were elders of the people and judges; and they condemned her to death.

42 Then Susanna cried out with a loud voice, and said, "O eternal God, who dost discern what is secret, who art aware of all things before they come to be, [43]thou knowest that these men have borne false witness against me. And now I am to die! Yet I have

15–27: The attempted seduction. 17: *Oil and* (perfumed) *ointments* were used after bathing. **22:** The Mosaic law prescribed *death* as punishment for the unfaithful wife (Lev.20.10; Dt.22.22). **23:** Compare Joseph's reply to his tempter (Gen.39.9).
  28–43: Susanna falsely accused and condemned to death. 34: The judges play the part of witnesses by laying their hands on the head of the accused (Lev.24.14). **35:** *She . . . looked up toward heaven*, appealing her cause to a higher tribunal (vv. 42–43). **41:** Since, according to Jewish law, a witness could not be the judge, the sentence of death is passed by the credulous *assembly*. **42:** *God, who dost discern what is secret*, Ps.33.13–15; Pr.15.11; Heb.4.13.

done none of the things that they have wickedly invented against me!"

44 The Lord heard her cry. [45]And as she was being led away to be put to death, God aroused the holy spirit of a young lad named Daniel; [46]and he cried with a loud voice, "I am innocent of the blood of this woman."

47 All the people turned to him, and said, "What is this that you have said?" [48]Taking his stand in the midst of them, he said, "Are you such fools, you sons of Israel? Have you condemned a daughter of Israel without examination and without learning the facts? [49]Return to the place of judgment. For these men have borne false witness against her."

50 Then all the people returned in haste. And the elders said to him, "Come, sit among us and inform us, for God has given you that right." [51]And Daniel said to them, "Separate them far from each other, and I will examine them."

52 When they were separated from each other, he summoned one of them and said to him, "You old relic of wicked days, your sins have now come home, which you have committed in the past, [53]pronouncing unjust judgments, condemning the innocent and letting the guilty go free, though the Lord said, 'Do not put to death an innocent and righteous person.' [54]Now then, if you really saw her, tell me this: Under what tree did you see them being intimate with each other?" He answered, "Under a mastic tree."[a] [55]And Daniel said, "Very well! You have lied against your own head, for the angel of God has received the sen-

tence from God and will immediately cut[a] you in two."

56 Then he put him aside, and commanded them to bring the other. And he said to him, "You offspring of Canaan and not of Judah, beauty has deceived you and lust has perverted your heart. [57]This is how you both have been dealing with the daughters of Israel, and they were intimate with you through fear; but a daughter of Judah would not endure your wickedness. [58]Now then, tell me: Under what tree did you catch them being intimate with each other?" He answered, "Under an evergreen oak."[b] [59]And Daniel said to him, "Very well! You also have lied against your own head, for the angel of God is waiting with his sword to saw[b] you in two, that he may destroy you both."

60 Then all the assembly shouted loudly and blessed God, who saves those who hope in him. [61]And they rose against the two elders, for out of their own mouths Daniel had convicted them of bearing false witness; [62]and they did to them as they had wickedly planned to do to their neighbor; acting in accordance with the law of Moses, they put them to death. Thus innocent blood was saved that day.

63 And Hilkiah and his wife praised God for their daughter Susanna, and so did Joakim her husband and all her kindred, because nothing shameful was found in her. [64]And from that day onward Daniel had a great reputation among the people.

a The Greek words for *mastic tree* and *cut* are so similar that the use of *cut* is ironic wordplay
b The Greek words for *evergreen oak* and *saw* are so similar that the use of *saw* is ironic wordplay

---

44–59: Susanna acquitted. 50: Here *the elders* are obviously not the two who had testified, but their colleagues on the bench. **53:** Ex.23.7. **54–59:** The wordplay of the original (see notes *a* and *b*) may be represented in English by the paraphrase, "Under a *clove* tree . . . the angel will *cleave* you"; "under a *yew* tree . . . the angel will *hew* you asunder."

60–62: The two elders condemned to death. 62: *The law of Moses*, concerning false witnesses (Dt.19.16–21).

BEL AND THE DRAGON

This addition to the Greek text of the book of Daniel comprises two popular tales, both designed to ridicule the folly of idolatry and to discredit heathen priestcraft. The first story tells of the great statue of Bel, the patron deity of Babylon, which every night devours huge quantities of food and drink and thus proves itself to be a living god. By clever detective work Daniel unmasks the chicanery of Bel's priests. The second story tells of Daniel's refusal to worship a monstrous dragon as a god, and his killing it with a ridiculous concoction of pitch, fat, and hair. The Babylonians, enraged by the death of their god, demand that Daniel be thrown into the lions' den. He is kept safe among the lions for six days, and is provided with food brought from Judea by the prophet Habakkuk. On the seventh day the king removes Daniel and throws into the den his enemies, who are immediately devoured.

The religious teaching of these stories, bizarre and fantastic as they appear to us today, is that those who worship the true and living God will be sustained in every kind of trial.

In the Greek manuscripts of Daniel the account of Bel and the Dragon is added at the close of ch. 12 of Daniel. In the Latin Vulgate it forms ch. 14, the story of Susanna being ch. 13. Concerning date and original language, see the first part of the Introduction to the Prayer of Azariah and the Song of the Three Young Men.

WHEN KING ASTYAGES WAS LAID with his fathers, Cyrus the Persian received his kingdom. ²And Daniel was a companion of the king, and was the most honored of his friends.

3 Now the Babylonians had an idol called Bel, and every day they spent on it twelve bushels of fine flour and forty sheep and fifty gallons of wine. ⁴The king revered it and went every day to worship it. But Daniel worshiped his own God.

5 And the king said to him, "Why do you not worship Bel?" He answered, "Because I do not revere manmade idols, but the living God, who created heaven and earth and has dominion over all flesh."

6 The king said to him, "Do you not think that Bel is a living God? Do you not see how much he eats and drinks every day?" ⁷Then Daniel laughed, and said, "Do not be deceived, O king; for this is but clay inside and brass outside, and it never ate or drank anything."

8 Then the king was angry, and he called his priests and said to them, "If you do not tell me who is eating these provisions, you shall die. ⁹But if you prove that Bel is eating them, Daniel shall die, because he blasphemed against Bel." And Daniel said to the king, "Let it be done as you have said."

10 Now there were seventy priests of Bel, besides their wives and children. And the king went with Daniel into the temple of Bel. ¹¹And the priests of Bel said, "Behold, we are going outside; you yourself, O king, shall set forth the food and mix and place the wine, and shut the door and seal it with your signet. ¹²And when you return in the morning, if you do not find that Bel has eaten it all, we will die; or else Daniel will, who is telling lies about us." ¹³They were unconcerned, for beneath the table they had made a hidden entrance, through which they used to go in regularly and consume the provisions. ¹⁴When they had gone out, the king

1–2: Introduction. 1: *Cyrus the Persian* (Dan.6.28) became king of Babylon in 538 B.C.

3–22: The story of Bel. 3: *Bel*, or Bel-Marduk (compare Merodach, Jer.50.2), was the chief god in the Babylonian pantheon. Several ancient sources testify to the enormous quantities of sacrifices presented to Marduk in the daily ritual. **7:** Daniel ridicules the king's argument: clay and brass do not eat (Sir.30.19). **11:** Dan.6.17. Archaeologists have found great numbers of Babylonian signets.

set forth the food for Bel. Then Daniel ordered his servants to bring ashes and they sifted them throughout the whole temple in the presence of the king alone. Then they went out, shut the door and sealed it with the king's signet, and departed. ¹⁵In the night the priests came with their wives and children, as they were accustomed to do, and ate and drank everything.

16 Early in the morning the king rose and came, and Daniel with him. ¹⁷And the king said, "Are the seals unbroken, Daniel?" He answered, "They are unbroken, O king." ¹⁸As soon as the doors were opened, the king looked at the table, and shouted in a loud voice, "You are great, O Bel; and with you there is no deceit, none at all."

19 Then Daniel laughed, and restrained the king from going in, and said, "Look at the floor, and notice whose footsteps these are." ²⁰The king said, "I see the footsteps of men and women and children."

21 Then the king was enraged, and he seized the priests and their wives and children; and they showed him the secret doors through which they were accustomed to enter and devour what was on the table. ²²Therefore the king put them to death, and gave Bel over to Daniel, who destroyed it and its temple.

23 There was also a great dragon, which the Babylonians revered. ²⁴And the king said to Daniel, "You cannot deny that this is a living god; so worship him." ²⁵Daniel said, "I will worship the Lord my God, for he is the living God. ²⁶But if you, O king, will

give me permission, I will slay the dragon without sword or club." The king said, "I give you permission."

27 Then Daniel took pitch, fat, and hair, and boiled them together and made cakes, which he fed to the dragon. The dragon ate them, and burst open. And Daniel said, "See what you have been worshiping!"

28 When the Babylonians heard it, they were very indignant and conspired against the king, saying, "The king has become a Jew; he has destroyed Bel, and slain the dragon, and slaughtered the priests." ²⁹Going to the king, they said, "Hand Daniel over to us, or else we will kill you and your household." ³⁰The king saw that they were pressing him hard, and under compulsion he handed Daniel over to them.

31 They threw Daniel into the lions' den, and he was there for six days. ³²There were seven lions in the den, and every day they had been given two human bodies and two sheep; but these were not given to them now, so that they might devour Daniel.

33 Now the prophet Habakkuk was in Judea. He had boiled pottage and had broken bread into a bowl, and was going into the field to take it to the reapers. ³⁴But the angel of the Lord said to Habakkuk, "Take the dinner which you have to Babylon, to Daniel, in the lions' den." ³⁵Habakkuk said, "Sir, I have never seen Babylon, and I know nothing about the den." ³⁶Then the angel of the Lord took him by the crown of his head, and lifted him by his hair and set him down in Babylon, right over the den, with the rushing sound of the wind itself.

37 Then Habakkuk shouted,

16–22: The fraud detected (compare Dan.2.12; 6.24). **22:** According to ancient historians it was Xerxes who destroyed Bel's temple.

23–42: The story of the dragon. 23: *A great dragon*, that is, a live serpent worshiped as a god (compare Num.21.8–9; 2 Kg.18.4). **26:** *Permission* was granted because the king believed in the immortality of the serpent-god. **31–32:** The second time that Daniel is put in *the lions' den* (Dan.6.16–24).

33–39: The intervention of Habakkuk. 33: The author intends to identify this Habakkuk with the Minor Prophet of that name; chronologically, however, such an identification is impossible. **36:** *Hair*, Ezek.8.3. **37:** 1 Kg.17.4.

"Daniel! Daniel! Take the dinner which God has sent you." [38]And Daniel said, "Thou hast remembered me, O God, and hast not forsaken those who love thee." [39]So Daniel arose and ate. And the angel of God immediately returned Habakkuk to his own place.

40 On the seventh day the king came to mourn for Daniel. When he came to the den he looked in, and there sat Daniel. [41]And the king shouted with a loud voice, "Thou art great, O Lord God of Daniel, and there is no other besides thee." [42]And he pulled Daniel*a* out, and threw into the den the men who had attempted his destruction, and they were devoured immediately before his eyes.

a Gk *him*

40–42: Daniel's liberation. 41: Compare Dan.6.26–27.

THE PRAYER OF MANASSEH

One of the finest pieces in the Apocrypha is the little classic of penitential devotion known as the Prayer of Manasseh. Constructed in accord with the best liturgical forms and full without being protracted, this beautiful prayer breathes throughout a spirit of deep and genuine religious feeling.

According to 2 Chr.33.11–13, Manasseh, the wicked king of Judah, while in exile composed a prayer entreating divine forgiveness for his many sins. The Old Testament account also refers to two literary works that contained Manasseh's prayer (2 Chr.33.18–19). Since neither of these has survived, it is not surprising that some devout Jew undertook to remedy the loss by drawing up such a prayer as might have been used by the wicked though now repentant king. Henceforth the name Manasseh was associated in Jewish tradition not only with the grossest acts of idolatry (2 Chr.33.1–9), but also with the efficacy of genuine repentance in securing divine forgiveness. It may be that the unknown author also had in mind the practical use of the prayer in providing a suitable penitential devotion for those of his countrymen who, having fallen into idolatry, could be reclaimed from the error of their way.

The date of composition of the Prayer is difficult to determine. Though there is no positive evidence, many scholars place it sometime during the last two centuries B.C. Whether it was composed originally in Hebrew, Aramaic, or Greek is disputed; today it survives in Greek, Latin, Syriac, Armenian, and Ethiopic. The Latin translation of the Prayer in the Vulgate Bible (which since the Council of Trent has been put into an Appendix) is entirely different from the Old Latin translation, and is of much more recent origin.

O LORD ALMIGHTY,
God of our fathers,
of Abraham and Isaac and Jacob
and of their righteous posterity;
²thou who hast made heaven and
earth
with all their order;
³who hast shackled the sea by thy
word of command,
who hast confined the deep
and sealed it with thy terrible
and glorious name;
⁴at whom all things shudder,
and tremble before thy power,
⁵for thy glorious splendor cannot be
borne,
and the wrath of thy threat to
sinners is irresistible;
⁶yet immeasurable and unsearchable
is thy promised mercy,
⁷ for thou art the Lord Most High,
of great compassion, long-suffering,
and very merciful,
and repentest over the evils of
men.
Thou, O Lord, according to thy
great goodness
hast promised repentance and
forgiveness
to those who have sinned against
thee;
and in the multitude of thy
mercies
thou hast appointed repentance
for sinners,
that they may be saved.
⁸Therefore thou, O Lord, God of
the righteous,
hast not appointed repentance
for the righteous,
for Abraham and Isaac and
Jacob, who did not sin against
thee,
but thou hast appointed
repentance for me, who am
a sinner.

1–8: Invocation and ascription of praise to God, whose majesty is displayed in creation (vv. 1–4), and whose mercy grants repentance to sinners (vv. 6–8). **1:** *God of our fathers,* Ex.3.15–16; Dan.2.23; Acts 3.13. **2:** *All their order,* splendor and orderly array. **3:** *Shackled the sea,* Job 38.8–11. **7:** The second part of this verse (*Thou, O Lord . . . may be saved*) is preserved in the later Greek manuscripts and in the Latin and Syriac versions. **8:** *Not . . . for the righteous,* Lk.5.32. *For me . . . a sinner,* Lk.18.13.

9For the sins I have committed are
more in number than the
sand of the sea;
my transgressions are multiplied,
O Lord, they are multiplied!
I am unworthy to look up and see
the height of heaven
because of the multitude of my
iniquities.
10I am weighted down with many
an iron fetter,
so that I am rejected because of
my sins,
and I have no relief;
for I have provoked thy wrath
and have done what is evil in
thy sight,
setting up abominations and
multiplying offenses.
11And now I bend the knee of my
heart,
beseeching thee for thy
kindness.

12I have sinned, O Lord, I have
sinned,
and I know my transgressions.
13I earnestly beseech thee,
forgive me, O Lord, forgive me!
Do not destroy me with my
transgressions!
Do not be angry with me for ever
or lay up evil for me;
do not condemn me to the
depths of the earth.
For thou, O Lord, art the God of
those who repent,
14 and in me thou wilt manifest
thy goodness;
for, unworthy as I am, thou wilt
save me in thy great mercy,
15 and I will praise thee continually
all the days of my life.
For all the host of heaven sings
thy praise,
and thine is the glory for ever.
Amen.

9–10: Personal confession of sin. For the background see 2 Kg.21.1–18; 2 Chr.33.1–20.

11–15a: Supplication for pardon. 11: *Knee of my heart*, an expression indicating special depth of feeling. **12:** *I know my transgressions*, compare Ps.19.12. **13:** *The depths of the earth*, probably Sheol or Hades is meant (Ps.63.9).

15b: Concluding doxology. *Host of heaven*, multitude of angelic beings (2 Chr.18.18; Lk.2.13).

MACCABEES

First Maccabees has come down to us in Greek, and also in Latin and several other versions derived from the Greek, the original Hebrew having been lost at an early time. The book was probably written shortly after the death of John Hyrcanus I (high priest 134–104 B.C.), since it refers to the chronicles of John's reign (16.23–24). Some scholars, however, think that chs. 14–16 are an addition made not long after A.D. 70, in which case the rest of the book may have been written about 140 B.C.

The author of 1 Maccabees was probably a Palestinian Jew who lived in Jerusalem. He modeled his work on the historical books of the Old Testament, particularly the books of Kings and Chronicles. After an introduction briefly sketching the conquests of Alexander the Great (336–323 B.C.), the division of his empire, and the origin of the Seleucid Empire (1.1–10), he recounts the principal events of Judea's history from the accession of Antiochus IV (175 B.C.) to the reign of John Hyrcanus I, which marked the period of the successful struggle for Jewish independence.

The style of 1 Maccabees is plain and straightforward and the book is generally an excellent historical source, though the order of events frequently differs from that in 2 Maccabees and it is not always certain which is to be preferred. Though the author (unlike the author of 2 Maccabees) records no miraculous interventions from heaven, he obviously sees the hand of God operative in the victories of Judas Maccabeus and his family. The letters of kings and others that are included are essential to the story, and, whether or not they are genuine copies of historical documents, they appear to be based on reliable information. The book also preserves portions of several contemporary poems (e.g. 1.24–28, 36–40; 2.7–13; 3.3–9, 45, 50–53; 14.4–15).

AFTER ALEXANDER SON OF PHILIP, the Macedonian, who came from the land of Kittim, had defeated[a] Darius, king of the Persians and the Medes, he succeeded him as king. (He had previously become king of Greece.) [2]He fought many battles, conquered strongholds, and put to death the kings of the earth. [3]He advanced to the ends of the earth, and plundered many nations. When the earth became quiet before him, he was exalted, and his heart was lifted up. [4]He gathered a very strong army and ruled over countries, nations, and princes, and they became tributary to him.

[5]After this he fell sick and perceived that he was dying. [6]So he summoned his most honored officers, who had been brought up with him from youth, and divided his kingdom among them while he was still alive. [7]And after Alexander had reigned twelve years, he died.

[8]Then his officers began to rule, each in his own place. [9]They all put on crowns after his death, and so did their sons after them for many years; and they caused many evils on the earth.

[10]From them came forth a sinful root, Antiochus Epiphanes, son of Antiochus the king; he had been a hostage in Rome. He began to reign

a Greek adds and he defeated

1.1–10: Introduction. A summary of history from Alexander to Antiochus IV. **1:** *Alexander the Great* (356–323 B.C.), son of Philip of Macedon, who had conquered *Kittim* (Greece), swept through Asia Minor, and *defeated Darius* III at Issus (333 B.C.) and at Gaugamela (331 B.C.). **3:** After taking Egypt, Mesopotamia, and Persia he advanced to the *ends of the earth* (to Bactria and India). *He was exalted,* i.e. he accepted divine honors. **4:** He planned a universal empire dominated by Greek culture. **5:** *He fell sick* in Babylon. **8–9:** By 275 B.C. three dynasties were established, the Antigonids of Macedonia, the Ptolemies of Egypt, and the Seleucids of Syria. **10:** *Sinful root,* Is.11.10; Dan.11.7. *Antiochus* IV, who took the name

in the one hundred and thirty-seventh year of the kingdom of the Greeks.*b*

11 In those days lawless men came forth from Israel, and misled many, saying, "Let us go and make a covenant with the Gentiles round about us, for since we separated from them many evils have come upon us." 12This proposal pleased them, 13and some of the people eagerly went to the king. He authorized them to observe the ordinances of the Gentiles. 14So they built a gymnasium in Jerusalem, according to Gentile custom, 15and removed the marks of circumcision, and abandoned the holy covenant. They joined with the Gentiles and sold themselves to do evil.

16 When Antiochus saw that his kingdom was established, he determined to become king of the land of Egypt, that he might reign over both kingdoms. 17So he invaded Egypt with a strong force, with chariots and elephants and cavalry and with a large fleet. 18He engaged Ptolemy king of Egypt in battle, and Ptolemy turned and fled before him, and many were wounded and fell. 19And they captured the fortified cities in the land of Egypt, and he plundered the land of Egypt.

20 After subduing Egypt, Antiochus returned in the one hundred and forty-third year.*c* He went up against Israel and came to Jerusalem with a strong force. 21He arrogantly entered the sanctuary and took the golden altar, the lampstand for the light, and all its utensils. 22He took also the table for the bread of the Presence, the cups for drink offerings, the bowls, the golden censers, the curtain, the crowns, and the gold decoration on the front of the temple; he stripped it all off. 23He took the silver and the gold, and the costly vessels; he took also the hidden treasures which he found. 24Taking them all, he departed to his own land.

He committed deeds of murder,
   and spoke with great arrogance.
25Israel mourned deeply in every
   community,
26   rulers and elders groaned,
maidens and young men became
   faint,
   the beauty of the women faded.
27Every bridegroom took up the
   lament;
   she who sat in the bridal chamber
   was mourning.
28Even the land shook for its
   inhabitants,
   and all the house of Jacob was
   clothed with shame.

29 Two years later the king sent to the cities of Judah a chief collector of tribute, and he came to Jerusalem with a large force. 30Deceitfully he spoke peaceable words to them, and they believed him; but he suddenly fell upon the city, dealt it a severe blow, and

b 175 B.C.   *c* 169 B.C.

Epiphanes ("god manifest"), reigned 175–164 B.C.; he was *son of Antiochus* III the Great (223–187 B.C.), who had wrested Palestine from Egypt at the battle of Paneas in 198 B.C. but lost most of Asia Minor to Rome at Magnesia in 190 B.C. (compare Dan.11.18). Because of this defeat the son *had been a hostage in Rome. One hundred and thirty-seventh year* of the Seleucid era; reckoning of this era varied in different places; dates given in the margin (notes *b*, *c*, etc.) are approximate.

1.11–15: The paganizing program. Greek culture had penetrated Palestine peacefully, but now enthusiasts introduced Greek religion (2 Macc.4.11–17). **11:** *Lawless men*, willing to abandon Judaism, led by Jason, whom Antiochus appointed in place of his brother Onias III (2 Macc.4.7). *Evils*, loss of business and prestige because relations with Syria were not close. **14:** *A gymnasium*, see 2 Macc.4.9–10 n.

1.16–40: Antiochus invades Egypt and Palestine. Invasion of Egypt is followed by plundering of the temple in Jerusalem (2 Macc.5.1,11–26). **17:** The Syrian army had *elephants*, though the treaty of Apamea with Rome (188 B.C.) had forbidden this. **18:** *Ptolemy* VI Philometor reigned 180–145 B.C. **20:** *Antiochus returned* because the Roman envoy, Popilius Laenas, threatened him with war if he annexed Egypt. **24–28:** Fragment of a contemporary poem. **28:** *The house*

destroyed many people of Israel. ³¹He plundered the city, burned it with fire, and tore down its houses and its surrounding walls. ³²And they took captive the women and children, and seized the cattle. ³³Then they fortified the city of David with a great strong wall and strong towers, and it became their citadel. ³⁴And they stationed there a sinful people, lawless men. These strengthened their position; ³⁵they stored up arms and food, and collecting the spoils of Jerusalem they stored them there, and became a great snare.

³⁶It became an ambush against the sanctuary,
    an evil adversary of Israel
      continually.
³⁷On every side of the sanctuary
    they shed innocent blood;
    they even defiled the sanctuary.
³⁸Because of them the residents of
      Jerusalem fled;
    she became a dwelling of
      strangers;
  she became strange to her
      offspring,
    and her children forsook her.
³⁹Her sanctuary became desolate as
      a desert;
    her feasts were turned into
      mourning,
  her sabbaths into a reproach,
    her honor into contempt.
⁴⁰Her dishonor now grew as great as
      her glory;
    her exaltation was turned into
      mourning.

41 Then the king wrote to his whole kingdom that all should be one people, ⁴²and that each should give up his customs. ⁴³All the Gentiles accepted the command of the king. Many even from Israel gladly adopted his religion;

they sacrificed to idols and profaned the sabbath. ⁴⁴And the king sent letters by messengers to Jerusalem and the cities of Judah; he directed them to follow customs strange to the land, ⁴⁵to forbid burnt offerings and sacrifices and drink offerings in the sanctuary, to profane sabbaths and feasts, ⁴⁶to defile the sanctuary and the priests, ⁴⁷to build altars and sacred precincts and shrines for idols, to sacrifice swine and unclean animals, ⁴⁸and to leave their sons uncircumcised. They were to make themselves abominable by everything unclean and profane, ⁴⁹so that they should forget the law and change all the ordinances. ⁵⁰"And whoever does not obey the command of the king shall die."

51 In such words he wrote to his whole kingdom. And he appointed inspectors over all the people and commanded the cities of Judah to offer sacrifice, city by city. ⁵²Many of the people, every one who forsook the law, joined them, and they did evil in the land; ⁵³they drove Israel into hiding in every place of refuge they had.

54 Now on the fifteenth day of Chislev, in the one hundred and forty-fifth year,ᵈ they erected a desolating sacrilege upon the altar of burnt offering. They also built altars in the surrounding cities of Judah, ⁵⁵and burned incense at the doors of the houses and in the streets. ⁵⁶The books of the law which they found they tore to pieces and burned with fire. ⁵⁷Where the book of the covenant was found in the possession of any one, or if any one adhered to the law, the decree of the king condemned him to death. ⁵⁸They kept using violence against Israel, against those found month after month

ᵈ 167 B.C.

---

of Jacob, Israel, the Jewish people. **33:** *City of David*, the Ophel hill south of the temple area (2 Sam.5.7). **34:** The *sinful people* were irreligious Jews. **36-40:** Poetic fragment (compare Pss.74; 79).

   1.41-64: Desecration of the temple. The first outright religious persecution of the Jews, which is also reflected in the book of Daniel (compare 2 Macc. 6.1-11). **41-42:** *His whole kingdom*, Syria, Palestine, Mesopotamia, Persia, and parts of Asia Minor. *One people*, unified in language, religion, culture, and even dress; Judaism, with its revealed law and rejection of other gods, opposed this. **47:** Jews had no *idols* and regarded *swine* as *unclean*. **54:** *Chislev*, approximately December. The *desolating sacrilege* (Dan.11.31; 12.11; 2 Macc.6.2) was an altar to

in the cities. [59]And on the twenty-fifth day of the month they offered sacrifice on the altar which was upon the altar of burnt offering. [60]According to the decree, they put to death the women who had their children circumcised, [61]and their families and those who circumcised them; and they hung the infants from their mothers' necks.

62 But many in Israel stood firm and were resolved in their hearts not to eat unclean food. [63]They chose to die rather than to be defiled by food or to profane the holy covenant; and they did die. [64]And very great wrath came upon Israel.

2 In those days Mattathias the son of John, son of Simeon, a priest of the sons of Joarib, moved from Jerusalem and settled in Modein. [2]He had five sons, John surnamed Gaddi, [3]Simon called Thassi, [4]Judas called Maccabeus, [5]Eleazar called Avaran, and Jonathan called Apphus. [6]He saw the blasphemies being committed in Judah and Jerusalem, [7]and said,

"Alas! Why was I born to see
    this,
the ruin of my people, the ruin
    of the holy city,
and to dwell there when it was
    given over to the enemy,
the sanctuary given over to
    aliens?
[8]Her temple has become like a man
    without honor;[e]
[9] her glorious vessels have been
    carried into captivity.
Her babes have been killed in her
    streets,

her youths by the sword of the
    foe.
[10]What nation has not inherited her
    palaces[f]
and has not seized her spoils?
[11]All her adornment has been taken
    away;
no longer free, she has become
    a slave.
[12]And behold, our holy place, our
    beauty,
and our glory have been laid
    waste;
the Gentiles have profaned it.
[13] Why should we live any longer?"

14 And Mattathias and his sons rent their clothes, put on sackcloth, and mourned greatly.

15 Then the king's officers who were enforcing the apostasy came to the city of Modein to make them offer sacrifice. [16]Many from Israel came to them; and Mattathias and his sons were assembled. [17]Then the king's officers spoke to Mattathias as follows: "You are a leader, honored and great in this city, and supported by sons and brothers. [18]Now be the first to come and do what the king commands, as all the Gentiles and the men of Judah and those that are left in Jerusalem have done. Then you and your sons will be numbered among the friends of the king, and you and your sons will be honored with silver and gold and many gifts."

19 But Mattathias answered and said in a loud voice: "Even if all the nations that live under the rule of the

---

e The text of this verse is uncertain
f Other authorities read *has not had a part in her kingdom*

Olympian Zeus and perhaps a statue of him. **59:** *Offered sacrifice*, probably of swine (2 Macc. 6.4–5). **60–64:** 2 Macc. chs. 6–7, and 4 Macc. contain stories of martyrdoms. *Chose to die rather than to be defiled by food*, compare Dan.3.8–18. *Wrath came upon Israel*, as a punishment for sin (2 Macc.6.12–16).

  2.1–48: Revolt of Mattathias. 1: The family of *Mattathias* is known as Hasmoneans (see p. 295), from a traditional ancestor Hashmonia. *Joarib* was first in the list of divisions of priests (1 Chr.24.7; Neh.11.10). *Modein*, on the road to Beth-horon, about seventeen miles northwest of Jerusalem. **2–5:** *Simon*, third of the family to rule (chs. 13–16). *Maccabeus*, probably from a Hebrew word meaning "hammer." The other surnames are of uncertain derivation. *Jonathan*, successor of Judas (chs. 9–12). **7–13:** Poetic fragment; compare Pss.44; 74; 79; and the book of Lamentations. **14:** *Rent their clothes*, *put on sackcloth*, signs of mourning (Gen.37.34). **18:** *The friends of the king* were a special class of potentates and courtiers who wore distinctive dress

king obey him, and have chosen to do his commandments, departing each one from the religion of his fathers, [20]yet I and my sons and my brothers will live by the covenant of our fathers. [21]Far be it from us to desert the law and the ordinances. [22]We will not obey the king's words by turning aside from our religion to the right hand or to the left."

23 When he had finished speaking these words, a Jew came forward in the sight of all to offer sacrifice upon the altar in Modein, according to the king's command. [24]When Mattathias saw it, he burned with zeal and his heart was stirred. He gave vent to righteous anger; he ran and killed him upon the altar. [25]At the same time he killed the king's officer who was forcing them to sacrifice, and he tore down the altar. [26]Thus he burned with zeal for the law, as Phinehas did against Zimri the son of Salu.

27 Then Mattathias cried out in the city with a loud voice, saying: "Let every one who is zealous for the law and supports the covenant come out with me!" [28]And he and his sons fled to the hills and left all that they had in the city.

29 Then many who were seeking righteousness and justice went down to the wilderness to dwell there, [30]they, their sons, their wives, and their cattle, because evils pressed heavily upon them. [31]And it was reported to the king's officers, and to the troops in Jerusalem the city of David, that men who had rejected the king's command had gone down to the hiding places in the wilderness. [32]Many pursued them, and overtook them; they encamped opposite them and prepared for battle against them on the sabbath day.

[33]And they said to them, "Enough of this! Come out and do what the king commands, and you will live." [34]But they said, "We will not come out, nor will we do what the king commands and so profane the sabbath day." [35]Then the enemy[g] hastened to attack them. [36]But they did not answer them or hurl a stone at them or block up their hiding places, [37]for they said, "Let us all die in our innocence; heaven and earth testify for us that you are killing us unjustly." [38]So they attacked them on the sabbath, and they died, with their wives and children and cattle, to the number of a thousand persons.

39 When Mattathias and his friends learned of it, they mourned for them deeply. [40]And each said to his neighbor: "If we all do as our brethren have done and refuse to fight with the Gentiles for our lives and our ordinances, they will quickly destroy us from the earth." [41]So they made this decision that day: "Let us fight against every man who comes to attack us on the sabbath day; let us not all die as our brethren died in their hiding places."

42 Then there united with them a company of Hasideans, mighty warriors of Israel, every one who offered himself willingly for the law. [43]And all who became fugitives to escape their troubles joined them and reinforced them. [44]They organized an army, and struck down sinners in their anger and lawless men in their wrath; the survivors fled to the Gentiles for safety. [45]And Mattathias and his friends went about and tore down the altars; [46]they forcibly circumcised all the uncircumcised boys that they found within the borders of Israel. [47]They hunted down

g Gk *they*

---

and insignia. **23:** Elsewhere in chs. 1–13, "man of Israel" is used instead of the term *Jew*, which here perhaps means "Judean." **24:** *His heart*, literally "his kidneys," which were considered the seat of deliberation. **26:** *As Phinehas did*, Num.25.6–15. **28:** 2 Macc.5.27. **29–30:** In *the wilderness* of Judea they found *hiding places* in grottoes and caves (Jg.20.47). **37:** 1.63. **41:** The earliest statement of the principle that one may profane one sabbath in order to keep all the others. **42:** *Hasideans*, "the pious," a group not concerned for Jewish nationalism but only for the religious law. At first they resisted passively (1.62–63; 2.37), but now turned to violent action.

the arrogant men, and the work prospered in their hands. [48]They rescued the law out of the hands of the Gentiles and kings, and they never let the sinner gain the upper hand.

[49] Now the days drew near for Mattathias to die, and he said to his sons: "Arrogance and reproach have now become strong; it is a time of ruin and furious anger. [50]Now, my children, show zeal for the law, and give your lives for the covenant of our fathers.

[51] "Remember the deeds of the fathers, which they did in their generations; and receive great honor and an everlasting name. [52]Was not Abraham found faithful when tested, and it was reckoned to him as righteousness? [53]Joseph in the time of his distress kept the commandment, and became lord of Egypt. [54]Phinehas our father, because he was deeply zealous, received the covenant of everlasting priesthood. [55]Joshua, because he fulfilled the command, became a judge in Israel. [56]Caleb, because he testified in the assembly, received an inheritance in the land. [57]David, because he was merciful, inherited the throne of the kingdom for ever. [58]Elijah because of great zeal for the law was taken up into heaven. [59]Hananiah, Azariah, and Mishael believed and were saved from the flame. [60]Daniel because of his innocence was delivered from the mouth of the lions.

[61] "And so observe, from generation to generation, that none who put their trust in him will lack strength. [62]Do not fear the words of a sinner, for his splendor will turn into dung and worms. [63]Today he will be exalted, but tomorrow he will not be found, because he has returned to the dust, and his plans will perish. [64]My children, be courageous and grow strong in the law, for by it you will gain honor.

[65] "Now behold, I know that Simeon your brother is wise in counsel; always listen to him; he shall be your father. [66]Judas Maccabeus has been a mighty warrior from his youth; he shall command the army for you and fight the battle against the peoples.[h] [67]You shall rally about you all who observe the law, and avenge the wrong done to your people. [68]Pay back the Gentiles in full, and heed what the law commands."

[69] Then he blessed them, and was gathered to his fathers. [70]He died in the one hundred and forty-sixth year[i] and was buried in the tomb of his fathers at Modein. And all Israel mourned for him with great lamentation.

3 Then Judas his son, who was called Maccabeus, took command in his place. [2]All his brothers and all who had joined his father helped him; they gladly fought for Israel.
[3]He extended the glory of his people.
Like a giant he put on his
    breastplate;
he girded on his armor of war and
    waged battles,
    protecting the host by his sword.
[4]He was like a lion in his deeds,
    like a lion's cub roaring for
    prey.
[5]He searched out and pursued the
    lawless;
he burned those who troubled
    his people.
[6]Lawless men shrank back for fear
    of him;
all the evildoers were
    confounded;

h Or *of the people*
i 166 B.C.

2.49–70: **Death of Mattathias.** 52: *Faithful when tested,* Gen.22.15–18. *Reckoned to him,* Gen.15.6; Rom.4.3. 53: *Joseph,* Gen. chs. 39–45. 54: *Phinehas,* v. 26. 55–56: *Joshua . . . Caleb,* Num.13.1–14.12; 26.65; Jos.1.1–9. 57: *Merciful,* or perhaps "loyal" (2 Sam.7.16; Pss.89.35–37; 132.11–12). 58: 2 Kg.2.9–12. 59–60: Dan.3.8–30; 6.1–24. 63: Ps.37.10, 35–36. 69: *Gathered to his fathers,* buried with his ancestors (Jg.2.10).
3.1–12: **Defeat of Apollonius.** 3–9: From a contemporary poem. 4: *Like a lion,* Hos.5.14.

and deliverance prospered by his hand.

⁷He embittered many kings,
but he made Jacob glad by his deeds,
and his memory is blessed for ever.

⁸He went through the cities of Judah;
he destroyed the ungodly out of the land;^{*j*}
thus he turned away wrath from Israel.

⁹He was renowned to the ends of the earth;
he gathered in those who were perishing.

10 But Apollonius gathered together Gentiles and a large force from Samaria to fight against Israel. ¹¹When Judas learned of it, he went out to meet him, and he defeated and killed him. Many were wounded and fell, and the rest fled. ¹²Then they seized their spoils; and Judas took the sword of Apollonius, and used it in battle the rest of his life.

13 Now when Seron, the commander of the Syrian army, heard that Judas had gathered a large company, including a body of faithful men who stayed with him and went out to battle, ¹⁴he said, "I will make a name for myself and win honor in the kingdom. I will make war on Judas and his companions, who scorn the king's command." ¹⁵And again a strong army of ungodly men went up with him to help him, to take vengeance on the sons of Israel.

16 When he approached the ascent of Beth-horon, Judas went out to meet him with a small company. ¹⁷But when they saw the army coming to meet them, they said to Judas, "How can we, few as we are, fight against so great and strong a multitude? And we are faint, for we have eaten nothing today." ¹⁸Judas replied, "It is easy for many to be hemmed in by few, for in the sight of Heaven there is no difference between saving by many or by few. ¹⁹It is not on the size of the army that victory in battle depends, but strength comes from Heaven. ²⁰They come against us in great pride and lawlessness to destroy us and our wives and our children, and to despoil us; ²¹but we fight for our lives and our laws. ²²He himself will crush them before us; as for you, do not be afraid of them."

23 When he finished speaking, he rushed suddenly against Seron and his army, and they were crushed before him. ²⁴They pursued them^{*k*} down the descent of Beth-horon to the plain; eight hundred of them fell, and the rest fled into the land of the Philistines. ²⁵Then Judas and his brothers began to be feared, and terror fell upon the Gentiles round about them. ²⁶His fame reached the king, and the Gentiles talked of the battles of Judas.

27 When King Antiochus heard these reports, he was greatly angered; and he sent and gathered all the forces of his kingdom, a very strong army. ²⁸And he opened his coffers and gave a year's pay to his forces, and ordered them to be ready for any need. ²⁹Then he saw that the money in the treasury was exhausted, and that the revenues from the country were small because of the dissension and disaster which he had caused in the land by abolishing the laws that had existed from the earli-

j Gk *it*
k Other authorities read *him*

8: *He turned away wrath,* i.e. God's punishment, through his exploits (2 Macc.7.38). **10:** *Apollonius,* according to Josephus (*Antiquities*. XII. v. 5; vii.1), was governor of Samaria.

3.13–26: Battle of Beth-horon. This was Judas' first great victory. **16:** *The ascent of Beth-horon* was a route from the coastal plain to the Judean highlands. The town is about twelve miles northwest of Jerusalem. **18:** The word *Heaven* was used to avoid pronouncing God's name (compare "he himself," v. 22, and see Sus.9 n.). *By many or by few,* 1 Sam.14.6. **24:** *Land of the Philistines,* the coastal plain.

3.27–4.35: Campaigns of Lysias. Antiochus IV goes to Persia; Judas defeats Lysias at Emmaus and Beth-zur. **28:** *Any need* implies that Seleucid power was beginning to decline.

est days. [30]He feared that he might not have such funds as he had before for his expenses and for the gifts which he used to give more lavishly than preceding kings. [31]He was greatly perplexed in mind, and determined to go to Persia and collect the revenues from those regions and raise a large fund.

32 He left Lysias, a distinguished man of royal lineage, in charge of the king's affairs from the river Euphrates to the borders of Egypt. [33]Lysias was also to take care of Antiochus his son until he returned. [34]And he turned over to Lysias[*l*] half of his troops and the elephants, and gave him orders about all that he wanted done. As for the residents of Judea and Jerusalem, [35]Lysias was to send a force against them to wipe out and destroy the strength of Israel and the remnant of Jerusalem; he was to banish the memory of them from the place, [36]settle aliens in all their territory, and distribute their land. [37]Then the king took the remaining half of his troops and departed from Antioch his capital in the one hundred and forty-seventh year.[*m*] He crossed the Euphrates river and went through the upper provinces.

38 Lysias chose Ptolemy the son of Dorymenes, and Nicanor and Gorgias, mighty men among the friends of the king, [39]and sent with them forty thousand infantry and seven thousand cavalry to go into the land of Judah and destroy it, as the king had commanded. [40]So they departed with their entire force, and when they arrived they encamped near Emmaus in the plain. [41]When the traders of the region heard what was said of them, they took silver and gold in immense amounts, and fet-

ters,[*n*] and went to the camp to get the sons of Israel for slaves. And forces from Syria and the land of the Philistines joined with them.

42 Now Judas and his brothers saw that misfortunes had increased and that the forces were encamped in their territory. They also learned what the king had commanded to do to the people to cause their final destruction. [43]But they said to one another, "Let us repair the destruction of our people, and fight for our people and the sanctuary." [44]And the congregation assembled to be ready for battle, and to pray and ask for mercy and compassion.

[45]Jerusalem was uninhabited like a
    wilderness;
  not one of her children went in
    or out.
The sanctuary was trampled down,
  and the sons of aliens held the
    citadel;
  it was a lodging place for the
    Gentiles.
Joy was taken from Jacob;
  the flute and the harp ceased to
    play.

46 So they assembled and went to Mizpah, opposite Jerusalem, because Israel formerly had a place of prayer in Mizpah. [47]They fasted that day, put on sackcloth and sprinkled ashes on their heads, and rent their clothes. [48]And they opened the book of the law to inquire into those matters about which the Gentiles were consulting the images of their idols. [49]They also brought the garments of the priesthood and the first fruits and the tithes, and

l Gk *him*   *m* 165 B.C.
n Syr: Gk *slaves*

30: Antiochus was noted for his extravagance (see 2 Macc.4.30 n.). **33:** *Antiochus* V Eupator, *his son*, was only nine years old; he reigned 164–162 B.C. **36:** *Settle aliens*, as the Assyrians had done (2 Kg.17.24). **37:** *Antioch*, modern Antakya, was built by Seleucus I in 300 B.C. and expanded by Antiochus IV. *Upper provinces*, Persia. **38:** *Ptolemy*, known as Macron (2 Macc. 10.12). *Nicanor*, 2 Macc.8.9. *Gorgias*, 2 Macc.10.14. **40:** *Emmaus* (not the Emmaus of Lk.24.13), was about twenty-five miles west of Jerusalem. **41:** Some pro-Syrian Jews joined Antiochus' army. **45:** Compare Ps.74; Is.24.8. **46:** *Mizpah*, perhaps en-Nebi Samwil, seven miles northwest of Jerusalem, but sometimes identified with Tell en-Nasbeh, nine miles north of the city. **48:** They expected guidance from *the book of the law*, the Pentateuch, while the Greeks sought oracles from *their idols*. **49:** *Tithes* were brought to Jerusalem and there distributed (Neh.10.35–

they stirred up the Nazirites who had completed their days; ⁵⁰and they cried aloud to Heaven, saying,

"What shall we do with these?
　Where shall we take them?
⁵¹Thy sanctuary is trampled down
　and profaned,
　and thy priests mourn in
　humiliation.
⁵²And behold, the Gentiles are
　assembled against us to
　destroy us;
　thou knowest what they plot
　against us.
⁵³How will we be able to withstand
　them,
　if thou dost not help us?"

54 Then they sounded the trumpets and gave a loud shout. ⁵⁵After this Judas appointed leaders of the people, in charge of thousands and hundreds and fifties and tens. ⁵⁶And he said to those who were building houses, or were betrothed, or were planting vineyards, or were fainthearted, that each should return to his home, according to the law. ⁵⁷Then the army marched out and encamped to the south of Emmaus.

58 And Judas said, "Gird yourselves and be valiant. Be ready early in the morning to fight with these Gentiles who have assembled against us to destroy us and our sanctuary. ⁵⁹It is better for us to die in battle than to see the misfortunes of our nation and of the sanctuary. ⁶⁰But as his will in heaven may be, so he will do."

4 Now Gorgias took five thousand infantry and a thousand picked cavalry, and this division moved out by night ²to fall upon the camp of the Jews and attack them suddenly. Men from the citadel were his guides. ³But Judas heard of it, and he and his mighty men moved out to attack the king's force in Emmaus ⁴while the

division was still absent from the camp. ⁵When Gorgias entered the camp of Judas by night, he found no one there, so he looked for them in the hills, because he said, "These men are fleeing from us."

6 At daybreak Judas appeared in the plain with three thousand men, but they did not have armor and swords such as they desired. ⁷And they saw the camp of the Gentiles, strong and fortified, with cavalry round about it; and these men were trained in war. ⁸But Judas said to the men who were with him, "Do not fear their numbers or be afraid when they charge. ⁹Remember how our fathers were saved at the Red Sea, when Pharaoh with his forces pursued them. ¹⁰And now let us cry to Heaven, to see whether he will favor us and remember his covenant with our fathers and crush this army before us today. ¹¹Then all the Gentiles will know that there is one who redeems and saves Israel."

12 When the foreigners looked up and saw them coming against them, ¹³they went forth from their camp to battle. Then the men with Judas blew their trumpets ¹⁴and engaged in battle. The Gentiles were crushed and fled into the plain, ¹⁵and all those in the rear fell by the sword. They pursued them to Gazara, and to the plains of Idumea, and to Azotus and Jamnia; and three thousand of them fell. ¹⁶Then Judas and his force turned back from pursuing them, ¹⁷and he said to the people, "Do not be greedy for plunder, for there is a battle before us; ¹⁸Gorgias and his force are near us in the hills. But stand now against our enemies and fight them, and afterward seize the plunder boldly."

19 Just as Judas was finishing this speech, a detachment appeared, com-

---

38). *Nazirites*, Num.6.1–21. **50–53**: V. 45. **54**: *Trumpets*, to summon the army (Num.10.1–10). **55**: In Moses' day such *leaders* assisted in civic administration (Ex.18.25); here, as in the Essene *War Scroll* from Qumran, they have a military function (2 Macc.8.22–23). **56**: Dt.20.5–8. **4.2**: *Men from the citadel*, Jewish refugees opposed to Judas. **9**: Ex.14.21–29. **15**: The pursuit went in all directions. *Gazara*, or Gezer (Jos.21.21; 1 Kg.9.17), was five miles northwest of Emmaus. *Idumea* was far to the south. *Azotus*, or Ashdod, and *Jamnia*, lay west and southwest. **17–18**: Judas maintained discipline (2 Macc.8.26). **19**: *The hills*, the Judean highland.

ing out of the hills. [20]They saw that their army[o] had been put to flight, and that the Jews[o] were burning the camp, for the smoke that was seen showed what had happened. [21]When they perceived this they were greatly frightened, and when they also saw the army of Judas drawn up in the plain for battle, [22]they all fled into the land of the Philistines. [23]Then Judas returned to plunder the camp, and they seized much gold and silver, and cloth dyed blue and sea purple, and great riches. [24]On their return they sang hymns and praises to Heaven, for he is good, for his mercy endures for ever. [25]Thus Israel had a great deliverance that day.

26 Those of the foreigners who escaped went and reported to Lysias all that had happened. [27]When he heard it, he was perplexed and discouraged, for things had not happened to Israel as he had intended, nor had they turned out as the king had commanded him. [28]But the next year he mustered sixty thousand picked infantrymen and five thousand cavalry to subdue them. [29]They came into Idumea and encamped at Beth-zur, and Judas met them with ten thousand men.

30 When he saw that the army was strong, he prayed, saying, "Blessed art thou, O Savior of Israel, who didst crush the attack of the mighty warrior by the hand of thy servant David, and didst give the camp of the Philistines into the hands of Jonathan, the son of Saul, and of the man who carried his armor. [31]So do thou hem in this army by the hand of thy people Israel, and let them be ashamed of their troops and their cavalry. [32]Fill them with cowardice; melt the boldness of their strength; let them tremble in their destruction. [33]Strike them down with the sword of those who love thee, and let all who know thy name praise thee with hymns."

34 Then both sides attacked, and there fell of the army of Lysias five thousand men; they fell in action.[p] [35]And when Lysias saw the rout of his troops and observed the boldness which inspired those of Judas, and how ready they were either to live or to die nobly, he departed to Antioch and enlisted mercenaries, to invade Judea again with an even larger army.

36 Then said Judas and his brothers, "Behold, our enemies are crushed; let us go up to cleanse the sanctuary and dedicate it." [37]So all the army assembled and they went up to Mount Zion. [38]And they saw the sanctuary desolate, the altar profaned, and the gates burned. In the courts they saw bushes sprung up as in a thicket, or as on one of the mountains. They saw also the chambers of the priests in ruins. [39]Then they rent their clothes, and mourned with great lamentation, and sprinkled themselves with ashes. [40]They fell face down on the ground, and sounded the signal on the trumpets, and cried out to Heaven. [41]Then Judas detailed men to fight against those in the citadel until he had cleansed the sanctuary.

42 He chose blameless priests devoted to the law, [43]and they cleansed the sanctuary and removed the defiled stones to an unclean place. [44]They deliberated what to do about the altar of burnt offering, which had been profaned. [45]And they thought it best to tear it down, lest it bring reproach upon them, for the Gentiles had defiled it.

o Gk *they*
p Or *and some fell on the opposite side*

24: *Heaven*, see 3.18 n. **26–35:** The account in 2 Macc.11.1–12 puts the rout of Lysias after the death of Timothy. **28:** *The next year*, perhaps as late as autumn, 164 B.C. **29:** *Beth-zur*, about twenty miles south of Jerusalem on the road to Hebron. Lysias decided to attack Jerusalem from the south. **30–35:** The account in 2 Macc.11.6–15 agrees that Judas won the battle, but states that there was a negotiated peace.

4.36–61: Rededication of the temple. 38: *Chambers of the priests* perhaps surrounded the sanctuary on three sides. **41:** *The citadel* (1.33–35) was occupied by a Syrian garrison until the

So they tore down the altar, [46]and stored the stones in a convenient place on the temple hill until there should come a prophet to tell what to do with them. [47]Then they took unhewn[q] stones, as the law directs, and built a new altar like the former one. [48]They also rebuilt the sanctuary and the interior of the temple, and consecrated the courts. [49]They made new holy vessels, and brought the lampstand, the altar of incense, and the table into the temple. [50]Then they burned incense on the altar and lighted the lamps on the lampstand, and these gave light in the temple. [51]They placed the bread on the table and hung up the curtains. Thus they finished all the work they had undertaken.

52 Early in the morning on the twenty-fifth day of the ninth month, which is the month of Chislev, in the one hundred and forty-eighth year,[r] [53]they rose and offered sacrifice, as the law directs, on the new altar of burnt offering which they had built. [54]At the very season and on the very day that the Gentiles had profaned it, it was dedicated with songs and harps and lutes and cymbals. [55]All the people fell on their faces and worshiped and blessed Heaven, who had prospered them. [56]So they celebrated the dedication of the altar for eight days, and offered burnt offerings with gladness; they offered a sacrifice of deliverance and praise. [57]They decorated the front of the temple with golden crowns and small shields; they restored the gates and the chambers for the priests, and furnished them with doors. [58]There

was very great gladness among the people, and the reproach of the Gentiles was removed.

59 Then Judas and his brothers and all the assembly of Israel determined that every year at that season the days of the dedication of the altar should be observed with gladness and joy for eight days, beginning with the twenty-fifth day of the month of Chislev.

60 At that time they fortified Mount Zion with high walls and strong towers round about, to keep the Gentiles from coming and trampling them down as they had done before. [61]And he stationed a garrison there to hold it. He also[s] fortified Beth-zur, so that the people might have a stronghold that faced Idumea.

5 When the Gentiles round about heard that the altar had been built and the sanctuary dedicated as it was before, they became very angry, [2]and they determined to destroy the descendants of Jacob who lived among them. So they began to kill and destroy among the people. [3]But Judas made war on the sons of Esau in Idumea, at Akrabattene, because they kept lying in wait for Israel. He dealt them a heavy blow and humbled them and despoiled them. [4]He also remembered the wickedness of the sons of Baean, who were a trap and a snare to the people and ambushed them on the highways. [5]They were shut up by him in their towers; and he encamped against them, vowed their complete

q Gk *whole*
r 164 B.C.
s Gk adds *to hold it*

time of Simon (13.49–52). **46:** Malachi was regarded as the last *prophet;* though such men as John Hyrcanus I and John the Baptist were thought to have prophetic gifts, this was not universally recognized. **47:** Ex.20.25; Dt.27.5–6. **50:** *Burned incense . . . lighted the lamps,* Ex.30:7–8. **51:** *The bread,* of the Presence (Ex.25.30). **52–59:** Judas set the rededication of the temple exactly three years after its pollution (1.54) and three and a half years after Antiochus' capture of Jerusalem (Dan.7.25; but see 2 Macc.10.3). The Hanukkah festival, celebrated *for eight days* like Hezekiah's reconsecration (2 Chr.29.17), commemorates this event.

5.1–68: Campaigns in all directions. Judas now attacked Idumea in the south (vv. 3–5, 65), Ammon and Gilead east of the Jordan (vv. 6–13, 24–51), Galilee in the north (vv. 21–23), and the coastal plain. These events may have occurred after the death of Antiochus IV (6.16). **2:** *Descendants of Jacob,* Israelites or Jews. **3:** *Sons of Esau,* Edomites or Idumeans, south of the Dead Sea. *Akrabattene,* perhaps on the border between Idumea and Judea. **4:** *Baean,*

destruction, and burned with fire their[t] towers and all who were in them. [6]Then he crossed over to attack the Ammonites, where he found a strong band and many people with Timothy as their leader. [7]He engaged in many battles with them and they were crushed before him; he struck them down. [8]He also took Jazer and its villages; then he returned to Judea.

9 Now the Gentiles in Gilead gathered together against the Israelites who lived in their territory, and planned to destroy them. But they fled to the stronghold of Dathema, [10]and sent to Judas and his brothers a letter which said, "The Gentiles around us have gathered together against us to destroy us. [11]They are preparing to come and capture the stronghold to which we have fled, and Timothy is leading their forces. [12]Now then come and rescue us from their hands, for many of us have fallen, [13]and all our brethren who were in the land of Tob have been killed; the enemy[u] have captured their wives and children and goods, and have destroyed about a thousand men there."

14 While the letter was still being read, behold, other messengers, with their garments rent, came from Galilee and made a similar report; [15]they said that against them had gathered together men of Ptolemais and Tyre and Sidon, and all Galilee of the Gentiles,[v] "to annihilate us." [16]When Judas and the people heard these messages, a great assembly was called to determine what they should do for their brethren who were in distress and were being attacked by enemies.[w] [17]Then Judas

said to Simon his brother, "Choose your men and go and rescue your brethren in Galilee; I and Jonathan my brother will go to Gilead." [18]But he left Joseph, the son of Zechariah, and Azariah, a leader of the people, with the rest of the forces, in Judea to guard it; [19]and he gave them this command, "Take charge of this people, but do not engage in battle with the Gentiles until we return." [20]Then three thousand men were assigned to Simon to go to Galilee, and eight thousand to Judas for Gilead.

21 So Simon went to Galilee and fought many battles against the Gentiles, and the Gentiles were crushed before him. [22]He pursued them to the gate of Ptolemais, and as many as three thousand of the Gentiles fell, and he despoiled them. [23]Then he took the Jews[x] of Galilee and Arbatta, with their wives and children, and all they possessed, and led them to Judea with great rejoicing.

24 Judas Maccabeus and Jonathan his brother crossed the Jordan and went three days' journey into the wilderness. [25]They encountered the Nabateans, who met them peaceably and told them all that had happened to their brethren in Gilead: [26]"Many of them have been shut up in Bozrah and Bosor, in Alema and Chaspho, Maked and Carnaim"—all these cities were strong and large—[27]"and some have been shut up in the other cities of Gilead; the enemy[y] are getting ready

t Gk *her*
u Gk *they*
v Gk *aliens*
w Gk *them*
x Gk *those*
y Gk *they*

---

probably in Transjordan (Num.32.3). **6:** *Ammonites*, a Semitic people east of the Jordan near the present Amman. **8:** *Jazer*, west of Amman, fifteen miles north of Heshbon (Num.32.3). **9:** *Gilead*, east of the Jordan between the Yarmuk and the Arnon (Jos.22.9). *Dathema*, possibly el-Hosn, in Gilead opposite Beisan; or Ramtha, now near the Syrian border. **13:** *Land of Tob*, possibly Hippos, twelve miles southeast of the Sea of Galilee (Jg.11.3; 2 Macc.12.17). **15:** *Ptolemais*, or Acco (Jg.1.31), now Acre, north of Haifa on the coast. *Tyre and Sidon*, farther north in Lebanon. As yet few Jews lived in *Galilee of the Gentiles* (Is.9.1; Mt.4.15). **23:** *Arbatta*, either near the Sea of Galilee, or the Arabah depression south of the Dead Sea (Dt.1.7; Jos. 11.16). **25:** *Nabateans*, or Nebaioth (Gen.25.13), an Aramaic-speaking people who occupied the desert east of Palestine as far north as Palmyra. **26:** *Bozrah*, southeast of Dera'a (Is.63.1; Jer.48.24). *Bosor*, Bezer in the desert (Dt.4.43). *Alema*, unidentified. *Chaspho* and *Maked*, cities

to attack the strongholds tomorrow and take and destroy all these men in one day."

28 Then Judas and his army quickly turned back by the wilderness road to Bozrah; and he took the city, and killed every male by the edge of the sword; then he seized all its spoils and burned it with fire. ²⁹He departed from there at night, and they went all the way to the stronghold of Dathema.ᶻ ³⁰At dawn they looked up, and behold, a large company, that could not be counted, carrying ladders and engines of war to capture the stronghold, and attacking the Jews within.ᵃ ³¹So Judas saw that the battle had begun and that the cry of the city went up to Heaven with trumpets and loud shouts, ³²and he said to the men of his forces, "Fight today for your brethren!" ³³Then he came up behind them in three companies, who sounded their trumpets and cried aloud in prayer. ³⁴And when the army of Timothy realized that it was Maccabeus, they fled before him, and he dealt them a heavy blow. As many as eight thousand of them fell that day.

35 Next he turned aside to Alema,ᵇ and fought against it and took it; and he killed every male in it, plundered it, and burned it with fire. ³⁶From there he marched on and took Chaspho, Maked, and Bosor, and the other cities of Gilead.

37 After these things Timothy gathered another army and encamped opposite Raphon, on the other side of the stream. ³⁸Judas sent men to spy out the camp, and they reported to him, "All the Gentiles around us have gathered to him; it is a very large force. ³⁹They also have hired Arabs to help them, and they are encamped across the stream, ready to come and fight

against you." And Judas went to meet them.

40 Now as Judas and his army drew near to the stream of water, Timothy said to the officers of his forces, "If he crosses over to us first, we will not be able to resist him, for he will surely defeat us. ⁴¹But if he shows fear and camps on the other side of the river, we will cross over to him and defeat him." ⁴²When Judas approached the stream of water, he stationed the scribes of the people at the stream and gave them this command, "Permit no man to encamp, but make them all enter the battle." ⁴³Then he crossed over against them first, and the whole army followed him. All the Gentiles were defeated before him, and they threw away their arms and fled into the sacred precincts at Carnaim. ⁴⁴But he took the city and burned the sacred precincts with fire, together with all who were in them. Thus Carnaim was conquered; they could stand before Judas no longer.

45 Then Judas gathered together all the Israelites in Gilead, the small and the great, with their wives and children and goods, a very large company, to go to the land of Judah. ⁴⁶So they came to Ephron. This was a large and very strong city on the road, and they could not go round it to the right or to the left; they had to go through it. ⁴⁷But the men of the city shut them out and blocked up the gates with stones. ⁴⁸And Judas sent them this friendly message, "Let us pass through your land to get to our land. No one will do you harm; we will simply pass by on foot." But they refused to open to him. ⁴⁹Then Judas ordered proclamation to be made to the army that each should

z Greek lacks *of Dathema*. See verse 9
a Gk *and they were attacking them*
b The name is uncertain

---

of Gilead (v. 36). *Carnaim*, Gen.14.5; Am.6.13; 2 Macc.12.21,26. **28:** *Killed every male*, Gen. 34.25. **37:** *The stream*, a tributary of the Yarmuk. **39:** *Arabs* were not usually hostile to the Jews but could be *hired* as mercenaries. **40–41:** Judas heard Timothy's order or decided to make a surprise attack (compare 1 Sam.14.7–10). **43:** *Sacred precincts*, of Atargatis, the Syrian fish goddess (2 Macc.12.26). **46:** *Ephron*, eight miles east of the Jordan, opposite Beth-shan (v. 52), and west of Irbid (Arbela). **48–51:** Num.21.21–24.

encamp where he was. ⁵⁰So the men
of the forces encamped, and he fought
against the city all that day and all the
night, and the city was delivered into
his hands. ⁵¹He destroyed every male
by the edge of the sword, and razed
and plundered the city. Then he passed
through the city over the slain.

52 And they crossed the Jordan into
the large plain before Beth-shan. ⁵³And
Judas kept rallying the laggards and
encouraging the people all the way till
he came to the land of Judah. ⁵⁴So
they went up to Mount Zion with gladness and joy, and offered burnt offerings, because not one of them had
fallen before they returned in safety.

55 Now while Judas and Jonathan
were in Gilead and Simon his brother
was in Galilee before Ptolemais,
⁵⁶Joseph, the son of Zechariah, and
Azariah, the commanders of the forces,
heard of their brave deeds and of the
heroic war they had fought. ⁵⁷So they
said, "Let us also make a name for
ourselves; let us go and make war on
the Gentiles around us." ⁵⁸And they
issued orders to the men of the forces
that were with them, and they marched
against Jamnia. ⁵⁹And Gorgias and his
men came out of the city to meet them
in battle. ⁶⁰Then Joseph and Azariah
were routed, and were pursued to the
borders of Judea; as many as two
thousand of the people of Israel fell
that day. ⁶¹Thus the people suffered a
great rout because, thinking to do a
brave deed, they did not listen to Judas
and his brothers. ⁶²But they did not
belong to the family of those men
through whom deliverance was given
to Israel.

63 The man Judas and his brothers

were greatly honored in all Israel and
among all the Gentiles, wherever their
name was heard. ⁶⁴Men gathered to
them and praised them.

65 Then Judas and his brothers
went forth and fought the sons of
Esau in the land to the south. He
struck Hebron and its villages and tore
down its strongholds and burned its
towers round about. Then he marched
off to go into the land of the Philistines,
and passed through Marisa.ᶜ ⁶⁷On that
day some priests, who wished to do a
brave deed, fell in battle, for they went
out to battle unwisely. ⁶⁸But Judas
turned aside to Azotus in the land of
the Philistines; he tore down their
altars, and the graven images of their
gods he burned with fire; he plundered
the cities and returned to the land of
Judah.

6 King Antiochus was going through
the upper provinces when he heard
that Elymais in Persia was a city famed
for its wealth in silver and gold. ²Its
temple was very rich, containing golden
shields, breastplates, and weapons left
there by Alexander, the son of Philip,
the Macedonian king who first reigned
over the Greeks. ³So he came and tried
to take the city and plunder it, but he
could not, because his plan became
known to the men of the city ⁴and they
withstood him in battle. So he fled and
in great grief departed from there to
return to Babylon.

5 Then some one came to him in
Persia and reported that the armies
which had gone into the land of Judah
had been routed; ⁶that Lysias had gone
first with a strong force, but had turned

c Other authorities read *Samaria*

52: *The large plain,* between the Jordan and Mt. Gilboa. *Beth-shan,* Beisan, about eighteen
miles south of the Sea of Galilee (Jg.1.27; 1 Kg.4.12). **58:** *Jamnia,* 4.15. **62:** Only *the family*
of the Hasmoneans is regarded as divinely chosen to save Israel. **65:** *Sons of Esau,* Edomites.
Hebron, the old capital of David, twenty miles south of Jerusalem (Gen.23.2; 2 Sam.2.11).
66: *Marisa,* or Mareshah (Jos.15.44), near Beit-Jibrin.

6.1–17: Death of Antiochus IV and accession of Antiochus V (2 Macc. ch. 9). **1:** *The upper
provinces,* Persia and Mesopotamia (3.31–37). *Elymais,* biblical Elam or Susiana; but according
to 2 Macc. 9.2 the incident occurred in Persepolis. **2:** *Its temple* was that of Nanea (2 Macc.
1.13–16), or Anahita, identified with Artemis. **5:** *In Persia,* perhaps at Ecbatana (2 Macc.9.3).
According to Polybius (*History,* XXXI. 11) the king took sick and died at Tabae (perhaps Gabae,

and fled before the Jews;*d* that the Jews*e* had grown strong from the arms, supplies, and abundant spoils which they had taken from the armies they had cut down; [7]that they had torn down the abomination which he had erected upon the altar in Jerusalem; and that they had surrounded the sanctuary with high walls as before, and also Beth-zur, his city.

8 When the king heard this news, he was astounded and badly shaken. He took to his bed and became sick from grief, because things had not turned out for him as he had planned. [9]He lay there for many days, because deep grief continually gripped him, and he concluded that he was dying. [10]So he called all his friends and said to them, "Sleep departs from my eyes and I am downhearted with worry. [11]I said to myself, 'To what distress I have come! And into what a great flood I now am plunged! For I was kind and beloved in my power.' [12]But now I remember the evils I did in Jerusalem. I seized all her vessels of silver and gold; and I sent to destroy the inhabitants of Judah without good reason. [13]I know that it is because of this that these evils have come upon me; and behold, I am perishing of deep grief in a strange land."

14 Then he called for Philip, one of his friends, and made him ruler over all his kingdom. [15]He gave him the crown and his robe and the signet, that he might guide Antiochus his son and bring him up to be king. [16]Thus Antiochus the king died there in the one hundred and forty-ninth year.*f* [17]And when Lysias learned that the king was dead, he set up Antiochus the king's*g* son to reign. Lysias*h* had

brought him up as a boy, and he named him Eupator.

18 Now the men in the citadel kept hemming Israel in around the sanctuary. They were trying in every way to harm them and strengthen the Gentiles. [19]So Judas decided to destroy them, and assembled all the people to besiege them. [20]They gathered together and besieged the citadel*i* in the one hundred and fiftieth year;*j* and he built siege towers and other engines of war. [21]But some of the garrison escaped from the siege and some of the ungodly Israelites joined them. [22]They went to the king and said, "How long will you fail to do justice and to avenge our brethren? [23]We were happy to serve your father, to live by what he said and to follow his commands. [24]For this reason the sons of our people besieged the citadel*k* and became hostile to us; moreover, they have put to death as many of us as they have caught, and they have seized our inheritances. [25]And not against us alone have they stretched out their hands, but also against all the lands on their borders. [26]And behold, today they have encamped against the citadel in Jerusalem to take it; they have fortified both the sanctuary and Beth-zur; [27]and unless you quickly prevent them, they will do still greater things, and you will not be able to stop them."

28 The king was enraged when he heard this. He assembled all his friends, the commanders of his forces and those in authority.*l* [29]And mercenary forces came to him from other

d Gk *them*   *e* Gk *they*
f 163 B.C.   *g* Gk *his*
h Gk *he*   *i* Gk *it*   *j* 162 B.C.
k The Greek text underlying *the sons . . . the citadel* is uncertain
l Gk *those over the reins*

---

modern Isfahan). **7:** *The abomination*, statue of a pagan god. **8–9:** *Deep grief*, perhaps insanity; according to 2 Macc.9.5–12 he was stricken with a loathsome physical malady. **12:** *Her vessels*, Dan.5.2. **14–15:** *Philip . . . ruler*, Lysias, satrap in the west, had previously been given this commission (3.32). *The signet*, a symbol of transfer of authority to the regent. **16:** 2 Macc.11.33 implies that Antiochus IV had died before the restoration of the temple at Jerusalem. **17:** The word *Eupator* means "of a good father."

6.18–54: Attack on the citadel and second battle at Beth-zur. The citadel was equally important to the Syrians and to Judas, for without it the Seleucid monarchy could not maintain sovereignty in Palestine. **21:** *Ungodly*, i.e. pro-Greek. **28–30:** Lysias' second campaign is here

kingdoms and from islands of the seas. [30]The number of his forces was a hundred thousand foot soldiers, twenty thousand horsemen, and thirty-two elephants accustomed to war. [31]They came through Idumea and encamped against Beth-zur, and for many days they fought and built engines of war; but the Jews[m] sallied out and burned these with fire, and fought manfully.

32 Then Judas marched away from the citadel and encamped at Beth-zechariah, opposite the camp of the king. [33]Early in the morning the king rose and took his army by a forced march along the road to Beth-zechariah, and his troops made ready for battle and sounded their trumpets. [34]They showed the elephants the juice of grapes and mulberries, to arouse them for battle. [35]And they distributed the beasts among the phalanxes; with each elephant they stationed a thousand men armed with coats of mail, and with brass helmets on their heads; and five hundred picked horsemen were assigned to each beast. [36]These took their position beforehand wherever the beast was; wherever it went they went with it, and they never left it. [37]And upon the elephants[n] were wooden towers, strong and covered; they were fastened upon each beast by special harness, and upon each were four[o] armed men who fought from there, and also its Indian driver. [38]The rest of the horsemen were stationed on either side, on the two flanks of the army, to harass the enemy while being themselves protected by the phalanxes. [39]When the sun shone upon the shields of gold and brass, the hills were ablaze with them and gleamed like flaming torches.

40 Now a part of the king's army was spread out on the high hills, and some troops were on the plain, and they advanced steadily and in good order. [41]All who heard the noise made by their multitude, by the marching of the multitude and the clanking of their arms, trembled, for the army was very large and strong. [42]But Judas and his army advanced to the battle, and six hundred men of the king's army fell. [43]And Eleazar, called Avaran, saw that one of the beasts was equipped with royal armor. It was taller than all the others, and he supposed that the king was upon it. [44]So he gave his life to save his people and to win for himself an everlasting name. [45]He courageously ran into the midst of the phalanx to reach it; he killed men right and left, and they parted before him on both sides. [46]He got under the elephant, stabbed it from beneath, and killed it; but it fell to the ground upon him and there he died. [47]And when the Jews[p] saw the royal might and the fierce attack of the forces, they turned away in flight.

48 The soldiers of the king's army went up to Jerusalem against them, and the king encamped in Judea and at Mount Zion. [49]He made peace with the men of Beth-zur, and they evacuated the city, because they had no provisions there to withstand a siege, since it was a sabbatical year for the land. [50]So the king took Beth-zur and stationed a guard there to hold it. [51]Then he encamped before the sanctuary for many days. He set up siege towers, engines of war to throw fire

m Gk *they*   *n* Gk *them*
o Cn: Some authorities read *thirty;* others *thirty-two*
p Gk *they*

dated 162 B.C. (v. 20), but in 2 Macc.13.1 a year earlier. **31:** Judas had won the first battle at *Beth-zur* (4.29–34) and had fortified it (4.61). **32:** *Beth-zechariah* was six miles from Beth-zur and ten miles southwest of Jerusalem. **34-35:** *The juice* may have been to simulate blood; but *elephants* were sometimes given wine to madden them. Here the animals were used to force an opening in the ranks. *Phalanxes,* the Greek infantry formation, eight to eighteen men deep, highly disciplined and mobile. The Seleucids could muster twenty thousand of such infantry. **43:** *Eleazar,* brother of Judas (2.5). **48:** *Mount Zion,* south of the temple (1.33). **49:** The garrison was promised immunity if it surrendered. Every seventh year the land had to lie fallow (Ex.23.11; Lev.25.3–7). This *sabbatical year* was apparently 162 B.C. (v. 20) or possibly a year earlier.

and stones, machines to shoot arrows, and catapults. [52]The Jews[q] also made engines of war to match theirs, and fought for many days. [53]But they had no food in storage,[r] because it was the seventh year; those who found safety in Judea from the Gentiles had consumed the last of the stores. [54]Few men were left in the sanctuary, because famine had prevailed over the rest and they had been scattered, each to his own place.

55 Then Lysias heard that Philip, whom King Antiochus while still living had appointed to bring up Antiochus his son to be king, [56]had returned from Persia and Media with the forces that had gone with the king, and that he was trying to seize control of the government. [57]So he quickly gave orders to depart, and said to the king, to the commanders of the forces, and to the men, "We daily grow weaker, our food supply is scant, the place against which we are fighting is strong, and the affairs of the kingdom press urgently upon us. [58]Now then let us come to terms with these men, and make peace with them and with all their nation, [59]and agree to let them live by their laws as they did before; for it was on account of their laws which we abolished that they became angry and did all these things."

60 The speech pleased the king and the commanders, and he sent to the Jews[s] an offer of peace, and they accepted it. [61]So the king and the commanders gave them their oath. On

these conditions the Jews[t] evacuated the stronghold. [62]But when the king entered Mount Zion and saw what a strong fortress the place was, he broke the oath he had sworn and gave orders to tear down the wall all around. [63]Then he departed with haste and returned to Antioch. He found Philip in control of the city, but he fought against him, and took the city by force.

7 In the one hundred and fifty-first[u] year Demetrius the son of Seleucus set forth from Rome, sailed with a few men to a city by the sea, and there began to reign. [2]As he was entering the royal palace of his fathers, the army seized Antiochus and Lysias to bring them to him. [3]But when this act became known to him, he said, "Do not let me see their faces!" [4]So the army killed them, and Demetrius took his seat upon the throne of his kingdom.

5 Then there came to him all the lawless and ungodly men of Israel; they were led by Alcimus, who wanted to be high priest. [6]And they brought to the king this accusation against the people: "Judas and his brothers have destroyed all your friends, and have driven us out of our land. [7]Now then send a man whom you trust; let him go and see all the ruin which Judas[v] has brought upon us and upon the land of the king, and let him punish them and all who help them."

q Gk *they*
r Other authorities read *in the sanctuary*
s Gk *them*   t Gk *they*
u 161 B.C.   v Gk *he*

6.55–63: **Lysias makes peace.** The return of Philip caused a diversion; Lysias abandoned the siege and restored Jewish religious rights. **55:** *Philip* had received the symbols of sovereignty (v. 15), though Antiochus IV had previously appointed Lysias. **59:** Judea had generally accepted Seleucid rule until Antiochus IV began his program of hellenization, though there was always a faction engaged in intrigue with Egypt. **62:** Judas had also built a citadel on *Mount Zion*; its wall was now destroyed.

7.1–4: **Demetrius I becomes king** (2 Macc.14.1–2). **1:** *Demetrius* I Soter (reigned 162–150 B.C.) was *son of Seleucus* IV Philopator, elder brother of Antiochus IV. When Rome demanded hostages (1.10), Antiochus IV was sent to Rome; later when Seleucus became king, his son Demetrius replaced Antiochus. On the latter's death, he vainly petitioned the senate to be released. Subsequently he escaped from Rome with a small group of men and landed in Tripolis, *a city by the sea* (2 Macc.14.1). **2:** *Antiochus*, that is, Antiochus V Eupator (6.17). **3:** *Do not let me see their faces*, a signal for the murder.

7.5–25: **Alcimus as high priest.** Legitimate high priests were descended from a particular

8 So the king chose Bacchides, one of the king's friends, governor of the province Beyond the River; he was a great man in the kingdom and was faithful to the king. [9]And he sent him, and with him the ungodly Alcimus, whom he made high priest; and he commanded him to take vengeance on the sons of Israel. [10]So they marched away and came with a large force into the land of Judah; and he sent messengers to Judas and his brothers with peaceable but treacherous words. [11]But they paid no attention to their words, for they saw that they had come with a large force.

12 Then a group of scribes appeared in a body before Alcimus and Bacchides to ask for just terms. [13]The Hasideans were the first among the sons of Israel to seek peace from them, [14]for they said, "A priest of the line of Aaron has come with the army, and he will not harm us." [15]And he spoke peaceable words to them and swore this oath to them, "We will not seek to injure you or your friends." [16]So they trusted him; but he seized sixty of them and killed them in one day, in accordance with the word which was written,

[17]"The flesh of thy saints and their blood
    they poured out round about
      Jerusalem,
and there was none to bury them."

[18]Then the fear and dread of them fell upon all the people, for they said, "There is no truth or justice in them, for they have violated the agreement and the oath which they swore."

19 Then Bacchides departed from Jerusalem and encamped in Beth-zaith. And he sent and seized many of the men who had deserted to him,[w] and some of the people, and killed them and threw them into the great pit. [20]He placed Alcimus in charge of the country and left with him a force to help him; then Bacchides went back to the king.

21 Alcimus strove for the high priesthood, [22]and all who were troubling their people joined him. They gained control of the land of Judah and did great damage in Israel. [23]And Judas saw all the evil that Alcimus and those with him had done among the sons of Israel; it was more than the Gentiles had done. [24]So Judas[x] went out into all the surrounding parts of Judea, and took vengeance on the men who had deserted, and he prevented those in the city[y] from going out into the country. [25]When Alcimus saw that Judas and those with him had grown strong, and realized that he could not withstand them, he returned to the king and brought wicked charges against them.

26 Then the king sent Nicanor, one of his honored princes, who hated and detested Israel, and he commanded him to destroy the people. [27]So Nicanor came to Jerusalem with a large force, and treacherously sent to Judas and his brothers this peaceable message, [28]"Let there be no fighting between me and you; I shall come with a few men to see you face to face in

w Or *many of his men who had deserted*
x Gk *he*
y Gk *they were prevented*

---

family. Antiochus IV appointed Jason in place of his brother Onias III (2 Macc.4.7); Jason was in turn supplanted by Menelaus (2 Macc.4.23–26), who was put to death about 162 B.C., after having officiated for ten years (2 Macc.13.1–8). Either Onias III or his son Onias IV, last legitimate claimant, fled to Egypt and established a temple at Heliopolis (Cairo). *Alcimus*, or Jakim (2 Macc.14.3), was not a member of the high-priestly family; he belonged to the hellenizing faction and was willing to further Demetrius' plans. **8:** *Beyond the River*, the province west of the Euphrates (Ezra 4.11). **12–14:** *The Hasideans* (2.42), probably the same as the *group of scribes*, had no political ambitions and were content to live under Syrian rule if they were permitted to keep the Mosaic law. **17:** Ps.79.2–3. All ancients regarded an unburied dead body with horror, and to leave foes unburied was the ultimate outrage. **19:** *Beth-zaith*, perhaps three miles north of Beth-zur; or Bezetha, north of the temple area in Jerusalem.

7.26–50: Defeat of Nicanor. The last of Judas' great victories (2 Macc.14.12–15.36). **26:** According to Josephus (*Antiquities*, XII. x. 4), *Nicanor* was one of the men who had escaped from

peace." 29 So he came to Judas, and
they greeted one another peaceably.
But the enemy were ready to seize
Judas. 30 It became known to Judas
that Nicanor[x] had come to him with
treacherous intent, and he was afraid
of him and would not meet him again.
31 When Nicanor learned that his plan
had been disclosed, he went out to
meet Judas in battle near Caphar-
salama. 32 About five hundred men of
the army of Nicanor fell, and the rest[z]
fled into the city of David.

33 After these events Nicanor went
up to Mount Zion. Some of the priests
came out of the sanctuary, and some
of the elders of the people, to greet him
peaceably and to show him the burnt
offering that was being offered for the
king. 34 But he mocked them and
derided them and defiled them and
spoke arrogantly, 35 and in anger he
swore this oath, "Unless Judas and his
army are delivered into my hands this
time, then if I return safely I will burn
up this house." And he went out in
great anger. 36 Then the priests went in
and stood before the altar and the
temple, and they wept and said,

37 "Thou didst choose this house to
be called by thy name,
and to be for thy people a house
of prayer and supplication.
38 Take vengeance on this man and
on his army,
and let them fall by the sword;
remember their blasphemies,
and let them live no longer."

39 Now Nicanor went out from
Jerusalem and encamped in Beth-
horon, and the Syrian army joined
him. 40 And Judas encamped in Adasa
with three thousand men. Then Judas
prayed and said, 41 "When the messengers from the king spoke blasphemy,
thy angel went forth and struck down
one hundred and eighty-five thousand
of the Assyrians.[a] 42 So also crush this
army before us today; let the rest learn
that Nicanor[b] has spoken wickedly
against thy sanctuary, and judge him
according to this wickedness." 43 So
the armies met in battle on the thirteenth day of the month of Adar. The
army of Nicanor was crushed, and he
himself was the first to fall in the battle.
44 When his army saw that Nicanor had
fallen, they threw down their arms and
fled. 45 The Jews[c] pursued them a day's
journey, from Adasa as far as Gazara,
and as they followed kept sounding
the battle call on the trumpets. 46 And
men came out of all the villages of
Judea round about, and they outflanked the enemy[d] and drove them
back to their pursuers,[e] so that they all
fell by the sword; not even one of them
was left. 47 Then the Jews[f] seized the
spoils and the plunder, and they cut
off Nicanor's head and the right hand
which he had so arrogantly stretched
out, and brought them and displayed
them just outside Jerusalem. 48 The
people rejoiced greatly and celebrated
that day as a day of great gladness.
49 And they decreed that this day
should be celebrated each year on the
thirteenth day of Adar. 50 So the land
of Judah had rest for a few days.

8 Now Judas heard of the fame of
the Romans, that they were very

x Gk *he* *z* Gk *they*
a Gk *of them* *b* Gk *he* *c* Gk *they*
d Gk *them* *e* Gk *these* *f* Gk *they*

Rome with Demetrius (see 7.1 n.). **30:** Judas never trusted the Syrians (vv. 10–11). **31:** *Caphar-salama*, perhaps Khirbet Deir Sellam, about five miles northeast of Jerusalem. **33:** The Jews customarily offered sacrifices to God for the welfare of their rulers. **37–38:** Compare 1 Kg.8.29,43; Pss.68.16; 87.1–2. **40:** *Adasa*, about seven miles from Beth-horon on the road to Jerusalem. **41:** 2 Kg.19.35. **43:** *Adar*, roughly March, in 161 B.C. (see 2 Macc.15.36 n.). **45:** *Gazara*, Gezer (4.15). **47:** *Head . . . right hand*, in punishment for blasphemy and for raising his hand against the temple (2 Macc.15.32). **49:** 2 Macc.15.36. This festival, which came to be called Nicanor Day, was one of the days on which the Jews prohibited mourning (compare 13.52).

8.1–32: Treaty with Rome. The author of 1 Maccabees emphasizes friendly relations between Rome and the Jews because the Romans checked the ambitions of the Seleucids. After 190 B.C. Rome steadily increased her influence in the Near East and Syrian power declined. **1:** *The*

strong and were well-disposed toward all who made an alliance with them, that they pledged friendship to those who came to them, [2]and that they were very strong. Men told him of their wars and of the brave deeds which they were doing among the Gauls, how they had defeated them and forced them to pay tribute, [3]and what they had done in the land of Spain to get control of the silver and gold mines there, [4]and how they had gained control of the whole region by their planning and patience, even though the place was far distant from them. They also subdued the kings who came against them from the ends of the earth, until they crushed them and inflicted great disaster upon them; the rest paid them tribute every year. [5]Philip, and Perseus king of the Macedonians,[g] and the others who rose up against them, they crushed in battle and conquered. [6]They also defeated Antiochus the Great, king of Asia, who went to fight against them with a hundred and twenty elephants and with cavalry and chariots and a very large army. He was crushed by them; [7]they took him alive and decreed that he and those who should reign after him should pay a heavy tribute and give hostages and surrender some of their best provinces, [8]the country of India and Media and Lydia. These they took from him and gave to Eumenes the king. [9]The Greeks planned to come and destroy them, [10]but this became known to them, and they sent a general against the Greeks[h]

and attacked them. Many of them were wounded and fell, and the Romans[i] took captive their wives and children; they plundered them, conquered the land, tore down their strongholds, and enslaved them to this day. [11]The remaining kingdoms and islands, as many as ever opposed them, they destroyed and enslaved; [12]but with their friends and those who rely on them they have kept friendship. They have subdued kings far and near, and as many as have heard of their fame have feared them. [13]Those whom they wish to help and to make kings, they make kings, and those whom they wish they depose; and they have been greatly exalted. [14]Yet for all this not one of them has put on a crown or worn purple as a mark of pride, [15]but they have built for themselves a senate chamber, and every day three hundred and twenty senators constantly deliberate concerning the people, to govern them well. [16]They trust one man each year to rule over them and to control all their land; they all heed the one man, and there is no envy or jealousy among them.

17 So Judas chose Eupolemus the son of John, son of Accos, and Jason the son of Eleazar, and sent them to Rome to establish friendship and alliance, [18]and to free themselves from the yoke; for they saw that the kingdom of the Greeks was completely enslaving Israel. [19]They went to Rome, a very long journey; and they entered the

g Or Kittim   h Gk them   i Gk they

Romans had made an alliance with kings in Asia Minor and Egypt. **2:** Two nations of *Gauls* were *defeated*, those of upper Italy in 190 B.C., and the Galatians of Asia Minor in 189 B.C. **3–4:** Rome conquered the Carthaginian colonies of *Spain*, not *the whole region*, in the Second Punic War. **5:** *Philip*, defeated at Cynoscephalae in 197 B.C.; *Perseus*, his son, last Macedonian king, beaten at Pydna in 168 B.C. **6–8:** *Antiochus* was not captured, but had to *give hostages* (7.1). *India* was not part of his domain; he kept *Media*, but he surrendered *Lydia* and other parts of Asia Minor. *Eumenes* II of Pergamum was given much of Seleucid Asia Minor. **9:** *The Greeks*, possibly the Macedonians (v. 5), or the Achaean league somewhat later. **12:** This is the estimate of a partisan; it is not true that they always *kept friendship*. **14:** *A crown*, Rome wanted no king, but magistrates, senators, and knights wore *purple* borders on their garments. **15:** *Every day*, actually senate meetings were held three times a month, and on the festivals. **16:** *One man*, in reality there were two consuls, and *envy and jealousy* were constant. The author of 1 Maccabees idealizes the Romans because their republican institutions were congenial to the Jews. **17:** *Eupolemus*, 2 Macc.4.11. *Accos*, a priestly family (Ezra 2.61).

senate chamber and spoke as follows: ²⁰"Judas, who is also called Maccabeus, and his brothers and the people of the Jews have sent us to you to establish alliance and peace with you, that we may be enrolled as your allies and friends." ²¹The proposal pleased them, ²²and this is a copy of the letter which they wrote in reply, on bronze tablets, and sent to Jerusalem to remain with them there as a memorial of peace and alliance:

23 "May all go well with the Romans and with the nation of the Jews at sea and on land for ever, and may sword and enemy be far from them. ²⁴If war comes first to Rome or to any of their allies in all their dominion, ²⁵the nation of the Jews shall act as their allies wholeheartedly, as the occasion may indicate to them. ²⁶And to the enemy who makes war they shall not give or supply grain, arms, money, or ships, as Rome has decided; and they shall keep their obligations without receiving any return. ²⁷In the same way, if war comes first to the nation of the Jews, the Romans shall willingly act as their allies, as the occasion may indicate to them. ²⁸And to the enemy allies shall be given no grain, arms, money, or ships, as Rome has decided; and they shall keep these obligations and do so without deceit. ²⁹Thus on these terms the Romans make a treaty with the Jewish people. ³⁰If after these terms are in effect both parties shall determine to add or delete anything, they shall do so at their discretion, and any addition or deletion that they may make shall be valid.

31 "And concerning the wrongs which King Demetrius is doing to them we have written to him as follows, 'Why have you made your yoke heavy upon our friends and allies the Jews? ³²If now they appeal again for help against you, we will defend their rights and fight you on sea and on land.' "

9 When Demetrius heard that Nicanor and his army had fallen in battle, he sent Bacchides and Alcimus into the land of Judah a second time, and with them the right wing of the army. ²They went by the road which leads to Gilgal and encamped against Mesaloth in Arbela, and they took it and killed many people. ³In the first month of the one hundred and fifty-second year*ʲ* they encamped against Jerusalem; ⁴then they marched off and went to Berea with twenty thousand foot soldiers and two thousand cavalry.

5 Now Judas was encamped in Elasa, and with him were three thousand picked men. ⁶When they saw the huge number of the enemy forces, they were greatly frightened, and many slipped away from the camp, until no more than eight hundred of them were left.

7 When Judas saw that his army had slipped away and the battle was imminent, he was crushed in spirit, for he had no time to assemble them. ⁸He became faint, but he said to those who were left, "Let us rise and go up against our enemies. We may be able to fight them." ⁹But they tried to dissuade him, saying, "We are not able. Let us rather

j 160 B.C.

22: Important documents were often inscribed *on bronze tablets*. 23–30: The treaty letter begins with the conventional formula and is drawn up as though the two parties were equals, and Judea a sovereign state. 31–32: This postscript was not part of the treaty, and is correctly omitted from it by Josephus (*Antiquities*, XII. x. 6); there is no evidence that the Romans helped Judas against Demetrius.

9.1–22: Death of Judas. Continual Syrian pressure weakened Judas' forces, which were a guerrilla band facing a highly organized army. Judas decided that it was better to fall in battle than to withdraw. 1–2: *Bacchides*, 7.8. *Alcimus*, see 7.5 n. Josephus (*Antiquities*, XII. xi. 1) says that they started from Antioch, camped at Arbela in Galilee (not *Gilgal*), besieged refugees in the caves, and went on toward Jerusalem. *Mesaloth*, perhaps the Hebrew word for "steps," i.e. ascents to *Arbela*. 4: *Berea*, perhaps el-Bireh, opposite Ramallah, ten miles north of Jerusalem. 5: *Elasa* has not been identified.

save our own lives now, and let us come back with our brethren and fight them; we are too few." [10]But Judas said, "Far be it from us to do such a thing as to flee from them. If our time has come, let us die bravely for our brethren, and leave no cause to question our honor."

11 Then the army of Bacchides[k] marched out from the camp and took its stand for the encounter. The cavalry was divided into two companies, and the slingers and the archers went ahead of the army, as did all the chief warriors. [12]Bacchides was on the right wing. Flanked by the two companies, the phalanx advanced to the sound of the trumpets; and the men with Judas also blew their trumpets. [13]The earth was shaken by the noise of the armies, and the battle raged from morning till evening.

14 Judas saw that Bacchides and the strength of his army were on the right; then all the stouthearted men went with him, [15]and they crushed the right wing, and he pursued them as far as Mount Azotus. [16]When those on the left wing saw that the right wing was crushed, they turned and followed close behind Judas and his men. [17]The battle became desperate, and many on both sides were wounded and fell. [18]Judas also fell, and the rest fled.

19 Then Jonathan and Simon took Judas their brother and buried him in the tomb of their fathers at Modein, [20]and wept for him. And all Israel made great lamentation for him; they mourned many days and said,
[21]"How is the mighty fallen,
  the savior of Israel!"

[22]Now the rest of the acts of Judas, and his wars and the brave deeds that he did, and his greatness, have not been recorded, for they were very many.

23 After the death of Judas, the lawless emerged in all parts of Israel; all the doers of injustice appeared. [24]In those days a very great famine occurred, and the country deserted with them to the enemy. [25]And Bacchides chose the ungodly and put them in charge of the country. [26]They sought and searched for the friends of Judas, and brought them to Bacchides, and he took vengeance on them and made sport of them. [27]Thus there was great distress in Israel, such as had not been since the time that prophets ceased to appear among them.

28 Then all the friends of Judas assembled and said to Jonathan, [29]"Since the death of your brother Judas there has been no one like him to go against our enemies and Bacchides, and to deal with those of our nation who hate us. [30]So now we have chosen you today to take his place as our ruler and leader, to fight our battle." [31]And Jonathan at that time accepted the leadership and took the place of Judas his brother.

32 When Bacchides learned of this, he tried to kill him. [33]But Jonathan and Simon his brother and all who were with him heard of it, and they fled into the wilderness of Tekoa and camped by the water of the pool of Asphar. [34]Bacchides found this out on the sabbath day, and he with all his army crossed the Jordan.

k Gk *the army*

15: *Mount Azotus*, perhaps el-'Asur, six miles northeast of el-Bireh; Ashdod (4.15) is too far away. 19: *Modein*, 2.1, 70; 13.27–30. 21: 2 Sam.1.19. 22: The expression *Now the rest of the acts* imitates the style of Hebrew chronicles (1 Kg.11.41).

9.23–73: Jonathan becomes leader and defeats Bacchides. 23: *The lawless*, i.e. the pro-Syrian element. 24: *The country*, the majority of the nation, or perhaps the rural population; resistance now seemed futile. 25: *The ungodly*, i.e. hellenized Jews. 27: *Prophets ceased*, see 4.46 n. 31: *We have chosen you*, Judas was self-appointed, but *Jonathan* was elected by his peers; he became leader about 160 or 159 B.C. and high priest in 152 (10.21). 33: *Tekoa*, five miles southeast of Bethlehem (Am. 1.1); *the wilderness* reached from here to the Dead Sea. *The pool of Asphar* may be three miles south of Tekoa. 34: *Bacchides* thought the Jews might be surprised *on the sabbath day*. He apparently came from Jerusalem, *crossed the Jordan*, and camped on the east

35 And Jonathan[l] sent his brother as leader of the multitude and begged the Nabateans, who were his friends, for permission to store with them the great amount of baggage which they had. [36]But the sons of Jambri from Medeba came out and seized John and all that he had, and departed with it.

37 After these things it was reported to Jonathan and Simon his brother, "The sons of Jambri are celebrating a great wedding, and are conducting the bride, a daughter of one of the great nobles of Canaan, from Nadabath with a large escort." [38]And they remembered the blood of John their brother, and went up and hid under cover of the mountain. [39]They raised their eyes and looked, and saw a tumultuous procession with much baggage; and the bridegroom came out with his friends and his brothers to meet them with tambourines and musicians and many weapons. [40]Then they rushed upon them from the ambush and began killing them. Many were wounded and fell, and the rest fled to the mountain; and they took all their goods. [41]Thus the wedding was turned into mourning and the voice of their musicians into a funeral dirge. [42]And when they had fully avenged the blood of their brother, they returned to the marshes of the Jordan.

43 When Bacchides heard of this, he came with a large force on the sabbath day to the banks of the Jordan. [44]And Jonathan said to those with him, "Let us rise up now and fight for our lives, for today things are not as they were before. [45]For look! the battle is in front of us and behind us; the water of the Jordan is on this side and on that, with marsh and thicket; there is no place to turn. [46]Cry out now to Heaven that you may be delivered from the hands of our enemies." [47]So the battle began, and Jonathan stretched out his hand to strike Bacchides, but he eluded him and went to the rear. [48]Then Jonathan and the men with him leaped into the Jordan and swam across to the other side, and the enemy[m] did not cross the Jordan to attack them. [49]And about one thousand of Bacchides' men fell that day.

50 Bacchides[n] then returned to Jerusalem and built strong cities in Judea: the fortress in Jericho, and Emmaus, and Beth-horon, and Bethel, and Timnath, and[o] Pharathon, and Tephon, with high walls and gates and bars. [51]And he placed garrisons in them to harass Israel. [52]He also fortified the city of Beth-zur, and Gazara, and the citadel, and in them he put troops and stores of food. [53]And he took the sons of the leading men of the land as hostages and put them under guard in the citadel at Jerusalem.

54 In the one hundred and fifty-third year,[p] in the second month, Alcimus gave orders to tear down the wall of the inner court of the sanctuary. He tore down the work of the prophets! [55]But he only began to tear it down, for at that time Alcimus was stricken and his work was hindered; his mouth was stopped and he was paralyzed, so that he could no longer say a word or give commands concerning his house.

l Gk *he*
m Gk *they*   *n* Gk *he*
o Some authorities omit *and*
p 159 B.C.

---

side. **35**: *His brother*, John (v. 36; 2.2). *The Nabateans*, see 5.25 n. **36**: *Sons of Jambri*, evidently a Nabatean tribe. *Medeba* or Madeba, twelve miles southeast of the north end of the Dead Sea. **37**: *Nadabath*, perhaps Nebo, a little north of Medeba (Num.33.47; Dt.32.49). **38**: *Blood of John*, the sequel to v. 36 was the murder of John and all his companions (Josephus, *Antiquities*, XIII. i. 2). **45**: The Jews were apparently on the east side of the Jordan, between the river and the Syrian forces. **50–53**: Bacchides established forces and garrisons to prevent guerrilla operations. *Emmaus*, see 3.40 n. *Beth-horon*, see 3.16 n. *Bethel*, now Beitin, about twelve miles north of Jerusalem. *Timnath*, perhaps twelve miles northwest of Bethel. *Pharathon*, six miles southwest of Shechem or Nablus. *Tephon*, Tappuah, twenty-five miles north of Jerusalem. *Beth-zur*, see 4.29 n. *Gazara*, see 4.15 n. **54**: *The wall of the inner court* separated this part from the rest of the temple mount, which was open to Gentiles. Pagans were now to have access to *the sanctuary*.

⁵⁶And Alcimus died at that time in great agony. ⁵⁷When Bacchides saw that Alcimus was dead, he returned to the king, and the land of Judah had rest for two years.

58 Then all the lawless plotted and said, "See! Jonathan and his men are living in quiet and confidence. So now let us bring Bacchides back, and he will capture them all in one night." ⁵⁹And they went and consulted with him. ⁶⁰He started to come with a large force, and secretly sent letters to all his allies in Judea, telling them to seize Jonathan and his men; but they were unable to do it, because their plan became known. ⁶¹And Jonathan's men*q* seized about fifty of the men of the country who were leaders in this treachery, and killed them.

62 Then Jonathan with his men, and Simon, withdrew to Bethbasi in the wilderness; he rebuilt the parts of it that had been demolished, and they fortified it. ⁶³When Bacchides learned of this, he assembled all his forces, and sent orders to the men of Judea. ⁶⁴Then he came and encamped against Bethbasi; he fought against it for many days and made machines of war.

65 But Jonathan left Simon his brother in the city, while he went out into the country; and he went with only a few men. ⁶⁶He struck down Odomera and his brothers and the sons of Phasiron in their tents. ⁶⁷Then he*r* began to attack and went into battle with his forces; and Simon and his men sallied out from the city and set fire to the machines of war. ⁶⁸They

fought with Bacchides, and he was crushed by them. They distressed him greatly, for his plan and his expedition had been in vain. ⁶⁹So he was greatly enraged at the lawless men who had counseled him to come into the country, and he killed many of them. Then he decided to depart to his own land.

70 When Jonathan learned of this, he sent ambassadors to him to make peace with him and obtain release of the captives. ⁷¹He agreed, and did as he said; and he swore to Jonathan*s* that he would not try to harm him as long as he lived. ⁷²He restored to him the captives whom he had formerly taken from the land of Judah; then he turned and departed to his own land, and came no more into their territory. ⁷³Thus the sword ceased from Israel. And Jonathan dwelt in Michmash. And Jonathan began to judge the people, and he destroyed the ungodly out of Israel.

10 In the one hundred and sixtieth year*t* Alexander Epiphanes, the son of Antiochus, landed and occupied Ptolemais. They welcomed him, and there he began to reign. ²When Demetrius the king heard of it, he assembled a very large army and marched out to meet him in battle. ³And Demetrius sent Jonathan a letter in peaceable words to honor him; ⁴for he said, "Let us act first to make peace with him*u* before he makes peace with Alexander against us, ⁵for he will re-

q Gk *they*   *r* Other authorities read *they*
s Gk *him*   *t* 152 B.C.
u Gk *them*

The prophets, Haggai and Zechariah had built the second temple. **56:** *Alcimus* had been high priest for about two years (7.5). **57:** *He returned*, believing that with the fortresses garrisoned the situation was stable; his departure gave Jonathan a free hand. **61:** *Fifty . . . leaders*, probably the hellenizers (see v. 25 n.). **62:** *Bethbasi*, perhaps Khirbet Beit-Bassa, about three miles northeast of Tekoa. **66:** *Odomera . . . sons of Phasiron*, probably bedouin sheikhs. **68:** *He was crushed*, for Simon attacked by surprise and *Bacchides* had depended heavily on the war machines (v. 67). **72:** Josephus says that there was an exchange of prisoners (*Antiquities*, XIII. i. 6). **73:** *Thus the sword ceased*, for about seven years, until the events of 10.69. *Michmash*, now Mukhmas, eight miles northeast of Jerusalem (1 Sam.14.5–23). *To judge the people*, as a natural leader, like Samuel and those in the book of Judges.

10.1–21: Alexander Balas appoints Jonathan high priest. 1: *Alexander* I *Epiphanes*, who came from Ephesus and whose given name was Balas (or Ba'al), posed as *the son of Antiochus* IV. He claimed the kingship from 150 B.C. onward, and reigned until about 145. Attalus II of Perga-

member all the wrongs which we did to him and to his brothers and his nation." [6]So Demetrius[v] gave him authority to recruit troops, to equip them with arms, and to become his ally; and he commanded that the hostages in the citadel should be released to him.

7 Then Jonathan came to Jerusalem and read the letter in the hearing of all the people and of the men in the citadel. [8]They were greatly alarmed when they heard that the king had given him authority to recruit troops. [9]But the men in the citadel released the hostages to Jonathan, and he returned them to their parents.

10 And Jonathan dwelt in Jerusalem and began to rebuild and restore the city. [11]He directed those who were doing the work to build the walls and encircle Mount Zion with squared stones, for better fortification; and they did so.

12 Then the foreigners who were in the strongholds that Bacchides had built fled; [13]each left his place and departed to his own land. [14]Only in Beth-zur did some remain who had forsaken the law and the commandments, for it served as a place of refuge.

15 Now Alexander the king heard of all the promises which Demetrius had sent to Jonathan, and men told him of the battles that Jonathan[w] and his brothers had fought, of the brave deeds that they had done, and of the troubles that they had endured. [16]So he said, "Shall we find another such man? Come now, we will make him our friend and ally." [17]And he wrote a

letter and sent it to him, in the following words:

18 "King Alexander to his brother Jonathan, greeting. [19]We have heard about you, that you are a mighty warrior and worthy to be our friend. [20]And so we have appointed you to-day to be the high priest of your nation; you are to be called the king's friend" (and he sent him a purple robe and a golden crown) "and you are to take our side and keep friendship with us."

21 So Jonathan put on the holy garments in the seventh month of the one hundred and sixtieth year,[x] at the feast of tabernacles, and he recruited troops and equipped them with arms in abundance. [22]When Demetrius heard of these things he was grieved and said, [23]"What is this that we have done? Alexander has gotten ahead of us in forming a friendship with the Jews to strengthen himself. [24]I also will write them words of encouragement and promise them honor and gifts, that I may have their help." [25]So he sent a message to them in the following words:

"King Demetrius to the nation of the Jews, greeting. [26]Since you have kept your agreement with us and have continued your friendship with us, and have not sided with our enemies, we have heard of it and rejoiced. [27]And now continue still to keep faith with us, and we will repay you with good for what you do for us. [28]We will grant you many immunities and give you gifts.

v Gk *he*   *w* Gk *he*   *x* 152 B.C.

---

mum and Ptolemy VI persuaded the Roman senate to recognize him. **6:** *Gave him authority*, as a local prince or governor, but not independence. *The hostages*, 9.53. The Syrians held the citadel at Jerusalem. **10:** *Jonathan* now left Michmash. **11:** Lysias had ordered the wall of the Jewish fortress torn down (6.62). **14:** *Some*, i.e. hellenized Jews opposed to the Hasmoneans. **18–20:** *Alexander*, hearing of Demetrius' letter, decided to outbid him. Until the time of Antiochus IV, the hereditary high priest had been confirmed but not appointed by the ruler; now Alexander appointed Jonathan and made him one of his friends (see 2.18 n.); the Jews had not elected him. **21:** *The holy garments*, Ex.28.1–39; 39:1–26. *Tabernacles*, a seven day festival held in September (Lev.23.33–43), had come to be associated with the hope of victory over the Gentiles (Zech.14.16–19).

10.22–50: Demetrius' offer to the Jews; his defeat. 25: The letter was addressed *to the nation*, ignoring Jonathan. Demetrius thought that he could drive a wedge between leader and people.

29 "And now I free you and exempt all the Jews from payment of tribute and salt tax and crown levies, ³⁰and instead of collecting the third of the grain and the half of the fruit of the trees that I should receive, I release them from this day and henceforth. I will not collect them from the land of Judah or from the three districts added to it from Samaria and Galilee, from this day and for all time. ³¹And let Jerusalem and her environs, her tithes and her revenues, be holy and free from tax. ³²I release also my control of the citadel in Jerusalem and give it to the high priest, that he may station in it men of his own choice to guard it. ³³And every one of the Jews taken as a captive from the land of Judah into any part of my kingdom, I set free without payment; and let all officials cancel also the taxes on their cattle.

34 "And all the feasts and sabbaths and new moons and appointed days, and the three days before a feast and the three after a feast—let them all be days of immunity and release for all the Jews who are in my kingdom. ³⁵No one shall have authority to exact anything from them or annoy any of them about any matter.

36 "Let Jews be enrolled in the king's forces to the number of thirty thousand men, and let the maintenance be given them that is due to all the forces of the king. ³⁷Let some of them be stationed in the great strongholds of the king, and let some of them be put in positions of trust in the kingdom. Let their officers and leaders be of their own number, and let them live by their own laws, just as the king has commanded in the land of Judah.

38 "As for the three districts that have been added to Judea from the country of Samaria, let them be so annexed to Judea that they are considered to be under one ruler and obey no other authority but the high priest. ³⁹Ptolemais and the land adjoining it I have given as a gift to the sanctuary in Jerusalem, to meet the necessary expenses of the sanctuary. ⁴⁰I also grant fifteen thousand shekels of silver yearly out of the king's revenues from appropriate places. ⁴¹And all the additional funds which the government officials have not paid as they did in the first years,[y] they shall give from now on for the service of the temple.[z] ⁴²Moreover, the five thousand shekels of silver which my officials[a] have received every year from the income of the services of the temple, this too is canceled, because it belongs to the priests who minister there. ⁴³And whoever takes refuge at the temple in Jerusalem, or in any of its precincts, because he owes money to the king or has any debt, let him be released and receive back all his property in my kingdom.

44 "Let the cost of rebuilding and restoring the structures of the sanctuary be paid from the revenues of the king. ⁴⁵And let the cost of rebuilding the walls of Jerusalem and fortifying it round about, and the cost of rebuilding the walls in Judea, also be paid from the revenues of the king."

46 When Jonathan and the people heard these words, they did not believe or accept them, because they remembered the great wrongs which

y The Greek text of this verse is uncertain
z Gk *house*   a Gk *they*

29–30: *All the Jews* in the Seleucid realm, not merely in Judea. *Tribute*, direct taxes proportionate to individual wealth. *Salt tax*, on salt from the marshes and the Dead Sea. *Crown levies*, fixed amounts of money. *The three districts* (11.34) that Alexander the Great had transferred from Samaria to Judea and Antiochus IV had reassigned to Samaria were now restored (v. 38). **32:** *Release* of *control of the citadel* would free Jerusalem from military domination. **34:** *Appointed days*, other public festivals. **36–37:** Opening the army and the civil service to Jews might strengthen their loyalty to the crown. **39:** *Ptolemais* was in the hands of Alexander (v. 1). This was an invitation to the Jews to help Demetrius recapture it. **41:** *The additional funds* were grants once made to the temple by Ptolemaic and Seleucid kings, but *not paid* since the time of Antiochus IV. **44–45:** Here Demetrius followed the custom of Persian kings (Ezra 6.8; 7.20).

Demetrius[b] had done in Israel and how he had greatly oppressed them. [47]They favored Alexander, because he had been the first to speak peaceable words to them, and they remained his allies all his days.

48 Now Alexander the king assembled large forces and encamped opposite Demetrius. [49]The two kings met in battle, and the army of Demetrius fled, and Alexander[c] pursued him and defeated them. [50]He pressed the battle strongly until the sun set, and Demetrius fell on that day.

51 Then Alexander sent ambassadors to Ptolemy king of Egypt with the following message: [52]"Since I have returned to my kingdom and have taken my seat on the throne of my fathers, and established my rule—for I crushed Demetrius and gained control of our country; [53]I met him in battle, and he and his army were crushed by us, and we have taken our seat on the throne of his kingdom— [54]now therefore let us establish friendship with one another; give me now your daughter as my wife, and I will become your son-in-law, and will make gifts to you and to her in keeping with your position."

55 Ptolemy the king replied and said, "Happy was the day on which you returned to the land of your fathers and took your seat on the throne of their kingdom. [56]And now I will do for you as you wrote, but meet me at Ptolemais, so that we may see one another, and I will become your father-in-law, as you have said."

57 So Ptolemy set out from Egypt, he and Cleopatra his daughter, and came to Ptolemais in the one hundred and sixty-second year.[d] [58]Alexander the king met him, and Ptolemy[e] gave him Cleopatra his daughter in marriage, and celebrated her wedding at Ptolemais with great pomp, as kings do.

59 Then Alexander the king wrote to Jonathan to come to meet him. [60]So he went with pomp to Ptolemais and met the two kings; he gave them and their friends silver and gold and many gifts, and found favor with them. [61]A group of pestilent men from Israel, lawless men, gathered together against him to accuse him; but the king paid no attention to them. [62]The king gave orders to take off Jonathan's garments and to clothe him in purple, and they did so. [63]The king also seated him at his side; and he said to his officers, "Go forth with him into the middle of the city and proclaim that no one is to bring charges against him about any matter, and let no one annoy him for any reason." [64]And when his accusers saw the honor that was paid him, in accordance with the proclamation, and saw him clothed in purple, they all fled. [65]Thus the king honored him and enrolled him among his chief friends, and made him general and governor of the province. [66]And Jonathan returned to Jerusalem in peace and gladness.

67 In the one hundred and sixty-fifth year[f] Demetrius the son of Demetrius came from Crete to the land of his fathers. [68]When Alexander the king heard of it, he was greatly grieved and returned to Antioch. [69]And Demetrius appointed Apollonius the governor of Coelesyria, and he

b Gk *he*
c Other authorities read *Alexander fled, and Demetrius*
d 150 B.C.   e Gk *he*   f 147 B.C.

47: *Alexander* was also recognized as king by the Jews' allies, the Romans. **50**: *Demetrius fell* probably in 150 B.C. (v. 57).

10.51–66: Alexander's relations with Egypt and Judea. 51: *Ptolemy* VI Philometor (1.18). **55**: *Ptolemy* recognized Alexander as legitimate (see 10.1–21 n.). **57**: *Cleopatra* III, who later married her uncle, Ptolemy VIII. **62**: A change of *garments* often signified honor or dishonor (Zech.3.3–5; Mt.22.11–14). **65**: *Chief friends*, see 2.18 n. *General and governor*, with military and civil authority.

10.67–89: Victories of Jonathan. 67: *Demetrius* II *the son of Demetrius* I disputed the throne with Alexander and later with Tryphon and Antiochus VI; in 138 B.C. he was taken captive by the Parthians. He reigned again from 129 till his death in 125 B.C. **69**: *Coelesyria*, meaning

assembled a large force and encamped against Jamnia. Then he sent the following message to Jonathan the high priest:

70 "You are the only one to rise up against us, and I have become a laughingstock and reproach because of you. Why do you assume authority against us in the hill country? ⁷¹If you now have confidence in your forces, come down to the plain to meet us, and let us match strength with each other there, for I have with me the power of the cities. ⁷²Ask and learn who I am and who the others are that are helping us. Men will tell you that you cannot stand before us, for your fathers were twice put to flight in their own land. ⁷³And now you will not be able to withstand my cavalry and such an army in the plain, where there is no stone or pebble, or place to flee."

74 When Jonathan heard the words of Apollonius, his spirit was aroused. He chose ten thousand men and set out from Jerusalem, and Simon his brother met him to help him. ⁷⁵He encamped before Joppa, but the men of the city closed its gates, for Apollonius had a garrison in Joppa. ⁷⁶So they fought against it, and the men of the city became afraid and opened the gates, and Jonathan gained possession of Joppa.

77 When Apollonius heard of it, he mustered three thousand cavalry and a large army, and went to Azotus as though he were going farther. At the same time he advanced into the plain, for he had a large troop of cavalry and put confidence in it. ⁷⁸Jonathanᵍ pursued him to Azotus, and the armies engaged in battle. ⁷⁹Now Apollonius had secretly left a thousand cavalry behind them. ⁸⁰Jonathan learned that there was an ambush behind him, for they surrounded his army and shot arrows at his men from early morning till late afternoon. ⁸¹But his men stood fast, as Jonathan commanded, and the enemy'sʰ horses grew tired.

82 Then Simon brought forward his force and engaged the phalanx in battle (for the cavalry was exhausted); they were overwhelmed by him and fled, ⁸³and the cavalry was dispersed in the plain. They fled to Azotus and entered Beth-dagon, the temple of their idol, for safety. ⁸⁴But Jonathan burned Azotus and the surrounding towns and plundered them; and the temple of Dagon, and those who had taken refuge in it he burned with fire. ⁸⁵The number of those who fell by the sword, with those burned alive, came to eight thousand men.

86 Then Jonathan departed from there and encamped against Askalon, and the men of the city came out to meet him with great pomp. ⁸⁷And Jonathan and those with him returned to Jerusalem with much booty. ⁸⁸When Alexander the king heard of these things, he honored Jonathan still more; ⁸⁹and he sent to him a golden buckle, such as it is the custom to give to the kinsmen of kings. He also gave him Ekron and all its environs as his possession.

‖ Then the king of Egypt gathered great forces, like the sand by the seashore, and many ships; and he tried to get possession of Alexander's kingdom by trickery and add it to his

g Gk *he*   *h* Gk *their*

"hollow Syria," originally designated the country between the Lebanon and anti-Lebanon mountains; here it is Palestine and Transjordan, including the coast. *Jamnia*, 4.15. **72:** *Twice put to flight*, 6.54; 9.18. **74:** Jonathan now had forces for more than guerrilla engagements (v. 65); he had troops organized as phalanxes (v. 82). **75:** *Joppa*, now Jaffa, a seaport near Jamnia and forty miles from Jerusalem. **82:** *His force* had been held in reserve and was fresh. **83:** *Beth-dagon*, house of Dagon, the Philistine grain god (Jg.16.23). **86:** *Askalon*, about twelve miles north of Gaza. **89:** *Ekron*, northernmost of the Philistine cities, was given to Jonathan as a personal possession, and its taxes were assigned to him.

11.1–19: Invasion of Ptolemy VI and victory of Demetrius II. 1: Josephus says that Ptolemy came to aid Alexander, his son-in-law, but that the latter plotted against Ptolemy's life (*Antiq-*

own kingdom. ²He set out for Syria with peaceable words, and the people of the cities opened their gates to him and went to meet him, for Alexander the king had commanded them to meet him, since he was Alexander's*ⁱ* father-in-law. ³But when Ptolemy entered the cities he stationed forces as a garrison in each city.

4 When he*ʲ* approached Azotus, they showed him the temple of Dagon burned down, and Azotus and its suburbs destroyed, and the corpses lying about, and the charred bodies of those whom Jonathan*ᵏ* had burned in the war, for they had piled them in heaps along his route. ⁵They also told the king what Jonathan had done, to throw blame on him; but the king kept silent. ⁶Jonathan met the king at Joppa with pomp, and they greeted one another and spent the night there. ⁷And Jonathan went with the king as far as the river called Eleutherus; then he returned to Jerusalem.

8 So King Ptolemy gained control of the coastal cities as far as Seleucia by the sea, and he kept devising evil designs against Alexander. ⁹He sent envoys to Demetrius the king, saying, "Come, let us make a covenant with each other, and I will give you in marriage my daughter who was Alexander's wife, and you shall reign over your father's kingdom. ¹⁰For I now regret that I gave him my daughter, for he has tried to kill me." ¹¹He threw blame on Alexander*ˡ* because he coveted his kingdom. ¹²So he took his daughter away from him and gave her

to Demetrius. He was estranged from Alexander, and their enmity became manifest.

13 Then Ptolemy entered Antioch and put on the crown of Asia. Thus he put two crowns upon his head, the crown of Egypt and that of Asia. ¹⁴Now Alexander the king was in Cilicia at that time, because the people of that region were in revolt. ¹⁵And Alexander heard of it and came against him in battle. Ptolemy marched out and met him with a strong force, and put him to flight. ¹⁶So Alexander fled into Arabia to find protection there, and King Ptolemy was exalted. ¹⁷And Zabdiel the Arab cut off the head of Alexander and sent it to Ptolemy. ¹⁸But King Ptolemy died three days later, and his troops in the strongholds were killed by the inhabitants of the strongholds. ¹⁹So Demetrius became king in the one hundred and sixty-seventh year.*ᵐ*

20 In those days Jonathan assembled the men of Judea to attack the citadel in Jerusalem, and he built many engines of war to use against it. ²¹But certain lawless men who hated their nation went to the king and reported to him that Jonathan was besieging the citadel. ²²When he heard this he was angry, and as soon as he heard it he set out and came to Ptolemais; and he wrote Jonathan not to continue the siege, but to meet him for a conference at Ptolemais as quickly as possible.

i Gk *his*
j Other ancient authorities read *they*
k Gk *he*
l Gk *him*
m 145 B.C.

---

uities, XIII. iv. 5–6). **5**: *Kept silent*, he had not yet broken with Alexander, and was not ready to commit himself. **7**: *Eleutherus*, now Nahr el-Kebir, north of Tripolis. **8**: *Seleucia* in Pieria, the main port for Antioch, near the mouth of the Orontes. **9**: *My daughter*, Cleopatra III (10.57). **13**: According to Josephus, the army proclaimed *Ptolemy* as king, but he persuaded the people of Antioch to support Demetrius. **14**: *Cilicia*, on the south coast of Turkey, always closely related to Syria, and the only section of Asia Minor then part of the Seleucid Empire. **15**: *Ptolemy marched out*, according to Josephus (*Antiquities*, XIII. iv. 8) with his son-in-law, Demetrius, who had already married Cleopatra. **16**: *Arabia* here includes the country east of Aleppo and Damascus. **18**: *Ptolemy died* of wounds suffered in the victory over Alexander. **19**: *Demetrius* had claimed to be *king* since 150 B.C. (see 10.67 n.).

11.20–37: Agreement between Demetrius II and Jonathan. 20: Demetrius I had once promised to turn *the citadel* over to the high priest (10.32), but he refused to recognize Jonathan as such because the latter had supported Alexander. Now Jonathan resolved to attack the citadel and

23 When Jonathan heard this, he gave orders to continue the siege; and he chose some of the elders of Israel and some of the priests, and put himself in danger, [24]for he went to the king at Ptolemais, taking silver and gold and clothing and numerous other gifts. And he won his favor. [25]Although certain lawless men of his nation kept making complaints against him, [26]the king treated him as his predecessors had treated him; he exalted him in the presence of all his friends. [27]He confirmed him in the high priesthood and in as many other honors as he had formerly had, and made him to be regarded as one of his chief friends. [28]Then Jonathan asked the king to free Judea and the three districts of Samaria[n] from tribute, and promised him three hundred talents. [29]The king consented, and wrote a letter to Jonathan about all these things; its contents were as follows:

30 "King Demetrius to Jonathan his brother and to the nation of the Jews, greeting. [31]This copy of the letter which we wrote concerning you to Lasthenes our kinsman we have written to you also, so that you may know what it says. [32]'King Demetrius to Lasthenes his father, greeting. [33]To the nation of the Jews, who are our friends and fulfil their obligations to us, we have determined to do good, because of the good will they show toward us. [34]We have confirmed as their possession both the territory of Judea and the three districts of Aphairema and Lydda and Rathamin; the latter, with all the region bordering them, were added to Judea from Samaria. To all those who offer sacrifice in Jerusalem, we have granted release from[o] the royal taxes which the king formerly received from them each year, from the crops of the land and the fruit of the trees. [35]And the other payments henceforth due to us of the tithes, and the taxes due to us, and the salt pits and the crown taxes due to us—from all these we shall grant them release. [36]And not one of these grants shall be canceled from this time forth for ever. [37]Now therefore take care to make a copy of this, and let it be given to Jonathan and put up in a conspicuous place on the holy mountain.' "

38 Now when Demetrius the king saw that the land was quiet before him and that there was no opposition to him, he dismissed all his troops, each man to his own place, except the foreign troops which he had recruited from the islands of the nations. So all the troops who had served his fathers hated him. [39]Now Trypho had formerly been one of Alexander's supporters. He saw that all the troops were murmuring against Demetrius. So he went to Imalkue the Arab, who was bringing up Antiochus, the young son of Alexander, [40]and insistently urged him to hand Antiochus[p] over to him, to become king in place of his father. He also reported to Imalkue[p] what Demetrius had done and told of the hatred which the troops of Demetrius[p] had for him; and he stayed there many days.

41 Now Jonathan sent to Demetrius the king the request that he remove the troops of the citadel from Jerusalem, and the troops in the strongholds; for they kept fighting against Israel. [42]And Demetrius sent this message to

n Cn: Gk *the three districts and Samaria*
o Or *Samaria, for all those who offer sacrifice in Jerusalem, in place of*
p Gk *him*

---

make Judea independent. **23–24:** Jonathan decided to *continue the siege* so as to negotiate from strength, but his dangerous visit and gifts showed that he was willing to make terms. **27:** 10.20. **30–37:** The letter repeats earlier promises (10.25–45), but says nothing of the citadel. **31:** *Lasthenes*, probably governor of Coelesyria. **34:** *The three districts*, 10.30,38. *Aphairema*, probably et-Taiyibeh, four miles northeast of Bethel, the Ephraim of Jn.11.54. *Lydda*, or Lod, east of Jaffa. *Rathamin*, perhaps Ramathaim-zophim (1 Sam.1.1), the Arimathea of Mk.15.43. **11.38–52: Jonathan's aid to Demetrius. 38:** *Demetrius* in overconfidence reduced his army, probably to save money. This made him unpopular. **42–43:** At last Demetrius seemed to agree

Jonathan, "Not only will I do these things for you and your nation, but I will confer great honor on you and your nation, if I find an opportunity. [43]Now then you will do well to send me men who will help me, for all my troops have revolted." [44]So Jonathan sent three thousand stalwart men to him at Antioch, and when they came to the king, the king rejoiced at their arrival.

45 Then the men of the city assembled within the city, to the number of a hundred and twenty thousand, and they wanted to kill the king. [46]But the king fled into the palace. Then the men of the city seized the main streets of the city and began to fight. [47]So the king called the Jews to his aid, and they all rallied about him and then spread out through the city; and they killed on that day as many as a hundred thousand men. [48]They set fire to the city and seized much spoil on that day, and they saved the king. [49]When the men of the city saw that the Jews had gained control of the city as they pleased, their courage failed and they cried out to the king with this entreaty, [50]"Grant us peace, and make the Jews stop fighting against us and our city." [51]And they threw down their arms and made peace. So the Jews gained glory in the eyes of the king and of all the people in his kingdom, and they returned to Jerusalem with much spoil.

52 So Demetrius the king sat on the throne of his kingdom, and the land was quiet before him. [53]But he broke his word about all that he had promised; and he became estranged from Jonathan and did not repay the favors which Jonathan[q] had done him, but oppressed him greatly.

54 After this Trypho returned, and with him the young boy Antiochus, who began to reign and put on the crown. [55]All the troops that Demetrius had cast off gathered around him, and they fought against Demetrius,[r] and he fled and was routed. [56]And Trypho captured the elephants[s] and gained control of Antioch. [57]Then the young Antiochus wrote to Jonathan, saying, "I confirm you in the high priesthood and set you over the four districts and make you one of the friends of the king." [58]And he sent him gold plate and a table service, and granted him the right to drink from gold cups and dress in purple and wear a gold buckle. [59]Simon his brother he made governor from the Ladder of Tyre to the borders of Egypt.

60 Then Jonathan set forth and traveled beyond the river and among the cities, and all the army of Syria gathered to him as allies. When he came to Askalon, the people of the city met him and paid him honor. [61]From there he departed to Gaza, but the men of Gaza shut him out. So he besieged it and burned its suburbs with fire and plundered them. [62]Then the people of Gaza pleaded with Jonathan, and he made peace with them, and took the sons of their rulers as hostages and sent them to Jerusalem. And he passed through the country as far as Damascus.

63 Then Jonathan heard that the officers of Demetrius had come to

q Gk *he*   *r* Gk *him*   *s* Gk *beasts*

(compare v. 53) to evacuate the citadel and other fortresses. **45–47:** *Men of the city*, a mob, not an army. *Jews*, Judeans (see 2.23 n.).

11.53–74: Estrangement of Demetrius and Jonathan. 53: Josephus says that Demetrius now demanded tribute as before (*Antiquities*, XIII. v. 3). **54:** *Antiochus* VI Epiphanes, son of Alexander Balas, reigned nominally from about 145 to 142 B.C. **55:** *All the troops*, v. 38. **57:** *The four districts*, the three of v. 34 and probably Ekron (10.89). **58:** *Gold cups*, Est.1.7. *Gold buckle*, sign of being a friend of the king (see 2.18 n.). **59:** *The Ladder of Tyre*, the coastline between Ptolemais and Tyre. *The borders of Egypt*, probably Wadi el-Arish. **60:** *The river*, Jordan. **61:** *Gaza*, southernmost of the Philistine cities, near the Egyptian border (Jg.16.1). **62:** *Damascus*, outside Jonathan's control, but his influence extended nearly that far. **63:** *Kadesh*, northwest of Lake Huleh or Merom (Jg.4.9).

Kadesh in Galilee with a large army, intending to remove him from office. [64]He went to meet them, but left his brother Simon in the country. [65]Simon encamped before Beth-zur and fought against it for many days and hemmed it in. [66]Then they asked him to grant them terms of peace, and he did so. He removed them from there, took possession of the city, and set a garrison over it.

[67]Jonathan and his army encamped by the waters of Gennesaret. Early in the morning they marched to the plain of Hazor, [68]and behold, the army of the foreigners met him in the plain; they had set an ambush against him in the mountains, but they themselves met him face to face. [69]Then the men in ambush emerged from their places and joined battle. [70]All the men with Jonathan fled; not one of them was left except Mattathias the son of Absalom and Judas the son of Chalphi, commanders of the forces of the army. [71]Jonathan rent his garments and put dust on his head, and prayed. [72]Then he turned back to the battle against the enemy[t] and routed them, and they fled. [73]When his men who were fleeing saw this, they returned to him and joined him in the pursuit as far as Kadesh, to their camp, and there they encamped. [74]As many as three thousand of the foreigners fell that day. And Jonathan returned to Jerusalem.

12 Now when Jonathan saw that the time was favorable for him, he chose men and sent them to Rome to confirm and renew the friendship with them. [2]He also sent letters to the same effect to the Spartans and to other places. [3]So they went to Rome and entered the senate chamber and said, "Jonathan the high priest and the Jewish nation have sent us to renew the former friendship and alliance with them." [4]And the Romans[u] gave them letters to the people in every place, asking them to provide for the envoys[v] safe conduct to the land of Judah.

5 This is a copy of the letter which Jonathan wrote to the Spartans: [6]"Jonathan the high priest, the senate of the nation, the priests, and the rest of the Jewish people to their brethren the Spartans, greeting. [7]Already in time past a letter was sent to Onias the high priest from Arius,[w] who was king among you, stating that you are our brethren, as the appended copy shows. [8]Onias welcomed the envoy with honor, and received the letter, which contained a clear declaration of alliance and friendship. [9]Therefore, though we have no need of these things, since we have as encouragement the holy books which are in our hands, [10]we have undertaken to send to renew our brotherhood and friendship with you, so that we may not become estranged from you, for considerable time has passed since you sent your letter to us. [11]We therefore remember you constantly on every occasion, both in our feasts and on other appropriate days, at the sacrifices which we offer and in our prayers, as it is right and proper to remember brethren. [12]And we rejoice in your glory. [13]But as for ourselves, many afflictions and many wars have encircled us; the kings round about us have waged war against us. [14]We were unwilling to annoy you and our other allies and friends with these wars, [15]for we have the help which comes from Heaven for our aid; and we were delivered from our enemies and our enemies were humbled. [16]We there-

t Gk *them*
u Gk *they*
v Gk *them*
w Vg Compare verse 20: Gk *Darius*

67: *The waters of Gennesaret*, the Sea of Galilee. *Hazor*, southwest of Lake Huleh (Jos.11.1). **12.1–23**: **Alliances with the Romans and Spartans** (compare ch. 8). **2**: *The Spartans* had not joined the Achaean league against Rome. **4**: *The Romans* continued the old alliance in order to keep Syria weak. **6**: *The senate*, over which the high priest presided; it corresponds to the later council or Sanhedrin (Mk.14.55). **7**: *Onias* I, high priest 320–290 B.C. *Arius*, king of Sparta

fore have chosen Numenius the son of Antiochus and Antipater the son of Jason, and have sent them to Rome to renew our former friendship and alliance with them. [17]We have commanded them to go also to you and greet you and deliver to you this letter from us concerning the renewal of our brotherhood. [18]And now please send us a reply to this."

19 This is a copy of the letter which they sent to Onias: [20]"Arius, king of the Spartans, to Onias the high priest, greeting. [21]It has been found in writing concerning the Spartans and the Jews that they are brethren and are of the family of Abraham. [22]And now that we have learned this, please write us concerning your welfare; [23]we on our part write to you that your cattle and your property belong to us, and ours belong to you. We therefore command that our envoys[x] report to you accordingly."

24 Now Jonathan heard that the commanders of Demetrius had returned, with a larger force than before, to wage war against him. [25]So he marched away from Jerusalem and met them in the region of Hamath, for he gave them no opportunity to invade his own country. [26]He sent spies to their camp, and they returned and reported to him that the enemy[y] were being drawn up in formation to fall upon the Jews[z] by night. [27]So when the sun set, Jonathan commanded his men to be alert and to keep their arms at hand so as to be ready all night for battle, and he stationed outposts around the camp. [28]When the enemy heard that Jonathan and his men were prepared for battle, they were

afraid and were terrified at heart; so they kindled fires in their camp and withdrew.[a] [29]But Jonathan and his men did not know it until morning, for they saw the fires burning. [30]Then Jonathan pursued them, but he did not overtake them, for they had crossed the Eleutherus river. [31]So Jonathan turned aside against the Arabs who are called Zabadeans, and he crushed them and plundered them. [32]Then he broke camp and went to Damascus, and marched through all that region.

33 Simon also went forth and marched through the country as far as Askalon and the neighboring strongholds. He turned aside to Joppa and took it by surprise, [34]for he had heard that they were ready to hand over the stronghold to the men whom Demetrius had sent. And he stationed a garrison there to guard it.

35 When Jonathan returned he convened the elders of the people and planned with them to build strongholds in Judea, [36]to build the walls of Jerusalem still higher, and to erect a high barrier between the citadel and the city to separate it from the city, in order to isolate it so that its garrison[b] could neither buy nor sell. [37]So they gathered together to build up the city; part of the wall on the valley to the east had fallen, and he repaired the section called Chaphenatha. [38]And Simon built Adida in the Shephelah; he fortified it and installed gates with bolts.

39 Then Trypho attempted to become king of Asia and put on the crown, and to raise his hand against

x Gk *they*
y Gk *they*
z Gk *them*
a Other ancient authorities omit *and withdrew*
b Gk *they*

309–265 B.C. **21:** *Brethren ... of the family of Abraham*, compare v. 7; such a tradition was evidently current in the East.

12.24–53: Jonathan captured by Trypho. 24–25: Jonathan met the Syrians at the border of Judea to prevent an invasion. *Hamath*, on the Orontes, modern Hama in Syria. **28:** *Kindled fires*, so that Jonathan would think they were still in camp. **30:** *The Eleutherus* is too far north (see 11.7 n.); perhaps the Orontes. **31:** *Zabadeans*, perhaps people northwest of Damascus. **36:** The purpose was to starve out the garrison. **37:** *The valley to the east*, the Kidron (1 Kg.2.37; Jn.18.1); here the slope was sometimes steep. The location of *Chaphenatha* is unknown. **38:** *Adida*, about three miles east of Lydda (Ezra 2.33; Neh.7.37). *Shephelah*, the foothill country

[253]

Antiochus the king. [40]He feared that Jonathan might not permit him to do so, but might make war on him, so he kept seeking to seize and kill him, and he marched forth and came to Beth-shan. [41]Jonathan went out to meet him with forty thousand picked fighting men, and he came to Beth-shan. [42]When Trypho saw that he had come with a large army, he was afraid to raise his hand against him. [43]So he received him with honor and commended him to all his friends, and he gave him gifts and commanded his friends and his troops to obey him as they would himself. [44]Then he said to Jonathan, "Why have you wearied all these people when we are not at war? [45]Dismiss them now to their homes and choose for yourself a few men to stay with you, and come with me to Ptolemais. I will hand it over to you as well as the other strongholds and the remaining troops and all the officials, and will turn round and go home. For that is why I am here."

[46]Jonathan[c] trusted him and did as he said; he sent away the troops, and they returned to the land of Judah. [47]He kept with himself three thousand men, two thousand of whom he left in Galilee, while a thousand accompanied him. [48]But when Jonathan entered Ptolemais, the men of Ptolemais closed the gates and seized him, and all who had entered with him they killed with the sword.

[49]Then Trypho sent troops and cavalry into Galilee and the Great Plain to destroy all Jonathan's soldiers. [50]But they realized that Jonathan[c] had been seized and had perished along with his men, and they encouraged one another and kept marching in close formation, ready for battle. [51]When their pursuers saw that they would fight for their lives, they turned back. [52]So they all reached the land of Judah safely, and they mourned for Jonathan and his companions and were in great fear; and all Israel mourned deeply. [53]And all the nations round about them tried to destroy them, for they said, "They have no leader or helper. Now therefore let us make war on them and blot out the memory of them from among men."

[13] Simon heard that Trypho had assembled a large army to invade the land of Judah and destroy it, [2]and he saw that the people were trembling and fearful. So he went up to Jerusalem, and gathering the people together [3]he encouraged them, saying to them, "You yourselves know what great things I and my brothers and the house of my father have done for the laws and the sanctuary; you know also the wars and the difficulties which we have seen. [4]By reason of this all my brothers have perished for the sake of Israel, and I alone am left. [5]And now, far be it from me to spare my life in any time of distress, for I am not better than my brothers. [6]But I will avenge my nation and the sanctuary and your wives and children, for all the nations have gathered together out of hatred to destroy us."

[7]The spirit of the people was rekindled when they heard these words, [8]and they answered in a loud voice, "You are our leader in place of Judas and Jonathan your brother. [9]Fight our battles, and all that you say to us we will do." [10]So he assembled all the warriors and hastened to complete the walls of Jerusalem, and he fortified it on every side. [11]He sent Jonathan the son of Absalom to Joppa, and with him

c Gk he

---

between the coastal plain and the central highlands. **40:** *Beth-shan*, see 5.52 n. **45:** *The other strongholds*, probably along the coast. **52:** *They mourned*, because of the supposition that Jonathan had been slain; but see 13.23.

    13.1–30: Simon becomes leader; death of Jonathan. 1: *Simon* (2.3) was governor of the coastal area (11.59). **4:** Eleazar, Judah, and John had died (6.46; 9.18,42), and Simon supposed that Jonathan had been slain. **7–8:** Jonathan had been chosen by his friends (9.28–30); *the people* now elected Simon *leader*, but not yet high priest (compare 14.41). **11:** *Jonathan the son of*

a considerable army; he drove out its occupants and remained there.

12 Then Trypho departed from Ptolemais with a large army to invade the land of Judah, and Jonathan was with him under guard. [13]And Simon encamped in Adida, facing the plain. [14]Trypho learned that Simon had risen up in place of Jonathan his brother, and that he was about to join battle with him, so he sent envoys to him and said, [15]"It is for the money that Jonathan your brother owed the royal treasury, in connection with the offices he held, that we are detaining him. [16]Send now a hundred talents of silver and two of his sons as hostages, so that when released he will not revolt against us, and we will release him."

17 Simon knew that they were speaking deceitfully to him, but he sent to get the money and the sons, lest he arouse great hostility among the people, who might say, [18]"Because Simon[d] did not send him the money and the sons, he perished." [19]So he sent the sons and the hundred talents, but Trypho[e] broke his word and did not release Jonathan.

20 After this Trypho came to invade the country and destroy it, and he circled around by the way to Adora. But Simon and his army kept marching along opposite him to every place he went. [21]Now the men in the citadel kept sending envoys to Trypho urging him to come to them by way of the wilderness and to send them food. [22]So Trypho got all his cavalry ready to go, but that night a very heavy snow fell, and he did not go because of the snow. He marched off and went into the land of Gilead. [23]When he approached Baskama, he killed Jonathan, and he

was buried there. [24]Then Trypho turned back and departed to his own land.

25 And Simon sent and took the bones of Jonathan his brother, and buried him in Modein, the city of his fathers. [26]All Israel bewailed him with great lamentation, and mourned for him many days. [27]And Simon built a monument over the tomb of his father and his brothers; he made it high that it might be seen, with polished stone at the front and back. [28]He also erected seven pyramids, opposite one another, for his father and mother and four brothers. [29]And for the pyramids[f] he devised an elaborate setting, erecting about them great columns, and upon the columns he put suits of armor for a permanent memorial, and beside the suits of armor carved ships, so that they could be seen by all who sail the sea. [30]This is the tomb which he built in Modein; it remains to this day.

31 Trypho dealt treacherously with the young king Antiochus; he killed him [32]and became king in his place, putting on the crown of Asia; and he brought great calamity upon the land. [33]But Simon built up the strongholds of Judea and walled them all around, with high towers and great walls and gates and bolts, and he stored food in the strongholds. [34]Simon also chose men and sent them to Demetrius the king with a request to grant relief to the country, for all that Trypho did was to plunder. [35]Demetrius the king sent him a favorable reply to this request, and wrote him a letter as follows, [36]"King Demetrius to Simon, the high

d Gk *I*   *e* Gk *he*
f Gk *for these*

Absalom, perhaps a brother of Mattathias (11.70). **15–16:** He regarded *Jonathan* as a vassal of Syria who had to pay for *the offices he held* (11.57). **20:** *Adora*, or Adoraim, now Dura, five miles southwest of Hebron (2 Chr.11.9). **22–23:** *He marched off*, south of the Dead Sea. *Baskama*, possibly northeast of the Sea of Galilee. *He killed Jonathan*, late in 143 or early in 142 B.C. **25:** *Modein*, 2.1; 9.19. **28:** *Pyramids*, following Egyptian fashion. **29:** *Carved ships*, symbols claiming domination of the sea, found also on coins of Herod and Archelaus.

13.31–53: Simon makes Judea independent. 31–32: *He killed him*, probably in 142 B.C. *Antiochus* VI was about seven years old and had reigned since 145 (11.54). *Became king*, about 142 or 141 B.C. **34:** *Demetrius* II (see 10.67 n.) now disputed the throne with Trypho. **36–40:** The letter, addressed to *the elders and nation* and to *Simon* as head of a priestly state, recognizes

priest and friend of kings, and to the elders and nation of the Jews, greeting. [37]We have received the gold crown and the palm branch which you[g] sent, and we are ready to make a general peace with you and to write to our officials to grant you release from tribute. [38]All the grants that we have made to you remain valid, and let the strongholds that you have built be your possession. [39]We pardon any errors and offenses committed to this day, and cancel the crown tax which you owe; and whatever other tax has been collected in Jerusalem shall be collected no longer. [40]And if any of you are qualified to be enrolled in our bodyguard,[h] let them be enrolled, and let there be peace between us."

41 In the one hundred and seventieth year[i] the yoke of the Gentiles was removed from Israel, [42]and the people began to write in their documents and contracts, "In the first year of Simon the great high priest and commander and leader of the Jews."

43 In those days Simon[j] encamped against Gazara[k] and surrounded it with troops. He made a siege engine, brought it up to the city, and battered and captured one tower. [44]The men in the siege engine leaped out into the city, and a great tumult arose in the city. [45]The men in the city, with their wives and children, went up on the wall with their clothes rent, and they cried out with a loud voice, asking Simon to make peace with them; [46]they said, "Do not treat us according to our wicked acts but according to your mercy." [47]So Simon reached an agreement with them and stopped fighting against them. But he expelled

them from the city and cleansed the houses in which the idols were, and then entered it with hymns and praise. [48]He cast out of it all uncleanness, and settled in it men who observed the law. He also strengthened its fortifications and built in it a house for himself.

49 The men in the citadel at Jerusalem were prevented from going out to the country and back to buy and sell. So they were very hungry, and many of them perished from famine. [50]Then they cried to Simon to make peace with them, and he did so. But he expelled them from there and cleansed the citadel from its pollutions. [51]On the twenty-third day of the second month, in the one hundred and seventy-first year,[l] the Jews[m] entered it with praise and palm branches, and with harps and cymbals and stringed instruments, and with hymns and songs, because a great enemy had been crushed and removed from Israel. [52]And Simon[n] decreed that every year they should celebrate this day with rejoicing. He strengthened the fortifications of the temple hill alongside the citadel, and he and his men dwelt there. [53]And Simon saw that John his son had reached manhood, so he made him commander of all the forces, and he dwelt in Gazara.

14 In the one hundred and seventy-second year[o] Demetrius the king assembled his forces and marched into Media to secure help, so that he could make war against Trypho.

g The word *you* in verses 37–40 is plural
h Or *court*
i 142 B.C.
j Gk *he*
k Cn: Gk *Gaza*
l 141 B.C.
m Gk *they*
n Gk *he*
o 140 B.C.

sovereignty (compare v. 42). The weakness of Demetrius II made possible a great diplomatic victory. **42:** The new era, replacing the Seleucid era, is a mark of sovereignty. It is debated whether Simon was the first of the Hasmoneans to strike coins. **43:** A Greek inscription hostile to Simon has been found at *Gazara.* **47–48:** The later Hasmoneans continued the policy of settling Jews in strategic places. **49–50:** *The men in the citadel,* probably Trypho's men, did not surrender until starved out. **51:** *The second month,* Iyyar or May. *Palm branches* symbolized victory (2 Macc.10.7). **52:** *Celebrate this day,* see 7.49 n. **53:** *John* Hyrcanus reigned as high priest 134–104 B.C.

14.1–24: Capture of Demetrius II. 1: Other historians date this invasion in 138 B.C., the year

²When Arsaces the king of Persia and Media heard that Demetrius had invaded his territory, he sent one of his commanders to take him alive. ³And he went and defeated the army of Demetrius, and seized him and took him to Arsaces, who put him under guard.

⁴The land^p had rest all the days of
   Simon.
   He sought the good of his
      nation;
   his rule was pleasing to them,
      as was the honor shown him, all
         his days.
⁵To crown all his honors he took
      Joppa for a harbor,
   and opened a way to the isles of
      the sea.
⁶He extended the borders of his
      nation,
   and gained full control of the
      country.
⁷He gathered a host of captives;
   he ruled over Gazara and
      Beth-zur and the citadel,
   and he removed its uncleanness
      from it;
   and there was none to oppose
      him.
⁸They tilled their land in peace;
   the ground gave its increase,
   and the trees of the plains their
      fruit.
⁹Old men sat in the streets;
   they all talked together of good
      things;
   and the youths donned the
      glories and garments of war.
¹⁰He supplied the cities with food,
   and furnished them with the
      means of defense,
   till his renown spread to the ends
      of the earth.

¹¹He established peace in the land,
   and Israel rejoiced with great joy.
¹²Each man sat under his vine and
      his fig tree,
   and there was none to make
      them afraid.
¹³No one was left in the land to fight
      them,
   and the kings were crushed in
      those days.
¹⁴He strengthened all the humble of
      his people;
   he sought out the law,
   and did away with every lawless
      and wicked man.
¹⁵He made the sanctuary glorious,
   and added to the vessels of the
      sanctuary.

16 It was heard in Rome, and as far away as Sparta, that Jonathan had died, and they were deeply grieved. ¹⁷When they heard that Simon his brother had become high priest in his place, and that he was ruling over the country and the cities in it, ¹⁸they wrote to him on bronze tablets to renew with him the friendship and alliance which they had established with Judas and Jonathan his brothers. ¹⁹And these were read before the assembly in Jerusalem.

20 This is a copy of the letter which the Spartans sent: "The rulers and the city of the Spartans to Simon the high priest and to the elders and the priests and the rest of the Jewish people, our brethren, greeting. ²¹The envoys who were sent to our people have told us about your glory and honor, and we rejoiced at their coming. ²²And what they said we have recorded in our public decrees, as follows, 'Numenius the son of Antiochus and Antipater the

p Other authorities add *of Judah*

---

in which he was captured. *Media*, lying west of Tehran, was still claimed by the Seleucids. **2–3**: *Arsaces* VI Mithradates I (171–138 B.C.), founder of the Parthian Empire, treated Demetrius kindly and later married him to his sister.

14.4–15: A contemporary poem of rejoicing. **5–7**: 13.41–53. *A harbor*, important for trade connections with the sea (13.11). *The isles of the sea*, Cyprus, Rhodes, and Crete. **12**: 1 Kg.4.25; Mic.4.4.

14.16–24: Alliances with Rome and Sparta. Simon was perhaps the first high priest recognized by the Roman senate as ruler of the Jews. **19**: *The assembly*, the people as a whole. **22**: *Numenius* and *Antipater*, 12.16.

son of Jason, envoys of the Jews, have come to us to renew their friendship with us. ²³It has pleased our people to receive these men with honor and to put a copy of their words in the public archives, so that the people of the Spartans may have a record of them. And they have sent a copy of this to Simon the high priest.' "

24 After this Simon sent Numenius to Rome with a large gold shield weighing a thousand minas, to confirm the alliance with the Romans.*q*

25 When the people heard these things they said, "How shall we thank Simon and his sons? ²⁶For he and his brothers and the house of his father have stood firm; they have fought and repulsed Israel's enemies and established its freedom." ²⁷So they made a record on bronze tablets and put it upon pillars on Mount Zion.

This is a copy of what they wrote: "On the eighteenth day of Elul, in the one hundred and seventy-second year,*r* which is the third year of Simon the great high priest, ²⁸in Asaramel,*s* in the great assembly of the priests and the people and the rulers of the nation and the elders of the country, the following was proclaimed to us:

29 "Since wars often occurred in the country, Simon the son of Mattathias, a priest of the sons*t* of Joarib, and his brothers, exposed themselves to danger and resisted the enemies of their nation, in order that their sanctuary and the law might be preserved; and they brought great glory to their nation. ³⁰Jonathan rallied the*u* nation, and became their high priest, and was gathered to his people. ³¹And when their enemies decided to invade their

country and lay hands on their sanctuary, ³²then Simon rose up and fought for his nation. He spent great sums of his own money; he armed the men of his nation's forces and paid them wages. ³³He fortified the cities of Judea, and Beth-zur on the borders of Judea, where formerly the arms of the enemy had been stored, and he placed there a garrison of Jews. ³⁴He also fortified Joppa, which is by the sea, and Gazara, which is on the borders of Azotus, where the enemy formerly dwelt. He settled Jews there, and provided in those cities*v* whatever was necessary for their restoration.

35 "The people saw Simon's faithfulness*w* and the glory which he had resolved to win for his nation, and they made him their leader and high priest, because he had done all these things and because of the justice and loyalty which he had maintained toward his nation. He sought in every way to exalt his people. ³⁶And in his days things prospered in his hands, so that the Gentiles were put out of the*x* country, as were also the men in the city of David in Jerusalem, who had built themselves a citadel from which they used to sally forth and defile the environs of the sanctuary and do great damage to its purity. ³⁷He settled Jews in it, and fortified it for the safety of the country and of the city, and built the walls of Jerusalem higher.

38 "In view of these things King Demetrius confirmed him in the high priesthood, ³⁹and he made him one of

q Gk *them*   *r* 140 B.C.
s This word resembles the Hebrew words for *the court of the people of God* or *the prince of the people of God*
t The Greek text of this phrase is uncertain
u Gk *their*   *v* Gk *them*
w Other authorities read *conduct*   *x* Gk *their*

24: *Weighing a thousand minas*, an obvious exaggeration; a Greek mina is over 15 ounces (troy).
14.25–49: **Simon elected high priest, military commander, and ruler.** The formal document of vv. 27–49 served as a constitution for the new state of Judea. **27–28:** *Bronze tablets*, see 8.22 n. *Mount Zion*, 1.33; 4.37. *Elul*, August–September. *Third year*, see 13.42 n. *The great assembly*, or synagogue, represented all "states" or classes. In theory the high priest held his office by divine appointment, indicated by descent from a particular family. Since there was no legitimate claimant, Simon was legitimized by a democratic process (v. 41). **29:** *Sons of Joarib*, see 2.1 n. **30:** The decree recognizes in retrospect the office of *Jonathan*, first Hasmonean *high priest*. **32:** Use of *his own money* had not been previously mentioned. **33–34:** 13.43–48; 14.3–7. **35:** The high priest must have moral responsibility along with his powers. **36–37:** 1.34; 4.41,60;

the king's[y] friends and paid him high honors. [40]For he had heard that the Jews were addressed by the Romans as friends and allies and brethren, and that the Romans[z] had received the envoys of Simon with honor.

41 "And[a] the Jews and their priests decided that Simon should be their leader and high priest for ever, until a trustworthy prophet should arise, [42]and that he should be governor over them and that he should take charge of the sanctuary and appoint men over its tasks and over the country and the weapons and the strongholds, and that he should take charge of the sanctuary, [43]and that he should be obeyed by all, and that all contracts in the country should be written in his name, and that he should be clothed in purple and wear gold.

44 "And none of the people or priests shall be permitted to nullify any of these decisions or to oppose what he says, or to convene an assembly in the country without his permission, or to be clothed in purple or put on a gold buckle. [45]Whoever acts contrary to these decisions or nullifies any of them shall be liable to punishment."

46 And all the people agreed to grant Simon the right to act in accord with these decisions. [47]So Simon accepted and agreed to be high priest, to be commander and ethnarch of the Jews and priests, and to be protector of them all.[b] [48]And they gave orders to inscribe this decree upon bronze tablets, to put them up in a conspicuous place in the precincts of the sanctuary, [49]and to deposit copies of them in the treasury, so that Simon and his sons might have them.

15 Antiochus, the son of Demetrius the king, sent a letter from the islands of the sea to Simon, the priest and ethnarch of the Jews, and to all the nation; [2]its contents were as follows: "King Antiochus to Simon the high priest and ethnarch and to the nation of the Jews, greeting. [3]Whereas certain pestilent men have gained control of the kingdom of our fathers, and I intend to lay claim to the kingdom so that I may restore it as it formerly was, and have recruited a host of mercenary troops and have equipped warships, [4]and intend to make a landing in the country so that I may proceed against those who have destroyed our country and those who have devastated many cities in my kingdom, [5]now therefore I confirm to you all the tax remissions that the kings before me have granted you, and release from all the other payments from which they have released you. [6]I permit you to mint your own coinage as money for your country, [7]and I grant freedom to Jerusalem and the sanctuary. All the weapons which you have prepared and the strongholds which you have built and now hold shall remain yours. [8]Every debt you owe to the royal treasury and any such future debts shall be canceled for you from henceforth and for all time. [9]When we gain control of our kingdom, we will bestow great honor upon you and your nation and the temple, so that your glory

y Gk *his*   z Gk *they*
a Gk *honor; and that*
b Or *to preside over them all*

6.18; 13.49–52. **41–43:** The office was to be hereditary in Simon's family, but since this was an act of the nation rather than of God, a *trustworthy prophet* might annul or confirm the decision (see 4.46 n.). *Clothed in purple and wear gold*, like a king or head of state. From Alexander Janneus onwards (103–76 B.C.), the Hasmoneans assumed the title of king. **46–47:** In this social contract, both the people and Simon accept the conditions. *Ethnarch*, civil magistrate. **49:** The *treasury* in the temple served as a national archive.

15.1–14: Arrival of Antiochus VII. 1: *Antiochus VII* (known as Sidetes because reared at Side in Pamphylia), younger brother of Demetrius II, reigned 138–129 B.C. After his brother's capture he married Cleopatra III (10.57–58; 11.12). **3:** *Pestilent men*, Trypho and his faction. **5:** He reaffirms his brother's grants (13.39). **6:** *To mint your own coinage* was legal recognition of independence. When the Seleucids permitted subject cities to coin money, it bore the king's name. **7–8:** 13.38–39.

will become manifest in all the earth."

10 In the one hundred and seventy-fourth year[c] Antiochus set out and invaded the land of his fathers. All the troops rallied to him, so that there were few with Trypho. [11]Antiochus pursued him, and he came in his flight to Dor, which is by the sea; [12]for he knew that troubles had converged upon him, and his troops had deserted him. [13]So Antiochus encamped against Dor, and with him were a hundred and twenty thousand warriors and eight thousand cavalry. [14]He surrounded the city, and the ships joined battle from the sea; he pressed the city hard from land and sea, and permitted no one to leave or enter it.

15 Then Numenius and his companions arrived from Rome, with letters to the kings and countries, in which the following was written: [16]"Lucius, consul of the Romans, to King Ptolemy, greeting. [17]The envoys of the Jews have come to us as our friends and allies to renew our ancient friendship and alliance. They had been sent by Simon the high priest and by the people of the Jews, [18]and have brought a gold shield weighing a thousand minas. [19]We therefore have decided to write to the kings and countries that they should not seek their harm or make war against them and their cities and their country, or make alliance with those who war against them. [20]And it has seemed good to us to accept the shield from them. [21]Therefore if any pestilent men have fled to you from their country, hand them over to Simon the high priest, that he may punish them according to their law."

22 The consul[d] wrote the same thing to Demetrius the king and to Attalus and Ariarathes and Arsaces, [23]and to all the countries, and to Sampsames,[e] and to the Spartans, and to Delos, and to Myndos, and to Sicyon, and to Caria, and to Samos, and to Pamphylia, and to Lycia, and to Halicarnassus, and to Rhodes, and to Phaselis, and to Cos, and to Side, and to Aradus and Gortyna and Cnidus and Cyprus and Cyrene. [24]They also sent a copy of these things to Simon the high priest.

25 Antiochus the king besieged Dor anew,[f] continually throwing his forces against it and making engines of war; and he shut Trypho up and kept him from going out or in. [26]And Simon sent to Antiochus[g] two thousand picked men, to fight for him, and silver and gold and much military equipment. [27]But he refused to receive them, and he broke all the agreements he formerly had made with Simon,[g] and became estranged from him. [28]He sent to him Athenobius, one of his friends, to confer with him, saying, "You hold control of Joppa and Gazara and the citadel in Jerusalem; they are cities of my kingdom. [29]You have devastated their territory, you have done great damage in the land, and you have taken possession of many places in my kingdom. [30]Now then, hand over the cities which you have seized and the tribute money of the places which you have conquered outside the borders of Judea; [31]or else give me for them five hundred talents of silver, and for the destruction that you have caused and

c 138 B.C.   d Gk He
e The name is uncertain
f Or *on the second day*
g Gk *him*

10: He first landed in Seleucia (11.8), where Cleopatra was living. 11: *Dor*, about nine miles north of Caesarea (Jg.1.27). 13: The numbers are probably exaggerated.
  15.15–24: Renewal of alliance with Rome. 16: If the letter is genuine, this is *Lucius* Calpurnius Piso, consul 140–139 B.C. *Ptolemy* VII Physcon reigned 145–116 B.C. 18: *Shield*, see 14.24 n. 22–23: *Demetrius* II was still a prisoner in Parthia; the Romans had not recognized Antiochus VII. *Attalus* II, king of Pergamum 159–138 B.C.; *Ariarathes* V, king of Cappadocia 162–130 B.C. *Delos* in the Cyclades and the other localities were free states in Greece, the Greek islands and Asia Minor. *Cyrene*, capital of Libya.
  15.25–16.10: War with Antiochus VII. 27: Josephus says that Antiochus accepted this aid (*Antiquities*, XIII. vii, 2). 28: *Cities of my kingdom*, this contradicts v. 7. 30: *Outside . . . Judea*,

the tribute money of the cities, five hundred talents more. Otherwise we will come and conquer you."

32 So Athenobius the friend of the king came to Jerusalem, and when he saw the splendor of Simon, and the sideboard with its gold and silver plate, and his great magnificence, he was amazed. He reported to him the words of the king, [33]but Simon gave him this reply: "We have neither taken foreign land nor seized foreign property, but only the inheritance of our fathers, which at one time had been unjustly taken by our enemies. [34]Now that we have the opportunity, we are firmly holding the inheritance of our fathers. [35]As for Joppa and Gazara, which you demand, they were causing great damage among the people and to our land; for them we will give a hundred talents." Athenobius[h] did not answer him a word, [36]but returned in wrath to the king and reported to him these words and the splendor of Simon and all that he had seen. And the king was greatly angered.

37 Now Trypho embarked on a ship and escaped to Orthosia. [38]Then the king made Cendebeus commander-in-chief of the coastal country, and gave him troops of infantry and cavalry. [39]He commanded him to encamp against Judea, and commanded him to build up Kedron and fortify its gates, and to make war on the people; but the king pursued Trypho. [40]So Cendebeus came to Jamnia and began to provoke the people and invade Judea and take the people captive and kill them. [41]He built up Kedron and stationed there horsemen and troops, so that they might go out and make raids along the highways of Judea, as the king had ordered him.

16 John went up from Gazara and reported to Simon his father what Cendebeus had done. [2]And Simon called in his two older sons Judas and John, and said to them: "I and my brothers and the house of my father have fought the wars of Israel from our youth until this day, and things have prospered in our hands so that we have delivered Israel many times. [3]But now I have grown old, and you by His mercy are mature in years. Take my place and my brother's, and go out and fight for our nation, and may the help which comes from Heaven be with you."

4 So John[i] chose out of the country twenty thousand warriors and horsemen, and they marched against Cendebeus and camped for the night in Modein. [5]Early in the morning they arose and marched into the plain, and behold, a large force of infantry and horsemen was coming to meet them; and a stream lay between them. [6]Then he and his army lined up against them. And he saw that the soldiers were afraid to cross the stream, so he crossed over first; and when his men saw him, they crossed over after him. [7]Then he divided the army and placed the horsemen in the midst of the infantry, for the cavalry of the enemy were very numerous. [8]And they sounded the trumpets, and Cendebeus and his army were put to flight, and many of them were wounded and fell; the rest fled into the stronghold. [9]At that time Judas the brother of John was wounded, but John pursued them until Cendebeus[j] reached Kedron, which he had built. [10]They also fled into the towers that were in the fields of Azotus,

h Gk *He*   *i* Other authorities read *he*
j Gk *he*

---

perhaps the districts of 11.34; but compare v. 8. **33**: The Hasmoneans claimed that all Palestine had always belonged by right to the Jews. **35**: *Joppa and Gazara*, 12.33; 13.43–48. **37**: *Orthosia*, a few miles north of Tripolis; from there Trypho went to Apamea, where he was besieged and slain. **39–40**: *Kedron*, perhaps Gedereth, southwest of Ekron (Jos.15.41). The plan was to control the coastal plain and recover Gazara and Joppa. **16.1**: *John* Hyrcanus I commanded Gazara (13.53). **4**: *Horsemen* are now for the first time part of the Judean army. **7**: The cavalry were unseasoned, and he protected their flanks. **8**: *The stronghold*, Kedron (15.39). **10**: *Azotus*, destroyed by Jonathan (10.84).

and John[j] burned it with fire, and about two thousand of them fell. And he returned to Judea safely.

11 Now Ptolemy the son of Abubus had been appointed governor over the plain of Jericho, and he had much silver and gold, [12]for he was son-in-law of the high priest. [13]His heart was lifted up; he determined to get control of the country, and made treacherous plans against Simon and his sons, to do away with them. [14]Now Simon was visiting the cities of the country and attending to their needs, and he went down to Jericho with Mattathias and Judas his sons, in the one hundred and seventy-seventh year,[k] in the eleventh month, which is the month of Shebat. [15]The son of Abubus received them treacherously in the little stronghold called Dok, which he had built; he gave them a great banquet, and hid men there. [16]When Simon and his sons were drunk, Ptolemy and his men rose up, took their weapons, and rushed in against Simon in the banquet hall, and they killed him and his two sons and some of his servants. [17]So he committed an act of great treachery and returned evil for good.

18 Then Ptolemy wrote a report about these things and sent it to the king, asking him to send troops to aid him and to turn over to him the cities and the country. [19]He sent other men to Gazara to do away with John; he sent letters to the captains asking them to come to him so that he might give them silver and gold and gifts; [20]and he sent other men to take possession of Jerusalem and the temple hill. [21]But some one ran ahead and reported to John at Gazara that his father and brothers had perished, and that "he has sent men to kill you also." [22]When he heard this, he was greatly shocked; and he seized the men who came to destroy him and killed them, for he had found out that they were seeking to destroy him.

23 The rest of the acts of John and his wars and the brave deeds which he did, and the building of the walls which he built, and his achievements, [24]behold, they are written in the chronicles of his high priesthood, from the time that he became high priest after his father.

j Gk *he*
k 134 B.C.

16.11–24: Death of Simon and accession of John Hyrcanus I. 11: *Plain of Jericho*, the fertile region north of the Dead Sea. **12:** *The high priest*, Simon. **14:** *Shebat*, February-March. **15:** *Dok*, 'Ain Duq, three miles northwest of Jericho. **18:** *The king*, Antiochus VII. **23:** *John* was high priest 134–104 B.C. When Antiochus later besieged Jerusalem, John was defeated but made peace and accompanied the king on an expedition to Parthia, where Antiochus was killed. Afterward he gained control of most of Palestine, and forced the Idumeans to adopt Judaism. Late in his reign the Pharisees turned against him and demanded that he give up the high priesthood. **24:** *The chronicles* have been lost.

THE SECOND BOOK OF THE

MACCABEES

Second Maccabees is an epitome or abridgment (2.23–28) of a five volume history, now lost, written by a certain Jason of Cyrene. Both Jason's work and 2 Maccabees were evidently composed in Greek, in which language the latter has been preserved. Jason narrated the events of Jewish history from the time of the high priest Onias III and the Syrian king Seleucus IV to the defeat of Nicanor's army (from about 180 to 161 B.C.), thus paralleling 1 Macc.1.10–7.50.

The purpose of Jason was to interpret history theologically. One of his favorite themes is the sanctity of the temple. He is the first writer known to us who celebrates the deeds of the martyrs, though there is a foreshadowing of such an interest in the book of Daniel. He also seems to be the first to teach clearly that the world was created out of nothing (7.28). He believed that the saints in heaven interceded for men on earth (15.11–16), and that the living might pray and offer sacrifices for the dead (12.43–45). His book includes accounts of marvelous portents and the miraculous intervention of angels. Jason seems not to have been a Pharisee; he may reflect the ideas of Jews at Antioch or possibly Alexandria.

The epitomist added chs. 1–2, 15.37–39, and several pretentious comments elsewhere. Sometimes there are signs of careless abbreviation, and he may have rearranged some incidents. Jason's history was probably not written before 110 B.C., and 2 Maccabees, as we have it, may have been composed some time during the first century B.C. It often supplements the information contained in 1 Maccabees, but its historical veracity is, on the whole, less trustworthy than that of 1 Maccabees.

THE JEWISH BRETHREN IN JERUSALEM and those in the land of Judea, To their Jewish brethren in Egypt, Greeting, and good peace.

2 May God do good to you, and may he remember his covenant with Abraham and Isaac and Jacob, his faithful servants. ³May he give you all a heart to worship him and to do his will with a strong heart and a willing spirit. ⁴May he open your heart to his law and his commandments, and may he bring peace. ⁵May he hear your prayers and be reconciled to you, and may he not forsake you in time of evil. ⁶We are now praying for you here.

7 In the reign of Demetrius, in the one hundred and sixty-ninth year,ᵃ we Jews wrote to you, in the critical distress which came upon us in those years after Jason and his company revolted from the holy land and the kingdom ⁸and burned the gate and shed innocent blood. We besought the Lord and we were heard, and we offered sacrifice and cereal offering, and we lighted the lamps and we set out the loaves. ⁹And now see that you keep the feast of booths in the month of Chislev, in the one hundred and eighty-eighth year.ᵇ

a 143 B.C.
b 124 B.C.

1.1–9: Letter to the Jews in Egypt. The epitomist, who abridged the history of Jason of Cyrene (2.23), includes two letters urging that the new festival be kept (v. 9). The first is addressed to the large Jewish community that had lived in Egypt since Alexander the Great (1 Macc.1.1). 1: Greek letters usually began with the word *greeting*, and Jewish ones with *peace* (Rom.1.7). 2: Gen.15.18; 26.3; 35.12; Lev.26.27–45. 5: To live outside Judea was thought of as divine punishment. 7: The previous letter was in the reign of Demetrius II (see 1 Macc. 10.67 n.). *The critical distress* was the capture and murder of the high priest Jonathan (1 Macc. 12.48; see 13.23 n.). *Jason and his company*, 4.7–22. *The kingdom*, rule of the legitimate high priests. 8: *Burned the gate*, 1 Macc.4.38. *Shed innocent blood*, 1 Macc.1.60–61. *We were heard*, i.e. by God, when Simon made Judea independent (1 Macc.13.1–42). 9: *The feast of booths* would properly be kept in September (Lev.23.33–43). This refers to Hanukkah, celebrated on the 25th of *Chislev* (November-December), commemorating Judas Maccabeus' restoration of the temple (10.1–8; 1 Macc.4.59). Palestinian Jews now wished the Egyptian Jews to observe the feast in 124 B.C., when they wrote.

10 Those in Jerusalem and those in Judea and the senate and Judas,

To Aristobulus, who is of the family of the anointed priests, teacher of Ptolemy the king, and to the Jews in Egypt,

Greeting, and good health.

11 Having been saved by God out of grave dangers we thank him greatly for taking our side against the king.[c] ¹²For he drove out those who fought against the holy city. ¹³For when the leader reached Persia with a force that seemed irresistible, they were cut to pieces in the temple of Nanea by a deception employed by the priests of Nanea. ¹⁴For under pretext of intending to marry her, Antiochus came to the place together with his friends, to secure most of its treasures as a dowry. ¹⁵When the priests of the temple of Nanea had set out the treasures and Antiochus had come with a few men inside the wall of the sacred precinct, they closed the temple as soon as he entered it. ¹⁶Opening the secret door in the ceiling, they threw stones and struck down the leader and his men, and dismembered them and cut off their heads and threw them to the people outside. ¹⁷Blessed in every way be our God, who has brought judgment upon those who have behaved impiously.

18 Since on the twenty-fifth day of Chislev we shall celebrate the purification of the temple, we thought it necessary to notify you, in order that you also may celebrate the feast of booths and the feast of the fire given when Nehemiah, who built the temple and the altar, offered sacrifices.

19 For when our fathers were being led captive to Persia, the pious priests of that time took some of the fire of the altar and secretly hid it in the hollow of a dry cistern, where they took such precautions that the place was unknown to any one. ²⁰But after many years had passed, when it pleased God, Nehemiah, having been commissioned by the king of Persia, sent the descendants of the priests who had hidden the fire to get it. And when they reported to us that they had not found fire but thick liquid, he ordered them to dip it out and bring it. ²¹And when the materials for the sacrifices were presented, Nehemiah ordered the priests to sprinkle the liquid on the wood and what was laid upon it. ²²When this was done and some time had passed and the sun, which had been clouded over, shone out, a great fire blazed up, so that all marveled. ²³And while the sacrifice was being consumed, the priests offered prayer—the priests and every one. Jonathan led, and the rest responded, as did Nehemiah. ²⁴The prayer was to this effect:

"O Lord, Lord God, Creator of all things, who art awe-inspiring and strong and just and merciful, who alone art King and art kind, ²⁵who alone art bountiful, who alone art just and al-

c Cn: Gk *as those who array themselves against a king*

1.10–2.18: Letter to Aristobulus. The purpose of the letter is to show why the new eight day festival should be kept, though it had not been prescribed by the Mosaic law. Nehemiah's rededication of the temple was a precedent (1.18–36). **10:** *The senate,* see 1 Macc.12.6 n. *The anointed priests,* descendants of Zadok (2 Chr.31.10), from whom high priests were chosen. One branch of these came to Egypt with Ptolemy I. *The king,* Ptolemy VII Physcon, who reigned 145–116 B.C. **11:** *Grave dangers,* in the time of king Antiochus IV (4.7). **13:** *The leader,* Antiochus IV, died later; his forces *were cut to pieces* (9.1–4; 1 Macc.6.1–4). *Nanea,* a Syrian goddess equated with Artemis or Aphrodite and the Persian Anahita. **14:** *Marry her,* the goddess, so as to obtain a large *dowry* from the treasures at her temple (compare 9.2; 1 Macc.6.1–4). **18:** *The feast of booths,* compare 1 Macc.10.21; 1 Kg.8.2; Neh.8.13–18. *The feast of the fire,* vv. 19–36. Fire and light are associated with Hanukkah, which is celebrated with a nine-branched candlestick. A Talmudic tradition tells of a small amount of oil that burned miraculously for a long time till new oil could be consecrated. **19:** *Persia,* actually Babylonia (2 Kg.24.14), later part of the Persian empire. **20:** *Nehemiah . . . commissioned,* Neh.2.7–8; his book does not contain the legend of the fire. *Thick liquid,* naphtha or petroleum (v. 36). **22:** 1 Kg.18.33–38.

mighty and eternal, who dost rescue Israel from every evil, who didst choose the fathers and consecrate them, [26]accept this sacrifice on behalf of all thy people Israel and preserve thy portion and make it holy. [27]Gather together our scattered people, set free those who are slaves among the Gentiles, look upon those who are rejected and despised, and let the Gentiles know that thou art our God. [28]Afflict those who oppress and are insolent with pride. [29]Plant thy people in thy holy place, as Moses said."

30 Then the priests sang the hymns. [31]And when the materials of the sacrifice were consumed, Nehemiah ordered that the liquid that was left should be poured upon large stones. [32]When this was done, a flame blazed up; but when the light from the altar shone back, it went out. [33]When this matter became known, and it was reported to the king of the Persians that, in the place where the exiled priests had hidden the fire, the liquid had appeared with which Nehemiah and his associates had burned the materials of the sacrifice, [34]the king investigated the matter, and enclosed the place and made it sacred. [35]And with those persons whom the king favored he exchanged many excellent gifts. [36]Nehemiah and his associates called this "nephthar," which means purification, but by most people it is called naphtha.[d]

2 One finds in the records that Jeremiah the prophet ordered those who were being deported to take some of the fire, as has been told, [2]and that the prophet after giving them the law instructed those who were being de-

ported not to forget the commandments of the Lord, nor to be led astray in their thoughts upon seeing the gold and silver statues and their adornment. [3]And with other similar words he exhorted them that the law should not depart from their hearts.

4 It was also in the writing that the prophet, having received an oracle, ordered that the tent and the ark should follow with him, and that he went out to the mountain where Moses had gone up and had seen the inheritance of God. [5]And Jeremiah came and found a cave, and he brought there the tent and the ark and the altar of incense, and he sealed up the entrance. [6]Some of those who followed him came up to mark the way, but could not find it. [7]When Jeremiah learned of it, he rebuked them and declared: "The place shall be unknown until God gathers his people together again and shows his mercy. [8]And then the Lord will disclose these things, and the glory of the Lord and the cloud will appear, as they were shown in the case of Moses, and as Solomon asked that the place should be specially consecrated."

9 It was also made clear that being possessed of wisdom Solomon[e] offered sacrifice for the dedication and completion of the temple. [10]Just as Moses prayed to the Lord, and fire came down from heaven and devoured the sacrifices, so also Solomon prayed, and the fire came down and consumed the whole burnt offerings. [11]And Moses said, "They were consumed because the sin offering had not been eaten."

d Gk *nephthai*　　*e* Gk *he*

25: *Who didst choose,* Gen.12.1–3; 22.15–18; Dt.14.2; Mal.1.2. **26:** *Thy portion,* Israel (Dt.32.9). *Holy,* Lev.19.2. **27:** *Gather together,* Ps.147.2; Jer.23.8; Sir.36.11; Bar.5.6. **28:** *Afflict . . . insolent,* 1 Sam.2.3–4; Lk.1.51–52. **29:** *As Moses said,* Dt.30.5. **34:** Localities where miracles occurred were *enclosed* as *sacred.* The Persians considered fire holy. **36:** *Nephthar* is an otherwise unknown word. **2.1:** No such *records* are known. *Jeremiah* remained in Judea after the exile (Jer.29.1–23; 40.1–42.7). **4:** Solomon brought the *tent* to Jerusalem with the ark (1 Kg.8.4). There is no further record in the Old Testament of the tent, but the ark was kept in the first temple; according to a later tradition Jeremiah concealed the ark after the temple was destroyed in 587–6 B.C. *The mountain,* Nebo (Dt.32.49). **8:** *The glory* and *the cloud* indicate God's direct presence (Ex.16.10; Mk.9.2–8). *Solomon,* 1 Kg.8.11. **9:** Solomon's *wisdom,* 1 Kg. 3.3–28; 4.29–34. *Offered sacrifice,* 1 Kg.8.62–64. **10:** *Moses prayed,* Lev.9.24. *Solomon,* 2 Chr.

¹²Likewise Solomon also kept the eight days.

13 The same things are reported in the records and in the memoirs of Nehemiah, and also that he founded a library and collected the books about the kings and prophets, and the writings of David, and letters of kings about votive offerings. ¹⁴In the same way Judas also collected all the books that had been lost on account of the war which had come upon us, and they are in our possession. ¹⁵So if you have need of them, send people to get them for you.

16 Since, therefore, we are about to celebrate the purification, we write to you. Will you therefore please keep the days? ¹⁷It is God who has saved all his people, and has returned the inheritance to all, and the kingship and priesthood and consecration, ¹⁸as he promised through the law. For we have hope in God that he will soon have mercy upon us and will gather us from everywhere under heaven into his holy place, for he has rescued us from great evils and has purified the place.

19 The story of Judas Maccabeus and his brothers, and the purification of the great temple, and the dedication of the altar, ²⁰and further the wars against Antiochus Epiphanes and his son Eupator, ²¹and the appearances which came from heaven to those who strove zealously on behalf of Judaism, so that though few in number they seized the whole land and pursued the barbarian hordes, ²²and recovered the temple famous throughout the world and freed the city and restored the laws that were about to be abolished, while the Lord with great kindness became gracious to them—²³all this, which has been set forth by Jason of Cyrene in five volumes, we shall attempt to condense into a single book. ²⁴For considering the flood of numbers involved and the difficulty there is for those who wish to enter upon the narratives of history because of the mass of material, ²⁵we have aimed to please those who wish to read, to make it easy for those who are inclined to memorize, and to profit all readers. ²⁶For us who have undertaken the toil of abbreviating, it is no light matter but calls for sweat and loss of sleep, ²⁷just as it is not easy for one who prepares a banquet and seeks the benefit of others. However, to secure the gratitude of many we will gladly endure the uncomfortable toil, ²⁸leaving the responsibility for exact details to the compiler, while devoting our effort to arriving at the outlines of the condensation. ²⁹For as the master builder of a new house must be concerned with the whole construction, while the one who undertakes its painting and decoration has to consider only what is suitable for its adornment, such in my judgment is the case with us. ³⁰It is the duty of the original historian to occupy the ground and to discuss matters from every side and to take trouble with details, ³¹but the one who

---

7.1. **11**: The meaning is obscure, but see Lev.10.16–19. **12**: *Eight days*, 1 Kg.8.65; 2 Chr.7.9. **13**: *The memoirs of Nehemiah*, Neh. ch. 8. There is no record that *he founded a library*, but the Pentateuch was canonized in his time, and part of *the books . . . and the writings of David* were perhaps collected then. *Votive offerings*, made to the temple (Ezra 7.15–20). **14**: *Judas* Maccabeus may have *collected all the books* remaining after the destruction in the time of Antiochus IV (1 Macc.1.56–57). **16**: 1.18. **17**: *The kingship*, independence; the Hasmoneans were not yet called kings. **18**: 1.27; Dt.30.3.

2.19–32: The epitomist's preface. This is like Polonius' long speech in *Hamlet:* "Since brevity is the soul of wit . . . I will be brief" (compare v. 31). He summarizes parts of the book (vv. 19–22): *wars against Antiochus* IV (4.7–10.9) and *his son* Antiochus V *Eupator* (10.10–13.26) and explains that he is condensing the work of *Jason* (vv. 23–24; see the Introduction to 2 Maccabees). **20–21**: *Appearances*, (Gr. *epiphaneiai*), true divine manifestations, in contrast to Antiochus' boastful title *Epiphanes*, "god manifest." *Judaism*, first known use of this term for the religion, in contrast to Hellenism (4.13).

recasts the narrative should be allowed to strive for brevity of expression and to forego exhaustive treatment. [32]At this point therefore let us begin our narrative, adding only so much to what has already been said; for it is foolish to lengthen the preface while cutting short the history itself.

3 While the holy city was inhabited in unbroken peace and the laws were very well observed because of the piety of the high priest Onias and his hatred of wickedness, [2]it came about that the kings themselves honored the place and glorified the temple with the finest presents, [3]so that even Seleucus, the king of Asia, defrayed from his own revenues all the expenses connected with the service of the sacrifices. [4]But a man named Simon, of the tribe of Benjamin, who had been made captain of the temple, had a disagreement with the high priest about the administration of the city market; [5]and when he could not prevail over Onias he went to Apollonius of Tarsus,[f] who at that time was governor of Coelesyria and Phoenicia. [6]He reported to him that the treasury in Jerusalem was full of untold sums of money, so that the amount of the funds could not be reckoned, and that they did not belong to the account of the sacrifices, but that it was possible for them to fall under the control of the king. [7]When Apollonius met the king, he told him of the money about which he had been informed. The king[g] chose

Heliodorus, who was in charge of his affairs, and sent him with commands to effect the removal of the aforesaid money. [8]Heliodorus at once set out on his journey, ostensibly to make a tour of inspection of the cities of Coelesyria and Phoenicia, but in fact to carry out the king's purpose.

9 When he had arrived at Jerusalem and had been kindly welcomed by the high priest of[h] the city, he told about the disclosure that had been made and stated why he had come, and he inquired whether this really was the situation. [10]The high priest explained that there were some deposits belonging to widows and orphans, [11]and also some money of Hyrcanus, son of Tobias, a man of very prominent position, and that it totaled in all four hundred talents of silver and two hundred of gold. To such an extent the impious Simon had misrepresented the facts. [12]And he said that it was utterly impossible that wrong should be done to those people who had trusted in the holiness of the place and in the sanctity and inviolability of the temple which is honored throughout the whole world. [13]But Heliodorus, because of the king's commands which he had, said that this money must in any case be confiscated for the king's treasury. [14]So he set a day and went in to direct the inspection of these funds.

There was no little distress through-

f Gk *Apollonius son of Tharseas*
g Gk *He*
h Some authorities read *and*

3.1–4.6: Simon's plot against Onias. 1: Jerusalem was not *in unbroken peace*, though quieter than in later years. *The high priest Onias* III, son of Simon the Just (Sir.50.1–21), ruled before 175 B.C. He turned against Syria and collaborated with Egypt, while his cousins, the family of Tobias, to which Simon (v. 4) belonged, were pro-Syrian. **2:** *The kings*, i.e. the Ptolemies of Egypt and Antiochus III the Great (reigned 233–187 B.C.). **3:** *Seleucus* IV Philopator, son of Antiochus III, reigned 187–175 B.C. The events of 3.1–4.6 were in his reign. He was assassinated by Heliodorus (v. 7). **4:** *Simon* was a grandson of Tobias, who married a sister of Onias II. When Onias II refused to pay tribute to Egypt, Ptolemy III took away his civil authority and appointed Joseph, son of Tobias, *captain of the temple*. His son Simon succeeded him. **5:** *Tarsus*, capital of Cilicia (Acts 9.11), then part of the Seleucid empire. *Coelesyria*, see 1 Macc. 10.69 n. *Apollonius* was removed from office at the death of Seleucus IV in 175 B.C. **7:** *Heliodorus*, see v. 5 n. **9:** *The high priest*, Onias III. **11:** *Hyrcanus*, actually son of Joseph and half-brother of Simon (v. 4), was pro-Egyptian. He fled east of the Jordan after 198 B.C. and built the fortress of 'Araq el-Emir. He committed suicide on the accession of Antiochus IV in 175 B.C. *Simon had misrepresented the facts* only in part; Onias and Hyrcanus probably withheld tribute.

out the whole city. [15]The priests prostrated themselves before the altar in their priestly garments and called toward heaven upon him who had given the law about deposits, that he should keep them safe for those who had deposited them. [16]To see the appearance of the high priest was to be wounded at heart, for his face and the change in his color disclosed the anguish of his soul. [17]For terror and bodily trembling had come over the man, which plainly showed to those who looked at him the pain lodged in his heart. [18]People also hurried out of their houses in crowds to make a general supplication because the holy place was about to be brought into contempt. [19]Women, girded with sackcloth under their breasts, thronged the streets. Some of the maidens who were kept indoors ran together to the gates, and some to the walls, while others peered out of the windows. [20]And holding up their hands to heaven, they all made entreaty. [21]There was something pitiable in the prostration of the whole populace and the anxiety of the high priest in his great anguish.

22 While they were calling upon the Almighty Lord that he would keep what had been entrusted safe and secure for those who had entrusted it, [23]Heliodorus went on with what had been decided. [24]But when he arrived at the treasury with his bodyguard, then and there the Sovereign of spirits and of all authority caused so great a manifestation that all who had been so bold as to accompany him were astounded by the power of God, and became faint with terror. [25]For there appeared to them a magnificently caparisoned horse, with a rider of frightening mien, and it rushed furiously at Heliodorus and struck at him with its front hoofs. Its rider was seen to have armor and weapons of gold.

[26]Two young men also appeared to him, remarkably strong, gloriously beautiful and splendidly dressed, who stood on each side of him and scourged him continuously, inflicting many blows on him. [27]When he suddenly fell to the ground and deep darkness came over him, his men took him up and put him on a stretcher [28]and carried him away, this man who had just entered the aforesaid treasury with a great retinue and all his bodyguard but was now unable to help himself; and they recognized clearly the sovereign power of God. [29]While he lay prostrate, speechless because of the divine intervention and deprived of any hope of recovery, [30]they praised the Lord who had acted marvelously for his own place. And the temple, which a little while before was full of fear and disturbance, was filled with joy and gladness, now that the Almighty Lord had appeared.

31 Quickly some of Heliodorus' friends asked Onias to call upon the Most High and to grant life to one who was lying quite at his last breath. [32]And the high priest, fearing that the king might get the notion that some foul play had been perpetrated by the Jews with regard to Heliodorus, offered sacrifice for the man's recovery. [33]While the high priest was making the offering of atonement, the same young men appeared again to Heliodorus, dressed in the same clothing, and they stood and said, "Be very grateful to Onias the high priest, since for his sake the Lord has granted you your life. [34]And see that you, who have been scourged by heaven, report to all men the majestic power of God." Having said this they vanished.

35 Then Heliodorus offered sacrifice to the Lord and made very great vows to the Savior of his life, and having bidden Onias farewell, he marched off

---

18: Temples, whether pagan or Jewish, were considered inviolate. 19: *Sackcloth,* a sign of mourning and penitence. *Maidens* were usually *kept indoors* until their marriage. 20: *Holding up their hands,* the ancient gesture of prayer (1 Kg.8.54; 1 Tim.2.8). 24: *Manifestation,* see 2.21 n. 29: *Speechless,* Lk.1.20. 31: *The Most High* (Gen.14.18), a title often used by non-Jews

with his forces to the king. ³⁶And he bore testimony to all men of the deeds of the supreme God, which he had seen with his own eyes. ³⁷When the king asked Heliodorus what sort of person would be suitable to send on another mission to Jerusalem, he replied, ³⁸"If you have any enemy or plotter against your government, send him there, for you will get him back thoroughly scourged, if he escapes at all, for there certainly is about the place some power of God. ³⁹For he who has his dwelling in heaven watches over that place himself and brings it aid, and he strikes and destroys those who come to do it injury." ⁴⁰This was the outcome of the episode of Heliodorus and the protection of the treasury.

4 The previously mentioned Simon, who had informed about the money against*ⁱ* his own country, slandered Onias, saying that it was he who had incited Heliodorus and had been the real cause of the misfortune. ²He dared to designate as a plotter against the government the man who was the benefactor of the city, the protector of his fellow countrymen, and a zealot for the laws. ³When his hatred progressed to such a degree that even murders were committed by one of Simon's approved agents, ⁴Onias recognized that the rivalry was serious and that Apollonius, the son of Menestheus*ʲ* and governor of Coelesyria and Phoenicia, was intensifying the malice of

Simon. ⁵So he betook himself to the king, not accusing his fellow citizens but having in view the welfare, both public and private, of all the people. ⁶For he saw that without the king's attention public affairs could not again reach a peaceful settlement, and that Simon would not stop his folly.

7 When Seleucus died and Antiochus who was called Epiphanes succeeded to the kingdom, Jason the brother of Onias obtained the high priesthood by corruption, ⁸promising the king at an interview*ᵏ* three hundred and sixty talents of silver and, from another source of revenue, eighty talents. ⁹In addition to this he promised to pay one hundred and fifty more if permission were given to establish by his authority a gymnasium and a body of youth for it, and to enrol the men of Jerusalem as citizens of Antioch. ¹⁰When the king assented and Jason*ˡ* came to office, he at once shifted his countrymen over to the Greek way of life. ¹¹He set aside the existing royal concessions to the Jews, secured through John the father of Eupolemus, who went on the mission to establish friendship and alliance with the Romans; and he destroyed the lawful ways of living and introduced new customs contrary to the law. ¹²For with alacrity he founded a gymnasium right under the citadel, and he induced the noblest of the

i Gk *and*
j Vg Compare verse 21: Greek uncertain
k Or *by a petition*   *l* Gk *he*

(Dan.3.26; Mk.5.7). **4.1–6:** Intrigues concerning the high priesthood. *Simon* (see 3.4 n.) was disturbed because *Onias* and *Heliodorus* were now friends. The latter may already have planned to kill Seleucus IV and wanted the high priest's good will. *Apollonius*, in favor with Seleucus, continued to support Simon. **5:** Before Onias arrived in Antioch, Seleucus had already been assassinated by Heliodorus (175 B.C.).
    4.7–22: Jason as high priest. 7: *Antiochus* IV *Epiphanes*, "god manifest," called Epimanes, "madman," by his enemies, was brother of Seleucus IV, and *succeeded to the kingdom* despite Heliodorus' attempt at revolution. He reigned 175–164 B.C. He had great ability but intense passion and pride (1 Macc.1.1–10). *Jason the brother of Onias* III (3.1), originally named Joshua, took a Greek name. **9–10:** Like Alexander the Great and his successors, Antiochus promoted *the Greek way of life* in order to strengthen his kingdom through cultural unity; this involved worship of other gods. *A gymnasium and a body of youth for it* were necessary *to enrol the men of Jerusalem as citizens of Antioch*, so that the city could coin money and have honors and commercial advantages. **11:** *Royal concessions*, granted by Antiochus III (3.2) The mission of *Eupolemus* (1 Macc.8.17) was later. *Destroyed*, 1 Macc.1.15,44–50. **12:** The broad-brimmed *Greek hat* was worn by the god Hermes; headgear has usually had national or

young men[m] to wear the Greek hat.
[13]There was such an extreme of Hellenization and increase in the adoption of foreign ways because of the surpassing wickedness of Jason, who was ungodly and no high priest, [14]that the priests were no longer intent upon their service at the altar. Despising the sanctuary and neglecting the sacrifices, they hastened to take part in the unlawful proceedings in the wrestling arena after the call to the discus, [15]disdaining the honors prized by their fathers and putting the highest value upon Greek forms of prestige. [16]For this reason heavy disaster overtook them, and those whose ways of living they admired and wished to imitate completely became their enemies and punished them. [17]For it is no light thing to show irreverence to the divine laws—a fact which later events will make clear.

18 When the quadrennial games were being held at Tyre and the king was present, [19]the vile Jason sent envoys, chosen as being Antiochian citizens from Jerusalem, to carry three hundred silver drachmas for the sacrifice to Hercules. Those who carried the money, however, thought best not to use it for sacrifice, because that was inappropriate, but to expend it for another purpose. [20]So this money was intended by the sender for the sacrifice to Hercules, but by the decision of its carriers it was applied to the construction of triremes.

21 When Apollonius the son of Menestheus was sent to Egypt for the coronation[n] of Philometor as king, Antiochus learned that Philometor[o] had become hostile to his government, and he took measures for his own security. Therefore upon arriving at Joppa he proceeded to Jerusalem. [22]He was welcomed magnificently by Jason and the city, and ushered in with a blaze of torches and with shouts. Then he marched into Phoenicia.

23 After a period of three years Jason sent Menelaus, the brother of the previously mentioned Simon, to carry the money to the king and to complete the records of essential business. [24]But he, when presented to the king, extolled him with an air of authority, and secured the high priesthood for himself, outbidding Jason by three hundred talents of silver. [25]After receiving the king's orders he returned, possessing no qualification for the high priesthood, but having the hot temper of a cruel tyrant and the rage of a savage wild beast. [26]So Jason, who after supplanting his own brother was supplanted by another man, was driven as a fugitive into the land of Ammon. [27]And Menelaus held the office, but he did not pay regularly any of the money promised to the king. [28]When Sostratus the captain of the citadel kept requesting payment, for the collection of the revenue was his responsibility, the two of them were summoned by the king on account of this issue. [29]Menelaus left his own brother Lysimachus as deputy in the high priesthood, while Sostratus left Crates, the commander of the Cyprian troops.

30 While such was the state of

m Some authorities add *subjecting them*
n The exact meaning of the Greek word is uncertain
o Gk *he*

religious significance in the East. **13:** *Hellenization,* Greek religion and culture (see vv. 9–10 n.). *No high priest,* because he got the office by bribery and did not keep the Mosaic law. **18:** *Tyre,* an important port north of Palestine (Jos.19.29; 1 Kg.7.13); *quadrennial games* had been held there as early as the time of Alexander the Great. **19:** *Hercules,* the Greek name of the god Melkart of Tyre. **20:** *Triremes,* war vessels manned by three benches of rowers. **21:** *Apollonius,* v. 4. *The coronation* of Ptolemy VI *Philometor* occurred about 172 B.C., some time after the death of his mother, Cleopatra I, and he ruled until 146 or 145 B.C. His advisers abandoned Cleopatra's policy, became *hostile* to Syria, and claimed Palestine. *Joppa,* the port forty miles from Jerusalem. **22:** *Phoenicia,* the coastal plain.

4.23–50: Menelaus as high priest. 23: *Menelaus* reigned from about 172 to 162 B.C., when he was executed (13.3–8) and replaced by Alcimus (14.3–14). **26:** *Land of Ammon,* east of the Jordan, near the present Amman. **29:** *The Cyprian troops* were mercenaries. **30:** *Mallus* was

affairs, it happened that the people of
Tarsus and of Mallus revolted because
their cities had been given as a present
to Antiochis, the king's concubine.
31 So the king went hastily to settle the
trouble, leaving Andronicus, a man of
high rank, to act as his deputy. 32 But
Menelaus, thinking he had obtained a
suitable opportunity, stole some of the
gold vessels of the temple and gave
them to Andronicus; other vessels, as
it happened, he had sold to Tyre and
the neighboring cities. 33 When Onias
became fully aware of these acts he
publicly exposed them, having first
withdrawn to a place of sanctuary at
Daphne near Antioch. 34 Therefore
Menelaus, taking Andronicus aside,
urged him to kill Onias. Andronicus[p]
came to Onias, and resorting to
treachery offered him sworn pledges
and gave him his right hand, and in
spite of his suspicion persuaded Onias[q]
to come out from the place of sanctuary; then, with no regard for justice,
he immediately put him out of the way.
35 For this reason not only Jews, but
many also of other nations, were
grieved and displeased at the unjust
murder of the man. 36 When the king
returned from the region of Cilicia, the
Jews in the city[r] appealed to him with
regard to the unreasonable murder of
Onias, and the Greeks shared their
hatred of the crime. 37 Therefore
Antiochus was grieved at heart and
filled with pity, and wept because of
the moderation and good conduct of
the deceased; 38 and inflamed with
anger, he immediately stripped off the
purple robe from Andronicus, tore off
his garments, and led him about the
whole city to that very place where he
had committed the outrage against
Onias, and there he dispatched the
bloodthirsty fellow. The Lord thus
repaid him with the punishment he
deserved.

39 When many acts of sacrilege had
been committed in the city by Lysimachus with the connivance of Menelaus, and when report of them had
spread abroad, the populace gathered
against Lysimachus, because many of
the gold vessels had already been
stolen. 40 And since the crowds were
becoming aroused and filled with anger,
Lysimachus armed about three thousand men and launched an unjust attack, under the leadership of a certain
Auranus, a man advanced in years and
no less advanced in folly. 41 But when
the Jews[s] became aware of Lysimachus' attack, some picked up stones,
some blocks of wood, and others took
handfuls of the ashes that were lying
about, and threw them in wild confusion at Lysimachus and his men. 42 As
a result, they wounded many of them,
and killed some, and put them all to
flight; and the temple robber himself
they killed close by the treasury.

43 Charges were brought against
Menelaus about this incident. 44 When
the king came to Tyre, three men sent
by the senate presented the case before
him. 45 But Menelaus, already as good
as beaten, promised a substantial bribe
to Ptolemy son of Dorymenes to win
over the king. 46 Therefore Ptolemy,
taking the king aside into a colonnade
as if for refreshment, induced the king
to change his mind. 47 Menelaus, the

p Gk *He* *q* Gk *him*
r Or *in each city*
s Gk *they*

---

on the Pyramus river east of *Tarsus* (3.5). Hellenistic kings often provided a wife or *concubine* with a regular income by giving her a city. Antiochus, being extravagant (see 1 Macc.3.30 n.), was often in need of money. **32:** *Gave them*, either to pay tribute or as a bribe. **33:** *Daphne*, about five miles from *Antioch*, had a *place of sanctuary* to Apollo and Artemis. **35:** *Unjust murder*, he had been lured from a place protected by the gods. **38:** *Stripped off the purple robe*, degrading him before execution. **39:** *The city*, Jerusalem. *Menelaus* was still in Antioch. **42:** *The temple robber*, Lysimachus. **44:** *The senate*, see 1 Macc.12.6 n. **45:** *Dorymenes* had fought for Ptolemy IV against Antiochus III; his son *Ptolemy* had been governor of Cyprus and deserted to Antiochus IV (see 10.12–13 n.). **47:** The *Scythians* (Col.3.11) lived in what is now southern Russia and were proverbial for their brutality.

cause of all the evil, he acquitted of the charges against him, while he sentenced to death those unfortunate men, who would have been freed uncondemned if they had pleaded even before Scythians. [48]And so those who had spoken for the city and the villages[t] and the holy vessels quickly suffered the unjust penalty. [49]Therefore even the Tyrians, showing their hatred of the crime, provided magnificently for their funeral. [50]But Menelaus, because of the cupidity of those in power, remained in office, growing in wickedness, having become the chief plotter against his fellow citizens.

5 About this time Antiochus made his second invasion of Egypt. [2]And it happened that over all the city, for almost forty days, there appeared golden-clad horsemen charging through the air, in companies fully armed with lances and drawn swords—[3]troops of horsemen drawn up, attacks and counterattacks made on this side and on that, brandishing of shields, massing of spears, hurling of missiles, the flash of golden trappings, and armor of all sorts. [4]Therefore all men prayed that the apparition might prove to have been a good omen.

[5]When a false rumor arose that Antiochus was dead, Jason took no less than a thousand men and suddenly made an assault upon the city. When the troops upon the wall had been forced back and at last the city was being taken, Menelaus took refuge in the citadel. [6]But Jason kept relentlessly slaughtering his fellow citizens,

not realizing that success at the cost of one's kindred is the greatest misfortune, but imagining that he was setting up trophies of victory over enemies and not over fellow countrymen. [7]He did not gain control of the government, however; and in the end got only disgrace from his conspiracy, and fled again into the country of the Ammonites. [8]Finally he met a miserable end. Accused[u] before Aretas the ruler of the Arabs, fleeing from city to city, pursued by all men, hated as a rebel against the laws, and abhorred as the executioner of his country and his fellow citizens, he was cast ashore in Egypt; [9]and he who had driven many from their own country into exile died in exile, having embarked to go to the Lacedaemonians in hope of finding protection because of their kinship. [10]He who had cast out many to lie unburied had no one to mourn for him; he had no funeral of any sort and no place in the tomb of his fathers.

[11]When news of what had happened reached the king, he took it to mean that Judea was in revolt. So, raging inwardly, he left Egypt and took the city by storm. [12]And he commanded his soldiers to cut down relentlessly every one they met and to slay those who went into the houses. [13]Then there was killing of young and old, destruction of boys, women, and children, and slaughter of virgins and infants. [14]Within the total of three days eighty thousand were destroyed, forty thousand in hand-to-hand fight-

t Other authorities read *the people*
u Cn: Gk *Imprisoned*

5.1–27: Antiochus IV desecrates the temple. 1: *Second invasion*, in 169 B.C.; perhaps the writer regards the coming of the Seleucid army into Palestine in 171 B.C. (4.21–22) as the first invasion. We would speak of them as the first and second phases of the invasion (compare 1 Macc.1.16–19). **2–4:** 3.25–26. *The city*, Jerusalem. **5–8:** *Jason* was an Oniad and pro-Egyptian (see 3.1 n.). Thinking *that Antiochus was dead*, he planned, with Egyptian help, to recover the high priesthood. He was opposed by *Menelaus* the Tobiad (4.23) and also by the Jews loyal to Judaism; he massacred people of both factions. *Ammonites*, 4.26. *Aretas*, king of Nabatean Arabia, south and east of Palestine; his capital was at Petra. **9–10:** Rejected in Egypt, Jason fled to Sparta (1 Macc.12.7). *Unburied*, see 1 Macc.7.17 n.; 1 Kg.13.22. **11–14:** So confused was the situation that Antiochus thought all *Judea was in revolt*. He was *raging inwardly* because the Romans had forced him out of Egypt (see 1 Macc.1.20 n.); both his foreign and his domestic programs were collapsing. **11:** *The city*, Jerusalem.

ing; and as many were sold into slavery as were slain.

15 Not content with this, Antiochus[v] dared to enter the most holy temple in all the world, guided by Menelaus, who had become a traitor both to the laws and to his country. [16]He took the holy vessels with his polluted hands, and swept away with profane hands the votive offerings which other kings had made to enhance the glory and honor of the place. [17]Antiochus was elated in spirit, and did not perceive that the Lord was angered for a little while because of the sins of those who dwelt in the city, and that therefore he was disregarding the holy place. [18]But if it had not happened that they were involved in many sins, this man would have been scourged and turned back from his rash act as soon as he came forward, just as Heliodorus was, whom Seleucus the king sent to inspect the treasury. [19]But the Lord did not choose the nation for the sake of the holy place, but the place for the sake of the nation. [20]Therefore the place itself shared in the misfortunes that befell the nation and afterward participated in its benefits; and what was forsaken in the wrath of the Almighty was restored again in all its glory when the great Lord became reconciled.

21 So Antiochus carried off eighteen hundred talents from the temple, and hurried away to Antioch, thinking in his arrogance that he could sail on the land and walk on the sea, because his mind was elated. [22]And he left governors to afflict the people: at Jerusalem, Philip, by birth a Phrygian and in character more barbarous than the man who appointed him; [23]and at Gerizim, Andronicus; and besides these Menelaus, who lorded it over his fellow citizens worse than the others did. In his malice toward the Jewish citizens,[w] [24]Antiochus[x] sent Apollonius, the captain of the Mysians, with an army of twenty-two thousand, and commanded him to slay all the grown men and to sell the women and boys as slaves. [25]When this man arrived in Jerusalem, he pretended to be peaceably disposed and waited until the holy sabbath day; then, finding the Jews not at work, he ordered his men to parade under arms. [26]He put to the sword all those who came out to see them, then rushed into the city with his armed men and killed great numbers of people.

27 But Judas Maccabeus, with about nine others, got away to the wilderness, and kept himself and his companions alive in the mountains as wild animals do; they continued to live on what grew wild, so that they might not share in the defilement.

6 Not long after this, the king sent an Athenian[y] senator[z] to compel the Jews to forsake the laws of their fathers and cease to live by the laws of God, [2]and also to pollute the temple in Jerusalem and call it the temple of Olympian Zeus, and to call the one in Gerizim the temple of Zeus the Friend of Strangers, as did the people who dwelt in that place.

v Gk he
w Or worse than the others did in his malice toward the Jewish citizens. x Gk he
y Some authorities read Antiochian
z Or Geron an Athenian

15–23a: The temple had been pillaged after the first Egyptian invasion (1 Macc.1.21–28). *Angered for a little while*, not permanently (compare 6.12–16). **21:** *His arrogance* was that of a god manifest (see 4.7 n.). **22–23:** *Philip*, probably not the later regent (9.29). *Andronicus* (4.31) was now made governor of Samaria. **24–26:** *Antiochus sent Apollonius* about two years after the events of vv. 15–23 (see 1 Macc.1.29). Loyal Jews did not yet fight on the *sabbath* (1 Macc.2.32–41). **27:** *Judas Maccabeus*, the third son of Mattathias, of the Hasmonean family (1 Macc.2.1–28). *The defilement*, 4.11; 1 Macc.1.48, 63.

6.1–6: Campaign against Judaism. What had been voluntary (4.9–17) was now enforced (see 1 Macc.1.41–64 n.). **2:** *Olympian Zeus* was now identified with the God of Israel and probably with Antiochus. *To pollute the temple*, they set up a statue or pagan altar (1 Macc.1.54). The Samaritans, descendants of the ten northern tribes and Assyrian settlers (2 Kg.17.6,24), had

3 Harsh and utterly grievous was the onslaught of evil. [4]For the temple was filled with debauchery and reveling by the Gentiles, who dallied with harlots and had intercourse with women within the sacred precincts, and besides brought in things for sacrifice that were unfit. [5]The altar was covered with abominable offerings which were forbidden by the laws. [6]A man could neither keep the sabbath, nor observe the feasts of his fathers, nor so much as confess himself to be a Jew.

7 On the monthly celebration of the king's birthday, the Jews[a] were taken, under bitter constraint, to partake of the sacrifices; and when the feast of Dionysus came, they were compelled to walk in the procession in honor of Dionysus, wearing wreaths of ivy. [8]At the suggestion of Ptolemy a decree was issued to the neighboring Greek cities, that they should adopt the same policy toward the Jews and make them partake of the sacrifices, [9]and should slay those who did not choose to change over to Greek customs. One could see, therefore, the misery that had come upon them. [10]For example, two women were brought in for having circumcised their children. These women they publicly paraded about the city, with their babies hung at their breasts, then hurled them down headlong from the wall. [11]Others who had assembled in the caves near by, to observe the seventh day secretly, were betrayed to Philip and were all burned together, because their piety kept them from defending themselves, in view of their regard for that most holy day.

12 Now I urge those who read this book not to be depressed by such calamities, but to recognize that these punishments were designed not to destroy but to discipline our people. [13]In fact, not to let the impious alone for long, but to punish them immediately, is a sign of great kindness. [14]For in the case of the other nations the Lord waits patiently to punish them until they have reached the full measure of their sins; but he does not deal in this way with us, [15]in order that he may not take vengeance on us afterward when our sins have reached their height. [16]Therefore he never withdraws his mercy from us. Though he disciplines us with calamities, he does not forsake his own people. [17]Let what we have said serve as a reminder; we must go on briefly with the story.

18 Eleazar, one of the scribes in high position, a man now advanced in age and of noble presence, was being forced to open his mouth to eat swine's flesh. [19]But he, welcoming death with honor rather than life with pollution, went up to the rack of his own accord, spitting out the flesh, [20]as men ought to go who have the courage to refuse things that it is not right to taste, even for the natural love of life.

21 Those who were in charge of that unlawful sacrifice took the man aside, because of their long acquaintance with him, and privately urged him to bring meat of his own providing, proper for him to use, and pretend that he was eating the flesh of the sacrificial meal which had been commanded by the king, [22]so that by doing this he might be saved from death, and be treated kindly on account of his old

a Gk *they*

---

built the temple on Mount *Gerizim*. **4**: *Intercourse . . . sacred precincts*, as in Syrian fertility cults (see Let. Jer.6.11 n. and 6.43 n.). *Things unfit*, swine (Lev.11.7; 1 Macc.1.47). **6**: 1 Macc. 1.45–51. *Jew*, originally "Judean"; here "one loyal to the religion" (Judaism, 2.21).

   6.7–17: The first martyrdoms. Chs. 6–7 are the earliest martyrologies, a type of writing popular subsequently in Christianity, designed to encourage the faithful when persecuted. **7**: *Dionysus*, god of wine and the grape harvest; *ivy* was one of his symbols. **8**: *Ptolemy*, see 4.45 n. *The same policy toward the Jews* outside Judea. **12–17**: The victories of Israel's enemies are explained as God's corrective punishment, always followed by mercy (compare Is.54.7–8).

   6.18–31: Martyrdom of Eleazar. The story is told more elaborately in 4 Maccabees. **18**: *Scribes*, scholars learned in the Mosaic law, not necessarily priests. **19**: *Of his own accord*, like

friendship with them. [23]But making a high resolve, worthy of his years and the dignity of his old age and the gray hairs which he had reached with distinction and his excellent life even from childhood, and moreover according to the holy God-given law, he declared himself quickly, telling them to send him to Hades.

24 "Such pretense is not worthy of our time of life," he said, "lest many of the young should suppose that Eleazar in his ninetieth year has gone over to an alien religion, [25]and through my pretense, for the sake of living a brief moment longer, they should be led astray because of me, while I defile and disgrace my old age. [26]For even if for the present I should avoid the punishment of men, yet whether I live or die I shall not escape the hands of the Almighty. [27]Therefore, by manfully giving up my life now, I will show myself worthy of my old age [28]and leave to the young a noble example of how to die a good death willingly and nobly for the revered and holy laws."

When he had said this, he went[b] at once to the rack. [29]And those who a little before had acted toward him with good will now changed to ill will, because the words he had uttered were in their opinion sheer madness.[c] [30]When he was about to die under the blows, he groaned aloud and said: "It is clear to the Lord in his holy knowledge that, though I might have been saved from death, I am enduring terrible sufferings in my body under this beating, but in my soul I am glad to suffer these things because I fear him."

31 So in this way he died, leaving in his death an example of nobility and a memorial of courage, not only to the young but to the great body of his nation.

7 It happened also that seven brothers and their mother were arrested and were being compelled by the king, under torture with whips and cords, to partake of unlawful swine's flesh. [2]One of them, acting as their spokesman, said, "What do you intend to ask and learn from us? For we are ready to die rather than transgress the laws of our fathers."

3 The king fell into a rage, and gave orders that pans and caldrons be heated. [4]These were heated immediately, and he commanded that the tongue of their spokesman be cut out and that they scalp him and cut off his hands and feet, while the rest of the brothers and the mother looked on. [5]When he was utterly helpless, the king[d] ordered them to take him to the fire, still breathing, and to fry him in a pan. The smoke from the pan spread widely, but the brothers[e] and their mother encouraged one another to die nobly, saying, [6]"The Lord God is watching over us and in truth has compassion on us, as Moses declared in his song which bore witness against the people to their faces, when he said, 'And he will have compassion on his servants.'"

7 After the first brother had died in this way, they brought forward the second for their sport. They tore off the skin of his head with the hair, and asked him, "Will you eat rather than have your body punished limb by limb?" [8]He replied in the language of his fathers, and said to them, "No." Therefore he in turn underwent tortures as the first brother had done. [9]And when he was at his last breath, he said, "You accursed wretch, you dismiss us from this present life, but the King of the universe will raise us

b Other authorities read *was dragged*
c The Greek text of this verse is uncertain
d Gk *he*　　*e* Gk *they*

---

many later martyrs. **29:** Pagans often regarded the martyrs as deluded fanatics. **30:** *Fear*, revere (Job 28.28; Ps.19.9).
　7.1–42: Martyrdom of seven brothers and their mother. This story is the principal subject of 4 Maccabees. **2:** Dan.3.16–18. **6:** Dt.32.36. **7:** *Their sport*, Mk.15.17–20; Jn.19.2–3; Heb.11.36. **9:** God is often addressed in Jewish prayer as *King of the universe*. The doctrine of resurrection

up to an everlasting renewal of life, because we have died for his laws."

10 After him, the third was the victim of their sport. When it was demanded, he quickly put out his tongue and courageously stretched forth his hands, [11]and said nobly, "I got these from Heaven, and because of his laws I disdain them, and from him I hope to get them back again." [12]As a result the king himself and those with him were astonished at the young man's spirit, for he regarded his sufferings as nothing.

13 When he too had died, they maltreated and tortured the fourth in the same way. [14]And when he was near death, he said, "One cannot but choose to die at the hands of men and to cherish the hope that God gives of being raised again by him. But for you there will be no resurrection to life!"

15 Next they brought forward the fifth and maltreated him. [16]But he looked at the king,[f] and said, "Because you have authority among men, mortal though you are, you do what you please. But do not think that God has forsaken our people. [17]Keep on, and see how his mighty power will torture you and your descendants!"

18 After him they brought forward the sixth. And when he was about to die, he said, "Do not deceive yourself in vain. For we are suffering these things on our own account, because of our sins against our own God. Therefore[g] astounding things have happened. [19]But do not think that you will go unpunished for having tried to fight against God!"

20 The mother was especially admirable and worthy of honorable memory. Though she saw her seven sons perish within a single day, she bore it with good courage because of her hope in the Lord. [21]She encouraged each of them in the language of their fathers. Filled with a noble spirit, she fired her woman's reasoning with a man's courage, and said to them, [22]"I do not know how you came into being in my womb. It was not I who gave you life and breath, nor I who set in order the elements within each of you. [23]Therefore the Creator of the world, who shaped the beginning of man and devised the origin of all things, will in his mercy give life and breath back to you again, since you now forget yourselves for the sake of his laws."

24 Antiochus felt that he was being treated with contempt, and he was suspicious of her reproachful tone. The youngest brother being still alive, Antiochus[h] not only appealed to him in words, but promised with oaths that he would make him rich and enviable if he would turn from the ways of his fathers, and that he would take him for his friend and entrust him with public affairs. [25]Since the young man would not listen to him at all, the king called the mother to him and urged her to advise the youth to save himself. [26]After much urging on his part, she undertook to persuade her son. [27]But, leaning close to him, she spoke in their native tongue as follows, deriding the cruel tyrant: "My son, have pity on me. I carried you nine months in my womb, and nursed you for three years, and have reared you and brought you up to this point in your life, and have taken care of you.[i] [28]I beseech you, my child, to look at the heaven and the earth and see everything that is in them, and recognize that God did not make them out of things that existed.[j]

f Gk *him*
g Lat: other authorities omit *Therefore*
h Gk *he*
i Or *have borne the burden of your education*
j Or *God made them out of things that did not exist*

---

is now clearly stated (Dan.12.2; Mt.19.29; Lk.18.30). **11:** The whole body will be restored (Rom.8.23). **14:** The wicked will have *no resurrection to life* (Dan.12.2; Rev.20.14–15). **17:** Antiochus IV died in misery and his son was murdered (9.5–28). **18–19:** 6.12–16. **21:** *The language of their fathers*, Aramaic or possibly Hebrew. **22–23:** The hope of resurrection depends entirely on *the Creator* and his mercy. **27:** Children were often *nursed . . . for three years*. **28:** God made all things out of nothing, by his will and creative power, not from previously

Thus also mankind comes into being. [29]Do not fear this butcher, but prove worthy of your brothers. Accept death, so that in God's mercy I may get you back again with your brothers."

30 While she was still speaking, the young man said, "What are you[k] waiting for? I will not obey the king's command, but I obey the command of the law that was given to our fathers through Moses. [31]But you,[l] who have contrived all sorts of evil against the Hebrews, will certainly not escape the hands of God. [32]For we are suffering because of our own sins. [33]And if our living Lord is angry for a little while, to rebuke and discipline us, he will again be reconciled with his own servants. [34]But you, unholy wretch, you most defiled of all men, do not be elated in vain and puffed up by uncertain hopes, when you raise your hand against the children of heaven. [35]You have not yet escaped the judgment of the almighty, all-seeing God. [36]For our brothers after enduring a brief suffering have drunk[m] of everflowing life under God's covenant; but you, by the judgment of God, will receive just punishment for your arrogance. [37]I, like my brothers, give up body and life for the laws of our fathers, appealing to God to show mercy soon to our nation and by afflictions and plagues to make you confess that he alone is God, [38]and through me and my brothers to bring to an end the wrath of the Almighty which has justly fallen on our whole nation."

39 The king fell into a rage, and handled him worse than the others, being exasperated at his scorn. [40]So he died in his integrity, putting his whole trust in the Lord.

41 Last of all, the mother died, after her sons.

42 Let this be enough, then, about the eating of sacrifices and the extreme tortures.

8 But Judas, who was also called Maccabeus, and his companions secretly entered the villages and summoned their kinsmen and enlisted those who had continued in the Jewish faith, and so they gathered about six thousand men. [2]They besought the Lord to look upon the people who were oppressed by all, and to have pity on the temple which had been profaned by ungodly men, [3]and to have mercy on the city which was being destroyed and about to be leveled to the ground, and to hearken to the blood that cried out to him, [4]and to remember also the lawless destruction of the innocent babies and the blasphemies committed against his name, and to show his hatred of evil.

5 As soon as Maccabeus got his army organized, the Gentiles could not withstand him, for the wrath of the Lord had turned to mercy. [6]Coming without warning, he would set fire to towns and villages. He captured strategic positions and put to flight not a few of the enemy. [7]He found the nights most advantageous for such attacks. And talk of his valor spread everywhere.

8 When Philip saw that the man was gaining ground little by little, and that he was pushing ahead with more frequent successes, he wrote to Ptolemy, the governor of Coelesyria and Phoenicia, for aid to the king's government. [9]And Ptolemy[n] promptly ap-

k The Greek here for *you* is plural
l The Greek here for *you* is singular
m Cn: Gk *fallen*   *n* Gk *he*

existing matter (Heb.11.3). **31**: The Jews of Antioch called themselves *Hebrews*. **33**: 5.17; 6.12–16. **36**: The martyrs already enjoy *life*. *God's covenant* with Abraham (Gen.12.1–3; 15.5–6; 17.4–8) is believed to guarantee the resurrection of his descendants (compare Mk.12.26–27). **37**: Martyrs often prayed that their enemies would *confess that he alone is God* (compare 9.12).

8.1–7: Judas begins the revolt; after prayer (vv. 2–4) he begins guerrilla warfare (vv. 5–7).

8.8–29: First victory over Nicanor. Judas assembled his forces at Mizpah and attacked Gorgias' army at Emmaus (see 1 Macc.3.40 n.). **8**: *Philip*, see 5.22 n. *Ptolemy* (see 4.45 n.), appointed by Lysias after Antiochus had left for Persia (1 Macc.3.38). **9**: *Gorgias*, not Nicanor,

pointed Nicanor the son of Patroclus, one of the king's chief friends, and sent him, in command of no fewer than twenty thousand Gentiles of all nations, to wipe out the whole race of Judea. He associated with him Gorgias, a general and a man of experience in military service. ¹⁰Nicanor determined to make up for the king the tribute due to the Romans, two thousand talents, by selling the captured Jews into slavery. ¹¹And he immediately sent to the cities on the seacoast, inviting them to buy Jewish slaves and promising to hand over ninety slaves for a talent, not expecting the judgment from the Almighty that was about to overtake him.

12 Word came to Judas concerning Nicanor's invasion; and when he told his companions of the arrival of the army, ¹³those who were cowardly and distrustful of God's justice ran off and got away. ¹⁴Others sold all their remaining property, and at the same time besought the Lord to rescue those who had been sold by the ungodly Nicanor before he ever met them, ¹⁵if not for their own sake, yet for the sake of the covenants made with their fathers, and because he had called them by his holy and glorious name. ¹⁶But Maccabeus gathered his men together, to the number of six thousand, and exhorted them not to be frightened by the enemy and not to fear the great multitude of Gentiles who were wickedly coming against them, but to fight nobly, ¹⁷keeping before their eyes the lawless outrage which the Gentiles*ᵒ* had committed against the holy place, and the torture of the derided city, and besides,

the overthrow of their ancestral way of life. ¹⁸"For they trust to arms and acts of daring," he said, "but we trust in the Almighty God, who is able with a single nod to strike down those who are coming against us and even the whole world."

19 Moreover, he told them of the times when help came to their ancestors; both the time of Sennacherib, when one hundred and eighty-five thousand perished, ²⁰and the time of the battle with the Galatians that took place in Babylonia, when eight thousand in all went into the affair, with four thousand Macedonians; and when the Macedonians were hard pressed, the eight thousand, by the help that came to them from heaven, destroyed one hundred and twenty thousand and took much booty.

21 With these words he filled them with good courage and made them ready to die for their laws and their country; then he divided his army into four parts. ²²He appointed his brothers also, Simon and Joseph and Jonathan, each to command a division, putting fifteen hundred men under each. ²³Besides, he appointed Eleazar to read aloud*ᵖ* from the holy book, and gave the watchword, "God's help"; then, leading the first division himself, he joined battle with Nicanor.

24 With the Almighty as their ally, they slew more than nine thousand of the enemy, and wounded and disabled most of Nicanor's army, and forced them all to flee. ²⁵They captured the money of those who had come to buy

o Gk *they*
p The Greek text of this clause is uncertain

---

is the principal figure in 1 Macc.3.38–4.25. **10:** Since the battle of Magnesia (see 1 Macc.1.10 n.) the Seleucids had been forced to pay *tribute;* perhaps the *two thousand talents* represented the last instalment. **11:** Slave traders accompanied the expedition (compare 8.34 and 1 Macc.3.41). **13:** Compare 1 Macc.3.56. **14:** They *sold . . . property* so as to escape and join Judas' army. **15:** *Covenants,* with the patriarchs and at Sinai (see 1.24–29 n.; Ex.19.5–6). *Called them by his . . . name,* as God's people (Dt.28.10). **17:** *Lawless outrage,* 5.15–16. *Ancestral way of life,* or government under true high priests. **19:** 2 Kg.19.35. **20:** *The Galatians* from Asia Minor often served as mercenaries. Jewish forces evidently aided Antiochus III and *the Macedonians.* **22:** *Simon,* high priest 142–134 B.C., and *Jonathan,* from 160 to 143 or 142 B.C. *Joseph,* called John in 1 Macc.2.2; 9.36. **23:** *Eleazar,* another brother, was killed at Beth-zechariah (1 Macc. 2.5; 6.43–46). The motto *"God's help"* is prescribed by the Qumran *War Scroll* for one of the

them as slaves. After pursuing them for some distance, they were obliged to return because the hour was late. ²⁶For it was the day before the sabbath, and for that reason they did not continue their pursuit. ²⁷And when they had collected the arms of the enemy and stripped them of their spoils, they kept the sabbath, giving great praise and thanks to the Lord, who had preserved them for that day and allotted it to them as the beginning of mercy. ²⁸After the sabbath they gave some of the spoils to those who had been tortured and to the widows and orphans, and distributed the rest among themselves and their children. ²⁹When they had done this, they made common supplication and besought the merciful Lord to be wholly reconciled with his servants.

30 In encounters with the forces of Timothy and Bacchides they killed more than twenty thousand of them and got possession of some exceedingly high strongholds, and they divided very much plunder, giving to those who had been tortured and to the orphans and widows, and also to the aged, shares equal to their own. ³¹Collecting the arms of the enemy,*q* they stored them all carefully in strategic places, and carried the rest of the spoils to Jerusalem. ³²They killed the commander of Timothy's forces, a most unholy man, and one who had greatly troubled the Jews. ³³While they were celebrating the victory in the city of their fathers, they burned those who had set fire to the sacred gates, Callisthenes and some others, who had fled into one little

house; so these received the proper recompense for their impiety.*r*

34 The thrice-accursed Nicanor, who had brought the thousand merchants to buy the Jews, ³⁵having been humbled with the help of the Lord by opponents whom he regarded as of the least account, took off his splendid uniform and made his way alone like a runaway slave across the country till he reached Antioch, having succeeded chiefly in the destruction of his own army! ³⁶Thus he who had undertaken to secure tribute for the Romans by the capture of the people of Jerusalem proclaimed that the Jews had a Defender, and that therefore the Jews were invulnerable, because they followed the laws ordained by him.

9 About that time, as it happened, Antiochus had retreated in disorder from the region of Persia. ²For he had entered the city called Persepolis, and attempted to rob the temples and control the city. Therefore the people rushed to the rescue with arms, and Antiochus and his men were defeated,*s* with the result that Antiochus was put to flight by the inhabitants and beat a shameful retreat. ³While he was in Ecbatana, news came to him of what had happened to Nicanor and the forces of Timothy. ⁴Transported with rage, he conceived the idea of turning upon the Jews the injury done by those who had put him to flight; so he ordered his charioteer to drive without stopping until he com-

q Gk *their arms*
r The Greek text of this verse is uncertain
s Gk *they were defeated*

---

banners of the army returning from battle. **25:** *Slaves,* vv. 11, 34. **26:** Gorgias and his army were in the hills (1 Macc.4.16–18). **27–29:** The victory was a sign of God's favor, but the campaign had not yet been won (6.12–16; 1 Macc.4.19–25).

8.30–36: Other victories (1 Macc.5.37–44 tells of a battle against *Timothy* at Raphon). **30:** *Bacchides,* 1 Macc.7.8. **33:** *City of their fathers,* Jerusalem, with its *sacred gates,* Judas' ancestral home (1 Macc.2.1). **34:** *Thrice-accursed,* 15.3; Ad. Est.16.15.

9.1–12: Antiochus' illness (1 Macc.6.1–16). Here this story is placed before the purification of the temple (10.1–8; 1 Macc.4.36–61), Judas' southern campaigns (10.14–38; 1 Macc. ch. 5), and Lysias' first expedition (11.1–15; 1 Macc.4.26–35). **1:** *Antiochus* went to *Persia* to strengthen his authority there and to get funds. **2:** *Persepolis,* near Shiraz, the capital of Persia, founded by Darius I. **3:** Antiochus was on his way to Babylon (1 Macc.6.4) but went north by way of *Ecbatana,* Hamadan. **4:** 5.11; 7.3.

pleted the journey. But the judgment of heaven rode with him! For in his arrogance he said, "When I get there I will make Jerusalem a cemetery of Jews."

5 But the all-seeing Lord, the God of Israel, struck him an incurable and unseen blow. As soon as he ceased speaking he was seized with a pain in his bowels for which there was no relief and with sharp internal tortures —⁶and that very justly, for he had tortured the bowels of others with many and strange inflictions. ⁷Yet he did not in any way stop his insolence, but was even more filled with arrogance, breathing fire in his rage against the Jews, and giving orders to hasten the journey. And so it came about that he fell out of his chariot as it was rushing along, and the fall was so hard as to torture every limb of his body. ⁸Thus he who had just been thinking that he could command the waves of the sea, in his superhuman arrogance, and imagining that he could weigh the high mountains in a balance, was brought down to earth and carried in a litter, making the power of God manifest to all. ⁹And so the ungodly man's body swarmed with worms, and while he was still living in anguish and pain, his flesh rotted away, and because of his stench the whole army felt revulsion at his decay. ¹⁰Because of his intolerable stench no one was able to carry the man who a little while before had thought that he could touch the stars of heaven. ¹¹Then it was that, broken in spirit, he began to lose much of his arrogance and to come to his senses under the scourge of God, for he was tortured with pain every moment. ¹²And when he could not endure his own stench, he uttered these words: "It is right to be subject to God, and

no mortal should think that he is equal to God."ᵗ

13 Then the abominable fellow made a vow to the Lord, who would no longer have mercy on him, stating ¹⁴that the holy city, which he was hastening to level to the ground and to make a cemetery, he was now declaring to be free; ¹⁵and the Jews, whom he had not considered worth burying but had planned to throw out with their children to the beasts, for the birds to pick, he would make, all of them, equal to citizens of Athens; ¹⁶and the holy sanctuary, which he had formerly plundered, he would adorn with the finest offerings; and the holy vessels he would give back, all of them, many times over; and the expenses incurred for the sacrifices he would provide from his own revenues; ¹⁷and in addition to all this he also would become a Jew and would visit every inhabited place to proclaim the power of God. ¹⁸But when his sufferings did not in any way abate, for the judgment of God had justly come upon him, he gave up all hope for himself and wrote to the Jews the following letter, in the form of a supplication. This was its content:

19 "To his worthy Jewish citizens, Antiochus their king and general sends hearty greetings and good wishes for their health and prosperity. ²⁰If you and your children are well and your affairs are as you wish, I am glad. As my hope is in heaven, ²¹I remember with affection your esteem and good will. On my way back from the region of Persia I suffered an annoying illness, and I have deemed it necessary to take thought for the general security of all. ²²I do not despair of my condition, for I have good hope of recovering from my illness, ²³but I observed that my fa-

t Or *think thoughts proper only to God*

5: See 1 Macc.6.9 n.   **8:** *Command the waves*, like Xerxes invading Greece. *Weigh the high mountains*, like God (see 5.21 n.; Is.40.12).   **9:** *Worms*, Acts 12.23.
   9.13–29: Repentance and death of Antiochus. 15: *Citizens of Athens* were proud of their heritage, though the city no longer had actual power. **16:** 5.16. **17:** 7.37; Dan.4.31–35. **19–27:** The letter is no supplication (v. 18); it is addressed to Jews loyal to the king and bids them support his *son Antiochus* V (vv. 25–27). **23:** *My father*, Antiochus III (see 3.3 n.), who *appointed*

ther, on the occasions when he made expeditions into the upper country, appointed his successor, ²⁴so that, if anything unexpected happened or any unwelcome news came, the people throughout the realm would not be troubled, for they would know to whom the government was left. ²⁵Moreover, I understand how the princes along the borders and the neighbors to my kingdom keep watching for opportunities and waiting to see what will happen. So I have appointed my son Antiochus to be king, whom I have often entrusted and commended to most of you when I hastened off to the upper provinces; and I have written to him what is written here. ²⁶I therefore urge and beseech you to remember the public and private services rendered to you and to maintain your present good will, each of you, toward me and my son. ²⁷For I am sure that he will follow my policy and will treat you with moderation and kindness."

28 So the murderer and blasphemer, having endured the most intense suffering, such as he had inflicted on others, came to the end of his life by a most pitiable fate, among the mountains in a strange land. ²⁹And Philip, one of his courtiers, took his body home; then, fearing the son of Antiochus, he betook himself to Ptolemy Philometor in Egypt.

10 Now Maccabeus and his followers, the Lord leading them on, recovered the temple and the city; ²and they tore down the altars which had been built in the public square by the foreigners, and also destroyed the sacred precincts. ³They purified the sanctuary, and made another altar of sacrifice; then, striking fire out of flint, they offered sacrifices, after a lapse of two years, and they burned incense and lighted lamps and set out the bread of the Presence. ⁴And when they had done this, they fell prostrate and besought the Lord that they might never again fall into such misfortunes, but that, if they should ever sin, they might be disciplined by him with forbearance and not be handed over to blasphemous and barbarous nations. ⁵It happened that on the same day on which the sanctuary had been profaned by the foreigners, the purification of the sanctuary took place, that is, on the twenty-fifth day of the same month, which was Chislev. ⁶And they celebrated it for eight days with rejoicing, in the manner of the feast of booths, remembering how not long before, during the feast of booths, they had been wandering in the mountains and caves like wild animals. ⁷Therefore bearing ivy-wreathed wands and beautiful branches and also fronds of palm, they offered hymns of thanksgiving to him who had given success to the purifying of his own holy place. ⁸They decreed by public ordinance and vote that the whole nation of the Jews should observe these days every year.

Seleucus IV as *his successor. The upper country*, Babylonia and Persia (1 Macc.3.37). **28:** Antiochus IV *died among the mountains*, perhaps at Gabae or Isfahan (see 1 Macc.6.5 n.). **29:** *Philip* was perhaps Antiochus V's guardian (see 1 Macc.6.14–15 n.). *Fearing* Lysias, viceroy in the west, rather than *the son of Antiochus*, who was a child, he went over to Syria's enemy, *Ptolemy* VI (see 4.21 n.). Josephus says that Philip took over the Seleucid government and was later killed (*Antiquities*, XII. ix. 7).
10.1–9: Purification of the temple (compare 1 Macc.4.36–61). **1:** They *recovered the temple*, desecrated by Antiochus (6.2–4; 1 Macc.1.54), *and the city*, except for the citadel (1 Macc.4.60; 6.18). **2:** *The altars* had been used for pagan worship. **3:** They *purified the sanctuary* by removing the desecrated stones (1 Macc.1.44–46). The reference to *striking fire out of flint* ignores the legends of 1.19–2.1. *Two years*, according to 1 Macc.1.54 and 4.52 it was three years. The *incense, lamps*, and *bread of the Presence*, prescribed by Ex.30.7–8; 25.30. **4:** 5.17–20; 6.12–16. **5–6:** *Chislev*, December, 164 B.C. (see 1 Macc.4.52–59 n.). At the normal time of *the feast of booths*, in September, *they had been wandering* like their ancestors (Lev.23.43) and could not celebrate it. **7:** *Ivy-wreathed wands*, here in honor of God (compare 6.7). *Branches* were carried

9 Such then was the end of Antiochus, who was called Epiphanes.

10 Now we will tell what took place under Antiochus Eupator, who was the son of that ungodly man, and will give a brief summary of the principal calamities of the wars. [11]This man, when he succeeded to the kingdom, appointed one Lysias to have charge of the government and to be chief governor of Coelesyria and Phoenicia. [12]Ptolemy, who was called Macron, took the lead in showing justice to the Jews because of the wrong that had been done to them, and attempted to maintain peaceful relations with them. [13]As a result he was accused before Eupator by the king's friends. He heard himself called a traitor at every turn, because he had abandoned Cyprus, which Philometor had entrusted to him, and had gone over to Antiochus Epiphanes. Unable to command the respect due his office,*u* he took poison and ended his life.

14 When Gorgias became governor of the region, he maintained a force of mercenaries, and at every turn kept on warring against the Jews. [15]Besides this, the Idumeans, who had control of important strongholds, were harassing the Jews; they received those who were banished from Jerusalem, and endeavored to keep up the war. [16]But Maccabeus and his men, after making solemn supplication and beseeching God to fight on their side, rushed to the strongholds of the Idumeans. [17]Attacking them vigorously, they gained possession of the places, and beat off all who fought upon the wall, and slew those whom they encountered, killing no fewer than twenty thousand.

18 When no less than nine thousand took refuge in two very strong towers well equipped to withstand a siege, [19]Maccabeus left Simon and Joseph, and also Zacchaeus and his men, a force sufficient to besiege them; and he himself set off for places where he was more urgently needed. [20]But the men with Simon, who were money-hungry, were bribed by some of those who were in the towers, and on receiving seventy thousand drachmas let some of them slip away. [21]When word of what had happened came to Maccabeus, he gathered the leaders of the people, and accused these men of having sold their brethren for money by setting their enemies free to fight against them. [22]Then he slew these men who had turned traitor, and immediately captured the two towers. [23]Having success at arms in everything he undertook, he destroyed more than twenty thousand in the two strongholds.

24 Now Timothy, who had been defeated by the Jews before, gathered a tremendous force of mercenaries and collected the cavalry from Asia in no small number. He came on, intending to take Judea by storm. [25]As he drew near, Maccabeus and his men sprinkled dust upon their heads and girded their loins with sackcloth, in supplication to God. [26]Falling upon the steps before the altar, they besought him to be gracious to them and to be an enemy to their enemies and an adversary to their

u Cn: the Greek text here is uncertain

---

in procession at the feast of booths. *Fronds of palm* symbolize victory (1 Macc.13.51; Jn.12.13).
    10.10–13: Antiochus V and Ptolemy Macron. 10–11: *Antiochus* V *Eupator* (9.25), son of Antiochus IV, reigned from 164 to 162 B.C., when he was murdered by order of Demetrius I. He was about nine years old; his father had *appointed . . . Lysias* as regent (1 Macc.3.32–33).
    12–13: *Ptolemy* had changed allegiance from Egypt to Syria (see 4.45 n.; 6.8); now he was friendly *to the Jews.*
    10.14–23: Attacks on the Idumeans (1 Macc.5.1–3,9–54). **14:** *Gorgias* succeeded Ptolemy. **15:** *Idumeans,* or Edomites (see 1 Macc.5.3 n.); John Hyrcanus later forced them to adopt Judaism. *Those . . . banished,* supporters of Menelaus. **19:** *Urgently needed,* perhaps in Ammon and Gilead (1 Macc.5.6–13).
    10.24–38: Victory over Timothy. 24: They met *Timothy* (8.30) *at dawn* (v. 28) at Dathema east of the Jordan (1 Macc.5.28–34). **26:** Ex.23.22.

adversaries, as the law declares. ²⁷And rising from their prayer they took up their arms and advanced a considerable distance from the city; and when they came near to the enemy they halted. ²⁸Just as dawn was breaking, the two armies joined battle, the one having as pledge of success and victory not only their valor but their reliance upon the Lord, while the other made rage their leader in the fight.

29 When the battle became fierce, there appeared to the enemy from heaven five resplendent men on horses with golden bridles, and they were leading the Jews. ³⁰Surrounding Maccabeus and protecting him with their own armor and weapons, they kept him from being wounded. And they showered arrows and thunderbolts upon the enemy, so that, confused and blinded, they were thrown into disorder and cut to pieces. ³¹Twenty thousand five hundred were slaughtered, besides six hundred horsemen.

32 Timothy himself fled to a stronghold called Gazara, especially well garrisoned, where Chaereas was commander. ³³Then Maccabeus and his men were glad, and they besieged the fort for four days. ³⁴The men within, relying on the strength of the place, blasphemed terribly and hurled out wicked words. ³⁵But at dawn of the fifth day, twenty young men in the army of Maccabeus, fired with anger because of the blasphemies, bravely stormed the wall and with savage fury cut down every one they met. ³⁶Others who came up in the same way wheeled around against the defenders and set fire to the towers; they kindled fires and burned the blasphemers alive. Others broke open the gates and let in the rest of the force, and they occupied the city. ³⁷They killed Timothy, who was hidden in a cistern, and his brother Chaereas, and Apollophanes. ³⁸When they had accomplished these things, with hymns and thanksgivings they blessed the Lord who shows great kindness to Israel and gives them the victory.

11 Very soon after this, Lysias, the king's guardian and kinsman, who was in charge of the government, being vexed at what had happened, ²gathered about eighty thousand men and all his cavalry and came against the Jews. He intended to make the city a home for Greeks, ³and to levy tribute on the temple as he did on the sacred places of the other nations, and to put up the high priesthood for sale every year. ⁴He took no account whatever of the power of God, but was elated with his ten thousands of infantry, and his thousands of cavalry, and his eighty elephants. ⁵Invading Judea, he approached Beth-zur, which was a fortified place about five leaguesᵛ from Jerusalem, and pressed it hard.

6 When Maccabeus and his men got word that Lysiasᵂ was besieging the strongholds, they and all the people, with lamentations and tears, besought the Lord to send a good angel to save Israel. ⁷Maccabeus himself was the first to take up arms, and he urged the others to risk their lives with him to aid their brethren. Then they eagerly rushed off together. ⁸And there, while they were still near Jerusalem, a horseman appeared at their head, clothed in white and brandishing weapons of gold. ⁹And they all together praised the

v About twenty miles. The text is uncertain here
w Gk *he*

29: 3.24–26. **31:** *Twenty thousand five hundred*, compare the number of fatalities mentioned in 8.30; 10.17,23. **32–38:** The fort of *Gazara* (1 Macc.4.15; 7.45) was well garrisoned; Simon captured it much later (1 Macc.13.43–48). **37:** *They killed Timothy;* but a Timothy reappears in 12.2, 18–25 (compare 1 Macc.5.11–40).

11.1–15: Victory over Lysias at Beth-zur. This probably occurred before the dedication of the temple (1 Macc.4.26–35). **1:** *Lysias*, see 10.10–13 n. **3:** In many Greek cults the *priesthood* was *for sale every year;* Antiochus IV had twice disposed of the Jewish high priesthood (4.7,24). **4:** *Elephants*, see 1 Macc.1.17 n.; 6.34–35 n. **5:** *Beth-zur*, about twenty miles south of Jerusalem on the road to Hebron. **6:** *Good angel*, Ex.23.20; Jos.5.13–15; Jg.6.11; 2 Kg.19.35.

merciful God, and were strengthened in heart, ready to assail not only men but the wildest beasts or walls of iron. ¹⁰They advanced in battle order, having their heavenly ally, for the Lord had mercy on them. ¹¹They hurled themselves like lions against the enemy, and slew eleven thousand of them and sixteen hundred horsemen, and forced all the rest to flee. ¹²Most of them got away stripped and wounded, and Lysias himself escaped by disgraceful flight. ¹³And as he was not without intelligence, he pondered over the defeat which had befallen him, and realized that the Hebrews were invincible because the mighty God fought on their side. So he sent to them ¹⁴and persuaded them to settle everything on just terms, promising that he would persuade the king, constraining him to be their friend.ˣ ¹⁵Maccabeus, having regard for the common good, agreed to all that Lysias urged. For the king granted every request in behalf of the Jews which Maccabeus delivered to Lysias in writing.

16 The letter written to the Jews by Lysias was to this effect:

"Lysias to the people of the Jews, greeting. ¹⁷John and Absalom, who were sent by you, have delivered your signed communication and have asked about the matters indicated therein. ¹⁸I have informed the king of everything that needed to be brought before him, and he has agreed to what was possible. ¹⁹If you will maintain your good will toward the government, I will endeavor for the future to help promote your welfare. ²⁰And concerning these matters and their details, I have ordered these men and my representatives to confer with you. ²¹Farewell. The one hundred and forty-eighth year,ʸ Dioscorinthius twenty-fourth."

22 The king's letter ran thus:

"King Antiochus to his brother Lysias, greeting. ²³Now that our father has gone on to the gods, we desire that the subjects of the kingdom be undisturbed in caring for their own affairs. ²⁴We have heard that the Jews do not consent to our father's change to Greek customs but prefer their own way of living and ask that their own customs be allowed them. ²⁵Accordingly, since we choose that this nation also be free from disturbance, our decision is that their temple be restored to them and that they live according to the customs of their ancestors. ²⁶You will do well, therefore, to send word to them and give them pledges of friendship, so that they may know our policy and be of good cheer and go on happily in the conduct of their own affairs."

27 To the nation the king's letter was as follows:

"King Antiochus to the senate of the Jews and to the other Jews, greeting. ²⁸If you are well, it is as we desire. We also are in good health. ²⁹Menelaus has informed us that you wish to return home and look after your own affairs. ³⁰Therefore those who go home by the thirtieth day of Xanthicus will have our pledge of friendship and full permission ³¹for the Jews to enjoy

x The Greek text here is corrupt   y 164 B.C.

13–15: According to 1 Macc.4.35 no peace was made, but Lysias returned to Antioch for reinforcements. He may have heard of Antiochus' death and hastened home to take control. **11.16–38: Letters of Lysias, Antiochus V, and the Romans.** If Lysias heard of Philip's plot (see 9.29 n.), he may have wished to gain time through friendly gestures to the Jews. **16:** He wrote *to the people;* he did not recognize Judas' authority. **19:** Part of the Jews had *good will toward the government.* **21:** The date is early December, 164 B.C., before Judas rededicated the temple (1 Macc.4.52). **23:** *Our father,* Antiochus IV, *has gone on to the gods;* in his lifetime he had been worshiped. **25:** 1 Macc.4.36–61 says nothing of this, but Lysias may have instructed the citadel garrison not to interfere with the temple. **27:** The letter *to the senate* (1.10) and people ignores Judas (compare vv. 16–21). **29:** *Menelaus* had gone to Antioch and advised the king to let the Jews *return* to Jerusalem. He was now sent back (v. 32), hoping to regain the high priesthood. **30:** *Xanthicus,* March-April. **31:** *Their own food and laws,* 1 Macc.1.47–49. The

their own food and laws, just as formerly, and none of them shall be molested in any way for what he may have done in ignorance. [32]And I have also sent Menelaus to encourage you. [33]Farewell. The one hundred and forty-eighth year,[z] Xanthicus fifteenth."

34 The Romans also sent them a letter, which read thus:

"Quintus Memmius and Titus Manius, envoys of the Romans, to the people of the Jews, greeting. [35]With regard to what Lysias the kinsman of the king has granted you, we also give consent. [36]But as to the matters which he decided are to be referred to the king, as soon as you have considered them, send some one promptly, so that we may make proposals appropriate for you. For we are on our way to Antioch. [37]Therefore make haste and send some men, so that we may have your judgment. [38]Farewell. The one hundred and forty-eighth year,[a] Xanthicus fifteenth."

12 When this agreement had been reached, Lysias returned to the king, and the Jews went about their farming.

2 But some of the governors in various places, Timothy and Apollonius the son of Gennaeus, as well as Hieronymus and Demophon, and in addition to these Nicanor the governor of Cyprus, would not let them live quietly and in peace. [3]And some men of Joppa did so ungodly a deed as this: they invited the Jews who lived among them to embark, with their wives and children, on boats which they had provided, as though there were no ill will to the Jews;[b] [4]and this was done by public vote of the city. And when they accepted, because they wished to live peaceably and suspected nothing, the men of Joppa[c] took them out to sea and drowned them, not less than two hundred. [5]When Judas heard of the cruelty visited on his countrymen, he gave orders to his men [6]and, calling upon God the righteous Judge, attacked the murderers of his brethren. He set fire to the harbor by night, and burned the boats, and massacred those who had taken refuge there. [7]Then, because the city's gates were closed, he withdrew, intending to come again and root out the whole community of Joppa. [8]But learning that the men in Jamnia meant in the same way to wipe out the Jews who were living among them, [9]he attacked the people of Jamnia by night and set fire to the harbor and the fleet, so that the glow of the light was seen in Jerusalem, thirty miles[d] distant.

10 When they had gone more than a mile[e] from there, on their march against Timothy, not less than five thousand Arabs with five hundred horsemen attacked them. [11]After a hard fight Judas and his men won the victory, by the help of God. The defeated nomads besought Judas to grant them pledges of friendship, promising to give him cattle and to help his people[f] in all other ways. [12]Judas, thinking that they might really be useful in many ways, agreed to make peace with them; and after receiving his pledges they departed to their tents.

13 He also attacked a certain city which was strongly fortified with

z 164 B.C.   a 164 B.C.
b Gk *them*   c Gk *they*
d Gk *two hundred and forty stadia*
e Gk *nine stadia*   f Gk *them*

---

words *in ignorance* imply that the king still maintained his claims and merely granted pardon (1 Macc.13.39). **34–37:** The *envoys* acted as intermediaries in *matters . . . referred to the king* that were still under negotiation.

12.1–16: Attacks on Joppa, Jamnia, and Caspin (the section 11.1–12.1 is out of place, and 12.2 resumes the narrative of 10.31). **1:** Palestinian Jews lived by *farming.* **2:** *Timothy,* 8.30–33; 10.24–37. *Apollonius,* not the Apollonius of 4.21. *Nicanor* is called *governor of Cyprus;* it was under Egypt's rule till 58 B.C., but Syria may have claimed it after the defection of Ptolemy Macron (10.13). There may have been two Nicanors (see 14.12 n.). **8:** *Jamnia,* about twelve miles south of Joppa. **13:** *Caspin,* perhaps Chaspho (1 Macc.5.36). **15:** Jos.6.1–21.

earthworks[g] and walls, and inhabited by all sorts of Gentiles. Its name was Caspin. [14]And those who were within, relying on the strength of the walls and on their supply of provisions, behaved most insolently toward Judas and his men, railing at them and even blaspheming and saying unholy things. [15]But Judas and his men, calling upon the great Sovereign of the world, who without battering-rams or engines of war overthrew Jericho in the days of Joshua, rushed furiously upon the walls. [16]They took the city by the will of God, and slaughtered untold numbers, so that the adjoining lake, a quarter of a mile[h] wide, appeared to be running over with blood.

[17] When they had gone ninety-five miles[i] from there, they came to Charax, to the Jews who are called Toubiani. [18]They did not find Timothy in that region, for he had by then departed from the region without accomplishing anything, though in one place he had left a very strong garrison. [19]Dositheus and Sosipater, who were captains under Maccabeus, marched out and destroyed those whom Timothy had left in the stronghold, more than ten thousand men. [20]But Maccabeus arranged his army in divisions, set men[j] in command of the divisions, and hastened after Timothy, who had with him a hundred and twenty thousand infantry and two thousand five hundred cavalry. [21]When Timothy learned of the approach of Judas, he sent off the women and the children and also the baggage to a place called Carnaim; for that place was hard to besiege and difficult of access because of the narrowness of all the approaches. [22]But when Judas' first division appeared, terror and fear came over the enemy at the manifestation to them of him who sees all things; and they rushed

off in flight and were swept on, this way and that, so that often they were injured by their own men and pierced by the points of their swords. [23]And Judas pressed the pursuit with the utmost vigor, putting .the sinners to the sword, and destroyed as many as thirty thousand men.

[24] Timothy himself fell into the hands of Dositheus and Sosipater and their men. With great guile he besought them to let him go in safety, because he held the parents of most of them and the brothers of some and no consideration would be shown them. [25]And when with many words he had confirmed his solemn promise to restore them unharmed, they let him go, for the sake of saving their brethren.

[26] Then Judas[k] marched against Carnaim and the temple of Atargatis, and slaughtered twenty-five thousand people. [27]After the rout and destruction of these, he marched also against Ephron, a fortified city where Lysias dwelt with multitudes of people of all nationalities.[l] Stalwart young men took their stand before the walls and made a vigorous defense; and great stores of war engines and missiles were there. [28]But the Jews[m] called upon the Sovereign who with power shatters the might of his enemies, and they got the city into their hands, and killed as many as twenty-five thousand of those who were within it.

[29] Setting out from there, they hastened to Scythopolis, which is seventy-five miles[n] from Jerusalem. [30]But when the Jews who dwelt there bore witness to the good will which the people of Scythopolis had shown them and their kind treatment of them

g The Greek text here is uncertain
h Gk *two stadia*
i Gk *seven hundred and fifty stadia*
j Gk *them*   k Gk *he*
l The Greek text of this sentence is uncertain
m Gk *they*   n Gk *six hundred stadia*

12.17–31: Battles in the northeast (the account supplements 1 Macc.5.9–32). **17:** *Toubiani,* perhaps men of Tob (1 Macc.5.13). **18:** *One place,* perhaps Bozrah, southeast of Tob (1 Macc. 5.28). **21:** *Carnaim,* a little north of Dera'a in Syria (Gen.14.5; 1 Macc.5.26). **26:** *Atargatis,* the Syrian goddess to whom fish were sacred. **27:** He *marched* south *against Ephron,* eight miles east of the Jordan, opposite Scythopolis (v. 29; 1 Macc.5.46–51). **29:** *Scythopolis,* ancient

in times of misfortune, [31]they thanked them and exhorted them to be well disposed to their race in the future also. Then they went up to Jerusalem, as the feast of weeks was close at hand.

32 After the feast called Pentecost, they hastened against Gorgias, the governor of Idumea. [33]And he came out with three thousand infantry and four hundred cavalry. [34]When they joined battle, it happened that a few of the Jews fell. [35]But a certain Dositheus, one of Bacenor's men, who was on horseback and was a strong man, caught hold of Gorgias, and grasping his cloak was dragging him off by main strength, wishing to take the accursed man alive, when one of the Thracian horsemen bore down upon him and cut off his arm; so Gorgias escaped and reached Marisa.

36 As Esdris and his men had been fighting for a long time and were weary, Judas called upon the Lord to show himself their ally and leader in the battle. [37]In the language of their fathers he raised the battle cry, with hymns; then he charged against Gorgias' men when they were not expecting it, and put them to flight.

38 Then Judas assembled his army and went to the city of Adullam. As the seventh day was coming on, they purified themselves according to the custom, and they kept the sabbath there.

39 On the next day, as by that time it had become necessary, Judas and his men went to take up the bodies of the fallen and to bring them back to lie with their kinsmen in the sepulchres of their fathers. [40]Then under the tunic of every one of the dead they found sacred tokens of the idols of Jamnia, which the law forbids the Jews to wear. And it became clear to all that this was why these men had fallen. [41]So they all blessed the ways of the Lord, the righteous Judge, who reveals the things that are hidden; [42]and they turned to prayer, beseeching that the sin which had been committed might be wholly blotted out. And the noble Judas exhorted the people to keep themselves free from sin, for they had seen with their own eyes what had happened because of the sin of those who had fallen. [43]He also took up a collection, man by man, to the amount of two thousand drachmas of silver, and sent it to Jerusalem to provide for a sin offering. In doing this he acted very well and honorably, taking account of the resurrection. [44]For if he were not expecting that those who had fallen would rise again, it would have been superfluous and foolish to pray for the dead. [45]But if he was looking to the splendid reward that is laid up for those who fall asleep in godliness, it was a holy and pious thought. Therefore he made atonement for the dead, that they might be delivered from their sin.

13 In the one hundred and forty-ninth year[o] word came to Judas

o 163 B.C.

Beth-shan, then and later an important city (see 1 Macc.5.52 n.). **31**: The *feast of weeks* or Pentecost was at the time of the wheat harvest, seven weeks after Passover, and was celebrated in Jerusalem (Ex.34.22–24; Dt.16.9–12).

12.32–38: Battle with Gorgias. 35: *Marisa*, in the foothills southwest of Jerusalem near Beit-Jibrin (see 1 Macc.5.66 n.). **36**: *Esdris*, evidently a division leader (v. 20); the author of 2 Maccabees has abbreviated his source. **38**: *City of Adullam*, northeast of Marisa (Jos.12.15; 15.35). *They kept the sabbath*, when it was not necessary to fight (8.27; see 1 Macc.2.41 n.).

12.39–45: Burial of the dead. The author believed that many had been killed because they wore *sacred tokens* of pagan gods *which the law forbids* (v. 40; Dt.7.25–26), but Josephus says (*Antiquities*, XII. viii. 6) this reverse befell them because they had disobeyed Judas' instructions not to join battle before his arrival. This is the first known statement of the doctrine that a *sin offering* and prayer make *atonement* for the sins of *the dead* (v. 45), and it is justified by the hope that *those who had fallen would rise again* (vv. 43–44; 7.11; 14.46). *Fall asleep*, die (1 Cor.15.20).

13.1–8: Death of Menelaus. 1–2: *Antiochus* and *Lysias*, see 10.10–11 n. *Chariots armed with*

and his men that Antiochus Eupator was coming with a great army against Judea, ²and with him Lysias, his guardian, who had charge of the government. Each of them had a Greek force of one hundred and ten thousand infantry, five thousand three hundred cavalry, twenty-two elephants, and three hundred chariots armed with scythes.

3 Menelaus also joined them and with utter hypocrisy urged Antiochus on, not for the sake of his country's welfare, but because he thought that he would be established in office. ⁴But the King of kings aroused the anger of Antiochus against the scoundrel; and when Lysias informed him that this man was to blame for all the trouble, he ordered them to take him to Beroea and to put him to death by the method which is the custom in that place. ⁵For there is a tower in that place, fifty cubits high, full of ashes, and it has a rim running around it which on all sides inclines precipitously into the ashes. ⁶There they all push to destruction any man guilty of sacrilege or notorious for other crimes. ⁷By such a fate it came about that Menelaus the lawbreaker died, without even burial in the earth. ⁸And this was eminently just; because he had committed many sins against the altar whose fire and ashes were holy, he met his death in ashes.

9 The king with barbarous arrogance was coming to show to the Jews things far worse than those that had been done[p] in his father's time. ¹⁰But when Judas heard of this, he ordered the people to call upon the Lord day and night, now if ever to help those who were on the point of being deprived of the law and their country and the holy temple, ¹¹and not to let the people who had just begun to revive fall into the hands of the blasphemous Gentiles. ¹²When they had all joined in the same petition and had besought the merciful Lord with weeping and fasting and lying prostrate for three days without ceasing, Judas exhorted them and ordered them to stand ready.

13 After consulting privately with the elders, he determined to march out and decide the matter by the help of God before the king's army could enter Judea and get possession of the city. ¹⁴So, committing the decision to the Creator of the world and exhorting his men to fight nobly to the death for the laws, temple, city, country, and commonwealth, he pitched his camp near Modein. ¹⁵He gave his men the watchword, "God's victory," and with a picked force of the bravest young men, he attacked the king's pavilion at night and slew as many as two thousand men in the camp. He stabbed[q] the leading elephant and its rider. ¹⁶In the end they filled the camp with terror and confusion and withdrew in triumph. ¹⁷This happened, just as day was dawning, because the Lord's help protected him.

18 The king, having had a taste of the daring of the Jews, tried strategy in attacking their positions. ¹⁹He advanced against Beth-zur, a strong fortress of the Jews, was turned back, attacked again,[r] and was defeated. ²⁰Judas sent in to the garrison what-

p Or *the worst of the things that had been done*
q The Greek text here is uncertain
r Or *faltered*

---

scythes to cut down foot soldiers had been used since the days of the Persian Empire. **4:** *The King of kings*, God (Rev.19.16). What *aroused* his *anger* is not known (but see 4.27). *Beroea*, now Aleppo in northern Syria. *The method* of execution (vv. 5–6) was Persian.

13.9–17: Preliminary skirmish. 12: Jews employed such acts of penitence particularly when there was danger of sacrilege (3.15; 10.4; 1 Macc.4.40). **14:** The Syrian army had invaded Judea from the south, through Idumea (1 Macc.6.31). Judas first *pitched his camp near Modein* to watch the Syrian line along the coast. The first battle occurred at Beth-zechariah (1 Macc.6.32–47). **15:** "*God's victory*," see 8.23 n. Eleazar *stabbed the leading elephant* (1 Macc.6.43–46). **16:** According to 1 Macc.6.47 the Jews fled.

13.18–26: Attack on Beth-zur. 19: The Syrians were defeated in the first attempt (1 Macc.

ever was necessary. [21]But Rhodocus, a man from the ranks of the Jews, gave secret information to the enemy; he was sought for, caught, and put in prison. [22]The king negotiated a second time with the people in Beth-zur, gave pledges, received theirs, withdrew, attacked Judas and his men, was defeated; [23]he got word that Philip, who had been left in charge of the government, had revolted in Antioch; he was dismayed, called in the Jews, yielded and swore to observe all their rights, settled with them and offered sacrifice, honored the sanctuary and showed generosity to the holy place. [24]He received Maccabeus, left Hegemonides as governor from Ptolemais to Gerar, [25]and went to Ptolemais. The people of Ptolemais were indignant over the treaty; in fact they were so angry that they wanted to annul its terms.[s] [26]Lysias took the public platform, made the best possible defense, convinced them, appeased them, gained their good will, and set out for Antioch. This is how the king's attack and withdrawal turned out.

14 Three years later, word came to Judas and his men that Demetrius, the son of Seleucus, had sailed into the harbor of Tripolis with a strong army and a fleet, [2]and had taken possession of the country, having made away with Antiochus and his guardian Lysias.

3 Now a certain Alcimus, who had formerly been high priest but had wilfully defiled himself in the times of separation, realized that there was no way for him to be safe or to have access again to the holy altar, [4]and went to King Demetrius in about the one hundred and fifty-first year,[t] presenting to him a crown of gold and a palm, and besides these some of the customary olive branches from the temple. During that day he kept quiet. [5]But he found an opportunity that furthered his mad purpose when he was invited by Demetrius to a meeting of the council and was asked about the disposition and intentions of the Jews. He answered:

6 "Those of the Jews who are called Hasideans, whose leader is Judas Maccabeus, are keeping up war and stirring up sedition, and will not let the kingdom attain tranquillity. [7]Therefore I have laid aside my ancestral glory—I mean the high priesthood—and have now come here, [8]first because I am genuinely concerned for the interests of the king, and second because I have regard also for my fellow citizens. For through the folly of those whom I have mentioned our whole nation is now in no small misfortune. [9]Since you are acquainted, O king, with the details of this matter, deign to take thought for our country and our hard-pressed nation with the gracious kindness which you show to all. [10]For as long as Judas lives, it is impossible for the government to find peace."

11 When he had said this, the rest of the king's friends, who were hostile to Judas, quickly inflamed Demetrius still more. [12]And he immediately chose Nicanor, who had been in command of

s The Greek text of this clause is uncertain
t 161 B.C.

6.31). **21–22:** The garrison surrendered because of lack of food (1 Macc.6.49); possibly this was the *secret information.* **23:** *Philip,* see 9.29 n.; 1 Macc.6.14–15,55–56. **24:** *Gerar,* south of Gaza on the coastal plain. **26:** 1 Macc.6.63.

14.1–10: Accession of Demetrius I (1 Macc.7.1–7). **1:** *Three years later,* about 161 B.C. *Demetrius* I Soter, *the son of Seleucus* IV, reigned 162–150. *Tripolis,* see 1 Macc.7.1 n. **2:** *Antiochus . . . Lysias,* 1 Macc.7.3–4. **3:** *Alcimus* may not have *been high priest. Defiled,* 4.11–15. **4:** 1 Macc.7.5–7 may record an earlier visit. *Crown,* emblem of sovereignty; the *palm,* victory. **6:** *Hasideans,* see 1 Macc.2.42 n. **7:** *Ancestral glory,* he claimed legitimate succession. **8:** See 1 Macc.1.11 n.

14.11–14: Appointment of Nicanor and Alcimus. This story omits the expedition of Bacchides (1 Macc.7.8–25). Josephus says that *Nicanor* had escaped from Rome with Demetrius (*Antiqui-*

the elephants, appointed him governor of Judea, and sent him off ¹³with orders to kill Judas and scatter his men, and to set up Alcimus as high priest of the greatest temple. ¹⁴And the Gentiles throughout Judea, who had fled before^u Judas, flocked to join Nicanor, thinking that the misfortunes and calamities of the Jews would mean prosperity for themselves.

15 When the Jews^v heard of Nicanor's coming and the gathering of the Gentiles, they sprinkled dust upon their heads and prayed to him who established his own people for ever and always upholds his own heritage by manifesting himself. ¹⁶At the command of the leader, they^w set out from there immediately and engaged them in battle at a village called Dessau.^x ¹⁷Simon, the brother of Judas, had encountered Nicanor, but had been temporarily^y checked because of the sudden consternation created by the enemy.

18 Nevertheless Nicanor, hearing of the valor of Judas and his men and their courage in battle for their country, shrank from deciding the issue by bloodshed. ¹⁹Therefore he sent Posidonius and Theodotus and Mattathias to give and receive pledges of friendship. ²⁰When the terms had been fully considered, and the leader had informed the people, and it appeared that they were of one mind, they agreed to the covenant. ²¹And the leaders^z set a day on which to meet by themselves. A chariot came forward from each army; seats of honor were set in place; ²²Judas posted armed men in readiness at key places to prevent sudden treachery on the part of the enemy; they held the proper conference.

23 Nicanor stayed on in Jerusalem and did nothing out of the way, but

dismissed the flocks of people that had gathered. ²⁴And he kept Judas always in his presence; he was warmly attached to the man. ²⁵And he urged him to marry and have children; so he married, settled down, and shared the common life.

26 But when Alcimus noticed their good will for one another, he took the covenant that had been made and went to Demetrius. He told him that Nicanor was disloyal to the government, for he had appointed that conspirator against the kingdom, Judas, to be his successor. ²⁷The king became excited and, provoked by the false accusations of that depraved man, wrote to Nicanor, stating that he was displeased with the covenant and commanding him to send Maccabeus to Antioch as a prisoner without delay.

28 When this message came to Nicanor, he was troubled and grieved that he had to annul their agreement when the man had done no wrong. ²⁹Since it was not possible to oppose the king, he watched for an opportunity to accomplish this by a stratagem. ³⁰But Maccabeus, noticing that Nicanor was more austere in his dealings with him and was meeting him more rudely than had been his custom, concluded that this austerity did not spring from the best motives. So he gathered not a few of his men, and went into hiding from Nicanor.

31 When the latter became aware that he had been cleverly outwitted by the man, he went to the great^a and holy temple while the priests were offering the customary sacrifices, and com-

u The Greek text is uncertain
v Gk *they*
w Gk *he*
x The name is uncertain
y Other authorities read *slowly*
z Gk *they*
a Gk *greatest*

ties, xii. x. 4); if he is the person in 8.9–36 he must have gone from Syria to Rome to assist the escape.

14.15–36: Nicanor seeks friendship with Judas. 15: *Sprinkled dust,* Jos.7.6. **16:** *The leader,* Judas, or possibly Nicanor. *Dessau,* perhaps Adasa (1 Macc.7.40–45). **20–21:** *The leader,* Nicanor. *The people,* his army. Afterward *the leaders,* Nicanor and Judas, met. **22:** 1 Macc.7.12–18. **24:** *Warmly attached* only so long as things went well (compare vv. 31–33). **26:** *Alcimus* failed to get civil power and feared that *Judas* would be made his *successor* as high priest.

manded them to hand the man over.
³²And when they declared on oath that
they did not know where the man was
whom he sought, ³³he stretched out his
right hand toward the sanctuary, and
swore this oath: "If you do not hand
Judas over to me as a prisoner, I will
level this precinct of God to the
ground and tear down the altar, and
I will build here a splendid temple to
Dionysus."

34 Having said this, he went away.
Then the priests stretched forth their
hands toward heaven and called upon
the constant Defender of our nation,
in these words: ³⁵"O Lord of all, who
hast need of nothing, thou wast pleased
that there be a temple for thy habitation among us; ³⁶so now, O holy One,
Lord of all holiness, keep undefiled for
ever this house that has been so
recently purified."

37 A certain Razis, one of the elders
of Jerusalem, was denounced to Nicanor as a man who loved his fellow
citizens and was very well thought
of and for his good will was called
father of the Jews. ³⁸For in former
times, when there was no mingling
with the Gentiles, he had been accused
of Judaism, and for Judaism he had
with all zeal risked body and life.
³⁹Nicanor, wishing to exhibit the enmity which he had for the Jews, sent
more than five hundred soldiers to
arrest him; ⁴⁰for he thought that by
arresting[b] him he would do them an
injury. ⁴¹When the troops were about
to capture the tower and were forcing
the door of the courtyard, they ordered
that fire be brought and the doors
burned. Being surrounded, Razis[c] fell
upon his own sword, ⁴²preferring to die
nobly rather than to fall into the hands
of sinners and suffer outrages unworthy
of his noble birth. ⁴³But in the heat of

the struggle he did not hit exactly, and
the crowd was now rushing in through
the doors. He bravely ran up on the
wall, and manfully threw himself down
into the crowd. ⁴⁴But as they quickly
drew back, a space opened and he fell
in the middle of the empty space.
⁴⁵Still alive and aflame with anger, he
rose, and though his blood gushed
forth and his wounds were severe he
ran through the crowd; and standing
upon a steep rock, ⁴⁶with his blood
now completely drained from him, he
tore out his entrails, took them with
both hands and hurled them at the
crowd, calling upon the Lord of life
and spirit to give them back to him
again. This was the manner of his
death.

15 When Nicanor heard that Judas
and his men were in the region
of Samaria, he made plans to attack
them with complete safety on the day
of rest. ²And when the Jews who were
compelled to follow him said, "Do not
destroy so savagely and barbarously,
but show respect for the day which he
who sees all things has honored and
hallowed above other days," ³the
thrice-accursed wretch asked if there
were a sovereign in heaven who had
commanded the keeping of the sabbath
day. ⁴And when they declared, "It is
the living Lord himself, the Sovereign
in heaven, who ordered us to observe
the seventh day," ⁵he replied, "And
I am a sovereign also, on earth, and I
command you to take up arms and
finish the king's business." Nevertheless, he did not succeed in carrying out
his abominable design.

6 This Nicanor in his utter boastfulness and arrogance had determined to
erect a public monument of victory

b The Greek text here is uncertain
c Gk *he*

33: *Stretched out his right hand . . . and swore*, 15.32–33. *Dionysus*, 6.7. **35–36:** 1 Kg.8.27–30. *Purified*, 10.1–8.

14.37–46: Death of Razis. A martyrology in the style of 6.18–7.42. **37:** *Elders*, 13.13. **46:** He expected his body to be restored in the resurrection (7.11).

15.1–36: Death of Nicanor (1 Macc.7.39–50). **1:** *Nicanor* camped at Beth-horon, and *Judas* was at Adasa, between Beth-horon and Jerusalem. **2:** *The Jews* in Nicanor's army wished to honor the sabbath. **3:** *Thrice-accursed*, 8.34. **4–5:** Ex.20.8–11; Dan.3.16–18.

over Judas and his men. ⁷But Maccabeus did not cease to trust with all confidence that he would get help from the Lord. ⁸And he exhorted his men not to fear the attack of the Gentiles, but to keep in mind the former times when help had come to them from heaven, and now to look for the victory which the Almighty would give them. ⁹Encouraging them from the law and the prophets, and reminding them also of the struggles they had won, he made them the more eager. ¹⁰And when he had aroused their courage, he gave his orders, at the same time pointing out the perfidy of the Gentiles and their violation of oaths. ¹¹He armed each of them not so much with confidence in shields and spears as with the inspiration of brave words, and he cheered them all by relating a dream, a sort of vision,ᵈ which was worthy of belief.

12 What he saw was this: Onias, who had been high priest, a noble and good man, of modest bearing and gentle manner, one who spoke fittingly and had been trained from childhood in all that belongs to excellence, was praying with outstretched hands for the whole body of the Jews. ¹³Then likewise a man appeared, distinguished by his gray hair and dignity, and of marvelous majesty and authority. ¹⁴And Onias spoke, saying, "This is a man who loves the brethren and prays much for the people and the holy city, Jeremiah, the prophet of God." ¹⁵Jeremiah stretched out his right hand and gave to Judas a golden sword, and as he gave it he addressed him thus: ¹⁶"Take this holy sword, a gift from God, with which you will strike down your adversaries."

17 Encouraged by the words of Judas, so noble and so effective in arousing valor and awaking manliness in the souls of the young, they determined not to carry on a campaign but to attack bravely, and to decide the matter, by fighting hand to hand with all courage, because the city and the sanctuary and the temple were in danger. ¹⁸Their concern for wives and children, and also for brethren and relatives, lay upon them less heavily; their greatest and first fear was for the consecrated sanctuary. ¹⁹And those who had to remain in the city were in no little distress, being anxious over the encounter in the open country.

20 When all were now looking forward to the coming decision, and the enemy was already close at hand with their army drawn up for battle, the elephantsᵉ strategically stationed and the cavalry deployed on the flanks, ²¹Maccabeus, perceiving the hosts that were before him and the varied supply of arms and the savagery of the elephants,ᵉ stretched out his hands toward heaven and called upon the Lord who works wonders; for he knew that it is not by arms, but as the Lordᶠ decides, that he gains the victory for those who deserve it. ²²And he called upon him in these words: "O Lord, thou didst send thy angel in the time of Hezekiah king of Judea, and he slew fully a hundred and eighty-five thousand in the camp of Sennacherib. ²³So now, O Sovereign of the heavens, send a good angel to carry terror and trembling before us. ²⁴By the might of thy arm may these blasphemers who come against thy holy people be struck down." With these words he ended his prayer.

d The Greek text here is uncertain
e Gk *beasts*
f Gk *he*

8: 1 Macc.7.41. **9:** *The law and the prophets*, the first two major divisions of the Old Testament, were now regarded as scripture (compare the Prologue to Sirach; see 2 Esd.14.45 n.); not all the other books had been collected. **10:** *Violation of oaths*, 11.27–32; 14.20–28. **12:** *Onias*, 3.1–40. **14:** The writer believed that saints like *Jeremiah* were alive even before the resurrection. **15–16:** The *golden sword* was a sign that God approved the Jews' self-defense on the sabbath. **18:** *First fear*, compare 14.33. **20:** *Elephants*, to break through the Jewish infantry; the *cavalry* protected the *flanks* of the Syrian infantry. **22–23:** See 11.6 n.; 2 Kg.19.35.

25 Nicanor and his men advanced with trumpets and battle songs; ²⁶and Judas and his men met the enemy in battle with invocation to God and prayers. ²⁷So, fighting with their hands and praying to God in their hearts, they laid low no less than thirty-five thousand men, and were greatly gladdened by God's manifestation.

28 When the action was over and they were returning with joy, they recognized Nicanor, lying dead, in full armor. ²⁹Then there was shouting and tumult, and they blessed the Sovereign Lord in the language of their fathers. ³⁰And the man who was ever in body and soul the defender of his fellow citizens, the man who maintained his youthful good will toward his countrymen, ordered them to cut off Nicanor's head and arm and carry them to Jerusalem. ³¹And when he arrived there and had called his countrymen together and stationed the priests before the altar, he sent for those who were in the citadel. ³²He showed them the vile Nicanor's head and that profane man's arm, which had been boastfully stretched out against the holy house of the Almighty; ³³and he cut out the tongue of the ungodly Nicanor and said that he would give it piecemeal to the birds and hang up these rewards of his folly opposite the sanctuary. ³⁴And they all, looking to heaven, blessed the Lord who had manifested himself, saying, "Blessed is he who has kept his own place undefiled." ³⁵And he hung Nicanor's head from the citadel, a clear and conspicuous sign to every one of the help of the Lord. ³⁶And they all decreed by public vote never to let this day go unobserved, but to celebrate the thirteenth day of the twelfth month—which is called Adar in the Syrian language—the day before Mordecai's day.

37 This, then, is how matters turned out with Nicanor. And from that time the city has been in the possession of the Hebrews. So I too will here end my story. ³⁸If it is well told and to the point, that is what I myself desired; if it is poorly done and mediocre, that was the best I could do. ³⁹For just as it is harmful to drink wine alone, or, again, to drink water alone, while wine mixed with water is sweet and delicious and enhances one's enjoyment, so also the style of the story delights the ears of those who read the work. And here will be the end.

25: *Battle songs,* such as Pss.68.1–3; 83. **29:** *Language of their fathers,* Hebrew or Aramaic. **31:** *The citadel* on the Ophel hill was held by Syrians (1 Macc.1.33; 6.18); but the Jews had built another fort (1 Macc.4.60). **32:** *Head . . . arm,* 14.33. **35:** 1 Sam.31.9; Jdt.14.1; 1 Macc.7.47. **36:** The *twelfth month* (February–March) was *called Adar in the Syrian language* (that is, in Aramaic) and also in Hebrew. If there was but one month of Adar in this year (probably 161 B.C.), it was *the day before Mordecai's day,* but in some years a second month of Adar was intercalated to harmonize the calendar. Nicanor's day was observed up to A.D. 70 (see 1 Macc.7.49 n.).

15.37–39: Conclusion. The epitomist wrote some time before the Jewish war (A.D. 66–70), when Jerusalem was still in Jewish hands. **37:** *Hebrews,* see 7.31 n. **39:** To *drink wine alone* was a mark of the drunkard or spendthrift. *Water alone* was the drink of the poor, or of certain Greek philosophers, or those who like the Rechabites were forbidden wine (Jer.35.5–10). *The style* will delight *the ears of those who read,* because in antiquity it was the custom to read literary works aloud, even to oneself.

THE THIRD BOOK OF THE

MACCABEES

The title of the book known as 3 Maccabees is a misnomer, for the contents deal not with the exploits of the Maccabean heroes, but with the struggles of Egyptian Jews who suffered under Ptolemy IV Philopator (221–203 B.C.), half a century prior to the Maccabean period and the persecution of Palestinian Jewry under Antiochus IV Epiphanes (175–164 B.C.). The book, which was written in Greek by an unknown Alexandrian Jew during the first century B.C., has been transmitted in manuscripts of the Greek Septuagint as well as of the Syriac Peshitta and in most manuscripts of the Armenian Bible. It is not, however, included in the Latin Vulgate. This may explain why the book has been accorded canonical status in Eastern Christendom, whereas in the Western Churches, both Roman and Reformed, it is regarded as apocryphal.

The author of 3 Maccabees describes the attempt made by Ptolemy IV Philopator to enter the holy of holies in the temple at Jerusalem, and his miraculous repulse (1.1–2.24). Having returned to Egypt, he determines to wreak his vengeance on the Jews of Egypt for his humiliation in Jerusalem. He alters not only their political status but also attempts to impose upon them the pagan cult of Dionysus (2.25–33). Unable to compel the great majority of the Jews to renounce their ancestral religion, he orders cruel and unusual punishments, and even death for all who refuse to apostatize (3.1–5.51). Finally, after Eleazar, an aged priest, prays earnestly for his people (6.1–25), through divine intervention the king repents and becomes the patron of the Jews, who return in safety and rejoicing to their homes (6.16–7.23).

The book was obviously written to console, exhort, and teach Egyptian Jews, who during the first century B.C. were several times threatened by efforts of the Roman administration to alter their civic status. The author intends to inspire faith in the providence of God (4.21) by recounting how the Jews had been delivered from similar tribulations in the past.

The style of the book is pseudoclassical, utilizing many uncommon and poetical words. Sentences are awkwardly constructed and full of repetitions. The author often exaggerates, and when in descriptions he attempts to introduce purple passages of rhetoric, he succeeds only in producing bombast and bathos.

Whether the events the author describes are fictional or real—and several names, places, and events can be corroborated in classical authors—3 Maccabees is significant for its religious message. The book represents the most orthodox type of Judaism, with its unswerving devotion to the Mosaic law and the temple cultus, as well as its emphasis upon the special position of the chosen people.

W HEN PHILOPATOR LEARNED FROM those who returned that the regions which he had controlled had been seized by Antiochus, he gave orders to all his forces, both infantry and cavalry, took with him his sister Arsinoë, and marched out to the region near Raphia, where Antiochus's supporters were encamped. ² But a certain Theodotus, determined to carry out the plot he had devised, took with him the best of the Ptolemaic arms that had been previously issued to him,[a] and crossed over by night to the tent of Ptolemy, intending single-handed to kill him and thereby end the war.

a Or the best of the Ptolemaic soldiers previously put under his command

---

1.1–7: The battle of Raphia (217 B.C.). The abruptness with which the book opens and the use of the Greek conjunctive particle *de* indicate that the introduction to 3 Macc. has not survived (see also 2.25 n.). **1:** Ptolemy IV *Philopator* was king of Egypt 221–203 B.C. *From those who returned*, fugitives who had escaped. *Antiochus* III, later called the Great, was king of Syria 223–187 B.C. *Raphia*, a city of Palestine, three miles from Gaza and not far from the Egyptian frontier. *Arsinoë*, Ptolemy's sister, who became his wife, was later put to death at the instigation of her husband. **2:** *Theodotus* had been chief commander of the Egyptian forces in Syria, but

3 But Dositheus, known as the son of Drimylus, a Jew by birth who later changed his religion and apostatized from the ancestral traditions, had led the king away and arranged that a certain insignificant man should sleep in the tent; and so it turned out that this man incurred the vengeance meant for the king.*b* 4 When a bitter fight resulted, and matters were turning out rather in favor of Antiochus, Arsinoë went to the troops with wailing and tears, her locks all disheveled, and exhorted them to defend themselves and their children and wives bravely, promising to give them each two minas of gold if they won the battle. 5 And so it came about that the enemy was routed in the action, and many captives also were taken. 6 Now that he had foiled the plot, Ptolemy*c* decided to visit the neighboring cities and encourage them. 7 By doing this, and by endowing their sacred enclosures with gifts, he strengthened the morale of his subjects.

8 Since the Jews had sent some of their council and elders to greet him, to bring him gifts of welcome, and to congratulate him on what had happened, he was all the more eager to visit them as soon as possible. 9 After he had arrived in Jerusalem, he offered sacrifice to the supreme God*d* and made thank-offerings and did what was fitting for the holy place.*e* Then, upon entering the place and being impressed by its excellence and its beauty, 10 he marveled at the good order of the temple, and conceived a desire to enter the holy of holies. 11 When they said that this was not permitted, because not even members of their own nation were allowed to enter, nor even all of the priests, but only the high priest who was pre-eminent over all, and he only once a year, the king was by no means persuaded. 12 Even after the law had been read to him, he did not cease to maintain that he ought to enter, saying, "Even if those men are deprived of this honor, I ought not to be." 13 And he inquired why, when he entered every other temple,*f* no one there had stopped him. 14 And someone heedlessly said that it was wrong to take this as a sign in itself. 15 "But since this has happened," the king*g* said, "why should not I at least enter, whether they wish it or not?"

16 Then the priests in all their vestments prostrated themselves and entreated the supreme God*h* to aid in the present situation and to avert the violence of this evil design, and they filled the temple with cries and tears; 17 and those who remained behind in the city were agitated and hurried out, supposing that something mysterious was occurring. 18 The virgins who had been enclosed in their chambers rushed out with their mothers, sprinkled their hair with dust,*i* and filled the streets with groans and lamentations. 19 Those women who had recently been arrayed

b Gk *that one*   *c* Gk *he*   *d* Gk *the greatest God*
e Gk *the place*   *f* Or *entered the temple precincts*
g Gk *he*   *h* Gk *the greatest God*
i Other ancient authorities add *and ashes*

subsequently became disaffected and deserted to Antiochus III (so Polybius, v.40). **3:** A *Dositheus* is mentioned in Hibeh papyrus 90 as priest of Alexander in 222 B.C. **5:** According to Polybius (v.86.5–6) Antiochus lost nearly 10,000 infantry, 300 cavalry, and 4,000 prisoners; Ptolemy 1,500 infantry and 700 cavalry.

1.8–15: Ptolemy attempts to enter the sanctuary at Jerusalem. 9: Reference to *the supreme God*, Greek *megistos theos*, occurs frequently in 3 Macc. (1.9,16; 3.11; 4.16; 5.25; 7.22) as well as in 2 Macc. (3.36). That the pagan Ptolemy should have offered *sacrifice* to the God of the Jews was not an unusual practice in an age of religious syncretism. *The place*, a surrogate for "the temple" in 3 Macc. and other Jewish literature. **10:** Ptolemy's eagerness to inspect the interior of the temple may have been motivated by his curiosity concerning its architecture, for he considered himself a connoisseur of the arts. **11:** *High priest . . . once a year*, Ex.30.10; Lev.16.2, 11–12,15,34; Heb.9.7; Josephus, *Ant.* XII.iii.3.

1.16–28: Jewish reaction to Ptolemy's determination to enter the sanctuary. It is possible that because of religious superstition many regarded Ptolemy's desire as an evil omen of something calamitous that would befall them. **18:** *Virgins*, 2 Macc.3.19. **19:** *Bridal chambers*, Jl.2.16;

for marriage abandoned the bridal chambers prepared for wedded union, and, neglecting proper modesty, in a disorderly rush flocked together in the city. [20] Mothers and nurses abandoned even newborn children here and there, some in houses and some in the streets, and without a backward look they crowded together at the most high temple. [21] Various were the supplications of those gathered there because of what the king was profanely plotting. [22] In addition, the bolder of the citizens would not tolerate the completion of his plans or the fulfillment of his intended purpose. [23] They shouted to their fellows to take arms and die courageously for the ancestral law, and created a considerable disturbance in the holy place;[j] and being barely restrained by the old men and the elders,[k] they resorted to the same posture of supplication as the others. [24] Meanwhile the crowd, as before, was engaged in prayer, [25] while the elders near the king tried in various ways to change his arrogant mind from the plan that he had conceived. [26] But he, in his arrogance, took heed of nothing, and began now to approach, determined to bring the aforesaid plan to a conclusion. [27] When those who were around him observed this, they turned, together with our people, to call upon him who has all power to defend them in the present trouble and not to overlook this unlawful and haughty deed. [28] The continuous, vehement, and concerted cry of the crowds[l] resulted in an immense uproar; [29] for it seemed that not only the men but also the walls and the whole earth around echoed, because indeed all at that time[m] preferred death to the profanation of the place.

2 Then the high priest Simon, facing the sanctuary, bending his knees and extending his hands with calm dignity, prayed as follows:[n] [2] "Lord, Lord, king of the heavens, and sovereign of all creation, holy among the holy ones, the only ruler, almighty, give attention to us who are suffering grievously from an impious and profane man, puffed up in his audacity and power. [3] For you, the creator of all things and the governor of all, are a just Ruler, and you judge those who have done anything in insolence and arrogance. [4] You destroyed those who in the past committed injustice, among whom were even giants who trusted in their strength and boldness, whom you destroyed by bringing upon them a boundless flood. [5] You consumed with fire and sulphur the men of Sodom who acted arrogantly, who were notorious for their vices;[o] and you made them an example to those who should come afterward. [6] You made known your mighty power by inflicting many and varied punishments on the audacious Pharaoh who had enslaved your holy people Israel. [7] And when he pursued them with chariots and a mass of troops, you overwhelmed him in the depths of the sea, but carried through safely those who had put their confidence in you, the Ruler over the whole creation. [8] And when they had seen works of your hands, they praised

j Gk *the place*
k Other ancient authorities read *priests*
l Other ancient authorities read *vehement cry of the assembled crowds*
m Other ancient authorities omit *at that time*
n Other ancient authorities omit verse 1
o Other ancient authorities read *secret in their vices*

2 Esd.16.33,34; Bar.2.23. **21:** *Various* with respect to the persons offering prayer. **23:** *Die courageously for the ancestral law,* 1 Macc.2.40; 3.21; 13.3–4; 2 Macc.8.21.

2.1–20: The prayer of Simon, the high priest. This was probably Simon II, son of Onias II and high priest about 219–196 B.C. (see Sir.50.1 n.). The prayer is in classic Jewish form which, like Eleazar's prayer in 6.1–15, follows the pattern of Pss.105 and 106 in addressing God in terms of his power, glory, and great works reflected in historical deliverances of Israel. **2:** *Holy among the holy ones,* Is.57.15 LXX. **3:** Ex.18.11; Ps.31.23. **4:** *Giants,* Jdt.16.7; Wis.14.6; Sir.16.7; Bar.3.26; 1 Enoch 7.2; 15.8. **5:** *Sodom,* Gen.19.24; Dt.29.23; Wis.10.7. *An example,* 2 Pet.2.6. **6:** *Power,* Ex.9.16; Rom.9.17. *Varied punishments,* Ex. chs. 5–12. **7:** *Overwhelmed him,* Ex. 14.21–28. **8:** *They praised,* Ex.15.1–21; Wis.19.8–9; 1 Macc.4.9. **9:** *Boundless and immeasurable*

you, the Almighty. [9] You, O King, when you had created the boundless and immeasurable earth, chose this city and sanctified this place for your name, though you have no need of anything; and when you had glorified it by your magnificent manifestation,[p] you made it a firm foundation for the glory of your great and honored name. [10] And because you love the house of Israel, you promised that if we should have reverses, and tribulation should overtake us, you would listen to our petition when we come to this place and pray. [11] And indeed you are faithful and true. [12] And because oftentimes when our fathers were oppressed you helped them in their humiliation, and rescued them from great evils, [13] see now, O holy King, that because of our many and great sins we are crushed with suffering, subjected to our enemies, and overtaken by helplessness. [14] In our downfall this audacious and profane man undertakes to violate the holy place on earth dedicated to your glorious name. [15] For your dwelling, the heaven of heavens, is unapproachable by man. [16] But because you graciously bestowed your glory upon your people Israel, you sanctified this place. [17] Do not punish us for the defilement committed by these men, or call us to account for this profanation, lest the transgressors boast in their wrath or exult in the arrogance of their tongue, saying, [18] 'We have trampled down the house of the sanctuary as offensive houses[q] are trampled down.' [19] Wipe away our sins and disperse our errors, and reveal your mercy at this hour. [20] Speedily let your mercies overtake us, and put praises in the mouth of those who are downcast and broken in spirit, and give us peace."

21 Thereupon God, who oversees all things, the first Father of all, holy among the holy ones, having heard the lawful supplication, scourged him who had exalted himself in insolence and audacity. [22] He shook him on this side and that as a reed is shaken by the wind, so that he lay helpless on the ground and, besides being paralyzed in his limbs, was unable even to speak, since he was smitten[r] by a righteous judgment. [23] Then both friends and bodyguards, seeing the severe punishment that had overtaken him, and fearing lest he should lose his life, quickly dragged him out, panic-stricken in their exceedingly great fear. [24] After a while he recovered, and though he had been punished, he by no means repented, but went away uttering bitter threats.

25 When he arrived in Egypt, he increased in his deeds of malice, abetted by the previously mentioned drinking companions and comrades, who were strangers to everything just. [26] He was not content with his uncounted licentious deeds, but he also continued with such audacity that he framed evil reports in the various localities; and many of his friends, intently observing the king's purpose,

p Or *epiphany*
q Or *the houses of the abominations*
r Other ancient authorities read *pierced*

---

earth, Bar.3.24–25. *This city*, Jerusalem. *Place*, see 1.9 n.; 1 Kg.9.3. *No need of anything*, Acts 17.25; 2 Macc.14.35–36. **10:** *Promised . . . you would listen*, Dt.4.30; 30.1–6; 1 Kg.8.33–34, 48–50. **12:** *Our fathers . . . you . . . received*, 1 Sam.12.10–11; Ps.22.4–5; 106.43; Neh.9.28. **14:** *Glorious name*, Jdt.9.8. **15:** *The heaven of heavens*, 1 Kg.8.27; Is.66.1. *Unapproachable by man*, Pr.30.4; Is.57.15; Bar.3.29. **18:** *Trampled down*, Is.10.10–11; Dan.8.13. **19:** *Wipe away our sins*, Ps.51.2,9. **20:** *Mercies*, Ps.79.8,13.

2.21–24: The punishment of Ptolemy. 21: *Holy ones*, see Is.57.15 LXX. **22:** *Paralyzed*, compare the punishment of Heliodorus (2 Macc.3.22–30) and of Antiochus (2 Macc.9.4–7). **23:** *Friends*, the higher officers and courtiers of the king (see 4 Macc.8.5 n.). *Lose his life*, 2 Macc.3.31. **24:** *By no means repented*, 2 Macc.9.7.

2.25–33: Hostile measures against the Jews of Alexandria. 25: Inasmuch as these *companions* have not, in fact, been *previously mentioned* in the present text of 3 Macc., we have additional evidence that the opening section has been lost (see 1.1–7 n.). **26:** *Friends*, see v.23 n.

themselves also followed his will.
²⁷ He proposed to inflict public disgrace upon the Jewish community,ˢ and he set up a stoneᵗ on the tower in the courtyard with this inscription: ²⁸ "None of those who do not sacrifice shall enter their sanctuaries, and all Jews shall be subjected to a registration involving poll tax and to the status of slaves. Those who object to this are to be taken by force and put to death; ²⁹ those who are registered are also to be branded on their bodies by fire with the ivy-leaf symbol of Dionysus, and they shall also be reduced to their former limited status." ³⁰ In order that he might not appear to be an enemy to all, he inscribed below: "But if any of them prefer to join those who have been initiated into the mysteries, they shall have equal citizenship with the Alexandrians."

31 Now some, however, with an obvious abhorrence of the price to be exacted for maintaining the religion of their city,ᵘ readily gave themselves up, since they expected to enhance their reputation by their future association with the king. ³² But the majority acted firmly with a courageous spirit and did not depart from their religion; and by paying money in exchange for life they confidently attempted to save themselves from the registration. ³³ They remained resolutely hopeful of obtaining help, and they abhorred those who separated themselves from them, considering them to be enemies of the Jewish nation,ᵛ and depriving them of common fellowship and mutual help.

3 When the impious king comprehended this situation, he became so infuriated that not only was he enraged against those Jews who lived in Alexandria, but was still more bitterly hostile toward those in the countryside; and he ordered that all should promptly be gathered into one place, and put to death by the most cruel means. ² While these matters were being arranged, a hostile rumor was circulated against the Jewish nationᵛ by men who conspired to do them ill, a pretext being given by a report that they hindered othersᵂ from the observance of their customs. ³ The Jews, however, continued to maintain good will and unswerving loyalty toward the dynasty; ⁴ but because they worshiped God and conducted themselves by his law, they kept their separateness with respect to foods. For this reason they appeared hateful to some; ⁵ but since they adorned their style of life with the good deeds of upright people, they were established in good repute among all men. ⁶ Nevertheless those of other races paid no heed to their good service to their nation, which was common talk among all; ⁷ instead they gossiped about the differences in worship and foods, alleging that these people were loyal neither to the king nor to his authorities, but were hostile and greatly opposed to his government. So they attached no ordinary reproach to them.

8 The Greeks in the city, though wronged in no way, when they saw an

s Gk *the nation*   t Gk *stele*
u The Greek text of this clause is uncertain
v Gk *the nation*   w Gk *them*

28: *Registration*, a rare Greek word (*laographia*), which has been found in Greek papyri from Egypt, refers to a list of all people of the lower classes and of the slaves. **29:** Such branding in honor of a deity was not uncommon in ancient times (compare Rev.7.3; 13.16–17). According to 2 Macc.6.7 Antiochus introduced the worship of Dionysus into Jerusalem. **32:** *Paying money*, as bribes. **33:** *Depriving them of . . . fellowship*, 2 Jn.10–11.

   3.1–10: The Jews and their neighbors. 1: The distinction between Jews in *Alexandria* and those in the *country* is made also in 4.11–12. **2:** The *rumor* (Est.3.8) maliciously represents the Jews as hostile to the best interests of the state. **4:** *Separateness with respect to foods*, for a defense of the observance of Jewish dietary rules, see the *Letter of Aristeas*, §§128–166. **5:** Dt.4.5; Col.4.5; 1 Th.4.12. **7:** For similar charges see Est.3.8; Ad. Est.13.4–5. **8:** *The Greeks*, the nobler, cultivated class, in distinction from "those of other races" (v.6).

unexpected tumult around these people and the crowds that suddenly were forming, were not strong enough to help them, for they lived under tyranny. They did try to console them, being grieved at the situation, and expected that matters would change; [9] for such a great community ought not be left to its fate when it had committed no offense. [10] And already some of their neighbors and friends and business associates had taken some of them aside privately and were pledging to protect them and to exert more earnest efforts for their assistance.

11 Then the king, boastful of his present good fortune, and not considering the might of the supreme God,[x] but assuming that he would persevere constantly in his same purpose, wrote this letter against them: [12] "King Ptolemy Philopator to his generals and soldiers in Egypt and all its districts, greetings and good health. [13] I myself and our government are faring well. [14] When our expedition took place in Asia, as you yourselves know, it was brought to conclusion, according to plan, by the gods' deliberate alliance with us in battle, [15] and we considered that we should not rule the nations inhabiting Coele-Syria and Phoenicia by the power of the spear but should cherish them with clemency and great benevolence, gladly treating them well. [16] And when we had granted very great revenues to the temples in the cities, we came on to Jerusalem also, and went up to honor the temple of those wicked people, who never cease from their folly. [17] They accepted our presence by word, but insincerely by deed, because when we proposed to enter their inner temple and honor it with magnificent and most beautiful offerings, [18] they were carried away by their traditional conceit, and excluded us from entering; but they were spared the exercise of our power because of the benevolence which we have toward all. [19] By maintaining their manifest ill-will toward us, they become the only people among all nations who hold their heads high in defiance of kings and their own benefactors, and are unwilling to regard any action as sincere.

20 "But we, when we arrived in Egypt victorious, accommodated ourselves to their folly and did as was proper, since we treat all nations with benevolence. [21] Among other things, we made known to all our amnesty toward their compatriots here, both because of their alliance with us and the myriad affairs liberally entrusted to them from the beginning; and we ventured to make a change, by deciding both to deem them worthy of Alexandrian citizenship and to make them participants in our regular religious rites.[y] [22] But in their innate malice they took this in a contrary spirit, and disdained what is good. Since they incline constantly to evil, [23] they not only spurn the priceless citizenship, but also both by speech and by silence they abominate those few among them who are sincerely disposed toward us; in every situation, in accordance with their infamous way of life, they secretly suspect that we may soon alter our policy. [24] Therefore, fully convinced by these indications that they are ill-disposed toward us in every way, we have taken precautions lest, if a sudden disorder should later arise against us, we should have these impious people behind our backs as traitors and barbarous enemies. [25] Therefore we have given orders that, as soon as this letter shall arrive, you are to send to

x Gk *the greatest God*
y Other ancient authorities read *partners of our regular priests*

3.11–30: Ptolemy orders the arrest of all Jews in his kingdom. 11: *Assuming that he would persevere*, a reference to the calamity that came upon him by which he forgot his own previous commands (5.27–28). 15: *Benevolence*, Greek *philanthropia* (see vv.18,20), was regarded as a major political virtue during the Hellenistic (and Byzantine) period. 18: *Excluded*, 1.10–12. 21: For the confidence reposed in Jews, see 6.25 and Josephus, *Ant.* XIX.v.2. 24: *Behind our*

us those who live among you, together with their wives and children, with insulting and harsh treatment, and bound securely with iron fetters, to suffer the sure and shameful death that befits enemies. [26] For when these all have been punished, we are sure that for the remaining time the government will be established for ourselves in good order and in the best state. [27] But whoever shelters any of the Jews, old people or children or even infants, will be tortured to death with the most hateful torments, together with his family. [28] Any one willing to give information will receive the property of the one who incurs the punishment, and also two thousand drachmas from the royal treasury, and will be awarded his freedom.[z] [29] Every place detected sheltering a Jew is to be made unapproachable and burned with fire, and shall become useless for all time to any mortal creature." [30] The letter was written in the above form.

4 In every place, then, where this decree arrived, a feast at public expense was arranged for the Gentiles with shouts and gladness, for the inveterate enmity which had long ago been in their minds was now made evident and outspoken. [2] But among the Jews there was incessant mourning, lamentation, and tearful cries; everywhere their hearts were burning, and they groaned because of the unexpected destruction that had suddenly been decreed for them. [3] What district or city, or what habitable place at all, or what streets were not filled with mourning and wailing for them? [4] For with such a harsh and ruthless spirit were they being sent off, all together, by the generals in the several cities, that at the sight of their unusual punish-

ments, even some of their enemies, perceiving the common object of pity before their eyes, reflected upon the uncertainty of life and shed tears at the most miserable expulsion of these people. [5] For a multitude of grayheaded old men, sluggish and bent with age, was being led away, forced to march at a swift pace by the violence with which they were driven in such a shameful manner. [6] And young women who had just entered the bridal chamber to share married life exchanged joy for wailing, their myrrh-perfumed hair sprinkled with ashes, and were carried away unveiled, all together raising a lament instead of a wedding song, as they were torn by the harsh treatment of the heathen.[a] [7] In bonds and in public view they were violently dragged along as far as the place of embarkation. [8] Their husbands, in the prime of youth, their necks encircled with ropes instead of garlands, spent the remaining days of their marriage festival in lamentations instead of good cheer and youthful revelry, seeing death immediately before them.[b] [9] They were brought on board like wild animals, driven under the constraint of iron bonds; some were fastened by the neck to the benches of the boats, others had their feet secured by unbreakable fetters, [10] and in addition they were confined under a solid deck, so that with their eyes in total darkness, they should undergo treatment befitting traitors during the whole voyage.

11 When these men had been brought to the place called Schedia, and the voyage was concluded as the king had decreed, he commanded that they

z Gk *crowned with freedom*
a One ancient authority reads *as though torn by heathen whelps*
b Gk *seeing Hades already lying at their feet*

---

backs, Ex.1.10. **28:** *Awarded his freedom,* another rendering is "crowned at the Eleutheria" (a festival of Dionysus; see 2.29 n.). **29:** *Useless for all time,* Ad. Est.16.24.
    4.1–21: The Jews brought to Alexandria and imprisoned. 1: *Enmity* on the part of native-born Egyptians for the Jews is assumed in 3 Macc.; contrast 3.8. **2:** *Mourning, lamentation, and tearful cries,* Est.4.3. **4:** *Unusual punishments,* 2 Macc.9.6. **6:** *Young women,* 1 Macc.1.26–27. **11:** *Schedia,* a promontory about three miles from Alexandria. *The hippodrome* was situated at the east or Canobic gate of Alexandria; according to Strabo (XVII.1.10, 16) a canal joined Schedia and the Canobic gate. *Inside . . . the city,* implies that Jews living in Alexandria (see

should be enclosed in the hippodrome which had been built with a monstrous perimeter wall in front of the city, and which was well suited to make them an obvious spectacle to all coming back into the city and to those from the city[c] going out into the country, so that they could neither communicate with the king's forces nor in any way claim to be inside the circuit of the city.[d] 12 And when this had happened, the king, hearing that the Jews' compatriots from the city frequently went out in secret to lament bitterly the ignoble misfortune of their brothers, 13 ordered in his rage that these men be dealt with in precisely the same fashion as the others, not omitting any detail of their punishment. 14 The entire race was to be registered individually, not for the hard labor that has been briefly mentioned before, but to be tortured with the outrages that he had ordered, and at the end to be destroyed in the space of a single day. 15 The registration of these people was therefore conducted with bitter haste and zealous intentness from the rising of the sun till its setting, and though uncompleted it stopped after forty days.

16 The king was greatly and continually filled with joy, organizing feasts in honor of all his idols, with a mind alienated from truth and with a profane mouth, praising speechless things that are not able even to communicate or to come to one's help, and uttering improper words against the supreme God.[e] 17 But after the previously mentioned interval of time the scribes declared to the king that they were no longer able to take the census of the Jews because of their innumerable multitude, 18 although most of

them were still in the country, some still residing in their homes, and some at the place;[f] the task was impossible for all the generals in Egypt. 19 After he had threatened them severely, charging that they had been bribed to contrive a means of escape, he was clearly convinced about the matter 20 when they said and proved that both the paper[g] and the pens they used for writing had already given out. 21 But this was an act of the invincible providence of him who was aiding the Jews from heaven.

5 Then the king, completely inflexible, was filled with overpowering anger and wrath; so he summoned Hermon, keeper of the elephants, 2 and ordered him on the following day to drug all the elephants – five hundred in number – with large handfuls of frankincense and plenty of unmixed wine, and to drive them in, maddened by the lavish abundance of liquor, so that the Jews might meet their doom. 3 When he had given these orders he returned to his feasting, together with those of his friends and of the army who were especially hostile toward the Jews. 4 And Hermon, keeper of the elephants, proceeded faithfully to carry out the orders. 5 The servants in charge of the Jews[h] went out in the evening and bound the hands of the wretched people and arranged for their continued custody through the night, convinced that the whole nation would experience its final destruction. 6 For to the Gentiles it appeared that the Jews were left

c Gk *those of them*
d Or *claim protection of the walls;* Greek obscure
e Gk *the greatest God*
f Other ancient authorities read *on the way*
g Or *paper factory*   *h* Gk *them*

v.12, *compatriots from the city*) had been thus far unmolested (yet compare 3.1). **14:** *Mentioned before,* see 2.28. **15:** *Forty days,* see 2 Macc.5.2. **16:** *Feasts,* Dan.5.4. *Supreme God,* see 1.9 n. **17:** *Their innumerable multitude,* an obvious hyperbole. **19:** *Bribed,* see 2.32. **21:** *Was aiding,* the author prepares his readers to expect that a vigilant Providence will provide further help *from heaven.*

5.1–51: Ptolemy orders the execution of the Jews, but is twice thwarted (vv.12,27–28). **2:** *Five hundred elephants* is an exaggeration; Ptolemy had seventy-three elephants at the battle of Raphia. **3:** *Returned to his feasting,* 4.16. **5:** *Bound the hands,* according to 3.25 they had already been bound securely, but perhaps their hands had been loosened when the Jews were enclosed

without any aid, [7] because in their bonds they were forcibly confined on every side. But with tears and a voice hard to silence they all called upon the Almighty Lord and Ruler of all power, their merciful God and Father, praying [8] that he avert with vengeance the evil plot against them and in a glorious manifestation rescue them from the fate now prepared for them. [9] So their entreaty ascended fervently to heaven.

10 Hermon, however, when he had drugged the pitiless elephants until they had been filled with a great abundance of wine and satiated with frankincense, presented himself at the courtyard early in the morning to report to the king about these preparations. [11] But the Lord[i] sent upon the king a portion of sleep, that beneficence which from the beginning, night and day, is bestowed by him who grants it to whomever he wishes. [12] And by the action of the Lord he was overcome by so pleasant and deep a sleep[j] that he quite failed in his lawless purpose and was completely frustrated in his inflexible plan. [13] Then the Jews, since they had escaped the appointed hour, praised their holy God and again begged him who is easily reconciled to show the might of his all-powerful hand to the arrogant Gentiles.

14 But now, since it was nearly the middle of the tenth hour, the person who was in charge of the invitations, seeing that the guests were assembled, approached the king and nudged him. [15] And when he had with difficulty roused him, he pointed out that the hour of the banquet was already slipping by, and he gave him an account of the situation. [16] The king, after considering this, returned to his drinking, and ordered those present for the banquet to recline opposite him. [17] When this was done he urged them to give themselves over to revelry and to make the present[k] portion of the banquet joyful by celebrating all the more. [18] After the party had been going on for some time, the king summoned Hermon and with sharp threats demanded to know why the Jews had been allowed to remain alive through the present day. [19] But when he, with the corroboration of his friends, pointed out that while it was still night he had carried out completely the order given him, [20] the king,[l] possessed by a savagery worse than that of Phalaris, said that the Jews[m] were benefited by today's sleep, "but," he added, "tomorrow without delay prepare the elephants in the same way for the destruction of the lawless Jews!" [21] When the king had spoken, all those present readily and joyfully with one accord gave their approval, and each departed to his own home. [22] But they did not so much employ the duration of the night in sleep as in devising all sorts of insults for those they thought to be doomed.

23 Then, as soon as the cock had crowed in the early morning, Hermon, having equipped[n] the beasts, began to move them along in the great colonnade. [24] The crowds of the city had been assembled for this most pitiful spectacle and they were eagerly waiting for daybreak. [25] But the Jews, at their last gasp, since the time had run out, stretched their hands toward heaven and with most tearful supplication and mournful dirges implored the supreme God[o] to help them again at once. [26] The rays of the sun were not yet shed abroad, and while the king was receiving his friends, Hermon arrived and invited him to come out,

i Gk *he*
j Other ancient authorities add *from evening to the ninth hour*
k Other ancient authorities read *delayed* (Gk *untimely*)
l Gk *he*   *m* Gk *they*   *n* Or *armed*
o Gk *the greatest God*

within the hippodrome (see 5.49 n.). **7**: The title *Father* is also given to God in Tob.13.4; Wis.11.10. **8**: *Glorious manifestation*, 2 Macc.2.21. **11**: The divine gift of *sleep* is extolled in the Latin poets (Seneca, *Hercules Furens* 1066 ff.; Statius, *Silvae* v.4) compare Ps.127.2. **14**: *Middle of the tenth hour*, 3:30 p.m. **19**: *Friends*, see 2.23 n. **20**: *Phalaris*, tyrant of Agrigentum (c. 570–554 B.C.) whose cruelty was proverbial (Polybius XII.25). **23**: *The great colonnade* was no

indicating that what the king desired was ready for action. [27] But he, upon receiving the report and being struck by the unusual invitation to come out – since he had been completely overcome by incomprehension – inquired what the matter was for which this had been so zealously completed for him. [28] This was the act of God who rules over all things, for he had implanted in the king's mind a forgetfulness of the things he had previously devised. [29] Then Hermon and all the king's friends pointed out that the beasts and the armed forces were ready, "O king, according to your eager purpose."[p] [30] But at these words he was filled with an overpowering wrath, because by the providence of God his whole mind had been deranged in regard to these matters; and with a threatening look he said, [31] "Were your parents or children present, I would have prepared them to be a rich feast for the savage beasts instead of the Jews, who give me no ground for complaint and have exhibited to an extraordinary degree a full and firm loyalty to my ancestors. [32] In fact you would have been deprived of life instead of these, were it not for an affection arising from our nurture in common and your usefulness." [33] So Hermon suffered an unexpected and dangerous threat, and his eyes wavered and his face fell. [34] The king's friends one by one sullenly slipped away and dismissed[q] the assembled people, each to his own occupation. [35] Then the Jews, upon hearing what the king had said, praised the manifest Lord God, King of kings, since this also was his aid which they had received.

36 The king, however, reconvened the party in the same manner and urged the guests to return to their celebrating. [37] After summoning Hermon he said in a threatening tone, "How many times, you poor wretch, must I give you orders about these things? [38] Equip[r] the elephants now once more for the destruction of the Jews tomorrow!" [39] But the officials who were at table with him, wondering at his instability of mind, remonstrated as follows: [40] "O king, how long will you try us, as though we are idiots, ordering now for a third time that they be destroyed, and again revoking your decree in the matter?[s] [41] As a result the city is in a tumult because of its expectation; it is crowded with masses of people, and also in constant danger of being plundered." [42] Upon this the king, a Phalaris in everything and filled with madness, took no account of the changes of mind which had come about within him for the protection of the Jews, and he firmly swore an irrevocable oath that he would send them to death[t] without delay, mangled by the knees and feet of the beasts, [43] and would also march against Judea and rapidly level it to the ground with fire and spear, and by burning to the ground the temple inaccessible to him[u] would quickly render it forever empty of those who offered sacrifices there. [44] Then the friends and officers departed with great joy, and they confidently posted the armed forces at the places in the city most favorable for keeping guard. [45] Now when the beasts had been brought virtually to a state of madness, so to speak, by the very fragrant draughts of wine mixed with frankincense and had been equipped with frightful devices, the elephant keeper [46] entered at about dawn into the courtyard – the city now being filled with countless masses of people

p Other ancient authorities read *pointed to the beasts and the armed forces, saying, "They are ready, O king, according to your eager purpose."*
q Other ancient authorities read *he dismissed*
r Or *Arm*
s Other ancient authorities read *when the matter is in hand*
t Gk *Hades*   u Gk *us*

doubt some well-known place in Alexandria. **28**: *The act of God*, Pr.21.1. **29**: An interpolation in several Greek manuscripts indicates that though Ptolemy was moved by compassion and determined to release the Jews, Hermon influenced him to proceed with his plans to destroy them. **41**: The revolutionary character of the Alexandrians in ancient times is well known. **42**: *Phalaris*, see v. 20 n. **45**: The *frightful devices* were probably scythes, knives, and other

crowding their way into the hippodrome – and urged the king on to the matter at hand. [47] So he, when he had filled his impious mind with a deep rage, rushed out in full force along with the beasts, wishing to witness, with invulnerable heart and with his own eyes, the grievous and pitiful destruction of the aforementioned people. [48] And when the Jews saw the dust raised by the elephants going out at the gate and by the following armed forces, as well as by the trampling of the crowd, and heard the loud and tumultuous noise, [49] they thought that this was their last moment of life, the end of their most miserable suspense, and giving way to lamentation and groans they kissed each other, embracing relatives and falling into one another's arms[v] – parents and children, mothers and daughters, and others with babies at their breasts who were drawing their last milk. [50] Not only this, but when they considered the help which they had received before from heaven they prostrated themselves with one accord on the ground, removing the babies from their breasts, [51] and cried out in a very loud voice, imploring the Ruler over every power to manifest himself and be merciful to them, as they stood now at the gates of death.[w]

6 Then a certain Eleazar, famous among the priests of the country, who had attained a ripe old age and throughout his life had been adorned with every virtue, directed the elders around him to cease calling upon the holy God and prayed as follows: [2] "King of great power, Almighty God Most High, governing all creation with mercy, [3] look upon the descendants of Abraham, O Father, upon the children of the sainted Jacob, a people of your consecrated portion who are perishing as foreigners in a foreign land. [4] Pharaoh with his abundance of chariots, the former ruler of this Egypt, exalted with lawless insolence and boastful tongue, you destroyed together with his arrogant army by drowning them in the sea, manifesting the light of your mercy upon the nation of Israel. [5] Sennacherib exulting in his countless forces, oppressive king of the Assyrians, who had already gained control of the whole world by the spear and was lifted up against your holy city, speaking grievous words with boasting and insolence, you, O Lord, broke in pieces, showing your power to many nations. [6] The three companions in Babylon who had voluntarily surrendered their lives to the flames so as not to serve vain things, you rescued unharmed, even to a hair, moistening the fiery furnace with dew and turning the flame against all their enemies. [7] Daniel, who through envious slanders was cast down into the ground to lions as food for wild beasts, you brought up to the light unharmed. [8] And Jonah, wasting away in the belly of a huge, sea-born monster, you, Father, watched over and restored[x] unharmed to all his family. [9] And now, you who hate insolence, all-merciful and protector of all, reveal yourself quickly to those of the nation of

v Gk *falling upon their necks*   w Gk *Hades*
x Other ancient authorities read *rescued and restored;* others, *recognized and restored;* others, *mercifully restored*

---

military equipment attached to the different parts of the bodies of the elephants. **49:** *Embracing*, but according to 6.27 they are still bound. **50–51:** The author continues to build up his thesis that God was the only resort for the captives, and that their hope would not be frustrated. **51:** *Gates of death*, Ps.9.13; 107.18.

6.1–15: The Prayer of Eleazar. Like Simon's prayer in 2.1–20, it is plainly Jewish in form and style, containing doxology, thanksgiving for God's earlier interventions in Israel's history, and petition for a new miracle. The emphasis is on the exclusiveness and separate standing of Israel before God (v.3). Eleazar expects God's intervention, not on account of Israel's virtues or merits, but because of divine mercy. **1:** *Eleazar*, a favorite name for a Jewish hero (2 Macc.6.18). *Priests*, perhaps those of the Jewish temple at Leontopolis. **4:** *Pharaoh*, Ex.14.28. **5:** Sennacherib, 2 Kg.18.13; 19.35–37. **6:** *Three companions in Babylon*, Dan.3.22,27; S. of 3 Y.22–27. **7:** *Daniel*, Dan.6.22. **8:** *Jonah*, Jon.2.10. **11:** Ps.115.2. **15:** *As you have said*, Lev.26.44.

Israel*ʸ* – who are being outrageously
treated by the abominable and lawless
Gentiles. ¹⁰ Even if our lives have
become entangled in impieties in our
exile, rescue us from the hand of the
enemy, and destroy us, Lord, by
whatever fate you choose. ¹¹ Let not
the vain-minded praise their vanities*ᶻ* at
the destruction of your beloved people,
saying, 'Not even their god has rescued
them.' ¹² But you, O Eternal One,
who have all might and all power,
watch over us now and have mercy
upon us who by the senseless insolence
of the lawless are being deprived of
life in the manner of traitors. ¹³ And
let the Gentiles cower today in fear of
your invincible might, O honored
One, who have power to save the
nation of Jacob. ¹⁴ The whole throng
of infants and their parents entreat
you with tears. ¹⁵ Let it be shown to
all the Gentiles that you are with us,
O Lord, and have not turned your
face from us; but just as you have
said, 'Not even when they were in the
land of their enemies did I neglect
them,' so accomplish it, O Lord."

16 Just as Eleazar was ending his
prayer, the king arrived at the hippodrome with the beasts and all the
arrogance of his forces. ¹⁷ And when the
Jews observed this they raised great
cries to heaven so that even the nearby
valleys resounded with them and
brought an uncontrollable terror upon
the army. ¹⁸ Then the most glorious,
almighty, and true God revealed his
holy face and opened the heavenly
gates, from which two glorious angels
of fearful aspect descended, visible
to all but the Jews. ¹⁹ They opposed
the forces of the enemy and filled them
with confusion and terror, binding
them with immovable shackles. ²⁰ Even
the king began to shudder bodily, and

he forgot his sullen insolence. ²¹ The
beasts turned back upon the armed
forces following them and began
trampling and destroying them. ²² Then
the king's anger was turned to pity and
tears because of the things that he had
devised beforehand. ²³ For when he
heard the shouting and saw them all
fallen headlong to destruction, he
wept and angrily threatened his friends,
saying, ²⁴ "You are committing treason
and surpassing tyrants in cruelty; and
even me, your benefactor, you are now
attempting to deprive of dominion and
life by secretly devising acts of no
advantage to the kingdom. ²⁵ Who is it
that has taken each man from his home
and senselessly gathered here those
who faithfully have held the fortresses
of our country? ²⁶ Who is it that has so
lawlessly encompassed with outrageous
treatment those who from the beginning differed from*ᵃ* all nations in their
goodwill toward us and often have
accepted willingly the worst of human
dangers? ²⁷ Loose and untie their
unjust bonds! Send them back to their
homes in peace, begging pardon for
your former actions!*ᵇ* ²⁸ Release the
sons of the almighty and living God of
heaven, who from the time of our
ancestors until now has granted an
unimpeded and notable stability to
our government." ²⁹ These then were
the things he said; and the Jews,
immediately released, praised their
holy God and Savior, since they now
had escaped death.

30 Then the king, when he had
returned to the city, summoned the
official in charge of the revenues and
ordered him to provide to the Jews
both wines and everything else needed

y Other ancient authorities read to the saints of Israel
z Or bless their vain gods   a Or excelled above
b Other ancient authorities read revoking your former
  commands

6.16–29: The Jews are delivered, and the king now favors them. 18: *Most glorious,* Greek
megalodoxos, compare 1 Enoch 14.20 and Testament of Levi 3.4, where God is called "the
Great Glory." *Angels of fearful aspect,* for similar terror-inspiring apparitions, see Wis.17.3,15;
18.17; 2 Macc.3.25–29; 10.29. *Visible to all but the Jews,* Dan.10.7; Acts 9.7; 22.6–9. **21:** *The
beasts turned* upon the king's own *forces,* a detail found also in Josephus's account (*Against
Apion,* ii.5), compare Ps.7.15–16; 9.15–16; 35.8; 57.6. **25:** *Faithfully,* contrast the king's language
in 3.24. **28:** *Sons of . . . God,* Wis.18.13.

for a festival of seven days, deciding that they should celebrate their rescue with all joyfulness in that same place in which they had expected to meet their destruction. [31] Accordingly those disgracefully treated and near to death,[c] or rather, who stood at its gates, arranged for a banquet of deliverance instead of a bitter and lamentable death, and full of joy they apportioned to celebrants the place which had been prepared for their destruction and burial. [32] They ceased their chanting of dirges and took up the song of their fathers, praising God, their Savior and worker of wonders.[d] Putting an end to all mourning and wailing, they formed choruses[e] as a sign of peaceful joy. [33] Likewise also the king, after convening a great banquet to celebrate these events, gave thanks to heaven unceasingly and lavishly for the unexpected rescue which he[f] had experienced. [34] And those who had previously believed that the Jews would be destroyed and become food for birds, and had joyfully registered them, groaned as they themselves were overcome by disgrace, and their fire-breathing boldness was ignominiously[g] quenched. [35] But the Jews, when they had arranged the aforementioned choral group, as we have said before, passed the time in feasting to the accompaniment of joyous thanksgiving and psalms. [36] And when they had ordained a public rite for these things in their whole community and for their descendants, they instituted the observance of the aforesaid days as a festival, not for drinking and gluttony, but because of the deliverance that

had come to them through God. [37] Then they petitioned the king, asking for dismissal to their homes. [38] So their registration was carried out from the twenty-fifth of Pachon to the fourth of Epeiph,[h] for forty days; and their destruction was set for the fifth to the seventh of Epeiph,[i] the three days [39] on which the Lord of all most gloriously revealed his mercy and rescued them all together and unharmed. [40] Then they feasted, provided with everything by the king, until the fourteenth day,[j] on which also they made the petition for their dismissal. [41] The king granted their request at once and wrote the following letter for them to the generals in the cities, magnanimously expressing his concern:

7 "King Ptolemy Philopator to the generals in Egypt and all in authority in his government, greetings and good health. [2] We ourselves and our children are faring well, the great God guiding our affairs according to our desire. [3] Certain of our friends, frequently urging us with malicious intent, persuaded us to gather together the Jews of the kingdom in a body and to punish them with barbarous penalties as traitors; [4] for they declared that our government would never be firmly established until this was accomplished, because of the ill-will which these people had toward all nations. [5] They also led them out with harsh treatment as slaves, or rather as traitors, and, girding themselves with

c Gk Hades
d Other ancient authorities read *praising Israel and the wonder-working God;* or *praising Israel's Savior, the wonder-working God*
e Or *choral groups*
f Other ancient authorities read *they*
g Other ancient authorities read *completely*
h May 20–June 28   i June 29–July 1   j July 8

6.30–41: The Jews celebrate their deliverance. 32: *The song of their fathers,* perhaps Ps.136, which was used earlier as a hymn of thanksgiving (1 Chr.16.41; 2 Chr.5.13; 7.3; Ezra 3.11). **34:** *Food for birds,* Gen.40.19; Ezek.39.4; 2 Macc.9.15. **36:** The institution of Jewish festivals is a common feature at this period (compare Est.9.15; 1 Macc.4.56; 7.49; 13.51; 2 Macc.10.6; 15.36). **38:** *Epeiph,* or Epiphi.

7.1–9: Ptolemy's letter on behalf of the Jews. 2: *Children,* Philopator had only one legitimate son, born in 209–8, who reigned later as Ptolemy V Epiphanes (203–181 B.C.). Either the author had no knowledge of Philopator's family life, or the king referred in general terms to include all members of his court. **3:** The king seeks to exonerate himself, blaming others. **4:** *Ill-will,* 3.2,7; Est.3.8; Ad. Est.13.4–5. **5:** *Scythian custom,* see 2 Macc.4.47 n.; 4 Macc.10.7 n.

a cruelty more savage than that of Scythian custom, they tried without any inquiry or examination to put them to death. [6] But we very severely threatened them for these acts, and in accordance with the clemency which we have toward all men we barely spared their lives. Since we have come to realize that the God of heaven surely defends the Jews, always taking their part as a father does for his children, [7] and since we have taken into account the friendly and firm goodwill which they had toward us and our ancestors, we justly have acquitted them of every charge of whatever kind. [8] We also have ordered each and every one to return to his own home, with no one in any place*k* doing them harm at all or reproaching them for the irrational things that have happened. [9] For you should know that if we devise any evil against them or cause them any grief at all, we always shall have not man but the Ruler over every power, the Most High God, in everything and inescapably as an antagonist to avenge such acts. Farewell."

10 Upon receiving this letter the Jews did not immediately hurry to make their departure, but they requested of the king that at their own hands those of the Jewish nation who had willfully transgressed against the holy God and the law of God should receive the punishment they deserved. [11] For they declared that those who for the belly's sake had transgressed the divine commandments would never be favorably disposed toward the king's government. [12] The king*l* then, admitting and approving the truth of what they said, granted them a general license so that freely and without royal authority or supervision they might destroy those everywhere in his kingdom who had transgressed the law of God. [13] When they had applauded him in fitting manner, their priests and the whole multitude shouted the Hallelujah and joyfully departed. [14] And so on their way they punished and put to a public and shameful death any whom they met of their fellow-countrymen who had become defiled. [15] In that day they put to death more than three hundred men; and they kept the day as a joyful festival, since they had destroyed the profaners. [16] But those who had held fast to God even to death and had received the full enjoyment of deliverance began their departure from the city, crowned with all sorts of very fragrant flowers, joyfully and loudly giving thanks to the one God of their fathers, the eternal Savior*m* of Israel, in words of praise and all kinds of melodious songs.

17 When they had arrived at Ptolemais, called "rose-bearing" because of a characteristic of the place, the fleet waited for them, in accord with the common desire, for seven days. [18] There they celebrated their deliverance,*n* for the king had generously provided all things to them for their journey, to each as far as his own house. [19] And when they had landed in peace with appropriate thanksgiving, there too in like manner they decided to observe these days as a joyous festival during the time of their stay. [20] Then, after inscribing them as holy on a pillar and dedicating a place of

k Other ancient authorities read *way*   *l* Gk *He*
m Other ancient authorities read *the holy Savior;* others, *the holy One*
n Gk *they made a cup of deliverance*

6: *Threatened them,* that is, the enemies of the Jews. *Father,* 5.7 n.; Ps.103.13. **8:** *In any place* through which the Jews might pass on their return.

7.10–23: The Jews punish the renegades and return home. 10: *They requested of the king,* in the later periods of their history the Jews were obliged to seek permission from their foreign rulers to execute their own laws pertaining to capital punishment (Dt.13.6–18; Est.8.8–11; Jn.18.31. **13:** *Hallelujah,* Tob.13.18. **16:** Bar.5.6,8. **17:** This *Ptolemais* was probably not the city of this name near Thebes in Upper Egypt, but "Ptolemais at the harbor" in the Arsinoite nome, about twelve miles from present-day Cairo. *Rose-bearing* is not elsewhere applied to Ptolemais. **20:** *And sea,* there was no sea to cross in Egypt.

prayer at the site of the festival, they departed unharmed, free, and overjoyed, since at the king's command they had been brought safely by land and sea and river each to his own place. [21] They also possessed greater prestige among their enemies, being held in honor and awe; and they were not subject at all to confiscation of their belongings by any one. [22] Besides they all recovered all of their property, in accordance with the registration, so that those who held any restored it to them with extreme fear.[o] So the supreme God perfectly performed great deeds for their deliverance. [23] Blessed be the Deliverer of Israel through all times! Amen.

[o] Other ancient authorities read *a very large supplement*

THE FOURTH BOOK OF THE

MACCABEES

The book known as 4 Maccabees is included in important manuscripts of the Greek Bible, and was early translated into Syriac. Although never canonized, it has deeply influenced the preaching and piety of the Eastern Churches.

At one time 4 Maccabees was attributed to Josephus and given the title *On the Supremacy of Reason*. This describes it well, for it is a diatribe or lecture, or perhaps a panegyric, on religious reason, as exemplified by the story of the martyrdoms of Eleazar, the seven brothers, and their mother. Its traditional title was no doubt adopted because the account is an expansion of 2 Macc.6.12–7.42, and the story belongs to the Maccabean period.

The book is a classic example of the interpretation of Judaism in terms of Greek philosophy. The ideas are Stoic (with some significant differences), and so is the terminology. The treatise was written originally in Greek, and in the florid Asiatic style. Possibly it was first delivered as an oration at a festival commemorating the Maccabean martyrs or at the Feast of Dedication (1.10; 3.19; 14.9; compare Jn.10.22).

The author's theology is genuinely Jewish but with two special characteristics. The martyrdoms are a substitutionary atonement that expiates the nation's sin and purifies the land (1.11; 17.21; 18.4). The martyrs are immediately immortal, received by the patriarchs and living in God (7.19; 16.25).

The book was evidently written in the period A.D. 20–54, when Cilicia was joined to Syria and Phoenicia as a single province (4.2), and it is tempting to date it to the reign of Caligula (A.D. 37–41), who had proposed to violate the Jerusalem temple (compare 4.5–14).

Alexandria has been proposed as the place of composition, and Jerusalem cannot be excluded. Antioch, however, has the best claim, for the martyrs might have been brought to the royal capital (5.1), and in Antioch the Jews were called "Hebrews," as in this book.

THE SUBJECT THAT I AM ABOUT TO discuss is most philosophical, that is, whether devout reason is sovereign over the emotions. So it is right for me to advise you to pay earnest attention to philosophy. ² For the subject is essential to everyone who is seeking knowledge, and in addition it includes the praise of the highest virtue – I mean, of course, rational judgment. ³ If, then, it is evident that reason rules over those emotions that hinder self-control, namely, gluttony and lust, ⁴ it is also clear that it masters the emotions that hinder one from justice, such as malice, and those that stand in the way of courage, namely anger, fear, and pain. ⁵ Some might perhaps ask, "If reason rules the emotions, why is it not sovereign over forgetfulness and ignorance?" Their attempt at argument is ridiculous!*ᵃ* ⁶ For reason does not rule its own emotions, but those that are opposed to justice, courage, and self-control;*ᵇ* and it is not for the purpose of destroying them, but so that one may not give way to them.

⁷ I could prove to you from many and various examples that reason*ᶜ* is dominant over the emotions, ⁸ but I can demonstrate it best from the noble bravery of those who died for the sake

a Or *They are attempting to make my argument ridiculous!*
b Other ancient authorities add *and rational judgment*
c Other ancient authorities read *devout reason*

1.1–3.18: Philosophical introduction. The principal thesis is stated in vv.3–12, which concludes with a short doxology, and is developed further in 1.13–3.18. **1**: *Devout*, Greek *eusebēs*, religious or pious; compare 5.7,31. **2–4**: *Rational judgment . . . self-control . . . justice . . . courage*, the four cardinal virtues of the Platonic and Stoic traditions. **5**: The objection is dealt with in 2.24–3.1. **8**: *Eleazar*, 2 Macc.6.18; 3 Macc.6.1. **10**: Compare 3.19 and see Introduction.

of virtue, Eleazar and the seven brothers and their mother. [9] All of these, by despising sufferings that bring death, demonstrated that reason controls the emotions. [10] On this anniversary[d] it is fitting for me to praise for their virtues those who, with their mother, died for the sake of nobility and goodness, but I would also call them blessed for the honor in which they are held. [11] For all people, even their torturers, marveled at their courage and endurance, and they became the cause of the downfall of tyranny over their nation. By their endurance they conquered the tyrant, and thus their native land was purified through them. [12] I shall shortly have an opportunity to speak of this; but, as my custom is, I shall begin by stating my main principle, and then I shall turn to their story, giving glory to the all-wise God.

13 Our inquiry, accordingly, is whether reason is sovereign over the emotions. [14] We shall decide just what reason is and what emotion is, how many kinds of emotions there are, and whether reason rules over all these. [15] Now reason is the mind that with sound logic prefers the life of wisdom. [16] Wisdom, next, is the knowledge of divine and human matters and the causes of these. [17] This, in turn, is education in the law, by which we learn divine matters reverently and human affairs to our advantage. [18] Now the kinds of wisdom are rational judgment, justice, courage, and self-control. [19] Rational judgment is supreme over all of these, since by means of it reason rules over the emotions. [20] The two most comprehensive types[e] of the emotions are pleasure and pain; and each of these is

by nature concerned with both body and soul. [21] The emotions of both pleasure and pain have many consequences. [22] Thus desire precedes pleasure and delight follows it. [23] Fear precedes pain and sorrow comes after. [24] Anger, as a man will see if he reflects on this experience, is an emotion embracing pleasure and pain. [25] In pleasure there exists even a malevolent tendency, which is the most complex of all the emotions. [26] In the soul it is boastfulness, covetousness, thirst for honor, rivalry, and malice; [27] in the body, indiscriminate eating, gluttony, and solitary gormandizing.

28 Just as pleasure and pain are two plants growing from the body and the soul, so there are many offshoots of these plants,[f] [29] each of which the master cultivator, reason, weeds and prunes and ties up and waters and thoroughly irrigates, and so tames the jungle of habits and emotions. [30] For reason is the guide of the virtues, but over the emotions it is sovereign.

Observe now first of all that rational judgment is sovereign over the emotions by virtue of the restraining power of self-control. [31] Self-control, then, is dominance over the desires. [32] Some desires are mental, others are physical, and reason obviously rules over both. [33] Otherwise how is it that when we are attracted to forbidden foods we abstain from the pleasure to be had from them? Is it not because reason is able to rule over appetites? I for one think so. [34] Therefore when we crave seafood and fowl and animals and all sorts of foods that are forbidden to us by the law, we abstain because of domination by reason. [35] For the

---

d Gk *At this time*   *e* Or *sources*
f Other ancient authorities read *these emotions*

11: *Tyranny*, the attempt of Antiochus IV (4.15) to impose pagan worship on the Jewish *nation*; see 5.1 n. *Purified*, the idea of expiation is developed further in 6.28–29; 17.21. **17:** *Education in the law*, Jews regarded the Mosaic law as philosophical and the highest form of education (see 11.21 n.; 18.6–19 n.). *We learn . . . to our advantage*, compare the Stoic definition of wisdom in Cicero's *Tusculan Disputations* iv.25.57. **18:** The four *kinds* are found also in Wis.8.7. **24:** *As a man . . . experience*, the Greek is obscure. **27:** Job 31.17. **33:** *Reason is able to rule over appetites*, in Judaism, desires are not to be extirpated, as Stoics taught, but are to be controlled; compare v.6; Mishnah *P. Aboth* 4.1. **34:** *Seafood*, Lev.11.1–31; Dt.14.3–21; Acts 10.10–14.

emotions of the appetites are restrained, checked by the temperate mind, and all the impulses of the body are bridled by reason.

2 And why is it amazing that the desires of the mind for the enjoyment of beauty are rendered powerless? [2] It is for this reason, certainly, that the temperate Joseph is praised, because by mental effort[g] he overcame sexual desire. [3] For when he was young and in his prime for intercourse, by his reason he nullified the frenzy[h] of the passions. [4] Not only is reason proved to rule over the frenzied urge of sexual desire, but also over every desire.[i] [5] Thus the law says, "You shall not covet your neighbor's wife . . . or anything that is your neighbor's." [6] In fact, since the law has told us not to covet, I could prove to you all the more that reason is able to control desires.

Just so it is with the emotions that hinder one from justice. [7] Otherwise how could it be that someone who is habitually a solitary gormandizer, a glutton, or even a drunkard can learn a better way, unless reason is clearly lord of the emotions? [8] Thus, as soon as a man adopts a way of life in accordance with the law, even though he is a lover of money, he is forced to act contrary to his natural ways and to lend without interest to the needy and to cancel the debt when the seventh year arrives. [9] If one is greedy, he is ruled by the law through his reason so that he neither gleans his harvest nor gathers the last grapes from the vineyard.

In all other matters we can recognize that reason rules the emotions. [10] For the law prevails even over affection for parents, so that virtue is not abandoned for their sakes. [11] It is superior to love for one's wife, so that one rebukes her when she breaks the law. [12] It takes precedence over love for children, so that one punishes them for misdeeds. [13] It is sovereign over the relationship of friends, so that one rebukes friends when they act wickedly. [14] Do not consider it paradoxical when reason, through the law, can prevail even over enmity. The fruit trees of the enemy are not cut down, but one preserves the property of enemies from the destroyers and helps raise up what has fallen.[j]

15 It is evident that reason rules even[k] the more violent emotions: lust for power, vainglory, boasting, arrogance, and malice. [16] For the temperate mind repels all these malicious emotions, just as it repels anger – for it is sovereign over even this. [17] When Moses was angry with Dathan and Abiram he did nothing against them in anger, but controlled his anger by reason. [18] For, as I have said, the temperate mind is able to get the better of the emotions, to correct some, and to render others powerless. [19] Why else did Jacob, our most wise father, censure the households of Simeon and Levi for their irrational slaughter of the entire tribe of the Shechemites, saying, "Cursed be their anger"? [20] For if reason could not control anger, he would not have spoken thus. [21] Now when God fashioned man, he planted in him emotions and inclinations, [22] but at the same time he enthroned the mind among the senses as a sacred governor over them all. [23] To the mind he gave the law; and one who lives subject to this

g Other ancient authorities add *in reasoning*
h Or *gadfly*
i Or *all covetousness*
j Or *the beasts that have fallen* (Ex 23.4–5 LXX)
k Other ancient authorities read *through*

2.1: *Enjoyment of beauty* refers to sexual desire but also suggests the concept of *eros* in Plato's *Symposium*. **2:** *Joseph*, Gen.39.7–12. **8:** *Lend without interest*, to other Jews, Ex.22.25. *Seventh year*, Dt.15.1–3. **9:** Lev.19.9–10; Dt.20.19–20. **11–12:** Mt.10.37; Lk.14.26. **14:** Dt.20.19–20; Ex.23.4–5; Josephus, *Against Apion* ii.211–212. **17:** *Dathan and Abiram*, Num.16.1–35; Sir.45.18. **19:** Gen.49.7. **21:** According to rabbinic Judaism, God *planted* the good and the evil *inclinations* in man; the latter is to be controlled, and in itself is not essentially evil. **23:** *Will rule a kingdom*, according to the Stoics and Philo, the wise man is a king. Compare the different concept of the

will rule a kingdom that is temperate, just, good, and courageous.

24 How is it then, one might say, that if reason is master of the emotions, it does not control forgetfulness and ignorance? [1] This notion is entirely ridiculous; for it is evident that reason rules not over its own emotions, but over those of the body. [2] No one of us can eradicate that kind of desire, but reason can provide a way for us not to be enslaved by desire. [3] No one of us[l] can eradicate anger from the mind, but reason can help to deal with anger. [4] No one of us can eradicate malice, but reason can fight at our side so that we are not overcome by malice. [5] For reason does not uproot the emotions but is their antagonist.

6 Now this can be explained more clearly by the story of King David's thirst. [7] David had been attacking the Philistines all day long, and together with the soldiers of his nation had slain many of them. [8] Then when evening fell, he[m] came, sweating and quite exhausted, to the royal tent, around which the whole army of our ancestors had encamped. [9] Now all the rest were at supper, [10] but the king was extremely thirsty, and although springs were plentiful there, he could not satisfy his thirst from them. [11] But a certain irrational desire for the water in the enemy's territory tormented and inflamed him, undid and consumed him. [12] When his guards complained bitterly because of the king's craving, two staunch young soldiers, respecting[n]

the king's desire, armed themselves fully, and taking a pitcher climbed over the enemy's ramparts. [13] Eluding the sentinels at the gates, they went searching throughout the enemy camp [14] and found the spring, and from it boldly brought the king a drink. [15] But David,[o] although he was burning with thirst, considered it an altogether fearful danger to his soul to drink what was regarded as equivalent to blood. [16] Therefore, opposing reason to desire, he poured out the drink as an offering to God. [17] For the temperate mind can conquer the drives of the emotions and quench the flames of frenzied desires; [18] it can overthrow bodily agonies even when they are extreme, and by nobility of reason spurn all domination by the emotions.

19 The present occasion now invites us to a narrative demonstration of temperate reason.

20 At a time when our fathers were enjoying profound peace because of their observance of the law and were prospering, so that even Seleucus Nicanor, king of Asia, had both appropriated money to them for the temple service and recognized their commonwealth – [21] just at that time certain men attempted a revolution against the public harmony and caused many and various disasters.

4 Now there was a certain Simon, a political opponent of the noble and good man, Onias, who then held

l Gk *you*
m Other ancient authorities read *he hurried and*
n Or *embarrassed because of*   *o* Gk *he*

---

reign of the saints in 1 Cor.4.8; 6.2–3; 1 Pet.2.9. **3.1:** *Those of the body*, but the emotions of vv. 2–4 are those of the mind; thus 1.6 would fit better here.

   3.6–18: King David's thirst. Some details are different in 2 Sam.23.13–17; 1 Chr.11.15–19. **7:** *Philistines*, literally "foreigners"; in the Greek Bible this word usually translates the Hebrew word "Philistines". **15:** *Equivalent to blood*, 2 Sam.23.17, "Shall I drink the blood . . .?" **17:** *Frenzied desires*, in Greek mythology the *oistros* was the gadfly that tormented Io, and it became a symbol of uncontrolled sexual desire.

   3.19–4.14: Attempt on the temple treasury. Compare 2 Macc.3.1–40. **19:** *The present occasion*, perhaps when 4 Macc. was first read publicly (see Introduction). **20:** *Profound peace*, see 2 Macc.3.1 n. *Seleucus Nicanor*, the author is confused. Seleucus I Nicator ruled 305/304–281/280 B.C.; the king who is meant here is Seleucus IV Philopator, 187–175 B.C. (see 2 Macc.3.3 n.). **4.1:** *Simon*, 2 Macc.3.4 n. *Onias* III, 2 Macc.3.1 n. Life tenure of *the high priesthood* was the regular rule until the first century A.D. when the Roman procurators disregarded it, Jn.18.13 n.;

the high priesthood for life. When despite all manner of slander he was unable to injure Onias in the eyes of the nation, he fled the country with the purpose of betraying it. [2] So he came to Apollonius, governor of Syria, Phoenicia, and Cilicia, and said, [3] "I have come here because I am loyal to the king's government, to report that in the Jerusalem treasuries there are deposited tens of thousands in private funds, which are not the property of the temple but belong to King Seleucus." [4] When Apollonius learned the details of these things, he praised Simon for his service to the king and went up to Seleucus to inform him of the rich treasure. [5] On receiving authority to deal with this matter, he proceeded quickly to our country accompanied by the accursed Simon and a very strong military force. [6] He said that he had come with the king's authority to seize the private funds in the treasury. [7] The people indignantly protested his words, considering it outrageous that those who had committed deposits to the sacred treasury should be deprived of them, and did all that they could to prevent it. [8] But, uttering threats, Apollonius went on to the temple. [9] While the priests together with women and children were imploring God in the temple to shield the holy place that was being treated so contemptuously, [10] and while Apollonius was going up with his armed forces to seize the money, angels on horseback with lightning flashing from their weapons appeared from heaven, instilling in them great fear and trembling. [11] Then Apollonius fell down half dead in the temple area

that was open to all, stretched out his hands toward heaven, and with tears besought the Hebrews to pray for him and propitiate the wrath of the heavenly army. [12] For he said that he had committed a sin deserving of death, and that if he were delivered he would praise the blessedness of the holy place before all people. [13] Moved by these words, Onias the high priest, although otherwise he had scruples about doing so, prayed for him lest King Seleucus suppose that Apollonius had been overcome by human treachery and not by divine justice. [14] So Apollonius, having been preserved beyond all expectations, went away to report to the king what had happened to him.

15 When King Seleucus died, his son Antiochus Epiphanes succeeded to the throne, an arrogant and terrible man, [16] who removed Onias from the priesthood and appointed Onias's[p] brother Jason as high priest. [17] Jason[q] agreed that if the office were conferred upon him he would pay the king three thousand six hundred and sixty talents annually. [18] So the king appointed him high priest and ruler of the nation. [19] Jason[q] changed the nation's way of life and altered its form of government in complete violation of the law, [20] so that not only was a gymnasium constructed at the very citadel[r] of our native land, but also the temple service was abolished. [21] The divine justice was angered by these acts and caused Antiochus himself to make war on them. [22] For when he was warring against Ptolemy in Egypt, he heard that a rumor of his death had spread

p Gk *his*   *q* Gk *He*   *r* Or *high place*

Josephus, *Ant.*XVIII.ii.2; xx.10. **2:** *Cilicia* was joined to Syria and Phoenicia as one province only in A.D. 20–54; 2 Macc.3.5 is more accurate. **3:** *Private funds* were often deposited in temples, as in a bank. **5:** *Authority*, but according to 2 Macc. 3.7–8, Heliodorus was put in command. **6:** *Private funds* in the Jerusalem temple, see Josephus, *B.J.*I.xiii.9; VI.v.2. **10:** Compare 3 Macc. 2.21–24; 6.18.
4.15–26: Antiochus's persecution of the Jews. Compare 1 Macc.1.20–64; 2 Macc.5.11–6.11. **15:** *Antiochus* IV *Epiphanes* was the brother of *Seleucus* IV, and son of Antiochus III; see 1 Macc.1.10 n. **16:** *Jason*, 2 Macc.4.7 n. **20:** *At the very citadel*, more probably "under the citadel," as in 2 Macc.4.12. **21:** *The divine justice*, a theological interpretation of 2 Macc.4.16–17. **22:** *Ptolemy* VI Philometor (180–145 B.C.), 1 Macc.1.16–19.

and that the people of Jerusalem had rejoiced greatly. He speedily marched against them, [23] and after he had plundered them he issued a decree that if any of them should be found observing the ancestral law they should die. [24] When, by means of his decrees, he had not been able in any way to put an end to the people's observance of the law, but saw that all his threats and punishments were being disregarded, [25] even to the point that women, because they had circumcised their sons, were thrown headlong from heights along with their infants, though they had known beforehand that they would suffer this – [26] when, then, his decrees were despised by the people, he himself, through torture, tried to compel everyone in the nation to eat defiling foods and to renounce Judaism.

5 The tyrant Antiochus, sitting in state with his counselors on a certain high place, and with his armed soldiers standing about him, [2] ordered the guards to seize each and every Hebrew and to compel them to eat pork and food sacrificed to idols. [3] If any were not willing to eat defiling food, they were to be broken on the wheel and killed. [4] And when many persons had been rounded up, one man, Eleazar by name, leader of the flock, was brought[s] before the king. He was a man of priestly family, learned in the law, advanced in age, and known to many in the tyrant's court because of his philosophy.[t]

[5] When Antiochus saw him he said, [6] "Before I begin to torture you, old man, I would advise you to save yourself by eating pork, [7] for I respect your age and your gray hairs. Although you have had them for so long a time, it does not seem to me that you are a philosopher when you observe the religion of the Jews. [8] Why, when nature has granted it to us, should you abhor eating the very excellent meat of this animal? [9] It is senseless not to enjoy delicious things that are not shameful, and wrong to spurn the gifts of nature. [10] It seems to me that you will do something even more senseless if, by holding a vain opinion concerning the truth, you continue to despise me to your own hurt. [11] Will you not awaken from your foolish philosophy, dispel your futile reasonings, adopt a mind appropriate to your years, philosophize according to the truth of what is beneficial, [12] and have compassion on your old age by honoring my humane advice? [13] For consider this, that if there is some power watching over this religion of yours, it will excuse you from any transgression that arises out of compulsion."

14 When the tyrant urged him in this fashion to eat meat unlawfully, Eleazar asked to have a word. [15] When he had received permission to speak, he began to address the people as follows: [16] "We, O Antiochus, who have been persuaded to govern our lives by the divine law, think that there is no compulsion more powerful than our obedience to the law. [17] Therefore

---

s Or *was the first of the flock to be brought*
t Other authorities read *his advanced age*

5.1–7.23: Martyrdom of Eleazar. Compare 2 Macc.6.18–31. **1:** *Tyrant*, in Greek usually with a bad connotation, denoting not a legitimate monarch but one who rules by force. *Sitting in state*, perhaps in Jerusalem; but early Christian tradition located this in Antioch, and a church was erected there in honor of the martyrs. **2:** Jews regarded the eating of *pork and food sacrificed to idols* as idolatry and profanation of the divine name because it was a public defiance of God's law; compare 1 Cor.10.6–22. **3:** *Defiling*, the Greek word, peculiar to 4 Macc., implies that forbidden foods were polluted and particularly odious. **4:** *Eleazar* may mean "God has helped"; it is the same name as Lazarus (Lk.16.20; Jn.11.1) and serves as a symbol for a man of great piety; compare 3 Macc.6.1; 2 Macc.8.23 n. **7–8:** A Stoic *philosopher* regarded the distinctions of national religions and laws, such as those of Judaism, as unimportant, whereas Jews considered the Mosaic law to be the highest philosophy; compare 1.17 n. Stoics also taught that one should live according to *nature*. **7:** *Religion*, Greek *thrēskeia*, religious practice or cult; compare v. 31. **13:** *Some power watching over*, a Greek philosophical expression; compare

we consider that we should not transgress it in any respect. ¹⁸ Even if, as you suppose, our law were not truly divine and we had wrongly held it to be divine, not even so would it be right for us to invalidate our reputation for piety. ¹⁹ Therefore do not suppose that it would be a petty sin if we were to eat defiling food; ²⁰ to transgress the law in matters either small or great is of equal seriousness, ²¹ for in either case the law is equally despised. ²² You scoff at our philosophy as though living by it were irrational, ²³ but it teaches us self-control, so that we master all pleasures and desires, and it also trains us in courage, so that we endure any suffering willingly; ²⁴ it instructs us in justice, so that in all our dealings we act impartially,ᵘ and it teaches us piety, so that with proper reverence we worship the only real God.

25 "Therefore we do not eat defiling food; for since we believe that the law was established by God, we know that in the nature of things the Creator of the world in giving us the law has shown sympathy toward us. ²⁶ He has permitted us to eat what will be most suitable for our lives,ᵛ but he has forbidden us to eat meats that would be contrary to this. ²⁷ It would be tyrannical for you to compel us not only to transgress the law, but also to eat in such a way that you may deride us for eating defiling foods, which are most hateful to us. ²⁸ But you shall have no such occasion to laugh at me, ²⁹ nor will I transgress the sacred oaths of my ancestors concerning the keeping of the law, ³⁰ not even if you gouge out my eyes and burn my entrails. ³¹ I am not so old and cowardly as not to be young in reason on behalf of piety. ³² Therefore get your torture

wheels ready and fan the fire more vehemently! ³³ I do not so pity my old age as to break the ancestral law by my own act. ³⁴ I will not play false to you, O law that trained me, nor will I renounce you, beloved self-control. ³⁵ I will not put you to shame, philosophical reason, nor will I reject you, honored priesthood and knowledge of the law. ³⁶ You, O king, shallʷ not stain the honorable mouth of my old age, nor my long life lived lawfully. ³⁷ The fathers will receive me as pure, as one who does not fear your violence even to death. ³⁸ You may tyrannize the ungodly, but you shall not dominate my religious principles either by word or by deed."

6 When Eleazar in this manner had made eloquent response to the exhortations of the tyrant, the guards who were standing by dragged him violently to the instruments of torture. ² First they stripped the old man, who remained adorned with the gracefulness of his piety. ³ And after they had tied his arms on each side they scourged him, ⁴ while a herald opposite him cried out, "Obey the king's commands!" ⁵ But the courageous and noble man, as a true Eleazar, was unmoved, as though being tortured in a dream; ⁶ yet while the old man's eyes were raised to heaven, his flesh was being torn by scourges, his blood flowing, and his sides were being cut to pieces. ⁷ And though he fell to the ground because his body could not endure the agonies, he kept his reason upright and unswerving. ⁸ One of the cruel guards rushed at him and began to kick him in the side to make him get up again after he fell. ⁹ But he

---

u Or so that we hold in balance all our habitual inclinations v Or souls w Gk You shall

---

2 Macc.7.35; 9.5; 3 Macc.2.21. **23–24:** *Self-control . . . courage . . . justice,* cardinal virtues (see 1.2–4 n.). In Xenophon's *Memorabilia,* and sometimes in Philo, *piety* or religion is the fourth virtue. **27:** *Deride us,* because this would bring discredit on the Jewish people, the Mosaic law, and the God who gave it. God's name must be hallowed (Mt.6.9). **31:** *Piety,* Greek *eusebeia,* proper reverence toward God (see v. 7 n.; 1.1 n.). No single Greek word corresponds to the English word "religion." **37:** 13.17; 17.12; Mk.12.26–27. Immortality of the martyrs is implied in 9.22; 2 Macc.7.36. **6.5:** *True Eleazar,* see 5.4 n. **6:** *Eyes . . . to heaven,* a natural gesture in prayer, particularly that of a martyr. Compare v. 26 and Stephen's supplication in Acts 7.55.

bore the pains and scorned the punishment, and endured the tortures. [10] And like a noble athlete the old man, while being beaten, was victorious over his torturers; [11] in fact, with his face bathed in sweat, and gasping heavily for breath, he amazed even his torturers by his courageous spirit.

12 At that point, partly out of pity for his old age, [13] partly out of sympathy from their acquaintance with him, partly out of admiration for his endurance, some of the king's retinue came to him and said, [14] "Eleazar, why are you so irrationally destroying yourself through these evil things? [15] We will set before you some cooked meat; save yourself by pretending to eat pork."

16 But Eleazar, as though more bitterly tormented by this counsel, cried out: [17] "May we, the children of Abraham,[x] never think so basely that out of cowardice we feign a role unbecoming to us! [18] For it would be irrational if we, who have lived in accordance with truth to old age and have maintained in accordance with law the reputation of such a life, should now change our course [19] and ourselves become a pattern of impiety to the young, in becoming an example of the eating of defiling food. [20] It would be shameful if we should survive for a little while and during that time be a laughing stock to all for our cowardice, [21] and if we should be despised by the tyrant as unmanly, and not protect our divine law even to death. [22] Therefore, O children of Abraham, die nobly for your religion! [23] And you, guards of the tyrant, why do you delay?"

24 When they saw that he was so courageous in the face of the afflictions, and that he had not been changed by their compassion, the guards brought him to the fire. [25] There they burned him with maliciously contrived instruments, threw him down, and poured stinking liquids into his nostrils. [26] When he was now burned to his very bones and about to expire, he lifted up his eyes to God and said, [27] "You know, O God, that though I might have saved myself, I am dying in burning torments for the sake of the law. [28] Be merciful to your people, and let our punishment suffice for them. [29] Make my blood their purification, and take my life in exchange for theirs." [30] And after he said this, the holy man died nobly in his tortures, and by reason he resisted even to the very tortures of death for the sake of the law.

31 Admittedly, then, devout reason is sovereign over the emotions. [32] For if the emotions had prevailed over reason, we would have testified to their domination. [33] But now that reason has conquered the emotions, we properly attribute to it the power to govern. [34] And it is right for us to acknowledge the dominance of reason when it masters even external agonies. It would be ridiculous to deny it.[y] [35] And I have proved not only that reason has mastered agonies, but also that it masters pleasures and in no respect yields to them.

7 For like a most skilful pilot, the reason of our father Eleazar steered the ship of religion over the sea of the emotions, [2] and though buffeted by the stormings of the tyrant and overwhelmed by the mighty waves of tortures, [3] in no way did he turn the rudder of religion until he sailed into the haven of immortal victory. [4] No

x Or *O children of Abraham*
y Syr: Greek obscure

10: *Noble athlete*, 1 Cor.9.24–27; Heb.12.1. **17–21:** See 5.27 n. **23:** *Why do you delay?* Compare 9.1; 2 Macc.7.30. **29:** *In exchange*, Greek *antipsychon*, a word used by the martyr Ignatius of Antioch in his letters. Compare 1.11; 9.24; 12.17; 17.21–22; 18.4; Mk.10.45. The idea of expiation derives ultimately from Is.53.5–12 and is also found in the Qumran *Manual of Discipline*. **31:** The transition from religious language in vv. 27–29 to the philosophical note of *devout reason* is abrupt; but for this author the two are one. **7.1–3:** The metaphor of the *pilot* and *the ship*, common in Greek literature, recurs in 13.6–7 and in 15.31–32 as a reference to

city besieged with many ingenious war machines has ever held out as did that most holy man. Although his sacred life was consumed by tortures and racks, he conquered the besiegers with the shield of his devout reason. [5] For in setting his mind firm like a jutting cliff, our father Eleazar broke the maddening waves of the emotions. [6] O priest, worthy of the priesthood, you neither defiled your sacred teeth nor profaned your stomach, which had room only for reverence and purity, by eating defiling foods. [7] O man in harmony with the law and philosopher of divine life! [8] Such should be those who are administrators of the law, shielding it with their own blood and noble sweat in sufferings even to death. [9] You, father, strengthened our loyalty to the law through your glorious endurance, and you did not abandon the holiness which you praised, but by your deeds you made your words of divine[z] philosophy credible. [10] O aged man, more powerful than tortures; O elder, fiercer than fire; O supreme king over the passions, Eleazar! [11] For just as our father Aaron, armed with the censer, ran through the multitude of the people and conquered the fiery[a] angel, [12] so the descendant of Aaron, Eleazar, though being consumed by the fire, remained unmoved in his reason. [13] Most amazing, indeed, though he was an old man, his body no longer tense and firm,[b] his muscles flabby, his sinews feeble, he became young again [14] in spirit through reason; and by reason like that of Isaac he rendered the many-headed rack ineffective. [15] O man of blessed age and of venerable gray hair and of law-abiding life,

whom the faithful seal of death has perfected!

16 If, therefore, because of piety an aged man despised tortures even to death, most certainly devout reason is governor of the emotions. [17] Some perhaps might say, "Not every one has full command of his emotions, because not every one has prudent reason." [18] But as many as attend to religion with a whole heart, these alone are able to control the passions of the flesh, [19] since they believe that they, like our patriarchs Abraham and Isaac and Jacob, do not die to God, but live in God.[c] [20] No contradiction therefore arises when some persons appear to be dominated by their emotions because of the weakness of their reason. [21] What person who lives as a philosopher by the whole rule of philosophy, and trusts in God, [22] and knows that it is blessed to endure any suffering for the sake of virtue, would not be able to overcome the emotions through godliness? [23] For only the wise and courageous man is lord of his emotions.

8 For this is why even the very young, by following a philosophy in accordance with devout reason, have prevailed over the most painful instruments of torture. [2] For when the tyrant was conspicuously defeated in his first attempt, being unable to compel an aged man to eat defiling foods, then in violent rage he commanded that others of the Hebrew captives be brought, and that any who ate defiling food should be freed after eating, but if any were to refuse, these should be tortured even more cruelly.

z Other ancient authorities omit *divine*
a Other ancient authorities omit *fiery*
b Gk *the tautness of the body already loosed*
c Or *to God*

Noah's ark; compare 1 Pet.3.20. **6:** *Defiled . . . profaned*, the Jewish concept was realistic, as though a physical infection were incurred (see 2 Macc. 6.20); contrast Mk.7.15; Acts 10.13–15. **8:** *Administrators*, literally "those who make (or create) something"; the Greek is obscure. A rabbi or priest was responsible for maintenance of the law in the community (Mal.2.7). **9:** *Credible*, in both Judaism and Stoicism, the ultimate test is the conformity of one's deeds to one's profession. **10:** *Eleazar*, see 5.4 n. **11:** Num.16.46–50. **14:** Compare 2 Cor.4.7–18. *Isaac*, Gen.22.1–14. **19:** *Abraham and Isaac and Jacob* are living (Mk.12.26). *Live in God*, or "to God," a similar expression is found in Lk.20.38; Rom.6.10; 14.8; Gal.2.19. Compare 16.25.

3 When the tyrant had given these orders, seven brothers – handsome, modest, noble, and accomplished in every way – were brought before him along with their aged mother. ⁴ When the tyrant saw them, grouped about their mother as if in a chorus, he was pleased with them. And struck by their appearance and nobility, he smiled at them, and summoned them nearer and said, ⁵ "Young men, I admire each and every one of you in a kindly manner, and greatly respect the beauty and the number of such brothers. Not only do I advise you not to display the same madness as that of the old man who has just been tortured, but I also exhort you to yield to me and enjoy my friendship. ⁶ Just as I am able to punish those who disobey my orders, so I can be a benefactor to those who obey me. ⁷ Trust me, then, and you will have positions of authority in my government if you will renounce the ancestral tradition of your national life. ⁸ And enjoy your youth by adopting the Greek way of life and by changing your manner of living. ⁹ But if by disobedience you rouse my anger, you will compel me to destroy each and every one of you with dreadful punishments through tortures. ¹⁰ Therefore take pity on yourselves. Even I, your enemy, have compassion for your youth and handsome appearance. ¹¹ Will you not consider this, that if you disobey, nothing remains for you but to die on the rack?"

12 When he had said these things, he ordered the instruments of torture to be brought forward so as to persuade them out of fear to eat the defiling food. ¹³ And when the guards had placed before them wheels and joint-dislocators, rack and hooks[d] and catapults[e] and caldrons, braziers and thumbscrews and iron claws and wedges and bellows, the tyrant resumed speaking: ¹⁴ "Be afraid, young fellows, and whatever justice you revere will be merciful to you when you transgress under compulsion."

15 But when they had heard the inducements and saw the dreadful devices, not only were they not afraid, but they also opposed the tyrant with their own philosophy, and by their right reasoning nullified his tyranny. ¹⁶ Let us consider, on the other hand, what arguments might have been used if some of them had been cowardly and unmanly. Would they not have been these? ¹⁷ "O wretches that we are and so senseless! Since the king has summoned and exhorted us to accept kind treatment if we obey him, ¹⁸ why do we take pleasure in vain resolves and venture upon a disobedience that brings death? ¹⁹ O men and brothers, should we not fear the instruments of torture and consider the threats of torments, and give up this vain opinion and this arrogance that threatens to destroy us? ²⁰ Let us take pity on our youth and have compassion on our mother's age; ²¹ and let us seriously consider that if we disobey we are dead! ²² Also, divine justice will excuse us for fearing the king when we are under compulsion. ²³ Why do we banish ourselves from this most pleasant life and deprive

d Greek obscure
e Here and elsewhere in 4 Macc. an instrument of torture

8.1–9.9: **The seven brothers defy the tyrant.** This account is an amplification of 2 Macc.7.1–2. **3:** *Accomplished*, or graceful, the Greek ideal of physical beauty joined to perfect education. **4:** A Greek *chorus* was a company of dancers, who often moved in a circle and spoke lines in unison; compare 14.7. **5:** *Beauty*, see 2.1 n. *Friendship*, almost a technical term, because the "friends" of a Hellenistic king were employed in the government; see v.7 and 3 Macc.2.23 n. **6:** *Benefactor*, a title often adopted by Hellenistic monarchs; in Lk.22.25 it seems ironical, as here. **8:** *Adopting the Greek way of life*, Antiochus could have believed sincerely that this was the highest civilization and that Judaism was "superstition." Thus it is a tragic conflict between two points of view. **13:** *Hooks*, these and some of the other instruments of torture cannot be described precisely; compare 11.10. **14:** *Justice*, a philosophical way of speaking of God. **15:** *Nullified his tyranny*, Epictetus the Stoic taught that, while the tyrant might chain a man's leg or cut off his head, he could neither chain nor cut off his moral purpose (*Discourses* i.18.17).

ourselves of this delightful world?
²⁴ Let us not struggle against compulsion*ᶠ* nor take hollow pride in
being put to the rack. ²⁵ Not even the
law itself would arbitrarily slay us for
fearing the instruments of torture.
²⁶ Why does such contentiousness excite
us and such a fatal stubbornness please
us, when we can live in peace if we obey
the king?"

27 But the youths, though about to
be tortured, neither said any of these
things nor even seriously considered
them. ²⁸ For they were contemptuous
of the emotions and sovereign over
agonies, ²⁹ so that as soon as the
tyrant had ceased counseling them to
eat defiling food, all with one voice
together, as from one mind, said:

9 "Why do you delay, O tyrant?
For we are ready to die rather
than transgress our ancestral commandments; ² we are obviously putting
our forefathers to shame unless we
should practice ready obedience to the
law and to Moses*ᵍ* our counselor.
³ Tyrant and counselor of lawlessness,
in your hatred for us do not pity us
more than we pity ourselves.*ʰ* ⁴ For we
consider this pity of yours which
insures our safety through transgression
of the law to be more grievous than
death itself. ⁵ You are trying to terrify
us by threatening us with death by
torture, as though a short time ago
you learned nothing from Eleazar.
⁶ And if the aged men of the Hebrews
because of their religion lived piously*ⁱ*
while enduring torture, it would be
even more fitting that we young men
should die despising your coercive
tortures, which our aged instructor
also overcame. ⁷ Therefore, tyrant, put
us to the test; and if you take our lives
because of our religion, do not suppose

that you can injure us by torturing us.
⁸ For we, through this severe suffering
and endurance, shall have the prize of
virtue and shall be with God, for
whom we suffer; ⁹ but you, because of
your bloodthirstiness toward us, will
deservedly undergo from the divine
justice eternal torment by fire."

10 When they had said these things
the tyrant not only was angry, as at
those who are disobedient, but also
was enraged, as at those who are ungrateful. ¹¹ Then at his command the
guards brought forward the eldest,
and having torn off his tunic, they
bound his hands and arms with thongs
on each side. ¹² When they had worn
themselves out beating him with
scourges, without accomplishing anything, they placed him upon the wheel.
¹³ When the noble youth was stretched
out around this, his limbs were dislocated, ¹⁴ and though broken in every
member he denounced the tyrant,
saying, ¹⁵ "Most abominable tyrant,
enemy of heavenly justice, savage of
mind, you are mangling me in this
manner, not because I am a murderer,
or as one who acts impiously, but
because I protect the divine law."
¹⁶ And when the guards said, "Agree
to eat so that you may be released
from the tortures," ¹⁷ he replied,
"You abominable lackeys, your wheel
is not so powerful as to strangle my
reason. Cut my limbs, burn my flesh,
and twist my joints. ¹⁸ Through all
these tortures I will convince you that
sons of the Hebrews alone are invincible where virtue is concerned."
¹⁹ While he was saying these things,
they spread fire under him, and while

f Or *fate*
g Other ancient authorities read *knowledge*
h Greek obscure
i One manuscript reads *died*

25: *The law* would not condemn them for *fearing*; but a Jew could not be excused for committing idolatry, even under duress (see 5.2 n.). **29:** *With one voice*, as if they were a chorus (see
8.4 n.). **9.6:** *Aged men*, the plural may refer to Hebrew prophets such as Isaiah, who, according
to Jewish tradition, were also martyred; compare Heb.11.35–37. **7:** *Do not suppose that you can
injure us*, a Stoic principle; suffering cannot affect the wise man's essential nature. **8:** *Prize of
virtue*, an athletic metaphor; compare 6.10; Wis.10.12; 1 Cor.9.24.

9.10–25: Martyrdom of the eldest. The details do not agree with the earlier account in 2
Macc.7.3–6; here the author allows himself the freedom of an historical novelist. **17:** See v.7 n.

fanning the flames[j] they tightened the wheel further. [20] The wheel was completely smeared with blood, and the heap of coals was being quenched by the drippings of gore, and pieces of flesh were falling off the axles of the machine. [21] Although the ligaments joining his bones were already severed, the courageous youth, worthy[k] of Abraham, did not groan, [22] but as though transformed by fire into immortality he nobly endured the rackings. [23] "Imitate me, brothers," he said. "Do not leave your post in my struggle[l] or renounce our courageous brotherhood. [24] Fight the sacred and noble battle for religion. Thereby the just Providence of our ancestors may become merciful to our nation and take vengeance on the accursed tyrant." [25] When he had said this, the saintly youth broke the thread of life.

26 While all were marveling at his courageous spirit, the guards brought in the next eldest, and after fitting themselves with iron gauntlets having sharp hooks, they bound him to the torture machine and catapult. [27] Before torturing him, they inquired if he were willing to eat, and they heard his noble decision.[m] [28] These leopard-like beasts tore out his sinews with the iron hands, flayed all his flesh up to his chin, and tore away his scalp. But he steadfastly endured this agony and said, [29] "How sweet is any kind of death for the religion of our fathers!" [30] To the tyrant he said, "Do you not think, you most savage tyrant, that

you are being tortured more than I, as you see the arrogant design of your tyranny being defeated by our endurance for the sake of religion? [31] I lighten my pain by the joys that come from virtue, [32] but you suffer torture by the threats that come from impiety. You will not escape, most abominable tyrant, the judgments of the divine wrath."

10 When he too had endured a glorious death, the third was led in, and many repeatedly urged him to save himself by tasting the meat. [2] But he shouted, "Do you not know that the same father begot me and those who died, and the same mother bore me, and that I was brought up on the same teachings? [3] I do not renounce the noble kinship that binds me to my brothers."[n] [5] Enraged by the man's boldness, they disjointed his hands and feet with their instruments, dismembering him by prying his limbs from their sockets, [6] and breaking his fingers and arms and legs and elbows. [7] Since they were not able in any way to break his spirit,[o] they abandoned the instruments[p] and scalped him with their fingernails in Scythian fashion. [8] They immediately brought him to the wheel, and while his vertebrae were being dislocated upon it he saw his

j Greek obscure   k Other authorities read *a son*
l Other authorities read *post for ever*
m Other ancient authorities read *having heard his noble decision they tore him to shreds*
n Some ancient authorities add verse 4: *So if you have any instrument of torture, apply it to my body; for you cannot touch my soul, even if you wish.*
o Gk *strangle him*
p Other ancient authorities read *they tore off his skin*

22: *Transformed*, the same Greek verb is used in Phil.3.21; synonymous verbs in 1 Cor.15.51–52; 2 Cor.3.18. *Immortality*, literally "incorruption," "that which is imperishable," as in 17.12; 1 Cor.15.53. Here the author comes close to the Greek doctrine that the soul is by nature immortal, but his emphasis is on reward and punishment after this life, compare Lk.16.19–31; 23.43. This is in contrast to the doctrine of the resurrection expressed in 2 Macc.12.44–45. **23:** *Brotherhood*, referring to the immediate family, but kinship with the whole Jewish nation may be implied. **24:** *Fight*, compare 2 Tim.4.7. *Accursed*, Greek *alastōr*, a word from the Greek tragedies.

9.26–12.19: Martyrdom of the other brothers. These stories follow 2 Macc.7.7–40 in general, but are made more vivid and sensational. **28:** *Beasts*, 1 Cor.15.32. **29:** *How sweet*, compare 2 Macc.6.30. One may compare the letter to the Romans by the Christian martyr Ignatius and also the Latin saying, *Dulce et decorum est pro patria mori.* **10.4:** *You cannot touch my soul*, see 9.7 n. and compare Mt.10.28; Lk.12.4–5. **5:** *Boldness*, Acts 4.13; 2 Cor.3.12. Freedom of speech was one of the ideals of Greek democracy. **7:** *Scythian fashion*, the Scythians were

own flesh torn all around and drops of blood flowing from his entrails. [9] When he was about to die, he said, [10] "We, most abominable tyrant, are suffering because of our godly training and virtue, [11] but you, because of your impiety and bloodthirstiness, will undergo unceasing torments."

[12] When he also had died in a manner worthy of his brothers, they dragged in the fourth, saying, [13] "As for you, do not give way to the same insanity as your brothers, but obey the king and save yourself." [14] But he said to them, "You do not have a fire hot enough to make me play the coward. [15] No, by the blessed death of my brothers, by the eternal destruction of the tyrant, and by the everlasting life of the pious, I will not renounce our noble brotherhood. [16] Contrive tortures, tyrant, so that you may learn from them that I am a brother to those who have just been tortured." [17] When he heard this, the bloodthirsty, murderous, and utterly abominable Antiochus gave orders to cut out his tongue. [18] But he said, "Even if you remove my organ of speech, God hears also those who are mute. [19] See, here is my tongue; cut it off, for in spite of this you will not make our reason speechless. [20] Gladly, for the sake of God, we let our bodily members be mutilated. [21] God will visit you swiftly, for you are cutting out a tongue that has been melodious with divine hymns."

‖ When this one died also, after being cruelly tortured, the fifth leaped up, saying, [2] "I will not refuse, tyrant, to be tortured for the sake of virtue. [3] I have come of my own accord, so that by murdering me you will incur punishment from the heavenly justice for even more crimes. [4] Hater of virtue, hater of mankind, for what

act of ours are you destroying us in this way? [5] Is it because[q] we revere the Creator of all things and live according to his virtuous law? [6] But these deeds deserve honors, not tortures."[r] [9] While he was saying these things, the guards bound him and dragged him to the catapult; [10] they tied him to it on his knees, and fitting iron clamps on them, they twisted his back[s] around the wedge on the wheel,[t] so that he was completely curled back like a scorpion, and all his members were disjointed. [11] In this condition, gasping for breath and in anguish of body, [12] he said, "Tyrant, they are splendid favors that you grant us against your will, because through these noble sufferings you give us an opportunity to show our endurance for the law."

[13] After he too had died, the sixth, a mere boy, was led in. When the tyrant inquired whether he was willing to eat and be released, he said, [14] "I am younger in age than my brothers, but I am their equal in mind. [15] Since to this end we were born and bred, we ought likewise to die for the same principles. [16] So if you intend to torture me for not eating defiling foods, go on torturing!" [17] When he had said this, they led him to the wheel. [18] He was carefully stretched tight upon it, his back was broken, and he was roasted[u] from underneath. [19] To his back they applied sharp spits that had been heated in the fire, and pierced his ribs so that his entrails were burned through. [20] While being tortured he said, "O contest befitting holiness, in which so many of us brothers have been summoned to an arena of suffer-

q Other ancient authorities read *Or does it seem evil to you that*
r Other authorities add verses 7 and 8: [7] *If of course you had human feelings and had hope of salvation from God—* [8] *but, as it is, you are a stranger to God and persecute those who serve him."*
s Gk *loins*   t Greek obscure
u Other ancient authorities add *by fire*

---

notorious for their barbarous cruelty (2 Macc.4.47; 3 Macc.7.5). **15**: *Everlasting life*, or glorious life; see 9.22 n. *Brotherhood*, see 9.23; the seven brothers and their mother represent the entire Jewish nation. **19**: 2 Macc.7.10. **11.3**: A new idea; he welcomes torture so that the tyrant may be punished the more. **7**: *Human feelings*, ironical because the compassion expressed in 12.2 was genuine but did not go far enough. **10**: *Wedge on the wheel*, it is not certain how the wheel was constructed. **13–27**: 2 Macc.7.18–19. **20**: *Contest*, compare 6.10. *Arena*, literally "gymnasium."

ings for religion, and in which we have not been defeated! ²¹ For the religious knowledge, O tyrant, is invincible. ²² I also, equipped with nobility, will die with my brothers, ²³ and I myself will bring a great avenger upon you, you inventor of tortures and enemy of those who are truly devout. ²⁴ We six boys have paralyzed your tyranny! ²⁵ Since you have not been able to persuade us to change our mind or to force us to eat defiling foods, is not this your downfall? ²⁶ Your fire is cold to us, and the catapults painless, and your violence powerless. ²⁷ For it is not the guards of the tyrant but those of the divine law that are set over us; therefore, unconquered, we hold fast to reason."

12 When he also, thrown into the caldron, had died a blessed death, the seventh and youngest of all came forward. ² Even though the tyrant had been fearfully reproached by the brothers, he felt strong compassion for this child when he saw that he was already in fetters. He summoned him to come nearer and tried to console him, saying, ³ "You see the result of your brothers' stupidity, for they died in torments because of their disobedience. ⁴ You too, if you do not obey, will be miserably tortured and die before your time, ⁵ but if you yield to persuasion you will be my friend and a leader in the government of the kingdom." ⁶ When he had so pleaded, he sent for the boy's mother to show compassion on her who had been bereaved of so many sons and to influence her to persuade the surviving son to obey and save himself. ⁷ But

when his mother had exhorted him in the Hebrew language, as we shall tell a little later, ⁸ he said, "Let me loose, let me speak to the king and to all his friends that are with him." ⁹ Extremely pleased by the boy's declaration, they freed him at once. ¹⁰ Running to the nearest of the braziers, ¹¹ he said, "You profane tyrant, most impious of all the wicked, since you have received good things and also your kingdom from God, were you not ashamed to murder his servants and torture on the wheel those who practice religion? ¹² Because of this, justice has laid up for you intense and eternal fire and tortures, and these throughout all time*ᵛ* will never let you go. ¹³ As a man, were you not ashamed, you most savage beast, to cut out the tongues of men who have feelings like yours and are made of the same elements as you, and to maltreat and torture them in this way? ¹⁴ Surely they by dying nobly fulfilled their service to God, but you will wail bitterly for having slain without cause the contestants for virtue." ¹⁵ Then because he too was about to die, he said, ¹⁶ "I do not desert the excellent example*ʷ* of my brothers, ¹⁷ and I call on the God of our fathers to be merciful to our nation;*ˣ* ¹⁸ but on you he will take vengeance both in this present life and when you are dead." ¹⁹ After he had uttered these imprecations, he flung himself into the braziers and so ended his life.*ʸ*

v Gk *throughout the whole age*
w Other ancient authorities read *the witness*
x Other ancient authorities read *my race*
y Gk *and so gave up;* other ancient authorities read *gave up his spirit* or *his soul*

21: *Religious knowledge,* or science. In Greek thought true knowledge almost always leads to virtue; in Judaism, knowledge of the Mosaic law at least predisposes one toward it; see 1.17 n.; 18.6–19 n. **25:** *Downfall,* see 8.15 n. **26:** *Painless,* compare Heb.12.2, "despising the shame." **12.2:** *The tyrant* could feel *strong compassion;* see 8.10. **5:** *Friend,* see 8.5 n. **7:** *Hebrew language,* or perhaps Aramaic, as in Acts 21.40; compare 2 Macc.7.21,27. Many Palestinians, and certainly the author's first readers, spoke Greek. *A little later,* for dramatic effect, the author postpones the speech to 16.16–23. **11:** *Those who practice,* Greek *askētas,* almost "the athletes of religion"; compare v.14 and Philo, *On Dreams* i.59. **13:** *Feelings like yours,* a Stoic idea, found also in Wis.7.1–6; Acts 14.15. **14:** *Contestants,* see 11.20 n. **19:** *Flung himself,* as the mother does in 17.1. The remaining defenders of Masada at the end of the Jewish War of A.D. 66–73 killed one another. Jews, like Stoics, approved of suicide in certain circumstances.

13 Since, then, the seven brothers despised sufferings even unto death, everyone must concede that devout reason is sovereign over the emotions. [2] For if they had been slaves to their emotions and had eaten defiling food, we would say that they had been conquered by these emotions. [3] But in fact it was not so. Instead, by reason, which is praised before God, they prevailed over their emotions. [4] The supremacy of the mind over these cannot be overlooked, for the brothers[z] mastered both emotions and pains. [5] How then can one fail to confess the sovereignty of right reason over emotion in those who were not turned back by fiery agonies? [6] For just as towers jutting out over harbors hold back the threatening waves and make it calm for those who sail into the inner basin, [7] so the seven-towered right reason of the youths, by fortifying the harbor of religion, conquered the tempest of the emotions. [8] For they constituted a holy chorus of religion and encouraged one another, saying, [9] "Brothers, let us die like brothers for the sake of the law; let us imitate the three youths in Assyria who despised the same ordeal of the furnace. [10] Let us not be cowardly in the demonstration of our piety." [11] While one said, "Courage, brother," another said, "Bear up nobly," [12] and another reminded them, "Remember whence you came, and the father by whose hand Isaac would have submitted to being slain for the sake of religion." [13] Each of them and all of them together looking at one another, cheerful and undaunted, said, "Let us with all our hearts consecrate ourselves to God, who gave us our lives,[a] and let us use our bodies as a bulwark for the law. [14] Let us not fear him who thinks he is killing us, [15] for great is the struggle of the soul and the danger of eternal torment lying before those who transgress the commandment of God. [16] Therefore let us put on the full armor of self-control, which is divine reason. [17] For if we so die,[b] Abraham and Isaac and Jacob will welcome us, and all the fathers will praise us." [18] Those who were left behind said to each of the brothers who were being dragged away, "Do not put us to shame, brother, or betray the brothers who have died before us."

19 You are not ignorant of the affection of brotherhood, which the divine and all-wise Providence has bequeathed through the fathers to their descendants and which was implanted in the mother's womb. [20] There each of the brothers dwelt the same length of time and was shaped during the same period of time; and growing from the same blood and through the same life, they were brought to the light of day. [21] When they were born after an equal time of gestation, they drank milk from the same fountains. For such embraces brotherly-loving souls are nourished; [22] and they grow stronger from this common nurture and daily companionship, and from both general education and our discipline in the law of God.

23 Therefore, when sympathy and brotherly affection had been so established, the brothers were the more sympathetic to one another. [24] Since they had been educated by the same law and trained in the same virtues and brought up in right living, they loved one another all the more. [25] A common zeal for nobility expanded their goodwill and harmony toward one another, [26] because, with the aid of their religion, they rendered their brotherly love more fervent. [27] But although nature and companionship

z Gk *they*   a Or *souls*
b Other ancient authorities read *suffer*

13.1–14.10: **Philosophical interpretation.** Compare 6.31–35. **13.8:** *Chorus*, see 8.4 n.; 14.7. **9:** Dan. ch. 3. **12:** *Remember whence you came*, Is.51.1–2. *The father* and *Isaac*, 15.28; Gen.22.1–19; Wis.10.5. Their story became a favorite theme for Christians (Heb.11.17–19). **13:** *Each of them and all of them together*, as in a Greek chorus (see 8.4 n.). **14:** Mt.10.28; Lk.12.4. **17:** 5.37 n.; compare Lk.16.22. **19:** *Affection*, Greek *philtra*, a magical charm believed to produce love.

and virtuous habits had augmented the affection of brotherhood, those who were left endured for the sake of religion, while watching their brothers being maltreated and tortured to

14 death. [1] Furthermore, they encouraged them to face the torture, so that they not only despised their agonies, but also mastered the emotions of brotherly love.

2 O reason,[c] more royal than kings and freer than the free! [3] O sacred and harmonious concord of the seven brothers on behalf of religion! [4] None of the seven youths proved coward or shrank from death, [5] but all of them, as though running the course toward immortality, hastened to death by torture. [6] Just as the hands and feet are moved in harmony with the guidance of the mind, so those holy youths, as though moved by an immortal spirit of devotion, agreed to go to death for its sake. [7] O most holy seven, brothers in harmony! For just as the seven days of creation move in choral dance around religion, [8] so these youths, forming a chorus, encircled the sevenfold fear of tortures and dissolved it. [9] Even now, we ourselves shudder as we hear of the tribulations of these young men; they not only saw what was happening, yes, not only heard the direct word of threat, but also bore the sufferings patiently, and in agonies of fire at that. [10] What could be more excruciatingly painful than this? For the power of fire is intense and swift, and it consumed their bodies quickly.

11 Do not consider it amazing that reason had full command over these men in their tortures, since the mind of woman despised even more diverse agonies, [12] for the mother of the seven young men bore up under the rackings of each one of her children.

13 Observe how complex is a mother's love for her children, which draws everything toward an emotion felt in her inmost parts. [14] Even unreasoning animals, like mankind, have a sympathy and parental love for their offspring. [15] For example, among birds, the ones that are tame protect their young by building on the housetops, [16] and the others, by building in precipitous chasms and in holes and tops of trees, hatch the nestlings and ward off the intruder. [17] If they are not able to keep him away, they do what they can to help their young by flying in circles around them in the anguish of love, and warning them with their own calls. [18] And why is it necessary to demonstrate sympathy for children by the example of unreasoning animals, [19] since even bees at the time for making honeycombs defend themselves against intruders and as though with an iron dart sting those who approach their hive and defend it even to the death? [20] But sympathy for her children did not sway the mother of the young men; she was of the same mind as Abraham.

15 O reason of the children, tyrant over the emotions! O religion, more desirable to the mother than her children! [2] Two courses were open to this mother, that of religion, and that of preserving her seven sons for a time, as the tyrant had promised. [3] She loved religion more, religion that preserves them for eternal life according to God's promise. [4] In what manner might I express the emotions of parents who love their children? We impress upon the character of a small child a wondrous likeness both of mind and of form. Especially is this true of mothers, who because of their birthpangs have a deeper sympathy toward

c Or O minds

14.5: 9.8 n.; Heb.12.1. **8:** *Sevenfold fear,* the Greek here is obscure. **9:** *Even now,* see 3.19 n.
   14.11–17.1: The mother of the seven. Her death is merely mentioned in 2 Macc.7.41; here it is made the climax of the oration. **14.14:** The analogy between *unreasoning animals* and *mankind* (vv. 14–19) was a theme of popular Greek philosophy. **20:** *Did not sway,* the mother's constancy is the supreme proof of the dominance of religious reason. *Abraham* had offered Isaac; see 13.12 n. **15.2:** *Two courses,* the two ways of Jer.21.8 became a pattern of Jewish thought.

their offspring than do the fathers.
[5] Considering that mothers are the
weaker sex and give birth to many,
they are the more devoted to their
children.[d] [6] The mother of the seven
boys, more than any other mother,
loved her children. In seven pregnancies
she had implanted in herself tender love
toward them, [7] and because of the
many pains she suffered with each of
them she had sympathy for them;
[8] yet because of the fear of God she
disdained the temporary safety of her
children. [9] Not only so, but also
because of the nobility of her sons and
their ready obedience to the law she
felt a greater tenderness toward them.
[10] For they were righteous and self-
controlled and brave and magnan-
imous, and loved their brothers and
their mother, so that they obeyed
her even to death in keeping the
ordinances. [11] Nevertheless, though so
many factors influenced the mother to
suffer with them out of love for her
children, in the case of none of them
were the various tortures strong enough
to pervert her reason. [12] Instead, the
mother urged them on, each child
singly and all together, to death for
the sake of religion. [13] O sacred nature
and affection of parental love, yearning
of parents toward offspring, nurture,
and indomitable suffering by mothers!
[14] This mother, who saw them tortured
and burned one by one, because of
religion did not change her attitude.
[15] She watched the flesh of her children
consumed by fire, their toes and
fingers scattered[e] on the ground, and
the flesh of the head to the chin exposed like masks. [16] O mother, tried
now by more bitter pains than even the
birth-pangs you suffered for them!
[17] O woman, who alone gave birth to
such complete devotion! [18] When the
first-born breathed his last it did not
turn you aside, nor when the second
in torments looked at you piteously,

nor when the third expired; [19] nor
did you weep when you looked at the
eyes of each one in his tortures gazing
boldly at the same agonies, and saw
in their nostrils signs of the approach
of death. [20] When you saw the flesh
of children burned upon the flesh of
other children, severed hands upon
hands, scalped heads upon heads, and
corpses fallen on other corpses and
when you saw the place filled with
many spectators of the torturings, you
did not shed tears. [21] Neither the
melodies of sirens nor the songs of
swans attract the attention of their
hearers as did the voices of the children
in torture calling to their mother.
[22] How great and how many torments
the mother then suffered as her sons
were tortured on the wheel and with
the hot irons! [23] But devout reason,
giving her heart a man's courage in the
very midst of her emotions, strengthened her to disregard her temporal
love for her children.

24 Although she witnessed the destruction of seven children and the
ingenious and various rackings, this
noble mother disregarded all these[f]
because of faith in God. [25] For as in
the council chamber of her own soul
she saw mighty advocates – nature,
family, parental love, and the rackings
of her children – [26] this mother held
two ballots, one bearing death and the
other deliverance for her children.
[27] She did not approve the deliverance
which would preserve the seven sons
for a short time, [28] but as the daughter
of God-fearing Abraham she remembered his fortitude.

29 O mother of the nation, vindicator
of the law and champion of religion,
who carried away the prize of the contest in your heart! [30] O more noble

---

d Or *For to the degree that mothers are weaker and the
more children they bear, the more they are devoted to
their children.*
e Or *quivering*
f Other ancient authorities read *having bidden them
farewell surrendered them*

Religion, 5.31 n. **4**: *Of mind and of form*, a Stoic idea. **13**: *Indomitable suffering*, actually it is
the mother who is *indomitable* in spite of her *love* and *suffering*. **17**: *Gave birth*, includes the idea
of spiritual birth; compare 16.13 n.; 17.6; Gal.4.19. **25–26**: *Ballots*, as though she were in the
council chamber of a Greek city. **28**: See 13.12 n. **31**: *Noah's ark*, see 7.1–3 n.; also Wis.14.6.

than males in steadfastness, and more manly than men in endurance! [31] Just as Noah's ark, carrying the world in the universal flood, stoutly endured the waves, [32] so you, O guardian of the law, overwhelmed from every side by the flood of your emotions and the violent winds, the torture of your sons, endured nobly and withstood the wintry storms that assail religion.

16 If, then, a woman, advanced in years and mother of seven sons, endured seeing her children tortured to death, it must be admitted that devout reason is sovereign over the emotions. [2] Thus I have demonstrated not only that men have ruled over the emotions, but also that a woman has despised the fiercest tortures. [3] The lions surrounding Daniel were not so savage, nor was the raging fiery furnace of Mishael so intensely hot, as was her innate parental love, inflamed as she saw her seven sons tortured in such varied ways. [4] But the mother quenched so many and such great emotions by devout reason.

[5] Consider this also. If this woman, though a mother, had been fainthearted, she would have mourned over them and perhaps have spoken as follows: [6] "O how wretched am I and many times unhappy! After bearing seven children, I am now the mother of none! [7] O seven childbirths all in vain, seven profitless pregnancies, fruitless nurturings and wretched nursings! [8] In vain, my sons, I endured many birth-pangs for you, and the more grievous anxieties of your upbringing. [9] Alas for my children, some unmarried, others married and without offspring.[g] I shall not see your children or have the happiness of being called grandmother. [10] Alas, I who had so many and beautiful children am a widow and alone, with many sorrows.[h] [11] Nor when I die, shall I have any of my sons to bury me."

[12] Yet the sacred and God-fearing mother did not wail with such a lament for any of them, nor did she dissuade any of them from dying, nor did she grieve as they were dying, [13] but, as though having a mind like adamant and giving rebirth for immortality to the whole number of her sons, she implored them and urged them on to death for the sake of religion. [14] O mother, soldier of God in the cause of religion, elder and woman! By steadfastness you have conquered even a tyrant, and in word and deed you have proved more powerful than a man. [15] For when you and your sons were arrested together, you stood and watched Eleazar being tortured, and said to your sons in the Hebrew language, [16] "My sons, noble is the contest to which you are called to bear witness for the nation. Fight zealously for our ancestral law. [17] For it would be shameful if, while an aged man endures such agonies for the sake of religion, you young men were to be terrified by tortures. [18] Remember that it is through God that you have had a share in the world and have enjoyed life, [19] and therefore you ought to endure any suffering for the sake of God. [20] For his sake also our father Abraham was zealous to sacrifice his son Isaac, the ancestor of our nation; and when Isaac saw his father's hand wielding a sword and descending upon him, he did not cower. [21] And Daniel the righteous was thrown to the lions, and Hananiah, Azariah, and Mishael were hurled into the fiery furnace and endured it for the sake of God. [22] You too must have the same faith in God and not be grieved. [23] It is unreasonable for people who have religious knowledge not to withstand pain."

[24] By these words the mother of the seven encouraged and persuaded each of her sons to die rather than violate

g Gk *without benefit*   h Or *much to be pitied*

16.3: *Daniel,* Dan.6.1–24. *Mishael,* Dan.1.7; 3.19–30. **11:** *Any . . . sons to bury me,* for both Jews and Greeks a supreme calamity. **13:** *Giving rebirth for immortality,* see 15.17 n.; Jn.3.5. **15:** *Hebrew language,* see 12.7 n. **16–23:** Compare this more rhetorical speech with 2 Macc.7.27–29. **16:** *Contest,* 6.10; 11.20. **20:** *Isaac,* see 13.12 n. **21:** *Daniel,* v. 3. *Hananiah, Azariah, and Mishael,*

God's commandment. [25] They knew also that those who die for the sake of God live in God,[i] as do Abraham and Isaac and Jacob and all the patriarchs.

17 Some of the guards said that when she also was about to be seized and put to death she threw herself into the flames so that no one might touch her body.

2 O mother, who with your seven sons nullified the violence of the tyrant, frustrated his evil designs, and showed the courage of your faith! [3] Nobly set like a roof on the pillars of your sons, you held firm and unswerving against the earthquake of the tortures. [4] Take courage, therefore, O holy-minded mother, maintaining firm an enduring hope in God. [5] The moon in heaven, with the stars, does not stand so august as you, who, after lighting the way of your star-like seven sons to piety, stand in honor before God and are firmly set in heaven with them. [6] For your children were true descendants of father Abraham.[j]

7 If it were possible for us to paint the history of your piety as an artist might, would not those who first beheld it have shuddered as they saw the mother of the seven children enduring their varied tortures to death for the sake of religion? [8] Indeed it would be proper to inscribe upon their tomb these words as a reminder to the people of our nation:[k]

9 "Here lie buried an aged priest and an aged woman and seven sons, because of the violence of the tyrant who wished to destroy the way of life of the Hebrews. [10] They vindicated their nation, looking to God and enduring torture even to death."

11 Truly the contest in which they were engaged was divine, [12] for on that day virtue gave the awards and tested them for their endurance. The prize was immortality in endless life. [13] Eleazar was the first contestant, the mother of the seven sons entered the competition, and the brothers contended. [14] The tyrant was the antagonist, and the world and the human race were the spectators. [15] Reverence for God was victor and gave the crown to its own athletes. [16] Who did not admire the athletes of the divine[l] legislation? Who were not amazed?

17 The tyrant himself and all his council marveled at their[m] endurance, [18] because of which they now stand before the divine throne and live through blessed eternity. [19] For Moses says, "All who are consecrated are under your hands." [20] These, then, who have been consecrated for the sake of God,[n] are honored, not only with this honor, but also by the fact that because of them our enemies did not rule over our nation, [21] the tyrant was punished, and the homeland purified – they having become, as it were, a ransom for the sin of our nation. [22] And through the blood of

i Or to God
j Gk For your childbearing was from Abraham the father; other authorities read For . . . Abraham the servant
k Or as a memorial to the heroes of our people
l Other authorities read true
m Other authorities add virtue and
n Other ancient authorities omit for the sake of God

Dan. ch. 3. **25:** *Live in God*, see 7.19 n. **17.1:** *Threw herself*, compare 12.19; 2 Macc.7.41. *Touch her body*, this would be a violation of her chastity.

17.2–18.5: Panegyric on the mother. The author has already pronounced encomiums on Eleazar (7.1–15), the brothers (14.2–10), and the mother (ch. 15), sometimes addressing them directly. The oration now comes to its climax. **3:** *Roof . . . pillars . . . earthquake*, metaphors appropriate to Antioch, where there were frequent earthquakes, but applicable also to Palestine. **5:** Stoics regarded *the stars* as living beings; for Jews the language was metaphorical. *Lighting the way*, mystical language; compare Jn.12.35–36,46. **6:** *True descendants*, compare 15.28; 13.12 n.; the giving of new birth is like Isaac's return from impending death; compare Heb. 11.17–19. **7:** *Possible*, or "permitted." At this time the Jews may have taken the commandment of Ex.20.4 strictly. **9:** *Way of life*, Greek *politeia*, "commonwealth." **11–12:** *Contest . . . awards . . . prize*, 6.10; 11.20. **21:** *Ransom*, see 6.29 n. **22:** *Through the blood*, Rom.3.25; *expiation*,

those devout ones and their death as an expiation, divine Providence preserved Israel that previously had been afflicted.

23 For the tyrant Antiochus, when he saw the courage of their virtue and their endurance under the tortures, proclaimed them to his soldiers as an example for their own endurance, [24] and this made them brave and courageous for infantry battle and siege, and he ravaged and conquered all his enemies.

18 O Israelite children, offspring of the seed of Abraham, obey this law and exercise piety in every way, [2] knowing that devout reason is master of all emotions, not only of sufferings from within, but also of those from without.

3 Therefore those who gave over their bodies in suffering for the sake of religion were not only admired by men, but also were deemed worthy to share in a divine inheritance. [4] Because of them the nation gained peace, and by reviving observance of the law in the homeland they ravaged the enemy. [5] The tyrant Antiochus was both punished on earth and is being chastised after his death. Since in no way whatever was he able to compel the Israelites to become pagans and to abandon their ancestral customs, he left Jerusalem and marched against the Persians.

6 The mother of the seven sons expressed also these principles to her children: [7] "I was a pure virgin and did not go outside my father's house; but I guarded the rib from which woman was made.[o] [8] No seducer corrupted me on a desert plain, nor did the destroyer, the deceitful serpent, defile the purity of my virginity. [9] In the time of my maturity I remained with my husband, and when these sons had grown up their father died. A happy man was he, who lived out his life with good children, and did not have the grief of bereavement. [10] While he was still with you, he taught you the law and the prophets. [11] He read to you about Abel slain by Cain, and Isaac who was offered as a burnt offering, and of Joseph in prison. [12] He told you of the zeal of Phineas, and he taught you about Hananiah, Azariah, and Mishael in the fire. [13] He praised Daniel in the den of the lions and blessed him. [14] He reminded you of the scripture of Isaiah, which says, 'Even though you go through the fire, the flame shall not consume you.' [15] He sang to you songs of the psalmist David, who said, 'Many are the afflictions of the righteous.' [16] He recounted to you Solomon's proverb, 'There is a tree of life for those who do his will.' [17] He confirmed the saying of Ezekiel, 'Shall these dry bones live?' [18] For he did not forget to teach you the song that Moses taught, which says, [19] 'I kill and I make alive: this is your life and the length of your days.'"

20 O bitter was that day–and yet not bitter – when that bitter tyrant of the Greeks quenched fire with fire

o Gk *the rib that was built* (Gen 2.22 LXX)

Greek *hilastērion*, as in Rom.3.25; compare Heb.9.11–15; 1 Pet.1.19; 1 Jn.1.7. **24:** *Ravaged and conquered*, but Antiochus was not successful, and died in Babylon (1 Macc.6.1–16). **18.1–5:** The exhortation seems repetitious after 17.7–24, but it is the author's method to employ recurrent themes. **5:** *Marched against the Persians*, 17.24 n. The second sentence in this verse does not fit well with the first.

18.6–19: The mother's last words. Compare 2 Macc.7.22–29. The mother is the supreme heroine of the story. This is a quiet passage after the highly emotional parts, designed to move the reader to reflection. Jewish education began in the home, and the mother's influence was always important. **7:** *Rib*, Gen.2.22. **8:** *Desert plain*, Dt.22.25–27. In such places women were in danger from men and also from demons, who were believed to inhabit the wilderness. **11:** *Abel*, Gen.4.2–15. *Isaac*, Gen.22.1–19. *Joseph*, Gen.39.1–23. **12:** *Phineas*, Num.25.1–9. *Hananiah*, 16.21. **13:** *Daniel*, Dan.6.1–24. **14:** Is.43.2. **15:** Ps.34.19. **16:** Pr.3.18, modified slightly. **17:** Ezek. 37.2–3. **19:** Dt.32.39; 30.20.

18.20–24: Conclusion. This peroration sums up many previous themes set forth in 4 Macc.

in his cruel caldrons, and in his burning rage brought those seven sons of the daughter of Abraham to the catapult and back again to more[p] tortures, [21] pierced the pupils of their eyes and cut out their tongues, and put them to death with various tortures. [22] For these crimes divine justice pursued and will pursue the accursed tyrant. [23] But the sons of Abraham with their victorious mother are gathered together into the chorus of the fathers, and have received pure and immortal[q] souls from God, [24] to whom be glory for ever and ever. Amen.

[p] Other ancient authorities read *to all his*
[q] Other ancient authorities read *victorious*

23: *Abraham*, 13.12 n. *Chorus*, see 8.4 n. *Immortal*, see 9.22 n. **24:** Compare Rom.11.36; 16.27; 2 Tim.4.18; Heb.13.21.

PSALM 151

Besides the 150 psalms comprising the Book of Psalms in the Masoretic text of the Hebrew Bible, a supernumerary psalm ascribed to David is included in manuscripts of the Greek Septuagint. The scribe of codex Sinaiticus regarded it as part of the Psalter, for his subscription reads "The 151 Psalms of David." On the other hand, in codex Alexandrinus and most other manuscripts of the Septuagint the psalm is excluded from the Psalter proper by the title which identifies the psalm to be "outside the number [of the 150 psalms]." Besides being in the Greek Bible, the psalm is current also in several other ancient versions, including the Old Latin, Syriac, Armenian, Ethiopic, and Arabic.

In 1956 a fragmentary leather scroll from Qumran Cave XI was found which contains portions of the Hebrew text of about thirty-five canonical psalms (not all in the traditional sequence) along with several non-canonical psalms. One of these latter is a somewhat enlarged form of what has been known as Ps.151. A translation of the Hebrew text, made by J. A. Sanders, the original editor of the scroll, in *Discoveries in the Judaean Desert of Jordan*, Vol. IV (Oxford, 1965), is given here for purposes of comparison with the Septuagint form of the psalm. It should be mentioned that the Hebrew script presents several palaeographical and philological uncertainties not yet satisfactorily resolved by scholars.

A Hallelujah of David the Son of Jesse.

1 Smaller was I than my brothers
    and the youngest of the sons of my father,
So he made me shepherd of his flock
    and ruler over his kids.

2 My hands have made an instrument
    and my fingers a lyre;
And [so] have I rendered glory to the Lord,
    thought I, within my soul.

3 The mountains do not witness to him,
    nor do the hills proclaim;
The trees have cherished my words
    and the flock my works.

4 For who can proclaim and who can bespeak
    and who can recount the deeds of the Lord?
Everything has God seen,
    everything has he heard and he has heeded.

5 He sent his prophet to anoint me,
    Samuel to make me great;
My brothers went out to meet him,
    handsome of figure and appearance.

6 Though they were tall of stature
    and handsome by their hair,
The Lord God chose
    them not.

7 But he sent and took me from behind the flock
    and anointed me with holy oil,
And he made me leader of his people
    and ruler over the sons of his covenant.

In the line following the Hebrew text of this psalm another psalm (with its heading) begins, of which only two poorly preserved lines remain. Apparently they celebrate David's victory over Goliath; Sanders's translation is as follows:

> At the beginning of David's power after
> the prophet of God had anointed him.

> ¹ Then I [saw] a Philistine
> uttering defiances from the r[anks of the Philistines].

It thus appears that the Greek text of Ps.151 is a condensed recension of what was originally two separate psalms in Hebrew.

PSALM 151

This psalm is ascribed to David as his own composition (though it is outside the number[a]), after he had fought in single combat with Goliath.

I WAS SMALL AMONG MY BROTHERS,
and youngest in my father's house;
I tended my father's sheep.

² My hands made a harp,
my fingers fashioned a lyre.

³ And who will declare it to my
Lord?
The Lord himself; it is he who
hears.[b]

⁴ It was he who sent his messenger[c]

and took me from my father's
sheep,
and anointed me with his
anointing oil.

⁵ My brothers were handsome and
tall,
but the Lord was not pleased
with them.

⁶ I went out to meet the Philistine,[d]
and he cursed me by his idols.

⁷ But I drew his own sword;
I beheaded him, and removed
reproach from the people of
Israel.

a Other authorities add *of the one hundred fifty* (psalms)
b Some witnesses add *everything;* others add *me;* others read *who will hear me*
c Or *angel*
d Or *foreigner*

1: *Small . . . youngest*, 1 Sam.16.7 and 11. *Tended . . . sheep*, 1 Sam.16.11. One form of the Syriac version continues, "and I met a lion and also a wolf, and I killed them and tore them in pieces" (compare 1 Sam.17.34–36). **2**: *My hands made a harp*, 2 Chr.29.26. **4**: *Anointed me*, 1 Sam.16.13; Ps.89.20. *Took me from my father's sheep*, Ps.78.70. **5**: *The Lord was not pleased with them*, 1 Sam.16.7–10. **6**: *He cursed . . . by his idols*, 1 Sam.17.43. Certain manuscripts of the Old Latin, Arabic, and Ethiopic versions continue, with minor deviations: "And I slung three stones at him in the middle of his forehead, and laid him low by the might of the Lord." According to 1 Sam.17.49–50 David felled Goliath with only one stone. **7**: *His own sword*, 1 Sam.17.51.

CHRONOLOGICAL TABLES OF RULERS

The Seleucid Dynasty

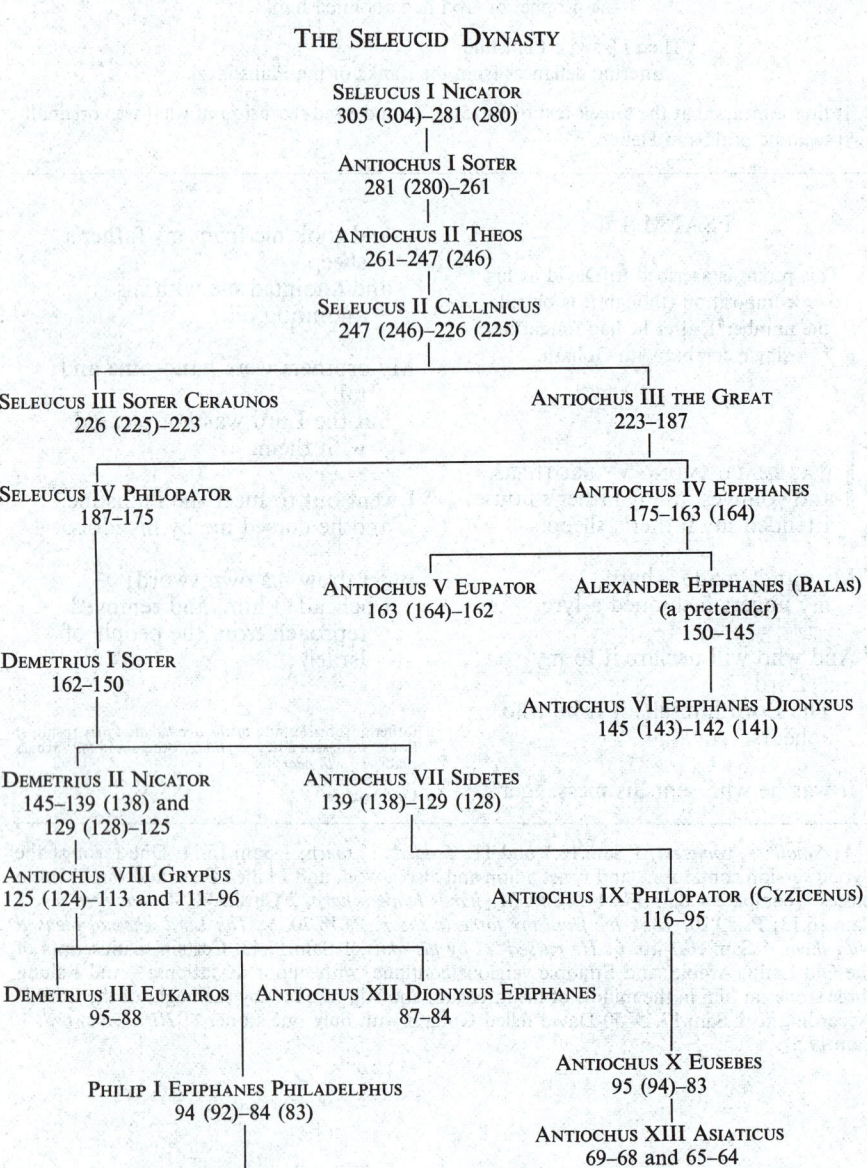

Seleucus I Nicator
305 (304)–281 (280)

Antiochus I Soter
281 (280)–261

Antiochus II Theos
261–247 (246)

Seleucus II Callinicus
247 (246)–226 (225)

Seleucus III Soter Ceraunos
226 (225)–223

Antiochus III the Great
223–187

Seleucus IV Philopator
187–175

Antiochus IV Epiphanes
175–163 (164)

Antiochus V Eupator
163 (164)–162

Alexander Epiphanes (Balas)
(a pretender)
150–145

Demetrius I Soter
162–150

Antiochus VI Epiphanes Dionysus
145 (143)–142 (141)

Demetrius II Nicator
145–139 (138) and
129 (128)–125

Antiochus VII Sidetes
139 (138)–129 (128)

Antiochus VIII Grypus
125 (124)–113 and 111–96

Antiochus IX Philopator (Cyzicenus)
116–95

Demetrius III Eukairos
95–88

Antiochus XII Dionysus Epiphanes
87–84

Antiochus X Eusebes
95 (94)–83

Philip I Epiphanes Philadelphus
94 (92)–84 (83)

Antiochus XIII Asiaticus
69–68 and 65–64

Philip II
67–66

The House of the Maccabees (Hasmoneans)

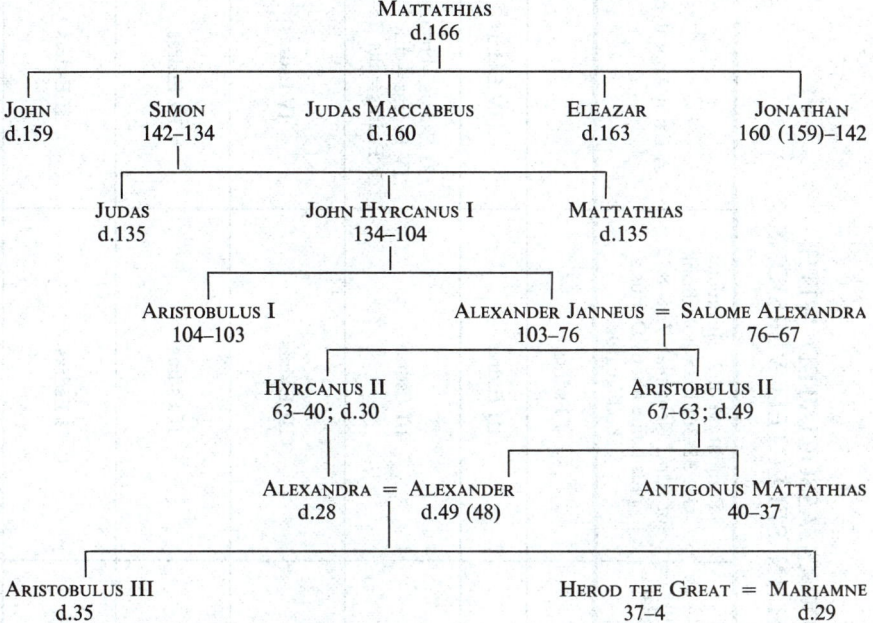

These two family trees include the names of the more important rulers. The presence of short parallel lines between two names indicates marriage. The date of an individual's death or the dates of his rule are in some cases disputed, and alternative possibilities are given within parentheses. All the dates are B.C. Besides the standard works on the chronology of the inter-testamental period, special mention should be made of F. M. Heichelheim's "Chronological Table from 323–30 B.C." in *Proceedings of the IX International Congress of Papyrology*, Oslo, 1958, pp. 163–182 (also published separately by the Norwegian Universities Press). Seleucus I became king in the seventh year of the Seleucid era; see A. J. Sachs and D. J. Wiseman, "A Babylonian King List of the Hellenistic Period," *Iraq*, xvi (1954), p. 205. Syria became a Roman province in 64 B.C., and Pompey conquered Jerusalem in 63 B.C.

TITLES GIVEN TO BOOKS ASSOCIATED WITH EZRA AND NEHEMIAH IN SELECTED VERSIONS

Version \ Document	Old Testament Book of Ezra	Old Testament Book of Nehemiah	Paraphrase of 2 Chronicles chs. 35–36; the whole Book of Ezra; Nehemiah 7.38–8.12; plus a tale about Darius's bodyguards	A Latin Apocalypse
Greek Bible (Septuagint)	II Esdras		I Esdras	
Latin Vulgate Bible	I Esdras	II Esdras	III Esdras	IV Esdras
Many later Latin Manuscripts	I Esdras		III Esdras	II Esdras=chs. 1–2 IV Esdras=chs. 3–14 V Esdras=chs. 15–16
Douay English Version (1609–1610)	I Esdras	II Esdras	III Esdras	IV Esdras
Russian Bible, Moscow Patriarchate (1956)	I Esdras	Nehemiah	II Esdras	III Esdras
King James and Revised Standard Versions	The Book of Ezra	The Book of Nehemiah	I Esdras	II Esdras

INDEX TO THE ANNOTATIONS

The following index lists important persons, places, and ideas which are mentioned in the general introduction and the annotations. In order to gain the fullest information, the verse (or verses) of the passage of the Apocrypha as well as the annotation itself should be read, and all cross references should be consulted.

NOTES

THE NEW OXFORD

BIBLE MAPS

*Prepared by the Cartographic Department
of Oxford University Press,
and based on the Oxford Bible Atlas.*

MAP 1

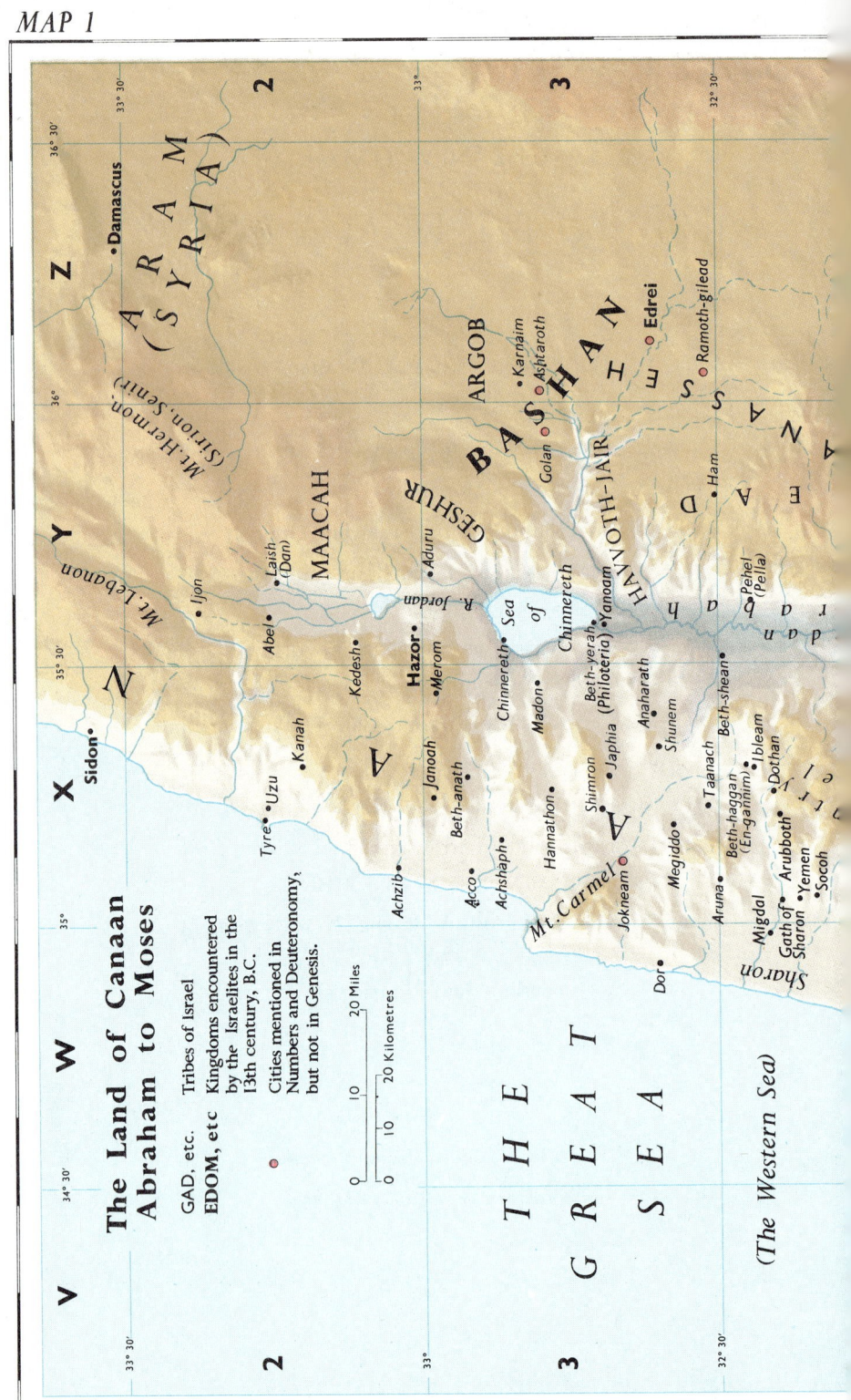

The Land of Canaan Abraham to Moses

GAD, etc.   Tribes of Israel

EDOM, etc   Kingdoms encountered by the Israelites in the 13th century, B.C.

●   Cities mentioned in Numbers and Deuteronomy, but not in Genesis.

THE GREAT SEA

(The Western Sea)

MAP 1

© Oxford University Press

OUTER BORDER SHOWS 10 MILE SUBDIVISIONS

MAP 2

The Exodus

—— Probable route of the Exodus
– – – Alternative routes
········· Line of border fortresses

| 0 | 20 | 40 Miles |
| 0 | 20 | 40 Kilometres |

SEA

Rabbah

Shittim
Heshbon
Mt. Nebo
Medeba

32°
34°

T

Gezer
Bethel
Ai
Jericho
Jerusalem

Ashdod
Libnah
Azekah
Lachish

Plain of Philistia
CANAAN

Gaza
Hebron
Salt
Sea
Dibon
R. Arnon

Debir
Juttah

Raphia
Gerar

Kir-hareseth

Beer-sheba
ARAD?

Hormah
Arad?

Philistines
Brook of Egypt
The Negeb

Shur
Wilderness
of Zin
Hazazon-tamar

Way to Shur
Azmon
Bene-jaakan
(Beeroth)
Bozrah

Mt. Sinai?
(Jebel Helal)
Hazar-addar
Punon

us
route
Kadesh-barnea
(Meribah)
Oboth

2

Sela
Teman

The Arabah
E D O M
Line of border fortresses

The King's Highway
Alternative Exodus route

Wilderness
of
Paran

Ezion-geber
3

S I N A I

Wilderness
of Sin?

ophkah?
erabit el-Khadim)

M I D I A N

Red Sea (Gulf of Aqaba)

4

Mt. Sinai?
(Mt Horeb)
T
U
© Oxford University Press

ILE SUBDIVISIONS

MAP 3

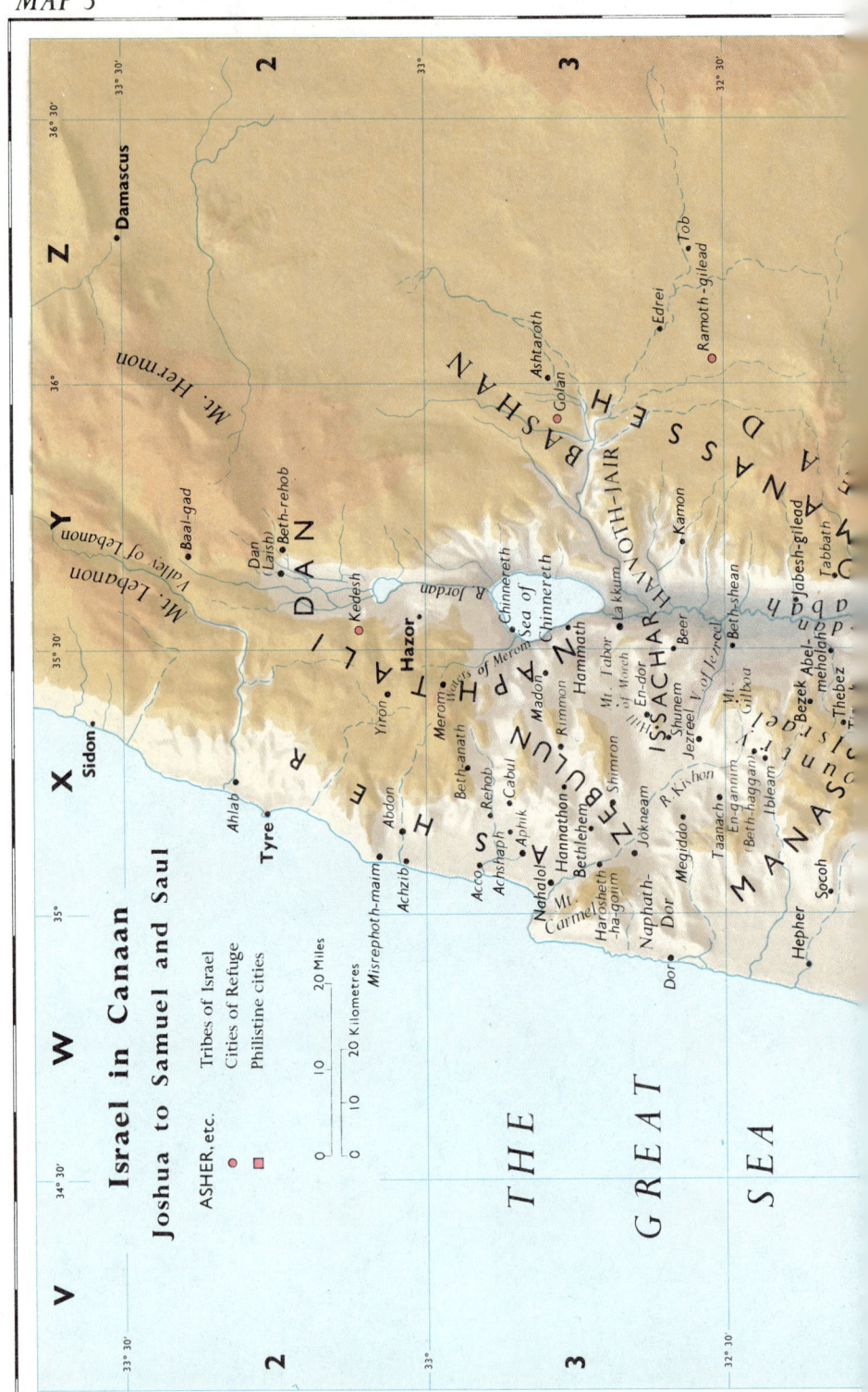

Israel in Canaan — Joshua to Samuel and Saul

MAP 3

OUTER BORDER SHOWS 10 MILE SUBDIVISIONS

© Oxford University Press

MAP 4

The United Monarchy

ISRAEL, JUDAH   Hebrew kingdoms
ASHER, etc.   Israelite tribes
SYRIA, etc.   Non-Israelite peoples
    ▣   Places fortified by Solomon
   I–XII   Solomon's administrative
         districts (1 Kgs. 4. 7–19)

0   10   20 Miles
0   10   20 Kilometres

Sidon

Tyre

ZOBAH

Damascus

S Y R I A (ARAM)

Mt. Lebanon

Mt. Hermon

BETH–REHOB

Abel-beth-maacah

Dan

Beth-rehob

MAACAH

B A S H A N

ARGOB

GESHUR

S I D O N I A N S

A S H E R

Hazor

Merom

VIII

IX

Acco

Cabul

R. Jordan

N A P H T A L I

Z E B U L U N

Sea of Chinnereth

Mt. Carmel

Jokneam (Jokmeam)

Dor

IV

R. Kishon

X

ISSACHAR

HAVVOTH–JAIR

G I L E A D

Helam

Lo-debar

VI

Megiddo

Jezreel

V. of Jezreel

Taanach

Mt. Gilboa

V

Beth-shean

Rogelim

Ramoth-gilead

Tob

T H E

G R E A T

S E A

of Sharon

I S R A E L

III

Arubboth

Hepher

Socoh

Abel-meholah

Thebez

R. Jordan

Jabesh-gilead

VII

MAP 4

OUTER BORDER SHOWS 10 MILE SUBDIVISIONS

MAP 5

MAP 5

OUTER BORDER SHOWS 10 MILE SUBDIVISIONS

© Oxford University Press

MAP 6

Black S

PHRYGIA

Gomer
(Gimarrai)

Gordion •

Meshech
(Mushki)

R. Halys

Tubal
(Tab

Usiana

LYDIA

R. Hermus

Sardis
(Sepharad)

Mus

R. Maeander

CILICIA
(KHILAKKU) Kue

JAVAN

HATTINA

Rhodes

Cyprus
(Iadanna)

Crete
(Caphtor)

Arvad •

Ka
Riblc

Gebal (Byblos) •

The Great Sea

Berytus •

Helbon

(The Upper Sea, the Western Sea)

Sidon •

Dam

Tyre •

Ushu

Acco •

Haura

Samaria •

ISRAEL

Jerusalem

AMMON

JUDAH MOAB

Migdol

Sais •

Zoan
(Tanis)

Pelusium

Gaza •
Raphia •

Libya

Tahpanhes

Athribis •

EDOM
• Sela

Memphis
(Noph)

Heliopolis
(On)

• Ezion-geber
(Elath)

Sinai

Hermopolis •

EGYPT

Lycopolis
(Siut)

Red Sea

Thebes •

Syene •

ETHIOPIA

E

F

G

OUTER BORDER S

MAP 6

The Near East

in the time of the

Assyrian Empire

Approximate extent of Assyrian domination in the latter part of the 8th. century.

(Later, under Esarhaddon (681-669), Assyria conquered Egypt.)

0   100   200 Miles

0   100   200 Kilometres

Caspian Sea

ARARAT (URARTU)

L. Van •Turushpa (Tuspar)

Nairi

L. Urmia Minni (Mannai)

A S S Y R I A

Haran Gozan •Dur-sharrukin
-eden •Nineveh •Arbela
(-adini) Calah *Upper Zab*

R. Euphrates *R. Habor* Asshur• *Lower Zab* •Arrapkha

MADAI (MEDES)

•Ecbatana

R. Tigris *R. Diyala* *R. Adhaim*

E L A M

Sippar•
Cuthah• Pekod (Puqudu)
Babylon• •Susa (Shushan)
Borsippa• •Nippur

BABYLONIA

Erech (Uruk)• •Larsa
Ur•

d a r
l r i)

A R A B I A

•Dumah

The Lower (Eastern) Sea

HEBA
SABA)

MAP 7

The Near East
in the time of the
Persian Empire

MAP 7

Caucasus Mountains

R. Cyrus

R. Araxes

COLCHI
(ECH)

zus
IECH)

Hyrcanian
Sea

(Caspian Sea)

ARMENIA
(URARTU)

L. Van

L. Urmia

sibis

ASSYRIA
Nineveh • Arbela

Asshur • • Arrapkha
R. Tigris

rates

R.

MEDIA

HYRCANIA

Astrabad Zadrakarta
(Gorgan) (Turang Tepe)
•(Damghan)

PARTHIA

Rages
(Rhagae)

Ecbatana
(Achmetha)

• Bisitun
(Behistun)

SAGARTIA

BABYLONIA
• Eshnunna
Sippar • Der •

Babylon
Borsippa •
Nippur

E L A M
(SUSIANA)

• Susa
(Shushan)

• Gabae
(Isfahan)

Erech (Uruk)
Larsa
• Ur

Parsagarda
(Pasargadae)
Persepolis •

PERSIS
(PERSIA)

ARABIA

Lower Sea (Persian Gulf)

0   100   200 Miles

0   100   200 Kilometres

© Oxford University Press

MILE SUBDIVISIONS

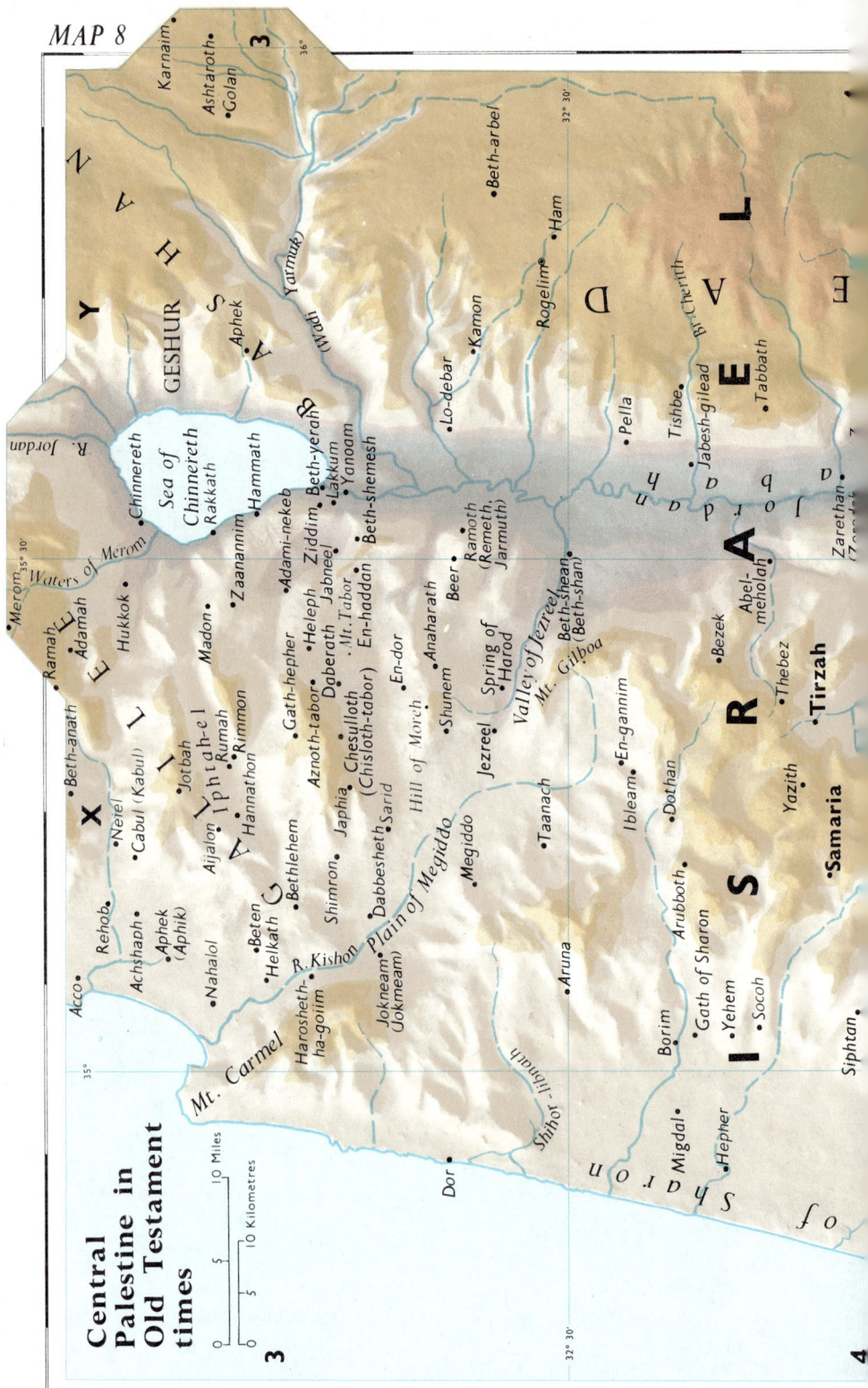

MAP 8

MAP 9

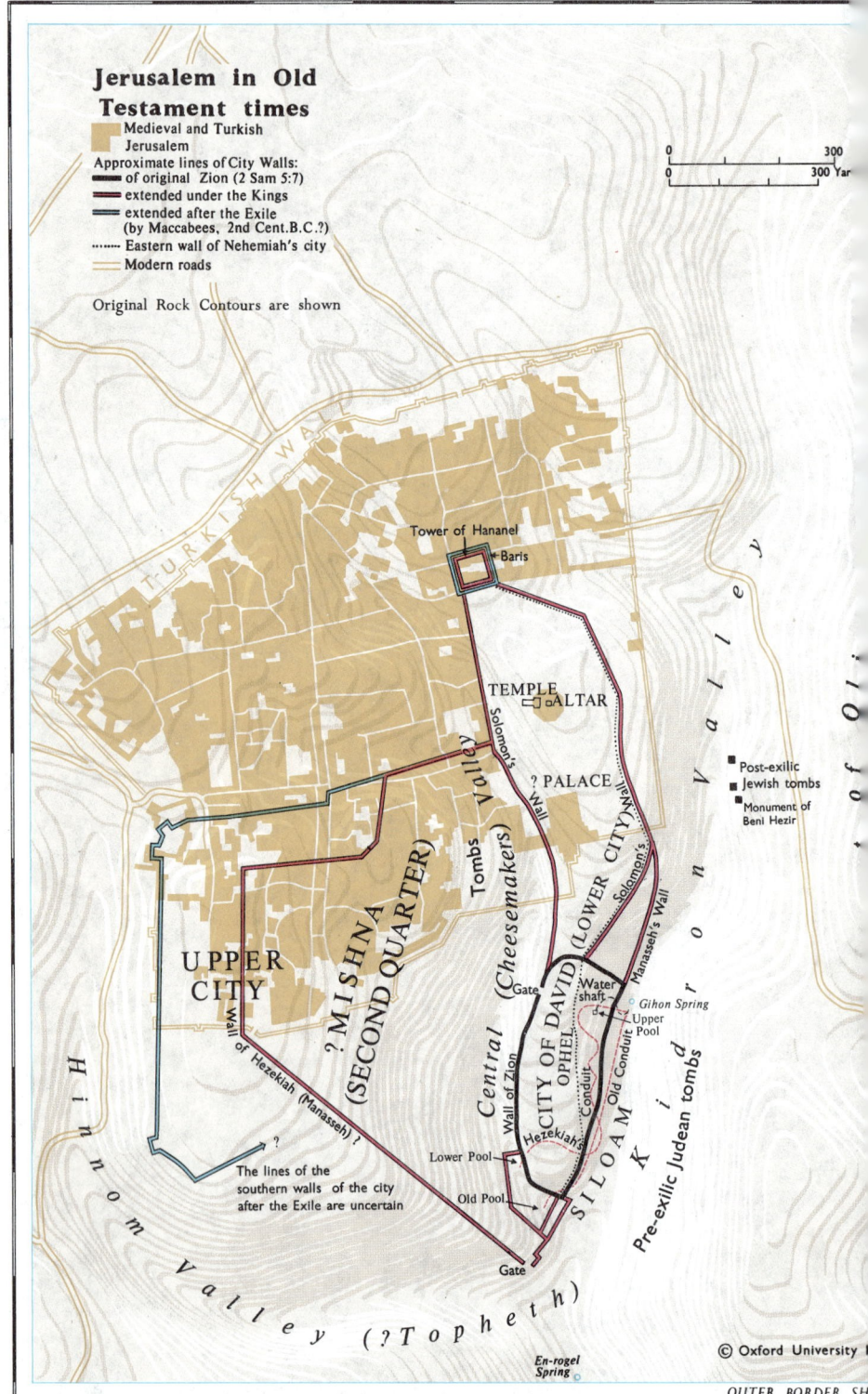

Jerusalem in Old Testament times

Medieval and Turkish Jerusalem

Approximate lines of City Walls:
- of original Zion (2 Sam 5:7)
- extended under the Kings
- extended after the Exile (by Maccabees, 2nd Cent.B.C.?)
- Eastern wall of Nehemiah's city
- Modern roads

Original Rock Contours are shown

Tower of Hananel

Baris

TEMPLE ☐ ALTAR

? PALACE

Post-exilic Jewish tombs

Monument of Beni Hezir

Solomon's Valley

Tombs

Central (Cheesemakers) Valley

Solomon's Wall

Solomon's Wall

Manasseh's Wall

(LOWER CITY)

UPPER CITY

?MISHNA (SECOND QUARTER)

Wall of Hezekiah (Manasseh) ?

Wall of Zion

Gate

CITY OF DAVID

OPHEL

Water shaft

Gihon Spring

Upper Pool

Conduit

Old Conduit

Hezekiah's Conduit

Lower Pool

SILOAM

Pre-exilic Judean tombs

Kidron Valley

of Oli·

Hinnom Valley

?

The lines of the southern walls of the city after the Exile are uncertain

Old Pool

Gate

Valley (?Topheth)

En-rogel Spring

© Oxford University

OUTER BORDER SH

MAP 9

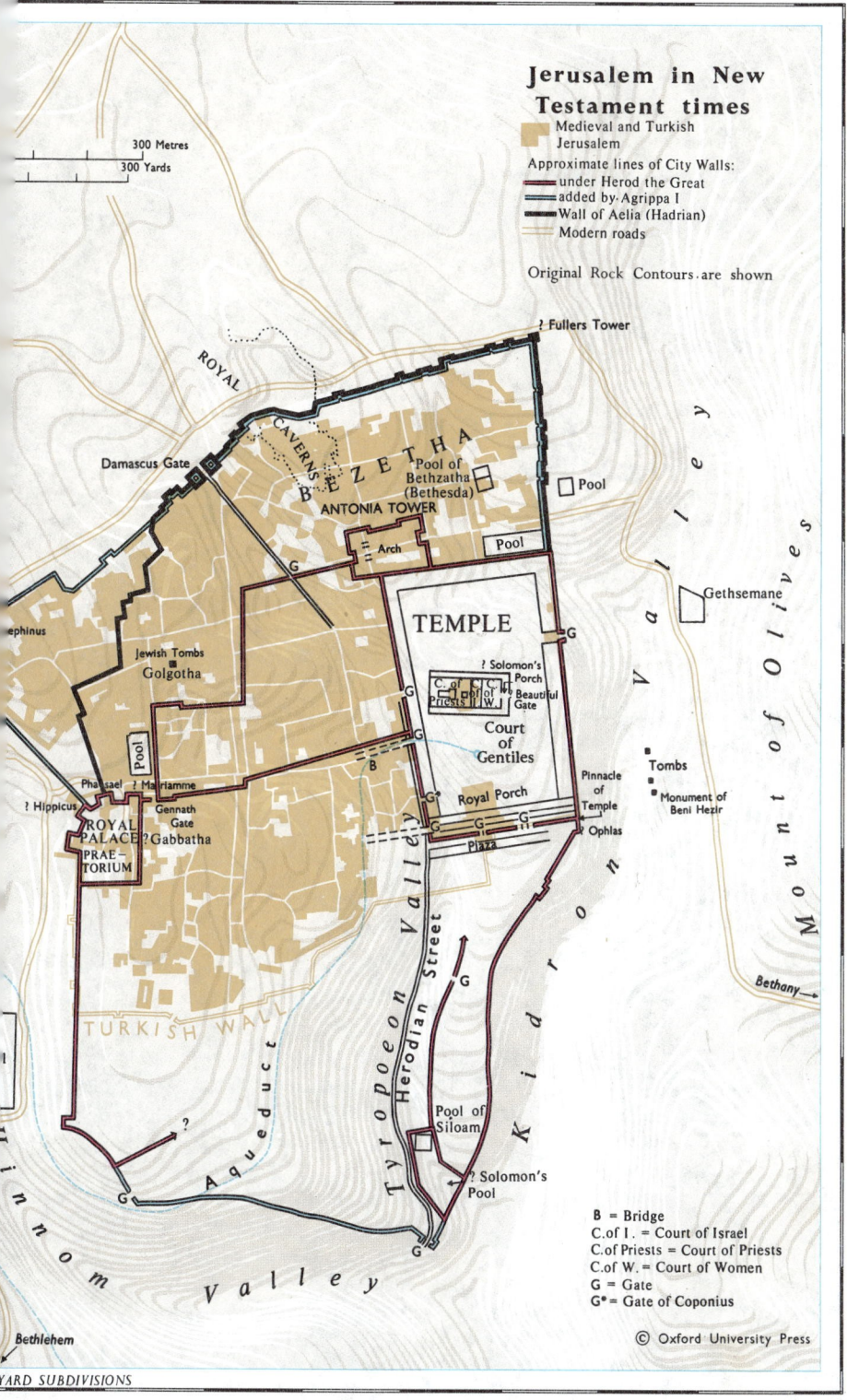

Jerusalem in New Testament times

Medieval and Turkish Jerusalem

Approximate lines of City Walls:
- under Herod the Great
- added by Agrippa I
- Wall of Aelia (Hadrian)
- Modern roads

Original Rock Contours are shown

B = Bridge
C. of I. = Court of Israel
C. of Priests = Court of Priests
C. of W. = Court of Women
G = Gate
G* = Gate of Coponius

© Oxford University Press

YARD SUBDIVISIONS

MAP 10

MAP 10

MAP 11

MAP 11

P   O   L   I   S

4

5

Gerasa ▲

Philadelphia ▲
(Rabbah)

© Oxford University Press

A   N   D

P   E   R   E   A

Brook Cherith

Pella ▲

Herod

Amathus

R. Jabbok

Antipas)

Zia •

Gadara •

• Esbus

Betharamphtha
(Livias Julias)

Salim ○
Aenon ○

J o r d a n

Coreae •

Alexandrium ▣

Phasaelis •

Archelais •

Jericho ●

Cyprus ▣

(Kh. Qumran:
settlement of
Dead Sea sect)

Ginae •

Bemeselis •

(Wadi Farah)

Acrabbein •

Selo (Shiloh) •

Taurus •

Sebaste ○
(Samaria)

Mt. Ebal •
Sychar •
Tirathana •

Mahnayim •

Anathu Borceus •

Ephraim •
(Aphairema)

Michmash •

Anatoth •

Mt. Scopus •
Bethphage ○

Neapolis ●

Mt. Gerizim •
Pharaton •

Arus •

Tephon •

Berzetho •
Gophna •

Bethel •

Berea •
Alalon? •

Adasa •

Capharsalama •

Bethany ○

A

S   A   M   A   R   I   A

Roman   administration)   (under

Thamna (Timnath) •

Ilon •

Sappho •

Lower Beth-horon •
Upper Beth-horon •

Gabaon •

Gabath Saul •

Colonia Amasa
(Emmaus)? •

Jerusalem ●

J   U   D   E   A

Narbata •

Gitta •

Yishub •

Capparetaea •

Tower of
Aphek •

Ratamin
(Arimathea)? •

Adida •

Modein •

Gazara •

Emmaus •
(Nicopolis)

Cariathiareim •

Capnarsaba •

P l a i n   o f   S h a r o n

Kanah •

Brook
(Pegai)

Antipatris ○

Lydda ●

Apollonia •
Sozusa •

Joppa ●

Jamnia •

R. Belus

Kedron •
(Kedron)

4

5

MAP 12

Paul's 1st Journey

Paul's 2nd Journey

Paul's 3rd Journey

MAP 12

S c y t h i a n s

BOSPORAN KINGDOM

Seven Churches of Asia (Rev. 1–3)
Boundary of Roman Empire (c.A.D. 65)
Provincial boundaries (c.A.D. 65)
ASIA,etc. Roman Provinces
Selected Roman roads (route between Rome and the East)

Chersonesus

E u x i n e   S e a
(Pontus   Euxinus)

0 100 200 Miles
0 100 200 Kilometres

Amastris
Sinope
...ea.
PONTUS
Amisus
Side
Trapezus
COLCHIS

Gangra
Amasea
Comana

K I N G D O M
O F
A R M E N I A

...laeum
Ancyra
Tavium
GALATIA
Artaxata
R. Araxes

Gordium
Pessinus
R. Halys

Lesser Armenia
L.Van
Tigranocerta

MEDIA ATROPATENE

Caesarea (Mazaca)
CAPPADOCIA
...Antioch
Archelais
Melitene
L. Urmia
GORDYENE
ADIABENE

Iconium
Lystra
Derbe
Commagene
Samosata
Nisibis
Ninus
Arbela

CILICIA
Tarsus
OSROENE
Edessa
Carrhae (Haran)

Cilicia Trachea
Zeugma
Europus (Carchemish)
(and SYRIA)

PARTHIAN

Seleucia
Antioch
Nicephorium

MESOPOTAMIA

M E D I A

R E
R. Orontes
Apamea
Epiphania
R. Euphrates
Dura-Europus

E M P I R E

CYPRUS
Salamis
Emesa
Palmyra

...aphos
Tripolis
Arca
ELAM →

Berytus
Seleucia
Ctesiphon

Sidon
Damascus
4

Tyre
Caesarea Philippi
Babylon

Ptolemais
Tiberias
Caesarea
Samaria
A r a b i a n
D e s e r t

Joppa
Jerusalem
Kingdom

Gaza
Judea

Pelusium

Nabataean
Petra
Dumah

...liopolis
...ylon
...phis

Aila (Aelana)

Mt. Sinai

Red Sea

Tema

The Background of the New Testament
Rome and the East
(including Paul's Journeys)

© Oxford University Press

INDEX TO MAPS

Index to maps

Index to maps

Index to maps

MAPS AND INDEX
PRINTED IN GREAT BRITAIN
BY COOK, HAMMOND & KELL LTD.
LONDON

THE NEW OXFORD
APOCRYPHA MAPS

*Prepared by the Cartographic Department
of the Clarendon Press, Oxford.*

Palestine in Persian-Hellenistic times

V · 34° 30' · 35° · X Sidon • · PHOENICIA · 35° 30' · Y · Mt. Lebanon · 36° · Z · 36° 30'

33° 30'

• Damascus · 33° 30'

2 · 2

Tyre •

0 · 10 · 20 Miles
0 · 10 · 20 Kilometres

Ladder of Tyre

Mt. Hermon

Kedesh •

Achzib •

33° · Hazor • · R. Jordan · Seleucia • · GAULANITIS · • Maked · 33°

Ptolemais
(Acco) •

THE

• Baskama

GALILEE

Taricheae · Lake · Chaspho · Carnaim · • Raphon
Arbela • · Gennesaret · (Casphor, · (Carnion) · • Dathema · • Bosor
Caspin) · • Gamala · (Diathema)

GREAT

• Shihin
(Asochis)

Susithah (Hippos)

3 · • Alema · 3

SEA

Mt. Carmel · Beth-yerah
(Philoteria)

Abila •

The Great Plain

Gadara •

Dor • · ARBATTA · • Arbela

Ephron •

Strato's Tower • · 32° 30' · Bozrah
(Bosora) • · 32° 30'

(Mediterranean
Sea) · • Narbata

Beth-shan
(Scythopolis) · GILEAD

• Pella

• Dothan

The Near East in the Hellenistic Period
Ptolemaic & Seleucid Empires

Trapezus

H   J   K   L

R. Cyrus

R. Araxes

H Y R C A N I A N

S e a

ARMENIA

L. Van

L. Urmia

Nisibis

Gaugamela

Arbela

Astrabad (Gorgan)

Zadrakarta (Turang Tepe)

Hecatompylus (?)

HYRCANIA

M E D I A

PARTHIA

Euphrates

Dura-Europus

R. Tigris

Rages (Rhagae)

Ecbatana

C

E

U

S

E

L

E

Ctesiphon

Seleucia

Babylon

BABYLONIA

Nippur

M

Uruk

Gabae

SUSIANA

Susa

P

D

I

R

Parsagarda

Persepolis

PERSIS

E

A

B

I

A

M

P e r s i a n   G u l f

H   J   K

© Oxford University Press.

INDEX TO MAPS